THE OFFICIAL®
2008 PRICE GUIDE TO
BASKETBALL
CARDS

DR. JAMES BECKETT

SEVENTEENTH EDITION

HOUSE OF COLLECTIBLES
Random House Reference
New York

House of Collectibles is a registered trademark and the colophon is a trademark of Random House, Inc.

Published by:
House of Collectibles
Random House Information Group
New York, New York

www.houseofcollectibles.com

Distributed by The Random House Information Group,
a division of Random House, Inc.,
New York, and simultaneously in Canada by
Random House of Canada Limited, Toronto.

www.randomhouse.com

Printed in the United States of America

ISSN: 1062-6980

ISBN: 978-0-375-72254-7

10 9 8 7 6 5 4 3 2 1

Seventeenth Edition: November 2007

Table of Contents

Table of Contents

Table of Contents

About the Author

Jim Beckett, the leading authority on sports card values in the United States, conducts a wide range of activities in the world of sports. He possesses one of the finest collections of sports cards and autographs in the world, has made numerous appearances on radio and television, and has been frequently cited in many national publications. He was awarded the first "Special Achievement Award" for Contributions to the Hobby by the National Sports Collectors Convention in 1980, the "Jock Jaspersen Award" for Hobby Dedication in 1983, and the "Buck Barker Spirit of the Hobby Award" in 1991.

Dr. Beckett is the author of *Beckett Baseball Card Price Guide, The Official Price Guide to Baseball Cards, The Sport Americana Price Guide to Baseball Collectibles, The Sport Americana Baseball Memorabilia and Autograph Price Guide, Beckett Football Card Price Guide, The Official Price Guide to Football Cards, Beckett Hockey Card Price Guide, The Official Price Guide to Hockey Cards, Beckett Basketball Card Price Guide, The Official Price Guide to Basketball Cards,* and *The Sport Americana Baseball Card Alphabetical Checklist.* In addition, he is the founder, publisher, and editor of *Beckett Baseball, Beckett Basketball, Beckett Football, Beckett Hockey,* and *Beckett Racing* magazines.

Jim Beckett received his Ph.D. in Statistics from Southern Methodist University in 1975. Prior to starting Beckett Publications in 1984, Dr. Beckett served as an Associate Professor of Statistics at Bowling Green State University and as a vice president of a consulting firm in Dallas, Texas. He currently resides in Dallas.

How to Use This Book

Isn't it great? Every year this book gets bigger and bigger with all the new sets coming out. But even more exciting is that every year there are more attractive choices and, subsequently, more interest in the cards we love so much. This edition has been enhanced and expanded from the previous edition. The cards you collect—who appears on them, what they look like, where they are from, and (most important to most of you) what their current values are —are enumerated within. Many of the features contained in the other Beckett Price Guides have been incorporated into this volume since condition grading, terminology, and many other aspects of collecting are common to card collecting in general. We hope you find the book both interesting and useful in your collecting pursuits.

The Beckett Guide has been successful where other attempts have failed because it is complete, current, and valid. This price guide contains not just one, but two prices by condition for all the basketball cards listed, which account for most of the basketball cards in existence. The prices were added to the card lists just prior to printing and reflect not the author's opinions or desires but the going retail prices for each card, based on the marketplace (sports memorabilia conventions and shows, sports card shops, hobby papers, internet autions, current mail-order catalogs, local club meetings, auction results, and other firsthand reports of actually realized prices).

What is the best price guide available on the market today? Of course, card sellers will prefer the price guide with the highest prices, while card buyers will naturally prefer the one with the lowest prices. Accuracy, however, is the true test. Use the price guide used by more collectors and dealers than all the others combined. Look for the Beckett name. I won't put my name on anything I won't stake my reputation on. Not the lowest and not the highest—but the most accurate, with integrity.

To facilitate your use of this book, read the complete introductory section on the following pages before going to the pricing pages. Every collectible field has its own terminology; we've tried to capture most of these terms and definitions in our glossary. Please read carefully the section on grading and the condition of your cards, as you will not be able to determine which price column is appropriate for a given card without first knowing its condition.

Introduction

Welcome to the exciting world of sports card collecting, one of America's most popular avocations. You have made a good choice in buying this book, since it will open up to you the entire spectrum of this field in the simplest, most concise way.

The growth of *Beckett Baseball, Beckett Basketball, Beckett Football, Beckett Hockey,* and *Beckett Racing* is another indication of the unprecedented popularity of sports cards. Founded in 1984 by Dr. James Beckett—the author of this price guide—*Beckett Baseball* contains the most extensive and accepted monthly Price Guide, collectible glossy superstar covers, colorful feature articles, a "Hot List," Convention Calendar, tips for beginners, "Readers Write" letters to and responses from the editor, information on errors and varieties, autograph collecting tips and profiles of the sport's hottest stars. Published every month, *BB* is the hobby's largest paid circulation periodical. The other five magazines were built on the success of *BB*.

So collecting sports cards—while still pursued as a hobby with youthful exuberance by kids in the neighborhood—has also taken on the trappings of an industry, with thousands of full- and part-time card dealers, as well as vendors of supplies, clubs, and conventions. In fact, each year since 1980 thousands of hobbyists have assembled for a National Sports Collectors Convention, at which hundreds of dealers have displayed their wares, seminars have been conducted, autographs penned by sports notables, and millions of cards changed hands.

The Beckett Guide is the best annual guide available to the exciting world of basketball cards. Read it and use it. May your enjoyment and your card collection increase in the coming months and years.

How to Collect

Each collection is personal and reflects the individuality of its owner. There are no set rules on how to collect cards. Since card collecting is a hobby or leisurely pastime, what you collect, how much you collect, and how much time and money you spend collecting are entirely up to you. The funds you have available for collecting and your own personal taste should determine how you collect. The information and ideas presented here are intended to help you get the most enjoyment from this hobby.

It is impossible to collect every card ever produced. Therefore, beginners as well as intermediate and advanced collectors usually specialize their collections in some way. One of the reasons this hobby is popular is that individual collectors can define and tailor their collecting methods to match their own tastes. To give you some ideas of the various approaches to collecting, we will list some of the more popular areas of specialization.

Many collectors select complete sets from particular years. For example, they may concentrate on assembling complete sets from all the years since their birth or from when they became avid sports fans. They may try to collect a card for every player during that specified period of time. Many others wish to acquire only certain players. Usually such players are the superstars of the sport, but occasionally collectors will specialize in all the cards of players who attended a particular college or came from a certain town. Some collectors are only interested in the first cards or Rookie cards of certain players.

Another fun way to collect cards is by team. Most fans have a favorite team, and it is natural for that loyalty to be translated into a desire for cards of the players on that particular team. For most of the recent years, team sets (all the cards from a given team for that year) are readily available at a reasonable price. *The Sport Americana Team Football and Basketball Card Checklist* will open up this aspect of the field to the collector.

Obtaining Cards

Several avenues are open to card collectors. Cards still can be purchased in the traditional way: by the pack at the local discount, grocery, or convenience store. But there are also thousands of card shops across the country that specialize in selling cards individually or by the pack, box, or set. Another alternative is the thousands of card shows held each month around the country, which feature anywhere from five to 800 tables of sports cards and memorabilia for sale.

For many years, it has been possible to purchase complete sets of cards through mail-order advertisers found in traditional sports media publications, such as *The Sporting News, Basketball Digest, Street & Smith* yearbooks, and others. These sets also are advertised in the card collecting periodicals. Many collectors will begin by subscribing to at least one of the hobby periodicals, all of which have good up-to-date information. In fact, subscription offers can be found in the advertising section of this book.

Most serious card collectors obtain old (and new) cards from one or more of several main sources: (1) trading or buying from other collectors or dealers; (2) responding to sale or auction ads in the hobby publications; (3) buying at a local hobby store; (4) attending sports collectibles shows or conventions; and/or (5) purchasing cards over the Internet.

We advise that you try all five methods since each has its own distinct advantages: (1) trading is a great way to make new friends; (2) hobby periodicals help you keep up with what's going on (including when and where the conventions are happening); (3) stores provide the opportunity to enjoy personalized service and to consider a great diversity of material in a relaxed sports-oriented atmosphere; (4) shows allow you to choose from multiple dealers and thousands of cards under one roof in a competitive situation; and (5) the Internet allows a collector to purchase cards from just about anywhere in the world.

Preserving Your Cards

Cards are fragile. They must be handled properly in order to retain their value. Careless handling can easily result in creased or bent cards. It is, however, not recommended that tweezers or tongs be used to pick up your cards since such utensils might mar or indent card surfaces and thus reduce those cards' conditions and values. In general, your cards should be directly handled as little as possible. This is sometimes easier said than done.

Although there are still many who use custom boxes, storage trays, or even shoeboxes, plastic sheets are the preferred method of many collectors for storing cards. A collection stored in plastic pages in a three-ring album allows you to view your collection at any time without the need to touch the card itself. Cards can also be kept in single holders (of various types and thicknesses) designed for the enjoyment of each card individually. For a large collection, some collectors may use a combination of the above methods. When purchasing plastic sheets for your cards, be sure that you find the pocket size that fits the cards snugly. Don't put your 1969-70 Topps in a sheet designed to fit 1992-93 Topps.

Most hobby and collectibles shops and virtually all collectors' conventions will have these plastic pages available in quantity for the various sizes offered, or you can purchase them directly from the advertisers at the back of this book. Also, remember that pocket size isn't the only factor to consider when looking for plastic sheets. Other factors such as safety, economy, appearance, availability, or personal preference also may indicate which types of sheets a collector may want to buy.

Damp, sunny, and/or hot conditions—no, this is not a weather forecast—are three elements to avoid in extremes if you are interested in preserving your collection. Too much (or too little) humidity can cause gradual deterioration of a card. Direct, bright sun (or fluorescent light) over time will bleach out the color of a card. Extreme heat accelerates the decomposition of the card. On the other hand, many cards have lasted more than 50 years without much scientific intervention. So be cautious, even if the above factors typically present a problem only when in the extreme. It never hurts to be prudent.

Collecting vs. Investing

Collecting individual players and collecting complete sets are both popular vehicles for investment and speculation. Most investors and speculators stock up on complete sets or on quantities of players that they think have good investment potential.

There is obviously no guarantee in this book, or anywhere else for that matter, that cards will outperform the stock market or other investment alternatives in the future. After all, basketball cards do not pay quarterly dividends and cards cannot be sold at their "current values" as easily as stocks or bonds.

Nevertheless, investors have noticed a favorable long-term trend in the past performance of sports collectibles, and certain cards and sets have outperformed just about any other investment in certain years. Many hobbyists maintain that the best investment is and always will be the building of a collection, which traditionally has held up better than outright speculation.

Some of the obvious questions are, Which cards? When to buy? When to sell? The best investment you can make is in your own education. The more you know about your collection and collecting in general, the more informed the decisions you will be able to make. We're not selling investment tips. We're selling information about the current value of basketball cards. It's up to you to use that information to your best advantage.

Glossary/Legend

Our glossary defines terms frequently used in card collecting. Many of these terms are also common to other types of sports memorabilia collecting. Some terms may have several meanings depending on use and context.

ABA—American Basketball Association.
ACC—Accomplishment.
ACO—Assistant Coach Card.
AL—Active Leader.
ART—All-Rookie Team.
AS—All-Star.
ASA—All-Star Advice.
ASW—All-Star Weekend.
AUTO/AU—Autograph.
AW—Award Winner.

B—Bronze.

BC—Bonus Card.

BRICK—A group or "lot" or cards, usually 50 or more having common characteristics, that is, intended to be bought, sold, or traded as a unit.

BT—Beam Team or Breakaway Threats.

CB—Collegiate Best.

CBA—Continental Basketball Association.

CL—Checklist Card. A card that lists in order the cards and players in the set or series. Older checklist cards in mint condition that have not been checked off are very desirable and command large premiums.

CO—Coach Card.

COIN—A small disc of metal or plastic portraying a player in its center.

COLLECTOR—A person who engages in the hobby of collecting cards primarily for his/her own enjoyment, with any profit motive being secondary.

COMBINATION CARD—A single card depicting two, or more players (not including team cards).

COMMON CARD—The typical card of any set.

CONVENTION ISSUE—A set produced in conjunction with a sports collectibles convention to commemorate or promote the show. Most recent convention issues could also be classified as promo sets.

COR—Corrected Card. A version of an error card that was fixed by the manufacturer.

COUPON—See Tab.

CY—City Lights.

DEALER—A person who engages in buying, selling, and trading sports collectibles or supplies. A dealer may also be a collector, but as a dealer, he anticipates a profit.

DIE-CUT—A card with part of its stock partially cut for ornamental reasons.

DISC—A circular-shaped card.

DISPLAY SHEET—A clear, plastic page that is punched for insertion into a binder (with standard three-ring spacing) containing pockets for displaying cards. Many different styles of sheets exist with pockets of varying sizes to hold the many differing card formats. The vast majority of current cards measure 2 1/2 by 3 1/2 inches and fit in nine-pocket sheets.

DP—Double Print. A card that was printed in approximately double the quantity compared to other cards in the same series. Or, Draft Pick card.

ERR—Error card. A card with erroneous information, spelling, or depiction on either side of the card. Most errors are never corrected by the producing card company.

EXCH—A Card that is inserted into packs that can be redeemed for something else—usually a set or autograph.

FIN—Finals.

FLB—Flashback.

FPM—Future Playoff MVPs.

FSL—Future Scoring Leaders.

FULL SHEET—A complete sheet of cards that has not been cut into individual cards by the manufacturer. Also called an uncut sheet.

G—Gold.

GQ—Gentleman's Quarterly.

GRA—Grace.

HL—Highlight Card.

HOF—Hall of Fame, or Hall of Famer (also abbreviated HOFer).

HOR—Horizontal pose on a card, as opposed to the standard vertical orientation found on most cards.

IA—In Action Card. A special type of card depicting a player in an action photo, such as the 1982 Topps cards.

INSERT—A card of a different type, e.g., a poster, or any other sports collectible contained and sold in the same package along with a card or cards of a major set.

IS—Inside Stuff.

ISSUE—Synonymous with set, but usually used in conjunction with a manufacturer, e.g., a Topps issue.

JSY—Jersey Card.

JWA—John Wooden Award.

KID—Kid Picture Card.

LEGITIMATE ISSUE—A set produced to promote or boost sales of a product or service, e.g., bubble gum, cereal, cigarettes, etc. Most collector issues are not legitimate issues in this sense.

LID—A circular-shaped card (possibly with tab) that forms the top of the container for the product being promoted.

MAG—Magic of SkyBox cards.

MAJOR SET—A set produced by a national manufacturer of cards, containing a large number of cards. Usually 100 or more different cards comprise a major set.

MC—Members Choice.

MEM—Memorial.

MINI—A small card or stamp (the 1991-92 SkyBox Canadian set, for example).

MO—McDonald's Open.

MVP—Most Valuable Player.

NNO—No Number on Back.

NY—New York.

OBVERSE—The front, face, or pictured side of the card.

OLY—Olympic Card.

PANEL—An extended card that is composed of multiple individual cards.

PC—Poster Card.

PERIPHERAL SET—A loosely defined term that applies to any nonregular issue set. This term most often is used to describe food issue, giveaway, regional, or sendaway sets that contain a fairly small number of cards and are not accepted by the hobby as major sets.

PF—Pacific Finest.

POY—Player of the Year.

PREMIUM—A card, sometimes on photographic stock, that is purchased or obtained in conjunction with (or redeemed for) another card or product. This term applies mainly to older products, as newer cards distributed in this manner are generally lumped together as peripheral sets.

PREMIUM CARDS—A class of products introduced recently, intended to have higher-quality card stock and photography than regular cards, but with more limited production and higher cost. Determining what is and isn't a premium card is somewhat subjective.

PROMOTIONAL SET—A set, usually containing a small number of cards, issued by a national card producer and distributed in limited quantities or to a select group of people, such as major show attendees or dealers with wholesale accounts. Presumably, the purpose of a promo set is to stir up demand for an upcoming set. Also called a preview, prototype, promo, or test set.

QP—Quadruple Print. A card that was printed in approximately four times the quantity compared to other cards in the same series.

RARE—A card or series of cards of very limited availability. Unfortunately, "rare" is a subjective term sometimes used indiscriminately. Using strict definitions, rare cards are harder to obtain than scarce cards.

RC—Rookie Card.

REGIONAL—A card issued and distributed only in a limited geographical area of the country. The producer may or may not be a major, national producer of trading cards. The key is whether the set was distributed nationally in any form or not.

REVERSE—The back or narrative side of the card.

REV NEG—Reversed or flopped photo side of the card. This is a common type of error card, but only some are corrected.

RIS—Rising Star.

ROY—Rookie of the Year.

S—Silver.

SA—Super Action Card. Similar to an In Action Card.

SAL—SkyBox Salutes.

SASE—Self-addressed, stamped envelope.

SCARCE—A card or series of cards of limited availability. This subjective term is sometimes used indiscriminately to promote or hype value. Using strict definitions, scarce cards are easier to obtain than rare cards.

SERIES—The entire set of cards issued by a particular producer in a particular year, e.g., the 1978-79 Topps series. Also, within a particular set, series can refer to a group of (consecutively numbered) cards printed at the same time, e.g., the first series of the 1972-73 Topps set (#1 through #132).

SET—One each of an entire run of cards of the same type, produced by a particular manufacturer during a single season. In other words, if you have a complete set of 1989-90 Fleer cards, then you have every card from #1 up to and including #132; i.e., all the different cards that were produced.

SHOOT—Shooting Star.

SHOW—A large gathering of dealers and collectors at a single location for the purpose of buying, selling, and trading sports cards and memorabilia. Conventions are open to the public and sometimes also feature autograph guests, door prizes, films, contests, etc. (Or, Showcase, as in 1996-97 Flair Showcase.)

SKED—Schedules.

SP—Single or Short Print. A card which was printed in a lesser quantity compared to the other cards in the same series (also see Double Print). This term can be used only in a relative sense and in reference to one particular set. For instance, the 1989-90 Hoops Pistons Championship card (#353A) is less common than the other cards in that set, but it isn't necessarily scarcer than regular cards of any other set.

SPECIAL CARD—A card that portrays something other than a single player or team.

SS—Star Stats.

STANDARD SIZE—The standard size for sports cards is 2 1/2 by 3 1/2 inches. All exceptions, such as 1969-70 Topps, are noted in card descriptions.

STAR CARD—A card that portrays a player of some repute, usually determined by his ability, but sometimes referring to sheer popularity.

STAY—Stay in School.

STICKER—A card-like item with a removable layer that can be affixed to another surface. Example: 1986-87 through 1989-90 Fleer bonus cards.

STOCK—The cardboard or paper on which the card is printed.

STY—Style.

SUPERSTAR CARD—A card that portrays a superstar, e.g., a Hall of Fame member or a player whose current performance may eventually warrant serious Hall of Fame consideration.

SY—Schoolyard Stars.

TC—Team Card or Team Checklist Card.

TD—Triple Double. A term used for having double-digit totals in three categories.

TAB — A card portion set off from the rest of the card, usually with perforations, that may be removed without damaging the central character or event depicted by the card.

TEAM CARD—A card that depicts an entire team, notably the 1989-90 and 1990-91 NBA Hoops Detroit Pistons championship cards and the 1991-92 NBA Hoops subset.

TEST SET—A set, usually containing a small number of cards, issued by a national producer and distributed in a limited section of the country or to a select group of people. Presumably, the purpose of a test set is to measure market appeal for a particular type of card. Also called a promo or prototype set.

TFC—Team Fact Card.

TL—Team Leader.

TO—Tip-Off.

TR—Traded Card.

TRIB—Tribune.

TRV—Trivia.

TT—Team Tickets Card.

UER—Uncorrected Error Card.

USA—Team USA.

VAR—Variation Card. One of two or more cards from the same series, with the same card number (or player with identical pose, if the series is unnumbered) differing from one another in some aspect, from the printing, stock, or other feature of the card. This is often caused when the manufacturer of the cards notices an error in a particular card, corrects the error, and then resumes the print run. In this case there will be two versions or variations of the same card. Sometimes one of the variations is relatively scarce. Variations also can result from accidental or deliberate design changes, information updates, photo substitutions, etc.

VERT—Vertical pose on a card.

XRC—Extended Rookie Card. A player's first appearance on a card, but issued in a set that was not distributed nationally or in packs. In basketball sets, this term refers only to the 1983, '84, and '85 Star Company sets.

YB—Yearbook.

20A—Twenty Assist Club.

50P—Fifty point Club.

6M—Sixth Man.

!—Condition-sensitive card or set (see Grading Your Cards).

*—Multisport set.

Understanding Card Values

Determining Value

Why are some cards more valuable than others? Obviously, the economic laws of supply and demand are applicable to card collecting, just as they are to any other field where a commodity is bought, sold, or traded in a free, unregulated market.

Supply (the number of cards available on the market) is less than the total number of cards originally produced, since attrition diminishes that original quantity of cards. Each year a percentage of cards is typically thrown away, destroyed, or otherwise lost to collectors. This percentage is much, much smaller today than it was in the past, because more and more people have become increasingly aware of the value of their cards.

For those who collect only mint condition cards, the supply of older cards can be quite small indeed. Until recently, collectors were not so conscious of the need to preserve the condition of their cards. For this reason, it is difficult to know exactly how many 1957-58 Topps cards are currently available, mint or otherwise. It is generally accepted that there are fewer 1957-58 Topps cards available than 1969-70, 1979-80, or 1992-93 Topps cards. If demand were equal for each of these sets, the law of supply and demand would increase the price for the least available sets.

Demand, however, is never equal for all sets, so price correlations can be complicated. The demand for a card is influenced by many factors. These include (1) the age of the card; (2) the number of cards printed; (3) the player(s) portrayed on the card; (4) the attractiveness and popularity of the set; and (5) the physical condition of the card.

In general, (1) the older the card, (2) the fewer the number of the cards printed, (3) the more famous, popular, and talented the player, (4) the more attractive and popular the set, and (5) the better the condition of the card, the higher the value of the card will be. There are exceptions to all but one of these factors: the condition of the card. Given two cards similar in all respects except condition, the one in the best condition will always be valued higher.

While those guidelines help to establish the value of a card, the countless exceptions and peculiarities make it impossible to develop any simple, direct mathematical formula to determine card values.

Regional Variation

Since the market for cards varies from region to region, card prices of local players may be higher. This is known as a regional premium. How significant the premium is—and if there is any premium at all—depends on the local popularity of the team and the player.

The largest regional premiums usually do not apply to superstars, who often are so well-known nationwide that the prices of their key cards are too high for local dealers to realize a premium.

Lesser stars often command the strongest premiums. Their popularity is concentrated in their home region, creating local demand that greatly exceeds overall demand.

Regional premiums can apply to popular retired players, and sometimes can be found in the areas where the players grew up or starred in college in addition to where they played.

A regional discount is the converse of a regional premium. Regional discounts occur when a player has been so popular in his region for so long that local collectors and dealers have accumulated quantities of his cards. The abundant supply may make the cards available in that area at the lowest prices anywhere.

Set Prices

A somewhat paradoxical situation exists in the price of a complete set versus the combined cost of the individual cards in the set. In nearly every case, the sum of the prices for the individual cards is higher than the cost for the complete set. This is prevalent especially in cards of the past few years. The reasons for this apparent anomaly stem from the habits of collectors and from the carrying costs to dealers. Today, each card in a set normally is produced in the same quantity as all others in its set.

Many collectors pick up only stars, superstars, and particular teams. As a result, the dealer is left with a shortage of certain player cards and an abundance of others. He therefore incurs an expense in simply "carrying" these less desirable cards in stock. On the other hand, if he sells a complete set, he gets rid of large numbers of cards at one time. For this reason, he generally is willing to receive less money for a complete set. By doing this, he recovers all of his costs and also makes a profit.

Set prices do not include rare card varieties, unless specifically stated. Of course, the prices for sets do include one example of each type for the given set, but this is the least expensive variety.

For some sets, a complete set price is not listed. This is due to sets currently not trading on the market as such. Usually, the sets that have low serial number print runs do not have complete set prices.

Scarce Series

Only a select few pre-1990 basketball sets contain scarce series: 1948 Bowman; 1970-71 and 1972-73 Topps; and 1983-84, 1984-85, and 1985-86 Star. The 1948 Bowman set was printed on two 36-card sheets, the second of which was issued in significantly lower quantities. The two Topps scarce series are only marginally tougher to aquire than the set as a whole. The Star Company scarcities relate to particular team sets that, to different extents, were less widely distributed.

We are always looking for information or photographs of printing sheets of cards for research. Each year, we try to update the hobby's knowledge of distribution anomalies. Please contact us at the address in this book if you have firsthand knowledge that would be helpful in this pursuit.

Grading Your Cards

Each hobby has its own grading terminology—stamps, coins, comic books, record collecting, etc. Collectors of sports cards are no exception. The one invariable criterion for determining the value of a card is its condition: The better the condition of the card, the more valuable it is. Condition grading, however, is subjective. Individual card dealers and collectors differ in the strictness of their grading, but the stated condition of a card should be determined without regard to whether it is being bought or sold.

No allowance is made for age. A 1961-62 Fleer card is judged by the same standards as a 1991-92 Fleer card. But there are specific sets and cards that are condition-sensitive (marked with "!" in the price guide) because of their border color, consistently poor centering, or other factors. Such cards and sets sometimes command premiums above the listed percentages in Mint condition.

Centering

Current centering terminology uses numbers representing the percentage of border on either side of the main design. Obviously, centering is diminished in importance for borderless cards such as Stadium Club.

Slightly Off-Center (60/40) - A slightly off-center card is one that upon close inspection is found to have one border wider than the opposite border. This degree once was offensive only to purists, but now some hobbyists try to avoid cards that are anything other than perfectly centered.

Off-Center (70/30) - An off-center card has one border that is noticeably more than twice as wide as the opposite border.

Badly Off-Center (80/20 or worse) - A badly off-center card has virtually no border on one side of the card.

Centering

Well-center

Slightly off-center

Off-center

Badly off-center

Miscut

Miscut - A miscut card actually shows part of the adjacent card in its larger border, and consequently a corresponding amount of its card is cut off.

Corner Wear

Corner wear is the most scrutinized grading criteria in the hobby. These are the major categories of corner wear:

Corner with a slight touch of wear - The corner still is sharp, but there is a slight touch of wear showing. On a dark-bordered card, this shows as a dot of white.

Fuzzy corner - The corner still comes to a point, but the point has just begun to fray. A slightly "dinged" corner is considered the same as a fuzzy corner.

Slightly rounded corner - The fraying of the corner has increased to where there is only a hint of a point. Mild layering may be evident. A "dinged" corner is considered the same as a slightly rounded corner.

Rounded corner - The point is completely gone. Some layering is noticeable.

Badly rounded corner - The corner is completely round and rough. Severe layering is evident.

Creases

A third common defect is the crease. The degree of creasing in a card is difficult to show in a drawing or picture. On giving the specific condition of an expensive card for sale, the seller should also note any creases. Creases can be categorized by severity according to the following scale:

Light Crease - A light crease is a crease that is barely noticeable upon close inspection. In fact, when cards are in plastic sheets or holders, a light crease may not be seen (until the card is taken out of the holder). A light crease on the front is much more serious than a light crease only on the back of the card.

Medium Crease - A medium crease is noticeable when held and studied at arm's length by the naked eye, but does not overly detract from the appearance of the card. It is an obvious crease, but not one that breaks the picture surface of the card.

Heavy Crease - A heavy crease is one that has torn or broken through the card's picture surface, e.g., puts a tear in the photo surface.

Alterations

Deceptive Trimming - This occurs when someone alters the card in order to (1) shave off edge wear, (2) improve the sharpness of the corners, or (3) improve centering. Obviously, the objective is to falsely increase the perceived value of the card to an unsuspecting buyer. The shrinkage is usually evident only if the trimmed card is compared to an adjacent full-size card or if the trimmed card is itself measured.

Obvious Trimming - Obvious trimming is noticeable and unfortunate. It is usually performed by non-collectors who give no thought to the present or future value of their cards.

Deceptively Retouched Borders - This occurs when the borders (especially on those cards with dark borders) are touched up on the edges and corners with Magic Marker or crayons of appropriate color in order to make the card appear to be in mint condition.

Categorization of Defects

Miscellaneous Flaws

The following are common minor flaws that, depending on severity, lower a card's condition by one to four grades and often render it no better than Excellent-Mint (see Condition Guide): bubbles (lumps in surface), gum and wax stains, diamond cutting (slanted borders), notching, off-centered backs, paper wrinkles, scratched-off cartoons or puzzles on back, rubber band marks, scratches, surface impressions, and warping.

The following are common serious flaws that, depending on severity, lower a card's condition at least four grades and often render it no better than Good: chemical or sun fading, erasure marks, mildew, miscutting (severe off-centering), holes, bleached or retouched borders, tape marks, tears, trimming, water or coffee stains, and writing.

Condition Guide

Grades

Mint (Mt) - A card with no flaws or wear. The card has four perfect corners, 55/45 or better centering from top to bottom and from left to right, original gloss, smooth edges, and original color borders. A mint card does not have print spots, or color or focus imperfections.

Near Mint-Mint (NrMt-Mt) - A card with one minor flaw. Any one of the following would lower a mint card to near mint-mint: one corner with a slight touch of wear, barely noticeable print spots, or color or focus imperfections. The card must have 60/40 or better centering in both directions, original gloss, smooth edges, and original color borders.

Near Mint (NrMt) - A card with one minor flaw. Any one of the following would lower a mint card to near mint: one fuzzy corner or two to four corners with slight touches of wear, 70/30 to 60/40 centering, slightly rough edges, minor print spots, or color or focus imperfections. The card must have original gloss and original color borders.

Excellent-Mint (ExMt) - A card with two or three fuzzy, but not rounded, corners and centering no worse than 80/20. The card may have no more than two of the following: slightly rough edges, very slightly discolored borders, minor print spots, or color or focus imperfections. The card must have original gloss.

Excellent (Ex) - A card with four fuzzy but definitely not rounded corners and centering no worse than 80/20. The card may have a small amount of original gloss lost, rough edges, slightly discolored borders and minor print spots, color or focus imperfections.

Very Good (Vg) - A card that has been handled but not abused: Factors may include slightly rounded corners with slight layering, slight notching on edges, a significant amount of gloss lost from the surface but no scuffing, and moderate discoloration of borders. The card may have a few light creases.

Good (G), Fair (F), Poor (P) - A well-worn, mishandled, or abused card: Factors may include badly rounded and layered corners, scuffing, most or all original gloss missing, seriously discolored borders, moderate or heavy creases, and one or more serious flaws. The grade of good, fair, or poor depends on the severity of wear and flaws. Good, fair, and poor cards generally are used only as fillers.

The most widely used grades are defined above. Obviously, many cards will not perfectly fit one of these definitions. Therefore, categories between the major grades known as in-between grades are used, such as Good to Very Good (G-Vg), Very Good to Excellent (VgEx), and Excellent-Mint to Near Mint (ExMt-NrMt). Such grades indicate a card with all qualities of the lower category but with at least a few qualities of the higher category.

This price guide book lists each card and set in two grades, with the bottom grade valued at about 40-45% of the top grade.

The value of cards that fall between the listed columns can also be calculated using a percentage of the top grade. For example, a card that falls between the top and middle grades (Ex, ExMt, or NrMt in most cases) will generally be valued at anywhere from 50% to 90% of the top grade.

Similarly, a card that falls between the middle and bottom grades (G-Vg, Vg, or VgEx in most cases) will generally be valued at anywhere from 20% to 40% of the top grade.

There are also cases where cards are in better condition than the top grade or worse than the bottom grade. Cards that grade worse than the lowest grade are generally valued at 5-10% of the top grade.

When a card exceeds the top grade by one—such as NrMt-Mt when the top grade is NrMt, or mint when the top grade is NrMt-Mt—a premium of up to 50% is possible, with 10-20% the usual norm.

When a card exceeds the top grade by two—such as mint when the top grade is NrMt, or NrMt-Mt when the top grade is ExMt—a premium of 25-50% is the usual norm. But certain condition-sensitive cards or sets, particularly those from the pre-war era, can bring premiums of up to 100% or even more.

Unopened packs, boxes, and factory-collated sets are considered mint in their unknown (and presumed perfect) state. Once opened, however, each card can be graded (and valued) in its own right by taking into account any defects that may be present in spite of the fact that the card has never been handled.

Selling Your Cards

Just about every collector sells cards or will sell cards at some point. Someday you may be interested in selling your duplicates or maybe even your whole collection. You may sell to other collectors, friends, or dealers. You may even sell cards you purchased from a certain dealer back to that same dealer. In any event, it helps to know some of the mechanics of the typical transaction between buyer and seller.

Dealers will buy cards in order to resell them to other collectors who are interested in them. Dealers will always pay a higher percentage for items that (in their opinion) can be resold quickly, and a much lower percentage for those items that are perceived as having low demand and hence are slow moving. In either case, dealers must buy at a price that allows for business expense and a profit margin.

If you have cards for sale, the best advice I can give is that you get several offers for your cards—either from card shops or at a card show—and take the best offer, all things considered. Note, the "best" offer may not be the one for the highest amount. And remember, if a dealer really wants your cards, he won't let you get away without making his best competitive offer. Another alternative is to place your cards in an auction as one or several lots.

Many people think nothing of going into a department store and paying $15 for an item of clothing for which the store paid $5. But if you were selling your $15 card to a dealer and he offered you $5 for it, you might think his mark-up unreasonable. To complete the analogy, most department stores (and card dealers) that consistently pay $10 for $15 items eventually go out of business. An exception is when the dealer has lined up a willing buyer for the item(s) you are attempting to sell, or if the cards are so hot that it's likely he'll have to hold the cards for only a short period of time.

In those cases, an offer of up to 75% of book value still will allow the dealer to make a reasonable profit considering the short time he will need to hold the merchandise. In general, however, most cards and collections will bring offers in the range of 25-50% of retail price. Also consider that most material from the past five to 10 years is plentiful. If that's what you're selling, don't be surprised if your best offer is well below that range.

Interesting Notes

The first card numerically of an issue is the single card most likely to obtain excessive wear. Consequently, you typically will find the price on the #1 card (in NrMt or mint condition) somewhat higher than might otherwise be the case. Similarly, but to a lesser extent (because normally the less important, reverse side of the card is the one exposed), the last card numerically in an issue also is prone to abnormal wear. This extra wear and tear occurs because the first and last cards are exposed to the elements (human element included) more than any other cards. They are generally end cards in any brick formations, rubber bandings, stackings on wet surfaces, and similar arrangements.

Sports cards have no intrinsic value. The value of a card, like the value of other collectibles, can be determined only by you and your enjoyment in viewing and possessing these cardboard treasures.

Remember, the buyer ultimately determines the price of each card. You are the determining price factor because you have the ability to say "no" to the price of any card by not exchanging your hard-earned money for a given card. When the cost of a trading card exceeds the enjoyment you will receive from it, your answer should be "no." We assess and report the prices. You set them!

We are always interested in receiving the price input of collectors and dealers from around the country. We happily credit all contributors. We welcome your opinions, since your contributions assist us in ensuring a better guide each year. If you would like to join our survey list for future editions of this book and others authored by Dr. Beckett, please send your name and address to Dr. James Beckett, 15850 Dallas Parkway, Dallas, Texas 75248.

History of Basketball Cards

The earliest basketball collectibles known are team postcards issued at the turn of the twentieth century. Many of these postcards feature collegiate or high school teams of that day. Postcards were intermittently issued throughout the first half of the twentieth century, with the bulk of them coming out in the 1920s and '30s. Unfortunately, the cataloging of these collectibles is sporadic at best. In addition, many collectors consider these postcards as more memorabilia than trading cards, thus their exclusion from this book.

In 1910, College Athlete felts (catalog number B-33) made their debut. Of a total of 270 felts, 20 featured basketball players.

The first true basketball trading cards were issued by Murad cigarettes in 1911. The "College Series" cards depict a number of various sports and colleges, including four basketball cards (Luther, Northwestern, Williams, and Xavier). In addition to these small (2-by-3-inch) cards, Murad issued a large (8-by-5-inch) basketball card featuring Williams College (catalog number T-6) as part of another multisport set.

The first basketball cards ever to be issued in gum packs were distributed in 1933 by Goudey in its multisport Sport Kings set, which was the first issue to list individual and professional players. Four cards from the complete 48-card set feature original Celtics basketball players Nat Holman, Ed Wachter, Joe Lapchick, and Eddie Burke.

The period of growth that the National Basketball Association experienced from 1948 to 1951 marked the first initial boom, both for that sport and the cards that chronicle it. In 1948, Bowman created the first trading card set exclusively devoted to basketball cards, ushering in the modern era of hoops collectibles. The 72-card Bowman set contains the Rookie card of HOFer George Mikan, one of the most valuable, and important, basketball cards in the hobby. Mikan, pro basketball's first dominant big man, set the stage for Bill

Russell, Wilt Chamberlain, and all the other legendary centers who have played the game since.

In addition to the Bowman release, Topps included 11 basketball cards in its 252-card multisport 1948 Magic Photo set. Five of the cards feature individual players (including collegiate great "Easy" Ed Macauley), another five feature colleges, and one additional card highlights a Manhattan-Dartmouth game. These 11 cards represent Topp's first effort to produce basketball trading cards. Kellogg's also created an 18-card multisport set of trading cards in 1948 that was inserted into boxes of Pep cereal. The only basketball card in the set features Mikan. Throughout 1948 and 1949, the Exhibit Supply Company of Chicago issued oversized thick-stock multisport trading cards in conjunction with the 1948 Olympic games. Six basketball players were featured, including HOFers Mikan and Joe Fulks, among others. The cards were distributed through penny arcade machines.

In 1950-51, Scott's Chips issued a 13-card set featuring the Minneapolis Lakers. The cards were issued in Scott's Potato and Cheese Potato Chip boxes. The cards are extremely scarce today due to the fact that many were redeemed back in 1950-51 in exchange for game tickets and signed team pictures. This set contains possibly the scarcest Mikan issue in existence. In 1951, a Philadelphia-based meat company called Berk Ross issued a four-series, 72-card multisport set. The set contains five different basketball players, including the first cards of HOFers Bob Cousy and Bill Sharman.

General Mills issued an oversized six-card multisport set on the backs of Wheaties cereal boxes in 1951. The only basketball player featured in the set is Mikan.

In 1952, Wheaties expanded the cereal box set to 30 cards, including six issues featuring basketball players of that day. Of these six cards, two feature Mikan (a portrait and an action shot). The 1952 cards are significantly smaller than the previous year's issue. That same year, the 32-card Bread for Health set was issued. The set was one of the few trading card issues of that decade exclusively devoted to the sport of basketball. The cards are actually bread end labels and were probably meant to be housed in an album. To date, the only companies known to have issued this set are Fisher's Bread in the New Jersey, New York, and Pennsylvania areas and NBC Bread in the Michigan area.

One must skip ahead to 1957-58 to find the next major basketball issue, again produced by Topps. Its 80-card basketball set from that year is recognized within the hobby as the second major modern basketball issue, including Rookie cards of all-time greats such as Bill Russell, Bob Cousy, and Bob Pettit.

In 1960, Post cereal created a nine-card multisport set by devoting most of the back of the actual cereal boxes to full-color picture frames of the athletes. HOFers Cousy and Pettit are the two featured basketball players.

In 1961-62, Fleer issued the third major modern basketball set. The 66-card set contains the Rookie cards of all-time greats such as Wilt Chamberlain, Oscar Robertson, and Jerry West. That same year, Bell Brand Potato Chips inserted trading cards (one per bag) featuring the L.A. Lakers team of that year and including scarce, early issues of HOFers West and Elgin Baylor.

From 1963 to 1968 no major companies manufactured basketball cards. Kahn's (an Ohio-based meat company) issued small regional basketball sets from 1957-58 through 1965-66 (including the first cards of Jerry West and Oscar Robertson in its 1960-61 set). All the Kahn's sets feature members of the Cincinnati Royals, except for the few issues featuring the Lakers' West.

In 1968, Topps printed a very limited quantity of standard-size black-and-white test issue cards, preluding its 1969-70 nationwide return to the basketball card market.

The 1969-70 Topps set began a 13-year run of producing nationally distributed basketball card sets which ended in 1981-82. This was about the time the league's popularity bottomed out and was about to begin its ascent to the lofty level it's at today. Topp's run included several sets that are troublesome for today's collectors. The 1969-70, 1970-71, and 1976-77 sets are larger than standard size, thus making them hard to store and preserve. The 1980-81 set consists of standard-size panels containing three cards each. Completing and cataloging the 1980-81 set (which features the classic Larry Bird RC/Magic Johnson RC/Julius Erving panel) is challenging, to say the least.

In 1983, this basketball card void was filled by the Star Company, a small company which issued three attractive sets of basketball cards, along with a plethora of peripheral sets. Star's 1983-84 premiere offering was issued in four groups, with the first series (cards 1-100) very difficult to obtain, as many of the early team subsets were miscut and destroyed before release. The 1984-85 and 1985-86 sets were more widely and evenly distributed. Even so, players' initial appearances on any of the three Star Company sets are considered Extended Rookie cards, not regular Rookie cards, because of the relatively limited distribution. Chief among these is Michael Jordan's 1984-85 Star XRC, the most valuable sports card issued in a 1980s major set.

Then, in 1986, Fleer took over the rights to produce cards for the NBA. Their 1986-87, 1987-88, and 1988-89 sets each contain 132 attractive, colorful cards depicting mostly stars and superstars. They were sold in the familiar wax pack format (12 cards and one sticker per pack). Fleer increased its set size to 168 in 1989-90, and was joined by NBA Hoops, which produced a 300-card first series (containing David Robinson's only Rookie card) and a 52-card second series. The demand for all three Star Company sets, along with the first four Fleer sets and the premiere NBA Hoops set, skyrocketed during the early part of 1990.

The basketball card market stabilized somewhat in 1990-91, with both Fleer and Hoops stepping up production substantially. A new major set, SkyBox, also made a splash in the market with its unique "high-tech" cards featuring computer-generated backgrounds. Because of overproduction, none of the three major 1990-91 sets have experienced significant price growth, although the increased competition has led to higher quality and more innovative products.

Another milestone in 1990-91 was the first-time inclusion of current rookies in update sets (NBA Hoops and SkyBox Series II, Fleer Update). The NBA Hoops and SkyBox issues contain just the 11 lottery picks, while Fleer's 100-card boxed set includes all rookies of any significance. A small company called "Star Pics" (not to be confused with Star Company) tried to fill this niche by printing a 70-card set in late 1990, but because the set was not licensed by the NBA, it is not considered a major set by the majority of collectors. It does, however, contain the first nationally distributed cards of 1990-91 rookies such as Derrick Coleman and Kendall Gill, among others.

In 1991-92, the draft pick set market that Star Pics opened in 1990-91 expanded to include several competitors. More significantly, that season brought with it the three established NBA card brands plus Upper Deck, known throughout the hobby for its high-quality card stock and photography in other sports. Upper Deck's first basketball set probably captured NBA action better than any previous set. But its value—like all other major 1990-91 and 1991-92 NBA sets—declined because of overproduction.

On the bright side, the historic entrance of NBA players to Olympic competition kept interest in basketball cards going long after the Chicago Bulls won their second straight NBA championship. So for at least one year, the basketball card market—probably the most seasonal of the four major team sports—remained in the spotlight for an extended period of time.

The 1992-93 season will be remembered as the year of Shaq—the debut campaign of the most heralded rookie in many years. Shaquille O'Neal headlined the most promising rookie class in NBA history, sparking unprecedented interest in basketball cards. Among O'Neal's many talented rookie companions were Alonzo Mourning, Jim Jackson, and Latrell Sprewell.

Classic Games, known primarily for producing draft picks and minor league baseball cards, signed O'Neal to an exclusive contract through 1992, thus postponing the appearances of O'Neal's NBA-licensed cards.

Shaquille's Classic and NBA cards, particularly the inserts, became some of the most sought-after collectibles in years. As a direct result of O'Neal and his fellow rookie standouts, the basketball card market achieved a new level of popularity in 1993.

The hobby rode that crest of popularity throughout the 1993-94 season. Michael Jordan may have retired, but his absence only spurred interest in some of his tougher inserts. Another strong rookie class followed Shaq, and Reggie Miller elevated his collectibility to a superstar level. Hakeem Olajuwon, by leading the Rockets to an NBA title, boosted his early cards to levels surpassed only by Jordan.

No new cardmakers came on board, but super premium Topps Finest raised the stakes, and the parallel set came into its own.

In 1994-95, the return of Michael Jordan, coupled with the high impact splash of Detroit Pistons rookie Grant Hill, kept collector interest high. In addition, the NBA granted all the licensed manufacturers the opportunity to create a fourth brand of basketball cards that year, allowing each company to create a selection of clearly defined niche products at different price points. The manufacturers also expanded the calendar release dates, with 1994-95 cards being released on a consistent basis from August, 1994, all the way through June, 1995. The super-premium card market expanded greatly as the battle for the best-selling five-dollar (or more) pack reached epic levels by season's end. The key new super premium products included the premier of SP, Embossed, and Emotion. This has continued through 1996 with the release of SPx, which contained only one card per pack.

The collecting year of 1996-97 brought even more to the table with a prominent motif of tough parallel sets and an influx of autographs available at lower ratio pulls. One of the greatest rookie classes in some time also carried the collecting season with players showing great promise: Allen Iverson, Kobe Bryant, Stephon Marbury, Antoine Walker, and Shareef Abdur-Rahim. Topps Chrome was also introduced, bringing about a rookie frenzy not seen since the 1986-87 Fleer set.

In 1997-98, Kobe Bryant was deemed the next Michael Jordan and his cards escalated in value throughout the year. In addition, a stronger than expected rookie class gave collectors some new blood to chase after, including Tim Duncan, Keith Van Horn, Ron Mercer, and Tim Thomas. Autographs and serial-numbered inserts were the key inserts to chase featuring numbering as low as one of one.

The 1998-99 season brought about a huge change in basketball. The players' strike crushed a growing basketball market and sent manufacturers scrambling. On top of this, Michael Jordan decided to retire (again), sending another direct hit to the hobby. Many releases were cut back—or cut period. There was a bright spot once the season began though—a great rookie class led by Vince Carter. The hobby benefited by combining the great class with shorter print run products. The top of the class was the 1998-99 SP Authentic release, which serially numbered the rookies to 3500. The San Antonio Spurs were crowned NBA Champions, leading to a spike in Tim Duncan cards. The top hobby card of the season was the SP Authentic Vince Carter RC.

If the beginning of the 1998-99 season was at rock bottom, the 1999-00 season was one of transition. Vince Carter became the new hobby hero and the NBA Champion L.A. Lakers helped the state of the hobby with their two horses, Kobe Bryant and Shaquille O'Neal. Another solid rookie class emerged, led by Steve Francis and Elton Brand, who shared Rookie of the Year honors. The 1999-00 card releases all combined elements of short-printed or serially numbered rookies, autographs, and game-worn materials. SP Authentic again led the way for consumer dollars, but many other brands also did extremely well, including E-X, Flair Showcase, and SPx, which combined rookie serial-numbered cards with autographs. The top hobby card of the season was the SPx Steve Francis RC, which was autographed to 500.

The year of 2000-01 releases will definitely leave its mark on the face of basketball cards for years to come. Noteworthy points of interest include the first one-per-pack graded insert in Upper Deck Ultimate Collection, the first one-per-pack memorabilia release in SP Game Floor, and the first one-per-box autographed jersey in Fleer Legacy. While these concepts have become commonplace over the course of the last year and a half, more than two years ago, notions such as these were unheard of.

Rookie cards were all the rage this year, and were available in several different formats and pricing tiers. It looks as though the sequentially numbered rookie has worked its way in as a hobby staple, as have autographed and memorabilia rookie issues. The uniqueness of 2000-01's releases is both staggering and impressive, as it is comforting to know that our hobby is still pointed in the right direction.

It also appears that 2000-01 marks a changing of the guard as far as basketball heroes are concerned. It is rather unfeasible to compare anyone in today's basketball game to the stature and legend that Michael Jordan has built for himself throughout the past two decades, but several young heroes are working their way up into our daily sports repertoire. As Michael Jordan sales begin to slow, Kobe Bryant, the L.A. Lakers' cast and crew, and Allen Iverson continue to build steam and fill the derelict space left by our hobby idol.

The release year of 2001-02 followed in the footsteps of previous years, as nearly every set issued had some type of memorabilia and/or autographed element to it. The hobby was shaken into somewhat of a frenzy as Michael Jordan rose up out of retirement (again), this time as a mentor and a player of the young Washington Wizards squad. Base Michael Jordan card values dominated sets, and at one point, $10 to $12 was a common value on the high end; and the explosive volume of sales provided the biggest boost as far as hobby dollars is concerned. Notable releases this year include Topps Pristine for its pack-in-a-pack-in-a-pack concept, encased uncirculated cards, and the use of new playoff-related materials such as towels. Upper Deck followed the comeback of Michael Jordan with several commemorative issues such as MJ Jersey Collection, and MJ's Back Jerseys which were inserted in several brands at the beginning of the release season. Fleer and Topps rejuvenated the market for parallel sets as Fleer issued two memorabilia parallels with its E-X release, and Topps made waves with the Topps Chrome Refractors Black Border set. A soft rookie crop as of the end of 2001-02 card releases had an impact on newer sales; the emergence of young stars such as Mike Bibby, Dirk Nowitzki, and Paul Pierce had collectors stammering for cardboard of players, who, since their rookie issues, had gone unnoticed, and dominated the market toward the end of the season.

2002-03 paved the way for the globalization of basketball trading cards. The 2002 NBA Draft boasts the highest number of foreign players drafted in the first round with ten, and the biggest push towards international card collecting was the number one draft choice, Yao Ming. Unlike most big men drafted, Ming had the ability to come in right away and put up good numbers for his Houston squad. Then, Ming coupled with Amare Stoudemire, a high-school draftee for Phoenix provided the perfect one-two punch to breathe some life back into the hobby, which had died off after the retirement of Michael Jordan in 1997 and the NBA lockout in 1998.

Additional Reading

Each year Beckett Publications produces comprehensive annual price guides for each of the five major sports: *Beckett Baseball Card Price Guide*, *Beckett Football Card Price Guide*, *Beckett Basketball Card Price Guide*, *Beckett Hockey Card Price Guide and Alpahabetical Checklist*, and *Beckett Racing Card and Die Cast Price Guide*. The aim of these annual guides is to provide information and accurate pricing on a wide array of sports cards, ranging from main issues by the major card manufacturers to various regional, promotional, and food issues. Also, alphabetical checklists, such as *Beckett Basketball Card Alphabetical Checklist #1*, are published to assist the collector in identifying all the cards of a particular player. The seasoned collector will find these tools valuable sources of information that will enable him/her to pursue his/her hobby interests.

In addition, abridged editions of the Beckett Price Guides have been published for each of three major sports as part of the House of Collectibles series: *The Official Price Guide to Baseball Cards*, *The Official Price Guide to Football Cards*, and *The Official Price Guide to Basketball Cards*. Published in a convenient mass-market paperback format, these price guides provide information and accurate pricing on all the main issues by the major card manufacturers.

Prices in This Guide

Prices found in this guide reflect current retail rates just prior to the printing of this book. They do not reflect the FOR SALE prices of the author, the publisher, the distributors, the advertisers, or any card dealers associated with this guide. No one is obligated in any way to buy, sell, or trade his or her cards based on these prices. The price listings were compiled by the author from actual buy/sell transactions at sports conventions, sports card shops, buy/sell advertisements in the hobby papers, for-sale prices from dealer catalogs and price lists, and discussions with leading hobbyists in the U.S. and Canada. All prices are in U.S. dollars. Prices marked .00 are either not available or are not priced becuase of their rarity.

Acknowledgments

A great deal of diligence, hard work, and dedicated effort went into this year's volume. The high standards to which we hold ourselves, however, could not have been met without the expert input and generous amount of time contributed by many people. Our sincere thanks are extended to each and every one of them.

A complete list of these invaluable contributors appears after the price guide.

2003-04 Bazooka

PEJA STOJAKOVIC

❑	COMP.SET w/o RC's (220)	30.00	12.50
❑	COMMON CARD (1-220)	.20	.08
❑	COMMON ROOKIE (221-275)	1.50	.60
❑	COMMON BAZ.JOE (276-288)	1.50	.60

❑ CARDS 1, 3, 23, 31, 66, 72, 90, 223, 226, 227
228, 240, 243, 244, 245, 250, 252, 260, 270,
AND 275 HAVE HOME & AWAY VERSIONS
B VERSION AWAY SAME VALUE AS A

❑	1A	Tracy McGrady	1.50	.60
❑	1B	Tracy McGrady	1.50	.60
❑	2	DaJuan Wagner	.40	.15
❑	3A	Allen Iverson	1.25	.50
❑	3B	Allen Iverson	1.25	.50
❑	4	Stromile Swift	.40	.15
❑	5	Jalen Rose	.60	.25
❑	6	Morris Peterson	.40	.15
❑	7	Lamar Odom	.60	.25
❑	8	Kobe Bryant	2.50	1.00
❑	9	Chauncey Billups	.40	.15
❑	10	Jason Kidd	1.00	.40
❑	11	Yao Ming	1.50	.60
❑	12	Stephon Marbury	.60	.25
❑	13	Ricky Davis	.60	.25
❑	14	Andrei Kirilenko	.60	.25
❑	15	Courtney Alexander	.40	.15
❑	16	Brad Miller	.60	.25
❑	17	Bobby Jackson	.40	.15
❑	18	Rashard Lewis	.60	.25
❑	19	Juwan Howard	.40	.15
❑	20	Allan Houston	.40	.15
❑	21	Kevin Garnett	1.25	.50
❑	22	Jason Terry	.60	.25
❑	23A	Jason Richardson		
❑	23B	Jason Richardson		
❑	24	Jerry Stackhouse	.60	.25
❑	25	Tyson Chandler	.60	.25
❑	26	Drew Gooden	.40	.15
❑	27	Jason Williams	.40	.15
❑	28	Eddie Jones	.60	.25
❑	29	Quentin Richardson	.40	.15
❑	30	Rasheed Wallace	.60	.25
❑	31A	Shawn Marion	.60	.25
❑	31B	Shawn Marion	.60	.25
❑	32	Malik Rose	.20	.08
❑	33	Ben Wallace	.60	.25
❑	34	Paul Pierce	.60	.25
❑	35	Matt Harpring	.60	.25
❑	36	Eddie Griffin	.40	.15
❑	37	Toni Kukoc	.40	.15
❑	38	Mike Bibby	.60	.25
❑	39	Kwame Brown	.40	.15
❑	40	Kurt Thomas	.40	.15
❑	41	Dirk Nowitzki	1.00	.40
❑	42	Theo Ratliff	.20	.08
❑	43	Ray Allen	.60	.25
❑	44	Michael Finley	.60	.25
❑	45	Lucious Harris	.20	.08
❑	46	Anfernee Hardaway	.60	.25
❑	47	Christian Laettner	.40	.15
❑	48	Manu Ginobili	.60	.25
❑	49	Tayshaun Prince	.40	.15
❑	50	Shaquille O'Neal	1.50	.60
❑	51	Vladimir Radmanovic	.20	.08
❑	52	Calbert Cheaney	.20	.08
❑	53	Eric Snow	.40	.15
❑	54	Pau Gasol	.60	.25
❑	55	Dikembe Mutombo	.40	.15
❑	56	Alvin Williams	.20	.08
❑	57	Corliss Williamson	.40	.15
❑	58	Kedrick Brown	.20	.08
❑	59	Jamaal Tinsley	.60	.25
❑	60	Chris Webber	.60	.25
❑	61	Donyell Marshall	.60	.25
❑	62	Darrell Armstrong	.20	.08
❑	63	Kenny Thomas	.20	.08
❑	64	Mehmet Okur	.20	.08
❑	65	Carlos Boozer	.60	.25
❑	66A	Kenyon Martin	.60	.25
❑	66B	Kenyon Martin		
❑	67	Speedy Claxton	.20	.08
❑	68	Brent Barry	.40	.15
❑	69	Ron Artest	.40	.15
❑	70	Elton Brand	.60	.25
❑	71	Troy Hudson	.20	.08
❑	72A	Steve Nash	.60	.25
❑	72B	Steve Nash	.60	.25
❑	73	Tony Parker	.60	.25
❑	74	Earl Boykins	.40	.15
❑	75	Kerry Kittles	.20	.08
❑	76	Shawn Bradley	.20	.08
❑	77	Tony Delk	.20	.08
❑	78	Zydrunas Ilgauskas	.40	.15
❑	79	Doug Christie	.40	.15
❑	80	Amare Stoudemire	1.25	.50
❑	81	Rick Fox	.40	.15
❑	82	Brian Skinner	.20	.08
❑	83	Jamal Mashburn	.40	.15
❑	84	Qyntel Woods	.20	.08
❑	85	Rafer Alston	.20	.08
❑	86	Derek Anderson	.40	.15
❑	87	Andre Miller	.40	.15
❑	88	Antoine Walker	.60	.25
❑	89	Frank Williams	.20	.08
❑	90A	Vince Carter	1.50	.60
❑	90B	Vince Carter	1.50	.60
❑	91	Donnell Harvey	.20	.08
❑	92	Rael Lafrentz	.40	.15
❑	93	Desmond Mason	.40	.15
❑	94	Rodney Rogers	.20	.08
❑	95	Juan Dixon	.40	.15
❑	96	Kareem Rush	.40	.15
❑	97	Bryon Russell	.20	.08
❑	98	Shandon Anderson	.20	.08
❑	99	Gordan Giricek	.40	.15
❑	100	Tim Duncan	1.25	.50
❑	101	Zach Randolph	.60	.25
❑	102	Malik Allen	.20	.08
❑	103	Richard Hamilton	.60	.25
❑	104	Maurice Taylor	.20	.08
❑	105	Marko Jaric	.20	.08
❑	106	Joe Smith	.40	.15
❑	107	Peja Stojakovic	.60	.25
❑	108	Othella Harrington	.20	.08
❑	109	Anthony Carter	.20	.08
❑	110	Wally Szczerbiak	.40	.15
❑	111	Troy Murphy	.60	.25
❑	112	Shareef Abdur-Rahim	.60	.25
❑	113	Reggie Miller	.60	.25
❑	114	Vin Baker	.20	.08
❑	115	Brian Scalabrine	.20	.08
❑	116	Eric Piatkowski	.40	.15
❑	117	Cuttino Mobley	.40	.15
❑	118	Erick Dampier	.20	.08
❑	119	Walter Mccarty	.20	.08
❑	120	Caron Butler	.60	.25
❑	121	Keyon Dooling	.20	.08
❑	122	Michael Redd	.60	.25
❑	123	Kenny Anderson	.40	.15
❑	124	P.J. Brown	.20	.08
❑	125	Devean George	.40	.15
❑	126	Joe Johnson	.40	.15
❑	127	Adrian Griffin	.20	.08
❑	128	Bonzi Wells	.40	.15
❑	129	Rasual Butler	.20	.08
❑	130	Baron Davis	.60	.25
❑	131	Wesley Person	.20	.08
❑	132	Shammond Williams	.20	.08
❑	133	Tyronn Lue	.20	.08
❑	134	Brian Grant	.40	.15
❑	135	Elden Campbell	.20	.08
❑	136	Glen Rice	.40	.15
❑	137	Michael Olowokandi	.20	.08
❑	138	Anthony Peeler	.20	.08
❑	139	Steven Hunter	.20	.08
❑	140	Eddy Curry	.40	.15
❑	141	Jerome James	.20	.08
❑	142	Travis Best	.20	.08
❑	143	Nazr Mohammed	.20	.08
❑	144	Tony Battie	.20	.08
❑	145	Scot Pollard	.20	.08
❑	146	Stanislav Medvedenko	.20	.08
❑	147	Jim Jackson	.20	.08
❑	148	Marcus Camby	.40	.15
❑	149	Marcus Haislip	.20	.08
❑	150	Glenn Robinson	.60	.25
❑	151	Jerome Williams	.20	.08
❑	152	Greg Ostertag	.20	.08
❑	153	Stephen Jackson	.20	.08
❑	154	David Wesley	.20	.08
❑	155	Sam Cassell	.60	.25
❑	156	Hedo Turkoglu	.40	.15
❑	157	Al Harrington	.40	.15
❑	158	John Salmons	.20	.08
❑	159	Nikoloz Tskitishvili	.20	.08
❑	160	Samaki Walker	.20	.08
❑	161	Jake Tsakalidis	.20	.08
❑	162	Tim Thomas	.40	.15
❑	163	Ronald Murray	.40	.15
❑	164	Alonzo Mourning	.40	.15
❑	165	Chris Jefferies	.20	.08
❑	166	Darius Miles	.60	.25
❑	167	Kendall Gill	.20	.08
❑	168	Lonny Baxter	.20	.08
❑	169	Jonathan Bender	.40	.15
❑	170	Antawn Jamison	.60	.25
❑	171	Keon Clark	.40	.15
❑	172	Chris Wilcox	.40	.15
❑	173	Brendan Haywood	.20	.08
❑	174	Predrag Drobnjak	.20	.08
❑	175	Nene	.40	.15
❑	176	Casey Jacobsen	.20	.08
❑	177	Marcus Fizer	.40	.15
❑	178	Howard Eisley	.20	.08
❑	179	Damon Stoudamire	.40	.15
❑	180	Gary Payton	.60	.25
❑	181	Shane Battier	.60	.25
❑	182	Desagana Diop	.20	.08
❑	183	Antonio Davis	.20	.08
❑	184	Keith Van Horn	.60	.25
❑	185	Corey Maggette	.40	.15
❑	186	Jarron Collins	.20	.08
❑	187	James Posey	.40	.15
❑	188	Latrell Sprewell	.60	.25
❑	189	Aaron McKie	.20	.08
❑	190	Vlade Divac	.40	.15
❑	191	Pat Garrity	.20	.08
❑	192	Eric Williams	.20	.08
❑	193	Radoslav Nesterovic	.40	.15
❑	194	Dan Gadzuric	.20	.08
❑	195	Moochie Norris	.20	.08
❑	196	Clifford Robinson	.20	.08
❑	197	Richard Jefferson	.40	.15
❑	198	Lorenzen Wright	.20	.08
❑	199	Nick Van Exel	.60	.25
❑	200	Gilbert Arenas	.60	.25
❑	201	Robert Horry	.40	.15
❑	202	Scottie Pippen	1.00	.40
❑	203	Jon Barry	.20	.08
❑	204	Derrick Coleman	.20	.08
❑	205	Ron Mercer	.20	.08
❑	206	DeShawn Stevenson	.20	.08
❑	207	Ruben Patterson	.40	.15
❑	208	Rodney White	.20	.08
❑	209	Jamal Crawford	.40	.15
❑	210	Jermaine O'Neal	.60	.25
❑	211	Eduardo Najera	.40	.15
❑	212	Dan Dickau	.20	.08
❑	213	Antonio McDyess	.60	.25
❑	214	J.R. Bremer	.20	.08
❑	215	Dion Glover	.20	.08
❑	216	Lamond Murray	.20	.08
❑	217	Larry Hughes	.40	.15
❑	218	Mike Miller	.60	.25
❑	219	Mike Dunleavy	.40	.15
❑	220	Karl Malone	.60	.25
❑	221	David West RC	1.50	.60
❑	222	Steve Blake RC	1.50	.60
❑	223A	LeBron James RC	15.00	6.00

❑ 223B LeBron James RC	15.00	6.00
❑ 224 Keith Bogans RC	1.50	.60
❑ 225 Josh Howard RC	2.50	1.00
❑ 226A Chris Kaman RC	1.50	.60
❑ 226B Chris Kaman RC	1.50	.60
❑ 227A Marcus Banks RC	1.50	.60
❑ 227B Marcus Banks RC	1.50	.60
❑ 228A Chris Bosh RC	4.00	1.50
❑ 228B Chris Bosh RC	3.00	1.25
❑ 229 Troy Bell RC	1.50	.60
❑ 230 Luke Walton RC	1.50	.60
❑ 231 Francisco Elson RC	1.50	.60
❑ 232 Ndudi Ebi RC	1.50	.60
❑ 233 Maurice Williams RC	1.50	.60
❑ 234 Kendrick Perkins RC	1.50	.60
❑ 235 Dahntay Jones RC	1.50	.60
❑ 236 Jason Kapono RC	1.50	.60
❑ 237 Kyle Korver RC	2.50	1.00
❑ 238 Josh Moore RC	1.50	.60
❑ 239 Travis Hansen RC	1.50	.60
❑ 240A Carmelo Anthony RC	6.00	2.50
❑ 240B Carmelo Anthony RC	6.00	2.50
❑ 241 Keith McLeod RC	1.50	.60
❑ 242 Zoran Planinic RC	1.50	.60
❑ 243A Jarvis Hayes RC	1.50	.60
❑ 243B Jarvis Hayes RC	1.50	.60
❑ 244A Mickael Pietrus RC	1.50	.60
❑ 244B Mickael Pietrus RC	1.50	.60
❑ 245A Mike Sweetney RC	1.50	.60
❑ 245B Mike Sweetney RC	1.50	.60
❑ 246 Jerome Beasley RC	1.50	.60
❑ 247 Zaza Pachulia RC	1.50	.60
❑ 248 Ben Handlogten RC	1.50	.60
❑ 249 Torraye Braggs RC	1.50	.60
❑ 250A Nick Collison RC	1.50	.60
❑ 250B Nick Collison RC	1.50	.60
❑ 251 Reece Gaines RC	1.50	.60
❑ 252A Dwyane Wade Dribble RC	8.00	3.00
❑ 252B Dwyane Wade Layup RC	6.00	2.50
❑ 253 Devin Brown RC	1.50	.60
❑ 254 Leandro Barbosa RC	2.00	.75
❑ 255 Boris Diaw RC	2.00	.75
❑ 256 Aleksandar Pavlovic RC	2.00	.75
❑ 257 Udonis Haslem RC	1.50	.60
❑ 258 Brian Cook RC	1.50	.60
❑ 259 Maciej Lampe RC	1.50	.60
❑ 260A T.J. Ford RC	2.00	.75
❑ 260B T.J. Ford RC	2.00	.75
❑ 261 Matt Carroll RC	1.50	.60
❑ 262 James Jones RC	1.50	.60
❑ 263 Brandon Hunter RC	1.50	.60
❑ 264 Luke Ridnour RC	2.00	.75
❑ 265 Theron Smith RC	1.50	.60
❑ 266 Jon Stefansson RC	1.50	.60
❑ 267 Zarko Cabarkapa RC	1.50	.60
❑ 268 Marquis Daniels RC	3.00	1.25
❑ 269 Willie Green RC	1.50	.60
❑ 270A Kirk Hinrich RC	2.50	1.00
❑ 270B Kirk Hinrich RC	2.50	1.00
❑ 271 Linton Johnson RC	1.50	.60
❑ 272 Travis Outlaw RC	1.50	.60
❑ 273 James Lang RC	1.50	.60
❑ 274 Slavko Vranes RC	1.50	.60
❑ 275A Darko Milicic RC	2.50	1.00
❑ 275B Darko Milicic RC	2.50	1.00
❑ 276 LeBron James BAZ	12.00	5.00
❑ 277 Darko Milicic BAZ	2.00	.75
❑ 278 Carmelo Anthony BAZ	4.00	1.50
❑ 279 Chris Bosh BAZ	2.50	1.00
❑ 280 Dwyane Wade BAZ	5.00	2.00
❑ 281 Chris Kaman BAZ	1.50	.60
❑ 282 Kirk Hinrich BAZ	2.00	.75
❑ 283 T.J. Ford BAZ	2.50	1.00
❑ 284 Mike Sweetney BAZ	1.50	.60
❑ 285 Jarvis Hayes BAZ	1.50	.60
❑ 286 Mickael Pietrus BAZ	1.50	.60
❑ 287 Nick Collison BAZ	1.50	.60
❑ 288 Marcus Banks BAZ	1.50	.60

2004-05 Bazooka

❑ COMP.SET w/o RC's (165)	25.00	10.00
❑ COMMON CARD (1-165)	.20	.08
❑ COMMON ROOKIE (166-220)	1.50	.60
❑ 1 Shaquille O'Neal	1.50	.60
❑ 2 Marquis Daniels	.60	.25
❑ 3 Ben Wallace	.60	.25

YAO MING

❑ 4 Jarvis Hayes	.40	.15
❑ 5 Gerald Wallace	.40	.15
❑ 6 Fred Jones	.20	.08
❑ 7 Pau Gasol	.60	.25
❑ 8 Latrell Sprewell	.60	.25
❑ 9 Steve Francis	.60	.25
❑ 10 Mike Bibby	.60	.25
❑ 11 Chris Bosh	.60	.25
❑ 12 Steve Nash	.60	.25
❑ 13 Kirk Hinrich	.60	.25
❑ 14 Richard Jefferson	.60	.25
❑ 15 Zach Randolph	.60	.25
❑ 16 Willie Green	.20	.08
❑ 17 Al Harrington	.40	.15
❑ 18 Rashard Lewis	.40	.15
❑ 19 Ricky Davis	.60	.25
❑ 20 Dwyane Wade	2.00	.75
❑ 21 Tim Duncan	1.25	.50
❑ 22 Eddy Curry	.40	.15
❑ 23 Andre Miller	.40	.15
❑ 24 Chris Wilcox	.40	.15
❑ 25 Bobby Jackson	.40	.15
❑ 26 Stephen Jackson	.20	.08
❑ 27 Shane Battier	.60	.25
❑ 28 Antawn Jamison	.60	.25
❑ 29 Brent Barry	.40	.15
❑ 30 Stephon Marbury	.60	.25
❑ 31 Gordan Giricek	.40	.15
❑ 32 Jamal Mashburn	.40	.15
❑ 33 Allen Iverson	1.25	.50
❑ 34 Paul Pierce	.60	.25
❑ 35 Mike Dunleavy	.40	.15
❑ 36 Gary Payton	.60	.25
❑ 37 Brad Miller	.60	.25
❑ 38 Eric Snow	.40	.15
❑ 39 Theo Ratliff	.20	.08
❑ 40 Richard Hamilton	.40	.15
❑ 41 Dirk Nowitzki	1.00	.40
❑ 42 Elton Brand	.60	.25
❑ 43 Reggie Miller	.60	.25
❑ 44 Baron Davis	.60	.25
❑ 45 Jerome Williams	.20	.08
❑ 46 Stromile Swift	.40	.15
❑ 47 Andrei Kirilenko	.60	.25
❑ 48 Jason Richardson	.60	.25
❑ 49 Larry Hughes	.40	.15
❑ 50 Yao Ming	1.50	.60
❑ 51 Tim Thomas	.40	.15
❑ 52 Erick Dampier	.40	.15
❑ 53 Keith Van Horn	.40	.15
❑ 54 Grant Hill	.60	.25
❑ 55 Shareef Abdur-Rahim	.60	.25
❑ 56 Amare Stoudemire	1.25	.50
❑ 57 David Wesley	.20	.08
❑ 58 Chris Kaman	.40	.15
❑ 59 Caron Butler	.60	.25
❑ 60 Kenyon Martin	.60	.25
❑ 61 Ray Allen	.60	.25
❑ 62 Jerry Stackhouse	.60	.25
❑ 63 Jason Kapono	.20	.08
❑ 64 Mark Blount	.20	.08
❑ 65 Hedo Turkoglu	.60	.25
❑ 66 Carlos Boozer	.60	.25
❑ 67 Kenny Thomas	.20	.08
❑ 68 Manu Ginobili	.60	.25
❑ 69 Kobe Bryant	2.50	1.00
❑ 70 Vince Carter	1.50	.60
❑ 71 Troy Murphy	.60	.25

❑ 72 Maurice Taylor	.20	.08
❑ 73 Earl Boykins	.40	.15
❑ 74 Boris Diaw	.20	.08
❑ 75 Kerry Kittles	.20	.08
❑ 76 Jamaal Tinsley	.60	.25
❑ 77 Lamar Odom	.60	.25
❑ 78 Jamaal Magloire	.20	.08
❑ 79 Wally Szczerbiak	.40	.15
❑ 80 Tayshaun Prince	.40	.15
❑ 81 Mehmet Okur	.20	.08
❑ 82 Eddie Jones	.60	.25
❑ 83 Voshon Lenard	.20	.08
❑ 84 Jamal Crawford	.40	.15
❑ 85 Marko Jaric	.40	.15
❑ 86 Ron Mercer	.20	.08
❑ 87 Steve Smith	.40	.15
❑ 88 Antoine Walker	.60	.25
❑ 89 Kurt Thomas	.40	.15
❑ 90 Ron Artest	.40	.15
❑ 91 Luke Walton	.40	.15
❑ 92 Dajuan Wagner	.40	.15
❑ 93 Luke Ridnour	.40	.15
❑ 94 Nene	.40	.15
❑ 95 Josh Howard	.40	.15
❑ 96 Juwan Howard	.40	.15
❑ 97 David West	.40	.15
❑ 98 Jonathan Bender	.40	.15
❑ 99 Tony Parker	.60	.25
❑ 100 LeBron James	4.00	1.50
❑ 101 Chris Webber	.60	.25
❑ 102 Cuttino Mobley	.40	.15
❑ 103 Rasheed Wallace	.60	.25
❑ 104 Marcus Banks	.40	.15
❑ 105 Ronald Murray	.20	.08
❑ 106 Quentin Richardson	.40	.15
❑ 107 Antonio McDyess	.20	.08
❑ 108 Sam Cassell	.60	.25
❑ 109 Allan Houston	.40	.15
❑ 110 Leandro Barbosa	.40	.15
❑ 111 Joe Smith	.40	.15
❑ 112 Jason Kidd	1.00	.40
❑ 113 Aleksandar Pavlovic	.20	.08
❑ 114 Bruce Bowen	.20	.08
❑ 115 Carmelo Anthony	1.25	.50
❑ 116 Kwame Brown	.40	.15
❑ 117 Mickael Pietrus	.40	.15
❑ 118 Tony Battie	.20	.08
❑ 119 Joe Johnson	.40	.15
❑ 120 Damon Stoudamire	.40	.15
❑ 121 Kevin Garnett	1.25	.50
❑ 122 Michael Redd	.40	.15
❑ 123 Doug Christie	.40	.15
❑ 124 Darrell Armstrong	.20	.08
❑ 125 James Posey	.40	.15
❑ 126 Jim Jackson	.20	.08
❑ 127 Udonis Haslem	.40	.15
❑ 128 Drew Gooden	.40	.15
❑ 129 Rasho Nesterovic	.40	.15
❑ 130 Jermaine O'Neal	.60	.25
❑ 131 Shawn Marion	.60	.25
❑ 132 Samuel Dalembert	.20	.08
❑ 133 Marcus Camby	.40	.15
❑ 134 Devean George	.40	.15
❑ 135 Darius Miles	.60	.25
❑ 136 Michael Olowokandi	.20	.08
❑ 137 Mike Miller	.60	.25
❑ 138 Kareem Rush	.20	.08
❑ 139 Jalen Rose	.60	.25
❑ 140 Chauncey Billups	.60	.25
❑ 141 Jason Williams	.40	.15
❑ 142 Derek Fisher	.40	.15
❑ 143 Donyell Marshall	.40	.15
❑ 144 Alonzo Mourning	.40	.15
❑ 145 T.J. Ford	.60	.25
❑ 146 Tony Delk	.20	.08
❑ 147 Gilbert Arenas	.60	.25
❑ 148 Glenn Robinson	.40	.15
❑ 149 Peja Stojakovic	.60	.25
❑ 150 Tracy McGrady	1.50	.60
❑ 151 Rafer Alston	.20	.08
❑ 152 Nazr Mohammed	.20	.08
❑ 153 Corey Maggette	.40	.15
❑ 154 Michael Doleac	.20	.08
❑ 155 Zydrunas Ilgauskas	.40	.15
❑ 156 Troy Hudson	.20	.08
❑ 157 Vladimir Radmanovic	.20	.08

158	Jason Collins	.20	.08
159	Dikembe Mutombo	.40	.15
160	Bonzi Wells	.40	.15
161	Jason Terry	.60	.25
162	Tyson Chandler	.60	.25
163	Desmond Mason	.40	.15
164	Carlos Arroyo	1.00	.40
165	Darko Milicic	.40	.15
166	Ben Gordon RC	6.00	2.50
167	Kevin Martin RC	2.50	1.00
168	Jackson Vroman RC	1.50	.60
169	Delonte West RC	3.00	1.25
170	Dorell Wright RC	2.50	1.00
171	Erik Daniels RC	1.50	.60
172	Josh Childress RC	2.00	.75
173	Anderson Varejao RC	2.00	.75
174	Andre Emmett RC	1.50	.60
175	Chris Duhon RC	2.50	1.00
176	Bernard Robinson RC	1.50	.60
177	D.J. Mbenga RC	1.50	.60
178	Kirk Snyder RC	1.50	.60
179	Damien Wilkins RC	1.50	.60
180	Andre Iguodala RC	4.00	1.50
181	Nenad Krstic RC	2.00	.75
182	Pape Sow RC	1.50	.60
183	Maurice Evans RC	1.50	.60
184	John Edwards RC	1.50	.60
185	Andres Nocioni RC	2.00	.75
186	Arthur Johnson RC	1.50	.60
187	Beno Udrih RC	2.50	1.00
188	Andris Biedrins RC	2.50	1.00
189	Kris Humphries RC	1.50	.60
190	Trevor Ariza RC	2.00	.75
191	Devin Harris RC	2.50	1.00
192	J.R. Smith RC	3.00	1.25
193	Romain Sato RC	1.50	.60
194	Lionel Chalmers RC	1.50	.60
195	Al Jefferson RC	4.00	1.50
196	Josh Smith RC	3.00	1.25
197	Antonio Burks RC	1.50	.60
198	Tim Pickett RC	1.50	.60
199	Justin Reed RC	1.50	.60
200	Emeka Okafor RC	6.00	2.50
201	Sebastian Telfair RC	1.50	.60
202	Sasha Vujacic RC	1.50	.60
203	Royal Ivey RC	1.50	.60
204	Rafael Araujo RC	1.50	.60
205	Ibrahim Kutluay RC	1.50	.60
206	Matt Freije RC	1.50	.60
207	Jared Reiner RC	1.50	.60
208	Luis Flores RC	1.50	.60
209	Robert Swift RC	1.50	.60
210	Shaun Livingston RC	2.50	1.00
211	Peter John Ramos RC	1.50	.60
212	Luke Jackson RC	1.50	.60
213	Luol Deng RC	3.00	1.25
214	Jameer Nelson RC	2.50	1.00
215	Tony Allen RC	2.00	.75
216	Josh Davis RC	1.50	.60
217	Yuta Tabuse RC	3.00	1.25
218	Donta Smith RC	1.50	.60
219	David Harrison RC	1.50	.60
220	Dwight Howard RC	5.00	2.00

2005-06 Bazooka

ELTON BRAND

COMPLETE SET (220)		40.00	15.00
COMMON CARD (1-165)		.20	.08
COMMON ROOKIE (166-215)		1.50	.60

	COMMON CELEB. (216-220)	2.00	.75
1	Gilbert Arenas	.60	.25
2	Josh Smith	.60	.25
3	Carlos Boozer	.40	.15
4	Al Jefferson	.60	.25
5	Jalen Rose	.60	.25
6	Primoz Brezec	.20	.08
7	Rashard Lewis	.60	.25
8	Ben Gordon	1.25	.50
9	Tony Parker	.60	.25
10	Drew Gooden	.40	.15
11	Mike Bibby	.60	.25
12	Josh Howard	.40	.15
13	Sebastian Telfair	.40	.15
14	Earl Boykins	.40	.15
15	Joe Johnson	.40	.15
16	Rasheed Wallace	.60	.25
17	Marc Jackson	.20	.08
18	Baron Davis	.60	.25
19	Dwight Howard	.75	.30
20	Tracy McGrady	1.50	.60
21	Trevor Ariza	.40	.15
22	David Harrison	.20	.08
23	J.R. Smith	.40	.15
24	Chris Kaman	.40	.15
25	Richard Jefferson	.40	.15
26	Chris Mihm	.20	.08
27	Sam Cassell	.60	.25
28	Mike Miller	.60	.25
29	Joe Smith	.40	.15
30	Dwyane Wade	2.00	.75
31	Tony Allen	.40	.15
32	Antawn Jamison	.60	.25
33	Eddy Curry	.40	.15
34	Rafael Araujo	.60	.25
35	Jerry Stackhouse	.60	.25
36	Manu Ginobili	.60	.25
37	Antonio McDyess	.40	.15
38	Zach Randolph	.60	.25
39	Mike James	.20	.08
40	Chris Webber	.60	.25
41	Bobby Simmons	.20	.08
42	Jamal Crawford	.40	.15
43	Pau Gasol	.60	.25
44	Brian Scalabrine	.20	.08
45	Desmond Mason	.40	.15
46	Tyronn Lue	.20	.08
47	Andrei Kirilenko	.60	.25
48	Luke Ridnour	.40	.15
49	Gerald Wallace	.40	.15
50	LeBron James	4.00	1.50
51	Peja Stojakovic	.60	.25
52	Andre Miller	.40	.15
53	Quentin Richardson	.40	.15
54	Mike Dunleavy	.40	.15
55	Steve Francis	.60	.25
56	Stephen Jackson	.40	.15
57	P.J. Brown	.20	.08
58	Caron Butler	.40	.15
59	Keith Van Horn	.40	.15
60	Shaquille O'Neal	1.50	.60
61	Josh Childress	.40	.15
62	Michael Doleac	.20	.08
63	Lamar Odom	.60	.25
64	Stephon Marbury	.60	.25
65	Chris Duhon	.40	.15
66	Shaun Livingston	.60	.25
67	Eric Snow	.40	.15
68	Travis Outlaw	.20	.08
69	Ron Artest	.40	.15
70	Emeka Okafor	1.00	.40
71	Chauncey Billups	.60	.25
72	Jason Williams	.40	.15
73	Jameer Nelson	.40	.15
74	Eduardo Najera	.40	.15
75	Speedy Claxton	.20	.08
76	Kirk Snyder	.20	.08
77	Rafer Alston	.20	.08
78	Kobe Bryant	2.50	1.00
79	Michael Redd	.60	.25
80	Tim Duncan	1.25	.50
81	Tayshaun Prince	.60	.25
82	Brendan Haywood	.20	.08
83	Kyle Korver	.60	.25
84	Tony Delk	.20	.08
85	Luol Deng	.60	.25

86	Elton Brand	.60	.25
87	Jason Richardson	.60	.25
88	Antoine Walker	.60	.25
89	Ray Allen	.60	.25
90	Yao Ming	1.50	.60
91	Damon Jones	.40	.15
92	Anderson Varejao	.40	.15
93	Kurt Thomas	.40	.15
94	Latrell Sprewell	.60	.25
95	Cuttino Mobley	.40	.15
96	Chris Wilcox	.20	.08
97	Devin Harris	.60	.25
98	Jared Jeffries	.20	.08
99	Nenad Krstic	.40	.15
100	Steve Nash	.60	.25
101	Reggie Evans	.20	.08
102	Ben Wallace	.60	.25
103	Allen Iverson	1.25	.50
104	Bruce Bowen	.40	.15
105	Paul Pierce	.60	.25
106	Shareef Abdur-Rahim	.60	.25
107	Vladimir Radmanovic	.20	.08
108	Michael Finley	.60	.25
109	Brent Barry	.40	.15
110	Carmelo Anthony	1.25	.50
111	Andre Iguodala	.60	.25
112	Shane Battier	.40	.15
113	Richard Hamilton	.60	.25
114	Kenny Thomas	.20	.08
115	Tyson Chandler	.40	.15
116	Jim Jackson	.40	.15
117	David Wesley	.20	.08
118	Grant Hill	.60	.25
119	Wally Szczerbiak	.40	.15
120	Dirk Nowitzki	1.00	.40
121	Udonis Haslem	.20	.08
122	Jason Hart	.20	.08
123	Marcus Camby	.40	.15
124	Kirk Hinrich	.60	.25
125	Jermaine O'Neal	.60	.25
126	Derek Fisher	.60	.25
127	Donyell Marshall	.20	.08
128	Darius Miles	.60	.25
129	Kenyon Martin	.40	.15
130	Jason Kidd	1.00	.40
131	Marquis Daniels	.40	.15
132	Kevin Garnett	1.25	.50
133	Juwan Howard	.40	.15
134	Shawn Marion	.60	.25
135	Morris Peterson	.40	.15
136	Kevin Martin	.40	.15
137	Gary Payton	.60	.25
138	Maurice Williams	.20	.08
139	Eddie Jones	.40	.15
140	Vince Carter	1.50	.60
141	Lorenzen Wright	.20	.08
142	Dan Dickau	.20	.08
143	Chucky Atkins	.20	.08
144	Mike Sweetney	.40	.15
145	Corey Maggette	.40	.15
146	Hedo Turkoglu	.40	.15
147	Jamaal Tinsley	.40	.15
148	Samuel Dalembert	.40	.15
149	Bob Sura	.40	.15
150	Amare Stoudemire	1.25	.50
151	Troy Murphy	.60	.25
152	Joel Przybilla	.20	.08
153	Carlos Arroyo	1.00	.40
154	Brad Miller	.60	.25
155	Jason Terry	.60	.25
156	Beno Udrih	.40	.15
157	Zydrunas Ilgauskas	.40	.15
158	Nick Collison	.20	.08
159	Andres Nocioni	.40	.15
160	Chris Bosh	.60	.25
161	Brevin Knight	.20	.08
162	Mehmet Okur	.40	.15
163	Ricky Davis	.60	.25
164	Larry Hughes	.60	.25
165	Al Harrington	.40	.15
166	Chris Paul RC	6.00	2.50
167	Danny Granger RC	2.00	.75
168	Jarrett Jack RC	1.50	.60
169	Wayne Simien RC	2.00	.75
170	Deron Williams RC	5.00	2.00
171	Ryan Gomes RC	1.50	.60

☐ 172	Daniel Ewing RC	2.00	.75
☐ 173	Sean May RC	1.50	.60
☐ 174	Alan Anderson RC	1.50	.60
☐ 175	Hakim Warrick RC	3.00	1.25
☐ 176	Francisco Garcia RC	2.00	.75
☐ 177	Nate Robinson RC	2.50	1.00
☐ 178	Luther Head RC	2.00	.75
☐ 179	Joey Graham RC	1.50	.60
☐ 180	Marvin Williams RC	3.00	1.25
☐ 181	Antoine Wright RC	1.50	.60
☐ 182	Andrew Bynum RC	5.00	2.00
☐ 183	Johan Petro RC	1.50	.60
☐ 184	Louis Williams RC	1.50	.60
☐ 185	Andray Blatche RC	1.50	.60
☐ 186	Sarunas Jasikevicius RC	2.00	.75
☐ 187	Ike Diogu RC	2.00	.75
☐ 188	Channing Frye RC	2.50	1.00
☐ 189	Julius Hodge RC	1.50	.60
☐ 190	Rashad McCants RC	3.00	1.25
☐ 191	Yaroslav Korolev RC	1.50	.60
☐ 192	C.J. Miles RC	1.50	.60
☐ 193	Brandon Bass RC	1.50	.60
☐ 194	Travis Diener RC	1.50	.60
☐ 195	Monta Ellis RC	2.50	1.00
☐ 196	Linas Kleiza RC	1.50	.60
☐ 197	Gerald Green RC	5.00	2.00
☐ 198	Jason Maxiell RC	1.50	.60
☐ 199	David Lee RC	2.50	1.00
☐ 200	Andrew Bogut RC	2.00	.75
☐ 201	Salim Stoudamire RC	2.50	1.00
☐ 202	Raymond Felton RC	3.00	1.25
☐ 203	Martell Webster RC	1.50	.60
☐ 204	Chris Taft RC	1.50	.60
☐ 205	Charlie Villanueva RC	2.50	1.00
☐ 206	Lawrence Roberts RC	1.50	.60
☐ 207	Ersan Ilyasova RC	1.50	.60
☐ 208	Martynas Andriuskevicius RC	1.50	.60
☐ 209	Bracey Wright RC	2.00	.75
☐ 210	Von Wafer RC	1.50	.60
☐ 211	Eddie Basden RC	1.50	.60
☐ 212	Dijon Thompson RC	1.50	.60
☐ 213	Robert Whaley RC	1.50	.60
☐ 214	Matt Walsh RC	1.50	.60
☐ 215	Ricky Sanchez RC	1.50	.60
☐ 216	Jay-Z	5.00	2.00
☐ 217	Sharon Elizabeth	2.00	.75
☐ 218	Christie Brinkley	2.00	.75
☐ 219	Jenny McCarthy	2.00	.75
☐ 220	Carmen Electra	2.00	.75

1998-99 Black Diamond

☐	COMPLETE SET (120)	80.00	40.00
☐	COMPLETE SET w/o RC (90)	40.00	20.00
☐	COMMON MJ (1-13/22)	3.00	1.25
☐	COMMON CARD (14-90)	.30	.10
☐	COMMON ROOKIE (91-120)	2.00	.75
☐ 1	Michael Jordan	3.00	1.25
☐ 2	Michael Jordan	3.00	1.25
☐ 3	Michael Jordan	3.00	1.25
☐ 4	Michael Jordan	3.00	1.25
☐ 5	Michael Jordan	3.00	1.25
☐ 6	Michael Jordan	3.00	1.25
☐ 7	Michael Jordan	3.00	1.25
☐ 8	Michael Jordan	3.00	1.25
☐ 9	Michael Jordan	3.00	1.25
☐ 10	Michael Jordan	3.00	1.25
☐ 11	Michael Jordan	3.00	1.25
☐ 12	Michael Jordan	3.00	1.25

☐ 13	Michael Jordan	3.00	1.25
☐ 14	Dikembe Mutombo	.60	.25
☐ 15	Steve Smith	.60	.25
☐ 16	Mookie Blaylock	.30	.10
☐ 17	Antoine Walker	1.00	.40
☐ 18	Kenny Anderson	.60	.25
☐ 19	Ron Mercer	.50	.20
☐ 20	Glen Rice	.60	.25
☐ 21	Derrick Coleman	.30	.10
☐ 22	Michael Jordan	3.00	1.25
☐ 23	Toni Kukoc	.60	.25
☐ 24	Brent Barry	.60	.25
☐ 25	Brevin Knight	.30	.10
☐ 26	Derek Anderson	.75	.30
☐ 27	Shawn Kemp	.60	.25
☐ 28	Shawn Bradley	.30	.10
☐ 29	Michael Finley	1.00	.40
☐ 30	Nick Van Exel	1.00	.40
☐ 31	Chauncey Billups	.60	.25
☐ 32	Antonio McDyess	.60	.25
☐ 33	Grant Hill	1.00	.40
☐ 34	Jerry Stackhouse	1.00	.40
☐ 35	Bison Dele	.30	.10
☐ 36	John Starks	.60	.25
☐ 37	Chris Mills	.30	.10
☐ 38	Scottie Pippen	1.50	.60
☐ 39	Hakeem Olajuwon	1.00	.40
☐ 40	Charles Barkley	1.25	.50
☐ 41	Antonio Davis	.30	.10
☐ 42	Reggie Miller	1.00	.40
☐ 43	Mark Jackson	.60	.25
☐ 44	Eddie Jones	1.00	.40
☐ 45	Shaquille O'Neal	2.50	1.00
☐ 46	Kobe Bryant	4.00	1.50
☐ 47	Rodney Rogers	.30	.10
☐ 48	Maurice Taylor	.50	.20
☐ 49	Tim Hardaway	.60	.25
☐ 50	Jamal Mashburn	.60	.25
☐ 51	Alonzo Mourning	.60	.25
☐ 52	Ray Allen	1.00	.40
☐ 53	Terrell Brandon	.60	.25
☐ 54	Glenn Robinson	.60	.25
☐ 55	Joe Smith	.60	.25
☐ 56	Stephon Marbury	1.00	.40
☐ 57	Kevin Garnett	2.00	.75
☐ 58	Kerry Kittles	.30	.10
☐ 59	Jayson Williams	.30	.10
☐ 60	Keith Van Horn	1.00	.40
☐ 61	Patrick Ewing	1.00	.40
☐ 62	Allan Houston	.60	.25
☐ 63	Latrell Sprewell	1.00	.40
☐ 64	Anfernee Hardaway	1.00	.40
☐ 65	Horace Grant	.60	.25
☐ 66	Allen Iverson	2.00	.75
☐ 67	Tim Thomas	.60	.25
☐ 68	Jason Kidd	1.50	.60
☐ 69	Danny Manning	.30	.10
☐ 70	Tom Gugliotta	.30	.10
☐ 71	Damon Stoudamire	.60	.25
☐ 72	Rasheed Wallace	1.00	.40
☐ 73	Isaiah Rider	.30	.10
☐ 74	Corliss Williamson	.60	.25
☐ 75	Chris Webber	1.00	.40
☐ 76	Tim Duncan	1.50	.60
☐ 77	David Robinson	1.00	.40
☐ 78	Sean Elliott	.60	.25
☐ 79	Gary Payton	1.00	.40
☐ 80	Vin Baker	.60	.25
☐ 81	John Wallace	.30	.10
☐ 82	Tracy McGrady	2.50	1.00
☐ 83	Jeff Hornacek	.60	.25
☐ 84	Karl Malone	1.00	.40
☐ 85	John Stockton	1.00	.40
☐ 86	Bryant Reeves	.30	.10
☐ 87	Shareef Abdur-Rahim	1.00	.40
☐ 88	Rod Strickland	.30	.10
☐ 89	Juwan Howard	.60	.25
☐ 90	Mitch Richmond	.60	.25
☐ 91	Michael Olowokandi RC	2.00	.75
☐ 92	Dirk Nowitzki RC	12.00	6.00
☐ 93	Raef LaFrentz RC	2.00	.75
☐ 94	Mike Bibby RC	6.00	2.50
☐ 95	Ricky Davis RC	4.00	1.50
☐ 96	Jason Williams RC	5.00	2.00
☐ 97	Al Harrington RC	3.00	1.25
☐ 98	Bonzi Wells RC	5.00	2.00

☐ 99	Keon Clark RC	2.00	.75
☐ 100	Rashard Lewis RC	5.00	2.00
☐ 101	Paul Pierce RC	6.00	2.50
☐ 102	Antawn Jamison RC	6.00	2.50
☐ 103	Nazr Mohammed RC	.60	.25
☐ 104	Brian Skinner RC	1.25	.50
☐ 105	Corey Benjamin RC	1.25	.50
☐ 106	Peja Stojakovic RC	5.00	2.00
☐ 107	Bryce Drew RC	1.25	.50
☐ 108	Matt Harpring RC	2.50	1.00
☐ 109	Toby Bailey RC	.50	.20
☐ 110	Tyronn Lue RC	1.50	.60
☐ 111	Michael Dickerson RC	2.50	1.00
☐ 112	Roshown McLeod RC	.60	.25
☐ 113	Felipe Lopez RC	1.50	.60
☐ 114	Michael Doleac RC	1.25	.50
☐ 115	Ruben Patterson RC	2.50	1.00
☐ 116	Robert Traylor RC	1.25	.50
☐ 117	Sam Jacobson RC	.50	.20
☐ 118	Larry Hughes RC	4.00	1.50
☐ 119	Pat Garrity RC	.60	.25
☐ 120	Vince Carter RC	15.00	6.00

1999-00 Black Diamond

☐	COMPLETE SET (120)	50.00	25.00
☐	COMPLETE SET w/o RC (90)	25.00	12.50
☐	COMMON CARD (1-90)	.25	.08
☐	COMMON ROOKIE (91-120)	.50	.20
☐ 1	Dikembe Mutombo	.50	.20
☐ 2	Alan Henderson	.25	.08
☐ 3	Roshown McLeod	.25	.08
☐ 4	Kenny Anderson	.50	.20
☐ 5	Paul Pierce	1.00	.40
☐ 6	Antoine Walker	.75	.30
☐ 7	Eddie Jones	.75	.30
☐ 8	Elden Campbell	.25	.08
☐ 9	David Wesley	.25	.08
☐ 10	Toni Kukoc	.50	.20
☐ 11	Randy Brown	.25	.08
☐ 12	Dickey Simpkins	.25	.08
☐ 13	Shawn Kemp	.50	.20
☐ 14	Zydrunas Ilgauskas	.50	.20
☐ 15	Brevin Knight	.25	.08
☐ 16	Michael Finley	.75	.30
☐ 17	Dirk Nowitzki	1.50	.60
☐ 18	Robert Pack	.25	.08
☐ 19	Antonio McDyess	.50	.20
☐ 20	Nick Van Exel	.75	.30
☐ 21	Ron Mercer	.50	.20
☐ 22	Grant Hill	.75	.30
☐ 23	Lindsey Hunter	.25	.08
☐ 24	Jerry Stackhouse	.75	.30
☐ 25	Antawn Jamison	1.25	.50
☐ 26	John Starks	.50	.20
☐ 27	Donyell Marshall	.50	.20
☐ 28	Hakeem Olajuwon	.75	.30
☐ 29	Charles Barkley	1.00	.40
☐ 30	Cuttino Mobley	.75	.30
☐ 31	Reggie Miller	.75	.30
☐ 32	Rik Smits	.50	.20
☐ 33	Jalen Rose	.75	.30
☐ 34	Maurice Taylor	.50	.20
☐ 35	Tyrone Nesby RC	.25	.08
☐ 36	Michael Olowokandi	.50	.20
☐ 37	Shaquille O'Neal	2.00	.75
☐ 38	Kobe Bryant	3.00	1.25
☐ 39	Glen Rice	.50	.20
☐ 40	P.J. Brown	.25	.08

❑ 41	Tim Hardaway	.50	.20
❑ 42	Alonzo Mourning	.50	.20
❑ 43	Jamal Mashburn	.50	.20
❑ 44	Glenn Robinson	.75	.30
❑ 45	Ray Allen	.75	.30
❑ 46	Tim Thomas	.50	.20
❑ 47	Kevin Garnett	1.50	.60
❑ 48	Joe Smith	.50	.20
❑ 49	Terrell Brandon	.50	.20
❑ 50	Stephon Marbury	.75	.30
❑ 51	Jayson Williams	.75	.30
❑ 52	Keith Van Horn	.75	.30
❑ 53	Latrell Sprewell	.75	.30
❑ 54	Allan Houston	.50	.20
❑ 55	Patrick Ewing	.75	.30
❑ 56	Marcus Camby	.50	.20
❑ 57	Darrell Armstrong	.25	.08
❑ 58	Bo Outlaw	.25	.08
❑ 59	Michael Doleac	.25	.08
❑ 60	Allen Iverson	1.50	.60
❑ 61	Theo Ratliff	.50	.20
❑ 62	Larry Hughes	.75	.30
❑ 63	Anfernee Hardaway	.75	.30
❑ 64	Jason Kidd	1.25	.50
❑ 65	Tom Gugliotta	.50	.20
❑ 66	Brian Grant	.50	.20
❑ 67	Damon Stoudamire	.50	.20
❑ 68	Rasheed Wallace	.75	.30
❑ 69	Jason Williams	.75	.30
❑ 70	Chris Webber	.75	.30
❑ 71	Vlade Divac	.50	.20
❑ 72	Tim Duncan	1.50	.60
❑ 73	David Robinson	.75	.30
❑ 74	Avery Johnson	.25	.08
❑ 75	Sean Elliott	.50	.20
❑ 76	Gary Payton	.75	.30
❑ 77	Vin Baker	.50	.20
❑ 78	Brent Barry	.50	.20
❑ 79	Vince Carter	2.00	.75
❑ 80	Tracy McGrady	2.00	.75
❑ 81	Doug Christie	.50	.20
❑ 82	Karl Malone	.75	.30
❑ 83	John Stockton	.75	.30
❑ 84	Bryon Russell	.25	.08
❑ 85	Shareef Abdur-Rahim	.75	.30
❑ 86	Mike Bibby	.75	.30
❑ 87	Felipe Lopez	.25	.08
❑ 88	Juwan Howard	.50	.20
❑ 89	Rod Strickland	.25	.08
❑ 90	Mitch Richmond	.50	.20
❑ 91	Elton Brand RC	3.00	1.25
❑ 92	Steve Francis RC	3.00	1.25
❑ 93	Baron Davis RC	5.00	2.00
❑ 94	Lamar Odom RC	2.50	1.00
❑ 95	Jonathan Bender RC	2.50	1.00
❑ 96	Wally Szczerbiak RC	2.50	1.00
❑ 97	Richard Hamilton RC	2.50	1.00
❑ 98	Andre Miller RC	2.50	1.00
❑ 99	Shawn Marion RC	3.00	1.25
❑ 100	Jason Terry RC	1.50	.60
❑ 101	Trajan Langdon RC	1.00	.40
❑ 102	A.Radojevic RC	.50	.20
❑ 103	Corey Maggette RC	2.50	1.00
❑ 104	William Avery RC	1.00	.40
❑ 105	Ron Artest RC	1.50	.60
❑ 106	Adrian Griffin RC	.75	.30
❑ 107	James Posey RC	.75	.30
❑ 108	Quincy Lewis RC	.75	.30
❑ 109	Dion Glover RC	.75	.30
❑ 110	Jeff Foster RC	.75	.30
❑ 111	Kenny Thomas RC	1.00	.40
❑ 112	Devean George RC	1.25	.50
❑ 113	Tim James RC	.75	.30
❑ 114	Vonteego Cummings RC	1.00	.40
❑ 115	Jumaine Jones RC	1.25	.50
❑ 116	Scott Padgett RC	.75	.30
❑ 117	Obinna Ekezie RC	.60	.25
❑ 118	Ryan Robertson RC	.60	.25
❑ 119	Chucky Atkins RC	1.00	.40
❑ 120	A.J. Bramlett RC	.50	.20

2000-01 Black Diamond

❑ COMP.SET w/o SP's (90)	20.00	8.00
❑ COMMON CARD (1-90)	.25	.08
❑ COMMON GEM (91-100)	3.00	1.25
❑ COMMON GEM (101-110)	4.00	1.50

❑ COMMON GEM (111-120)		4.00	1.50
❑ COMMON JSY (121-126)		8.00	3.00
❑ COMMON JSY (127-132)		10.00	4.00
❑ 1	Dikembe Mutombo	.50	.20
❑ 2	Alan Henderson	.25	.08
❑ 3	Jason Terry	.75	.30
❑ 4	Paul Pierce	.75	.30
❑ 5	Antoine Walker	.75	.30
❑ 6	Kenny Anderson	.50	.20
❑ 7	Jamal Mashburn	.50	.20
❑ 8	Derrick Coleman	.25	.08
❑ 9	Baron Davis	.75	.30
❑ 10	Elton Brand	.75	.30
❑ 11	Ron Artest	.50	.20
❑ 12	Ron Mercer	.50	.20
❑ 13	Lamond Murray	.25	.08
❑ 14	Andre Miller	.50	.20
❑ 15	Matt Harpring	.75	.30
❑ 16	Michael Finley	.75	.30
❑ 17	Dirk Nowitzki	1.25	.50
❑ 18	Steve Nash	.75	.30
❑ 19	Antonio McDyess	.50	.20
❑ 20	Nick Van Exel	.75	.30
❑ 21	Raef LaFrentz	.50	.20
❑ 22	Jerry Stackhouse	.75	.30
❑ 23	Joe Smith	.50	.20
❑ 24	Chucky Atkins	.25	.08
❑ 25	Antawn Jamison	.75	.30
❑ 26	Larry Hughes	.75	.30
❑ 27	Chris Mills	.25	.08
❑ 28	Steve Francis	.75	.30
❑ 29	Hakeem Olajuwon	.75	.30
❑ 30	Cuttino Mobley	.50	.20
❑ 31	Reggie Miller	.75	.30
❑ 32	Jalen Rose	.75	.30
❑ 33	Jermaine O'Neal	.75	.30
❑ 34	Austin Croshere	.50	.20
❑ 35	Lamar Odom	.75	.30
❑ 36	Corey Maggette	.50	.20
❑ 37	Jeff McInnis	.25	.08
❑ 38	Kobe Bryant	3.00	1.25
❑ 39	Shaquille O'Neal	2.00	.75
❑ 40	Ron Harper	.50	.20
❑ 41	Isaiah Rider	.50	.20
❑ 42	Eddie Jones	.75	.30
❑ 43	Tim Hardaway	.50	.20
❑ 44	Brian Grant	.50	.20
❑ 45	Glenn Robinson	.75	.30
❑ 46	Sam Cassell	.75	.30
❑ 47	Ray Allen	.75	.30
❑ 48	Kevin Garnett	1.50	.60
❑ 49	Terrell Brandon	.50	.20
❑ 50	Wally Szczerbiak	.50	.20
❑ 51	Stephon Marbury	.75	.30
❑ 52	Keith Van Horn	.75	.30
❑ 53	Kendall Gill	.25	.08
❑ 54	Latrell Sprewell	.75	.30
❑ 55	Allan Houston	.50	.20
❑ 56	Marcus Camby	.50	.20
❑ 57	Grant Hill	.75	.30
❑ 58	Tracy McGrady	2.00	.75
❑ 59	Darrell Armstrong	.25	.08
❑ 60	Allen Iverson	1.50	.60
❑ 61	Toni Kukoc	.50	.20
❑ 62	Theo Ratliff	.50	.20
❑ 63	Jason Kidd	1.25	.50
❑ 64	Shawn Marion	.75	.30
❑ 65	Anfernee Hardaway	.75	.30

❑ 66	Scottie Pippen	1.25	.50
❑ 67	Rasheed Wallace	.75	.30
❑ 68	Damon Stoudamire	.50	.20
❑ 69	Steve Smith	.50	.20
❑ 70	Chris Webber	.75	.30
❑ 71	Jason Williams	.50	.20
❑ 72	Peja Stojakovic	.75	.30
❑ 73	Tim Duncan	1.50	.60
❑ 74	David Robinson	.75	.30
❑ 75	Derek Anderson	.50	.20
❑ 76	Gary Payton	.75	.30
❑ 77	Patrick Ewing	.75	.30
❑ 78	Rashard Lewis	.50	.20
❑ 79	Vince Carter	2.00	.75
❑ 80	Mark Jackson	.25	.08
❑ 81	Antonio Davis	.25	.08
❑ 82	Karl Malone	.75	.30
❑ 83	John Stockton	.75	.30
❑ 84	Bryon Russell	.25	.08
❑ 85	Shareef Abdur-Rahim	.75	.30
❑ 86	Michael Dickerson	.50	.20
❑ 87	Mike Bibby	.75	.30
❑ 88	Mitch Richmond	.50	.20
❑ 89	Richard Hamilton	.50	.20
❑ 90	Juwan Howard	.50	.20
❑ 91	Eduardo Najera RC	4.00	1.50
❑ 92	Eddie House RC	3.00	1.25
❑ 93	Michael Redd RC	5.00	2.00
❑ 94	Ruben Wolkowyski RC	3.00	1.25
❑ 95	Dan Langhi RC	3.00	1.25
❑ 96	Mark Madsen RC	3.00	1.25
❑ 97	Speedy Claxton RC	3.00	1.25
❑ 98	Iakovos Tsakalidis RC	3.00	1.25
❑ 99	Dragan Tarlac RC	3.00	1.25
❑ 100	Donnell Harvey RC	3.00	1.25
❑ 101	Etan Thomas RC	4.00	1.50
❑ 102	Hidayet Turkoglu RC	6.00	2.50
❑ 103	Mike Penberthy RC	4.00	1.50
❑ 104	Paul McPherson RC	4.00	1.50
❑ 105	Jason Collier RC	6.00	2.50
❑ 106	Hanno Mottola RC	4.00	1.50
❑ 107	A.J. Guyton RC	4.00	1.50
❑ 108	Daniel Santiago RC	4.00	1.50
❑ 109	Lavor Postell RC	4.00	1.50
❑ 110	Erick Barkley RC	4.00	1.50
❑ 111	Chris Porter RC	4.00	1.50
❑ 112	Mateen Cleaves RC	4.00	1.50
❑ 113	Marc Jackson RC	4.00	1.50
❑ 114	Joel Przybilla RC	4.00	1.50
❑ 115	Courtney Alexander RC	4.00	1.50
❑ 116	Khalid El-Amin RC	4.00	1.50
❑ 117	Keyon Dooling RC	4.00	1.50
❑ 118	Desmond Mason RC	4.00	1.50
❑ 119	Stephen Jackson RC	5.00	2.00
❑ 120	Morris Peterson RC	6.00	2.50
❑ 121	Jerome Moiso JSY RC	8.00	3.00
❑ 122	Jamal Crawford JSY RC	12.00	5.00
❑ 123	DeShawn Stevenson JSY RC	8.00	3.00
❑ 124	Quentin Richardson JSY RC	12.00	5.00
❑ 125	Marcus Fizer JSY RC	8.00	3.00
❑ 126	Mike Miller JSY RC	12.00	5.00
❑ 127	Jamaal Magloire JSY RC	10.00	4.00
❑ 128	Chris Mihm JSY RC	10.00	4.00
❑ 129	DerMarr Johnson JSY RC	10.00	4.00
❑ 130	Stromile Swift JSY RC	10.00	4.00
❑ 131	Darius Miles JSY RC	15.00	6.00
❑ 132	Kenyon Martin JSY RC	20.00	8.00

2003-04 Black Diamond

❑ COMMON CARD (1-84)	.20	.08
❑ COMMON CARD (85-117)	.25	.10
❑ COMMON ROOKIE (118-126)	3.00	1.25
❑ COMMON CARD (127-147)	2.00	.75
❑ COMMON ROOKIE (148-168)	4.00	1.50
❑ COMMON CARD (169-183)	8.00	3.00
❑ COMMON ROOKIE (184-198)	10.00	4.00
KORVER AND KITTLES HAVE 2 CARDS		
❑ 1 Carlos Boozer	.60	.25
❑ 2 Dajuan Wagner	.40	.15
❑ 3 Steve Francis	.60	.25
❑ 4 Michael Finley	.60	.25
❑ 5 Jalen Rose	.60	.25
❑ 6 Kenyon Martin	.50	.20
❑ 7 Quentin Richardson	.40	.15
❑ 8 Antoine Walker	.60	.25
❑ 9 Drew Gooden	.40	.15

☐ 10 Mike Bibby	.60	.25
☐ 11 Zydrunas Ilgauskas	.40	.15
☐ 12 Dan Dickau	.20	.08
☐ 13 Steve Nash	.60	.25
☐ 14 Eduardo Najera	.40	.15
☐ 15 Joe Smith	.40	.15
☐ 16 Pau Gasol	.60	.25
☐ 17 Anthony Mason	.20	.08
☐ 18 Lamar Odom	.60	.25
☐ 19 Sam Cassell	.60	.25
☐ 20 Marko Jaric	.40	.15
☐ 21 Marcus Fizer	.40	.15
☐ 22 Jay Williams	.60	.25
☐ 23 Jason Richardson	.60	.25
☐ 24 Richard Jefferson	.40	.15
☐ 25 Gerald Wallace	.20	.08
☐ 26 Reggie Evans	.20	.08
☐ 27 Jerome Williams	.20	.08
☐ 28 Grant Hill	.60	.25
☐ 29 Darrell Armstrong	.20	.08
☐ 30 Rasheed Wallace	.40	.15
☐ 31 Shane Battier	.60	.25
☐ 32 Richard Hamilton	.40	.15
☐ 33 Antonio Davis	.20	.08
☐ 34 Ray Allen	.60	.25
☐ 35 Terrell Brandon	.20	.08
☐ 36 Tim Thomas	.40	.15
☐ 37 Al Harrington	.40	.15
☐ 38 Brian Grant	.40	.15
☐ 39 Zeljko Rebraca	.20	.08
☐ 40 Kerry Kittles	.40	.15
☐ 41 Maurice Taylor	.20	.08
☐ 42 Jerry Stackhouse	.60	.25
☐ 43 Nikoloz Tskitishvili	.20	.08
☐ 44 Derrick Coleman	.40	.15
☐ 45 Raef LaFrentz	.40	.15
☐ 46 Dale Davis	.20	.08
☐ 47 Andrei Kirilenko	.60	.25
☐ 48 Melvin Ely	.20	.08
☐ 49 Speedy Claxton	.20	.08
☐ 50 Mike Miller	.60	.25
☐ 51 Scot Pollard	.20	.08
☐ 52 Popeye Jones	.20	.08
☐ 53 Wesley Person	.20	.08
☐ 54 Chris Wilcox	.40	.15
☐ 55 Dikembe Mutombo	.40	.15
☐ 56 Toni Kukoc	.40	.15
☐ 57 Eddie Griffin	.20	.08
☐ 58 Kedrick Brown	.20	.08
☐ 59 Eddie Jones	.60	.25
☐ 60 Jon Barry	.20	.08
☐ 61 Jonathan Bender	.40	.15
☐ 62 Larry Hughes	.40	.15
☐ 63 Rodney White	.20	.08
☐ 64 Eddy Curry	.40	.15
☐ 65 Theo Ratliff	.40	.15
☐ 66 Jamaal Tinsley	.60	.25
☐ 67 Zach Randolph	.60	.25
☐ 68 Alvin Williams	.20	.08
☐ 69 Derek Fisher	.60	.25
☐ 70 Vin Baker	.40	.15
☐ 71 Juan Dixon	.40	.15
☐ 72 Devean George	.40	.15
☐ 73 Damon Stoudamire	.40	.15
☐ 74 Joe Johnson	.20	.08
☐ 75 Jared Jeffries	.20	.08
☐ 76 Cuttino Mobley	.40	.15
☐ 77 Vladimir Radmanovic	.20	.08

☐ 78 Ron Mercer	.20	.08
☐ 79 Kenny Thomas	.20	.08
☐ 80 Nazr Mohammed	.20	.08
☐ 81 Donyell Marshall	.60	.25
☐ 82 Lorenzen Wright	.20	.08
☐ 83 Nick Van Exel	.60	.25
☐ 84 Jason Terry	.60	.25
☐ 85 Ben Wallace	1.00	.40
☐ 86 Glenn Robinson	1.00	.40
☐ 87 Gilbert Arenas	1.00	.40
☐ 88 Caron Butler	1.00	.40
☐ 89 Marcus Camby	.40	.15
☐ 90 Jason Kidd	1.50	.60
☐ 91 Antawn Jamison	1.00	.40
☐ 92 Rashard Lewis	1.00	.40
☐ 93 Juwan Howard	.60	.25
☐ 94 Andre Miller	.60	.25
☐ 95 Hedo Turkoglu	1.00	.40
☐ 96 Jason Williams	.60	.25
☐ 97 Chauncey Billups	.60	.25
☐ 98 P.J. Brown	.25	.10
☐ 99 Tyson Chandler	1.00	.40
☐ 100 Jamal Mashburn	.60	.25
☐ 101 Bonzi Wells	.60	.25
☐ 102 Brad Miller	1.00	.40
☐ 103 Gordan Giricek	.60	.25
☐ 104 Nene	.60	.25
☐ 105 Mike Dunleavy	.60	.25
☐ 106 Kerry Kittles	.25	.10
☐ 107 Jamaal Magloire	.25	.10
☐ 108 Desmond Mason	.60	.25
☐ 109 Corey Maggette	.60	.25
☐ 110 Michael Olowokandi	.25	.10
☐ 111 Tayshaun Prince	.60	.25
☐ 112 Earl Boykins	.60	.25
☐ 113 Allan Houston	.60	.25
☐ 114 Morris Peterson	.60	.25
☐ 115 Ricky Davis	1.00	.40
☐ 116 Keith Van Horn	1.00	.40
☐ 117 Shareef Abdur-Rahim	1.00	.40
☐ 118 Willie Green RC	3.00	1.25
☐ 119 Kyle Korver RC	5.00	2.00
☐ 120 Brandon Hunter RC	3.00	1.25
☐ 121 Keith Bogans RC	3.00	1.25
☐ 122 Maurice Williams RC	3.00	1.25
☐ 123 James Lang RC	3.00	1.25
☐ 124 Zaur Pachulia RC	3.00	1.25
☐ 125 Slavko Vranes RC	3.00	1.25
☐ 126 Theron Smith RC	3.00	1.25
☐ 127 Paul Pierce	2.00	.75
☐ 128 Alonzo Mourning	2.00	.75
☐ 129 Elton Brand	2.00	.75
☐ 130 Manu Ginobili	2.00	.75
☐ 131 Peja Stojakovic	2.00	.75
☐ 132 Latrell Sprewell	2.00	.75
☐ 133 Baron Davis	2.00	.75
☐ 134 Stephon Marbury	2.00	.75
☐ 135 Darius Miles	2.00	.75
☐ 136 Antonio McDyess	2.00	.75
☐ 137 Jermaine O'Neal	2.00	.75
☐ 138 Scottie Pippen	3.00	1.25
☐ 139 Wally Szczerbiak	2.00	.75
☐ 140 Chris Webber	2.00	.75
☐ 141 Reggie Miller	2.00	.75
☐ 142 Tony Parker	2.00	.75
☐ 143 Karl Malone	2.00	.75
☐ 144 David Robinson	2.00	.75
☐ 145 Matt Harpring	2.00	.75
☐ 146 Shawn Marion	2.00	.75
☐ 147 Tim Duncan	4.00	1.50
☐ 148 Dwyane Wade RC	15.00	6.00
☐ 149 Chris Kaman RC	4.00	1.50
☐ 150 Chris Bosh RC	10.00	4.00
☐ 151 Mickael Pietrus RC	4.00	1.50
☐ 152 Boris Diaw RC	5.00	2.00
☐ 153 Marcus Banks RC	4.00	1.50
☐ 154 Troy Bell RC	4.00	1.50
☐ 155 Zarko Cabarkapa RC	4.00	1.50
☐ 156 David West RC	4.00	1.50
☐ 157 Zoran Planinic RC	4.00	1.50
☐ 158 Aleksandar Pavlovic RC	5.00	2.00
☐ 159 Jerome Beasley RC	4.00	1.50
☐ 160 Kyle Korver	6.00	2.50
☐ 161 Travis Hansen RC	4.00	1.50
☐ 162 Steve Blake RC	4.00	1.50
☐ 163 Leandro Barbosa RC	6.00	2.50

☐ 164 Kendrick Perkins RC	4.00	1.50
☐ 165 Kirk Penney RC	4.00	1.50
☐ 166 Maciej Lampe RC	4.00	1.50
☐ 167 Jason Kapono RC	4.00	1.50
☐ 168 Luke Walton RC	4.00	1.50
☐ 169 Gary Payton	8.00	3.00
☐ 170 Wilt Chamberlain	10.00	4.00
☐ 171 Tracy McGrady	10.00	4.00
☐ 172 Amare Stoudemire	8.00	3.00
☐ 173 Vince Carter	10.00	4.00
☐ 174 Shaquille O'Neal	10.00	4.00
☐ 175 Larry Bird	20.00	8.00
☐ 176 Julius Erving	10.00	4.00
☐ 177 Magic Johnson	10.00	4.00
☐ 178 Dirk Nowitzki	8.00	3.00
☐ 179 Yao Ming	10.00	4.00
☐ 180 Allen Iverson	10.00	4.00
☐ 181 Kevin Garnett	10.00	4.00
☐ 182 Kobe Bryant	15.00	6.00
☐ 183 Michael Jordan	25.00	10.00
☐ 184 LeBron James RC	80.00	40.00
☐ 185 Darko Milicic RC	10.00	4.00
☐ 186 Carmelo Anthony RC	30.00	12.50
☐ 187 T.J. Ford RC	10.00	4.00
☐ 188 Mike Sweetney RC	10.00	4.00
☐ 189 Kirk Hinrich RC	12.00	5.00
☐ 190 Nick Collison RC	10.00	4.00
☐ 191 Travis Outlaw RC	10.00	4.00
☐ 192 Jarvis Hayes RC	10.00	4.00
☐ 193 Luke Ridnour RC	10.00	4.00
☐ 194 Reece Gaines RC	10.00	4.00
☐ 195 Ndudi Ebi RC	10.00	4.00
☐ 196 Dahntay Jones RC	10.00	4.00
☐ 197 Brian Cook RC	10.00	4.00
☐ 198 Josh Howard RC	15.00	6.00

2004-05 Black Diamond

☐ COMP.SET w/o SP's (84)	20.00	8.00
☐ COMMON SINGLE (1-84)	.20	.08
☐ COMMON DOUBLE (85-126)	1.00	.40
☐ COMMON TRIPLE (127-147)	2.50	1.00
☐ COMMON QUAD (148-162)	8.00	3.00
☐ COMMON RC TRIPLE (163-183)	6.00	2.50
☐ COMMON RC QUAD (184-198)	10.00	4.00
☐ 1 Tony Delk	.20	.08
☐ 2 Boris Diaw	.20	.08
☐ 3 Chris Crawford	.20	.08
☐ 4 Ricky Davis	.75	.30
☐ 5 Jiri Welsch	.50	.20
☐ 6 Raef LaFrentz	.50	.20
☐ 7 Jason Kapono	.50	.20
☐ 8 Brevin Knight	.20	.08
☐ 9 Bernard Robinson RC	3.00	1.25
☐ 10 Jahidi White	.20	.08
☐ 11 Tyson Chandler	.75	.30
☐ 12 Antonio Davis	.50	.20
☐ 13 Andres Nocioni RC	4.00	1.40
☐ 14 Dajuan Wagner	.50	.20
☐ 15 Zydrunas Ilgauskas	.50	.20
☐ 16 Jeff McInnis	.20	.08
☐ 17 Josh Howard	.75	.30
☐ 18 Marquis Daniels	.75	.30
☐ 19 Jason Terry	.75	.30
☐ 20 Andre Miller	.50	.20
☐ 21 Earl Boykins	.50	.20
☐ 22 Carlos Delfino	.20	.08
☐ 23 Ben Wallace	.75	.30
☐ 24 Tayshaun Prince	.50	.20

25	Mickael Pietrus	.50	.20
26	Mike Dunleavy	.50	.20
27	Speedy Claxton	.20	.20
28	Jim Jackson	.20	.08
29	Juwan Howard	.50	.20
30	Maurice Taylor	.20	.08
31	Tyronn Lue	.20	.08
32	Jamaal Tinsley	.75	.30
33	Stephen Jackson	.20	.08
34	Fred Jones	.20	.08
35	Kerry Kittles	.20	.08
36	Marko Jaric	.50	.20
37	Chris Kaman	.50	.20
38	Caron Butler	.50	.20
39	Kareem Rush	.50	.20
40	Mike Miller	.50	.20
41	James Posey	.50	.20
42	Stromile Swift	.50	.20
43	Eddie Jones	.75	.30
44	Udonis Haslem	.20	.08
45	Matt Freije RC	3.00	1.25
46	T.J. Ford	3.00	1.25
47	Toni Kukoc	.50	.20
48	Joe Smith	.50	.20
49	Michael Olowokandi	.50	.20
50	Wally Szczerbiak	.50	.20
51	Troy Hudson	.20	.08
52	Aaron Williams	.20	.08
53	Alonzo Mourning	.75	.30
54	Nenad Krstic RC	4.00	1.50
55	Jamal Mashburn	.50	.20
56	David Wesley	.20	.08
57	Tim Pickett RC	3.00	1.25
58	Trevor Ariza RC	4.00	1.50
59	Tim Thomas	.50	.20
60	Grant Hill	.75	.30
61	Hedo Turkoglu	.75	.30
62	Kelvin Cato	.20	.08
63	Kenny Thomas	.50	.20
64	Aaron McKie	.50	.20
65	Joe Johnson	.50	.20
66	Quentin Richardson	.50	.20
67	Damon Stoudamire	.50	.20
68	Derek Anderson	.50	.20
69	Nick Van Exel	.75	.30
70	Doug Christie	.50	.20
71	Bobby Jackson	.75	.30
72	Malik Rose	.20	.08
73	Rasho Nesterovic	.50	.20
74	Romain Sato RC	3.00	1.25
75	Ronald Murray	.20	.08
76	Luke Ridnour	.50	.20
77	Pape Sow RC	3.00	1.25
78	Rafer Alston	.20	.08
79	Morris Peterson	.50	.20
80	Matt Harpring	.75	.30
81	Mehmet Okur	.20	.08
82	Larry Hughes	.50	.20
83	Jarvis Hayes	.50	.20
84	Kwame Brown	.50	.20
85	Antoine Walker	1.00	.40
86	Al Harrington	1.00	.40
87	Gary Payton	1.00	.40
88	Gerald Wallace	1.00	.40
89	Eddy Curry	1.00	.40
90	Kirk Hinrich	1.00	.40
91	Drew Gooden	1.00	.40
92	Michael Finley	1.00	.40
93	Jerry Stackhouse	1.00	.40
94	Kenyon Martin	1.00	.40
95	Nene	1.00	.40
96	Chauncey Billups	1.00	.40
97	Richard Hamilton	1.00	.40
98	Derek Fisher	1.00	.40
99	Reggie Miller	1.00	.40
100	Ron Artest	1.00	.40
101	Corey Maggette	1.00	.40
102	Lamar Odom	1.00	.40
103	Karl Malone	1.00	.40
104	Jason Williams	1.00	.40
105	Bonzi Wells	1.00	.40
106	Desmond Mason	1.00	.40
107	Sam Cassell	1.00	.40
108	Jamaal Magloire	1.00	.40
109	Jamal Crawford	1.00	.40
110	Allan Houston	1.00	.40
111	Cuttino Mobley	1.00	.40
112	Glenn Robinson	1.00	.40
113	Shawn Marion	1.00	.40
114	Darius Miles	1.00	.40
115	Zach Randolph	1.00	.40
116	Chris Webber	1.00	.40
117	Mike Bibby	1.00	.40
118	Brad Miller	1.00	.40
119	Manu Ginobili	1.00	.40
120	Rashard Lewis	1.00	.40
121	Jalen Rose	1.00	.40
122	Chris Bosh	1.00	.40
123	Carlos Boozer	1.00	.40
124	Carlos Arroyo	1.50	.60
125	Gilbert Arenas	1.00	.40
126	Antawn Jamison	1.00	.40
127	Paul Pierce	2.50	1.00
128	Dirk Nowitzki	4.00	1.50
129	Rasheed Wallace	2.50	1.00
130	Jason Richardson	2.50	1.00
131	Jermaine O'Neal	2.50	1.00
132	Elton Brand	2.50	1.00
133	Pau Gasol	2.50	1.00
134	Dwyane Wade	8.00	3.00
135	Michael Redd	2.50	1.00
136	Latrell Sprewell	2.50	1.00
137	Richard Jefferson	2.50	1.00
138	Baron Davis	2.50	1.00
139	Stephon Marbury	2.50	1.00
140	Steve Francis	2.50	1.00
141	Steve Nash	2.50	1.00
142	Shareef Abdur-Rahim	2.50	1.00
143	Peja Stojakovic	2.50	1.00
144	Tony Parker	2.50	1.00
145	Ray Allen	2.50	1.00
146	Vince Carter	2.50	1.00
147	Andrei Kirilenko	2.50	1.00
148	Larry Bird	20.00	8.00
149	Michael Jordan	25.00	10.00
150	LeBron James	8.00	3.00
151	Carmelo Anthony	8.00	3.00
152	Tracy McGrady	10.00	4.00
153	Yao Ming	10.00	4.00
154	Kobe Bryant	15.00	6.00
155	Magic Johnson	12.00	5.00
156	Shaquille O'Neal	10.00	4.00
157	Kevin Garnett	8.00	3.00
158	Jason Kidd	8.00	3.00
159	Allen Iverson	8.00	3.00
160	Julius Erving	10.00	4.00
161	Amare Stoudemire	8.00	3.00
162	Tim Duncan	8.00	3.00
163	Andris Biedrins RC	10.00	4.00
164	Robert Swift RC	6.00	2.50
165	Al Jefferson RC	12.00	5.00
166	Kirk Snyder RC	6.00	2.50
167	Dorell Wright RC	10.00	4.00
168	Pavel Podkolzine RC	6.00	2.50
169	Viktor Khryapa RC	6.00	2.50
170	Delonte West RC	6.00	2.50
171	Tony Allen RC	6.00	2.50
172	Kevin Martin RC	8.00	3.00
173	Sasha Vujacic RC	6.00	2.50
174	Beno Udrih RC	8.00	3.00
175	David Harrison RC	6.00	2.50
176	Anderson Varejao RC	8.00	3.00
177	Jackson Vroman RC	6.00	2.50
178	Peter John Ramos RC	6.00	2.50
179	Lionel Chalmers RC	6.00	2.50
180	Andre Emmett RC	6.00	2.50
181	Yuta Tabuse RC	10.00	4.00
182	Trevor Ariza RC	6.00	2.50
183	Chris Duhon RC	6.00	2.50
184	Dwight Howard RC	25.00	10.00
185	Emeka Okafor RC	30.00	12.50
186	Ben Gordon RC	30.00	12.50
187	Shaun Livingston RC	12.00	5.00
188	Devin Harris RC	12.00	5.00
189	Josh Childress RC	10.00	4.00
190	Luol Deng RC	15.00	6.00
191	Andre Iguodala RC	20.00	8.00
192	Luke Jackson RC	10.00	4.00
193	Sebastian Telfair RC	8.00	3.00
194	Kris Humphries RC	10.00	4.00
195	Josh Smith RC	15.00	6.00
196	J.R. Smith RC	15.00	6.00
197	Jameer Nelson RC	12.00	5.00
198	Rafael Araujo RC	10.00	4.00

1948 Bowman

	COMPLETE SET (72)	8000.00	6000.00
	COMMON CARD (1-36)	60.00	40.00
	COMMON CARD (37-72)	90.00	60.00
1	Ernie Calverley RC !	150.00	75.00
2	Ralph Hamilton	60.00	40.00
3	Gale Bishop	60.00	40.00
4	Fred Lewis RC	75.00	50.00
5	Basketball Play	50.00	30.00
6	Bob Feerick RC	75.00	50.00
7	John Logan	60.00	40.00
8	Mel Riebe	60.00	40.00
9	Andy Phillip RC	100.00	50.00
10	Bob Davies RC !	100.00	50.00
11	Basketball Play	50.00	30.00
12	Kenny Sailors RC	60.00	40.00
13	Paul Armstrong	60.00	40.00
14	Howard Dallmar RC	75.00	50.00
15	Bruce Hale RC	75.00	50.00
16	Sid Hertzberg	60.00	40.00
17	Basketball Play	50.00	30.00
18	Red Rocha	60.00	40.00
19	Eddie Ehlers	60.00	40.00
20	Ellis(Gene) Vance	60.00	40.00
21	Fuzzy Levane RC	75.00	50.00
22	Earl Shannon	60.00	40.00
23	Basketball Play	50.00	30.00
24	Leo(Crystal) Klier	60.00	40.00
25	George Senesky	60.00	40.00
26	Price Brookfield	60.00	40.00
27	John Norlander	60.00	40.00
28	Don Putman	60.00	40.00
29	Basketball Play	50.00	30.00
30	Jack Garfinkel	60.00	40.00
31	Chuck Gilmur	60.00	40.00
32	Red Holzman RC !	225.00	125.00
33	Jack Smiley	60.00	40.00
34	Joe Fulks RC !	150.00	90.00
35	Basketball Play	50.00	30.00
36	Hal Tidrick	60.00	40.00
37	Don(Swede) Carlson	90.00	60.00
38	Buddy Jeanette RC CO	135.00	80.00
39	Ray Kuka	90.00	60.00
40	Stan Miasek	90.00	60.00
41	Basketball Play	75.00	50.00
42	George Nostrand	90.00	60.00
43	Chuck Halbert RC	125.00	75.00
44	Arnie Johnson	90.00	60.00
45	Bob Doll	90.00	60.00
46	Bones McKinney RC	135.00	80.00
47	Basketball Play	75.00	50.00
48	Ed Sadowski	125.00	75.00
49	Bob Kinney	90.00	60.00
50	Charles(Hawk) Black	90.00	60.00
51	Jack Dwan	75.00	50.00
52	Connie Simmons RC	125.00	75.00
53	Basketball Play	50.00	30.00
54	Bud Palmer RC	150.00	100.00
55	Max Zaslofsky RC !	200.00	125.00
56	Lee Roy Robbins	90.00	60.00
57	Arthur Spector	90.00	60.00
58	Arnie Risen RC	150.00	90.00
59	Basketball Play	75.00	50.00
60	Ariel Maughan	90.00	60.00
61	Dick O'Keefe	90.00	60.00
62	Herman Schaefer	90.00	60.00
63	John Mahnken	90.00	60.00

#	Player		
❏ 64	Tommy Byrnes	90.00	60.00
❏ 65	Basketball Play	75.00	50.00
❏ 66	Jim Pollard RC !	250.00	125.00
❏ 67	. Lee Mogus	90.00	60.00
❏ 68	Lee Knorek	90.00	60.00
❏ 69	George Mikan RC !	2250.00	1500.00
❏ 70	Walter Budko	90.00	60.00
❏ 71	Basketball Play	75.00	50.00
❏ 72	Carl Braun RC !	400.00	200.00

2003-04 Bowman

#	Player		
❏	COMP.SET w/o RC's (110)	40.00	15.00
❏	COMMON CARD (1-110)	.20	.08
❏	COMMON ROOKIE (111-146)	4.00	1.50
❏	COMMON AU RC (148-156)	40.00	15.00
❏	CARD 147 NOT RELEASED		
❏ 1	Yao Ming	2.00	.75
❏ 2	Glenn Robinson	.75	.30
❏ 3	Antoine Walker	.75	.30
❏ 4	Jalen Rose	.75	.30
❏ 5	Ricky Davis	.75	.30
❏ 6	Juwan Howard	.50	.20
❏ 7	Kwame Brown	.50	.20
❏ 8	Mike Bibby	.75	.30
❏ 9	Wally Szczerbiak	.50	.20
❏ 10	Allen Iverson	1.50	.60
❏ 11	Shareef Abdur-Rahim	.75	.30
❏ 12	Jamal Mashburn	.50	.20
❏ 13	Stephon Marbury	.75	.30
❏ 14	Desmond Mason	.50	.20
❏ 15	Gordan Giricek	.50	.20
❏ 16	Caron Butler	.75	.30
❏ 17	Jermaine O'Neal	.75	.30
❏ 18	Kenyon Martin	.75	.30
❏ 19	Andrei Kirilenko	.75	.30
❏ 20	Dirk Nowitzki	1.25	.50
❏ 21	Richard Hamilton	.50	.20
❏ 22	Troy Murphy	.75	.30
❏ 23	Shawn Marion	.75	.30
❏ 24	Allan Houston	.50	.20
❏ 25	Keith Van Horn	.50	.20
❏ 26	Brian Grant	.50	.20
❏ 27	Mike Miller	.50	.20
❏ 28	Chris Webber	.75	.30
❏ 29	Brent Barry	.50	.20
❏ 30	Elton Brand	.75	.30
❏ 31	Juan Dixon	.75	.30
❏ 32	Karl Malone	.75	.30
❏ 33	Darrell Armstrong	.20	.08
❏ 34	Rasheed Wallace	.75	.30
❏ 35	Michael Redd	.75	.30
❏ 36	Rashard Lewis	.50	.20
❏ 37	Ron Artest	.50	.20
❏ 38	P.J. Brown	.20	.08
❏ 39	Eddie Griffin	.50	.20
❏ 40	Tim Duncan	1.50	.60
❏ 41	Kurt Thomas	.50	.20
❏ 42	Raef Lafrentz	.20	.08
❏ 43	Ben Wallace	.75	.30
❏ 44	Lamar Odom	.75	.30
❏ 45	Vince Carter	2.00	.75
❏ 46	Derek Anderson	.50	.20
❏ 47	Stromile Swift	.50	.20
❏ 48	Bobby Jackson	.50	.20
❏ 49	Richard Jefferson	.50	.20
❏ 50	Shaquille O'Neal	2.00	.75
❏ 51	Calbert Cheaney	.20	.08
❏ 52	Troy Hudson	.20	.08
❏ 53	Ray Allen	.75	.30
❏ 54	Howard Eisley	.20	.08
❏ 55	Alonzo Mourning	.50	.20
❏ 56	Sam Cassell	.75	.30
❏ 57	Derrick Coleman	.20	.08
❏ 58	Andre Miller	.50	.20
❏ 59	Antawn Jamison	.75	.30
❏ 60	Kevin Garnett	1.50	.60
❏ 61	Steve Francis	.75	.30
❏ 62	Tyson Chandler	.75	.30
❏ 63	Drew Gooden	.50	.20
❏ 64	Scottie Pippen	1.25	.50
❏ 65	Pau Gasol	.75	.30
❏ 66	Steve Nash	.75	.30
❏ 67	DaJuan Wagner	.50	.20
❏ 68	Jason Terry	.75	.30
❏ 69	Reggie Miller	.75	.30
❏ 70	Tracy McGrady	2.00	.75
❏ 71	Nene Hilario	.50	.20
❏ 72	Morris Peterson	.50	.20
❏ 73	Peja Stojakovic	.75	.30
❏ 74	Eddie Jones	.75	.30
❏ 75	Tony Parker	.75	.30
❏ 76	Corliss Williamson	.50	.20
❏ 77	Vladimir Radmanovic	.20	.08
❏ 78	Amare Stoudemire	1.50	.60
❏ 79	Tony Delk	.20	.08
❏ 80	Jason Kidd	1.25	.50
❏ 81	Gary Payton	.75	.30
❏ 82	Corey Maggette	.75	.30
❏ 83	Darius Miles	.75	.30
❏ 84	Cuttino Mobley	.50	.20
❏ 85	Eric Snow	.50	.20
❏ 86	Matt Harpring	.75	.30
❏ 87	Manu Ginobili	.75	.30
❏ 88	Latrell Sprewell	.75	.30
❏ 89	Alvin Williams	.20	.08
❏ 90	Paul Pierce	.75	.30
❏ 91	Anfernee Hardaway	.75	.30
❏ 92	Gilbert Arenas	.75	.30
❏ 93	Jerry Stackhouse	.75	.30
❏ 94	Tim Thomas	.50	.20
❏ 95	Nikoloz Tskitishvili	.20	.08
❏ 96	Doug Christie	.50	.20
❏ 97	Zydrunas Ilgauskas	.50	.20
❏ 98	Jamaal Tinsley	.75	.30
❏ 99	Theo Ratliff	.50	.20
❏ 100	Kobe Bryant	3.00	1.25
❏ 101	Chauncey Billups	.50	.20
❏ 102	Michael Finley	.75	.30
❏ 103	Jason Williams	.50	.20
❏ 104	Bonzi Wells	.50	.20
❏ 105	Voshon Lenard	.20	.08
❏ 106	Jason Richardson	.75	.30
❏ 107	Baron Davis	.75	.30
❏ 108	Radoslav Nesterovic	.50	.20
❏ 109	Eddy Curry	.50	.20
❏ 110	Michael Olowokandi	.20	.08
❏ 111	Josh Howard RC	6.00	2.50
❏ 112	Mario Austin RC	4.00	1.50
❏ 113	Rick Rickert RC	4.00	1.50
❏ 114	Tommy Smith RC	4.00	1.50
❏ 115	Dahntay Jones RC	4.00	1.50
❏ 116	Ndudi Ebi RC	4.00	1.50
❏ 117	Maurice Williams RC	4.00	1.50
❏ 118	Kendrick Perkins RC	4.00	1.50
❏ 119	Steve Blake RC	4.00	1.50
❏ 120	David West RC	4.00	1.50
❏ 121	Chris Kaman RC	4.00	1.50
❏ 122	Keith Bogans RC	4.00	1.50
❏ 123	LeBron James RC	35.00	15.00
❏ 124	Devin Brown RC	4.00	1.50
❏ 125	Jason Kapono RC	4.00	1.50
❏ 126	Zoran Planinic RC	4.00	1.50
❏ 127	Zaur Pachulia RC	4.00	1.50
❏ 128	Malick Badiane RC	4.00	1.50
❏ 129	Kyle Korver RC	6.00	2.50
❏ 130	Darko Milicic RC	5.00	2.00
❏ 131	Troy Bell RC	4.00	1.50
❏ 132	Luke Walton RC	3.00	1.25
❏ 133	Mike Sweetney RC	4.00	1.50
❏ 134	Jarvis Hayes RC	4.00	1.50
❏ 135	Leandro Barbosa RC	6.00	2.50
❏ 136	Carlos Delfino RC	4.00	1.50
❏ 137	Sofoklis Schortsanitis RC	5.00	2.00
❏ 138	Slavko Vranes RC	4.00	1.50
❏ 139	Travis Hansen RC	4.00	1.50
❏ 140	Carmelo Anthony RC	12.00	5.00
❏ 141	Reece Gaines RC	4.00	1.50
❏ 142	Maciej Lampe RC	4.00	1.50
❏ 143	Travis Outlaw RC	4.00	1.50
❏ 144	Jerome Beasley RC	4.00	1.50
❏ 145	Mickael Pietrus RC	4.00	1.50
❏ 146	Brian Cook RC	4.00	1.50
❏ 148	Kirk Hinrich AU RC	80.00	40.00
❏ 149	Dwyane Wade AU RC	150.00	75.00
❏ 150	Marcus Banks AU RC	25.00	10.00
❏ 151	Nick Collison AU RC	25.00	10.00
❏ 152	Boris Diaw AU RC	40.00	15.00
❏ 153	Chris Bosh AU RC	40.00	15.00
❏ 154	T.J. Ford AU RC	30.00	12.50
❏ 155	Luke Ridnour AU RC	25.00	10.00
❏ 156	A.Pavlovic AU RC	30.00	12.50
❏ 157	Z.Cabarkapa AU RC	25.00	10.00

2004-05 Bowman

#	Player		
❏	COMP.SET w/o RC's (110)	40.00	15.00
❏	COMMON CARD (1-110)	.20	.08
❏	COMMON ROOKIE (111-146)	2.50	1.00
❏	COMMON AU RC (147-156)	20.00	8.00
❏ 1	Yao Ming	2.00	.75
❏ 2	Eddy Curry	.50	.20
❏ 3	Stephon Marbury	.75	.30
❏ 4	Chris Webber	.75	.30
❏ 5	Jason Kidd	1.25	.50
❏ 6	Cuttino Mobley	.50	.20
❏ 7	Jermaine O'Neal	.75	.30
❏ 8	Kobe Bryant	3.00	1.25
❏ 9	Tony Parker	.75	.30
❏ 10	Gary Payton	.75	.30
❏ 11	T.J. Ford	.50	.20
❏ 12	Tim Duncan	1.50	.60
❏ 13	Glenn Robinson	.75	.30
❏ 14	Jason Richardson	.75	.30
❏ 15	Carmelo Anthony	1.50	.60
❏ 16	Pau Gasol	.75	.30
❏ 17	Kirk Hinrich	.75	.30
❏ 18	Kenyon Martin	.50	.20
❏ 19	Jamal Crawford	.50	.20
❏ 20	Elton Brand	.75	.30
❏ 21	Kevin Garnett	1.50	.60
❏ 22	Michael Redd	.50	.20
❏ 23	LeBron James	5.00	2.00
❏ 24	Andre Miller	.50	.20
❏ 25	Peja Stojakovic	.50	.20
❏ 26	Jarvis Hayes	.50	.20
❏ 27	David Wesley	.20	.08
❏ 28	Jason Kapono	.50	.20
❏ 29	Corey Maggette	.50	.20
❏ 30	Rasheed Wallace	.75	.30
❏ 31	Nene	.50	.20
❏ 32	Amare Stoudemire	1.50	.60
❏ 33	Allen Iverson	1.50	.60
❏ 34	Shaquille O'Neal	2.00	.75
❏ 35	Mike Dunleavy	.50	.20
❏ 36	Steve Nash	.75	.30
❏ 37	Brad Miller	.50	.20
❏ 38	Chris Bosh	.75	.30
❏ 39	Boris Diaw	.20	.08
❏ 40	Steve Francis	.75	.30
❏ 41	Dirk Nowitzki	1.25	.50
❏ 42	Jason Williams	.50	.20
❏ 43	Gilbert Arenas	.75	.30
❏ 44	Keith Van Horn	.75	.30

☐ 45	Jamal Mashburn	.50	.20
☐ 46	Derek Fisher	.75	.30
☐ 47	Andrei Kirilenko	.75	.30
☐ 48	Ricky Davis	.75	.30
☐ 49	Gerald Wallace	.50	.20
☐ 50	Tracy McGrady	2.00	.75
☐ 51	Zach Randolph	.75	.30
☐ 52	Rafer Alston	.20	.08
☐ 53	Bobby Jackson	.50	.20
☐ 54	Desmond Mason	.50	.20
☐ 55	Tim Thomas	.50	.20
☐ 56	Jamaal Tinsley	.50	.20
☐ 57	Kwame Brown	.50	.20
☐ 58	Chauncey Billups	.50	.20
☐ 59	Brandon Hunter	.20	.08
☐ 60	Reggie Miller	.75	.30
☐ 61	Samuel Dalembert	.20	.08
☐ 62	James Posey	.50	.20
☐ 63	Erick Dampier	.20	.08
☐ 64	Carlos Arroyo	1.25	.50
☐ 65	Reece Gaines	.20	.08
☐ 66	Darko Milicic	.50	.20
☐ 67	Sam Cassell	.75	.30
☐ 68	Dwyane Wade	2.50	1.00
☐ 69	Allan Houston	.50	.20
☐ 70	Ray Allen	.75	.30
☐ 71	Tyson Chandler	.75	.30
☐ 72	Bonzi Wells	.50	.20
☐ 73	Jalen Rose	.75	.30
☐ 74	Marquis Daniels	.75	.30
☐ 75	Zydrunas Ilgauskas	.50	.20
☐ 76	Tayshaun Prince	.50	.20
☐ 77	Lamar Odom	.75	.30
☐ 78	Luke Ridnour	.50	.20
☐ 79	Joe Johnson	.50	.20
☐ 80	Vince Carter	2.00	.75
☐ 81	Antoine Walker	.75	.30
☐ 82	Shareef Abdur-Rahim	.75	.30
☐ 83	Richard Jefferson	.50	.20
☐ 84	Maurice Taylor	.20	.08
☐ 85	Chris Kaman	.50	.20
☐ 86	Marcus Banks	.20	.08
☐ 87	Mike Bibby	.75	.30
☐ 88	Latrell Sprewell	.75	.30
☐ 89	Rashard Lewis	.75	.30
☐ 90	Baron Davis	.75	.30
☐ 91	Caron Butler	.75	.30
☐ 92	Michael Finley	.75	.30
☐ 93	Mike Miller	.75	.30
☐ 94	Al Harrington	.50	.20
☐ 95	Quentin Richardson	.50	.20
☐ 96	Jamaal Magloire	.20	.08
☐ 97	Darius Miles	.75	.30
☐ 98	Jeff Foster	.20	.08
☐ 99	Karl Malone	.75	.30
☐ 100	Shawn Marion	.75	.30
☐ 101	Antawn Jamison	.75	.30
☐ 102	Manu Ginobili	.75	.30
☐ 103	Ben Wallace	.75	.30
☐ 104	Paul Pierce	.75	.30
☐ 105	Mike Sweetney	.50	.20
☐ 106	Ron Artest	.50	.20
☐ 107	Michael Olowokandi	.20	.08
☐ 108	Jason Terry	.75	.30
☐ 109	Gordan Giricek	.50	.20
☐ 110	Carlos Boozer	.75	.30
☐ 111	Romain Sato RC	2.50	1.00
☐ 112	Chris Duhon RC	4.00	1.50
☐ 113	Ben Gordon RC	10.00	4.00
☐ 114	Matt Freije RC	2.50	1.00
☐ 115	Al Jefferson RC	6.00	2.50
☐ 116	Beno Udrih RC	4.00	1.50
☐ 117	Kirk Snyder RC	2.50	1.00
☐ 118	Anderson Varejao RC	3.00	1.25
☐ 119	Devin Harris RC	4.00	1.50
☐ 120	Tony Allen RC	.75	.30
☐ 121	Ha Seung-Jin RC	2.50	1.00
☐ 122	J.R. Smith RC	5.00	2.00
☐ 123	Blake Stepp RC	2.50	1.00
☐ 124	Jameer Nelson RC	4.00	1.50
☐ 125	Kris Humphries RC	2.50	1.00
☐ 126	Josh Childress RC	3.00	1.25
☐ 127	Tim Pickett RC	2.50	1.00
☐ 128	Delonte West RC	3.00	1.25
☐ 129	Dwight Howard RC	8.00	3.00
☐ 130	Luke Jackson RC	2.50	1.00

☐ 131	Rickey Paulding RC	2.50	1.00
☐ 132	Andre Emmett RC	2.50	1.00
☐ 133	Josh Smith RC	5.00	2.00
☐ 134	Antonio Burks RC	2.50	1.00
☐ 135	Ricky Minard RC	2.50	1.00
☐ 136	Lionel Chalmers RC	2.50	1.00
☐ 137	Shaun Livingston RC	4.00	1.50
☐ 138	Trevor Ariza RC	3.00	1.25
☐ 139	Sergei Lishouk RC	2.50	1.00
☐ 140	Pape Sow RC	2.50	1.00
☐ 141	Rashad Wright RC	2.50	1.00
☐ 142	Jackson Vroman RC	2.50	1.00
☐ 143	Luis Flores RC	2.50	1.00
☐ 144	Royal Ivey RC	2.50	1.00
☐ 145	Kevin Martin RC	4.00	1.50
☐ 146	Andre Iguodala RC	6.00	2.50
☐ 147	Andris Biedrins AU RC	25.00	10.00
☐ 148	Pavel Podkolzine AU RC	15.00	6.00
☐ 149	Luol Deng AU RC	30.00	12.50
☐ 150	Robert Swift AU RC	15.00	6.00
☐ 151	Sebastian Telfair AU RC	15.00	6.00
☐ 152	Emeka Okafor AU RC	50.00	20.00
☐ 153	Dorell Wright AU RC	30.00	12.50
☐ 154	Sasha Vujacic AU RC	15.00	6.00
☐ 155	Rafael Araujo AU RC	15.00	6.00
☐ 156	David Harrison AU RC	15.00	6.00

2005-06 Bowman

☐	COMP.SET w/o RC's (110)	40.00	15.00
☐	COMMON CARD (1-110)	.20	.08
☐	COMMON ROOKIE (111-146)	2.00	.75
☐	COMMON CELEBRITY (147-151)	6.00	2.50
☐	COMMON AU RC (152-161)	12.00	5.00
☐ 1	Steve Nash	.75	.30
☐ 2	Primoz Brezec	.20	.08
☐ 3	Baron Davis	.75	.30
☐ 4	Al Harrington	.50	.20
☐ 5	Caron Butler	.50	.20
☐ 6	Marcus Camby	.20	.08
☐ 7	Carlos Boozer	.50	.20
☐ 8	Ben Gordon	1.50	.60
☐ 9	Stephen Jackson	.50	.20
☐ 10	Dirk Nowitzki	1.25	.50
☐ 11	Nenad Krstic	.50	.20
☐ 12	Jason Richardson	.75	.30
☐ 13	Brendan Haywood	.20	.08
☐ 14	Chauncey Billups	.50	.20
☐ 15	Corey Maggette	.50	.20
☐ 16	Peja Stojakovic	.75	.30
☐ 17	Grant Hill	.75	.30
☐ 18	Pau Gasol	.75	.30
☐ 19	Vladimir Radmanovic	.20	.08
☐ 20	Jason Kidd	1.25	.50
☐ 21	Tim Duncan	1.50	.60
☐ 22	David Harrison	.20	.08
☐ 23	LeBron James	5.00	2.00
☐ 24	Udonis Haslem	.75	.30
☐ 25	Dan Dickau	.20	.08
☐ 26	Cuttino Mobley	.50	.20
☐ 27	Chris Bosh	.75	.30
☐ 28	Sebastian Telfair	.50	.20
☐ 29	Latrell Sprewell	.75	.30
☐ 30	Emeka Okafor	1.25	.50
☐ 31	Mike James	.20	.08
☐ 32	Trevor Ariza	.50	.20
☐ 33	Larry Hughes	.50	.20
☐ 34	Desmond Mason	.50	.20
☐ 35	Tayshaun Prince	.75	.30

☐ 36	Manu Ginobili	.75	.30
☐ 37	Mike Bibby	.75	.30
☐ 38	Andre Iguodala	.75	.30
☐ 39	Jamaal Magloire	.20	.08
☐ 40	Amare Stoudemire	1.50	.60
☐ 41	Rafer Alston	.20	.08
☐ 42	Elton Brand	.75	.30
☐ 43	Steve Francis	.75	.30
☐ 44	Rashard Lewis	.75	.30
☐ 45	Lorenzen Wright	.20	.08
☐ 46	Kirk Hinrich	.75	.30
☐ 47	Andrei Kirilenko	.75	.30
☐ 48	Brad Miller	.75	.30
☐ 49	Jamal Crawford	.50	.20
☐ 50	Shaquille O'Neal	2.00	.75
☐ 51	Shaun Livingston	.75	.30
☐ 52	Troy Murphy	.50	.20
☐ 53	Drew Gooden	.50	.20
☐ 54	Paul Pierce	.75	.30
☐ 55	Vince Carter	2.00	.75
☐ 56	Wally Szczerbiak	.50	.20
☐ 57	Antawn Jamison	.75	.30
☐ 58	Marquis Daniels	.50	.20
☐ 59	Gerald Wallace	.50	.20
☐ 60	Ray Allen	.75	.30
☐ 61	Jamaal Tinsley	.50	.20
☐ 62	Shane Battier	.75	.30
☐ 63	Zydrunas Ilgauskas	.50	.20
☐ 64	Mehmet Okur	.20	.08
☐ 65	Rasheed Wallace	.75	.30
☐ 66	Maurice Williams	.20	.08
☐ 67	Josh Howard	.50	.20
☐ 68	Zach Randolph	.75	.30
☐ 69	Kobe Bryant	3.00	1.25
☐ 70	Tracy McGrady	2.00	.75
☐ 71	Luke Ridnour	.50	.20
☐ 72	Damon Jones	.50	.20
☐ 73	Tony Allen	.50	.20
☐ 74	Mike Miller	.75	.30
☐ 75	Sam Cassell	.75	.30
☐ 76	Ben Wallace	.75	.30
☐ 77	Mike Sweetney	.50	.20
☐ 78	Eddy Curry	.50	.20
☐ 79	Michael Redd	.75	.30
☐ 80	Carmelo Anthony	1.50	.60
☐ 81	Dwight Howard	1.00	.40
☐ 82	Josh Smith	.75	.30
☐ 83	Richard Jefferson	.50	.20
☐ 84	Richard Hamilton	.50	.20
☐ 85	Chris Webber	.75	.30
☐ 86	Shawn Marion	.75	.30
☐ 87	Jalen Rose	.75	.30
☐ 88	Bob Sura	.50	.20
☐ 89	Mike Dunleavy	.50	.20
☐ 90	Dwyane Wade	2.50	1.00
☐ 91	Gary Payton	.75	.30
☐ 92	Luol Deng	.75	.30
☐ 93	Kenyon Martin	.75	.30
☐ 94	Beno Udrih	.50	.20
☐ 95	J.R. Smith	.50	.20
☐ 96	Lamar Odom	.75	.30
☐ 97	Andre Miller	.50	.20
☐ 98	Jermaine O'Neal	.75	.30
☐ 99	Yao Ming	2.00	.75
☐ 100	Allen Iverson	1.50	.60
☐ 101	Quentin Richardson	.50	.20
☐ 102	Gilbert Arenas	.75	.30
☐ 103	Stephon Marbury	.75	.30
☐ 104	Antoine Walker	.75	.30
☐ 105	Jameer Nelson	.50	.20
☐ 106	Joel Przybilla	.20	.08
☐ 107	Devin Harris	.75	.30
☐ 108	Tony Parker	.75	.30
☐ 109	Josh Childress	.50	.20
☐ 110	Kevin Garnett	1.50	.60
☐ 111	Chris Paul RC	12.00	5.00
☐ 112	Danny Granger RC	1.50	.60
☐ 113	Antoine Wright RC	2.00	.75
☐ 114	Joey Graham RC	2.00	.75
☐ 115	Wayne Simien RC	3.00	1.25
☐ 116	Channing Frye RC	4.00	1.50
☐ 117	Charlie Villanueva RC	4.00	1.50
☐ 118	Francisco Garcia RC	3.00	1.25
☐ 119	Ike Diogu RC	3.00	1.25
☐ 120	Jarrett Jack RC	2.00	.75
☐ 121	Robert Whaley RC	2.00	.75

#	Card	Hi	Lo
❏ 122	C.J. Miles RC	2.00	.75
❏ 123	Ryan Gomes RC	2.00	.75
❏ 124	Nate Robinson RC	4.00	1.50
❏ 125	Daniel Ewing RC	3.00	1.25
❏ 126	Andray Blatche RC	2.00	.75
❏ 127	Luther Head RC	5.00	2.00
❏ 128	Julius Hodge RC	3.00	1.25
❏ 129	Lawrence Roberts RC	2.00	.75
❏ 130	Jason Maxiell RC	3.00	1.25
❏ 131	Martynas Andriuskevicius RC	2.00	.75
❏ 132	Ersan Ilyasova RC	2.00	.75
❏ 133	Martell Webster RC	2.00	.75
❏ 134	Andrew Bynum RC	6.00	2.50
❏ 135	Louis Williams RC	2.00	.75
❏ 136	Johan Petro RC	2.00	.75
❏ 137	Brandon Bass RC	2.00	.75
❏ 138	Travis Diener RC	2.00	.75
❏ 139	Bracey Wright RC	3.00	1.25
❏ 140	Marvin Williams RC	6.00	2.50
❏ 141	Eddie Basden RC	2.00	.75
❏ 142	Von Wafer RC	2.00	.75
❏ 143	David Lee RC	3.00	1.25
❏ 144	Linas Kleiza RC	2.00	.75
❏ 145	Luke Schenscher RC	2.00	.75
❏ 146	Yaroslav Korolev RC	2.00	.75
❏ 147	Carmen Electra	6.00	2.50
❏ 148	Christie Brinkley	6.00	2.50
❏ 149	Shannon Elizabeth	6.00	2.50
❏ 150	Jenny McCarthy	6.00	2.50
❏ 151	Jay-Z	6.00	2.50
❏ 152	Raymond Felton AU RC	20.00	8.00
❏ 153	Gerald Green AU RC	30.00	12.50
❏ 154	Rashad McCants AU RC	20.00	8.00
❏ 155	Andrew Bogut AU RC	15.00	6.00
❏ 156	Chris Taft AU RC	12.00	5.00
❏ 157	Sarunas Jasikevicius AU RC	20.00	8.00
❏ 158	Hakim Warrick AU RC	30.00	12.50
❏ 159	Deron Williams AU RC	40.00	15.00
❏ 160	Sean May AU RC	10.00	4.00
❏ 161	Monta Ellis AU RC	25.00	10.00
❏ DSBS	A.Bogut/A.Smith AU/100	250.00	125.00

2006-07 Bowman

#	Player	Hi	Lo
❏ 1	Gilbert Arenas	.75	.30
❏ 2	Delonte West	.50	.20
❏ 3	Gerald Wallace	.75	.30
❏ 4	Ike Diogu	.50	.20
❏ 5	Mike Miller	.75	.30
❏ 6	Kobe Bryant	3.00	1.25
❏ 7	Richard Hamilton	.50	.20
❏ 8	Vince Carter	2.00	.75
❏ 9	Elton Brand	.75	.30
❏ 10	Boris Diaw	.50	.20
❏ 11	Carmelo Anthony	1.50	.60
❏ 12	Jermaine O'Neal	.75	.30
❏ 13	Al Harrington	.25	.10
❏ 14	Dwight Howard	1.00	.40
❏ 15	Chris Bosh	.75	.30
❏ 16	Ben Gordon	1.50	.60
❏ 17	Josh Howard	.50	.20
❏ 18	Yao Ming	2.00	.75
❏ 19	David West	.25	.10
❏ 20	Tim Duncan	1.50	.60
❏ 21	Andre Iguodala	.75	.30
❏ 22	LeBron James	5.00	2.00
❏ 23	Channing Frye	.50	.20
❏ 24	Antoine Walker	.75	.30
❏ 25	Ricky Davis	.75	.30
❏ 26	Lamar Odom	.75	.30
❏ 27	Amare Stoudemire	1.50	.60
❏ 28	Mike Bibby	.75	.30
❏ 29	Allen Iverson	1.50	.60
❏ 30	Marvin Williams	1.00	.40
❏ 31	Wally Szczerbiak	.50	.20
❏ 32	Ben Wallace	.75	.30
❏ 33	Nenad Krstic	.50	.20
❏ 34	Derron Williams	.75	.30
❏ 35	Troy Murphy	.75	.30
❏ 36	Raymond Felton	1.00	.40
❏ 37	Jason Terry	.75	.30
❏ 38	Zach Randolph	.75	.30
❏ 39	Pau Gasol	.75	.30
❏ 40	Larry Hughes	.50	.20
❏ 41	Luol Deng	.75	.30
❏ 42	Steve Francis	.75	.30
❏ 43	Chauncey Billups	.75	.30
❏ 44	Smush Parker	.25	.10
❏ 45	Shareef Abdur-Rahim	.75	.30
❏ 46	Andrei Kirilenko	.75	.30
❏ 47	Shawn Marion	.75	.30
❏ 48	Darko Milicic	.75	.30
❏ 49	Shaquille O'Neal	2.00	.75
❏ 50	Kevin Garnett	1.50	.60
❏ 51	Michael Finley	.75	.30
❏ 52	Peja Stojakovic	.75	.30
❏ 53	Michael Redd	.75	.30
❏ 54	Desmond Mason	.25	.10
❏ 55	Luke Ridnour	.50	.20
❏ 56	Kenyon Martin	.75	.30
❏ 57	Morris Peterson	.50	.20
❏ 58	Chris Kaman	.25	.10
❏ 59	Jason Richardson	.75	.30
❏ 60	Jason Kidd	1.25	.50
❏ 61	Carlos Boozer	.50	.20
❏ 62	Rashad McCants	1.00	.40
❏ 63	Nate Robinson	.75	.30
❏ 64	Devin Harris	.75	.30
❏ 65	Andrew Bogut	1.00	.40
❏ 66	Chris Duhon	.25	.10
❏ 67	Drew Gooden	.50	.20
❏ 68	Manu Ginobili	.75	.30
❏ 69	Jameer Nelson	.50	.20
❏ 70	Corey Maggette	.50	.20
❏ 71	Charlie Villanueva	.75	.30
❏ 72	Shane Battier	.75	.30
❏ 73	Udonis Haslem	.75	.30
❏ 74	Tracy McGrady	2.00	.75
❏ 75	Bobby Simmons	.25	.10
❏ 76	Baron Davis	.75	.30
❏ 77	Zydrunas Ilgauskas	.25	.10
❏ 78	Danny Granger	.50	.20
❏ 79	Hakim Warrick	.50	.20
❏ 80	Josh Smith	.75	.30
❏ 81	Tayshaun Prince	.75	.30
❏ 82	Rashard Lewis	.75	.30
❏ 83	Luther Head	.50	.20
❏ 84	Andre Miller	.50	.20
❏ 85	T.J. Ford	.50	.20
❏ 86	Sebastian Telfair	.50	.20
❏ 87	Dirk Nowitzki	1.25	.50
❏ 88	Kwame Brown	.50	.20
❏ 89	Antawn Jamison	.75	.30
❏ 90	Ron Artest	.75	.30
❏ 91	Mehmet Okur	.25	.10
❏ 92	Emeka Okafor	.75	.30
❏ 93	Sam Cassell	.75	.30
❏ 94	Chris Paul	2.00	.75
❏ 95	Chris Webber	.75	.30
❏ 96	Richard Jefferson	.50	.20
❏ 97	Dwyane Wade	2.50	1.00
❏ 98	Tony Parker	.75	.30
❏ 99	Paul Pierce	.75	.30
❏ 100	Marcus Camby	.25	.10
❏ 101	Ray Allen	.75	.30
❏ 102	Stephon Marbury	.75	.30
❏ 103	Rasheed Wallace	.75	.30
❏ 104	Brad Miller	.75	.30
❏ 105	Kirk Hinrich	.75	.30
❏ 106	Steve Nash	.75	.30
❏ 107	Sarunas Jasikevicius	.50	.20
❏ 108	Darius Miles	.75	.30
❏ 109	Joe Johnson	.50	.20
❏ 110	Caron Butler	.50	.20
❏ 111	John Wooden CO	3.00	1.25
❏ 112	Ben Howland CO	2.50	1.00
❏ 113	Jim Calhoun CO	2.50	1.00
❏ 114	Jim Boeheim CO	2.50	1.00
❏ 115	Roy Williams CO	2.50	1.00
❏ 116	LaMarcus Aldridge RC	5.00	2.00
❏ 117	Marcus Vinicius RC	2.50	1.00
❏ 118	Sergio Rodriguez RC	2.50	1.00
❏ 119	Will Blalock RC	2.50	1.00
❏ 120	Paul Millsap RC	4.00	1.50
❏ 121	Leon Powe RC	2.50	1.00
❏ 122	Rudy Gay RC	5.00	2.00
❏ 123	Tyrus Thomas RC	4.00	1.50
❏ 124	Brandon Roy RC	6.00	2.50
❏ 125	J.R. Pinnock RC	2.50	1.00
❏ 126	Kevin Pittsnogle RC	3.00	1.25
❏ 127	Mile Ilic RC	2.50	1.00
❏ 128	Mardy Collins RC	2.50	1.00
❏ 129	Craig Smith RC	2.50	1.00
❏ 130	Jordan Farmar RC	4.00	1.50
❏ 431	Quincy Douby RC	2.50	1.00
❏ 132	James Augustine RC	2.50	1.00
❏ 133	Josh Boone RC	2.50	1.00
❏ 134	Shannon Brown RC	3.00	1.25
❏ 135	David Noel RC	2.50	1.00
❏ 136	Kyle Lowry RC	4.00	1.50
❏ 137	Ryan Hollins RC	2.50	1.00
❏ 138	Renaldo Balkman RC	2.50	1.00
❏ 139	James White RC	2.50	1.00
❏ 140	Damir Markota RC	2.50	1.00
❏ 141	Paul Davis RC	2.50	1.00
❏ 142	Alexander Johnson RC	2.50	1.00
❏ 143	Steve Novak RC	2.50	1.00
❏ 144	P.J. Tucker RC	2.50	1.00
❏ 145	Saer Sene RC	2.50	1.00
❏ 146	Bobby Jones RC	2.50	1.00
❏ 147	Cedric Simmons RC	2.50	1.00
❏ 148	Allan Ray RC	2.50	1.00
❏ 149	Solomon Jones RC	2.50	1.00
❏ 150	Ronnie Brewer RC	5.00	2.00
❏ 151	Thabo Sefolosha RC	3.00	1.25
❏ 152	Maurice Ager RC	3.00	1.25
❏ 153	Daniel Gibson RC	6.00	2.50
❏ 154	Shawne Williams RC	3.00	1.25
❏ 155	Dee Brown RC	4.00	1.50
❏ 156	Andrea Bargnani RC	6.00	2.50
❏ 157	Patrick O'Bryant RC	2.50	1.00
❏ 158	Shelden Williams RC	4.00	1.50
❏ 159	Hilton Armstrong RC	2.50	1.00
❏ 160	Adam Morrison RC	6.00	2.50
❏ 161	Rodney Carney RC	3.00	1.25
❏ 162	Randy Foye RC	6.00	2.50
❏ 163	Rajon Rondo RC	5.00	2.00
❏ 164	Marcus Williams RC	3.00	1.25
❏ 165	J.J. Redick RC	5.00	2.00

2003-04 Bowman Chrome

	Hi	Lo
❏ COMP.SET w/o RC's (110)	80.00	30.00
❏ COMMON CARD (1-110)	.40	.15
❏ COMMON ROOKIE (111-147)	8.00	3.00
❏ COMMON AU RC (148-157)	40.00	15.00
❏ 148-157 AU RC STATED ODDS 1:385		
❏ 148-157 AU PRINT RUN 250 SER.#'d SETS		
❏ CARD 147 NOT RELEASED		
❏ 1 Yao Ming	4.00	1.50
❏ 2 Green Robinson	1.25	.50
❏ 3 Antoine Walker	1.25	.50
❏ 4 Jalen Rose	1.25	.50
❏ 5 Ricky Davis	1.25	.50

#	Player		
6	Juwan Howard	.75	.30
7	Kwame Brown	1.25	.50
8	Mike Bibby	1.25	.50
9	Wally Szczerbiak	.75	.30
10	Allen Iverson	2.50	1.00
11	Shareef Abdur-Rahim	1.25	.50
12	Jamal Mashburn	.75	.30
13	Stephon Marbury	1.25	.50
14	Desmond Mason	.75	.30
15	Gordan Giricek	.75	.30
16	Caron Butler	1.25	.50
17	Jermaine O'Neal	1.25	.50
18	Kenyon Martin	1.25	.50
19	Andrei Kirilenko	1.25	.50
20	Dirk Nowitzki	2.00	.75
21	Richard Hamilton	.75	.30
22	Troy Murphy	.75	.30
23	Shawn Marion	1.25	.50
24	Allan Houston	.75	.30
25	Keith Van Horn	1.25	.50
26	Brian Grant	.75	.30
27	Mike Miller	1.25	.50
28	Chris Webber	1.25	.50
29	Brent Barry	.75	.30
30	Elton Brand	1.25	.50
31	Juan Dixon	.75	.30
32	Karl Malone	1.25	.50
33	Darrell Armstrong	.40	.15
34	Rasheed Wallace	1.25	.50
35	Michael Redd	1.25	.50
36	Rashard Lewis	1.25	.50
37	Ron Artest	.75	.30
38	P.J. Brown	.40	.15
39	Eddie Griffin	.75	.30
40	Tim Duncan	2.50	1.00
41	Kurt Thomas	.75	.30
42	Raef Lafrentz	.75	.30
43	Ben Wallace	1.25	.50
44	Lamar Odom	1.25	.50
45	Vince Carter	3.00	1.25
46	Derek Anderson	.75	.30
47	Stromile Swift	.75	.30
48	Bobby Jackson	.75	.30
49	Richard Jefferson	.75	.30
50	Shaquille O'Neal	3.00	1.25
51	Calbert Cheaney	.40	.15
52	Troy Hudson	.40	.15
53	Ray Allen	1.25	.50
54	Howard Eisley	.40	.15
55	Alonzo Mourning	.75	.30
56	Sam Cassell	1.25	.50
57	Derrick Coleman	.40	.15
58	Andre Miller	.75	.30
59	Antawn Jamison	1.25	.50
60	Kevin Garnett	2.50	1.00
61	Steve Francis	1.25	.50
62	Tyson Chandler	1.25	.50
63	Drew Gooden	.75	.30
64	Scottie Pippen	2.00	.75
65	Pau Gasol	1.25	.50
66	Steve Nash	1.25	.50
67	DaJuan Wagner	.75	.30
68	Jason Terry	1.25	.50
69	Reggie Miller	1.25	.50
70	Tracy McGrady	3.00	1.25
71	Nene Hilario	.75	.30
72	Morris Peterson	.75	.30
73	Peja Stojakovic	1.25	.50
74	Eddie Jones	1.25	.50
75	Tony Parker	1.25	.50
76	Corliss Williamson	.75	.30
77	Vladimir Radmanovic	.40	.15
78	Amare Stoudemire	4.00	1.50
79	Tony Delk	.40	.15
80	Jason Kidd	2.00	.75
81	Gary Payton	1.25	.50
82	Corey Maggette	.75	.30
83	Darius Miles	.75	.30
84	Cuttino Mobley	.75	.30
85	Eric Snow	.75	.30
86	Matt Harpring	1.25	.50
87	Manu Ginobili	1.25	.50
88	Latrell Sprewell	1.25	.50
89	Alvin Williams	.40	.15
90	Paul Pierce	1.25	.50
91	Anfernee Hardaway	1.25	.50

#	Player		
92	Gilbert Arenas	1.25	.50
93	Jerry Stackhouse	1.25	.50
94	Tim Thomas	.75	.30
95	Nikoloz Tskitishvili	.40	.15
96	Doug Christie	.75	.30
97	Zydrunas Ilgauskas	.75	.30
98	Jamaal Tinsley	1.25	.50
99	Theo Ratliff	.75	.30
100	Kobe Bryant	5.00	2.00
101	Chauncey Billups	.75	.30
102	Michael Finley	1.25	.50
103	Jason Williams	.75	.30
104	Bonzi Wells	.75	.30
105	Voshon Lenard	.40	.15
106	Jason Richardson	1.25	.50
107	Baron Davis	1.25	.50
108	Radoslav Nesterovic	.75	.30
109	Eddy Curry	.75	.30
110	Michael Olowokandi	.40	.15
111	Josh Howard RC	12.00	5.00
112	Mario Austin RC	8.00	3.00
113	Rick Rickert RC	8.00	3.00
114	Tommy Smith RC	8.00	3.00
115	Dahntay Jones RC	8.00	3.00
116	Ndudi Ebi RC	8.00	3.00
117	Maurice Williams RC	8.00	3.00
118	Kendrick Perkins RC	8.00	3.00
119	Steve Blake RC	8.00	3.00
120	David West RC	8.00	3.00
121	Chris Kaman RC	8.00	3.00
122	Keith Bogans RC	8.00	3.00
123	LeBron James RC	60.00	25.00
124	Devin Brown RC	8.00	3.00
125	Jason Kapono RC	8.00	3.00
126	Zoran Planinic RC	8.00	3.00
127	Zaur Pachulia RC	8.00	3.00
128	Malick Badiane RC	8.00	3.00
129	Kyle Korver RC	12.00	5.00
130	Darko Milicic RC	12.00	5.00
131	Troy Bell RC	8.00	3.00
132	Luke Walton RC	8.00	3.00
133	Mike Sweetney RC	8.00	3.00
134	Jarvis Hayes RC	8.00	3.00
135	Leandro Barbosa RC	12.00	5.00
136	Carlos Delfino RC	8.00	3.00
137	Sofoklis Schortsanitis RC	10.00	4.00
138	Slavko Vranes RC	8.00	3.00
139	Travis Hansen RC	8.00	3.00
140	Carmelo Anthony RC	25.00	10.00
141	Reece Gaines RC	8.00	3.00
142	Maciej Lampe RC	8.00	3.00
143	Travis Outlaw RC	8.00	3.00
144	Jerome Beasley RC	8.00	3.00
145	Mickael Pietrus RC	8.00	3.00
146	Brian Cook RC	8.00	3.00
148	Kirk Hinrich AU RC	120.00	60.00
149	Dwyane Wade AU RC	400.00	200.00
150	Marcus Banks AU RC	40.00	15.00
151	Nick Collison AU RC	30.00	12.50
152	Boris Diaw AU RC	50.00	20.00
153	Chris Bosh AU RC	150.00	75.00
154	T.J. Ford AU RC	80.00	40.00
155	Luke Ridnour AU RC	40.00	15.00
156	A.Pavlovic AU RC	40.00	15.00
157	Zarko Cabarkapa AU RC	30.00	12.50

2004-05 Bowman Chrome

#	Player		
	COMP.SET w/o RC's (110)	60.00	25.00
	COMMON CARD (1-110)	.40	.15
	COMMON ROOKIE (111-146)	5.00	2.00
	COMMON AU RC (147-156)	40.00	15.00
1	Yao Ming	3.00	1.00
2	Eddy Curry	.75	.30
3	Stephon Marbury	1.25	.50
4	Chris Webber	1.25	.50
5	Jason Kidd	2.00	.75
6	Cuttino Mobley	.75	.30
7	Jermaine O'Neal	1.25	.50
8	Kobe Bryant	5.00	2.00
9	Tony Parker	1.25	.50
10	Gary Payton	1.25	.50
11	T.J. Ford	.75	.30
12	Tim Duncan	2.50	1.00
13	Glenn Robinson	1.25	.50
14	Jason Richardson	1.25	.50
15	Carmelo Anthony	2.50	1.00
16	Pau Gasol	1.25	.50
17	Kirk Hinrich	1.25	.50
18	Kenyon Martin	1.25	.50
19	Jamal Crawford	.75	.30
20	Elton Brand	1.25	.50
21	Kevin Garnett	2.50	1.00
22	Michael Redd	.75	.30
23	LeBron James	8.00	3.00
24	Andre Miller	.75	.30
25	Peja Stojakovic	1.25	.50
26	Jarvis Hayes	.75	.30
27	David Wesley	.40	.15
28	Jason Kapono	.75	.30
29	Corey Maggette	.75	.30
30	Rasheed Wallace	1.25	.50
31	Nene	.75	.30
32	Amare Stoudemire	2.50	1.00
33	Allen Iverson	2.50	1.00
34	Shaquille O'Neal	3.00	1.25
35	Mike Dunleavy	.75	.30
36	Steve Nash	1.25	.50
37	Brad Miller	1.25	.50
38	Chris Bosh	1.25	.50
39	Boris Diaw	.40	.15
40	Steve Francis	1.25	.50
41	Dirk Nowitzki	2.00	.75
42	Jason Williams	.75	.30
43	Gilbert Arenas	1.25	.50
44	Keith Van Horn	1.25	.50
45	Jamal Mashburn	.75	.30
46	Derek Fisher	1.25	.50
47	Andrei Kirilenko	1.25	.50
48	Ricky Davis	1.25	.50
49	Gerald Wallace	.75	.30
50	Tracy McGrady	3.00	1.25
51	Zach Randolph	1.25	.50
52	Rafer Alston	.40	.15
53	Bobby Jackson	.75	.30
54	Desmond Mason	.75	.30
55	Tim Thomas	.75	.30
56	Jamaal Tinsley	1.25	.50
57	Kwame Brown	.75	.30
58	Chauncey Billups	.75	.30
59	Brandon Hunter	.40	.15
60	Reggie Miller	1.25	.50
61	Samuel Dalembert	.40	.15
62	James Posey	.75	.30
63	Erick Dampier	.75	.30
64	Carlos Arroyo	2.00	.75
65	Reece Gaines	.40	.15
66	Darko Milicic	.75	.30
67	Sam Cassell	1.25	.50
68	Dwyane Wade	4.00	1.50
69	Allan Houston	.75	.30
70	Ray Allen	1.25	.50
71	Tyson Chandler	1.25	.50
72	Bonzi Wells	.75	.30
73	Jalen Rose	1.25	.50
74	Marquis Daniels	.75	.30
75	Zydrunas Ilgauskas	.75	.30
76	Tayshaun Prince	.75	.30
77	Lamar Odom	1.25	.50
78	Luke Ridnour	.75	.30
79	Joe Johnson	.40	.15
80	Vince Carter	3.00	1.25
81	Antoine Walker	1.25	.50
82	Shareef Abdur-Rahim	1.25	.50

#	Player		
83	Richard Jefferson	.75	.30
84	Maurice Taylor	.40	.15
85	Chris Kaman	.75	.30
86	Marcus Banks	.75	.30
87	Mike Bibby	1.25	.50
88	Latrell Sprewell	1.25	.50
89	Rashard Lewis	1.25	.50
90	Baron Davis	1.25	.50
91	Caron Butler	1.25	.50
92	Michael Finley	1.25	.50
93	Mike Miller	1.25	.50
94	Al Harrington	.75	.30
95	Quentin Richardson	.75	.30
96	Jamaal Magloire	.40	.15
97	Darius Miles	1.25	.50
98	Jeff Foster	.40	.15
99	Karl Malone	1.25	.50
100	Shawn Marion	1.25	.50
101	Antawn Jamison	1.25	.50
102	Manu Ginobili	1.25	.50
103	Ben Wallace	1.25	.50
104	Paul Pierce	1.25	.50
105	Mike Sweetney	.75	.30
106	Ron Artest	.75	.30
107	Michael Olowokandi	.40	.15
108	Jason Terry	1.25	.50
109	Gordan Giricek	.75	.30
110	Carlos Boozer	1.25	.50
111	Romain Sato RC	5.00	2.00
112	Chris Duhon RC	10.00	4.00
113	Ben Gordon RC	20.00	8.00
114	Matt Freije RC	5.00	2.00
115	Al Jefferson RC	10.00	4.00
116	Beno Udrih RC	8.00	3.00
117	Kirk Snyder RC	5.00	2.00
118	Anderson Varejao RC	6.00	2.50
119	Devin Harris RC	8.00	3.00
120	Tony Allen RC	6.00	2.50
121	Ha Seung-Jin RC	5.00	2.00
122	J.R. Smith RC	10.00	4.00
123	Blake Stepp RC	5.00	2.00
124	Jameer Nelson RC	8.00	3.00
125	Kris Humphries RC	5.00	2.00
126	Josh Childress RC	6.00	2.50
127	Tim Pickett RC	5.00	2.00
128	Delonte West RC	10.00	4.00
129	Dwight Howard RC	15.00	6.00
130	Luke Jackson RC	5.00	2.00
131	Rickey Paulding RC	5.00	2.00
132	Andre Emmett RC	5.00	2.00
133	Josh Smith RC	10.00	4.00
134	Antonio Burks RC	5.00	2.00
135	Ricky Minard RC	5.00	2.00
136	Lionel Chalmers RC	5.00	2.00
137	Shaun Livingston RC	8.00	3.00
138	Trevor Ariza RC	6.00	2.50
139	Sergei Lishouk RC	5.00	2.00
140	Pape Sow RC	5.00	2.00
141	Rashad Wright RC	5.00	2.00
142	Jackson Vroman RC	5.00	2.00
143	Luis Flores RC	5.00	2.00
144	Royal Ivey RC	5.00	2.00
145	Kevin Martin RC	8.00	3.00
146	Andre Iguodala RC	12.00	5.00
147	Andris Biedrins AU RC	50.00	20.00
148	Pavel Podkolzine AU RC	30.00	12.50
149	Luol Deng AU RC	80.00	40.00
150	Robert Swift AU RC	30.00	12.50
151	Sebastian Telfair AU RC	40.00	15.00
152	Emeka Okafor AU RC	120.00	60.00
153	Dorell Wright AU RC	60.00	30.00
154	Sasha Vujacic AU RC	30.00	12.50
155	Rafael Araujo AU RC	30.00	12.50
156	David Harrison AU RC	30.00	12.50

2005-06 Bowman Chrome

	COMP.SET w/o RC's (110)	60.00	25.00
	COMMON CARD (1-110)	.50	.20
	COMMON ROOKIE (111-146)	5.00	2.00
	COMMON CELEBRITY (147-151)	10.00	4.00
	COMMON AU RC (152-161)	25.00	10.00
1	Steve Nash		
2	Primoz Brezec	.50	.20
3	Baron Davis	1.50	.60
4	Al Harrington	1.00	.40
5	Caron Butler	1.00	.40
6	Marcus Camby	.50	.20
7	Carlos Boozer	1.00	.40
8	Ben Gordon	3.00	1.25
9	Stephen Jackson	.50	.20
10	Dirk Nowitzki	2.50	1.00
11	Nenad Krstic	1.00	.40
12	Jason Richardson	1.50	.60
13	Brendan Haywood	.50	.20
14	Chauncey Billups	1.50	.60
15	Corey Maggette	1.00	.40
16	Peja Stojakovic	1.50	.60
17	Grant Hill	1.50	.60
18	Pau Gasol	1.50	.60
19	Vladimir Radmanovic	.50	.20
20	Jason Kidd	2.50	1.00
21	Tim Duncan	3.00	1.25
22	David Harrison	.50	.20
23	LeBron James	10.00	4.00
24	Udonis Haslem	1.50	.60
25	Dan Dickau	.50	.20
26	Cuttino Mobley	1.00	.40
27	Chris Bosh	1.50	.60
28	Sebastian Telfair	1.00	.40
29	Latrell Sprewell	1.50	.60
30	Emeka Okafor	2.50	1.00
31	Mike James	.50	.20
32	Trevor Ariza	1.00	.40
33	Larry Hughes	1.00	.40
34	Desmond Mason	1.00	.40
35	Tayshaun Prince	1.50	.60
36	Manu Ginobili	1.50	.60
37	Mike Bibby	1.50	.60
38	Andre Iguodala	1.50	.60
39	Jamaal Magloire	.50	.20
40	Amare Stoudemire	3.00	1.25
41	Rafer Alston	.50	.20
42	Elton Brand	1.50	.60
43	Steve Francis	1.50	.60
44	Rashard Lewis	1.50	.60
45	Lorenzen Wright	.50	.20
46	Kirk Hinrich	1.50	.60
47	Andrei Kirilenko	1.50	.60
48	Brad Miller	1.50	.60
49	Jamal Crawford	1.00	.40
50	Shaquille O'Neal	4.00	1.50
51	Shaun Livingston	1.50	.60
52	Troy Murphy	1.50	.60
53	Drew Gooden	1.00	.40
54	Paul Pierce	1.50	.60
55	Vince Carter	4.00	1.50
56	Wally Szczerbiak	1.00	.40
57	Antawn Jamison	1.50	.60
58	Marquis Daniels	1.00	.40
59	Gerald Wallace	1.50	.60
60	Ray Allen	1.50	.60
61	Jamaal Tinsley	1.00	.40
62	Shane Battier	1.50	.60
63	Zydrunas Ilgauskas	1.00	.40
64	Mehmet Okur	.50	.20
65	Rasheed Wallace	1.50	.60
66	Maurice Williams	.50	.20
67	Josh Howard	1.00	.40
68	Zach Randolph	1.50	.60
69	Kobe Bryant	6.00	2.50
70	Tracy McGrady	4.00	1.50
71	Luke Ridnour	1.00	.40
72	Damon Jones	.50	.20
73	Tony Allen	1.00	.40
74	Mike Miller	1.50	.60
75	Sam Cassell	1.50	.60
76	Ben Wallace	1.50	.60
77	Mike Sweetney	1.00	.40
78	Eddy Curry	1.00	.40
79	Michael Redd	1.50	.60
80	Carmelo Anthony	3.00	1.25
81	Dwight Howard	2.00	.75
82	Josh Smith	1.50	.60
83	Richard Jefferson	1.00	.40
84	Richard Hamilton	1.50	.60
85	Chris Webber	1.50	.60
86	Shawn Marion	1.50	.60
87	Jalen Rose	1.50	.60
88	Bob Sura	1.00	.40
89	Mike Dunleavy	1.00	.40
90	Dwyane Wade	5.00	2.00
91	Gary Payton	1.50	.60
92	Luol Deng	1.50	.60
93	Kenyon Martin	1.50	.60
94	Beno Udrih	1.00	.40
95	J.R. Smith	1.00	.40
96	Lamar Odom	1.50	.60
97	Andre Miller	1.00	.40
98	Jermaine O'Neal	1.50	.60
99	Yao Ming	4.00	1.50
100	Allen Iverson	3.00	1.25
101	Quentin Richardson	1.00	.40
102	Gilbert Arenas	1.50	.60
103	Stephon Marbury	1.50	.60
104	Antoine Walker	1.50	.60
105	Jameer Nelson	1.00	.40
106	Joel Przybilla	.50	.20
107	Devin Harris	1.50	.60
108	Tony Parker	1.50	.60
109	Josh Childress	1.00	.40
110	Kevin Garnett	3.00	1.25
111	Chris Paul RC	25.00	10.00
112	Danny Granger RC	6.00	2.50
113	Antoine Wright RC	5.00	2.00
114	Joey Graham RC	5.00	2.00
115	Wayne Simien RC	6.00	2.50
116	Channing Frye RC	10.00	4.00
117	Charlie Villanueva RC	8.00	3.00
118	Francisco Garcia RC	6.00	2.50
119	Ike Diogu RC	6.00	2.50
120	Jarrett Jack RC	5.00	2.00
121	Robert Whaley RC	5.00	2.00
122	C.J. Miles RC	5.00	2.00
123	Ryan Gomes RC	5.00	2.00
124	Nate Robinson RC	8.00	3.00
125	Daniel Ewing RC	5.00	2.00
126	Andray Blatche RC	5.00	2.00
127	Luther Head RC	10.00	4.00
128	Julius Hodge RC	5.00	2.00
129	Lawrence Roberts RC	5.00	2.00
130	Jason Maxiell RC	6.00	2.50
131	Martynas Andriuskevicius RC	5.00	2.00
132	Ersan Ilyasova RC	5.00	2.00
133	Martell Webster RC	5.00	2.00
134	Andrew Bynum RC	15.00	6.00
135	Louis Williams RC	5.00	2.00
136	Johan Petro RC	5.00	2.00
137	Brandon Bass RC	5.00	2.00
138	Travis Diener RC	5.00	2.00
139	Bracey Wright RC	5.00	2.00
140	Marvin Williams RC	12.00	5.00
141	Eddie Basden RC	5.00	2.00
142	Von Wafer RC	5.00	2.00
143	David Lee RC	8.00	3.00
144	Linas Kleiza RC	5.00	2.00
145	Luke Schenscher RC	5.00	2.00
146	Yaroslav Korolev RC	5.00	2.00
147	Carmen Electra	10.00	4.00
148	Christie Brinkley	10.00	4.00
149	Shannon Elizabeth	10.00	4.00
150	Jenny McCarthy	10.00	4.00
151	Jay-Z	10.00	4.00
152	Raymond Felton AU RC	40.00	15.00
153	Gerald Green AU RC	60.00	25.00
154	Rashad McCants AU RC	40.00	15.00
155	Andrew Bogut AU RC	40.00	15.00
156	Chris Taft AU RC	25.00	10.00
157	S.Jaskevicius AU RC	40.00	15.00
158	Hakim Warrick AU RC	50.00	20.00
159	Deron Williams AU RC	150.00	75.00

❑ 160	Sean May AU RC	20.00	8.00
❑ 161	Monta Ellis AU RC	60.00	25.00

2006-07 Bowman Chrome

❑ 1	Gilbert Arenas	1.50	.60
❑ 2	Delonte West	1.00	.40
❑ 3	Gerald Wallace	1.50	.60
❑ 4	Ike Diogu	1.00	.40
❑ 5	Mike Miller	1.50	.60
❑ 6	Kobe Bryant	6.00	2.50
❑ 7	Richard Hamilton	1.00	.40
❑ 8	Vince Carter	4.00	1.50
❑ 9	Elton Brand	1.50	.60
❑ 10	Boris Diaw	1.00	.40
❑ 11	Carmelo Anthony	3.00	1.25
❑ 12	Jermaine O'Neal	1.50	.60
❑ 13	Al Harrington	.50	.20
❑ 14	Dwight Howard	2.00	.75
❑ 15	Chris Bosh	1.50	.60
❑ 16	Ben Gordon	3.00	1.25
❑ 17	Josh Howard	1.00	.40
❑ 18	Yao Ming	4.00	1.50
❑ 19	David West	.50	.20
❑ 20	Tim Duncan	3.00	1.25
❑ 21	Andre Iguodala	1.50	.60
❑ 22	LeBron James	10.00	4.00
❑ 23	Channing Frye	1.00	.40
❑ 24	Antoine Walker	1.50	.60
❑ 25	Ricky Davis	1.50	.60
❑ 26	Lamar Odom	1.50	.60
❑ 27	Amare Stoudemire	3.00	1.25
❑ 29	Mike Bibby	1.50	.60
❑ 29	Allen Iverson	3.00	1.25
❑ 30	Marvin Williams	2.00	.75
❑ 31	Wally Szczerbiak	1.00	.40
❑ 32	Ben Wallace	1.50	.60
❑ 33	Nenad Krstic	1.00	.40
❑ 34	Deron Williams	1.50	.60
❑ 35	Troy Murphy	1.50	.60
❑ 36	Raymond Felton	2.00	.75
❑ 37	Jason Terry	1.50	.60
❑ 38	Zach Randolph	1.50	.60
❑ 39	Pau Gasol	1.50	.60
❑ 40	Larry Hughes	1.00	.40
❑ 41	Luol Deng	1.50	.60
❑ 42	Steve Francis	1.50	.60
❑ 43	Chauncey Billups	1.50	.60
❑ 44	Smush Parker	.50	.20
❑ 45	Shareef Abdur-Rahim	1.50	.60
❑ 46	Andrei Kirilenko	1.50	.60
❑ 47	Shawn Marion	1.50	.60
❑ 48	Darko Milicic	1.50	.60
❑ 49	Shaquille O'Neal	4.00	1.25
❑ 50	Kevin Garnett	3.00	1.25
❑ 51	Michael Finley	1.50	.60
❑ 52	Peja Stojakovic	1.50	.60
❑ 53	Michael Redd	1.50	.60
❑ 54	Desmond Mason	.50	.20
❑ 55	Luke Ridnour	1.00	.40
❑ 56	Kenyon Martin	1.50	.60
❑ 57	Morris Peterson	1.00	.40
❑ 58	Chris Kaman	.50	.20
❑ 59	Jason Richardson	1.50	.60
❑ 60	Jason Kidd	2.50	1.00
❑ 61	Carlos Boozer	1.00	.40
❑ 62	Rashad McCants	2.00	.75
❑ 63	Nate Robinson	1.50	.60
❑ 64	Devin Harris	1.50	.60
❑ 65	Andrew Bogut	2.00	.75
❑ 66	Chris Duhon	.50	.20
❑ 67	Drew Gooden	1.00	.40
❑ 68	Manu Ginobili	1.50	.60
❑ 69	Jameer Nelson	1.00	.40
❑ 70	Corey Maggette	1.00	.40
❑ 71	Charlie Villanueva	1.50	.60
❑ 72	Shane Battier	1.50	.60
❑ 73	Udonis Haslem	1.50	.60
❑ 74	Tracy McGrady	4.00	1.50
❑ 75	Bobby Simmons	.50	.20
❑ 76	Baron Davis	1.50	.60
❑ 77	Zydrunas Ilgauskas	.50	.20
❑ 78	Danny Granger	1.00	.40
❑ 79	Hakim Warrick	1.00	.40
❑ 80	Josh Smith	1.50	.60
❑ 81	Tayshaun Prince	1.50	.60
❑ 82	Rashard Lewis	1.50	.60
❑ 83	Luther Head	1.00	.40
❑ 84	Andre Miller	1.00	.40
❑ 85	T.J. Ford	1.00	.40
❑ 86	Sebastian Telfair	1.00	.40
❑ 87	Dirk Nowitzki	2.50	1.00
❑ 88	Kwame Brown	1.00	.40
❑ 89	Antawn Jamison	1.50	.60
❑ 90	Ron Artest	1.00	.40
❑ 91	Mehmet Okur	.50	.20
❑ 92	Emeka Okafor	1.50	.60
❑ 93	Sam Cassell	1.50	.60
❑ 94	Chris Paul	4.00	1.50
❑ 95	Chris Webber	1.50	.60
❑ 96	Richard Jefferson	1.00	.40
❑ 97	Dwyane Wade	5.00	2.00
❑ 98	Tony Parker	1.50	.60
❑ 99	Paul Pierce	1.50	.60
❑ 100	Marcus Camby	.50	.20
❑ 101	Ray Allen	1.50	.60
❑ 102	Stephon Marbury	1.50	.60
❑ 103	Rasheed Wallace	1.50	.60
❑ 104	Brad Miller	1.50	.60
❑ 105	Kirk Hinrich	1.50	.60
❑ 106	Steve Nash	1.50	.60
❑ 107	Sarunas Jasikevicius	1.00	.40
❑ 108	Darius Miles	1.50	.60
❑ 109	Joe Johnson	1.00	.40
❑ 110	Caron Butler	1.00	.40
❑ 111	John Wooden CO	6.00	2.50
❑ 112	Ben Howland CO	5.00	2.00
❑ 113	Jim Calhoun CO	5.00	2.00
❑ 114	Jim Boeheim CO	5.00	2.00
❑ 115	Roy Williams CO	5.00	2.00
❑ 116	LaMarcus Aldridge RC	10.00	4.00
❑ 117	Marcus Vinicius RC	5.00	2.00
❑ 118	Sergio Rodriguez RC	5.00	2.00
❑ 119	Will Blalock RC	5.00	2.00
❑ 120	Paul Millsap RC	8.00	3.00
❑ 121	Leon Powe RC	5.00	2.00
❑ 122	Rudy Gay RC	10.00	4.00
❑ 123	Tyrus Thomas RC	8.00	3.00
❑ 124	Brandon Roy RC	12.00	5.00
❑ 125	J.R. Pinnock RC	5.00	2.00
❑ 126	Kevin Pittsnogle B AU RC	12.00	5.00
❑ 127	Mile Ilic C AU RC	12.00	5.00
❑ 128	Mardy Collins B AU RC	12.00	5.00
❑ 129	Craig Smith C AU RC	12.00	5.00
❑ 130	Jordan Farmar B AU RC	50.00	20.00
❑ 131	Quincy Douby B AU RC	12.00	5.00
❑ 132	James Augustine B AU RC	12.00	5.00
❑ 133	Josh Boone B AU RC	12.00	5.00
❑ 134	Shannon Brown B AU RC	12.00	5.00
❑ 135	David Noel B AU RC	12.00	5.00
❑ 136	Kyle Lowry B AU RC	12.00	5.00
❑ 137	Ryan Hollins C AU RC	12.00	5.00
❑ 138	Renaldo Balkman B AU RC	12.00	5.00
❑ 139	James White C AU RC	12.00	5.00
❑ 140	Damir Markota C AU RC	12.00	5.00
❑ 141	Paul Davis B AU RC	12.00	5.00
❑ 142	Alexander Johnson C AU RC	12.00	5.00
❑ 143	Steve Novak B AU RC	12.00	5.00
❑ 144	P.J. Tucker B AU RC	12.00	5.00
❑ 145	Saer Sene B AU RC	12.00	5.00
❑ 146	Bobby Jones B AU RC	12.00	5.00
❑ 147	Cedric Simmons C AU RC	12.00	5.00
❑ 148	Allan Ray C AU RC	12.00	5.00
❑ 149	Solomon Jones B AU RC	12.00	5.00
❑ 150	Ronnie Brewer A AU RC	15.00	6.00
❑ 151	Thabo Sefolosha B AU RC	40.00	15.00
❑ 152	Maurice Ager B AU RC	12.00	5.00
❑ 153	Daniel Gibson C AU RC	40.00	20.00
❑ 154	Shawne Williams B AU RC	15.00	6.00
❑ 155	Dee Brown B AU RC	20.00	8.00
❑ 156	Andrea Bargnani A AU RC	70.00	35.00
❑ 157	Patrick O'Bryant A AU RC	12.00	5.00
❑ 158	Shelden Williams A AU RC	15.00	6.00
❑ 159	Hilton Armstrong A AU RC	12.00	5.00
❑ 160	Adam Morrison A AU RC	75.00	35.00
❑ 161	Rodney Carney B AU RC	12.00	5.00
❑ 162	Randy Foye A AU RC	60.00	30.00
❑ 163	Rajon Rondo B AU RC	15.00	6.00
❑ 164	Marcus Williams A AU RC	30.00	12.50
❑ 165	J.J. Redick A AU RC	50.00	20.00

2006-07 Bowman Elevation

❑ 1	Dwyane Wade	5.00	2.00
❑ 2	Elton Brand	1.50	.60
❑ 3	Dwight Howard	2.00	.75
❑ 4	Chris Bosh	1.50	.60
❑ 5	Baron Davis	1.50	.60
❑ 6	Marcus Camby	.50	.20
❑ 7	Rashard Lewis	1.50	.60
❑ 8	Paul Pierce	1.50	.60
❑ 9	Jermaine O'Neal	1.50	.60
❑ 10	Gilbert Arenas	1.50	.60
❑ 11	Larry Hughes	1.00	.40
❑ 12	Manu Ginobili	1.50	.60
❑ 13	Lamar Odom	1.50	.60
❑ 14	Ron Artest	1.00	.40
❑ 15	Carmelo Anthony	3.00	1.25
❑ 16	Deron Williams	1.50	.60
❑ 17	Gerald Wallace	1.50	.60
❑ 18	Peja Stojakovic	1.50	.60
❑ 19	Vince Carter	4.00	1.50
❑ 20	Kevin Garnett	3.00	1.25
❑ 21	Yao Ming	4.00	1.50
❑ 22	Josh Howard	1.00	.40
❑ 23	Michael Redd	1.50	.60
❑ 24	Eddy Curry	1.00	.40
❑ 25	Shawn Marion	1.50	.60
❑ 26	Luol Deng	1.50	.60
❑ 27	Ben Wallace	1.50	.60
❑ 28	Sam Cassell	1.50	.60
❑ 29	Steve Francis	1.50	.60
❑ 30	Ray Allen	1.50	.60
❑ 31	Andre Iguodala	1.50	.60
❑ 32	Shaquille O'Neal	4.00	1.50
❑ 33	Pau Gasol	1.50	.60
❑ 34	Jason Richardson	1.50	.60
❑ 35	Ricky Davis	1.50	.60
❑ 36	Joe Johnson	1.00	.40
❑ 37	Dirk Nowitzki	2.50	1.00
❑ 38	Richard Hamilton	1.00	.40
❑ 39	Troy Murphy	1.50	.60
❑ 40	Charlie Villanueva	1.50	.60
❑ 41	T.J. Ford	1.00	.40
❑ 42	Zydrunas Ilgauskas	.50	.20
❑ 43	Andrei Kirilenko	1.50	.60
❑ 44	Chris Paul	4.00	1.50
❑ 45	Grant Hill	1.50	.60
❑ 46	Kobe Bryant	6.00	2.50
❑ 47	Tim Duncan	3.00	1.25
❑ 48	Raymond Felton	2.00	.75
❑ 49	Antawn Jamison	1.50	.60
❑ 50	Jason Kidd	2.50	1.00
❑ 51	Shareef Abdur-Rahim	1.50	.60

□	#	Player		
□	52	Shane Battier	1.50	.60
□	53	Kirk Hinrich	1.50	.60
□	54	Jason Terry	1.50	.60
□	55	Mehmet Okur	.50	.20
□	56	Stephon Marbury	1.50	.60
□	57	Steve Nash	1.50	.60
□	58	Mike Bibby	1.50	.60
□	59	Sebastian Telfair	1.00	.40
□	60	Richard Jefferson	1.00	.40
□	61	Andre Miller	1.00	.40
□	62	Delonte West	1.00	.40
□	63	Tracy McGrady	4.00	1.50
□	64	Rasheed Wallace	1.50	.60
□	65	Al Harrington	.50	.20
□	66	Emeka Okafor	1.50	.60
□	67	Caron Butler	1.00	.40
□	68	Andrew Bogut	2.00	.75
□	69	Tony Parker	1.50	.60
□	70	Zach Randolph	1.50	.60
□	71	Allen Iverson	3.00	1.25
□	72	David West	.50	.20
□	73	Chris Webber	1.50	.60
□	74	Ben Gordon	3.00	1.25
□	75	Corey Maggette	1.00	.40
□	76	Sarunas Jasikevicius	1.00	.40
□	77	Chauncey Billups	1.50	.60
□	78	Amare Stoudemire	3.00	1.25
□	79	Luke Ridnour	1.00	.40
□	80	LeBron James	10.00	4.00
□	81	Kenyon Martin	1.50	.60
□	82	Marko Jaric	.50	.20
□	83	Antoine Walker	1.50	.60
□	84	J.R. Smith	1.00	.40
□	85	Mike Miller	1.50	.60
□	86	Channing Frye	1.00	.40
□	87	Smush Parker	.50	.20
□	88	Wally Szczerbiak	1.00	.40
□	89	Morris Peterson	1.00	.40
□	90	Luther Head	1.00	.40
□	91	Randy Foye RC	10.00	4.00
□	92	Daniel Gibson RC	12.00	5.00
□	93	Hassan Adams RC	6.00	2.50
□	94	Hilton Armstrong RC	5.00	2.00
□	95	Marcus Williams RC	5.00	2.50
□	96	Paul Davis RC	5.00	2.00
□	97	Quincy Douby RC	5.00	2.00
□	98	Ronnie Brewer RC	6.00	2.50
□	99	Rodney Carney RC	5.00	2.00
□	100	Rudy Gay RC	10.00	4.00
□	101	Adam Morrison RC	12.00	5.00
□	102	Rajon Rondo RC	6.00	2.50
□	103	Steve Novak RC	5.00	2.00
□	104	Craig Smith RC	5.00	2.00
□	105	Leon Powe RC	5.00	2.00
□	106	James White RC	5.00	2.00
□	107	Josh Boone RC	5.00	2.00
□	108	J.J. Redick RC	10.00	4.00
□	109	Shelden Williams RC	6.00	2.50
□	110	Alexander Johnson RC	5.00	2.00
□	111	Guillermo Diaz RC	5.00	2.00
□	112	Maurice Ager RC	5.00	2.00
□	113	Jordan Farmar RC	10.00	4.00
□	114	Mardy Collins RC	5.00	2.00
□	115	Ryan Hollins RC	5.00	2.00
□	116	Kyle Lowry RC	5.00	2.00
□	117	James Augustine RC	5.00	2.00
□	118	Shawne Williams RC	6.00	2.50
□	119	LaMarcus Aldridge RC	12.00	5.00
□	120	Patrick O'Bryant RC	5.00	2.00
□	121	Cedric Simmons RC	5.00	2.00
□	122	P.J. Tucker RC	5.00	2.00
□	123	Brandon Roy RC	15.00	6.00
□	124	Tyrus Thomas RC	15.00	6.00
□	125	Andrea Bargnani RC	12.00	5.00
□	126	Dee Brown RC	8.00	3.00
□	127	Denham Brown RC	5.00	2.00
□	128	Saer Sene RC	5.00	2.00
□	129	Thabo Sefolosha RC	8.00	3.00
□	130	Shannon Brown RC	5.00	2.00

2002-03 Bowman Signature Edition

□	COMMON CARD	.60	.25
□	COMMON ROOKIE	12.00	5.00
□	SE-AI Allen Iverson	4.00	1.50

□	SE-AJ	Antawn Jamison	2.00	.75
□	SE-AK	Andrei Kirilenko	2.00	.75
□	SE-AM	Alonzo Mourning	2.00	.75
□	SE-AS	Stoudemire JSY AU RC	120.00	60.00
□	SE-AW	Antoine Walker	2.00	.75
□	SE-AKM	Antonio McDyess	1.25	.50
□	SE-ALM	Andre Miller	1.25	.50
□	SE-BD	Baron Davis	2.00	.75
□	SE-BN	Bostjan Nachbar JSY AU RC	12.00	5.00
□	SE-BW	Ben Wallace	2.00	.75
□	SE-CB	Curtis Borchardt JSY AU RC	12.00	5.00
□	SE-CM	Cuttino Mobley	1.25	.50
□	SE-CO	Chris Owens AU RC	12.00	5.00
□	SE-CT	Cezary Trybanski AU RC	12.00	5.00
□	SE-CW	Chris Wilcox JSY AU RC	20.00	8.00
□	SE-CBO	C.Boozer JSY AU RC	30.00	12.50
□	SE-CBU	Caron Butler JSY AU RC	25.00	10.00
□	SE-CJA	C.Jacobsen JSY AU RC	12.00	5.00
□	SE-CLE	C.Laettner JSY AU RC	12.00	5.00
□	SE-DD	Dan Dickau AU RC	12.00	5.00
□	SE-DN	Dirk Nowitzki	3.00	1.25
□	SE-DW	D.Wagner JSY AU RC	15.00	6.00
□	SE-DGA	D.Gadzuric JSY AU RC	12.00	5.00
□	SE-DGO	D.Gooden JSY AU RC	30.00	12.50
□	SE-DLM	Darius Miles	2.00	.75
□	SE-EB	Elton Brand	2.00	.75
□	SE-EC	Eddy Curry	2.00	.75
□	SE-EG	Manu Ginobili AU RC	60.00	25.00
□	SE-EJ	Eddie Jones	2.00	.75
□	SE-ER	E.Rentzias AU RC	12.00	5.00
□	SE-FJ	Fred Jones JSY AU RC	12.00	5.00
□	SE-FR	Frank Williams AU RC	12.00	5.00
□	SE-GG	Gordan Giricek AU RC	20.00	8.00
□	SE-GP	Gary Payton	2.00	.75
□	SE-GR	Glenn Robinson	2.00	.75
□	SE-JB	J.R. Bremer AU RC	12.00	5.00
□	SE-JD	Juan Dixon JSY AU RC	25.00	10.00
□	SE-JJ	J.Jeffries JSY AU RC	15.00	6.00
□	SE-JK	Jason Kidd	3.00	1.25
□	SE-JM	Jamal Mashburn	1.25	.50
□	SE-JO	Jermaine O'Neal	2.00	.75
□	SE-JP	Jannero Pargo JSY AU RC	12.00	5.00
□	SE-JS	John Salmons JSY AU RC	12.00	5.00
□	SE-JT	Jamaal Tinsley	1.50	.60
□	SE-JAW	Jay Williams/1249 RC	8.00	3.00
□	SE-JDS	Jerry Stackhouse	2.00	.75
□	SE-JOS	John Stockton	2.00	.75
□	SE-JWE	Jiri Welsch AU RC	12.00	5.00
□	SE-JWI	Jerome Williams	.60	.25
□	SE-KB	Kobe Bryant	8.00	3.00
□	SE-KG	Kevin Garnett	4.00	1.50
□	SE-KM	Karl Malone	2.00	.75
□	SE-KR	K.Rush JSY AU RC	25.00	10.00
□	SE-KS	Kenny Satterfield	.60	.25
□	SE-KLM	Kenyon Martin	2.00	.75
□	SE-LS	Latrell Sprewell	2.00	.75
□	SE-MB	Mike Bibby	2.00	.75
□	SE-MD	M.Dunleavy JSY AU RC	25.00	10.00
□	SE-ME	Melvin Ely JSY AU RC	12.00	5.00
□	SE-MH	M.Haislip JSY AU RC	12.00	5.00
□	SE-MO	Mehmet Okur AU RC	12.00	5.00
□	SE-MCW	Chris Webber	2.00	.75
□	SE-MJA	Marko Jaric AU RC	15.00	6.00
□	SE-MJJ	Michael Jordan	12.00	5.00
□	SE-NH	N.Hilario JSY AU RC	30.00	12.50
□	SE-NT	N.Tskitishvili JSY AU RC	12.00	5.00
□	SE-PG	Pau Gasol	2.00	.75
□	SE-PP	Paul Pierce	2.00	.75

□	SE-PS	Peja Stojakovic	2.00	.75
□	SE-PSA	P.Savovic JSY AU RC	12.00	5.00
□	SE-QR	Quentin Richardson	1.25	.50
□	SE-RA	Ray Allen	2.00	.75
□	SE-RA	R.Archibald JSY AU RC	15.00	6.00
□	SE-RB	Rasual Butler JSY AU RC	15.00	6.00
□	SE-RJ	Richard Jefferson	2.00	.75
□	SE-RL	Rashard Lewis	1.25	.50
□	SE-RW	Rasheed Wallace	2.00	.75
□	SE-RCH	Richard Hamilton	1.25	.50
□	SE-RHU	R.Humphrey JSY AU RC	12.00	5.00
□	SE-RMA	R.Mason JSY AU RC	12.00	5.00
□	SE-RMU	R.Murray JSY AU RC	40.00	15.00
□	SE-SA	Shareef Abdur-Rahim	2.00	.75
□	SE-SC	Sam Clancy JSY AU RC	12.00	5.00
□	SE-SF	Steve Francis	2.00	.75
□	SE-SM	Stephon Marbury	2.00	.75
□	SE-SN	Steve Nash	2.00	.75
□	SE-SO	Shaquille O'Neal	5.00	2.00
□	SE-SCB	Shane Battier	2.00	.75
□	SE-SDM	Shawn Marion	2.00	.75
□	SE-TC	Tyson Chandler	2.00	.75
□	SE-TD	Tim Duncan	5.00	1.50
□	SE-TP	T.Prince JSY AU RC	40.00	15.00
□	SE-TP	Tony Parker	2.00	.75
□	SE-TS	Tamar Slay AU RC	12.00	5.00
□	SE-TLM	Tracy McGrady	5.00	2.00
□	SE-VC	Vince Carter	5.00	2.00
□	SE-VY	V.Yarbrough JSY AU RC	12.00	5.00
□	SE-WS	Wally Szczerbiak	1.25	.50
□	SE-YM	Yao Ming AU RC	200.00	100.00

2003-04 Bowman Signature Edition

□	COMP.SET w/o SP's (55)	60.00	25.00
□	COMMON CARD (1-55)	.60	.25
□	SEMISTARS 1-55	1.25	.50
□	UNLISTED STARS 1-55	2.00	.75
□	COMMON ROOKIE (56-60)	6.00	2.50
□	UNLESS NOTED BELOW		
□	COMMON AU RC (61-76)	12.00	5.00
□	COMMON JSY AU RC (77-105)	15.00	6.00
□	COMMON AU RC (106-118)	10.00	4.00
□	1 Tracy McGrady	5.00	2.00
□	2 Baron Davis	2.00	.75
□	3 Allen Iverson	4.00	1.50
□	4 Bonzi Wells	2.00	.75
□	5 Tony Parker	2.00	.75
□	6 Morris Peterson	1.25	.50
□	7 Jerry Stackhouse	2.00	.75
□	8 Jason Terry	2.00	.75
□	9 Tyson Chandler	2.00	.75
□	10 Dirk Nowitzki	3.00	1.25
□	11 Nene	1.25	.50
□	12 Antawn Jamison	2.00	.75
□	13 Richard Hamilton	1.25	.50
□	14 Steve Francis	2.00	.75
□	15 Jermaine O'Neal	2.00	.75
□	16 Elton Brand	2.00	.75
□	17 Mike Miller	2.00	.75
□	18 Caron Butler	2.00	.75
□	19 Gary Payton	2.00	.75
□	20 Shaquille O'Neal	5.00	2.00
□	21 Kevin Garnett	4.00	1.50
□	22 Desmond Mason	1.25	.50
□	23 Jamal Mashburn	1.25	.50
□	24 Drew Gooden	1.25	.50
□	25 Eric Snow	1.25	.50

#	Player		
26	Shawn Marion	2.00	.75
27	Peja Stojakovic	2.00	.75
28	Karl Malone	2.00	.75
29	Shareef Abdur-Rahim	2.00	.75
30	Paul Pierce	2.00	.75
31	Dajuan Wagner	1.25	.50
32	Steve Nash	2.00	.75
33	Ben Wallace	2.00	.75
34	Jason Richardson	2.00	.75
35	Yao Ming	5.00	2.00
36	Ron Artest	1.25	.50
37	Andre Miller	1.25	.50
38	Kobe Bryant	8.00	3.00
39	Pau Gasol	2.00	.75
40	Tim Duncan	4.00	1.50
41	Ray Allen	2.00	.75
42	Vince Carter	5.00	2.00
43	Andrei Kirilenko	2.00	.75
44	Chris Webber	2.00	.75
45	Rasheed Wallace	2.00	.75
46	Amare Stoudemire	4.00	1.50
47	Latrell Sprewell	2.00	.75
48	Kenyon Martin	2.00	.75
49	Wally Szczerbiak	1.25	.50
50	Jason Kidd	3.00	1.25
51	Eddie Jones	2.00	.75
52	Jalen Rose	2.00	.75
53	Ricky Davis	2.00	.75
54	Antoine Walker	2.00	.75
55	Allan Houston	1.25	.50
56	Lebron James RC	80.00	30.00
57	Darko Milicic RC	10.00	4.00
58	Chris Kaman RC	6.00	2.50
59	Kyle Korver RC	10.00	4.00
60	Willie Green RC	6.00	2.50
61	James Lang AU RC	12.00	5.00
62	Carl English AU RC	12.00	5.00
63	Devin Brown AU RC	12.00	5.00
64	Theron Smith AU RC	12.00	5.00
65	Rick Rickert AU RC	12.00	5.00
66	Z.Cabarkapa AU RC	12.00	5.00
67	D.Zimmerman AU RC	12.00	5.00
68	A.Pavlovic AU RC	15.00	6.00
69	Malick Badiane AU RC	12.00	5.00
70	Boris Diaw AU RC	20.00	8.00
71	Zaur Pachulia AU RC	12.00	5.00
72	Zoran Planinic AU RC	12.00	5.00
73	Carlos Delfino AU RC	12.00	5.00
74	Maciej Lampe AU RC	12.00	5.00
75	S.Schortsanitis AU RC	25.00	10.00
76	Mario Austin AU RC	12.00	5.00
77	C.Anthony/1170 JSY AU RC	100.00	50.00
78	Chris Bosh JSY AU RC	50.00	20.00
79	D.Wade JSY AU RC	225.00	125.00
80	Kirk Hinrich JSY AU RC	40.00	15.00
81	T.J. Ford JSY AU RC	30.00	12.50
82	D.West/1245 JSY AU RC	15.00	6.00
83	Marcus Banks JSY AU RC	15.00	6.00
84	Dahntay Jones JSY AU RC	15.00	6.00
85	Luke Ridnour JSY AU RC	25.00	10.00
86	Reece Gaines JSY AU RC	15.00	6.00
87	T.Outlaw/1075 JSY AU RC	15.00	6.00
88	B.Cook/1063 JSY AU RC	15.00	6.00
89	Troy Bell JSY AU RC	15.00	6.00
90	Ndudi Ebi JSY AU RC	20.00	8.00
91	K.Perkins/1238 JSY AU RC	15.00	6.00
92	L.Barbosa JSY AU RC	25.00	10.00
93	J.Howard/1111 JSY AU RC	40.00	15.00
94	Slavko Vranes JSY AU RC	15.00	6.00
95	Jason Kapono JSY AU RC	15.00	6.00
96	Luke Walton JSY AU RC	25.00	10.00
97	M.Williams/1172 JSY AU RC	15.00	6.00
98	M.Bonner/960 JSY AU RC	15.00	6.00
99	Travis Hansen JSY AU RC	15.00	6.00
100	Steve Blake JSY AU RC	15.00	6.00
101	Keith Bogans JSY AU RC	15.00	6.00
102	Mike Sweetney JSY AU RC	15.00	6.00
103	Jarvis Hayes JSY AU RC	15.00	6.00
104	Mickael Pietrus JSY AU RC	20.00	8.00
105	Nick Collison JSY AU RC	20.00	8.00
106	Jerome Beasley AU RC		
107	James Jones AU RC	10.00	4.00
108	Brandon Hunter AU RC	10.00	4.00
109	Tommy Smith AU RC	10.00	4.00
110	Marcus Hatten AU RC	10.00	4.00
111	Koko Archibong AU RC	10.00	4.00
112	Ime Udoka AU RC	12.00	5.00
113	Eric Chenowith AU RC	10.00	4.00
114	Stephane Pelle AU RC	10.00	4.00
115	Marquis Daniels AU RC	25.00	10.00
116	Paccelis Morlende AU RC	10.00	4.00
117	George Williams AU RC	10.00	4.00
118	Udonis Haslem AU RC	15.00	6.00

2004-05 Bowman Signature Edition

#	Player		
	COMP.SET w/o SP's (55)	60.00	25.00
	COMMON CARD (1-55)	.60	.25
	COMMON JSY AU RC (58-86)	15.00	6.00
	COMMON AU RC (87-103)	8.00	3.00
1	Kevin Garnett	4.00	1.50
2	Eddy Curry	1.25	.50
3	Ben Wallace	2.00	.75
4	Cuttino Mobley	1.25	.50
5	Vince Carter	5.00	2.00
6	Bonzi Wells	1.25	.50
7	Jermaine O'Neal	2.00	.75
8	Kobe Bryant	8.00	3.00
9	Stephon Marbury	2.00	.75
10	Mike Bibby	2.00	.75
11	Yao Ming	5.00	2.00
12	Richard Jefferson	1.25	.50
13	Steve Nash	2.00	.75
14	Luke Ridnour	1.25	.50
15	Carmelo Anthony	4.00	1.50
16	Pau Gasol	2.00	.75
17	Amare Stoudemire	4.00	1.50
18	Chris Webber	2.00	.75
19	Sam Cassell	2.00	.75
20	Tracy McGrady	5.00	2.00
21	Tim Duncan	4.00	1.50
22	Michael Redd	1.25	.50
23	LeBron James	12.00	5.00
24	Baron Davis	2.00	.75
25	Zach Randolph	2.00	.75
26	Peja Stojakovic	2.00	.75
27	Lamar Odom	2.00	.75
28	Michael Finley	2.00	.75
29	Zydrunas Ilgauskas	1.25	.50
30	Rasheed Wallace	1.25	.50
31	Mike Sweetney	1.25	.50
32	Elton Brand	2.00	.75
33	Steve Francis	2.00	.75
34	Paul Pierce	2.00	.75
35	Ray Allen	2.00	.75
36	Tony Parker	2.00	.75
37	Gerald Wallace	1.25	.50
38	Chris Bosh	2.00	.75
39	Desmond Mason	1.25	.50
40	Allen Iverson	4.00	1.50
41	Dirk Nowitzki	3.00	1.25
42	Antoine Walker	1.25	.50
43	Ron Artest	1.25	.50
44	Jamaal Magloire	.60	.25
45	Kirk Hinrich	2.00	.75
46	Jason Richardson	2.00	.75
47	Andrei Kirilenko	2.00	.75
48	Kenyon Martin	2.00	.75
49	Carlos Boozer	2.00	.75
50	Shaquille O'Neal	5.00	2.00
51	Shawn Marion	2.00	.75
52	Kwame Brown	1.25	.50
53	Corey Maggette	1.25	.50
54	Dwyane Wade	6.00	2.50
55	Jason Kidd	3.00	1.25
56	Dwight Howard JSY AU RC	15.00	6.00
57	Andre Iguodala JSY AU RC	12.00	5.00
58	Andre Emmett JSY AU RC	10.00	4.00
59	Al Jefferson JSY AU RC	25.00	10.00
60	A.Varejao JSY AU RC	12.00	5.00
61	Ben Gordon JSY AU RC	50.00	20.00
62	David Harrison JSY AU RC	10.00	4.00
63	Delonte West JSY AU RC	20.00	8.00
64	Devin Harris JSY AU RC	15.00	6.00
65	Dorell Wright JSY AU RC	20.00	8.00
66	Ha Seung-Jin JSY AU RC	10.00	4.00
67	J.R. Smith JSY AU RC	20.00	8.00
68	Jackson Vroman JSY AU RC	10.00	4.00
69	Jameer Nelson JSY AU RC	15.00	6.00
70	Kris Humphries JSY AU RC	10.00	4.00
71	Josh Smith JSY AU RC	20.00	8.00
72	Kevin Martin JSY AU RC	20.00	8.00
73	Kirk Snyder JSY AU RC	10.00	4.00
74	Trevor Ariza JSY AU RC	12.00	5.00
75	Lionel Chalmers JSY AU RC	10.00	4.00
76	Luke Jackson JSY AU RC	10.00	4.00
77	Luol Deng JSY AU RC	25.00	10.00
78	Rafael Araujo JSY AU RC	10.00	4.00
79	Rickey Paulding JSY AU RC	10.00	4.00
80	SebastianTelfair JSY AU RC	10.00	4.00
81	S.Livingston JSY AU RC	15.00	6.00
82	Tony Allen JSY AU RC	12.00	5.00
83	Josh Childress JSY AU RC	12.00	5.00
84	Emeka Okafor JSY AU RC	50.00	20.00
85	Ber.Robinson JSY AU RC	10.00	4.00
86	Chris Duhon JSY AU RC	15.00	6.00
87	Blake Stepp AU RC	8.00	3.00
88	Andris Biedrins AU RC	12.00	5.00
89	Donta Smith AU RC	8.00	3.00
90	Beno Udrih AU RC	15.00	6.00
91	Justin Reed AU RC	8.00	3.00
92	Pavel Podkolzine AU RC	8.00	3.00
93	Matt Freije AU RC	8.00	3.00
94	Pape Sow AU RC	8.00	3.00
95	Antonio Burks AU RC	8.00	3.00
96	Rashad Wright AU RC	8.00	3.00
97	Ricky Minard AU RC	8.00	3.00
98	Robert Swift AU RC	8.00	3.00
99	Romain Sato AU RC	8.00	3.00
100	Sasha Vujacic AU RC	8.00	3.00
102	Tim Pickett AU RC	8.00	3.00
103	Yuta Tabuse AU RC	25.00	10.00

2006-07 Bowman Sterling

#	Player		
1	Ben Wallace JSY	10.00	4.00
2	Jason Richardson JSY	10.00	4.00
3	Steve Nash JSY	15.00	6.00
4	Pau Gasol JSY	10.00	4.00
5	Carmelo Anthony JSY	15.00	6.00
6	Kevin Garnett JSY	12.00	5.00
7	Tim Duncan JSY	12.00	5.00
8	Chauncey Billups JSY	10.00	4.00
9	Chris Paul JSY	12.00	5.00
10	Kobe Bryant JSY	25.00	10.00
11	Tony Parker JSY	10.00	4.00
12	Shaquille O'Neal JSY	20.00	8.00
13	Allen Iverson JSY	15.00	6.00
14	Dirk Nowitzki JSY	12.00	5.00
15	Paul Pierce JSY	12.00	5.00
16	Tracy McGrady JSY	12.00	5.00
17	Channing Frye JSY	10.00	4.00
18	Amare Stoudemire JSY	12.00	5.00

❑ 19	Dwight Howard JSY	12.00	5.00
❑ 20	Dwyane Wade JSY	20.00	8.00
❑ 21	Yao Ming JSY	12.00	5.00
❑ 22	Andrei Kirilenko JSY	10.00	4.00
❑ 23	Gilbert Arenas JSY	10.00	4.00
❑ 24	Shawn Marion JSY	10.00	4.00
❑ 25	Bob Lanier JSY	10.00	4.00
❑ 26	Pete Maravich JSY	40.00	20.00
❑ 27	Bill Walton JSY	12.00	5.00
❑ 28	Dennis Rodman JSY	15.00	6.00
❑ 29	Magic Johnson JSY	20.00	8.00
❑ 30	John Stockton JSY	12.00	5.00
❑ 31	Larry Bird JSY AU	120.00	60.00
❑ 32	Rick Barry JSY AU	40.00	20.00
❑ 33	Isiah Thomas JSY AU	30.00	12.50
❑ 34	Dominique Wilkins JSY AU	40.00	20.00
❑ 35	Ben Gordon JSY AU	40.00	20.00
❑ 36	Raymond Felton JSY AU	20.00	8.00
❑ 37	T.J. Ford JSY AU	20.00	8.00
❑ 38	Josh Howard JSY AU	20.00	8.00
❑ 39	Dwyane Wade JSY AU	60.00	30.00
❑ 40	Andre Iguodala JSY AU	20.00	8.00
❑ 41	Tarence Kinsey RC	6.00	2.50
❑ 42	Mickael Gelabale RC	6.00	2.50
❑ 43	Kelenna Azubuike RC	8.00	3.00
❑ 44	Pops Mensah-Bonsu RC	6.00	2.50
❑ 45	Walter Herrmann RC	8.00	3.00
❑ 46	Tyrus Thomas RC	20.00	8.00
❑ 47	Lynn Greer RC	6.00	2.50
❑ 48	Leon Powe RC	6.00	2.50
❑ 49	Yakhouba Diawara RC	6.00	2.50
❑ 50	Jose Barea RC	6.00	2.50
❑ 51	Saer Sene JSY RC	8.00	3.00
❑ 52	Steve Novak JSY RC	8.00	3.00
❑ 53	Josh Boone JSY RC	8.00	3.00
❑ 54	James White JSY RC	8.00	3.00
❑ 55	Rudy Gay JSY RC	15.00	6.00
❑ 56	David Noel JSY RC	8.00	3.00
❑ 57	Allan Ray JSY RC	8.00	3.00
❑ 58	Paul Davis JSY RC	8.00	3.00
❑ 59	Shawne Williams JSY RC	10.00	4.00
❑ 60	LaMarcus Aldridge JSY RC	20.00	8.00
❑ 61	Mardy Collins JSY RC	8.00	3.00
❑ 62	Solomon Jones JSY RC	8.00	3.00
❑ 63	Craig Smith JSY RC	8.00	3.00
❑ 64	Rajon Rondo JSY RC	10.00	4.00
❑ 65	Jorge Garbajosa JSY RC	15.00	6.00
❑ 66	Patrick O'Bryant JSY RC	8.00	3.00
❑ 67	Dee Brown JSY RC	10.00	4.00
❑ 68	Brandon Roy JSY RC	25.00	10.00
❑ 69	Bobby Jones JSY RC	8.00	3.00
❑ 70	Kyle Lowry JSY RC	8.00	3.00
❑ 71	Paul Millsap AU RC	15.00	6.00
❑ 72	Vassilis Spanoulis AU RC	12.00	5.00
❑ 73	Daniel Gibson AU RC	30.00	12.00
❑ 74	Marcus Vinicius AU RC	12.00	5.00
❑ 75	Ronnie Brewer AU RC	15.00	6.00
❑ 76	Damir Markota AU RC	12.00	5.00
❑ 77	Hilton Armstrong AU RC	12.00	5.00
❑ 78	Shannon Brown AU RC	12.00	5.00
❑ 79	Mile Ilic AU RC	12.00	5.00
❑ 80	Alexander Johnson AU RC	12.00	5.00
❑ 81	Will Blalock AU RC	12.00	5.00
❑ 82	P.J. Tucker AU RC	12.00	5.00
❑ 83	Sergio Rodriguez AU RC	12.00	5.00
❑ 84	Jordan Farmar AU RC	25.00	10.00
❑ 85	Renaldo Balkman AU RC	12.00	5.00
❑ 86	Quincy Douby AU RC	12.00	5.00
❑ 87	Hassan Adams AU RC	15.00	6.00
❑ 88	Chris Quinn AU RC	12.00	5.00
❑ 89	James Augustine AU RC	12.00	5.00
❑ 90	Ryan Hollins AU RC	12.00	5.00
❑ 91	J.J. Redick JSY AU RC	25.00	10.00
❑ 92	Adam Morrison JSY AU RC	30.00	12.00
❑ 93	Maurice Ager JSY AU RC	12.00	5.00
❑ 94	Shelden Williams JSY AU RC	15.00	6.00
❑ 95	Marcus Williams JSY AU RC	15.00	6.00
❑ 96	Andrea Bargnani JSY AU RC	50.00	20.00
❑ 97	Thabo Sefolosha JSY AU RC	20.00	8.00
❑ 98	Randy Foye JSY AU RC	25.00	10.00
❑ 99	Cedric Simmons JSY AU RC	12.00	5.00
❑ 100	Rodney Carney JSY AU RC	12.00	5.00

1996-97 Bowman's Best

❑	COMPLETE SET (125)	50.00	25.00
❑	COMMON CARD (1-80/TB1-20)	.40	.15
❑	COMMON ROOKIE (R1-R25)	.50	.20
❑ 1	Scottie Pippen	2.00	.75
❑ 2	Glen Rice	.75	.30
❑ 3	Bryant Stith	.40	.15
❑ 4	Dino Radja	.40	.15
❑ 5	Horace Grant	.75	.30
❑ 6	Mahmoud Abdul-Rauf	.40	.15
❑ 7	Mookie Blaylock	.40	.15
❑ 8	Clifford Robinson	.40	.15
❑ 9	Vin Baker	.75	.30
❑ 10	Grant Hill	1.25	.50
❑ 11	Terrell Brandon	.75	.30
❑ 12	P.J. Brown	.40	.15
❑ 13	Kendall Gill	.40	.15
❑ 14	Brent Barry	.40	.15
❑ 15	Hakeem Olajuwon	1.25	.50
❑ 16	Allan Houston	.75	.30
❑ 17	Elden Campbell	.40	.15
❑ 18	Latrell Sprewell	1.25	.50
❑ 19	Jerry Stackhouse	1.50	.60
❑ 20	Robert Horry	.75	.30
❑ 21	Mitch Richmond	.75	.30
❑ 22	Gary Payton	1.25	.50
❑ 23	Rik Smits	.75	.30
❑ 24	Jim Jackson	.40	.15
❑ 25	Damon Stoudamire	1.25	.50
❑ 26	Bobby Phills	.40	.15
❑ 27	Chris Webber	1.25	.50
❑ 28	Shawn Bradley	.40	.15
❑ 29	Arvydas Sabonis	.75	.30
❑ 30	John Stockton	1.25	.50
❑ 31	Anfernee Hardaway	1.25	.50
❑ 32	Christian Laettner	.75	.30
❑ 33	Juwan Howard	.75	.30
❑ 34	Anthony Mason	.75	.30
❑ 35	Tom Gugliotta	.40	.15
❑ 36	Avery Johnson	.40	.15
❑ 37	Cedric Ceballos	.40	.15
❑ 38	Patrick Ewing	1.25	.50
❑ 39	Joe Smith	.75	.30
❑ 40	Dennis Rodman	2.50	1.00
❑ 41	Alonzo Mourning	.75	.30
❑ 42	Kevin Garnett	2.50	1.00
❑ 43	Antonio McDyess	1.25	.50
❑ 44	Detlef Schrempf	.75	.30
❑ 45	Reggie Miller	1.25	.50
❑ 46	Charles Barkley	1.50	.60
❑ 47	Derrick Coleman	.75	.30
❑ 48	Brian Grant	1.25	.50
❑ 49	Kenny Anderson	.40	.15
❑ 50	Otis Thorpe	.40	.15
❑ 51	Rod Strickland	.40	.15
❑ 52	Eric Williams	.40	.15
❑ 53	Rony Seikaly	.40	.15
❑ 54	Danny Manning	.75	.30
❑ 55	Karl Malone	1.25	.50
❑ 56	B.J. Armstrong	.40	.15
❑ 57	Greg Anthony	.40	.15
❑ 58	Larry Johnson	.75	.30
❑ 59	Loy Vaught	.40	.15
❑ 60	Sean Elliott	.75	.30
❑ 61	Dikembe Mutombo	.75	.30
❑ 62	Clarence Weatherspoon	.40	.15
❑ 63	Jamal Mashburn	.75	.30
❑ 64	Bryant Reeves	.40	.15
❑ 65	Vlade Divac	.40	.15
❑ 66	Shawn Kemp	.75	.30
❑ 67	LaPhonso Ellis	.40	.15
❑ 68	Tyrone Hill	.40	.15
❑ 69	David Robinson	1.25	.50
❑ 70	Shaquille O'Neal	3.00	1.25
❑ 71	Doug Christie	.75	.30
❑ 72	Jayson Williams	.75	.30
❑ 73	Michael Finley	1.50	.60
❑ 74	Tim Hardaway	.75	.30
❑ 75	Clyde Drexler	1.25	.50
❑ 76	Joe Dumars	1.25	.50
❑ 77	Glenn Robinson	1.25	.50
❑ 78	Dana Barros	.40	.15
❑ 79	Jason Kidd	2.00	.75
❑ 80	Michael Jordan	8.00	4.00
❑ R1	Allen Iverson RC	12.00	5.00
❑ R2	Stephon Marbury RC	4.00	1.50
❑ R3	Shareef Abdur-Rahim RC	4.00	1.50
❑ R4	Marcus Camby RC	2.00	.75
❑ R5	Ray Allen RC	5.00	2.00
❑ R6	Antoine Walker RC	4.00	1.50
❑ R7	Lorenzen Wright RC	.50	.20
❑ R8	Kerry Kittles RC	1.50	.60
❑ R9	Samaki Walker RC	.50	.20
❑ R10	Tony Delk RC	.50	.20
❑ R11	Vitaly Potapenko RC	.50	.20
❑ R12	Jerome Williams RC	1.50	.60
❑ R13	Todd Fuller RC	.50	.20
❑ R14	Erick Dampier RC	1.50	.60
❑ R15	Derek Fisher RC	2.50	1.00
❑ R16	Donald Whiteside RC	.50	.20
❑ R17	John Wallace RC	.50	.20
❑ R18	Steve Nash RC	8.00	3.00
❑ R19	Brian Evans RC	.50	.20
❑ R20	Jermaine O'Neal RC	4.00	1.50
❑ R21	Roy Rogers RC	.50	.20
❑ R22	Priest Lauderdale RC	.50	.20
❑ R23	Kobe Bryant RC	25.00	10.00
❑ R24	Martin Muursepp RC	.50	.20
❑ R25	Zydrunas Ilgauskas RC	1.00	.40
❑ TB1	Avery Johnson RET	.40	.15
❑ TB2	Chris Webber RET	1.25	.50
❑ TB3	Sean Elliott RET	.40	.15
❑ TB4	Joe Dumars RET	.75	.30
❑ TB5	Grant Hill RET	1.25	.50
❑ TB6	Gary Payton RET	.75	.30
❑ TB7	Shawn Kemp RET	.40	.15
❑ TB8	S.O'Neal Lakers RET	1.25	.50
❑ TB9	Eddie Jones RET	.75	.30
❑ TB10	John Wallace RET	.75	.30
❑ TB11	Patrick Ewing RET	.75	.30
❑ TB12	Jerry Stackhouse RET	.50	.20
❑ TB13	Allen Iverson RET	2.50	1.00
❑ TB14	Latrell Sprewell RET	1.25	.50
❑ TB15	Dino Radja RET	.40	.15
❑ TB16	David Wesley RET	.40	.15
❑ TB17	Joe Smith RET	.40	.15
❑ TB18	Damon Stoudamire RET	.75	.30
❑ TB19	Marcus Camby RET	.75	.30
❑ TB20	Juwan Howard RET	.40	.15

1997-98 Bowman's Best

❑	COMPLETE SET (125)	40.00	15.00
❑	COMMON CARD (1-100)	.25	.08
❑	COMMON ROOKIE (101-125)	.30	.10
❑ 1	Scottie Pippen	1.25	.50

❑ 2	Michael Finley	.75	.30
❑ 3	David Wesley	.25	.08
❑ 4	Brent Barry	.50	.20
❑ 5	Gary Payton	.75	.30
❑ 6	Christian Laettner	.50	.20
❑ 7	Grant Hill	.75	.30
❑ 8	Glenn Robinson	.75	.30
❑ 9	Reggie Miller	.75	.30
❑ 10	Tyus Edney	.25	.08
❑ 11	Jim Jackson	.25	.08
❑ 12	John Stockton	.75	.30
❑ 13	Karl Malone	.75	.30
❑ 14	Samaki Walker	.25	.08
❑ 15	Bryant Stith	.25	.08
❑ 16	Clyde Drexler	.75	.30
❑ 17	Danny Ferry	.25	.08
❑ 18	Shawn Bradley	.25	.08
❑ 19	Bryant Reeves	.25	.08
❑ 20	John Starks	.75	.30
❑ 21	Joe Dumars	.50	.20
❑ 22	Checklist	.25	.08
❑ 23	Antonio McDyess	.50	.20
❑ 24	Jeff Hornacek	.50	.20
❑ 25	Terrell Brandon	.50	.20
❑ 26	Kendall Gill	.25	.08
❑ 27	LaPhonso Ellis	.25	.08
❑ 28	Shaquille O'Neal	2.00	.75
❑ 29	Mahmoud Abdul-Rauf	.25	.08
❑ 30	Eric Williams	.25	.08
❑ 31	Lorenzen Wright	.25	.08
❑ 32	Shareef Abdur-Rahim	1.25	.50
❑ 33	Avery Johnson	.25	.08
❑ 34	Juwan Howard	.50	.20
❑ 35	Vin Baker	.50	.20
❑ 36	Dikembe Mutombo	.50	.20
❑ 37	Patrick Ewing	.75	.30
❑ 38	Allen Iverson	2.00	.75
❑ 39	Alonzo Mourning	.50	.20
❑ 40	Travis Knight	.25	.08
❑ 41	Ray Allen	.75	.30
❑ 42	Detlef Schrempf	.50	.20
❑ 43	Kevin Johnson	.50	.20
❑ 44	David Robinson	.75	.30
❑ 45	Tim Hardaway	.50	.20
❑ 46	Shawn Kemp	.50	.20
❑ 47	Marcus Camby	.50	.20
❑ 48	Rony Seikaly	.25	.08
❑ 49	Eddie Jones	.75	.30
❑ 50	Rik Smits	.50	.20
❑ 51	Jayson Williams	.25	.08
❑ 52	Malik Sealy	.25	.08
❑ 53	Chris Mullin	.75	.30
❑ 54	Larry Johnson	.50	.20
❑ 55	Isaiah Rider	.50	.20
❑ 56	Dennis Rodman	.75	.30
❑ 57	Bob Sura	.25	.08
❑ 58	Hakeem Olajuwon	.75	.30
❑ 59	Steve Smith	.50	.20
❑ 60	Michael Jordan	5.00	2.00
❑ 61	Jerry Stackhouse	.75	.30
❑ 62	Joe Smith	.50	.20
❑ 63	Walt Williams	.25	.08
❑ 64	Anthony Peeler	.25	.08
❑ 65	Charles Barkley	1.00	.40
❑ 66	Erick Dampier	.50	.20
❑ 67	Horace Grant	.50	.20
❑ 68	Anthony Mason	.50	.20
❑ 69	Anfernee Hardaway	.75	.30
❑ 70	Elden Campbell	.25	.08
❑ 71	Cedric Ceballos	.25	.08
❑ 72	Allan Houston	.50	.20
❑ 73	Kerry Kittles	.75	.30
❑ 74	Antoine Walker	1.00	.40
❑ 76	Sean Elliott	.50	.20
❑ 76	Jamal Mashburn	.50	.20
❑ 77	Mitch Richmond	.50	.20
❑ 78	Damon Stoudamire	.50	.20
❑ 79	Tom Gugliotta	.50	.20
❑ 80	Jason Kidd	1.25	.50
❑ 81	Chris Webber	.75	.30
❑ 82	Glen Rice	.50	.20
❑ 83	Loy Vaught	.25	.08
❑ 84	Olden Polynice	.25	.08
❑ 85	Kenny Anderson	.50	.20
❑ 86	Stephon Marbury	1.00	.40
❑ 87	Calbert Cheaney	.25	.08

❑ 88	Kobe Bryant	3.00	1.25
❑ 89	Arvydas Sabonis	.50	.20
❑ 90	Kevin Garnett	1.50	.60
❑ 91	Grant Hill BP	.75	.30
❑ 92	Clyde Drexler BP	.50	.20
❑ 93	Patrick Ewing BP	.50	.20
❑ 94	Shawn Kemp BP	.25	.08
❑ 95	Shaquille O'Neal BP	.75	.30
❑ 96	Michael Jordan BP	2.50	1.00
❑ 97	Karl Malone BP	.75	.30
❑ 98	Allen Iverson BP	1.00	.40
❑ 99	Shareef Abdur-Rahim BP	.60	.25
❑ 100	Dikembe Mutombo BP	.25	.08
❑ 101	Bobby Jackson RC	1.00	.40
❑ 102	Tony Battle RC	.60	.25
❑ 103	Keith Booth RC	.30	.10
❑ 104	Keith Van Horn RC	1.50	.60
❑ 105	Paul Grant RC	.30	.10
❑ 106	Tim Duncan RC	5.00	2.00
❑ 107	Scot Pollard RC	.50	.20
❑ 108	Maurice Taylor RC	1.00	.40
❑ 109	Antonio Daniels RC	.60	.25
❑ 110	Austin Croshere RC	1.00	.40
❑ 111	Tracy McGrady RC	8.00	3.00
❑ 112	Charles O'Bannon RC	.30	.10
❑ 113	Rodrick Rhodes RC	.30	.10
❑ 114	Johnny Taylor RC	.30	.10
❑ 115	Danny Fortson RC	.75	.30
❑ 116	Chauncey Billups RC	2.50	1.00
❑ 117	Tim Thomas RC	2.00	.75
❑ 118	Derek Anderson RC	1.25	.50
❑ 119	Ed Gray RC	.30	.10
❑ 120	Jacque Vaughn RC	.50	.20
❑ 121	Kelvin Cato RC	.50	.20
❑ 122	Tariq Abdul-Wahad RC	.50	.20
❑ 123	Ron Mercer RC	1.00	.40
❑ 124	Brevin Knight RC	.75	.30
❑ 125	Adonal Foyle RC	.50	.20

1998-99 Bowman's Best

❑	COMPLETE SET (125)	100.00	50.00
❑	COMPLETE SET w/o SP (100)	20.00	10.00
❑	COMMON CARD (1-100)	.25	.10
❑	COMMON ROOKIE (101-125)	.75	.30
❑ 1	Jason Kidd	1.25	.50
❑ 2	Dikembe Mutombo	.50	.20
❑ 3	Chris Mullin	.75	.30
❑ 4	Terrell Brandon	.50	.20
❑ 5	Cedric Ceballos	.25	.08
❑ 6	Rod Strickland	.25	.08
❑ 7	Darrell Armstrong	.25	.08
❑ 8	Anfernee Hardaway	.75	.30
❑ 9	Eddie Jones	.75	.30
❑ 10	Allen Iverson	1.50	.60
❑ 11	Kenny Anderson	.50	.20
❑ 12	Toni Kukoc	.50	.20
❑ 13	Lawrence Funderburke	.25	.08
❑ 14	P.J. Brown	.25	.08
❑ 15	Jeff Hornacek	.50	.20
❑ 16	Mookie Blaylock	.25	.08
❑ 17	Avery Johnson	.25	.08
❑ 18	Donyell Marshall	.50	.20
❑ 19	Detlef Schrempf	.50	.20
❑ 20	Joe Dumars	.75	.30
❑ 21	Charles Barkley	1.00	.40
❑ 22	Maurice Taylor	.40	.15
❑ 23	Chauncey Billups	.50	.20
❑ 24	Lee Mayberry	.25	.08

❑ 25	Glen Rice	.50	.20
❑ 26	John Stockton	.75	.30
❑ 27	Rik Smits	.50	.20
❑ 28	Laphonso Ellis	.25	.08
❑ 29	Kerry Kittles	.25	.08
❑ 30	Damon Stoudamire	.50	.20
❑ 31	Kevin Garnett	1.50	.60
❑ 32	Chris Mills	.25	.08
❑ 33	Kendall Gill	.25	.08
❑ 34	Tim Thomas	.50	.20
❑ 35	Derek Anderson	.60	.25
❑ 36	Billy Owens	.25	.08
❑ 37	Bobby Jackson	.50	.20
❑ 38	Allan Houston	.50	.20
❑ 39	Horace Grant	.50	.20
❑ 40	Ray Allen	.75	.30
❑ 41	Shawn Bradley	.25	.08
❑ 42	Arvydas Sabonis	.50	.20
❑ 43	Rex Chapman	.25	.08
❑ 44	Larry Johnson	.50	.20
❑ 45	Jayson Williams	.25	.08
❑ 46	Joe Smith	.50	.20
❑ 47	Ron Mercer	.40	.15
❑ 48	Rodney Rogers	.25	.08
❑ 49	Corliss Williamson	.50	.20
❑ 50	Tim Duncan	1.25	.50
❑ 51	Rasheed Wallace	.75	.30
❑ 52	Vin Baker	.50	.20
❑ 53	Reggie Miller	.75	.30
❑ 54	Patrick Ewing	.75	.30
❑ 55	Michael Finley	.75	.30
❑ 56	Bryant Reeves	.25	.08
❑ 57	Glenn Robinson	.50	.20
❑ 58	Walter McCarty	.25	.08
❑ 59	Brent Barry	.50	.20
❑ 60	John Starks	.50	.20
❑ 61	Clarence Weatherspoon	.25	.08
❑ 62	Calbert Cheaney	.25	.08
❑ 63	Lamond Murray	.25	.08
❑ 64	Zydrunas Ilgauskas	.50	.20
❑ 65	Anthony Mason	.50	.20
❑ 66	Bryon Russell	.25	.08
❑ 67	Dean Garrett	.25	.08
❑ 68	Tom Gugliotta	.25	.08
❑ 69	Dennis Rodman	.50	.20
❑ 70	Keith Van Horn	.75	.30
❑ 71	Jamal Mashburn	.50	.20
❑ 72	Steve Smith	.50	.20
❑ 73	David Wesley	.25	.08
❑ 74	Chris Webber	.75	.30
❑ 75	Isaiah Rider	.25	.08
❑ 76	Stephon Marbury	.75	.30
❑ 77	Tim Hardaway	.50	.20
❑ 78	Jerry Stackhouse	.75	.30
❑ 79	John Wallace	.25	.08
❑ 80	Karl Malone	.75	.30
❑ 81	Juwan Howard	.50	.20
❑ 82	Antonio McDyess	.50	.20
❑ 83	David Robinson	.75	.30
❑ 84	Bobby Phills	.25	.08
❑ 85	Scottie Pippen	1.25	.50
❑ 86	Brevin Knight	.25	.08
❑ 87	Alan Henderson	.25	.08
❑ 88	Kobe Bryant	3.00	1.25
❑ 89	Shawn Kemp	.50	.20
❑ 90	Antoine Walker	.75	.30
❑ 91	Tracy McGrady	2.00	.75
❑ 92	Hakeem Olajuwon	.75	.30
❑ 93	Mark Jackson	.50	.20
❑ 94	Bison Dele	.25	.08
❑ 95	Gary Payton	.75	.30
❑ 96	Ron Harper	.50	.20
❑ 97	Shareef Abdur-Rahim	.75	.30
❑ 98	Alonzo Mourning	.50	.20
❑ 99	Grant Hill	.75	.30
❑ 100	Shaquille O'Neal	2.00	.75
❑ 101	Michael Olowokandi RC	2.50	1.00
❑ 102	Mike Bibby RC	8.00	3.00
❑ 103	Raef LaFrentz RC	2.50	1.00
❑ 104	Antawn Jamison RC	8.00	3.00
❑ 105	Vince Carter RC	20.00	8.00
❑ 106	Robert Traylor RC	1.50	.60
❑ 107	Jason Williams RC	6.00	2.50
❑ 108	Larry Hughes RC	5.00	2.00
❑ 109	Dirk Nowitzki RC	15.00	6.00
❑ 110	Paul Pierce RC	8.00	3.00

❑ 111 Bonzi Wells RC	6.00	2.50
❑ 112 Michael Doleac RC	1.50	.60
❑ 113 Keon Clark RC	2.50	1.00
❑ 114 Michael Dickerson RC	3.00	1.25
❑ 115 Matt Harpring RC	2.50	1.00
❑ 116 Bryce Drew RC	1.50	.60
❑ 117 Pat Garrity RC	1.00	.40
❑ 118 Roshown McLeod RC	1.00	.40
❑ 119 Ricky Davis RC	5.00	2.00
❑ 120 Brian Skinner RC	1.50	.60
❑ 121 Tyronn Lue RC	2.00	.75
❑ 122 Felipe Lopez RC	2.00	.75
❑ 123 Al Harrington RC	4.00	1.50
❑ 124 Corey Benjamin RC	1.50	.60
❑ 125 Nazr Mohammed RC	.75	.30

1999-00 Bowman's Best

❑ COMPLETE SET (133)	60.00	30.00
❑ COMMON CARD (1-100)	.25	.08
❑ COMMON ROOKIE (101-133)	.50	.20
❑ 1 Vince Carter	2.00	.75
❑ 2 Dikembe Mutombo	.50	.20
❑ 3 Steve Nash	.75	.30
❑ 4 Matt Harpring	.75	.30
❑ 5 Stephon Marbury	.75	.30
❑ 6 Chris Webber	.75	.30
❑ 7 Jason Kidd	1.25	.50
❑ 8 Theo Ratliff	.50	.20
❑ 9 Damon Stoudamire	.50	.20
❑ 10 Shareef Abdur-Rahim	.75	.30
❑ 11 Rod Strickland	.50	.20
❑ 12 Jeff Hornacek	.50	.20
❑ 13 Vin Baker	.50	.20
❑ 14 Joe Smith	.50	.20
❑ 15 Alonzo Mourning	.50	.20
❑ 16 Isaiah Rider	.25	.08
❑ 17 Shaquille O'Neal	2.00	.75
❑ 18 Chris Mullin	.75	.30
❑ 19 Charles Barkley	1.00	.40
❑ 20 Grant Hill	.75	.30
❑ 21 Chris Mills	.25	.08
❑ 22 Antonio McDyess	.25	.08
❑ 23 Brevin Knight	.25	.08
❑ 24 Toni Kukoc	.50	.20
❑ 25 Antoine Walker	.75	.30
❑ 26 Eddie Jones	.75	.30
❑ 27 Tim Thomas	.50	.20
❑ 28 Latrell Sprewell	.75	.30
❑ 29 Larry Hughes	.75	.30
❑ 30 Tim Duncan	1.50	.60
❑ 31 Horace Grant	.50	.20
❑ 32 John Stockton	.50	.20
❑ 33 Mike Bibby	.75	.30
❑ 34 Mitch Richmond	.50	.20
❑ 35 Allan Houston	.50	.20
❑ 36 Terrell Brandon	.50	.20
❑ 37 Glenn Robinson	.50	.20
❑ 38 Tyrone Nesby RC	.25	.08
❑ 39 Glen Rice	.75	.30
❑ 40 Hakeem Olajuwon	.75	.30
❑ 41 Jerry Stackhouse	.75	.30
❑ 42 Elden Campbell	.25	.08
❑ 43 Ron Harper	.50	.20
❑ 44 Kenny Anderson	.50	.20
❑ 45 Michael Finley	.75	.30
❑ 46 Scottie Pippen	1.25	.50
❑ 47 Lindsey Hunter	.25	.08
❑ 48 Michael Olowokandi	.50	.20
❑ 49 P.J. Brown	.25	.08
❑ 50 Keith Van Horn	.75	.30
❑ 51 Michael Doleac	.25	.08
❑ 52 Anfernee Hardaway	.75	.30
❑ 53 Rasheed Wallace	.75	.30
❑ 54 Nick Anderson	.25	.08
❑ 55 Gary Payton	.75	.30
❑ 56 Tracy McGrady	2.00	.75
❑ 57 Ray Allen	.75	.30
❑ 58 Kobe Bryant	3.00	1.25
❑ 59 Ron Mercer	.50	.20
❑ 60 Shawn Kemp	.50	.20
❑ 61 Anthony Mason	.50	.20
❑ 62 Tim Hardaway	.50	.20
❑ 63 Antawn Jamison	1.25	.50
❑ 64 Mark Jackson	.50	.20
❑ 65 Tom Gugliotta	.25	.08
❑ 66 Marcus Camby	.50	.20
❑ 67 Kerry Kittles	.25	.08
❑ 68 Vlade Divac	.50	.20
❑ 69 Avery Johnson	.25	.08
❑ 70 Karl Malone	.75	.30
❑ 71 Juwan Howard	.50	.20
❑ 72 Alan Henderson	.25	.08
❑ 73 Hersey Hawkins	.50	.20
❑ 74 Darrell Armstrong	.25	.08
❑ 75 Allen Iverson	1.50	.60
❑ 76 Maurice Taylor	.50	.20
❑ 77 Gary Trent	.25	.08
❑ 78 John Starks	.50	.20
❑ 79 Paul Pierce	.75	.30
❑ 80 Kevin Garnett	1.50	.60
❑ 81 Patrick Ewing	.75	.30
❑ 82 Steve Smith	.50	.20
❑ 83 Jason Williams	.75	.30
❑ 84 David Robinson	.75	.30
❑ 85 Charles Oakley	.25	.08
❑ 86 Bryant Reeves	.25	.08
❑ 87 Nick Van Exel	.75	.30
❑ 88 Reggie Miller	.75	.30
❑ 89 Chris Gatling	.25	.08
❑ 90 Brian Grant	.50	.20
❑ 91 Allen Iverson BP	.50	.20
❑ 92 Tim Duncan BP	.75	.30
❑ 93 Keith Van Horn BP	.25	.08
❑ 94 Kevin Garnett BP	.75	.30
❑ 95 Kobe Bryant BP	1.50	.60
❑ 96 Elton Brand BP	1.50	.60
❑ 97 Baron Davis BP	1.50	.60
❑ 98 Lamar Odom BP	1.25	.50
❑ 99 Wally Szczerbiak BP	1.25	.50
❑ 100 Jason Terry BP	.75	.30
❑ 101 Elton Brand RC	3.00	1.25
❑ 102 Steve Francis RC	3.00	1.25
❑ 103 Baron Davis RC	5.00	2.00
❑ 104 Lamar Odom RC	2.50	1.00
❑ 105 Jonathan Bender RC	2.50	1.00
❑ 106 Wally Szczerbiak RC	2.50	1.00
❑ 107 Richard Hamilton RC	2.50	1.00
❑ 108 Andre Miller RC	2.50	1.00
❑ 109 Shawn Marion RC	3.00	1.25
❑ 110 Jason Terry RC	1.50	.60
❑ 111 Trajan Langdon RC	1.00	.40
❑ 112 A.Radojevic RC	.75	.30
❑ 113 Corey Maggette RC	2.50	1.00
❑ 114 William Avery RC	1.00	.40
❑ 115 DeMarco Johnson RC	.60	.25
❑ 116 Ron Artest RC	1.50	.60
❑ 117 Cal Bowdler RC	.75	.30
❑ 118 James Posey RC	1.50	.60
❑ 119 Quincy Lewis RC	.75	.30
❑ 120 Dion Glover RC	.75	.30
❑ 121 Jeff Foster RC	.75	.30
❑ 122 Kenny Thomas RC	1.00	.40
❑ 123 Devean George RC	1.25	.50
❑ 124 Tim James RC	.75	.30
❑ 125 Vonteego Cummings RC	1.00	.40
❑ 126 Jumaine Jones RC	1.25	.50
❑ 127 Scott Padgett RC	.75	.30
❑ 128 Anthony Carter RC	1.50	.60
❑ 129 Chris Herren RC	.50	.20
❑ 130 Todd MacCulloch RC	.75	.30
❑ 131 John Celestand RC	.50	.20
❑ 132 Adrian Griffin RC	.75	.30
❑ 133 Mirsad Turkcan RC	.50	.20

2000-01 Bowman's Best

❑ COMPLETE SET w/o RC (100)	30.00	15.00
❑ COMMON CARD (1-100)	.25	.08
❑ COMMON ROOKIE (101-133)	2.50	1.00
❑ 1 Allen Iverson	1.50	.60
❑ 2 Darrell Armstrong	.25	.08
❑ 3 Kendall Gill	.25	.08
❑ 4 Marcus Camby	.50	.20
❑ 5 Glen Rice	.50	.20
❑ 6 Eddie Jones	.75	.30
❑ 7 Wally Szczerbiak	.50	.20
❑ 8 Antawn Jamison	.75	.30
❑ 9 Raef LaFrentz	.50	.20
❑ 10 Steve Francis	.75	.30
❑ 11 Tracy McGrady	2.00	.75
❑ 12 Brian Grant	.50	.20
❑ 13 Vlade Divac	.50	.20
❑ 14 Gary Payton	.75	.30
❑ 15 Vince Carter	2.00	.75
❑ 16 John Stockton	.75	.30
❑ 17 Mike Bibby	.50	.20
❑ 18 Derek Anderson	.50	.20
❑ 19 Juwan Howard	.50	.20
❑ 20 Allan Houston	.50	.20
❑ 21 Kevin Garnett	1.50	.60
❑ 22 Michael Olowokandi	.25	.08
❑ 23 Maurice Taylor	.25	.08
❑ 24 Jerry Stackhouse	.75	.30
❑ 25 Nick Van Exel	.75	.30
❑ 26 Andre Miller	.50	.20
❑ 27 Michael Finley	.50	.20
❑ 28 Jamal Mashburn	.50	.20
❑ 29 Ron Mercer	.50	.20
❑ 30 Jim Jackson	.25	.08
❑ 31 Kenny Anderson	.50	.20
❑ 32 Karl Malone	.75	.30
❑ 33 Rod Strickland	.25	.08
❑ 34 Shaquille O'Neal	2.00	.75
❑ 35 Glenn Robinson	.50	.20
❑ 36 Keith Van Horn	.75	.30
❑ 37 Grant Hill	.75	.30
❑ 38 Eric Snow	.50	.20
❑ 39 Anfernee Hardaway	.75	.30
❑ 40 Scottie Pippen	1.25	.50
❑ 41 Jason Williams	.50	.20
❑ 42 Elton Brand	.75	.30
❑ 43 Stephon Marbury	.75	.30
❑ 44 David Robinson	.75	.30
❑ 45 Antonio Davis	.25	.08
❑ 46 Michael Dickerson	.50	.20
❑ 47 Mitch Richmond	.50	.20
❑ 48 Rashard Lewis	.50	.20
❑ 49 Jermaine O'Neal	.75	.30
❑ 50 Tim Duncan	1.50	.60
❑ 51 Tom Gugliotta	.25	.08
❑ 52 Theo Ratliff	.50	.20
❑ 53 Joe Smith	.50	.20
❑ 54 Tim Thomas	.50	.20
❑ 55 Brevin Knight	.25	.08
❑ 56 Dale Davis	.25	.08
❑ 57 Cuttino Mobley	.50	.20
❑ 58 Cedric Ceballos	.25	.08
❑ 59 Christian Laettner	.50	.20
❑ 60 Dirk Nowitzki	1.25	.50
❑ 61 Paul Pierce	.50	.20
❑ 62 Derrick Coleman	.25	.08
❑ 63 Dikembe Mutombo	.50	.20

64	Lamond Murray	.25	.08	117B	Desmond Mason RC	2.50	1.00	12	Isiah Thomas	.20	.07
65	Antonio McDyess	.50	.20	117C	Desmond Mason RC	2.50	1.00	13	Kendall Gill	.10	.02
66	Reggie Miller	.75	.30	118A	Quentin Richardson RC	10.00	4.00	14	Jeff Hornacek	.10	.02
67	Hakeem Olajuwon	.75	.30	118B	Quentin Richardson RC	10.00	4.00	15	Latrell Sprewell	.20	.07
68	Corey Maggette	.50	.20	118C	Quentin Richardson RC	10.00	4.00	16	Lucious Harris	.05	.01
69	Lamar Odom	.75	.30	119A	Jamaal Magloire RC	2.50	1.00	17	Chris Mullin	.20	.07
70	Larry Hughes	.50	.20	119B	Jamaal Magloire RC	2.50	1.00	18	John Williams	.05	.01
71	Anthony Mason	.50	.20	119C	Jamaal Magloire RC	2.50	1.00	19	Tony Campbell	.05	.01
72	Sam Cassell	.75	.30	120A	Speedy Claxton RC	2.50	1.00	20	LaPhonso Ellis	.05	.01
73	Terrell Brandon	.50	.20	120B	Speedy Claxton RC	2.50	1.00	21	Gerald Wilkins	.05	.01
74	Latrell Sprewell	.75	.30	120C	Speedy Claxton RC	2.50	1.00	22	Clyde Drexler	.20	.07
75	Kobe Bryant	3.00	1.25	121A	Morris Peterson RC	6.00	2.50	23	Michael Jordan BB	2.50	1.00
76	Tim Hardaway	.50	.20	121B	Morris Peterson RC	6.00	2.50	24	George Lynch	.05	.01
77	Mark Jackson	.25	.08	121C	Morris Peterson RC	6.00	2.50	25	Mark Price	.05	.01
78	Vin Baker	.50	.20	122A	Donnell Harvey RC	2.50	1.00	26	James Robinson	.05	.01
79	Jonathan Bender	.75	.30	122B	Donnell Harvey RC	2.50	1.00	27	Elmore Spencer	.05	.01
80	Chris Webber	.75	.30	122C	Donnell Harvey RC	2.50	1.00	28	Stacey King	.05	.01
81	Rasheed Wallace	.75	.30	123A	DeShawn Stevenson RC	2.50	1.00	29	Corie Blount	.05	.01
82	Shawn Marion	.75	.30	123B	DeShawn Stevenson RC	2.50	1.00	30	Dell Curry	.05	.01
83	Toni Kukoc	.50	.20	123C	DeShawn Stevenson RC	2.50	1.00	31	Reggie Miller	.20	.07
84	Patrick Ewing	.75	.30	124A	Dalibor Bagaric RC	2.50	1.00	32	Karl Malone	.30	.10
85	Ray Allen	.75	.30	124B	Dalibor Bagaric RC	2.50	1.00	33	Scottie Pippen	.60	.25
86	Isaiah Rider	.50	.20	124C	Dalibor Bagaric RC	2.50	1.00	34	Hakeem Olajuwon	.30	.10
87	Danny Fortson	.25	.08	125A	Iakovos Tsakalidis RC	2.50	1.00	35	Clarence Weatherspoon	.05	.01
88	Jerome Williams	.25	.08	125B	Iakovos Tsakalidis RC	2.50	1.00	36	Kevin Edwards	.05	.01
89	Shawn Kemp	.50	.20	125C	Iakovos Tsakalidis RC	2.50	1.00	37	Pete Myers	.05	.01
90	Ron Artest	.50	.20	126A	Mamadou N'Diaye RC	2.50	1.00	38	Jeff Turner	.05	.01
91	P.J. Brown	.25	.08	126B	Mamadou N'Diaye RC	2.50	1.00	39	Ennis Whatley	.05	.01
92	Baron Davis	.75	.30	126C	Mamadou N'Diaye RC	2.50	1.00	40	Calbert Cheaney	.05	.01
93	Antoine Walker	.75	.30	127A	Lavor Postell RC	2.50	1.00	41	Glen Rice	.10	.02
94	Jason Terry	.75	.30	127B	Lavor Postell RC	2.50	1.00	42	Vin Baker	.20	.07
95	Jalen Rose	.75	.30	127C	Lavor Postell RC	2.50	1.00	43	Grant Long	.05	.01
96	Avery Johnson	.25	.08	128A	Erick Barkley RC	2.50	1.00	44	Derrick Coleman	.10	.02
97	Shareef Abdur-Rahim	.75	.30	128B	Erick Barkley RC	2.50	1.00	45	Rik Smits	.05	.01
98	Bryon Russell	.25	.08	128C	Erick Barkley RC	2.50	1.00	46	Chris Smith	.05	.01
99	Richard Hamilton	.50	.20	129A	Mark Madsen RC	2.50	1.00	47	Carl Herrera	.05	.01
100	Jason Kidd	1.25	.50	129B	Mark Madsen RC	2.50	1.00	48	Bob Martin	.05	.01
101A	Kenyon Martin RC	12.00	5.00	129C	Mark Madsen RC	2.50	1.00	49	Terrell Brandon	.10	.02
101B	Kenyon Martin RC	12.00	5.00	130A	Khalid El-Amin RC	2.50	1.00	50	David Robinson	.30	.10
101C	Kenyon Martin RC	12.00	5.00	130B	Khalid El-Amin RC	2.50	1.00	51	Danny Ferry	.05	.01
102A	Stromile Swift RC	6.00	2.50	130C	Khalid El-Amin RC	2.50	1.00	52	Buck Williams	.05	.01
102B	Stromile Swift RC	6.00	2.50	131A	A.J. Guyton RC	2.50	1.00	53	Josh Grant	.05	.01
102C	Stromile Swift RC	6.00	2.50	131B	A.J. Guyton RC	2.50	1.00	54	Ed Pinckney	.05	.01
103A	Darius Miles RC	12.00	5.00	131C	A.J. Guyton RC	2.50	1.00	55	Dikembe Mutombo	.10	.02
103B	Darius Miles RC	12.00	5.00	132A	Stephen Jackson RC	5.00	2.00	56	Clifford Robinson	.10	.02
103C	Darius Miles RC	12.00	5.00	132B	Stephen Jackson RC	5.00	2.00	57	Luther Wright	.05	.01
104A	Marcus Fizer RC	2.50	1.00	132C	Stephen Jackson RC	5.00	2.00	58	Scott Burrell	.05	.01
104B	Marcus Fizer RC	2.50	1.00	133A	Michael Redd RC	6.00	2.50	59	Stacey Augmon	.05	.01
104C	Marcus Fizer RC	2.50	1.00	133B	Michael Redd RC	6.00	2.50	60	Jeff Malone	.05	.01
105A	Mike Miller RC	2.50	1.00	133C	Michael Redd RC	6.00	2.50	61	Byron Houston	.05	.01
105B	Mike Miller RC	2.50	1.00	LCP1	Draft Picks	10.00	4.00	62	Anthony Peeler	.05	.01
105C	Mike Miller RC	2.50	1.00					63	Michael Adams	.05	.01
106A	DerMarr Johnson RC	2.50	1.00					64	Negele Knight	.05	.01
106B	DerMarr Johnson RC	2.50	1.00		**1994-95 Collector's**			65	Terry Cummings	.05	.01
106C	DerMarr Johnson RC	2.50	1.00		**Choice**			66	Christian Laettner	.10	.02
107A	Chris Mihm RC	2.50	1.00					67	Tracy Murray	.05	.01
107B	Chris Mihm RC	2.50	1.00					68	Sedale Threatt	.05	.01
107C	Chris Mihm RC	2.50	1.00					69	Dan Majerle	.10	.02
108A	Jamal Crawford RC	3.00	1.25					70	Frank Brickowski	.05	.01
108B	Jamal Crawford RC	3.00	1.25					71	Ken Norman	.05	.01
108C	Jamal Crawford RC	3.00	1.25					72	Charles Smith	.05	.01
109A	Joel Przybilla RC	2.50	1.00					73	Adam Keefe	.05	.01
109B	Joel Przybilla RC	2.50	1.00					74	P.J. Brown	.05	.01
109C	Joel Przybilla RC	2.50	1.00					75	Kevin Duckworth	.05	.01
110A	Keyon Dooling RC	2.50	1.00					76	Shawn Bradley	.10	.02
110B	Keyon Dooling RC	2.50	1.00					77	Darnell Mee	.05	.01
110C	Keyon Dooling RC	2.50	1.00					78	Nick Anderson	.05	.01
111A	Jerome Moiso RC	2.50	1.00					79	Mark West	.05	.01
111B	Jerome Moiso RC	2.50	1.00					80	B.J. Armstrong	.05	.01
111C	Jerome Moiso RC	2.50	1.00					81	Dennis Scott	.05	.01
112A	Etan Thomas RC	2.50	1.00					82	Lindsey Hunter	.10	.02
112B	Etan Thomas RC	2.50	1.00					83	Derek Strong	.05	.01
112C	Etan Thomas RC	2.50	1.00		COMPLETE SET (420)	30.00	15.00	84	Mike Brown	.05	.01
113A	Courtney Alexander RC	5.00	2.00		COMPLETE SERIES 1 (210)	12.00	6.00	85	Antonio Harvey	.05	.01
113B	Courtney Alexander RC	5.00	2.00		COMPLETE SERIES 2 (210)	18.00	9.00	86	Anthony Bonner	.05	.01
113C	Courtney Alexander RC	5.00	2.00	1	Anfernee Hardaway	.50	.20	87	Sam Cassell	.20	.07
114A	Mateen Cleaves RC	2.50	1.00	2	Mark Macon	.05	.01	88	Harold Miner	.05	.01
114B	Mateen Cleaves RC	2.50	1.00	3	Steve Smith	.10	.02	89	Spud Webb	.10	.02
114C	Mateen Cleaves RC	2.50	1.00	4	Chris Webber	.50	.20	90	Mookie Blaylock	.05	.01
115A	Jason Collier RC	4.00	1.50	5	Donald Royal	.05	.01	91	Greg Anthony	.05	.01
115B	Jason Collier RC	4.00	1.50	6	Avery Johnson	.05	.01	92	Richard Petruska	.05	.01
115C	Jason Collier RC	4.00	1.50	7	Kevin Johnson	.10	.02	93	Sean Rooks	.05	.01
116A	Hidayet Turkoglu RC	8.00	3.00	8	Doug Christie	.05	.01	94	Kevin Johnson	.05	.01
116B	Hidayet Turkoglu RC	8.00	3.00	9	Derrick McKey	.05	.01	95	Randy Brown	.05	.01
116C	Hidayet Turkoglu RC	8.00	3.00	10	Dennis Rodman	.40	.15	96	Orlando Woolridge	.05	.01
117A	Desmond Mason RC	2.50	1.00	11	Scott Skiles UER	.05	.01	97	Charles Oakley	.05	.01

❑ 98	Craig Ehlo	.05	.01
❑ 99	Derek Harper	.05	.01
❑ 100	Doug Edwards	.05	.01
❑ 101	Muggsy Bogues	.10	.02
❑ 102	Mitch Richmond	.05	.07
❑ 103	Mahmoud Abdul-Rauf	.05	.01
❑ 104	Joe Dumars	.20	.07
❑ 105	Eric Riley	.05	.01
❑ 106	Terry Mills	.05	.01
❑ 107	Toni Kukoc	.30	.10
❑ 108	Jon Koncak	.05	.01
❑ 109	Haywoode Workman	.05	.01
❑ 110	Todd Day	.05	.01
❑ 111	Detlef Schrempf	.10	.02
❑ 112	David Wesley	.05	.01
❑ 113	Mark Jackson	.05	.01
❑ 114	Doug Overton	.05	.01
❑ 115	Vinny Del Negro	.05	.01
❑ 116	Loy Vaught	.05	.01
❑ 117	Mike Peplowski	.05	.01
❑ 118	Bimbo Coles	.05	.01
❑ 119	Rex Walters	.05	.01
❑ 120	Sherman Douglas	.05	.01
❑ 121	David Benoit	.05	.01
❑ 122	John Salley	.05	.01
❑ 123	Cedric Ceballos	.05	.01
❑ 124	Chris Mills	.10	.02
❑ 125	Robert Horry	.10	.02
❑ 126	Johnny Newman	.05	.01
❑ 127	Malcolm Mackey	.05	.01
❑ 128	Terry Dehere	.05	.01
❑ 129	Dino Radja	.05	.01
❑ 130	Tree Rollins	.05	.01
❑ 131	Xavier McDaniel	.05	.01
❑ 132	Bobby Hurley	.05	.01
❑ 133	Alonzo Mourning	.25	.08
❑ 134	Isaiah Rider	.10	.01
❑ 135	Antoine Carr	.05	.01
❑ 136	Robert Pack	.05	.01
❑ 137	Walt Williams	.05	.01
❑ 138	Tyrone Corbin	.05	.01
❑ 139	Popeye Jones	.05	.01
❑ 140	Shawn Kemp	.30	.10
❑ 141	Thurl Bailey	.05	.01
❑ 142	James Worthy	.20	.07
❑ 143	Scott Haskin	.05	.01
❑ 144	Hubert Davis	.05	.01
❑ 145	A.C. Green	.10	.02
❑ 146	Dale Davis	.05	.01
❑ 147	Nate McMillan	.05	.01
❑ 148	Chris Morris	.05	.01
❑ 149	Will Perdue	.05	.01
❑ 150	Felton Spencer	.05	.01
❑ 151	Rod Strickland	.10	.02
❑ 152	Blue Edwards	.05	.01
❑ 153	John Williams	.05	.01
❑ 154	Rodney Rogers	.05	.01
❑ 155	Acie Earl	.05	.01
❑ 156	Hersey Hawkins	.10	.02
❑ 157	Jamal Mashburn	.20	.07
❑ 158	Don MacLean	.05	.01
❑ 159	Micheal Williams	.05	.01
❑ 160	Kenny Gattison	.05	.01
❑ 161	Rich King	.05	.01
❑ 162	Allan Houston	.30	.10
❑ 163	Hoop-it up	.05	.01
❑ 164	Hoop-it up	.05	.01
❑ 165	Hoop-it up	.05	.01
❑ 166	Danny Manning TO	.05	.01
❑ 167	Robert Parish TO	.05	.01
❑ 168	Alonzo Mourning TO	.20	.07
❑ 169	Scottie Pippen TO	.30	.10
❑ 170	Mark Price TO	.05	.01
❑ 171	Jamal Mashburn TO	.10	.02
❑ 172	Dikembe Mutombo TO	.05	.01
❑ 173	Joe Dumars TO	.10	.02
❑ 174	Chris Webber TO	.25	.08
❑ 175	Hakeem Olajuwon TO	.20	.07
❑ 176	Reggie Miller TO	.10	.02
❑ 177	Ron Harper TO	.05	.01
❑ 178	Nick Van Exel TO	.10	.02
❑ 179	Steve Smith TO	.05	.01
❑ 180	Vin Baker TO	.10	.02
❑ 181	Isaiah Rider TO	.05	.01
❑ 182	Derrick Coleman TO	.05	.01
❑ 183	Patrick Ewing TO	.10	.02
❑ 184	Shaquille O'Neal TO	.40	.15
❑ 185	Clarence Weatherspoon	.05	.01
❑ 186	Charles Barkley TO	.20	.07
❑ 187	Clyde Drexler TO	.10	.02
❑ 188	Mitch Richmond TO	.10	.02
❑ 189	David Robinson TO	.20	.07
❑ 190	Shawn Kemp TO	.20	.07
❑ 191	Karl Malone TO	.20	.07
❑ 192	Tom Gugliotta TO	.05	.01
❑ 193	Kenny Anderson ASA	.05	.01
❑ 194	Alonzo Mourning ASA	.20	.07
❑ 195	Mark Price ASA	.05	.01
❑ 196	John Stockton ASA	.20	.07
❑ 197	Shaquille O'Neal ASA	.40	.15
❑ 198	Latrell Sprewell ASA	.20	.07
❑ 199	Charles Barkley PRO	.20	.07
❑ 200	Chris Webber PRO	.25	.08
❑ 201	Patrick Ewing PRO	.10	.02
❑ 202	Dennis Rodman PRO	.20	.07
❑ 203	Shawn Kemp PRO	.20	.07
❑ 204	Michael Jordan PRO	1.25	.50
❑ 205	Shaquille O'Neal PRO	.40	.15
❑ 206	Larry Johnson PRO	.05	.01
❑ 207	Tim Hardaway CL	.05	.01
❑ 208	John Stockton CL	.20	.07
❑ 209	Harold Miner CL	.05	.01
❑ 210	B.J. Armstrong CL	.05	.01
❑ 211	Vernon Maxwell	.05	.01
❑ 212	John Stockton	.25	.10
❑ 213	Luc Longley	.05	.01
❑ 214	Sam Perkins	.10	.02
❑ 215	Pooh Richardson	.05	.01
❑ 216	Tyrone Corbin	.05	.01
❑ 217	Mario Elie	.05	.01
❑ 218	Bobby Phills	.05	.01
❑ 219	Grant Hill RC	1.00	.40
❑ 220	Gary Payton	.30	.10
❑ 221	Tom Hammonds	.05	.01
❑ 222	Danny Ainge	.05	.01
❑ 223	Gary Grant	.05	.01
❑ 224	Jim Jackson	.10	.02
❑ 225	Chris Gatling	.05	.01
❑ 226	Sergei Bazarevich	.05	.01
❑ 227	Tony Dumas RC	.05	.01
❑ 228	Andrew Lang	.05	.01
❑ 229	Wesley Person RC	.05	.07
❑ 230	Terry Porter	.05	.01
❑ 231	Duane Causwell	.05	.01
❑ 232	Shaquille O'Neal	1.00	.40
❑ 233	Antonio Davis	.05	.01
❑ 234	Charles Barkley	.30	.10
❑ 235	Tony Massenburg	.05	.01
❑ 236	Ricky Pierce	.05	.01
❑ 237	Scott Skiles	.05	.01
❑ 238	Jalen Rose RC	.75	.30
❑ 239	Charlie Ward RC	.20	.07
❑ 240	Michael Jordan COMM	1.25	.50
❑ 241	Elden Campbell	.05	.01
❑ 242	Bill Cartwright	.05	.01
❑ 243	Armon Gilliam	.05	.01
❑ 244	Rick Fox	.05	.01
❑ 245	Tim Breaux	.05	.01
❑ 246	Monty Williams RC	.05	.01
❑ 247	Dominique Wilkins	.20	.07
❑ 248	Robert Parish	.10	.02
❑ 249	Mark Jackson	.05	.01
❑ 250	Jason Kidd RC	2.00	.75
❑ 251	Andres Guibert	.05	.01
❑ 252	Matt Geiger	.05	.01
❑ 253	Stanley Roberts	.05	.01
❑ 254	Jack Haley	.05	.01
❑ 255	David Wingate	.05	.01
❑ 256	John Crotty	.05	.01
❑ 257	Brian Grant RC	.50	.20
❑ 258	Otis Thorpe	.05	.01
❑ 259	Clifford Rozier RC	.05	.01
❑ 260	Grant Long	.05	.01
❑ 261	Eric Mobley RC	.05	.01
❑ 262	Dickey Simpkins RC	.05	.01
❑ 263	J.R. Reid	.05	.01
❑ 264	Kevin Willis	.05	.01
❑ 265	Scott Brooks	.05	.01
❑ 266	Glenn Robinson RC	.60	.25
❑ 267	Dana Barros	.05	.01
❑ 268	Ken Norman	.05	.01
❑ 269	Herb Williams	.05	.01
❑ 270	Dee Brown	.05	.01
❑ 271	Steve Kerr	.05	.01
❑ 272	Jon Barry	.05	.01
❑ 273	Sean Elliott	.10	.02
❑ 274	Elliot Perry	.05	.01
❑ 275	Kenny Smith	.05	.01
❑ 276	Sean Rooks	.05	.01
❑ 277	Gheorghe Muresan	.05	.01
❑ 278	Juwan Howard RC	.50	.20
❑ 279	Steve Smith	.10	.02
❑ 280	Anthony Bowie	.05	.01
❑ 281	Moses Malone	.05	.07
❑ 282	Olden Polynice	.05	.01
❑ 283	Jo Jo English	.05	.01
❑ 284	Marty Conlon	.05	.01
❑ 285	Sam Mitchell	.05	.01
❑ 286	Doug West	.05	.01
❑ 287	Cedric Ceballos	.05	.01
❑ 288	Lorenzo Williams	.05	.01
❑ 289	Harold Ellis	.05	.01
❑ 290	Doc Rivers	.10	.02
❑ 291	Keith Tower	.05	.01
❑ 292	Mark Bryant	.05	.01
❑ 293	Oliver Miller	.05	.01
❑ 294	Michael Adams	.05	.01
❑ 295	Tree Rollins	.05	.01
❑ 296	Eddie Jones RC	1.00	.40
❑ 297	Malik Sealy	.05	.01
❑ 298	Blue Edwards	.05	.01
❑ 299	Brooks Thompson RC	.05	.01
❑ 300	Benoit Benjamin	.05	.01
❑ 301	Avery Johnson	.05	.01
❑ 302	Larry Johnson	.10	.02
❑ 303	John Starks	.05	.01
❑ 304	Byron Scott	.10	.02
❑ 305	Eric Murdock	.05	.01
❑ 306	Jay Humphries	.05	.01
❑ 307	Kenny Anderson	.10	.02
❑ 308	Brian Williams	.05	.01
❑ 309	Nick Van Exel	.20	.07
❑ 310	Tim Hardaway	.20	.07
❑ 311	Lee Mayberry	.05	.01
❑ 312	Vlade Divac	.05	.01
❑ 313	Donyell Marshall RC	.20	.07
❑ 314	Anthony Mason	.10	.02
❑ 315	Danny Manning	.10	.02
❑ 316	Tyrone Hill	.05	.01
❑ 317	Vincent Askew	.05	.01
❑ 318	Khalid Reeves RC	.05	.01
❑ 319	Ron Harper	.10	.02
❑ 320	Brent Price	.05	.01
❑ 321	Byron Houston	.05	.01
❑ 322	Lamond Murray RC	.10	.02
❑ 323	Bryant Stith	.05	.01
❑ 324	Tom Gugliotta	.10	.02
❑ 325	Jerome Kersey	.05	.01
❑ 326	B.J. Tyler RC	.05	.01
❑ 327	Antonio Lang	.05	.01
❑ 328	Carlos Rogers RC	.05	.01
❑ 329	Wayman Tisdale	.05	.01
❑ 330	Kevin Gamble	.05	.01
❑ 331	Eric Piatkowski RC	.05	.01
❑ 332	Mitchell Butler	.05	.01
❑ 333	Patrick Ewing	.20	.07
❑ 334	Doug Smith	.05	.01
❑ 335	Joe Kleine	.05	.01
❑ 336	Keith Jennings	.05	.01
❑ 337	Bill Curley RC	.05	.01
❑ 338	Johnny Newman	.05	.01
❑ 339	Howard Eisley RC	.05	.01
❑ 340	Willie Anderson	.05	.01
❑ 341	Aaron McKie RC	.50	.20
❑ 342	Tom Chambers	.05	.01
❑ 343	Scott Williams	.05	.01
❑ 344	Harvey Grant	.05	.01
❑ 345	Billy Owens	.05	.01
❑ 346	Sharone Wright RC	.05	.01
❑ 347	Michael Cage	.05	.01
❑ 348	Vern Fleming	.05	.01
❑ 349	Darrin Hancock RC	.05	.01
❑ 350	Matt Fish	.05	.01
❑ 351	Rony Seikaly	.05	.01
❑ 352	Victor Alexander	.05	.01
❑ 353	Anthony Miller RC	.05	.01
❑ 354	Horace Grant	.10	.02
❑ 355	Jayson Williams	.10	.02

#	Player		
❏ 356	Dale Ellis	.05	.01
❏ 357	Sarunas Marciulionis	.05	.01
❏ 358	Anthony Avent	.05	.01
❏ 359	Rex Chapman	.05	.01
❏ 360	Askia Jones RC	.05	.01
❏ 361	Bo Outlaw RC	.05	.01
❏ 362	Chuck Person	.05	.01
❏ 363	Danny Schayes	.05	.01
❏ 364	Morlon Wiley	.05	.01
❏ 365	Dontonio Wingfield RC	.05	.01
❏ 366	Tony Smith	.05	.01
❏ 367	Bill Wennington	.05	.01
❏ 368	Bryon Russell	.05	.01
❏ 369	Geert Hammink	.05	.01
❏ 370	Eric Montross RC	.05	.01
❏ 371	Cliff Levingston	.05	.01
❏ 372	Stacey Augmon BP	.05	.01
❏ 373	Eric Montross BP	.05	.01
❏ 374	Alonzo Mourning BP	.20	.07
❏ 375	Scottie Pippen BP	.30	.10
❏ 376	Mark Price BP	.05	.01
❏ 377	Jason Kidd BP	.75	.30
❏ 378	Jalen Rose BP	.10	.02
❏ 379	Grant Hill BP	.40	.15
❏ 380	Latrell Sprewell BP	.20	.07
❏ 381	Hakeem Olajuwon BP	.20	.07
❏ 382	Reggie Miller BP	.10	.02
❏ 383	Lamond Murray BP	.05	.01
❏ 384	Eddie Jones BP	.50	.20
❏ 385	Khalid Reeves BP	.05	.01
❏ 386	Glenn Robinson BP	.30	.10
❏ 387	Donyell Marshall BP	.10	.02
❏ 388	Derrick Coleman BP	.05	.01
❏ 389	Patrick Ewing BP	.10	.02
❏ 390	Shaquille O'Neal BP	.40	.15
❏ 391	Sharone Wright BP	.05	.01
❏ 392	Charles Barkley BP	.20	.07
❏ 393	Aaron McKie BP	.10	.02
❏ 394	Brian Grant BP	.10	.02
❏ 395	David Robinson BP	.20	.07
❏ 396	Shawn Kemp BP	.20	.07
❏ 397	Karl Malone BP	.20	.07
❏ 398	Tom Gugliotta BP	.05	.01
❏ 399	Hakeem Olajuwon TRIV	.20	.07
❏ 400	Shaquille O'Neal TRIV	.40	.15
❏ 401	Chris Webber TRIV	.25	.08
❏ 402	Michael Jordan TRIV	1.25	.50
❏ 403	David Robinson TRIV	.20	.07
❏ 404	Shawn Kemp TRIV	.20	.07
❏ 405	Patrick Ewing TRIV	.10	.02
❏ 406	Charles Barkley TRIV	.20	.07
❏ 407	Glenn Robinson DC	.30	.10
❏ 408	Jason Kidd DC	.75	.30
❏ 409	Grant Hill DC	.40	.15
❏ 410	Donyell Marshall DC	.10	.02
❏ 411	Sharone Wright DC	.05	.01
❏ 412	Lamond Murray DC	.05	.01
❏ 413	Brian Grant DC	.10	.02
❏ 414	Eric Montross DC	.05	.01
❏ 415	Eddie Jones DC	.50	.20
❏ 416	Carlos Rogers DC	.05	.01
❏ 417	Shawn Kemp CL	.05	.01
❏ 418	Bobby Hurley CL	.05	.01
❏ 419	Shawn Bradley CL	.05	.01
❏ 420	Michael Jordan CL	.75	.30

1995-96 Collector's Choice

❏	COMPLETE SET (410)	35.00	17.50
❏	COMP.FACTORY SET (419)	35.00	25.00
❏	COMPLETE SERIES 1 (210)	15.00	7.50
❏	COMPLETE SERIES 2 (200)	20.00	10.00
❏ 1	Rod Strickland	.15	.05
❏ 2	Larry Johnson	.25	.08
❏ 3	Mahmoud Abdul-Rauf	.15	.05
❏ 4	Joe Dumars	.40	.15
❏ 5	Jason Kidd	1.25	.50
❏ 6	Avery Johnson	.15	.05
❏ 7	Dee Brown	.15	.05
❏ 8	Brian Williams	.15	.05
❏ 9	Nick Van Exel	.40	.15
❏ 10	Dennis Rodman	.25	.08
❏ 11	Rony Seikaly	.15	.05
❏ 12	Harvey Grant	.15	.05
❏ 13	Craig Ehlo	.15	.05
❏ 14	Derek Harper	.25	.08
❏ 15	Oliver Miller	.15	.05
❏ 16	Dennis Scott	.15	.05
❏ 17	Ed Pinckney	.15	.05
❏ 18	Eric Piatkowski	.25	.08
❏ 19	B.J. Armstrong	.15	.05
❏ 20	Tyrone Hill	.15	.05
❏ 21	Malik Sealy	.15	.05
❏ 22	Clyde Drexler	.40	.15
❏ 23	Aaron McKie	.25	.08
❏ 24	Harold Miner	.15	.05
❏ 25	Bobby Hurley	.15	.05
❏ 26	Dell Curry	.15	.05
❏ 27	Micheal Williams	.15	.05
❏ 28	Adam Keefe	.15	.05
❏ 29	Antonio Harvey	.15	.05
❏ 30	Billy Owens	.15	.05
❏ 31	Nate McMillan	.15	.05
❏ 32	J.R. Reid	.15	.05
❏ 33	Grant Hill	.50	.20
❏ 34	Charles Barkley	.40	.15
❏ 35	Tyrone Corbin	.15	.05
❏ 36	Don MacLean	.15	.05
❏ 37	Kenny Smith	.15	.05
❏ 38	Juwan Howard	.40	.15
❏ 39	Charles Smith	.15	.05
❏ 40	Shawn Kemp	.25	.08
❏ 41	Dana Barros	.15	.05
❏ 42	Vin Baker	.25	.08
❏ 43	Armon Gilliam	.15	.05
❏ 44	Spud Webb	.25	.08
❏ 45	Michael Jordan	2.50	1.00
❏ 46	Scott Williams	.15	.05
❏ 47	Vlade Divac	.25	.08
❏ 48	Roy Tarpley	.15	.05
❏ 49	Bimbo Coles	.15	.05
❏ 50	David Robinson	.40	.15
❏ 51	Terry Dehere	.15	.05
❏ 52	Bobby Phills	.15	.05
❏ 53	Sherman Douglas	.15	.05
❏ 54	Rodney Rogers	.15	.05
❏ 55	Detlef Schrempf	.25	.08
❏ 56	Calbert Cheaney	.15	.05
❏ 57	Tom Gugliotta	.15	.05
❏ 58	Jeff Turner	.15	.05
❏ 59	Mookie Blaylock	.15	.05
❏ 60	Bill Curley	.15	.05
❏ 61	Chris Dudley	.15	.05
❏ 62	Popeye Jones	.15	.05
❏ 63	Scott Burrell	.15	.05
❏ 64	Dale Davis	.15	.05
❏ 65	Mitchell Butler	.15	.05
❏ 66	Pervis Ellison	.15	.05
❏ 67	Todd Day	.15	.05
❏ 68	Carl Herrera	.15	.05
❏ 69	Jeff Hornacek	.25	.08
❏ 70	Vincent Askew	.15	.05
❏ 71	A.C. Green	.25	.08
❏ 72	Kevin Gamble	.15	.05
❏ 73	Chris Gatling	.15	.05
❏ 74	Otis Thorpe	.15	.05
❏ 75	Michael Cage	.15	.05
❏ 76	Carlos Rogers	.15	.05
❏ 77	Gheorghe Muresan	.15	.05
❏ 78	Olden Polynice	.15	.05
❏ 79	Grant Long	.15	.05
❏ 80	Allan Houston	.25	.08
❏ 81	Bo Outlaw	.15	.05
❏ 82	Clarence Weatherspoon	.15	.05

#	Player		
❏ 83	Tony Dumas	.15	.05
❏ 84	Herb Williams	.15	.05
❏ 85	P.J. Brown	.15	.05
❏ 86	Robert Horry	.25	.08
❏ 87	Byron Scott	.15	.05
❏ 88	Horace Grant	.25	.08
❏ 89	Dominique Wilkins	.40	.15
❏ 90	Doug West	.15	.05
❏ 91	Antoine Carr	.15	.05
❏ 92	Dickey Simpkins	.15	.05
❏ 93	Elden Campbell	.15	.05
❏ 94	Kevin Johnson	.25	.08
❏ 95	Rex Chapman	.15	.05
❏ 96	John Williams	.15	.05
❏ 97	Tim Hardaway	.25	.08
❏ 98	Rik Smits	.25	.08
❏ 99	Rex Walters	.15	.05
❏ 100	Robert Parish	.25	.08
❏ 101	Isaiah Rider	.15	.05
❏ 102	Sarunas Marciulionis	.15	.05
❏ 103	Andrew Lang	.15	.05
❏ 104	Eric Mobley	.15	.05
❏ 105	Randy Brown	.15	.05
❏ 106	John Stockton	.50	.20
❏ 107	Lamond Murray	.15	.05
❏ 108	Will Perdue	.15	.05
❏ 109	Wayman Tisdale	.15	.05
❏ 110	John Starks	.25	.08
❏ 111	John Salley	.15	.05
❏ 112	Lucious Harris	.15	.05
❏ 113	Jeff Malone	.15	.05
❏ 114	Anthony Bowie	.15	.05
❏ 115	Vinny Del Negro	.15	.05
❏ 116	Michael Adams	.15	.05
❏ 117	Chris Mullin	.40	.15
❏ 118	Benoit Benjamin	.15	.05
❏ 119	Byron Houston	.15	.05
❏ 120	LaPhonso Ellis	.15	.05
❏ 121	Doug Overton	.15	.05
❏ 122	Jerome Kersey	.15	.05
❏ 123	Greg Minor	.15	.05
❏ 124	Christian Laettner	.25	.08
❏ 125	Mark Price	.25	.08
❏ 126	Kevin Willis	.15	.05
❏ 127	Kenny Anderson	.25	.08
❏ 128	Marty Conlon	.15	.05
❏ 129	Blue Edwards	.15	.05
❏ 130	Danny Schayes	.15	.05
❏ 131	Duane Ferrell	.15	.05
❏ 132	Charles Oakley	.15	.05
❏ 133	Brian Grant	.40	.15
❏ 134	Reggie Williams	.15	.05
❏ 135	Steve Kerr	.25	.08
❏ 136	Khalid Reeves	.15	.05
❏ 137	David Benoit	.15	.05
❏ 138	Derrick Coleman	.15	.05
❏ 139	Anthony Peeler	.15	.05
❏ 140	Jim Jackson	.15	.05
❏ 141	Stacey Augmon	.15	.05
❏ 142	Sam Cassell	.40	.15
❏ 143	Derrick McKey	.15	.05
❏ 144	Danny Ferry	.15	.05
❏ 145	Anfernee Hardaway	.40	.15
❏ 146	Clifford Robinson	.15	.05
❏ 147	B.J. Tyler	.15	.05
❏ 148	Mark West	.15	.05
❏ 149	David Wingate	.15	.05
❏ 150	Willie Anderson	.15	.05
❏ 151	Hersey Hawkins	.15	.05
❏ 152	Bryant Stith	.15	.05
❏ 153	Dan Majerle	.25	.08
❏ 154	Chris Smith	.15	.05
❏ 155	Donyell Marshall	.25	.08
❏ 156	Loy Vaught	.15	.05
❏ 157	Reggie Miller	.40	.15
❏ 158	Hubert Davis	.15	.05
❏ 159	Ron Harper	.25	.08
❏ 160	Lee Mayberry	.15	.05
❏ 161	Eddie Jones	.50	.20
❏ 162	Shawn Bradley	.15	.05
❏ 163	Nick Anderson	.15	.05
❏ 164	Ervin Johnson	.15	.05
❏ 165	Walt Williams	.15	.05
❏ 166	Steve Smith FF	.15	.05
❏ 167	Dino Radja FF	.15	.05
❏ 168	Alonzo Mourning FF	.15	.05

#	Player		
169	Michael Jordan FF	1.25	.50
170	Tyrone Hill FF	.15	.05
171	Jamal Mashburn FF	.15	.05
172	Dikembe Mutombo FF	.15	.05
173	Grant Hill FF w/Jordan	.50	.20
174	Latrell Sprewell FF	.40	.15
175	Hakeem Olajuwon FF	.25	.08
176	Reggie Miller FF	.25	.08
177	Pooh Richardson FF	.15	.05
178	Cedric Ceballos FF	.15	.05
179	Glen Rice FF	.15	.05
180	Glenn Robinson FF	.25	.08
181	Isaiah Rider FF	.15	.05
182	Derrick Coleman FF	.15	.05
183	Patrick Ewing FF	.25	.08
184	Shaquille O'Neal FF	.40	.15
185	Dana Barros FF	.15	.05
186	Dan Majerle FF	.15	.05
187	Clifford Robinson FF	.15	.05
188	Mitch Richmond FF	.15	.05
189	David Robinson FF	.25	.08
190	Gary Payton FF	.25	.08
191	Oliver Miller FF	.15	.05
192	Karl Malone FF	.40	.15
193	Kevin Pritchard FF	.15	.05
194	Chris Webber FF	.40	.15
195	Michael Jordan PD	1.25	.50
196	Hakeem Olajuwon PD	.25	.08
197	Vin Baker PD	.25	.08
198	Grant Hill PD	.40	.15
199	Clyde Drexler PD	.25	.08
200	Chris Webber PD	.40	.15
201	Shawn Kemp PD	.15	.05
202	Shaquille O'Neal PD	.40	.15
203	Stacey Augmon PD	.15	.05
204	David Benoit PD	.15	.05
205	Rodney Rogers PD	.15	.05
206	Latrell Sprewell PD	.40	.15
207	Brian Grant PD	.25	.08
208	Lamond Murray PD	.15	.05
209	Shawn Kemp CL	.15	.05
210	Michael Jordan CL	.60	.25
211	Cory Alexander RC	.15	.05
212	Vernon Maxwell	.15	.05
213	George Lynch	.15	.05
214	Terry Mills	.15	.05
215	Scottie Pippen	.60	.25
216	Donald Royal	.15	.05
217	Wesley Person	.15	.05
218	Antonio Davis	.15	.05
219	Glenn Robinson	.40	.15
220	Jerry Stackhouse RC	1.25	.50
221	James Robinson	.15	.05
222	Chris Mills	.15	.05
223	Chuck Person	.15	.05
224	Duane Causwell	.15	.05
225	Gary Payton	.40	.15
226	Eric Montross	.15	.05
227	Felton Spencer	.15	.05
228	Scott Skiles	.15	.05
229	Latrell Sprewell	.40	.15
230	Sedale Threatt	.15	.05
231	Mark Bryant	.15	.05
232	Buck Williams	.15	.05
233	Brian Williams	.15	.05
234	Sharone Wright	.15	.05
235	Karl Malone	.50	.20
236	Kevin Edwards	.15	.05
237	Muggsy Bogues	.25	.08
238	Mario Elie	.15	.05
239	Rasheed Wallace RC	1.00	.40
240	George Zidek RC	.15	.05
241	Cedric Ceballos	.15	.05
242	Alan Henderson RC	.40	.15
243	Joe Kleine	.15	.05
244	Patrick Ewing	.40	.15
245	Sasha Danilovic RC	.15	.05
246	Bill Wennington	.15	.05
247	Steve Smith	.25	.08
248	Bryant Stith	.15	.05
249	Dino Radja	.15	.05
250	Monty Williams	.15	.05
251	Andrew DeClercq RC	.15	.05
252	Sean Elliott	.15	.05
253	Rick Fox	.15	.05
254	Lionel Simmons	.15	.05
255	Dikembe Mutombo	.25	.08
256	Lindsey Hunter	.15	.05
257	Terrell Brandon	.25	.08
258	Shawn Respert RC	.15	.05
259	Rodney Rogers	.15	.05
260	Bryon Russell	.15	.05
261	David Wesley	.15	.05
262	Ken Norman	.15	.05
263	Mitch Richmond	.25	.08
264	Sam Perkins	.25	.08
265	Hakeem Olajuwon	.40	.15
266	Brian Shaw	.15	.05
267	B.J. Armstrong	.15	.05
268	Jalen Rose	.50	.20
269	Bryant Reeves RC	.40	.15
270	Cherokee Parks RC	.15	.05
271	Dennis Rodman	.25	.08
272	Kendall Gill	.15	.05
273	Elliot Perry	.15	.05
274	Anthony Mason	.25	.08
275	Kevin Garnett RC	2.00	.75
276	Damon Stoudamire RC	.75	.30
277	Lawrence Moten RC	.15	.05
278	Ed O'Bannon RC	.15	.05
279	Toni Kukoc	.25	.08
280	Greg Ostertag RC	.15	.05
281	Tom Hammonds	.15	.05
282	Yinka Dare	.15	.05
283	Michael Smith	.15	.05
284	Clifford Rozier	.15	.05
285	Gary Trent RC	.15	.05
286	Shaquille O'Neal	1.00	.40
287	Luc Longley	.15	.05
288	Bob Sura RC	.15	.05
289	Dana Barros	.15	.05
290	Lorenzo Williams	.15	.05
291	Haywoode Workman	.15	.05
292	Randolph Childress RC	.15	.05
293	Doc Rivers	.25	.08
294	Chris Webber	.50	.20
295	Kurt Thomas RC	.25	.08
296	Greg Anthony	.15	.05
297	Tyus Edney RC	.15	.05
298	Danny Manning	.25	.08
299	Brent Barry RC	.40	.15
300	Joe Smith RC	.60	.25
301	Pooh Richardson	.15	.05
302	Mark Jackson	.15	.05
303	Richard Dumas	.15	.05
304	Michael Finley RC	1.00	.40
305	Theo Ratliff RC	.50	.20
306	Gary Grant	.15	.05
307	Jamal Mashburn	.25	.08
308	Corliss Williamson RC	.40	.15
309	Eric Williams RC	.25	.08
310	Zan Tabak	.15	.05
311	Eric Murdock	.15	.05
312	Sherrell Ford RC	.15	.05
313	Terry Davis	.15	.05
314	Vern Fleming	.15	.05
315	Jason Caffey RC	.25	.08
316	Mario Bennett RC	.15	.05
317	David Vaughn RC	.15	.05
318	Loren Meyer RC	.15	.05
319	Travis Best RC	.15	.05
320	Byron Scott	.15	.05
321	Mookie Blaylock SR	.15	.05
322	Dee Brown SR	.15	.05
323	Alonzo Mourning SR	.15	.05
324	Michael Jordan SR	1.25	.50
325	Terrell Brandon SR	.15	.05
326	Jim Jackson SR	.15	.05
327	Dikembe Mutombo SR	.15	.05
328	Grant Hill SR	.40	.15
329	Joe Smith SR	.40	.15
330	Clyde Drexler SR	.25	.08
331	Reggie Miller SR	.25	.08
332	Lamond Murray SR	.15	.05
333	Nick Van Exel SR	.25	.08
334	Glen Rice SR	.15	.05
335	Glenn Robinson SR	.25	.08
336	Christian Laettner SR	.15	.05
337	Kenny Anderson SR	.15	.05
338	Patrick Ewing SR	.25	.08
339	Shaquille O'Neal SR	.40	.15
340	Jerry Stackhouse SR	.60	.30
341	Charles Barkley SR	.40	.15
342	Clifford Robinson SR	.15	.05
343	Brian Grant SR	.25	.08
344	David Robinson SR	.25	.08
345	Shawn Kemp SR	.15	.05
346	Damon Stoudamire SR	.50	.20
347	Karl Malone SR	.40	.15
348	Bryant Reeves SR	.25	.08
349	Juwan Howard SR	.25	.08
350	N.Anderson/D.Brown PT	.15	.05
351	Rik Smits PT	.15	.05
352	H.Williams/T.Tolbert PT	.15	.05
353	Michael Jordan PT	1.25	.50
354	David Robinson PT	.25	.08
355	T.Porter/K.Johnson PT	.15	.05
356	Clyde Drexler PT	.25	.08
357	Cedric Ceballos PT	.15	.05
358	Horace Grant/Group PT	.15	.05
359	Reggie Miller PT	.15	.05
360	A.Johnson/N.Van Exel PT	.25	.08
361	H.Olajuwon/R.Horry PT	.40	.15
362	Rik Smits PT	.15	.05
363	D.Rob/H.Olajuwon PT	.40	.15
364	Robert Horry PT	.15	.05
365	Kenny Smith PT	.15	.05
366	Stacey Augmon LOVE	.15	.05
367	Sherman Douglas LOVE	.15	.05
368	Larry Johnson LOVE	.15	.05
369	Scottie Pippen LOVE	.40	.15
370	Tyrone Hill LOVE	.15	.05
371	Jamal Mashburn LOVE	.15	.05
372	Mahmoud Abdul-Rauf LOVE	.15	.05
373	Grant Hill LOVE	.40	.15
374	Latrell Sprewell LOVE	.40	.15
375	Sam Cassell LOVE	.15	.05
376	Rik Smits LOVE	.15	.05
377	Terry Dehere LOVE	.15	.05
378	Eddie Jones LOVE	.40	.15
379	Billy Owens LOVE	.15	.05
380	Vin Baker LOVE	.15	.05
381	Isaiah Rider LOVE	.15	.05
382	Kenny Anderson LOVE	.15	.05
383	John Starks LOVE	.15	.05
384	Anfernee Hardaway LOVE	.25	.08
385	Sharone Wright LOVE	.15	.05
386	Charles Barkley LOVE	.40	.15
387	Clifford Robinson LOVE	.15	.05
388	Walt Williams LOVE	.15	.05
389	Sean Elliott LOVE	.15	.05
390	Gary Payton LOVE	.25	.08
391	Carlos Rogers LOVE	.15	.05
392	John Stockton LOVE	.40	.15
393	Greg Anthony LOVE	.15	.05
394	Chris Webber LOVE	.40	.15
395	Gary Payton PG	.25	.08
396	Mookie Blaylock PG	.15	.05
397	Charles Barkley PG	.40	.15
398	Grant Hill PG	.40	.15
399	Anfernee Hardaway PG	.25	.08
400	Kenny Anderson PG	.15	.05
401	Mark Jackson PG	.15	.05
402	Karl Malone PG	.40	.15
403	Avery Johnson PG	.15	.05
404	Larry Johnson 40	.15	.05
405	Nick Van Exel 40	.15	.05
406	Vin Baker 40	.15	.05
407	Jason Kidd 40	.40	.15
408	David Robinson 40	.25	.08
409	Shawn Kemp CL	.60	.25
410	Michael Jordan CL	.60	.25
NNO	Bulls Fact.Set Comm.	3.00	3.00

1996-97 Collector's Choice

COMPLETE SET (400)	30.00	30.00
COMP.FACT.SET (406)	35.00	15.00
COMPLETE SERIES 1 (200)	15.00	7.50
COMPLETE SERIES 2 (200)	15.00	7.50
COMMON CARD (1-400)	.15	.05
COMMON PENNY! (113-117)	.30	.10
COMMON UPDATE SET (30)	12.00	6.00
COMMON UPDATE (401-430)	.40	.15
1 Mookie Blaylock	.15	.05
2 Grant Long	.15	.05
3 Christian Laettner	.25	.08

#	Player		
4	Craig Ehlo	.15	.05
5	Ken Norman	.15	.05
6	Stacey Augmon	.15	.05
7	Dana Barros	.15	.05
8	Dino Radja	.15	.05
9	Rick Fox	.15	.05
10	Eric Montross	.15	.05
11	David Wesley	.15	.05
12	Eric Williams	.15	.05
13	Glen Rice	.25	.08
14	Dell Curry	.15	.05
15	Matt Geiger	.15	.05
16	Scott Burrell	.15	.05
17	George Zidek	.15	.05
18	Muggsy Bogues	.15	.05
19	Ron Harper	.25	.08
20	Steve Kerr	.25	.08
21	Toni Kukoc	.25	.08
22	Dennis Rodman	.25	.08
23	Michael Jordan	2.50	1.00
24	Luc Longley	.15	.05
25	M.Jordan/V.Divac Bulls VT	1.25	.50
26	M.Jordan Bulls VT	1.25	.50
27	L.Longley Bulls VT	.15	.05
28	S.Pippen Bulls VT	.40	.15
29	T.Kukoc/J.Howard Bulls VT	.25	.08
30	Terrell Brandon	.25	.08
31	Bobby Phills	.15	.05
32	Tyrone Hill	.15	.05
33	Michael Cage	.15	.05
34	Bob Sura	.15	.05
35	Tony Dumas	.15	.05
36	Jim Jackson	.15	.05
37	Loren Meyer	.15	.05
38	Cherokee Parks	.15	.05
39	Jamal Mashburn	.25	.08
40	Popeye Jones	.15	.05
41	LaPhonso Ellis	.15	.05
42	Jalen Rose	.40	.15
43	Antonio McDyess	.25	.08
44	Tom Hammonds	.15	.05
45	Mahmoud Abdul-Rauf	.15	.05
46	Dale Ellis	.15	.05
47	Joe Dumars	.40	.15
48	Theo Ratliff	.25	.08
49	Lindsey Hunter	.15	.05
50	Terry Mills	.15	.05
51	Don Reid	.15	.05
52	B.J. Armstrong	.15	.05
53	Bimbo Coles	.15	.05
54	Joe Smith	.25	.08
55	Chris Mullin	.40	.15
56	Rony Seikaly	.15	.05
57	Donyell Marshall	.25	.08
58	Hakeem Olajuwon	.40	.15
59	Robert Horry	.25	.08
60	Mario Elie	.15	.05
61	Mark Bryant	.15	.05
62	Chucky Brown	.15	.05
63	Rik Smits	.25	.08
64	Derrick McKey	.15	.05
65	Eddie Johnson	.15	.05
66	Mark Jackson	.15	.05
67	Ricky Pierce	.15	.05
68	Travis Best	.15	.05
69	Rodney Rogers	.15	.05
70	Brent Barry	.15	.05
71	Lamond Murray	.15	.05
72	Eric Piatkowski	.25	.08
73	Pooh Richardson	.15	.05
74	Cedric Ceballos	.15	.05
75	Eddie Jones	.40	.15
76	Anthony Peeler	.15	.05
77	George Lynch	.15	.05
78	Vlade Divac	.15	.05
79	Rex Chapman	.15	.05
80	Sasha Danilovic	.15	.05
81	Kurt Thomas	.25	.08
82	Keith Askins	.15	.05
83	Walt Williams	.15	.05
84	Vin Baker	.25	.08
85	Shawn Respert	.15	.05
86	Sherman Douglas	.15	.05
87	Marty Conlon	.15	.05
88	Johnny Newman	.15	.05
89	Kevin Garnett	.75	.30
90	Andrew Lang	.15	.05
91	Terry Porter	.15	.05
92	Sam Mitchell	.15	.05
93	Tom Gugliotta	.15	.05
94	Spud Webb	.15	.05
95	Kendall Gill	.15	.05
96	Vern Fleming	.15	.05
97	Shawn Bradley	.15	.05
98	Yinka Dare	.15	.05
99	Jayson Williams	.25	.08
100	Kevin Edwards	.15	.05
101	Charles Oakley	.15	.05
102	Anthony Mason	.25	.08
103	John Starks	.25	.08
104	J.R. Reid	.15	.05
105	Hubert Davis	.15	.05
106	Gary Grant	.15	.05
107	Nick Anderson	.15	.05
108	Donald Royal	.15	.05
109	Brian Shaw	.15	.05
110	Brooks Thompson	.15	.05
111	Anfernee Hardaway	.30	.10
112	Dennis Scott	.15	.05
113	Anfernee Hardaway PEN	.30	.10
114	Anfernee Hardaway PEN	.30	.10
115	Anfernee Hardaway PEN	.30	.10
116	Anfernee Hardaway PEN	.30	.10
117	Anfernee Hardaway PEN	.30	.10
118	Derrick Coleman	.25	.08
119	Rex Walters	.15	.05
120	Sean Higgins	.15	.05
121	Clarence Weatherspoon	.15	.05
122	Jerry Stackhouse	.40	.15
123	Elliot Perry	.15	.05
124	Wayman Tisdale	.15	.05
125	Wesley Person	.15	.05
126	Charles Barkley	.50	.20
127	A.C. Green	.25	.08
128	Harvey Grant	.15	.05
129	Arvydas Sabonis	.25	.08
130	Aaron McKie	.15	.05
131	Gary Trent	.15	.05
132	Buck Williams	.15	.05
133	Billy Owens	.15	.05
134	Brian Grant	.40	.15
135	Corliss Williamson	.25	.08
136	Tyus Edney	.15	.05
137	Olden Polynice	.15	.05
138	Avery Johnson	.15	.05
139	Vinny Del Negro	.15	.05
140	Sean Elliott	.25	.08
141	Chuck Person	.15	.05
142	Will Perdue	.15	.05
143	Nate McMillan	.15	.05
144	Vincent Askew	.15	.05
145	Detlef Schrempf	.25	.08
146	Hersey Hawkins	.25	.08
147	Sharone Wright	.15	.05
148	Zan Tabak	.15	.05
149	Oliver Miller	.15	.05
150	Doug Christie	.25	.08
151	Damon Stoudamire	.40	.15
152	Jeff Hornacek	.25	.08
153	Chris Morris	.15	.05
154	Antoine Carr	.15	.05
155	Karl Malone	.40	.15
156	Adam Keefe	.15	.05
157	Greg Anthony	.15	.05
158	Blue Edwards	.15	.05
159	Bryant Reeves	.15	.05
160	Anthony Avent	.15	.05
161	Lawrence Moten	.15	.05
162	Calbert Cheaney	.15	.05
163	Chris Webber	.40	.15
164	Tim Legler	.15	.05
165	Gheorghe Muresan	.15	.05
166	Stacey Augmon FUND	.15	.05
167	Dee Brown FUND	.15	.05
168	Glen Rice FUND	.15	.05
169	Scottie Pippen FUND	.40	.15
170	Danny Ferry FUND	.15	.05
171	Jason Kidd FUND	.40	.15
172	LaPhonso Ellis FUND	.15	.05
173	Grant Hill FUND	.40	.15
174	Chris Mullin FUND	.25	.08
175	Clyde Drexler FUND	.25	.08
176	Rik Smits FUND	.15	.05
177	Loy Vaught FUND	.15	.05
178	Nick Van Exel FUND	.15	.05
179	Alonzo Mourning FUND	.15	.05
180	Glenn Robinson FUND	.25	.08
181	Isaiah Rider FUND	.15	.05
182	Ed O'Bannon FUND	.15	.05
183	Patrick Ewing FUND	.25	.08
184	Shaquille O'Neal FUND	.40	.15
185	Derrick Coleman FUND	.15	.05
186	Danny Manning FUND	.15	.05
187	Clifford Robinson FUND	.15	.05
188	Mitch Richmond FUND	.15	.05
189	David Robinson FUND	.25	.08
190	Shawn Kemp FUND	.15	.05
191	Oliver Miller FUND	.15	.05
192	John Stockton FUND	.50	.20
193	Greg Anthony FUND	.15	.05
194	Rasheed Wallace FUND	.40	.15
195	Michael Jordan FUND	1.25	.50
196	M.Jordan/M.Geiger CL	.40	.15
197	E.Jones/A.McDyess CL	.15	.05
198	A.Hardaway/K.Garnett CL	.40	.15
199	D.Stoudamire/J.Howard CL	.15	.05
200	D.Robinson/C.Mullin CL	.15	.05
201	Alan Henderson	.15	.05
202	Steve Smith	.25	.08
203	Donnie Boyce RC	.15	.05
204	Priest Lauderdale RC	.15	.05
205	Dikembe Mutombo	.25	.08
206	Dee Brown	.15	.05
207	Junior Burrough	.15	.05
208	Todd Day	.15	.05
209	Pervis Ellison	.15	.05
210	Greg Minor	.15	.05
211	Antoine Walker RC	1.25	.50
212	Rafael Addison	.15	.05
213	Tony Delk RC	.40	.15
214	Vlade Divac	.15	.05
215	Anthony Goldwire	.15	.05
216	Anthony Mason	.25	.08
217	Dickey Simpkins	.15	.05
218	Randy Brown	.15	.05
219	Jud Buechler	.15	.05
220	Jason Caffey	.15	.05
221	Scottie Pippen	.60	.25
222	Bill Wennington	.15	.05
223	Danny Ferry	.15	.05
224	Antonio Lang	.15	.05
225	Chris Mills	.15	.05
226	Vitaly Potapenko RC	.15	.05
227	Terry Davis	.15	.05
228	Chris Gatling	.15	.05
229	Jason Kidd	.60	.25
230	George McCloud	.15	.05
231	Eric Montross	.15	.05
232	Samaki Walker RC	.15	.05
233	Mark Jackson	.15	.05
234	Ervin Johnson	.15	.05
235	Sarunas Marciulionis	.15	.05
236	Eric Murdock	.15	.05
237	Ricky Pierce	.15	.05
238	Bryant Stith	.15	.05
239	Stacey Augmon	.15	.05
240	Grant Hill	.40	.15
241	Otis Thorpe	.25	.08
242	Jerome Williams RC	.40	.15
243	Andrew DeClercq	.15	.05

❑	Card	Hi	Lo
244	Todd Fuller RC	.15	.05
245	Mark Price	.25	.08
246	Clifford Rozier	.15	.05
247	Latrell Sprewell	.40	.15
248	Charles Barkley	.50	.20
249	Clyde Drexler	.40	.15
250	Othella Harrington RC	.40	.15
251	Sam Mack	.15	.05
252	Kevin Willis	.15	.05
253	Erick Dampier RC	.40	.15
254	Antonio Davis	.15	.05
255	Dale Davis	.15	.05
256	Duane Ferrell	.15	.05
257	Reggie Miller	.40	.15
258	Jalen Rose	.40	.15
259	Reggie Williams	.15	.05
260	Terry Dehere	.15	.05
261	Bo Outlaw	.15	.05
262	Stanley Roberts	.15	.05
263	Malik Sealy	.15	.05
264	Loy Vaught	.15	.05
265	Lorenzen Wright RC	.25	.08
266	Corie Blount	.15	.05
267	Kobe Bryant RC	4.00	1.50
268	Elden Campbell	.15	.05
269	Derek Fisher RC	.60	.25
270	Shaquille O'Neal	1.00	.40
271	Nick Van Exel	.40	.15
272	P.J. Brown	.15	.05
273	Tim Hardaway	.25	.08
274	Voshon Lenard RC	.25	.08
275	Dan Majerle	.25	.08
276	Alonzo Mourning	.25	.08
277	Martin Muursepp RC	.15	.05
278	Ray Allen RC	1.25	.50
279	Elliot Perry	.15	.05
280	Glenn Robinson	.40	.15
281	Stephon Marbury RC	1.25	.50
282	Cherokee Parks	.15	.05
283	Doug West	.15	.05
284	Micheal Williams	.15	.05
285	Kerry Kittles RC	.40	.15
286	Ed O'Bannon	.15	.05
287	Robert Pack	.15	.05
288	Khalid Reeves	.15	.05
289	David Benoit	.15	.05
290	Patrick Ewing	.40	.15
291	Allan Houston	.25	.08
292	Larry Johnson	.25	.08
293	Dontae' Jones RC	.15	.05
294	Walter McCarty RC	.15	.05
295	John Wallace RC	.40	.15
296	Charlie Ward	.15	.05
297	Brian Evans RC	.15	.05
298	Horace Grant	.25	.08
299	Jon Koncak	.15	.05
300	Felton Spencer	.15	.05
301	Allen Iverson RC	2.00	.75
302	Don MacLean	.15	.05
303	Scott Williams	.15	.05
304	Sam Cassell	.40	.15
305	Michael Finley	.25	.08
306	Robert Horry	.25	.08
307	Kevin Johnson	.25	.08
308	Joe Kleine	.15	.05
309	Danny Manning	.25	.08
310	Steve Nash RC	3.00	1.25
311	John Williams	.15	.05
312	Kenny Anderson	.25	.08
313	Randolph Childress	.15	.05
314	Chris Dudley	.15	.05
315	Jermaine O'Neal RC	1.25	.50
316	Isaiah Rider	.25	.08
317	Clifford Robinson	.15	.05
318	Rasheed Wallace	.50	.20
319	Mahmoud Abdul-Rauf	.15	.05
320	Duane Causwell	.15	.05
321	Bobby Hurley	.15	.05
322	Mitch Richmond	.25	.08
323	Lionel Simmons	.15	.05
324	Michael Smith	.15	.05
325	Dominique Wilkins	.40	.15
326	Cory Alexander	.15	.05
327	Greg Anderson	.15	.05
328	Carl Herrera	.15	.05
329	David Robinson	.40	.15
330	Charles Smith	.15	.05
331	Craig Ehlo	.15	.05
332	Sherrell Ford	.15	.05
333	Shawn Kemp	.25	.08
334	Jim McIlvaine	.15	.05
335	Gary Payton	.40	.15
336	Sam Perkins	.25	.08
337	Eric Snow RC	.25	.08
338	David Wingate	.15	.05
339	Marcus Camby RC	.50	.20
340	Acie Earl	.15	.05
341	Carlos Rogers	.15	.05
342	Greg Ostertag	.15	.05
343	Bryon Russell	.15	.05
344	John Stockton	.50	.20
345	Jamie Watson	.15	.05
346	Shareef Abdur-Rahim RC	1.25	.50
347	Doug Edwards	.15	.05
348	George Lynch	.15	.05
349	Eric Mobley	.15	.05
350	Anthony Peeler	.15	.05
351	Roy Rogers RC	.15	.05
352	Juwan Howard	.25	.08
353	Harvey Grant	.15	.05
354	Tracy Murray	.15	.05
355	Rod Strickland	.15	.05
356	A.Hardaway/M.Jordan ONE	1.25	.50
357	H.Olajuwon/S.O'Neal ONE	.60	.25
358	J.Smith/S.Kemp ONE	.15	.05
359	D.Schrempf/T.Kukoc ONE	.25	.08
360	J.Jackson/Stackhouse ONE	.40	.15
361	Bryant/Abdur-Rahim ONE	1.00	.40
362	N.Anderson/M.Jordan AJ	.75	.30
363	J.Dumars/M.Jordan AJ	.75	.30
364	J.Starks/M.Jordan AJ	.75	.30
365	R.Miller/M.Jordan AJ	1.00	.40
366	G.Payton/M.Jordan AJ	1.00	.40
367	Mookie Blaylock PLAY	.15	.05
368	D.Radja/Fox/Wesley PLAY	.15	.05
369	Glen Rice PLAY	.15	.05
370	M.Jordan/S.Pippen PLAY	1.25	.50
371	Terrell Brandon PLAY	.15	.05
372	Jason Kidd PLAY	.40	.15
373	Antonio McDyess PLAY	.25	.08
374	Grant Hill PLAY	.40	.15
375	Joe Smith PLAY	.15	.05
376	Barkley/Olaj/Drexler PLAY	.75	.30
377	Reggie Miller PLAY	.25	.08
378	L.A. Clippers PLAY	.15	.05
379	Nick Van Exel PLAY	.15	.05
380	Alonzo Mourning PLAY	.15	.05
381	Ray Allen PLAY	.60	.25
382	Stephon Marbury PLAY	.75	.30
383	Shawn Bradley PLAY	.15	.05
384	Patrick Ewing PLAY	.25	.08
385	Anfernee Hardaway PLAY	.25	.08
386	Jerry Stackhouse PLAY	.40	.15
387	Danny Manning PLAY	.15	.05
388	Clifford Robinson PLAY	.15	.05
389	Tyus Edney PLAY	.15	.05
390	San Antonio Spurs PLAY	.15	.05
391	Shawn Kemp PLAY	.15	.05
392	Toronto Raptors PLAY	.15	.05
393	John Stockton PLAY	.50	.20
394	Greg Anthony PLAY	.15	.05
395	Gheorghe Muresan PLAY	.15	.05
396	Checklist	.15	.05
397	Checklist	.15	.05
398	Checklist	.15	.05
399	Checklist	.15	.05
400	Checklist	.15	.05
401	Henry James TRADE	.40	.15
402	Shawn Bradley TRADE	.40	.15
403	Sasha Danilovic TRADE	.40	.15
404	Michael Finley TRADE	1.25	.50
405	A.C. Green TRADE	.60	.25
406	Derek Harper TRADE	.40	.15
407	Khalid Reeves TRADE	.40	.15
408	Aaron McKie TRADE	.60	.25
409	Matt Maloney TRADE	.40	.15
410	Darrick Martin TRADE	.40	.15
411	Robert Horry TRADE	.60	.25
412	Travis Knight TRADE	.40	.15
413	Isaac Austin TRADE	.40	.15
414	Jamal Mashburn TRADE	.60	.25
415	Armon Gilliam TRADE	.40	.15
416	Chris Carr TRADE	.40	.15
417	Dean Garrett TRADE	.40	.15
418	Shane Heal TRADE	.40	.15
419	Sam Cassell TRADE	1.00	.40
420	Chris Gatling TRADE	.40	.15
421	Jim Jackson TRADE	.40	.15
422	Chris Childs TRADE	.40	.15
423	Rony Seikaly TRADE	.40	.15
424	Gerald Wilkins TRADE	.40	.15
425	Cedric Ceballos TRADE	.40	.15
426	Tony Dumas TRADE	.40	.15
427	Jason Kidd TRADE	2.50	1.00
428	Popeye Jones TRADE	.40	.15
429	Walt Williams TRADE	.40	.15
430	Jason Jackson TRADE	.60	.25
NNO	Update Trade Card	15.00	6.00
NNO	Michael Jordan 5x7 MM		
NNO	Michael Jordan 5x7 DD		

1997-98 Collector's Choice

❑		Hi	Lo
	COMPLETE SET (400)	30.00	15.00
	COMP.FACTORY SET (415)	40.00	25.00
	COMPLETE SERIES 1 (200)	15.00	7.50
	COMPLETE SERIES 2 (200)	15.00	7.50
1	Mookie Blaylock	.15	.05
2	Dikembe Mutombo	.25	.08
3	Eldridge Recasner	.15	.05
4	Christian Laettner	.25	.08
5	Tyrone Corbin	.15	.05
6	Antoine Walker	.50	.20
7	Eric Williams	.15	.05
8	Dana Barros	.15	.05
9	David Wesley	.15	.05
10	Dino Radja	.15	.05
11	Vlade Divac	.25	.08
12	Dell Curry	.15	.05
13	Muggsy Bogues	.15	.05
14	Tony Smith	.15	.05
15	Glen Rice	.25	.08
16	Anthony Mason	.25	.08
17	Dennis Rodman	.50	.20
18	Brian Williams	.15	.05
19	Toni Kukoc	.25	.08
20	Jason Caffey	.15	.05
21	Steve Kerr	.15	.05
22	Luc Longley	.15	.05
23	Michael Jordan	2.50	1.00
24	Chris Mills	.15	.05
25	Tyrone Hill	.15	.05
26	Vitaly Potapenko	.15	.05
27	Bob Sura	.15	.05
28	Robert Pack	.15	.05
29	Ed O'Bannon	.15	.05
30	Michael Finley	.40	.15
31	Shawn Bradley	.15	.05
32	Khalid Reeves	.15	.05
33	Antonio McDyess	.25	.08
34	Ervin Johnson	.15	.05
35	Dale Ellis	.15	.05
36	Bryant Stith	.15	.05
37	Tom Hammonds	.15	.05
38	Otis Thorpe	.25	.08
39	Lindsey Hunter	.15	.05
40	Grant Long	.15	.05
41	Aaron McKie	.25	.08
42	Randolph Childress	.15	.05
43	Scott Burrell	.15	.05

No.	Player			No.	Player			No.	Player		
44	Bimbo Coles	.15	.05	130	Shawn Kemp	.25	.08	216	David Wesley	.15	.05
45	B.J. Armstrong	.15	.05	131	Hersey Hawkins	.15	.05	217	Ron Harper	.25	.08
46	Mark Price	.25	.08	132	Nate McMillan	.15	.05	218	Scottie Pippen	.60	.25
47	Latrell Sprewell	.40	.15	133	Craig Ehlo	.15	.05	219	Scott Burrell	.15	.05
48	Felton Spencer	.15	.05	134	Detlef Schrempf	.25	.08	220	Keith Booth RC	.15	.05
49	Charles Barkley	.40	.15	135	Sam Perkins	.25	.08	221	Bill Wennington	.15	.05
50	Mario Elie	.15	.05	136	Sharone Wright	.15	.05	222	Shawn Kemp	.25	.08
51	Clyde Drexler	.40	.15	137	Doug Christie	.25	.08	223	Zydrunas Ilgauskas	.25	.08
52	Kevin Willis	.25	.08	138	Popeye Jones	.15	.05	224	Brevin Knight RC	.25	.08
53	Antonio Davis	.15	.05	139	Shawn Respert	.15	.05	225	Danny Ferry	.15	.05
54	Reggie Miller	.40	.15	140	Marcus Camby	.40	.15	226	Derek Anderson RC	.40	.15
55	Dale Davis	.15	.05	141	Adam Keefe	.15	.05	227	Wesley Person	.15	.05
56	Mark Jackson	.25	.08	142	Karl Malone	.40	.15	228	A.C. Green	.25	.08
57	Erick Dampier	.25	.08	143	John Stockton	.50	.20	229	Samaki Walker	.15	.05
58	Pooh Richardson	.15	.05	144	Greg Ostertag	.15	.05	230	Hubert Davis	.15	.05
59	Terry Dehere	.15	.05	145	Chris Morris	.15	.05	231	Erick Strickland RC	.25	.08
60	Brent Barry	.25	.08	146	Shareef Abdur-Rahim	.60	.25	232	Dennis Scott	.15	.05
61	Loy Vaught	.15	.05	147	Roy Rogers	.15	.05	233	Tony Battie RC	.40	.15
62	Lorenzen Wright	.15	.05	148	George Lynch	.15	.05	234	LaPhonso Ellis	.15	.05
63	Eddie Jones	.40	.15	149	Anthony Peeler	.15	.05	235	Eric Williams	.15	.05
64	Kobe Bryant	1.50	.60	150	Lee Mayberry	.15	.05	236	Bobby Jackson RC	1.00	.40
65	Elden Campbell	.15	.05	151	Calbert Cheaney	.15	.05	237	Anthony Goldwire	.15	.05
66	Corie Blount	.15	.05	152	Harvey Grant	.15	.05	238	Danny Fortson RC	.25	.08
67	Shaquille O'Neal	1.00	.40	153	Rod Strickland	.15	.05	239	Joe Dumars	.40	.15
68	Dan Majerle	.25	.08	154	Tracy Murray	.15	.05	240	Grant Hill	.40	.15
69	P.J. Brown	.15	.05	155	Chris Webber	.40	.15	241	Malik Sealy	.15	.05
70	Tim Hardaway	.25	.08	156	Mookie Blaylock/Hawks GN	.15	.05	242	Brian Williams	.15	.05
71	Isaac Austin	.15	.05	157	A.Walker/Celtics GN	.40	.15	243	Theo Ratliff	.15	.05
72	Jamal Mashburn	.25	.08	158	Glen Rice/Hornets GN	.25	.08	244	Scot Pollard RC	.25	.08
73	Ray Allen	.40	.15	159	M.Jordan/Bulls GN	1.25	.50	245	Erick Dampier	.25	.08
74	Glenn Robinson	.40	.15	160	Tyrone Hill/Cavaliers GN	.15	.05	246	Duane Ferrell	.15	.05
75	Armon Gilliam	.15	.05	161	Shawn Bradley/Mavericks GN	.15	.05	247	Joe Smith	.25	.08
76	Johnny Newman	.15	.05	162	Antonio McDyess/Nuggets GN	.25	.08	248	Todd Fuller	.15	.05
77	Elliot Perry	.15	.05	163	G.Hill/Pistons GN	.25	.08	249	Adonal Foyle RC	.25	.08
78	Sherman Douglas	.15	.05	164	Latrell Sprewell/Warriors GN	.15	.05	250	Othella Harrington	.15	.05
79	Doug West	.15	.05	165	H.Olajuwon/Rockets GN	.40	.15	251	Matt Maloney	.15	.05
80	Kevin Garnett	.75	.30	166	Reggie Miller/Pacers GN	.25	.08	252	Hakeem Olajuwon	.40	.15
81	Sam Mitchell	.15	.05	167	Loy Vaught/Clippers GN	.15	.05	253	Rodrick Rhodes RC	.15	.05
82	Tom Gugliotta	.25	.08	168	E.Jones/Lakers GN	.40	.15	254	Eddie Johnson	.15	.05
83	Terry Porter	.15	.05	169	Tim Hardaway/Heat GN	.15	.05	255	Brent Price	.15	.05
84	Chris Carr	.15	.05	170	Vin Baker/Bucks GN	.15	.05	256	Austin Croshere RC	.30	.12
85	Kevin Edwards	.15	.05	171	K.Garnett/T'wolves GN	.60	.25	257	Derrick McKey	.15	.05
86	Jayson Williams	.15	.05	172	Kendall Gill/Nets GN	.15	.05	258	Chris Mullin	.40	.15
87	Kendall Gill	.15	.05	173	Patrick Ewing/Knicks GN	.25	.08	259	Rik Smits	.25	.08
88	Kerry Kittles	.40	.15	174	A.Hardaway/Magic GN	.25	.08	260	Jalen Rose	.40	.15
89	Chris Gatling	.15	.05	175	A.Iverson/76ers GN	.40	.15	261	Darrick Martin	.15	.05
90	John Starks	.25	.08	176	J.Kidd/Suns GN	.40	.15	262	Lamond Murray	.15	.05
91	Charlie Ward	.15	.05	177	Rasheed Wallace/Trail Blazers GN	.25	.08	263	Maurice Taylor RC	.30	.12
92	Larry Johnson	.25	.08	178	Mitch Richmond/Kings GN	.25	.08	264	Rodney Rogers	.15	.05
93	Charles Oakley	.15	.05	179	Sean Elliott/Spurs GN	.15	.05	265	James Robinson	.15	.05
94	Chris Childs	.15	.05	180	G.Payton/SuperSonics GN	.40	.15	266	Rick Fox	.25	.08
95	Allan Houston	.25	.08	181	D.Stoudamire/Raptors GN	.40	.15	267	Nick Van Exel	.40	.15
96	Horace Grant	.25	.08	182	Karl Malone/Jazz GN	.40	.15	268	Sean Rooks	.15	.05
97	Darrell Armstrong	.15	.05	183	S.Abdur-Rahim/Griz. GN	.25	.08	269	Derek Fisher	.40	.15
98	Rony Seikaly	.15	.05	184	C.Webber/Wizards GN	.25	.08	270	Jon Barry	.15	.05
99	Dennis Scott	.15	.05	185	M.Jordan/97 Finals GN	1.25	.50	271	Robert Horry	.25	.08
100	Anfernee Hardaway	.40	.15	186	Michael Jordan C23	1.00	.40	272	Terry Mills	.15	.05
101	Brian Shaw	.15	.05	187	Michael Jordan C23	1.00	.40	273	Charles Smith RC	.15	.05
102	Jerry Stackhouse	.40	.15	188	Michael Jordan C23	1.00	.40	274	Alonzo Mourning	.25	.08
103	Rex Walters	.15	.05	189	Michael Jordan C23	1.00	.40	275	Voshon Lenard	.15	.05
104	Don MacLean	.15	.05	190	Michael Jordan C23	1.00	.40	276	Todd Day	.15	.05
105	Derrick Coleman	.15	.05	191	Michael Jordan C23	1.00	.40	277	Ervin Johnson	.15	.05
106	Lucious Harris	.15	.05	192	Michael Jordan C23	1.00	.40	278	Terrell Brandon	.25	.08
107	Clarence Weatherspoon	.15	.05	193	Michael Jordan C23	1.00	.40	279	Michael Curry	.15	.05
108	Cedric Ceballos	.15	.05	194	Michael Jordan C23	1.00	.40	280	Andrew Lang	.15	.05
109	Danny Manning	.25	.08	195	Michael Jordan C23	1.00	.40	281	Tyrone Hill	.15	.05
110	Jason Kidd	.60	.25	196	Checklist #1	.15	.05	282	Stephon Marbury	.50	.20
111	Loren Meyer	.15	.05	197	Checklist #2	.15	.05	283	Cherokee Parks	.15	.05
112	Wesley Person	.15	.05	198	Checklist #3	.15	.05	284	Stanley Roberts	.15	.05
113	Steve Nash	.40	.15	199	Checklist #4	.15	.05	285	Paul Grant RC	.15	.05
114	Isaiah Rider	.25	.08	200	Checklist #5	.15	.05	286	David Benoit	.15	.05
115	Stacey Augmon	.15	.05	201	Steve Smith	.25	.08	287	Lucious Harris	.15	.05
116	Arvydas Sabonis	.25	.08	202	Chris Crawford RC	.15	.05	288	Don MacLean	.15	.05
117	Kenny Anderson	.25	.08	203	Ed Gray RC	.15	.05	289	Sam Cassell	.40	.15
118	Jermaine O'Neal	.60	.25	204	Alan Henderson	.15	.05	290	Keith Van Horn RC	.50	.20
119	Gary Trent	.15	.05	205	Walter McCarty	.15	.05	291	Patrick Ewing	.40	.15
120	Michael Smith	.15	.05	206	Dee Brown	.15	.05	292	Walter McCarty	.15	.05
121	Kevin Gamble	.15	.05	207	Chauncey Billups RC	1.25	.50	293	Chris Dudley	.15	.05
122	Olden Polynice	.15	.05	208	Ron Mercer RC	.40	.15	294	Chris Mills	.15	.05
123	Billy Owens	.15	.05	209	Travis Knight	.15	.05	295	Buck Williams	.15	.05
124	Corliss Williamson	.15	.05	210	Andrew DeClercq	.15	.05	296	Nick Anderson	.15	.05
125	Cory Alexander	.15	.05	211	Tyus Edney	.15	.05	297	Derek Strong	.15	.05
126	Vinny Del Negro	.15	.05	212	Matt Geiger	.15	.05	298	Gerald Wilkins	.15	.05
127	Sean Elliott	.25	.08	213	Tony Delk	.15	.05	299	Johnny Taylor RC	.15	.05
128	Will Perdue	.15	.05	214	J.R. Reid	.15	.05	300	Derek Harper	.25	.08
129	Carl Herrera	.15	.05	215	Bobby Phills	.15	.05	301	Anthony Parker RC	.15	.05

302	Allen Iverson	1.00	.40
303	Jim Jackson	.15	.05
304	Eric Montross	.15	.05
305	Tim Thomas RC	.60	.25
306	Kebu Stewart RC	.15	.05
307	Rex Chapman	.15	.05
308	Tom Chambers	.15	.05
309	Kevin Johnson	.25	.08
310	John Williams	.15	.05
311	Clifford Robinson	.15	.05
312	Antonio McDyess	.25	.08
313	Rasheed Wallace	.40	.15
314	Brian Grant	.25	.08
315	Dontonio Wingfield	.15	.05
316	Kelvin Cato RC	.40	.05
317	Mahmoud Abdul-Rauf	.15	.05
318	Lawrence Funderburke RC	.25	.08
319	Mitch Richmond	.25	.08
320	Tariq Abdul-Wahad RC	.25	.08
321	Terry Dehere	.15	.05
322	Michael Stewart RC	.15	.05
323	Tim Duncan RC	1.50	.60
324	Avery Johnson	.15	.05
325	David Robinson	.40	.15
326	Charles Smith	.15	.05
327	Chuck Person	.15	.05
328	Monty Williams	.15	.05
329	Jim McIlvaine	.15	.05
330	Gary Payton	.40	.15
331	Eric Snow	.25	.08
332	Dale Ellis	.15	.05
333	Vin Baker	.25	.08
334	Walt Williams	.15	.05
335	Tracy McGrady RC	2.00	.75
336	Damon Stoudamire	.25	.08
337	Carlos Rogers	.15	.05
338	John Wallace	.15	.05
339	Shandon Anderson	.15	.05
340	Jeff Hornacek	.15	.05
341	Howard Eisley	.15	.05
342	Jacque Vaughn RC	.25	.08
343	Bryon Russell	.15	.05
344	Antoine Carr	.15	.05
345	Antonio Daniels RC	.40	.15
346	Pete Chilcutt	.15	.05
347	Blue Edwards	.15	.05
348	Bryant Reeves	.15	.05
349	Chris Robinson RC	.15	.05
350	Otis Thorpe	.15	.05
351	Tim Legler	.15	.05
352	Juwan Howard	.25	.08
353	God Shammgod RC	.15	.05
354	Gheorghe Muresan	.15	.05
355	Chris Whitney	.15	.05
356	Dikembe Mutombo HP	.15	.05
357	Antoine Walker HP	.40	.15
358	Glen Rice HP	.15	.05
359	Scottie Pippen HP	.30	.10
360	Derek Anderson HP	.20	.08
361	Michael Finley HP	.25	.08
362	LaPhonso Ellis HP	.15	.05
363	Grant Hill HP	.40	.15
364	Joe Smith HP	.15	.05
365	Charles Barkley HP	.40	.15
366	Reggie Miller HP	.25	.08
367	Loy Vaught HP	.15	.05
368	Shaquille O'Neal HP	.40	.15
369	Alonzo Mourning HP	.25	.08
370	Glenn Robinson HP	.25	.08
371	Kevin Garnett HP	.50	.20
372	Kendall Gill HP	.15	.05
373	Allan Houston HP	.15	.05
374	Anfernee Hardaway HP	.25	.08
375	Tim Thomas HP	.30	.10
376	Jason Kidd HP	.30	.10
377	Kenny Anderson HP	.15	.05
378	Mitch Richmond HP	.15	.05
379	Tim Duncan HP	.75	.40
380	Gary Payton HP	.25	.08
381	Marcus Camby HP	.25	.08
382	Karl Malone HP	.40	.15
383	Shareef Abdur-Rahim HP	.30	.10
384	Chris Webber HP	.25	.08
385	Michael Jordan HP	1.25	.50
386	Michael Jordan MM	1.00	.40
387	Michael Jordan MM	1.00	.40
388	Michael Jordan MM	1.00	.40
389	Michael Jordan MM	1.00	.40
390	Michael Jordan MM	1.00	.40
391	Michael Jordan MM	1.00	.40
392	Michael Jordan MM	1.00	.40
393	Michael Jordan MM	1.00	.40
394	Michael Jordan MM	1.00	.40
395	Michael Jordan MM	1.00	.40
396	Checklist #1	.15	.05
397	Checklist #2	.15	.05
398	Checklist #3	.15	.05
399	Checklist #4	.15	.05
400	Checklist #5	.15	.05

1994-95 Emotion

	COMPLETE SET (121)	50.00	25.00
1	Stacey Augmon	.15	.05
2	Mookie Blaylock	.15	.05
3	Steve Smith	.30	.10
4	Greg Minor RC	.15	.05
5	Eric Montross RC	.15	.05
6	Dino Radja	.15	.05
7	Dominique Wilkins	.60	.25
8	Muggsy Bogues	.30	.10
9	Larry Johnson	.30	.10
10	Alonzo Mourning	.75	.30
11	B.J. Armstrong	.15	.05
12	Toni Kukoc	1.00	.40
13	Scottie Pippen	2.00	.75
14	Dickey Simpkins RC	.15	.05
15	Tyrone Hill	.15	.05
16	Chris Mills	.30	.10
17	Mark Price	.15	.05
18	Tony Dumas RC	.15	.05
19	Jim Jackson	.30	.10
20	Jason Kidd RC	6.00	2.50
21	Jamal Mashburn	.60	.25
22	LaPhonso Ellis	.15	.05
23	Dikembe Mutombo	.30	.10
24	Rodney Rogers	.15	.05
25	Jalen Rose RC	2.50	1.00
26	Bill Curley RC	.15	.05
27	Joe Dumars	.60	.25
28	Grant Hill RC	4.00	1.50
29	Tim Hardaway	.60	.25
30	Donyell Marshall RC	.60	.25
31	Chris Mullin	.60	.25
32	Carlos Rogers RC	.15	.05
33	Clifford Rozier RC	.15	.05
34	Latrell Sprewell	.60	.25
35	Sam Cassell	.60	.25
36	Clyde Drexler w/Hakeem	.60	.25
37	Robert Horry	.30	.10
38	Hakeem Olajuwon	1.00	.40
39	Mark Jackson	.15	.05
40	Reggie Miller	.60	.25
41	Rik Smits	.15	.05
42	Lamond Murray RC	.30	.10
43	Eric Piatkowski RC	.15	.05
44	Loy Vaught	.15	.05
45	Cedric Ceballos	.15	.05
46	Eddie Jones RC	3.00	1.25
47	George Lynch	.15	.05
48	Nick Van Exel	.60	.25
49	Harold Miner	.15	.05
50	Khalid Reeves RC	.15	.05
51	Glen Rice	.30	.10
52	Kevin Willis	.15	.05
53	Vin Baker	.60	.25
54	Eric Mobley RC	.15	.05
55	Eric Murdock	.15	.05
56	Glenn Robinson RC	2.00	.75
57	Tom Gugliotta	.30	.10
58	Christian Laettner	.30	.10
59	Isaiah Rider	.30	.10
60	Kenny Anderson	.30	.10
61	Derrick Coleman	.30	.10
62	Yinka Dare	.15	.05
63	Patrick Ewing	.60	.25
64	John Starks	.15	.05
65	Charlie Ward RC	.60	.25
66	Monty Williams RC	.15	.05
67	Nick Anderson	.15	.05
68	Horace Grant	.30	.10
69	Anfernee Hardaway	1.50	.60
70	Shaquille O'Neal	3.00	1.25
71	Brooks Thompson	.15	.05
72	Dana Barros	.15	.05
73	Shawn Bradley	.15	.05
74	B.J. Tyler	.15	.05
75	Clarence Weatherspoon	.15	.05
76	Sharone Wright RC	.15	.05
77	Charles Barkley	1.00	.40
78	Kevin Johnson	.30	.10
79	Dan Majerle	.30	.10
80	Danny Manning	.30	.10
81	Wesley Person RC	.60	.25
82	Aaron McKie RC	1.00	.40
83	Clifford Robinson	.30	.10
84	Rod Strickland	.30	.10
85	Brian Grant RC	1.50	.60
86	Bobby Hurley	.15	.05
87	Mitch Richmond	.60	.25
88	Sean Elliott	.30	.10
89	David Robinson	1.00	.40
90	Dennis Rodman	1.25	.50
91	Shawn Kemp	1.00	.40
92	Gary Payton	1.00	.40
93	Dontonio Wingfield	.15	.05
94	Jeff Hornacek	.30	.10
95	Karl Malone	1.00	.40
96	John Stockton	.60	.25
97	Calbert Cheaney	.15	.05
98	Juwan Howard RC	1.50	.60
99	Chris Webber	1.50	.60
100	Michael Jordan	12.00	5.00
101	Brian Grant ROO	.30	.10
102	Grant Hill ROO	1.50	.60
103	Juwan Howard ROO	1.25	.50
104	Eddie Jones ROO	1.50	.60
105	Jason Kidd ROO	4.00	1.50
106	Eric Montross ROO	.15	.05
107	Lamond Murray ROO	.15	.05
108	Wesley Person ROO	.30	.10
109	Glenn Robinson ROO	1.00	.40
110	Sharone Wright ROO	.15	.05
111	Anfernee Hardaway MAS	.75	.30
112	Shawn Kemp MAS	.60	.25
113	Karl Malone MAS	.60	.25
114	Alonzo Mourning MAS	.60	.25
115	Shaquille O'Neal MAS	1.25	.50
116	Hakeem Olajuwon MAS	.60	.25
117	Scottie Pippen MAS	1.00	.40
118	David Robinson MAS	.60	.25
119	Latrell Sprewell MAS	.60	.25
120	Chris Webber MAS	.75	.30
121	Checklist	.15	.05
NNO	Hill SkyMotion Exch.	40.00	20.00
NNO	Grant Hill David Robinson Promo	2.50	1.00

1995-96 E-XL

	COMPLETE SET (100)	50.00	20.00
1	Stacey Augmon	.40	.15
2	Mookie Blaylock	.40	.15
3	Christian Laettner	.75	.30
4	Dana Barros	.40	.15
5	Dino Radja	.40	.15
6	Eric Williams RC	.75	.30
7	Kenny Anderson	.75	.30
8	Larry Johnson	.75	.30
9	Glen Rice	.75	.30
10	Michael Jordan	8.00	3.00
11	Toni Kukoc	.75	.30

❑ 12	Scottie Pippen	2.00	.75
❑ 13	Dennis Rodman	.75	.30
❑ 14	Terrell Brandon	.75	.30
❑ 15	Bobby Phills	.40	.15
❑ 16	Bob Sura RC	.75	.30
❑ 17	Jim Jackson	.40	.15
❑ 18	Jason Kidd	4.00	1.50
❑ 19	Jamal Mashburn	.75	.30
❑ 20	Mahmoud Abdul-Rauf	.40	.15
❑ 21	Antonio McDyess RC	2.50	1.00
❑ 22	Dikembe Mutombo	.75	.30
❑ 23	Joe Dumars	1.25	.50
❑ 24	Grant Hill	1.50	.60
❑ 25	Allan Houston	.75	.30
❑ 26	Joe Smith RC	2.00	.75
❑ 27	Latrell Sprewell	1.25	.50
❑ 28	Kevin Willis	.75	.30
❑ 29	Sam Cassell	1.25	.50
❑ 30	Clyde Drexler	1.25	.50
❑ 31	Robert Horry	.75	.30
❑ 32	Hakeem Olajuwon	1.25	.50
❑ 33	Derrick McKey	.40	.15
❑ 34	Reggie Miller	1.25	.50
❑ 35	Rik Smits	.75	.30
❑ 36	Brent Barry RC	1.25	.50
❑ 37	Loy Vaught	.40	.15
❑ 38	Brian Williams	.40	.15
❑ 39	Cedric Ceballos	.40	.15
❑ 40	Magic Johnson	2.00	.75
❑ 41	Nick Van Exel	1.25	.50
❑ 42	Tim Hardaway	.75	.30
❑ 43	Alonzo Mourning	.75	.30
❑ 44	Kurt Thomas RC	.75	.30
❑ 45	Walt Williams	.40	.15
❑ 46	Vin Baker	.75	.30
❑ 47	Shawn Respert RC	.40	.15
❑ 48	Glenn Robinson	1.25	.50
❑ 49	Kevin Garnett RC	6.00	2.50
❑ 50	Tom Gugliotta	.40	.15
❑ 51	Isaiah Rider	.40	.15
❑ 52	Shawn Bradley	.40	.15
❑ 53	Chris Childs	.40	.15
❑ 54	Ed O'Bannon RC	.40	.15
❑ 55	Patrick Ewing	1.25	.50
❑ 56	Anthony Mason	.75	.30
❑ 57	Charles Oakley	.75	.30
❑ 58	Horace Grant	.75	.30
❑ 59	Anfernee Hardaway	1.25	.50
❑ 60	Shaquille O'Neal	3.00	1.25
❑ 61	Derrick Coleman	.40	.15
❑ 62	Jerry Stackhouse RC	4.00	1.50
❑ 63	Clarence Weatherspoon	.40	.15
❑ 64	Charles Barkley	1.50	.60
❑ 65	Michael Finley RC	3.00	1.25
❑ 66	Kevin Johnson	.75	.30
❑ 67	Clifford Robinson	.40	.15
❑ 68	Arvydas Sabonis RC	1.50	.60
❑ 69	Rod Strickland	.40	.15
❑ 70	Tyus Edney RC	.40	.15
❑ 71	Billy Owens	.40	.15
❑ 72	Mitch Richmond	.75	.30
❑ 73	Sean Elliott	.75	.30
❑ 74	Avery Johnson	.40	.15
❑ 75	David Robinson	1.25	.50
❑ 76	Shawn Kemp	.75	.30
❑ 77	Gary Payton	1.25	.50
❑ 78	Detlef Schrempf	.75	.30
❑ 79	Tracy Murray	.40	.15

❑ 80	Damon Stoudamire RC	2.50	1.00
❑ 81	Sharone Wright	.40	.15
❑ 82	Jeff Hornacek	.75	.30
❑ 83	Karl Malone	1.50	.60
❑ 84	John Stockton	1.50	.60
❑ 85	Greg Anthony	.40	.15
❑ 86	Bryant Reeves RC	1.25	.50
❑ 87	Byron Scott	.40	.15
❑ 88	Juwan Howard	1.25	.50
❑ 89	Gheorghe Muresan	.40	.15
❑ 90	Rasheed Wallace RC	3.00	1.25
❑ 91	Steve Smith UNT	.40	.15
❑ 92	Dikembe Mutombo UNT	.40	.15
❑ 93	Brent Barry UNT	.75	.30
❑ 94	Glenn Robinson UNT	.75	.30
❑ 95	Armon Gilliam UNT	.40	.15
❑ 96	Nick Anderson UNT	.40	.15
❑ 97	Gary Trent UNT	.40	.15
❑ 98	Brian Grant UNT	.75	.30
❑ 99	Bryant Reeves UNT	.75	.30
❑ 100	Checklist	.40	.15
❑ NNO	Grant Hill Promo	2.50	1.00

2004-05 E-XL

❑ COMP SET w/o SP's (70)		40.00	15.00
❑ COMMON CARD (1-70)		.25	.10
❑ COMMON ROOKIE (71-94)		6.00	2.50
❑ COMMON ROOKIE (95-107)		4.00	1.50
❑ 1	Dwyane Wade	3.00	1.25
❑ 2	Kobe Bryant	4.00	1.50
❑ 3	Mike Bibby	1.00	.40
❑ 4	Michael Finley	1.00	.40
❑ 5	Jamal Mashburn	.60	.25
❑ 6	Carmelo Anthony	2.00	.75
❑ 7	Jason Kidd	1.50	.60
❑ 8	Andrei Kirilenko	1.00	.40
❑ 9	Ron Artest	.60	.25
❑ 10	Peja Stojakovic	1.00	.40
❑ 11	Yao Ming	2.50	1.00
❑ 12	Shawn Marion	.60	.25
❑ 13	Desmond Mason	.60	.25
❑ 14	Paul Pierce	1.00	.40
❑ 15	Pau Gasol	1.00	.40
❑ 16	Tim Duncan	2.00	.75
❑ 17	Andre Miller	.60	.25
❑ 18	Allan Houston	.60	.25
❑ 19	Ben Wallace	1.00	.40
❑ 20	Stephon Marbury	1.00	.40
❑ 21	Gilbert Arenas	1.00	.40
❑ 22	Luke Walton	.60	.25
❑ 23	Rashard Lewis	1.00	.40
❑ 24	Elton Brand	1.00	.40
❑ 25	Zach Randolph	1.00	.40
❑ 26	Eddy Curry	.60	.25
❑ 27	Richard Jefferson	.60	.25
❑ 28	Kirk Hinrich	1.00	.40
❑ 29	Jason Terry	1.00	.40
❑ 30	Ray Allen	1.00	.40
❑ 31	Mike Dunleavy	.60	.25
❑ 32	Glenn Robinson	1.00	.40
❑ 33	Darko Milicic	.60	.25
❑ 34	Steve Francis	1.00	.40
❑ 35	Antawn Jamison	1.00	.40
❑ 36	Jason Williams	.60	.25
❑ 37	Tracy McGrady	2.50	1.00
❑ 38	Steve Nash	1.00	.40
❑ 39	Gary Payton	1.00	.40
❑ 40	Sam Cassell	1.00	.40

❑ 41	Gerald Wallace	.60	.25
❑ 42	Shaquille O'Neal	2.50	1.00
❑ 43	Tony Parker	1.00	.40
❑ 44	Richard Hamilton	.60	.25
❑ 45	Kenyon Martin	1.00	.40
❑ 46	Baron Davis	1.00	.40
❑ 47	Jarvis Hayes	.60	.25
❑ 48	Chris Kaman	.60	.25
❑ 49	Manu Ginobili	1.00	.40
❑ 50	Jermaine O'Neal	1.00	.40
❑ 51	Amare Stoudemire	2.00	.75
❑ 52	Latrell Sprewell	1.00	.40
❑ 53	LeBron James	6.00	2.50
❑ 54	Michael Redd	.60	.25
❑ 55	Chris Bosh	1.00	.40
❑ 56	Juwan Howard	.60	.25
❑ 57	Jason Richardson	1.00	.40
❑ 58	Allen Iverson	2.00	.75
❑ 59	Antoine Walker	1.00	.40
❑ 60	Eddie Jones	1.00	.40
❑ 61	Carlos Arroyo	1.50	.60
❑ 62	Lamar Odom	1.00	.40
❑ 63	Chris Webber	1.00	.40
❑ 64	Drew Gooden	.60	.25
❑ 65	Jamaal Magloire	.25	.10
❑ 66	Dirk Nowitzki	1.50	.60
❑ 67	Kevin Garnett	2.00	.75
❑ 68	Vince Carter	2.50	1.00
❑ 69	Reggie Miller	1.00	.40
❑ 70	Shareef Abdur-Rahim	1.00	.40
❑ 71	Emeka Okafor RC	25.00	10.00
❑ 72	Pavel Podkolzine RC	6.00	2.50
❑ 73	Kirk Snyder RC	6.00	2.50
❑ 74	Ben Gordon RC	25.00	10.00
❑ 75	Devin Harris RC	10.00	4.00
❑ 76	Josh Childress RC	8.00	3.00
❑ 77	Dorell Wright RC	10.00	4.00
❑ 78	Dwight Howard RC	20.00	8.00
❑ 79	Andre Iguodala RC	15.00	6.00
❑ 80	Viktor Khryapa RC	6.00	2.50
❑ 81	Al Jefferson RC	15.00	6.00
❑ 82	Kevin Martin RC	10.00	4.00
❑ 83	Delonte West RC	12.00	5.00
❑ 84	Josh Smith RC	12.00	5.00
❑ 85	Luol Deng RC	12.00	5.00
❑ 86	Kris Humphries RC	6.00	2.50
❑ 87	Sebastian Telfair RC	6.00	2.50
❑ 88	Rafael Araujo RC	8.00	3.00
❑ 89	Jameer Nelson RC	10.00	4.00
❑ 90	Shaun Livingston RC	10.00	4.00
❑ 91	Andris Biedrins RC	10.00	4.00
❑ 92	Robert Swift RC	6.00	2.50
❑ 93	Luke Jackson RC	6.00	2.50
❑ 94	J.R. Smith RC	12.00	5.00
❑ 95	Tony Allen RC	4.00	1.50
❑ 96	Sasha Vujacic RC	4.00	1.50
❑ 97	David Harrison RC	4.00	1.50
❑ 98	Anderson Varejao RC	5.00	2.00
❑ 99	Jackson Vroman RC	4.00	1.50
❑ 100	Peter John Ramos RC	6.00	2.50
❑ 101	Lionel Chalmers RC	4.00	1.50
❑ 102	Donta Smith RC	4.00	1.50
❑ 103	Andre Emmett RC	4.00	1.50
❑ 104	Trevor Ariza RC	5.00	2.00
❑ 105	Tim Pickett RC	4.00	1.50
❑ 106	Bernard Robinson RC	4.00	1.50
❑ 107	Matt Freije RC	4.00	1.50

1996-97 E-X2000

❑ COMPLETE SET (82)		120.00	60.00
❑ COMMON CARD (1-82)		.60	.25
❑ COMMON ROOKIE		2.00	.75
❑ 1	Christian Laettner	1.50	.60
❑ 2	Dikembe Mutombo	1.50	.60
❑ 3	Steve Smith	1.50	.60
❑ 4	Antoine Walker RC	10.00	4.00
❑ 5	David Wesley	.60	.25
❑ 6	Tony Delk RC	2.00	.75
❑ 7	Anthony Mason	1.50	.60
❑ 8	Glen Rice	1.50	.60
❑ 9	Michael Jordan	15.00	7.50
❑ 10	Scottie Pippen	3.00	1.25
❑ 11	Dennis Rodman	1.50	.60
❑ 12	Terrell Brandon	1.50	.60
❑ 13	Chris Mills	.60	.25
❑ 14	Shawn Bradley	.60	.25

#	Player		
15	Michael Finley	2.50	1.00
16	Dale Ellis	.60	.25
17	Antonio McDyess	1.50	.60
18	Joe Dumars	2.00	.75
19	Grant Hill	2.00	.75
20	Chris Mullin	2.00	.75
21	Joe Smith	1.50	.60
22	Latrell Sprewell	2.00	.75
23	Charles Barkley	2.50	1.00
24	Clyde Drexler	2.00	.75
25	Hakeem Olajuwon	2.00	.75
26	Erick Dampier RC	2.50	1.00
27	Reggie Miller	2.00	.75
28	Loy Vaught	.60	.25
29	Lorenzen Wright RC	2.00	.75
30	Kobe Bryant RC	60.00	25.00
31	Eddie Jones	2.00	.75
32	Shaquille O'Neal	5.00	2.00
33	Nick Van Exel	2.00	.75
34	Tim Hardaway	1.50	.60
35	Jamal Mashburn	1.50	.60
36	Alonzo Mourning	1.50	.60
37	Ray Allen RC	10.00	4.00
38	Vin Baker	1.50	.60
39	Glenn Robinson	2.00	.75
40	Kevin Garnett	4.00	1.50
41	Tom Gugliotta	.60	.25
42	Stephon Marbury RC	8.00	3.00
43	Kendall Gill	.60	.25
44	Jim Jackson	.60	.25
45	Kerry Kittles RC	2.50	1.00
46	Patrick Ewing	2.00	.75
47	Larry Johnson	1.50	.60
48	John Wallace RC	2.00	.75
49	Nick Anderson	.60	.25
50	Horace Grant	1.50	.60
51	Anfernee Hardaway	2.00	.75
52	Derrick Coleman	1.50	.60
53	Allen Iverson RC	25.00	10.00
54	Jerry Stackhouse	3.00	1.25
55	Cedric Ceballos	.60	.25
56	Kevin Johnson	1.50	.60
57	Jason Kidd	3.00	1.25
58	Clifford Robinson	.60	.25
59	Arvydas Sabonis	1.50	.60
60	Rasheed Wallace	2.50	1.00
61	Mahmoud Abdul-Rauf	.60	.25
62	Brian Grant	2.00	.75
63	Mitch Richmond	1.50	.60
64	Sean Elliott	1.50	.60
65	David Robinson	2.00	.75
66	Dominique Wilkins	2.00	.75
67	Shawn Kemp	1.50	.60
68	Gary Payton	2.00	.75
69	Detlef Schrempf	1.50	.60
70	Marcus Camby RC	4.00	1.50
71	Damon Stoudamire	2.00	.75
72	Walt Williams	.60	.25
73	Shandon Anderson RC	2.50	1.00
74	Karl Malone	2.00	.75
75	John Stockton	2.00	.75
76	Shareef Abdur-Rahim RC	10.00	4.00
77	Bryant Reeves	.60	.25
78	Roy Rogers RC	2.00	.75
79	Juwan Howard	1.50	.60
80	Chris Webber	2.00	.75
81	Checklist	.60	.25
82	Checklist	.60	.25

NNO Grant Hill		
Blow-Up/3000	15.00	6.00
NNO G.Hill Emerald AU	200.00	100.00
NNO Grant Hill		
Promo	2.50	1.00

1997-98 E-X2001

#	Player		
	COMPLETE SET (82)	60.00	25.00
	COMMON CARD (1-61)	.40	.15
	COMMON ROOKIE (62-80)	.75	.30
1	Grant Hill	1.25	.50
2	Kevin Garnett	2.50	1.00
3	Allen Iverson	3.00	1.25
4	Anfernee Hardaway	1.25	.50
5	Dennis Rodman	.75	.30
6	Shawn Kemp	.75	.30
7	Shaquille O'Neal	3.00	1.25
8	Kobe Bryant	6.00	2.50
9	Michael Jordan	8.00	3.00
10	Marcus Camby	1.25	.50
11	Scottie Pippen	2.00	.75
12	Antoine Walker	1.25	.50
13	Stephon Marbury	1.50	.60
14	Shareef Abdur-Rahim	2.00	.75
15	Jerry Stackhouse	1.25	.50
16	Eddie Jones	1.25	.50
17	Charles Barkley	1.50	.60
18	David Robinson	1.25	.50
19	Karl Malone	1.25	.50
20	Damon Stoudamire	.75	.30
21	Patrick Ewing	1.25	.50
22	Kerry Kittles	1.25	.50
23	Gary Payton	1.25	.50
24	Glenn Robinson	1.25	.50
25	Hakeem Olajuwon	1.25	.50
26	John Starks	.75	.30
27	John Stockton	1.25	.50
28	Vin Baker	.75	.30
29	Reggie Miller	1.25	.50
30	Clyde Drexler	1.25	.50
31	Alonzo Mourning	.75	.30
32	Juwan Howard	.75	.30
33	Ray Allen	1.25	.50
34	Christian Laettner	.75	.30
35	Terrell Brandon	.75	.30
36	Sean Elliott	.75	.30
37	Rod Strickland	.40	.15
38	Rodney Rogers	.40	.15
39	Donyell Marshall	.75	.30
40	David Wesley	.40	.15
41	Sam Cassell	1.25	.50
42	Cedric Ceballos	.40	.15
43	Mahmoud Abdul-Rauf	.40	.15
44	Rik Smits	.75	.30
45	Lindsey Hunter	.40	.15
46	Michael Finley	1.25	.50
47	Steve Smith	.75	.30
48	Larry Johnson	.75	.30
49	Dikembe Mutombo	.75	.30
50	Tom Gugliotta	.75	.30
51	Joe Dumars	1.25	.50
52	Glen Rice	.75	.30
53	Bryant Reeves	.40	.15
54	Tim Hardaway	.75	.30
55	Isaiah Rider	.75	.30
56	Rasheed Wallace	1.25	.50
57	Jason Kidd	2.00	.75
58	Joe Smith	.75	.30
59	Chris Webber	1.25	.50
60	Mitch Richmond	.75	.30
61	Antonio McDyess	.75	.30
62	Bobby Jackson RC	2.50	1.00
63	Derek Anderson RC	3.00	1.25
64	Kelvin Cato RC	1.25	.50
65	Jacque Vaughn RC	1.00	.40
66	Tariq Abdul-Wahad RC	1.00	.40
67	Johnny Taylor RC	.75	.30
68	Chris Anstey RC	.75	.30
69	Maurice Taylor RC	2.00	.75
70	Antonio Daniels RC	1.25	.50
71	Chauncey Billups RC	5.00	2.00
72	Austin Croshere RC	2.00	.75
73	Brevin Knight RC	1.25	.50
74	Keith Van Horn RC	3.00	1.25
75	Tim Duncan RC	12.00	5.00
76	Danny Fortson RC	1.50	.60
77	Tim Thomas RC	4.00	1.50
78	Tony Battie RC	1.25	.50
79	Tracy McGrady RC	12.00	5.00
80	Ron Mercer RC	2.50	1.00
81	Checklist (1-82)	.40	.15
82	Checklist (inserts)	.40	.15
S1	Grant Hill SAMPLE	3.00	1.25

1998-99 E-X Century

#	Player		
	COMPLETE SET (1-90)	100.00	40.00
	COMMON CARD (1-60)	.30	.10
	COMMON ROOKIE (61-90)	.75	.30
1	Keith Van Horn	1.00	.40
2	Scottie Pippen	1.50	.60
3	Tim Thomas	.60	.25
4	Stephon Marbury	1.00	.40
5	Allen Iverson	2.00	.75
6	Grant Hill	1.00	.40
7	Tim Duncan	1.50	.60
8	Latrell Sprewell	1.00	.40
9	Ron Mercer	.50	.20
10	Kobe Bryant	4.00	1.50
11	Antoine Walker	1.00	.40
12	Reggie Miller	1.00	.40
13	Kevin Garnett	2.00	.75
14	Shaquille O'Neal	2.50	1.00
15	Karl Malone	1.00	.40
16	Dennis Rodman	1.00	.40
17	Tracy McGrady	2.50	1.00
18	Anfernee Hardaway	1.00	.40
19	Shareef Abdur-Rahim	1.00	.40
20	Marcus Camby	.60	.25
21	Eddie Jones	.60	.25
22	Vin Baker	.60	.25
23	Charles Barkley	1.00	.40
24	Patrick Ewing	1.00	.40
25	Jason Kidd	1.50	.60
26	Mitch Richmond	.60	.25
27	Tim Hardaway	.60	.25
28	Glen Rice	.60	.25
29	Shawn Kemp	1.00	.40
30	John Stockton	1.00	.40
31	Ray Allen	1.00	.40
32	Brevin Knight	.30	.10
33	David Robinson	1.00	.40
34	Juwan Howard	.60	.25
35	Alonzo Mourning	.60	.25
36	Hakeem Olajuwon	1.00	.40
37	Gary Payton	1.00	.40
38	Damon Stoudamire	.60	.25

#	Player		
❏ 39	Steve Smith	.60	.25
❏ 40	Chris Webber	1.00	.40
❏ 41	Michael Finley	1.00	.40
❏ 42	Jayson Williams	.30	.15
❏ 43	Maurice Taylor	.50	.20
❏ 44	Jalen Rose	1.00	.40
❏ 45	Sam Cassell	1.00	.40
❏ 46	Jerry Stackhouse	1.00	.40
❏ 47	Toni Kukoc	.60	.25
❏ 48	Charles Oakley	.30	.10
❏ 49	Jim Jackson	.30	.10
❏ 50	Dikembe Mutombo	.60	.25
❏ 51	Wesley Person	.30	.10
❏ 52	Antonio Daniels	.30	.10
❏ 53	Isaiah Rider	.30	.10
❏ 54	Tom Gugliotta	.30	.10
❏ 55	Antonio McDyess	.60	.25
❏ 56	Jeff Hornacek	.60	.25
❏ 57	Joe Dumars	1.00	.40
❏ 58	Jamal Mashburn	.60	.25
❏ 59	Donyell Marshall	.60	.25
❏ 60	Glenn Robinson	.60	.25
❏ 61	Jelani McCoy RC	.75	.30
❏ 62	Peja Stojakovic RC	6.00	2.50
❏ 63	Randell Jackson RC	.75	.30
❏ 64	Brad Miller RC	8.00	3.00
❏ 65	Corey Benjamin RC	1.50	.60
❏ 66	Toby Bailey RC	.75	.30
❏ 67	Naz Mohammed RC	1.00	.40
❏ 68	Dirk Nowitzki RC	15.00	6.00
❏ 69	Andrae Patterson RC	.75	.30
❏ 70	Michael Dickerson RC	3.00	1.25
❏ 71	Cory Carr RC	.75	.30
❏ 72	Brian Skinner RC	1.50	.60
❏ 73	Pat Garrity RC	1.00	.40
❏ 74	Ricky Davis RC	5.00	2.00
❏ 75	Roshown McLeod RC	1.00	.40
❏ 76	Matt Harpring RC	2.50	1.00
❏ 77	Jason Williams RC	6.00	2.50
❏ 78	Keon Clark RC	2.50	1.00
❏ 79	Al Harrington RC	4.00	1.50
❏ 80	Felipe Lopez RC	2.00	.75
❏ 81	Michael Doleac RC	1.50	.60
❏ 82	Paul Pierce RC	8.00	3.00
❏ 83	Robert Traylor RC	1.50	.60
❏ 84	Raef LaFrentz RC	2.50	1.00
❏ 85	Michael Olowokandi RC	2.50	1.00
❏ 86	Mike Bibby RC	8.00	3.00
❏ 87	Antawn Jamison RC	8.00	3.00
❏ 88	Bonzi Wells RC	6.00	2.50
❏ 89	Vince Carter RC	25.00	10.00
❏ 90	Larry Hughes RC	5.00	2.00

1999-00 E-X

#	Player		
❏	COMPLETE SET (90)	120.00	60.00
❏	COMPLETE SET w/o RC (60)	30.00	15.00
❏	COMMON CARD (1-60)	.30	.10
❏	COMMON ROOKIE (61-90)	1.25	.50
❏ 1	Stephon Marbury	1.00	.40
❏ 2	Antawn Jamison	1.50	.60
❏ 3	Patrick Ewing	1.00	.40
❏ 4	Nick Anderson	.30	.10
❏ 5	Charles Barkley	1.25	.50
❏ 6	Marcus Camby	.60	.25
❏ 7	Ron Mercer	.60	.25
❏ 8	Avery Johnson	.30	.10
❏ 9	Maurice Taylor	.30	.10
❏ 10	Isaiah Rider	.30	.10
❏ 11	Dirk Nowitzki	2.00	.75
❏ 12	Damon Stoudamire	.60	.25
❏ 13	Alonzo Mourning	.60	.25
❏ 14	Jason Kidd	1.50	.60
❏ 15	Juwan Howard	.60	.25
❏ 16	Vince Carter	2.50	1.00
❏ 17	Tim Duncan	2.00	.75
❏ 18	Paul Pierce	1.00	.40
❏ 19	Tim Hardaway	.60	.25
❏ 20	Grant Hill	1.00	.40
❏ 21	Keith Van Horn	1.00	.40
❏ 22	Shaquille O'Neal	2.50	1.00
❏ 23	Jason Williams	1.00	.40
❏ 24	Shareef Abdur-Rahim	1.00	.40
❏ 25	Kobe Bryant	4.00	1.50
❏ 26	David Robinson	1.00	.40
❏ 27	Anfernee Hardaway	1.00	.40
❏ 28	Vin Baker	.60	.25
❏ 29	Hakeem Olajuwon	1.00	.40
❏ 30	Michael Olowokandi	.60	.25
❏ 31	Mike Bibby	1.00	.40
❏ 32	Tracy McGrady	2.50	1.00
❏ 33	Antoine Walker	1.00	.40
❏ 34	Larry Hughes	1.00	.40
❏ 35	Chris Webber	1.00	.40
❏ 36	Ray Allen	1.00	.40
❏ 37	Danny Fortson	.30	.10
❏ 38	Shawn Kemp	.60	.25
❏ 39	Michael Doleac	.30	.10
❏ 40	Gary Payton	1.00	.40
❏ 41	Toni Kukoc	.60	.25
❏ 42	Kevin Garnett	2.00	.75
❏ 43	Steve Smith	.60	.25
❏ 44	Scottie Pippen	1.50	.60
❏ 45	Allen Iverson	2.00	.75
❏ 46	Latrell Sprewell	1.00	.40
❏ 47	Matt Harpring	1.00	.40
❏ 48	Lindsey Hunter	.30	.10
❏ 49	Karl Malone	1.00	.40
❏ 50	Michael Finley	1.00	.40
❏ 51	Jerry Stackhouse	1.00	.40
❏ 52	Cedric Ceballos	.30	.10
❏ 53	Brent Barry	.60	.25
❏ 54	Elden Campbell	.30	.10
❏ 55	Glenn Robinson	1.00	.40
❏ 56	Eddie Jones	1.00	.40
❏ 57	Reggie Miller	1.00	.40
❏ 58	Mitch Richmond	.60	.25
❏ 59	Raef LaFrentz	.60	.25
❏ 60	John Starks	.60	.25
❏ 61	Elton Brand RC	8.00	3.00
❏ 62	William Avery RC	2.50	1.00
❏ 63	Cal Bowdler RC	2.00	.75
❏ 64	Dion Glover RC	2.00	.75
❏ 65	Lamar Odom RC	6.00	2.50
❏ 66	Richard Hamilton RC	6.00	2.50
❏ 67	Kenny Thomas RC	2.50	1.00
❏ 68	Shawn Marion RC	8.00	3.00
❏ 69	Baron Davis RC	10.00	4.00
❏ 70	Wally Szczerbiak RC	8.00	3.00
❏ 71	Scott Padgett RC	2.00	.75
❏ 72	Jason Terry RC	4.00	1.50
❏ 73	Trajan Langdon RC	2.50	1.00
❏ 74	Andre Miller RC	6.00	2.50
❏ 75	Jeff Foster RC	2.00	.75
❏ 76	Tim James RC	2.00	.75
❏ 77	A.Radojevic RC	1.25	.50
❏ 78	Quincy Lewis RC	2.00	.75
❏ 79	James Posey RC	4.00	1.50
❏ 80	Steve Francis RC	8.00	3.00
❏ 81	Jonathan Bender RC	6.00	2.50
❏ 82	Corey Maggette RC	6.00	2.50
❏ 83	Obinna Ekezie RC	1.50	.60
❏ 84	Laron Profit RC	2.00	.75
❏ 85	Devean George RC	3.00	1.25
❏ 86	Ron Artest RC	4.00	1.50
❏ 87	Rafer Alston RC	2.50	1.00
❏ 88	Vonteego Cummings RC	2.50	1.00
❏ 89	Evan Eschmeyer RC	1.25	.50
❏ 90	Jumaine Jones RC	3.00	1.25
❏ S16	Vince Carter PROMO	2.50	1.00

2000-01 E-X

#	Player		
❏	COMPLETE SET w/o RC (100)	40.00	20.00
❏	COMMON CARD (1-100)	.30	.10

#	Player		
❏	COMMON ROOKIE (101-130)	4.00	1.50
❏ 1	Dikembe Mutombo	.60	.25
❏ 2	Jim Jackson	.30	.10
❏ 3	Jason Terry	1.00	.40
❏ 4	Kenny Anderson	.60	.25
❏ 5	Antoine Walker	1.00	.40
❏ 6	Paul Pierce	1.00	.40
❏ 7	Jamal Mashburn	.60	.25
❏ 8	Baron Davis	1.00	.40
❏ 9	Derrick Coleman	.30	.10
❏ 10	Elton Brand	1.00	.40
❏ 11	Ron Artest	.60	.25
❏ 12	Andre Miller	.60	.25
❏ 13	Brevin Knight	.30	.10
❏ 14	Trajan Langdon	.60	.25
❏ 15	Lamond Murray	.30	.10
❏ 16	Dirk Nowitzki	1.50	.60
❏ 17	Michael Finley	1.00	.40
❏ 18	Nick Van Exel	1.00	.40
❏ 19	Antonio McDyess	.60	.25
❏ 20	Raef LaFrentz	.60	.25
❏ 21	Tariq Abdul-Wahad	.30	.10
❏ 22	Cedric Ceballos	.30	.10
❏ 23	Jerry Stackhouse	1.00	.40
❏ 24	Jerome Williams	.30	.10
❏ 25	Larry Hughes	.60	.25
❏ 26	Antawn Jamison	1.00	.40
❏ 27	Mookie Blaylock	.30	.10
❏ 28	Steve Francis	1.00	.40
❏ 29	Hakeem Olajuwon	1.00	.40
❏ 30	Maurice Taylor	.30	.10
❏ 31	Jonathan Bender	.60	.25
❏ 32	Reggie Miller	1.00	.40
❏ 33	Austin Croshere	.60	.25
❏ 34	Travis Best	.30	.10
❏ 35	Jalen Rose	1.00	.40
❏ 36	Lamar Odom	1.00	.40
❏ 37	Corey Maggette	.60	.25
❏ 38	Shaquille O'Neal	2.50	1.00
❏ 39	Kobe Bryant	4.00	1.50
❏ 40	Horace Grant	.60	.25
❏ 41	Isaiah Rider	.60	.25
❏ 42	Brian Grant	.60	.25
❏ 43	Eddie Jones	1.00	.40
❏ 44	Tim Hardaway	.60	.25
❏ 45	Anthony Mason	.60	.25
❏ 46	Glenn Robinson	1.00	.40
❏ 47	Ray Allen	1.00	.40
❏ 48	Sam Cassell	1.00	.40
❏ 49	Tim Thomas	.60	.25
❏ 50	Kevin Garnett	2.00	.75
❏ 51	Terrell Brandon	.60	.25
❏ 52	Joe Smith	.60	.25
❏ 53	Wally Szczerbiak	.60	.25
❏ 54	Chauncey Billups	.60	.25
❏ 55	Stephon Marbury	1.00	.40
❏ 56	Keith Van Horn	1.00	.40
❏ 57	Kerry Kittles	.30	.10
❏ 58	Allan Houston	.60	.25
❏ 59	Latrell Sprewell	1.00	.40
❏ 60	Larry Johnson	.60	.25
❏ 61	Glen Rice	.60	.25
❏ 62	Grant Hill	1.00	.40
❏ 63	Tracy McGrady	2.50	1.00
❏ 64	Darrell Armstrong	.30	.10
❏ 65	Allen Iverson	2.00	.75
❏ 66	Toni Kukoc	.60	.25
❏ 67	Theo Ratliff	.60	.25

#				#				#		
68	Jason Kidd	1.50	.60	COMMON ROOKIE (101-130)	2.50	1.00		86 Sam Cassell	1.00	.40
69	Anfernee Hardaway	1.00	.40	1 Shareef Abdur-Rahim	1.00	.40		87 Cliff Robinson	.60	.25
70	Tom Gugliotta	.30	.10	2 DerMarr Johnson	.60	.25		88 Patrick Ewing	1.00	.40
71	Clifford Robinson	.30	.10	3 Jason Terry	1.00	.40		89 Tim Duncan	1.00	.40
72	Shawn Kemp	.60	.25	4 Paul Pierce	1.00	.40		90 Marcus Camby	.60	.25
73	Scottie Pippen	1.50	.60	5 Antoine Walker	1.00	.40		91 Brian Grant	.60	.25
74	Rasheed Wallace	1.00	.40	6 Baron Davis	1.00	.40		92 Kobe Bryant	4.00	1.50
75	Steve Smith	.60	.25	7 Jamal Mashburn	.60	.25		93 Ron Mercer	.60	.25
76	Chris Webber	1.00	.40	8 Chris Mihm	.60	.25		94 Reggie Miller	1.00	.40
77	Jason Williams	.60	.25	9 Andre Miller	.60	.25		95 Shaquille O'Neal	2.50	1.00
78	Peja Stojakovic	1.00	.40	10 Dirk Nowitzki	1.50	.60		96 Kevin Garnett	2.00	.75
79	Tim Duncan	2.00	.75	11 Michael Finley	1.00	.40		97 Scottie Pippen	1.50	.60
80	David Robinson	1.00	.40	12 Raef LaFrentz	.60	.25		98 Michael Jordan	15.00	6.00
81	Sean Elliott	.60	.25	13 Antonio McDyess	.60	.25		99 Steve Nash	1.00	.40
82	Derek Anderson	.60	.25	14 Jerry Stackhouse	1.00	.40		100 Derek Anderson —	.60	.25
83	Vin Baker	.60	.25	15 Antawn Jamison	1.00	.40		101 Kedrick Brown/1750 RC	2.50	1.00
84	Rashard Lewis	.60	.25	16 Steve Francis	1.00	.40		102 Joseph Forte/1750 RC	6.00	2.50
85	Gary Payton	1.00	.40	17 Jalen Rose	1.00	.40		103 Joe Johnson/1250 RC	10.00	4.00
86	Patrick Ewing	1.00	.40	18 Elton Brand	1.00	.40		104 Kirk Haston/1750 RC	2.50	1.00
87	Vince Carter	2.50	1.00	19 Darius Miles	1.25	.50		105 Tyson Chandler/750 RC	12.00	5.00
88	Mark Jackson	.30	.10	20 Lamar Odom	1.00	.40		106 Eddy Curry/1250 RC	6.00	2.50
89	Antonio Davis	.30	.10	21 Mitch Richmond	.60	.25		107 D.Diop/1750 RC	2.50	1.00
90	Karl Malone	1.00	.40	22 Michael Dickerson	.60	.25		108 T.Hassell/1250 RC	2.50	1.00
91	John Stockton	1.00	.40	23 Stromile Swift	.60	.25		109 Z.Rebraca/1250 RC	2.50	1.00
92	Bryon Russell	.30	.10	24 Alonzo Mourning	.60	.25		110 Rodney White/1750 RC	3.00	1.25
93	Donyell Marshall	.60	.25	25 Courtney Alexander	.60	.25		111 Troy Murphy/1250 RC	6.00	2.50
94	Shareef Abdur-Rahim	1.00	.40	26 Ray Allen	1.00	.40		112 J.Richardson/750 RC	10.00	4.00
95	Mike Bibby	1.00	.40	27 Glenn Robinson	.60	.25		113 Eddie Griffin/750 RC	4.00	1.50
96	Michael Dickerson	.60	.25	28 Terrell Brandon	.60	.25		114 Terence Morris/1750 RC	2.50	1.00
97	Mitch Richmond	.60	.25	29 Wally Szczerbiak	.60	.25		115 Oscar Torres/1250 RC	3.00	1.25
98	Juwan Howard	.60	.25	30 Joe Smith	.60	.25		116 Jamaal Tinsley/750 RC	8.00	3.00
99	Richard Hamilton	.60	.25	31 Jason Kidd	1.50	.60		117 Pau Gasol/750 RC	20.00	8.00
100	Rod Strickland	.30	.10	32 Kenyon Martin	1.00	.40		118 Shane Battier/750 RC	8.00	3.00
101	DerMarr Johnson RC	4.00	1.50	33 Keith Van Horn	1.00	.40		119 B.Armstrong/750 RC	4.00	1.50
102	Kenyon Martin RC	15.00	6.00	34 Grant Hill	1.00	.40		120 R.Jefferson/750 RC	6.00	2.50
103	Marcus Fizer RC	4.00	1.50	35 Tracy McGrady	2.50	1.00		121 Steven Hunter/1250 RC	3.00	1.25
104	Courtney Alexander RC	4.00	1.50	36 Mike Miller	1.00	.40		122 S.Dalembert/1750 RC	2.50	1.00
105	Stromile Swift RC	8.00	3.00	37 Allen Iverson	2.00	.75		123 Z.Randolph/1250 RC	10.00	4.00
106	Darius Miles RC	15.00	6.00	38 Speedy Claxton	.60	.25		124 G.Wallace/1750 RC	5.00	2.00
107	Mike Miller RC	12.00	5.00	39 Dikembe Mutombo	.60	.25		125 Tony Parker/750 RC	20.00	8.00
108	Jamal Crawford RC	4.00	1.50	40 Tom Gugliotta	.30	.10		126 V.Radmanovic/1250 RC	4.00	1.50
109	Speedy Claxton RC	4.00	1.50	41 Penny Hardaway	1.00	.40		127 Michael Bradley/1750 RC	2.50	1.00
110	Quentin Richardson RC	15.00	6.00	42 Stephon Marbury	1.00	.40		128 Jarron Collins/1750 RC	2.50	1.00
111	Keyon Dooling RC	4.00	1.50	43 Shawn Marion	1.00	.40		129 Andrei Kirilenko/750 RC	15.00	6.00
112	Desmond Mason RC	4.00	1.50	44 Rasheed Wallace	1.00	.40		130 Kwame Brown/750 RC	6.00	2.50
113	Mateen Cleaves RC	4.00	1.50	45 Peja Stojakovic	1.00	.40				
114	Morris Peterson RC	8.00	3.00	46 Mike Bibby	1.00	.40				
115	Hidayet Turkoglu RC	10.00	4.00	47 Chris Webber	1.00	.40		**2003-04 E-X**		
116	Donnell Harvey RC	4.00	1.50	48 David Robinson	1.00	.40				
117	Jerome Moiso RC	4.00	1.50	49 Vin Baker	.60	.25				
118	Jason Collier RC	6.00	2.50	50 Rashard Lewis	.60	.25				
119	Jamaal Magloire RC	4.00	1.50	51 Desmond Mason	.60	.25				
120	Erick Barkley RC	4.00	1.50	52 Gary Payton	1.00	.40				
121	Etan Thomas RC	4.00	1.50	53 Vince Carter	2.50	1.00				
122	DeShawn Stevenson RC	4.00	1.50	54 Antonio Davis	.30	.10				
123	Dan Langhi RC	4.00	1.50	55 Hakeem Olajuwon	1.00	.40				
124	Mark Madsen RC	4.00	1.50	56 Morris Peterson	.60	.25				
125	Khalid El-Amin RC	4.00	1.50	57 Karl Malone	1.00	.40				
126	Lavor Postell RC	4.00	1.50	58 DeShawn Stevenson	.60	.25				
127	Eddie House RC	4.00	1.50	59 John Stockton	1.00	.40				
128	Michael Redd RC	6.00	2.50	60 Richard Hamilton	.60	.25				
129	Chris Porter RC	4.00	1.50	61 Corey Maggette	.60	.25				
130	Mike Smith RC	4.00	1.50	62 Steve Smith	.60	.25				
				63 Tim Duncan	.60	.25				
	2001-02 E-X			64 Lindsey Hunter	.30	.10				
				65 Jermaine O'Neal	1.00	.40				
				66 Cuttino Mobley	.60	.25				
				67 Nick Van Exel	1.00	.40				
				68 Juwan Howard	.60	.25				
				69 James Posey	.60	.25				
				70 David Wesley	.30	.10				
				71 Marcus Fizer	.60	.25				

				72 Jumaine Jones	.60	.25				
				73 Tim Hardaway	.60	.25				
				74 Danny Fortson	.30	.10				
				75 Jonathan Bender	.60	.25				
				76 Quentin Richardson	.60	.25				
				77 Eddie House	.60	.25		COMP.SET w/o SP's (72)	50.00	20.00
				78 Kurt Thomas	.60	.25		COMMON CARD (1-72)	.25	.10
				79 Anthony Mason	.60	.25		COMMON ROOKIE (73-102)	6.00	2.50
				80 Theo Ratliff	.60	.25		1 Shareef Abdur-Rahim	1.00	.40
				81 Allan Houston	.60	.25		2 Ray Allen	1.00	.40
				82 Latrell Sprewell	1.00	.40		3 Gilbert Arenas	1.00	.40
				83 Jason Williams	.60	.25		4 Ron Artest	.60	.25
				84 Eddie Jones	1.00	.40		5 Mike Bibby	1.00	.40
				85 Damon Stoudamire	.60	.25		6 Chauncey Billups	.60	.25
COMPLETE SET (130)		500.00	250.00					7 Elton Brand	1.00	.40
COMP.SET w/o SP's (100)		50.00	25.00					8 Kwame Brown	.60	.25
COMMON CARD (1-100)		.30	.10					9 Kobe Bryant	4.00	1.50

10 Caron Butler	1.00	.40
11 Vince Carter	2.50	1.00
12 Eddy Curry	.60	.25
13 Ricky Davis	1.00	.40
14 Baron Davis	1.00	.40
15 Tim Duncan	2.00	.75
16 Michael Finley	1.00	.40
17 Steve Francis	1.00	.40
18 Kevin Garnett	2.00	.75

❑ 19	Pau Gasol	1.00	.40
❑ 20	Manu Ginobili	1.00	.40
❑ 21	Drew Gooden	.60	.25
❑ 22	Nene	.60	.25
❑ 23	Grant Hill	1.00	.40
❑ 24	Allan Houston	.60	.25
❑ 25	Juwan Howard	.60	.25
❑ 26	Zydrunas Ilgauskas	.60	.25
❑ 27	Allen Iverson	2.00	.75
❑ 28	Antawn Jamison	1.00	.40
❑ 29	Richard Jefferson	.60	.25
❑ 30	Eddie Jones	1.00	.40
❑ 31	Jason Kidd	1.50	.60
❑ 32	Andrei Kirilenko	1.00	.40
❑ 33	Rashard Lewis	1.00	.40
❑ 34	Corey Maggette	.60	.25
❑ 35	Karl Malone	1.00	.40
❑ 36	Stephon Marbury	1.00	.40
❑ 37	Shawn Marion	1.00	.40
❑ 38	Kenyon Martin	1.00	.40
❑ 39	Jamal Mashburn	.60	.25
❑ 40	Tracy McGrady	2.50	1.00
❑ 41	Reggie Miller	1.00	.40
❑ 42	Mike Miller	1.00	.40
❑ 43	Yao Ming	2.50	1.00
❑ 44	Cuttino Mobley	.60	.25
❑ 45	Steve Nash	.60	.25
❑ 46	Dirk Nowitzki	1.50	.60
❑ 47	Jermaine O'Neal	1.00	.40
❑ 48	Shaquille O'Neal	2.50	1.00
❑ 49	Tony Parker	1.00	.40
❑ 50	Gary Payton	1.00	.40
❑ 51	Morris Peterson	.60	.25
❑ 52	Paul Pierce	1.00	.40
❑ 53	Scottie Pippen	1.50	.60
❑ 54	Tayshaun Prince	.60	.25
❑ 55	Vladimir Radmanovic	.25	.10
❑ 56	Michael Redd	1.00	.40
❑ 57	Jason Richardson	1.00	.40
❑ 58	Glenn Robinson	1.00	.40
❑ 59	Jalen Rose	1.00	.40
❑ 60	Latrell Sprewell	1.00	.40
❑ 61	Jerry Stackhouse	.60	.25
❑ 62	Peja Stojakovic	1.00	.40
❑ 63	Amare Stoudemire	2.00	.75
❑ 64	Wally Szczerbiak	.60	.25
❑ 65	Jason Terry	1.00	.40
❑ 66	Keith Van Horn	1.00	.40
❑ 67	Dajuan Wagner	.60	.25
❑ 68	Antoine Walker	1.00	.40
❑ 69	Ben Wallace	1.00	.40
❑ 70	Rasheed Wallace	1.00	.40
❑ 71	Chris Webber	1.00	.40
❑ 72	Bonzi Wells	1.00	.40
❑ 73	Carmelo Anthony RC	25.00	10.00
❑ 74	Ndudi Ebi RC	6.00	3.00
❑ 75	Luke Ridnour RC	8.00	3.00
❑ 76	Josh Howard RC	10.00	4.00
❑ 77	Marcus Banks RC	6.00	2.50
❑ 78	Zarko Cabarkapa RC	6.00	2.50
❑ 79	Kendrick Perkins RC	6.00	2.50
❑ 80	Leandro Barbosa RC	10.00	4.00
❑ 81	David West RC	6.00	2.50
❑ 82	Boris Diaw RC	8.00	3.00
❑ 83	Carlos Delfino RC	6.00	2.50
❑ 84	Mickael Pietrus RC	6.00	2.50
❑ 85	Troy Bell RC	6.00	2.50
❑ 86	Reece Gaines RC	6.00	2.50
❑ 87	Brian Cook RC	6.00	2.50
❑ 88	Kirk Hinrich RC	8.00	3.00
❑ 89	Travis Outlaw RC	6.00	2.50
❑ 90	Dwyane Wade RC	25.00	10.00
❑ 91	Luke Walton RC	6.00	2.50
❑ 92	Chris Bosh RC	15.00	6.00
❑ 93	Jarvis Hayes RC	6.00	2.50
❑ 94	Maciej Lampe RC	6.00	2.50
❑ 95	Mike Sweetney RC	6.00	2.50
❑ 96	Sofoklis Schortsanitis RC	8.00	3.00
❑ 97	Dahntay Jones RC	6.00	2.50
❑ 98	Nick Collison RC	6.00	2.50
❑ 99	Chris Kaman RC	6.00	2.50
❑ 100	Darko Milicic RC	10.00	4.00
❑ 101	T.J. Ford RC	8.00	3.00
❑ 102	LeBron James RC	80.00	40.00

2006-07 E-X

❑ 1	Joe Johnson	.75	.30
❑ 2	Paul Pierce	1.25	.50
❑ 3	Emeka Okafor	1.25	.50
❑ 4	Michael Jordan	8.00	3.00
❑ 5	Ben Gordon	2.50	1.00
❑ 6	LeBron James	8.00	3.00
❑ 7	Dirk Nowitzki	2.00	.75
❑ 8	Jason Terry	1.25	.50
❑ 9	Carmelo Anthony	2.50	1.00
❑ 10	Chauncey Billups	1.25	.50
❑ 11	Ben Wallace	1.25	.50
❑ 12	Baron Davis	1.25	.50
❑ 13	Jason Richardson	1.25	.50
❑ 14	Yao Ming	3.00	1.25
❑ 15	Jermaine O'Neal	1.25	.50
❑ 16	Elton Brand	1.25	.50
❑ 17	Kobe Bryant	5.00	2.00
❑ 18	Pau Gasol	1.25	.50
❑ 19	Tracy McGrady	3.00	1.25
❑ 20	Shaquille O'Neal	3.00	1.25
❑ 21	Dwyane Wade	4.00	1.50
❑ 22	Andrew Bogut	1.50	.60
❑ 23	Kevin Garnett	2.50	1.00
❑ 24	Vince Carter	3.00	1.25
❑ 25	Jason Kidd	2.00	.75
❑ 26	Chris Paul	3.00	1.25
❑ 27	Stephon Marbury	1.25	.50
❑ 28	Dwight Howard	1.50	.60
❑ 29	Allen Iverson	2.50	1.00
❑ 30	Steve Nash	1.25	.50
❑ 31	Shawn Marion	1.25	.50
❑ 32	Martell Webster	.75	.30
❑ 33	Mike Bibby	1.25	.50
❑ 34	Ron Artest	.75	.30
❑ 35	Tim Duncan	2.50	1.00
❑ 36	Manu Ginobili	1.25	.50
❑ 37	Ray Allen	1.25	.50
❑ 38	Chris Bosh	1.25	.50
❑ 39	Andrei Kirilenko	1.25	.50
❑ 40	Gilbert Arenas	1.25	.50
❑ 41	J.J. Redick/99 RC	25.00	10.00
❑ 42	Adam Morrison/99 RC	30.00	12.50
❑ 43	Jorge Garbajosa/99 RC	20.00	8.00
❑ 44	Saer Sene/99 RC	20.00	8.00
❑ 45	Renaldo Balkman/99 RC	25.00	10.00
❑ 46	Thabo Sefolosha/99 RC	20.00	8.00
❑ 47	Kevin Pittsnogle/899 AU RC	20.00	8.00
❑ 48	Daniel Gibson/899 AU RC	40.00	20.00
❑ 49	Dee Brown/899 AU RC	20.00	8.00
❑ 50	Sergio Rodriguez/899 AU RC	12.00	5.00
❑ 51	Bobby Jones/899 AU RC	12.00	5.00
❑ 52	Craig Smith/899 AU RC	12.00	5.00
❑ 53	David Noel/899 AU RC	12.00	5.00
❑ 54	Denham Brown/899 AU RC	12.00	5.00
❑ 55	James White/899 AU RC	12.00	5.00
❑ 56	Paul Davis/899 AU RC	12.00	5.00
❑ 57	P.J. Tucker/899 AU RC	12.00	5.00
❑ 58	Solomon Jones/899 AU RC	12.00	5.00
❑ 59	Steve Novak/899 AU RC	12.00	5.00
❑ 60	Allan Ray/899 AU RC	12.00	5.00
❑ 61	Jordan Farmar/899 AU RC	30.00	12.00
❑ 62	Josh Boone/899 AU RC	12.00	5.00
❑ 63	Mardy Collins/899 AU RC	12.00	5.00
❑ 64	Rodney Carney/399 AU RC	15.00	6.00
❑ 65	Quincy Douby/399 AU RC	20.00	8.00
❑ 66	Shannon Brown/399 AU RC	20.00	8.00

❑ 67	Rajon Rondo/399 AU RC	20.00	8.00
❑ 68	Maurice Ager/399 AU RC	15.00	6.00
❑ 69	Ronnie Brewer/399 AU RC	20.00	8.00
❑ 70	Marcus Williams/399 AU RC	20.00	8.00
❑ 71	Kyle Lowry/399 AU RC	15.00	6.00
❑ 72	Cedric Simmons/399 AU RC	15.00	6.00
❑ 73	Patrick O'Bryant/399 AU RC	20.00	8.00
❑ 74	Hilton Armstrong/399 AU RC	15.00	6.00
❑ 75	Rudy Gay/199 AU RC	50.00	20.00
❑ 76	Brandon Roy/199 AU RC	80.00	40.00
❑ 77	Shelden Williams/199 AU RC	20.00	8.00
❑ 78	Tyrus Thomas/199 AU RC	75.00	30.00
❑ 79	LaMarcus Aldridge/199 AU RC	75.00	30.00
❑ 80	Andrea Bargnani/199 AU RC	80.00	40.00

2003-04 Exquisite Collection

❑	COMMON CARD (1-42)	15.00	6.00
❑	COMMON ROOKIE (44-73)	50.00	20.00
❑ 1	Jason Terry	30.00	12.50
❑ 2	Paul Pierce	40.00	15.00
❑ 3	Michael Jordan	325.00	200.00
❑ 4	Kirk Hinrich RC	175.00	100.00
❑ 5	Dajuan Wagner	25.00	10.00
❑ 6	Dirk Nowitzki	60.00	25.00
❑ 7	Steve Nash	60.00	25.00
❑ 8	Andre Miller	25.00	10.00
❑ 9	Ben Wallace	30.00	12.50
❑ 10	Jason Richardson	30.00	12.50
❑ 11	Steve Francis	30.00	12.50
❑ 12	Yao Ming	75.00	30.00
❑ 13	Jermaine O'Neal	30.00	12.50
❑ 14	Elton Brand	30.00	12.50
❑ 15	Kobe Bryant	150.00	75.00
❑ 16	Gary Payton	30.00	12.50
❑ 17	Shaquille O'Neal	100.00	50.00
❑ 18	Pau Gasol	30.00	12.50
❑ 19	Lamar Odom	30.00	12.50
❑ 20	T.J. Ford RC	100.00	50.00
❑ 21	Kevin Garnett	75.00	30.00
❑ 22	Latrell Sprewell	30.00	12.50
❑ 23	Jason Kidd	50.00	20.00
❑ 24	Richard Jefferson	25.00	10.00
❑ 25	Baron Davis	30.00	12.50
❑ 26	Allan Houston	25.00	10.00
❑ 27	Stephon Marbury	30.00	12.50
❑ 28	Tracy McGrady	120.00	60.00
❑ 29	Allen Iverson	160.00	80.00
❑ 30	Shawn Marion	30.00	12.50
❑ 31	Amare Stoudemire	50.00	20.00
❑ 32	Shareef Abdur-Rahim	30.00	12.50
❑ 33	Mike Bibby	30.00	12.50
❑ 34	Chris Webber	40.00	15.00
❑ 35	Tim Duncan	100.00	50.00
❑ 36	Manu Ginobili	75.00	30.00
❑ 37	Ray Allen	30.00	12.50
❑ 38	Nick Collison RC	60.00	20.00
❑ 39	Vince Carter	80.00	40.00
❑ 40	Andrei Kirilenko	40.00	15.00
❑ 41	Gilbert Arenas	40.00	15.00
❑ 42	Jerry Stackhouse	25.00	10.00
❑ 43	U.Haslem JSY AU RC	400.00	200.00
❑ 44	M.Williams JSY AU RC	200.00	100.00
❑ 45	Keith Bogans JSY AU RC	60.00	25.00
❑ 46	T.Hansen JSY AU RC	60.00	25.00
❑ 47	J.Kapono JSY AU RC	100.00	50.00
❑ 48	Z.Pachulia JSY AU RC	75.00	30.00
❑ 49	Z.Cabarkapa JSY AU RC	75.00	30.00

❑ 50 Kyle Korver JSY AU RC	100.00	50.00
❑ 51 Luke Walton JSY AU RC	150.00	75.00
❑ 52 Maciej Lampe JSY AU RC	80.00	40.00
❑ 53 Josh Howard JSY AU RC	450.00	275.00
❑ 54 L.Barbosa JSY AU RC	375.00	225.00
❑ 55 K.Perkins JSY AU RC	160.00	80.00
❑ 56 Ndudi Ebi JSY AU RC	80.00	40.00
❑ 57 J.Beasley JSY AU RC	50.00	20.00
❑ 58 Brian Cook JSY AU RC	80.00	40.00
❑ 59 Travis Outlaw JSY AU RC	120.00	60.00
❑ 60 Z.Planinic JSY AU RC	60.00	25.00
❑ 61 Boris Diaw JSY AU RC	325.00	175.00
❑ 62 Steve Blake JSY AU RC	80.00	40.00
❑ 63 A.Pavlovic JSY AU RC	80.00	40.00
❑ 64 David West JSY AU RC	200.00	100.00
❑ 65 M.Sweetney JSY AU RC	80.00	30.00
❑ 66 Troy Bell JSY AU RC	60.00	25.00
❑ 67 R.Gaines JSY AU RC	50.00	20.00
❑ 68 Luke Ridnour JSY AU RC	160.00	80.00
❑ 69 Marcus Banks JSY AU RC	150.00	75.00
❑ 70 Dahntay Jones JSY AU RC	60.00	25.00
❑ 71 T.M.Pietrus JSY AU RC	160.00	80.00
❑ 72 Chris Kaman JSY AU RC	200.00	100.00
❑ 73 Jarvis Hayes JSY AU RC	80.00	30.00
❑ 74 D.Wade JSY AU RC	6000.00	4000.00
❑ 75 Chris Bosh JSY AU RC	2200.00	1800.00
❑ 76 C.Anthony JSY AU RC	3500.00	2800.00
❑ 77 Darko Milicic JSY AU RC	850.00	500.00
❑ 78 L.James JSY AU RC	12000.00	9000.00

2004-05 Exquisite Collection

❑ COMMON JSY AU RC LEV 2 (43-84)	50.00	20.00
❑ COMMON AU RC LEV 2 (43-84)	40.00	15.00
❑ 1 Al Harrington	15.00	6.00
❑ 2 Paul Pierce	15.00	6.00
❑ 3 Emeka Okafor RC	80.00	40.00
❑ 4 Michael Jordan	180.00	90.00
❑ 5 LeBron James	120.00	60.00
❑ 6 Dirk Nowitzki	25.00	10.00
❑ 7 Carmelo Anthony	25.00	10.00
❑ 8 Kenyon Martin	15.00	6.00
❑ 9 Richard Hamilton	15.00	6.00
❑ 10 Ben Wallace	15.00	6.00
❑ 11 Jason Richardson	15.00	6.00
❑ 12 Yao Ming	30.00	12.50
❑ 13 Tracy McGrady	30.00	12.50
❑ 14 Reggie Miller	15.00	6.00
❑ 15 Corey Maggette	15.00	6.00
❑ 16 Kobe Bryant	60.00	25.00
❑ 17 Lamar Odom	15.00	6.00
❑ 18 Pau Gasol	15.00	6.00
❑ 19 Dwyane Wade	40.00	15.00
❑ 20 Shaquille O'Neal	40.00	15.00
❑ 21 Michael Redd	15.00	6.00
❑ 22 Kevin Garnett	25.00	10.00
❑ 23 Vince Carter	30.00	12.50
❑ 24 Jason Kidd	25.00	10.00
❑ 25 Baron Davis	15.00	6.00
❑ 26 Jamaal Magloire	12.00	5.00
❑ 27 Stephon Marbury	15.00	6.00
❑ 28 Steve Francis	15.00	6.00
❑ 29 Allen Iverson	100.00	50.00
❑ 30 Amare Stoudemire	25.00	10.00
❑ 31 Shawn Marion	15.00	6.00
❑ 32 Shareef Abdur-Rahim	15.00	6.00
❑ 33 Peja Stojakovic	15.00	6.00
❑ 34 Mike Bibby	15.00	6.00
❑ 35 Tim Duncan	30.00	12.50
❑ 36 Tony Parker	15.00	6.00
❑ 37 Ray Allen	15.00	6.00
❑ 38 Chris Bosh	15.00	6.00
❑ 39 Andrei Kirilenko	15.00	6.00
❑ 40 Carlos Boozer	15.00	6.00
❑ 41 Gilbert Arenas	15.00	6.00
❑ 42 Antawn Jamison	15.00	6.00
❑ 43 Andre Emmett JSY AU RC	50.00	20.00
❑ 44 Jameer Nelson JSY AU RC	200.00	100.00
❑ 45 S.Livingston JSY AU RC	200.00	100.00
❑ 46 Delonte West JSY AU RC	200.00	100.00
❑ 47 Trevor Ariza AU RC	40.00	15.00
❑ 48 Tony Allen JSY AU RC	120.00	60.00
❑ 49 Luke Jackson JSY AU RC	60.00	30.00
❑ 50 Dorell Wright JSY AU RC	200.00	100.00
❑ 51 Nenad Krstic JSY AU RC	100.00	50.00
❑ 52 Al Jefferson JSY RC	500.00	300.00
❑ 53 J.R. Smith JSY AU RC	300.00	150.00
❑ 54 Rafael Araujo JSY AU RC	60.00	30.00
❑ 55 Andris Biedrins JSY AU RC	150.00	75.00
❑ 56 Josh Smith JSY AU RC	300.00	150.00
❑ 57 Ha Seung-Jin JSY AU RC	60.00	30.00
❑ 58 B.Robinson JSY AU RC	60.00	30.00
❑ 59 Kevin Martin JSY AU RC	350.00	200.00
❑ 60 David Harrison JSY AU RC	60.00	30.00
❑ 61 Kris Humphries JSY AU RC	60.00	30.00
❑ 62 A.Varejao JSY AU RC	60.00	30.00
❑ 63 Jackson Vroman JSY AU RC	50.00	20.00
❑ 64 Sebastian Telfair JSY AU RC	100.00	50.00
❑ 65 Chris Duhon JSY AU RC	100.00	50.00
❑ 66 Kirk Snyder JSY AU RC	60.00	25.00
❑ 67 Andres Nocioni AU RC	100.00	50.00
❑ 68 Antonio Burks AU RC	40.00	15.00
❑ 69 Beno Udrih AU RC	50.00	20.00
❑ 70 D.J. Mbenga AU RC	40.00	15.00
❑ 71 Lionel Chalmers JSY AU RC	50.00	20.00
❑ 72 Robert Swift AU RC	40.00	15.00
❑ 73 Sasha Vujacic JSY AU RC	50.00	20.00
❑ 74 Donta Smith AU RC	40.00	15.00
❑ 75 Peter John Ramos AU RC	40.00	15.00
❑ 76 Justin Reed AU RC	60.00	30.00
❑ 77 Pape Sow AU RC	40.00	15.00
❑ 78 Pavel Podkolzin AU RC	40.00	15.00
❑ 79 Viktor Khryapa AU RC	40.00	15.00
❑ 80 John Edwards AU RC	40.00	15.00
❑ 81 Royal Ivey AU RC	40.00	15.00
❑ 82 Damien Wilkins AU RC	40.00	15.00
❑ 83 Erik Daniels AU RC	40.00	15.00
❑ 84 Luis Flores AU RC	40.00	15.00
❑ 85 Andre Iguodala JSY AU RC	900.00	600.00
❑ 86 Josh Childress JSY AU RC	300.00	150.00
❑ 87 Devin Harris JSY AU RC	300.00	200.00
❑ 88 Ben Gordon JSY AU RC	1100.00	900.00
❑ 89 Luol Deng JSY AU RC EXCH	600.00	400.00
❑ 90 Dwight Howard JSY AU RC	3000.00	2500.00

2005-06 Exquisite Collection

❑ 1 Joe Johnson	10.00	4.00
❑ 2 Paul Pierce	15.00	6.00
❑ 3 Emeka Okafor	25.00	10.00
❑ 4 Ben Gordon	20.00	10.00
❑ 5 Michael Jordan	200.00	100.00
❑ 6 LeBron James	120.00	60.00
❑ 7 Dirk Nowitzki	25.00	10.00
❑ 8 Carmelo Anthony	32.00	12.00
❑ 9 Kenyon Martin	16.00	6.00
❑ 10 Chauncey Billups	16.00	6.00
❑ 11 Ben Wallace	16.00	6.00
❑ 12 Jason Richardson	16.00	6.00
❑ 13 Tracy McGrady	40.00	16.00
❑ 14 Yao Ming	40.00	16.00
❑ 15 Jermaine O'Neal	16.00	6.00
❑ 16 Elton Brand	16.00	6.00
❑ 17 Kobe Bryant	60.00	24.00
❑ 18 Pau Gasol	16.00	6.00
❑ 19 Shaquille O'Neal	40.00	16.00
❑ 20 Dwyane Wade	50.00	20.00
❑ 21 Michael Redd	16.00	6.00
❑ 22 Kevin Garnett	32.00	12.00
❑ 23 Vince Carter	40.00	16.00
❑ 24 Jason Kidd	25.00	10.00
❑ 25 J.R. Smith	10.00	4.00
❑ 26 Stephon Marbury	16.00	6.00
❑ 27 Quentin Richardson	10.00	4.00
❑ 28 Steve Francis	16.00	6.00
❑ 29 Dwight Howard	25.00	10.00
❑ 30 Allen Iverson	60.00	25.00
❑ 31 Chris Webber	16.00	6.00
❑ 32 Steve Nash	16.00	6.00
❑ 33 Amare Stoudemire	32.00	12.00
❑ 34 Zach Randolph	15.00	6.00
❑ 35 Mike Bibby	16.00	6.00
❑ 36 Peja Stojakovic	16.00	6.00
❑ 37 Tim Duncan	32.00	12.00
❑ 38 Tony Parker	16.00	6.00
❑ 39 Ray Allen	16.00	6.00
❑ 40 Chris Bosh	16.00	6.00
❑ 41 Andrei Kirilenko	16.00	6.00
❑ 42 Gilbert Arenas	16.00	6.00
❑ 43 A.Bogut JSY AU RC/99	550.00	300.00
❑ 44 M.Williams JSY AU RC/99	800.00	400.00
❑ 45 D.Williams JSY AU RC/99	1200.00	900.00
❑ 46 C.Paul JSY AU RC/99	2500.00	2000.00
❑ 47 R.Felton JSY AU RC/99	600.00	300.00
❑ 48 C.Frye JSY AU RC/99	400.00	200.00
❑ 49 M.Webster JSY AU RC	200.00	100.00
❑ 50 C.Villanueva JSY AU RC	200.00	100.00
❑ 51 Ike Diogu AU RC	100.00	50.00
❑ 52 Andrew Bynum JSY AU RC	400.00	200.00
❑ 53 Sean May JSY AU RC	100.00	50.00
❑ 54 Rashad McCants JSY AU RC	200.00	100.00
❑ 55 Antoine Wright JSY AU RC	75.00	30.00
❑ 56 Joey Graham JSY AU RC	75.00	30.00
❑ 57 Danny Granger JSY AU RC	200.00	100.00
❑ 58 Gerald Green JSY AU RC	350.00	200.00
❑ 59 Hakim Warrick JSY AU RC	150.00	75.00
❑ 60 Julius Hodge JSY AU RC	80.00	40.00
❑ 61 Nate Robinson JSY AU RC	120.00	60.00
❑ 62 Jarrett Jack JSY AU RC	100.00	50.00
❑ 63 Francisco Garcia JSY AU RC	100.00	50.00
❑ 64 Luther Head JSY AU RC	120.00	60.00
❑ 65 Johan Petro JSY AU RC	80.00	40.00
❑ 66 Jason Maxiell JSY AU RC	80.00	40.00
❑ 67 Linas Kleiza JSY AU RC	80.00	40.00
❑ 68 Wayne Simien JSY AU RC	120.00	60.00
❑ 69 David Lee JSY AU RC	150.00	75.00
❑ 70 Salim Stoudamire JSY AU RC	100.00	50.00
❑ 71 Daniel Ewing JSY AU RC	80.00	40.00
❑ 72 Brandon Bass JSY AU RC	80.00	40.00
❑ 73 C.J. Miles JSY AU RC	80.00	40.00
❑ 74 Ersan Ilyasova JSY AU RC	80.00	40.00
❑ 75 Travis Diener JSY AU RC	80.00	40.00
❑ 76 Monta Ellis JSY AU RC	450.00	300.00
❑ 77 Chris Taft JSY AU RC	80.00	40.00
❑ 78 M.Andriuskevicius JSY AU RC	80.00	40.00
❑ 79 Louis Williams JSY AU RC	150.00	75.00
❑ 80 Andray Blatche JSY AU RC	120.00	60.00
❑ 81 Ryan Gomes JSY AU RC	100.00	50.00
❑ 82 S.Jasikevicius JSY AU RC	80.00	40.00
❑ 83 Yaroslav Korolev AU RC	40.00	15.00
❑ 84 Von Wafer AU RC	40.00	15.00
❑ 85 Orien Greene AU RC	40.00	15.00
❑ 86 Robert Whaley AU RC	40.00	15.00
❑ 87 Dijon Thompson AU RC	40.00	15.00
❑ 88 Bracey Wright AU RC	40.00	15.00
❑ 89 Amir Johnson AU RC	60.00	30.00
❑ 90 Ronny Turiaf AU RC	120.00	60.00
❑ 91 James Singleton AU RC	40.00	15.00
❑ 92 James Singleton AU RC	40.00	15.00
❑ 93 Alex Acker AU RC	40.00	15.00
❑ 94 Chuck Hayes AU RC	40.00	15.00
❑ 95 Lawrence Roberts AU RC	40.00	15.00
❑ 96 Stephen Graham AU RC	40.00	15.00

1993-94 Finest

#	Player		
	COMPLETE SET (220)	100.00	40.00
1	Michael Jordan	12.00	6.00
2	Larry Bird	2.50	1.00
3	Shaquille O'Neal	5.00	2.00
4	Benoit Benjamin	.25	.08
5	Ricky Pierce	.25	.08
6	Ken Norman	.25	.08
7	Victor Alexander	.25	.08
8	Mark Jackson	.40	.15
9	Mark West	.25	.08
10	Don MacLean	.25	.08
11	Reggie Miller	.75	.30
12	Sarunas Marciulionis	.25	.08
13	Craig Ehlo	.25	.08
14	Toni Kukoc RC	4.00	1.50
15	Glen Rice	.40	.15
16	Otis Thorpe	.25	.08
17	Reggie Williams	.25	.08
18	Charles Smith	.25	.08
19	Micheal Williams	.25	.08
20	Tom Chambers	.25	.08
21	David Robinson	1.50	.60
22	Jamal Mashburn RC	5.00	2.00
23	Clifford Robinson	.40	.15
24	Acie Earl RC	.25	.08
25	Danny Ferry	.25	.08
26	Bobby Hurley RC	.40	.15
27	Eddie Johnson	.25	.08
28	Detlef Schrempf	.40	.15
29	Mike Brown	.25	.08
30	Latrell Sprewell	2.50	1.00
31	Derek Harper	.40	.15
32	Stacey Augmon	.25	.08
33	Pooh Richardson	.25	.08
34	Larry Krystkowiak	.25	.08
35	Pervis Ellison	.25	.08
36	Jeff Malone	.25	.08
37	Sean Elliott	.40	.15
38	John Paxson	.25	.08
39	Robert Parish	.40	.15
40	Mark Aguirre	.25	.08
41	Danny Ainge	.40	.15
42	Brian Shaw	.25	.08
43	LaPhonso Ellis	.25	.08
44	Carl Herrera	.25	.08
45	Terry Cummings	.25	.08
46	Chris Dudley	.25	.08
47	Anthony Mason	.40	.15
48	Chris Morris	.25	.08
49	Todd Day	.25	.08
50	Nick Van Exel RC	6.00	2.50
51	Larry Nance	.40	.15
52	Derrick McKey	.25	.08
53	Muggsy Bogues	.40	.15
54	Andrew Lang	.25	.08
55	Chuck Person	.25	.08
56	Michael Adams	.25	.08
57	Spud Webb	.40	.15
58	Scott Skiles	.25	.08
59	A.C. Green	.40	.15
60	Terry Mills	.25	.08
61	Xavier McDaniel	.25	.08
62	B.J. Armstrong	.25	.08
63	Donald Hodge	.25	.08
64	Gary Grant	.25	.08
65	Billy Owens	.25	.08
66	Greg Anthony	.25	.08
67	Jay Humphries	.25	.08
68	Lionel Simmons	.25	.08
69	Dana Barros	.25	.08
70	Steve Smith	.75	.30
71	Ervin Johnson RC	.40	.15
72	Sleepy Floyd	.25	.08
73	Blue Edwards	.25	.08
74	Clyde Drexler	.75	.30
75	Elden Campbell	.25	.08
76	Hakeem Olajuwon	1.50	.60
77	Clarence Weatherspoon	.25	.08
78	Kevin Willis	.25	.08
79	Isaiah Rider RC	4.00	1.50
80	Derrick Coleman	.40	.15
81	Nick Anderson	.40	.15
82	Bryant Stith	.25	.08
83	Johnny Newman	.25	.08
84	Calbert Cheaney RC	1.50	.60
85	Oliver Miller	.25	.08
86	Loy Vaught	.25	.08
87	Isiah Thomas	.75	.30
88	Dee Brown	.25	.08
89	Horace Grant	.40	.15
90	Patrick Ewing AF	.40	.15
91	Clarence Weatherspoon AF	.25	.08
92	Rony Seikaly AF	.25	.08
93	Dino Radja AF	.25	.08
94	Kenny Anderson AF	.25	.08
95	John Starks AF	.25	.08
96	Tom Gugliotta AF	.40	.15
97	Steve Smith AF	.40	.15
98	Derrick Coleman AF	.25	.08
99	Shaquille O'Neal AF	3.00	1.25
100	Brad Daugherty CF	.25	.08
101	Horace Grant CF	.25	.08
102	Dominique Wilkins CF	.40	.15
103	Joe Dumars CF	.40	.15
104	Alonzo Mourning CF	.75	.30
105	Scottie Pippen CF	2.50	1.00
106	Reggie Miller CF	.40	.15
107	Mark Price CF	.25	.08
108	Ken Norman CF	.25	.08
109	Larry Johnson CF	.40	.15
110	Jamal Mashburn MF	.75	.30
111	Christian Laettner MF	.25	.08
112	Karl Malone MF	.75	.30
113	Dennis Rodman MF	.75	.30
114	Mahmoud Abdul-Rauf MF	.25	.08
115	Hakeem Olajuwon MF	.75	.30
116	Jim Jackson MF	.25	.08
117	John Stockton MF	.40	.15
118	David Robinson MF	.75	.30
119	Dikembe Mutombo MF	.40	.15
120	Vlade Divac PF	.25	.08
121	Dan Majerle PF	.25	.08
122	Chris Mullin PF	.40	.15
123	Shawn Kemp PF	.75	.30
124	Danny Manning PF	.25	.08
125	Charles Barkley PF	.75	.30
126	Mitch Richmond PF	.40	.15
127	Tim Hardaway PF	.40	.15
128	Detlef Schrempf PF	.25	.08
129	Clyde Drexler PF	.40	.15
130	Christian Laettner	.40	.15
131	Rodney Rogers RC	2.00	.75
132	Rik Smits	.40	.15
133	Chris Mills RC	2.00	.75
134	Corie Blount RC	.25	.08
135	Mookie Blaylock	.40	.15
136	Jim Jackson	.40	.15
137	Tom Gugliotta	.75	.30
138	Dennis Scott	.25	.08
139	Vin Baker RC	4.00	1.50
140	Gary Payton	1.50	.60
141	Sedale Threatt	.25	.08
142	Orlando Woolridge	.25	.08
143	Avery Johnson	.25	.08
144	Charles Oakley	.40	.15
145	Harvey Grant	.25	.08
146	Bimbo Coles	.25	.08
147	Vernon Maxwell	.25	.08
148	Danny Manning	.40	.15
149	Hersey Hawkins	.40	.15
150	Kevin Gamble	.25	.08
151	Johnny Dawkins	.25	.08
152	Olden Polynice	.25	.08
153	Kevin Edwards	.25	.08
154	Willie Anderson	.25	.08
155	Wayman Tisdale	.25	.08
156	Popeye Jones RC	.25	.08
157	Dan Majerle	.40	.15
158	Rex Chapman	.25	.08
159	Shawn Kemp UER 136	1.50	.60
160	Eric Murdock	.25	.08
161	Randy White	.25	.08
162	Larry Johnson	.75	.30
163	Dominique Wilkins	.75	.30
164	Dikembe Mutombo	.75	.30
165	Patrick Ewing	.75	.30
166	Jerome Kersey	.25	.08
167	Dale Davis	.25	.08
168	Ron Harper	.40	.15
169	Sam Cassell RC	6.00	2.50
170	Bill Cartwright	.25	.08
171	John Williams	.25	.08
172	Dino Radja	.25	.08
173	Dennis Rodman	2.00	.75
174	Kenny Anderson	.40	.15
175	Robert Horry	.40	.15
176	Chris Mullin	.75	.30
177	John Salley	.25	.08
178	Scott Burrell RC	1.50	.60
179	Mitch Richmond	.75	.30
180	Lee Mayberry	.25	.08
181	James Worthy	.75	.30
182	Rick Fox	.25	.08
183	Kevin Johnson	.40	.15
184	Lindsey Hunter RC	2.00	.75
185	Marlon Maxey	.25	.08
186	Sam Perkins	.40	.15
187	Kevin Duckworth	.25	.08
188	Jeff Hornacek	.40	.15
189	Anfernee Hardaway RC	12.00	5.00
190	Rex Walters RC	.25	.08
191	Mahmoud Abdul-Rauf	.25	.08
192	Terry Dehere RC	.25	.08
193	Brad Daugherty	.25	.08
194	John Starks	.40	.15
195	Rod Strickland	.40	.15
196	Luther Wright RC	.25	.08
197	Vlade Divac	.40	.15
198	Tim Hardaway	.75	.30
199	Joe Dumars	.75	.30
200	Charles Barkley	1.50	.60
201	Alonzo Mourning	1.50	.60
202	Doug West	.25	.08
203	Anthony Avent	.25	.08
204	Lloyd Daniels	.25	.08
205	Mark Price	.25	.08
206	Rumeal Robinson	.25	.08
207	Kendall Gill	.40	.15
208	Scottie Pippen	3.00	1.25
209	Kenny Smith	.25	.08
210	Walt Williams	.25	.08
211	Hubert Davis	.25	.08
212	Chris Webber RC	25.00	10.00
213	Rony Seikaly	.25	.08
214	Sam Bowie	.25	.08
215	Karl Malone	1.50	.60
216	Malik Sealy	.25	.08
217	Dale Ellis	.25	.08
218	Harold Miner	.25	.08
219	John Stockton	.75	.30
220	Shawn Bradley RC	2.00	.75

1994-95 Finest

#	Player		
	COMPLETE SET (1-331)	250.00	125.00
	COMP.SERIES 1 (165)	100.00	50.00
	COMP.SERIES 2 (166)	150.00	75.00
	COMMON CARD (1-165)	.60	.25
	COMMON CARD (166-331)	.30	.10
1	Chris Mullin CY	1.25	.50
2	Anthony Mason CY	.60	.25
3	John Salley CY	.60	.25
4	Jamal Mashburn CY	1.25	.50
5	Mark Jackson CY	.60	.25
6	Mario Elie CY	.60	.25
7	Kenny Anderson CY	.60	.25
8	Rod Strickland CY	.60	.25
9	Kenny Smith CY	.60	.25
10	Olden Polynice CY	.60	.25
11	Derek Harper	.60	.25

GRANT HILL

#	Player		
12	Danny Ainge	.60	.25
13	Dino Radja	.60	.25
14	Eric Murdock	.60	.25
15	Sean Rooks	.60	.25
16	Dell Curry	.60	.25
17	Victor Alexander	.60	.25
18	Rodney Rogers	.60	.25
19	John Salley	.60	.25
20	Brad Daugherty	.60	.25
21	Elmore Spencer	.60	.25
22	Mitch Richmond	2.50	1.00
23	Rex Walters	.60	.25
24	Antonio Davis	.60	.25
25	B.J. Armstrong	.60	.25
26	Andrew Lang	.60	.25
27	Carl Herrera	.60	.25
28	Kevin Edwards	.60	.25
29	Micheal Williams	.60	.25
30	Clyde Drexler	2.50	1.00
31	Dana Barros	.60	.25
32	Shaquille O'Neal	12.00	5.00
33	Patrick Ewing	2.50	1.00
34	Charles Barkley	4.00	1.50
35	J.R. Reid	.60	.25
36	Lindsey Hunter	1.25	.50
37	Jeff Malone	.60	.25
38	Rik Smits	.60	.25
39	Brian Williams	.60	.25
40	Shawn Kemp	4.00	1.50
41	Terry Porter	.60	.25
42	James Worthy	2.50	1.00
43	Rex Chapman	.60	.25
44	Stanley Roberts	.60	.25
45	Chris Smith	.60	.25
46	Dee Brown	.60	.25
47	Chris Gatling	.60	.25
48	Donald Hodge	.60	.25
49	Bimbo Coles	.60	.25
50	Derrick Coleman	1.25	.50
51	Muggsy Bogues CY	.60	.25
52	Reggie Williams CY	.60	.25
53	David Wingate CY	.60	.25
54	Sam Cassell CY	2.50	1.00
55	Sherman Douglas CY	.60	.25
56	Keith Jennings	.60	.25
57	Kenny Gattison	.60	.25
58	Brent Price	.60	.25
59	Luc Longley	.60	.25
60	Jamal Mashburn	2.50	1.00
61	Doug West	.60	.25
62	Walt Williams	.60	.25
63	Tracy Murray	.60	.25
64	Robert Pack	.60	.25
65	Johnny Dawkins	.60	.25
66	Vin Baker	2.50	1.00
67	Sam Cassell	2.50	1.00
68	Dale Davis	.60	.25
69	Terrell Brandon	1.25	.50
70	Billy Owens	.60	.25
71	Ervin Johnson	.60	.25
72	Allan Houston	4.00	1.50
73	Craig Ehlo	.60	.25
74	Loy Vaught	.60	.25
75	Scottie Pippen	8.00	4.00
76	Sam Bowie	.60	.25
77	Anthony Mason	1.25	.50
78	Felton Spencer	.60	.25
79	P.J. Brown	.60	.25
80	Christian Laettner	1.25	.50
81	Todd Day	.60	.25
82	Sean Elliott	1.25	.50
83	Grant Long	.60	.25
84	Xavier McDaniel	.60	.25
85	David Benoit	.60	.25
86	Larry Stewart	.60	.25
87	Donald Royal	.60	.25
88	Duane Causwell	.60	.25
89	Vlade Divac	.60	.25
90	Derrick McKey	.60	.25
91	Kevin Johnson	1.25	.50
92	LaPhonso Ellis	.60	.25
93	Jerome Kersey	.60	.25
94	Muggsy Bogues	1.25	.50
95	Tom Gugliotta	1.25	.50
96	Jeff Hornacek	1.25	.50
97	Kevin Willis	.60	.25
98	Chris Mills	1.25	.50
99	Sam Perkins	1.25	.50
100	Alonzo Mourning	3.00	1.25
101	Derrick Coleman CY	.60	.25
102	Glen Rice CY	.60	.25
103	Kevin Willis CY	.60	.25
104	Chris Webber CY	3.00	1.25
105	Terry Mills CY	.60	.25
106	Tim Hardaway CY	1.25	.50
107	Nick Anderson CY	.60	.25
108	Terry Cummings CY	.60	.25
109	Hersey Hawkins CY	.60	.25
110	Ken Norman CY	.60	.25
111	Nick Anderson	.60	.25
112	Tim Perry	.60	.25
113	Terry Dehere	.60	.25
114	Chris Morris	.60	.25
115	Alvin Williams	.60	.25
116	Jon Barry	.60	.25
117	Rony Seikaly	.60	.25
118	Detlef Schrempf	1.25	.50
119	Terry Cummings	.60	.25
120	Chris Webber	6.00	2.50
121	David Wingate	.60	.25
122	Popeye Jones	.60	.25
123	Sherman Douglas	.60	.25
124	Greg Anthony	.60	.25
125	Mookie Blaylock	.60	.25
126	Don MacLean	.60	.25
127	Lionel Simmons	.60	.25
128	Scott Brooks	.60	.25
129	Jeff Turner	.60	.25
130	Bryant Stith	.60	.25
131	Shawn Bradley	.60	.25
132	Byron Scott	1.25	.50
133	Doug Christie	1.25	.50
134	Dennis Rodman	5.00	2.00
135	Dan Majerle	1.25	.50
136	Gary Grant	.60	.25
137	Bryon Russell	.60	.25
138	Will Perdue	.60	.25
139	Gheorghe Muresan	.60	.25
140	Kendall Gill	1.25	.50
141	Isaiah Rider	1.25	.50
142	Terry Mills	.60	.25
143	Willie Anderson	.60	.25
144	Hubert Davis	.60	.25
145	Lucious Harris	.60	.25
146	Spud Webb	.60	.25
147	Glen Rice	1.25	.50
148	Dennis Scott	.60	.25
149	Robert Horry	1.25	.50
150	John Stockton	2.50	1.00
151	Stacey Augmon CY	.60	.25
152	Chris Mills CY	.60	.25
153	Elden Campbell CY	.60	.25
154	Jay Humphries CY	.60	.25
155	Reggie Miller CY	1.25	.50
156	George Lynch	.60	.25
157	Tyrone Hill	.60	.25
158	Lee Mayberry	.60	.25
159	Jon Koncak	.60	.25
160	Joe Dumars	2.50	1.00
161	Vernon Maxwell	.60	.25
162	Joe Kleine	.60	.25
163	Acie Earl	.60	.25
164	Steve Kerr	.60	.25
165	Rod Strickland	1.25	.50
166	Glenn Robinson RC	10.00	4.00
167	Anfernee Hardaway	4.00	1.50
168	Latrell Sprewell	2.50	1.00
169	Sergei Bazarevich	.30	.10
170	Hakeem Olajuwon	2.00	.75
171	Nick Van Exel	1.25	.50
172	Buck Williams	.30	.10
173	Antoine Carr	.30	.10
174	Corie Blount	.30	.10
175	Dominique Wilkins	1.25	.50
176	Yinka Dare	.30	.10
177	Byron Houston	.30	.10
178	LaSalle Thompson	.30	.10
179	Doug Smith	.30	.10
180	David Robinson	2.00	.75
181	Eric Piatkowski RC	.30	.10
182	Scott Skiles	.30	.10
183	Scott Burrell	.30	.10
184	Mark West	.30	.10
185	Billy Owens	.30	.10
186	Brian Grant RC	5.00	2.00
187	Scott Williams	.30	.10
188	Gerald Madkins	.30	.10
189	Reggie Williams	.30	.10
190	Danny Manning	.60	.25
191	Mike Brown	.30	.10
192	Charles Smith	.30	.10
193	Elden Campbell	.30	.10
194	Ricky Pierce	.30	.10
195	Karl Malone	2.00	.75
196	Brooks Thompson	.30	.10
197	Alaa Abdelnaby	.30	.10
198	Tyrone Corbin	.30	.10
199	Johnny Newman	.30	.10
200	Grant Hill CB	6.00	2.50
201	Kenny Anderson CB	.30	.10
202	Olden Polynice CB	.30	.10
203	Horace Grant CB	.30	.10
204	Muggsy Bogues CB	.30	.10
205	Mark Price CB	.30	.10
206	Tom Gugliotta CB	.30	.10
207	Christian Laettner CB	.30	.10
208	Eric Montross CB	.30	.10
209	Sam Cassell CB	1.25	.50
210	Charles Oakley CB	.30	.10
211	Harold Ellis CB	.30	.10
212	Nate McMillan CB	.30	.10
213	Chuck Person CB	.30	.10
214	Harold Miner CB	.30	.10
215	Clarence Weatherspoon CB	.30	.10
216	Robert Parish CB	.60	.25
217	Michael Cage CB	.30	.10
218	Kenny Smith CB	.30	.10
219	Larry Krystkowiak CB	.30	.10
220	Dikembe Mutombo CB	.60	.25
221	Wayman Tisdale CB	.30	.10
222	Kevin Duckworth CB	.30	.10
223	Vern Fleming CB	.30	.10
224	Eric Mobley RC	.30	.10
225	Patrick Ewing CB	.60	.25
226	Clifford Robinson CB	.30	.10
227	Eric Murdock CB	.30	.10
228	Derrick Coleman CB	.30	.10
229	Otis Thorpe CB	.30	.10
230	Alonzo Mourning CB	1.25	.50
231	Donyell Marshall CB	.60	.25
232	Dikembe Mutombo CB	.30	.10
233	Rony Seikaly CB	.30	.10
234	Chris Mullin CB	.60	.25
235	Reggie Miller	1.25	.50
236	Benoit Benjamin	.30	.10
237	Sean Rooks	.30	.10
238	Terry Davis	.30	.10
239	Anthony Avent	.30	.10
240	Grant Hill RC	30.00	12.50
241	Randy Woods	.30	.10
242	Tom Chambers	.30	.10
243	Michael Adams	.30	.10
244	Monty Williams RC	.30	.10
245	Chris Mullin	1.25	.50
246	Bill Wennington	.30	.10
247	Mark Jackson	.30	.10
248	Blue Edwards	.30	.10
249	Jalen Rose RC	10.00	4.00
250	Glenn Robinson CB	1.50	.50
251	Kevin Willis CB	.30	.10

❏ 252	B.J. Armstrong CB	.30	.10
❏ 253	Jim Jackson CB	.30	.10
❏ 254	Steve Smith CB	.30	.10
❏ 255	Chris Webber CB	1.50	.60
❏ 256	Glen Rice CB	.30	.10
❏ 257	Derek Harper CB	.30	.10
❏ 258	Jalen Rose CB	2.00	.75
❏ 259	Juwan Howard CB	1.25	.50
❏ 260	Kenny Anderson	.60	.25
❏ 261	Calbert Cheaney	.30	.10
❏ 262	Bill Cartwright	.30	.10
❏ 263	Mario Elie	.30	.10
❏ 264	Chris Dudley	.30	.10
❏ 265	Jim Jackson	.60	.25
❏ 266	Antonio Harvey	.30	.10
❏ 267	Bill Curley RC	.30	.10
❏ 268	Moses Malone	1.25	.50
❏ 269	A.C. Green	.60	.25
❏ 270	Larry Johnson	.60	.25
❏ 271	Marty Conlon	.30	.10
❏ 272	Greg Graham	.30	.10
❏ 273	Eric Montross RC	.30	.10
❏ 274	Stacey King	.30	.10
❏ 275	Charles Barkley CB	1.25	.50
❏ 276	Chris Morris CB	.30	.10
❏ 277	Robert Horry CB	.60	.25
❏ 278	Dominique Wilkins CB	.60	.25
❏ 279	Latrell Sprewell CB	1.25	.50
❏ 280	Shaquille O'Neal CB	3.00	1.25
❏ 281	Wesley Person CB	.60	.25
❏ 282	Mahmoud Abdul-Rauf CB	.30	.10
❏ 283	Jamal Mashburn CB	.60	.25
❏ 284	Dale Ellis CB	.30	.10
❏ 285	Gary Payton	2.00	.75
❏ 286	Jason Kidd RC	25.00	10.00
❏ 287	Ken Norman	.30	.10
❏ 288	Juwan Howard RC	5.00	2.00
❏ 289	Lamond Murray RC	2.00	1.00
❏ 290	Clifford Robinson	.60	.25
❏ 291	Frank Brickowski	.30	.10
❏ 292	Adam Keefe	.30	.10
❏ 293	Ron Harper	.60	.25
❏ 294	Tom Hammonds	.30	.10
❏ 295	Otis Thorpe	.30	.10
❏ 296	Rick Mahorn	.30	.10
❏ 297	Alton Lister	.30	.10
❏ 298	Vinny Del Negro	.30	.10
❏ 299	Danny Ferry	.30	.10
❏ 300	John Starks	.30	.10
❏ 301	Duane Ferrell	.30	.10
❏ 302	Hersey Hawkins	.60	.25
❏ 303	Khalid Reeves RC	.30	.10
❏ 304	Anthony Peeler	.30	.10
❏ 305	Tim Hardaway	1.25	.50
❏ 306	Rick Fox	.30	.10
❏ 307	Jay Humphries	.30	.10
❏ 308	Brian Shaw	.30	.10
❏ 309	Danny Schayes	.30	.10
❏ 310	Stacey Augmon	.30	.10
❏ 311	Oliver Miller	.30	.10
❏ 312	Pooh Richardson	.30	.10
❏ 313	Donyell Marshall RC	5.00	2.00
❏ 314	Aaron McKie RC	5.00	2.00
❏ 315	Mark Price	.30	.10
❏ 316	B.J. Tyler RC	.30	.10
❏ 317	Olden Polynice	.30	.10
❏ 318	Avery Johnson	.30	.10
❏ 319	Derek Strong	.30	.10
❏ 320	Toni Kukoc	2.00	.75
❏ 321	Charlie Ward RC	4.00	1.50
❏ 322	Wesley Person RC	4.00	1.50
❏ 323	Eddie Jones RC	10.00	4.00
❏ 324	Horace Grant	.60	.25
❏ 325	Mahmoud Abdul-Rauf	.30	.10
❏ 326	Sharone Wright RC	.30	.10
❏ 327	Kevin Gamble	.30	.10
❏ 328	Sarunas Marciulionis	.30	.10
❏ 329	Harvey Grant	.30	.10
❏ 330	Bobby Hurley	.60	.25
❏ 331	Michael Jordan	15.00	6.00

1995-96 Finest

❏	COMPLETE SET (251)	220.00	120.00
❏	COMP.SERIES 1 (140)	180.00	100.00
❏	COMP.SERIES 2 (111)	40.00	20.00
❏	COMMON CARD (1-250/252)	.75	.30

❏	COMMON ROOKIE	1.50	.60
❏ 1	Hakeem Olajuwon	2.50	1.00
❏ 2	Stacey Augmon	.75	.30
❏ 3	John Starks	1.50	.60
❏ 4	Sharone Wright	.75	.30
❏ 5	Jason Kidd	8.00	3.00
❏ 6	Lamond Murray	.75	.30
❏ 7	Kenny Anderson	1.50	.60
❏ 8	James Robinson	.75	.30
❏ 9	Wesley Person	.75	.30
❏ 10	Latrell Sprewell	2.50	1.00
❏ 11	Sean Elliott	1.50	.60
❏ 12	Greg Anthony	.75	.30
❏ 13	Kendall Gill	.75	.30
❏ 14	Mark Jackson	1.50	.60
❏ 15	John Stockton	3.00	1.25
❏ 16	Steve Smith	1.50	.60
❏ 17	Bobby Hurley	.75	.30
❏ 18	Ervin Johnson	.75	.30
❏ 19	Elden Campbell	.75	.30
❏ 20	Vin Baker	1.50	.60
❏ 21	Micheal Williams	.75	.30
❏ 22	Steve Kerr	1.50	.60
❏ 23	Kevin Duckworth	.75	.30
❏ 24	Willie Anderson	.75	.30
❏ 25	Joe Dumars	2.50	1.00
❏ 26	Dale Ellis	.75	.30
❏ 27	Bimbo Coles	.75	.30
❏ 28	Nick Anderson	.75	.30
❏ 29	Dee Brown	.75	.30
❏ 30	Tyrone Hill	.75	.30
❏ 31	Reggie Miller	2.50	1.00
❏ 32	Shaquille O'Neal	6.00	2.50
❏ 33	Brian Grant	2.50	1.00
❏ 34	Charles Barkley	3.00	1.25
❏ 35	Cedric Ceballos	.75	.30
❏ 36	Rex Walters	.75	.30
❏ 37	Kenny Smith	.75	.30
❏ 38	Popeye Jones	.75	.30
❏ 39	Harvey Grant	.75	.30
❏ 40	Gary Payton	2.50	1.00
❏ 41	John Williams	.75	.30
❏ 42	Sherman Douglas	.75	.30
❏ 43	Oliver Miller	.75	.30
❏ 44	Kevin Willis	1.50	.60
❏ 45	Isaiah Rider	.75	.30
❏ 46	Gheorghe Muresan	.75	.30
❏ 47	Blue Edwards	.75	.30
❏ 48	Jeff Hornacek	1.50	.60
❏ 49	J.R. Reid	.75	.30
❏ 50	Glenn Robinson	2.50	1.00
❏ 51	Dell Curry	.75	.30
❏ 52	Greg Graham	.75	.30
❏ 53	Ron Harper	1.50	.60
❏ 54	Derek Harper	1.50	.60
❏ 55	Dikembe Mutombo	1.50	.60
❏ 56	Terry Mills	.75	.30
❏ 57	Victor Alexander	.75	.30
❏ 58	Malik Sealy	.75	.30
❏ 59	Vincent Askew	.75	.30
❏ 60	Mitch Richmond	1.50	.60
❏ 61	Duane Ferrell	.75	.30
❏ 62	Dickey Simpkins	.75	.30
❏ 63	Pooh Richardson	.75	.30
❏ 64	Khalid Reeves	.75	.30
❏ 65	Dino Radja	.75	.30
❏ 66	Lee Mayberry	.75	.30
❏ 67	Kenny Gattison	.75	.30

❏ 68	Joe Kleine	.75	.30
❏ 69	Tony Dumas	.75	.30
❏ 70	Nick Van Exel	2.50	1.00
❏ 71	Armon Gilliam	.75	.30
❏ 72	Craig Ehlo	.75	.30
❏ 73	Adam Keefe	.75	.30
❏ 74	Chris Dudley	.75	.30
❏ 75	Clyde Drexler	2.50	1.00
❏ 76	Jeff Turner	.75	.30
❏ 77	Calbert Cheaney	.75	.30
❏ 78	Vinny Del Negro	.75	.30
❏ 79	Tim Perry	.75	.30
❏ 80	Tim Hardaway	1.50	.60
❏ 81	B.J. Armstrong	.75	.30
❏ 82	Muggsy Bogues	1.50	.60
❏ 83	Mark Macon	.75	.30
❏ 84	Doug West	.75	.30
❏ 85	Jalen Rose	3.00	1.25
❏ 86	Chris Mills	.75	.30
❏ 87	Charles Oakley	.75	.30
❏ 88	Andrew Lang	.75	.30
❏ 89	Olden Polynice	.75	.30
❏ 90	Sam Cassell	2.50	1.00
❏ 91	Todd Day	.75	.30
❏ 92	P.J. Brown	.75	.30
❏ 93	Benoit Benjamin	.75	.30
❏ 94	Sam Perkins	1.50	.60
❏ 95	Eddie Jones	3.00	1.25
❏ 96	Robert Parish	1.50	.60
❏ 97	Avery Johnson	.75	.30
❏ 98	Lindsey Hunter	.75	.30
❏ 99	Billy Owens	.75	.30
❏ 100	Shawn Bradley	.75	.30
❏ 101	Dale Davis	.75	.30
❏ 102	Terry Dehere	.75	.30
❏ 103	A.C. Green	1.50	.60
❏ 104	Christian Laettner	1.50	.60
❏ 105	Horace Grant	1.50	.60
❏ 106	Rony Seikaly	.75	.30
❏ 107	Reggie Williams	.75	.30
❏ 108	Toni Kukoc	1.50	.60
❏ 109	Terrell Brandon	1.50	.60
❏ 110	Clifford Robinson	.75	.30
❏ 111	Joe Smith RC	5.00	2.00
❏ 112	Antonio McDyess RC	10.00	4.00
❏ 113	Jerry Stackhouse RC	15.00	6.00
❏ 114	Rasheed Wallace RC	12.00	5.00
❏ 115	Kevin Garnett RC	70.00	30.00
❏ 116	Bryant Reeves RC	2.50	1.00
❏ 117	Damon Stoudamire RC	6.00	2.50
❏ 118	Shawn Respert RC	.75	.30
❏ 119	Ed O'Bannon RC	1.50	.60
❏ 120	Kurt Thomas RC	1.50	.60
❏ 121	Gary Trent RC	3.00	1.25
❏ 122	Cherokee Parks RC	1.50	.60
❏ 123	Corliss Williamson RC	3.00	1.25
❏ 124	Eric Williams RC	1.50	.60
❏ 125	Brent Barry RC	2.50	1.00
❏ 126	Alan Henderson RC	3.00	1.25
❏ 127	Bob Sura RC	1.50	.60
❏ 128	Theo Ratliff RC	5.00	2.50
❏ 129	Randolph Childress RC	1.50	.60
❏ 130	Jason Caffey RC	1.50	.60
❏ 131	Michael Finley RC	12.00	5.00
❏ 132	George Zidek RC	1.50	.60
❏ 133	Travis Best RC	1.50	.60
❏ 134	Loren Meyer RC	1.50	.60
❏ 135	David Vaughn RC	1.50	.60
❏ 136	Sherrell Ford RC	1.50	.60
❏ 137	Mario Bennett RC	1.50	.60
❏ 138	Greg Ostertag RC	1.50	.60
❏ 139	Cory Alexander RC	1.50	.60
❏ 140	Checklist (1-110) UER misnumbered 111	.75	.30
❏ 141	Chucky Brown	.75	.30
❏ 142	Eric Mobley	.75	.30
❏ 143	Tom Hammonds	.75	.30
❏ 144	Chris Webber	3.00	1.25
❏ 145	Carlos Rogers	.75	.30
❏ 146	Chuck Person	.75	.30
❏ 147	Brian Williams	.75	.30
❏ 148	Sam Gamble	.75	.30
❏ 149	Dennis Rodman	1.50	.60
❏ 150	Pervis Ellison	.75	.30
❏ 151	Jayson Williams	.75	.30
❏ 152	Buck Williams	.75	.30

#	Player		
153	Allan Houston	1.50	.60
154	Tom Gugliotta	.75	.30
155	Charles Smith	.75	.30
156	Chris Gatling	.75	.30
157	Darrin Hancock	.75	.30
158	Blue Edwards	.75	.30
159	Shawn Kemp	1.50	.60
160	Michael Cage	.75	.30
161	Sedale Threatt	.75	.30
162	Byron Scott	.75	.30
163	Elliot Perry	.75	.30
164	Jim Jackson	.75	.30
165	Wayman Tisdale	.75	.30
166	Vernon Maxwell	.75	.30
167	Brian Shaw	.75	.30
168	Haywoode Workman	.75	.30
169	Mookie Blaylock	.75	.30
170	Donald Royal	.75	.30
171	Lorenzo Williams	.75	.30
172	Eric Piatkowski	1.50	.60
173	Sarunas Marciulionis	.75	.30
174	Otis Thorpe	.75	.30
175	Rex Chapman	.75	.30
176	Felton Spencer	.75	.30
177	John Salley	.75	.30
178	Pete Chilcutt	.75	.30
179	Scottie Pippen	4.00	1.50
180	Robert Pack	.75	.30
181	Dana Barros	.75	.30
182	Mahmoud Abdul-Rauf	.75	.30
183	Eric Murdock	.75	.30
184	Anthony Mason	1.50	.60
185	Will Perdue	.75	.30
186	Jeff Malone	.75	.30
187	Anthony Peeler	.75	.30
188	Chris Childs	.75	.30
189	Glen Rice	1.50	.60
190	Grant Hill	3.00	1.25
191	Michael Smith	.75	.30
192	Sean Rooks	.75	.30
193	Clifford Rozier	.75	.30
194	Rik Smits	1.50	.60
195	Spud Webb	1.50	.60
196	Nate McKie	1.50	.60
197	Nate McMillan	.75	.30
198	Bobby Phills	.75	.30
199	Dennis Scott	.75	.30
200	Mark West	.75	.30
201	George McCloud	.75	.30
202	B.J. Tyler	.75	.30
203	Lionel Simmons	.75	.30
204	Loy Vaught	.75	.30
205	Kevin Edwards	.75	.30
206	Eric Montross	.75	.30
207	Kenny Gattison	.75	.30
208	Mario Elie	.75	.30
209	Karl Malone	3.00	1.25
210	Ken Norman	.75	.30
211	Antonio Davis	.75	.30
212	Doc Rivers	1.50	.60
213	Hubert Davis	.75	.30
214	Jamal Mashburn	1.50	.60
215	Donyell Marshall	1.50	.60
216	Sasha Danilovic RC	.75	.30
217	Danny Manning	1.50	.60
218	Scott Burrell	.75	.30
219	Vlade Divac	1.50	.60
220	Marty Conlon	.75	.30
221	Clarence Weatherspoon	.75	.30
222	Terry Porter	.75	.30
223	Luc Longley	.75	.30
224	Juwan Howard	2.50	1.00
225	Danny Ferry	.75	.30
226	Rod Strickland	.75	.30
227	Bryant Stith	.75	.30
228	Derrick McKey	.75	.30
229	Michael Jordan	15.00	6.00
230	Jamie Watson	.75	.30
231	Rick Fox	1.50	.60
232	Scott Williams	.75	.30
233	Larry Johnson	1.50	.60
234	Anthony Hardaway	2.50	1.00
235	Hersey Hawkins	.75	.30
236	Robert Horry	.75	.30
237	Kevin Johnson	1.50	.60
238	Rodney Rogers	.75	.30
239	Detlef Schrempf	1.50	.60
240	Derrick Coleman	.75	.30
241	Walt Williams	.75	.30
242	LaPhonso Ellis	.75	.30
243	Patrick Ewing	2.50	1.00
244	Grant Long	.75	.30
245	David Robinson	2.50	1.00
246	Chris Mullin	2.50	1.00
247	Alonzo Mourning	1.50	.60
248	Dan Majerle	1.50	.60
249	Johnny Newman	.75	.30
250	Chris Morris	.75	.30
252	Magic Johnson	4.00	1.50

1996-97 Finest

COMPLETE SET (291)	600.00	300.00
COMPLETE SERIES 1 (146)	350.00	150.00
COMPLETE SERIES 2 (145)	300.00	150.00
COMP.BRONZE SET (200)	140.00	70.00
COMP.BRONZE SER.1 (100)	100.00	50.00
COMP.BRONZE SER.2 (100)	40.00	20.00
COMMON BRONZE	.40	.15
COMMON BRONZE RC	1.25	.50
COMP.SILVER SET (54)	120.00	60.00
COMP.SILVER SER.1 (27)	40.00	20.00
COMP.SILVER SER.2 (27)	80.00	40.00
COMMON SILVER	1.25	.50
COMP.GOLD SET (37)	400.00	200.00
COMP.GOLD SER.1 (19)	200.00	100.00
COMP.GOLD SER.2 (18)	200.00	100.00
COMMON GOLD	4.00	1.50

#	Player		
1	Scottie Pippen B	2.00	.75
2	Tim Legler B	.40	.15
3	Rex Walters B	.40	.15
4	Calbert Cheaney B	.40	.15
5	Dennis Rodman B	.75	.30
6	Tyrone Hill B	.40	.15
8	Dell Curry B	.40	.15
9	Olden Polynice B	.40	.15
10	John Wallace B RC	1.50	.60
11	Martin Muursepp B RC	1.25	.50
12	Chuck Person B	.40	.15
13	Grant Hill B	1.25	.50
14	Shawn Kemp B	.75	.30
15	B.J. Armstrong B	.40	.15
16	Gary Trent B	.40	.15
17	Scott Williams B	.40	.15
18	Dino Radja B	.40	.15
19	Roy Rogers B RC	1.25	.50
20	Tony Delk B RC	2.50	1.00
21	Clifford Robinson B	.40	.15
22	Ray Allen B RC	8.00	3.00
23	Clyde Drexler B	1.25	.50
24	Elliot Perry B	.40	.15
25	Gary Payton B	1.25	.50
26	Dale Davis B	.40	.15
27	Horace Grant B	.75	.30
28	Brian Evans B RC	1.25	.50
29	Joe Smith B	.75	.30
30	Reggie Miller B	1.25	.50
31	Jermaine O'Neal B RC	8.00	3.00
32	Avery Johnson B	.40	.15
33	Ed O'Bannon B	.40	.15
34	Cedric Ceballos B	.40	.15
35	Jamal Mashburn B	.75	.30
36	Micheal Williams B	.40	.15
37	Detlef Schrempf B	.75	.30
38	Damon Stoudamire B	1.25	.50
39	Jason Kidd B	2.00	.75
40	Tom Gugliotta B	.40	.15
41	Arvydas Sabonis B	.75	.30
42	Samaki Walker B RC	1.25	.50
43	Derek Fisher B RC	4.00	1.50
44	Patrick Ewing B	1.25	.50
45	Bryant Reeves B	.40	.15
46	Mookie Blaylock B	.40	.15
47	George Zidek B	.40	.15
48	Jerry Stackhouse B	1.50	.60
49	Vin Baker B	.75	.30
50	Michael Jordan B	8.00	3.00
51	Terrell Brandon B	.75	.30
52	Karl Malone B	1.25	.50
53	Lorenzen Wright B RC	1.25	.50
54	S.Abdur-Rahim B RC	5.00	2.00
55	Kurt Thomas B	.75	.30
56	Glen Rice B	.75	.30
57	Shawn Bradley B	.40	.15
58	Todd Fuller B RC	1.25	.50
59	Dale Ellis B	.40	.15
60	David Robinson B	1.25	.50
61	Doug Christie B	.75	.30
62	Stephon Marbury B RC	8.00	3.00
63	Hakeem Olajuwon B	1.25	.50
64	Lindsey Hunter B	.40	.15
65	Anfernee Hardaway B	1.25	.50
66	Kevin Garnett B	2.50	1.00
67	Kendall Gill B	.40	.15
68	Sean Elliott B	.75	.30
69	Allen Iverson B RC	15.00	6.00
70	Erick Dampier B RC	1.25	.50
71	Jerome Williams B RC	2.50	1.00
72	Charles Jones B	.40	.15
73	Danny Manning B	.75	.30
74	Kobe Bryant B RC	40.00	20.00
75	Steve Nash B RC	12.00	5.00
76	Sam Perkins B	.75	.30
77	Horace Grant B	.75	.30
78	Alonzo Mourning B	.75	.30
79	Kerry Kittles B RC	2.50	1.00
80	LaPhonso Ellis B	.40	.15
81	Michael Finley B	1.50	.60
82	Marcus Camby B RC	3.00	1.25
83	Antonio McDyess B	.75	.30
84	Antoine Walker B RC	8.00	3.00
85	Juwan Howard B	.75	.30
86	Bryon Russell B	.40	.15
87	Walter McCarty B RC	1.25	.50
88	Priest Lauderdale B RC	1.25	.50
89	C.Weatherspoon B	.40	.15
90	John Stockton B	1.25	.50
91	Mitch Richmond B	.75	.30
92	Dontae' Jones B RC	1.25	.50
93	Michael Smith B	.40	.15
94	Brent Barry B	.40	.15
95	Chris Mills B	.40	.15
96	Dee Brown B	.40	.15
97	Terry Dehere B	.40	.15
98	Danny Ferry B	.40	.15
99	Gheorghe Muresan B	.40	.15
100	Checklist B	.40	.15
101	Jim Jackson S	1.25	.50
102	Cedric Ceballos S	1.25	.50
103	Glen Rice S	2.50	1.00
104	Tom Gugliotta S	1.25	.50
105	Mario Elie S	1.25	.50
106	Nick Anderson S	1.25	.50
107	Glenn Robinson S	2.50	1.00
108	Terrell Brandon S	2.50	1.00
109	Tim Hardaway S	2.50	1.00
110	John Stockton S	4.00	1.50
111	Brent Barry S	1.25	.50
112	Mookie Blaylock S	1.25	.50
113	Tyus Edney S	1.25	.50
114	Gary Payton S	4.00	1.50
115	Joe Smith S	2.50	1.00
116	Karl Malone S	4.00	1.50
117	Dino Radja S	1.25	.50
118	Alonzo Mourning S	2.50	1.00
119	Bryant Stith S	1.25	.50
120	Derrick McKey S	1.25	.50
121	Clyde Drexler S	4.00	1.50
122	Michael Finley S	5.00	2.00
123	Sean Elliott S	2.50	1.00
124	Hakeem Olajuwon S	4.00	1.50

❏ 125	Joe Dumars S	4.00	1.50
❏ 126	Shawn Bradley S	1.25	.50
❏ 127	Michael Jordan S	25.00	10.00
❏ 128	Latrell Sprewell S	10.00	4.00
❏ 129	Anfernee Hardaway S	10.00	4.00
❏ 130	Grant Hill S	10.00	4.00
❏ 131	Damon Stoudamire G	10.00	4.00
❏ 132	David Robinson G	10.00	4.00
❏ 133	Scottie Pippen G	15.00	6.00
❏ 135	Jason Kidd G	15.00	6.00
❏ 136A	Jeff Hornacek G	4.00	1.50
❏ 136B	Patrick Ewing G UER	10.00	4.00
❏ 136C	Christian Laettner B UER	6.00	2.50
❏ 137	Jerry Stackhouse G	12.00	5.00
❏ 138	Kevin Garnett G	20.00	8.00
❏ 139	Mitch Richmond G	6.00	2.50
❏ 140	Juwan Howard G	6.00	2.50
❏ 141	Reggie Miller G	10.00	4.00
❏ 142	Christian Laettner G	6.00	2.50
❏ 143	Vin Baker G	6.00	2.50
❏ 144	Shawn Kemp G	6.00	2.50
❏ 145	Dennis Rodman G	6.00	2.50
❏ 146	Shaquille O'Neal G	25.00	10.00
❏ 147	Mookie Blaylock B	.40	.15
❏ 148	Derek Harper B	.40	.15
❏ 149	Gerald Wilkins B	.40	.15
❏ 150	Adam Keefe B	.40	.15
❏ 151	Billy Owens B	.40	.15
❏ 152	Terrell Brandon B	.75	.30
❏ 153	Antonio Davis B	.40	.15
❏ 154	Muggsy Bogues B	.40	.15
❏ 155	Cherokee Parks B	.40	.15
❏ 156	Rasheed Wallace B	1.50	.60
❏ 157	Lee Mayberry B	.40	.15
❏ 158	Craig Ehlo B	.40	.15
❏ 159	Todd Fuller B	.40	.15
❏ 160	Charles Barkley B	1.50	.60
❏ 161	Glenn Robinson B	1.25	.50
❏ 162	Charles Oakley B	.40	.15
❏ 163	Chris Webber B	1.25	.50
❏ 164	Frank Brickowski B	.40	.15
❏ 165	Mark Jackson B	.40	.15
❏ 166	Jayson Williams B	.75	.30
❏ 167	Clarence Weatherspoon B	.40	.15
❏ 168	Toni Kukoc B	.75	.30
❏ 169	Alan Henderson B	.40	.15
❏ 170	Tony Delk B	.75	.30
❏ 171	Jamal Mashburn B	.75	.30
❏ 172	Vinny Del Negro B	.40	.15
❏ 173	Greg Ostertag B	.40	.15
❏ 174	Shawn Bradley B	.40	.15
❏ 175	Gheorghe Muresan B	.40	.15
❏ 176	Brent Price B	.40	.15
❏ 177	Rick Fox B	.40	.15
❏ 178	Stacey Augmon B	.40	.15
❏ 179	P.J. Brown B	.40	.15
❏ 180	Jim Jackson B	.40	.15
❏ 181	Hersey Hawkins B	.75	.30
❏ 182	Danny Manning B	.75	.30
❏ 183	Dennis Scott B	.40	.15
❏ 184	Tom Gugliotta B	.40	.15
❏ 185	Tyrone Hill B	.40	.15
❏ 186	Malik Sealy B	.40	.15
❏ 187	John Starks B	.75	.30
❏ 188	Mark Price B	.75	.30
❏ 189	Elden Campbell B	.40	.15
❏ 190	Mahmoud Abdul-Rauf B	.40	.15
❏ 191	Will Perdue B	.40	.15
❏ 192	Nate McMillan B	.40	.15
❏ 193	Robert Horry B	.75	.30
❏ 194	Dino Radja B	.40	.15
❏ 195	Loy Vaught B	.40	.15
❏ 196	Dikembe Mutombo B	.75	.30
❏ 197	Eric Montross B	.40	.15
❏ 198	Sasha Danilovic B	.40	.15
❏ 199	Kenny Anderson B	.40	.15
❏ 200	Sean Elliott B	.75	.30
❏ 201	Mark West B	.40	.15
❏ 202	Vlade Divac B	.40	.15
❏ 203	Joe Dumars B	1.25	.50
❏ 204	Allan Houston B	.75	.30
❏ 205	Kevin Garnett B	2.50	1.00
❏ 206	Rod Strickland B	.40	.15
❏ 207	Robert Parish B	.75	.30
❏ 208	Jalen Rose B	1.25	.50
❏ 209	Armon Gilliam B	.40	.15
❏ 210	Kerry Kittles B	1.25	.50
❏ 211	Derrick Coleman B	.75	.30
❏ 212	Greg Anthony B	.40	.15
❏ 213	Joe Smith B	.75	.30
❏ 214	Steve Smith B	.75	.30
❏ 215	Tim Hardaway B	.75	.30
❏ 216	Tyus Edney B	.40	.15
❏ 217	Steve Nash B	1.50	.60
❏ 218	Anthony Mason B	.75	.30
❏ 219	Otis Thorpe B	.40	.15
❏ 220	Eddie Jones B	1.25	.50
❏ 221	Rik Smits B	.75	.30
❏ 222	Isaiah Rider B	.75	.30
❏ 223	Bobby Phills B	.40	.15
❏ 224	Antoine Walker B	1.25	.50
❏ 225	Rod Strickland B	.40	.15
❏ 226	Hubert Davis B	.40	.15
❏ 227	Eric Williams B	.40	.15
❏ 228	Danny Manning B	.75	.30
❏ 229	Dominique Wilkins B	1.25	.50
❏ 230	Brian Shaw B	.40	.15
❏ 231	Larry Johnson B	.75	.30
❏ 232	Kevin Willis B	.40	.15
❏ 233	Bryant Stith B	.40	.15
❏ 234	Blue Edwards B	.40	.15
❏ 235	Robert Pack B	.40	.15
❏ 236	Brian Grant B	1.25	.50
❏ 237	Latrell Sprewell B	1.25	.50
❏ 238	Glen Rice B	.75	.30
❏ 239	Jerome Williams B	1.25	.50
❏ 240	Allen Iverson B	4.00	1.50
❏ 241	Popeye Jones B	.40	.15
❏ 242	Clifford Robinson B	.40	.15
❏ 243	Shaquille O'Neal B	4.00	1.50
❏ 244	Vitaly Potapenko B RC	1.25	.50
❏ 245	Ervin Johnson B	.40	.15
❏ 246	Checklist	.40	.15
❏ 247	Scottie Pippen S	6.00	2.50
❏ 248	Jason Kidd S	6.00	2.50
❏ 249	Antonio McDyess S	2.50	1.00
❏ 250	Latrell Sprewell S	4.00	1.50
❏ 251	Lorenzen Wright S	1.25	.50
❏ 252	Ray Allen S	8.00	3.00
❏ 253	Stephon Marbury S	6.00	2.50
❏ 254	Patrick Ewing S	4.00	1.50
❏ 255	Anfernee Hardaway S	4.00	1.50
❏ 256	Kenny Anderson S	1.25	.50
❏ 257	David Robinson S	4.00	1.50
❏ 258	Marcus Camby S	4.00	1.50
❏ 259	S.Abdur-Rahim S	8.00	3.00
❏ 260	Dennis Rodman S	2.50	1.00
❏ 261	Juwan Howard S	2.50	1.00
❏ 262	Damon Stoudamire S	4.00	1.50
❏ 263	Shawn Kemp S	2.50	1.00
❏ 264	Mitch Richmond S	2.50	1.00
❏ 265	Jerry Stackhouse S	5.00	2.00
❏ 266	Horace Grant S	2.50	1.00
❏ 267	Kerry Kittles S	1.25	.50
❏ 268	Vin Baker S	2.50	1.00
❏ 269	Kobe Bryant S	80.00	40.00
❏ 270	Reggie Miller S	4.00	1.50
❏ 271	Grant Hill S	8.00	3.00
❏ 272	Oliver Miller S	1.25	.50
❏ 273	Chris Webber S	2.50	1.00
❏ 274	Dikembe Mutombo G	6.00	2.50
❏ 275	Antonio McDyess G	6.00	2.50
❏ 276	Clyde Drexler G	10.00	4.00
❏ 277	Brent Barry G	4.00	1.50
❏ 278	Tim Hardaway G	6.00	2.50
❏ 279	Glenn Robinson G	6.00	2.50
❏ 280	Allen Iverson G	25.00	10.00
❏ 281	Hakeem Olajuwon G	10.00	4.00
❏ 282	Marcus Camby G	10.00	4.00
❏ 283	John Stockton G	10.00	4.00
❏ 284	S.Abdur-Rahim G	15.00	6.00
❏ 285	Karl Malone G	10.00	4.00
❏ 286	Gary Payton G	10.00	4.00
❏ 287	Stephon Marbury G	12.00	5.00
❏ 288	Alonzo Mourning G	6.00	2.50
❏ 289	Shaquille O'Neal G	8.00	3.00
❏ 290	Charles Barkley G	12.00	5.00
❏ 291	Michael Jordan G	60.00	25.00

1997-98 Finest

❏	COMPLETE SET (326)	750.00	375.00
❏	COMPLETE SERIES 1 (173)	350.00	175.00
❏	COMPLETE SERIES 2 (153)	400.00	200.00
❏	COMP.BRONZE SET (220)	100.00	50.00
❏	COMP.BRONZE SER.1 (120)	60.00	30.00
❏	COMP.BRONZE SER.2 (100)	50.00	25.00
❏	COMMON BRONZE	.30	.10
❏	COMMON BRONZE RC	.60	.25
❏	COMP.SILVER SET (66)	150.00	75.00
❏	COMP.SILVER SER.1 (33)	80.00	40.00
❏	COMP.SILVER SER.2 (33)	60.00	30.00
❏	COMMON SILVER	1.00	.40
❏	COMP.GOLD SET (40)	500.00	250.00
❏	COMP.GOLD SER.1 (20)	200.00	100.00
❏	COMP.GOLD SER.2 (20)	300.00	150.00
❏	COMMON GOLD	4.00	1.50
❏ 1	Scottie Pippen B	1.50	.60
❏ 2	Tim Hardaway B	.60	.25
❏ 3	Bo Outlaw B	.30	.10
❏ 4	Rik Smits B	.30	.10
❏ 5	Dale Ellis B	.30	.10
❏ 6	Clyde Drexler B	1.00	.40
❏ 7	Steve Smith B	.60	.25
❏ 8	Nick Anderson B	.30	.10
❏ 9	Juwan Howard B	.60	.25
❏ 10	Cedric Ceballos B	.30	.10
❏ 11	Shawn Bradley B	.30	.10
❏ 12	Loy Vaught B	.30	.10
❏ 13	Todd Day B	.30	.10
❏ 14	Glen Rice B	.60	.25
❏ 15	Bryant Stith B	.30	.10
❏ 16	Bob Sura B	.30	.10
❏ 17	Derrick McKey B	.30	.10
❏ 18	Ray Allen B	1.00	.40
❏ 19	Stephon Marbury B	1.25	.50
❏ 20	David Robinson B	1.00	.40
❏ 21	Anthony Peeler B	.30	.10
❏ 22	Isaiah Rider B	.60	.25
❏ 23	Mookie Blaylock B	.30	.10
❏ 24	Damon Stoudamire B	.60	.25
❏ 25	Rod Strickland B	.30	.10
❏ 26	Glenn Robinson B	1.00	.40
❏ 27	Chris Webber B	1.00	.40
❏ 28	Christian Laettner B	.60	.25
❏ 29	Joe Dumars B	1.00	.40
❏ 30	Mark Price B	.60	.25
❏ 31	Jamal Mashburn B	.60	.25
❏ 32	Danny Manning B	.60	.25
❏ 33	John Stockton B	1.00	.40
❏ 34	Detlef Schrempf B	.60	.25
❏ 35	Tyus Edney B	.30	.10
❏ 36	Chris Childs B	.30	.10
❏ 37	Dana Barros B	.30	.10
❏ 38	Bobby Phills B	.30	.10
❏ 39	Michael Jordan B	6.00	2.50
❏ 40	Grant Hill B	1.00	.40
❏ 41	Brent Barry B	.60	.25
❏ 42	Rony Seikaly B	.30	.10
❏ 43	Shareef Abdur-Rahim B	1.50	.60
❏ 44	Dominique Wilkins B	1.00	.40
❏ 45	Vin Baker B	.60	.25
❏ 46	Kendall Gill B	.30	.10
❏ 47	Muggsy Bogues B	.60	.25
❏ 48	Hakeem Olajuwon B	1.00	.40
❏ 49	Reggie Miller B	1.00	.40
❏ 50	Shaquille O'Neal B	2.50	1.00

#	Player		
51	Antonio McDyess B	.60	.25
52	Michael Finley B	1.00	.40
53	Jerry Stackhouse B	1.00	.40
54	Brian Grant B	.60	.25
55	Greg Anthony B	.30	.10
56	Patrick Ewing B	1.00	.40
57	Allen Iverson B	2.50	1.00
58	Rasheed Wallace B	1.00	.40
59	Shawn Kemp B	.60	.25
60	Bryant Reeves B	.30	.10
61	Kevin Garnett B	2.00	.75
62	Allan Houston B	.60	.25
63	Stacey Augmon B	.30	.10
64	Rick Fox B	.60	.25
65	Derek Harper B	.30	.10
66	Lindsey Hunter B	.30	.10
67	Eddie Jones B	1.00	.40
68	Joe Smith B	.60	.25
69	Alonzo Mourning B	.60	.25
70	LaPhonso Ellis B	.30	.10
71	Tyrone Hill B	.30	.10
72	Charles Barkley B	1.25	.50
73	Malik Sealy B	.30	.10
74	Shandon Anderson B	.30	.10
75	Arvydas Sabonis B	.60	.25
76	Tom Gugliotta B	.60	.25
77	Anfernee Hardaway B	1.00	.40
78	Sean Elliott B	.60	.25
79	Marcus Camby B	1.00	.40
80	Gary Payton B	1.00	.40
81	Kerry Kittles B	1.00	.40
82	Dikembe Mutombo B	.60	.25
83	Antoine Walker B	1.25	.50
84	Terrell Brandon B	.60	.25
85	Otis Thorpe B	.30	.10
86	Mark Jackson B	.30	.10
87	A.C. Green B	.60	.25
88	John Starks B	.60	.25
89	Kenny Anderson B	.60	.25
90	Karl Malone B	1.00	.40
91	Mitch Richmond B	.60	.25
92	Derrick Coleman B	.30	.10
93	Horace Grant B	.60	.25
94	John Williams B	.30	.10
95	Jason Kidd B	1.50	.60
96	Mahmoud Abdul-Rauf B	.30	.10
97	Walt Williams B	.30	.10
98	Anthony Mason B	.60	.25
99	Latrell Sprewell B	1.00	.40
100	Checklist	.30	.10
101	Tim Duncan B RC	12.00	5.00
102	Keith Van Horn B RC	2.50	1.00
103	Chauncey Billups B RC	5.00	2.00
104	Antonio Daniels B RC	1.25	.50
105	Tony Battie B RC	1.25	.50
106	Tim Thomas B RC	4.00	1.50
107	Tracy McGrady B RC	15.00	6.00
108	Adonal Foyle B RC	.75	.30
109	Maurice Taylor B RC	2.00	.75
110	Austin Croshere B RC	2.00	.75
111	Bobby Jackson B RC	2.00	.75
112	Olivier Saint-Jean B RC	.60	.25
113	John Thomas B RC	.60	.25
114	Derek Anderson B RC	2.50	1.00
115	Brevin Knight B RC	1.50	.60
116	Charles Smith B RC	.60	.25
117	Johnny Taylor B RC	.60	.25
118	Jacque Vaughn B RC	.75	.30
119	Anthony Parker B RC	.60	.25
120	Paul Grant B RC	.60	.25
121	Stephon Marbury S	4.00	1.50
122	Terrell Brandon S	2.00	.75
123	Dikembe Mutombo S	2.00	.75
124	Patrick Ewing S	3.00	1.25
125	Scottie Pippen S	5.00	2.00
126	Antoine Walker S	4.00	1.50
127	Karl Malone S	3.00	1.25
128	Sean Elliott S	2.00	.75
129	Chris Webber S	3.00	1.25
130	Shawn Kemp S	2.00	.75
131	Hakeem Olajuwon S	3.00	1.25
132	Tim Hardaway S	2.00	.75
133	Glen Rice S	2.00	.75
134	Vin Baker S	2.00	.75
135	Jim Jackson S	1.00	.40
136	Kevin Garnett S	6.00	2.50
137	Kobe Bryant S	15.00	6.00
138	Damon Stoudamire S	2.00	.75
139	Larry Johnson S	2.00	.75
140	Latrell Sprewell S	3.00	1.25
141	Lorenzen Wright S	1.00	.40
142	Toni Kukoc S	2.00	.75
143	Allen Iverson S	8.00	3.00
144	Elden Campbell S	1.00	.40
145	Tom Gugliotta S	2.00	.75
146	David Robinson S	3.00	1.25
147	Jayson Williams S	1.00	.40
148	Shaquille O'Neal S	8.00	3.00
149	Grant Hill S	3.00	1.25
150	Reggie Miller S	3.00	1.25
151	Clyde Drexler S	3.00	1.25
152	Ray Allen S	1.25	.50
153	Eddie Jones S	3.00	1.25
154	Michael Jordan S	80.00	40.00
155	Dominique Wilkins S	12.00	5.00
156	Charles Barkley S	15.00	6.00
157	Jerry Stackhouse S	12.00	5.00
158	Juwan Howard S	8.00	3.00
159	Marcus Camby S	12.00	5.00
160	Christian Laettner S	8.00	3.00
161	Anthony Mason S	8.00	3.00
162	Joe Smith S	8.00	3.00
163	Kerry Kittles S	12.00	5.00
164	Mitch Richmond S	8.00	3.00
165	Shareef Abdur-Rahim S	20.00	10.00
166	Alonzo Mourning S	8.00	3.00
167	Dennis Rodman S	8.00	3.00
168	Antonio McDyess S	8.00	3.00
169	Shawn Bradley S	4.00	1.50
170	Anfernee Hardaway S	12.00	5.00
171	Jason Kidd S	20.00	10.00
172	Gary Payton S	12.00	5.00
173	John Stockton S	12.00	5.00
174	Allan Houston S	.60	.25
175	Bob Sura S	.30	.10
176	Clyde Drexler S	1.00	.40
177	Glenn Robinson S	1.00	.40
178	Joe Smith S	.60	.25
179	Larry Johnson S	.60	.25
180	Mitch Richmond S	.60	.25
181	Rony Seikaly S	.30	.10
182	Tyrone Hill S	.30	.10
183	Allen Iverson S	2.50	1.00
184	Brent Barry S	.60	.25
185	Damon Stoudamire S	.60	.25
186	Grant Hill S	1.00	.40
187	John Stockton S	1.00	.40
188	Latrell Sprewell S	1.00	.40
189	Mookie Blaylock S	.30	.10
190	Samaki Walker S	.30	.10
191	Vin Baker S	.60	.25
192	Alonzo Mourning S	.60	.25
193	Brevin Knight B	.60	.25
194	Danny Manning B	.60	.25
195	Hakeem Olajuwon B	1.00	.40
196	Johnny Taylor B	.30	.10
197	Lorenzen Wright B	.30	.10
198	Olden Polynice B	.30	.10
199	Scottie Pippen B	1.50	.60
200	Lindsey Hunter B	.30	.10
201	Anfernee Hardaway B	1.00	.40
202	Greg Anthony B	.30	.10
203	David Robinson B	1.00	.40
204	Horace Grant B	.60	.25
205	Calbert Cheaney B	.30	.10
206	Loy Vaught B	.30	.10
207	Tariq Abdul-Wahad B	.30	.10
208	Sean Elliott B	.60	.25
209	Rodney Rogers B	.30	.10
210	Anthony Mason B	.60	.25
211	Bryant Reeves B	.30	.10
212	David Wesley B	.30	.10
213	Isaiah Rider B	.60	.25
214	Karl Malone B	1.00	.40
215	Mahmoud Abdul-Rauf B	.30	.10
216	Patrick Ewing B	1.00	.40
217	Shaquille O'Neal B	2.50	1.00
218	Antoine Walker B	1.25	.50
219	Charles Barkley B	1.25	.50
220	Dennis Rodman B	.60	.25
221	Jamal Mashburn B	.60	.25
222	Kendall Gill B	.30	.10
223	Malik Sealy B	.30	.10
224	Rasheed Wallace B	1.00	.40
225	Shareef Abdur-Rahim B	1.50	.60
226	Antonio Daniels B	.60	.25
227	Charles Oakley B	.60	.25
228	Derek Anderson B	.60	.25
229	Jason Kidd B	1.50	.60
230	Kenny Anderson B	.60	.25
231	Marcus Camby B	1.00	.40
232	Ray Allen B	1.00	.40
233	Shawn Bradley B	.30	.10
234	Antonio McDyess B	.60	.25
235	Chauncey Billups B	.75	.30
236	Detlef Schrempf B	.60	.25
237	Jayson Williams B	.30	.10
238	Kerry Kittles B	1.00	.40
239	Jalen Rose B	1.00	.40
240	Reggie Miller B	1.00	.40
241	Shawn Kemp B	.60	.25
242	Arvydas Sabonis B	.60	.25
243	Tom Gugliotta B	.60	.25
244	Dikembe Mutombo B	.60	.25
245	Jeff Hornacek B	.60	.25
246	Kevin Garnett B	2.00	.75
247	Matt Maloney B	.30	.10
248	Rex Chapman B	.30	.10
249	Stephon Marbury B	1.25	.50
250	Austin Croshere B	.50	.20
251	Chris Childs B	.30	.10
252	Eddie Jones B	1.00	.40
253	Jerry Stackhouse B	1.00	.40
254	Kevin Johnson B	.60	.25
255	Maurice Taylor B	.75	.30
256	Chris Mullin B	1.00	.40
257	Terrell Brandon B	.60	.25
258	Avery Johnson B	.30	.10
259	Chris Webber B	1.00	.40
260	Gary Payton B	1.00	.40
261	Jim Jackson B	.30	.10
262	Kobe Bryant B	5.00	2.00
263	Michael Finley B	1.00	.40
264	Rod Strickland B	.30	.10
265	Tim Hardaway B	.60	.25
266	B.J. Armstrong B	.30	.10
267	Christian Laettner B	.60	.25
268	Glen Rice B	.60	.25
269	Joe Dumars B	1.00	.40
270	LaPhonso Ellis B	.30	.10
271	Michael Jordan B	6.00	2.50
272	Ron Mercer B RC	2.00	.75
273	Checklist B	.30	.10
274	Anfernee Hardaway S	3.00	1.25
275	Dennis Rodman S	2.00	.75
276	Gary Payton S	3.00	1.25
277	Jamal Mashburn S	2.00	.75
278	Shareef Abdur-Rahim S	5.00	2.00
279	Steve Smith S	2.00	.75
280	Tony Battie S	2.00	.75
281	Alonzo Mourning S	2.00	.75
282	Bobby Jackson S	1.00	.40
283	Christian Laettner S	2.00	.75
284	Jerry Stackhouse S	3.00	1.25
285	Terrell Brandon S	2.00	.75
286	Chauncey Billups S	2.50	1.00
287	Michael Jordan S	20.00	10.00
288	Glenn Robinson S	3.00	1.25
289	Jason Kidd S	5.00	2.00
290	Joe Smith S	2.00	.75
291	Michael Finley S	3.00	1.25
292	Rod Strickland S	1.00	.40
293	Ron Mercer S	1.50	.60
294	Tracy McGrady S	6.00	2.50
295	Adonal Foyle S	1.00	.40
296	Marcus Camby S	3.00	1.25
297	John Stockton S	3.00	1.25
298	Kerry Kittles S	1.25	.50
299	Mitch Richmond S	2.00	.75
300	Shawn Bradley S	1.00	.40
301	Anthony Mason S	2.00	.75
302	Antonio Daniels S	2.00	.75
303	Antonio McDyess S	2.00	.75
304	Charles Barkley S	4.00	1.50
305	Keith Van Horn S	3.00	1.25
306	Tim Duncan S	5.00	2.00
307	Dikembe Mutombo G	8.00	3.00
308	Grant Hill G	12.00	5.00

309	Shaquille O'Neal G	30.00	12.50
310	Keith Van Horn G	12.00	5.00
311	Shawn Kemp G	8.00	3.00
312	Antoine Walker G	15.00	6.00
313	Hakeem Olajuwon G	12.00	5.00
314	Vin Baker G	8.00	3.00
315	Patrick Ewing G	12.00	5.00
316	Tracy McGrady G	20.00	8.00
317	Glen Rice G	8.00	3.00
318	Reggie Miller G	12.00	5.00
319	Kevin Garnett G	25.00	10.00
320	Allen Iverson G	30.00	12.50
321	Karl Malone G	12.00	5.00
322	Scottie Pippen G	20.00	10.00
323	Kobe Bryant G	50.00	20.00
324	Stephon Marbury G	15.00	6.00
325	Tim Duncan G	15.00	6.00
326	Chris Webber G	12.00	5.00
P67	Eddie Jones	2.00	.75
P68	Joe Smith	2.00	.75

1998-99 Finest

COMPLETE SET (250)		100.00	50.00
COMPLETE SERIES 1 (125)		30.00	15.00
COMPLETE SERIES 2 (125)		60.00	25.00
COMMON CARD (1-225)		.30	.10
COMMON ROOKIE (226-250)		.60	.25
1	Chris Mills	.30	.10
2	Matt Maloney	.30	.10
3	Sam Mitchell	.30	.10
4	Corliss Williamson	.60	.25
5	Bryant Reeves	.30	.10
6	Juwan Howard	.60	.25
7	Eddie Jones	1.00	.40
8	Ray Allen	1.00	.40
9	Larry Johnson	.60	.25
10	Travis Best	.30	.10
11	Isaiah Rider	.30	.10
12	Hakeem Olajuwon	1.00	.40
13	Gary Trent	.30	.10
14	Kevin Garnett	2.00	.75
15	Dikembe Mutombo	.60	.25
16	Brevin Knight	.30	.10
17	Keith Van Horn	1.00	.40
18	Theo Ratliff	.60	.25
19	Tim Hardaway	.60	.25
20	Blue Edwards	.30	.10
21	David Wesley	.30	.10
22	Jaren Jackson	.30	.10
23	Nick Anderson	.30	.10
24	Rodney Rogers	.30	.10
25	Antonio Davis	.30	.10
26	Clarence Weatherspoon	.30	.10
27	Kelvin Cato	.30	.10
28	Tracy McGrady	2.50	1.00
29	Mookie Blaylock	.30	.10
30	Ron Harper	.60	.25
31	Allan Houston	.60	.25
32	Brian Williams	.30	.10
33	John Stockton	1.00	.40
34	Hersey Hawkins	.30	.10
35	Donyell Marshall	.60	.25
36	Mark Strickland	.30	.10
37	Rod Strickland	.30	.10
38	Cedric Ceballos	.30	.10
39	Danny Fortson	.30	.10
40	Shaquille O'Neal	2.50	1.00
41	Kendall Gill	.30	.10
42	Allen Iverson	2.00	.75
43	Travis Knight	.30	.10
44	Cedric Henderson	.30	.10
45	Steve Kerr	.60	.25
46	Antonio McDyess	.60	.25
47	Darrick Martin	.30	.10
48	Shandon Anderson	.30	.10
49	Shareef Abdur-Rahim	1.00	.40
50	Antoine Carr	.30	.10
51	Jason Kidd	1.50	.60
52	Calbert Cheaney	.30	.10
53	Antoine Walker	1.00	.40
54	Greg Anthony	.30	.10
55	Jeff Hornacek	.60	.25
56	Reggie Miller	1.00	.40
57	Lawrence Funderburke	.30	.10
58	Derek Strong	.30	.10
59	Robert Horry	.60	.25
60	Shawn Bradley	.30	.10
61	Matt Bullard	.30	.10
62	Terrell Brandon	.60	.25
63	Dan Majerle	.60	.25
64	Jim Jackson	.30	.10
65	Anthony Peeler	.30	.10
66	Bo Outlaw	.30	.10
67	Khalid Reeves	.30	.10
68	Toni Kukoc	.60	.25
69	Mario Elie	.30	.10
70	Derek Anderson	.75	.30
71	Jalen Rose	1.00	.40
72	Tyrone Corbin	.30	.10
73	Anthony Mason	.60	.25
74	Lamond Murray	.30	.10
75	Tom Gugliotta	.30	.10
76	Arvydas Sabonis	.60	.25
77	Brian Shaw	.30	.10
78	Rick Fox	.30	.10
79	Danny Manning	.30	.10
80	Lindsey Hunter	.30	.10
81	Michael Jordan	6.00	3.00
82	LaPhonso Ellis	.30	.10
83	David Robinson	1.00	.40
84	Christian Laettner	.60	.25
85	Armon Gilliam	.30	.10
86	Sherman Douglas	.30	.10
87	Charlie Ward	.30	.10
88	Shawn Kemp	.60	.25
89	Gary Payton	1.00	.40
90	Doug Christie	.60	.25
91	Voshon Lenard	.30	.10
92	Detlef Schrempf	.60	.25
93	Walter McCarty	.30	.10
94	Sam Cassell	1.00	.40
95	Jerry Stackhouse	1.00	.40
96	Billy Owens	.30	.10
97	Matt Geiger	.30	.10
98	Avery Johnson	.30	.10
99	Bobby Jackson	.30	.10
100	Rex Chapman	.30	.10
101	Andrew DeClercq	.30	.10
102	Vlade Divac	.60	.25
103	Erick Strickland	.30	.10
104	Dean Garrett	.30	.10
105	Grant Long	.30	.10
106	Adonal Foyle	.30	.10
107	Isaac Austin	.30	.10
108	Michael Curry	.30	.10
109	Darrell Armstrong	.30	.10
110	Aaron McKie	.60	.25
111	Stacey Augmon	.30	.10
112	Anthony Johnson	.30	.10
113	Vinny Del Negro	.30	.10
114	Reggie Slater	.30	.10
115	Lee Mayberry	.30	.10
116	Tracy Murray	.30	.10
117	Scottie Pippen	1.50	.60
118	Sam Perkins	.30	.10
119	Derek Fisher	1.00	.40
120	Mark Bryant	.30	.10
121	Dale Davis	.60	.25
122	B.J. Armstrong	.30	.10
123	Charles Barkley	1.25	.50
124	Horace Grant	.60	.25
125	Checklist	.30	.10
126	Alonzo Mourning	.60	.25
127	Kerry Kittles	.30	.10
128	Eldridge Recasner	.30	.10
129	Dell Curry	.30	.10
130	Jamal Mashburn	.60	.25
131	Eric Piatkowski	.60	.25
132	Othella Harrington	.30	.10
133	Pete Chilcutt	.30	.10
134	Dennis Rodman	.60	.25
135	Patrick Ewing	1.00	.40
136	Danny Schayes	.30	.10
137	John Williams	.30	.10
138	Joe Smith	.60	.25
139	Tariq Abdul-Wahad	.30	.10
140	Vin Baker	.60	.25
141	Elden Campbell	.30	.10
142	Chris Carr	.30	.10
143	John Starks	.60	.25
144	Felton Spencer	.30	.10
145	Mark Jackson	.60	.25
146	Dana Barros	.30	.10
147	Eric Williams	.30	.10
148	Wesley Person	.30	.10
149	Joe Dumars	1.00	.40
150	Steve Smith	.60	.25
151	Randy Brown	.30	.10
152	A.C. Green	.60	.25
153	Dee Brown	.30	.10
154	Brian Grant	.60	.25
155	Tim Thomas	.60	.25
156	Howard Eisley	.30	.10
157	Malik Sealy	.30	.10
158	Maurice Taylor	.50	.20
159	Tyrone Hill	.30	.10
160	Chris Gatling	.30	.10
161	Rodrick Rhodes	.30	.10
162	Muggsy Bogues	.60	.25
163	Kenny Anderson	.60	.25
164	Zydrunas Ilgauskas	.60	.25
165	Grant Hill	1.00	.40
166	Lorenzen Wright	.30	.10
167	Tony Battie	.30	.10
168	Bobby Phills	.30	.10
169	Michael Finley	1.00	.40
170	Anfernee Hardaway	1.00	.40
171	Terry Porter	.30	.10
172	P.J. Brown	.30	.10
173	Clifford Robinson	.30	.10
174	Olden Polynice	.30	.10
175	Kobe Bryant	4.00	1.50
176	Sean Elliott	.30	.10
177	Latrell Sprewell	1.00	.40
178	Rik Smits	.60	.25
179	Darrell Armstrong	.30	.10
180	Stephon Marbury	1.00	.40
181	Brent Price	.30	.10
182	Danny Fortson	.30	.10
183	Vitaly Potapenko	.30	.10
184	Anthony Parker	.30	.10
185	Glenn Robinson	.60	.25
186	Erick Dampier	.60	.25
187	George McCloud	.30	.10
188	Rasheed Wallace	1.00	.40
189	Aaron Williams	.30	.10
190	Tim Duncan	1.50	.60
191	Chauncey Billups	.60	.25
192	Jim McIlvaine	.30	.10
193	Chris Mullin	1.00	.40
194	George Lynch	.30	.10
195	Damon Stoudamire	.60	.25
196	Bryon Russell	.30	.10
197	Luc Longley	.30	.10
198	Ron Mercer	.50	.20
199	Alan Henderson	.30	.10
200	Jayson Williams	.30	.10
201	Ben Wallace	1.00	.40
202	Elliot Perry	.30	.10
203	Walt Williams	.30	.10
204	Cherokee Parks	.30	.10
205	Brent Barry	.60	.25
206	Hubert Davis	.30	.10
207	Terry Davis	.30	.10
208	Loy Vaught	.30	.10
209	Adam Keefe	.30	.10
210	Karl Malone	1.00	.40
211	Chuck Person	.30	.10
212	Chris Childs	.30	.10
213	Rony Seikaly	.30	.10

□	Player		
214	Ervin Johnson	.30	.10
215	Derrick McKey	.30	.10
216	Jerome Williams	.30	.10
217	Glen Rice	.60	.25
218	Steve Nash	1.00	.40
219	Nick Van Exel	1.00	.40
220	Chris Webber	1.00	.40
221	Marcus Camby	.60	.25
222	Antonio Daniels	.30	.10
223	Mitch Richmond	.60	.25
224	Otis Thorpe	.30	.10
225	Charles Oakley	.30	.10
226	Michael Olowokandi RC	1.50	.60
227	Mike Bibby RC	8.00	3.00
228	Raef LaFrentz RC	1.50	.60
229	Antawn Jamison RC	5.00	2.00
230	Vince Carter RC	15.00	6.00
231	Robert Traylor RC	1.25	.50
232	Jason Williams RC	4.00	1.50
233	Larry Hughes RC	3.00	1.25
234	Dirk Nowitzki RC	12.00	5.00
235	Paul Pierce RC	5.00	2.00
236	Bonzi Wells RC	4.00	1.50
237	Michael Doleac RC	1.25	.50
238	Keon Clark RC	1.50	.60
239	Michael Dickerson RC	2.00	.75
240	Matt Harpring RC	2.00	1.00
241	Bryce Drew RC	1.25	.50
242	Pat Garrity RC	.75	.30
243	Roshown McLeod RC	.75	.30
244	Ricky Davis RC	3.00	1.25
245	Brian Skinner RC	1.25	.50
246	Tyronn Lue RC	1.25	.50
247	Felipe Lopez RC	1.25	.50
248	Sam Jacobson RC	.60	.25
249	Corey Benjamin RC	1.25	.50
250	Nazr Mohammed RC	.75	.30
PP5	Eddie Jones		

1999-00 Finest

COMPLETE SET (266)		280.00	140.00
COMPLETE SERIES 1 (133)		80.00	40.00
COMPLETE SERIES 2 (133)		200.00	100.00
COMP.SERIES 2 w/o RC (118)		50.00	25.00
COMMON CARD (1-266)		.30	.10
COMMON ROOKIE (110-124)		4.00	1.50
COMMON ROOKIE (252-266)		4.00	1.50
COMMON SUBSET		.40	.15

□	Player		
1	Shareef Abdur-Rahim	1.00	.40
2	Kevin Willis	.30	.10
3	Sean Elliott	.60	.25
4	Vlade Divac	.60	.25
5	Tom Gugliotta	.30	.10
6	Matt Harpring	1.00	.40
7	Kerry Kittles	.30	.10
8	Joe Smith	.60	.25
9	Jamal Mashburn	.60	.25
10	Tyrone Nesby RC	.30	.10
11	Alan Henderson	.30	.10
12	Vitaly Potapenko	.30	.10
13	Dickey Simpkins	.30	.10
14	Michael Finley	1.00	.40
15	Lindsey Hunter	.30	.10
16	Antawn Jamison	1.50	.60
17	Reggie Miller	1.00	.40
18	Maurice Taylor	.60	.25
19	Clarence Weatherspoon	.30	.10
20	Sam Mitchell	.30	.10
21	Latrell Sprewell	1.00	.40
22	Michael Doleac	.30	.10
23	Rex Chapman	.30	.10
24	Peja Stojakovic	1.25	.50
25	Vladimir Stepania	.30	.10
26	Tracy McGrady	2.50	1.00
27	Cherokee Parks	.30	.10
28	LaPhonso Ellis	.30	.10
29	Hakeem Olajuwon	1.00	.40
30	Adonal Foyle	.30	.10
31	Bryant Stith	.30	.10
32	Andrew DeClercq	.30	.10
33	Toni Kukoc	.60	.25
34	Kenny Anderson	.60	.25
35	Mike Bibby	1.00	.40
36	Glen Rice	.60	.25
37	Avery Johnson	.30	.10
38	Arvydas Sabonis	.60	.25
39	Kornel David RC	.30	.10
40	Hubert Davis	.30	.10
41	Grant Hill	1.00	.40
42	Donyell Marshall	.60	.25
43	Jalen Rose	1.00	.40
44	Derrick Coleman	.60	.25
45	P.J. Brown	.30	.10
46	Vin Baker	.60	.25
47	Clifford Robinson	.30	.10
48	Allan Houston	.60	.25
49	Kendall Gill	.30	.10
50	Matt Geiger	.30	.10
51	Larry Hughes	1.00	.40
52	Corliss Williamson	.60	.25
53	Darrell Armstrong	.30	.10
54	Bobby Jackson	.60	.25
55	Bryon Russell	.30	.10
56	Juwan Howard	.60	.25
57	Dikembe Mutombo	.60	.25
58	Eddie Jones	1.00	.40
59	Randy Brown	.30	.10
60	Dirk Nowitzki	2.00	.75
61	Jerome Williams	.30	.10
62	Scottie Pippen	1.50	.60
63	Dale Davis	.30	.10
64	Kobe Bryant	4.00	1.50
65	Robert Traylor	.30	.10
66	Tim Hardaway	.60	.25
67	Michael Olowokandi	.60	.25
68	Walter McCarty	.30	.10
69	Damon Stoudamire	.60	.25
70	Othella Harrington	.30	.10
71	Chauncey Billups	.60	.25
72	John Starks	.60	.25
73	Ricky Davis	.60	.25
74	Glenn Robinson	1.00	.40
75	Dean Garrett	.30	.10
76	Chris Childs	.30	.10
77	Shawn Kemp	.60	.25
78	Allen Iverson	2.00	.75
79	Brian Grant	.60	.25
80	David Robinson	1.00	.40
81	Tracy Murray	.30	.10
82	Howard Eisley	.30	.10
83	Doug Christie	.60	.25
84	Gary Payton	1.00	.40
85	John Stockton	1.00	.40
86	Rod Strickland	.30	.10
87	Tyrone Corbin	.30	.10
88	Antonio Daniels	.30	.10
89	Dee Brown	.30	.10
90	Antoine Walker	1.00	.40
91	Theo Ratliff	.60	.25
92	Larry Johnson	.60	.25
93	Stephon Marbury	1.00	.40
94	Brevin Knight	.30	.10
95	Antonio McDyess	.60	.25
96	Bison Dele	.30	.10
97	Cuttino Mobley	1.00	.40
98	Haywoode Workman	.30	.10
99	J.R. Reid	.30	.10
100	Travis Best	.30	.10
101	Chris Webber GEM	1.50	.60
102	Grant Hill GEM	.75	.30
103	Kevin Garnett GEM	3.00	1.25
104	Jason Kidd GEM	2.50	1.00
105	Gary Payton GEM	1.00	.40
106	Shaquille O'Neal GEM	4.00	1.50
107	Alonzo Mourning GEM	.75	.30
108	Karl Malone GEM	1.50	.60
109	John Stockton GEM	.75	.30
110	Elton Brand RC	6.00	2.50
111	Baron Davis RC	8.00	3.00
112	A.Radojevic RC	1.50	.60
113	Cal Bowdler RC	1.50	.60
114	Jumaine Jones RC	1.50	.60
115	Jason Terry RC	3.00	1.25
116	Trajan Langdon RC	2.00	.75
117	Dion Glover RC	1.50	.60
118	Jeff Foster RC	1.50	.60
119	Lamar Odom RC	5.00	2.00
120	Wally Szczerbiak RC	5.00	2.00
121	Shawn Marion RC	6.00	2.50
122	Kenny Thomas RC	2.00	.75
123	Devean George RC	2.50	1.00
124	Scott Padgett RC	1.50	.60
125	Tim Duncan SEN	3.00	1.25
126	Jason Williams SEN	.60	.25
127	Paul Pierce SEN	1.00	.40
128	Kobe Bryant SEN	6.00	2.50
129	Keith Van Horn SEN	1.00	.40
130	Vince Carter SEN	4.00	1.50
131	Matt Harpring SEN	.75	.30
132	Antawn Jamison SEN	2.50	1.00
133	Tracy McGrady SEN	4.00	1.50
134	Tim Duncan	2.00	.75
135	Tariq Abdul-Wahad	.30	.10
136	Luc Longley	.30	.10
137	Steve Smith	.60	.25
138	Alonzo Mourning	.60	.25
139	Kevin Garnett	2.00	.75
140	Christian Laettner	.60	.25
141	Rik Smits	.60	.25
142	Cedric Henderson	.30	.10
143	Jim Jackson	.30	.10
144	Dan Majerle	.60	.25
145	Bryant Reeves	.30	.10
146	Antonio Davis	.30	.10
147	Michael Smith	.30	.10
148	Charlie Ward	.30	.10
149	Chris Mullin	1.00	.40
150	Danny Manning	.30	.10
151	Eric Williams	.30	.10
152	Hersey Hawkins	.60	.25
153	Isaiah Rider	.30	.10
154	Shandon Anderson	.30	.10
155	Jason Kidd	1.50	.60
156	Chris Whitney	.30	.10
157	Brent Barry	.60	.25
158	Patrick Ewing	1.00	.40
159	George Lynch	.30	.10
160	Dickey Simpkins	.30	.10
161	Derek Anderson	.50	.20
162	Ron Mercer	.60	.25
163	David Wesley	.30	.10
164	Mookie Blaylock	.30	.10
165	Terrell Brandon	.60	.25
166	Detlef Schrempf	.60	.25
167	Olden Polynice	.30	.10
168	Jayson Williams	.30	.10
169	Eric Piatkowski	.30	.10
170	A.C. Green	.60	.25
171	Chris Mills	.30	.10
172	Chris Webber	1.00	.40
173	Jeff Hornacek	.60	.25
174	Calbert Cheaney	.30	.10
175	Wesley Person	.30	.10
176	Corey Benjamin	.30	.10
177	Loy Vaught	.30	.10
178	Keith Closs	.30	.10
179	Bo Outlaw	.30	.10
180	Mitch Richmond	.60	.25
181	Charles Oakley	.30	.10
182	Felipe Lopez	.30	.10
183	Eric Snow	.60	.25
184	Paul Pierce	1.00	.40
185	Elden Campbell	.30	.10
186	Shaquille O'Neal	2.50	1.00
187	Charles Barkley	1.25	.50
188	Mark Jackson	.60	.25
189	Scott Burrell	.30	.10
190	Anfernee Hardaway	1.00	.40
191	Samaki Walker	.30	.10
192	Karl Malone	1.00	.40

❑ 193 Jermaine O'Neal	1.00	.40
❑ 194 Mario Elie	.30	.10
❑ 195 Malik Sealy	.30	.10
❑ 196 Voshon Lenard	.30	.10
❑ 197 Chris Gatling	.30	.10
❑ 198 Walt Williams	.30	.10
❑ 199 Nick Van Exel	1.00	.40
❑ 200 Bimbo Coles	.30	.10
❑ 201 John Wallace	.30	.10
❑ 202 Anthony Mason	.60	.25
❑ 203 Steve Nash	1.00	.40
❑ 204 Erick Dampier	.60	.25
❑ 205 Cedric Ceballos	.30	.10
❑ 206 Derek Fisher	1.00	.40
❑ 207 Marcus Camby	.60	.25
❑ 208 Tyrone Hill	.30	.10
❑ 209 Nick Anderson	.30	.10
❑ 210 Sam Cassell	1.00	.40
❑ 211 Raef LaFrentz	.60	.25
❑ 212 Ruben Patterson	.60	.25
❑ 213 Rick Fox	.60	.25
❑ 214 Jason Williams	1.00	.40
❑ 215 Vince Carter	2.50	1.00
❑ 216 Michael Dickerson	.60	.25
❑ 217 Steve Kerr	.60	.25
❑ 218 Rasheed Wallace	1.00	.40
❑ 219 Keith Van Horn	1.00	.40
❑ 220 Bob Sura	.30	.10
❑ 221 Ray Allen	1.00	.40
❑ 222 Jerry Stackhouse	1.00	.40
❑ 223 Shawn Bradley	.30	.10
❑ 224 Horace Grant	.60	.25
❑ 225 Tim Duncan USA	3.00	1.25
❑ 226 Kevin Garnett USA	3.00	1.25
❑ 227 Jason Kidd USA	2.50	1.00
❑ 228 Steve Smith USA	.40	.15
❑ 229 Allan Houston USA	.75	.30
❑ 230 Tom Gugliotta USA	.40	.15
❑ 231 Gary Payton USA	.75	.30
❑ 232 Tim Hardaway USA	.75	.30
❑ 233 Vin Baker USA	.40	.15
❑ 234 Karl Malone CAT	1.00	.40
❑ 235 Vince Carter CAT	4.00	1.50
❑ 236 Jason Williams CAT	.75	.30
❑ 237 Alonzo Mourning CAT	.75	.30
❑ 238 Anfernee Hardaway CAT	2.00	.75
❑ 239 Mitch Richmond CAT	.75	.30
❑ 240 Steve Smith CAT	.75	.30
❑ 241 Charles Barkley CAT	1.25	.50
❑ 242 Ron Mercer CAT	.75	.30
❑ 243 Shaquille O'Neal EDGE	4.00	1.50
❑ 244 Jason Kidd EDGE	2.50	1.00
❑ 245 Kevin Garnett EDGE	3.00	1.25
❑ 246 Tim Duncan EDGE	3.00	1.25
❑ 247 Ray Allen EDGE	1.50	.60
❑ 248 Chris Webber EDGE	1.50	.60
❑ 249 Jerry Stackhouse EDGE	.75	.30
❑ 250 Keith Van Horn EDGE	.75	.30
❑ 251 Patrick Ewing EDGE	.75	.30
❑ 252 Steve Francis RC	30.00	12.50
❑ 253 Jonathan Bender RC	20.00	8.00
❑ 254 Richard Hamilton RC	20.00	8.00
❑ 255 Andre Miller RC	20.00	8.00
❑ 256 Corey Maggette RC	20.00	8.00
❑ 257 William Avery RC	8.00	3.00
❑ 258 Ron Artest RC	12.00	5.00
❑ 259 James Posey RC	10.00	4.00
❑ 260 Quincy Lewis RC	5.00	2.00
❑ 261 Tim James RC	6.00	2.50
❑ 262 Vonteego Cummings RC	8.00	3.00
❑ 263 Anthony Carter RC	12.00	5.00
❑ 264 Mirsad Turkcan RC	4.00	1.50
❑ 265 Adrian Griffin RC	6.00	2.50
❑ 266 Ryan Robertson RC	5.00	2.00
❑ PP1 Reggie Miller Promo		.40

2000-01 Finest

❑ COMPLETE SET (173)	275.00	150.00
❑ COMPLETE SET w/o SP (125)	40.00	20.00
❑ COMMON CARD (1-173)	.30	.10
❑ COMMON ROOKIE (126-150)	6.00	2.50
❑ 1 Shaquille O'Neal	2.50	1.00
❑ 2 P.J. Brown	.30	.10
❑ 3 Joe Smith	.60	.25
❑ 4 Kendall Gill	.30	.10
❑ 5 Corey Maggette	.60	.25

KEVIN GARNETT

❑ 6 Marcus Camby	.60	.25
❑ 7 Toni Kukoc	.60	.25
❑ 8 Kobe Bryant	1.00	1.50
❑ 9 David Robinson	1.00	.40
❑ 10 Ruben Patterson	.60	.25
❑ 11 Allen Iverson	2.00	.75
❑ 12 Glenn Robinson	.60	.25
❑ 13 Anthony Carter	.60	.25
❑ 14 Jonathan Bender	.60	.25
❑ 15 Vince Carter	2.50	1.00
❑ 16 Jerry Stackhouse	1.00	.40
❑ 17 Raef LaFrentz	.60	.25
❑ 18 Dikembe Mutombo	.60	.25
❑ 19 Baron Davis	1.00	.40
❑ 20 Kenny Anderson	.60	.25
❑ 21 Corey Benjamin	.30	.10
❑ 22 Cedric Ceballos	.30	.10
❑ 23 Christian Laettner	.60	.25
❑ 24 Shandon Anderson	.30	.10
❑ 25 Rik Smits	.30	.10
❑ 26 Michael Olowokandi	.30	.10
❑ 27 Sam Cassell	1.00	.40
❑ 28 Tom Gugliotta	.30	.10
❑ 29 Jason Williams	.60	.25
❑ 30 Avery Johnson	.30	.10
❑ 31 Karl Malone	1.00	.40
❑ 32 Paul Pierce	1.00	.40
❑ 33 Grant Hill	1.00	.40
❑ 34 Nick Anderson	.30	.10
❑ 35 Alan Henderson	.30	.10
❑ 36 Eddie Jones	1.00	.40
❑ 37 Ron Artest	.60	.25
❑ 38 Brevin Knight	.30	.10
❑ 39 Keon Clark	.60	.25
❑ 40 Elton Brand	1.00	.40
❑ 41 Reggie Miller	1.00	.40
❑ 42 Steve Francis	1.00	.40
❑ 43 Derek Anderson	.60	.25
❑ 44 Alonzo Mourning	.60	.25
❑ 45 Terrell Brandon	.60	.25
❑ 46 Larry Johnson	.60	.25
❑ 47 Keith Van Horn	1.00	.40
❑ 48 Jason Kidd	1.50	.60
❑ 49 Scottie Pippen	1.50	.60
❑ 50 Gary Payton	1.00	.40
❑ 51 Robert Pack	.30	.10
❑ 52 Adrian Griffin	.30	.10
❑ 53 Jim Jackson	.30	.10
❑ 54 Leonard Murray	.30	.10
❑ 55 Larry Hughes	.60	.25
❑ 56 Dirk Nowitzki	1.50	.60
❑ 57 Vonteego Cummings	.30	.10
❑ 58 Jalen Rose	1.00	.40
❑ 59 Arvydas Sabonis	.30	.10
❑ 60 Kerry Kittles	.30	.10
❑ 61 Kevin Garnett	2.00	.75
❑ 62 Latrell Sprewell	1.00	.40
❑ 63 Shawn Marion	1.00	.40
❑ 64 Darrell Armstrong	.30	.10
❑ 65 Ron Mercer	.60	.25
❑ 66 Damon Stoudamire	.60	.25
❑ 67 Tracy McGrady	2.50	1.00
❑ 68 Theo Ratliff	.60	.25
❑ 69 Lamar Odom	1.00	.40
❑ 70 Charlie Ward	.30	.10
❑ 71 John Amaechi	.30	.10

❑ 74 Quincy Lewis	.30	.10
❑ 75 Othella Harrington	.30	.10
❑ 76 Doug Christie	.60	.25
❑ 77 Richard Hamilton	.60	.25
❑ 78 Donyell Marshall	.60	.25
❑ 79 Vlade Divac	.60	.25
❑ 80 Clifford Robinson	.30	.10
❑ 81 Sean Elliott	.60	.25
❑ 82 Rashard Lewis	.60	.25
❑ 83 Wally Szczerbiak	.60	.25
❑ 84 Dale Davis	.30	.10
❑ 85 Kelvin Cato	.30	.10
❑ 86 Cuttino Mobley	.60	.25
❑ 87 Travis Best	.30	.10
❑ 88 Robert Horry	.60	.25
❑ 89 Maurice Taylor	.30	.10
❑ 90 Jamal Mashburn	.60	.25
❑ 91 Tim Thomas	.60	.25
❑ 92 Stephon Marbury	1.00	.40
❑ 93 Patrick Ewing	1.00	.40
❑ 94 Eric Snow	.60	.25
❑ 95 Anfernee Hardaway	1.00	.40
❑ 96 Steve Smith	.60	.25
❑ 97 Chris Webber	1.00	.40
❑ 98 Rodney Rogers	.30	.10
❑ 99 John Stockton	1.00	.40
❑ 100 Tim Duncan	2.00	.75
❑ 101 Ray Allen	1.00	.40
❑ 102 Glen Rice	.60	.25
❑ 103 Bryon Russell	.30	.10
❑ 104 Tim Hardaway	.60	.25
❑ 105 Allan Houston	.60	.25
❑ 106 Rasheed Wallace	1.00	.40
❑ 107 Vin Baker	.60	.25
❑ 108 Michael Dickerson	.60	.25
❑ 109 Juwan Howard	.60	.25
❑ 110 Hakeem Olajuwon	1.00	.40
❑ 111 Shareef Abdur-Rahim	1.00	.40
❑ 112 Rod Strickland	.30	.10
❑ 113 Hersey Hawkins	.30	.10
❑ 114 Jason Terry	1.00	.40
❑ 115 Anthony Mason	.60	.25
❑ 116 Mike Bibby	1.00	.40
❑ 117 Shawn Kemp	.60	.25
❑ 118 Derrick Coleman	.30	.10
❑ 119 Antoine Walker	1.00	.40
❑ 120 Antawn Jamison	1.00	.40
❑ 121 Michael Finley	1.00	.40
❑ 122 Antonio McDyess	.60	.25
❑ 123 Nick Van Exel	1.00	.40
❑ 124 Mitch Richmond	.60	.25
❑ 125 Lindsey Hunter	.30	.10
❑ 126 Kenyon Martin RC	15.00	6.00
❑ 127 Stromile Swift RC	8.00	3.00
❑ 128 Darius Miles RC	15.00	6.00
❑ 129 Marcus Fizer RC	6.00	2.50
❑ 130 Mike Miller RC	12.00	5.00
❑ 131 DerMarr Johnson RC	6.00	2.50
❑ 132 Chris Mihm RC	6.00	2.50
❑ 133 Jamal Crawford RC	8.00	3.00
❑ 134 Joel Przybilla RC	6.00	2.50
❑ 135 Keyon Dooling RC	6.00	2.50
❑ 136 Jerome Moiso RC	6.00	2.50
❑ 137 Etan Thomas RC	6.00	2.50
❑ 138 Courtney Alexander RC	6.00	2.50
❑ 139 Mateen Cleaves RC	6.00	2.50
❑ 140 Jason Collier RC	8.00	3.00
❑ 141 Desmond Mason RC	6.00	2.50
❑ 142 Quentin Richardson RC	12.00	5.00
❑ 143 Jamaal Magloire RC	6.00	2.50
❑ 144 Speedy Claxton RC	6.00	2.50
❑ 145 Morris Peterson RC	8.00	3.00
❑ 146 Donnell Harvey RC	6.00	2.50
❑ 147 DeShawn Stevenson RC	6.00	2.50
❑ 148 Mamadou N'diaye RC	6.00	2.50
❑ 149 Erick Barkley RC	6.00	2.50
❑ 150 Mark Madsen RC	6.00	2.50
❑ 151 A.Iverson/S.Marbury OTM	1.50	.60
❑ 152 V.Carter/K.Bryant OTM	3.00	1.25
❑ 153 K.Garnett/Abdur-Rahim OTM	2.50	1.00
❑ 154 T.McGrady/S.Pippen OTM	4.00	1.50
❑ 155 T.Duncan/E.Brand OTM	3.00	1.25
❑ 156 S.Francis/D.Robinson OTM	2.50	1.00
❑ 157 C.Webber/K.Malone OTM	1.00	.40
❑ 158 A.Mourning/P.Ewing OTM	1.00	.40
❑ 159 L.Sprewell/E.Jones OTM	1.00	.40

160	J.Kidd/J.Stockton OTM	1.50	.60
161	R.Miller/A.Houston OTM	1.00	.40
162	R.Wallace/A.Walker OTM	1.00	.40
163	J.Stackhouse/J.Rose OTM	1.00	.40
164	Shaquille O'Neal GEM	6.00	2.50
165	Kobe Bryant GEM	10.00	4.00
166	Vince Carter GEM	6.00	2.50
167	Kevin Garnett GEM	5.00	2.00
168	Jason Williams GEM	2.00	.75
169	Tracy McGrady GEM	5.00	2.00
170	Steve Francis GEM	3.00	1.25
171	Tim Duncan GEM	5.00	2.00
172	Elton Brand GEM	2.00	.75
173	Grant Hill GEM	2.50	1.00

2002-03 Finest

Dirk Nowitzki

	COMP.DRAFT SET (10)	450.00	250.00
	COMMON CARD (1-100)	.25	.10
	COMMON AU (101-120)	12.00	5.00
	COMMON (121-156)	12.00	5.00
	COMMON AU (157-177)	12.00	5.00
1	Dirk Nowitzki	1.50	.60
2	Jason Terry	1.00	.40
3	Marcus Camby	.60	.25
4	Joe Johnson	1.00	.40
5	Shawn Marion	1.00	.40
6	Andrei Kirilenko	1.00	.40
7	Jamal Mashburn	.60	.25
8	Andre Miller	.60	.25
9	Jason Williams	.60	.25
10	Tony Delk	.25	.10
11	Tyson Chandler	1.00	.40
12	Jason Richardson	1.00	.40
13	Derek Fisher	1.00	.40
14	Troy Hudson	.25	.10
15	Kerry Kittles	.25	.10
16	Peja Stojakovic	1.00	.40
17	Kurt Thomas	.60	.25
18	Jamaal Tinsley	1.00	.40
19	Matt Harpring	1.00	.40
20	Kenny Thomas	.25	.10
21	Kwame Brown	.60	.25
22	Antonio Davis	.25	.10
23	David Robinson	1.00	.40
24	Keith Van Horn	1.00	.40
25	Howard Eisley	.25	.10
26	Jalen Rose	1.00	.40
27	Chauncey Billups	.25	.10
28	Corey Maggette	.60	.25
29	Pau Gasol	1.00	.40
30	Desmond Mason	.60	.25
31	Brian Grant	.60	.25
32	Eddie Griffin	.60	.25
33	Voshon Lenard	.25	.10
34	Al Harrington	.60	.25
35	Calbert Cheaney	.25	.10
36	Malik Rose	.25	.10
37	Bonzi Wells	.60	.25
38	Pat Garrity	.25	.10
39	P.J. Brown	.25	.10
40	Ray Allen	1.00	.40
41	Karl Malone	1.00	.40
42	Steve Nash	1.00	.40
43	Antawn Jamison	1.00	.40
44	Ron Artest	.60	.25
45	Shane Battier	1.00	.40
46	Gary Payton	1.00	.40
47	Kobe Bryant	4.00	1.50

48	Lucious Harris	.25	.10
49	Richard Hamilton	.25	.10
50	Darius Miles	1.00	.40
51	Marcus Fizer	.60	.25
52	Antoine Walker	1.00	.40
53	Juwan Howard	.60	.25
54	Eddie Jones	1.00	.40
55	Kenyon Martin	1.00	.40
56	Derek Anderson	.60	.25
57	Stephen Jackson	.25	.10
58	Vince Carter	2.00	.75
59	Larry Hughes	.60	.25
60	Doug Christie	.60	.25
61	Derrick Coleman	.25	.10
62	Michael Finley	1.00	.40
63	Wally Szczerbiak	.60	.25
64	David Wesley	.25	.10
65	Brad Miller	1.00	.40
66	Clifford Robinson	.25	.10
67	Shandon Anderson	.25	.10
68	Stephon Marbury	1.00	.40
69	Bobby Jackson	.60	.25
70	Brent Barry	.60	.25
71	Ruben Patterson	.25	.10
72	Rashard Lewis	1.00	.40
73	Tony Battie	.25	.10
74	Ben Wallace	1.00	.40
75	Theo Ratliff	.60	.25
76	Ricky Davis	1.00	.40
77	Nick Van Exel	1.00	.40
78	Mike Miller	1.00	.40
79	Sam Cassell	1.00	.40
80	Malik Allen	.25	.10
81	Mike Bibby	1.00	.40
82	Scottie Pippen	1.50	.60
83	Dikembe Mutombo	.60	.25
84	Latrell Sprewell	1.00	.40
85	Predrag Drobnjak	.25	.10
86	Joe Smith	.60	.25
87	Aaron Mckie	.60	.25
88	Jamaal Magloire	.60	.25
89	Keon Clark	.60	.25
90	Eric Williams	.25	.10
91	Raef Lafrentz	.60	.25
92	Troy Murphy	1.00	.40
93	Rick Fox	.60	.25
94	Michael Redd	1.00	.40
95	Radoslav Nesterovic	.60	.25
96	Donyell Marshall	1.00	.40
97	Elton Brand	1.00	.40
98	Robert Horry	.60	.25
99	Zydrunas Ilgauskas	.60	.25
100	Michael Jordan	8.00	3.00
101	Juaquin Hawkins AU RC	10.00	4.00
102	Dan Dickau AU RC	12.00	5.00
103	Jiri Welsh AU EXCH	10.00	4.00
104	John Salmons AU	10.00	4.00
105	Tamar Slay AU RC	10.00	4.00
106	Melvin Ely AU RC	10.00	4.00
107	Jared Jeffries AU RC	15.00	6.00
108	J.Harrington AU RC	10.00	4.00
109	M.Haislip AU EXCH	10.00	4.00
110	Qyntel Woods AU RC	15.00	6.00
111	R.Humphrey AU RC	10.00	4.00
112	J.R. Bremer AU RC	10.00	4.00
113	A.Rigadeau AU RC	10.00	4.00
114	Jay Williams RC*	6.00	2.50
115	Pat Burke AU RC	10.00	4.00
116	Smush Parker AU RC	40.00	15.00
117	Juan Dixon AU RC	25.00	10.00
118	V.Yarbrough AU RC	10.00	4.00
119	M.Okur AU EXCH	15.00	6.00
120	Rasual Butler AU RC	12.00	5.00
121	Baron Davis JSY	12.00	5.00
122	S.Abdur-Rahim JSY	12.00	5.00
123	Gilbert Arenas JSY	12.00	5.00
124	Travis Best JSY	12.00	5.00
125	Vlade Divac JSY	12.00	5.00
126	Tim Duncan JSY	20.00	8.00
127	Jason Kidd JSY	15.00	6.00
128	Kevin Garnett JSY	20.00	8.00
129	A.Hardaway JSY	12.00	5.00
130	Allen Iverson JSY	20.00	8.00
131	Cuttino Mobley JSY	12.00	5.00
132	Steve Francis JSY	12.00	5.00
133	Jermaine O'Neal JSY	12.00	5.00

134	Lamar Odom JSY	12.00	5.00
135	M.Olowokandi JSY	12.00	5.00
136	Paul Pierce JSY	12.00	5.00
137	Reggie Miller JSY	12.00	5.00
138	Chris Webber JSY	12.00	5.00
139	Richard Jefferson JSY	12.00	5.00
140	Allan Houston JSY	12.00	5.00
141	Glenn Robinson JSY	12.00	5.00
142	Jerome Williams JSY	12.00	5.00
143	John Stockton JSY	12.00	5.00
144	Rasheed Wallace JSY	12.00	5.00
145	Eric Snow JSY	12.00	5.00
146	Tracy McGrady JSY	25.00	10.00
147	S.O'Neal JSY	25.00	10.00
148	J.Stackhouse JSY	12.00	5.00
149	Morris Peterson JSY	12.00	5.00
150	D.Armstrong JSY	12.00	5.00
151	Tony Parker JSY	12.00	5.00
152	V.Radmanovic JSY	12.00	5.00
153	Anthony Mason JSY	12.00	5.00
154	Charles Oakley JSY	12.00	5.00
155	Grant Hill JSY	12.00	5.00
156	Vin Baker JSY	12.00	5.00
157	Chris Jefferies AU RC	12.00	5.00
158	Drew Gooden AU RC	30.00	12.50
159	C.Jacobsen AU RC	12.00	5.00
160	Kareem Rush AU RC	20.00	8.00
161	B.Nachbar AU RC	10.00	4.00
162	T.Prince AU RC	25.00	10.00
163	Manu Ginobili RC*	50.00	20.00
164	Gordan Giricek AU RC	20.00	8.00
165	Raul Lopez AU RC	10.00	4.00
166	Dan Gadzuric AU RC	10.00	4.00
167	Marko Jaric AU	12.00	5.00
168	Lonny Baxter AU RC	10.00	4.00
169	Yao Ming AU RC	120.00	60.00
170	Mike Dunleavy AU RC	25.00	10.00
171	Caron Butler AU RC	30.00	12.50
172	Nene Hilario AU RC	20.00	8.00
173	A.Stoudemire AU RC	80.00	40.00
174	N.Tskitishvili AU RC	15.00	6.00
175	Fred Jones AU RC	12.00	5.00
176	D.Wagner AU RC	25.00	10.00
177	Carlos Boozer AU RC	40.00	15.00
178	LeBron James XRC	160.00	80.00
179	Darko Milicic XRC	25.00	10.00
180	Carmelo Anthony XRC	60.00	25.00
181	Chris Bosh XRC	25.00	10.00
182	Dwyane Wade XRC	50.00	20.00
183	Chris Kaman XRC	12.00	5.00
184	Kirk Hinrich XRC	20.00	8.00
185	T.J. Ford XRC	20.00	-8.00
186	Mike Sweetney XRC	12.00	5.00
187	Jarvis Hayes XRC	12.00	5.00

2003-04 Finest

	COMP.SET w/o SP's (100)	40.00	15.00
	COMMON CARD (1-100)	.25	.10
	COMMON JSY (101-130)	10.00	4.00
	COMMON ROOKIE (131-143)	6.00	2.50
	COMMON AU (144-172)	12.00	5.00
	COMMON JSY (173-185)	10.00	4.00
1	Zach Randolph	1.00	.40
2	Keith Van Horn	1.00	.40
3	Steve Francis	1.00	.40
4	Al Harrington	.60	.25
5	Jason Kidd	1.50	.60
6	Jamaal Tinsley	1.00	.40

#	Player		
7	Lamar Odom	1.00	.40
8	Antoine Walker	1.00	.40
9	Tony Parker	1.00	.40
10	Jamal Mashburn	.60	.25
11	Desmond Mason	.60	.25
12	Carlos Arroyo	1.50	.60
13	Chris Andersen	.25	.10
14	Chris Wilcox	.60	.25
15	Vince Carter	2.50	1.00
16	Peja Stojakovic	1.00	.40
17	Qyntel Woods	.25	.10
18	Mike Dunleavy	.60	.25
19	Sam Cassell	1.00	.40
20	Allan Houston	.60	.25
21	Speedy Claxton	.25	.10
22	Rafer Alston	.25	.10
23	Michael Finley	1.00	.40
24	Richard Jefferson	.60	.25
25	Larry Hughes	.60	.25
26	Pau Gasol	1.00	.40
27	Maurice Taylor	.25	.10
28	Donyell Marshall	1.00	.40
29	Darrell Armstrong	.25	.10
30	Latrell Sprewell	1.00	.40
31	Reggie Miller	1.00	.40
32	Stephon Marbury	1.00	.40
33	Antawn Jamison	1.00	.40
34	DerMarr Johnson	.25	.10
35	Shareef Abdur-Rahim	1.00	.40
36	Tony Battie	.25	.10
37	Kwame Brown	.60	.25
38	Fred Jones	.25	.10
39	Jamal Crawford	.60	.25
40	Kurt Thomas	.60	.25
41	Eric Snow	.60	.25
42	Andre Miller	.60	.25
43	Ray Allen	1.00	.40
44	Caron Butler	1.00	.40
45	Corliss Williamson	.60	.25
46	Kenny Thomas	.25	.10
47	Jason Terry	1.00	.40
48	Ronald Murray	.25	.10
49	Richard Hamilton	.60	.25
50	Elton Brand	1.00	.40
51	Ron Artest	.60	.25
52	Jerome Williams	.25	.10
53	Ricky Davis	1.00	.40
54	Brent Barry	.60	.25
55	Dikembe Mutombo	.60	.25
56	Earl Boykins	.60	.25
57	Brad Miller	1.00	.40
58	Shane Battier	.60	.25
59	Tyson Chandler	1.00	.40
60	Kelvin Cato	.25	.10
61	Shawn Marion	1.00	.40
62	Bobby Jackson	.60	.25
63	Corey Maggette	.60	.25
64	Antonio McDyess	.60	.25
65	Drew Gooden	.60	.25
66	Mike Miller	1.00	.40
67	Darius Miles	.60	.25
68	Stephen Jackson	.25	.10
69	Cuttino Mobley	.60	.25
70	Gary Payton	1.00	.40
71	Toni Kukoc	.60	.25
72	Eddie Jones	1.00	.40
73	Gilbert Arenas	1.00	.40
74	Matt Harpring	1.00	.40
75	Marko Jaric	.60	.25
76	Bonzi Wells	.60	.25
77	Nick Van Exel	1.00	.40
78	Quentin Richardson	.60	.25
79	Rasho Nesterovic	.60	.25
80	Steve Nash	1.00	.40
81	Morris Peterson	.60	.25
82	Nikoloz Tskitishvili	.25	.10
83	Damon Stoudamire	.60	.25
84	Bruce Bowen	.25	.10
85	Brian Grant	.60	.25
86	Jalen Rose	1.00	.40
87	Jerry Stackhouse	1.00	.40
88	Kobe Bryant	4.00	1.50
89	Eddy Curry	.60	.25
90	Tim Thomas	.60	.25
91	Erick Dampier	.25	.10
92	Jason Williams	.60	.25
93	Troy Murphy	1.00	.40
94	Kerry Kittles	.25	.10
95	Zydrunas Ilgauskas	.60	.25
96	Theo Ratliff	.60	.25
97	Samuel Dalembert	.25	.10
98	Jeff McInnis	.25	.10
99	Juwan Howard	.60	.25
100	Joe Johnson	.60	.25
101	Paul Pierce JSY	10.00	4.00
102	Ben Wallace JSY	10.00	4.00
103	Yao Ming JSY	15.00	6.00
104	Jermaine O'Neal JSY	10.00	4.00
105	Rashard Lewis JSY	10.00	4.00
106	Karl Malone JSY	10.00	4.00
107	Allen Iverson JSY	12.00	5.00
108	Mike Bibby JSY	10.00	4.00
109	Rasheed Wallace JSY	10.00	4.00
110	Nene JSY	10.00	4.00
111	Tracy McGrady JSY	15.00	6.00
112	Andrei Kirilenko JSY	10.00	4.00
113	Manu Ginobili JSY	10.00	4.00
114	Kenyon Martin JSY	10.00	4.00
115	Amare Stoudemire JSY	12.00	5.00
116	Baron Davis JSY	10.00	4.00
117	Michael Olowokandi JSY	10.00	4.00
118	Carlos Boozer JSY	10.00	4.00
119	Jason Richardson JSY	10.00	4.00
120	Dirk Nowitzki JSY	12.00	5.00
121	Chauncey Billups JSY	10.00	4.00
122	Chris Webber JSY	10.00	4.00
123	Glenn Robinson JSY/807	10.00	4.00
124	Kevin Garnett JSY	12.00	5.00
125	Michael Redd JSY	10.00	4.00
126	David Wesley JSY	10.00	4.00
127	Tayshaun Prince JSY	10.00	4.00
128	Jamaal Magloire JSY	10.00	4.00
129	Tim Duncan JSY	12.00	5.00
130	Shaquille O'Neal JSY	15.00	6.00
131	Darko Milicic RC	10.00	4.00
132	Chris Kaman RC	6.00	2.50
133	LeBron James RC	100.00	50.00
134	Richie Frahm RC	6.00	2.50
135	Steve Blake RC	6.00	2.50
136	Zaza Pachulia RC	6.00	2.50
137	Keith Bogans RC	6.00	2.50
138	Kirk Hinrich AU RC	40.00	15.00
139	Jarvis Hayes RC	6.00	2.50
140	Zarko Cabarkapa AU RC	12.00	5.00
141	Zoran Planinic AU RC	12.00	5.00
142	Udonis Haslem RC	10.00	4.00
143	David West RC	6.00	2.50
144	Boris Diaw AU RC	25.00	12.50
145	Travis Outlaw AU RC EXCH	12.00	5.00
146	Brian Cook AU RC	12.00	5.00
147	Ndudi Ebi AU RC	12.00	5.00
148	Josh Howard AU RC	40.00	15.00
149	Jason Kapono AU RC	12.00	5.00
150	Luke Walton AU RC	20.00	8.00
151	Travis Hansen AU RC	12.00	5.00
152	Willie Green AU RC	12.00	5.00
153	Maurice Williams AU RC	12.00	5.00
154	Francisco Elson AU RC	12.00	5.00
155	Kyle Korver AU RC	25.00	10.00
156	Marquis Daniels AU RC	30.00	12.50
157	Chris Bosh AU RC	60.00	25.00
158	Dwyane Wade AU RC	200.00	100.00
159	Aleksandar Pavlovic AU RC	15.00	6.00
160	Mike Sweetney AU RC	12.00	5.00
161	Marcus Banks AU RC	12.00	5.00
162	Luke Ridnour AU RC	25.00	10.00
163	Carmelo Anthony AU RC	120.00	60.00
164	Mickael Pietrus AU RC	12.00	5.00
165	Reece Gaines AU RC	12.00	5.00
166	Kendrick Perkins AU RC	12.00	5.00
167	Troy Bell AU RC	12.00	5.00
168	Leandro Barbosa AU RC	25.00	10.00
169	Dahntay Jones AU RC	12.00	5.00
170	T.J. Ford AU RC	40.00	15.00
171	Nick Collison AU RC	12.00	5.00
172	Theron Smith AU RC	12.00	5.00
173	Dwight Howard XRC	30.00	12.50
174	Emeka Okafor XRC	20.00	8.00
175	Ben Gordon XRC	50.00	20.00
176	Shaun Livingston XRC	15.00	6.00
177	Devin Harris XRC	15.00	6.00
178	Josh Childress XRC	10.00	4.00
179	Luol Deng XRC	20.00	8.00
180	Rafael Araujo XRC	10.00	4.00
181	Andre Iguodala XRC	20.00	8.00
182	Andris Biedrins XRC	10.00	4.00
183	Kirk Snyder XRC	10.00	4.00
184	Josh Smith XRC	20.00	8.00
185	Sebastian Telfair XRC	10.00	4.00

2004-05 Finest

#			
	COMP.SET w/o SP's (100)	40.00	15.00
	COMMON CARD (131-160)	5.00	2.00
1	Richard Hamilton	.60	.25
2	Mike Dunleavy	.60	.25
3	Jamaal Tinsley	1.00	.40
4	Corey Maggette	.60	.25
5	Zach Randolph	1.00	.40
6	Desmond Mason	.60	.25
7	Marc Jackson	.60	.25
8	Kobe Bryant	4.00	1.50
9	Mike Bibby	1.00	.40
10	Vince Carter	2.50	1.00
11	Bonzi Wells	.60	.25
12	Ricky Davis	1.00	.40
13	Steve Nash	1.00	.40
14	Rashard Lewis	1.00	.40
15	Eddy Curry	.60	.25
16	Carlos Boozer	1.00	.40
17	Brad Miller	1.00	.40
18	Kurt Thomas	.60	.25
19	Shareef Abdur-Rahim	1.00	.40
20	Grant Hill	1.00	.40
21	Jason Hart	.25	.10
22	Larry Hughes	.60	.25
23	Lebron James	6.00	2.50
24	Udonis Haslem	.25	.10
25	David Wesley	.25	.10
26	Kenny Thomas	.25	.10
27	Marcus Camby	.60	.25
28	Michael Redd	1.00	.40
29	Rasho Nesterovic	.60	.25
30	Keith Van Horn	1.00	.40
31	Reggie Miller	1.00	.40
32	Stephon Marbury	1.00	.40
33	Donyell Marshall	1.00	.40
34	Jermaine O'Neal	1.00	.40
35	Antoine Walker	1.00	.40
36	Rasheed Wallace	1.00	.40
37	Antonio Daniels	.25	.10
38	Damon Jones	.25	.10
39	Caron Butler	1.00	.40
40	Shawn Marion	1.00	.40
41	Lee Nailon	.25	.10
42	Damon Stoudamire	.60	.25
43	Bob Sura	.25	.10
44	Mehmet Okur	.60	.25
45	Shane Battier	1.00	.40
46	Michael Finley	1.00	.40
47	Doug Christie	.60	.25
48	Eddie Jones	1.00	.40
49	Speedy Claxton	.25	.10
50	Wally Szczerbiak	.60	.25
51	Primoz Brezec	.25	.10
52	Marko Jaric	.60	.25
53	Antonio McDyess	1.00	.40
54	Jeff McInnis	.25	.10
55	Tony Parker	1.00	.40
56	Rafer Alston	.25	.10
57	Troy Murphy	1.00	.40

#	Player		
58	Chris Mihm	.25	.10
59	Jarvis Hayes	.25	.10
60	Marquis Daniels	1.00	.40
61	Jamal Crawford	.60	.25
62	Morris Peterson	.60	.25
63	Luke Ridnour	.60	.25
64	Mike Miller	1.00	.40
65	Carlos Arroyo	1.50	.60
66	Gary Payton	1.00	.40
67	Joe Johnson	.60	.25
68	Latrell Sprewell	1.00	.40
69	Allan Houston	.60	.25
70	Earl Boykins	.60	.25
71	Brendan Haywood	.25	.10
72	Baron Davis	.60	.25
73	Fred Jones	.25	.10
74	Joe Smith	.60	.25
75	Jalen Rose	1.00	.40
76	Eddie Griffin	.25	.10
77	Lamar Odom	1.00	.40
78	Theo Ratliff	.25	.10
79	Gordan Giricek	.60	.25
80	Maurice Williams	.25	.10
81	Tayshaun Prince	.60	.25
82	Kyle Korver	.60	.25
83	Andre Miller	.60	.25
84	Chris Wilcox	.60	.25
85	Alonzo Mourning	.60	.25
86	Gilbert Arenas	1.00	.40
87	Zydrunas Ilgauskas	.60	.25
88	Jamaal Magloire	.25	.10
89	Jason Williams	.60	.25
90	Chucky Atkins	.25	.10
91	Jeff Foster	.25	.10
92	Kareem Rush	.60	.25
93	Sam Cassell	1.00	.40
94	Josh Howard	.60	.25
95	Tyronn Lue	.25	.10
96	Vladimir Radmanovic	.25	.10
97	Chauncey Billups	.60	.25
98	Brent Barry	.25	.10
99	Paul Pierce	1.00	.40
100	Dwyane Wade	3.00	1.25
101	Al Harrington JSY	8.00	3.00
102	Antawn Jamison JSY	8.00	3.00
103	Kirk Hinrich JSY	8.00	3.00
104	Tim Duncan JSY	12.00	5.00
105	Gerald Wallace JSY	8.00	3.00
106	Dirk Nowitzki JSY	10.00	4.00
107	Chris Webber JSY	8.00	3.00
108	Jason Kidd JSY	10.00	4.00
109	Carmelo Anthony JSY	12.00	5.00
110	Tracy McGrady JSY	15.00	6.00
111	Elton Brand JSY	8.00	3.00
112	Pau Gasol JSY	8.00	3.00
113	Jason Richardson JSY	8.00	3.00
114	Chris Bosh JSY	8.00	3.00
115	Kevin Garnett JSY	12.00	5.00
116	Steve Francis JSY	8.00	3.00
117	Richard Jefferson JSY	8.00	3.00
118	Baron Davis JSY	8.00	3.00
119	Manu Ginobili JSY	8.00	3.00
120	Shaquille O'Neal JSY	15.00	6.00
121	Amare Stoudemire JSY	12.00	5.00
122	Yao Ming JSY	15.00	6.00
123	Kenyon Martin JSY	8.00	3.00
124	Allen Iverson JSY	12.00	5.00
125	Peja Stojakovic JSY	8.00	3.00
126	Drew Gooden JSY	8.00	3.00
127	Ray Allen JSY	8.00	3.00
128	Ben Wallace JSY	8.00	3.00
129	Andrei Kirilenko JSY	8.00	3.00
130	Quentin Richardson JSY	8.00	3.00
131	Larry Bird	15.00	6.00
132	George Gervin	5.00	2.00
133	Walt Frazier	5.00	2.00
134	Oscar Robertson	6.00	2.50
135	Elgin Baylor	5.00	2.00
136	Moses Malone	6.00	2.50
137	Pete Maravich	25.00	10.00
138	Bob Cousy	6.00	2.50
139	Earl Monroe	5.00	2.00
140	Kareem Abdul-Jabbar	8.00	3.00
141	Isiah Thomas	5.00	2.00
142	Kevin McHale	6.00	2.50
143	Bill Walton	6.00	2.50

#	Player		
144	John Havlicek	6.00	2.50
145	Rick Barry	5.00	2.00
146	Wilt Chamberlain	10.00	4.00
147	Bill Russell	6.00	2.50
148	Willis Reed	5.00	2.00
149	Julius Erving	8.00	3.00
150	Drazen Petrovic	8.00	3.00
151	Andre Iguodala RC	10.00	4.00
152	Luke Jackson RC	5.00	2.00
153	Kirk Snyder RC	5.00	2.00
154	Kevin Martin RC	6.00	2.50
155	Antonio Burks RC	5.00	2.00
156	Robert Swift RC	5.00	2.00
157	Dorell Wright RC	8.00	3.00
158	David Harrison RC	5.00	2.00
159	Dwight Howard RC	15.00	6.00
160	Al Jefferson RC	10.00	4.00
161	Justin Reed AU RC	20.00	8.00
162	Shaun Livingston AU RC	30.00	12.50
163	Luol Deng AU RC	30.00	12.50
164	Josh Smith AU RC	30.00	12.50
165	Jameer Nelson AU RC	30.00	12.50
166	Pavel Podkolzin AU RC	20.00	8.00
167	Emeka Okafor AU RC	50.00	20.00
168	Kris Humphries AU RC	20.00	8.00
169	J.R. Smith AU RC	30.00	12.50
170	Sebastian Telfair AU RC	20.00	8.00
171	Sasha Vujacic AU RC	20.00	8.00
172	Tony Allen AU RC	25.00	10.00
173	Romain Sato AU RC	20.00	8.00
174	Ben Gordon AU RC	60.00	25.00
175	Devin Harris AU RC	30.00	12.50
176	Josh Childress AU RC	20.00	8.00
177	Andre Barrett AU RC	20.00	8.00
178	Jackson Vroman AU RC	20.00	8.00
179	Lionel Chalmers AU RC	20.00	8.00
180	Delonte West AU RC	40.00	15.00
181	Nenad Krstic AU RC	25.00	10.00
182	Donta Smith AU RC	20.00	8.00
183	Chris Duhon AU RC	30.00	12.50
184	Peter John Ramos AU RC	20.00	8.00
185	Bernard Robinson AU RC	20.00	8.00
186	Beno Udrih AU RC	25.00	10.00
187	Andris Biedrins AU RC	30.00	12.50
188	Trevor Ariza AU RC	25.00	10.00
189	Rafael Araujo AU RC	20.00	8.00
190	Andres Nocioni AU RC	25.00	10.00
191	Draft Pick #1	30.00	12.50
192	Draft Pick #2	40.00	15.00
193	Draft Pick #3	25.00	10.00
194	Chris Paul	30.00	12.50
195	Draft Pick #5	20.00	8.00
196	Draft Pick #6	15.00	6.00
197	Draft Pick #7	12.00	5.00
198	Draft Pick #8	10.00	4.00
199	Draft Pick #9	10.00	4.00
200	Draft Pick #10	12.00	5.00
201	Draft Pick #11	8.00	3.00
202	Draft Pick #12	6.00	2.50
203	Draft Pick #13	20.00	8.00
204	Draft Pick #14	20.00	8.00
205	Draft Pick #15	10.00	4.00
206	Draft Pick #16	10.00	4.00
207	Draft Pick #17	10.00	4.00
208	Draft Pick #18	25.00	10.00
209	Draft Pick #19	15.00	6.00
210	Draft Pick #20	12.00	5.00
211	Draft Pick #21	10.00	4.00
212	Draft Pick #22	6.00	2.50
213	Draft Pick #23	10.00	4.00
214	Draft Pick #24	20.00	8.00
215	Daniel Ewing	6.00	2.50
216	Draft Pick #26	6.00	2.50
217	Draft Pick #27	6.00	2.50
218	Draft Pick #28	6.00	2.50
219	Draft Pick #29	8.00	3.00
220	Draft Pick #30	6.00	2.50

2005-06 Finest

COMP.SET w/o SP's (100)	40.00	15.00
COMMON CARD (1-100)	.25	.10
COMMON CELEB (101-105)	6.00	2.50
COMMON ROOKIE (106-125)	4.00	1.50
COMMON RC (126-139)	12.00	5.00
COMMON DRAFT EXCH (140-169)		
1 Shaquille O'Neal	2.50	1.00

#	Player		
2	Eddy Curry	.60	.25
3	Ben Wallace	1.00	.40
4	Wally Szczerbiak	.60	.25
5	Richard Jefferson	.60	.25
6	Josh Howard	.60	.25
7	Grant Hill	1.00	.40
8	Desmond Mason	.30	.10
9	Corey Maggette	.60	.25
10	Caron Butler	.60	.25
11	Andrei Kirilenko	1.00	.40
12	Al Harrington	.30	.10
13	Tony Parker	1.00	.40
14	Stephon Marbury	1.00	.40
15	Rafer Alston	.30	.10
16	Marquis Daniels	.60	.25
17	Luke Ridnour		
18	Kirk Hinrich		
19	Jason Kidd		
20	Morris Peterson	.60	.25
21	Yao Ming	2.50	1.00
22	Nenad Krstic	.60	.25
23	Mehmet Okur	.30	.10
24	Shareef Abdur-Rahim	1.00	.40
25	Rashard Lewis	1.00	.40
26	Luol Deng	1.00	.40
27	Elton Brand	1.00	.40
28	Dirk Nowitzki	1.50	.60
29	Bobby Simmons	.30	.10
30	Antawn Jamison	1.00	.40
31	Tracy McGrady	2.50	1.00
32	Steve Francis	1.00	.40
33	Kobe Bryant	4.00	1.50
34	Jason Richardson	1.00	.40
35	J.R. Smith	.60	.25
36	Tayshaun Prince	1.00	.40
37	Chauncey Billups	1.00	.40
38	Allen Iverson	2.00	.75
39	Ricky Davis	1.00	.40
40	Josh Smith	1.00	.40
41	Brad Miller	1.00	.40
42	Zach Randolph	1.00	.40
43	Troy Murphy	1.00	.40
44	Shawn Marion	1.00	.40
45	Pau Gasol	1.00	.40
46	Lamar Odom	1.00	.40
47	Drew Gooden	.60	.25
48	Darius Miles	1.00	.40
49	Chris Bosh	1.00	.40
50	Antoine Walker	1.00	.40
51	Amare Stoudemire	2.00	.75
52	Rasheed Wallace	1.00	.40
53	Emeka Okafor	1.50	.60
54	Steve Nash	1.00	.40
55	Sam Cassell	1.00	.40
56	Michael Finley	1.00	.40
57	Manu Ginobili	.60	.25
58	Mike Dunleavy	.60	.25
59	Jason Terry	1.00	.40
60	Jalen Rose	.75	.30
61	Ron Artest	.60	.25
62	Marcus Camby	.30	.10
63	Udonis Haslem	1.00	.40
64	Kenyon Martin	1.00	.40
65	Gerald Wallace	.60	.25
66	David West	.60	.25
67	Samuel Dalembert	.30	.10
68	Jermaine O'Neal	1.00	.40
69	Dwight Howard	1.25	.50

☐ 70	T.J. Ford	.60	.25	☐ 156 Draft Pick #17	8.00	3.00	☐ 50 Chris Gatling	.15	.05
☐ 71	Smush Parker	.30	.10	☐ 157 Draft Pick #18	8.00	3.00	☐ 51 Billy Owens	.15	.05
☐ 72	Sebastian Telfair	.60	.25	☐ 158 Draft Pick #19	8.00	3.00	☐ 52 Latrell Sprewell	.50	.20
☐ 73	Ray Allen	1.00	.40	☐ 159 Draft Pick #20	8.00	3.00	☐ 53 Chris Webber	1.25	.50
☐ 74	Michael Redd	1.00	.40	☐ 160 Draft Pick #21	8.00	3.00	☐ 54 Sam Cassell	.50	.20
☐ 75	Larry Hughes	.60	.25	☐ 161 Draft Pick #22	8.00	3.00	☐ 55 Carl Herrera	.15	.05
☐ 76	Jamaal Tinsley	.60	.25	☐ 162 Draft Pick #23	8.00	3.00	☐ 56 Robert Horry	.30	.10
☐ 77	Chris Duhon	.60	.25	☐ 163 Draft Pick #24	8.00	3.00	☐ 57 Hakeem Olajuwon	.75	.30
☐ 78	Baron Davis	1.00	.40	☐ 164 Draft Pick #25	10.00	4.00	☐ 58 Kenny Smith	.15	.05
☐ 79	Andre Iguodala	1.00	.40	☐ 165 Draft Pick #26	10.00	4.00	☐ 59 Otis Thorpe	.15	.05
☐ 80	Paul Pierce	1.00	.40	☐ 166 Draft Pick #27	8.00	3.00	☐ 60 Antonio Davis	.15	.05
☐ 81	Zydrunas Ilgauskas	.30	.10	☐ 167 Draft Pick #28	8.00	3.00	☐ 61 Dale Davis	.15	.05
☐ 82	Tim Duncan	2.00	.75	☐ 168 Draft Pick #29	8.00	3.00	☐ 62 Reggie Miller	.50	.20
☐ 83	Shane Battier	1.00	.40	☐ 169 Draft Pick #30	8.00	3.00	☐ 63 Byron Scott	.30	.10
☐ 84	Peja Stojakovic	1.00	.40				☐ 64 Rik Smits	.15	.05
☐ 85	LeBron James	6.00	2.50	**1994-95 Flair**			☐ 65 Haywoode Workman	.15	.05
☐ 86	Kevin Garnett	2.00	.75				☐ 66 Terry Dehere	.15	.05
☐ 87	Chris Webber	1.00	.40				☐ 67 Harold Ellis	.15	.05
☐ 88	Carmelo Anthony	2.00	.75				☐ 68 Gary Grant	.15	.05
☐ 89	Vince Carter	2.50	1.00				☐ 69 Elmore Spencer	.15	.05
☐ 90	Stephen Jackson	.60	.25				☐ 70 Loy Vaught	.15	.05
☐ 91	Richard Hamilton	.60	.25				☐ 71 Elden Campbell	.15	.05
☐ 92	Mike Bibby	1.00	.40				☐ 72 Doug Christie	.30	.05
☐ 93	Marko Jaric	.30	.10				☐ 73 Vlade Divac	.15	.05
☐ 94	Jamal Crawford	.60	.25				☐ 74 George Lynch	.15	.05
☐ 95	Gilbert Arenas	1.00	.40				☐ 75 Anthony Peeler	.15	.05
☐ 96	Dwyane Wade	3.00	1.25				☐ 76 Nick Van Exel	.50	.20
☐ 97	Delonte West	.60	.25				☐ 77 James Worthy	.50	.20
☐ 98	Ben Gordon	2.00	.75				☐ 78 Bimbo Coles	.15	.05
☐ 99	Andre Miller	.60	.25				☐ 79 Harold Miner	.15	.05
☐ 100	Joe Johnson	.60	.25				☐ 80 John Salley	.15	.05
☐ 101	Jay-Z	6.00	2.50				☐ 81 Rony Seikaly	.15	.05
☐ 102	Shannon Elizabeth	6.00	2.50				☐ 82 Steve Smith	.30	.10
☐ 103	Jenny McCarthy	6.00	2.50	☐ COMPLETE SET (326)	50.00	25.00	☐ 83 Vin Baker	.50	.20
☐ 104	Carmen Electra	6.00	2.50	☐ COMPLETE SERIES 1 (175)	15.00	7.50	☐ 84 Jon Barry	.15	.05
☐ 105	Christie Brinkley	6.00	2.50	☐ COMPLETE SERIES 2 (151)	30.00	15.00	☐ 85 Todd Day	.15	.05
☐ 106	Chris Paul RC	15.00	6.00	☐ 1 Stacey Augmon	.15	.05	☐ 86 Lee Mayberry	.15	.05
☐ 107	Channing Frye RC	5.00	2.00	☐ 2 Mookie Blaylock	.15	.05	☐ 87 Eric Murdock	.15	.05
☐ 108	Ike Diogu RC	5.00	2.00	☐ 3 Craig Ehlo	.15	.05	☐ 88 Mike Brown	.15	.05
☐ 109	Marvin Williams RC	8.00	3.00	☐ 4 Jon Koncak	.15	.05	☐ 89 Christian Laettner	.30	.10
☐ 110	Rashad McCants RC	8.00	3.00	☐ 5 Andrew Lang	.15	.05	☐ 90 Isaiah Rider	.30	.10
☐ 111	Luther Head RC	5.00	2.00	☐ 6 Dee Brown	.15	.05	☐ 91 Doug West	.15	.05
☐ 112	Gerald Green RC	8.00	3.00	☐ 7 Sherman Douglas	.15	.05	☐ 92 Micheal Williams	.15	.05
☐ 113	Salim Stoudamire RC	5.00	2.00	☐ 8 Acie Earl	.15	.05	☐ 93 Kenny Anderson	.30	.10
☐ 114	Jose Calderon RC	4.00	1.50	☐ 9 Rick Fox	.15	.05	☐ 94 Benoit Benjamin	.15	.05
☐ 115	Andrew Bynum RC	10.00	4.00	☐ 10 Kevin Gamble	.15	.05	☐ 95 P.J. Brown	.15	.05
☐ 116	Wayne Simien RC	5.00	2.00	☐ 11 Xavier McDaniel	.15	.05	☐ 96 Derrick Coleman	.30	.10
☐ 117	Chris Taft RC	4.00	1.50	☐ 12 Dino Radja	.15	.05	☐ 97 Kevin Edwards	.15	.05
☐ 118	Ryan Gomes RC	4.00	1.50	☐ 13 Tony Bennett	.15	.05	☐ 98 Hubert Davis	.15	.05
☐ 119	Martell Webster RC	4.00	1.50	☐ 14 Dell Curry	.15	.05	☐ 99 Patrick Ewing	.50	.20
☐ 120	Johan Petro RC	4.00	1.50	☐ 15 Kenny Gattison	.15	.05	☐ 100 Derek Harper	.15	.05
☐ 121	Antoine Wright RC	4.00	1.50	☐ 16 Hersey Hawkins	.30	.10	☐ 101 Anthony Mason	.30	.10
☐ 122	Jarrett Jack RC	4.00	1.50	☐ 17 Larry Johnson	.30	.10	☐ 102 Charles Oakley	.15	.05
☐ 123	Daniel Ewing RC	5.00	2.00	☐ 18 Alonzo Mourning	.60	.25	☐ 103 Charles Smith	.15	.05
☐ 124	Joey Graham RC	4.00	1.50	☐ 19 David Wingate	.15	.05	☐ 104 John Starks	.15	.05
☐ 125	Nate Robinson RC	6.00	2.50	☐ 20 B.J. Armstrong	.15	.05	☐ 105 Nick Anderson	.15	.05
☐ 126	Andrew Bogut AU RC	25.00	10.00	☐ 21 Steve Kerr	.15	.05	☐ 106 Anfernee Hardaway	1.25	.50
☐ 127	Raymond Felton AU RC	25.00	10.00	☐ 22 Toni Kukoc	.75	.30	☐ 107 Shaquille O'Neal	2.50	1.00
☐ 128	Francisco Garcia AU RC	15.00	6.00	☐ 23 Pete Myers	.15	.05	☐ 108 Dennis Scott	.15	.05
☐ 129	Danny Granger AU RC	20.00	8.00	☐ 24 Scottie Pippen	1.50	.60	☐ 109 Jeff Turner	.15	.05
☐ 130	Orien Greene AU RC	12.00	5.00	☐ 25 Bill Wennington	.15	.05	☐ 110 Dana Barros	.15	.05
☐ 131	Sarunas Jasikevicius AU RC	15.00	6.00	☐ 26 Terrell Brandon	.30	.10	☐ 111 Shawn Bradley	.15	.05
☐ 132	Linas Kleiza AU RC	12.00	5.00	☐ 27 Brad Daugherty	.15	.05	☐ 112 Jeff Malone	.15	.05
☐ 133	David Lee AU RC	20.00	8.00	☐ 28 Tyrone Hill	.15	.05	☐ 113 Tim Perry	.15	.05
☐ 134	Sean May AU RC	15.00	6.00	☐ 29 Bobby Phills	.15	.05	☐ 114 Clarence Weatherspoon	.15	.05
☐ 135	Fabricio Oberto AU RC	12.00	5.00	☐ 30 Mark Price	.15	.05	☐ 115 Danny Ainge	.15	.05
☐ 136	Charlie Villanueva AU RC	20.00	8.00	☐ 31 Gerald Wilkins	.15	.05	☐ 116 Charles Barkley	.75	.30
☐ 137	Hakim Warrick AU RC	25.00	10.00	☐ 32 John Williams	.15	.05	☐ 117 A.C. Green	.30	.10
☐ 138	James Singleton AU RC	12.00	5.00	☐ 33 Lucious Harris	.15	.05	☐ 118 Kevin Johnson	.30	.10
☐ 139	Deron Williams AU RC	40.00	15.00	☐ 34 Jim Jackson	.30	.10	☐ 119 Dan Majerle	.15	.05
☐ 140	Draft Pick #1	12.00	5.00	☐ 35 Jamal Mashburn	.50	.20	☐ 120 Clyde Drexler	.50	.20
☐ 141	Draft Pick #2	12.00	5.00	☐ 36 Sean Rooks	.15	.05	☐ 121 Harvey Grant	.15	.05
☐ 142	Draft Pick #3	30.00	12.50	☐ 37 Doug Smith	.15	.05	☐ 122 Jerome Kersey	.15	.05
☐ 143	Draft Pick #4	12.00	5.00	☐ 38 Mahmoud Abdul-Rauf	.15	.05	☐ 123 Clifford Robinson	.15	.10
☐ 144	Draft Pick #5	12.00	5.00	☐ 39 LaPhonso Ellis	.15	.05	☐ 124 Rod Strickland	.30	.10
☐ 145	Draft Pick #6	25.00	10.00	☐ 40 Dikembe Mutombo	.30	.10	☐ 125 Buck Williams	.15	.05
☐ 146	Draft Pick #7	15.00	6.00	☐ 41 Robert Pack	.15	.05	☐ 126 Randy Brown	.15	.05
☐ 147	Draft Pick #8	15.00	6.00	☐ 42 Rodney Rogers	.15	.05	☐ 127 Olden Polynice	.15	.05
☐ 148	Draft Pick #9	12.00	5.00	☐ 43 Brian Williams	.15	.05	☐ 128 Mitch Richmond	.50	.20
☐ 149	Draft Pick #10	12.00	5.00	☐ 44 Reggie Williams	.15	.05	☐ 129 Lionel Simmons	.15	.05
☐ 150	Draft Pick #11	20.00	8.00	☐ 45 Joe Dumars	.50	.20	☐ 130 Spud Webb	.15	.05
☐ 151	Draft Pick #12	10.00	4.00	☐ 46 Allan Houston	.75	.30	☐ 131 Walt Williams	.15	.05
☐ 152	Draft Pick #13	10.00	4.00	☐ 47 Lindsey Hunter	.30	.10	☐ 132 Willie Anderson	.15	.05
☐ 153	Draft Pick #14	12.00	5.00	☐ 48 Terry Mills	.15	.05	☐ 133 Vinny Del Negro	.15	.05
☐ 154	Draft Pick #15	8.00	3.00	☐ 49 Victor Alexander	.15	.05	☐ 134 Sean Elliott	.30	.10
☐ 155	Draft Pick #16	8.00	3.00				☐ 135 Avery Johnson	.15	.05

#	Player		
❏ 136	J.R. Reid	.15	.05
❏ 137	David Robinson	.75	.30
❏ 138	Dennis Rodman	1.00	.40
❏ 139	Kendall Gill	.30	.10
❏ 140	Ervin Johnson	.15	.05
❏ 141	Shawn Kemp	.75	.30
❏ 142	Nate McMillan	.15	.05
❏ 143	Gary Payton	.75	.30
❏ 144	Sam Perkins	.30	.10
❏ 145	David Benoit	.15	.05
❏ 146	Jeff Hornacek	.30	.10
❏ 147	Jay Humphries	.15	.05
❏ 148	Karl Malone	.75	.30
❏ 149	Bryon Russell	.15	.05
❏ 150	Felton Spencer	.15	.05
❏ 151	John Stockton	.50	.20
❏ 152	Rex Chapman	.15	.05
❏ 153	Calbert Cheaney	.15	.05
❏ 154	Tom Gugliotta	.30	.10
❏ 155	Don MacLean	.15	.05
❏ 156	Gheorghe Muresan	.15	.05
❏ 157	Doug Overton	.15	.05
❏ 158	Brent Price	.15	.05
❏ 159	Derrick Coleman USA	.15	.05
❏ 160	Joe Dumars USA	.30	.10
❏ 161	Tim Hardaway USA	.30	.10
❏ 162	Kevin Johnson USA	.15	.05
❏ 163	Larry Johnson USA	.15	.05
❏ 164	Shawn Kemp USA	.50	.20
❏ 165	Dan Majerle USA	.15	.05
❏ 166	Reggie Miller USA	.30	.10
❏ 167	Alonzo Mourning USA	.50	.20
❏ 168	Shaquille O'Neal USA	1.00	.40
❏ 169	Mark Price USA	.15	.05
❏ 170	Steve Smith USA	.15	.05
❏ 171	Isiah Thomas USA	.30	.10
❏ 172	Dominique Wilkins USA	.30	.10
❏ 173	Checklist	.15	.05
❏ 174	Checklist	.15	.05
❏ 175	Checklist	.15	.05
❏ 176	Tyrone Corbin	.15	.05
❏ 177	Grant Long	.15	.05
❏ 178	Ken Norman	.15	.05
❏ 179	Steve Smith	.30	.10
❏ 180	Blue Edwards	.15	.05
❏ 181	Pervis Ellison	.15	.05
❏ 182	Greg Minor RC	.15	.05
❏ 183	Eric Montross RC	.15	.05
❏ 184	Derek Strong	.15	.05
❏ 185	David Wesley	.15	.05
❏ 186	Dominique Wilkins	.50	.20
❏ 187	Michael Adams	.15	.05
❏ 188	Muggsy Bogues	.30	.10
❏ 189	Scott Burrell	.15	.05
❏ 190	Darrin Hancock	.15	.05
❏ 191	Robert Parish	.30	.10
❏ 192	Jud Buechler	.15	.05
❏ 193	Ron Harper	.30	.10
❏ 194	Larry Krystkowiak	.15	.05
❏ 195	Will Perdue	.15	.05
❏ 196	Dickey Simpkins RC	.15	.05
❏ 197	Michael Cage	.15	.05
❏ 198	Tony Campbell	.15	.05
❏ 199	Danny Ferry	.15	.05
❏ 200	Chris Mills	.30	.10
❏ 201	Popeye Jones	.15	.05
❏ 202	Jason Kidd RC	5.00	2.00
❏ 203	Roy Tarpley	.15	.05
❏ 204	Lorenzo Williams	.15	.05
❏ 205	Dale Ellis	.15	.05
❏ 206	Tom Hammonds	.15	.05
❏ 207	Jalen Rose RC	2.00	.75
❏ 208	Reggie Slater	.15	.05
❏ 209	Bryant Stith	.15	.05
❏ 210	Rafael Addison	.15	.05
❏ 211	Bill Curley RC	.15	.05
❏ 212	Johnny Dawkins	.15	.05
❏ 213	Grant Hill RC	3.00	1.25
❏ 214	Mark Macon	.15	.05
❏ 215	Oliver Miller	.15	.05
❏ 216	Ivano Newbill	.15	.05
❏ 217	Mark West	.15	.05
❏ 218	Tom Gugliotta	.15	.10
❏ 219	Tim Hardaway	.50	.20
❏ 220	Keith Jennings	.15	.05
❏ 221	Dwayne Morton	.15	.05
❏ 222	Chris Mullin	.50	.20
❏ 223	Ricky Pierce	.15	.05
❏ 224	Carlos Rogers RC	.15	.05
❏ 225	Clifford Rozier RC	.15	.05
❏ 226	Rony Seikaly	.15	.05
❏ 227	Tim Breaux	.15	.05
❏ 228	Scott Brooks	.15	.05
❏ 229	Mario Elie	.15	.05
❏ 230	Vernon Maxwell	.15	.05
❏ 231	Zan Tabak	.15	.05
❏ 232	Mark Jackson	.15	.05
❏ 233	Derrick McKey	.15	.05
❏ 234	Tony Massenburg	.15	.05
❏ 235	Lamond Murray RC	.30	.10
❏ 236	Bo Outlaw	.15	.05
❏ 237	Eric Piatkowski RC	.15	.05
❏ 238	Pooh Richardson	.15	.05
❏ 239	Malik Sealy	.15	.05
❏ 240	Cedric Ceballos	.15	.05
❏ 241	Eddie Jones RC	2.50	1.00
❏ 242	Anthony Miller	.15	.05
❏ 243	Tony Smith	.15	.05
❏ 244	Sedale Threatt	.15	.05
❏ 245	Ledell Eackles	.15	.05
❏ 246	Kevin Gamble	.15	.05
❏ 247	Matt Geiger	.15	.05
❏ 248	Brad Lohaus	.15	.05
❏ 249	Billy Owens	.15	.05
❏ 250	Khalid Reeves RC	.15	.05
❏ 251	Glen Rice	.30	.10
❏ 252	Kevin Willis	.15	.05
❏ 253	Marty Conlon	.15	.05
❏ 254	Eric Mobley RC	.15	.05
❏ 255	Johnny Newman	.15	.05
❏ 256	Ed Pinckney	.15	.05
❏ 257	Glenn Robinson RC	1.50	.60
❏ 258	Pat Durham	.15	.05
❏ 259	Howard Eisley	.15	.05
❏ 260	Winston Garland	.15	.05
❏ 261	Stacey King	.15	.05
❏ 262	Donyell Marshall RC	.50	.20
❏ 263	Sean Rooks	.15	.05
❏ 264	Chris Smith	.15	.05
❏ 265	Chris Childs RC	.50	.20
❏ 266	Sleepy Floyd	.15	.05
❏ 267	Armon Gilliam	.15	.05
❏ 268	Sean Higgins	.15	.05
❏ 269	Rex Walters	.15	.05
❏ 270	Greg Anthony	.15	.05
❏ 271	Charlie Ward RC	.50	.20
❏ 272	Herb Williams	.15	.05
❏ 273	Monty Williams RC	.15	.05
❏ 274	Anthony Avent	.15	.05
❏ 275	Anthony Bowie	.15	.05
❏ 276	Horace Grant	.30	.10
❏ 277	Donald Royal	.15	.05
❏ 278	Brian Shaw	.15	.05
❏ 279	Brooks Thompson RC	.15	.05
❏ 280	Derrick Alston	.15	.05
❏ 281	Willie Burton	.15	.05
❏ 282	Greg Graham	.15	.05
❏ 283	B.J. Tyler RC	.15	.05
❏ 284	Scott Williams	.15	.05
❏ 285	Sharone Wright RC	.15	.05
❏ 286	Joe Kleine	.15	.05
❏ 287	Danny Manning	.30	.10
❏ 288	Elliot Perry	.15	.05
❏ 289	Wesley Person RC	.50	.20
❏ 290	Trevor Ruffin RC	.15	.05
❏ 291	Wayman Tisdale	.15	.05
❏ 292	Mark Bryant	.15	.05
❏ 293	Chris Dudley	.15	.05
❏ 294	Aaron McKie RC	1.00	.40
❏ 295	Tracy Murray	.15	.05
❏ 296	Terry Porter	.15	.05
❏ 297	James Robinson	.15	.05
❏ 298	Alaa Abdelnaby	.15	.05
❏ 299	Duane Causwell	.15	.05
❏ 300	Brian Grant RC	1.25	.50
❏ 301	Bobby Hurley	.15	.05
❏ 302	Michael Smith RC	.15	.05
❏ 303	Terry Cummings	.15	.05
❏ 304	Moses Malone	.50	.20
❏ 305	Julius Nwosu	.15	.05
❏ 306	Chuck Person	.15	.05
❏ 307	Doc Rivers	.30	.10
❏ 308	Vincent Askew	.15	.05
❏ 309	Sarunas Marciulionis	.15	.05
❏ 310	Detlef Schrempf	.30	.10
❏ 311	Dontonio Wingfield	.15	.05
❏ 312	Antoine Carr	.15	.05
❏ 313	Tom Chambers	.15	.05
❏ 314	John Crotty	.15	.05
❏ 315	Adam Keefe	.15	.05
❏ 316	Jamie Watson RC	.15	.05
❏ 317	Mitchell Butler	.15	.05
❏ 318	Kevin Duckworth	.15	.05
❏ 319	Juwan Howard RC	1.25	.50
❏ 320	Jim McIlvaine	.15	.05
❏ 321	Scott Skiles	.15	.05
❏ 322	Anthony Tucker RC	.15	.05
❏ 323	Chris Webber	1.25	.50
❏ 324	Checklist	.15	.05
❏ 325	Checklist	.15	.05
❏ 326	Michael Jordan	10.00	5.00

1995-96 Flair

❏	COMPLETE SET (250)	80.00	40.00
❏	COMPLETE SERIES 1 (150)	40.00	20.00
❏	COMPLETE SERIES 2 (100)	40.00	20.00
❏	COMMON CARD (1-150)	.60	.25
❏	COMMON CARD (151-250)	.40	.15
❏ 1	Stacey Augmon	.60	.25
❏ 2	Mookie Blaylock	.60	.25
❏ 3	Grant Long	.60	.25
❏ 4	Steve Smith	1.50	.60
❏ 5	Dee Brown	.60	.25
❏ 6	Sherman Douglas	.60	.25
❏ 7	Eric Montross	.60	.25
❏ 8	Dino Radja	.60	.25
❏ 9	David Wesley	.60	.25
❏ 10	Muggsy Bogues	1.50	.60
❏ 11	Scott Burrell	.60	.25
❏ 12	Dell Curry	.60	.25
❏ 13	Larry Johnson	1.50	.60
❏ 14	Alonzo Mourning	1.50	.60
❏ 15	Michael Jordan	12.00	6.00
❏ 16	Steve Kerr	1.50	.60
❏ 17	Toni Kukoc	1.50	.60
❏ 18	Scottie Pippen	3.00	1.25
❏ 19	Terrell Brandon	.60	.25
❏ 20	Tyrone Hill	.60	.25
❏ 21	Chris Mills	.60	.25
❏ 22	Bobby Phills	.60	.25
❏ 23	Mark Price	1.50	.60
❏ 24	John Williams	.60	.25
❏ 25	Jim Jackson	.60	.25
❏ 26	Popeye Jones	.60	.25
❏ 27	Jason Kidd	6.00	2.50
❏ 28	Jamal Mashburn	1.50	.60
❏ 29	Lorenzo Williams	.60	.25
❏ 30	Mahmoud Abdul-Rauf	.60	.25
❏ 31	Dikembe Mutombo	1.50	.60
❏ 32	Robert Pack	.60	.25
❏ 33	Jalen Rose	2.50	1.00
❏ 34	Bryant Stith	.60	.25
❏ 35	Reggie Williams	.60	.25
❏ 36	Joe Dumars	2.00	.75
❏ 37	Grant Hill	2.50	1.00
❏ 38	Allan Houston	1.50	.60
❏ 39	Lindsey Hunter	.60	.25
❏ 40	Terry Mills	.60	.25
❏ 41	Chris Gatling	1.50	.60
❏ 42	Tim Hardaway	1.50	.60

#	Player		
❑ 43	Donyell Marshall	1.50	.60
❑ 44	Chris Mullin	2.00	.75
❑ 45	Carlos Rogers	.60	.25
❑ 46	Clifford Rozier	.60	.25
❑ 47	Latrell Sprewell	2.00	.75
❑ 48	Sam Cassell	2.00	.75
❑ 49	Clyde Drexler	2.00	.75
❑ 50	Mario Elie	.60	.25
❑ 51	Robert Horry	1.50	.60
❑ 52	Hakeem Olajuwon	2.00	.75
❑ 53	Kenny Smith	.60	.25
❑ 54	Antonio Davis	.60	.25
❑ 55	Dale Davis	.60	.25
❑ 56	Mark Jackson	1.50	.60
❑ 57	Derrick McKey	.60	.25
❑ 58	Reggie Miller	2.00	.75
❑ 59	Rik Smits	1.50	.60
❑ 60	Lamond Murray	.60	.25
❑ 61	Pooh Richardson	.60	.25
❑ 62	Malik Sealy	.60	.25
❑ 63	Loy Vaught	.60	.25
❑ 64	Elden Campbell	.60	.25
❑ 65	Cedric Ceballos	.60	.25
❑ 66	Vlade Divac	1.50	.60
❑ 67	Eddie Jones	2.50	1.00
❑ 68	Nick Van Exel	2.00	.75
❑ 69	Bimbo Coles	.60	.25
❑ 70	Billy Owens	.60	.25
❑ 71	Khalid Reeves	.60	.25
❑ 72	Glen Rice	1.50	.60
❑ 73	Kevin Willis	1.50	.60
❑ 74	Vin Baker	1.50	.60
❑ 75	Todd Day	.60	.25
❑ 76	Eric Murdock	.60	.25
❑ 77	Glenn Robinson	2.00	.75
❑ 78	Tom Gugliotta	.60	.25
❑ 79	Christian Laettner	1.50	.60
❑ 80	Isaiah Rider	.60	.25
❑ 81	Doug West	.60	.25
❑ 82	Kenny Anderson	1.50	.60
❑ 83	P.J. Brown	.60	.25
❑ 84	Derrick Coleman	.60	.25
❑ 85	Armon Gilliam	.60	.25
❑ 86	Chris Morris	.60	.25
❑ 87	Hubert Davis	.60	.25
❑ 88	Patrick Ewing	2.00	.75
❑ 89	Derek Harper	1.50	.60
❑ 90	Anthony Mason	1.50	.60
❑ 91	Charles Oakley	.60	.25
❑ 92	Charles Smith	.60	.25
❑ 93	John Starks	1.50	.60
❑ 94	Nick Anderson	.60	.25
❑ 95	Horace Grant	1.50	.60
❑ 96	Anfernee Hardaway	2.00	.75
❑ 97	Shaquille O'Neal	5.00	2.00
❑ 98	Dennis Scott	.60	.25
❑ 99	Brian Shaw	.60	.25
❑ 100	Dana Barros	.60	.25
❑ 101	Shawn Bradley	.60	.25
❑ 102	Clarence Weatherspoon	.60	.25
❑ 103	Sharone Wright	.60	.25
❑ 104	Charles Barkley	2.50	1.00
❑ 105	A.C. Green	1.50	.60
❑ 106	Kevin Johnson	1.50	.60
❑ 107	Dan Majerle	1.50	.60
❑ 108	Danny Manning	1.50	.60
❑ 109	Elliot Perry	.60	.25
❑ 110	Wesley Person	.60	.25
❑ 111	Terry Porter	.60	.25
❑ 112	Clifford Robinson	.60	.25
❑ 113	Rod Strickland	.60	.25
❑ 114	Otis Thorpe	.60	.25
❑ 115	Buck Williams	.60	.25
❑ 116	Brian Grant	2.00	.75
❑ 117	Bobby Hurley	.60	.25
❑ 118	Olden Polynice	.60	.25
❑ 119	Mitch Richmond	1.50	.60
❑ 120	Walt Williams	.60	.25
❑ 121	Vinny Del Negro	.60	.25
❑ 122	Sean Elliott	1.50	.60
❑ 123	Avery Johnson	.60	.25
❑ 124	David Robinson	2.00	.75
❑ 125	Dennis Rodman	1.50	.60
❑ 126	Shawn Kemp	1.50	.60
❑ 127	Nate McMillan	.60	.25
❑ 128	Gary Payton	2.00	.75
❑ 129	Sam Perkins	1.50	.60
❑ 130	Detlef Schrempf	1.50	.60
❑ 131	B.J. Armstrong	.60	.25
❑ 132	Jerome Kersey	.60	.25
❑ 133	Oliver Miller	.60	.25
❑ 134	John Salley	.60	.25
❑ 135	David Benoit	.60	.25
❑ 136	Antoine Carr	.60	.25
❑ 137	Jeff Hornacek	1.50	.60
❑ 138	Karl Malone	2.50	1.00
❑ 139	John Stockton	2.50	1.00
❑ 140	Greg Anthony	.60	.25
❑ 141	Benoit Benjamin	.60	.25
❑ 142	Blue Edwards	.60	.25
❑ 143	Byron Scott	.60	.25
❑ 144	Calbert Cheaney	.60	.25
❑ 145	Juwan Howard	2.00	.75
❑ 146	Gheorghe Muresan	.60	.25
❑ 147	Scott Skiles	.60	.25
❑ 148	Chris Webber	2.50	1.00
❑ 149	Checklist	.60	.25
❑ 150	Checklist	.60	.25
❑ 151	Stacey Augmon	.40	.15
❑ 152	Mookie Blaylock	.40	.15
❑ 153	Andrew Lang	.40	.15
❑ 154	Steve Smith	.75	.30
❑ 155	Dana Barros	.40	.15
❑ 156	Rick Fox	.75	.30
❑ 157	Kendall Gill	.40	.15
❑ 158	Khalid Reeves	.40	.15
❑ 159	Glen Rice	.75	.30
❑ 160	Dennis Rodman	1.50	.60
❑ 161	Dan Majerle	.75	.30
❑ 162	Tony Dumas	.40	.15
❑ 163	Dale Ellis	.40	.15
❑ 164	Otis Thorpe	.40	.15
❑ 165	Rony Seikaly	.40	.15
❑ 166	Sam Cassell	1.25	.50
❑ 167	Clyde Drexler	1.25	.50
❑ 168	Robert Horry	.75	.30
❑ 169	Hakeem Olajuwon	2.00	.75
❑ 170	Ricky Pierce	.40	.15
❑ 171	Rodney Rogers	.40	.15
❑ 172	Brian Williams	.40	.15
❑ 173	Magic Johnson	2.00	.75
❑ 174	Alonzo Mourning	.75	.30
❑ 175	Lee Mayberry	.40	.15
❑ 176	Terry Porter	.40	.15
❑ 177	Shawn Bradley	.40	.15
❑ 178	Jayson Williams	.40	.15
❑ 179	Gary Grant	.40	.15
❑ 180	Jon Koncak	.40	.15
❑ 181	Derrick Coleman	.60	.25
❑ 182	Vernon Maxwell	.40	.15
❑ 183	John Williams	.40	.15
❑ 184	Aaron McKie	1.50	.60
❑ 185	Michael Smith	.40	.15
❑ 186	Chuck Person	.40	.15
❑ 187	Hersey Hawkins	.40	.15
❑ 188	Shawn Kemp	1.50	.60
❑ 189	Gary Payton	2.00	.75
❑ 190	Detlef Schrempf	.75	.30
❑ 191	Chris Morris	.40	.15
❑ 192	Robert Pack	.40	.15
❑ 193	Willie Anderson EXP	.40	.15
❑ 194	Oliver Miller EXP	.40	.15
❑ 195	Alan Robertson EXP	.40	.15
❑ 196	Greg Anthony EXP	.40	.15
❑ 197	Blue Edwards EXP	.40	.15
❑ 198	Byron Scott EXP	.40	.15
❑ 199	Cory Alexander RC	.40	.15
❑ 200	Brent Barry RC	1.25	.50
❑ 201	Travis Best RC	.60	.25
❑ 202	Jason Caffey RC	.75	.30
❑ 203	Sasha Danilovic RC	.40	.15
❑ 204	Tyus Edney RC	.40	.15
❑ 205	Michael Finley RC	3.00	1.25
❑ 206	Kevin Garnett RC	6.00	2.50
❑ 207	Alan Henderson RC	1.25	.50
❑ 208	Antonio McDyess RC	2.50	1.00
❑ 209	Loren Meyer RC	.40	.15
❑ 210	Lawrence Moten RC	.40	.15
❑ 211	Ed O'Bannon RC	.40	.15
❑ 212	Greg Ostertag RC	.40	.15
❑ 213	Cherokee Parks RC	.40	.15
❑ 214	Theo Ratliff RC	1.50	.60
❑ 215	Bryant Reeves RC	1.25	.50
❑ 216	Shawn Respert RC	.60	.25
❑ 217	Arvydas Sabonis RC	1.50	.60
❑ 218	Joe Smith RC	2.00	.75
❑ 219	Jerry Stackhouse RC	4.00	1.50
❑ 220	Damon Stoudamire RC	2.50	1.00
❑ 221	Bob Sura RC	.75	.30
❑ 222	Kurt Thomas RC	.75	.30
❑ 223	Gary Trent RC	.40	.15
❑ 224	David Vaughn RC	.40	.15
❑ 225	Rasheed Wallace RC	3.00	1.25
❑ 226	Eric Williams RC	.75	.30
❑ 227	Corliss Williamson RC	1.25	.50
❑ 228	George Zidek RC	.40	.15
❑ 229	Vin Baker STY	.40	.15
❑ 230	Charles Barkley STY	1.25	.50
❑ 231	Patrick Ewing STY	.75	.30
❑ 232	Anfernee Hardaway STY	1.50	.60
❑ 233	Grant Hill STY	1.25	.50
❑ 234	Larry Johnson STY	.40	.15
❑ 235	Michael Jordan STY	4.00	1.50
❑ 236	Jason Kidd STY	2.00	.75
❑ 237	Karl Malone STY	1.25	.50
❑ 238	Jamal Mashburn STY	.40	.15
❑ 239	Reggie Miller STY	.75	.30
❑ 240	Shaquille O'Neal STY	1.50	.60
❑ 241	Scottie Pippen STY	1.25	.50
❑ 242	Mitch Richmond STY	.40	.15
❑ 243	Clifford Robinson STY	.40	.15
❑ 244	David Robinson STY	.75	.30
❑ 245	Glenn Robinson STY	.75	.30
❑ 246	John Stockton STY	1.25	.50
❑ 247	Nick Van Exel STY	.40	.15
❑ 248	Chris Webber STY	1.25	.50
❑ 249	Checklist	.40	.15
❑ 250	Checklist	.40	.15

1996-97 Flair Showcase Row 2

❑	COMPLETE SET (90)	60.00	25.00
❑ 1	Anfernee Hardaway	1.50	.60
❑ 2	Mitch Richmond	1.00	.40
❑ 3	Allen Iverson RC	8.00	3.00
❑ 4	Charles Barkley	2.00	.75
❑ 5	Juwan Howard	1.00	.40
❑ 6	David Robinson	1.50	.60
❑ 7	Gary Payton	1.50	.60
❑ 8	Kerry Kittles RC	1.50	.60
❑ 9	Dennis Rodman	1.00	.40
❑ 10	Shaquille O'Neal	4.00	1.50
❑ 11	Stephon Marbury RC	4.00	1.50
❑ 12	John Stockton	1.50	.60
❑ 13	Glenn Robinson	1.50	.60
❑ 14	Hakeem Olajuwon	1.50	.60
❑ 15	Jason Kidd	2.50	1.00
❑ 16	Jerry Stackhouse	2.00	.75
❑ 17	Joe Smith	1.00	.40
❑ 18	Reggie Miller	1.50	.60
❑ 19	Grant Hill	3.00	1.25
❑ 20	Damon Stoudamire	1.50	.60
❑ 21	Kevin Garnett	3.00	1.25
❑ 22	Clyde Drexler	1.50	.60
❑ 23	Michael Jordan	10.00	5.00
❑ 24	Antonio McDyess	1.00	.40
❑ 25	Chris Webber	1.50	.60
❑ 26	Antoine Walker RC	4.00	1.50
❑ 27	Scottie Pippen	2.50	1.00
❑ 28	Karl Malone	1.50	.60

□			
□ 29	Shareef Abdur-Rahim RC	4.00	1.50
□ 30	Shawn Kemp	1.00	.40
□ 31	Kobe Bryant RC	12.00	5.00
□ 32	Derrick Coleman	1.00	.40
□ 33	Alonzo Mourning	1.00	.40
□ 34	Anthony Mason	1.00	.40
□ 35	Ray Allen RC	3.00	1.25
□ 36	Arvydas Sabonis	1.00	.40
□ 37	Brian Grant	1.50	.60
□ 38	Bryant Reeves	.50	.20
□ 39	Christian Laettner	1.00	.40
□ 40	Tom Gugliotta	.50	.20
□ 41	Latrell Sprewell	1.50	.60
□ 42	Erick Dampier RC	1.50	.60
□ 43	Gheorghe Muresan	.50	.20
□ 44	Glen Rice	1.00	.40
□ 45	Patrick Ewing	1.50	.60
□ 46	Jim Jackson	.50	.20
□ 47	Michael Finley	2.00	.75
□ 48	Toni Kukoc	1.00	.40
□ 49	Marcus Camby RC	2.00	.75
□ 50	Kenny Anderson	.50	.20
□ 51	Mark Price	1.00	.40
□ 52	Tim Hardaway	1.00	.40
□ 53	Mookie Blaylock	.50	.20
□ 54	Steve Smith	1.00	.40
□ 55	Terrell Brandon	1.00	.40
□ 56	Lorenzen Wright RC	1.00	.40
□ 57	Sasha Danilovic	.50	.20
□ 58	Jeff Hornacek	1.00	.40
□ 59	Eddie Jones	1.50	.60
□ 60	Vin Baker	1.00	.40
□ 61	Chris Childs	.50	.20
□ 62	Clifford Robinson	.50	.20
□ 63	Anthony Peeler	.50	.20
□ 64	Dino Radja	.50	.20
□ 65	Joe Dumars	1.50	.60
□ 66	Loy Vaught	.50	.20
□ 67	Rony Seikaly	.50	.20
□ 68	Vitaly Potapenko RC	.50	.20
□ 69	Chris Gatling	.50	.20
□ 70	Dale Ellis	.50	.20
□ 71	Allan Houston	1.00	.40
□ 72	Doug Christie	1.00	.40
□ 73	LaPhonso Ellis	.50	.20
□ 74	Kendall Gill	.50	.20
□ 75	Rik Smits	1.00	.40
□ 76	Bobby Phills	.50	.20
□ 77	Malik Sealy	.50	.20
□ 78	Sean Elliott	1.00	.40
□ 79	Vlade Divac	.50	.20
□ 80	David Wesley	.50	.20
□ 81	Dominique Wilkins	1.50	.60
□ 82	Danny Manning	1.00	.40
□ 83	Detlef Schrempf	1.00	.40
□ 84	Hersey Hawkins	1.00	.40
□ 85	Lindsey Hunter	.50	.20
□ 86	Mahmoud Abdul-Rauf	.50	.20
□ 87	Shawn Bradley	.50	.20
□ 88	Horace Grant	1.00	.40
□ 89	Cedric Ceballos	.50	.20
□ 90	Jamal Mashburn	1.00	.40
□ NNO	Jerry Stackhouse Promo		
	3-card strip	3.00	1.25

1997-98 Flair Showcase Row 3

□ COMPLETE SET (80)		50.00	25.00
□ 1	Michael Jordan	10.00	4.00
□ 2	Grant Hill	1.50	.60
□ 3	Allen Iverson	4.00	1.50
□ 4	Kevin Garnett	3.00	1.25
□ 5	Tim Duncan RC	6.00	2.50
□ 6	Shawn Kemp	1.00	.40
□ 7	Shaquille O'Neal	4.00	1.50
□ 8	Antoine Walker	2.00	.75
□ 9	Shareef Abdur-Rahim	2.50	1.00
□ 10	Damon Stoudamire	1.00	.40
□ 11	Anfernee Hardaway	1.50	.60
□ 12	Keith Van Horn RC	2.00	.75
□ 13	Dennis Rodman	1.00	.40
□ 14	Ron Mercer RC	1.50	.60
□ 15	Stephon Marbury	2.00	.75
□ 16	Scottie Pippen	2.50	1.00
□ 17	Kerry Kittles	1.50	.60
□ 18	Kobe Bryant	6.00	2.50
□ 19	Marcus Camby	1.50	.60
□ 20	Chauncey Billups RC	4.00	1.50
□ 21	Tracy McGrady RC	8.00	3.00
□ 22	Joe Smith	1.00	.40
□ 23	Brevin Knight RC	1.00	.40
□ 24	Danny Fortson RC	1.00	.40
□ 25	Tim Thomas RC	2.50	1.00
□ 26	Gary Payton	1.50	.60
□ 27	David Robinson	1.50	.60
□ 28	Hakeem Olajuwon	1.50	.60
□ 29	Antonio Daniels RC	1.50	.60
□ 30	Antonio McDyess	1.50	.60
□ 31	Eddie Jones	1.50	.60
□ 32	Adonal Foyle RC	1.00	.40
□ 33	Glenn Robinson	1.50	.60
□ 34	Charles Barkley	2.00	.75
□ 35	Vin Baker	1.00	.40
□ 36	Jerry Stackhouse	1.50	.60
□ 37	Ray Allen	1.50	.60
□ 38	Derek Anderson RC	1.00	.40
□ 39	Isaac Austin	.50	.20
□ 40	Tony Battie RC	1.50	.60
□ 41	Tariq Abdul-Wahad RC	1.00	.40
□ 42	Dikembe Mutombo	1.00	.40
□ 43	Clyde Drexler	1.50	.60
□ 44	Chris Mullin	1.50	.60
□ 45	Tim Hardaway	1.00	.40
□ 46	Terrell Brandon	1.00	.40
□ 47	John Stockton	1.50	.60
□ 48	Patrick Ewing	1.50	.60
□ 49	Horace Grant	1.00	.40
□ 50	Tom Gugliotta	1.00	.40
□ 51	Mookie Blaylock	.50	.20
□ 52	Mitch Richmond	1.00	.40
□ 53	Anthony Mason	1.00	.40
□ 54	Michael Finley	1.50	.60
□ 55	Jason Kidd	2.50	1.00
□ 56	Karl Malone	1.50	.60
□ 57	Reggie Miller	1.50	.60
□ 58	Steve Smith	1.00	.40
□ 59	Glen Rice	1.00	.40
□ 60	Bryant Stith	.50	.20
□ 61	Loy Vaught	.50	.20
□ 62	Brian Grant	1.00	.40
□ 63	Joe Dumars	1.50	.60
□ 64	Juwan Howard	1.00	.40
□ 65	Rik Smits	1.00	.40
□ 66	Alonzo Mourning	1.00	.40
□ 67	Allan Houston	1.00	.40
□ 68	Chris Webber	1.50	.60
□ 69	Kendall Gill	.50	.20
□ 70	Rony Seikaly	.50	.20
□ 71	Kenny Anderson	1.00	.40
□ 72	John Wallace	.50	.20
□ 73	Bryant Reeves	.50	.20
□ 74	Brian Williams	.50	.20
□ 75	Larry Johnson	1.00	.40
□ 76	Shawn Bradley	.50	.20
□ 77	Kevin Johnson	1.00	.40
□ 78	Rod Strickland	.50	.20
□ 79	Rodney Rogers	.50	.20
□ 80	Rasheed Wallace	1.50	.60
□ NNO	Grant Hill Promo	1.50	.60

1998-99 Flair Showcase Row 3

□ COMPLETE SET (90)		50.00	20.00
□ COMMON CARD (1-90)		.25	.08
□ COMMON ROOKIE		.50	.20
□ 1	Keith Van Horn	.75	.30
□ 1A	K.Van Horn Promo	1.00	.40
□ 2	Kobe Bryant	3.00	1.25
□ 3	Tim Duncan	1.25	.50
□ 4	Kevin Garnett	1.50	.60
□ 5	Grant Hill	.75	.30
□ 6	Allen Iverson	1.50	.60
□ 7	Shaquille O'Neal	2.00	.75
□ 8	Antoine Walker	.75	.30
□ 9	Shareef Abdur-Rahim	.75	.30
□ 10	Stephon Marbury	.75	.30
□ 11	Ray Allen	.75	.30
□ 12	Shawn Kemp	.50	.20
□ 13	Tim Thomas	.50	.20
□ 14	Scottie Pippen	1.25	.50
□ 15	Latrell Sprewell	.75	.30
□ 16	Dirk Nowitzki RC	8.00	3.00
□ 17	Antawn Jamison RC	4.00	1.50
□ 18	Anfernee Hardaway	.75	.30
□ 19	Larry Hughes RC	2.50	1.00
□ 20	Robert Traylor RC	1.00	4.00
□ 21	Kerry Kittles	.50	.20
□ 22	Ron Mercer	.40	.15
□ 23	Michael Olowokandi RC	1.25	.50
□ 24	Jason Kidd	1.00	.40
□ 25	Vince Carter RC	10.00	4.00
□ 26	Charles Barkley	.75	.30
□ 27	Antonio McDyess	.50	.20
□ 28	Mike Bibby RC	4.00	1.50
□ 29	Paul Pierce RC	4.00	1.50
□ 30	Raef LaFrentz RC	1.25	.50
□ 31	Reggie Miller	.75	.30
□ 32	Michael Finley	.75	.30
□ 33	Eddie Jones	.75	.30
□ 34	Tim Hardaway	.50	.20
□ 35	Glenn Robinson	.50	.20
□ 36	Brevin Knight	.25	.08
□ 37	Gary Payton	.75	.30
□ 38	David Robinson	.75	.30
□ 39	Karl Malone	.75	.30
□ 40	Derek Anderson	.60	.25
□ 41	Patrick Ewing	.75	.30
□ 42	Juwan Howard	.50	.20
□ 43	Jayson Williams	.25	.08
□ 44	Terrell Brandon	.50	.20
□ 45	Hakeem Olajuwon	.75	.30
□ 46	Isaac Austin	.25	.08
□ 47	Glen Rice	.50	.20
□ 48	Maurice Taylor	.40	.15
□ 49	Damon Stoudamire	.50	.20
□ 50	Brian Skinner RC	1.00	4.00
□ 51	Nazr Mohammed RC	.50	.20
□ 52	Tom Gugliotta	.25	.08
□ 53	Al Harrington RC	2.00	.75
□ 54	Pat Garrity RC	.60	.25
□ 55	Jason Williams RC	3.00	1.25
□ 56	Tracy McGrady	1.50	.60
□ 57	Keon Clark RC	1.25	.50
□ 58	Vin Baker	.50	.20
□ 59	Bonzi Wells RC	3.00	1.25
□ 60	John Stockton	.75	.30
□ 61	Isaiah Rider	.25	.08

#	Player		
62	Alonzo Mourning	.50	.20
63	Allan Houston	.50	.20
64	Dennis Rodman	.50	.20
65	Felipe Lopez RC	1.00	.40
66	Joe Smith	.50	.20
67	Chris Webber	.75	.30
68	Mitch Richmond	.50	.20
69	Brent Barry	.50	.20
70	Mookie Blaylock	.25	.08
71	Donyell Marshall	.50	.20
72	Anthony Mason	.50	.20
73	Rod Strickland	.25	.08
74	Roshown McLeod RC	.60	.25
75	Matt Harpring RC	2.00	.75
76	Detlef Schrempf	.50	.20
77	Michael Dickerson RC	1.50	.60
78	Michael Doleac RC	1.00	4.00
79	John Starks	.50	.20
80	Ricky Davis RC	2.00	.75
81	Steve Smith	.50	.20
82	Voshon Lenard	.25	.08
83	Toni Kukoc	.50	.20
84	Steve Nash	.75	.30
85	Vlade Divac	.50	.20
86	Rasheed Wallace	.75	.30
87	Bryon Russell	.25	.08
88	Antonio Daniels	.25	.08
89	Rik Smits	.50	.20
90	Joe Dumars	.75	.30

1999-00 Flair Showcase

	COMPLETE SET (130)	300.00	150.00
	COMPLETE SET w/o RC (100)	30.00	15.00
	COMMON CARD (1-100)	.30	.10
	COMMON ROOKIE (101-130)	2.00	.75
1	Vince Carter	2.50	1.00
2	Anfernee Hardaway	1.00	.40
3	Nick Van Exel	1.00	.40
4	Kerry Kittles	.30	.10
5	Michael Doleac	.30	.10
6	Sean Elliott	.60	.25
7	Shaquille O'Neal	2.50	1.00
8	Avery Johnson	.30	.10
9	Brian Grant	.60	.25
10	Jerome Williams	.30	.10
11	Larry Hughes	1.00	.40
12	Jerry Stackhouse	1.00	.40
13	Alonzo Mourning	.60	.25
14	Antonio McDyess	.60	.25
15	Jason Kidd	1.50	.60
16	Bryon Russell	.30	.10
17	Hakeem Olajuwon	1.00	.40
18	Juwan Howard	.60	.25
19	Paul Pierce	1.00	.40
20	Vin Baker	.60	.25
21	Larry Johnson	.30	.10
22	Gary Trent	.30	.10
23	Jayson Williams	.30	.10
24	Tim Hardaway	.60	.25
25	Dirk Nowitzki	2.00	.75
26	Jamal Mashburn	.60	.25
27	Glenn Robinson	1.00	.40
28	Shawn Bradley	.30	.10
29	Tom Gugliotta	.30	.10
30	Vlade Divac	.60	.25
31	David Robinson	1.00	.40
32	Matt Geiger	.30	.10
33	Grant Hill	1.00	.40

#	Player		
34	Maurice Taylor	.60	.25
35	Toni Kukoc	.60	.25
36	Cedric Ceballos	.30	.10
37	Patrick Ewing	1.00	.40
38	Ray Allen	1.00	.40
39	Michael Finley	1.00	.40
40	Robert Traylor	.30	.10
41	Brevin Knight	.30	.10
42	Marcus Camby	.60	.25
43	Sam Cassell	1.00	.40
44	Antawn Jamison	1.50	.60
45	Steve Smith	.60	.25
46	Darrell Armstrong	.30	.10
47	Mookie Blaylock	.30	.10
48	Derek Anderson	.60	.25
49	Hersey Hawkins	.60	.25
50	Kobe Bryant	4.00	1.50
51	Shawn Kemp	.60	.25
52	Scottie Pippen	1.50	.60
53	Chris Webber	1.00	.40
54	Damon Stoudamire	.60	.25
55	Donyell Marshall	.60	.25
56	Isaiah Rider	.30	.10
57	Karl Malone	1.00	.40
58	Kevin Garnett	2.00	.75
59	Mario Elie	.30	.10
60	Michael Dickerson	.60	.25
61	Jahidi White	.30	.10
62	Joe Smith	.60	.25
63	Kenny Anderson	.60	.25
64	Reggie Miller	1.00	.40
65	Ruben Patterson	.60	.25
66	Shareef Abdur-Rahim	1.00	.40
67	Allen Iverson	2.00	.75
68	Glen Rice	.60	.25
69	Nick Anderson	.30	.10
70	Rex Chapman	.30	.10
71	Ron Mercer	.60	.25
72	Tim Duncan	2.00	.75
73	Al Harrington	1.00	.40
74	Brent Barry	.60	.25
75	Eddie Jones	1.00	.40
76	Mike Bibby	1.00	.40
77	Anthony Mason	.60	.25
78	Michael Olowokandi	.60	.25
79	Matt Harpring	1.00	.40
80	Stephon Marbury	1.00	.40
81	Tracy McGrady	2.50	1.00
82	Allan Houston	.60	.25
83	Lindsey Hunter	.30	.10
84	Tariq Abdul-Wahad	.30	.10
85	Antoine Walker	1.00	.40
86	Charles Barkley	1.25	.50
87	Gary Payton	1.00	.40
88	John Stockton	1.00	.40
89	Mitch Richmond	.60	.25
90	Terrell Brandon	.60	.25
91	Charles Oakley	.30	.10
92	Bryant Reeves	.30	.10
93	Dikembe Mutombo	.60	.25
94	Elden Campbell	.30	.10
95	Jalen Rose	1.00	.40
96	Jason Williams	1.00	.40
97	Keith Van Horn	1.00	.40
98	Latrell Sprewell	1.00	.40
99	Rael LaFrentz	.60	.25
100	Rasheed Wallace	1.00	.40
101	Cal Bowdler RC	3.00	1.25
102	Dion Glover RC	3.00	1.25
103	Jason Terry RC	6.00	2.50
104	Adrian Griffin RC	3.00	1.25
105	Baron Davis RC	15.00	6.00
106	Michael Ruffin RC	2.50	1.00
107	Elton Brand RC	12.00	5.00
108	Ron Artest RC	6.00	2.50
109	Andre Miller RC	10.00	4.00
110	Trajan Langdon RC	4.00	1.50
111	James Posey RC	6.00	2.50
112	Vonteego Cummings RC	4.00	1.50
113	Kenny Thomas RC	4.00	1.50
114	Steve Francis RC	12.00	5.00
115	Jonathan Bender RC	10.00	4.00
116	Lamar Odom RC	10.00	4.00
117	Devean George RC	5.00	2.00
118	Tim James RC	3.00	1.25
119	Anthony Carter RC	6.00	2.50

#	Player		
120	Wally Szczerbiak RC	10.00	4.00
121	William Avery RC	4.00	1.50
122	Evan Eschmeyer RC	2.00	.75
123	Corey Maggette RC	10.00	4.00
124	Jumaine Jones RC	3.00	1.25
125	Shawn Marion RC	15.00	6.00
126	Ryan Robertson RC	2.50	1.00
127	A.Radojevic RC	2.00	.75
128	Quincy Lewis RC	3.00	1.25
129	Scott Padgett RC	3.00	1.25
130	Richard Hamilton RC	10.00	4.00
P1	Vince Carter PROMO	2.50	1.00

2001-02 Flair

	COMP.SET w/o SP's (90)	50.00	25.00
	COMMON CARDS (1-121)	.30	.10
	COMMON ROOKIE (91-120)	1.50	.60
1	Tracy McGrady	2.50	1.00
2	Derek Fisher	1.00	.40
3	Allen Iverson	2.00	.75
4	Chris Webber	1.00	.40
5	Jalen Rose	1.00	.40
6	Kenyon Martin	1.00	.40
7	Jermaine O'Neal	1.00	.40
8	Kobe Bryant	4.00	1.50
9	Bryon Russell	.30	.10
10	Wally Szczerbiak	.60	.25
11	Damon Stoudamire	.60	.25
12	John Stockton	1.00	.40
13	Glenn Robinson	.60	.25
14	Steve Francis	1.00	.40
15	Vince Carter	2.50	1.00
16	Peja Stojakovic	1.00	.40
17	Rick Fox	.60	.25
18	Allan Houston	.60	.25
19	Danny Fortson	.30	.10
20	Gary Payton	1.00	.40
21	Darius Miles	1.00	.40
22	Kevin Garnett	2.00	.75
23	Marcus Camby	.60	.25
24	Desmond Mason	.60	.25
25	Tim Duncan	2.00	.75
26	Jamal Mashburn	.60	.25
27	Andre Miller	.60	.25
28	Antonio McDyess	.60	.25
29	Morris Peterson	.60	.25
30	Rasheed Wallace	1.00	.40
31	Shawn Marion	1.00	.40
32	Karl Malone	1.00	.40
33	Grant Hill	1.00	.40
34	Shaquille O'Neal	2.50	1.00
35	Hakeem Olajuwon	1.00	.40
36	Corliss Williamson	.60	.25
37	Paul Pierce	1.00	.40
38	Antonio Davis	.30	.10
39	Antonio Daniels	.30	.10
40	Ray Allen	1.00	.40
41	Dirk Nowitzki	1.50	.60
42	Jerry Stackhouse	1.00	.40
43	Donyell Marshall	.60	.25
44	Brian Grant	.60	.25
45	Rael LaFrentz	.60	.25
46	Corey Maggette	.60	.25
47	Mike Miller	1.00	.40
48	Jason Williams	.60	.25
49	Jahidi White	.30	.10
50	David Robinson	1.00	.40
51	Shareef Abdur-Rahim	1.00	.40

52 Anfernee Hardaway	1.00	.40
53 Baron Davis	1.00	.40
54 DerMarr Johnson	.60	.25
55 Dikembe Mutombo	.60	.25
56 David Wesley	.30	.10
57 Chris Mihm	.60	.25
58 Michael Finley	1.00	.40
59 Eddie House	.60	.25
60 Stromile Swift	.60	.25
61 Courtney Alexander	.60	.25
62 Ron Mercer	.60	.25
63 Cuttino Mobley	.60	.25
64 Tim Thomas	.60	.25
65 Eddie Jones	1.00	.40
66 Lamar Odom	1.00	.40
67 Terrell Brandon	.60	.25
68 Rashard Lewis	.60	.25
69 Antoine Walker	1.00	.40
70 Latrell Sprewell	1.00	.40
71 Sam Cassell	1.00	.40
72 Mike Bibby	1.00	.40
73 Speedy Claxton	.60	.25
74 Steve Nash	1.00	.40
75 Mark Jackson	.60	.25
76 Ron Artest	.60	.25
77 Matt Harpring	1.00	.40
78 Wang Zhizhi	1.00	.40
79 Nazr Mohammed	.30	.10
80 Jason Terry	1.00	.40
81 Nick Van Exel	1.00	.40
82 Reggie Miller	1.00	.40
83 Joe Smith	.60	.25
84 Jason Kidd	1.50	.60
85 Richard Hamilton	.60	.25
86 Antawn Jamison	1.00	.40
87 Alonzo Mourning	.60	.25
88 Stephon Marbury	1.00	.40
89 Scottie Pippen	1.50	.60
90 Elton Brand	1.00	.40
91 Kwame Brown RC	4.00	1.50
92 Eddie Griffin RC	3.00	1.25
93 Tyson Chandler RC	8.00	3.00
94 Omar Cook	1.50	.60
95 Loren Woods RC	1.50	.60
96 Alton Ford RC	1.50	.60
97 Shane Battier RC	4.00	1.50
98 Joe Johnson RC	8.00	3.00
99 Rodney White RC	2.50	1.00
100 Pau Gasol RC	10.00	4.00
101 Zach Randolph RC	8.00	3.00
102 Vladimir Radmanovic RC	2.00	.75
103 Brendan Haywood RC	3.00	1.25
104 Michael Bradley RC	1.50	.60
105 Tony Parker RC	12.00	5.00
106 Jason Richardson RC	6.00	2.50
107 Gerald Wallace RC	5.00	2.00
108 Damone Brown RC	1.50	.60
109 Richard Jefferson RC	6.00	2.50
110 Rookie Exchange		
111 DeSagana Diop RC	1.50	.60
112 Brandon Armstrong RC	3.00	1.25
113 Troy Murphy RC	4.00	1.50
114 Kedrick Brown RC	1.50	.60
115 Kirk Haston RC	2.50	1.00
116 Gilbert Arenas RC	10.00	4.00
117 Jeryl Sasser RC	2.50	1.00
118 Jamaal Tinsley RC	4.00	1.50
119 Terence Morris RC	2.50	1.00
120 Michael Wright	1.50	.60
121 Michael Jordan	15.00	6.00

2002-03 Flair

COMP.SET w/o SP's (90)	50.00	25.00
COMMON CARD (1-90)	.20	.10
COMMON ROOKIE (91-120)	5.00	2.00
1 Tracy McGrady	2.50	1.00
2 Jamal Mashburn	.60	.25
3 Allen Iverson	2.00	.75
4 Alonzo Mourning	.60	.25
5 Joe Smith	.60	.25
6 Wang Zhizhi	1.00	.40
7 Karl Malone	1.00	.40
8 Keith Van Horn	1.00	.40
9 Joseph Forte	.60	.25
10 Peja Stojakovic	.60	.25

11 Juwan Howard	.60	.25
12 Brian Grant	.60	.25
13 Glenn Robinson	1.00	.40
14 Antonio McDyess	.60	.25
15 Vince Carter	2.50	1.00
16 Pau Gasol	1.00	.40
17 Bonzi Wells	.60	.25
18 Chucky Atkins	.30	.10
19 Shane Battier	1.00	.40
20 Steve Nash	1.00	.40
21 Kevin Garnett	2.00	.75
22 Antawn Jamison	1.00	.40
23 Hidayet Turkoglu	1.00	.40
24 Kenyon Martin	1.00	.40
25 Cuttino Mobley	.60	.25
26 Steve Nash	1.00	.40
27 Morris Peterson	.60	.25
28 Jason Richardson	1.00	.40
29 Antoine Walker	1.00	.40
30 Rasheed Wallace	1.00	.40
31 Tim Duncan	2.00	.75
32 Paul Pierce	1.00	.40
33 Ben Wallace	1.00	.40
34 Jason Kidd	1.50	.60
35 Gary Payton	1.00	.40
36 Mike Miller	1.00	.40
37 Kobe Bryant	4.00	1.50
38 Baron Davis	1.00	.40
39 Steve Smith	.60	.25
40 Reggie Miller	1.00	.40
41 Dirk Nowitzki	1.50	.60
42 Rashard Lewis	.60	.25
43 Andre Miller	.60	.25
44 David Wesley	.30	.10
45 Ray Allen	1.00	.40
46 Tyson Chandler	1.00	.40
47 Jamaal Tinsley	1.00	.40
48 Grant Hill	1.00	.40
49 Richard Jefferson	.60	.25
50 Latrell Sprewell	1.00	.40
51 Jason Terry	1.00	.40
52 Alvin Williams	.30	.10
53 Vin Baker	.60	.25
54 Robert Horry	.60	.25
55 Eddie Jones	1.00	.40
56 Andrei Kirilenko	1.00	.40
57 Darius Miles	1.00	.40
58 Kedrick Brown	.60	.25
59 Jermaine O'Neal	1.00	.40
60 David Robinson	1.00	.40
61 Jason Williams	.60	.25
62 Wally Szczerbiak	.60	.25
63 Mike Bibby	1.00	.40
64 Shawn Marion	1.00	.40
65 Shaquille O'Neal	2.50	1.00
66 Michael Redd	1.00	.40
67 Chris Webber	1.00	.40
68 Quentin Richardson	.60	.25
69 Michael Jordan	8.00	3.00
70 Jamaal Magloire	.30	.10
71 Radoslav Nesterovic	.60	.25
72 Eddy Curry	1.00	.40
73 Michael Finley	1.00	.40
74 Eddie Griffin	.60	.25
75 Aaron McKie	.60	.25
76 Tony Parker	1.00	.40
77 Shareef Abdur-Rahim	1.00	.40
78 Jalen Rose	1.00	.40

79 Jerry Stackhouse	1.00	.40
80 Jumaine Jones	.60	.25
81 Toni Kukoc	.60	.25
82 Vladimir Radmanovic	.60	.25
83 Zach Randolph	1.00	.40
84 John Stockton	1.00	.40
85 Mengke Bateer	1.00	.40
86 Dikembe Mutombo	.60	.25
87 Elton Brand	1.00	.40
88 Allan Houston	.60	.25
89 Joe Johnson	1.00	.40
90 Kwame Brown	.60	.25
91 Rookie Exchange	30.00	12.50
92 Jay Williams RC	5.00	2.00
93 Mike Dunleavy RC	8.00	3.00
94 Drew Gooden RC	12.00	5.00
95 DaJuan Wagner RC	6.00	2.50
96 Caron Butler RC	8.00	3.00
97 Jared Jeffries RC	5.00	2.00
98 Nene Hilario RC	6.00	2.50
99 Chris Wilcox RC	6.00	2.50
100 Nikoloz Tskitishvili RC	6.00	2.50
101 Kareem Rush RC	6.00	2.50
102 Curtis Borchardt RC	5.00	2.00
103 Qyntel Woods RC	5.00	2.00
104 Melvin Ely RC	5.00	2.00
105 Marcus Haislip RC	5.00	2.00
106 Carlos Boozer RC	10.00	4.00
107 Bostjan Nachbar RC	5.00	2.00
108 Amare Stoudemire RC	20.00	8.00
109 Frank Williams RC	5.00	2.00
110 Jiri Welsch RC	5.00	2.00
111 Fred Jones RC	5.00	2.00
112 Juan Dixon RC	8.00	3.00
113 Ryan Humphrey RC	5.00	2.00
114 Casey Jacobsen RC	5.00	2.00
115 Tayshaun Prince RC	6.00	2.50
116 Dan Dickau RC	5.00	2.00
117 Rookie Exchange	5.00	2.00
118 John Salmons RC	5.00	2.00
119 Manu Ginobili RC	15.00	6.00
119B Rookie Exchange	5.00	2.00
120 Rookie Exchange	5.00	2.00

2003-04 Flair

COMP.SET w/o SP's (90)	40.00	15.00
COMMON CARD (1-90)	.20	.08
COMMON ROOKIE (91-120)	4.00	1.50
1 Jerry Stackhouse	.75	.30
2 Eddie Griffin	.50	.20
3 Jermaine O'Neal	.75	.30
4 Kobe Bryant	3.00	1.25
5 Juwan Howard	.50	.20
6 Alonzo Mourning	.50	.20
7 Kenny Thomas	.20	.08
8 Steve Francis	.75	.30
9 Radoslav Nesterovic	.50	.20
10 Morris Peterson	.50	.20
11 DeShawn Stevenson	.20	.08
12 Steve Francis	.75	.30
13 Andrei Kirilenko	.75	.30
14 Kwame Brown	.50	.20
15 Tim Duncan	1.50	.60
16 Yao Ming	2.00	.75
17 Jamaal Tinsley	.75	.30
18 Shaquille O'Neal	2.00	.75
19 Tracy McGrady	2.00	.75
20 Dirk Nowitzki	1.25	.50

❑ 21	Marcus Camby	.50	.20
❑ 22	Elton Brand	.75	.30
❑ 23	Latrell Sprewell	.75	.30
❑ 24	Grant Hill	.75	.30
❑ 25	Shawn Marion	.75	.30
❑ 26	Rasheed Wallace	.75	.30
❑ 27	Ray Allen	.75	.30
❑ 28	Antonio Davis	.20	.08
❑ 29	Antoine Walker	.75	.30
❑ 30	Ricky Davis	.75	.30
❑ 31	Jason Kidd	1.25	.50
❑ 32	Tony Parker	.75	.30
❑ 33	Paul Pierce	.75	.30
❑ 34	Gary Payton	.75	.30
❑ 35	Kenyon Martin	.75	.30
❑ 36	Dale Davis		.20
❑ 37	Vladimir Radmanovic	.20	.08
❑ 38	Matt Harpring	.75	.30
❑ 39	Shareef Abdur-Rahim	.75	.30
❑ 40	Antawn Jamison	.75	.30
❑ 41	Eddie Jones	.75	.30
❑ 42	Jamaal Magloire	.20	.08
❑ 43	Jason Richardson	.75	.30
❑ 44	Jonathan Bender	.50	.20
❑ 45	Chris Wilcox	.50	.20
❑ 46	Manu Ginobili	.75	.30
❑ 47	Chauncey Billups	.50	.20
❑ 48	Jamal Mashburn	.50	.20
❑ 49	Joe Smith	.50	.20
❑ 50	Aaron McKie	.50	.20
❑ 51	Theo Ratliff	.50	.20
❑ 52	Eddy Curry	.50	.20
❑ 53	Ron Artest	.50	.20
❑ 54	Quentin Richardson	.50	.20
❑ 55	Karl Malone	.75	.30
❑ 56	Pau Gasol	.75	.30
❑ 57	Dan Dickau	.20	.08
❑ 58	Darius Miles	.75	.30
❑ 59	Ben Wallace	.75	.30
❑ 60	Cuttino Mobley	.50	.20
❑ 61	Lamar Odom	.75	.30
❑ 62	Shane Battier	.75	.30
❑ 63	Allan Houston	.50	.20
❑ 64	Peja Stojakovic	.75	.30
❑ 65	Dajuan Wagner	.50	.20
❑ 66	Caron Butler	.75	.30
❑ 67	Keith Van Horn	.75	.30
❑ 68	Vincent Yarbrough	.20	.08
❑ 69	Tim Thomas	.50	.20
❑ 70	Troy Hudson	.20	.08
❑ 71	Amare Stoudemire	1.50	.60
❑ 72	Bobby Jackson	.50	.20
❑ 73	Bonzi Wells	.50	.20
❑ 74	Steve Nash	.75	.30
❑ 75	Gilbert Arenas	.75	.30
❑ 76	Glenn Robinson	.75	.30
❑ 77	Jalen Rose	.75	.30
❑ 78	Michael Finley	.75	.30
❑ 79	Nene	.50	.20
❑ 80	Kevin Garnett	1.50	.60
❑ 81	Richard Jefferson	.50	.20
❑ 82	Baron Davis	.75	.30
❑ 83	Mike Bibby	.75	.30
❑ 84	Tyson Chandler	.75	.30
❑ 85	Michael Redd	.75	.30
❑ 86	Mike Dunleavy	.50	.20
❑ 87	Drew Gooden	.50	.20
❑ 88	Allen Iverson	1.50	.60
❑ 89	Vince Carter	2.00	.75
❑ 90	Larry Hughes	.50	.20
❑ 91	Josh Howard RC	6.00	2.50
❑ 92	Maciej Lampe RC	4.00	1.50
❑ 93	Zarko Cabarkapa RC	4.00	1.50
❑ 94	LeBron James RC	50.00	20.00
❑ 95	Reece Gaines RC	4.00	1.50
❑ 96	Jarvis Hayes RC	4.00	1.50
❑ 97	Mickael Pietrus RC	4.00	1.50
❑ 98	T.J. Ford RC	5.00	2.00
❑ 99	Zoran Planinic RC	4.00	1.50
❑ 100	Luke Ridnour RC	5.00	2.00
❑ 101	Boris Diaw RC	4.00	1.50
❑ 102	Nick Collison RC	4.00	1.50
❑ 103	Travis Outlaw RC	4.00	1.50
❑ 104	Carmelo Anthony RC	15.00	6.00
❑ 105	Chris Kaman RC	4.00	1.50
❑ 106	Mike Sweetney RC	4.00	1.50
❑ 107	Kendrick Perkins RC	4.00	1.50
❑ 108	Jason Kapono RC	4.00	1.50
❑ 109	Troy Bell RC	4.00	1.50
❑ 110	Chris Bosh RC	10.00	4.00
❑ 111	Jerome Beasley RC	4.00	1.50
❑ 112	Darko Milicic RC	6.00	2.50
❑ 113	Dwyane Wade RC	15.00	6.00
❑ 114	David West RC	4.00	1.50
❑ 115	Kirk Hinrich RC	6.00	2.50
❑ 116	Dahntay Jones RC	4.00	1.50
❑ 117	Leandro Barbosa RC	6.00	2.50
❑ 118	Marcus Banks RC	4.00	1.50
❑ 119	Luke Walton RC	4.00	1.50
❑ 120	Ndudi Ebi RC	4.00	1.50

2004-05 Flair

	COMP.SET w/o SP's (60)	70.00	30.00
	COMMON CARD (1-60)	.50	.20
	COMMON ROOKIE (61-90)	5.00	2.00
❑ 1	Gilbert Arenas	1.50	.60
❑ 2	Richard Hamilton	1.00	.40
❑ 3	Stephon Marbury	1.50	.60
❑ 4	Tony Parker	1.50	.60
❑ 5	Michael Redd	1.00	.40
❑ 6	Latrell Sprewell	1.50	.60
❑ 7	Willie Green	.50	.20
❑ 8	Joe Johnson	1.00	.40
❑ 9	Lamar Odom	1.50	.60
❑ 10	Tim Duncan	3.00	1.25
❑ 11	Ben Wallace	1.50	.60
❑ 12	Elton Brand	1.50	.60
❑ 13	Allen Iverson	3.00	1.25
❑ 14	Andrei Kirilenko	1.50	.60
❑ 15	Dirk Nowitzki	2.50	1.00
❑ 16	Paul Pierce	1.50	.60
❑ 17	Mike Dunleavy	1.00	.40
❑ 18	Zach Randolph	1.50	.60
❑ 19	David West	1.00	.40
❑ 20	Corey Maggette	1.00	.40
❑ 21	Dwyane Wade	5.00	2.00
❑ 22	Chris Bosh	1.50	.60
❑ 23	Michael Finley	1.50	.60
❑ 24	Kevin Garnett	3.00	1.25
❑ 25	Allan Houston	1.00	.40
❑ 26	Antawn Jamison	1.50	.60
❑ 27	Jermaine O'Neal	1.50	.60
❑ 28	Alonzo Mourning	1.50	.60
❑ 29	Gerald Wallace	1.00	.40
❑ 30	Jason Williams	1.00	.40
❑ 31	Tyronn Lue	.50	.20
❑ 32	Pau Gasol	1.50	.60
❑ 33	Jason Kidd	2.50	1.00
❑ 34	Shareef Abdur-Rahim	1.50	.60
❑ 35	LeBron James	10.00	4.00
❑ 36	Shaquille O'Neal	4.00	1.50
❑ 37	Jason Richardson	1.50	.60
❑ 38	Rasheed Wallace	1.50	.60
❑ 39	Nene	1.00	.40
❑ 40	Tracy McGrady	4.00	1.50
❑ 41	Kenyon Martin	1.00	.40
❑ 42	Peja Stojakovic	1.50	.60
❑ 43	Amare Stoudemire	3.00	1.25
❑ 44	Carmelo Anthony	3.00	1.25
❑ 45	Steve Francis	1.50	.60
❑ 46	Antoine Walker	1.50	.60
❑ 47	Reggie Miller	1.50	.60
❑ 48	Mike Bibby	1.50	.60
❑ 49	Sam Cassell	1.50	.60
❑ 50	Richard Jefferson	1.00	.40
❑ 51	Jason Kapono	1.00	.40
❑ 52	Dajuan Wagner	1.00	.40
❑ 53	Kobe Bryant	6.00	2.50
❑ 54	Kenyon Martin	1.50	.60
❑ 55	T.J. Ford	1.00	.40
❑ 56	Ray Allen	1.50	.60
❑ 57	Vince Carter	4.00	1.50
❑ 58	Yao Ming	4.00	1.50
❑ 59	Baron Davis	1.50	.60
❑ 60	Joe Smith	1.00	.40
❑ 61	Luol Deng RC	10.00	4.00
❑ 62	J.R. Smith RC	10.00	4.00
❑ 63	Josh Childress RC	6.00	2.50
❑ 64	Shaun Livingston RC	8.00	3.00
❑ 65	Rafael Araujo RC	5.00	2.00
❑ 66	Devin Harris RC	10.00	4.00
❑ 67	Kevin Martin RC	8.00	3.00
❑ 68	Sasha Vujacic RC	5.00	2.00
❑ 69	Robert Swift RC	5.00	2.00
❑ 70	Andris Biedrins RC	8.00	3.00
❑ 71	Kirk Snyder RC	5.00	2.00
❑ 72	Jameer Nelson RC	8.00	3.00
❑ 73	Tony Allen RC	6.00	2.50
❑ 74	Chris Duhon RC	8.00	3.00
❑ 75	David Harrison RC	5.00	2.00
❑ 76	Andre Iguodala RC	12.00	5.00
❑ 77	Josh Smith RC	10.00	4.00
❑ 78	Andre Emmett RC	5.00	2.00
❑ 79	Luke Jackson RC	5.00	2.00
❑ 80	Dorell Wright RC	8.00	3.00
❑ 81	Ben Gordon RC	20.00	8.00
❑ 82	Dwight Howard RC	15.00	6.00
❑ 83	Kris Humphries RC	5.00	2.00
❑ 84	Al Jefferson RC	12.00	5.00
❑ 85	Jackson Vroman RC	5.00	2.00
❑ 86	Beno Udrih RC	8.00	3.00
❑ 87	Trevor Ariza RC	6.00	2.50
❑ 88	Sebastian Telfair RC	5.00	2.00
❑ 89	Emeka Okafor RC	20.00	8.00
❑ 90	Peter John Ramos RC	5.00	2.00

2003-04 Flair Final Edition

ROOKIE CLASS

	COMP.SET w/o SP's (65)	30.00	12.50
	COMMON CARD (1-65)	.20	.08
	COMMON ROOKIE (66-90)	5.00	2.00
❑ 1	Allen Iverson	1.50	.60
❑ 2	Juwan Howard	.50	.20
❑ 3	Stephen Jackson	.20	.08
❑ 4	Manu Ginobili	.75	.30
❑ 5	Steve Nash	.75	.30
❑ 6	Jason Terry	.75	.30
❑ 7	Tayshaun Prince	.50	.20
❑ 8	Stephon Marbury	.75	.30
❑ 9	Eddie Jones	.75	.30
❑ 10	Reggie Miller	.75	.30
❑ 11	Baron Davis	.75	.30
❑ 12	Donyell Marshall	.50	.20
❑ 13	Mike Bibby	.75	.30
❑ 14	Kobe Bryant	3.00	1.25
❑ 15	Jason Richardson	.75	.30
❑ 16	Cuttino Mobley	.50	.20
❑ 17	Andre Miller	.50	.20
❑ 18	Corey Maggette	.50	.20
❑ 19	Michael Finley	.75	.30
❑ 20	Jason Kidd	1.25	.50
❑ 21	Lamar Odom	.75	.30

☐ 22	Tracy McGrady	2.00	.75
☐ 23	Peja Stojakovic	.75	.30
☐ 24	Richard Jefferson	.50	.20
☐ 25	Rasheed Wallace	.75	.30
☐ 26	Eddy Curry	.50	.20
☐ 27	Ben Wallace	.75	.30
☐ 28	Rashard Lewis	.75	.30
☐ 29	Sam Cassell	.75	.30
☐ 30	Anfernee Hardaway	.75	.30
☐ 31	Carlos Boozer	.75	.30
☐ 32	Jamal Crawford	.50	.20
☐ 33	Dirk Nowitzki	1.25	.50
☐ 34	Steve Francis	.75	.30
☐ 35	Chris Webber	.75	.30
☐ 36	Elton Brand	.75	.30
☐ 37	Michael Redd	.50	.20
☐ 38	Jason Williams	.50	.20
☐ 39	Nene	.50	.20
☐ 40	Nick Van Exel	.75	.30
☐ 41	Amare Stoudemire	1.50	.60
☐ 42	Latrell Sprewell	.75	.30
☐ 43	Tony Parker	.75	.30
☐ 44	Keith Van Horn	.75	.30
☐ 45	Pau Gasol	.75	.30
☐ 46	Andrei Kirilenko	.75	.30
☐ 47	Shareef Abdur-Rahim	.75	.30
☐ 48	Tim Thomas	.50	.20
☐ 49	Jerry Stackhouse	.75	.30
☐ 50	Jermaine O'Neal	.75	.30
☐ 51	Jamal Mashburn	.50	.20
☐ 52	Matt Harpring	.50	.20
☐ 53	Damon Stoudamire	.50	.20
☐ 54	Zydrunas Ilgauskas	.50	.20
☐ 55	Kevin Garnett	1.50	.60
☐ 56	Tim Duncan	1.50	.60
☐ 57	Yao Ming	2.00	.75
☐ 58	Kenyon Martin	.75	.30
☐ 59	Paul Pierce	.75	.30
☐ 60	Ron Artest	.50	.20
☐ 61	Vince Carter	2.00	.75
☐ 62	Shaquille O'Neal	2.00	.75
☐ 63	Shawn Marion	.75	.30
☐ 64	Gilbert Arenas	.75	.30
☐ 65	Ray Allen	.75	.30
☐ 66	Chris Bosh RC	15.00	6.00
☐ 67	Brian Cook RC	5.00	2.00
☐ 68	Luke Ridnour RC	8.00	3.00
☐ 69	Willie Green RC	5.00	2.00
☐ 70	Zarko Cabarkapa RC	5.00	2.00
☐ 71	Maurice Williams RC	5.00	2.00
☐ 72	Luke Walton RC	5.00	2.00
☐ 73	David West RC	5.00	2.00
☐ 74	Mickael Pietrus RC	5.00	2.00
☐ 75	LeBron James RC	60.00	30.00
☐ 76	Marcus Banks RC	5.00	2.00
☐ 77	Keith Bogans RC	5.00	2.00
☐ 78	Darko Milicic RC	10.00	4.00
☐ 79	Jarvis Hayes RC	5.00	2.00
☐ 80	Josh Howard RC	10.00	4.00
☐ 81	Chris Kaman RC	5.00	2.00
☐ 82	Mike Sweetney RC	5.00	2.00
☐ 83	Carmelo Anthony RC	20.00	8.00
☐ 84	Travis Outlaw RC	5.00	2.00
☐ 85	Kyle Korver RC	5.00	2.00
☐ 86	Boris Diaw RC	6.00	2.50
☐ 87	Dwyane Wade RC	25.00	10.00
☐ 88	Troy Bell RC	5.00	2.00
☐ 89	T.J. Ford RC	8.00	3.00
☐ 90	Kirk Hinrich RC	10.00	4.00

1961-62 Fleer

☐	COMPLETE SET (66)	4000.00	2800.00
☐ 1	Al Attles RC !	125.00	75.00
☐ 2	Paul Arizin	50.00	30.00
☐ 3	Elgin Baylor RC !	250.00	150.00
☐ 4	Walt Bellamy RC !	60.00	40.00
☐ 5	Arlen Bockhorn	15.00	10.00
☐ 6	Bob Boozer RC !	25.00	15.00
☐ 7	Carl Braun	30.00	18.00
☐ 8	Wilt Chamberlain RC !	800.00	400.00
☐ 9	Larry Costello	20.00	12.00
☐ 10	Bob Cousy !	200.00	125.00
☐ 11	Walter Dukes	20.00	12.00
☐ 12	Wayne Embry RC	40.00	25.00
☐ 13	Dave Gambee	15.00	10.00
☐ 14	Tom Gola	40.00	25.00

☐ 15	Sihugo Green RC	20.00	12.00
☐ 16	Hal Greer RC	80.00	50.00
☐ 17	Richie Guerin RC	40.00	20.00
☐ 18	Cliff Hagan	50.00	30.00
☐ 19	Tom Heinsohn	100.00	60.00
☐ 20	Bailey Howell RC	50.00	30.00
☐ 21	Rod Hundley	75.00	45.00
☐ 22	K.C. Jones RC	110.00	65.00
☐ 23	Sam Jones RC	110.00	65.00
☐ 24	Phil Jordan	15.00	10.00
☐ 25	John/Red Kerr	50.00	30.00
☐ 26	Rudy LaRusso RC	40.00	25.00
☐ 27	George Lee	15.00	10.00
☐ 28	Bob Leonard	25.00	15.00
☐ 29	Clyde Lovellette	50.00	30.00
☐ 30	John McCarthy	15.00	10.00
☐ 31	Tom Meschery RC	25.00	15.00
☐ 32	Willie Naulls	25.00	15.00
☐ 33	Don Ohl RC	25.00	15.00
☐ 34	Bob Pettit	90.00	50.00
☐ 35	Frank Ramsey	40.00	25.00
☐ 36	Oscar Robertson RC !	400.00	250.00
☐ 37	Guy Rodgers RC	25.00	15.00
☐ 38	Bill Russell !	400.00	250.00
☐ 39	Dolph Schayes	55.00	35.00
☐ 40	Frank Selvy	20.00	12.00
☐ 41	Gene Shue	25.00	15.00
☐ 42	Jack Twyman	40.00	25.00
☐ 43	Jerry West RC !	500.00	350.00
☐ 44	Len Wilkens RC UER !	175.00	100.00
☐ 45	Paul Arizin IA	25.00	15.00
☐ 46	Elgin Baylor IA	100.00	65.00
☐ 47	Wilt Chamberlain IA !	400.00	250.00
☐ 48	Larry Costello IA	20.00	12.00
☐ 49	Bob Cousy IA UER	125.00	75.00
☐ 50	Walter Dukes IA	15.00	10.00
☐ 51	Tom Gola IA	25.00	15.00
☐ 52	Richie Guerin IA	20.00	12.00
☐ 53	Cliff Hagan IA	25.00	15.00
☐ 54	Tom Heinsohn IA	50.00	30.00
☐ 55	Bailey Howell IA	25.00	15.00
☐ 56	John/Red Kerr IA	30.00	18.00
☐ 57	Rudy LaRusso IA	20.00	12.00
☐ 58	Clyde Lovellette IA	30.00	18.00
☐ 59	Bob Pettit IA	50.00	30.00
☐ 60	Frank Ramsey IA	25.00	15.00
☐ 61	Oscar Robertson IA !	175.00	100.00
☐ 62	Bill Russell IA !	200.00	100.00
☐ 63	Dolph Schayes IA	35.00	20.00
☐ 64	Gene Shue IA	20.00	12.00
☐ 65	Jack Twyman IA	25.00	15.00
☐ 66	Jerry West IA !	300.00	175.00

1986-87 Fleer

☐	COMPLETE w/Stickers (143)	1000.00	600.00
☐	COMP.SET (132)	800.00	500.00
☐ 1	Kareem Abdul-Jabbar	15.00	6.00
☐ 2	Alvan Adams	2.00	.75
☐ 3	Mark Aguirre RC	3.00	1.25
☐ 4	Danny Ainge RC	8.00	4.00
☐ 5	John Bagley RC**	2.00	.75
☐ 6	Thurl Bailey RC**	2.00	.75
☐ 7	Charles Barkley RC	50.00	20.00
☐ 8	Benoit Benjamin RC	2.50	1.00
☐ 9	Larry Bird !	30.00	15.00
☐ 10	Otis Birdsong	2.00	.75
☐ 11	Rolando Blackman RC	2.50	1.00
☐ 12	Manute Bol RC	2.00	.75

☐ 14	Joe Barry Carroll	2.00	.75
☐ 15	Tom Chambers RC	4.00	1.50
☐ 16	Maurice Cheeks	2.00	.75
☐ 17	Michael Cooper	2.50	1.00
☐ 18	Wayne Cooper	2.00	.75
☐ 19	Pat Cummings	2.00	.75
☐ 20	Terry Cummings RC	3.00	1.25
☐ 21	Adrian Dantley	2.50	1.00
☐ 22	Brad Davis RC**	2.00	.75
☐ 23	Walter Davis	2.00	.75
☐ 24	Darryl Dawkins	2.50	1.00
☐ 25	Larry Drew	2.00	.75
☐ 26	Clyde Drexler RC	25.00	10.00
☐ 27	Joe Dumars RC	15.00	6.00
☐ 28	Mark Eaton RC**	2.00	.75
☐ 29	James Edwards	2.00	.75
☐ 30	Alex English	2.50	1.00
☐ 31	Julius Erving	15.00	6.00
☐ 32	Patrick Ewing RC !	40.00	15.00
☐ 33	Vern Fleming RC**	2.00	.75
☐ 34	Sleepy Floyd RC**	2.00	.75
☐ 35	World B. Free	2.00	.75
☐ 36	George Gervin	4.00	1.50
☐ 37	Artis Gilmore	2.50	1.00
☐ 38	Mike Gminski	2.00	.75
☐ 39	Rickey Green	2.00	.75
☐ 40	Sidney Green	2.00	.75
☐ 41	David Greenwood	2.00	.75
☐ 42	Darrell Griffith	2.00	.75
☐ 43	Bill Hanzlik	2.00	.75
☐ 44	Derek Harper RC !	6.00	3.00
☐ 45	Gerald Henderson	2.00	.75
☐ 46	Roy Hinson	2.00	.75
☐ 47	Craig Hodges RC**	2.00	.75
☐ 48	Phil Hubbard	2.00	.75
☐ 49	Jay Humphries RC**	2.00	.75
☐ 50	Dennis Johnson	2.50	1.00
☐ 51	Eddie Johnson RC	2.50	1.00
☐ 52	Frank Johnson RC**	2.00	.75
☐ 53	Magic Johnson	20.00	8.00
☐ 54	Marques Johnson	2.00	.75
☐ 55	Steve Johnson UER	2.00	.75
☐ 56	Vinnie Johnson	2.00	.75
☐ 57	Michael Jordan RC !	650.00	350.00
☐ 58	Clark Kellogg RC**	2.00	.75
☐ 59	Albert King	2.00	.75
☐ 60	Bill Laimbeer	2.50	1.00
☐ 61	Bill Laimbeer	2.50	1.00
☐ 62	Allen Leavell	2.00	.75
☐ 63	Fat Lever RC**	2.00	.75
☐ 64	Alton Lister	2.00	.75
☐ 65	Lewis Lloyd	2.00	.75
☐ 66	Maurice Lucas	2.00	.75
☐ 67	Jeff Malone RC	2.00	.75
☐ 68	Karl Malone RC	40.00	15.00
☐ 69	Moses Malone	3.00	1.25
☐ 70	Cedric Maxwell	2.00	.75
☐ 71	Rodney McCray RC**	2.00	.75
☐ 72	Xavier McDaniel RC	2.50	1.00
☐ 73	Kevin McHale	3.00	1.25
☐ 74	Mike Mitchell	2.00	.75
☐ 75	Sidney Moncrief	2.50	1.00
☐ 76	Johnny Moore	2.00	.75
☐ 77	Chris Mullin RC !	25.00	10.00
☐ 78	Larry Nance RC	4.00	1.50
☐ 79	Calvin Natt	2.00	.75
☐ 80	Norm Nixon	2.00	.75
☐ 81	Charles Oakley RC	6.00	3.00

82 Hakeem Olajuwon RC	30.00	12.50
83 Louis Orr	2.00	.75
84 Robert Parish	3.00	1.25
85 Jim Paxson	2.00	.75
86 Sam Perkins RC	6.00	2.50
87 Ricky Pierce RC	2.50	1.00
88 Paul Pressey RC**	2.00	.75
89 Kurt Rambis RC	2.00	.75
90 Robert Reid	2.00	.75
91 Doc Rivers RC	6.00	2.50
92 Alvin Robertson RC	2.00	.75
93 Cliff Robinson	2.00	.75
94 Tree Rollins	2.00	.75
95 Dan Roundfield	2.00	.75
96 Jeff Ruland	2.00	.75
97 Ralph Sampson RC	2.50	1.00
98 Danny Schayes RC**	2.00	.75
99 Byron Scott RC	4.00	1.50
100 Purvis Short	2.00	.75
101 Jerry Sichting	2.00	.75
102 Jack Sikma	2.00	.75
103 Derek Smith	2.00	.75
104 Larry Smith	2.00	.75
105 Rory Sparrow	2.00	.75
106 Steve Stipanovich	2.00	.75
107 Terry Teagle	2.00	.75
108 Reggie Theus	2.50	1.00
109 Isiah Thomas RC !	25.00	10.00
110 LaSalle Thompson RC**	2.00	.75
111 Mychal Thompson	2.00	.75
112 Sedale Threatt RC**	2.00	.75
113 Wayman Tisdale RC	2.50	1.00
114 Andrew Toney	2.00	.75
115 Kelly Tripucka RC	2.00	.75
116 Mel Turpin	2.00	.75
117 Kiki Vandeweghe RC	2.50	1.00
118 Jay Vincent	2.00	.75
119 Bill Walton	4.00	1.50
120 Spud Webb RC !	6.00	3.00
121 Dominique Wilkins RC !	30.00	12.50
122 Gerald Wilkins RC	2.50	1.00
123 Buck Williams RC	4.00	1.50
124 Gus Williams	2.00	.75
125 Herb Williams RC**	2.00	.75
126 Kevin Willis RC	6.00	2.50
127 Randy Wittman	2.00	.75
128 Al Wood	2.00	.75
129 Mike Woodson	2.00	.75
130 Orlando Woolridge RC**	2.00	.75
131 James Worthy RC	20.00	8.00
132 Checklist 1-132	20.00	8.00

1987-88 Fleer

COMPLETE w/Stickers (143)	300.00	175.00
COMPLETE SET (132)	200.00	100.00
1 Kareem Abdul-Jabbar !	8.00	3.00
2 Alvan Adams	1.50	.60
3 Mark Aguirre	2.00	.75
4 Danny Ainge	2.00	.75
5 John Bagley	1.50	.60
6 Thurl Bailey UER	1.50	.60
7 Greg Ballard	1.50	.60
8 Gene Banks	1.50	.60
9 Charles Barkley	15.00	6.00
10 Benoit Benjamin	1.50	.60
11 Larry Bird !	20.00	8.00
12 Rolando Blackman	1.50	.60
13 Manute Bol	1.50	.60
14 Tony Brown	1.50	.60
15 Michael Cage RC**	1.50	.60
16 Joe Barry Carroll	1.50	.60
17 Bill Cartwright	2.00	.75
18 Terry Catledge RC	1.50	.60
19 Tom Chambers	1.50	.60
20 Maurice Cheeks	1.50	.60
21 Michael Cooper	2.00	.75
22 Dave Corzine	1.50	.60
23 Terry Cummings	2.00	.75
24 Adrian Dantley	1.50	.60
25 Brad Daugherty RC	2.50	1.00
26 Walter Davis	1.50	.60
27 Johnny Dawkins RC	1.50	.60
28 James Donaldson	1.50	.60
29 Larry Drew	1.50	.60
30 Clyde Drexler	12.00	5.00
31 Joe Dumars	4.00	1.50
32 Mark Eaton	1.50	.60
33 Dale Ellis RC	2.50	1.00
34 Alex English	2.00	.75
35 Julius Erving	12.00	5.00
36 Mike Evans	1.50	.60
37 Patrick Ewing	10.00	4.00
38 Vern Fleming	1.50	.60
39 Sleepy Floyd	1.50	.60
40 Artis Gilmore	2.00	.75
41 Mike Gminski UER	1.50	.60
42 A.C.Green RC	6.00	2.50
43 Rickey Green	1.50	.60
44 Sidney Green	1.50	.60
45 David Greenwood	1.50	.60
46 Darrell Griffith	1.50	.60
47 Bill Hanzlik	1.50	.60
48 Derek Harper	2.00	.75
49 Ron Harper RC	6.00	2.50
50 Gerald Henderson	1.50	.60
51 Roy Hinson	1.50	.60
52 Craig Hodges	1.50	.60
53 Phil Hubbard	1.50	.60
54 Dennis Johnson	1.50	.60
55 Eddie Johnson	2.00	.75
56 Magic Johnson	25.00	12.50
57 Steve Johnson	1.50	.60
58 Vinnie Johnson	1.50	.60
59 Michael Jordan	60.00	25.00
60 Jerome Kersey RC**	1.50	.60
61 Bill Laimbeer	2.00	.75
62 Lafayette Lever UER	1.50	.60
63 Cliff Levingston RC**	1.50	.60
64 Alton Lister	1.50	.60
65 John Long	1.50	.60
66 John Lucas	1.50	.60
67 Jeff Malone	1.50	.60
68 Karl Malone	15.00	6.00
69 Moses Malone	2.50	1.00
70 Cedric Maxwell	1.50	.60
71 Tim McCormick	1.50	.60
72 Rodney McCray	1.50	.60
73 Xavier McDaniel	1.50	.60
74 Kevin McHale	2.50	1.00
75 Nate McMillan RC	2.50	1.00
76 Sidney Moncrief	1.50	.60
77 Chris Mullin	4.00	1.50
78 Larry Nance	2.00	.75
79 Charles Oakley	2.50	1.00
80 Hakeem Olajuwon	15.00	6.00
81 Robert Parish	2.50	1.00
82 Jim Paxson	1.50	.60
83 John Paxson RC	2.50	1.00
84 Sam Perkins	2.50	1.00
85 Chuck Person RC	2.50	1.00
86 Jim Petersen	1.50	.60
87 Ricky Pierce	1.50	.60
88 Ed Pinckney RC	1.50	.60
89 Terry Porter RC	2.50	1.00
90 Paul Pressey	1.50	.60
91 Robert Reid	1.50	.60
92 Doc Rivers	2.50	1.00
93 Alvin Robertson	1.50	.60
94 Tree Rollins	1.50	.60
95 Ralph Sampson	1.50	.60
96 Mike Sanders	1.50	.60
97 Detlef Schrempf RC	10.00	4.00
98 Byron Scott	2.00	.75
99 Jerry Sichting	1.50	.60
100 Jack Sikma	1.50	.60
101 Larry Smith	1.50	.60
102 Rory Sparrow	1.50	.60
103 Steve Stipanovich	1.50	.60
104 Jon Sundvold	1.50	.60
105 Reggie Theus	2.00	.75
106 Isiah Thomas	6.00	2.50
107 LaSalle Thompson	1.50	.60
108 Mychal Thompson	1.50	.60
109 Otis Thorpe	5.00	2.00
110 Sedale Threatt	1.50	.60
111 Wayman Tisdale	1.50	.60
112 Kelly Tripucka	1.50	.60
113 Trent Tucker RC**	1.50	.60
114 Terry Tyler	1.50	.60
115 Darnell Valentine	1.50	.60
116 Kiki Vandeweghe	1.50	.60
117 Darrell Walker RC**	1.50	.60
118 Dominique Wilkins	4.00	1.50
119 Gerald Wilkins	1.50	.60
120 Buck Williams	2.00	.75
121 Herb Williams	1.50	.60
122 John Williams RC	1.50	.60
123 Hot Rod Williams RC	2.00	.75
124 Kevin Willis	1.50	.60
125 David Wingate RC	1.50	.60
126 Randy Wittman	1.50	.60
127 Leon Wood	1.50	.60
128 Mike Woodson	1.50	.60
129 Orlando Woolridge	1.50	.60
130 James Worthy	4.00	1.50
131 Danny Young RC**	1.50	.60
132 Checklist 1-132	10.00	4.00

1988-89 Fleer

COMPLETE w/Stickers (143)	200.00	100.00
COMPLETE SET (132)	150.00	75.00
1 Antoine Carr RC**	.75	.30
2 Cliff Levingston	.50	.20
3 Doc Rivers	.75	.30
4 Spud Webb	.75	.30
5 Dominique Wilkins	1.50	.60
6 Kevin Willis	.75	.30
7 Randy Wittman	.50	.20
8 Danny Ainge	.75	.30
9 Larry Bird	10.00	4.00
10 Dennis Johnson	.50	.20
11 Kevin McHale	1.50	.60
12 Robert Parish	1.50	.60
13 Muggsy Bogues RC	2.00	.75
14 Dell Curry RC	1.50	.60
15 Dave Corzine	.50	.20
16 Horace Grant RC	5.00	2.00
17 Michael Jordan	30.00	12.50
18 Charles Oakley	.75	.30
19 John Paxson	.75	.30
20 Scottie Pippen RC !	25.00	10.00
21 Brad Sellers RC	.50	.20
22 Brad Daugherty	.50	.20
23 Ron Harper	.75	.30
24 Larry Nance	.50	.20
25 Mark Price RC	2.00	.75
26 Hot Rod Williams	.50	.20
27 Mark Aguirre	.50	.20
28 Rolando Blackman	.50	.20
29 James Donaldson	.50	.20
30 Derek Harper	.75	.30
31 Sam Perkins	.75	.30

#	Player		
32	Roy Tarpley RC	.50	.20
33	Michael Adams RC	.50	.20
34	Alex English	.75	.30
35	Lafayette Lever	.50	.20
36	Blair Rasmussen RC	.50	.20
37	Danny Schayes	.50	.20
38	Jay Vincent	.50	.20
39	Adrian Dantley	.50	.20
40	Joe Dumars	1.50	.60
41	Vinnie Johnson	.50	.20
42	Bill Laimbeer	.75	.30
43	Dennis Rodman RC !	12.00	5.00
44	John Salley RC	.75	.30
45	Isiah Thomas	1.50	.60
46	Winston Garland RC	.50	.20
47	Rod Higgins	.50	.20
48	Chris Mullin	1.50	.60
49	Ralph Sampson	.50	.20
50	Joe Barry Carroll	.50	.20
51	Sleepy Floyd	.50	.20
52	Rodney McCray	.50	.20
53	Hakeem Olajuwon	5.00	2.00
54	Purvis Short	.50	.20
55	Vern Fleming	.50	.20
56	John Long	.50	.20
57	Reggie Miller RC !	20.00	8.00
58	Chuck Person	.75	.30
59	Steve Stipanovich	.50	.20
60	Wayman Tisdale	.50	.20
61	Benoit Benjamin	.50	.20
62	Michael Cage	.50	.20
63	Mike Woodson	.50	.20
64	Kareem Abdul-Jabbar	4.00	1.50
65	Michael Cooper	.50	.20
66	A.C.Green	.75	.30
67	Magic Johnson	10.00	4.00
68	Byron Scott	.50	.30
69	Mychal Thompson	.50	.20
70	James Worthy	1.50	.60
71	Duane Washington	.50	.20
72	Kevin Williams	.50	.20
73	Randy Breuer RC**	.50	.20
74	Terry Cummings	.75	.30
75	Paul Pressey	.50	.20
76	Jack Sikma	.50	.20
77	John Bagley	.50	.20
78	Roy Hinson	.50	.20
79	Buck Williams	.75	.30
80	Patrick Ewing	3.00	1.25
81	Sidney Green	.50	.20
82	Mark Jackson	2.50	1.00
83	Kenny Walker RC	.50	.20
84	Gerald Wilkins	.50	.20
85	Charles Barkley	5.00	2.00
86	Maurice Cheeks	.50	.20
87	Mike Gminski	.50	.20
88	Cliff Robinson	.50	.20
89	Armon Gilliam RC	1.50	.60
90	Eddie Johnson	.50	.20
91	Mark West RC	.50	.20
92	Clyde Drexler	3.00	1.25
93	Kevin Duckworth RC	.50	.20
94	Steve Johnson	.50	.20
95	Jerome Kersey	.50	.20
96	Terry Porter	.50	.20
97	Joe Kleine RC	.50	.20
98	Reggie Theus	.75	.30
99	Otis Thorpe	.75	.30
100	Kenny Smith RC	1.50	.60
101	Greg Anderson RC	.50	.20
102	Walter Berry RC	.50	.20
103	Frank Brickowski RC	.50	.20
104	Johnny Dawkins	.50	.20
105	Alvin Robertson	.50	.20
106	Tom Chambers	.50	.20
107	Dale Ellis	.75	.30
108	Xavier McDaniel	.50	.20
109	Derrick McKey RC	1.50	.60
110	Nate McMillan UER	.50	.20
111	Thurl Bailey	.50	.20
112	Mark Eaton	.50	.20
113	Bobby Hansen RC**	.50	.20
114	Karl Malone	5.00	2.00
115	John Stockton RC !	20.00	8.00
116	Bernard King	.50	.20
117	Jeff Malone	.50	.20
118	Moses Malone	1.50	.60
119	John Williams	.50	.20
120	Michael Jordan AS	15.00	6.00
121	Mark Jackson AS	1.50	.60
122	Byron Scott AS	.50	.20
123	Magic Johnson AS	4.00	1.50
124	Larry Bird AS	5.00	2.00
125	Dominique Wilkins AS	.75	.30
126	Hakeem Olajuwon AS	2.00	.75
127	John Stockton AS	5.00	2.00
128	Alvin Robertson AS	.50	.20
129	Charles Barkley AS	2.00	.75
130	Patrick Ewing AS	1.50	.60
131	Mark Eaton AS	.50	.20
132	Checklist 1-132	.50	.20

1989-90 Fleer

#	Player		
	COMPLETE w/Stickers (179)	50.00	20.00
	COMPLETE SET (168)	30.00	15.00
1	John Battle RC	.15	.05
2	Jon Koncak RC	.15	.05
3	Cliff Levingston	.15	.05
4	Moses Malone	.50	.20
5	Doc Rivers	.25	.08
6	Spud Webb	.25	.08
7	Dominique Wilkins	.50	.20
8	Larry Bird	3.00	1.25
9	Dennis Johnson	.15	.05
10	Reggie Lewis RC	.75	.30
11	Kevin McHale	.50	.20
12	Robert Parish	.25	.08
13	Ed Pinckney	.15	.05
14	Brian Shaw RC	.50	.20
15	Rex Chapman RC	.75	.30
16	Kurt Rambis	.15	.05
17	Robert Reid	.15	.05
18	Kelly Tripucka	.15	.05
19	Bill Cartwright UER	.15	.05
20	Horace Grant	.25	.08
21	Michael Jordan	15.00	6.00
22	John Paxson	.15	.05
23	Scottie Pippen	5.00	2.00
24	Brad Sellers	.15	.05
25	Brad Daugherty	.15	.05
26	Craig Ehlo RC**	.15	.05
27	Ron Harper	.25	.08
28	Larry Nance	.25	.08
29	Mark Price	.25	.08
30	Mike Sanders	.15	.05
31A	Hot Rod Williams ERR		
31B	Hot Rod Williams COR	.15	.05
32	Rolando Blackman	.15	.05
33	Adrian Dantley	.15	.05
34	James Donaldson	.15	.05
35	Derek Harper	.25	.08
36	Sam Perkins	.25	.08
37	Herb Williams	.15	.05
38	Michael Adams	.15	.05
39	Walter Davis	.15	.05
40	Alex English	.15	.05
41	Lafayette Lever	.15	.05
42	Blair Rasmussen	.15	.05
43	Danny Schayes	.15	.05
44	Mark Aguirre	.15	.05
45	Joe Dumars	.50	.20
46	James Edwards	.15	.05
47	Vinnie Johnson	.15	.05
48	Bill Laimbeer	.25	.08
49	Dennis Rodman	3.00	1.25
50	Isiah Thomas	.50	.20
51	John Salley	.15	.05
52	Manute Bol	.15	.05
53	Winston Garland	.15	.05
54	Rod Higgins	.15	.05
55	Chris Mullin	.50	.20
56	Mitch Richmond RC	4.00	1.50
57	Terry Teagle	.15	.05
58	Derrick Chievous UER	.15	.05
59	Sleepy Floyd	.15	.05
60	Tim McCormick	.15	.05
61	Hakeem Olajuwon	1.25	.50
62	Otis Thorpe	.25	.08
63	Mike Woodson	.15	.05
64	Vern Fleming	.15	.05
65	Reggie Miller	2.00	.75
66	Chuck Person	.25	.08
67	Detlef Schrempf	.25	.08
68	Rik Smits RC	1.00	.40
69	Benoit Benjamin	.15	.05
70	Gary Grant RC	.15	.05
71	Danny Manning RC	1.00	.40
72	Ken Norman RC	.15	.05
73	Charles Smith RC	.50	.20
74	Reggie Williams RC	.15	.05
75	Michael Cooper	.15	.05
76	A.C.Green	.25	.08
77	Magic Johnson	2.50	1.00
78	Byron Scott	.25	.08
79	Mychal Thompson	.15	.05
80	James Worthy	.50	.20
81	Kevin Edwards RC	.15	.05
82	Grant Long RC	.15	.05
83	Rony Seikaly RC	.50	.20
84	Rory Sparrow	.15	.05
85	Greg Anderson UER	.15	.05
86	Jay Humphries	.15	.05
87	Larry Krystkowiak RC	.15	.05
88	Ricky Pierce	.15	.05
89	Paul Pressey	.15	.05
90	Alvin Robertson	.15	.05
91	Jack Sikma	.15	.05
92	Steve Johnson	.15	.05
93	Rick Mahorn	.15	.05
94	David Rivers	.15	.05
95	Joe Barry Carroll	.15	.05
96	Lester Conner UER	.15	.05
97	Roy Hinson	.15	.05
98	Mike McGee	.15	.05
99	Chris Morris RC	.25	.08
100	Patrick Ewing	.75	.30
101	Mark Jackson	.25	.08
102	Johnny Newman RC	.15	.05
103	Charles Oakley	.25	.08
104	Rod Strickland RC	2.50	1.00
105	Trent Tucker	.15	.05
106	Kiki Vandeweghe	.15	.05
107A	Gerald Wilkins	.15	.05
107B	Gerald Wilkins	.15	.05
108	Terry Catledge	.15	.05
109	Dave Corzine	.15	.05
110	Scott Skiles RC	.25	.08
111	Reggie Theus	.25	.08
112	Ron Anderson RC**	.15	.05
113	Charles Barkley	1.25	.50
114	Scott Brooks RC	.15	.05
115	Maurice Cheeks	.15	.05
116	Mike Gminski	.15	.05
117	Hersey Hawkins RC	1.00	.40
118	Christian Welp	.15	.05
119	Tom Chambers	.15	.05
120	Armon Gilliam	.15	.05
121	Jeff Hornacek RC	1.00	.40
122	Eddie Johnson	.25	.08
123	Kevin Johnson RC	1.50	.60
124	Dan Majerle RC	1.00	.40
125	Mark West	.15	.05
126	Richard Anderson	.15	.05
127	Mark Bryant RC	.15	.05
128	Clyde Drexler	.75	.30
129	Kevin Duckworth	.15	.05
130	Jerome Kersey	.15	.05
131	Terry Porter	.15	.05
132	Buck Williams	.25	.08
133	Danny Ainge	.25	.08

☐ 134	Ricky Berry	.15	.05	☐ 29	Will Perdue	.05	.01	☐ 113 Tyrone Corbin	.05	.01

#	Player		
☐ 134	Ricky Berry	.15	.05
☐ 135	Rodney McCray	.15	.05
☐ 136	Jim Petersen	.15	.05
☐ 137	Harold Pressley	.15	.05
☐ 138	Kenny Smith	.15	.05
☐ 139	Wayman Tisdale	.15	.05
☐ 140	Willie Anderson RC	.15	.05
☐ 141	Frank Brickowski	.15	.05
☐ 142	Terry Cummings	.25	.08
☐ 143	Johnny Dawkins	.15	.05
☐ 144	Vernon Maxwell RC	.75	.30
☐ 145	Michael Cage	.15	.05
☐ 146	Dale Ellis	.25	.08
☐ 147	Alton Lister	.15	.05
☐ 148	Xavier McDaniel	.15	.05
☐ 149	Derrick McKey	.15	.05
☐ 150	Nate McMillan	.25	.08
☐ 151	Thurl Bailey	.15	.05
☐ 152	Mark Eaton	.15	.05
☐ 153	Darrell Griffith	.15	.05
☐ 154	Eric Leckner	.15	.05
☐ 155	Karl Malone	1.25	.50
☐ 156	John Stockton	2.00	.75
☐ 157	Mark Alarie	.15	.05
☐ 158	Ledell Eackles RC	.15	.05
☐ 159	Bernard King	.15	.05
☐ 160	Jeff Malone	.15	.05
☐ 161	Darrell Walker	.15	.05
☐ 162A	John Williams ERR		
☐ 162B	John Williams COR	.15	.05
☐ 163	Malone/Stockton/Eaton AS	.50	.20
☐ 164	H.Olajuwon/C.Drexler AS	.50	.20
☐ 165	ASG:Wilkins/M.Malone	.50	.20
☐ 166	ASG:Daugh/Price/Nance	.15	.05
☐ 167	ASG:Ewing/M.Jackson	.50	.20
☐ 168	Checklist 1-168	.15	.05

1990-91 Fleer

☐	COMPLETE SET (198)	6.00	3.00
☐ 1	John Battle UER	.05	.01
☐ 2	Cliff Levingston	.05	.01
☐ 3	Moses Malone	.15	.05
☐ 4	Kenny Smith	.08	.01
☐ 5	Spud Webb	.08	.01
☐ 6	Dominique Wilkins	.15	.05
☐ 7	Kevin Willis	.08	.01
☐ 8	Larry Bird	.60	.25
☐ 9	Dennis Johnson	.05	.01
☐ 10	Joe Kleine	.05	.01
☐ 11	Reggie Lewis	.08	.01
☐ 12	Kevin McHale	.08	.01
☐ 13	Robert Parish	.08	.01
☐ 14	Jim Paxson	.08	.01
☐ 15	Ed Pinckney	.05	.01
☐ 16	Muggsy Bogues	.08	.01
☐ 17	Rex Chapman	.15	.05
☐ 18	Dell Curry	.05	.01
☐ 19	Armon Gilliam	.05	.01
☐ 20	J.R.Reid RC	.08	.01
☐ 21	Kelly Tripucka	.05	.01
☐ 22	B.J.Armstrong RC	.05	.01
☐ 23A	Bill Cartwright ERR		
☐ 23B	Bill Cartwright COR	.05	.01
☐ 24	Horace Grant	.05	.01
☐ 25	Craig Hodges	.05	.01
☐ 26	Michael Jordan	4.00	1.50
☐ 27	Stacey King RC	.05	.01
☐ 28	John Paxson	.08	.01

☐ 29	Will Perdue	.05	.01
☐ 30	Scottie Pippen	.60	.25
☐ 31	Brad Daugherty	.05	.01
☐ 32	Craig Ehlo	.05	.01
☐ 33	Danny Ferry RC	.08	.01
☐ 34	Steve Kerr	.15	.05
☐ 35	Larry Nance	.08	.01
☐ 36	Mark Price	.08	.01
☐ 37	Hot Rod Williams	.05	.01
☐ 38	Rolando Blackman	.05	.01
☐ 39A	Adrian Dantley ERR		
☐ 39B	Adrian Dantley COR	.05	.01
☐ 40	Brad Davis	.05	.01
☐ 41	James Donaldson UER	.05	.01
☐ 42	Derek Harper	.08	.01
☐ 43	Sam Perkins UER	.08	.01
☐ 44	Bill Wennington	.05	.01
☐ 45	Herb Williams	.05	.01
☐ 46	Michael Adams	.05	.01
☐ 47	Walter Davis	.08	.01
☐ 48	Alex English UER	.08	.01
☐ 49	Bill Hanzlik	.05	.01
☐ 50	Lafayette Lever UER	.05	.01
☐ 51	Todd Lichti RC	.05	.01
☐ 52	Blair Rasmussen	.05	.01
☐ 53	Danny Schayes	.05	.01
☐ 54	Mark Aguirre	.05	.01
☐ 55	Joe Dumars	.15	.05
☐ 56	James Edwards	.05	.01
☐ 57	Vinnie Johnson	.05	.01
☐ 58	Bill Laimbeer	.08	.01
☐ 59	Dennis Rodman	.40	.15
☐ 60	John Salley	.05	.01
☐ 61	Isiah Thomas	.15	.05
☐ 62	Manute Bol	.05	.01
☐ 63	Tim Hardaway RC	1.00	.40
☐ 64	Rod Higgins	.05	.01
☐ 65	Sarun.Marciulionis RC	.05	.01
☐ 66	Chris Mullin	.15	.05
☐ 67	Mitch Richmond	.20	.07
☐ 68	Terry Teagle	.05	.01
☐ 69	Anthony Bowie RC	.05	.01
☐ 70	Sleepy Floyd	.05	.01
☐ 71	Buck Johnson	.05	.01
☐ 72	Vernon Maxwell	.05	.01
☐ 73	Hakeem Olajuwon	.25	.08
☐ 74	Otis Thorpe	.05	.01
☐ 75	Mitchell Wiggins	.05	.01
☐ 76	Vern Fleming	.05	.01
☐ 77	George McCloud RC	.15	.05
☐ 78	Reggie Miller	.20	.07
☐ 79	Chuck Person	.08	.01
☐ 80	Mike Sanders	.05	.01
☐ 81	Detlef Schrempf	.08	.01
☐ 82	Rik Smits	.15	.05
☐ 83	LaSalle Thompson	.05	.01
☐ 84	Benoit Benjamin	.05	.01
☐ 85	Winston Garland	.05	.01
☐ 86	Ron Harper	.08	.01
☐ 87	Danny Manning	.08	.01
☐ 88	Ken Norman	.05	.01
☐ 89	Charles Smith	.05	.01
☐ 90	Michael Cooper	.05	.01
☐ 91	Vlade Divac RC	.40	.15
☐ 92	A.C. Green	.08	.01
☐ 93	Magic Johnson	.50	.20
☐ 94	Byron Scott	.08	.01
☐ 95	Mychal Thompson UER	.05	.01
☐ 96	Orlando Woolridge	.05	.01
☐ 97	James Worthy	.15	.05
☐ 98	Sherman Douglas RC	.08	.01
☐ 99	Kevin Edwards	.05	.01
☐ 100	Grant Long	.05	.01
☐ 101	Glen Rice RC	.60	.25
☐ 102	Rony Seikaly / Michael Jordan UER	.08	.01
☐ 103	Billy Thompson	.05	.01
☐ 104	Jeff Grayer RC	.05	.01
☐ 105	Jay Humphries	.05	.01
☐ 106	Ricky Pierce	.05	.01
☐ 107	Paul Pressey	.05	.01
☐ 108	Fred Roberts	.05	.01
☐ 109	Alvin Robertson	.05	.01
☐ 110	Jack Sikma	.05	.01
☐ 111	Randy Breuer	.05	.01
☐ 112	Tony Campbell	.05	.01

☐ 113	Tyrone Corbin	.05	.01
☐ 114	Sam Mitchell RC	.05	.01
☐ 115	Tod Murphy UER	.05	.01
☐ 116	Pooh Richardson RC	.08	.01
☐ 117	Mookie Blaylock RC	.25	.08
☐ 118	Sam Bowie	.05	.01
☐ 119	Lester Conner	.05	.01
☐ 120	Dennis Hopson	.05	.01
☐ 121	Chris Morris	.08	.01
☐ 122	Charles Shackleford	.05	.01
☐ 123	Purvis Short	.05	.01
☐ 124	Maurice Cheeks	.08	.01
☐ 125	Patrick Ewing	.15	.05
☐ 126	Mark Jackson	.08	.01
☐ 127A	Johnny Newman ERR	.40	.15
☐ 127B	Johnny Newman COR	.05	.01
☐ 128	Charles Oakley	.08	.01
☐ 129	Trent Tucker	.05	.01
☐ 130	Kenny Walker	.05	.01
☐ 131	Gerald Wilkins	.05	.01
☐ 132	Nick Anderson RC	.25	.08
☐ 133	Terry Catledge	.05	.01
☐ 134	Sidney Green	.05	.01
☐ 135	Otis Smith	.05	.01
☐ 136	Reggie Theus	.08	.01
☐ 137	Sam Vincent	.05	.01
☐ 138	Ron Anderson	.05	.01
☐ 139	Charles Barkley	.25	.08
☐ 140	Scott Brooks UER	.05	.01
☐ 141	Johnny Dawkins	.05	.01
☐ 142	Mike Gminski	.05	.01
☐ 143	Hersey Hawkins	.08	.01
☐ 144	Rick Mahorn	.05	.01
☐ 145	Derek Smith	.05	.01
☐ 146	Tom Chambers	.08	.01
☐ 147	Jeff Hornacek	.08	.01
☐ 148	Eddie Johnson	.08	.01
☐ 149	Kevin Johnson	.15	.05
☐ 150A	Dan Majerle ERR 1988	.75	.30
☐ 150B	Dan Majerle COR 1989	.15	.05
☐ 151	Tim Perry	.05	.01
☐ 152	Kurt Rambis	.05	.01
☐ 153	Mark West	.05	.01
☐ 154	Clyde Drexler	.15	.05
☐ 155	Kevin Duckworth	.05	.01
☐ 156	Byron Irvin	.05	.01
☐ 157	Jerome Kersey	.05	.01
☐ 158	Terry Porter	.05	.01
☐ 159	Clifford Robinson RC	.25	.08
☐ 160	Buck Williams	.08	.01
☐ 161	Danny Young	.05	.01
☐ 162	Danny Ainge	.08	.01
☐ 163	Antoine Carr	.05	.01
☐ 164	Pervis Ellison RC	.08	.01
☐ 165	Rodney McCray	.05	.01
☐ 166	Harold Pressley	.05	.01
☐ 167	Wayman Tisdale	.05	.01
☐ 168	Willie Anderson	.05	.01
☐ 169	Frank Brickowski	.05	.01
☐ 170	Terry Cummings	.08	.01
☐ 171	Sean Elliott RC	.30	.10
☐ 172	David Robinson	.50	.20
☐ 173	Rod Strickland	.15	.05
☐ 174	David Wingate	.05	.01
☐ 175	Dana Barros	.15	.05
☐ 176	Michael Cage UER	.05	.01
☐ 177	Dale Ellis	.08	.01
☐ 178	Shawn Kemp RC	1.50	.60
☐ 179	Xavier McDaniel	.05	.01
☐ 180	Derrick McKey	.05	.01
☐ 181	Nate McMillan	.05	.01
☐ 182	Thurl Bailey	.05	.01
☐ 183	Mike Brown	.05	.01
☐ 184	Mark Eaton	.05	.01
☐ 185	Blue Edwards RC	.05	.01
☐ 186	Bobby Hansen	.05	.01
☐ 187	Eric Leckner	.05	.01
☐ 188	Karl Malone	.25	.08
☐ 189	John Stockton	.20	.07
☐ 190	Mark Alarie	.05	.01
☐ 191	Ledell Eackles	.05	.01
☐ 192A	Harvey Grant FFC Black	.75	.30
☐ 192B	Harvey Grant FFC White	.05	.01
☐ 193	Tom Hammonds RC	.05	.01
☐ 194	Bernard King	.05	.01
☐ 195	Jeff Malone	.05	.01

1990-91 Fleer Update

❏ COMPLETE SET (100)		8.00	3.00
❏ U1 Jon Koncak		.05	.01
❏ U2 Tim McCormick		.05	.01
❏ U3 Doc Rivers		.15	.05
❏ U4 Rumeal Robinson RC		.05	.01
❏ U5 Trevor Wilson		.05	.01
❏ U6 Dee Brown RC		.30	.10
❏ U7 Dave Popson		.05	.01
❏ U8 Kevin Gamble FFC		.05	.01
❏ U9 Brian Shaw		.30	.10
❏ U10 Michael Smith		.05	.01
❏ U11 Kendall Gill RC		.60	.25
❏ U12 Johnny Newman		.05	.01
❏ U13 Steve Scheffler RC		.05	.01
❏ U14 Dennis Hopson		.05	.01
❏ U15 Cliff Levingston		.05	.01
❏ U16 Chucky Brown RC		.05	.01
❏ U17 John Morton		.05	.01
❏ U18 Gerald Paddio RC		.05	.01
❏ U19 Alex English		.05	.01
❏ U20 Fat Lever		.05	.01
❏ U21 Rodney McCray		.05	.01
❏ U22 Roy Tarpley		.05	.01
❏ U23 Randy White RC		.05	.01
❏ U24 Anthony Cook RC		.05	.01
❏ U25 Chris Jackson RC		.30	.10
❏ U26 Marcus Liberty RC		.05	.01
❏ U27 Orlando Woolridge		.05	.01
❏ U28 William Bedford RC		.05	.01
❏ U29 Lance Blanks RC		.05	.01
❏ U30 Scott Hastings		.05	.01
❏ U31 Tyrone Hill RC		.15	.05
❏ U32 Les Jepsen RC		.05	.01
❏ U33 Steve Johnson		.05	.01
❏ U34 Kevin Pritchard		.05	.01
❏ U35 Dave Jamerson RC		.05	.01
❏ U36 Kenny Smith		.05	.01
❏ U37 Greg Dreiling RC		.05	.01
❏ U38 Kenny Williams RC		.05	.01
❏ U39 Micheal Williams FFC UER		.15	.05
❏ U40 Gary Grant		.05	.01
❏ U41 Bo Kimble RC		.05	.01
❏ U42 Loy Vaught RC		.50	.20
❏ U43 Elden Campbell RC		.60	.25
❏ U44 Sam Perkins		.15	.05
❏ U45 Tony Smith RC		.05	.01
❏ U46 Terry Teagle		.05	.01
❏ U47 Willie Burton RC		.05	.01
❏ U48 Bimbo Coles RC		.30	.10
❏ U49 Terry Davis RC		.05	.01
❏ U50 Alec Kessler RC		.05	.01
❏ U51 Greg Anderson		.05	.01
❏ U52 Frank Brickowski		.05	.01
❏ U53 Steve Henson RC		.05	.01
❏ U54 Brad Lohaus		.05	.01
❏ U55 Danny Schayes		.05	.01
❏ U56 Gerald Glass RC		.05	.01
❏ U57 Felton Spencer RC		.15	.05
❏ U58 Doug West RC		.15	.05
❏ U59 Jud Buechler RC		.15	.05
❏ U60 Derrick Coleman RC		.60	.25
❏ U61 Tate George RC		.05	.01
❏ U62 Reggie Theus		.15	.05

❏ U63 Greg Grant RC		.05	.01
❏ U64 Jerrod Mustaf RC		.05	.01
❏ U65 Eddie Lee Wilkins RC**		.05	.01
❏ U66 Michael Ansley		.05	.01
❏ U67 Jerry Reynolds		.05	.01
❏ U68 Dennis Scott RC		.40	.15
❏ U69 Manute Bol		.05	.01
❏ U70 Armon Gilliam		.05	.01
❏ U71 Brian Oliver		.05	.01
❏ U72 Kenny Payne RC		.05	.01
❏ U73 Jayson Williams RC		1.00	.40
❏ U74 Kenny Battle RC		.05	.01
❏ U75 Cedric Ceballos RC		.50	.20
❏ U76 Negele Knight RC		.05	.01
❏ U77 Xavier McDaniel		.05	.01
❏ U78 Alaa Abdelnaby RC		.05	.01
❏ U79 Danny Ainge		.15	.05
❏ U80 Mark Bryant		.05	.01
❏ U81 Drazen Petrovic RC		.15	.05
❏ U82 Anthony Bonner RC		.05	.01
❏ U83 Duane Causwell RC		.05	.01
❏ U84 Bobby Hansen		.05	.01
❏ U85 Eric Leckner		.05	.01
❏ U86 Travis Mays RC		.05	.01
❏ U87 Lionel Simmons RC		.15	.05
❏ U88 Sidney Green		.05	.01
❏ U89 Tony Massenburg RC		.05	.01
❏ U90 Paul Pressey		.05	.01
❏ U91 Dwayne Schintzius RC		.05	.01
❏ U92 Gary Payton RC		6.00	2.50
❏ U93 Olden Polynice		.05	.01
❏ U94 Jeff Malone		.05	.01
❏ U95 Walter Palmer		.05	.01
❏ U96 Delaney Rudd		.05	.01
❏ U97 Pervis Ellison		.15	.05
❏ U98 A.J.English RC		.05	.01
❏ U99 Greg Foster RC		.15	.05
❏ U100 Checklist 1-100		.05	.01

1991-92 Fleer

❏ COMPLETE SET (400)		10.00	5.00
❏ COMPLETE SERIES 1 (240)		5.00	2.50
❏ COMPLETE SERIES 2 (160)		5.00	2.50
❏ 1 John Battle		.05	.01
❏ 2 Jon Koncak		.05	.01
❏ 3 Rumeal Robinson		.05	.01
❏ 4 Spud Webb		.08	.01
❏ 5 Bob Weiss CO		.05	.01
❏ 6 Dominique Wilkins		.15	.05
❏ 7 Kevin Willis		.05	.01
❏ 8 Larry Bird		.60	.25
❏ 9 Dee Brown		.05	.01
❏ 10 Chris Ford CO		.05	.01
❏ 11 Kevin Gamble		.05	.01
❏ 12 Reggie Lewis		.08	.01
❏ 13 Kevin McHale		.08	.01
❏ 14 Robert Parish		.08	.01
❏ 15 Ed Pinckney		.05	.01
❏ 16 Brian Shaw		.05	.01
❏ 17 Muggsy Bogues		.08	.01
❏ 18 Rex Chapman		.05	.01
❏ 19 Dell Curry		.05	.01
❏ 20 Kendall Gill		.08	.01
❏ 21 Eric Leckner		.05	.01
❏ 22 Gene Littles CO		.05	.01
❏ 23 Johnny Newman		.05	.01
❏ 24 J.R. Reid		.05	.01
❏ 25 B.J.Armstrong		.05	.01

❏ 26 Bill Cartwright		.05	.01
❏ 27 Horace Grant		.08	.01
❏ 28 Phil Jackson CO		.08	.01
❏ 29 Michael Jordan		2.00	.75
❏ 30 Cliff Levingston		.05	.01
❏ 31 John Paxson		.05	.01
❏ 32 Will Perdue		.05	.01
❏ 33 Scottie Pippen		.50	.20
❏ 34 Brad Daugherty		.05	.01
❏ 35 Craig Ehlo		.05	.01
❏ 36 Danny Ferry		.05	.01
❏ 37 Larry Nance		.05	.01
❏ 38 Mark Price		.05	.01
❏ 39 Darnell Valentine		.05	.01
❏ 40 Hot Rod Williams		.05	.01
❏ 41 Lenny Wilkens CO		.08	.01
❏ 42 Richie Adubato CO		.05	.01
❏ 43 Rolando Blackman		.05	.01
❏ 44 James Donaldson		.05	.01
❏ 45 Derek Harper		.05	.01
❏ 46 Rodney McCray		.05	.01
❏ 47 Randy White		.05	.01
❏ 48 Herb Williams		.05	.01
❏ 49 Chris Jackson		.05	.01
❏ 50 Marcus Liberty		.05	.01
❏ 51 Todd Lichti		.05	.01
❏ 52 Blair Rasmussen		.05	.01
❏ 53 Paul Westhead CO		.05	.01
❏ 54 Reggie Williams		.05	.01
❏ 55 Joe Wolf		.05	.01
❏ 56 Orlando Woolridge		.05	.01
❏ 57 Mark Aguirre		.05	.01
❏ 58 Chuck Daly CO		.08	.01
❏ 59 Joe Dumars		.15	.05
❏ 60 James Edwards		.05	.01
❏ 61 Vinnie Johnson		.05	.01
❏ 62 Bill Laimbeer		.08	.01
❏ 63 Dennis Rodman		.30	.10
❏ 64 Isiah Thomas		.15	.05
❏ 65 Tim Hardaway		.25	.08
❏ 66 Rod Higgins		.05	.01
❏ 67 Tyrone Hill		.08	.01
❏ 68 Sarunas Marciulionis		.05	.01
❏ 69 Chris Mullin		.15	.05
❏ 70 Don Nelson CO		.08	.01
❏ 71 Mitch Richmond		.15	.05
❏ 72 Tom Tolbert		.05	.01
❏ 73 Don Chaney CO		.05	.01
❏ 74 Eric(Sleepy) Floyd		.05	.01
❏ 75 Buck Johnson		.05	.01
❏ 76 Vernon Maxwell		.05	.01
❏ 77 Hakeem Olajuwon		.25	.08
❏ 78 Kenny Smith		.05	.01
❏ 79 Larry Smith		.05	.01
❏ 80 Otis Thorpe		.08	.01
❏ 81 Vern Fleming		.05	.01
❏ 82 Bob Hill RC CO		.08	.01
❏ 83 Reggie Miller		.15	.05
❏ 84 Chuck Person		.05	.01
❏ 85 Detlef Schrempf		.08	.01
❏ 86 Rik Smits		.08	.01
❏ 87 LaSalle Thompson		.05	.01
❏ 88 Micheal Williams		.05	.01
❏ 89 Gary Grant		.05	.01
❏ 90 Ron Harper		.08	.01
❏ 91 Bo Kimble		.05	.01
❏ 92 Danny Manning		.08	.01
❏ 93 Ken Norman		.05	.01
❏ 94 Olden Polynice		.05	.01
❏ 95 Mike Schuler CO		.05	.01
❏ 96 Charles Smith		.05	.01
❏ 97 Vlade Divac		.08	.01
❏ 98 Mike Dunleavy CO		.05	.01
❏ 99 A.C. Green		.08	.01
❏ 100 Magic Johnson		.50	.20
❏ 101 Sam Perkins		.08	.01
❏ 102 Byron Scott		.08	.01
❏ 103 Terry Teagle		.05	.01
❏ 104 James Worthy		.15	.05
❏ 105 Willie Burton		.05	.01
❏ 106 Bimbo Coles		.05	.01
❏ 107 Sherman Douglas		.05	.01
❏ 108 Kevin Edwards		.05	.01
❏ 109 Grant Long		.05	.01
❏ 110 Kevin Loughery CO		.05	.01
❏ 111 Glen Rice		.15	.05

Top of second column:

❏ 196 Darrell Walker		.05	.01
❏ 197 Checklist 1-99		.05	.01
❏ 198 Checklist 100-198		.05	.01

#	Player		
112	Rony Seikaly	.05	.01
113	Frank Brickowski	.05	.01
114	Dale Ellis	.08	.01
115	Del Harris CO	.05	.01
116	Jay Humphries	.05	.01
117	Fred Roberts	.05	.01
118	Alvin Robertson	.05	.01
119	Danny Schayes	.05	.01
120	Jack Sikma	.05	.01
121	Tony Campbell	.05	.01
122	Tyrone Corbin	.05	.01
123	Sam Mitchell	.05	.01
124	Tod Murphy	.05	.01
125	Pooh Richardson	.05	.01
126	Jimmy Rodgers CO	.05	.01
127	Felton Spencer	.05	.01
128	Mookie Blaylock	.08	.01
129	Sam Bowie	.05	.01
130	Derrick Coleman	.08	.01
131	Chris Dudley	.05	.01
132	Bill Fitch CO	.05	.01
133	Chris Morris	.05	.01
134	Drazen Petrovic	.08	.01
135	Maurice Cheeks	.05	.01
136	Patrick Ewing	.15	.05
137	Mark Jackson	.05	.01
138	Charles Oakley	.08	.01
139	Pat Riley CO	.08	.01
140	Trent Tucker	.05	.01
141	Kiki Vandeweghe	.05	.01
142	Gerald Wilkins	.05	.01
143	Nick Anderson	.06	.01
144	Terry Catledge	.05	.01
145	Matt Guokas CO	.05	.01
146	Jerry Reynolds	.05	.01
147	Dennis Scott	.08	.01
148	Scott Skiles	.05	.01
149	Otis Smith	.05	.01
150	Ron Anderson	.05	.01
151	Charles Barkley	.25	.08
152	Johnny Dawkins	.05	.01
153	Armon Gilliam	.05	.01
154	Hersey Hawkins	.05	.01
155	Jim Lynam CO	.05	.01
156	Rick Mahorn	.05	.01
157	Brian Oliver	.05	.01
158	Tom Chambers	.08	.01
159	Cotton Fitzsimmons CO	.05	.01
160	Jeff Hornacek	.08	.01
161	Kevin Johnson	.15	.05
162	Negele Knight	.05	.01
163	Dan Majerle	.08	.01
164	Xavier McDaniel	.05	.01
165	Mark West	.05	.01
166	Rick Adelman CO	.05	.01
167	Danny Ainge	.08	.01
168	Clyde Drexler	.15	.05
169	Kevin Duckworth	.05	.01
170	Jerome Kersey	.05	.01
171	Terry Porter	.05	.01
172	Clifford Robinson	.08	.01
173	Buck Williams	.05	.01
174	Antoine Carr	.05	.01
175	Duane Causwell	.05	.01
176	Jim Les RC	.05	.01
177	Travis Mays	.05	.01
178	Dick Motta CO	.05	.01
179	Lionel Simmons	.05	.01
180	Rory Sparrow	.05	.01
181	Wayman Tisdale	.05	.01
182	Willie Anderson	.05	.01
183	Larry Brown CO	.05	.01
184	Terry Cummings	.05	.01
185	Sean Elliott	.08	.01
186	Paul Pressey	.05	.01
187	David Robinson	.30	.10
188	Rod Strickland	.15	.05
189	Benoit Benjamin	.05	.01
190	Eddie Johnson	.05	.01
191	K.C. Jones CO	.08	.01
192	Shawn Kemp	.40	.15
193	Derrick McKey	.05	.01
194	Gary Payton	.40	.15
195	Ricky Pierce	.05	.01
196	Sedale Threatt	.05	.01
197	Thurl Bailey	.05	.01
198	Mark Eaton	.05	.01
199	Blue Edwards	.05	.01
200	Jeff Malone	.05	.01
201	Karl Malone	.25	.08
202	Jerry Sloan CO	.08	.01
203	John Stockton	.15	.05
204	Ledell Eackles	.05	.01
205	Pervis Ellison	.05	.01
206	A.J. English	.05	.01
207	Harvey Grant	.05	.01
208	Bernard King	.05	.01
209	Wes Unseld CO	.08	.01
210	Kevin Johnson AS	.08	.01
211	Michael Jordan AS	1.00	.40
212	Dominique Wilkins AS	.08	.01
213	Charles Barkley AS	.15	.05
214	Hakeem Olajuwon AS	.15	.05
215	Patrick Ewing AS	.08	.01
216	Tim Hardaway AS	.15	.05
217	John Stockton AS	.08	.01
218	Chris Mullin AS	.08	.01
219	Karl Malone AS	.15	.05
220	Michael Jordan LL	1.00	.40
221	John Stockton LL	.08	.01
222	Alvin Robertson LL	.05	.01
223	Hakeem Olajuwon LL	.15	.05
224	Buck Williams LL	.05	.01
225	David Robinson LL	.15	.05
226	Reggie Miller LL	.08	.01
227	Blue Edwards SD	.05	.01
228	Dee Brown SD	.05	.01
229	Rex Chapman SD	.05	.01
230	Kenny Smith SD	.05	.01
231	Shawn Kemp SD	.15	.05
232	Kendall Gill SD	.05	.01
233	M.Jordan/Group ASG	.50	.20
234	'91 All Star Game	.15	.05
235	'91 All Star Game	.05	.01
236	P.Ewing/K.Malone ASG	.05	.01
237	Superstars/Group ASG	.25	.08
238	M.Jordan/Group ASG	.50	.20
239	Checklist 1-120	.05	.01
240	Checklist 121-240	.05	.01
241	Stacey Augmon RC	.15	.05
242	Maurice Cheeks	.05	.01
243	Paul Graham RC	.05	.01
244	Rodney Monroe RC	.05	.01
245	Blair Rasmussen	.05	.01
246	Alexander Volkov	.05	.01
247	John Bagley	.05	.01
248	Rick Fox RC	.15	.05
249	Rickey Green	.05	.01
250	Joe Kleine	.05	.01
251	Stojko Vrankovic	.05	.01
252	Allan Bristow CO	.05	.01
253	Kenny Gattison	.05	.01
254	Mike Gminski	.05	.01
255	Larry Johnson RC	.60	.25
256	Bobby Hansen	.05	.01
257	Craig Hodges	.05	.01
258	Stacey King	.05	.01
259	Scott Williams RC	.05	.01
260	John Battle	.05	.01
261	Winston Bennett	.05	.01
262	Terrell Brandon RC	.50	.20
263	Henry James	.05	.01
264	Steve Kerr	.08	.01
265	Jimmy Oliver RC	.05	.01
266	Brad Davis	.05	.01
267	Terry Davis	.05	.01
268	Donald Hodge RC	.05	.01
269	Mike Iuzzolino RC	.05	.01
270	Fat Lever	.05	.01
271	Doug Smith RC	.05	.01
272	Greg Anderson	.05	.01
273	Kevin Brooks RC	.05	.01
274	Walter Davis	.05	.01
275	Winston Garland	.05	.01
276	Mark Macon RC	.05	.01
277	Dikembe Mutombo RC	.60	.25
277B	D.Mutombo RC 91-92	.60	.25
278	William Bedford	.05	.01
279	Lance Blanks	.05	.01
280	John Salley	.05	.01
281	Charles Thomas RC	.05	.01
282	Darrell Walker	.05	.01
283	Orlando Woolridge	.05	.01
284	Victor Alexander RC	.05	.01
285	Vincent Askew RC	.05	.01
286	Mario Elie RC	.15	.05
287	Alton Lister	.05	.01
288	Billy Owens RC	.15	.05
289	Matt Bullard RC	.05	.01
290	Carl Herrera RC	.05	.01
291	Tree Rollins	.05	.01
292	John Turner	.05	.01
293	Dale Davis RC	.15	.05
294	Sean Green RC	.05	.01
295	Kenny Williams	.05	.01
296	James Edwards	.05	.01
297	LeRon Ellis RC	.05	.01
298	Doc Rivers	.08	.01
299	Loy Vaught	.08	.01
300	Elden Campbell	.08	.01
301	Jack Haley	.05	.01
302	Keith Owens	.05	.01
303	Tony Smith	.05	.01
304	Sedale Threatt	.05	.01
305	Keith Askins RC	.05	.01
306	Alec Kessler	.05	.01
307	John Morton	.05	.01
308	Alan Ogg	.05	.01
309	Steve Smith RC	.60	.25
310	Lester Conner	.05	.01
311	Jeff Grayer	.05	.01
312	Frank Hamblen CO	.05	.01
313	Steve Henson	.05	.01
314	Larry Krystkowiak	.05	.01
315	Moses Malone	.15	.05
316	Thurl Bailey	.05	.01
317	Randy Breuer	.05	.01
318	Scott Brooks	.05	.01
319	Gerald Glass	.05	.01
320	Luc Longley RC	.15	.05
321	Doug West	.05	.01
322	Kenny Anderson RC	.30	.10
323	Tate George	.05	.01
324	Terry Mills RC	.15	.05
325	Greg Anthony RC	.15	.05
326	Anthony Mason RC	.30	.10
327	Tim McCormick	.05	.01
328	Xavier McDaniel	.05	.01
329	Brian Quinnett	.05	.01
330	John Starks RC	.15	.05
331	Stanley Roberts RC	.05	.01
332	Jeff Turner	.05	.01
333	Sam Vincent	.05	.01
334	Brian Williams RC	.15	.05
335	Manute Bol	.05	.01
336	Kenny Payne	.05	.01
337	Charles Shackleford	.05	.01
338	Jayson Williams	.15	.05
339	Cedric Ceballos	.08	.01
340	Andrew Lang	.05	.01
341	Jerrod Mustaf	.05	.01
342	Tim Perry	.05	.01
343	Kurt Rambis	.05	.01
344	Alaa Abdelnaby	.05	.01
345	Robert Pack RC	.08	.01
346	Danny Young	.05	.01
347	Anthony Bonner	.05	.01
348	Pete Chilcutt RC	.05	.01
349	Rex Hughes CO	.05	.01
350	Mitch Richmond	.15	.05
351	Dwayne Schintzius	.05	.01
352	Spud Webb	.08	.01
353	Antoine Carr	.05	.01
354	Sidney Green	.05	.01
355	Vinnie Johnson	.05	.01
356	Greg Sutton	.05	.01
357	Dana Barros	.05	.01
358	Michael Cage	.05	.01
359	Marty Conlon RC	.05	.01
360	Rich King RC	.05	.01
361	Nate McMillan	.05	.01
362	David Benoit RC	.08	.01
363	Mike Brown	.05	.01
364	Tyrone Corbin	.05	.01
365	Eric Murdock RC	.05	.01
366	Delaney Rudd	.05	.01
367	Michael Adams	.05	.01
368	Tom Hammonds	.05	.01

☐ 369 Larry Stewart RC	.05	.01
☐ 370 Andre Turner	.05	.01
☐ 371 David Wingate	.05	.01
☐ 372 Dominique Wilkins TL	.08	.01
☐ 373 Larry Bird TL	.30	.10
☐ 374 Rex Chapman TL	.05	.01
☐ 375 Michael Jordan TL	1.00	.40
☐ 376 Brad Daugherty TL	.05	.01
☐ 377 Derek Harper TL	.05	.01
☐ 378 Dikembe Mutombo TL	.15	.05
☐ 379 Joe Dumars TL	.08	.01
☐ 380 Chris Mullin TL	.08	.01
☐ 381 Hakeem Olajuwon TL	.15	.05
☐ 382 Chuck Person TL	.05	.01
☐ 383 Charles Smith TL	.05	.01
☐ 384 James Worthy TL	.08	.01
☐ 385 Glen Rice TL	.08	.01
☐ 386 Alvin Robertson TL	.05	.01
☐ 387 Tony Campbell TL	.05	.01
☐ 388 Derrick Coleman TL	.05	.01
☐ 389 Patrick Ewing TL	.08	.01
☐ 390 Scott Skiles TL	.05	.01
☐ 391 Charles Barkley TL	.15	.05
☐ 392 Kevin Johnson TL	.08	.01
☐ 393 Clyde Drexler TL	.08	.01
☐ 394 Lionel Simmons TL	.05	.01
☐ 395 David Robinson TL	.15	.05
☐ 396 Ricky Pierce TL	.05	.01
☐ 397 John Stockton TL	.08	.01
☐ 398 Michael Adams TL	.05	.01
☐ 399 Checklist	.05	.01
☐ 400 Checklist	.05	.01

1992-93 Fleer

☐ COMPLETE SET (444)	30.00	15.00
☐ COMPLETE SERIES 1 (264)	15.00	7.50
☐ COMPLETE SERIES 2 (180)	15.00	7.50
☐ 1 Stacey Augmon	.10	.02
☐ 2 Duane Ferrell	.05	.01
☐ 3 Paul Graham	.05	.01
☐ 4A Jon Koncak	.05	.01
☐ 4B Jon Koncak	.05	.01
☐ 5 Blair Rasmussen	.05	.01
☐ 6 Rumeal Robinson	.05	.01
☐ 7 Bob Weiss CO	.05	.01
☐ 8 Dominique Wilkins	.25	.08
☐ 9 Kevin Willis	.05	.01
☐ 10 John Bagley	.05	.01
☐ 11 Larry Bird	1.00	.40
☐ 12 Dee Brown	.05	.01
☐ 13 Chris Ford CO	.05	.01
☐ 14 Rick Fox	.10	.02
☐ 15 Kevin Gamble	.05	.01
☐ 16 Reggie Lewis	.10	.02
☐ 17 Kevin McHale	.25	.08
☐ 18 Robert Parish	.10	.02
☐ 19 Ed Pinckney	.05	.01
☐ 20 Muggsy Bogues	.10	.02
☐ 21 Allan Bristow CO	.05	.01
☐ 22 Dell Curry	.05	.01
☐ 23 Kenny Gattison	.05	.01
☐ 24 Kendall Gill	.10	.02
☐ 25 Larry Johnson	.30	.10
☐ 26 Johnny Newman	.05	.01
☐ 27 J.R. Reid	.05	.01
☐ 28 B.J. Armstrong	.05	.01
☐ 29 Bill Cartwright	.05	.01
☐ 30 Horace Grant	.10	.02

☐ 31 Phil Jackson CO	.10	.02
☐ 32 Michael Jordan	3.00	1.25
☐ 33 Stacey King	.05	.01
☐ 34 Cliff Levingston	.05	.01
☐ 35 John Paxson	.05	.01
☐ 36 Scottie Pippen	.75	.30
☐ 37 Scott Williams	.05	.01
☐ 38 John Battle	.05	.01
☐ 39 Terrell Brandon	.25	.08
☐ 40 Brad Daugherty	.05	.01
☐ 41 Craig Ehlo	.05	.01
☐ 42 Larry Nance	.05	.01
☐ 43 Mark Price	.05	.01
☐ 44 Mike Sanders	.05	.01
☐ 45 Lenny Wilkens CO	.10	.02
☐ 46 John Hot Rod Williams	.05	.01
☐ 47 Richie Adubato CO	.05	.01
☐ 48 Terry Davis	.05	.01
☐ 49 Derek Harper	.10	.02
☐ 50 Donald Hodge	.05	.01
☐ 51 Mike Iuzzolino	.05	.01
☐ 52 Rodney McCray	.05	.01
☐ 53 Doug Smith	.05	.01
☐ 54 Greg Anderson	.05	.01
☐ 55 Winston Garland	.05	.01
☐ 56 Dan Issel CO	.05	.01
☐ 57 Chris Jackson	.05	.01
☐ 58 Marcus Liberty	.05	.01
☐ 59 Mark Macon	.05	.01
☐ 60 Dikembe Mutombo	.30	.10
☐ 61 Reggie Williams	.05	.01
☐ 62 Mark Aguirre	.05	.01
☐ 63 Joe Dumars	.25	.08
☐ 64 Bill Laimbeer	.10	.02
☐ 65 Olden Polynice	.05	.01
☐ 66 Dennis Rodman	.50	.20
☐ 67 Ron Rothstein CO	.05	.01
☐ 68 John Salley	.05	.01
☐ 69 Isiah Thomas	.25	.08
☐ 70 Darrell Walker	.05	.01
☐ 71 Orlando Woolridge	.05	.01
☐ 72 Victor Alexander	.05	.01
☐ 73 Mario Elie	.10	.02
☐ 74 Tim Hardaway	.30	.10
☐ 75 Tyrone Hill	.05	.01
☐ 76 Sarunas Marciulionis	.05	.01
☐ 77 Chris Mullin	.25	.08
☐ 78 Don Nelson CO	.10	.02
☐ 79 Billy Owens	.10	.02
☐ 80 Sleepy Floyd UER	.05	.01
☐ 81 Avery Johnson	.05	.01
☐ 82 Buck Johnson	.05	.01
☐ 83 Vernon Maxwell	.05	.01
☐ 84 Hakeem Olajuwon	.40	.15
☐ 85 Kenny Smith	.05	.01
☐ 86 Otis Thorpe	.10	.02
☐ 87 Rudy Tomjanovich CO	.10	.02
☐ 88 Dale Davis	.10	.02
☐ 89 Vern Fleming	.05	.01
☐ 90 Bob Hill CO	.05	.01
☐ 91 Reggie Miller	.25	.08
☐ 92 Chuck Person	.05	.01
☐ 93 Detlef Schrempf	.10	.02
☐ 94 Rik Smits	.10	.02
☐ 95 LaSalle Thompson	.05	.01
☐ 96 Micheal Williams	.05	.01
☐ 97 Larry Brown CO	.10	.02
☐ 98 James Edwards	.05	.01
☐ 99 Gary Grant	.05	.01
☐ 100 Ron Harper	.10	.02
☐ 101 Danny Manning	.10	.02
☐ 102 Ken Norman	.05	.01
☐ 103 Doc Rivers	.10	.02
☐ 104 Charles Smith	.05	.01
☐ 105 Loy Vaught	.05	.01
☐ 106 Elden Campbell	.10	.02
☐ 107 Vlade Divac	.10	.02
☐ 108 A.C. Green	.10	.02
☐ 109 Sam Perkins	.10	.02
☐ 110 Randy Pfund RC CO	.05	.01
☐ 111 Byron Scott	.10	.02
☐ 112 Terry Teagle	.05	.01
☐ 113 Sedale Threatt	.05	.01
☐ 114 James Worthy	.25	.08
☐ 115 Willie Burton	.05	.01
☐ 116 Bimbo Coles	.05	.01

☐ 117 Kevin Edwards	.05	.01
☐ 118 Grant Long	.05	.01
☐ 119 Kevin Loughery CO	.05	.01
☐ 120 Glen Rice	.25	.08
☐ 121 Rony Seikaly	.05	.01
☐ 122 Brian Shaw	.05	.01
☐ 123 Steve Smith	.30	.10
☐ 124 Frank Brickowski	.05	.01
☐ 125 Mike Dunleavy CO	.05	.01
☐ 126 Blue Edwards	.05	.01
☐ 127 Moses Malone	.25	.08
☐ 128 Eric Murdock	.05	.01
☐ 129 Fred Roberts	.05	.01
☐ 130 Alvin Robertson	.05	.01
☐ 131 Thurl Bailey	.05	.01
☐ 132 Tony Campbell	.05	.01
☐ 133 Gerald Glass	.05	.01
☐ 134 Luc Longley	.10	.02
☐ 135 Sam Mitchell	.05	.01
☐ 136 Pooh Richardson	.05	.01
☐ 137 Jimmy Rodgers CO	.05	.01
☐ 138 Felton Spencer	.05	.01
☐ 139 Doug West	.05	.01
☐ 140 Kenny Anderson	.25	.08
☐ 141 Mookie Blaylock	.10	.02
☐ 142 Sam Bowie	.05	.01
☐ 143 Derrick Coleman	.10	.02
☐ 144 Chuck Daly CO	.10	.02
☐ 145 Terry Mills	.05	.01
☐ 146 Chris Morris	.05	.01
☐ 147 Drazen Petrovic	.05	.01
☐ 148 Greg Anthony	.05	.01
☐ 149 Rolando Blackman	.05	.01
☐ 150 Patrick Ewing	.25	.08
☐ 151 Mark Jackson	.10	.02
☐ 152 Anthony Mason	.25	.08
☐ 153 Xavier McDaniel	.05	.01
☐ 154 Charles Oakley	.10	.02
☐ 155 Pat Riley CO	.10	.02
☐ 156 John Starks	.10	.02
☐ 157 Gerald Wilkins	.05	.01
☐ 158 Nick Anderson	.10	.02
☐ 159 Anthony Bowie	.05	.01
☐ 160 Terry Catledge	.05	.01
☐ 161 Matt Guokas CO	.05	.01
☐ 162 Stanley Roberts	.05	.01
☐ 163 Dennis Scott	.10	.02
☐ 164 Scott Skiles	.05	.01
☐ 165 Brian Williams	.05	.01
☐ 166 Ron Anderson	.05	.01
☐ 167 Manute Bol	.05	.01
☐ 168 Johnny Dawkins	.05	.01
☐ 169 Armon Gilliam	.05	.01
☐ 170 Hersey Hawkins	.10	.02
☐ 171 Jeff Hornacek	.10	.02
☐ 172 Andrew Lang	.05	.01
☐ 173 Doug Moe CO	.05	.01
☐ 174 Tim Perry	.05	.01
☐ 175 Jeff Ruland	.05	.01
☐ 176 Charles Shackleford	.05	.01
☐ 177 Danny Ainge	.10	.02
☐ 178 Charles Barkley	.40	.15
☐ 179 Cedric Ceballos	.10	.02
☐ 180 Tom Chambers	.05	.01
☐ 181 Kevin Johnson	.25	.08
☐ 182 Dan Majerle	.10	.02
☐ 183 Mark West UER	.05	.01
☐ 184 Paul Westphal CO	.05	.01
☐ 185 Rick Adelman CO	.05	.01
☐ 186 Clyde Drexler	.25	.08
☐ 187 Kevin Duckworth	.05	.01
☐ 188 Jerome Kersey	.05	.01
☐ 189 Robert Pack	.05	.01
☐ 190 Terry Porter	.05	.01
☐ 191 Cliff Robinson	.10	.02
☐ 192 Rod Strickland	.25	.08
☐ 193 Buck Williams	.10	.02
☐ 194 Anthony Bonner	.05	.01
☐ 195 Duane Causwell	.05	.01
☐ 196 Mitch Richmond	.25	.08
☐ 197 Garry St.Jean RC CO	.05	.01
☐ 198 Lionel Simmons	.05	.01
☐ 199 Wayman Tisdale	.05	.01
☐ 200 Spud Webb	.10	.02
☐ 201 Willie Anderson	.05	.01
☐ 202 Antoine Carr	.05	.01

❏ 203	Terry Cummings	.10	.02	❏ 289	Dennis Rodman SD	.25	.08	❏ 375	Lee Mayberry RC	.05	.01
❏ 204	Sean Elliott	.10	.02	❏ 290	Blue Edwards SD	.05	.01	❏ 376	Eric Murdock	.05	.01
❏ 205	Dale Ellis	.05	.01	❏ 291	Patrick Ewing SD	.10	.02	❏ 377	Danny Schayes	.05	.01
❏ 206	Vinnie Johnson	.05	.01	❏ 292	Larry Johnson SD	.25	.08	❏ 378	Lance Blanks	.05	.01
❏ 207	David Robinson	.40	.15	❏ 293	Jerome Kersey SD	.05	.01	❏ 379	Christian Laettner RC	.50	.20
❏ 208	Jerry Tarkanian RC	.05	.01	❏ 294	Hakeem Olajuwon SD	.25	.08	❏ 380	Bob McCann RC	.05	.01
❏ 209	Benoit Benjamin	.05	.01	❏ 295	Stacey Augmon SD	.05	.01	❏ 381	Chuck Person	.05	.01
❏ 210	Michael Cage	.05	.01	❏ 296	Derrick Coleman SD	.05	.01	❏ 382	Brad Sellers	.05	.01
❏ 211	Eddie Johnson	.05	.01	❏ 297	Kendall Gill SD	.05	.01	❏ 383	Chris Smith RC	.05	.01
❏ 212	George Karl CO	.10	.02	❏ 298	Shaquille O'Neal SD	3.00	1.25	❏ 384	Micheal Williams	.05	.01
❏ 213	Shawn Kemp	.50	.20	❏ 299	Scottie Pippen SD	.40	.15	❏ 385	Rafael Addison	.05	.01
❏ 214	Derrick McKey	.05	.01	❏ 300	Darryl Dawkins SD	.10	.02	❏ 386	Chucky Brown	.05	.01
❏ 215	Nate McMillan	.05	.01	❏ 301	Mookie Blaylock	.10	.02	❏ 387	Chris Dudley	.05	.01
❏ 216	Gary Payton	.50	.20	❏ 302	Adam Keefe RC	.05	.01	❏ 388	Tate George	.05	.01
❏ 217	Ricky Pierce	.05	.01	❏ 303	Travis Mays	.05	.01	❏ 389	Rick Mahorn	.05	.01
❏ 218	David Benoit	.05	.01	❏ 304	Morlon Wiley	.05	.01	❏ 390	Rumeal Robinson	.05	.01
❏ 219	Mike Brown	.05	.01	❏ 305	Sherman Douglas	.05	.01	❏ 391	Jayson Williams	.10	.02
❏ 220	Tyrone Corbin	.05	.01	❏ 306	Joe Kleine	.05	.01	❏ 392	Eric Anderson RC	.05	.01
❏ 221	Mark Eaton	.05	.01	❏ 307	Xavier McDaniel	.05	.01	❏ 393	Rolando Blackman	.05	.01
❏ 222	Jay Humphries	.05	.01	❏ 308	Tony Bennett RC	.05	.01	❏ 394	Tony Campbell	.05	.01
❏ 223	Larry Krystkowiak	.05	.01	❏ 309	Tom Hammonds	.05	.01	❏ 395	Hubert Davis RC	.10	.02
❏ 224	Jeff Malone	.05	.01	❏ 310	Kevin Lynch	.05	.01	❏ 396	Doc Rivers	.10	.02
❏ 225	Karl Malone	.40	.15	❏ 311	Alonzo Mourning RC	1.50	.60	❏ 397	Charles Smith	.05	.01
❏ 226	Jerry Sloan CO	.10	.02	❏ 312	David Wingate	.05	.01	❏ 398	Herb Williams	.05	.01
❏ 227	John Stockton	.25	.08	❏ 313	Rodney McCray	.05	.01	❏ 399	Litterial Green RC	.05	.01
❏ 228	Michael Adams	.05	.01	❏ 314	Will Perdue	.05	.01	❏ 400	Greg Kite	.05	.01
❏ 229	Rex Chapman	.05	.01	❏ 315	Trent Tucker	.05	.01	❏ 401	Shaquille O'Neal RC	6.00	2.50
❏ 230	Ledell Eackles	.05	.01	❏ 316	Corey Williams RC	.05	.01	❏ 402	Jerry Reynolds	.05	.01
❏ 231	Pervis Ellison	.05	.01	❏ 317	Danny Ferry	.05	.01	❏ 403	Jeff Turner	.05	.01
❏ 232	A.J. English	.05	.01	❏ 318	Jay Guidinger RC	.05	.01	❏ 404	Greg Grant	.05	.01
❏ 233	Harvey Grant	.05	.01	❏ 319	Jerome Lane	.05	.01	❏ 405	Jeff Hornacek	.10	.02
❏ 234	LaBradford Smith	.05	.01	❏ 320	Gerald Wilkins	.05	.01	❏ 406	Andrew Lang	.05	.01
❏ 235	Larry Stewart	.05	.01	❏ 321	Steve Bardo RC	.05	.01	❏ 407	Kenny Payne	.05	.01
❏ 236	Wes Unseld CO	.10	.02	❏ 322	Walter Bond RC	.05	.01	❏ 408	Tim Perry	.05	.01
❏ 237	David Wingate	.05	.01	❏ 323	Brian Howard RC	.05	.01	❏ 409	C.Weatherspoon RC	.25	.08
❏ 238	Michael Jordan LL	1.50	.60	❏ 324	Tracy Moore RC	.05	.01	❏ 410	Danny Ainge	.10	.02
❏ 239	Dennis Rodman LL	.25	.08	❏ 325	Sean Rooks RC	.05	.01	❏ 411	Charles Barkley	.40	.15
❏ 240	John Stockton LL	.10	.02	❏ 326	Randy White	.05	.01	❏ 412	Negele Knight	.05	.01
❏ 241	Buck Williams LL	.05	.01	❏ 327	Kevin Brooks	.05	.01	❏ 413	Oliver Miller RC	.10	.02
❏ 242	Mark Price LL	.05	.01	❏ 328	LaPhonso Ellis RC	.25	.08	❏ 414	Jerrod Mustaf	.05	.01
❏ 243	Dana Barros LL	.05	.01	❏ 329	Scott Hastings	.05	.01	❏ 415	Mark Bryant	.05	.01
❏ 244	David Robinson LL	.25	.08	❏ 330	Todd Lichti	.05	.01	❏ 416	Mario Elie	.10	.02
❏ 245	Chris Mullin LL	.10	.02	❏ 331	Robert Pack	.05	.01	❏ 417	Dave Johnson RC	.05	.01
❏ 246	Michael Jordan MVP	1.50	.60	❏ 332	Bryant Stith RC	.10	.02	❏ 418	Tracy Murray RC	.10	.02
❏ 247	Larry Johnson ROY	.25	.08	❏ 333	Gerald Glass	.05	.01	❏ 419	Reggie Smith RC	.05	.01
❏ 248	David Robinson POY	.25	.08	❏ 334	Terry Mills	.05	.01	❏ 420	Rod Strickland	.25	.08
❏ 249	Detlef Schrempf	.05	.01	❏ 335	Isaiah Morris RC	.05	.01	❏ 421	Randy Brown	.05	.01
❏ 250	Clyde Drexler PV	.10	.02	❏ 336	Mark Randall	.05	.01	❏ 422	Pete Chilcutt	.05	.01
❏ 251	Tim Hardaway PV	.25	.08	❏ 337	Danny Young	.05	.01	❏ 423	Jim Les	.05	.01
❏ 252	Kevin Johnson PV	.10	.02	❏ 338	Chris Gatling	.05	.01	❏ 424	Walt Williams RC	.25	.08
❏ 253	Larry Johnson PV	.25	.08	❏ 339	Jeff Grayer	.05	.01	❏ 425	Lloyd Daniels RC	.05	.01
❏ 254	Scottie Pippen PV	.40	.15	❏ 340	Byron Houston RC	.05	.01	❏ 426	Vinny Del Negro	.05	.01
❏ 255	Isiah Thomas PV	.10	.02	❏ 341	Kelvin Jennings RC	.05	.01	❏ 427	Dale Ellis	.05	.01
❏ 256	Larry Bird SY	.50	.20	❏ 342	Alton Lister	.05	.01	❏ 428	Sidney Green	.05	.01
❏ 257	Brad Daugherty SY	.05	.01	❏ 343	Latrell Sprewell RC	2.00	.75	❏ 429	Avery Johnson	.05	.01
❏ 258	Kevin Johnson SY	.10	.02	❏ 344	Scott Brooks	.05	.01	❏ 430	Dana Barros	.05	.01
❏ 259	Larry Johnson SY	.25	.08	❏ 345	Matt Bullard	.05	.01	❏ 431	Rich Kelley	.05	.01
❏ 260	Scottie Pippen SY	.40	.15	❏ 346	Carl Herrera	.05	.01	❏ 432	Isaac Austin RC	.10	.02
❏ 261	Dennis Rodman SY	.25	.08	❏ 347	Robert Horry RC	.25	.08	❏ 433	John Crotty RC	.05	.01
❏ 262	Checklist 1	.05	.01	❏ 348	Tree Rollins	.05	.01	❏ 434	Stephen Howard RC	.05	.01
❏ 263	Checklist 2	.05	.01	❏ 349	Greg Dreiling	.05	.01	❏ 435	Jay Humphries	.05	.01
❏ 264	Checklist 3	.05	.01	❏ 350	George McCloud	.05	.01	❏ 436	Larry Krystkowiak	.05	.01
❏ 265	Charles Barkley SD	.25	.08	❏ 351	Sam Mitchell	.05	.01	❏ 437	Tom Gugliotta RC	.75	.30
❏ 266	Shawn Kemp SD	.25	.08	❏ 352	Pooh Richardson	.05	.01	❏ 438	Buck Johnson	.05	.01
❏ 267	Dan Majerle SD	.05	.01	❏ 353	Malik Sealy RC	.10	.02	❏ 439	Charles Jones	.05	.01
❏ 268	Karl Malone SD	.25	.08	❏ 354	Kenny Williams	.05	.01	❏ 440	Don MacLean RC	.05	.01
❏ 269	Buck Williams SD	.05	.01	❏ 355	Jaren Jackson RC	.10	.02	❏ 441	Doug Overton	.05	.01
❏ 270	Clyde Drexler SD	.10	.02	❏ 356	Mark Jackson	.05	.01	❏ 442	Brent Price RC	.10	.02
❏ 271	Sean Elliott SD	.05	.01	❏ 357	Stanley Roberts	.05	.01	❏ 443	Checklist 1	.05	.01
❏ 272	Ron Harper SD	.05	.01	❏ 358	Elmore Spencer RC	.05	.01	❏ 444	Checklist 2	.05	.01
❏ 273	Michael Jordan SD	1.50	.60	❏ 359	Kiki Vandeweghe	.05	.01	❏ SD266	Shawn Dunk Augmon AU	120.00	60.00
❏ 274	James Worthy SD	.10	.02	❏ 360	John S. Williams	.05	.01	❏ SD277	Kenny Walker AU	40.00	15.00
❏ 275	Cedric Ceballos SD	.05	.01	❏ 361	Randy Woods RC	.05	.01	❏ SD300	Darryl Dawkins AU	40.00	25.00
❏ 276	Larry Nance SD	.05	.01	❏ 362	Duane Cooper RC	.05	.01	❏ NNO	Slam Dunk Wrapper Exch.	3.00	1.25
❏ 277	Kenny Walker SD	.05	.01	❏ 363	James Edwards	.05	.01				
❏ 278	Spud Webb SD	.05	.01	❏ 364	Anthony Peeler RC	.05	.02	**1993-94 Fleer**			
❏ 279	Dominique Wilkins SD	.10	.02	❏ 365	Tony Smith	.05	.01				
❏ 280	Terrell Brandon SD	.10	.02	❏ 366	Keith Askins	.05	.01	❏	COMPLETE SET (400)	20.00	10.00
❏ 281	Dee Brown SD	.05	.01	❏ 367	Matt Geiger RC	.10	.02	❏	COMPLETE SERIES 1 (240)	10.00	5.00
❏ 282	Kevin Johnson SD	.10	.02	❏ 368	Alec Kessler	.05	.01	❏	COMPLETE SERIES 2 (160)	10.00	5.00
❏ 283	Doc Rivers SD	.05	.01	❏ 369	Harold Miner RC	.10	.02	❏ 1	Stacey Augmon	.05	.01
❏ 284	Byron Scott SD	.05	.01	❏ 370	John Salley	.05	.01	❏ 2	Mookie Blaylock	.10	.02
❏ 285	Manute Bol SD	.05	.01	❏ 371	Anthony Avent RC	.05	.01	❏ 3	Duane Ferrell	.05	.01
❏ 286	Dikembe Mutombo SD	.25	.08	❏ 372	Todd Day RC	.10	.02	❏ 4	Paul Graham	.05	.01
❏ 287	Robert Parish SD	.05	.01	❏ 373	Blue Edwards	.05	.01	❏ 5	Adam Keefe	.05	.01
❏ 288	David Robinson SD	.25	.08	❏ 374	Brad Lohaus	.05	.01	❏ 6	Jon Koncak	.05	.01
								❏ 7	Dominique Wilkins	.25	.08

☐ 8	Kevin Willis	.05	.01
☐ 9	Alaa Abdelnaby	.05	.01
☐ 10	Dee Brown	.05	.01
☐ 11	Sherman Douglas	.05	.01
☐ 12	Rick Fox	.05	.01
☐ 13	Kevin Gamble	.05	.01
☐ 14	Reggie Lewis	.10	.02
☐ 15	Xavier McDaniel	.05	.01
☐ 16	Robert Parish	.10	.02
☐ 17	Muggsy Bogues	.10	.02
☐ 18	Dell Curry	.05	.01
☐ 19	Kenny Gattison	.05	.01
☐ 20	Kendall Gill	.10	.02
☐ 21	Larry Johnson	.25	.08
☐ 22	Alonzo Mourning	.40	.15
☐ 23	Johnny Newman	.05	.01
☐ 24	David Wingate	.05	.01
☐ 25	B.J.Armstrong	.05	.01
☐ 26	Bill Cartwright	.05	.01
☐ 27	Horace Grant	.10	.02
☐ 28	Michael Jordan	3.00	1.25
☐ 29	Stacey King	.05	.01
☐ 30	John Paxson	.05	.01
☐ 31	Will Perdue	.05	.01
☐ 32	Scottie Pippen	.75	.30
☐ 33	Scott Williams	.05	.01
☐ 34	Terrell Brandon	.10	.02
☐ 35	Brad Daugherty	.05	.01
☐ 36	Craig Ehlo	.05	.01
☐ 37	Danny Ferry	.05	.01
☐ 38	Larry Nance	.05	.01
☐ 39	Mark Price	.05	.01
☐ 40	Mike Sanders	.05	.01
☐ 41	Gerald Wilkins	.05	.01
☐ 42	John Williams	.05	.01
☐ 43	Terry Davis	.05	.01
☐ 44	Derek Harper	.10	.02
☐ 45	Mike Iuzzolino	.05	.01
☐ 46	Jim Jackson	.10	.02
☐ 47	Sean Rooks	.05	.01
☐ 48	Doug Smith	.05	.01
☐ 49	Randy White	.05	.01
☐ 50	Mahmoud Abdul-Rauf	.05	.01
☐ 51	LaPhonso Ellis	.05	.01
☐ 52	Marcus Liberty	.05	.01
☐ 53	Mark Macon	.05	.01
☐ 54	Dikembe Mutombo	.25	.08
☐ 55	Robert Pack	.05	.01
☐ 56	Bryant Stith	.05	.01
☐ 57	Reggie Williams	.05	.01
☐ 58	Mark Aguirre	.05	.01
☐ 59	Joe Dumars	.25	.08
☐ 60	Bill Laimbeer	.05	.01
☐ 61	Terry Mills	.05	.01
☐ 62	Olden Polynice	.05	.01
☐ 63	Alvin Robertson	.05	.01
☐ 64	Dennis Rodman	.50	.20
☐ 65	Isiah Thomas	.25	.08
☐ 66	Victor Alexander	.05	.01
☐ 67	Tim Hardaway	.25	.08
☐ 68	Tyrone Hill	.05	.01
☐ 69	Byron Houston	.05	.01
☐ 70	Sarunas Marciulionis	.05	.01
☐ 71	Chris Mullin	.10	.02
☐ 72	Billy Owens	.05	.01
☐ 73	Latrell Sprewell	.60	.25
☐ 74	Scott Brooks	.05	.01
☐ 75	Matt Bullard	.05	.01

☐ 76	Carl Herrera	.05	.01
☐ 77	Robert Horry	.10	.02
☐ 78	Vernon Maxwell	.05	.01
☐ 79	Hakeem Olajuwon	.40	.15
☐ 80	Kenny Smith	.05	.01
☐ 81	Otis Thorpe	.10	.02
☐ 82	Dale Davis	.05	.01
☐ 83	Vern Fleming	.05	.01
☐ 84	George McCloud	.05	.01
☐ 85	Reggie Miller	.25	.08
☐ 86	Sam Mitchell	.05	.01
☐ 87	Pooh Richardson	.05	.01
☐ 88	Detlef Schrempf	.10	.02
☐ 89	Rik Smits	.10	.02
☐ 90	Gary Grant	.05	.01
☐ 91	Ron Harper	.10	.02
☐ 92	Mark Jackson	.10	.02
☐ 93	Danny Manning	.10	.02
☐ 94	Ken Norman	.05	.01
☐ 95	Stanley Roberts	.05	.01
☐ 96	Loy Vaught	.05	.01
☐ 97	John Williams	.05	.01
☐ 98	Elden Campbell	.05	.01
☐ 99	Doug Christie	.10	.02
☐ 100	Duane Cooper	.05	.01
☐ 101	Vlade Divac	.10	.02
☐ 102	A.C. Green	.10	.02
☐ 103	Anthony Peeler	.05	.01
☐ 104	Sedale Threatt	.05	.01
☐ 105	James Worthy	.25	.08
☐ 106	Bimbo Coles	.05	.01
☐ 107	Grant Long	.05	.01
☐ 108	Harold Miner	.05	.01
☐ 109	Glen Rice	.10	.02
☐ 110	John Salley	.05	.01
☐ 111	Rony Seikaly	.05	.01
☐ 112	Brian Shaw	.05	.01
☐ 113	Steve Smith	.25	.08
☐ 114	Anthony Avent	.05	.01
☐ 115	Jon Barry	.05	.01
☐ 116	Frank Brickowski	.05	.01
☐ 117	Todd Day	.05	.01
☐ 118	Blue Edwards	.05	.01
☐ 119	Brad Lohaus	.05	.01
☐ 120	Lee Mayberry	.05	.01
☐ 121	Eric Murdock	.05	.01
☐ 122	Thurl Bailey	.05	.01
☐ 123	Christian Laettner	.10	.02
☐ 124	Luc Longley	.10	.02
☐ 125	Chuck Person	.05	.01
☐ 126	Felton Spencer	.05	.01
☐ 127	Doug West	.05	.01
☐ 128	Micheal Williams	.05	.01
☐ 129	Rafael Addison	.05	.01
☐ 130	Kenny Anderson	.10	.02
☐ 131	Sam Bowie	.05	.01
☐ 132	Chucky Brown	.05	.01
☐ 133	Derrick Coleman	.10	.02
☐ 134	Chris Dudley	.05	.01
☐ 135	Chris Morris	.05	.01
☐ 136	Rumeal Robinson	.05	.01
☐ 137	Greg Anthony	.05	.01
☐ 138	Rolando Blackman	.05	.01
☐ 139	Tony Campbell	.05	.01
☐ 140	Hubert Davis	.05	.01
☐ 141	Patrick Ewing	.25	.08
☐ 142	Anthony Mason	.10	.02
☐ 143	Charles Oakley	.10	.02
☐ 144	Doc Rivers	.05	.01
☐ 145	Charles Smith	.05	.01
☐ 146	John Starks	.10	.02
☐ 147	Nick Anderson	.10	.02
☐ 148	Anthony Bowie	.05	.01
☐ 149	Shaquille O'Neal	1.25	.60
☐ 150	Donald Royal	.05	.01
☐ 151	Dennis Scott	.05	.01
☐ 152	Scott Skiles	.05	.01
☐ 153	Tom Tolbert	.05	.01
☐ 154	Jeff Turner	.05	.01
☐ 155	Ron Anderson	.05	.01
☐ 156	Johnny Dawkins	.05	.01
☐ 157	Hersey Hawkins	.10	.02
☐ 158	Jeff Hornacek	.10	.02
☐ 159	Andrew Lang	.05	.01
☐ 160	Tim Perry	.05	.01
☐ 161	Clarence Weatherspoon	.05	.01

☐ 162	Danny Ainge	.10	.02
☐ 163	Charles Barkley	.40	.15
☐ 164	Cedric Ceballos	.10	.02
☐ 165	Tom Chambers	.05	.01
☐ 166	Richard Dumas	.05	.01
☐ 167	Kevin Johnson	.10	.02
☐ 168	Negele Knight	.05	.01
☐ 169	Dan Majerle	.10	.02
☐ 170	Oliver Miller	.05	.01
☐ 171	Mark West	.05	.01
☐ 172	Mark Bryant	.05	.01
☐ 173	Clyde Drexler	.25	.08
☐ 174	Kevin Duckworth	.05	.01
☐ 175	Mario Elie	.05	.01
☐ 176	Jerome Kersey	.05	.01
☐ 177	Terry Porter	.05	.01
☐ 178	Cliff Robinson	.10	.02
☐ 179	Rod Strickland	.10	.02
☐ 180	Buck Williams	.05	.01
☐ 181	Anthony Bonner	.05	.01
☐ 182	Duane Causwell	.05	.01
☐ 183	Mitch Richmond	.25	.08
☐ 184	Lionel Simmons	.05	.01
☐ 185	Wayman Tisdale	.05	.01
☐ 186	Spud Webb	.10	.02
☐ 187	Walt Williams	.05	.01
☐ 188	Antoine Carr	.05	.01
☐ 189	Terry Cummings	.05	.01
☐ 190	Lloyd Daniels	.05	.01
☐ 191	Vinny Del Negro	.05	.01
☐ 192	Sean Elliott	.10	.02
☐ 193	Dale Ellis	.05	.01
☐ 194	Avery Johnson	.05	.01
☐ 195	J.R. Reid	.05	.01
☐ 196	David Robinson	.40	.15
☐ 197	Michael Cage	.05	.01
☐ 198	Eddie Johnson	.05	.01
☐ 199	Shawn Kemp	.40	.15
☐ 200	Derrick McKey	.05	.01
☐ 201	Nate McMillan	.05	.01
☐ 202	Gary Payton	.40	.15
☐ 203	Sam Perkins	.10	.02
☐ 204	Ricky Pierce	.05	.01
☐ 205	David Benoit	.05	.01
☐ 206	Tyrone Corbin	.05	.01
☐ 207	Mark Eaton	.05	.01
☐ 208	Jay Humphries	.05	.01
☐ 209	Larry Krystkowiak	.05	.01
☐ 210	Jeff Malone	.05	.01
☐ 211	Karl Malone	.40	.15
☐ 212	John Stockton	.25	.08
☐ 213	Michael Adams	.05	.01
☐ 214	Rex Chapman	.05	.01
☐ 215	Pervis Ellison	.05	.01
☐ 216	Harvey Grant	.05	.01
☐ 217	Tom Gugliotta	.25	.08
☐ 218	Buck Johnson	.05	.01
☐ 219	LaBradford Smith	.05	.01
☐ 220	Larry Stewart	.05	.01
☐ 221	B.J. Armstrong LL	.05	.01
☐ 222	Cedric Ceballos LL	.05	.01
☐ 223	Larry Johnson LL	.10	.02
☐ 224	Michael Jordan LL	1.50	.60
☐ 225	Hakeem Olajuwon LL	.25	.08
☐ 226	Mark Price LL	.05	.01
☐ 227	Dennis Rodman LL	.25	.08
☐ 228	John Stockton LL	.10	.02
☐ 229	Charles Barkley AW	.25	.08
☐ 230	Hakeem Olajuwon AW	.25	.08
☐ 231	Shaquille O'Neal AW	.50	.20
☐ 232	Clifford Robinson AW	.05	.01
☐ 233	Shawn Kemp PV	.25	.08
☐ 234	Alonzo Mourning PV	.25	.08
☐ 235	Hakeem Olajuwon PV	.25	.08
☐ 236	John Stockton PV	.10	.02
☐ 237	Dominique Wilkins PV	.10	.02
☐ 238	Checklist 1-85	.05	.01
☐ 239	Checklist 86-165	.05	.01
☐ 240	Checklist 166-240 UER	.05	.01
☐ 241	Doug Edwards RC	.05	.01
☐ 242	Craig Ehlo	.05	.01
☐ 243	Andrew Lang	.05	.01
☐ 244	Ennis Whatley	.05	.01
☐ 245	Chris Corchiani	.05	.01
☐ 246	Acie Earl RC	.05	.01
☐ 247	Jimmy Oliver	.05	.01

❑ 248	Ed Pinckney	.05	.01
❑ 249	Dino Radja RC	.05	.01
❑ 250	Matt Wenstrom RC	.05	.01
❑ 251	Tony Bennett	.05	.01
❑ 252	Scott Burrell RC	.25	.08
❑ 253	LeRon Ellis	.05	.01
❑ 254	Hersey Hawkins	.10	.02
❑ 255	Eddie Johnson	.05	.01
❑ 256	Corie Blount RC	.05	.01
❑ 257	Jo Jo English RC	.05	.01
❑ 258	Dave Johnson	.05	.01
❑ 259	Steve Kerr	.10	.02
❑ 260	Toni Kukoc RC	1.00	.40
❑ 261	Pete Myers	.05	.01
❑ 262	Bill Wennington	.05	.01
❑ 263	John Battle	.05	.01
❑ 264	Tyrone Hill	.05	.01
❑ 265	Gerald Madkins RC	.05	.01
❑ 266	Chris Mills RC	.25	.08
❑ 267	Bobby Phills	.05	.01
❑ 268	Greg Dreiling	.05	.01
❑ 269	Lucious Harris RC	.05	.01
❑ 270	Donald Hodge	.05	.01
❑ 271	Popeye Jones RC	.05	.01
❑ 272	Tim Legler RC	.05	.01
❑ 273	Fat Lever	.05	.01
❑ 274	Jamal Mashburn RC	.60	.25
❑ 275	Darren Morningstar RC	.05	.01
❑ 276	Tom Hammonds	.05	.01
❑ 277	Darnell Mee RC	.05	.01
❑ 278	Rodney Rogers RC	.25	.08
❑ 279	Brian Williams	.05	.01
❑ 280	Greg Anderson	.05	.01
❑ 281	Sean Elliott	.10	.02
❑ 282	Allan Houston RC	1.00	.40
❑ 283	Lindsey Hunter RC	.25	.08
❑ 284	Marcus Liberty	.05	.01
❑ 285	Mark Macon	.05	.01
❑ 286	David Wood	.05	.01
❑ 287	Jud Buechler	.05	.01
❑ 288	Chris Gatling	.05	.01
❑ 289	Josh Grant RC	.05	.01
❑ 290	Jeff Grayer	.05	.01
❑ 291	Avery Johnson	.05	.01
❑ 292	Chris Webber RC	2.50	1.00
❑ 293	Sam Cassell RC	1.00	.40
❑ 294	Mario Elie	.05	.01
❑ 295	Richard Petruska RC	.05	.01
❑ 296	Eric Riley RC	.05	.01
❑ 297	Antonio Davis RC	.30	.10
❑ 298	Scott Haskin RC	.05	.01
❑ 299	Derrick McKey	.05	.01
❑ 300	Byron Scott	.10	.02
❑ 301	Malik Sealy	.05	.01
❑ 302	LaSalle Thompson	.05	.01
❑ 303	Kenny Williams	.05	.01
❑ 304	Haywoode Workman	.05	.01
❑ 305	Mark Aguirre	.05	.01
❑ 306	Terry Dehere RC	.05	.01
❑ 307	Bob Martin RC	.05	.01
❑ 308	Elmore Spencer	.05	.01
❑ 309	Tom Tolbert	.05	.01
❑ 310	Randy Woods	.05	.01
❑ 311	Sam Bowie	.05	.01
❑ 312	James Edwards	.05	.01
❑ 313	Antonio Harvey RC	.05	.01
❑ 314	George Lynch RC	.05	.01
❑ 315	Tony Smith	.05	.01
❑ 316	Nick Van Exel RC	.75	.30
❑ 317	Manute Bol	.05	.01
❑ 318	Willie Burton	.05	.01
❑ 319	Matt Geiger	.05	.01
❑ 320	Alec Kessler	.05	.01
❑ 321	Vin Baker RC	.60	.25
❑ 322	Ken Norman	.05	.01
❑ 323	Danny Schayes	.05	.01
❑ 324	Derek Strong RC	.05	.01
❑ 325	Mike Brown	.05	.01
❑ 326	Brian Davis RC	.05	.01
❑ 327	Tellis Frank	.05	.01
❑ 328	Marlon Maxey	.05	.01
❑ 329	Isaiah Rider RC	.50	.20
❑ 330	Chris Smith	.05	.01
❑ 331	Benoit Benjamin	.05	.01
❑ 332	P.J.Brown RC	.25	.08
❑ 333	Kevin Edwards	.05	.01

❑ 334	Armon Gilliam	.05	.01
❑ 335	Rick Mahorn	.05	.01
❑ 336	Dwayne Schintzius	.05	.01
❑ 337	Rex Walters RC	.05	.01
❑ 338	David Wesley RC	.25	.08
❑ 339	Jayson Williams	.10	.02
❑ 340	Anthony Bonner	.05	.01
❑ 341	Herb Williams	.05	.01
❑ 342	Litterial Green	.05	.01
❑ 343	Anfernee Hardaway RC	2.00	.75
❑ 344	Greg Kite	.05	.01
❑ 345	Larry Krystkowiak	.05	.01
❑ 346	Todd Lichti	.05	.01
❑ 347	Keith Tower RC	.05	.01
❑ 348	Dana Barros	.05	.01
❑ 349	Shawn Bradley RC	.25	.08
❑ 350	Michael Curry RC	.05	.01
❑ 351	Greg Graham RC	.05	.01
❑ 352	Warren Kidd RC	.05	.01
❑ 353	Moses Malone	.25	.08
❑ 354	Orlando Woolridge	.05	.01
❑ 355	Duane Cooper	.05	.01
❑ 356	Joe Courtney RC	.05	.01
❑ 357	A.C. Green	.10	.02
❑ 358	Frank Johnson	.05	.01
❑ 359	Joe Kleine	.05	.01
❑ 360	Malcolm Mackey RC	.05	.01
❑ 361	Jerrod Mustaf	.05	.01
❑ 362	Chris Dudley	.05	.01
❑ 363	Harvey Grant	.05	.01
❑ 364	Tracy Murray	.05	.01
❑ 365	James Robinson RC	.05	.01
❑ 366	Reggie Smith	.05	.01
❑ 367	Kevin Thompson RC	.05	.01
❑ 368	Randy Breuer	.05	.01
❑ 369	Randy Brown	.05	.01
❑ 370	Evers Burns RC	.05	.01
❑ 371	Pete Chilcutt	.05	.01
❑ 372	Bobby Hurley RC	.10	.02
❑ 373	Jim Les	.05	.01
❑ 374	Mike Peplowski RC	.05	.01
❑ 375	Willie Anderson	.05	.01
❑ 376	Sleepy Floyd	.05	.01
❑ 377	Negele Knight	.05	.01
❑ 378	Dennis Rodman	.50	.20
❑ 379	Chris Whitney RC	.05	.01
❑ 380	Vincent Askew	.05	.01
❑ 381	Kendall Gill	.10	.02
❑ 382	Ervin Johnson RC	.10	.02
❑ 383	Chris King RC	.05	.01
❑ 384	Rich King	.05	.01
❑ 385	Steve Scheffler	.05	.01
❑ 386	Detlef Schrempf	.10	.02
❑ 387	Tom Chambers	.05	.01
❑ 388	John Crotty	.05	.01
❑ 389	Bryon Russell RC	.25	.08
❑ 390	Felton Spencer	.05	.01
❑ 391	Luther Wright RC	.05	.01
❑ 392	Mitchell Butler RC	.05	.01
❑ 393	Calbert Cheaney RC	.10	.02
❑ 394	Kevin Duckworth	.05	.01
❑ 395	Don MacLean	.05	.01
❑ 396	Gheorghe Muresan RC	.25	.08
❑ 397	Doug Overton	.05	.01
❑ 398	Brent Price	.05	.01
❑ 399	Checklist	.05	.01
❑ 400	Checklist	.05	.01

1994-95 Fleer

❑ COMPLETE SET (390)		24.00	12.00
❑ COMPLETE SERIES 1 (240)		12.00	6.00
❑ COMPLETE SERIES 2 (150)		12.00	6.00
❑ 1	Stacey Augmon	.05	.01
❑ 2	Mookie Blaylock	.05	.01
❑ 3	Craig Ehlo	.05	.01
❑ 4	Duane Ferrell	.05	.01
❑ 5	Adam Keefe	.05	.01
❑ 6	Jon Koncak	.05	.01
❑ 7	Andrew Lang	.05	.01
❑ 8	Danny Manning	.10	.02
❑ 9	Kevin Willis	.05	.01
❑ 10	Dee Brown	.05	.01
❑ 11	Sherman Douglas	.05	.01
❑ 12	Acie Earl	.05	.01
❑ 13	Rick Fox	.05	.01
❑ 14	Kevin Gamble	.05	.01

❑ 15	Xavier McDaniel	.05	.01
❑ 16	Robert Parish	.10	.02
❑ 17	Ed Pinckney	.05	.01
❑ 18	Dino Radja	.05	.01
❑ 19	Muggsy Bogues	.10	.02
❑ 20	Frank Brickowski	.05	.01
❑ 21	Scott Burrell	.05	.01
❑ 22	Dell Curry	.05	.01
❑ 23	Kenny Gattison	.05	.01
❑ 24	Hersey Hawkins	.10	.02
❑ 25	Eddie Johnson	.05	.01
❑ 26	Larry Johnson	.10	.02
❑ 27	Alonzo Mourning	.30	.10
❑ 28	David Wingate	.05	.01
❑ 29	B.J. Armstrong	.05	.01
❑ 30	Horace Grant	.10	.02
❑ 31	Steve Kerr	.05	.01
❑ 32	Toni Kukoc	.40	.15
❑ 33	Luc Longley	.05	.01
❑ 34	Pete Myers	.05	.01
❑ 35	Scottie Pippen	.75	.30
❑ 36	Bill Wennington	.05	.01
❑ 37	Scott Williams	.05	.01
❑ 38	Terrell Brandon	.10	.02
❑ 39	Brad Daugherty	.05	.01
❑ 40	Tyrone Hill	.05	.01
❑ 41	Chris Mills	.10	.02
❑ 42	Larry Nance	.05	.01
❑ 43	Bobby Phills	.05	.01
❑ 44	Mark Price	.05	.01
❑ 45	Gerald Wilkins	.05	.01
❑ 46	John Williams	.05	.01
❑ 47	Lucious Harris	.05	.01
❑ 48	Donald Hodge	.05	.01
❑ 49	Jim Jackson	.10	.02
❑ 50	Popeye Jones	.05	.01
❑ 51	Tim Legler	.05	.01
❑ 52	Fat Lever	.05	.01
❑ 53	Jamal Mashburn	.25	.08
❑ 54	Sean Rooks	.05	.01
❑ 55	Doug Smith	.05	.01
❑ 56	Mahmoud Abdul-Rauf	.05	.01
❑ 57	LaPhonso Ellis	.05	.01
❑ 58	Dikembe Mutombo	.10	.02
❑ 59	Robert Pack	.05	.01
❑ 60	Rodney Rogers	.05	.01
❑ 61	Bryant Stith	.05	.01
❑ 62	Brian Williams	.05	.01
❑ 63	Reggie Williams	.05	.01
❑ 64	Greg Anderson	.05	.01
❑ 65	Joe Dumars	.25	.08
❑ 66	Sean Elliott	.10	.02
❑ 67	Allan Houston	.40	.15
❑ 68	Lindsey Hunter	.10	.02
❑ 69	Terry Mills	.05	.01
❑ 70	Victor Alexander	.05	.01
❑ 71	Chris Gatling	.05	.01
❑ 72	Tim Hardaway	.25	.08
❑ 73	Keith Jennings	.05	.01
❑ 74	Avery Johnson	.05	.01
❑ 75	Chris Mullin	.25	.08
❑ 76	Billy Owens	.05	.01
❑ 77	Latrell Sprewell	.25	.08
❑ 78	Chris Webber	.60	.25
❑ 79	Scott Brooks	.05	.01
❑ 80	Sam Cassell	.25	.08
❑ 81	Mario Elie	.05	.01
❑ 82	Carl Herrera	.05	.01

83	Robert Horry	.10	.02
84	Vernon Maxwell	.05	.01
85	Hakeem Olajuwon	.40	.15
86	Kenny Smith	.05	.01
87	Otis Thorpe	.05	.01
88	Antonio Davis	.05	.01
89	Dale Davis	.05	.01
90	Vern Fleming	.05	.01
91	Derrick McKey	.05	.01
92	Reggie Miller	.25	.08
93	Pooh Richardson	.05	.01
94	Byron Scott	.10	.02
95	Rik Smits	.05	.01
96	Haywoode Workman	.05	.01
97	Terry Dehere	.05	.01
98	Harold Ellis	.05	.01
99	Gary Grant	.05	.01
100	Ron Harper	.10	.02
101	Mark Jackson	.05	.01
102	Stanley Roberts	.05	.01
103	Elmore Spencer	.05	.01
104	Loy Vaught	.05	.01
105	Dominique Wilkins	.25	.08
106	Elden Campbell	.05	.01
107	Doug Christie	.10	.02
108	Vlade Divac	.05	.01
109	George Lynch	.05	.01
110	Anthony Peeler	.05	.01
111	Tony Smith	.05	.01
112	Sedale Threatt	.05	.01
113	Nick Van Exel	.25	.08
114	James Worthy	.25	.08
115	Bimbo Coles	.05	.01
116	Grant Long	.05	.01
117	Harold Miner	.05	.01
118	Glen Rice	.10	.02
119	John Salley	.05	.01
120	Rony Seikaly	.05	.01
121	Brian Shaw	.05	.01
122	Steve Smith	.10	.02
123	Vin Baker	.25	.08
124	Jon Barry	.05	.01
125	Todd Day	.05	.01
126	Blue Edwards	.05	.01
127	Lee Mayberry	.05	.01
128	Eric Murdock	.05	.01
129	Ken Norman	.05	.01
130	Derek Strong	.05	.01
131	Thurl Bailey	.05	.01
132	Stacey King	.05	.01
133	Christian Laettner	.10	.02
134	Chuck Person	.05	.01
135	Isaiah Rider	.10	.02
136	Chris Smith	.05	.01
137	Doug West	.05	.01
138	Micheal Williams	.05	.01
139	Kenny Anderson	.10	.02
140	Benoit Benjamin	.05	.01
141	P.J. Brown	.05	.01
142	Derrick Coleman	.10	.02
143	Kevin Edwards	.05	.01
144	Armon Gilliam	.05	.01
145	Chris Morris	.05	.01
146	Johnny Newman	.05	.01
147	Greg Anthony	.05	.01
148	Anthony Bonner	.05	.01
149	Hubert Davis	.05	.01
150	Patrick Ewing	.25	.08
151	Derek Harper	.05	.01
152	Anthony Mason	.10	.02
153	Charles Oakley	.05	.01
154	Doc Rivers	.10	.02
155	Charles Smith	.05	.01
156	John Starks	.05	.01
157	Nick Anderson	.05	.01
158	Anthony Avent	.05	.01
159	Anfernee Hardaway	.60	.25
160	Shaquille O'Neal	1.25	.50
161	Donald Royal	.05	.01
162	Dennis Scott	.05	.01
163	Scott Skiles	.05	.01
164	Jeff Turner	.05	.01
165	Dana Barros	.05	.01
166	Shawn Bradley	.05	.01
167	Greg Graham	.05	.01
168	Eric Leckner	.05	.01
169	Jeff Malone	.05	.01
170	Moses Malone	.25	.08
171	Tim Perry	.05	.01
172	Clarence Weatherspoon	.05	.01
173	Orlando Woolridge	.05	.01
174	Danny Ainge	.05	.01
175	Charles Barkley	.40	.15
176	Cedric Ceballos	.05	.01
177	A.C. Green	.10	.02
178	Kevin Johnson	.10	.02
179	Joe Kleine	.05	.01
180	Dan Majerle	.10	.02
181	Oliver Miller	.05	.01
182	Mark West	.05	.01
183	Clyde Drexler	.25	.08
184	Harvey Grant	.05	.01
185	Jerome Kersey	.05	.01
186	Tracy Murray	.05	.01
187	Terry Porter	.05	.01
188	Clifford Robinson	.10	.02
189	James Robinson	.05	.01
190	Rod Strickland	.10	.02
191	Buck Williams	.05	.01
192	Duane Causwell	.05	.01
193	Bobby Hurley	.05	.01
194	Olden Polynice	.05	.01
195	Mitch Richmond	.25	.08
196	Lionel Simmons	.05	.01
197	Wayman Tisdale	.05	.01
198	Spud Webb	.05	.01
199	Walt Williams	.05	.01
200	Trevor Wilson	.05	.01
201	Willie Anderson	.05	.01
202	Antoine Carr	.05	.01
203	Terry Cummings	.05	.01
204	Vinny Del Negro	.05	.01
205	Dale Ellis	.05	.01
206	Negele Knight	.05	.01
207	J.R. Reid	.05	.01
208	David Robinson	.40	.15
209	Dennis Rodman	.50	.20
210	Vincent Askew	.05	.01
211	Michael Cage	.05	.01
212	Kendall Gill	.10	.02
213	Shawn Kemp	.40	.15
214	Nate McMillan	.05	.01
215	Gary Payton	.40	.15
216	Sam Perkins	.10	.02
217	Ricky Pierce	.05	.01
218	Detlef Schrempf	.10	.02
219	David Benoit	.05	.01
220	Tom Chambers	.05	.01
221	Tyrone Corbin	.05	.01
222	Jeff Hornacek	.10	.02
223	Jay Humphries	.05	.01
224	Karl Malone	.40	.15
225	Bryon Russell	.05	.01
226	Felton Spencer	.05	.01
227	John Stockton	.25	.08
228	Michael Adams	.05	.01
229	Rex Chapman	.05	.01
230	Calbert Cheaney	.05	.01
231	Kevin Duckworth	.05	.01
232	Pervis Ellison	.05	.01
233	Tom Gugliotta	.10	.02
234	Don MacLean	.05	.01
235	Gheorghe Muresan	.05	.01
236	Brent Price	.05	.01
237	Toronto Raptors Logo	.05	.01
238	Checklist	.05	.01
239	Checklist	.05	.01
240	Checklist	.05	.01
241	Sergei Bazarevich	.05	.01
242	Tyrone Corbin	.05	.01
243	Grant Long	.05	.01
244	Ken Norman	.05	.01
245	Steve Smith	.10	.02
246	Fred Vinson	.05	.01
247	Blue Edwards	.05	.01
248	Greg Minor RC	.05	.01
249	Eric Montross RC	.05	.01
250	Derek Strong	.05	.01
251	David Wesley	.05	.01
252	Dominique Wilkins	.25	.08
253	Michael Adams	.05	.01
254	Tony Bennett	.05	.01
255	Darrin Hancock RC	.05	.01
256	Robert Parish	.10	.02
257	Corie Blount	.05	.01
258	Jud Buechler	.05	.01
259	Greg Foster	.05	.01
260	Ron Harper	.10	.02
261	Larry Krystkowiak	.05	.01
262	Will Perdue	.05	.01
263	Dickey Simpkins RC	.05	.01
264	Michael Cage	.05	.01
265	Tony Campbell	.05	.01
266	Terry Davis	.05	.01
267	Tony Dumas RC	.05	.01
268	Jason Kidd RC	2.50	1.00
269	Roy Tarpley	.05	.01
270	Morlon Wiley	.05	.01
271	Lorenzo Williams	.05	.01
272	Dale Ellis	.05	.01
273	Tom Hammonds	.05	.01
274	Cliff Levingston	.05	.01
275	Darnell Mee	.05	.01
276	Jalen Rose RC	1.00	.40
277	Reggie Slater	.05	.01
278	Bill Curley RC	.05	.01
279	Johnny Dawkins	.05	.01
280	Grant Hill RC	1.25	.50
281	Eric Leckner	.05	.01
282	Mark Macon	.05	.01
283	Oliver Miller	.05	.01
284	Mark West	.05	.01
285	Manute Bol	.05	.01
286	Tom Gugliotta	.10	.02
287	Ricky Pierce	.05	.01
288	Carlos Rogers RC	.05	.01
289	Clifford Rozier RC	.05	.01
290	Rony Seikaly	.05	.01
291	Tim Breaux	.05	.01
292	Chris Jent	.05	.01
293	Eric Riley	.05	.01
294	Zan Tabak	.05	.01
295	Duane Ferrell	.05	.01
296	Mark Jackson	.05	.01
297	John Williams	.05	.01
298	Matt Fish	.05	.01
299	Tony Massenburg	.05	.01
300	Lamond Murray RC	.10	.02
301	Bo Outlaw RC	.05	.01
302	Eric Piatkowski RC	.05	.01
303	Pooh Richardson	.05	.01
304	Randy Woods	.05	.01
305	Sam Bowie	.05	.01
306	Cedric Ceballos	.05	.01
307	Antonio Harvey	.05	.01
308	Eddie Jones RC	1.25	.50
309	Anthony Miller RC	.05	.01
310	Ledell Eackles	.05	.01
311	Kevin Gamble	.05	.01
312	Brad Lohaus	.05	.01
313	Billy Owens	.05	.01
314	Khalid Reeves RC	.05	.01
315	Kevin Willis	.05	.01
316	Marty Conlon	.05	.01
317	Eric Mobley RC	.05	.01
318	Johnny Newman	.05	.01
319	Ed Pinckney	.05	.01
320	Glenn Robinson RC	.75	.30
321	Mike Brown	.05	.01
322	Pat Durham	.05	.01
323	Howard Eisley RC	.05	.01
324	Andres Guibert	.05	.01
325	Donyell Marshall RC	.25	.08
326	Sean Rooks	.05	.01
327	Yinka Dare RC	.05	.01
328	Sleepy Floyd	.05	.01
329	Sean Higgins	.05	.01
330	Rick Mahorn	.05	.01
331	Rex Walters	.05	.01
332	Jayson Williams	.10	.02
333	Charlie Ward RC	.25	.08
334	Herb Williams	.05	.01
335	Monty Williams RC	.05	.01
336	Anthony Bowie	.05	.01
337	Horace Grant	.10	.02
338	Geert Hammink	.05	.01
339	Tree Rollins	.05	.01
340	Brian Shaw	.05	.01

#	Player		
341	Brooks Thompson RC	.05	.01
342	Derrick Alston RC	.05	.01
343	Willie Burton	.05	.01
344	Jaren Jackson RC	.05	.01
345	B.J.Tyler RC	.05	.01
346	Scott Williams	.05	.01
347	Sharone Wright RC	.05	.01
348	Antonio Lang RC	.05	.01
349	Danny Manning	.10	.02
350	Elliot Perry	.05	.01
351	Wesley Person RC	.25	.08
352	Trevor Ruffin	.05	.01
353	Danny Schayes	.05	.01
354	Aaron Swinson RC	.05	.01
355	Wayman Tisdale	.05	.01
356	Mark Bryant	.05	.01
357	Chris Dudley	.05	.01
358	James Edwards	.05	.01
359	Aaron McKie RC	.50	.20
360	Alaa Abdelnaby	.05	.01
361	Frank Brickowski	.05	.01
362	Randy Brown	.05	.01
363	Brian Grant RC	.60	.25
364	Michael Smith RC	.05	.01
365	Henry Turner	.05	.01
366	Sean Elliott	.10	.02
367	Avery Johnson	.05	.01
368	Moses Malone	.25	.08
369	Julius Nwosu	.05	.01
370	Chuck Person	.05	.01
371	Chris Whitney	.05	.01
372	Bill Cartwright	.05	.01
373	Byron Houston	.05	.01
374	Ervin Johnson	.05	.01
375	Sarunas Marciulionis	.05	.01
376	Antoine Carr	.05	.01
377	John Crotty	.05	.01
378	Adam Keefe	.05	.01
379	Jamie Watson RC	.05	.01
380	Mitchell Butler	.05	.01
381	Juwan Howard RC	.60	.25
382	Jim McIlvaine RC	.05	.01
383	Doug Overton	.05	.01
384	Scott Skiles	.05	.01
385	Larry Stewart	.05	.01
386	Kenny Walker	.05	.01
387	Chris Webber	.60	.25
388	Vancouver Grizzlies	.05	.01
389	Checklist	.05	.01
390	Checklist	.05	.01

1995-96 Fleer

COMPLETE SET (350)		40.00	20.00
COMPLETE SERIES 1 (200)		20.00	10.00
COMPLETE SERIES 2 (150)		20.00	10.00
1	Stacey Augmon	.15	.05
2	Mookie Blaylock	.15	.05
3	Craig Ehlo	.15	.05
4	Andrew Lang	.15	.05
5	Grant Long	.15	.05
6	Ken Norman	.15	.05
7	Steve Smith	.30	.10
8	Dee Brown	.15	.05
9	Sherman Douglas	.15	.05
10	Eric Montross	.15	.05
11	Dino Radja	.15	.05
12	David Wesley	.15	.05
13	Dominique Wilkins	.50	.20
14	Muggsy Bogues	.30	.10
15	Scott Burrell	.15	.05
16	Dell Curry	.15	.05
17	Hersey Hawkins	.15	.05
18	Larry Johnson	.30	.10
19	Alonzo Mourning	.30	.10
20	Robert Parish	.30	.10
21	B.J. Armstrong	.15	.05
22	Michael Jordan	3.00	1.25
23	Steve Kerr	.30	.10
24	Toni Kukoc	.30	.10
25	Will Perdue	.15	.05
26	Scottie Pippen	.75	.30
27	Dickey Simpkins	.30	.10
28	Tyrone Hill	.15	.05
29	Chris Mills	.15	.05
30	Bobby Phills	.15	.05
31	Mark Price	.30	.10
32	John Williams	.15	.05
33	Lucious Harris	.15	.05
34	Jim Jackson	.15	.05
35	Popeye Jones	.15	.05
36	Jason Kidd	1.50	.60
37	Jamal Mashburn	.30	.10
38	George McCloud	.15	.05
39	Roy Tarpley	.15	.05
40	Lorenzo Williams	.15	.05
41	Mahmoud Abdul-Rauf	.15	.05
42	Dale Ellis	.15	.05
43	LaPhonso Ellis	.15	.05
44	Dikembe Mutombo	.30	.10
45	Robert Pack	.15	.05
46	Rodney Rogers	.15	.05
47	Jalen Rose	.60	.25
48	Bryant Stith	.15	.05
49	Reggie Williams	.15	.05
50	Joe Dumars	.50	.20
51	Grant Hill	.60	.25
52	Allan Houston	.30	.10
53	Lindsey Hunter	.15	.05
54	Oliver Miller	.15	.05
55	Terry Mills	.15	.05
56	Mark West	.15	.05
57	Chris Gatling	.15	.05
58	Tim Hardaway	.30	.10
59	Donyell Marshall	.15	.05
60	Chris Mullin	.50	.20
61	Carlos Rogers	.15	.05
62	Clifford Rozier	.15	.05
63	Rony Seikaly	.15	.05
64	Latrell Sprewell	.50	.20
65	Sam Cassell	.50	.20
66	Clyde Drexler	.50	.20
67	Mario Elie	.15	.05
68	Carl Herrera	.15	.05
69	Robert Horry	.30	.10
70	Vernon Maxwell	.15	.05
71	Hakeem Olajuwon	.50	.20
72	Kenny Smith	.15	.05
73	Dale Davis	.15	.05
74	Mark Jackson	.30	.10
75	Derrick McKey	.15	.05
76	Reggie Miller	.50	.20
77	Sam Mitchell	.15	.05
78	Byron Scott	.15	.05
79	Rik Smits	.30	.10
80	Terry Dehere	.15	.05
81	Tony Massenburg	.15	.05
82	Lamond Murray	.15	.05
83	Pooh Richardson	.15	.05
84	Malik Sealy	.15	.05
85	Loy Vaught	.15	.05
86	Elden Campbell	.15	.05
87	Cedric Ceballos	.15	.05
88	Vlade Divac	.30	.10
89	Eddie Jones	.60	.25
90	Anthony Peeler	.15	.05
91	Sedale Threatt	.15	.05
92	Nick Van Exel	.50	.20
93	Bimbo Coles	.15	.05
94	Matt Geiger	.15	.05
95	Billy Owens	.15	.05
96	Khalid Reeves	.15	.05
97	Glen Rice	.30	.10
98	John Salley	.15	.05
99	Kevin Willis	.30	.10
100	Vin Baker	.30	.10
101	Marty Conlon	.15	.05
102	Todd Day	.15	.05
103	Lee Mayberry	.15	.05
104	Eric Murdock	.15	.05
105	Glenn Robinson	.50	.20
106	Winston Garland	.15	.05
107	Tom Gugliotta	.15	.05
108	Christian Laettner	.30	.10
109	Isaiah Rider	.30	.10
110	Sean Rooks	.15	.05
111	Doug West	.15	.05
112	Kenny Anderson	.30	.10
113	Benoit Benjamin	.15	.05
114	P.J. Brown	.15	.05
115	Derrick Coleman	.15	.05
116	Armon Gilliam	.15	.05
117	Chris Morris	.15	.05
118	Rex Walters	.15	.05
119	Hubert Davis	.15	.05
120	Patrick Ewing	.50	.20
121	Derek Harper	.30	.10
122	Anthony Mason	.30	.10
123	Charles Oakley	.15	.05
124	Charles Smith	.15	.05
125	John Starks	.30	.10
126	Nick Anderson	.15	.05
127	Anthony Bowie	.15	.05
128	Horace Grant	.30	.10
129	Anfernee Hardaway	.50	.20
130	Shaquille O'Neal	1.25	.50
131	Donald Royal	.15	.05
132	Dennis Scott	.15	.05
133	Brian Shaw	.15	.05
134	Derrick Alston	.15	.05
135	Dana Barros	.15	.05
136	Shawn Bradley	.15	.05
137	Willie Burton	.15	.05
138	Clarence Weatherspoon	.15	.05
139	Scott Williams	.15	.05
140	Sharone Wright	.15	.05
141	Danny Ainge	.15	.05
142	Charles Barkley	.60	.25
143	A.C. Green	.30	.10
144	Kevin Johnson	.30	.10
145	Dan Majerle	.30	.10
146	Danny Manning	.15	.05
147	Elliot Perry	.15	.05
148	Wesley Person	.15	.05
149	Wayman Tisdale	.15	.05
150	Chris Dudley	.15	.05
151	Jerome Kersey	.15	.05
152	Aaron McKie	.15	.05
153	Terry Porter	.15	.05
154	Clifford Robinson	.15	.05
155	James Robinson	.15	.05
156	Rod Strickland	.15	.05
157	Otis Thorpe	.15	.05
158	Buck Williams	.15	.05
159	Brian Grant	.50	.20
160	Bobby Hurley	.15	.05
161	Olden Polynice	.15	.05
162	Mitch Richmond	.30	.10
163	Michael Smith	.15	.05
164	Spud Webb	.30	.10
165	Walt Williams	.15	.05
166	Terry Cummings	.15	.05
167	Vinny Del Negro	.15	.05
168	Sean Elliott	.30	.10
169	Avery Johnson	.15	.05
170	Chuck Person	.15	.05
171	J.R. Reid	.15	.05
172	Doc Rivers	.30	.10
173	David Robinson	.50	.20
174	Dennis Rodman	.30	.10
175	Vincent Askew	.15	.05
176	Kendall Gill	.15	.05
177	Shawn Kemp	.30	.10
178	Sarunas Marciulionis	.15	.05
179	Nate McMillan	.15	.05
180	Gary Payton	.50	.20
181	Sam Perkins	.30	.10
182	Detlef Schrempf	.15	.05
183	David Benoit	.15	.05
184	Antoine Carr	.15	.05
185	Blue Edwards	.15	.05

☐ 186	Jeff Hornacek	.30	.10
☐ 187	Adam Keefe	.15	.05
☐ 188	Karl Malone	.60	.25
☐ 189	Felton Spencer	.15	.05
☐ 190	John Stockton	.60	.25
☐ 191	Rex Chapman	.15	.05
☐ 192	Calbert Cheaney	.15	.05
☐ 193	Juwan Howard	.50	.20
☐ 194	Don MacLean	.15	.05
☐ 195	Gheorghe Muresan	.15	.05
☐ 196	Scott Skiles	.15	.05
☐ 197	Chris Webber	.60	.25
☐ 198	Checklist	.15	.05
☐ 199	Checklist	.15	.05
☐ 200	Checklist	.15	.05
☐ 201	Stacey Augmon	.15	.05
☐ 202	Mookie Blaylock	.15	.05
☐ 203	Grant Long	.15	.05
☐ 204	Ken Norman	.15	.05
☐ 205	Steve Smith	.30	.10
☐ 206	Spud Webb	.30	.10
☐ 207	Dana Barros	.15	.05
☐ 208	Rick Fox	.30	.10
☐ 209	Kendall Gill	.15	.05
☐ 210	Khalid Reeves	.15	.05
☐ 211	Glen Rice	.30	.10
☐ 212	Luc Longley	.15	.05
☐ 213	Dennis Rodman	.30	.10
☐ 214	Dan Majerle	.15	.05
☐ 215	Tony Dumas	.15	.05
☐ 216	Tom Hammonds	.15	.05
☐ 217	Elmore Spencer	.15	.05
☐ 218	Otis Thorpe	.15	.05
☐ 219	B.J. Armstrong	.15	.05
☐ 220	Sam Cassell	.50	.20
☐ 221	Clyde Drexler	.50	.20
☐ 222	Mario Elie	.15	.05
☐ 223	Robert Horry	.30	.10
☐ 224	Hakeem Olajuwon	.50	.20
☐ 225	Kenny Smith	.15	.05
☐ 226	Antonio Davis	.15	.05
☐ 227	Eddie Johnson	.15	.05
☐ 228	Ricky Pierce	.15	.05
☐ 229	Eric Piatkowski	.10	.02
☐ 230	Rodney Rogers	.15	.05
☐ 231	Brian Williams	.15	.05
☐ 232	Corie Blount	.15	.05
☐ 233	George Lynch	.15	.05
☐ 234	Kevin Gamble	.15	.05
☐ 235	Alonzo Mourning	.30	.10
☐ 236	Eric Mobley	.15	.05
☐ 237	Terry Porter	.15	.05
☐ 238	Micheal Williams	.15	.05
☐ 239	Kevin Edwards	.15	.05
☐ 240	Vern Fleming	.15	.05
☐ 241	Charlie Ward	.15	.05
☐ 242	Jon Koncak	.15	.05
☐ 243	Richard Dumas	.15	.05
☐ 244	Jeff Malone	.15	.05
☐ 245	Vernon Maxwell	.15	.05
☐ 246	John Williams	.15	.05
☐ 247	Harvey Grant	.15	.05
☐ 248	Dontonio Wingfield	.15	.05
☐ 249	Tyrone Corbin	.15	.05
☐ 250	Sarunas Marciulionis	.15	.05
☐ 251	Will Perdue	.15	.05
☐ 252	Hersey Hawkins	.15	.05
☐ 253	Ervin Johnson	.15	.05
☐ 254	Shawn Kemp	.30	.10
☐ 255	Gary Payton	.50	.20
☐ 256	Sam Perkins	.15	.05
☐ 257	Detlef Schrempf	.30	.10
☐ 258	Chris Morris	.15	.05
☐ 259	Robert Pack	.15	.05
☐ 260	Willie Anderson ET	.15	.05
☐ 261	Jimmy King ET	.15	.05
☐ 262	Oliver Miller ET	.15	.05
☐ 263	Tracy Murray ET	.15	.05
☐ 264	Ed Pinckney ET	.15	.05
☐ 265	Alvin Robertson ET	.15	.05
☐ 266	Carlos Rogers ET	.15	.05
☐ 267	John Salley ET	.15	.05
☐ 268	Damon Stoudamire ET	.60	.25
☐ 269	Zan Tabak ET	.15	.05
☐ 270	Ashraf Amaya ET	.15	.05
☐ 271	Greg Anthony ET	.15	.05
☐ 272	Benoit Benjamin ET	.15	.05
☐ 273	Blue Edwards ET	.15	.05
☐ 274	Kenny Gattison ET	.15	.05
☐ 275	Antonio Harvey ET	.15	.05
☐ 276	Chris King ET	.15	.05
☐ 277	Lawrence Moten ET	.15	.05
☐ 278	Bryant Reeves ET	.30	.10
☐ 279	Byron Scott ET	.15	.05
☐ 280	Cory Alexander RC	.15	.05
☐ 281	Jerome Allen RC	.15	.05
☐ 282	Brent Barry RC	.50	.20
☐ 283	Mario Bennett RC	.15	.05
☐ 284	Travis Best RC	.15	.05
☐ 285	Junior Burrough RC	.15	.05
☐ 286	Jason Caffey RC	.30	.10
☐ 287	Randolph Childress RC	.15	.05
☐ 288	Sasha Danilovic RC	.15	.05
☐ 289	Mark Davis RC	.15	.05
☐ 290	Tyus Edney RC	.15	.05
☐ 291	Michael Finley RC	1.25	.50
☐ 292	Sherrell Ford RC	.15	.05
☐ 293	Kevin Garnett RC	2.50	1.25
☐ 294	Alan Henderson RC	.50	.20
☐ 295	Frankie King RC	.15	.05
☐ 296	Jimmy King RC	.15	.05
☐ 297	Donny Marshall RC	.15	.05
☐ 298	Antonio McDyess RC	1.00	.40
☐ 299	Loren Meyer RC	.15	.05
☐ 300	Lawrence Moten RC	.15	.05
☐ 301	Ed O'Bannon RC	.15	.05
☐ 302	Greg Ostertag RC	.15	.05
☐ 303	Cherokee Parks RC	.15	.05
☐ 304	Theo Ratliff RC	.60	.25
☐ 305	Bryant Reeves RC	.50	.20
☐ 306	Shawn Respert RC	.15	.05
☐ 307	Lou Roe RC	.15	.05
☐ 308	Arvydas Sabonis RC	.60	.25
☐ 309	Joe Smith RC	.75	.30
☐ 310	Jerry Stackhouse RC	1.50	.60
☐ 311	Damon Stoudamire RC	1.00	.40
☐ 312	Bob Sura RC	.15	.05
☐ 313	Kurt Thomas RC	.30	.10
☐ 314	Gary Trent RC	.15	.05
☐ 315	David Vaughn RC	.15	.05
☐ 316	Rasheed Wallace RC	1.25	.50
☐ 317	Eric Williams RC	.30	.10
☐ 318	Corliss Williamson RC	.50	.20
☐ 319	George Zidek RC	.15	.05
☐ 320	Mookie Blaylock FF	.15	.05
☐ 321	Dino Radja FF	.15	.05
☐ 322	Larry Johnson FF	.15	.05
☐ 323	Michael Jordan FF	1.50	.60
☐ 324	Tyrone Hill FF	.15	.05
☐ 325	Jason Kidd FF	.75	.30
☐ 326	Dikembe Mutombo FF	.15	.05
☐ 327	Grant Hill FF	.50	.20
☐ 328	Joe Smith FF	.30	.10
☐ 329	Hakeem Olajuwon FF	.30	.10
☐ 330	Reggie Miller FF	.30	.10
☐ 331	Loy Vaught FF	.15	.05
☐ 332	Nick Van Exel FF	.15	.05
☐ 333	Alonzo Mourning FF	.15	.05
☐ 334	Glenn Robinson FF	.30	.10
☐ 335	Kevin Garnett FF	1.00	.40
☐ 336	Kenny Anderson FF	.15	.05
☐ 337	Patrick Ewing FF	.30	.10
☐ 338	Shaquille O'Neal FF	.50	.20
☐ 339	Jerry Stackhouse FF	.75	.30
☐ 340	Charles Barkley FF	.30	.10
☐ 341	Clifford Robinson FF	.15	.05
☐ 342	Mitch Richmond FF	.15	.05
☐ 343	David Robinson FF	.30	.10
☐ 344	Shawn Kemp FF	.15	.05
☐ 345	Damon Stoudamire FF	.60	.25
☐ 346	Karl Malone FF	.30	.10
☐ 347	Bryant Reeves FF	.30	.10
☐ 348	Chris Webber FF	.30	.10
☐ 349	Checklist (201-319)	.15	.05
☐ 350	Checklist (320-350/Ins.)	.15	.05

1996-97 Fleer

☐	COMPLETE SET (300)	35.00	17.50
☐	COMPLETE SERIES 1 (150)	15.00	7.50
☐	COMPLETE SERIES 2 (150)	20.00	10.00
☐ 1	Stacey Augmon	.15	.05
☐ 2	Mookie Blaylock	.15	.05
☐ 3	Christian Laettner	.30	.10
☐ 4	Grant Long	.15	.05
☐ 5	Steve Smith	.30	.10
☐ 6	Rick Fox	.15	.05
☐ 7	Dino Radja	.15	.05
☐ 8	Eric Williams	.15	.05
☐ 9	Kenny Anderson	.15	.05
☐ 10	Dell Curry	.15	.05
☐ 11	Larry Johnson	.30	.10
☐ 12	Glen Rice	.30	.10
☐ 13	Michael Jordan	3.00	1.25
☐ 14	Toni Kukoc	.30	.10
☐ 15	Scottie Pippen	.75	.30
☐ 16	Dennis Rodman	.75	.30
☐ 17	Terrell Brandon	.15	.05
☐ 18	Chris Mills	.15	.05
☐ 19	Bobby Phills	.15	.05
☐ 20	Bob Sura	.15	.05
☐ 21	Jim Jackson	.15	.05
☐ 22	Jason Kidd	.75	.30
☐ 23	Jamal Mashburn	.30	.10
☐ 24	George McCloud	.15	.05
☐ 25	Mahmoud Abdul-Rauf	.15	.05
☐ 26	Antonio McDyess	.30	.10
☐ 27	Dikembe Mutombo	.30	.10
☐ 28	Jalen Rose	.50	.20
☐ 29	Bryant Stith	.15	.05
☐ 30	Joe Dumars	.50	.20
☐ 31	Grant Hill	.50	.20
☐ 32	Allan Houston	.30	.10
☐ 33	Theo Ratliff	.30	.10
☐ 34	Otis Thorpe	.15	.05
☐ 35	Chris Mullin	.30	.10
☐ 36	Joe Smith	.30	.10
☐ 37	Latrell Sprewell	.50	.20
☐ 38	Kevin Willis	.15	.05
☐ 39	Sam Cassell	.15	.05
☐ 40	Clyde Drexler	.50	.20
☐ 41	Robert Horry	.15	.05
☐ 42	Hakeem Olajuwon	.50	.20
☐ 43	Dale Davis	.15	.05
☐ 44	Mark Jackson	.15	.05
☐ 45	Derrick McKey	.15	.05
☐ 46	Reggie Miller	.50	.20
☐ 47	Rik Smits	.30	.10
☐ 48	Brent Barry	.15	.05
☐ 49	Malik Sealy	.15	.05
☐ 50	Loy Vaught	.15	.05
☐ 51	Brian Williams	.15	.05
☐ 52	Elden Campbell	.15	.05
☐ 53	Cedric Ceballos	.15	.05
☐ 54	Vlade Divac	.15	.05
☐ 55	Eddie Jones	.50	.20
☐ 56	Nick Van Exel	.50	.20
☐ 57	Tim Hardaway	.30	.10
☐ 58	Alonzo Mourning	.30	.10
☐ 59	Kurt Thomas	.15	.05
☐ 60	Walt Williams	.15	.05
☐ 61	Vin Baker	.30	.10
☐ 62	Sherman Douglas	.15	.05
☐ 63	Glenn Robinson	.50	.20
☐ 64	Kevin Garnett	1.00	.40
☐ 65	Tom Gugliotta	.15	.05
☐ 66	Isaiah Rider	.15	.05
☐ 67	Shawn Bradley	.15	.05
☐ 68	Chris Childs	.15	.05
☐ 69	Armon Gilliam	.15	.05
☐ 70	Ed O'Bannon	.15	.05

#	Player		
☐ 71	Patrick Ewing	.50	.20
☐ 72	Derek Harper	.15	.05
☐ 73	Anthony Mason	.30	.10
☐ 74	Charles Oakley	.15	.05
☐ 75	John Starks	.30	.10
☐ 76	Nick Anderson	.15	.05
☐ 77	Horace Grant	.30	.10
☐ 78	Anfernee Hardaway	.50	.20
☐ 79	Shaquille O'Neal	1.25	.50
☐ 80	Dennis Scott	.15	.05
☐ 81	Derrick Coleman	.30	.10
☐ 82	Vernon Maxwell	.15	.05
☐ 83	Jerry Stackhouse	.60	.25
☐ 84	Clarence Weatherspoon	.15	.05
☐ 85	Charles Barkley	.60	.25
☐ 86	Michael Finley	.60	.25
☐ 87	Kevin Johnson	.30	.10
☐ 88	Wesley Person	.15	.05
☐ 89	Clifford Robinson	.15	.05
☐ 90	Arvydas Sabonis	.30	.10
☐ 91	Rod Strickland	.15	.05
☐ 92	Gary Trent	.15	.05
☐ 93	Tyus Edney	.15	.05
☐ 94	Brian Grant	.50	.20
☐ 95	Billy Owens	.15	.05
☐ 96	Mitch Richmond	.50	.20
☐ 97	Vinny Del Negro	.15	.05
☐ 98	Sean Elliott	.30	.10
☐ 99	Avery Johnson	.15	.05
☐ 100	David Robinson	.50	.20
☐ 101	Hersey Hawkins	.30	.10
☐ 102	Shawn Kemp	.30	.10
☐ 103	Gary Payton	.50	.20
☐ 104	Detlef Schrempf	.30	.10
☐ 105	Oliver Miller	.15	.05
☐ 106	Tracy Murray	.15	.05
☐ 107	Damon Stoudamire	.50	.20
☐ 108	Sharone Wright	.15	.05
☐ 109	Jeff Hornacek	.30	.10
☐ 110	Karl Malone	.50	.20
☐ 111	John Stockton	.50	.20
☐ 112	Greg Anthony	.15	.05
☐ 113	Bryant Reeves	.15	.05
☐ 114	Byron Scott	.15	.05
☐ 115	Calbert Cheaney	.15	.05
☐ 116	Juwan Howard	.30	.10
☐ 117	Gheorghe Muresan	.15	.05
☐ 118	Rasheed Wallace	.60	.25
☐ 119	Chris Webber	.50	.20
☐ 120	Mookie Blaylock	.15	.05
☐ 121	Dino Radja HL	.15	.05
☐ 122	Larry Johnson HL	.15	.05
☐ 123	Michael Jordan HL	1.50	.60
☐ 124	Terrell Brandon HL	.15	.05
☐ 125	Jason Kidd HL	.40	.15
☐ 126	Antonio McDyess HL	.15	.05
☐ 127	Grant Hill HL	.30	.10
☐ 128	Latrell Sprewell HL	.50	.20
☐ 129	Hakeem Olajuwon HL	.30	.10
☐ 130	Reggie Miller HL	.30	.10
☐ 131	Loy Vaught HL	.15	.05
☐ 132	Cedric Ceballos HL	.15	.05
☐ 133	Alonzo Mourning HL	.15	.05
☐ 134	Vin Baker HL	.15	.05
☐ 135	Isaiah Rider HL	.15	.05
☐ 136	Armon Gilliam HL	.15	.05
☐ 137	Patrick Ewing HL	.30	.10
☐ 138	Shaquille O'Neal HL	.50	.20
☐ 139	Jerry Stackhouse HL	.30	.10
☐ 140	Charles Barkley HL	.50	.20
☐ 141	Clifford Robinson HL	.15	.05
☐ 142	Mitch Richmond HL	.15	.05
☐ 143	David Robinson HL	.30	.10
☐ 144	Shawn Kemp HL	.15	.05
☐ 145	Damon Stoudamire HL	.30	.10
☐ 146	Karl Malone HL	.30	.10
☐ 147	Bryant Reeves HL	.15	.05
☐ 148	Juwan Howard HL	.15	.05
☐ 149	Checklist	.15	.05
☐ 150	Checklist	.15	.05
☐ 151	Alan Henderson	.15	.05
☐ 152	Priest Lauderdale RC	.15	.05
☐ 153	Dikembe Mutombo	.30	.10
☐ 154	Dana Barros	.15	.05
☐ 155	Todd Day	.15	.05
☐ 156	Brett Szabo RC	.15	.05

#	Player		
☐ 157	Antoine Walker RC	1.00	.40
☐ 158	Scott Burrell	.15	.05
☐ 159	Tony Delk RC	.50	.20
☐ 160	Vlade Divac	.15	.05
☐ 161	Matt Geiger	.15	.05
☐ 162	Anthony Mason	.30	.10
☐ 163	Malik Rose RC	.15	.05
☐ 164	Ron Harper	.30	.10
☐ 165	Steve Kerr	.30	.10
☐ 166	Luc Longley	.15	.05
☐ 167	Danny Ferry	.15	.05
☐ 168	Tyrone Hill	.15	.05
☐ 169	Vitaly Potapenko RC	.15	.05
☐ 170	Tony Dumas	.15	.05
☐ 171	Chris Gatling	.15	.05
☐ 172	Oliver Miller	.15	.05
☐ 173	Eric Montross	.15	.05
☐ 174	Samaki Walker RC	.15	.05
☐ 175	Darvin Ham RC	.15	.05
☐ 176	Mark Jackson	.15	.05
☐ 177	Ervin Johnson	.15	.05
☐ 178	Stacey Augmon	.15	.05
☐ 179	Joe Dumars	.50	.20
☐ 180	Grant Hill	.50	.20
☐ 181	Grant Long	.15	.05
☐ 182	Terry Mills	.15	.05
☐ 183	Otis Thorpe	.15	.05
☐ 184	Jerome Williams RC	.50	.20
☐ 185	B.J. Armstrong	.15	.05
☐ 186	Todd Fuller RC	.15	.05
☐ 187	Ray Owes RC	.15	.05
☐ 188	Mark Price	.30	.10
☐ 189	Felton Spencer	.15	.05
☐ 190	Charles Barkley	.60	.25
☐ 191	Mario Elie	.15	.05
☐ 192	Othella Harrington RC	.30	.10
☐ 193	Matt Maloney RC	.30	.10
☐ 194	Brent Price	.15	.05
☐ 195	Kevin Willis	.15	.05
☐ 196	Travis Best	.15	.05
☐ 197	Erick Dampier RC	.50	.20
☐ 198	Antonio Davis	.15	.05
☐ 199	Jalen Rose	.50	.20
☐ 200	Pooh Richardson	.15	.05
☐ 201	Rodney Rogers	.15	.05
☐ 202	Lorenzen Wright RC	.30	.10
☐ 203	Kobe Bryant RC	6.00	2.50
☐ 204	Derek Fisher RC	.75	.30
☐ 205	Travis Knight RC	.15	.05
☐ 206	Shaquille O'Neal	1.25	.50
☐ 207	Byron Scott	.15	.05
☐ 208	P.J. Brown	.15	.05
☐ 209	Sasha Danilovic	.15	.05
☐ 210	Dan Majerle	.30	.10
☐ 211	Martin Muursepp RC	.15	.05
☐ 212	Ray Allen RC	1.50	.60
☐ 213	Armon Gilliam	.15	.05
☐ 214	Andrew Lang	.15	.05
☐ 215	Moochie Norris RC	.15	.05
☐ 216	Kevin Garnett	1.00	.40
☐ 217	Tom Gugliotta	.15	.05
☐ 218	Shane Heal RC	.15	.05
☐ 219	Stephon Marbury RC	1.50	.60
☐ 220	Stojko Vrankovic	.15	.05
☐ 221	Kerry Kittles RC	.50	.20
☐ 222	Robert Pack	.15	.05
☐ 223	Jayson Williams	.30	.10
☐ 224	Allan Houston	.30	.10
☐ 225	Larry Johnson	.30	.10
☐ 226	Dontae' Jones RC	.15	.05
☐ 227	Walter McCarty RC	.15	.05
☐ 228	John Wallace RC	.30	.10
☐ 229	Charlie Ward	.15	.05
☐ 230	Brian Evans RC	.15	.05
☐ 231	Amal McCaskill RC	.15	.05
☐ 232	Brian Shaw	.15	.05
☐ 233	Mark Davis	.15	.05
☐ 234	Lucious Harris	.15	.05
☐ 235	Allen Iverson RC	2.50	1.00
☐ 236	Sam Cassell	.30	.10
☐ 237	Robert Horry	.30	.10
☐ 238	Danny Manning	.30	.10
☐ 239	Steve Nash RC	4.00	1.50
☐ 240	Kevin Ollie RC	.15	.05
☐ 241	Aleksandar Djordjevic RC	.15	.05
☐ 242	Jermaine O'Neal RC	1.50	.60

#	Player		
☐ 243	Isaiah Rider	.30	.10
☐ 244	Rasheed Wallace	.60	.25
☐ 245	Mahmoud Abdul-Rauf	.15	.05
☐ 246	Michael Smith	.15	.05
☐ 247	Corliss Williamson	.30	.10
☐ 248	Vernon Maxwell	.15	.05
☐ 249	Charles Smith	.15	.05
☐ 250	Dominique Wilkins	.50	.20
☐ 251	Craig Ehlo	.15	.05
☐ 252	Jim McIlvaine	.15	.05
☐ 253	Sam Perkins	.30	.10
☐ 254	Marcus Camby RC	.60	.25
☐ 255	Popeye Jones	.15	.05
☐ 256	Donald Whiteside RC	.15	.05
☐ 257	Walt Williams	.15	.05
☐ 258	Jeff Hornacek	.30	.10
☐ 259	Karl Malone	.50	.20
☐ 260	Bryon Russell	.15	.05
☐ 261	John Stockton	.50	.20
☐ 262	Shareef Abdur-Rahim RC	1.50	.60
☐ 263	Anthony Peeler	.15	.05
☐ 264	Roy Rogers RC	.15	.05
☐ 265	Tim Legler	.15	.05
☐ 266	Tracy Murray	.15	.05
☐ 267	Rod Strickland	.15	.05
☐ 268	Ben Wallace RC	3.00	1.25
☐ 269	Kevin Garnett CB	.50	.20
☐ 270	Allan Houston CB	.15	.05
☐ 271	Eddie Jones CB	.30	.10
☐ 272	Jamal Mashburn CB	.15	.05
☐ 273	Antonio McDyess CB	.15	.05
☐ 274	Glenn Robinson CB	.30	.10
☐ 275	Joe Smith CB	.15	.05
☐ 276	Steve Smith CB	.15	.05
☐ 277	Jerry Stackhouse CB	.50	.20
☐ 278	Damon Stoudamire CB	.30	.10
☐ 279	Hakeem Olajuwon CB	.30	.10
☐ 280	Charles Barkley AS	.30	.10
☐ 281	Patrick Ewing AS	.30	.10
☐ 282	Michael Jordan AS	1.50	.60
☐ 283	Clyde Drexler AS	.30	.10
☐ 284	Karl Malone AS	.30	.10
☐ 285	John Stockton AS	.30	.10
☐ 286	David Robinson AS	.30	.10
☐ 287	Scottie Pippen AS	.40	.15
☐ 288	Shawn Kemp AS	.15	.05
☐ 289	Shaquille O'Neal AS	.50	.20
☐ 290	Mitch Richmond AS	.15	.05
☐ 291	Reggie Miller AS	.30	.10
☐ 292	Alonzo Mourning AS	.15	.05
☐ 293	Gary Payton AS	.30	.10
☐ 294	Anfernee Hardaway AS	.30	.10
☐ 295	Grant Hill AS	.30	.10
☐ 296	Dennis Rodman AS	.15	.05
☐ 297	Juwan Howard AS	.15	.05
☐ 298	Jason Kidd AS	.40	.15
☐ 299	Checklist	.15	.05
☐ 300	Checklist	.15	.05

1997-98 Fleer

☐ COMPLETE SET (350)		40.00	20.00
☐ COMPLETE SERIES 1 (200)		20.00	10.00
☐ COMPLETE SERIES 2 (150)		20.00	10.00
☐ 1	Anfernee Hardaway	.50	.20
☐ 2	Mitch Richmond	.30	.10
☐ 3	Allen Iverson	1.25	.50
☐ 4	Chris Webber	.50	.20
☐ 5	Sasha Danilovic	.15	.05

#	Player		
❏ 6	Avery Johnson	.15	.05
❏ 7	Kenny Anderson	.30	.10
❏ 8	Antoine Walker	.60	.25
❏ 9	Nick Van Exel	.50	.20
❏ 10	Mookie Blaylock	.15	.05
❏ 11	Wesley Person	.15	.05
❏ 12	Vlade Divac	.30	.10
❏ 13	Glenn Robinson	.50	.20
❏ 14	Chris Mills	.15	.05
❏ 15	Latrell Sprewell	.50	.20
❏ 16	Jayson Williams	.15	.05
❏ 17	Travis Best	.15	.05
❏ 18	Charlie Ward	.15	.05
❏ 19	Theo Ratliff	.15	.05
❏ 20	Gary Payton	.50	.20
❏ 21	Marcus Camby	.50	.20
❏ 22	Clyde Drexler	.50	.20
❏ 23	Michael Jordan	3.00	1.25
❏ 24	Antonio McDyess	.30	.10
❏ 25	Stephon Marbury	.60	.25
❏ 26	Isaac Austin	.15	.05
❏ 27	Shareef Abdur-Rahim	.75	.30
❏ 28	Malik Sealy	.15	.05
❏ 29	Arvydas Sabonis	.30	.10
❏ 30	Kerry Kittles	.50	.20
❏ 31	Reggie Miller	.50	.20
❏ 32	Karl Malone	.50	.20
❏ 33	Grant Hill	.50	.20
❏ 34	Hakeem Olajuwon	.50	.20
❏ 35	Danny Ferry	.15	.05
❏ 36	Dominique Wilkins	.50	.20
❏ 37	Armon Gilliam	.15	.05
❏ 38	Danny Manning	.30	.10
❏ 39	Larry Johnson	.30	.10
❏ 40	Dino Radja	.15	.05
❏ 41	Jason Caffey	.15	.05
❏ 42	Jerry Stackhouse	.50	.20
❏ 43	Alonzo Mourning	.30	.10
❏ 44	Shawn Bradley	.15	.05
❏ 45	Bo Outlaw	.15	.05
❏ 46	Bryon Russell	.15	.05
❏ 47	Doug West	.15	.05
❏ 48	Lawrence Moten	.15	.05
❏ 49	Dale Ellis	.15	.05
❏ 50	Kobe Bryant	2.00	.75
❏ 51	Carlos Rogers	.15	.05
❏ 52	Todd Fuller	.15	.05
❏ 53	Tyus Edney	.15	.05
❏ 54	Horace Grant	.30	.10
❏ 55	Dikembe Mutombo	.30	.10
❏ 56	Jim McIlvaine	.15	.05
❏ 57	Harvey Grant	.15	.05
❏ 58	Dean Garrett	.15	.05
❏ 59	Samaki Walker	.15	.05
❏ 60	Johnny Newman	.15	.05
❏ 61	Antonio Davis	.15	.05
❏ 62	Jamal Mashburn	.30	.10
❏ 63	Muggsy Bogues	.30	.10
❏ 64	Rod Strickland	.15	.05
❏ 65	Craig Ehlo	.15	.05
❏ 66	Rex Walters	.15	.05
❏ 67	Bob Sura	.15	.05
❏ 68	Travis Knight	.15	.05
❏ 69	Toni Kukoc	.30	.10
❏ 70	Antoine Carr	.15	.05
❏ 71	Mario Elie	.15	.05
❏ 72	Popeye Jones	.15	.05
❏ 73	David Wesley	.15	.05
❏ 74	John Wallace	.15	.05
❏ 75	Calbert Cheaney	.15	.05
❏ 76	Grant Long	.15	.05
❏ 77	Will Perdue	.15	.05
❏ 78	Rasheed Wallace	.50	.20
❏ 79	Chris Gatling	.15	.05
❏ 80	Corliss Williamson	.30	.10
❏ 81	B.J. Armstrong	.15	.05
❏ 82	Brian Shaw	.15	.05
❏ 83	Darrick Martin	.15	.05
❏ 84	Vinny Del Negro	.15	.05
❏ 85	Tony Delk	.15	.05
❏ 86	Greg Anthony	.15	.05
❏ 87	Mark Davis	.15	.05
❏ 88	Anthony Goldwire	.15	.05
❏ 89	Rex Chapman	.15	.05
❏ 90	Stojko Vrankovic	.15	.05
❏ 91	Dennis Rodman	.30	.10
❏ 92	Detlef Schrempf	.30	.10
❏ 93	Henry James	.15	.05
❏ 94	Tracy Murray	.15	.05
❏ 95	Voshon Lenard	.15	.05
❏ 96	Sharone Wright	.15	.05
❏ 97	Ed O'Bannon	.15	.05
❏ 98	Gerald Wilkins	.15	.05
❏ 99	Kevin Willis	.30	.10
❏ 100	Shaquille O'Neal	1.25	.50
❏ 101	Jim Jackson	.15	.05
❏ 102	Mark Price	.30	.10
❏ 103	Patrick Ewing	.50	.20
❏ 104	Lorenzen Wright	.15	.05
❏ 105	Tyrone Hill	.15	.05
❏ 106	Ray Allen	.50	.20
❏ 107	Jermaine O'Neal	.75	.30
❏ 108	Anthony Mason	.30	.10
❏ 109	Mahmoud Abdul-Rauf	.15	.05
❏ 110	Terry Mills	.15	.05
❏ 111	Gheorghe Muresan	.15	.05
❏ 112	Mark Jackson	.30	.10
❏ 113	Greg Ostertag	.15	.05
❏ 114	Kevin Johnson	.30	.10
❏ 115	Anthony Peeler	.15	.05
❏ 116	Rony Seikaly	.15	.05
❏ 117	Keith Askins	.15	.05
❏ 118	Todd Day	.15	.05
❏ 119	Chris Mills	.15	.05
❏ 120	Chris Carr	.15	.05
❏ 121	Erick Strickland RC	.30	.10
❏ 122	Elden Campbell	.15	.05
❏ 123	Elliot Perry	.15	.05
❏ 124	Pooh Richardson	.15	.05
❏ 125	Juwan Howard	.30	.10
❏ 126	Ervin Johnson	.15	.05
❏ 127	Eric Montross	.15	.05
❏ 128	Otis Thorpe	.15	.05
❏ 129	Hersey Hawkins	.15	.05
❏ 130	Bimbo Coles	.15	.05
❏ 131	Olden Polynice	.15	.05
❏ 132	Christian Laettner	.30	.10
❏ 133	Sean Elliott	.30	.10
❏ 134	Othella Harrington	.15	.05
❏ 135	Erick Dampier	.15	.05
❏ 136	Vitaly Potapenko	.15	.05
❏ 137	Doug Christie	.30	.10
❏ 138	Luc Longley	.15	.05
❏ 139	Clarence Weatherspoon	.15	.05
❏ 140	Gary Trent	.15	.05
❏ 141	Shandon Anderson	.15	.05
❏ 142	Sam Perkins	.30	.10
❏ 143	Derek Harper	.30	.10
❏ 144	Robert Horry	.30	.10
❏ 145	Roy Rogers	.15	.05
❏ 146	John Starks	.30	.10
❏ 147	Tyrone Corbin	.15	.05
❏ 148	Andrew Lang	.15	.05
❏ 149	Derek Strong	.15	.05
❏ 150	Joe Smith	.30	.10
❏ 151	Ron Harper	.30	.10
❏ 152	Sam Cassell	.50	.20
❏ 153	Brent Barry	.15	.05
❏ 154	LaPhonso Ellis	.15	.05
❏ 155	Matt Geiger	.15	.05
❏ 156	Steve Nash	.50	.20
❏ 157	Michael Smith	.15	.05
❏ 158	Eric Williams	.15	.05
❏ 159	Tom Gugliotta	.30	.10
❏ 160	Monty Williams	.15	.05
❏ 161	Lindsey Hunter	.15	.05
❏ 162	Oliver Miller	.15	.05
❏ 163	Brent Price	.15	.05
❏ 164	Derrick McKey	.15	.05
❏ 165	Robert Pack	.15	.05
❏ 166	Derrick Coleman	.15	.05
❏ 167	Isaiah Rider	.30	.10
❏ 168	Dan Majerle	.30	.10
❏ 169	Jeff Hornacek	.30	.10
❏ 170	Terrell Brandon	.30	.10
❏ 171	Nate McMillan	.15	.05
❏ 172	Cedric Ceballos	.15	.05
❏ 173	Derek Fisher	.50	.20
❏ 174	Rodney Rogers	.15	.05
❏ 175	Blue Edwards	.15	.05
❏ 176	Brooks Thompson	.15	.05
❏ 177	Sherman Douglas	.15	.05
❏ 178	Sam Mitchell	.15	.05
❏ 179	Charles Oakley	.30	.10
❏ 180	Greg Minor	.15	.05
❏ 181	Chris Mullin	.50	.20
❏ 182	P.J. Brown	.15	.05
❏ 183	Stacey Augmon	.15	.05
❏ 184	Don MacLean	.15	.05
❏ 185	Aaron McKie	.30	.10
❏ 186	Dale Davis	.15	.05
❏ 187	Vernon Maxwell	.15	.05
❏ 188	Dell Curry	.15	.05
❏ 189	Kendall Gill	.15	.05
❏ 190	Billy Owens	.15	.05
❏ 191	Steve Kerr	.30	.10
❏ 192	Matt Maloney	.15	.05
❏ 193	Dennis Scott	.15	.05
❏ 194	A.C. Green	.30	.10
❏ 195	George McCloud	.15	.05
❏ 196	Walt Williams	.15	.05
❏ 197	Eldridge Recasner	.15	.05
❏ 198	Checklist (Hawks/Bucks)	.15	.05
❏ 199	Checklist (T'wolves/Wizards)	.15	.05
❏ 200	Checklist (inserts)	.15	.05
❏ 201	Tim Duncan RC	2.00	.75
❏ 202	Tim Thomas RC	.75	.30
❏ 203	Clifford Rozier	.15	.05
❏ 204	Bryant Reeves	.15	.05
❏ 205	Glen Rice	.30	.10
❏ 206	Darrell Armstrong	.15	.05
❏ 207	Juwan Howard	.30	.10
❏ 208	John Stockton	.50	.20
❏ 209	Antonio McDyess	.30	.10
❏ 210	James Cotton RC	.15	.05
❏ 211	Brian Grant	.15	.05
❏ 212	Chris Whitney	.15	.05
❏ 213	Antonio Davis	.15	.05
❏ 214	Kendall Gill	.15	.05
❏ 215	Adonal Foyle RC	.30	.10
❏ 216	Dean Garrett	.15	.05
❏ 217	Dennis Scott	.15	.05
❏ 218	Zydrunas Ilgauskas	.30	.10
❏ 219	Antonio Daniels RC	.50	.20
❏ 220	Derek Harper	.30	.10
❏ 221	Travis Knight	.15	.05
❏ 222	Bobby Hurley	.15	.05
❏ 223	Greg Anderson	.15	.05
❏ 224	Rod Strickland	.15	.05
❏ 225	David Benoit	.15	.05
❏ 226	Tracy McGrady RC	2.50	1.00
❏ 227	Brian Williams	.15	.05
❏ 228	James Robinson	.15	.05
❏ 229	Randy Brown	.15	.05
❏ 230	Greg Foster	.15	.05
❏ 231	Reggie Miller	.50	.20
❏ 232	Eric Montross	.15	.05
❏ 233	Malik Rose	.15	.05
❏ 234	Charles Barkley	.60	.25
❏ 235	Tony Battie RC	.50	.20
❏ 236	Terry Mills	.15	.05
❏ 237	Jerald Honeycutt RC	.15	.05
❏ 238	Bubba Wells RC	.15	.05
❏ 239	John Wallace	.15	.05
❏ 240	Jason Kidd	.75	.30
❏ 241	Mark Price	.30	.10
❏ 242	Ron Mercer RC	.50	.20
❏ 243	Derrick Coleman	.15	.05
❏ 244	Fred Hoiberg	.15	.05
❏ 245	Wesley Person	.15	.05
❏ 246	Eddie Jones	.50	.20
❏ 247	Allan Houston	.30	.10
❏ 248	Keith Van Horn RC	.60	.25
❏ 249	Johnny Newman	.15	.05
❏ 250	Kevin Garnett	1.00	.40
❏ 251	Latrell Sprewell	.50	.20
❏ 252	Tracy Murray	.15	.05
❏ 253	Charles O'Bannon RC	.15	.05
❏ 254	Lamond Murray	.15	.05
❏ 255	Jerry Stackhouse	.50	.20
❏ 256	Rik Smits	.30	.10
❏ 257	Alan Henderson	.15	.05
❏ 258	Tariq Abdul-Wahad RC	.30	.10
❏ 259	Nick Anderson	.15	.05
❏ 260	Calbert Cheaney	.15	.05
❏ 261	Scottie Pippen	.75	.30
❏ 262	Rodrick Rhodes RC	.15	.05
❏ 263	Derek Anderson RC	.50	.20

❑ 264	Dana Barros	.15	.05
❑ 265	Todd Day	.15	.05
❑ 266	Michael Finley	.50	.20
❑ 267	Kevin Edwards	.15	.05
❑ 268	Terrell Brandon	.30	.10
❑ 269	Bobby Phills	.15	.05
❑ 270	Kelvin Cato RC	.50	.20
❑ 271	Vin Baker	.30	.10
❑ 272	Eric Washington RC	.50	.20
❑ 273	Jim Jackson	.15	.05
❑ 274	Joe Dumars	.50	.20
❑ 275	David Robinson	.50	.20
❑ 276	Jayson Williams	.15	.05
❑ 277	Travis Best	.15	.05
❑ 278	Kurt Thomas	.30	.10
❑ 279	Otis Thorpe	.15	.05
❑ 280	Damon Stoudamire	.30	.10
❑ 281	John Williams	.15	.05
❑ 282	Loy Vaught	.15	.05
❑ 283	Bo Outlaw	.15	.05
❑ 284	Todd Fuller	.15	.05
❑ 285	Terry Dehere	.15	.05
❑ 286	Clarence Weatherspoon	.15	.05
❑ 287	Danny Fortson RC	.30	.10
❑ 288	Howard Eisley	.15	.05
❑ 289	Steve Smith	.30	.10
❑ 290	Chris Webber	.50	.20
❑ 291	Shawn Kemp	.50	.10
❑ 292	Sam Cassell	.50	.20
❑ 293	Rick Fox	.30	.10
❑ 294	Walter McCarty	.15	.05
❑ 295	Mark Jackson	.30	.10
❑ 296	Chris Mills	.15	.05
❑ 297	Jacque Vaughn RC	.30	.10
❑ 298	Shawn Respert	.15	.05
❑ 299	Scott Burrell	.15	.05
❑ 300	Allen Iverson	1.25	.50
❑ 301	Charles Smith RC	.15	.05
❑ 302	Ervin Johnson	.15	.05
❑ 303	Hubert Davis	.15	.05
❑ 304	Eddie Johnson	.15	.05
❑ 305	Erick Dampier	.30	.10
❑ 306	Eric Williams	.15	.05
❑ 307	Anthony Johnson RC	.15	.05
❑ 308	David Wesley	.15	.05
❑ 309	Eric Piatkowski	.30	.10
❑ 310	Austin Croshere RC	.40	.15
❑ 311	Malik Sealy	.15	.05
❑ 312	George McCloud	.15	.05
❑ 313	Anthony Parker RC	.15	.05
❑ 314	Cedric Henderson RC	.30	.10
❑ 315	John Thomas RC	.15	.05
❑ 316	Cory Alexander	.15	.05
❑ 317	Johnny Taylor RC	.15	.05
❑ 318	Chris Mullin	.50	.20
❑ 319	J.R. Reid	.15	.05
❑ 320	George Lynch	.15	.05
❑ 321	Lawrence Funderburke RC	.30	.10
❑ 322	God Shammgod RC	.15	.05
❑ 323	Bobby Jackson RC	.75	.30
❑ 324	Khalid Reeves	.15	.05
❑ 325	Zan Tabak	.15	.05
❑ 326	Chris Gatling	.15	.05
❑ 327	Alvin Williams RC	.15	.05
❑ 328	Scot Pollard RC	.30	.10
❑ 329	Kerry Kittles	.50	.20
❑ 330	Tim Hardaway	.30	.10
❑ 331	Maurice Taylor RC	.40	.15
❑ 332	Keith Booth RC	.15	.05
❑ 333	Chris Morris	.15	.05
❑ 334	Bryant Stith	.15	.05
❑ 335	Terry Cummings	.15	.05
❑ 336	Ed Gray RC	.15	.05
❑ 337	Eric Snow	.30	.10
❑ 338	Clifford Robinson	.15	.05
❑ 339	Chris Dudley	.15	.05
❑ 340	Chauncey Billups RC	1.25	.50
❑ 341	Paul Grant RC	.15	.05
❑ 342	Tyrone Hill	.15	.05
❑ 343	Joe Smith	.30	.10
❑ 344	Sean Rooks	.15	.05
❑ 345	Harvey Grant	.15	.05
❑ 346	Dale Davis	.15	.05
❑ 347	Brevin Knight RC	.15	.05
❑ 348	Serge Zwikker RC	.15	.05

❑ 349	Checklist (Hawks/Kings)	.15	.05
❑ 350	Checklist (Spurs/Wizards/Inserts)	.15	.05

1998-99 Fleer

❑ COMPLETE SET (150)		20.00	10.00
❑ 1	Kobe Bryant	2.00	.75
❑ 2	Corliss Williamson	.30	.10
❑ 3	Allen Iverson	1.00	.40
❑ 4	Michael Finley	.60	.25
❑ 5	Juwan Howard	.30	.10
❑ 6	Marcus Camby	.30	.10
❑ 7	Toni Kukoc	.30	.10
❑ 8	Antoine Walker	.60	.25
❑ 9	Stephon Marbury	.60	.25
❑ 10	Tim Hardaway	.30	.10
❑ 11	Zydrunas Ilgauskas	.30	.10
❑ 12	John Stockton	.60	.25
❑ 13	Glenn Robinson	.30	.10
❑ 14	Isaiah Rider	.15	.05
❑ 15	Danny Fortson	.15	.05
❑ 16	Donyell Marshall	.30	.10
❑ 17	Chris Mullin	.60	.25
❑ 18	Shareef Abdur-Rahim	.60	.25
❑ 19	Bobby Phills	.15	.05
❑ 20	Gary Payton	.60	.25
❑ 21	Derrick Coleman	.15	.05
❑ 22	Larry Johnson	.30	.10
❑ 23	Michael Jordan	3.00	1.25
❑ 24	Danny Manning	.15	.05
❑ 25	Nick Anderson	.15	.05
❑ 26	Chris Gatling	.15	.05
❑ 27	Steve Smith	.30	.10
❑ 28	Chris Whitney	.15	.05
❑ 29	Terrell Brandon	.30	.10
❑ 30	Rasheed Wallace	.60	.25
❑ 31	Reggie Miller	.60	.25
❑ 32	Karl Malone	.60	.25
❑ 33	Grant Hill	.60	.25
❑ 34	Hakeem Olajuwon	.60	.25
❑ 35	Erick Dampier	.15	.05
❑ 36	Vin Baker	.30	.10
❑ 37	Tim Thomas	.30	.10
❑ 38	Mark Price	.15	.05
❑ 39	Shawn Bradley	.15	.05
❑ 40	Calbert Cheaney	.15	.05
❑ 41	Glen Rice	.30	.10
❑ 42	Kevin Willis	.15	.05
❑ 43	Chris Carr	.15	.05
❑ 44	Keith Van Horn	.60	.25
❑ 45	Jamal Mashburn	.30	.10
❑ 46	Eddie Jones	.60	.25
❑ 47	Brevin Knight	.15	.05
❑ 48	Olden Polynice	.15	.05
❑ 49	Bobby Jackson	.30	.10
❑ 50	David Robinson	.60	.25
❑ 51	Patrick Ewing	.60	.25
❑ 52	Samaki Walker	.15	.05
❑ 53	Antonio Daniels	.15	.05
❑ 54	Rodney Rogers	.15	.05
❑ 55	Dikembe Mutombo	.30	.10
❑ 56	Tracy McGrady	1.25	.50
❑ 57	Walt Williams	.15	.05
❑ 58	Walter McCarty	.15	.05
❑ 59	Detlef Schrempf	.30	.10
❑ 60	Ervin Johnson	.15	.05
❑ 61	Michael Smith	.15	.05
❑ 62	Clifford Robinson	.15	.05
❑ 63	Brian Williams	.15	.05

❑ 64	Shandon Anderson	.15	.05
❑ 65	P.J. Brown	.15	.05
❑ 66	Scottie Pippen	.75	.30
❑ 67	Anthony Peeler	.15	.05
❑ 68	Tony Delk	.15	.05
❑ 69	David Wesley	.15	.05
❑ 70	John Starks	.30	.10
❑ 71	Nick Van Exel	.60	.25
❑ 72	Kerry Kittles	.15	.05
❑ 73	Tony Battie	.15	.05
❑ 74	Lamond Murray	.15	.05
❑ 75	Anfernee Hardaway	.60	.25
❑ 76	Jalen Rose	.60	.25
❑ 77	Derek Anderson	.50	.20
❑ 78	Avery Johnson	.15	.05
❑ 79	Michael Stewart	.15	.05
❑ 80	Brian Shaw	.15	.05
❑ 81	Chauncey Billups	.30	.10
❑ 82	Kenny Anderson	.30	.10
❑ 83	Bryon Russell	.15	.05
❑ 84	Jason Kidd	.75	.30
❑ 85	Tyrone Hill	.15	.05
❑ 86	Jim McIlvaine	.15	.05
❑ 87	Brian Grant	.30	.10
❑ 88	Bryant Stith	.15	.05
❑ 89	Brent Price	.15	.05
❑ 90	John Wallace	.15	.05
❑ 91	Dennis Rodman	.30	.10
❑ 92	Alonzo Mourning	.30	.10
❑ 93	Bimbo Coles	.15	.05
❑ 94	Chris Anstey	.15	.05
❑ 95	Lindsey Hunter	.15	.05
❑ 96	Ed Gray	.15	.05
❑ 97	Chris Mills	.15	.05
❑ 98	Rick Fox	.15	.05
❑ 99	Lorenzen Wright	.15	.05
❑ 100	Kevin Garnett	1.00	.40
❑ 101	Shawn Kemp	.30	.10
❑ 102	Mark Jackson	.30	.10
❑ 103	Sam Cassell	.60	.25
❑ 104	Monty Williams	.15	.05
❑ 105	Ron Mercer	.20	.08
❑ 106	Bryant Reeves	.15	.05
❑ 107	Tracy Murray	.15	.05
❑ 108	Ray Allen	.60	.25
❑ 109	Maurice Taylor	.25	.08
❑ 110	Jerome Williams	.15	.05
❑ 111	Horace Grant	.30	.10
❑ 112	Tariq Abdul-Wahad	.15	.05
❑ 113	Travis Knight	.15	.05
❑ 114	Kendall Gill	.15	.05
❑ 115	Aaron McKie	.15	.05
❑ 116	Dean Garrett	.15	.05
❑ 117	Jeff Hornacek	.30	.10
❑ 118	Todd Fuller	.15	.05
❑ 119	Arvydas Sabonis	.30	.10
❑ 120	Voshon Lenard	.15	.05
❑ 121	Steve Nash	.60	.25
❑ 122	Cedric Henderson	.15	.05
❑ 123	Rodrick Rhodes	.15	.05
❑ 124	Mookie Blaylock	.15	.05
❑ 125	Hersey Hawkins	.15	.05
❑ 126	Doug Christie	.30	.10
❑ 127	Eric Piatkowski	.15	.05
❑ 128	Sean Elliott	.30	.10
❑ 129	Anthony Mason	.30	.10
❑ 130	Allan Houston	.30	.10
❑ 131	Antonio Davis	.15	.05
❑ 132	Hubert Davis	.15	.05
❑ 133	Rod Strickland PF	.15	.05
❑ 134	Jason Kidd PF	.60	.25
❑ 135	Mark Jackson PF	.15	.05
❑ 136	Marcus Camby PF	.15	.05
❑ 137	Dikembe Mutombo PF	.15	.05
❑ 138	Shawn Bradley PF	.15	.05
❑ 139	Dennis Rodman PF	.15	.05
❑ 140	Jayson Williams PF	.15	.05
❑ 141	Tim Duncan PF	.50	.20
❑ 142	Michael Jordan PF	1.50	.60
❑ 143	Shaquille O'Neal PF	.75	.30
❑ 144	Karl Malone PF	.60	.25
❑ 145	Mookie Blaylock PF	.15	.05
❑ 146	Brevin Knight PF	.15	.05
❑ 147	Doug Christie PF	.30	.10
❑ 148	Checklist	.15	.05
❑ 149	Checklist	.15	.05

☐ 150 Checklist	.15	.05
☐ S44 Keith Van Horn SAMPLE	1.00	.40

1999-00 Fleer

☐ COMPLETE SET (220)	30.00	15.00
☐ COMMON CARD (1-200)	.15	.05
☐ COMMON ROOKIE (201-220)	.25	.08
☐ 1 Vince Carter	1.25	.50
☐ 2 Kobe Bryant	2.00	.75
☐ 3 Keith Van Horn	.50	.20
☐ 4 Tim Duncan	1.00	.40
☐ 5 Grant Hill	.50	.20
☐ 6 Kevin Garnett	1.00	.40
☐ 7 Anfernee Hardaway	.50	.20
☐ 8 Jason Williams	.50	.20
☐ 9 Paul Pierce	.50	.20
☐ 10 Mookie Blaylock	.15	.05
☐ 11 Shawn Bradley	.15	.05
☐ 12 Kenny Anderson	.15	.05
☐ 13 Chauncey Billups	.30	.10
☐ 14 Elden Campbell	.15	.05
☐ 15 Jason Caffey	.15	.05
☐ 16 Brent Barry	.30	.10
☐ 17 Charles Barkley	.60	.25
☐ 18 Derek Anderson	.30	.10
☐ 19 Darrick Martin	.15	.05
☐ 20 Bison Dele	.15	.05
☐ 21 Rick Fox	.30	.10
☐ 22 Antonio Davis	.15	.05
☐ 23 Terrell Brandon	.30	.10
☐ 24 P.J. Brown	.15	.05
☐ 25 Toby Bailey	.15	.05
☐ 26 Ray Allen	.30	.10
☐ 27 Brian Grant	.30	.10
☐ 28 Scott Burrell	.15	.05
☐ 29 Tariq Abdul-Wahad	.15	.05
☐ 30 Marcus Camby	.30	.10
☐ 31 John Stockton	.50	.20
☐ 32 Nick Anderson	.15	.05
☐ 33 Antonio Daniels	.15	.05
☐ 34 Matt Geiger	.15	.05
☐ 35 Vin Baker	.30	.10
☐ 36 Dee Brown	.15	.05
☐ 37 Shandon Anderson	.15	.05
☐ 38 Calbert Cheaney	.15	.05
☐ 39 Shareef Abdur-Rahim	.50	.20
☐ 40 LaPhonso Ellis	.15	.05
☐ 41 Cedric Ceballos	.15	.05
☐ 42 Tony Battie	.15	.05
☐ 43 Keon Clark	.30	.10
☐ 44 Derrick Coleman	.30	.10
☐ 45 Erick Dampier	.15	.05
☐ 46 Corey Benjamin	.15	.05
☐ 47 Michael Dickerson	.30	.10
☐ 48 Cedric Henderson	.15	.05
☐ 49 Lamond Murray	.15	.05
☐ 50 Horace Grant	.30	.10
☐ 51 Shaquille O'Neal	1.25	.50
☐ 52 Dale Davis	.15	.05
☐ 53 Dean Garrett	.15	.05
☐ 54 Tim Hardaway	.30	.10
☐ 55 Gerald Brown RC	.15	.05
☐ 56 Sam Cassell	.50	.20
☐ 57 Jim Jackson	.15	.05
☐ 58 Kendall Gill	.15	.05
☐ 59 Eric Williams	.15	.05
☐ 60 Chris Childs	.15	.05
☐ 61 Vlade Divac	.30	.10
☐ 62 Darrell Armstrong	.15	.05
☐ 63 Mario Elie	.15	.05
☐ 64 Tyrone Hill	.15	.05
☐ 65 Dale Ellis	.15	.05
☐ 66 Doug Christie	.30	.10
☐ 67 Howard Eisley	.15	.05
☐ 68 Juwan Howard	.30	.10
☐ 69 Mike Bibby	.50	.20
☐ 70 Alan Henderson	.15	.05
☐ 71 Michael Finley	.50	.20
☐ 72 Dana Barros	.15	.05
☐ 73 Danny Fortson	.15	.05
☐ 74 Ricky Davis	.30	.10
☐ 75 Adonal Foyle	.15	.05
☐ 76 Cory Carr	.15	.05
☐ 77 Bryce Drew	.15	.05
☐ 78 Shawn Kemp	.30	.10
☐ 79 Tyrone Nesby RC	.15	.05
☐ 80 Lindsey Hunter	.15	.05
☐ 81 Ruben Patterson	.30	.10
☐ 82 Al Harrington	.50	.20
☐ 83 Bobby Jackson	.30	.10
☐ 84 Dan Majerle	.30	.10
☐ 85 Rex Chapman	.15	.05
☐ 86 Dell Curry	.15	.05
☐ 87 Walt Williams	.15	.05
☐ 88 Kerry Kittles	.15	.05
☐ 89 Isaiah Rider	.15	.05
☐ 90 Patrick Ewing	.50	.20
☐ 91 Lawrence Funderburke	.15	.05
☐ 92 Isaac Austin	.15	.05
☐ 93 Sean Elliott	.30	.10
☐ 94 Larry Hughes	.50	.20
☐ 95 Hersey Hawkins	.30	.10
☐ 96 Tracy McGrady	1.25	.50
☐ 97 Jeff Hornacek	.30	.10
☐ 98 Randell Jackson	.15	.05
☐ 99 J.R. Henderson	.15	.05
☐ 100 Roshown McLeod	.15	.05
☐ 101 Steve Nash	.50	.20
☐ 102 Ron Mercer	.30	.10
☐ 103 Raef LaFrentz	.30	.10
☐ 104 Eddie Jones	.50	.20
☐ 105 Antawn Jamison	.75	.30
☐ 106 Kornel David RC	.15	.05
☐ 107 Othella Harrington	.15	.05
☐ 108 Brevin Knight	.15	.05
☐ 109 Michael Olowokandi	.30	.10
☐ 110 Christian Laettner	.30	.10
☐ 111 J.R. Reid	.15	.05
☐ 112 Reggie Miller	.50	.20
☐ 113 Andrae Patterson	.15	.05
☐ 114 Jamal Mashburn	.30	.10
☐ 115 Glenn Robinson	.50	.20
☐ 116 Pat Garrity	.15	.05
☐ 117 Stephon Marbury	.50	.20
☐ 118 Arvydas Sabonis	.30	.10
☐ 119 Allan Houston	.30	.10
☐ 120 Peja Stojakovic	.60	.25
☐ 121 Michael Doleac	.15	.05
☐ 122 Avery Johnson	.15	.05
☐ 123 Allen Iverson	1.00	.40
☐ 124 Rashard Lewis	.50	.20
☐ 125 Charles Oakley	.15	.05
☐ 126 Karl Malone	.50	.20
☐ 127 Tracy Murray	.15	.05
☐ 128 Felipe Lopez	.15	.05
☐ 129 Dikembe Mutombo	.30	.10
☐ 130 Dirk Nowitzki	1.00	.40
☐ 131 Vitaly Potapenko	.15	.05
☐ 132 Antonio McDyess	.30	.10
☐ 133 Anthony Mason	.30	.10
☐ 134 Donyell Marshall	.15	.05
☐ 135 Ron Harper	.30	.10
☐ 136 Cuttino Mobley	.30	.10
☐ 137 Wesley Person	.15	.05
☐ 138 Rodney Rogers	.15	.05
☐ 139 Jerry Stackhouse	.50	.20
☐ 140 Glen Rice	.30	.10
☐ 141 Chris Mullin	.50	.20
☐ 142 Anthony Peeler	.15	.05
☐ 143 Alonzo Mourning	.30	.10
☐ 144 Tom Gugliotta	.30	.10
☐ 145 Tim Thomas	.30	.10
☐ 146 Damon Stoudamire	.30	.10
☐ 147 Jayson Williams	.15	.05
☐ 148 Larry Johnson	.30	.10
☐ 149 Chris Webber	.50	.20
☐ 150 Matt Harpring	.50	.20
☐ 151 David Robinson	.50	.20
☐ 152 George Lynch	.15	.05
☐ 153 Gary Payton	.50	.20
☐ 154 John Wallace	.15	.05
☐ 155 Greg Ostertag	.15	.05
☐ 156 Mitch Richmond	.30	.10
☐ 157 Cherokee Parks	.15	.05
☐ 158 Steve Smith	.30	.10
☐ 159 Gary Trent	.15	.05
☐ 160 Antoine Walker	.50	.20
☐ 161 Johnny Taylor	.15	.05
☐ 162 Brad Miller	.50	.20
☐ 163 Chris Mills	.15	.05
☐ 164 Charles Jones	.15	.05
☐ 165 Hakeem Olajuwon	.50	.20
☐ 166 Bob Sura	.15	.05
☐ 167 Brian Skinner	.15	.05
☐ 168 Korleone Young	.15	.05
☐ 169 Tyronn Lue	.30	.10
☐ 170 Jalen Rose	.50	.20
☐ 171 Joe Smith	.30	.10
☐ 172 Clarence Weatherspoon	.15	.05
☐ 173 Jason Kidd	.75	.30
☐ 174 Robert Traylor	.15	.05
☐ 175 Rasheed Wallace	.50	.20
☐ 176 Latrell Sprewell	.50	.20
☐ 177 Corliss Williamson	.30	.10
☐ 178 Bo Outlaw	.15	.05
☐ 179 Malik Rose	.15	.05
☐ 180 Nazr Mohammed	.15	.05
☐ 181 Olden Polynice	.15	.05
☐ 182 Kevin Willis	.15	.05
☐ 183 Bryon Russell	.15	.05
☐ 184 Bryant Reeves	.15	.05
☐ 185 Rod Strickland	.15	.05
☐ 186 Samaki Walker	.15	.05
☐ 187 Nick Van Exel	.50	.20
☐ 188 David Wesley	.15	.05
☐ 189 John Starks	.30	.10
☐ 190 Toni Kukoc	.30	.10
☐ 191 Scottie Pippen	.75	.30
☐ 192 Zydrunas Ilgauskas	.30	.10
☐ 193 Maurice Taylor	.30	.10
☐ 194 Rik Smits	.30	.10
☐ 195 Clifford Robinson	.15	.05
☐ 196 Bonzi Wells	.50	.20
☐ 197 Charlie Ward	.15	.05
☐ 198 Detlef Schrempf	.30	.10
☐ 199 Theo Ratliff	.30	.10
☐ 200 Rodrick Rhodes	.15	.05
☐ 201 Ron Artest RC	.75	.30
☐ 202 William Avery RC	.50	.20
☐ 203 Elton Brand RC	1.50	.60
☐ 204 Baron Davis RC	3.00	1.25
☐ 205 Jumaine Jones RC	.75	.30
☐ 206 Andre Miller RC	1.25	.50
☐ 207 Lee Nailon RC	.25	.08
☐ 208 James Posey RC	.75	.30
☐ 209 Jason Terry RC	.75	.30
☐ 210 Kenny Thomas RC	.50	.20
☐ 211 Steve Francis RC	1.50	.60
☐ 212 Wally Szczerbiak RC	1.25	.50
☐ 213 Richard Hamilton RC	1.25	.50
☐ 214 Jonathan Bender RC	1.25	.50
☐ 215 Shawn Marion RC	1.50	.60
☐ 216 A.Radojevic RC	.25	.08
☐ 217 Tim James RC	.40	.15
☐ 218 Trajan Langdon RC	.50	.20
☐ 219 Lamar Odom RC	1.25	.50
☐ 220 Corey Maggette RC	1.50	.60
☐ NNO Checklist 1	.15	.05
☐ NNO Checklist #2	.15	.05
☐ NNO Checklist #1	.15	.05

2000-01 Fleer

☐ COMMON CARD (1-300)	.15	.05
☐ COMMON ROOKIE (227-271)	.50	.20
☐ 1 Lamar Odom	.30	.10
☐ 2 Christian Laettner	.30	.10
☐ 3 Michael Olowokandi	.15	.05
☐ 4 Anthony Carter	.30	.10
☐ 5 Steve Francis	.50	.20
☐ 6 Darvin Ham	.15	.05

7	Mitch Richmond	.30	.10
8	Corliss Williamson	.30	.10
9	Jason Terry	.50	.20
10	Brian Grant	.30	.10
11	Peja Stojakovic	.50	.20
12	Rick Fox	.30	.10
13	Tyrone Hill	.15	.05
14	Chauncey Billups	.30	.10
15	Otis Thorpe	.15	.05
16	Richard Hamilton	.30	.10
17	Ervin Johnson	.15	.05
18	Jim Jackson	.15	.05
19	Theo Ratliff	.30	.10
20	Doug Christie	.30	.10
21	Jalen Rose	.50	.20
22	John Wallace	.15	.05
23	Ruben Patterson	.30	.10
24	Steve Nash	.50	.20
25	Toni Kukoc	.30	.10
26	Anthony Peeler	.15	.05
27	Ray Allen	.50	.20
28	Adonal Foyle	.15	.05
29	Chris Whitney	.15	.05
30	Nick Van Exel	.50	.20
31	Sean Elliott	.30	.10
32	Erick Strickland	.15	.05
33	Jerry Stackhouse	.50	.20
34	Antawn Jamison	.50	.20
35	Grant Hill	.50	.20
36	Antonio Daniels	.15	.05
37	Karl Malone	.50	.20
38	Keith Van Horn	.50	.20
39	Ron Harper	.30	.10
40	Stephon Marbury	.50	.20
41	Bryon Russell	.15	.05
42	Corey Maggette	.30	.10
43	Hersey Hawkins	.15	.05
44	Vince Carter	1.25	.50
45	Paul Pierce	.50	.20
46	Mikki Moore	.15	.05
47	Othella Harrington	.15	.05
48	Erick Dampier	.30	.10
49	Jerome Williams	.15	.05
50	Nick Anderson	.15	.05
51	Tim Hardaway	.30	.10
52	Allan Houston	.30	.10
53	Tyrone Nesby	.15	.05
54	Brevin Knight	.15	.05
55	Chris Mills	.15	.05
56	Ron Artest	.30	.10
57	Walt Williams	.15	.05
58	Duane Causwell	.15	.05
59	Bonzi Wells	.30	.10
60	Rasheed Wallace	.50	.20
61	Dikembe Mutombo	.30	.10
62	Jahidi White	.15	.05
63	Chris Webber	.50	.20
64	Tony Battie	.15	.05
65	Mahmoud Abdul-Rauf	.15	.05
66	Monty Williams	.15	.05
67	Charlie Ward	.15	.05
68	David Robinson	.50	.20
69	Eric Snow	.30	.10
70	Jermaine O'Neal	.50	.20
71	Kurt Thomas	.30	.10
72	James Posey	.30	.10
73	Travis Best	.15	.05
74	Jonathan Bender	.30	.10
75	John Stockton	.50	.20
76	Jacque Vaughn	.15	.05
77	Ron Mercer	.30	.10
78	Shawn Marion	.50	.20
79	Larry Johnson	.30	.10
80	Maurice Taylor	.15	.05
81	Clifford Robinson	.15	.05
82	Scot Pollard	.15	.05
83	Patrick Ewing	.50	.20
84	Terrell Brandon	.30	.10
85	Horace Grant	.30	.10
86	Vin Baker	.30	.10
87	Al Harrington	.30	.10
88	Larry Hughes	.30	.10
89	David Wesley	.15	.05
90	Wally Szczerbiak	.30	.10
91	Charles Oakley	.15	.05
92	Tim Thomas	.30	.10
93	Mookie Blaylock	.15	.05
94	Jamal Mashburn	.30	.10
95	Roshown McLeod	.15	.05
96	John Starks	.30	.10
97	Rodney Rogers	.15	.05
98	Juwan Howard	.30	.10
99	Isaiah Rider	.30	.10
100	Rashard Lewis	.30	.10
101	Dion Glover	.15	.05
102	Johnny Newman	.15	.05
103	Avery Johnson	.15	.05
104	Darrell Armstrong	.15	.05
105	Eric Williams	.15	.05
106	Gary Payton	.50	.20
107	Antonio Davis	.15	.05
108	Dirk Nowitzki	.75	.30
109	Trajan Langdon	.30	.10
110	Michael Dickerson	.30	.10
111	Joe Smith	.30	.10
112	Rod Strickland	.15	.05
113	Shawn Kemp	.30	.10
114	Voshon Lenard	.15	.05
115	Marcus Camby	.30	.10
116	Matt Harpring	.50	.20
117	Isaac Austin	.15	.05
118	Malik Rose	.15	.05
119	Pat Garrity	.15	.05
120	Kenny Thomas	.15	.05
121	LaPhonso Ellis	.15	.05
122	Danny Fortson	.15	.05
123	Elton Brand	.50	.20
124	Jason Williams	.30	.10
125	Kobe Bryant	2.00	.75
126	Tariq Abdul-Wahad	.15	.05
127	Tracy McGrady	1.25	.50
128	Matt Geiger	.15	.05
129	Antoine Walker	.50	.20
130	Michael Finley	.50	.20
131	Andre Miller	.30	.10
132	Robert Horry	.15	.05
133	Donyell Marshall	.30	.10
134	Shareef Abdur-Rahim	.50	.20
135	Vonteego Cummings	.15	.05
136	Anthony Mason	.30	.10
137	Mike Bibby	.50	.20
138	Raef LaFrentz	.30	.10
139	Glen Rice	.50	.20
140	Chris Gatling	.15	.05
141	Latrell Sprewell	.50	.20
142	Austin Croshere	.30	.10
143	Kenny Anderson	.30	.10
144	Elden Campbell	.15	.05
145	Jason Kidd	.75	.30
146	Michael Doleac	.15	.05
147	Muggsy Bogues	.30	.10
148	Tim Duncan	1.00	.40
149	Samaki Walker	.15	.05
150	Gary Trent	.15	.05
151	Kevin Garnett	1.00	.40
152	Allen Iverson	1.00	.40
153	Anfernee Hardaway	.50	.20
154	Robert Traylor	.15	.05
155	Scottie Pippen	.75	.30
156	Shaquille O'Neal	1.25	.50
157	Vlade Divac	.30	.10
158	Lucious Harris	.15	.05
159	Keon Clark	.30	.10
160	Bo Outlaw	.15	.05
161	P.J. Brown	.15	.05
162	Derrick Coleman	.15	.05
163	Mark Jackson	.15	.05
164	Lamond Murray	.15	.05
165	Dan Majerle	.30	.10
166	Eddie Jones	.50	.20
167	Cedric Ceballos	.15	.05
168	Kendall Gill	.15	.05
169	Tom Gugliotta	.15	.05
170	Jeff McInnis	.15	.05
171	Steve Smith	.30	.10
172	Kevin Willis	.15	.05
173	Lindsey Hunter	.15	.05
174	Derek Anderson	.30	.10
175	Shandon Anderson	.15	.05
176	Adrian Griffin	.15	.05
177	Baron Davis	.50	.20
178	Radoslav Nesterovic	.30	.10
179	Glenn Robinson	.50	.20
180	Sam Cassell	.50	.20
181	Chucky Atkins	.15	.05
182	Arvydas Sabonis	.30	.10
183	Damon Stoudamire	.30	.10
184	Antonio McDyess	.30	.10
185	Derek Fisher	.50	.20
186	Bryant Reeves	.15	.05
187	Hakeem Olajuwon	.50	.20
188	Kerry Kittles	.15	.05
189	Alan Henderson	.15	.05
190	Sam Perkins	.30	.10
191	Felipe Lopez	.15	.05
192	Tracy Murray	.15	.05
193	Shammond Williams	.15	.05
194	Vitaly Potapenko	.15	.05
195	John Amaechi	.15	.05
196	Quincy Lewis	.15	.05
197	Reggie Miller	.50	.20
198	Cuttino Mobley	.30	.10
199	Rex Chapman	.15	.05
200	Dale Davis	.15	.05
201	Andrew DeClercq	.15	.05
202	Kelvin Cato	.15	.05
203	Jon Barry	.15	.05
204	Greg Anthony	.15	.05
205	Brent Barry	.30	.10
206	Derrick McKey	.15	.05
207	Vince Carter UH	.60	.25
208	David Robinson UH	.30	.10
209	Eric Snow UH	.15	.05
210	Ray Allen UH	.30	.10
211	Lamar Odom UH	.50	.20
212	Dikembe Mutombo UH	.15	.05
213	Brevin Knight UH	.15	.05
214	Vin Baker UH	.30	.10
215	Antoine Walker UH	.30	.10
216	Mitch Richmond UH	.15	.05
217	Elton Brand UH	.50	.20
218	Jerome Williams UH	.15	.05
219	Keith Van Horn UH	.30	.10
220	Nick Van Exel UH	.15	.05
221	Shaquille O'Neal UH	.60	.25
222	Allan Houston UH	.15	.05
223	Shareef Abdur-Rahim UH	.30	.10
224	Karl Malone UH	.50	.20
225	Terrell Brandon UH	.15	.05
226	Eddie Jones UH	.30	.10
227	Stromile Swift RC	1.00	.40
228	Dalibor Bagaric RC	.50	.20
229	Erick Barkley RC	.50	.20
230	Mike Miller RC	1.50	.60
231	Kenyon Martin RC	2.00	.75
232	Michael Redd RC	1.25	.50
233	Darius Miles RC	1.50	.60
234	Chris Mihm RC	.50	.20
235	Brian Cardinal RC	.50	.20
236	Khalid El-Amin RC	.50	.20
237	Hanno Mottola RC	.50	.20
238	Jamaal Magloire RC	.50	.20
239	Courtney Alexander RC	.50	.20
240	Mamadou N'Diaye RC	.50	.20
241	Chris Porter RC	.50	.20
242	Quentin Richardson RC	1.25	.50
243	Eddie House RC	.50	.20
244	Joel Przybilla RC	.50	.20
245	Soumaila Samake RC	.50	.20
246	Speedy Claxton RC	.50	.20

#	Player		
247	Desmond Mason RC	.50	.20
248	Mike Smith RC	.50	.20
249	Lavor Postell RC	.50	.20
250	Ruben Garces RC	.50	.20
251	DeShawn Stevenson RC	.50	.20
252	Hidayet Turkoglu RC	1.50	.60
253	Keyon Dooling RC	.50	.20
254	Dan Langhi RC	.50	.20
255	Mateen Cleaves RC	.50	.20
256	Donnell Harvey RC	.50	.20
257	DerMarr Johnson RC	.50	.20
258	Jason Collier RC	1.00	.40
259	Jake Voskuhl RC	.50	.20
260	Mark Madsen RC	.50	.20
261	Pepe Sanchez RC	.50	.20
262	Morris Peterson RC	1.00	.40
263	Daniel Santiago RC	.50	.20
264	Etan Thomas RC	.50	.20
265	A.J. Guyton RC	.50	.20
266	Marcus Fizer RC	.50	.20
267	Jamal Crawford RC	.60	.25
268	Jerome Moiso RC	.50	.20
269	Olumide Oyedeji RC	.50	.20
270	Paul McPherson RC	.50	.20
271	Eduardo Najera RC	.75	.30
272	Dallas Mavericks CL	.15	.05
273	Denver Nuggets CL	.15	.05
274	Houston Rockets CL	.30	.10
275	Minnesota Timberwolves CL	.30	.10
276	San Antonio Spurs CL	.30	.10
277	Utah Jazz CL	.30	.10
278	Vancouver Grizzlies CL	.30	.10
279	Golden State Warriors CL	.30	.10
280	Los Angeles Clippers CL	.50	.20
281	Los Angeles Lakers CL	.50	.20
282	Phoenix Suns CL	.30	.10
283	Portland Trail Blazers CL	.30	.10
284	Sacramento Kings CL	.30	.10
285	Seattle Supersonics CL	.30	.10
286	Boston Celtics CL	.15	.05
287	Miami Heat CL	.30	.10
288	New Jersey Nets CL	.30	.10
289	New York Knicks CL	.30	.10
290	Orlando Magic CL	.50	.20
291	Philadelphia 76ers CL	.30	.10
292	Washington Wizards CL	.15	.05
293	Atlanta Hawks CL	.15	.05
294	Charlotte Hornets CL	.15	.05
295	Chicago Bulls CL	.30	.10
296	Cleveland Cavaliers CL	.15	.05
297	Detroit Pistons CL	.15	.05
298	Indiana Pacers CL	.30	.10
299	Milwaukee Bucks CL	.15	.05
300	Toronto Raptors CL	.50	.20
NNO	V.Carter OSR Retail		
NNO	V.Carter OSR Sticker	5.00	2.00
NNO	V.Carter OSR/1986	20.00	8.00
NNO	V.Carter OSR AU/15		

2006-07 Fleer

BARON DAVIS

#	Player		
1	Josh Childress	.40	.15
2	Al Harrington	.20	.07
3	Joe Johnson	.40	.15
4	Tyronn Lue	.20	.07
5	Josh Smith	.60	.25
6	Salim Stoudamire	.40	.15
7	Marvin Williams	.75	.30
8	Tony Allen	.40	.15
9	Dan Dickau	.20	.07
10	Al Jefferson	.60	.25
11	Michael Olowokandi	.20	.07
12	Paul Pierce	.60	.25
13	Wally Szczerbiak	.40	.15
14	Gerald Green	.75	.30
15	Raymond Felton	.75	.30
16	Brevin Knight	.20	.07
17	Sean May	.40	.15
18	Emeka Okafor	.60	.25
19	Othella Harrington	.20	.07
20	Gerald Wallace	.60	.25
21	Tyson Chandler	.60	.25
22	Luol Deng	.60	.25
23	Chris Duhon	.20	.07
24	Ben Gordon	1.25	.50
25	Kirk Hinrich	.60	.25
26	Mike Sweetney	.20	.07
27	Michael Jordan	4.00	1.50
28	Drew Gooden	.40	.15
29	Larry Hughes	.40	.15
30	Zydrunas Ilgauskas	.40	.15
31	Damon Jones	.20	.07
32	LeBron James	4.00	1.50
33	Donyell Marshall	.20	.07
34	Anderson Varejao	.40	.15
35	Erick Dampier	.20	.07
36	Marquis Daniels	.40	.15
37	Devin Harris	.60	.25
38	Josh Howard	.40	.15
39	Dirk Nowitzki	1.00	.40
40	Jerry Stackhouse	.60	.25
41	Jason Terry	.60	.25
42	Carmelo Anthony	1.25	.50
43	Marcus Camby	.20	.07
44	Reggie Evans	.20	.07
45	Kenyon Martin	.60	.25
46	Andre Miller	.40	.15
47	Eduardo Najera	.20	.07
48	Nene	.20	.07
49	Chauncey Billups	.60	.25
50	Richard Hamilton	.40	.15
51	Jason Maxiell	.20	.07
52	Antonio McDyess	.20	.07
53	Tayshaun Prince	.40	.15
54	Ben Wallace	.60	.25
55	Rasheed Wallace	.60	.25
56	Baron Davis	.60	.25
57	Ike Diogu	.40	.15
58	Mike Dunleavy	.40	.15
59	Derek Fisher	.40	.15
60	Adonal Foyle	.20	.07
61	Troy Murphy	.60	.25
62	Jason Richardson	.60	.25
63	Rafer Alston	.20	.07
64	Chuck Hayes	.20	.07
65	Luther Head	.40	.15
66	Juwan Howard	.40	.15
67	Tracy McGrady	1.50	.60
68	Stromile Swift	.40	.15
69	Yao Ming	1.50	.60
70	Austin Croshere	.20	.07
71	Danny Granger	.40	.15
72	Sarunas Jasikevicius	.40	.15
73	Stephen Jackson	.40	.15
74	Jermaine O'Neal	.60	.25
75	Peja Stojakovic	.60	.25
76	Jamaal Tinsley	.40	.15
77	Elton Brand	.60	.25
78	Sam Cassell	.60	.25
79	Chris Kaman	.20	.07
80	Yaroslav Korolev	.20	.07
81	Shaun Livingston	.50	.20
82	Corey Maggette	.40	.15
83	Cuttino Mobley	.20	.07
84	Kwame Brown	.40	.15
85	Kobe Bryant	2.50	1.00
86	Andrew Bynum	.40	.15
87	Devean George	.40	.15
88	Lamar Odom	.60	.25
89	Ronny Turiaf	.20	.07
90	Luke Walton	.20	.07
91	Shane Battier	.60	.25
92	Pau Gasol	.60	.25
93	Bobby Jackson	.20	.07
94	Mike Miller	.60	.25
95	Lawrence Roberts	.20	.07
96	Damon Stoudamire	.40	.15
97	Hakim Warrick	.40	.15
98	Alonzo Mourning	.40	.15
99	Shaquille O'Neal	1.50	.60
100	Gary Payton	.60	.25
101	Wayne Simien	.40	.15
102	Dwyane Wade	2.00	.75
103	Antoine Walker	.40	.15
104	Jason Williams	.40	.15
105	Andrew Bogut	.75	.30
106	T.J. Ford	.40	.15
107	Jamaal Magloire	.20	.07
108	Michael Redd	.60	.25
109	Bobby Simmons	.20	.07
110	Maurice Williams	.20	.07
111	Mark Blount	.20	.07
112	Ricky Davis	.60	.25
113	Kevin Garnett	1.25	.50
114	Eddie Griffin	.20	.07
115	Troy Hudson	.20	.07
116	Rashad McCants	.75	.30
117	Vince Carter	1.50	.60
118	Jason Collins	.20	.07
119	Richard Jefferson	.40	.15
120	Jason Kidd	1.00	.40
121	Nenad Krstic	.40	.15
122	Jeff McInnis	.20	.07
123	Antoine Wright	.20	.07
124	Brandon Bass	.20	.07
125	David West	.20	.07
126	Desmond Mason	.20	.07
127	Chris Paul	1.50	.60
128	J.R. Smith	.40	.15
129	Kirk Snyder	.20	.07
130	Jamal Crawford	.20	.07
131	Steve Francis	.60	.25
132	Channing Frye	.40	.15
133	Stephon Marbury	.60	.25
134	Quentin Richardson	.40	.15
135	Nate Robinson	.60	.25
136	Jalen Rose	.50	.20
137	Carlos Arroyo	1.00	.40
138	Keyon Dooling	.20	.07
139	Grant Hill	.60	.25
140	Dwight Howard	.75	.30
141	Darko Milicic	.60	.25
142	Jameer Nelson	.40	.15
143	DeShawn Stevenson	.20	.07
144	Samuel Dalembert	.20	.07
145	Steven Hunter	.20	.07
146	Andre Iguodala	.60	.25
147	Allen Iverson	1.25	.50
148	Kyle Korver	.60	.25
149	Chris Webber	.60	.25
150	Leandro Barbosa	.40	.15
151	Raja Bell	.20	.07
152	Boris Diaw	.40	.15
153	Shawn Marion	.60	.25
154	Steve Nash	.60	.25
155	Amare Stoudemire	1.25	.50
156	Kurt Thomas	.20	.07
157	Steve Blake	.20	.07
158	Juan Dixon	.20	.07
159	Joel Przybilla	.20	.07
160	Zach Randolph	.60	.25
161	Travis Outlaw	.20	.07
162	Sebastian Telfair	.40	.15
163	Martell Webster	.40	.15
164	Shareef Abdur-Rahim	.60	.25
165	Ron Artest	.40	.15
166	Mike Bibby	.60	.25
167	Francisco Garcia	.20	.07
168	Brad Miller	.60	.25
169	Kenny Thomas	.20	.07
170	Bonzi Wells	.40	.15
171	Bruce Bowen	.20	.07
172	Tim Duncan	1.25	.50

#	Player		
❏ 173	Michael Finley	.60	.25
❏ 174	Manu Ginobili	.60	.25
❏ 175	Tony Parker	.60	.25
❏ 176	Ray Allen	.60	.25
❏ 177	Danny Fortson	.20	.07
❏ 178	Rashard Lewis	.60	.25
❏ 179	Luke Ridnour	.40	.15
❏ 180	Robert Swift	.20	.07
❏ 181	Chris Wilcox	.20	.07
❏ 182	Chris Bosh	.60	.25
❏ 183	Jose Calderon	.40	.15
❏ 184	Joey Graham	.40	.15
❏ 185	Pape Sow	.20	.07
❏ 186	Charlie Villanueva	.60	.25
❏ 187	Morris Peterson	.40	.15
❏ 188	Carlos Boozer	.40	.15
❏ 189	Gordan Giricek	.20	.07
❏ 190	Kris Humphries	.20	.07
❏ 191	Andrei Kirilenko	.60	.25
❏ 192	Mehmet Okur	.20	.07
❏ 193	Deron Williams	.60	.25
❏ 194	Gilbert Arenas	.60	.25
❏ 195	Andray Blatche	.20	.07
❏ 196	Caron Butler	.40	.15
❏ 197	Brendan Haywood	.20	.07
❏ 198	Antawn Jamison	.60	.25
❏ 199	Etan Thomas	.20	.07
❏ 200	Antonio Daniels	.20	.07
❏ 201	Tyrus Thomas RC	3.00	1.25
❏ 202	Adam Morrison RC	4.00	1.50
❏ 203	LaMarcus Aldridge RC	3.00	1.25
❏ 204	Rudy Gay RC	3.00	1.25
❏ 205	Andrea Bargnani RC	4.00	1.50
❏ 206	Rodney Carney RC	2.00	.75
❏ 207	Alexander Johnson RC	1.50	.60
❏ 208	Brandon Roy RC	4.00	1.50
❏ 209	Patrick O'Bryant RC	2.00	.75
❏ 210	Randy Foye RC	4.00	1.50
❏ 211	Ronnie Brewer RC	3.00	1.25
❏ 212	Mardy Collins RC	1.50	.60
❏ 213	Shelden Williams RC	2.00	.75
❏ 214	J.J. Redick RC	3.00	1.25
❏ 215	Hilton Armstrong RC	1.50	.60
❏ 216	Marcus Williams RC	2.00	.75
❏ 217	Rajon Rondo RC	3.00	1.25
❏ 218	Cedric Simmons RC	1.50	.60
❏ 219	Bobby Jones RC	1.50	.60
❏ 220	Jordan Farmar RC	3.00	1.25
❏ 221	Maurice Ager RC	2.00	.75
❏ 222	David Noel RC	1.50	.60
❏ 223	James White RC	1.50	.60
❏ 224	Leon Powe RC	1.50	.60
❏ 225	Paul Millsap RC	2.50	1.00
❏ 226	Josh Boone RC	1.50	.60
❏ 227	Kevin Pittsnogle RC	2.00	.75
❏ 228	Daniel Gibson RC	4.00	1.50
❏ 229	Hassan Adams RC	2.00	.75
❏ 230	Kyle Lowry RC	2.50	1.00
❏ 231	Renaldo Balkman RC	1.50	.60
❏ 232	Dee Brown RC	2.50	1.00
❏ 233	Shawne Williams RC	2.00	.75
❏ 234	P.J. Tucker RC	1.50	.60
❏ 235	Craig Smith RC	1.50	.60
❏ 236	Paul Davis RC	1.50	.60
❏ 237	Pops Mensah-Bonsu RC	1.50	.60
❏ 238	Denham Brown RC	1.50	.60
❏ 239	Ryan Hollins RC	1.50	.60
❏ 240	Allan Ray RC	1.50	.60
❏ 241	Saer Sene RC	1.50	.60
❏ 242	Shannon Brown RC	2.00	.75
❏ 243	Thabo Sefolosha RC	2.00	.75
❏ 244	Quincy Douby RC	2.00	.75
❏ 245	Solomon Jones RC	1.50	.60
❏ 246	Damir Markota RC	1.50	.60
❏ 247	Steve Novak RC	1.50	.60
❏ 248	Will Blalock RC	1.50	.60
❏ 249	Tarence Kinsey RC	1.50	.60
❏ 250	Vassilis Spanoulis RC	1.50	.60

2004 Fleer Authentix Player Autographs

#	Player		
❏ NNO	Ben Gordon/100	30.00	12.50
❏ NNO	Ben Gordon/75	40.00	15.00
❏ NNO	Ben Gordon JSY/100	40.00	15.00
❏ NNO	Ben Gordon/50	50.00	20.00
❏ NNO	Ben Wallace/100	25.00	10.00
❏ NNO	Jerry Stackhouse/126	12.00	5.00
❏ NNO	Jerry Stackhouse/50	15.00	6.00
❏ NNO	Jerry Stackhouse/50	25.00	10.00
❏ NNO	Jerry Stackhouse/25		
❏ NNO	Marcus Banks/75		
❏ NNO	Sebastian Telfair/250	15.00	6.00
❏ NNO	Sebastian Telfair/50	25.00	10.00
❏ NNO	Vince Carter/300	40.00	15.00
❏ NNO	Vince Carter/150	50.00	20.00

2005 Fleer Authentix Player Autographs

#	Player		
❏ BG1	Ben Gordon/300	25.00	10.00
❏ BG2	Ben Gordon/100	30.00	12.50
❏ BG3	Ben Gordon/100	30.00	12.50
❏ BG4	Ben Gordon/75	40.00	15.00
❏ DG1	Drew Gooden/300	12.00	5.00
❏ DG2	Drew Gooden/150	15.00	6.00
❏ TP	Tayshaun Prince/50	20.00	8.00
❏ TP1	Tayshaun Prince/300		
❏ BGJ1	Ben Gordon JSY/100	40.00	15.00
❏ BGJ2	Ben Gordon JSY/25		
❏ TPJ	Tayshaun Prince JSY/25		

2001-02 Fleer Authentix

#	Player		
❏	COMP. SET w/o SP'S	40.00	
❏	COMMON CARD (1-100)	.25	.08
❏	COMMON ROOKIE (101-135)	3.00	1.25
❏ 1	Vince Carter	2.00	.75
❏ 2	Terrell Brandon	.50	.20
❏ 3	Raef LaFrentz	.50	.20
❏ 4	Iakovos Tsakalidis	.25	.08
❏ 5	Elton Brand	.75	.30
❏ 6	David Robinson	.75	.30
❏ 7	Lamar Odom	.75	.30
❏ 8	Larry Hughes	.50	.20
❏ 9	Gary Payton	.75	.30
❏ 10	Rick Fox	.50	.20
❏ 11	Jamal Mashburn	.50	.20
❏ 12	Brian Grant	.50	.20
❏ 13	David Wesley	.25	.08
❏ 14	Steve Smith	.50	.20
❏ 15	Corey Maggette	.50	.20
❏ 16	Michael Jordan	12.00	5.00
❏ 17	Wally Szczerbiak	.50	.20
❏ 18	Antoine Walker	.75	.30
❏ 19	Marcus Camby	.50	.20
❏ 20	Rasheed Wallace	.75	.30
❏ 21	Travis Best	.25	.08
❏ 22	Theo Ratliff	.50	.20
❏ 23	LaPhonso Ellis	.25	.08
❏ 24	Dirk Nowitzki	1.25	.50
❏ 25	Kurt Thomas	.50	.20
❏ 26	Tim Duncan	1.50	.60
❏ 27	Tim Duncan	1.50	.60
❏ 28	Eddie House	.50	.20
❏ 29	Ron Mercer	.50	.20
❏ 30	Allan Houston	.50	.20

#	Player		
❏ 31	Trajan Langdon	.25	.08
❏ 32	Karl Malone	.75	.30
❏ 33	Glenn Robinson	.75	.30
❏ 34	Wang Zhizhi	.75	.30
❏ 35	Jason Kidd	1.25	.50
❏ 36	Maurice Taylor	.50	.20
❏ 37	Chris Webber	.75	.30
❏ 38	Michael Dickerson	.50	.20
❏ 39	Paul Pierce	.75	.30
❏ 40	Bonzi Wells	.50	.20
❏ 41	Antawn Jamison	.75	.30
❏ 42	Rashard Lewis	.50	.20
❏ 43	Reggie Miller	.75	.30
❏ 44	Patrick Ewing	.75	.30
❏ 45	Marcus Fizer	.50	.20
❏ 46	Aaron McKie	.50	.20
❏ 47	Marc Jackson	.50	.20
❏ 48	Desmond Mason	.50	.20
❏ 49	Jermaine O'Neal	.75	.30
❏ 50	DeShawn Stevenson	.50	.20
❏ 51	John Stockton	.75	.30
❏ 52	Tim Thomas	.50	.20
❏ 53	Andre Miller	.50	.20
❏ 54	Jumaine Jones	.50	.20
❏ 55	Nick Van Exel	.75	.30
❏ 56	Damon Stoudamire	.50	.20
❏ 57	Stephon Marbury	.75	.30
❏ 58	Clifford Robinson	.25	.08
❏ 59	Hidayet Turkoglu	.50	.20
❏ 60	Kobe Bryant	3.00	1.25
❏ 61	Richard Hamilton	.50	.20
❏ 62	Stromile Swift	.50	.20
❏ 63	Chris Mihm	.50	.20
❏ 64	Tracy McGrady	2.00	.75
❏ 65	Jalen Rose	.75	.30
❏ 66	Morris Peterson	.50	.20
❏ 67	Alonzo Mourning	.50	.20
❏ 68	Courtney Alexander	.50	.20
❏ 69	Michael Finley	.75	.30
❏ 70	Shawn Marion	.75	.30
❏ 71	Darius Miles	.75	.30
❏ 72	Antonio Davis	.25	.08
❏ 73	Ray Allen	.75	.30
❏ 74	Shareef Abdur-Rahim	.75	.30
❏ 75	Kevin Garnett	1.50	.60
❏ 76	Latrell Sprewell	.75	.30
❏ 77	Antonio McDyess	.50	.20
❏ 78	Derek Anderson	.50	.20
❏ 79	Derek Fisher	.75	.30
❏ 80	Jason Terry	.75	.30
❏ 81	Eddie Jones	.75	.30
❏ 82	Hakeem Olajuwon	.75	.30
❏ 83	Toni Kukoc	.50	.20
❏ 84	Sam Cassell	.75	.30
❏ 85	Jamal Crawford	.50	.20
❏ 86	Allen Iverson	1.50	.60
❏ 87	Steve Nash	.75	.30
❏ 88	Dikembe Mutombo	.50	.20
❏ 89	Shaquille O'Neal	2.00	.75
❏ 90	Jerome Moiso	.50	.20
❏ 91	Kenyon Martin	.75	.30
❏ 92	Chucky Atkins	.25	.08
❏ 93	Grant Hill	.75	.30
❏ 94	Jerry Stackhouse	.75	.30
❏ 95	Jason Williams	.50	.20
❏ 96	Baron Davis	.75	.30
❏ 97	Mike Miller	.75	.30
❏ 98	Joe Smith	.50	.20
❏ 99	Peja Stojakovic	.75	.30
❏ 100	Cuttino Mobley	.50	.20
❏ 101	Kwame Brown	5.00	2.00
❏ 102	Jason Collins RC	3.00	1.25
❏ 103	Willie Solomon RC	3.00	1.25
❏ 104	Brendan Haywood RC	4.00	1.50
❏ 105	Jeff Trepagnier RC	3.00	1.25
❏ 106	Eddie Griffin RC	3.00	1.25
❏ 107	Joseph Forte RC	6.00	2.50
❏ 108	Rodney White RC	4.00	1.50
❏ 109	Jeryl Sasser RC	3.00	1.25
❏ 110	Samuel Dalembert RC	3.00	1.25
❏ 111	Shane Battier RC	5.00	2.00
❏ 112	Tony Parker RC	12.00	5.00
❏ 113	DeSagana Diop RC	3.00	1.25
❏ 114	Steven Hunter RC	3.00	1.25
❏ 115	Trenton Hassell RC	5.00	2.00

#	Player		
116	Michael Bradley RC	3.00	1.25
117	Brian Scalabrine RC	3.00	1.25
118	Troy Murphy RC	6.00	2.50
119	Brandon Armstrong RC	4.00	1.50
120	Pau Gasol RC	12.00	5.00
121	Gerald Wallace RC	5.00	2.00
122	Jason Richardson RC	8.00	3.00
123	Joe Johnson RC	10.00	4.00
124	Loren Woods RC	3.00	1.25
125	Vladimir Radmanovic RC	4.00	1.50
126	Jamaal Tinsley RC	5.00	2.00
127	Omar Cook RC	3.00	1.25
128	Kedrick Brown RC	3.00	1.25
129	Terence Morris RC	3.00	1.25
130	Richard Jefferson RC	8.00	3.00
131	Gilbert Arenas RC	12.00	5.00
132	Tyson Chandler RC	8.00	3.00
133	Kirk Haston RC	3.00	1.25
134	Eddy Curry RC	8.00	3.00
135	Zach Randolph RC	10.00	4.00

2002-03 Fleer Authentix

#	Player		
	COMPLETE (135)	250.00	125.00
	COMP.SET w/o SPs (100)	40.00	15.00
	COMMON CARD (1-100)	.20	.08
	COMMON ROOKIE (101-135)	5.00	2.00
1	Vince Carter	2.00	.75
2	Bobby Jackson	.50	.20
3	Cuttino Mobley	.50	.20
4	John Stockton	.75	.30
5	Jamal Mashburn	.50	.20
6	Ben Wallace	.75	.30
7	Tim Duncan	1.50	.60
8	Richard Jefferson	.50	.20
9	Clifford Robinson	.20	.08
10	Gary Payton	.75	.30
11	Terrell Brandon	.50	.20
12	Michael Finley	.75	.30
13	Rasheed Wallace	.75	.30
14	Jason Williams	.50	.20
15	Andre Miller	.50	.20
16	Shawn Marion	.75	.30
17	Kobe Bryant	3.00	1.25
18	Jason Terry	.75	.30
19	Latrell Sprewell	.75	.30
20	Jerry Stackhouse	.75	.30
21	Tony Parker	.75	.30
22	Ray Allen	.75	.30
23	Dirk Nowitzki	1.25	.50
24	Chris Webber	.75	.30
25	Rick Fox	.50	.20
26	Jermaine O'Neal	.75	.30
27	Karl Malone	.75	.30
28	Allan Houston	.50	.20
29	Jason Richardson	.75	.30
30	Morris Peterson	.50	.20
31	Kevin Garnett	1.50	.60
32	Antawn Jamison	.75	.30
33	Rashard Lewis	.50	.20
34	Jason Kidd	1.25	.50
35	Joe Smith	.50	.20
36	David Robinson	.75	.30
37	Brian Grant	.50	.20
38	Lamond Murray	.20	.08
39	Damon Stoudamire	.50	.20
40	Shane Battier	.75	.30
41	Eddy Curry	.75	.30
42	Dikembe Mutombo	.50	.20
43	Jamaal Tinsley	.75	.30
44	Courtney Alexander	.50	.20
45	Wally Szczerbiak	.50	.20
46	Antonio McDyess	.50	.20
47	Mike Bibby	.75	.30
48	Alonzo Mourning	.50	.20
49	Tyson Chandler	.75	.30
50	Stephon Marbury	.75	.30
51	Sam Cassell	.75	.30
52	Steve Nash	.75	.30
53	Bonzi Wells	.50	.20
54	Pau Gasol	.75	.30
55	Rodney Rogers	.20	.08
56	Allen Iverson	1.50	.60
57	Derek Fisher	.75	.30
58	Travis Best	.20	.08
59	Aaron McKie	.50	.20
60	Darius Miles	.75	.30
61	Richard Hamilton	.50	.20
62	Marcus Camby	.50	.20
63	Eddie Griffin	.50	.20
64	Antonio Davis	.20	.08
65	David Wesley	.20	.08
66	Stromile Swift	.50	.20
67	Brent Barry	.50	.20
68	Glenn Robinson	.75	.30
69	Antoine Walker	.75	.30
70	Tracy McGrady	2.00	.75
71	Steve Smith	.50	.20
72	Michael Jordan	6.00	2.50
73	Mike Miller	.75	.30
74	DeShawn Stevenson	.20	.08
75	Raef LaFrentz	.50	.20
76	Al Harrington	.50	.20
77	Vlade Divac	.50	.20
78	Eddie Jones	.75	.30
79	Wesley Person	.20	.08
80	Kenny Anderson	.50	.20
81	Elton Brand	.75	.30
82	Jalen Rose	.75	.30
83	Joe Johnson	.75	.30
84	Shaquille O'Neal	2.00	.75
85	Paul Pierce	.75	.30
86	Grant Hill	.75	.30
87	Steve Francis	.75	.30
88	Keon Clark	.50	.20
89	Baron Davis	.75	.30
90	Tim Thomas	.50	.20
91	Shareef Abdur-Rahim	.75	.30
92	Kenyon Martin	.75	.30
93	Juwan Howard	.50	.20
94	Peja Stojakovic	.75	.30
95	Lamar Odom	.75	.30
96	Toni Kukoc	.50	.20
97	Darrell Armstrong	.20	.08
98	Reggie Miller	.75	.30
99	Andrei Kirilenko	.75	.30
100	Keith Van Horn	.75	.30
101	Rookie Exchange	6.00	2.50
102	Jay Williams RC	5.00	2.00
103	Mike Dunleavy RC	6.00	2.50
104	Drew Gooden RC	10.00	4.00
105	Nikoloz Tskitishvili RC	5.00	2.00
106	Caron Butler RC	8.00	3.00
107	Chris Wilcox RC	5.00	2.00
108	DaJuan Wagner RC	6.00	2.50
109	Nene Hilario RC	5.00	2.00
110	Qyntel Woods RC	5.00	2.00
111	Jared Jeffries RC	5.00	2.00
112	Tamar Slay RC	5.00	2.00
113	Marcus Haislip RC	5.00	2.00
114	Kareem Rush RC	5.00	2.00
115	Bostjan Nachbar RC	5.00	2.00
116	Melvin Ely RC	5.00	2.00
117	Jiri Welsch RC	5.00	2.00
118	Amare Stoudemire RC	20.00	8.00
119	Frank Williams RC	5.00	2.00
120	Rasual Butler RC	5.00	2.00
121	Dan Dickau RC	5.00	2.00
122	Carlos Boozer RC	8.00	3.00
123	Roger Mason RC	5.00	2.00
124	Corsley Edwards RC	5.00	2.00
125	Robert Archibald RC	5.00	2.00
126	John Salmons RC	5.00	2.00
127	Rod Grizzard RC	5.00	2.00
128	Dan Gadzuric RC	5.00	2.00
129	Sam Clancy RC	5.00	2.00
130	Fred Jones RC	5.00	2.00
131	Casey Jacobsen RC	5.00	2.00
132	Ryan Humphrey RC	5.00	2.00
133	Vincent Yarbrough RC	5.00	2.00
134	Juan Dixon RC	6.00	2.50
135	Tayshaun Prince RC	6.00	2.50

2003-04 Fleer Authentix

#	Player		
	COMP.SET w/o SP's (1-100)	40.00	15.00
	COMMON CARD (1-100)	.20	.08
	COMMON ROOKIE (101-130)	4.00	1.50
1	Vince Carter	2.00	.75
2	David Wesley	.20	.08
3	Eddie Griffin	.50	.20
4	Andrei Kirilenko	.75	.30
5	Kerry Kittles	.20	.08
6	Tayshaun Prince	.75	.30
7	Tim Duncan	1.50	.60
8	Troy Hudson	.20	.08
9	Ben Wallace	.75	.30
10	Manu Ginobili	.75	.30
11	Gary Payton	.75	.30
12	Dajuan Wagner	.50	.20
13	Stephon Marbury	.75	.30
14	Shane Battier	.50	.20
15	Zydrunas Ilgauskas	.50	.20
16	Eric Snow	.50	.20
17	Andre Miller	.50	.20
18	Shareef Abdur-Rahim	.75	.30
19	Kurt Thomas	.50	.20
20	Vincent Yarbrough	.20	.08
21	Mike Bibby	.75	.30
22	Desmond Mason	.50	.20
23	Steve Nash	.75	.30
24	Rasheed Wallace	.75	.30
25	Kobe Bryant	3.00	1.25
26	Cuttino Mobley	.50	.20
27	Matt Harpring	.75	.30
28	Jamal Mashburn	.50	.20
29	Mike Dunleavy	.50	.20
30	Antonio Davis	.20	.08
31	Michael Redd	.75	.30
32	Richard Hamilton	.50	.20
33	Predrag Drobnjak	.20	.08
34	Kevin Garnett	1.50	.60
35	Nene	.50	.20
36	Bobby Jackson	.50	.20
37	Jason Williams	.50	.20
38	Ricky Davis	.75	.30
39	Shawn Marion	.75	.30
40	Kareem Rush	.50	.20
41	Eddy Curry	.50	.20
42	Gordan Giricek	.50	.20
43	Brad Miller	.50	.20
44	Kwame Brown	.50	.20
45	Sam Cassell	.75	.30
46	Juwan Howard	.50	.20
47	Peja Stojakovic	.75	.30
48	Brian Grant	.50	.20
49	Al Harrington	.50	.20
50	Allen Iverson	1.50	.60
51	Caron Butler	.75	.30
52	Dirk Nowitzki	1.25	.50
53	Zach Randolph	.75	.30
54	Pau Gasol	.50	.20
55	Tony Delk	.20	.08
56	Grant Hill	.75	.30

❑ 57	Shaquille O'Neal	2.00	.75
❑ 58	Tyson Chandler	.75	.30
❑ 59	Tracy McGrady	2.00	.75
❑ 60	Ron Artest	.50	.20
❑ 61	Jerry Stackhouse	.75	.30
❑ 62	Jamaal Magloire	.20	.08
❑ 63	Jason Richardson	.75	.30
❑ 64	Morris Peterson	.50	.20
❑ 65	Richard Jefferson	.50	.20
❑ 66	Kenny Thomas	.20	.08
❑ 67	Tony Parker	.75	.30
❑ 68	Eddie Jones	.75	.30
❑ 69	Paul Pierce	.75	.30
❑ 70	Drew Gooden	.50	.20
❑ 71	Jermaine O'Neal	.75	.30
❑ 72	Juan Dixon	.50	.20
❑ 73	Baron Davis	.75	.30
❑ 74	Antawn Jamison	.75	.30
❑ 75	Rashard Lewis	.75	.30
❑ 76	Nick Van Exel	.75	.30
❑ 77	Bonzi Wells	.50	.20
❑ 78	Speedy Claxton	.50	.20
❑ 79	Carlos Boozer	.75	.30
❑ 80	Amare Stoudemire	1.50	.60
❑ 81	Elton Brand	.75	.30
❑ 82	Jalen Rose	.75	.30
❑ 83	Keith Van Horn	.75	.30
❑ 84	Corey Maggette	.50	.20
❑ 85	Antoine Walker	.75	.30
❑ 86	Latrell Sprewell	.75	.30
❑ 87	Yao Ming	2.00	.75
❑ 88	Glenn Robinson	.75	.30
❑ 89	Jason Kidd	1.25	.50
❑ 90	Gilbert Arenas	.75	.30
❑ 91	Ray Allen	.75	.30
❑ 92	Wally Szczerbiak	.50	.20
❑ 93	Michael Finley	.75	.30
❑ 94	Chris Webber	.75	.30
❑ 95	Reggie Miller	.75	.30
❑ 96	Jason Terry	.75	.30
❑ 97	Allan Houston	.50	.20
❑ 98	Steve Francis	.75	.30
❑ 99	Karl Malone	.75	.30
❑ 100	Kenyon Martin	.75	.30
❑ 101	Carmelo Anthony RC	20.00	8.00
❑ 102	Troy Bell RC	4.00	1.50
❑ 103	T.J. Ford RC	5.00	2.00
❑ 104	LeBron James RC	60.00	30.00
❑ 105	Travis Outlaw RC	4.00	1.50
❑ 106	Mike Sweetney RC	4.00	1.50
❑ 107	Aleksandar Pavlovic RC	5.00	2.00
❑ 108	Dahntay Jones RC	4.00	1.50
❑ 109	Chris Bosh RC	10.00	4.00
❑ 110	Boris Diaw RC	5.00	2.00
❑ 111	Jarvis Hayes RC	4.00	1.50
❑ 112	Brian Cook RC	4.00	1.50
❑ 113	Luke Ridnour RC	5.00	2.00
❑ 114	David West RC	4.00	1.50
❑ 115	Zoran Planinic RC	4.00	1.50
❑ 116	Zarko Cabarkapa RC	4.00	1.50
❑ 117	Marcus Banks RC	4.00	1.50
❑ 118	Kirk Hinrich RC	6.00	2.50
❑ 119	Darko Milicic RC	6.00	2.50
❑ 120	Sofoklis Schortsanitis RC	5.00	2.00
❑ 121	Ndudi Ebi RC	4.00	1.50
❑ 122	Kendrick Perkins RC	4.00	1.50
❑ 123	Leandro Barbosa RC	6.00	2.50
❑ 124	Nick Collison RC	4.00	1.50
❑ 125	Reece Gaines RC	4.00	1.50
❑ 126	Chris Kaman RC	4.00	1.50
❑ 127	Mickael Pietrus RC	4.00	1.50
❑ 128	Dwyane Wade RC	25.00	10.00
❑ 129	Josh Howard RC	6.00	2.50

2004-05 Fleer Authentix

❑ COMPLETE SET (137)			
❑ COMP.SET w/o SPs (100)		40.00	15.00
❑ COMMON CARD (1-100)		.20	.08
❑ COMMON ROOKIE (101-129)		4.00	1.50
❑ 101-129 RC PRINT RUN 750 SER.#'d SETS			
❑ COMMON ROOKIE (130-140)			
❑ 130-140 RC PRINT RUN 200 SER.#'d SETS			
❑ 1	Allen Iverson	1.50	.60
❑ 2	Allan Houston	.50	.20
❑ 3	Jermaine O'Neal	.75	.30

❑ 4	Andrei Kirilenko	.75	.30
❑ 5	Baron Davis	.75	.30
❑ 6	Rasheed Wallace	.75	.30
❑ 7	Manu Ginobili	.75	.30
❑ 8	Kenyon Martin	.75	.30
❑ 9	Richard Hamilton	.50	.20
❑ 10	Tony Parker	.75	.30
❑ 11	Keith Van Horn	.75	.30
❑ 12	Steve Nash	.75	.30
❑ 13	Darius Miles	.75	.30
❑ 14	Jason Williams	.50	.20
❑ 15	Carlos Boozer	.75	.30
❑ 16	Amare Stoudemire	1.50	.60
❑ 17	Kobe Bryant	3.00	1.25
❑ 18	Jason Terry	.75	.30
❑ 19	Stephon Marbury	.75	.30
❑ 20	Ben Wallace	.75	.30
❑ 21	Tim Duncan	1.50	.60
❑ 22	Michael Redd	.50	.20
❑ 23	Antoine Walker	.75	.30
❑ 24	Shareef Abdur-Rahim	.75	.30
❑ 25	Luke Walton	.50	.20
❑ 26	Reggie Miller	.75	.30
❑ 27	Antawn Jamison	.75	.30
❑ 28	Anfernee Hardaway	.75	.30
❑ 29	Yao Ming	2.00	.75
❑ 30	Chris Bosh	.75	.30
❑ 31	Latrell Sprewell	.75	.30
❑ 32	Mike Dunleavy	.50	.20
❑ 33	Luke Ridnour	.50	.20
❑ 34	Kevin Garnett	1.50	.60
❑ 35	Darko Milicic	.50	.20
❑ 36	Bobby Jackson	.50	.20
❑ 37	Caron Butler	.75	.30
❑ 38	Dirk Nowitzki	1.25	.50
❑ 39	Joe Johnson	.50	.20
❑ 40	Pau Gasol	.75	.30
❑ 41	Kirk Hinrich	.75	.30
❑ 42	Willie Green	.20	.08
❑ 43	Jamaal Tinsley	.75	.30
❑ 44	Jarvis Hayes	.50	.20
❑ 45	Sam Cassell	.75	.30
❑ 46	Nene	.50	.20
❑ 47	Mike Bibby	.75	.30
❑ 48	Lamar Odom	.75	.30
❑ 49	LeBron James	5.00	2.00
❑ 50	Marquis Daniels	.75	.30
❑ 51	T.J. Ford	.50	.20
❑ 52	Michael Finley	.75	.30
❑ 53	Zach Randolph	.75	.30
❑ 54	Bonzi Wells	.50	.20
❑ 55	Stephen Jackson	.75	.30
❑ 56	Gary Payton	.75	.30
❑ 57	Jason Kapono	.20	.08
❑ 58	Glenn Robinson	.75	.30
❑ 59	Elton Brand	.75	.30
❑ 60	Jerry Stackhouse	.75	.30
❑ 61	Jamaal Magloire	.20	.08
❑ 62	Tracy McGrady	2.00	.75
❑ 63	Jalen Rose	.75	.30
❑ 64	Kerry Kittles	.50	.20
❑ 65	Nick Van Exel	.75	.30
❑ 66	Rashard Lewis	.75	.30
❑ 67	Desmond Mason	.50	.20
❑ 68	Gerald Wallace	.50	.20
❑ 69	Drew Gooden	.50	.20
❑ 70	Corey Maggette	.50	.20
❑ 71	Gilbert Arenas	.75	.30

❑ 73	Tim Thomas	.50	.20
❑ 74	Jason Richardson	.75	.30
❑ 75	Ray Allen	.75	.30
❑ 76	Carmelo Anthony	1.50	.60
❑ 77	Peja Stojakovic	.75	.30
❑ 78	Dwyane Wade	2.50	1.00
❑ 79	Dajuan Wagner	.50	.20
❑ 80	Shawn Marion	.75	.30
❑ 81	Shaquille O'Neal	2.00	.75
❑ 82	Eddy Curry	.75	.30
❑ 83	Samuel Dalembert	.20	.08
❑ 84	Karl Malone	.75	.30
❑ 85	Ricky Davis	.75	.30
❑ 86	Steve Francis	.75	.30
❑ 87	Juwan Howard	.50	.20
❑ 88	Carlos Arroyo	1.25	.50
❑ 89	Jamal Mashburn	.50	.20
❑ 90	Mickael Pietrus	.50	.20
❑ 91	Vince Carter	2.00	.75
❑ 92	Jason Kidd	1.25	.50
❑ 93	Andre Miller	.50	.20
❑ 94	Chris Webber	.75	.30
❑ 95	Chris Kaman	.50	.20
❑ 96	Paul Pierce	.75	.30
❑ 97	Cuttino Mobley	.50	.20
❑ 98	Ron Artest	.50	.20
❑ 99	Matt Harpring	.75	.30
❑ 100	Richard Jefferson	.50	.20
❑ 101	Albert Miralles RC	4.00	1.50
❑ 102	Chris Duhon RC	8.00	3.00
❑ 103	Ha Seung-Jin RC	4.00	1.50
❑ 104	Antonio Burks RC	4.00	1.50
❑ 105	Andre Emmett RC	4.00	1.50
❑ 106	Donta Smith RC	4.00	1.50
❑ 107	Lionel Chalmers RC	4.00	1.50
❑ 108	Rickey Paulding RC	4.00	1.50
❑ 109	Jackson Vroman RC	4.00	1.50
❑ 110	Anderson Varejao RC	5.00	2.00
❑ 111	Beno Udrih RC	6.00	2.50
❑ 112	Sasha Vujacic RC	4.00	1.50
❑ 113	Kevin Martin RC	6.00	2.50
❑ 114	Tony Allen RC	5.00	2.00
❑ 115	Delonte West RC	8.00	3.00
❑ 116	Sergei Monia RC	4.00	1.50
❑ 117	Romain Sato RC	4.00	1.50
❑ 118	Jameer Nelson RC	6.00	2.50
❑ 119	Josh Smith RC	8.00	3.00
❑ 120	Kirk Snyder RC	4.00	1.50
❑ 121	Robert Swift RC	4.00	1.50
❑ 122	Andre Iguodala RC	10.00	4.00
❑ 123	Rafael Araujo RC	4.00	1.50
❑ 124	Luol Deng RC	8.00	3.00
❑ 125	Josh Childress RC	5.00	2.00
❑ 126	Ben Gordon RC	15.00	6.00
❑ 127	Emeka Okafor RC	15.00	6.00
❑ 128	Dwight Howard RC	12.00	5.00
❑ 129	Harrison RC/Bird AU EXCH	75.00	30.00
❑ 130	Livingston RC/E.Baylor AU	30.00	12.50
❑ 131	D.Harris RC/D.Nelson AU	30.00	12.50
❑ 132	L.Jackson RC/P.Silas AU	20.00	8.00
❑ 133	A.Biedrins RC/C.Mullin AU	50.00	20.00
❑ 134	S.Telfair RC/M.Cheeks AU	20.00	8.00
❑ 135	K.Humphries RC/J.Sloan AU	50.00	20.00
❑ 136	A.Jefferson RC/J.Kidd AU	40.00	15.00
❑ 137	J.R.Smith RC/B.Scott AU	50.00	20.00
❑ 138	D.Wright RC/P.Riley AU	30.00	12.50
❑ 139	T.Ariza RC/I.Thomas AU	40.00	15.00

2002 Fleer Authentix WNBA

❑ COMPLETE SET (120)		150.00	75.00
❑ COMPLETE SET w/o RC's (100)		30.00	12.50
❑ COMMON CARD (1-100)		.50	.25
❑ COMMON ROOKIE (101-120)		6.00	2.50
❑ 1	Jackie Stiles	3.00	1.25
❑ 2	Taj McWilliams-Franklin	.60	.25
❑ 3	Allison Feaster	.60	.25
❑ 4	Sheryl Swoopes	3.00	1.25
❑ 5	Edwina Brown	.60	.25
❑ 6	DeLisha Milton	.60	.25
❑ 7	Tonya Edwards	.60	.25
❑ 8	Svetlana Abrosimova	.60	.25
❑ 9	Alicia Thompson	.60	.25
❑ 10	Kristen Rasmussen	.60	.25
❑ 11	Marie Ferdinand	.60	.25

❑ 12 Coco Miller	.60	.25
❑ 13 Tari Phillips	.60	.25
❑ 14 Kristin Folkl	.60	.25
❑ 15 Annie Burgess	.60	.25
❑ 16 Elaine Powell	.60	.25
❑ 17 Jamie Redd	.60	.25
❑ 18 Sophia Witherspoon	.60	.25
❑ 19 Shannon Johnson	.60	.25
❑ 20 Amanda Lassiter	.60	.25
❑ 21 Dawn Staley	2.00	.75
❑ 22 Dominique Canty	.60	.25
❑ 23 Jessie Hicks	.60	.25
❑ 24 Mwadi Mabika	.60	.25
❑ 25 Georgia Schweitzer	.60	.25
❑ 26 Lauren Jackson	2.00	.75
❑ 27 Natalie Williams	2.00	.75
❑ 28 Tynesha Lewis	.60	.25
❑ 29 Rushia Brown	.60	.25
❑ 30 Tamicha Jackson	.60	.25
❑ 31 Chasity Melvin	.60	.25
❑ 32 Chamique Holdsclaw	3.00	1.25
❑ 33 Michelle Marciniak	.60	.25
❑ 34 Lynn Pride	.60	.25
❑ 35 Tammy Sutton-Brown	.60	.25
❑ 36 Sandy Brondello	2.00	.75
❑ 37 Semeka Randall	.60	.25
❑ 38 Tammy Jackson	.60	.25
❑ 39 Ukari Figgs	.60	.25
❑ 40 Ruthie Bolton	2.00	.75
❑ 41 Lisa Harrison	.60	.25
❑ 42 Kate Starbird	2.00	.75
❑ 43 Katie Douglas	.60	.25
❑ 44 Coquese Washington	.60	.25
❑ 45 Sheri Sam	.60	.25
❑ 46 Vickie Johnson	.60	.25
❑ 47 Latasha Byears	.60	.25
❑ 48 Erin Buescher	.60	.25
❑ 49 Ann Wauters	1.25	.50
❑ 50 Kedra Holland-Corn	.60	.25
❑ 51 Astou Ndiaye-Diatta	.60	.25
❑ 52 Kara Wolters	.60	.25
❑ 53 Tully Bevilaqua	.60	.25
❑ 54 Simone Edwards	.60	.25
❑ 55 Vicky Bullett	.60	.25
❑ 56 Nykesha Sales	.60	.25
❑ 57 Crystal Robinson	.60	.25
❑ 58 Tina Thompson	2.00	.75
❑ 59 Lisa Leslie	3.00	1.25
❑ 60 Deanna Nolan	.60	.25
❑ 61 Jennifer Gillom	1.25	.50
❑ 62 Nadine Malcolm	.60	.25
❑ 63 Merlakia Jones	.60	.25
❑ 64 Rebecca Lobo	2.00	.75
❑ 65 Tamecka Dixon	.60	.25
❑ 66 Yolanda Griffith	2.00	.75
❑ 67 Teresa Weatherspoon	2.00	.75
❑ 68 Penny Taylor	.60	.25
❑ 69 Brooke Wyckoff	1.25	.50
❑ 70 Murriel Page	.60	.25
❑ 71 Adrienne Goodson	.60	.25
❑ 72 Camille Cooper	.60	.25
❑ 73 Kamila Vodichkova	.60	.25
❑ 74 Jennifer Azzi	2.00	.75
❑ 75 Katie Smith	2.00	.75
❑ 76 Kristen Veal	.60	.25
❑ 77 Tamika Catchings	2.50	1.00
❑ 78 Clarisse Machanguana	.60	.25
❑ 79 Wendy Palmer	1.25	.50
❑ 80 Ticha Penicheiro	1.25	.50
❑ 81 Becky Hammon	1.25	.50
❑ 82 Jennifer Rizzotti	1.25	.50
❑ 83 Helen Luz	.60	.25
❑ 84 Adrain Williams	.60	.25
❑ 85 Tamika Whitmore	.60	.25
❑ 86 Sylvia Crawley	.60	.25
❑ 87 Edna Campbell	.60	.25
❑ 88 Sonja Henning	.60	.25
❑ 89 Vedrana Grgin	.60	.25
❑ 90 Tracy Reid	.60	.25
❑ 91 Betty Lennox	1.25	.50
❑ 92 Andrea Stinson	.60	.25
❑ 93 Tangela Smith	.60	.25
❑ 94 Margo Dydek	.60	.25
❑ 95 Nikki McCray	1.25	.50
❑ 96 Sue Wicks	.60	.25
❑ 97 Olympia Scott-Richardson	.60	.25
❑ 98 Ruth Riley	.60	.25
❑ 99 Janeth Arcain	.60	.25
❑ 100 Rita Williams	.60	.25
❑ 101 Sue Bird RC	60.00	25.00
❑ 102 Swin Cash RC	15.00	6.00
❑ 103 S.Dales-Schuman RC	15.00	6.00
❑ 104 Asjha Jones RC	12.00	5.00
❑ 105 Nikki Teasley RC	10.00	4.00
❑ 106 Tamika Williams RC	12.00	5.00
❑ 107 Sheila Lambert RC	6.00	2.50
❑ 108 Lindsey Yamasaki RC	10.00	4.00
❑ 109 Shaunzinski Gortman RC	6.00	2.50
❑ 110 Michelle Snow RC	20.00	8.00
❑ 111 Danielle Crockrom RC	10.00	4.00
❑ 112 Hamchetou Maiga RC	6.00	2.50
❑ 113 Tawana McDonald RC	8.00	3.00
❑ 114 LaNeishea Caulfield RC	8.00	3.00
❑ 115 Tamara Moore RC	10.00	4.00
❑ 116 Rosalind Ross RC	6.00	2.50
❑ 117 Zuzi Klimesova RC	10.00	4.00
❑ 118 Lenae Williams RC	8.00	3.00
❑ 119 Iziane Castro Marques RC	6.00	2.50
❑ 120 Ayana Walker RC	8.00	3.00

2000-01 Fleer Authority

❑ COMPLETE SET (141)	160.00	80.00
❑ COMP.SET w/o SP's (110)	25.00	10.00
❑ COMMON CARD (1-110)	.15	.05
❑ COMMON ROOKIE (111-141)	4.00	1.50
❑ 1 Dikembe Mutombo	.20	.07
❑ 2 Cuttino Mobley	.20	.07
❑ 3 Brian Grant	.20	.07
❑ 4 Grant Hill	.40	.15
❑ 5 Jim Jackson	.15	.05
❑ 6 Derek Anderson	.20	.07
❑ 7 Jerry Stackhouse	.40	.15
❑ 8 Eddie Jones	.40	.15
❑ 9 Tracy McGrady	2.00	.75
❑ 10 Vin Baker	.20	.07
❑ 11 Jason Terry	.40	.15
❑ 12 Jerome Williams	.15	.05
❑ 13 Tim Hardaway	.20	.07
❑ 14 Darrell Armstrong	.15	.05
❑ 15 Rashard Lewis	.20	.07
❑ 16 Kenny Anderson	.20	.07
❑ 17 Larry Hughes	.20	.07
❑ 18 Anthony Mason	.20	.07
❑ 19 Allen Iverson	1.50	.60
❑ 20 Gary Payton	.40	.15
❑ 21 Antoine Walker	.40	.15
❑ 22 Antawn Jamison	.40	.15
❑ 23 Glenn Robinson	.20	.07
❑ 24 Toni Kukoc	.20	.07
❑ 25 Ruben Patterson	.20	.07
❑ 26 Paul Pierce	.40	.15
❑ 27 Mookie Blaylock	.15	.05
❑ 28 Ray Allen	.40	.15
❑ 29 Theo Ratliff	.20	.07
❑ 30 Vince Carter	2.00	.75
❑ 31 Jamal Mashburn	.20	.07
❑ 32 Steve Francis	.40	.15
❑ 33 Sam Cassell	.40	.15
❑ 34 Jason Kidd	1.25	.50
❑ 35 Mark Jackson	.15	.05
❑ 36 Baron Davis	.40	.15
❑ 37 Hakeem Olajuwon	.40	.15
❑ 38 Darvin Ham	.15	.05
❑ 39 Anfernee Hardaway	.40	.15
❑ 40 Antonio Davis	.15	.05
❑ 41 Derrick Coleman	.15	.05
❑ 42 Maurice Taylor	.15	.05
❑ 43 Kevin Garnett	1.50	.60
❑ 44 Tom Gugliotta	.15	.05
❑ 45 Karl Malone	.40	.15
❑ 46 Elton Brand	.40	.15
❑ 47 Jonathan Bender	.20	.07
❑ 48 Terrell Brandon	.20	.07
❑ 49 Clifford Robinson	.15	.05
❑ 50 John Stockton	.40	.15
❑ 51 Ron Artest	.20	.07
❑ 52 Reggie Miller	.40	.15
❑ 53 Joe Smith	.20	.07
❑ 54 Shawn Kemp	.20	.07
❑ 55 Bryon Russell	.15	.05
❑ 56 Andre Miller	.20	.07
❑ 57 Austin Croshere	.20	.07
❑ 58 Wally Szczerbiak	.20	.07
❑ 59 Scottie Pippen	1.25	.50
❑ 60 Donyell Marshall	.20	.07
❑ 61 Brevin Knight	.15	.05
❑ 62 Travis Best	.15	.05
❑ 63 Chauncey Billups	.20	.07
❑ 64 Rasheed Wallace	.40	.15
❑ 65 Shareef Abdur-Rahim	.40	.15
❑ 66 Trajan Langdon	.20	.07
❑ 67 Jalen Rose	.40	.15
❑ 68 Stephon Marbury	.40	.15
❑ 69 Steve Smith	.20	.07
❑ 70 Mike Bibby	.40	.15
❑ 71 Lamond Murray	.15	.05
❑ 72 Lamar Odom	.40	.15
❑ 73 Keith Van Horn	.20	.07
❑ 74 Chris Webber	.40	.15
❑ 75 Michael Dickerson	.20	.07
❑ 76 Dirk Nowitzki	1.25	.50
❑ 77 Corey Maggette	.20	.07
❑ 78 Kerry Kittles	.15	.05
❑ 79 Jason Williams	.20	.07
❑ 80 Mitch Richmond	.20	.07
❑ 81 Michael Finley	.40	.15
❑ 82 Shaquille O'Neal	2.00	.75
❑ 83 Allan Houston	.20	.07
❑ 84 Peja Stojakovic	.40	.15
❑ 85 Juwan Howard	.20	.07
❑ 86 Nick Van Exel	.40	.15
❑ 87 Kobe Bryant	3.00	1.25
❑ 88 Latrell Sprewell	.40	.15
❑ 89 Tim Duncan	1.50	.60
❑ 90 Richard Hamilton	.20	.07
❑ 91 Antonio McDyess	.20	.07
❑ 92 Glen Rice	.20	.07
❑ 93 Larry Johnson	.20	.07
❑ 94 David Robinson	.40	.15
❑ 95 Rod Strickland	.15	.05
❑ 96 Rael LaFrentz	.15	.05
❑ 97 Ron Harper	.20	.07
❑ 98 Patrick Ewing	.40	.15
❑ 99 Sean Elliot	.20	.07
❑ 100 Tariq Abdul-Wahad	.15	.05
❑ 101 Chucky Atkins	.15	.05
❑ 102 Marcus Camby	.20	.07
❑ 103 Corliss Williamson	.20	.07
❑ 104 Rodney Rogers	.15	.05
❑ 105 Othella Harrington	.15	.05
❑ 106 Alan Henderson	.15	.05
❑ 107 David Wesley	.15	.05

#	Player		
108	Michael Doleac	.20	.07
109	Doug Christie	.20	.07
110	Vitaly Potapenko	.15	.05
111	DerMarr Johnson RC	4.00	1.50
112	Jamal Crawford RC	5.00	2.00
113	Morris Peterson RC	5.00	2.00
114	Erick Barkley RC	4.00	1.50
115	Kenyon Martin RC	12.00	5.00
116	Joel Przybilla RC	4.00	1.50
117	Speedy Claxton RC	4.00	1.50
118	Hidayet Turkoglu RC	6.00	2.50
119	Etan Thomas RC	4.00	1.50
120	Eddie House RC	4.00	1.50
121	Marcus Fizer RC	4.00	1.50
122	Quentin Richardson RC	6.00	2.50
123	Donnell Harvey RC	4.00	1.50
124	DeShawn Stevenson RC	4.00	1.50
125	Chris Mihm RC	4.00	1.50
126	Courtney Alexander RC	4.00	1.50
127	Keyon Dooling RC	4.00	1.50
128	Jerome Moiso RC	4.00	1.50
129	Stephen Jackson RC	5.00	2.00
130	Chris Porter RC	4.00	1.50
131	Stromile Swift RC	6.00	2.50
132	Desmond Mason RC	4.00	1.50
133	Jason Collier RC	5.00	2.00
134	Mark Madsen RC	4.00	1.50
135	Mamadou N'Diaye RC	4.00	1.50
136	Darius Miles RC	10.00	4.00
137	Mateen Cleaves RC	4.00	1.50
138	Jamaal Magloire RC	4.00	1.50
139	Khalid El-Amin RC	4.00	1.50
140	Mike Miller RC	8.00	3.00
141	Marc Jackson RC	4.00	1.50
NNO	Fleer/BGS Redemption	8.00	3.00

2003-04 Fleer Avant

Shaquille O'Neal / Lakers

#	Player		
	COMP.SET w/o SP's	40.00	15.00
	COMMON USA (57-64)	5.00	2.00
	COMMON ROOKIE (65-90)	4.00	1.50
1	Ben Wallace	1.50	.60
2	Glenn Robinson	1.50	.60
3	Pau Gasol	1.50	.60
4	Keon Clark	.50	.20
5	Kobe Bryant	6.00	2.50
6	Morris Peterson	1.00	.40
7	Steve Francis	1.50	.60
8	Amare Stoudemire	3.00	1.25
9	Mike Dunleavy Jr.	1.00	.40
10	Kevin Garnett	3.00	1.25
11	Yao Ming	4.00	1.50
12	Stephon Marbury	1.50	.60
13	Jason Richardson	1.50	.60
14	Rasheed Wallace	1.50	.60
15	Tayshaun Prince	1.00	.40
16	Steve Nash	1.50	.60
17	Jamal Mashburn	1.00	.40
18	Reggie Miller	1.50	.60
19	Chris Webber	1.50	.60
20	Andre Miller	1.00	.40
21	Peja Stojakovic	1.50	.60
22	Nene	1.00	.40
23	Manu Ginobili	1.50	.60
24	Bonzi Wells	1.00	.40
25	Lamar Odom	1.50	.60
26	Kwame Brown	1.00	.40
27	Caron Butler	1.50	.60
28	Gilbert Arenas	1.50	.60
29	Dirk Nowitzki	2.50	1.00
30	Allan Houston	1.00	.40
31	Michael Finley	1.50	.60
32	Drew Gooden	1.00	.40
33	Shareef Abdur-Rahim	1.50	.60
34	Michael Redd	1.50	.60
35	Jerry Stackhouse	1.50	.60
36	Scottie Pippen	2.50	1.00
37	Latrell Sprewell	1.50	.60
38	Ron Artest	1.00	.40
39	Derrick Coleman	.50	.20
40	Eddy Curry	1.00	.40
41	Wally Szczerbiak	1.00	.40
42	Dajuan Wagner	1.00	.40
43	Baron Davis	1.50	.60
44	Karl Malone	1.50	.60
45	Andrei Kirilenko	1.50	.60
46	Paul Pierce	1.50	.60
47	Desmond Mason	1.00	.40
48	Shaquille O'Neal	4.00	1.50
49	Rashard Lewis	1.50	.60
50	Ricky Davis	1.50	.60
51	Kerry Kittles	.50	.20
52	Quentin Richardson	1.00	.40
53	Tony Parker	1.50	.60
54	Elton Brand	1.50	.60
55	Richard Jefferson	1.00	.40
56	Kenyon Martin	1.50	.60
57	Ray Allen	1.50	.60
58	Mike Bibby	1.50	.60
59	Tim Duncan	8.00	3.00
60	Allen Iverson	8.00	3.00
61	Jason Kidd	6.00	2.50
62	Tracy McGrady	10.00	4.00
63	Jermaine O'Neal	1.50	.60
64	Larry Brown EXCH	8.00	3.00
65	LeBron James RC	8.00	40.00
66	Darko Milicic RC	8.00	3.00
67	Carmelo Anthony RC	20.00	8.00
68	Chris Bosh RC	12.00	5.00
69	Dwyane Wade RC	25.00	10.00
70	Chris Kaman RC	4.00	1.50
71	Kirk Hinrich RC	8.00	3.00
72	T.J. Ford RC	6.00	2.50
73	Mike Sweetney RC	4.00	1.50
74	Jarvis Hayes RC	4.00	1.50
75	Mickael Pietrus RC	4.00	1.50
76	Travis Hansen RC	4.00	1.50
77	Marcus Banks RC	4.00	1.50
78	Luke Ridnour RC	6.00	2.50
79	Reece Gaines RC	4.00	1.50
80	Troy Bell RC	4.00	1.50
81	Zarko Cabarkapa RC	4.00	1.50
82	David West RC	4.00	1.50
83	Aleksandar Pavlovic RC	4.00	1.50
84	Dahntay Jones RC	4.00	1.50
85	Boris Diaw RC	5.00	2.00
86	Zoran Planinic RC	4.00	1.50
87	Travis Outlaw RC	4.00	1.50
88	Brian Cook RC	4.00	1.50
89	Maciej Lampe RC	4.00	1.50
90	Nick Collison RC	4.00	1.50

2002-03 Fleer Box Score

#	Player		
	COMP.SET w/o SP's (135)	30.00	12.50
	COMMON CARD (1-135)	.25	.10
	COMMON RC (136-150)	2.50	1.00
	RS SEALED SET (151-180)	25.00	10.00
	COMMON RS (151-180)	2.50	1.00
	AS SEALED SET (181-210)	20.00	8.00
	AW SEALED SET (211-240)	20.00	8.00
1	Kwame Brown	.60	.25
2	Eddy Curry	1.00	.40
3	Allen Iverson	2.00	.75
4	Elton Brand	1.00	.40
5	Jason Kidd	1.50	.60
6	Kedrick Brown	.60	.25
7	Elden Campbell	.25	.10
8	Jason Richardson	1.00	.40
9	Shawn Marion	1.00	.40
10	John Stockton	1.00	.40
11	Theo Ratliff	.60	.25
12	Marcus Fizer	.60	.25
13	Tony Parker	1.00	.40
14	Michael Redd	1.00	.40
15	Vince Carter	2.50	1.00
16	Aaron McKie	.60	.25
17	Michael Finley	1.00	.40
18	Rashard Lewis	.60	.25
19	Steve Nash	1.00	.40
20	Reggie Miller	1.00	.40
21	Tim Duncan	2.00	.75
22	Marcus Camby	.60	.25
23	Michael Jordan	8.00	3.00
24	Donnell Harvey	.25	.10
25	Michael Dickerson	.25	.10
26	James Posey	.60	.25
27	Vin Baker	.60	.25
28	Antonio McDyess	.60	.25
29	Mike Miller	1.00	.40
30	Karl Malone	1.00	.40
31	Corliss Williamson	.60	.25
32	Derek Anderson	.60	.25
33	Scottie Pippen	1.50	.60
34	Paul Pierce	1.00	.40
35	Steve Francis	1.00	.40
36	Terrell Brandon	.25	.10
37	Cuttino Mobley	.60	.25
38	Ron Artest	.60	.25
39	Jonathan Bender	.60	.25
40	Ron Mercer	.60	.25
41	Dirk Nowitzki	1.50	.60
42	Jermaine O'Neal	1.00	.40
43	Ray Allen	1.00	.40
44	Jason Terry	1.00	.40
45	Pau Gasol	1.00	.40
46	Lamar Odom	1.00	.40
47	P.J. Brown	.25	.10
48	Kurt Thomas	.60	.25
49	Grant Hill	1.00	.40
50	David Robinson	1.00	.40
51	Rasheed Wallace	1.00	.40
52	Antawn Jamison	1.00	.40
53	Juwan Howard	.60	.25
54	Andre Miller	.60	.25
55	Kenyon Martin	1.00	.40
56	Jason Williams	.60	.25
57	Travis Best	.25	.10
58	Brian Grant	.60	.25
59	Keith Van Horn	1.00	.40
60	Alonzo Mourning	.60	.25
61	Rod Strickland	.25	.10
62	Jamaal Tinsley	1.00	.40
63	Sam Cassell	1.00	.40
64	Jalen Rose	1.00	.40
65	Tim Thomas	.60	.25
66	Eddie Griffin	.60	.25
67	Kevin Garnett	2.00	.75
68	Darrell Armstrong	.25	.10
69	Joe Smith	.60	.25
70	Wally Szczerbiak	.60	.25
71	Richard Jefferson	.60	.25
72	Chauncey Billups	.60	.25
73	Kerry Kittles	.25	.10
74	Stromile Swift	.60	.25
75	Dikembe Mutombo	.60	.25
76	Courtney Alexander	.60	.25
77	Tony Delk	.25	.10
78	Baron Davis	1.00	.40
79	Ricky Davis	.60	.25
80	Vlade Divac	.60	.25
81	Allan Houston	.60	.25
82	Richard Hamilton	.60	.25
83	Moochie Norris	.25	.10

#	Player		
84	Quentin Richardson	.60	.25
85	Charlie Ward	.25	.10
86	Troy Hudson	.25	.10
87	Pat Garrity	.25	.10
88	Kobe Bryant	4.00	1.50
89	Tracy McGrady	2.50	1.00
90	Clifford Robinson	.25	.10
91	Glenn Robinson	1.00	.40
92	Todd MacCulloch	.25	.10
93	Lamond Murray	.25	.10
94	Eric Snow	.60	.25
95	Eddie Jones	1.00	.40
96	Tom Gugliotta	.25	.10
97	Anfernee Hardaway	1.00	.40
98	Stephon Marbury	1.00	.40
99	Antoine Walker	1.00	.40
100	Gilbert Arenas	1.00	.40
101	Ruben Patterson	.60	.25
102	Shane Battier	1.00	.40
103	David Wesley	.25	.10
104	Damon Stoudamire	.60	.25
105	Shaquille O'Neal	2.50	1.00
106	Bonzi Wells	.60	.25
107	Mike Bibby	1.00	.40
108	Jamal Mashburn	.60	.25
109	Peja Stojakovic	1.00	.40
110	Latrell Sprewell	1.00	.40
111	Chris Webber	1.00	.40
112	Alvin Williams	.25	.10
113	Trenton Hassell	.25	.10
114	Derek Fisher	1.00	.40
115	Malik Rose	.25	.10
116	Kenny Anderson	.60	.25
117	Zydrunas Ilgauskas	.60	.25
118	Raef LaFrentz	.60	.25
119	Gary Payton	1.00	.40
120	Vladimir Radmanovic	.60	.25
121	Darius Miles	1.00	.40
122	Antonio Davis	.25	.10
123	Larry Hughes	.60	.25
124	Maurice Taylor	.25	.10
125	Morris Peterson	.60	.25
126	Nick Van Exel	1.00	.40
127	Ira Newble	.25	.10
128	Eric Williams	.25	.10
129	Andrei Kirilenko	1.00	.40
130	Ben Wallace	1.00	.40
131	Tyson Chandler	1.00	.40
132	Desmond Mason	.60	.25
133	Shareef Abdur-Rahim	1.00	.40
134	Danny Fortson	.25	.10
135	Jerry Stackhouse	1.00	.40
136	Yao Ming RC	20.00	8.00
137	Juan Dixon RC	4.00	1.50
138	Caron Butler RC	5.00	2.00
139	Drew Gooden RC	6.00	2.50
140	DaJuan Wagner RC	4.00	1.50
141	Jared Jeffries RC	3.00	1.25
142	Pat Burke RC	2.50	1.00
143	Kareem Rush RC	3.00	1.25
144	Ryan Humphrey RC	2.50	1.00
145	Manu Ginobili RC	10.00	4.00
146	Predrag Savovic RC	2.50	1.00
147	Marcus Haislip RC	2.50	1.00
148	John Salmons RC	2.50	1.00
149	Fred Jones RC	2.50	1.00
150	Roger Mason RC	2.50	1.00
151	Jay Williams RC	3.00	1.25
152	Mike Dunleavy RC	3.00	1.25
153	Carlos Boozer RC	4.00	1.50
154	Dan Dickau RC	2.50	1.00
155	Tayshaun Prince RS RC	3.00	1.25
156	Nene Hilario RS RC	2.50	1.00
157	Amare Stoudemire RS RC	10.00	4.00
158	Frank Williams RS RC	2.50	1.00
159	Chris Wilcox RS RC	2.50	1.00
160	Robert Archibald RS RC	2.50	1.00
161	Lonny Baxter RS RC	2.50	1.00
162	Curtis Borchardt RS RC	2.50	1.00
163	Sam Clancy RS RC	2.50	1.00
164	Melvin Ely RS RC	2.50	1.00
165	Dan Gadzuric RS RC	2.50	1.00
166	Smush Parker RS RC	4.00	1.50
167	Chris Jefferies RS RC	2.50	1.00
168	Nikoloz Tskitishvili RS RC	2.50	1.00
169	Casey Jacobsen RS RC	2.50	1.00
170	Ronald Murray RS RC	4.00	1.50
171	Gordan Giricek RS RC	2.50	1.00
172	Rasual Butler RS RC	2.50	1.00
173	Jannero Pargo RS RC	2.50	1.00
174	Bostjan Nachbar RS RC	2.50	1.00
175	Jiri Welsch RS RC	2.50	1.00
176	Qyntel Woods RS RC	2.50	1.00
177	Vincent Yarbrough RS RC	2.50	1.00
178	Raul Lopez RS RC	2.50	1.00
179	Mehmet Okur RS RC	2.50	1.00
180	Reggie Evans RS RC	2.50	1.00
181	Karl Malone AS	1.00	.40
182	Michael Jordan AS	8.00	3.00
183	Glen Rice AS	.60	.25
184	John Stockton AS	1.00	.40
185	David Robinson AS	1.00	.40
186	Shaquille O'Neal AS	2.50	1.00
187	Dikembe Mutombo AS	.60	.25
188	Gary Payton AS	1.00	.40
189	Alonzo Mourning AS	.60	.25
190	Scottie Pippen AS	1.50	.60
191	Grant Hill AS	1.00	.40
192	Vin Baker AS	.60	.25
193	Kevin Garnett AS	2.00	.75
194	Jason Kidd AS	1.50	.60
195	Reggie Miller AS	1.00	.40
196	Ray Allen AS	1.00	.40
197	Kobe Bryant AS	4.00	1.50
198	Tim Duncan AS	2.00	.75
199	Chris Webber AS	.60	.25
200	Anfernee Hardaway AS	1.00	.40
201	Latrell Sprewell AS	1.00	.40
202	Vince Carter AS	2.50	1.00
203	Allen Iverson AS	2.00	.75
204	Eddie Jones AS	1.00	.40
205	Antoine Walker AS	1.00	.40
206	Michael Finley AS	1.00	.40
207	Tracy McGrady AS	2.50	1.00
208	Jerry Stackhouse AS	1.00	.40
209	Glenn Robinson AS	1.00	.40
210	Allan Houston AS	.60	.25
211	Baron Davis AW	1.00	.40
212	Tony Parker AW	1.00	.40
213	Rick Fox AW	.60	.25
214	Steve Nash AW	1.00	.40
215	Jamaal Magloire AW	.60	.25
216	Wang Zhizhi AW	1.00	.40
217	Mengke Bateer AW	1.00	.40
218	Dirk Nowitzki AW	1.50	.60
219	Jake Tsakalidis AW	.25	.10
220	Adonal Foyle AW	.25	.10
221	Marko Jaric AW	.25	.10
222	Arvydas Sabonis AW	.25	.10
223	Eduardo Najera AW	.60	.25
224	Michael Olowokandi AW	.25	.10
225	Darius Miles AW	1.00	.40
226	Andrei Kirilenko AW	1.00	.40
227	Mamadou N'diaye AW	.25	.10
228	DeSagana Diop AW	.25	.10
229	Rasho Nesterovic AW	.60	.25
230	Pau Gasol AW	1.00	.40
231	Vladimir Radmanovic AW	.60	.25
232	Hidayet Turkoglu AW	.60	.25
233	Tim Duncan AW	2.00	.75
234	Peja Stojakovic AW	1.00	.40
235	Toni Kukoc AW	.60	.25
236	Zeljko Rebraca AW	.60	.25
237	Vlade Divac AW	.60	.25
238	Dikembe Mutombo AW	.60	.25
239	Shareef Abdur-Rahim AW	1.00	.40
240	Jason Richardson AW	1.00	.40

1998-99 Fleer Brilliants

	COMPLETE SET (125)		25.00
	COMPLETE SET w/o SP (100)	30.00	15.00
	COMMON CARD (1-100)	.25	.08
	COMMON ROOKIE (101-125)	.50	.20
1	Tim Duncan	1.50	.60
2	Dikembe Mutombo	.30	.10
3	Steve Nash	.50	.20
4	Charles Barkley	1.25	.50
5	Eddie Jones	.50	.20
6	Ray Allen	.50	.20
7	Stephon Marbury	.50	.20
8	Anfernee Hardaway	.50	.20
9	Gary Payton	.50	.20
10	Ron Mercer	.25	.08
11	Nick Van Exel	.50	.20
12	Brent Barry	.30	.10
13	Allan Houston	.30	.10
14	Avery Johnson	.25	.08
15	Shareef Abdur-Rahim	.50	.20
16	Rod Strickland	.25	.08
17	Vin Baker	.30	.10
18	Patrick Ewing	.50	.20
19	Maurice Taylor	.25	.08
20	Shawn Kemp	.30	.10
21	Michael Finley	.50	.20
22	Reggie Miller	.50	.20
23	Joe Smith	.30	.10
24	Toni Kukoc	.30	.10
25	Blue Edwards	.25	.08
26	Joe Dumars	.50	.20
27	Tom Gugliotta	.25	.08
28	Terrell Brandon	.30	.10
29	Erick Dampier	.25	.08
30	Antonio McDyess	.30	.10
31	Donyell Marshall	.30	.10
32	Jeff Hornacek	.30	.10
33	David Wesley	.25	.08
34	Derek Anderson	.40	.15
35	Ron Harper	.30	.10
36	John Starks	.30	.10
37	Kenny Anderson	.30	.10
38	Anthony Mason	.30	.10
39	Brevin Knight	.25	.08
40	Antoine Walker	.50	.20
41	Mookie Blaylock	.25	.08
42	LaPhonso Ellis	.25	.08
43	Tim Hardaway	.30	.10
44	Jim Jackson	.25	.08
45	Matt Maloney	.25	.08
46	Lamond Murray	.25	.08
47	Voshon Lenard	.25	.08
48	Isaiah Rider	.25	.08
49	Tracy Murray	.25	.08
50	Grant Hill	1.00	.40
51	Vlade Divac	.30	.10
52	Glenn Robinson	.30	.10
53	Tony Battie	.25	.08
54	Bobby Jackson	.25	.08
55	Jayson Williams	.25	.08
56	Doug Christie	.30	.10
57	Glen Rice	.30	.10
58	Tim Thomas	.50	.20
59	Lindsey Hunter	.25	.08
60	Scottie Pippen	1.50	.60
61	Marcus Camby	.30	.10
61B	K.Van Horn Promo	.30	.10
62	Clifford Robinson	.25	.08
63	John Wallace	.25	.08
64	Larry Johnson	.25	.08
65	Bryon Russell	.25	.08
66	Isaac Austin	.25	.08
67	Sam Cassell	.50	.20
68	Allen Iverson	2.00	.75
69	Chauncey Billups	.30	.10
70	Kobe Bryant	4.00	1.50
71	Kevin Willis	.25	.08
72	Jason Kidd	1.50	.60
73	Chris Webber	.50	.20
74	Rasheed Wallace	.50	.20
75	Karl Malone	.50	.20

#	Player		
76	Shawn Bradley	.25	.08
77	Kerry Kittles	.25	.08
78	Mitch Richmond	.30	.10
79	Antonio Daniels	.25	.08
80	Kevin Garnett	2.00	.75
81	Nick Anderson	.25	.08
82	David Robinson	.50	.20
83	Jamal Mashburn	.30	.10
84	Rodney Rogers	.25	.08
85	Michael Stewart	.25	.08
86	Rik Smits	.30	.10
87	Billy Owens	.25	.08
88	Damon Stoudamire	.30	.10
89	Theo Ratliff	.25	.08
90	Keith Van Horn	.50	.20
91	Hakeem Olajuwon	.50	.20
92	Alonzo Mourning	.30	.10
93	Steve Smith	.30	.10
94	Mark Jackson	.30	.10
95	Cedric Ceballos	.25	.08
96	Bryant Reeves	.25	.08
97	Juwan Howard	.30	.10
98	Detlef Schrempf	.30	.10
99	John Stockton	.50	.20
100	Shaquille O'Neal	2.50	1.00
101	Michael Olowokandi RC	1.25	.50
102	Mike Bibby RC	4.00	1.50
103	Raef LaFrentz RC	1.25	.50
104	Antawn Jamison RC	4.00	1.50
105	Vince Carter RC	8.00	3.00
106	Robert Traylor RC	1.00	.40
107	Jason Williams RC	3.00	1.25
108	Larry Hughes RC	2.50	1.00
109	Dirk Nowitzki RC	10.00	4.00
110	Paul Pierce RC	5.00	2.00
111	Bonzi Wells RC	3.00	1.25
112	Michael Doleac RC	1.00	.40
113	Keon Clark RC	1.25	.50
114	Michael Dickerson RC	1.50	.60
115	Matt Harpring RC	1.25	.50
116	Bryce Drew RC	1.00	.40
117	Pat Garrity RC	1.00	.40
118	Roshown McLeod RC	1.00	.40
119	Ricky Davis RC	2.50	1.00
120	Rashard Lewis RC	3.00	1.25
121	Tyronn Lue RC	1.00	.40
122	Al Harrington RC	2.00	.75
123	Corey Benjamin RC	1.00	.40
124	Felipe Lopez RC	1.00	.40
125	Korleone Young RC	1.00	.40

2001-02 Fleer Exclusive

#	Player		
	COMPLETE SET (149)	700.00	350.00
	COMP.SET w/o SP's (120)	60.00	30.00
	COMMON CARD (1-100)	.20	.10
	COMMON MO (101-120)	.25	.08
1	Vince Carter	2.50	1.00
2	Tracy McGrady	2.50	1.00
3	Dikembe Mutombo	.60	.25
4	Kobe Bryant	4.00	1.50
5	Baron Davis	1.00	.40
6	Alonzo Mourning	.60	.25
7	Allan Houston	.60	.25
8	Paul Pierce	1.00	.40
9	Jason Williams	.60	.25
10	Marcus Camby	.60	.25
11	Jason Terry	1.00	.40
12	Anfernee Hardaway	1.00	.40
13	Cuttino Mobley	.60	.25
14	Kenyon Martin	1.00	.40
15	Rashard Lewis	.60	.25
16	Darius Miles	1.00	.40
17	Jamal Mashburn	.60	.25
18	Derek Fisher	1.00	.40
19	Sam Cassell	1.00	.40
20	Antonio McDyess	.60	.25
21	John Stockton	1.00	.40
22	Andre Miller	.60	.25
23	Shawn Marion	1.00	.40
24	Steve Nash	1.00	.40
25	Kevin Garnett	2.00	.75
26	Peja Stojakovic	1.00	.40
27	Dirk Nowitzki	1.50	.60
28	Chris Webber	1.00	.40
29	Shaquille O'Neal	2.50	1.00
30	Stephon Marbury	1.00	.40
31	Eddie Jones	1.00	.40
32	Raef LaFrentz	.60	.25
33	Wally Szczerbiak	.60	.25
34	Richard Hamilton	.60	.25
35	Michael Finley	1.00	.40
36	Jason Kidd	1.50	.60
37	Courtney Alexander	.60	.25
38	Glenn Robinson	1.00	.40
39	Tim Duncan	2.00	.75
40	Steve Francis	1.00	.40
41	Stromile Swift	.60	.25
42	Desmond Mason	.60	.25
43	Shareef Abdur-Rahim	1.00	.40
44	Terrell Brandon	.60	.25
45	Antawn Jamison	1.00	.40
46	Latrell Sprewell	1.00	.40
47	Mateen Cleaves	.60	.25
48	Karl Malone	1.00	.40
49	Lamar Odom	1.00	.40
50	Grant Hill	1.00	.40
51	Reggie Miller	1.00	.40
52	Ray Allen	1.00	.40
53	David Robinson	1.00	.40
54	Elton Brand	1.00	.40
55	Jerry Stackhouse	1.00	.40
56	Brian Grant	.60	.25
57	Hakeem Olajuwon	1.00	.40
58	Jalen Rose	1.00	.40
59	Allen Iverson	2.00	.75
60	Darrell Armstrong	.30	.10
61	Joe Smith	.60	.25
62	Anthony Mason	.60	.25
63	Mike Bibby	1.00	.40
64	Gary Payton	1.00	.40
65	Glen Rice	.60	.25
66	Shandon Anderson	.30	.10
67	Antoine Walker	.60	.25
68	Tim Thomas	.60	.25
69	Patrick Ewing	1.00	.40
70	Ben Wallace	1.00	.40
71	Corey Maggette	.60	.25
72	Larry Hughes	.60	.25
73	Scottie Pippen	1.50	.60
74	Michael Doleac	.30	.10
75	Clifford Robinson	.30	.10
76	Aaron McKie	.60	.25
77	Marc Jackson	.60	.25
78	Tom Gugliotta	.30	.10
79	James Posey	.60	.25
80	Moochie Norris	.30	.10
81	Speedy Claxton	.30	.10
82	Michael Redd	1.00	.40
83	Rasheed Wallace	1.00	.40
84	Juwan Howard	.60	.25
85	Nick Van Exel	1.00	.40
86	Toni Kukoc	.60	.25
87	Jamaal Magloire	.60	.25
88	Jermaine O'Neal	1.00	.40
89	Anthony Peeler	.30	.10
90	Marcus Fizer	.60	.25
91	Jumaine Jones	.60	.25
92	Kendall Gill	.30	.10
93	Antonio Daniels	.30	.10
94	DerMarr Johnson	.30	.10
95	Mitch Richmond	.30	.10
96	Antonio Davis	.30	.10
97	Ron Mercer	.60	.25
98	Keyon Dooling	.60	.25
99	Morris Peterson	.60	.25
100	Derek Anderson	.60	.25
101	Allen Iverson MO	1.50	.60
102	Glenn Robinson MO	.50	.20
103	Tim Duncan MO	1.50	.60
104	Shaquille O'Neal MO	2.00	.75
105	Vince Carter MO	2.00	.75
106	Tracy McGrady MO	2.00	.75
107	Jason Kidd MO	1.25	.50
108	Karl Malone MO	1.00	.40
109	Michael Jordan MO	15.00	6.00
110	Shareef Abdur-Rahim MO	.75	.30
111	Grant Hill MO	.75	.30
112	Stephon Marbury MO	.75	.30
113	Michael Finley MO	.75	.30
114	Antoine Walker MO	.75	.30
115	Kobe Bryant MO	3.00	1.25
116	Dirk Nowitzki MO	1.25	.50
117	Alonzo Mourning MO	.50	.20
118	John Stockton MO	1.00	.40
119	Kevin Garnett MO	1.50	.60
120	Eddie Jones MO	.75	.30
121	Steven Hunter/500 RC	10.00	4.00
122	Tony Parker/500 RC	20.00	8.00
123	Zach Randolph/478 RC	20.00	8.00
124	R.Jefferson/500 RC	20.00	8.00
125	Kedrick Brown/433 RC	10.00	4.00
126	Kwame Brown/472 RC	15.00	6.00
127	B.Armstrong/500 RC	12.00	5.00
128	Pau Gasol/474 RC	40.00	15.00
129	Troy Murphy/500 RC	15.00	6.00
130	Rodney White/500 RC	12.00	5.00
131	Jamaal Tinsley/500 RC	12.00	5.00
132	Jeryl Sasser/500 RC	10.00	4.00
133	Eddie Griffin/500 RC	12.00	5.00
134	Michael Bradley/476 RC	10.00	4.00
135	V.Radmanovic/500 RC	12.00	5.00
136	J.Richardson/388 RC	25.00	10.00
137	Shane Battier/500 RC	12.00	5.00
138	Joe Johnson/300 RC	30.00	12.50
139	Andrei Kirilenko/500 RC	20.00	8.00
140	Kirk Haston/500 RC	10.00	4.00
141	Jason Collins/500 RC	10.00	4.00
142	Tyson Chandler/500 RC	20.00	8.00
143	DeSagana Diop/499 RC	12.00	5.00
144	Gerald Wallace/467 RC	15.00	6.00
145	Joseph Forte/450 RC	12.00	5.00
146	B.Haywood/500 RC	12.00	5.00
147	S.Dalembert/360 RC	10.00	4.00
148	Eddy Curry/500 RC	20.00	8.00
149	Primoz Brezec/500 RC	12.00	5.00

1999-00 Fleer Focus

#	Player		
	COMPLETE SET (150)	150.00	75.00
	COMPLETE SET w/o SP (100)	20.00	10.00
	COMMON CARD (1-100)	.25	.08
	COMMON ROOKIE (101-150)	1.25	.50
1	Anfernee Hardaway	.75	.30
2	Derek Anderson	.50	.20
3	Jayson Williams	.25	.08
4	Ron Mercer	.50	.20
5	Jerry Stackhouse	.75	.30
6	Tariq Abdul-Wahad	.25	.08
7	Sean Elliott	.50	.20
8	Lindsey Hunter	.25	.08
9	Larry Johnson	.50	.20
10	Steve Smith	.50	.20
11	Raef LaFrentz	.50	.20

❑ 12	Jalen Rose	.75	.30
❑ 13	Stephon Marbury	.75	.30
❑ 14	Detlef Schrempf	.50	.20
❑ 15	Rod Strickland	.25	.08
❑ 16	Paul Pierce	.75	.30
❑ 17	Maurice Taylor	.50	.20
❑ 18	Allen Iverson	1.50	.60
❑ 19	Mitch Richmond	.50	.20
❑ 20	Gary Trent	.25	.08
❑ 21	Reggie Miller	.75	.30
❑ 22	Kerry Kittles	.25	.08
❑ 23	Rasheed Wallace	.75	.30
❑ 24	Steve Nash	.75	.30
❑ 25	Scottie Pippen	1.25	.50
❑ 26	Joe Smith	.50	.20
❑ 27	Jason Williams	.75	.30
❑ 28	Michael Finley	.75	.30
❑ 29	Hakeem Olajuwon	.75	.30
❑ 30	Kevin Garnett	1.50	.60
❑ 31	Darrell Armstrong	.25	.08
❑ 32	David Robinson	.75	.30
❑ 33	Anthony Mason	.50	.20
❑ 34	Jamal Mashburn	.50	.20
❑ 35	Gary Payton	.75	.30
❑ 36	Bryon Russell	.25	.08
❑ 37	Cedric Ceballos	.50	.20
❑ 38	Michael Dickerson	.50	.20
❑ 39	Robert Traylor	.25	.08
❑ 40	Vin Baker	.50	.20
❑ 41	Shawn Kemp	.50	.20
❑ 42	Charles Barkley	1.00	.40
❑ 43	Glenn Robinson	.75	.30
❑ 44	Vince Carter	2.00	.75
❑ 45	Zydrunas Ilgauskas	.50	.20
❑ 46	Sam Cassell	.50	.20
❑ 47	Tracy McGrady	2.00	.75
❑ 48	Chris Mills	.25	.08
❑ 49	Antawn Jamison	1.25	.50
❑ 50	Nick Anderson	.25	.08
❑ 51	Avery Johnson	.25	.08
❑ 52	Brent Barry	.25	.08
❑ 53	Alonzo Mourning	.50	.20
❑ 54	Karl Malone	.75	.30
❑ 55	Toni Kukoc	.50	.20
❑ 56	Ray Allen	.75	.30
❑ 57	Charles Oakley	.25	.08
❑ 58	Cuttino Mobley	.75	.30
❑ 59	Kenny Anderson	.50	.20
❑ 60	Tom Gugliotta	.25	.08
❑ 61	Antoine Walker	.75	.30
❑ 62	Kobe Bryant	3.00	1.25
❑ 63	Larry Hughes	.75	.30
❑ 64	Vlade Divac	.50	.20
❑ 65	Juwan Howard	.50	.20
❑ 66	Isaiah Rider	.25	.08
❑ 67	Antonio McDyess	.50	.20
❑ 68	Rik Smits	.50	.20
❑ 69	Keith Van Horn	.75	.30
❑ 70	Doug Christie	.50	.20
❑ 71	Elden Campbell	.25	.08
❑ 72	Shaquille O'Neal	2.00	.75
❑ 73	Matt Geiger	.25	.08
❑ 74	Chris Webber	.75	.30
❑ 75	Troy Hudson	.25	.08
❑ 76	Eddie Jones	.75	.30
❑ 77	Tim Hardaway	.50	.20
❑ 78	Hersey Hawkins	.50	.20
❑ 79	Shareef Abdur-Rahim	.50	.20
❑ 80	Christian Laettner	.50	.20
❑ 81	Latrell Sprewell	.50	.20
❑ 82	Damon Stoudamire	.50	.20
❑ 83	Jason Caffey	.25	.08
❑ 84	Michael Olowokandi	.50	.20
❑ 85	Horace Grant	.50	.20
❑ 86	Grant Hill	.75	.30
❑ 87	Patrick Ewing	.75	.30
❑ 88	Clifford Robinson	.25	.08
❑ 89	Ricky Davis	.50	.20
❑ 90	Glen Rice	.50	.20
❑ 91	Matt Harpring	.75	.30
❑ 92	Mike Bibby	.75	.30
❑ 93	Dikembe Mutombo	.50	.20
❑ 94	Chris Mullin	.50	.20
❑ 95	Marcus Camby	.50	.20
❑ 96	Jason Kidd	1.25	.50
❑ 97	John Starks	.50	.20
❑ 98	Terrell Brandon	.50	.20
❑ 99	Tim Duncan	1.50	.60
❑ 100	John Stockton	.75	.30
❑ 101	Ron Artest RC	4.00	1.50
❑ 101A	Ron Artest SP	8.00	3.00
❑ 102	William Avery RC	2.50	1.00
❑ 102A	William Avery SP	6.00	2.50
❑ 103	Jonathan Bender RC	6.00	2.50
❑ 103A	Jonathan Bender SP	12.00	5.00
❑ 104	Cal Bowdler RC	2.00	.75
❑ 104A	Cal Bowdler SP	5.00	2.00
❑ 105	Elton Brand RC	10.00	4.00
❑ 105A	Elton Brand SP	20.00	8.00
❑ 106	Vonteego Cummings RC	2.50	1.00
❑ 106A	Vonteego Cummings SP	4.00	1.50
❑ 107	Baron Davis RC	6.00	2.50
❑ 107A	Baron Davis SP	12.00	5.00
❑ 108	Jeff Foster RC	2.00	.75
❑ 108A	Jeff Foster SP	4.00	1.50
❑ 109	Steve Francis RC	10.00	4.00
❑ 109A	Steve Francis SP	25.00	10.00
❑ 110	Devean George RC	3.00	1.25
❑ 110A	Devean George SP	6.00	2.50
❑ 111	Dion Glover RC	2.00	.75
❑ 111A	Dion Glover SP	4.00	1.50
❑ 112	Richard Hamilton RC	6.00	2.50
❑ 112A	Richard Hamilton SP	10.00	4.00
❑ 113	Tim James RC	2.00	.75
❑ 113A	Tim James SP	5.00	2.00
❑ 114	Trajan Langdon RC	2.50	1.00
❑ 114A	Trajan Langdon SP	5.00	2.00
❑ 115	Quincy Lewis RC	2.00	.75
❑ 115A	Quincy Lewis SP	4.00	1.50
❑ 116	Corey Maggette RC	6.00	2.50
❑ 116A	Corey Maggette SP	12.00	5.00
❑ 117	Shawn Marion RC	10.00	4.00
❑ 117A	Shawn Marion SP	20.00	8.00
❑ 118	Andre Miller RC	6.00	2.50
❑ 118A	Andre Miller SP	12.00	5.00
❑ 119	Lamar Odom RC	8.00	3.00
❑ 119A	Lamar Odom SP	15.00	6.00
❑ 120	Scott Padgett RC	2.00	.75
❑ 120A	Scott Padgett SP	4.00	1.50
❑ 121	James Posey RC	4.00	1.50
❑ 121A	James Posey SP	8.00	3.00
❑ 122	A.Radojevic RC	1.25	.50
❑ 122A	Aleksandar Radojevic SP	2.50	1.00
❑ 123	Wally Szczerbiak RC	6.00	2.50
❑ 123A	Wally Szczerbiak SP	12.00	5.00
❑ 124	Jason Terry RC	4.00	1.50
❑ 124A	Jason Terry SP	8.00	3.00
❑ 125	Kenny Thomas RC	2.50	1.00
❑ 125A	Kenny Thomas SP	4.00	1.50
❑ 126	Jumaine Jones RC	2.50	1.00
❑ 126A	Jumaine Jones SP	3.00	1.25
❑ 127	Rick Hughes RC	1.25	.50
❑ 127A	Rick Hughes SP	2.50	1.00
❑ 128	John Celestand RC	2.00	.75
❑ 128A	John Celestand SP	4.00	1.50
❑ 129	Adrian Griffin RC	2.00	.75
❑ 129A	Adrian Griffin SP	3.00	1.25
❑ 130	Michael Ruffin RC	1.50	.60
❑ 130A	Michael Ruffin SP	3.00	1.25
❑ 131	Chris Herren RC	1.25	.50
❑ 131A	Chris Herren SP	2.50	1.00
❑ 132	Evan Eschmeyer RC	1.25	.50
❑ 132A	Evan Eschmeyer SP	2.50	1.00
❑ 133	Tim Young RC	1.25	.50
❑ 133A	Tim Young SP	2.50	1.00
❑ 134	Obinna Ekezie RC	1.50	.60
❑ 134A	Obinna Ekezie SP	3.00	1.25
❑ 135	Laron Profit RC	2.00	.75
❑ 135A	Laron Profit SP	4.00	1.50
❑ 136	A.J. Bramlett RC	1.25	.50
❑ 136A	A.J. Bramlett SP	2.50	1.00
❑ 137	Eddie Robinson RC	4.00	1.50
❑ 137A	Eddie Robinson SP	8.00	3.00
❑ 138	Ryan Bowen RC	1.25	.50
❑ 138A	Ryan Bowen SP	2.50	1.00
❑ 139	Chucky Atkins RC	2.50	1.00
❑ 139A	Chucky Atkins SP	5.00	2.00
❑ 140	Ryan Robertson RC	1.50	.60
❑ 140A	Ryan Robertson SP	3.00	1.25
❑ 141	Derrick Dial RC	1.25	.50
❑ 141A	Derrick Dial SP	2.50	1.00
❑ 142	Todd MacCulloch RC	2.00	.75
❑ 142A	Todd MacCulloch SP	4.00	1.50
❑ 143	DeMarco Johnson RC	1.50	.60
❑ 143A	DeMarco Johnson SP	3.00	1.25
❑ 144	Anthony Carter RC	4.00	1.50
❑ 144A	Anthony Carter SP	10.00	4.00
❑ 145	Lazaro Borrell RC	1.25	.50
❑ 145A	Lazaro Borrell SP	2.50	1.00
❑ 146	Rafer Alston RC	2.50	1.00
❑ 146A	Rafer Alston SP	5.00	2.00
❑ 147	Nikita Morgunov RC	1.25	.50
❑ 147A	Nikita Morgunov SP	2.50	1.00
❑ 148	Rodney Buford RC	1.25	.50
❑ 148A	Rodney Buford SP	2.50	1.00
❑ 149	Milt Palacio RC	1.25	.50
❑ 149A	Milt Palacio SP	2.50	1.00
❑ 150	Jermaine Jackson RC	1.25	.50
❑ 150A	Jermaine Jackson SP	2.50	1.00

2000-01 Fleer Focus

❑ COMPLETE SET w/o RC (200)		40.00	20.00
❑ COMMON CARD (1-180/217-236)		.25	.08
❑ COMMON ROOKIE (181-216)		.50	.20
❑ 1	Vince Carter	2.00	.75
❑ 2	Shawn Marion	.75	.30
❑ 3	Muggsy Bogues	.50	.20
❑ 4	Dikembe Mutombo	.50	.20
❑ 5	Stephon Marbury	.75	.30
❑ 6	Michael Dickerson	.50	.20
❑ 7	Andre Miller	.50	.20
❑ 8	Toni Kukoc	.50	.20
❑ 9	Nick Van Exel	.75	.30
❑ 10	Aaron Williams	.25	.08
❑ 11	Derrick Coleman	.25	.08
❑ 12	Wally Szczerbiak	.50	.20
❑ 13	Rodney Rogers	.25	.08
❑ 14	Tom Gugliotta	.25	.08
❑ 15	Vonteego Cummings	.25	.08
❑ 16	Cedric Ceballos	.25	.08
❑ 17	Malik Rose	.25	.08
❑ 18	Shawn Bradley	.25	.08
❑ 19	Shandon Anderson	.25	.08
❑ 20	Jacque Vaughn	.25	.08
❑ 21	Jamie Feick	.25	.08
❑ 22	Shawn Kemp	.50	.20
❑ 23	Monty Williams	.25	.08
❑ 24	Allan Houston	.50	.20
❑ 25	Chauncey Billups	.50	.20
❑ 26	Vlade Divac	.50	.20
❑ 27	Othella Harrington	.25	.08
❑ 28	Dale Davis	.25	.08
❑ 29	Charlie Ward	.25	.08
❑ 30	Hakeem Olajuwon	.75	.30
❑ 31	Ray Allen	.75	.30
❑ 32	Lamar Odom	.75	.30
❑ 33	Shaquille O'Neal	2.00	.75
❑ 34	Chris Childs	.25	.08
❑ 35	Nick Anderson	.25	.08
❑ 36	Keon Clark	.50	.20
❑ 37	Danny Fortson	.25	.08
❑ 38	Sam Mitchell	.25	.08
❑ 39	Travis Best	.25	.08
❑ 40	Chris Webber	.75	.30
❑ 41	Brent Barry	.50	.20
❑ 42	Scottie Pippen	1.25	.50
❑ 43	Reggie Miller	.75	.30
❑ 44	Bryant Reeves	.25	.08
❑ 45	Bobby Jackson	.50	.20
❑ 46	Antonio McDyess	.50	.20

❏ 47	Elden Campbell	.25	.08	❏ 133	Chris Carr	.25	.08	❏ 219	Grant Hill 20	.75	.30
❏ 48	Kenny Anderson	.50	.20	❏ 134	Jonathan Bender	.50	.20	❏ 220	Vince Carter 20	.75	.30
❏ 49	Christian Laettner	.25	.20	❏ 135	Paul Pierce	.75	.30	❏ 221	Karl Malone 20	.75	.30
❏ 50	Darrell Armstrong	.25	.08	❏ 136	Dan Majerle	.50	.20	❏ 222	Chris Webber 20	.50	.20
❏ 51	Vinny Del Negro	.25	.08	❏ 137	Ron Artest	.50	.20	❏ 223	Gary Payton 20	.50	.20
❏ 52	Quincy Lewis	.25	.08	❏ 138	Jermaine O'Neal	.75	.30	❏ 224	Jerry Stackhouse 20	.50	.20
❏ 53	Peja Stojakovic	.75	.30	❏ 139	Chris Whitney	.25	.08	❏ 225	Tim Duncan 20	.75	.30
❏ 54	Matt Geiger	.25	.08	❏ 140	Anthony Carter	.50	.20	❏ 226	Kevin Garnett 20	.60	.25
❏ 55	Larry Hughes	.50	.20	❏ 141	Gary Payton	.75	.30	❏ 227	Michael Finley 20	.50	.20
❏ 56	Tracy McGrady	2.00	.75	❏ 142	Kevin Garnett	1.50	.60	❏ 228	Kobe Bryant 20	1.25	.50
❏ 57	Tim Hardaway	.50	.20	❏ 143	Kevin Willis	.25	.08	❏ 229	Stephon Marbury 20	.50	.20
❏ 58	Brevin Knight	.25	.08	❏ 144	Charles Oakley	.25	.08	❏ 230	Ray Allen 20	.50	.20
❏ 59	Michael Finley	.75	.30	❏ 145	Larry Johnson	.50	.20	❏ 231	Alonzo Mourning 20	.50	.20
❏ 60	Jason Kidd	1.25	.50	❏ 146	Bonzi Wells	.50	.20	❏ 232	Glenn Robinson 20	.25	.08
❏ 61	Matt Harpring	.75	.30	❏ 147	Clifford Robinson	.25	.08	❏ 233	Antoine Walker 20	.50	.20
❏ 62	Antawn Jamison	.75	.30	❏ 148	Chucky Atkins	.25	.08	❏ 234	Shareef Abdur-Rahim 20	.50	.20
❏ 63	Wesley Person	.25	.08	❏ 149	Brian Grant	.50	.20	❏ 235	Elton Brand 20	.50	.20
❏ 64	Antonio Davis	.25	.08	❏ 150	Voshon Lenard	.25	.08	❏ 236	Eddie Jones 20	.75	.30
❏ 65	Roshown McLeod	.25	.08	❏ 151	Antoine Walker	.75	.30				
❏ 66	Anthony Peeler	.25	.08	❏ 152	Cuttino Mobley	.50	.20		**2001-02 Fleer Focus**		
❏ 67	Grant Hill	.75	.30	❏ 153	Robert Horry	.50	.20				
❏ 68	Michael Olowokandi	.25	.08	❏ 154	Tracy Murray	.25	.08				
❏ 69	Kerry Kittles	.25	.08	❏ 155	Kobe Bryant	3.00	1.25				
❏ 70	Elton Brand	.75	.30	❏ 156	Joe Smith	.50	.20				
❏ 71	Tariq Abdul-Wahad	.25	.08	❏ 157	Jaren Jackson	.25	.08				
❏ 72	Aaron McKie	.50	.20	❏ 158	Scott Williams	.25	.08				
❏ 73	Andrew DeClercq	.25	.08	❏ 159	Allen Iverson	1.50	.60				
❏ 74	Anfernee Hardaway	.75	.30	❏ 160	Rashard Lewis	.50	.20				
❏ 75	Bimbo Coles	.25	.08	❏ 161	Chris Mills	.25	.08				
❏ 76	Terrell Brandon	.50	.20	❏ 162	Karl Malone	.75	.30				
❏ 77	Jalen Rose	.75	.30	❏ 163	John Amaechi	.25	.08				
❏ 78	Radoslav Nesterovic	.50	.20	❏ 164	Jason Terry	.75	.30				
❏ 79	Howard Eisley	.25	.08	❏ 165	Ruben Patterson	.50	.20				
❏ 80	Steve Smith	.50	.20	❏ 166	Austin Croshere	.50	.20				
❏ 81	Arvydas Sabonis	.50	.20	❏ 167	Maurice Taylor	.25	.08				
❏ 82	Jim Jackson	.50	.20	❏ 168	Rod Strickland	.25	.08				
❏ 83	Corey Maggette	.50	.20	❏ 169	Clarence Weatherspoon	.25	.08		COMP.SET w/o SP's (100)	40.00	20.00
❏ 84	James Posey	.50	.20	❏ 170	Lindsey Hunter	.25	.08	❏ 1	COMMON CARD 1-100	.25	.08
❏ 85	LaPhonso Ellis	.25	.08	❏ 171	David Wesley	.25	.08	❏ 1	COMMON ROOKIE (101-130)	2.00	.75
❏ 86	Eric Snow	.50	.20	❏ 172	Jerry Stackhouse	.75	.30	❏ 1	Vince Carter	2.00	.75
❏ 87	Mikki Moore	.25	.08	❏ 173	Scott Burrell	.25	.08	❏ 2	Steve Nash	.75	.30
❏ 88	Baron Davis	.75	.30	❏ 174	John Stockton	.75	.30	❏ 3	Anthony Mason	.50	.20
❏ 89	Jason Williams	.50	.20	❏ 175	Vitaly Potapenko	.25	.08	❏ 4	Avery Johnson	.25	.08
❏ 90	Mike Bibby	.75	.30	❏ 176	Dirk Nowitzki	1.25	.50	❏ 5	Peja Stojakovic	.75	.30
❏ 91	Marcus Camby	.50	.20	❏ 177	Vin Baker	.50	.20	❏ 6	Shaquille O'Neal	2.00	.75
❏ 92	Bryon Russell	.25	.08	❏ 178	Rick Fox	.50	.20	❏ 7	Jason Kidd	1.25	.50
❏ 93	Steve Francis	.75	.30	❏ 179	Mookie Blaylock	.25	.08	❏ 8	Steve Smith	.50	.20
❏ 94	Sam Cassell	.75	.30	❏ 180	Felipe Lopez	.25	.08	❏ 9	Kobe Bryant	3.00	1.25
❏ 95	Rasheed Wallace	.75	.30	❏ 181	Chris Mihm A RC	.50	.20	❏ 10	Eddie Robinson	.50	.20
❏ 96	Keith Van Horn	.75	.30	❏ 182	Mamadou N'Diaye A RC	.50	.20	❏ 11	Allan Houston	.50	.20
❏ 97	Eddie Jones	.75	.30	❏ 183	Joel Przybilla A RC	.50	.20	❏ 12	Larry Hughes	.50	.20
❏ 98	Corliss Williamson	.50	.20	❏ 184	Jamaal Magloire A RC	.50	.20	❏ 13	Gary Payton	.75	.30
❏ 99	Ron Mercer	.50	.20	❏ 185	Iakovos Tsakalidis A RC	.50	.20	❏ 14	Alonzo Mourning	.50	.20
❏ 100	Sean Elliott	.50	.20	❏ 186	Etan Thomas A RC	.50	.20	❏ 15	Baron Davis	.75	.30
❏ 101	Shareef Abdur-Rahim	.75	.30	❏ 187	Mark Madsen A RC	.50	.20	❏ 16	Speedy Claxton	.50	.20
❏ 102	Glen Rice	.50	.20	❏ 188	Hanno Mottola B RC	1.00	.40	❏ 17	Hakeem Olajuwon	.75	.30
❏ 103	Patrick Ewing	.75	.30	❏ 189	Donnell Harvey B RC	.50	.20	❏ 18	Anthony Carter	.50	.20
❏ 104	Adrian Griffin	.25	.08	❏ 190	Jason Collier B RC	1.00	.40	❏ 19	Raef LaFrentz	.50	.20
❏ 105	David Robinson	.75	.30	❏ 191	Eduardo Najera B RC	1.50	.60	❏ 20	Dikembe Mutombo	.50	.20
❏ 106	Isaac Austin	.25	.08	❏ 192	Jerome Moiso B RC	.50	.20	❏ 21	Moochie Norris	.25	.08
❏ 107	Anthony Mason	.50	.20	❏ 193	Mateen Cleaves C RC	.50	.20	❏ 22	Karl Malone	.75	.30
❏ 108	P.J. Brown	.25	.08	❏ 194	Keyon Dooling C RC	.50	.20	❏ 23	Darrell Armstrong	.25	.08
❏ 109	Kendall Gill	.25	.08	❏ 195	Speedy Claxton C RC	.50	.20	❏ 24	Allen Iverson	1.50	.60
❏ 110	Tyrone Nesby	.25	.08	❏ 196	Erick Barkley C RC	.50	.20	❏ 25	Danny Fortson	.25	.08
❏ 111	Damon Stoudamire	.50	.20	❏ 197	A.J. Guyton C RC	.50	.20	❏ 26	Antonio Davis	.50	.20
❏ 112	Latrell Sprewell	.75	.30	❏ 198	Jamal Crawford C RC	.60	.25	❏ 27	Eddie Jones	.75	.30
❏ 113	Tim Duncan	1.50	.60	❏ 199	Dan Langhi D RC	.50	.20	❏ 28	Patrick Ewing	.75	.30
❏ 114	Glenn Robinson	.50	.20	❏ 200	Desmond Mason D RC	.50	.20	❏ 29	Stephon Marbury	.75	.30
❏ 115	John Wallace	.25	.08	❏ 201	Chris Porter D RC	.90	.20	❏ 30	Cuttino Mobley	.50	.20
❏ 116	Erick Strickland	.25	.08	❏ 202	Corey Hightower D RC	.50	.20	❏ 31	Morris Peterson	.50	.20
❏ 117	Doug Christie	.50	.20	❏ 203	Morris Peterson D RC	4.00	1.50	❏ 32	Glenn Robinson	.75	.30
❏ 118	Juwan Howard	.50	.20	❏ 204	Mark Karcher D RC	.50	.20	❏ 33	Paul Pierce	.75	.30
❏ 119	Tim Thomas	.50	.20	❏ 205	Courtney Alexander E RC	1.00	.40	❏ 34	Shawn Marion	.75	.30
❏ 120	Tyrone Hill	.25	.08	❏ 206	Quentin Richardson E RC	4.00	1.50	❏ 35	Jermaine O'Neal	.75	.30
❏ 121	Avery Johnson	.25	.08	❏ 207	DeShawn Stevenson E RC	.50		❏ 36	Donyell Marshall	.50	.20
❏ 122	Jerome Williams	.25	.08	❏ 208	Michael Redd E RC	2.00	.75	❏ 37	Chauncey Billups	.50	.20
❏ 123	Mitch Richmond	.50	.20	❏ 209	Chris Carrawell E RC	.50	.20	❏ 38	Tracy McGrady	2.00	.75
❏ 124	Hersey Hawkins	.25	.08	❏ 210	Hidayet Turkoglu E RC	6.00	2.50	❏ 39	Vlade Divac	.50	.20
❏ 125	Donyell Marshall	.50	.20	❏ 211	Kenyon Martin F RC	10.00	4.00	❏ 40	Lamar Odom	.75	.30
❏ 126	Derek Anderson	.50	.20	❏ 212	Marcus Fizer F RC	4.00	1.50	❏ 41	Chris Mihm	.50	.20
❏ 127	Jamal Mashburn	.50	.20	❏ 213	Darius Miles F RC	8.00	3.00	❏ 42	Kenyon Martin	.75	.30
❏ 128	Richard Hamilton	.50	.20	❏ 214	Mike Miller F RC	6.00	2.50	❏ 43	Antonio McDyess	.50	.20
❏ 129	Alonzo Mourning	.50	.20	❏ 215	DerMarr Johnson F RC	.50	.20	❏ 44	Mike Bibby	.75	.30
❏ 130	Kelvin Cato	.25	.08	❏ 216	Stromile Swift F RC	6.00	2.50	❏ 45	Darius Miles	.75	.30
❏ 131	Lamond Murray	.25	.08	❏ 217	Shaquille O'Neal 20	.75	.30				
❏ 132	Bo Outlaw	.25	.08	❏ 218	Allen Iverson 20	.60	.25				

❑ 46	Wesley Person	.25	.08
❑ 47	Mark Jackson	.50	.20
❑ 48	Nick Van Exel	.75	.30
❑ 49	Tim Duncan	1.50	.60
❑ 50	Sam Cassell	.75	.30
❑ 51	Jason Terry	.75	.30
❑ 52	Bonzi Wells	.50	.20
❑ 53	Al Harrington	.50	.20
❑ 54	Richard Hamilton	.50	.20
❑ 55	Wally Szczerbiak	.50	.20
❑ 56	Toni Kukoc	.50	.20
❑ 57	Rasheed Wallace	.75	.30
❑ 58	Reggie Miller	.75	.30
❑ 59	Courtney Alexander	.50	.20
❑ 60	Terrell Brandon	.50	.20
❑ 61	Dirk Nowitzki	1.25	.50
❑ 62	Chris Webber	.75	.30
❑ 63	Lindsey Hunter	.25	.08
❑ 64	Andre Miller	.50	.20
❑ 65	Clifford Robinson	.25	.08
❑ 66	David Robinson	.75	.30
❑ 67	Stromile Swift	.50	.20
❑ 68	Nazr Mohammed	.25	.08
❑ 69	Kurt Thomas	.50	.20
❑ 70	Corliss Williamson	.50	.20
❑ 71	Rashard Lewis	.50	.20
❑ 72	Lorenzen Wright	.25	.08
❑ 73	David Wesley	.25	.08
❑ 74	Derrick Coleman	.25	.08
❑ 75	Jerry Stackhouse	.75	.30
❑ 76	Antonio Daniels	.25	.08
❑ 77	Mitch Richmond	.50	.20
❑ 78	Ron Mercer	.50	.20
❑ 79	Latrell Sprewell	.75	.30
❑ 80	Antawn Jamison	.75	.30
❑ 81	Desmond Mason	.50	.20
❑ 82	Jason Williams	.50	.20
❑ 83	Jamal Mashburn	.50	.20
❑ 84	Grant Hill	.75	.30
❑ 85	Elton Brand	.75	.30
❑ 86	Brian Grant	.50	.20
❑ 87	Antoine Walker	.75	.30
❑ 88	Anfernee Hardaway	.75	.30
❑ 89	Steve Francis	.75	.30
❑ 90	John Stockton	.75	.30
❑ 91	Ray Allen	.75	.30
❑ 92	Tim Hardaway	.50	.20
❑ 93	Derek Anderson	.50	.20
❑ 94	Jalen Rose	.75	.30
❑ 95	Michael Jordan	15.00	6.00
❑ 96	Kevin Garnett	1.50	.60
❑ 97	Shareef Abdur-Rahim	.75	.30
❑ 98	Tony Delk	.50	.20
❑ 99	Quentin Richardson	.50	.20
❑ 100	Michael Finley	.75	.30
❑ 101	Jamaal Tinsley RC	3.00	1.25
❑ 102	Zach Randolph RC	6.00	2.50
❑ 103	Kedrick Brown RC	2.00	.75
❑ 104	Kirk Haston RC	2.00	.75
❑ 105	Tyson Chandler RC	6.00	2.50
❑ 106	Shane Battier RC	3.00	1.25
❑ 107	Richard Jefferson RC	3.00	1.25
❑ 108	Gerald Wallace RC	4.00	1.50
❑ 109	DeSagana Diop RC	2.00	.75
❑ 110	R.Bountje-Bountje RC	2.00	.75
❑ 111	Rodney White RC	2.50	1.00
❑ 112	Eddie Griffin RC	2.50	1.00
❑ 113	Pau Gasol RC	8.00	3.00
❑ 114	Tony Parker RC	8.00	3.00
❑ 115	Kwame Brown RC	4.00	1.50
❑ 116	Vladimir Radmanovic RC	2.50	1.00
❑ 117	Troy Murphy RC	4.00	1.50
❑ 118	Loren Woods RC	2.00	.75
❑ 119	Joe Johnson RC	6.00	2.50
❑ 120	Brandon Armstrong RC	2.50	1.00
❑ 121	Trenton Hassell RC	3.00	1.25
❑ 122	Andrei Kirilenko RC	6.00	2.50
❑ 123	Jason Richardson RC	6.00	2.50
❑ 124	Jason Collins RC	2.00	.75
❑ 125	Jeryl Sasser RC	2.00	.75
❑ 126	Michael Bradley RC	2.00	.75
❑ 127	Eddy Curry RC	6.00	2.50
❑ 128	Joseph Forte RC	5.00	2.00
❑ 129	Brendan Haywood RC	2.50	1.00
❑ 130	Zeljko Rebraca RC	2.00	.75

2003-04 Fleer Focus

❑	COMP.SET w/o SP's	30.00	12.50
❑	COMMON ROOKIE (121-160)	6.00	2.50
❑ 1	Allan Houston	.50	.20
❑ 2	Manu Ginobili	.75	.30
❑ 3	Allen Iverson	1.50	.60
❑ 4	Kenyon Martin	.75	.30
❑ 5	Rasho Nesterovic	.50	.20
❑ 6	Tracy McGrady	2.00	.75
❑ 7	Drew Gooden	.50	.20
❑ 8	Tony Parker	.75	.30
❑ 9	Troy Murphy	.75	.30
❑ 10	Alonzo Mourning	.50	.20
❑ 11	Rasual Butler	.50	.20
❑ 12	Alvin Williams	.20	.08
❑ 13	Troy Hudson	.20	.08
❑ 14	Gary Payton	.75	.30
❑ 15	Tyson Chandler	.75	.30
❑ 16	Ray Allen	.75	.30
❑ 17	Amare Stoudemire	2.00	.75
❑ 18	Chauncey Billups	.50	.20
❑ 19	Gilbert Arenas	.75	.30
❑ 20	Eddie Jones	.75	.30
❑ 21	Vince Carter	2.00	.75
❑ 22	Kobe Bryant	3.00	1.25
❑ 23	Reggie Miller	.75	.30
❑ 24	Vincent Yarbrough	.20	.08
❑ 25	Kevin Garnett	1.50	.60
❑ 26	Andre Miller	.50	.20
❑ 27	Glenn Robinson	.75	.30
❑ 28	Kurt Thomas	.50	.20
❑ 29	Vladimir Radmanovic	.20	.08
❑ 30	Richard Jefferson	.50	.20
❑ 31	Andrei Kirilenko	.75	.30
❑ 32	Wally Szczerbiak	.50	.20
❑ 33	Gordan Giricek	.50	.20
❑ 34	Kwame Brown	.50	.20
❑ 35	Yao Ming	2.00	.75
❑ 36	Devean George	.50	.20
❑ 37	Richard Hamilton	.50	.20
❑ 38	Anfernee Hardaway	.75	.30
❑ 39	Grant Hill	.75	.30
❑ 40	Zach Randolph	.75	.30
❑ 41	Dirk Nowitzki	1.25	.50
❑ 42	Zydrunas Ilgauskas	.50	.20
❑ 43	Antawn Jamison	.75	.30
❑ 44	J.R. Bremer	.20	.08
❑ 45	Latrell Sprewell	.75	.30
❑ 46	Ron Artest	.50	.20
❑ 47	Antoine Walker	.75	.30
❑ 48	Eddy Curry	.50	.20
❑ 49	Larry Hughes	.50	.20
❑ 50	Jalen Rose	.75	.30
❑ 51	Matt Harpring	.75	.30
❑ 52	Sam Cassell	.75	.30
❑ 53	Antonio McDyess	.50	.20
❑ 54	Jamaal Tinsley	.50	.20
❑ 55	Mehmet Okur	.20	.08
❑ 56	Scottie Pippen	1.25	.50
❑ 57	Antonio Davis	.20	.08
❑ 58	Jamaal Magloire	.20	.08
❑ 59	Michael Olowokandi	.20	.08
❑ 60	Shane Battier	.75	.30
❑ 61	Desmond Mason	.50	.20
❑ 62	Baron Davis	.75	.30
❑ 63	Jamal Mashburn	.50	.20
❑ 64	Michael Redd	.75	.30

❑ 65	Shaquille O'Neal	2.00	.75
❑ 66	Ben Wallace	.75	.30
❑ 67	Jason Terry	.75	.30
❑ 68	Michael Finley	.75	.30
❑ 69	Shareef Abdur-Rahim	.75	.30
❑ 70	Bobby Jackson	.50	.20
❑ 71	Jason Williams	.50	.20
❑ 72	Mike Bibby	.75	.30
❑ 73	Shawn Marion	.75	.30
❑ 74	Ricky Davis	.75	.30
❑ 75	Bonzi Wells	.50	.20
❑ 76	Jason Kidd	1.25	.50
❑ 77	Mike Miller	.75	.30
❑ 78	Stephen Jackson	.20	.08
❑ 79	Brad Miller	.75	.30
❑ 80	Jason Richardson	.75	.30
❑ 81	Mike Dunleavy Jr.	.50	.20
❑ 82	Stephon Marbury	.75	.30
❑ 83	Brian Grant	.50	.20
❑ 84	Jay Williams	.50	.20
❑ 85	Morris Peterson	.50	.20
❑ 86	Steve Nash	.75	.30
❑ 87	Carlos Boozer	.75	.30
❑ 88	Jermaine O'Neal	.75	.30
❑ 89	Nene	.50	.20
❑ 90	Eric Snow	.50	.20
❑ 91	Steve Francis	.75	.30
❑ 92	Caron Butler	.75	.30
❑ 93	Jerry Stackhouse	.75	.30
❑ 94	Nick Van Exel	.75	.30
❑ 95	Tayshaun Prince	.50	.20
❑ 96	Calbert Cheaney	.20	.08
❑ 97	Pau Gasol	.75	.30
❑ 98	Theo Ratliff	.50	.20
❑ 99	Chris Webber	.75	.30
❑ 100	Juan Dixon	.50	.20
❑ 101	Paul Pierce	.75	.30
❑ 102	Tim Thomas	.50	.20
❑ 103	Eddie Griffin	.50	.20
❑ 104	Corey Maggette	.50	.20
❑ 105	Juwan Howard	.50	.20
❑ 106	Peja Stojakovic	.75	.30
❑ 107	Tim Duncan	1.50	.60
❑ 108	Keith Van Horn	.75	.30
❑ 109	Cuttino Mobley	.50	.20
❑ 110	Kareem Rush	.50	.20
❑ 111	Predrag Drobnjak	.20	.08
❑ 112	Tony Delk	.20	.08
❑ 113	Dajuan Wagner	.50	.20
❑ 114	Karl Malone	.75	.30
❑ 115	Rashard Lewis	.50	.20
❑ 116	David Wesley	.20	.08
❑ 117	Rasheed Wallace	.75	.30
❑ 118	Derrick Coleman	.20	.08
❑ 119	Donnell Harvey	.20	.08
❑ 120	Elton Brand	.75	.30
❑ 121	Carmelo Anthony RC	25.00	10.00
❑ 122	Keith Bogans RC	6.00	2.50
❑ 123	Leandro Barbosa RC	10.00	4.00
❑ 124	Troy Bell RC	6.00	2.50
❑ 125	Chris Bosh RC	15.00	6.00
❑ 126	Zarko Cabarkapa RC	6.00	2.50
❑ 127	Jason Kapono RC	6.00	2.50
❑ 128	Nick Collison RC	6.00	2.50
❑ 129	Boris Diaw-Riffiod RC	6.00	2.50
❑ 130	Marcus Banks RC	6.00	2.50
❑ 131	T.J. Ford RC	10.00	4.00
❑ 132	Reece Gaines RC	6.00	2.50
❑ 133	Travis Hansen RC	6.00	2.50
❑ 134	Jarvis Hayes RC	6.00	2.50
❑ 135	Kirk Hinrich RC	12.00	5.00
❑ 136	Josh Howard RC	8.00	3.00
❑ 137	LeBron James RC	60.00	30.00
❑ 138	Dahntay Jones RC	6.00	2.50
❑ 139	Chris Kaman RC	6.00	2.50
❑ 140	Maciej Lampe RC	6.00	2.50
❑ 141	Darko Milicic RC	12.00	5.00
❑ 142	Travis Outlaw RC	6.00	2.50
❑ 143	Mickael Pietrus RC	6.00	2.50
❑ 144	Rick Rickert RC	6.00	2.50
❑ 145	Luke Ridnour RC	10.00	4.00
❑ 146	Sofoklis Schortsanitis RC	8.00	3.00
❑ 147	Mike Sweetney RC	6.00	2.50
❑ 148	Dwyane Wade RC	25.00	10.00
❑ 149	Luke Walton RC	6.00	2.50
❑ 150	David West RC	6.00	2.50

❑ 151	Zoran Planinic RC	6.00 2.50
❑ 152	Ndudi Ebi RC	6.00 2.50
❑ 153	Aleksandar Pavlovic RC	6.00 2.50
❑ 154	Kendrick Perkins RC	6.00 2.50
❑ 155	Maurice Williams RC	6.00 2.50
❑ 156	Jerome Beasley RC	6.00 2.50
❑ 157	Slavko Vranes RC	6.00 2.50
❑ 158	Zaur Pachulia RC	6.00 2.50
❑ 159	Carlos Delfino RC	6.00 2.50
❑ 160	Brian Cook RC	6.00 2.50

1999-00 Fleer Force

❑ COMPLETE SET (235)		250.00 125.00
❑ COMPLETE SET w/o RC (200)		30.00 15.00
❑ COMMON CARD (1-200)		.25 .08
❑ COMMON ROOKIE (201-235)		3.00 1.25
❑ 1	Vince Carter	2.00 .75
❑ 2	Kobe Bryant	3.00 1.25
❑ 3	Keith Van Horn	.75 .30
❑ 4	Tim Duncan	1.50 .60
❑ 5	Grant Hill	.75 .30
❑ 6	Kevin Garnett	1.50 .60
❑ 7	Anfernee Hardaway	.75 .30
❑ 8	Jason Williams	.75 .30
❑ 9	Paul Pierce	.75 .30
❑ 10	Mookie Blaylock	.25 .08
❑ 11	Shawn Bradley	.25 .08
❑ 12	Kenny Anderson	.50 .20
❑ 13	Chauncey Billups	.25 .08
❑ 14	Elden Campbell	.25 .08
❑ 15	Jason Caffey	.25 .08
❑ 16	Brent Barry	.50 .20
❑ 17	Charles Barkley	1.00 .40
❑ 18	Derek Anderson	.50 .20
❑ 19	Darrick Martin	.25 .08
❑ 20	Michael Curry	.25 .08
❑ 21	Rick Fox	.50 .20
❑ 22	Antonio Davis	.25 .08
❑ 23	Terrell Brandon	.50 .20
❑ 24	P.J. Brown	.25 .08
❑ 25	Toby Bailey	.25 .08
❑ 26	Ray Allen	.75 .30
❑ 27	Brian Grant	.50 .20
❑ 28	Scott Burrell	.25 .08
❑ 29	Tariq Abdul-Wahad	.25 .08
❑ 30	Marcus Camby	.50 .20
❑ 31	John Stockton	.75 .30
❑ 32	Nick Anderson	.25 .08
❑ 33	Jamie Feick RC	3.00 1.25
❑ 34	Matt Geiger	.25 .08
❑ 35	Vin Baker	.50 .20
❑ 36	Dee Brown	.25 .08
❑ 37	Shandon Anderson	.25 .08
❑ 38	Vernon Maxwell	.25 .08
❑ 39	Shareef Abdur-Rahim	.75 .30
❑ 40	LaPhonso Ellis	.25 .08
❑ 41	Cedric Ceballos	.25 .08
❑ 42	Tony Battie	.25 .08
❑ 43	Keon Clark	.50 .20
❑ 44	Derrick Coleman	.25 .08
❑ 45	Erick Dampier	.25 .08
❑ 46	Corey Benjamin	.25 .08
❑ 47	Michael Dickerson	.50 .20
❑ 48	Cedric Henderson	.25 .08
❑ 49	Lamond Murray	.25 .08
❑ 50	Jerome Williams	.25 .08
❑ 51	Shaquille O'Neal	2.00 .75
❑ 52	Dale Davis	.25 .08
❑ 53	Dean Garrett	.25 .08
❑ 54	Tim Hardaway	.50 .20
❑ 55	Dennis Rodman	.50 .20
❑ 56	Sam Cassell	.75 .30
❑ 57	Jim Jackson	.25 .08
❑ 58	Kendall Gill	.25 .08
❑ 59	Eric Williams	.25 .08
❑ 60	Chris Childs	.25 .08
❑ 61	Vlade Divac	.50 .20
❑ 62	Darrell Armstrong	.25 .08
❑ 63	Mario Elie	.25 .08
❑ 64	Jaren Jackson	.25 .08
❑ 65	Dale Ellis	.25 .08
❑ 66	Doug Christie	.50 .20
❑ 67	Howard Eisley	.25 .08
❑ 68	Juwan Howard	.50 .20
❑ 69	Mike Bibby	.75 .30
❑ 70	Alan Henderson	.25 .08
❑ 71	Michael Finley	.75 .30
❑ 72	Dana Barros	.25 .08
❑ 73	Troy Hudson	.25 .08
❑ 74	Ricky Davis	.50 .20
❑ 75	John Amaechi RC	.75 .30
❑ 76	Erick Strickland	.25 .08
❑ 77	Bryce Drew	.25 .08
❑ 78	Shawn Kemp	.50 .20
❑ 79	Tyrone Nesby RC	.25 .08
❑ 80	Lindsey Hunter	.25 .08
❑ 81	Ruben Patterson	.25 .08
❑ 82	Al Harrington	.75 .30
❑ 83	Bobby Jackson	.50 .20
❑ 84	Dan Majerle	.50 .20
❑ 85	Rex Chapman	.25 .08
❑ 86	Dell Curry	.25 .08
❑ 87	Robert Pack	.25 .08
❑ 88	Kerry Kittles	.25 .08
❑ 89	Isaiah Rider	.25 .08
❑ 90	Patrick Ewing	.75 .30
❑ 91	Lawrence Funderburke	.25 .08
❑ 92	Isaac Austin	.25 .08
❑ 93	Sean Elliott	.50 .20
❑ 94	Larry Hughes	.75 .30
❑ 95	Jelani McCoy	.25 .08
❑ 96	Tracy McGrady	2.00 .75
❑ 97	Jeff Hornacek	.50 .20
❑ 98	Jahidi White	.25 .08
❑ 99	Danny Manning	.25 .08
❑ 100	Roshown McLeod	.25 .08
❑ 101	Steve Nash	.75 .30
❑ 102	Ron Mercer	.50 .20
❑ 103	Rael LaFrentz	.50 .20
❑ 104	Eddie Jones	.75 .30
❑ 105	Antawn Jamison	1.25 .50
❑ 106	Chucky Atkins RC	.50 .20
❑ 107	Othella Harrington	.25 .08
❑ 108	Brevin Knight	.25 .08
❑ 109	Michael Olowokandi	.50 .20
❑ 110	Christian Laettner	.50 .20
❑ 111	J.R. Reid	.25 .08
❑ 112	Reggie Miller	.75 .30
❑ 113	Lazaro Borrell RC	3.00 1.25
❑ 114	Jamal Mashburn	.50 .20
❑ 115	Glenn Robinson	.75 .30
❑ 116	Pat Garrity	.25 .08
❑ 117	Stephon Marbury	.75 .30
❑ 118	Arvydas Sabonis	.50 .20
❑ 119	Allan Houston	.50 .20
❑ 120	Peja Stojakovic	1.00 .40
❑ 121	Michael Doleac	.25 .08
❑ 122	Avery Johnson	.25 .08
❑ 123	Allen Iverson	1.50 .60
❑ 124	Rashard Lewis	.75 .30
❑ 125	Charles Oakley	.25 .08
❑ 126	Karl Malone	.75 .30
❑ 127	Tracy Murray	.25 .08
❑ 128	Felipe Lopez	.25 .08
❑ 129	Dikembe Mutombo	.50 .20
❑ 130	Dirk Nowitzki	1.50 .60
❑ 131	Vitaly Potapenko	.25 .08
❑ 132	Antonio McDyess	.50 .20
❑ 133	Anthony Mason	.50 .20
❑ 134	Donyell Marshall	.50 .20
❑ 135	Dickey Simpkins	.25 .08
❑ 136	Cuttino Mobley	.75 .30
❑ 137	Wesley Person	.25 .08
❑ 138	Rodney Rogers	.25 .08
❑ 139	Jerry Stackhouse	.75 .30
❑ 140	Glen Rice	.50 .20
❑ 141	Chris Mullin	.75 .30
❑ 142	Anthony Peeler	.25 .08
❑ 143	Alonzo Mourning	.50 .20
❑ 144	Tom Gugliotta	.25 .08
❑ 145	Tim Thomas	.50 .20
❑ 146	Damon Stoudamire	.50 .20
❑ 147	Jayson Williams	.25 .08
❑ 148	Larry Johnson	.50 .20
❑ 149	Chris Webber	.75 .30
❑ 150	Matt Harpring	.75 .30
❑ 151	David Robinson	.75 .30
❑ 152	George Lynch	.25 .08
❑ 153	Gary Payton	.75 .30
❑ 154	John Wallace	.25 .08
❑ 155	Greg Ostertag	.25 .08
❑ 156	Mitch Richmond	.50 .20
❑ 157	Cherokee Parks	.25 .08
❑ 158	Steve Smith	.50 .20
❑ 159	Gary Trent	.25 .08
❑ 160	Antoine Walker	.75 .30
❑ 161	Chris Herren RC	.25 .08
❑ 162	Ron Harper	.50 .20
❑ 163	Chris Mills	.25 .08
❑ 164	Fred Hoiberg	.25 .08
❑ 165	Hakeem Olajuwon	.75 .30
❑ 166	Bob Sura	.25 .08
❑ 167	Brian Skinner	.25 .08
❑ 168	Loy Vaught	.25 .08
❑ 169	A.C. Green	.25 .08
❑ 170	Jalen Rose	.75 .30
❑ 171	Joe Smith	.50 .20
❑ 172	Clarence Weatherspoon	.25 .08
❑ 173	Jason Kidd	1.25 .50
❑ 174	Robert Traylor	.25 .08
❑ 175	Rasheed Wallace	.75 .30
❑ 176	Latrell Sprewell	.75 .30
❑ 177	Corliss Williamson	.50 .20
❑ 178	Bo Outlaw	.25 .08
❑ 179	Malik Rose	.25 .08
❑ 180	Nazr Mohammed	.25 .08
❑ 181	Eric Murdock	.25 .08
❑ 182	Kevin Willis	.25 .08
❑ 183	Bryon Russell	.25 .08
❑ 184	Bryant Reeves	.25 .08
❑ 185	Rod Strickland	.25 .08
❑ 186	Samaki Walker	.25 .08
❑ 187	Nick Van Exel	.75 .30
❑ 188	David Wesley	.25 .08
❑ 189	Dan Starks	.50 .20
❑ 190	Toni Kukoc	.50 .20
❑ 191	Scottie Pippen	1.25 .50
❑ 192	Johnny Newman	.25 .08
❑ 193	Maurice Taylor	.50 .20
❑ 194	Rik Smits	.50 .20
❑ 195	Clifford Robinson	.25 .08
❑ 196	Bonzi Wells	.75 .30
❑ 197	Charlie Ward	.25 .08
❑ 198	Detlef Schrempf	.50 .20
❑ 199	Theo Ratliff	.50 .20
❑ 200	Kelvin Cato	.25 .08
❑ 201	Ron Artest RC	10.00 4.00
❑ 202	William Avery RC	6.00 2.50
❑ 203	Elton Brand RC	20.00 8.00
❑ 204	Baron Davis RC	20.00 8.00
❑ 205	Jumaine Jones RC	6.00 2.50
❑ 206	Andre Miller RC	15.00 6.00
❑ 207	Eddie Robinson RC	10.00 4.00
❑ 208	James Posey RC	10.00 4.00
❑ 209	Jason Terry RC	10.00 4.00
❑ 210	Kenny Thomas RC	6.00 2.50
❑ 211	Steve Francis RC	20.00 8.00
❑ 212	Wally Szczerbiak RC	15.00 6.00
❑ 213	Richard Hamilton RC	15.00 6.00
❑ 214	Jonathan Bender RC	15.00 6.00
❑ 215	Shawn Marion RC	20.00 8.00
❑ 216	A.Radojevic RC	3.00 1.25
❑ 217	Tim James RC	5.00 2.00
❑ 218	Trajan Langdon RC	6.00 2.50
❑ 219	Lamar Odom RC	20.00 8.00
❑ 220	Corey Maggette RC	15.00 6.00
❑ 221	Dion Glover RC	5.00 2.00
❑ 222	Cal Bowdler RC	5.00 2.00
❑ 223	Vonteego Cummings RC	6.00 2.50
❑ 224	Devean George RC	8.00 3.00

#	Player		
☐ 225	Anthony Carter RC	10.00	4.00
☐ 226	Laron Profit RC	6.00	2.50
☐ 227	Quincy Lewis RC	5.00	2.00
☐ 228	John Celestand RC	5.00	2.00
☐ 229	Obinna Ekezie RC	4.00	1.50
☐ 230	Scott Padgett RC	5.00	2.00
☐ 231	Michael Ruffin RC	4.00	1.50
☐ 232	Jeff Foster RC	5.00	2.00
☐ 233	Jermaine Jackson RC	3.00	1.25
☐ 234	Adrian Griffin RC	5.00	2.00
☐ 235	Todd MacCulloch RC	5.00	2.00
☐ NNO	V.Carter Sgt.	20.00	8.00
☐ NNO	V.Carter Sgt. AU	100.00	50.00

2001-02 Fleer Force

☐ COMPLETE SET (180)		250.00	100.00
☐ COMPLETE SET w/o SP's (150)		50.00	20.00
☐ COMMON CARD (1-180)		.25	.08
☐ COMMON ROOKIE (101-130)		2.50	1.00
☐ 1	Vince Carter	2.00	.75
☐ 2	Allan Houston	.50	.20
☐ 3	Steve Francis	.75	.30
☐ 4	Karl Malone	.75	.30
☐ 5	Joe Smith	.50	.20
☐ 6	Rael LaFrentz	.50	.20
☐ 7	David Robinson	.75	.30
☐ 8	Tim Thomas	.50	.20
☐ 9	Antonio McDyess	.50	.20
☐ 10	Steve Smith	.50	.20
☐ 11	Eddie Jones	.75	.30
☐ 12	Jumaine Jones	.50	.20
☐ 13	Derek Anderson	.50	.20
☐ 14	Shaquille O'Neal	2.00	.75
☐ 15	Eddie Robinson	.50	.20
☐ 16	Stephon Marbury	.75	.30
☐ 17	Darius Miles	.75	.30
☐ 18	Toni Kukoc	.50	.20
☐ 19	Latrell Sprewell	.75	.30
☐ 20	Wang Zhizhi	.75	.30
☐ 21	Tim Duncan	1.50	.60
☐ 22	Eddie House	.50	.20
☐ 23	Chris Mihm	.50	.20
☐ 24	Rasheed Wallace	.75	.30
☐ 25	Kobe Bryant	3.00	1.25
☐ 26	Kenny Thomas	.25	.08
☐ 27	John Stockton	.75	.30
☐ 28	Mike Bibby	.75	.30
☐ 29	Larry Hughes	.50	.20
☐ 30	Antonio Davis	.25	.08
☐ 31	Ray Allen	.75	.30
☐ 32	Corliss Williamson	.50	.20
☐ 33	Desmond Mason	.75	.30
☐ 34	Sam Cassell	.75	.30
☐ 35	Dirk Nowitzki	1.25	.50
☐ 36	Chris Webber	.75	.30
☐ 37	Michael Dickerson	.50	.20
☐ 38	Ron Mercer	.50	.20
☐ 39	Iakovos Tsakalidis	.25	.08
☐ 40	Derek Fisher	.75	.30
☐ 41	Baron Davis	.75	.30
☐ 42	Allen Iverson	1.50	.60
☐ 43	Avery Johnson	.25	.08
☐ 44	Courtney Alexander	.50	.20
☐ 45	Alonzo Mourning	.50	.20
☐ 46	Steve Nash	.75	.30
☐ 47	Hidayet Turkoglu	.50	.20
☐ 48	Jason Williams	.50	.20
☐ 49	David Wesley	.25	.08
☐ 50	Dikembe Mutombo	.50	.20
☐ 51	LaPhonso Ellis	.25	.08
☐ 52	Trajan Langdon	.25	.08
☐ 53	Damon Stoudamire	.50	.20
☐ 54	Rick Fox	.50	.20
☐ 55	Paul Pierce	.75	.30
☐ 56	Tracy McGrady	2.00	.75
☐ 57	Lamar Odom	.75	.30
☐ 58	Antoine Walker	.75	.30
☐ 59	Mike Miller	.75	.30
☐ 60	Jermaine O'Neal	.75	.30
☐ 61	Michael Jordan	15.00	6.00
☐ 62	Jason Kidd	1.25	.50
☐ 63	Marc Jackson	.50	.20
☐ 64	Hakeem Olajuwon	.75	.30
☐ 65	Kevin Garnett	1.50	.60
☐ 66	Nick Van Exel	.75	.30
☐ 67	Rashard Lewis	.50	.20
☐ 68	Brian Grant	.50	.20
☐ 69	Keith Van Horn	.75	.30
☐ 70	Grant Hill	.75	.30
☐ 71	Reggie Miller	.75	.30
☐ 72	Richard Hamilton	.50	.20
☐ 73	Marcus Camby	.50	.20
☐ 74	Clifford Robinson	.25	.08
☐ 75	Gary Payton	.75	.30
☐ 76	Andre Miller	.50	.20
☐ 77	Bonzi Wells	.50	.20
☐ 78	Stromile Swift	.50	.20
☐ 79	Marcus Fizer	.50	.20
☐ 80	Shawn Marion	.75	.30
☐ 81	Elton Brand	.75	.30
☐ 82	Jamal Mashburn	.50	.20
☐ 83	Aaron McKie	.50	.20
☐ 84	Corey Maggette	.50	.20
☐ 85	Jason Terry	.75	.30
☐ 86	Anfernee Hardaway	.75	.30
☐ 87	Antawn Jamison	.75	.30
☐ 88	Morris Peterson	.50	.20
☐ 89	Wally Szczerbiak	.50	.20
☐ 90	Jerry Stackhouse	.75	.30
☐ 91	Shareef Abdur-Rahim	.75	.30
☐ 92	Glenn Robinson	.75	.30
☐ 93	Michael Finley	.75	.30
☐ 94	Peja Stojakovic	.75	.30
☐ 95	Jalen Rose	.75	.30
☐ 96	Theo Ratliff	.50	.20
☐ 97	Kurt Thomas	.50	.20
☐ 98	Cuttino Mobley	.50	.20
☐ 99	DeShawn Stevenson	.50	.20
☐ 100	Terrell Brandon	.50	.20
☐ 101	Kwame Brown RC	4.00	1.50
☐ 102	Tyson Chandler RC	6.00	2.50
☐ 103	Pau Gasol RC	10.00	4.00
☐ 104	Eddy Curry RC	6.00	2.50
☐ 105	Jason Richardson RC	6.00	2.50
☐ 106	Shane Battier RC	4.00	1.50
☐ 107	Eddie Griffin RC	2.50	1.00
☐ 108	DeSagana Diop RC	2.50	1.00
☐ 109	Rodney White RC	3.00	1.25
☐ 110	Joe Johnson RC	10.00	4.00
☐ 111	Kedrick Brown RC	2.50	1.00
☐ 112	Vladimir Radmanovic RC	3.00	1.25
☐ 113	Richard Jefferson RC	4.00	1.50
☐ 114	Troy Murphy RC	5.00	2.00
☐ 115	Steven Hunter RC	2.50	1.00
☐ 116	Kirk Haston RC	2.50	1.00
☐ 117	Michael Bradley RC	2.50	1.00
☐ 118	Jason Collins RC	2.50	1.00
☐ 119	Zach Randolph RC	8.00	3.00
☐ 120	Brendan Haywood RC	3.00	1.25
☐ 121	Joseph Forte RC	5.00	2.00
☐ 122	Jeryl Sasser RC	2.50	1.00
☐ 123	Brandon Armstrong RC	3.00	1.25
☐ 124	Andrei Kirilenko RC	6.00	2.50
☐ 125	Gerald Wallace RC	5.00	2.00
☐ 126	Samuel Dalembert RC	2.50	1.00
☐ 127	Jamaal Tinsley RC	4.00	1.50
☐ 128	Tony Parker RC	10.00	4.00
☐ 129	Loren Woods RC	2.50	1.00
☐ 130	Primoz Brezec RC	3.00	1.25
☐ 131	Dion Glover	.25	.08
☐ 132	Moochie Norris	.25	.08
☐ 133	Mark Jackson	.50	.20
☐ 134	Bryon Russell	.25	.08
☐ 135	Danny Fortson	.25	.08
☐ 136	Kenyon Martin	.75	.30
☐ 137	Alvin Williams	.25	.08
☐ 138	Erick Dampier	.50	.20
☐ 139	Clarence Weatherspoon	.25	.08
☐ 140	Brent Barry	.50	.20
☐ 141	Lamond Murray	.25	.08
☐ 142	Lindsey Hunter	.25	.08
☐ 143	Speedy Claxton	.50	.20
☐ 144	James Posey	.50	.20
☐ 145	Anthony Mason	.50	.20
☐ 146	Mateen Cleaves	.50	.20
☐ 147	Kenny Anderson	.50	.20
☐ 148	Travis Best	.25	.08
☐ 149	Patrick Ewing	.75	.30
☐ 150	Dana Barros	.25	.08
☐ 151	Lorenzen Wright	.25	.08
☐ 152	Rodney Rogers	.25	.08
☐ 153	Brad Miller	.75	.30
☐ 154	Anthony Peeler	.25	.08
☐ 155	Antonio Daniels	.25	.08
☐ 156	Tim Hardaway	.50	.20
☐ 157	Quentin Richardson	.50	.20
☐ 158	Darrell Armstrong	.25	.08
☐ 159	Nazr Mohammed	.25	.08
☐ 160	Todd MacCulloch	.25	.08
☐ 161	Ruben Patterson	.50	.20
☐ 162	Wesley Person	.25	.08
☐ 163	Jeff McInnis	.25	.08
☐ 164	Vin Baker	.50	.20
☐ 165	George McCloud	.25	.08
☐ 166	Chris Gatling	.25	.08
☐ 167	Derrick Coleman	.25	.08
☐ 168	Elden Campbell	.25	.08
☐ 169	Glen Rice	.50	.20
☐ 170	Donyell Marshall	.25	.08
☐ 171	Juwan Howard	.50	.20
☐ 172	Mitch Richmond	.50	.20
☐ 173	Tom Gugliotta	.25	.08
☐ 174	Chucky Atkins	.25	.08
☐ 175	Michael Redd	.75	.30
☐ 176	Malik Rose	.25	.08
☐ 177	Lee Nailon	.25	.08
☐ 178	Al Harrington	.50	.20
☐ 179	Matt Harpring	.75	.30
☐ 180	Tyronn Lue	.25	.08

2000-01 Fleer Futures

☐ COMPLETE SET (250)		80.00	40.00
☐ COMPLETE SET w/o RCs (200)		25.00	12.50
☐ COMMON CARD (1-200)		.20	.07
☐ COMMON EVEN RC (201-250)		.25	.08
☐ COMMON ODD RC (201-250)		.50	.20
☐ 1	Vince Carter	1.50	.60
☐ 2	Dan Majerle	.40	.15
☐ 3	George McCloud	.20	.07
☐ 4	Radoslav Nesterovic	.40	.15
☐ 5	Corey Maggette	.40	.15
☐ 6	Derek Anderson	.40	.15
☐ 7	Ray Allen	.60	.25
☐ 8	Greg Ostertag	.20	.07
☐ 9	Cedric Ceballos	.20	.07
☐ 10	Danny Fortson	.20	.07
☐ 11	Roshown McLeod	.20	.07
☐ 12	Christian Laettner	.40	.15
☐ 13	Avery Johnson	.20	.07
☐ 14	Michael Curry	.20	.07
☐ 15	Michael Curry	.20	.07
☐ 16	Chris Whitney	.20	.07

#	Player		
❑ 17	Anthony Mason	.40	.15
❑ 18	Antonio McDyess	.40	.15
❑ 19	Vitaly Potapenko	.20	.07
❑ 20	Shaquille O'Neal	1.50	.60
❑ 21	David Robinson	.60	.25
❑ 22	Tyrone Hill	.20	.07
❑ 23	Otis Thorpe	.20	.07
❑ 24	Reggie Miller	.60	.25
❑ 25	Kevin Garnett	1.25	.50
❑ 26	Michael Dickerson	.40	.15
❑ 27	John Amaechi	.20	.07
❑ 28	Jason Kidd	1.00	.40
❑ 29	Ron Artest	.40	.15
❑ 30	Muggsy Bogues	.40	.15
❑ 31	Antawn Jamison	.60	.25
❑ 32	Brian Grant	.40	.15
❑ 33	Stephon Marbury	.60	.25
❑ 34	William Avery	.20	.07
❑ 35	Paul Pierce	.60	.25
❑ 36	Marcus Camby	.40	.15
❑ 37	Kevin Willis	.20	.07
❑ 38	Dikembe Mutombo	.40	.15
❑ 39	Rashard Lewis	.40	.15
❑ 40	Allan Houston	.40	.15
❑ 41	Hakeem Olajuwon	.60	.25
❑ 42	Rod Strickland	.20	.07
❑ 43	Derrick Coleman	.20	.07
❑ 44	Tariq Abdul-Wahad	.20	.07
❑ 45	Terrell Brandon	.40	.15
❑ 46	Michael Olowokandi	.40	.15
❑ 47	Robert Horry	.40	.15
❑ 48	Kelvin Cato	.20	.07
❑ 49	Eric Williams	.20	.07
❑ 50	Glen Rice	.40	.15
❑ 51	Carlos Rogers	.20	.07
❑ 52	Allen Iverson	1.25	.50
❑ 53	P.J. Brown	.20	.07
❑ 54	Jalen Rose	.60	.25
❑ 55	Damon Stoudamire	.40	.15
❑ 56	Damon Jones RC	.25	.08
❑ 57	Darrell Armstrong	.20	.07
❑ 58	Samaki Walker	.20	.07
❑ 59	John Stockton	.60	.25
❑ 60	Chucky Atkins	.20	.07
❑ 61	Rasheed Wallace	.60	.25
❑ 62	Jason Terry	.60	.25
❑ 63	Aaron Williams	.20	.07
❑ 64	Steve Nash	.60	.25
❑ 65	Antoine Walker	.60	.25
❑ 66	Patrick Ewing	.60	.25
❑ 67	Cuttino Mobley	.40	.15
❑ 68	Aaron McKie	.40	.15
❑ 69	Jamal Mashburn	.40	.15
❑ 70	Scottie Pippen	1.00	.40
❑ 71	Bryant Reeves	.20	.07
❑ 72	Isaiah Rider	.40	.15
❑ 73	Jaren Jackson	.20	.07
❑ 74	Lindsey Hunter	.20	.07
❑ 75	Jacque Vaughn	.20	.07
❑ 76	Travis Best	.20	.07
❑ 77	Vinny Del Negro	.20	.07
❑ 78	Othella Harrington	.20	.07
❑ 79	Michael Finley	.60	.25
❑ 80	Brent Barry	.40	.15
❑ 81	Brevin Knight	.20	.07
❑ 82	Kurt Thomas	.40	.15
❑ 83	Mark Jackson	.20	.07
❑ 84	Richard Hamilton	.40	.15
❑ 85	Anthony Carter	.40	.15
❑ 86	Matt Harpring	.40	.15
❑ 87	Bobby Jackson	.40	.15
❑ 88	Jerome Williams	.40	.15
❑ 89	Jahidi White	.20	.07
❑ 90	Lorenzen Wright	.20	.07
❑ 91	Kerry Kittles	.20	.07
❑ 92	Anthony Peeler	.20	.07
❑ 93	Kenny Anderson	.40	.15
❑ 94	Latrell Sprewell	.60	.25
❑ 95	Maurice Taylor	.20	.07
❑ 96	Toni Kukoc	.40	.15
❑ 97	Eddie Robinson	.20	.07
❑ 98	Voshon Lenard	.20	.07
❑ 99	Sam Mitchell	.20	.07
❑ 100	Isaac Austin	.20	.07
❑ 101	Michael Doleac	.20	.07
❑ 102	Andre Miller	.40	.15
❑ 103	Jason Williams	.40	.15
❑ 104	Charles Oakley	.20	.07
❑ 105	Mitch Richmond	.40	.15
❑ 106	Bruce Bowen	.20	.07
❑ 107	Keith Van Horn	.60	.25
❑ 108	Wally Szczerbiak	.40	.15
❑ 109	Tony Battie	.20	.07
❑ 110	Larry Johnson	.40	.15
❑ 111	Shandon Anderson	.20	.07
❑ 112	Sam Cassell	.60	.25
❑ 113	David Wesley	.20	.07
❑ 114	James Posey	.40	.15
❑ 115	Bonzi Wells	.40	.15
❑ 116	Mike Bibby	.60	.25
❑ 117	Andrew DeClercq	.20	.07
❑ 118	Clifford Robinson	.20	.07
❑ 119	Corliss Williamson	.40	.15
❑ 120	Antonio Davis	.20	.07
❑ 121	Eddie Jones	.60	.25
❑ 122	Jamie Feick	.20	.07
❑ 123	Anfernee Hardaway	.60	.25
❑ 124	Adrian Griffin	.20	.07
❑ 125	Erick Strickland	.20	.07
❑ 126	Doug Christie	.40	.15
❑ 127	Scot Pollard	.20	.07
❑ 128	Sam Perkins	.40	.15
❑ 129	Raef LaFrentz	.40	.15
❑ 130	Dale Davis	.20	.07
❑ 131	Tyrone Nesby	.20	.07
❑ 132	Rick Fox	.40	.15
❑ 133	Tom Gugliotta	.20	.07
❑ 134	Glenn Robinson	.60	.25
❑ 135	Quincy Lewis	.20	.07
❑ 136	Austin Croshere	.40	.15
❑ 137	Shawn Kemp	.40	.15
❑ 138	Lamar Odom	.60	.25
❑ 139	Tim Duncan	1.25	.50
❑ 140	Tim Thomas	.40	.15
❑ 141	Bryon Russell	.20	.07
❑ 142	Jermaine O'Neal	.60	.25
❑ 143	Erick Dampier	.40	.15
❑ 144	Shareef Abdur-Rahim	.60	.25
❑ 145	Bo Outlaw	.20	.07
❑ 146	Gary Payton	.60	.25
❑ 147	Chris Gatling	.20	.07
❑ 148	Vlade Divac	.40	.15
❑ 149	Ben Wallace	.60	.25
❑ 150	Larry Hughes	.40	.15
❑ 151	Ron Mercer	.40	.15
❑ 152	Karl Malone	.60	.25
❑ 153	Jonathan Bender	.40	.15
❑ 154	Mookie Blaylock	.20	.07
❑ 155	Jim Jackson	.20	.07
❑ 156	Chris Crawford	.20	.07
❑ 157	Vin Baker	.40	.15
❑ 158	Lamond Murray	.20	.07
❑ 159	Charlie Ward	.20	.07
❑ 160	Steve Francis	.60	.25
❑ 161	Cherokee Parks	.20	.07
❑ 162	Baron Davis	.60	.25
❑ 163	Keon Clark	.40	.15
❑ 164	Ruben Patterson	.40	.15
❑ 165	Tracy McGrady	1.50	.60
❑ 166	Antonio Daniels	.20	.07
❑ 167	Scott Williams	.20	.07
❑ 168	John Starks	.40	.15
❑ 169	Jerry Stackhouse	.60	.25
❑ 170	Vonteego Cummings	.20	.07
❑ 171	LaPhonso Ellis	.20	.07
❑ 172	Dirk Nowitzki	1.00	.40
❑ 173	Horace Grant	.40	.15
❑ 174	Wesley Person	.20	.07
❑ 175	Peja Stojakovic	.60	.25
❑ 176	Eric Snow	.40	.15
❑ 177	Juwan Howard	.40	.15
❑ 178	Tim Hardaway	.40	.15
❑ 179	Kendall Gill	.20	.07
❑ 180	Chauncey Billups	.40	.15
❑ 181	Kobe Bryant	2.50	1.00
❑ 182	Sean Elliott	.20	.07
❑ 183	Donyell Marshall	.40	.15
❑ 184	Al Harrington	.40	.15
❑ 185	Arvydas Sabonis	.40	.15
❑ 186	Grant Hill	.60	.25
❑ 187	Malik Rose	.20	.07
❑ 188	Nazr Mohammed	.20	.07
❑ 189	Elden Campbell	.20	.07
❑ 190	Nick Van Exel	.60	.25
❑ 191	Steve Smith	.40	.15
❑ 192	Sean Rooks	.20	.07
❑ 193	Monty Williams	.20	.07
❑ 194	Elton Brand	.60	.25
❑ 195	Chris Webber	.60	.25
❑ 196	Mikki Moore	.20	.07
❑ 197	Chris Mills	.20	.07
❑ 198	Alan Henderson	.20	.07
❑ 199	Shawn Bradley	.20	.07
❑ 200	Shawn Marion	.60	.25
❑ 201	Hidayet Turkoglu RC	4.00	1.50
❑ 202	Iakovos Tsakalidis RC	.25	.08
❑ 203	Kenyon Martin RC	5.00	2.00
❑ 204	Mamadou N'Diaye RC	.25	.08
❑ 205	Stromile Swift RC	3.00	1.25
❑ 206	Pepe Sanchez RC	.25	.08
❑ 207	Chris Mihm RC	.50	.20
❑ 208	Lavor Postell RC	.25	.08
❑ 209	Marcus Fizer RC	.50	.20
❑ 210	Ruben Garces RC	.25	.08
❑ 211	Courtney Alexander RC	.50	.20
❑ 212	A.J. Guyton RC	.25	.08
❑ 213	Darius Miles RC	4.00	1.50
❑ 214	Ademola Okulaja RC	.25	.08
❑ 215	Jerome Moiso RC	.50	.20
❑ 216	Khalid El-Amin RC	.50	.20
❑ 217	Joel Przybilla RC	.25	.08
❑ 218	Mike Smith RC	.25	.08
❑ 219	DerMarr Johnson RC	.50	.20
❑ 220	Soumaila Samake RC	.25	.08
❑ 221	Mike Miller RC	4.00	1.50
❑ 222	Eddie House RC	.25	.08
❑ 223	Quentin Richardson RC	4.00	1.50
❑ 224	Eduardo Najera RC	.60	.25
❑ 225	Morris Peterson RC	3.00	1.25
❑ 226	Hanno Mottola RC	.25	.08
❑ 227	Speedy Claxton RC	.50	.20
❑ 228	Ruben Wolkowyski RC	.25	.08
❑ 229	Keyon Dooling RC	.50	.20
❑ 230	Olumide Oyedeji RC	.25	.08
❑ 231	Mark Madsen RC	.50	.20
❑ 232	Mike Penberthy RC	.25	.08
❑ 233	Mateen Cleaves RC	.50	.20
❑ 234	Brian Cardinal RC	.25	.08
❑ 235	Etan Thomas RC	.50	.20
❑ 236	Garth Joseph RC	.25	.08
❑ 237	Jason Collier RC	1.00	.40
❑ 238	Paul McPherson RC	.25	.08
❑ 239	Erick Barkley RC	.50	.20
❑ 240	Stephen Jackson RC	.75	.30
❑ 241	Desmond Mason RC	.50	.20
❑ 242	Jason Hart RC	.25	.08
❑ 243	Jamal Crawford RC	.60	.25
❑ 244	Daniel Santiago RC	.25	.08
❑ 245	DeShawn Stevenson RC	.50	.20
❑ 246	Stanislav Medvedenko RC	.25	.08
❑ 247	Donnell Harvey RC	.50	.20
❑ 248	Chris Porter RC	.25	.08
❑ 249	Jamaal Magloire RC	.50	.20
❑ 250	Dalibor Bagaric RC	.25	.08

2000-01 Fleer Game Time

JASON KIDD

❑	COMPLETE SET w/o RC (90)	25.00	12.50
❑	COMMON CARD (1-90)	.20	.07
❑	COMMON ROOKIE (91-120)	1.25	.50
❑ 1	Vince Carter	2.00	.75

#	Player		
2	Raef LaFrentz	.50	.20
3	Kobe Bryant	3.00	1.25
4	Toni Kukoc	.50	.20
5	Bonzi Wells	.50	.20
6	Rashard Lewis	.50	.20
7	Karl Malone	.75	.30
8	Juwan Howard	.50	.20
9	Lindsey Hunter	.25	.08
10	Alonzo Mourning	.50	.20
11	Larry Hughes	.50	.20
12	Austin Croshere	.50	.20
13	Charles Oakley	.25	.08
14	Patrick Ewing	.75	.30
15	Vlade Divac	.50	.20
16	Michael Finley	.75	.30
17	Tim Hardaway	.50	.20
18	Jason Kidd	1.25	.50
19	Cal Bowdler	.25	.08
20	Dirk Nowitzki	1.25	.50
21	Terrell Brandon	.50	.20
22	Allan Houston	.50	.20
23	Theo Ratliff	.50	.20
24	Chris Webber	.75	.30
25	Shawn Kemp	.50	.20
26	Jalen Rose	.75	.30
27	Bryon Russell	.25	.08
28	Jahidi White	.25	.08
29	Trajan Langdon	.50	.20
30	Baron Davis	.75	.30
31	Cuttino Mobley	.50	.20
32	Wally Szczerbiak	.50	.20
33	Michael Dickerson	.50	.20
34	Andre Miller	.50	.20
35	Michael Olowokandi	.25	.08
36	Ray Allen	.75	.30
37	Latrell Sprewell	.75	.30
38	Jason Williams	.50	.20
39	Mikki Moore	.25	.08
40	Shawn Marion	.75	.30
41	Radoslav Nesterovic	.50	.20
42	Ron Artest	.50	.20
43	Vonteego Cummings	.25	.08
44	Anfernee Hardaway	.75	.30
45	Jerome Williams	.25	.08
46	John Stockton	.75	.30
47	Antawn Jamison	.75	.30
48	Grant Hill	.75	.30
49	Elden Campbell	.25	.08
50	Steve Francis	.75	.30
51	Jamie Feick	.25	.08
52	Gary Payton	.75	.30
53	Elton Brand	.75	.30
54	Eddie Jones	.75	.30
55	Tom Gugliotta	.25	.08
56	Richard Hamilton	.50	.20
57	Dion Glover	.25	.08
58	Shaquille O'Neal	2.00	.75
59	Kevin Garnett	1.50	.60
60	Paul Pierce	.75	.30
61	Brian Grant	.50	.20
62	Tim Thomas	.50	.20
63	Tracy McGrady	2.00	.75
64	Jonathan Bender	.50	.20
65	Adrian Griffin	.25	.08
66	Lamar Odom	.75	.30
67	Rasheed Wallace	.75	.30
68	Mike Bibby	.75	.30
69	Glenn Robinson	.75	.30
70	Eddie Robinson	.50	.20
71	Robert Horry	.50	.20
72	Jerry Stackhouse	.75	.30
73	Stephon Marbury	.75	.30
74	Marcus Camby	.50	.20
75	Scottie Pippen	1.25	.50
76	David Robinson	.75	.30
77	Jason Terry	.75	.30
78	Reggie Miller	.75	.30
79	Larry Johnson	.50	.20
80	Antonio Daniels	.25	.08
81	Shareef Abdur-Rahim	.75	.30
82	Robert Patterson	.50	.20
83	Nick Van Exel	.75	.30
84	Keith Van Horn	.75	.30
85	Antonio Davis	.25	.08
86	Antoine Walker	.75	.30
87	Allen Iverson	1.50	.60
88	Antonio McDyess	.50	.20
89	Tim Duncan	1.50	.60
90	Hakeem Olajuwon	.75	.30
91	Jamaal Magloire RC	1.25	.50
92	DerMarr Johnson RC	1.25	.50
93	Jerome Moiso RC	1.25	.50
94	Marcus Fizer RC	1.25	.50
95	Jamal Crawford RC	1.50	.60
96	Chris Mihm RC	1.25	.50
97	Donnell Harvey RC	1.25	.50
98	Courtney Alexander RC	1.25	.50
99	Etan Thomas RC	1.25	.50
100	Mamadou N'diaye RC	1.25	.50
101	Mateen Cleaves RC	1.25	.50
102	Chris Porter RC	1.25	.50
103	Jason Collier RC	2.00	.75
104	Keyon Dooling RC	1.25	.50
105	Darius Miles RC	6.00	2.50
106	Mark Madsen RC	1.25	.50
107	Eddie House RC	1.25	.50
108	Joel Przybilla RC	1.25	.50
109	Kenyon Martin RC	8.00	3.00
110	Mike Miller RC	5.00	2.00
111	Speedy Claxton RC	1.25	.50
112	Iakovos Tsakalidis RC	1.25	.50
113	Erick Barkley RC	1.25	.50
114	Hidayet Turkoglu RC	4.00	1.50
115	Eduardo Najera RC	2.00	.75
116	Desmond Mason RC	1.25	.50
117	Morris Peterson RC	3.00	1.25
118	DeShawn Stevenson RC	1.25	.50
119	Stromile Swift RC	3.00	1.25
120	Mike Smith RC	1.25	.50

2000-01 Fleer Genuine

	COMPLETE SET w/o RC (100)	40.00	20.00
	COMMON CARD (1-100)	.30	.10
	COMMON ROOKIE (101-130)	4.00	1.50
1	Vince Carter	2.50	1.00
2	Glenn Robinson	1.00	.40
3	Rasheed Wallace	1.00	.40
4	Michael Dickerson	.60	.25
5	Mikki Moore	.30	.10
6	Wally Szczerbiak	.60	.25
7	Shawn Marion	1.00	.40
8	Dan Majerle	.60	.25
9	Trajan Langdon	.60	.25
10	Chauncey Billups	.60	.25
11	Jason Kidd	1.50	.60
12	Derrick Coleman	.30	.10
13	Jason Terry	1.00	.40
14	Eddie Jones	1.00	.40
15	Scottie Pippen	1.50	.60
16	Mike Bibby	1.00	.40
17	Ron Mercer	.60	.25
18	Hakeem Olajuwon	1.00	.40
19	Patrick Ewing	1.00	.40
20	Ruben Patterson	.60	.25
21	Kenny Anderson	.60	.25
22	Alonzo Mourning	.60	.25
23	Steve Smith	.60	.25
24	Juwan Howard	.60	.25
25	Antoine Walker	1.00	.40
26	Kobe Bryant	4.00	1.50
27	Chris Webber	1.00	.40
28	Mitch Richmond	.60	.25
29	Paul Pierce	1.00	.40
30	Shaquille O'Neal	2.50	1.00
31	Jason Williams	.60	.25
32	Richard Hamilton	.60	.25
33	Michael Finley	1.00	.40
34	Jalen Rose	1.00	.40
35	Grant Hill	1.00	.40
36	John Stockton	1.00	.40
37	Vitaly Potapenko	.30	.10
38	Glen Rice	.60	.25
39	Vlade Divac	.60	.25
40	Jahidi White	.30	.10
41	Baron Davis	1.00	.40
42	Michael Olowokandi	.30	.10
43	Tim Duncan	2.00	.75
44	Rod Strickland	.30	.10
45	Jamal Mashburn	.60	.25
46	Lamar Odom	1.00	.40
47	David Robinson	1.00	.40
48	Travis Best	.30	.10
49	Raef LaFrentz	.60	.25
50	Keith Van Horn	1.00	.40
51	Vonteego Cummings	.30	.10
52	Jerome Williams	.30	.10
53	Kevin Garnett	2.00	.75
54	Anfernee Hardaway	1.00	.40
55	Antonio McDyess	.60	.25
56	Reggie Miller	1.00	.40
57	Tracy McGrady	2.50	1.00
58	Bryon Russell	.30	.10
59	Nick Van Exel	1.00	.40
60	Allen Iverson	2.00	.75
61	Karl Malone	1.00	.40
62	David Wesley	.30	.10
63	Bob Sura	.30	.10
64	Stephon Marbury	1.00	.40
65	Antonio Daniels	.30	.10
66	Shawn Kemp	.60	.25
67	Cuttino Mobley	.60	.25
68	Marcus Camby	.60	.25
69	Gary Payton	1.00	.40
70	Dikembe Mutombo	.60	.25
71	Tim Hardaway	.60	.25
72	Bonzi Wells	.60	.25
73	Shareef Abdur-Rahim	1.00	.40
74	Brevin Knight	.30	.10
75	Steve Francis	1.00	.40
76	Allan Houston	.60	.25
77	Dion Glover	.30	.10
78	Dirk Nowitzki	1.50	.60
79	Jonathan Bender	.60	.25
80	Darrell Armstrong	.30	.10
81	Antonio Davis	.30	.10
82	Jerry Stackhouse	1.00	.40
83	Terrell Brandon	.60	.25
84	Tom Gugliotta	.30	.10
85	Sean Elliott	.60	.25
86	Elton Brand	1.00	.40
87	Larry Hughes	.60	.25
88	Kerry Kittles	.30	.10
89	Vin Baker	.60	.25
90	Donyell Marshall	.60	.25
91	Tim Thomas	.60	.25
92	Toni Kukoc	.60	.25
93	Charles Oakley	.30	.10
94	Andre Miller	.60	.25
95	Austin Croshere	.60	.25
96	Latrell Sprewell	1.00	.40
97	Mark Jackson	.30	.10
98	Antawn Jamison	1.00	.40
99	Ray Allen	1.00	.40
100	Theo Ratliff	.60	.25
101	Chris Mihm RC	4.00	1.50
102	Mateen Cleaves RC	4.00	1.50
103	Etan Thomas RC	4.00	1.50
104	Morris Peterson RC	6.00	2.50
105	Jamal Crawford RC	5.00	2.00
106	Darius Miles RC	10.00	4.00
107	Desmond Mason RC	4.00	1.50
108	Joel Przybilla RC	4.00	1.50
109	Mike Miller RC	10.00	4.00
110	Quentin Richardson RC	8.00	3.00
111	Jason Collier RC	5.00	2.00
112	Keyon Dooling RC	4.00	1.50
113	Courtney Alexander RC	5.00	2.00
114	Eddie House RC	4.00	1.50
115	DerMarr Johnson RC	4.00	1.50
116	Michael Redd RC	6.00	2.50

❏ 117	Mark Madsen RC	4.00	1.50
❏ 118	Stromile Swift RC	6.00	2.50
❏ 119	Mamadou N'Diaye RC	4.00	1.50
❏ 120	DeShawn Stevenson RC	4.00	1.50
❏ 121	Hidayet Turkoglu RC	10.00	4.00
❏ 122	Stephen Jackson RC	6.00	2.50
❏ 123	Marcus Fizer RC	4.00	1.50
❏ 124	Khalid El-Amin RC	4.00	1.50
❏ 125	Speedy Claxton RC	4.00	1.50
❏ 126	Hanno Mottola RC	4.00	1.50
❏ 127	Jerome Moiso RC	4.00	1.50
❏ 128	Jamaal Magloire RC	4.00	1.50
❏ 129	Donnell Harvey RC	4.00	1.50
❏ 130	Kenyon Martin RC	12.00	5.00
❏ NNO	V.Carter Main Man	50.00	20.00
❏ NNO	V.Carter Main Man AU	600.00	300.00

2001-02 Fleer Genuine

❏	COMMON CARD (1-120)	.30	.10
❏	COMMON ROOKIE (121-150)	2.50	1.00
❏ 1	Larry Hughes	.60	.25
❏ 2	Wally Szczerbiak	.60	.25
❏ 3	Jahidi White	.30	.10
❏ 4	Aaron McKie	.60	.25
❏ 5	Antonio McDyess	.60	.25
❏ 6	Tom Gugliotta	.30	.10
❏ 7	Elton Brand	1.00	.40
❏ 8	Lamar Odom	1.00	.40
❏ 9	Chris Webber	1.00	.40
❏ 10	Ron Artest	.60	.25
❏ 11	Gary Payton	1.00	.40
❏ 12	Brian Grant	.60	.25
❏ 13	Steve Nash	1.00	.40
❏ 14	DerMarr Johnson	.60	.25
❏ 15	Vince Carter	2.50	1.00
❏ 16	Kurt Thomas	.60	.25
❏ 17	Cuttino Mobley	.60	.25
❏ 18	Marc Jackson	.60	.25
❏ 19	Stromile Swift	.60	.25
❏ 20	Grant Hill	1.00	.40
❏ 21	Rael LaFrentz	.60	.25
❏ 22	Marcus Fizer	.60	.25
❏ 23	Antonio Davis	.30	.10
❏ 24	John Starks	.60	.25
❏ 25	Trajan Langdon	.30	.10
❏ 26	Jason Williams	.60	.25
❏ 27	Toni Kukoc	.60	.25
❏ 28	Morris Peterson	.60	.25
❏ 29	Allen Iverson	2.00	.75
❏ 30	Andre Miller	.60	.25
❏ 31	Larry Johnson	.60	.25
❏ 32	Vitaly Potapenko	.30	.10
❏ 33	Tim Thomas	.60	.25
❏ 34	Eddie House	.60	.25
❏ 35	Juwan Howard	.60	.25
❏ 36	Joel Przybilla	.60	.25
❏ 37	John Stockton	1.00	.40
❏ 38	Michael Finley	1.00	.40
❏ 39	Hidayet Turkoglu	.60	.25
❏ 40	Keith Van Horn	1.00	.40
❏ 41	Shawn Marion	1.00	.40
❏ 42	Derek Fisher	1.00	.40
❏ 43	Terrell Brandon	.60	.25
❏ 44	Jamal Mashburn	.60	.25
❏ 45	Shareef Abdur-Rahim	1.00	.40
❏ 46	Brevin Knight	.30	.10
❏ 47	Antoine Walker	1.00	.40
❏ 48	Mateen Cleaves	.60	.25

❏ 49	Alonzo Mourning	.60	.25
❏ 50	Jermaine O'Neal	1.00	.40
❏ 51	Kenyon Martin	.60	.40
❏ 52	Steve Smith	.60	.25
❏ 53	Jerry Stackhouse	1.00	.40
❏ 54	Mike Bibby	1.00	.40
❏ 55	Latrell Sprewell	.60	.25
❏ 56	Iakovos Tsakalidis	.30	.10
❏ 57	Sam Cassell	.60	.40
❏ 58	Michael Dickerson	.60	.25
❏ 59	Alan Henderson	.30	.10
❏ 60	Allan Houston	.60	.25
❏ 61	Patrick Ewing	1.00	.40
❏ 62	Joe Smith	.60	.25
❏ 63	Rick Fox	.60	.25
❏ 64	Tracy McGrady	2.50	1.00
❏ 65	Scottie Pippen	1.50	.60
❏ 66	Chauncey Billups	.60	.25
❏ 67	Voshon Lenard	.30	.10
❏ 68	Jalen Rose	1.00	.40
❏ 69	Derrick Coleman	.30	.10
❏ 70	Shaquille O'Neal	2.50	1.00
❏ 71	Anfernee Hardaway	1.00	.40
❏ 72	Derek Anderson	.60	.25
❏ 73	Travis Best	.30	.10
❏ 74	Darius Miles	1.00	.40
❏ 75	Glenn Robinson	1.00	.40
❏ 76	Darrell Armstrong	.30	.10
❏ 77	Dirk Nowitzki	1.50	.60
❏ 78	Stephon Marbury	1.00	.40
❏ 79	Tyronn Lue	.30	.10
❏ 80	Bonzi Wells	.60	.25
❏ 81	Mike Miller	1.00	.40
❏ 82	Tim Duncan	2.00	.75
❏ 83	Tim Hardaway	.60	.25
❏ 84	Desmond Mason	.60	.25
❏ 85	Ray Allen	1.00	.40
❏ 86	Sean Elliott	.60	.25
❏ 87	David Wesley	.30	.10
❏ 88	Rasheed Wallace	.60	.25
❏ 89	Kevin Garnett	2.00	.75
❏ 90	Dikembe Mutombo	.60	.25
❏ 91	Baron Davis	1.00	.40
❏ 92	Donyell Marshall	.60	.25
❏ 93	Eddie Jones	1.00	.40
❏ 94	Vin Baker	.60	.25
❏ 95	Peja Stojakovic	1.00	.40
❏ 96	Antawn Jamison	1.00	.40
❏ 97	Maurice Taylor	.60	.25
❏ 98	Courtney Alexander	.60	.25
❏ 99	Steve Francis	1.00	.40
❏ 100	Chris Mihm	.60	.25
❏ 101	Kobe Bryant	4.00	1.50
❏ 102	Hakeem Olajuwon	1.00	.40
❏ 103	Richard Hamilton	.60	.25
❏ 104	Karl Malone	1.00	.40
❏ 105	Chucky Atkins	.30	.10
❏ 106	Eric Snow	.60	.25
❏ 107	Ruben Patterson	.60	.25
❏ 108	David Robinson	1.00	.40
❏ 109	Bryon Russell	.30	.10
❏ 110	Jason Terry	1.00	.40
❏ 111	Jason Kidd	1.50	.60
❏ 112	Charles Oakley	.30	.10
❏ 113	Wang Zhizhi	1.00	.40
❏ 114	Quentin Richardson	.60	.25
❏ 115	Clarence Weatherspoon	.30	.10
❏ 116	Nick Van Exel	1.00	.40
❏ 117	Reggie Miller	1.00	.40
❏ 118	Marcus Camby	.60	.25
❏ 119	Corey Maggette	.60	.25
❏ 120	Paul Pierce	1.00	.40
❏ 121	Kwame Brown RC	5.00	2.00
❏ 122	Eddie Griffin RC	3.00	1.25
❏ 123	Eddy Curry RC	10.00	4.00
❏ 124	Jamaal Tinsley RC	5.00	2.00
❏ 125	Jason Richardson RC	20.00	8.00
❏ 126	Shane Battier RC	5.00	2.00
❏ 127	Troy Murphy RC	5.00	2.00
❏ 128	Richard Jefferson RC	8.00	3.00
❏ 129	DeSagana Diop RC	2.50	1.00
❏ 130	Tyson Chandler RC	10.00	4.00
❏ 131	Joe Johnson RC	8.00	3.00
❏ 132	Zach Randolph RC	10.00	4.00
❏ 133	Gerald Wallace RC	6.00	2.50
❏ 134	Loren Woods RC	2.50	1.00

❏ 135	Jason Collins RC	2.50	1.00
❏ 136	Rodney White RC	2.50	1.00
❏ 137	Jeryl Sasser RC	3.00	1.25
❏ 138	Kirk Haston RC	2.50	1.00
❏ 139	Pau Gasol RC	10.00	4.00
❏ 140	Kedrick Brown RC	2.50	1.00
❏ 141	Steven Hunter RC	2.50	1.00
❏ 142	Michael Bradley RC	2.50	1.00
❏ 143	Joseph Forte RC	6.00	2.50
❏ 144	Brandon Armstrong RC	4.00	1.50
❏ 145	Samuel Dalembert RC	2.50	1.00
❏ 146	Trenton Hassell RC	4.00	1.50
❏ 147	Gilbert Arenas RC	4.00	1.50
❏ 148	Omar Cook RC	2.50	1.00
❏ 149	Tony Parker RC	12.00	5.00
❏ 150	Terence Morris RC	2.50	1.00

2002-03 Fleer Genuine

❏	COMPLETE SET (135)	275.00	150.00
❏	COMP.SET w/o SP's (100)	40.00	20.00
❏	COMMON CARD (1-100)	.25	.08
❏	COMMON ROOKIE (101-135)	3.00	1.25
❏ 1	Shaquille O'Neal	2.00	.75
❏ 2	Allen Iverson	1.50	.60
❏ 3	Jerry Stackhouse	.75	.30
❏ 4	Kobe Bryant	3.00	1.25
❏ 5	Jason Kidd	1.25	.50
❏ 6	Andre Miller	.50	.20
❏ 7	David Robinson	.75	.30
❏ 8	John Stockton	.75	.30
❏ 9	Glenn Robinson	.75	.30
❏ 10	Chauncey Billups	.50	.20
❏ 11	Chris Webber	.75	.30
❏ 12	Antawn Jamison	.75	.30
❏ 13	Sam Cassell	.75	.30
❏ 14	Vlade Divac	.50	.20
❏ 15	P.J. Brown	.25	.08
❏ 16	Robert Horry	.50	.20
❏ 17	Eric Snow	.50	.20
❏ 18	Popeye Jones	.25	.08
❏ 19	Paul Pierce	.75	.30
❏ 20	Eddie Griffin	.50	.20
❏ 21	Marcus Camby	.50	.20
❏ 22	Gary Payton	.75	.30
❏ 23	Michael Jordan	5.00	2.00
❏ 24	Shareef Abdur-Rahim	.75	.30
❏ 25	Anfernee Hardaway	.75	.30
❏ 26	Michael Finley	.75	.30
❏ 27	Steve Nash	.75	.30
❏ 28	Shane Battier	.75	.30
❏ 29	Stephon Marbury	.75	.30
❏ 30	Dirk Nowitzki	1.25	.50
❏ 31	Pau Gasol	.75	.30
❏ 32	Shawn Marion	.75	.30
❏ 33	Rodney Rogers	.25	.08
❏ 34	Steve Smith	.50	.20
❏ 35	Darrell Armstrong	.25	.08
❏ 36	Alvin Williams	.25	.08
❏ 37	Nick Van Exel	.75	.30
❏ 38	Jason Williams	.50	.20
❏ 39	Ruben Patterson	.50	.20
❏ 40	Juwan Howard	.50	.20
❏ 41	Brian Grant	.50	.20
❏ 42	Damon Stoudamire	.50	.20
❏ 43	Antonio McDyess	.50	.20
❏ 44	Eddie Jones	.75	.30
❏ 45	Rasheed Wallace	.75	.30
❏ 46	Larry Hughes	.50	.20

□	#	Player		
□	47	Wally Szczerbiak	.50	.20
□	48	Tony Parker	.75	.30
□	49	Ron Artest	.50	.20
□	50	Kevin Garnett	1.50	.60
□	51	Tim Duncan	1.50	.60
□	52	Marcus Fizer	.50	.20
□	53	Darius Miles	.75	.30
□	54	Grant Hill	.75	.30
□	55	Andrei Kirilenko	.75	.30
□	56	Jalen Rose	.75	.30
□	57	Lamar Odom	.75	.30
□	58	Tracy McGrady	2.00	.75
□	59	Karl Malone	.75	.30
□	60	Jason Terry	.75	.30
□	61	Steve Francis	.75	.30
□	62	Kenyon Martin	.75	.30
□	63	Brent Barry	.50	.20
□	64	Antoine Walker	.75	.30
□	65	Reggie Miller	.75	.30
□	66	Allan Houston	.50	.20
□	67	Vince Carter	2.00	.75
□	68	Toni Kukoc	.50	.20
□	69	Lamond Murray	.25	.08
□	70	Jason Richardson	.75	.30
□	71	Rick Fox	.50	.20
□	72	Kerry Kittles	.25	.08
□	73	Dikembe Mutombo	.50	.20
□	74	Tyson Chandler	.75	.30
□	75	Richard Hamilton	.75	.30
□	76	Elden Campbell	.25	.08
□	77	Jermaine O'Neal	.75	.30
□	78	Mike Miller	.75	.30
□	79	Morris Peterson	.50	.20
□	80	Jamal Mashburn	.50	.20
□	81	Elton Brand	.75	.30
□	82	Kurt Thomas	.50	.20
□	83	Antonio Davis	.25	.08
□	84	Ben Wallace	.75	.30
□	85	Anthony Mason	.50	.20
□	86	Peja Stojakovic	.75	.30
□	87	Kenny Anderson	.50	.20
□	88	Cuttino Mobley	.50	.20
□	89	Keith Van Horn	.75	.30
□	90	Rashard Lewis	.50	.20
□	91	Clifford Robinson	.25	.08
□	92	Ray Allen	.75	.30
□	93	Mike Bibby	.75	.30
□	94	Baron Davis	.75	.30
□	95	Jamaal Tinsley	.75	.30
□	96	Latrell Sprewell	.75	.30
□	97	Jon Barry	.25	.08
□	98	Desmond Mason	.50	.20
□	99	Alonzo Mourning	.50	.20
□	100	Bonzi Wells	.50	.20
□	101	Jay Williams RC	5.00	2.00
□	102	Mike Dunleavy RC	6.00	2.50
□	103	Amare Stoudemire RC	15.00	6.00
□	104	Caron Butler RC	10.00	4.00
□	105	Jared Jeffries RC	4.00	1.50
□	106	Fred Jones RC	4.00	1.50
□	107	Bostjan Nachbar RC	3.00	1.25
□	108	Jiri Welsch RC	3.00	1.25
□	109	Juan Dixon RC	6.00	2.50
□	110	Curtis Borchardt RC	3.00	1.25
□	111	Kareem Rush RC	4.00	1.50
□	112	Qyntel Woods RC	4.00	1.50
□	113	Casey Jacobsen RC	3.00	1.25
□	114	Frank Williams RC	3.00	1.25
□	115	John Salmons RC	3.00	1.25
□	116	Dan Dickau RC	3.00	1.25
□	117	DaJuan Wagner RC	6.00	2.50
□	118	Drew Gooden EXCH	10.00	4.00
□	119	Nikoloz Tskitishvili EXCH	4.00	1.50
□	120	Yao Ming RC	25.00	10.00
□	120A	Yao Ming EXCH		
□	121	Nene Hilario EXCH	5.00	2.00
□	122	Chris Wilcox EXCH	5.00	2.00
□	123	Melvin Ely EXCH	3.00	1.25
□	124	Marcus Haislip EXCH	3.00	1.25
□	125	Ryan Humphrey EXCH	3.00	1.25
□	126	Tayshaun Prince EXCH	5.00	2.00
□	127	Tito Maddox EXCH	3.00	1.25
□	128	Chris Jefferies EXCH	3.00	1.25
□	129	Manu Ginobili RC	10.00	4.00
□	130	Roger Mason EXCH	3.00	1.25
□	131	Robert Archibald EXCH	3.00	1.25
□	132	Vincent Yarbrough EXCH	3.00	1.25
□	133	Dan Gadzuric EXCH	3.00	1.25
□	134	Carlos Boozer EXCH	6.00	2.50
□	135	Rasual Butler EXCH	3.00	1.25

2003-04 Fleer Genuine Insider

		COMP SET w/o SP's (100)	30.00	12.50
□		COMMON ROOKIE (101-110)	5.00	2.00
□		COMMON ROOKIE (111-140)	3.00	1.25
□		COMMON ROOKIE (131-140)	5.00	2.00
□	1	Shareef Abdur-Rahim	.75	.30
□	2	Andre Miller	.50	.20
□	3	Reggie Miller	.75	.30
□	4	Michael Redd	.75	.30
□	5	Allan Houston	.50	.20
□	6	Mike Bibby	.75	.30
□	7	Kwame Brown	.75	.30
□	8	Earl Boykins	.50	.20
□	9	Ron Artest	.50	.20
□	10	Eddie Jones	.75	.30
□	11	Zach Randolph	.75	.30
□	12	Derek Anderson	.50	.20
□	13	Andrei Kirilenko	.75	.30
□	14	Carlos Boozer	.75	.30
□	15	Yao Ming	2.00	.75
□	16	Pau Gasol	.75	.30
□	17	Jamal Mashburn	.50	.20
□	18	Shawn Marion	.75	.30
□	19	Vince Carter	2.00	.75
□	20	Eddy Curry	.50	.20
□	21	Mike Dunleavy Jr.	.50	.20
□	22	Kobe Bryant	3.00	1.25
□	23	Tim Thomas	.50	.20
□	24	Drew Gooden	.75	.30
□	25	Tim Duncan	1.50	.60
□	26	Dajuan Wagner	.50	.20
□	27	Speedy Claxton	.20	.08
□	28	Karl Malone	.75	.30
□	29	Jason Kidd	1.25	.50
□	30	Kenny Thomas	.20	.08
□	31	Vladimir Radmanovic	.20	.08
□	32	Tyson Chandler	.75	.30
□	33	Jason Richardson	.75	.30
□	34	Quentin Richardson	.50	.20
□	35	Kerry Kittles	.20	.08
□	36	Derrick Coleman	.20	.08
□	37	Manu Ginobili	.75	.30
□	38	Paul Pierce	.75	.30
□	39	Ben Wallace	.75	.30
□	40	Corey Maggette	.50	.20
□	41	Sam Cassell	.50	.20
□	42	Hidayet Turkoglu	.75	.30
□	43	Peja Stojakovic	.75	.30
□	44	Gilbert Arenas	.75	.30
□	45	Dirk Nowitzki	1.25	.50
□	46	Al Harrington	.50	.20
□	47	Caron Butler	.75	.30
□	48	Baron Davis	.75	.30
□	49	Rasheed Wallace	.75	.30
□	50	Morris Peterson	.50	.20
□	51	Steve Nash	.75	.30
□	52	Steve Francis	.75	.30
□	53	Lamar Odom	.75	.30
□	54	Jamaal Magloire	.20	.08
□	55	Amare Stoudemire	1.50	.60
□	56	Antonio Davis	.20	.08
□	57	Dan Dickau	.20	.08
□	58	Cuttino Mobley	.50	.20
□	59	Jason Williams	.50	.20
□	60	David Wesley	.20	.08
□	61	Stephon Marbury	.75	.30
□	62	Ray Allen	.75	.30
□	63	Scottie Pippen	1.25	.50
□	64	Nick Van Exel	.75	.30
□	65	Shaquille O'Neal	2.00	.75
□	66	Richard Jefferson	.50	.20
□	67	Allen Iverson	1.50	.60
□	68	Tony Parker	.75	.30
□	69	Jason Terry	.75	.30
□	70	Nenà	.50	.20
□	71	Marko Jaric	.50	.20
□	72	Troy Hudson	.20	.08
□	73	Malik Rose	.20	.08
□	74	Bobby Jackson	.50	.20
□	75	Jerry Stackhouse	.75	.30
□	76	Voshon Lenard	.20	.08
□	77	Richard Hamilton	.50	.20
□	78	Scot Pollard	.20	.08
□	79	Latrell Sprewell	.75	.30
□	80	Tracy McGrady	2.00	.75
□	81	Chris Webber	.75	.30
□	82	Rael LaFrentz	.50	.20
□	83	Tayshaun Prince	.50	.20
□	84	Elton Brand	.75	.30
□	85	Kevin Garnett	1.50	.60
□	86	Keon Clark	.50	.20
□	87	Brad Miller	.75	.30
□	88	Alvin Williams	.20	.08
□	89	Michael Finley	.75	.30
□	90	Jermaine O'Neal	.75	.30
□	91	Desmond Mason	.75	.30
□	92	Keith Van Horn	.75	.30
□	93	Bonzi Wells	.75	.30
□	94	Matt Harpring	.75	.30
□	95	Darius Miles	.50	.20
□	96	Eddie Griffin	.50	.20
□	97	Shane Battier	.75	.30
□	98	Kenyon Martin	.75	.30
□	99	Glenn Robinson	.75	.30
□	100	Rashard Lewis	.75	.30
□	101	Carmelo Anthony RC	20.00	8.00
□	102	Troy Bell RC	5.00	2.00
□	103	T.J. Ford RC	6.00	2.50
□	104	LeBron James RC	60.00	30.00
□	105	Mike Sweetney RC	5.00	2.00
□	106	Chris Bosh RC	12.00	5.00
□	107	Jarvis Hayes RC	5.00	2.00
□	108	Darko Milicic RC	8.00	3.00
□	109	Chris Kaman RC	5.00	2.00
□	110	Dwyane Wade RC	25.00	10.00
□	111	Udonis Haslem RC	3.00	1.25
□	112	Josh Howard RC	5.00	2.00
□	113	Mickael Pietrus RC	3.00	1.25
□	114	Reece Gaines RC	3.00	1.25
□	115	Nick Collison RC	3.00	1.25
□	116	Leandrinho Barbosa RC	5.00	2.00
□	117	Kendrick Perkins RC	3.00	1.25
□	118	Ndudi Ebi RC	3.00	1.25
□	119	Willie Green RC	3.00	1.25
□	120	Kirk Hinrich RC	5.00	2.00
□	121	Marcus Banks RC	3.00	1.25
□	122	Zarko Cabarkapa RC	3.00	1.25
□	123	Zoran Planinic RC	3.00	1.25
□	124	David West RC	3.00	1.25
□	125	Luke Ridnour RC	4.00	1.50
□	126	Brian Cook RC	3.00	1.25
□	127	Boris Diaw RC	4.00	1.50
□	128	Dahntay Jones RC	3.00	1.25
□	129	Maciej Lampe RC	3.00	1.25
□	130	Travis Outlaw RC	3.00	1.25
□	131	Ben Handlogten MM RC	5.00	2.00
□	132	Jerome Beasley MM RC	5.00	2.00
□	133	Marquis Daniels MM RC	10.00	4.00
□	134	Luke Walton MM RC	5.00	2.00
□	135	Aleksandar Pavlovic MM RC	5.00	2.00
□	136	Matt Carroll MM RC	5.00	2.00
□	137	Curtis Borchardt MM	5.00	2.00
□	138	Jason Kapono MM RC	5.00	2.00
□	139	Steve Blake MM RC	5.00	2.00
□	140	Keith Bogans MM RC	5.00	2.00

2004-05 Fleer Genuine

☐ COMP.SET w/o SP's (100)	40.00	15.00
☐ COMMON CARD (1-100)	.20	.08
☐ COMMON ROOKIE (101-110)	6.00	2.50
☐ COMMON ROOKIE (111-135)	5.00	2.00
☐ 1 Rasheed Wallace	.75	.30
☐ 2 Larry Hughes	.50	.20
☐ 3 Allen Iverson	1.50	.60
☐ 4 Josh Howard	.50	.20
☐ 5 Bonzi Wells	.20	.08
☐ 6 Jamaal Magloire	.20	.08
☐ 7 Luke Ridnour	.50	.20
☐ 8 Chauncey Billups	.50	.20
☐ 9 Dwyane Wade	2.50	1.00
☐ 10 Amare Stoudemire	1.50	.60
☐ 11 Earl Boykins	.50	.20
☐ 12 Damon Jones	.20	.08
☐ 13 Marquis Daniels	.75	.30
☐ 14 Luke Walton	.50	.20
☐ 15 Jamal Crawford	.50	.20
☐ 16 Corliss Williamson	.50	.20
☐ 17 Vince Carter	2.00	.75
☐ 18 Antoine Walker	.75	.30
☐ 19 Jason Richardson	.75	.30
☐ 20 Jason Kidd	1.25	.50
☐ 21 Peja Stojakovic	.75	.30
☐ 22 Jeff McInnis	.20	.08
☐ 23 Lamar Odom	.75	.30
☐ 24 Allan Houston	.50	.20
☐ 25 Jalen Rose	.75	.30
☐ 26 LeBron James	5.00	2.00
☐ 27 Caron Butler	.75	.30
☐ 28 Stephon Marbury	.75	.30
☐ 29 Carlos Arroyo	1.25	.50
☐ 30 Zydrunas Ilgauskas	.50	.20
☐ 31 Kobe Bryant	3.00	1.25
☐ 32 Steve Francis	.75	.30
☐ 33 Carlos Boozer	.75 *	.30
☐ 34 Primoz Brezec	.20	.08
☐ 35 Reggie Miller	.75	.30
☐ 36 Sam Cassell	.75	.30
☐ 37 Ray Allen	.75	.30
☐ 38 Drew Gooden	.50	.20
☐ 39 Chris Wilcox	.50	.20
☐ 40 Grant Hill	.75	.30
☐ 41 Andrei Kirilenko	.75	.30
☐ 42 Kirk Hinrich	.75	.30
☐ 43 Corey Maggette	.50	.20
☐ 44 Cuttino Mobley	.50	.20
☐ 45 Gilbert Arenas	.75	.30
☐ 46 Tyson Chandler	.75	.30
☐ 47 Elton Brand	.75	.30
☐ 48 Samuel Dalembert	.20	.08
☐ 49 Jarvis Hayes	.50	.20
☐ 50 Ben Wallace	.75	.30
☐ 51 Shawn Marion	.75	.30
☐ 52 Michael Redd	.50	.20
☐ 53 Richard Hamilton	.50	.20
☐ 54 Desmond Mason	.50	.20
☐ 55 Steve Nash	.75	.30
☐ 56 Antawn Jamison	.75	.30
☐ 57 Kareem Rush	.50	.20
☐ 58 Jermaine O'Neal	.75	.30
☐ 59 Keith Van Horn	.50	.20
☐ 60 Rashard Lewis	1.00	.75
☐ 61 Gerald Wallace	.50	.20
☐ 62 Jamaal Tinsley	.75	.30

☐ 63 Vladimir Radmanovic	.20	.08
☐ 64 Predrag Drobnjak	.20	.08
☐ 65 Mike Dunleavy	.50	.20
☐ 66 Baron Davis	.75	.30
☐ 67 Mike Bibby	.75	.30
☐ 68 Ricky Davis	.75	.30
☐ 69 Tracy McGrady	2.00	.75
☐ 70 Richard Jefferson	.50	.20
☐ 71 Chris Webber	.75	.30
☐ 72 Michael Finley	.75	.30
☐ 73 Pau Gasol	.75	.30
☐ 74 David West	.50	.20
☐ 75 Chris Bosh	.75	.30
☐ 76 Gary Payton	.75	.30
☐ 77 Yao Ming	2.00	.75
☐ 78 Wally Szczerbiak	.50	.20
☐ 79 Tim Duncan	1.50	.60
☐ 80 Keith Bogans	.20	.08
☐ 81 Stephen Jackson	.20	.08
☐ 82 Kevin Garnett	1.50	.60
☐ 83 Tony Parker	.75	.30
☐ 84 Kenyon Martin	.75	.30
☐ 85 Shaquille O'Neal	2.00	.75
☐ 86 Shareef Abdur-Rahim	.75	.30
☐ 87 Al Harrington	.50	.20
☐ 88 Adonal Foyle	.20	.08
☐ 89 Brian Scalabrine	.20	.08
☐ 90 Brad Miller	.75	.30
☐ 91 Carmelo Anthony	1.50	.60
☐ 92 Udonis Haslem	.20	.08
☐ 93 Zach Randolph	.75	.30
☐ 94 Paul Pierce	.75	.30
☐ 95 Maurice Taylor	.20	.08
☐ 96 Latrell Sprewell	.75	.30
☐ 97 Manu Ginobili	.75	.30
☐ 98 Dirk Nowitzki	1.25	.50
☐ 99 Jason Williams	.50	.20
☐ 100 Nick Van Exel	.75	.30
☐ 101 Charles Barkley	8.00	3.00
☐ 102 Jerry West	6.00	2.50
☐ 103 Magic Johnson	12.00	5.00
☐ 104 Kareem Abdul-Jabbar	8.00	3.00
☐ 105 Pete Maravich	25.00	10.00
☐ 106 Maurice Cheeks	6.00	2.50
☐ 107 Alex English	5.00	2.00
☐ 108 George Mikan	6.00	2.50
☐ 109 Wilt Chamberlain	8.00	3.00
☐ 110 Dominique Wilkins	5.00	2.00
☐ 111 Josh Childress RC	5.00	2.00
☐ 112 Josh Smith RC	8.00	3.00
☐ 113 Al Jefferson RC	10.00	4.00
☐ 114 Delonte West RC	5.00	2.00
☐ 115 Tony Allen RC	5.00	2.00
☐ 116 Emeka Okafor RC	15.00	6.00
☐ 117 Chris Duhon RC	6.00	2.50
☐ 118 Ben Gordon RC	15.00	6.00
☐ 119 Luol Deng RC	8.00	3.00
☐ 120 Andres Nocioni RC	5.00	2.00
☐ 121 David Harrison RC	5.00	2.00
☐ 122 Devin Harris RC	6.00	2.50
☐ 123 Shaun Livingston RC	6.00	2.50
☐ 124 Dorell Wright RC	6.00	2.50
☐ 125 J.R. Smith RC	8.00	3.00
☐ 126 Trevor Ariza RC	5.00	2.00
☐ 127 Dwight Howard RC	12.00	5.00
☐ 128 Jameer Nelson RC	6.00	2.50
☐ 129 Andre Iguodala RC	10.00	4.00
☐ 130 Sebastian Telfair RC	4.00	1.50
☐ 131 Kevin Martin RC	6.00	2.50
☐ 132 Ha Seung-Jin RC	5.00	2.00
☐ 133 Rafael Araujo RC	5.00	2.00
☐ 134 Kirk Snyder RC	5.00	2.00
☐ 135 Beno Udrih RC	6.00	2.50

2000-01 Fleer Glossy

☐ COMP.SET w/o SP's (200)	30.00	12.50
☐ COMMON CARD (1-200)	.25	.08
☐ COMMON ROOKIE (201-210)	4.00	1.50
☐ COMMON ROOKIE (211-235)	3.00	1.25
☐ COMMON ROOKIE (236-245)	3.00	1.25
☐ 1 Lamar Odom	.75	.30
☐ 2 Christian Laettner	.50	.20
☐ 3 Michael Olowokandi	.25	.08
☐ 4 Anthony Carter	.50	.20
☐ 5 Steve Francis	.75	.30

☐ 6 Darvin Ham	.25	.08
☐ 7 Mitch Richmond	.50	.20
☐ 8 Corliss Williamson	.50	.20
☐ 9 Jason Terry	.75	.30
☐ 10 Brian Grant	.50	.20
☐ 11 Peja Stojakovic	.75	.30
☐ 12 Rick Fox	.50	.20
☐ 13 Tyrone Hill	.25	.08
☐ 14 Chauncey Billups	.50	.20
☐ 15 Otis Thorpe	.25	.08
☐ 16 Richard Hamilton	.50	.20
☐ 17 Ervin Johnson	.25	.08
☐ 18 Jim Jackson	.25	.08
☐ 19 Theo Ratliff	.50	.20
☐ 20 Doug Christie	.50	.20
☐ 21 Jalen Rose	.75	.30
☐ 22 John Wallace	.25	.08
☐ 23 Ruben Patterson	.50	.20
☐ 24 Steve Nash	.75	.30
☐ 25 Toni Kukoc	.50	.20
☐ 26 Anthony Peeler	.25	.08
☐ 27 Ray Allen	.75	.30
☐ 28 Chris Mills	.25	.08
☐ 29 Chris Whitney	.25	.08
☐ 30 Nick Van Exel	.50	.20
☐ 31 Sean Elliott	.50	.20
☐ 32 Erick Strickland	.25	.08
☐ 33 Jerry Stackhouse	.75	.30
☐ 34 Antawn Jamison	.75	.30
☐ 35 Grant Hill	.75	.30
☐ 36 Antonio Daniels	.25	.08
☐ 37 Karl Malone	.75	.30
☐ 38 Keith Van Horn	.50	.20
☐ 39 Ron Harper	.25	.08
☐ 40 Stephon Marbury	.75	.30
☐ 41 Bryon Russell	.25	.08
☐ 42 Corey Maggette	.50	.20
☐ 43 Hersey Hawkins	.25	.08
☐ 44 Vince Carter	2.00	.75
☐ 45 Paul Pierce	.75	.30
☐ 46 Mikki Moore	.25	.08
☐ 47 Othella Harrington	.25	.08
☐ 48 Erick Dampier	.50	.20
☐ 49 Jerome Williams	.25	.08
☐ 50 Nick Anderson	.25	.08
☐ 51 Tim Hardaway	.50	.20
☐ 52 Allan Houston	.50	.20
☐ 53 Tyrone Nesby	.25	.08
☐ 54 Brevin Knight	.25	.08
☐ 55 Chris Mills	.25	.08
☐ 56 Ron Artest	.50	.20
☐ 57 Walt Williams	.25	.08
☐ 58 Duane Causwell	.25	.08
☐ 59 Bonzi Wells	.50	.20
☐ 60 Nate Huddleston	.75	.30
☐ 61 Dikembe Mutombo	.50	.20
☐ 62 Jahidi White	.25	.08
☐ 63 Chris Webber	.75	.30
☐ 64 Tony Battie	.25	.08
☐ 65 Mahmoud Abdul-Rauf	.25	.08
☐ 66 Monty Williams	.25	.08
☐ 67 Charlie Ward	.25	.08
☐ 68 David Robinson	.75	.30
☐ 69 Eric Snow	.50	.20
☐ 70 Jermaine O'Neal	.75	.30
☐ 71 Kurt Thomas	.50	.20
☐ 72 James Posey	.50	.20
☐ 73 Travis Best	.25	.08

#	Player		
74	Jonathan Bender	.50	.20
75	John Stockton	.75	.30
76	Jacque Vaughn	.25	.08
77	Ron Mercer	.50	.20
78	Shawn Marion	.75	.30
79	Larry Johnson	.50	.20
80	Maurice Taylor	.25	.08
81	Clifford Robinson	.25	.08
82	Scot Pollard	.25	.08
83	Patrick Ewing	.75	.30
84	Terrell Brandon	.50	.20
85	Horace Grant	.50	.20
86	Vin Baker	.50	.20
87	Al Harrington	.50	.20
88	Larry Hughes	.50	.20
89	David Wesley	.25	.08
90	Wally Szczerbiak	.50	.20
91	Charles Oakley	.25	.08
92	Tim Thomas	.50	.20
93	Mookie Blaylock	.25	.08
94	Jamal Mashburn	.50	.20
95	Roshown McLeod	.25	.08
96	John Starks	.50	.20
97	Rodney Rogers	.25	.08
98	Juwan Howard	.50	.20
99	Isaiah Rider	.50	.20
100	Rashard Lewis	.25	.08
101	Dion Glover	.25	.08
102	Johnny Newman	.25	.08
103	Avery Johnson	.25	.08
104	Darrell Armstrong	.25	.08
105	Eric Williams	.25	.08
106	Gary Payton	.75	.30
107	Antonio Davis	.25	.08
108	Dirk Nowitzki	1.25	.50
109	Trajan Langdon	.50	.20
110	Michael Dickerson	.50	.20
111	Joe Smith	.50	.20
112	Rod Strickland	.50	.20
113	Shawn Kemp	.50	.20
114	Voshon Lenard	.25	.08
115	Marcus Camby	.50	.20
116	Matt Harpring	.75	.30
117	Isaac Austin	.25	.08
118	Malik Rose	.25	.08
119	Pat Garrity	.25	.08
120	Kenny Thomas	.25	.08
121	LaPhonso Ellis	.25	.08
122	Danny Fortson	.25	.08
123	Elton Brand	.75	.30
124	Jason Williams	.50	.20
125	Kobe Bryant	3.00	1.25
126	Tariq Abdul-Wahad	.25	.08
127	Tracy McGrady	2.00	.75
128	Matt Geiger	.25	.08
129	Antoine Walker	.75	.30
130	Michael Finley	.75	.30
131	Andre Miller	.50	.20
132	Robert Horry	.50	.20
133	Donyell Marshall	.50	.20
134	Shareef Abdur-Rahim	.75	.30
135	Vonteego Cummings	.25	.08
136	Anthony Mason	.50	.20
137	Mike Bibby	.75	.30
138	Raef LaFrentz	.50	.20
139	Glen Rice	.50	.20
140	Chris Gatling	.25	.08
141	Latrell Sprewell	.75	.30
142	Austin Croshere	.25	.08
143	Kenny Anderson	.50	.20
144	Elden Campbell	.25	.08
145	Jason Kidd	1.25	.50
146	Michael Doleac	.25	.08
147	Muggsy Bogues	.25	.08
148	Tim Duncan	1.50	.60
149	Samaki Walker	.25	.08
150	Gary Trent	.25	.08
151	Kevin Garnett	1.50	.60
152	Allen Iverson	1.50	.60
153	Anfernee Hardaway	.75	.30
154	Robert Traylor	.25	.08
155	Scottie Pippen	1.25	.50
156	Shaquille O'Neal	2.00	.75
157	Vlade Divac	.50	.20
158	Lucious Harris	.25	.08
159	Keon Clark	.50	.20
160	Bo Outlaw	.25	.08
161	P.J. Brown	.25	.08
162	Derrick Coleman	.25	.08
163	Mark Jackson	.25	.08
164	Lamond Murray	.25	.08
165	Dan Majerle	.50	.20
166	Eddie Jones	.75	.30
167	Cedric Ceballos	.25	.08
168	Kendall Gill	.25	.08
169	Tom Gugliotta	.25	.08
170	Jeff McInnis	.25	.08
171	Steve Smith	.50	.20
172	Kevin Willis	.25	.08
173	Lindsey Hunter	.25	.08
174	Derek Anderson	.50	.20
175	Shandon Anderson	.25	.08
176	Adrian Griffin	.25	.08
177	Baron Davis	.75	.30
178	Radoslav Nesterovic	.25	.08
179	Glenn Robinson	.75	.30
180	Sam Cassell	.75	.30
181	Chucky Atkins	.25	.08
182	Arydas Sabonis	.50	.20
183	Damon Stoudamire	.50	.20
184	Antonio McDyess	.50	.20
185	Derek Fisher	.75	.30
186	Bryant Reeves	.25	.08
187	Hakeem Olajuwon	.75	.30
188	Kerry Kittles	.25	.08
189	Alan Henderson	.25	.08
190	Sam Perkins	.25	.08
191	Felipe Lopez	.50	.20
192	Tracy Murray	.25	.08
193	Shammond Williams	.25	.08
194	Vitaly Potapenko	.25	.08
195	John Amaechi	.25	.08
196	Quincy Lewis	.25	.08
197	Reggie Miller	.50	.20
198	Cuttino Mobley	.50	.20
199	Rex Chapman	.25	.08
200	Dale Davis	.25	.08
201	Stromile Swift RC	8.00	3.00
202	Stephen Jackson RC	6.00	2.50
203	Erick Barkley RC	4.00	1.50
204	Mike Miller RC	10.00	4.00
205	Kenyon Martin RC	12.00	5.00
206	Michael Redd RC	8.00	3.00
207	Darius Miles RC	10.00	4.00
208	Chris Mihm RC	4.00	1.50
209	Brian Cardinal RC	4.00	1.50
210	Khalid El-Amin RC	4.00	1.50
211	Hanno Mottola RC	3.00	1.25
212	Jamaal Magloire RC	3.00	1.25
213	Courtney Alexander RC	4.00	1.50
214	Mamadou N'Diaye RC	3.00	1.25
215	Chris Porter RC	3.00	1.25
216	Quentin Richardson RC	6.00	2.50
217	Eddie House RC	3.00	1.25
218	Joel Przybilla RC	3.00	1.25
219	Soumaila Samake RC	3.00	1.25
220	Speedy Claxton RC	3.00	1.25
221	Desmond Mason RC	3.00	1.25
222	Mike Smith RC	3.00	1.25
223	Lavor Postell RC	3.00	1.25
224	Pepe Sanchez RC	3.00	1.25
225	DeShawn Stevenson RC	3.00	1.25
226	Hidayet Turkoglu RC	6.00	2.50
227	Keyon Dooling RC	3.00	1.25
228	Dan Langhi RC	3.00	1.25
229	Mateen Cleaves RC	3.00	1.25
230	Donnell Harvey RC	3.00	1.25
231	DerMarr Johnson RC	3.00	1.25
232	Jason Collier RC	5.00	2.00
233	Jake Voskuhl RC	3.00	1.25
234	Mark Madsen RC	3.00	1.25
235	Jabari Smith RC	3.00	1.25
236	Morris Peterson RC	6.00	2.50
237	Daniel Santiago RC	3.00	1.25
238	Etan Thomas RC	3.00	1.25
239	A.J. Guyton RC	3.00	1.25
240	Marcus Fizer RC	3.00	1.25
241	Jamal Crawford RC	4.00	1.50
242	Jerome Moiso RC	3.00	1.25
243	Olumide Oyedeji RC	3.00	1.25
244	Paul McPherson RC	3.00	1.25
245	Eduardo Najera RC	4.00	1.50
246	Marc Jackson AU EXCH	10.00	4.00
247	Mike Penberthy AU	8.00	3.00
248	Dragan Tarlac AU	8.00	3.00
249	Ruben Wolkowyski AU	8.00	3.00
250	Iakovos Tsakalidis AU	10.00	4.00
251	Ruben Garces AU	8.00	3.00
NNO	Rookie AU EXCH		

2006-07 Fleer Hot Prospects

1	Joe Johnson	.60	.25
2	Marvin Williams	1.25	.50
3	Tony Allen	.60	.25
4	Paul Pierce	1.00	.40
5	Raymond Felton	1.25	.50
6	Emeka Okafor	1.00	.40
7	Ben Gordon	2.00	.75
8	Michael Jordan	6.00	2.50
9	Zydrunas Ilgauskas	.30	.12
10	LeBron James	6.00	2.50
11	Devin Harris	1.00	.40
12	Dirk Nowitzki	1.50	.60
13	Carmelo Anthony	2.00	.75
14	Nene	.30	.12
15	Chauncey Billups	1.00	.40
16	Ben Wallace	1.00	.40
17	Baron Davis	1.00	.40
18	Troy Murphy	1.00	.40
19	Tracy McGrady	2.50	1.00
20	Yao Ming	2.50	1.00
21	Jermaine O'Neal	1.00	.40
22	Peja Stojakovic	1.00	.40
23	Corey Maggette	.60	.25
24	Sam Cassell	1.00	.40
25	Kobe Bryant	4.00	1.50
26	Lamar Odom	1.00	.40
27	Pau Gasol	1.00	.40
28	Hakim Warrick	.60	.25
29	Shaquille O'Neal	2.50	1.00
30	Dwyane Wade	3.00	1.25
31	T.J. Ford	.60	.25
32	Michael Redd	1.00	.40
33	Kevin Garnett	2.00	.75
34	Troy Hudson	.30	.12
35	Vince Carter	2.50	1.00
36	Jason Kidd	1.50	.60
37	Desmond Mason	.30	.12
38	Chris Paul	2.50	1.00
39	Stephon Marbury	1.00	.40
40	Nate Robinson	1.00	.40
41	Grant Hill	1.00	.40
42	Darko Milicic	1.00	.40
43	Andre Iguodala	1.00	.40
44	Allen Iverson	2.00	.75
45	Steve Nash	1.00	.40
46	Amare Stoudemire	2.00	.75
47	Zach Randolph	1.00	.40
48	Sebastian Telfair	.60	.25
49	Ron Artest	.60	.25
50	Mike Bibby	1.00	.40
51	Tim Duncan	2.00	.75
52	Manu Ginobili	1.00	.40
53	Ray Allen	1.00	.40
54	Rashard Lewis	1.00	.40
55	Chris Bosh	1.00	.40
56	Charlie Villanueva	1.00	.40
57	Andrei Kirilenko	1.00	.40
58	Deron Williams	1.00	.40

#	Player		
59	Gilbert Arenas	1.00	.40
60	Antawn Jamison	1.00	.40
61	Ronnie Brewer JSY AU RC	40.00	15.00
62	LaMarcus Aldridge JSY AU RC	60.00	25.00
63	Tyrus Thomas JSY AU RC	80.00	40.00
64	Shelden Williams JSY AU RC	30.00	12.00
65	Cedric Simmons JSY AU RC	25.00	10.00
66	Randy Foye JSY AU RC	50.00	20.00
67	Rudy Gay JSY AU RC	50.00	20.00
68	Patrick O'Bryant JSY AU RC	25.00	10.00
69	Rodney Carney JSY AU RC	25.00	10.00
70	Hilton Armstrong JSY AU RC	25.00	10.00
71	Denham Brown JSY AU RC	15.00	6.00
72	Dee Brown JSY AU RC	25.00	10.00
73	Allan Ray JSY AU RC	20.00	8.00
74	Shawne Williams JSY AU RC	30.00	12.50
75	Quincy Douby JSY AU RC	15.00	6.00
76	Renaldo Balkman JSY AU RC	25.00	10.00
77	Rajon Rondo JSY AU RC	20.00	8.00
78	Marcus Williams JSY AU RC	20.00	8.00
79	Josh Boone JSY AU RC	15.00	6.00
80	Kyle Lowry JSY AU RC	15.00	6.00
81	Shannon Brown JSY AU RC	15.00	6.00
82	Jordan Farmar JSY AU RC	40.00	15.00
83	Maurice Ager JSY AU RC	15.00	6.00
84	Mardy Collins JSY AU RC	15.00	6.00
85	P.J. Tucker JSY AU RC	15.00	6.00
86	James White JSY AU RC	15.00	6.00
87	Steve Novak JSY AU RC	15.00	6.00
88	Solomon Jones JSY AU RC	15.00	6.00
89	Paul Davis JSY AU RC	15.00	6.00
90	Thabo Sefolosha AU RC	20.00	8.00
91	Craig Smith AU RC	12.00	5.00
92	Bobby Jones AU RC	12.00	5.00
93	David Noel AU RC	12.00	5.00
94	Andrea Bargnani AU RC/50	75.00	30.00
95	James Augustine AU RC	12.00	5.00
96	Daniel Gibson AU RC	30.00	12.00
97	Brandon Roy AU RC/150	80.00	40.00
98	Ryan Hollins AU RC	12.00	5.00
99	Hassan Adams AU RC	12.00	5.00
100	Pops Mensah-Bonsu AU RC	12.00	5.00
101	Will Blalock AU RC	12.00	5.00
102	Damir Markota AU RC	12.00	5.00
103	Saer Sene AU RC	12.00	5.00
104	Alexander Johnson RC	6.00	2.50
105	Leon Powe RC	6.00	2.50
106	J.J. Redick RC	12.00	5.00
107	Adam Morrison RC	15.00	6.00
108	Paul Millsap RC	12.00	5.00
109	J.R. Pinnock RC	6.00	2.50
110	Jorge Garbajosa RC	12.00	5.00
111	Vassilis Spanoulis RC	6.00	2.50
112	Yakhouba Diawara RC	6.00	2.50

2002-03 Fleer Hot Shots

	COMP. SET w/o SP's (168)	40.00	15.00
	COMMON CARD (1-168)	.20	.08
	COMMON ROOKIE (169-195)	12.00	5.00
	COMMON ROOKIE (196-201)	15.00	6.00
	COMMON ROOKIE (202-207)	5.00	2.00
	RC CARDS HAVE SHIRT UNLESS NOTED		
1	Shareef Abdur-Rahim	.75	.30
2	Kedrick Brown	.50	.20
3	Trenton Hassell	.50	.20
4	Raef LaFrentz	.50	.20
5	Donnell Harvey	.20	.08
6	Danny Fortson	.20	.08

#	Player		
7	Maurice Taylor	.20	.08
8	Wang Zhizhi	.75	.30
9	Malik Allen	.20	.08
10	Tim Thomas	.50	.20
11	Jason Kidd	1.25	.50
12	Jamaal Magloire	.20	.08
13	Grant Hill	.75	.30
14	Anfernee Hardaway	.75	.30
15	Bonzi Wells	.50	.20
16	Malik Rose	.20	.08
17	Antonio Davis	.20	.08
18	John Stockton	.75	.30
19	Theo Ratliff	.50	.20
20	Paul Pierce	.75	.30
21	Jalen Rose	.75	.30
22	Eduardo Najera	.50	.20
23	Chauncey Billups	.75	.30
24	Antawn Jamison	.75	.30
25	Jonathan Bender	.20	.08
26	Rick Fox	.50	.20
27	Brian Grant	.50	.20
28	Kevin Garnett	1.50	.60
29	Kenyon Martin	.50	.20
30	Allan Houston	.50	.20
31	Tracy McGrady	2.00	.75
32	Stephon Marbury	.75	.30
33	Mike Bibby	.75	.30
34	Predrag Drobnjak	.20	.08
35	Lamond Murray	.20	.08
36	Kwame Brown	.50	.20
37	Glenn Robinson	.75	.30
38	Antoine Walker	.75	.30
39	Zydrunas Ilgauskas	.50	.20
40	Clifford Robinson	.20	.08
41	Dirk Nowitzki	1.25	.50
42	Troy Murphy	.50	.20
43	Al Harrington	.50	.20
44	Shaquille O'Neal	2.00	.75
45	Eddie House	.20	.08
46	Troy Hudson	.20	.08
47	Rodney Rogers	.20	.08
48	Latrell Sprewell	.75	.30
49	Allen Iverson	1.50	.60
50	Derek Anderson	.50	.20
51	Vlade Divac	.50	.20
52	Rashard Lewis	.50	.20
53	Morris Peterson	.75	.30
54	Jerry Stackhouse	.75	.30
55	Jason Terry	.75	.30
56	Tyson Chandler	.75	.30
57	Jumaine Jones	.50	.20
58	Nick Van Exel	.75	.30
59	Ben Wallace	.75	.30
60	Jason Richardson	.75	.30
61	Ron Mercer	.50	.20
62	Shane Battier	.75	.30
63	Eddie Jones	.75	.30
64	Joe Smith	.50	.20
65	Courtney Alexander	.20	.08
66	Kurt Thomas	.50	.20
67	Todd MacCulloch	.20	.08
68	Ruben Patterson	.20	.08
69	Tim Duncan	1.50	.60
70	Gary Payton	.75	.30
71	Jarron Collins	.20	.08
72	Vin Baker	.50	.20
73	Eddy Curry	.75	.30
74	Michael Finley	.75	.30
75	Marcus Camby	.50	.20
76	Corliss Williamson	.50	.20
77	Steve Francis	.75	.30
78	Jermaine O'Neal	.75	.30
79	Michael Dickerson	.20	.08
80	Alonzo Mourning	.75	.30
81	Rod Strickland	.20	.08
82	Elden Campbell	.20	.08
83	Charlie Ward	.20	.08
84	Aaron McKie	.20	.08
85	Scottie Pippen	1.25	.50
86	Tony Parker	.75	.30
87	Vladimir Radmanovic	.50	.20
88	Matt Harpring	.75	.30
89	Eddie Griffin	.20	.08
90	Michael Olowokandi	.20	.08
91	Stromile Swift	.50	.20
92	Michael Redd	.75	.30

#	Player		
93	Richard Jefferson	.50	.20
94	Baron Davis	.75	.30
95	Pat Garrity	.20	.08
96	Tom Gugliotta	.20	.08
97	Arvydas Sabonis	.20	.08
98	David Robinson	.75	.30
99	Michael Bradley	.50	.20
100	Karl Malone	.75	.30
101	J.Terry/G.Robinson	.75	.30
102	T.Delk/P.Pierce	.50	.20
103	J.Rose/M. Fizer	.50	.20
104	D.Miles/R.Davis	.75	.30
105	S.Nash/D.Nowitzki	1.00	.40
106	K.Satterfield/J.Howard	.50	.20
107	R.Hamilton/B.Wallace	.75	.30
108	G.Arenas/A.Jamison	.75	.30
109	M.Norris/C.Mobley	.50	.20
110	J.Tinsley/R.Miller	.50	.20
111	A.Miller/L.Odom	.50	.20
112	D.Fisher/K.Bryant	1.50	.60
113	J.Williams/S.Battier	.75	.30
114	T.Best/E.Jones	.50	.20
115	S.Cassell/R.Allen	.50	.20
116	T.Brandon/W.Szczerbiak	.50	.20
117	K.Kittles/R.Jefferson	.50	.20
118	D.Wesley/J.Mashburn	.50	.20
119	L.Sprewell/A.McDyess	.50	.20
120	D.Armstrong/M.Miller	.50	.20
121	E.Snow/K.Van Horn	.50	.20
122	S.Marbury/S.Marion	.50	.20
123	D.Stoudamire/R.Wallace	.50	.20
124	M.Bibby/C.Webber	.75	.30
125	T.Parker/D.Robinson	.75	.30
126	K.Anderson/R.Lewis	.50	.20
127	A.Williams/V.Carter	.75	.30
128	J.Stockton/K.Malone	.75	.30
129	L.Hughes/M.Jordan	2.50	1.00
130	Joe Johnson AS	.50	.20
131	Andrei Kirilenko AS	.50	.20
132	Brendan Haywood AS	.50	.20
133	Zeljko Rebraca AS	.50	.20
134	Quentin Richardson AS	.75	.30
135	Chris Mihm AS	.20	.08
136	Darius Miles AS	.75	.30
137	Desmond Mason AS	.50	.20
138	Hidayet Turkoglu AS	.50	.20
139	Jason Richardson AS	.75	.30
140	Gerald Wallace AS	.75	.30
141	Steve Francis AS	.75	.30
142	Steve Nash AS	.75	.30
143	Peja Stojakovic AS	.75	.30
144	Ray Allen AS	.75	.30
145	Mike Miller AS	.75	.30
146	Pau Gasol AS	.75	.30
147	Steve Smith AS	.75	.30
148	Paul Pierce AS	.75	.30
149	Derek Fisher AS	.75	.30
150	Cuttino Mobley AS	.50	.20
151	Dikembe Mutombo AS	.50	.20
152	Vince Carter AS	2.00	.75
153	Antoine Walker AS	.75	.30
154	Allen Iverson AS	1.25	.60
155	Michael Jordan AS	6.00	2.50
156	Shaquille O'Neal AS	2.00	.75
157	Tim Duncan AS	1.50	.60
158	Kevin Garnett AS	1.50	.60
159	Kobe Bryant AS	3.00	1.25
160	Shareef Abdur-Rahim AS	.75	.30
161	Baron Davis AS	.75	.30
162	Jason Kidd AS	1.25	.50
163	Tracy McGrady AS	2.00	.75
164	Jermaine O'Neal AS	.75	.30
165	Elton Brand AS	.75	.30
166	Gary Payton AS	.75	.30
167	Wally Szczerbiak AS	.50	.20
168	Chris Webber AS	.75	.30
169	Yao Ming Jsy RC	80.00	40.00
170	Fred Jones RC	12.00	5.00
171	Ryan Humphrey RC	12.00	5.00
172	D.Gooden Hat/300 RC	20.00	8.00
173	Nikoloz Tskitishvili RC	12.00	5.00
174	C.Butler Shorts/350 RC	15.00	6.00
175	Vincent Yarbrough RC	12.00	5.00
176	DaJuan Wagner RC	12.00	5.00
177	Nene Hilario RC	12.00	5.00
178	Qyntel Woods/350 RC	12.00	5.00

❏ 179	Jared Jeffries RC	12.00	5.00
❏ 180	Casey Jacobsen RC	12.00	5.00
❏ 181	M.Haislip Hat/300 RC	12.00	5.00
❏ 182	Kareem Rush RC	15.00	6.00
❏ 183	Predrag Savovic RC	12.00	5.00
❏ 184	Melvin Ely RC	12.00	5.00
❏ 185	Amare Stoudmire RC	40.00	15.00
❏ 186	John Salmons RC	12.00	5.00
❏ 187	Chris Jefferies RC	12.00	5.00
❏ 188	Juan Dixon RC	20.00	8.00
❏ 189	Carlos Boozer RC	25.00	10.00
❏ 190	Roger Mason/350 RC	12.00	5.00
❏ 191	Ronald Murray/350 RC	15.00	6.00
❏ 192	Tayshaun Prince RC	15.00	6.00
❏ 193	Chris Wilcox/350 RC	12.00	5.00
❏ 194	Sam Clancy RC	12.00	5.00
❏ 195	Dan Gadzuric RC	12.00	5.00
❏ 196	D.Dickau RC/Carter Jsy	15.00	6.00
❏ 197	F.Williams RC/Carter Jsy	15.00	6.00
❏ 198	Dunleavy RC/VC Jsy/350	20.00	8.00
❏ 199	J.Will RC/Carter Jsy/350	10.00	4.00
❏ 200	Borchardt RC/Carter Jsy/350	15.00	6.00
❏ 201	Giricek RC/Carter Jsy/350	15.00	6.00
❏ 202	Pat Burke RC	5.00	2.00
❏ 203	Reggie Evans RC	5.00	2.00
❏ 204	Rasual Butler RC	5.00	2.00
❏ 205	Jiri Welsch RC	5.00	2.00
❏ 206	Mehmet Okur RC	5.00	2.00
❏ 207	Jannero Pargo RC	5.00	2.00

2000-01 Fleer Legacy

❏	COMP.SET w/o SP's (90)	50.00	20.00
❏	COMMON CARD (1-90)	.30	.10
❏	COMMON ROOKIE (91-115)	5.00	2.00
❏	COMMON JSY RC (91-115)	10.00	4.00
❏ 1	Vince Carter	2.50	1.00
❏ 2	Tim Duncan	2.00	.75
❏ 3	Darrell Armstrong	.30	.10
❏ 4	Chauncey Billups	.60	.25
❏ 5	Shawn Kemp	.60	.25
❏ 6	Stephon Marbury	1.00	.40
❏ 7	Dan Majerle	.60	.25
❏ 8	Antawn Jamison	1.00	.40
❏ 9	Hakeem Olajuwon	1.00	.40
❏ 10	Kobe Bryant	4.00	1.50
❏ 11	Paul Pierce	1.00	.40
❏ 12	Patrick Ewing	1.00	.40
❏ 13	Steve Francis	1.00	.40
❏ 14	Latrell Sprewell	1.00	.40
❏ 15	Andre Miller	.60	.25
❏ 16	Gary Payton	1.00	.40
❏ 17	Michael Finley	1.00	.40
❏ 18	Brian Grant	.60	.25
❏ 19	Scottie Pippen	1.50	.60
❏ 20	Antonio Davis	.30	.10
❏ 21	Jason Williams	.60	.25
❏ 22	Chris Gatling	.30	.10
❏ 23	David Robinson	1.00	.40
❏ 24	John Stockton	1.00	.40
❏ 25	Matt Harpring	1.00	.40
❏ 26	Rashard Lewis	1.00	.40
❏ 27	Dirk Nowitzki	6.00	2.50
❏ 28	Alan Henderson	.30	.10
❏ 29	Rasheed Wallace	1.00	.40
❏ 30	Ben Wallace	1.00	.40
❏ 31	Chris Webber	1.00	.40
❏ 32	Elton Brand	1.00	.40
❏ 33	Anfernee Hardaway	1.00	.40

❏ 34	Isaiah Rider	.30	.10
❏ 35	Baron Davis	1.00	.40
❏ 36	Eric Snow	.60	.25
❏ 37	Tom Gugliotta	.30	.10
❏ 38	Grant Hill	1.00	.40
❏ 39	Lamar Odom	1.00	.40
❏ 40	Kevin Garnett	2.00	.75
❏ 41	Reggie Miller	1.00	.40
❏ 42	Karl Malone	1.00	.40
❏ 43	Ray Allen	1.00	.40
❏ 44	Derek Anderson	.60	.25
❏ 45	Glen Rice	.60	.25
❏ 46	Antonio McDyess	.60	.25
❏ 47	Eddie Jones	1.00	.40
❏ 48	Mitch Richmond	.60	.25
❏ 49	Mark Jackson	.60	.25
❏ 50	Larry Johnson	.60	.25
❏ 51	Ron Mercer	.60	.25
❏ 52	Jason Kidd	1.50	.60
❏ 53	Voshon Lenard	.30	.10
❏ 54	Rick Fox	.60	.25
❏ 55	Rod Strickland	.30	.10
❏ 56	Jalen Rose	1.00	.40
❏ 57	Tracy McGrady	2.50	1.00
❏ 58	Dikembe Mutombo	.60	.25
❏ 59	Richard Hamilton	.60	.25
❏ 60	Jerry Stackhouse	1.00	.40
❏ 61	Peja Stojakovic	1.00	.40
❏ 62	Sam Cassell	1.00	.40
❏ 63	Sean Elliott	.60	.25
❏ 64	Keith Van Horn	1.00	.40
❏ 65	Mike Bibby	1.00	.40
❏ 66	Larry Hughes	.60	.25
❏ 67	Nick Van Exel	1.00	.40
❏ 68	Michael Dickerson	.30	.10
❏ 69	Terrell Brandon	.60	.25
❏ 70	Chucky Atkins	.30	.10
❏ 71	John Starks	.60	.25
❏ 72	Glenn Robinson	1.00	.40
❏ 73	Cuttino Mobley	.60	.25
❏ 74	Shaquille O'Neal	2.50	1.00
❏ 75	Shareef Abdur-Rahim	1.00	.40
❏ 76	Danny Fortson	.30	.10
❏ 77	Austin Croshere	.60	.25
❏ 78	Jamal Mashburn	.60	.25
❏ 79	Kenny Anderson	.60	.25
❏ 80	Shawn Marion	1.00	.40
❏ 81	Travis Best	.30	.10
❏ 82	Derrick Coleman	.30	.10
❏ 83	Toni Kukoc	.60	.25
❏ 84	Allen Iverson	2.00	.75
❏ 85	Allan Houston	.60	.25
❏ 86	Antoine Walker	1.00	.40
❏ 87	Wally Szczerbiak	.60	.25
❏ 88	Raef LaFrentz	.60	.25
❏ 89	Tim Hardaway	.60	.25
❏ 90	Juwan Howard	.60	.25
❏ 91	Kenyon Martin JSY RC	20.00	8.00
❏ 92	Stromile Swift RC	6.00	2.50
❏ 93	Darius Miles JSY RC	15.00	6.00
❏ 94	Mike Miller JSY RC	12.00	5.00
❏ 95	Marcus Fizer RC	5.00	2.00
❏ 96	Jerome Moiso JSY RC	10.00	4.00
❏ 97	DerMarr Johnson JSY RC	10.00	4.00
❏ 98	Quentin Richardson JSY RC	15.00	6.00
❏ 99	Morris Peterson JSY RC	10.00	4.00
❏ 100	Jamaal Magloire RC	5.00	2.00
❏ 101	Mateen Cleaves RC	5.00	2.00
❏ 102	Hidayet Turkoglu RC	8.00	3.00
❏ 103	Chris Mihm JSY RC	5.00	2.00
❏ 104	Courtney Alexander RC	5.00	2.00
❏ 105	Joel Przybilla RC	5.00	2.00
❏ 106	Speedy Claxton JSY RC	10.00	4.00
❏ 107	Keyon Dooling JSY RC	10.00	4.00
❏ 108	Desmond Mason JSY RC	10.00	4.00
❏ 109	Jamal Crawford RC	6.00	2.50
❏ 110	DeShawn Stevenson RC	5.00	2.00
❏ 111	Stephen Jackson RC	6.00	2.50
❏ 112	Marc Jackson RC	5.00	2.00
❏ 113	Hanno Mottola JSY RC	10.00	4.00
❏ 114	Eduardo Najera RC	6.00	2.50
❏ 115	Wang Zhizhi RC	12.00	5.00
❏	WUSA1 Vince Carter/600	100.00	50.00

2001-02 Fleer Marquee

❏	COMPLETE SET w/o SPs	40.00	20.00
❏	COMMON ROOKIE (116-125)	3.00	1.25
❏ 1	DerMarr Johnson	.50	.20
❏ 2	Darius Miles	.75	.30
❏ 3	Michael Jordan	15.00	6.00
❏ 4	Speedy Claxton	.50	.20
❏ 5	Stromile Swift	.50	.20
❏ 6	Michael Finley	.75	.30
❏ 7	Kurt Thomas	.50	.20
❏ 8	Tim Duncan	1.50	.60
❏ 9	Kenyon Martin	.75	.30
❏ 10	Jermaine O'Neal	.75	.30
❏ 11	Elton Brand	.75	.30
❏ 12	Jamal Mashburn	.50	.20
❏ 13	Jumaine Jones	.50	.20
❏ 14	Stephon Marbury	.75	.30
❏ 15	Eddie Jones	.75	.30
❏ 16	Antonio McDyess	.50	.20
❏ 17	Tim Thomas	.50	.20
❏ 18	Gary Payton	.75	.30
❏ 19	Latrell Sprewell	.75	.30
❏ 20	Grant Hill	.75	.30
❏ 21	Jason Terry	.75	.30
❏ 22	Marcus Fizer	.50	.20
❏ 23	Anthony Mason	.50	.20
❏ 24	Bonzi Wells	.50	.20
❏ 25	Sam Cassell	.75	.30
❏ 26	Jerry Stackhouse	.75	.30
❏ 27	Hidayet Turkoglu	.50	.20
❏ 28	Morris Peterson	.50	.20
❏ 29	John Stockton	.75	.30
❏ 30	Dikembe Mutombo	.50	.20
❏ 31	Mitch Richmond	.50	.20
❏ 32	Andre Miller	.50	.20
❏ 33	Joe Smith	.50	.20
❏ 34	Mike Bibby	.75	.30
❏ 35	Wally Szczerbiak	.50	.20
❏ 36	Steve Francis	.75	.30
❏ 37	Nazr Mohammed	.25	.08
❏ 38	Antoine Walker	.75	.30
❏ 39	Courtney Alexander	.50	.20
❏ 40	Shawn Marion	.75	.30
❏ 41	Jamal Mashburn	.50	.20
❏ 42	Steve Nash	.75	.30
❏ 43	Antonio Davis	.25	.08
❏ 44	Steve Smith	.50	.20
❏ 45	Jason Kidd	1.25	.50
❏ 46	Reggie Miller	.75	.30
❏ 47	Quentin Richardson	.50	.20
❏ 48	Baron Davis	.75	.30
❏ 49	Juwan Howard	.50	.20
❏ 50	Rasheed Wallace	.75	.30
❏ 51	Brian Grant	.50	.20
❏ 52	Nick Van Exel	.75	.30
❏ 53	Donyell Marshall	.50	.20
❏ 54	Vin Baker	.50	.20
❏ 55	Allan Houston	.50	.20
❏ 56	Mike Miller	.75	.30
❏ 57	Shaquille O'Neal	2.00	.75
❏ 58	Ron Mercer	.50	.20
❏ 59	Lindsey Hunter	.25	.08
❏ 60	Peja Stojakovic	.75	.30
❏ 61	Ray Allen	.75	.30
❏ 62	Antawn Jamison	.75	.30
❏ 63	Theo Ratliff	.50	.20
❏ 64	Vince Carter	2.00	.75

#	Player		
65	DeShawn Stevenson	.50	.20
66	Allen Iverson	1.50	.60
67	Derek Fisher	.75	.30
68	Dirk Nowitzki	1.25	.50
69	Keith Van Horn	.75	.30
70	David Robinson	.75	.30
71	Terrell Brandon	.50	.20
72	Cuttino Mobley	.50	.20
73	Shareef Abdur-Rahim	.75	.30
74	Paul Pierce	.75	.30
75	Elden Campbell	.25	.08
76	Anfernee Hardaway	.75	.30
77	Alonzo Mourning	.50	.20
78	Raef LaFrentz	.50	.20
79	Richard Hamilton	.50	.20
80	Rashard Lewis	.50	.20
81	Marcus Camby	.50	.20
82	Jalen Rose	.75	.30
83	Lamar Odom	.75	.30
84	David Wesley	.25	.08
85	James Posey	.50	.20
86	Derek Anderson	.50	.20
87	Glenn Robinson	.50	.20
88	Clifford Robinson	.25	.08
89	Kerry Kittles	.25	.08
90	Hakeem Olajuwon	.75	.30
91	Patrick Ewing	.75	.30
92	Tracy McGrady	2.00	.75
93	Kobe Bryant	3.00	1.25
94	Chris Mihm	.50	.20
95	Lorenzen Wright	.25	.08
96	Chris Webber	.75	.30
97	Kevin Garnett	1.50	.60
98	Larry Hughes	.50	.20
99	Keyon Dooling	.50	.20
100	Karl Malone	.75	.30
101	Joe Johnson RC	6.00	2.50
102	Tyson Chandler RC	6.00	2.50
103	Eddy Curry RC	5.00	2.00
104	Jason Richardson RC	5.00	2.00
105	Troy Murphy RC	4.00	1.50
106	Eddie Griffin RC	3.00	1.25
107	Jamaal Tinsley RC	3.00	1.25
108	Pau Gasol RC	8.00	3.00
109	Shane Battier RC	3.00	1.25
110	Richard Jefferson RC	3.00	1.25
111	Steven Hunter RC	2.00	.75
112	Tony Parker RC	8.00	3.00
113	Vladimir Radmanovic RC	2.50	1.00
114	Andrei Kirilenko RC	6.00	2.50
115	Kwame Brown RC	3.00	1.25
116	S.Dalembert RC/D.Brown RC	3.00	1.25
117	J.Forte RC/Ke.Brown RC	3.00	1.25
118	Randolph RC/R.Boumtje RC	6.00	2.50
119	O.Torres RC/T.Morris RC	3.00	1.25
120	A.Ford RC/K.Satterfield RC	4.00	1.50
121	R.White RC/Z.Rebraca RC	3.00	1.25
122	T.Hassell RC/E.Watson RC	3.00	1.25
123	D.Diop RC/P.Brezec RC	4.00	1.50
124	E.Brown RC/G.Wallace RC	3.00	1.25
125	L.Woods RC/B.Haywood RC	3.00	1.25
126	Mengke Bateer RC	8.00	3.00
NNO	Vince Carter AU/113	100.00	50.00

2001-02 Fleer Maximum

	COMPLETE SET (220)	300.00	125.00
	COMP.SET w/o SP's (180)	40.00	15.00
	COMMON CARD (1-180)	.20	.07

#	Player		
	COMMON ROOKIE (181-220)	2.50	1.00
	CARTER AU NOT INCLUDED IN SET PRICE		
1	Ray Allen	.60	.25
2	Elton Brand	.60	.25
3	Grant Hill	.60	.25
4	Tracy McGrady	1.50	.60
5	Chris Webber	.60	.25
6	Latrell Sprewell	.60	.25
7	Paul Pierce	.60	.25
8	Jason Kidd	.60	.25
9	Shaquille O'Neal	1.50	.60
10	Stephon Marbury	.60	.25
11	Steve Francis	.60	.25
12	Vince Carter	1.50	.60
13	Allen Iverson	1.25	.50
14	Kevin Garnett	1.25	.50
15	Eddie Jones	.60	.25
16	Antoine Walker	.60	.25
17	Kobe Bryant	2.50	1.00
18	Avery Johnson	.20	.07
19	Damon Stoudamire	.40	.15
20	Kurt Thomas	.40	.15
21	Aaron McKie	.40	.15
22	Chris Whitney	.20	.07
23	David Robinson	.60	.25
24	Erick Dampier	.40	.15
25	Jumaine Jones	.40	.15
26	Radoslav Nesterovic	.40	.15
27	Robert Horry	.40	.15
28	Ben Wallace	.60	.25
29	Christian Laettner	.40	.15
30	Eddie Robinson	.40	.15
31	Alvin Williams	.20	.07
32	Mart Harpring	.60	.25
33	Terrell Brandon	.40	.15
34	Tim Duncan	1.25	.50
35	Bonzi Wells	.40	.15
36	Clarence Weatherspoon	.20	.07
37	George McCloud	.20	.07
38	Jermaine O'Neal	.60	.25
39	Al Harrington	.40	.15
40	Antawn Jamison	.60	.25
41	John Amaechi	.20	.07
42	Rod Strickland	.20	.07
43	Stacey Augmon	.20	.07
44	Dion Glover	.20	.07
45	Michael Dickerson	.40	.15
46	Anfernee Hardaway	.60	.25
47	Rashard Lewis	.40	.15
48	Shawn Bradley	.20	.07
49	Todd MacCulloch	.20	.07
50	Antonio McDyess	.40	.15
51	Darrell Armstrong	.20	.07
52	Jalen Rose	.60	.25
53	Mike Bibby	.60	.25
54	P.J. Brown	.20	.07
55	Quincy Lewis	.20	.07
56	Doug Christie	.40	.15
57	Elden Campbell	.20	.07
58	James Posey	.40	.15
59	Karl Malone	.60	.25
60	Patrick Ewing	.60	.25
61	Sam Cassell	.60	.25
62	Baron Davis	.60	.25
63	Corey Maggette	.40	.15
64	Donyell Marshall	.40	.15
65	Ervin Johnson	.20	.07
66	Horace Grant	.40	.15
67	Nick Van Exel	.60	.25
68	Vlade Divac	.40	.15
69	Allan Houston	.40	.15
70	Antonio Davis	.20	.07
71	Dale Davis	.20	.07
72	Eduardo Najera	.40	.15
73	Kenny Anderson	.40	.15
74	Kevin Willis	.20	.07
75	LaPhonso Ellis	.20	.07
76	Anthony Mason	.40	.15
77	Greg Ostertag	.20	.07
78	Jamal Mashburn	.40	.15
79	Jeff McInnis	.20	.07
80	Peja Stojakovic	.60	.25
81	Scott Williams	.20	.07
82	Bryon Russell	.20	.07
83	Chucky Atkins	.20	.07

#	Player		
84	Darius Miles	.60	.25
85	David Wesley	.20	.07
86	Hidayet Turkoglu	.40	.15
87	Mark Pope	.20	.07
88	Dana Barros	.20	.07
89	Glenn Robinson	.40	.15
90	John Stockton	.60	.25
91	Lamar Odom	.60	.25
92	Mike Miller	.60	.25
93	Ron Artest	.40	.15
94	Adonal Foyle	.20	.07
95	Andre Miller	.20	.07
96	Eric Snow	.40	.15
97	Stanislav Medvedenko	.20	.07
98	Steve Smith	.40	.15
99	Wally Szczerbiak	.40	.15
100	Chris Mihm	.40	.15
101	Danny Fortson	.20	.07
102	Dikembe Mutombo	.40	.15
103	Joe Smith	.40	.15
104	Lindsey Hunter	.20	.07
105	Malik Rose	.20	.07
106	Austin Croshere	.20	.07
107	Chris Gatling	.20	.07
108	Hakeem Olajuwon	.60	.25
109	Mark Jackson	.40	.15
110	Milt Palacio	.20	.07
111	Ruben Patterson	.40	.15
112	Steve Nash	.60	.25
113	Brian Grant	.40	.15
114	Dirk Nowitzki	1.00	.40
115	Jeff Foster	.20	.07
116	Morris Peterson	.40	.15
117	Scottie Pippen	1.50	.60
118	Lamond Murray	.20	.07
119	Larry Hughes	.40	.15
120	Shareef Abdur-Rahim	.60	.25
121	Tony Delk	.20	.07
122	Vin Baker	.40	.15
123	Art Long	.20	.07
124	Kenyon Martin	.60	.25
125	Michael Finley	.60	.25
126	Stromile Swift	.40	.15
127	Toni Kukoc	.40	.15
128	Alonzo Mourning	.40	.15
129	Charlie Ward	.20	.07
130	Eric Williams	.20	.07
131	Jerome Williams	.20	.07
132	Raef LaFrentz	.40	.15
133	Rasheed Wallace	.60	.25
134	Reggie Miller	.60	.25
135	Cuttino Mobley	.40	.15
136	Desmond Mason	.40	.15
137	Jason Williams	.40	.15
138	Keith Van Horn	.60	.25
139	Nazr Mohammed	.20	.07
140	Shawn Marion	.60	.25
141	Tim Hardaway	.40	.15
142	Anthony Carter	.20	.07
143	Danny Manning	.20	.07
144	Derek Anderson	.40	.15
145	Jason Terry	.60	.25
146	Kenny Thomas	.20	.07
147	Othella Harrington	.20	.07
148	Corliss Williamson	.40	.15
149	Derek Fisher	.60	.25
150	Ricky Davis	.40	.15
151	Stephen Jackson	.40	.15
152	Tyrone Nesby	.20	.07
153	Calvin Booth	.20	.07
154	Emanual Davis	.20	.07
155	Kerry Kittles	.20	.07
156	Marc Jackson	.20	.07
157	Samaki Walker	.20	.07
158	Tom Gugliotta	.20	.07
159	Wesley Person	.20	.07
160	Antonio Daniels	.20	.07
161	Charles Oakley	.20	.07
162	Chauncey Billups	.40	.15
163	Derrick Coleman	.20	.07
164	Jerry Stackhouse	.60	.25
165	Michael Jordan	10.00	4.00
166	Quentin Richardson	.40	.15
167	Gary Payton	.60	.25
168	Iakovos Tsakalidis	.20	.07
169	Juwan Howard	.40	.15

☐ 170	Lorenzen Wright	.20	.07
☐ 171	Marcus Camby	.40	.15
☐ 172	Maurice Taylor	.40	.15
☐ 173	Jacque Vaughn	.20	.07
☐ 174	Bruce Bowen	.20	.07
☐ 175	Clifford Robinson	.20	.07
☐ 176	Michael Olowokandi	.40	.15
☐ 177	Richard Hamilton	.40	.15
☐ 178	Ron Mercer	.40	.15
☐ 179	Speedy Claxton	.40	.15
☐ 180	Tim Thomas	.40	.15
☐ 181	Joe Johnson HW RC	8.00	3.00
☐ 182	Pau Gasol HW RC	10.00	4.00
☐ 183	Kwame Brown HW RC	4.00	1.50
☐ 184	Zach Randolph HW RC	8.00	3.00
☐ 185	Jason Richardson HW RC	6.00	2.50
☐ 186	Jamaal Tinsley HW RC	4.00	1.50
☐ 187	Oscar Torres HW RC	3.00	1.25
☐ 188	Rodney White HW RC	3.00	1.25
☐ 189	Kedrick Brown HW RC	2.50	1.00
☐ 190	Tony Parker HW RC	10.00	4.00
☐ 191	Samuel Dalembert HW RC	2.50	1.00
☐ 192	Shane Battier HW RC	4.00	1.50
☐ 193	Loren Woods HW RC	2.50	1.00
☐ 194	Richard Jefferson HW RC	4.00	1.50
☐ 195	Jeff Trepagnier HW RC	2.50	1.00
☐ 196	Terence Morris HW RC	2.50	1.00
☐ 197	Eddie Griffin TC RC	3.00	1.25
☐ 198	Primoz Brezec TC RC	3.00	1.25
☐ 199	V.Radmanovic TC RC	3.00	1.25
☐ 200	Gerald Wallace TC RC	5.00	2.00
☐ 201	Alton Ford TC RC	3.00	1.25
☐ 202	Steven Hunter TC RC	2.50	1.00
☐ 203	Michael Bradley TC RC	2.50	1.00
☐ 204	B.Armstrong TC RC	3.00	1.25
☐ 205	Jamaal Tinsley TC RC	4.00	1.50
☐ 206	Bobby Simmons TC RC	2.50	1.00
☐ 207	Zeljko Rebraca TC RC	2.50	1.00
☐ 208	Tony Parker TC RC	10.00	4.00
☐ 209	Troy Murphy TC RC	5.00	2.00
☐ 210	Kwame Brown TC RC	4.00	1.50
☐ 211	Andrei Kirilenko TC RC	6.00	2.50
☐ 212	Trenton Hassell TC RC	4.00	1.50
☐ 213	Pau Gasol TC RC	10.00	4.00
☐ 214	Tang Hamilton TC RC	2.50	1.00
☐ 215	Joseph Forte TC RC	6.00	2.50
☐ 216	Eddy Curry TC RC	6.00	2.50
☐ 217	DeSagana Diop TC RC	2.50	1.00
☐ 218	Joe Johnson TC RC	5.00	2.00
☐ 219	Tyson Chandler TC RC	6.00	2.50
☐ 220	Jason Collins TC RC	2.50	1.00
☐ NNO	V.Carter AU/375	100.00	50.00

1999-00 Fleer Mystique

☐	COMPLETE SET (150)	150.00	75.00
☐	COMPLETE SET w/o SP (100)	30.00	15.00
☐	COMMON CARD (1-100)	.30	.10
☐	COMMON ROOKIE (101-140)	1.25	.50
☐	COMMON STAR (141-150)	2.00	.75
☐ 1	Allen Iverson	2.00	.75
☐ 2	Grant Hill	1.00	.40
☐ 3	Antawn Jamison	1.50	.60
☐ 4	Glenn Robinson	1.00	.40
☐ 5	Kenny Anderson	.60	.25
☐ 6	Dikembe Mutombo	.60	.25
☐ 7	Gary Trent	.30	.10
☐ 8	Brevin Knight	.30	.10
☐ 9	Chucky Brown	.30	.10

☐ 10	Derek Anderson	.60	.25
☐ 11	Ricky Davis	.60	.25
☐ 12	Chris Webber	1.00	.40
☐ 13	Jalen Rose	1.00	.40
☐ 14	Antoine Walker	1.00	.40
☐ 15	Michael Dickerson	.60	.25
☐ 16	Tim Hardaway	.60	.25
☐ 17	Toni Kukoc	.60	.25
☐ 18	Rael LaFrentz	.60	.25
☐ 19	Anthony Mason	.60	.25
☐ 20	John Stockton	1.00	.40
☐ 21	Hakeem Olajuwon	1.00	.40
☐ 22	Shaquille O'Neal	2.50	1.00
☐ 23	Scottie Pippen	1.50	.60
☐ 24	Maurice Taylor	.60	.25
☐ 25	Tariq Abdul-Wahad	.30	.10
☐ 26	Tracy McGrady	2.50	1.00
☐ 27	Joe Smith	.60	.25
☐ 28	Rod Strickland	.30	.10
☐ 29	Ruben Patterson	.60	.25
☐ 30	Tom Gugliotta	.30	.10
☐ 31	Ray Allen	1.00	.40
☐ 32	Elden Campbell	.30	.10
☐ 33	Lindsey Hunter	.30	.10
☐ 34	Larry Johnson	.60	.25
☐ 35	Michael Olowokandi	.60	.25
☐ 36	Mario Elie	.30	.10
☐ 37	Anfernee Hardaway	1.00	.40
☐ 38	Juwan Howard	.60	.25
☐ 39	Karl Malone	1.00	.40
☐ 40	Alonzo Mourning	.60	.25
☐ 41	Billy Owens	.30	.10
☐ 42	Mitch Richmond	.60	.25
☐ 43	Darrell Armstrong	.30	.10
☐ 44	Jason Williams	1.00	.40
☐ 45	Mookie Blaylock	.30	.10
☐ 46	Gary Payton	1.00	.40
☐ 47	Brian Grant	.60	.25
☐ 48	Paul Pierce	1.00	.40
☐ 49	Michael Finley	1.00	.40
☐ 50	Reggie Miller	1.00	.40
☐ 51	Corliss Williamson	.60	.25
☐ 52	Shandon Anderson	.30	.10
☐ 53	Stephon Marbury	1.00	.40
☐ 54	Sam Cassell	1.00	.40
☐ 55	Bryon Russell	.30	.10
☐ 56	Rasheed Wallace	1.00	.40
☐ 57	Jayson Williams	.30	.10
☐ 58	Damon Stoudamire	.60	.25
☐ 59	Terrell Brandon	.60	.25
☐ 60	Loy Vaught	.30	.10
☐ 61	Kobe Bryant	4.00	1.50
☐ 62	Vlade Divac	.60	.25
☐ 63	Derek Fisher	1.00	.40
☐ 64	Isaiah Rider	.30	.10
☐ 65	Eddie Jones	1.00	.40
☐ 66	Kevin Garnett	2.00	.75
☐ 67	David Robinson	1.00	.40
☐ 68	Marcus Camby	.60	.25
☐ 69	Glen Rice	.60	.25
☐ 70	Mike Bibby	1.00	.40
☐ 71	Patrick Ewing	1.00	.40
☐ 72	Robert Traylor	.30	.10
☐ 73	Tim Duncan	2.00	.75
☐ 74	Michael Doleac	.30	.10
☐ 75	Steve Smith	.60	.25
☐ 76	Allan Houston	.60	.25
☐ 77	Jamal Mashburn	.60	.25
☐ 78	Brent Barry	.60	.25
☐ 79	Charles Barkley	1.25	.50
☐ 80	Ron Mercer	.60	.25
☐ 81	Jerry Stackhouse	1.00	.40
☐ 82	Keith Van Horn	1.00	.40
☐ 83	Hersey Hawkins	.60	.25
☐ 84	Avery Johnson	.30	.10
☐ 85	Cedric Ceballos	.30	.10
☐ 86	P.J. Brown	.30	.10
☐ 87	Doug Christie	.60	.25
☐ 88	Shawn Kemp	.60	.25
☐ 89	Dirk Nowitzki	2.00	.75
☐ 90	Erick Dampier	.60	.25
☐ 91	Antonio McDyess	.60	.25
☐ 92	Mark Jackson	.60	.25
☐ 93	Clifford Robinson	.30	.10
☐ 94	Vince Carter	2.50	1.00
☐ 95	Shareef Abdur-Rahim	1.00	.40

☐ 96	Vin Baker	.60	.25
☐ 97	Larry Hughes	1.00	.40
☐ 98	Jason Kidd	1.50	.60
☐ 99	Kerry Kittles	.30	.10
☐ 100	Latrell Sprewell	1.00	.40
☐ 101	Lamar Odom RC	6.00	2.50
☐ 102	Elton Brand RC	8.00	3.00
☐ 103	Baron Davis RC	10.00	4.00
☐ 104	Jason Terry RC	4.00	1.50
☐ 105	Corey Maggette RC	6.00	2.50
☐ 106	Wally Szczerbiak RC	6.00	2.50
☐ 107	Richard Hamilton RC	6.00	2.50
☐ 108	Milt Palacio RC	1.25	.50
☐ 109	Ron Artest RC	4.00	1.50
☐ 110	Eddie Robinson RC	4.00	1.50
☐ 111	Jumaine Jones RC	2.50	1.00
☐ 112	Andre Miller RC	6.00	2.50
☐ 113	Chucky Atkins RC	2.50	1.00
☐ 114	Kenny Thomas RC	2.50	1.00
☐ 115	Scott Padgett RC	2.00	.75
☐ 116	Devean George RC	3.00	1.25
☐ 117	Tim Young RC	1.25	.50
☐ 118	Tim James RC	2.00	.75
☐ 119	Quincy Lewis RC	2.00	.75
☐ 120	James Posey RC	4.00	1.50
☐ 121	Shawn Marion RC	8.00	3.00
☐ 122	A.Radojevic RC	1.25	.50
☐ 123	Trajan Langdon RC	2.50	1.00
☐ 124	Laron Profit RC	2.00	.75
☐ 125	Jonathan Bender RC	6.00	2.50
☐ 126	William Avery RC	2.50	1.00
☐ 127	Cal Bowdler RC	2.00	.75
☐ 128	Dion Glover RC	2.00	.75
☐ 129	Jeff Foster RC	2.00	.75
☐ 130	Steve Francis RC	8.00	3.00
☐ 131	Adrian Griffin RC	2.00	.75
☐ 132	Vonteego Cummings RC	2.50	1.00
☐ 133	Rafer Alston RC	2.50	1.00
☐ 134	Michael Ruffin RC	1.50	.60
☐ 135	Chris Herren RC	2.00	.75
☐ 136	Jermaine Jackson RC	1.25	.50
☐ 137	Lazaro Borrell RC	1.25	.50
☐ 138	Obinna Ekezie RC	1.50	.60
☐ 139	Rick Hughes RC	1.25	.50
☐ 140	Todd MacCulloch RC	2.00	.75
☐ 141	Kobe Bryant STAR	12.00	5.00
☐ 142	Vince Carter STAR	8.00	3.00
☐ 143	Tim Duncan STAR	6.00	2.50
☐ 144	Kevin Garnett STAR	6.00	2.50
☐ 145	Allen Iverson STAR	6.00	2.50
☐ 146	Keith Van Horn STAR		
☐ 147	Grant Hill STAR	2.00	.75
☐ 148	Stephon Marbury STAR	2.00	.75
☐ 149	Antoine Walker STAR	2.50	1.00
☐ 150	Shaquille O'Neal STAR	8.00	3.00

2000-01 Fleer Mystique

☐	COMPLETE SET w/o RC (100)	30.00	15.00
☐	COMMON CARD (1-100)	.25	.08
☐	COMMON ROOKIE (101-106)	8.00	3.00
☐	COMMON ROOKIE (107-112)	5.00	2.00
☐	COMMON ROOKIE (113-117)	4.00	1.50
☐	COMMON ROOKIE (118-124)	2.50	1.00
☐	COMMON ROOKIE (125-130)	1.50	.60
☐	COMMON ROOKIE (131-136)	1.25	.50
☐ 1	Shaquille O'Neal	2.00	.75
☐ 2	Gary Payton	.75	.30
☐ 3	Nick Van Exel	.75	.30

#	Player		
4	Alonzo Mourning	.50	.20
5	Shawn Marion	.75	.30
6	Rod Strickland	.25	.08
7	Mookie Blaylock	.25	.08
8	Terrell Brandon	.50	.20
9	Bryon Russell	.25	.08
10	Jerry Stackhouse	.75	.30
11	Glenn Robinson	.75	.30
12	Rasheed Wallace	.75	.30
13	Tracy McGrady	2.00	.75
14	Raef LaFrentz	.50	.20
15	P.J. Brown	.25	.08
16	Anfernee Hardaway	.75	.30
17	Mike Bibby	.75	.30
18	Elden Campbell	.25	.08
19	Steve Francis	.75	.30
20	Keith Van Horn	.75	.30
21	Karl Malone	.75	.30
22	Dirk Nowitzki	1.25	.50
23	Glen Rice	.50	.20
24	Tom Gugliotta	.25	.08
25	Avery Johnson	.25	.08
26	Michael Finley	.75	.30
27	Theo Ratliff	.50	.20
28	Juwan Howard	.50	.20
29	Anthony Carter	.50	.20
30	Kobe Bryant	3.00	1.25
31	Toni Kukoc	.50	.20
32	Jason Terry	.75	.30
33	Elton Brand	.75	.30
34	Reggie Miller	.75	.30
35	Latrell Sprewell	.75	.30
36	Adrian Griffin	.25	.08
37	Cuttino Mobley	.50	.20
38	Maurice Taylor	.25	.08
39	Allen Iverson	1.50	.60
40	Tim Duncan	1.50	.60
41	Andre Miller	.50	.20
42	Antonio Davis	.25	.08
43	Howard Eisley	.25	.08
44	Vlade Divac	.50	.20
45	Brevin Knight	.25	.08
46	Lamar Odom	.75	.30
47	Ron Mercer	.50	.20
48	Jason Williams	.50	.20
49	Antawn Jamison	.75	.30
50	Wally Szczerbiak	.50	.20
51	Chris Webber	.75	.30
52	Larry Hughes	.50	.20
53	Kevin Garnett	1.50	.60
54	Michael Dickerson	.50	.20
55	Chucky Atkins	.25	.08
56	Jalen Rose	.75	.30
57	John Amaechi	.25	.08
58	Shareef Abdur-Rahim	.75	.30
59	Shawn Kemp	.50	.20
60	Derek Anderson	.50	.20
61	Darrell Armstrong	.25	.08
62	Vin Baker	.50	.20
63	Paul Pierce	.75	.30
64	Donyell Marshall	.50	.20
65	Jamie Feick	.25	.08
66	Travis Best	.25	.08
67	Baron Davis	.75	.30
68	Hakeem Olajuwon	.75	.30
69	Joe Smith	.50	.20
70	Ruben Patterson	.50	.20
71	Antonio McDyess	.50	.20
72	Jamal Mashburn	.50	.20
73	Jason Kidd	1.25	.50
74	Eddie Jones	.75	.30
75	Kenny Thomas	.25	.08
76	Marcus Camby	.50	.20
77	Doug Christie	.50	.20
78	Ron Artest	.50	.20
79	Mark Jackson	.25	.08
80	Allan Houston	.50	.20
81	John Stockton	.75	.30
82	Jerome Williams	.50	.20
83	Tim Thomas	.50	.20
84	Alan Henderson	.25	.08
85	Antoine Walker	.75	.30
86	Robert Horry	.50	.20
87	Stephon Marbury	.75	.30
88	David Robinson	.75	.30
89	Lindsey Hunter	.25	.08
90	Richard Hamilton	.50	.20
91	Damon Stoudamire	.50	.20
92	Dikembe Mutombo	.50	.20
93	Anthony Mason	.50	.20
94	Austin Croshere	.50	.20
95	Patrick Ewing	.75	.30
96	Mitch Richmond	.50	.20
97	Grant Hill	.75	.30
98	Ray Allen	.75	.30
99	Scottie Pippen	1.25	.50
100	Vince Carter	2.00	.75
101	Kenyon Martin A RC	15.00	6.00
102	Stromile Swift A RC	10.00	4.00
103	Darius Miles A RC	12.00	5.00
104	Marcus Fizer A RC	8.00	3.00
105	Mike Miller A RC	12.00	5.00
106	DerMarr Johnson A RC	8.00	3.00
107	Chris Mihm B RC	5.00	2.00
108	Jamal Crawford B RC	6.00	2.50
109	Joel Przybilla B RC	5.00	2.00
110	Keyon Dooling B RC	5.00	2.00
111	Jerome Moiso B RC	5.00	2.00
112	Etan Thomas B RC	4.00	1.50
113	Courtney Alexander C RC	5.00	2.00
114	Mateen Cleaves C RC	4.00	1.50
115	Jason Collier C RC	6.00	2.50
116	Hidayet Turkoglu C RC	6.00	2.50
117	Desmond Mason C RC	6.00	2.50
118	Quentin Richardson C RC	8.00	3.00
119	Jamaal Magloire D RC	2.50	1.00
120	Speedy Claxton D RC	2.50	1.00
121	Morris Peterson D RC	4.00	1.50
122	Donnell Harvey D RC	2.50	1.00
123	DeShawn Stevenson D RC	2.50	1.00
124	Mark Karcher D RC	2.50	1.00
125	Mamadou N'diaye E RC	1.50	.60
126	Erick Barkley E RC	1.50	.60
127	Mark Madsen E RC	1.50	.60
128	Corey Hightower E RC	1.50	.60
129	Dan McClintock E RC	1.50	.60
130	Soumaila Samake E RC	1.50	.60
131	Hanno Mottola F RC	1.25	.50
132	Chris Carrawell F RC	1.25	.50
133	Olumide Oyedeji F RC	1.25	.50
134	Michael Redd F RC	2.00	.75
135	Chris Porter F RC	1.25	.50
136	Jabari Smith F RC	1.25	.50

2003-04 Fleer Mystique

#	Player		
	COMP.SET w/o SP's (80)	40.00	15.00
	COMMON CARD (1-80)	.20	.08
	COMMON ROOKIE (81-120)	5.00	2.00
1	Eric Williams	.20	.08
2	Dirk Nowitzki	1.25	.50
3	Jason Richardson	.75	.30
4	Corey Maggette	.50	.20
5	Troy Hudson	.20	.08
6	Tracy McGrady	2.00	.75
7	Zach Randolph	.75	.30
8	Bobby Jackson	.50	.20
9	Dan Gadzuric	.20	.08
10	Kevin Garnett	1.50	.60
11	Manu Ginobili	.75	.30
12	Andrei Kirilenko	.75	.30
13	Richard Hamilton	.50	.20
14	Mike Bibby	.75	.30
15	Vince Carter	2.00	.75
16	Jermaine O'Neal	.75	.30
17	Antoine Walker	.75	.30
18	Jalen Rose	.75	.30
19	Dajuan Wagner	.50	.20
20	Nene	.50	.20
21	Jamaal Tinsley	.75	.30
22	Kobe Bryant	3.00	1.25
23	Shane Battier	.75	.30
24	Allan Houston	.50	.20
25	Jerry Stackhouse	.75	.30
26	Eddie Jones	.75	.30
27	Morris Peterson	.50	.20
28	Richard Jefferson	.50	.20
29	Tony Parker	.75	.30
30	Glenn Robinson	.75	.30
31	Ron Artest	.50	.20
32	Marcus Haislip	.20	.08
33	Drew Gooden	.50	.20
34	Keith Van Horn	.75	.30
35	Shareef Abdur-Rahim	.75	.30
36	Michael Redd	.75	.30
37	Stephon Marbury	.75	.30
38	Tim Duncan	1.50	.60
39	Eddie Griffin	.50	.20
40	Kwame Brown	.75	.30
41	Steve Francis	.75	.30
42	Vladimir Radmanovic	.20	.08
43	Kenyon Martin	.75	.30
44	Eddy Curry	.50	.20
45	Nikoloz Tskitishvili	.20	.08
46	Shaquille O'Neal	2.00	.75
47	Allen Iverson	1.50	.60
48	Jason Kidd	1.25	.50
49	Ben Wallace	.75	.30
50	Caron Butler	.75	.30
51	Dan Dickau	.20	.08
52	Baron Davis	.75	.30
53	Bruce Bowen	.20	.08
54	Amare Stoudemire	1.50	.60
55	Michael Finley	.75	.30
56	Jamal Mashburn	.50	.20
57	Pau Gasol	.75	.30
58	Shawn Marion	.75	.30
59	Rasheed Wallace	.75	.30
60	Chris Webber	.75	.30
61	Rodney White	.20	.08
62	Tayshaun Prince	.50	.20
63	Yao Ming	2.00	.75
64	Latrell Sprewell	.75	.30
65	Aaron McKie	.50	.20
66	Bonzi Wells	.75	.30
67	Hedo Turkoglu	.75	.30
68	Ray Allen	.75	.30
69	Matt Harpring	.75	.30
70	Paul Pierce	.75	.30
71	Darius Miles	.75	.30
72	Chris Wilcox	.50	.20
73	Steve Nash	.75	.30
74	Antawn Jamison	.75	.30
75	Juan Dixon	.75	.30
76	Peja Stojakovic	.75	.30
77	Antonio Davis	.20	.08
78	Kenny Thomas	.20	.08
79	Elton Brand	.75	.30
80	Gilbert Arenas	.75	.30
81	Mickael Pietrus RC	5.00	2.00
82	Keith Bogans RC	5.00	2.00
83	Dahntay Jones RC	5.00	2.00
84	Darko Milicic RC	8.00	3.00
85	Torraye Braggs RC	5.00	2.00
86	Troy Bell RC	5.00	2.00
87	Maciej Lampe RC	5.00	2.00
88	Kendrick Perkins RC	5.00	2.00
89	Kirk Hinrich RC	8.00	3.00
90	Jason Kapono RC	5.00	2.00
91	Udonis Haslem RC	5.00	2.00
92	James Lang RC	5.00	2.00
93	Willie Green RC	5.00	2.00
94	Travis Outlaw RC	5.00	2.00
95	Nick Collison RC	5.00	2.00
96	Jarvis Hayes RC	5.00	2.00
97	Boris Diaw RC	6.00	2.50
98	Chris Bosh RC	12.00	5.00
99	LeBron James RC	60.00	25.00
100	Zarko Cabarkapa RC	5.00	2.00
101	Travis Hansen RC	5.00	2.00
102	James Jones RC	5.00	2.00

□			
103	Aleksandar Pavlovic RC	6.00	2.50
104	Luke Walton RC	5.00	2.00
105	Maurice Williams RC	5.00	2.00
106	Linton Johnson RC	5.00	2.00
107	David West RC	5.00	2.00
108	Carmelo Anthony RC	20.00	8.00
109	T.J. Ford RC	6.00	2.50
110	Ndudi Ebi RC	5.00	2.00
111	Reece Gaines RC	5.00	2.00
112	Leandro Barbosa RC	8.00	3.00
113	Luke Ridnour RC	6.00	2.50
114	Brian Cook RC	5.00	2.00
115	Marcus Banks RC	5.00	2.00
116	Josh Howard RC	8.00	3.00
117	Chris Kaman RC	5.00	2.00
118	Zoran Planinic RC	5.00	2.00
119	Dwyane Wade RC	25.00	10.00
120	Mike Sweetney RC	5.00	2.00

2003-04 Fleer Patchworks

□			
	COMP.SET w/o SP's (90)	30.00	12.50
	COMMON CARD (1-90)	.20	.08
	COMMON ROOKIE (91-120)	3.00	1.25
1	Shareef Abdur-Rahim	.75	.30
2	Theo Ratliff	.50	.20
3	Jason Terry	.75	.30
4	Carlos Boozer	.75	.30
5	Paul Pierce	.75	.30
6	Ricky Davis	.75	.30
7	Tyson Chandler	.75	.30
8	Jamal Crawford	.75	.30
9	Eddy Curry	.50	.20
10	Darius Miles	.75	.30
11	Dajuan Wagner	.50	.20
12	Michael Finley	.75	.30
13	Steve Nash	.75	.30
14	Dirk Nowitzki	1.25	.50
15	Earl Boykins	.50	.20
16	Andre Miller	.50	.20
17	Nene	.50	.20
18	Richard Hamilton	.50	.20
19	Tayshaun Prince	.50	.20
20	Ben Wallace	.75	.30
21	Mike Dunleavy	.50	.20
22	Troy Murphy	.75	.30
23	Jason Richardson	.75	.30
24	Steve Francis	.75	.30
25	Yao Ming	2.00	.75
26	Cuttino Mobley	.50	.20
27	Maurice Taylor	.20	.08
28	Ron Artest	.50	.20
29	Reggie Miller	.75	.30
30	Jermaine O'Neal	.75	.30
31	Jamaal Tinsley	.75	.30
32	Elton Brand	.75	.30
33	Marko Jaric	.50	.20
34	Corey Maggette	.50	.20
35	Kobe Bryant	3.00	1.25
36	Karl Malone	.75	.30
37	Shaquille O'Neal	2.00	.75
38	Shane Battier	.75	.30
39	Pau Gasol	.75	.30
40	Jason Williams	.50	.20
41	Caron Butler	.75	.30
42	Lamar Odom	.75	.30
43	Desmond Mason	.50	.20
44	Michael Redd	.75	.30
45	Tim Thomas	.50	.20
46	Sam Cassell	.75	.30
47	Kevin Garnett	1.50	.60
48	Latrell Sprewell	.75	.30
49	Wally Szczerbiak	.50	.20
50	Richard Jefferson	.50	.20
51	Jason Kidd	1.25	.50
52	Kenyon Martin	.75	.30
53	Baron Davis	.75	.30
54	Jamal Mashburn	.50	.20
55	Jamaal Magloire	.20	.08
56	Allan Houston	.50	.20
57	Stephon Marbury	.75	.30
58	Kurt Thomas	.50	.20
59	Drew Gooden	.50	.20
60	Juwan Howard	.50	.20
61	Tracy McGrady	2.00	.75
62	Allen Iverson	1.50	.60
63	Aaron McKie	.50	.20
64	Glenn Robinson	.75	.30
65	Kenny Thomas	.20	.08
66	Shawn Marion	.75	.30
67	Antonio McDyess	.75	.30
68	Amare Stoudemire	1.50	.60
69	Zach Randolph	.75	.30
70	Damon Stoudamire	.50	.20
71	Rasheed Wallace	.75	.30
72	Qyntel Woods	.20	.08
73	Mike Bibby	.75	.30
74	Peja Stojakovic	.75	.30
75	Chris Webber	.75	.30
76	Tim Duncan	1.50	.60
77	Manu Ginobili	.75	.30
78	Tony Parker	.75	.30
79	Malik Rose	.20	.08
80	Ray Allen	.75	.30
81	Rashard Lewis	.75	.30
82	Vladimir Radmanovic	.20	.08
83	Vince Carter	2.00	.75
84	Donyell Marshall	.75	.30
85	Jalen Rose	.75	.30
86	Matt Harpring	.75	.30
87	Andrei Kirilenko	.75	.30
88	Gilbert Arenas	.75	.30
89	Larry Hughes	.50	.20
90	Jerry Stackhouse	.75	.30
91	Carmelo Anthony RC	10.00	4.00
92	Marcus Banks RC	3.00	1.25
93	Troy Bell RC	3.00	1.25
94	Chris Bosh RC	8.00	3.00
95	Zarko Cabarkapa RC	3.00	1.25
96	Nick Collison RC	3.00	1.25
97	Boris Diaw RC	4.00	1.50
98	Francisco Elson RC	3.00	1.25
99	T.J. Ford RC	4.00	1.50
100	Reece Gaines RC	3.00	1.25
101	Udonis Haslem RC	3.00	1.25
102	Jarvis Hayes RC	3.00	1.25
103	Kirk Hinrich RC	5.00	2.00
104	Josh Howard RC	5.00	2.00
105	LeBron James RC	40.00	15.00
106	Dahntay Jones RC	3.00	1.25
107	Chris Kaman RC	3.00	1.25
108	Jason Kapono RC	3.00	1.25
109	Raul Lopez RC	3.00	1.25
110	Darko Milicic RC	5.00	2.00
111	Zaur Pachulia RC	3.00	1.25
112	Mickael Pietrus RC	3.00	1.25
113	Zoran Planinic RC	3.00	1.25
114	Luke Ridnour RC	4.00	1.50
115	Darius Songaila RC	3.00	1.25
116	Mike Sweetney RC	3.00	1.25
117	Dwyane Wade RC	12.00	5.00
118	Luke Walton RC	5.00	2.00
119	David West RC	3.00	1.25
120	Maurice Williams RC	3.00	1.25

2001-02 Fleer Platinum

□			
	COMPLETE SET (250)	300.00	150.00
	COMP.SET w/o SP's (200)	20.00	8.00
	COMMON CARD (1-200)	.20	.07
	COMMON HL (201-220)	2.50	1.00
	COMMON ROOKIE (221-250)	2.50	1.00
1	Tyrone Hill	.20	.07
2	Sam Cassell	.60	.25

□			
3	Elton Brand	.60	.25
4	Andre Miller	.40	.15
5	Vitaly Potapenko	.20	.07
6	Lamar Odom	.60	.25
7	Mike Bibby	.60	.25
8	Alan Henderson	.20	.07
9	Dan Majerle	.40	.15
10	Donyell Marshall	.40	.15
11	Jason Williams	.40	.15
12	Glen Rice	.40	.15
13	Kobe Bryant	2.50	1.00
14	Pat Garrity	.20	.07
15	Shawn Bradley	.20	.07
16	Aaron Williams	.20	.07
17	Antonio McDyess	.40	.15
18	Jonathan Bender	.40	.15
19	Ben Wallace	.60	.25
20	Vince Carter	1.50	.60
21	Maurice Taylor	.40	.15
22	Antonio Daniels	.20	.07
23	Rodney Rogers	.20	.07
24	Patrick Ewing	.60	.25
25	Chauncey Billups	.40	.15
26	Steve Smith	.40	.15
27	Antawn Jamison	.60	.25
28	Mitch Richmond	.40	.15
29	Jumaine Jones	.40	.15
30	Glenn Robinson	.40	.15
31	Ron Mercer	.40	.15
32	Jelani McCoy	.20	.07
33	Paul Pierce	.60	.25
34	Jeff McInnis	.20	.07
35	Michael Dickerson	.40	.15
36	Toni Kukoc	.40	.15
37	Anthony Mason	.40	.15
38	Jamal Mashburn	.40	.15
39	John Stockton	.60	.25
40	Peja Stojakovic	.60	.25
41	Charlie Ward	.20	.07
42	Donnell Harvey	.40	.15
43	Darrell Armstrong	.20	.07
44	Michael Finley	.60	.25
45	Kerry Kittles	.20	.07
46	Voshon Lenard	.20	.07
47	Reggie Miller	.60	.25
48	Joe Smith	.40	.15
49	Antonio Davis	.20	.07
50	Hakeem Olajuwon	.60	.25
51	David Robinson	.60	.25
52	Tony Delk	.20	.07
53	Gary Payton	.60	.25
54	Kevin Garnett	1.25	.50
55	Arvydas Sabonis	.40	.15
56	Larry Hughes	.40	.15
57	Richard Hamilton	.40	.15
58	Aaron McKie	.40	.15
59	Tim Thomas	.40	.15
60	Ron Artest	.40	.15
61	Matt Harpring	.60	.25
62	Kenny Anderson	.40	.15
63	Quentin Richardson	.40	.15
64	Damon Jones	.20	.07
65	Theo Ratliff	.20	.07
66	Brian Grant	.40	.15
67	Eddie Robinson	.40	.15
68	Karl Malone	.60	.25
69	Bobby Jackson	.40	.15
70	Larry Johnson	.40	.15

#	Player		
❏ 71	Shareef Abdur-Rahim	.60	.25
❏ 72	Grant Hill	.60	.25
❏ 73	Eduardo Najera	.40	.15
❏ 74	Keith Van Horn	.60	.25
❏ 75	Nick Van Exel	.60	.25
❏ 76	Jalen Rose	.60	.25
❏ 77	Jerry Stackhouse	.60	.25
❏ 78	Jerome Williams	.20	.07
❏ 79	Cuttino Mobley	.40	.15
❏ 80	Derek Anderson	.40	.15
❏ 81	Anfernee Hardaway	.60	.25
❏ 82	Rashard Lewis	.40	.15
❏ 83	Terrell Brandon	.40	.15
❏ 84	Scottie Pippen	1.00	.40
❏ 85	Danny Fortson	.20	.07
❏ 86	Jahidi White	.20	.07
❏ 87	Eric Snow	.40	.15
❏ 88	Ervin Johnson	.20	.07
❏ 89	Marcus Fizer	.20	.07
❏ 90	Lamond Murray	.20	.07
❏ 91	Antoine Walker	.60	.25
❏ 92	Keyon Dooling	.40	.15
❏ 93	Bryant Reeves	.40	.15
❏ 94	Hanno Mottola	.40	.15
❏ 95	Tim Hardaway	.40	.15
❏ 96	David Wesley	.20	.07
❏ 97	John Starks	.40	.15
❏ 98	Hidayet Turkoglu	.40	.15
❏ 99	Allan Houston	.40	.15
❏ 100	Rick Fox	.40	.15
❏ 101	Bo Outlaw	.20	.07
❏ 102	Juwan Howard	.40	.15
❏ 103	Kendall Gill	.20	.07
❏ 104	Raef LaFrentz	.40	.15
❏ 105	Austin Croshere	.40	.15
❏ 106	Chucky Atkins	.20	.07
❏ 107	Morris Peterson	.40	.15
❏ 108	Shandon Anderson	.20	.07
❏ 109	Sean Elliott	.40	.15
❏ 110	Tom Gugliotta	.40	.15
❏ 111	Vin Baker	.40	.15
❏ 112	Wally Szczerbiak	.40	.15
❏ 113	Rasheed Wallace	.60	.25
❏ 114	Vonteego Cummings	.20	.07
❏ 115	Christian Laettner	.40	.15
❏ 116	Dikembe Mutombo	.40	.15
❏ 117	Lindsey Hunter	.20	.07
❏ 118	Jamal Crawford	.40	.15
❏ 119	Jim Jackson	.20	.07
❏ 120	Bryant Stith	.20	.07
❏ 121	Corey Maggette	.40	.15
❏ 122	Mahmoud Abdul-Rauf	.20	.07
❏ 123	Lorenzen Wright	.20	.07
❏ 124	Alonzo Mourning	.40	.15
❏ 125	Jamaal Magloire	.20	.07
❏ 126	Bryon Russell	.20	.07
❏ 127	Vlade Divac	.40	.15
❏ 128	Marcus Camby	.40	.15
❏ 129	Derek Fisher	.40	.15
❏ 130	Mike Miller	.60	.25
❏ 131	Steve Nash	.60	.25
❏ 132	Kenyon Martin	.60	.25
❏ 133	James Posey	.40	.15
❏ 134	Travis Best	.20	.07
❏ 135	Corliss Williamson	.20	.07
❏ 136	Alvin Williams	.20	.07
❏ 137	Walt Williams	.20	.07
❏ 138	Malik Rose	.20	.07
❏ 139	Clifford Robinson	.20	.07
❏ 140	Ruben Patterson	.40	.15
❏ 141	LaPhonso Ellis	.20	.07
❏ 142	Rod Strickland	.20	.07
❏ 143	Marc Jackson	.40	.15
❏ 144	Hubert Davis	.20	.07
❏ 145	Speedy Claxton	.40	.15
❏ 146	Scott Williams	.20	.07
❏ 147	Tyronn Lue	.20	.07
❏ 148	Chris Mihm	.40	.15
❏ 149	George Lynch	.20	.07
❏ 150	Michael Olowokandi	.40	.15
❏ 151	Nazr Mohammed	.20	.07
❏ 152	Eddie House	.20	.07
❏ 153	Elden Campbell	.20	.07
❏ 154	DeShawn Stevenson	.40	.15
❏ 155	Doug Christie	.40	.15
❏ 156	Kurt Thomas	.40	.15
❏ 157	Robert Horry	.40	.15
❏ 158	Radoslav Nesterovic	.40	.15
❏ 159	Wang Zhizhi	.60	.25
❏ 160	Stephen Jackson	.40	.15
❏ 161	George McCloud	.20	.07
❏ 162	Jermaine O'Neal	.60	.25
❏ 163	Mateen Cleaves	.20	.07
❏ 164	Charles Oakley	.20	.07
❏ 165	Kenny Thomas	.20	.07
❏ 166	Terry Porter	.20	.07
❏ 167	Iakovos Tsakalidis	.20	.07
❏ 168	Shammond Williams	.20	.07
❏ 169	Anthony Peeler	.20	.07
❏ 170	Damon Stoudamire	.40	.15
❏ 171	Chris Porter	.40	.15
❏ 172	Chris Whitney	.20	.07
❏ 173	Raja Bell RC	.75	.30
❏ 174	Darvin Ham	.20	.07
❏ 175	A.J. Guyton	.40	.15
❏ 176	Trajan Langdon	.40	.15
❏ 177	Jerome Moiso	.40	.15
❏ 178	Anthony Carter	.20	.07
❏ 179	P.J. Brown	.20	.07
❏ 180	Danny Manning	.20	.07
❏ 181	Scot Pollard	.20	.07
❏ 182	Mark Jackson	.40	.15
❏ 183	Mark Madsen	.20	.07
❏ 184	Michael Doleac	.20	.07
❏ 185	Calvin Booth	.20	.07
❏ 186	Kevin Willis	.20	.07
❏ 187	Al Harrington	.40	.15
❏ 188	Mikki Moore	.20	.07
❏ 189	Keon Clark	.40	.15
❏ 190	Moochie Norris	.20	.07
❏ 191	Ron Harper	.40	.15
❏ 192	Danny Ferry	.20	.07
❏ 193	Jacque Vaughn	.20	.07
❏ 194	Derrick Coleman	.20	.07
❏ 195	Brent Barry	.40	.15
❏ 196	Dion Glover	.20	.07
❏ 197	Felipe Lopez	.20	.07
❏ 198	Shawn Kemp	.40	.15
❏ 199	Mookie Blaylock	.20	.07
❏ 200	Bonzi Wells	.40	.15
❏ 201	Vince Carter HL	6.00	2.50
❏ 202	Ray Allen HL	2.50	1.00
❏ 203	Darius Miles HL	.60	.25
❏ 204	Shaquille O'Neal HL	5.00	2.00
❏ 205	Stromile Swift HL	.60	.25
❏ 206	DerMarr Johnson HL	2.50	1.00
❏ 207	Eddie Jones HL	2.50	1.00
❏ 208	Chris Webber HL	.60	.25
❏ 209	Latrell Sprewell HL	.60	.25
❏ 210	Tracy McGrady HL	6.00	2.50
❏ 211	Dirk Nowitzki HL	4.00	1.50
❏ 212	Stephon Marbury HL	2.50	1.00
❏ 213	Steve Francis HL	.60	.25
❏ 214	Tim Duncan HL	5.00	2.00
❏ 215	Jason Kidd HL	4.00	1.50
❏ 216	Shawn Marion HL	.60	.25
❏ 217	Desmond Mason HL	2.50	1.00
❏ 218	Courtney Alexander HL	2.50	1.00
❏ 219	Baron Davis HL	2.50	1.00
❏ 220	Allen Iverson HL	5.00	2.00
❏ 221	Joe Johnson RC	8.00	3.00
❏ 222	Kedrick Brown RC	2.50	1.00
❏ 223	Joseph Forte RC	3.00	1.25
❏ 224	Kirk Haston RC	2.50	1.00
❏ 225	Tyson Chandler RC	6.00	2.50
❏ 226	Eddy Curry RC	6.00	2.50
❏ 227	DeSagana Diop RC	2.50	1.00
❏ 228	Jeff Trepagnier RC	2.50	1.00
❏ 229	Oscar Torres RC	3.00	1.25
❏ 230	Rodney White RC	2.50	1.00
❏ 231	Jason Richardson RC	6.00	2.50
❏ 232	Troy Murphy RC	5.00	2.00
❏ 233	Eddie Griffin RC	3.00	1.25
❏ 234	Jamaal Tinsley RC	4.00	1.50
❏ 235	Pau Gasol RC	10.00	4.00
❏ 236	Shane Battier RC	4.00	1.50
❏ 237	Richard Jefferson RC	6.00	2.50
❏ 238	Jason Collins RC	2.50	1.00
❏ 239	Brendan Haywood RC	2.50	1.00
❏ 240	Steven Hunter RC	2.50	1.00
❏ 241	Zach Randolph RC	6.00	2.50
❏ 242	Gerald Wallace RC	5.00	2.00
❏ 243	Tony Parker RC	10.00	4.00
❏ 244	Vladimir Radmanovic RC	3.00	1.25
❏ 245	Michael Bradley RC	2.50	1.00
❏ 246	Andrei Kirilenko RC	6.00	2.50
❏ 247	Kwame Brown RC	5.00	2.00
❏ 248	Alton Ford RC	2.00	.75
❏ 249	Zeljko Rebraca RC	2.50	1.00
❏ 250	Trenton Hassell RC	4.00	1.50

2002-03 Fleer Platinum

❏	COMP.SET w/o SP's (160)	40.00	15.00
❏	COMMON CARD (1-160)	.20	.08
❏	COMMON ROOKIE (161-170)	3.00	1.25
❏	COMMON ROOKIE (171-180)	6.00	2.50
❏	COMMON ROOKIE (181-190)	8.00	3.00
❏	COMMON ROOKIE (191-200)	10.00	4.00
❏ 1	Vince Carter	2.00	.75
❏ 2	Lamar Odom	.75	.30
❏ 3	Darrell Armstrong	.20	.08
❏ 4	Kwame Brown	.50	.20
❏ 5	Ron Artest	.50	.20
❏ 6	Kurt Thomas	.50	.20
❏ 7	Jerry Stackhouse	.75	.30
❏ 8	Eddie Griffin	.50	.20
❏ 9	David Wesley	.20	.08
❏ 10	Morris Peterson	.50	.20
❏ 11	Jon Barry	.20	.08
❏ 12	Troy Hudson	.20	.08
❏ 13	Kenny Anderson	.50	.20
❏ 14	Corliss Williamson	.50	.20
❏ 15	Kevin Garnett	1.50	.60
❏ 16	Desmond Mason	.50	.20
❏ 17	Lucious Harris	.20	.08
❏ 18	Steve Smith	.50	.20
❏ 19	Nick Van Exel	.75	.30
❏ 20	Tyson Chandler	.75	.30
❏ 21	Shane Battier	.75	.30
❏ 22	Rasheed Wallace	.75	.30
❏ 23	Donyell Marshall	.75	.30
❏ 24	Anfernee Hardaway	.75	.30
❏ 25	Antoine Walker	.75	.30
❏ 26	Kobe Bryant	3.00	1.50
❏ 27	Keith Van Horn	.75	.30
❏ 28	Elton Brand	.75	.30
❏ 29	Grant Hill	.75	.30
❏ 30	Elden Campbell	.20	.08
❏ 31	Jason Richardson	.75	.30
❏ 32	Wally Szczerbiak	.50	.20
❏ 33	Speedy Claxton	.20	.08
❏ 34	Voshon Lenard	.20	.08
❏ 35	Eddie Jones	.75	.30
❏ 36	Bonzi Wells	.50	.20
❏ 37	Jalen Rose	.75	.30
❏ 38	Jason Williams	.50	.20
❏ 39	Tom Gugliotta	.20	.08
❏ 40	Juwan Howard	.50	.20
❏ 41	Michael Redd	.75	.30
❏ 42	David Robinson	.75	.30
❏ 43	Steve Nash	.75	.30
❏ 44	Vlade Divac	.50	.20
❏ 45	Avery Johnson	.20	.08
❏ 46	Scottie Pippen	1.25	.50
❏ 47	Eric Williams	.20	.08
❏ 48	Derek Fisher	.75	.30
❏ 49	Tony Battie	.20	.08
❏ 50	Rick Fox	.50	.20
❏ 51	Theo Ratliff	.50	.20
❏ 52	Corey Maggette	.50	.20

#	Player		
53	Jermaine O'Neal	.75	.30
54	Bryon Russell	.20	.08
55	Steve Francis	.75	.30
56	Jamal Mashburn	.50	.20
57	Jerome Williams	.20	.08
58	Gilbert Arenas	.75	.30
59	Joe Smith	.50	.20
60	Brent Barry	.50	.20
61	Marcus Camby	.50	.20
62	Toni Kukoc	.50	.20
63	Tim Duncan	1.50	.60
64	Ira Newble	.20	.08
65	Brian Grant	.50	.20
66	Jason Terry	.50	.20
67	Andre Miller	.50	.20
68	Mike Miller	.75	.30
69	Troy Murphy	.75	.30
70	P.J. Brown	.20	.08
71	Jason Richardson	.75	.30
72	Glenn Robinson	.75	.30
73	Richard Jefferson	.75	.30
74	Richard Hamilton	.50	.20
75	Jason Kidd	1.25	.50
76	Rashard Lewis	.75	.30
77	Kenny Satterfield	.20	.08
78	Terrell Brandon	.50	.20
79	Dirk Nowitzki	1.25	.50
80	Chris Webber	.75	.30
81	Michael Finley	.75	.30
82	Malik Allen	.20	.08
83	Bobby Jackson	.50	.20
84	Darius Miles	.75	.30
85	Kendall Gill	.20	.08
86	Damon Stoudamire	.50	.20
87	Shammond Williams	.20	.08
88	Stephon Marbury	.75	.30
89	Shareef Abdur-Rahim	.75	.30
90	Charlie Ward	.20	.08
91	Michael Jordan	6.00	2.50
92	Jamaal Magloire	.20	.08
93	Karl Malone	.75	.30
94	Kerry Kittles	.20	.08
95	Lindsey Hunter	.20	.08
96	Gary Payton	.75	.30
97	Travis Best	.20	.08
98	Derek Anderson	.50	.20
99	Stromile Swift	.50	.20
100	Shaquille O'Neal	2.00	.75
101	Derrick Coleman	.20	.08
102	DeShawn Stevenson	.20	.08
103	Jamaal Tinsley	.75	.30
104	Latrell Sprewell	.75	.30
105	Larry Hughes	.50	.20
106	Eddy Curry	.75	.30
107	Shawn Marion	.75	.30
108	Paul Pierce	.75	.30
109	Samaki Walker	.20	.08
110	Allen Iverson	1.50	.60
111	Michael Olowokandi	.20	.08
112	Tracy McGrady	2.00	.75
113	Shawn Bradley	.20	.08
114	Reggie Miller	.75	.30
115	Antonio McDyess	.50	.20
116	Calbert Cheany	.20	.08
117	Al Harrington	.50	.20
118	Allan Houston	.50	.20
119	Andrei Kirilenko	.75	.30
120	Courtney Alexander	.20	.08
121	Alvin Williams	.20	.08
122	Antawn Jamison	.75	.30
123	Dikembe Mutombo	.50	.20
124	Tony Parker	.75	.30
125	Raef LaFrentz	.50	.20
126	Ray Allen	.75	.30
127	Peja Stojakovic	.75	.30
128	Zydrunas Ilgauskas	.50	.20
129	Gerald Wallace	.75	.30
130	Ruben Patterson	.50	.20
131	Pau Gasol	.75	.30
132	Joe Johnson	.75	.30
133	Aaron McKie	.50	.20
134	Walter McCarty	.20	.08
135	Baron Davis	.75	.30
136	Kenyon Martin	.75	.30
137	Antonio Davis	.20	.08
138	Ben Wallace	.75	.30
139	Sam Cassell	.75	.30
140	Mike Bibby	.75	.30
141	Cuttino Mobley	.50	.20
142	LaPhonso Ellis	.20	.08
143	Shandon Anderson	.20	.08
144	Hedo Turkoglu	.75	.30
145	Matt Harpring	.75	.30
146	Dion Glover	.20	.08
147	Tony Delk	.20	.08
148	Ricky Davis	.75	.30
149	James Posey	.50	.20
150	Chucky Atkins	.20	.08
151	Danny Fortson	.20	.08
152	Robert Horry	.50	.20
153	Radoslav Nesterovic	.50	.20
154	Pat Garrity	.20	.08
155	Todd MacCulloch	.20	.08
156	Eric Snow	.50	.20
157	Malik Rose	.20	.08
158	Vladimir Radmanovic	.50	.20
159	Trenton Hassell	.50	.20
160	Brad Miller	.75	.30
161	Kareem Rush RC	3.00	1.25
162	Nikoloz Tskitishvili RC	3.00	1.25
163	Nene Hilario RC	3.00	1.25
164	Marcus Haislip RC	3.00	1.25
165	Jiri Welsch RC	3.00	1.25
166	Dan Dickau RC	3.00	1.25
167	Vincent Yarbrough RC	3.00	1.25
168	Tito Maddox RC	3.00	1.25
169	Mike Dunleavy RC	4.00	1.50
170	Chris Wilcox RC	3.00	1.25
171	Jared Jeffries RC	6.00	2.50
172	Bostjan Nachbar RC	6.00	2.50
173	Frank Williams RC	6.00	2.50
174	Reggie Evans RC	6.00	2.50
175	Casey Jacobsen RC	6.00	2.50
176	Tayshaun Prince RC	6.00	2.50
177	Mike Batiste RC	6.00	2.50
178	Drew Gooden RC	8.00	3.00
179	DaJuan Wagner RC	6.00	2.50
180	Tamar Slay RC	6.00	2.50
181	Melvin Ely RC	8.00	3.00
182	Rasual Butler RC	8.00	3.00
183	Dan Gadzuric RC	8.00	3.00
184	Ryan Humphrey RC	8.00	3.00
185	Gordan Giricek RC	8.00	3.00
186	Mehmet Okur RC	8.00	3.00
187	Jay Williams RC	8.00	3.00
188	Caron Butler RC	12.00	5.00
189	Qyntel Woods RC	8.00	3.00
190	Amare Stoudemire RC	25.00	10.00
191	Yao Ming RC	60.00	30.00
192	Carlos Boozer RC	15.00	6.00
193	John Salmons RC	10.00	4.00
194	Fred Jones RC	10.00	4.00
195	Juan Dixon RC	12.00	5.00
196	Manu Ginobili RC	25.00	10.00
197	Pat Burke RC	10.00	4.00
198	Smush Parker RC	15.00	6.00
199	Lonny Baxter RC	10.00	4.00
200	Ronald Murray RC	12.00	5.00

2003-04 Fleer Platinum

Shane Battier
Guard/Forward, No. 31

COMMON CARD (1-170)	.20	.08
COMMON ROOKIE (171-180)	2.50	1.00
COMMON ROOKIE (181-190)	4.00	1.50
COMMON ROOKIE (191-200)	5.00	2.00

#	Player		
1	Shane Battier	.60	.25
2	Brad Miller	.60	.25
3	Jason Kidd	1.00	.40
4	Nick Van Exel	.60	.25
5	David Wesley	.20	.08
6	Corey Maggette	.40	.15
7	Juan Dixon	.40	.15
8	Jamaal Tinsley	.60	.25
9	Stromile Swift	.40	.15
10	Dajuan Wagner	.40	.15
11	Joe Smith	.40	.15
12	Jermaine O'Neal	.60	.25
13	Steve Nash	.60	.25
14	Karl Malone	.60	.25
15	Vince Carter	1.50	.60
16	Antonio McDyess	.60	.25
17	Tim Thomas	.40	.15
18	Vladimir Radmanovic	.20	.08
19	Scottie Pippen	1.00	.40
20	Tracy McGrady	1.50	.60
21	Darius Miles	.60	.25
22	Toni Kukoc	.40	.15
23	Antonio Davis	.40	.15
24	Jamal Crawford	.40	.15
25	Rasho Nesterovic	.40	.15
26	Carlos Boozer	.60	.25
27	Cuttino Mobley	.40	.15
28	Larry Hughes	.40	.15
29	Alvin Williams	.20	.08
30	Andre Miller	.40	.15
31	Amare Stoudemire	1.25	.50
32	Eric Williams	.20	.08
33	Pau Gasol	.60	.25
34	Kenyon Martin	.60	.25
35	Elton Brand	.60	.25
36	Charlie Ward	.20	.08
37	Andrei Kirilenko	.60	.25
38	Aaron McKie	.40	.15
39	Maurice Taylor	.20	.08
40	Baron Davis	.60	.25
41	Dirk Nowitzki	1.00	.40
42	Gary Payton	.60	.25
43	Grant Hill	.60	.25
44	Jalen Rose	.60	.25
45	Allan Houston	.40	.15
46	Erick Dampier	.20	.08
47	Brian Grant	.40	.15
48	Wally Szczerbiak	.40	.15
49	Greg Ostertag	.20	.08
50	Gilbert Arenas	.60	.25
51	Kenny Anderson	.40	.15
52	Juwan Howard	.40	.15
53	Jason Terry	.60	.25
54	Raef LaFrentz	.40	.15
55	Ricky Davis	.60	.25
56	Kobe Bryant	2.50	1.00
57	Chris Webber	.60	.25
58	P.J. Brown	.20	.08
59	Nene	.40	.15
60	Kenny Thomas	.20	.08
61	Mike Bibby	.60	.25
62	Chris Wilcox	.40	.15
63	Anfernee Hardaway	.60	.25
64	Drew Gooden	.60	.25
65	Rodney White	.20	.08
66	Shareef Abdur-Rahim	.40	.15
67	Quentin Richardson	.40	.15
68	Ben Wallace	.60	.25
69	Latrell Sprewell	.60	.25
70	Shaquille O'Neal	1.50	.60
71	Vin Baker	.40	.15
72	Tony Parker	.60	.25
73	Stephen Jackson	.20	.08
74	Ray Allen	.60	.25
75	Eric Snow	.40	.15
76	Jason Richardson	.60	.25
77	Shammond Williams	.20	.08
78	Tayshaun Prince	.60	.25
79	Antawn Jamison	.60	.25
80	Derek Fisher	.40	.15
81	Jeff Foster	.20	.08
82	Kwame Brown	.60	.25
83	Yao Ming	1.50	.60
84	Rasheed Wallace	.60	.25
85	Tyson Chandler	.60	.25
86	Mike Dunleavy	.40	.15

#	Player		
87	Alan Henderson	.20	.08
88	Rashard Lewis	.60	.25
89	Jamaal Magloire	.20	.08
90	Stephon Marbury	.60	.25
91	DeShawn Stevenson	.20	.08
92	Damon Stoudamire	.40	.15
93	Eddy Curry	.40	.15
94	Peja Stojakovic	.60	.25
95	Glenn Robinson	.60	.25
96	Mike Miller	.60	.25
97	Richard Hamilton	.40	.15
98	Kevin Garnett	1.25	.50
99	Zach Randolph	.60	.25
100	Tony Delk	.20	.08
101	Clifford Robinson	.20	.08
102	Steve Francis	.60	.25
103	Curtis Borchardt	.20	.08
104	Jerry Stackhouse	.60	.25
105	Desmond Mason	.40	.15
106	Chauncey Billups	.40	.15
107	Sam Cassell	.40	.15
108	Michael Finley	.60	.25
109	Hedo Turkoglu	.60	.25
110	Ronald Murray	.40	.15
111	Allen Iverson	1.25	.50
112	Richard Jefferson	.40	.15
113	Theo Ratliff	.40	.15
114	Ron Artest	.40	.15
115	Doug Christie	.40	.15
116	Lamar Odom	.60	.25
117	Lamond Murray	.20	.08
118	Bonzi Wells	.40	.15
119	Caron Butler	.60	.25
120	Marcus Camby	.40	.15
121	Manu Ginobili	.60	.25
122	Paul Pierce	.60	.25
123	Troy Hudson	.20	.08
124	Jim Jackson	.20	.08
125	Keith Van Horn	.60	.25
126	Reggie Miller	.60	.25
127	Tim Duncan	1.25	.50
128	Shawn Marion	.60	.25
129	Eddie Jones	.60	.25
130	Matt Harpring	.60	.25
131	Elden Campbell	.20	.08
132	Marko Jaric	.40	.15
133	John Wallace	.20	.08
134	Erick Strickland	.20	.08
135	Voshon Lenard	.20	.08
136	Aaron Williams	.20	.08
137	Qyntel Woods	.40	.15
138	Kelvin Cato	.20	.08
139	Michael Curry	.20	.08
140	Vlade Divac	.40	.15
141	Jason Hart	.20	.08
142	Nazr Mohammed UH	.20	.08
143	Mike James UH	.20	.08
144	Jerome Williams UH	.20	.08
145	Zydrunas Ilgauskas UH	.40	.15
146	Antoine Walker UH	.60	.25
147	Earl Boykins UH	.40	.15
148	Mehmet Okur UH	.20	.08
149	Brian Cardinal UH	.20	.08
150	Bostjan Nachbar UH	.20	.08
151	Al Harrington UH	.40	.15
152	Eddie House UH	.20	.08
153	Devean George UH	.20	.08
154	Jason Williams UH	.40	.15
155	Rafer Alston UH	.20	.08
156	Michael Redd UH	.60	.25
157	Gary Trent UH	.20	.08
158	Kerry Kittles UH	.20	.08
159	Jamal Mashburn UH	.40	.15
160	Kurt Thomas UH	.20	.08
161	Tyronn Lue UH	.20	.08
162	Derrick Coleman UH	.20	.08
163	Joe Johnson UH	.40	.15
164	Dale Davis UH	.20	.08
165	Bobby Jackson UH	.20	.08
166	Malik Rose UH	.20	.08
167	Brent Barry UH	.40	.15
168	Donyell Marshall UH	.60	.25
169	Carlos Arroyo UH	1.00	.40
170	Etan Thomas UH	.20	.08
171	Zoran Planinic RC	2.50	1.00
172	Jason Kapono RC	2.50	1.00
173	Zarko Cabarkapa RC	2.50	1.00
174	Darko Milicic RC	4.00	1.50
175	Aleksandar Pavlovic RC	3.00	1.25
176	Marcus Banks RC	2.50	1.00
177	Willie Green RC	2.50	1.00
178	Udonis Haslem RC	2.50	1.00
179	Nick Collison RC	2.50	1.00
180	Chris Kaman RC	2.50	1.00
181	T.J. Ford RC	5.00	2.00
182	Travis Outlaw RC	4.00	1.50
183	LeBron James RC	40.00	20.00
184	Troy Bell RC	4.00	1.50
185	Reece Gaines RC	4.00	1.50
186	David West RC	4.00	1.50
187	Kirk Hinrich RC	6.00	2.50
188	Chris Bosh RC	8.00	3.00
189	Leandro Barbosa RC	6.00	2.50
190	Dwyane Wade RC	15.00	6.00
191	Mike Sweetney RC	5.00	2.00
192	Darius Songaila RC	5.00	2.00
193	Luke Ridnour RC	6.00	2.50
194	Carmelo Anthony RC	15.00	6.00
195	Jarvis Hayes RC	5.00	2.00
196	Mickael Pietrus RC	5.00	2.00
197	Dahntay Jones RC	5.00	2.00
198	Josh Howard RC	8.00	3.00
199	Maciej Lampe RC	5.00	2.00
200	Luke Walton RC	5.00	2.00

2000-01 Fleer Premium

	COMPLETE SET w/o RC (200)	40.00	20.00
	COMMON CARD (1-200)	.25	.08
	COMMON ROOKIE (201-241)	2.00	.75
1	Vince Carter	2.00	.75
2	Kobe Bryant	3.00	1.25
3	Jermaine Jackson	.25	.08
4	Lamar Odom	.75	.30
5	Robert Traylor	.25	.08
6	Jason Kidd	1.25	.50
7	Rashard Lewis	.50	.20
8	Ron Artest	.50	.20
9	Grant Hill	.75	.30
10	Kenny Thomas	.25	.08
11	Anthony Carter	.50	.20
12	Kerry Kittles	.25	.08
13	Pat Garrity	.25	.08
14	David Robinson	.75	.30
15	Bryant Reeves	.25	.08
16	Fred Hoiberg	.25	.08
17	Jerry Stackhouse	.75	.30
18	Donyell Marshall	.50	.20
19	Ron Harper	.50	.20
20	Scott Burrell	.25	.08
21	Ron Mercer	.25	.08
22	Avery Johnson	.25	.08
23	Jacque Vaughn	.25	.08
24	Adrian Griffin	.25	.08
25	Antonio McDyess	.50	.20
26	Adonal Foyle	.25	.08
27	Derek Fisher	.75	.30
28	Terrell Brandon	.50	.20
29	Matt Harpring	.75	.30
30	Nazr Mohammed	.25	.08
31	Tom Gugliotta	.25	.08
32	Scott Padgett	.25	.08
33	Detlef Schrempf	.50	.20
34	Dirk Nowitzki	1.25	.50
35	Mookie Blaylock	.25	.08
36	James Posey	.50	.20
37	Latrell Sprewell	.75	.30
38	Michael Doleac	.25	.08
39	Damon Stoudamire	.50	.20
40	Tim Duncan	1.50	.60
41	John Stockton	.75	.30
42	Danny Fortson	.25	.08
43	Raef LaFrentz	.25	.08
44	Steve Francis	.75	.30
45	Travis Knight	.25	.08
46	Kevin Garnett	1.50	.60
47	Mitch Richmond	.50	.20
48	Olden Polynice	.25	.08
49	Derrick Coleman	.25	.08
50	Ervin Johnson	.25	.08
51	Shandon Anderson	.25	.08
52	Jamal Mashburn	.50	.20
53	Joe Smith	.50	.20
54	Bo Outlaw	.25	.08
55	Clifford Robinson	.25	.08
56	Scottie Pippen	1.25	.50
57	Chris Webber	.75	.30
58	Doug Christie	.50	.20
59	Michael Dickerson	.50	.20
60	Anthony Mason	.50	.20
61	Shawn Bradley	.25	.08
62	Reggie Miller	.75	.30
63	P.J. Brown	.25	.08
64	Wally Szczerbiak	.50	.20
65	Keon Clark	.50	.20
66	Anthony Peeler	.25	.08
67	Doug West	.25	.08
68	Antoine Walker	.75	.30
69	Trajan Langdon	.50	.20
70	Mark Jackson	.50	.20
71	Sam Cassell	.75	.30
72	Kurt Thomas	.50	.20
73	Ruben Patterson	.50	.20
74	Alvin Williams	.25	.08
75	Juwan Howard	.50	.20
76	Baron Davis	.75	.30
77	Otis Thorpe	.25	.08
78	Austin Croshere	.50	.20
79	Tony Delk	.25	.08
80	William Avery	.25	.08
81	Matt Geiger	.25	.08
82	Richard Hamilton	.50	.20
83	Ricky Davis	.50	.20
84	Hubert Davis	.25	.08
85	Jalen Rose	.75	.30
86	Theo Ratliff	.50	.20
87	Bobby Jackson	.50	.20
88	Glenn Robinson	.75	.30
89	Kendall Gill	.25	.08
90	Laron Profit	.25	.08
91	Brad Miller	.50	.20
92	Cedric Ceballos	.25	.08
93	Arvydas Sabonis	.50	.20
94	Vitaly Potapenko	.25	.08
95	Rod Strickland	.25	.08
96	Erick Dampier	.50	.20
97	Ryan Bowen	.25	.08
98	Dale Davis	.25	.08
99	Larry Johnson	.50	.20
100	John Thomas	.25	.08
101	Rodney Rogers	.25	.08
102	Ray Allen	.75	.30
103	Isaac Austin	.25	.08
104	Radoslav Nesterovic	.50	.20
105	Tariq Abdul-Wahad	.25	.08
106	Jonathan Bender	.50	.20
107	Tim Hardaway	.50	.20
108	Jamie Feick	.25	.08
109	Toni Kukoc	.50	.20
110	Tyrone Corbin	.25	.08
111	Aleksandar Radojevic	.25	.08
112	Tony Battie	.25	.08
113	Andre Miller	.50	.20
114	Derek Anderson	.50	.20
115	Tim Thomas	.50	.20
116	Corey Maggette	.50	.20
117	Rasheed Wallace	.75	.30
118	Shammond Williams	.25	.08
119	Charlie Ward	.25	.08
120	Paul Pierce	.75	.30
121	Shawn Kemp	.50	.20

#	Player		
122	Darrell Armstrong	.25	.08
123	Fred Vinson	.25	.08
124	Jim Jackson	.25	.08
125	Steve Nash	.75	.30
126	Michael Stewart	.25	.08
127	Maurice Taylor	.25	.08
128	Michael Ruffin	.25	.08
129	Vlade Divac	.50	.20
130	LaPhonso Ellis	.25	.08
131	Eddie Jones	.75	.30
132	Hakeem Olajuwon	.75	.30
133	Rick Fox	.50	.20
134	Patrick Ewing	.75	.30
135	Brian Grant	.50	.20
136	Jaren Jackson	.25	.08
137	Christian Laettner	.50	.20
138	Greg Ostertag	.25	.08
139	Anfernee Hardaway	.75	.30
140	Nick Van Exel	.75	.30
141	Jason Caffey	.25	.08
142	Michael Olowokandi	.25	.08
143	Darvin Ham	.25	.08
144	Calbert Cheaney	.25	.08
145	Steve Smith	.50	.20
146	Jason Williams	.50	.20
147	Jelani McCoy	.25	.08
148	Karl Malone	.75	.30
149	Dikembe Mutombo	.50	.20
150	Wesley Person	.25	.08
151	Kelvin Cato	.25	.08
152	Alonzo Mourning	.50	.20
153	Terry Mills	.25	.08
154	Allen Iverson	1.50	.60
155	Bonzi Wells	.50	.20
156	Antonio Daniels	.25	.08
157	Shareef Abdur-Rahim	.75	.30
158	Randy Brown	.25	.08
159	Mike Bibby	.75	.30
160	Travis Best	.25	.08
161	Dan Majerle	.25	.08
162	Aaron McKie	.50	.20
163	Jason Terry	.75	.30
164	Michael Finley	.75	.30
165	Antonio Davis	.25	.08
166	Lindsey Hunter	.25	.08
167	Cuttino Mobley	.50	.20
168	Glen Rice	.50	.20
169	Stephon Marbury	.75	.30
170	Sean Elliott	.50	.20
171	Cedric Henderson	.25	.08
172	Eric Snow	.50	.20
173	Othella Harrington	.25	.08
174	Vonteego Cummings	.25	.08
175	John Amaechi	.25	.08
176	Allan Houston	.50	.20
177	Shawn Marion	.75	.30
178	Scot Pollard	.25	.08
179	Elton Brand	.75	.30
180	Jacque Vaughn	.25	.08
181	Larry Hughes	.50	.20
182	Shaquille O'Neal	2.00	.75
183	Keith Van Horn	.75	.30
184	Terry Porter	.25	.08
185	Quincy Lewis	.25	.08
186	Alan Henderson	.25	.08
187	Brevin Knight	.25	.08
188	Walt Williams	.25	.08
189	Clarence Weatherspoon	.25	.08
190	Marcus Camby	.50	.20
191	Corliss Williamson	.25	.08
192	Gary Payton	.75	.30
193	Felipe Lopez	.25	.08
194	Elden Campbell	.25	.08
195	Jerome Williams	.25	.08
196	Antawn Jamison	.75	.30
197	Gerard King	.25	.08
198	Andrae Patterson	.25	.08
199	Vin Baker	.50	.20
200	Tracy McGrady	2.00	.75
201	Chris Carrawell RC	2.00	.75
202	Eduardo Najera RC	5.00	2.00
203	Olumide Oyedeji RC	2.00	.75
204	Hanno Mottola RC	2.00	.75
205	Dan McClintock RC	2.00	.75
206	Jacquay Walls RC	2.00	.75
207	Corey Hightower RC	2.00	.75
208	Jamal Crawford RC	2.50	1.00
209	Soumaila Samake RC	2.00	.75
210	Michael Redd RC	5.00	2.00
211	Jason Hart RC	2.00	.75
212	Mark Karcher RC	2.00	.75
213	Chris Porter RC	2.00	.75
214	Eddie House RC	2.00	.75
215	Jabari Smith RC	2.00	.75
216	Dan Langhi RC	2.00	.75
217	Desmond Mason RC	2.00	.75
218	Darius Miles RC	10.00	4.00
219	Donnell Harvey RC	2.00	.75
220	DeShawn Stevenson RC	2.00	.75
221	Kenyon Martin RC	12.00	5.00
222	Joel Przybilla RC	2.00	.75
223	Keyon Dooling RC	2.00	.75
224	Speedy Claxton RC	2.00	.75
225	Jerome Moiso RC	2.00	.75
226	Hidayet Turkoglu RC	8.00	3.00
227	Mark Madsen RC	2.00	.75
228	Morris Peterson RC	6.00	2.50
229	Courtney Alexander RC	4.00	1.50
230	Etan Thomas RC	2.00	.75
231	Mateen Cleaves RC	2.00	.75
232	Stromile Swift RC	6.00	2.50
233	Marcus Fizer RC	2.00	.75
234	Quentin Richardson RC	10.00	4.00
235	Jason Collier RC	3.00	1.25
236	Jamaal Magloire RC	2.00	.75
237	Erick Barkley RC	2.00	.75
238	DerMarr Johnson RC	2.00	.75
239	Chris Mihm RC	2.00	.75
240	Mamadou N'diaye RC	2.00	.75
241	Mike Miller RC	10.00	4.00

2001-02 Fleer Premium

COMPLETE SET (185)		350.00	175.00
COMP.SET w/o SP's (1-150)		40.00	20.00
COMMON CARD (1-150)		.75	.30
COMMON ROOKIE (151-185)		2.50	1.00
1	Shareef Abdur-Rahim	.75	.30
2	Charlie Ward	.25	.08
3	Anfernee Hardaway	.75	.30
4	Robert Horry	.50	.20
5	Michael Jordan	15.00	6.00
6	Trajan Langdon	.25	.08
7	Dan Majerle	.50	.20
8	Tracy McGrady	2.00	.75
9	Alonzo Mourning	.50	.20
10	Gary Payton	.75	.30
11	Erick Barkley	.50	.20
12	Jerry Stackhouse	.75	.30
13	Vince Carter	2.00	.75
14	Speedy Claxton	.50	.20
15	DerMarr Johnson	.50	.20
16	Bryon Russell	.25	.08
17	Derrick Coleman	.25	.08
18	Kevin Willis	.25	.08
19	Dirk Nowitzki	1.25	.50
20	Derek Anderson	.50	.20
21	Tim Hardaway	.50	.20
22	Avery Johnson	.25	.08
23	Quincy Lewis	.25	.08
24	Shawn Marion	.75	.30
25	Joe Smith	.50	.20
26	Tim Thomas	.50	.20
27	Bonzi Wells	.50	.20
28	Ron Artest	.75	.30
29	Elton Brand	.75	.30
30	Mateen Cleaves	.50	.20
31	Marcus Fizer	.50	.20
32	Ervin Johnson	.25	.08
33	Mark Madsen	.50	.20
34	Andre Miller	.50	.20
35	Nazr Mohammed	.25	.08
36	Dikembe Mutombo	.50	.20
37	Ben Wallace	.75	.30
38	Scottie Pippen	1.25	.50
39	Theo Ratliff	.50	.20
40	Hidayet Turkoglu	.50	.20
41	Alvin Williams	.25	.08
42	Corey Maggette	.50	.20
43	Steve Francis	.75	.30
44	Dean Garrett	.25	.08
45	Wally Szczerbiak	.50	.20
46	Brent Barry	.50	.20
47	Vlade Divac	.50	.20
48	LaPhonso Ellis	.25	.08
49	Tyrone Hill	.25	.08
50	Toni Kukoc	.50	.20
51	George Lynch	.25	.08
52	Antonio McDyess	.50	.20
53	Paul Pierce	.75	.30
54	Mitch Richmond	.50	.20
55	Latrell Sprewell	.75	.30
56	Otis Thorpe	.25	.08
57	Ray Allen	.75	.30
58	Mike Bibby	.75	.30
59	P.J. Brown	.25	.08
60	Allan Houston	.50	.20
61	Stephon Marbury	.75	.30
62	Aaron McKie	.50	.20
63	Reggie Miller	.75	.30
64	Eduardo Najera	.50	.20
65	Eddie Robinson	.50	.20
66	John Stockton	.75	.30
67	Chris Webber	.75	.30
68	Kenny Anderson	.50	.20
69	Alan Henderson	.25	.08
70	Dan Langhi	.25	.08
71	Rashard Lewis	.50	.20
72	Donyell Marshall	.50	.20
73	Charles Oakley	.25	.08
74	Stephen Jackson	.50	.20
75	Clarence Weatherspoon	.25	.08
76	David Wesley	.25	.08
77	Kobe Bryant	3.00	1.25
78	Tom Gugliotta	.25	.08
79	Darius Miles	.75	.30
80	Cuttino Mobley	.50	.20
81	Jason Terry	.75	.30
82	Shandon Anderson	.25	.08
83	Antonio Daniels	.25	.08
84	Larry Hughes	.50	.20
85	Rael LaFrentz	.50	.20
86	Kenyon Martin	.75	.30
87	Lamar Odom	.75	.30
88	Jermaine O'Neal	.75	.30
89	Glenn Robinson	.75	.30
90	Damon Stoudamire	.50	.20
91	Eddie House	.50	.20
92	Antonio Davis	.25	.08
93	Rick Fox	.50	.20
94	Allen Iverson	1.50	.60
95	Chris Mihm	.50	.20
96	Hakeem Olajuwon	.75	.30
97	Clifford Robinson	.25	.08
98	Derek Fisher	.75	.30
99	Joel Przybilla	.50	.20
100	Sean Rooks	.25	.08
101	Jason Kidd	1.25	.50
102	Antoine Walker	.75	.30
103	Jason Williams	.50	.20
104	Jamal Mashburn	.50	.20
105	Courtney Alexander	.50	.20
106	Vin Baker	.50	.20
107	Chauncey Billups	.50	.20
108	Marcus Camby	.50	.20
109	Kevin Garnett	1.50	.60
110	Juwan Howard	.50	.20
111	Marc Jackson	.50	.20
112	Karl Malone	.75	.30
113	Ricky Davis	.50	.20
114	Desmond Mason	.50	.20

#	Player		
115	Jerome Moiso	.50	.20
116	Steve Nash	.75	.30
117	Quentin Richardson	.50	.20
118	Peja Stojakovic	.75	.30
119	Rasheed Wallace	.75	.30
120	Travis Best	.25	.08
121	Terrell Brandon	.50	.20
122	Austin Croshere	.50	.20
123	Tony Delk	.25	.08
124	Anthony Mason	.50	.20
125	Patrick Ewing	.75	.30
126	Brian Grant	.50	.20
127	Bobby Jackson	.50	.20
128	Eddie Jones	.75	.30
129	Popeye Jones	.25	.08
130	Brevin Knight	.25	.08
131	Mike Miller	.75	.30
132	Shaquille O'Neal	2.00	.75
133	Morris Peterson	.50	.20
134	Mookie Blaylock	.25	.08
135	David Robinson	.75	.30
136	John Starks	.50	.20
137	Stromile Swift	.50	.20
138	Nick Van Exel	.75	.30
139	Keith Van Horn	.75	.30
140	Antawn Jamison	.75	.30
141	Kurt Thomas	.50	.20
142	Sam Cassell	.75	.30
143	Tim Duncan	1.50	.60
144	Baron Davis	.75	.30
145	Jerome Williams	.25	.08
146	Michael Finley	.75	.30
147	Richard Hamilton	.50	.20
148	Grant Hill	.75	.30
149	Jalen Rose	.75	.30
150	Steve Smith	.50	.20
151	Kwame Brown RC	5.00	2.00
152	Jeryl Sasser RC	2.50	1.00
153	Shane Battier RC	5.00	2.00
154	Gilbert Arenas RC	20.00	8.00
156	Jarron Collins RC	2.50	1.00
156	Jamaal Tinsley RC	5.00	2.00
157	Brandon Armstrong RC	4.00	1.50
158	Michael Bradley RC	2.50	1.00
159	Tyson Chandler RC	8.00	3.00
160	Joseph Forte RC	5.00	2.00
161	Brendan Haywood RC	4.00	1.50
162	Joe Johnson RC	10.00	4.00
163	Vladimir Radmanovic RC	4.00	1.50
164	Gerald Wallace RC	6.00	2.50
165	Steven Hunter RC	2.50	1.00
166	Richard Jefferson RC	8.00	3.00
167	DeSagana Diop RC	2.50	1.00
168	Terence Morris RC	2.50	1.00
169	Jason Richardson RC	8.00	3.00
170	Jeff Trepagnier RC	2.50	1.00
171	Kirk Haston RC	2.50	1.00
172	Eddy Curry RC	8.00	3.00
173	Eddie Griffin RC	3.00	1.25
174	Omar Cook RC	2.50	1.00
175	Pau Gasol RC	12.00	5.00
176	Troy Murphy RC	6.00	2.50
177	Trenton Hassell RC	5.00	2.00
178	Kedrick Brown RC	2.50	1.00
179	Zeljko Rebraca RC	2.50	1.00
180	Tony Parker RC	12.00	5.00
181	Rodney White RC	4.00	1.50
182	Jason Collins RC	2.50	1.00
183	Samuel Dalembert RC	2.50	1.00
184	Zach Randolph RC	10.00	4.00
185	Will Solomon RC	2.50	1.00

2002-03 Fleer Premium

	COMP.SET w/o SP's (110)	40.00	15.00
	COMMON ROOKIE (111-140)	4.00	1.50
1	Tracy McGrady	2.00	.75
2	Tim Duncan	1.50	.60
3	Shaquille O'Neal	2.00	.75
4	Jason Kidd	1.25	.50
5	Kobe Bryant	3.00	1.25
6	Kevin Garnett	1.50	.60
7	Chris Webber	.75	.30
8	Dirk Nowitzki	1.25	.50
9	Gary Payton	.75	.30
10	Allen Iverson	1.50	.60

#	Player		
11	Ben Wallace	.75	.30
12	Jermaine O'Neal	.75	.30
13	Dikembe Mutombo	.50	.20
14	Paul Pierce	.75	.30
15	Steve Nash	.75	.30
16	Pau Gasol	.75	.30
17	Jason Richardson	.75	.30
18	Tony Parker	.75	.30
19	Andrei Kirilenko	.75	.30
20	Shane Battier	.75	.30
21	Jamaal Tinsley	.75	.30
22	Richard Jefferson	.50	.20
23	Joe Johnson	.75	.30
24	Eddie Griffin	.50	.20
25	Zeljko Rebraca	.50	.20
26	Vladimir Radmanovic	.50	.20
27	Damon Stoudamire	.50	.20
28	Eddie Jones	.75	.30
29	Tyson Chandler	.75	.30
30	Karl Malone	.75	.30
31	David Wesley	.25	.08
32	Steve Francis	.75	.30
33	Hakeem Olajuwon	.75	.30
34	Baron Davis	.75	.30
35	Antonio McDyess	.50	.20
36	Mike Bibby	.75	.30
37	Bonzi Wells	.50	.20
38	Ray Allen	.75	.30
39	Doug Christie	.50	.20
40	Richard Hamilton	.50	.20
41	Grant Hill	.75	.30
42	Elton Brand	.75	.30
43	Gilbert Arenas	.75	.30
44	Vlade Divac	.50	.20
45	Sam Cassell	.75	.30
46	Jalen Rose	.75	.30
47	Peja Stojakovic	.75	.30
48	Glenn Robinson	.75	.30
49	Ricky Davis	.50	.20
50	Antonio Daniels	.25	.08
51	Tim Thomas	.50	.20
52	Andre Miller	.50	.20
53	Stephon Marbury	.75	.30
54	Robert Horry	.50	.20
55	Tony Delk	.25	.08
56	David Robinson	.75	.30
57	Radoslav Nesterovic	.50	.20
58	Lamond Murray	.50	.20
59	Brent Barry	.50	.20
60	Wally Szczerbiak	.50	.20
61	Lee Nailon	.25	.08
62	Rashard Lewis	.50	.20
63	Kenyon Martin	.75	.30
64	Michael Finley	.75	.30
65	John Stockton	.75	.30
66	Allan Houston	.50	.20
67	Terrell Brandon	.50	.20
68	Donyell Marshall	.50	.20
69	Marcus Camby	.50	.20
70	Cuttino Mobley	.50	.20
71	Shawn Marion	.75	.30
72	Jason Williams	.50	.20
73	Rodney Rogers	.25	.08
74	Scottie Pippen	1.25	.50
75	Brian Grant	.50	.20
76	Clifford Robinson	.25	.08
77	Antoine Walker	.75	.30
78	Michael Dickerson	.25	.08

#	Player		
79	Latrell Sprewell	.75	.30
80	Ron Artest	.50	.20
81	Shareef Abdur-Rahim	.75	.30
82	Michael Jordan	6.00	2.50
83	Mike Miller	.75	.30
84	Corey Maggette	.50	.20
85	Antawn Jamison	.75	.30
86	Rasheed Wallace	.75	.30
87	Alonzo Mourning	.50	.20
88	Eddy Curry	.75	.30
89	Derrick Coleman	.25	.08
90	Joe Smith	.50	.20
91	Darius Miles	.75	.30
92	Nick Van Exel	.75	.30
93	Derek Fisher	.75	.30
94	Nazr Mohammed	.25	.08
95	Morris Peterson	.50	.20
96	Jamal Mashburn	.50	.20
97	Jerry Stackhouse	.75	.30
98	Kwame Brown	.50	.20
99	Darrell Armstrong	.25	.08
100	Reggie Miller	.75	.30
101	Desmond Mason	.50	.20
102	Antonio Davis	.25	.08
103	Elden Campbell	.25	.08
104	Voshon Lenard	.25	.08
105	Eric Snow	.50	.20
106	Lamar Odom	.75	.30
107	Toni Kukoc	.50	.20
108	Vince Carter	2.00	.75
109	Keith Van Horn	.50	.20
110	Juwan Howard	.50	.20
111	Jay Williams RC	5.00	2.00
112	Rookie Exchange	20.00	8.00
113	Mike Dunleavy RC	6.00	2.50
114	Drew Gooden RC	10.00	4.00
115	Nikoloz Tskitishvili RC	4.00	1.50
116	DaJuan Wagner RC	6.00	2.50
117	Nene Hilario RC	4.00	1.50
118	Chris Wilcox RC	5.00	2.00
119	Amare Stoudemire RC	15.00	6.00
120	Caron Butler RC	8.00	3.00
121	Rookie Exchange	4.00	1.50
122	Marcus Haislip RC	4.00	1.50
123	Jared Jeffries RC	4.00	1.50
124	Fred Jones RC	4.00	1.50
125	Bostjan Nachbar RC	4.00	1.50
126	Jiri Welsch RC	4.00	1.50
127	Juan Dixon RC	6.00	2.50
128	Curtis Borchardt RC	4.00	1.50
129	Ryan Humphrey RC	4.00	1.50
130	Kareem Rush RC	5.00	2.00
131	Qyntel Woods RC	4.00	1.50
132	Casey Jacobsen RC	4.00	1.50
133	Tayshaun Prince RC	5.00	2.00
134	Carlos Boozer RC	15.00	6.00
135	Frank Williams RC	4.00	1.50
136	John Salmons RC	4.00	1.50
137	Rookie Exchange	4.00	1.50
138	Dan Dickau RC	4.00	1.50
139	Manu Ginobili RC	4.00	1.50
140	Roger Mason RC	4.00	1.50

2001-02 Fleer Shoebox

	COMP.SET w/o SP's (150)	40.00	20.00
	COMMON CARD (1-150)	.25	.08
	COMMON ROOKIE (151-180)	2.00	.75
1	Tariq Abdul-Wahad	.25	.08

#	Player		
2	Glen Rice	.50	.20
3	Derek Anderson	.50	.20
4	Desmond Mason	.50	.20
5	Al Harrington	.50	.20
6	Mitch Richmond	.50	.20
7	Felipe Lopez	.25	.08
8	Andre Miller	.50	.20
9	Jerry Stackhouse	.75	.30
10	Jalen Rose	.75	.30
11	Lindsey Hunter	.25	.08
12	Tim Thomas	.50	.20
13	Wally Szczerbiak	.50	.20
14	Vince Carter	2.00	.75
15	Nick Van Exel	.75	.30
16	Jon Barry	.25	.08
17	Aaron McKie	.50	.20
18	Iakovos Tsakalidis	.25	.08
19	Chris Webber	.75	.30
20	Karl Malone	.75	.30
21	Shareef Abdur-Rahim	.75	.30
22	Baron Davis	.75	.30
23	Michael Doleac	.25	.08
24	Jermaine O'Neal	.75	.30
25	Elton Brand	.75	.30
26	Glenn Robinson	.75	.30
27	Tracy McGrady	2.00	.75
28	Allen Iverson	1.50	.60
29	Anfernee Hardaway	.75	.30
30	Scot Pollard	.25	.08
31	David Robinson	.75	.30
32	John Stockton	.75	.30
33	Jason Williams	.50	.20
34	Voshon Lenard	.25	.08
35	Shaquille O'Neal	2.00	.75
36	Grant Hill	.75	.30
37	Shawn Marion	.75	.30
38	Vin Baker	.50	.20
39	Raef LaFrentz	.50	.20
40	Steve Francis	.75	.30
41	Michael Dickerson	.50	.20
42	Hidayet Turkoglu	.50	.20
43	Patrick Ewing	.75	.30
44	Dirk Nowitzki	1.25	.50
45	Keyon Dooling	.50	.20
46	Marcus Camby	.50	.20
47	Bonzi Wells	.50	.20
48	Tim Duncan	1.50	.60
49	Jamaal Magloire	.50	.20
50	Rick Fox	.50	.20
51	Kendall Gill	.25	.08
52	Michael Redd	.75	.30
53	Keith Van Horn	.75	.30
54	Eric Snow	.50	.20
55	Theo Ratliff	.50	.20
56	Clifford Robinson	.25	.08
57	Moochie Norris	.25	.08
58	Alonzo Mourning	.50	.20
59	Joe Smith	.50	.20
60	Brent Barry	.50	.20
61	Alvin Williams	.25	.08
62	Antoine Walker	.75	.30
63	Antonio McDyess	.50	.20
64	Derek Fisher	.75	.30
65	Ron Mercer	.50	.20
66	Hakeem Olajuwon	.75	.30
67	Jamal Crawford	.50	.20
68	Chris Mihm	.50	.20
69	Ben Wallace	.75	.30
70	Brian Grant	.50	.20
71	Kevin Garnett	1.50	.60
72	Shandon Anderson	.25	.08
73	Shawn Bradley	.25	.08
74	Danny Fortson	.25	.08
75	Jeff McInnis	.25	.08
76	LaPhonso Ellis	.25	.08
77	Sam Cassell	.75	.30
78	Rasheed Wallace	.75	.30
79	Malik Rose	.25	.08
80	Jahidi White	.25	.08
81	Milt Palacio	.25	.08
82	Tim Hardaway	.50	.20
83	Antonio Daniels	.25	.08
84	Tyronn Lue	.25	.08
85	Cuttino Mobley	.50	.20
86	DerMarr Johnson	.50	.20
87	Lamond Murray	.25	.08
88	Larry Hughes	.50	.20
89	Reggie Miller	.75	.30
90	Lorenzen Wright	.25	.08
91	Eddie Jones	.75	.30
92	Anthony Mason	.50	.20
93	Todd MacCulloch	.25	.08
94	Speedy Claxton	.50	.20
95	Mateen Cleaves	.50	.20
96	Gary Payton	.75	.30
97	Morris Peterson	.50	.20
98	Mike Miller	.75	.30
99	Hanno Mottola	.50	.20
100	Steve Nash	.75	.30
101	Stromile Swift	.50	.20
102	Ray Allen	.75	.30
103	Mark Jackson	.50	.20
104	Stephon Marbury	.75	.30
105	Mike Bibby	.75	.30
106	Rashard Lewis	.50	.20
107	Jason Kidd	1.25	.50
108	P.J. Brown	.25	.08
109	Kobe Bryant	3.00	1.25
110	Tom Gugliotta	.25	.08
111	Richard Hamilton	.50	.20
112	Antawn Jamison	.75	.30
113	Lamar Odom	.75	.30
114	Kurt Thomas	.50	.20
115	Robert Horry	.50	.20
116	Dikembe Mutombo	.50	.20
117	Tony Delk	.25	.08
118	Peja Stojakovic	.75	.30
119	Donyell Marshall	.50	.20
120	Paul Pierce	.75	.30
121	Michael Finley	.75	.30
122	Quentin Richardson	.50	.20
123	Kenyon Martin	.75	.30
124	Allan Houston	.50	.20
125	Scottie Pippen	1.25	.50
126	Steve Smith	.50	.20
127	Bryon Russell	.25	.08
128	James Posey	.50	.20
129	Terrell Brandon	.50	.20
130	Toni Kukoc	.50	.20
131	Stephen Jackson	.50	.20
132	Marc Jackson	.50	.20
133	Kelvin Cato	.25	.08
134	Travis Best	.25	.08
135	David Wesley	.25	.08
136	Anthony Carter	.50	.20
137	Michael Jordan	12.00	5.00
138	Darrell Armstrong	.25	.08
139	Matt Harpring	.75	.30
140	Antonio Davis	.25	.08
141	Courtney Alexander	.50	.20
142	Jamal Mashburn	.50	.20
143	Jason Terry	.75	.30
144	Marcus Fizer	.50	.20
145	Juwan Howard	.50	.20
146	Darius Miles	.75	.30
147	Latrell Sprewell	.75	.30
148	Damon Stoudamire	.50	.20
149	John Starks	.50	.20
150	Jumaine Jones	.50	.20
151	Kedrick Brown RC	2.00	.75
152	Trenton Hassell RC	3.00	1.25
153	Kwame Brown RC	5.00	2.00
154	Terence Morris RC	2.00	.75
155	Richard Jefferson RC	3.00	1.25
156	Vladimir Radmanovic RC	2.50	1.00
157	Brandon Armstrong RC	2.50	1.00
158	Kirk Haston RC	2.00	.75
159	Eddie Griffin RC	2.50	1.00
160	Steven Hunter RC	2.00	.75
161	Troy Murphy RC	4.00	1.50
162	Andrei Kirilenko RC	5.00	2.00
163	Jeryl Sasser RC	2.00	.75
164	Michael Bradley RC	2.00	.75
165	Rodney White RC	2.50	1.00
166	Loren Woods RC	2.00	.75
167	Zach Randolph RC	6.00	2.50
168	Joe Johnson RC	6.00	2.50
169	Eddy Curry RC	5.00	2.00
170	Jason Richardson RC	5.00	2.00
171	DeSagana Diop RC	2.00	.75
172	Jamaal Tinsley RC	3.00	1.25
173	Pau Gasol RC	8.00	3.00
174	Jason Collins RC	2.00	.75
175	Zeljko Rebraca RC	2.00	.75
176	Shane Battier RC	3.00	1.25
177	Gerald Wallace RC	4.00	1.50
178	Joseph Forte RC	5.00	2.00
179	Tyson Chandler RC	5.00	2.00
180	Tony Parker RC	8.00	3.00

2000-01 Fleer Showcase

	COMPLETE SET w/o RCs (90)	30.00	15.00
	COMMON CARD (1-90)	.30	.10
	COMMON ROOKIE (91-100)	10.00	4.00
	COMMON ROOKIE (101-110)	5.00	2.00
	COMMON ROOKIE (111-121)	4.00	1.50
1	Vince Carter	2.50	1.00
2	Lamar Odom	1.00	.40
3	Larry Hughes	.60	.25
4	Brian Grant	.60	.25
5	Bryon Russell	.30	.10
6	Allan Houston	.60	.25
7	Juwan Howard	.60	.25
8	Cuttino Mobley	.60	.25
9	Keith Van Horn	1.00	.40
10	Mike Bibby	1.00	.40
11	Jerome Williams	.30	.10
12	Ray Allen	1.00	.40
13	Antonio Davis	.30	.10
14	Adrian Griffin	.30	.10
15	Dan Majerle	.60	.25
16	Rasheed Wallace	1.00	.40
17	Antonio McDyess	.60	.25
18	Tim Thomas	.60	.25
19	Theo Ratliff	.60	.25
20	Charles Oakley	.30	.10
21	Nick Van Exel	1.00	.40
22	Glenn Robinson	1.00	.40
23	Cal Bowdler	.30	.10
24	Raef LaFrentz	.60	.25
25	Terrell Brandon	.60	.25
26	Allen Iverson	2.00	.75
27	Patrick Ewing	1.00	.40
28	Ron Artest	.60	.25
29	Michael Olowokandi	.30	.10
30	Derek Anderson	.60	.25
31	Dirk Nowitzki	1.50	.60
32	Wally Szczerbiak	.60	.25
33	Gary Payton	1.00	.40
34	Michael Finley	1.00	.40
35	Chauncey Billups	.30	.10
36	Jason Kidd	1.50	.60
37	Rashard Lewis	.60	.25
38	Andre Miller	.60	.25
39	Kevin Garnett	2.00	.75
40	Tim Duncan	2.00	.75
41	Jalen Rose	1.00	.40
42	Marcus Camby	.60	.25
43	Richard Hamilton	.60	.25
44	Austin Croshere	.60	.25
45	Latrell Sprewell	1.00	.40
46	Shawn Marion	1.00	.40
47	Jahidi White	.30	.10
48	Elton Brand	1.00	.40
49	Reggie Miller	1.00	.40
50	David Robinson	1.00	.40
51	Trajan Langdon	.30	.10
52	Jonathan Bender	.60	.25
53	Antonio Daniels	.30	.10
54	Jason Terry	1.00	.40

❏ 55	Eddie Jones	1.00	.40
❏ 56	Mitch Richmond	.60	.25
❏ 57	Antoine Walker	1.00	.40
❏ 58	Robert Horry	.60	.25
❏ 59	Tracy McGrady	2.50	1.00
❏ 60	Scottie Pippen	1.50	.60
❏ 61	Jerry Stackhouse	1.00	.40
❏ 62	Zydrunas Ilgauskas	.60	.25
❏ 63	Toni Kukoc	.60	.25
❏ 64	Karl Malone	1.00	.40
❏ 65	Baron Davis	1.00	.40
❏ 66	Shaquille O'Neal	2.50	1.00
❏ 67	Vlade Divac	.60	.25
❏ 68	Eddie Robinson	.30	.10
❏ 69	Dion Glover	.30	.10
❏ 70	Jason Williams	.60	.25
❏ 71	Steve Francis	1.00	.40
❏ 72	Glen Rice	.60	.25
❏ 73	Clifford Robinson	.30	.10
❏ 74	Shareef Abdur-Rahim	1.00	.40
❏ 75	Hakeem Olajuwon	1.00	.40
❏ 76	Paul Pierce	1.00	.40
❏ 77	Tim Hardaway	.60	.25
❏ 78	Darrell Armstrong	.30	.10
❏ 79	Bonzi Wells	.60	.25
❏ 80	Antawn Jamison	1.00	.40
❏ 81	Stephon Marbury	1.00	.40
❏ 82	Tony Delk	.30	.10
❏ 83	Michael Dickerson	.60	.25
❏ 84	Jamal Mashburn	.60	.25
❏ 85	Kobe Bryant	4.00	1.50
❏ 86	Grant Hill	1.00	.40
❏ 87	Chris Webber	1.00	.40
❏ 88	Vonteego Cummings	.30	.10
❏ 89	Jamie Feick	.30	.10
❏ 90	John Stockton	1.00	.40
❏ 91	Kenyon Martin RC	25.00	10.00
❏ 92	Stromile Swift RC	15.00	6.00
❏ 93	Darius Miles RC	20.00	8.00
❏ 94	Marcus Fizer RC	10.00	4.00
❏ 95	Mike Miller RC	20.00	8.00
❏ 96	DerMarr Johnson RC	10.00	4.00
❏ 97	Chris Mihm RC	10.00	4.00
❏ 98	Jamal Crawford RC	15.00	6.00
❏ 99	Joel Przybilla RC	10.00	4.00
❏ 100	Keyon Dooling RC	10.00	4.00
❏ 101	Jerome Moiso RC	5.00	2.00
❏ 102	Etan Thomas RC	5.00	2.00
❏ 103	Courtney Alexander RC	10.00	4.00
❏ 104	Mateen Cleaves RC	5.00	2.00
❏ 105	Jason Collier RC	8.00	3.00
❏ 106	Hidayet Turkoglu RC	6.00	2.50
❏ 107	Desmond Mason RC	5.00	2.00
❏ 108	Quentin Richardson RC	6.00	2.50
❏ 109	Jamaal Magloire RC	5.00	2.00
❏ 110	Speedy Claxton RC	5.00	2.00
❏ 111	Morris Peterson RC	6.00	2.50
❏ 112	Donnell Harvey RC	4.00	1.50
❏ 113	DeShawn Stevenson RC	4.00	1.50
❏ 114	Dalibor Bagaric RC	4.00	1.50
❏ 115	Mamadou N'Diaye RC	4.00	1.50
❏ 116	Erick Barkley RC	4.00	1.50
❏ 117	Mark Madsen RC	4.00	1.50
❏ 118	Chris Porter RC	4.00	1.50
❏ 119	Brian Cardinal RC	4.00	1.50
❏ 120	Iakovos Tsakalidis RC	4.00	1.50
❏ 121	Marc Jackson RC	5.00	2.00

2001-02 Fleer Showcase

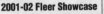

❏ COMPLETE SET (123)		400.00	200.00
❏ COMP.SET w/o SP's (86)		50.00	20.00
❏ COMMON AVANT(87-91/123)		20.00	8.00
❏ COMMON AVANT (92-97)		20.00	8.00
❏ COMMON ROOKIE (98-112)		4.00	1.50
❏ COMMON ROOKIE (113-122)		3.00	1.25
❏ CARTER AU/150 NOT INCL.IN SET PRICE			
❏ 1	Grant Hill	1.00	.40
❏ 2	Elton Brand	1.00	.40
❏ 3	Sam Cassell	1.00	.40
❏ 4	John Stockton	1.00	.40
❏ 5	James Posey	.60	.25
❏ 6	Eddie Jones	1.00	.40
❏ 7	Damon Stoudamire	.60	.25
❏ 8	Nick Van Exel	1.00	.40
❏ 9	Brian Grant	.60	.25
❏ 10	Mike Miller	1.00	.40

❏ 11	Steve Smith	.60	.25
❏ 12	Michael Finley	1.00	.40
❏ 13	Peja Stojakovic	1.00	.40
❏ 14	DerMarr Johnson	.60	.25
❏ 15	Reggie Miller	1.00	.40
❏ 16	Quentin Richardson	.60	.25
❏ 17	Latrell Sprewell	1.00	.40
❏ 18	Richard Hamilton	.60	.25
❏ 19	Michael Doleac	.30	.10
❏ 20	Derek Fisher	1.00	.40
❏ 21	Marcus Camby	.60	.25
❏ 22	Stephon Marbury	1.00	.40
❏ 23	Bryon Russell	.30	.10
❏ 24	Jumaine Jones	.60	.25
❏ 25	Anfernee Hardaway	1.00	.40
❏ 26	P.J. Brown	.30	.10
❏ 27	Marc Jackson	.60	.25
❏ 28	Dikembe Mutombo	.60	.25
❏ 29	Andre Miller	.60	.25
❏ 30	Robert Horry	.60	.25
❏ 31	Tom Gugliotta	.30	.10
❏ 32	David Robinson	1.00	.40
❏ 33	Ron Mercer	.60	.25
❏ 34	Shawn Marion	1.00	.40
❏ 35	Ron Artest	.60	.25
❏ 36	Jason Williams	.60	.25
❏ 37	Scottie Pippen	1.50	.60
❏ 38	Jerry Stackhouse	1.00	.40
❏ 39	Stromile Swift	.60	.25
❏ 40	Rasheed Wallace	1.00	.40
❏ 41	Alonzo Mourning	.60	.25
❏ 42	Eddie Robinson	.60	.25
❏ 43	Shareef Abdur-Rahim	1.00	.40
❏ 44	Wally Szczerbiak	.60	.25
❏ 45	Antonio Davis	.30	.10
❏ 46	Glen Rice	.60	.25
❏ 47	Jason Kidd	1.50	.60
❏ 48	Gary Payton	1.00	.40
❏ 49	Steve Nash	1.00	.40
❏ 50	Lamar Odom	1.00	.40
❏ 51	Glenn Robinson	1.00	.40
❏ 52	Mike Bibby	1.00	.40
❏ 53	Hakeem Olajuwon	.60	.25
❏ 54	Theo Ratliff	.60	.25
❏ 55	Kenyon Martin	1.00	.40
❏ 56	Jamal Mashburn	.60	.25
❏ 57	Larry Hughes	.60	.25
❏ 58	Speedy Claxton	.60	.25
❏ 59	Rashard Lewis	.60	.25
❏ 60	Rael LaFrentz	.60	.25
❏ 61	Antonio Daniels	.30	.10
❏ 62	Jason Terry	1.00	.40
❏ 63	Jalen Rose	1.00	.40
❏ 64	Terrell Brandon	.60	.25
❏ 65	Karl Malone	1.00	.40
❏ 66	Antonio McDyess	.60	.25
❏ 67	Anthony Carter	.60	.25
❏ 68	Tim Hardaway	.60	.25
❏ 69	Antoine Walker	1.00	.40
❏ 70	Cuttino Mobley	.60	.25
❏ 71	Allan Houston	.60	.25
❏ 72	Desmond Mason	.60	.25
❏ 73	Kurt Thomas	.60	.25
❏ 74	Juwan Howard	.60	.25
❏ 75	Tim Thomas	.60	.25
❏ 76	Tracy McGrady	2.50	1.00
❏ 77	Dirk Nowitzki	1.50	.60
❏ 78	Tim Duncan	2.00	.75

❏ 79	Chris Webber	1.00	.40
❏ 80	Steve Francis	1.00	.40
❏ 81	Paul Pierce	1.00	.40
❏ 82	Darius Miles	1.00	.40
❏ 83	Ray Allen	1.00	.40
❏ 84	Baron Davis	1.00	.40
❏ 85	Antawn Jamison	1.00	.40
❏ 86	Michael Jordan	15.00	6.00
❏ 87	Vince Carter AVANT	20.00	8.00
❏ 87A	V.Carter AU/150	120.00	60.00
❏ 88	Kobe Bryant AVANT	30.00	12.50
❏ 89	Allen Iverson AVANT	20.00	8.00
❏ 90	Kevin Garnett AVANT	20.00	8.00
❏ 91	S.O'Neal AVANT	20.00	8.00
❏ 92	K.Brown AVANT RC	20.00	8.00
❏ 93	E.Griffin AVANT RC	20.00	8.00
❏ 94	E.Curry AVANT RC	20.00	8.00
❏ 95	S.Battier AVANT RC	20.00	8.00
❏ 96	J.Johnson AVANT RC	30.00	12.50
❏ 97	T.Chandler AVANT RC	20.00	8.00
❏ 98	Jason Richardson RC	10.00	4.00
❏ 99	Zach Randolph RC	12.00	8.00
❏ 100	Rodney White RC	5.00	2.00
❏ 101	Pau Gasol RC	12.00	5.00
❏ 102	Jamaal Tinsley RC	6.00	2.50
❏ 103	Troy Murphy RC	8.00	3.00
❏ 104	Richard Jefferson RC	6.00	2.50
❏ 105	DeSagana Diop RC	4.00	1.50
❏ 106	Joseph Forte RC	8.00	3.00
❏ 107	Gerald Wallace RC	8.00	3.00
❏ 108	Loren Woods RC	4.00	1.50
❏ 109	Jason Collins RC	4.00	1.50
❏ 110	Jeryl Sasser RC	4.00	1.50
❏ 111	Zeljko Rebraca RC	4.00	1.50
❏ 112	Kirk Haston RC	4.00	1.50
❏ 113	Kedrick Brown RC	3.00	1.25
❏ 114	Steven Hunter RC	4.00	1.50
❏ 115	Michael Bradley RC	3.00	1.25
❏ 116	Brandon Armstrong RC	4.00	1.50
❏ 117	Samuel Dalembert RC	4.00	1.50
❏ 118	Primoz Brezec RC	5.00	2.00
❏ 119	Andrei Kirilenko RC	8.00	3.00
❏ 120	Vladimir Radmanovic RC	4.00	1.50
❏ 121	Ratko Varda RC	4.00	1.50
❏ 122	Brendan Haywood RC	5.00	2.00
❏ 123	Wang Zhizhi AVANT	15.00	6.00

2002-03 Fleer Showcase

❏ COMP. SET w/o SP's (100)		30.00	12.50
❏ COMMON CARD (1-100)		.25	.10
❏ COMM.AVANT.ROW 2 (101-112)		4.00	1.50
❏ COMM.AVANT.ROW 0 (113-118)			
❏ COMM.RC AVANT (119-124)		10.00	4.00
❏ COMMON ROOKIE (125-148)		15.00	6.00
❏ 1	Michael Jordan	6.00	2.50
❏ 2	Shareef Abdur-Rahim	1.00	.40
❏ 3	Jalen Rose	1.00	.40
❏ 4	Antonio McDyess	.25	.10
❏ 5	Malik Rose	.25	.10
❏ 6	Juwan Howard	.25	.10
❏ 7	Jason Williams	.60	.25
❏ 8	Darrell Armstrong	.25	.10
❏ 9	Karl Malone	1.00	.40
❏ 10	Jason Terry	1.00	.40
❏ 11	David Wesley	.25	.10
❏ 12	David Robinson	1.00	.40
❏ 13	Gary Payton	1.00	.40
❏ 14	Quentin Richardson	.60	.25

#	Player		
15	Allan Houston	.60	.25
16	Alvin Williams	.25	.10
17	Jamal Mashburn	.60	.25
18	Theo Ratliff	.60	.25
19	Tyson Chandler	1.00	.40
20	Gilbert Arenas	1.00	.40
21	Dikembe Mutombo	.60	.25
22	Calbert Cheaney	.25	.10
23	Rodney Rogers	.25	.10
24	Shane Battier	1.00	.40
25	Mike Miller	1.00	.40
26	John Stockton	1.00	.40
27	Mengke Bateer	.25	.10
28	Andre Miller	.60	.25
29	Sam Cassell	1.00	.40
30	Anfernee Hardaway	1.00	.40
31	Keith Van Horn	1.00	.40
32	Tony Battie	.25	.10
33	Derek Fisher	1.00	.40
34	Grant Hill	1.00	.40
35	Andrei Kirilenko	1.00	.40
36	Toni Kukoc	.60	.25
37	Jerry Stackhouse	1.00	.40
38	Latrell Sprewell	1.00	.40
39	Morris Peterson	1.00	.40
40	Darius Miles	1.00	.40
41	Eddie Jones	1.00	.40
42	Stephon Marbury	1.00	.40
43	Brent Barry	.60	.25
44	DeShawn Stevenson	.25	.10
45	Brian Grant	.60	.25
46	Derrick Coleman	.25	.10
47	Richard Hamilton	.60	.25
48	Jason Richardson	1.00	.40
49	Kerry Kittles	.25	.10
50	Desmond Mason	.60	.25
51	Stromile Swift	.60	.25
52	Richard Jefferson	.60	.25
53	Vladimir Radmanovic	.60	.25
54	Lamond Murray	.25	.10
55	Troy Murphy	.60	.25
56	Kenyon Martin	1.00	.40
57	Vlade Divac	.60	.25
58	Chris Mihm	.25	.10
59	Eddie Griffin	.60	.25
60	Marc Jackson	.60	.25
61	Peja Stojakovic	1.00	.40
62	Vin Baker	.60	.25
63	Cuttino Mobley	.60	.25
64	Joe Smith	.60	.25
65	Damon Stoudamire	.60	.25
66	Eddy Curry	1.00	.40
67	Alonzo Mourning	.60	.25
68	Aaron McKie	.60	.25
69	Kwame Brown	.60	.25
70	Raef LaFrentz	.60	.25
71	Jermaine O'Neal	1.00	.40
72	Terrell Brandon	.60	.25
73	Bonzi Wells	.60	.25
74	Steve Nash	1.00	.40
75	Jamaal Tinsley	.60	.25
76	Wally Szczerbiak	.60	.25
77	Scottie Pippen	1.50	.60
78	Michael Finley	1.00	.40
79	Reggie Miller	1.00	.40
80	Glenn Robinson	1.00	.40
81	Rasheed Wallace	1.00	.40
82	Antoine Walker	1.00	.40
83	Robert Horry	.60	.25
84	Kurt Thomas	.60	.25
85	Antonio Davis	.25	.10
86	Nick Van Exel	1.00	.40
87	Al Harrington	.60	.25
88	Tony Delk	.25	.10
89	Joe Johnson	.60	.25
90	Chauncey Billups	.60	.25
91	P.J. Brown	.25	.10
92	Tony Parker	1.00	.40
93	Antawn Jamison	1.00	.40
94	Courtney Alexander	.60	.25
95	Kenny Anderson	.60	.25
96	Clifford Robinson	.25	.10
97	Lamar Odom	1.00	.40
98	Anthony Carter	.60	.25
99	Shawn Marion	1.00	.40
100	Hidayet Turkoglu	1.00	.40

#	Player		
101	Paul Pierce AVANT	4.00	1.50
102	Dirk Nowitzki AVANT	4.00	1.50
103	Ben Wallace AVANT	4.00	1.50
104	Steve Francis AVANT	4.00	1.50
105	Pau Gasol AVANT	4.00	1.50
106	Ray Allen AVANT	4.00	1.50
107	Kevin Garnett AVANT	5.00	2.00
108	Jason Kidd AVANT	4.00	1.50
109	Baron Davis AVANT	4.00	1.50
110	Mike Bibby AVANT	4.00	1.50
111	Chris Webber AVANT	4.00	1.50
112	Tim Duncan AVANT	5.00	2.00
113	Kobe Bryant AVANT	15.00	6.00
114	Shaquille O'Neal AVANT	10.00	4.00
115	Tracy McGrady AVANT	10.00	4.00
116	Allen Iverson AVANT	8.00	3.00
117	Vince Carter AVANT	10.00	4.00
118	Elton Brand AVANT	5.00	2.00
119	J.Williams AVANT RC	5.00	2.00
120	Yao Ming AVANT RC	50.00	20.00
121	M.Dunleavy AVANT RC	5.00	2.00
122	D.Wagner AVANT RC	5.00	2.00
123	C.Butler AVANT RC	12.00	5.00
124	D.Gooden AVANT RC	15.00	6.00
125	Manu Ginobli RC	15.00	6.00
126	Mehmet Okur RC	5.00	2.00
127	Nene Hilario RC	6.00	2.50
128	Nikoloz Tskitishvili RC	6.00	2.50
129	Tayshaun Prince RC	8.00	3.00
130	Bostjan Nachbar RC	5.00	2.00
131	Fred Jones RC	5.00	2.00
132	Melvin Ely RC	5.00	2.00
133	Chris Wilcox RC	6.00	2.50
134	Kareem Rush RC	6.00	2.50
135	Marcus Haislip RC	5.00	2.00
136	Frank Williams RC	5.00	2.00
137	Ryan Humphrey RC	5.00	2.00
138	John Salmons RC	5.00	2.00
139	Casey Jacobsen RC	5.00	2.00
140	Amare Stoudemire RC	25.00	10.00
141	Qyntel Woods RC	6.00	2.50
142	Chris Jefferies RC	5.00	2.00
143	Juan Dixon RC	8.00	3.00
144	Jared Jeffries RC	5.00	2.00
145	Lenny Baxter RC	5.00	2.00
146	Dan Dickau RC	5.00	2.00
147	Carlos Boozer RC	10.00	4.00
148	Vincent Yarbrough RC	5.00	2.00

2003-04 Fleer Showcase

#	Player		
	COMP.SET w/o SP's (100)	40.00	15.00
	COMMON SP (91-100)	5.00	2.00
	COMMON ROOKIE (101-130)	5.00	2.00
1	Jason Richardson	1.00	.40
2	Andrei Kirilenko	1.00	.40
3	Steve Francis	1.00	.40
4	Shareef Abdur-Rahim	1.00	.40
5	Ben Wallace	1.00	.40
6	Predrag Drobnjak	.25	.10
7	Jalen Rose	1.00	.40
8	Rashard Lewis	1.00	.40
9	Darius Miles	1.00	.40
10	Bobby Jackson	.60	.25
11	Steve Nash	1.00	.40
12	Gilbert Arenas	1.00	.40
13	Aaron McKie	.60	.25
14	Reggie Miller	1.00	.40
15	Elton Brand	1.00	.40

#	Player		
16	Allan Houston	.60	.25
17	Pau Gasol	1.00	.40
18	Jamaal Magloire	.25	.10
19	Eddie Jones	1.00	.40
20	Richard Jefferson	.60	.25
21	Wally Szczerbiak	.60	.25
22	Antonio McDyess	.60	.25
23	Michael Redd	1.00	.40
24	Grant Hill	1.00	.40
25	Jason Williams	.60	.25
26	Rasheed Wallace	1.00	.40
27	Andre Miller	.60	.25
28	Peja Stojakovic	1.00	.40
29	Cuttino Mobley	.60	.25
30	David Robinson	1.00	.40
31	Richard Hamilton	.60	.25
32	Morris Peterson	.60	.25
33	Karl Malone	1.00	.40
34	Zydrunas Ilgauskas	.60	.25
35	Jerry Stackhouse	1.00	.40
36	Eddy Curry	1.00	.40
37	Sam Cassell	1.00	.40
38	Troy Hudson	.25	.10
39	Jason Terry	1.00	.40
40	Kenyon Martin	1.00	.40
41	Bonzi Wells	.60	.25
42	Donnell Harvey	.25	.10
43	Tracy McGrady	2.50	1.00
44	Allen Iverson	2.00	.75
45	Jermaine O'Neal	1.00	.40
46	Larry Hughes	.60	.25
47	Scottie Pippen	1.50	.60
48	Antonio Davis	.25	.10
49	Chris Webber	1.00	.40
50	Vladimir Radmanovic	.25	.10
51	Glenn Robinson	1.00	.40
52	Antoine Walker	1.00	.40
53	Ricky Davis	1.00	.40
54	Michael Finley	1.00	.40
55	Nick Van Exel	1.00	.40
56	Tayshaun Prince	.60	.25
57	Antawn Jamison	1.00	.40
58	Jamal Mashburn	.60	.25
59	Jamaal Tinsley	.60	.25
60	Kerry Kittles	.25	.10
61	Derek Fisher	1.00	.40
62	Radoslav Nesterovic	.60	.25
63	Mike Miller	1.00	.40
64	Gary Payton	1.00	.40
65	Brian Grant	.60	.25
66	Baron Davis	1.00	.40
67	Shane Battier	1.00	.40
68	Latrell Sprewell	1.00	.40
69	Keith Van Horn	1.00	.40
70	Eddie Griffin	.60	.25
71	Stephon Marbury	1.00	.40
72	Chauncey Billups	.60	.25
73	Shawn Marion	1.00	.40
74	Juwan Howard	.60	.25
75	Mike Bibby	1.00	.40
76	DaJuan Wagner	.60	.25
77	Tony Parker	1.00	.40
78	Tyson Chandler	1.00	.40
79	Ray Allen	1.00	.40
80	Matt Harpring	1.00	.40
81	Kwame Brown	.60	.25
82	Troy Murphy	.60	.25
83	Ron Artest	.60	.25
84	Corey Maggette	.60	.25
85	Tony Delk	.25	.10
86	Jamal Crawford	.25	.10
87	Vince Carter	2.50	1.00
88	Kevin Garnett	2.00	.75
89	Jason Kidd	1.50	.60
90	Paul Pierce	5.00	2.00
91	Nene SP	5.00	2.00
92	Drew Gooden SP	5.00	2.00
93	Caron Butler SP	5.00	2.00
94	Manu Ginobili SP	5.00	2.00
95	Dirk Nowitzki SP	5.00	2.00
96	Yao Ming SP	8.00	3.00
97	Amare Stoudemire SP	6.00	2.50
98	Kobe Bryant SP	12.00	5.00
99	Tim Duncan SP	6.00	2.50
100	Shaquille O'Neal SP	8.00	3.00
101	T.J. Ford RC	5.00	2.50

❏ 102	Chris Bosh RC	15.00	6.00
❏ 103	Boris Diaw RC	6.00	2.50
❏ 104	Luke Ridnour RC	6.00	2.50
❏ 105	Zoran Planinic RC	5.00	2.00
❏ 106	Josh Howard RC	8.00	3.00
❏ 107	Darko Milicic EXCH	8.00	3.00
❏ 108	Dahntay Jones RC	5.00	2.00
❏ 109	Mike Sweetney RC	4.00	1.50
❏ 110	Kirk Hinrich RC	8.00	3.00
❏ 111	Marcus Banks RC	4.00	1.50
❏ 112	Travis Outlaw RC	5.00	2.00
❏ 113	Brian Cook RC	5.00	2.00
❏ 114	Mario Austin RC	5.00	2.00
❏ 115	Dwyane Wade RC	25.00	10.00
❏ 116	Chris Kaman RC	5.00	2.00
❏ 117	Zarko Cabarkapa RC	5.00	2.00
❏ 118	Ndudi Ebi RC	5.00	2.00
❏ 119	Mickael Pietrus RC	5.00	2.00
❏ 120	Carmelo Anthony RC	20.00	8.00
❏ 121	Kendrick Perkins RC	5.00	2.00
❏ 122	Troy Bell RC	5.00	2.00
❏ 123	Maciej Lampe RC	5.00	2.00
❏ 124	Carlos Delfino RC	5.00	2.00
❏ 125	Leandro Barbosa RC	8.00	3.00
❏ 126	Sofoklis Schortsanitis RC	6.00	2.50
❏ 127	Reece Gaines RC	5.00	2.00
❏ 128	Nick Collison RC	5.00	2.00
❏ 129	David West RC	5.00	2.00
❏ 130	LeBron James RC	60.00	30.00

2004-05 Fleer Showcase

❏	COMP.SET w/o SP's (90)	40.00	15.00
❏	COMMON CARD (1-90)	.20	.08
❏	COMMON ROOKIE/199	12.00	5.00
❏	COMMON ROOKIE/499	6.00	2.50
❏	COMMON ROOKIE/699	5.00	2.00
❏ 1	Kirk Hinrich	.75	.30
❏ 2	Shaquille O'Neal	2.00	.75
❏ 3	Allen Iverson	1.50	.60
❏ 4	Carlos Arroyo	1.25	.50
❏ 5	Darko Milicic	.50	.20
❏ 6	Sam Cassell	.50	.20
❏ 7	Peja Stojakovic	.75	.30
❏ 8	Ben Wallace	.75	.30
❏ 9	T.J. Ford	.50	.20
❏ 10	Chris Webber	.75	.30
❏ 11	LeBron James	5.00	2.00
❏ 12	Karl Malone	.75	.30
❏ 13	Glenn Robinson	.75	.30
❏ 14	Jarvis Hayes	.50	.20
❏ 15	Bob Sura	.20	.08
❏ 16	Yao Ming	2.00	.75
❏ 17	Baron Davis	.75	.30
❏ 18	Rashard Lewis	.75	.30
❏ 19	Carlos Boozer	.75	.30
❏ 20	Pau Gasol	.75	.30
❏ 21	Tim Duncan	1.50	.60
❏ 22	Gilbert Arenas	.75	.30
❏ 23	Dajuan Wagner	.50	.20
❏ 24	Bonzi Wells	.50	.20
❏ 25	Dirk Nowitzki	1.25	.50
❏ 26	Jason Williams	.50	.20
❏ 27	Amare Stoudemire	1.50	.60
❏ 28	Gerald Wallace	.50	.20
❏ 29	Corey Maggette	.50	.20
❏ 30	Tim Thomas	.50	.20
❏ 31	Andrei Kirilenko	.75	.30
❏ 32	Steve Nash	.75	.30
❏ 33	Caron Butler	.75	.30
❏ 34	Shawn Marion	.75	.30
❏ 35	Michael Finley	.75	.30
❏ 36	Dwyane Wade	2.50	1.00
❏ 37	Joe Johnson	.75	.30
❏ 38	Carmelo Anthony	1.50	.60
❏ 39	Lamar Odom	.75	.30
❏ 40	Darius Miles	.75	.30
❏ 41	Mike Dunleavy	.50	.20
❏ 42	Jason Kidd	1.25	.50
❏ 43	Manu Ginobili	.75	.30
❏ 44	Jason Richardson	.75	.30
❏ 45	Latrell Sprewell	.75	.30
❏ 46	Willie Green	.20	.08
❏ 47	Theron Smith	.20	.08
❏ 48	Elton Brand	.75	.30
❏ 49	Tracy McGrady	2.00	.75
❏ 50	Matt Harpring	.75	.30
❏ 51	Eddy Curry	.50	.20
❏ 52	Chris Kaman	.50	.20
❏ 53	Drew Gooden	.50	.20
❏ 54	Stephen Jackson	.20	.08
❏ 55	Mickael Pietrus	.50	.20
❏ 56	Kenyon Martin	.75	.30
❏ 57	Tony Parker	.75	.30
❏ 58	Paul Pierce	.75	.30
❏ 59	Cuttino Mobley	.50	.20
❏ 60	Jamal Mashburn	.50	.20
❏ 61	Luke Ridnour	.50	.20
❏ 62	Jamal Crawford	.50	.20
❏ 63	Kobe Bryant	3.00	1.25
❏ 64	Keith Bogans	.20	.08
❏ 65	Jerry Stackhouse	.50	.20
❏ 66	Ricky Davis	.75	.30
❏ 67	Jermaine O'Neal	.75	.30
❏ 68	Jamaal Magloire	.20	.08
❏ 69	Vince Carter	2.00	.75
❏ 70	Jason Kapono	.50	.20
❏ 71	Ron Artest	.50	.20
❏ 72	Allan Houston	.50	.20
❏ 73	Chris Bosh	.75	.30
❏ 74	Rasheed Wallace	.75	.30
❏ 75	Kevin Garnett	1.50	.60
❏ 76	Mike Bibby	.75	.30
❏ 77	Jason Terry	.75	.30
❏ 78	Steve Francis	.75	.30
❏ 79	Richard Jefferson	.75	.30
❏ 80	Ray Allen	.75	.30
❏ 81	Andre Miller	.50	.20
❏ 82	Desmond Mason	.50	.20
❏ 83	Zach Randolph	.75	.30
❏ 84	Marcus Banks	.50	.20
❏ 85	Reggie Miller	.75	.30
❏ 86	Stephon Marbury	.75	.30
❏ 87	Jalen Rose	.75	.30
❏ 88	Nene	.50	.20
❏ 89	Michael Redd	.50	.20
❏ 90	Shareef Abdur-Rahim	.75	.30
❏ 91	Emeka Okafor/199 RC	50.00	20.00
❏ 92	Jameer Nelson/199 RC	20.00	8.00
❏ 93	Dwight Howard/199 RC	40.00	15.00
❏ 94	Josh Smith/199 RC	25.00	10.00
❏ 95	Pavel Podkolzine/699 RC	5.00	2.00
❏ 96	Shaun Livingston/199 RC	20.00	8.00
❏ 97	Andre Iguodala/199 RC	30.00	12.50
❏ 98	Luol Deng/199 RC	25.00	10.00
❏ 99	Delonte West/699 RC	10.00	4.00
❏ 100	Andris Biedrins/699 RC	6.00	2.50
❏ 101	Sasha Vujacic/499 RC	6.00	2.50
❏ 102	Kris Humphries/499 RC	6.00	2.50
❏ 103	Ben Gordon/199 RC	60.00	25.00
❏ 104	Robert Swift/499 RC	6.00	2.50
❏ 105	Al Jefferson/499 RC	15.00	6.00
❏ 106	Sergei Monia/499 RC	6.00	2.50
❏ 107	Devin Harris/499 RC	10.00	4.00
❏ 108	Luke Jackson/499 RC	6.00	2.50
❏ 109	Anderson Varejao/499 RC	8.00	3.00
❏ 110	Sebastian Telfair/199 RC	15.00	6.00
❏ 111	Josh Childress/199 RC	15.00	6.00
❏ 112	J.R. Smith/499 RC	10.00	4.00
❏ 113	Viktor Khryapa/699 RC	5.00	2.00
❏ 114	Rafael Araujo/499 RC	6.00	2.50
❏ 115	Dorell Wright/499 RC	8.00	3.00
❏ 116	Ha Seung-Jin/499 RC	5.00	2.00
❏ 117	Tony Allen/699 RC	6.00	2.50
❏ 118	Kirk Snyder/699 RC	5.00	2.00
❏ 119	Chris Duhon/699 RC	10.00	4.00
❏ 120	Beno Udrih/699 RC	8.00	3.00

2004-05 Fleer Sweet Sigs

❏	COMP.SET w/o SP's (75)	40.00	15.00
❏	COMMON CARD (1-75)	.20	.08
❏	COMMON ROOKIE (76-100)	4.00	1.50
❏ 1	Kirk Hinrich	.75	.30
❏ 2	Ron Artest	.50	.20
❏ 3	T.J. Ford	.50	.20
❏ 4	Stephon Marbury	.75	.30
❏ 5	Antawn Jamison	.75	.30
❏ 6	Jason Richardson	.75	.30
❏ 7	Dwyane Wade	2.50	1.00
❏ 8	Shawn Marion	.75	.30
❏ 9	Jermaine O'Neal	.75	.30
❏ 10	Ricky Davis	.75	.30
❏ 11	Richard Hamilton	.75	.30
❏ 12	Karl Malone	.75	.30
❏ 13	Jason Williams	.75	.30
❏ 14	Lamar Odom	.75	.30
❏ 15	Allan Houston	.50	.20
❏ 16	Allen Iverson	1.50	.60
❏ 17	Peja Stojakovic	.75	.30
❏ 18	Jarvis Hayes	.50	.20
❏ 19	Stephen Jackson	.20	.08
❏ 20	Richard Jefferson	.50	.20
❏ 21	Jahidi White	.20	.08
❏ 22	Carmelo Anthony	1.50	.60
❏ 23	Baron Davis	.75	.30
❏ 24	Dajuan Wagner	.50	.20
❏ 25	Nene	.50	.20
❏ 26	Ben Wallace	.75	.30
❏ 27	Latrell Sprewell	.75	.30
❏ 28	Ray Allen	.75	.30
❏ 29	Andrei Kirilenko	.75	.30
❏ 30	Antoine Walker	.75	.30
❏ 31	Marcus Banks	.50	.20
❏ 32	Pau Gasol	.75	.30
❏ 33	Tony Parker	.75	.30
❏ 34	Vince Carter	2.00	.75
❏ 35	Mike Bibby	.75	.30
❏ 36	Jim Jackson	.20	.08
❏ 37	Shaquille O'Neal	2.50	1.00
❏ 38	Bonzi Wells	.50	.20
❏ 39	Paul Pierce	.75	.30
❏ 40	Jason Kapono	.50	.20
❏ 41	Reggie Miller	.75	.30
❏ 42	Drew Gooden	.50	.20
❏ 43	Shareef Abdur-Rahim	.75	.30
❏ 44	Chris Bosh	.75	.30
❏ 45	Steve Nash	.75	.30
❏ 46	Elton Brand	.75	.30
❏ 47	Kevin Garnett	1.50	.60
❏ 48	Kenyon Martin	.75	.30
❏ 49	Jamal Crawford	.50	.20
❏ 50	Dirk Nowitzki	1.25	.50
❏ 51	Yao Ming	2.00	.75
❏ 52	Jamaal Magloire	.20	.08
❏ 53	Tim Duncan	1.50	.60
❏ 54	Gilbert Arenas	.75	.30
❏ 55	Steve Francis	.75	.30
❏ 56	Corey Maggette	.50	.20
❏ 57	Caron Butler	.75	.30
❏ 58	Michael Redd	.50	.20
❏ 59	Kyle Korver	.75	.30
❏ 60	Amare Stoudemire	1.50	.60
❏ 61	Carlos Boozer	.75	.30

❑ 62 Darko Milicic	.50	.20
❑ 63 Kobe Bryant	3.00	1.25
❑ 64 Tracy McGrady	2.00	.75
❑ 65 Zach Randolph	.75	.30
❑ 66 Luke Ridnour	.50	.20
❑ 67 Carlos Arroyo	1.25	.50
❑ 68 Michael Finley	.75	.30
❑ 69 Mickael Pietrus	.50	.20
❑ 70 Darius Miles	.75	.30
❑ 71 Chris Webber	.75	.30
❑ 72 Eddy Curry	.50	.20
❑ 73 Jason Kidd	1.25	.50
❑ 74 Manu Ginobili	.75	.30
❑ 75 LeBron James	5.00	2.00
❑ 76 Emeka Okafor RC	15.00	6.00
❑ 77 Rafael Araujo RC	4.00	1.50
❑ 78 Andre Iguodala RC	10.00	4.00
❑ 79 Kris Humphries RC	4.00	1.50
❑ 80 Kevin Martin RC	6.00	2.50
❑ 81 Delonte West RC	4.00	1.50
❑ 82 Pavel Podkolzine RC	4.00	1.50
❑ 83 Al Jefferson RC	10.00	4.00
❑ 84 Shaun Livingston RC	6.00	2.50
❑ 85 Luke Jackson RC	4.00	1.50
❑ 86 Dorell Wright RC	6.00	2.50
❑ 87 Andris Biedrins RC	8.00	3.00
❑ 88 Sasha Vujacic RC	4.00	1.50
❑ 89 Jameer Nelson RC	6.00	2.50
❑ 90 Dwight Howard RC	12.00	5.00
❑ 91 Robert Swift RC	4.00	1.50
❑ 92 Josh Childress RC	5.00	2.00
❑ 93 Luol Deng RC	8.00	3.00
❑ 94 J.R. Smith RC	8.00	3.00
❑ 95 Kirk Snyder RC	4.00	1.50
❑ 96 Josh Smith RC	8.00	3.00
❑ 97 Devin Harris RC	6.00	2.50
❑ 98 Viktor Khryapa RC	4.00	1.50
❑ 99 Ben Gordon RC	15.00	6.00
❑ 100 Sebastian Telfair RC	4.00	1.50

2004-05 Fleer Throwbacks

❑ COMP.SET w/o RC's (65)	40.00	15.00
❑ COMMON CARD (1-65)	.20	.08
❑ SEMISTARS 1-65	.50	.20
❑ UNLISTED STARS 1-65	.75	.30
❑ COMMON ROOKIE (66-76)	8.00	3.00
❑ 66-76 RC PRINT RUN 50 SER.#'d SETS		
❑ COMMON JSY RC (77-100)	10.00	4.00
❑ 77-100 JSY RC PRINT RUN 499 #'d SETS		
❑ 1 Baron Davis	.75	.30
❑ 2 Willie Green	.20	.08
❑ 3 Allen Iverson	1.50	.60
❑ 4 Jason Williams	.50	.20
❑ 5 Kevin Garnett	1.50	.60
❑ 6 Jason Richardson	.75	.30
❑ 7 Lamar Odom	.75	.30
❑ 8 Ben Wallace	.75	.30
❑ 9 Steve Nash	.75	.30
❑ 10 Kobe Bryant	3.00	1.25
❑ 11 Kenyon Martin	.75	.30
❑ 12 Jermaine O'Neal	.75	.30
❑ 13 Tracy McGrady	2.00	.75
❑ 14 Darko Milic	.50	.20
❑ 15 Pau Gasol	.75	.30
❑ 16 Darius Miles	.75	.30
❑ 17 Ray Allen	.75	.30
❑ 18 Michael Redd	.75	.30

❑ 19 Chris Bosh	.75	.30
❑ 20 Peja Stojakovic	.75	.30
❑ 21 Tim Duncan	1.50	.60
❑ 22 Corey Maggette	.50	.20
❑ 23 LeBron James	5.00	2.00
❑ 24 Antoine Walker	.75	.30
❑ 25 Stephon Marbury	.75	.30
❑ 26 Carlos Boozer	.75	.30
❑ 27 Jason Kapono	.50	.20
❑ 28 Grant Hill	.75	.30
❑ 29 Mike Bibby	.75	.30
❑ 30 Jamaal Magloire	.20	.08
❑ 31 Rashard Lewis	.75	.30
❑ 32 Jason Kidd	1.25	.50
❑ 33 Al Harrington	.50	.20
❑ 34 Steve Francis	.75	.30
❑ 35 Kirk Hinrich	.75	.30
❑ 36 Amare Stoudemire	1.50	.60
❑ 37 Gilbert Arenas	.75	.30
❑ 38 Allan Houston	.50	.20
❑ 39 Eddy Curry	.50	.20
❑ 40 Latrell Sprewell	.75	.30
❑ 41 Mickael Pietrus	.50	.20
❑ 42 Zach Randolph	.75	.30
❑ 43 Shaquille O'Neal	2.00	.75
❑ 44 Jason Terry	.75	.30
❑ 45 Richard Hamilton	.50	.20
❑ 46 Karl Malone	.75	.30
❑ 47 Elton Brand	.75	.30
❑ 48 Richard Jefferson	.75	.30
❑ 49 Andrei Kirilenko	.75	.30
❑ 50 Reggie Miller	.75	.30
❑ 51 Yao Ming	2.00	.75
❑ 52 Gary Payton	.75	.30
❑ 53 Dirk Nowitzki	1.25	.50
❑ 54 Dwyane Wade	2.50	1.00
❑ 55 Carmelo Anthony	1.50	.60
❑ 56 Tony Parker	.75	.30
❑ 57 T.J. Ford	.50	.20
❑ 58 Vince Carter	2.00	.75
❑ 59 Paul Pierce	.75	.30
❑ 60 Drew Gooden	.50	.20
❑ 61 Antawn Jamison	.75	.30
❑ 62 Manu Ginobili	.75	.30
❑ 63 Chris Webber	.75	.30
❑ 64 Shawn Marion	.75	.30
❑ 65 Jerry Stackhouse	.75	.30
❑ 66 Andris Biedrins RC	12.00	5.00
❑ 67 Robert Swift RC	8.00	3.00
❑ 68 Pavel Podkolzin RC	8.00	3.00
❑ 69 Kevin Martin RC	10.00	4.00
❑ 70 Beno Udrih RC	10.00	4.00
❑ 71 David Harrison RC	8.00	3.00
❑ 72 Victor Khryapa RC	8.00	3.00
❑ 73 Jackson Vroman RC	8.00	3.00
❑ 74 Emeka Okafor RC	20.00	8.00
❑ 75 Andre Emmett RC	8.00	3.00
❑ 76 Andres Nocioni RC	10.00	4.00
❑ 77 Dwight Howard JSY RC	20.00	8.00
❑ 78 Ben Gordon JSY RC	25.00	10.00
❑ 79 Shaun Livingston JSY RC	10.00	4.00
❑ 80 David Harrison JSY RC	10.00	4.00
❑ 81 Josh Childress JSY RC	10.00	4.00
❑ 82 Luol Deng JSY RC	12.00	5.00
❑ 83 Rafael Araujo JSY RC	10.00	4.00
❑ 84 Andre Iguodala JSY RC	15.00	6.00
❑ 85 Luke Jackson JSY RC	10.00	4.00
❑ 86 Sebastian Telfair JSY RC	6.00	2.50
❑ 87 Kris Humphries JSY RC	10.00	4.00
❑ 88 Al Jefferson JSY RC	15.00	6.00
❑ 89 Kirk Snyder JSY RC	10.00	4.00
❑ 90 Josh Smith JSY RC	12.00	5.00
❑ 91 JR Smith JSY RC	10.00	4.00
❑ 92 Dorell Wright JSY RC	10.00	4.00
❑ 93 Jameer Nelson JSY RC	10.00	4.00
❑ 94 Chris Duhon JSY RC	10.00	4.00
❑ 95 Delonte West JSY RC	10.00	4.00
❑ 96 Tony Allen JSY RC	10.00	4.00
❑ 97 Anderson Varejao JSY RC	10.00	4.00
❑ 98 Lionel Chalmers JSY RC	10.00	4.00
❑ 99 Bernard Robinson JSY RC	10.00	4.00
❑ 100 Trevor Ariza JSY RC	10.00	4.00

2002-03 Fleer Tradition

❑ COMPLETE SET (300)	80.00	30.00
❑ COMMON CARD (1-270)	.20	.08
❑ COMMON ROOKIE (271-300)	2.50	1.00
❑ 1 Shareef Abdur-Rahim	.60	.25
❑ 2 Dion Glover	.20	.08
❑ 3 Theo Ratliff	.40	.15
❑ 4 Nazr Mohammed	.20	.08
❑ 5 Ira Newble	.20	.08
❑ 6 Alan Henderson	.20	.08
❑ 7 Vin Baker	.40	.15
❑ 8 Tony Battie	.20	.08
❑ 9 Eric Williams	.20	.08
❑ 10 Shammond Williams	.20	.08
❑ 11 Walter McCarty	.20	.08
❑ 12 Bruno Sundov	.20	.08
❑ 13 Donyell Marshall	.40	.15
❑ 14 Marcus Fizer	.40	.15
❑ 15 Eddie Robinson	.40	.15
❑ 16 Trenton Hassell	.40	.15
❑ 17 Ricky Davis	.40	.15
❑ 18 Jumaine Jones	.20	.08
❑ 19 Chris Mihm	.20	.08
❑ 20 Zydrunas Ilgauskas	.40	.15
❑ 21 Tyrone Hill	.20	.08
❑ 22 Adrian Griffin	.20	.08
❑ 23 Nick Van Exel	.60	.25
❑ 24 Raef LaFrentz	.40	.15
❑ 25 Eduardo Najera	.40	.15
❑ 26 Shawn Bradley	.20	.08
❑ 27 Evan Eschmeyer	.20	.08
❑ 28 Walt Williams	.20	.08
❑ 29 Raja Bell	.20	.08
❑ 30 Marcus Camby	.40	.15
❑ 31 Donnell Harvey	.20	.08
❑ 32 Kenny Satterfield	.20	.08
❑ 33 Rodney White	.40	.15
❑ 34 Chris Whitney	.20	.08
❑ 35 Clifford Robinson	.20	.08
❑ 36 Zeljko Rebraca	.20	.08
❑ 37 Corliss Williamson	.40	.15
❑ 38 Chucky Atkins	.20	.08
❑ 39 Jon Barry	.20	.08
❑ 40 Michael Curry	.20	.08
❑ 41 Erick Dampier	.40	.15
❑ 42 Danny Fortson	.20	.08
❑ 43 Adonal Foyle	.20	.08
❑ 44 Troy Murphy	.40	.15
❑ 45 Bob Sura	.20	.08
❑ 46 Moochie Norris	.20	.08
❑ 47 Kenny Thomas	.20	.08
❑ 48 Terence Morris	.20	.08
❑ 49 Glen Rice	.40	.15
❑ 50 Maurice Taylor	.20	.08
❑ 51 Erick Strickland	.20	.08
❑ 52 Al Harrington	.40	.15
❑ 53 Ron Artest	.40	.15
❑ 54 Austin Croshere	.20	.08
❑ 55 Ron Mercer	.40	.15
❑ 56 Brad Miller	.60	.25
❑ 57 Lamar Odom	.60	.25
❑ 58 Keyon Dooling	.20	.08
❑ 59 Corey Maggette	.40	.15
❑ 60 Michael Olowokandi	.20	.08
❑ 61 Stanislav Medvedenko	.20	.08
❑ 62 Rick Fox	.40	.15
❑ 63 Derek Fisher	.60	.25

#	Player		
64	Samaki Walker	.20	.08
65	Robert Horry	.40	.15
66	Mark Madsen	.20	.08
67	Wesley Person	.20	.08
68	Michael Dickerson	.20	.08
69	Lorenzen Wright	.20	.08
70	Brevin Knight	.20	.08
71	Travis Best	.20	.08
72	Brian Grant	.40	.15
73	Eddie Jones	.60	.25
74	LaPhonso Ellis	.20	.08
75	Anthony Carter	.40	.15
76	Tim Thomas	.40	.15
77	Toni Kukoc	.40	.15
78	Anthony Mason	.40	.15
79	Ervin Johnson	.20	.08
80	Joel Przybilla	.20	.08
81	Rod Strickland	.20	.08
82	Terrell Brandon	.40	.15
83	Anthony Peeler	.20	.08
84	Joe Smith	.40	.15
85	Gary Trent	.20	.08
86	Rasho Nesterovic	.40	.15
87	Loren Woods	.40	.15
88	Felipe Lopez	.20	.08
89	Dikembe Mutombo	.40	.15
90	Rodney Rogers	.20	.08
91	Jason Collins	.20	.08
92	Kerry Kittles	.20	.08
93	Lucious Harris	.20	.08
94	Aaron Williams	.20	.08
95	Jamal Mashburn	.40	.15
96	David Wesley	.20	.08
97	Elden Campbell	.20	.08
98	Jerome Moiso	.20	.08
99	P.J. Brown	.20	.08
100	George Lynch	.20	.08
101	Robert Traylor	.20	.08
102	Antonio McDyess	.40	.15
103	Kurt Thomas	.40	.15
104	Clarence Weatherspoon	.20	.08
105	Charlie Ward	.20	.08
106	Lavor Postell	.20	.08
107	Shandon Anderson	.20	.08
108	Michael Doleac	.20	.08
109	Othella Harrington	.20	.08
110	Darrell Armstrong	.20	.08
111	Steven Hunter	.20	.08
112	Pat Garrity	.20	.08
113	Horace Grant	.40	.15
114	Jacque Vaughn	.20	.08
115	Jeryl Sasser	.20	.08
116	Todd MacCulloch	.20	.08
117	Greg Buckner	.20	.08
118	Eric Snow	.40	.15
119	Samuel Dalembert	.40	.15
120	Monty Williams	.20	.08
121	Stephon Marbury	.60	.25
122	Anfernee Hardaway	.40	.15
123	Tom Gugliotta	.20	.08
124	Iakovos Tsakalidis	.20	.08
125	Bo Outlaw	.20	.08
126	Damon Stoudamire	.40	.15
127	Jeff McInnis	.20	.08
128	Derek Anderson	.40	.15
129	Antonio Daniels	.20	.08
130	Dale Davis	.20	.08
131	Zach Randolph	.60	.25
132	Bobby Jackson	.40	.15
133	Chris Webber	.60	.25
134	Vlade Divac	.40	.15
135	Keon Clark	.20	.08
136	Doug Christie	.40	.15
137	Scot Pollard	.20	.08
138	Mengke Bateer	.60	.25
139	David Robinson	.60	.25
140	Steve Smith	.40	.15
141	Malik Rose	.20	.08
142	Speedy Claxton	.20	.08
143	Danny Ferry	.20	.08
144	Brent Barry	.20	.08
145	Joseph Forte	.40	.15
146	Vladimir Radmanovic	.40	.15
147	Kenny Anderson	.20	.08
148	Predrag Drobnjak	.20	.08
149	Calvin Booth	.20	.08
150	Ansu Sesay	.20	.08
151	Voshon Lenard	.20	.08
152	Lamond Murray	.20	.08
153	Antonio Davis	.20	.08
154	Lindsey Hunter	.20	.08
155	Michael Bradley	.40	.15
156	Jerome Williams	.20	.08
157	Alvin Williams	.20	.08
158	Mamadou N'diaye	.20	.08
159	Raul Lopez	.20	.08
160	John Stockton	.60	.25
161	Mark Jackson	.20	.08
162	DeShawn Stevenson	.20	.08
163	Calbert Cheaney	.20	.08
164	Matt Harpring	.60	.25
165	Jarron Collins	.20	.08
166	Tyronn Lue	.20	.08
167	Bryon Russell	.20	.08
168	Larry Hughes	.40	.15
169	Brendan Haywood	.40	.15
170	Christian Laettner	.40	.15
171	Glenn Robinson	.60	.25
172	Tony Delk	.20	.08
173	Antoine Walker	.60	.25
174	Jalen Rose	.60	.25
175	Jamal Crawford	.40	.15
176	DeSagana Diop	.40	.15
177	Michael Finley	.60	.25
178	Dirk Nowitzki	1.00	.40
179	Juwan Howard	.40	.15
180	Chauncey Billups	.40	.15
181	Richard Hamilton	.40	.15
182	Antawn Jamison	.60	.25
183	Steve Francis	.60	.25
184	Eddie Griffin	.40	.15
185	Jonathan Bender	.40	.15
186	Reggie Miller	.60	.25
187	Elton Brand	.60	.25
188	Marco Jaric	.20	.08
189	Kobe Bryant	2.50	1.00
190	Shaquille O'Neal	1.50	.60
191	Jason Williams	.40	.15
192	Stromile Swift	.40	.15
193	Alonzo Mourning	.40	.15
194	Malik Allen	.20	.08
195	Sam Cassell	.60	.25
196	Ray Allen	.60	.25
197	Wally Szczerbiak	.40	.15
197B	Vince Carter Promo	2.50	1.00
198	Jason Kidd	1.00	.40
199	Kenyon Martin	.60	.25
200	Courtney Alexander	.40	.15
201	Baron Davis	.60	.25
202	Allan Houston	.40	.15
203	Grant Hill	.60	.25
204	Aaron McKie	.40	.15
205	Keith Van Horn	.60	.25
206	Shawn Marion	.60	.25
207	Joe Johnson	.40	.15
208	Scottie Pippen	1.00	.40
209	Rasheed Wallace	.60	.25
210	Peja Stojakovic	.60	.25
211	Hidayet Turkoglu	.60	.25
212	Tony Parker	.60	.25
213	Tim Duncan	1.25	.50
214	Gary Payton	.60	.25
215	Desmond Mason	.40	.15
216	Vince Carter	1.50	.60
217	Karl Malone	.60	.25
218	Andrei Kirilenko	.60	.25
219	Jerry Stackhouse	.60	.25
220	Michael Jordan	5.00	2.00
221	DerMarr Johnson	.20	.08
222	Kedrick Brown	.40	.15
223	Eddy Curry	.60	.25
224	Tyson Chandler	.60	.25
225	Darius Miles	.60	.25
226	Wang ZhiZhi	.60	.25
227	James Posey	.40	.15
228	Ben Wallace	.60	.25
229	Jason Richardson	.60	.25
230	Gilbert Arenas	.60	.25
231	Eddie Griffin	.40	.15
232	Jermaine O'Neal	.60	.25
233	Quentin Richardson	.40	.15
234	Devean George	.40	.15
235	Shane Battier	.60	.25
236	Pau Gasol	.60	.25
237	Eddie House	.20	.08
238	Michael Redd	.60	.25
239	Troy Hudson	.20	.08
240	Richard Jefferson	.40	.15
241	Jamal Magloire	.20	.08
242	Mike Miller	.60	.25
243	Joe Johnson	.40	.15
244	Ruben Patterson	.40	.15
245	Gerald Wallace	.40	.15
246	Tony Parker	.60	.25
247	Rashard Lewis	.40	.15
248	Morris Peterson	.40	.15
249	Andrei Kirilenko	.60	.25
250	Kwame Brown	.40	.15
251	Jason Terry	.60	.25
252	Paul Pierce	.60	.25
253	Darius Miles	.60	.25
254	Steve Nash	.60	.25
255	Cuttino Mobley	.40	.15
256	Jamaal Tinsley	.60	.25
257	Andre Miller	.40	.15
258	Shaquille O'Neal	1.50	.60
259	Kobe Bryant	2.50	1.00
260	Kevin Garnett	1.50	.60
261	Kenyon Martin	.60	.25
262	Latrell Sprewell	.60	.25
263	Tracy McGrady	1.50	.60
264	Allen Iverson	1.25	.50
265	Shawn Marion	.60	.25
266	Bonzi Wells	.40	.15
267	Mike Bibby	.60	.25
268	Tim Duncan	1.25	.50
269	Vince Carter	1.50	.60
270	Michael Jordan	5.00	2.00
271	Ming/Williams/Dunlvy RC	4.00	1.50
272	Ginobili/Prince/Gircek RC	5.00	2.00
273	Jeffries/Williams/Pargo RC	2.50	1.00
274	Wilcox/Dixon/Baxter RC	2.50	1.00
275	Wagnr/Dickau/Ginbili RC	3.00	1.25
276	Ely/Jefferies/Maddox RC	2.50	1.00
277	Evans/Brner/Williams RC	4.00	1.50
278	Butler/Haislip/Hmphry RC	2.50	1.00
279	Archbld/Burke/Huffmn RC	2.50	1.00
280	Goodn/Amare/Woods RC	4.00	1.50
281	Nachbr/Welsch/Savovic RC	2.50	1.00
282	Borchrdt/Jacobsn/Gadzu RC	2.50	1.00
283	Clancy/Okur/Sampson RC	2.50	1.00
284	Prince/Rush/Salmons RC	4.00	1.50
285	Ming/Tskitishvili/Hilario RC	8.00	3.00
286	Wagner/Woods/Slay RC	1.50	.60
287	Ely/Haislip/Jones RC	2.50	1.00
288	Butler/Ginobili/Haislip RC	3.00	1.25
289	Mason/Yrbrogh/Dickau RC	2.50	1.00
290	Murray/Owens/Parker RC	6.00	2.50
291	Butler/Pargo/Giricek RC	2.50	1.00
292	Goodn/Tskitishvili/Wagnr RC		1.25
293	Hilario/Ginobili/Amare RC	6.00	2.50
294	Jay Will/Hmphry/Woods RC	2.00	.75
295	Ming/Stoudamire/Rush RC	15.00	6.00
296	Tskitishvili/Butler/Dixon RC	2.50	1.00
297	Wilcox/Jones/Nachbar RC	3.00	1.25
298	Dunlvy/Hilario/Jacobsn RC	2.50	1.00
299	Jeffries/Dixon/Boozer RC	2.00	.75
300	Boozer/Jay Will/Dunlvy RC	2.50	1.00

2003-04 Fleer Tradition

#			
	COMP.SET w/o RC's (260)	50.00	20.00
	COMMON CARD (1-260)	.20	.08
	COMMON ROOKIE (261-290)	2.50	1.00
	COMMON TRIPLE (291-300)	4.00	1.50
1	Shareef Abdur-Rahim	.60	.25
2	Vince Carter	1.50	.60
3	Kevin Garnett	1.25	.50
4	Bobby Jackson	.40	.15
5	Courtney Alexander	.20	.08
6	Tracy McGrady	1.50	.60
7	Paul Pierce	.60	.25
8	Sam Cassell	.60	.25
9	Maurice Taylor	.20	.08
10	Pat Garrity	.20	.08
11	Casey Jacobsen	.20	.08
12	Malik Allen	.20	.08
13	Aaron McKie	.40	.15

DIRK NOWITZKI · MAVERICKS

#	Player		
14	Tyson Chandler	.60	.25
15	Scottie Pippen	1.00	.40
16	Jason Terry	.60	.25
17	Pau Gasol	.60	.25
18	Antawn Jamison	.60	.25
19	Stanislav Medvedenko	.20	.08
20	Ray Allen	.60	.25
21	James Posey	.40	.15
22	Calbert Cheaney	.20	.08
23	Devean George	.40	.15
24	Tim Thomas	.40	.15
25	Marko Jaric	.40	.15
26	Ron Mercer	.20	.08
27	Rafer Alston	.20	.08
28	Tayshaun Prince	.40	.15
29	Doug Christie	.40	.15
30	Kendall Gill	.20	.08
31	Kurt Thomas	.40	.15
32	Richard Jefferson	.60	.25
33	Darius Miles	.60	.25
34	Kenny Anderson	.40	.15
35	Keon Clark	.40	.15
36	Vladimir Radmanovic	.20	.08
37	Kenny Thomas	.20	.08
38	Manu Ginobili	.60	.25
39	Jared Jeffries	.20	.08
40	Brad Miller	.60	.25
41	Derek Anderson	.40	.15
42	Zach Randolph	.60	.25
43	Speedy Claxton	.20	.08
44	Jamaal Tinsley	.60	.25
45	Gordan Giricek	.40	.15
46	Joe Johnson	.40	.15
47	Mike Miller	.60	.25
48	Shandon Anderson	.20	.08
49	Theo Ratliff	.20	.08
50	Derrick Coleman	.20	.08
51	Dion Glover	.20	.08
52	Nikoloz Tskitishvili	.20	.08
53	Jumaine Jones	.40	.15
54	Gilbert Arenas	.60	.25
55	Reggie Miller	.60	.25
56	Michael Redd	.40	.15
57	Jason Collins	.20	.08
58	Drew Gooden	.40	.15
59	Hidayet Turkoglu	.60	.25
60	Eddie Jones	.60	.25
61	Andre Miller	.40	.15
62	Darrell Armstrong	.20	.08
63	Glen Rice	.40	.15
64	Jarron Collins	.20	.08
65	Nick Van Exel	.60	.25
66	Brian Grant	.40	.15
67	Shawn Kemp	.20	.08
68	Yao Ming	1.50	.60
69	Ron Artest	.40	.15
70	Jamal Crawford	.20	.08
71	Jason Richardson	.60	.25
72	Eddie Griffin	.20	.08
73	Keith Van Horn	.60	.25
74	Jason Kidd	1.00	.40
75	Cuttino Mobley	.40	.15
76	Brent Barry	.40	.15
77	Eddy Curry	.40	.15
78	Quentin Richardson	.40	.15
79	Dajuan Wagner	.40	.15
80	Tom Gugliotta	.20	.08
81	Andrei Kirilenko	.60	.25
82	Shane Battier	.60	.25
83	Alonzo Mourning	.40	.15
84	Clifford Robinson	.20	.08
85	Erick Dampier	.40	.15
86	Antoine Walker	.60	.25
87	Marcus Haislip	.20	.08
88	Kerry Kittles	.20	.08
89	Lonny Baxter	.20	.08
90	Troy Murphy	.60	.25
91	Glenn Robinson	.60	.25
92	Ricky Davis	.60	.25
93	Richard Hamilton	.40	.15
94	Ben Wallace	.60	.25
95	Toni Kukoc	.40	.15
96	Raja Bell	.20	.08
97	Dikembe Mutombo	.40	.15
98	Eddie Robinson	.40	.15
99	Antonio Davis	.20	.08
100	Anfernee Hardaway	.60	.25
101	Rasheed Wallace	.60	.25
102	Christian Laettner	.40	.15
103	Eduardo Najera	.40	.15
104	Jonathan Bender	.40	.15
105	Rodney Rogers	.20	.08
106	Baron Davis	.60	.25
107	Chris Webber	.60	.25
108	Matt Harpring	.60	.25
109	Raef LaFrentz	.40	.15
110	Steve Nash	.60	.25
111	Travis Best	.20	.08
112	Tony Delk	.20	.08
113	Malik Rose	.20	.08
114	Al Harrington	.40	.15
115	Bonzi Wells	.40	.15
116	Voshon Lenard	.20	.08
117	Radoslav Nesterovic	.40	.15
118	Mike Bibby	.60	.25
119	Dan Dickau	.20	.08
120	Jalen Rose	.60	.25
121	Lucious Harris	.20	.08
122	David Wesley	.20	.08
123	Rashard Lewis	.60	.25
124	Ira Newble	.20	.08
125	Chauncey Billups	.40	.15
126	Kareem Rush	.40	.15
127	Michael Dickerson	.20	.08
128	Walt Williams	.20	.08
129	Donnell Harvey	.20	.08
130	Tyronn Lue	.20	.08
131	Carlos Boozer	.60	.25
132	Moochie Norris	.20	.08
133	John Salmons	.20	.08
134	Vlade Divac	.40	.15
135	Shammond Williams	.20	.08
136	Brendan Haywood	.20	.08
137	George Lynch	.20	.08
138	Dirk Nowitzki	1.00	.40
139	Bruce Bowen	.40	.15
140	Brian Skinner	.20	.08
141	Juan Dixon	.40	.15
142	Eric Williams	.20	.08
143	Grant Hill	.60	.25
144	Corey Maggette	.40	.15
145	Earl Boykins	.40	.15
146	Lamar Odom	.60	.25
147	Keyon Dooling	.20	.08
148	Joe Smith	.40	.15
149	Corliss Williamson	.20	.08
150	Robert Horry	.40	.15
151	Jamaal Magloire	.20	.08
152	Mehmet Okur	.20	.08
153	Elton Brand	.60	.25
154	Steve Smith	.40	.15
155	Predrag Drobnjak	.20	.08
156	Allan Houston	.40	.15
157	Jerome Williams	.20	.08
158	Karl Malone	.60	.25
159	Michael Olowokandi	.20	.08
160	Terrell Brandon	.20	.08
161	Eric Snow	.40	.15
162	Tim Duncan	1.25	.50
163	Juwan Howard	.40	.15
164	Jason Williams	.40	.15
165	Stephon Marbury	.60	.25
166	J.R. Bremer	.20	.08
167	Shaquille O'Neal	1.50	.60
168	Mike Dunleavy	.40	.15
169	Latrell Sprewell	.60	.25
170	Troy Hudson	.20	.08
171	Alvin Williams	.20	.08
172	Shawn Marion	.60	.25
173	Jermaine O'Neal	.60	.25
174	P.J. Brown	.20	.08
175	Howard Eisley	.20	.08
176	Jerry Stackhouse	.60	.25
177	Qyntel Woods	.20	.08
178	Larry Hughes	.40	.15
179	Donyell Marshall	.40	.15
180	Greg Ostertag	.20	.08
181	Kwame Brown	.40	.15
182	Reggie Evans	.20	.08
183	DeShawn Stevenson	.20	.08
184	Lorenzen Wright	.20	.08
185	Lindsey Hunter	.20	.08
186	Kenyon Martin	.60	.25
187	Kobe Bryant	2.50	1.00
188	Scott Padgett	.20	.08
189	Michael Finley	.60	.25
190	Peja Stojakovic	.60	.25
191	Zydrunas Ilgauskas	.40	.15
192	Vincent Yarbrough	.20	.08
193	Jamal Mashburn	.40	.15
194	Smush Parker	.60	.25
195	Caron Butler	.60	.25
196	Derek Fisher	.60	.25
197	Damon Stoudamire	.40	.15
198	Nene Hilario	.40	.15
199	Allen Iverson	1.25	.50
200	Anthony Mason	.20	.08
201	Rasual Butler	.40	.15
202	Tony Parker	.60	.25
203	Marcus Fizer	.40	.15
204	Amare Stoudemire	1.50	.60
205	Marc Jackson	.40	.15
206	Desmond Mason	.40	.15
207	Marcus Camby	.40	.15
208	Ruben Patterson	.40	.15
209	Bob Sura	.20	.08
210	Rick Fox	.40	.15
211	Jim Jackson	.20	.08
212	Walter McCarty	.20	.08
213	Gary Payton	.60	.25
214	Elden Campbell	.20	.08
215	Steve Francis	.60	.25
216	Stromile Swift	.40	.15
217	Stephen Jackson	.20	.08
218	Antonio McDyess	.40	.15
219	Morris Peterson	.40	.15
220	Wally Szczerbiak	.40	.15
221	Tim Duncan AW	1.25	.50
222	Amare Stoudemire AW	1.50	.60
223	Bobby Jackson AW	.40	.15
224	Ben Wallace AW	.60	.25
225	Gilbert Arenas AW	.60	.25
226	Tracy McGrady AW	1.50	.60
227	Kobe Bryant AW	2.50	1.00
228	Kevin Garnett AW	1.25	.50
229	Shaquille O'Neal AW	1.50	.60
230	Yao Ming AW	1.50	.60
231	Stephon Marbury BS	.60	.25
232	Ron Artest BS	.20	.08
233	Troy Hudson BS	.20	.08
234	Ray Allen BS	.60	.25
235	Matt Harpring BS	.60	.25
236	Jermaine O'Neal BS	.60	.25
237	Jason Kidd BS	1.00	.40
238	Jason Williams BS	.40	.15
239	Zydrunas Ilgauskas BS	.40	.15
240	Jamal Mashburn BS	.40	.15
241	Yao Ming BS	1.50	.60
242	Peja Stojakovic BS	.60	.25
243	Tony Parker BS	.60	.25
244	Caron Butler BS	.60	.25
245	Amare Stoudemire BS	1.50	.60
246	Troy Murphy BS	.60	.25
247	Nene Hilario BS	.40	.15
248	Allen Iverson BS	1.25	.50
249	Kobe Bryant BS	2.50	1.00
250	Tim Duncan BS	1.25	.50
251	Tracy McGrady BS	1.50	.60
252	Kevin Garnett BS	1.25	.50
253	Drew Gooden BS	.40	.15

#	Player		
❑ 254	Kenyon Martin BS	.60	.25
❑ 255	Dirk Nowitzki BS	1.00	.40
❑ 256	Paul Pierce BS	.60	.25
❑ 257	Steve Francis BS	.60	.25
❑ 258	Steve Nash BS	.60	.25
❑ 259	Gary Payton BS	.60	.25
❑ 260	Chris Webber BS	.40	.15
❑ 261	LeBron James RC	15.00	6.00
❑ 262	Darko Milicic RC	3.00	1.25
❑ 263	Carmelo Anthony RC	6.00	2.50
❑ 264	Chris Bosh RC	5.00	2.00
❑ 265	Dwyane Wade RC	8.00	3.00
❑ 266	Chris Kaman RC	2.50	1.00
❑ 267	Kirk Hinrich RC	4.00	1.50
❑ 268	T.J. Ford RC	3.00	1.25
❑ 269	Mike Sweetney RC	2.50	1.00
❑ 270	Mickael Pietrus RC	2.50	1.00
❑ 271	Jarvis Hayes RC	2.50	1.00
❑ 272	Nick Collison RC	2.50	1.00
❑ 273	Marcus Banks RC	3.00	1.25
❑ 274	Luke Ridnour RC	3.00	1.25
❑ 275	Reece Gaines RC	2.50	1.00
❑ 276	Troy Bell RC	2.50	1.00
❑ 277	Zarko Cabarkapa RC	2.50	1.00
❑ 278	David West RC	2.50	1.00
❑ 279	Luke Walton RC	2.50	1.00
❑ 280	Dahntay Jones RC	2.50	1.00
❑ 281	Boris Diaw RC	3.00	1.25
❑ 282	Zoran Planinic RC	2.50	1.00
❑ 283	Travis Outlaw RC	2.50	1.00
❑ 284	Brian Cook RC	2.50	1.00
❑ 285	Jason Kapono RC	2.50	1.00
❑ 286	Ndudi Ebi RC	2.50	1.00
❑ 287	Kendrick Perkins RC	2.50	1.00
❑ 288	Leandro Barbosa RC	4.00	1.50
❑ 289	Josh Howard RC	4.00	1.50
❑ 290	Maciej Lampe RC	2.50	1.00
❑ 291	James/Darko/Melo	25.00	10.00
❑ 292	Sweetney/Bosh/Hayes	5.00	2.00
❑ 293	Hinrich/Collison/Kaman	4.00	1.50
❑ 294	Sweetney/West/Cook	4.00	1.50
❑ 295	Kaman/Bosh/Darko	4.00	1.50
❑ 296	Ford/Wade/Hinrich	10.00	4.00
❑ 297	Pietrus/Jones/Gaines	4.00	1.50
❑ 298	Ford/Banks/Ridnour	5.00	2.00
❑ 299	Pietrus/Zarko/Hayes	4.00	1.50
❑ 300	LeBron/Melo/Wade	30.00	12.50

2004-05 Fleer Tradition

#	Player		
❑	COMPLETE SET (268)		
❑	COMP.SET w/o RC's (220)	50.00	20.00
❑	COMMON CARD (1-208)	.20	.08
❑	SEMISTARS 1-208		
❑	UNLISTED STARS 1-208	.60	.25
❑	COMMON AW (209-220)	1.25	.50
❑	COMMON ROOKIE (221-250)	2.00	.75
❑	RC STATED ODDS 1:4		
❑	COMMON RC TRIO (251-268)	4.00	1.50
❑	TRIO STATED ODDS 1:18		
❑ 1	Jonathan Bender	.40	.15
❑ 2	Boris Diaw	.20	.08
❑ 3	Eddie Robinson	.20	.08
❑ 4	Jason Richardson	.60	.25
❑ 5	Bonzi Wells	.40	.15
❑ 6	Elden Campbell	.20	.08
❑ 7	P.J. Brown	.20	.08
❑ 8	Ray Allen	.60	.25
❑ 9	Theron Smith	.20	.08
❑ 10	Darko Milicic	.40	.15
❑ 11	Bob Sura	.20	.08
❑ 12	Sam Cassell	.60	.25
❑ 13	Cuttino Mobley	.40	.15
❑ 14	Andrei Kirilenko	.60	.25
❑ 15	Rael LaFrentz	.40	.15
❑ 16	Aleksandar Pavlovic	.20	.08
❑ 17	Carmelo Anthony	2.00	.75
❑ 18	Mickael Pietrus	.40	.15
❑ 19	James Posey	.40	.15
❑ 20	Nazr Mohammed	.20	.08
❑ 21	Jalen Rose	.60	.25
❑ 22	Jiri Welsch	.40	.15
❑ 23	Drew Gooden	.40	.15
❑ 24	Nene	.40	.15
❑ 25	Troy Murphy	.60	.25
❑ 26	Mike Miller	.60	.25
❑ 27	T.J. Ford	.40	.15
❑ 28	Allan Houston	.40	.15
❑ 29	Donyell Marshall	.60	.25
❑ 30	Chris Crawford	.20	.08
❑ 31	Eric Snow	.40	.15
❑ 32	Marcus Camby	.40	.15
❑ 33	Devean George	.40	.15
❑ 34	Eric Williams	.20	.08
❑ 35	Kurt Thomas	.40	.15
❑ 36	Rashard Lewis	.60	.25
❑ 37	Alvin Williams	.20	.08
❑ 38	David West	.40	.15
❑ 39	Shawn Marion	.60	.25
❑ 40	Mark Blount	.20	.08
❑ 41	Dikembe Mutombo	.40	.15
❑ 42	Stephen Jackson	.20	.08
❑ 43	Rasual Butler	.20	.08
❑ 44	Michael Redd	.60	.25
❑ 45	Jason Kidd	1.00	.40
❑ 46	Malik Rose	.20	.08
❑ 47	Chris Bosh	.60	.25
❑ 48	Antonio Daniels	.20	.08
❑ 49	Doug Christie	.40	.15
❑ 50	Stephon Marbury	.60	.25
❑ 51	Gary Payton	.60	.25
❑ 52	Michael Finley	.60	.25
❑ 53	Ben Wallace	.60	.25
❑ 54	Jason Williams	.40	.15
❑ 55	Michael Olowokandi	.20	.08
❑ 56	Steve Francis	.60	.25
❑ 57	Chris Webber	.60	.25
❑ 58	Tim Duncan	1.25	.50
❑ 59	Carlos Arroyo	1.00	.40
❑ 60	Eddie House	.20	.08
❑ 61	Mike Bibby	.60	.25
❑ 62	Tony Parker	.60	.25
❑ 63	Matt Harpring	.60	.25
❑ 64	Richard Hamilton	.40	.15
❑ 65	Corey Maggette	.40	.15
❑ 66	Damon Jones	.20	.08
❑ 67	Keith Bogans	.20	.08
❑ 68	Willie Green	.20	.08
❑ 69	Kirk Hinrich	.60	.25
❑ 70	Jerry Stackhouse	.60	.25
❑ 71	Chris Kaman	.20	.08
❑ 72	Lamar Odom	.60	.25
❑ 73	Dwyane Wade	2.00	.75
❑ 74	Kevin Garnett	1.25	.50
❑ 75	Allen Iverson	1.25	.50
❑ 76	Theo Ratliff	.40	.15
❑ 77	Shareef Abdur-Rahim	.60	.25
❑ 78	Gilbert Arenas	.60	.25
❑ 79	Jamal Sampson	.20	.08
❑ 80	Josh Howard	.40	.15
❑ 81	Latrell Sprewell	.60	.25
❑ 82	Kyle Korver	.40	.15
❑ 83	Brad Miller	.60	.25
❑ 84	Rasho Nesterovic	.40	.15
❑ 85	Larry Hughes	.40	.15
❑ 86	Eddy Curry	.40	.15
❑ 87	Rasheed Wallace	.60	.25
❑ 88	Chris Wilcox	.40	.15
❑ 89	Mark Madsen	.20	.08
❑ 90	Kenny Thomas	.20	.08
❑ 91	Zach Randolph	.60	.25
❑ 92	Juan Dixon	.40	.15
❑ 93	Tyson Chandler	.60	.25
❑ 94	Stromile Swift	.40	.15
❑ 95	Udonis Haslem	.20	.08
❑ 96	Jason Collins	.20	.08
❑ 97	Glenn Robinson	.60	.25
❑ 98	Darius Miles	.60	.25
❑ 99	Jared Jeffries	.20	.08
❑ 100	Bobby Jackson	.40	.15
❑ 101	Jahidi White	.20	.08
❑ 102	Dirk Nowitzki	1.00	.40
❑ 103	Wally Szczerbiak	.40	.15
❑ 104	John Salmons	.20	.08
❑ 105	Kwame Brown	.40	.15
❑ 106	Jason Kapono	.40	.15
❑ 107	Chauncey Billups	.40	.15
❑ 108	Shane Battier	.60	.25
❑ 109	Samuel Dalembert	.20	.08
❑ 110	Manu Ginobili	.60	.25
❑ 111	Anfernee Hardaway	.60	.25
❑ 112	Yao Ming	1.50	.60
❑ 113	Eric Piatkowski	.20	.08
❑ 114	Vlade Divac	.40	.15
❑ 115	Ron Mercer	.20	.08
❑ 116	Quentin Richardson	.40	.15
❑ 117	Derek Anderson	.40	.15
❑ 118	Jarvis Hayes	.40	.15
❑ 119	Antonio Davis	.20	.08
❑ 120	Erick Dampier	.40	.15
❑ 121	Antonio McDyess	.40	.15
❑ 122	Fred Jones	.20	.08
❑ 123	Damon Stoudamire	.40	.15
❑ 124	Jason Collier	.20	.08
❑ 125	Frank Williams	.20	.08
❑ 126	Kobe Bryant	2.50	1.00
❑ 127	Keith Van Horn	.60	.25
❑ 128	Darrell Armstrong	.20	.08
❑ 129	Steve Nash	.60	.25
❑ 130	Nick Collison	.40	.15
❑ 131	Ricky Davis	.60	.25
❑ 132	Tracy McGrady	1.50	.60
❑ 133	Shaquille O'Neal	1.50	.60
❑ 134	Desmond Mason	.40	.15
❑ 135	Richard Jefferson	.40	.15
❑ 136	Casey Jacobsen	.20	.08
❑ 137	Ronald Murray	.20	.08
❑ 138	Rafer Alston	.20	.08
❑ 139	Tony Delk	.20	.08
❑ 140	LeBron James	4.00	1.50
❑ 141	Earl Boykins	.40	.15
❑ 142	Speedy Claxton	.20	.08
❑ 143	Jamaal Tinsley	.60	.25
❑ 144	Elton Brand	.60	.25
❑ 145	Jamaal Magloire	.20	.08
❑ 146	Jamal Crawford	.40	.15
❑ 147	Peja Stojakovic	.60	.25
❑ 148	Bruce Bowen	.20	.08
❑ 149	Paul Pierce	.60	.25
❑ 150	Jason Terry	.60	.25
❑ 151	Kenyon Martin	.60	.25
❑ 152	Maurice Taylor	.20	.08
❑ 153	Toni Kukoc	.40	.15
❑ 154	Aaron Williams	.20	.08
❑ 155	Tony Battie	.20	.08
❑ 156	Leandro Barbosa	.40	.15
❑ 157	Carlos Boozer	.60	.25
❑ 158	Brevin Knight	.20	.08
❑ 159	Marquis Daniels	.60	.25
❑ 160	Jim Jackson	.20	.08
❑ 161	Caron Butler	.60	.25
❑ 162	Troy Hudson	.20	.08
❑ 163	DeShawn Stevenson	.20	.08
❑ 164	Nick Van Exel	.60	.25
❑ 165	Antawn Jamison	.60	.25
❑ 166	Marcus Banks	.40	.15
❑ 167	Derek Fisher	.60	.25
❑ 168	Juwan Howard	.40	.15
❑ 169	Reggie Miller	.60	.25
❑ 170	Joe Smith	.40	.15
❑ 171	Alonzo Mourning	.40	.15
❑ 172	Mike Sweetney	.20	.08
❑ 173	Mehmet Okur	.20	.08
❑ 174	Brent Barry	.40	.15
❑ 175	Al Harrington	.40	.15
❑ 176	Dajuan Wagner	.20	.08
❑ 177	Voshon Lenard	.20	.08
❑ 178	Jermaine O'Neal	.60	.25
❑ 179	Bobby Simmons	.20	.08
❑ 180	Karl Malone	.60	.25
❑ 181	Dan Gadzuric	.20	.08

#	Player		
❑ 182	David Wesley	.20	.08
❑ 183	Tim Thomas	.40	.15
❑ 184	Amare Stoudemire	1.25	.50
❑ 185	Morris Peterson	.40	.15
❑ 186	Fred Hoiberg	.20	.08
❑ 187	Jeff McInnis	.20	.08
❑ 188	Andre Miller	.40	.15
❑ 189	Mike Dunleavy	.40	.15
❑ 190	Ron Artest	.40	.15
❑ 191	Kerry Kittles	.20	.08
❑ 192	Baron Davis	.60	.25
❑ 193	Vince Carter	1.50	.60
❑ 194	Gerald Wallace	.40	.15
❑ 195	Tayshaun Prince	.40	.15
❑ 196	Marko Jaric	.40	.15
❑ 197	Luke Walton	.40	.15
❑ 198	Eddie Jones	.60	.25
❑ 199	Hedo Turkoglu	.60	.25
❑ 200	Joe Johnson	.40	.15
❑ 201	Vladimir Radmanovic	.20	.08
❑ 202	Gordan Giricek	.40	.15
❑ 203	Antoine Walker	.60	.25
❑ 204	Zydrunas Ilgauskas	.40	.15
❑ 205	Clifford Robinson	.20	.08
❑ 206	Pau Gasol	.60	.25
❑ 207	Jamal Mashburn	.40	.15
❑ 208	Luke Ridnour	.40	.15
❑ 209	Kevin Garnett AW	1.50	.60
❑ 210	LeBron James AW	5.00	2.00
❑ 211	Jason Kidd AW	1.25	.50
❑ 212	Kobe Bryant AW	3.00	1.25
❑ 213	Shaquille O'Neal AW	2.00	.75
❑ 214	Tim Duncan AW	1.50	.60
❑ 215	Ron Artest AW	1.25	.50
❑ 216	Dwyane Wade AW	2.50	1.00
❑ 217	Kirk Hinrich AW	1.25	.50
❑ 218	Chris Bosh AW	1.25	.50
❑ 219	Carmelo Anthony AW	1.50	.60
❑ 220	Antawn Jamison AW	1.25	.50
❑ 221	Dwight Howard RC	6.00	2.50
❑ 222	Emeka Okafor RC	8.00	3.00
❑ 223	Ben Gordon RC	8.00	3.00
❑ 224	Shaun Livingston RC	3.00	1.25
❑ 225	Devin Harris RC	3.00	1.25
❑ 226	Josh Childress RC	2.50	1.00
❑ 227	Luol Deng RC	4.00	1.50
❑ 228	Rafael Araujo RC	2.00	.75
❑ 229	Andre Iguodala RC	5.00	2.00
❑ 230	Luke Jackson RC	1.25	.50
❑ 231	Andris Biedrins RC	3.00	1.25
❑ 232	Robert Swift RC	2.00	.75
❑ 233	Sebastian Telfair RC	3.00	1.25
❑ 234	Kris Humphries RC	2.00	.75
❑ 235	Al Jefferson RC	5.00	2.00
❑ 236	Kirk Snyder RC	2.00	.75
❑ 237	Josh Smith RC	4.00	1.50
❑ 238	J.R. Smith RC	4.00	1.50
❑ 239	Dorell Wright RC	3.00	1.25
❑ 240	Jameer Nelson RC	3.00	1.25
❑ 241	Pavel Podkolzine RC	2.00	.75
❑ 242	Nenad Krstic RC	2.50	1.00
❑ 243	Andres Nocioni RC	2.50	1.00
❑ 244	Delonte West RC	4.00	1.50
❑ 245	Tony Allen RC	2.50	1.00
❑ 246	Kevin Martin RC	4.00	1.50
❑ 247	Sasha Vujacic RC	2.00	.75
❑ 248	Beno Udrih RC	3.00	1.25
❑ 249	David Harrison RC	2.00	.75
❑ 250	Anderson Varejao RC	2.50	1.00
❑ 251	Okafor/Gordon/Howard	12.00	5.00
❑ 252	Howard/Kasun RC/Nelson	3.00	1.50
❑ 253	Allen/Jefferson/West	8.00	3.00
❑ 254	Deng/Duhon/Gordon	10.00	4.00
❑ 255	Nocioni/Martin/Telfair	4.00	1.50
❑ 256	Childress/Ivey RC/Smith	4.00	1.50
❑ 257	Harris/Nelson/Telfair	4.00	1.50
❑ 258	Chalmers RC/Burks RC Emmett RC	4.00	1.50
❑ 259	Deng/Duhon RC/Pickett RC	5.00	2.00
❑ 260	Childress/Jackson/Iguodala	4.00	1.50
❑ 261	Livingston/Howard/Swift	3.00	1.25
❑ 262	Smith/Jefferson/Telfair	4.00	1.50
❑ 263	Livingston/Wright/Smith	3.00	1.25
❑ 264	Reed RC/Vroman RC Ramos RC	4.00	1.50
❑ 265	Podkolzine/Biedrins/Krstic	4.00	1.50
❑ 266	Vujacic/Tabuse RC/Udrih	6.00	2.50
❑ 267	Araujo/Humphries/Snyder	4.00	1.50
❑ 268	Robinson RC/Sow RC/Ariza RC	4.00	1.50

2000-01 Fleer Triple Crown

❑	COMPLETE SET w/o RC (200)	25.00	12.50
❑	COMMON CARD (41-240)	.20	.07
❑	COMMON ROOKIE (1-40/241)	.60	.25
❑ 1	Quentin Richardson RC	3.00	1.25
❑ 2	Khalid El-Amin RC	.60	.25
❑ 3	Courtney Alexander RC	1.25	.50
❑ 4	Mike Penberthy RC	.60	.25
❑ 5	DerMarr Johnson RC	.60	.25
❑ 6	A.J. Guyton RC	.60	.25
❑ 7	Erick Barkley RC	.60	.25
❑ 8	Jamal Crawford RC	.75	.30
❑ 9	Hidayet Turkoglu RC	2.50	1.00
❑ 10	Michael Redd RC	2.00	.75
❑ 11	Stromile Swift RC	2.50	1.00
❑ 12	Eddie House RC	.60	.25
❑ 13	Keyon Dooling RC	.60	.25
❑ 14	Lavor Postell RC	.60	.25
❑ 15	Mateen Cleaves RC	.60	.25
❑ 16	Morris Peterson RC	2.50	1.00
❑ 17	DeShawn Stevenson RC	.60	.25
❑ 18	Darius Miles RC	3.00	1.25
❑ 19	Hanno Mottola RC	.60	.25
❑ 20	Jerome Moiso RC	.60	.25
❑ 21	Desmond Mason RC	.60	.25
❑ 22	Jason Collier RC	.75	.30
❑ 23	Ruben Wolkowyski RC	.60	.25
❑ 24	Eduardo Najera RC	1.50	.60
❑ 25	Kenyon Martin RC	4.00	1.50
❑ 26	Marcus Fizer RC	.60	.25
❑ 27	Etan Thomas RC	.60	.25
❑ 28	Mark Madsen RC	.60	.25
❑ 29	Pepe Sanchez RC	.60	.25
❑ 30	Brian Cardinal RC	.60	.25
❑ 31	Chris Porter RC	.60	.25
❑ 32	Dan Langhi RC	.60	.25
❑ 33	Mike Miller RC	3.00	1.25
❑ 34	Chris Mihm RC	.60	.25
❑ 35	Mamadou N'Diaye RC	.60	.25
❑ 36	Dragan Tarlac RC	.60	.25
❑ 37	Iakovos Tsakalidis RC	.60	.25
❑ 38	Stephen Jackson RC	2.00	.75
❑ 39	Jamaal Magloire RC	.60	.25
❑ 40	Joel Przybilla RC	.60	.25
❑ 41	Adrian Griffin	.20	.07
❑ 42	Allan Houston	.40	.15
❑ 43	Mahmoud Abdul-Rauf	.20	.07
❑ 44	Avery Johnson	.20	.07
❑ 45	Damon Stoudamire	.40	.15
❑ 46	Jim Jackson	.20	.07
❑ 47	Jason Williams	.40	.15
❑ 48	Jason Kidd	1.00	.40
❑ 49	Ray Allen	.60	.25
❑ 50	Baron Davis	.60	.25
❑ 51	Mark Jackson	.20	.07
❑ 52	Darrick Martin	.20	.07
❑ 53	Derek Fisher	.60	.25
❑ 54	Anthony Peeler	.20	.07
❑ 55	Vince Carter	1.50	.60
❑ 56	Tim Hardaway	.40	.15
❑ 57	Richard Hamilton	.40	.15
❑ 58	Malik Rose	.20	.07
❑ 59	Antonio Daniels	.20	.07
❑ 60	Lindsey Hunter	.20	.07
❑ 61	William Avery	.20	.07
❑ 62	Reggie Miller	.60	.25
❑ 63	Shareef Abdur-Rahim	.60	.25
❑ 64	Travis Best	.20	.07
❑ 65	John Stockton	.60	.25
❑ 66	Kenny Anderson	.40	.15
❑ 67	Trajan Langdon	.20	.07
❑ 68	Sam Cassell	.60	.25
❑ 69	Chucky Atkins	.20	.07
❑ 70	Laron Profit	.20	.07
❑ 71	Andre Miller	.40	.15
❑ 72	Erick Strickland	.20	.07
❑ 73	Ron Artest	.40	.15
❑ 74	Kobe Bryant	2.50	1.00
❑ 75	Ricky Davis	.40	.15
❑ 76	Allen Iverson	1.25	.50
❑ 77	Steve Smith	.40	.15
❑ 78	Alvin Williams	.20	.07
❑ 79	Randy Brown	.20	.07
❑ 80	Michael Dickerson	.40	.15
❑ 81	Tyronn Lue	.40	.15
❑ 82	Bonzi Wells	.40	.15
❑ 83	Felipe Lopez	.20	.07
❑ 84	Steve Francis	.60	.25
❑ 85	Jaren Jackson	.20	.07
❑ 86	Anthony Carter	.40	.15
❑ 87	Mitch Richmond	.40	.15
❑ 88	Sherman Douglas	.20	.07
❑ 89	Cuttino Mobley	.40	.15
❑ 90	Mario Elie	.20	.07
❑ 91	Tariq Abdul-Wahad	.20	.07
❑ 92	Ron Mercer	.40	.15
❑ 93	Jalen Rose	.60	.25
❑ 94	Mike Bibby	.60	.25
❑ 95	Voshon Lenard	.20	.07
❑ 96	Derek Anderson	.40	.15
❑ 97	Kendall Gill	.20	.07
❑ 98	Muggsy Bogues	.20	.07
❑ 99	Eddie Jones	.60	.25
❑ 100	Larry Hughes	.40	.15
❑ 101	Latrell Sprewell	.60	.25
❑ 102	Stephon Marbury	.60	.25
❑ 103	Eric Piatkowski	.20	.07
❑ 104	Brevin Knight	.20	.07
❑ 105	Isaiah Rider	.40	.15
❑ 106	Wesley Person	.20	.07
❑ 107	Nick Van Exel	.60	.25
❑ 108	Dell Curry	.20	.07
❑ 109	Tony Delk	.40	.15
❑ 110	Glen Rice	.40	.15
❑ 111	Bobby Jackson	.40	.15
❑ 112	Kerry Kittles	.20	.07
❑ 113	John Starks	.40	.15
❑ 114	Gary Payton	.60	.25
❑ 115	Mookie Blaylock	.20	.07
❑ 116	David Wesley	.20	.07
❑ 117	Rod Strickland	.20	.07
❑ 118	Terrell Brandon	.20	.07
❑ 119	Steve Nash	.60	.25
❑ 120	Moochie Norris	.20	.07
❑ 121	Eric Snow	.40	.15
❑ 122	Chauncey Billups	.40	.15
❑ 123	Darrell Armstrong	.20	.07
❑ 124	Ron Harper	.40	.15
❑ 125	Dion Glover	.20	.07
❑ 126	Vin Baker	.40	.15
❑ 127	Terry Mills	.20	.07
❑ 128	Joe Smith	.40	.15
❑ 129	Kurt Thomas	.40	.15
❑ 130	Dirk Nowitzki	1.00	.40
❑ 131	Sean Elliott	.20	.07
❑ 132	Jerome Williams	.20	.07
❑ 133	Larry Johnson	.40	.15
❑ 134	LaPhonso Ellis	.20	.07
❑ 135	Pat Garrity	.20	.07
❑ 136	Lawrence Funderburke	.20	.07
❑ 137	Elton Brand	.60	.25
❑ 138	Rashard Lewis	.40	.15
❑ 139	Shawn Kemp	.40	.15
❑ 140	Elden Campbell	.20	.07
❑ 141	Christian Laettner	.40	.15
❑ 142	Al Harrington	.40	.15
❑ 143	Billy Owens	.20	.07
❑ 144	Wally Szczerbiak	.40	.15
❑ 145	Jonathan Bender	.40	.15

#	Player		
146	Karl Malone	.60	.25
147	Andrew DeClercq	.20	.07
148	Danny Manning	.40	.15
149	Antoine Walker	.60	.25
150	Jason Caffey	.20	.07
151	P.J. Brown	.20	.07
152	Matt Harpring	.60	.25
153	Mark Strickland	.20	.07
154	Theo Ratliff	.40	.15
155	Ruben Patterson	.40	.15
156	Tom Gugliotta	.20	.07
157	Derrick Coleman	.20	.07
158	Lorenzen Wright	.20	.07
159	Tracy McGrady	1.50	.60
160	Quincy Lewis	.20	.07
161	Tony Battie	.20	.07
162	Keith Van Horn	.60	.25
163	Paul Pierce	.60	.25
164	Glenn Robinson	.60	.25
165	John Wallace	.20	.07
166	Popeye Jones	.20	.07
167	Kevin Garnett	1.25	.50
168	Donyell Marshall	.40	.15
169	Michael Finley	.60	.25
170	Nick Anderson	.20	.07
171	Danny Fortson	.20	.07
172	Keon Clark	.40	.15
173	Juwan Howard	.40	.15
174	Brian Grant	.40	.15
175	Marcus Camby	.40	.15
176	Scottie Pippen	1.00	.40
177	Shawn Marion	.60	.25
178	Lamar Odom	.60	.25
179	Charles Oakley	.20	.07
180	Tim James	.20	.07
181	Eric Williams	.20	.07
182	Tim Duncan	1.25	.50
183	Andrae Patterson	.20	.07
184	Toni Kukoc	.40	.15
185	Chris Mullin	.60	.25
186	Alan Henderson	.20	.07
187	Maurice Taylor	.20	.07
188	Chris Webber	.60	.25
189	Jamal Mashburn	.40	.15
190	Rodney Rogers	.20	.07
191	Loy Vaught	.20	.07
192	Carlos Rogers	.20	.07
193	Grant Hill	.60	.25
194	George Lynch	.20	.07
195	Antonio McDyess	.40	.15
196	Tim Thomas	.40	.15
197	Roshown McLeod	.20	.07
198	Antawn Jamison	.60	.25
199	Clifford Robinson	.20	.07
200	Corey Maggette	.40	.15
201	Horace Grant	.20	.07
202	David Benoit	.20	.07
203	Cedric Ceballos	.20	.07
204	Antonio Davis	.20	.07
205	Lamond Murray	.20	.07
206	Jerry Stackhouse	.60	.25
207	Jermaine O'Neal	.40	.15
208	Anthony Mason	.40	.15
209	Cedric Henderson	.20	.07
210	Corliss Williamson	.40	.15
211	Austin Croshere	.40	.15
212	Radoslav Nesterovic	.40	.15
213	Hakeem Olajuwon	.60	.25
214	Nazr Mohammed	.20	.07
215	David Robinson	.60	.25
216	Jeff McInnis	.20	.07
217	Brad Miller	.60	.25
218	Evan Eschmeyer	.20	.07
219	Jelani McCoy	.20	.07
220	Sean Rooks	.20	.07
221	Dikembe Mutombo	.40	.15
222	Othella Harrington	.20	.07
223	John Amaechi	.20	.07
224	Erick Dampier	.40	.15
225	Calvin Booth	.20	.07
226	Adonal Foyle	.20	.07
227	Michael Doleac	.20	.07
228	Michael Olowokandi	.20	.07
229	Matt Geiger	.20	.07
230	Vlade Divac	.40	.15
231	Bryant Reeves	.20	.07
232	Shaquille O'Neal	1.50	.60
233	Todd Fuller	.20	.07
234	Arvydas Sabonis	.40	.15
235	Jim McIlvaine	.20	.07
236	Isaac Austin	.20	.07
237	Raef LaFrentz	.40	.15
238	Rasheed Wallace	.60	.25
239	Kelvin Cato	.20	.07
240	Patrick Ewing	.60	.25
241	Marc Jackson RC	3.00	1.25

2001 Fleer WNBA

LISA LESLIE

#	Player		
	COMP.SET w/o REDEM. (165)	30.00	15.00
	COMMON CARD	.50	.20
	COMMON ROOKIE (1-165)	.75	.30
	COMMON ROOKIE (166-204)	15.00	6.00
1	Lisa Leslie	2.00	.75
2	Andrea Stinson	1.00	.40
3	Tammy Jackson	.50	.20
4	Nicky McCrimmon RC	.75	.30
5	Vickie Johnson	.50	.20
6	Maria Stepanova	.50	.20
7	Michelle Edwards	1.00	.40
8	Tausha Mills	.50	.20
9	Edwina Brown	.50	.20
10	Jurgita Streimikyte	.50	.20
11	Keitha Dickerson RC	.75	.30
12	Taj McWilliams-Franklin	.50	.20
13	DeMya Walker	.50	.20
14	Adrienne Goodson	.50	.20
15	Eva Nemcova	1.00	.40
16	Danielle McCulley RC	.75	.30
17	Shannon Johnson	.50	.20
18	Margo Dydek	.50	.20
19	Mery Andrade	.50	.20
20	Marlies Askamp	.50	.20
21	Adrain Williams	.50	.20
22	Sonja Henning	.50	.20
23	Astou Ndiaye-Diatta	.50	.20
24	Latasha Byears	.50	.20
25	Kate Paye RC	.75	.30
26	Yolanda Griffith	1.50	.60
27	Kate Starbird	1.50	.60
28	Jennifer Rizzotti	1.00	.40
29	Umeki Webb	.50	.20
30	Tari Phillips	.50	.20
31	Tully Bevilacqua RC	.75	.30
32	Murriel Page	.50	.20
33	Tricia Bader Binford	.50	.20
34	Sheryl Swoopes	3.00	1.25
35	Debbie Black	.50	.20
36	Teresa Weatherspoon	1.50	.60
37	Alisa Burras	.50	.20
38	Stacey Lovelace RC	.75	.30
39	Helen Darling	.50	.20
40	Tina Thompson	1.50	.60
41	Katrina Colleton	.50	.20
42	Tamika Whitmore	.50	.20
43	Sylvia Crawley	.50	.20
44	Jamie Redd RC	.75	.30
45	Tracy Reid	.50	.20
46	Janeth Arcain	.50	.20
47	Stacey Frese RC	.75	.30
48	Grace Daley	.50	.20
49	Bridget Pettis	.50	.20
50	Katy Steding	.50	.20
51	Beth Cunningham	.50	.20
52	Vicki Hall RC	.75	.30
53	Amaya Valdemoro	.50	.20
54	Milena Flores	.50	.20
55	Sue Wicks	.50	.20
56	Michelle Marciniak	.50	.20
57	Tracy Henderson	.50	.20
58	Kisha Ford	.50	.20
59	Jannon Roland	.50	.20
60	Vanessa Nygaard RC	.75	.30
61	Pollyanna Johns RC	.75	.30
62	Gordana Grubin	.50	.20
63	Shantia Owens	.50	.20
64	Cintia dos Santos	.50	.20
65	Lynn Pride	.50	.20
66	Robin Threatt RC	.75	.30
67	Claudia Maria das Neves	.50	.20
68	Chantel Tremitiere	.50	.20
69	Betty Lennox	1.00	.40
70	Ruthie Bolton-Holifield	1.50	.60
71	Korie Hlede	.50	.20
72	Dominique Canty	.50	.20
73	Alicia Thompson	.50	.20
74	Kristin Folkl	.50	.20
75	Elaine Powell	.50	.20
76	Cindy Blodgett	.50	.20
77	Charlotte Smith	.50	.20
78	Mwadi Mabika	.50	.20
79	Marina Ferragut RC	.75	.30
80	Brandy Reed	.50	.20
81	Quacy Barnes	.50	.20
82	Chamique Holdsclaw	3.00	1.25
83	Dawn Staley	1.50	.60
84	Nekeshia Henderson RC	.75	.30
85	Rhonda Mapp	.50	.20
86	Becky Hammon	1.00	.40
87	Edna Campbell	.50	.20
88	Nikki McCray	1.00	.40
89	Anna DeForge	.50	.20
90	Rita Williams	.50	.20
91	Andrea Lloyd Curry	.50	.20
92	Nykesha Sales	.50	.20
93	Stacy Clinesmith RC	.75	.30
94	LaTonya Johnson	.50	.20
95	Markita Aldridge	.50	.20
96	Shalonda Enis	.50	.20
97	Wendy Palmer	1.00	.40
98	Tameeka Dixon	.50	.20
99	Katie Smith	1.50	.60
100	Tonya Edwards	.50	.20
101	Lady Hardmon	.50	.20
102	Dalma Ivanyi	.50	.20
103	Tiffany Travis RC	.75	.30
104	Tiffani Johnson RC	.75	.30
105	DeLisha Milton	.50	.20
106	Rebecca Lobo	1.50	.60
107	Michele Timms	1.50	.60
108	Andrea Garner RC	.75	.30
109	Andrea Nagy	.50	.20
110	Summer Erb	.50	.20
111	Ukari Figgs	.50	.20
112	Jennifer Gillom	1.00	.40
113	Kedra Holland-Corn	.50	.20
114	Natalie Williams	1.50	.60
115	Clarisse Machanguana	.50	.20
116	E.C. Hill RC	.75	.30
117	Lisa Harrison	.50	.20
118	Tangela Smith	.50	.20
119	Vicky Bullett	.50	.20
120	Ann Wauters	1.00	.40
121	Marla Brumfield RC	.75	.30
122	Carla McGhee	.50	.20
123	Sophia Witherspoon	.50	.20
124	Tamicha Jackson	.50	.20
125	Kara Wolters	.50	.20
126	Maylana Martin	.50	.20
127	Tiffany McCain RC	.75	.30
128	Naomi Mulitauaopele	.50	.20
129	Chasity Melvin	.50	.20
130	Stephanie McCarty	1.00	.40
131	Sheri Sam	.50	.20
132	Adrienne Johnson	.50	.20
133	Jennifer Azzi	1.50	.60
134	Allison Feaster	.50	.20
135	Elena Tornikidou RC	.75	.30
136	Sonja Tate	.50	.20
137	Michelle Brogan RC	.75	.30
138	Ticha Penicheiro	1.00	.40

☐ 139	Keisha Anderson	.50	.20
☐ 140	Merlakia Jones	.50	.20
☐ 141	Monica Maxwell	.50	.20
☐ 142	Kristen Rasmussen RC	.75	.30
☐ 143	Stacey Thomas	.50	.20
☐ 144	Kamila Vodichkova	.50	.20
☐ 145	Angie Braziel	.50	.20
☐ 146	Olympia Scott-Richardson	.50	.20
☐ 147	Vedrana Grgin RC	.75	.30
☐ 148	Shanele Stires	.50	.20
☐ 149	Coquese Washington	.50	.20
☐ 150	Crystal Robinson	.50	.20
☐ 151	Texlan Quinney	.50	.20
☐ 152	Michelle Cleary RC	.75	.30
☐ 153	La'Keshia Frett	.50	.20
☐ 154	Jessie Hicks	.50	.20
☐ 155	Katrina Hibbert	.50	.20
☐ 156	Cass Bauer	.50	.20
☐ 157	Jessica Bibby	.50	.20
☐ 158	Shea Mahoney RC	.75	.30
☐ 159	Charmin Smith	.50	.20
☐ 160	Oksana Zakaulzhnaya	.50	.20
☐ 161	Tonya Washington	.50	.20
☐ 162	Rushia Brown	.50	.20
☐ 163	Amy Herrig RC	.75	.30
☐ 164	Tara Williams	.50	.20
☐ 165	Sandy Brondello	1.50	.60
☐ 166	Tammy Sutton-Brown	15.00	6.00
☐ 167	Kelly Miller	15.00	6.00
☐ 168	Penny Taylor	15.00	6.00
☐ 169	Kelly Santos	15.00	6.00
☐ 170	Deanna Nolan	15.00	6.00
☐ 171	Jae Kingi	15.00	6.00
☐ 172	Amanda Lassiter	15.00	6.00
☐ 173	Trisha Stafford-Odom	15.00	6.00
☐ 174	Tynesa Lewis	15.00	6.00
☐ 175	Tamika Catchings	20.00	8.00
☐ 176	Kelly Schumaker	15.00	6.00
☐ 177	Niele Ivey	15.00	6.00
☐ 178	Nicole Levandusky	15.00	6.00
☐ 179	Wendy Willits	15.00	6.00
☐ 180	Ruth Riley	15.00	6.00
☐ 181	Levys Torres	15.00	6.00
☐ 182	Janell Burse	15.00	6.00
☐ 183	Svetlana Abrosimova	15.00	6.00
☐ 184	Erin Buescher	15.00	6.00
☐ 185	Georgia Schweitzer	15.00	6.00
☐ 186	Camille Cooper	15.00	6.00
☐ 187	Brooke Wyckoff	15.00	6.00
☐ 188	Jaclyn Johnson	15.00	6.00
☐ 189	Tawona Alehaleem	15.00	6.00
☐ 190	Katie Douglas	15.00	6.00
☐ 191	Jaynetta Saunders	15.00	6.00
☐ 192	Kristen Veal	15.00	6.00
☐ 193	Jenny Mowe	15.00	6.00
☐ 194	Jackie Stiles	30.00	12.50
☐ 195	LaQuanda Barksdale	15.00	6.00
☐ 196	Lauren Jackson	50.00	20.00
☐ 197	Semeka Randall	15.00	6.00
☐ 198	Michaela Pavlickova	15.00	6.00
☐ 199	Marie Ferdinand	15.00	6.00
☐ 200	Shea Ralph	15.00	6.00
☐ 201	Cara Consuegra	15.00	6.00
☐ 202	Tamara Stocks	15.00	6.00
☐ 203	Coco Miller	15.00	6.00
☐ 204	Helen Luz	15.00	6.00

2001 Greats of the Game

☐	COMPLETE SET (84)	50.00	20.00
☐	COMMON CARD (1-84)	.75	.30
☐	COMMON QC (76-83)	3.00	1.25
☐ 1	Adolph Rupp	.75	.30
☐ 2	Alonzo Mourning	.75	.30
☐ 3	Antawn Jamison	1.50	.60
☐ 4	Antoine Walker	1.50	.60
☐ 5	Bill Walton	1.50	.60
☐ 6	Bob Cousy	1.50	.60
☐ 7	Bob Lanier	1.50	.60
☐ 8	Bobby Cremins	.75	.30
☐ 9	Bobby Hurley	1.50	.60
☐ 10	Bobby Knight	2.00	.75
☐ 11	Cazzie Russell	.75	.30
☐ 12	Charlie Ward	.75	.30
☐ 13	Christian Laettner	2.00	.75
☐ 14	Clyde Drexler	.75	.30
☐ 15	Danny Ainge	.75	.30
☐ 16	Danny Ferry	2.00	.75
☐ 17	Danny Manning	2.00	.75
☐ 18	Darrell Griffith	.75	.30
☐ 19	Dave Cowens	.75	.30
☐ 20	David Robinson	1.50	.60
☐ 21	David Thompson	2.00	.75
☐ 22	Dean Smith	.75	.30
☐ 23	Don Haskins	.75	.30
☐ 24	Eddie Jones	.75	.30
☐ 25	Elvin Hayes	.75	.30
☐ 26	Gene Keady	.75	.30
☐ 27	George Mikan	1.50	.60
☐ 28	Glen Rice	.75	.30
☐ 29	Hakeem Olajuwon	1.50	.60
☐ 30	Isiah Thomas	1.50	.60
☐ 31	Jalen Rose	.75	.30
☐ 32	Jamal Mashburn	.75	.30
☐ 33	James Worthy	1.50	.60
☐ 34	Jerry Stackhouse	1.50	.60
☐ 35	Jerry Lucas	.75	.30
☐ 36	Jerry Tarkanian	.75	.30
☐ 37	Jerry West	.75	.30
☐ 38	Jim Valvano	1.50	.60
☐ 39	Joe Smith	.75	.30
☐ 40	John Thompson	.75	.30
☐ 41	John Havlicek	1.50	.60
☐ 42	John Wooden	1.50	.60
☐ 43	John Lucas	.75	.30
☐ 44	Kareem Abdul-Jabbar	2.50	1.00
☐ 45	Keith Van Horn	1.50	.60
☐ 46	Kent Benson	.75	.30
☐ 47	Kerry Kittles	.75	.30
☐ 48	Lamar Odom	1.50	.60
☐ 49	Larry Bird	5.00	2.00
☐ 50	Larry Johnson	.75	.30
☐ 51	Lefty Driesell	2.00	.75
☐ 52	Lenny Wilkens	1.50	.60
☐ 53	Lou Carnesecca	.75	.30
☐ 54	Marques Johnson	.75	.30
☐ 55	Mateen Cleaves	1.50	.60
☐ 56	Mike Bibby	1.50	.60
☐ 57	Mike Krzyzewski	2.00	.75
☐ 58	Mychal Thompson	.75	.30
☐ 59	Nate Archibald	.75	.30
☐ 60	Pat Riley	1.50	.60
☐ 61	Paul Arizin	1.50	.60
☐ 62	Pete Maravich	2.00	.75
☐ 63	Phil Ford	1.50	.60
☐ 64	Ralph Sampson	.75	.30
☐ 65	Ray Meyer	.75	.30
☐ 66	Rick Pitino	2.00	.75
☐ 67	Rick Barry	.75	.30
☐ 68	Rollie Massimino	.75	.30
☐ 69	Sam Jones	.75	.30
☐ 70	Sidney Moncrief	.75	.30
☐ 71	Spud Webb	.75	.30
☐ 72	Steve Alford	1.50	.60
☐ 73	Vince Carter	2.00	.75
☐ 74	Walt Frazier	2.00	.75
☐ 75	Wilt Chamberlain	3.00	1.25
☐ 76	Carol Blazejowski QC	3.00	1.25
☐ 77	Cynthia Cooper QC	3.00	1.25
☐ 78	Chamique Holdsclaw QC	3.00	1.25
☐ 79	Lisa Leslie QC	3.00	1.25
☐ 80	Nancy Lieberman QC	3.00	1.25
☐ 81	Rebecca Lobo QC	3.00	1.25
☐ 82	Cheryl Miller QC	3.00	1.25

☐ 83	Sheryl Swoopes QC	4.00	1.50
☐ 84	Marcus Camby	.75	.30

2005-06 Greats of the Game

☐	COMP.SET w/o SP's (100)	80.00	40.00
☐	COMMON CARD (1-100)	1.50	.60
☐	SEMISTARS	1.50	.60
☐	UNLISTED STARS	3.00	1.25
☐	COMMON AU RC (101-152)	30.00	12.50
☐	COMMON ROOKIE (153-169)	8.00	3.00
☐	101-169 PRINT RUN 99 SER.#'d SETS		
☐ 1	Earl Monroe	1.50	.60
☐ 2	World Free	1.50	.60
☐ 3	James Worthy	1.50	.60
☐ 4	Bob McAdoo	1.50	.60
☐ 5	Connie Hawkins	1.50	.60
☐ 6	John Starks	1.50	.60
☐ 7	Byron Scott	1.50	.60
☐ 8	Brad Daugherty	1.50	.60
☐ 9	Chris Ford	1.50	.60
☐ 10	Jamaal Wilkes	1.50	.60
☐ 11	Julius Erving	3.00	1.25
☐ 12	Joe Carroll	1.50	.60
☐ 13	Bill Laimbeer	3.00	1.25
☐ 14	Bill Walton	1.50	.60
☐ 15	Brian Winters	1.50	.60
☐ 16	David Robinson	3.00	1.25
☐ 17	Horace Grant	1.50	.60
☐ 18	Bob Pettit	1.50	.60
☐ 19	Dan Roundfield	1.50	.60
☐ 20	Kenny Walker	1.50	.60
☐ 21	Kenny Smith	1.50	.60
☐ 22	Thurl Bailey	1.50	.60
☐ 23	Cedric Maxwell	1.50	.60
☐ 24	Joe Dumars	1.50	.60
☐ 25	Adrian Dantley	1.50	.60
☐ 26	Dale Ellis	1.50	.60
☐ 27	John Stockton	3.00	1.25
☐ 28	Bob Lanier	1.50	.60
☐ 29	Bernard King	3.00	1.25
☐ 30	Jerry Lucas	1.50	.60
☐ 31	Bill Russell	4.00	1.50
☐ 32	Hal Greer	1.50	.60
☐ 33	Billy Cunningham	1.50	.60
☐ 34	Jack Sikma	1.50	.60
☐ 35	Michael Cooper	1.50	.60
☐ 36	David Thompson	3.00	1.25
☐ 37	Kareem Abdul-Jabbar	4.00	1.50
☐ 38	Bill Sharman	3.00	1.25
☐ 39	George Gervin	1.50	.60
☐ 40	Kiki Vandeweghe	1.50	.60
☐ 41	Calvin Murphy	1.50	.60
☐ 42	Darryl Dawkins	1.50	.60
☐ 43	Vern Mikkelsen	1.50	.60
☐ 44	Dee Brown	1.50	.60
☐ 45	Dennis Rodman	4.00	1.50
☐ 46	Bobby Jones	1.50	.60
☐ 47	Hakeem Olajuwon	3.00	1.25
☐ 48	Alvin Robertson	1.50	.60
☐ 49	Dennis Johnson	1.50	.60
☐ 50	Clyde Drexler	3.00	1.25
☐ 51	Anthony Mason	1.50	.60
☐ 52	Larry Bird	8.00	3.00
☐ 53	LeBron James	8.00	3.00
☐ 54	Magic Johnson	4.00	1.50
☐ 55	Manute Bol	1.50	.60

#	Player		
❏ 56	Mookie Blaylock	1.50	.60
❏ 57	Mark Eaton	1.50	.60
❏ 58	Kevin McHale	3.00	1.25
❏ 59	Maurice Cheeks	1.50	.60
❏ 60	Maurice Lucas	1.50	.60
❏ 61	Michael Jordan	8.00	3.00
❏ 62	Michael Ray Richardson	1.50	.60
❏ 63	B.J. Armstrong	1.50	.60
❏ 64	ML Carr	3.00	1.25
❏ 65	Muggsy Bogues	1.50	.60
❏ 66	Nate Archibald	1.50	.60
❏ 67	Glen Rice	1.50	.60
❏ 68	Nate Thurmond	1.50	.60
❏ 69	Norm Nixon	1.50	.60
❏ 70	Bob Love	1.50	.60
❏ 71	Paul Arizin	1.50	.60
❏ 72	Ralph Sampson	1.50	.60
❏ 73	Rolando Blackman	1.50	.60
❏ 74	Reggie Theus	1.50	.60
❏ 75	Mitch Richmond	1.50	.60
❏ 76	Robert Parish	3.00	1.25
❏ 77	Paul Westphal	3.00	1.25
❏ 78	Sam Perkins	1.50	.60
❏ 79	Scottie Pippen	4.00	1.50
❏ 80	Sean Elliott	1.50	.60
❏ 81	Spud Webb	1.50	.60
❏ 82	Steve Kerr	1.50	.60
❏ 83	Tom Chambers	1.50	.60
❏ 84	Walt Bellamy	1.50	.60
❏ 85	Walt Frazier	1.50	.60
❏ 86	Jeff Hornacek	1.50	.60
❏ 87	Danny Manning	1.50	.60
❏ 88	Wes Unseld	1.50	.60
❏ 89	Geoff Petrie	1.50	.60
❏ 90	Xavier McDaniel	1.50	.60
❏ 91	Chris Mullin	1.50	.60
❏ 92	Buck Williams CC	1.50	.60
❏ 93	Dave Bing CC	1.50	.60
❏ 94	John Havlicek CC	3.00	1.25
❏ 95	Karl Malone CC	3.00	1.25
❏ 96	Artis Gilmore CC	1.50	.60
❏ 97	Doug Moe CC	1.50	.60
❏ 98	Doug Collins CC	1.50	.60
❏ 99	Chuck Daly CC	1.50	.60
❏ 100	Bob Knight CC	3.00	1.25
❏ 101	Alex Acker AU RC	30.00	12.50
❏ 102	Amir Johnson AU RC	60.00	25.00
❏ 103	Andray Blatche AU RC	50.00	20.00
❏ 104	Andrew Bogut AU RC	120.00	60.00
❏ 105	Andrew Bynum AU RC	100.00	50.00
❏ 106	Antoine Wright AU RC	30.00	12.50
❏ 107	Yaroslav Korolev AU RC	40.00	15.00
❏ 108	Bracey Wright AU RC	30.00	12.50
❏ 109	Brandon Bass AU RC	30.00	12.50
❏ 110	C.J. Miles AU RC	40.00	15.00
❏ 111	Channing Frye AU RC	100.00	50.00
❏ 112	Charlie Villanueva AU RC	100.00	50.00
❏ 113	Chris Paul AU RC	650.00	400.00
❏ 114	Chris Taft AU RC	30.00	12.50
❏ 115	Chuck Hayes AU RC	30.00	12.50
❏ 116	Daniel Ewing AU RC	40.00	15.00
❏ 117	Danny Granger AU RC	75.00	30.00
❏ 118	David Lee AU RC	100.00	50.00
❏ 119	Deron Williams AU EXCH	325.00	250.00
❏ 120	Dijon Thompson AU RC	30.00	12.50
❏ 121	Ersan Ilyasova AU RC	40.00	15.00
❏ 122	Francisco Garcia RC	30.00	12.50
❏ 123	Gerald Green AU RC	200.00	100.00
❏ 124	Hakim Warrick AU RC	120.00	60.00
❏ 125	Ike Diogu AU RC	50.00	20.00
❏ 126	Jarrett Jack AU RC	50.00	20.00
❏ 127	Jason Maxiell AU RC	40.00	15.00
❏ 128	Joey Graham AU RC	40.00	15.00
❏ 129	Johan Petro AU RC	25.00	12.50
❏ 130	Julius Hodge AU RC	30.00	10.00
❏ 131	Lawrence Roberts AU RC	30.00	12.50
❏ 132	Linas Kleiza AU RC	30.00	12.50
❏ 133	Louis Williams AU RC	50.00	20.00
❏ 134	Luther Head AU RC	60.00	25.00
❏ 135	Martell Webster AU RC	50.00	20.00
❏ 136	M.Andriuskevicius AU RC	30.00	12.50
❏ 137	Marvin Williams AU RC	250.00	125.00
❏ 138	Monta Ellis AU RC	300.00	200.00
❏ 139	Nate Robinson AU RC	60.00	25.00
❏ 140	Orien Greene AU RC	30.00	12.50
❏ 141	Rashad McCants AU EXCH	75.00	35.00
❏ 142	Raymond Felton AU RC	225.00	125.00
❏ 143	Robert Whaley AU RC	30.00	12.50
❏ 144	Ronny Turiaf AU RC	100.00	50.00
❏ 145	Ryan Gomes AU RC	50.00	20.00
❏ 146	Salim Stoudamire AU RC	80.00	40.00
❏ 147	Sarunas Jasikevicius AU EXCH	30.00	12.50
❏ 148	Sean May AU RC	100.00	50.00
❏ 149	Stephen Graham AU RC	30.00	12.50
❏ 150	Travis Diener AU RC	30.00	12.50
❏ 151	Von Wafer AU RC	30.00	12.50
❏ 152	Wayne Simien AU RC	50.00	20.00
❏ 153	Shavlik Randolph RC	8.00	3.00
❏ 154	Alan Anderson RC	8.00	3.00
❏ 155	Andre Owens RC	8.00	3.00
❏ 156	Anthony Roberson RC	8.00	3.00
❏ 157	Arvydas Macijauskas RC	8.00	3.00
❏ 158	Boniface N'Dong RC	8.00	3.00
❏ 159	Devin Green RC	8.00	3.00
❏ 160	Donell Taylor RC	8.00	3.00
❏ 161	Earl Barron RC	8.00	3.00
❏ 162	Esteban Batista RC	8.00	3.00
❏ 163	Fabricio Oberto RC	8.00	3.00
❏ 164	Rawle Marshall RC	8.00	3.00
❏ 165	James Singleton RC	8.00	3.00
❏ 166	Jose Calderon RC	8.00	3.00
❏ 167	Josh Powell RC	8.00	3.00
❏ 168	Kevin Burleson RC	8.00	3.00
❏ 169	Ronnie Price RC	8.00	3.00

1989-90 Hoops

MITCH RICHMOND — WARRIORS

❏ COMPLETE SET (352)	25.00	12.50
❏ COMPLETE SERIES 1 (300)	20.00	10.00
❏ COMPLETE SERIES 2 (52)	5.00	2.50
❏ COMMON CARD (1-352)	.05	.01
❏ COMMON SP	.15	.05
❏ 1 Joe Dumars	.25	.08
❏ 2 Tree Rollins	.05	.01
❏ 3 Kenny Walker	.05	.01
❏ 4 Mychal Thompson	.05	.01
❏ 5 Alvin Robertson SP	.15	.05
❏ 6 Vinny Del Negro RC	.25	.08
❏ 7 Greg Anderson SP	.15	.05
❏ 8 Rod Strickland RC	.75	.30
❏ 9 Ed Pinckney	.05	.01
❏ 10 Dale Ellis	.10	.02
❏ 11 Chuck Daly RC	.25	.08
❏ 12 Eric Leckner	.05	.01
❏ 13 Charles Davis	.05	.01
❏ 14 Cotton Fitzsimmons CO	.05	.01
❏ 15 Byron Scott	.10	.02
❏ 16 Derrick Chievous	.05	.01
❏ 17 Reggie Lewis RC	.25	.08
❏ 18 Jim Paxson	.05	.01
❏ 19 Tony Campbell RC	.05	.01
❏ 20 Rolando Blackman	.05	.01
❏ 21 Michael Jordan AS	1.50	.60
❏ 22 Cliff Levingston	.05	.01
❏ 23 Roy Tarpley	.05	.01
❏ 24 Harold Pressley UER	.05	.01
❏ 25 Larry Nance	.10	.02
❏ 26 Chris Morris RC	.10	.02
❏ 27 Bob Hansen UER	.05	.01
❏ 28 Mark Price AS	.05	.01
❏ 29 Reggie Miller	.60	.25
❏ 30 Karl Malone	.40	.15
❏ 31 Sidney Lowe SP	.15	.05
❏ 32 Ron Anderson	.05	.01
❏ 33 Mike Gminski	.05	.01
❏ 34 Scott Brooks RC	.05	.01
❏ 35 Kevin Johnson RC	.50	.20
❏ 36 Mark Bryant RC	.05	.01
❏ 37 Rik Smits RC	.30	.10
❏ 38 Tim Perry RC	.05	.01
❏ 39 Ralph Sampson	.05	.01
❏ 40 Danny Manning RC	.30	.10
❏ 41 Kevin Edwards RC	.05	.01
❏ 42 Paul Mokeski	.05	.01
❏ 43 Dale Ellis AS	.05	.01
❏ 44 Walter Berry	.05	.01
❏ 45 Chuck Person	.10	.02
❏ 46 Rick Mahorn SP	.15	.05
❏ 47 Joe Kleine	.05	.01
❏ 48 Brad Daugherty AS	.05	.01
❏ 49 Mike Woodson	.05	.01
❏ 50 Brad Daugherty	.05	.01
❏ 51 Shelton Jones SP	.15	.05
❏ 52 Michael Adams	.05	.01
❏ 53 Wes Unseld RC	.15	.05
❏ 54 Rex Chapman RC	.25	.08
❏ 55 Kelly Tripucka	.05	.01
❏ 56 Rickey Green	.05	.01
❏ 57 Frank Johnson SP	.15	.05
❏ 58 Johnny Newman RC	.05	.01
❏ 59 Billy Thompson	.05	.01
❏ 60 Stu Jackson CO	.05	.01
❏ 61 Walter Davis	.05	.01
❏ 62 Brian Shaw RC SP	.25	.08
❏ 63 Gerald Wilkins	.05	.01
❏ 64 Armon Gilliam	.05	.01
❏ 65 Maurice Cheeks SP	.25	.08
❏ 66 Jack Sikma	.05	.01
❏ 67 Harvey Grant RC	.05	.01
❏ 68 Jim Lynam CO	.05	.01
❏ 69 Clyde Drexler AS	.10	.02
❏ 70 Xavier McDaniel	.05	.01
❏ 71 Danny Young	.05	.01
❏ 72 Fennis Dembo	.05	.01
❏ 73 Mark Acres SP	.15	.05
❏ 74 Brad Lohaus RC SP	.15	.05
❏ 75 Manute Bol	.05	.01
❏ 76 Purvis Short	.05	.01
❏ 77 Allen Leavell	.05	.01
❏ 78 Johnny Dawkins SP	.15	.05
❏ 79 Paul Pressey	.05	.01
❏ 80 Patrick Ewing	.25	.08
❏ 81 Bill Wennington RC	.05	.01
❏ 82 Danny Schayes	.05	.01
❏ 83 Derek Smith	.05	.01
❏ 84 Moses Malone AS	.10	.02
❏ 85 Jeff Malone	.05	.01
❏ 86 Otis Smith RC SP	.15	.05
❏ 87 Trent Tucker	.05	.01
❏ 88 Robert Reid	.05	.01
❏ 89 John Bagley	.05	.01
❏ 90 Chris Mullin	.25	.08
❏ 91 Tom Garrick	.05	.01
❏ 92 Willis Reed CO SP	.25	.08
❏ 93 Dave Corzine SP	.15	.05
❏ 94 Mark Alarie	.05	.01
❏ 95 Mark Aguirre	.05	.01
❏ 96 Charles Barkley	.20	.07
❏ 97 Sidney Green SP	.15	.05
❏ 98 Kevin Willis	.10	.02
❏ 99 Dave Hoppen	.05	.01
❏ 100 Terry Cummings SP	.25	.08
❏ 101 Dwayne Washington SP	.15	.05
❏ 102 Larry Brown CO	.10	.02
❏ 103 Kevin Duckworth	.05	.01
❏ 104 Uwe Blab SP	.15	.05
❏ 105 Terry Porter	.05	.01
❏ 106 Craig Ehlo RC**	.05	.01
❏ 107 Don Casey CO	.05	.01
❏ 108 Pat Riley CO	.05	.01
❏ 109 John Salley	.05	.01
❏ 110 Charles Barkley	.40	.15
❏ 111 Sam Bowie SP	.15	.05
❏ 112 Earl Cureton	.05	.01
❏ 113 Craig Hodges UER	.05	.01
❏ 114 Benoit Benjamin	.05	.01
❏ 115A Spud Webb 9/27/89	.25	.08
❏ 115B Spud Webb 9/26/85	.10	.02
❏ 116 Karl Malone AS	.25	.08
❏ 117 Sleepy Floyd	.05	.01
❏ 118 Hot Rod Williams	.05	.01

#	Player		
119	Michael Holton	.05	.01
120	Alex English	.05	.01
121	Dennis Johnson	.05	.01
122	Wayne Cooper SP	.15	.05
123A	Don Chaney CO	.05	.01
123B	Don Chaney CO	.05	.01
124	A.C. Green	.10	.02
125	Adrian Dantley	.05	.01
126	Del Harris CO	.05	.01
127	Dick Harter CO	.05	.01
128	Reggie Williams RC	.05	.01
129	Bill Hanzlik	.05	.01
130	Dominique Wilkins	.25	.08
131	Herb Williams	.05	.01
132	Steve Johnson SP	.15	.05
133	Alex English AS	.05	.01
134	Darrell Walker	.05	.01
135	Bill Laimbeer	.10	.02
136	Fred Roberts RC**	.05	.01
137	Hersey Hawkins RC	.30	.10
138	David Robinson SP RC!	10.00	4.00
139	Brad Sellers SP	.15	.05
140	John Stockton	.60	.25
141	Grant Long RC	.05	.01
142	Marc Iavaroni SP	.15	.05
143	Steve Alford RC SP	.25	.08
144	Jeff Lamp SP	.15	.05
145	Buck Williams AS	.25	.08
146	Mark Jackson AS	.05	.01
147	Jim Petersen	.05	.01
148	Steve Stipanovich SP	.15	.05
149	Sam Vincent RC SP	.15	.05
150	Larry Bird	1.00	.40
151	Jon Koncak RC	.05	.01
152	Olden Polynice RC	.10	.02
153	Randy Breuer	.05	.01
154	John Battle RC	.05	.01
155	Mark Eaton	.05	.01
156	Kevin McHale AS UER	.10	.02
157	Jerry Sichting SP	.15	.05
158	Pat Cummings SP	.15	.05
159	Patrick Ewing AS	.15	.05
160	Mark Price	.10	.02
161	Jerry Reynolds CO	.05	.01
162	Ken Norman RC	.05	.01
163	John Bagley SP UER	.15	.05
164	Christian Welp SP	.15	.05
165	Reggie Theus SP	.25	.08
166	Magic Johnson AS	.40	.15
167	John Long UER	.05	.01
168	Larry Smith SP	.15	.05
169	Charles Shackleford RC	.05	.01
170	Tom Chambers	.10	.02
171A	John MacLeod CO SP	.15	.05
171B	John MacLeod CO	.05	.01
172	Ron Rothstein CO	.05	.01
173	Joe Wolf	.05	.01
174	Mark Eaton AS	.05	.01
175	Jon Sundvold	.05	.01
176	Scott Hastings SP	.15	.05
177	Isiah Thomas AS	.10	.02
178	Hakeem Olajuwon AS	.25	.08
179	Mike Fratello CO	.10	.02
180	Hakeem Olajuwon	.40	.15
181	Randolph Keys	.05	.01
182	Richard Anderson UER	.05	.01
183	Dan Majerle RC	.30	.10
184	Derek Harper	.10	.02
185	Robert Parish	.10	.02
186	Ricky Berry SP	.15	.05
187	Michael Cooper	.10	.02
188	Vinnie Johnson	.10	.02
189	James Donaldson	.05	.01
190	Clyde Drexler	.25	.08
191	Jay Vincent SP	.15	.05
192	Nate McMillan	.05	.01
193	Kevin Duckworth AS	.05	.01
194	Ledell Eackles RC	.05	.01
195	Eddie Johnson	.10	.02
196	Terry Teagle	.05	.01
197	Tom Chambers AS	.05	.01
198	Joe Barry Carroll	.05	.01
199	Dennis Hopson RC	.05	.01
200	Michael Jordan	3.00	1.50
201	Jerome Lane RC	.05	.01
202	Greg Kite RC**	.05	.01
203	David Rivers SP	.15	.05
204	Sylvester Gray	.05	.01
205	Ron Harper	.10	.02
206	Frank Brickowski	.05	.01
207	Rory Sparrow	.05	.01
208	Gerald Henderson	.05	.01
209	Rod Higgins UER	.05	.01
210	James Worthy	.25	.08
211	Dennis Rodman	1.00	.40
212	Ricky Pierce	.05	.01
213	Charles Oakley	.10	.02
214	Steve Colter	.05	.01
215	Danny Ainge	.10	.02
216	Lenny Wilkens CO UER	.10	.02
217	Larry Nance AS	.05	.01
218	Muggsy Bogues	.10	.02
219	James Worthy AS	.10	.02
220	Lafayette Lever	.05	.01
221	Quintin Dailey SP	.15	.05
222	Lester Conner	.05	.01
223	Jose Ortiz	.05	.01
224	Micheal Williams RC SP U	.25	.08
225	Wayman Tisdale	.05	.01
226	Mike Sanders SP	.15	.05
227	Jim Farmer SP	.15	.05
228	Mark West	.05	.01
229	Jeff Hornacek AS	.30	.10
230	Chris Mullin AS	.10	.02
231	Vern Fleming	.05	.01
232	Kenny Smith	.05	.01
233	Derrick McKey	.05	.01
234	Dominique Wilkins AS	.10	.02
235	Willie Anderson RC	.05	.01
236	Keith Lee SP	.15	.05
237	Buck Johnson RC	.05	.01
238	Randy Wittman	.05	.01
239	Terry Catledge SP	.15	.05
240	Bernard King	.05	.01
241	Darrell Griffith	.05	.01
242	Horace Grant	.10	.02
243	Rony Seikaly RC	.25	.08
244	Scottie Pippen	1.50	.60
245	Michael Cage UER	.05	.01
246	Kurt Rambis	.05	.01
247	Morlon Wiley RC SP	.15	.05
248	Ronnie Grandison	.05	.01
249	Scott Skiles RC SP	.25	.08
250	Isiah Thomas	.25	.08
251	Thurl Bailey	.05	.01
252	Doc Rivers	.10	.02
253	Stuart Gray SP	.15	.05
254	John Williams	.05	.01
255	Bill Cartwright	.05	.01
256	Terry Cummings AS	.05	.01
257	Rodney McCray	.05	.01
258	Larry Krystkowiak RC	.05	.01
259	Will Perdue RC	.05	.01
260	Mitch Richmond RC	1.25	.50
261	Blair Rasmussen	.05	.01
262	Charles Smith RC	.25	.08
263	Tyrone Corbin RC SP	.15	.05
264	Kelvin Upshaw	.05	.01
265	Otis Thorpe	.10	.02
266	Phil Jackson CO	.25	.08
267	Jerry Sloan CO	.10	.02
268	John Shasky	.05	.01
269A	B. Bickerstaff CO SP	.15	.05
269B	B. Bickerstaff CO	.05	.01
270	Magic Johnson	.75	.30
271	Vernon Maxwell RC	.05	.01
272	Tim McCormick	.05	.01
273	Don Nelson CO	.10	.02
274	Gary Grant RC	.05	.01
275	Sidney Moncrief SP	.15	.05
276	Roy Hinson	.05	.01
277	Jimmy Rodgers CO	.05	.01
278	Antoine Carr	.05	.01
279A	Orlando Woolridge SP	.15	.05
279B	Orlando Woolridge	.05	.01
280	Kevin McHale	.25	.08
281	LaSalle Thompson	.05	.01
282	Detlef Schrempf	.10	.02
283	Doug Moe CO	.05	.01
284A	James Edwards	.05	.01
284B	James Edwards	.05	.01
285	Jerome Kersey	.05	.01
286	Sam Perkins	.10	.02
287	Sedale Threatt	.05	.01
288	Tim Kempton SP	.15	.05
289	Mark McNamara	.05	.01
290	Moses Malone	.25	.08
291	Rick Adelman CO UER	.05	.01
292	Dick Versace CO	.05	.01
293	Alton Lister SP	.15	.05
294	Winston Garland	.05	.01
295	Kiki Vandeweghe	.05	.01
296	Brad Davis	.05	.01
297	John Stockton AS	.25	.08
298	Jay Humphries	.05	.01
299	Dell Curry	.05	.01
300	Mark Jackson	.10	.02
301	Morlon Wiley	.05	.01
302	Reggie Theus	.10	.02
303	Otis Smith	.05	.01
304	Tod Murphy RC	.05	.01
305	Sidney Lowe	.05	.01
306	Shelton Jones	.05	.01
307	Mark Acres	.05	.01
308	Terry Catledge	.05	.01
309	Larry Smith	.05	.01
310	David Robinson IA	2.00	.75
311	Johnny Dawkins	.05	.01
312	Terry Cummings	.10	.02
313	Sidney Lowe	.05	.01
314	Bill Musselman CO	.05	.01
315	Buck Williams	.10	.02
316	Mel Turpin	.05	.01
317	Scott Hastings	.05	.01
318	Scott Skiles	.10	.02
319	Tyrone Corbin	.05	.01
320	Maurice Cheeks	.05	.01
321	Matt Guokas CO	.05	.01
322	Jeff Turner	.05	.01
323	David Wingate	.05	.01
324	Steve Johnson	.05	.01
325	Alton Lister	.05	.01
326	Ken Bannister	.05	.01
327	Bill Fitch CO UER	.05	.01
328	Sam Vincent	.05	.01
329	Larry Drew	.05	.01
330	Rick Mahorn	.05	.01
331	Christian Welp	.05	.01
332	Brad Lohaus	.05	.01
333	Frank Johnson	.05	.01
334	Jim Farmer	.05	.01
335	Wayne Cooper	.05	.01
336	Mike Brown RC	.05	.01
337	Sam Bowie	.05	.01
338	Kevin Gamble RC	.05	.01
339	Jerry Ice Reynolds RC	.05	.01
340	Mike Sanders	.05	.01
341	Bill Jones UER	.05	.01
342	Greg Anderson	.05	.01
343	Dave Corzine	.05	.01
344	Micheal Williams UER	.05	.01
345	Jay Vincent	.05	.01
346	David Rivers	.05	.01
347	Caldwell Jones UER	.05	.01
348	Brad Sellers	.05	.01
349	Scott Roth	.05	.01
350	Alvin Robertson	.05	.01
351	Steve Kerr RC	.50	.20
352	Stuart Gray	.05	.01
353A	Pistons Champions SP	4.00	1.50
353B	Pistons Champions	.50	.20

1990-91 Hoops

	COMPLETE SET (440)	15.00	7.50
	COMPLETE SERIES 1 (336)	10.00	5.00
	COMPLETE SERIES 2 (104)	5.00	2.50
	COMMON CARD (1-440)	.05	.01
	COMMON SP	.10	.02
1	Charles Barkley AS SP	.25	.08
2	Larry Bird AS SP	.60	.25
3	Joe Dumars AS SP	.15	.05
4	Patrick Ewing AS SP	.15	.05
5	Michael Jordan AS SP	2.00	.75
6	Kevin McHale AS SP	.08	.01
7	Reggie Miller AS SP	.15	.05
8	Robert Parish AS SP	.10	.02
9	Scottie Pippen AS SP	.60	.25
10	Dennis Rodman AS SP	.40	.15

❑ 11 Isiah Thomas AS SP	.15	.05
❑ 12 Dominique Wilkins AS SP	.15	.05
❑ 13A AS CL: ERR NNO SP	.25	.10
❑ 13B AS CL: COR SP	.10	.02
❑ 14 Rolando Blackman AS SP	.10	.02
❑ 15 Tom Chambers AS SP	.10	.02
❑ 16 Clyde Drexler AS SP	.08	.01
❑ 17 A.C. Green SP	.10	.02
❑ 18 Magic Johnson AS SP	.50	.20
❑ 19 Kevin Johnson AS SP	.15	.05
❑ 20 Lafayette Lever AS SP	.10	.02
❑ 21 Karl Malone AS SP	.25	.08
❑ 22 Chris Mullin AS SP	.15	.05
❑ 23 Hakeem Olajuwon AS SP	.25	.08
❑ 24 David Robinson AS SP	.50	.20
❑ 25 John Stockton AS SP	.20	.07
❑ 26 James Worthy AS SP	.15	.05
❑ 27 John Battle	.05	.01
❑ 28 Jon Koncak	.05	.01
❑ 29 Cliff Levingston SP	.05	.01
❑ 30 John Long SP	.10	.02
❑ 31 Moses Malone	.15	.05
❑ 32 Doc Rivers	.08	.01
❑ 33 Kenny Smith SP	.10	.02
❑ 34 Alexander Volkov	.05	.01
❑ 35 Spud Webb	.08	.01
❑ 36 Dominique Wilkins	.15	.05
❑ 37 Kevin Willis	.08	.01
❑ 38 John Bagley	.05	.01
❑ 39 Larry Bird	.60	.25
❑ 40 Kevin Gamble	.05	.01
❑ 41 Dennis Johnson SP	.05	.01
❑ 42 Joe Kleine	.05	.01
❑ 43 Reggie Lewis	.08	.01
❑ 44 Kevin McHale	.08	.01
❑ 45 Robert Parish	.08	.01
❑ 46 Jim Paxson SP	.08	.01
❑ 47 Ed Pinckney	.05	.01
❑ 48 Brian Shaw	.15	.05
❑ 49 Richard Anderson SP	.10	.02
❑ 50 Muggsy Bogues	.08	.01
❑ 51 Rex Chapman	.15	.05
❑ 52 Dell Curry	.05	.01
❑ 53 Kenny Gattison RC	.05	.01
❑ 54 Armon Gilliam	.05	.01
❑ 55 Dave Hoppen	.05	.01
❑ 56 Randolph Keys	.05	.01
❑ 57 J.R.Reid RC	.05	.01
❑ 58 Robert Reid SP	.10	.02
❑ 59 Kelly Tripucka	.05	.01
❑ 60 B.J.Armstrong RC	.05	.01
❑ 61 Bill Cartwright	.05	.01
❑ 62 Charles Davis SP	.10	.02
❑ 63 Horace Grant	.08	.01
❑ 64 Craig Hodges	.05	.01
❑ 65 Michael Jordan	2.00	.75
❑ 66 Stacey King RC	.05	.01
❑ 67 John Paxson	.08	.01
❑ 68 Will Perdue	.05	.01
❑ 69 Scottie Pippen	.60	.25
❑ 70 Winston Bennett	.05	.01
❑ 71 Chucky Brown RC	.05	.01
❑ 72 Derrick Chievous	.05	.01
❑ 73 Brad Daugherty	.05	.01
❑ 74 Craig Ehlo	.05	.01
❑ 75 Steve Kerr	.15	.05
❑ 76 Paul Mokeski SP	.10	.02
❑ 77 John Morton	.05	.01

❑ 78 Larry Nance	.05	.01
❑ 79 Mark Price	.08	.01
❑ 80 Hot Rod Williams	.05	.01
❑ 81 Steve Alford	.05	.01
❑ 82 Rolando Blackman	.05	.01
❑ 83 Adrian Dantley SP	.05	.01
❑ 84 Brad Davis	.05	.01
❑ 85 James Donaldson	.05	.01
❑ 86 Derek Harper	.08	.01
❑ 87 Sam Perkins SP	.08	.01
❑ 88 Roy Tarpley	.05	.01
❑ 89 Bill Wennington SP	.10	.02
❑ 90 Herb Williams	.05	.01
❑ 91 Michael Adams	.05	.01
❑ 92 Joe Barry Carroll SP	.10	.02
❑ 93 Walter Davis UER	.05	.01
❑ 94 Alex English SP	.05	.01
❑ 95 Bill Hanzlik	.05	.01
❑ 96 Jerome Lane	.05	.01
❑ 97 Lafayette Lever SP	.10	.02
❑ 98 Todd Lichti RC	.05	.01
❑ 99 Blair Rasmussen	.05	.01
❑ 100 Danny Schayes SP	.10	.02
❑ 101 Mark Aguirre	.05	.01
❑ 102 William Bedford RC	.05	.01
❑ 103 Joe Dumars	.15	.05
❑ 104 James Edwards SP	.05	.01
❑ 105 Scott Hastings	.05	.01
❑ 106 Gerald Henderson SP	.10	.02
❑ 107 Vinnie Johnson	.05	.01
❑ 108 Bill Laimbeer	.08	.01
❑ 109 Dennis Rodman	.40	.15
❑ 110 John Salley	.05	.01
❑ 111 Isiah Thomas	.15	.05
❑ 112 Manute Bol SP	.10	.02
❑ 113 Tim Hardaway SP	1.00	.40
❑ 114 Rod Higgins	.05	.01
❑ 115 Sarun.Marciulionis RC	.05	.01
❑ 116 Chris Mullin	.15	.05
❑ 117 Jim Petersen	.05	.01
❑ 118 Mitch Richmond	.20	.07
❑ 119 Mike Smrek	.05	.01
❑ 120 Terry Teagle SP	.10	.02
❑ 121 Tom Tolbert RC	.05	.01
❑ 122 Christian Welp SP	.10	.02
❑ 123 Byron Dinkins SP	.10	.02
❑ 124 Eric(Sleepy) Floyd	.05	.01
❑ 125 Buck Johnson	.05	.01
❑ 126 Vernon Maxwell	.05	.01
❑ 127 Hakeem Olajuwon	.25	.08
❑ 128 Larry Smith	.05	.01
❑ 129 Otis Thorpe	.08	.01
❑ 130 Mitchell Wiggins SP	.10	.02
❑ 131 Mike Woodson	.05	.01
❑ 132 Greg Dreiling SP	.05	.01
❑ 133 Vern Fleming	.05	.01
❑ 134 Rickey Green SP	.10	.02
❑ 135 Reggie Miller	.25	.08
❑ 136 Chuck Person	.08	.01
❑ 137 Mike Sanders	.05	.01
❑ 138 Detlef Schrempf	.08	.01
❑ 139 Rik Smits	.15	.05
❑ 140 LaSalle Thompson	.05	.01
❑ 141 Randy Wittman	.05	.01
❑ 142 Benoit Benjamin	.05	.01
❑ 143 Winston Garland	.05	.01
❑ 144 Tom Garrick	.05	.01
❑ 145 Gary Grant	.05	.01
❑ 146 Ron Harper	.08	.01
❑ 147 Danny Manning	.08	.01
❑ 148 Jeff Martin	.05	.01
❑ 149 Ken Norman	.05	.01
❑ 150 David Rivers SP	.10	.02
❑ 151 Charles Smith	.05	.01
❑ 152 Joe Wolf SP	.10	.02
❑ 153 Michael Cooper SP	.10	.02
❑ 154 Vlade Divac RC	.40	.15
❑ 155 Larry Drew	.05	.01
❑ 156 A.C. Green	.08	.01
❑ 157 Magic Johnson	.50	.20
❑ 158 Mark McNamara SP	.10	.02
❑ 159 Byron Scott	.08	.01
❑ 160 Mychal Thompson	.05	.01
❑ 161 Jay Vincent SP	.10	.02
❑ 162 Orlando Woolridge SP	.10	.02
❑ 163 James Worthy	.15	.05

❑ 164 Sherman Douglas RC	.08	.01
❑ 165 Kevin Edwards	.05	.01
❑ 166 Tellis Frank SP	.10	.02
❑ 167 Grant Long	.05	.01
❑ 168 Glen Rice RC	.60	.25
❑ 169A Rony Seikaly Athens	.08	.01
❑ 169B Rony Seikaly Beirut	.08	.01
❑ 170 Rory Sparrow SP	.10	.02
❑ 171A Jon Sundvold	.05	.01
❑ 171B Billy Thompson	.05	.01
❑ 172A Billy Thompson	.05	.01
❑ 172B Jon Sundvold	.05	.01
❑ 173 Greg Anderson	.05	.01
❑ 174 Jeff Grayer RC	.05	.01
❑ 175 Jay Humphries	.05	.01
❑ 176 Frank Kornet	.05	.01
❑ 177 Larry Krystkowiak	.05	.01
❑ 178 Brad Lohaus	.05	.01
❑ 179 Ricky Pierce	.05	.01
❑ 180 Paul Pressey SP	.10	.02
❑ 181 Fred Roberts	.05	.01
❑ 182 Alvin Robertson	.05	.01
❑ 183 Jack Sikma	.05	.01
❑ 184 Randy Breuer	.05	.01
❑ 185 Tony Campbell	.05	.01
❑ 186 Tyrone Corbin	.05	.01
❑ 187 Sidney Lowe SP	.10	.02
❑ 188 Sam Mitchell RC	.05	.01
❑ 189 Tod Murphy	.05	.01
❑ 190 Pooh Richardson RC	.08	.01
❑ 191 Scott Roth SP	.05	.01
❑ 192 Brad Sellers SP	.10	.02
❑ 193 Mookie Blaylock RC	.25	.08
❑ 194 Sam Bowie	.05	.01
❑ 195 Lester Conner	.05	.01
❑ 196 Derrick Gervin	.05	.01
❑ 197 Jack Haley RC	.05	.01
❑ 198 Roy Hinson	.05	.01
❑ 199 Dennis Hopson SP	.10	.02
❑ 200 Chris Morris	.08	.01
❑ 201 Purvis Short SP	.10	.02
❑ 202 Maurice Cheeks	.05	.01
❑ 203 Patrick Ewing	.15	.05
❑ 204 Stuart Gray	.05	.01
❑ 205 Mark Jackson	.08	.01
❑ 206 Johnny Newman SP	.10	.02
❑ 207 Charles Oakley	.08	.01
❑ 208 Trent Tucker	.05	.01
❑ 209 Kiki Vandeweghe	.05	.01
❑ 210 Kenny Walker	.05	.01
❑ 211 Eddie Lee Wilkins	.05	.01
❑ 212 Gerald Wilkins	.05	.01
❑ 213 Mark Acres	.05	.01
❑ 214 Nick Anderson RC	.25	.08
❑ 215 Michael Ansley UER	.05	.01
❑ 216 Terry Catledge	.05	.01
❑ 217 Dave Corzine SP	.10	.02
❑ 218 Sidney Green SP	.10	.02
❑ 219 Jerry Reynolds	.05	.01
❑ 220 Scott Skiles	.08	.01
❑ 221 Otis Smith	.05	.01
❑ 222 Reggie Theus SP	.08	.01
❑ 223A S.Vincent w/M.Jordan	1.50	.60
❑ 223B Sam Vincent	.05	.01
❑ 224 Ron Anderson	.05	.01
❑ 225 Charles Barkley	.25	.08
❑ 226 Scott Brooks SP UER	.10	.02
❑ 227 Johnny Dawkins	.05	.01
❑ 228 Mike Gminski	.05	.01
❑ 229 Hersey Hawkins	.08	.01
❑ 230 Rick Mahorn	.05	.01
❑ 231 Derek Smith SP	.10	.02
❑ 232 Bob Thornton	.05	.01
❑ 233 Kenny Battle RC	.05	.01
❑ 234A Tom Chambers Forward		
❑ 234B Tom Chambers Guard	.05	.01
❑ 235 Greg Grant RC SP	.10	.02
❑ 236 Jeff Hornacek	.08	.01
❑ 237 Eddie Johnson	.08	.01
❑ 238A Kevin Johnson Guard	.15	.05
❑ 238B Kevin Johnson Forward	.15	.05
❑ 239 Dan Majerle	.15	.05
❑ 240 Tim Perry	.05	.01
❑ 241 Kurt Rambis	.05	.01
❑ 242 Mark West	.05	.01
❑ 243 Mark Bryant	.05	.01

#	Player		
244	Wayne Cooper	.05	.01
245	Clyde Drexler	.15	.05
246	Kevin Duckworth	.05	.01
247	Jerome Kersey	.05	.01
248	Drazen Petrovic RC	.08	.01
249A	Terry Porter ERR	.50	.20
249B	Terry Porter COR	.05	.01
250	Clifford Robinson SP	.25	.08
251	Buck Williams	.05	.01
252	Danny Young	.05	.01
253	Danny Ainge SP UER	.08	.01
254	Randy Allen SP	.10	.02
255	Antoine Carr	.05	.01
256	Vinny Del Negro SP	.10	.02
257	Pervis Ellison RC SP	.10	.02
258	Greg Kite SP	.10	.02
259	Rodney McCray SP	.10	.02
260	Harold Pressley SP	.10	.02
261	Ralph Sampson	.05	.01
262	Wayman Tisdale	.05	.01
263	Willie Anderson	.05	.01
264	Uwe Blab SP	.10	.02
265	Frank Brickowski SP	.10	.02
266	Terry Cummings	.05	.01
267	Sean Elliott RC	.30	.10
268	Caldwell Jones SP	.10	.02
269	Johnny Moore SP	.10	.02
270	David Robinson	.50	.20
271	Rod Strickland	.15	.05
272	Reggie Williams	.05	.01
273	David Wingate SP	.10	.02
274	Dana Barros RC	.15	.05
275	Michael Cage SP	.05	.01
276	Quintin Dailey	.05	.01
277	Dale Ellis	.08	.01
278	Steve Johnson SP	.10	.02
279	Shawn Kemp RC	1.50	.60
280	Xavier McDaniel	.05	.01
281	Derrick McKey	.05	.01
282	Nate McMillan	.08	.01
283	Olden Polynice	.05	.01
284	Sedale Threatt	.05	.01
285	Thurl Bailey	.05	.01
286	Mike Brown	.05	.01
287	Mark Eaton UER	.05	.01
288	Blue Edwards RC	.05	.01
289	Darrell Griffith	.05	.01
290	Bobby Hansen SP	.10	.02
291	Eric Leckner SP	.10	.02
292	Karl Malone	.25	.08
293	Delaney Rudd	.05	.01
294	John Stockton	.20	.07
295	Mark Alarie	.05	.01
296	Ledell Eackles SP	.10	.02
297	Harvey Grant	.05	.01
298A	Tom Hammonds RC w/o	.05	.01
298B	Tom Hammonds RC w/star	.05	.01
299	Charles Jones	.05	.01
300	Bernard King	.10	.02
301	Jeff Malone SP	.10	.02
302	Mel Turpin SP	.10	.02
303	Darrell Walker	.05	.01
304	John Williams	.05	.01
305	Bob Weiss CO	.05	.01
306	Chris Ford CO	.05	.01
307	Gene Littles CO	.05	.01
308	Phil Jackson CO	.15	.05
309	Lenny Wilkens CO	.08	.01
310	Richie Adubato CO	.05	.01
311	Doug Moe CO SP	.10	.02
312	Chuck Daly CO	.08	.01
313	Don Nelson CO	.08	.01
314	Don Chaney CO	.05	.01
315	Dick Versace CO	.05	.01
316	Mike Schuler CO	.05	.01
317	Pat Riley CO SP	.15	.05
318	Ron Rothstein CO	.05	.01
319	Del Harris CO	.05	.01
320	Bill Musselman CO	.05	.01
321	Bill Fitch CO	.05	.01
322	Stu Jackson CO	.05	.01
323	Matt Guokas CO	.05	.01
324	Jim Lynam CO	.05	.01
325	Cotton Fitzsimmons CO	.05	.01
326	Rick Adelman CO	.05	.01
327	Dick Motta CO	.05	.01
328	Larry Brown CO	.08	.01
329	K.C. Jones CO	.05	.01
330	Jerry Sloan CO	.08	.01
331	Wes Unseld CO	.05	.01
332	Checklist 1 SP	.10	.02
333	Checklist 2 SP	.10	.02
334	Checklist 3 SP	.10	.02
335	Checklist 4 SP	.10	.02
336	Danny Ferry SP RC	.25	.08
337	NBA Final Game 1	.15	.05
338	NBA Final Game 2	.15	.05
339	NBA Final Game 3	.15	.05
340	NBA Final Game 4	.08	.01
341A	Pistons Win ERR w/o	.05	.01
341B	Pistons Win COR Sports	.05	.01
342	Pistons Back to Back UER	.05	.01
343	K.C. Jones CO	.05	.01
344	Wes Unseld CO	.05	.01
345	Don Nelson CO	.08	.01
346	Bob Weiss CO	.05	.01
347	Chris Ford CO	.05	.01
348	Phil Jackson CO	.15	.05
349	Lenny Wilkens CO	.08	.01
350	Don Chaney CO	.05	.01
351	Mike Dunleavy CO	.05	.01
352	Matt Guokas CO	.05	.01
353	Rick Adelman CO	.05	.01
354	Jerry Sloan CO	.08	.01
355	Dominique Wilkins TC	.08	.01
356	Larry Bird TC	.30	.10
357	Rex Chapman TC	.05	.01
358	Michael Jordan TC	1.00	.40
359	Mark Price TC	.05	.01
360	Rolando Blackman TC	.05	.01
361	Michael Adams TC UER	.05	.01
362	Joe Dumars TC	.08	.01
363	Chris Mullin TC	.08	.01
364	Hakeem Olajuwon TC	.15	.05
365	Reggie Miller TC	.15	.05
366	Danny Manning TC	.05	.01
367	Magic Johnson TC	.25	.08
368	Rony Seikaly TC	.05	.01
369	Alvin Robertson TC	.05	.01
370	Pooh Richardson TC	.05	.01
371	Chris Morris TC	.05	.01
372	Patrick Ewing TC	.15	.05
373	Nick Anderson TC	.15	.05
374	Charles Barkley TC	.08	.01
375	Kevin Johnson TC	.08	.01
376	Clyde Drexler TC	.08	.01
377	Wayman Tisdale TC	.05	.01
378	David Robinson TC	.25	.08
378B	David Robinson TC half	.30	.10
379	Xavier McDaniel TC	.05	.01
380	Karl Malone TC	.15	.05
381	Bernard King TC	.05	.01
382	M.Jordan Playground	1.00	.40
383	Karl Malone Legends	.15	.05
384	V.Divac/Marciulionis	.05	.01
385	M.Johnson/M.Jordan	1.00	.40
386	Johnny Newman	.05	.01
387	Dell Curry	.05	.01
388	Patrick Ewing DFO	.08	.01
389	Isiah Thomas DFO	.08	.01
390	Derrick Coleman	.30	.10
391	Gary Payton TC	1.50	.60
392	Chris Jackson RC	.08	.01
393	Dennis Scott RC	.20	.07
394	Kendall Gill RC	.30	.10
395	Felton Spencer RC	.08	.01
396	Lionel Simmons RC	.08	.01
397	Bo Kimble RC	.05	.01
398	Willie Burton RC	.05	.01
399	Rumeal Robinson RC	.05	.01
400	Tyrone Hill RC	.05	.01
401	Tim McCormick	.05	.01
402	Sidney Moncrief	.05	.01
403	Johnny Newman	.05	.01
404	Dennis Hopson	.05	.01
405	Cliff Levingston	.05	.01
406A	Danny Ferry ERR NPO	.10	.02
406B	Danny Ferry COR	.15	.05
407	Alex English	.05	.01
408	Lafayette Lever	.05	.01
409	Rodney McCray	.05	.01
410	Mike Dunleavy CO	.05	.01
411	Orlando Woolridge	.05	.01
412	Joe Wolf	.05	.01
413	Tree Rollins	.05	.01
414	Kenny Smith	.05	.01
415	Sam Perkins	.08	.01
416	Terry Teagle	.05	.01
417	Frank Brickowski	.05	.01
418	Danny Schayes	.05	.01
419	Scott Brooks	.05	.01
420	Reggie Theus	.05	.01
421	Greg Grant	.05	.01
422	Paul Westhead CO	.05	.01
423	Greg Kite	.05	.01
424	Manute Bol	.05	.01
425	Rickey Green	.05	.01
426	Ed Nealy	.05	.01
427	Danny Ainge	.08	.01
428	Bobby Hansen	.05	.01
429	Eric Leckner	.05	.01
430	Rory Sparrow	.05	.01
431	Bill Wennington	.05	.01
432	Paul Pressey	.05	.01
433	David Greenwood	.05	.01
434	Mark McNamara	.05	.01
435	Sidney Green	.05	.01
436	Dave Corzine	.05	.01
437	Jeff Malone	.05	.01
438	Pervis Ellison	.08	.01
439	Checklist 5	.05	.01
440	Checklist 6	.05	.01
NNO	D.Robinson/ART NoStats	1.25	.50
NNO	D.Robinson/ART Stats	5.00	2.50

1991-92 Hoops

PATRICK EWING

#	Player		
	COMPLETE SET (590)	25.00	12.50
	COMPLETE SERIES 1 (330)	10.00	5.00
	COMPLETE SERIES 2 (260)	15.00	7.50
1	John Battle	.05	.01
2	Moses Malone	.25	.08
3	Sidney Moncrief	.05	.01
4	Doc Rivers	.10	.02
5	Rumeal Robinson UER	.05	.01
6	Spud Webb	.10	.02
7	Dominique Wilkins	.25	.08
8	Kevin Willis	.05	.01
9	Larry Bird	1.00	.40
10	Dee Brown FHC	.05	.01
11	Kevin Gamble	.05	.01
12	Joe Kleine	.05	.01
13	Reggie Lewis	.10	.02
14	Kevin McHale	.10	.02
15	Robert Parish	.10	.02
16	Ed Pinckney	.05	.01
17	Brian Shaw	.05	.01
18	Muggsy Bogues	.10	.02
19	Rex Chapman	.10	.02
20	Dell Curry	.05	.01
21	Kendall Gill	.10	.02
22	Mike Gminski	.05	.01
23	Johnny Newman	.05	.01
24	J.R. Reid	.05	.01
25	Kelly Tripucka	.05	.01
26	B.J.Armstrong	.05	.01
27	Bill Cartwright	.05	.01
28	Horace Grant	.10	.02
29	Craig Hodges	.05	.01
30	Michael Jordan	3.00	1.25
31	Stacey King	.05	.01

#	Player		
❏ 32	Cliff Levingston	.05	.01
❏ 33	John Paxson	.05	.01
❏ 34	Scottie Pippen	.75	.30
❏ 35	Chucky Brown	.05	.01
❏ 36	Brad Daugherty	.05	.01
❏ 37	Craig Ehlo	.05	.01
❏ 38	Danny Ferry	.05	.01
❏ 39	Larry Nance	.10	.02
❏ 40	Mark Price	.05	.01
❏ 41	Darnell Valentine	.05	.01
❏ 42	Hot Rod Williams	.05	.01
❏ 43	Rolando Blackman	.05	.01
❏ 44	Brad Davis	.05	.01
❏ 45	James Donaldson	.05	.01
❏ 46	Derek Harper	.10	.02
❏ 47	Fat Lever	.05	.01
❏ 48	Rodney McCray	.05	.01
❏ 49	Roy Tarpley	.05	.01
❏ 50	Herb Williams	.05	.01
❏ 51	Michael Adams	.05	.01
❏ 52	Chris Jackson	.05	.01
❏ 53	Jerome Lane	.05	.01
❏ 54	Todd Lichti	.05	.01
❏ 55	Blair Rasmussen	.05	.01
❏ 56	Reggie Williams	.05	.01
❏ 57	Joe Wolf	.05	.01
❏ 58	Orlando Woolridge	.05	.01
❏ 59	Mark Aguirre	.05	.01
❏ 60	Joe Dumars	.25	.08
❏ 61	James Edwards	.05	.01
❏ 62	Vinnie Johnson	.05	.01
❏ 63	Bill Laimbeer	.10	.02
❏ 64	Dennis Rodman	.50	.20
❏ 65	John Salley	.05	.01
❏ 66	Isiah Thomas	.40	.15
❏ 67	Tim Hardaway	.40	.15
❏ 68	Rod Higgins	.05	.01
❏ 69	Tyrone Hill	.10	.02
❏ 70	Alton Lister	.05	.01
❏ 71	Sarunas Marciulionis	.05	.01
❏ 72	Chris Mullin	.25	.08
❏ 73	Mitch Richmond	.25	.08
❏ 74	Tom Tolbert	.05	.01
❏ 75	Eric(Sleepy) Floyd	.05	.01
❏ 76	Buck Johnson	.05	.01
❏ 77	Vernon Maxwell	.05	.01
❏ 78	Hakeem Olajuwon	.40	.15
❏ 79	Kenny Smith	.05	.01
❏ 80	Larry Smith	.05	.01
❏ 81	Otis Thorpe	.10	.02
❏ 82	David Wood RC	.05	.01
❏ 83	Vern Fleming	.05	.01
❏ 84	Reggie Miller	.25	.08
❏ 85	Chuck Person	.05	.01
❏ 86	Mike Sanders	.05	.01
❏ 87	Detlef Schrempf	.10	.02
❏ 88	Rik Smits	.05	.01
❏ 89	LaSalle Thompson	.05	.01
❏ 90	Micheal Williams	.05	.01
❏ 91	Winston Garland	.05	.01
❏ 92	Gary Grant	.05	.01
❏ 93	Ron Harper	.10	.02
❏ 94	Danny Manning	.10	.02
❏ 95	Jeff Martin	.05	.01
❏ 96	Ken Norman	.05	.01
❏ 97	Olden Polynice	.05	.01
❏ 98	Charles Smith	.05	.01
❏ 99	Vlade Divac	.10	.02
❏ 100	A.C. Green	.10	.02
❏ 101	Magic Johnson	.75	.30
❏ 102	Sam Perkins	.10	.02
❏ 103	Byron Scott	.10	.02
❏ 104	Terry Teagle	.05	.01
❏ 105	Mychal Thompson	.05	.01
❏ 106	James Worthy	.25	.08
❏ 107	Willie Burton	.05	.01
❏ 108	Bimbo Coles FHC	.05	.01
❏ 109	Terry Davis	.05	.01
❏ 110	Sherman Douglas	.05	.01
❏ 111	Kevin Edwards	.05	.01
❏ 112	Alec Kessler	.05	.01
❏ 113	Glen Rice	.25	.08
❏ 114	Rony Seikaly	.05	.01
❏ 115	Frank Brickowski	.05	.01
❏ 116	Dale Ellis	.10	.02
❏ 117	Jay Humphries	.05	.01
❏ 118	Brad Lohaus	.05	.01
❏ 119	Fred Roberts	.05	.01
❏ 120	Alvin Robertson	.05	.01
❏ 121	Danny Schayes	.05	.01
❏ 122	Jack Sikma	.05	.01
❏ 123	Randy Breuer	.05	.01
❏ 124	Tony Campbell	.05	.01
❏ 125	Tyrone Corbin	.05	.01
❏ 126	Gerald Glass	.05	.01
❏ 127	Sam Mitchell	.05	.01
❏ 128	Tod Murphy	.05	.01
❏ 129	Pooh Richardson	.05	.01
❏ 130	Felton Spencer	.05	.01
❏ 131	Mookie Blaylock	.10	.02
❏ 132	Sam Bowie	.05	.01
❏ 133	Jud Buechler	.05	.01
❏ 134	Derrick Coleman	.10	.02
❏ 135	Chris Dudley	.05	.01
❏ 136	Chris Morris	.05	.01
❏ 137	Drazen Petrovic	.10	.02
❏ 138	Reggie Theus	.10	.02
❏ 139	Maurice Cheeks	.05	.01
❏ 140	Patrick Ewing	.25	.08
❏ 141	Mark Jackson	.05	.01
❏ 142	Charles Oakley	.10	.02
❏ 143	Trent Tucker	.05	.01
❏ 144	Kiki Vandeweghe	.05	.01
❏ 145	Kenny Walker	.05	.01
❏ 146	Gerald Wilkins	.05	.01
❏ 147	Nick Anderson	.10	.02
❏ 148	Michael Ansley	.05	.01
❏ 149	Terry Catledge	.05	.01
❏ 150	Jerry Reynolds	.05	.01
❏ 151	Dennis Scott	.10	.02
❏ 152	Scott Skiles	.05	.01
❏ 153	Otis Smith	.05	.01
❏ 154	Sam Vincent	.05	.01
❏ 155	Ron Anderson	.05	.01
❏ 156	Charles Barkley	.40	.15
❏ 157	Manute Bol	.05	.01
❏ 158	Johnny Dawkins	.05	.01
❏ 159	Armon Gilliam	.05	.01
❏ 160	Rickey Green	.05	.01
❏ 161	Hersey Hawkins	.10	.02
❏ 162	Rick Mahorn	.05	.01
❏ 163	Tom Chambers	.05	.01
❏ 164	Jeff Hornacek	.10	.02
❏ 165	Kevin Johnson	.25	.08
❏ 166	Andrew Lang	.05	.01
❏ 167	Dan Majerle	.10	.02
❏ 168	Xavier McDaniel	.05	.01
❏ 169	Kurt Rambis	.05	.01
❏ 170	Mark West	.05	.01
❏ 171	Danny Ainge	.10	.02
❏ 172	Mark Bryant	.05	.01
❏ 173	Walter Davis	.05	.01
❏ 174	Clyde Drexler	.25	.08
❏ 175	Kevin Duckworth	.05	.01
❏ 176	Jerome Kersey	.05	.01
❏ 177	Terry Porter	.05	.01
❏ 178	Clifford Robinson	.10	.02
❏ 179	Buck Williams	.05	.01
❏ 180	Anthony Bonner	.05	.01
❏ 181	Antoine Carr	.05	.01
❏ 182	Duane Causwell	.05	.01
❏ 183	Bobby Hansen	.05	.01
❏ 184	Travis Mays	.05	.01
❏ 185	Lionel Simmons	.05	.01
❏ 186	Rory Sparrow	.05	.01
❏ 187	Wayman Tisdale	.05	.01
❏ 188	Willie Anderson	.05	.01
❏ 189	Terry Cummings	.05	.01
❏ 190	Sean Elliott	.10	.02
❏ 191	Sidney Green	.05	.01
❏ 192	David Greenwood	.05	.01
❏ 193	Paul Pressey	.05	.01
❏ 194	David Robinson	.50	.20
❏ 195	Dwayne Schintzius	.05	.01
❏ 196	Rod Strickland	.25	.08
❏ 197	Benoit Benjamin	.05	.01
❏ 198	Michael Cage	.05	.01
❏ 199	Eddie Johnson	.10	.02
❏ 200	Shawn Kemp	.60	.25
❏ 201	Derrick McKey	.05	.01
❏ 202	Gary Payton	.60	.25
❏ 203	Ricky Pierce	.05	.01
❏ 204	Sedale Threatt	.05	.01
❏ 205	Thurl Bailey	.05	.01
❏ 206	Mike Brown	.05	.01
❏ 207	Mark Eaton	.05	.01
❏ 208	Blue Edwards UER	.05	.01
❏ 209	Darrell Griffith	.05	.01
❏ 210	Jeff Malone	.05	.01
❏ 211	Karl Malone	.40	.15
❏ 212	John Stockton	.25	.08
❏ 213	Ledell Eackles	.05	.01
❏ 214	Pervis Ellison	.05	.01
❏ 215	A.J. English	.05	.01
❏ 216	Harvey Grant	.05	.01
❏ 217	Charles Jones	.05	.01
❏ 218	Bernard King	.05	.01
❏ 219	Darrell Walker	.05	.01
❏ 220	John Williams	.05	.01
❏ 221	Bob Weiss CO	.05	.01
❏ 222	Chris Ford CO	.05	.01
❏ 223	Gene Littles CO	.05	.01
❏ 224	Phil Jackson CO	.10	.02
❏ 225	Lenny Wilkens CO	.10	.02
❏ 226	Richie Adubato CO	.05	.01
❏ 227	Paul Westhead CO	.05	.01
❏ 228	Chuck Daly CO	.10	.02
❏ 229	Don Nelson CO	.10	.02
❏ 230	Don Chaney CO	.05	.01
❏ 231	Bob Hill RC CO	.05	.01
❏ 232	Mike Schuler CO	.05	.01
❏ 233	Mike Dunleavy CO	.05	.01
❏ 234	Kevin Loughery CO	.05	.01
❏ 235	Del Harris CO	.05	.01
❏ 236	Jimmy Rodgers CO	.05	.01
❏ 237	Bill Fitch CO	.05	.01
❏ 238	Pat Riley CO	.10	.02
❏ 239	Matt Guokas CO	.05	.01
❏ 240	Jim Lynam CO	.05	.01
❏ 241	Cotton Fitzsimmons CO	.05	.01
❏ 242	Rick Adelman CO	.05	.01
❏ 243	Dick Motta CO	.05	.01
❏ 244	Larry Brown CO	.05	.01
❏ 245	K.C. Jones CO	.10	.02
❏ 246	Jerry Sloan CO	.10	.02
❏ 247	Wes Unseld CO	.10	.02
❏ 248	Charles Barkley AS	.25	.08
❏ 249	Brad Daugherty AS	.05	.01
❏ 250	Joe Dumars AS	.10	.02
❏ 251	Patrick Ewing AS	.10	.02
❏ 252	Hersey Hawkins AS	.05	.01
❏ 253	Michael Jordan AS	1.50	.60
❏ 254	Bernard King AS	.05	.01
❏ 255	Kevin McHale AS	.05	.01
❏ 256	Robert Parish AS	.05	.01
❏ 257	Ricky Pierce AS	.05	.01
❏ 258	Alvin Robertson AS	.05	.01
❏ 259	Dominique Wilkins AS	.10	.02
❏ 260	Chris Ford CO AS	.05	.01
❏ 261	Tom Chambers AS	.05	.01
❏ 262	Clyde Drexler AS	.10	.02
❏ 263	Kevin Duckworth AS	.05	.01
❏ 264	Tim Hardaway AS	.25	.08
❏ 265	Kevin Johnson AS	.10	.02
❏ 266	Magic Johnson AS	.40	.15
❏ 267	Karl Malone AS	.25	.08
❏ 268	Chris Mullin AS	.10	.02
❏ 269	Terry Porter AS	.05	.01
❏ 270	David Robinson AS	.25	.08
❏ 271	John Stockton AS	.10	.02
❏ 272	James Worthy AS	.10	.02
❏ 273	Rick Adelman CO AS	.05	.01
❏ 274	Atlanta Hawks	.05	.01
❏ 275	Boston Celtics	.05	.01
❏ 276	Charlotte Hornets	.05	.01
❏ 277	Chicago Bulls	.05	.01
❏ 278	Cleveland Cavaliers	.05	.01
❏ 279	Dallas Mavericks	.05	.01
❏ 280	Denver Nuggets	.05	.01
❏ 281	Detroit Pistons	.05	.01
❏ 282	Golden State Warriors	.05	.01
❏ 283	Houston Rockets	.05	.01
❏ 284	Indiana Pacers	.05	.01
❏ 285	Los Angeles Clippers	.05	.01
❏ 286	Los Angeles Lakers	.05	.01
❏ 287	Miami Heat	.05	.01
❏ 288	Milwaukee Bucks	.05	.01
❏ 289	Minnesota Timberwolves	.05	.01

#	Player	Price 1	Price 2
290	New Jersey Nets	.05	.01
291	New York Knicks	.05	.01
292	Orlando Magic	.05	.01
293	Philadelphia 76ers	.05	.01
294	Phoenix Suns	.05	.01
295	Portland Trail Blazers	.05	.01
296	Sacramento Kings	.05	.01
297	San Antonio Spurs	.05	.01
298	Seattle Supersonics	.05	.01
299	Utah Jazz	.05	.01
300	Washington Bullets	.05	.01
301	Centennial Lord	.05	.01
302	Kevin Johnson IS	.10	.02
303	Reggie Miller IS	.10	.02
304	Hakeem Olajuwon IS	.25	.08
305	Robert Parish IS	.05	.01
306	M.Jordan/K.Malone LL	1.00	.40
307	3-Point FG Percent	.05	.01
308	R.Miller/J.Malone LL	.10	.02
309	Olajuwon/D.Robinson LL	.25	.08
310	Steals League Leaders	.05	.01
311	D.Robinson/Rodman LL	.50	.20
312	J.Stockton/M.Johnson LL	.10	.02
313	Field Goal Percent	.10	.02
314	Larry Bird MS	.50	.20
315	A.English/M.Malone	.10	.02
316	Magic Johnson MS	.40	.15
317	Michael Jordan MS	1.50	.60
318	Moses Malone	.10	.02
319	Larry Bird YB	.50	.20
320	Maurice Cheeks	.05	.01
321	Magic Johnson YB	.40	.15
322	Bernard King	.05	.01
323	Moses Malone	.10	.02
324	Robert Parish	.05	.01
325	All-Star Jam	.10	.02
326	All-Star Jam	.10	.02
327	David Robinson DON'T	.25	.08
328	Checklist 1	.05	.01
329	Checklist 2 UER	.05	.01
330	Checklist 3 UER	.05	.01
331	Maurice Cheeks	.05	.01
332	Duane Ferrell	.05	.01
333	Jon Koncak	.05	.01
334	Gary Leonard	.05	.01
335	Travis Mays	.05	.01
336	Blair Rasmussen	.05	.01
337	Alexander Volkov	.05	.01
338	John Bagley	.05	.01
339	Rickey Green UER	.05	.01
340	Derek Smith	.05	.01
341	Stojko Vrankovic	.05	.01
342	Anthony Frederick RC	.05	.01
343	Kenny Gattison	.05	.01
344	Eric Leckner	.05	.01
345	Will Perdue	.05	.01
346	Scott Williams RC	.05	.01
347	John Battle	.05	.01
348	Winston Bennett	.05	.01
349	Henry James	.05	.01
350	Steve Kerr	.10	.02
351	John Morton	.05	.01
352	Terry Davis	.05	.01
353	Randy White	.05	.01
354	Greg Anderson	.05	.01
355	Anthony Cook	.05	.01
356	Walter Davis	.05	.01
357	Winston Garland	.05	.01
358	Scott Hastings	.05	.01
359	Marcus Liberty	.05	.01
360	William Bedford	.05	.01
361	Lance Blanks	.05	.01
362	Brad Sellers	.05	.01
363	Darrell Walker	.05	.01
364	Orlando Woolridge	.05	.01
365	Vincent Askew RC	.05	.01
366	Mario Elie RC	.25	.08
367	Jim Petersen	.05	.01
368	Matt Bullard RC	.05	.01
369	Gerald Henderson	.05	.01
370	Dave Jamerson	.05	.01
371	Tree Rollins	.05	.01
372	Greg Dreiling	.05	.01
373	George McCloud	.05	.01
374	Kenny Williams	.05	.01
375	Randy Wittman	.05	.01
376	Tony Brown	.05	.01
377	Lanard Copeland	.05	.01
378	James Edwards	.05	.01
379	Bo Kimble	.05	.01
380	Doc Rivers	.10	.02
381	Loy Vaught	.05	.01
382	Elden Campbell FHC	.25	.08
383	Jack Haley	.05	.01
384	Tony Smith	.05	.01
385	Sedale Threatt	.05	.01
386	Keith Askins RC	.05	.01
387	Grant Long	.05	.01
388	Alan Ogg	.05	.01
389	Jon Sundvold	.05	.01
390	Lester Conner	.05	.01
391	Jeff Grayer	.05	.01
392	Steve Henson	.05	.01
393	Larry Krystkowiak	.05	.01
394	Moses Malone	.25	.08
395	Scott Brooks	.05	.01
396	Tellis Frank	.05	.01
397	Doug West	.05	.01
398	Rafael Addison RC	.05	.01
399	Dave Feitl RC	.05	.01
400	Tate George	.05	.01
401	Terry Mills RC	.25	.08
402	Tim McCormick	.05	.01
403	Xavier McDaniel	.05	.01
404	Anthony Mason RC	.50	.20
405	Brian Quinnett	.05	.01
406	John Starks RC	.25	.08
407	Mark Acres	.05	.01
408	Greg Kite	.05	.01
409	Jeff Turner	.05	.01
410	Morlon Wiley	.05	.01
411	Dave Hoppen	.05	.01
412	Brian Oliver	.05	.01
413	Kenny Payne	.05	.01
414	Charles Shackleford	.05	.01
415	Mitchell Wiggins	.05	.01
416	Jayson Williams	.25	.08
417	Cedric Ceballos	.10	.02
418	Negele Knight FHC	.05	.01
419	Andrew Lang	.05	.01
420	Jerrod Mustaf	.05	.01
421	Ed Nealy	.05	.01
422	Tim Perry	.05	.01
423	Alaa Abdelnaby	.05	.01
424	Wayne Cooper	.05	.01
425	Danny Young	.05	.01
426	Dennis Hopson	.05	.01
427	Les Jepsen	.05	.01
428	Jim Les RC	.05	.01
429	Mitch Richmond	.25	.08
430	Dwayne Schintzius	.05	.01
431	Spud Webb	.10	.02
432	Jud Buechler	.05	.01
433	Antoine Carr	.05	.01
434	Tom Garrick	.05	.01
435	Sean Higgins RC	.05	.01
436	Avery Johnson	.10	.02
437	Tony Massenburg	.05	.01
438	Dana Barros	.05	.01
439	Quintin Dailey	.05	.01
440	Bart Kofoed RC	.05	.01
441	Nate McMillan	.05	.01
442	Delaney Rudd	.05	.01
443	Michael Adams	.05	.01
444	Mark Alarie	.05	.01
445	Greg Foster	.05	.01
446	Tom Hammonds	.05	.01
447	Andre Turner	.05	.01
448	David Wingate	.05	.01
449	Dominique Wilkins SC	.10	.02
450	Kevin Willis SC	.05	.01
451	Larry Bird SC	.50	.20
452	Robert Parish SC	.05	.01
453	Rex Chapman SC	.05	.01
454	Kendall Gill SC	.05	.01
455	Michael Jordan SC	1.50	.60
456	Scottie Pippen SC	.40	.15
457	Brad Daugherty SC	.05	.01
458	Larry Nance SC	.05	.01
459	Rolando Blackman SC	.05	.01
460	Derek Harper SC	.05	.01
461	Chris Jackson SC	.05	.01
462	Todd Lichti SC	.05	.01
463	Joe Dumars SC	.10	.02
464	Isiah Thomas SC	.10	.02
465	Tim Hardaway SC	.25	.08
466	Chris Mullin SC	.10	.02
467	Hakeem Olajuwon SC	.25	.08
468	Otis Thorpe SC	.05	.01
469	Reggie Miller SC	.10	.02
470	Detlef Schrempf SC	.05	.01
471	Ron Harper SC	.05	.01
472	Charles Smith SC	.05	.01
473	Magic Johnson SC	.40	.15
474	James Worthy SC	.10	.02
475	Sherman Douglas SC	.05	.01
476	Rony Seikaly SC	.05	.01
477	Jay Humphries SC	.05	.01
478	Alvin Robertson SC	.05	.01
479	Tyrone Corbin SC	.05	.01
480	Pooh Richardson SC	.05	.01
481	Sam Bowie SC	.05	.01
482	Derrick Coleman SC	.05	.01
483	Patrick Ewing SC	.10	.02
484	Charles Oakley SC	.05	.01
485	Dennis Scott SC	.05	.01
486	Scott Skiles SC	.05	.01
487	Charles Barkley SC	.25	.08
488	Hersey Hawkins SC	.05	.01
489	Tom Chambers SC	.05	.01
490	Kevin Johnson SC	.10	.02
491	Clyde Drexler SC	.10	.02
492	Terry Porter SC	.05	.01
493	Lionel Simmons SC	.05	.01
494	Wayman Tisdale SC	.05	.01
495	Terry Cummings SC	.05	.01
496	David Robinson SC	.25	.08
497	Shawn Kemp SC	.25	.08
498	Ricky Pierce SC	.05	.01
499	Karl Malone SC	.25	.08
500	John Stockton SC	.10	.02
501	Harvey Grant SC	.05	.01
502	Bernard King SC	.05	.01
503	Travis Mays Art	.05	.01
504	Kevin McHale Art	.05	.01
505	Muggsy Bogues Art	.05	.01
506	Scottie Pippen TC	.40	.15
507	Brad Daugherty TC	.05	.01
508	Derek Harper Art	.05	.01
509	Chris Jackson Art	.05	.01
510	Isiah Thomas TC	.10	.02
511	Tim Hardaway TC	.25	.08
512	Otis Thorpe Art	.05	.01
513	Chuck Person Art	.05	.01
514	Ron Harper Art	.05	.01
515	James Worthy Art	.10	.02
516	Sherman Douglas Art	.05	.01
517	Dale Ellis Art	.05	.01
518	Tony Campbell Art	.05	.01
519	Derrick Coleman TC	.05	.01
520	Gerald Wilkins Art	.05	.01
521	Scott Skiles Art	.05	.01
522	Manute Bol Art	.05	.01
523	Tom Chambers Art	.05	.01
524	Terry Porter Art	.05	.01
525	Lionel Simmons TC	.05	.01
526	Sean Elliott TC	.05	.01
527	Shawn Kemp TC	.25	.08
528	John Stockton TC	.10	.02
529	Harvey Grant Art	.05	.01
530	Michael Adams	.05	.01
531	Charles Barkley AL	.25	.08
532	Larry Bird AL	.50	.20
533	Maurice Cheeks	.05	.01
534	Mark Eaton	.05	.01
535	Magic Johnson AL	.40	.15
536	Michael Jordan AL	1.50	.60
537	Moses Malone	.10	.02
538	NBA Finals Game 1	.05	.01
539	S.Pippen/J.Worthy FIN	.25	.08
540	NBA Finals Game 3	.05	.01
541	NBA Finals Game 4	.05	.01
542	Michael Jordan FIN	1.50	.60
543	Michael Jordan FIN	1.50	.60
544	Otis Smith	.05	.01
545	Jeff Turner	.05	.01
546	Larry Johnson RC	1.00	.40
547	Kenny Anderson RC	.50	.20

❏ 548	Billy Owens RC	.25	.08
❏ 549	Dikembe Mutombo RC	1.00	.40
❏ 550	Steve Smith RC	1.00	.40
❏ 551	Doug Smith RC	.05	.01
❏ 552	Luc Longley RC	.25	.08
❏ 553	Mark Macon RC	.05	.01
❏ 554	Stacey Augmon RC	.05	.08
❏ 555	Brian Williams RC	.25	.08
❏ 556	Terrell Brandon RC	.75	.30
❏ 557	Walter Davis	.05	.01
❏ 558	Vern Fleming	.05	.01
❏ 559	Joe Kleine	.05	.01
❏ 560	Jon Koncak	.05	.01
❏ 561	Sam Perkins	.05	.01
❏ 562	Alvin Robertson	.05	.01
❏ 563	Wayman Tisdale	.05	.01
❏ 564	Jeff Turner	.05	.01
❏ 565	Willie Anderson	.05	.01
❏ 566	Stacey Augmon USA	.25	.08
❏ 567	Bimbo Coles	.05	.01
❏ 568	Jeff Grayer	.05	.01
❏ 569	Hersey Hawkins	.05	.01
❏ 570	Dan Majerle USA	.05	.01
❏ 571	Danny Manning USA	.05	.01
❏ 572	J.R. Reid	.05	.01
❏ 573	Mitch Richmond USA	.50	.20
❏ 574	Charles Smith	.05	.01
❏ 575	Charles Barkley USA	.75	.30
❏ 576	Larry Bird USA	2.00	.75
❏ 577	Patrick Ewing USA	.50	.20
❏ 578	Magic Johnson USA	1.50	.60
❏ 579	Michael Jordan USA	6.00	3.00
❏ 580	Karl Malone USA	.75	.30
❏ 581	Chris Mullin USA	.25	.08
❏ 582	Scottie Pippen USA	1.50	.60
❏ 583	David Robinson USA	1.00	.40
❏ 584	John Stockton USA	.50	.20
❏ 585	Chuck Daly CO	.10	.02
❏ 586	Lenny Wilkens CO	.10	.02
❏ 587	P.J.Carlesimo RC USA CO	.05	.01
❏ 588	Mike Krzyzewski USA RC	.40	.15
❏ 589	Checklist Card 1	.05	.01
❏ 590	Checklist Card 2	.05	.01
❏ CC1	Naismith Special	1.00	.40
❏ XX	Head of the Class	20.00	10.00
❏ NNO	Centennial Sendaway Card	.50	.20
❏ NNO	Team USA Title Card	1.00	.40

1992-93 Hoops

❏	COMPLETE SET (490)	35.00	17.50
❏	COMPLETE SERIES 1 (350)	15.00	7.50
❏	COMPLETE SERIES 2 (140)	20.00	10.00
❏	COMMON CARD (1-350)	.05	.01
❏	COMMON CARD (351-490)	.10	.02
	BAR.PLASTIC PRICED UNDER SKYBOX VALUE		
❏ 1	Stacey Augmon	.10	.02
❏ 2	Maurice Cheeks	.05	.01
❏ 3	Duane Ferrell	.05	.01
❏ 4	Paul Graham	.05	.01
❏ 5	Jon Koncak	.05	.01
❏ 6	Blair Rasmussen	.05	.01
❏ 7	Rumeal Robinson	.05	.01
❏ 8	Dominique Wilkins	.25	.08
❏ 9	Kevin Willis	.05	.01
❏ 10	Larry Bird	1.00	.40
❏ 11	Dee Brown	.05	.01
❏ 12	Sherman Douglas	.05	.01
❏ 13	Rick Fox	.10	.02
❏ 14	Kevin Gamble	.05	.01
❏ 15	Reggie Lewis	.10	.02
❏ 16	Kevin McHale	.25	.08
❏ 17	Robert Parish	.10	.02
❏ 18	Ed Pinckney UER	.05	.01
❏ 19	Muggsy Bogues	.10	.02
❏ 20	Dell Curry	.05	.01
❏ 21	Kenny Gattison	.05	.01
❏ 22	Kendall Gill	.10	.02
❏ 23	Mike Gminski	.05	.01
❏ 24	Larry Johnson	.30	.10
❏ 25	Johnny Newman	.05	.01
❏ 26	J.R. Reid	.05	.01
❏ 27	B.J. Armstrong	.05	.01
❏ 28	Bill Cartwright	.05	.01
❏ 29	Horace Grant	.10	.02
❏ 30	Michael Jordan	3.00	1.25
❏ 31	Stacey King	.05	.01
❏ 32	John Paxson	.05	.01
❏ 33	Will Perdue	.05	.01
❏ 34	Scottie Pippen	.75	.30
❏ 35	Scott Williams	.05	.01
❏ 36	John Battle	.05	.01
❏ 37	Terrell Brandon	.25	.08
❏ 38	Brad Daugherty	.05	.01
❏ 39	Craig Ehlo	.05	.01
❏ 40	Danny Ferry	.05	.01
❏ 41	Henry James	.05	.01
❏ 42	Larry Nance	.05	.01
❏ 43	Mark Price	.05	.01
❏ 44	Hot Rod Williams	.05	.01
❏ 45	Rolando Blackman	.05	.01
❏ 46	Terry Davis	.05	.01
❏ 47	Derek Harper	.10	.02
❏ 48	Mike Iuzzolino	.05	.01
❏ 49	Fat Lever	.05	.01
❏ 50	Rodney McCray	.05	.01
❏ 51	Doug Smith	.05	.01
❏ 52	Randy White	.05	.01
❏ 53	Herb Williams	.05	.01
❏ 54	Greg Anderson	.05	.01
❏ 55	Winston Garland	.05	.01
❏ 56	Chris Jackson	.05	.01
❏ 57	Marcus Liberty	.05	.01
❏ 58	Todd Lichti	.05	.01
❏ 59	Mark Macon	.05	.01
❏ 60	Dikembe Mutombo	.30	.10
❏ 61	Reggie Williams	.05	.01
❏ 62	Mark Aguirre	.05	.01
❏ 63	William Bedford	.05	.01
❏ 64	Joe Dumars	.25	.08
❏ 65	Bill Laimbeer	.10	.02
❏ 66	Dennis Rodman	.50	.20
❏ 67	John Salley	.05	.01
❏ 68	Isiah Thomas	.25	.08
❏ 69	Darrell Walker	.05	.01
❏ 70	Orlando Woolridge	.05	.01
❏ 71	Victor Alexander	.05	.01
❏ 72	Mario Elie	.10	.02
❏ 73	Chris Gatling	.05	.01
❏ 74	Tim Hardaway	.30	.10
❏ 75	Tyrone Hill	.05	.01
❏ 76	Alton Lister	.05	.01
❏ 77	Sarunas Marciulionis	.05	.01
❏ 78	Chris Mullin	.25	.08
❏ 79	Billy Owens	.10	.02
❏ 80	Matt Bullard	.05	.01
❏ 81	Sleepy Floyd	.05	.01
❏ 82	Avery Johnson	.05	.01
❏ 83	Buck Johnson	.05	.01
❏ 84	Vernon Maxwell	.05	.01
❏ 85	Hakeem Olajuwon	.40	.15
❏ 86	Kenny Smith	.05	.01
❏ 87	Larry Smith	.05	.01
❏ 88	Otis Thorpe	.10	.02
❏ 89	Dale Davis	.05	.01
❏ 90	Vern Fleming	.05	.01
❏ 91	George McCloud	.05	.01
❏ 92	Reggie Miller	.25	.08
❏ 93	Chuck Person	.05	.01
❏ 94	Detlef Schrempf	.10	.02
❏ 95	Rik Smits	.10	.02
❏ 96	LaSalle Thompson	.05	.01
❏ 97	Micheal Williams	.05	.01
❏ 98	James Edwards	.05	.01
❏ 99	Gary Grant	.05	.01
❏ 100	Ron Harper	.10	.02
❏ 101	Danny Manning	.10	.02
❏ 102	Ken Norman	.05	.01
❏ 103	Olden Polynice	.05	.01
❏ 104	Doc Rivers	.10	.02
❏ 105	Charles Smith	.05	.01
❏ 106	Loy Vaught	.05	.01
❏ 107	Elden Campbell	.10	.02
❏ 108	Vlade Divac	.10	.02
❏ 109	A.C. Green	.10	.02
❏ 110	Sam Perkins	.10	.02
❏ 111	Byron Scott	.10	.02
❏ 112	Tony Smith	.05	.01
❏ 113	Terry Teagle	.05	.01
❏ 114	Sedale Threatt	.05	.01
❏ 115	James Worthy	.25	.08
❏ 116	Willie Burton	.05	.01
❏ 117	Bimbo Coles	.05	.01
❏ 118	Kevin Edwards	.05	.01
❏ 119	Alec Kessler	.05	.01
❏ 120	Grant Long	.05	.01
❏ 121	Glen Rice	.25	.08
❏ 122	Rony Seikaly	.05	.01
❏ 123	Brian Shaw	.05	.01
❏ 124	Steve Smith	.30	.10
❏ 125	Frank Brickowski	.05	.01
❏ 126	Dale Ellis	.05	.01
❏ 127	Jeff Grayer	.05	.01
❏ 128	Jay Humphries	.05	.01
❏ 129	Larry Krystkowiak	.05	.01
❏ 130	Moses Malone	.25	.08
❏ 131	Fred Roberts	.05	.01
❏ 132	Alvin Robertson	.05	.01
❏ 133	Danny Schayes	.05	.01
❏ 134	Thurl Bailey	.05	.01
❏ 135	Scott Brooks	.05	.01
❏ 136	Tony Campbell	.05	.01
❏ 137	Gerald Glass	.05	.01
❏ 138	Luc Longley	.10	.02
❏ 139	Sam Mitchell	.05	.01
❏ 140	Pooh Richardson	.05	.01
❏ 141	Felton Spencer	.05	.01
❏ 142	Doug West	.05	.01
❏ 143	Rafael Addison	.05	.01
❏ 144	Kenny Anderson	.25	.08
❏ 145	Mookie Blaylock	.10	.02
❏ 146	Sam Bowie	.05	.01
❏ 147	Derrick Coleman	.10	.02
❏ 148	Chris Dudley	.05	.01
❏ 149	Terry Mills	.05	.01
❏ 150	Chris Morris	.05	.01
❏ 151	Drazen Petrovic	.05	.01
❏ 152	Greg Anthony	.05	.01
❏ 153	Patrick Ewing	.25	.08
❏ 154	Mark Jackson	.10	.02
❏ 155	Anthony Mason	.25	.08
❏ 156	Xavier McDaniel	.05	.01
❏ 157	Charles Oakley	.10	.02
❏ 158	John Starks	.10	.02
❏ 159	Gerald Wilkins	.05	.01
❏ 160	Nick Anderson	.10	.02
❏ 161	Terry Catledge	.05	.01
❏ 162	Jerry Reynolds	.05	.01
❏ 163	Stanley Roberts	.05	.01
❏ 164	Dennis Scott	.10	.02
❏ 165	Scott Skiles	.05	.01
❏ 166	Jeff Turner	.05	.01
❏ 167	Sam Vincent	.05	.01
❏ 168	Brian Williams	.05	.01
❏ 169	Ron Anderson	.05	.01
❏ 170	Charles Barkley	.40	.15
❏ 171	Manute Bol	.05	.01
❏ 172	Johnny Dawkins	.05	.01
❏ 173	Armon Gilliam	.05	.01
❏ 174	Hersey Hawkins	.10	.02
❏ 175	Brian Oliver	.05	.01
❏ 176	Charles Shackleford	.05	.01
❏ 177	Jayson Williams	.10	.02
❏ 178	Cedric Ceballos	.10	.02
❏ 179	Tom Chambers	.05	.01
❏ 180	Jeff Hornacek	.10	.02
❏ 181	Kevin Johnson	.25	.08
❏ 182	Negele Knight	.05	.01
❏ 183	Andrew Lang	.05	.01
❏ 184	Dan Majerle	.10	.02
❏ 185	Tim Perry	.05	.01

❏ 186	Mark West	.05	.01
❏ 187	Alaa Abdelnaby	.05	.01
❏ 188	Danny Ainge	.10	.02
❏ 189	Clyde Drexler	.25	.08
❏ 190	Kevin Duckworth	.05	.01
❏ 191	Jerome Kersey	.05	.01
❏ 192	Robert Pack	.05	.01
❏ 193	Terry Porter	.05	.01
❏ 194	Cliff Robinson	.10	.02
❏ 195	Buck Williams	.10	.02
❏ 196	Anthony Bonner	.05	.01
❏ 197	Duane Causwell	.05	.01
❏ 198	Pete Chilcutt	.05	.01
❏ 199	Dennis Hopson	.05	.01
❏ 200	Mitch Richmond	.25	.08
❏ 201	Lionel Simmons	.05	.01
❏ 202	Wayman Tisdale	.05	.01
❏ 203	Spud Webb	.10	.02
❏ 204	Willie Anderson	.05	.01
❏ 205	Antoine Carr	.05	.01
❏ 206	Terry Cummings	.10	.02
❏ 207	Sean Elliott	.10	.02
❏ 208	Sidney Green	.05	.01
❏ 209	David Robinson	.40	.15
❏ 210	Rod Strickland	.25	.08
❏ 211	Greg Sutton	.05	.01
❏ 212	Dana Barros	.05	.01
❏ 213	Benoit Benjamin	.05	.01
❏ 214	Michael Cage	.05	.01
❏ 215	Eddie Johnson	.05	.01
❏ 216	Shawn Kemp	.50	.20
❏ 217	Derrick McKey	.05	.01
❏ 218	Nate McMillan	.05	.01
❏ 219	Gary Payton	.50	.20
❏ 220	Ricky Pierce	.05	.01
❏ 221	David Benoit	.05	.01
❏ 222	Mike Brown	.05	.01
❏ 223	Tyrone Corbin	.05	.01
❏ 224	Mark Eaton	.05	.01
❏ 225	Blue Edwards	.05	.01
❏ 226	Jeff Malone	.05	.01
❏ 227	Karl Malone	.40	.15
❏ 228	Eric Murdock	.05	.01
❏ 229	John Stockton	.25	.08
❏ 230	Michael Adams	.05	.01
❏ 231	Rex Chapman	.05	.01
❏ 232	Ledell Eackles	.05	.01
❏ 233	Pervis Ellison	.05	.01
❏ 234	A.J. English	.05	.01
❏ 235	Harvey Grant	.05	.01
❏ 236	Charles Jones	.05	.01
❏ 237	LaBradford Smith	.05	.01
❏ 238	Larry Stewart	.05	.01
❏ 239	Bob Weiss CO	.05	.01
❏ 240	Chris Ford CO	.05	.01
❏ 241	Allan Bristow CO	.05	.01
❏ 242	Phil Jackson CO	.10	.02
❏ 243	Lenny Wilkens CO	.10	.02
❏ 244	Richie Adubato CO	.05	.01
❏ 245	Dan Issel CO	.05	.01
❏ 246	Ron Rothstein CO	.05	.01
❏ 247	Don Nelson CO	.10	.02
❏ 248	Rudy Tomjanovich CO	.10	.02
❏ 249	Bob Hill CO	.05	.01
❏ 250	Larry Brown CO	.10	.02
❏ 251	Randy Pfund RC CO	.05	.01
❏ 252	Kevin Loughery CO	.05	.01
❏ 253	Mike Dunleavy CO	.05	.01
❏ 254	Jimmy Rodgers CO	.05	.01
❏ 255	Chuck Daly CO	.10	.02
❏ 256	Pat Riley CO	.10	.02
❏ 257	Matt Guokas CO	.05	.01
❏ 258	Doug Moe CO	.05	.01
❏ 259	Paul Westphal CO	.10	.02
❏ 260	Rick Adelman CO	.05	.01
❏ 261	Garry St.Jean RC CO	.05	.01
❏ 262	Jerry Tarkanian RC	.05	.01
❏ 263	George Karl CO	.10	.02
❏ 264	Jerry Sloan CO	.10	.02
❏ 265	Wes Unseld CO	.10	.02
❏ 266	Atlanta Hawks	.05	.01
❏ 267	Boston Celtics	.05	.01
❏ 268	Charlotte Hornets	.05	.01
❏ 269	Chicago Bulls	.05	.01
❏ 270	Cleveland Cavaliers	.05	.01
❏ 271	Dallas Mavericks	.05	.01
❏ 272	Denver Nuggets	.05	.01
❏ 273	Detroit Pistons	.05	.01
❏ 274	Golden State Warriors	.05	.01
❏ 275	Houston Rockets	.05	.01
❏ 276	Indiana Pacers	.05	.01
❏ 277	Los Angeles Clippers	.05	.01
❏ 278	Los Angeles Lakers	.05	.01
❏ 279	Miami Heat	.05	.01
❏ 280	Milwaukee Bucks	.05	.01
❏ 281	Minnesota Timberwolves	.05	.01
❏ 282	New Jersey Nets	.05	.01
❏ 283	New York Knicks	.05	.01
❏ 284	Orlando Magic	.05	.01
❏ 285	Philadelphia 76ers	.05	.01
❏ 286	Phoenix Suns	.05	.01
❏ 287	Portland Trail Blazers	.05	.01
❏ 288	Sacramento Kings	.05	.01
❏ 289	San Antonio Spurs	.05	.01
❏ 290	Seattle Supersonics	.05	.01
❏ 291	Utah Jazz	.05	.01
❏ 292	Washington Bullets	.05	.01
❏ 293	Michael Adams AS	.05	.01
❏ 294	Charles Barkley AS	.25	.08
❏ 295	Brad Daugherty AS	.05	.01
❏ 296	Joe Dumars AS	.10	.02
❏ 297	Patrick Ewing AS	.10	.02
❏ 298	Michael Jordan AS	1.50	.60
❏ 299	Reggie Lewis AS	.05	.01
❏ 300	Scottie Pippen AS	.40	.15
❏ 301	Mark Price AS	.05	.01
❏ 302	Dennis Rodman AS	.25	.08
❏ 303	Isiah Thomas AS	.10	.02
❏ 304	Kevin Willis AS	.05	.01
❏ 305	Phil Jackson CO AS	.10	.02
❏ 306	Clyde Drexler AS	.10	.02
❏ 307	Tim Hardaway AS	.25	.08
❏ 308	Jeff Hornacek AS	.05	.01
❏ 309	Magic Johnson AS	.40	.15
❏ 310	Dan Majerle AS	.05	.01
❏ 311	Karl Malone AS	.25	.08
❏ 312	Chris Mullin AS	.10	.02
❏ 313	Dikembe Mutombo AS	.25	.08
❏ 314	Hakeem Olajuwon AS	.25	.08
❏ 315	David Robinson AS	.25	.08
❏ 316	John Stockton AS	.10	.02
❏ 317	Otis Thorpe AS	.05	.01
❏ 318	James Worthy AS	.10	.02
❏ 319	Don Nelson CO AS	.10	.02
❏ 320	M.Jordan/K.Malone LL	1.00	.40
❏ 321	Three-Point Field	.05	.01
❏ 322	M.Price/L.Bird LL	.30	.10
❏ 323	D.Robinson/H.Olajuwon LL	.25	.08
❏ 324	J.Stockton/M.Williams LL	.25	.08
❏ 325	D.Rodman/K.Willis LL	.25	.08
❏ 326	J.Stockton/K.Johnson LL	.25	.08
❏ 327	Field Goal Percent	.05	.01
❏ 328	Magic Moments 1980	.25	.08
❏ 329	Magic Moments 1985	.25	.08
❏ 330	Magic Moments 1987&1988	.25	.08
❏ 331	Magic Numbers	.25	.10
❏ 332	Drazen Petrovic	.05	.01
❏ 333	Patrick Ewing SI	.10	.02
❏ 334	David Robinson STAY	.25	.08
❏ 335	Kevin Johnson STAY	.10	.02
❏ 336	Charles Barkley USA	.25	.08
❏ 337	Larry Bird USA	.50	.20
❏ 338	Clyde Drexler USA	.10	.02
❏ 339	Patrick Ewing USA	.10	.02
❏ 340	Magic Johnson USA	.40	.15
❏ 341	Michael Jordan USA	1.50	.60
❏ 342	Christian Laettner USA RC	.50	.20
❏ 343	Karl Malone USA	.25	.08
❏ 344	Chris Mullin USA	.10	.02
❏ 345	Scottie Pippen USA	.40	.15
❏ 346	David Robinson USA	.25	.08
❏ 347	John Stockton USA	.10	.02
❏ 348	Checklist 1	.05	.01
❏ 349	Checklist 2	.05	.01
❏ 350	Checklist 3	.05	.01
❏ 351	Mookie Blaylock	.20	.07
❏ 352	Adam Keefe RC	.10	.02
❏ 353	Travis Mays	.10	.02
❏ 354	Morlon Wiley	.10	.02
❏ 355	Joe Kleine	.10	.02
❏ 356	Bart Kofoed	.10	.02
❏ 357	Xavier McDaniel	.10	.02
❏ 358	Tony Bennett RC	.10	.02
❏ 359	Tom Hammonds	.10	.02
❏ 360	Kenny Lynch	.10	.02
❏ 361	Alonzo Mourning RC	2.50	1.00
❏ 362	Rodney McCray	.10	.02
❏ 363	Trent Tucker	.10	.02
❏ 364	Corey Williams RC	.10	.02
❏ 365	Steve Kerr	.20	.07
❏ 366	Jerome Lane	.10	.02
❏ 367	Bobby Phills RC	.40	.15
❏ 368	Mike Sanders	.10	.02
❏ 369	Gerald Wilkins	.10	.02
❏ 370	Donald Hodge	.10	.02
❏ 371	Brian Howard RC	.10	.02
❏ 372	Tracy Moore RC	.10	.02
❏ 373	Sean Rooks RC	.10	.02
❏ 374	Kevin Brooks	.10	.02
❏ 375	LaPhonso Ellis RC	.40	.15
❏ 376	Scott Hastings	.10	.02
❏ 377	Robert Pack	.10	.02
❏ 378	Bryant Stith RC	.20	.07
❏ 379	Robert Werdann RC	.10	.02
❏ 380	Lance Blanks	.10	.02
❏ 381	Terry Mills	.10	.02
❏ 382	Isaiah Morris RC	.10	.02
❏ 383	Olden Polynice	.10	.02
❏ 384	Brad Sellers	.10	.02
❏ 385	Jud Buechler	.10	.02
❏ 386	Jeff Grayer	.10	.02
❏ 387	Byron Houston RC	.10	.02
❏ 388	Keith Jennings RC	.10	.02
❏ 389	Latrell Sprewell RC	3.00	1.25
❏ 390	Scott Brooks	.10	.02
❏ 391	Carl Herrera	.10	.02
❏ 392	Robert Horry RC	.40	.15
❏ 393	Tree Rollins	.10	.02
❏ 394	Kennard Winchester	.10	.02
❏ 395	Greg Dreiling	.10	.02
❏ 396	Sean Green	.10	.02
❏ 397	Sam Mitchell	.10	.02
❏ 398	Pooh Richardson	.10	.02
❏ 399	Malik Sealy RC	.20	.07
❏ 400	Kenny Williams	.10	.02
❏ 401	Jaren Jackson RC	.20	.07
❏ 402	Mark Jackson	.20	.07
❏ 403	Stanley Roberts	.10	.02
❏ 404	Elmore Spencer RC	.10	.02
❏ 405	Kiki Vandeweghe	.10	.02
❏ 406	John Williams	.10	.02
❏ 407	Randy Woods RC	.10	.02
❏ 408	Alex Blackwell RC	.10	.02
❏ 409	Duane Cooper RC	.10	.02
❏ 410	Anthony Peeler RC	.20	.07
❏ 411	Keith Askins	.10	.02
❏ 412	Matt Geiger RC	.20	.07
❏ 413	Harold Miner RC	.20	.07
❏ 414	John Salley	.10	.02
❏ 415	Alaa Abdelnaby	.10	.02
❏ 416	Todd Day RC	.10	.02
❏ 417	Blue Edwards	.10	.02
❏ 418	Brad Lohaus	.10	.02
❏ 419	Lee Mayberry RC	.10	.02
❏ 420	Eric Murdock	.10	.02
❏ 421	Christian Laettner RC	.75	.30
❏ 422	Bob McCann RC	.10	.02
❏ 423	Chuck Person	.10	.02
❏ 424	Chris Smith RC	.10	.02
❏ 425	Gundars Vetra RC	.10	.02
❏ 426	Micheal Williams	.10	.02
❏ 427	Chucky Brown	.10	.02
❏ 428	Tate George	.10	.02
❏ 429	Rick Mahorn	.10	.02
❏ 430	Rumeal Robinson	.10	.02
❏ 431	Jayson Williams	.20	.07
❏ 432	Eric Anderson RC	.10	.02
❏ 433	Rolando Blackman	.20	.07
❏ 434	Tony Campbell	.10	.02
❏ 435	Hubert Davis RC	.20	.07
❏ 436	Bo Kimble	.10	.02
❏ 437	Doc Rivers	.20	.07
❏ 438	Charles Smith	.10	.02
❏ 439	Anthony Bowie	.10	.02
❏ 440	Litteral Green RC	.10	.02
❏ 441	Greg Kite	.10	.02
❏ 442	Shaquille O'Neal RC	10.00	4.00
❏ 443	Donald Royal	.10	.02

444	Greg Grant	.10	.02
445	Jeff Hornacek	.20	.07
446	Andrew Lang	.10	.02
447	Kenny Payne	.10	.02
448	Tim Perry	.10	.02
449	C.Weatherspoon RC	.40	.15
450	Danny Ainge	.20	.07
451	Charles Barkley	.60	.25
452	Tim Kempton	.10	.02
453	Oliver Miller RC	.20	.07
454	Mark Bryant	.10	.02
455	Mario Elie	.20	.07
456	Dave Johnson RC	.10	.02
457	Tracy Murray RC	.20	.07
458	Rod Strickland	.40	.15
459	Vincent Askew	.10	.02
460	Randy Brown	.10	.02
461	Marty Conlon	.10	.02
462	Jim Les	.10	.02
463	Walt Williams RC	.40	.15
464	William Bedford	.10	.02
465	Lloyd Daniels RC	.10	.02
466	Vinny Del Negro	.10	.02
467	Dale Ellis	.10	.02
468	Larry Smith	.10	.02
469	David Wood	.10	.02
470	Rich King	.10	.02
471	Isaac Austin RC	.20	.07
472	John Crotty RC	.10	.02
473	Stephen Howard RC	.10	.02
474	Jay Humphries	.10	.02
475	Larry Krystkowiak	.10	.02
476	Tom Gugliotta RC	1.25	.50
477	Buck Johnson	.10	.02
478	Don MacLean RC	.10	.02
479	Doug Overton	.10	.02
480	Brent Price RC w/Mark	.20	.07
481	David Robinson TRV	.40	.15
482	Magic Johnson TRV	.60	.25
483	John Stockton TRV	.20	.07
484	Patrick Ewing TRV	.20	.07
485	D.Rob/Ew/Stock/Mag TRV	.40	.15
486	John Stockton STAY	.20	.07
487	Ahmad Rashad	.20	.07
488	Rookie Checklist	.10	.02
489	Checklist 1	.10	.02
490	Checklist 2	.10	.02
AC1	P.Ewing Art Card	.50	.20
SU1	J.Stockton Game AU	200.00	100.00
SU1	J.Stockton Game	1.50	.60
TR1	M.Jordan/C.Drexler FIN	3.00	1.25
NNO	M.Johnson Comm	1.00	.40
NNO	M.Johnson Comm AU	150.00	75.00
NNO	P.Ewing Game	.50	.20
NNO	P.Ewing Game AU	160.00	80.00

1993-94 Hoops

COMPLETE SET (421)		20.00	10.00
COMPLETE SERIES 1 (300)		12.00	6.00
COMPLETE SERIES 2 (121)		8.00	4.00
BEWARE COUNTERFEIT BIRD/MAGIC AU			
1	Stacey Augmon	.05	.01
2	Mookie Blaylock	.10	.02
3	Duane Ferrell	.05	.01
4	Paul Graham	.05	.01
5	Adam Keefe	.05	.01
6	Blair Rasmussen	.05	.01
7	Dominique Wilkins	.25	.08
8	Kevin Willis	.05	.01
9	Alaa Abdelnaby	.05	.01
10	Dee Brown	.05	.01
11	Sherman Douglas	.05	.01
12	Rick Fox	.05	.01
13	Kevin Gamble	.05	.01
14	Joe Kleine	.05	.01
15	Xavier McDaniel	.05	.01
16	Robert Parish	.10	.02
17	Tony Bennett	.05	.01
18	Muggsy Bogues	.10	.02
19	Dell Curry	.05	.01
20	Kenny Gattison	.05	.01
21	Kendall Gill	.05	.01
22	Larry Johnson	.25	.08
23	Alonzo Mourning	.40	.15
24	Johnny Newman	.05	.01
25	B.J. Armstrong	.05	.01
26	Bill Cartwright	.05	.01
27	Horace Grant	.10	.02
28	Michael Jordan	3.00	1.25
29	Stacey King	.05	.01
30	John Paxson	.05	.01
31	Will Perdue	.05	.01
32	Scottie Pippen	.75	.30
33	Scott Williams	.05	.01
34	Moses Malone	.25	.08
35	John Battle	.05	.01
36	Terrell Brandon	.10	.02
37	Brad Daugherty	.05	.01
38	Craig Ehlo	.05	.01
39	Danny Ferry	.05	.01
40	Larry Nance	.05	.01
41	Mark Price	.05	.01
42	Gerald Wilkins	.05	.01
43	John Williams	.05	.01
44	Terry Davis	.05	.01
45	Derek Harper	.10	.02
46	Donald Hodge	.05	.01
47	Mike Iuzzolino	.05	.01
48	Jim Jackson	.10	.02
49	Sean Rooks	.05	.01
50	Doug Smith	.05	.01
51	Randy White	.05	.01
52	Mahmoud Abdul-Rauf	.05	.01
53	LaPhonso Ellis	.05	.01
54	Marcus Liberty	.05	.01
55	Mark Macon	.05	.01
56	Dikembe Mutombo	.25	.08
57	Robert Pack	.05	.01
58	Bryant Stith	.05	.01
59	Reggie Williams	.05	.01
60	Mark Aguirre	.05	.01
61	Joe Dumars	.25	.08
62	Bill Laimbeer	.05	.01
63	Terry Mills	.05	.01
64	Olden Polynice	.05	.01
65	Alvin Robertson	.05	.01
66	Dennis Rodman	.50	.20
67	Isiah Thomas	.25	.08
68	Victor Alexander	.05	.01
69	Tim Hardaway	.25	.08
70	Tyrone Hill	.05	.01
71	Byron Houston	.05	.01
72	Sarunas Marciulionis	.05	.01
73	Chris Mullin	.25	.08
74	Billy Owens	.05	.01
75	Latrell Sprewell	.60	.25
76	Scott Brooks	.05	.01
77	Matt Bullard	.05	.01
78	Carl Herrera	.05	.01
79	Robert Horry	.10	.02
80	Vernon Maxwell	.05	.01
81	Hakeem Olajuwon	.40	.15
82	Kenny Smith	.05	.01
83	Otis Thorpe	.10	.02
84	Dale Davis	.05	.01
85	Vern Fleming	.05	.01
86	George McCloud	.05	.01
87	Reggie Miller	.25	.08
88	Sam Mitchell	.05	.01
89	Pooh Richardson	.05	.01
90	Detlef Schrempf	.10	.02
91	Malik Sealy	.05	.01
92	Rik Smits	.10	.02
93	Gary Grant	.05	.01
94	Ron Harper	.10	.02
95	Mark Jackson	.10	.02
96	Danny Manning	.10	.02
97	Ken Norman	.05	.01
98	Stanley Roberts	.05	.01
99	Elmore Spencer	.05	.01
100	Loy Vaught	.05	.01
101	John Williams	.05	.01
102	Randy Woods	.05	.01
103	Benoit Benjamin	.05	.01
104	Elden Campbell	.05	.01
105	Doug Christie	.10	.02
106	Vlade Divac	.10	.02
107	Anthony Peeler	.05	.01
108	Tony Smith	.05	.01
109	Sedale Threatt	.05	.01
110	James Worthy	.25	.08
111	Bimbo Coles	.05	.01
112	Grant Long	.05	.01
113	Harold Miner	.05	.01
114	Glen Rice	.10	.02
115	John Salley	.05	.01
116	Rony Seikaly	.05	.01
117	Brian Shaw	.05	.01
118	Steve Smith	.25	.08
119	Anthony Avent	.05	.01
120	Jon Barry	.05	.01
121	Frank Brickowski	.05	.01
122	Todd Day	.05	.01
123	Blue Edwards	.05	.01
124	Brad Lohaus	.05	.01
125	Lee Mayberry	.05	.01
126	Eric Murdock	.05	.01
127	Derek Strong RC	.05	.01
128	Thurl Bailey	.05	.01
129	Christian Laettner	.10	.02
130	Luc Longley	.10	.02
131	Marlon Maxey	.05	.01
132	Chuck Person	.05	.01
133	Chris Smith	.05	.01
134	Doug West	.05	.01
135	Micheal Williams	.05	.01
136	Rafael Addison	.05	.01
137	Kenny Anderson	.10	.02
138	Sam Bowie	.05	.01
139	Chucky Brown	.05	.01
140	Derrick Coleman	.10	.02
141	Chris Morris	.05	.01
142	Rumeal Robinson	.05	.01
143	Greg Anthony	.05	.01
144	Rolando Blackman	.05	.01
145	Hubert Davis	.05	.01
146	Patrick Ewing	.25	.08
147	Anthony Mason	.10	.02
148	Charles Oakley	.05	.01
149	Doc Rivers	.10	.02
150	Charles Smith	.05	.01
151	John Starks	.10	.02
152	Nick Anderson	.10	.02
153	Anthony Bowie	.05	.01
154	Litterial Green	.05	.01
155	Shaquille O'Neal	1.25	.50
156	Donald Royal	.05	.01
157	Dennis Scott	.05	.01
158	Scott Skiles	.05	.01
159	Tom Tolbert	.05	.01
160	Jeff Turner	.05	.01
161	Ron Anderson	.05	.01
162	Johnny Dawkins	.05	.01
163	Hersey Hawkins	.10	.02
164	Jeff Hornacek	.10	.02
165	Andrew Lang	.05	.01
166	Tim Perry	.05	.01
167	Clarence Weatherspoon	.05	.01
168	Danny Ainge	.10	.02
169	Charles Barkley	.40	.15
170	Cedric Ceballos	.05	.01
171	Richard Dumas	.05	.01
172	Kevin Johnson	.10	.02
173	Dan Majerle	.10	.02
174	Oliver Miller	.05	.01
175	Mark West	.05	.01
176	Clyde Drexler	.25	.08
177	Kevin Duckworth	.05	.01
178	Mario Elie	.05	.01
179	Dave Johnson	.05	.01

#	Player		
180	Jerome Kersey	.05	.01
181	Tracy Murray	.05	.01
182	Terry Porter	.05	.01
183	Cliff Robinson	.10	.02
184	Rod Strickland	.10	.02
185	Buck Williams	.05	.01
186	Anthony Bonner	.05	.01
187	Randy Brown	.05	.01
188	Duane Causwell	.05	.01
189	Pete Chilcutt	.05	.01
190	Mitch Richmond	.25	.08
191	Lionel Simmons	.05	.01
192	Wayman Tisdale	.05	.01
193	Spud Webb	.10	.02
194	Walt Williams	.05	.01
195	Willie Anderson	.05	.01
196	Antoine Carr	.05	.01
197	Terry Cummings	.05	.01
198	Lloyd Daniels	.05	.01
199	Sean Elliott	.10	.02
200	Dale Ellis	.05	.01
201	Avery Johnson	.05	.01
202	J.R. Reid	.05	.01
203	David Robinson	.40	.15
204	Dana Barros	.05	.01
205	Michael Cage	.05	.01
206	Eddie Johnson	.05	.01
207	Shawn Kemp	.40	.15
208	Derrick McKey	.05	.01
209	Nate McMillan	.05	.01
210	Gary Payton	.40	.15
211	Sam Perkins	.10	.02
212	Ricky Pierce	.05	.01
213	David Benoit	.05	.01
214	Tyrone Corbin	.05	.01
215	Mark Eaton	.05	.01
216	Jay Humphries	.05	.01
217	Jeff Malone	.05	.01
218	Karl Malone	.40	.15
219	John Stockton	.25	.08
220	Michael Adams	.05	.01
221	Rex Chapman	.05	.01
222	Pervis Ellison	.05	.01
223	Harvey Grant	.05	.01
224	Tom Gugliotta	.25	.08
225	Don MacLean	.05	.01
226	Doug Overton	.05	.01
227	Brent Price	.05	.01
228	LaBradford Smith	.05	.01
229	Larry Stewart	.05	.01
230	Lenny Wilkens CO	.10	.02
231	Chris Ford CO	.05	.01
232	Allan Bristow CO	.05	.01
233	Phil Jackson CO	.10	.02
234	Mike Fratello CO	.10	.02
235	Quinn Buckner CO	.05	.01
236	Dan Issel CO	.05	.01
237	Don Chaney CO	.05	.01
238	Don Nelson CO	.10	.02
239	Rudy Tomjanovich CO	.10	.02
240	Larry Brown CO	.05	.01
241	Bob Weiss CO	.05	.01
242	Randy Pfund CO	.05	.01
243	Kevin Loughery CO	.05	.01
244	Mike Dunleavy CO	.05	.01
245	Sidney Lowe CO	.05	.01
246	Chuck Daly CO	.10	.02
247	Pat Riley CO	.10	.02
248	Brian Hill CO	.05	.01
249	Fred Carter CO	.05	.01
250	Paul Westphal CO	.05	.01
251	Rick Adelman CO	.05	.01
252	Garry St. Jean CO	.05	.01
253	John Lucas CO	.05	.01
254	George Karl CO	.10	.02
255	Jerry Sloan CO	.10	.02
256	Wes Unseld CO	.05	.01
257	Michael Jordan AS	1.50	.60
258	Isiah Thomas AS	.10	.02
259	Scottie Pippen AS	.40	.15
260	Larry Johnson AS	.10	.02
261	Dominique Wilkins AS	.10	.02
262	Joe Dumars AS	.10	.02
263	Mark Price AS	.05	.01
264	Shaquille O'Neal AS	.50	.20
265	Patrick Ewing AS	.10	.02
266	Larry Nance AS	.05	.01
267	Detlef Schrempf AS	.05	.01
268	Brad Daugherty AS	.05	.01
269	Charles Barkley AS	.25	.08
270	Clyde Drexler AS	.10	.02
271	Sean Elliott AS	.05	.01
272	Tim Hardaway AS	.10	.02
273	Shawn Kemp AS	.25	.08
274	Dan Majerle AS	.05	.01
275	Karl Malone AS	.25	.08
276	Danny Manning AS	.05	.01
277	Hakeem Olajuwon AS	.25	.08
278	Terry Porter AS	.05	.01
279	David Robinson AS	.25	.08
280	John Stockton AS	.10	.02
281	East Team Photo	.05	.01
282	West Team Photo	.05	.01
283	Jordan/Wilkins/Malone LL	.75	.30
284	Rodman/O'Neal/Mut. LL	.50	.20
285	Field Goal Percentage	.05	.01
286	Stock./Hardaway/Skiles LL	.10	.02
287	Price/A-Rauf/L.Johnson LL	.05	.01
288	3-point FG Percentage	.05	.01
289	Jordan/Blaylock/Stock. LL	.75	.30
290	Olajuwon/O'Neal/Mut. LL	.40	.15
291	D.Robinson BOYS/GIRLS	.10	.02
292	Tribune 1	.05	.01
293	Scottie Pippen TRIB	.40	.15
294	Tribune 3	.05	.01
295	Charles Barkley TRIB	.05	.01
296	Richard Dumas TRIB	.05	.01
297	Tribune 2	.05	.01
298	Checklist 1	.05	.01
299	Checklist 2	.05	.01
300	Checklist 3	.05	.01
301	Craig Ehlo	.05	.01
302	Jon Koncak	.05	.01
303	Andrew Lang	.05	.01
304	Chris Corchiani	.05	.01
305	Acie Earl RC	.05	.01
306	Dino Radja RC	.05	.01
307	Scott Burrell RC	.25	.08
308	Hersey Hawkins	.10	.02
309	Eddie Johnson	.05	.01
310	David Wingate	.05	.01
311	Corie Blount RC	.05	.01
312	Steve Kerr	.10	.02
313	Toni Kukoc RC	1.00	.40
314	Pete Myers	.05	.01
315	Jay Guidinger	.05	.01
316	Tyrone Hill	.05	.01
317	Gerald Madkins RC	.05	.01
318	Chris Mills RC	.25	.08
319	Bobby Phills	.05	.01
320	Lucious Harris RC	.05	.01
321	Popeye Jones RC	.05	.01
322	Fat Lever	.05	.01
323	Jamal Mashburn RC	.60	.30
324	Darren Morningstar RC	.05	.01
325	Kevin Brooks	.05	.01
326	Tom Hammonds	.05	.01
327	Darnell Mee RC	.05	.01
328	Rodney Rogers RC	.25	.08
329	Brian Williams	.05	.01
330	Greg Anderson	.05	.01
331	Sean Elliott	.10	.02
332	Allan Houston RC	1.00	.40
333	Lindsey Hunter RC	.25	.08
334	David Wood UER	.05	.01
335	Jud Buechler	.05	.01
336	Chris Gatling	.05	.01
337	Josh Grant RC	.05	.01
338	Jeff Grayer	.05	.01
339	Keith Jennings	.05	.01
340	Avery Johnson	.05	.01
341	Chris Webber RC	2.50	1.00
342	Sam Cassell RC	1.00	.40
343	Mario Elie	.05	.01
344	Eric Riley RC	.05	.01
345	Antonio Davis RC	.30	.10
347	Gerald Paddio	.05	.01
348	LaSalle Thompson	.05	.01
350	Mark Aguirre	.05	.01
351	Terry Dehere RC	.05	.01
352	Henry James	.05	.01
353	Sam Bowie	.05	.01
354	George Lynch RC	.05	.01
355	Kurt Rambis	.05	.01
356	Nick Van Exel RC	.75	.30
357	Trevor Wilson	.05	.01
358	Keith Askins	.05	.01
359	Manute Bol	.05	.01
360	Willie Burton	.05	.01
361	Matt Geiger	.05	.01
362	Alec Kessler	.05	.01
363	Vin Baker RC	.60	.25
364	Ken Norman	.05	.01
365	Danny Schayes	.05	.01
366	Mike Brown	.05	.01
367	Isaiah Rider RC	.50	.20
368	Benoit Benjamin	.05	.01
369	P.J.Brown RC	.25	.08
370	Kevin Edwards	.05	.01
371	Armon Gilliam	.05	.01
372	Rick Mahorn	.05	.01
373	Dwayne Schintzius	.05	.01
374	Rex Walters RC	.05	.01
375	Jayson Williams	.10	.02
376	Eric Anderson	.05	.01
377	Anthony Bonner	.05	.01
378	Tony Campbell	.05	.01
379	Herb Williams	.05	.01
380	Anfernee Hardaway RC	2.00	.75
381	Greg Kite	.05	.01
382	Larry Krystkowiak	.05	.01
383	Todd Lichti	.05	.01
384	Dana Barros	.05	.01
385	Shawn Bradley RC	.25	.08
386	Greg Graham RC	.05	.01
387	Warren Kidd RC	.05	.01
388	Eric Leckner	.05	.01
389	Moses Malone	.25	.08
390	A.C. Green	.10	.02
391	Frank Johnson	.05	.01
392	Joe Kleine	.05	.01
393	Malcolm Mackey RC	.05	.01
394	Jerrod Mustaf	.05	.01
395	Mark Bryant	.05	.01
396	Chris Dudley	.05	.01
397	Harvey Grant	.05	.01
398	James Robinson RC	.05	.01
399	Reggie Smith	.05	.01
400	Randy Brown	.05	.01
401	Bobby Hurley RC	.10	.02
402	Jim Les	.05	.01
403	Vinny Del Negro	.05	.01
404	Sleepy Floyd	.05	.01
405	Dennis Rodman	.50	.20
406	Chris Whitney RC	.05	.01
407	Vincent Askew	.05	.01
408	Kendall Gill	.10	.02
409	Ervin Johnson RC	.10	.02
410	Rich King	.05	.01
411	Detlef Schrempf	.10	.02
412	Tom Chambers	.05	.01
413	John Crotty	.05	.01
414	Felton Spencer	.05	.01
415	Luther Wright RC	.05	.01
416	Calbert Cheaney RC	.10	.02
417	Kevin Duckworth	.05	.01
418	Gheorghe Muresan RC	.25	.08
419	Checklist 1	.05	.01
420	Checklist 2	.05	.01
421	Rookie Checklist	.05	.01
DR1	D.Robinson Comm	.40	.15
MB1	Magic/Bird Comm	.50	.20
MB1A	Magic/Bird Comm AU	250.00	125.00
NNO	D.Robinson Comm AU	80.00	40.00
NNO	D.Robinson Exp.Vouch.	10.00	5.00
NNO	Magic/Bird Exp.Vouch.	30.00	18.00

1994-95 Hoops

	COMPLETE SET (450)	24.00	12.00
	COMPLETE SERIES 1 (300)	12.00	6.00
	COMPLETE SERIES 2 (150)	12.00	6.00
1	Stacey Augmon	.05	.01
2	Mookie Blaylock	.05	.01
3	Doug Edwards	.05	.01
4	Craig Ehlo	.05	.01

#	Player		
5	Jon Koncak	.05	.01
6	Danny Manning	.10	.02
7	Kevin Willis	.05	.01
8	Dee Brown	.05	.01
9	Sherman Douglas	.05	.01
10	Acie Earl	.05	.01
11	Kevin Gamble	.05	.01
12	Xavier McDaniel	.05	.01
13	Robert Parish	.10	.02
14	Dino Radja	.05	.01
15	Tony Bennett	.05	.01
16	Muggsy Bogues	.10	.02
17	Scott Burrell	.05	.01
18	Dell Curry	.05	.01
19	Hersey Hawkins	.10	.02
20	Eddie Johnson	.05	.01
21	Larry Johnson	.10	.02
22	Alonzo Mourning	.30	.10
23	B.J. Armstrong	.05	.01
24	Corie Blount	.05	.01
25	Bill Cartwright	.05	.01
26	Horace Grant	.10	.02
27	Toni Kukoc	.40	.15
28	Luc Longley	.05	.01
29	Pete Myers	.05	.01
30	Scottie Pippen	.75	.30
31	Scott Williams	.05	.01
32	Terrell Brandon	.10	.02
33	Brad Daugherty	.05	.01
34	Tyrone Hill	.05	.01
35	Chris Mills	.10	.02
36	Larry Nance	.05	.01
37	Bobby Phills	.05	.01
38	Mark Price	.05	.01
39	Gerald Wilkins	.05	.01
40	John Williams	.05	.01
41	Terry Davis	.05	.01
42	Lucious Harris	.05	.01
43	Jim Jackson	.10	.02
44	Popeye Jones	.05	.01
45	Tim Legler	.05	.01
46	Jamal Mashburn	.25	.08
47	Sean Rooks	.05	.01
48	Mahmoud Abdul-Rauf	.05	.01
49	LaPhonso Ellis	.05	.01
50	Dikembe Mutombo	.10	.02
51	Robert Pack	.05	.01
52	Rodney Rogers	.05	.01
53	Bryant Stith	.05	.01
54	Brian Williams	.05	.01
55	Reggie Williams	.05	.01
56	Greg Anderson	.05	.01
57	Joe Dumars	.25	.08
58	Sean Elliott	.10	.02
59	Allan Houston	.40	.15
60	Lindsey Hunter	.10	.02
61	Mark Macon	.05	.01
62	Terry Mills	.05	.01
63	Victor Alexander	.05	.01
64	Chris Gatling	.05	.01
65	Tim Hardaway	.25	.08
66	Avery Johnson	.05	.01
67	Sarunas Marciulionis	.05	.01
68	Chris Mullin	.25	.08
69	Billy Owens	.05	.01
70	Latrell Sprewell	.25	.08
71	Chris Webber	.60	.25
72	Matt Bullard	.05	.01
73	Sam Cassell	.25	.08
74	Mario Elie	.05	.01
75	Carl Herrera	.05	.01
76	Robert Horry	.10	.02
77	Vernon Maxwell	.05	.01
78	Hakeem Olajuwon	.40	.15
79	Kenny Smith	.05	.01
80	Otis Thorpe	.05	.01
81	Antonio Davis	.05	.01
82	Dale Davis	.05	.01
83	Vern Fleming	.05	.01
84	Scott Haskin	.05	.01
85	Derrick McKey	.05	.01
86	Reggie Miller	.25	.08
87	Byron Scott	.10	.02
88	Rik Smits	.05	.01
89	Haywoode Workman	.05	.01
90	Terry Dehere	.05	.01
91	Harold Ellis	.05	.01
92	Gary Grant	.05	.01
93	Ron Harper	.10	.02
94	Mark Jackson	.05	.01
95	Stanley Roberts	.05	.01
96	Loy Vaught	.05	.01
97	Dominique Wilkins	.25	.08
98	Elden Campbell	.05	.01
99	Doug Christie	.10	.02
100	Vlade Divac	.05	.01
101	Reggie Jordan	.05	.01
102	George Lynch	.05	.01
103	Anthony Peeler	.05	.01
104	Sedale Threatt	.05	.01
105	Nick Van Exel	.25	.08
106	James Worthy	.25	.08
107	Bimbo Coles	.05	.01
108	Matt Geiger	.05	.01
109	Grant Long	.05	.01
110	Harold Miner	.05	.01
111	Glen Rice	.10	.02
112	John Salley	.05	.01
113	Rony Seikaly	.05	.01
114	Brian Shaw	.05	.01
115	Steve Smith	.10	.02
116	Vin Baker	.25	.08
117	Jon Barry	.05	.01
118	Todd Day	.05	.01
119	Lee Mayberry	.05	.01
120	Eric Murdock	.05	.01
121	Ken Norman	.05	.01
122	Mike Brown	.05	.01
123	Stacey King	.05	.01
124	Christian Laettner	.10	.02
125	Chuck Person	.10	.02
126	Isaiah Rider	.10	.02
127	Chris Smith	.05	.01
128	Doug West	.05	.01
129	Micheal Williams	.05	.01
130	Kenny Anderson	.10	.02
131	Benoit Benjamin	.05	.01
132	P.J. Brown	.05	.01
133	Derrick Coleman	.10	.02
134	Kevin Edwards	.05	.01
135	Armon Gilliam	.05	.01
136	Chris Morris	.05	.01
137	Rex Walters	.05	.01
138	David Wesley	.05	.01
139	Greg Anthony	.05	.01
140	Anthony Bonner	.05	.01
141	Hubert Davis	.05	.01
142	Patrick Ewing	.25	.08
143	Derek Harper	.05	.01
144	Anthony Mason	.10	.02
145	Charles Oakley	.05	.01
146	Charles Smith	.05	.01
147	John Starks	.05	.01
148	Nick Anderson	.05	.01
149	Anthony Avent	.05	.01
150	Anthony Bowie	.05	.01
151	Anfernee Hardaway	.60	.25
152	Shaquille O'Neal	1.25	.50
153	Donald Royal	.05	.01
154	Dennis Scott	.05	.01
155	Scott Skiles	.05	.01
156	Jeff Turner	.05	.01
157	Dana Barros	.05	.01
158	Shawn Bradley	.05	.01
159	Greg Graham	.05	.01
160	Warren Kidd	.05	.01
161	Eric Leckner	.05	.01
162	Jeff Malone	.05	.01
163	Tim Perry	.05	.01
164	Clarence Weatherspoon	.05	.01
165	Danny Ainge	.05	.01
166	Charles Barkley	.40	.15
167	Cedric Ceballos	.05	.01
168	A.C. Green	.10	.02
169	Kevin Johnson	.10	.02
170	Malcolm Mackey	.05	.01
171	Dan Majerle	.10	.02
172	Oliver Miller	.05	.01
173	Mark West	.05	.01
174	Clyde Drexler	.25	.08
175	Chris Dudley	.05	.01
176	Harvey Grant	.05	.01
177	Tracy Murray	.05	.01
178	Terry Porter	.05	.01
179	Clifford Robinson	.10	.02
180	James Robinson	.05	.01
181	Rod Strickland	.10	.02
182	Buck Williams	.05	.01
183	Duane Causwell	.05	.01
184	Bobby Hurley	.05	.01
185	Olden Polynice	.05	.01
186	Mitch Richmond	.25	.08
187	Lionel Simmons	.05	.01
188	Wayman Tisdale	.05	.01
189	Spud Webb	.05	.01
190	Walt Williams	.05	.01
191	Willie Anderson	.05	.01
192	Lloyd Daniels	.05	.01
193	Vinny Del Negro	.05	.01
194	Dale Ellis	.05	.01
195	J.R. Reid	.05	.01
196	David Robinson	.40	.15
197	Dennis Rodman	.50	.20
198	Kendall Gill	.10	.02
199	Ervin Johnson	.05	.01
200	Shawn Kemp	.40	.15
201	Chris King	.05	.01
202	Nate McMillan	.05	.01
203	Gary Payton	.40	.15
204	Sam Perkins	.10	.02
205	Ricky Pierce	.05	.01
206	Detlef Schrempf	.10	.02
207	David Benoit	.05	.01
208	Tom Chambers	.05	.01
209	Tyrone Corbin	.05	.01
210	Jeff Hornacek	.10	.02
211	Karl Malone	.40	.15
212	Bryon Russell	.05	.01
213	Felton Spencer	.05	.01
214	John Stockton	.25	.08
215	Luther Wright	.05	.01
216	Michael Adams	.05	.01
217	Mitchell Butler	.05	.01
218	Rex Chapman	.05	.01
219	Calbert Cheaney	.05	.01
220	Pervis Ellison	.05	.01
221	Tom Gugliotta	.10	.02
222	Don MacLean	.05	.01
223	Gheorghe Muresan	.05	.01
224	Kenny Anderson AS	.05	.01
225	B.J. Armstrong AS	.05	.01
226	Mookie Blaylock AS	.05	.01
227	Derrick Coleman AS	.05	.01
228	Patrick Ewing AS	.10	.02
229	Horace Grant AS	.05	.01
230	Alonzo Mourning AS	.25	.08
231	Shaquille O'Neal AS	.50	.20
232	Charles Oakley AS	.05	.01
233	Scottie Pippen AS	.40	.15
234	Mark Price AS	.05	.01
235	John Starks AS	.05	.01
236	Dominique Wilkins AS	.10	.02
237	East Team	.05	.01
238	Charles Barkley AS	.25	.08
239	Clyde Drexler AS	.10	.02
240	Kevin Johnson AS	.05	.01
241	Shawn Kemp AS	.25	.08
242	Karl Malone AS	.25	.08
243	Danny Manning AS	.05	.01
244	Hakeem Olajuwon AS	.25	.08

❑ 245	Gary Payton AS	.25	.08
❑ 246	Mitch Richmond AS	.10	.02
❑ 247	Clifford Robinson AS	.05	.01
❑ 248	David Robinson AS	.25	.08
❑ 249	Latrell Sprewell AS	.25	.08
❑ 250	John Stockton AS	.10	.02
❑ 251	West Team	.05	.01
❑ 252	Tracy Murray LL	.05	.01
❑ 253	John Stockton LL	.10	.02
❑ 254	Mutombo/Olaj/D.Rob LL	.25	.08
❑ 255	Mahmoud Abdul-Rauf LL	.05	.01
❑ 256	Rodman/O'Neal/Willis LL	.40	.15
❑ 257	D.Rob/O'Neal/Olaj LL	.40	.15
❑ 258	Nate McMillan LL	.25	.08
❑ 259	Chris Webber AW	.05	.01
❑ 260	Hakeem Olajuwon AW	.25	.08
❑ 261	Hakeem Olajuwon AW	.25	.08
❑ 262	Dell Curry AW	.05	.01
❑ 263	Scottie Pippen AW	.40	.15
❑ 264	Anfernee Hardaway AW	.30	.10
❑ 265	Don MacLean AW	.05	.01
❑ 266	Hakeem Olajuwon FIN	.05	.01
❑ 267	Derek Harper FINALS	.05	.01
❑ 268	Sam Cassell TRIB	.05	.01
❑ 269	Hakeem Olajuwon TRIB	.25	.08
❑ 270	Patrick Ewing TRIB	.10	.02
❑ 271	Carl Herrera FINALS	.05	.01
❑ 272	Vernon Maxwell FINALS	.05	.01
❑ 273	Hakeem Olajuwon FIN	.25	.08
❑ 274	Lenny Wilkens CO	.10	.02
❑ 275	Chris Ford CO	.05	.01
❑ 276	Allan Bristow CO	.05	.01
❑ 277	Phil Jackson CO	.10	.02
❑ 278	Mike Fratello CO	.10	.02
❑ 279	Dick Motta CO	.05	.01
❑ 280	Dan Issel CO	.10	.02
❑ 281	Don Chaney CO	.05	.01
❑ 282	Don Nelson CO	.10	.02
❑ 283	Rudy Tomjanovich CO	.10	.02
❑ 284	Larry Brown CO	.10	.02
❑ 285	Del Harris CO UER	.05	.01
❑ 286	Kevin Loughery CO	.05	.01
❑ 287	Mike Dunleavy CO	.05	.01
❑ 288	Sidney Lowe CO	.05	.01
❑ 289	Pat Riley CO	.10	.02
❑ 290	Brian Hill CO	.05	.01
❑ 291	John Lucas CO	.10	.02
❑ 292	Paul Westphal CO	.05	.01
❑ 293	Garry St. Jean CO	.05	.01
❑ 294	George Karl CO	.10	.02
❑ 295	Jerry Sloan CO	.10	.02
❑ 296	Magic Johnson COMM	.75	.30
❑ 297	Denzel Washington SPEC	.10	.02
❑ 298	Checklist	.05	.01
❑ 299	Checklist	.05	.01
❑ 300	Checklist	.05	.01
❑ 301	Serge Bazarevich	.05	.01
❑ 302	Tyrone Corbin	.05	.01
❑ 303	Grant Long	.05	.01
❑ 304	Ken Norman	.05	.01
❑ 305	Steve Smith	.10	.02
❑ 306	Blue Edwards	.05	.01
❑ 307	Greg Minor RC	.05	.01
❑ 308	Eric Montross RC	.05	.01
❑ 309	Dominique Wilkins	.25	.08
❑ 310	Michael Adams	.05	.01
❑ 311	Darrin Hancock RC	.05	.01
❑ 312	Robert Parish	.10	.02
❑ 313	Ron Harper	.10	.02
❑ 314	Dickey Simpkins RC	.05	.01
❑ 315	Michael Cage	.05	.01
❑ 316	Tony Dumas RC	.05	.01
❑ 317	Jason Kidd RC	3.00	1.25
❑ 318	Roy Tarpley	.05	.01
❑ 319	Dale Ellis	.05	.01
❑ 320	Jalen Rose RC	1.00	.40
❑ 321	Bill Curley RC	.05	.01
❑ 322	Grant Hill RC	1.25	.50
❑ 323	Oliver Miller	.05	.01
❑ 324	Mark West	.05	.01
❑ 325	Tom Gugliotta	.10	.02
❑ 326	Ricky Pierce	.05	.01
❑ 327	Carlos Rogers RC	.05	.01
❑ 328	Clifford Rozier RC	.05	.01
❑ 329	Rony Seikaly	.05	.01
❑ 330	Tim Breaux	.05	.01
❑ 331	Duane Ferrell	.05	.01
❑ 332	Mark Jackson	.05	.01
❑ 333	Lamond Murray RC	.10	.02
❑ 334	Bo Outlaw RC	.05	.01
❑ 335	Eric Piatkowski RC	.05	.01
❑ 336	Pooh Richardson	.05	.01
❑ 337	Malik Sealy	.05	.01
❑ 338	Cedric Ceballos	.05	.01
❑ 339	Eddie Jones RC	1.25	.50
❑ 340	Anthony Miller RC	.05	.01
❑ 341	Kevin Gamble	.05	.01
❑ 342	Benoit Benjamin	.05	.01
❑ 343	Billy Owens	.05	.01
❑ 344	Khalid Reeves RC	.05	.01
❑ 345	Kevin Willis	.05	.01
❑ 346	Eric Mobley RC	.05	.01
❑ 347	Johnny Newman	.05	.01
❑ 348	Ed Pinckney	.05	.01
❑ 349	Glenn Robinson RC	.75	.30
❑ 350	Howard Eisley RC	.05	.01
❑ 351	Donnell Marshall RC	.25	.08
❑ 352	Yinka Dare RC	.05	.01
❑ 353	Charlie Ward RC	.25	.08
❑ 354	Monty Williams RC	.05	.01
❑ 355	Horace Grant	.10	.02
❑ 356	Brian Shaw	.05	.01
❑ 357	Brooks Thompson RC	.05	.01
❑ 358	Derrick Alston RC	.05	.01
❑ 359	B.J.Tyler RC	.05	.01
❑ 360	Scott Williams	.05	.01
❑ 361	Sharone Wright RC	.05	.01
❑ 362	Antonio Lang RC	.05	.01
❑ 363	Danny Manning	.10	.02
❑ 364	Wesley Person RC	.25	.08
❑ 365	Wayman Tisdale	.05	.01
❑ 366	Trevor Ruffin RC	.05	.01
❑ 367	Aaron McKie RC	.50	.20
❑ 368	Brian Grant RC	.60	.25
❑ 369	Michael Smith RC	.05	.01
❑ 370	Sean Elliott	.10	.02
❑ 371	Avery Johnson	.05	.01
❑ 372	Chuck Person	.05	.01
❑ 373	Bill Cartwright	.05	.01
❑ 374	Sarunas Marciulionis	.05	.01
❑ 375	Dontonio Wingfield RC	.05	.01
❑ 376	Antoine Carr	.05	.01
❑ 377	Jamie Watson RC	.05	.01
❑ 378	Juwan Howard RC	.60	.25
❑ 379	Jim McIlvaine RC	.05	.01
❑ 380	Scott Skiles	.05	.01
❑ 381	Anthony Tucker RC	.05	.01
❑ 382	Chris Webber	.60	.25
❑ 383	Bill Fitch CO	.05	.01
❑ 384	Bill Blair CO	.05	.01
❑ 385	Butch Beard CO	.05	.01
❑ 386	P.J. Carlesimo CO	.05	.01
❑ 387	Bob Hill CO	.05	.01
❑ 388	Jim Lynam CO	.05	.01
❑ 389	Checklist 4	.05	.01
❑ 390	Checklist 5	.05	.01
❑ 391	Atlanta Hawks TC	.05	.01
❑ 392	Boston Celtics TC	.05	.01
❑ 393	Charlotte Hornets TC	.05	.01
❑ 394	Chicago Bulls TC	.05	.01
❑ 395	Cleveland Cavaliers TC	.05	.01
❑ 396	Dallas Mavericks TC	.05	.01
❑ 397	Denver Nuggets TC	.05	.01
❑ 398	Detroit Pistons TC	.05	.01
❑ 399	Golden State	.05	.01
❑ 400	Houston Rockets TC	.05	.01
❑ 401	Indiana Pacers TC	.05	.01
❑ 402	Los Angeles Clippers TC	.05	.01
❑ 403	Los Angeles Lakers TC	.05	.01
❑ 404	Miami Heat TC	.05	.01
❑ 405	Milwaukee Bucks TC	.05	.01
❑ 406	Minnesota	.05	.01
❑ 407	New Jersey Nets TC	.05	.01
❑ 408	New York Knicks TC	.05	.01
❑ 409	Orlando Magic TC	.05	.01
❑ 410	Philadelphia 76ers TC	.05	.01
❑ 411	Phoenix Suns TC	.05	.01
❑ 412	Portland Trail	.05	.01
❑ 413	Sacramento Kings TC	.05	.01
❑ 414	San Antonio Spurs TC	.05	.01
❑ 415	Seattle SuperSonics TC	.05	.01
❑ 416	Utah Jazz TC	.05	.01
❑ 417	Washington Bullets TC	.05	.01
❑ 418	Toronto Raptors TC	.05	.01
❑ 419	Vancouver Grizzlies TC	.05	.01
❑ 420	NBA Logo Card	.05	.01
❑ 421	G.Rob/C.Webber TOP	.25	.08
❑ 422	J.Kidd/S.Bradley TOP	.50	.20
❑ 423	G.Hill/A.Hardaway TOP	.50	.20
❑ 424	D.Marshall/J.Mashburn TO	.25	.08
❑ 425	J.Howard/I.Rider TOP	.25	.08
❑ 426	S.Wright/C.Cheaney TOP	.05	.01
❑ 427	L.Murray/B.Hurley TOP	.05	.01
❑ 428	B.Grant/V.Baker TOP	.25	.08
❑ 429	E.Montross/R.Rogers TOP	.05	.01
❑ 430	E.Jones/L.Hunter TOP	.30	.10
❑ 431	Craig Ehlo GM	.05	.01
❑ 432	Dino Radja GM	.05	.01
❑ 433	Toni Kukoc GM	.25	.08
❑ 434	Mark Price GM	.05	.01
❑ 435	Latrell Sprewell GM	.25	.08
❑ 436	Sam Cassell GM	.25	.08
❑ 437	Vernon Maxwell GM	.05	.01
❑ 438	Haywoode Workman GM	.05	.01
❑ 439	Harold Ellis GM	.05	.01
❑ 440	Cedric Ceballos GM	.05	.01
❑ 441	Vlade Divac GM	.05	.01
❑ 442	Nick Van Exel GM	.10	.02
❑ 443	John Starks GM	.05	.01
❑ 444	Scott Williams GM	.05	.01
❑ 445	Clifford Robinson GM	.05	.01
❑ 446	Spud Webb GM	.05	.01
❑ 447	Avery Johnson GM	.05	.01
❑ 448	Dennis Rodman GM	.25	.08
❑ 449	Sarunas Marciulionis GM	.05	.01
❑ 450	Nate McMillan GM	.05	.01
❑ NNO	Shaq Sheet Wrap.Exch. AU	400.00	200.00
❑ NNO	G.Hill Wrapper Exch.	4.00	1.50
❑ NNO	Shaq Sheet Wrap.Exch.	30.00	15.00

1995-96 Hoops

❑	COMPLETE SET (400)	35.00	17.50
❑	COMPLETE SERIES 1 (250)	20.00	10.00
❑	COMPLETE SERIES 2 (150)	15.00	7.50
❑ 1	Stacey Augmon	.15	.05
❑ 2	Mookie Blaylock	.15	.05
❑ 3	Craig Ehlo	.15	.05
❑ 4	Andrew Lang	.15	.05
❑ 5	Grant Long	.15	.05
❑ 6	Ken Norman	.15	.05
❑ 7	Steve Smith	.30	.10
❑ 8	Dee Brown	.15	.05
❑ 9	Sherman Douglas	.15	.05
❑ 10	Pervis Ellison	.15	.05
❑ 11	Eric Montross	.15	.05
❑ 12	Dino Radja	.15	.05
❑ 13	Dominique Wilkins	.50	.20
❑ 14	Muggsy Bogues	.30	.10
❑ 15	Scott Burrell	.15	.05
❑ 16	Dell Curry	.15	.05
❑ 17	Hersey Hawkins	.15	.05
❑ 18	Larry Johnson	.30	.10
❑ 19	Alonzo Mourning	.30	.10
❑ 20	B.J. Armstrong	.15	.05
❑ 21	Michael Jordan	3.00	1.25
❑ 22	Toni Kukoc	.30	.10
❑ 23	Will Perdue	.15	.05
❑ 24	Scottie Pippen	.75	.30
❑ 25	Dickey Simpkins	.15	.05
❑ 26	Terrell Brandon	.30	.10

#	Player		
27	Tyrone Hill	.15	.05
28	Chris Mills	.15	.05
29	Bobby Phills	.15	.05
30	Mark Price	.30	.10
31	John Williams	.15	.05
32	Tony Dumas	.15	.05
33	Jim Jackson	.15	.05
34	Popeye Jones	.15	.05
35	Jason Kidd	1.50	.60
36	Jamal Mashburn	.30	.10
37	Roy Tarpley	.15	.05
38	Mahmoud Abdul-Rauf	.15	.05
39	LaPhonso Ellis	.15	.05
40	Dikembe Mutombo	.30	.10
41	Robert Pack	.15	.05
42	Rodney Rogers	.15	.05
43	Jalen Rose	.60	.25
44	Bryant Stith	.15	.05
45	Joe Dumars	.50	.20
46	Grant Hill	.60	.25
47	Allan Houston	.30	.10
48	Lindsey Hunter	.15	.05
49	Oliver Miller	.15	.05
50	Terry Mills	.15	.05
51	Chris Gatling	.15	.05
52	Tim Hardaway	.30	.10
53	Donyell Marshall	.30	.10
54	Chris Mullin	.50	.20
55	Carlos Rogers	.15	.05
56	Clifford Rozier	.15	.05
57	Rony Seikaly	.15	.05
58	Latrell Sprewell	.50	.20
59	Sam Cassell	.50	.20
60	Clyde Drexler	.50	.20
61	Robert Horry	.30	.10
62	Vernon Maxwell	.50	.20
63	Hakeem Olajuwon	.15	.05
64	Kenny Smith	.15	.05
65	Dale Davis	.15	.05
66	Mark Jackson	.30	.10
67	Derrick McKey	.15	.05
68	Reggie Miller	.50	.20
69	Byron Scott	.15	.05
70	Rik Smits	.30	.10
71	Terry Dehere	.15	.05
72	Lamond Murray	.30	.10
73	Eric Piatkowski	.30	.10
74	Pooh Richardson	.15	.05
75	Malik Sealy	.15	.05
76	Loy Vaught	.15	.05
77	Elden Campbell	.15	.05
78	Cedric Ceballos	.15	.05
79	Vlade Divac	.30	.10
80	Eddie Jones	.60	.25
81	Sedale Threatt	.15	.05
82	Nick Van Exel	.50	.20
83	Bimbo Coles	.15	.05
84	Harold Miner	.15	.05
85	Billy Owens	.15	.05
86	Khalid Reeves	.15	.05
87	Glen Rice	.30	.10
88	Kevin Willis	.30	.10
89	Vin Baker	.30	.10
90	Marty Conlon	.15	.05
91	Todd Day	.15	.05
92	Eric Mobley	.15	.05
93	Eric Murdock	.15	.05
94	Glenn Robinson	.50	.20
95	Winston Garland	.15	.05
96	Tom Gugliotta	.30	.10
97	Christian Laettner	.30	.10
98	Isaiah Rider	.15	.05
99	Sean Rooks	.15	.05
100	Doug West	.15	.05
101	Kenny Anderson	.30	.10
102	Benoit Benjamin	.15	.05
103	Derrick Coleman	.15	.05
104	Kevin Edwards	.15	.05
105	Armon Gilliam	.15	.05
106	Chris Morris	.15	.05
107	Patrick Ewing	.50	.20
108	Derek Harper	.30	.10
109	Anthony Mason	.30	.10
110	Charles Oakley	.15	.05
111	Charles Smith	.15	.05
112	John Starks	.30	.10
113	Monty Williams	.15	.05
114	Nick Anderson	.15	.05
115	Horace Grant	.30	.10
116	Anfernee Hardaway	.50	.20
117	Shaquille O'Neal	1.25	.50
118	Dennis Scott	.15	.05
119	Brian Shaw	.15	.05
120	Dana Barros	.15	.05
121	Shawn Bradley	.15	.05
122	Willie Burton	.15	.05
123	Jeff Malone	.15	.05
124	Clarence Weatherspoon	.15	.05
125	Sharone Wright	.15	.05
126	Charles Barkley	.60	.25
127	A.C. Green	.30	.10
128	Kevin Johnson	.30	.10
129	Dan Majerle	.30	.10
130	Danny Manning	.30	.10
131	Elliot Perry	.15	.05
132	Wesley Person	.15	.05
133	Chris Dudley	.15	.05
134	Clifford Robinson	.15	.05
135	James Robinson	.15	.05
136	Rod Strickland	.15	.05
137	Otis Thorpe	.15	.05
138	Buck Williams	.15	.05
139	Brian Grant	.50	.20
140	Olden Polynice	.15	.05
141	Mitch Richmond	.30	.10
142	Michael Smith	.15	.05
143	Spud Webb	.30	.10
144	Walt Williams	.15	.05
145	Vinny Del Negro	.15	.05
146	Sean Elliott	.30	.10
147	Avery Johnson	.15	.05
148	Chuck Person	.15	.05
149	David Robinson	.50	.20
150	Dennis Rodman	.30	.10
151	Kendall Gill	.15	.05
152	Ervin Johnson	.15	.05
153	Shawn Kemp	.30	.10
154	Nate McMillan	.15	.05
155	Gary Payton	.50	.20
156	Detlef Schrempf	.30	.10
157	Dontonio Wingfield	.15	.05
158	David Benoit	.15	.05
159	Jeff Hornacek	.30	.10
160	Karl Malone	.60	.25
161	Felton Spencer	.15	.05
162	John Stockton	.60	.25
163	Jamie Watson	.15	.05
164	Rex Chapman	.15	.05
165	Calbert Cheaney	.15	.05
166	Juwan Howard	.50	.20
167	Don MacLean	.15	.05
168	Gheorghe Muresan	.15	.05
169	Scott Skiles	.15	.05
170	Chris Webber	.60	.25
171	Lenny Wilkens CO	.30	.10
172	Allan Bristow CO	.15	.05
173	Phil Jackson CO	.30	.10
174	Mike Fratello CO	.30	.10
175	Dick Motta CO	.15	.05
176	Bernie Bickerstaff CO	.15	.05
177	Doug Collins CO	.15	.05
178	Rick Adelman CO	.15	.05
179	Rudy Tomjanovich CO	.30	.10
180	Larry Brown CO	.30	.10
181	Bill Fitch CO	.15	.05
182	Del Harris CO	.15	.05
183	Mike Dunleavy CO	.15	.05
184	Bill Blair CO	.15	.05
185	Butch Beard CO	.15	.05
186	Pat Riley CO	.30	.10
187	Brian Hill CO	.15	.05
188	John Lucas CO	.30	.10
189	Paul Westphal CO	.15	.05
190	P.J. Carlesimo CO	.15	.05
191	Garry St. Jean CO	.15	.05
192	Bob Hill CO	.15	.05
193	George Karl CO	.30	.10
194	Brendan Malone CO	.15	.05
195	Jerry Sloan CO	.15	.05
196	Kevin Pritchard	.15	.05
197	Jim Lynam CO	.15	.05
198	Brian Grant SS	.30	.10
199	Grant Hill SS	.30	.10
200	Juwan Howard SS	.30	.10
201	Eddie Jones SS	.50	.20
202	Jason Kidd SS	.75	.30
203	Donyell Marshall SS	.30	.10
204	Eric Montross SS	.15	.05
205	Glenn Robinson SS	.30	.10
206	Jalen Rose SS	.50	.20
207	Sharone Wright SS	.15	.05
208	Dana Barros MS	.15	.05
209	Joe Dumars MS	.30	.10
210	A.C. Green MS	.15	.05
211	Grant Hill MS	.50	.20
212	Karl Malone MS	.50	.20
213	Reggie Miller MS	.30	.10
214	Glen Rice MS	.15	.05
215	John Stockton MS	.30	.10
216	Lenny Wilkens MS	.30	.10
217	Dominique Wilkins MS	.30	.10
218	Kenny Anderson BB	.15	.05
219	Mookie Blaylock BB	.15	.05
220	Larry Johnson BB	.15	.05
221	Shawn Kemp BB	.15	.05
222	Toni Kukoc BB	.15	.05
223	Jamal Mashburn BB	.15	.05
224	Glen Rice BB	.15	.05
225	Mitch Richmond BB	.15	.05
226	Latrell Sprewell BB	.50	.20
227	Rod Strickland BB	.15	.05
228	Michael Adams PL	.15	.05
229	Craig Ehlo PL	.15	.05
230	Mario Elie PL	.15	.05
231	Anthony Mason PL	.15	.05
232	John Starks PL	.15	.05
233	Muggsy Bogues CA	.15	.05
234	Joe Dumars CA	.30	.10
235	LaPhonso Ellis CA	.15	.05
236	Patrick Ewing CA	.30	.10
237	Grant Hill CA	.50	.20
238	Kevin Johnson CA	.15	.05
239	Dan Majerle CA	.15	.05
240	Karl Malone CA	.30	.10
241	Hakeem Olajuwon CA	.30	.10
242	David Robinson CA	.30	.10
243	Dana Barros TT	.15	.05
244	Scott Burrell TT	.15	.05
245	Reggie Miller TT	.30	.10
246	Glen Rice TT	.15	.05
247	John Stockton TT	.50	.20
248	Checklist #1	.15	.05
249	Checklist #2	.15	.05
250	Checklist #3	.15	.05
251	Alan Henderson RC	.50	.20
252	Junior Burrough RC	.15	.05
253	Eric Williams RC	.30	.10
254	George Zidek RC	.15	.05
255	Jason Caffey RC	.30	.10
256	Donny Marshall RC	.15	.05
257	Bob Sura RC	.30	.10
258	Loren Meyer RC	.15	.05
259	Cherokee Parks RC	.30	.10
260	Antonio McDyess RC	1.00	.40
261	Theo Ratliff RC	.60	.25
262	Lou Roe RC	.15	.05
263	Andrew DeClercq RC	.15	.05
264	Joe Smith RC	.75	.30
265	Travis Best RC	.15	.05
266	Brent Barry RC	.50	.20
267	Frankie King RC	.15	.05
268	Sasha Danilovic RC	.15	.05
269	Kurt Thomas RC	.30	.10
270	Shawn Respert RC	.30	.10
271	Jerome Allen RC	.15	.05
272	Kevin Garnett RC	2.50	1.25
273	Ed O'Bannon RC	.15	.05
274	David Vaughn RC	.15	.05
275	Jerry Stackhouse RC	1.50	.60
276	Mario Bennett RC	.15	.05
277	Michael Finley RC	1.25	.50
278	Randolph Childress RC	.15	.05
279	Arvydas Sabonis RC	.60	.25
280	Gary Trent RC	.15	.05
281	Tyus Edney RC	.15	.05
282	Corliss Williamson RC	.50	.20
283	Cory Alexander RC	.15	.05
284	Sherrell Ford RC	.15	.05

285	Jimmy King RC	.15	.05
286	Damon Stoudamire RC	1.00	.40
287	Greg Ostertag RC	.15	.05
288	Lawrence Moten RC	.15	.05
289	Bryant Reeves RC	.50	.20
290	Rasheed Wallace RC	1.25	.50
291	Spud Webb	.30	.10
292	Dana Barros	.15	.05
293	Rick Fox	.30	.10
294	Kendall Gill	.15	.05
295	Khalid Reeves	.15	.05
296	Glen Rice	.30	.10
297	Luc Longley	.15	.05
298	Dennis Rodman	.30	.10
299	Dan Majerle	.30	.10
300	Lorenzo Williams	.15	.05
301	Dale Ellis	.15	.05
302	Reggie Williams	.15	.05
303	Otis Thorpe	.15	.05
304	B.J. Armstrong	.15	.05
305	Pete Chilcutt	.15	.05
306	Mario Elie	.15	.05
307	Antonio Davis	.15	.05
308	Ricky Pierce	.15	.05
309	Rodney Rogers	.15	.05
310	Brian Williams	.15	.05
311	Corie Blount	.15	.05
312	George Lynch	.15	.05
313	Alonzo Mourning	.30	.10
314	Lee Mayberry	.15	.05
315	Terry Porter	.15	.05
316	P.J. Brown	.15	.05
317	Hubert Davis	.15	.05
318	Charlie Ward	.15	.05
319	Jon Koncak	.15	.05
320	Derrick Coleman	.15	.05
321	Richard Dumas	.15	.05
322	Vernon Maxwell	.15	.05
323	Wayman Tisdale	.15	.05
324	Dontonio Wingfield	.15	.05
325	Tyrone Corbin	.15	.05
326	Bobby Hurley	.15	.05
327	Will Perdue	.15	.05
328	J.R. Reid	.15	.05
329	Hersey Hawkins	.15	.05
330	Sam Perkins	.30	.10
331	Adam Keefe	.15	.05
332	Chris Morris	.15	.05
333	Robert Pack	.15	.05
334	M.L. Carr CO	.15	.05
335	Pat Riley CO	.30	.10
336	Don Nelson CO	.30	.10
337	Brian Winters CO	.15	.05
338	Willie Anderson ET	.15	.05
339	Acie Earl ET	.15	.05
340	Jimmy King ET	.15	.05
341	Oliver Miller ET	.15	.05
342	Tracy Murray ET	.15	.05
343	Ed Pinckney ET	.15	.05
344	Alvin Robertson ET	.15	.05
345	Carlos Rogers ET	.15	.05
346	John Salley ET	.15	.05
347	Damon Stoudamire ET	.60	.25
348	Zan Tabak ET	.15	.05
349	Greg Anthony ET	.15	.05
350	Blue Edwards ET	.15	.05
351	Kenny Gattison ET	.15	.05
352	Antonio Harvey ET	.15	.05
353	Chris King ET	.15	.05
354	Darrick Martin ET	.15	.05
355	Lawrence Moten ET	.15	.05
356	Bryant Reeves ET	.30	.10
357	Byron Scott ET	.15	.05
358	Michael Jordan ES	1.50	.60
359	Dikembe Mutombo ES	.15	.05
360	Grant Hill ES	.30	.10
361	Robert Horry ES	.15	.05
362	Alonzo Mourning ES	.15	.05
363	Vin Baker ES	.15	.05
364	Isaiah Rider ES	.15	.05
365	Charles Oakley ES	.15	.05
366	Shaquille O'Neal ES	.50	.20
367	Jerry Stackhouse ES	.75	.30
368	Clarence Weatherspoon ES	.15	.05
369	Charles Barkley ES	.50	.20
370	Sean Elliott ES	.15	.05
371	Shawn Kemp ES	.15	.05
372	Chris Webber ES	.30	.10
373	Spud Webb RH	.15	.05
374	Muggsy Bogues RH	.15	.05
375	Toni Kukoc RH	.15	.05
376	Dennis Rodman RH	.15	.05
377	Jamal Mashburn RH	.15	.05
378	Jalen Rose RH	.50	.20
379	Clyde Drexler RH	.30	.10
380	Mark Jackson RH	.15	.05
381	Cedric Ceballos RH	.15	.05
382	Nick Van Exel RH	.15	.05
383	John Starks RH	.15	.05
384	Vernon Maxwell RH	.15	.05
385	Shawn Kemp RH	.15	.05
386	Gary Payton RH	.15	.05
387	Karl Malone RH	.50	.20
388	Mookie Blaylock WD	.15	.05
389	Muggsy Bogues WD	.15	.05
390	Jason Kidd WD	.75	.30
391	Tim Hardaway WD	.15	.05
392	Nick Van Exel WD	.15	.05
393	Kenny Anderson WD	.15	.05
394	Anfernee Hardaway WD	.30	.10
395	Rod Strickland WD	.15	.05
396	Avery Johnson WD	.15	.05
397	John Stockton WD	.50	.20
398	Grant Hill SPEC	.50	.20
399	Checklist (251-367)	.15	.05
400	Checklist (368-400/Ins.)	.15	.05
NNO	G.Hill Co-ROY Exch.	12.00	5.00
NNO	G.Hill Sweepstakes	.60	.25
NNO	G.Hill Tribute	25.00	10.00

1996-97 Hoops

COMPLETE SET (350)		30.00	15.00
COMPLETE SERIES 1 (200)		15.00	7.50
COMPLETE SERIES 2 (150)		15.00	7.50
1	Stacey Augmon	.15	.05
2	Mookie Blaylock	.15	.05
3	Alan Henderson	.15	.05
4	Christian Laettner	.30	.10
5	Grant Long	.15	.05
6	Steve Smith	.30	.10
7	Dana Barros	.15	.05
8	Todd Day	.15	.05
9	Rick Fox	.15	.05
10	Eric Montross	.15	.05
11	Dino Radja	.15	.05
12	Eric Williams	.15	.05
13	Kenny Anderson	.15	.05
14	Scott Burrell	.15	.05
15	Dell Curry	.15	.05
16	Matt Geiger	.15	.05
17	Larry Johnson	.30	.10
18	Glen Rice	.30	.10
19	Ron Harper	.30	.10
20	Michael Jordan	3.00	1.25
21	Steve Kerr	.30	.10
22	Toni Kukoc	.30	.10
23	Luc Longley	.15	.05
24	Scottie Pippen	.75	.30
25	Dennis Rodman	.30	.10
26	Terrell Brandon	.30	.10
27	Danny Ferry	.15	.05
28	Tyrone Hill	.15	.05
29	Chris Mills	.15	.05
30	Bobby Phills	.15	.05

31	Bob Sura	.15	.05
32	Tony Dumas	.15	.05
33	Jim Jackson	.15	.05
34	Popeye Jones	.15	.05
35	Jason Kidd	.75	.30
36	Jamal Mashburn	.30	.10
37	George McCloud	.15	.05
38	Cherokee Parks	.15	.05
39	Mahmoud Abdul-Rauf	.15	.05
40	LaPhonso Ellis	.15	.05
41	Antonio McDyess	.30	.10
42	Dikembe Mutombo	.30	.10
43	Jalen Rose	.50	.20
44	Bryant Stith	.15	.05
45	Joe Dumars	.50	.20
46	Grant Hill	.50	.20
47	Allan Houston	.30	.10
48	Lindsey Hunter	.15	.05
49	Terry Mills	.15	.05
50	Theo Ratliff	.30	.10
51	Otis Thorpe	.15	.05
52	B.J. Armstrong	.15	.05
53	Donyell Marshall	.30	.10
54	Chris Mullin	.50	.20
55	Joe Smith	.30	.10
56	Rony Seikaly	.15	.05
57	Latrell Sprewell	.50	.20
58	Mark Bryant	.15	.05
59	Sam Cassell	.50	.20
60	Clyde Drexler	.50	.20
61	Mario Elie	.15	.05
62	Robert Horry	.30	.10
63	Hakeem Olajuwon	.50	.20
64	Travis Best	.15	.05
65	Antonio Davis	.15	.05
66	Mark Jackson	.15	.05
67	Derrick McKey	.15	.05
68	Reggie Miller	.50	.20
69	Rik Smits	.30	.10
70	Brent Barry	.15	.05
71	Terry Dehere	.15	.05
72	Pooh Richardson	.15	.05
73	Rodney Rogers	.15	.05
74	Loy Vaught	.15	.05
75	Brian Williams	.15	.05
76	Elden Campbell	.15	.05
77	Cedric Ceballos	.15	.05
78	Vlade Divac	.15	.05
79	Eddie Jones	.50	.20
80	Anthony Peeler	.15	.05
81	Nick Van Exel	.30	.10
82	Sasha Danilovic	.15	.05
83	Tim Hardaway	.30	.10
84	Alonzo Mourning	.30	.10
85	Kurt Thomas	.15	.05
86	Walt Williams	.15	.05
87	Vin Baker	.30	.10
88	Sherman Douglas	.15	.05
89	Johnny Newman	.15	.05
90	Shawn Respert	.15	.05
91	Glenn Robinson	.50	.20
92	Kevin Garnett	1.00	.40
93	Tom Gugliotta	.15	.05
94	Andrew Lang	.15	.05
95	Sam Mitchell	.15	.05
96	Isaiah Rider	.30	.10
97	Shawn Bradley	.15	.05
98	P.J. Brown	.15	.05
99	Chris Childs	.15	.05
100	Armon Gilliam	.15	.05
101	Ed O'Bannon	.15	.05
102	Jayson Williams	.30	.10
103	Hubert Davis	.15	.05
104	Patrick Ewing	.50	.20
105	Anthony Mason	.30	.10
106	Charles Oakley	.15	.05
107	John Starks	.30	.10
108	Charlie Ward	.15	.05
109	Nick Anderson	.15	.05
110	Horace Grant	.30	.10
111	Anfernee Hardaway	.50	.20
112	Shaquille O'Neal	1.25	.50
113	Dennis Scott	.15	.05
114	Brian Shaw	.15	.05
115	Derrick Coleman	.30	.10
116	Vernon Maxwell	.15	.05

❏ 117	Trevor Ruffin	.15	.05
❏ 118	Jerry Stackhouse	.60	.25
❏ 119	Clarence Weatherspoon	.15	.05
❏ 120	Charles Barkley	.60	.25
❏ 121	Michael Finley	.60	.25
❏ 122	A.C. Green	.30	.10
❏ 123	Kevin Johnson	.30	.10
❏ 124	Danny Manning	.30	.10
❏•125	Wesley Person	.15	.05
❏ 126	John Williams	.15	.05
❏ 127	Harvey Grant	.15	.05
❏ 128	Aaron McKie	.30	.10
❏ 129	Clifford Robinson	.15	.05
❏ 130	Arvydas Sabonis	.30	.10
❏ 131	Rod Strickland	.15	.05
❏ 132	Gary Trent	.15	.05
❏ 133	Tyus Edney	.15	.05
❏ 134	Brian Grant	.50	.20
❏ 135	Billy Owens	.15	.05
❏ 136	Olden Polynice	.15	.05
❏ 137	Mitch Richmond	.30	.10
❏ 138	Corliss Williamson	.30	.10
❏ 139	Vinny Del Negro	.15	.05
❏ 140	Sean Elliott	.30	.10
❏ 141	Avery Johnson	.15	.05
❏ 142	Chuck Person	.15	.05
❏ 143	David Robinson	.50	.20
❏ 144	Charles Smith	.15	.05
❏ 145	Sherrell Ford	.15	.05
❏ 146	Hersey Hawkins	.30	.10
❏ 147	Shawn Kemp	.30	.10
❏ 148	Nate McMillan	.15	.05
❏ 149	Gary Payton	.50	.20
❏ 150	Detlef Schrempf	.30	.10
❏ 151	Oliver Miller	.15	.05
❏ 152	Tracy Murray	.15	.05
❏ 153	Carlos Rogers	.15	.05
❏ 154	Damon Stoudamire	.50	.20
❏ 155	Zan Tabak	.15	.05
❏ 156	Sharone Wright	.15	.05
❏ 157	Antoine Carr	.15	.05
❏ 158	Jeff Hornacek	.30	.10
❏ 159	Adam Keefe	.15	.05
❏ 160	Karl Malone	.50	.20
❏ 161	Chris Morris	.15	.05
❏ 162	John Stockton	.50	.20
❏ 163	Greg Anthony	.15	.05
❏ 164	Blue Edwards	.15	.05
❏ 165	Chris King	.15	.05
❏ 166	Lawrence Moten	.15	.05
❏ 167	Bryant Reeves	.15	.05
❏ 168	Byron Scott	.15	.05
❏ 169	Calbert Cheaney	.15	.05
❏ 170	Juwan Howard	.30	.10
❏ 171	Tim Legler	.15	.05
❏ 172	Gheorghe Muresan	.15	.05
❏ 173	Rasheed Wallace	.60	.25
❏ 174	Chris Webber	.50	.20
❏ 175	Steve Smith BF	.15	.05
❏ 176	Michael Jordan BF	1.50	.60
❏ 177	Scottie Pippen BF	.30	.10
❏ 178	Dennis Rodman BF	.15	.05
❏ 179	Allan Houston BF	.15	.05
❏ 180	Hakeem Olajuwon BF	.30	.10
❏ 181	Patrick Ewing BF	.15	.05
❏ 182	Anfernee Hardaway BF	.30	.10
❏ 183	Shaquille O'Neal BF	.50	.20
❏ 184	Charles Barkley BF	.50	.20
❏ 185	Arvydas Sabonis BF	.15	.05
❏ 186	David Robinson BF	.30	.10
❏ 187	Shawn Kemp BF	.30	.10
❏ 188	Gary Payton BF	.15	.05
❏ 189	Karl Malone BF	.30	.10
❏ 190	Kenny Anderson PLA	.15	.05
❏ 191	Toni Kukoc PLA	.15	.05
❏ 192	Brent Barry PLA	.15	.05
❏ 193	Cedric Ceballos PLA	.15	.05
❏ 194	Shawn Bradley PLA	.15	.05
❏ 195	Charles Oakley PLA	.15	.05
❏ 196	Dennis Scott PLA	.15	.05
❏ 197	Clifford Robinson PLA	.15	.05
❏ 198	Mitch Richmond PLA	.15	.05
❏ 199	Checklist		
❏ 200	Checklist	.15	.05
❏ 201	Dikembe Mutombo	.30	.10
❏ 202	Dee Brown	.15	.05

❏ 203	David Wesley	.15	.05
❏ 204	Vlade Divac	.15	.05
❏ 205	Anthony Mason	.30	.10
❏ 206	Chris Gatling	.15	.05
❏ 207	Eric Montross	.15	.05
❏ 208	Ervin Johnson	.15	.05
❏ 209	Stacey Augmon	.15	.05
❏ 210	Joe Dumars	.50	.20
❏ 211	Grant Hill	.50	.20
❏ 212	Charles Barkley	.60	.25
❏ 213	Jalen Rose	.50	.20
❏ 214	Lamond Murray	.15	.05
❏ 215	Shaquille O'Neal	1.25	.50
❏ 216	P.J. Brown	.15	.05
❏ 217	Dan Majerle	.30	.10
❏ 218	Armon Gilliam	.15	.05
❏ 219	Andrew Lang	.15	.05
❏ 220	Kevin Garnett	1.00	.40
❏ 221	Tom Gugliotta	.30	.10
❏ 222	Cherokee Parks	.15	.05
❏ 223	Doug West	.15	.05
❏ 224	Kendall Gill	.15	.05
❏ 225	Robert Pack	.15	.05
❏ 226	Allan Houston	.30	.10
❏ 227	Larry Johnson	.30	.10
❏ 228	Rony Seikaly	.15	.05
❏ 229	Gerald Wilkins	.15	.05
❏ 230	Michael Cage	.15	.05
❏ 231	Lucious Harris	.15	.05
❏ 232	Sam Cassell	.50	.20
❏ 233	Robert Horry	.30	.10
❏ 234	Kenny Anderson	.15	.05
❏ 235	Isaiah Rider	.30	.10
❏ 236	Rasheed Wallace	.60	.25
❏ 237	Mahmoud Abdul-Rauf	.15	.05
❏ 238	Vernon Maxwell	.15	.05
❏ 239	Dominique Wilkins	.50	.20
❏ 240	Jim McIlvaine	.15	.05
❏ 241	Hubert Davis	.15	.05
❏ 242	Popeye Jones	.15	.05
❏ 243	Walt Williams	.15	.05
❏ 244	Karl Malone	.50	.20
❏ 245	John Stockton	.50	.20
❏ 246	Anthony Peeler	.15	.05
❏ 247	Tracy Murray	.15	.05
❏ 248	Rod Strickland	.15	.05
❏ 249	Lenny Wilkens CO	.30	.10
❏ 250	M.L. Carr CO	.15	.05
❏ 251	Dave Cowens CO	.15	.05
❏ 252	Phil Jackson CO	.30	.10
❏ 253	Mike Fratello CO	.30	.10
❏ 254	Jim Cleamons CO	.15	.05
❏ 255	Dick Motta CO	.15	.05
❏ 256	Doug Collins CO	.15	.05
❏ 257	Rick Adelman CO	.15	.05
❏ 258	Rudy Tomjanovich CO	.30	.10
❏ 259	Larry Brown CO	.30	.10
❏ 260	Bill Fitch CO	.15	.05
❏ 261	Del Harris CO	.15	.05
❏ 262	Pat Riley CO	.30	.10
❏ 263	Chris Ford CO	.15	.05
❏ 264	Flip Saunders CO	.15	.05
❏ 265	John Calipari CO	.30	.10
❏ 266	Jeff Van Gundy CO	.15	.05
❏ 267	Brian Hill CO	.15	.05
❏ 268	Johnny Davis CO	.15	.05
❏ 269	Danny Ainge CO	.30	.10
❏ 270	P.J. Carlesimo CO	.15	.05
❏ 271	Garry St. Jean CO	.15	.05
❏ 272	Bob Hill CO	.15	.05
❏ 273	George Karl CO	.30	.10
❏ 274	Darrell Walker CO	.15	.05
❏ 275	Jerry Sloan CO	.30	.10
❏ 276	Brian Winters CO	.15	.05
❏ 277	Jim Lynam CO	.15	.05
❏ 278	Shareef Abdur-Rahim RC	1.50	.60
❏ 279	Ray Allen RC	1.50	.60
❏ 280	Shandon Anderson RC	.30	.10
❏ 281	Kobe Bryant RC	8.00	3.00
❏ 282	Marcus Camby RC	.60	.25
❏ 283	Erick Dampier RC	.15	.05
❏ 284	Emanual Davis RC	.15	.05
❏ 285	Tony Delk RC	.50	.20
❏ 286	Brian Evans RC	.15	.05
❏ 287	Derek Fisher RC	.75	.30
❏ 288	Todd Fuller RC	.15	.05

❏ 289	Dean Garrett RC	.15	.05
❏ 290	Reggie Geary RC	.15	.05
❏ 291	Darvin Ham RC	.15	.05
❏ 292	Othella Harrington RC	.50	.20
❏ 293	Shane Heal RC	.15	.05
❏ 294	Mark Hendrickson RC	.15	.05
❏ 295	Allen Iverson RC	2.50	1.00
❏ 296	Dontae' Jones RC	.15	.05
❏ 297	Kerry Kittles RC	.50	.20
❏ 298	Priest Lauderdale RC	.15	.05
❏ 299	Matt Maloney RC	.30	.10
❏ 300	Stephon Marbury RC	1.50	.60
❏ 301	Walter McCarty RC	.15	.05
❏ 302	Jeff McInnis RC	.15	.05
❏ 303	Martin Muursepp RC	.15	.05
❏ 304	Steve Nash RC	4.00	1.50
❏ 305	Moochie Norris RC	.30	.10
❏ 306	Jermaine O'Neal RC	1.50	.60
❏ 307	Vitaly Potapenko RC	.15	.05
❏ 308	Virginius Praskevicius RC	.15	.05
❏ 309	Roy Rogers RC	.15	.05
❏ 310	Malik Rose RC	.30	.10
❏ 311	James Scott RC	.15	.05
❏ 312	Antoine Walker RC	1.50	.60
❏ 313	Samaki Walker RC	.15	.05
❏ 314	Ben Wallace RC	3.00	1.25
❏ 315	John Wallace RC	.50	.20
❏ 316	Jerome Williams RC	.50	.20
❏ 317	Lorenzen Wright RC	.30	.10
❏ 318	Charles Barkley ST	.50	.20
❏ 319	Derrick Coleman ST	.15	.05
❏ 320	Michael Finley ST	.50	.20
❏ 321	Stephon Marbury ST	1.00	.40
❏ 322	Reggie Miller ST	.30	.10
❏ 323	Alonzo Mourning ST	.15	.05
❏ 324	Shaquille O'Neal ST	.50	.20
❏ 325	Gary Payton ST	.30	.10
❏ 326	Dennis Rodman ST	.15	.05
❏ 327	Damon Stoudamire ST	.30	.10
❏ 328	Vin Baker CBG	.15	.05
❏ 329	Clyde Drexler CBG	.30	.10
❏ 330	Patrick Ewing CBG	.30	.10
❏ 331	Anfernee Hardaway CBG	.30	.10
❏ 332	Grant Hill CBG	.50	.20
❏ 333	Juwan Howard CBG	.15	.05
❏ 334	Larry Johnson CBG	.15	.05
❏ 335	Michael Jordan CBG	1.50	.60
❏ 336	Shawn Kemp CBG	.15	.05
❏ 337	Jason Kidd CBG	.30	.10
❏ 338	Karl Malone CBG	.50	.20
❏ 339	Reggie Miller CBG	.15	.05
❏ 340	Hakeem Olajuwon CBG	.30	.10
❏ 341	Scottie Pippen CBG	.30	.10
❏ 342	Mitch Richmond CBG	.15	.05
❏ 343	David Robinson CBG	.30	.10
❏ 344	Dennis Rodman CBG	.30	.10
❏ 345	Joe Smith CBG	.15	.05
❏ 346	Jerry Stackhouse CBG	.30	.10
❏ 347	John Stockton CBG	.50	.20
❏ 348	Jerry Stackhouse BG	.50	.20
❏ 349	Checklist (201-350/inserts)	.15	.05
❏ 350	Checklist (inserts)	.15	.05
❏ NNO	G.Hill/J.Stackhouse Promo	2.00	.75
❏ NNO	G.Hill Z-Force Preview	10.00	4.00

1997-98 Hoops

ANFERNEE HARDAWAY

❏ COMPLETE SET (330)	30.00	15.00
❏ COMPLETE SERIES 1 (165)	12.00	6.00

#	Player		
❑	COMPLETE SERIES 2 (165)	18.00	9.00
❑ 1	Michael Jordan LL	1.50	.60
❑ 2	Dennis Rodman LL	.15	.05
❑ 3	Mark Jackson LL	.30	.10
❑ 4	Shawn Bradley LL	.15	.05
❑ 5	Glen Rice LL	.15	.05
❑ 6	Mookie Blaylock LL	.15	.05
❑ 7	Gheorghe Muresan LL	.15	.05
❑ 8	Mark Price LL	.30	.10
❑ 9	Tyrone Corbin	.15	.05
❑ 10	Christian Laettner	.30	.10
❑ 11	Priest Lauderdale	.15	.05
❑ 12	Dikembe Mutombo	.30	.10
❑ 13	Steve Smith	.30	.10
❑ 14	Todd Day	.15	.05
❑ 15	Rick Fox	.30	.10
❑ 16	Brett Szabo	.15	.05
❑ 17	Antoine Walker	.60	.25
❑ 18	David Wesley	.15	.05
❑ 19	Muggsy Bogues	.30	.10
❑ 20	Dell Curry	.15	.05
❑ 21	Tony Delk	.15	.05
❑ 22	Anthony Mason	.30	.10
❑ 23	Glen Rice	.30	.10
❑ 24	Malik Rose	.15	.05
❑ 25	Steve Kerr	.30	.10
❑ 26	Toni Kukoc	.30	.10
❑ 27	Luc Longley	.15	.05
❑ 28	Robert Parish	.30	.10
❑ 29	Scottie Pippen	.75	.30
❑ 30	Dennis Rodman	.30	.10
❑ 31	Terrell Brandon	.30	.10
❑ 32	Danny Ferry	.15	.05
❑ 33	Tyrone Hill	.15	.05
❑ 34	Bobby Phills	.15	.05
❑ 35	Vitaly Potapenko	.15	.05
❑ 36	Shawn Bradley	.15	.05
❑ 37	Sasha Danilovic	.15	.05
❑ 38	Derek Harper	.30	.10
❑ 39	Martin Muursepp	.15	.05
❑ 40	Robert Pack	.15	.05
❑ 41	Khalid Reeves	.15	.05
❑ 42	Vincent Askew	.15	.05
❑ 43	Dale Ellis	.15	.05
❑ 44	LaPhonso Ellis	.15	.05
❑ 45	Antonio McDyess	.30	.10
❑ 46	Bryant Stith	.15	.05
❑ 47	Joe Dumars	.50	.20
❑ 48	Grant Hill	.50	.20
❑ 49	Lindsey Hunter	.15	.05
❑ 50	Aaron McKie	.30	.10
❑ 51	Theo Ratliff	.15	.05
❑ 52	Scott Burrell	.15	.05
❑ 53	Todd Fuller	.15	.05
❑ 54	Chris Mullin	.50	.20
❑ 55	Mark Price	.30	.10
❑ 56	Joe Smith	.30	.10
❑ 57	Latrell Sprewell	.50	.20
❑ 58	Clyde Drexler	.50	.20
❑ 59	Mario Elie	.15	.05
❑ 60	Othella Harrington	.15	.05
❑ 61	Matt Maloney	.15	.05
❑ 62	Hakeem Olajuwon	.50	.20
❑ 63	Kevin Willis	.30	.10
❑ 64	Travis Best	.15	.05
❑ 65	Erick Dampier	.30	.10
❑ 66	Antonio Davis	.15	.05
❑ 67	Dale Davis	.15	.05
❑ 68	Mark Jackson	.30	.10
❑ 69	Reggie Miller	.50	.20
❑ 70	Brent Barry	.30	.10
❑ 71	Darrick Martin	.15	.05
❑ 72	Bo Outlaw	.15	.05
❑ 73	Loy Vaught	.15	.05
❑ 74	Lorenzen Wright	.15	.05
❑ 75	Kobe Bryant	2.00	.75
❑ 76	Derek Fisher	.50	.20
❑ 77	Robert Horry	.30	.10
❑ 78	Eddie Jones	.50	.20
❑ 79	Travis Knight	.15	.05
❑ 80	George McCloud	.15	.05
❑ 81	Shaquille O'Neal	1.25	.50
❑ 82	P.J. Brown	.15	.05
❑ 83	Tim Hardaway	.30	.10
❑ 84	Voshon Lenard	.15	.05
❑ 85	Jamal Mashburn	.30	.10
❑ 86	Alonzo Mourning	.30	.10
❑ 87	Ray Allen	.50	.20
❑ 88	Vin Baker	.30	.10
❑ 89	Sherman Douglas	.15	.05
❑ 90	Armon Gilliam	.15	.05
❑ 91	Glenn Robinson	.50	.20
❑ 92	Kevin Garnett	1.00	.40
❑ 93	Dean Garrett	.15	.05
❑ 94	Tom Gugliotta	.30	.10
❑ 95	Stephon Marbury	.60	.25
❑ 96	Doug West	.15	.05
❑ 97	Chris Gatling	.15	.05
❑ 98	Kendall Gill	.15	.05
❑ 99	Kerry Kittles	.50	.20
❑ 100	Jayson Williams	.15	.05
❑ 101	Chris Childs	.15	.05
❑ 102	Patrick Ewing	.50	.20
❑ 103	Allan Houston	.30	.10
❑ 104	Larry Johnson	.30	.10
❑ 105	Charles Oakley	.30	.10
❑ 106	John Starks	.30	.10
❑ 107	John Wallace	.15	.05
❑ 108	Nick Anderson	.15	.05
❑ 109	Horace Grant	.30	.10
❑ 110	Anfernee Hardaway	.50	.20
❑ 111	Rony Seikaly	.15	.05
❑ 112	Derek Strong	.15	.05
❑ 113	Derrick Coleman	.15	.05
❑ 114	Allen Iverson	1.25	.50
❑ 115	Doug Overton	.15	.05
❑ 116	Jerry Stackhouse	.50	.20
❑ 117	Rex Walters	.15	.05
❑ 118	Cedric Ceballos	.15	.05
❑ 119	Kevin Johnson	.30	.10
❑ 120	Jason Kidd	.75	.30
❑ 121	Steve Nash	.25	.05
❑ 122	Wesley Person	.15	.05
❑ 123	Kenny Anderson	.30	.10
❑ 124	Jermaine O'Neal	.75	.30
❑ 125	Isaiah Rider	.30	.10
❑ 126	Arvydas Sabonis	.30	.10
❑ 127	Gary Trent	.15	.05
❑ 128	Tyus Edney	.15	.05
❑ 129	Brian Grant	.30	.10
❑ 130	Olden Polynice	.15	.05
❑ 131	Mitch Richmond	.30	.10
❑ 132	Corliss Williamson	.15	.05
❑ 133	Vinny Del Negro	.15	.05
❑ 134	Sean Elliott	.30	.10
❑ 135	Avery Johnson	.15	.05
❑ 136	Will Perdue	.15	.05
❑ 137	Dominique Wilkins	.50	.20
❑ 138	Craig Ehlo	.15	.05
❑ 139	Hersey Hawkins	.15	.05
❑ 140	Shawn Kemp	.30	.10
❑ 141	Jim McIlvaine	.15	.05
❑ 142	Sam Perkins	.30	.10
❑ 143	Detlef Schrempf	.30	.10
❑ 144	Marcus Camby	.50	.20
❑ 145	Doug Christie	.30	.10
❑ 146	Popeye Jones	.15	.05
❑ 147	Damon Stoudamire	.30	.10
❑ 148	Walt Williams	.15	.05
❑ 149	Jeff Hornacek	.30	.10
❑ 150	Karl Malone	.50	.20
❑ 151	Greg Ostertag	.15	.05
❑ 152	Bryon Russell	.15	.05
❑ 153	John Stockton	.50	.20
❑ 154	Shareef Abdur-Rahim	.75	.30
❑ 155	Greg Anthony	.15	.05
❑ 156	Anthony Peeler	.15	.05
❑ 157	Bryant Reeves	.15	.05
❑ 158	Roy Rogers	.15	.05
❑ 159	Calbert Cheaney	.15	.05
❑ 160	Juwan Howard	.30	.10
❑ 161	Gheorghe Muresan	.15	.05
❑ 162	Rod Strickland	.15	.05
❑ 163	Chris Webber	.50	.20
❑ 164	Checklist	.15	.05
❑ 165	Checklist	.15	.05
❑ 166	Tim Duncan RC	2.00	.75
❑ 167	Chauncey Billups RC	1.25	.50
❑ 168	Keith Van Horn RC	.60	.25
❑ 169	Tracy McGrady RC	2.50	1.00
❑ 170	John Thomas RC	.15	.05
❑ 171	Tim Thomas RC	.75	.30
❑ 172	Ron Mercer RC	.50	.20
❑ 173	Scot Pollard RC	.30	.10
❑ 174	Jason Lawson RC	.15	.05
❑ 175	Keith Booth RC	.15	.05
❑ 176	Adonal Foyle RC	.30	.10
❑ 177	Bubba Wells RC	.15	.05
❑ 178	Derek Anderson RC	.50	.20
❑ 179	Rodrick Rhodes RC	.15	.05
❑ 180	Kelvin Cato RC	.50	.20
❑ 181	Serge Zwikker RC	.15	.05
❑ 182	Ed Gray RC	.15	.05
❑ 183	Brevin Knight RC	.30	.10
❑ 184	Alvin Williams RC	.15	.05
❑ 185	Paul Grant RC	.15	.05
❑ 186	Austin Croshere RC	.40	.15
❑ 187	Chris Crawford RC	.15	.05
❑ 188	Anthony Johnson RC	.15	.05
❑ 189	James Cotton RC	.15	.05
❑ 190	James Collins RC	.15	.05
❑ 191	Tony Battie RC	.50	.20
❑ 192	Tariq Abdul-Wahad RC	.30	.10
❑ 193	Danny Fortson RC	.30	.10
❑ 194	Maurice Taylor RC	.40	.15
❑ 195	Bobby Jackson RC	.75	.30
❑ 196	Charles Smith RC	.15	.05
❑ 197	Johnny Taylor RC	.15	.05
❑ 198	Jerald Honeycutt RC	.15	.05
❑ 199	Marko Milic RC	.15	.05
❑ 200	Anthony Parker RC	.15	.05
❑ 201	Jacque Vaughn RC	.30	.10
❑ 202	Antonio Daniels RC	.50	.20
❑ 203	Charles O'Bannon RC	.15	.05
❑ 204	God Shammgod RC	.15	.05
❑ 205	Kebu Stewart RC	.15	.05
❑ 206	Mookie Blaylock	.15	.05
❑ 207	Chucky Brown	.15	.05
❑ 208	Alan Henderson	.15	.05
❑ 209	Dana Barros	.15	.05
❑ 210	Tyus Edney	.15	.05
❑ 211	Travis Knight	.15	.05
❑ 212	Walter McCarty	.15	.05
❑ 213	Vlade Divac	.30	.10
❑ 214	Matt Geiger	.15	.05
❑ 215	Bobby Phills	.15	.05
❑ 216	J.R. Reid	.15	.05
❑ 217	David Wesley	.15	.05
❑ 218	Scott Burrell	.15	.05
❑ 219	Ron Harper	.30	.10
❑ 220	Michael Jordan	3.00	1.25
❑ 221	Bill Wennington	.15	.05
❑ 222	Mitchell Butler	.15	.05
❑ 223	Zydrunas Ilgauskas	.30	.10
❑ 224	Shawn Kemp	.30	.10
❑ 225	Wesley Person	.15	.05
❑ 226	Shawnelle Scott RC	.15	.05
❑ 227	Bob Sura	.15	.05
❑ 228	Hubert Davis	.15	.05
❑ 229	Michael Finley	.50	.20
❑ 230	Dennis Scott	.15	.05
❑ 231	Erick Strickland RC	.30	.10
❑ 232	Samaki Walker	.15	.05
❑ 233	Dean Garrett	.15	.05
❑ 234	Priest Lauderdale	.15	.05
❑ 235	Eric Williams	.15	.05
❑ 236	Grant Long	.15	.05
❑ 237	Malik Sealy	.15	.05
❑ 238	Brian Williams	.15	.05
❑ 239	Muggsy Bogues	.30	.10
❑ 240	Bimbo Coles	.15	.05
❑ 241	Brian Shaw	.15	.05
❑ 242	Joe Smith	.30	.10
❑ 243	Latrell Sprewell	.50	.20
❑ 244	Charles Barkley	.60	.25
❑ 245	Emanual Davis	.15	.05
❑ 246	Brent Price	.15	.05
❑ 247	Reggie Miller	.50	.20
❑ 248	Chris Mullin	.50	.20
❑ 249	Jalen Rose	.50	.20
❑ 250	Rik Smits	.30	.10
❑ 251	Mark West	.15	.05
❑ 252	Lamond Murray	.15	.05
❑ 253	Pooh Richardson	.15	.05
❑ 254	Rodney Rogers	.15	.05
❑ 255	Stojko Vrankovic	.15	.05
❑ 256	Jon Barry	.15	.05
❑ 257	Corie Blount	.15	.05

❏ 258	Elden Campbell	.15	.05
❏ 259	Rick Fox	.30	.10
❏ 260	Nick Van Exel	.50	.20
❏ 261	Isaac Austin	.15	.05
❏ 262	Dan Majerle	.30	.10
❏ 263	Terry Mills	.15	.05
❏ 264	Mark Strickland RC	.15	.05
❏ 265	Terrell Brandon	.30	.10
❏ 266	Tyrone Hill	.15	.05
❏ 267	Ervin Johnson	.15	.05
❏ 268	Andrew Lang	.15	.05
❏ 269	Elliot Perry	.15	.05
❏ 270	Chris Carr	.15	.05
❏ 271	Reggie Jordan	.15	.05
❏ 272	Sam Mitchell	.15	.05
❏ 273	Stanley Roberts	.15	.05
❏ 274	Michael Cage	.15	.05
❏ 275	Sam Cassell	.50	.20
❏ 276	Lucious Harris	.15	.05
❏ 277	Kerry Kittles	.50	.20
❏ 278	Don MacLean	.15	.05
❏ 279	Chris Dudley	.15	.05
❏ 280	Chris Mills	.15	.05
❏ 281	Charlie Ward	.15	.05
❏ 282	Buck Williams	.15	.05
❏ 283	Herb Williams	.15	.05
❏ 284	Derek Harper	.30	.10
❏ 285	Mark Price	.30	.10
❏ 286	Gerald Wilkins	.15	.05
❏ 287	Allen Iverson	1.25	.50
❏ 288	Jim Jackson	.15	.05
❏ 289	Eric Montross	.15	.05
❏ 290	Jerry Stackhouse	.50	.20
❏ 291	Clarence Weatherspoon	.15	.05
❏ 292	Tom Chambers	.15	.05
❏ 293	Rex Chapman	.15	.05
❏ 294	Danny Manning	.30	.10
❏ 295	Antonio McDyess	.30	.10
❏ 296	Clifford Robinson	.15	.05
❏ 297	Stacey Augmon	.15	.05
❏ 298	Brian Grant	.30	.10
❏ 299	Rasheed Wallace	.50	.20
❏ 300	Mahmoud Abdul-Rauf	.15	.05
❏ 301	Terry Dehere	.15	.05
❏ 302	Billy Owens	.15	.05
❏ 303	Michael Smith	.15	.05
❏ 304	Cory Alexander	.15	.05
❏ 305	Chuck Person	.15	.05
❏ 306	David Robinson	.50	.20
❏ 307	Charles Smith	.15	.05
❏ 308	Monty Williams	.15	.05
❏ 309	Vin Baker	.30	.10
❏ 310	Jerome Kersey	.15	.05
❏ 311	Nate McMillan	.15	.05
❏ 312	Gary Payton	.50	.20
❏ 313	Eric Snow	.30	.10
❏ 314	Carlos Rogers	.15	.05
❏ 315	Zan Tabak	.15	.05
❏ 316	John Wallace	.15	.05
❏ 317	Sharone Wright	.15	.05
❏ 318	Shandon Anderson	.15	.05
❏ 319	Antoine Carr	.15	.05
❏ 320	Howard Eisley	.15	.05
❏ 321	Chris Morris	.15	.05
❏ 322	Pete Chilcutt	.15	.05
❏ 323	George Lynch	.15	.05
❏ 324	Chris Robinson	.15	.05
❏ 325	Otis Thorpe	.15	.05
❏ 326	Harvey Grant	.15	.05
❏ 327	Darvin Ham	.15	.05
❏ 328	Juwan Howard	.30	.10
❏ 329	Ben Wallace	.50	.20
❏ 330	Chris Webber	.50	.20
❏ NNO	Grant Hill Promo	.50	.20

1998-99 Hoops

❏	COMPLETE SET (167)	20.00	10.00
❏ 1	Kobe Bryant	2.00	.75
❏ 2	Glenn Robinson	.30	.10
❏ 3	Derek Anderson	.40	.15
❏ 4	Terry Dehere	.15	.05
❏ 5	Jalen Rose	.50	.20
❏ 6	Zydrunas Ilgauskas	.30	.10
❏ 7	Scott Williams	.15	.05
❏ 8	Toni Kukoc	.30	.10
❏ 9	John Stockton	.50	.20

❏ 10	Kevin Garnett	1.00	.40
❏ 11	Jerome Williams	.15	.05
❏ 12	Anthony Mason	.30	.10
❏ 13	Harvey Grant	.15	.05
❏ 14	Mookie Blaylock	.15	.05
❏ 15	Tyrone Hill	.15	.05
❏ 16	Dale Davis	.30	.10
❏ 17	Eric Washington	.15	.05
❏ 18	Aaron McKie	.30	.10
❏ 19	Jermaine O'Neal	.50	.20
❏ 20	Anfernee Hardaway	.50	.20
❏ 21	Derrick Coleman	.15	.05
❏ 22	Allan Houston	.30	.10
❏ 23	Michael Jordan	3.00	1.25
❏ 24	Jason Kidd	.75	.30
❏ 25	Tyrone Corbin	.15	.05
❏ 26	Jacque Vaughn	.15	.05
❏ 27	Bobby Jackson	.30	.10
❏ 28	Chris Anstey	.15	.05
❏ 29	Brent Barry	.30	.10
❏ 30	Shareef Abdur-Rahim	.50	.20
❏ 31	Jeff Hornacek	.30	.10
❏ 32	Ed Gray	.15	.05
❏ 33	Grant Hill	.50	.20
❏ 34	Steve Smith	.30	.10
❏ 35	Rony Seikaly	.15	.05
❏ 36	Mark Jackson	.30	.10
❏ 37	Shawn Bradley	.15	.05
❏ 38	Corie Blount	.15	.05
❏ 39	Erick Dampier	.30	.10
❏ 40	Kerry Kittles	.15	.05
❏ 41	David Wesley	.15	.05
❏ 42	Horace Grant	.30	.10
❏ 43	Bobby Hurley	.15	.05
❏ 44	Tariq Abdul-Wahad	.15	.05
❏ 45	Brian Williams	.15	.05
❏ 46	Ray Allen	.50	.20
❏ 47	Kenny Anderson	.30	.10
❏ 48	Rodrick Rhodes	.15	.05
❏ 49	Greg Foster	.15	.05
❏ 50	Tim Duncan	.75	.30
❏ 51	Steve Nash	.50	.20
❏ 52	Kelvin Cato	.15	.05
❏ 53	Donyell Marshall	.30	.10
❏ 54	Marcus Camby	.30	.10
❏ 55	Kevin Willis	.15	.05
❏ 56	Michael Finley	.50	.20
❏ 57	Muggsy Bogues	.30	.10
❏ 58	Mark Price	.30	.10
❏ 59	Larry Johnson	.30	.10
❏ 60	Karl Malone	.50	.20
❏ 61	Greg Ostertag	.15	.05
❏ 62	Sean Elliott	.30	.10
❏ 63	Johnny Taylor	.15	.05
❏ 64	Howard Eisley	.15	.05
❏ 65	Chris Childs	.15	.05
❏ 66	Walt Williams	.15	.05
❏ 67	Tracy Murray	.15	.05
❏ 68	Patrick Ewing	.50	.20
❏ 69	Olden Polynice	.15	.05
❏ 70	Allen Iverson	1.00	.40
❏ 71	David Robinson	.50	.20
❏ 72	Calbert Cheaney	.15	.05
❏ 73	Lamond Murray	.15	.05
❏ 74	Scot Pollard	.15	.05
❏ 75	Alonzo Mourning	.30	.10
❏ 76	Tracy McGrady	1.25	.50
❏ 77	Jim McIlvaine	.15	.05

❏ 78	Bob Sura	.15	.05
❏ 79	Anthony Peeler	.15	.05
❏ 80	Keith Van Horn	.50	.20
❏ 81	Maurice Taylor	.20	.08
❏ 82	Charles Smith	.15	.05
❏ 83	Dikembe Mutombo	.30	.10
❏ 84	Nick Anderson	.15	.05
❏ 85	Austin Croshere	.40	.15
❏ 86	Armon Gilliam	.15	.05
❏ 87	Eddie Jones	.50	.20
❏ 88	Glen Rice	.30	.10
❏ 89	Sam Cassell	.50	.20
❏ 90	Stephon Marbury	.50	.20
❏ 91	Elliot Perry UER	.15	.05
❏ 92	Jamal Mashburn	.30	.10
❏ 93	Adonal Foyle	.15	.05
❏ 94	Avery Johnson	.15	.05
❏ 95	Micheal Williams	.15	.05
❏ 96	Danny Fortson	.15	.05
❏ 97	Brevin Knight	.15	.05
❏ 98	Ron Harper	.30	.10
❏ 99	Chauncey Billups	.30	.10
❏ 100	Shaquille O'Neal	1.25	.50
❏ 101	Brent Price	.15	.05
❏ 102	Tim Thomas	.50	.20
❏ 103	Khalid Reeves	.15	.05
❏ 104	Chris Gatling	.15	.05
❏ 105	Terry Cummings	.15	.05
❏ 106	Vin Baker	.30	.10
❏ 107	Bryant Reeves	.15	.05
❏ 108	John Starks	.30	.10
❏ 109	Juwan Howard	.15	.05
❏ 110	Antoine Walker	.50	.20
❏ 111	Rodney Rogers	.15	.05
❏ 112	Nick Van Exel	.50	.20
❏ 113	Chris Whitney	.15	.05
❏ 114	Bobby Phills	.15	.05
❏ 115	Travis Knight	.15	.05
❏ 116	Robert Horry	.30	.10
❏ 117	Erick Strickland	.15	.05
❏ 118	Dontae Jones	.15	.05
❏ 119	Tony Battie	.15	.05
❏ 120	Lindsey Hunter	.15	.05
❏ 121	Reggie Miller	.50	.20
❏ 122	John Wallace	.15	.05
❏ 123	Ron Mercer	.25	.10
❏ 124	Antonio Daniels	.15	.05
❏ 125	Paul Grant	.15	.05
❏ 126	Voshon Lenard	.15	.05
❏ 127	Shawn Kemp	.30	.10
❏ 128	Antonio Davis	.15	.05
❏ 129	Hakeem Olajuwon	.50	.20
❏ 130	Danny Manning	.15	.05
❏ 131	Bimbo Coles	.15	.05
❏ 132	Tim Hardaway	.30	.10
❏ 133	Lorenzo Williams	.15	.05
❏ 134	Dan Majerle	.15	.05
❏ 135	Bryant Stith	.15	.05
❏ 136	Randy Brown	.15	.05
❏ 137	Hubert Davis	.15	.05
❏ 138	Gary Payton	.50	.20
❏ 139	Rasheed Wallace	.50	.20
❏ 140	Chris Robinson	.15	.05
❏ 141	Doug Christie	.30	.10
❏ 142	Brian Grant	.30	.10
❏ 143	Isaiah Rider	.15	.05
❏ 144	Kendall Gill	.15	.05
❏ 145	Lorenzen Wright	.15	.05
❏ 146	Ervin Johnson	.15	.05
❏ 147	Monty Williams	.15	.05
❏ 148	Keith Closs	.15	.05
❏ 149	Tony Delk	.15	.05
❏ 150	Hersey Hawkins	.15	.05
❏ 151	Dean Garrett	.15	.05
❏ 152	Cedric Henderson	.15	.05
❏ 153	Detlef Schrempf	.30	.10
❏ 154	Dana Barros	.15	.05
❏ 155	Dee Brown	.15	.05
❏ 156	Jayson Williams SO	.15	.05
❏ 157	Charles Barkley SO	.50	.20
❏ 158	Damon Stoudamire SO	.15	.05
❏ 159	Scottie Pippen SO	.50	.20
❏ 160	Joe Smith SO	.15	.05
❏ 161	Antonio McDyess SO	.15	.05
❏ 162	Jerry Stackhouse SO	.30	.10
❏ 163	Dennis Rodman SO	.15	.05

164	Shaquille O'Neal SO	.50	.20
165	Grant Hill SO	.30	.10
166	Checklist	.15	.05
167	Checklist	.15	.05

1999-00 Hoops

	COMPLETE SET (185)	30.00	15.00
	COMMON CARD (1-165)	.15	.05
	COMMON ROOKIE (166-185)	.25	.08
1	Paul Pierce	.50	.20
2	Ray Allen	.50	.20
3	Jason Williams	.50	.20
4	Sean Elliott	.30	.10
5	Al Harrington	.50	.20
6	Bobby Phills	.15	.05
7	Tyronn Lue	.30	.10
8	James Cotton	.15	.05
9	Anthony Peeler	.15	.05
10	LaPhonso Ellis	.15	.05
11	Voshon Lenard	.15	.05
12	Kornel David RC	.15	.05
13	Michael Finley	.50	.20
14	Danny Fortson	.15	.05
15	Antawn Jamison	.75	.30
16	Reggie Miller	.50	.20
17	Shaquille O'Neal	1.25	.50
18	P.J. Brown	.15	.05
19	Roshown McLeod	.15	.05
20	Larry Johnson	.30	.10
21	Rashard Lewis	.50	.20
22	Tracy McGrady	1.25	.50
23	Peja Stojakovic	.60	.25
24	Tracy Murray	.15	.05
25	Gary Payton	.50	.20
26	Ricky Davis	.30	.10
27	Kobe Bryant	2.00	.75
28	Avery Johnson	.15	.05
29	Kevin Garnett	1.00	.40
30	Charles Jones	.15	.05
31	Brevin Knight	.15	.05
32	Lindsey Hunter	.15	.05
33	Felipe Lopez	.15	.05
34	Rik Smits	.30	.10
35	Maurice Taylor	.30	.10
36	Corey Benjamin	.15	.05
37	Ervin Johnson	.15	.05
38	Steve Smith	.30	.10
39	Austin Croshere	.30	.10
40	Matt Geiger	.15	.05
41	Tom Gugliotta	.15	.05
42	Radoslav Nesterovic RC	.50	.20
43	Juwan Howard	.30	.10
44	Keon Clark	.30	.10
45	Latrell Sprewell	.50	.20
46	George Lynch	.15	.05
47	Greg Ostertag	.15	.05
48	J.R. Henderson	.15	.05
49	Kerry Kittles	.15	.05
50	Matt Harpring	.50	.20
51	Duane Causwell	.15	.05
52	Andrae Patterson	.15	.05
53	Jerry Stackhouse	.50	.20
54	Adonal Foyle	.15	.05
55	Bryce Drew	.15	.05
56	Chris Childs	.15	.05
57	Charles Smith	.15	.05
58	Rony Seikaly	.15	.05
59	Chauncey Billups	.30	.10
60	Grant Hill	.50	.20
61	Marion Garnett RC	.15	.05
62	Tim Hardaway	.30	.10
63	Vlade Divac	.30	.10
64	Chris Gatling	.15	.05
65	Glenn Robinson	.50	.20
66	Michael Olowokandi	.30	.10
67	Elliot Perry	.15	.05
68	Howard Eisley	.15	.05
69	Glen Rice	.30	.10
70	Marcus Camby	.30	.10
71	Theo Ratliff	.30	.10
72	Brian Skinner	.15	.05
73	Kenny Anderson	.30	.10
74	Jamal Mashburn	.30	.10
75	Vladimir Stepania	.15	.05
76	Jayson Williams	.15	.05
77	Brian Grant	.30	.10
78	Raef LaFrentz	.30	.10
79	John Starks	.30	.10
80	Mike Bibby	.50	.20
81	Stephon Marbury	.50	.20
82	Armon Gilliam	.15	.05
83	Sam Jacobson	.15	.05
84	Derrick Coleman	.30	.10
85	Allan Houston	.30	.10
86	Miles Simon	.15	.05
87	Allen Iverson	1.00	.40
88	Derek Anderson	.30	.10
89	Chris Anstey	.15	.05
90	Larry Hughes	.50	.20
91	Vitaly Potapenko	.15	.05
92	Cherokee Parks	.15	.05
93	Donyell Marshall	.30	.10
94	Danny Manning	.15	.05
95	Bryon Russell	.15	.05
96	Randell Jackson	.15	.05
97	Antoine Walker	.50	.20
98	Dirk Nowitzki	1.00	.40
99	Karl Malone	.50	.20
100	Vince Carter	1.25	.50
101	Eddie Jones	.50	.20
102	Bryant Stith	.15	.05
103	Korleone Young	.15	.05
104	Tim Duncan	1.00	.40
105	Jerome Kersey	.15	.05
106	Bonzi Wells	.50	.20
107	Wesley Person	.15	.05
108	Steve Nash	.50	.20
109	Tyrone Nesby RC	.15	.05
110	Doug Christie	.30	.10
111	David Robinson	.50	.20
112	Ruben Patterson	.30	.10
113	Dikembe Mutombo	.30	.10
114	Ron Mercer	.30	.10
115	Elden Campbell	.15	.05
116	Kevin Willis	.15	.05
117	Hakeem Olajuwon	.50	.20
118	Shawn Kemp	.30	.10
119	Eric Montross	.15	.05
120	Shareef Abdur-Rahim	.50	.20
121	Bob Sura	.15	.05
122	James Robinson	.15	.05
123	Shawn Bradley	.15	.05
124	Robert Traylor	.15	.05
125	Dean Garrett	.15	.05
126	Keith Van Horn	.50	.20
127	Patrick Ewing	.50	.20
128	Isaac Austin	.15	.05
129	Jason Kidd	.75	.30
130	Isaiah Rider	.30	.10
131	Jerome James RC	.15	.05
132	John Stockton	.50	.20
133	Jason Caffey	.15	.05
134	Bryant Reeves	.15	.05
135	Michael Dickerson	.30	.10
136	Chris Mullin	.50	.20
137	Rasheed Wallace	.50	.20
138	Cuttino Mobley	.50	.20
139	Antonio McDyess	.30	.10
140	Chris Webber	.50	.20
141	Jelani McCoy	.15	.05
142	Damon Stoudamire	.50	.20
143	Gerald Brown	.15	.05
144	Cory Carr	.15	.05
145	Brent Barry	.30	.10
146	Alan Henderson	.15	.05
147	Nazr Mohammed	.15	.05
148	Bison Dele	.15	.05
149	Scottie Pippen	.75	.30
150	Michael Doleac	.15	.05
151	Nick Anderson	.15	.05
152	Alonzo Mourning	.30	.10
153	Jahidi White	.15	.05
154	Jalen Rose	.50	.20
155	Brad Miller	.50	.20
156	Andrew DeClercq	.15	.05
157	Erick Strickland	.15	.05
158	Toni Kukoc	.30	.10
159	Pat Garrity	.15	.05
160	Bobby Jackson	.30	.10
161	Steve Kerr	.30	.10
162	Toby Bailey	.15	.05
163	Charles Oakley	.15	.05
164	Rod Strickland	.15	.05
165	Rodrick Rhodes	.15	.05
166	Ron Artest RC	.75	.30
167	William Avery RC	.50	.20
168	Elton Brand RC	1.50	.60
169	Baron Davis RC	3.00	1.25
170	John Celestand RC	.40	.15
171	Jumaine Jones RC	.50	.20
172	Andre Miller RC	1.25	.50
173	Lee Nailon RC	.25	.08
174	James Posey RC	.75	.30
175	Jason Terry RC	.75	.30
176	Kenny Thomas RC	.50	.20
177	Steve Francis RC	1.50	.60
178	Wally Szczerbiak RC	1.25	.50
179	Richard Hamilton RC	1.25	.50
180	Jonathan Bender RC	1.25	.50
181	Shawn Marion RC	1.50	.60
182	A.Radojevic RC	.25	.08
183	Tim James RC	.40	.15
184	Trajan Langdon RC	.50	.20
185	Corey Maggette RC	1.25	.50

2004-05 Hoops

	COMP.SET w/o SP's (165)	40.00	15.00
	COMMON CARD (1-165)	.20	.08
	COMMON HH (166-175)	8.00	3.00
	COMMON ROOKIE (176-200)	3.00	1.25
	CARDS 168-170 NOT RELEASED		
1	Dwyane Wade	2.00	.75
2	Vince Carter	1.50	.60
3	Luke Walton	.40	.15
4	Alonzo Mourning	.60	.25
5	Antoine Walker	.60	.25
6	Jerry Stackhouse	.60	.25
7	Chris Wilcox	.40	.15
8	Udonis Haslem	.20	.08
9	Michael Redd	.60	.25
10	Darius Miles	.60	.25
11	Jarvis Hayes	.40	.15
12	Kirk Hinrich	.60	.25
13	Tayshaun Prince	.40	.15
14	Caron Butler	.60	.25
15	Sam Cassell	.60	.25
16	Kurt Thomas	.40	.15
17	Bruce Bowen	.20	.08
18	Jared Jeffries	.20	.08
19	Keith Bogans	.20	.08
20	Chauncey Billups	.40	.15
21	Lamar Odom	.60	.25

#	Player		
❏ 22	Fred Hoiberg	.20	.08
❏ 23	Cuttino Mobley	.40	.15
❏ 24	Manu Ginobili	.60	.25
❏ 25	Juan Dixon	.40	.15
❏ 26	Predrag Drobnjak	.20	.08
❏ 27	Nene	.40	.15
❏ 28	Elton Brand	.60	.25
❏ 29	Rasual Butler	.20	.08
❏ 30	Nick Van Exel	.60	.25
❏ 31	Carlos Arroyo	1.00	.40
❏ 32	Zydrunas Ilgauskas	.40	.15
❏ 33	Troy Murphy	.60	.25
❏ 34	Jason Williams	.40	.15
❏ 35	Jason Kidd	1.00	.40
❏ 36	Samuel Dalembert	.20	.08
❏ 37	Vladimir Radmanovic	.20	.08
❏ 38	Kenny Anderson	.20	.08
❏ 39	Kenyon Martin	.60	.25
❏ 40	Jamaal Tinsley	.60	.25
❏ 41	Damon Jones	.20	.08
❏ 42	Shareef Abdur-Rahim	.60	.25
❏ 43	Ricky Davis	.60	.25
❏ 44	Earl Boykins	.40	.15
❏ 45	Austin Croshere	.20	.08
❏ 46	Keith Van Horn	.60	.25
❏ 47	Theo Ratliff	.40	.15
❏ 48	Mehmet Okur	.20	.08
❏ 49	Paul Pierce	.60	.25
❏ 50	Marcus Camby	.40	.15
❏ 51	Stephen Jackson	.20	.08
❏ 52	Maurice Williams	.20	.08
❏ 53	Brad Miller	.60	.25
❏ 54	Carlos Boozer	.60	.25
❏ 55	Dirk Nowitzki	1.00	.40
❏ 56	Dikembe Mutombo	.40	.15
❏ 57	James Posey	.60	.25
❏ 58	Baron Davis	.60	.25
❏ 59	Shawn Marion	.60	.25
❏ 60	Ronald Murray	.20	.08
❏ 61	Gary Payton	.60	.25
❏ 62	Andre Miller	.40	.15
❏ 63	Reggie Miller	.60	.25
❏ 64	Zaza Pachulia	.40	.15
❏ 65	Bobby Jackson	.40	.15
❏ 66	Peja Stojakovic	.60	.25
❏ 67	Jiri Welsch	.40	.15
❏ 68	Darko Milicic	.60	.25
❏ 69	Ron Artest	.40	.15
❏ 70	T.J. Ford	.40	.15
❏ 71	Andrei Kirilenko	.60	.25
❏ 72	Jason Kapono	.40	.15
❏ 73	Jermaine O'Neal	.60	.25
❏ 74	Desmond Mason	.40	.15
❏ 75	Chris Webber	.60	.25
❏ 76	Morris Peterson	.40	.15
❏ 77	Ben Wallace	.60	.25
❏ 78	Antonio Davis	.20	.08
❏ 79	Slava Medvedenko	.20	.08
❏ 80	Brian Scalabrine	.20	.08
❏ 81	Jamal Crawford	.40	.15
❏ 82	Josh Howard	.40	.15
❏ 83	Tyson Chandler	.60	.25
❏ 84	Rasheed Wallace	.60	.25
❏ 85	Chris Mihm	.20	.08
❏ 86	Latrell Sprewell	.40	.15
❏ 87	Mike Sweetney	.40	.15
❏ 88	Robert Horry	.40	.15
❏ 89	Michael Finley	.60	.25
❏ 90	Bostjan Nachbar	.20	.08
❏ 91	Allan Houston	.40	.15
❏ 92	Joe Johnson	.40	.15
❏ 93	Jalen Rose	.60	.25
❏ 94	Marquis Daniels	.40	.15
❏ 95	Tyronn Lue	.20	.08
❏ 96	Stephon Marbury	.60	.25
❏ 97	Quentin Richardson	.40	.15
❏ 98	Chris Bosh	.60	.25
❏ 99	Dajuan Wagner	.20	.08
❏ 100	Derek Fisher	.60	.25
❏ 101	Devean George	.20	.08
❏ 102	Zoran Planinic	.20	.08
❏ 103	Corliss Williamson	.20	.08
❏ 104	Brent Barry	.40	.15
❏ 105	Drew Gooden	.40	.15
❏ 106	Clifford Robinson	.20	.08
❏ 107	Shane Battier	.60	.25
❏ 108	P.J. Brown	.20	.08
❏ 109	Willie Green	.20	.08
❏ 110	Nick Collison	.20	.08
❏ 111	Al Harrington	.40	.15
❏ 112	Carmelo Anthony	1.25	.50
❏ 113	Corey Maggette	.40	.15
❏ 114	Eddie Jones	.60	.25
❏ 115	Zach Randolph	.60	.25
❏ 116	Raja Bell	.20	.08
❏ 117	Jeff McInnis	.20	.08
❏ 118	Yao Ming	1.50	.60
❏ 119	Brian Cardinal	.20	.08
❏ 120	Jamaal Magloire	.20	.08
❏ 121	Kyle Korver	.40	.15
❏ 122	Luke Ridnour	.40	.15
❏ 123	Jason Terry	.60	.25
❏ 124	Maurice Taylor	.20	.08
❏ 125	Bonzi Wells	.40	.15
❏ 126	David West	.40	.15
❏ 127	Amare Stoudemire	1.25	.50
❏ 128	Ray Allen	.60	.25
❏ 129	Eddy Curry	.40	.15
❏ 130	Richard Hamilton	.40	.15
❏ 131	Kobe Bryant	2.50	1.00
❏ 132	Kevin Garnett	1.25	.50
❏ 133	Steve Francis	.60	.25
❏ 134	Tim Duncan	1.25	.50
❏ 135	Larry Hughes	.40	.15
❏ 136	LeBron James	4.00	1.50
❏ 137	Adonal Foyle	.20	.08
❏ 138	Pau Gasol	.60	.25
❏ 139	Richard Jefferson	.40	.15
❏ 140	Allen Iverson	1.25	.50
❏ 141	Antonio Daniels	.20	.08
❏ 142	Eric Williams	.20	.08
❏ 143	Primoz Brezec	.20	.08
❏ 144	Jason Richardson	.40	.15
❏ 145	Chris Kaman	.40	.15
❏ 146	Troy Hudson	.20	.08
❏ 147	Hedo Turkoglu	.60	.25
❏ 148	Tony Parker	.60	.25
❏ 149	Gilbert Arenas	.60	.25
❏ 150	Eric Snow	.40	.15
❏ 151	Tracy McGrady	1.50	.60
❏ 152	Stromile Swift	.20	.08
❏ 153	Dan Dickau	.20	.08
❏ 154	Steve Nash	.60	.25
❏ 155	Rashard Lewis	.40	.15
❏ 156	Gerald Wallace	.40	.15
❏ 157	Mike Dunleavy	.40	.15
❏ 158	Bobby Simmons	.20	.08
❏ 159	Wally Szczerbiak	.40	.15
❏ 160	Grant Hill	.60	.25
❏ 161	Mike Bibby	.60	.25
❏ 162	Antawn Jamison	.60	.25
❏ 163	Antonio McDyess	.20	.08
❏ 164	Shaquille O'Neal	1.50	.60
❏ 165	Rafer Alston	.20	.08
❏ 166	Charles Barkley HH	8.00	3.00
❏ 167	David Robinson HH	12.00	5.00
❏ 171	Larry Bird HH	20.00	8.00
❏ 172	Scottie Pippen HH	12.00	5.00
❏ 173	Isiah Thomas HH	12.00	5.00
❏ 174	Kevin McHale HH	8.00	3.00
❏ 175	Dominique Wilkins HH	8.00	3.00
❏ 176	Josh Childress RC	4.00	1.50
❏ 177	Josh Smith RC	6.00	2.50
❏ 178	Al Jefferson RC	8.00	3.00
❏ 179	Delonte West RC	6.00	2.50
❏ 180	Tony Allen RC	4.00	1.50
❏ 181	Emeka Okafor RC	12.00	5.00
❏ 182	Bernard Robinson RC	3.00	1.25
❏ 183	Ben Gordon RC	12.00	5.00
❏ 184	Luol Deng RC	6.00	2.50
❏ 185	Andres Nocioni RC	4.00	1.50
❏ 186	Luke Jackson RC	8.00	3.00
❏ 187	Devin Harris RC	6.00	2.50
❏ 188	Andris Biedrins RC	5.00	2.00
❏ 189	Shaun Livingston RC	5.00	2.00
❏ 190	Dorell Wright RC	5.00	2.00
❏ 191	J.R. Smith RC	8.00	3.00
❏ 192	Trevor Ariza RC	3.00	1.25
❏ 193	Dwight Howard RC	10.00	4.00
❏ 194	Jameer Nelson RC	5.00	2.00
❏ 195	Andre Iguodala RC	8.00	3.00
❏ 196	Sebastian Telfair RC	3.00	1.25
❏ 197	Kevin Martin RC	5.00	2.00
❏ 198	David Harrison RC	3.00	1.25
❏ 199	Rafael Araujo RC	3.00	1.25
❏ 200	Kirk Snyder RC	3.00	1.25

2005-06 Hoops

#	Player		
❏	COMPLETE SET (184)	50.00	20.00
❏	COMMON CARD (1-142)	.20	.08
❏	COMMON ROOKIE (143-184)	1.50	.60
❏ 1	Josh Childress	.40	.15
❏ 2	Al Harrington	.40	.15
❏ 3	Josh Smith	.60	.25
❏ 4	Tony Delk	.20	.08
❏ 5	Joe Johnson	.40	.15
❏ 6	Al Jefferson	.60	.25
❏ 7	Paul Pierce	.60	.25
❏ 8	Ricky Davis	.60	.25
❏ 9	Tony Allen	.40	.15
❏ 10	Dan Dickau	.20	.08
❏ 11	Keith Bogans	.20	.08
❏ 12	Emeka Okafor	1.00	.40
❏ 13	Kareem Rush	.20	.08
❏ 14	Gerald Wallace	.40	.15
❏ 15	Primoz Brezec	.20	.08
❏ 16	Ben Gordon	1.25	.50
❏ 17	Luol Deng	.60	.25
❏ 18	Kirk Hinrich	.60	.25
❏ 19	Chris Duhon	.40	.15
❏ 20	Michael Jordan	4.00	1.50
❏ 21	LeBron James	4.00	1.50
❏ 22	Larry Hughes	.40	.15
❏ 23	Donyell Marshall	.20	.08
❏ 24	Drew Gooden	.40	.15
❏ 25	Zydrunas Ilgauskas	.40	.15
❏ 26	Erick Dampier	.20	.08
❏ 27	Jason Terry	.60	.25
❏ 28	Josh Howard	.40	.15
❏ 29	Dirk Nowitzki	1.00	.40
❏ 30	Jerry Stackhouse	.60	.25
❏ 31	Carmelo Anthony	1.25	.50
❏ 32	Marcus Camby	.40	.15
❏ 33	Nene	.40	.15
❏ 34	Kenyon Martin	.60	.25
❏ 35	Chauncey Billups	.60	.25
❏ 36	Richard Hamilton	.60	.25
❏ 37	Ben Wallace	.60	.25
❏ 38	Rasheed Wallace	.60	.25
❏ 39	Tayshaun Prince	.60	.25
❏ 40	Baron Davis	.60	.25
❏ 41	Mike Dunleavy	.40	.15
❏ 42	Mickael Pietrus	.20	.08
❏ 43	Jason Richardson	.60	.25
❏ 44	Tracy McGrady	1.50	.60
❏ 45	Yao Ming	1.50	.60
❏ 46	Stromile Swift	.40	.15
❏ 47	Bob Sura	.20	.08
❏ 48	Jermaine O'Neal	.60	.25
❏ 49	Ron Artest	.60	.25
❏ 50	Fred Jones	.40	.15
❏ 51	Stephen Jackson	.40	.15
❏ 52	Corey Maggette	.40	.15
❏ 53	Elton Brand	.60	.25
❏ 54	Shaun Livingston	.60	.25
❏ 55	Chris Wilcox	.20	.08
❏ 56	Chris Kaman	.40	.15
❏ 57	Kobe Bryant	2.50	1.00
❏ 58	Lamar Odom	.60	.25
❏ 59	Kwame Brown	.40	.15

#	Player		
60	Luke Walton	.40	.15
61	Devean George	.20	.08
62	Pau Gasol	.60	.25
63	Shane Battier	.60	.25
64	Bobby Jackson	.40	.15
65	Eddie Jones	.40	.15
66	Lorenzen Wright	.20	.08
67	Shaquille O'Neal	1.50	.60
68	Dwyane Wade	2.00	.75
69	Antoine Walker	.60	.25
70	Jason Williams	.40	.15
71	James Posey	.20	.08
72	T.J. Ford	.40	.15
73	Dan Gadzuric	.20	.08
74	Desmond Mason	.40	.15
75	Michael Redd	.60	.25
76	Kevin Garnett	1.25	.50
77	Sam Cassell	.60	.25
78	Eddie Griffin	.20	.08
79	Wally Szczerbiak	.40	.15
80	Michael Olowokandi	.20	.08
81	Jeff McInnis	.20	.08
82	Vince Carter	1.50	.60
83	Jason Kidd	1.00	.40
84	Richard Jefferson	.40	.15
85	Clifford Robinson	.20	.08
86	P.J. Brown	.20	.08
87	Jamaal Magloire	.20	.08
88	J.R. Smith	.40	.15
89	Speedy Claxton	.20	.08
90	Jamal Crawford	.40	.15
91	Stephon Marbury	.60	.25
92	Quentin Richardson	.40	.15
93	Mike Sweetney	.40	.15
94	Malik Rose	.20	.08
95	Steve Francis	.60	.25
96	Dwight Howard	.75	.30
97	Keyon Dooling	.20	.08
98	Grant Hill	.60	.25
99	Jameer Nelson	.40	.15
100	Allen Iverson	1.25	.50
101	Samuel Dalembert	.40	.15
102	Chris Webber	.60	.25
103	Andre Iguodala	.60	.25
104	Kyle Korver	.60	.25
105	Steve Nash	.60	.25
106	Shawn Marion	.60	.25
107	Amare Stoudemire	1.25	.50
108	Kurt Thomas	.40	.15
109	Darius Miles	.60	.25
110	Zach Randolph	.60	.25
111	Sebastian Telfair	.40	.15
112	Ruben Patterson	.20	.08
113	Joel Przybilla	.20	.08
114	Mike Bibby	.60	.25
115	Peja Stojakovic	.60	.25
116	Brad Miller	.60	.25
117	Bonzi Wells	.40	.15
118	Tim Duncan	1.25	.50
119	Manu Ginobili	.60	.25
120	Tony Parker	.60	.25
121	Robert Horry	.40	.15
122	Bruce Bowen	.40	.15
123	Ray Allen	.60	.25
124	Rashard Lewis	.60	.25
125	Vladimir Radmanovic	.20	.08
126	Luke Ridnour	.40	.15
127	Reggie Evans	.20	.08
128	Chris Bosh	.60	.25
129	Morris Peterson	.40	.15
130	Rafer Alston	.20	.08
131	Rafael Araujo	.20	.08
132	Jalen Rose	.40	.15
133	Carlos Boozer	.40	.15
134	Gordan Giricek	.20	.08
135	Matt Harpring	.60	.25
136	Andrei Kirilenko	.60	.25
137	Mehmet Okur	.20	.08
138	Gilbert Arenas	.60	.25
139	Antawn Jamison	.60	.25
140	Caron Butler	.40	.15
141	Antonio Daniels	.20	.08
142	Brendan Haywood	.20	.08
143	Sarunas Jasikevicius RC	2.50	1.00
144	Ryan Gomes RC	1.50	.60
145	Andray Blatche RC	1.50	.60

#	Player		
146	Bracey Wright RC	1.50	.60
147	Louis Williams RC	1.50	.60
148	Martynas Andriuskevicius RC	1.50	.60
149	Chris Taft RC	1.50	.60
150	Monta Ellis RC	3.00	1.25
151	Travis Diener RC	1.50	.60
152	Ersan Ilyasova RC	1.50	.60
153	Yaroslav Korolev RC	1.50	.60
154	C.J. Miles RC	1.50	.60
155	Brandon Bass RC	1.50	.60
156	Daniel Ewing RC	1.50	.60
157	Salim Stoudamire RC	2.50	1.00
158	David Lee RC	2.50	1.00
159	Wayne Simien RC	2.50	1.00
160	Linas Kleiza RC	1.50	.60
161	Jason Maxiell RC	1.50	.60
162	Johan Petro RC	1.50	.60
163	Luther Head RC	2.50	1.00
164	Francisco Garcia RC	2.50	1.00
165	Jarrett Jack RC	1.50	.60
166	Nate Robinson RC	3.00	1.25
167	Julius Hodge RC	2.50	1.00
168	Hakim Warrick RC	4.00	1.50
169	Gerald Green RC	5.00	2.00
170	Danny Granger RC	3.00	1.25
171	Joey Graham RC	1.50	.60
172	Antoine Wright RC	1.50	.60
173	Rashad McCants RC	4.00	1.50
174	Sean May RC	2.00	.75
175	Andrew Bynum RC	6.00	2.50
176	Ike Diogu RC	2.50	1.00
177	Channing Frye RC	2.50	1.00
178	Charlie Villanueva RC	3.00	1.25
179	Martell Webster RC	1.50	.60
180	Raymond Felton RC	4.00	1.50
181	Chris Paul RC	10.00	4.00
182	Deron Williams RC	6.00	2.50
183	Marvin Williams RC	5.00	2.00
184	Andrew Bogut RC	5.00	2.00

1999-00 Hoops Decade

STEVE FRANCIS — ROCKETS

COMPLETE SET (180)		30.00	15.00
COMMON CARD (1-180)		.25	.05
COMMON ROOKIE		.25	.08
1	David Robinson	.50	.20
2	Mookie Blaylock	.15	.05
3	Jaren Jackson	.15	.05
4	Andre Miller RC	1.25	.50
5	Michael Olowokandi	.30	.10
6	Glenn Robinson	.50	.20
7	Steve Smith	.30	.10
8	Eric Snow	.30	.10
9	Antoine Walker	.50	.20
10	Nick Anderson	.15	.05
11	Jonathan Bender RC	1.25	.50
12	Sean Elliott	.30	.10
13	Danny Fortson	.15	.05
14	Adonal Foyle	.15	.05
15	Richard Hamilton RC	1.25	.50
16	Shawn Kemp	.30	.10
17	Christian Laettner	.30	.10
18	Rashard Lewis	.50	.20
19	Danny Manning	.15	.05
20	Mitch Richmond	.30	.10
21	Shawn Bradley	.15	.05
22	Tim Duncan	1.00	.40
23	Tim Hardaway	.30	.10
24	Antawn Jamison	.75	.30

#	Player		
25	Jeff Hornacek	.30	.10
26	Jumaine Jones RC	.50	.20
27	Corey Maggette RC	1.25	.50
28	Vitaly Potapenko	.15	.05
29	Jerry Stackhouse	.50	.20
30	Jason Terry RC	.75	.30
31	Baron Davis RC	3.00	1.25
32	Matt Harpring	.50	.20
33	Glen Rice	.30	.10
34	Vladimir Stepania	.15	.05
35	Jayson Williams	.15	.05
36	Wally Szczerbiak RC	1.25	.50
37	Michael Doleac	.15	.05
38	Hersey Hawkins	.30	.10
39	Allan Houston	.30	.10
40	Hakeem Olajuwon	.50	.20
41	Damon Stoudamire	.30	.10
42	Jelani McCoy	.15	.05
43	A.Radojevic RC	.25	.08
44	Cal Bowdler RC	.40	.15
45	Tyronn Lue	.30	.10
46	Andrae Patterson	.15	.05
47	Karl Malone	.50	.20
48	Alonzo Mourning	.30	.10
49	Vince Carter	1.25	.50
50	Darrell Armstrong	.15	.05
51	Terrell Brandon	.30	.10
52	John Celestand RC	.40	.15
53	Grant Hill	.50	.20
54	Stephon Marbury	.50	.20
55	Tracy McGrady	1.25	.50
56	Reggie Miller	.50	.20
57	Clifford Robinson	.15	.05
58	Arvydas Sabonis	.30	.10
59	William Avery RC	.50	.20
60	Calbert Cheaney	.15	.05
61	Jermaine Jackson RC	.25	.08
62	Allen Iverson	1.00	.40
63	Larry Johnson	.30	.10
64	Toni Kukoc	.30	.10
65	Raef LaFrentz	.30	.10
66	Isaiah Rider	.15	.05
67	Jeff Foster RC	.40	.15
68	Juwan Howard	.30	.10
69	Kerry Kittles	.15	.05
70	Brevin Knight	.15	.05
71	Voshon Lenard	.15	.05
72	Latrell Sprewell	.50	.20
73	Maurice Taylor	.30	.10
74	Chris Webber	.50	.20
75	Jerome Williams	.15	.05
76	Scott Padgett RC	.40	.15
77	Vin Baker	.30	.10
78	Chris Childs	.15	.05
79	Erick Dampier	.30	.10
80	Anfernee Hardaway	.50	.20
81	Jamal Mashburn	.30	.10
82	Todd Fuller	.15	.05
83	Eric Piatkowski	.30	.10
84	Gary Trent	.15	.05
85	Kevin Garnett	1.00	.40
86	Chris Mullin	.50	.20
87	Charles Oakley	.15	.05
88	Detlef Schrempf	.30	.10
89	Elton Brand RC	1.50	.60
90	Patrick Ewing	.50	.20
91	Devean George RC	.60	.25
92	Brian Grant	.30	.10
93	Larry Hughes	.50	.20
94	Dan Majerle	.30	.10
95	Shawn Marion RC	1.50	.60
96	Cuttino Mobley	.50	.20
97	Paul Pierce	.50	.20
98	Bryant Reeves	.15	.05
99	Keith Van Horn	.50	.20
100	Corliss Williamson	.30	.10
101	Tariq Abdul-Wahad	.15	.05
102	Brent Barry	.30	.10
103	Elden Campbell	.15	.05
104	Mark Jackson	.30	.10
105	Lamond Murray	.15	.05
106	Bryon Russell	.15	.05
107	Jason Williams	.30	.10
108	Ray Allen	.50	.20
109	Ron Artest RC	.75	.30
110	Charles Barkley	.60	.25

#	Player		
111	Cedric Ceballos	.15	.05
112	Jason Kidd	.75	.30
113	Donyell Marshall	.30	.10
114	John Stockton	.50	.20
115	Mike Bibby	.50	.20
116	Ricky Davis	.30	.10
117	Steve Francis RC	1.50	.60
118	Tom Gugliotta	.15	.05
119	Laron Profit RC	.40	.15
120	Joe Smith	.30	.10
121	Doug Christie	.30	.10
122	Kenny Anderson	.30	.10
123	Michael Dickerson	.30	.10
124	Zydrunas Ilgauskas	.30	.10
125	Bobby Jackson	.30	.10
126	Quincy Lewis RC	.40	.15
127	Shandon Anderson	.15	.05
128	Bo Outlaw	.15	.05
129	Scottie Pippen	.75	.30
130	Rodney Rogers	.15	.05
131	Rik Smits	.30	.10
132	Chauncey Billups	.30	.10
133	Chris Crawford	.15	.05
134	Kornel David RC	.15	.05
135	Tony Delk	.15	.05
136	Kendall Gill	.15	.05
137	Trajan Langdon RC	.50	.20
138	Ron Mercer	.30	.10
139	Othella Harrington	.15	.05
140	Gheorghe Muresan	.15	.05
141	Isaac Austin	.15	.05
142	Dion Glover RC	.40	.15
143	Avery Johnson *	.15	.05
144	Antonio McDyess	.30	.10
145	Steve Nash	.50	.20
146	Tyrone Nesby RC	.15	.05
147	Shaquille O'Neal	1.25	.50
148	James Posey RC	.75	.30
149	Rod Strickland	.15	.05
150	Kobe Bryant	2.00	.75
151	Michael Finley	.50	.20
152	Anthony Mason	.30	.10
153	Dikembe Mutombo	.30	.10
154	John Starks	.30	.10
155	Kenny Thomas RC	.50	.20
156	Matt Geiger	.15	.05
157	Tim James RC	.40	.15
158	Eddie Jones	.50	.20
159	Lamar Odom RC	1.25	.50
160	Nick Van Exel	.50	.20
161	Sam Cassell	.50	.20
162	Vonteego Cummings RC	.50	.20
163	Lindsey Hunter	.15	.05
164	Dirk Nowitzki	1.00	.40
165	Gary Payton	.50	.20
166	Shareef Abdur-Rahim	.50	.20
167	Jalen Rose	.50	.20
168	Robert Traylor	.15	.05
169	Derek Anderson	.30	.10
170	Corey Benjamin	.15	.05
171	Marcus Camby	.30	.10
172	Vlade Divac	.30	.10
173	Mario Elie	.15	.05
174	Felipe Lopez	.15	.05
175	Rafer Alston RC	.75	.30
176	Antonio Davis	.15	.05
177	Howard Eisley	.15	.05
178	Theo Ratliff	.30	.10
179	Tim Thomas	.30	.10
180	Rasheed Wallace	.50	.20

2000-01 Hoops Hot Prospects

COMPLETE SET w/o RC (120)		40.00	20.00
COMMON CARD (1-120)		.30	.10
COMMON ROOKIE (121-145)		5.00	2.00
1	Vince Carter	2.50	1.00
2	Wesley Person	.30	.10
3	Juwan Howard	.60	.25
4	Rodney Rogers	.30	.10
5	Tim Duncan	2.00	.75
6	Rasheed Wallace	1.00	.40
7	Anthony Peeler	.30	.10
8	John Amaechi	.30	.10
9	Tim Hardaway	.60	.25

#	Player		
10	Mark Jackson	.30	.10
11	Latrell Sprewell	1.00	.10
12	Kevin Garnett	2.00	.75
13	Alonzo Mourning	.60	.25
14	Alan Henderson	.30	.10
15	Anfernee Hardaway	1.00	.40
16	Clifford Robinson	.30	.10
17	Mike Bibby	1.00	.40
18	Allen Iverson	2.00	.75
19	Terrell Brandon	.60	.25
20	Jerry Stackhouse	1.00	.40
21	Brian Grant	.60	.25
22	Lamond Murray	.30	.10
23	Nick Anderson	.30	.10
24	Alan Henderson	.30	.10
25	Bryon Russell	.30	.10
26	Elton Brand	1.00	.40
27	Antawn Jamison	1.00	.40
28	Mitch Richmond	.60	.25
29	Marcus Camby	.60	.25
30	Raef LaFrentz	.60	.25
31	Damon Stoudamire	.60	.25
32	Vin Baker	.60	.25
33	Allan Houston	.60	.25
34	Doug Christie	.60	.25
35	Stephon Marbury	1.00	.40
36	Tim Thomas	.60	.25
37	Tracy McGrady	2.50	1.00
38	Shareef Abdur-Rahim	1.00	.40
39	Eddie Jones	1.00	.40
40	Glenn Robinson	1.00	.40
41	Sam Cassell	1.00	.40
42	Dan Majerle	.60	.25
43	Maurice Taylor	.30	.10
44	Anthony Mason	.60	.25
45	Dirk Nowitzki	1.50	.60
46	Kobe Bryant	4.00	1.50
47	Kerry Kittles	.30	.10
48	Derrick Coleman	.30	.10
49	Cuttino Mobley	.60	.25
50	Nick Van Exel	1.00	.40
51	LaPhonso Ellis	.30	.10
52	Kendall Gill	.30	.10
53	Hakeem Olajuwon	1.00	.40
54	Rashard Lewis	.60	.25
55	Dale Davis	.30	.10
56	Keith Van Horn	1.00	.40
57	Michael Finley	1.00	.40
58	Othella Harrington	.30	.10
59	Gary Payton	1.00	.40
60	Michael Dickerson	.60	.25
61	Voshon Lenard	.30	.10
62	Patrick Ewing	1.00	.40
63	Ron Mercer	.60	.25
64	Kenny Anderson	.60	.25
65	Shaquille O'Neal	2.50	1.00
66	Tariq Abdul-Wahad	.30	.10
67	Antonio Davis	.30	.10
68	Rick Fox	.60	.25
69	Lamar Odom	1.00	.40
70	Derek Anderson	.60	.25
71	Vitaly Potapenko	.30	.10
72	Karl Malone	1.00	.40
73	Wally Szczerbiak	.60	.25
74	Jason Williams	.60	.25
75	Steve Francis	1.00	.40
76	John Starks	.60	.25
77	Ron Artest	.60	.25

#	Player		
78	Grant Hill	1.00	.40
79	Theo Ratliff	.60	.25
80	Antonio McDyess	.60	.25
81	Antoine Walker	1.00	.40
82	Sean Elliott	.60	.25
83	Ruben Patterson	.60	.25
84	Ray Allen	1.00	.40
85	Tom Gugliotta	.30	.10
86	Scottie Pippen	1.50	.60
87	Jim Jackson	.30	.10
88	Joe Smith	.60	.25
89	Reggie Miller	1.00	.40
90	Richard Hamilton	.60	.25
91	Paul Pierce	1.00	.40
92	Mookie Blaylock	.30	.10
93	Glen Rice	.60	.25
94	P.J. Brown	.30	.10
95	Avery Johnson	.30	.10
96	John Stockton	1.00	.40
97	Tyrone Hill	.30	.10
98	Tracy Murray	.30	.10
99	Darrell Armstrong	.30	.10
100	Steve Smith	.60	.25
101	Shawn Kemp	.60	.25
102	Jalen Rose	1.00	.40
103	Vonteego Cummings	.30	.10
104	Larry Hughes	.60	.25
105	Charles Oakley	.30	.10
106	Rod Strickland	.30	.10
107	Christian Laettner	.60	.25
108	Baron Davis	1.00	.40
109	Jamal Mashburn	.60	.25
110	Lindsey Hunter	.30	.10
111	Toni Kukoc	.60	.25
112	Austin Croshere	.60	.25
113	Chris Webber	1.00	.40
114	Vlade Divac	.60	.25
115	Andre Miller	.60	.25
116	Larry Johnson	.60	.25
117	Jason Kidd	1.50	.60
118	David Robinson	1.00	.40
119	Donyell Marshall	.60	.25
120	Jason Terry	1.00	.40
121	Kenyon Martin RC	12.00	5.00
122	Stromile Swift RC	8.00	3.00
123	Chris Mihm RC	5.00	2.00
124	Marcus Fizer RC	5.00	2.00
125	Courtney Alexander RC	5.00	2.00
126	Darius Miles RC	10.00	4.00
127	Jerome Moiso RC	5.00	2.00
128	Joel Przybilla RC	5.00	2.00
129	DerMarr Johnson RC	5.00	2.00
130	Mike Miller RC	8.00	3.00
131	Quentin Richardson RC	8.00	3.00
132	Morris Peterson RC	8.00	3.00
133	Speedy Claxton RC	5.00	2.00
134	Keyon Dooling RC	5.00	2.00
135	Mark Madsen RC	5.00	2.00
136	Mateen Cleaves RC	5.00	2.00
137	Etan Thomas RC	5.00	2.00
138	Jason Collier RC	6.00	2.50
139	Erick Barkley RC	5.00	2.00
140	Desmond Mason RC	5.00	2.00
141	Mamadou N'diaye RC	5.00	2.00
142	DeShawn Stevenson RC	5.00	2.00
143	Donnell Harvey RC	5.00	2.00
144	Jamaal Magloire RC	5.00	2.00
145	Hidayet Turkoglu RC	5.00	2.00

2001-02 Hoops Hot Prospects

COMP.SET w/o SP's (80)		40.00	20.00
COMMON CARD (1-80)		.30	.10
COMMON ROOKIE (81-120)		6.00	2.50
1	Vince Carter	2.50	1.00
2	John Stockton	1.00	.40
3	Steve Smith	.60	.25
4	Kevin Garnett	2.00	.75
5	Larry Hughes	.60	.25
6	Ron Mercer	.60	.25
7	Marcus Fizer	.60	.25
8	Rashard Lewis	.60	.25
9	Mike Miller	1.00	.40
10	Darius Miles	1.00	.40
11	Michael Finley	1.00	.40

❏ 12	Marcus Camby	.60	.25
❏ 13	Morris Peterson	.60	.25
❏ 14	Shawn Marion	1.00	.40
❏ 15	Alonzo Mourning	.60	.25
❏ 16	Jamal Mashburn	.60	.25
❏ 17	Michael Jordan	15.00	6.00
❏ 18	Jason Williams	.60	.25
❏ 19	Latrell Sprewell	1.00	.40
❏ 20	Reggie Miller	1.00	.40
❏ 21	Glenn Robinson	1.00	.40
❏ 22	Steve Francis	1.00	.40
❏ 23	Antoine Walker	1.00	.40
❏ 24	Stromile Swift	.60	.25
❏ 25	Damon Stoudamire	.60	.25
❏ 26	Allan Houston	.60	.25
❏ 27	Kobe Bryant	4.00	1.50
❏ 28	Dirk Nowitzki	1.50	.60
❏ 29	Iakovos Tsakalidis	.30	.10
❏ 30	Gary Payton	1.00	.40
❏ 31	Allen Iverson	2.00	.75
❏ 32	Eddie Jones	1.00	.40
❏ 33	Mateen Cleaves	1.00	.40
❏ 34	Nick Van Exel	1.00	.40
❏ 35	Terrell Brandon	.60	.25
❏ 36	Wally Szczerbiak	.60	.25
❏ 37	Jalen Rose	1.00	.40
❏ 38	Elton Brand	1.00	.40
❏ 39	DerMarr Johnson	.60	.25
❏ 40	Peja Stojakovic	1.00	.40
❏ 41	Jason Kidd	1.50	.60
❏ 42	Sam Cassell	1.00	.40
❏ 43	Cuttino Mobley	.60	.25
❏ 44	Toni Kukoc	.60	.25
❏ 45	DeShawn Stevenson	.60	.25
❏ 46	David Robinson	1.00	.40
❏ 47	Grant Hill	1.00	.40
❏ 48	Shaquille O'Neal	2.50	1.00
❏ 49	Andre Miller	.60	.25
❏ 50	Corey Maggette	.60	.25
❏ 51	Jason Terry	1.00	.40
❏ 52	Aaron McKie	.60	.25
❏ 53	Eddie House	.60	.25
❏ 54	Steve Nash	1.00	.40
❏ 55	Clifford Robinson	.30	.10
❏ 56	Chris Webber	1.00	.40
❏ 57	Kenyon Martin	1.00	.40
❏ 58	Jermaine O'Neal	1.00	.40
❏ 59	Baron Davis	1.00	.40
❏ 60	Mitch Richmond	1.00	.40
❏ 61	Antawn Jamison	1.00	.40
❏ 62	Paul Pierce	1.00	.40
❏ 63	Shareef Abdur-Rahim	1.00	.40
❏ 64	Rasheed Wallace	1.00	.40
❏ 65	Ray Allen	1.00	.40
❏ 66	Lamar Odom	1.00	.40
❏ 67	Chris Mihm	.60	.25
❏ 68	Raef LaFrentz	.60	.25
❏ 69	Patrick Ewing	1.00	.40
❏ 70	Tracy McGrady	2.50	1.00
❏ 71	Derek Fisher	1.00	.40
❏ 72	Jerry Stackhouse	1.00	.40
❏ 73	Antonio McDyess	.60	.25
❏ 74	Karl Malone	1.00	.40
❏ 75	Dikembe Mutombo	.60	.25
❏ 76	Hakeem Olajuwon	1.00	.40
❏ 77	David Wesley	.30	.10
❏ 78	Courtney Alexander	.60	.25
❏ 79	Tim Duncan	2.00	.75

❏ 80	Stephon Marbury	1.00	.40
❏ 81	Kwame Brown JSY RC	10.00	4.00
❏ 82	Tyson Chandler JSY RC	10.00	4.00
❏ 83	Pau Gasol JSY RC	20.00	8.00
❏ 84	Eddy Curry JSY RC	10.00	4.00
❏ 85	J.Richardson JSY/300 RC	15.00	6.00
❏ 86	Shane Battier JSY RC	8.00	3.00
❏ 87	E.Griffin JSY/300 RC	8.00	3.00
❏ 88	DeSagana Diop JSY RC	6.00	2.50
❏ 89	Rodney White JSY RC	6.00	2.50
❏ 90	J.Johnson JSY/300 RC	50.00	20.00
❏ 91	Ke.Brown JSY/300 RC	6.00	2.50
❏ 92	V.Radmanovic JSY RC	6.00	2.50
❏ 93	Richard Jefferson JSY RC	12.00	5.00
❏ 94	Troy Murphy JSY RC	10.00	4.00
❏ 95	Steven Hunter JSY RC	6.00	2.50
❏ 96	Kirk Haston JSY RC	6.00	2.50
❏ 97	Michael Bradley JSY RC	6.00	2.50
❏ 98	Jason Collins JSY RC	6.00	2.50
❏ 99	Zach Randolph JSY RC	15.00	6.00
❏ 100	Brendan Haywood JSY RC	6.00	2.50
❏ 101	Joseph Forte JSY RC	6.00	2.50
❏ 102	Jeryl Sasser JSY RC	6.00	2.50
❏ 103	B.Armstrong JSY/300 RC	6.00	2.50
❏ 104	Andrei Kirilenko JSY RC	15.00	6.00
❏ 105	Primos Brezec JSY RC	6.00	2.50
❏ 106	S.Dalembert JSY/300 RC	12.00	5.00
❏ 107	Jamaal Tinsley JSY RC	6.00	2.50
❏ 108	Tony Parker JSY RC	25.00	10.00

2002-03 Hoops Hot Prospects

❏ COMP.SET w/o SP's (80).		50.00	20.00
❏ COMMON JSY RC (81-108)		15.00	6.00
❏ COMMON ROOKIE (109-120)		10.00	4.00
❏ 1	Vince Carter	3.00	1.25
❏ 2	Chris Webber	1.00	.40
❏ 3	Latrell Sprewell	1.00	.40
❏ 4	Brian Grant	.60	.25
❏ 5	Jerry Stackhouse	1.00	.40
❏ 6	Joe Smith	.60	.25
❏ 7	Jason Terry	1.00	.40
❏ 8	Shawn Marion	1.00	.40
❏ 9	Wally Szczerbiak	.60	.25
❏ 10	Reggie Miller	1.00	.40
❏ 11	Steve Nash	1.00	.40
❏ 12	Karl Malone	1.00	.40
❏ 13	Damon Stoudamire	.60	.25
❏ 14	Jamal Mashburn	.60	.25
❏ 15	Kobe Bryant	4.00	1.50
❏ 16	Paul Pierce	1.00	.40
❏ 17	Tony Parker	1.00	.40
❏ 18	Mike Miller	1.00	.40
❏ 19	Sam Cassell	1.00	.40
❏ 20	Eddie Griffin	.60	.25
❏ 21	Jason Williams	1.00	.40
❏ 22	Jason Richardson	1.00	.40
❏ 23	Antoine Walker	1.00	.40
❏ 24	Tim Duncan	2.00	.75
❏ 25	Baron Davis	1.00	.40
❏ 26	Glenn Robinson	1.00	.40
❏ 27	Darius Miles	1.00	.40
❏ 28	Dirk Nowitzki	1.50	.60
❏ 29	John Stockton	1.00	.40
❏ 30	Allen Iverson	2.00	.75
❏ 31	Richard Jefferson	.60	.25
❏ 32	Rick Fox	.60	.25
❏ 33	Ben Wallace	1.00	.40

❏ 34	Michael Jordan	8.00	3.00
❏ 35	Rasheed Wallace	1.00	.40
❏ 36	Alonzo Mourning	.60	.25
❏ 37	Steve Francis	1.00	.40
❏ 38	Jalen Rose	1.00	.40
❏ 39	Rashard Lewis	.60	.25
❏ 40	Tracy McGrady	2.50	1.00
❏ 41	David Wesley	.25	.10
❏ 42	Pau Gasol	1.00	.40
❏ 43	Antawn Jamison	1.00	.40
❏ 44	Shareef Abdur-Rahim	1.00	.40
❏ 45	Mike Bibby	1.00	.40
❏ 46	Dikembe Mutombo	.60	.25
❏ 47	Kevin Garnett	2.00	.75
❏ 48	Elton Brand	1.00	.40
❏ 49	Lamond Murray	.25	.10
❏ 50	Morris Peterson	.60	.25
❏ 51	Joe Johnson	.60	.25
❏ 52	Kenyon Martin	1.00	.40
❏ 53	Shaquille O'Neal	2.50	1.00
❏ 54	Antonio McDyess	.60	.25
❏ 55	Vin Baker	.60	.25
❏ 56	Marcus Camby	.60	.25
❏ 57	Ray Allen	1.00	.40
❏ 58	Jermain O'Neal	1.00	.40
❏ 59	Eddy Curry	1.00	.40
❏ 60	David Robinson	1.00	.40
❏ 61	Clifford Robinson	.25	.10
❏ 62	Rodney Rogers	.25	.10
❏ 63	Peja Stojakovic	1.00	.40
❏ 64	Allan Houston	.60	.25
❏ 65	Shane Battier	1.00	.40
❏ 66	Jamaal Tinsley	1.00	.40
❏ 67	Michael Finley	1.00	.40
❏ 68	Kenny Anderson	.60	.25
❏ 69	Stephon Marbury	1.00	.40
❏ 70	Terrell Brandon	.60	.25
❏ 71	Lamar Odom	1.00	.40
❏ 72	Raef LaFrentz	.60	.25
❏ 73	Jamaal Magloire	.25	.10
❏ 74	Bonzi Wells	.60	.25
❏ 75	Jason Kidd	1.50	.60
❏ 76	Cuttino Mobley	.60	.25
❏ 77	Tyson Chandler	1.00	.40
❏ 78	Gary Payton	1.00	.40
❏ 79	Grant Hill	1.00	.40
❏ 80	Eddie Jones	1.00	.40
❏ 81	Yao Ming JSY RC	80.00	40.00
❏ 82	Fred Jones JSY RC	15.00	6.00
❏ 83	R.Humphrey JSY RC	15.00	6.00
❏ 84	Drew Gooden JSY RC	30.00	12.50
❏ 85	N.Tskitishvili JSY RC	15.00	6.00
❏ 86	Caron Butler JSY RC	25.00	10.00
❏ 87	V.Yarbrough JSY RC	15.00	6.00
❏ 88	DaJ.Wagner JSY RC	20.00	8.00
❏ 89	Nene Hilario JSY RC	25.00	10.00
❏ 90	Qyntel Woods JSY RC	15.00	6.00
❏ 91	Jared Jeffries JSY RC	15.00	6.00
❏ 92	C.Jacobsen JSY RC	15.00	6.00
❏ 93	Marcus Haislip JSY RC	15.00	6.00
❏ 94	Kareem Rush JSY RC	15.00	6.00
❏ 95	P.Savovic JSY RC	15.00	6.00
❏ 96	Melvin Ely JSY RC	15.00	6.00
❏ 97	Steve Logan JSY RC	15.00	6.00
❏ 98	A.Stoudemire JSY RC	60.00	30.00
❏ 99	John Salmons JSY RC	15.00	6.00
❏ 100	Chris Jefferies JSY RC	20.00	8.00
❏ 101	Juan Dixon JSY RC	20.00	8.00
❏ 102	Carlos Boozer JSY RC	25.00	10.00
❏ 103	Roger Mason JSY RC	15.00	6.00
❏ 104	Rod Grizzard JSY RC	15.00	6.00
❏ 105	T.Prince JSY RC	20.00	8.00
❏ 106	Chris Wilcox JSY RC	20.00	8.00
❏ 107	Sam Clancy JSY RC	20.00	8.00
❏ 108	Dan Gadzuric JSY RC	15.00	6.00
❏ 109	Dan Dickau/900 RC	10.00	4.00
❏ 110	Jay Williams/900 RC	10.00	4.00
❏ 111	Mike Dunleavy/900 RC	8.00	3.00
❏ 112	Robert Archibald/900 RC	10.00	4.00
❏ 113	Curtis Borchardt/900 RC	10.00	4.00
❏ 114	Bostjan Nachbar/900 RC	10.00	4.00
❏ 115	Jiri Welsch/1500 RC	10.00	4.00
❏ 116	Frank Williams/1500 RC	10.00	4.00
❏ 117	Rasual Butler/1500 RC	10.00	4.00
❏ 118	Tamar Slay/1500 RC	10.00	4.00

❑ 119 Ronald Murray/1500 RC	10.00	4.00
❑ 120 Corsley Edwards/1500 RC	10.00	4.00

2003-04 Hoops Hot Prospects

❑ COMP. SET w/o SP's	40.00	15.00
❑ COMMON CARD (1-80)	.25	.10
❑ COMMON AU RC (81-87)	12.00	5.00
❑ COMMON JSY RC (88-94)	12.00	5.00
❑ COMMON JSY AU RC (95-111)	25.00	10.00
❑ COMMON ROOKIE (112-117)	8.00	3.00
❑ WHITE HOT ONE OF ONE's EXIST		
❑ WHITE HOT UNPRICED DUE TO SCARCITY		
❑ 1 Shareef Abdur-Rahim	1.00	.40
❑ 2 Mike Bibby	1.00	.40
❑ 3 Allan Houston	.60	.25
❑ 4 Pau Gasol	1.00	.40
❑ 5 Tayshaun Prince	.60	.25
❑ 6 Darius Miles	1.00	.40
❑ 7 Ray Allen	1.00	.40
❑ 8 Amare Stoudemire	2.00	.75
❑ 9 Latrell Sprewell	1.00	.40
❑ 10 Jamaal Tinsley	1.00	.40
❑ 11 Nene	.60	.25
❑ 12 Matt Harpring	1.00	.40
❑ 13 Bonzi Wells	.60	.25
❑ 14 Alonzo Mourning	.60	.25
❑ 15 Elton Brand	1.00	.40
❑ 16 Paul Pierce	1.00	.40
❑ 17 Tony Parker	1.00	.40
❑ 18 Glenn Robinson	1.00	.40
❑ 19 Marcus Haislip	.25	.10
❑ 20 Eddie Griffin	.60	.25
❑ 21 Jamaal Magloire	.25	.10
❑ 22 Gilbert Arenas	1.00	.40
❑ 23 Antoine Walker	1.00	.40
❑ 24 Manu Ginobili	1.00	.40
❑ 25 Jamal Mashburn	.60	.25
❑ 26 Michael Redd	1.00	.40
❑ 27 Ron Artest	1.00	.40
❑ 28 Steve Nash	1.00	.40
❑ 29 Andrei Kirilenko	1.00	.40
❑ 30 Stephon Marbury	1.00	.40
❑ 31 Richard Jefferson	.60	.25
❑ 32 Kobe Bryant	4.00	1.50
❑ 33 Cuttino Mobley	.60	.25
❑ 34 Juan Dixon	.60	.25
❑ 35 Rasheed Wallace	1.00	.40
❑ 36 Eddie Jones	1.00	.40
❑ 37 Steve Francis	1.00	.40
❑ 38 Dajuan Wagner	.60	.25
❑ 39 Vladimir Radmanovic	.25	.10
❑ 40 Drew Gooden	.60	.25
❑ 41 Baron Davis	1.00	.40
❑ 42 Mike Miller	1.00	.40
❑ 43 Jason Richardson	1.00	.40
❑ 44 Dan Dickau	.25	.10
❑ 45 Chris Webber	1.00	.40
❑ 46 Kenny Thomas	.25	.10
❑ 47 Kevin Garnett	2.00	.75
❑ 48 Reggie Miller	1.00	.40
❑ 49 Dirk Nowitzki	1.50	.60
❑ 50 Vince Carter	2.50	1.00
❑ 51 Zach Randolph	1.00	.40
❑ 52 Jason Kidd	1.50	.60
❑ 53 Shaquille O'Neal	2.50	1.00
❑ 54 Nikoloz Tskitishvili	.25	.10
❑ 55 Jerry Stackhouse	1.00	.40
❑ 56 Tracy McGrady	2.50	1.00
❑ 57 Desmond Mason	.60	.25
❑ 58 Yao Ming	2.50	1.00
❑ 59 Jalen Rose	1.00	.40
❑ 60 Tim Duncan	2.00	.75
❑ 61 Ben Wallace	1.00	.40
❑ 62 Mike Dunleavy	.60	.25
❑ 63 Peja Stojakovic	1.00	.40
❑ 64 Keith Van Horn	1.00	.40
❑ 65 Karl Malone	1.00	.40
❑ 66 Jermaine O'Neal	1.00	.40
❑ 67 Michael Finley	1.00	.40
❑ 68 Morris Peterson	.60	.25
❑ 69 Shawn Marion	1.00	.40
❑ 70 John Salmons	.25	.10
❑ 71 Chris Wilcox	.60	.25
❑ 72 Rodney White	.25	.10
❑ 73 Kwame Brown	.60	.25
❑ 74 Bobby Jackson	.60	.25
❑ 75 Kenyon Martin	1.00	.40
❑ 76 Antawn Jamison	1.00	.40
❑ 77 Eddy Curry	.60	.25
❑ 78 Bruce Bowen	.25	.10
❑ 79 Allen Iverson	2.00	.75
❑ 80 Caron Butler	1.00	.40
❑ 81 Boris Diaw AU RC	20.00	8.00
❑ 82 Quinton Ross AU RC	12.00	5.00
❑ 83 Matt Carroll AU RC	12.00	5.00
❑ 84 Travis Hansen AU RC	12.00	5.00
❑ 85 Zaur Pachulia AU RC	12.00	5.00
❑ 86 Zarko Cabarkapa AU RC	12.00	5.00
❑ 87 Maciej Lampe AU RC	12.00	5.00
❑ 88 Ndudi Ebi JSY RC	15.00	6.00
❑ 89 Jarvis Hayes JSY RC	20.00	8.00
❑ 90 Steve Blake JSY RC	12.00	5.00
❑ 91 Keith Bogans JSY RC	12.00	5.00
❑ 92 Reece Gaines JSY RC	12.00	5.00
❑ 93 Chris Kaman JSY RC	20.00	8.00
❑ 94 Slavko Vranes JSY RC	12.00	5.00
❑ 95 C.Anthony JSY AU RC	160.00	80.00
❑ 96 Troy Bell JSY AU RC	25.00	10.00
❑ 97 Travis Outlaw JSY AU RC	25.00	10.00
❑ 98 M.Sweetney JSY AU RC	25.00	10.00
❑ 99 Dahntay Jones JSY AU RC	25.00	10.00
❑ 100 Chris Bosh JSY AU RC	120.00	60.00
❑ 101 Brian Cook JSY AU RC	25.00	10.00
❑ 102 Luke Ridnour JSY AU RC	30.00	12.50
❑ 103 David West JSY AU RC	25.00	10.00
❑ 104 Banks JSY AU RC EXCH	25.00	10.00
❑ 105 Ken.Perkins JSY AU RC	25.00	10.00
❑ 106 Barbosa JSY AU RC EXCH	40.00	15.00
❑ 107 M.Pietrus JSY AU RC	25.00	10.00
❑ 108 D.Wade JSY AU RC	250.00	125.00
❑ 109 Howard JSY AU RC EXCH	50.00	20.00
❑ 110 J.Kapono JSY AU RC	20.00	8.00
❑ 111 Luke Walton JSY AU RC	20.00	8.00
❑ 112 LeBron James RC	50.00	20.00
❑ 113 T.J. Ford RC	8.00	3.00
❑ 114 Zoran Planinic RC	8.00	3.00
❑ 115 Darko Milicic RC	10.00	4.00
❑ 116 Kirk Hinrich RC	10.00	4.00
❑ 117 Nick Collison RC	8.00	3.00

2004-05 Hoops Hot Prospects

❑ COMP. SET w/o SP's (70)	40.00	15.00
❑ COMMON CARD (1-70)	.25	.10
❑ COMMON JSY AU RC (71-90)	25.00	10.00
❑ COMMON JSY RC (91-100)	15.00	6.00
❑ COMMON ROOKIE (100-110)	5.00	2.00
❑ 1 Dwyane Wade	2.00	.75
❑ 2 Chris Bosh	1.00	.40
❑ 3 Peja Stojakovic	1.00	.40
❑ 4 Darius Miles	1.00	.40
❑ 5 Drew Gooden	.60	.25
❑ 6 Latrell Sprewell	1.00	.40
❑ 7 Caron Butler	1.00	.40
❑ 8 Shaquille O'Neal	2.50	1.00
❑ 9 Reggie Miller	1.00	.40
❑ 10 Corey Maggette	.60	.25
❑ 11 Tracy McGrady	2.50	1.00
❑ 12 Ben Wallace	1.00	.40
❑ 13 Steve Nash	1.00	.40
❑ 14 Paul Pierce	1.00	.40
❑ 15 Jarvis Hayes	.60	.25
❑ 16 Ray Allen	1.00	.40
❑ 17 Chris Webber	1.00	.40
❑ 18 Amare Stoudemire	2.00	.75
❑ 19 Pau Gasol	1.00	.40
❑ 20 Jermaine O'Neal	1.00	.40
❑ 21 Yao Ming	2.50	1.00
❑ 22 Richard Hamilton	.60	.25
❑ 23 Kirk Hinrich	1.00	.40
❑ 24 Antoine Walker	1.00	.40
❑ 25 Carlos Arroyo	1.50	.60
❑ 26 Luke Ridnour	.60	.25
❑ 27 Mike Bibby	1.00	.40
❑ 28 Tim Duncan	2.00	.75
❑ 29 Shareef Abdur-Rahim	1.00	.40
❑ 30 Willie Green	.25	.10
❑ 31 Jamaal Magloire	.25	.10
❑ 32 Stephen Jackson	.60	.25
❑ 33 Karl Malone	1.00	.40
❑ 34 Elton Brand	1.00	.40
❑ 35 Jason Richardson	1.00	.40
❑ 36 Steve Francis	1.00	.40
❑ 37 Jason Kidd	1.50	.60
❑ 38 Kevin Garnett	2.00	.75
❑ 39 Jason Williams	.60	.25
❑ 40 Ron Artest	.60	.25
❑ 41 Darko Milicic	.60	.25
❑ 42 Carmelo Anthony	2.50	1.00
❑ 43 Carlos Boozer	1.00	.40
❑ 44 Michael Finley	1.00	.40
❑ 45 Marcus Fizer	.25	.10
❑ 46 Ricky Davis	1.00	.40
❑ 47 Andrei Kirilenko	1.00	.40
❑ 48 Tony Parker	1.00	.40
❑ 49 Shawn Marion	1.00	.40
❑ 50 Allan Houston	1.00	.40
❑ 51 Kenyon Martin	1.00	.40
❑ 52 T.J. Ford	.60	.25
❑ 53 Nene	.60	.25
❑ 54 LeBron James	6.00	2.50
❑ 55 Eddy Curry	1.00	.40
❑ 56 Jason Terry	1.00	.40
❑ 57 Vince Carter	2.50	1.00
❑ 58 Zach Randolph	1.00	.40
❑ 59 Allen Iverson	2.00	.75
❑ 60 Stephon Marbury	1.00	.40
❑ 61 Richard Jefferson	1.00	.40
❑ 62 Baron Davis	1.00	.40
❑ 63 Michael Redd	1.00	.40
❑ 64 Lamar Odom	1.00	.40
❑ 65 Kobe Bryant	4.00	1.50
❑ 66 Mickael Pietrus	.60	.25
❑ 67 Dirk Nowitzki	1.50	.60
❑ 68 Dajuan Wagner	.60	.25
❑ 69 Jason Kapono	.60	.25
❑ 70 Antawn Jamison	1.00	.40
❑ 71 B.Gordon JSY AU RC/350	120.00	60.00
❑ 72 Livingston JSY AU RC/350	60.00	30.00
❑ 73 Dev.Harris JSY AU RC/150	100.00	50.00
❑ 74 J.Childress JSY AU RC/150	50.00	25.00
❑ 75 Luol Deng JSY AU RC/350	80.00	40.00
❑ 76 R.Araujo JSY AU RC/350	25.00	10.00
❑ 77 L.Jackson JSY AU RC/150	25.00	10.00
❑ 78 Andris Biedrins JSY AU RC		
❑ 79 Y.Tabuse JSY AU RC/350	30.00	12.50
❑ 80 S.Telfair JSY AU RC/350	25.00	10.00
❑ 81 Humphries JSY AU RC/350	25.00	10.00
❑ 82 Kirk Snyder JSY AU RC/150	12.50	
❑ 83 Josh Smith JSY AU RC/150	80.00	40.00
❑ 84 J.R. Smith JSY AU RC/350	50.00	20.00

☐	85 D.Wright JSY AU RC/350	30.00	12.50
☐	86 J.Nelson JSY AU RC/350	50.00	20.00
☐	87 D.West JSY AU RC/350	25.00	10.00
☐	88 Tony Allen JSY AU RC/350	25.00	10.00
☐	89 Seung-Jin JSY AU RC/350	25.00	10.00
☐	90 A.Jefferson JSY AU RC/150	80.00	40.00
☐	91 Dwight Howard JSY RC	40.00	15.00
☐	92 Andre Iguodala JSY RC	40.00	15.00
☐	93 Jackson Vroman JSY RC	15.00	6.00
☐	94 Lionel Chalmers JSY RC	15.00	6.00
☐	95 Kevin Martin JSY RC	30.00	12.50
☐	96 Sasha Vujacic RC	15.00	6.00
☐	97 Andre Emmett JSY RC	15.00	6.00
☐	98 David Harrison RC	15.00	6.00
☐	99 A.Varejao JSY RC	15.00	6.00
☐	100 Chris Duhon RC	30.00	12.50
☐	101 Emeka Okafor RC	20.00	8.00
☐	102 Viktor Khryapa RC	5.00	2.00
☐	103 Peter John Ramos RC	5.00	2.00
☐	104 Sergei Monia RC	5.00	2.00
☐	105 Beno Udrih RC	8.00	3.00
☐	106 Pavel Podkolzine RC	5.00	2.00
☐	107 Trevor Ariza RC	6.00	2.50
☐	108 Royal Ivey RC	5.00	2.00
☐	109 Bernard Robinson RC	5.00	2.00
☐	110 Robert Swift RC	5.00	2.00

2002-03 Hoops Stars

☐	COMP. SET w/o RC's (170)	30.00	12.50
☐	COMMON CARD (1-170)	.20	.08
☐	COMMON ROOKIE (171-200)	2.50	1.00
☐	1 Tracy McGrady	2.00	.75
☐	2 Kevin Garnett	1.50	.60
☐	3 Allen Iverson	1.50	.50
☐	4 Keith Van Horn	.75	.30
☐	5 Kwame Brown	.50	.20
☐	6 Alan Henderson	.50	.20
☐	7 Kenny Anderson	.50	.20
☐	8 Antoine Walker	.75	.30
☐	9 Tony Delk	.20	.08
☐	10 Tony Battie	.20	.08
☐	11 Wally Szczerbiak	.50	.20
☐	12 Paul Pierce	.75	.30
☐	13 Glenn Robinson	.75	.30
☐	14 Tim Thomas	.50	.20
☐	15 Vince Carter	2.00	.75
☐	16 Pau Gasol	.75	.30
☐	17 Eddy Curry	.75	.30
☐	18 Darrell Armstrong	.20	.08
☐	19 Sam Cassell	.75	.30
☐	20 Darius Miles	.75	.30
☐	21 Jason Richardson	.75	.30
☐	22 Elton Brand	.75	.30
☐	23 Michael Jordan	6.00	2.50
☐	24 Andre Miller	.50	.20
☐	25 Anfernee Hardaway	.75	.30
☐	26 Steve Nash	.75	.30
☐	27 Ron Artest	.50	.20
☐	28 Rael LaFrentz	.50	.20
☐	29 Troy Hudson	.20	.08
☐	30 Rasheed Wallace	.75	.30
☐	31 Ricky Davis	.50	.20
☐	32 Juwan Howard	.50	.20
☐	33 Steve Francis	.75	.30
☐	34 Shaquille O'Neal	.75	.30
☐	35 James Posey	.50	.20
☐	36 DeShawn Stevenson	.20	.08
☐	37 Clifford Robinson	.20	.08
☐	38 Jerry Stackhouse	.75	.30
☐	39 Chauncey Billups	.50	.20
☐	40 Mike Bibby	.75	.30
☐	41 Dirk Nowitzki	1.25	.50
☐	42 Corliss Williamson	.50	.20
☐	43 Antawn Jamison	.75	.30
☐	44 Jamal Mashburn	.50	.20
☐	45 Danny Fortson	.20	.08
☐	46 Reggie Miller	.75	.30
☐	47 Scottie Pippen	1.25	.50
☐	48 Donnell Harvey	.20	.08
☐	49 Moochie Norris	.20	.08
☐	50 Corey Maggette	.50	.20
☐	51 Eddie Griffin	.50	.20
☐	52 Karl Malone	.75	.30
☐	53 Maurice Taylor	.20	.08
☐	54 Al Harrington	.50	.20
☐	55 Kenyon Martin	.75	.30
☐	56 Nick Van Exel	.75	.30
☐	57 Jermaine O'Neal	.75	.30
☐	58 Anthony Mason	.50	.20
☐	59 Jamaal Tinsley	.75	.30
☐	60 Chris Mihm	.20	.08
☐	61 Lamar Odom	.75	.30
☐	62 Cuttino Mobley	.50	.20
☐	63 Michael Olowokandi	.20	.08
☐	64 Michael Finley	.75	.30
☐	65 Anthony Peeler	.20	.08
☐	66 Mengke Bateer	.75	.30
☐	67 Rick Fox	.50	.20
☐	68 Steve Smith	.50	.20
☐	69 Robert Horry	.50	.20
☐	70 Devean George	.20	.08
☐	71 Jason Williams	.50	.20
☐	72 Stromile Swift	.50	.20
☐	73 Marcus Fizer	.20	.08
☐	74 Michael Dickerson	.20	.08
☐	75 Shane Battier	.75	.30
☐	76 Larry Hughes	.75	.30
☐	77 Brian Skinner	.20	.08
☐	78 Eddie Jones	.75	.30
☐	79 Malik Allen	.20	.08
☐	80 Ray Allen	.75	.30
☐	81 Jumaine Jones	.50	.20
☐	82 Donyell Marshall	.50	.20
☐	83 Toni Kukoc	.50	.20
☐	84 Michael Redd	.75	.30
☐	85 Ron Mercer	.50	.20
☐	86 Terrell Brandon	.50	.20
☐	87 Latrell Sprewell	.75	.30
☐	88 Kobe Bryant	3.00	1.25
☐	89 Kurt Thomas	.50	.20
☐	90 Rasho Nesterovic	.20	.08
☐	91 Shareef Abdur-Rahim	.75	.30
☐	92 Eduardo Najera	.20	.08
☐	93 Jamaal Magloire	.20	.08
☐	94 Antonio Davis	.20	.08
☐	95 Rodney Rogers	.20	.08
☐	96 Jason Collins	.20	.08
☐	97 Marcus Camby	.50	.20
☐	98 Joe Smith	.20	.08
☐	99 Richard Jefferson	.50	.20
☐	100 Gilbert Arenas	.75	.30
☐	101 Courtney Alexander	.50	.20
☐	102 David Wesley	.20	.08
☐	103 Baron Davis	.75	.30
☐	104 Elden Campbell	.20	.08
☐	105 Jason Kidd	1.25	.50
☐	106 P.J. Brown	.20	.08
☐	107 Rashard Lewis	.50	.20
☐	108 Alvin Williams	.20	.08
☐	109 Kerry Kittles	.20	.08
☐	110 Charlie Ward	.20	.08
☐	111 Kedrick Brown	.50	.20
☐	112 Shandon Anderson	.20	.08
☐	113 Grant Hill	.75	.30
☐	114 Tyson Chandler	.75	.30
☐	115 Brent Barry	.20	.08
☐	116 Travis Best	.20	.08
☐	117 Mike Miller	.75	.30
☐	118 Aaron McKie	.50	.20
☐	119 Theo Ratliff	.50	.20
☐	120 Todd MacCulloch	.20	.08
☐	121 Trenton Hassell	.20	.08
☐	122 Vin Baker	.50	.20
☐	123 Dion Glover	.20	.08
☐	124 Stephon Marbury	.75	.30
☐	125 Ben Wallace	.75	.30
☐	126 Glen Rice	.50	.20
☐	127 Joe Johnson	.50	.20
☐	128 Chris Webber	.75	.30
☐	129 Damon Stoudamire	.50	.20
☐	130 Voshon Lenard	.20	.08
☐	131 Troy Murphy	.50	.20
☐	132 Desmond Mason	.50	.20
☐	133 Ruben Patterson	.20	.08
☐	134 John Stockton	.75	.30
☐	135 Bobby Jackson	.50	.20
☐	136 Shawn Marion	.75	.30
☐	137 Jarron Collins	.20	.08
☐	138 Tom Gugliotta	.20	.08
☐	139 Doug Christie	.50	.20
☐	140 Zeljko Rebraca	.20	.08
☐	141 Tim Duncan	1.50	.60
☐	142 David Robinson	.75	.30
☐	143 Tony Parker	.75	.30
☐	144 Derek Fisher	.75	.30
☐	145 Speedy Claxton	.50	.20
☐	146 Eric Snow	.50	.20
☐	147 Gary Payton	.75	.30
☐	148 Pat Garrity	.20	.08
☐	149 Joseph Forte	.20	.08
☐	150 Derek Anderson	.50	.20
☐	151 Vladimir Radmanovic	.50	.20
☐	152 Samuel Dalembert	.20	.08
☐	153 Allan Houston	.50	.20
☐	154 Jalen Rose	.75	.30
☐	155 Dikembe Mutombo	.50	.20
☐	156 Jerome Williams	.20	.08
☐	157 Antonio McDyess	.50	.20
☐	158 Morris Peterson	.50	.20
☐	159 Bonzi Wells	.50	.20
☐	160 Hedo Turkoglu	.75	.30
☐	161 Gerald Wallace	.75	.30
☐	162 Andrei Kirilenko	.75	.30
☐	163 Matt Harpring	.75	.30
☐	164 Peja Stojakovic	.75	.30
☐	165 Zydrunas Ilgauskas	.50	.20
☐	166 Richard Hamilton	.50	.20
☐	167 Brian Grant	.50	.20
☐	168 Christian Laettner	.50	.20
☐	169 Jason Terry	.75	.30
☐	170 Alonzo Mourning	.50	.20
☐	171 Yao Ming RC	20.00	8.00
☐	172 Jay Williams RC	3.00	1.25
☐	173 Mike Dunleavy RC	4.00	1.50
☐	174 Chris Wilcox RC	3.00	1.25
☐	175 Amare Stoudemire RC	12.00	5.00
☐	176 Fred Jones RC	2.50	1.00
☐	177 Caron Butler RC	5.00	2.00
☐	178 Melvin Ely RC	2.50	1.00
☐	179 Drew Gooden RC	4.00	1.50
☐	180 DaJuan Wagner RC	4.00	1.50
☐	181 Jared Jeffries RC	2.50	1.00
☐	182 Nikoloz Tskitishvili RC	2.50	1.00
☐	183 Nene Hilario RC	2.50	1.00
☐	184 Dan Dickau RC	2.50	1.00
☐	185 Marcus Haislip RC	2.50	1.00
☐	186 Gordan Giricek RC	3.00	1.25
☐	187 Jiri Welsch RC	2.50	1.00
☐	188 Juan Dixon RC	4.00	1.50
☐	189 Curtis Borchardt RC	2.50	1.00
☐	190 Ryan Humphrey RC	2.50	1.00
☐	191 Kareem Rush RC	3.00	1.25
☐	192 Qyntel Woods RC	2.50	1.00
☐	193 Casey Jacobsen RC	2.50	1.00
☐	194 Tayshaun Prince RC	3.00	1.25
☐	195 Frank Williams RC	2.50	1.00
☐	196 Pat Burke RC	2.50	1.00
☐	197 Chris Jefferies RC	2.50	1.00
☐	198 Carlos Boozer RC	5.00	2.00
☐	199 Manu Ginobili RC	12.00	5.00
☐	200 Vincent Yarbrough RC	2.50	1.00

1999 Hoops WNBA

☐	COMPLETE SET (110)	15.00	6.00
☐	1 Cynthia Cooper RC	1.50	.60
☐	2 Houston vs. Phoenix PR	.50	.20
☐	3 Houston vs. Phoenix PR	.50	.20
☐	4 Houston vs. Phoenix PR	.50	.20
☐	5 Houston vs. Charlotte PR	.50	.20
☐	6 Phoenix vs. Cleveland PR	.50	.20

❑ 7	Cynthia Cooper LL	1.50	.60
❑ 8	Lisa Leslie LL	1.50	.60
❑ 9	Isabelle Fijalkowski LL	.50	.20
❑ 10	Eva Nemcova LL	1.00	.40
❑ 11	Sandy Brondello LL	1.00	.40
❑ 12	Ticha Penicheiro LL	1.00	.40
❑ 13	Teresa Weatherspoon LL	1.00	.40
❑ 14	Margo Dydek LL	1.00	.40
❑ 15	Andrea Kuklova	.50	.20
❑ 16	Christy Smith	.50	.20
❑ 17	Penny Moore	1.00	.40
❑ 18	Octavia Blue RC	.50	.20
❑ 19	Vickie Johnson	1.00	.40
❑ 20	Latasha Byears	1.00	.40
❑ 21	Vicky Bullett	1.00	.40
❑ 22	Franthea Price RC	.50	.20
❑ 23	Tina Thompson	1.50	.60
❑ 24	Teresa Weatherspoon	1.50	.60
❑ 25	Maria Stepanova RC	.50	.20
❑ 26	Merlakia Jones	1.00	.40
❑ 27	Razija Mujanovic RC	.50	.20
❑ 28	Rhonda Mapp	.50	.20
❑ 29	Kristi Harrower RC	.50	.20
❑ 30	Penny Toler	1.00	.40
❑ 31	Margo Dydek RC	1.00	.40
❑ 32	Kim Perrot	1.50	.60
❑ 33	Cindy Brown	1.00	.40
❑ 34	Eva Nemcova	1.00	.40
❑ 35	Quacy Barnes	.50	.20
❑ 36	Tracy Reid RC	1.00	.40
❑ 37	Chantel Tremitiere	.50	.20
❑ 38	Lady Hardmon	.50	.20
❑ 39	Michelle Griffiths RC	.50	.20
❑ 40	Sheryl Swoopes	3.00	1.25
❑ 41	Sandy Brondello RC	2.00	.75
❑ 42	Andrea Stinson	1.00	.40
❑ 43	Marlies Askamp RC	1.00	.40
❑ 44	Rachael Sporn RC	1.00	.40
❑ 45	Nikki McCray	.50	.20
❑ 46	Andrea Congreaves	1.00	.40
❑ 47	Toni Foster	1.00	.40
❑ 48	Kim Williams	.50	.20
❑ 49	Carla Porter RC	1.00	.40
❑ 50	Jamila Wideman	.50	.20
❑ 51	Isabelle Fijalkowski	.50	.20
❑ 52	Korie Hlede RC	1.00	.40
❑ 53	Tora Suber	1.00	.40
❑ 54	Sue Wicks	.50	.20
❑ 55	C.Washington RC	.50	.20
❑ 56	Sharon Manning	.50	.20
❑ 57	Tammy Jackson	.50	.20
❑ 58	Tangela Smith	.50	.20
❑ 59	Suzie McConnell-Serio	1.00	.40
❑ 60	Lisa Leslie	2.00	.75
❑ 61	Wendy Palmer	1.00	.40
❑ 62	Adia Barnes RC	.50	.20
❑ 63	La'Shawn Brown RC	.50	.20
❑ 64	Janeth Arcain	.50	.20
❑ 65	Ruthie Bolton-Holifield	1.50	.60
❑ 66	Bridget Pettis	.50	.20
❑ 67	Pamela McGee	1.00	.40
❑ 68	Rebecca Lobo	1.50	.60
❑ 69	Cindy Blodgett RC	1.00	.40
❑ 70	Rita Williams	1.00	.40
❑ 71	Mwadi Mabika	.50	.20
❑ 72	Sophia Witherspoon	1.00	.40
❑ 73	Janice Braxton	.50	.20
❑ 74	Cynthia Cooper	3.00	1.25

❑ 75	Tammi Reiss	1.00	.40
❑ 76	Umeki Webb	.50	.20
❑ 77	Kym Hampton	1.00	.40
❑ 78	LaTonya Johnson RC	1.00	.40
❑ 79	Michele Timms	1.50	.60
❑ 80	Kisha Ford	.50	.20
❑ 81	Monica Lamb RC	1.00	.40
❑ 82	Keri Chaconas RC	.50	.20
❑ 83	Elena Baranova	1.00	.40
❑ 84	Linda Burgess	.50	.20
❑ 85	Tamecka Dixon	1.00	.40
❑ 86	Heidi Burge	.50	.20
❑ 87	Michelle Edwards	1.00	.40
❑ 88	Yolanda Moore RC	.50	.20
❑ 89	Ticha Penicheiro RC	2.00	.75
❑ 90	A.Santos de Oliveira RC	1.00	.40
❑ 91	Rushia Brown	.50	.20
❑ 92	Lynette Woodard	1.00	.40
❑ 93	Katrina Colleton RC	.50	.20
❑ 94	Bridgette Gordon	1.00	.40
❑ 95	Jennifer Gillom	1.00	.40
❑ 96	Murriel Page	1.00	.40
❑ 97	O.Scott-Richardson	.50	.20
❑ 98	Adrienne Johnson RC	1.50	.60
❑ 99	G.Branzova FP RC	.50	.20
❑ 100	Allison Feaster FP	.50	.20
❑ 101	Brandy Reed FP RC	1.50	.60
❑ 102	Katie Smith FP RC	2.00	.75
❑ 103	Natalie Williams FP RC	2.50	1.00
❑ 104	Jennifer Azzi FP RC	2.00	.75
❑ 105	C.Holdsclaw FP RC	5.00	2.00
❑ 106	Dawn Staley FP RC	2.00	.75
❑ 107	Nykesha Sales FP RC	1.50	.60
❑ 108	Kristin Folkl FP RC	1.50	.60
❑ 109	Checklist	.50	.20
❑ 110	Checklist	.50	.20

1995-96 Metal

❑	COMPLETE SET (220)	40.00	20.00
❑	COMPLETE SERIES 1 (120)	20.00	10.00
❑	COMPLETE SERIES 2 (100)	20.00	10.00
❑ 1	Stacey Augmon	.25	.08
❑ 2	Mookie Blaylock	.25	.08
❑ 3	Grant Long	.25	.08
❑ 4	Steve Smith	.50	.20
❑ 5	Dee Brown	.25	.08
❑ 6	Sherman Douglas	.25	.08
❑ 7	Eric Montross	.25	.08
❑ 8	Dino Radja	.25	.08
❑ 9	Muggsy Bogues	.50	.20
❑ 10	Scott Burrell	.25	.08
❑ 11	Larry Johnson	.50	.20
❑ 12	Alonzo Mourning	1.00	.40
❑ 13	Michael Jordan	5.00	2.50
❑ 14	Toni Kukoc	.50	.20
❑ 15	Scottie Pippen	1.25	.50
❑ 16	Terrell Brandon	.50	.20
❑ 17	Tyrone Hill	.25	.08
❑ 18	Mark Price	.50	.20
❑ 19	John Williams	.25	.08
❑ 20	Jim Jackson	.25	.08
❑ 21	Popeye Jones	.25	.08
❑ 22	Jason Kidd	2.50	1.00
❑ 23	Jamal Mashburn	.50	.20
❑ 24	Mahmoud Abdul-Rauf	.25	.08
❑ 25	Dikembe Mutombo	.50	.20
❑ 26	Robert Pack	.25	.08
❑ 27	Jalen Rose	1.25	.50

❑ 28	Joe Dumars	.75	.30
❑ 29	Grant Hill	1.00	.40
❑ 30	Lindsey Hunter	.25	.08
❑ 31	Terry Mills	.25	.08
❑ 32	Tim Hardaway	.50	.20
❑ 33	Donyell Marshall	.50	.20
❑ 34	Chris Mullin	.75	.30
❑ 35	Clifford Rozier	.25	.08
❑ 36	Latrell Sprewell	.75	.30
❑ 37	Sam Cassell	.75	.30
❑ 38	Clyde Drexler	.75	.30
❑ 39	Robert Horry	.50	.20
❑ 40	Hakeem Olajuwon	.75	.30
❑ 41	Kenny Smith	.25	.08
❑ 42	Dale Davis	.25	.08
❑ 43	Mark Jackson	.50	.20
❑ 44	Derrick McKey	.25	.08
❑ 45	Reggie Miller	.75	.30
❑ 46	Rik Smits	.50	.20
❑ 47	Lamond Murray	.25	.08
❑ 48	Pooh Richardson	.25	.08
❑ 49	Malik Sealy	.25	.08
❑ 50	Loy Vaught	.25	.08
❑ 51	Elden Campbell	.25	.08
❑ 52	Cedric Ceballos	.25	.08
❑ 53	Vlade Divac	.50	.20
❑ 54	Eddie Jones	1.00	.40
❑ 55	Nick Van Exel	.75	.30
❑ 56	Bimbo Coles	.25	.08
❑ 57	Billy Owens	.25	.08
❑ 58	Khalid Reeves	.25	.08
❑ 59	Glen Rice	.50	.20
❑ 60	Kevin Willis	.25	.08
❑ 61	Vin Baker	.50	.20
❑ 62	Todd Day	.25	.08
❑ 63	Eric Murdock	.25	.08
❑ 64	Glenn Robinson	.75	.30
❑ 65	Tom Gugliotta	.50	.20
❑ 66	Christian Laettner	.50	.20
❑ 67	Isaiah Rider	.25	.08
❑ 68	Kenny Anderson	.50	.20
❑ 69	P.J. Brown	.25	.08
❑ 70	Derrick Coleman	.25	.08
❑ 71	Patrick Ewing	.75	.30
❑ 72	Anthony Mason	.50	.20
❑ 73	Charles Oakley	.25	.08
❑ 74	John Starks	.50	.20
❑ 75	Nick Anderson	.25	.08
❑ 76	Horace Grant	.50	.20
❑ 77	Anfernee Hardaway	.75	.30
❑ 78	Shaquille O'Neal	2.00	.75
❑ 79	Dennis Scott	.25	.08
❑ 80	Dana Barros	.25	.08
❑ 81	Shawn Bradley	.25	.08
❑ 82	Clarence Weatherspoon	.25	.08
❑ 83	Sharone Wright	.25	.08
❑ 84	Charles Barkley	1.00	.40
❑ 85	Kevin Johnson	.50	.20
❑ 86	Dan Majerle	.50	.20
❑ 87	Danny Manning	.50	.20
❑ 88	Wesley Person	.25	.08
❑ 89	Clifford Robinson	.25	.08
❑ 90	Rod Strickland	.25	.08
❑ 91	Otis Thorpe	.25	.08
❑ 92	Buck Williams	.25	.08
❑ 93	Brian Grant	.75	.30
❑ 94	Olden Polynice	.25	.08
❑ 95	Mitch Richmond	.50	.20
❑ 96	Walt Williams	.25	.08
❑ 97	Sean Elliott	.50	.20
❑ 98	Avery Johnson	.25	.08
❑ 99	David Robinson	.75	.30
❑ 100	Dennis Rodman	.50	.20
❑ 101	Shawn Kemp	.50	.20
❑ 102	Nate McMillan	.25	.08
❑ 103	Gary Payton	.75	.30
❑ 104	Detlef Schrempf	.50	.20
❑ 105	B.J. Armstrong	.25	.08
❑ 106	Oliver Miller	.25	.08
❑ 107	John Salley	.25	.08
❑ 108	David Benoit	.25	.08
❑ 109	Jeff Hornacek	.50	.20
❑ 110	Karl Malone	1.00	.40
❑ 111	John Stockton	1.00	.40
❑ 112	Greg Anthony	.25	.08
❑ 113	Benoit Benjamin	.25	.08

#	Player		
114	Byron Scott	.25	.08
115	Calbert Cheaney	.25	.08
116	Juwan Howard	.75	.30
117	Gheorghe Muresan	.25	.08
118	Chris Webber	1.00	.40
119	Checklist	.25	.08
120	Checklist	.25	.08
121	Stacey Augmon	.25	.08
122	Mookie Blaylock	.25	.08
123	Alan Henderson RC	.75	.30
124	Andrew Lang	.25	.08
125	Ken Norman	.25	.08
126	Steve Smith	.50	.20
127	Dana Barros	.25	.08
128	Rick Fox	.50	.20
129	Eric Williams RC	.50	.20
130	Kendall Gill	.25	.08
131	Khalid Reeves	.25	.08
132	Glen Rice	.50	.20
133	George Zidek RC	.25	.08
134	Dennis Rodman	.50	.20
135	Danny Ferry	.25	.08
136	Dan Majerle	.50	.20
137	Chris Mills	.25	.08
138	Bobby Phills	.25	.08
139	Bob Sura RC	.50	.20
140	Tony Dumas	.25	.08
141	Dale Ellis	.25	.08
142	Don MacLean	.25	.08
143	Antonio McDyess RC	1.50	.60
144	Bryant Stith	.25	.08
145	Allan Houston	.50	.20
146	Theo Ratliff RC	1.00	.40
147	Otis Thorpe	.25	.08
148	B.J. Armstrong	.25	.08
149	Rony Seikaly	.25	.08
150	Joe Smith RC	1.25	.50
151	Sam Cassell	.75	.30
152	Clyde Drexler	.75	.30
153	Robert Horry	.25	.08
154	Hakeem Olajuwon	.75	.30
155	Antonio Davis	.25	.08
156	Ricky Pierce	.25	.08
157	Brent Barry RC	.75	.30
158	Terry Dehere	.25	.08
159	Rodney Rogers	.25	.08
160	Brian Williams	.25	.08
161	Magic Johnson	1.25	.50
162	Sasha Danilovic RC	.25	.08
163	Alonzo Mourning	.50	.20
164	Kurt Thomas RC	.50	.20
165	Sherman Douglas	.25	.08
166	Shawn Respert RC	.50	.20
167	Kevin Garnett RC	4.00	1.50
168	Terry Porter	.25	.08
169	Shawn Bradley	.25	.08
170	Kevin Edwards	.25	.08
171	Ed O'Bannon RC	.25	.08
172	Jayson Williams	.25	.08
173	Derek Harper	.50	.20
174	Charles Smith	.25	.08
175	Brian Shaw	.25	.08
176	Derrick Coleman	.25	.08
177	Vernon Maxwell	.25	.08
178	Trevor Ruffin	.25	.08
179	Jerry Stackhouse RC	2.50	1.00
180	Michael Finley RC	2.00	.75
181	A.C. Green	.50	.20
182	John Williams	.25	.08
183	Aaron McKie	.25	.08
184	Arvydas Sabonis RC	1.00	.40
185	Gary Trent RC	.25	.08
186	Tyus Edney RC	.25	.08
187	Sarunas Marciulionis	.25	.08
188	Michael Smith	.25	.08
189	Corliss Williamson RC	.50	.20
190	Vinny Del Negro	.25	.08
191	Hersey Hawkins	.25	.08
192	Shawn Kemp	.50	.20
193	Gary Payton	.75	.30
194	Sam Perkins	.50	.20
195	Detlef Schrempf	.25	.08
196	Willie Anderson	.25	.08
197	Oliver Miller	.25	.08
198	Tracy Murray	.25	.08
199	Alvin Robertson	.25	.08
200	Damon Stoudamire RC	1.50	.60
201	Chris Morris	.25	.08
202	Greg Anthony	.25	.08
203	Blue Edwards	.25	.08
204	Eric Murdock	.25	.08
205	Bryant Reeves RC	.75	.30
206	Byron Scott	.25	.08
207	Robert Pack	.25	.08
208	Rasheed Wallace RC	2.00	.75
209	Anfernee Hardaway NB	.50	.20
210	Grant Hill NB	.75	.30
211	Larry Johnson NB	.50	.20
212	Michael Jordan NB	2.50	1.00
213	Jason Kidd NB	1.25	.50
214	Karl Malone NB	.75	.30
215	Shaquille O'Neal NB	.75	.30
216	Scottie Pippen NB	.75	.30
217	David Robinson NB	.50	.20
218	Glenn Robinson NB	.50	.20
219	Checklist	.25	.08
220	Checklist	.25	.08

1996-97 Metal

COMPLETE SET (250)	45.00	25.00
COMPLETE SERIES 1 (150)	25.00	15.00
COMPLETE SERIES 2 (100)	20.00	10.00

#	Player		
1	Mookie Blaylock	.25	.08
2	Christian Laettner	.25	.08
3	Steve Smith	.50	.20
4	Dana Barros	.25	.08
5	Rick Fox	.25	.08
6	Dino Radja	.25	.08
7	Eric Williams	.25	.08
8	Dell Curry	.25	.08
9	Matt Geiger	.25	.08
10	Glen Rice	.50	.20
11	Michael Jordan	5.00	2.50
12	Toni Kukoc	.50	.20
13	Luc Longley	.25	.08
14	Scottie Pippen	1.25	.50
15	Dennis Rodman	.50	.20
16	Terrell Brandon	.25	.08
17	Danny Ferry	.25	.08
18	Chris Mills	.25	.08
19	Bobby Phills	.25	.08
20	Bob Sura	.25	.08
21	Jim Jackson	.50	.20
22	Jason Kidd	1.25	.50
23	Jamal Mashburn	.50	.20
24	George McCloud	.25	.08
25	LaPhonso Ellis	.25	.08
26	Antonio McDyess	.50	.20
27	Bryant Stith	.25	.08
28	Joe Dumars	.75	.30
29	Grant Hill	1.50	.60
30	Theo Ratliff	.50	.20
31	Otis Thorpe	.25	.08
32	Chris Mullin	.75	.30
33	Joe Smith	.75	.30
34	Latrell Sprewell	.75	.30
35	Sam Cassell	.50	.20
36	Clyde Drexler	.75	.30
37	Robert Horry	.25	.08
38	Hakeem Olajuwon	.75	.30
39	Antonio Davis	.25	.08
40	Dale Davis	.25	.08
41	Derrick McKey	.25	.08
42	Reggie Miller	.75	.30
43	Rik Smits	.50	.20
44	Brent Barry	.25	.08
45	Malik Sealy	.25	.08
46	Loy Vaught	.25	.08
47	Elden Campbell	.25	.08
48	Cedric Ceballos	.25	.08
49	Eddie Jones	.75	.30
50	Nick Van Exel	.75	.30
51	Sasha Danilovic	.25	.08
52	Tim Hardaway	.50	.20
53	Alonzo Mourning	.50	.20
54	Kurt Thomas	.50	.20
55	Vin Baker	.50	.20
56	Sherman Douglas	.25	.08
57	Glenn Robinson	.75	.30
58	Kevin Garnett	1.50	.60
59	Tom Gugliotta	.25	.08
60	Doug West	.25	.08
61	Shawn Bradley	.25	.08
62	Ed O'Bannon	.25	.08
63	Jayson Williams	.50	.20
64	Patrick Ewing	.75	.30
65	Charles Oakley	.50	.20
66	John Starks	.50	.20
67	Nick Anderson	.25	.08
68	Horace Grant	.50	.20
69	Anfernee Hardaway-	.75	.30
70	Dennis Scott	.25	.08
71	Brian Shaw	.25	.08
72	Derrick Coleman	.25	.08
73	Jerry Stackhouse	.60	.25
74	Clarence Weatherspoon	.25	.08
75	Charles Barkley	1.00	.40
76	Michael Finley	1.00	.40
77	Kevin Johnson	.50	.20
78	Wesley Person	.25	.08
79	Aaron McKie	.25	.08
80	Clifford Robinson	.25	.08
81	Arvydas Sabonis	.50	.20
82	Gary Trent	.25	.08
83	Tyus Edney	.25	.08
84	Brian Grant	.75	.30
85	Billy Owens	.25	.08
86	Olden Polynice	.25	.08
87	Mitch Richmond	.50	.20
88	Vinny Del Negro	.25	.08
89	Sean Elliott	.50	.20
90	Avery Johnson	.25	.08
91	David Robinson	.75	.30
92	Hersey Hawkins	.50	.20
93	Shawn Kemp	.50	.20
94	Gary Payton	.75	.30
95	Sam Perkins	.50	.20
96	Detlef Schrempf	.50	.20
97	Doug Christie	.50	.20
98	Damon Stoudamire	.75	.30
99	Sharone Wright	.25	.08
100	Jeff Hornacek	.50	.20
101	Karl Malone	.75	.30
102	John Stockton	.75	.30
103	Greg Anthony	.25	.08
104	Blue Edwards	.25	.08
105	Bryant Reeves	.25	.08
106	Juwan Howard	.50	.20
107	Gheorghe Muresan	.25	.08
108	Chris Webber	.75	.30
109	Kenny Anderson OTM	.25	.08
110	Stacey Augmon OTM	.25	.08
111	Chris Childs OTM	.25	.08
112	Vlade Divac OTM	.25	.08
113	Allan Houston OTM	.25	.08
114	Mark Jackson OTM	.25	.08
115	Larry Johnson OTM	.25	.08
116	Grant Long OTM	.25	.08
117	Anthony Mason OTM	.25	.08
118	Dikembe Mutombo OTM	.50	.20
119	Shaquille O'Neal OTM	.75	.30
120	Isaiah Rider OTM	.25	.08
121	Rod Strickland OTM	.25	.08
122	Rasheed Wallace OTM	.75	.30
123	Jalen Rose OTM	.25	.08
124	Anfernee Hardaway MET	.50	.20
125	Tim Hardaway MET	.25	.08
126	Allan Houston MET	.25	.08
127	Eddie Jones MET	.50	.20
128	Michael Jordan MET	2.50	1.00

129	Reggie Miller MET	.50	.20
130	Glen Rice MET	.25	.08
131	Mitch Richmond MET	.25	.08
132	Steve Smith MET	.25	.08
133	John Stockton MET	.75	.30
134	Stephon Marbury FF RC	2.00	.75
135	S.Abdur-Rahim FF RC	2.50	1.00
136	Ray Allen FF RC	2.50	1.00
137	Kobe Bryant FF RC	10.00	4.00
138	Steve Nash FF RC	5.00	2.00
139	Grant Hill MS	.50	.20
140	Jason Kidd MS	.60	.25
141	Karl Malone MS	.75	.30
142	Hakeem Olajuwon MS	.50	.20
143	Shaquille O'Neal MS	.75	.30
144	Gary Payton MS	.50	.20
145	Scottie Pippen MS	.60	.25
146	Jerry Stackhouse MS	.75	.30
147	Damon Stoudamire MS	.25	.08
148	Rod Strickland MS	.25	.08
149	Checklist (1-102)	.25	.08
150	Checklist (103-150/inserts)	.25	.08
151	Tyrone Corbin	.25	.08
152	Dikembe Mutombo	.50	.20
153	Antoine Walker RC	2.00	.75
154	David Wesley	.25	.08
155	Vlade Divac	.25	.08
156	Anthony Mason	.50	.20
157	Ron Harper	.50	.20
158	Steve Kerr	.50	.20
159	Robert Parish	.50	.20
160	Tyrone Hill	.25	.08
161	Vitaly Potapenko RC	.25	.08
162	Sam Cassell	.75	.30
163	Chris Gatling	.25	.08
164	Samaki Walker RC	.25	.08
165	Dale Ellis	.25	.08
166	Mark Jackson	.25	.08
167	Ervin Johnson	.25	.08
168	Grant Hill	.75	.30
169	Lindsey Hunter	.25	.08
170	Todd Fuller RC	.25	.08
171	Mark Price	.25	.20
172	Charles Barkley	1.00	.40
173	Othella Harrington RC	.75	.30
174	Matt Maloney RC	.50	.20
175	Kevin Willis	.25	.08
176	Travis Best	.25	.08
177	Erick Dampier RC	.75	.30
178	Jalen Rose	.75	.30
179	Rodney Rogers	.25	.08
180	Lorenzan Wright RC	.50	.20
181	Kobe Bryant	6.00	2.50
182	Robert Horry	.25	.08
183	Shaquille O'Neal	2.00	.75
184	P.J. Brown	.25	.08
185	Dan Majerle	.50	.20
186	Ray Allen	1.25	.50
187	Armon Gilliam	.25	.08
188	Andrew Lang	.25	.08
189	Stephon Marbury	1.00	.40
190	Stojko Vrankovic	.25	.08
191	Kendall Gill	.25	.08
192	Kerry Kittles RC	.75	.30
193	Robert Pack	.25	.08
194	Chris Childs	.25	.08
195	Allan Houston	.50	.20
196	Larry Johnson	.50	.20
197	John Wallace RC	.75	.30
198	Rony Seikaly	.25	.08
199	Gerald Wilkins	.25	.08
200	Lucious Harris	.25	.08
201	Allen Iverson RC	5.00	2.00
202	Cedric Ceballos	.25	.08
203	Jason Kidd	1.25	.50
204	Danny Manning	.50	.20
205	Steve Nash	1.00	.40
206	Kenny Anderson	.25	.08
207	Isaiah Rider	.50	.20
208	Rasheed Wallace	1.00	.40
209	Mahmoud Abdul-Rauf	.25	.08
210	Corliss Williamson	.50	.20
211	Vernon Maxwell	.25	.08
212	Dominique Wilkins	.75	.30
213	Craig Ehlo	.25	.08
214	Jim McIlvaine	.25	.08

215	Marcus Camby RC	1.00	.40
216	Hubert Davis	.25	.08
217	Walt Williams	.25	.08
218	Shandon Anderson RC	.50	.20
219	Bryon Russell	.25	.08
220	Shareef Abdur-Rahim	1.25	.50
221	Roy Rogers RC	.25	.08
222	Tracy Murray	.25	.08
223	Rod Strickland	.25	.08
224	Kevin Garnett MET	.75	.30
225	Karl Malone MET	.75	.30
226	Alonzo Mourning MET	.25	.08
227	Hakeem Olajuwon MET	.50	.20
228	Gary Payton MET	.50	.20
229	Scottie Pippen MET	.60	.25
230	David Robinson MET	.50	.20
231	Dennis Rodman MET	.25	.08
232	Latrell Sprewell MET	.75	.30
233	Jerry Stackhouse MET	.75	.30
234	Marcus Camby FF	.75	.30
235	Todd Fuller FF	.25	.08
236	Allen Iverson FF	2.00	.75
237	Kerry Kittles FF	.75	.30
238	Roy Rogers FF	.25	.08
239	Anfernee Hardaway MS	.50	.20
240	Juwan Howard MS	.25	.08
241	Michael Jordan MS	2.50	1.00
242	Shawn Kemp MS	.25	.08
243	Gary Payton MS	.50	.20
244	Mitch Richmond MS	.25	.08
245	Glenn Robinson MS	.50	.20
246	John Stockton MS	.75	.30
247	Damon Stoudamire MS	.50	.20
248	Chris Webber MS	.50	.20
249	Checklist	.25	.08
250	Checklist	.25	.08

1999-00 Metal

	COMPLETE SET (180)	50.00	25.00
	COMMON CARD (1-150)	.15	.05
	COMMON ROOKIE (151-180)	.50	.20
1	Vince Carter	1.25	.50
2	Stephon Marbury	.50	.20
3	David Robinson	.50	.20
4	Ray Allen	.50	.20
5	P.J. Brown	.15	.05
6	Shawn Kemp	.30	.10
7	Cedric Ceballos	.15	.05
8	Dale Ellis	.15	.05
9	Rodney Rogers	.15	.05
10	Chris Gatling	.15	.05
11	Bryant Reeves	.15	.05
12	Al Harrington	.50	.20
13	Brent Barry	.30	.10
14	Brevin Knight	.15	.05
15	Radoslav Nesterovic RC	1.00	.40
16	Tom Gugliotta	.15	.05
17	Charles Barkley	.60	.25
18	Cuttino Mobley	.50	.20
19	Corliss Williamson	.30	.10
20	Henry Williams	.30	.10
21	Mike Bibby	.50	.20
22	Pat Garrity	.15	.05
23	Kelvin Cato	.15	.05
24	Alan Henderson	.15	.05
25	Alvin Williams	.15	.05
26	Antonio McDyess	.30	.10
27	Damon Stoudamire	.30	.10

28	Kerry Kittles	.15	.05
29	Michael Olowokandi	.30	.10
30	Brent Price	.15	.05
31	Fred Hoiberg	.15	.05
32	Glenn Robinson	.50	.20
33	Hakeem Olajuwon	.50	.20
34	Monty Williams	.15	.05
35	Terry Porter	.15	.05
36	Allen Iverson	1.00	.40
37	Juwan Howard	.30	.10
38	Mario Elie	.15	.05
39	Mookie Blaylock	.15	.05
40	Sam Cassell	.50	.20
41	Toni Kukoc	.30	.10
42	Anthony Mason	.30	.10
43	George Lynch	.15	.05
44	John Starks	.30	.10
45	Malik Rose	.15	.05
46	Rod Strickland	.15	.05
47	Tim Thomas	.30	.10
48	Howard Eisley	.15	.05
49	Kenny Anderson	.30	.10
50	Kurt Thomas	.15	.05
51	Lindsey Hunter	.15	.05
52	Rick Fox	.30	.10
53	Vlade Divac	.30	.10
54	Avery Johnson	.15	.05
55	Dale Ellis	.15	.05
56	Donyell Marshall	.30	.10
57	Elden Campbell	.15	.05
58	Larry Hughes	.50	.20
59	Mitch Richmond	.30	.10
60	Chris Mills	.15	.05
61	David Wesley	.15	.05
62	Gary Payton	.50	.20
63	Isaac Austin	.15	.05
64	Robert Traylor	.15	.05
65	Theo Ratliff	.30	.10
66	Antawn Jamison	.75	.30
67	Eddie Jones	.50	.20
68	Kevin Garnett	1.00	.40
69	Matt Geiger	.15	.05
70	Vernon Maxwell	.15	.05
71	Antonio Davis	.15	.05
72	Dirk Nowitzki	1.00	.40
73	Johnny Newman	.15	.05
74	Maurice Taylor	.30	.10
75	Steve Smith	.30	.10
76	Derek Anderson	.30	.10
77	Doug Christie	.30	.10
78	Erick Strickland	.15	.05
79	Keith Van Horn	.50	.20
80	Luc Longley	.15	.05
81	Alonzo Mourning	.30	.10
82	Christian Laettner	.30	.10
83	Jamal Mashburn	.30	.10
84	Jon Barry	.15	.05
85	Patrick Ewing	.50	.20
86	Shareef Abdur-Rahim	.50	.20
87	Vitaly Potapenko	.15	.05
88	Darrell Armstrong	.15	.05
89	Eric Williams	.15	.05
90	Jerome Williams	.15	.05
91	Nick Anderson	.15	.05
92	Othella Harrington	.15	.05
93	Tim Hardaway	.30	.10
94	Eric Piatkowski	.30	.10
95	Isaiah Rider	.15	.05
96	Kendall Gill	.15	.05
97	Rasheed Wallace	.50	.20
98	Robert Pack	.15	.05
99	Tracy McGrady	1.25	.50
100	Allan Houston	.30	.10
101	Brian Grant	.30	.10
102	Dikembe Mutombo	.30	.10
103	Karl Malone	.50	.20
104	Nick Van Exel	.50	.20
105	Shaquille O'Neal	1.25	.50
106	Chris Anstey	.15	.05
107	Michael Dickerson	.30	.10
108	Shandon Anderson	.15	.05
109	Tariq Abdul-Wahad	.15	.05
110	Tim Duncan	1.00	.40
111	Voshon Lenard	.15	.05
112	Bimbo Coles	.15	.05
113	Detlef Schrempf	.30	.10

❏ 114	John Stockton	.50	.20
❏ 115	Kobe Bryant	2.00	.75
❏ 116	Latrell Sprewell	.50	.20
❏ 117	Raef LaFrentz	.30	.10
❏ 118	Antoine Walker	.50	.20
❏ 119	Bryon Russell	.15	.05
❏ 120	Derek Fisher	.50	.20
❏ 121	Jason Williams	.50	.20
❏ 122	Jerry Stackhouse	.50	.20
❏ 123	Larry Johnson	.30	.10
❏ 124	Clifford Robinson	.15	.05
❏ 125	Horace Grant	.30	.10
❏ 126	Malik Sealy	.15	.05
❏ 127	Michael Finley	.50	.20
❏ 128	Rik Smits	.30	.10
❏ 129	Dell Curry	.15	.05
❏ 130	Jim Jackson	.15	.05
❏ 131	Ron Mercer	.30	.10
❏ 132	Scott Burrell	.15	.05
❏ 133	Scottie Pippen	.75	.30
❏ 134	Troy Hudson	.15	.05
❏ 135	Anfernee Hardaway	.50	.20
❏ 136	Anthony Peeler	.15	.05
❏ 137	Jalen Rose	.50	.20
❏ 138	Lamond Murray	.15	.05
❏ 139	Ruben Patterson	.30	.10
❏ 140	Chris Webber	.50	.20
❏ 141	Glen Rice	.30	.10
❏ 142	Grant Hill	.50	.20
❏ 143	Jeff Hornacek	.30	.10
❏ 144	Marcus Camby	.30	.10
❏ 145	Paul Pierce	.50	.20
❏ 146	Bob Sura	.15	.05
❏ 147	Jason Kidd	.75	.30
❏ 148	Reggie Miller	.50	.20
❏ 149	Terrell Brandon	.30	.10
❏ 150	Vin Baker	.30	.10
❏ 151	Lamar Odom RC	2.50	1.00
❏ 152	Steve Francis RC	3.00	1.25
❏ 153	Elton Brand RC	3.00	1.25
❏ 154	Wally Szczerbiak RC	2.50	1.00
❏ 155	Adrian Griffin RC	.75	.30
❏ 156	Andre Miller RC	2.50	1.00
❏ 157	Jason Terry RC	1.50	.60
❏ 158	Richard Hamilton RC	2.50	1.00
❏ 159	Ron Artest RC	1.50	.60
❏ 160	Shawn Marion RC	3.00	1.25
❏ 161	James Posey RC	1.50	.60
❏ 162	Greg Buckner RC	.50	.20
❏ 163	Chucky Atkins RC	1.00	.40
❏ 164	Corey Maggette RC	2.50	1.00
❏ 165	Todd MacCulloch RC	.75	.30
❏ 166	Baron Davis RC	5.00	2.00
❏ 167	Trajan Langdon RC	1.00	.40
❏ 168	Bruno Sundov RC	.50	.20
❏ 169	Scott Padgett RC	.75	.30
❏ 170	Vonteego Cummings RC	1.00	.40
❏ 171	Ryan Bowen RC	.50	.20
❏ 172	Jonathan Bender RC	2.50	1.00
❏ 173	Jermaine Jackson RC	.50	.20
❏ 174	Devean George RC	1.25	.50
❏ 175	Chris Herren RC	.50	.20
❏ 176	Rodney Buford RC	.50	.20
❏ 177	Laron Profit RC	.75	.30
❏ 178	Mirsad Turkcan RC	.50	.20
❏ 179	Eddie Robinson RC	1.50	.60
❏ 180	Anthony Carter RC	1.50	.60

1997-98 Metal Universe

❏ COMPLETE SET (125)		25.00	12.50
❏ 1	Charles Barkley	1.00	.40
❏ 2	Dell Curry	.25	.08
❏ 3	Derek Fisher	.75	.30
❏ 4	Derek Harper	.50	.20
❏ 5	Avery Johnson	.25	.08
❏ 6	Steve Smith	.50	.20
❏ 7	Alonzo Mourning	.50	.20
❏ 8	Rod Strickland	.25	.08
❏ 9	Chris Mullin	.75	.30
❏ 10	Rony Seikaly	.25	.08
❏ 11	Vin Baker	.50	.20
❏ 12	Austin Croshere RC	.60	.25
❏ 13	Vinny Del Negro	.25	.08
❏ 14	Sherman Douglas	.25	.08
❏ 15	Priest Lauderdale	.25	.08

❏ 16	Cedric Ceballos	.25	.08
❏ 17	LaPhonso Ellis	.25	.08
❏ 18	Luc Longley	.25	.08
❏ 19	Brian Grant	.50	.20
❏ 20	Allen Iverson	2.00	.75
❏ 21	Anthony Mason	.50	.20
❏ 22	Bryant Reeves	.25	.08
❏ 23	Michael Jordan	5.00	2.00
❏ 24	Dale Ellis	.25	.08
❏ 25	Terrell Brandon	.50	.20
❏ 26	Patrick Ewing	.75	.30
❏ 27	Allan Houston	.50	.20
❏ 28	Damon Stoudamire	.50	.20
❏ 29	Loy Vaught	.25	.08
❏ 30	Walt Williams	.25	.08
❏ 31	Shareef Abdur-Rahim	1.25	.50
❏ 32	Mario Elie	.25	.08
❏ 33	Juwan Howard	.50	.20
❏ 34	Tom Gugliotta	.50	.20
❏ 35	Glen Rice	.50	.20
❏ 36	Isaiah Rider	.50	.20
❏ 37	Arvydas Sabonis	.50	.20
❏ 38	Derrick Coleman	.25	.08
❏ 39	Kevin Willis	.25	.08
❏ 40	Kendall Gill	.25	.08
❏ 41	John Wallace	.25	.08
❏ 42	Tracy McGrady RC	4.00	1.50
❏ 43	Travis Best	.25	.08
❏ 44	Malik Rose	.25	.08
❏ 45	Anfernee Hardaway	.75	.30
❏ 46	Roy Rogers	.25	.08
❏ 47	Kerry Kittles	.50	.20
❏ 48	Matt Maloney	.25	.08
❏ 49	Antonio McDyess	.50	.20
❏ 50	Shaquille O'Neal	2.00	.75
❏ 51	George McCloud	.25	.08
❏ 52	Wesley Person	.25	.08
❏ 53	Shawn Bradley	.25	.08
❏ 54	Antonio Davis	.25	.08
❏ 55	P.J. Brown	.25	.08
❏ 56	Joe Dumars	.75	.30
❏ 57	Horace Grant	.50	.20
❏ 58	Steve Kerr	.50	.20
❏ 59	Hakeem Olajuwon	.75	.30
❏ 60	Tim Hardaway	.50	.20
❏ 61	Toni Kukoc	.50	.20
❏ 62	Ron Mercer RC	.75	.30
❏ 63	Gary Payton	.75	.30
❏ 64	Grant Hill	.75	.30
❏ 65	Detlef Schrempf	.50	.20
❏ 66	Tim Duncan RC	3.00	1.25
❏ 67	Shawn Kemp	.50	.20
❏ 68	Voshon Lenard	.25	.08
❏ 69	Othella Harrington	.25	.08
❏ 70	Hersey Hawkins	.25	.08
❏ 71	Lindsey Hunter	.25	.08
❏ 72	Antoine Walker	1.00	.40
❏ 73	Jamal Mashburn	.50	.20
❏ 74	Kenny Anderson	.50	.20
❏ 75	Todd Day	.25	.08
❏ 76	Todd Fuller	.25	.08
❏ 77	Jermaine O'Neal	1.25	.50
❏ 78	David Robinson	.75	.30
❏ 79	Erick Dampier	.25	.08
❏ 80	Keith Van Horn RC	1.00	.40
❏ 81	Kobe Bryant	3.00	1.25
❏ 82	Chris Childs	.25	.08
❏ 83	Scottie Pippen	1.25	.50

❏ 84	Marcus Camby	.75	.30
❏ 85	Danny Ferry	.25	.08
❏ 86	Jeff Hornacek	.50	.20
❏ 87	Bo Outlaw	.25	.08
❏ 88	Larry Johnson	.50	.20
❏ 89	Tony Delk	.25	.08
❏ 90	Stephon Marbury	1.00	.40
❏ 91	Robert Pack	.25	.08
❏ 92	Chris Webber	.75	.30
❏ 93	Clyde Drexler	.75	.30
❏ 94	Eddie Jones	.75	.30
❏ 95	Jerry Stackhouse	.75	.30
❏ 96	Tyrone Hill	.25	.08
❏ 97	Karl Malone	.75	.30
❏ 98	Reggie Miller	.75	.30
❏ 99	Bryon Russell	.25	.08
❏ 100	Dale Davis	.25	.08
❏ 101	Steve Nash	.75	.30
❏ 102	Vitaly Potapenko	.25	.08
❏ 103	Nick Anderson	.25	.08
❏ 104	Ray Allen	.75	.30
❏ 105	Sean Elliott	.50	.20
❏ 106	Dikembe Mutombo	.50	.20
❏ 107	Dennis Rodman	.50	.20
❏ 108	Lorenzen Wright	.25	.08
❏ 109	Kevin Garnett	1.50	.60
❏ 110	Christian Laettner	.50	.20
❏ 111	Mitch Richmond	.50	.20
❏ 112	Joe Smith	.50	.20
❏ 113	Jason Kidd	1.25	.50
❏ 114	Glenn Robinson	.75	.30
❏ 115	Mark Price	.25	.08
❏ 116	Mark Jackson	.50	.20
❏ 117	Bobby Phills	.25	.08
❏ 118	John Starks	.50	.20
❏ 119	John Stockton	.75	.30
❏ 120	Mookie Blaylock	.25	.08
❏ 121	Dean Garrett	.25	.08
❏ 122	Olden Polynice	.25	.08
❏ 123	Latrell Sprewell	.75	.30
❏ 124	Checklist	.25	.08
❏ 125	Checklist	.25	.08

1998-99 Metal Universe

❏ COMPLETE SET (125)		25.00	12.50
❏ 1	Michael Jordan	5.00	2.00
❏ 2	Mario Elie	.25	.08
❏ 3	Voshon Lenard	.25	.08
❏ 4	John Starks	.50	.20
❏ 5	Juwan Howard	.50	.20
❏ 6	Michael Finley	.75	.30
❏ 7	Bobby Jackson	.50	.20
❏ 8	Glenn Robinson	.50	.20
❏ 9	Antonio McDyess	.50	.20
❏ 10	Marcus Camby	.50	.20
❏ 11	Zydrunas Ilgauskas	.50	.20
❏ 12	LaPhonso Ellis	.25	.08
❏ 13	Terrell Brandon	.25	.08
❏ 14	Rex Chapman	.25	.08
❏ 15	Rod Strickland	.25	.08
❏ 16	Dennis Rodman	.50	.20
❏ 17	Clarence Weatherspoon	.25	.08
❏ 18	P.J. Brown	.25	.08
❏ 19	Anfernee Hardaway	.75	.30
❏ 20	Dikembe Mutombo	.50	.20
❏ 21	Gary Trent	.25	.08
❏ 22	Patrick Ewing	.75	.30
❏ 23	Sam Mack	.25	.08

#	Player		
24	Scottie Pippen	1.25	.50
25	Shaquille O'Neal	2.00	.75
26	Donyell Marshall	.50	.20
27	Bo Outlaw	.25	.08
28	Isaiah Rider	.25	.08
29	Detlef Schrempf	.50	.20
30	Mark Price	.50	.20
31	Jim Jackson	.25	.08
32	Eddie Jones	.75	.30
33	Allen Iverson	1.50	.60
34	Corliss Williamson	.50	.20
35	Tim Duncan	1.25	.50
36	Ron Harper	.50	.20
37	Tony Delk	.25	.08
38	Derek Fisher	.75	.30
39	Kendall Gill	.25	.08
40	Theo Ratliff	.50	.20
41	Kelvin Cato	.25	.08
42	Antoine Walker	.75	.30
43	Lamond Murray	.25	.08
44	Avery Johnson	.25	.08
45	John Stockton	.75	.30
46	David Wesley	.25	.08
47	Brian Williams	.25	.08
48	Elden Campbell	.25	.08
49	Sam Cassell	.75	.30
50	Grant Hill	.75	.30
51	Tracy McGrady	2.00	.75
52	Glen Rice	.50	.20
53	Kobe Bryant	3.00	1.25
54	Cherokee Parks	.25	.08
55	John Wallace	.25	.08
56	Bobby Phills	.25	.08
57	Jerry Stackhouse	.75	.30
58	Lorenzen Wright	.25	.08
59	Stephon Marbury	.75	.30
60	Shandon Anderson	.25	.08
61	Jeff Hornacek	.50	.20
62	Joe Dumars	.75	.30
63	Tom Gugliotta	.50	.20
64	Johnny Newman	.25	.08
65	Kevin Garnett	1.50	.60
66	Clifford Robinson	.25	.08
67	Dennis Scott	.25	.08
68	Anthony Mason	.50	.20
69	Rodney Rogers	.25	.08
70	Bryon Russell	.25	.08
71	Maurice Taylor	.40	.15
72	Mookie Blaylock	.25	.08
73	Shawn Bradley	.25	.08
74	Matt Maloney	.25	.08
75	Karl Malone	.75	.30
76	Larry Johnson	.50	.20
77	Calbert Cheaney	.25	.08
78	Steve Smith	.50	.20
79	Toni Kukoc	.50	.20
80	Reggie Miller	.75	.30
81	Jayson Williams	.50	.20
82	Gary Payton	.75	.30
83	George Lynch	.25	.08
84	Wesley Person	.25	.08
85	Charles Barkley	1.00	.40
86	Tim Hardaway	.50	.20
87	Darrell Armstrong	.25	.08
88	Rasheed Wallace	.75	.30
89	Tariq Abdul-Wahad	.25	.08
90	Kenny Anderson	.50	.20
91	Chris Mullin	.75	.30
92	Keith Van Horn	.75	.30
93	Hersey Hawkins	.25	.08
94	Billy Owens	.25	.08
95	Ron Mercer	.40	.15
96	Rik Smits	.50	.20
97	David Robinson	.75	.30
98	Derek Anderson	.60	.25
99	Danny Fortson	.25	.08
100	Jason Kidd	1.25	.50
101	Sean Elliott	.50	.20
102	Chauncey Billups	.50	.20
103	Tyrone Hill	.25	.08
104	Alan Henderson	.25	.08
105	Chris Anstey	.25	.08
106	Hakeem Olajuwon	.75	.30
107	Allan Houston	.50	.20
108	Bryant Reeves	.25	.08
109	Anthony Johnson	.25	.08
110	Shawn Kemp	.50	.20
111	Brevin Knight	.25	.08
112	A.C. Green	.50	.20
113	Ray Allen	.75	.30
114	Tim Thomas	.50	.20
115	Walter McCarty	.25	.08
116	Jalen Rose	.75	.30
117	Kerry Kittles	.25	.08
118	Vin Baker	.50	.20
119	Shareef Abdur-Rahim	.75	.30
120	Alonzo Mourning	.50	.20
121	Joe Smith	.50	.20
122	Tracy Murray	.25	.08
123	Damon Stoudamire	.50	.20
124	Checklist	.25	.08
125	Checklist	.25	.08
NNO	Grant Hill SAMPLE	1.50	.60

1997-98 Metal Universe Championship

#	Player		
	COMPLETE SET (100)	25.00	12.50
1	Shaquille O'Neal	2.00	.75
2	Chris Webber	.25	.08
3	Tariq Abdul-Wahad RC	.50	.20
4	Adonal Foyle RC	.50	.20
5	Kendall Gill	.25	.08
6	Vin Baker	.50	.20
7	Chauncey Billups RC	1.50	.60
8	Bobby Jackson RC	1.00	.40
9	Keith Van Horn RC	1.00	.40
10	Avery Johnson	.25	.08
11	Juwan Howard	.50	.20
12	Steve Smith	.50	.20
13	Alonzo Mourning	.50	.20
14	Anfernee Hardaway	.75	.30
15	Sean Elliott	.50	.20
16	Danny Fortson RC	.50	.20
17	John Stockton	.75	.30
18	John Thomas RC	.25	.08
19	Lorenzen Wright	.25	.08
20	Mark Price	.50	.20
21	Rasheed Wallace	.75	.30
22	Ray Allen	.75	.30
23	Michael Jordan	5.00	2.00
24	John Wallace	.25	.08
25	Bryant Reeves	.25	.08
26	Allen Iverson	2.00	.75
27	Antoine Walker	1.00	.40
28	Terrell Brandon	.50	.20
29	Damon Stoudamire	.50	.20
30	Antonio Daniels RC	.75	.30
31	Corey Beck	.25	.08
32	Tyrone Hill	.25	.08
33	Grant Hill	.75	.30
34	Tim Thomas RC	1.25	.50
35	Clifford Robinson	.25	.08
36	Tracy McGrady RC	4.00	1.50
37	Chris Webber	.75	.30
38	Austin Croshere RC	.60	.25
39	Reggie Miller	.75	.30
40	Derek Anderson RC	.75	.30
41	Kevin Garnett	1.50	.60
42	Kevin Johnson	.50	.20
43	Antonio McDyess	.50	.20
44	Brevin Knight RC	.50	.20
45	Charles Barkley	1.00	.40
46	Tom Gugliotta	.25	.08
47	Jason Kidd	1.25	.50
48	Marcus Camby	.75	.30
49	God Shammgod RC	.25	.08
50	Wesley Person	.25	.08
51	Clyde Drexler	.75	.30
52	Paul Grant RC	.25	.08
53	Rod Strickland	.25	.08
54	Tony Delk	.25	.08
55	Stephon Marbury	1.00	.40
56	Detlef Schrempf	.50	.20
57	Joe Smith	.50	.20
58	Sam Cassell	.75	.30
59	Gary Payton	.75	.30
60	Chris Crawford RC	.25	.08
61	Hakeem Olajuwon	.75	.30
62	Dennis Rodman	.50	.20
63	Eddie Jones	.75	.30
64	Mitch Richmond	.50	.20
65	David Wesley	.25	.08
66	Tony Battie RC	.75	.30
67	Isaac Austin	.25	.08
68	Isaiah Rider	.50	.20
69	Jacque Vaughn RC	.50	.20
70	Tim Hardaway	.50	.20
71	Darrell Armstrong	.25	.08
72	Tim Duncan RC	3.00	1.25
73	Glen Rice	.50	.20
74	Bubba Wells RC	.25	.08
75	Maurice Taylor RC	.60	.25
76	Kelvin Cato RC	.75	.30
77	Shareef Abdur-Rahim	1.25	.50
78	Shawn Kemp	.50	.20
79	Michael Finley	.75	.30
80	Chris Mullin	.75	.30
81	Ron Mercer RC	.75	.30
82	Brian Williams	.25	.08
83	Kerry Kittles	.75	.30
84	David Robinson	.75	.30
85	Scottie Pippen	1.25	.50
86	Kobe Bryant	3.00	1.25
87	Anthony Johnson RC	.25	.08
88	Karl Malone	.75	.30
89	Mookie Blaylock	.25	.08
90	Joe Dumars	.75	.30
91	Patrick Ewing	.75	.30
92	Bobby Phills	.25	.08
93	Dennis Scott	.25	.08
94	Rodney Rogers	.25	.08
95	Jim Jackson	.25	.08
96	Kenny Anderson	.50	.20
97	Jerry Stackhouse	.75	.30
98	Larry Johnson	.50	.20
99	Checklist	.25	.08
100	Checklist	.25	.08

1997 Pinnacle Inside WNBA

#	Player		
	COMPLETE SET (81)	80.00	40.00
1	Lisa Leslie	8.00	4.00
2	Cynthia Cooper	15.00	6.00
3	Rebecca Lobo RC	4.00	1.50
4	Michele Timms RC	4.00	2.00
5	Ruthie Bolton-Holifield RC	3.00	1.50
6	Michelle Edwards RC	1.25	.50
7	Vicky Bullett RC	1.00	.40
8	Tammi Reiss RC	1.00	.40
9	Penny Toler RC	1.00	.40
10	Tia Jackson RC	.30	.10
11	Rhonda Mapp RC	.60	.25

❏ 12 Elena Baranova RC	2.00	.75
❏ 13 Tina Thompson RC	8.00	3.00
❏ 14 Merlakia Jones RC	1.00	.40
❏ 15 Tora Suber RC	1.00	.40
❏ 16 Sophia Witherspoon RC	1.00	.40
❏ 17 Tajama Abraham RC	.30	.10
❏ 18 Jessie Hicks RC	.30	.10
❏ 19 Tina Nicholson RC	.30	.10
❏ 20 Tiffany Woosley RC	.30	.10
❏ 21 Chantel Tremitiere RC	.30	.10
❏ 22 Daedra Charles RC	.30	.10
❏ 23 Nancy Lieberman-Cline RC	2.50	1.00
❏ 24 Denique Graves RC	.30	.10
❏ 25 Toni Foster RC	1.00	.40
❏ 26 Sheryl Swoopes RC	15.00	6.00
❏ 27 Kym Hampton RC	1.00	.40
❏ 28 Sharon Manning RC	.30	.10
❏ 29 Janice Lawrence Braxton RC	.30	.10
❏ 30 Sue Wicks RC	1.00	.40
❏ 31 Lady Hardmon RC	.30	.10
❏ 32 Jamila Wideman RC	1.00	.40
❏ 33 Bridgette Gordon RC	.30	.10
❏ 34 Lynette Woodard RC	1.50	.60
❏ 35 Kim Perrot RC	5.00	2.50
❏ 36 Teresa Weatherspoon RC	6.00	3.00
❏ 37 Andrea Stinson RC	1.50	.60
❏ 38 Janeth Arcain RC	.30	.10
❏ 39 Pamela McGee RC	1.00	.40
❏ 40 Tamecka Dixon RC	1.00	.40
❏ 41 Wendy Palmer RC	2.00	.75
❏ 42 Umeki Webb RC	.30	.10
❏ 43 Isabelle Fijalkowski RC	.30	.10
❏ 44 Jennifer Gillom RC	2.00	.75
❏ 45 Latasha Byears RC	.30	.10
❏ 46 Haixia Zheng RC	.30	.10
❏ 47 Kisha Ford RC	.30	.10
❏ 48 Eva Nemcova RC	1.25	.60
❏ 49 Penny Moore RC	1.00	.40
❏ 50 Mwadi Mabika RC	.30	.10
❏ 51 Kim Williams RC	.30	.10
❏ 52 Wanda Guyton RC	.30	.10
❏ 53 Vickie Johnson RC	1.00	.40
❏ 54 Deborah Carter RC	.30	.10
❏ 55 Bridget Pettis RC	.30	.10
❏ 56 Andrea Congreaves RC	.30	.10
❏ 57 Haixia Zheng HS	.30	.10
❏ 58 Tammi Reiss HS	.30	.20
❏ 59 Jennifer Gillom HS	.75	.30
❏ 60 Bridgette Gordon HS	.30	.10
❏ 61 Janice Lawrence Braxton HS	.30	.10
❏ 62 Cynthia Cooper HS	3.00	1.25
❏ 63 Teresa Weatherspoon HS	.50	.20
❏ 64 Elena Baranova HS	.75	.30
❏ 65 N. Lieberman-Cline HS	1.00	.40
❏ 66 Andrea Congreaves HS	.30	.10
❏ 67 Sophia Witherspoon HS	1.00	.40
❏ 68 Vicky Bullett HS	1.00	.40
❏ 69 R.Bolton-Holifield HS	1.50	.60
❏ 70 Tina Thompson HS	.75	.30
❏ 71 Lynette Woodard HS	.60	.25
❏ 72 Jamila Wideman HS	.60	.25
❏ 73 Lisa Leslie SG	2.00	.75
❏ 74 Wendy Palmer SG	.75	.30
❏ 75 Michele Timms SG	.60	.25
❏ 76 R.Bolton-Holifield SG	1.50	.60
❏ 77 Andrea Stinson SG	.60	.25
❏ 78 Lynette Woodard SG	.60	.25
❏ 79 Cynthia Cooper SG	3.00	1.25
❏ 80 Rebecca Lobo SG	1.50	.60
❏ 81 Checklist		

1998 Pinnacle WNBA

❏ COMPLETE SET (85)	30.00	12.50
❏ 1 Rhonda Blades RC	1.25	.50
❏ 2 Lisa Leslie	2.50	1.00
❏ 3 Jennifer Gillom	1.25	.50
❏ 4 Ruthie Bolton-Holifield	2.00	.75
❏ 5 Wendy Palmer	1.25	.50
❏ 6 Sophia Witherspoon	2.00	.75
❏ 7 Eva Nemcova	1.25	.50
❏ 8 Andrea Stinson	1.25	.50
❏ 9 Heidi Burge RC	.60	.25
❏ 10 Cynthia Cooper	4.00	1.50
❏ 11 Christy Smith RC	.60	.25
❏ 12 Penny Moore	1.25	.50

❏ 13 Penny Toler	1.25	.50
❏ 14 Bridget Pettis	.60	.25
❏ 15 Tora Suber	1.25	.50
❏ 16 Elena Baranova	1.25	.50
❏ 17 Rebecca Lobo	2.00	.75
❏ 18 Isabelle Fijalkowski	.60	.25
❏ 19 Vicky Bullett	1.25	.50
❏ 20 Tina Thompson	2.00	.75
❏ 21 Andrea Kuklova RC	.60	.25
❏ 22 Rita Williams RC	1.25	.50
❏ 23 Tamecka Dixon	1.25	.50
❏ 24 Michele Timms	2.00	.75
❏ 25 Bridgette Gordon	1.25	.50
❏ 26 Tammi Reiss	1.25	.50
❏ 27 Kym Hampton	2.00	.75
❏ 28 Janice Braxton	.60	.25
❏ 29 Rhonda Mapp	1.25	.50
❏ 30 Janeth Arcain	1.25	.50
❏ 31 Lynette Woodard	1.25	.50
❏ 32 Tammy Jackson RC	.60	.25
❏ 33 Haixia Zheng	.60	.25
❏ 34 Toni Foster	1.25	.50
❏ 35 Chantel Tremitiere	1.25	.50
❏ 36 Vickie Johnson	1.25	.50
❏ 37 Michelle Edwards	1.25	.50
❏ 38 Wanda Guyton	.60	.25
❏ 39 Kim Perrot	2.00	.75
❏ 40 Sheryl Swoopes	4.00	1.50
❏ 41 Merlakia Jones	2.00	.75
❏ 42 Teresa Weatherspoon	2.00	.75
❏ 43 Kim Williams	.60	.25
❏ 44 Lady Hardmon	.60	.25
❏ 45 Latasha Byears	1.25	.50
❏ 46 Umeki Webb	.60	.25
❏ 47 Pamela McGee	1.25	.50
❏ 48 Nikki McCray RC	3.00	1.50
❏ 49 Cindy Brown RC	2.00	.75
❏ 50 Tiffany Woosley	.60	.25
❏ 51 Andrea Congreaves	1.25	.50
❏ 52 Jamila Wideman	2.00	.75
❏ 53 Mwadi Mabika	.60	.25
❏ 54 Murriel Page RC	1.25	.50
❏ 55 Mikiko Hagiwara RC	.60	.25
❏ 56 Linda Burgess RC	1.25	.50
❏ 57 Olympia Scott RC	.60	.25
❏ 58 Dena Head RC	.60	.25
❏ 59 Quacy Barnes RC	.60	.25
❏ 60 S.McConnell-Serio RC	2.00	.75
❏ 61 Trena Trice RC	.60	.25
❏ 62 Rushia Brown RC	.60	.25
❏ 63 Kisha Ford	.60	.25
❏ 64 Sharon Manning	.60	.25
❏ 65 Tangela Smith RC	.60	.25
❏ 66 Jim Lewis CO	1.25	.50
❏ 67 N.Lieberman-Cline CO	2.00	.75
❏ 68 Van Chancellor CO	.60	.25
❏ 69 Denise Taylor CO	1.25	.50
❏ 70 Heidi VanDerveer CO	1.25	.50
❏ 71 Marynell Meadors CO	1.25	.50
❏ 72 Linda Hill-MacDonald CO	1.25	.50
❏ 73 Nancy Darsch CO	1.25	.50
❏ 74 Cheryl Miller CO	3.00	1.50
❏ 75 Julie Rousseau CO	1.25	.50
❏ 76 Rebecca Lobo P	1.25	.50
❏ 77 Jennifer Gillom P	1.25	.50
❏ 78 Janeth Arcain P	1.25	.50
❏ 79 Rhonda Mapp P	1.25	.50
❏ 80 Cynthia Cooper P	2.00	.75

❏ 81 Tina Thompson P	1.25	.50
❏ 82 Kym Hampton P	.60	.25
❏ 83 Cynthia Cooper P	2.00	.75
❏ 84 Checklist	.60	.25
❏ 85 Checklist	.60	.25
❏ S66 Sheryl Swoopes	2.00	.75

2006-07 Press Pass Legends

❏ 1 Ronnie Brewer	3.00	1.25
❏ 2 J.J. Redick	3.00	1.25
❏ 3 Shelden Williams	2.00	.75
❏ 4 Adam Morrison	4.00	1.50
❏ 5 Rajon Rondo	3.00	1.25
❏ 6 Tyrus Thomas	3.00	1.25
❏ 7 Rodney Carney	2.00	.75
❏ 8 Shawne Williams	2.00	.75
❏ 9 Maurice Ager	2.00	.75
❏ 10 Shannon Brown	2.00	.75
❏ 11 Cedric Simmons	1.50	.60
❏ 12 Mardy Collins	1.50	.60
❏ 13 LaMarcus Aldridge	3.00	1.25
❏ 14 Hilton Armstrong	1.50	.60
❏ 15 Rudy Gay	3.00	1.25
❏ 16 Marcus Williams	2.00	.75
❏ 17 Randy Foye	4.00	1.50
❏ 18 Brandon Roy	4.00	1.50
❏ 19 Sidney Moncrief	1.50	.60
❏ 20 Nate Thurmond	1.50	.60
❏ 21 Larry Nance	1.50	.60
❏ 22 Sue Bird	5.00	2.00
❏ 23 Diana Taurasi	5.00	2.00
❏ 24 Jay Bilas	1.50	.60
❏ 25 Sleepy Floyd	1.50	.60
❏ 26 Dominique Wilkins	2.00	.75
❏ 27 Clyde Drexler	1.50	.60
❏ 28 Elvin Hayes	1.50	.60
❏ 29 Hakeem Olajuwon	1.50	.60
❏ 30 Steve Alford	1.50	.60
❏ 31 Calbert Cheaney	1.50	.60
❏ 32 Scott May	1.50	.60
❏ 33 Isiah Thomas	1.50	.60
❏ 34 Larry Bird	6.00	2.50
❏ 35 Connie Hawkins	1.50	.60
❏ 36 Danny Manning	1.50	.60
❏ 37 Jo Jo White	1.50	.60
❏ 38 Rex Chapman	1.50	.60
❏ 39 Dan Issel	1.50	.60
❏ 40 Pat Riley	2.00	.75
❏ 41 Pete Maravich	12.00	5.00
❏ 42 Wes Unseld	1.50	.60
❏ 43 Rick Barry	1.50	.60
❏ 44 Lou Hudson	1.50	.60
❏ 45 David Robinson	2.00	.75
❏ 46 Spud Webb	1.50	.60
❏ 47 David Thompson	1.50	.60
❏ 48 Brad Daugherty	1.50	.60
❏ 49 Bob McAdoo	1.50	.60
❏ 50 Sam Perkins	1.50	.60
❏ 51 Kenny Smith	1.50	.60
❏ 52 Bill Laimbeer	1.50	.60
❏ 53 Adrian Dantley	1.50	.60
❏ 54 John Havlicek	1.50	.60
❏ 55 A.C. Green	1.50	.60
❏ 56 Bill Russell	4.00	1.60
❏ 57 Walt Frazier	1.50	.60
❏ 58 Mark Jackson	1.50	.60
❏ 59 Bernard King	1.50	.60

❑ 60 Henry Bibby	1.50	.60
❑ 61 Bill Walton	1.50	.60
❑ 62 Stacey Augmon	1.50	.60
❑ 63 Reggie Theus	1.50	.60
❑ 64 Ralph Sampson	1.50	.60
❑ 65 Jerry West	2.00	.75
❑ 66 Dean Smith	1.50	.60
❑ 67 Digger Phelps	1.50	.60
❑ 68 John Wooden	1.50	.60
❑ 69 Jerry Tarkanian	1.50	.60
❑ 70 Larry Bird CL	3.00	1.25

2005-06 Reflections

❑ COMP.SET w/o RC's (100)	50.00	20.00
❑ COMMON CARD (1-100)	.50	.20
❑ COMMON ROOKIE (101-150)	5.00	2.00
❑ 1 Al Harrington	1.00	.40
❑ 2 Josh Smith	1.50	.60
❑ 3 Josh Childress	1.00	.40
❑ 4 Joe Johnson	1.00	.40
❑ 5 Paul Pierce	1.50	.60
❑ 6 Antoine Walker	1.50	.60
❑ 7 Gary Payton	1.50	.60
❑ 8 Al Jefferson	1.50	.60
❑ 9 Emeka Okafor	2.50	1.00
❑ 10 Primoz Brezec	.50	.20
❑ 11 Gerald Wallace	1.00	.40
❑ 12 Michael Jordan	10.00	4.00
❑ 13 Ben Gordon	3.00	1.25
❑ 14 Luol Deng	1.50	.60
❑ 15 Kirk Hinrich	1.50	.60
❑ 16 LeBron James	10.00	4.00
❑ 17 Dajuan Wagner	.50	.20
❑ 18 Drew Gooden	1.00	.40
❑ 19 Larry Hughes	1.00	.40
❑ 20 Dirk Nowitzki	2.50	1.00
❑ 21 Jason Terry	1.50	.60
❑ 22 Michael Finley	1.50	.60
❑ 23 Jerry Stackhouse	1.50	.60
❑ 24 Andre Miller	1.00	.40
❑ 25 Carmelo Anthony	3.00	1.25
❑ 26 Kenyon Martin	1.50	.60
❑ 27 Earl Boykins	1.00	.40
❑ 28 Rasheed Wallace	1.50	.60
❑ 29 Ben Wallace	1.00	.40
❑ 30 Richard Hamilton	1.00	.40
❑ 31 Chauncey Billups	1.50	.60
❑ 32 Baron Davis	1.50	.60
❑ 33 Derek Fisher	1.50	.60
❑ 34 Jason Richardson	1.50	.60
❑ 35 Tracy McGrady	4.00	1.50
❑ 36 Yao Ming	4.00	1.50
❑ 37 Juwan Howard	1.00	.40
❑ 38 Jermaine O'Neal	1.50	.60
❑ 39 Ron Artest	1.50	.60
❑ 40 Jamaal Tinsley	1.00	.40
❑ 41 Corey Maggette	1.00	.40
❑ 42 Elton Brand	1.50	.60
❑ 43 Shaun Livingston	1.50	.60
❑ 44 Kobe Bryant	6.00	2.50
❑ 45 Brian Cook	.50	.20
❑ 46 Lamar Odom	1.50	.60
❑ 47 Mike Miller	1.50	.60
❑ 48 Pau Gasol	1.50	.60
❑ 49 Shane Battier	1.50	.60
❑ 50 Shaquille O'Neal	4.00	1.50
❑ 51 Dwyane Wade	5.00	2.00
❑ 52 Udonis Haslem	1.50	.60
❑ 53 Joe Smith	1.00	.40
❑ 54 Michael Redd	1.50	.60
❑ 55 Desmond Mason	.50	.20
❑ 56 Kevin Garnett	3.00	1.25
❑ 57 Wally Szczerbiak	1.00	.40
❑ 58 Sam Cassell	1.50	.60
❑ 59 Vince Carter	4.00	1.50
❑ 60 Jason Kidd	2.50	1.00
❑ 61 Richard Jefferson	1.00	.40
❑ 62 Jamaal Magloire	.50	.20
❑ 63 J.R. Smith	1.00	.40
❑ 64 Bostjan Nachbar	.50	.20
❑ 65 Allan Houston	1.00	.40
❑ 66 Stephon Marbury	1.50	.60
❑ 67 Jamal Crawford	1.00	.40
❑ 68 Dwight Howard	2.00	.75
❑ 69 Grant Hill	1.50	.60
❑ 70 Jameer Nelson	1.00	.40
❑ 71 Steve Francis	1.50	.60
❑ 72 Allen Iverson	3.00	1.25
❑ 73 Andre Iguodala	1.50	.60
❑ 74 Chris Webber	1.50	.60
❑ 75 Samuel Dalembert	1.00	.40
❑ 76 Amare Stoudemire	3.00	1.25
❑ 77 Steve Nash	1.50	.60
❑ 78 Quentin Richardson	1.00	.40
❑ 79 Shawn Marion	1.00	.40
❑ 80 Damon Stoudamire	1.00	.40
❑ 81 Zach Randolph	1.50	.60
❑ 82 Sebastian Telfair	1.00	.40
❑ 83 Peja Stojakovic	1.50	.60
❑ 84 Mike Bibby	1.50	.60
❑ 85 Cuttino Mobley	1.00	.40
❑ 86 Manu Ginobili	1.50	.60
❑ 87 Tim Duncan	3.00	1.25
❑ 88 Tony Parker	1.50	.60
❑ 89 Ray Allen	1.50	.60
❑ 90 Rashard Lewis	1.50	.60
❑ 91 Luke Ridnour	1.00	.40
❑ 92 Ronald Murray	.50	.20
❑ 93 Chris Bosh	1.50	.60
❑ 94 Morris Peterson	1.00	.40
❑ 95 Rafael Araujo	1.00	.40
❑ 96 Andrei Kirilenko	1.50	.60
❑ 97 Raul Lopez	.50	.20
❑ 98 Carlos Boozer	1.00	.40
❑ 99 Antawn Jamison	1.50	.60
❑ 100 Gilbert Arenas	1.50	.60
❑ 101 Travis Diener RC	5.00	2.00
❑ 102 Julius Hodge RC	6.00	2.50
❑ 103 David Lee RC	8.00	3.00
❑ 104 Sarunas Jasikevicius RC	6.00	2.50
❑ 105 Jason Maxiell RC	5.00	2.00
❑ 106 Luther Head RC	6.00	2.50
❑ 107 Amir Johnson RC	5.00	2.00
❑ 108 Linas Kleiza RC	5.00	2.00
❑ 109 Uros Slokar RC	5.00	2.00
❑ 110 Andray Blatche RC	5.00	2.00
❑ 111 Sean May RC	4.00	1.50
❑ 112 Alex Acker RC	5.00	2.00
❑ 113 Nate Robinson RC	8.00	3.00
❑ 114 Brandon Bass RC	5.00	2.00
❑ 115 Ike Diogu RC	6.00	2.50
❑ 116 Daniel Ewing RC	5.00	2.00
❑ 117 Salim Stoudamire RC	6.00	2.50
❑ 118 Dijon Thompson RC	5.00	2.00
❑ 119 Danny Granger RC	8.00	3.00
❑ 120 Chris Taft RC	5.00	2.00
❑ 121 Louis Williams RC	5.00	2.00
❑ 122 Channing Frye RC	6.00	2.50
❑ 123 Francisco Garcia RC	6.00	2.50
❑ 124 Ryan Gomes RC	5.00	2.00
❑ 125 Von Wafer RC	5.00	2.00
❑ 126 Jarrett Jack RC	5.00	2.00
❑ 127 Lawrence Roberts RC	5.00	2.00
❑ 128 Ricky Sanchez RC	5.00	2.00
❑ 129 C.J. Miles RC	5.00	2.00
❑ 130 Ersan Ilyasova RC	5.00	2.00
❑ 131 Robert Whaley RC	5.00	2.00
❑ 132 Monta Ellis RC	10.00	4.00
❑ 133 Bracey Wright RC	5.00	2.00
❑ 134 Johan Petro RC	5.00	2.00
❑ 135 Will Bynum RC	5.00	2.00
❑ 136 Andrew Bynum RC	15.00	6.00
❑ 137 Martynas Andriuskevicius RC	5.00	2.00
❑ 138 Charlie Villanueva RC	6.00	2.50
❑ 139 Antoine Wright RC	5.00	2.00
❑ 140 Joey Graham RC	5.00	2.00
❑ 141 Wayne Simien RC	6.00	2.50
❑ 142 Hakim Warrick RC	10.00	4.00
❑ 143 Gerald Green RC	12.00	5.00
❑ 144 Marvin Williams RC	12.00	5.00
❑ 145 Deron Williams RC	20.00	8.00
❑ 146 Rashad McCants RC	8.00	3.00
❑ 147 Martell Webster RC	5.00	2.00
❑ 148 Raymond Felton RC	8.00	3.00
❑ 149 Chris Paul RC	25.00	10.00
❑ 150 Andrew Bogut RC	8.00	3.00

2006-07 Reflections

❑ 1 Josh Childress	1.00	.40
❑ 2 Joe Johnson	1.00	.40
❑ 3 Marvin Williams	2.00	.75
❑ 4 Dan Dickau	.50	.20
❑ 5 Paul Pierce	1.50	.60
❑ 6 Wally Szczerbiak	2.00	.75
❑ 7 Raymond Felton	1.50	.60
❑ 8 Emeka Okafor	1.50	.60
❑ 9 Kareem Rush	.50	.20
❑ 10 Gerald Wallace	1.50	.60
❑ 11 Tyson Chandler	1.50	.60
❑ 12 Luol Deng	1.50	.60
❑ 13 Ben Gordon	3.00	1.25
❑ 14 Michael Jordan	10.00	4.00
❑ 15 Larry Hughes	1.00	.40
❑ 16 Zydrunas Ilgauskas	.50	.20
❑ 17 LeBron James	10.00	4.00
❑ 18 Donyell Marshall	.50	.20
❑ 19 Marquis Daniels	1.00	.40
❑ 20 Josh Howard	1.00	.40
❑ 21 Dirk Nowitzki	2.50	1.00
❑ 22 Jason Terry	1.50	.60
❑ 23 Carmelo Anthony	3.00	1.25
❑ 24 Earl Boykins	.50	.20
❑ 25 Marcus Camby	.50	.20
❑ 26 Kenyon Martin	1.50	.60
❑ 27 Chauncey Billups	1.50	.60
❑ 28 Richard Hamilton	1.00	.40
❑ 29 Rasheed Wallace	1.50	.60
❑ 30 Baron Davis	1.50	.60
❑ 31 Ike Diogu	1.00	.40
❑ 32 Mike Dunleavy	1.00	.40
❑ 33 Troy Murphy	1.50	.60
❑ 34 Luther Head	1.00	.40
❑ 35 Tracy McGrady	4.00	1.50
❑ 36 Yao Ming	4.00	1.50
❑ 37 Jermaine O'Neal	1.50	.60
❑ 38 Peja Stojakovic	1.50	.60
❑ 39 Jamaal Tinsley	1.00	.40
❑ 40 Chris Kaman	.50	.20
❑ 41 Sam Cassell	1.50	.60
❑ 42 Shaun Livingston	1.25	.50
❑ 43 Cuttino Mobley	1.00	.40
❑ 44 Kobe Bryant	6.00	2.50
❑ 45 Devean George	1.00	.40
❑ 46 Lamar Odom	1.50	.60
❑ 47 Pau Gasol	1.50	.60
❑ 48 Bobby Jackson	.50	.20
❑ 49 Mike Miller	1.50	.60
❑ 50 Shaquille O'Neal	4.00	1.50
❑ 51 Dwyane Wade	5.00	2.00
❑ 52 Jason Williams	1.00	.40
❑ 53 Andrew Bogut	2.00	.75
❑ 54 T.J. Ford	1.00	.40

☐ 55 Michael Redd	1.50	.60
☐ 56 Ricky Davis	1.50	.60
☐ 57 Kevin Garnett	3.00	1.25
☐ 58 Troy Hudson	.50	.20
☐ 59 Vince Carter	4.00	1.50
☐ 60 Jason Collins	.50	.20
☐ 61 Richard Jefferson	1.00	.40
☐ 62 Jason Kidd	2.50	1.00
☐ 63 Desmond Mason	.50	.20
☐ 64 Chris Paul	4.00	1.50
☐ 65 J.R. Smith	1.00	.40
☐ 66 Steve Francis	1.50	.60
☐ 67 Channing Frye	1.00	.40
☐ 68 Stephon Marbury	1.50	.60
☐ 69 Dwight Howard	2.00	.75
☐ 70 Darko Milicic	1.50	.60
☐ 71 Jameer Nelson	1.00	.40
☐ 72 Andre Iguodala	1.50	.60
☐ 73 Allen Iverson	3.00	1.25
☐ 74 Chris Webber	1.50	.60
☐ 75 Boris Diaw	1.00	.40
☐ 76 Shawn Marion	1.50	.60
☐ 77 Steve Nash	1.50	.60
☐ 78 Amare Stoudemire	3.00	1.25
☐ 79 Juan Dixon	.50	.20
☐ 80 Darius Miles	1.00	.40
☐ 81 Sebastian Telfair	1.00	.40
☐ 82 Ron Artest	1.00	.40
☐ 83 Mike Bibby	1.50	.60
☐ 84 Brad Miller	1.50	.60
☐ 85 Tim Duncan	3.00	1.25
☐ 86 Manu Ginobili	1.50	.60
☐ 87 Robert Horry	1.00	.40
☐ 88 Tony Parker	1.50	.60
☐ 89 Ray Allen	1.50	.60
☐ 90 Rashard Lewis	1.50	.60
☐ 91 Luke Ridnour	1.00	.40
☐ 92 Chris Bosh	1.50	.60
☐ 93 Joey Graham	1.00	.40
☐ 94 Charlie Villanueva	1.50	.60
☐ 95 Carlos Boozer	1.00	.40
☐ 96 Andrei Kirilenko	1.50	.60
☐ 97 Deron Williams	1.50	.60
☐ 98 Gilbert Arenas	1.50	.60
☐ 99 Caron Butler	1.50	.60
☐ 100 Antawn Jamison	1.50	.60
☐ 101 Adam Morrison RC	15.00	6.00
☐ 102 Tyrus Thomas RC	20.00	8.00
☐ 103 Rudy Gay RC	12.00	5.00
☐ 104 Andrea Bargnani RC	15.00	6.00
☐ 105 LaMarcus Aldridge RC	15.00	6.00
☐ 106 Brandon Roy RC	20.00	8.00
☐ 107 Randy Foye RC	12.00	5.00
☐ 108 Marcus Williams RC	8.00	3.00
☐ 109 Rodney Carney RC	6.00	2.50
☐ 110 Shelden Williams RC	8.00	3.00
☐ 111 Patrick O'Bryant RC	4.00	1.50
☐ 112 Cedric Simmons RC	4.00	1.50
☐ 113 Jordan Farmar RC	8.00	3.00
☐ 114 J.J. Redick RC	8.00	3.00
☐ 115 Terence Kinsey RC	4.00	1.50
☐ 116 Kevin Pittsnogle RC	4.00	1.50
☐ 117 Ronnie Brewer RC	5.00	2.00
☐ 118 Shawne Williams RC	5.00	2.00
☐ 119 Allan Ray RC	4.00	1.50
☐ 120 Shannon Brown RC	4.00	1.50
☐ 121 Kyle Lowry RC	4.00	1.50
☐ 122 Marty Collins RC	4.00	1.50
☐ 123 Hilton Armstrong RC	4.00	1.50
☐ 124 Maurice Ager RC	4.00	1.50
☐ 125 Quincy Douby RC	4.00	1.50
☐ 126 Rajon Rondo RC	6.00	2.50
☐ 127 Mike Gansey RC	5.00	2.00
☐ 128 Joel Freeland RC	5.00	2.00
☐ 129 Josh Boone RC	5.00	2.00
☐ 130 Saer Sene RC	5.00	2.00
☐ 131 Denham Brown RC	5.00	2.00
☐ 132 Renaldo Balkman RC	5.00	2.00
☐ 133 Will Blalock RC	5.00	2.00
☐ 134 David Noel RC	5.00	2.00
☐ 135 Steve Novak RC	5.00	2.00
☐ 136 Solomon Jones RC	5.00	2.00
☐ 137 Dee Brown RC	8.00	3.00
☐ 138 Hassan Adams RC	6.00	2.50
☐ 139 Bobby Jones RC	5.00	2.00
☐ 140 Thabo Sefolosha RC	8.00	3.00

☐ 141 James White RC	5.00	2.00
☐ 142 Paul Davis RC	5.00	2.00
☐ 143 P.J. Tucker RC	5.00	2.00
☐ 144 Ryan Hollins RC	5.00	2.00
☐ 145 Damir Markota RC	5.00	2.00
☐ 146 Leon Powe RC	5.00	2.00
☐ 147 James Augustine RC	5.00	2.00
☐ 148 Alexander Johnson RC	5.00	2.00
☐ 149 Daniel Gibson RC	12.00	5.00

1990-91 SkyBox

SAM PERKINS

☐ COMPLETE SET (423)	20.00	10.00
☐ COMPLETE SERIES 1 (300)	12.00	6.00
☐ COMPLETE SERIES 2 (123)	8.00	4.00
☐ COMMON CARD (1-300)	.05	.01
☐ COMMON CARD (301-423)	.10	.02
☐ COMMON SP	.10	.02
☐ 1 John Battle	.05	.01
☐ 2 Duane Ferrell RC SP	.10	.02
☐ 3 Jon Koncak	.05	.01
☐ 4 Cliff Levingston SP	.10	.02
☐ 5 John Long SP	.10	.02
☐ 6 Moses Malone	.25	.08
☐ 7 Doc Rivers	.10	.02
☐ 8 Kenny Smith SP	.10	.02
☐ 9 Alexander Volkov	.05	.01
☐ 10 Spud Webb	.10	.02
☐ 11 Dominique Wilkins	.25	.08
☐ 12 Kevin Willis	.10	.02
☐ 13 John Bagley	.05	.01
☐ 14 Larry Bird	1.00	.30
☐ 15 Kevin Gamble	.05	.01
☐ 16 Dennis Johnson SP	.10	.02
☐ 17 Joe Kleine	.05	.01
☐ 18 Reggie Lewis	.10	.02
☐ 19 Kevin McHale	.10	.02
☐ 20 Robert Parish	.10	.02
☐ 21 Jim Paxson SP	.10	.02
☐ 22 Ed Pinckney	.05	.01
☐ 23 Brian Shaw	.25	.08
☐ 24 Michael Smith	.05	.01
☐ 25 Richard Anderson SP	.10	.02
☐ 26 Muggsy Bogues	.25	.08
☐ 27 Rex Chapman	.05	.01
☐ 28 Dell Curry	.05	.01
☐ 29 Armon Gilliam	.05	.01
☐ 30 Michael Holton SP	.10	.02
☐ 31 Dave Hoppen	.05	.01
☐ 32 J.R.Reid RC	.05	.01
☐ 33 Robert Reid SP	.10	.02
☐ 34 Brian Rowsom SP	.10	.02
☐ 35 Kelly Tripucka	.05	.01
☐ 36 Micheal Williams SP UER	.10	.02
☐ 37 B.J.Armstrong RC	.10	.02
☐ 38 Bill Cartwright	.05	.01
☐ 39 Horace Grant	.10	.02
☐ 40 Craig Hodges	.05	.01
☐ 41 Michael Jordan	3.00	1.50
☐ 42 Stacey King RC	.05	.01
☐ 43 Ed Nealy SP	.10	.02
☐ 44 John Paxson	.05	.01
☐ 45 Will Perdue	.05	.01
☐ 46 Scottie Pippen	1.00	.40
☐ 47 Jeff Sanders RC SP	.10	.02
☐ 48 Winston Bennett	.05	.01
☐ 49 Chucky Brown RC	.05	.01
☐ 50 Brad Daugherty	.05	.01
☐ 51 Craig Ehlo	.05	.01

☐ 52 Steve Kerr	.25	.08
☐ 53 Paul Mokeski SP	.10	.02
☐ 54 John Morton	.05	.01
☐ 55 Larry Nance	.05	.01
☐ 56 Mark Price	.10	.02
☐ 57 Tree Rollins SP	.10	.02
☐ 58 Hot Rod Williams	.05	.01
☐ 59 Steve Alford	.05	.01
☐ 60 Rolando Blackman	.05	.01
☐ 61 Adrian Dantley SP	.05	.01
☐ 62 Brad Davis	.05	.01
☐ 63 James Donaldson	.05	.01
☐ 64 Derek Harper	.10	.02
☐ 65 Anthony Jones SP	.10	.02
☐ 66 Sam Perkins SP	.10	.02
☐ 67 Roy Tarpley	.05	.01
☐ 68 Bill Wennington SP	.10	.02
☐ 69 Randy White RC	.05	.01
☐ 70 Herb Williams	.05	.01
☐ 71 Michael Adams	.05	.01
☐ 72 Joe Barry Carroll SP	.10	.02
☐ 73 Walter Davis	.05	.01
☐ 74 Alex English SP	.10	.02
☐ 75 Bill Hanzlik SP	.10	.02
☐ 76 Tim Kempton SP	.10	.02
☐ 77 Jerome Lane	.05	.01
☐ 78 Lafayette Lever SP	.10	.02
☐ 79 Todd Lichti RC	.05	.01
☐ 80 Blair Rasmussen	.05	.01
☐ 81 Danny Schayes SP	.10	.02
☐ 82 Mark Aguirre	.05	.01
☐ 83 William Bedford SP	.10	.02
☐ 84 Joe Dumars	.25	.08
☐ 85 James Edwards	.05	.01
☐ 86 David Greenwood SP	.10	.02
☐ 87 Scott Hastings	.05	.01
☐ 88 Gerald Henderson SP	.10	.02
☐ 89 Vinnie Johnson	.05	.01
☐ 90 Bill Laimbeer	.05	.01
☐ 91 Dennis Rodman	.60	.25
☐ 91B Dennis Rodman Left	1.00	.40
☐ 92 John Salley	.05	.01
☐ 93 Isiah Thomas	.25	.08
☐ 94 Manute Bol SP	.10	.02
☐ 95 Tim Hardaway RC	1.50	.60
☐ 96 Rod Higgins	.05	.01
☐ 97 Sarun.Marciulionis RC	.05	.01
☐ 98 Chris Mullin	.25	.08
☐ 99 Jim Petersen	.05	.01
☐ 100 Mitch Richmond	.30	.10
☐ 101 Mike Smrek	.05	.01
☐ 102 Terry Teagle SP	.10	.02
☐ 103 Tom Tolbert RC	.05	.01
☐ 104 Kelvin Upshaw SP	.10	.02
☐ 105 Anthony Bowie RC SP	.10	.02
☐ 106 Adrian Caldwell	.05	.01
☐ 107 Eric(Sleepy) Floyd	.05	.01
☐ 108 Buck Johnson	.05	.01
☐ 109 Vernon Maxwell	.05	.01
☐ 110 Hakeem Olajuwon	.40	.15
☐ 111 Larry Smith	.05	.01
☐ 112A Otis Thorpe ERR	1.50	.60
☐ 112B Otis Thorpe COR	.10	.02
☐ 113A M. Wiggins SP ERR	1.50	.60
☐ 113B M. Wiggins SP COR	.10	.02
☐ 114 Vern Fleming	.05	.01
☐ 115 Rickey Green SP	.10	.02
☐ 116 George McCloud RC	.25	.08
☐ 117 Reggie Miller	.30	.10
☐ 118A Dyron Nix SP ERR	1.50	.60
☐ 118B Dyron Nix SP COR	.10	.02
☐ 119 Chuck Person	.10	.02
☐ 120 Mike Sanders	.05	.01
☐ 121 Detlef Schrempf	.10	.02
☐ 122 Rik Smits	.25	.08
☐ 123 LaSalle Thompson	.05	.01
☐ 124 Benoit Benjamin	.05	.01
☐ 125 Winston Garland	.05	.01
☐ 126 Tom Garrick	.05	.01
☐ 127 Gary Grant	.05	.01
☐ 128 Ron Harper	.10	.02
☐ 129 Danny Manning	.10	.02
☐ 130 Jeff Martin	.05	.01
☐ 131 Ken Norman	.05	.01
☐ 132 Charles Smith	.05	.01
☐ 133 Joe Wolf SP	.10	.02

#	Card	Val1	Val2
134	Michael Cooper SP	.10	.02
135	Vlade Divac RC	.60	.25
136	Larry Drew	.05	.01
137	A.C. Green	.10	.02
138	Magic Johnson	.75	.30
139	Mark McNamara SP	.10	.02
140	Byron Scott	.10	.02
141	Mychal Thompson	.05	.01
142	Orlando Woolridge SP	.10	.02
143	James Worthy	.25	.08
144	Terry Davis SP	.05	.01
145	Sherman Douglas RC	.10	.02
146	Kevin Edwards	.05	.01
147	Tellis Frank SP	.10	.02
148	Scott Haffner SP	.10	.02
149	Grant Long	.05	.01
150	Glen Rice RC	1.00	.40
151	Rony Seikaly	.10	.02
152	Rory Sparrow SP	.10	.02
153	Jon Sundvold	.05	.01
154	Billy Thompson	.05	.01
155	Greg Anderson	.05	.01
156	Ben Coleman SP	.10	.02
157	Jeff Grayer RC	.05	.01
158	Jay Humphries	.05	.01
159	Frank Kornet	.05	.01
160	Larry Krystkowiak	.05	.01
161	Brad Lohaus	.05	.01
162	Ricky Pierce	.05	.01
163	Paul Pressey SP	.10	.02
164	Fred Roberts	.05	.01
165	Alvin Robertson	.05	.01
166	Jack Sikma	.05	.01
167	Randy Breuer	.05	.01
168	Tony Campbell	.05	.01
169	Tyrone Corbin	.05	.01
170	Sidney Lowe SP	.10	.02
171	Sam Mitchell RC	.05	.01
172	Tod Murphy	.05	.01
173	Pooh Richardson RC	.10	.02
174	Donald Royal RC SP	.10	.02
175	Brad Sellers SP	.10	.02
176	Mookie Blaylock RC	.40	.15
177	Sam Bowie	.05	.01
178	Lester Conner	.05	.01
179	Derrick Gervin	.05	.01
180	Jack Haley SP	.10	.02
181	Roy Hinson	.05	.01
182	Dennis Hopson SP	.10	.02
183	Chris Morris	.10	.02
184	Pete Myers RC SP	.10	.02
185	Purvis Short SP	.10	.02
186	Maurice Cheeks	.05	.01
187	Patrick Ewing	.25	.08
188	Stuart Gray	.05	.01
189	Mark Jackson	.10	.02
190	Johnny Newman SP	.10	.02
191	Charles Oakley	.05	.01
192	Brian Quinnett SP	.05	.01
193	Trent Tucker	.05	.01
194	Kiki Vandeweghe	.05	.01
195	Kenny Walker	.05	.01
196	Eddie Lee Wilkins SP	.05	.01
197	Gerald Wilkins	.05	.01
198	Mark Acres	.05	.01
199	Nick Anderson RC	.40	.15
200	Michael Ansley	.05	.01
201	Terry Catledge	.05	.01
202	Dave Corzine SP	.10	.02
203	Sidney Green SP	.10	.02
204	Jerry Reynolds SP	.10	.02
205	Scott Skiles	.05	.01
206	Otis Smith	.05	.01
207	Reggie Theus SP	.10	.01
208	Jeff Turner	.05	.01
209	Sam Vincent	.05	.01
210	Ron Anderson	.05	.01
211	Charles Barkley	.40	.15
212	Scott Brooks SP	.10	.02
213	Lanard Copeland SP	.10	.02
214	Johnny Dawkins	.05	.01
215	Mike Gminski	.05	.01
216	Hersey Hawkins	.10	.02
217	Rick Mahorn	.05	.01
218	Derek Smith SP	.10	.02
219	Bob Thornton	.05	.01
220	Tom Chambers	.05	.01
221	Greg Grant RC SP	.10	.02
222	Jeff Hornacek	.10	.02
223	Eddie Johnson	.10	.02
224A	Kevin Johnson Lower	.25	.08
224B	Kevin Johnson Upper	.25	.08
225	Andrew Lang RC	.25	.08
226	Dan Majerle	.25	.08
227	Mike McGee SP	.10	.02
228	Tim Perry	.05	.01
229	Kurt Rambis	.05	.01
230	Mark West	.05	.01
231	Mark Bryant	.05	.01
232	Wayne Cooper	.05	.01
233	Clyde Drexler	.25	.08
234	Kevin Duckworth	.05	.01
235	Byron Irvin SP	.10	.02
236	Jerome Kersey	.05	.01
237	Drazen Petrovic RC	.30	.10
238	Terry Porter	.05	.01
239	Clifford Robinson RC	.40	.15
240	Buck Williams	.10	.02
241	Danny Young	.05	.01
242	Danny Ainge SP	.10	.02
243	Randy Allen SP	.10	.02
244A	Antoine Carr SP	.15	.05
244B	Antoine Carr	.05	.01
245	Vinny Del Negro SP	.10	.02
246	Pervis Ellison RC SP	.10	.02
247	Greg Kite SP	.10	.02
248	Rodney McCray SP	.10	.02
249	Harold Pressley SP	.10	.02
250	Ralph Sampson	.05	.01
251	Wayman Tisdale	.05	.01
252	Willie Anderson	.05	.01
253	Uwe Blab SP	.10	.02
254	Frank Brickowski SP	.10	.02
255	Terry Cummings	.05	.01
256	Sean Elliott RC	.50	.20
257	Caldwell Jones SP	.10	.02
258	Johnny Moore SP	.10	.02
259	Zarko Paspalj SP	.10	.02
260	David Robinson	.75	.30
261	Rod Strickland	.25	.08
262	David Wingate SP	.10	.02
263	Dana Barros RC	.25	.06
264	Michael Cage	.05	.01
265	Quintin Dailey	.05	.01
266	Dale Ellis	.10	.02
267	Steve Johnson SP	.10	.02
268	Shawn Kemp RC	2.50	1.00
269	Xavier McDaniel	.05	.01
270	Derrick McKey	.05	.01
271A	Nate McMillan SP ERR	.20	.07
271B	Nate McMillan COR	.10	.02
272	Olden Polynice	.05	.01
273	Sedale Threatt	.05	.01
274	Thurl Bailey	.05	.01
275	Mike Brown	.05	.01
276	Mark Eaton	.05	.01
277	Blue Edwards RC	.05	.01
278	Darrell Griffith	.05	.01
279	Bobby Hansen SP	.10	.02
280	Eric Johnson	.05	.01
281	Eric Leckner SP	.10	.02
282	Karl Malone	.40	.15
283	Delaney Rudd	.05	.01
284	John Stockton	.30	.10
285	Mark Alarie	.05	.01
286	Steve Colter SP	.10	.02
287	Ledell Eackles SP	.10	.02
288	Harvey Grant	.05	.01
289	Tom Hammonds RC	.05	.01
290	Charles Jones	.05	.01
291	Bernard King	.10	.02
292	Jeff Malone SP	.10	.02
293	Darrell Walker	.05	.01
294	John Williams	.05	.01
295	Checklist 1 SP	.10	.02
296	Checklist 2 SP	.10	.02
297	Checklist 3 SP	.10	.02
298	Checklist 4 SP	.10	.02
299	Checklist 5 SP	.10	.02
300	Danny Ferry SP RC	.50	.20
301	Bob Weiss CO	.10	.02
302	Chris Ford CO	.10	.02
303	Gene Littles CO	.10	.02
304	Phil Jackson CO	.30	.10
305	Lenny Wilkens CO	.30	.10
306	Richie Adubato CO	.10	.02
307	Paul Westhead CO	.10	.02
308	Chuck Daly CO	.30	.10
309	Don Nelson CO	.30	.10
310	Don Chaney CO	.10	.02
311	Dick Versace CO	.10	.02
312	Mike Schuler CO	.10	.02
313	Mike Dunleavy CO	.10	.02
314	Ron Rothstein CO	.10	.02
315	Del Harris CO	.10	.02
316	Bill Musselman CO	.10	.02
317	Bill Fitch CO	.10	.02
318	Stu Jackson CO	.10	.02
319	Matt Guokas CO	.10	.02
320	Jim Lynam CO	.10	.02
321	Cotton Fitzsimmons CO	.10	.02
322	Rick Adelman CO	.10	.02
323	Dick Motta CO	.10	.02
324	Larry Brown CO	.10	.02
325	K.C. Jones CO	.30	.10
326	Jerry Sloan CO	.30	.10
327	Wes Unseld CO	.10	.02
328	Atlanta Hawks TC	.10	.02
329	Boston Celtics TC	.10	.02
330	Charlotte Hornets TC	.10	.02
331	Chicago Bulls TC	.30	.10
332	Cleveland Cavaliers TC	.10	.02
333	Dallas Mavericks TC	.10	.02
334	Denver Nuggets TC	.10	.02
335	Detroit Pistons TC	.10	.02
336	Golden State Warriors TC	.10	.02
337	Houston Rockets TC	.10	.02
338	Indiana Pacers TC	.10	.02
339	Los Angeles Clippers TC	.10	.02
340	Los Angeles Lakers TC	.10	.02
341	Miami Heat TC	.10	.02
342	Milwaukee Bucks TC	.10	.02
343	Minnesota Timberwolves TC	.10	.02
344	New Jersey Nets TC	.10	.02
345	New York Knicks TC	.10	.02
346	Orlando Magic TC	.10	.02
347	Philadelphia 76ers TC	.10	.02
348	Phoenix Suns TC	.10	.02
349	Portland Trail Blazers TC	.10	.02
350	Sacramento Kings TC	.10	.02
351	San Antonio Spurs TC	.10	.02
352	Seattle SuperSonics TC	.10	.02
353	Utah Jazz TC	.10	.02
354	Washington Bullets TC	.10	.02
355	Rumeal Robinson RC	.10	.02
356	Kendall Gill RC	1.25	.50
357	Chris Jackson RC	.60	.25
358	Tyrone Hill RC	.50	.20
359	Bo Kimble RC	.10	.02
360	Willie Burton RC	.10	.02
361	Felton Spencer RC	.30	.10
362	Derrick Coleman RC	1.25	.50
363	Dennis Scott RC	.75	.30
364	Lionel Simmons RC	.30	.10
365	Gary Payton RC	5.00	2.00
366	Tim McCormick	.10	.02
367	Sidney Moncrief	.10	.02
368	Kenny Gattison RC	.10	.02
369	Randolph Keys	.10	.02
370	Johnny Newman	.10	.02
371	Dennis Hopson	.10	.02
372	Cliff Levingston	.10	.02
373	Derrick Chievous	.10	.02
374	Danny Ferry	.30	.10
375	Alex English	.10	.02
376	Lafayette Lever	.10	.02
377	Rodney McCray	.10	.02
378	T.R. Dunn	.10	.02
379	Corey Gaines	.10	.02
380	Avery Johnson	.75	.30
381	Joe Wolf	.10	.02
382	Orlando Woolridge	.10	.02
383	Tree Rollins	.10	.02
384	Steve Johnson	.10	.02
385	Kenny Smith	.10	.02
386	Mike Woodson	.10	.02
387	Greg Dreiling RC	.10	.02
388	Micheal Williams	.30	.10

❏ 389 Randy Wittman	.10	.02
❏ 390 Ken Bannister	.10	.02
❏ 391 Sam Perkins	.30	.07
❏ 392 Terry Teagle	.10	.02
❏ 393 Milt Wagner	.10	.02
❏ 394 Frank Brickowski	.10	.02
❏ 395 Danny Schayes	.10	.02
❏ 396 Scott Brooks	.10	.02
❏ 397 Doug West RC	.30	.10
❏ 398 Chris Dudley RC	.30	.10
❏ 399 Reggie Theus	.30	.10
❏ 400 Greg Grant	.10	.02
❏ 401 Greg Kite	.10	.02
❏ 402 Mark McNamara	.10	.02
❏ 403 Manute Bol	.10	.02
❏ 404 Rickey Green	.10	.02
❏ 405 Kenny Battle RC	.10	.02
❏ 406 Ed Nealy	.10	.02
❏ 407 Danny Ainge	.30	.10
❏ 408 Steve Colter	.10	.02
❏ 409 Bobby Hansen	.10	.02
❏ 410 Eric Leckner	.10	.02
❏ 411 Rory Sparrow	.10	.02
❏ 412 Bill Wennington	.10	.02
❏ 413 Sidney Green	.10	.02
❏ 414 David Greenwood	.10	.02
❏ 415 Paul Pressey	.10	.02
❏ 416 Reggie Williams	.10	.02
❏ 417 Dave Corzine	.10	.02
❏ 418 Jeff Malone	.10	.02
❏ 419 Pervis Ellison	.10	.02
❏ 420 Byron Irvin	.10	.02
❏ 421 Checklist 1	.10	.02
❏ 422 Checklist 2	.10	.02
❏ 423 Checklist 3	.10	.02
❏ NNO SkyBox Salutes the NBA	5.00	2.00

1991-92 SkyBox

❏ COMPLETE SET (659)	60.00	30.00
❏ COMPLETE SERIES 1 (350)	20.00	10.00
❏ COMPLETE SERIES 2 (309)	40.00	20.00
❏ 1 John Battle	.05	.01
❏ 2 Duane Ferrell	.05	.01
❏ 3 Jon Koncak	.05	.01
❏ 4 Moses Malone	.40	.15
❏ 5 Tim McCormick	.05	.01
❏ 6 Sidney Moncrief	.05	.01
❏ 7 Doc Rivers	.20	.07
❏ 8 Rumeal Robinson UER	.05	.01
❏ 9 Spud Webb	.20	.07
❏ 10 Dominique Wilkins	.40	.15
❏ 11 Kevin Willis	.05	.01
❏ 12 Larry Bird	1.50	.60
❏ 13 Dee Brown FSBC	.05	.01
❏ 14 Kevin Gamble	.05	.01
❏ 15 Joe Kleine	.05	.01
❏ 16 Reggie Lewis	.20	.07
❏ 17 Kevin McHale	.20	.07
❏ 18 Robert Parish	.20	.07
❏ 19 Ed Pinckney	.05	.01
❏ 20 Brian Shaw	.05	.01
❏ 21 Michael Smith	.05	.01
❏ 22 Stojko Vrankovic	.05	.01
❏ 23 Muggsy Bogues	.20	.07
❏ 24 Rex Chapman	.20	.07
❏ 25 Dell Curry	.05	.01
❏ 26 Kenny Gattison	.05	.01
❏ 27 Kendall Gill	.20	.07

❏ 28 Mike Gminski	.05	.01
❏ 29 Randolph Keys	.05	.01
❏ 30 Eric Leckner	.05	.01
❏ 31 Johnny Newman	.05	.01
❏ 32 J.R. Reid	.05	.01
❏ 33 Kelly Tripucka	.05	.01
❏ 34 B.J.Armstrong	.05	.01
❏ 35 Bill Cartwright	.05	.01
❏ 36 Horace Grant	.20	.07
❏ 37 Craig Hodges	.05	.01
❏ 38 Dennis Hopson	.05	.01
❏ 39 Michael Jordan	5.00	2.00
❏ 40 Stacey King	.05	.01
❏ 41 Cliff Levingston	.05	.01
❏ 42 John Paxson	.05	.01
❏ 43 Will Perdue	.05	.01
❏ 44 Scottie Pippen	1.25	.50
❏ 45 Winston Bennett	.05	.01
❏ 46 Chucky Brown	.05	.01
❏ 47 Brad Daugherty	.05	.01
❏ 48 Craig Ehlo	.05	.01
❏ 49 Danny Ferry	.05	.01
❏ 50 Steve Kerr	.20	.07
❏ 51 John Morton	.05	.01
❏ 52 Larry Nance	.20	.07
❏ 53 Mark Price	.05	.01
❏ 54 Darnell Valentine	.05	.01
❏ 55 John Williams	.05	.01
❏ 56 Steve Alford	.05	.01
❏ 57 Rolando Blackman	.05	.01
❏ 58 Brad Davis	.05	.01
❏ 59 James Donaldson	.05	.01
❏ 60 Derek Harper	.20	.07
❏ 61 Fat Lever	.05	.01
❏ 62 Rodney McCray	.05	.01
❏ 63 Roy Tarpley	.05	.01
❏ 64 Kelvin Upshaw	.05	.01
❏ 65 Randy White	.05	.01
❏ 66 Herb Williams	.05	.01
❏ 67 Michael Adams	.05	.01
❏ 68 Greg Anderson	.05	.01
❏ 69 Anthony Cook	.05	.01
❏ 70 Chris Jackson	.05	.01
❏ 71 Jerome Lane	.05	.01
❏ 72 Marcus Liberty	.05	.01
❏ 73 Todd Lichti	.05	.01
❏ 74 Blair Rasmussen	.05	.01
❏ 75 Reggie Williams	.05	.01
❏ 76 Joe Wolf	.05	.01
❏ 77 Orlando Woolridge	.05	.01
❏ 78 Mark Aguirre	.05	.01
❏ 79 William Bedford	.05	.01
❏ 80 Lance Blanks	.05	.01
❏ 81 Joe Dumars	.40	.15
❏ 82 James Edwards	.05	.01
❏ 83 Scott Hastings	.05	.01
❏ 84 Vinnie Johnson	.05	.01
❏ 85 Bill Laimbeer	.20	.07
❏ 86 Dennis Rodman	.75	.30
❏ 87 John Salley	.05	.01
❏ 88 Isiah Thomas	.40	.15
❏ 89 Mario Elie RC	.40	.15
❏ 90 Tim Hardaway	.60	.25
❏ 91 Rod Higgins	.05	.01
❏ 92 Tyrone Hill	.20	.07
❏ 93 Les Jepsen	.05	.01
❏ 94 Alton Lister	.05	.01
❏ 95 Sarunas Marciulionis	.05	.01
❏ 96 Chris Mullin	.40	.15
❏ 97 Jim Petersen	.05	.01
❏ 98 Mitch Richmond	.40	.15
❏ 99 Tom Tolbert	.05	.01
❏ 100 Adrian Caldwell	.05	.01
❏ 101 Eric(Sleepy) Floyd	.05	.01
❏ 102 Dave Jamerson	.05	.01
❏ 103 Buck Johnson	.05	.01
❏ 104 Vernon Maxwell	.05	.01
❏ 105 Hakeem Olajuwon	.60	.25
❏ 106 Kenny Smith	.05	.01
❏ 107 Larry Smith	.05	.01
❏ 108 Otis Thorpe	.20	.07
❏ 109 Kenard Winchester RC	.05	.01
❏ 110 David Wood RC	.05	.01
❏ 111 Greg Dreiling	.05	.01
❏ 112 Vern Fleming	.05	.01
❏ 113 George McCloud	.05	.01

❏ 114 Reggie Miller	.40	.15
❏ 115 Chuck Person	.05	.01
❏ 116 Mike Sanders	.05	.01
❏ 117 Detlef Schrempf	.20	.07
❏ 118 Rik Smits	.05	.01
❏ 119 LaSalle Thompson	.05	.01
❏ 120 Kenny Williams	.05	.01
❏ 121 Micheal Williams	.05	.01
❏ 122 Ken Bannister	.05	.01
❏ 123 Winston Garland	.05	.01
❏ 124 Gary Grant	.05	.01
❏ 125 Ron Harper	.20	.07
❏ 126 Bo Kimble	.05	.01
❏ 127 Danny Manning	.20	.07
❏ 128 Jeff Martin	.05	.01
❏ 129 Ken Norman	.05	.01
❏ 130 Olden Polynice	.05	.01
❏ 131 Charles Smith	.05	.01
❏ 132 Loy Vaught	.05	.01
❏ 133 Elden Campbell	.20	.07
❏ 134 Vlade Divac	.20	.07
❏ 135 Larry Drew	.05	.01
❏ 136 A.C. Green	.20	.07
❏ 137 Magic Johnson	1.25	.50
❏ 138 Sam Perkins	.20	.07
❏ 139 Byron Scott	.05	.01
❏ 140 Tony Smith	.05	.01
❏ 141 Terry Teagle	.05	.01
❏ 142 Mychal Thompson	.05	.01
❏ 143 James Worthy	.40	.15
❏ 144 Willie Burton	.05	.01
❏ 145 Bimbo Coles FSBC	.05	.01
❏ 146 Terry Davis	.05	.01
❏ 147 Sherman Douglas	.05	.01
❏ 148 Kevin Edwards	.05	.01
❏ 149 Alec Kessler	.05	.01
❏ 150 Grant Long	.05	.01
❏ 151 Glen Rice	.40	.15
❏ 152 Rony Seikaly	.05	.01
❏ 153 Jon Sundvold	.05	.01
❏ 154 Billy Thompson	.05	.01
❏ 155 Frank Brickowski	.05	.01
❏ 156 Lester Conner	.05	.01
❏ 157 Jeff Grayer	.05	.01
❏ 158 Jay Humphries	.05	.01
❏ 159 Larry Krystkowiak	.05	.01
❏ 160 Brad Lohaus	.05	.01
❏ 161 Dale Ellis	.20	.07
❏ 162 Fred Roberts	.05	.01
❏ 163 Alvin Robertson	.05	.01
❏ 164 Danny Schayes	.05	.01
❏ 165 Jack Sikma	.05	.01
❏ 166 Randy Breuer	.05	.01
❏ 167 Scott Brooks	.05	.01
❏ 168 Tony Campbell	.05	.01
❏ 169 Tyrone Corbin	.05	.01
❏ 170 Gerald Glass	.05	.01
❏ 171 Sam Mitchell	.05	.01
❏ 172 Tod Murphy	.05	.01
❏ 173 Pooh Richardson	.05	.01
❏ 174 Felton Spencer	.05	.01
❏ 175 Bob Thornton	.05	.01
❏ 176 Doug West	.05	.01
❏ 177 Mookie Blaylock	.20	.07
❏ 178 Sam Bowie	.05	.01
❏ 179 Jud Buechler	.05	.01
❏ 180 Derrick Coleman	.20	.07
❏ 181 Chris Dudley	.05	.01
❏ 182 Tate George	.05	.01
❏ 183 Jack Haley	.05	.01
❏ 184 Terry Mills RC	.40	.15
❏ 185 Chris Morris	.05	.01
❏ 186 Drazen Petrovic	.20	.07
❏ 187 Reggie Theus	.20	.07
❏ 188 Maurice Cheeks	.05	.01
❏ 189 Patrick Ewing	.40	.15
❏ 190 Mark Jackson	.20	.07
❏ 191 Jerrod Mustaf FSBC	.05	.01
❏ 192 Charles Oakley	.05	.01
❏ 193 Brian Quinnett	.05	.01
❏ 194 John Starks RC	.40	.15
❏ 195 Trent Tucker	.05	.01
❏ 196 Kiki Vandeweghe	.05	.01
❏ 197 Kenny Walker	.05	.01
❏ 198 Gerald Wilkins	.05	.01
❏ 199 Mark Acres	.05	.01

200	Nick Anderson	.20	.07
201	Michael Ansley	.05	.01
202	Terry Catledge	.05	.01
203	Greg Kite	.05	.01
204	Jerry Reynolds	.05	.01
205	Dennis Scott	.20	.07
206	Scott Skiles	.05	.01
207	Otis Smith	.05	.01
208	Jeff Turner	.05	.01
209	Sam Vincent	.05	.01
210	Ron Anderson	.05	.01
211	Charles Barkley	.60	.25
212	Manute Bol	.05	.01
213	Johnny Dawkins	.05	.01
214	Armon Gilliam	.05	.01
215	Rickey Green	.05	.01
216	Hersey Hawkins	.20	.07
217	Rick Mahorn	.05	.01
218	Brian Oliver	.05	.01
219	Andre Turner	.05	.01
220	Jayson Williams	.40	.15
221	Joe Barry Carroll	.05	.01
222	Cedric Ceballos	.20	.07
223	Tom Chambers	.05	.01
224	Jeff Homacek	.20	.07
225	Kevin Johnson	.40	.15
226	Negele Knight FSBC	.05	.01
227	Andrew Lang	.05	.01
228	Dan Majerle	.20	.07
229	Xavier McDaniel	.05	.01
230	Kurt Rambis	.05	.01
231	Mark West	.05	.01
232	Alaa Abdelnaby	.05	.01
233	Danny Ainge	.20	.07
234	Mark Bryant	.05	.01
235	Wayne Cooper	.05	.01
236	Walter Davis	.05	.01
237	Clyde Drexler	.40	.15
238	Kevin Duckworth	.05	.01
239	Jerome Kersey	.05	.01
240	Terry Porter	.05	.01
241	Clifford Robinson	.20	.07
242	Buck Williams	.05	.01
243	Anthony Bonner	.05	.01
244	Antoine Carr	.05	.01
245	Duane Causwell	.05	.01
246	Bobby Hansen	.05	.01
247	Jim Les RC	.05	.01
248	Travis Mays	.05	.01
249	Ralph Sampson	.05	.01
250	Lionel Simmons	.05	.01
251	Rory Sparrow	.05	.01
252	Wayman Tisdale	.05	.01
253	Bill Wennington	.05	.01
254	Willie Anderson	.05	.01
255	Terry Cummings	.05	.01
256	Sean Elliott	.20	.07
257	Sidney Green	.05	.01
258	David Greenwood	.05	.01
259	Avery Johnson	.20	.07
260	Paul Pressey	.05	.01
261	David Robinson	.75	.30
262	Dwayne Schintzius	.05	.01
263	Rod Strickland	.40	.15
264	David Wingate	.05	.01
265	Dana Barros	.05	.01
266	Benoit Benjamin	.05	.01
267	Michael Cage	.05	.01
268	Quintin Dailey	.05	.01
269	Ricky Pierce	.05	.01
270	Eddie Johnson	.20	.07
271	Shawn Kemp	1.00	.40
272	Derrick McKey	.05	.01
273	Nate McMillan	.05	.01
274	Gary Payton	1.00	.40
275	Sedale Threatt	.05	.01
276	Thurl Bailey	.05	.01
277	Mike Brown	.05	.01
278	Tony Brown	.05	.01
279	Mark Eaton	.05	.01
280	Blue Edwards	.05	.01
281	Darrell Griffith	.05	.01
282	Jeff Malone	.05	.01
283	Karl Malone	.60	.25
284	Delaney Rudd	.05	.01
285	John Stockton	.40	.15
286	Andy Toolson	.05	.01
287	Mark Alarie	.05	.01
288	Ledell Eackles	.05	.01
289	Pervis Ellison	.05	.01
290	A.J. English	.05	.01
291	Harvey Grant	.05	.01
292	Tom Hammonds	.05	.01
293	Charles Jones	.05	.01
294	Bernard King	.05	.01
295	Darrell Walker	.05	.01
296	John Williams	.05	.01
297	Haywoode Workman RC	.20	.07
298	Muggsy Bogues	.05	.01
299	Lester Conner	.05	.01
300	Michael Adams	.05	.01
301	Chris Mullin Minutes	.20	.07
302	Otis Thorpe	.05	.01
303	Rich/Hard/Mullin TRIO	.40	.15
304	Darrell Walker	.05	.01
305	Jerome Lane	.05	.01
306	John Stockton Assists	.20	.07
307	Michael Jordan Points	2.50	1.00
308	Michael Adams	.05	.01
309	Larry Smith	.05	.01
310	Scott Skiles	.05	.01
311	H.Olajuwon/D.Robinson	.40	.15
312	Alvin Robertson	.05	.01
313	Stay in School Jam	.05	.01
314	Craig Hodges	.05	.01
315	Dee Brown SD	.05	.01
316	Charles Barkley AS-MVP	.40	.15
317	Behind the Scenes	.40	.15
318	Derrick Coleman ART	.05	.01
319	Lionel Simmons ART	.05	.01
320	Dennis Scott ART	.05	.01
321	Kendall Gill ART	.05	.01
322	Dee Brown ART	.05	.01
323	Magic Johnson GQ	.60	.25
324	Hakeem Olajuwon GQ	.40	.15
325	K.Willis/D.Wilkins GQ	.20	.07
326	K.Willis/D.Wilkins GQ	.20	.07
327	Gerald Wilkins	.05	.01
328	Centennial Logo Card	.05	.01
329	Old-Fashioned Ball	.05	.01
330	Women Take the Court	.05	.01
331	The Peach Basket	.05	.01
332	Dr.James Naismith	.20	.07
333	M.Johnson/M.Jordan IA	2.00	.75
334	Michael Jordan IA	2.50	1.00
335	Vlade Divac	.05	.01
336	John Paxson	.05	.01
337	Bulls Team/M.Jordan	1.25	.50
338	Language Arts	.05	.01
339	Mathematics	.05	.01
340	Vocational Education	.05	.01
341	Social Studies	.05	.01
342	Physical Education	.05	.01
343	Art	.05	.01
344	Science	.05	.01
345	Checklist 1 (1-60)	.05	.01
346	Checklist 2 (61-120)	.05	.01
347	Checklist 3 (121-180)	.05	.01
348	Checklist 4 (181-244)	.05	.01
349	Checklist 5 (245-305)	.05	.01
350	Checklist 6 (306-350)	.05	.01
351	Atlanta Hawks	.05	.01
352	Boston Celtics	.05	.01
353	Charlotte Hornets	.05	.01
354	Chicago Bulls	.05	.01
355	Cleveland Cavaliers	.05	.01
356	Dallas Mavericks	.05	.01
357	Denver Nuggets	.05	.01
358	Detroit Pistons	.05	.01
359	Golden State Warriors	.05	.01
360	Houston Rockets	.05	.01
361	Indiana Pacers	.05	.01
362	Los Angeles Clippers	.05	.01
363	Los Angeles Lakers	.05	.01
364	Miami Heat	.05	.01
365	Milwaukee Bucks	.05	.01
366	Minnesota Timberwolves	.05	.01
367	New Jersey Nets	.05	.01
368	New York Knicks	.05	.01
369	Orlando Magic	.05	.01
370	Philadelphia 76ers	.05	.01
371	Phoenix Suns	.05	.01
372	Portland Trail Blazers	.05	.01
373	Sacramento Kings	.05	.01
374	San Antonio Spurs	.05	.01
375	Seattle Supersonics	.05	.01
376	Utah Jazz	.05	.01
377	Washington Bullets	.05	.01
378	Bob Weiss CO	.05	.01
379	Chris Ford CO	.05	.01
380	Allan Bristow CO	.05	.01
381	Phil Jackson CO	.20	.07
382	Lenny Wilkens CO	.20	.07
383	Richie Adubato CO	.05	.01
384	Paul Westhead CO	.05	.01
385	Chuck Daly CO	.20	.07
386	Don Nelson CO	.20	.07
387	Don Chaney CO	.05	.01
388	Bob Hill CO	.05	.01
389	Mike Schuler CO	.05	.01
390	Mike Dunleavy CO	.05	.01
391	Kevin Loughery CO	.05	.01
392	Del Harris CO	.05	.01
393	Jimmy Rodgers CO	.05	.01
394	Bill Fitch CO	.05	.01
395	Pat Riley CO	.20	.07
396	Matt Guokas CO	.05	.01
397	Jim Lynam CO	.05	.01
398	Cotton Fitzsimmons CO	.05	.01
399	Rick Adelman CO	.05	.01
400	Dick Motta CO	.05	.01
401	Larry Brown CO	.05	.01
402	K.C. Jones CO	.20	.07
403	Jerry Sloan CO	.20	.07
404	Wes Unseld CO	.20	.07
405	Mo Cheeks GF	.05	.01
406	Celtics/Dee Brown GF	.05	.01
407	Rex Chapman GF	.05	.01
408	Michael Jordan GF.	2.50	1.00
409	John Williams GF	.05	.01
410	James Donaldson GF	.05	.01
411	Dikembe Mutombo GF	.40	.15
412	Pistons/Isiah GF	.20	.07
413	Warriors/Hardaway GF	.40	.15
414	Hakeem Olajuwon GF	.40	.15
415	Pacers/Schrempf GF	.05	.01
416	Danny Manning GF	.05	.01
417	Magic Johnson GF	.60	.25
418	Bimbo Coles GF	.05	.01
419	Alvin Robertson GF	.05	.01
420	Sam Mitchell GF	.05	.01
421	Sam Bowie GF	.05	.01
422	Mark Jackson GF	.05	.01
423	Orlando Magic	.05	.01
424	Charles Barkley GF	.40	.15
425	Suns/Majerle GF	.05	.01
426	Robert Pack GF	.05	.01
427	Wayman Tisdale GF	.05	.01
428	David Robinson GF	.40	.15
429	Nate McMillan GF	.05	.01
430	Jazz/Karl Malone GF	.40	.15
431	Michael Adams SM	.05	.01
432	Duane Ferrell SM	.05	.01
433	Kevin McHale SM	.05	.01
434	Dell Curry SM	.05	.01
435	B.J.Armstrong SM	.05	.01
436	John Williams SM	.05	.01
437	Brad Davis SM	.05	.01
438	Marcus Liberty SM	.05	.01
439	Mark Aguirre SM	.05	.01
440	Rod Higgins SM	.05	.01
441	Eric(Sleepy) Floyd SM	.05	.01
442	Detlef Schrempf SM	.05	.01
443	Loy Vaught SM	.05	.01
444	Terry Teagle SM	.05	.01
445	Kevin Edwards SM	.05	.01
446	Dale Ellis SM	.05	.01
447	Tod Murphy SM	.05	.01
448	Chris Dudley SM	.05	.01
449	Mark Jackson SM	.05	.01
450	Jerry Reynolds SM	.05	.01
451	Ron Anderson SM	.05	.01
452	Dan Majerle SM	.05	.01
453	Danny Ainge SM	.05	.01
454	Jim Les SM	.05	.01
455	Paul Pressey SM	.05	.01
456	Ricky Pierce SM	.05	.01
457	Mike Brown SM	.05	.01

458	Ledell Eackles SM	.05	.01
459	D.Wilkins/Willis TW	.20	.07
460	L.Bird/R.Parish TW	.40	.15
461	R.Chapman/Gill TW	.05	.01
462	M.Jordan/S.Pippen TW	1.50	.60
463	Cleveland Cavaliers	.05	.01
464	Dallas Mavericks	.05	.01
465	Denver Nuggets	.05	.01
466	I.Thomas/Laimbeer TW	.20	.07
467	T.Hardaway/C.Mullin TW	.20	.07
468	Houston Rockets	.05	.01
469	P.Miller/D.Schrempf TW	.20	.07
470	Los Angeles Clippers	.05	.01
471	M.Johnson/J.Worthy TW	.40	.15
472	G.Rice/Seikaly TW	.40	.15
473	Milwaukee Bucks	.05	.01
474	Minnesota Timberwolves	.05	.01
475	D.Coleman/Bowie TW	.05	.01
476	P.Ewing/Oakley TW	.20	.07
477	Orlando Magic	.05	.01
478	C.Barkley/Hawkins TW	.40	.15
479	K.Johnson/Chambers TW	.20	.07
480	C.Drexler/Porter TW	.40	.15
481	L.Simmons/Tisdale TW	.05	.01
482	T.Cummings/Elliott TW	.05	.01
483	Seattle Supersonics	.05	.01
484	K.Malone/J.Stockton TW	.40	.15
485	Washington Bullets	.05	.01
486	Rumeal Robinson RS	.05	.01
487	Dee Brown RIS	.05	.01
488	Kendall Gill RIS	.05	.01
489	B.J.Armstrong RIS	.05	.01
490	Danny Ferry RS	.05	.01
491	Randy White RS	.05	.01
492	Chris Jackson RS	.05	.01
493	Lance Blanks RS	.05	.01
494	Tim Hardaway RS	.40	.15
495	Vernon Maxwell RS	.05	.01
496	Micheal Williams RS	.05	.01
497	Charles Smith RS	.05	.01
498	Vlade Divac RS	.05	.01
499	Willie Burton RS	.05	.01
500	Jeff Grayer RS	.05	.01
501	Pooh Richardson RS	.05	.01
502	Derrick Coleman RIS	.05	.01
503	John Starks RIS	.20	.07
504	Dennis Scott RIS	.05	.01
505	Hersey Hawkins RS	.05	.01
506	Negele Knight RS	.05	.01
507	Cliff Robinson RIS	.05	.01
508	Lionel Simmons RIS	.05	.01
509	David Robinson RIS	.40	.15
510	Gary Payton RS	.50	.20
511	Blue Edwards RS	.05	.01
512	Harvey Grant RS	.05	.01
513	Larry Johnson RC	1.50	.60
514	Kenny Anderson RC	.75	.30
515	Billy Owens RC	.05	.01
516	Dikembe Mutombo RC	1.50	.60
517	Steve Smith RC	1.50	.60
518	Doug Smith RC	.05	.01
519	Luc Longley RC	.40	.15
520	Mark Macon RC	.05	.01
521	Stacey Augmon RC	.40	.15
522	Brian Williams RC	.40	.15
523	Terrell Brandon RC	1.25	.50
524	The Ball	.05	.01
525	The Basket	.05	.01
526	The 24-second Shot	.05	.01
527	The Game Program	.05	.01
528	The Championship Gift	.05	.01
529	Championship Trophy	.05	.01
530	Charles Barkley USA	1.25	.50
531	Larry Bird USA	3.00	1.25
532	Patrick Ewing USA	.75	.30
533	Magic Johnson USA	2.50	1.00
534	Michael Jordan USA	8.00	3.00
535	Karl Malone USA	1.25	.50
536	Chris Mullin USA	.40	.15
537	Scottie Pippen USA	2.50	1.00
538	David Robinson USA	1.50	.60
539	John Stockton USA	.75	.30
540	Chuck Daly CO USA	.20	.07
541	P.J.Carlesimo RC USA CO	.05	.01
542	M.Krzyzewski CO USA RC	.60	.25
543	Lenny Wilkens CO USA	.20	.07
544	Team USA 1	2.50	1.00
545	Team USA 2	2.50	1.00
546	Team USA 3	2.50	1.00
547	Willie Anderson USA	.05	.01
548	Stacey Augmon USA	.40	.15
549	Bimbo Coles USA	.05	.01
550	Jeff Grayer USA	.05	.01
551	Hersey Hawkins USA	.05	.01
552	Dan Majerle USA	.05	.01
553	Danny Manning USA	.05	.01
554	J.R. Reid USA	.05	.01
555	Mitch Richmond USA	.75	.30
556	Charles Smith USA	.05	.01
557	Vern Fleming USA	.05	.01
558	Joe Kleine USA	.05	.01
559	Jon Koncak USA	.05	.01
560	Sam Perkins USA	.05	.01
561	Alvin Robertson USA	.05	.01
562	Wayman Tisdale USA	.05	.01
563	Jeff Turner USA	.05	.01
564	Tony Campbell USA	.05	.01
565	Joe Dumars USA	.20	.07
566	Horace Grant USA	.05	.01
567	Reggie Lewis MAG	.05	.01
568	Hakeem Olajuwon MAG	.40	.15
569	Sam Perkins	.05	.01
570	Chuck Person	.05	.01
571	Buck Williams	.05	.01
572	Michael Jordan SAL	2.50	1.00
573	Bernard King	.05	.01
574	Moses Malone	.20	.07
575	Robert Parish	.05	.01
576	Pat Riley CO	.20	.07
577	Dee Brown SM	.05	.01
578	Rex Chapman	.05	.01
579	Clyde Drexler SKM	.20	.07
580	Blue Edwards	.05	.01
581	Ron Harper	.05	.01
582	Kevin Johnson SKM	.20	.07
583	Michael Jordan SKM	2.50	1.00
584	Shawn Kemp SKM	.75	.30
585	Xavier McDaniel	.05	.01
586	Scottie Pippen SKM	.60	.25
587	Kenny Smith	.05	.01
588	Dominique Wilkins SKM	.20	.07
589	Michael Adams	.05	.01
590	Danny Ainge	.05	.01
591	Larry Bird SS	.75	.30
592	Dale Ellis	.05	.01
593	Hersey Hawkins	.05	.01
594	Jeff Hornacek	.05	.01
595	Jeff Malone	.05	.01
596	Reggie Miller SS	.20	.07
597	Chris Mullin SS	.20	.07
598	John Paxson	.05	.01
599	Drazen Petrovic SS	.05	.01
600	Ricky Pierce	.05	.01
601	Mark Price SS	.05	.01
602	Dennis Scott SS	.05	.01
603	Manute Bol	.05	.01
604	Jerome Kersey	.05	.01
605	Charles Oakley	.05	.01
606	Scottie Pippen SMALL	.60	.25
607	Terry Porter	.05	.01
608	Dennis Rodman SMALL	.40	.15
609	Sedale Threatt	.05	.01
610	Business	.05	.01
611	Engineering	.05	.01
612	Law	.05	.01
613	Liberal Arts	.05	.01
614	Medicine	.05	.01
615	Maurice Cheeks	.05	.01
616	Travis Mays	.05	.01
617	Blair Rasmussen	.05	.01
618	Alexander Volkov	.05	.01
619	Rickey Green	.05	.01
620	Bobby Hansen	.05	.01
621	John Battle	.05	.01
622	Terry Davis	.05	.01
623	Walter Davis	.05	.01
624	Winston Garland	.05	.01
625	Scott Hastings	.05	.01
626	Brad Sellers	.05	.01
627	Darrell Walker	.05	.01
628	Orlando Woolridge	.05	.01
629	Tony Brown	.05	.01
630	James Edwards	.05	.01
631	Doc Rivers	.20	.07
632	Jack Haley	.05	.01
633	Sedale Threatt	.05	.01
634	Moses Malone	.40	.15
635	Thurl Bailey	.05	.01
636	Rafael Addison RC	.05	.01
637	Tim McCormick	.05	.01
638	Xavier McDaniel	.05	.01
639	Charles Shackleford	.05	.01
640	Mitchell Wiggins	.05	.01
641	Jerrod Mustaf	.05	.01
642	Dennis Hopson	.05	.01
643	Les Jepsen	.05	.01
644	Mitch Richmond	.40	.15
645	Dwayne Schintzius	.05	.01
646	Spud Webb	.20	.07
647	Jud Buechler	.05	.01
648	Antoine Carr	.05	.01
649	Tyrone Corbin	.05	.01
650	Michael Adams	.05	.01
651	Ralph Sampson	.05	.01
652	Andre Turner	.05	.01
653	David Wingate	.05	.01
654	Checklist %%S-	.05	.01
655	Checklist %%S-	.05	.01
656	Checklist %%Y-	.05	.01
657	Checklist %%B-	.05	.01
658	Checklist %%O-	.05	.01
659	Checklist %%X-	.05	.01
NNO	Clyde Drexler USA	75.00	40.00
NNO	Team USA Card	12.00	6.00

1992-93 SkyBox

Danny

COMPLETE SET (413)	50.00	25.00
COMPLETE SERIES 1 (327)	30.00	15.00
COMPLETE SERIES 2 (86)	20.00	10.00
COMMON SP RC	.50	.20
1 Stacey Augmon	.25	.08
2 Maurice Cheeks	.10	.02
3 Duane Ferrell	.10	.02
4 Paul Graham	.10	.02
5 Jon Koncak	.10	.02
6 Blair Rasmussen	.10	.02
7 Rumeal Robinson	.10	.02
8 Dominique Wilkins	.50	.20
9 Kevin Willis	.10	.02
10 Larry Bird	2.00	.75
11 Dee Brown	.10	.02
12 Sherman Douglas	.10	.02
13 Rick Fox	.25	.08
14 Kevin Gamble	.10	.02
15 Reggie Lewis	.25	.08
16 Kevin McHale	.50	.20
17 Robert Parish	.25	.08
18 Ed Pinckney	.10	.02
19 Muggsy Bogues	.25	.08
20 Dell Curry	.10	.02
21 Kenny Gattison	.10	.02
22 Kendall Gill	.25	.08
23 Mike Gminski	.10	.02
24 Tom Hammonds	.10	.02
25 Larry Johnson	.60	.25
26 Johnny Newman	.10	.02
27 J.R. Reid	.10	.02
28 B.J. Armstrong	.10	.02
29 Bill Cartwright	.10	.02
30 Horace Grant	.25	.08

31	Michael Jordan	6.00	2.50
32	Stacey King	.10	.02
33	John Paxson	.10	.02
34	Will Perdue	.10	.02
35	Scottie Pippen	1.50	.60
36	Scott Williams	.10	.02
37	John Battle	.10	.02
38	Terrell Brandon	.50	.20
39	Brad Daugherty	.10	.02
40	Craig Ehlo	.10	.02
41	Danny Ferry	.10	.02
42	Henry James	.10	.02
43	Larry Nance	.10	.02
44	Mark Price	.10	.02
45	Mike Sanders	.10	.02
46	Hot Rod Williams	.10	.02
47	Rolando Blackman	.10	.02
48	Terry Davis	.10	.02
49	Derek Harper	.25	.08
50	Donald Hodge	.10	.02
51	Mike Iuzzolino	.10	.02
52	Fat Lever	.10	.02
53	Rodney McCray	.10	.02
54	Doug Smith	.10	.02
55	Randy White	.10	.02
56	Herb Williams	.10	.02
57	Greg Anderson	.10	.02
58	Walter Davis	.10	.02
59	Winston Garland	.10	.02
60	Chris Jackson	.10	.02
61	Marcus Liberty	.10	.02
62	Todd Lichti	.10	.02
63	Mark Macon	.10	.02
64	Dikembe Mutombo	.60	.25
65	Reggie Williams	.10	.02
66	Mark Aguirre	.10	.02
67	William Bedford	.10	.02
68	Lance Blanks	.10	.02
69	Joe Dumars	.50	.20
70	Bill Laimbeer	.25	.08
71	Dennis Rodman	1.00	.40
72	John Salley	.10	.02
73	Isiah Thomas	.50	.20
74	Darrell Walker	.10	.02
75	Orlando Woolridge	.10	.02
76	Victor Alexander	.10	.02
77	Mario Elie	.25	.08
78	Chris Gatling	.10	.02
79	Tim Hardaway	.60	.25
80	Tyrone Hill	.10	.02
81	Alton Lister	.10	.02
82	Sarunas Marciulionis	.10	.02
83	Chris Mullin	.50	.20
84	Billy Owens	.25	.08
85	Matt Bullard	.10	.02
86	Sleepy Floyd	.10	.02
87	Avery Johnson	.10	.02
88	Buck Johnson	.10	.02
89	Vernon Maxwell	.10	.02
90	Hakeem Olajuwon	.75	.30
91	Kenny Smith	.10	.02
92	Larry Smith	.10	.02
93	Otis Thorpe	.25	.08
94	Dale Davis	.10	.02
95	Vern Fleming	.10	.02
96	George McCloud	.10	.02
97	Reggie Miller	.50	.20
98	Chuck Person	.10	.02
99	Detlef Schrempf	.25	.08
100	Rik Smits	.25	.08
101	LaSalle Thompson	.10	.02
102	Micheal Williams	.10	.02
103	James Edwards	.10	.02
104	Gary Grant	.10	.02
105	Ron Harper	.25	.08
106	Bo Kimble	.10	.02
107	Danny Manning	.25	.08
108	Ken Norman	.10	.02
109	Olden Polynice	.10	.02
110	Doc Rivers	.25	.08
111	Charles Smith	.10	.02
112	Loy Vaught	.25	.08
113	Elden Campbell	.25	.08
114	Vlade Divac	.25	.08
115	A.C. Green	.25	.08
116	Jack Haley	.10	.02
117	Sam Perkins	.25	.08
118	Byron Scott	.25	.08
119	Tony Smith	.10	.02
120	Sedale Threatt	.10	.02
121	James Worthy	.50	.20
122	Keith Askins	.10	.02
123	Willie Burton	.10	.02
124	Bimbo Coles	.10	.02
125	Kevin Edwards	.10	.02
126	Alec Kessler	.10	.02
127	Grant Long	.10	.02
128	Glen Rice	.50	.20
129	Rony Seikaly	.10	.02
130	Brian Shaw	.10	.02
131	Steve Smith	.60	.25
132	Frank Brickowski	.10	.02
133	Dale Ellis	.10	.02
134	Jeff Grayer	.10	.02
135	Jay Humphries	.10	.02
136	Larry Krystkowiak	.10	.02
137	Moses Malone	.50	.20
138	Fred Roberts	.10	.02
139	Alvin Robertson	.10	.02
140	Danny Schayes	.10	.02
141	Thurl Bailey	.10	.02
142	Scott Brooks	.10	.02
143	Tony Campbell	.10	.02
144	Gerald Glass	.10	.02
145	Luc Longley	.25	.08
146	Sam Mitchell	.10	.02
147	Pooh Richardson	.10	.02
148	Felton Spencer	.10	.02
149	Doug West	.10	.02
150	Rafael Addison	.10	.02
151	Kenny Anderson	.50	.20
152	Mookie Blaylock	.25	.08
153	Sam Bowie	.10	.02
154	Derrick Coleman	.25	.08
155	Chris Dudley	.10	.02
156	Tate George	.10	.02
157	Terry Mills	.10	.02
158	Chris Morris	.10	.02
159	Drazen Petrovic	.10	.02
160	Greg Anthony	.10	.02
161	Patrick Ewing	.50	.20
162	Mark Jackson	.25	.08
163	Anthony Mason	.50	.20
164	Tim McCormick	.10	.02
165	Xavier McDaniel	.10	.02
166	Charles Oakley	.25	.08
167	John Starks	.25	.08
168	Gerald Wilkins	.10	.02
169	Nick Anderson	.25	.08
170	Terry Catledge	.10	.02
171	Jerry Reynolds	.10	.02
172	Stanley Roberts	.10	.02
173	Dennis Scott	.25	.08
174	Scott Skiles	.10	.02
175	Jeff Turner	.10	.02
176	Sam Vincent	.10	.02
177	Brian Williams	.10	.02
178	Ron Anderson	.10	.02
179	Charles Barkley	.75	.30
180	Manute Bol	.10	.02
181	Johnny Dawkins	.10	.02
182	Armon Gilliam	.10	.02
183	Greg Grant	.10	.02
184	Hersey Hawkins	.25	.08
185	Brian Oliver	.10	.02
186	Charles Shackleford	.10	.02
187	Jayson Williams	.10	.02
188	Cedric Ceballos	.25	.08
189	Tom Chambers	.10	.02
190	Jeff Hornacek	.25	.08
191	Kevin Johnson	.50	.20
192	Negele Knight	.10	.02
193	Andrew Lang	.10	.02
194	Dan Majerle	.25	.08
195	Jerrod Mustaf	.10	.02
196	Tim Perry	.10	.02
197	Mark West	.10	.02
198	Alaa Abdelnaby	.10	.02
199	Danny Ainge	.25	.08
200	Mark Bryant	.10	.02
201	Clyde Drexler	.50	.20
202	Kevin Duckworth	.10	.02
203	Jerome Kersey	.10	.02
204	Robert Pack	.10	.02
205	Terry Porter	.10	.02
206	Cliff Robinson	.25	.08
207	Buck Williams	.25	.08
208	Anthony Bonner	.10	.02
209	Randy Brown	.10	.02
210	Duane Causwell	.10	.02
211	Pete Chilcutt	.10	.02
212	Dennis Hopson	.10	.02
213	Jim Les	.10	.02
214	Mitch Richmond	.50	.20
215	Lionel Simmons	.10	.02
216	Wayman Tisdale	.10	.02
217	Spud Webb	.25	.08
218	Willie Anderson	.10	.02
219	Antoine Carr	.10	.02
220	Terry Cummings	.25	.08
221	Sean Elliott	.25	.08
222	Sidney Green	.10	.02
223	Vinnie Johnson	.10	.02
224	David Robinson	.75	.30
225	Rod Strickland	.50	.20
226	Greg Sutton	.10	.02
227	Dana Barros	.10	.02
228	Benoit Benjamin	.10	.02
229	Michael Cage	.10	.02
230	Eddie Johnson	.10	.02
231	Shawn Kemp	1.00	.40
232	Derrick McKey	.10	.02
233	Nate McMillan	.10	.02
234	Gary Payton	1.00	.40
235	Ricky Pierce	.10	.02
236	David Benoit	.10	.02
237	Mike Brown	.10	.02
238	Tyrone Corbin	.10	.02
239	Mark Eaton	.10	.02
240	Blue Edwards	.10	.02
241	Jeff Malone	.10	.02
242	Karl Malone	.75	.30
243	Eric Murdock	.10	.02
244	John Stockton	.50	.20
245	Michael Adams	.10	.02
246	Rex Chapman	.10	.02
247	Ledell Eackles	.10	.02
248	Pervis Ellison	.10	.02
249	A.J. English	.10	.02
250	Harvey Grant	.10	.02
251	Charles Jones	.10	.02
252	Bernard King	.10	.02
253	LaBradford Smith	.10	.02
254	Larry Stewart	.10	.02
255	Bob Weiss CO	.10	.02
256	Chris Ford CO	.10	.02
257	Allan Bristow CO	.10	.02
258	Phil Jackson CO	.25	.08
259	Lenny Wilkens CO	.25	.08
260	Richie Adubato CO	.10	.02
261	Dan Issel CO	.10	.02
262	Ron Rothstein CO	.10	.02
263	Don Nelson CO	.25	.08
264	Rudy Tomjanovich CO	.25	.08
265	Bob Hill CO	.10	.02
266	Larry Brown CO	.25	.08
267	Randy Pfund RC CO	.10	.02
268	Kevin Loughery CO	.10	.02
269	Mike Dunleavy CO	.10	.02
270	Jimmy Rodgers CO	.10	.02
271	Chuck Daly CO	.25	.08
272	Pat Riley CO	.25	.08
273	Matt Guokas CO	.10	.02
274	Doug Moe CO	.10	.02
275	Paul Westphal CO	.10	.02
276	Rick Adelman CO	.10	.02
277	Garry St.Jean RC CO	.10	.02
278	Jerry Tarkanian RC	.10	.02
279	George Karl CO	.25	.08
280	Jerry Sloan CO	.25	.08
281	Wes Unseld CO	.25	.08
282	Dominique Wilkins TT	.25	.08
283	Reggie Lewis TT	.10	.02
284	Kendall Gill TT	.10	.02
285	Horace Grant TT	.10	.02
286	Brad Daugherty TT	.10	.02
287	Derek Harper TT	.10	.02
288	Chris Jackson TT	.10	.02

289	Isiah Thomas TT	.25	.08
290	Chris Mullin TT	.25	.08
291	Kenny Smith TT	.10	.02
292	Reggie Miller TT	.25	.08
293	Ron Harper TT	.10	.02
294	Vlade Divac TT	.10	.02
295	Glen Rice TT	.25	.08
296	Moses Malone TT	.25	.08
297	Doug West TT	.10	.02
298	Derrick Coleman TT	.10	.02
299	Patrick Ewing TT	.25	.08
300	Scott Skiles TT	.10	.02
301	Hersey Hawkins TT	.10	.02
302	Kevin Johnson TT	.10	.02
303	Cliff Robinson TT	.10	.02
304	Spud Webb TT	.10	.02
305	David Robinson TT	.50	.20
305A	Dav.Robinson ERR 299	.50	.20
306	Shawn Kemp TT	.50	.20
307	John Stockton TT	.25	.08
308	Pervis Ellison TT	.10	.02
309	Craig Hodges AS	.10	.02
310	Magic Johnson AS MVP	.75	.30
311	Cedric Ceballos AS	.10	.02
312	D.Rodman/Group AS	.50	.20
313	K.Malone/Group AS	.50	.20
314	Michael Jordan MVP	3.00	1.25
315	Clyde Drexler FINALS	.25	.08
316	Western Conference	.10	.02
317	Scottie Pippen FINALS	.75	.30
318	NBA Champs	.10	.02
319	L.Johnson/D.Mut. ART	.50	.20
320	NBA Stay in School	.10	.02
321	Boys and Girls	.10	.02
322	Checklist 1	.10	.02
323	Checklist 2	.10	.02
324	Checklist 3	.10	.02
325	Checklist 4	.10	.02
326	Checklist 5	.10	.02
327	Checklist 6	.10	.02
328	Adam Keefe SP RC	.10	.02
329	Sean Rooks SP RC	.10	.02
330	Xavier McDaniel	.10	.02
331	Kiki Vandeweghe	.10	.02
332	Alonzo Mourning SP RC	3.00	1.25
333	Rodney McCray	.10	.02
334	Gerald Wilkins	.10	.02
335	Tony Bennett SP RC	.10	.02
336	LaPhonso Ellis SP RC	.50	.20
337	Bryant Stith SP RC	.50	.20
338	Isaiah Morris SP RC	.10	.02
339	Olden Polynice	.10	.02
340	Jeff Grayer	.10	.02
341	Byron Houston SP RC	.10	.02
342	Latrell Sprewell SP RC	4.00	1.50
343	Scott Brooks	.10	.02
344	Frank Johnson	.10	.02
345	Robert Horry SP RC	.50	.20
346	David Wood	.10	.02
347	Sam Mitchell	.10	.02
348	Pooh Richardson	.10	.02
349	Malik Sealy SP RC	.50	.20
350	Morlon Wiley	.10	.02
351	Mark Jackson	.25	.08
352	Stanley Roberts	.10	.02
353	Elmore Spencer SP RC	.10	.02
354	John Williams	.10	.02
355	Randy Woods SP RC	.10	.02
356	James Edwards	.10	.02
357	Jeff Sanders	.10	.02
358	Magic Johnson	1.50	.60
359	Anthony Peeler SP RC	.50	.20
360	Harold Miner SP RC	.50	.20
361	John Salley	.10	.02
362	Alaa Abdelnaby	.10	.02
363	Todd Day SP RC	.50	.20
364	Blue Edwards	.10	.02
365	Lee Mayberry SP RC	.10	.02
366	Eric Murdock	.10	.02
367	Mookie Blaylock	.25	.08
368	Anthony Avent RC	.10	.02
369	Christian Laettner SP RC	1.00	.40
370	Chuck Person	.10	.02
371	Chris Smith SP RC	.10	.02
372	Micheal Williams	.10	.02
373	Rolando Blackman	.10	.02
374	Tony Campbell UER	.10	.02
375	Hubert Davis SP RC	.50	.20
376	Travis Mays	.10	.02
377	Doc Rivers	.25	.08
378	Charles Smith	.10	.02
379	Rumeal Robinson	.10	.02
380	Vinny Del Negro	.10	.02
381	Steve Kerr	.25	.08
382	Shaquille O'Neal SP RC	12.00	5.00
383	Donald Royal	.10	.02
384	Jeff Hornacek	.25	.08
385	Andrew Lang	.10	.02
386	Tim Perry UER	.10	.02
387	C.Weatherspoon SP RC	.50	.20
388	Danny Ainge	.25	.08
389	Charles Barkley	.75	.30
390	Tim Kempton	.10	.02
391	Oliver Miller SP RC	.50	.20
392	Dave Johnson SP RC	.50	.20
393	Tracy Murray SP RC	.50	.20
394	Rod Strickland	.50	.20
395	Marty Conlon	.10	.02
396	Walt Williams SP RC	.50	.20
397	Lloyd Daniels RC	.10	.02
398	Dale Ellis	.10	.02
399	Dave Hoppen	.10	.02
400	Larry Smith	.10	.02
401	Doug Overton	.10	.02
402	Isaac Austin RC	.25	.08
403	Jay Humphries	.10	.02
404	Larry Krystkowiak	.10	.02
405	Tom Gugliotta SP RC	1.50	.60
406	Buck Johnson	.10	.02
407	Don MacLean SP RC	.50	.20
408	Marlon Maxey SP RC	.50	.20
409	Corey Williams SP RC	.50	.20
410	Special Olympics	.25	.08
411	Checklist 1	.10	.02
412	Checklist 2	.10	.02
413	Checklist 3	.10	.02
NNO	David Robinson AU	100.00	50.00
NNO	Admiral Comes Prepared	4.00	1.50
NNO	Magic Johnson AU	200.00	100.00
NNO	Head of the Class	30.00	15.00
NNO	Magic Never Ends	6.00	3.00

1993-94 SkyBox Premium

	COMPLETE SET (341)	30.00	15.00
	COMPLETE SERIES 1 (191)	15.00	7.50
	COMPLETE SERIES 2 (150)	15.00	7.50
1	Checklist	.05	.01
2	Checklist	.05	.01
3	Checklist	.05	.01
4	Larry Johnson PO	.15	.05
5	Alonzo Mourning PO	.30	.10
6	Hakeem Olajuwon PO	.30	.10
7	Brad Daugherty PO	.05	.01
8	Oliver Miller PO	.05	.01
9	David Robinson PO	.30	.10
10	Patrick Ewing PO	.15	.05
11	Ricky Pierce PO	.05	.01
12	Sam Perkins PO	.05	.01
13	John Starks PO	.05	.01
14	Michael Jordan PO	2.00	.75
15	Dan Majerle PO	.05	.01
16	Scottie Pippen PO	.50	.20
17	Shawn Kemp PO	.30	.10
18	Charles Barkley PO	.30	.10
19	Horace Grant PO	.05	.01
20	Kevin Johnson PO	.05	.01
21	John Paxson PO	.05	.01
22	Inside Stuff	.30	.10
23	NBA On NBC	.05	.01
24	Stacey Augmon	.05	.01
25	Mookie Blaylock	.15	.05
26	Craig Ehlo	.05	.01
27	Adam Keefe	.05	.01
28	Dominique Wilkins	.30	.10
29	Kevin Willis	.05	.01
30	Dee Brown	.05	.01
31	Sherman Douglas	.05	.01
32	Rick Fox	.05	.01
33	Kevin Gamble	.05	.01
34	Xavier McDaniel	.05	.01
35	Robert Parish	.15	.05
36	Muggsy Bogues	.15	.05
37	Dell Curry	.05	.01
38	Kendall Gill	.15	.05
39	Larry Johnson	.30	.10
40	Alonzo Mourning	.50	.20
41	Johnny Newman	.05	.01
42	B.J. Armstrong	.05	.01
43	Bill Cartwright	.05	.01
44	Horace Grant	.15	.05
45	Michael Jordan	4.00	1.50
46	John Paxson	.05	.01
47	Scottie Pippen	1.00	.40
48	Scott Williams	.05	.01
49	Terrell Brandon	.15	.05
50	Brad Daugherty	.05	.01
51	Larry Nance	.05	.01
52	Mark Price	.15	.05
53	Gerald Wilkins	.05	.01
54	John Williams	.05	.01
55	Terry Davis	.05	.01
56	Derek Harper	.15	.05
57	Jim Jackson	.50	.20
58	Sean Rooks	.05	.01
59	Doug Smith	.05	.01
60	Mahmoud Abdul-Rauf	.05	.01
61	LaPhonso Ellis	.05	.01
62	Mark Macon	.05	.01
63	Dikembe Mutombo	.30	.10
64	Bryant Stith	.05	.01
65	Reggie Williams	.05	.01
66	Joe Dumars	.30	.10
67	Bill Laimbeer	.05	.01
68	Terry Mills	.05	.01
69	Alvin Robertson	.05	.01
70	Dennis Rodman	.60	.25
71	Isiah Thomas	.30	.10
72	Victor Alexander	.05	.01
73	Tim Hardaway	.30	.10
74	Tyrone Hill	.05	.01
75	Sarunas Marciulionis	.05	.01
76	Chris Mullin	.30	.10
77	Billy Owens	.05	.01
78	Latrell Sprewell	.75	.30
79	Robert Horry	.05	.01
80	Vernon Maxwell	.05	.01
81	Hakeem Olajuwon	.50	.20
82	Kenny Smith	.05	.01
83	Otis Thorpe	.15	.05
84	Dale Davis	.05	.01
85	Reggie Miller	.30	.10
86	Pooh Richardson	.05	.01
87	Detlef Schrempf	.15	.05
88	Malik Sealy	.05	.01
89	Rik Smits	.15	.05
90	Ron Harper	.15	.05
91	Mark Jackson	.15	.05
92	Danny Manning	.15	.05
93	Stanley Roberts	.05	.01
94	Loy Vaught	.15	.05
95	Randy Woods	.05	.01
96	Sam Bowie	.05	.01
97	Doug Christie	.15	.05
98	Vlade Divac	.15	.05
99	Anthony Peeler	.05	.01
100	Sedale Threatt	.05	.01
101	James Worthy	.30	.10
102	Grant Long	.05	.01
103	Harold Miner	.05	.01
104	Glen Rice	.15	.05

105	John Salley	.05	.01
106	Rony Seikaly	.05	.01
107	Steve Smith	.30	.10
108	Anthony Avent	.05	.01
109	Jon Barry	.05	.01
110	Frank Brickowski	.05	.01
111	Blue Edwards	.05	.01
112	Todd Day	.05	.01
113	Lee Mayberry	.05	.01
114	Eric Murdock	.05	.01
115	Thurl Bailey	.05	.01
116	Christian Laettner	.15	.05
117	Chuck Person	.05	.01
118	Doug West	.05	.01
119	Micheal Williams	.05	.01
120	Kenny Anderson	.15	.05
121	Benoit Benjamin	.05	.01
122	Derrick Coleman	.15	.05
123	Chris Morris	.05	.01
124	Rumeal Robinson	.05	.01
125	Rolando Blackman	.05	.01
126	Patrick Ewing	.30	.10
127	Anthony Mason	.15	.05
128	Charles Oakley	.15	.05
129	Doc Rivers	.05	.01
130	Charles Smith	.05	.01
131	John Starks	.15	.05
132	Nick Anderson	.15	.05
133	Shaquille O'Neal	1.50	.60
134	Donald Royal	.05	.01
135	Dennis Scott	.05	.01
136	Scott Skiles	.05	.01
137	Brian Williams	.05	.01
138	Johnny Dawkins	.05	.01
139	Hersey Hawkins	.15	.05
140	Jeff Hornacek	.05	.01
141	Andrew Lang	.05	.01
142	Tim Perry	.05	.01
143	Clarence Weatherspoon	.05	.01
144	Danny Ainge	.15	.05
145	Charles Barkley	.50	.20
146	Cedric Ceballos	.15	.05
147	Kevin Johnson	.15	.05
148	Oliver Miller	.05	.01
149	Dan Majerle	.15	.05
150	Clyde Drexler	.30	.10
151	Harvey Grant	.05	.01
152	Jerome Kersey	.05	.01
153	Terry Porter	.05	.01
154	Clifford Robinson	.15	.05
155	Rod Strickland	.15	.05
156	Buck Williams	.05	.01
157	Mitch Richmond	.30	.10
158	Lionel Simmons	.05	.01
159	Wayman Tisdale	.05	.01
160	Spud Webb	.15	.05
161	Walt Williams	.05	.01
162	Antoine Carr	.05	.01
163	Lloyd Daniels	.05	.01
164	Sean Elliott	.15	.05
165	Dale Ellis	.05	.01
166	Avery Johnson	.05	.01
167	J.R. Reid	.05	.01
168	David Robinson	.50	.20
169	Shawn Kemp	.50	.20
170	Derrick McKey	.05	.01
171	Nate McMillan	.05	.01
172	Gary Payton	.50	.20
173	Sam Perkins	.15	.05
174	Ricky Pierce	.05	.01
175	Tyrone Corbin	.05	.01
176	Jay Humphries	.05	.01
177	Jeff Malone	.05	.01
178	Karl Malone	.50	.20
179	John Stockton	.30	.10
180	Michael Adams	.05	.01
181	Kevin Duckworth	.05	.01
182	Pervis Ellison	.05	.01
183	Tom Gugliotta	.30	.10
184	Don MacLean	.05	.01
185	Brent Price	.05	.01
186	George Lynch RC	.05	.01
187	Rex Walters RC	.05	.01
188	Shawn Bradley RC	.05	.01
189	Ervin Johnson RC	.15	.05
190	Luther Wright RC	.05	.01
191	Calbert Cheaney RC	.15	.05
192	Craig Ehlo	.05	.01
193	Duane Ferrell	.05	.01
194	Paul Graham	.05	.01
195	Andrew Lang	.05	.01
196	Chris Corchiani	.05	.01
197	Acie Earl RC	.05	.01
198	Dino Radja RC	.05	.01
199	Ed Pinckney	.05	.01
200	Tony Bennett	.05	.01
201	Scott Burrell RC	.30	.10
202	Kenny Gattison	.05	.01
203	Hersey Hawkins	.15	.05
204	Eddie Johnson	.05	.01
205	Corie Blount RC	.05	.01
206	Steve Kerr	.15	.05
207	Toni Kukoc RC	1.25	.50
208	Pete Myers	.05	.01
209	Danny Ferry	.05	.01
210	Tyrone Hill	.05	.01
211	Gerald Madkins RC	.05	.01
212	Chris Mills RC	.30	.10
213	Lucious Harris RC	.05	.01
214	Popeye Jones RC	.05	.01
215	Jamal Mashburn RC	.75	.30
216	Darnell Mee RC	.05	.01
217	Rodney Rogers RC	.30	.10
218	Brian Williams	.05	.01
219	Greg Anderson	.05	.01
220	Sean Elliott	.15	.05
221	Allan Houston RC	1.25	.50
222	Lindsey Hunter RC	.30	.10
223	Chris Gatling	.05	.01
224	Josh Grant RC	.05	.01
225	Keith Jennings	.05	.01
226	Avery Johnson	.05	.01
227	Chris Webber RC	3.00	1.25
228	Sam Cassell RC	1.25	.50
229	Mario Elie	.05	.01
230	Richard Petruska RC	.05	.01
231	Eric Riley RC	.05	.01
232	Antonio Davis RC	.40	.15
233	Scott Haskin RC	.05	.01
234	Derrick McKey	.05	.01
235	Mark Aguirre	.05	.01
236	Terry Dehere RC	.05	.01
237	Gary Grant	.05	.01
238	Randy Woods	.05	.01
239	Sam Bowie	.05	.01
240	Elden Campbell	.05	.01
241	Nick Van Exel RC	1.00	.40
242	Manute Bol	.05	.01
243	Brian Shaw	.05	.01
244	Vin Baker RC	.75	.30
245	Brad Lohaus	.05	.01
246	Ken Norman	.05	.01
247	Derek Strong RC	.05	.01
248	Danny Schayes	.05	.01
249	Mike Brown	.05	.01
250	Luc Longley	.15	.05
251	Isaiah Rider RC	.60	.25
252	Kevin Edwards	.05	.01
253	Armon Gilliam	.05	.01
254	Greg Anthony	.05	.01
255	Anthony Bonner	.05	.01
256	Tony Campbell	.05	.01
257	Hubert Davis	.05	.01
258	Litterial Green	.05	.01
259	Anfernee Hardaway RC	2.50	1.00
260	Larry Krystkowiak	.05	.01
261	Todd Lichti	.05	.01
262	Dana Barros	.05	.01
263	Greg Graham RC	.05	.01
264	Warren Kidd RC	.05	.01
265	Moses Malone	.30	.10
266	A.C. Green	.15	.05
267	Joe Kleine	.05	.01
268	Malcolm Mackey RC	.05	.01
269	Mark Bryant	.05	.01
270	Chris Dudley	.05	.01
271	Harvey Grant	.05	.01
272	James Robinson RC	.05	.01
273	Duane Causwell	.05	.01
274	Bobby Hurley RC	.15	.05
275	Jim Les	.05	.01
276	Willie Anderson	.05	.01
277	Terry Cummings	.05	.01
278	Vinny Del Negro	.05	.01
279	Sleepy Floyd	.05	.01
280	Dennis Rodman	.60	.25
281	Vincent Askew	.05	.01
282	Kendall Gill	.15	.05
283	Steve Scheffler	.05	.01
284	Detlef Schrempf	.15	.05
285	David Benoit	.05	.01
286	Tom Chambers	.05	.01
287	Felton Spencer	.05	.01
288	Rex Chapman	.05	.01
289	Kevin Duckworth	.05	.01
290	Gheorghe Muresan RC	.30	.10
291	Kenny Walker	.05	.01
292	Andrew Lang CF	.05	.01
293	D.Radja/A.Earl CF	.05	.01
294	Eddie Johnson CF	.05	.01
295	T.Kukoc/C.Blount CF	.30	.10
296	Tyrone Hill CF	.05	.01
297	J.Mashburn/P.Jones CF	.30	.10
298	Darnell Mee CF	.05	.01
299	L.Hunter/A.Houston CF	.15	.05
300	C.Webber/A.Johnson CF	.60	.25
301	Sam Cassell CF	.30	.10
302	Derrick McKey CF	.05	.01
303	Terry Dehere CF	.05	.01
304	N.Van Exel/G.Lynch CF	.30	.10
305	Harold Miner CF	.05	.01
306	K.Norman/V.Baker CF	.15	.05
307	M.Brown/I.Rider CF	.15	.05
308	Kevin Edwards CF	.05	.01
309	Hubert Davis CF	.05	.01
310	A.Hardaway/L.Kryst. CF	1.00	.40
311	M.Malone/S.Bradley CF	.30	.10
312	Joe Kleine CF	.05	.01
313	Harvey Grant CF	.05	.01
314	B.Hurley/M.Richmond CF	.30	.10
315	S.Floyd/D.Rodman CF	.30	.10
316	Kendall Gill CF	.05	.01
317	Felton Spencer CF	.05	.01
318	C.Cheaney/Duckworth CF	.05	.01
319	Karl Malone PC	.30	.10
320	Alonzo Mourning PC	.30	.10
321	Scottie Pippen PC	.50	.20
322	Mark Price PC	.05	.01
323	LaPhonso Ellis PC	.15	.05
324	Joe Dumars PC	.15	.05
325	Chris Mullin PC	.15	.05
326	Ron Harper PC	.05	.01
327	Glen Rice PC	.05	.01
328	Christian Laettner PC	.05	.01
329	Kenny Anderson PC	.05	.01
330	John Starks PC	.05	.01
331	Shaquille O'Neal PC	.60	.25
332	Charles Barkley PC	.30	.10
333	Clifford Robinson PC	.05	.01
334	Clyde Drexler PC	.15	.05
335	Mitch Richmond PC	.15	.05
336	David Robinson PC	.30	.10
337	Shawn Kemp PC	.30	.10
338	John Stockton PC	.15	.05
339	Checklist 4	.05	.01
340	Checklist 5	.05	.01
341	Checklist 6	.05	.01
DP4	Jim Jackson 1992	1.50	.60
DP17	Doug Christie 1992	.40	.15
NNO	Expired HOC Exchange	1.50	.60
NNO	Head of Class Card	30.00	15.00

1994-95 SkyBox Premium

	COMPLETE SET (350)	30.00	15.00
	COMPLETE SERIES 1 (200)	15.00	7.50
	COMPLETE SERIES 2 (150)	15.00	7.50
	COMMON CARD (1-200)	.10	.02
	COMMON CARD (201-350)	.10	.01
1	Stacey Augmon	.10	.02
2	Mookie Blaylock	.10	.02
3	Doug Edwards	.10	.02
4	Craig Ehlo	.10	.02
5	Adam Keefe	.10	.02
6	Danny Manning	.20	.07
7	Kevin Willis	.10	.02
8	Dee Brown	.10	.02
9	Sherman Douglas	.10	.02

❏ 10 Acie Earl	.10	.02
❏ 11 Kevin Gamble	.10	.02
❏ 12 Xavier McDaniel	.10	.02
❏ 13 Dino Radja	.10	.02
❏ 14 Muggsy Bogues	.20	.07
❏ 15 Scott Burrell	.10	.02
❏ 16 Dell Curry	.10	.02
❏ 17 LeRon Ellis	.10	.02
❏ 18 Hersey Hawkins	.20	.07
❏ 19 Larry Johnson	.20	.07
❏ 20 Alonzo Mourning	.50	.20
❏ 21 B.J. Armstrong	.10	.02
❏ 22 Corie Blount	.10	.02
❏ 23 Horace Grant	.20	.07
❏ 24 Toni Kukoc	.60	.25
❏ 25 Luc Longley	.10	.02
❏ 26 Scottie Pippen	1.25	.50
❏ 27 Scott Williams	.10	.02
❏ 28 Terrell Brandon	.20	.07
❏ 29 Brad Daugherty	.10	.02
❏ 30 Tyrone Hill	.10	.02
❏ 31 Chris Mills	.20	.07
❏ 32 Bobby Phills	.10	.02
❏ 33 Mark Price	.20	.07
❏ 34 Gerald Wilkins	.10	.02
❏ 35 Lucious Harris	.10	.02
❏ 36 Jim Jackson	.20	.07
❏ 37 Popeye Jones	.10	.02
❏ 38 Jamal Mashburn	.40	.15
❏ 39 Sean Rooks	.10	.02
❏ 40 Mahmoud Abdul-Rauf	.10	.02
❏ 41 LaPhonso Ellis	.10	.02
❏ 42 Dikembe Mutombo	.20	.07
❏ 43 Robert Pack	.10	.02
❏ 44 Rodney Rogers	.10	.02
❏ 45 Bryant Stith	.10	.02
❏ 46 Reggie Williams	.10	.02
❏ 47 Joe Dumars	.40	.15
❏ 48 Sean Elliott	.20	.07
❏ 49 Allan Houston	.60	.25
❏ 50 Lindsey Hunter	.20	.07
❏ 51 Terry Mills	.10	.02
❏ 52 Victor Alexander	.10	.02
❏ 53 Tim Hardaway	.40	.15
❏ 54 Chris Mullin	.40	.15
❏ 55 Billy Owens	.10	.02
❏ 56 Latrell Sprewell	.40	.15
❏ 57 Chris Webber	1.00	.40
❏ 58 Sam Cassell	.40	.15
❏ 59 Carl Herrera	.10	.02
❏ 60 Robert Horry	.20	.07
❏ 61 Vernon Maxwell	.10	.02
❏ 62 Hakeem Olajuwon	.60	.25
❏ 63 Kenny Smith	.10	.02
❏ 64 Otis Thorpe	.10	.02
❏ 65 Antonio Davis	.10	.02
❏ 66 Dale Davis	.10	.02
❏ 67 Derrick McKey	.10	.02
❏ 68 Reggie Miller	.40	.15
❏ 69 Pooh Richardson	.10	.02
❏ 70 Rik Smits	.10	.02
❏ 71 Haywoode Workman	.10	.02
❏ 72 Terry Dehere	.10	.02
❏ 73 Harold Ellis	.10	.02
❏ 74 Ron Harper	.20	.07
❏ 75 Mark Jackson	.10	.02
❏ 76 Loy Vaught	.10	.02
❏ 77 Dominique Wilkins	.40	.15

❏ 78 Elden Campbell	.10	.02
❏ 79 Doug Christie	.20	.07
❏ 80 Vlade Divac	.10	.02
❏ 81 George Lynch	.10	.02
❏ 82 Anthony Peeler	.10	.02
❏ 83 Sedale Threatt	.10	.02
❏ 84 Nick Van Exel	.40	.15
❏ 85 Harold Miner	.10	.02
❏ 86 Glen Rice	.20	.07
❏ 87 John Salley	.10	.02
❏ 88 Rony Seikaly	.10	.02
❏ 89 Brian Shaw	.10	.02
❏ 90 Steve Smith	.10	.02
❏ 91 Vin Baker	.40	.15
❏ 92 Jon Barry	.10	.02
❏ 93 Todd Day	.10	.02
❏ 94 Blue Edwards	.10	.02
❏ 95 Lee Mayberry	.10	.02
❏ 96 Eric Murdock	.10	.02
❏ 97 Mike Brown	.10	.02
❏ 98 Stacey King	.10	.02
❏ 99 Christian Laettner	.20	.07
❏ 100 Isaiah Rider	.20	.07
❏ 101 Doug West	.10	.02
❏ 102 Micheal Williams	.10	.02
❏ 103 Kenny Anderson	.20	.07
❏ 104 P.J. Brown	.10	.02
❏ 105 Derrick Coleman	.20	.07
❏ 106 Kevin Edwards	.10	.02
❏ 107 Chris Morris	.10	.02
❏ 108 Rex Walters	.10	.02
❏ 109 Hubert Davis	.10	.02
❏ 110 Patrick Ewing	.40	.15
❏ 111 Derek Harper	.10	.02
❏ 112 Anthony Mason	.20	.07
❏ 113 Charles Oakley	.10	.02
❏ 114 Charles Smith	.10	.02
❏ 115 John Starks	.10	.02
❏ 116 Nick Anderson	.10	.02
❏ 117 Anfernee Hardaway	1.00	.40
❏ 118 Shaquille O'Neal	2.00	.75
❏ 119 Donald Royal	.10	.02
❏ 120 Dennis Scott	.10	.02
❏ 121 Scott Skiles	.10	.02
❏ 122 Dana Barros	.10	.02
❏ 123 Shawn Bradley	.10	.02
❏ 124 Johnny Dawkins	.10	.02
❏ 125 Greg Graham	.10	.02
❏ 126 Clarence Weatherspoon	.10	.02
❏ 127 Danny Ainge	.10	.02
❏ 128 Charles Barkley	.60	.25
❏ 129 Cedric Ceballos	.10	.02
❏ 130 A.C. Green	.20	.07
❏ 131 Kevin Johnson	.20	.07
❏ 132 Dan Majerle	.20	.07
❏ 133 Oliver Miller	.10	.02
❏ 134 Clyde Drexler	.40	.15
❏ 135 Harvey Grant	.10	.02
❏ 136 Tracy Murray	.10	.02
❏ 137 Terry Porter	.10	.02
❏ 138 Clifford Robinson	.20	.07
❏ 139 James Robinson	.10	.02
❏ 140 Rod Strickland	.20	.07
❏ 141 Bobby Hurley	.10	.02
❏ 142 Olden Polynice	.10	.02
❏ 143 Mitch Richmond	.40	.15
❏ 144 Lionel Simmons	.10	.02
❏ 145 Wayman Tisdale	.10	.02
❏ 146 Spud Webb	.10	.02
❏ 147 Walt Williams	.10	.02
❏ 148 Willie Anderson	.10	.02
❏ 149 Vinny Del Negro	.10	.02
❏ 150 Dale Ellis	.10	.02
❏ 151 J.R. Reid	.10	.02
❏ 152 David Robinson	.60	.25
❏ 153 Dennis Rodman	.75	.30
❏ 154 Kendall Gill	.20	.07
❏ 155 Shawn Kemp	.60	.25
❏ 156 Nate McMillan	.10	.02
❏ 157 Gary Payton	.60	.25
❏ 158 Sam Perkins	.20	.07
❏ 159 Ricky Pierce	.10	.02
❏ 160 Detlef Schrempf	.20	.07
❏ 161 David Benoit	.10	.02
❏ 162 Tyrone Corbin	.10	.02
❏ 163 Jeff Hornacek	.20	.07

❏ 164 Jay Humphries	.10	.02
❏ 165 Karl Malone	.60	.25
❏ 166 Bryon Russell	.10	.02
❏ 167 Felton Spencer	.10	.02
❏ 168 John Stockton	.40	.15
❏ 169 Michael Adams	.10	.02
❏ 170 Rex Chapman	.10	.02
❏ 171 Calbert Cheaney	.10	.02
❏ 172 Pervis Ellison	.10	.02
❏ 173 Tom Gugliotta	.20	.07
❏ 174 Don MacLean	.10	.02
❏ 175 Gheorghe Muresan	.10	.02
❏ 176 Charles Barkley PO	.40	.15
❏ 177 Charles Oakley NBC	.10	.02
❏ 178 Hakeem Olajuwon PO	.40	.15
❏ 179 Dikembe Mutombo NBC	.10	.02
❏ 180 Scottie Pippen PO	.60	.25
❏ 181 Sam Cassell NBC	.40	.15
❏ 182 Karl Malone NBC	.40	.15
❏ 183 Reggie Miller PO	.20	.07
❏ 184 Patrick Ewing PO	.20	.07
❏ 185 Vernon Maxwell NBC	.10	.02
❏ 186 A.Hardaway/S.Smith DD	.40	.15
❏ 187 S.O'Neal/C.Webber DD	.40	.15
❏ 188 R.Rogers/J.Mashburn DD	.10	.02
❏ 189 Toni Kukoc DD	.20	.07
❏ 190 Lindsey Hunter DD	.10	.02
❏ 191 L.Sprewell/J.Jackson DD	.20	.07
❏ 192 C.Weatherspoon/V.Baker DD	.20	.07
❏ 193 Calbert Cheaney DD	.10	.02
❏ 194 Isaiah Rider DD	.20	.07
❏ 195 Sam Cassell DD	.10	.02
❏ 196 Gheorghe Muresan DD	.10	.02
❏ 197 LaPhonso Ellis DD	.10	.02
❏ 198 USA Basketball Card	.10	.02
❏ 199 Checklist	.10	.02
❏ 200 Checklist	.10	.02
❏ 201 Sergei Bazarevich	.05	.01
❏ 202 Tyrone Corbin	.05	.01
❏ 203 Grant Long	.05	.01
❏ 204 Ken Norman	.05	.01
❏ 205 Steve Smith	.10	.02
❏ 206 Blue Edwards	.05	.01
❏ 207 Greg Minor RC	.05	.01
❏ 208 Eric Montross RC	.05	.01
❏ 209 Dominique Wilkins	.25	.08
❏ 210 Michael Adams	.05	.01
❏ 211 Kenny Gattison	.05	.01
❏ 212 Darrin Hancock	.05	.01
❏ 213 Robert Parish	.10	.02
❏ 214 Ron Harper	.10	.02
❏ 215 Steve Kerr	.05	.01
❏ 216 Will Perdue	.05	.01
❏ 217 Dickey Simpkins RC	.05	.01
❏ 218 John Battle	.05	.01
❏ 219 Michael Cage	.05	.01
❏ 220 Tony Dumas RC	.05	.01
❏ 221 Jason Kidd RC	2.50	1.00
❏ 222 Roy Tarpley	.05	.01
❏ 223 Dale Ellis	.05	.01
❏ 224 Jalen Rose RC	1.00	.40
❏ 225 Bill Curley RC	.05	.01
❏ 226 Grant Hill RC	1.25	.50
❏ 227 Oliver Miller	.05	.01
❏ 228 Mark West	.05	.01
❏ 229 Tom Gugliotta	.10	.02
❏ 230 Ricky Pierce	.05	.01
❏ 231 Carlos Rogers RC	.05	.01
❏ 232 Clifford Rozier RC	.05	.01
❏ 233 Rony Seikaly	.05	.01
❏ 234 Tim Breaux	.05	.01
❏ 235 Duane Ferrell	.05	.01
❏ 236 Mark Jackson	.05	.01
❏ 237 Byron Scott	.10	.02
❏ 238 John Williams	.05	.01
❏ 239 Lamond Murray RC	.05	.01
❏ 240 Eric Piatkowski RC	.05	.01
❏ 241 Pooh Richardson	.05	.01
❏ 242 Malik Sealy	.05	.01
❏ 243 Cedric Ceballos	.05	.01
❏ 244 Eddie Jones RC	1.25	.50
❏ 245 Anthony Miller RC	.05	.01
❏ 246 Tony Smith	.05	.01
❏ 247 Kevin Gamble	.05	.01
❏ 248 Brad Lohaus	.05	.01
❏ 249 Billy Owens	.05	.01

250	Khalid Reeves RC	.05	.01
251	Kevin Willis	.05	.01
252	Eric Mobley RC	.05	.01
253	Johnny Newman	.05	.01
254	Ed Pinckney	.05	.01
255	Glenn Robinson RC	.75	.30
256	Howard Eisley	.05	.01
257	Donyell Marshall RC	.25	.08
258	Yinka Dare RC	.05	.01
259	Sean Higgins	.05	.01
260	Jayson Williams	.10	.02
261	Charlie Ward RC	.25	.08
262	Monty Williams RC	.05	.01
263	Horace Grant	.10	.02
264	Brian Shaw	.05	.01
265	Brooks Thompson RC	.05	.01
266	Derrick Alston RC	.05	.01
267	B.J. Tyler RC	.05	.01
268	Scott Williams	.05	.01
269	Sharone Wright RC	.05	.01
270	Antonio Lang RC	.05	.01
271	Danny Manning	.10	.02
272	Wesley Person RC	.25	.08
273	Trevor Ruffin RC	.05	.01
274	Wayman Tisdale	.05	.01
275	Jerome Kersey	.05	.01
276	Aaron McKie RC	.50	.20
277	Frank Brickowski	.05	.01
278	Brian Grant RC	.60	.25
279	Michael Smith RC	.05	.01
280	Terry Cummings	.05	.01
281	Sean Elliott	.10	.02
282	Avery Johnson	.05	.01
283	Moses Malone	.25	.08
284	Chuck Person	.05	.01
285	Vincent Askew	.05	.01
286	Bill Cartwright	.05	.01
287	Sarunas Marciulionis	.05	.01
288	Dontonio Wingfield RC	.05	.01
289	Jay Humphries	.05	.01
290	Adam Keefe	.05	.01
291	Jamie Watson RC	.05	.01
292	Kevin Duckworth	.05	.01
293	Juwan Howard RC	.60	.25
294	Jim McIlvaine	.05	.01
295	Scott Skiles	.05	.01
296	Anthony Tucker RC	.05	.01
297	Chris Webber	.60	.25
298	Checklist 201-265	.05	.01
299	Checklist 266-345	.05	.01
300	Checklist 346-350/Inserts	.05	.01
301	Vin Baker SSL	.10	.02
302	Charles Barkley SSL	.25	.08
303	Derrick Coleman SSL	.05	.01
304	Clyde Drexler SSL	.10	.02
305	LaPhonso Ellis SSL	.05	.01
306	Larry Johnson SSL	.05	.01
307	Shawn Kemp SSL	.25	.08
308	Karl Malone SSL	.25	.08
309	Jamal Mashburn SSL	.10	.02
310	Scottie Pippen SSL	.40	.15
311	Dominique Wilkins SSL	.10	.02
312	Walt Williams SSL	.05	.01
313	Sharone Wright SSL	.05	.01
314	B.J. Armstrong SSH	.05	.01
315	Joe Dumars SSH	.10	.02
316	Tony Dumas SSH	.05	.01
317	Tim Hardaway SSH	.10	.02
318	Toni Kukoc SSH	.25	.08
319	Danny Manning SSH	.05	.01
320	Reggie Miller SSH	.10	.02
321	Chris Mullin SSH	.10	.02
322	Wesley Person SSH	.05	.01
323	John Starks SSH	.05	.01
324	John Stockton SSH	.10	.02
325	Clarence Weatherspoon SSH	.05	.01
326	Shawn Bradley SSW	.05	.01
327	Vlade Divac SSW	.05	.01
328	Patrick Ewing SSW	.10	.02
329	Christian Laettner SSW	.05	.01
330	Eric Montross SSW	.05	.01
331	Gheorghe Muresan SSW	.05	.01
332	Dikembe Mutombo SSW	.05	.01
333	Hakeem Olajuwon SSW	.25	.08
334	Robert Parish SSW	.05	.01
335	David Robinson SSW	.25	.08

336	Dennis Rodman SSW	.25	.08
337	Rony Seikaly SSW	.05	.01
338	Rik Smits SSW	.10	.02
339	Kenny Anderson SPI	.05	.01
340	Dee Brown SPI	.05	.01
341	Bobby Hurley SPI	.05	.01
342	Kevin Johnson SPI	.05	.01
343	Jason Kidd SPI	1.00	.40
344	Gary Payton SPI	.25	.08
345	Mark Price SPI	.05	.01
346	Khalid Reeves SPI	.05	.01
347	Jalen Rose SPI	.10	.02
348	Latrell Sprewell SPI	.25	.08
349	B.J. Tyler SPI	.05	.01
350	Charlie Ward SPI	.10	.02
GHO	Grant Hill Gold	12.00	5.00
NNO	Grant Hill Hoops JUMBO	6.00	2.50
NNO	Grant Hill SkyBox JUMBO	6.00	2.50
NNO	H.Olajuwon Gold	10.00	4.00
NNO	G.Hill Slammin' Univ. JUMBO	6.00	2.50
NNO	Emotion Sheet A	30.00	20.00
NNO	Emotion Sheet B	30.00	20.00
NNO	Exp.Emotion Exch.A	1.00	.40
NNO	Exp.Emotion Exch.B	1.00	.40
NNO	Exp.Emotion Exch.C	1.00	.40
NNO	Exp.3rd Prize Game Card	.25	.08
NNO	Olajuwon/D.Rob AU	300.00	150.00
NNO	M.Johnson Exch.Card	5.00	2.00
NNO	Three-Card Panel Exch.	4.00	1.50

1995-96 SkyBox Premium

	COMPLETE SET (301)	35.00	17.50
	COMPLETE SERIES 1 (150)	15.00	7.50
	COMPLETE SERIES 2 (151)	20.00	10.00
1	Stacey Augmon	.20	.07
2	Mookie Blaylock	.20	.07
3	Grant Long	.20	.07
4	Steve Smith	.40	.15
5	Dee Brown	.20	.07
6	Sherman Douglas	.20	.07
7	Eric Montross	.20	.07
8	Dino Radja	.20	.07
9	Dominique Wilkins	.60	.25
10	Muggsy Bogues	.40	.15
11	Scott Burrell	.20	.07
12	Dell Curry	.20	.07
13	Larry Johnson	.40	.15
14	Alonzo Mourning	.40	.15
15	Michael Jordan	4.00	1.50
16	Steve Kerr	.40	.15
17	Toni Kukoc	.40	.15
18	Scottie Pippen	1.00	.40
19	Terrell Brandon	.40	.15
20	Tyrone Hill	.20	.07
21	Chris Mills	.20	.07
22	Mark Price	.40	.15
23	John Williams	.20	.07
24	Tony Dumas	.20	.07
25	Jim Jackson	.20	.07
26	Popeye Jones	.20	.07
27	Jason Kidd	2.00	.75
28	Jamal Mashburn	.40	.15
29	LaPhonso Ellis	.20	.07
30	Dikembe Mutombo	.40	.15
31	Robert Pack	.20	.07
32	Jalen Rose	.75	.30
33	Bryant Stith	.20	.07
34	Joe Dumars	.60	.25

35	Grant Hill	.75	.30
36	Allan Houston	.40	.15
37	Lindsey Hunter	.20	.07
38	Chris Gatling	.20	.07
39	Tim Hardaway	.40	.15
40	Donyell Marshall	.40	.15
41	Chris Mullin	.60	.25
42	Carlos Rogers	.20	.07
43	Latrell Sprewell	.60	.25
44	Sam Cassell	.60	.25
45	Clyde Drexler	.40	.15
46	Robert Horry	.40	.15
47	Hakeem Olajuwon	.60	.25
48	Kenny Smith	.20	.07
49	Dale Davis	.20	.07
50	Mark Jackson	.40	.15
51	Reggie Miller	.60	.25
52	Rik Smits	.40	.15
53	Lamond Murray	.20	.07
54	Eric Piatkowski	.40	.15
55	Pooh Richardson	.20	.07
56	Rodney Rogers	.20	.07
57	Loy Vaught	.20	.07
58	Elden Campbell	.20	.07
59	Cedric Ceballos	.20	.07
60	Vlade Divac	.40	.15
61	Eddie Jones	.75	.30
62	Anthony Peeler	.20	.07
63	Nick Van Exel	.60	.25
64	Bimbo Coles	.20	.07
65	Billy Owens	.20	.07
66	Khalid Reeves	.20	.07
67	Glen Rice	.40	.15
68	Kevin Willis	.20	.07
69	Vin Baker	.40	.15
70	Todd Day	.20	.07
71	Eric Murdock	.20	.07
72	Glenn Robinson	.60	.25
73	Tom Gugliotta	.40	.15
74	Christian Laettner	.40	.15
75	Isaiah Rider	.20	.07
76	Doug West	.20	.07
77	Kenny Anderson	.40	.15
78	P.J. Brown	.20	.07
79	Derrick Coleman	.40	.15
80	Armon Gilliam	.20	.07
81	Patrick Ewing	.60	.25
82	Derek Harper	.40	.15
83	Anthony Mason	.20	.07
84	Charles Oakley	.20	.07
85	John Starks	.20	.07
86	Nick Anderson	.20	.07
87	Horace Grant	.40	.15
88	Anfernee Hardaway	.60	.25
89	Shaquille O'Neal	1.50	.60
90	Dana Barros	.20	.07
91	Shawn Bradley	.20	.07
92	Clarence Weatherspoon	.20	.07
93	Sharone Wright	.20	.07
94	Charles Barkley	.75	.30
95	Kevin Johnson	.40	.15
96	Dan Majerle	.40	.15
97	Danny Manning	.40	.15
98	Wesley Person	.20	.07
99	Clifford Robinson	.20	.07
100	Rod Strickland	.20	.07
101	Otis Thorpe	.20	.07
102	Buck Williams	.20	.07
103	Brian Grant	.60	.25
104	Olden Polynice	.20	.07
105	Mitch Richmond	.40	.15
106	Walt Williams	.20	.07
107	Vinny Del Negro	.20	.07
108	Sean Elliott	.40	.15
109	Avery Johnson	.20	.07
110	David Robinson	.60	.25
111	Dennis Rodman	.40	.15
112	Shawn Kemp	.60	.25
113	Gary Payton	.60	.25
114	Sam Perkins	.20	.07
115	Detlef Schrempf	.40	.15
116	David Benoit	.20	.07
117	Jeff Hornacek	.40	.15
118	Karl Malone	.75	.30
119	John Stockton	.75	.30
120	Calbert Cheaney	.20	.07

121	Juwan Howard	.60	.25
122	Don MacLean	.20	.07
123	Gheorghe Muresan	.20	.07
124	Chris Webber	.75	.30
125	Robert Horry FC	.20	.07
126	Mark Jackson FC	.20	.07
127	Steve Smith FC	.20	.07
128	Lamond Murray FC	.20	.07
129	Christian Laettner FC	.20	.07
130	Kenny Anderson FC	.20	.07
131	Anthony Mason FC	.20	.07
132	Kevin Johnson FC	.20	.07
133	Jeff Hornacek FC	.20	.07
134	Larry Johnson TP	.20	.07
135	Popeye Jones TP	.20	.07
136	Allan Houston TP	.20	.07
137	Chris Gatling TP	.20	.07
138	Sam Cassell TP	.20	.07
139	Anthony Peeler TP	.20	.07
140	Vin Baker TP	.20	.07
141	Dana Barros TP	.20	.07
142	Gheorghe Muresan TP	.20	.07
143	Toronto Raptors	.20	.07
144	Vancouver Grizzlies	.20	.07
145	G.Rice/M.Bogues EXP	.40	.15
146	N.Anderson/C.Laettner EXP	.20	.07
147	John Salley TF	.20	.07
148	Greg Anthony TF	.20	.07
149	Checklist #1	.20	.07
150	Checklist #2	.20	.07
151	Craig Ehlo	.20	.07
152	Spud Webb	.40	.15
153	Dana Barros	.20	.07
155	Kendall Gill	.20	.07
156	Khalid Reeves	.20	.07
157	Glen Rice	.40	.15
158	Luc Longley	.20	.07
159	Dennis Rodman	.40	.15
160	Dickey Simpkins	.20	.07
161	Danny Ferry	.20	.07
162	Dan Majerle	.40	.15
163	Bobby Phills	.20	.07
164	Lucious Harris	.20	.07
165	George McCloud	.20	.07
166	Mahmoud Abdul-Rauf	.20	.07
167	Don MacLean	.20	.07
168	Reggie Williams	.20	.07
169	Terry Mills	.20	.07
170	Otis Thorpe	.20	.07
171	B.J. Armstrong	.20	.07
172	Rony Seikaly	.20	.07
173	Chucky Brown	.20	.07
174	Mario Elie	.20	.07
175	Antonio Davis	.20	.07
176	Ricky Pierce	.20	.07
177	Terry Dehere	.20	.07
178	Rodney Rogers	.20	.07
179	Malik Sealy	.20	.07
180	Brian Williams	.20	.07
181	Sedale Threatt	.20	.07
182	Alonzo Mourning	.40	.15
183	Lee Mayberry	.20	.07
184	Sean Rooks	.20	.07
185	Shawn Bradley	.20	.07
186	Kevin Edwards	.20	.07
187	Hubert Davis	.20	.07
188	Charles Smith	.20	.07
189	Charlie Ward	.20	.07
190	Dennis Scott	.20	.07
191	Brian Shaw	.20	.07
192	Derrick Coleman	.20	.07
193	Richard Dumas	.20	.07
194	Vernon Maxwell	.20	.07
195	A.C. Green	.40	.15
196	Elliot Perry	.20	.07
197	John Williams	.20	.07
198	Aaron McKie	.40	.15
199	Bobby Hurley	.20	.07
200	Michael Smith UER front Mike Smith	.20	.07
201	J.R. Reid	.20	.07
202	Hersey Hawkins	.20	.07
203	Willie Anderson	.20	.07
204	Oliver Miller	.20	.07
205	Tracy Murray	.20	.07
206	Alvin Robertson	.20	.07
207	Carlos Rogers UER	.20	.07
208	John Salley	.20	.07
209	Zan Tabak	.20	.07
210	Adam Keefe	.20	.07
211	Chris Morris	.20	.07
212	Greg Anthony	.20	.07
213	Blue Edwards	.20	.07
214	Kenny Gattison	.20	.07
215	Antonio Harvey	.20	.07
216	Chris King	.20	.07
217	Byron Scott	.20	.07
218	Robert Pack	.20	.07
219	Alan Henderson RC	.60	.25
220	Eric Williams RC	.20	.15
221	George Zidek RC	.20	.07
222	Jason Caffey RC	.40	.15
223	Bob Sura RC	.40	.15
224	Cherokee Parks RC	.20	.07
225	Antonio McDyess RC	1.25	.50
226	Theo Ratliff RC	.75	.30
227	Joe Smith RC	1.00	.40
228	Travis Best RC	.20	.07
229	Brent Barry RC	.60	.25
230	Sasha Danilovic RC	.20	.07
231	Kurt Thomas RC	.40	.15
232	Shawn Respert RC	.20	.07
233	Kevin Garnett RC	3.00	1.50
234	Ed O'Bannon RC	.20	.07
235	Jerry Stackhouse RC	2.00	.75
236	Michael Finley RC	1.50	.60
237	Mario Bennett RC	.20	.07
238	Randolph Childress RC	.20	.07
239	Arvydas Sabonis RC	.75	.30
240	Gary Trent RC	.20	.07
241	Tyus Edney RC	.20	.07
242	Corliss Williamson RC	.60	.25
243	Cory Alexander RC	.20	.07
244	Damon Stoudamire RC	1.25	.50
245	Greg Ostertag RC	.20	.07
246	Lawrence Moten RC	.20	.07
247	Bryant Reeves RC	.60	.25
248	Rasheed Wallace RC	1.50	.60
249	Muggsy Bogues HR	.20	.07
250	Dell Curry HR	.20	.07
251	Scottie Pippen HR	.40	.15
252	Danny Ferry HR	.20	.07
253	Mahmoud Abdul-Rauf HR	.20	.07
254	Joe Dumars HR	.40	.15
255	Tim Hardaway HR	.20	.07
256	Chris Mullin HR	.20	.07
257	Hakeem Olajuwon HR	.40	.15
258	Kenny Smith HR	.20	.07
259	Reggie Miller HR	.40	.15
260	Rik Smits HR	.20	.07
261	Vlade Divac HR	.20	.07
262	Doug West HR	.20	.07
263	Patrick Ewing HR	.40	.15
264	Charles Oakley HR	.20	.07
265	Nick Anderson HR	.20	.07
266	Dennis Scott HR	.20	.07
267	Jeff Turner HR	.20	.07
268	Charles Barkley HR	.60	.25
269	Kevin Johnson HR	.20	.07
270	Clifford Robinson HR	.20	.07
271	Buck Williams HR	.20	.07
272	Lionel Simmons HR	.20	.07
273	David Robinson HR	.40	.15
274	Gary Payton HR	.40	.15
275	Karl Malone HR	.60	.25
276	John Stockton HR	.60	.25
277	Steve Smith ELE	.20	.07
278	Michael Jordan ELE	2.00	.75
279	Jim Jackson ELE	.20	.07
280	Jason Kidd ELE	1.00	.40
281	Jamal Mashburn ELE	.20	.07
282	Dikembe Mutombo ELE	.20	.07
283	Grant Hill ELE	.60	.25
284	Tim Hardaway ELE	.20	.07
285	Clyde Drexler ELE	.40	.15
286	Cedric Ceballos ELE	.20	.07
287	Gary Payton ELE	.40	.15
288	Billy Owens ELE	.20	.07
289	Vin Baker ELE	.20	.07
290	Glenn Robinson ELE	.40	.15
291	Kenny Anderson ELE	.20	.07
292	Anfernee Hardaway ELE	.40	.15
293	Shaquille O'Neal ELE	.60	.25
294	Charles Barkley ELE	.20	.25
295	Rod Strickland ELE	.20	.07
296	Mitch Richmond ELE	.20	.07
297	Juwan Howard ELE	.40	.15
298	Chris Webber ELE	.60	.25
299	Checklist #1	.20	.07
300	Checklist #2	.20	.07
301	Magic Johnson	1.00	.40
PR	Grant Hill JUMBO	6.00	2.50
NNO	G.Hill Melt.Exch	25.00	10.00
NNO	J.Stackhouse Melt.Exch	30.00	12.50

1996-97 SkyBox Premium

COMPLETE SET (281)	35.00	20.00
COMPLETE SERIES 1 (131)	25.00	12.50
COMPLETE SERIES 2 (150)	15.00	7.50
1 Mookie Blaylock	.20	.07
2 Alan Henderson	.20	.07
3 Christian Laettner	.40	.15
4 Dikembe Mutombo	.40	.15
5 Steve Smith	.40	.15
6 Dana Barros	.20	.07
7 Rick Fox	.20	.07
8 Dino Radja	.20	.07
9 Antoine Walker RC	2.00	.75
10 Eric Williams	.20	.07
11 Dell Curry	.20	.07
12 Tony Delk RC	.60	.25
13 Matt Geiger	.20	.07
14 Glen Rice	.40	.15
15 Ron Harper	.20	.07
16 Michael Jordan	4.00	1.50
17 Toni Kukoc	.40	.15
18 Scottie Pippen	1.00	.40
19 Dennis Rodman	.40	.15
20 Terrell Brandon	.40	.15
21 Danny Ferry	.20	.07
22 Chris Mills	.20	.07
23 Bobby Phills	.20	.07
24 Vitaly Potapenko RC	.20	.07
25 Jim Jackson	.20	.07
26 Jason Kidd	1.00	.40
27 Jamal Mashburn	.40	.15
28 George McCloud	.20	.07
29 Samaki Walker RC	.20	.07
30 LaPhonso Ellis	.20	.07
31 Antonio McDyess	.40	.15
32 Bryant Stith	.20	.07
33 Joe Dumars	.60	.25
34 Grant Hill	.60	.25
35 Lindsey Hunter	.20	.07
36 Theo Ratliff	.40	.15
37 Otis Thorpe	.20	.07
38 Todd Fuller RC	.20	.07
39 Chris Mullin	.60	.25
40 Joe Smith	.40	.15
41 Latrell Sprewell	.60	.25
42 Charles Barkley	.75	.30
43 Clyde Drexler	.60	.25
44 Mario Elie	.20	.07
45 Hakeem Olajuwon	.60	.25
46 Erick Dampier RC	.60	.25
47 Dale Davis	.20	.07
48 Derrick McKey	.20	.07
49 Reggie Miller	.60	.25
50 Rik Smits	.40	.15
51 Brent Barry	.20	.07

52	Rodney Rogers	.20	.07
53	Loy Vaught	.20	.07
54	Lorenzen Wright RC	.40	.15
55	Kobe Bryant RC	10.00	4.00
56	Cedric Ceballos	.20	.07
57	Eddie Jones	.60	.25
58	Shaquille O'Neal	1.50	.60
59	Nick Van Exel	.60	.25
60	Tim Hardaway	.40	.15
61	Alonzo Mourning	.40	.15
62	Kurt Thomas	.40	.15
63	Ray Allen RC	2.50	1.00
64	Vin Baker	.40	.15
65	Shawn Respert	.20	.07
66	Glenn Robinson	.60	.25
67	Kevin Garnett	1.25	.50
68	Tom Gugliotta	.20	.07
69	Stephon Marbury RC	2.00	.75
70	Sam Mitchell	.20	.07
71	Shawn Bradley	.20	.07
72	Kendall Gill	.20	.07
73	Kerry Kittles RC	.60	.25
74	Ed O'Bannon	.20	.07
75	Patrick Ewing	.60	.25
76	Larry Johnson	.40	.15
77	Charles Oakley	.20	.07
78	John Starks	.40	.15
79	John Wallace RC	.60	.25
80	Nick Anderson	.20	.07
81	Horace Grant	.40	.15
82	Anfernee Hardaway	.60	.25
83	Dennis Scott	.20	.07
84	Derrick Coleman	.40	.15
85	Allen Iverson RC	4.00	1.50
86	Jerry Stackhouse	.75	.30
87	Clarence Weatherspoon	.20	.07
88	Michael Finley	.75	.30
89	Robert Horry	.40	.15
90	Kevin Johnson	.40	.15
91	Steve Nash RC	5.00	2.00
92	Wesley Person	.20	.07
93	Aaron McKie	.20	.07
94	Jermaine O'Neal RC	2.00	.75
95	Clifford Robinson	.20	.07
96	Arvydas Sabonis	.40	.15
97	Gary Trent	.20	.07
98	Tyus Edney	.20	.07
99	Brian Grant	.60	.25
100	Mitch Richmond	.40	.15
101	Billy Owens	.20	.07
102	Corliss Williamson	.20	.07
103	Vinny Del Negro	.20	.07
104	Sean Elliott	.40	.15
105	Avery Johnson	.20	.07
106	Chuck Person	.20	.07
107	David Robinson	.60	.25
108	Hersey Hawkins	.20	.07
109	Shawn Kemp	.40	.15
110	Gary Payton	.60	.25
111	Sam Perkins	.40	.15
112	Detlef Schrempf	.40	.15
113	Marcus Camby RC	.75	.30
114	Carlos Rogers	.20	.07
115	Damon Stoudamire	.60	.25
116	Zan Tabak	.20	.07
117	Antoine Carr	.20	.07
118	Jeff Hornacek	.40	.15
119	Karl Malone	.60	.25
120	Chris Morris	.20	.07
121	John Stockton	.40	.15
122	Shareef Abdur-Rahim RC	2.00	.75
123	Greg Anthony	.20	.07
124	Bryant Reeves	.20	.07
125	Roy Rogers RC	.20	.07
126	Calbert Cheaney	.20	.07
127	Juwan Howard	.40	.15
128	Gheorghe Muresan	.20	.07
129	Chris Webber	.60	.25
130	Checklist	.20	.07
131	Checklist	.20	.07
132	Jon Barry	.20	.07
133	Christian Laettner	.40	.15
134	Dikembe Mutombo	.40	.15
135	Dee Brown	.20	.07
136	Todd Day	.20	.07
137	David Wesley	.20	.07
138	Vlade Divac	.20	.07
139	Anthony Goldwire	.20	.07
140	Anthony Mason	.40	.15
141	Jason Caffey	.20	.07
142	Luc Longley	.20	.07
143	Tyrone Hill	.20	.07
144	Antonio Lang	.20	.07
145	Sam Cassell	.60	.25
146	Chris Gatling	.20	.07
147	Eric Montross	.20	.07
148	Ervin Johnson	.20	.07
149	Sarunas Marciulionis	.20	.07
150	Stacey Augmon	.20	.07
151	Grant Long	.20	.07
152	Terry Mills	.20	.07
153	Kenny Smith	.20	.07
154	B.J. Armstrong	.20	.07
155	Bimbo Coles	.20	.07
156	Charles Barkley	.75	.30
157	Brent Price	.20	.07
158	Duane Ferrell	.20	.07
159	Jalen Rose	.60	.25
160	Terry Dehere	.20	.07
161	Bo Outlaw	.20	.07
162	Corie Blount	.20	.07
163	Shaquille O'Neal	1.50	.60
164	Rumeal Robinson	.20	.07
165	P.J. Brown	.20	.07
166	Ronnie Grandison	.20	.07
167	Sherman Douglas	.20	.07
168	Johnny Newman	.20	.07
169	James Robinson	.20	.07
170	Doug West	.20	.07
171	Robert Pack	.20	.07
172	Khalid Reeves	.20	.07
173	Chris Childs	.20	.07
174	Allan Houston	.40	.15
175	Charlie Ward	.20	.07
176	Darrell Armstrong RC	2.00	.75
177	Gerald Wilkins	.20	.07
178	Lucious Harris	.20	.07
179	Robert Horry	.40	.15
180	Danny Manning	.40	.15
181	Kenny Anderson	.20	.07
182	Isaiah Rider	.40	.15
183	Rasheed Wallace	.75	.30
184	Mahmoud Abdul-Rauf	.20	.07
185	Cory Alexander	.20	.07
186	Vernon Maxwell	.20	.07
187	Dominique Wilkins	.60	.25
188	Nate McMillan	.20	.07
189	Larry Stewart	.20	.07
190	Doug Christie	.40	.15
191	Hubert Davis	.20	.07
192	Walt Williams	.20	.07
193	Adam Keefe	.20	.07
194	Greg Ostertag	.20	.07
195	John Stockton	.60	.25
196	George Lynch	.20	.07
197	Lee Mayberry	.20	.07
198	Tracy Murray	.20	.07
199	Rod Strickland	.20	.07
200	Shareef Abdur-Rahim ROO	1.00	.40
201	Ray Allen ROO	1.00	.40
202	Shandon Anderson ROO RC	.40	.15
203	Kobe Bryant ROO	3.00	1.25
204	Marcus Camby ROO	.40	.15
205	Erick Dampier ROO	.20	.07
206	Emanual Davis ROO RC	.20	.07
207	Tony Delk ROO	.40	.15
208	Brian Evans ROO RC	.20	.07
209	Derek Fisher ROO RC	1.00	.40
210	Todd Fuller ROO	.20	.07
211	Dean Garrett ROO RC	.20	.07
212	Reggie Geary ROO RC	.20	.07
213	Darvin Ham ROO RC	.20	.07
214	Othella Harrington ROO RC	.40	.15
215	Shane Heal ROO RC	.20	.07
216	Allen Iverson ROO	1.50	.60
217	Dontae' Jones ROO RC	.20	.07
218	Kerry Kittles ROO	.60	.25
219	Fred Lauderdale ROO RC	.20	.07
220	Randy Livingston ROO RC	.20	.07
221	Matt Maloney ROO RC	.20	.07
222	Stephon Marbury ROO	1.25	.50
223	Walter McCarty ROO RC	.20	.07
224	Amal McCaskill ROO RC	.20	.07
225	Jeff McInnis ROO RC	.20	.07
226	Martin Muursepp ROO RC	.20	.07
227	Steve Nash ROO	.75	.30
228	Ruben Nembhard ROO RC	.20	.07
229	Jermaine O'Neal ROO	.75	.30
230	Vitaly Potapenko ROO	.20	.07
231	Virginas Praskevicius ROO RC	.20	.07
232	Roy Rogers ROO	.20	.07
233	Malik Rose ROO RC	.40	.15
234	Antoine Walker ROO	1.50	.60
235	Samaki Walker ROO	.20	.07
236	Ben Wallace ROO RC	4.00	1.50
237	John Wallace ROO	.40	.15
238	Jerome Williams ROO RC	.60	.25
239	Lorenzen Wright ROO	.20	.07
240	Sam Cassell PM	.20	.07
241	Anfernee Hardaway PM	.40	.15
242	Tim Hardaway PM	.20	.07
243	Grant Hill PM	.40	.15
244	Allan Houston PM	.20	.07
245	Juwan Howard PM	.20	.07
246	Kevin Johnson PM	.40	.15
247	Michael Jordan PM	2.00	.75
248	Jason Kidd PM	.50	.20
249	Karl Malone PM	.60	.25
250	Reggie Miller PM	.40	.15
251	Gary Payton PM	.40	.15
252	Wesley Person PM	.20	.07
253	Glen Rice PM	.40	.15
254	David Robinson PM	.40	.15
255	Steve Smith PM	.20	.07
256	Latrell Sprewell PM	.60	.25
257	Jerry Stackhouse PM	.60	.25
258	Rod Strickland PM	.20	.07
259	Nick Van Exel PM	.40	.15
260	Charles Barkley DT	.60	.25
261	Dale Davis DT	.20	.07
262	Patrick Ewing DT	.40	.15
263	Michael Finley DT	.60	.25
264	Chris Gatling DT	.20	.07
265	Armon Gilliam DT	.20	.07
266	Tyrone Hill DT	.20	.07
267	Robert Horry DT	.20	.07
268	Mark Jackson DT	.20	.07
269	Shawn Kemp DT	.20	.07
270	Jamal Mashburn DT	.20	.07
271	Antony Mason DT	.20	.07
272	Alonzo Mourning DT	.20	.07
273	Dikembe Mutombo DT	.20	.07
274	Shaquille O'Neal DT	.60	.25
275	Isaiah Rider DT	.20	.07
276	Dennis Rodman DT	.60	.25
277	Damon Stoudamire DT	.40	.15
278	Chris Webber DT	.40	.15
279	Jayson Williams DT	.20	.07
280	Checklist	.20	.07
281	Checklist	.20	.07
NNO	Jerry Stackhouse Promo	2.00	.75

1997-98 SkyBox Premium

	COMPLETE SET (250)	90.00	50.00
	COMPLETE SERIES 1 (125)	25.00	12.50
	COMPLETE SERIES 2 (125)	70.00	40.00
1	Grant Hill	.75	.30
2	Matt Maloney	.25	.08
3	Vinny Del Negro	.25	.08
4	Kevin Willis	.50	.20

5	Mark Jackson	.50	.20
6	Ray Allen	.75	.30
7	Derrick Coleman	.25	.08
8	Isaiah Rider	.50	.20
9	Rod Strickland	.25	.08
10	Danny Ferry	.25	.08
11	Antonio Davis	.25	.08
12	Glenn Robinson	.75	.30
13	Cedric Ceballos	.25	.08
14	Sean Elliott	.50	.20
15	Walt Williams	.25	.08
16	Glen Rice	.50	.20
17	Clyde Drexler	.75	.30
18	Sherman Douglas	.25	.08
19	Othella Harrington	.25	.08
20	John Stockton	.75	.30
21	Priest Lauderdale	.25	.08
22	Khalid Reeves	.25	.08
23	Kobe Bryant	3.00	1.25
24	Vin Baker UER	.50	.20
25	Steve Nash	.75	.30
26	Jeff Hornacek	.50	.20
27	Tyrone Corbin	.25	.08
28	Charles Barkley	1.00	.40
29	Michael Jordan	5.00	2.00
30	Latrell Sprewell	.75	.30
31	Anfernee Hardaway	.75	.30
32	Steve Kerr	.50	.20
33	Joe Smith	.50	.20
34	Jermaine O'Neal	1.25	.50
35	Ron Mercer RC	.60	.25
36	Antonio McDyess	.50	.20
37	Patrick Ewing	.75	.30
38	Avery Johnson	.25	.08
39	Toni Kukoc	.50	.20
40	Sam Perkins	.50	.20
41	Voshon Lenard	.25	.08
42	Detlef Schrempf	.50	.20
43	Horace Grant	.50	.20
44	Luc Longley	.25	.08
45	Todd Fuller	.25	.08
46	Tim Hardaway	.50	.20
47	Nick Anderson	.25	.08
48	Scottie Pippen	1.25	.50
49	Lindsey Hunter	.25	.08
50	Shawn Kemp	.50	.20
51	Larry Johnson	.50	.20
52	Shawn Bradley	.25	.08
53	Martin Muursepp	.25	.08
54	Jamal Mashburn	.50	.20
55	John Starks	.50	.20
56	Rony Seikaly	.25	.08
57	Gary Payton	.75	.30
58	Juwan Howard	.50	.20
59	Vitaly Potapenko	.25	.08
60	Reggie Miller	.75	.30
61	Alonzo Mourning	.50	.20
62	Roy Rogers	.25	.08
63	Antoine Walker	1.00	.40
64	Joe Dumars	.75	.30
65	Allan Houston	.50	.20
66	Hersey Hawkins	.25	.08
67	Dell Curry	.25	.08
68	Tony Delk	.25	.08
69	Mookie Blaylock	.25	.08
70	Derek Harper	.50	.20
71	Loy Vaught	.25	.08
72	Tom Gugliotta	.50	.20
73	Mitch Richmond	.50	.20
74	Dikembe Mutombo	.50	.20
75	Tony Battie RC	.75	.30
76	Derek Fisher	.75	.30
77	Jason Kidd	1.25	.50
78	Shareef Abdur-Rahim	1.25	.50
79	Tracy McGrady RC	5.00	2.00
80	Anthony Mason	.50	.20
81	Mario Elie	.25	.08
82	Karl Malone	.75	.30
83	Mark Price	.50	.20
84	Steve Smith	.50	.20
85	LaPhonso Ellis	.25	.08
86	Robert Horry	.25	.08
87	Wesley Person	.25	.08
88	Marcus Camby	.75	.30
89	Antonio Daniels RC	.75	.30
90	Eddie Jones	.75	.30
91	Gary Trent	.25	.08
92	Danny Fortson RC	.75	.30
93	Chris Childs	.25	.08
94	David Robinson	.75	.30
95	Bryant Reeves	.25	.08
96	Chris Webber	.75	.30
97	P.J. Brown	.25	.08
98	Tyrone Hill	.25	.08
99	Dale Davis	.25	.08
100	Allen Iverson	2.00	.75
101	Jerry Stackhouse	.75	.30
102	Arvydas Sabonis	.50	.20
103	Damon Stoudamire	.50	.20
104	Tim Thomas RC	1.50	.60
105	Christian Laettner	.50	.20
106	Robert Pack	.25	.08
107	Lorenzen Wright	.25	.08
108	Olden Polynice	.25	.08
109	Terrell Brandon	.50	.20
110	Theo Ratliff	.25	.08
111	Kevin Garnett	1.50	.60
112	Tim Duncan RC	4.00	1.50
113	Bryon Russell	.25	.08
114	Chauncey Billups RC	2.50	1.00
115	Dale Ellis	.25	.08
116	Shaquille O'Neal	2.00	.75
117	Keith Van Horn RC	1.25	.50
118	Kenny Anderson	.50	.20
119	Dennis Rodman	.50	.20
120	Hakeem Olajuwon	.75	.30
121	Stephon Marbury	1.00	.40
122	Kendall Gill	.25	.08
123	Kerry Kittles	.75	.30
124	Checklist	.25	.08
125	Checklist	.25	.08
126	Anthony Johnson RC	.25	.08
127	Chris Anstey RC	.25	.08
128	Dean Garrett	.25	.08
129	Rik Smits	.50	.20
130	Tracy Murray	.25	.08
131	Charles O'Bannon RC	.25	.08
132	Eldridge Recasner	.25	.08
133	Johnny Taylor RC	.25	.08
134	Priest Lauderdale	.25	.08
135	Rod Strickland	.25	.08
136	Alan Henderson	.25	.08
137	Austin Croshere RC	.60	.25
138	Buck Williams	.25	.08
139	Clifford Robinson	.25	.08
140	Darrell Armstrong	.25	.08
141	Dennis Scott	.25	.08
142	Carl Herrera	.25	.08
143	Maurice Taylor RC	.60	.25
144	Chris Gatling	.25	.08
145	Alvin Williams RC	.25	.08
146	Antonio McDyess	.50	.20
147	Chauncey Billups	.60	.25
148	George McCloud	.25	.08
149	George Lynch	.25	.08
150	John Thomas RC	.25	.08
151	Jayson Williams	.25	.08
152	Otis Thorpe	.25	.08
153	Serge Zwikker RC	.25	.08
154	Chris Crawford RC	.25	.08
155	Muggsy Bogues	.50	.20
156	Mark Jackson	.50	.20
157	Dontonio Wingfield	.25	.08
158	Rodrick Rhodes RC	.25	.08
159	Sam Cassell	.75	.30
160	Hubert Davis	.25	.08
161	Clarence Weatherspoon	.25	.08
162	Eddie Johnson	.25	.08
163	Jacque Vaughn RC	.50	.20
164	Mark Price	.50	.20
165	Terry Dehere	.25	.08
166	Travis Knight	.25	.08
167	Charles Smith	.25	.08
168	David Wesley	.25	.08
169	David Wingate	.25	.08
170	Todd Day	.25	.08
171	Adonal Foyle RC	.50	.20
172	Chris Mills	.25	.08
173	Paul Grant RC	.25	.08
174	Adam Keefe	.25	.08
175	Erick Dampier	.50	.20
176	Ervin Johnson	.25	.08
177	Lamond Murray	.25	.08
178	Vlade Divac	.50	.20
179	Bobby Phills	.25	.08
180	Brian Williams	.25	.08
181	Chris Dudley	.25	.08
182	Tyrone Hill	.25	.08
183	Donyell Marshall	.50	.20
184	Kevin Gamble	.25	.08
185	Scot Pollard RC	.50	.20
186	Cherokee Parks	.25	.08
187	Terry Mills	.25	.08
188	Glen Rice	.50	.20
189	Shawn Respert	.25	.08
190	Terrell Brandon	.50	.20
191	Keith Closs RC	.25	.08
192	Tariq Abdul-Wahad RC	.50	.20
193	Wesley Person	.25	.08
194	Chuck Person	.25	.08
195	Derek Anderson RC	.75	.30
196	Jon Barry	.25	.08
197	Chris Mullin	.75	.30
198	Ed Gray RC	.25	.08
199	Charlie Ward	.25	.08
200	Kelvin Cato RC	.75	.30
201	Michael Finley	.75	.30
202	Rick Fox	.50	.20
203	Scott Burrell	.25	.08
204	Vin Baker	.50	.20
205	Eric Snow	.50	.20
206	Isaac Austin	.25	.08
207	Keith Booth RC	.25	.08
208	Brian Grant	.50	.20
209	Chris Webber	.75	.30
210	Eric Williams	.25	.08
211	Jim Jackson	.25	.08
212	Anthony Parker RC	.25	.08
213	Brevin Knight RC	.75	.30
214	Cory Alexander	.25	.08
215	James Robinson	.25	.08
216	Bobby Jackson RC	1.25	.50
217	Bo Outlaw	.25	.08
218	God Shammgod RC	.25	.08
219	James Cotton RC	.25	.08
220	Jud Buechler	.25	.08
221	Shandon Anderson	.25	.08
222	Kevin Johnson	.50	.20
223	Chris Morris	.25	.08
224	Shareef Abdur-Rahim TS	2.50	1.00
225	Ray Allen TS	.75	.30
226	Kobe Bryant TS	6.00	2.50
227	Marcus Camby TS	.75	.30
228	Antonio Daniels TS	1.00	.40
229	Tim Duncan TS	3.00	1.25
230	Kevin Garnett TS	3.00	1.25
231	Anfernee Hardaway TS	2.00	.75
232	Grant Hill TS	1.50	.60
233	Allen Iverson TS	4.00	1.50
234	Bobby Jackson TS	.75	.30
235	Michael Jordan TS	10.00	5.00
236	Shawn Kemp TS	1.50	.60
237	Karl Malone TS	.75	.30
238	Stephon Marbury TS	2.50	1.00
239	Hakeem Olajuwon TS	1.50	.60
240	Shaquille O'Neal TS	4.00	1.50
241	Gary Payton TS	1.25	.50
242	Scottie Pippen TS	2.50	1.00
243	David Robinson TS	1.50	.60
244	Dennis Rodman TS	2.50	1.50
245	Jerry Stackhouse TS	1.00	.40
246	Damon Stoudamire TS	1.00	.40
247	Keith Van Horn TS	2.50	1.00
248	Antoine Walker TS	4.00	1.50
249	Grant Hill CL	.50	.20
250	Hakeem Olajuwon CL	.50	.20
NNO	A.Iverson Shoe Bronze	1.25	.50
NNO	A.Iverson Shoe Ruby	12.00	5.00
NNO	A.Iverson Shoe Gold	4.00	1.50
NNO	A.Iverson Shoe Silver	2.00	.75
NNO	A.Iverson Shoe Emerald	30.00	12.50

1998-99 SkyBox Premium

COMPLETE SET (265)	120.00	60.00
COMPLETE SET w/o SP (225)	40.00	20.00
COMPLETE SERIES 1 (125)	25.00	12.50
COMPLETE SERIES 2 (140)	100.00	50.00

	COMMON CARD (1-225)	.25	.08
	COMMON ROOKIE (226-265)	.75	.30
1	Tim Duncan	1.25	.50
2	Voshon Lenard	.25	.08
3	John Starks	.50	.20
4	Juwan Howard	.50	.20
5	Michael Finley	.75	.30
6	Bobby Jackson	.50	.20
7	Glenn Robinson	.50	.20
8	Antonio McDyess	.50	.20
9	Eric Williams	.25	.08
10	Zydrunas Ilgauskas	.50	.20
11	Terrell Brandon	.50	.20
12	Shandon Anderson	.25	.08
13	Rod Strickland	.25	.08
14	Dennis Rodman	.50	.20
15	Clarence Weatherspoon	.25	.08
16	P.J. Brown	.25	.08
17	Anfernee Hardaway	.75	.30
18	Dikembe Mutombo	.50	.20
19	Patrick Ewing	.75	.30
20	Scottie Pippen	1.25	.50
21	Shaquille O'Neal	2.00	.75
22	Donyell Marshall	.50	.20
23	Michael Jordan	5.00	2.00
24	Mark Price	.50	.20
25	Jim Jackson	.25	.08
26	Isaiah Rider	.25	.08
27	Eddie Jones	.75	.30
28	Detlef Schrempf	.50	.20
29	Corliss Williamson	.50	.20
30	Bo Outlaw	.25	.08
31	Allen Iverson	1.50	.60
32	Luc Longley	.25	.08
33	Theo Ratliff	.25	.08
34	Antoine Walker	.75	.30
35	Lamond Murray	.25	.08
36	Avery Johnson	.25	.08
37	John Stockton	.75	.30
38	David Wesley	.25	.08
39	Elden Campbell	.25	.08
40	Grant Hill	.75	.30
41	Sam Cassell	.75	.30
42	Tracy McGrady	2.00	.75
43	Glen Rice	.50	.20
44	Kobe Bryant	3.00	1.25
45	John Wallace	.25	.08
46	Bobby Phills	.25	.08
47	Jerry Stackhouse	.75	.30
48	Stephon Marbury	.75	.30
49	Jeff Hornacek	.50	.20
50	Tom Gugliotta	.25	.08
51	Joe Dumars	.75	.30
52	Johnny Newman	.25	.08
53	Kevin Garnett	1.50	.60
54	Dennis Scott	.25	.08
55	Anthony Mason	.50	.20
56	Rodney Rogers	.25	.08
57	Bryon Russell	.25	.08
58	Maurice Taylor	.40	.15
59	Mookie Blaylock	.25	.08
60	Shawn Bradley	.25	.08
61	Matt Maloney	.25	.08
62	Karl Malone	.75	.30
63	Larry Johnson	.50	.20
64	Calbert Cheaney	.25	.08
65	Steve Smith	.50	.20
66	Toni Kukoc	.50	.20
67	Reggie Miller	.75	.30
68	Jayson Williams	.25	.08
69	Gary Payton	.75	.30
70	Sean Elliott	.50	.20
71	Charles Barkley	1.00	.40
72	Tim Hardaway	.50	.20
73	Rasheed Wallace	.75	.30
74	Tariq Abdul-Wahad	.25	.08
75	Kenny Anderson	.50	.20
76	Chris Mullin	.75	.30
77	Keith Van Horn	.75	.30
78	Hersey Hawkins	.25	.08
79	Ron Mercer	.40	.15
80	Rik Smits	.50	.20
81	David Robinson	.75	.30
82	Derek Anderson	.60	.25
83	Danny Fortson	.25	.08
84	Jason Kidd	1.25	.50
85	Chauncey Billups	.50	.20
86	Chris Anstey	.25	.08
87	Hakeem Olajuwon	.75	.30
88	Bryant Reeves	.25	.08
89	Anthony Johnson	.25	.08
90	Shawn Kemp	.50	.20
91	Brevin Knight	.25	.08
92	Ray Allen	.75	.30
93	Tim Thomas	.50	.20
94	Jalen Rose	.50	.20
95	Kerry Kittles	.25	.08
96	Vin Baker	.50	.20
97	Shareef Abdur-Rahim	.75	.30
98	Alonzo Mourning	.50	.20
99	Joe Smith	.50	.20
100	Damon Stoudamire	.50	.20
101	Alan Henderson	.25	.08
102	Walter McCarty	.25	.08
103	Vlade Divac	.50	.20
104	Wesley Person	.25	.08
105	A.C. Green	.25	.08
106	Malik Sealy	.25	.08
107	Carl Thomas	.25	.08
108	Brent Price	.25	.08
109	Mark Jackson	.50	.20
110	Lorenzen Wright	.25	.08
111	Derek Fisher	.75	.30
112	Michael Smith	.25	.08
113	Tyrone Hill	.25	.08
114	Cherokee Parks	.25	.08
115	Kendall Gill	.25	.08
116	Darrell Armstrong	.25	.08
117	Derrick Coleman	.25	.08
118	Rex Chapman	.25	.08
119	Arvydas Sabonis	.50	.20
120	Billy Owens	.25	.08
121	Sam Perkins	.25	.08
122	Gary Trent	.25	.08
123	Sam Mack	.25	.08
124	Tracy Murray	.25	.08
125	Allan Houston	.50	.20
126	Mitch Richmond	.50	.20
127	Carl Herrera	.25	.08
128	Ron Harper	.25	.08
129	Gary Trent	.25	.08
130	Chris Webber	.75	.30
131	Antonio Daniels	.25	.08
132	Charles Oakley	.25	.08
133	Marcus Camby	.50	.20
134	Tony Battie	.25	.08
135	Otis Thorpe	.25	.08
136	Dale Davis	.50	.20
137	Chuck Person	.25	.08
138	Ervin Johnson	.25	.08
139	Jamal Mashburn	.50	.20
140	Brian Grant	.50	.20
141	Chris Mills	.25	.08
142	Doug Christie	.50	.20
143	George McCloud	.25	.08
144	Todd Fuller	.25	.08
145	Jerome Williams	.25	.08
146	Chauncey Billups	.50	.20
147	Dean Garrett	.25	.08
148	Robert Pack	.25	.08
149	Clarence Weatherspoon	.25	.08
150	Tim Legler	.25	.08
151	Bob Sura	.25	.08
152	B.J. Armstrong	.25	.08
153	Charlie Ward	.25	.08
154	Rony Seikaly	.25	.08
155	Chris Carr	.25	.08
156	Eldridge Recasner	.25	.08
157	Michael Stewart	.25	.08
158	Jim McIlvaine	.25	.08
159	Adam Keefe	.25	.08
160	Antonio Davis	.25	.08
161	Lawrence Funderburke	.25	.08
162	Greg Ostertag	.25	.08
163	Dan Majerle	.50	.20
164	Dale Ellis	.25	.08
165	Greg Anthony	.25	.08
166	Chris Whitney	.25	.08
167	Eric Piatkowski	.50	.20
168	Tom Gugliotta	.25	.08
169	Luc Longley	.25	.08
170	Antonio McDyess	.50	.20
171	George Lynch	.25	.08
172	Dell Curry	.25	.08
173	Johnny Newman	.25	.08
174	Christian Laettner	.50	.20
175	Steve Kerr	.50	.20
176	Popeye Jones	.25	.08
177	Brent Barry	.50	.20
178	Billy Owens	.25	.08
179	Cherokee Parks	.25	.08
180	Derek Harper	.25	.08
181	Howard Eisley	.25	.08
182	Matt Geiger	.25	.08
183	Darrick Martin	.25	.08
184	Isaac Austin	.25	.08
185	Dennis Scott	.25	.08
186	Derrick Coleman	.25	.08
187	Sam Perkins	.25	.08
188	Latrell Sprewell	.75	.30
189	Jud Buechler	.25	.08
190	Jason Caffey	.25	.08
191	Vlade Divac	.50	.20
192	Travis Best	.25	.08
193	Loy Vaught	.25	.08
194	Mario Elie	.25	.08
195	Ed Gray	.25	.08
196	Joe Smith	.50	.20
197	John Starks	.50	.20
198	Anthony Johnson	.25	.08
199	Kurt Thomas	.50	.20
200	Chris Dudley	.25	.08
201	Shareef Abdur-Rahim NF	.50	.20
202	Ray Allen NF	.50	.20
203	Vin Baker NF	.25	.08
204	Charles Barkley NF	.25	.08
205	Kobe Bryant NF	1.50	.60
206	Tim Duncan NF	.75	.30
207	Anfernee Hardaway NF	.25	.08
208	Grant Hill NF	.75	.30
209	Allen Iverson NF	1.25	.50
210	Jason Kidd NF	.75	.30
211	Shawn Kemp NF	.25	.08
212	Shaquille O'Neal NF	1.00	.40
213	Kerry Kittles NF	.25	.08
214	Karl Malone NF	.25	.08
215	Stephon Marbury NF	.75	.30
216	Ron Mercer NF	.20	.06
217	Reggie Miller NF	.25	.08
218	Kevin Garnett NF	.75	.30
219	Gary Payton NF	.25	.08
220	Scottie Pippen NF	.75	.30
221	David Robinson NF	.25	.08
222	Hakeem Olajuwon NF	.25	.08
223	Damon Stoudamire NF	.25	.08
224	Keith Van Horn NF	.25	.08
225	Antoine Walker NF	.25	.08
226	Cory Carr RC	.75	.30
227	Cuttino Mobley RC	6.00	2.50
228	Miles Simon RC	.75	.30
229	J.R. Henderson RC	.75	.30
230	Jason Williams RC	5.00	2.00
231	Felipe Lopez RC	1.50	.60
232	Shammond Williams RC	3.00	1.25
233	Ricky Davis RC	5.00	2.00
234	Vince Carter RC	15.00	6.00
235	Antawn Jamison RC	6.00	2.50
236	Ryan Stack RC	.75	.30
237	Nazr Mohammed RC	1.00	.40
238	Sam Jacobson RC	.75	.30

239	Larry Hughes RC	4.00	1.50
240	Ruben Patterson RC	2.50	1.00
241	Al Harrington RC	3.00	1.25
242	Ansu Sesay RC	.75	.30
243	Vladimir Stepania RC	.75	.30
244	Matt Harpring RC	2.00	.75
245	Andrae Patterson RC	.75	.30
246	Pat Garrity RC	1.00	.40
247	Bonzi Wells RC	5.00	2.00
248	Bryce Drew RC	1.50	.60
249	Toby Bailey RC	.75	.30
250	Michael Doleac RC	1.50	.60
251	Michael Dickerson RC	2.50	1.00
252	Peja Stojakovic	5.00	2.00
253	Robert Traylor RC	1.50	.60
254	Tyronn Lue RC	2.00	.75
255	Dirk Nowitzki RC	12.00	6.00
256	Raef LaFrentz RC	2.00	.75
257	Jelani McCoy RC	.75	.30
258	Michael Olowokandi RC	2.00	.75
259	Brian Skinner RC	1.50	.60
260	Keon Clark RC	1.50	.60
261	Roshown McLeod RC	1.00	.40
262	Mike Bibby RC	6.00	2.50
263	Paul Pierce RC	6.00	2.50
264	Tyson Wheeler RC	.75	.30
265	Corey Benjamin RC	1.50	.60

1999-00 SkyBox Premium

COMPLETE SET (150)	120.00	60.00
COMPLETE SET w/o SP (125)	40.00	15.00
COMMON CARD (1-100)	.25	.08
COMMON ROOKIE (101-125)	.30	.10
COMMON SP (101-125)	1.25	.50

1	Vince Carter	2.00	.75
2	Nick Anderson	.25	.08
3	Isaiah Rider	.25	.08
4	Mitch Richmond	.25	.08
5	Danny Fortson	.25	.08
6	Kenny Anderson	.50	.20
7	Reggie Miller	.75	.30
8	Tracy McGrady	2.00	.75
9	Steve Nash	.75	.30
10	Robert Traylor	.25	.08
11	Tom Gugliotta	.25	.08
12	Steve Smith	.50	.20
13	Jalen Rose	.75	.30
14	Kerry Kittles	.25	.08
15	Nick Van Exel	.75	.30
16	Raef LaFrentz	.50	.20
17	Damon Stoudamire	.50	.20
18	Gary Trent	.25	.08
19	Jayson Williams	.25	.08
20	Brian Grant	.50	.20
21	Rod Strickland	.25	.08
22	Larry Hughes	.75	.30
23	Derek Anderson	.50	.20
24	Hakeem Olajuwon	.75	.30
25	Ray Allen	.75	.30
26	Gary Payton	.75	.30
27	Michael Finley	.75	.30
28	Keith Van Horn	.75	.30
29	Clifford Robinson	.25	.08
30	Shawn Kemp	.50	.20
31	Glenn Robinson	.50	.20
32	Theo Ratliff	.25	.08
33	Lindsey Hunter	.25	.08
34	Chris Webber	.75	.30
35	Grant Hill	.75	.30
36	Vlade Divac	.50	.20
37	Paul Pierce	.75	.30
38	Tyrone Nesby RC	.25	.08
39	Larry Johnson	.50	.20
40	Bryon Russell	.25	.08
41	Antoine Walker	.75	.30
42	Michael Olowokandi	.50	.20
43	John Stockton	.75	.30
44	Elden Campbell	.25	.08
45	Christian Laettner	.50	.20
46	Maurice Taylor	.50	.20
47	Shareef Abdur-Rahim	.75	.30
48	Ricky Davis	.50	.20
49	Jerry Stackhouse	.75	.30
50	Kobe Bryant	3.00	1.25
51	Jason Williams	.75	.30
52	Mike Bibby	.75	.30
53	Eddie Jones	.75	.30
54	Antawn Jamison	1.25	.50
55	Shaquille O'Neal	2.00	.75
56	Tim Duncan	1.50	.60
57	Cherokee Parks	.25	.08
58	Antonio McDyess	.50	.20
59	Rasheed Wallace	.75	.30
60	Anthony Mason	.50	.20
61	Chris Mills	.25	.08
62	Glen Rice	.50	.20
63	Latrell Sprewell	.75	.30
64	Darrell Armstrong	.25	.08
65	Sean Elliott	.50	.20
66	Juwan Howard	.50	.20
67	Brent Barry	.50	.20
68	John Starks	.50	.20
69	Tim Hardaway	.50	.20
70	Marcus Camby	.50	.20
71	Anfernee Hardaway	.75	.30
72	Avery Johnson	.25	.08
73	Tariq Abdul-Wahad	.25	.08
74	Charles Barkley	1.00	.40
75	Stephon Marbury	.75	.30
76	Jamal Mashburn	.75	.30
77	Matt Harpring	.75	.30
78	David Robinson	.75	.30
79	Cedric Ceballos	.25	.08
80	Terrell Brandon	.50	.20
81	Jason Kidd	1.25	.50
82	Toni Kukoc	.50	.20
83	Michael Dickerson	.50	.20
84	Alonzo Mourning	.50	.20
85	Kevin Garnett	1.50	.60
86	Matt Geiger	.25	.08
87	Vin Baker	.50	.20
88	Dikembe Mutombo	.50	.20
89	Hersey Hawkins	.50	.20
90	Joe Smith	.50	.20
91	Charles Oakley	.25	.08
92	Ron Mercer	.50	.20
93	Rik Smits	.50	.20
94	Patrick Ewing	.75	.30
95	Karl Malone	.75	.30
96	Scottie Pippen	1.25	.50
97	Zydrunas Ilgauskas	.50	.20
98	Sam Cassell	.75	.30
99	Detlef Schrempf	.50	.20
100	Allen Iverson	1.50	.60
101	Elton Brand RC	2.00	.75
101A	Elton Brand SP	8.00	3.00
102	Steve Francis RC	2.00	.75
102A	Steve Francis SP	10.00	4.00
103	Baron Davis RC	3.00	1.25
103A	Baron Davis RC	6.00	2.50
104	Lamar Odom RC	1.00	.40
104A	Lamar Odom SP	6.00	2.50
105	Jonathan Bender RC	1.50	.60
105A	Jonathan Bender SP	4.00	1.50
106	Wally Szczerbiak RC	1.50	.60
106A	Wally Szczerbiak SP	6.00	2.50
107	Richard Hamilton RC	2.00	.75
107A	Richard Hamilton SP	5.00	2.00
108	Andre Miller RC	1.50	.60
108A	Andre Miller SP	6.00	2.50
109	Shawn Marion RC	2.00	.75
109A	Shawn Marion SP	8.00	3.00
110	Jason Terry RC	1.00	.40
110A	Jason Terry SP	4.00	1.50
111	Trajan Langdon RC	.60	.25
111A	Trajan Langdon SP	2.50	1.00
112	A.Radojevic RC	.30	.10
112A	A.Radojevic SP	1.25	.50
113	Corey Maggette RC	1.50	.60
113A	Corey Maggette SP	6.00	2.50
114	William Avery RC	.60	.25
114A	William Avery SP	2.50	1.00
115	Vonteego Cummings RC	.60	.25
115A	Vonteego Cummings SP	2.50	1.00
116	Ron Artest RC	1.00	.40
116A	Ron Artest SP	4.00	1.50
117	Cal Bowdler RC	.50	.20
117A	Cal Bowdler SP	1.50	.60
118	James Posey RC	1.00	.40
118A	James Posey SP	4.00	1.50
119	Quincy Lewis RC	.50	.20
119A	Quincy Lewis SP	1.50	.60
120	Dion Glover RC	.50	.20
120A	Dion Glover SP	1.50	.60
121	Jeff Foster RC	.50	.20
121A	Jeff Foster SP	1.50	.60
122	Kenny Thomas RC	.60	.25
122A	Kenny Thomas SP	2.50	1.00
123	Devean George RC	.75	.30
123A	Devean George SP	3.00	1.25
124	Scott Padgett RC	.50	.20
124A	Scott Padgett SP	1.50	.60
125	Tim James RC	.50	.20
125A	Tim James SP	2.00	.75

2004-05 Skybox Premium

COMP.SET w/ SP's (75)	40.00	15.00
COMMON CARD (1-75)	.25	.10
COMMON ROOKIE (76-100)	5.00	2.00

1	Dwyane Wade	3.00	1.25
2	Rashard Lewis	1.00	.40
3	Jermaine O'Neal	1.00	.40
4	Ben Wallace	1.00	.40
5	Steve Francis	1.00	.40
6	Lamar Odom	1.00	.40
7	Jason Richardson	1.00	.40
8	Jarvis Hayes	.60	.25
9	Carmelo Anthony	2.00	.75
10	Tony Parker	1.00	.40
11	Eddy Curry	.60	.25
12	Nene	.60	.25
13	Kevin Garnett	2.00	.75
14	Darius Miles	1.00	.40
15	Elton Brand	1.00	.40
16	Zach Randolph	1.00	.40
17	Mike Dunleavy	.60	.25
18	Dajuan Wagner	.60	.25
19	Steve Nash	1.00	.40
20	Ron Artest	1.00	.40
21	Ricky Davis	1.00	.40
22	Antawn Jamison	1.00	.40
23	Jamaal Magloire	.60	.25
24	T.J. Ford	.60	.25
25	Amare Stoudemire	2.00	.75
26	Jason Kapono	.60	.25
27	Shawn Marion	1.00	.40
28	Corliss Williamson	.60	.25
29	Reggie Miller	1.00	.40
30	Desmond Mason	.60	.25
31	Pau Gasol	1.00	.40
32	Baron Davis	1.00	.40
33	Allen Iverson	2.00	.75

Paul Pierce

☐ 34	Darko Milicic	.60	.25
☐ 35	Ray Allen	1.00	.40
☐ 36	Jason Williams	.60	.25
☐ 37	Michael Redd	1.00	.40
☐ 38	Yao Ming	2.50	1.00
☐ 39	Antoine Walker	1.00	.40
☐ 40	Jason Terry	1.00	.40
☐ 41	Sam Cassell	1.00	.40
☐ 42	Richard Jefferson	.60	.25
☐ 43	Manu Ginobili	1.50	.60
☐ 44	Dirk Nowitzki	1.50	.60
☐ 45	Peja Stojakovic	1.00	.40
☐ 46	Samuel Dalembert	.25	.10
☐ 47	Latrell Sprewell	1.00	.40
☐ 48	Gerald Wallace	.60	.25
☐ 49	Andrei Kirilenko	1.00	.40
☐ 50	Nick Van Exel	1.00	.40
☐ 51	Jalen Rose	1.00	.40
☐ 52	Shaquille O'Neal	2.50	1.00
☐ 53	Shareef Abdur-Rahim	1.00	.40
☐ 54	Tracy McGrady	2.50	1.00
☐ 55	Rasheed Wallace	1.00	.40
☐ 56	Cuttino Mobley	.60	.25
☐ 57	Jason Kidd	1.50	.60
☐ 58	Chris Webber	1.00	.40
☐ 59	Paul Pierce	1.00	.40
☐ 60	Mike Bibby	1.00	.40
☐ 61	Allan Houston	.60	.25
☐ 62	Kobe Bryant	4.00	1.50
☐ 63	Kenyon Martin	1.00	.40
☐ 64	LeBron James	6.00	2.50
☐ 65	Tim Duncan	2.00	.75
☐ 66	Stephon Marbury	1.00	.40
☐ 67	Kirk Hinrich	1.00	.40
☐ 68	Chris Bosh	1.00	.40
☐ 69	Corey Maggette	.60	.25
☐ 70	Vince Carter	2.50	1.00
☐ 71	Caron Butler	1.00	.40
☐ 72	Stephen Jackson	.25	.10
☐ 73	Carlos Boozer	1.00	.40
☐ 74	Michael Finley	1.00	.40
☐ 75	Jamal Crawford	.60	.25
☐ 76	Dwight Howard RC	12.00	5.00
☐ 77	Emeka Okafor RC	15.00	6.00
☐ 78	Ben Gordon RC	20.00	8.00
☐ 79	Shaun Livingston RC	6.00	2.50
☐ 80	Devin Harris RC	6.00	2.50
☐ 81	Josh Childress RC	5.00	2.00
☐ 82	Luol Deng RC	8.00	3.00
☐ 83	Rafael Araujo RC	5.00	2.00
☐ 84	Andre Iguodala RC	10.00	4.00
☐ 85	Luke Jackson RC	5.00	2.00
☐ 86	Andris Biedrins RC	5.00	2.00
☐ 87	Robert Swift RC	5.00	2.00
☐ 88	Sebastian Telfair RC	4.00	1.50
☐ 89	Kris Humphries RC	5.00	2.00
☐ 90	Al Jefferson RC	10.00	4.00
☐ 91	Kirk Snyder RC	5.00	2.00
☐ 92	Josh Smith RC	8.00	3.00
☐ 93	J.R. Smith RC	8.00	3.00
☐ 94	Dorell Wright RC	8.00	3.00
☐ 95	Jameer Nelson RC	6.00	2.50
☐ 96	Bernard Robinson RC	5.00	2.00
☐ 97	Andre Emmett RC	5.00	2.00
☐ 98	Delonte West RC	5.00	2.00
☐ 99	Tony Allen RC	5.00	2.00
☐ 100	Kevin Martin RC	6.00	2.50

1999-00 SkyBox APEX

☐	COMPLETE SET (163)	80.00	40.00
☐	COMPLETE SET w/o RC (150)	25.00	12.50
☐	COMMON CARD (1-150)	.25	.08
☐	COMMON ROOKIE (151-163)	.75	.30
☐ 1	Paul Pierce	.75	.30
☐ 2	Stephon Marbury	.75	.30
☐ 3	Chris Webber	.75	.30
☐ 4	Kobe Bryant	3.00	1.25
☐ 5	David Robinson	.75	.30
☐ 6	Gary Payton	.75	.30
☐ 7	Kornel David RC	.25	.08
☐ 8	Glenn Robinson	.50	.20
☐ 9	Nick Van Exel	.75	.30
☐ 10	Jelani McCoy	.25	.08
☐ 11	Charles Oakley	.25	.08
☐ 12	Michael Finley	.75	.30
☐ 13	Steve Smith	.50	.20
☐ 14	Arvydas Sabonis	.50	.20
☐ 15	Cuttino Mobley	.75	.30
☐ 16	Eric Piatkowski	.50	.20
☐ 17	Bobby Jackson	.50	.20
☐ 18	Keith Van Horn	.75	.30
☐ 19	Shaquille O'Neal	2.00	.75
☐ 20	Karl Malone	.75	.30
☐ 21	Allan Houston	.50	.20
☐ 22	Ron Mercer	.50	.20
☐ 23	Vince Carter	2.00	.75
☐ 24	Lindsey Hunter	.25	.08
☐ 25	Scottie Pippen	1.25	.50
☐ 26	Wesley Person	.25	.08
☐ 27	Vitaly Potapenko	.25	.08
☐ 28	Glen Rice	.50	.20
☐ 29	Tyrone Nesby RC	.25	.08
☐ 30	Detlef Schrempf	.50	.20
☐ 31	Clifford Robinson	.25	.08
☐ 32	Joe Smith	.50	.20
☐ 33	P.J. Brown	.25	.08
☐ 34	Christian Laettner	.50	.20
☐ 35	Avery Johnson	.25	.08
☐ 36	Kevin Garnett	1.50	.60
☐ 37	Jason Kidd	1.25	.50
☐ 38	Kenny Anderson	.50	.20
☐ 39	Shawn Kemp	.50	.20
☐ 40	Bison Dele	.25	.08
☐ 41	Rodney Rogers	.25	.08
☐ 42	Jamal Mashburn	.50	.20
☐ 43	Grant Hill	.75	.30
☐ 44	Larry Johnson	.50	.20
☐ 45	Darrell Armstrong	.25	.08
☐ 46	Shandon Anderson	.25	.08
☐ 47	Kendall Gill	.25	.08
☐ 48	Jason Williams	.50	.20
☐ 49	Tom Gugliotta	.50	.20
☐ 50	Ray Allen	.75	.30
☐ 51	Sam Mitchell	.25	.08
☐ 52	Brent Barry	.50	.20
☐ 53	Antawn Jamison	1.25	.50
☐ 54	Chris Mullin	.75	.30
☐ 55	Alan Henderson	.25	.08
☐ 56	Derek Anderson	.50	.20
☐ 57	Tim Thomas	.50	.20
☐ 58	Anfernee Hardaway	.75	.30
☐ 59	Pat Garrity	.25	.08
☐ 60	Corliss Williamson	.25	.08
☐ 61	Gary Trent	.25	.08
☐ 62	Greg Ostertag	.25	.08
☐ 63	Vin Baker	.50	.20
☐ 64	LaPhonso Ellis	.25	.08
☐ 65	Brevin Knight	.25	.08
☐ 66	Rick Fox	.25	.08
☐ 67	Bryant Reeves	.25	.08
☐ 68	Mark Jackson	.50	.20
☐ 69	John Starks	.50	.20
☐ 70	Robert Traylor	.25	.08
☐ 71	Maurice Taylor	.50	.20
☐ 72	Hersey Hawkins	.50	.20
☐ 73	Zydrunas Ilgauskas	.50	.20
☐ 74	Charles Barkley	1.00	.40
☐ 75	Isaac Austin	.25	.08
☐ 76	Mike Bibby	.75	.30
☐ 77	Michael Olowokandi	.50	.20
☐ 78	Brian Grant	.50	.20
☐ 79	Felipe Lopez	.25	.08
☐ 80	Chris Crawford	.25	.08
☐ 81	Dee Brown	.25	.08
☐ 82	Antoine Walker	.75	.30
☐ 83	Vlade Divac	.50	.20
☐ 84	Rod Strickland	.25	.08
☐ 85	Dickey Simpkins	.25	.08
☐ 86	Donyell Marshall	.50	.20
☐ 87	Larry Hughes	.75	.30
☐ 88	Rasheed Wallace	.75	.30
☐ 89	Erick Dampier	.50	.20
☐ 90	Kerry Kittles	.25	.08
☐ 91	Mitch Richmond	.50	.20
☐ 92	Isaiah Rider	.25	.08
☐ 93	Bobby Phills	.25	.08
☐ 94	Dirk Nowitzki	1.50	.60
☐ 95	Cedric Henderson	.25	.08
☐ 96	Howard Eisley	.25	.08
☐ 97	Toni Kukoc	.50	.20
☐ 98	Jalen Rose	.75	.30
☐ 99	Michael Doleac	.25	.08
☐ 100	Matt Geiger	.25	.08
☐ 101	Bryon Russell	.25	.08
☐ 102	Alvin Williams	.25	.08
☐ 103	Shawn Bradley	.25	.08
☐ 104	Latrell Sprewell	.75	.30
☐ 105	Vernon Maxwell	.25	.08
☐ 106	Tim Hardaway	.50	.20
☐ 107	Peja Stojakovic	1.00	.40
☐ 108	Tracy Murray	.25	.08
☐ 109	Theo Ratliff	.50	.20
☐ 110	Dikembe Mutombo	.50	.20
☐ 111	Alonzo Mourning	.50	.20
☐ 112	Raef LaFrentz	.50	.20
☐ 113	Marcus Camby	.50	.20
☐ 114	Eddie Jones	.75	.30
☐ 115	Chauncey Billups	.50	.20
☐ 116	Jayson Williams	.25	.08
☐ 117	Anthony Mason	.50	.20
☐ 118	Tracy McGrady	2.00	.75
☐ 119	John Stockton	.75	.30
☐ 120	Matt Harpring	.75	.30
☐ 121	Mario Elie	.25	.08
☐ 122	Juwan Howard	.50	.20
☐ 123	Antonio McDyess	.50	.20
☐ 124	Ricky Davis	.50	.20
☐ 125	Reggie Miller	.75	.30
☐ 126	Allen Iverson	1.50	.60
☐ 127	Terrell Brandon	.50	.20
☐ 128	Hakeem Olajuwon	.75	.30
☐ 129	Damon Stoudamire	.50	.20
☐ 130	Randy Brown	.25	.08
☐ 131	Cedric Ceballos	.25	.08
☐ 132	Jerry Stackhouse	.75	.30
☐ 133	Michael Dickerson	.50	.20
☐ 134	Rik Smits	.50	.20
☐ 135	Cherokee Parks	.25	.08
☐ 136	Tim Duncan	1.50	.60
☐ 137	Shareef Abdur-Rahim	.75	.30
☐ 138	Derek Fisher	.75	.30
☐ 139	Bo Outlaw	.25	.08
☐ 140	Eric Snow	.50	.20
☐ 141	Jaren Jackson	.25	.08
☐ 142	Tony Battie	.25	.08
☐ 143	Derrick Coleman	.50	.20
☐ 144	Corey Benjamin	.25	.08
☐ 145	Steve Nash	.75	.30
☐ 146	Mookie Blaylock	.50	.20
☐ 147	Voshon Lenard	.25	.08
☐ 148	Vinny Del Negro	.25	.08
☐ 149	Jeff Hornacek	.50	.20
☐ 150	Patrick Ewing	.75	.30
☐ 151	Elton Brand RC	5.00	2.00
☐ 152	Steve Francis RC	5.00	2.00
☐ 153	Baron Davis RC	6.00	2.50
☐ 154	Lamar Odom RC	4.00	1.50
☐ 155	Jonathan Bender RC	4.00	1.50
☐ 156	Wally Szczerbiak RC	4.00	1.50
☐ 157	Richard Hamilton RC	3.00	1.25
☐ 158	Andre Miller RC	4.00	1.50
☐ 159	Shawn Marion RC	5.00	2.00
☐ 160	Jason Terry RC	2.50	1.00
☐ 161	Trajan Langdon RC	.75	.30
☐ 162	A.Radojevic RC	.75	.30
☐ 163	Corey Maggette RC	4.00	1.50
☐ P2	Stephon Marbury PROMO	1.25	.50
☐ NNO	K.Van Horn AU JSY/50	200.00	100.00

2003-04 Skybox Autographics

COMP. SET w/o SP's (45)	30.00	12.50
COMMON CARD (1-45)	.25	.10
COMMON ROOKIE (46-90)	4.00	1.50
1 Vince Carter	2.50	1.00
2 Kobe Bryant	4.00	1.50
3 Tony Parker	1.00	.40
4 Richard Hamilton	.60	.25
5 Jamal Mashburn	.60	.25
6 Paul Pierce	1.00	.40
7 Allan Houston	.60	.25
8 Carlos Boozer	.60	.25
9 Michael Redd	1.00	.40
10 Chris Webber	1.00	.40
11 Yao Ming	2.50	1.00
12 Tracy McGrady	2.50	1.00
13 Zach Randolph	1.00	.40
14 Ben Wallace	1.00	.40
15 Kenyon Martin	1.00	.40
16 Ray Allen	1.00	.40
17 Jermaine O'Neal	1.00	.40
18 Bonzi Wells	.60	.25
19 Ron Artest	.60	.25
20 Peja Stojakovic	1.00	.40
21 Dirk Nowitzki	1.50	.60
22 Desmond Mason	.60	.25
23 Morris Peterson	.60	.25
24 Eddy Curry	.60	.25
25 Kevin Garnett	2.00	.75
26 Rashard Lewis	1.00	.40
27 Jason Richardson	1.00	.40
28 Amare Stoudemire	2.00	.75
29 Steve Francis	1.00	.40
30 Allen Iverson	2.00	.75
31 Jason Terry	1.00	.40
32 Pau Gasol	1.00	.40
33 Manu Ginobili	1.00	.40
34 Reggie Miller	1.00	.40
35 Cuttino Mobley	.60	.25
36 Mike Bibby	1.00	.40
37 Mike Dunleavy	.60	.25
38 Jason Kidd	1.50	.60
39 Shareef Abdur-Rahim	1.00	.40
40 Elton Brand	1.00	.40
41 Kwame Brown	1.00	.40
42 Shaquille O'Neal	2.50	1.00
43 Tim Duncan	2.00	.75
44 Nene	.60	.25
45 Baron Davis	1.00	.40
46 Boris Diaw RC	5.00	2.00
47 Luke Walton RC	4.00	1.50
48 Willie Green RC	4.00	1.50
49 Marcus Banks RC	4.00	1.50
50 Dahntay Jones RC	4.00	1.50
51 Leandro Barbosa RC	6.00	2.50
52 Josh Howard RC	6.00	2.50
53 Ndudi Ebi RC	4.00	1.50
54 Chris Bosh RC	10.00	4.00
55 Carmelo Anthony RC	12.00	5.00
56 Zoran Planinic RC	4.00	1.50
57 Aleksandar Pavlovic RC	5.00	2.00
58 Marquis Daniels RC	8.00	3.00
59 Keith McLeod RC	4.00	1.50
60 Ben Handlogten RC	4.00	1.50
61 Francisco Elson RC	4.00	1.50
62 David West RC	4.00	1.50
63 Maurice Williams RC	4.00	1.50
64 Brian Cook RC	4.00	1.50
65 Keith Bogans RC	4.00	1.50
66 Kendrick Perkins RC	4.00	1.50
67 Troy Bell RC	4.00	1.50
68 Kyle Korver RC	6.00	2.50
69 Mickael Pietrus RC	4.00	1.50
70 Maciej Lampe RC	4.00	1.50
71 Steve Blake RC	4.00	1.50
72 Chris Kaman RC	4.00	1.50
73 Curtis Borchardt RC	4.00	1.50
74 Kirk Hinrich RC	6.00	2.50
75 Dwyane Wade RC	15.00	6.00
76 Zarko Cabarkapa RC	4.00	1.50
77 LeBron James RC	40.00	15.00
78 Jerome Beasley RC	4.00	1.50
79 Nick Collison RC	4.00	1.50
80 Linton Johnson RC	4.00	1.50
81 Udonis Haslem RC	4.00	1.50
82 Travis Outlaw RC	4.00	1.50
83 Jason Kapono RC	4.00	1.50
84 T.J. Ford RC	5.00	2.00
85 Luke Ridnour RC	5.00	2.00
86 Darko Milicic RC	6.00	2.50
87 Mike Sweetney RC	4.00	1.50
88 Jarvis Hayes RC	4.00	1.50
89 Josh Moore RC	4.00	1.50
90 Reece Gaines RC	4.00	1.50

2004-05 Skybox Autographics

COMP. SET w/o SP's (60)	40.00	15.00
COMMON CARD (1-60)	.25	.10
COMMON ROOKIE (61-105)	4.00	1.50
1 Dwyane Wade	3.00	1.25
2 Derek Fisher	1.00	.40
3 Latrell Sprewell	1.00	.40
4 Peja Stojakovic	1.00	.40
5 LeBron James	6.00	2.50
6 Elton Brand	1.00	.40
7 Allan Houston	.60	.25
8 Chris Bosh	1.00	.40
9 Carmelo Anthony	2.00	.75
10 Shaquille O'Neal	2.50	1.00
11 Steve Nash	1.00	.40
12 Antawn Jamison	1.00	.40
13 Darko Milicic	.60	.25
14 Michael Redd	.60	.25
15 Shawn Marion	1.00	.40
16 Dirk Nowitzki	1.50	.60
17 Kobe Bryant	4.00	1.50
18 Steve Francis	1.00	.40
19 Carlos Boozer	1.00	.40
20 Karl Malone	1.00	.40
21 T.J. Ford	.60	.25
22 Darius Miles	1.00	.40
23 Paul Pierce	1.00	.40
24 Jermaine O'Neal	1.00	.40
25 Baron Davis	1.00	.40
26 Tony Parker	1.00	.40
27 Kirk Hinrich	1.00	.40
28 Chris Kaman	.60	.25
29 Stephon Marbury	1.00	.40
30 Rashard Lewis	1.00	.40
31 Ben Wallace	1.00	.40
32 Antoine Walker	1.00	.40
33 Amare Stoudemire	2.00	.75
34 Gary Payton	1.00	.40
35 Yao Ming	2.50	1.00
36 Richard Jefferson	.60	.25
37 Tim Duncan	2.00	.75
38 Drew Gooden	.60	.25
39 Lamar Odom	1.00	.40
40 Grant Hill	1.00	.40
41 Vince Carter	2.50	1.00
42 Michael Finley	1.00	.40
43 Jason Williams	.60	.25
44 Samuel Dalembert	.25	.10
45 Andrei Kirilenko	1.00	.40
46 Jason Kapono	.60	.25
47 Reggie Miller	1.00	.40
48 Jamaal Magloire	.25	.10
49 Ray Allen	1.00	.40
50 Kenyon Martin	1.00	.40
51 Pau Gasol	1.00	.40
52 Allen Iverson	2.00	.75
53 Gilbert Arenas	1.00	.40
54 Jason Richardson	1.00	.40
55 Kevin Garnett	2.00	.75
56 Zach Randolph	1.00	.40
57 Al Harrington	.60	.25
58 Tracy McGrady	2.50	1.00
59 Jason Kidd	1.50	.60
60 Chris Webber	1.00	.40
61 Andris Biedrins RC	6.00	2.50
62 Robert Swift RC	4.00	1.50
63 Pavel Podkolzine RC	4.00	1.50
64 Kevin Martin RC	6.00	2.50
65 Beno Udrih RC	6.00	2.50
66 David Harrison RC	4.00	1.50
67 Andre Emmett RC	4.00	1.50
68 Emeka Okafor RC	15.00	6.00
69 Dwight Howard RC	12.00	5.00
70 Ben Gordon RC	15.00	6.00
71 Shaun Livingston RC	6.00	2.50
72 Devin Harris RC	6.00	2.50
73 Josh Childress RC	5.00	2.00
74 Luol Deng RC	8.00	3.00
75 Rafael Araujo RC	4.00	1.50
76 Andre Iguodala RC	10.00	4.00
77 Luke Jackson RC	5.00	2.00
78 Sebastian Telfair RC	4.00	1.50
79 Kris Humphries RC	4.00	1.50
80 Al Jefferson RC	10.00	4.00
81 Kirk Snyder RC	4.00	1.50
82 Josh Smith RC	8.00	3.00
83 J.R. Smith RC	8.00	3.00
84 Dorell Wright RC	6.00	2.50
85 Jameer Nelson RC	6.00	2.50
86 Delonte West RC	8.00	3.00
87 Tony Allen RC	5.00	2.00
88 Sasha Vujacic RC	4.00	1.50
89 Andres Nocioni RC	5.00	2.00
90 Royal Ivey RC	4.00	1.50
91 Trevor Ariza RC	5.00	2.00
92 Chris Duhon RC	6.00	2.50
93 John Edwards RC	4.00	1.50
94 Jackson Vroman RC	4.00	1.50
95 Quinton Ross RC	4.00	1.50
96 Erik Daniels RC	4.00	1.50
97 Anderson Varejao RC	5.00	2.00
98 Lionel Chalmers RC	4.00	1.50
99 Carlos Delfino RC		
100 Jared Reiner RC	4.00	1.50
101 Bernard Robinson RC	4.00	1.50
102 Peter John Ramos RC	4.00	1.50
103 D.J. Mbenga RC	4.00	1.50
104 Mario Kasun RC	4.00	1.50
105 Nenad Krstic RC	5.00	2.00

1999-00 SkyBox Dominion

COMPLETE SET (220)	40.00	20.00
COMMON CARD (1-200)	.15	.05
COMMON ROOKIE (201-220)	.30	.10
1 Jason Williams	.50	.20
2 Isaiah Rider	.15	.05
3 Tim Hardaway	.30	.10
4 Isaac Austin	.15	.05
5 Joe Smith	.30	.10
6 Mitch Richmond	.30	.10
7 Sam Mitchell	.15	.05
8 Terrell Brandon	.30	.10
9 Grant Long	.15	.05

10	Shaquille O'Neal	1.25	.50
11	Derrick Coleman	.30	.10
12	Rod Strickland	.15	.05
13	J.R. Reid	.15	.05
14	Tyrone Corbin	.15	.05
15	Jeff Hornacek	.30	.10
16	Malik Rose	.15	.05
17	Terry Davis	.15	.05
18	Theo Ratliff	.30	.10
19	Kevin Willis	.15	.05
20	Raef LaFrentz	.30	.10
21	Othella Harrington	.15	.05
22	Marcus Camby	.30	.10
23	Keon Clark	.30	.10
24	Robert Pack	.15	.05
25	Sam Mack	.15	.05
26	Shawn Kemp	.30	.10
27	Nick Anderson	.15	.05
28	Bill Wennington	.15	.05
29	Steve Smith	.30	.10
30	Kobe Bryant	2.00	.75
31	Bobby Phills	.15	.05
32	Cedric Ceballos	.15	.05
33	Derek Fisher	.50	.20
34	Doug Christie	.30	.10
35	Danny Manning	.15	.05
36	Eric Murdock	.15	.05
37	Glen Rice	.30	.10
38	Dikembe Mutombo	.30	.10
39	Jason Kidd	.75	.30
40	Cedric Henderson	.15	.05
41	Rasheed Wallace	.50	.20
42	Tim Duncan	1.00	.40
43	John Stockton	.50	.20
44	Dell Curry	.15	.05
45	Muggsy Bogues	.15	.05
46	Danny Fortson	.15	.05
47	Charles Oakley	.15	.05
48	Elden Campbell	.15	.05
49	Tony Massenburg	.15	.05
50	Kevin Garnett	1.00	.40
51	Cherokee Parks	.15	.05
52	LaPhonso Ellis	.15	.05
53	Sam Cassell	.50	.20
54	Shawn Bradley	.15	.05
55	David Robinson	.50	.20
56	Juwan Howard	.30	.10
57	Lindsey Hunter	.15	.05
58	Mark Jackson	.30	.10
59	Olden Polynice	.15	.05
60	Tracy McGrady	1.25	.50
61	Michael Finley	.50	.20
62	Matt Geiger	.15	.05
63	Maurice Taylor	.30	.10
64	Rex Chapman	.15	.05
65	Chris Mullin	.50	.20
66	Ray Allen	.50	.20
67	Bison Dele	.15	.05
68	Dickey Simpkins	.15	.05
69	Alvin Williams	.15	.05
70	Grant Hill	.50	.20
71	Mark Bryant	.15	.05
72	Adam Keefe	.15	.05
73	Alan Henderson	.15	.05
74	Eric Snow	.30	.10
75	Matt Harpring	.50	.20
76	Jalen Rose	.50	.20
77	Derek Harper	.30	.10
78	Kerry Kittles	.15	.05
79	Tony Battie	.15	.05
80	Larry Hughes	.30	.10
81	Arvydas Sabonis	.30	.10
82	Allan Houston	.30	.10
83	Tom Gugliotta	.15	.05
84	Reggie Miller	.50	.20
85	Dejuan Wheat	.15	.05
86	Pat Garrity	.15	.05
87	Karl Malone	.50	.20
88	Sam Perkins	.15	.05
89	Michael Olowokandi	.30	.10
90	Anfernee Hardaway	.50	.20
91	Bryant Reeves	.15	.05
92	Gary Trent	.15	.05
93	George Lynch	.15	.05
94	Scottie Pippen	.75	.30
95	Jerry Stackhouse	.50	.20
96	Kendall Gill	.15	.05
97	Vin Baker	.30	.10
98	Dale Davis	.15	.05
99	Charles Barkley	.60	.25
100	Allen Iverson	1.00	.40
101	Keith Van Horn	.50	.20
102	Andrew DeClercq	.15	.05
103	Michael Doleac	.15	.05
104	Chauncey Billups	.30	.10
105	Chris Mills	.15	.05
106	Lamond Murray	.15	.05
107	Glenn Robinson	.50	.20
108	Brian Grant	.30	.10
109	Christian Laettner	.30	.10
110	Antawn Jamison	.75	.30
111	Erick Dampier	.15	.05
112	Vernon Maxwell	.15	.05
113	Kenny Anderson	.30	.10
114	Clarence Weatherspoon	.15	.05
115	Corliss Williamson	.30	.10
116	Paul Pierce	.50	.20
117	Clifford Robinson	.15	.05
118	Damon Stoudamire	.30	.10
119	Dana Barros	.15	.05
120	Stephon Marbury	.50	.20
120B	Stephon Marbury Promo	.50	.20
121	Latrell Sprewell	.50	.20
122	Tyronn Lue	.30	.10
123	Walt Williams	.15	.05
124	P.J. Brown	.15	.05
125	Gary Payton	.50	.20
126	Nick Van Exel	.50	.20
127	Bryant Stith	.15	.05
128	Eric Piatkowski	.30	.10
129	Tyrone Nesby RC	.15	.05
130	Ron Mercer	.30	.10
131	Hersey Hawkins	.30	.10
132	Vlade Divac	.30	.10
133	Darrick Martin	.15	.05
134	Avery Johnson	.15	.05
135	Jaren Jackson	.15	.05
136	Brevin Knight	.15	.05
137	Wesley Person	.15	.05
138	Derek Anderson	.30	.10
139	Tim Thomas	.30	.10
140	Antonio McDyess	.30	.10
141	A.C. Green	.30	.10
142	Chris Webber	.50	.20
143	Scott Burrell	.15	.05
144	John Starks	.30	.10
145	Howard Eisley	.15	.05
146	Mike Bibby	.50	.20
147	Toni Kukoc	.30	.10
148	Eddie Jones	.50	.20
149	Otis Thorpe	.15	.05
150	Shareef Abdur-Rahim	.50	.20
151	Calbert Cheaney	.15	.05
152	Cuttino Mobley	.50	.20
153	Michael Dickerson	.30	.10
154	Sean Elliott	.30	.10
155	Terry Porter	.15	.05
156	Dana Garrett	.15	.05
157	Charlie Ward	.15	.05
158	Larry Johnson	.30	.10
159	Dan Majerle	.30	.10
160	Jayson Williams	.30	.10
161	Anthony Peeler	.15	.05
162	Ron Harper	.30	.10
163	Darrell Armstrong	.15	.05
164	Kurt Thomas	.30	.10
165	Brent Barry	.30	.10
166	Lawrence Funderburke	.15	.05
167	Terry Cummings	.15	.05
168	Jamal Mashburn	.30	.10
169	Robert Traylor	.15	.05
170	Greg Ostertag	.15	.05
171	Brad Miller	.50	.20
172	Mario Elie	.15	.05
173	Antoine Walker	.50	.20
174	Ricky Davis	.30	.10
175	Vince Carter	1.25	.50
176	Hakeem Olajuwon WT	.30	.10
177	Luc Longley WT	.15	.05
178	Tim Duncan WT	.50	.20
179	Rick Fox WT	.15	.05
181	Zydrunas Ilgauskas WT	.15	.05
181	Toni Kukoc WT	.15	.05
182	Felipe Lopez WT	.15	.05
183	Dikembe Mutombo WT	.15	.05
184	Steve Nash WT	.50	.20
185	Dirk Nowitzki WT	1.00	.40
186	Vitaly Potapenko WT	.15	.05
187	Detlef Schrempf WT	.15	.05
188	Rik Smits WT	.15	.05
189	Vladimir Stepania WT	.15	.05
190	Peja Stojakovic WT	.50	.20
191	Donyell Marshall 3FA	.30	.10
192	Shareef Abdur-Rahim 3FA	.30	.10
193	Michael Dickerson 3FA	.30	.10
194	Damon Stoudamire 3FA	.15	.05
195	Allen Iverson 3FA	.50	.20
196	Grant Hill 3FA	.30	.10
197	Scottie Pippen 3FA	.50	.20
198	Bryon Russell 3FA	.15	.05
199	Alonzo Mourning 3FA	.15	.05
200	Patrick Ewing 3FA	.30	.10
201	Ron Artest RC	1.00	.40
202	William Avery RC	.60	.25
203	Lamar Odom RC	1.50	.60
204	Baron Davis RC	3.00	1.25
205	John Celestand RC	.50	.20
206	Jumaine Jones RC	.60	.25
207	Andre Miller RC	1.50	.60
208	Elton Brand RC	2.00	.75
209	James Posey RC	1.00	.40
210	Jason Terry RC	1.00	.40
211	Kenny Thomas RC	.60	.25
212	Steve Francis RC	2.00	.75
213	Wally Szczerbiak RC	1.50	.60
214	Richard Hamilton RC	1.50	.60
215	Jonathan Bender RC	1.50	.60
216	Shawn Marion RC	1.25	.50
217	A.Radojevic RC	.30	.10
218	Tim James RC	.50	.20
219	Trajan Langdon RC	.60	.25
220	Corey Maggette RC	1.50	.60

2000 SkyBox Dominion WNBA

	COMPLETE SET (156)	25.00	10.00
1	Cynthia Cooper	3.00	1.25
2	Sue Wicks	.50	.20
3	Clarisse Machanguana RC	1.50	.60
4	Adrienne Goodson	.50	.20
5	Astou Ndiaye RC	1.50	.60
6	Crystal Robinson	.50	.20

❑ 7	Tora Suber	.50	.20	❑ 93	Becky Hammon RC	5.00	2.00	❑	COMMON ROOKIE (91-120)	4.00	1.50
❑ 8	Lady Hardmon	.50	.20	❑ 94	Amaya Valdemoro RC	1.50	.60	❑ 1	T.J. Ford	.50	.20
❑ 9	Maria Stepanova	.50	.20	❑ 95	Jennifer Gillom	1.00	.40	❑ 2	Pau Gasol	.75	.30
❑ 10	Mwadi Mabika	.50	.20	❑ 96	La'Keshia Frett RC	1.50	.60	❑ 3	Kirk Hinrich	.75	.30
❑ 11	Rebecca Lobo	1.50	.60	❑ 97	Markita Aldridge RC	1.50	.60	❑ 4	Shawn Marion	.75	.30
❑ 12	Ticha Penicheiro	1.00	.40	❑ 98	Natalie Williams	1.50	.60	❑ 5	Darius Miles	.50	.20
❑ 13	Vicky Bullett	.50	.20	❑ 99	Rhonda Mapp	.50	.20	❑ 6	Dirk Nowitzki	1.25	.50
❑ 14	Adia Barnes	.50	.20	❑ 100	Suzie McConnell-Serio	.50	.20	❑ 7	Paul Pierce	.75	.30
❑ 15	Andrea Stinson	1.00	.40	❑ 101	Tina Thompson	1.50	.60	❑ 8	Theron Smith	.20	.08
❑ 16	Sheryl Swoopes	3.00	1.25	❑ 102	Wanda Guyton	.50	.20	❑ 9	Rasheed Wallace	.75	.30
❑ 17	Heather Owen RC	1.50	.60	❑ 103	Lisa Harrison RC	1.50	.60	❑ 10	Kobe Bryant	3.00	1.25
❑ 18	Andrea Congreaves	.50	.20	❑ 104	Andrea Nagy RC	1.50	.60	❑ 11	Kevin Garnett	1.50	.60
❑ 19	Brandy Reed	.50	.20	❑ 105	Edna Campbell ED	.50	.20	❑ 12	Steve Nash	.75	.30
❑ 20	Dawn Staley	1.50	.60	❑ 106	Nina Bjedov ED RC	1.50	.60	❑ 13	Gilbert Arenas	.75	.30
❑ 21	Jennifer Rizzotti RC	2.00	.75	❑ 107	Sonja Henning ED RC	1.50	.60	❑ 14	Udonis Haslem	.20	.08
❑ 22	Latasha Byears	.50	.20	❑ 108	Toni Foster ED	.50	.20	❑ 15	Ben Wallace	.75	.30
❑ 23	Merlakia Jones	.50	.20	❑ 109	Angela Aycock ED RC	1.50	.60	❑ 16	Ray Allen	.75	.30
❑ 24	Niesa Johnson RC	1.50	.60	❑ 110	Charmin Smith ED RC	1.50	.60	❑ 17	Elton Brand	.50	.20
❑ 25	Rushia Brown	.50	.20	❑ 111	Chantel Tremitiere ED	.50	.20	❑ 18	Caron Butler	.75	.30
❑ 26	Taj McWilliams RC	1.50	.60	❑ 112	Gordana Grubin ED RC	1.50	.60	❑ 19	Drew Gooden	.50	.20
❑ 27	Wendy Palmer	1.00	.40	❑ 113	Kara Wolters ED	.50	.20	❑ 20	Richard Hamilton	.50	.20
❑ 28	Krystyna Lara RC	1.50	.60	❑ 114	Rita Williams ED	.50	.20	❑ 21	Grant Hill	.50	.20
❑ 29	Andrea Lloyd Curry RC	1.50	.60	❑ 115	Stephanie McCarty ED	1.00	.40	❑ 22	Jason Kapono	.50	.20
❑ 30	Carla McGhee	.50	.20	❑ 116	Monica Maxwell ED RC	1.50	.60	❑ 23	Tony Parker	.75	.30
❑ 31	Vicky Bullett	.50	.20	❑ 117	Debbie Black ED	.50	.20	❑ 24	Jalen Rose	.50	.20
❑ 32	Katie Smith	1.50	.60	❑ 118	Elena Baranova ED	1.00	.40	❑ 25	Amare Stoudemire	1.50	.60
❑ 33	Mery Andrade	.50	.20	❑ 119	Sharon Manning ED	.50	.20	❑ 26	Gerald Wallace	.50	.20
❑ 34	Nikki McCray	1.00	.40	❑ 120	Molly Goodenbour ED RC	1.50	.60	❑ 27	Jason Williams	.50	.20
❑ 35	Ruthie Bolton-Holifield	1.50	.60	❑ 121	Alisa Burras ED RC	1.50	.60	❑ 28	LeBron James	5.00	2.00
❑ 36	Tamecka Dixon	.50	.20	❑ 122	Mila Nikolich ED RC	1.50	.60	❑ 29	Jamal Crawford	.50	.20
❑ 37	Tracy Henderson RC	1.50	.60	❑ 123	Jamila Wideman ED	.50	.20	❑ 30	Earl Boykins	.50	.20
❑ 38	Yolanda Griffith	1.50	.60	❑ 124	Michele VanGorp ED	.50	.20	❑ 31	Michael Finley	.75	.30
❑ 39	LaTonya Johnson	.50	.20	❑ 125	Sophia Witherspoon ED	.50	.20	❑ 32	Chris Kaman	.50	.20
❑ 40	Coquese Washington	.50	.20	❑ 126	Tari Phillips ED	.50	.20	❑ 33	Stephon Marbury	.75	.30
❑ 41	Chamique Holdsclaw	3.00	1.25	❑ 127	Sheri Sam SM	.50	.20	❑ 34	Shaquille O'Neal	2.00	.75
❑ 42	Dominique Canty	2.00	.75	❑ 128	Mwadi Mabika SM	.50	.20	❑ 35	Antoine Walker	.75	.30
❑ 43	Kedra Holland-Corn	1.50	.60	❑ 129	Murriel Page SM	.50	.20	❑ 36	Ron Artest	.50	.20
❑ 44	Michele Timms	.50	.20	❑ 130	Latasha Byears SM	.50	.20	❑ 37	Samuel Dalembert	.20	.08
❑ 45	Nykesha Sales	.50	.20	❑ 131	Dominique Canty SM	1.00	.40	❑ 38	Reece Gaines	.50	.20
❑ 46	Shalonda Enis RC	1.50	.60	❑ 132	Crystal Robinson SM	.50	.20	❑ 39	Brian Cardinal	.75	.30
❑ 47	Tamika Whitmore RC	1.50	.60	❑ 133	Cynthia Cooper SM	1.50	.60	❑ 40	Desmond Mason	.50	.20
❑ 48	Tracy Reid	.50	.20	❑ 134	Ruthie Bolton-Holifield SM	1.00	.40	❑ 41	Jason Richardson	.75	.30
❑ 49	Kate Starbird	1.50	.60	❑ 135	Cindy Brown SM	.50	.20	❑ 42	Wally Szczerbiak	.50	.20
❑ 50	Amanda Wilson RC	.50	.20	❑ 136	Kristin Folkl SM	.50	.20	❑ 43	Bonzi Wells	.50	.20
❑ 51	Sonia Chase RC	1.50	.60	❑ 137	Jennifer Gillom SM	.50	.20	❑ 44	Tim Duncan	1.50	.60
❑ 52	Elaine Powell	.50	.20	❑ 138	Adrienne Goodson SM	.50	.20	❑ 45	Lamar Odom	.75	.30
❑ 53	Michelle Edwards	1.00	.40	❑ 139	Vickie Johnson SM	.50	.20	❑ 46	Jermaine O'Neal	.75	.30
❑ 54	Olympia Scott-Richardson	.50	.20	❑ 140	Merlakia Jones SM	.50	.20	❑ 47	Mickael Pietrus	.50	.20
❑ 55	Shannon Johnson	.50	.20	❑ 141	Rebecca Lobo SM	1.00	.40	❑ 48	Zach Randolph	.75	.30
❑ 56	Tammy Jackson	.50	.20	❑ 142	Nikki McCray SM	.50	.20	❑ 49	Joe Smith	.50	.20
❑ 57	Ukari Figgs	.50	.20	❑ 143	Suzie McConnell-Serio SM	.50	.20	❑ 50	Allan Houston	.50	.20
❑ 58	Linda Burgess	.50	.20	❑ 144	DeLisha Milton SM	.50	.20	❑ 51	Carmelo Anthony	1.50	.60
❑ 59	Angie Braziel RC	1.50	.60	❑ 145	Eva Nemcova SM	.50	.20	❑ 52	Manu Ginobili	.75	.30
❑ 60	Tricia Bader RC	1.50	.60	❑ 146	Wendy Palmer SM	.50	.20	❑ 53	Tyronn Lue	.20	.08
❑ 61	Adrienne Johnson	.50	.20	❑ 147	Brandy Reed SM	.50	.20	❑ 54	Tayshaun Prince	.50	.20
❑ 62	Chasity Melvin RC	1.50	.60	❑ 148	Nykesha Sales SM	.50	.20	❑ 55	Luke Ridnour	.50	.20
❑ 63	Korie Hlede	.50	.20	❑ 149	Andrea Stinson SM	.50	.20	❑ 56	Peja Stojakovic	.75	.30
❑ 64	Michelle Griffiths	.50	.20	❑ 150	Michele Timms SM	1.00	.40	❑ 57	Dwyane Wade	2.50	1.00
❑ 65	Penny Moore	.50	.20	❑ 151	Valerie Still SM	.50	.20	❑ 58	David West	.50	.20
❑ 66	Sheri Sam	.50	.20	❑ 152	Andrea Nagy SM	.50	.20	❑ 59	Allen Iverson	1.50	.60
❑ 67	Tangela Smith	.50	.20	❑ 153	Tonya Edwards SM	.50	.20	❑ 60	Richard Jefferson	.50	.20
❑ 68	Val Whiting	.50	.20	❑ 154	Taj McWilliams SM	.50	.20	❑ 61	Andrei Kirilenko	.75	.30
❑ 69	Angie Potthoff	.50	.20	❑ 155	K.Holland-Corn SM	.50	.20	❑ 62	Latrell Sprewell	.50	.20
❑ 70	Cindy Brown	.50	.20	❑ 156	Maria Stepanova SM	.50	.20	❑ 63	Jason Kidd	1.25	.50
❑ 71	Kristin Folkl	.50	.20					❑ 64	Baron Davis	.75	.30
❑ 72	Lisa Leslie	2.00	.75		**2004-05 Skybox Fresh Ink**			❑ 65	Al Harrington	.50	.20
❑ 73	Monica Lamb	.50	.20					❑ 66	Jarvis Hayes	.50	.20
❑ 74	Teresa Weatherspoon	1.50	.60					❑ 67	Gary Payton	.75	.30
❑ 75	Valerie Still RC	1.50	.60					❑ 68	Chris Webber	.75	.30
❑ 76	Tonya Edwards	.50	.20					❑ 69	Vince Carter	2.00	.75
❑ 77	Heather Quella RC	1.50	.60					❑ 70	Eric Williams	.20	.08
❑ 78	Cass Bauer RC	1.50	.60					❑ 71	Nene	.50	.20
❑ 79	Bridget Pettis	.50	.20					❑ 72	Chris Bosh	.75	.30
❑ 80	Cindy Blodgett	.50	.20					❑ 73	Sam Cassell	.75	.30
❑ 81	Janeth Arcain	.50	.20					❑ 74	Mike Dunleavy	.75	.30
❑ 82	Kym Hampton	.50	.20					❑ 75	Steve Francis	.75	.30
❑ 83	Margo Dydek	.50	.20					❑ 76	Antawn Jamison	.75	.30
❑ 84	Murriel Page	.50	.20					❑ 77	Joe Johnson	.50	.20
❑ 85	Sonja Tate	.50	.20					❑ 78	Corey Maggette	.50	.20
❑ 86	Vickie Johnson	.50	.20					❑ 79	Jamaal Magloire	.20	.08
❑ 87	Eva Nemcova	1.00	.40					❑ 80	Kenyon Martin	.75	.30
❑ 88	Charlotte Smith	.50	.20					❑ 81	Reggie Miller	.75	.30
❑ 89	Venus Lacy RC	1.50	.60					❑ 82	Yao Ming	2.00	.75
❑ 90	Polina Tzekova RC	1.50	.60	❑	COMP.SET w/o SP's (90)	40.00	15.00	❑ 83	Dajuan Wagner	.20	.08
❑ 91	Dalma Ivanyi RC	1.50	.60	❑	COMMON CARD (1-90)	.20	.08	❑ 84	Willie Green	.20	.08
❑ 92	Allison Feaster	.50	.20					❑ 85	Shareef Abdur-Rahim	.75	.30

2004-05 Skybox Fresh Ink

86	Tracy McGrady	2.00	.75
87	Carlos Arroyo	1.25	.50
88	Michael Redd	.75	.30
89	Alonzo Mourning	.50	.20
90	Mike Bibby	.75	.30
91	Luke Jackson RC	4.00	1.50
92	Matt Freije RC	4.00	1.50
93	Kevin Martin RC	6.00	2.50
94	Josh Smith RC	8.00	3.00
95	Kris Humphries RC	4.00	1.50
96	Trevor Ariza RC	5.00	2.00
97	Shaun Livingston RC	6.00	2.50
98	Pavel Podkolzin RC	4.00	1.50
99	Kirk Snyder RC	4.00	1.50
100	Beno Udrih RC	6.00	2.50
101	Tony Allen RC	5.00	2.00
102	Chris Duhon RC	6.00	2.50
103	Josh Childress RC	5.00	2.00
104	David Harrison RC	4.00	1.50
105	Al Jefferson RC	10.00	4.00
106	Rafael Araujo RC	4.00	1.50
107	Andre Emmett RC	4.00	1.50
108	Devin Harris RC	6.00	2.50
109	Andre Iguodala RC	10.00	4.00
110	Emeka Okafor RC	15.00	6.00
111	Dorell Wright RC	6.00	2.50
112	Luol Deng RC	8.00	3.00
113	Dwight Howard RC	12.00	5.00
114	J.R. Smith RC	8.00	3.00
115	Sasha Vujacic RC	4.00	1.50
116	Jameer Nelson RC	6.00	2.50
117	Robert Swift RC	4.00	1.50
118	Sebastian Telfair RC	4.00	1.50
119	Andris Biedrins RC	6.00	2.50
120	Ben Gordon RC	15.00	6.00

1999-00 SkyBox Impact

	COMPLETE SET (200)	25.00	12.50
	COMMON CARD (1-200)	.15	.05
	COMMON ROOKIE	.20	.07
1	Tim Duncan	.75	.30
2	Doug Christie	.25	.08
3	Mark Jackson	.25	.08
4	Paul Pierce	.40	.15
5	James Posey RC	.60	.25
6	Steve Smith	.25	.08
7	Charlie Ward	.15	.05
8	Elton Brand RC	1.25	.50
9	Grant Long	.15	.05
10	Grant Hill	.40	.15
11	Christian Laettner	.25	.08
12	Corey Maggette RC	1.00	.40
13	Scot Pollard	.15	.05
14	Robert Traylor	.15	.05
15	Nick Anderson	.15	.05
16	Pat Garrity	.15	.05
17	Hersey Hawkins	.15	.05
18	Troy Hudson	.15	.05
19	Charles Oakley	.15	.05
20	Gary Payton	.40	.15
21	Rik Smits	.25	.08
22	Muggsy Bogues	.25	.08
23	Dale Davis	.15	.05
24	Larry Johnson	.25	.08
25	Antonio McDyess	.25	.08
26	Alonzo Mourning	.25	.08
27	Scottie Pippen	.60	.25
28	Rod Strickland	.15	.05

29	Antoine Walker	.40	.15
30	Allen Iverson	.75	.30
31	Sam Cassell	.40	.15
32	Mookie Blaylock	.15	.05
33	Jim Jackson	.15	.05
34	Brevin Knight	.15	.05
35	Anthony Peeler	.15	.05
36	Bryon Russell	.15	.05
37	Maurice Taylor	.25	.08
38	Elden Campbell	.15	.05
39	Austin Croshere	.25	.08
40	Keith Van Horn	.40	.15
41	Raef LaFrentz	.25	.08
42	Jamal Mashburn	.25	.08
43	Jermaine O'Neal	.40	.15
44	Glenn Robinson	.40	.15
45	Mitch Richmond	.25	.08
46	Keon Clark	.25	.08
47	Derrick Coleman	.15	.05
48	Patrick Ewing	.40	.15
49	Brian Grant	.25	.08
50	Kobe Bryant	1.50	.60
51	Dan Majerle	.25	.08
52	Ruben Patterson	.25	.08
53	Walt Williams	.15	.05
54	Chris Childs	.15	.05
55	Baron Davis RC	2.00	.75
56	Richard Hamilton RC	1.00	.40
57	Voshon Lenard	.15	.05
58	Vernon Maxwell	.15	.05
59	Hakeem Olajuwon	.40	.15
60	Jason Williams	.40	.15
61	Gary Trent	.15	.05
62	Kenny Anderson	.25	.08
63	Shawn Bradley	.15	.05
64	Obinna Ekezie RC	.25	.08
65	Tom Gugliotta	.15	.05
66	Ron Harper	.25	.08
67	Corey Benjamin	.15	.05
68	Donyell Marshall	.25	.08
69	David Robinson	.40	.15
70	Stephon Marbury	.40	.15
71	Marcus Camby	.25	.08
72	Horace Grant	.25	.08
73	Tim Hardaway	.25	.08
74	Greg Foster	.15	.05
75	Cuttino Mobley	.40	.15
76	Rodney Buford RC	.20	.07
77	Clifford Robinson	.15	.05
78	Isaac Austin	.15	.05
79	Robert Pack	.15	.05
80	Eddie Jones	.40	.15
81	Shawn Marion RC	1.25	.50
82	Anthony Mason	.25	.08
83	Oliver Miller	.15	.05
84	Dirk Nowitzki	.75	.30
85	Jayson Williams	.15	.05
86	Brent Barry	.25	.08
87	P.J. Brown	.15	.05
88	Kevin Duckworth	.15	.05
89	Jim McIlvaine	.15	.05
90	Steve Francis RC	1.25	.50
91	Bryant Reeves	.15	.05
92	Jerry Stackhouse	.40	.15
93	Allan Houston	.25	.08
94	Kevin Garnett	.75	.30
95	Karl Malone	.40	.15
96	David Wesley	.15	.05
97	Eddie Robinson RC	.60	.25
98	Ben Wallace	.40	.15
99	Chris Webber	.40	.15
100	Lamar Odom RC	1.00	.40
101	Shandon Anderson	.15	.05
102	Terrell Brandon	.25	.08
103	Jeff Hornacek	.25	.08
104	Terry Mills	.15	.05
105	Tyrone Nesby RC	.15	.05
106	Bo Outlaw	.15	.05
107	Peja Stojakovic	.50	.20
108	Ron Artest RC	.60	.25
109	Tony Battie	.15	.05
110	Cedric Ceballos	.15	.05
111	Anfernee Hardaway	.40	.15
112	Othella Harrington	.15	.05
113	Rick Hughes RC	.20	.07
114	Loy Vaught	.15	.05

115	Malik Rose	.15	.05
116	Vin Baker	.25	.08
117	Charles Barkley	.50	.20
118	Michael Finley	.40	.15
119	Adrian Griffin RC	.30	.10
120	Jason Kidd	.60	.25
121	Gheorghe Muresan	.15	.05
122	Cherokee Parks	.15	.05
123	Glen Rice	.25	.08
124	Bimbo Coles	.15	.05
125	Andrew DeClercq	.15	.05
126	Matt Geiger	.15	.05
127	Bobby Jackson	.25	.08
128	Michael Olowokandi	.25	.08
129	Greg Ostertag	.15	.05
130	Tracy McGrady	1.00	.40
131	Rodney Rogers	.15	.05
132	Juwan Howard	.25	.08
133	Terry Cummings	.15	.05
134	Mario Elie	.15	.05
135	Trajan Langdon RC	.40	.15
136	George Lynch	.15	.05
137	Roshown McLeod	.15	.05
138	Joe Smith	.25	.08
139	John Stockton	.40	.15
140	Ray Allen	.40	.15
141	Vince Carter	1.00	.40
142	Al Harrington	.40	.15
143	Ron Mercer	.25	.08
144	Vitaly Potapenko	.15	.05
145	Arvydas Sabonis	.25	.08
146	Latrell Sprewell	.40	.15
147	Aaron Williams	.15	.05
148	Shareef Abdur-Rahim	.40	.15
149	Vonteego Cummings RC	.15	.05
150	Shaquille O'Neal	1.00	.40
151	Derek Fisher	.40	.15
152	Todd MacCulloch RC	.30	.10
153	Andre Miller RC	1.00	.40
154	Dikembe Mutombo	.25	.08
155	Ervin Johnson	.15	.05
156	Michael Dickerson	.25	.08
157	A.C. Green	.25	.08
158	Kevin Willis	.15	.05
159	Kerry Kittles	.15	.05
160	Damon Stoudamire	.25	.08
161	Eric Snow	.25	.08
162	Bob Sura	.15	.05
163	Jason Terry RC	.60	.25
164	Derek Anderson	.25	.08
165	Randy Brown	.15	.05
166	Vlade Divac	.25	.08
167	Chris Gatling	.15	.05
168	Lindsey Hunter	.15	.05
169	Tim Thomas	.25	.08
170	Antawn Jamison	.60	.25
171	Alan Henderson	.15	.05
172	Larry Hughes	.40	.15
173	Shawn Kemp	.40	.15
174	Radoslav Nesterovic RC	.50	.20
175	Scott Padgett	.25	.08
176	Brian Skinner	.15	.05
177	Jerome Williams	.15	.05
178	Corliss Williamson	.25	.08
179	Sean Elliott	.15	.05
180	Wally Szczerbiak RC	1.00	.40
181	Toni Kukoc	.25	.08
182	Chucky Atkins RC	.40	.15
183	Jalen Rose	.40	.15
184	Nick Van Exel	.40	.15
185	Rasheed Wallace	.40	.15
186	Avery Johnson	.15	.05
187	Jamie Feick RC	.20	.07
188	Adonal Foyle	.15	.05
189	Devean George RC	.50	.20
190	Mike Bibby	.40	.15
191	Lamond Murray	.15	.05
192	Billy Owens	.15	.05
193	Isaiah Rider	.15	.05
194	Darrell Armstrong	.15	.05
195	Antonio Davis	.15	.05
196	Dale Ellis	.15	.05
197	Tim Young RC	.20	.07
198	Roy Rogers	.15	.05
199	Terry Porter	.15	.05
200	Reggie Miller	.40	.15

❏ P141	Vince Carter PROMO	1.50	.60
❏ NNO	V.Carter COMM	12.00	5.00
❏ NNO	V.Carter AU/15		

2003-04 Skybox LE

❏	COMP.SET w/o SP's (110)	30.00	12.50
❏	COMMON CARD (1-110)	.20	.08
❏	COMMON ROOKIE (111-160)	6.00	2.50
❏ 1	Jason Terry	.75	.30
❏ 2	Antoine Walker	.75	.30
❏ 3	Paul Pierce	.75	.30
❏ 4	Eddy Curry	.50	.20
❏ 5	Ricky Davis	.75	.30
❏ 6	Jamal Crawford	.50	.20
❏ 7	Raef LaFrentz	.50	.20
❏ 8	Darius Miles	.75	.30
❏ 9	Ray Allen	.75	.30
❏ 10	Sam Cassell	.75	.30
❏ 11	Andre Miller	.50	.20
❏ 12	Dirk Nowitzki	1.25	.50
❏ 13	Zach Randolph	.75	.30
❏ 14	Tim Duncan	1.50	.60
❏ 15	Gary Payton	.75	.30
❏ 16	Ben Wallace	.75	.30
❏ 17	Michael Finley	.75	.30
❏ 18	David Wesley	.20	.08
❏ 19	Nick Van Exel	.75	.30
❏ 20	Marcus Camby	.50	.20
❏ 21	Gilbert Arenas	.75	.30
❏ 22	Marcus Haislip	.20	.08
❏ 23	Cuttino Mobley	.50	.20
❏ 24	Tayshaun Prince	.50	.20
❏ 25	Chris Webber	.75	.30
❏ 26	Reggie Miller	.75	.30
❏ 27	Chauncey Billups	.50	.20
❏ 28	Quentin Richardson	.50	.20
❏ 29	Mike Dunleavy	.50	.20
❏ 30	Karl Malone	.75	.30
❏ 31	Yao Ming	2.00	.75
❏ 32	Tyson Chandler	.75	.30
❏ 33	Jason Williams	.50	.20
❏ 34	Eddie Griffin	.50	.20
❏ 35	Eddie Jones	.75	.30
❏ 36	Jamaal Tinsley	.75	.30
❏ 37	Michael Redd	.75	.30
❏ 38	Elton Brand	.75	.30
❏ 39	Rashard Lewis	.75	.30
❏ 40	Vince Carter	2.00	.75
❏ 41	Wally Szczerbiak	.50	.20
❏ 42	Chris Wilcox	.50	.20
❏ 43	Kenyon Martin	.75	.30
❏ 44	Shaquille O'Neal	2.00	.75
❏ 45	Baron Davis	.75	.30
❏ 46	Pau Gasol	.75	.30
❏ 47	Dikembe Mutombo	.50	.20
❏ 48	Shane Battier	.75	.30
❏ 49	Drew Gooden	.75	.30
❏ 50	Lamar Odom	.75	.30
❏ 51	Glenn Robinson	.75	.30
❏ 52	Tim Thomas	.50	.20
❏ 53	Shawn Marion	.75	.30
❏ 54	Kevin Garnett	1.50	.60
❏ 55	Stephon Marbury	.75	.30
❏ 56	Rasheed Wallace	.75	.30
❏ 57	Troy Hudson	.20	.08
❏ 58	Mike Bibby	.75	.30
❏ 59	Jason Kidd	1.25	.50
❏ 60	Tony Parker	.75	.30

❏ 61	Andrei Kirilenko	.75	.30
❏ 62	Manu Ginobili	.75	.30
❏ 63	Kerry Kittles	.20	.08
❏ 64	Brent Barry	.50	.20
❏ 65	Allan Houston	.50	.20
❏ 66	Morris Peterson	.50	.20
❏ 67	Tracy McGrady	2.00	.75
❏ 68	Matt Harpring	.75	.30
❏ 69	Erick Dampier	.20	.08
❏ 70	Jerry Stackhouse	.50	.20
❏ 71	John Salmons	.20	.08
❏ 72	Stephen Jackson	.20	.08
❏ 73	Scottie Pippen	1.25	.50
❏ 74	Dajuan Wagner	.50	.20
❏ 75	Keon Clark	.20	.08
❏ 76	Carlos Boozer	.75	.30
❏ 77	Steve Nash	.75	.30
❏ 78	Nene	.50	.20
❏ 79	Keith Van Horn	.75	.30
❏ 80	Earl Boykins	.50	.20
❏ 81	Richard Hamilton	.50	.20
❏ 82	Jason Richardson	.75	.30
❏ 83	Steve Francis	.75	.30
❏ 84	Jermaine O'Neal	.75	.30
❏ 85	Ron Artest	.50	.20
❏ 86	Corey Maggette	.50	.20
❏ 87	Kwame Brown	.75	.30
❏ 88	Kobe Bryant	3.00	1.25
❏ 89	Mike Miller	.75	.30
❏ 90	Caron Butler	.75	.30
❏ 91	Desmond Mason	.50	.20
❏ 92	Latrell Sprewell	.75	.30
❏ 93	Richard Jefferson	.50	.20
❏ 94	Jamal Mashburn	.50	.20
❏ 95	Troy Murphy	.75	.30
❏ 96	Peja Stojakovic	.75	.30
❏ 97	Allen Iverson	1.50	.60
❏ 98	Amare Stoudemire	1.50	.60
❏ 99	Rasho Nesterovic	.50	.20
❏ 100	Bonzi Wells	.50	.20
❏ 101	Bobby Jackson	.50	.20
❏ 102	Anfernee Hardaway	.75	.30
❏ 103	Larry Hughes	.50	.20
❏ 104	Shareef Abdur-Rahim	.75	.30
❏ 105	Hedo Turkoglu	.75	.30
❏ 106	Alvin Williams	.20	.08
❏ 107	Qyntel Woods	.20	.08
❏ 108	Brad Miller	.75	.30
❏ 109	Jalen Rose	.75	.30
❏ 110	Antonio Davis	.20	.08
❏ 111	David West RC	6.00	2.50
❏ 112	Boris Diaw RC	8.00	3.00
❏ 113	Travis Hansen RC	6.00	2.50
❏ 114	Marcus Banks RC	6.00	2.50
❏ 115	Kendrick Perkins RC	6.00	2.50
❏ 116	Darius Songaila RC	6.00	2.50
❏ 117	Kirk Hinrich/99 RC	80.00	40.00
❏ 118	LeBron James/99 RC	750.00	450.00
❏ 119	Jason Kapono RC	6.00	2.50
❏ 120	Josh Howard RC	10.00	4.00
❏ 121	Marquis Daniels RC	12.00	5.00
❏ 122	Carmelo Anthony/99 RC	150.00	75.00
❏ 123	Darko Milicic/99 RC	30.00	12.50
❏ 124	Zaur Pachulia RC	6.00	2.50
❏ 125	Mickael Pietrus RC	6.00	2.50
❏ 126	Ben Handlogten RC	6.00	2.50
❏ 127	James Jones RC	6.00	2.50
❏ 128	Chris Kaman RC	6.00	2.50
❏ 129	Josh Moore RC	6.00	2.50
❏ 130	Brian Cook RC	6.00	2.50
❏ 131	Luke Walton RC	8.00	3.00
❏ 132	Troy Bell RC	6.00	2.50
❏ 133	Dahntay Jones RC	6.00	2.50
❏ 134	Dwyane Wade/99 RC	200.00	100.00
❏ 135	Udonis Haslem RC	6.00	2.50
❏ 136	T.J. Ford/99 RC	60.00	25.00
❏ 137	Ndudi Ebi RC	6.00	2.50
❏ 138	Zoran Planinic RC	6.00	2.50
❏ 139	Raul Lopez	6.00	2.50
❏ 140	Francisco Elson RC	6.00	2.50
❏ 141	Mike Sweetney RC	6.00	2.50
❏ 142	Maciej Lampe RC	6.00	2.50
❏ 143	Slavko Vranes RC	6.00	2.50
❏ 144	Keith Bogans/99 RC	20.00	10.00
❏ 145	Reece Gaines RC	6.00	2.50
❏ 146	Willie Green RC	6.00	2.50

❏ 147	Kyle Korver RC	10.00	4.00
❏ 148	Zarko Cabarkapa RC	6.00	2.50
❏ 149	Leandro Barbosa RC	10.00	4.00
❏ 150	Travis Outlaw RC	6.00	2.50
❏ 151	Curtis Borchardt	6.00	2.50
❏ 152	Alex Garcia RC	6.00	2.50
❏ 153	Richie Frahm RC	6.00	2.50
❏ 154	Nick Collison RC	6.00	2.50
❏ 155	Luke Ridnour/99 RC	60.00	25.00
❏ 156	Chris Bosh/99 RC	150.00	75.00
❏ 157	Aleksandar Pavlovic RC	8.00	3.00
❏ 158	Maurice Williams RC	6.00	2.50
❏ 159	Jarvis Hayes/99 RC	30.00	12.50
❏ 160	Steve Blake RC	6.00	2.50

2004-05 Skybox LE

❏	COMMON CARD (1-75)	.20	.08
❏	COMMON ROOKIE/499	8.00	3.00
❏	COMMON ROOKIE/499	5.00	2.00
❏ 1	Tony Parker	.75	.30
❏ 2	Vince Carter	2.00	.75
❏ 3	Al Harrington	.50	.20
❏ 4	Dwyane Wade	2.50	1.00
❏ 5	Latrell Sprewell	.75	.30
❏ 6	Michael Finley	.75	.30
❏ 7	Caron Butler	.75	.30
❏ 8	Zach Randolph	.75	.30
❏ 9	Peja Stojakovic	.75	.30
❏ 10	Eddy Curry	.50	.20
❏ 11	Allen Iverson	1.50	.60
❏ 12	Kirk Hinrich	.75	.30
❏ 13	Jason Williams	.50	.20
❏ 14	Hedo Turkoglu	.75	.30
❏ 15	Manu Ginobili	.75	.30
❏ 16	Eddie House	.20	.08
❏ 17	Reggie Miller	.75	.30
❏ 18	Steve Francis	.75	.30
❏ 19	LeBron James	5.00	2.00
❏ 20	Dirk Nowitzki	1.25	.50
❏ 21	Stephon Marbury	.75	.30
❏ 22	Ray Allen	.75	.30
❏ 23	Carmelo Anthony	1.50	.60
❏ 24	Lamar Odom	.75	.30
❏ 25	Jamaal Magloire	.50	.20
❏ 26	Shareef Abdur-Rahim	.75	.30
❏ 27	Chris Webber	.75	.30
❏ 28	Jason Richardson	.75	.30
❏ 29	Richard Jefferson	.75	.30
❏ 30	Richard Hamilton	.50	.20
❏ 31	Alonzo Mourning	.75	.30
❏ 32	Chris Bosh	.75	.30
❏ 33	Mike Dunleavy	.50	.20
❏ 34	Andrei Kirilenko	.75	.30
❏ 35	Tracy McGrady	2.00	.75
❏ 36	T.J. Ford	.50	.20
❏ 37	Jason Kidd	1.25	.50
❏ 38	Carlos Arroyo	.50	.20
❏ 39	Rasheed Wallace	.75	.30
❏ 40	Gilbert Arenas	.75	.30
❏ 41	Kenyon Martin	.75	.30
❏ 42	Tim Duncan	1.50	.60
❏ 43	Yao Ming	2.00	.75
❏ 44	Carlos Boozer	.75	.30
❏ 45	Michael Redd	.75	.30
❏ 46	Larry Hughes	.50	.20
❏ 47	Antoine Walker	.75	.30
❏ 48	Kevin Garnett	1.50	.60
❏ 49	Willie Green	.20	.08

❏ 50	Tyson Chandler	.75	.30
❏ 51	Elton Brand	.75	.30
❏ 52	Allan Houston	.50	.20
❏ 53	Shawn Marion	.75	.30
❏ 54	Ricky Davis	.75	.30
❏ 55	Shaquille O'Neal	2.00	.75
❏ 56	Steve Nash	.75	.30
❏ 57	Jarvis Hayes	.50	.20
❏ 58	Zydrunas Ilgauskas	.50	.20
❏ 59	Corey Maggette	.50	.20
❏ 60	Ben Wallace	.75	.30
❏ 61	Darius Miles	.75	.30
❏ 62	Drew Gooden	.50	.20
❏ 63	Pau Gasol	.75	.30
❏ 64	Jamal Crawford	.50	.20
❏ 65	Gary Payton	.75	.30
❏ 66	Jermaine O'Neal	.75	.30
❏ 67	Jason Kapono	.50	.20
❏ 68	Marquis Daniels	.75	.30
❏ 69	Kobe Bryant	3.00	1.25
❏ 70	Baron Davis	.75	.30
❏ 71	Mike Bibby	.75	.30
❏ 72	Rashard Lewis	.75	.30
❏ 73	Paul Pierce	.75	.30
❏ 74	Sam Cassell	.75	.30
❏ 75	Amare Stoudemire	1.50	.60
❏ 76	Dwight Howard/99 RC	25.00	10.00
❏ 77	Emeka Okafor/99 RC	30.00	12.50
❏ 78	Ben Gordon/99 RC	30.00	12.50
❏ 79	Shaun Livingston/99 RC	12.00	5.00
❏ 80	Devin Harris/99 RC	12.00	5.00
❏ 81	Josh Childress/99 RC	10.00	4.00
❏ 82	Luol Deng/99 RC	15.00	6.00
❏ 83	Rafael Araujo/99 RC	8.00	3.00
❏ 84	Andre Iguodala/99 RC	20.00	8.00
❏ 85	Luke Jackson/99 RC	8.00	3.00
❏ 86	Andris Biedrins/99 RC	12.00	5.00
❏ 87	Robert Swift RC	5.00	2.00
❏ 88	Sebastian Telfair/99 RC	6.00	2.50
❏ 89	Kris Humphries RC	5.00	2.00
❏ 90	Al Jefferson RC	12.00	5.00
❏ 91	Kirk Snyder RC	5.00	2.00
❏ 92	Josh Smith/99 RC	15.00	6.00
❏ 93	J.R. Smith/99 RC	15.00	6.00
❏ 94	Dorell Wright RC	8.00	3.00
❏ 95	Jameer Nelson/99 RC		
❏ 96	Pavel Podkolzine RC	5.00	2.00
❏ 97	Nenad Krstic RC	6.00	2.50
❏ 98	Andres Nocioni/99 RC	10.00	4.00
❏ 99	Delonte West RC	10.00	4.00
❏ 100	Tony Allen RC	6.00	2.50
❏ 101	Kevin Martin RC	8.00	3.00
❏ 102	Sasha Vujacic/99 RC	8.00	3.00
❏ 103	Beno Udrih RC	8.00	3.00
❏ 104	David Harrison RC	5.00	2.00
❏ 105	Anderson Varejao/99 RC	10.00	4.00
❏ 106	Jackson Vroman RC	5.00	2.00
❏ 107	Peter John Ramos RC	5.00	2.00
❏ 108	Lionel Chalmers RC	5.00	2.00
❏ 109	Donta Smith RC	5.00	2.00
❏ 110	Andre Emmett RC	5.00	2.00
❏ 111	Antonio Burks RC	5.00	2.00
❏ 112	Royal Ivey RC	5.00	2.00
❏ 113	Chris Duhon/99 RC	12.00	5.00
❏ 114	Erik Daniels RC	5.00	2.00
❏ 115	Justin Reed RC	5.00	2.00
❏ 116	Horace Jenkins RC	5.00	2.00
❏ 117	D.J. Mbenga RC	5.00	2.00
❏ 118	Trevor Ariza RC	6.00	2.50
❏ 119	Tim Pickett RC	5.00	2.00
❏ 120	Bernard Robinson RC	5.00	2.00
❏ 121	Ibrahim Kutluay RC	5.00	2.00
❏ 122	Romain Sato RC	5.00	2.00
❏ 123	Luis Flores RC	5.00	2.00
❏ 124	Damien Wilkins RC	5.00	2.00
❏ 125	Yuta Tabuse/99 RC		

1998-99 SkyBox Molten Metal

❏ COMPLETE SET (150)		80.00	40.00
❏ COMMON CARD (1-100)		.10	.02
❏ COMMON ROOKIE		.60	.25
❏ COMMON CARD (101-130)		.15	.05
❏ COMMON CARD (131-150)		.50	.20
❏ 1	Maurice Taylor	.12	.04

❏ 2	Bison Dele	.10	.02
❏ 3	Anthony Mason	.15	.05
❏ 4	John Starks	.15	.05
❏ 5	Anthony Johnson	.10	.02
❏ 6	Calbert Cheaney	.10	.02
❏ 7	Roshown McLeod RC	.60	.25
❏ 8	Jalen Rose	.25	.08
❏ 9	Kelvin Cato	.10	.02
❏ 10	Walter McCarty	.10	.02
❏ 11	Isaac Austin	.10	.02
❏ 12	Arvydas Sabonis	.15	.05
❏ 13	David Wesley	.10	.02
❏ 14	Jim Jackson	.10	.02
❏ 15	Elden Campbell	.10	.02
❏ 16	Michael Doleac RC	1.25	.50
❏ 17	Chris Webber	.25	.08
❏ 18	Mitch Richmond	.15	.05
❏ 19	Johnny Newman	.10	.02
❏ 20	Jayson Williams	.10	.02
❏ 21	George Lynch	.10	.02
❏ 22	Ron Harper	.15	.05
❏ 23	Donyell Marshall	.15	.05
❏ 24	Derek Fisher	.25	.08
❏ 25	Matt Harpring RC	2.00	.75
❏ 26	Jason Williams RC	5.00	2.00
❏ 27	Toni Kukoc	.15	.05
❏ 28	Clarence Weatherspoon	.10	.02
❏ 29	Eddie Jones	.25	.08
❏ 30	Bo Outlaw	.10	.02
❏ 31	Zydrunas Ilgauskas	.15	.05
❏ 32	Michael Dickerson RC	2.50	1.00
❏ 33	Tyronn Lue RC	1.50	.60
❏ 34	Theo Ratliff	.15	.05
❏ 35	Dirk Nowitzki RC	12.00	6.00
❏ 36	Robert Traylor RC	1.25	.50
❏ 37	Gary Trent	.10	.02
❏ 38	Wesley Person	.10	.02
❏ 39	Bryce Drew RC	1.25	.50
❏ 40	P.J. Brown	.10	.02
❏ 41	Joe Smith	.15	.05
❏ 42	Avery Johnson	.10	.02
❏ 43	Chris Anstey	.10	.02
❏ 44	Mario Elie	.10	.02
❏ 45	Voshon Lenard	.10	.02
❏ 46	Rex Chapman	.10	.02
❏ 47	Hersey Hawkins	.10	.02
❏ 48	Shawn Bradley	.10	.02
❏ 49	Matt Maloney	.10	.02
❏ 50	Dan Majerle	.15	.05
❏ 51	Pat Garrity RC	.75	.30
❏ 52	Sam Perkins	.10	.02
❏ 53	Mookie Blaylock	.10	.02
❏ 54	Al Harrington RC	3.00	1.25
❏ 55	Clifford Robinson	.10	.02
❏ 56	Alan Henderson	.10	.02
❏ 57	Chris Mullin	.25	.08
❏ 58	Dennis Scott	.10	.02
❏ 59	A.C. Green	.15	.05
❏ 60	Tyrone Hill	.10	.02
❏ 61	Chauncey Billups	.15	.05
❏ 62	Michael Finley	.25	.08
❏ 63	Terrell Brandon	.15	.05
❏ 64	Detlef Schrempf	.15	.05
❏ 65	Bonzi Wells RC	5.00	2.00
❏ 66	Larry Johnson	.15	.05
❏ 67	Bryant Reeves	.10	.02
❏ 68	Rael LaFrentz RC	2.00	.75
❏ 69	Kendall Gill	.10	.02

❏ 70	Bryon Russell	.10	.02
❏ 71	Bobby Phills	.10	.02
❏ 72	Tony Delk	.10	.02
❏ 73	Lorenzen Wright	.10	.02
❏ 74	Keon Clark RC	2.00	.75
❏ 75	Billy Owens	.10	.02
❏ 76	Tracy Murray	.10	.02
❏ 77	Bobby Jackson	.15	.05
❏ 78	Sam Cassell	.25	.08
❏ 79	Corliss Williamson	.15	.05
❏ 80	Jeff Hornacek	.15	.05
❏ 81	LaPhonso Ellis	.10	.02
❏ 82	Sam Mitchell	.10	.02
❏ 83	Sean Elliott	.15	.05
❏ 84	John Wallace	.10	.02
❏ 85	Dikembe Mutombo	.15	.05
❏ 86	Rik Smits	.15	.05
❏ 87	Isaiah Rider	.10	.02
❏ 88	Joe Dumars	.25	.08
❏ 89	Allan Houston	.15	.05
❏ 90	Sam Mack	.10	.02
❏ 91	Paul Pierce RC	6.00	2.50
❏ 92	Lamond Murray	.10	.02
❏ 93	Rasheed Wallace	.25	.08
❏ 94	Danny Fortson	.10	.02
❏ 95	Cherokee Parks	.10	.02
❏ 96	Antonio Daniels	.10	.02
❏ 97	Shandon Anderson	.10	.02
❏ 98	Ricky Davis RC	4.00	1.50
❏ 99	Rodney Rogers	.10	.02
❏ 100	Tariq Abdul-Wahad	.15	.05
❏ 101	Glenn Robinson	.20	.07
❏ 102	Ron Mercer	.15	.06
❏ 103	Alonzo Mourning	.20	.07
❏ 104	Marcus Camby	.20	.07
❏ 105	Steve Smith	.20	.07
❏ 106	Tim Hardaway	.20	.07
❏ 107	Rod Strickland	.15	.05
❏ 108	Reggie Miller	.40	.15
❏ 109	Juwan Howard	.20	.07
❏ 110	Hakeem Olajuwon	.40	.15
❏ 111	John Stockton	.25	.08
❏ 112	Antonio McDyess	.20	.07
❏ 113	Charles Barkley	1.00	.40
❏ 114	Karl Malone	.25	.08
❏ 115	Jerry Stackhouse	.40	.15
❏ 116	Tracy McGrady	2.00	.75
❏ 117	Brevin Knight	.15	.05
❏ 118	Gary Payton	.40	.15
❏ 119	Derek Anderson	.30	.12
❏ 120	Glen Rice	.20	.07
❏ 121	David Robinson	.40	.15
❏ 122	Vin Baker	.20	.07
❏ 123	Tom Gugliotta	.15	.05
❏ 124	Patrick Ewing	.40	.15
❏ 125	Ray Allen	.40	.15
❏ 126	Anfernee Hardaway	.40	.15
❏ 127	Jason Kidd	1.25	.50
❏ 128	Kenny Anderson	.20	.07
❏ 129	Kerry Kittles	.15	.05
❏ 130	Tim Thomas	.20	.07
❏ 131	Shareef Abdur-Rahim	1.50	.60
❏ 132	Mike Bibby RC	8.00	3.00
❏ 133	Kobe Bryant	6.00	2.50
❏ 134	Vince Carter RC	15.00	6.00
❏ 135	Tim Duncan	2.50	1.00
❏ 136	Kevin Garnett	3.00	1.25
❏ 137	Grant Hill	.25	.08
❏ 138	Larry Hughes RC	5.00	2.00
❏ 139	Allen Iverson	3.00	1.25
❏ 140	Antawn Jamison RC	8.00	3.00
❏ 141	Michael Jordan	10.00	4.00
❏ 142	Shawn Kemp	1.00	.50
❏ 143	Stephon Marbury	1.50	.60
❏ 144	Michael Olowokandi RC	2.50	1.00
❏ 145	Shaquille O'Neal	4.00	1.50
❏ 146	Scottie Pippen	2.50	1.00
❏ 147	Dennis Rodman	1.00	.50
❏ 148	Damon Stoudamire	1.00	.50
❏ 149	Keith Van Horn	1.50	.60
❏ 150	Antoine Walker	1.50	.60

1998-99 SkyBox Thunder

❏ COMPLETE SET (127)		25.00	10.00
❏ 1	Kerry Kittles	.15	.05
❏ 2	Larry Johnson	.30	.10

☐ 3	Hakeem Olajuwon	.50	.20
☐ 4	Glenn Robinson	.30	.10
☐ 5	Alonzo Mourning	.30	.10
☐ 6	Reggie Miller	.50	.20
☐ 7	Toni Kukoc	.30	.10
☐ 8	Corliss Williamson	.30	.10
☐ 9	Nick Van Exel	.50	.20
☐ 10	Mookie Blaylock	.15	.05
☐ 11	Michael Smith	.15	.05
☐ 12	Avery Johnson	.15	.05
☐ 13	Brian Williams	.15	.05
☐ 14	Doug Christie	.30	.10
☐ 15	Danny Fortson	.15	.05
☐ 16	Michael Stewart	.15	.05
☐ 17	Anthony Peeler	.15	.05
☐ 18	Cedric Henderson	.15	.05
☐ 19	Lamond Murray	.15	.05
☐ 20	Walt Williams	.15	.05
☐ 21	Samaki Walker	.15	.05
☐ 22	David Wesley	.15	.05
☐ 23	Maurice Taylor	.25	.10
☐ 24	Todd Fuller	.15	.05
☐ 25	Jeff Hornacek	.30	.10
☐ 26	Danny Manning	.15	.05
☐ 27	Detlef Schrempf	.30	.10
☐ 28	Nick Anderson	.15	.05
☐ 29	Ron Harper	.30	.10
☐ 30	Brian Shaw	.15	.05
☐ 31	Bryant Stith	.15	.05
☐ 32	Chris Whitney	.15	.05
☐ 33	Patrick Ewing	.50	.20
☐ 34	Travis Knight	.15	.05
☐ 35	Tracy McGrady	1.25	.50
☐ 36	Dan Majerle	.30	.10
☐ 37	Dale Davis	.30	.10
☐ 38	Kelvin Cato	.15	.05
☐ 39	Zydrunas Ilgauskas	.30	.10
☐ 40	Sean Elliott	.30	.10
☐ 41	Tony Delk	.15	.05
☐ 42	Bobby Phills	.15	.05
☐ 43	Clifford Robinson	.15	.05
☐ 44	Shawn Bradley	.15	.05
☐ 45	Aaron McKie	.30	.10
☐ 46	Mark Jackson	.15	.05
☐ 47	P.J. Brown	.15	.05
☐ 48	Armon Gilliam	.15	.05
☐ 49	Erl Gray	.15	.05
☐ 50	Olden Polynice	.15	.05
☐ 51	Kendall Gill	.15	.05
☐ 52	Bryon Russell	.15	.05
☐ 53	Dale Ellis	.15	.05
☐ 54	Mark Price	.30	.10
☐ 55	Donyell Marshall	.30	.10
☐ 56	John Starks	.30	.10
☐ 57	Jerome Williams	.15	.05
☐ 58	Rodney Rogers	.15	.05
☐ 59	Michael Finley	.50	.20
☐ 60	Marcus Camby	.30	.10
☐ 61	Chris Anstey	.15	.05
☐ 62	Rodrick Rhodes	.15	.05
☐ 63	Derek Anderson	.40	.15
☐ 64	Jermaine O'Neal	.50	.20
☐ 65	Glen Rice	.30	.10
☐ 66	Bryant Reeves	.15	.05
☐ 67	Jalen Rose	.50	.20
☐ 68	Calbert Cheaney	.15	.05
☐ 69	Steve Smith	.30	.10
☐ 70	Shandon Anderson	.15	.05
☐ 71	Tony Battie	.15	.05
☐ 72	Kenny Anderson	.30	.10
☐ 73	Tim Hardaway	.30	.10
☐ 74	Antonio Daniels	.15	.05
☐ 75	Charles Barkley	.60	.25
☐ 76	Chauncey Billups	.30	.10
☐ 77	Lindsey Hunter	.15	.05
☐ 78	Terrell Brandon	.30	.10
☐ 79	Anthony Mason	.30	.10
☐ 80	Elden Campbell	.15	.05
☐ 81	Rasheed Wallace	.50	.20
☐ 82	Erick Dampier	.30	.10
☐ 83	Tracy Murray	.15	.05
☐ 84	Sam Cassell	.50	.20
☐ 85	Bobby Jackson	.30	.10
☐ 86	Horace Grant	.30	.10
☐ 87	Brent Price	.15	.05
☐ 88	Allan Houston	.30	.10
☐ 89	Brevin Knight	.15	.05
☐ 90	Steve Nash	.50	.20
☐ 91	Lorenzen Wright	.15	.05
☐ 92	Hubert Davis	.15	.05
☐ 93	Walter McCarty	.15	.05
☐ 94	Jamal Mashburn	.30	.10
☐ 95	Dikembe Mutombo	.30	.10
☐ 96	Chris Carr	.15	.05
☐ 97	Tariq Abdul-Wahad	.15	.05
☐ 98	Chris Mullin	.50	.20
☐ 99	Charlie Ward	.15	.05
☐ 100	Tim Thomas	.30	.10
☐ 101	Tim Duncan	1.00	.40
☐ 102	Antoine Walker	.60	.25
☐ 103	Stephon Marbury	.60	.25
☐ 104*	Ray Allen	.60	.25
☐ 105	Shawn Kemp	.40	.15
☐ 106	Michael Jordan	4.00	1.50
☐ 107	Gary Payton	.60	.25
☐ 108	Kobe Bryant	2.50	1.00
☐ 109	Karl Malone	.60	.25
☐ 110	Kevin Garnett	1.00	.40
☐ 111	Jason Kidd	1.00	.40
☐ 112	Dennis Rodman	.40	.15
☐ 113	Grant Hill	.50	.20
☐ 114	Keith Van Horn	.60	.25
☐ 115	Shareef Abdur-Rahim	.60	.25
☐ 116	Ron Mercer	.30	.12
☐ 117	Allen Iverson	1.25	.50
☐ 118	Shaquille O'Neal	1.50	.60
☐ 119	Anfernee Hardaway	.60	.25
☐ 120	Scottie Pippen	1.00	.40
☐ 121	David Robinson	.60	.25
☐ 122	Vin Baker	.40	.15
☐ 123	John Stockton	.50	.20
☐ 124	Eddie Jones	.60	.25
☐ 125	Juwan Howard	.40	.15
☐ 126	Checklist	.15	.05
☐ 127	Checklist	.15	.05
☐ NNO	Grant Hill SAMPLE		

1994-95 SP

☐	COMPLETE SET (165)	30.00	15.00
☐	COMMON FOIL RC (1-30)	.50	.20
☐	COMMON CARD (31-165)	.15	.05
☐ 1	Glenn Robinson FOIL RC	2.50	1.00
☐ 2	Jason Kidd FOIL RC	8.00	3.00
☐ 3	Grant Hill FOIL RC	5.00	2.00
☐ 4	Donyell Marshall FOIL RC	.75	.30
☐ 5	Juwan Howard FOIL RC	1.50	.60
☐ 6	Sharone Wright FOIL RC	.50	.20
☐ 7	Lamond Murray FOIL RC	.50	.20
☐ 8	Brian Grant FOIL RC	2.00	.75
☐ 9	Eric Montross FOIL RC	.50	.20
☐ 10	Eddie Jones FOIL RC	3.00	1.25
☐ 11	Carlos Rogers FOIL RC	.50	.20
☐ 12	Khalid Reeves FOIL RC	.50	.20
☐ 13	Jalen Rose FOIL RC	3.00	1.25
☐ 14	Eric Piatkowski FOIL RC	.50	.20
☐ 15	Clifford Rozier FOIL RC	.50	.20
☐ 16	Aaron McKie FOIL RC	1.50	.60
☐ 17	Eric Mobley FOIL RC	.50	.20
☐ 18	Tony Dumas FOIL RC	.50	.20
☐ 19	B.J. Tyler FOIL RC	.50	.20
☐ 20	Dickey Simpkins FOIL RC	.50	.20
☐ 21	Bill Curley FOIL RC	.50	.20
☐ 22	Wesley Person FOIL RC	.75	.30
☐ 23	Monty Williams FOIL RC	.50	.20
☐ 24	Greg Minor FOIL RC	.50	.20
☐ 25	Charlie Ward FOIL RC	.50	.20
☐ 26	Brooks Thompson FOIL RC	.50	.20
☐ 27	Trevor Ruffin FOIL RC	.50	.20
☐ 28	Derrick Alston FOIL RC	.50	.20
☐ 29	Michael Smith FOIL RC	.50	.20
☐ 30	Dontonio Wingfield FOIL RC	.50	.20
☐ 31	Stacey Augmon	.15	.05
☐ 32	Steve Smith	.25	.08
☐ 33	Mookie Blaylock	.15	.05
☐ 34	Grant Long	.15	.05
☐ 35	Ken Norman	.15	.05
☐ 36	Dominique Wilkins	.50	.20
☐ 37	Dino Radja	.15	.05
☐ 38	Dee Brown	.15	.05
☐ 39	David Wesley	.15	.05
☐ 40	Rick Fox	.15	.05
☐ 41	Alonzo Mourning	.60	.25
☐ 42	Larry Johnson	.25	.08
☐ 43	Hersey Hawkins	.25	.08
☐ 44	Scott Burrell	.15	.05
☐ 45	Muggsy Bogues	.25	.08
☐ 46	Scottie Pippen	1.50	.60
☐ 47	Toni Kukoc	.75	.30
☐ 48	B.J. Armstrong	.15	.05
☐ 49	Will Perdue	.15	.05
☐ 50	Ron Harper	.25	.08
☐ 51	Mark Price	.15	.05
☐ 52	Tyrone Hill	.15	.05
☐ 53	Chris Mills	.25	.08
☐ 54	John Williams	.15	.05
☐ 55	Bobby Phills	.15	.05
☐ 56	Jim Jackson	.25	.08
☐ 57	Jamal Mashburn	.50	.20
☐ 58	Popeye Jones	.15	.05
☐ 59	Roy Tarpley	.15	.05
☐ 60	Lorenzo Williams	.15	.05
☐ 61	Mahmoud Abdul-Rauf	.15	.05
☐ 62	Rodney Rogers	.15	.05
☐ 63	Bryant Stith	.15	.05
☐ 64	Dikembe Mutombo	.25	.08
☐ 65	Robert Pack	.15	.05
☐ 66	Joe Dumars	.50	.20
☐ 67	Terry Mills	.15	.05
☐ 68	Oliver Miller	.15	.05
☐ 69	Lindsey Hunter	.25	.08
☐ 70	Mark West	.15	.05
☐ 71	Latrell Sprewell	.50	.20
☐ 72	Tim Hardaway	.50	.20
☐ 73	Ricky Pierce	.15	.05
☐ 74	Rony Seikaly	.15	.05
☐ 75	Tom Gugliotta	.25	.08
☐ 76	Hakeem Olajuwon	.75	.30
☐ 77	Clyde Drexler	.50	.20
☐ 78	Vernon Maxwell	.15	.05
☐ 79	Robert Horry	.25	.08
☐ 80	Sam Cassell	.50	.20
☐ 81	Reggie Miller	.50	.20
☐ 82	Rik Smits	.15	.05
☐ 83	Derrick McKey	.15	.05
☐ 84	Mark Jackson	.15	.05
☐ 85	Dale Davis	.15	.05
☐ 86	Loy Vaught	.15	.05
☐ 87	Terry Dehere	.15	.05
☐ 88	Malik Sealy	.15	.05
☐ 89	Pooh Richardson	.15	.05
☐ 90	Tony Massenburg	.15	.05
☐ 91	Cedric Ceballos	.15	.05

❑ 92 Nick Van Exel	.50	.20
❑ 93 George Lynch	.15	.05
❑ 94 Vlade Divac	.15	.05
❑ 95 Elden Campbell	.15	.05
❑ 96 Glen Rice	.25	.08
❑ 97 Kevin Willis	.15	.05
❑ 98 Billy Owens	.15	.05
❑ 99 Bimbo Coles	.15	.05
❑ 100 Harold Miner	.15	.05
❑ 101 Vin Baker	.50	.20
❑ 102 Todd Day	.15	.05
❑ 103 Marty Conlon	.15	.05
❑ 104 Lee Mayberry	.15	.05
❑ 105 Eric Murdock	.15	.05
❑ 106 Isaiah Rider	.25	.08
❑ 107 Doug West	.15	.05
❑ 108 Christian Laettner	.25	.08
❑ 109 Sean Rooks	.15	.05
❑ 110 Stacey King	.15	.05
❑ 111 Derrick Coleman	.25	.08
❑ 112 Kenny Anderson	.25	.08
❑ 113 Chris Morris	.15	.05
❑ 114 Armon Gilliam	.15	.05
❑ 115 Benoit Benjamin	.15	.05
❑ 116 Patrick Ewing	.50	.20
❑ 117 Charles Oakley	.15	.05
❑ 118 John Starks	.15	.05
❑ 119 Derek Harper	.15	.05
❑ 120 Charles Smith	.15	.05
❑ 121 Shaquille O'Neal	2.50	1.00
❑ 122 Anfernee Hardaway	1.25	.50
❑ 123 Nick Anderson	.15	.05
❑ 124 Horace Grant	.25	.08
❑ 125 Donald Royal	.15	.05
❑ 126 Sharone Weatherspoon	.15	.05
❑ 127 Dana Barros	.15	.05
❑ 128 Jeff Malone	.15	.05
❑ 129 Willie Burton	.15	.05
❑ 130 Shawn Bradley	.15	.05
❑ 131 Charles Barkley	.75	.30
❑ 132 Kevin Johnson	.25	.08
❑ 133 Danny Manning	.25	.08
❑ 134 Dan Majerle	.25	.08
❑ 135 A.C. Green	.25	.08
❑ 136 Otis Thorpe	.15	.05
❑ 137 Clifford Robinson	.25	.08
❑ 138 Rod Strickland	.25	.08
❑ 139 Buck Williams	.15	.05
❑ 140 James Robinson	.15	.05
❑ 141 Mitch Richmond	.50	.20
❑ 142 Walt Williams	.15	.05
❑ 143 Olden Polynice	.15	.05
❑ 144 Spud Webb	.15	.05
❑ 145 Duane Causwell	.15	.05
❑ 146 David Robinson	.75	.30
❑ 147 Dennis Rodman	1.00	.40
❑ 148 Sean Elliott	.25	.08
❑ 149 Avery Johnson	.15	.05
❑ 150 J.R. Reid	.15	.05
❑ 151 Shawn Kemp	.75	.30
❑ 152 Gary Payton	.75	.30
❑ 153 Detlef Schrempf	.25	.08
❑ 154 Nate McMillan	.15	.05
❑ 155 Kendall Gill	.25	.08
❑ 156 Karl Malone	.75	.30
❑ 157 John Stockton	.50	.20
❑ 158 Jeff Hornacek	.25	.08
❑ 159 Felton Spencer	.15	.05
❑ 160 David Benoit	.15	.05
❑ 161 Chris Webber	1.25	.50
❑ 162 Rex Chapman	.15	.05
❑ 163 Don MacLean	.15	.05
❑ 164 Calbert Cheaney	.15	.05
❑ 165 Scott Skiles	.15	.05
❑ P23 M.Jordan Promo	10.00	4.00
❑ MJ1R M.Jordan Red	5.00	2.00
❑ MJ1S M.Jordan Silver	15.00	6.00

1995-96 SP

❑ COMPLETE SET (167)	30.00	15.00
❑ 1 Stacey Augmon	.25	.08
❑ 2 Mookie Blaylock	.25	.08
❑ 3 Andrew Lang	.25	.08
❑ 4 Steve Smith	.50	.20
❑ 5 Spud Webb	.50	.20
❑ 6 Dana Barros	.25	.08

❑ 7 Dee Brown	.25	.08
❑ 8 Todd Day	.25	.08
❑ 9 Rick Fox	.50	.20
❑ 10 Eric Montross	.25	.08
❑ 11 Dino Radja	.25	.08
❑ 12 Kenny Anderson	.25	.08
❑ 13 Scott Burrell	.25	.08
❑ 14 Dell Curry	.25	.08
❑ 15 Matt Geiger	.25	.08
❑ 16 Larry Johnson	.50	.20
❑ 17 Glen Rice	.50	.20
❑ 18 Steve Kerr	.50	.20
❑ 19 Toni Kukoc	.50	.20
❑ 20 Luc Longley	.25	.08
❑ 21 Scottie Pippen	1.25	.50
❑ 22 Dennis Rodman	.50	.20
❑ 23 Michael Jordan	5.00	2.50
❑ 24 Terrell Brandon	.50	.20
❑ 25 Michael Cage	.25	.08
❑ 26 Danny Ferry	.25	.08
❑ 27 Chris Mills	.25	.08
❑ 28 Bobby Phills	.25	.08
❑ 29 Tony Dumas	.25	.08
❑ 30 Jim Jackson	.25	.08
❑ 31 Popeye Jones	.25	.08
❑ 32 Jason Kidd	2.50	1.00
❑ 33 Jamal Mashburn	.50	.20
❑ 34 Mahmoud Abdul-Rauf	.25	.08
❑ 35 LaPhonso Ellis	.25	.08
❑ 36 Dikembe Mutombo	.50	.20
❑ 37 Jalen Rose	1.00	.40
❑ 38 Bryant Stith	.25	.08
❑ 39 Joe Dumars	.75	.30
❑ 40 Grant Hill	1.00	.40
❑ 41 Lindsey Hunter	.25	.08
❑ 42 Allan Houston	.50	.20
❑ 43 Otis Thorpe	.25	.08
❑ 44 B.J. Armstrong	.25	.08
❑ 45 Tim Hardaway	.50	.20
❑ 46 Chris Mullin	.75	.30
❑ 47 Latrell Sprewell	.75	.30
❑ 48 Rony Seikaly	.25	.08
❑ 49 Sam Cassell	.75	.30
❑ 50 Clyde Drexler	.75	.30
❑ 51 Robert Horry	.50	.20
❑ 52 Hakeem Olajuwon	.75	.30
❑ 53 Kevin Willis	.25	.08
❑ 54 Dale Davis	.25	.08
❑ 55 Derrick McKey	.25	.08
❑ 56 Reggie Miller	.75	.30
❑ 57 Ricky Pierce	.25	.08
❑ 58 Rik Smits	.50	.20
❑ 59 Lamond Murray	.25	.08
❑ 60 Rodney Rogers	.25	.08
❑ 61 Malik Sealy	.25	.08
❑ 62 Loy Vaught	.25	.08
❑ 63 Brian Williams	.25	.08
❑ 64 Elden Campbell	.25	.08
❑ 65 Cedric Ceballos	.25	.08
❑ 66 Magic Johnson	1.25	.50
❑ 67 Eddie Jones	1.00	.40
❑ 68 Nick Van Exel	.75	.30
❑ 69 Bimbo Coles	.25	.08
❑ 70 Alonzo Mourning	.50	.20
❑ 71 Billy Owens	.25	.08
❑ 72 Kevin Willis	.25	.08
❑ 73 Vin Baker	.50	.20
❑ 74 Benoit Benjamin	.25	.08

❑ 75 Sherman Douglas	.25	.08
❑ 76 Lee Mayberry	.25	.08
❑ 77 Glenn Robinson	.75	.30
❑ 78 Tom Gugliotta	.25	.08
❑ 79 Christian Laettner	.50	.20
❑ 80 Sam Mitchell	.25	.08
❑ 81 Terry Porter	.25	.08
❑ 82 Isaiah Rider	.25	.08
❑ 83 Shawn Bradley	.25	.08
❑ 84 P.J. Brown	.25	.08
❑ 85 Kendall Gill	.25	.08
❑ 86 Armon Gilliam	.25	.08
❑ 87 Jayson Williams	.25	.08
❑ 88 Patrick Ewing	.75	.30
❑ 89 Derek Harper	.50	.20
❑ 90 Anthony Mason	.50	.20
❑ 91 Charles Oakley	.25	.08
❑ 92 John Starks	.50	.20
❑ 93 Nick Anderson	.25	.08
❑ 94 Horace Grant	.50	.20
❑ 95 Anfernee Hardaway	.75	.30
❑ 96 Shaquille O'Neal	2.00	.80
❑ 97 Dennis Scott	.25	.08
❑ 98 Derrick Coleman	.25	.08
❑ 99 Vernon Maxwell	.25	.08
❑ 100 Trevor Ruffin	.25	.08
❑ 101 Clarence Weatherspoon	.25	.08
❑ 102 Sharone Wright	.25	.08
❑ 103 Charles Barkley	1.00	.40
❑ 104 A.C. Green	.50	.20
❑ 105 Kevin Johnson	.50	.20
❑ 106 Wesley Person	.25	.08
❑ 107 John Williams	.25	.08
❑ 108 Chris Dudley	.25	.08
❑ 109 Harvey Grant	.25	.08
❑ 110 Aaron McKie	.25	.08
❑ 111 Clifford Robinson	.25	.08
❑ 112 Rod Strickland	.25	.08
❑ 113 Brian Grant	.75	.30
❑ 114 Sarunas Marciulionis	.25	.08
❑ 115 Olden Polynice	.25	.08
❑ 116 Mitch Richmond	.50	.20
❑ 117 Walt Williams	.25	.08
❑ 118 Vinny Del Negro	.25	.08
❑ 119 Sean Elliott	.50	.20
❑ 120 Avery Johnson	.25	.08
❑ 121 Chuck Person	.25	.08
❑ 122 David Robinson	.75	.30
❑ 123 Hersey Hawkins	.25	.08
❑ 124 Shawn Kemp	.50	.20
❑ 125 Gary Payton	.75	.30
❑ 126 Sam Perkins	.50	.20
❑ 127 Detlef Schrempf	.50	.20
❑ 128 Oliver Miller	.25	.08
❑ 129 Tracy Murray	.25	.08
❑ 130 Ed Pinckney	.25	.08
❑ 131 Alvin Robertson	.25	.08
❑ 132 Zan Tabak	.25	.08
❑ 133 Jeff Hornacek	.50	.20
❑ 134 Adam Keefe	.25	.08
❑ 135 Karl Malone	1.00	.40
❑ 136 Chris Morris	.25	.08
❑ 137 John Stockton	1.00	.40
❑ 138 Greg Anthony	.25	.08
❑ 139 Blue Edwards	.25	.08
❑ 140 Kenny Gattison	.25	.08
❑ 141 Chris King	.25	.08
❑ 142 Byron Scott	.25	.08
❑ 143 Calbert Cheaney	.25	.08
❑ 144 Juwan Howard	.75	.30
❑ 145 Gheorghe Muresan	.25	.08
❑ 146 Robert Pack	.25	.08
❑ 147 Chris Webber	1.00	.40
❑ 148 Alan Henderson RC	.75	.30
❑ 149 Eric Williams RC	.50	.20
❑ 150 George Zidek RC	.25	.08
❑ 151 Bob Sura RC	.50	.20
❑ 152 Antonio McDyess RC	1.50	.60
❑ 153 Theo Ratliff RC	1.00	.40
❑ 154 Joe Smith RC	1.25	.50
❑ 155 Brent Barry RC	.75	.30
❑ 156 Sasha Danilovic RC	.25	.08
❑ 157 Kurt Thomas RC	.50	.20
❑ 158 Shawn Respert RC	.25	.08
❑ 159 Kevin Garnett RC	12.00	5.00
❑ 160 Ed O'Bannon RC	.25	.08

❏ 161 Jerry Stackhouse RC	5.00	2.00
❏ 162 Michael Finley RC	2.50	1.00
❏ 163 Arvydas Sabonis RC	1.00	.40
❏ 164 Cory Alexander RC	.25	.08
❏ 165 Damon Stoudamire RC	1.50	.60
❏ 166 Bryant Reeves RC	.75	.30
❏ 167 Rasheed Wallace RC	2.50	1.00
❏ C1 H.Olajuwon Comm.	12.00	5.00
❏ P23 Michael Jordan Promo	10.00	4.00

1996-97 SP

❏ COMPLETE SET (146)	35.00	17.50
❏ COMMON CARD (1-126)	.25	.08
❏ COMMON ROOKIE (127-146)	.25	.08
❏ 1 Mookie Blaylock	.25	.08
❏ 2 Christian Laettner	.50	.20
❏ 3 Dikembe Mutombo	.50	.20
❏ 4 Steve Smith	.50	.20
❏ 5 Dana Barros	.25	.08
❏ 6 Rick Fox	.25	.08
❏ 7 Dino Radja	.25	.08
❏ 8 Eric Williams	.25	.08
❏ 9 Dell Curry	.25	.08
❏ 10 Vlade Divac	.25	.08
❏ 11 Anthony Mason	.50	.20
❏ 12 Glen Rice	.50	.20
❏ 13 Scottie Pippen	1.25	.50
❏ 14 Toni Kukoc	.50	.20
❏ 15 Luc Longley	.25	.08
❏ 16 Michael Jordan	5.00	2.00
❏ 17 Dennis Rodman	.50	.20
❏ 18 Terrell Brandon	.25	.08
❏ 19 Tyrone Hill	.25	.08
❏ 20 Bobby Phills	.25	.08
❏ 21 Bob Sura	.25	.08
❏ 22 Chris Gatling	.25	.08
❏ 23 Jim Jackson	.25	.08
❏ 24 Sam Cassell	.75	.30
❏ 25 Jamal Mashburn	.50	.20
❏ 26 Dale Ellis	.25	.08
❏ 27 LaPhonso Ellis	.25	.08
❏ 28 Mark Jackson	.25	.08
❏ 29 Antonio McDyess	.50	.20
❏ 30 Bryant Stith	.25	.08
❏ 31 Joe Dumars	.75	.30
❏ 32 Grant Hill	.75	.30
❏ 33 Lindsey Hunter	.25	.08
❏ 34 Otis Thorpe	.25	.08
❏ 35 Chris Mullin	.75	.30
❏ 36 Mark Price	.50	.20
❏ 37 Joe Smith	.50	.20
❏ 38 Latrell Sprewell	.75	.30
❏ 39 Charles Barkley	1.00	.40
❏ 40 Clyde Drexler	.75	.30
❏ 41 Mario Elie	.25	.08
❏ 42 Hakeem Olajuwon	.75	.30
❏ 43 Travis Best	.25	.08
❏ 44 Dale Davis	.25	.08
❏ 45 Reggie Miller	.75	.30
❏ 46 Rik Smits	.50	.20
❏ 47 Pooh Richardson	.25	.08
❏ 48 Rodney Rogers	.25	.08
❏ 49 Malik Sealy	.25	.08
❏ 50 Loy Vaught	.25	.08
❏ 51 Elden Campbell	.25	.08
❏ 52 Robert Horry	.50	.20
❏ 53 Eddie Jones	.75	.30
❏ 54 Shaquille O'Neal	2.00	.75
❏ 55 Nick Van Exel	.75	.30
❏ 56 Sasha Danilovic	.25	.08
❏ 57 Tim Hardaway	.50	.20
❏ 58 Dan Majerle	.50	.20
❏ 59 Alonzo Mourning	.50	.20
❏ 60 Vin Baker	.50	.20
❏ 61 Sherman Douglas	.25	.08
❏ 62 Armon Gilliam	.25	.08
❏ 63 Glenn Robinson	.75	.30
❏ 64 Kevin Garnett	1.50	.60
❏ 65 Terry Porter	.25	.08
❏ 66 Tom Gugliotta	.25	.08
❏ 67 Doug West	.25	.08
❏ 68 Shawn Bradley	.25	.08
❏ 69 Kendall Gill	.25	.08
❏ 70 Robert Pack	.25	.08
❏ 71 Jayson Williams	.50	.20
❏ 72 Chris Childs	.25	.08
❏ 73 Patrick Ewing	.75	.30
❏ 74 Allan Houston	.50	.20
❏ 75 Larry Johnson	.50	.20
❏ 76 John Starks	.50	.20
❏ 77 Nick Anderson	.25	.08
❏ 78 Horace Grant	.50	.20
❏ 79 Anfernee Hardaway	.75	.30
❏ 80 Dennis Scott	.25	.08
❏ 81 Derrick Coleman	.25	.08
❏ 82 Mark Davis	.25	.08
❏ 83 Jerry Stackhouse	1.00	.40
❏ 84 Clarence Weatherspoon	.25	.08
❏ 85 Cedric Ceballos	.25	.08
❏ 86 Kevin Johnson	.50	.20
❏ 87 Jason Kidd	1.25	.50
❏ 88 Danny Manning	.50	.20
❏ 89 Wesley Person	.25	.08
❏ 90 Kenny Anderson	.25	.08
❏ 91 Isaiah Rider	.50	.20
❏ 92 Clifford Robinson	.25	.08
❏ 93 Arvydas Sabonis	.50	.20
❏ 94 Rasheed Wallace	1.00	.40
❏ 95 Mahmoud Abdul-Rauf	.25	.08
❏ 96 Brian Grant	.75	.30
❏ 97 Olden Polynice	.25	.08
❏ 98 Mitch Richmond	.75	.30
❏ 99 Corliss Williamson	.50	.20
❏ 100 Sean Elliott	.25	.08
❏ 101 Avery Johnson	.25	.08
❏ 102 David Robinson	.75	.30
❏ 103 Dominique Wilkins	.75	.30
❏ 104 Hersey Hawkins	.25	.08
❏ 105 Jim McIlvaine	.25	.08
❏ 106 Shawn Kemp	.50	.20
❏ 107 Gary Payton	.75	.30
❏ 108 Detlef Schrempf	.50	.20
❏ 109 Doug Christie	.25	.08
❏ 110 Popeye Jones	.25	.08
❏ 111 Damon Stoudamire	.75	.30
❏ 112 Walt Williams	.25	.08
❏ 113 Jeff Hornacek	.50	.20
❏ 114 Karl Malone	.75	.30
❏ 115 Greg Ostertag	.25	.08
❏ 116 Bryon Russell	.25	.08
❏ 117 John Stockton	.75	.30
❏ 118 Greg Anthony	.25	.08
❏ 119 Blue Edwards	.25	.08
❏ 120 Anthony Peeler	.25	.08
❏ 121 Bryant Reeves	.25	.08
❏ 122 Calbert Cheaney	.25	.08
❏ 123 Juwan Howard	.50	.20
❏ 124 Gheorghe Muresan	.25	.08
❏ 125 Rod Strickland	.25	.08
❏ 126 Chris Webber	.75	.30
❏ 127 Antoine Walker RC	4.00	1.50
❏ 128 Tony Delk RC	.75	.30
❏ 129 Vitaly Potapenko RC	.75	.30
❏ 130 Samaki Walker RC	.75	.30
❏ 131 Todd Fuller RC	.75	.30
❏ 132 Erick Dampier RC	.75	.30
❏ 133 Lorenzen Wright RC	.75	.30
❏ 134 Kobe Bryant RC	20.00	8.00
❏ 135 Derek Fisher RC	1.50	.60
❏ 136 Ray Allen RC	5.00	2.00
❏ 137 Stephon Marbury RC	3.00	1.25
❏ 138 Kerry Kittles RC	.75	.30
❏ 139 Walter McCarty RC	.75	.30
❏ 140 John Wallace RC	.75	.30
❏ 141 Allen Iverson RC	10.00	4.00
❏ 142 Steve Nash RC	12.00	5.00
❏ 143 Jermaine O'Neal RC	5.00	2.00
❏ 144 Marcus Camby RC	1.50	.60
❏ 145 Shareef Abdur-Rahim RC	4.00	1.50
❏ 146 Roy Rogers RC	.75	.30
❏ S16 M.Jordan Sample	5.00	2.00

1997-98 SP Authentic

❏ COMPLETE SET (176)	120.00	60.00
❏ COMMON CARD (1-176)	.40	.15
❏ COMMON ROOKIE	.75	.30
❏ 1 Steve Smith	.75	.30
❏ 2 Dikembe Mutombo	.75	.30
❏ 3 Christian Laettner	.75	.30
❏ 4 Mookie Blaylock	.40	.15
❏ 5 Alan Henderson	.40	.15
❏ 6 Antoine Walker	1.50	.60
❏ 7 Ron Mercer	3.00	1.25
❏ 8 Walter McCarty	.40	.15
❏ 9 Kenny Anderson	.75	.30
❏ 10 Travis Knight	.40	.15
❏ 11 Dana Barros	.40	.15
❏ 12 Glen Rice	.75	.30
❏ 13 Vlade Divac	.75	.30
❏ 14 Dell Curry	.40	.15
❏ 15 David Wesley	.40	.15
❏ 16 Bobby Phills	.40	.15
❏ 17 Anthony Mason	.75	.30
❏ 18 Toni Kukoc	.75	.30
❏ 19 Dennis Rodman	.75	.30
❏ 20 Ron Harper	.40	.15
❏ 21 Steve Kerr	.75	.30
❏ 22 Scottie Pippen	2.00	.75
❏ 23 Michael Jordan	8.00	4.00
❏ 24 Shawn Kemp	.75	.30
❏ 25 Wesley Person	.40	.15
❏ 26 Derek Anderson RC	4.00	1.50
❏ 27 Zydrunas Ilgauskas	.75	.30
❏ 28 Brevin Knight RC	1.50	.60
❏ 29 Michael Finley	1.25	.50
❏ 30 Shawn Bradley	.40	.15
❏ 31 A.C. Green	.75	.30
❏ 32 Hubert Davis	.40	.15
❏ 33 Dennis Scott	.40	.15
❏ 34 Tony Battie RC	1.50	.60
❏ 35 Bobby Jackson RC	8.00	3.00
❏ 36 LaPhonso Ellis	.40	.15
❏ 37 Bryant Stith	.40	.15
❏ 38 Dean Garrett	.40	.15
❏ 39 Danny Fortson RC	4.00	1.50
❏ 40 Grant Hill	1.25	.50
❏ 41 Brian Williams	.40	.15
❏ 42 Lindsey Hunter	.40	.15
❏ 43 Malik Sealy	.40	.15
❏ 44 Jerry Stackhouse	1.25	.50
❏ 45 Muggsy Bogues	.75	.30
❏ 46 Joe Smith	.75	.30
❏ 47 Donyell Marshall	.75	.30
❏ 48 Erick Dampier	.75	.30
❏ 49 Bimbo Coles	.40	.15
❏ 50 Charles Barkley	1.50	.60
❏ 51 Hakeem Olajuwon	1.25	.50
❏ 52 Clyde Drexler	1.25	.50
❏ 53 Kevin Willis	.75	.30
❏ 54 Mario Elie	.40	.15
❏ 55 Reggie Miller	1.25	.50
❏ 56 Rik Smits	.75	.30

❑ 57 Chris Mullin	1.25	.50
❑ 58 Antonio Davis	.40	.15
❑ 59 Dale Davis	.40	.15
❑ 60 Mark Jackson	.75	.30
❑ 61 Brent Barry	.75	.30
❑ 62 Loy Vaught	.40	.15
❑ 63 Rodney Rogers	.40	.15
❑ 64 Lamond Murray	.40	.15
❑ 65 Maurice Taylor RC	3.00	1.25
❑ 66 Shaquille O'Neal	3.00	1.25
❑ 67 Eddie Jones	1.25	.50
❑ 68 Kobe Bryant	5.00	2.00
❑ 69 Nick Van Exel	1.25	.50
❑ 70 Robert Horry	.75	.30
❑ 71 Tim Hardaway	.75	.30
❑ 72 Jamal Mashburn	.75	.30
❑ 73 Alonzo Mourning	.75	.30
❑ 74 Isaac Austin	.40	.15
❑ 75 P.J. Brown	.40	.15
❑ 76 Ray Allen	1.25	.50
❑ 77 Glenn Robinson	1.25	.50
❑ 78 Ervin Johnson	.40	.15
❑ 79 Terrell Brandon	.75	.30
❑ 80 Tyrone Hill	.40	.15
❑ 81 Stephon Marbury	1.50	.60
❑ 82 Kevin Garnett	2.50	1.00
❑ 83 Tom Gugliotta	.75	.30
❑ 84 Chris Carr	.40	.15
❑ 85 Cherokee Parks	.40	.15
❑ 86 Sam Cassell	1.25	.50
❑ 87 Chris Gatling	.40	.15
❑ 88 Kendall Gill	.40	.15
❑ 89 Keith Van Horn RC	4.00	1.50
❑ 90 Jayson Williams	.40	.15
❑ 91 Kerry Kittles	1.25	.50
❑ 92 Patrick Ewing	1.25	.50
❑ 93 Larry Johnson	.75	.30
❑ 94 Chris Childs	.40	.15
❑ 95 John Starks	.75	.30
❑ 96 Charles Oakley	.75	.30
❑ 97 Allan Houston	.75	.30
❑ 98 Mark Price	.75	.30
❑ 99 Anfernee Hardaway	1.25	.50
❑ 100 Rony Seikaly	.40	.15
❑ 101 Horace Grant	.75	.30
❑ 102 Bo Outlaw	.40	.15
❑ 103 Clarence Weatherspoon	.40	.15
❑ 104 Allen Iverson	3.00	1.25
❑ 105 Jim Jackson	.40	.15
❑ 106 Theo Ratliff	.40	.15
❑ 107 Tim Thomas RC	8.00	3.00
❑ 108 Danny Manning	.75	.30
❑ 109 Jason Kidd	2.00	.75
❑ 110 Kevin Johnson	.75	.30
❑ 111 Rex Chapman	.40	.15
❑ 112 Clifford Robinson	.40	.15
❑ 113 Antonio McDyess	.75	.30
❑ 114 Damon Stoudamire	.75	.30
❑ 115 Isaiah Rider	.75	.30
❑ 116 Arvydas Sabonis	.75	.30
❑ 117 Rasheed Wallace	1.25	.50
❑ 118 Brian Grant	.75	.30
❑ 119 Gary Trent	.40	.15
❑ 120 Mitch Richmond	.75	.30
❑ 121 Corliss Williamson	.75	.30
❑ 122 Lawrence Funderburke RC	1.00	.40
❑ 123 Olden Polynice	.40	.15
❑ 124 Billy Owens	.40	.15
❑ 125 Avery Johnson	.40	.15
❑ 126 Sean Elliott	.75	.30
❑ 127 David Robinson	1.25	.50
❑ 128 Tim Duncan RC !	25.00	10.00
❑ 129 Jaren Jackson	.40	.15
❑ 130 Detlef Schrempf	.75	.30
❑ 131 Gary Payton	1.25	.50
❑ 132 Vin Baker	.75	.30
❑ 133 Hersey Hawkins	.40	.15
❑ 134 Dale Ellis	.40	.15
❑ 135 Sam Perkins	.40	.15
❑ 136 Marcus Camby	1.25	.50
❑ 137 John Wallace	.40	.15
❑ 138 Doug Christie	.75	.30
❑ 139 Chauncey Billups RC	10.00	4.00
❑ 140 Walt Williams	.40	.15
❑ 141 Karl Malone	1.25	.50
❑ 142 Bryon Russell	.40	.15

❑ 143 Jeff Hornacek	.75	.30
❑ 144 Greg Ostertag	.40	.15
❑ 145 John Stockton	1.25	.50
❑ 146 Shandon Anderson	.40	.15
❑ 147 Shareef Abdur-Rahim	2.00	.75
❑ 148 Bryant Reeves	.40	.15
❑ 149 Antonio Daniels RC	1.50	.60
❑ 150 Otis Thorpe	.40	.15
❑ 151 Blue Edwards	.40	.15
❑ 152 Chris Webber	1.25	.50
❑ 153 Juwan Howard	.75	.30
❑ 154 Rod Strickland	.40	.15
❑ 155 Calbert Cheaney	.40	.15
❑ 156 Tracy Murray	.40	.15
❑ 157 Chauncey Billups FW	1.00	.40
❑ 158 Ed Gray FW RC	.75	.30
❑ 159 Tony Battie FW	1.00	.40
❑ 160 Keith Van Horn FW	2.00	.75
❑ 161 Cedric Henderson FW RC	1.00	.40
❑ 162 Kelvin Cato FW RC	1.50	.60
❑ 163 Tariq Abdul-Wahad FW RC	1.00	.40
❑ 164 Derek Anderson FW	1.25	.50
❑ 165 Tim Duncan FW	5.00	2.00
❑ 166 Tracy McGrady FW RC !	50.00	20.00
❑ 167 Ron Mercer FW	1.25	.50
❑ 168 Bobby Jackson FW	.75	.30
❑ 169 Antonio Daniels FW	1.00	.40
❑ 170 Zydrunas Ilgauskas FW	.75	.30
❑ 171 Maurice Taylor FW	.75	.30
❑ 172 Tim Thomas FW	2.00	.75
❑ 173 Brevin Knight FW	.75	.30
❑ 174 Lawrence Funderburke FW	.75	.30
❑ 175 Jacque Vaughn FW RC	1.00	.40
❑ 176 Danny Fortson FW	.75	.30
❑ SPA23 M.Jordan Promo	6.00	2.50

1998-99 SP Authentic

❑ COMPLETE SET w/o RC (90)	40.00	20.00
❑ COMMON MJ (1-10)	3.00	1.25
❑ COMMON CARD (11-90)	.30	.10
❑ COMMON ROOKIE (91-120)	4.00	1.50
❑ 1 Michael Jordan	3.00	1.25
❑ 2 Michael Jordan	3.00	1.25
❑ 3 Michael Jordan	3.00	1.25
❑ 4 Michael Jordan	3.00	1.25
❑ 5 Michael Jordan	3.00	1.25
❑ 6 Michael Jordan	3.00	1.25
❑ 7 Michael Jordan	3.00	1.25
❑ 8 Michael Jordan	3.00	1.25
❑ 9 Michael Jordan	3.00	1.25
❑ 10 Michael Jordan	3.00	1.25
❑ 11 Steve Smith	.60	.25
❑ 12 Dikembe Mutombo	.60	.25
❑ 13 Alan Henderson	.30	.10
❑ 14 Antoine Walker	1.00	.40
❑ 15 Ron Mercer	.50	.20
❑ 16 Kenny Anderson	.60	.25
❑ 17 Derrick Coleman	.30	.10
❑ 18 David Wesley	.30	.10
❑ 19 Glen Rice	.60	.25
❑ 20 Toni Kukoc	.60	.25
❑ 21 Ron Harper	.60	.25
❑ 22 Brent Barry	.60	.25
❑ 23 Shawn Kemp	.60	.25
❑ 24 Zydrunas Ilgauskas	.30	.10
❑ 25 Brevin Knight	.30	.10
❑ 26 Michael Finley	1.00	.40
❑ 27 Steve Nash	1.00	.40

❑ 28 Cedric Ceballos	.30	.10
❑ 29 Antonio McDyess	.60	.25
❑ 30 Nick Van Exel	1.00	.40
❑ 31 Grant Hill	1.00	.40
❑ 32 Jerry Stackhouse	1.00	.40
❑ 33 Bison Dele	.30	.10
❑ 34 John Starks	.60	.25
❑ 35 Chris Mills	.30	.10
❑ 36 Hakeem Olajuwon	1.00	.40
❑ 37 Charles Barkley	1.25	.50
❑ 38 Scottie Pippen	1.50	.60
❑ 39 Reggie Miller	1.00	.40
❑ 40 Chris Mullin	1.00	.40
❑ 41 Rik Smits	.60	.25
❑ 42 Lamond Murray	.30	.10
❑ 43 Maurice Taylor	.50	.20
❑ 44 Kobe Bryant	4.00	1.50
❑ 45 Dennis Rodman	.60	.25
❑ 46 Shaquille O'Neal	2.50	1.00
❑ 47 Alonzo Mourning	.60	.25
❑ 48 Tim Hardaway	.60	.25
❑ 49 Jamal Mashburn	.60	.25
❑ 50 Ray Allen	1.00	.40
❑ 51 Glenn Robinson	.60	.25
❑ 52 Terrell Brandon	.60	.25
❑ 53 Kevin Garnett	2.00	.75
❑ 54 Stephon Marbury	.60	.25
❑ 55 Joe Smith	.60	.25
❑ 56 Keith Van Horn	1.00	.40
❑ 57 Kendall Gill	.30	.10
❑ 58 Jayson Williams	.30	.10
❑ 59 Patrick Ewing	1.00	.40
❑ 60 Allan Houston	.60	.25
❑ 61 Larry Johnson	.60	.25
❑ 62 Anfernee Hardaway	1.00	.40
❑ 63 Horace Grant	.60	.25
❑ 64 Allen Iverson	2.00	.75
❑ 65 Tim Thomas	.60	.25
❑ 66 Jason Kidd	1.50	.60
❑ 67 Tom Gugliotta	.30	.10
❑ 68 Rex Chapman	.30	.10
❑ 69 Damon Stoudamire	.60	.25
❑ 70 Isaiah Rider	.30	.10
❑ 71 Rasheed Wallace	1.00	.40
❑ 72 Chris Webber	1.00	.40
❑ 73 Vlade Divac	.60	.25
❑ 74 Corliss Williamson	.60	.25
❑ 75 Tim Duncan	1.50	.60
❑ 76 David Robinson	1.00	.40
❑ 77 Sean Elliott	.30	.10
❑ 78 Detlef Schrempf	.60	.25
❑ 79 Vin Baker	.60	.25
❑ 80 Gary Payton	1.00	.40
❑ 81 Doug Christie	.60	.25
❑ 82 Tracy McGrady	2.50	1.00
❑ 83 Karl Malone	1.00	.40
❑ 84 John Stockton	1.00	.40
❑ 85 Jeff Hornacek	.30	.10
❑ 86 Shareef Abdur-Rahim	1.00	.40
❑ 87 Bryant Reeves	.30	.10
❑ 88 Juwan Howard	.60	.25
❑ 89 Mitch Richmond	.60	.25
❑ 90 Rod Strickland	.30	.10
❑ 91 Michael Olowokandi RC	6.00	2.50
❑ 92 Mike Bibby RC	30.00	12.50
❑ 93 Raef LaFrentz RC	12.00	5.00
❑ 94 Antawn Jamison RC	40.00	15.00
❑ 95 Vince Carter RC	100.00	50.00
❑ 96 Robert Traylor RC	5.00	2.00
❑ 97 Jason Williams RC	30.00	12.50
❑ 98 Larry Hughes RC	25.00	10.00
❑ 99 Dirk Nowitzki RC	60.00	25.00
❑ 100 Paul Pierce RC	40.00	15.00
❑ 101 Bonzi Wells RC	30.00	12.50
❑ 102 Michael Doleac RC	5.00	2.00
❑ 103 Keon Clark RC	15.00	6.00
❑ 104 Michael Dickerson RC	12.00	5.00
❑ 105 Matt Harpring RC	6.00	2.50
❑ 106 Bryce Drew RC	5.00	2.00
❑ 107 Pat Garrity RC	6.00	2.50
❑ 108 Roshown McLeod RC	6.00	2.50
❑ 109 Ricky Davis RC	20.00	8.00
❑ 110 Brian Skinner RC	5.00	2.00
❑ 111 Tyronn Lue RC	6.00	2.50
❑ 112 Felipe Lopez RC	6.00	2.50
❑ 113 Al Harrington RC	25.00	10.00

☐ 114	Sam Jacobson RC	4.00	1.50
☐ 115	Cory Carr RC	4.00	1.50
☐ 116	Corey Benjamin RC	6.00	2.50
☐ 117	Nazr Mohammed RC	6.00	2.50
☐ 118	Rashard Lewis RC	40.00	15.00
☐ 119	Peja Stojakovic RC	50.00	20.00
☐ 120	Andrae Patterson RC	4.00	1.50
☐ 23P	Michael Jordan PROMO	5.00	2.00

1999-00 SP Authentic

☐ COMPLETE SET w/o RC (90)		30.00	15.00
☐ COMMON CARD (1-90)		.30	.10
☐ COMMON ROOKIE (91-135)		10.00	4.00
☐ 1	Dikembe Mutombo	.60	.25
☐ 2	Jim Jackson	.30	.10
☐ 3	Alan Henderson	.30	.10
☐ 4	Antoine Walker	1.00	.40
☐ 5	Paul Pierce	1.00	.40
☐ 6	Kenny Anderson	.60	.25
☐ 7	Eddie Jones	1.00	.40
☐ 8	Derrick Coleman	.60	.25
☐ 9	Anthony Mason	.60	.25
☐ 10	Chris Carr	.30	.10
☐ 11	Hersey Hawkins	.60	.25
☐ 12	B.J. Armstrong	.30	.10
☐ 13	Shawn Kemp	.60	.25
☐ 14	Bob Sura	.30	.10
☐ 15	Lamond Murray	.30	.10
☐ 16	Michael Finley	1.00	.40
☐ 17	Cedric Ceballos	.30	.10
☐ 18	Dirk Nowitzki	2.00	.75
☐ 19	Erick Strickland	.30	.10
☐ 20	Antonio McDyess	.60	.25
☐ 21	Nick Van Exel	1.00	.40
☐ 22	Grant Hill	1.00	.40
☐ 23	Jerry Stackhouse	1.00	.40
☐ 24	Lindsey Hunter	.30	.10
☐ 25	Christian Laettner	.60	.25
☐ 26	Antawn Jamison	1.50	.60
☐ 27	Chris Mills	.30	.10
☐ 28	Larry Hughes	1.00	.40
☐ 29	Charles Barkley	1.25	.50
☐ 30	Hakeem Olajuwon	1.00	.40
☐ 31	Cuttino Mobley	1.00	.40
☐ 32	Reggie Miller	1.00	.40
☐ 33	Jalen Rose	1.00	.40
☐ 34	Rik Smits	.60	.25
☐ 35	Maurice Taylor	.60	.25
☐ 36	Derek Anderson	.60	.25
☐ 37	Tyrone Nesby RC	.30	.10
☐ 38	Kobe Bryant	4.00	1.50
☐ 39	Shaquille O'Neal	2.50	1.00
☐ 40	Glen Rice	.60	.25
☐ 41	Tim Hardaway	.60	.25
☐ 42	Alonzo Mourning	.60	.25
☐ 43	Jamal Mashburn	.60	.25
☐ 44	Ray Allen	1.00	.40
☐ 45	Sam Cassell	1.00	.40
☐ 46	Glenn Robinson	1.00	.40
☐ 47	Kevin Garnett	2.00	.75
☐ 48	Terrell Brandon	.60	.25
☐ 49	Joe Smith	.60	.25
☐ 50	Stephon Marbury	1.00	.40
☐ 51	Keith Van Horn	1.00	.40
☐ 52	Jamie Feick RC	.30	.10
☐ 53	Kerry Kittles	.30	.10
☐ 54	Allan Houston	.60	.25
☐ 55	Latrell Sprewell	1.00	.40

☐ 56	Patrick Ewing	1.00	.40
☐ 57	Darrell Armstrong	.30	.10
☐ 58	Ron Mercer	.60	.25
☐ 59	Michael Doleac	.30	.10
☐ 60	Allen Iverson	2.00	.75
☐ 61	Toni Kukoc	.60	.25
☐ 62	Eric Snow	.60	.25
☐ 63	Anfernee Hardaway	1.00	.40
☐ 64	Jason Kidd	1.50	.60
☐ 65	Tom Gugliotta	.30	.10
☐ 66	Scottie Pippen	1.50	.60
☐ 67	Steve Smith	.60	.25
☐ 68	Damon Stoudamire	.60	.25
☐ 69	Jason Williams	1.00	.40
☐ 70	Peja Stojakovic	1.25	.50
☐ 71	Chris Webber	1.00	.40
☐ 72	Vlade Divac	.60	.25
☐ 73	Tim Duncan	2.00	.75
☐ 74	David Robinson	1.00	.40
☐ 75	Avery Johnson	.30	.10
☐ 76	Gary Payton	1.00	.40
☐ 77	Vin Baker	.60	.25
☐ 78	Vernon Maxwell	.30	.10
☐ 79	Vince Carter	2.50	1.00
☐ 80	Tracy McGrady	2.50	1.00
☐ 81	Doug Christie	.60	.25
☐ 82	Karl Malone	1.00	.40
☐ 83	John Stockton	1.00	.40
☐ 84	Jeff Hornacek	.60	.25
☐ 85	Mike Bibby	1.00	.40
☐ 86	Shareef Abdur-Rahim	1.00	.40
☐ 87	Othella Harrington	.30	.10
☐ 88	Mitch Richmond	.60	.25
☐ 89	Juwan Howard	.60	.25
☐ 90	Rod Strickland	.30	.10
☐ 91	Elton Brand RC	25.00	10.00
☐ 92	Steve Francis RC	30.00	12.50
☐ 93	Baron Davis RC	60.00	25.00
☐ 94	Lamar Odom RC	30.00	12.50
☐ 95	Jonathan Bender RC	20.00	8.00
☐ 96	Wally Szczerbiak RC	25.00	10.00
☐ 97	Richard Hamilton RC	40.00	15.00
☐ 98	Andre Miller RC	25.00	10.00
☐ 99	Shawn Marion RC	40.00	15.00
☐ 100	Jason Terry RC	20.00	8.00
☐ 101	Trajan Langdon RC	12.00	5.00
☐ 102	A.Radojevic RC	8.00	3.00
☐ 103	Corey Maggette RC	25.00	10.00
☐ 104	William Avery RC	12.00	5.00
☐ 105	Ron Artest RC	12.00	5.00
☐ 106	James Posey RC	12.00	5.00
☐ 107	Quincy Lewis RC	12.00	5.00
☐ 108	Dion Glover RC	8.00	3.00
☐ 109	Kenny Thomas RC	12.00	5.00
☐ 110	Devean George RC	12.00	5.00
☐ 111	Tim James RC	8.00	3.00
☐ 112	Vonteego Cummings RC	12.00	5.00
☐ 113	Jumaine Jones RC	12.00	5.00
☐ 114	Scott Padgett RC	8.00	3.00
☐ 115	Adrian Griffin RC	8.00	3.00
☐ 116	Anthony Carter RC	12.00	5.00
☐ 117	Todd MacCulloch RC	8.00	3.00
☐ 118	Chucky Atkins RC	8.00	3.00
☐ 119	Obinna Ekezie RC	8.00	3.00
☐ 120	Eddie Robinson RC	12.00	5.00
☐ 121	Michael Ruffin RC	8.00	3.00
☐ 122	Laron Profit RC	8.00	3.00
☐ 123	Cal Bowdler RC	8.00	3.00
☐ 124	Chris Herren RC	8.00	3.00
☐ 125	Milt Palacio RC	8.00	3.00
☐ 126	Jeff Foster RC	8.00	3.00
☐ 127	Ryan Bowen RC	8.00	3.00
☐ 128	Tim Young RC	8.00	3.00
☐ 129	Derrick Dial RC	8.00	3.00
☐ 130	Greg Buckner RC	8.00	3.00
☐ 131	Rodney Buford RC	8.00	3.00
☐ 132	Evan Eschmeyer RC	8.00	3.00
☐ 133	Jermaine Jackson RC	8.00	3.00
☐ 134	John Celestand RC	8.00	3.00
☐ 135	Ryan Robertson RC	8.00	3.00
☐ KG	Kevin Garnett PROMO	2.00	.75

2000-01 SP Authentic

☐ COMP.SET w/o SP's (90)		25.00	10.00
☐ COMMON CARD (1-90)		.30	.10
☐ COMMON RC/500 (91-136)		25.00	10.00

☐ COMMON RC/1250 (91-136)		6.00	2.50
☐ COMMON RC/2000 (91-136)		5.00	2.00
☐ 1	Jason Terry	1.00	.40
☐ 2	Alan Henderson	.30	.10
☐ 3	Lorenzen Wright	.30	.10
☐ 4	Paul Pierce	1.00	.40
☐ 5	Antoine Walker	1.00	.40
☐ 6	Bryant Stith	.30	.10
☐ 7	Jamal Mashburn	.60	.25
☐ 8	Baron Davis	1.00	.40
☐ 9	David Wesley	.30	.10
☐ 10	Elton Brand	1.00	.40
☐ 11	Ron Artest	.60	.25
☐ 12	Ron Mercer	.60	.25
☐ 13	Andre Miller	.60	.25
☐ 14	Lamond Murray	.30	.10
☐ 15	Jim Jackson	.30	.10
☐ 16	Michael Finley	1.00	.40
☐ 17	Dirk Nowitzki	2.00	.75
☐ 18	Steve Nash	1.00	.40
☐ 19	Antonio McDyess	.60	.25
☐ 20	Nick Van Exel	1.00	.40
☐ 21	Raef LaFrentz	.60	.25
☐ 22	Jerry Stackhouse	1.00	.40
☐ 23	Chucky Atkins	.30	.10
☐ 24	Joe Smith	.60	.25
☐ 25	Antawn Jamison	1.00	.40
☐ 26	Larry Hughes	.60	.25
☐ 27	Mookie Blaylock	.30	.10
☐ 28	Steve Francis	1.00	.40
☐ 29	Hakeem Olajuwon	1.00	.40
☐ 30	Cuttino Mobley	.60	.25
☐ 31	Reggie Miller	1.00	.40
☐ 32	Jermaine O'Neal	1.00	.40
☐ 33	Jalen Rose	1.00	.40
☐ 34	Travis Best	.30	.10
☐ 35	Lamar Odom	1.00	.40
☐ 36	Corey Maggette	.60	.25
☐ 37	Eric Piatkowski	.60	.25
☐ 38	Shaquille O'Neal	2.50	1.00
☐ 39	Kobe Bryant	4.00	1.50
☐ 40	Isaiah Rider	.30	.10
☐ 41	Horace Grant	.60	.25
☐ 42	Eddie Jones	.60	.25
☐ 43	Brian Grant	.60	.25
☐ 44	Tim Hardaway	.60	.25
☐ 45	Ray Allen	1.00	.40
☐ 46	Glenn Robinson	1.00	.40
☐ 47	Sam Cassell	1.00	.40
☐ 48	Kevin Garnett	2.00	.75
☐ 49	Terrell Brandon	.60	.25
☐ 50	Chauncey Billups	.60	.25
☐ 51	Wally Szczerbiak	.60	.25
☐ 52	Stephon Marbury	1.00	.40
☐ 53	Keith Van Horn	1.00	.40
☐ 54	Aaron Williams	.30	.10
☐ 55	Latrell Sprewell	1.00	.40
☐ 56	Allan Houston	.60	.25
☐ 57	Glen Rice	.60	.25
☐ 58	Tracy McGrady	2.50	1.00
☐ 59	Grant Hill	1.00	.40
☐ 60	Darrell Armstrong	.30	.10
☐ 61	Allen Iverson	2.00	.75
☐ 62	Dikembe Mutombo	.60	.25
☐ 63	Aaron McKie	.60	.25
☐ 64	Jason Kidd	1.50	.60
☐ 65	Clifford Robinson	.30	.10
☐ 66	Shawn Marion	1.00	.40

#	Player	Price1	Price2
67	Damon Stoudamire	.60	.25
68	Steve Smith	.60	.25
69	Rasheed Wallace	1.00	.40
70	Chris Webber	1.00	.40
71	Jason Williams	.60	.25
72	Peja Stojakovic	1.00	.40
73	Tim Duncan	2.00	.75
74	David Robinson	1.00	.40
75	Derek Anderson	.60	.25
76	Gary Payton	1.00	.40
77	Rashard Lewis	.60	.25
78	Patrick Ewing	1.00	.40
79	Vince Carter	2.50	1.00
80	Charles Oakley	.30	.10
81	Antonio Davis	.30	.10
82	Karl Malone	1.00	.40
83	John Stockton	1.00	.40
84	John Starks	.60	.25
85	Shareef Abdur-Rahim	1.00	.40
86	Mike Bibby	1.00	.40
87	Michael Dickerson	.60	.25
88	Richard Hamilton	.60	.25
89	Mitch Richmond	.60	.25
90	Christian Laettner	.60	.25
91	K.Martin AU/500 RC	40.00	15.00
92	S.Swift AU/500 RC	20.00	8.00
93	Darius Miles AU/500 RC	30.00	12.50
94	Marcus Fizer/1250 RC	6.00	2.50
95	Mike Miller AU/500 RC	20.00	8.00
96	D.Johnson AU/500 RC	15.00	6.00
97	Chris Mihm/1250 RC	6.00	2.50
98	Jamal Crawford/1250 RC	10.00	4.00
99	Joel Przybilla/2000 RC	5.00	2.00
100	Keyon Dooling/1250 RC	6.00	2.50
101	Jerome Moiso/1250 RC	6.00	2.50
102	Etan Thomas/2000 RC	5.00	2.00
103	C.Alexander/1250 RC	5.00	2.00
104	Mateen Cleaves/1250 RC	6.00	2.50
105	Jason Collier/2000 RC	8.00	3.00
106	Hidayet Turkoglu/1250 RC	12.00	5.00
107	Desmond Mason/1250 RC	6.00	2.50
108	Q.Richardson/1250 RC	15.00	6.00
109	Jamaal Magloire/1250 RC	6.00	2.50
110	Speedy Claxton/2000 RC	5.00	2.00
111	Morris Peterson AU/500 RC	15.00	6.00
112	Donnell Harvey/2000 RC	5.00	2.00
113	D.Stevenson/1250 RC	6.00	2.50
114	I.Tsakalidis/2000 RC	5.00	2.00
115	Soumaila Samake/2000 RC	5.00	2.00
116	Erick Barkley/2000 RC	5.00	2.00
117	Mark Madsen/2000 RC	5.00	2.00
118	A.J. Guyton/1250 RC	5.00	2.00
119	Olumide Oyedeji/2000 RC	5.00	2.00
120	Eddie House/1250 RC	6.00	2.50
121	Eduardo Najera/2000 RC	8.00	3.00
122	Lavor Postell/2000 RC	5.00	2.00
123	Hanno Mottola/1250 RC	6.00	2.50
124	Ira Newble/2000 RC	5.00	2.00
125	Chris Porter/1250 RC	6.00	2.50
126	R.Wolkowyski/2000 RC	5.00	2.00
127	Pepe Sanchez/2000 RC	5.00	2.00
128	Stephen Jackson/1250 RC	10.00	4.00
129	Marc Jackson/2000 RC	6.00	2.50
130	Dragan Tarlac/2000 RC	5.00	2.00
131	Lee Nailon/2000 RC	5.00	2.00
132	Mike Penberthy/1250 RC	6.00	2.50
133	Mark Blount/2000 RC	5.00	2.00
134	Dan Langhi/2000 RC	5.00	2.00
135	Daniel Santiago/2000 RC	5.00	2.00
136	Wang Zhizhi AU/500 RC	25.00	10.00

2001-02 SP Authentic

	COMP.SET w/o SP's (90)	40.00	20.00
	COMMON CARD (1-165)	.30	.10
	COMMON ROOKIE (91-106)	6.00	2.50
	COMMON ROOKIE (107-115)	10.00	4.00
	COMMON ROOKIE (116-131)	10.00	4.00
	COMMON ROOKIE (132-140)	12.00	5.00
1	Shareef Abdur-Rahim	1.00	.40
2	Jason Terry	1.00	.40
3	Dion Glover	.30	.10
4	Paul Pierce	1.00	.40
5	Antoine Walker	1.00	.40
6	Kenny Anderson	.60	.25
7	Baron Davis	1.00	.40
8	David Wesley	.30	.10

#	Player	Price1	Price2
9	Jamal Mashburn	.60	.25
10	Jalen Rose	1.00	.40
11	Fred Hoiberg	.30	.10
12	Marcus Fizer	.60	.25
13	Andre Miller	.60	.25
14	Lamond Murray	.30	.10
15	Chris Mihm	.60	.25
16	Dirk Nowitzki	1.50	.60
17	Steve Nash	1.00	.40
18	Michael Finley	1.00	.40
19	Nick Van Exel	1.00	.40
20	Antonio McDyess	.60	.25
21	Juwan Howard	.60	.25
22	James Posey	.60	.25
23	Jerry Stackhouse	1.00	.40
24	Clifford Robinson	.30	.10
25	Ben Wallace	1.00	.40
26	Antawn Jamison	1.00	.40
27	Larry Hughes	.60	.25
28	Danny Fortson	.30	.10
29	Steve Francis	1.00	.40
30	Cuttino Mobley	.60	.25
31	Reggie Miller	1.00	.40
32	Al Harrington	.60	.25
33	Jermaine O'Neal	1.00	.40
34	Darius Miles	1.00	.40
35	Elton Brand	1.00	.40
36	Lamar Odom	1.00	.40
37	Corey Maggette	.60	.25
38	Kobe Bryant	4.00	1.50
39	Shaquille O'Neal	2.50	1.00
40	Rick Fox	.30	.10
41	Lindsey Hunter	.30	.10
42	Stromile Swift	.60	.25
43	Michael Dickerson	.60	.25
44	Jason Williams	.60	.25
45	Alonzo Mourning	.60	.25
46	Eddie Jones	1.00	.40
47	Anthony Carter	.60	.25
48	Ray Allen	1.00	.40
49	Glenn Robinson	1.00	.40
50	Sam Cassell	1.00	.40
51	Kevin Garnett	2.00	.75
52	Terrell Brandon	.60	.25
53	Wally Szczerbiak	.60	.25
54	Joe Smith	.60	.25
55	Jason Kidd	1.50	.60
56	Kenyon Martin	.60	.25
57	Mark Jackson	.60	.25
58	Allan Houston	.60	.25
59	Latrell Sprewell	1.00	.40
60	Marcus Camby	.60	.25
61	Tracy McGrady	2.50	1.00
62	Grant Hill	1.00	.40
63	Mike Miller	1.00	.40
64	Allen Iverson	2.00	.75
65	Dikembe Mutombo	.60	.25
66	Aaron McKie	.60	.25
67	Stephon Marbury	1.00	.40
68	Shawn Marion	1.00	.40
69	Anfernee Hardaway	1.00	.40
70	Rasheed Wallace	.60	.25
71	Bonzi Wells	.60	.25
72	Derek Anderson	.60	.25
73	Chris Webber	1.00	.40
74	Mike Bibby	.60	.25
75	Peja Stojakovic	.60	.25
76	Tim Duncan	2.00	.75

#	Player	Price1	Price2
77	David Robinson	1.00	.40
78	Antonio Daniels	.30	.10
79	Gary Payton	1.00	.40
80	Rashard Lewis	.60	.25
81	Desmond Mason	.60	.25
82	Vince Carter	2.50	1.00
83	Morris Peterson	.60	.25
84	Antonio Davis	.30	.10
85	Karl Malone	1.00	.40
86	John Stockton	1.00	.40
87	Donyell Marshall	.60	.25
88	Richard Hamilton	.60	.25
89	Courtney Alexander	.60	.25
90	Michael Jordan	15.00	6.00
91	Tierre Brown RC	5.00	2.00
92	Damone Brown RC	5.00	2.00
93	Michael Bradley RC	5.00	2.00
94	Kedrick Brown RC	5.00	2.00
95	Alton Ford RC	5.00	2.00
96	Jason Collins RC	5.00	2.00
97	Antonis Fotsis RC	5.00	2.00
98	Mengke Bateer RC	8.00	3.00
99	Trenton Hassell RC	6.00	2.50
100	Jamison Brewer RC	5.00	2.00
101	Bobby Simmons RC	5.00	2.00
102	Mike James RC	5.00	2.00
103	Oscar Torres RC	5.00	2.00
104	Brandon Armstrong RC	5.00	2.00
105	Will Solomon RC	5.00	2.00
106	Vladimir Radmanovic RC	6.00	2.50
107	Kirk Haston RC	10.00	4.00
108	Gerald Wallace RC	8.00	3.00
109	Andrei Kirilenko RC	20.00	8.00
110	Joseph Forte RC	12.00	5.00
111	Brendan Haywood RC	10.00	4.00
112	Zach Randolph RC	15.00	6.00
113	DeSagana Diop RC	5.00	2.00
114	Shane Battier RC	8.00	3.00
115	Pau Gasol RC	25.00	10.00
116	Alvin Jones AU RC	10.00	4.00
117	Zeljko Rebraca AU RC	10.00	4.00
118	Kenny Satterfield AU RC	10.00	4.00
119	Jarron Collins AU RC	10.00	4.00
120	R.Bountije-Boumtje AU RC	10.00	4.00
121	Loren Woods AU RC	10.00	4.00
122	Earl Watson AU RC	10.00	4.00
123	Jeff Trepagnier AU RC	10.00	4.00
124	Brian Scalabrine AU RC	10.00	4.00
125	Terence Morris AU RC	10.00	4.00
126	Gilbert Arenas AU RC	120.00	60.00
127	Samuel Dalembert AU RC	10.00	4.00
128	Jeryl Sasser AU RC	10.00	4.00
129	Rodney White AU RC	10.00	4.00
130	Eddie Griffin AU RC	12.00	5.00
131	Tyson Chandler AU RC	40.00	15.00
132	Steven Hunter AU RC	12.00	5.00
133	Troy Murphy AU RC	12.00	5.00
134	R.Jefferson AU RC	30.00	12.50
135	Joe Johnson AU RC	40.00	15.00
136	Eddy Curry AU RC	30.00	12.50
137	Jason Richardson AU RC	50.00	20.00
138	Tony Parker AU RC	40.00	15.00
139	Jamaal Tinsley AU RC	20.00	8.00
140	Kwame Brown AU RC	20.00	8.00
141	Paul Pierce SPEC	6.00	2.50
142	Tim Duncan SPEC	10.00	4.00
143	Stephon Marbury SPEC	6.00	2.50
144	Ray Allen SPEC	6.00	2.50
145	Ray Allen SPEC	6.00	2.50
146	Bonzi Wells SPEC	6.00	2.50
147	Kenyon Martin SPEC	6.00	2.50
148	Darius Miles SPEC	6.00	2.50
149	Baron Davis SPEC	6.00	2.50
150	Dirk Nowitzki SPEC	8.00	3.00
151	Antoine Walker SPEC	6.00	2.50
152	Mike Miller SPEC	6.00	2.50
153	Shawn Marion SPEC	6.00	2.50
154	Jason Kidd SPEC	8.00	3.00
155	Elton Brand SPEC	4.00	1.50
156	Antawn Jamison SPEC	6.00	2.50
157	Rashard Lewis SPEC	6.00	2.50
158	Steve Francis SPEC	6.00	2.50
159	Tracy McGrady SPEC	12.00	5.00
160	Kobe Bryant SPEC	25.00	10.00
161	Allen Iverson SPECT	12.00	5.00
162	Vince Carter SPECT	15.00	6.00

❑ 163 Shaquille O'Neal ™ SPECT	15.00	6.00
❑ 164 Kevin Garnett SPECT	12.00	5.00
❑ 165 Michael Jordan SPECT	40.00	15.00
❑ PROMO Michael Jordan	10.00	4.00

2002-03 SP Authentic

❑ COMP.SET w/SP's (100)	40.00	15.00
❑ COMMON CARD (1-100)	.25	.10
❑ COMMON (101-142)	5.00	2.00
❑ COMMON AU RC (143-174)	8.00	3.00
❑ COMMON ROOKIE (175-203)	5.00	2.00
❑ 1 Glenn Robinson	1.00	.40
❑ 2 Shareef Abdur-Rahim	1.00	.40
❑ 3 Jason Terry	1.00	.40
❑ 4 Theo Ratliff	.60	.25
❑ 5 Paul Pierce	1.00	.40
❑ 5A Paul Pierce AU	30.00	12.50
❑ 6 Antoine Walker	1.00	.40
❑ 6A Antoine Walker AU	25.00	10.00
❑ 7 Tony Delk	.25	.10
❑ 8 Vin Baker	.60	.25
❑ 9 Jalen Rose	1.00	.40
❑ 10 Eddy Curry	1.00	.40
❑ 11 Tyson Chandler	1.00	.40
❑ 11A Tyson Chandler AU	20.00	8.00
❑ 12 Marcus Fizer	.60	.25
❑ 12A M.Fizer AU EXCH	15.00	6.00
❑ 13 Darius Miles	1.00	.40
❑ 14 Zydrunas Ilgauskas	.60	.25
❑ 15 Dirk Nowitzki	1.50	.60
❑ 16 Michael Finley	1.00	.40
❑ 17 Steve Nash	1.00	.40
❑ 18 Raef LaFrentz	.60	.25
❑ 19 Juwan Howard	.60	.25
❑ 20 Rodney White	.60	.25
❑ 21 Ben Wallace	1.00	.40
❑ 22 Richard Hamilton	.60	.25
❑ 23 Chauncey Billups	.60	.25
❑ 24 Chucky Atkins	.25	.10
❑ 25 Jason Richardson	1.00	.40
❑ 26 Antawn Jamison	1.00	.40
❑ 27 Gilbert Arenas	1.00	.40
❑ 28 Steve Francis	1.00	.40
❑ 29 Cuttino Mobley	.60	.25
❑ 30 Jermaine O'Neal	1.00	.40
❑ 30A Jermaine O'Neal AU	25.00	10.00
❑ 31 Jamaal Tinsley	1.00	.40
❑ 32 Reggie Miller	1.00	.40
❑ 33 Ron Artest	.60	.25
❑ 34 Elton Brand	1.00	.40
❑ 35 Andre Miller	.60	.25
❑ 36 Michael Olowokandi	.25	.10
❑ 37 Kobe Bryant	4.00	1.50
❑ 38 Shaquille O'Neal	2.50	1.00
❑ 39 Robert Horry	.60	.25
❑ 40 Derek Fisher	1.00	.40
❑ 41 Pau Gasol	1.00	.40
❑ 42 Shane Battier	1.00	.40
❑ 43 Eddie Jones	1.00	.40
❑ 44 Brian Grant	.60	.25
❑ 45 Malik Allen	.25	.10
❑ 46 Gary Payton	1.00	.40
❑ 47 Sam Cassell	1.00	.40
❑ 48 Kevin Garnett	2.00	.75

❑ 49 Wally Szczerbiak	.60	.25
❑ 50 Troy Hudson	.25	.10
❑ 51 Radoslav Nesterovic	.60	.25
❑ 52 Jason Kidd	1.50	.60
❑ 53 Richard Jefferson	.60	.25
❑ 54 Kenyon Martin	1.00	.40
❑ 54A K.Martin AU EXCH	20.00	8.00
❑ 55 Kerry Kittles	.25	.10
❑ 56 Baron Davis	1.00	.40
❑ 57 Jamal Mashburn	.60	.25
❑ 58 David Wesley	.25	.10
❑ 59 P.J. Brown	.25	.10
❑ 60 Jamaal Magloire	.25	.10
❑ 60A Jamaal Magloire AU	12.00	5.00
❑ 61 Allan Houston	.60	.25
❑ 62 Kurt Thomas	.60	.25
❑ 63 Latrell Sprewell	1.00	.40
❑ 64 Clarence Weatherspoon	.25	.10
❑ 65 Tracy McGrady	2.50	1.00
❑ 66 Grant Hill	1.00	.40
❑ 67 Mike Miller	1.00	.40
❑ 67A Mike Miller AU	20.00	8.00
❑ 68 Allen Iverson	2.00	.75
❑ 69 Keith Van Horn	1.00	.40
❑ 70 Stephon Marbury	1.00	.40
❑ 71 Shawn Marion	1.00	.40
❑ 72 Anfernee Hardaway	1.00	.40
❑ 73 Rasheed Wallace	1.00	.40
❑ 74 Derek Anderson	.60	.25
❑ 75 Scottie Pippen	1.50	.60
❑ 76 Bonzi Wells	.60	.25
❑ 77 Chris Webber	1.00	.40
❑ 78 Mike Bibby	1.00	.40
❑ 78A Mike Bibby AU	25.00	10.00
❑ 79 Peja Stojakovic	1.00	.40
❑ 80 Hedo Turkoglu	1.00	.40
❑ 81 Vlade Divac	.60	.25
❑ 82 Tim Duncan	2.00	.75
❑ 83 David Robinson	1.00	.40
❑ 84 Tony Parker	1.00	.40
❑ 85 Steve Smith	.60	.25
❑ 86 Ray Allen	1.00	.40
❑ 87 Rashard Lewis	1.00	.40
❑ 88 Brent Barry	.60	.25
❑ 89 Elden Campbell	.25	.10
❑ 90 Vince Carter	2.50	1.00
❑ 91 Morris Peterson	.60	.25
❑ 92 Antonio Davis	.25	.10
❑ 93 Alvin Williams	.25	.10
❑ 94 Karl Malone	1.00	.40
❑ 95 John Stockton	1.00	.40
❑ 96 Andrei Kirilenko	1.00	.40
❑ 97 DeShawn Stevenson	.25	.10
❑ 97A DeShawn Stevenson AU	12.00	5.00
❑ 98 Jerry Stackhouse	1.00	.40
❑ 99 Michael Jordan	8.00	3.00
❑ 100 Kwame Brown	.60	.25
❑ 101 Kobe Bryant SPEC	8.00	3.00
❑ 102 Allen Iverson SPEC	6.00	2.50
❑ 103 Pau Gasol SPEC	5.00	2.00
❑ 104 Antoine Walker SPEC	5.00	2.00
❑ 105 J.O'Neal SPEC	5.00	2.00
❑ 106 Ray Allen SPEC	5.00	2.00
❑ 107 Baron Davis SPEC	5.00	2.00
❑ 108 Tim Duncan SPEC	6.00	2.50
❑ 109 Rashard Lewis SPEC	5.00	2.00
❑ 110 Michael Jordan SPEC	20.00	8.00
❑ 111 S.Marbury SPEC	5.00	2.00
❑ 112 S.Abdur-Rahim SPEC	5.00	2.00
❑ 113 Vince Carter SPEC	8.00	3.00
❑ 114 Allan Houston SPEC	5.00	2.00
❑ 115 Dirk Nowitzki SPEC	6.00	2.50
❑ 116 Grant Hill SPEC	5.00	2.00
❑ 117 Mike Bibby SPEC	5.00	2.00
❑ 118 Der.Anderson SPEC	5.00	2.00
❑ 119 Reggie Miller SPEC	5.00	2.00
❑ 120 Steve Francis SPEC	5.00	2.00
❑ 121 R.Jefferson SPEC	5.00	2.00
❑ 122 Ben Wallace SPEC	5.00	2.00
❑ 123 Jason Kidd SPEC	6.00	2.50
❑ 124 Jalen Rose SPEC	5.00	2.00

❑ 125 Paul Pierce SPEC	5.00	2.00
❑ 126 Michael Finley SPEC	5.00	2.00
❑ 127 J.Mashburn SPEC	5.00	2.00
❑ 128 Elton Brand SPEC	5.00	2.00
❑ 129 R.Wallace SPEC	5.00	2.00
❑ 130 Gary Payton SPEC	5.00	2.00
❑ 131 Tracy McGrady SPEC	8.00	3.00
❑ 132 Rich.Hamilton SPEC	5.00	2.00
❑ 133 Chris Webber SPEC	5.00	2.00
❑ 134 Karl Malone SPEC	5.00	2.00
❑ 135 Darius Miles SPEC	5.00	2.00
❑ 136 Shawn Marion SPEC	5.00	2.00
❑ 137 Kevin Garnett SPEC	6.00	2.50
❑ 138 Eddie Jones SPEC	5.00	2.00
❑ 139 J.Richardson SPEC	5.00	2.00
❑ 140 Glenn Robinson SPEC	5.00	2.00
❑ 141 J.Stackhouse SPEC	5.00	2.00
❑ 142 Shane Battier SPEC	5.00	2.00
❑ 143 Yao Ming AU RC	100.00	50.00
❑ 144 Jay Williams AU RC	15.00	6.00
❑ 145 Drew Gooden AU RC	20.00	8.00
❑ 146 N.Tskitishvili AU RC	10.00	4.00
❑ 147 D.Wagner AU RC	15.00	6.00
❑ 148 Nene Hilario AU RC	12.00	5.00
❑ 149 Chris Wilcox AU RC	12.00	5.00
❑ 150 A.Stoudemire AU RC	80.00	40.00
❑ 151 Caron Butler AU RC	20.00	8.00
❑ 152 Jared Jeffries AU RC	10.00	4.00
❑ 153 Melvin Ely AU RC	8.00	3.00
❑ 154 Marcus Haislip AU RC	8.00	3.00
❑ 155 Fred Jones AU RC	8.00	3.00
❑ 156 B.Nachbar AU RC	8.00	3.00
❑ 157 Jiri Welsch AU RC	8.00	3.00
❑ 158 Juan Dixon AU RC	15.00	6.00
❑ 159 C.Borchardt AU RC	8.00	3.00
❑ 160 R.Humphrey AU RC	8.00	3.00
❑ 161 Kareem Rush AU RC	12.00	5.00
❑ 162 Qyntel Woods AU RC	10.00	4.00
❑ 163 C.Jacobsen AU RC	8.00	3.00
❑ 164 T.Prince AU RC	15.00	6.00
❑ 165 Frank Williams AU RC	8.00	3.00
❑ 166 John Salmons AU RC	8.00	3.00
❑ 167 Chris Jefferies AU RC	8.00	3.00
❑ 168 Dan Dickau AU RC	8.00	3.00
❑ 169 Carlos Boozer AU RC	40.00	20.00
❑ 170 Marko Jaric AU	8.00	3.00
❑ 171 Sam Clancy AU RC	8.00	3.00
❑ 172 M.Ginobili AU RC	50.00	20.00
❑ 173 V.Yarbrough AU RC	8.00	3.00
❑ 174 Gordan Giricek AU RC	12.00	5.00
❑ 175 Predrag Savovic RC	5.00	2.00
❑ 176 Mike Dunleavy RC	8.00	3.00
❑ 177 Tamar Slay RC	5.00	2.00
❑ 178 Rasual Butler RC	5.00	2.00
❑ 179 Reggie Evans RC	5.00	2.00
❑ 180 Igor Rakocevic RC	5.00	2.00
❑ 181 Juaquin Hawkins RC	5.00	2.00
❑ 182 J.R. Bremer RC	5.00	2.00
❑ 183 Cezary Trybanski RC	5.00	2.00
❑ 184 Junior Harrington RC	5.00	2.00
❑ 185 Efthimios Rentzias RC	5.00	2.00
❑ 186 Smush Parker RC	10.00	4.00
❑ 187 Jamal Sampson RC	5.00	2.00
❑ 188 Roger Mason RC	5.00	2.00
❑ 189 Robert Archibald RC	5.00	2.00
❑ 190 Mehmet Okur RC	5.00	2.00
❑ 191 Dan Gadzuric RC	5.00	2.00
❑ 192 Pat Burke RC	5.00	2.00
❑ 193 Lonny Baxter RC	5.00	2.00
❑ 194 Tito Maddox RC	5.00	2.00
❑ 195 Jannero Pargo RC	6.00	2.50
❑ 196 Ronald Murray RC	12.00	5.00
❑ 197 Mike Wilks RC	5.00	2.00
❑ 198 Mike Batiste RC	5.00	2.00
❑ 199 Chris Owens RC	5.00	2.00
❑ 200 Raul Lopez RC	5.00	2.00
❑ 201 Antoine Rigaudeau RC	5.00	2.00
❑ 202 Ken Johnson RC	5.00	2.00
❑ 203 Maceo Baston RC	5.00	2.00
❑ NNO Michael Jordan PROMO	5.00	2.00

2003-04 SP Authentic

❏ COMP.SET w/o SP's (90)	40.00	15.00
❏ COMMON CARD (1-90)	.25	.10
❏ COMMON ROOKIE (91-132 & 144)	4.00	1.50
❏ COMMON ROOKIE (133-147)	6.00	2.50
❏ COMMON AU (148-153)	15.00	6.00
❏ COMMON AU RC (154-189)	12.00	5.00
❏ 1 Shareef Abdur-Rahim	1.00	.40
❏ 2 Theo Ratliff	.60	.25
❏ 3 Jason Terry	1.00	.40
❏ 4 Raef LaFrentz	.60	.25
❏ 5 Vin Baker	.60	.25
❏ 6 Paul Pierce	1.00	.40
❏ 7 Antonio Davis	.25	.10
❏ 8 Scottie Pippen	1.50	.60
❏ 9 Tyson Chandler	1.00	.40
❏ 10 Dajuan Wagner	.60	.25
❏ 11 Carlos Boozer	.60	.25
❏ 12 Zydrunas Ilgauskas	.60	.25
❏ 13 Dirk Nowitzki	1.50	.60
❏ 14 Antoine Walker	1.00	.40
❏ 15 Steve Nash	1.00	.40
❏ 16 Michael Finley	1.00	.40
❏ 17 Earl Boykins	.60	.25
❏ 18 Andre Miller	.60	.25
❏ 19 Nene	.60	.25
❏ 20 Chauncey Billups	.60	.25
❏ 21 Richard Hamilton	.60	.25
❏ 22 Ben Wallace	1.00	.40
❏ 23 Clifford Robinson	.25	.10
❏ 24 Jason Richardson	1.00	.40
❏ 25 Nick Van Exel	1.00	.40
❏ 26 Yao Ming	2.50	1.00
❏ 27 Cuttino Mobley	.60	.25
❏ 28 Steve Francis	1.00	.40
❏ 29 Jermaine O'Neal	1.00	.40
❏ 30 Reggie Miller	1.00	.40
❏ 31 Ron Artest	.60	.25
❏ 32 Elton Brand	1.00	.40
❏ 33 Corey Maggette	.60	.25
❏ 34 Quentin Richardson	.60	.25
❏ 35 Kobe Bryant	4.00	1.50
❏ 36 Karl Malone	1.00	.40
❏ 37 Gary Payton	1.00	.40
❏ 38 Shaquille O'Neal	2.50	1.00
❏ 39 Pau Gasol	1.00	.40
❏ 40 Bonzi Wells	.60	.25
❏ 41 Mike Miller	1.00	.40
❏ 42 Lamar Odom	1.00	.40
❏ 43 Eddie Jones	1.00	.40
❏ 44 Caron Butler	1.00	.40
❏ 45 Toni Kukoc	.60	.25
❏ 46 Desmond Mason	.60	.25
❏ 47 Michael Redd	1.00	.40
❏ 48 Latrell Sprewell	1.00	.40
❏ 49 Kevin Garnett	2.00	.75
❏ 50 Sam Cassell	1.00	.40
❏ 51 Richard Jefferson	.60	.25
❏ 52 Kenyon Martin	1.00	.40
❏ 53 Jason Kidd	1.50	.60
❏ 54 Jamal Mashburn	.60	.25
❏ 55 Baron Davis	1.00	.40
❏ 56 David Wesley	.25	.10
❏ 57 Allan Houston	.60	.25
❏ 58 Stephon Marbury	1.00	.40
❏ 59 Keith Van Horn	1.00	.40
❏ 60 Gordan Giricek	.60	.25
❏ 61 Drew Gooden	.60	.25
❏ 62 Tracy McGrady	2.50	1.00
❏ 63 Glenn Robinson	1.00	.40
❏ 64 Allen Iverson	2.00	.75
❏ 65 Eric Snow	.60	.25
❏ 66 Amare Stoudemire	2.00	.75
❏ 67 Antonio McDyess	1.00	.40
❏ 68 Shawn Marion	1.00	.40
❏ 69 Zach Randolph	1.00	.40
❏ 70 Damon Stoudamire	.60	.25
❏ 71 Rasheed Wallace	1.00	.40
❏ 72 Peja Stojakovic	1.00	.40
❏ 73 Chris Webber	1.00	.40
❏ 74 Mike Bibby	1.00	.40
❏ 75 Brad Miller	1.00	.40
❏ 76 Tony Parker	1.00	.40
❏ 77 Tim Duncan	2.00	.75
❏ 78 Manu Ginobili	1.00	.40
❏ 79 Vladimir Radmanovic	.25	.10
❏ 80 Ray Allen	1.00	.40
❏ 81 Rashard Lewis	1.00	.40
❏ 82 Morris Peterson	.60	.25
❏ 83 Vince Carter	2.50	1.00
❏ 84 Jalen Rose	1.00	.40
❏ 85 Andrei Kirilenko	1.00	.40
❏ 86 Matt Harpring	1.00	.40
❏ 87 Carlos Arroyo	4.00	1.50
❏ 88 Gilbert Arenas	1.00	.40
❏ 89 Larry Hughes	.60	.25
❏ 90 Jerry Stackhouse	1.00	.40
❏ 91 Kobe Bryant SPEC	10.00	4.00
❏ 92 Jason Kidd SPEC	4.00	1.50
❏ 93 Rasheed Wallace SPEC	4.00	1.50
❏ 94 Jalen Rose SPEC	4.00	1.50
❏ 95 Tim Duncan SPEC	5.00	2.00
❏ 96 S.Abdur-Rahim SPEC	4.00	1.50
❏ 97 Baron Davis SPEC	4.00	1.50
❏ 98 Pau Gasol SPEC	4.00	1.50
❏ 99 Allen Iverson SPEC	5.00	2.00
❏ 100 Yao Ming SPEC	6.00	2.50
❏ 101 Gary Payton SPEC	4.00	1.50
❏ 102 Ray Allen SPEC	4.00	1.50
❏ 103 Tracy McGrady SPEC	6.00	2.50
❏ 104 Amare Stoudemire SPEC	5.00	2.00
❏ 105 Tony Parker SPEC	4.00	1.50
❏ 106 Stephon Marbury SPEC	4.00	1.50
❏ 107 Richard Hamilton SPEC	4.00	1.50
❏ 108 Chris Webber SPEC	4.00	1.50
❏ 109 Elton Brand SPEC	4.00	1.50
❏ 110 Jerry Stackhouse SPEC	4.00	1.50
❏ 111 Andre Miller SPEC	4.00	1.50
❏ 112 Kevin Garnett SPEC	5.00	2.00
❏ 113 Jason Richardson SPEC	4.00	1.50
❏ 114 Allan Houston SPEC	4.00	1.50
❏ 115 Dajuan Wagner SPEC	4.00	1.50
❏ 116 Richard Jefferson SPEC	4.00	1.50
❏ 117 Shaquille O'Neal SPEC	6.00	2.50
❏ 118 Latrell Sprewell SPEC	4.00	1.50
❏ 119 Rashard Lewis SPEC	4.00	1.50
❏ 120 Steve Nash SPEC	4.00	1.50
❏ 121 Desmond Mason SPEC	4.00	1.50
❏ 122 Mike Bibby SPEC	4.00	1.50
❏ 123 Shawn Marion SPEC	4.00	1.50
❏ 124 Vince Carter SPEC	6.00	2.50
❏ 125 Caron Butler SPEC	4.00	1.50
❏ 126 Gilbert Arenas SPEC	4.00	1.50
❏ 127 Dirk Nowitzki SPEC	4.00	1.50
❏ 128 Paul Pierce SPEC	4.00	1.50
❏ 129 Jermaine O'Neal SPEC	4.00	1.50
❏ 130 Andrei Kirilenko SPEC	4.00	1.50
❏ 131 Michael Jordan SPEC	12.00	5.00
❏ 132 Steve Francis SPEC	4.00	1.50
❏ 133 T.J. Ford RC	8.00	3.00
❏ 134 Nick Hinrich RC	10.00	4.00
❏ 135 Nick Collison RC	6.00	2.50
❏ 136 Maurice Carter RC	6.00	2.50
❏ 137 Francisco Elson RC	6.00	2.50
❏ 138 Udonis Haslem RC	6.00	2.50
❏ 139 Jon Stefansson RC	6.00	2.50
❏ 140 Richie Frahm RC	6.00	2.50
❏ 141 Ronald Dupree RC	6.00	2.50
❏ 142 Josh Moore RC	6.00	2.50
❏ 143 Alex Garcia RC	6.00	2.50
❏ 144 Zach Randolph SPEC	4.00	1.50
❏ 145 Ben Handlogten RC	6.00	2.50
❏ 146 Devin Brown RC	6.00	2.50
❏ 147 Marquis Daniels RC	12.00	5.00
❏ 148 LeBron James AU RC	750.00	500.00
❏ 149 Darko Milicic AU RC	60.00	30.00
❏ 150 Carmelo Anthony AU RC	120.00	60.00
❏ 151 Chris Bosh AU RC	100.00	50.00
❏ 152 Dwyane Wade AU RC	250.00	125.00
❏ 153 Jarvis Hayes AU RC	15.00	6.00
❏ 154 Mickael Pietrus AU RC	12.00	5.00
❏ 155 Chris Kaman AU RC	12.00	5.00
❏ 156 Dahntay Jones AU RC	12.00	5.00
❏ 157 Marcus Banks AU RC	12.00	5.00
❏ 158 Luke Ridnour AU RC	20.00	8.00
❏ 159 Reece Gaines AU RC	12.00	5.00
❏ 160 Troy Bell AU RC	12.00	5.00
❏ 161 Mike Sweetney AU RC	12.00	5.00
❏ 162 David West AU RC	12.00	5.00
❏ 163 Aleksandar Pavlovic AU RC	15.00	6.00
❏ 164 Steve Blake AU RC	12.00	5.00
❏ 165 Boris Diaw AU RC	25.00	10.00
❏ 166 Zoran Planinic AU RC	12.00	5.00
❏ 167 Travis Outlaw AU RC	12.00	5.00
❏ 168 Brian Cook AU RC EXCH*	12.00	5.00
❏ 169 Jerome Beasley AU RC	12.00	5.00
❏ 170 Ndudi Ebi AU RC	12.00	5.00
❏ 171 Kendrick Perkins AU RC	12.00	5.00
❏ 172 Leandro Barbosa AU RC	25.00	10.00
❏ 173 Josh Howard AU RC	40.00	15.00
❏ 174 Maciej Lampe AU RC	12.00	5.00
❏ 175 Jason Kapono AU RC	12.00	5.00
❏ 176 Luke Walton AU RC	20.00	8.00
❏ 177 Slavko Vranes AU RC	12.00	5.00
❏ 178 Zarko Cabarkapa AU RC	12.00	5.00
❏ 179 Zaur Pachulia AU RC	12.00	5.00
❏ 180 Maurice Williams AU RC	12.00	5.00
❏ 181 Brandon Hunter AU RC	12.00	5.00
❏ 182 Keith Bogans AU RC	12.00	5.00
❏ 183 Travis Hansen AU RC	12.00	5.00
❏ 184 Theron Smith AU RC	12.00	5.00
❏ 185 Willie Green AU RC	12.00	5.00
❏ 186 James Jones AU RC	12.00	5.00
❏ 187 Kyle Korver AU RC	20.00	8.00
❏ 188 Udonis Haslem AU RC	12.00	5.00
❏ 189 James Lang AU RC	12.00	5.00

2004-05 SP Authentic

❏ COMP.SET w/o SP's (90)		
❏ COMMON CARD (1-90)	.25	.10
❏ COMMON SP (91-130)	5.00	2.00
❏ COMMON RC (131-140)	6.00	2.50
❏ COMMON AU RC (141-180)	10.00	4.00
❏ SIX AU VERSIONS FOR CARD 146		
❏ 1 Al Harrington	.60	.25
❏ 2 Antoine Walker	1.00	.40
❏ 3 Tony Delk	.25	.10
❏ 4 Gary Payton	1.00	.40
❏ 5 Mark Blount	.25	.10
❏ 6 Paul Pierce	1.00	.40
❏ 7 Kareem Rush	.60	.25
❏ 8 Gerald Wallace	.60	.25
❏ 9 Jason Kapono	.60	.25
❏ 10 Eddy Curry	.60	.25
❏ 11 Kirk Hinrich	1.00	.40
❏ 12 Tyson Chandler	1.00	.40
❏ 13 Drew Gooden	.60	.25
❏ 14 LeBron James	6.00	2.50
❏ 15 Zydrunas Ilgauskas	.60	.25
❏ 16 Dirk Nowitzki	1.50	.60
❏ 17 Jason Terry	1.00	.40

#	Player	Hi	Lo
18	Michael Finley	1.00	.40
19	Carmelo Anthony	2.00	.75
20	Kenyon Martin	1.00	.40
21	Andre Miller	.60	.25
22	Ben Wallace	1.00	.40
23	Chauncey Billups	.60	.25
24	Rasheed Wallace	1.00	.40
25	Derek Fisher	1.00	.40
26	Jason Richardson	1.00	.40
27	Speedy Claxton	.60	.25
28	Juwan Howard	.60	.25
29	Tracy McGrady	2.50	1.00
30	Yao Ming	2.50	1.00
31	Jermaine O'Neal	1.00	.40
32	Reggie Miller	1.00 -	.40
33	Fred Jones	.25	.10
34	Corey Maggette	.60	.25
35	Elton Brand	1.00	.40
36	Kerry Kittles	.25	.10
37	Caron Butler	1.00	.40
38	Kobe Bryant	4.00	1.50
39	Lamar Odom	1.00	.40
40	Bonzi Wells	.60	.25
41	Jason Williams	.60	.25
42	Pau Gasol	1.00	.40
43	Dwyane Wade	3.00	1.25
44	Eddie Jones	1.00	.40
45	Shaquille O'Neal	2.50	1.00
46	Desmond Mason	.60	.25
47	Keith Van Horn	1.00	.40
48	Michael Redd	.60	.25
49	Kevin Garnett	2.00	.75
50	Latrell Sprewell	1.00	.40
51	Sam Cassell	1.00	.40
52	Vince Carter	2.50	1.00
53	Jason Kidd	1.50	.60
54	Richard Jefferson	.60	.25
55	Baron Davis	1.00	.40
56	Jamaal Magloire	.25	.10
57	P.J. Brown	.25	.10
58	Allan Houston	.60	.25
59	Jamal Crawford	.60	.25
60	Stephon Marbury	1.00	.40
61	Hedo Turkoglu	1.00	.40
62	Grant Hill	1.00	.40
63	Steve Francis	1.00	.40
64	Allen Iverson	2.00	.75
65	Glenn Robinson	1.00	.40
66	Kyle Korver	1.00	.40
67	Amare Stoudemire	2.00	.75
68	Shawn Marion	1.00	.40
69	Steve Nash	1.00	.40
70	Darius Miles	1.00	.40
71	Shareef Abdur-Rahim	1.00	.40
72	Zach Randolph	1.00	.40
73	Chris Webber	1.00	.40
74	Mike Bibby	1.00	.40
75	Peja Stojakovic	1.00	.40
76	Manu Ginobili	1.00	.40
77	Tim Duncan	2.00	.75
78	Tony Parker	1.00	.40
79	Rashard Lewis	1.00	.40
80	Ray Allen	1.00	.40
81	Ronald Murray	.25	.10
82	Donyell Marshall	1.00	.40
83	Jalen Rose	1.00	.40
84	Chris Bosh	1.00	.40
85	Andrei Kirilenko	1.00	.40
86	Carlos Boozer	1.00	.40
87	Matt Harpring	1.00	.40
88	Antawn Jamison	1.00	.40
89	Gilbert Arenas	1.00	.40
90	Larry Hughes	.60	.25
91	Bill Russell ESS	6.00	2.50
92	Larry Bird ESS	12.00	5.00
93	Paul Pierce ESS	5.00	2.00
94	Michael Jordan ESS	15.00	6.00
95	LeBron James ESS	15.00	6.00
96	Dirk Nowitzki ESS	5.00	2.00
97	Carmelo Anthony ESS	5.00	2.00
98	Ben Wallace ESS	5.00	2.00
99	Isiah Thomas ESS	6.00	2.50
100	Tracy McGrady ESS	6.00	2.50
101	Yao Ming ESS	6.00	2.50
102	Jermaine O'Neal ESS	5.00	2.00
103	Reggie Miller ESS	5.00	2.00
104	Elton Brand ESS	5.00	2.00
105	Kareem Abdul-Jabbar ESS	8.00	3.00
106	Kobe Bryant ESS	8.00	3.00
107	Magic Johnson ESS	10.00	4.00
108	Wilt Chamberlain ESS	10.00	4.00
109	Pau Gasol ESS	5.00	2.00
110	Dwyane Wade ESS	8.00	3.00
111	Shaquille O'Neal ESS	6.00	2.50
112	Michael Redd ESS	5.00	2.00
113	Oscar Robertson ESS	8.00	3.00
114	Kevin Garnett ESS	5.00	2.00
115	Sam Cassell ESS	5.00	2.00
116	Jason Kidd ESS	5.00	2.00
117	Baron Davis ESS	5.00	2.00
118	Stephon Marbury ESS	5.00	2.00
119	Steve Francis ESS	5.00	2.00
120	Allen Iverson ESS	5.00	2.00
121	Julius Erving ESS	6.00	2.50
122	Amare Stoudemire ESS	5.00	2.00
123	Shawn Marion ESS	5.00	2.00
124	Chris Webber ESS	5.00	2.00
125	Peja Stojakovic ESS	5.00	2.00
126	Tim Duncan ESS	5.00	2.00
127	Ray Allen ESS	5.00	2.00
128	Vince Carter ESS	6.00	2.50
129	Andrei Kirilenko ESS	5.00	2.00
130	John Stockton ESS	6.00	2.50
131	Emeka Okafor RC	25.00	10.00
132	Mario Kasun RC	6.00	2.50
133	Andre Barrett RC	6.00	2.50
134	Ha Seung-Jin RC	6.00	2.50
135	Horace Jenkins RC	6.00	2.50
136	Tony Bobbitt RC	6.00	2.50
137	Luis Flores RC	6.00	2.50
138	John Edwards RC	6.00	2.50
139	Beno Udrih RC	8.00	3.00
140	Erik Daniels RC	6.00	2.50
141	Nenad Krstic AU RC	15.00	6.00
142	Yuta Tabuse AU RC	40.00	15.00
143	Pape Sow AU RC	12.00	5.00
144	Andres Nocioni AU RC	25.00	10.00
145	B.Robinson AU RC EXCH	12.00	5.00
146A	Michael Jordan AU		
146B	Dwight Howard AU		
146C	LeBron James AU		
146D	Steve Nash AU		
146E	Scottie Pippen AU		
146F	Larry Brown AU		
147	Trevor Ariza AU RC	12.00	5.00
148	Damien Wilkins AU RC	10.00	4.00
149	Justin Reed AU RC EXCH	10.00	4.00
150	Chris Duhon AU RC	15.00	6.00
151	Royal Ivey AU RC	10.00	4.00
152	Antonio Burks AU RC	10.00	4.00
153	Andre Emmett AU RC	10.00	4.00
154	Donta Smith AU RC	10.00	4.00
155	Lionel Chalmers AU RC	10.00	4.00
156	P.J. Ramos AU RC EXCH	10.00	4.00
157	Jackson Vroman AU RC	10.00	4.00
158	Anderson Varejao AU RC	12.00	5.00
159	David Harrison AU RC	10.00	4.00
160	D.J. Mbenga AU RC	10.00	4.00
161	Sasha Vujacic AU RC	10.00	4.00
162	Kevin Martin AU RC	15.00	6.00
163	Tony Allen AU RC	15.00	6.00
164	Delonte West AU RC EXCH	20.00	8.00
165	Romain Sato AU RC	10.00	4.00
166	Viktor Khryapa AU RC	10.00	4.00
167	Pavel Podkolzine AU RC	10.00	4.00
168	Jameer Nelson AU RC EXCH	20.00	8.00
169	Dorell Wright AU RC	10.00	4.00
170	J.R. Smith AU RC	40.00	15.00
171	Josh Smith AU RC EXCH	40.00	15.00
172	Kirk Snyder AU RC EXCH	10.00	4.00
173	Al Jefferson AU RC	60.00	25.00
174	Kris Humphries AU RC	10.00	4.00
175	Sebastian Telfair AU RC	15.00	6.00
176	Robert Swift AU RC	10.00	4.00
177	Andris Biedrins AU RC	15.00	6.00
178	Luke Jackson AU RC	10.00	4.00
179	Andre Iguodala AU RC	50.00	20.00
180	Rafael Araujo AU RC	10.00	4.00
181	Luol Deng AU RC	50.00	20.00
182	Josh Childress AU RC	20.00	8.00
183	Devin Harris AU RC EXCH	25.00	10.00
184	Shaun Livingston AU RC	25.00	10.00
185	Ben Gordon AU RC	120.00	60.00
186	D.Howard AU RC EXCH	160.00	80.00

2005-06 SP Authentic

		Hi	Lo
	COMP.SET w/o SP's (90)	40.00	15.00
	COMMON CARD (1-90)	.25	.10
	SEMISTARS	.60	.25
	UNLISTED STARS	1.00	.40
	COMMON AU RC (91-125)	12.00	5.00
	91-125 PRINT RUN 1299 SER.#'d SETS		
	91-125 #'d 1-100 ARE PATCH PARALLEL		
	COMMON AU RC (126-132)	15.00	6.00
	126-132 PRINT RUN 1299 SER.#'d SETS		
	COMMON ROOKIE (133-157)	8.00	3.00
	133-157 PRINT RUN 999 SER.#'d SETS		
1	Boris Diaw	.60	.25
2	Josh Childress	.60	.25
3	Josh Smith	1.00	.40
4	Antoine Walker	1.00	.40
5	Al Jefferson	1.00	.40
6	Paul Pierce	1.00	.40
7	Kareem Rush	.30	.10
8	Emeka Okafor	1.50	.60
9	Gerald Wallace	1.00	.40
10	Ben Gordon	2.00	.75
11	Kirk Hinrich	1.00	.40
12	Michael Jordan	6.00	2.50
13	Drew Gooden	.60	.25
14	LeBron James	6.00	2.50
15	Luke Jackson	.30	.10
16	Dirk Nowitzki	1.50	.60
17	Jason Terry	1.00	.40
18	Josh Howard	.60	.25
19	Nene Hilario	.30	.10
20	Carmelo Anthony	2.00	.75
21	Kenyon Martin	1.00	.40
22	Ben Wallace	1.00	.40
23	Chauncey Billups	1.00	.40
24	Rasheed Wallace	1.00	.40
25	Baron Davis	1.00	.40
26	Jason Richardson	1.00	.40
27	Mike Dunleavy	.60	.25
28	David Wesley	.30	.10
29	Tracy McGrady	2.50	1.00
30	Yao Ming	2.50	1.00
31	Jamaal Tinsley	.60	.25
32	Jermaine O'Neal	1.00	.40
33	Fred Jones	.60	.25
34	Corey Maggette	.60	.25
35	Elton Brand	1.00	.40
36	Shaun Livingston	.75	.30
37	Caron Butler	.60	.25
38	Kobe Bryant	4.00	1.50
39	Wilt Chamberlain	5.00	2.00
40	Jason Williams	.60	.25
41	Pau Gasol	1.00	.40
42	Shane Battier	1.00	.40
43	Udonis Haslem	1.00	.40
44	Dwyane Wade	3.00	1.25
45	Shaquille O'Neal	2.50	1.00
46	Desmond Mason	.30	.10
47	T.J. Ford	.60	.25
48	Michael Redd	1.00	.40
49	Kevin Garnett	2.00	.75
50	Wally Szczerbiak	.60	.25
51	Ndudi Ebi	.30	.10
52	Jason Kidd	1.50	.60
53	Richard Jefferson	.60	.25

❏ 54	Vince Carter	2.50	1.00
❏ 55	Lee Nailon	.30	.10
❏ 56	J.R. Smith	.60	.25
❏ 57	Jamaal Magloire	.30	.10
❏ 58	Jamal Crawford	.60	.25
❏ 59	Stephon Marbury	1.00	.40
❏ 60	Quentin Richardson	.60	.25
❏ 61	Dwight Howard	1.25	.50
❏ 62	Grant Hill	1.00	.40
❏ 63	Steve Francis	1.00	.40
❏ 64	Chris Webber	2.00	.75
❏ 65	Andre Iguodala	1.00	.40
❏ 66	Chris Webber	1.00	.40
❏ 67	Amare Stoudemire		
❏ 68	Shawn Marion	1.00	.40
❏ 69	Steve Nash	1.00	.40
❏ 70	Sebastian Telfair	.60	.25
❏ 71	Darius Miles	1.00	.40
❏ 72	Zach Randolph	1.00	.40
❏ 73	Brad Miller	1.00	.40
❏ 74	Mike Bibby	1.00	.40
❏ 75	Peja Stojakovic	1.00	.40
❏ 76	Manu Ginobili	1.00	.40
❏ 77	Tim Duncan	2.00	.75
❏ 78	Tony Parker	1.00	.40
❏ 79	Luke Ridnour	.60	.25
❏ 80	Ron Artest	1.00	.40
❏ 81	Ray Allen	1.00	.40
❏ 82	Chris Bosh	1.00	.40
❏ 83	Morris Peterson	1.00	.40
❏ 84	Jalen Rose	.75	.30
❏ 85	Andrei Kirilenko	1.00	.40
❏ 86	Carlos Boozer	.60	.25
❏ 87	John Stockton	4.00	1.50
❏ 88	Antawn Jamison	1.00	.40
❏ 89	Gilbert Arenas	1.00	.40
❏ 90	Brendan Haywood	2.00	.75
❏ 91	Andrew Bogut AU RC	25.00	10.00
❏ 92	Marvin Williams AU RC	40.00	15.00
❏ 93	Deron Williams AU RC	60.00	25.00
❏ 94	Chris Paul AU RC	120.00	60.00
❏ 95	Raymond Felton AU RC	30.00	12.50
❏ 96	Martell Webster AU RC	12.00	5.00
❏ 97	Charlie Villanueva AU RC	25.00	10.00
❏ 98	Channing Frye AU RC	20.00	8.00
❏ 99	Brandon Bass AU RC	12.00	5.00
❏ 100	Travis Diener AU RC	12.00	5.00
❏ 101	Andray Blatche AU RC	20.00	8.00
❏ 102	Monta Ellis AU RC	30.00	12.50
❏ 103	Sean May AU RC	15.00	6.00
❏ 104	Rashad McCants AU RC	25.00	10.00
❏ 105	Antoine Wright AU RC	12.00	5.00
❏ 106	Joey Graham AU RC	12.00	5.00
❏ 107	Danny Granger AU RC	15.00	6.00
❏ 108	Gerald Green AU RC	40.00	15.00
❏ 109	Hakim Warrick AU RC	30.00	12.50
❏ 110	Julius Hodge AU RC	12.00	5.00
❏ 111	Sarunas Jasikevicius AU RC	15.00	6.00
❏ 112	Martynas Andriuskevicius AU RC	12.00	5.00
❏ 113	Francisco Garcia AU RC	15.00	6.00
❏ 114	Luther Head AU RC	20.00	8.00
❏ 115	Nate Robinson AU RC	25.00	10.00
❏ 116	Jason Maxiell AU RC	12.00	5.00
❏ 117	Wayne Simien AU RC	20.00	8.00
❏ 118	David Lee AU RC	20.00	8.00
❏ 119	Daniel Ewing AU RC	12.00	5.00
❏ 120	Louis Williams AU RC	12.00	5.00
❏ 121	Salim Stoudamire AU RC	15.00	6.00
❏ 122	Jarrett Jack AU RC	12.00	5.00
❏ 123	Andrew Bynum AU RC	40.00	15.00
❏ 124	C.J. Miles AU RC	12.00	5.00
❏ 125	Irsan Ilyasova AU RC	12.00	5.00
❏ 126	Will Bynum AU RC	12.00	5.00
❏ 127	Lawrence Roberts AU RC	12.00	5.00
❏ 128	Dijon Thompson AU RC	12.00	5.00
❏ 129	Johan Petro AU RC	12.00	5.00
❏ 130	Bracey Wright AU RC	12.00	5.00
❏ 131	Ike Diogu AU RC	15.00	6.00
❏ 132	Ryan Gomes AU RC	12.00	5.00
❏ 133	Ronnie Price RC	8.00	3.00
❏ 134	Alan Anderson RC	8.00	3.00
❏ 135	Esteban Batista RC	8.00	3.00
❏ 136	Linas Kleiza RC	8.00	3.00
❏ 137	Eddie Basden RC	8.00	3.00
❏ 138	Josh Powell RC	8.00	3.00
❏ 139	Kevin Burleson RC	8.00	3.00
❏ 140	Von Wafer RC	8.00	3.00
❏ 141	Rawle Marshall RC	8.00	3.00
❏ 142	Gerald Fitch RC	8.00	3.00
❏ 143	Robert Whaley RC	8.00	3.00
❏ 144	Orien Greene RC	8.00	3.00
❏ 145	Fabricio Oberto RC	8.00	3.00
❏ 146	Amir Johnson RC	8.00	3.00
❏ 147	Shavlik Randolph RC	8.00	3.00
❏ 148	Arvydas Macijauskas RC	8.00	3.00
❏ 149	Alex Acker RC	8.00	3.00
❏ 150	James Singleton RC	8.00	3.00
❏ 151	Anthony Roberson RC	8.00	3.00
❏ 152	Earl Barron RC	8.00	3.00
❏ 153	Dwayne Jones RC	8.00	3.00
❏ 154	Sean Banks RC	8.00	3.00
❏ 155	Sharrod Ford RC	8.00	3.00
❏ 156	Andre Owens RC	8.00	3.00
❏ 157	Donell Taylor RC	8.00	3.00

2006-07 SP Authentic

❏ 1	Joe Johnson	.60	.25
❏ 2	Marvin Williams	1.25	.50
❏ 3	Josh Childress	.60	.25
❏ 4	Paul Pierce	1.00	.40
❏ 5	Sebastian Telfair	.60	.25
❏ 6	Gerald Green	1.25	.50
❏ 7	Emeka Okafor	1.00	.40
❏ 8	Raymond Felton	1.25	.50
❏ 9	Gerald Wallace	1.00	.40
❏ 10	Ben Wallace	1.00	.40
❏ 11	Ben Gordon	2.00	.75
❏ 12	Kirk Hinrich	1.00	.40
❏ 13	LeBron James	6.00	2.50
❏ 14	Zydrunas Ilgauskas	.30	.12
❏ 15	Drew Gooden	.60	.25
❏ 16	Jason Terry	1.00	.40
❏ 17	Dirk Nowitzki	1.50	.60
❏ 18	Devin Harris	1.00	.40
❏ 19	Carmelo Anthony	2.00	.75
❏ 20	Kenyon Martin	1.00	.40
❏ 21	Andre Miller	.60	.25
❏ 22	Chauncey Billups	1.00	.40
❏ 23	Richard Hamilton	.60	.25
❏ 24	Rasheed Wallace	1.00	.40
❏ 25	Jason Richardson	1.00	.40
❏ 26	Baron Davis	1.00	.40
❏ 27	Troy Murphy	1.00	.40
❏ 28	Tracy McGrady	2.50	1.00
❏ 29	Yao Ming	2.50	1.00
❏ 30	Shane Battier	1.00	.40
❏ 31	Jermaine O'Neal	1.00	.40
❏ 32	Sarunas Jasikevicius	.60	.25
❏ 33	Al Harrington	.30	.12
❏ 34	Elton Brand	1.00	.40
❏ 35	Sam Cassell	1.00	.40
❏ 36	Chris Kaman	.30	.12
❏ 37	Kobe Bryant	4.00	1.50
❏ 38	Lamar Odom	1.00	.40
❏ 39	Vladimir Radmanovic	.30	.12
❏ 40	Pau Gasol	1.00	.40
❏ 41	Hakim Warrick	.60	.25
❏ 42	Damon Stoudamire	.60	.25
❏ 43	Shaquille O'Neal	2.50	1.00
❏ 44	Dwyane Wade	3.00	1.25
❏ 45	Alonzo Mourning	1.00	.40
❏ 46	Andrew Bogut	1.25	.50
❏ 47	Charlie Villanueva	1.00	.40
❏ 48	Michael Redd	1.00	.40
❏ 49	Kevin Garnett	2.00	.75
❏ 50	Ricky Davis	1.00	.40
❏ 51	Rashad McCants	1.25	.50
❏ 52	Vince Carter	2.50	1.00
❏ 53	Jason Kidd	1.50	.60
❏ 54	Richard Jefferson	.60	.25
❏ 55	Chris Paul	2.50	1.00
❏ 56	Peja Stojakovic	1.00	.40
❏ 57	Tyson Chandler	1.00	.40
❏ 58	Stephon Marbury	1.00	.40
❏ 59	Channing Frye	.60	.25
❏ 60	Nate Robinson	1.00	.40
❏ 61	Grant Hill	1.00	.40
❏ 62	Dwight Howard	1.25	.50
❏ 63	Jameer Nelson	.60	.25
❏ 64	Allen Iverson	2.00	.75
❏ 65	Andre Iguodala	1.00	.40
❏ 66	Kyle Korver	1.00	.40
❏ 67	Steve Nash	1.00	.40
❏ 68	Amare Stoudemire	2.00	.75
❏ 69	Shawn Marion	1.00	.40
❏ 70	Jamaal Magloire	.30	.12
❏ 71	Martell Webster	.60	.25
❏ 72	Jarrett Jack	.60	.25
❏ 73	Mike Bibby	1.00	.40
❏ 74	Ron Artest	1.00	.40
❏ 75	Brad Miller	1.00	.40
❏ 76	Tony Parker	1.00	.40
❏ 77	Tim Duncan	2.00	.75
❏ 78	Manu Ginobili	1.00	.40
❏ 79	Ray Allen	1.00	.40
❏ 80	Rashard Lewis	.60	.25
❏ 81	Luke Ridnour	.60	.25
❏ 82	Chris Bosh	1.00	.40
❏ 83	T.J. Ford	.60	.25
❏ 84	Joey Graham	.60	.25
❏ 85	Carlos Boozer	.60	.25
❏ 86	Andrei Kirilenko	1.00	.40
❏ 87	Deron Williams	1.00	.40
❏ 88	Gilbert Arenas	1.00	.40
❏ 89	Antawn Jamison	1.00	.40
❏ 90	Andray Blatche	.30	.12
❏ 91	Adam Morrison RC	12.00	5.00
❏ 92	Alexander Johnson RC	5.00	2.00
❏ 93	J.J. Redick RC	10.00	4.00
❏ 94	Vassilis Spanoulis RC	5.00	2.00
❏ 95	Jorge Garbajosa RC	10.00	4.00
❏ 96	Leon Powe RC	5.00	2.00
❏ 97	Chris Quinn RC	5.00	2.00
❏ 98	Tarence Kinsey RC	5.00	2.00
❏ 99	Yakhouba Diawara RC	5.00	2.00
❏ 100	Robert Hite RC	5.00	2.00
❏ 101	Thabo Sefolosha RC	25.00	10.00
❏ 102	Ronnie Brewer AU RC	20.00	8.00
❏ 103	Cedric Simmons RC	15.00	6.00
❏ 104	Dee Brown AU RC EXCH	20.00	8.00
❏ 105	Craig Smith AU RC	15.00	6.00
❏ 106	Rodney Carney AU RC	15.00	6.00
❏ 107	Pops Mensah-Bonsu AU RC	15.00	6.00
❏ 108	Shawne Williams AU RC	20.00	8.00
❏ 109	Quincy Douby AU RC	15.00	6.00
❏ 110	Renaldo Balkman AU RC	15.00	6.00
❏ 111	Rajon Rondo AU RC	20.00	8.00
❏ 112	Marcus Williams AU RC	20.00	8.00
❏ 113	Josh Boone AU RC	15.00	6.00
❏ 114	Kyle Lowry AU RC	15.00	6.00
❏ 115	Shannon Brown AU RC	15.00	6.00
❏ 116	Jordan Farmar AU RC	30.00	12.00
❏ 117	Sergio Rodriguez AU RC	15.00	6.00
❏ 118	Maurice Ager AU RC	15.00	6.00
❏ 119	Mardy Collins AU RC	15.00	6.00
❏ 120	James White AU RC	15.00	6.00
❏ 121	Steve Novak AU RC	15.00	6.00
❏ 122	Solomon Jones AU RC	15.00	6.00
❏ 123	Andrea Bargnani AU RC EXCH	60.00	30.00
❏ 124	LaMarcus Aldridge AU RC	60.00	30.00
❏ 125	Tyrus Thomas AU RC	90.00	45.00
❏ 126	Shelden Williams AU RC	25.00	10.00
❏ 127	Brandon Roy AU RC	100.00	50.00
❏ 128	Randy Foye AU RC	40.00	15.00
❏ 129	Rudy Gay AU RC	40.00	15.00
❏ 130	Patrick O'Bryant AU RC	20.00	8.00
❏ 131	Saer Sene AU RC	20.00	8.00
❏ 132	Hilton Armstrong AU RC	20.00	8.00

1994-95 SP Championship

COMPLETE SET (135)	30.00	15.00
1 Mookie Blaylock RF	.10	.02
2 Dominique Wilkins RF	.20	.07
3 Alonzo Mourning RF	.40	.15
4 Michael Jordan RF	4.00	1.50
5 Mark Price RF	.10	.02
6 Jamal Mashburn RF	.20	.07
7 Dikembe Mutombo RF	.10	.02
8 Grant Hill RF	1.00	.40
9 Latrell Sprewell RF	.40	.15
10 Hakeem Olajuwon RF	.40	.15
11 Reggie Miller RF	.20	.07
12 Loy Vaught RF	.10	.02
13 Nick Van Exel RF	.20	.07
14 Glen Rice RF	.10	.02
15 Glenn Robinson RF	.60	.25
16 Isaiah Rider RF	.10	.02
17 Kenny Anderson RF	.10	.02
18 Patrick Ewing RF	.20	.07
19 Shaquille O'Neal RF	.75	.30
20 Dana Barros RF	.10	.02
21 Charles Barkley RF	.40	.15
22 Clifford Robinson RF	.10	.02
23 Mitch Richmond RF	.20	.07
24 David Robinson RF	.40	.15
25 Shawn Kemp RF	.40	.15
26 Karl Malone RF	.40	.15
27 Chris Webber RF	.50	.20
28 Stacey Augmon	.10	.02
29 Mookie Blaylock	.10	.02
30 Grant Long	.10	.02
31 Steve Smith	.20	.07
32 Dee Brown	.10	.02
33 Eric Montross RC	.10	.02
34 Dino Radja	.10	.02
35 Dominique Wilkins	.40	.15
36 Muggsy Bogues	.20	.07
37 Scott Burrell	.10	.02
38 Larry Johnson	.20	.07
39 Alonzo Mourning	.50	.20
40 B.J. Armstrong	.10	.02
41 Michael Jordan	8.00	4.00
42 Toni Kukoc	.60	.25
43 Scottie Pippen	1.25	.50
44 Tyrone Hill	.10	.02
45 Chris Mills	.20	.07
46 Mark Price	.10	.02
47 John Williams	.10	.02
48 Jim Jackson	.20	.07
49 Jason Kidd RC	4.00	1.50
50 Jamal Mashburn	.40	.15
51 Roy Tarpley	.10	.02
52 Mahmoud Abdul-Rauf	.10	.02
53 Dikembe Mutombo	.20	.07
54 Rodney Rogers	.10	.02
55 Bryant Stith	.10	.02
56 Joe Dumars	.40	.15
57 Grant Hill RC	2.00	.75
58 Lindsey Hunter	.20	.07
59 Terry Mills	.10	.02
60 Tim Hardaway	.40	.15
61 Donyell Marshall RC	.40	.15
62 Chris Mullin	.40	.15
63 Latrell Sprewell	.40	.15
64 Sam Cassell	.40	.15
65 Clyde Drexler	.40	.15
66 Vernon Maxwell	.10	.02
67 Hakeem Olajuwon	.60	.25
68 Dale Davis	.10	.02
69 Mark Jackson	.10	.02
70 Reggie Miller	.40	.15
71 Rik Smits	.10	.02
72 Terry Dehere	.10	.02
73 Lamond Murray RC	.20	.07
74 Pooh Richardson	.10	.02
75 Loy Vaught	.10	.02
76 Cedric Ceballos	.10	.02
77 Vlade Divac	.10	.02
78 Eddie Jones RC	2.00	.80
79 Nick Van Exel	.40	.15
80 Bimbo Coles	.10	.02
81 Billy Owens	.10	.02
82 Glen Rice	.20	.07
83 Kevin Willis	.10	.02
84 Vin Baker	.40	.15
85 Marty Conlon	.10	.02
86 Eric Murdock	.10	.02
87 Glenn Robinson RC	1.25	.50
88 Tom Gugliotta	.20	.07
89 Christian Laettner	.20	.07
90 Isaiah Rider	.20	.07
91 Doug West	.10	.02
92 Kenny Anderson	.20	.07
93 Benoit Benjamin	.10	.02
94 Derrick Coleman	.20	.07
95 Armon Gilliam	.10	.02
96 Patrick Ewing	.40	.15
97 Derek Harper	.10	.02
98 Charles Oakley	.10	.02
99 John Starks	.10	.02
100 Nick Anderson	.10	.02
101 Horace Grant	.20	.07
102 Anfernee Hardaway	1.00	.40
103 Shaquille O'Neal	2.00	.75
104 Dana Barros	.10	.02
105 Shawn Bradley	.10	.02
106 Clarence Weatherspoon	.10	.02
107 Sharone Wright RC	.10	.02
108 Charles Barkley	.60	.25
109 Kevin Johnson	.20	.07
110 Dan Majerle	.20	.07
111 Wesley Person RC	.40	.15
112 Terry Porter	.10	.02
113 Clifford Robinson	.20	.07
114 Rod Strickland	.20	.07
115 Buck Williams	.10	.02
116 Brian Grant RC	1.00	.40
117 Mitch Richmond	.40	.15
118 Spud Webb	.10	.02
119 Walt Williams	.10	.02
120 Vinny Del Negro	.10	.02
121 Sean Elliott	.20	.07
122 David Robinson	.60	.25
123 Dennis Rodman	.75	.30
124 Kendall Gill	.20	.07
125 Shawn Kemp	.60	.25
126 Gary Payton	.60	.25
127 Detlef Schrempf	.20	.07
128 David Benoit	.10	.02
129 Jeff Hornacek	.20	.07
130 Karl Malone	.60	.25
131 John Stockton	.40	.15
132 Rex Chapman	.10	.02
133 Calbert Cheaney	.10	.02
134 Juwan Howard RC	1.00	.40
135 Chris Webber	1.00	.40

1995-96 SP Championship

COMPLETE SET (146)	40.00	20.00
1 Stacey Augmon	.25	.08
2 Mookie Blaylock	.25	.08
3 Alan Henderson RC	.75	.30
4 Steve Smith	.50	.20
5 Dana Barros	.25	.08
6 Dee Brown	.25	.08
7 Eric Montross	.25	.08
8 Dino Radja	.25	.08
9 Eric Williams RC	.50	.20
10 Kenny Anderson	.50	.20
11 Larry Johnson	.50	.20
12 Glen Rice	.50	.20

13 George Zidek RC	.25	.08
14 Toni Kukoc	.50	.20
15 Scottie Pippen	1.25	.50
16 Dennis Rodman	.50	.20
17 Michael Jordan	5.00	2.00
18 Terrell Brandon	.50	.20
19 Danny Ferry	.25	.08
20 Chris Mills	.25	.08
21 Bobby Phills	.25	.08
22 Jim Jackson	.25	.08
23 Popeye Jones	.25	.08
24 Jason Kidd	2.50	1.00
25 Jamal Mashburn	.50	.20
26 Mahmoud Abdul-Rauf	.25	.08
27 Dale Ellis	.25	.08
28 Antonio McDyess RC	1.50	.60
29 Dikembe Mutombo	.50	.20
30 Joe Dumars	.75	.30
31 Grant Hill	1.00	.40
32 Allan Houston	.50	.20
33 Otis Thorpe	.25	.08
34 Tim Hardaway	.50	.20
35 Chris Mullin	.75	.30
36 Latrell Sprewell	.75	.30
37 Joe Smith RC	1.25	.50
38 Sam Cassell	.75	.30
39 Clyde Drexler	.75	.30
40 Robert Horry	.50	.20
41 Hakeem Olajuwon	.75	.30
42 Dale Davis	.25	.08
43 Derrick McKey	.25	.08
44 Reggie Miller	.75	.30
45 Rik Smits	.50	.20
46 Brent Barry RC	.75	.30
47 Lamond Murray	.25	.08
48 Loy Vaught	.25	.08
49 Brian Williams	.25	.08
50 Cedric Ceballos	.25	.08
51 Magic Johnson	1.25	.50
52 Eddie Jones	1.00	.40
53 Nick Van Exel	.75	.30
54 Sasha Danilovic RC	.25	.08
55 Alonzo Mourning	.50	.20
56 Billy Owens	.25	.08
57 Kevin Willis	.50	.20
58 Vin Baker	.50	.20
59 Sherman Douglas	.25	.08
60 Lee Mayberry	.25	.08
61 Glenn Robinson	.75	.30
62 Kevin Garnett RC	6.00	2.50
63 Tom Gugliotta	.25	.08
64 Christian Laettner	.50	.20
65 Isaiah Rider	.25	.08
66 Chris Childs	.25	.08
67 Kendall Gill	.25	.08
68 Armon Gilliam	.25	.08
69 Ed O'Bannon RC	.25	.08
70 Patrick Ewing	.75	.30
71 Derek Harper	.50	.20
72 Charles Oakley	.25	.08
73 John Starks	.50	.20
74 Horace Grant	.50	.20
75 Anfernee Hardaway	.75	.30
76 Shaquille O'Neal	2.00	.75
77 Dennis Scott	.25	.08
78 Derrick Coleman	.25	.08
79 Trevor Ruffin	.25	.08
80 Jerry Stackhouse RC	2.50	1.00

81	Clarence Weatherspoon	.25	.08
82	Charles Barkley	1.00	.40
83	Michael Finley RC	2.00	.75
84	Kevin Johnson	.50	.20
85	Danny Manning	.50	.20
86	Randolph Childress RC	.25	.08
87	Clifford Robinson	.25	.08
88	Arvydas Sabonis RC	1.00	.40
89	Rod Strickland	.25	.08
90	Tyus Edney RC	.25	.08
91	Brian Grant	.75	.30
92	Mitch Richmond	.50	.20
93	Walt Williams	.25	.08
94	Sean Elliott	.50	.20
95	Avery Johnson	.25	.08
96	Chuck Person	.25	.08
97	David Robinson	.75	.30
98	Shawn Kemp	.75	.30
99	Gary Payton	.75	.30
100	Sam Perkins	.50	.20
101	Detlef Schrempf	.50	.20
102	Ed Pinckney	.25	.08
103	Tracy Murray	.25	.08
104	Alvin Robertson	.25	.08
105	Damon Stoudamire RC	1.50	.60
106	Jeff Hornacek	.25	.08
107	Karl Malone	1.00	.40
108	Chris Morris	.25	.08
109	John Stockton	1.00	.40
110	Greg Anthony	.25	.08
111	Blue Edwards	.25	.08
112	Bryant Reeves RC	.75	.30
113	Byron Scott	.25	.08
114	Juwan Howard	.75	.30
115	Gheorghe Muresan	.25	.08
116	Rasheed Wallace RC	2.00	.75
117	Chris Webber	1.00	.40
118	Mookie Blaylock RP	.25	.08
119	Dana Barros RP	.25	.08
120	Larry Johnson RP	.50	.20
121	Michael Jordan RP	2.50	1.00
122	Terrell Brandon RP	.25	.08
123	Jason Kidd RP	1.25	.50
124	Mahmoud Abdul-Rauf RP	.25	.08
125	Grant Hill RP	.75	.30
126	Latrell Sprewell RP	.75	.30
127	Hakeem Olajuwon RP	.50	.20
128	Reggie Miller RP	.50	.20
129	Loy Vaught RP	.25	.08
130	Magic Johnson RP	.75	.30
131	Alonzo Mourning RP	.25	.08
132	Vin Baker RP	.25	.08
133	Tom Gugliotta RP	.25	.08
134	Ed O'Bannon RP	.25	.08
135	Patrick Ewing RP	.50	.20
136	Anfernee Hardaway RP	.50	.20
137	Jerry Stackhouse RP	1.25	.50
138	Charles Barkley RP	.25	.08
139	Clifford Robinson RP	.25	.08
140	Mitch Richmond RP	.50	.20
141	David Robinson RP	.50	.20
142	Shawn Kemp RP	.50	.20
143	Damon Stoudamire RP	1.00	.40
144	John Stockton RP	.75	.30
145	Bryant Reeves RP	.50	.20
146	Juwan Howard RP	.50	.20

2000-01 SP Game Floor

	COMMON CARD (1-60)	.75	.30
	COMMON ROOKIE (61-100)	1.50	.60
1	Jason Terry	2.50	1.00
2	Toni Kukoc	1.50	.60
3	Antoine Walker	2.50	1.00
4	Paul Pierce	2.50	1.00
5	Jamal Mashburn	1.50	.60
6	Baron Davis	2.50	1.00
7	Elton Brand	2.50	1.00
8	Ron Mercer	1.50	.60
9	Andre Miller	1.50	.60
10	Lamond Murray	.75	.30
11	Michael Finley	2.50	1.00
12	Dirk Nowitzki	4.00	1.50
13	Antonio McDyess	1.50	.60
14	Nick Van Exel	2.50	1.00
15	Jerry Stackhouse	2.50	1.00
16	Joe Smith	1.50	.60
17	Antawn Jamison	2.50	1.00
18	Larry Hughes	1.50	.60
19	Steve Francis	2.50	1.00
20	Maurice Taylor	1.50	.60
21	Jalen Rose	2.50	1.00
22	Reggie Miller	2.50	1.00
23	Lamar Odom	2.50	1.00
24	Corey Maggette	1.50	.60
25	Kobe Bryant	10.00	4.00
26	Shaquille O ™Neal	6.00	2.50
27	Horace Grant	1.50	.60
28	Eddie Jones	2.50	1.00
29	Tim Hardaway	1.50	.60
30	Glenn Robinson	2.50	1.00
31	Ray Allen	2.50	1.00
32	Kevin Garnett	5.00	2.00
33	Terrell Brandon	1.50	.60
34	Wally Szczerbiak	1.50	.60
35	Stephon Marbury	2.50	1.00
36	Keith Van Horn	2.50	1.00
37	Latrell Sprewell	2.50	1.00
38	Allan Houston	1.50	.60
39	Tracy McGrady	6.00	2.50
40	Darrell Armstrong	.75	.30
41	Allen Iverson	5.00	2.00
42	Dikembe Mutombo	1.50	.60
43	Jason Kidd	4.00	1.50
44	Shawn Marion	3.00	1.25
45	Rasheed Wallace	2.50	1.00
46	Damon Stoudamire	1.50	.60
47	Chris Webber	2.50	1.00
48	Jason Williams	1.50	.60
49	Tim Duncan	5.00	2.00
50	David Robinson	2.50	1.00
51	Gary Payton	2.50	1.00
52	Rashard Lewis	1.50	.60
53	Vince Carter	6.00	2.50
54	Charles Oakley	.75	.30
55	Karl Malone	2.50	1.00
56	John Stockton	2.50	1.00
57	Shareef Abdur-Rahim	2.50	1.00
58	Mike Bibby	2.50	1.00
59	Richard Hamilton	1.50	.60
60	Mitch Richmond	1.50	.60
61	Kenyon Martin RC	20.00	8.00
62	Marc Jackson RC	6.00	2.50
63	Darius Miles RC	15.00	6.00
64	Morris Peterson RC	10.00	4.00
65	Mike Miller RC	12.00	5.00
66	Quentin Richardson RC	25.00	10.00
67	DerMarr Johnson RC	6.00	2.50
68	Chris Mihm RC	6.00	2.50
69	Jamal Crawford RC	8.00	3.00
70	Joel Przybilla RC	6.00	2.50
71	Keyon Dooling RC	6.00	2.50
72	Jerome Moiso RC	6.00	2.50
73	Mike Penberthy RC	6.00	2.50
74	Courtney Alexander RC	6.00	2.50
75	Mateen Cleaves RC	6.00	2.50
76	Wang Zhizhi RC	6.00	2.50
77	Hidayet Turkoglu RC	10.00	4.00
78	Desmond Mason RC	6.00	2.50
79	Marcus Fizer RC	6.00	2.50
80	Jamaal Magloire RC	6.00	2.50
81	Stromile Swift RC	8.00	3.00
82	DeShawn Stevenson RC	6.00	2.50
83	Stephen Jackson RC	8.00	3.00
84	Erick Barkley RC	6.00	2.50
85	Mark Madsen RC	6.00	2.50
86	Dan Langhi RC	6.00	2.50
87	Hanno Mottola RC	6.00	2.50
88	Paul McPherson RC	6.00	2.50
89	Eddie House RC	6.00	2.50
90	Chris Porter RC	6.00	2.50
91	Jason Collier RC	6.00	2.50
92	Speedy Claxton RC	6.00	2.50
93	Ruben Wolkowyski RC	6.00	2.50
94	A.J. Guyton RC	6.00	2.50
95	Donnell Harvey RC	6.00	2.50
96	Ira Newble RC	6.00	2.50
97	Lee Nailon RC	6.00	2.50
98	Pepe Sanchez RC	6.00	2.50
99	Eduardo Najera RC	6.00	2.50
100	David Vanterpool RC	6.00	2.50

2002-03 SP Game Used

	COMMON CARD (1-102)	2.50	1.00
	COMMON JSY	12.00	5.00
	COMMON ROOKIE (103-144)	12.00	5.00
1	S.Abdur-Rahim JSY	15.00	6.00
2	DerMarr Johnson JSY	12.00	5.00
3	Jason Terry JSY	15.00	6.00
4	Antoine Walker JSY	15.00	6.00
5	Paul Pierce SP JSY	40.00	15.00
6	Kedrick Brown JSY	12.00	5.00
7	Tony Battie	2.50	1.00
8	Jamal Mashburn JSY	12.00	5.00
9	Baron Davis	5.00	2.00
10	David Wesley	2.50	1.00
11	Jalen Rose	5.00	2.00
12	Eddy Curry JSY	15.00	6.00
13	Tyson Chandler JSY	15.00	6.00
14	Marcus Fizer JSY	12.00	5.00
15	Lamond Murray	2.50	1.00
16	Andre Miller JSY	12.00	5.00
17	Chris Mihm JSY	12.00	5.00
18	Ricky Davis	3.00	1.25
19	Dirk Nowitzki	8.00	3.00
20	Michael Finley	5.00	2.00
21	Steve Nash	5.00	2.00
22	Nick Van Exel	5.00	2.00
23	Antonio McDyess JSY	12.00	5.00
24	Juwan Howard	3.00	1.25
25	James Posey	3.00	1.25
26	Jerry Stackhouse	5.00	2.00
27	Clifford Robinson	2.50	1.00
28	Ben Wallace	6.00	2.50
29	Antawn Jamison	6.00	2.50
30	J.Richardson SP JSY	15.00	6.00
31	Gilbert Arenas	5.00	2.00
32	Steve Francis	5.00	2.00
33	Cuttino Mobley	3.00	1.25
34	Eddie Griffin JSY	12.00	5.00
35	Reggie Miller JSY	15.00	6.00
36	Jermaine O'Neal	5.00	2.00
37	Jamaal Tinsley JSY	15.00	6.00
38	Elton Brand	5.00	2.00
39	Darius Miles JSY	15.00	6.00
40	Lamar Odom JSY	15.00	6.00
41	Corey Maggette JSY	15.00	6.00
42	Kobe Bryant SP JSY	80.00	30.00
43	Shaquille O'Neal	12.00	5.00
44	Derek Fisher	5.00	2.00
45	Devean George	3.00	1.25
46	Pau Gasol	5.00	2.00
47	Jason Williams	3.00	1.25

❏ 48	Shane Battier	5.00	2.00
❏ 49	Stromile Swift	3.00	1.25
❏ 50	Alonzo Mourning	3.00	1.25
❏ 51	Eddie Jones	5.00	2.00
❏ 52	Brian Grant	3.00	1.25
❏ 53	Ray Allen	5.00	2.00
❏ 54	Glenn Robinson	5.00	2.00
❏ 55	Sam Cassell	5.00	2.00
❏ 56	Kevin Garnett SP JSY	40.00	15.00
❏ 57	Wally Szczerbiak JSY	15.00	6.00
❏ 58	Terrell Brandon JSY	12.00	5.00
❏ 59	Chauncey Billups JSY	12.00	5.00
❏ 60	Jason Kidd SP	40.00	15.00
❏ 61	Richard Jefferson	3.00	1.25
❏ 62	Kenyon Martin JSY	12.00	5.00
❏ 63	B.Armstrong JSY	12.00	5.00
❏ 64	Keith Van Horn	5.00	2.00
❏ 65	Allan Houston	3.00	1.25
❏ 66	Latrell Sprewell	5.00	2.00
❏ 67	Kurt Thomas	3.00	1.25
❏ 68	Tracy McGrady	12.00	5.00
❏ 69	Mike Miller JSY	15.00	6.00
❏ 70	Darrell Armstrong JSY	12.00	5.00
❏ 71	Allen Iverson	25.00	10.00
❏ 72	D.Mutombo JSY	15.00	6.00
❏ 73	Aaron McKie	3.00	1.25
❏ 74	Stephon Marbury	5.00	2.00
❏ 75	Shawn Marion	5.00	2.00
❏ 76	Joe Johnson	12.00	5.00
❏ 77	Anfernee Hardaway	5.00	2.00
❏ 78	Rasheed Wallace	5.00	2.00
❏ 79	Damon Stoudamire	3.00	1.25
❏ 80	Scottie Pippen	8.00	3.00
❏ 81	Chris Webber	5.00	2.00
❏ 82	Peja Stojakovic	5.00	2.00
❏ 83	Mike Bibby	15.00	6.00
❏ 84	Gerald Wallace JSY	12.00	5.00
❏ 85	Tim Duncan	10.00	4.00
❏ 86	David Robinson	10.00	4.00
❏ 87	Tony Parker JSY	20.00	8.00
❏ 88	Gary Payton	5.00	2.00
❏ 89	Rashard Lewis	3.00	1.25
❏ 90	Desmond Mason	3.00	1.25
❏ 91	V.Radmanovic JSY	12.00	5.00
❏ 92	Morris Peterson	5.00	2.00
❏ 93	Antonio Davis	2.50	1.00
❏ 94	Vince Carter	12.00	5.00
❏ 95	Karl Malone	5.00	2.00
❏ 96	John Stockton JSY	20.00	8.00
❏ 97	Donyell Marshall	3.00	1.25
❏ 98	Andrei Kirilenko	5.00	2.00
❏ 99	Richard Hamilton	3.00	1.25
❏ 100	Michael Jordan SP JSY	300.00	150.00
❏ 101	C.Alexander JSY	12.00	5.00
❏ 102	Kwame Brown JSY	12.00	5.00
❏ 103	Jay Williams JSY	10.00	4.00
❏ 104	Yao Ming RC	80.00	40.00
❏ 105	Drew Gooden RC	20.00	8.00
❏ 106	DaJuan Wagner RC	12.00	5.00
❏ 107	Curtis Borchardt RC	12.00	5.00
❏ 108	Amare Stoudemire RC	40.00	15.00
❏ 109	Caron Butler RC	15.00	6.00
❏ 110	Jared Jeffries RC	6.00	2.50
❏ 111	Chris Wilcox RC	10.00	4.00
❏ 112	Qyntel Woods RC	8.00	3.00
❏ 113	Casey Jacobsen RC	15.00	6.00
❏ 114	Melvin Ely RC	6.00	2.50
❏ 115	Kareem Rush RC	8.00	3.00
❏ 116	Mike Dunleavy RC	12.00	5.00
❏ 117	Dan Dickau RC	5.00	2.00
❏ 118	Juan Dixon RC	10.00	4.00
❏ 119	Sam Clancy RC	12.00	5.00
❏ 120	Tayshaun Prince RC	10.00	4.00
❏ 121	Dan Gadzuric RC	12.00	5.00
❏ 122	Chris Jefferies RC	6.00	2.50
❏ 123	Steve Logan RC	15.00	6.00
❏ 124	Vincent Yarbrough RC	12.00	5.00
❏ 125	Fred Jones RC	8.00	3.00
❏ 126	Efthimios Rentzias RC	10.00	4.00
❏ 127	Nene Hilario RC	10.00	4.00
❏ 128	Rod Grizzard RC	12.00	5.00
❏ 129	Matt Barnes RC	12.00	5.00
❏ 130	Nikoloz Tskitishvili RC	10.00	4.00
❏ 131	Bostjan Nachbar RC	6.00	2.50
❏ 132	Marcus Haislip RC	12.00	5.00
❏ 133	Jamal Sampson RC	12.00	5.00
❏ 134	Frank Williams RC	5.00	2.00
❏ 135	Tito Maddox RC	12.00	5.00
❏ 136	Carlos Boozer RC	12.00	5.00
❏ 137	Jiri Welsch RC	12.00	5.00
❏ 138	John Salmons RC	12.00	5.00
❏ 139	Predrag Savovic RC	10.00	4.00
❏ 140	Marko Jaric	12.00	5.00
❏ 141	Robert Archibald RC	12.00	5.00
❏ 142	Manu Ginobili RC	30.00	12.50
❏ 143	Chris Owens RC	12.00	5.00
❏ 144	Ryan Humphrey RC	10.00	4.00

2003-04 SP Game Used

❏	COMMON CARD (1-94)	1.50	.60
❏	COMMON JSY (1-94)	10.00	4.00
❏	COMMON MJ TRIB (95-106)	25.00	10.00
❏	COMMON ROOKIE (107-148)	10.00	4.00
❏ 1	Shareef Abdur-Rahim	5.00	2.00
❏ 2	Glenn Robinson	5.00	2.00
❏ 3	Jason Terry JSY	10.00	4.00
❏ 4	Paul Pierce	5.00	2.00
❏ 5	Antoine Walker	5.00	2.00
❏ 6	Eddy Curry	5.00	2.00
❏ 7	Tyson Chandler JSY	10.00	4.00
❏ 8	Jalen Rose JSY	10.00	4.00
❏ 9	Jay Williams JSY	10.00	4.00
❏ 10	DaJuan Wagner JSY	10.00	4.00
❏ 11	Darius Miles JSY	10.00	4.00
❏ 12	Carlos Boozer JSY	10.00	4.00
❏ 13	Steve Nash	5.00	2.00
❏ 14	Michael Finley	5.00	2.00
❏ 15	Nick Van Exel	5.00	2.00
❏ 16	Dirk Nowitzki JSY	15.00	6.00
❏ 17	Rodney White	1.50	.60
❏ 18	Marcus Camby	3.00	1.25
❏ 19	Nikoloz Tskitishvili	3.00	1.25
❏ 20	Nene Hilario JSY	10.00	4.00
❏ 21	Richard Hamilton	3.00	1.25
❏ 22	Chauncey Billups	3.00	1.25
❏ 23	Ben Wallace	5.00	2.00
❏ 24	Gilbert Arenas	5.00	2.00
❏ 25	Troy Murphy	5.00	2.00
❏ 26	Jason Richardson JSY	10.00	4.00
❏ 27	Antawn Jamison JSY	10.00	4.00
❏ 28	Cuttino Mobley	3.00	1.25
❏ 29	Steve Francis	5.00	2.00
❏ 30	Eddie Griffin	3.00	1.25
❏ 31	Jermaine O'Neal	5.00	2.00
❏ 32	Reggie Miller	5.00	2.00
❏ 33	Jamaal Tinsley JSY	10.00	4.00
❏ 34	Lamar Odom	5.00	2.00
❏ 35	Chris Wilcox	3.00	1.25
❏ 36	Marko Jaric	3.00	1.25
❏ 37	Elton Brand JSY	10.00	4.00
❏ 38	Andre Miller JSY	10.00	4.00
❏ 39	Kobe Bryant	15.00	6.00
❏ 40	Shaquille O'Neal	12.00	5.00
❏ 41	Gary Payton	5.00	2.00
❏ 42	Kareem Rush JSY	10.00	4.00
❏ 43	Mike Miller	5.00	2.00
❏ 44	Shane Battier JSY	10.00	4.00
❏ 45	Pau Gasol JSY	10.00	4.00
❏ 46	Eddie Jones	5.00	2.00
❏ 47	Brian Grant	3.00	1.25
❏ 48	Caron Butler JSY	10.00	4.00
❏ 49	Joe Smith	3.00	1.25
❏ 50	Desmond Mason	3.00	1.25
❏ 51	Toni Kukoc	3.00	1.25
❏ 52	Wally Szczerbiak	3.00	1.25
❏ 53	Kevin Garnett JSY	20.00	8.00
❏ 54	Alonzo Mourning	3.00	1.25
❏ 55	Kenyon Martin	5.00	2.00
❏ 56	Jason Kidd JSY	15.00	6.00
❏ 57	Richard Jefferson JSY	10.00	4.00
❏ 58	Baron Davis	5.00	2.00
❏ 59	Jamal Mashburn JSY	10.00	4.00
❏ 60	Latrell Sprewell	5.00	2.00
❏ 61	Allan Houston	3.00	1.25
❏ 62	Antonio McDyess	3.00	1.25
❏ 63	Juwan Howard	3.00	1.25
❏ 64	Drew Gooden JSY	10.00	4.00
❏ 65	Tracy McGrady	25.00	10.00
❏ 66	Keith Van Horn	5.00	2.00
❏ 67	Aaron McKie	3.00	1.25
❏ 68	Allen Iverson JSY	20.00	8.00
❏ 69	Stephon Marbury	5.00	2.00
❏ 70	Shawn Marion	5.00	2.00
❏ 71	Anfernee Hardaway	5.00	2.00
❏ 72	Joe Johnson	3.00	1.25
❏ 73	Amare Stoudemire JSY	15.00	6.00
❏ 74	Rasheed Wallace	5.00	2.00
❏ 75	Scottie Pippen	8.00	3.00
❏ 76	Mike Bibby	5.00	2.00
❏ 77	Peja Stojakovic	5.00	2.00
❏ 78	Gerald Wallace	3.00	1.25
❏ 79	Chris Webber JSY	10.00	4.00
❏ 80	Tim Duncan	10.00	4.00
❏ 81	Manu Ginobili	5.00	2.00
❏ 82	Tony Parker JSY	10.00	4.00
❏ 83	Ray Allen	5.00	2.00
❏ 84	Rashard Lewis JSY	10.00	4.00
❏ 85	Morris Peterson	3.00	1.25
❏ 86	Antonio Davis	1.50	.60
❏ 87	Vince Carter	12.00	5.00
❏ 88	John Stockton JSY	10.00	4.00
❏ 89	Karl Malone JSY	10.00	4.00
❏ 90	Jerry Stackhouse	3.00	1.25
❏ 91	Michael Jordan	20.00	8.00
❏ 92	Michael Jordan JSY	150.00	75.00
❏ 93	Kobe Bryant JSY	40.00	15.00
❏ 94	Yao Ming JSY	25.00	10.00
❏ 95	M.Jordan Tribute	25.00	10.00
❏ 96	M.Jordan Tribute	25.00	10.00
❏ 97	M.Jordan Tribute	25.00	10.00
❏ 98	M.Jordan Tribute	25.00	10.00
❏ 99	M.Jordan Tribute	25.00	10.00
❏ 100	M.Jordan Tribute	25.00	10.00
❏ 101	M.Jordan Tribute	25.00	10.00
❏ 102	M.Jordan Tribute	25.00	10.00
❏ 103	M.Jordan Tribute	25.00	10.00
❏ 104	M.Jordan Tribute	25.00	10.00
❏ 105	M.Jordan Tribute	25.00	10.00
❏ 106	M.Jordan Tribute	25.00	10.00
❏ 107	Lebron James RC	120.00	60.00
❏ 108	Darko Milicic RC	15.00	6.00
❏ 109	Carmelo Anthony RC	40.00	15.00
❏ 110	Chris Bosh RC	30.00	12.50
❏ 111	Dwyane Wade RC	50.00	20.00
❏ 112	Chris Kaman RC	10.00	4.00
❏ 113	Kirk Hinrich RC	15.00	6.00
❏ 114	T.J. Ford RC	12.00	5.00
❏ 115	Mike Sweetney RC	10.00	4.00
❏ 116	Jarvis Hayes RC	10.00	4.00
❏ 117	Mickael Pietrus RC	10.00	4.00
❏ 118	Nick Collison RC	10.00	4.00
❏ 119	Marcus Banks RC	10.00	4.00
❏ 120	Luke Ridnour RC	12.00	5.00
❏ 121	Reece Gaines RC	10.00	4.00
❏ 122	Troy Bell RC	10.00	4.00
❏ 123	Zarko Cabarkapa RC	10.00	4.00
❏ 124	David West RC	10.00	4.00
❏ 125	Aleksandar Pavlovic RC	12.00	5.00
❏ 126	Dahntay Jones RC	10.00	4.00
❏ 127	Boris Diaw RC	10.00	4.00
❏ 128	Zoran Planinic RC	10.00	4.00
❏ 129	Travis Outlaw RC	10.00	4.00
❏ 130	Brian Cook RC	10.00	4.00
❏ 131	Carlos Delfino RC	10.00	4.00
❏ 132	Ndudi Ebi RC	10.00	4.00
❏ 133	Kendrick Perkins RC	10.00	4.00
❏ 134	Leandro Barbosa RC	15.00	6.00
❏ 135	Josh Howard RC	12.00	5.00
❏ 136	Maciej Lampe RC	10.00	4.00
❏ 137	Jason Kapono RC	10.00	4.00

❏ 138	Luke Walton RC	10.00	4.00
❏ 139	Jerome Beasley RC	10.00	4.00
❏ 140	Sofoklis Schortsanitis RC	12.00	5.00
❏ 141	Mario Austin RC	10.00	4.00
❏ 142	Travis Hansen RC	10.00	4.00
❏ 143	Steve Blake RC	10.00	4.00
❏ 144	Slavko Vranes RC	10.00	4.00
❏ 145	Zaur Pachulia RC	10.00	4.00
❏ 146	Keith Bogans RC	10.00	4.00
❏ 147	Matt Bonner RC	10.00	4.00
❏ 148	Maurice Williams RC	10.00	4.00

2004-05 SP Game Used

❏ COMMON CARD (1-60)		1.25	.50
❏ COMMON JSY (61-90)		8.00	3.00
❏ COMMON ROOKIE (91-132)		8.00	3.00
❏ COMMON LEBRON SIR (133-162)		10.00	4.00
❏ 1	Tony Delk	1.25	.50
❏ 2	Boris Diaw	1.25	.50
❏ 3	Ricky Davis	4.00	1.50
❏ 4	Gary Payton	2.50	1.00
❏ 5	Gerald Wallace	2.50	1.00
❏ 6	Jason Kapono	4.00	1.50
❏ 7	Tyson Chandler	4.00	1.50
❏ 8	Kirk Hinrich	4.00	1.50
❏ 9	Dajuan Wagner	2.50	1.00
❏ 10	Zydrunas Ilgauskas	4.00	1.50
❏ 11	Jerry Stackhouse	4.00	1.50
❏ 12	Michael Finley	4.00	1.50
❏ 13	Andre Miller	2.50	1.00
❏ 14	Nene	2.50	1.00
❏ 15	Richard Hamilton	2.50	1.00
❏ 16	Rasheed Wallace	4.00	1.50
❏ 17	Derek Fisher	4.00	1.50
❏ 18	Mike Dunleavy	2.50	1.00
❏ 19	Tracy McGrady	10.00	4.00
❏ 20	Jim Jackson	1.25	.50
❏ 21	Reggie Miller	4.00	1.50
❏ 22	Jermaine O'Neal	4.00	1.50
❏ 23	Elton Brand	4.00	1.50
❏ 24	Corey Maggette	2.50	1.00
❏ 25	Lamar Odom	4.00	1.50
❏ 26	Caron Butler	4.00	1.50
❏ 27	Pau Gasol	4.00	1.50
❏ 28	Bonzi Wells	2.50	1.00
❏ 29	Dwyane Wade	12.00	5.00
❏ 30	Shaquille O'Neal	10.00	4.00
❏ 31	Michael Redd	2.50	1.00
❏ 32	T.J. Ford	2.50	1.00
❏ 33	Latrell Sprewell	4.00	1.50
❏ 34	Sam Cassell	4.00	1.50
❏ 35	Jason Kidd	6.00	2.50
❏ 36	Richard Jefferson	2.50	1.00
❏ 37	Baron Davis	4.00	1.50
❏ 38	Jamaal Magloire	1.25	.50
❏ 39	Allan Houston	2.50	1.00
❏ 40	Stephon Marbury	4.00	1.50
❏ 41	Steve Francis	4.00	1.50
❏ 42	Cuttino Mobley	2.50	1.00
❏ 43	Glenn Robinson	4.00	1.50
❏ 44	Kenny Thomas	1.25	.50
❏ 45	Shawn Marion	4.00	1.50
❏ 46	Amare Stoudemire	8.00	3.00
❏ 47	Zach Randolph	4.00	1.50
❏ 48	Damon Stoudamire	4.00	1.50
❏ 49	Chris Webber	4.00	1.50
❏ 50	Peja Stojakovic	4.00	1.50
❏ 51	Manu Ginobili	4.00	1.50
❏ 52	Tim Duncan	8.00	3.00
❏ 53	Rashard Lewis	4.00	1.50
❏ 54	Ray Allen	4.00	1.50
❏ 55	Jalen Rose	4.00	1.50
❏ 56	Vince Carter	10.00	4.00
❏ 57	Carlos Boozer	4.00	1.50
❏ 58	Andrei Kirilenko	4.00	1.50
❏ 59	Larry Hughes	2.50	1.00
❏ 60	Gilbert Arenas	4.00	1.50
❏ 61	Paul Pierce JSY	8.00	3.00
❏ 62	Eddy Curry JSY	8.00	3.00
❏ 63	LeBron James JSY	50.00	20.00
❏ 64	Antawn Jamison JSY	8.00	3.00
❏ 65	Dirk Nowitzki JSY	12.00	5.00
❏ 66	Antoine Walker JSY	8.00	3.00
❏ 67	Carmelo Anthony JSY	20.00	8.00
❏ 68	Ben Wallace JSY	8.00	3.00
❏ 69	Jason Richardson JSY	8.00	3.00
❏ 70	Yao Ming JSY	15.00	6.00
❏ 71	Michael Jordan JSY	120.00	60.00
❏ 72	Kobe Bryant JSY	40.00	15.00
❏ 73	Quentin Richardson JSY	8.00	3.00
❏ 74	Jason Williams JSY	8.00	3.00
❏ 75	Eddie Jones JSY	8.00	3.00
❏ 76	Keith Van Horn JSY	8.00	3.00
❏ 77	Kevin Garnett JSY	12.00	5.00
❏ 78	Kenyon Martin JSY	8.00	3.00
❏ 79	Jamal Mashburn JSY	8.00	3.00
❏ 80	Kurt Thomas JSY	8.00	3.00
❏ 81	Juwan Howard JSY	8.00	3.00
❏ 82	Allen Iverson JSY	12.00	5.00
❏ 83	Joe Johnson JSY	8.00	3.00
❏ 84	Shareef Abdur-Rahim JSY	8.00	3.00
❏ 85	Mike Bibby JSY	8.00	3.00
❏ 86	Tony Parker JSY	8.00	3.00
❏ 87	Luke Ridnour JSY	8.00	3.00
❏ 88	Jalen Rose JSY	8.00	3.00
❏ 89	Gordan Giricek JSY	8.00	3.00
❏ 90	Juan Dixon JSY	8.00	3.00
❏ 91	Emeka Okafor RC	30.00	12.50
❏ 92	Dwight Howard RC	25.00	10.00
❏ 93	Shaun Livingston RC	12.00	5.00
❏ 94	Luol Deng RC	15.00	6.00
❏ 95	Ben Gordon RC	30.00	12.50
❏ 96	Devin Harris RC	12.00	5.00
❏ 97	Andre Iguodala RC	20.00	8.00
❏ 98	Andris Biedrins RC	15.00	6.00
❏ 99	Josh Childress RC	10.00	4.00
❏ 100	Josh Smith RC	15.00	6.00
❏ 101	Jameer Nelson RC	12.00	5.00
❏ 102	J.R. Smith RC	15.00	6.00
❏ 103	Sergei Monia RC	8.00	3.00
❏ 104	Sebastian Telfair RC	8.00	3.00
❏ 105	Pavel Podkolzine RC	8.00	3.00
❏ 106	Luke Jackson RC	8.00	3.00
❏ 107	Dorell Wright RC	12.00	5.00
❏ 108	Robert Swift RC	8.00	3.00
❏ 109	Anderson Varejao RC	10.00	4.00
❏ 110	Sasha Vujacic RC	8.00	3.00
❏ 111	Rafael Araujo RC	8.00	3.00
❏ 112	Al Jefferson RC	20.00	8.00
❏ 113	Kris Humphries RC	8.00	3.00
❏ 114	Kirk Snyder RC	8.00	3.00
❏ 115	Peter John Ramos RC	8.00	3.00
❏ 116	Beno Udrih RC	12.00	5.00
❏ 117	Viktor Khryapa RC	8.00	3.00
❏ 118	David Harrison RC	8.00	3.00
❏ 119	Trevor Ariza RC	10.00	4.00
❏ 120	Ha Seung-Jin RC	8.00	3.00
❏ 121	Kevin Martin RC	12.00	5.00
❏ 122	Delonte West RC	15.00	6.00
❏ 123	Blake Stepp RC	8.00	3.00
❏ 124	Chris Duhon RC	15.00	6.00
❏ 125	Tony Allen RC	10.00	4.00
❏ 126	Donta Smith RC	8.00	3.00
❏ 127	Andre Emmett RC	8.00	3.00
❏ 128	Royal Ivey RC	8.00	3.00
❏ 129	Nenad Krstic RC	12.00	5.00
❏ 130	Romain Sato RC	8.00	3.00
❏ 131	Antonio Burks RC	8.00	3.00
❏ 132	Lionel Chalmers RC	8.00	3.00
❏ 133	LeBron James SIR	10.00	4.00
❏ 134	LeBron James SIR	10.00	4.00
❏ 135	LeBron James SIR	10.00	4.00
❏ 136	LeBron James SIR	10.00	4.00
❏ 137	LeBron James SIR	10.00	4.00
❏ 138	LeBron James SIR	10.00	4.00
❏ 139	LeBron James SIR	10.00	4.00
❏ 140	LeBron James SIR	10.00	4.00
❏ 141	LeBron James SIR	10.00	4.00
❏ 142	LeBron James SIR	10.00	4.00
❏ 143	LeBron James SIR	10.00	4.00
❏ 144	LeBron James SIR	10.00	4.00
❏ 145	LeBron James SIR	10.00	4.00
❏ 146	LeBron James SIR	10.00	4.00
❏ 147	LeBron James SIR	10.00	4.00
❏ 148	LeBron James SIR	10.00	4.00
❏ 149	LeBron James SIR	10.00	4.00
❏ 150	LeBron James SIR	10.00	4.00
❏ 151	LeBron James SIR	10.00	4.00
❏ 152	LeBron James SIR	10.00	4.00
❏ 153	LeBron James SIR	10.00	4.00
❏ 154	LeBron James SIR	10.00	4.00
❏ 155	LeBron James SIR	10.00	4.00
❏ 156	LeBron James SIR	10.00	4.00
❏ 157	LeBron James SIR	10.00	4.00
❏ 158	LeBron James SIR	10.00	4.00
❏ 159	LeBron James SIR	10.00	4.00
❏ 160	LeBron James SIR	10.00	4.00
❏ 161	LeBron James SIR	10.00	4.00
❏ 162	LeBron James SIR	10.00	4.00

2005-06 SP Game Used

❏ COMMON CARD (1-100)		1.50	.60
❏ COMMON ROOKIE (101-150)		10.00	4.00
❏ 1	Al Harrington	1.50	.60
❏ 2	Josh Smith	1.50	.60
❏ 3	Josh Childress	1.50	.60
❏ 4	Joe Johnson	1.50	.60
❏ 5	Paul Pierce	2.50	1.00
❏ 6	Antoine Walker	2.50	1.00
❏ 7	Gary Payton	2.50	1.00
❏ 8	Al Jefferson	2.50	1.00
❏ 9	Emeka Okafor	4.00	1.50
❏ 10	Primoz Brezec	1.50	.60
❏ 11	Gerald Wallace	1.50	.60
❏ 12	Michael Jordan	15.00	6.00
❏ 13	Ben Gordon	5.00	2.00
❏ 14	Luol Deng	2.50	1.00
❏ 15	Eddy Curry	1.50	.60
❏ 16	LeBron James	15.00	6.00
❏ 17	Dajuan Wagner	1.50	.60
❏ 18	Drew Gooden	1.50	.60
❏ 19	Larry Hughes	1.50	.60
❏ 20	Dirk Nowitzki	4.00	1.50
❏ 21	Marquis Daniels	1.50	.60
❏ 22	Michael Finley	2.50	1.00
❏ 23	Jerry Stackhouse	2.50	1.00
❏ 24	Andre Miller	1.50	.60
❏ 25	Carmelo Anthony	5.00	2.00
❏ 26	Kenyon Martin	2.50	1.00
❏ 27	Nene	1.50	.60
❏ 28	Rasheed Wallace	2.50	1.00
❏ 29	Ben Wallace	2.50	1.00
❏ 30	Richard Hamilton	2.50	1.00
❏ 31	Chauncey Billups	2.50	1.00
❏ 32	Baron Davis	2.50	1.00
❏ 33	Derek Fisher	2.50	1.00
❏ 34	Jason Richardson	2.50	1.00
❏ 35	Tracy McGrady	6.00	2.50
❏ 36	Yao Ming	6.00	2.50
❏ 37	Juwan Howard	1.50	.60
❏ 38	Jermaine O'Neal	2.50	1.00
❏ 39	Ron Artest	1.50	.60

❑ 40	Jamaal Tinsley	1.50	.60
❑ 41	Corey Maggette	1.50	.60
❑ 42	Elton Brand	2.50	1.00
❑ 43	Shaun Livingston	2.50	1.00
❑ 44	Kobe Bryant	10.00	4.00
❑ 45	Brian Cook	1.50	.60
❑ 46	Lamar Odom	2.50	1.00
❑ 47	Bonzi Wells	1.50	.60
❑ 48	Pau Gasol	2.50	1.00
❑ 49	Shane Battier	2.50	1.00
❑ 50	Shaquille O'Neal	6.00	2.50
❑ 51	Dwyane Wade	8.00	3.00
❑ 52	Dorell Wright	1.50	.60
❑ 53	Eddie Jones	1.50	.60
❑ 54	Joe Smith	1.50	.60
❑ 55	Michael Redd	2.50	1.00
❑ 56	Desmond Mason	1.50	.60
❑ 57	Kevin Garnett	5.00	2.00
❑ 58	Wally Szczerbiak	2.50	1.00
❑ 59	Sam Cassell	2.50	1.00
❑ 60	Vince Carter	6.00	2.50
❑ 61	Jason Kidd	4.00	1.50
❑ 62	Richard Jefferson	1.50	.60
❑ 63	Jamaal Magloire	1.50	.60
❑ 64	J.R. Smith	1.50	.60
❑ 65	Bostjan Nachbar	1.50	.60
❑ 66	Allan Houston	1.50	.60
❑ 67	Stephon Marbury	2.50	1.00
❑ 68	Jamal Crawford	1.50	.60
❑ 69	Dwight Howard	3.00	1.25
❑ 70	Grant Hill	2.50	1.00
❑ 71	Jameer Nelson	1.50	.60
❑ 72	Steve Francis	2.50	1.00
❑ 73	Allen Iverson	5.00	2.00
❑ 74	Andre Iguodala	2.50	1.00
❑ 75	Chris Webber	2.50	1.00
❑ 76	Samuel Dalembert	1.50	.60
❑ 77	Amare Stoudemire	5.00	2.00
❑ 78	Steve Nash	2.50	1.00
❑ 79	Quentin Richardson	1.50	.60
❑ 80	Shawn Marion	1.50	.60
❑ 81	Darius Miles	2.50	1.00
❑ 82	Zach Randolph	2.50	1.00
❑ 83	Shareef Abdur-Rahim	2.50	1.00
❑ 84	Peja Stojakovic	2.50	1.00
❑ 85	Mike Bibby	2.50	1.00
❑ 86	Manu Ginobili	2.50	1.00
❑ 87	Tim Duncan	5.00	2.00
❑ 88	Tony Parker	2.50	1.00
❑ 89	Ray Allen	2.50	1.00
❑ 90	Rashard Lewis	2.50	1.00
❑ 91	Robert Swift	1.50	.60
❑ 92	Ronald Murray	1.50	.60
❑ 93	Chris Bosh	2.50	1.00
❑ 94	Morris Peterson	1.50	.60
❑ 95	Rafael Araujo	1.50	.60
❑ 96	Andrei Kirilenko	2.50	1.00
❑ 97	Raul Lopez	1.50	.60
❑ 98	Carlos Boozer	1.50	.60
❑ 99	Antawn Jamison	2.50	1.00
❑ 100	Gilbert Arenas	2.50	1.00
❑ 101	Andrew Bynum RC	30.00	12.50
❑ 102	Julius Hodge RC	12.00	5.00
❑ 103	David Lee RC	15.00	6.00
❑ 104	Sarunas Jasikevicius RC	12.00	5.00
❑ 105	Ike Diogu RC	12.00	5.00
❑ 106	Luther Head RC	12.00	5.00
❑ 107	Jason Maxiell RC	10.00	4.00
❑ 108	Linas Kleiza RC	10.00	4.00
❑ 109	Amir Johnson RC	10.00	4.00
❑ 110	Andray Blatche RC	10.00	4.00
❑ 111	Sean May RC	10.00	4.00
❑ 112	Alex Acker RC	10.00	4.00
❑ 113	Nate Robinson RC	12.00	5.00
❑ 114	Brandon Bass RC	10.00	4.00
❑ 115	Ricky Sanchez RC	10.00	4.00
❑ 116	Daniel Ewing RC	12.00	5.00
❑ 117	Salim Stoudamire RC	12.00	5.00
❑ 118	Dijon Thompson RC	10.00	4.00
❑ 119	Danny Granger RC	15.00	6.00
❑ 120	Raymond Felton RC	20.00	8.00
❑ 121	Louis Williams RC	10.00	4.00
❑ 122	Channing Frye RC	15.00	6.00
❑ 123	Francisco Garcia RC	12.00	5.00
❑ 124	Ryan Gomes RC	10.00	4.00
❑ 125	Ersan Ilyasova RC	10.00	4.00
❑ 126	Jarrett Jack RC	10.00	4.00
❑ 127	Lawrence Roberts RC	10.00	4.00
❑ 128	Bracey Wright RC	12.00	5.00
❑ 129	C.J. Miles RC	10.00	4.00
❑ 130	Will Bynum RC	10.00	4.00
❑ 131	Travis Diener RC	10.00	4.00
❑ 132	Monta Ellis RC	20.00	8.00
❑ 133	Martell Webster RC	10.00	4.00
❑ 134	Johan Petro RC	10.00	4.00
❑ 135	Uros Slokar RC	10.00	4.00
❑ 136	Von Wafer RC	10.00	4.00
❑ 137	Martynas Andriuskevicius RC	10.00	4.00
❑ 138	Charlie Villanueva RC	15.00	6.00
❑ 139	Antoine Wright RC	10.00	4.00
❑ 140	Joey Graham RC	10.00	4.00
❑ 141	Wayne Simien RC	12.00	5.00
❑ 142	Hakim Warrick RC	12.00	5.00
❑ 143	Gerald Green RC	30.00	12.50
❑ 144	Marvin Williams RC	20.00	8.00
❑ 145	Deron Williams RC	30.00	12.50
❑ 146	Rashad McCants RC	20.00	8.00
❑ 147	Robert Whaley RC	10.00	4.00
❑ 148	Chris Taft RC	10.00	4.00
❑ 149	Chris Paul RC	50.00	20.00
❑ 150	Andrew Bogut RC	12.00	5.00

2005-06 SP Game Used SIGnificance

❑ SIG 25	PRINT RUN 25 SER.#'d SETS		
❑ SIG 10	PRINT RUN 10 SER.#'d SETS		
❑ AB	Andray Blatche EXCH	12.00	5.00
❑ AH	Al Harrington	12.00	5.00
❑ AI	Andre Iguodala	20.00	8.00
❑ AJ	Antawn Jamison		
❑ AK0	Andrei Kirilenko ERR	30.00	12.50
❑ AL	Al Jefferson	20.00	8.00
❑ AM	Antonio McDyess	20.00	8.00
❑ AN	Martynas Andriuskevicius	12.00	5.00
❑ AR	Carlos Arroyo	40.00	15.00
❑ AW	Antoine Wright	12.00	5.00
❑ BB	Brandon Bass	12.00	5.00
❑ BD	Baron Davis	15.00	6.00
❑ BE	Bernard King	20.00	8.00
❑ BG	Ben Gordon	40.00	15.00
❑ BK	Bob Knight	60.00	25.00
❑ BL	Bill Laimbeer	40.00	20.00
❑ BM	Brad Miller	15.00	6.00
❑ BO	Andrew Bogut	15.00	6.00
❑ BU	Beno Udrih	15.00	6.00
❑ BW	Bracey Wright	12.00	5.00
❑ BY	Andrew Bynum	50.00	20.00
❑ CB	Carlos Boozer	15.00	6.00
❑ CD	Clyde Drexler		
❑ CF	Channing Frye	60.00	25.00
❑ CH	Chauncey Billups	25.00	10.00
❑ CJ	C.J. Miles	12.00	5.00
❑ CM	Corey Maggette	12.00	5.00
❑ CN	Curly Neal	50.00	20.00
❑ CO	Michael Cooper	20.00	8.00
❑ CP	Chris Paul	150.00	75.00
❑ CS	Chris Bosh	15.00	6.00
❑ CT	Chris Taft EXCH	15.00	6.00
❑ CV	Charlie Villanueva	50.00	20.00
❑ DA	Daniel Ewing	30.00	12.50
❑ DD	Dan Dickau	15.00	6.00
❑ DE	Desmond Mason	12.00	5.00
❑ DF	Derek Fisher	15.00	6.00
❑ DG	Danny Granger	40.00	15.00
❑ DH	Dwight Howard	25.00	10.00
❑ DL	David Lee	12.00	5.00
❑ DM	Darko Milicic EXCH	20.00	8.00
❑ DP	Dan Patrick EXCH	25.00	10.00
❑ DR	Dennis Rodman	80.00	40.00
❑ DS	Damon Stoudamire	12.00	5.00
❑ DT	Dijon Thompson	12.00	5.00
❑ DW	Deron Williams	60.00	25.00
❑ ED	Erik Daniels	12.00	5.00
❑ EH	Elvin Hayes	25.00	10.00
❑ EI	Ersan Ilyasova	12.00	5.00
❑ FG	Francisco Garcia	25.00	10.00
❑ GA	Gilbert Arenas	15.00	6.00
❑ GG	George Gervin	25.00	10.00
❑ GW	Gerald Wallace	15.00	6.00
❑ HO	Hakeem Olajuwon	50.00	20.00
❑ HW	Hakim Warrick	40.00	15.00
❑ ID	Ike Diogu	30.00	12.50
❑ IT	Isiah Thomas	40.00	15.00
❑ JA	Jamal Crawford	12.00	5.00
❑ JC	Josh Childress	12.00	5.00
❑ JD	Juan Dixon	12.00	5.00
❑ JG	Joey Graham	15.00	6.00
❑ JH	Julius Hodge	12.00	5.00
❑ JJ	Jarrett Jack	12.00	5.00
❑ JK	Jason Kidd	40.00	15.00
❑ JM	Jamaal Magloire EXCH	12.00	5.00
❑ JO	John Edwards	12.00	5.00
❑ JP	Johan Petro	15.00	6.00
❑ JR	J.R. Smith	20.00	8.00
❑ JV	Jackson Vroman	12.00	5.00
❑ JW	John Wooden	75.00	35.00
❑ KA	Jason Kapono	12.00	5.00
❑ KE	Kevin Martin	12.00	5.00
❑ KH	Kris Humphries	12.00	5.00
❑ KI	Kirk Hinrich	25.00	10.00
❑ KK	Kyle Korver	15.00	6.00
❑ KM	Kenny Mayne EXCH	25.00	10.00
❑ LA	Larry Brown	50.00	20.00
❑ LC	Linda Cohn EXCH	25.00	10.00
❑ LD	Luol Deng	20.00	8.00
❑ LF	Luis Flores	12.00	5.00
❑ LH	Luther Head	50.00	20.00
❑ LJ	LeBron James EXCH	250.00	125.00
❑ LO	Lamar Odom	20.00	8.00
❑ LR	Lawrence Roberts	12.00	5.00
❑ LU	Louis Williams EXCH	12.00	5.00
❑ LW	Lenny Wilkens	40.00	15.00
❑ MA	Marvin Williams	50.00	20.00
❑ MB	Mike Bibby	15.00	6.00
❑ MC	Mark Cuban EXCH	30.00	12.50
❑ MD	Marquis Daniels	12.00	5.00
❑ ME	Monta Ellis	15.00	6.00
❑ MI	Andre Miller	15.00	6.00
❑ MJ	Michael Jordan	450.00	225.00
❑ ML	Meadowlark Lemon	30.00	12.50
❑ MP	Morris Peterson	12.00	5.00
❑ MR	Michael Redd	15.00	6.00
❑ MW	Maurice Williams	12.00	5.00
❑ NR	Nate Robinson EXCH	40.00	15.00
❑ PG	Pau Gasol	15.00	6.00
❑ PS	Pape Sow	12.00	5.00
❑ QR	Quentin Richardson	12.00	5.00
❑ RF	Raymond Felton	60.00	25.00
❑ RJ	Richard Jefferson	12.00	5.00
❑ RM	Ronald Murray	12.00	5.00
❑ RT	Ronny Turiaf	30.00	12.50
❑ SB	Steve Blake	12.00	5.00
❑ SH	Shane Battier	15.00	6.00
❑ SV	Sasha Vujacic	12.00	5.00
❑ TA	Tony Allen	12.00	5.00
❑ TD	Travis Diener	12.00	5.00
❑ TR	Trevor Ariza	15.00	6.00
❑ UH	Udonis Haslem		
❑ VK	Viktor Khryapa	12.00	5.00
❑ VW	Von Wafer	12.00	5.00
❑ WE	Martell Webster	15.00	6.00
❑ WF	Walt Frazier	30.00	12.50
❑ WI	Jason Williams	40.00	15.00
❑ WR	Willis Reed	25.00	10.00
❑ WS	Wayne Simien	12.00	5.00
❑ ZC	Zarko Cabarkapa		

2006-07 SP Game Used

❑ 1	Al Harrington	.60	.25
❑ 2	Joe Johnson	1.25	.50
❑ 3	Salim Stoudamire	1.25	.50
❑ 4	Tony Allen	1.25	.50
❑ 5	Dan Dickau	.60	.25
❑ 6	Gerald Green	2.50	1.00
❑ 7	Michael Olowokandi	.60	.25
❑ 8	Brevin Knight	.60	.25
❑ 9	Peja Stojakovic	2.00	.75
❑ 10	Gerald Wallace	2.00	.75
❑ 11	Luol Deng	2.00	.75
❑ 12	Chris Duhon	.60	.25
❑ 13	Mike Sweetney	.60	.25
❑ 14	Drew Gooden	1.25	.50
❑ 15	Luke Jackson	.60	.25
❑ 16	Damon Jones	1.25	.50
❑ 17	Eric Snow	.60	.25
❑ 18	Erick Dampier	.60	.25
❑ 19	Marquis Daniels	1.25	.50
❑ 20	Jerry Stackhouse	2.00	.75
❑ 21	Jason Terry	2.00	.75
❑ 22	Earl Boykins	.60	.25
❑ 23	Marcus Camby	1.25	.50
❑ 24	Kenyon Martin	2.00	.75
❑ 25	Andre Miller	1.25	.50
❑ 26	Kelvin Cato	.60	.25
❑ 27	Lindsey Hunter	.60	.25
❑ 28	Antonio McDyess	.60	.25
❑ 29	Mike Dunleavy	1.25	.50
❑ 30	Derek Fisher	1.25	.50
❑ 31	Troy Murphy	2.00	.75
❑ 32	Rafer Alston	.60	.25
❑ 33	Juwan Howard	1.25	.50
❑ 34	Stromile Swift	.60	.25
❑ 35	Austin Croshere	.60	.25
❑ 36	Stephen Jackson	1.25	.50
❑ 37	Jamaal Tinsley	1.25	.50
❑ 38	Sam Cassell	2.00	.75
❑ 39	Chris Kaman	.60	.25
❑ 40	Yaroslav Korolev	.60	.25
❑ 41	Cuttino Mobley	1.25	.50
❑ 42	Devean George	1.25	.50
❑ 43	Smush Parker	.60	.25
❑ 44	Ronny Turiaf	.60	.25
❑ 45	Shane Battier	2.00	.75
❑ 46	Bobby Jackson	.60	.25
❑ 47	Mike Miller	2.00	.75
❑ 48	Damon Stoudamire	1.25	.50
❑ 49	Alonzo Mourning	2.00	.75
❑ 50	Gary Payton	2.00	.75
❑ 51	Dwyane Wade	6.00	2.50
❑ 52	Jason Williams	1.25	.50
❑ 53	T.J. Ford	1.25	.50
❑ 54	Jamaal Magloire	.60	.25
❑ 55	Maurice Williams	.60	.25
❑ 56	Marcus Banks	.60	.25
❑ 57	Eddie Griffin	.60	.25
❑ 58	Troy Hudson	.60	.25
❑ 59	Jason Collins	.60	.25
❑ 60	Nenad Krstic	1.25	.50
❑ 61	Antoine Wright	.60	.25
❑ 62	P.J. Brown	.60	.25
❑ 63	Speedy Claxton	.60	.25
❑ 64	Marc Jackson	.60	.25
❑ 65	Jamal Crawford	.60	.25
❑ 66	Eddy Curry	1.25	.50
❑ 67	Quentin Richardson	1.25	.50
❑ 68	Carlos Arroyo	3.00	1.25
❑ 69	Keyon Dooling	.60	.25
❑ 70	Darko Milicic	2.00	.75
❑ 71	Steven Hunter	.60	.25
❑ 72	Allen Iverson	4.00	1.50
❑ 73	Kyle Korver	2.00	.75
❑ 74	Raja Bell	.60	.25
❑ 75	Boris Diaw	1.25	.50
❑ 76	Kurt Thomas	.60	.25
❑ 77	Steve Blake	.60	.25
❑ 78	Darius Miles	2.00	.75
❑ 79	Joel Przybilla	.60	.25
❑ 80	Ha Seung-Jin	.60	.25
❑ 81	Shareef Abdur-Rahim	2.00	.75
❑ 82	Brad Miller	2.00	.75
❑ 83	Kenny Thomas	.60	.25
❑ 84	Bonzi Wells	1.25	.50
❑ 85	Brent Barry	.60	.25
❑ 86	Bruce Bowen	.60	.25
❑ 87	Michael Finley	2.00	.75
❑ 88	Robert Horry	1.25	.50
❑ 89	Luke Ridnour	1.25	.50
❑ 90	Robert Swift	.60	.25
❑ 91	Chris Wilcox	.60	.25
❑ 92	Rafael Araujo	.60	.25
❑ 93	Jose Calderon	1.25	.50
❑ 94	Mike James	.60	.25
❑ 95	Matt Harpring	1.25	.50
❑ 96	Kris Humphries	.60	.25
❑ 97	Jason Richardson	2.00	.75
❑ 98	Gilbert Arenas	2.00	.75
❑ 99	Antonio Daniels	.60	.25
❑ 100	Brendan Haywood	.60	.25
❑ 101	Josh Childress JSY	8.00	3.00
❑ 102	Josh Smith JSY	8.00	3.00
❑ 103	Marvin Williams JSY	8.00	3.00
❑ 104	Al Jefferson JSY	8.00	3.00
❑ 105	Paul Pierce JSY	8.00	3.00
❑ 106	Wally Szczerbiak JSY	8.00	3.00
❑ 107	Raymond Felton JSY	10.00	4.00
❑ 108	Sean May JSY	8.00	3.00
❑ 109	Emeka Okafor JSY	8.00	3.00
❑ 110	Tyson Chandler JSY	8.00	3.00
❑ 111	Ben Gordon JSY	10.00	4.00
❑ 112	Kirk Hinrich JSY	8.00	3.00
❑ 113	Michael Jordan JSY	75.00	30.00
❑ 114	Larry Hughes JSY	8.00	3.00
❑ 115	Zydrunas Ilgauskas JSY	8.00	3.00
❑ 116	LeBron James JSY	40.00	15.00
❑ 117	Devin Harris JSY	8.00	3.00
❑ 118	Josh Howard JSY	8.00	3.00
❑ 119	Dirk Nowitzki JSY	10.00	4.00
❑ 120	Carmelo Anthony JSY	10.00	4.00
❑ 121	Julius Hodge JSY	8.00	3.00
❑ 122	Linas Kleiza JSY	8.00	3.00
❑ 123	Chauncey Billups JSY	8.00	3.00
❑ 124	Tayshaun Prince JSY	8.00	3.00
❑ 125	Ben Wallace JSY	8.00	3.00
❑ 126	Rasheed Wallace JSY	8.00	3.00
❑ 127	Baron Davis JSY	8.00	3.00
❑ 128	Ike Diogu JSY	8.00	3.00
❑ 129	Jason Richardson JSY	8.00	3.00
❑ 130	Chris Taft JSY	8.00	3.00
❑ 131	Luther Head JSY	8.00	3.00
❑ 132	Tracy McGrady JSY	10.00	4.00
❑ 133	Yao Ming JSY	10.00	4.00
❑ 134	Danny Granger JSY	8.00	3.00
❑ 135	Sarunas Jasikevicius JSY	8.00	3.00
❑ 136	Jermaine O'Neal JSY	8.00	3.00
❑ 137	Peja Stojakovic SP JSY	8.00	3.00
❑ 138	Elton Brand JSY	8.00	3.00
❑ 139	Shaun Livingston JSY	8.00	3.00
❑ 140	Corey Maggette JSY	8.00	3.00
❑ 141	Kwame Brown JSY	8.00	3.00
❑ 142	Kobe Bryant JSY	25.00	10.00
❑ 143	Andrew Bynum JSY	8.00	3.00
❑ 144	Lamar Odom JSY	8.00	3.00
❑ 145	Pau Gasol JSY	8.00	3.00
❑ 146	Eddie Jones JSY	8.00	3.00
❑ 147	Hakim Warrick JSY	8.00	3.00
❑ 148	Shaquille O'Neal JSY	12.00	5.00
❑ 149	Wayne Simien JSY	8.00	3.00
❑ 150	Antoine Walker JSY	8.00	3.00
❑ 151	Andrew Bogut JSY	8.00	3.00
❑ 152	Ersan Ilyasova JSY	8.00	3.00
❑ 153	Michael Redd JSY	8.00	3.00
❑ 154	Ricky Davis JSY	8.00	3.00
❑ 155	Kevin Garnett JSY	10.00	4.00
❑ 156	Rashad McCants JSY	8.00	3.00
❑ 157	Bracey Wright JSY	8.00	3.00
❑ 158	Vince Carter JSY	12.00	5.00
❑ 159	Richard Jefferson JSY	8.00	3.00
❑ 160	Jason Kidd JSY	10.00	4.00
❑ 161	Jeff McInnis JSY	8.00	3.00
❑ 163	Chris Paul JSY	12.00	5.00
❑ 164	J.R. Smith JSY	8.00	3.00
❑ 165	David West JSY	8.00	3.00
❑ 166	Steve Francis JSY	8.00	3.00
❑ 167	Channing Frye JSY	8.00	3.00
❑ 168	Stephon Marbury JSY	8.00	3.00
❑ 169	Nate Robinson JSY	8.00	3.00
❑ 170	Grant Hill JSY	8.00	3.00
❑ 171	Dwight Howard JSY	10.00	4.00
❑ 172	Jameer Nelson JSY	8.00	3.00
❑ 173	Samuel Dalembert JSY	8.00	3.00
❑ 174	Andre Iguodala JSY	8.00	3.00
❑ 175	Chris Webber JSY	8.00	3.00
❑ 176	Shawn Marion JSY	8.00	3.00
❑ 177	Steve Nash JSY	8.00	3.00
❑ 178	Amare Stoudemire JSY	10.00	4.00
❑ 179	Zach Randolph JSY	8.00	3.00
❑ 180	Sebastian Telfair JSY	8.00	3.00
❑ 181	Martell Webster JSY	8.00	3.00
❑ 182	Ron Artest JSY	8.00	3.00
❑ 183	Mike Bibby JSY	8.00	3.00
❑ 184	Francisco Garcia JSY	8.00	3.00
❑ 185	Tim Duncan JSY	10.00	4.00
❑ 186	Manu Ginobili JSY	8.00	3.00
❑ 187	Tony Parker JSY	8.00	3.00
❑ 188	Ray Allen JSY	8.00	3.00
❑ 189	Rashard Lewis JSY	8.00	3.00
❑ 190	Johan Petro JSY	8.00	3.00
❑ 191	Chris Bosh JSY	8.00	3.00
❑ 192	Joey Graham JSY	8.00	3.00
❑ 193	Charlie Villanueva JSY	8.00	3.00
❑ 194	Carlos Boozer JSY	8.00	3.00
❑ 195	Andrei Kirilenko JSY	8.00	3.00
❑ 196	C.J. Miles JSY	8.00	3.00
❑ 197	Deron Williams JSY	8.00	3.00
❑ 198	Andray Blatche JSY	8.00	3.00
❑ 199	Caron Butler JSY	8.00	3.00
❑ 200	Antawn Jamison JSY	8.00	3.00
❑ 201	Andrea Bargnani RC	15.00	6.00
❑ 202	LaMarcus Aldridge RC	15.00	6.00
❑ 203	Adam Morrison RC	15.00	6.00
❑ 204	Tyrus Thomas RC	20.00	8.00
❑ 205	Shelden Williams RC	8.00	3.00
❑ 206	Brandon Roy RC	20.00	8.00
❑ 207	Randy Foye RC	12.00	5.00
❑ 208	Rudy Gay RC	12.00	5.00
❑ 209	Patrick O'Bryant RC	6.00	2.50
❑ 210	Saer Sene RC	6.00	2.50
❑ 211	J.J. Redick RC	12.00	5.00
❑ 212	Hilton Armstrong RC	6.00	2.50
❑ 213	Thabo Sefolosha RC	10.00	4.00
❑ 214	Ronnie Brewer RC	8.00	3.00
❑ 215	Cedric Simmons RC	6.00	2.50
❑ 216	Rodney Carney RC	6.00	2.50
❑ 217	Shawne Williams RC	6.00	2.50
❑ 218	Hassan Adams RC	8.00	3.00
❑ 219	Quincy Douby RC	6.00	2.50
❑ 220	Renaldo Balkman RC	6.00	2.50
❑ 221	Rajon Rondo RC	8.00	3.00
❑ 222	Marcus Williams RC	8.00	3.00
❑ 223	Josh Boone RC	6.00	2.50
❑ 224	Kyle Lowry RC	6.00	2.50
❑ 225	Shannon Brown RC	6.00	2.50
❑ 226	Jordan Farmar RC	12.00	5.00
❑ 227	Maurice Ager RC	6.00	2.50
❑ 228	Mardy Collins RC	6.00	2.50
❑ 229	Will Blalock RC	6.00	2.50
❑ 230	James White RC	6.00	2.50
❑ 231	Steve Novak RC	6.00	2.50
❑ 232	Solomon Jones RC	6.00	2.50
❑ 233	Paul Davis RC	6.00	2.50
❑ 234	P.J. Tucker RC	6.00	2.50
❑ 235	Craig Smith RC	6.00	2.50
❑ 236	Bobby Jones RC	6.00	2.50
❑ 237	David Noel RC	6.00	2.50
❑ 238	Denham Brown RC	6.00	2.50
❑ 239	James Augustine RC	6.00	2.50

❏ 240	Daniel Gibson RC	15.00	6.00
❏ 241	Ryan Hollins RC	6.00	2.50
❏ 242	Alexander Johnson RC	6.00	2.50
❏ 243	Dee Brown RC	10.00	4.00
❏ 244	Paul Millsap RC	12.00	5.00
❏ 245	Leon Powe RC	6.00	2.50
❏ 246	Mike Gansey RC	6.00	2.50
❏ 247	Tarence Kinsey RC	6.00	2.50
❏ 248	Damir Markota RC	6.00	2.50
❏ 249	J.R. Pinnock RC	6.00	2.50
❏ 250	Kevin Pittsnogle RC	6.00	2.50

2003-04 SP Signature Edition

#			
❏ COMP. SET w/o SP's (100)		80.00	30.00
❏ COMMON CARD (1-100)		.50	.20
❏ COMMON ROOKIE (101-142)		10.00	4.00
❏ MOST UNPRICED DUE TO SCARCITY			
❏ 1	Shareef Abdur-Rahim	1.50	.60
❏ 2	Jason Terry	1.50	.60
❏ 3	Theo Ratliff	1.00	.40
❏ 4	Raef LaFrentz	1.00	.40
❏ 5	Paul Pierce	1.50	.60
❏ 6	Larry Bird	6.00	2.50
❏ 7	Jalen Rose	1.50	.60
❏ 8	Scottie Pippen	2.00	.75
❏ 9	Michael Jordan	10.00	4.00
❏ 10	Dennis Rodman	2.00	.75
❏ 11	Dajuan Wagner	1.00	.40
❏ 12	Darius Miles	1.50	.60
❏ 13	Carlos Boozer	1.50	.60
❏ 14	Zydrunas Ilgauskas	1.00	.40
❏ 15	Dirk Nowitzki	2.00	.75
❏ 16	Steve Nash	1.50	.60
❏ 17	Antoine Walker	1.50	.60
❏ 18	Antawn Jamison	1.50	.60
❏ 19	Andre Miller	1.00	.40
❏ 20	Nene	1.00	.40
❏ 21	Nikoloz Tskitishvili	.50	.20
❏ 22	Ben Wallace	1.50	.60
❏ 23	Richard Hamilton	1.00	.40
❏ 24	Chauncey Billups	1.00	.40
❏ 25	Nick Van Exel	1.50	.60
❏ 26	Jason Richardson	1.50	.60
❏ 27	Mike Dunleavy	1.00	.40
❏ 28	Yao Ming	4.00	1.50
❏ 29	Steve Francis	1.50	.60
❏ 30	Cuttino Mobley	1.00	.40
❏ 31	Reggie Miller	1.50	.60
❏ 32	Jermaine O'Neal	1.50	.60
❏ 33	Jamaal Tinsley	1.50	.60
❏ 34	Chris Wilcox	.50	.20
❏ 35	Elton Brand	1.50	.60
❏ 36	Wang Zhizhi	1.50	.60
❏ 37	Corey Maggette	1.00	.40
❏ 38	Kobe Bryant	6.00	2.50
❏ 39	Shaquille O'Neal	4.00	1.50
❏ 40	Gary Payton	1.50	.60
❏ 41	Karl Malone	1.50	.60
❏ 42	Pau Gasol	1.50	.60
❏ 43	Shane Battier	1.50	.60
❏ 44	Mike Miller	1.50	.60
❏ 45	Caron Butler	1.50	.60
❏ 46	Eddie Jones	1.50	.60
❏ 47	Lamar Odom	1.50	.60
❏ 48	Brian Grant	1.00	.40
❏ 49	Desmond Mason	1.00	.40
❏ 50	Michael Redd	1.50	.60
❏ 51	Tim Thomas	1.00	.40
❏ 52	Wally Szczerbiak	1.00	.40
❏ 53	Kevin Garnett	3.00	1.25
❏ 54	Latrell Sprewell	1.50	.60
❏ 55	Sam Cassell	1.50	.60
❏ 56	Richard Jefferson	1.00	.40
❏ 57	Kenyon Martin	1.50	.60
❏ 58	Jason Kidd	2.00	.75
❏ 59	Alonzo Mourning	1.00	.40
❏ 60	Jamal Mashburn	1.00	.40
❏ 61	Baron Davis	1.50	.60
❏ 62	David Wesley	.50	.20
❏ 63	Allan Houston	1.00	.40
❏ 64	Keith Van Horn	1.50	.60
❏ 65	Antonio McDyess	1.50	.60
❏ 66	Gordan Giricek	1.00	.40
❏ 67	Tracy McGrady	4.00	1.50
❏ 68	Drew Gooden	1.50	.60
❏ 69	Grant Hill	1.50	.60
❏ 70	Glenn Robinson	1.50	.60
❏ 71	Allen Iverson	3.00	1.25
❏ 72	Julius Erving	4.00	1.50
❏ 73	Eric Snow	1.00	.40
❏ 74	Shawn Marion	1.50	.60
❏ 75	Amare Stoudemire	3.00	1.25
❏ 76	Stephon Marbury	1.50	.60
❏ 77	Damon Stoudamire	1.00	.40
❏ 78	Rasheed Wallace	1.50	.60
❏ 79	Derek Anderson	1.00	.40
❏ 80	Zach Randolph	1.50	.60
❏ 81	Mike Bibby	1.50	.60
❏ 82	Chris Webber	1.50	.60
❏ 83	Peja Stojakovic	1.50	.60
❏ 84	Brad Miller	1.50	.60
❏ 85	Tony Parker	1.50	.60
❏ 86	Tim Duncan	3.00	1.25
❏ 87	Manu Ginobili	1.50	.60
❏ 88	David Robinson	1.50	.60
❏ 89	Rashard Lewis	1.50	.60
❏ 90	Ray Allen	1.50	.60
❏ 91	Vladimir Radmanovic	.50	.20
❏ 92	Morris Peterson	1.00	.40
❏ 93	Vince Carter	4.00	1.50
❏ 94	Antonio Davis	.50	.20
❏ 95	Andrei Kirilenko	1.50	.60
❏ 96	Matt Harpring	1.50	.60
❏ 97	Jarron Collins	.50	.20
❏ 98	Gilbert Arenas	1.50	.60
❏ 99	Jerry Stackhouse	1.00	.40
❏ 100	Kwame Brown	1.50	.60
❏ 101	LeBron James RC	160.00	80.00
❏ 102	Darko Milicic RC	20.00	8.00
❏ 103	Carmelo Anthony RC	50.00	20.00
❏ 104	Chris Bosh RC	25.00	10.00
❏ 105	Dwyane Wade RC	50.00	20.00
❏ 106	Chris Kaman RC	10.00	4.00
❏ 107	Kirk Hinrich RC	20.00	8.00
❏ 108	T.J. Ford RC	15.00	6.00
❏ 109	Mike Sweetney RC	10.00	4.00
❏ 110	Jarvis Hayes RC	10.00	4.00
❏ 111	Mickael Pietrus RC	10.00	4.00
❏ 112	Nick Collison RC	10.00	4.00
❏ 113	Marcus Banks RC	10.00	4.00
❏ 114	Luke Ridnour RC	15.00	6.00
❏ 115	Reece Gaines RC	10.00	4.00
❏ 116	Troy Bell RC	10.00	4.00
❏ 117	Zarko Cabarkapa RC	10.00	4.00
❏ 118	David West RC	10.00	4.00
❏ 119	Aleksandar Pavlovic RC	12.00	5.00
❏ 120	Dahntay Jones RC	10.00	4.00
❏ 121	Boris Diaw RC	12.00	5.00
❏ 122	Zoran Planinic RC	10.00	4.00
❏ 123	Travis Outlaw RC	10.00	4.00
❏ 124	Brian Cook RC	10.00	4.00
❏ 125	James Lang RC	10.00	4.00
❏ 126	Ndudi Ebi RC	10.00	4.00
❏ 127	Kendrick Perkins RC	10.00	4.00
❏ 128	Leandro Barbosa RC	15.00	6.00
❏ 129	Josh Howard RC	20.00	8.00
❏ 130	Maciej Lampe RC	10.00	4.00
❏ 131	Jason Kapono RC	10.00	4.00
❏ 132	Luke Walton RC	12.00	5.00
❏ 133	Jerome Beasley RC	10.00	4.00
❏ 134	Willie Green RC	10.00	4.00
❏ 135	James Jones RC	10.00	4.00
❏ 136	Travis Hansen RC	10.00	4.00
❏ 137	Steve Blake RC	10.00	4.00
❏ 138	Slavko Vranes RC	10.00	4.00
❏ 139	Zaur Pachulia RC	10.00	4.00
❏ 140	Keith Bogans RC	10.00	4.00
❏ 141	Kyle Korver RC	20.00	8.00
❏ 142	Brandon Hunter RC	10.00	4.00
❏ 143	Kobe Bryant/8		
❏ 144	LeBron James/23		
❏ 145	Michael Jordan/23		
❏ 146	Darius Miles/21		
❏ 147	Yao Ming/11		
❏ 148	Gary Payton/20		
❏ 149	Tim Thomas/5		
❏ 150	Allan Houston/20		
❏ 151	Stephon Marbury/3		
❏ 152	Ray Allen/34	50.00	20.00
❏ 153	Paul Pierce/34	50.00	20.00
❏ 154	Carmelo Anthony/15		
❏ 155	Jamaal Tinsley/11		
❏ 156	Kirk Hinrich/12		
❏ 157	Jason Kidd/5		
❏ 158	Julius Erving/6		
❏ 159	Mike Bibby/10		
❏ 160	Andrei Kirilenko/47	25.00	10.00
❏ 161	T.J. Ford/11		
❏ 162	Nene/31	20.00	10.00
❏ 163	Elton Brand/42	25.00	10.00
❏ 164	Caron Butler/4		
❏ 165	Richard Jefferson/24		
❏ 166	Allen Iverson/3		
❏ 167	Peja Stojakovic/16		
❏ 168	Jerry Stackhouse/42	25.00	10.00
❏ 169	Jalen Rose/5		
❏ 170	Ben Wallace/3		
❏ 171	Darko Milicic/31	50.00	20.00
❏ 172	Lamar Odom/7		
❏ 173	Kenyon Martin/6		
❏ 174	Glenn Robinson/31	20.00	10.00
❏ 175	Tim Duncan/21		
❏ 176	Gilbert Arenas/10		
❏ 177	Scottie Pippen/33	100.00	50.00
❏ 178	Richard Hamilton/32	25.00	10.00
❏ 179	Corey Maggette/50	20.00	8.00
❏ 180	Dwyane Wade/3		
❏ 181	Baron Davis/1		
❏ 182	Amare Stoudemire/32	40.00	15.00
❏ 183	Tony Parker/9		
❏ 184	Shareef Abdur-Rahim/3		
❏ 185	Dirk Nowitzki/41	30.00	12.50
❏ 186	Steve Francis/3		
❏ 187	Magic Johnson/32	60.00	25.00
❏ 188	Michael Redd/22		
❏ 189	Keith Van Horn/2		
❏ 190	Rasheed Wallace/30	30.00	12.50
❏ 191	Nick Collison/4		
❏ 192	Jason Terry/31	25.00	10.00
❏ 193	Steve Nash/13		
❏ 194	Cuttino Mobley/5		
❏ 195	Karl Malone/11		
❏ 196	Kevin Garnett/21		
❏ 197	Tracy McGrady/1		
❏ 198	Bonzi Wells/6		
❏ 199	Rashard Lewis/7		
❏ 200	Antoine Walker/8		
❏ 201	Michael Finley/4		
❏ 202	Jermaine O'Neal/7		
❏ 203	Mike Miller/33	20.00	8.00
❏ 204	Wally Szczerbiak/10		
❏ 205	Gordan Giricek/7		
❏ 206	Chris Webber/4		
❏ 207	Morris Peterson/24		
❏ 208	Dajuan Wagner/2		
❏ 209	Jason Richardson/23		
❏ 210	Shaquille O'Neal/34	60.00	25.00
❏ 211	Desmond Mason/24		
❏ 212	Jamal Mashburn/24		
❏ 213	Shawn Marion/31	25.00	10.00
❏ 214	Manu Ginobili/20		
❏ 215	Larry Bird/33	150.00	75.00
❏ 216	Antawn Jamison/33	25.00	10.00
❏ 217	Reggie Miller/31	40.00	15.00
❏ 218	Pau Gasol/16		
❏ 219	Latrell Sprewell/8		
❏ 220	Drew Gooden/10		
❏ 221	Damon Stoudamire/3		
❏ 222	Vince Carter/15		

☐ 223 Spike Lee	4.00	1.50
☐ 224 Summer Sanders	3.00	1.25
☐ 225 Cheryl Miller	2.00	.75

2004-05 SP Signature Edition

Emeka Okafor

☐ COMMON CARD (1-100)	.50	.20
☐ COMMON JSY RC (101-142)	8.00	3.00
☐ COMMON ROOKIE (101-142)	5.00	2.00
☐ SOME NOT PRICED DUE TO SCARCITY		

☐ 1 Antoine Walker	1.50	.60
☐ 2 Al Harrington	1.00	.40
☐ 3 Boris Diaw	.50	.20
☐ 4 Paul Pierce	1.50	.60
☐ 5 Ricky Davis	1.50	.60
☐ 6 Gary Payton	1.50	.60
☐ 7 Gerald Wallace	1.00	.40
☐ 8 Emeka Okafor RC	12.00	5.00
☐ 9 Jahidi White	.50	.20
☐ 10 Eddy Curry	1.00	.40
☐ 11 Kirk Hinrich	1.50	.60
☐ 12 Michael Jordan	10.00	4.00
☐ 13 LeBron James	10.00	4.00
☐ 14 Dajuan Wagner	1.00	.40
☐ 15 Jeff McInnis	.50	.20
☐ 16 Drew Gooden	1.00	.40
☐ 17 Dirk Nowitzki	2.50	1.00
☐ 18 Michael Finley	1.50	.60
☐ 19 Jerry Stackhouse	1.50	.60
☐ 20 Jason Terry	1.50	.60
☐ 21 Kenyon Martin	1.50	.60
☐ 22 Andre Miller	1.00	.40
☐ 23 Carmelo Anthony	3.00	1.25
☐ 24 Nene	1.00	.40
☐ 25 Chauncey Billups	1.00	.40
☐ 26 Rasheed Wallace	1.50	.60
☐ 27 Ben Wallace	1.50	.60
☐ 28 Richard Hamilton	1.00	.40
☐ 29 Derek Fisher	1.50	.60
☐ 30 Jason Richardson	1.50	.60
☐ 31 Mike Dunleavy	1.00	.40
☐ 32 Yao Ming	4.00	1.50
☐ 33 Tracy McGrady	4.00	1.50
☐ 34 Juwan Howard	1.00	.40
☐ 35 Jermaine O'Neal	1.50	.60
☐ 36 Reggie Miller	1.50	.60
☐ 37 Ron Artest	1.00	.40
☐ 38 Jamaal Tinsley	1.50	.60
☐ 39 Elton Brand	1.50	.60
☐ 40 Corey Maggette	1.00	.40
☐ 41 Marko Jaric	.50	.20
☐ 42 Kerry Kittles	.50	.20
☐ 43 Kobe Bryant	6.00	2.50
☐ 44 Karl Malone	1.50	.60
☐ 45 Lamar Odom	1.50	.60
☐ 46 Caron Butler	1.50	.60
☐ 47 Pau Gasol	1.50	.60
☐ 48 Jason Williams	1.00	.40
☐ 49 Bonzi Wells	1.00	.40
☐ 50 Shaquille O'Neal	4.00	1.50
☐ 51 Dwyane Wade	5.00	2.00
☐ 52 Eddie Jones	1.50	.60
☐ 53 Michael Redd	1.50	.60
☐ 54 Desmond Mason	1.00	.40
☐ 55 T.J. Ford	1.00	.40
☐ 56 Latrell Sprewell	1.50	.60
☐ 57 Kevin Garnett	3.00	1.25

☐ 58 Sam Cassell	1.00	.40
☐ 59 Troy Hudson	.50	.20
☐ 60 Vince Carter	4.00	1.50
☐ 61 Richard Jefferson	1.50	.60
☐ 62 Jason Kidd	2.50	1.00
☐ 63 Jamal Mashburn	1.00	.40
☐ 64 Baron Davis	1.50	.60
☐ 65 Jamaal Magloire	.50	.20
☐ 66 Allan Houston	1.00	.40
☐ 67 Jamal Crawford	1.00	.40
☐ 68 Stephon Marbury	1.50	.60
☐ 69 Grant Hill	1.50	.60
☐ 70 Cuttino Mobley	1.00	.40
☐ 71 Steve Francis	1.50	.60
☐ 72 Glenn Robinson	1.50	.60
☐ 73 Allen Iverson	3.00	1.25
☐ 74 Kyle Korver	1.00	.40
☐ 75 Amare Stoudemire	3.00	1.25
☐ 76 Steve Nash	1.50	.60
☐ 77 Quentin Richardson	1.00	.40
☐ 78 Shawn Marion	1.50	.60
☐ 79 Shareef Abdur-Rahim	1.50	.60
☐ 80 Damon Stoudamire	1.00	.40
☐ 81 Zach Randolph	1.50	.60
☐ 82 Darius Miles	1.50	.60
☐ 83 Peja Stojakovic	1.50	.60
☐ 84 Chris Webber	1.50	.60
☐ 85 Mike Bibby	1.50	.60
☐ 86 Tony Parker	1.50	.60
☐ 87 Tim Duncan	3.00	1.25
☐ 88 Manu Ginobili	1.50	.60
☐ 89 Ronald Murray	1.00	.40
☐ 90 Ray Allen	1.50	.60
☐ 91 Rashard Lewis	1.50	.60
☐ 92 Chris Bosh	1.50	.60
☐ 93 Jalen Rose	1.50	.60
☐ 94 Rafer Alston	1.00	.40
☐ 95 Andrei Kirilenko	1.50	.60
☐ 96 Matt Harpring	1.50	.60
☐ 97 Carlos Boozer	1.50	.60
☐ 98 Gilbert Arenas	1.50	.60
☐ 99 Jarvis Hayes	1.00	.40
☐ 100 Antawn Jamison	1.50	.60
☐ 101 Dwight Howard JSY RC	25.00	10.00
☐ 102 Ben Gordon JSY RC	30.00	12.50
☐ 103 Shaun Livingston JSY RC	12.00	5.00
☐ 104 Devin Harris JSY RC	12.00	5.00
☐ 105 Josh Childress JSY RC	10.00	4.00
☐ 106 Luol Deng JSY RC	15.00	6.00
☐ 107 Rafael Araujo JSY RC	8.00	3.00
☐ 108 Andre Iguodala JSY RC	20.00	8.00
☐ 109 Luke Jackson JSY RC	8.00	3.00
☐ 110 Sebastian Telfair JSY RC	8.00	3.00
☐ 111 Kris Humphries JSY RC	8.00	3.00
☐ 112 Al Jefferson JSY RC	20.00	8.00
☐ 113 Kirk Snyder JSY RC	8.00	3.00
☐ 114 Josh Smith JSY RC	15.00	6.00
☐ 115 J.R. Smith JSY RC	15.00	6.00
☐ 116 Dorell Wright JSY RC	12.00	5.00
☐ 117 Jameer Nelson JSY RC	12.00	5.00
☐ 118 Delonte West JSY RC	15.00	6.00
☐ 119 Tony Allen JSY RC	8.00	3.00
☐ 120 Kevin Martin JSY RC	12.00	5.00
☐ 121 David Harrison JSY RC	8.00	3.00
☐ 122 Anderson Varejao JSY RC	10.00	4.00
☐ 123 Jackson Vroman JSY RC	8.00	3.00
☐ 124 Lionel Chalmers JSY RC	8.00	3.00
☐ 125 Andre Emmett JSY RC	8.00	3.00
☐ 126 Chris Duhon JSY RC	12.00	5.00
☐ 127 Bernard Robinson JSY RC	8.00	3.00
☐ 128 Tim Pickett RC	5.00	2.00
☐ 129 Nenad Krstic JSY RC	10.00	4.00
☐ 130 Andris Biedrins JSY RC	12.00	5.00
☐ 131 Robert Swift RC	5.00	2.00
☐ 132 Andres Nocioni RC	8.00	3.00
☐ 133 Justin Reed RC	5.00	2.00
☐ 134 Romain Sato RC	5.00	2.00
☐ 135 Sasha Vujacic JSY RC	5.00	2.00
☐ 136 Beno Udrih RC	8.00	3.00
☐ 137 Peter John Ramos JSY RC	8.00	3.00
☐ 138 Donta Smith JSY RC	5.00	2.00
☐ 139 Antonio Burks RC	5.00	2.00
☐ 140 Yuta Tabuse JSY RC	15.00	6.00
☐ 141 Trevor Ariza JSY RC	10.00	4.00
☐ 142 Matt Freije JSY RC	8.00	3.00
☐ 143 Drew Gooden/90	5.00	2.00

☐ 144 Elton Brand/42	15.00	6.00
☐ 145 Shawn Marion/31	20.00	8.00
☐ 146 Dwight Howard/12		
☐ 147 Shaun Livingston/14		
☐ 148 Dirk Nowitzki/41	15.00	6.00
☐ 149 Pau Gasol/16		
☐ 150 Steve Nash/13		
☐ 151 Eddy Curry/2		
☐ 152 Devin Harris/34	20.00	8.00
☐ 153 Bill Russell/6		
☐ 154 Tracy McGrady/1		
☐ 155 Baron Davis/1		
☐ 156 Tony Parker/9		
☐ 157 Rafer Alston/11		
☐ 158 Josh Smith/5		
☐ 159 Michael Finley/4		
☐ 160 Dwyane Wade/3		
☐ 161 Clyde Drexler/22		
☐ 162 Dajuan Wagner/2		
☐ 163 Josh Childress/1		
☐ 164 Carmelo Anthony/15		
☐ 165 Shaquille O'Neal/32	30.00	12.50
☐ 166 Shareef Abdur-Rahim/33	15.00	6.00
☐ 167 Jason Terry/31	15.00	6.00
☐ 168 Luol Deng/9		
☐ 169 Kenyon Martin/6		
☐ 170 Oscar Robertson/1		
☐ 171 Zach Randolph/50	12.00	5.00
☐ 172 Dave DeBusschere/22		
☐ 173 Andre Iguodala/4		
☐ 174 Gerald Wallace/3		
☐ 175 Kobe Bryant/8		
☐ 176 Gary Payton/20		
☐ 177 Antawn Jamison/4		
☐ 178 Chris Webber/4		
☐ 179 Ben Wallace/3		
☐ 180 Michael Redd/22		
☐ 181 Peja Stojakovic/16		
☐ 182 Walt Frazier/10		
☐ 183 Luke Jackson/33	15.00	6.00
☐ 184 Richard Hamilton/32	15.00	6.00
☐ 185 Kevin Garnett/21		
☐ 186 Mike Bibby/10		
☐ 187 Kirk Hinrich/12		
☐ 188 Sebastian Telfair/31	15.00	6.00
☐ 189 Isiah Thomas/11		
☐ 190 Latrell Sprewell/8		
☐ 191 David Robinson/50	30.00	12.50
☐ 192 Jerry Stackhouse/42	15.00	6.00
☐ 193 Kris Humphries/43	12.00	5.00
☐ 194 Dennis Rodman/91	15.00	6.00
☐ 195 Lamar Odom/7		
☐ 196 Julius Erving/6		
☐ 197 Gilbert Arenas/10		
☐ 198 Rasheed Lewis/7		
☐ 199 Michael Jordan/23		
☐ 200 Magic Johnson/32	40.00	15.00
☐ 201 Allen Iverson/3		
☐ 202 Jason Williams/2		
☐ 203 Chris Bosh/4		
☐ 204 Al Harrington/3		
☐ 205 Jason Richardson/23		
☐ 206 Jason Kidd/5		
☐ 207 George Gervin/44	20.00	8.00
☐ 208 Chauncey Billups/1		
☐ 209 Al Jefferson/8		
☐ 210 Bob Cousy/14		
☐ 211 Yao Ming/11		
☐ 212 Bernard King/30	20.00	8.00
☐ 213 Vince Carter/15		
☐ 214 Grant Hill/33	15.00	6.00
☐ 215 J.R. Smith/23		
☐ 216 LeBron James/23		
☐ 217 Wilt Chamberlain/13		
☐ 218 Amare Stoudemire/32	20.00	8.00
☐ 219 Steve Francis/3		
☐ 220 Ben Gordon/7		
☐ 221 Larry Bird/33	40.00	15.00
☐ 222 Reggie Miller/31	30.00	12.50
☐ 223 Stephon Marbury/3		
☐ 224 Andrei Kirilenko/47	15.00	6.00
☐ 225 Karl Malone/11		
☐ 226 Jameer Nelson/14		
☐ 227 Emeka Okafor/50		
☐ 228 Corey Maggette/50	12.00	5.00
☐ 229 Jamal Crawford/11		

#	Player	Hi	Lo
230	John Stockton/12		
231	Jamaal Magloire/21		
232	Antoine Walker/8		
233	Hakeem Olajuwon/34	15.00	6.00
234	Richard Jefferson/24		
235	Tim Duncan/21		
236	Ray Allen/34	25.00	10.00
237	Kirk Snyder/3		
238	Paul Pierce/34	20.00	8.00
239	Jermaine O'Neal/7		
240	Willis Reed/19		
241	Carlos Boozer/5		
242	Manu Ginobili/20		

2005-06 SP Signature Edition

#	Player	Hi	Lo
	COMPLETE SET (142)		
	COMP.SET w/o SP's (100)	100.00	50.00
	COMMON CARD (1-100)	.50	.20
	SEMISTARS (1-100)	1.00	.40
	UNLISTED STARS	1.50	.60
	COMMON ROOKIE (101-142)	8.00	3.00
	101-142 RC PRINT RUN 499 SER.#'d SETS		
1	Josh Smith	1.50	.60
2	Josh Childress	1.00	.40
3	Joe Johnson	1.00	.40
4	Paul Pierce	1.50	.60
5	Ricky Davis	1.50	.60
6	Al Jefferson	1.50	.60
7	Emeka Okafor	2.50	1.00
8	Kareem Rush	.50	.20
9	Gerald Wallace	1.50	.60
10	Michael Jordan	10.00	4.00
11	Ben Gordon	3.00	1.25
12	Luol Deng	1.50	.60
13	Kirk Hinrich	1.50	.60
14	LeBron James	10.00	4.00
15	Larry Hughes	1.00	.40
16	Zydrunas Ilgauskas	.50	.20
17	Donyell Marshall	.50	.20
18	Dirk Nowitzki	2.50	1.00
19	Jason Terry	1.50	.60
20	Josh Howard	1.00	.40
21	Devin Harris	.50	.20
22	Carmelo Anthony	3.00	1.25
23	Marcus Camby	.50	.20
24	Andre Miller	1.00	.40
25	Kenyon Martin	1.50	.60
26	Chauncey Billups	1.50	.60
27	Ben Wallace	1.50	.60
28	Richard Hamilton	1.00	.40
29	Jason Richardson	1.50	.60
30	Troy Murphy	1.50	.60
31	Baron Davis	1.50	.60
32	Tracy McGrady	4.00	1.50
33	Yao Ming	4.00	1.50
34	Stromile Swift	1.00	.40
35	Jermaine O'Neal	1.50	.60
36	Ron Artest	1.50	.60
37	Stephen Jackson	1.00	.40
38	Corey Maggette	1.00	.40
39	Shaun Livingston	1.25	.50
40	Chris Wilcox		
41	Elton Brand	1.50	.60
42	Kobe Bryant	6.00	2.50
43	Kwame Brown	1.50	.60
44	Lamar Odom	1.50	.60
45	Pau Gasol	1.50	.60
46	Damon Stoudamire	1.00	.40
47	Lorenzen Wright	.50	.20
48	Shaquille O'Neal	4.00	1.50
49	Dwyane Wade	5.00	2.00
50	Antoine Walker	1.50	.60
51	Jason Williams	1.00	.40
52	Desmond Mason	.50	.20
53	Michael Redd	1.50	.60
54	Maurice Williams	.50	.20
55	Kevin Garnett	3.00	1.25
56	Marko Jaric	.50	.20
57	Wally Szczerbiak	1.00	.40
58	Jason Kidd	2.50	1.00
59	Richard Jefferson	1.00	.40
60	Vince Carter	4.00	1.50
61	Jamaal Magloire	.50	.20
62	J.R. Smith	1.00	.40
63	Speedy Claxton	.50	.20
64	Stephon Marbury	1.50	.60
65	Quentin Richardson	1.00	.40
66	Mike Sweetney	1.00	.40
67	Grant Hill	1.50	.60
68	Dwight Howard	2.00	.75
69	Steve Francis	1.50	.60
70	Allen Iverson	3.00	1.25
71	Samuel Dalembert	.50	.20
72	Kyle Korver	1.50	.60
73	Chris Webber	1.50	.60
74	Steve Nash	1.50	.60
75	Amare Stoudemire	3.00	1.25
76	Shawn Marion	1.50	.60
77	Sebastian Telfair	1.00	.40
78	Zach Randolph	1.50	.60
79	Juan Dixon	.50	.20
80	Mike Bibby	1.50	.60
81	Peja Stojakovic	1.50	.60
82	Brad Miller	1.50	.60
83	Tim Duncan	3.00	1.25
84	Manu Ginobili	1.50	.60
85	Robert Horry	1.00	.40
86	Tony Parker	1.50	.60
87	Ray Allen	1.50	.60
88	Rashard Lewis	1.50	.60
89	Vladimir Radmanovic	.50	.20
90	Chris Bosh	1.50	.60
91	Rafer Alston	.50	.20
92	Jalen Rose	1.25	.50
93	Andrei Kirilenko	1.50	.60
94	Matt Harpring	1.50	.60
95	Carlos Boozer	1.00	.40
96	Mehmet Okur	1.50	.60
97	Gilbert Arenas	1.50	.60
98	Antawn Jamison	1.50	.60
99	Caron Butler	1.00	.40
100	Antonio Daniels	.50	.20
101	Andrew Bogut RC	15.00	6.00
102	Marvin Williams RC	15.00	6.00
103	Deron Williams RC	25.00	10.00
104	Chris Paul RC	30.00	12.00
105	Raymond Felton RC	15.00	6.00
106	Martell Webster RC	8.00	3.00
107	Charlie Villanueva RC	12.00	5.00
108	Channing Frye RC	12.00	5.00
109	Ike Diogu RC	10.00	4.00
110	Andrew Bynum RC	20.00	8.00
111	Sean May RC	12.00	5.00
112	Rashad McCants RC	15.00	6.00
113	Antoine Wright RC	8.00	3.00
114	Joey Graham RC	8.00	3.00
115	Danny Granger RC	12.00	5.00
116	Gerald Green RC	15.00	6.00
117	Hakim Warrick RC	15.00	6.00
118	Julius Hodge RC	10.00	4.00
119	Nate Robinson RC	12.00	5.00
120	Jarrett Jack RC	8.00	3.00
121	Francisco Garcia RC	10.00	4.00
122	Luther Head RC	10.00	4.00
123	Johan Petro RC	8.00	3.00
124	Jason Maxiell RC	8.00	3.00
125	Linas Kleiza RC	8.00	3.00
126	Wayne Simien RC	10.00	4.00
127	David Lee RC	12.00	5.00
128	Salim Stoudamire RC	10.00	4.00
129	Daniel Ewing RC	10.00	4.00
130	Brandon Bass RC	8.00	3.00
131	C.J. Miles RC	8.00	3.00
132	Ersan Ilyasova RC	8.00	3.00
133	Travis Diener RC	8.00	3.00
134	Monta Ellis RC	15.00	6.00
135	Chris Taft RC	8.00	3.00
136	Martynas Andriuskevicius RC	8.00	3.00
137	Louis Williams RC	8.00	3.00
138	Bracey Wright RC	8.00	3.00
139	Robert Whaley RC	8.00	3.00
140	Andray Blatche RC	8.00	3.00
141	Ryan Gomes RC	8.00	3.00
142	Sarunas Jasikevicius RC	10.00	4.00

2006-07 SP Signature Edition

#	Player	Hi	Lo
1	Josh Childress	1.50	.60
2	Joe Johnson	1.50	.60
3	Marvin Williams	3.00	1.25
4	Al Jefferson	2.50	1.00
5	Paul Pierce	2.50	1.00
6	Sebastian Telfair	1.50	.60
7	Raymond Felton	3.00	1.25
8	Emeka Okafor	2.50	1.00
9	Gerald Wallace	2.50	1.00
10	Ben Gordon	5.00	2.00
11	Kirk Hinrich	2.50	1.00
12	Ben Wallace	2.50	1.00
13	Drew Gooden	1.50	.60
14	LeBron James	15.00	6.00
15	Donyell Marshall	1.50	.60
16	Devin Harris	2.50	1.00
17	Josh Howard	1.50	.60
18	Dirk Nowitzki	4.00	1.50
19	Jason Terry	2.50	1.00
20	Carmelo Anthony	5.00	2.00
21	Kenyon Martin	2.50	1.00
22	J.R. Smith	2.50	1.00
23	Chauncey Billups	2.50	1.00
24	Rasheed Wallace	2.50	1.00
25	Baron Davis	2.50	1.00
26	Baron Davis	2.50	1.00
27	Troy Murphy	2.50	1.00
28	Jason Richardson	2.50	1.00
29	Rafer Alston	2.50	1.00
30	Shane Battier	2.50	1.00
31	Tracy McGrady	6.00	2.50
32	Yao Ming	6.00	2.50
33	Marquis Daniels	1.50	.60
34	Al Harrington	1.50	.60
35	Jermaine O'Neal	2.50	1.00
36	Elton Brand	2.50	1.00
37	Sam Cassell	2.50	1.00
38	Chris Kaman	1.50	.60
39	Corey Maggette	1.50	.60
40	Kobe Bryant	10.00	4.00
41	Lamar Odom	2.50	1.00
42	Kwame Brown	1.50	.60
43	Eddie Jones	1.50	.60
44	Mike Miller	2.50	1.00
45	Hakim Warrick	1.50	.60
46	Pau Gasol	2.50	1.00
47	Alonzo Mourning	1.50	.60
48	Shaquille O'Neal	6.00	2.50
49	Dwyane Wade	8.00	3.00
50	Jason Williams	1.50	.60
51	Andrew Bogut	3.00	1.25
52	Michael Redd	2.50	1.00
53	Charlie Villanueva	2.50	1.00
54	Kevin Garnett	5.00	2.00

❑ 55 Mike James	1.50	.60
❑ 56 Rashad McCants	3.00	1.25
❑ 57 Vince Carter	6.00	2.50
❑ 58 Richard Jefferson	1.50	.60
❑ 59 Jason Kidd	4.00	1.50
❑ 60 Tyson Chandler	2.50	1.00
❑ 61 Desmond Mason	1.50	.60
❑ 62 Chris Paul	6.00	2.50
❑ 63 Peja Stojakovic	2.50	1.00
❑ 64 Steve Francis	2.50	1.00
❑ 65 Stephon Marbury	2.50	1.00
❑ 66 Quentin Richardson	1.50	.60
❑ 67 Nate Robinson	2.50	1.00
❑ 68 Carlos Arroyo	4.00	1.50
❑ 69 Dwight Howard	3.00	1.25
❑ 70 Darko Milicic	2.50	1.00
❑ 71 Andre Iguodala	2.50	1.00
❑ 72 Allen Iverson	5.00	2.00
❑ 73 Kyle Korver	2.50	1.00
❑ 74 Chris Webber	2.50	1.00
❑ 75 Boris Diaw	1.50	.60
❑ 76 Shawn Marion	2.50	1.00
❑ 77 Steve Nash	2.50	1.00
❑ 78 Amare Stoudemire	5.00	2.00
❑ 79 Jamaal Magloire	1.50	.60
❑ 80 Zach Randolph	2.50	1.00
❑ 81 Martell Webster	1.50	.60
❑ 82 Ron Artest	1.50	.60
❑ 83 Brad Miller	2.50	1.00
❑ 84 Mike Bibby	2.50	1.00
❑ 85 Tim Duncan	5.00	2.00
❑ 86 Michael Finley	2.50	1.00
❑ 87 Manu Ginobili	2.50	1.00
❑ 88 Tony Parker	2.50	1.00
❑ 89 Ray Allen	2.50	1.00
❑ 90 Rashard Lewis	2.50	1.00
❑ 91 Luke Ridnour	1.50	.60
❑ 92 Chris Bosh	2.50	1.00
❑ 93 T.J. Ford	1.50	.60
❑ 94 Joey Graham	1.50	.60
❑ 95 Carlos Boozer	1.50	.60
❑ 96 Andrei Kirilenko	2.50	1.00
❑ 97 Deron Williams	2.50	1.00
❑ 98 Gilbert Arenas	2.50	1.00
❑ 99 Caron Butler	1.50	.60
❑ 100 Antawn Jamison	2.50	1.00
❑ 101 Andrea Bargnani RC	20.00	8.00
❑ 102 LaMarcus Aldridge RC	15.00	6.00
❑ 103 Adam Morrison RC	15.00	6.00
❑ 104 Tyrus Thomas RC	20.00	8.00
❑ 105 Shelden Williams RC	8.00	3.00
❑ 106 Brandon Roy RC	20.00	8.00
❑ 107 Randy Foye RC	12.00	5.00
❑ 108 Rudy Gay RC	12.00	5.00
❑ 109 Patrick O'Bryant RC	6.00	2.50
❑ 110 Saer Sene RC	6.00	2.50
❑ 111 J.J. Redick RC	12.00	5.00
❑ 112 Hilton Armstrong RC	6.00	2.50
❑ 113 Thabo Sefolosha RC	10.00	4.00
❑ 114 Ronnie Brewer RC	8.00	3.00
❑ 115 Cedric Simmons RC	6.00	2.50
❑ 116 Rodney Carney RC	6.00	2.50
❑ 117 Shawne Williams RC	8.00	3.00
❑ 118 Quincy Douby RC	6.00	2.50
❑ 119 Renaldo Balkman RC	6.00	2.50
❑ 120 Rajon Rondo RC	8.00	3.00
❑ 121 Marcus Williams RC	8.00	3.00
❑ 122 Josh Boone RC	6.00	2.50
❑ 123 Kyle Lowry RC	6.00	2.50
❑ 124 Shannon Brown RC	6.00	2.50
❑ 125 Jordan Farmar RC	12.00	5.00
❑ 126 Sergio Rodriguez RC	6.00	2.50
❑ 127 Maurice Ager RC	6.00	2.50
❑ 128 Mardy Collins RC	6.00	2.50
❑ 129 James White RC	6.00	2.50
❑ 130 Steve Novak RC	6.00	2.50
❑ 131 Solomon Jones RC	6.00	2.50
❑ 132 Paul Davis RC	6.00	2.50
❑ 133 P.J. Tucker RC	6.00	2.50
❑ 134 Craig Smith RC	6.00	2.50
❑ 135 Bobby Jones RC	6.00	2.50
❑ 136 David Noel RC	6.00	2.50
❑ 137 James Augustine RC	6.00	2.50
❑ 138 Daniel Gibson RC	15.00	6.00
❑ 139 Marcus Vinicius RC	6.00	2.50
❑ 140 Dee Brown RC	8.00	3.00
❑ 141 Ryan Hollins RC	6.00	2.50
❑ 142 Hassan Adams RC	8.00	3.00

1996 SPx

❑ COMPLETE SET (50)	60.00	30.00
❑ 1 Stacey Augmon	1.00	.40
❑ 2 Mookie Blaylock	1.00	.40
❑ 3 Eric Montross	1.00	.40
❑ 4 Eric Williams	1.00	.40
❑ 5 Larry Johnson	2.00	.75
❑ 6 George Zidek	1.00	.40
❑ 7 Jason Caffey	1.00	.40
❑ 8 Michael Jordan	20.00	10.00
❑ 9 Chris Mills	1.00	.40
❑ 10 Bob Sura	1.00	.40
❑ 11 Jason Kidd	5.00	2.00
❑ 12 Jamal Mashburn	2.00	.75
❑ 13 Antonio McDyess	3.00	1.25
❑ 14 Jalen Rose	3.00	1.25
❑ 15 Grant Hill	3.00	1.25
❑ 16 Theo Ratliff	2.00	.75
❑ 17 Joe Smith	2.00	.75
❑ 18 Latrell Sprewell	3.00	1.25
❑ 19 Hakeem Olajuwon	3.00	1.25
❑ 20 Reggie Miller	3.00	1.25
❑ 21 Rik Smits	2.00	.75
❑ 22 Brent Barry	1.00	.40
❑ 23 Lamond Murray	1.00	.40
❑ 24 Magic Johnson	5.00	2.00
❑ 25 Eddie Jones	3.00	1.25
❑ 26 Nick Van Exel	3.00	1.25
❑ 27 Alonzo Mourning	2.00	.75
❑ 28 Kurt Thomas	2.00	.75
❑ 29 Vin Baker	2.00	.75
❑ 30 Glenn Robinson	3.00	1.25
❑ 31 Kevin Garnett	6.00	2.50
❑ 32 Ed O'Bannon	1.00	.40
❑ 33 Patrick Ewing	3.00	1.25
❑ 34 Anfernee Hardaway	3.00	1.25
❑ 35 Shaquille O'Neal	8.00	3.00
❑ 36 Jerry Stackhouse	4.00	1.50
❑ 37 Charles Barkley	4.00	1.50
❑ 38 Michael Finley	4.00	1.50
❑ 39 Randolph Childress	1.00	.40
❑ 40 Gary Trent	1.00	.40
❑ 41 Brian Grant	3.00	1.25
❑ 42 Mitch Richmond	2.00	.75
❑ 43 David Robinson	3.00	1.25
❑ 44 Shawn Kemp	2.00	.75
❑ 45 Gary Payton	3.00	1.25
❑ 46 Damon Stoudamire	3.00	1.25
❑ 47 Karl Malone	3.00	1.25
❑ 48 John Stockton	3.00	1.25
❑ 49 Bryant Reeves	1.00	.40
❑ 50 Rasheed Wallace	4.00	1.50
❑ R1 Michael Jordan RB	12.00	5.00
❑ T1 Anfernee Hardaway TRIB	3.00	1.25
❑ NNO Anfernee Hardaway AU	50.00	20.00
❑ NNO A.Hardaway Expired	30.00	15.00
❑ NNO Michael Jordan AU	1400.00	800.00
❑ NNO M.Jordan Expired	1000.00	750.00

1997 SPx

❑ COMPLETE SET (50)	100.00	50.00
❑ 1 Mookie Blaylock	1.00	.40
❑ 2 Antoine Walker	4.00	1.50
❑ 3 Eric Williams	1.00	.40
❑ 4 Tony Delk	1.00	.40

❑ 5 Michael Jordan	20.00	8.00
❑ 6 Dennis Rodman	2.00	.75
❑ 7 Vitaly Potapenko	1.00	.40
❑ 8 Bob Sura	1.00	.40
❑ 9 Jamal Mashburn	2.00	.75
❑ 10 Samaki Walker	1.00	.40
❑ 11 Antonio McDyess	2.00	.75
❑ 12 Joe Dumars	3.00	1.25
❑ 13 Grant Hill	3.00	1.25
❑ 14 Joe Smith	2.00	.75
❑ 15 Latrell Sprewell	3.00	1.25
❑ 16 Charles Barkley	4.00	1.50
❑ 17 Hakeem Olajuwon	3.00	1.25
❑ 18 Erick Dampier	2.00	.75
❑ 19 Reggie Miller	3.00	1.25
❑ 20 Brent Barry	2.00	.75
❑ 21 Lorenzen Wright	1.00	.40
❑ 22 Kobe Bryant	20.00	8.00
❑ 23 Eddie Jones	3.00	1.25
❑ 24 Shaquille O'Neal	8.00	3.00
❑ 25 Alonzo Mourning	2.00	.75
❑ 26 Kurt Thomas	2.00	.75
❑ 27 Vin Baker	2.00	.75
❑ 28 Glenn Robinson	3.00	1.25
❑ 29 Kevin Garnett	6.00	2.50
❑ 30 Stephon Marbury	4.00	1.50
❑ 31 Kerry Kittles	3.00	1.25
❑ 32 Patrick Ewing	2.00	.75
❑ 33 Larry Johnson	2.00	.75
❑ 34 Anfernee Hardaway	3.00	1.25
❑ 35 Allen Iverson	10.00	4.00
❑ 36 Jerry Stackhouse	3.00	1.25
❑ 37 Kevin Johnson	2.00	.75
❑ 38 Steve Nash	3.00	1.25
❑ 39 Jermaine O'Neal	5.00	2.00
❑ 40 Mitch Richmond	2.00	.75
❑ 41 David Robinson	3.00	1.25
❑ 42 Shawn Kemp	2.00	.75
❑ 43 Gary Payton	3.00	1.25
❑ 44 Marcus Camby	3.00	1.25
❑ 45 Damon Stoudamire	2.00	.75
❑ 46 Karl Malone	3.00	1.25
❑ 47 John Stockton	3.00	1.25
❑ 48 Shareef Abdur-Rahim	5.00	2.00
❑ 49 Bryant Reeves	1.00	.40
❑ 50 Juwan Howard	2.00	.75
❑ SPX5 Michael Jordan Promo	15.00	6.00

1997-98 SPx

❑ COMPLETE SET (50)	75.00	40.00
❑ 1 Mookie Blaylock	.60	.25

2	Dikembe Mutombo	1.50	.60
3	Chauncey Billups RC	5.00	2.00
4	Antoine Walker	2.50	1.00
5	Glen Rice	1.50	.60
6	Michael Jordan	12.00	6.00
7	Scottie Pippen	3.00	1.25
8	Dennis Rodman	1.50	.60
9	Shawn Kemp	1.50	.60
10	Michael Finley	1.50	.60
11	Tony Battie RC	2.00	.75
12	LaPhonso Ellis	.60	.25
13	Grant Hill	2.00	.75
14	Joe Dumars	2.00	.75
15	Joe Smith	1.50	.60
16	Clyde Drexler	2.00	.75
17	Charles Barkley	2.50	1.00
18	Hakeem Olajuwon	2.00	.75
19	Reggie Miller	2.00	.75
20	Brent Barry	1.50	.60
21	Kobe Bryant	8.00	3.00
22	Shaquille O'Neal	5.00	2.00
23	Alonzo Mourning	1.50	.60
24	Glenn Robinson	2.00	.75
25	Kevin Garnett	4.00	1.50
26	Stephon Marbury	2.50	1.00
27	Keith Van Horn RC	3.00	1.25
28	Patrick Ewing	2.00	.75
29	Anfernee Hardaway	2.00	.75
30	Allen Iverson	5.00	2.00
31	Kevin Johnson	1.50	.60
32	Antonio McDyess	1.50	.60
33	Jason Kidd	3.00	1.25
34	Kenny Anderson	1.50	.60
35	Rasheed Wallace	2.00	.75
36	Mitch Richmond	1.50	.60
37	Tim Duncan RC	15.00	6.00
38	David Robinson	2.00	.75
39	Vin Baker	1.50	.60
40	Gary Payton	2.00	.75
41	Marcus Camby	1.50	.60
42	Tracy McGrady RC	20.00	8.00
43	Damon Stoudamire	1.50	.60
44	Karl Malone	2.00	.75
45	John Stockton	2.00	.75
46	Shareef Abdur-Rahim	3.00	1.25
47	Antonio Daniels RC	2.00	.75
48	Bryant Reeves	.60	.25
49	Juwan Howard	1.50	.60
50	Chris Webber	2.00	.75
T1	Piece of History Trade	200.00	125.00

1998-99 SPx Finite

COMPLETE SET w/o RC (90)	100.00	60.00
COMP.ST.POWER SET (60)	125.00	75.00
COMMON ST.POWER (91-150)	1.25	.50
COMP.SPx 2000 SET (30)	125.00	75.00
COMMON SPx 2000 (151-180)	2.00	.75
COMP.TP.FLIGHT SET (20)	100.00	60.00
COMMON TP.FLIGHT (181-200)	2.50	1.00
COMP.FIN.EXC.SET (10)	125.00	75.00
COMMON FIN.EXC. (201-210)	4.00	1.50
COMP.ROOKIE SET (28)	400.00	150.00
COMMON ROOKIE (211-240)	5.00	2.00
1 Tim Duncan	15.00	7.50
2 Hakeem Olajuwon	2.50	1.00
3 Keith Van Horn	2.50	1.00
4 Rasheed Wallace	2.50	1.00
5 Mookie Blaylock	.75	.30

6	Bobby Jackson	1.50	.60
7	Detlef Schrempf	1.50	.60
8	Antonio McDyess	1.50	.60
9	Lamond Murray	.75	.30
10	Chris Mullin	2.50	1.00
11	Zydrunas Ilgauskas	1.50	.60
12	Tracy Murray	.75	.30
13	Jerry Stackhouse	2.50	1.00
14	Avery Johnson	.75	.30
15	Larry Johnson	1.50	.60
16	Alan Henderson	.75	.30
17	David Wesley	.75	.30
18	Kevin Willis	.75	.30
19	Eddie Jones	2.50	1.00
20	Horace Grant	1.50	.60
21	Ray Allen	2.50	1.00
22	Derrick Coleman	.75	.30
23	Derek Anderson	2.00	.75
24	Tim Hardaway	1.50	.60
25	Danny Fortson	.75	.30
26	Tariq Abdul-Wahad	.75	.30
27	Charles Barkley	3.00	1.25
28	Sam Cassell	2.50	1.00
29	Kevin Garnett	5.00	2.00
30	Jeff Hornacek	1.50	.60
31	Isaac Austin	.75	.30
32	Allan Houston	1.50	.60
33	David Robinson	2.50	1.00
34	Tracy McGrady	6.00	2.50
35	LaPhonso Ellis	.75	.30
36	Shawn Kemp	1.50	.60
37	Glenn Robinson	1.50	.60
38	Shareef Abdur-Rahim	2.50	1.00
39	Vin Baker	1.50	.60
40	Rik Smits	1.50	.60
41	Jason Kidd	4.00	1.50
42	Erick Dampier	1.50	.60
43	Shawn Bradley	.75	.30
44	Anfernee Hardaway	2.50	1.00
45	John Stockton	2.50	1.00
46	Calbert Cheaney	.75	.30
47	Terrell Brandon	1.50	.60
48	Hubert Davis	.75	.30
49	Patrick Ewing	2.50	1.00
50	Kobe Bryant	10.00	4.00
51	Gary Payton	2.50	1.00
52	Marcus Camby	1.50	.60
53	Bryant Reeves	.75	.30
54	Reggie Miller	2.50	1.00
55	Antoine Walker	2.50	1.00
56	Scottie Pippen	4.00	1.50
57	Hersey Hawkins	.75	.30
58	John Starks	1.50	.60
59	Dikembe Mutombo	1.50	.60
60	Damon Stoudamire	1.50	.60
61	Rodney Rogers	.75	.30
62	Nick Anderson	.75	.30
63	Brian Williams	.75	.30
64	Ron Mercer	1.25	.50
65	Donyell Marshall	.75	.30
66	Glen Rice	1.50	.60
67	Michael Finley	2.50	1.00
68	Tim Duncan	4.00	1.50
69	Stephon Marbury	2.50	1.00
70	Antonio Daniels	.75	.30
71	Chauncey Billups	1.50	.60
72	Kerry Kittles	.75	.30
73	Brian Grant	.75	.30
74	Anthony Mason	1.50	.60
75	Allen Iverson	5.00	2.00
76	Juwan Howard	1.50	.60
77	Grant Hill	2.50	1.00
78	Tony Delk	.75	.30
79	Olden Polynice	.75	.30
80	Alonzo Mourning	1.50	.60
81	Karl Malone	2.50	1.00
82	Isaiah Rider	.75	.30
83	Shaquille O'Neal	6.00	2.50
84	Steve Smith	1.50	.60
85	Kenny Anderson	1.50	.60
86	Toni Kukoc	1.50	.60
87	Anthony Peeler	.75	.30
88	Tim Thomas	1.50	.60
89	Nick Van Exel	2.50	1.00
90	Jamal Mashburn	1.50	.60
91	Reggie Miller SP	4.00	1.50

92	Juwan Howard SP	2.50	1.00
93	Glen Rice SP	2.50	1.00
94	Grant Hill SP	4.00	1.50
95	Maurice Taylor SP	2.00	.75
96	Vin Baker SP	2.50	1.00
97	Tim Thomas SP	2.50	1.00
98	Bobby Jackson SP	1.25	.50
99	Damon Stoudamire SP	2.50	1.00
100	Michael Jordan SP	30.00	12.50
101	Eddie Jones SP	4.00	1.50
102	Keith Van Horn SP	4.00	1.50
103	Dikembe Mutombo SP	2.50	1.00
104	Brevin Knight SP	1.25	.50
105	Shawn Bradley SP	1.25	.50
106	Lamond Murray SP	1.25	.50
107	Tim Duncan SP	6.00	2.50
108	Bryant Reeves SP	1.25	.50
109	Antoine Walker SP	4.00	1.50
110	John Stockton SP	4.00	1.50
111	Nick Anderson SP	1.25	.50
112	Chris Mullin SP	4.00	1.50
113	Glenn Robinson SP	2.50	1.00
114	Kevin Garnett SP	8.00	3.00
115	Michael Stewart SP	1.25	.50
116	Antonio McDyess SP	2.50	1.00
117	Jim Jackson SP	1.25	.50
118	Chauncey Billups SP	1.25	.50
119	Sam Cassell SP	2.50	1.00
120	Dennis Rodman SP	2.50	1.00
121	Rasheed Wallace SP	2.50	1.00
122	Brian Williams SP	1.25	.50
123	Anfernee Hardaway SP	4.00	1.50
124	Scottie Pippen SP	6.00	2.50
125	Terrell Brandon SP	2.50	1.00
126	Michael Finley SP	4.00	1.50
127	Kerry Kittles SP	1.25	.50
128	Toni Kukoc SP	2.50	1.00
129	Hakeem Olajuwon SP	2.50	1.00
130	Tim Hardaway SP	2.50	1.00
131	Shareef Abdur-Rahim SP	4.00	1.50
132	Donyell Marshall SP	1.25	.50
133	David Robinson SP	4.00	1.50
134	LaPhonso Ellis SP	1.25	.50
135	Ray Allen SP	4.00	1.50
136	Nick Van Exel SP	4.00	1.50
137	Patrick Ewing SP	4.00	1.50
138	Anthony Mason SP	2.50	1.00
139	Shaquille O'Neal SP	10.00	4.00
140	Shawn Kemp SP	4.00	1.50
141	Stephon Marbury SP	4.00	1.50
142	Karl Malone SP	4.00	1.50
143	Allen Iverson SP	8.00	3.00
144	Kenny Anderson SP	2.50	1.00
145	Marcus Camby SP	4.00	1.50
146	Steve Smith SP	2.50	1.00
147	Gary Payton SP	4.00	1.50
148	Jason Kidd SP	6.00	2.50
149	Alonzo Mourning SP	4.00	1.50
150	Charles Barkley SP	5.00	2.00
151	Kobe Bryant SPx	25.00	10.00
152	Ron Mercer SPx	5.00	2.00
153	Maurice Taylor SPx	3.00	1.25
154	Tim Duncan SPx	15.00	6.00
155	Shareef Abdur-Rahim SPx	6.00	2.50
156	Eddie Jones SPx	6.00	2.50
157	Chauncey Billups SPx	2.00	.75
158	Derek Anderson SPx	5.00	2.00
159	Bobby Jackson SPx	2.00	.75
160	Stephon Marbury SPx	6.00	2.50
161	Anfernee Hardaway SPx	6.00	2.50
162	Zydrunas Ilgauskas SPx	4.00	1.50
163	Allen Iverson SPx	12.00	5.00
164	Antoine Walker SPx	6.00	2.50
165	Tracy McGrady SPx	15.00	6.00
166	Rasheed Wallace SPx	4.00	1.50
167	Jason Kidd SPx	10.00	4.00
168	Kevin Garnett SPx	12.00	5.00
169	Damon Stoudamire SPx	4.00	1.50
170	Brevin Knight SPx	2.00	.75
171	Tim Thomas SPx	4.00	1.50
172	Danny Fortson SPx	2.00	.75
173	Jermaine O'Neal SPx	6.00	2.50
174	Keith Van Horn SPx	6.00	2.50
175	Ray Allen SPx	6.00	2.50
176	Kerry Kittles SPx	2.00	.75
177	Vin Baker SPx	4.00	1.50

178	Allan Houston SPx	6.00	2.50
179	Alan Henderson SPx	2.00	.75
180	Bryon Russell SPx	2.00	.75
181	Michael Jordan TF	50.00	20.00
182	Maurice Taylor TF	4.00	1.50
183	Isaiah Rider TF	2.50	1.00
184	Antonio McDyess TF	5.00	2.00
185	Anfernee Hardaway TF	8.00	3.00
186	Glenn Robinson TF	5.00	2.00
187	Dikembe Mutombo TF	5.00	2.00
188	Shawn Kemp TF	5.00	2.00
189	Tracy McGrady TF	20.00	8.00
190	Reggie Miller TF	5.00	2.00
191	Derek Anderson TF	6.00	2.50
192	Allan Houston TF	8.00	3.00
193	Michael Finley TF	8.00	3.00
194	Nick Van Exel TF	8.00	3.00
195	Juwan Howard TF	5.00	2.00
196	LaPhonso Ellis TF	2.50	1.00
197	Ron Mercer TF	4.00	1.50
198	Glen Rice TF	5.00	2.00
199	Joe Smith TF	5.00	2.00
200	Kobe Bryant TF	30.00	12.50
201	Michael Jordan FE	80.00	40.00
202	Karl Malone FE	4.00	1.50
203	Hakeem Olajuwon FE	5.00	2.00
204	David Robinson FE	12.00	5.00
205	Shaquille O'Neal FE	30.00	12.50
206	John Stockton FE	12.00	5.00
207	Grant Hill FE	12.00	5.00
208	Tim Hardaway FE	8.00	3.00
209	Scottie Pippen FE	20.00	8.00
210	Gary Payton FE	12.00	5.00
211	Michael Olowokandi RC	6.00	2.50
212	Mike Bibby RC	20.00	8.00
213	Raef LaFrentz RC		
214	Antawn Jamison RC		
215	Vince Carter RC	80.00	40.00
216	Robert Traylor RC	5.00	2.00
217	Jason Williams RC	15.00	6.00
218	Larry Hughes RC		
219	Dirk Nowitzki RC	40.00	15.00
220	Paul Pierce RC	25.00	10.00
221	Bonzi Wells RC	15.00	6.00
222	Michael Doleac RC	5.00	2.00
223	Keon Clark RC	10.00	4.00
224	Michael Dickerson RC	12.00	5.00
225	Matt Harpring RC	8.00	3.00
226	Bryce Drew RC	5.00	2.00
227	Does not exist		
228	Does not exist		
229	Pat Garrity RC	5.00	2.00
230	Roshown McLeod RC	5.00	2.00
231	Ricky Davis RC	10.00	4.00
232	Brian Skinner RC	5.00	2.00
233	Tyronn Lue RC	8.00	3.00
234	Felipe Lopez RC	5.00	2.00
235	Al Harrington RC	12.00	5.00
236	Ruben Patterson RC	8.00	3.00
237	Jelani McCoy RC	5.00	2.00
238	Corey Benjamin RC	5.00	2.00
239	Nazr Mohammed RC	5.00	2.00
240	Rashard Lewis RC	20.00	8.00

1999-00 SPx

COMPLETE SET w/o RC (90)	30.00	18.00
COMMON CARD (1-90)	.40	.15
COMMON ROOKIE (91-120)	3.00	1.25

1	Dikembe Mutombo	.75	.30
2	Alan Henderson	.40	.15
3	Antoine Walker	1.25	.50
4	Paul Pierce	1.25	.50
5	Kenny Anderson	.75	.30
6	Eddie Jones	1.25	.50
7	David Wesley	.40	.15
8	Elden Campbell	.40	.15
9	Toni Kukoc	.75	.30
10	Dickey Simpkins	.40	.15
11	Shawn Kemp	.75	.30
12	Brevin Knight	.40	.15
13	Michael Finley	1.25	.50
14	Cedric Ceballos	.40	.15
15	Dirk Nowitzki	2.50	1.00
16	Antonio McDyess	.75	.30
17	Nick Van Exel	1.25	.50
18	Chauncey Billups	.75	.30
19	Grant Hill	1.25	.50
20	Jerry Stackhouse	1.25	.50
21	Bison Dele	.40	.15
22	Lindsey Hunter	.40	.15
23	Antawn Jamison	2.00	.75
24	Donyell Marshall	.75	.30
25	John Starks	.75	.30
26	Chris Mills	.40	.15
27	Hakeem Olajuwon	1.25	.50
28	Scottie Pippen	2.00	.75
29	Charles Barkley	1.50	.60
30	Reggie Miller	1.25	.50
31	Rik Smits	.75	.30
32	Jalen Rose	1.25	.50
33	Chris Mullin	1.25	.50
34	Maurice Taylor	.75	.30
35	Michael Olowokandi	.75	.30
36	Shaquille O'Neal	3.00	1.25
37	Kobe Bryant	5.00	2.00
38	Glen Rice	.75	.30
39	Tim Hardaway	.75	.30
40	Alonzo Mourning	.75	.30
41	Dan Majerle	.75	.30
42	P.J. Brown	.40	.15
43	Glenn Robinson	1.25	.50
44	Ray Allen	1.25	.50
45	Sam Cassell	1.25	.50
46	Tim Thomas	.75	.30
47	Kevin Garnett	2.50	1.00
48	Bobby Jackson	.75	.30
49	Joe Smith	.75	.30
50	Stephon Marbury	1.25	.50
51	Keith Van Horn	1.25	.50
52	Jayson Williams	.40	.15
53	Patrick Ewing	1.25	.50
54	Latrell Sprewell	1.25	.50
55	Allan Houston	.75	.30
56	Marcus Camby	.75	.30
57	Bo Outlaw	.40	.15
58	Darrell Armstrong	.40	.15
59	Allen Iverson	2.50	1.00
60	Theo Ratliff	.75	.30
61	Larry Hughes	1.25	.50
62	Jason Kidd	2.00	.75
63	Tom Gugliotta	.40	.15
64	Clifford Robinson	.40	.15
65	Brian Grant	.75	.30
66	Jermaine O'Neal	1.25	.50
67	Rasheed Wallace	1.25	.50
68	Damon Stoudamire	.75	.30
69	Jason Williams	1.25	.50
70	Chris Webber	1.25	.50
71	Vlade Divac	.75	.30
72	Avery Johnson	.40	.15
73	Tim Duncan	2.50	1.00
74	David Robinson	1.25	.50
75	Sean Elliott	.75	.30
76	Gary Payton	1.25	.50
77	Vin Baker	.75	.30
78	Jelani McCoy	.40	.15
79	Charles Oakley	.40	.15
80	Vince Carter	3.00	1.25
81	Tracy McGrady	3.00	1.25
82	Doug Christie	.75	.30
83	Karl Malone	1.25	.50
84	John Stockton	1.25	.50
85	Shareef Abdur-Rahim	1.25	.50
86	Bryant Reeves	.40	.15

87	Mike Bibby	1.25	.50
88	Juwan Howard	.75	.30
89	Mitch Richmond	.75	.30
90	Rod Strickland	.40	.15
91	Elton Brand RC	25.00	10.00
92	Steve Francis AU/500 RC	80.00	40.00
93	Baron Davis AU/500 RC	120.00	60.00
94	Lamar Odom RC	20.00	8.00
95	Jonathan Bender RC	15.00	6.00
96	W.Szczerbiak AU/500 RC	50.00	20.00
97	Richard Hamilton AU/500 RC	30.00	12.50
98	Andre Miller AU/500 RC	30.00	12.50
99	Shawn Marion AU/500 RC	60.00	12.50
100	Jason Terry AU RC	20.00	8.00
101	Trajan Langdon AU RC	8.00	3.00
102	Venson Hamilton RC	3.00	1.25
103	C.Maggette AU/500 RC	40.00	15.00
104	William Avery AU RC	8.00	3.00
105	Dion Glover RC	4.00	1.50
106	Ron Artest AU RC	25.00	10.00
107	Cal Bowdler RC	4.00	1.50
108	James Posey AU RC	12.00	5.00
109	Quincy Lewis AU RC	8.00	3.00
110	Devean George AU RC	15.00	6.00
111	Tim James AU RC	8.00	3.00
112	Vonteego Cummings RC	5.00	2.00
113	Jumaine Jones AU RC	10.00	4.00
114	Scott Padgett AU RC	8.00	3.00
115	Kenny Thomas RC	5.00	2.00
116	Jeff Foster RC	4.00	1.50
117	Ryan Robertson RC	4.00	1.50
118	Chris Herren AU RC	8.00	3.00
119	E.Eschmeyer AU RC	8.00	3.00
120	A.J. Bramlett AU RC	8.00	3.00
P32	Karl Malone	1.25	.50

2000-01 SPx

COMPLETE SET w/o RC (90)		40.00	20.00
COMMON CARD (1-90)		.40	.15
COMM. RC (91/93-98/138)		2.00	.75
COMMON RC (99-104)		4.00	1.50
COMMON RC (105-110)		6.00	2.50
COMM.RC (92/111-130/136-137)		8.00	3.00
COMMON RC (131-135)		10.00	4.00
1	Dikembe Mutombo	.75	.30
2	Jim Jackson	.40	.15
3	Jason Terry	1.25	.50
4	Paul Pierce	1.25	.50
5	Kenny Anderson	.75	.30
6	Antoine Walker	1.25	.50
7	Derrick Coleman	.40	.15
8	Baron Davis	1.25	.50
9	David Wesley	.40	.15
10	Elton Brand	1.25	.50
11	Ron Artest	.75	.30
12	Corey Benjamin	.40	.15
13	Lamond Murray	.75	.30
14	Lamond Murray	.40	.15
15	Andre Miller	.75	.30
16	Michael Finley	1.25	.50
17	Gary Trent	.40	.15
18	Dirk Nowitzki	2.00	.75
19	Antonio McDyess	.75	.30
20	Nick Van Exel	1.25	.50
21	Raef LaFrentz	.75	.30
22	Jerry Stackhouse	1.25	.50
23	Michael Curry	.40	.15
24	Jerome Williams	.40	.15

25	Larry Hughes	.75	.30
26	Antawn Jamison	1.25	.50
27	Mookie Blaylock	.40	.15
28	Hakeem Olajuwon	1.25	.50
29	Steve Francis	1.25	.50
30	Shandon Anderson	.40	.15
31	Reggie Miller	1.25	.50
32	Jalen Rose	1.25	.50
33	Austin Croshere	.75	.30
34	Lamar Odom	1.25	.50
35	Michael Olowokandi	.40	.15
36	Tyrone Nesby	.40	.15
37	Shaquille O'™Neal	3.00	1.25
38	Kobe Bryant	5.00	2.00
39	Robert Horry	.75	.30
40	Ron Harper	.75	.30
41	Alonzo Mourning	.75	.30
42	Eddie Jones	1.25	.50
43	Tim Hardaway	.75	.30
44	Glenn Robinson	1.25	.50
45	Sam Cassell	1.25	.50
46	Ray Allen	1.25	.50
47	Tim Thomas	.75	.30
48	Kevin Garnett	2.50	1.00
49	Terrell Brandon	.75	.30
50	Wally Szczerbiak	.75	.30
51	Keith Van Horn	1.25	.50
52	Stephon Marbury	1.25	.50
53	Jamie Feick	.40	.15
54	Latrell Sprewell	.75	.30
55	Marcus Camby	.75	.30
56	Allan Houston	.75	.30
57	Grant Hill	1.25	.50
58	Tracy McGrady	3.00	1.25
59	Darrell Armstrong	.40	.15
60	Allen Iverson	2.50	1.00
61	Toni Kukoc	.75	.30
62	Theo Ratliff	.75	.30
63	Anfernee Hardaway	1.25	.50
64	Jason Kidd	2.00	.75
65	Shawn Marion	.75	.30
66	Steve Smith	.75	.30
67	Rasheed Wallace	1.25	.50
68	Scottie Pippen	2.00	.75
69	Bonzi Wells	.75	.30
70	Jason Williams	.75	.30
71	Vlade Divac	.75	.30
72	Chris Webber	1.25	.50
73	David Robinson	1.25	.50
74	Sean Elliott	.75	.30
75	Tim Duncan	2.50	1.00
76	Gary Payton	1.25	.50
77	Rashard Lewis	.75	.30
78	Vin Baker	.75	.30
79	Vince Carter	3.00	1.25
80	Muggsy Bogues	.75	.30
81	Antonio Davis	.40	.15
82	Karl Malone	1.25	.50
83	John Stockton	1.25	.50
84	Bryon Russell	.40	.15
85	Shareef Abdur-Rahim	1.25	.50
86	Michael Dickerson	.75	.30
87	Mike Bibby	1.25	.50
88	Mitch Richmond	.75	.30
89	Richard Hamilton	.75	.30
90	Juwan Howard	.75	.30
91	Lavor Postell RC	2.00	.75
92	Mark Madsen JSY RC	6.00	2.50
93	Soumaila Samake RC	2.00	.75
94	Michael Redd RC	10.00	4.00
95	Paul McPherson RC	2.00	.75
96	Ruben Wolkowyski RC	2.00	.75
97	Daniel Santiago RC	2.00	.75
98	Pepe Sanchez RC	2.00	.75
99	Marc Jackson RC	4.00	1.50
100	Khalid El-Amin RC	4.00	1.50
101	Iakovos Tsakalidis RC	4.00	1.50
102	Jabari Smith RC	4.00	1.50
103	Jason Hart RC	4.00	1.50
104	Stephen Jackson RC	5.00	2.00
105	Eduardo Najera RC	10.00	4.00
106	Hanno Mottola RC	6.00	2.50
107	Eddie House RC	6.00	2.50
108	Dan Langhi RC	6.00	2.50
109	A.J. Guyton RC	6.00	2.50
110	Chris Porter RC	6.00	2.50
111	Mike Miller JSY RC	15.00	6.00
112	Keyon Dooling JSY RC	8.00	3.00
113	C.Alexander JSY RC EXCH	8.00	3.00
114	D.Mason JSY RC	8.00	3.00
115	J.Magloire JSY RC	8.00	3.00
116	D.Stevenson JSY RC	8.00	3.00
117	Dermarr Johnson JSY RC	8.00	3.00
117A	D.Johnson JSY RC EXCH	8.00	3.00
118	M.Cleaves JSY RC EXCH	8.00	3.00
119	Morris Peterson JSY RC	12.00	5.00
120	Jerome Moiso JSY RC	8.00	3.00
121	Donnell Harvey JSY RC	8.00	3.00
122	Q.Richardson JSY RC	12.00	5.00
123	J.Crawford JSY RC	12.00	5.00
124	Erick Barkley JSY RC	8.00	3.00
125	H.Turkoglu JSY RC	12.00	5.00
126	Etan Thomas JSY RC	8.00	3.00
127	M.Na'™Diaye JSY RC	8.00	3.00
128	Joel Przybilla JSY RC	8.00	3.00
129	Jason Collier JSY RC	12.00	5.00
130	Speedy Claxton JSY RC	8.00	3.00
131	Kenyon Martin JSY RC	40.00	15.00
132	Stromile Swift JSY RC	15.00	6.00
133	Darius Miles JSY RC	30.00	12.50
134	Marcus Fizer JSY RC	10.00	4.00
135	Chris Mihm JSY RC	10.00	4.00
136	I.Voskuhl JSY RC EXCH	8.00	3.00
137	P.Mickeal JSY RC EXCH	8.00	3.00
138	Dalibor Bagaric RC	2.00	.75

2001-02 SPx

COMPLETE SET (173)	3500.00	1250.00
COMP.SET w/o SP's (90)	60.00	30.00
COMMON CARD (1-90)	.40	.15
COMMON ROOKIE (91-105)	10.00	4.00
COMMON ROOKIE (106-111)	12.00	5.00
COMMON ROOKIE (121-140)	6.00	2.50

1	Jason Terry	1.25	.50
2	Shareef Abdur-Rahim	1.25	.50
3	DerMarr Johnson	.75	.30
4	Paul Pierce	1.25	.50
5	Antoine Walker	1.25	.50
6	Kenny Anderson	.75	.30
7	Baron Davis	1.25	.50
8	Jamal Mashburn	.75	.30
9	David Wesley	.40	.15
10	Ron Mercer	.75	.30
11	Ron Artest	.75	.30
12	Marcus Fizer	.75	.30
13	Andre Miller	.75	.30
14	Lamond Murray	.40	.15
15	Chris Mihm	.75	.30
16	Michael Finley	1.25	.50
17	Dirk Nowitzki	2.00	.75
18	Steve Nash	1.25	.50
19	Antonio McDyess	.75	.30
20	Nick Van Exel	1.25	.50
21	Rael LaFrentz	.75	.30
22	Jerry Stackhouse	1.25	.50
23	Chucky Atkins	.40	.15
24	Corliss Williamson	.75	.30
25	Antawn Jamison	1.25	.50
26	Larry Hughes	.75	.30
27	Chris Porter	.75	.30
28	Steve Francis	1.25	.50
29	Cuttino Mobley	.75	.30
30	Maurice Taylor	.75	.30
31	Reggie Miller	1.25	.50
32	Jalen Rose	1.25	.50
33	Jermaine O'™Neal	1.25	.50
34	Darius Miles	1.25	.50
35	Elton Brand	1.25	.50
36	Lamar Odom	1.25	.50
37	Quentin Richardson	.75	.30
38	Kobe Bryant	5.00	2.00
39	Shaquille O'™Neal	3.00	1.25
40	Rick Fox	.75	.30
41	Derek Fisher	1.25	.50
42	Stromile Swift	.75	.30
43	Jason Williams	.75	.30
44	Michael Dickerson	.75	.30
45	Alonzo Mourning	.75	.30
46	Eddie Jones	1.25	.50
47	Anthony Carter	.40	.15
48	Glenn Robinson	1.25	.50
49	Ray Allen	1.25	.50
50	Sam Cassell	1.25	.50
51	Kevin Garnett	2.50	1.00
52	Wally Szczerbiak	.75	.30
53	Terrell Brandon	.75	.30
54	Chauncey Billups	.75	.30
55	Kenyon Martin	1.25	.50
56	Keith Van Horn	1.25	.50
57	Jason Kidd	2.00	.75
58	Latrell Sprewell	1.25	.50
59	Allan Houston	.75	.30
60	Marcus Camby	.75	.30
61	Tracy McGrady	3.00	1.25
62	Mike Miller	1.25	.50
63	Grant Hill	1.25	.50
64	Allen Iverson	2.50	1.00
65	Dikembe Mutombo	.75	.30
66	Aaron McKie	.75	.30
67	Stephon Marbury	1.25	.50
68	Shawn Marion	1.25	.50
69	Tom Gugliotta	.40	.15
70	Rasheed Wallace	1.25	.50
71	Damon Stoudamire	.75	.30
72	Bonzi Wells	.75	.30
73	Chris Webber	1.25	.50
74	Peja Stojakovic	1.25	.50
75	Mike Bibby	1.25	.50
76	Tim Duncan	2.50	1.00
77	David Robinson	1.25	.50
78	Antonio Daniels	.40	.15
79	Gary Payton	1.25	.50
80	Rashard Lewis	.75	.30
81	Desmond Mason	.75	.30
82	Vince Carter	3.00	1.25
83	Morris Peterson	.75	.30
84	Antonio Davis	.40	.15
85	Karl Malone	1.25	.50
86	John Stockton	1.25	.50
87	Donyell Marshall	.75	.30
88	Richard Hamilton	.75	.30
89	Courtney Alexander	.75	.30
90	Michael Jordan	25.00	10.00
91A	Tony Parker JSY AU RC	40.00	15.00
91B	Tony Parker JSY AU RC	40.00	15.00
91C	Tony Parker JSY AU RC	40.00	15.00
92A	J.Tinsley JSY AU RC	20.00	8.00
92B	J.Tinsley JSY AU RC	20.00	8.00
92C	J.Tinsley JSY AU RC	20.00	8.00
93A	S.Dalembert JSY AU RC	10.00	4.00
93B	S.Dalembert JSY AU RC	10.00	4.00
93C	S.Dalembert JSY AU RC	10.00	4.00
94A	G.Wallace JSY AU RC	20.00	8.00
94B	G.Wallace JSY AU RC	20.00	8.00
94C	G.Wallace JSY AU RC	20.00	8.00
95A	B.Armstrong JSY AU RC	12.00	5.00
95B	B.Armstrong JSY AU RC	12.00	5.00
95C	B.Armstrong JSY AU RC	12.00	5.00
96A	Jeryl Sasser JSY AU RC	10.00	4.00
96B	Jeryl Sasser JSY AU RC	10.00	4.00
96C	Jeryl Sasser JSY AU RC	10.00	4.00
97A	Jas.Collins JSY AU RC	10.00	4.00
97B	Jas.Collins JSY AU RC	10.00	4.00
97C	Jas.Collins JSY AU RC	10.00	4.00
98A	M.Bradley JSY AU RC	10.00	4.00
98B	M.Bradley JSY AU RC	10.00	4.00
98C	M.Bradley JSY AU RC	10.00	4.00
99A	S.Hunter JSY AU RC	10.00	4.00
99B	S.Hunter JSY AU RC	10.00	4.00
99C	S.Hunter JSY AU RC	10.00	4.00

❏ 100A	T.Murphy JSY AU RC	15.00	6.00
❏ 100B	T.Murphy JSY AU RC	15.00	6.00
❏ 100C	T.Murphy JSY AU RC	15.00	6.00
❏ 101A	R.Jefferson JSY AU RC	25.00	10.00
❏ 101B	R.Jefferson JSY AU RC	25.00	10.00
❏ 101C	R.Jefferson JSY AU RC	25.00	10.00
❏ 102A	V.Radmanov JSY AU RC	12.00	5.00
❏ 102B	V.Radmanov JSY AU RC	12.00	5.00
❏ 102C	V.Radmanov JSY AU RC	12.00	5.00
❏ 103A	Ke.Brown JSY AU RC	10.00	4.00
❏ 103B	Ke.Brown JSY AU RC	10.00	4.00
❏ 103C	Ke.Brown JSY AU RC	10.00	4.00
❏ 104A	J.Johnson JSY AU RC	25.00	10.00
❏ 104B	J.Johnson JSY AU RC ERR	25.00	10.00
❏ 104C	J.Johnson JSY AU RC COR		
❏ 104D	J.Johnson JSY AU RC COR		
❏ 104E	J.Johnson JSY AU RC COR		
❏ 104F	J.Johnson JSY AU RC COR		
❏ 105A	Kirk Haston JSY AU RC	10.00	4.00
❏ 105B	Kirk Haston JSY AU RC	10.00	4.00
❏ 105C	Kirk Haston JSY AU RC	10.00	4.00
❏ 106A	R.White JSY RC	12.00	5.00
❏ 106B	R.White JSY RC	12.00	5.00
❏ 106C	R.White JSY RC	12.00	5.00
❏ 107A	Eddie Griffin JSY AU RC	25.00	10.00
❏ 107B	Eddie Griffin JSY AU RC	25.00	10.00
❏ 107C	Eddie Griffin JSY AU RC	25.00	10.00
❏ 108A	J.Richardson JSY AU RC	50.00	20.00
❏ 108B	J.Richardson JSY AU RC	50.00	20.00
❏ 108C	J.Richardson JSY AU RC	50.00	20.00
❏ 109A	Eddy Curry JSY AU RC	40.00	15.00
❏ 109B	Eddy Curry JSY AU RC	40.00	15.00
❏ 109C	Eddy Curry JSY AU RC	40.00	15.00
❏ 110A	T.Chandler JSY AU RC	40.00	15.00
❏ 110B	T.Chandler JSY AU RC	40.00	15.00
❏ 110C	T.Chandler JSY AU RC	40.00	15.00
❏ 111A	Kw.Brown JSY AU RC	25.00	10.00
❏ 111B	Kw.Brown JSY AU RC	25.00	10.00
❏ 111C	Kw.Brown JSY AU RC	25.00	10.00
❏ 121	Shane Battier RC	10.00	4.00
❏ 122	Brendan Haywood RC	10.00	4.00
❏ 123	Joseph Forte RC	10.00	4.00
❏ 124	Zach Randolph RC	20.00	8.00
❏ 125	DeSagana Diop RC	6.00	2.50
❏ 126	Damone Brown RC	6.00	2.50
❏ 127	Andrei Kirilenko RC	15.00	6.00
❏ 128	Trenton Hassell RC	10.00	4.00
❏ 129	Gilbert Arenas RC	40.00	15.00
❏ 130	Earl Watson RC	6.00	2.50
❏ 131	Kenny Satterfield RC	6.00	2.50
❏ 132	Will Solomon RC	6.00	2.50
❏ 133	Bobby Simmons RC	6.00	2.50
❏ 134	Brian Scalabrine RC	6.00	2.50
❏ 135	Charlie Bell RC	6.00	2.50
❏ 136	Zeljko Rebraca RC	6.00	2.50
❏ 137	Loren Woods RC	6.00	2.50
❏ 138	Terence Morris RC	6.00	2.50
❏ 139	Jamison Brewer RC	6.00	2.50
❏ 140	Pau Gasol RC	25.00	10.00
❏ NNO	Kobe Bryant Promo	5.00	2.00

2002-03 SPx

❏ COMP.SET w/o SP's (90)		60.00	25.00
❏ COMMON CARD (1-90)		.40	.15
❏ COMMON AU (91-110)		15.00	6.00
❏ COM. JSY AU RC (111-132)		12.00	5.00
❏ COMMON ROOKIE (133-138)		5.00	2.00
❏ COMMON ROOKIE (139-147)		5.00	2.00

❏ COMMON ROOKIE (148-162)		4.00	1.50
❏ 1	Shareef Abdur-Rahim	1.25	.50
❏ 2	Jason Terry	1.25	.50
❏ 3	Glenn Robinson	1.25	.50
❏ 4	Paul Pierce	1.25	.50
❏ 5	Antoine Walker	1.25	.50
❏ 6	Kedrick Brown	.75	.30
❏ 7	Vin Baker	.75	.30
❏ 8	Jalen Rose	1.25	.50
❏ 9	Tyson Chandler	1.25	.50
❏ 10	Eddy Curry	1.25	.50
❏ 11	Ricky Davis	.75	.30
❏ 12	Chris Mihm	.40	.15
❏ 13	Darius Miles	1.25	.50
❏ 14	Dirk Nowitzki	2.00	.75
❏ 15	Michael Finley	1.25	.50
❏ 16	Steve Nash	1.25	.50
❏ 17	Raef LaFrentz	.75	.30
❏ 18	James Posey	.40	.15
❏ 19	Juwan Howard	.75	.30
❏ 20	Richard Hamilton	.75	.30
❏ 21	Ben Wallace	1.25	.50
❏ 22	Chauncey Billups	.75	.30
❏ 23	Antawn Jamison	1.25	.50
❏ 24	Jason Richardson	1.25	.50
❏ 25	Steve Francis	1.25	.50
❏ 26	Eddie Griffin	.75	.30
❏ 27	Cuttino Mobley	.75	.30
❏ 28	Reggie Miller	1.25	.50
❏ 29	Jamaal Tinsley	1.25	.50
❏ 30	Jermaine O'Neal	1.25	.50
❏ 31	Elton Brand	1.25	.50
❏ 32	Andre Miller	.75	.30
❏ 33	Lamar Odom	1.25	.50
❏ 34	Kobe Bryant	5.00	2.00
❏ 35	Shaquille O'Neal	3.00	1.25
❏ 36	Robert Horry	.75	.30
❏ 37	Devean George	.75	.30
❏ 38	Pau Gasol	1.25	.50
❏ 39	Shane Battier	1.25	.50
❏ 40	Jason Williams	.75	.30
❏ 41	Alonzo Mourning	.75	.30
❏ 42	Eddie Jones	1.25	.50
❏ 43	Brian Grant	.75	.30
❏ 44	Ray Allen	1.25	.50
❏ 45	Tim Thomas	.75	.30
❏ 46	Kevin Garnett	2.50	1.00
❏ 47	Terrell Brandon	.75	.30
❏ 48	Wally Szczerbiak	.75	.30
❏ 49	Jason Kidd	2.00	.75
❏ 50	Richard Jefferson	.75	.30
❏ 51	Kenyon Martin	1.25	.50
❏ 52	Baron Davis	1.25	.50
❏ 53	Jamal Mashburn	.75	.30
❏ 54	David Wesley	.40	.15
❏ 55	P.J. Brown	.40	.15
❏ 56	Allan Houston	.75	.30
❏ 57	Antonio McDyess	.75	.30
❏ 58	Latrell Sprewell	1.25	.50
❏ 59	Tracy McGrady	4.00	1.50
❏ 60	Mike Miller	1.25	.50
❏ 61	Darrell Armstrong	.40	.15
❏ 62	Allen Iverson	2.50	1.00
❏ 63	Keith Van Horn	1.25	.50
❏ 64	Stephon Marbury	1.25	.50
❏ 65	Shawn Marion	1.25	.50
❏ 66	Anfernee Hardaway	1.25	.50
❏ 67	Rasheed Wallace	1.25	.50
❏ 68	Damon Stoudamire	.75	.30
❏ 69	Scottie Pippen	2.00	.75
❏ 70	Chris Webber	1.25	.50
❏ 71	Mike Bibby	1.25	.50
❏ 72	Peja Stojakovic	1.25	.50
❏ 73	Hidayet Turkoglu	1.25	.50
❏ 74	Tim Duncan	3.00	1.25
❏ 75	David Robinson	1.25	.50
❏ 76	Tony Parker	1.25	.50
❏ 77	Steve Smith	.75	.30
❏ 78	Gary Payton	1.25	.50
❏ 79	Rashard Lewis	.75	.30
❏ 80	Brent Barry	.75	.30
❏ 81	Desmond Mason	.75	.30
❏ 82	Vince Carter	4.00	1.50
❏ 83	Morris Peterson	.75	.30
❏ 84	Antonio Davis	.40	.15
❏ 85	Karl Malone	1.25	.50

❏ 86	John Stockton	1.25	.50
❏ 87	Andrei Kirilenko	1.25	.50
❏ 88	Jerry Stackhouse	1.25	.50
❏ 89	Michael Jordan	10.00	4.00
❏ 90	Kwame Brown	.75	.30
❏ 91	J.Richardson JSY AU	1.25	.50
❏ 92	Tyson Chandler JSY AU	20.00	8.00
❏ 93	Kenyon Martin JSY AU	40.00	15.00
❏ 94	G.Wallace JSY AU	20.00	8.00
❏ 95	K.Abdul-Jbbr JSY AU SP	150.00	75.00
❏ 96	Mo.Peterson JSY AU	20.00	8.00
❏ 97	Andre Miller JSY AU	20.00	8.00
❏ 98	Q.Richardson JSY AU	20.00	8.00
❏ 99	Mike Miller JSY AU	20.00	8.00
❏ 100	J.O'Neal JSY AU SP	40.00	15.00
❏ 101	Marcus Fizer JSY AU	20.00	8.00
❏ 102	Mike Bibby JSY AU	50.00	20.00
❏ 103	C.Billups JSY AU SP		
❏ 104	Lamar Odom JSY AU SP	40.00	15.00
❏ 105	Antoine Walker JSY AU	40.00	15.00
❏ 106	Paul Pierce JSY AU	40.00	15.00
❏ 107	Jason Kidd JSY AU SP	50.00	20.00
❏ 108	K.Garnett JSY AU SP		
❏ 109	K.Bryant JSY AU SP		
❏ 110	M.Jordan JSY AU SP		
❏ 111	Chris Jefferies JSY AU RC	12.00	5.00
❏ 112	John Salmons JSY AU RC	12.00	5.00
❏ 113	T.Prince JSY AU RC	25.00	10.00
❏ 114	C.Jacobsen JSY AU RC	12.00	5.00
❏ 115	Qyntel Woods JSY AU RC	15.00	6.00
❏ 116	Kareem Rush JSY AU RC	20.00	8.00
❏ 117	R.Humphrey JSY AU RC	12.00	5.00
❏ 118	Carlos Boozer JSY AU RC	40.00	15.00
❏ 119	Sam Clancy JSY AU RC	12.00	5.00
❏ 120	Fred Jones JSY AU RC	15.00	6.00
❏ 121	Marcus Haislip JSY AU RC	12.00	5.00
❏ 122	Melvin Ely JSY AU RC	12.00	5.00
❏ 123	Jared Jeffries JSY AU RC	15.00	6.00
❏ 124	Dan Gadzuric JSY AU RC	12.00	5.00
❏ 125	A.Stoudemire JSY AU RC	100.00	50.00
❏ 126	Caron Butler JSY AU RC	30.00	12.50
❏ 127	Nene Hilario JSY AU RC	25.00	10.00
❏ 128	D.Wagner JSY AU RC	25.00	10.00
❏ 129	N.Tskitishvili JSY AU RC	15.00	6.00
❏ 130	Drew Gooden JSY AU RC	30.00	12.50
❏ 131	Jay Williams JSY AU RC	20.00	8.00
❏ 132	Yao Ming JSY AU RC	180.00	90.00
❏ 133	Mike Dunleavy RC	10.00	4.00
❏ 134	Frank McCants RC	10.00	4.00
❏ 135	Jiri Welsch RC	5.00	2.00
❏ 136	Dan Dickau RC	5.00	2.00
❏ 137	Efthimios Rentzias RC	5.00	2.00
❏ 138	Chris Wilcox RC	8.00	3.00
❏ 139	Curtis Borchardt RC	5.00	2.00
❏ 140	Predrag Savovic RC	5.00	2.00
❏ 141	Tito Maddox RC	5.00	2.00
❏ 142	Roger Mason RC	5.00	2.00
❏ 143	Juan Dixon RC	5.00	2.00
❏ 144	Pat Burke RC	5.00	2.00
❏ 145	Marko Jaric	5.00	2.00
❏ 146	Gordan Giricek RC	6.00	2.50
❏ 147	Juaquin Hawkins RC	5.00	2.00
❏ 148	Vincent Yarbrough RC	4.00	1.50
❏ 149	Robert Archibald RC	4.00	1.50
❏ 150	Bostjan Nachbar RC	4.00	1.50
❏ 151	Jamal Sampson RC	4.00	1.50
❏ 152	Lonny Baxter RC	4.00	1.50
❏ 153	J.R. Bremer RC	4.00	1.50
❏ 154	Cezary Trybanski RC	4.00	1.50
❏ 155	Manu Ginobili RC	15.00	6.00
❏ 156	Raul Lopez RC	4.00	1.50
❏ 157	Rasual Butler RC	4.00	1.50
❏ 158	Tamar Slay RC	4.00	1.50
❏ 159	Ronald Murray RC	10.00	4.00
❏ 160	Igor Rakocevic RC	4.00	1.50
❏ 161	Reggie Evans RC	4.00	1.50
❏ 162	Jannero Pargo RC	4.00	1.50

2003-04 SPx

❏ COMP.SET w/o SP's (90)		60.00	25.00
❏ COMMON SPXCCL (91-132)		3.00	1.25
❏ COMMON ROOKIE (133-150)		8.00	3.00
❏ COMMON JSY AU (151-156)		30.00	12.50
❏ COMMON JSY AU RC (163-185)		12.00	5.00
❏ COMMON JSY AU (186-206)		30.00	12.50
❏ SOME UNPRICED DUE TO SCARCITY			

❏ 1	Shafreef Abdur-Rahim	1.25	.50
❏ 2	Jason Terry	1.25	.50
❏ 3	Theo Ratliff	.75	.30
❏ 4	Paul Pierce	1.25	.50
❏ 5	Raef LaFrentz	.75	.30
❏ 6	Vin Baker	.75	.30
❏ 7	Jalen Rose	1.25	.50
❏ 8	Tyson Chandler	1.25	.50
❏ 9	Michael Jordan	8.00	3.00
❏ 10	Dajuan Wagner	.75	.30
❏ 11	Darius Miles	1.25	.50
❏ 12	Carlos Boozer	1.25	.50
❏ 13	Dirk Nowitzki	2.00	.75
❏ 14	Antoine Walker	1.25	.50
❏ 15	Steve Nash	1.25	.50
❏ 16	Nene	.75	.30
❏ 17	Marcus Camby	.75	.30
❏ 18	Andre Miller	.75	.30
❏ 19	Richard Hamilton	.75	.30
❏ 20	Ben Wallace	1.25	.50
❏ 21	Chauncey Billups	.75	.30
❏ 22	Nick Van Exel	1.25	.50
❏ 23	Jason Richardson	1.25	.50
❏ 24	Speedy Claxton	.40	.15
❏ 25	Steve Francis	1.25	.50
❏ 26	Yao Ming	3.00	1.25
❏ 27	Cuttino Mobley	.75	.30
❏ 28	Reggie Miller	1.25	.50
❏ 29	Jamaal Tinsley	1.25	.50
❏ 30	Jermaine O'Neal	1.25	.50
❏ 31	Elton Brand	1.25	.50
❏ 32	Corey Maggette	.75	.30
❏ 33	Quentin Richardson	.75	.30
❏ 34	Kobe Bryant	5.00	2.00
❏ 35	Karl Malone	1.25	.50
❏ 36	Shaquille O'Neal	3.00	1.25
❏ 37	Gary Payton	1.25	.50
❏ 38	Pau Gasol	1.25	.50
❏ 39	Shane Battier	1.25	.50
❏ 40	Mike Miller	1.25	.50
❏ 41	Eddie Jones	1.25	.50
❏ 42	Lamar Odom	1.25	.50
❏ 43	Caron Butler	1.25	.50
❏ 44	Michael Redd	1.25	.50
❏ 45	Joe Smith	.75	.30
❏ 46	Desmond Mason	.75	.30
❏ 47	Kevin Garnett	2.50	1.00
❏ 48	Latrell Sprewell	1.25	.50
❏ 49	Michael Olowokandi	.40	.15
❏ 50	Jason Kidd	2.00	.75
❏ 51	Richard Jefferson	.75	.30
❏ 52	Kenyon Martin	1.25	.50
❏ 53	Baron Davis	1.25	.50
❏ 54	Jamal Mashburn	.75	.30
❏ 55	David Wesley	.40	.15
❏ 56	Allan Houston	.75	.30
❏ 57	Antonio McDyess	.75	.30
❏ 58	Keith Van Horn	1.25	.50
❏ 59	Tracy McGrady	3.00	1.25
❏ 60	Grant Hill	1.25	.50
❏ 61	Drew Gooden	.75	.30
❏ 62	Juwan Howard	.75	.30
❏ 63	Allen Iverson	2.50	1.00
❏ 64	Glenn Robinson	1.25	.50
❏ 65	Eric Snow	.75	.30
❏ 66	Stephon Marbury	1.25	.50
❏ 67	Shawn Marion	1.25	.50
❏ 68	Amare Stoudemire	2.50	1.00
❏ 69	Rasheed Wallace	1.25	.50
❏ 70	Bonzi Wells	.75	.30
❏ 71	Damon Stoudamire	.75	.30
❏ 72	Chris Webber	1.25	.50
❏ 73	Mike Bibby	1.25	.50
❏ 74	Peja Stojakovic	1.25	.50
❏ 75	Brad Miller	1.25	.50
❏ 76	Tim Duncan	2.50	1.00
❏ 77	Tony Parker	1.25	.50
❏ 78	Manu Ginobili	1.25	.50
❏ 79	Ray Allen	1.25	.50
❏ 80	Rashard Lewis	1.25	.50
❏ 81	Vladimir Radmanovic	.40	.15
❏ 82	Vince Carter	3.00	1.25
❏ 83	Morris Peterson	.75	.30
❏ 84	Antonio Davis	.40	.15
❏ 85	Raul Lopez	.40	.15
❏ 86	Matt Harpring	1.25	.50
❏ 87	Andrei Kirilenko	1.25	.50
❏ 88	Jerry Stackhouse	1.25	.50
❏ 89	Gilbert Arenas	1.25	.50
❏ 90	Larry Hughes	.75	.30
❏ 91	Allen Iverson	5.00	2.00
❏ 92	Dirk Nowitzki	4.00	1.50
❏ 93	Kobe Bryant	10.00	4.00
❏ 94	Michael Jordan	15.00	6.00
❏ 95	Vince Carter	6.00	2.50
❏ 96	Shaquille O'Neal	6.00	2.50
❏ 97	Yao Ming	6.00	2.50
❏ 98	Amare Stoudemire	5.00	2.00
❏ 99	Paul Pierce	3.00	1.25
❏ 100	Jason Richardson	3.00	1.25
❏ 101	Steve Francis	1.25	.50
❏ 102	Jermaine O'Neal	3.00	1.25
❏ 103	Karl Malone	3.00	1.25
❏ 104	Tracy McGrady	6.00	2.50
❏ 105	Stephon Marbury	3.00	1.25
❏ 106	Chris Webber	3.00	1.25
❏ 107	Tim Duncan	5.00	2.00
❏ 108	Ray Allen	3.00	1.25
❏ 109	Antoine Walker	3.00	1.25
❏ 110	Steve Nash	3.00	1.25
❏ 111	Elton Brand	3.00	1.25
❏ 112	Rashard Lewis	3.00	1.25
❏ 113	Jerry Stackhouse	3.00	1.25
❏ 114	Shawn Marion	3.00	1.25
❏ 115	Mike Bibby	3.00	1.25
❏ 116	Tony Parker	3.00	1.25
❏ 117	Michael Finley	3.00	1.25
❏ 118	Allan Houston	3.00	1.25
❏ 119	Richard Hamilton	3.00	1.25
❏ 120	Ben Wallace	3.00	1.25
❏ 121	Reggie Miller	3.00	1.25
❏ 122	Richard Jefferson	3.00	1.25
❏ 123	Glenn Robinson	3.00	1.25
❏ 124	Rasheed Wallace	3.00	1.25
❏ 125	Gilbert Arenas	3.00	1.25
❏ 126	Jason Kidd	4.00	1.50
❏ 127	Latrell Sprewell	3.00	1.25
❏ 128	Kevin Garnett	5.00	2.00
❏ 129	Caron Butler	3.00	1.25
❏ 130	Pau Gasol	3.00	1.25
❏ 131	Alonzo Mourning	3.00	1.25
❏ 132	Gary Payton	3.00	1.25
❏ 133	Kirk Hinrich RC	12.00	5.00
❏ 134	T.J. Ford RC	10.00	4.00
❏ 135	Nick Collison RC	8.00	3.00
❏ 136	Keith McLeod RC	8.00	3.00
❏ 137	Jon Stefansson RC	8.00	3.00
❏ 138	Britton Johnsen RC	8.00	3.00
❏ 139	Matt Carroll RC	8.00	3.00
❏ 140	Linton Johnson RC	8.00	3.00
❏ 141	Francisco Elson RC	8.00	3.00
❏ 142	Willie Green RC	8.00	3.00
❏ 143	Kyle Korver RC	12.00	5.00
❏ 144	Theron Smith RC	8.00	3.00
❏ 145	Brandon Hunter RC	8.00	3.00
❏ 146	Josh Moore RC	8.00	3.00
❏ 147	Marquis Daniels RC	15.00	6.00
❏ 148	James Lang RC	8.00	3.00
❏ 149	Udonis Haslem RC	8.00	3.00
❏ 150	Alex Garcia RC	8.00	3.00
❏ 151	L.James JSY AU RC	950.00	700.00
❏ 152	D.Milicic JSY AU RC	50.00	20.00
❏ 153	C.Anthony JSY AU RC	250.00	125.00
❏ 154	Chris Bosh JSY AU RC	120.00	60.00
❏ 155	D.Wade JSY AU RC	400.00	200.00
❏ 156	Chris Kaman JSY AU RC	30.00	12.50
❏ 157	Jarvis Hayes JSY AU RC	30.00	12.50
❏ 158	M.Pietrus JSY AU RC	15.00	6.00
❏ 159	D.Jones JSY AU RC	15.00	6.00
❏ 160	M.Banks JSY AU RC	15.00	6.00
❏ 161	Luke Ridnour JSY AU RC	30.00	12.50
❏ 162	R.Gaines JSY AU RC	12.00	5.00
❏ 163	Troy Bell JSY AU RC	12.00	5.00
❏ 164	M.Sweetney JSY AU RC	12.00	5.00
❏ 165	David West JSY AU RC	12.00	5.00
❏ 166	A.Pavlovic JSY AU RC	15.00	6.00
❏ 167	M.Williams JSY AU RC	12.00	5.00
❏ 168	Boris Diaw JSY AU RC	30.00	12.50
❏ 169	Z.Planinic JSY AU RC	12.00	5.00
❏ 170	Travis Outlaw JSY AU RC	12.00	5.00
❏ 171	Brian Cook JSY AU RC	12.00	5.00
❏ 172	J.Beasley JSY AU RC	12.00	5.00
❏ 173	Ndudi Ebi JSY AU RC	12.00	5.00
❏ 174	K.Perkins JSY AU RC	12.00	5.00
❏ 175	L.Barbosa JSY AU RC	30.00	12.50
❏ 176	J.Howard JSY AU RC	40.00	15.00
❏ 177	Maciej Lampe JSY AU RC	12.00	5.00
❏ 178	J.Kapono JSY AU RC	15.00	6.00
❏ 179	Luke Walton JSY AU RC	20.00	8.00
❏ 180	S.Vranes JSY AU RC	12.00	5.00
❏ 181	Z.Cabarkapa JSY AU RC	12.00	5.00
❏ 182	T.Hansen JSY AU RC	12.00	5.00
❏ 183	Steve Blake JSY AU RC	12.00	5.00
❏ 184	Zaur Pachulia JSY AU RC	12.00	5.00
❏ 185	Keith Bogans JSY AU RC	12.00	5.00
❏ 186	M.Jordan JSY AU/23		
❏ 187	Kobe Bryant JSY AU/25		
❏ 188	K.Garnett JSY AU/150	120.00	60.00
❏ 189	R.Jefferson JSY AU/215	30.00	12.50
❏ 190	G.Arenas JSY AU/215	40.00	15.00
❏ 191	A.Jamison JSY AU/215	30.00	12.50
❏ 192	T.McGrady JSY AU/50	150.00	75.00
❏ 193	S.Francis JSY AU/100	50.00	20.00
❏ 194	Ming JSY AU/100 EXCH	80.00	30.00
❏ 195	A.Stoudemire JSY AU/25	60.00	25.00
❏ 196	Abdur-Rahim JSY AU/242	30.00	12.50
❏ 197	Shane Battier JSY AU/280	30.00	12.50
❏ 198	Tony Parker JSY AU/300	30.00	12.50
❏ 199	Andre Miller JSY AU/215	30.00	12.50
❏ 200	Shawn Marion JSY AU/265	30.00	12.50
❏ 201	R.Hamilton JSY AU/215	40.00	15.00
❏ 202	Lamar Odom JSY AU/215	30.00	12.50
❏ 203	J.Stackhouse JSY AU/215	30.00	12.50
❏ 204	A.McDyess JSY AU/230		
❏ 205	Manu Ginobili JSY AU/300	40.00	15.00
❏ 206	Drew Gooden JSY AU/215	30.00	12.50

2004-05 SPx

❏ COMP.SET w/o SP's (90)	60.00	25.00
❏ COMMON CARD (1-90)	.40	.15
❏ COMMON ROOKIE (91-111)	8.00	3.00
❏ COMMON ROOKIE (112-117)	30.00	12.50
❏ COMMON JSY AU RC (108, 118-139)	12.00	05.00
❏ COMMON JSY AU RC (140-147)	10,00	4.00
❏ COMMON FLASH AU (148-168)	30.00	12.50
❏ 1 Antoine Walker	1.25	.50
❏ 2 Al Harrington	.75	.30
❏ 3 Boris Diaw	.40	.15
❏ 4 Paul Pierce	1.25	.50
❏ 5 Ricky Davis	1.25	.50
❏ 6 Gary Payton	1.25	.50
❏ 7 Jahidi White	.40	.15

8	Jason Kapono	.75	.30
9	Gerald Wallace	.75	.30
10	Eddy Curry	.75	.30
11	Kirk Hinrich	1.25	.50
12	Tyson Chandler	1.25	.50
13	LeBron James	8.00	3.00
14	Drew Gooden	1.25	.50
15	Dajuan Wagner	.75	.30
16	Dirk Nowitzki	2.00	.75
17	Michael Finley	1.25	.50
18	Jerry Stackhouse	1.25	.50
19	Carmelo Anthony	2.50	1.00
20	Kenyon Martin	1.25	.50
21	Nene	.75	.30
22	Chauncey Billups	.75	.30
23	Richard Hamilton	.75	.30
24	Ben Wallace	1.25	.50
25	Mike Dunleavy	.75	.30
26	Jason Richardson	1.25	.50
27	Derek Fisher	1.25	.50
28	Yao Ming	3.00	1.25
29	Jim Jackson	.40	.15
30	Tracy McGrady	3.00	1.25
31	Jermaine O'Neal	1.25	.50
32	Reggie Miller	1.25	.50
33	Stephen Jackson	.40	.15
34	Elton Brand	1.25	.50
35	Corey Maggette	.75	.30
36	Chris Kaman	.75	.30
37	Kobe Bryant	5.00	2.00
38	Chris Mihm	.40	.15
39	Lamar Odom	1.25	.50
40	Pau Gasol	1.25	.50
41	Jason Williams	.75	.30
42	Bonzi Wells	.75	.30
43	Shaquille O'Neal	3.00	1.25
44	Dwyane Wade	4.00	1.50
45	Eddie Jones	1.25	.50
46	Michael Redd	.75	.30
47	Desmond Mason	.75	.30
48	T.J. Ford	.75	.30
49	Latrell Sprewell	1.25	.50
50	Kevin Garnett	2.50	1.00
51	Sam Cassell	1.25	.50
52	Richard Jefferson	.75	.30
53	Alonzo Mourning	.40	.15
54	Jason Kidd	2.00	.75
55	Jamaal Mashburn	.75	.30
56	Baron Davis	1.25	.50
57	Jamaal Magloire	.40	.15
58	Allan Houston	.75	.30
59	Jamal Crawford	.75	.30
60	Stephon Marbury	1.25	.50
61	Cuttino Mobley	.75	.30
62	Hedo Turkoglu	.75	.30
63	Steve Francis	1.25	.50
64	Glenn Robinson	1.25	.50
65	Allen Iverson	2.50	1.00
66	Aaron McKie	.75	.30
67	Amare Stoudemire	2.50	1.00
68	Steve Nash	1.25	.50
69	Shawn Marion	1.25	.50
70	Shareef Abdur-Rahim	1.25	.50
71	Damon Stoudamire	.75	.30
72	Zach Randolph	1.25	.50
73	Peja Stojakovic	1.25	.50
74	Chris Webber	1.25	.50
75	Mike Bibby	1.25	.50
76	Tony Parker	1.25	.50
77	Tim Duncan	2.50	1.00
78	Manu Ginobili	1.25	.50
79	Ronald Murray	.40	.15
80	Ray Allen	1.25	.50
81	Rashard Lewis	1.25	.50
82	Chris Bosh	1.25	.50
83	Vince Carter	3.00	1.25
84	Jalen Rose	1.25	.50
85	Andrei Kirilenko	1.25	.50
86	Carlos Boozer	1.25	.50
87	Carlos Arroyo	1.50	.60
88	Gilbert Arenas	1.25	.50
89	Jarvis Hayes	.75	.30
90	Antawn Jamison	1.25	.50
91	Matt Freije RC	8.00	3.00
92	Horace Jenkins RC	8.00	3.00
93	Luis Flores RC	8.00	3.00
94	Jared Reiner RC	8.00	3.00
95	D.J. Mbenga RC	8.00	3.00
96	Pape Sow RC	8.00	3.00
97	Erik Daniels RC	8.00	3.00
98	Arthur Johnson RC	8.00	3.00
99	John Edwards RC	8.00	3.00
100	Andre Barrett RC	8.00	3.00
101	Romain Sato RC	8.00	3.00
102	Tim Pickett RC	8.00	3.00
103	Bernard Robinson RC	8.00	3.00
104	Justin Reed RC	8.00	3.00
105	Andres Nocioni RC	12.00	5.00
106	Awvee Storey RC	8.00	3.00
107	Damien Wilkins RC	8.00	3.00
108	Nenad Krstic JSY RC	15.00	6.00
109	Viktor Khryapa RC	8.00	3.00
110	Royal Ivey RC	8.00	3.00
111	Antonio Burks RC	8.00	3.00
112	Robert Swift RC	40.00	15.00
113	Trevor Ariza RC	50.00	20.00
114	Chris Duhon RC	60.00	25.00
115	Beno Udrih RC	60.00	25.00
116	Pavel Podkolzine RC	40.00	15.00
117	Emeka Okafor RC	80.00	40.00
118	Yuta Tabuse JSY AU RC	10.00	4.00
119	Andre Emmett JSY AU RC	10.00	4.00
120	Sasha Vujacic JSY AU RC	10.00	4.00
121	Lionel Chalmers JSY AU RC	10.00	4.00
122	J.R. Smith JSY AU RC	25.00	10.00
123	Dorell Wright JSY AU RC	12.00	5.00
124	Jameer Nelson JSY AU RC	20.00	8.00
125	Andris Biedrins JSY AU RC	15.00	6.00
126	Jackson Vroman JSY AU RC	10.00	4.00
127	A.Varejao JSY AU RC	15.00	6.00
128	Delonte West JSY AU RC	25.00	10.00
129	Tony Allen JSY AU RC	25.00	10.00
130	Kevin Martin JSY AU RC	20.00	8.00
131	Rafael Araujo JSY AU RC	10.00	4.00
132	David Harrison JSY AU RC	10.00	4.00
133	Kris Humphries JSY AU RC	10.00	4.00
134	Al Jefferson JSY AU RC	50.00	25.00
135	Kirk Snyder JSY AU RC	10.00	4.00
136	Peter J.Ramos JSY AU RC	10.00	4.00
137	Luke Jackson JSY AU RC	10.00	4.00
138	Dorta Smith JSY AU RC	10.00	4.00
139	Josh Smith JSY AU RC	25.00	10.00
140	Sebastian Telfair JSY AU RC	25.00	10.00
141	Andre Iguodala JSY AU RC	50.00	25.00
142	Luol Deng JSY AU RC	60.00	30.00
143	Josh Childress JSY AU RC	25.00	10.00
144	Devin Harris JSY AU RC	40.00	15.00
145	S.Livingston JSY AU RC	30.00	12.50
146	Ben Gordon JSY AU RC	60.00	30.00
147	D.Howard JSY AU RC	150.00	75.00
148	Kobe Bryant AU SP		
149	Pau Gasol AU	30.00	12.50
150	Jason Kidd AU	60.00	25.00
151	Richard Hamilton AU	50.00	20.00
152	Amare Stoudemire AU	60.00	25.00
153	Chauncey Billups AU	40.00	15.00
154	Mike Bibby AU	30.00	12.50
155	Jason Richardson AU	30.00	12.50
156	LeBron James AU SP		
157	Larry Bird AU SP		
158	Reggie Miller AU	80.00	40.00
159	Kevin Garnett AU		
160	Baron Davis AU	40.00	15.00
161	Carmelo Anthony AU		
162	Magic Johnson AU SP		
163	Tracy McGrady AU	100.00	50.00
164	Yao Ming AU	60.00	25.00
165	Michael Jordan AU SP		
166	Andrei Kirilenko AU	40.00	15.00
167	Stephon Marbury AU	40.00	15.00
168	Shawn Marion AU	30.00	12.50

2005-06 SPx

COMP.SET w/o SP's (90)		50.00	20.00
COMMON CARD (1-90)		.40	.15
COMMON ROOKIE (91-120)		5.00	2.00
COMMON JSY AU RC (121-146)		12.00	5.00
ASTERISK INDICATES EXCHANGE CARDS			
1	Josh Childress	.75	.30
2	Josh Smith	1.25	.50
3	Al Harrington	.75	.30
4	Antoine Walker	1.25	.50
5	Gary Payton	1.25	.50
6	Paul Pierce	1.25	.50
7	Kareem Rush	.40	.15
8	Emeka Okafor	2.00	.75
9	Gerald Wallace	.75	.30
10	Michael Jordan	8.00	3.00
11	Kirk Hinrich	1.25	.50
12	Ben Gordon	2.50	1.00
13	Drew Gooden	.75	.30
14	Larry Hughes	.75	.30
15	LeBron James	8.00	3.00
16	Zydrunas Ilgauskas	.75	.30
17	Dirk Nowitzki	2.00	.75
18	Jason Terry	1.25	.50
19	Michael Finley	1.25	.50
20	Carmelo Anthony	2.50	1.00
21	Kenyon Martin	1.25	.50
22	Andre Miller	.75	.30
23	Ben Wallace	1.25	.50
24	Chauncey Billups	1.25	.50
25	Richard Hamilton	.75	.30
26	Troy Murphy	1.25	.50
27	Jason Richardson	1.25	.50
28	Baron Davis	1.25	.50
29	Tracy McGrady	3.00	1.25
30	Yao Ming	3.00	1.25
31	David Wesley	.40	.15
32	Jermaine O'Neal	1.25	.50
33	Jamaal Tinsley	.75	.30
34	Ron Artest	1.25	.50
35	Corey Maggette	.75	.30
36	Elton Brand	1.25	.50
37	Bobby Simmons	.40	.15
38	Caron Butler	.75	.30
39	Kobe Bryant	5.00	2.00
40	Lamar Odom	1.25	.50
41	Mike Miller	1.25	.50
42	Jason Williams	.75	.30
43	Pau Gasol	1.25	.50
44	Dwyane Wade	4.00	1.50
45	Eddie Jones	.75	.30
46	Shaquille O'Neal	3.00	1.25
47	Desmond Mason	.75	.30
48	Keith Van Horn	1.25	.50
49	Michael Redd	1.25	.50
50	Kevin Garnett	2.50	1.00
51	Latrell Sprewell	1.25	.50
52	Sam Cassell	1.25	.50
53	Vince Carter	3.00	1.25
54	Jason Kidd	2.00	.75
55	Richard Jefferson	.75	.30
56	Dan Dickau	.40	.15
57	Jamaal Magloire	.40	.15
58	J.R. Smith	.75	.30
59	Jamal Crawford	.75	.30
60	Stephon Marbury	1.25	.50
61	Quentin Richardson	.75	.30
62	Dwight Howard	1.50	.60
63	Grant Hill	1.25	.50
64	Steve Francis	1.25	.50
65	Allen Iverson	2.50	1.00
66	Andre Iguodala	1.25	.50
67	Chris Webber	1.25	.50
68	Amare Stoudemire	2.50	1.00
69	Shawn Marion	1.25	.50
70	Steve Nash	1.25	.50
71	Damon Stoudamire	.75	.30

72	Shareef Abdur-Rahim	1.25	.50
73	Zach Randolph	1.25	.50
74	Brad Miller	1.25	.50
75	Mike Bibby	1.25	.50
76	Peja Stojakovic	1.25	.50
77	Manu Ginobili	1.25	.50
78	Tim Duncan	2.50	1.00
79	Tony Parker	1.25	.50
80	Rashard Lewis	1.25	.50
81	Ray Allen	1.25	.50
82	Luke Ridnour	.75	.30
83	Rafer Alston	.40	.15
84	Jalen Rose	1.25	.50
85	Chris Bosh	1.25	.50
86	Andrei Kirilenko	1.25	.50
87	Carlos Boozer	.75	.30
88	Matt Harpring	1.25	.50
89	Antawn Jamison	1.25	.50
90	Gilbert Arenas	1.25	.50
91	Bracey Wright RC	5.00	2.00
92	Chris Taft RC	5.00	2.00
93	Jose Calderon RC	5.00	2.00
94	Dijon Thompson RC	5.00	2.00
95	Esteban Batista RC	5.00	2.00
96	Linas Kleiza RC	5.00	2.00
97	Earl Barron RC	6.00	2.50
98	Ike Diogu RC	6.00	2.50
99	Alan Anderson RC	5.00	2.00
100	Shavlik Randolph RC	5.00	2.00
101	Eddie Basden RC	5.00	2.00
102	Johan Petro RC	5.00	2.00
103	Ersan Ilyasova RC	5.00	2.00
104	Dwayne Jones RC	5.00	2.00
105	Aaron Miles RC	5.00	2.00
106	James Singleton RC	5.00	2.00
107	Von Wafer RC	5.00	2.00
108	Josh Powell RC	5.00	2.00
109	Yaroslav Korolev RC	5.00	2.00
110	Ronnie Price RC	5.00	2.00
111	Andray Blatche RC	5.00	2.00
112	Robert Whaley RC	5.00	2.00
113	Donell Taylor RC	5.00	2.00
114	Orien Greene RC	5.00	2.00
115	Lawrence Roberts RC	5.00	2.00
116	Amir Johnson RC	5.00	2.00
117	Matt Walsh RC	5.00	2.00
118	Fabricio Oberto RC	5.00	2.00
119	Arvydas Macijauskas RC	5.00	2.00
120	Alex Acker RC	5.00	2.00
121	Salim Stoudamire JSY AU RC	12.00	5.00
122	Francisco Garcia JSY AU RC	12.00	5.00
123	Daniel Ewing JSY AU RC	12.00	5.00
124	N.Robinson JSY AU RC/99*	75.00	40.00
125	Luther Head JSY AU RC	12.00	5.00
126	Louis Williams JSY AU RC	12.00	5.00
127	Jarrett Jack JSY AU RC	12.00	5.00
128	J.Maxiell JSY AU RC/1453	12.00	5.00
129	Wayne Simien JSY AU RC	12.00	5.00
130	Julius Hodge JSY AU RC	12.00	5.00
131	C.J. Miles JSY AU RC	12.00	5.00
132	Andrew Bynum JSY AU RC	40.00	15.00
133	Monta Ellis JSY AU RC/99	450.00	300.00
134	Joey Graham JSY AU RC	12.00	5.00
135	Antoine Wright JSY AU RC	12.00	5.00
136	Sean May JSY AU RC/1458	12.00	5.00
137	Channing Frye JSY AU RC	20.00	8.00
138	Gerald Green JSY AU RC	40.00	15.00
139	S.Jasikevicius JSY AU RC	15.00	6.00
140	Danny Granger JSY AU RC	30.00	12.50
141	H.Warrick JSY AU RC/99*	60.00	25.00
142	David Lee JSY AU RC	20.00	8.00
143	Brandon Bass JSY AU RC	12.00	5.00
144	Ryan Gomes JSY AU RC	12.00	5.00
145	M.Andriuskevicius JSY AU RC	12.00	5.00
146	Travis Diener JSY AU RC*	12.00	5.00
147	Martell Webster JSY AU RC	20.00	8.00
148	Rashad McCants JSY AU RC	30.00	12.50
149	Deron Williams JSY AU RC	75.00	35.00
150	Charlie Villanueva JSY AU RC	30.00	12.50
151	Raymond Felton JSY AU RC	30.00	12.50
152	Chris Paul JSY AU RC	150.00	75.00
153	Chris Paul JSY AU RC	150.00	75.00
154	Marvin Williams JSY AU RC	50.00	20.00

2006-07 SPx

1	Joe Johnson	.75	.30
2	Salim Stoudamire	.75	.30
3	Marvin Williams	1.50	.60
4	Tony Allen	.75	.30
5	Al Jefferson	1.25	.50
6	Paul Pierce	1.25	.50
7	Raymond Felton	1.50	.60
8	Emeka Okafor	1.25	.50
9	Gerald Wallace	1.25	.50
10	Tyson Chandler	1.25	.50
11	Ben Gordon	2.50	1.00
12	Michael Jordan	8.00	3.00
13	Drew Gooden	.75	.30
14	Zydrunas Ilgauskas	.40	.15
15	LeBron James	8.00	3.00
16	Devin Harris	1.25	.50
17	Dirk Nowitzki	2.00	.75
18	Jason Terry	1.25	.50
19	Carmelo Anthony	2.50	1.00
20	Andre Miller	.75	.30
21	Eduardo Najera	.40	.15
22	Chauncey Billups	1.25	.50
23	Richard Hamilton	.75	.30
24	Ben Wallace	1.25	.50
25	Rasheed Wallace	1.25	.50
26	Baron Davis	1.25	.50
27	Troy Murphy	1.25	.50
28	Jason Richardson	1.25	.50
29	Rafer Alston	.40	.15
30	Tracy McGrady	3.00	1.25
31	Yao Ming	3.00	1.25
32	Sarunas Jasikevicius	.75	.30
33	Jermaine O'Neal	1.25	.50
34	Peja Stojakovic	1.25	.50
35	Elton Brand	1.25	.50
36	Sam Cassell	1.25	.50
37	Chris Kaman	.40	.15
38	Shaun Livingston	1.00	.40
39	Kobe Bryant	5.00	2.00
40	Lamar Odom	1.25	.50
41	Ronny Turiaf	.40	.15
42	Pau Gasol	1.25	.50
43	Mike Miller	1.25	.50
44	Damon Stoudamire	.75	.30
45	Shaquille O'Neal	3.00	1.25
46	Wayne Simien	.75	.30
47	Dwyane Wade	4.00	1.50
48	Jason Williams	.75	.30
49	Andrew Bogut	1.50	.60
50	T.J. Ford	.75	.30
51	Jamaal Magloire	.40	.15
52	Michael Redd	1.25	.50
53	Ricky Davis	1.25	.50
54	Kevin Garnett	2.50	1.00
55	Rashad McCants	1.50	.60
56	Vince Carter	3.00	1.25
57	Richard Jefferson	.75	.30
58	Jason Kidd	2.00	.75
59	Speedy Claxton	.40	.15
60	Desmond Mason	.40	.15
61	Chris Paul	3.00	1.25
62	Steve Francis	1.25	.50
63	Channing Frye	.75	.30
64	Stephon Marbury	1.25	.50
65	Nate Robinson	1.25	.50
66	Carlos Arroyo	2.00	.75

67	Grant Hill	1.25	.50
68	Dwight Howard	1.50	.60
69	Jameer Nelson	.75	.30
70	Andre Iguodala	1.25	.50
71	Allen Iverson	2.50	1.00
72	Chris Webber	1.25	.50
73	Boris Diaw	.75	.30
74	Shawn Marion	1.25	.50
75	Steve Nash	1.25	.50
76	Amare Stoudemire	2.50	1.00
77	Zach Randolph	1.25	.50
78	Sebastian Telfair	.75	.30
79	Martell Webster	.75	.30
80	Shareef Abdur-Rahim	1.25	.50
81	Ron Artest	.75	.30
82	Mike Bibby	1.25	.50
83	Brad Miller	1.25	.50
84	Tim Duncan	2.50	1.00
85	Michael Finley	1.25	.50
86	Manu Ginobili	1.25	.50
87	Tony Parker	1.25	.50
88	Ray Allen	1.25	.50
89	Rashard Lewis	1.25	.50
90	Chris Wilcox	.40	.15
91	Chris Bosh	1.25	.50
92	Joey Graham	.75	.30
93	Charlie Villanueva	1.25	.50
94	Carlos Boozer	.75	.30
95	Andrei Kirilenko	1.25	.50
96	C.J. Miles	.40	.15
97	Deron Williams	1.25	.50
98	Gilbert Arenas	1.25	.50
99	Caron Butler	.75	.30
100	Antawn Jamison	1.25	.50
101	Adam Morrison RC	12.00	5.00
102	Alexander Johnson RC	5.00	2.00
103	Damir Markota RC	5.00	2.00
104	J.J. Redick RC	10.00	4.00
105	Will Blalock RC	5.00	2.00
106	Leon Powe RC	5.00	2.00
107	Thabo Sefolosha RC	8.00	3.00
108	Pops Mensah-Bonsu RC	5.00	2.00
109	Robert Hite RC	5.00	2.00
110	Terence Kinsey RC	5.00	2.00
111	Vassilis Spanoulis RC	5.00	2.00
112	Yakhouba Diawara RC	5.00	2.00
113	Daniel Gibson RC	12.00	5.00
114	Hassan Adams RC	6.00	2.50
115	James Augustine RC	5.00	2.00
116	Chris Quinn RC	5.00	2.00
117	Mardy Collins RC	5.00	2.00
118	Paul Millsap RC	8.00	3.00
119	P.J. Tucker RC	5.00	2.00
120	Ryan Hollins RC	5.00	2.00
121	Saer Sene RC	5.00	2.00
122	Andrea Bargnani JSY AU RC	120.00	60.00
123	LaMarcus Aldridge JSY AU RC	90.00	45.00
124	Tyrus Thomas JSY AU RC	120.00	60.00
125	Shelden Williams JSY AU RC	60.00	30.00
126	Brandon Roy JSY AU RC	150.00	75.00
127	Randy Foye JSY AU RC	80.00	40.00
128	Paul Davis JSY AU RC	15.00	6.00
129	Solomon Jones JSY AU RC	15.00	6.00
130	David Noel JSY AU RC	15.00	6.00
131	Allan Ray JSY AU RC	15.00	6.00
132	Bobby Jones JSY AU RC	15.00	6.00
133	Cedric Simmons JSY AU RC	15.00	6.00
134	Dee Brown JSY AU RC	25.00	10.00
135	Shawne Williams JSY AU RC	20.00	8.00
136	Hilton Armstrong JSY AU RC	15.00	6.00
137	James White JSY AU RC	15.00	6.00
138	Jordan Farmar JSY AU RC	30.00	12.00
139	Josh Boone JSY AU RC	15.00	6.00
140	Kyle Lowry JSY AU RC	15.00	6.00
141	Marcus Williams JSY AU RC	20.00	8.00
142	Maurice Ager JSY AU RC	15.00	6.00
143	Patrick O'Bryant JSY AU RC	15.00	6.00
144	Quincy Douby JSY AU RC	15.00	6.00
145	Rajon Rondo JSY AU RC	20.00	8.00
146	Renaldo Balkman JSY AU RC	15.00	6.00
147	Rodney Carney JSY AU RC	15.00	6.00
148	Ronnie Brewer JSY AU RC	20.00	8.00
149	Rudy Gay JSY AU RC	50.00	20.00
150	Shannon Brown JSY AU RC	15.00	6.00
151	Steve Novak JSY AU RC	15.00	6.00
152	Craig Smith JSY AU RC	15.00	6.00

1992-93 Stadium Club

❏ COMPLETE SET (400)	50.00	25.00
❏ COMPLETE SERIES 1 (200)	20.00	10.00
❏ COMPLETE SERIES 2 (200)	30.00	15.00
❏ 1 Michael Jordan	8.00	4.00
❏ 2 Greg Anthony	.10	.02
❏ 3 Otis Thorpe	.30	.10
❏ 4 Jim Les	.10	.02
❏ 5 Kevin Willis	.10	.02
❏ 6 Derek Harper	.30	.10
❏ 7 Elden Campbell	.30	.10
❏ 8 A.J. English	.10	.02
❏ 9 Kenny Gattison	.10	.02
❏ 10 Drazen Petrovic	.10	.02
❏ 11 Chris Mullin	.60	.25
❏ 12 Mark Price	.10	.02
❏ 13 Karl Malone	1.00	.40
❏ 14 Gerald Glass	.10	.02
❏ 15 Negele Knight	.10	.02
❏ 16 Mark Macon	.10	.02
❏ 17 Michael Cage	.10	.02
❏ 18 Kevin Edwards	.10	.02
❏ 19 Sherman Douglas	.10	.02
❏ 20 Ron Harper	.30	.10
❏ 21 Cliff Robinson	.30	.10
❏ 22 Byron Scott	.30	.10
❏ 23 Antoine Carr	.10	.02
❏ 24 Greg Dreiling	.10	.02
❏ 25 Bill Laimbeer	.30	.10
❏ 26 Hersey Hawkins	.30	.10
❏ 27 Will Perdue	.10	.02
❏ 28 Todd Lichti	.10	.02
❏ 29 Gary Grant	.10	.02
❏ 30 Sam Perkins	.30	.10
❏ 31 Jayson Williams	.30	.10
❏ 32 Magic Johnson	2.00	.75
❏ 33 Larry Bird	2.50	1.00
❏ 34 Chris Morris	.10	.02
❏ 35 Nick Anderson	.30	.10
❏ 36 Scott Hastings	.10	.02
❏ 37 Ledell Eackles	.10	.02
❏ 38 Robert Pack	.10	.02
❏ 39 Dana Barros	.10	.02
❏ 40 Anthony Bonner	.10	.02
❏ 41 J.R. Reid	.10	.02
❏ 42 Tyrone Hill	.10	.02
❏ 43 Rik Smits	.30	.10
❏ 44 Kevin Duckworth	.10	.02
❏ 45 LaSalle Thompson	.10	.02
❏ 46 Brian Williams	.10	.02
❏ 47 Willie Anderson	.10	.02
❏ 48 Ken Norman	.10	.02
❏ 49 Mike Iuzzolino	.10	.02
❏ 50 Isiah Thomas	.60	.25
❏ 51 Alec Kessler	.10	.02
❏ 52 Johnny Dawkins	.10	.02
❏ 53 Avery Johnson	.10	.02
❏ 54 Stacey Augmon	.30	.10
❏ 55 Charles Oakley	.30	.10
❏ 56 Rex Chapman	.10	.02
❏ 57 Charles Shackleford	.10	.02
❏ 58 Jeff Ruland	.10	.02
❏ 59 Craig Ehlo	.10	.02
❏ 60 Jon Koncak	.10	.02
❏ 61 Danny Schayes	.10	.02
❏ 62 David Benoit	.10	.02
❏ 63 Robert Parish	.30	.10
❏ 64 Mookie Blaylock	.30	.10
❏ 65 Sean Elliott	.30	.10
❏ 66 Mark Aguirre	.10	.02
❏ 67 Scott Williams	.10	.02
❏ 68 Doug West	.10	.02
❏ 69 Kenny Anderson	.60	.25
❏ 70 Randy Brown	.10	.02
❏ 71 Muggsy Bogues	.30	.10
❏ 72 Spud Webb	.30	.10
❏ 73 Sedale Threatt	.10	.02
❏ 74 Chris Gatling	.10	.02
❏ 75 Derrick McKey	.10	.02
❏ 76 Sleepy Floyd	.10	.02
❏ 77 Chris Jackson	.10	.02
❏ 78 Thurl Bailey	.10	.02
❏ 79 Steve Smith	.75	.30
❏ 80 Jerrod Mustaf	.10	.02
❏ 81 Anthony Bowie	.10	.02
❏ 82 John Williams	.10	.02
❏ 83 Paul Graham	.10	.02
❏ 84 Willie Burton	.10	.02
❏ 85 Vernon Maxwell	.10	.02
❏ 86 Stacey King	.10	.02
❏ 87 B.J. Armstrong	.10	.02
❏ 88 Kevin Gamble	.10	.02
❏ 89 Terry Catledge	.10	.02
❏ 90 Jeff Malone	.10	.02
❏ 91 Sam Bowie	.10	.02
❏ 92 Orlando Woolridge	.10	.02
❏ 93 Steve Kerr	.30	.10
❏ 94 Eric Leckner	.10	.02
❏ 95 Loy Vaught	.10	.02
❏ 96 Jud Buechler	.10	.02
❏ 97 Doug Smith	.10	.02
❏ 98 Sidney Green	.10	.02
❏ 99 Jerome Kersey	.10	.02
❏ 100 Patrick Ewing	.60	.25
❏ 101 Ed Nealy	.10	.02
❏ 102 Shawn Kemp	1.25	.50
❏ 103 Luc Longley	.30	.10
❏ 104 George McCloud	.10	.02
❏ 105 Ron Anderson	.10	.02
❏ 106 Moses Malone	.60	.25
❏ 107 Tony Smith	.10	.02
❏ 108 Terry Porter	.10	.02
❏ 109 Blair Rasmussen	.10	.02
❏ 110 Bimbo Coles	.10	.02
❏ 111 Grant Long	.10	.02
❏ 112 John Battle	.10	.02
❏ 113 Brian Oliver	.10	.02
❏ 114 Tyrone Corbin	.10	.02
❏ 115 Benoit Benjamin	.10	.02
❏ 116 Rick Fox	.30	.10
❏ 117 Rafael Addison	.10	.02
❏ 118 Danny Young	.10	.02
❏ 119 Fat Lever	.10	.02
❏ 120 Terry Cummings	.30	.10
❏ 121 Felton Spencer	.10	.02
❏ 122 Joe Kleine	.10	.02
❏ 123 Johnny Newman	.10	.02
❏ 124 Gary Payton	1.25	.50
❏ 125 Kurt Rambis	.10	.02
❏ 126 Vlade Divac	.30	.10
❏ 127 John Paxson	.10	.02
❏ 128 Lionel Simmons	.10	.02
❏ 129 Randy Wittman	.10	.02
❏ 130 Winston Garland	.10	.02
❏ 131 Jerry Reynolds	.10	.02
❏ 132 Dell Curry	.10	.02
❏ 133 Fred Roberts	.10	.02
❏ 134 Michael Adams	.10	.02
❏ 135 Charles Jones	.10	.02
❏ 136 Frank Brickowski	.10	.02
❏ 137 Alton Lister	.10	.02
❏ 138 Horace Grant	.30	.10
❏ 139 Greg Sutton	.10	.02
❏ 140 John Starks	.30	.10
❏ 141 Detlef Schrempf	.30	.10
❏ 142 Rodney Monroe	.10	.02
❏ 143 Pete Chilcutt	.10	.02
❏ 144 Mike Brown	.10	.02
❏ 145 Rony Seikaly	.10	.02
❏ 146 Donald Hodge	.10	.02
❏ 147 Kevin McHale	.60	.25
❏ 148 Ricky Pierce	.10	.02
❏ 149 Brian Shaw	.10	.02
❏ 150 Reggie Williams	.10	.02
❏ 151 Kendall Gill	.30	.10
❏ 152 Tom Chambers	.10	.02
❏ 153 Jack Haley	.10	.02
❏ 154 Terrell Brandon	.60	.25
❏ 155 Dennis Scott	.30	.10
❏ 156 Mark Randall	.10	.02
❏ 157 Kenny Payne	.10	.02
❏ 158 Bernard King	.10	.02
❏ 159 Tate George	.10	.02
❏ 160 Scott Skiles	.10	.02
❏ 161 Pervis Ellison	.10	.02
❏ 162 Marcus Liberty	.10	.02
❏ 163 Rumeal Robinson	.10	.02
❏ 164 Anthony Mason	.60	.25
❏ 165 Les Jepsen	.10	.02
❏ 166 Kenny Smith	.10	.02
❏ 167 Randy White	.10	.02
❏ 168 Dee Brown	.10	.02
❏ 169 Chris Dudley	.10	.02
❏ 170 Armon Gilliam	.10	.02
❏ 171 Eddie Johnson	.10	.02
❏ 172 A.C. Green	.30	.10
❏ 173 Darrell Walker	.10	.02
❏ 174 Bill Cartwright	.10	.02
❏ 175 Mike Gminski	.10	.02
❏ 176 Tom Tolbert	.10	.02
❏ 177 Buck Williams	.30	.10
❏ 178 Mark Eaton	.10	.02
❏ 179 Danny Manning	.30	.10
❏ 180 Glen Rice	.60	.25
❏ 181 Sarunas Marciulionis	.10	.02
❏ 182 Danny Ferry	.10	.02
❏ 183 Chris Corchiani	.10	.02
❏ 184 Dan Majerle	.30	.10
❏ 185 Alvin Robertson	.10	.02
❏ 186 Vern Fleming	.10	.02
❏ 187 Kevin Lynch	.10	.02
❏ 188 John Williams	.10	.02
❏ 189 Checklist 1-100	.10	.02
❏ 190 Checklist 101-200	.10	.02
❏ 191 David Robinson MC	.60	.25
❏ 192 Larry Johnson MC	.60	.25
❏ 193 Derrick Coleman MC	.10	.02
❏ 194 Larry Bird MC	1.25	.50
❏ 195 Billy Owens MC	.10	.02
❏ 196 Dikembe Mutombo MC	.60	.25
❏ 197 Charles Barkley MC	.60	.25
❏ 198 Scottie Pippen MC	1.00	.40
❏ 199 Clyde Drexler MC	.30	.10
❏ 200 John Stockton MC	.30	.10
❏ 201 Shaquille O'Neal MC	8.00	3.00
❏ 202 Chris Mullin MC	.30	.10
❏ 203 Glen Rice MC	.30	.10
❏ 204 Isiah Thomas MC	.30	.10
❏ 205 Karl Malone MC	.60	.25
❏ 206 Christian Laettner MC	.60	.25
❏ 207 Patrick Ewing MC	.30	.10
❏ 208 Dominique Wilkins MC	.30	.10
❏ 209 Alonzo Mourning MC	1.25	.50
❏ 210 Michael Jordan MC	4.00	1.50
❏ 211 Tim Hardaway	.75	.30
❏ 212 Rodney McCray	.10	.02
❏ 213 Larry Johnson	.75	.30
❏ 214 Charles Smith	.10	.02
❏ 215 Kevin Brooks	.10	.02
❏ 216 Kevin Johnson	.60	.25
❏ 217 Duane Cooper RC	.10	.02
❏ 218 Christian Laettner RC	1.25	.50
❏ 219 Tim Perry	.10	.02
❏ 220 Hakeem Olajuwon	1.00	.40
❏ 221 Lee Mayberry RC	.10	.02
❏ 222 Mark Bryant	.10	.02
❏ 223 Robert Horry RC	.60	.25
❏ 224 Tracy Murray RC	.30	.10
❏ 225 Greg Grant	.10	.02
❏ 226 Rolando Blackman	.10	.02
❏ 227 James Edwards UER	.10	.02
❏ 228 Sean Green	.10	.02
❏ 229 Buck Johnson	.10	.02
❏ 230 Andrew Lang	.10	.02
❏ 231 Tracy Moore RC	.10	.02
❏ 232 Adam Keefe RC	.10	.02
❏ 233 Tony Campbell	.10	.02
❏ 234 Rod Strickland	.60	.25
❏ 235 Terry Mills	.10	.02

236	Billy Owens	.30	.10
237	Bryant Stith RC	.30	.10
238	Tony Bennett RC	.10	.02
239	David Wood	.10	.02
240	Jay Humphries	.10	.02
241	Doc Rivers	.30	.10
242	Wayman Tisdale	.10	.02
243	Litterial Green RC	.10	.02
244	Jon Barry	.30	.10
245	Brad Daugherty	.10	.02
246	Nate McMillan	.10	.02
247	Shaquille O'Neal RC	15.00	6.00
248	Chris Smith RC	.10	.02
249	Duane Ferrell	.10	.02
250	Anthony Peeler RC	.30	.10
251	Gundars Vetra RC	.10	.02
252	Danny Ainge	.30	.10
253	Mitch Richmond	.60	.25
254	Malik Sealy RC	.30	.10
255	Brent Price RC	.30	.10
256	Xavier McDaniel	.10	.02
257	Bobby Phills RC	.60	.25
258	Donald Royal	.10	.02
259	Olden Polynice	.10	.02
260	Dominique Wilkins	.60	.25
261	Larry Krystkowiak	.10	.02
262	Duane Causwell	.10	.02
263	Todd Day RC	.30	.10
264	Sam Mack RC	.30	.10
265	John Stockton	.60	.25
266	Eddie Lee Wilkins	.10	.02
267	Gerald Glass	.10	.02
268	Robert Pack	.10	.02
269	Gerald Wilkins	.10	.02
270	Reggie Lewis	.30	.10
271	Scott Brooks	.10	.02
272	Randy Woods RC	.10	.02
273	Dikembe Mutombo	.75	.30
274	Kiki Vandeweghe	.10	.02
275	Rich King	.10	.02
276	Jeff Turner	.10	.02
277	Vinny Del Negro	.10	.02
278	Marlon Maxey RC	.10	.02
279	Elmore Spencer RC	.10	.02
280	Cedric Ceballos	.30	.10
281	Alex Blackwell RC	.10	.02
282	Terry Davis	.10	.02
283	Morlon Wiley	.10	.02
284	Trent Tucker	.10	.02
285	Carl Herrera	.10	.02
286	Eric Anderson RC	.10	.02
287	Clyde Drexler	.60	.25
288	Tom Gugliotta RC	2.00	.75
289	Dale Ellis	.10	.02
290	Lance Blanks	.10	.02
291	Tom Hammonds	.10	.02
292	Eric Murdock	.10	.02
293	Walt Williams RC	.60	.25
294	Gerald Paddio	.10	.02
295	Brian Howard RC	.10	.02
296	Ken Williams	.10	.02
297	Alonzo Mourning RC	4.00	1.50
298	Larry Nance	.10	.02
299	Jeff Grayer	.10	.02
300	Dave Johnson RC	.10	.02
301	Bob McCann RC	.10	.02
302	Bart Kofoed	.10	.02
303	Anthony Cook	.10	.02
304	Radisav Curcic RC	.10	.02
305	John Crotty RC	.10	.02
306	Brad Sellers	.10	.02
307	Marcus Webb RC	.10	.02
308	Winston Garland	.10	.02
309	Walter Palmer	.10	.02
310	Rod Higgins	.10	.02
311	Travis Mays	.10	.02
312	Alex Stivrins RC	.10	.02
313	Greg Kite	.10	.02
314	Dennis Rodman	1.25	.50
315	Mike Sanders	.10	.02
316	Ed Pinckney	.10	.02
317	Harold Miner RC	.30	.10
318	Pooh Richardson	.10	.02
319	Oliver Miller RC	.30	.10
320	Latrell Sprewell RC	5.00	2.00
321	Anthony Pullard RC	.10	.02
322	Mark Randall	.10	.02
323	Jeff Hornacek	.10	.02
324	Rick Mahorn UER	.10	.02
325	Sean Rooks RC	.10	.02
326	Paul Pressey	.10	.02
327	James Worthy	.60	.25
328	Matt Bullard	.10	.02
329	Reggie Smith RC	.10	.02
330	Don MacLean RC	.10	.02
331	John Williams UER	.10	.02
332	Frank Johnson	.10	.02
333	Hubert Davis RC	.30	.10
334	Lloyd Daniels RC	.10	.02
335	Steve Bardo RC	.10	.02
336	Jeff Sanders	.10	.02
337	Tree Rollins	.10	.02
338	Micheal Williams	.10	.02
339	Lorenzo Williams RC	.10	.02
340	Harvey Grant	.10	.02
341	Avery Johnson	.10	.02
342	Bo Kimble	.10	.02
343	LaPhonso Ellis RC	.60	.25
344	Mookie Blaylock	.30	.10
345	Isaiah Morris RC	.10	.02
346	C.Weatherspoon RC	.60	.25
347	Manute Bol	.10	.02
348	Victor Alexander	.10	.02
349	Corey Williams RC	.10	.02
350	Byron Houston RC	.10	.02
351	Stanley Roberts	.10	.02
352	Anthony Avent RC	.10	.02
353	Vincent Askew	.10	.02
354	Herb Williams	.10	.02
355	J.R. Reid	.10	.02
356	Brad Lohaus	.10	.02
357	Reggie Miller	.60	.25
358	Blue Edwards	.10	.02
359	Tom Tolbert	.10	.02
360	Charles Barkley	1.00	.40
361	David Robinson	1.00	.40
362	Dale Davis	.10	.02
363	Robert Werdann RC	.10	.02
364	Chuck Person	.10	.02
365	Alaa Abdelnaby	.10	.02
366	Dave Jamerson	.10	.02
367	Scottie Pippen	2.00	.75
368	Mark Jackson	.30	.10
369	Keith Askins	.10	.02
370	Marty Conlon	.10	.02
371	Chucky Brown	.10	.02
372	LaBradford Smith	.10	.02
373	Tim Kempton	.10	.02
374	Sam Mitchell	.10	.02
375	John Salley	.10	.02
376	Mario Elie	.30	.10
377	Mark West	.10	.02
378	David Wingate	.10	.02
379	Jaren Jackson RC	.30	.10
380	Rumeal Robinson	.10	.02
381	Kennard Winchester	.10	.02
382	Walter Bond RC	.10	.02
383	Isaac Austin RC	.30	.10
384	Derrick Coleman	.30	.10
385	Larry Smith	.10	.02
386	Joe Dumars	.60	.25
387	Matt Geiger RC	.30	.10
388	Stephen Howard RC	.10	.02
389	William Bedford	.10	.02
390	Jayson Williams	.30	.10
391	Kurt Rambis	.10	.02
392	Keith Jennings RC	.10	.02
393	Steve Kerr UER	.30	.10
394	Larry Stewart	.10	.02
395	Danny Young	.10	.02
396	Doug Overton	.10	.02
397	Mark Acres	.10	.02
398	John Bagley	.10	.02
399	Checklist 201-300	.10	.02
400	Checklist 301-400	.10	.02

1993-94 Stadium Club

COMPLETE SET (360)		40.00	20.00
COMPLETE SERIES 1 (180)		20.00	10.00
COMPLETE SERIES 2 (180)		20.00	10.00
COMMON CARD (1-180)		.10	.02

	COMMON CARD (181-360)	.05	.01
1	Michael Jordan TD	2.50	1.00
2	Kenny Anderson TD	.10	.02
3	Steve Smith TD	.20	.07
4	Kevin Gamble TD	.10	.02
5	Detlef Schrempf TD	.10	.02
6	Larry Johnson TD	.20	.07
7	Brad Daugherty TD	.10	.02
8	Rumeal Robinson TD	.10	.02
9	Micheal Williams TD	.10	.02
10	David Robinson TD	.40	.15
11	Sam Perkins TD	.10	.02
12	Thurl Bailey TD	.10	.02
13	Sherman Douglas TD	.10	.02
14	Larry Stewart TD	.10	.02
15	Kevin Johnson TD	.20	.07
16	Bill Cartwright TD	.10	.02
17	Larry Nance TD	.10	.02
18	P.J.Brown RC	.40	.15
19	Tony Bennett	.10	.02
20	Robert Parish	.20	.07
21	David Benoit	.10	.02
22	Detlef Schrempf	.20	.07
23	Hubert Davis	.10	.02
24	Donald Hodge	.10	.02
25	Hersey Hawkins	.20	.07
26	Mark Jackson	.20	.07
27	Reggie Williams	.10	.02
28	Lionel Simmons	.10	.02
29	Ron Harper	.20	.07
30	Chris Mills RC	.40	.15
31	Danny Schayes	.10	.02
32	J.R. Reid	.10	.02
33	Willie Burton	.10	.02
34	Greg Anthony	.10	.02
35	Elden Campbell	.10	.02
36	Ervin Johnson RC	.20	.07
37	Scott Brooks	.10	.02
38	Johnny Newman	.10	.02
39	Rex Chapman	.10	.02
40	Chuck Person	.10	.02
41	John Williams	.10	.02
42	Anthony Bowie	.10	.02
43	Negele Knight	.10	.02
44	Tyrone Corbin	.10	.02
45	Jud Buechler	.10	.02
46	Adam Keefe	.10	.02
47	Glen Rice	.20	.07
48	Tracy Murray	.10	.02
49	Rick Mahorn	.10	.02
50	Vlade Divac	.20	.07
51	Eric Murdock	.10	.02
52	Isaiah Morris	.10	.02
53	Bobby Hurley RC	.20	.07
54	Mitch Richmond	.40	.15
55	Danny Ainge	.20	.07
56	Dikembe Mutombo	.40	.15
57	Jeff Hornacek	.20	.07
58	Tony Campbell	.10	.02
59	Vinny Del Negro	.10	.02
60	Xavier McDaniel HC	.10	.02
61	Scottie Pippen HC	.60	.25
62	Larry Nance HC	.10	.02
63	Dikembe Mutombo HC	.20	.07
64	Hakeem Olajuwon HC	.40	.15
65	Dominique Wilkins HC	.20	.07
66	Clarence Weatherspoon HC	.10	.02
67	Chris Morris HC	.10	.02

❏ 68	Patrick Ewing HC	.20	.07
❏ 69	Kevin Willis HC	.10	.02
❏ 70	Jon Barry	.10	.02
❏ 71	Jerry Reynolds	.10	.02
❏ 72	Sarunas Marciulionis	.10	.02
❏ 73	Mark West	.10	.02
❏ 74	B.J. Armstrong	.10	.02
❏ 75	Greg Kite	.10	.02
❏ 76	LaSalle Thompson	.10	.02
❏ 77	Randy White	.10	.02
❏ 78	Alaa Abdelnaby	.10	.02
❏ 79	Kevin Brooks	.10	.02
❏ 80	Vern Fleming	.10	.02
❏ 81	Doc Rivers	.20	.07
❏ 82	Shawn Bradley RC	.40	.15
❏ 83	Wayman Tisdale	.10	.02
❏ 84	Olden Polynice	.10	.02
❏ 85	Michael Cage	.10	.02
❏ 86	Harold Miner	.10	.02
❏ 87	Doug Smith	.10	.02
❏ 88	Tom Gugliotta	.40	.15
❏ 89	Hakeem Olajuwon	.60	.25
❏ 90	Loy Vaught	.10	.02
❏ 91	James Worthy	.40	.15
❏ 92	John Paxson	.10	.02
❏ 93	Jon Koncak	.10	.02
❏ 94	Lee Mayberry	.10	.02
❏ 95	Clarence Weatherspoon	.10	.02
❏ 96	Mark Eaton	.10	.02
❏ 97	Rex Walters RC	.10	.02
❏ 98	Alvin Robertson	.10	.02
❏ 99	Dan Majerle	.20	.07
❏ 100	Shaquille O'Neal	2.00	.75
❏ 101	Derrick Coleman TD	.10	.02
❏ 102	Hersey Hawkins TD	.10	.02
❏ 103	Scottie Pippen TD	.60	.25
❏ 104	Scott Skiles TD	.10	.02
❏ 105	Rod Strickland TD	.10	.02
❏ 106	Pooh Richardson TD	.10	.02
❏ 107	Tom Gugliotta TD	.20	.07
❏ 108	Mark Jackson TD	.10	.02
❏ 109	Dikembe Mutombo TD	.20	.07
❏ 110	Charles Barkley TD	.40	.15
❏ 111	Otis Thorpe TD	.10	.02
❏ 112	Malik Sealy	.10	.02
❏ 113	Mark Macon	.10	.02
❏ 114	Dee Brown	.10	.02
❏ 115	Nate McMillan	.10	.02
❏ 116	John Starks	.20	.07
❏ 117	Clyde Drexler	.40	.15
❏ 118	Antoine Carr	.10	.02
❏ 119	Doug West	.10	.02
❏ 120	Victor Alexander	.10	.02
❏ 121	Kenny Gattison	.10	.02
❏ 122	Spud Webb	.20	.07
❏ 123	Rumeal Robinson	.10	.02
❏ 124	Tim Kempton	.10	.02
❏ 125	Karl Malone	.60	.25
❏ 126	Randy Woods	.10	.02
❏ 127	Calbert Cheaney RC	.20	.07
❏ 128	Johnny Dawkins	.10	.02
❏ 129	Dominique Wilkins	.40	.15
❏ 130	Horace Grant	.20	.07
❏ 131	Bill Laimbeer	.10	.02
❏ 132	Kenny Smith	.10	.02
❏ 133	Sedale Threatt	.10	.02
❏ 134	Brian Shaw	.10	.02
❏ 135	Dennis Scott	.10	.02
❏ 136	Mark Bryant	.10	.02
❏ 137	Xavier McDaniel	.10	.02
❏ 138	David Wood	.10	.02
❏ 139	Luther Wright RC	.10	.02
❏ 140	Lloyd Daniels	.10	.02
❏ 141	Marlon Maxey UER	.10	.02
❏ 142	Pooh Richardson	.10	.02
❏ 143	Jeff Grayer	.10	.02
❏ 144	LaPhonso Ellis	.10	.02
❏ 145	Gerald Wilkins	.10	.02
❏ 146	Dell Curry	.10	.02
❏ 147	Duane Causwell	.10	.02
❏ 148	Tim Hardaway	.40	.15
❏ 149	Isiah Thomas	.40	.15
❏ 150	Doug Edwards RC	.10	.02
❏ 151	Anthony Peeler	.10	.02
❏ 152	Tate George	.10	.02
❏ 153	Terry Davis	.10	.02
❏ 154	Sam Perkins	.20	.07
❏ 155	John Salley	.10	.02
❏ 156	Vernon Maxwell	.10	.02
❏ 157	Anthony Avent	.10	.02
❏ 158	Clifford Robinson	.20	.07
❏ 159	Corie Blount RC	.10	.02
❏ 160	Gerald Paddio	.10	.02
❏ 161	Blair Rasmussen	.10	.02
❏ 162	Carl Herrera	.10	.02
❏ 163	Chris Smith	.10	.02
❏ 164	Pervis Ellison	.10	.02
❏ 165	Rod Strickland	.20	.07
❏ 166	Jeff Malone	.10	.02
❏ 167	Danny Ferry	.10	.02
❏ 168	Kevin Lynch	.10	.02
❏ 169	Michael Jordan	5.00	2.00
❏ 170	Derrick Coleman HC	.10	.02
❏ 171	Jerome Kersey HC	.10	.02
❏ 172	David Robinson HC	.40	.15
❏ 173	Shawn Kemp HC	.40	.15
❏ 174	Karl Malone HC	.40	.15
❏ 175	Shaquille O'Neal HC	.75	.30
❏ 176	Alonzo Mourning HC	.40	.15
❏ 177	Charles Barkley HC	.40	.15
❏ 178	Larry Johnson HC	.20	.07
❏ 179	Checklist 1-90	.10	.02
❏ 180	Checklist 91-180	.10	.02
❏ 181	Michael Jordan FF	2.00	.75
❏ 182	Dominique Wilkins FF	.15	.05
❏ 183	Dennis Rodman FF	.30	.10
❏ 184	Scottie Pippen FF	.50	.20
❏ 185	Larry Johnson FF	.15	.05
❏ 186	Karl Malone FF	.30	.10
❏ 187	Clarence Weatherspoon FF	.05	.01
❏ 188	Charles Barkley FF	.30	.10
❏ 189	Patrick Ewing FF	.20	.07
❏ 190	Derrick Coleman FF	.05	.01
❏ 191	LaBradford Smith	.05	.01
❏ 192	Derek Harper	.15	.05
❏ 193	Ken Norman	.05	.01
❏ 194	Rodney Rogers RC	.30	.10
❏ 195	Chris Dudley	.05	.01
❏ 196	Gary Payton	.50	.20
❏ 197	Andrew Lang	.05	.01
❏ 198	Billy Owens	.05	.01
❏ 199	Bryon Russell RC	.30	.10
❏ 200	Patrick Ewing	.30	.10
❏ 201	Stacey King	.05	.01
❏ 202	Grant Long	.05	.01
❏ 203	Sean Elliott	.15	.05
❏ 204	Muggsy Bogues	.15	.05
❏ 205	Kevin Edwards	.05	.01
❏ 206	Dale Davis	.05	.01
❏ 207	Dale Ellis	.05	.01
❏ 208	Terrell Brandon	.15	.05
❏ 209	Kevin Gamble	.05	.01
❏ 210	Robert Horry	.15	.05
❏ 211	Moses Malone	.40	.15
❏ 212	Gary Grant	.05	.01
❏ 213	Bobby Hurley	.15	.05
❏ 214	Larry Krystkowiak	.05	.01
❏ 215	A.C. Green	.15	.05
❏ 216	Christian Laettner	.15	.05
❏ 217	Orlando Woolridge	.05	.01
❏ 218	Craig Ehlo	.05	.01
❏ 219	Terry Porter	.05	.01
❏ 220	Mark Mashburn RC	1.00	.40
❏ 221	Kevin Duckworth	.05	.01
❏ 222	Shawn Kemp	.50	.20
❏ 223	Frank Brickowski	.05	.01
❏ 224	Chris Webber RC	3.00	1.25
❏ 225	Charles Oakley	.15	.05
❏ 226	Jay Humphries	.05	.01
❏ 227	Steve Kerr	.15	.05
❏ 228	Tim Perry	.05	.01
❏ 229	Sleepy Floyd	.05	.01
❏ 230	Bimbo Coles	.05	.01
❏ 231	Eddie Johnson	.05	.01
❏ 232	Terry Mills	.05	.01
❏ 233	Danny Manning	.15	.05
❏ 234	Isaiah Rider RC	.75	.30
❏ 235	Darnell Mee RC	.05	.01
❏ 236	Haywoode Workman	.05	.01
❏ 237	Scott Skiles	.05	.01
❏ 238	Otis Thorpe	.15	.05
❏ 239	Mike Peplowski RC	.05	.01
❏ 240	Eric Leckner	.05	.01
❏ 241	Johnny Newman	.05	.01
❏ 242	Benoit Benjamin	.05	.01
❏ 243	Doug Christie	.15	.05
❏ 244	Acie Earl RC	.05	.01
❏ 245	Luc Longley	.15	.05
❏ 246	Tyrone Hill	.05	.01
❏ 247	Allan Houston RC	1.25	.50
❏ 248	Joe Kleine	.05	.01
❏ 249	Mookie Blaylock	.15	.05
❏ 250	Anthony Bonner	.05	.01
❏ 251	Luther Wright	.05	.01
❏ 252	Todd Day	.05	.01
❏ 253	Kendall Gill	.15	.05
❏ 254	Mario Elie	.05	.01
❏ 255	Pete Myers	.05	.01
❏ 256	Jim Les	.05	.01
❏ 257	Stanley Roberts	.05	.01
❏ 258	Michael Adams	.05	.01
❏ 259	Hersey Hawkins	.15	.05
❏ 260	Shawn Bradley	.20	.07
❏ 261	Scott Haskin RC	.05	.01
❏ 262	Corie Blount	.05	.01
❏ 263	Charles Smith	.05	.01
❏ 264	Armon Gilliam	.05	.01
❏ 265	Jamal Mashburn NW	.30	.10
❏ 266	Anfernee Hardaway NW	1.25	.50
❏ 267	Shawn Bradley NW	.20	.07
❏ 268	Chris Webber NW	1.50	.60
❏ 269	Bobby Hurley NW	.05	.01
❏ 270	Isaiah Rider NW	.30	.10
❏ 271	Dino Radja NW	.05	.01
❏ 272	Chris Mills NW	.15	.05
❏ 273	Nick Van Exel NW	.30	.10
❏ 274	Lindsey Hunter NW UER	.20	.07
❏ 275	Toni Kukoc NW	.30	.10
❏ 276	Popeye Jones NW	.05	.01
❏ 277	Chris Mills	.40	.15
❏ 278	Ricky Pierce	.05	.01
❏ 279	Negele Knight	.05	.01
❏ 280	Kenny Walker	.05	.01
❏ 281	Nick Van Exel RC	1.00	.40
❏ 282	Derrick Coleman	.15	.05
❏ 283	Popeye Jones RC	.05	.01
❏ 284	Derrick McKey	.05	.01
❏ 285	Rick Fox	.05	.01
❏ 286	Jerome Kersey	.05	.01
❏ 287	Steve Smith	.30	.10
❏ 288	Brian Williams	.05	.01
❏ 289	Chris Mullin	.30	.10
❏ 290	Terry Cummings	.05	.01
❏ 291	Donald Royal	.05	.01
❏ 292	Alonzo Mourning	.50	.20
❏ 293	Mike Brown	.05	.01
❏ 294	Latrell Sprewell	.75	.30
❏ 295	Oliver Miller	.05	.01
❏ 296	Terry Dehere RC	.05	.01
❏ 297	Detlef Schrempf	.15	.05
❏ 298	Sam Bowie UER	.05	.01
❏ 299	Chris Morris	.05	.01
❏ 300	Scottie Pippen	1.00	.40
❏ 301	Warren Kidd RC	.05	.01
❏ 302	Don MacLean	.05	.01
❏ 303	Sean Rooks	.05	.01
❏ 304	Matt Geiger	.05	.01
❏ 305	Dennis Rodman	.60	.25
❏ 306	Reggie Miller	.30	.10
❏ 307	Vin Baker RC	.75	.30
❏ 308	Anfernee Hardaway RC	2.50	1.00
❏ 309	Lindsey Hunter RC	.30	.10
❏ 310	Stacey Augmon	.05	.01
❏ 311	Randy Brown	.05	.01
❏ 312	Anthony Mason	.15	.05
❏ 313	John Stockton	.30	.10
❏ 314	Sam Cassell RC	1.25	.50
❏ 315	Buck Williams	.05	.01
❏ 316	Bryant Stith	.05	.01
❏ 317	Brad Daugherty	.05	.01
❏ 318	Dino Radja RC	.05	.01
❏ 319	Rony Seikaly	.05	.01
❏ 320	Charles Barkley	.60	.25
❏ 321	Avery Johnson	.05	.01
❏ 322	Mahmoud Abdul-Rauf	.05	.01
❏ 323	Larry Johnson	.30	.10
❏ 324	Micheal Williams	.05	.01
❏ 325	Mark Aguirre	.05	.01

□	#	Player		
□	326	Jim Jackson	.15	.05
□	327	Antonio Harvey RC	.05	.01
□	328	David Robinson	.50	.20
□	329	Calbert Cheaney	.10	.02
□	330	Kenny Anderson	.20	.07
□	331	Walt Williams	.10	.02
□	332	Kevin Willis	.05	.01
□	333	Nick Anderson	.15	.05
□	334	Rik Smits	.15	.05
□	335	Joe Dumars	.40	.15
□	336	Toni Kukoc RC	1.25	.50
□	337	Harvey Grant	.05	.01
□	338	Tom Chambers	.05	.01
□	339	Blue Edwards	.05	.01
□	340	Mark Price	.05	.01
□	341	Ervin Johnson	.15	.05
□	342	Rolando Blackman	.05	.01
□	343	Scott Burrell RC	.30	.10
□	344	Gheorghe Muresan RC	.30	.10
□	345	Chris Corchiani UER 336	.05	.01
□	346	Richard Petruska RC	.05	.01
□	347	Dana Barros	.05	.01
□	348	Hakeem Olajuwon FF	.30	.10
□	349	Dee Brown FF	.05	.01
□	350	John Starks FF	.05	.01
□	351	Ron Harper FF	.05	.01
□	352	Chris Webber FF	1.50	.60
□	353	Dan Majerle FF	.15	.05
□	354	Clyde Drexler FF	.15	.05
□	355	Shawn Kemp FF	.30	.10
□	356	David Robinson FF	.30	.10
□	357	Chris Morris FF	.05	.01
□	358	Shaquille O'Neal FF	.60	.25
□	359	Checklist	.05	.01
□	360	Checklist	.05	.01

1994-95 Stadium Club

□	#	Player		
□		COMPLETE SET (362)	40.00	20.00
□		COMPLETE SERIES 1 (182)	20.00	10.00
□		COMPLETE SERIES 2 (180)	20.00	10.00
□	1	Patrick Ewing	.40	.15
□	2	Patrick Ewing TG	.15	.05
□	3	Bimbo Coles	.10	.02
□	4	Elden Campbell	.10	.02
□	5	Brent Price	.10	.02
□	6	Hubert Davis	.10	.02
□	7	Donald Royal	.10	.02
□	8	Tim Perry	.10	.02
□	9	Chris Webber	1.00	.40
□	10	Chris Webber TG	.50	.20
□	11	Brad Daugherty	.10	.02
□	12	P.J. Brown	.10	.02
□	13	Charles Barkley	.60	.25
□	14	Mario Elie	.10	.02
□	15	Tyrone Hill	.10	.02
□	16	Anfernee Hardaway	1.00	.40
□	17	Anfernee Hardaway TG	.50	.20
□	18	Toni Kukoc	.60	.25
□	19	Chris Morris	.10	.02
□	20	Gerald Wilkins	.10	.02
□	21	David Benoit	.10	.02
□	22	Kevin Duckworth	.10	.02
□	23	Derrick Coleman	.15	.05
□	24	Adam Keefe	.10	.02
□	25	Marlon Maxey	.10	.02
□	26	Vern Fleming	.10	.02
□	27	Jeff Malone	.10	.02
□	28	Rodney Rogers	.10	.02
□	29	Terry Mills	.10	.02
□	30	Doug West	.10	.02
□	31	Doug West TTG	.10	.02
□	32	Shaquille O'Neal	2.00	.75
□	33	Scottie Pippen	1.25	.50
□	34	Lee Mayberry	.10	.02
□	35	Dale Ellis	.10	.02
□	36	Cedric Ceballos	.10	.02
□	37	Lionel Simmons	.10	.02
□	38	Kenny Gattison	.10	.02
□	39	Popeye Jones	.10	.02
□	40	Jerome Kersey	.10	.02
□	41	Jerome Kersey TTG	.10	.02
□	42	Larry Stewart	.10	.02
□	43	Rod Strickland	.15	.05
□	44	Chris Mills	.15	.05
□	45	Latrell Sprewell	.40	.15
□	46	Haywoode Workman	.10	.02
□	47	Charles Smith	.10	.02
□	48	Detlef Schrempf	.15	.05
□	49	Gary Grant	.10	.02
□	50	Gary Grant TTG	.10	.02
□	51	Tom Chambers	.10	.02
□	52	J.R. Reid	.10	.02
□	53	Mookie Blaylock	.10	.02
□	54	Mookie Blaylock TTG	.10	.02
□	55	Rony Seikaly	.10	.02
□	56	Isaiah Rider	.15	.05
□	57	Isaiah Rider TTG	.10	.02
□	58	Nick Anderson	.10	.02
□	59	Victor Alexander	.10	.02
□	60	Lucious Harris	.10	.02
□	61	Mark Macon	.10	.02
□	62	Otis Thorpe	.10	.02
□	63	Randy Woods	.10	.02
□	64	Clyde Drexler	.40	.15
□	65	Dikembe Mutombo	.15	.05
□	66	Todd Day	.10	.02
□	67	Greg Anthony	.10	.02
□	68	Sherman Douglas	.10	.02
□	69	Chris Mullin	.40	.15
□	70	Kevin Johnson	.15	.05
□	71	Kendall Gill	.15	.05
□	72	Dennis Rodman	.75	.30
□	73	Dennis Rodman TG	.40	.15
□	74	Jeff Turner	.10	.02
□	75	John Stockton	.40	.15
□	76	John Stockton TTG	.15	.05
□	77	Doug Edwards	.10	.02
□	78	Jim Jackson	.15	.05
□	79	Hakeem Olajuwon	.60	.25
□	80	Glen Rice	.15	.05
□	81	Christian Laettner	.15	.05
□	82	Terry Porter	.10	.02
□	83	Joe Dumars	.40	.15
□	84	David Wingate	.10	.02
□	85	B.J. Armstrong	.10	.02
□	86	Derrick McKey	.10	.02
□	87	Elmore Spencer	.10	.02
□	88	Walt Williams	.10	.02
□	89	Shawn Bradley	.10	.02
□	90	Acie Earl	.10	.02
□	91	Acie Earl TTG	.10	.02
□	92	Randy Brown	.10	.02
□	93	Grant Long	.10	.02
□	94	Terry Dehere	.10	.02
□	95	Spud Webb	.10	.02
□	96	Lindsey Hunter	.15	.05
□	97	Blair Rasmussen	.10	.02
□	98	Tim Hardaway	.40	.15
□	99	Kevin Edwards	.10	.02
□	100	Patrick Ewing CT	.15	.05
□	101	Chuck Person CT	.40	.15
□	102	S.O'Neal/Abdul-Rauf CT	.40	.15
□	103	Rony Seikaly CT	.10	.02
□	104	H.Olajuwon/C.Drexler CT	.40	.15
□	105	Chris Mullin CT	.15	.05
□	106	R.Horry/L.Sprewell CT	.40	.15
□	107	Pooh Richardson CT	.15	.05
□	108	Dennis Scott CT	.10	.02
□	109	Kendall Gill CT	.10	.02
□	110	Scott Skiles CT	.10	.02
□	111	Terry Mills CT	.15	.05
□	112	Christian Laettner CT	.15	.05
□	113	Stacey Augmon CT	.10	.02
□	114	Sam Perkins CT	.15	.05
□	115	Carl Herrera	.10	.02
□	116	Sam Bowie	.10	.02
□	117	Gary Payton	.60	.25
□	118	Danny Ainge	.10	.02
□	119	Danny Ainge TTG	.10	.02
□	120	Luc Longley	.10	.02
□	121	Antonio Davis	.10	.02
□	122	Terry Cummings	.10	.02
□	123	Terry Cummings TTG	.10	.02
□	124	Mark Price	.10	.02
□	125	Jamal Mashburn	.40	.15
□	126	Mahmoud Abdul-Rauf	.10	.02
□	127	Charles Oakley	.10	.02
□	128	Steve Smith	.15	.05
□	129	Vin Baker	.40	.15
□	130	Robert Horry	.15	.05
□	131	Doug Christie	.10	.02
□	132	Wayman Tisdale	.10	.02
□	133	Wayman Tisdale TTG	.10	.02
□	134	Muggsy Bogues	.15	.05
□	135	Dino Radja	.10	.02
□	136	Jeff Hornacek	.15	.05
□	137	Gheorghe Muresan	.10	.02
□	138	Loy Vaught	.10	.02
□	139	Loy Vaught TTG	.10	.02
□	140	Benoit Benjamin	.10	.02
□	141	Johnny Dawkins	.10	.02
□	142	Allan Houston	.60	.25
□	143	Jon Barry	.10	.02
□	144	Reggie Miller	.40	.15
□	145	Kevin Willis	.10	.02
□	146	James Worthy	.40	.15
□	147	James Worthy TTG	.15	.05
□	148	Scott Burrell	.10	.02
□	149	Tom Gugliotta	.15	.05
□	150	LaPhonso Ellis	.10	.02
□	151	Doug Smith	.10	.02
□	152	A.C. Green	.15	.05
□	153	A.C. Green TTG	.10	.02
□	154	George Lynch	.10	.02
□	155	Sam Perkins	.15	.05
□	156	Corie Blount	.10	.02
□	157	Xavier McDaniel	.10	.02
□	158	Xavier McDaniel TTG	.10	.02
□	159	Eric Murdock	.10	.02
□	160	David Robinson	.60	.25
□	161	Karl Malone	.40	.15
□	162	Karl Malone TTG	.40	.15
□	163	Clarence Weatherspoon	.10	.02
□	164	Calbert Cheaney	.10	.02
□	165	Tom Hammonds	.10	.02
□	166	Tom Hammonds TTG	.10	.02
□	167	Alonzo Mourning	.50	.20
□	168	Clifford Robinson	.15	.05
□	169	Micheal Williams	.10	.02
□	170	Ervin Johnson	.10	.02
□	171	Mike Gminski	.10	.02
□	172	Jason Kidd RC	4.00	1.50
□	173	Anthony Bonner	.10	.02
□	174	Stacey King	.10	.02
□	175	Rex Chapman	.10	.02
□	176	Greg Graham	.10	.02
□	177	Stanley Roberts	.10	.02
□	178	Mitch Richmond	.40	.15
□	179	Eric Montross RC	.10	.02
□	180	Eddie Jones RC	2.00	.75
□	181	Grant Hill RC	2.00	.75
□	182	Donyell Marshall RC	.40	.15
□	183	Glenn Robinson RC	1.25	.50
□	184	Dominique Wilkins	.40	.15
□	185	Mark Price	.10	.02
□	186	Anthony Mason	.15	.05
□	187	Tyrone Corbin	.10	.02
□	188	Dale Davis	.10	.02
□	189	Nate McMillan	.10	.02
□	190	Jason Kidd	2.00	.75
□	191	John Salley	.10	.02
□	192	Keith Jennings	.10	.02
□	193	Mark Bryant	.10	.02
□	194	Sleepy Floyd	.10	.02
□	195	Grant Hill	1.00	.40
□	196	Joe Kleine	.10	.02
□	197	Anthony Peeler	.10	.02
□	198	Malik Sealy	.10	.02
□	199	Kenny Walker	.10	.02
□	200	Donyell Marshall	.40	.15

❑ 201 Vlade Divac AI	.10	.02
❑ 202 Dino Radja AI	.10	.02
❑ 203 Carl Herrera AI	.10	.02
❑ 204 Olden Polynice AI	.10	.02
❑ 205 Patrick Ewing AI	.15	.05
❑ 206 Willie Anderson	.10	.02
❑ 207 Mitch Richmond	.40	.15
❑ 208 John Crotty	.10	.02
❑ 209 Tracy Murray	.10	.02
❑ 210 Juwan Howard AI	1.00	.40
❑ 211 Robert Parish	.15	.05
❑ 212 Steve Kerr	.10	.02
❑ 213 Anthony Bowie	.10	.02
❑ 214 Tim Breaux	.10	.02
❑ 215 Sharone Wright RC	.10	.02
❑ 216 Brian Williams	.10	.02
❑ 217 Rick Fox	.10	.02
❑ 218 Harold Miner	.10	.02
❑ 219 Duane Ferrell	.10	.02
❑ 220 Lamond Murray RC	.15	.05
❑ 221 Blue Edwards	.10	.02
❑ 222 Bill Cartwright	.10	.02
❑ 223 Sergei Bazarevich	.10	.02
❑ 224 Herb Williams	.10	.02
❑ 225 Brian Grant RC	1.00	.40
❑ 226 Derek Harper BCT	.10	.02
❑ 227 Rod Strickland BCT	.40	.15
❑ 228 Kevin Johnson BCT	.10	.02
❑ 229 Lindsey Hunter BCT	.10	.02
❑ 230 T.Hardaway/Sprewell BCT	.15	.05
❑ 231 Bill Wennington	.10	.02
❑ 232 Brian Shaw	.10	.02
❑ 233 Jamie Watson RC	.10	.02
❑ 234 Chris Whitney	.10	.02
❑ 235 Eric Montross	.10	.02
❑ 236 Kenny Smith	.10	.02
❑ 237 Andrew Lang	.10	.02
❑ 238 Lorenzo Williams	.10	.02
❑ 239 Dana Barros	.10	.02
❑ 240 Eddie Jones	1.00	.40
❑ 241 Harold Ellis	.10	.02
❑ 242 James Edwards	.10	.02
❑ 243 Don MacLean	.10	.02
❑ 244 Ed Pinckney	.10	.02
❑ 245 Carlos Rogers RC	.10	.02
❑ 246 Michael Adams	.10	.02
❑ 247 Rex Walters	.10	.02
❑ 248 John Starks	.10	.02
❑ 249 Terrell Brandon	.15	.05
❑ 250 Khalid Reeves RC	.10	.02
❑ 251 Dominique Wilkins AI	.15	.05
❑ 252 Toni Kukoc AI	.40	.15
❑ 253 Rick Fox AI	.10	.02
❑ 254 Detlef Schrempf AI	.10	.02
❑ 255 Rik Smits AI	.10	.02
❑ 256 Johnny Dawkins	.10	.02
❑ 257 Dan Majerle	.15	.05
❑ 258 Mike Brown	.10	.02
❑ 259 Byron Scott	.15	.05
❑ 260 Jalen Rose RC	1.50	.60
❑ 261 Bryon Houston	.10	.02
❑ 262 Frank Brickowski	.10	.02
❑ 263 Vernon Maxwell	.10	.02
❑ 264 Craig Ehlo	.10	.02
❑ 265 Yinka Dare RC	.10	.02
❑ 266 Dee Brown	.10	.02
❑ 267 Felton Spencer	.10	.02
❑ 268 Harvey Grant	.10	.02
❑ 269 Nick Van Exel	.40	.15
❑ 270 Bob Martin	.10	.02
❑ 271 Hersey Hawkins	.15	.05
❑ 272 Scott Williams	.10	.02
❑ 273 Sarunas Marciulionis	.10	.02
❑ 274 Kevin Gamble	.10	.02
❑ 275 Clifford Rozier RC	.10	.02
❑ 276 B.J. Armstrong BCT	.10	.02
❑ 277 John Stockton BCT	.15	.05
❑ 278 Bobby Hurley BCT	.15	.05
❑ 279 A.Hardaway/J.D.Scott BCT	.30	.10
❑ 280 J.Kidd/J.Jackson BCT	.40	.15
❑ 281 Ron Harper	.15	.05
❑ 282 Chuck Person	.10	.02
❑ 283 John Williams	.10	.02
❑ 284 Robert Pack	.10	.02
❑ 285 Aaron McKie RC	.75	.30
❑ 286 Chris Smith	.10	.02

❑ 287 Horace Grant	.15	.05
❑ 288 Oliver Miller	.10	.02
❑ 289 Derek Harper	.10	.02
❑ 290 Eric Mobley RC	.10	.02
❑ 291 Scott Skiles	.10	.02
❑ 292 Olden Polynice	.10	.02
❑ 293 Mark Jackson	.10	.02
❑ 294 Wayman Tisdale	.10	.02
❑ 295 Tony Dumas RC	.10	.02
❑ 296 Bryon Russell	.10	.02
❑ 297 Vlade Divac	.10	.02
❑ 298 David Wesley	.10	.02
❑ 299 Askia Jones RC	.10	.02
❑ 300 B.J.Tyler RC	.10	.02
❑ 301 Hakeem Olajuwon AI	.40	.15
❑ 302 Luc Longley AI	.10	.02
❑ 303 Rony Seikaly AI	.10	.02
❑ 304 Sarunas Marciulionis AI	.10	.02
❑ 305 Dikembe Mutombo AI	.10	.02
❑ 306 Ken Norman	.10	.02
❑ 307 Dell Curry	.10	.02
❑ 308 Danny Ferry	.10	.02
❑ 309 Shawn Kemp	.60	.25
❑ 310 Dickey Simpkins RC	.10	.02
❑ 311 Johnny Newman	.10	.02
❑ 312 Dwayne Schintzius	.10	.02
❑ 313 Sean Elliott	.15	.05
❑ 314 Sean Rooks	.10	.02
❑ 315 Bill Curley RC	.10	.02
❑ 316 Bryant Stith	.10	.02
❑ 317 Pooh Richardson	.10	.02
❑ 318 Jim McIlvaine	.10	.02
❑ 319 Dennis Scott	.10	.02
❑ 320 Wesley Person RC	.40	.15
❑ 321 Bobby Hurley	.10	.02
❑ 322 Armon Gilliam	.10	.02
❑ 323 Rik Smits	.10	.02
❑ 324 Tony Smith	.10	.02
❑ 325 Monty Williams RC	.10	.02
❑ 326 G.Payton/K.Gill BCT	.40	.15
❑ 327 Mookie Blaylock BCT	.10	.02
❑ 328 Mark Jackson BCT	.15	.05
❑ 329 Sam Cassell BCT	.40	.15
❑ 330 Harold Miner BCT	.10	.02
❑ 331 Vinny Del Negro	.10	.02
❑ 332 Billy Owens	.10	.02
❑ 333 Mark West	.10	.02
❑ 334 Matt Geiger	.10	.02
❑ 335 Greg Minor RC	.10	.02
❑ 336 Larry Johnson	.15	.05
❑ 337 Donald Hodge	.10	.02
❑ 338 Aaron Williams RC	.10	.02
❑ 339 Jay Humphries	.10	.02
❑ 340 Charlie Ward RC	.40	.15
❑ 341 Scott Brooks	.10	.02
❑ 342 Stacey Augmon	.10	.02
❑ 343 Will Perdue	.10	.02
❑ 344 Dale Ellis	.10	.02
❑ 345 Brooks Thompson RC	.10	.02
❑ 346 Manute Bol	.10	.02
❑ 347 Kenny Anderson	.15	.05
❑ 348 Willie Burton	.10	.02
❑ 349 Michael Cage	.10	.02
❑ 350 Danny Manning	.15	.05
❑ 351 Ricky Pierce	.10	.02
❑ 352 Sam Cassell	.40	.15
❑ 353 Reggie Miller FG	.15	.05
❑ 354 David Robinson FG	.40	.15
❑ 355 Shaquille O'Neal FG	.75	.30
❑ 356 Scottie Pippen FG	.60	.25
❑ 357 Alonzo Mourning FG	.15	.05
❑ 358 Clarence Weatherspoon FG	.10	.02
❑ 359 Derrick Coleman FG	.10	.02
❑ 360 Charles Barkley FG	.40	.15
❑ 361 Karl Malone FG	.40	.15
❑ 362 Chris Webber FG	.50	.20

1995-96 Stadium Club

❑ COMPLETE SET (361)	50.00	25.00
❑ COMPLETE SERIES 1 (180)	25.00	15.00
❑ COMPLETE SERIES 2 (181)	25.00	10.00
❑ 1 Michael Jordan	5.00	2.00
❑ 2 Glenn Robinson	.75	.30
❑ 3 Jason Kidd	2.50	1.00
❑ 4 Clyde Drexler	.75	.30

❑ 5 Horace Grant	.50	.20
❑ 6 Allan Houston	.50	.20
❑ 7 Xavier McDaniel	.25	.08
❑ 8 Jeff Hornacek	.50	.20
❑ 9 Vlade Divac	.25	.08
❑ 10 Juwan Howard	.75	.30
❑ 11 Keith Jennings EXP	.25	.08
❑ 12 Grant Long	.25	.08
❑ 13 Jalen Rose	1.00	.40
❑ 14 Malik Sealy	.25	.08
❑ 15 Gary Payton	.75	.30
❑ 16 Danny Ferry	.25	.08
❑ 17 Glen Rice	.50	.20
❑ 18 Randy Brown	.25	.08
❑ 19 Greg Graham	.25	.08
❑ 20 Kenny Anderson	.50	.20
❑ 21 Aaron McKie	.50	.20
❑ 22 John Salley EXP	.25	.08
❑ 23 Darrin Hancock	.25	.08
❑ 24 Carlos Rogers	.25	.08
❑ 25 Vin Baker	.50	.20
❑ 26 Bill Wennington	.25	.08
❑ 27 Kenny Smith	.25	.08
❑ 28 Sherman Douglas	.25	.08
❑ 29 Terry Davis	.25	.08
❑ 30 Grant Hill	1.00	.40
❑ 31 Reggie Miller	.75	.30
❑ 32 Anfernee Hardaway	.75	.30
❑ 33 Patrick Ewing	.75	.30
❑ 34 Charles Barkley	1.00	.40
❑ 35 Eddie Jones	1.00	.40
❑ 36 Kevin Duckworth	.25	.08
❑ 37 Tom Hammonds	.25	.08
❑ 38 Craig Ehlo	.25	.08
❑ 39 Michael Williams	.25	.08
❑ 40 Alonzo Mourning	.50	.20
❑ 41 John Williams	.25	.08
❑ 42 Felton Spencer	.25	.08
❑ 43 Lamond Murray	.25	.08
❑ 44 Dontonio Wingfield EXP	.25	.08
❑ 45 Rik Smits	.25	.08
❑ 46 Donyell Marshall	.50	.20
❑ 47 Clarence Weatherspoon	.25	.08
❑ 48 Kevin Edwards	.25	.08
❑ 49 Charlie Ward	.25	.08
❑ 50 David Robinson	.75	.30
❑ 51 James Robinson	.25	.08
❑ 52 Bill Cartwright	.25	.08
❑ 53 Bobby Hurley	.25	.08
❑ 54 Kevin Gamble	.25	.08
❑ 55 B.J. Tyler EXP	.25	.08
❑ 56 Chris Smith	.25	.08
❑ 57 Wesley Person	.25	.08
❑ 58 Tim Breaux	.25	.08
❑ 59 Mitchell Butler	.25	.08
❑ 60 Toni Kukoc	.50	.20
❑ 61 Roy Tarpley	.25	.08
❑ 62 Todd Day	.25	.08
❑ 63 Anthony Peeler	.25	.08
❑ 64 Brian Williams	.25	.08
❑ 65 Muggsy Bogues	.50	.20
❑ 66 Jerome Kersey EXP	.25	.08
❑ 67 Eric Piatkowski	.50	.20
❑ 68 Tim Perry	.25	.08
❑ 69 Chris Gatling	.25	.08
❑ 70 Mark Price	.50	.20
❑ 71 Terry Mills	.25	.08
❑ 72 Anthony Avent	.25	.08

❏ 73	Matt Geiger	.25	.08	❏ 159	Harvey Grant	.25	.08	❏ 245	Lorenzo Williams	.25	.08
❏ 74	Walt Williams	.25	.08	❏ 160	Tim Hardaway	.50	.20	❏ 246	Haywoode Workman	.25	.08
❏ 75	Sean Elliott	.50	.20	❏ 161	Sarunas Marciulionis	.25	.08	❏ 247	Loy Vaught	.25	.08
❏ 76	Ken Norman	.25	.08	❏ 162	Khalid Reeves	.25	.08	❏ 248	Vernon Maxwell	.25	.08
❏ 77	Kendall Gill TA	.25	.08	❏ 163	Bo Outlaw	.25	.08	❏ 249	Lionel Simmons	.25	.08
❏ 78	Byron Houston	.25	.08	❏ 164	Dale Davis	.25	.08	❏ 250	Chris Childs	.25	.08
❏ 79	Rick Fox	.50	.20	❏ 165	Nick Van Exel	.75	.30	❏ 251	Mahmoud Abdul-Rauf	.25	.08
❏ 80	Derek Harper	.50	.20	❏ 166	Byron Scott EXP	.25	.08	❏ 252	Vincent Askew	.25	.08
❏ 81	Rod Strickland	.25	.08	❏ 167	Steve Smith	.50	.20	❏ 253	Chris Morris	.25	.08
❏ 82	Bryon Russell	.25	.08	❏ 168	Brian Grant	.75	.30	❏ 254	Elliot Perry	.25	.08
❏ 83	Antonio Davis	.25	.08	❏ 169	Avery Johnson	.25	.08	❏ 255	Dell Curry	.25	.08
❏ 84	Isaiah Rider	.25	.08	❏ 170	Dikembe Mutombo	.50	.20	❏ 256	Dana Barros	.25	.08
❏ 85	Kevin Johnson	.50	.20	❏ 171	Tom Gugliotta	.25	.08	❏ 257	Terrell Brandon	.50	.20
❏ 86	Derrick Coleman	.25	.08	❏ 172	Armon Gilliam	.25	.08	❏ 258	Monty Williams	.25	.08
❏ 87	Doug Overton	.25	.08	❏ 173	Shawn Bradley	.25	.08	❏ 259	Corie Blount	.25	.08
❏ 88	Hersey Hawkins TA	.25	.08	❏ 174	Herb Williams	.25	.08	❏ 260	B.J. Armstrong	.25	.08
❏ 89	Popeye Jones	.25	.08	❏ 175	Dino Radja	.25	.08	❏ 261	Jim McIlvaine	.25	.08
❏ 90	Dickey Simpkins	.25	.08	❏ 176	Billy Owens	.25	.08	❏ 262	Otis Thorpe	.25	.08
❏ 91	Rodney Rogers TA	.25	.08	❏ 177	Kenny Gattison EXP	.25	.08	❏ 263	Sean Rooks	.25	.08
❏ 92	Rex Chapman TA	.25	.08	❏ 178	J.R. Reid	.25	.08	❏ 264	Tony Massenburg	.25	.08
❏ 93	Spud Webb TA	.25	.08	❏ 179	Otis Thorpe	.25	.08	❏ 265	Steve Smith	.50	.20
❏ 94	Lee Mayberry	.25	.08	❏ 180	Sam Cassell	.75	.30	❏ 266	Ron Harper	.50	.20
❏ 95	Cedric Ceballos	.25	.08	❏ 181	Sam Cassell	.75	.30	❏ 267	Dale Ellis	.25	.08
❏ 96	Tyrone Hill	.25	.08	❏ 182	Pooh Richardson	.25	.08	❏ 268	Clyde Drexler	.75	.30
❏ 97	Bill Curley	.25	.08	❏ 183	Johnny Newman	.25	.08	❏ 269	Jamie Watson	.25	.08
❏ 98	Jeff Turner	.25	.08	❏ 184	Dennis Scott	.25	.08	❏ 270	Doc Rivers	.50	.20
❏ 99	Tyrone Corbin TA	.25	.08	❏ 185	Will Perdue	.25	.08	❏ 271	Derrick Alston	.25	.08
❏ 100	John Stockton	1.00	.40	❏ 186	Andrew Lang	.25	.08	❏ 272	Eric Mobley	.25	.08
❏ 101	Mookie Blaylock EC	.25	.08	❏ 187	Karl Malone	1.00	.40	❏ 273	Ricky Pierce	.25	.08
❏ 102	Dino Radja EC	.25	.08	❏ 188	Buck Williams	.25	.08	❏ 274	David Wesley	.25	.08
❏ 103	Alonzo Mourning EC	.50	.20	❏ 189	P.J. Brown	.25	.08	❏ 275	John Starks	.50	.20
❏ 104	Scottie Pippen EC	1.25	.50	❏ 190	Khalid Reeves	.25	.08	❏ 276	Chris Mullin	.75	.30
❏ 105	Terrell Brandon EC	.50	.20	❏ 191	Kevin Willis	.50	.20	❏ 277	Ervin Johnson	.25	.08
❏ 106	Jim Jackson EC	.25	.08	❏ 192	Robert Pack	.25	.08	❏ 278	Jamal Mashburn	.50	.20
❏ 107	Mahmoud Abdul-Rauf EC	.25	.08	❏ 193	Joe Dumars	.75	.30	❏ 279	Joe Kleine	.25	.08
❏ 108	Grant Hill EC	1.00	.40	❏ 194	Sam Perkins	.50	.20	❏ 280	Mitch Richmond	.50	.20
❏ 109	Tim Hardaway EC	.25	.08	❏ 195	Dan Majerle	.50	.20	❏ 281	Chris Mills	.25	.08
❏ 110	Hakeem Olajuwon EC	.50	.20	❏ 196	John Williams	.25	.08	❏ 282	Bimbo Coles	.25	.08
❏ 111	Rik Smits EC	.25	.08	❏ 197	Reggie Williams	.25	.08	❏ 283	Larry Johnson	.50	.20
❏ 112	Loy Vaught EC	.25	.08	❏ 198	Greg Anthony	.25	.08	❏ 284	Stanley Roberts	.25	.08
❏ 113	Vlade Divac EC	.25	.08	❏ 199	Steve Kerr	.50	.20	❏ 285	Rex Walters	.25	.08
❏ 114	Kevin Willis EC	.25	.08	❏ 200	Richard Dumas	.25	.08	❏ 286	Donald Royal	.25	.08
❏ 115	Glenn Robinson EC	.75	.30	❏ 201	Dee Brown	.25	.08	❏ 287	Benoit Benjamin	.25	.08
❏ 116	Christian Laettner EC	.50	.20	❏ 202	Zan Tabak	.25	.08	❏ 288	Chris Dudley	.25	.08
❏ 117	Derrick Coleman EC	.25	.08	❏ 203	David Wood	.25	.08	❏ 289	Elden Campbell	.25	.08
❏ 118	Patrick Ewing EC	.75	.30	❏ 204	Duane Causwell	.25	.08	❏ 290	Mookie Blaylock	.25	.08
❏ 119	Shaquille O'Neal EC	2.00	.75	❏ 205	Sedale Threatt	.25	.08	❏ 291	Hersey Hawkins	.25	.08
❏ 120	Dana Barros EC	.25	.08	❏ 206	Hubert Davis	.25	.08	❏ 292	Anthony Mason	.50	.20
❏ 121	Charles Barkley EC	.75	.30	❏ 207	Donald Hodge	.25	.08	❏ 293	Latrell Sprewell	.75	.30
❏ 122	Rod Strickland EC	.25	.08	❏ 208	Duane Ferrell	.25	.08	❏ 294	Harold Miner	.25	.08
❏ 123	Brian Grant EC	.75	.30	❏ 209	Sam Mitchell	.25	.08	❏ 295	Scott Williams	.25	.08
❏ 124	David Robinson EC	.50	.20	❏ 210	Adam Keefe	.25	.08	❏ 296	David Benoit	.25	.08
❏ 125	Shawn Kemp EC	.25	.08	❏ 211	Clifford Robinson	.25	.08	❏ 297	Christian Laettner	.50	.20
❏ 126	Oliver Miller EC	.25	.08	❏ 212	Rodney Rogers	.25	.08	❏ 298	LaPhonso Ellis	.25	.08
❏ 127	Karl Malone EC	.75	.30	❏ 213	Jayson Williams	.25	.08	❏ 299	Gheorghe Muresan	.25	.08
❏ 128	Benoit Benjamin EC	.25	.08	❏ 214	Brian Shaw	.25	.08	❏ 300	Kendall Gill	.25	.08
❏ 129	Chris Webber EC	.75	.30	❏ 215	Luc Longley	.25	.08	❏ 301	Eddie Johnson	.25	.08
❏ 130	Dan Majerle	.50	.20	❏ 216	Don MacLean	.25	.08	❏ 302	Terry Cummings	.25	.08
❏ 131	Calbert Cheaney	.25	.08	❏ 217	Rex Chapman	.25	.08	❏ 303	Chuck Person	.25	.08
❏ 132	Mark Jackson	.50	.20	❏ 218	Wayman Tisdale	.25	.08	❏ 304	Michael Smith	.25	.08
❏ 133	Greg Anthony EXP	.25	.08	❏ 219	Shawn Kemp	.50	.20	❏ 305	Mark West	.25	.08
❏ 134	Scott Burrell	.25	.08	❏ 220	Chris Webber	1.00	.40	❏ 306	Willie Anderson	.25	.08
❏ 135	Detlef Schrempf	.50	.20	❏ 221	Antonio Harvey	.25	.08	❏ 307	Pervis Ellison	.25	.08
❏ 136	Marty Conlon	.25	.08	❏ 222	Sarunas Marciulionis	.25	.08	❏ 308	Brian Williams	.25	.08
❏ 137	Rony Seikaly	.25	.08	❏ 223	Jeff Malone	.25	.08	❏ 309	Danny Manning	.50	.20
❏ 138	Olden Polynice	.25	.08	❏ 224	Chucky Brown	.25	.08	❏ 310	Hakeem Olajuwon	.75	.30
❏ 139	Terry Cummings	.25	.08	❏ 225	Greg Minor	.25	.08	❏ 311	Scottie Pippen	1.25	.50
❏ 140	Stacey Augmon	.25	.08	❏ 226	Clifford Rozier	.25	.08	❏ 312	Jon Koncak	.25	.08
❏ 141	Bryant Stith	.25	.08	❏ 227	Derrick McKey	.25	.08	❏ 313	Sasha Danilovic RC	.25	.08
❏ 142	Sean Higgins	.25	.08	❏ 228	Tony Dumas	.25	.08	❏ 314	Lucious Harris	.25	.08
❏ 143	Antoine Carr	.25	.08	❏ 229	Oliver Miller	.25	.08	❏ 315	Yinka Dare	.25	.08
❏ 144	Blue Edwards EXP	.25	.08	❏ 230	Charles Oakley	.25	.08	❏ 316	Eric Williams RC	.50	.20
❏ 145	A.C. Green	.50	.20	❏ 231	Fred Roberts	.25	.08	❏ 317	Gary Trent RC	.25	.08
❏ 146	Bobby Phills	.25	.08	❏ 232	Glen Rice	.50	.20	❏ 318	Theo Ratliff RC	1.00	.40
❏ 147	Terry Dehere	.25	.08	❏ 233	Terry Porter	.25	.08	❏ 319	Lawrence Moten RC	.25	.08
❏ 148	Sharone Wright	.25	.08	❏ 234	Mark Macon	.25	.08	❏ 320	Jerome Allen RC	.25	.08
❏ 149	Nick Anderson	.25	.08	❏ 235	Michael Cage	.25	.08	❏ 321	Tyus Edney RC	.25	.08
❏ 150	Jim Jackson	.25	.08	❏ 236	Eric Murdock	.25	.08	❏ 322	Loren Meyer RC	.25	.08
❏ 151	Eric Montross	.25	.08	❏ 237	Vinny Del Negro	.25	.08	❏ 323	Michael Finley RC	2.00	.75
❏ 152	Doug West	.25	.08	❏ 238	Spud Webb	.50	.20	❏ 324	Alan Henderson RC	.75	.30
❏ 153	Charles Smith	.25	.08	❏ 239	Mario Elie	.25	.08	❏ 325	Bob Sura RC	.50	.20
❏ 154	Will Perdue	.25	.08	❏ 240	Blue Edwards	.25	.08	❏ 326	Joe Smith RC	1.25	.50
❏ 155	Gerald Wilkins EXP	.25	.08	❏ 241	Dontonio Wingfield	.25	.08	❏ 327	Damon Stoudamire RC	1.50	.60
❏ 156	Robert Horry	.25	.08	❏ 242	Brooks Thompson	.25	.08	❏ 328	Sherrell Ford RC	.25	.08
❏ 157	Robert Parish	.50	.20	❏ 243	Alonzo Mourning	.50	.20	❏ 329	Jerry Stackhouse RC	2.50	1.00
❏ 158	Lindsey Hunter	.25	.08	❏ 244	Dennis Rodman	.50	.20	❏ 330	George Zidek RC	.25	.08

❑ 331	Brent Barry RC	.75	.30
❑ 332	Shawn Respert RC	.25	.08
❑ 333	Rasheed Wallace RC	2.00	.75
❑ 334	Antonio McDyess RC	1.50	.60
❑ 335	David Vaughn RC	.25	.08
❑ 336	Cory Alexander RC	.25	.08
❑ 337	Jason Caffey RC	.50	.20
❑ 338	Frankie King RC	.25	.08
❑ 339	Travis Best RC	.25	.08
❑ 340	Greg Ostertag RC	.25	.08
❑ 341	Ed O'Bannon RC	.25	.08
❑ 342	Kurt Thomas RC	.50	.20
❑ 343	Kevin Garnett RC	4.00	2.00
❑ 344	Bryant Reeves RC	.75	.30
❑ 345	Corliss Williamson RC	.75	.30
❑ 346	Cherokee Parks RC	.25	.08
❑ 347	Junior Burrough RC	.25	.08
❑ 348	Randolph Childress RC	.25	.08
❑ 349	Lou Roe RC	.25	.08
❑ 350	Mario Bennett RC	.25	.08
❑ 351	Dikembe Mutombo XP	.25	.08
❑ 352	Larry Johnson XP	.50	.20
❑ 353	Vlade Divac XP	.25	.08
❑ 354	Karl Malone XP	.75	.30
❑ 355	John Stockton XP	.75	.30
❑ 356	Alonzo Mourning TA	.25	.08
❑ 357	Glen Rice TA	.25	.08
❑ 358	Dan Majerle TA	.25	.08
❑ 359	John Williams TA	.25	.08
❑ 360	Mark Price TA	.25	.08
❑ 361	Magic Johnson	1.25	.50

1996-97 Stadium Club

❑ COMPLETE SET (180)		25.00	12.50
❑ COMPLETE SERIES 1 (90)		10.00	5.00
❑ COMPLETE SERIES 2 (90)		15.00	7.50
❑ 1	Scottie Pippen	1.25	.50
❑ 2	Dale Davis	.25	.08
❑ 3	Horace Grant	.50	.20
❑ 4	Gheorghe Muresan	.25	.08
❑ 5	Elliot Perry	.25	.08
❑ 6	Carlos Rogers	.25	.08
❑ 7	Glenn Robinson	.75	.30
❑ 8	Avery Johnson	.25	.08
❑ 9	Dee Brown	.25	.08
❑ 10	Grant Hill	.75	.30
❑ 11	Tyus Edney	.25	.08
❑ 12	Patrick Ewing	.75	.30
❑ 13	Jason Kidd	1.25	.50
❑ 14	Clifford Robinson	.25	.08
❑ 15	Robert Horry	.50	.20
❑ 16	Dell Curry	.25	.08
❑ 17	Terry Porter	.25	.08
❑ 18	Shaquille O'Neal	2.00	.75
❑ 19	Bryant Stith	.25	.08
❑ 20	Shawn Kemp	.50	.20
❑ 21	Kurt Thomas	.50	.20
❑ 22	Pooh Richardson	.25	.08
❑ 23	Bob Sura	.25	.08
❑ 24	Olden Polynice	.25	.08
❑ 25	Lawrence Moten	.25	.08
❑ 26	Kendall Gill	.25	.08
❑ 27	Cedric Ceballos	.25	.08
❑ 28	Latrell Sprewell	.75	.30
❑ 29	Christian Laettner	.50	.20
❑ 30	Jamal Mashburn	.50	.20
❑ 31	Jerry Stackhouse	1.00	.40
❑ 32	John Stockton	.75	.30

❑ 33	Arvydas Sabonis	.50	.20
❑ 34	Detlef Schrempf	.50	.20
❑ 35	Toni Kukoc	.50	.20
❑ 36	Sasha Danilovic	.25	.08
❑ 37	Dana Barros	.25	.08
❑ 38	Loy Vaught	.25	.08
❑ 39	John Starks	.50	.20
❑ 40	Marty Conlon	.25	.08
❑ 41	Antonio McDyess	.50	.20
❑ 42	Michael Finley	1.00	.40
❑ 43	Tom Gugliotta	.50	.20
❑ 44	Terrell Brandon	.50	.20
❑ 45	Derrick McKey	.25	.08
❑ 46	Damon Stoudamire	.75	.30
❑ 47	Elden Campbell	.25	.08
❑ 48	Luc Longley	.25	.08
❑ 49	B.J. Armstrong	.25	.08
❑ 50	Lindsey Hunter	.25	.08
❑ 51	Glen Rice	.50	.20
❑ 52	Shawn Respert	.25	.08
❑ 53	Cory Alexander	.25	.08
❑ 54	Tim Legler	.25	.08
❑ 55	Bryant Reeves	.25	.08
❑ 56	Anfernee Hardaway	.75	.30
❑ 57	Charles Barkley	1.00	.40
❑ 58	Mookie Blaylock	.25	.08
❑ 59	Kevin Garnett	1.50	.60
❑ 60	Hersey Hawkins	.50	.20
❑ 61	Ed O'Bannon	.25	.08
❑ 62	George Zidek	.25	.08
❑ 63	Mitch Richmond	.50	.20
❑ 64	Derrick Coleman	.50	.20
❑ 65	Chris Webber	.75	.30
❑ 66	Bobby Phills	.25	.08
❑ 67	Rik Smits	.50	.20
❑ 68	Jeff Hornacek	.50	.20
❑ 69	Sam Cassell	.75	.30
❑ 70	Gary Trent	.25	.08
❑ 71	LaPhonso Ellis	.25	.08
❑ 72	Oliver Miller	.25	.08
❑ 73	Rex Chapman	.25	.08
❑ 74	Jim Jackson	.25	.08
❑ 75	Eric Williams	.25	.08
❑ 76	Brent Barry	.25	.08
❑ 77	Nick Anderson	.25	.08
❑ 78	David Robinson	.75	.30
❑ 79	Calbert Cheaney	.25	.08
❑ 80	Joe Smith	.50	.20
❑ 81	Steve Kerr	.25	.08
❑ 82	Wayman Tisdale	.25	.08
❑ 83	Steve Smith	.25	.08
❑ 84	Clyde Drexler	.75	.30
❑ 85	Theo Ratliff	.50	.20
❑ 86	Charlie Ward	.25	.08
❑ 87	Karl Malone	.75	.30
❑ 88	Clarence Weatherspoon	.25	.08
❑ 89	Greg Anthony	.25	.08
❑ 90	Shawn Bradley	.25	.08
❑ 91	Otis Thorpe	.25	.08
❑ 92	Larry Johnson	.50	.20
❑ 93	Sharone Wright	.25	.08
❑ 94	Charles Barkley	1.00	.40
❑ 95	Wesley Person	.25	.08
❑ 96	Dikembe Mutombo	.50	.20
❑ 97	Eddie Jones	.75	.30
❑ 98	Juwan Howard	.50	.20
❑ 99	Grant Hill	.75	.30
❑ 100	Chris Carr RC	.25	.08
❑ 101	Michael Jordan	5.00	2.00
❑ 102	Vincent Askew	.25	.08
❑ 103	Gary Payton	.75	.30
❑ 104	Chris Mills	.25	.08
❑ 105	Reggie Miller	.75	.30
❑ 106	Don MacLean	.25	.08
❑ 107	John Stockton	.75	.30
❑ 108	Mahmoud Abdul-Rauf	.25	.08
❑ 109	P.J. Brown	.25	.08
❑ 110	Kenny Anderson	.25	.08
❑ 111	Mark Price	.50	.20
❑ 112	Derek Harper	.25	.08
❑ 113	Dino Radja	.25	.08
❑ 114	Terry Dehere	.25	.08
❑ 115	Mark Jackson	.25	.08
❑ 116	Vin Baker	.50	.20
❑ 117	Dennis Scott	.25	.08
❑ 118	Sean Elliott	.50	.20

❑ 119	Lee Mayberry	.25	.08
❑ 120	Vlade Divac	.25	.08
❑ 121	Joe Dumars	.75	.30
❑ 122	Isaiah Rider	.50	.20
❑ 123	Hakeem Olajuwon	.75	.30
❑ 124	Robert Pack	.25	.08
❑ 125	Jalen Rose	.75	.30
❑ 126	Allan Houston	.50	.20
❑ 127	Nate McMillan	.25	.08
❑ 128	Rod Strickland	.25	.08
❑ 129	Sean Rooks	.25	.08
❑ 130	Dennis Rodman	.50	.20
❑ 131	Alonzo Mourning	.50	.20
❑ 132	Danny Ferry	.25	.08
❑ 133	Sam Cassell	.75	.30
❑ 134	Brian Grant	.75	.30
❑ 135	Karl Malone	.75	.30
❑ 136	Chris Gatling	.25	.08
❑ 137	Tom Gugliotta	.25	.08
❑ 138	Hubert Davis	.25	.08
❑ 139	Lucious Harris	.25	.08
❑ 140	Rony Seikaly	.25	.08
❑ 141	Alan Henderson	.25	.08
❑ 142	Mario Elie	.25	.08
❑ 143	Vinny Del Negro	.25	.08
❑ 144	Harvey Grant	.25	.08
❑ 145	Muggsy Bogues	.25	.08
❑ 146	Rodney Rogers	.25	.08
❑ 147	Kevin Johnson	.50	.20
❑ 148	Anthony Peeler	.25	.08
❑ 149	Jon Koncak	.25	.08
❑ 150	Ricky Pierce	.25	.08
❑ 151	Todd Day	.25	.08
❑ 152	Tyrone Hill	.25	.08
❑ 153	Nick Van Exel	.75	.30
❑ 154	Rasheed Wallace	1.00	.40
❑ 155	Jayson Williams	.50	.20
❑ 156	Sherman Douglas	.25	.08
❑ 157	Bryon Russell	.25	.08
❑ 158	Ron Harper	.50	.20
❑ 159	Stacey Augmon	.25	.08
❑ 160	Antonio Davis	.25	.08
❑ 161	Tim Hardaway	.50	.20
❑ 162	Charles Oakley	.25	.08
❑ 163	Billy Owens	.25	.08
❑ 164	Sam Perkins	.50	.20
❑ 165	Chris Whitney	.25	.08
❑ 166	Matt Geiger	.25	.08
❑ 167	Andrew Lang	.25	.08
❑ 168	Danny Manning	.25	.08
❑ 169	Doug Christie	.50	.20
❑ 170	George Lynch	.25	.08
❑ 171	Malik Sealy	.25	.08
❑ 172	Eric Montross	.25	.08
❑ 173	Rick Fox	.25	.08
❑ 174	Chris Mullin	.75	.30
❑ 175	Ken Norman	.25	.08
❑ 176	Sarunas Marciulionis	.25	.08
❑ 177	Kevin Garnett	1.50	.60
❑ 178	Brian Shaw	.25	.08
❑ 179	Will Perdue	.25	.08
❑ 180	Scott Williams	.25	.08
❑ NNO	Checklist	.25	.08

1997-98 Stadium Club

❑ COMPLETE SET (240)		45.00	22.50
❑ COMPLETE SERIES 1 (120)		25.00	12.50
❑ COMPLETE SERIES 2 (120)		20.00	10.00

#	Player		
☐ 1	Scottie Pippen	1.25	.50
☐ 2	Bryon Russell	.25	.08
☐ 3	Muggsy Bogues	.50	.20
☐ 4	Gary Payton	.75	.30
☐ 5	Bulls - Team of the 90s	5.00	2.00
☐ 6	Corliss Williamson	.50	.20
☐ 7	Samaki Walker	.25	.08
☐ 8	Allan Houston	.50	.20
☐ 9	Ray Allen	.75	.30
☐ 10	Nick Van Exel	.75	.30
☐ 11	Chris Mullin	.75	.30
☐ 12	Popeye Jones	.25	.08
☐ 13	Horace Grant	.50	.20
☐ 14	Rik Smits	.50	.20
☐ 15	Wayman Tisdale	.25	.08
☐ 16	Donny Marshall	.25	.08
☐ 17	Rod Strickland	.25	.08
☐ 18	Rod Strickland	.25	.08
☐ 19	Greg Anthony	.25	.08
☐ 20	Lindsey Hunter	.25	.08
☐ 21	Glen Rice	.50	.20
☐ 22	Anthony Goldwire	.25	.08
☐ 23	Mahmoud Abdul-Rauf	.25	.08
☐ 24	Sean Elliott	.50	.20
☐ 25	Cory Alexander	.25	.08
☐ 26	Tyrone Corbin	.25	.08
☐ 27	Sam Perkins	.25	.08
☐ 28	Brian Shaw	.25	.08
☐ 29	Doug Christie	.50	.20
☐ 30	Mark Jackson	.50	.20
☐ 31	Christian Laettner	.50	.20
☐ 32	Damon Stoudamire	.50	.20
☐ 33	Eric Williams	.25	.08
☐ 34	Glenn Robinson	.75	.30
☐ 35	Brooks Thompson	.25	.08
☐ 36	Derrick Coleman	.25	.08
☐ 37	Theo Ratliff	.25	.08
☐ 38	Ron Harper	.50	.20
☐ 39	Hakeem Olajuwon	.75	.30
☐ 40	Mitch Richmond	.75	.30
☐ 41	Reggie Miller	.75	.30
☐ 42	Reggie Miller	.75	.30
☐ 43	Shaquille O'Neal	2.00	.75
☐ 44	Zydrunas Ilgauskas	.50	.20
☐ 45	Jamal Mashburn	.50	.20
☐ 46	Isaiah Rider	.50	.20
☐ 47	Tom Gugliotta	.50	.20
☐ 48	Rex Chapman	.25	.08
☐ 49	Lorenzen Wright	.25	.08
☐ 50	Pooh Richardson	.25	.08
☐ 51	Armon Gilliam	.25	.08
☐ 52	Kevin Johnson	.50	.20
☐ 53	Kerry Kittles	.75	.30
☐ 54	Kerry Kittles	.75	.30
☐ 55	Charles Oakley	.50	.20
☐ 56	Dennis Rodman	.50	.20
☐ 57	Greg Ostertag	.25	.08
☐ 58	Todd Fuller	.25	.08
☐ 59	Mark Davis	.25	.08
☐ 60	Erick Strickland RC	.50	.20
☐ 61	Clifford Robinson	.25	.08
☐ 62	Nate McMillan	.25	.08
☐ 63	Steve Kerr	.50	.20
☐ 64	Bob Sura	.25	.08
☐ 65	Danny Ferry	.25	.08
☐ 66	Loy Vaught	.25	.08
☐ 67	A.C. Green	.25	.08
☐ 68	John Stockton	.75	.30
☐ 69	Terry Mills	.25	.08
☐ 70	Voshon Lenard	.25	.08
☐ 71	Matt Maloney	.25	.08
☐ 72	Charlie Ward	.25	.08
☐ 73	Brent Barry	.50	.20
☐ 74	Chris Webber	.75	.30
☐ 75	Stephon Marbury	1.00	.40
☐ 76	Bryant Stith	.25	.08
☐ 77	Shareef Abdur-Rahim	1.25	.50
☐ 78	Sean Rooks	.25	.08
☐ 79	Rony Seikaly	.25	.08
☐ 80	Brent Price	.25	.08
☐ 81	Wesley Person	.25	.08
☐ 82	Michael Smith	.25	.08
☐ 83	Gary Trent	.25	.08
☐ 84	Dan Majerle	.50	.20
☐ 85	Rex Walters	.25	.08
☐ 86	Clarence Weatherspoon	.25	.08
☐ 87	Patrick Ewing	.75	.30
☐ 88	B.J. Armstrong	.25	.08
☐ 89	Travis Best	.25	.08
☐ 90	Steve Smith	.50	.20
☐ 91	Vitaly Potapenko	.25	.08
☐ 92	Derek Strong	.25	.08
☐ 93	Michael Finley	.75	.30
☐ 94	Will Perdue	.25	.08
☐ 95	Antoine Walker	1.00	.40
☐ 96	Chuck Person	.25	.08
☐ 97	Mookie Blaylock	.25	.08
☐ 98	Eric Snow	.50	.20
☐ 99	Tony Delk	.25	.08
☐ 100	Mario Elie	.25	.08
☐ 101	Terrell Brandon	.50	.20
☐ 102	Shawn Bradley	.25	.08
☐ 103	Latrell Sprewell	.75	.30
☐ 104	Latrell Sprewell	.75	.30
☐ 105	Tim Hardaway	.50	.20
☐ 106	Terry Porter	.25	.08
☐ 107	Darrell Armstrong	.25	.08
☐ 108	Rasheed Wallace	.75	.30
☐ 109	Vinny Del Negro	.25	.08
☐ 110	Tracy Murray	.25	.08
☐ 111	Lawrence Moten	.25	.08
☐ 112	Lamond Murray	.25	.08
☐ 113	Juwan Howard	.50	.20
☐ 114	Juwan Howard	.50	.20
☐ 115	Karl Malone	.75	.30
☐ 116	Aaron McKie	.50	.20
☐ 117	Shawn Respert	.25	.08
☐ 118	Michael Jordan	5.00	2.00
☐ 119	Shawn Kemp	.50	.20
☐ 120	Arvydas Sabonis	.50	.20
☐ 121	Tyus Edney	.25	.08
☐ 122	Bryant Reeves	.25	.08
☐ 123	Jason Kidd	1.25	.50
☐ 124	Dikembe Mutombo	.50	.20
☐ 125	Allen Iverson	2.00	.75
☐ 126	Allen Iverson	2.00	.75
☐ 127	Larry Johnson	.50	.20
☐ 128	Jerry Stackhouse	.75	.30
☐ 129	Kendall Gill	.25	.08
☐ 130	Kendall Gill	.25	.08
☐ 131	Vin Baker	.50	.20
☐ 132	Joe Dumars	.75	.30
☐ 133	Calbert Cheaney	.25	.08
☐ 134	Alonzo Mourning	.50	.20
☐ 135	Isaac Austin	.25	.08
☐ 136	Joe Smith	.50	.20
☐ 137	Elden Campbell	.25	.08
☐ 138	Kevin Garnett	1.50	.60
☐ 139	Malik Sealy	.25	.08
☐ 140	John Starks	.50	.20
☐ 141	Clyde Drexler	.75	.30
☐ 142	Matt Geiger	.25	.08
☐ 143	Mark Price	.50	.20
☐ 144	Buck Williams	.25	.08
☐ 145	Grant Hill	.75	.30
☐ 146	Kobe Bryant	3.00	1.25
☐ 147	Dale Ellis	.25	.08
☐ 148	Jason Caffey	.25	.08
☐ 149	Toni Kukoc	.50	.20
☐ 150	Avery Johnson	.25	.08
☐ 151	Alan Henderson	.25	.08
☐ 152	Walt Williams	.25	.08
☐ 153	Greg Minor	.25	.08
☐ 154	Calbert Cheaney	.25	.08
☐ 155	Vlade Divac	.50	.20
☐ 156	Greg Foster	.25	.08
☐ 157	LaPhonso Ellis	.25	.08
☐ 158	Charles Barkley	1.00	.40
☐ 159	Antonio Davis	.25	.08
☐ 160	Roy Rogers	.25	.08
☐ 161	Robert Horry	.50	.20
☐ 162	Sam Cassell	.75	.30
☐ 163	Chris Carr	.25	.08
☐ 164	Robert Pack	.25	.08
☐ 165	Sam Cassell	.75	.30
☐ 166	Rodney Rogers	.25	.08
☐ 167	Chris Childs	.25	.08
☐ 168	Shandon Anderson	.25	.08
☐ 169	Kenny Anderson	.50	.20
☐ 170	Anthony Mason	.50	.20
☐ 171	Olden Polynice	.25	.08
☐ 172	David Wingate	.25	.08
☐ 173	David Robinson	.75	.30
☐ 174	Billy Owens	.25	.08
☐ 175	Detlef Schrempf	.50	.20
☐ 176	Carlos Rogers	.25	.08
☐ 177	Marcus Camby	.75	.30
☐ 178	Dana Barros	.25	.08
☐ 179	Shandon Anderson	.25	.08
☐ 180	Jayson Williams	.25	.08
☐ 181	Eldridge Recasner	.25	.08
☐ 182	Doug West	.25	.08
☐ 183	Kevin Willis	.50	.20
☐ 184	Eddie Johnson	.25	.08
☐ 185	Derek Fisher	.75	.30
☐ 186	Eddie Jones	.75	.30
☐ 187	Sherman Douglas	.25	.08
☐ 188	Anthony Peeler	.25	.08
☐ 189	Danny Manning	.25	.08
☐ 190	Stacey Augmon	.25	.08
☐ 191	Hersey Hawkins	.25	.08
☐ 192	Michael Williams	.25	.08
☐ 193	Jeff Hornacek	.50	.20
☐ 194	Anfernee Hardaway		.30
☐ 195	Harvey Grant	.25	.08
☐ 196	Nick Anderson	.25	.08
☐ 197	Luc Longley	.25	.08
☐ 198	Andrew Lang	.25	.08
☐ 199	P.J. Brown	.25	.08
☐ 200	Cedric Ceballos	.25	.08
☐ 201	Tim Duncan RC	3.00	1.25
☐ 202	Ervin Johnson TRAN	.25	.08
☐ 203	Keith Van Horn RC	1.00	.40
☐ 204	David Wesley TRAN	.25	.08
☐ 205	Chauncey Billups RC	2.00	.75
☐ 206	Jim Jackson TRAN	.25	.08
☐ 207	Antonio Daniels RC	.75	.30
☐ 208	Travis Knight TRAN	.25	.08
☐ 209	Tony Battie RC	.75	.30
☐ 210	Bobby Phills TRAN	.25	.08
☐ 211	Bobby Jackson RC	1.00	.40
☐ 212	Otis Thorpe TRAN	.25	.08
☐ 213	Tim Thomas RC	1.25	.50
☐ 214	Chris Mullin TRAN	.50	.20
☐ 215	Adonal Foyle RC	.50	.20
☐ 216	Brian Williams TRAN	.25	.08
☐ 217	Tracy McGrady RC	4.00	1.50
☐ 218	Tyus Edney TRAN	.25	.08
☐ 219	Danny Fortson RC	.50	.20
☐ 220	Clifford Robinson TRAN	.25	.08
☐ 221	Olivier Saint-Jean RC	.25	.08
☐ 222	Vin Baker TRAN	.25	.08
☐ 223	Austin Croshere RC	.60	.25
☐ 224	John Wallace TRAN	.25	.08
☐ 225	Derek Anderson RC	.75	.30
☐ 226	Kelvin Cato RC	.75	.30
☐ 227	Maurice Taylor RC	.60	.25
☐ 228	Scot Pollard RC	.50	.20
☐ 229	John Thomas RC	.25	.08
☐ 230	Dean Garrett TRAN	.25	.08
☐ 231	Brevin Knight RC	.50	.20
☐ 232	Ron Mercer RC	.75	.30
☐ 233	Johnny Taylor RC	.25	.08
☐ 234	Antonio McDyess TRAN	.50	.20
☐ 235	Ed Gray RC	.25	.08
☐ 236	Terrell Brandon TRAN	.25	.08
☐ 237	Anthony Parker RC	.25	.08
☐ 238	Shawn Kemp TRAN	.25	.08
☐ 239	Paul Grant RC	.25	.08
☐ 240	Dennis Scott TRAN	.25	.08

1998-99 Stadium Club

☐	COMPLETE SET (240)	250.00	125.00
☐	COMPLETE SERIES 1 (120)	200.00	75.00
☐	COMP SERIES 1 w/o RC (100)	15.00	7.50
☐	COMPLETE SERIES 2 (120)	30.00	15.00
☐	COMMON CARD (1-240)	.25	.08
☐	COMMON CARD (101-120)	2.50	1.00
☐ 1	Eddie Jones	.75	.30
☐ 2	Matt Geiger	.25	.08
☐ 3	Ray Allen	.75	.30
☐ 4	Billy Owens	.25	.08
☐ 5	Larry Johnson	.50	.20
☐ 6	Jerry Stackhouse	.75	.30
☐ 7	Travis Best	.25	.08
☐ 8	Sam Cassell	.75	.30
☐ 9	Isaiah Rider	.25	.08

#	Player		
☐ 10	Walter McCarty	.25	.08
☐ 11	Hakeem Olajuwon	.75	.30
☐ 12	Detlef Schrempf	.50	.20
☐ 13	Chris Garner	.25	.08
☐ 14	Voshon Lenard	.25	.08
☐ 15	Kevin Garnett	1.50	.60
☐ 16	Doug Christie	.50	.20
☐ 17	Dikembe Mutombo	.50	.20
☐ 18	Terrell Brandon	.50	.20
☐ 19	Brevin Knight	.25	.08
☐ 20	Dan Majerle	.50	.20
☐ 21	Keith Van Horn	.75	.30
☐ 22	Jim Jackson	.25	.08
☐ 23	Theo Ratliff	.50	.20
☐ 24	Anthony Peeler	.25	.08
☐ 25	Tim Hardaway	.50	.20
☐ 26	Bo Outlaw	.25	.08
☐ 27	Blue Edwards	.25	.08
☐ 28	Khalid Reeves	.25	.08
☐ 29	David Wesley	.25	.08
☐ 30	Toni Kukoc	.50	.20
☐ 31	Jaren Jackson	.25	.08
☐ 32	Mario Elie	.25	.08
☐ 33	Nick Anderson	.25	.08
☐ 34	Derek Anderson	.60	.25
☐ 35	Rodney Rogers	.25	.08
☐ 36	Jalen Rose	.75	.30
☐ 37	Corliss Williamson	.50	.20
☐ 38	Tyrone Corbin	.25	.08
☐ 39	Antonio Davis	.25	.08
☐ 40	Chris Mills	.25	.08
☐ 41	Clarence Weatherspoon	.25	.08
☐ 42	George Lynch	.25	.08
☐ 43	Kelvin Cato	.25	.08
☐ 44	Anthony Mason	.50	.20
☐ 45	Tracy McGrady	2.00	.75
☐ 46	Lamond Murray	.25	.08
☐ 47	Mookie Blaylock	.25	.08
☐ 48	Tracy Murray	.25	.08
☐ 49	Ron Harper	.50	.20
☐ 50	Tom Gugliotta	.50	.20
☐ 51	Allan Houston	.50	.20
☐ 52	Arvydas Sabonis	.50	.20
☐ 53	Brian Williams	.25	.08
☐ 54	Brian Shaw	.25	.08
☐ 55	John Stockton	.75	.30
☐ 56	Rick Fox	.50	.20
☐ 57	Hersey Hawkins	.25	.08
☐ 58	Danny Manning	.50	.20
☐ 59	Chris Carr	.25	.08
☐ 60	Lindsey Hunter	.25	.08
☐ 61	Donyell Marshall	.50	.20
☐ 62	Michael Jordan	5.00	2.00
☐ 63	Mark Strickland	.25	.08
☐ 64	LaPhonso Ellis	.25	.08
☐ 65	Rod Strickland	.25	.08
☐ 66	David Robinson	.75	.30
☐ 67	Cedric Ceballos	.25	.08
☐ 68	Christian Laettner	.50	.20
☐ 69	Anthony Goldwire	.25	.08
☐ 70	Armon Gilliam	.25	.08
☐ 71	Shaquille O'Neal	2.00	.75
☐ 72	Sherman Douglas	.25	.08
☐ 73	Kendall Gill	.25	.08
☐ 74	Charlie Ward	.25	.08
☐ 75	Allen Iverson	1.50	.60
☐ 76	Shawn Kemp	.50	.20
☐ 77	Travis Knight	.25	.08
☐ 78	Gary Payton	.75	.30
☐ 79	Cedric Henderson	.25	.08
☐ 80	Matt Bullard	.25	.08
☐ 81	Steve Kerr	.50	.20
☐ 82	Shawn Bradley	.25	.08
☐ 83	Antonio McDyess	.50	.20
☐ 84	Robert Horry	.50	.20
☐ 85	Darrick Martin	.25	.08
☐ 86	Derek Strong	.25	.08
☐ 87	Shandon Anderson	.25	.08
☐ 88	Lawrence Funderburke	.25	.08
☐ 89	Brent Price	.25	.08
☐ 90	Reggie Miller	.75	.30
☐ 91	Shareef Abdur-Rahim	.75	.30
☐ 92	Jeff Hornacek	.50	.20
☐ 93	Antoine Carr	.25	.08
☐ 94	Greg Anthony	.25	.08
☐ 95	Rex Chapman	.25	.08
☐ 96	Antoine Walker	.75	.30
☐ 97	Bobby Jackson	.50	.20
☐ 98	Calbert Cheaney	.25	.08
☐ 99	Avery Johnson	.25	.08
☐ 100	Jason Kidd	1.25	.50
☐ 101	Michael Olowokandi RC	4.00	1.50
☐ 102	Mike Bibby RC	10.00	4.00
☐ 103	Raef LaFrentz RC	4.00	1.50
☐ 104	Antawn Jamison RC	25.00	10.00
☐ 105	Vince Carter RC	50.00	20.00
☐ 106	Robert Traylor RC	4.00	1.50
☐ 107	Jason Williams RC	10.00	4.00
☐ 108	Larry Hughes RC	5.00	2.00
☐ 109	Dirk Nowitzki RC	40.00	15.00
☐ 110	Paul Pierce RC	15.00	6.00
☐ 111	Bonzi Wells RC	8.00	3.00
☐ 112	Michael Doleac RC	4.00	1.50
☐ 113	Keon Clark RC	4.00	1.50
☐ 114	Michael Dickerson RC	5.00	2.00
☐ 115	Matt Harpring RC	4.00	1.50
☐ 116	Bryce Drew RC	4.00	1.50
☐ 117	Pat Garrity RC	2.50	1.00
☐ 118	Roshown McLeod RC	4.00	1.50
☐ 119	Ricky Davis RC	8.00	3.00
☐ 120	Brian Skinner RC	4.00	1.50
☐ 121	Dee Brown	.25	.08
☐ 122	Hubert Davis	.25	.08
☐ 123	Vitaly Potapenko	.25	.08
☐ 124	Ervin Johnson	.25	.08
☐ 125	Chris Gatling	.25	.08
☐ 126	Darrell Armstrong	.25	.08
☐ 127	Glen Rice	.50	.20
☐ 128	Ben Wallace	.75	.30
☐ 129	Sam Mitchell	.25	.08
☐ 130	Joe Dumars	.75	.30
☐ 131	Terry Davis	.25	.08
☐ 132	A.C. Green	.50	.20
☐ 133	Alan Henderson	.25	.08
☐ 134	Ron Mercer	.40	.15
☐ 135	Brian Grant	.25	.08
☐ 136	Chris Childs	.25	.08
☐ 137	Rony Seikaly	.25	.08
☐ 138	Pete Chilcutt	.25	.08
☐ 139	Anfernee Hardaway	.75	.30
☐ 140	Bryon Russell	.25	.08
☐ 141	Tim Thomas	.50	.20
☐ 142	Erick Dampier	.50	.20
☐ 143	Charles Barkley	1.00	.40
☐ 144	Mark Jackson	.50	.20
☐ 145	Bryant Reeves	.25	.08
☐ 146	Tyrone Hill	.25	.08
☐ 147	Rasheed Wallace	.75	.30
☐ 148	Tim Duncan	1.25	.50
☐ 149	Steve Smith	.50	.20
☐ 150	Alonzo Mourning	.50	.20
☐ 151	Danny Fortson	.25	.08
☐ 152	Aaron Williams	.25	.08
☐ 153	Andrew DeClercq	.25	.08
☐ 154	Elden Campbell	.25	.08
☐ 155	Don Reid	.25	.08
☐ 156	Rik Smits	.50	.20
☐ 157	Adonal Foyle	.25	.08
☐ 158	Muggsy Bogues	.50	.20
☐ 159	Chris Mullin	.75	.30
☐ 160	Randy Brown	.25	.08
☐ 161	Kenny Anderson	.50	.20
☐ 162	Tariq Abdul-Wahad	.25	.08
☐ 163	P.J. Brown	.25	.08
☐ 164	Jayson Williams	.25	.08
☐ 165	Grant Hill	.75	.30
☐ 166	Clifford Robinson	.25	.08
☐ 167	Damon Stoudamire	.50	.20
☐ 168	Aaron McKie	.50	.20
☐ 169	Erick Strickland	.25	.08
☐ 170	Kobe Bryant	3.00	1.25
☐ 171	Karl Malone	.75	.30
☐ 172	Eric Piatkowski	.25	.08
☐ 173	Rodrick Rhodes	.25	.08
☐ 174	Sean Elliott	.50	.20
☐ 175	John Wallace	.25	.08
☐ 176	Derek Fisher	.75	.30
☐ 177	Maurice Taylor	.40	.15
☐ 178	Wesley Person	.25	.08
☐ 179	Jamal Mashburn	.50	.20
☐ 180	Patrick Ewing	.75	.30
☐ 181	Howard Eisley	.25	.08
☐ 182	Michael Finley	.50	.20
☐ 183	Juwan Howard	.50	.20
☐ 184	Matt Maloney	.25	.08
☐ 185	Glenn Robinson	.50	.20
☐ 186	Zydrunas Ilgauskas	.50	.20
☐ 187	Dana Barros	.25	.08
☐ 188	Stacey Augmon	.25	.08
☐ 189	Bobby Phills	.25	.08
☐ 190	Kerry Kittles	.25	.08
☐ 191	Vin Baker	.50	.20
☐ 192	Stephon Marbury	.75	.30
☐ 193	Peja Stojakovic RC	1.50	.60
☐ 194	Michael Olowokandi	.60	.25
☐ 195	Mike Bibby	2.00	.75
☐ 196	Raef LaFrentz	.60	.25
☐ 197	Antawn Jamison	2.00	.75
☐ 198	Vince Carter	5.00	2.00
☐ 199	Robert Traylor	.25	.08
☐ 200	Jason Williams	1.50	.60
☐ 201	Larry Hughes	1.25	.50
☐ 202	Dirk Nowitzki	4.00	1.50
☐ 203	Paul Pierce	2.00	.75
☐ 204	Bonzi Wells	1.50	.60
☐ 205	Michael Doleac	.50	.20
☐ 206	Keon Clark	.75	.30
☐ 207	Michael Dickerson	.75	.30
☐ 208	Matt Harpring	.75	.30
☐ 209	Bryce Drew	.50	.20
☐ 210	Pat Garrity	.25	.08
☐ 211	Roshown McLeod	.75	.30
☐ 212	Ricky Davis	.75	.30
☐ 213	Brian Skinner	.50	.20
☐ 214	Tyronn Lue RC	.50	.20
☐ 215	Felipe Lopez RC	.50	.20
☐ 216	Al Harrington RC	1.00	.40
☐ 217	Sam Jacobson RC	.25	.08
☐ 218	Vladimir Stepania RC	.25	.08
☐ 219	Corey Benjamin RC	.75	.30
☐ 220	Nazr Mohammed RC	.50	.20
☐ 221	Tom Gugliotta TRAN	.25	.08
☐ 222	Derrick Coleman TRAN	.25	.08
☐ 223	Mitch Richmond TRAN	.50	.20
☐ 224	John Starks TRAN	.25	.08
☐ 225	Antonio McDyess TRAN	.50	.20
☐ 226	Joe Smith TRAN	.25	.08
☐ 227	Bobby Jackson TRAN	.25	.08
☐ 228	Luc Longley TRAN	.25	.08
☐ 229	Isaac Austin TRAN	.25	.08
☐ 230	Chris Webber TRAN	.50	.20
☐ 231	Chauncey Billups TRAN	.50	.20
☐ 232	Sam Perkins TRAN	.25	.08
☐ 233	Loy Vaught TRAN	.25	.08
☐ 234	Antonio Daniels TRAN	.25	.08
☐ 235	Brent Barry TRAN	.25	.08
☐ 236	Latrell Sprewell TRAN	.75	.30
☐ 237	Vlade Divac TRAN	.50	.20
☐ 238	Marcus Camby TRAN	.50	.20
☐ 239	Charles Oakley TRAN	.25	.08
☐ 240	Scottie Pippen TRAN	.50	.20

1999-00 Stadium Club

☐	COMPLETE SET (201)	80.00	40.00
☐	COMPLETE SET w/o RC (175)	40.00	20.00
☐	COMMON CARD (1-175)	.20	.07
☐	COMMON ROOKIE (176-201)	.60	.25
☐ 1	Allen Iverson	1.25	.50
☐ 2	Chris Crawford	.20	.07

❏ 3 Chris Webber	.60	.25
❏ 4 Antawn Jamison	1.00	.40
❏ 5 Karl Malone	.60	.25
❏ 6 Sam Cassell	.60	.25
❏ 7 Kerry Kittles	.20	.07
❏ 8 Tim Thomas	.40	.15
❏ 9 Chauncey Billups	.40	.15
❏ 10 Shawn Bradley	.20	.07
❏ 11 Alan Henderson	.20	.07
❏ 12 David Wesley	.20	.07
❏ 13 Glenn Robinson	.60	.25
❏ 14 Mitch Richmond	.40	.15
❏ 15 Luc Longley	.20	.07
❏ 16 Shareef Abdur-Rahim	.60	.25
❏ 17 Christian Laettner	.40	.15
❏ 18 Anthony Mason	.40	.15
❏ 19 Randy Brown	.20	.07
❏ 20 Charles Barkley	.75	.30
❏ 21 Bob Sura	.20	.07
❏ 22 Bobby Jackson	.40	.15
❏ 23 Arvydas Sabonis	.40	.15
❏ 24 Tracy Murray	.20	.07
❏ 25 Matt Harpring	.60	.25
❏ 26 Shawn Kemp	.40	.15
❏ 27 Travis Best	.20	.07
❏ 28 Ruben Patterson	.40	.15
❏ 29 Mike Bibby	.60	.25
❏ 30 Vlade Divac	.40	.15
❏ 31 Tyrone Hill	.20	.07
❏ 32 David Robinson	.60	.25
❏ 33 Keith Van Horn	.60	.25
❏ 34 Alvin Williams	.20	.07
❏ 35 Juwan Howard	.40	.15
❏ 36 Shaquille O'Neal	1.50	.60
❏ 37 Dale Davis	.20	.07
❏ 38 Alonzo Mourning	.40	.15
❏ 39 Michael Olowokandi	.40	.15
❏ 40 Jason Caffey	.20	.07
❏ 41 Andrew DeClercq	.20	.07
❏ 42 Jud Buechler	.20	.07
❏ 43 Toni Kukoc	.40	.15
❏ 44 Dikembe Mutombo	.40	.15
❏ 45 Steve Nash	.60	.25
❏ 46 Eddie Jones	.60	.25
❏ 47 Reggie Miller	.60	.25
❏ 48 Rick Fox	.40	.15
❏ 49 Larry Hughes	.60	.25
❏ 50 Tim Duncan	1.25	.50
❏ 51 Jerome Williams	.20	.07
❏ 52 Rod Strickland	.20	.07
❏ 53 Anthony Peeler	.20	.07
❏ 54 Greg Ostertag	.20	.07
❏ 55 Patrick Ewing	.60	.25
❏ 56 Grant Hill	.60	.25
❏ 57 Derrick Coleman	.40	.15
❏ 58 Raef LaFrentz	.40	.15
❏ 59 Mark Bryant	.20	.07
❏ 60 Rik Smits	.40	.15
❏ 61 Latrell Sprewell	.60	.25
❏ 62 John Starks	.40	.15
❏ 63 Brevin Knight	.20	.07
❏ 64 Cuttino Mobley	.60	.25
❏ 65 Clarence Weatherspoon	.20	.07
❏ 66 Marcus Camby	.40	.15
❏ 67 Stephon Marbury	.60	.25
❏ 68 Tom Gugliotta	.20	.07
❏ 69 Vince Carter	1.50	.60
❏ 70 Vladimir Stepania	.20	.07
❏ 71 Chris Mullin	.60	.25
❏ 72 Tyrone Nesby RC	.20	.07
❏ 73 Komel David RC	.20	.07
❏ 74 Elden Campbell	.20	.07
❏ 75 Lindsey Hunter	.20	.07
❏ 76 Chris Childs	.20	.07
❏ 77 Ervin Johnson	.20	.07
❏ 78 Rasheed Wallace	.60	.25
❏ 79 Jeff Hornacek	.40	.15
❏ 80 Matt Geiger	.20	.07
❏ 81 Antoine Walker	.60	.25
❏ 82 Jason Williams	.60	.25
❏ 83 Robert Horry	.40	.15
❏ 84 Jaren Jackson	.20	.07
❏ 85 Kendall Gill	.40	.15
❏ 86 Dan Majerle	.40	.15
❏ 87 Bobby Phills	.20	.07
❏ 88 Eric Piatkowski	.40	.15
❏ 89 Robert Traylor	.20	.07
❏ 90 Cory Carr	.20	.07
❏ 91 P.J. Brown	.20	.07
❏ 92 Terrell Brandon	.40	.15
❏ 93 Corliss Williamson	.40	.15
❏ 94 Bryant Reeves	.20	.07
❏ 95 Larry Johnson	.40	.15
❏ 96 Keith Closs	.20	.07
❏ 97 Gary Trent	.20	.07
❏ 98 Walter McCarty	.20	.07
❏ 99 Wesley Person	.20	.07
❏ 100 Chris Mills	.20	.07
❏ 101 Glen Rice	.40	.15
❏ 102 Peja Stojakovic	.75	.30
❏ 103 Jason Kidd	1.00	.40
❏ 104 Dirk Nowitzki	1.25	.50
❏ 105 Bryon Russell	.20	.07
❏ 106 Vin Baker	.40	.15
❏ 107 Darrell Armstrong	.20	.07
❏ 108 Eric Snow	.40	.15
❏ 109 Hakeem Olajuwon	.60	.25
❏ 110 Tracy McGrady	1.50	.60
❏ 111 Kenny Anderson	.40	.15
❏ 112 Jalen Rose	.60	.25
❏ 113 Greg Anthony	.20	.07
❏ 114 Tim Hardaway	.40	.15
❏ 115 Doug Christie	.40	.15
❏ 116 Allan Houston	.40	.15
❏ 117 Kobe Bryant	2.50	1.00
❏ 118 Kevin Garnett	1.25	.50
❏ 119 Vitaly Potapenko	.20	.07
❏ 120 Steve Kerr	.40	.15
❏ 121 Nick Van Exel	.60	.25
❏ 122 Jerry Stackhouse	.60	.25
❏ 123 Derek Fisher	.60	.25
❏ 124 Donyell Marshall	.40	.15
❏ 125 Mark Jackson	.40	.15
❏ 126 Ray Allen	.60	.25
❏ 127 Avery Johnson	.20	.07
❏ 128 Michael Doleac	.20	.07
❏ 129 Charles Oakley	.20	.07
❏ 130 Gary Payton	.60	.25
❏ 131 Theo Ratliff	.40	.15
❏ 132 Cedric Ceballos	.20	.07
❏ 133 Paul Pierce	.60	.25
❏ 134 Michael Finley	.60	.25
❏ 135 Malik Sealy	.20	.07
❏ 136 Brian Grant	.40	.15
❏ 137 John Stockton	.60	.25
❏ 138 Chris Whitney	.20	.07
❏ 139 Maurice Taylor	.40	.15
❏ 140 Antonio McDyess	.40	.15
❏ 141 Adrian Griffin RC	1.00	.40
❏ 142 Vernon Maxwell	.20	.07
❏ 143 Jamal Mashburn	.40	.15
❏ 144 Jayson Williams	.20	.07
❏ 145 Joe Smith	.40	.15
❏ 146 Clifford Robinson	.20	.07
❏ 147 Mario Elie	.20	.07
❏ 148 Damon Stoudamire	.40	.15
❏ 149 Felipe Lopez	.20	.07
❏ 150 Rex Chapman	.20	.07
❏ 151 Antonio Davis TRAN	.20	.07
❏ 152 Mookie Blaylock TRAN	.20	.07
❏ 153 Ron Mercer TRAN	.40	.15
❏ 154 Horace Grant TRAN	.40	.15
❏ 155 Steve Smith TRAN	.40	.15
❏ 156 Isaiah Rider TRAN	.20	.07
❏ 157 Tariq Abdul-Wahad TRAN	.20	.07
❏ 158 Michael Dickerson TRAN	.40	.15
❏ 159 Nick Anderson TRAN	.20	.07
❏ 160 Jim Jackson TRAN	.40	.15
❏ 161 Hersey Hawkins TRAN	.40	.15
❏ 162 Brent Barry TRAN	.20	.07
❏ 163 Shandon Anderson TRAN	.20	.07
❏ 164 Scottie Pippen TRAN	1.00	.40
❏ 165 Isaac Austin TRAN	.20	.07
❏ 166 Anfernee Hardaway TRAN	.60	.25
❏ 167 Natalie Williams USA	2.50	1.00
❏ 168 Teresa Edwards USA	2.00	.75
❏ 169 Yolanda Griffith USA	2.50	1.00
❏ 170 Nikki McCray USA	1.25	.50
❏ 171 Katie Smith USA	1.50	.60
❏ 172 Chamique Holdsclaw USA	8.00	3.00
❏ 173 Dawn Staley USA	2.00	.75
❏ 174 Ruthie Bolton-Holifield USA	1.25	.50
❏ 175 Lisa Leslie USA	2.00	.75
❏ 176 Elton Brand RC	4.00	1.50
❏ 177 Steve Francis RC	4.00	1.50
❏ 178 Baron Davis RC	5.00	2.00
❏ 179 Lamar Odom RC	3.00	1.25
❏ 180 Jonathan Bender RC	3.00	1.25
❏ 181 Wally Szczerbiak RC	3.00	1.25
❏ 182 Richard Hamilton RC	3.00	1.25
❏ 183 Andre Miller RC	3.00	1.25
❏ 184 Shawn Marion RC	4.00	1.50
❏ 185 Jason Terry RC	2.00	.75
❏ 186 Trajan Langdon RC	1.25	.50
❏ 187 A.Radojevic RC	.60	.25
❏ 188 Corey Maggette RC	3.00	1.25
❏ 189 William Avery RC	1.25	.50
❏ 190 DeMarco Johnson RC	.75	.30
❏ 191 Ron Artest RC	2.00	.75
❏ 192 Cal Bowdler RC	1.00	.40
❏ 193 James Posey RC	2.00	.75
❏ 194 Quincy Lewis RC	1.00	.40
❏ 195 Scott Padgett RC	1.00	.40
❏ 196 Jeff Foster RC	1.00	.40
❏ 197 Kenny Thomas RC	1.25	.50
❏ 198 Devean George RC	1.50	.60
❏ 199 Tim James RC	1.00	.40
❏ 200 Vonteego Cummings RC	1.25	.50
❏ 201 Jumaine Jones RC	1.25	.50

2000-01 Stadium Club

❏ COMPLETE SET (175)	60.00	30.00
❏ COMPLETE SET w/o RC (150)	25.00	12.50
❏ COMMON CARD (1-150)	.20	.07
❏ COMMON ROOKIE (151-175)	1.00	.40
❏ 1 Baron Davis	.60	.25
❏ 2 Adrian Griffin	.20	.07
❏ 3 Dikembe Mutombo	.40	.15
❏ 4 Andre Miller	.40	.15
❏ 5 Kenny Anderson	.40	.15
❏ 6 Keon Clark	.40	.15
❏ 7 Larry Hughes	.40	.15
❏ 8 Ruben Patterson	.20	.07
❏ 9 Shandon Anderson	.20	.07
❏ 10 Reggie Miller	.60	.25
❏ 11 Lamar Odom	.60	.25
❏ 12 John Stockton	.60	.25
❏ 13 Rod Strickland	.20	.07
❏ 14 Michael Dickerson	.40	.15
❏ 15 Quincy Lewis	.20	.07
❏ 16 Vin Baker	.40	.15
❏ 17 Vince Carter	1.50	.60

#	Player		
18	Avery Johnson	.20	.07
19	Michael Finley	.60	.25
20	Eric Snow	.40	.15
21	Kevin Garnett	1.25	.50
22	Rodney Rogers	.20	.07
23	Bonzi Wells	.40	.15
24	Jason Kidd	1.00	.40
25	Toni Kukoc	.40	.15
26	Darrell Armstrong	.20	.07
27	Larry Johnson	.40	.15
28	Kendall Gill	.20	.07
29	Wally Szczerbiak	.40	.15
30	Tim Thomas	.40	.15
31	Dan Majerle	.40	.15
32	Karl Malone	.60	.25
33	Juwan Howard	.40	.15
34	Kobe Bryant	2.50	1.00
35	Bryant Reeves	.20	.07
36	Cuttino Mobley	.40	.15
37	Mookie Blaylock	.20	.07
38	Jerome Williams	.20	.07
39	James Posey	.40	.15
40	Shawn Bradley	.20	.07
41	Tim Hardaway	.40	.15
42	Theo Ratliff	.40	.15
43	Damon Stoudamire	.40	.15
44	Derrick Coleman	.20	.07
45	Ron Artest	.40	.15
46	Antoine Walker	.60	.25
47	Jason Terry	.60	.25
48	Antonio McDyess	.40	.15
49	Jonathan Bender	.40	.15
50	Shaquille O'Neal	1.50	.60
51	Anthony Carter	.40	.15
52	Ray Allen	.60	.25
53	Joe Smith	.40	.15
54	Marcus Camby	.40	.15
55	Keith Van Horn	.60	.25
56	Charlie Ward	.20	.07
57	John Amaechi	.20	.07
58	Tom Gugliotta	.20	.07
59	Allan Houston	.40	.15
60	Anfernee Hardaway	.60	.25
61	Scottie Pippen	1.00	.40
62	Jason Williams	.40	.15
63	Steve Smith	.40	.15
64	David Robinson	.60	.25
65	Gary Payton	.60	.25
66	Robert Horry	.40	.15
67	Greg Ostertag	.20	.07
68	Mike Bibby	.60	.25
69	Tim Duncan	1.25	.50
70	Richard Hamilton	.40	.15
71	Bryon Russell	.20	.07
72	Charles Oakley	.40	.15
73	Rashard Lewis	.40	.15
74	Chris Webber	.60	.25
75	Arvydas Sabonis	.40	.15
76	Allen Iverson	1.25	.50
77	Bo Outlaw	.20	.07
78	Elden Campbell	.20	.07
79	Dirk Nowitzki	1.00	.40
80	Elton Brand	.60	.25
81	Brevin Knight	.20	.07
82	David Wesley	.20	.07
83	Raef LaFrentz	.40	.15
84	Antawn Jamison	.60	.25
85	Hakeem Olajuwon	.60	.25
86	Jamie Feick	.20	.07
87	Jalen Rose	.60	.25
88	Michael Olowokandi	.20	.07
89	Rick Fox	.40	.15
90	Austin Croshere	.40	.15
91	Glenn Robinson	.60	.25
92	Stephon Marbury	.60	.25
93	Clifford Robinson	.20	.07
94	Derek Fisher	.60	.25
95	Vlade Divac	.40	.15
96	Jim Jackson	.20	.07
97	Paul Pierce	.60	.25
98	Corey Benjamin	.20	.07
99	Lamond Murray	.20	.07
100	Steve Francis	.60	.25
101	Mitch Richmond	.40	.15
102	Othella Harrington	.20	.07
103	Nick Anderson	.20	.07

#	Player		
104	Antonio Davis	.20	.07
105	Ervin Johnson	.20	.07
106	Rasheed Wallace	.60	.25
107	Shawn Marion	.60	.25
108	Latrell Sprewell	.60	.25
109	Terrell Brandon	.40	.15
110	Sam Cassell	.60	.25
111	Shareef Abdur-Rahim	.60	.25
112	Travis Best	.20	.07
113	Tyrone Nesby	.20	.07
114	Alan Henderson	.20	.07
115	Vonteego Cummings	.20	.07
116	Kelvin Cato	.20	.07
117	Jerry Stackhouse	.60	.25
118	Nick Van Exel	.60	.25
119	Corliss Williamson TRAN	.20	.07
120	Doug Christie TRAN	.20	.07
121	Horace Grant TRAN	.40	.15
122	Glen Rice TRAN	.60	.25
123	Patrick Ewing TRAN	.60	.25
124	Dale Davis TRAN	.20	.07
125	Brian Grant TRAN	.40	.15
126	Shawn Kemp TRAN	.20	.07
127	Cedric Ceballos TRAN	.40	.15
128	Christian Laettner TRAN	.40	.15
129	Lindsey Hunter TRAN	.20	.07
130	Donyell Marshall TRAN	.40	.15
131	Robert Pack TRAN	.20	.07
132	Danny Fortson TRAN	.20	.07
133	Howard Eisley TRAN	.20	.07
134	Andrew DeClercq TRAN	.20	.07
135	Mark Jackson TRAN	.20	.07
136	Grant Hill TRAN	.40	.15
137	Tracy McGrady TRAN	1.50	.60
138	Maurice Taylor TRAN	.20	.07
139	Derek Anderson TRAN	.20	.07
140	Corey Maggette TRAN	.40	.15
141	Jermaine O'Neal TRAN	.60	.25
142	Ben Wallace TRAN	.60	.25
143	Ron Mercer TRAN	.20	.07
144	John Starks TRAN	.60	.25
145	Erick Strickland TRAN	.20	.07
146	Isaiah Rider TRAN	.40	.15
147	Eddie Jones TRAN	.40	.15
148	Anthony Mason TRAN	.20	.07
149	P.J. Brown TRAN	.20	.07
150	Jamal Mashburn TRAN	.40	.15
151	Kenyon Martin TRAN	4.00	1.50
152	Stromile Swift RC	2.00	.75
153	Darius Miles RC	3.00	1.25
154	Marcus Fizer RC	1.00	.40
155	Mike Miller RC	3.00	1.25
156	DerMarr Johnson RC	1.00	.40
157	Chris Mihm RC	1.00	.40
158	Jamal Crawford RC	1.25	.50
159	Joel Przybilla RC	1.00	.40
160	Keyon Dooling RC	1.00	.40
161	Jerome Moiso RC	1.00	.40
162	Etan Thomas RC	1.00	.40
163	Courtney Alexander RC	1.25	.50
164	Mateen Cleaves RC	1.00	.40
165	Jason Collier RC	1.00	.40
166	Desmond Mason RC	1.00	.40
167	Quentin Richardson RC	3.00	1.25
168	Jamaal Magloire RC	1.00	.40
169	Speedy Claxton RC	1.00	.40
170	Morris Peterson RC	2.00	.75
171	Donnell Harvey RC	1.00	.40
172	DeShawn Stevenson RC	1.00	.40
173	Mamadou N'Diaye RC	1.00	.40
174	Erick Barkley RC	1.00	.40
175	Mark Madsen RC	1.00	.40

2001-02 Stadium Club

	COMP.SET w/o SP's (101)	25.00	12.50
	COMMON CARD (1-134)	.20	.07
	COMMON ROOKIE (101-133)	2.00	.75
1	Dikembe Mutombo	.40	.15
2	Clifford Robinson	.20	.07
3	Bonzi Wells	.40	.15
4	Peja Stojakovic	.60	.25
5	Gary Payton	.60	.25
6	Morris Peterson	.40	.15
7	Patrick Ewing	.60	.25
8	Terrell Brandon	.40	.15
9	Tim Thomas	.40	.15

#	Player		
10	Kobe Bryant	2.50	1.00
11	Hakeem Olajuwon	.60	.25
12	Marc Jackson	.40	.15
13	Wang Zhizhi	.60	.25
14	Andre Miller	.40	.15
15	Elton Brand	.60	.25
16	Eddie Robinson	.40	.15
17	Jason Terry	.60	.25
18	Allan Houston	.40	.15
19	Grant Hill	.60	.25
20	Tim Duncan	1.25	.50
21	Kevin Garnett	1.25	.50
22	Jahidi White	.20	.07
23	Michael Dickerson	.40	.15
24	Karl Malone	.60	.25
25	Chris Webber	.60	.25
26	Scottie Pippen	1.00	.40
27	Latrell Sprewell	.60	.25
28	Keith Van Horn	.60	.25
29	Ray Allen	.60	.25
30	Alonzo Mourning	.40	.15
31	Lamar Odom	.60	.25
32	Jalen Rose	.60	.25
33	Ben Wallace	.60	.25
34	Shaquille O'Neal	1.50	.60
35	Antonio McDyess	.40	.15
36	Dirk Nowitzki	1.00	.40
37	Marcus Fizer	.40	.15
38	Jamal Mashburn	.40	.15
39	Paul Pierce	.60	.25
40	Derrick Johnson	.40	.15
41	Steve Nash	.60	.25
42	Jerry Stackhouse	.60	.25
43	Larry Hughes	.40	.15
44	Cuttino Mobley	.40	.15
45	Horace Grant	.40	.15
46	Eddie Jones	.60	.25
47	Wally Szczerbiak	.40	.15
48	Marcus Camby	.40	.15
49	Jamal Crawford	.40	.15
50	Vince Carter	1.50	.60
51	Donyell Marshall	.40	.15
52	Shareef Abdur-Rahim	.60	.25
53	Courtney Alexander	.40	.15
54	Kenny Anderson	.40	.15
55	Ron Mercer	.40	.15
56	Lamond Murray	.20	.07
57	Michael Finley	.60	.25
58	Raef LaFrentz	.40	.15
59	Reggie Miller	.60	.25
60	Steve Francis	.60	.25
61	Rick Fox	.40	.15
62	Tim Hardaway	.40	.15
63	Glenn Robinson	.60	.25
64	LaPhonso Ellis	.20	.07
65	Kenyon Martin	.60	.25
66	Jason Williams	.40	.15
67	Derek Anderson	.40	.15
68	Eric Snow	.40	.15
69	Darius Miles	.60	.25
70	Antawn Jamison	.60	.25
71	Mateen Cleaves	.40	.15
72	Jason Kidd	1.00	.40
73	Rasheed Wallace	.60	.25
74	Chris Porter	.40	.15
75	Tracy McGrady	1.50	.60
76	Aaron McKie	.40	.15
77	Baron Davis	.60	.25

78	Toni Kukoc	.40	.15
79	Antoine Walker	.60	.25
80	Shawn Marion	.60	.25
81	Mike Miller	.60	.25
82	Stephon Marbury	.60	.25
83	Glen Rice	.40	.15
84	David Robinson	.60	.25
85	Rashard Lewis	.40	.15
86	John Stockton	.60	.25
87	Stromile Swift	.40	.15
88	Richard Hamilton	.40	.15
89	Desmond Mason	.40	.15
90	Brian Grant	.40	.15
91	Keyon Dooling	.40	.15
92	Jermaine O'Neal	.60	.25
93	Nick Van Exel	.60	.25
94	Tom Gugliotta	.20	.07
95	Darrell Armstrong	.20	.07
96	Sam Cassell	.60	.25
97	Mike Bibby	.60	.25
98	DeShawn Stevenson	.40	.15
99	Antonio Davis	.20	.07
100	Allen Iverson	1.25	.50
101	Kwame Brown RC	5.00	2.00
102	Tyson Chandler RC	6.00	2.50
103	Pau Gasol RC	6.00	2.50
104	Eddy Curry RC	6.00	2.50
105	Jason Richardson RC	8.00	3.00
106	Shane Battier RC	3.00	1.25
107	Eddie Griffin RC	3.00	1.25
108	DeSagana Diop RC	2.00	.75
109	Rodney White RC	2.50	1.00
110	Joe Johnson RC	6.00	2.50
111	Kedrick Brown RC	2.00	.75
112	Vladimir Radmanovic RC	2.50	1.00
113	Richard Jefferson RC	6.00	2.50
114	Troy Murphy RC	4.00	1.50
115	Steven Hunter RC	2.00	.75
116	Kirk Haston RC	2.00	.75
117	Michael Bradley RC	2.00	.75
118	Jason Collins RC	2.50	1.00
119	Zach Randolph RC	6.00	2.50
120	Brendan Haywood RC	2.50	1.00
121	Joseph Forte RC	2.50	1.00
122	Jeryl Sasser RC	2.00	.75
123	Brandon Armstrong RC	2.50	1.00
124	Gerald Wallace RC	4.00	1.50
125	Samuel Dalembert RC	2.00	.75
126	Jamaal Tinsley RC	3.00	1.25
127	Tony Parker RC	8.00	3.00
128	Trenton Hassell RC	4.00	1.50
129	Gilbert Arenas RC	8.00	3.00
130	Omar Cook RC	2.00	.75
131	Jeff Trepagnier RC	2.00	.75
132	Loren Woods RC	2.00	.75
133	Terence Morris RC	2.00	.75
134	Michael Jordan	15.00	6.00

2002-03 Stadium Club

❑	COMPLETE SET (133)	100.00	50.00
❑	COMP.SET w/o SP's (100)	25.00	10.00
❑	COMMON CARD (1-100)	.20	.08
❑	COMMON ROOKIE (101-133)	2.00	.75
❑ 1	Shaquille O'Neal	1.50	.60
❑ 2	Pau Gasol	.60	.25
❑ 3	Allen Iverson	1.25	.50
❑ 4	Bonzi Wells	.40	.15
❑ 5	Mike Bibby	.60	.25

6	Rashard Lewis	.40	.15
7	Aaron McKie	.40	.15
8	Shane Battier	.60	.25
9	Kenyon Martin	.60	.25
10	Tim Duncan	1.25	.50
11	Richard Jefferson	.40	.15
12	Jalen Rose	.60	.25
13	Antoine Walker	.60	.25
14	Michael Finley	.60	.25
15	Clifford Robinson	.20	.08
16	Antawn Jamison	.60	.25
17	Reggie Miller	.60	.25
18	Elton Brand	.60	.25
19	Robert Horry	.40	.15
20	Kevin Garnett	1.25	.50
21	Baron Davis	.60	.25
22	Latrell Sprewell	.60	.25
23	Glenn Robinson	.60	.25
24	Wally Szczerbiak	.40	.15
25	Tracy McGrady	1.50	.60
26	Stephon Marbury	.60	.25
27	Rasheed Wallace	.60	.25
28	Doug Christie	.40	.15
29	Desmond Mason	.40	.15
30	Vince Carter	1.50	.60
31	Andrei Kirilenko	.60	.25
32	Richard Hamilton	.40	.15
33	Jamaal Tinsley	.60	.25
34	Steve Francis	.60	.25
35	Ben Wallace	.60	.25
36	Juwan Howard	.40	.15
37	Dirk Nowitzki	1.00	.40
38	Andre Miller	.40	.15
39	Elden Campbell	.20	.08
40	Paul Pierce	.60	.25
41	Shareef Abdur-Rahim	.60	.25
42	John Stockton	.60	.25
43	Gary Payton	.60	.25
44	David Robinson	.60	.25
45	Scottie Pippen	1.00	.40
46	Morris Peterson	.40	.15
47	Mike Miller	.60	.25
48	Marcus Camby	.40	.15
49	Joe Smith	.40	.15
50	Kobe Bryant	2.50	1.00
51	Alonzo Mourning	.40	.15
52	Ray Allen	.60	.25
53	Keith Van Horn	.60	.25
54	Grant Hill	.60	.25
55	Dikembe Mutombo	.40	.15
56	Shawn Marion	.60	.25
57	Peja Stojakovic	.60	.25
58	Tony Parker	.60	.25
59	Keon Clark	.40	.15
60	Brendan Haywood	.40	.15
61	Derek Anderson	.40	.15
62	Allan Houston	.40	.15
63	Brian Grant	.40	.15
64	Lamar Odom	.60	.25
65	Jermaine O'Neal	.60	.25
66	Kenny Anderson	.40	.15
67	Dermarr Johnson	.20	.08
68	Lamond Murray	.20	.08
69	Jason Richardson	.60	.25
70	Rodney Rogers	.20	.08
71	Rick Fox	.40	.15
72	Tim Thomas	.40	.15
73	Darrell Armstrong	.20	.08
74	Anfernee Hardaway	.60	.25
75	Chris Webber	.60	.25
76	Derrick Coleman	.20	.08
77	Karl Malone	.60	.25
78	Antonio Davis	.20	.08
79	Jason Terry	.60	.25
80	Wang Zhizhi	.60	.25
81	Steve Nash	.60	.25
82	Eddy Curry UER	.60	.25
83	Tim Hardaway	.40	.15
84	Corliss Williamson	.40	.15
85	Eddie Griffin	.40	.15
86	Darius Miles	.60	.25
87	Jason Williams	.40	.15
88	Sam Cassell	.60	.25
89	Kwame Brown	.60	.25
90	Jason Kidd	1.00	.40
91	Jamal Mashburn	.40	.15

92	Jamaal Magloire	.20	.08
93	Tyson Chandler	.60	.25
94	Jumaine Jones	.40	.15
95	Antonio McDyess	.40	.15
96	Jerry Stackhouse	.60	.25
97	Gilbert Arenas	.60	.25
98	Cuttino Mobley	.40	.15
99	Eddie Jones	.60	.25
100	Michael Jordan	6.00	2.50
101	Yao Ming RC	12.00	5.00
102	Jay Williams RC	2.50	1.00
103	Mike Dunleavy RC	4.00	1.50
104	Drew Gooden RC	4.00	1.50
105	Nikoloz Tskitishvili RC	2.00	.75
106	DaJuan Wagner RC	3.00	1.25
107	Nene Hilario RC	2.50	1.00
108	Chris Wilcox RC	2.50	1.00
109	Amare Stoudemire RC	10.00	4.00
110	Caron Butler RC	4.00	1.50
111	Jared Jeffries RC	2.00	.75
112	Melvin Ely RC	2.00	.75
113	Marcus Haislip RC	2.00	.75
114	Fred Jones RC	2.00	.75
115	Bostjan Nachbar RC	2.00	.75
116	Dan Dickau RC	2.00	.75
117	Juan Dixon RC	3.00	1.25
118	Dan Gadzuric RC	2.00	.75
119	Ryan Humphrey RC	2.00	.75
120	Kareem Rush RC	3.00	1.25
121	Qyntel Woods RC	2.00	.75
122	Casey Jacobsen RC	2.00	.75
123	Tayshaun Prince RC	2.50	1.00
124	Frank Williams RC	2.00	.75
125	John Salmons RC	2.00	.75
126	Chris Jefferies RC	2.00	.75
127	Sam Clancy RC	2.00	.75
128	Ronald Murray RC	3.00	1.25
129	Roger Mason RC	2.00	.75
130	Robert Archibald RC	2.00	.75
131	Vincent Yarbrough RC	2.00	.75
132	Darius Songaila RC	2.00	.75
133	Carlos Boozer RC	4.00	1.50

1999-00 Stadium Club Chrome

❑	COMPLETE SET (150)	80.00	30.00
❑	COMMON CARD (1-150)	.25	.08
❑	COMMON ROOKIE	.75	.30
❑ 1	Allen Iverson	1.50	.60
❑ 2	Chris Webber	.75	.30
❑ 3	Antawn Jamison	1.25	.30
❑ 4	Karl Malone	.75	.30
❑ 5	Sam Cassell	.75	.30
❑ 6	Kerry Kittles	.25	.08
❑ 7	Tim Thomas	.50	.20
❑ 8	Shawn Bradley	.25	.08
❑ 9	David Wesley	.25	.08
❑ 10	Glenn Robinson	.75	.30
❑ 11	Mitch Richmond	.50	.20
❑ 12	Shareef Abdur-Rahim	.75	.30
❑ 13	Christian Laettner	.50	.20
❑ 14	Anthony Mason	.50	.20
❑ 15	Randy Brown	.25	.08
❑ 16	Charles Barkley	1.00	.40
❑ 17	Bobby Jackson	.50	.20
❑ 18	Matt Harpring	.75	.30
❑ 19	Shawn Kemp	.50	.20
❑ 20	Ruben Patterson	.50	.20

21 Mike Bibby	.75	.30
22 Vlade Divac	.50	.20
23 David Robinson	.75	.30
24 Keith Van Horn	.75	.30
25 Juwan Howard	.50	.20
26 Shaquille O'Neal	2.00	.75
27 Alonzo Mourning	.50	.20
28 Michael Olowokandi	.50	.20
29 Andrew DeClercq	.25	.08
30 Toni Kukoc	.50	.20
31 Dikembe Mutombo	.50	.20
32 Steve Nash	.75	.30
33 Eddie Jones	.75	.30
34 Reggie Miller	.75	.30
35 Larry Hughes	.75	.30
36 Tim Duncan	1.50	.60
37 Jerome Williams	.25	.08
38 Rod Strickland	.25	.08
39 Patrick Ewing	.75	.30
40 Grant Hill	.75	.30
41 Derrick Coleman	.50	.20
42 Raef LaFrentz	.50	.20
43 Rik Smits	.50	.20
44 Latrell Sprewell	.75	.30
45 John Starks	.50	.20
46 Cuttino Mobley	.75	.30
47 Marcus Camby	.50	.20
48 Stephon Marbury	.75	.30
49 Tom Gugliotta	.25	.08
50 Vince Carter	2.00	.75
51 Chris Mullin	.75	.30
52 Tyrone Nesby RC	.25	.08
53 Elden Campbell	.25	.08
54 Lindsey Hunter	.25	.08
55 Rasheed Wallace	.75	.30
56 Jeff Hornacek	.50	.20
57 Matt Geiger	.25	.08
58 Antoine Walker	.75	.30
59 Jason Williams	.75	.30
60 Robert Horry	.50	.20
61 Kendall Gill	.25	.08
62 Dan Majerle	.25	.08
63 Robert Traylor	.25	.08
64 P.J. Brown	.25	.08
65 Terrell Brandon	.50	.20
66 Corliss Williamson	.25	.08
67 Bryant Reeves	.25	.08
68 Larry Johnson	.50	.20
69 Keith Closs	.25	.08
70 Walter McCarty	.25	.08
71 Wesley Person	.25	.08
72 Chris Mills	.25	.08
73 Glen Rice	.50	.20
74 Jason Kidd	1.25	.50
75 Dirk Nowitzki	1.50	.60
76 Bryon Russell	.25	.08
77 Vin Baker	.50	.20
78 Darrell Armstrong	.25	.08
79 Eric Snow	.50	.20
80 Hakeem Olajuwon	.75	.30
81 Tracy McGrady	2.00	.75
82 Kenny Anderson	.50	.20
83 Jalen Rose	.75	.30
84 Tim Hardaway	.50	.20
85 Doug Christie	.50	.20
86 Allan Houston	.50	.20
87 Kobe Bryant	3.00	1.25
88 Kevin Garnett	1.50	.60
89 Steve Kerr	.50	.20
90 Nick Van Exel	.75	.30
91 Jerry Stackhouse	.75	.30
92 Derek Fisher	.75	.30
93 Donyell Marshall	.50	.20
94 Mark Jackson	.50	.20
95 Ray Allen	.75	.30
96 Avery Johnson	.25	.08
97 Michael Doleac	.25	.08
98 Charles Oakley	.25	.08
99 Gary Payton	.75	.30
100 Theo Ratliff	.50	.20
101 Cedric Ceballos	.25	.08
102 Paul Pierce	.75	.30
103 Michael Finley	.75	.30
104 Brian Grant	.50	.20
105 John Stockton	.75	.30
106 Maurice Taylor	.50	.20

107 Antonio McDyess	.50	.20
108 Adrian Griffin RC	1.25	.50
109 Jamal Mashburn	.50	.20
110 Jayson Williams	.25	.08
111 Joe Smith	.25	.08
112 Clifford Robinson	.25	.08
113 Mario Elie	.25	.08
114 Damon Stoudamire	.50	.20
115 Felipe Lopez	.25	.08
116 Antonio Davis TRAN	.25	.08
117 Mookie Blaylock TRAN	.50	.20
118 Ron Mercer TRAN	.50	.20
119 Horace Grant TRAN	.50	.20
120 Steve Smith TRAN	.50	.20
121 Isaiah Rider TRAN	.25	.08
122 Tariq Abdul-Wahad TRAN	.50	.20
123 Michael Dickerson TRAN	.50	.20
124 Nick Anderson TRAN	.25	.08
125 Jim Jackson TRAN	.25	.08
126 Hersey Hawkins TRAN	.50	.20
127 Brent Barry TRAN	.25	.08
128 Shandon Anderson TRAN	.25	.08
129 Scottie Pippen TRAN	1.25	.50
130 Isaac Austin TRAN	.25	.08
131 Anfernee Hardaway TRAN	1.25	.50
132 Elton Brand RC	5.00	2.00
133 Steve Francis RC	5.00	2.00
134 Baron Davis RC	6.00	2.50
135 Lamar Odom RC	4.00	1.50
136 Jonathan Bender RC	4.00	1.50
137 Wally Szczerbiak RC	4.00	1.50
138 Richard Hamilton RC	4.00	1.50
139 Andre Miller RC	4.00	1.50
140 Shawn Marion RC	5.00	2.00
141 Jason Terry RC	3.00	1.25
142 Trajan Langdon RC	1.50	.60
143 A.Radojevic RC	.75	.30
144 Corey Maggette RC	4.00	1.50
145 William Avery RC	1.50	.60
146 Ron Artest RC	2.50	1.00
147 Cal Bowdler RC	1.25	.50
148 James Posey RC	2.50	1.00
149 Quincy Lewis RC	1.25	.50
150 Scott Padgett RC	1.25	.50

1983-84 Star

BOBBY JONES
Philadelphia 76ers

COMPLETE SET (275)	1500.00	1000.00
COMP.76ERS (1-12)	100.00	40.00
COMP.LAKERS (13-25)	500.00	300.00
COMP.CELTICS (26-37)	425.00	300.00
COMP.BUCKS (38-48)	50.00	25.00
COMP.MAVS (49-60)	425.00	200.00
COMP.KNICKS (61-72)	25.00	12.50
COMP.ROCKETS (73-84)	20.00	8.00
COMP.PISTONS (85-96)	165.00	65.00
COMP.BLAZERS (97-108)	225.00	150.00
COMP.SUNS (109-120)	20.00	8.00
COMP.CLIPPERS (121-132)	40.00	20.00
COMP.JAZZ (133-144)	20.00	8.00
COMP.NETS (145-156)	25.00	10.00
COMP.PACERS (157-168)	18.00	8.00
COMP.BULLS (169-180)	30.00	12.50
COMP.NUGGETS (181-192)	30.00	15.00
COMP.SONICS (193-203)	35.00	20.00
COMP.BULLETS (204-215)	25.00	10.00
COMP.KINGS (216-227)	20.00	8.00
COMP.CAVS (228-240)	25.00	10.00
COMP.SPURS (241-251)	25.00	10.00

COMP.WARRIORS (252-262)	20.00	8.00
COMP.HAWKS (263-275)	195.00	100.00
COMMON SP (1-25/38-48)	4.00	1.50
COMMON SP (26-37)	8.00	4.00
COMMON CARD (61-275)	2.00	.75
COMMON SP (49-60) !	18.00	9.00
*OPENED TEAM SETS: .75X to 1.0X		
1 Julius Erving SP !	55.00	25.00
2 Maurice Cheeks SP	10.00	5.00
3 Franklin Edwards	4.00	1.50
4 Marc Iavaroni	5.00	2.00
5 Clemon Johnson	4.00	1.50
6 Bobby Jones SP	10.00	5.00
7 Moses Malone SP	18.00	9.00
8 Leo Rautins	4.00	1.50
9 Clint Richardson	4.00	1.50
10 Sedale Threatt XRC SP	8.00	3.00
11 Andrew Toney XRC SP	12.00	5.00
12 Sam Williams	4.00	1.50
13 Magic Johnson SP !	70.00	35.00
14 Kareem Abdul-Jabbar SP	35.00	15.00
15 Michael Cooper SP	12.00	5.00
16 Calvin Garrett	4.00	1.50
17 Mitch Kupchak	5.00	2.00
18 Bob McAdoo SP	12.00	5.00
19 Mike McGee	4.00	1.50
20 Swen Nater	4.00	1.50
21 Kurt Rambis XRC SP	15.00	6.00
22 Byron Scott XRC SP	25.00	15.00
23 Larry Spriggs	4.00	1.50
24 Jamaal Wilkes SP	9.00	4.50
25 James Worthy XRC SP	50.00	30.00
26 Larry Bird SP !	300.00	175.00
27 Danny Ainge XRC SP !	50.00	30.00
28 Quinn Buckner	8.00	4.00
29 M.L. Carr	8.00	4.00
30 Carlos Clark	8.00	4.00
31 Gerald Henderson	8.00	4.00
32 Dennis Johnson SP	18.00	9.00
33 Cedric Maxwell SP	8.00	4.00
34 Kevin McHale SP	40.00	15.00
35 Robert Parish SP	35.00	15.00
36 Scott Wedman	8.00	4.00
37 Greg Kite XRC SP	8.00	4.00
38 Sidney Moncrief SP	15.00	7.50
39A Sidney Moncrief SP	20.00	8.00
39B Nate Archibald SP	15.00	7.50
40 Randy Breuer XRC SP	4.00	1.50
41 Junior Bridgeman	4.00	1.50
42 Harvey Catchings	4.00	1.50
43 Kevin Grevey	4.00	1.50
44 Marques Johnson	10.00	5.00
45 Bob Lanier	15.00	6.00
46 Alton Lister SP	4.00	1.50
47 Paul Mokeski XRC SP	4.00	1.50
48 Paul Pressey XRC SP	4.00	1.50
49 Mark Aguirre XRC SP	45.00	20.00
50 Rolando Blackman XRC SP	45.00	20.00
51 Pat Cummings	18.00	9.00
52 Brad Davis XRC SP	30.00	15.00
53 Dale Ellis XRC SP	45.00	20.00
54 Bill Garnett	18.00	9.00
55 Derek Harper XRC SP	50.00	30.00
56 Kurt Nimphius	18.00	9.00
57 Jim Spanarkel	18.00	9.00
58 Elston Turner	18.00	9.00
59 Jay Vincent XRC SP	40.00	20.00
60 Mark West XRC SP	20.00	10.00
61 Bernard King	8.00	4.00
62 Bill Cartwright	5.00	2.50
63 Len Elmore	3.00	1.25
64 Eric Fernsten	3.00	1.25
65 Ernie Grunfeld	3.00	1.25
66 Louis Orr	2.00	.75
67 Leonard Robinson	2.00	.75
68 Rory Sparrow XRC	3.00	1.25
69 Trent Tucker SP	4.00	1.50
70 Darrell Walker XRC	4.00	1.50
71 Marvin Webster	2.00	.75
72 Ray Williams	2.00	.75
73 Ralph Sampson XRC	8.00	3.00
74 James Bailey	2.00	.75
75 Phil Ford	2.00	.75
76 Elvin Hayes	9.00	4.50
77 Caldwell Jones	2.00	.75
78 Major Jones	2.00	.75

#	Player		
☐ 79	Allen Leavell	2.00	.75
☐ 80	Lewis Lloyd	2.00	.75
☐ 81	Rodney McCray XRC	3.00	1.25
☐ 82	Robert Reid	2.00	.75
☐ 83	Terry Teagle XRC	3.00	1.25
☐ 84	Wally Walker	2.00	.75
☐ 85	Kelly Tripucka XRC	3.00	1.25
☐ 86	Kent Benson	2.00	.75
☐ 87	Earl Cureton	2.00	.75
☐ 88	Lionel Hollins	3.00	1.25
☐ 89	Vinnie Johnson	3.00	1.25
☐ 90	Bill Laimbeer	6.00	2.50
☐ 91	Cliff Levingston XRC	4.00	1.50
☐ 92	John Long	2.00	.75
☐ 93	David Thirdkill	2.00	.75
☐ 94	Isiah Thomas XRC !	100.00	50.00
☐ 95	Ray Tolbert	2.00	.75
☐ 96	Terry Tyler	2.00	.75
☐ 97	Jim Paxson	4.00	1.50
☐ 98	Kenny Carr	2.00	.75
☐ 99	Wayne Cooper	2.00	.75
☐ 100	Clyde Drexler XRC !	180.00	90.00
☐ 101	Jeff Lamp XRC	5.00	2.00
☐ 102	Fat Lever XRC	5.00	2.00
☐ 103	Calvin Natt	2.00	.75
☐ 104	Audie Norris	2.00	.75
☐ 105	Tom Piotrowski	2.00	.75
☐ 106	Mychal Thompson	3.00	1.25
☐ 107	Darnell Valentine XRC	4.00	1.50
☐ 108	Pete Verhoeven	2.00	.75
☐ 109	Walter Davis	5.00	2.50
☐ 110	Alvan Adams	3.00	1.25
☐ 111	James Edwards	2.00	.75
☐ 112	Rod Foster XRC	3.00	1.25
☐ 113	Maurice Lucas	4.00	1.50
☐ 114	Kyle Macy	3.00	1.25
☐ 115	Larry Nance XRC	20.00	8.00
☐ 116	Charles Pittman	2.00	.75
☐ 117	Rick Robey	2.00	.75
☐ 118	Mike Sanders XRC	3.00	1.25
☐ 119	Alvin Scott	2.00	.75
☐ 120	Paul Westphal	8.00	3.00
☐ 121	Bill Walton	18.00	9.00
☐ 122	Michael Brooks	2.00	.75
☐ 123	Terry Cummings XRC	10.00	5.00
☐ 124	James Donaldson XRC	3.00	1.25
☐ 125	Craig Hodges XRC	4.00	2.00
☐ 126	Greg Kelser XRC	4.00	1.50
☐ 127	Hank McDowell	2.00	.75
☐ 128	Billy McKinney	2.00	.75
☐ 129	Norm Nixon	4.00	1.50
☐ 130	Ricky Pierce XRC UER	8.00	3.00
☐ 131	Derek Smith XRC	5.00	2.00
☐ 132	Jerome Whitehead	2.00	.75
☐ 133	Adrian Dantley	8.00	4.00
☐ 134	Mitchell Anderson	2.00	.75
☐ 135	Thurl Bailey XRC	5.00	2.00
☐ 136	Tom Boswell	2.00	.75
☐ 137	John Drew	2.00	.75
☐ 138	Mark Eaton XRC	5.00	2.50
☐ 139	Jerry Eaves	2.00	.75
☐ 140	Rickey Green XRC	4.00	1.50
☐ 141	Darrell Griffith	3.00	1.25
☐ 142	Bobby Hansen XRC	4.00	1.50
☐ 143	Rich Kelley	2.00	.75
☐ 144	Jeff Wilkins	2.00	.75
☐ 145	Buck Williams XRC	15.00	7.50
☐ 146	Otis Birdsong	2.00	.75
☐ 147	Darwin Cook	2.00	.75
☐ 148	Darryl Dawkins	5.00	2.50
☐ 149	Mike Gminski	3.00	1.25
☐ 150	Reggie Johnson	2.00	.75
☐ 151	Albert King XRC	2.00	.75
☐ 152	Mike O'Koren	2.00	.75
☐ 153	Kelvin Ransey	2.00	.75
☐ 154	Micheal Ray Richardson	2.00	.75
☐ 155	Clarence Walker	2.00	.75
☐ 156	Bill Willoughby	3.00	1.25
☐ 157	Steve Stipanovich XRC	4.00	1.50
☐ 158	Butch Carter	2.00	.75
☐ 159	Edwin Leroy Combs	2.00	.75
☐ 160	George L. Johnson	2.00	.75
☐ 161	Clark Kellogg XRC	4.00	1.50
☐ 162	Sidney Lowe XRC	3.00	1.25
☐ 163	Kevin McKenna	2.00	.75
☐ 164	Jerry Sichting XRC	3.00	1.25

#	Player		
☐ 165	Brook Steppe	2.00	.75
☐ 166	Jimmy Thomas	2.00	.75
☐ 167	Granville Waiters	3.00	1.25
☐ 168	Herb Williams XRC	4.00	1.50
☐ 169	Dave Corzine	3.00	1.25
☐ 170	Wallace Bryant	2.00	.75
☐ 171	Quintin Dailey XRC	3.00	1.25
☐ 172	Sidney Green XRC	3.00	1.25
☐ 173	David Greenwood	3.00	1.25
☐ 174	Rod Higgins XRC	4.00	1.50
☐ 175	Clarence Johnson	2.00	.75
☐ 176	Ronnie Lester	5.00	2.00
☐ 177	Jawann Oldham	2.00	.75
☐ 178	Ennis Whatley XRC	3.00	1.25
☐ 179	Mitchell Wiggins XRC	3.00	1.25
☐ 180	Orlando Woolridge XRC	4.00	1.50
☐ 181	Kiki Vandeweghe XRC	10.80	4.00
☐ 182	Richard Anderson	2.00	.75
☐ 183	Howard Carter	2.00	.75
☐ 184	T.R. Dunn	2.00	.75
☐ 185	Keith Edmonson	2.00	.75
☐ 186	Alex English	10.00	4.00
☐ 187	Mike Evans	2.00	.75
☐ 188	Bill Hanzlik XRC	4.00	1.50
☐ 189	Dan Issel	10.00	5.00
☐ 190	Anthony Roberts	2.00	.75
☐ 191	Danny Schayes XRC	5.00	2.00
☐ 192	Rob Williams	2.00	.75
☐ 193	Jack Sikma	4.00	1.50
☐ 194	Fred Brown	3.00	1.25
☐ 195	Tom Chambers XRC	15.00	7.50
☐ 196	Steve Hawes	2.00	.75
☐ 197	Steve Hayes	2.00	.75
☐ 198	Reggie King	2.00	.75
☐ 199	Scooter McCray	2.00	.75
☐ 200	Jon Sundvold XRC	3.00	1.25
☐ 201	Danny Vranes	2.00	.75
☐ 202	Gus Williams	3.00	1.25
☐ 203	Al Wood	2.00	.75
☐ 204	Jeff Ruland XRC	4.00	1.50
☐ 205	Greg Ballard	2.00	.75
☐ 206	Charles Davis	2.00	.75
☐ 207	Darren Daye	2.00	.75
☐ 208	Michael Gibson	2.00	.75
☐ 209	Frank Johnson XRC	4.00	1.50
☐ 210	Joe Kopicki	2.00	.75
☐ 211	Rick Mahorn	3.00	1.25
☐ 212	Jeff Malone XRC	8.00	3.00
☐ 213	Tom McMillen	3.00	1.25
☐ 214	Ricky Sobers	2.00	.75
☐ 215	Bryan Warrick	2.00	.75
☐ 216	Billy Knight	2.00	.75
☐ 217	Don Buse	2.00	.75
☐ 218	Larry Drew XRC	4.00	1.50
☐ 219	Eddie Johnson XRC	8.00	3.00
☐ 220	Joe Meriweather	2.00	.75
☐ 221	Larry Micheaux	2.00	.75
☐ 222	Ed Nealy XRC	3.00	1.25
☐ 223	Mark Olberding	2.00	.75
☐ 224	Dave Robisch	2.00	.75
☐ 225	Reggie Theus	4.00	1.50
☐ 226	LaSalle Thompson XRC	3.00	1.25
☐ 227	Mike Woodson	2.00	.75
☐ 228	World B.Free	4.00	1.50
☐ 229	John Bagley XRC	3.00	1.25
☐ 230	Jeff Cook	2.00	.75
☐ 231	Geoff Crompton	2.00	.75
☐ 232	John Garris	2.00	.75
☐ 233	Stewart Granger	2.00	.75
☐ 234	Roy Hinson XRC	3.00	1.25
☐ 235	Phil Hubbard	2.00	.75
☐ 236	Geoff Huston	2.00	.75
☐ 237	Ben Poquette	2.00	.75
☐ 238	Cliff Robinson	2.00	.75
☐ 239	Lonnie Shelton	3.00	1.25
☐ 240	Paul Thompson	2.00	.75
☐ 241	George Gervin	15.00	7.50
☐ 242	Gene Banks	3.00	1.25
☐ 243	Ron Brewer	2.00	.75
☐ 244	Artis Gilmore	5.00	2.50
☐ 245	Edgar Jones	2.00	.75
☐ 246	John Lucas	4.00	2.00
☐ 247A	Mike Mitchell ERR	3.00	1.25
☐ 247B	Mike Mitchell COR	5.00	2.50
☐ 248A	M.McNamara XRC ERR	3.00	1.25
☐ 248B	M.McNamara XRC COR	5.00	2.50

#	Player		
☐ 249	Johnny Moore	3.00	1.25
☐ 250	John Paxson XRC	10.00	5.00
☐ 251	Fred Roberts XRC	4.00	1.50
☐ 252	Joe Barry Carroll	2.00	.75
☐ 253	Mike Bratz	2.00	.75
☐ 254	Don Collins	2.00	.75
☐ 255	Lester Conner	2.00	.75
☐ 256	Chris Engler	2.00	.75
☐ 257	Sleepy Floyd XRC	6.00	3.00
☐ 258	Wallace Johnson	2.00	.75
☐ 259	Pace Mannion	2.00	.75
☐ 260	Purvis Short	2.00	.75
☐ 261	Larry Smith	2.00	.75
☐ 262	Darren Tillis	2.00	.75
☐ 263	Dominique Wilkins XRC !	165.00	85.00
☐ 264	Rickey Brown	2.00	.75
☐ 265	Johnny Davis	2.00	.75
☐ 266	Mike Glenn XRC	4.00	1.50
☐ 267	Scott Hastings XRC	3.00	1.25
☐ 268	Eddie Johnson	2.00	.75
☐ 269	Mark Landsberger	2.00	.75
☐ 270	Billy Paultz	2.00	.75
☐ 271	Doc Rivers XRC	15.00	7.50
☐ 272	Tree Rollins	2.00	.75
☐ 273	Dan Roundfield	2.00	.75
☐ 274	Sly Williams	2.00	.75
☐ 275	Randy Wittman XRC	4.00	1.50

1984-85 Star

☐ COMPLETE SET (288)	4500.00	3500.00
☐ COMP.CELTICS (1-12)	225.00	100.00
☐ COMP.CLIPPERS (13-24)	25.00	•10.00
☐ COMP.KNICKS (25-37)	20.00	8.00
☐ COMP.SUNS (38-51)	20.00	8.00
☐ COMP.PACERS SP (52-63)	35.00	20.00
☐ COMP.SPURS (64-75)	25.00	10.00
☐ COMP.HAWKS (76-87)	65.00	30.00
☐ COMP.NETS (88-100)	18.00	8.00
☐ COMP.BULLS (101-112)	2700.00	2000.00
☐ COMP.SONICS (113-124)	25.00	10.00
☐ COMP.BUCKS (125-136)	20.00	8.00
☐ COMP.NUGGETS (137-148)	20.00	8.00
☐ COMP.WARRIORS (149-160)	20.00	8.00
☐ COMP.BLAZERS (161-171)	90.00	45.00
☐ COMP.LAKERS (172-184)	125.00	65.00
☐ COMP.BULLETS (185-194)	20.00	8.00
☐ COMP.SC (195-200/281-288)	800.00	500.00
☐ COMP.76ERS (201-212)	240.00	125.00
☐ COMP.CAVS (213-224)	20.00	8.00
☐ COMP.JAZZ (225-236)	225.00	100.00
☐ COMP.ROCKETS (237-249)	250.00	100.00
☐ COMP.MAVS (250-260) !	40.00	20.00
☐ COMP.PISTONS (261-269)	40.00	15.00
☐ COMP.KINGS (270-280)	25.00	10.00
☐ COMMON CARD (1-51/64-288)	2.00	.75
☐ COMMON SP (52-63)	3.00	1.25
☐ *OPENED TEAM SETS: .75X to 1.0X		
☐ 1 Larry Bird	140.00	70.00
☐ 2 Danny Ainge	12.00	6.00
☐ 3 Quinn Buckner	2.00	.75
☐ 4 Rick Carlisle	7.00	3.00
☐ 5 M.L. Carr	2.00	.75
☐ 6 Dennis Johnson	5.00	2.50
☐ 7 Greg Kite	2.00	.75
☐ 8 Cedric Maxwell	2.00	.75
☐ 9 Kevin McHale	15.00	7.50
☐ 10 Robert Parish	12.00	6.00
☐ 11 Scott Wedman	2.00	.75

12	Larry Bird: MVP !	70.00	35.00
13	Marques Johnson	3.00	1.25
14	Junior Bridgeman	2.00	.75
15	Michael Cage XRC	4.00	1.50
16	Harvey Catchings	2.00	.75
17	James Donaldson	2.00	.75
18	Lancaster Gordon	2.00	.75
19	Jay Murphy	2.00	.75
20	Norm Nixon	3.00	1.25
21	Derek Smith	3.00	1.25
22	Bill Walton	15.00	7.50
23	Bryan Warrick	2.00	.75
24	Rory White	2.00	.75
25	Bernard King	6.00	3.00
26	James Bailey	2.00	.75
27	Ken Bannister	2.00	.75
28	Butch Carter	2.00	.75
29	Bill Cartwright	4.00	1.50
30	Pat Cummings	2.00	.75
31	Ernie Grunfeld	3.00	1.25
32	Louis Orr	2.00	.75
33	Leonard Robinson	2.00	.75
34	Rory Sparrow	2.00	.75
35	Trent Tucker	2.00	.75
36	Darrell Walker	3.00	1.25
37	Eddie Lee Wilkins XRC	3.00	1.25
38	Alvan Adams	3.00	1.25
39	Walter Davis	4.00	1.50
40	James Edwards	2.00	.75
41	Rod Foster	2.00	.75
42	Michael Holton	2.00	.75
43	Jay Humphries XRC	4.00	1.50
44	Charles Jones	2.00	.75
45	Maurice Lucas	3.00	1.25
46	Kyle Macy	3.00	1.25
47	Larry Nance	8.00	3.00
48	Charles Pittman	2.00	.75
49	Rick Robey	3.00	1.25
50	Mike Sanders	2.00	.75
51	Alvin Scott	2.00	.75
52	Clark Kellogg	4.00	1.50
53	Tony Brown	3.00	1.25
54	Devin Durrant	3.00	1.25
55	Vern Fleming XRC SP	3.00	1.25
56	Bill Garnett	3.00	1.25
57	Stuart Gray UER	3.00	1.25
58	Jerry Sichting	4.00	1.50
59	Terence Stansbury	4.00	1.50
60	Steve Stipanovich	4.00	1.50
61	Jimmy Thomas	3.00	1.25
62	Granville Waiters	5.00	2.00
63	Herb Williams SP	5.00	2.00
64	Artis Gilmore	6.00	3.00
65	Gene Banks	2.00	.75
66	Ron Brewer	2.00	.75
67	George Gervin	15.00	7.50
68	Edgar Jones	2.00	.75
69	Ozell Jones	2.00	.75
70	Mark McNamara	2.00	.75
71	Mike Mitchell	2.00	.75
72	Johnny Moore	2.00	.75
73	John Paxson	4.00	1.50
74	Fred Roberts	2.00	.75
75	Alvin Robertson XRC	4.00	1.50
76	Dominique Wilkins	45.00	20.00
77	Rickey Brown	2.00	.75
78	Antoine Carr XRC	4.00	1.50
79	Mike Glenn	2.00	.75
80	Scott Hastings	2.00	.75
81	Eddie Johnson	2.00	.75
82	Cliff Levingston	2.00	.75
83	Leo Rautins	2.00	.75
84	Doc Rivers	6.00	3.00
85	Tree Rollins	2.00	.75
86	Randy Wittman	2.00	.75
87	Sly Williams	2.00	.75
88	Darryl Dawkins	4.00	1.50
89	Otis Birdsong	2.00	.75
90	Darwin Cook	2.00	.75
91	Mike Gminski	2.00	.75
92	George L. Johnson	2.00	.75
93	Albert King	2.00	.75
94	Mike O'Koren	2.00	.75
95	Kelvin Ramsey	2.00	.75
96	M.R. Richardson	2.00	.75
97	Wayne Sappleton	2.00	.75
98	Jeff Turner XRC	5.00	2.00
99	Buck Williams	5.00	2.00
100	Michael Wilson	2.00	.75
101	Michael Jordan XRC !	2650.00	1800.00
102	Dave Corzine	4.00	1.50
103	Quintin Dailey	4.00	1.50
104	Sidney Green	4.00	1.50
105	David Greenwood	4.00	1.50
106	Rod Higgins	4.00	1.50
107	Steve Johnson	4.00	1.50
108	Caldwell Jones	4.00	1.50
109	Wes Matthews	5.00	2.00
110	Jawann Oldham	4.00	1.50
111	Ennis Whatley	4.00	1.50
112	Orlando Woolridge	4.00	1.50
113	Tom Chambers	4.00	1.50
114	Cory Blackwell	2.00	.75
115	Frank Brickowski XRC	4.00	1.50
116	Gerald Henderson	2.00	.75
117	Reggie King	2.00	.75
118	Tim McCormick XRC	4.00	1.50
119	John Schweitz	2.00	.75
120	Jack Sikma	4.00	1.50
121	Ricky Sobers	2.00	.75
122	Jon Sundvold	2.00	.75
123	Danny Vranes	2.00	.75
124	Al Wood	2.00	.75
125	Terry Cummings	5.00	2.00
126	Randy Breuer	2.00	.75
127	Charles Davis	2.00	.75
128	Mike Dunleavy	4.00	1.50
129	Kenny Fields	2.00	.75
130	Kevin Grevey	3.00	1.25
131	Craig Hodges	4.00	1.50
132	Alton Lister	2.00	.75
133	Larry Micheaux	2.00	.75
134	Paul Mokeski	2.00	.75
135	Sidney Moncrief	6.00	2.50
136	Paul Pressey	2.00	.75
137	Alex English	8.00	3.00
138	Wayne Cooper	2.00	.75
139	T.R. Dunn	2.00	.75
140	Mike Evans	2.00	.75
141	Bill Hanzlik	2.00	.75
142	Dan Issel	8.00	4.00
143	Joe Kopicki	2.00	.75
144	Fat Lever	3.00	1.25
145	Calvin Natt	2.00	.75
146	Danny Schayes	4.00	1.50
147	Elston Turner	2.00	.75
148	Willie White	2.00	.75
149	Purvis Short	2.00	.75
150	Chuck Aleksinas	2.00	.75
151	Mike Bratz	2.00	.75
152	Steve Burtt	2.00	.75
153	Lester Conner	2.00	.75
154	Sleepy Floyd	4.00	1.50
155	Mickey Johnson	2.00	.75
156	Gary Plummer	2.00	.75
157	Larry Smith	2.00	.75
158	Peter Thibeaux	2.00	.75
159	Jerome Whitehead	2.00	.75
160	Othell Wilson	2.00	.75
161	Kiki Vandeweghe	4.00	1.50
162	Sam Bowie XRC	8.00	3.00
163	Kenny Carr	2.00	.75
164	Steve Colter	2.00	.75
165	Clyde Drexler !	70.00	35.00
166	Audie Norris	2.00	.75
167	Jim Paxson	3.00	1.25
168	Tom Scheffler	2.00	.75
169	Bernard Thompson	2.00	.75
170	Mychal Thompson	3.00	1.25
171	Darnell Valentine	2.00	.75
172	Magic Johnson !	70.00	35.00
173	Kareem Abdul-Jabbar	35.00	20.00
174	Michael Cooper	5.00	2.00
175	Earl Jones	3.00	1.25
176	Mitch Kupchak	3.00	1.25
177	Ronnie Lester	4.00	1.50
178	Bob McAdoo	8.00	3.00
179	Mike McGee	2.00	.75
180	Kurt Rambis	5.00	2.00
181	Byron Scott	7.00	3.00
182	Larry Spriggs	2.00	.75
183	Jamaal Wilkes	5.00	2.00
184	James Worthy	15.00	6.00
185	Gus Williams	3.00	1.25
186	Greg Ballard	2.00	.75
187	Dudley Bradley	2.00	.75
188	Darren Daye	2.00	.75
189	Frank Johnson	2.00	.75
190	Charles Jones	2.00	.75
191	Rick Mahorn	3.00	1.25
192	Jeff Malone	4.00	1.50
193	Tom McMillen	3.00	1.25
194	Jeff Ruland	4.00	1.50
195	Michael Jordan OLY !	350.00	250.00
196	Vern Fleming OLY	4.00	1.50
197	Sam Perkins OLY	8.00	3.00
198	Alvin Robertson OLY	4.00	1.50
199	Jeff Turner OLY	5.00	2.00
200	Leon Wood OLY	5.00	2.00
201	Moses Malone	12.00	6.00
202	Charles Barkley XRC !	225.00	100.00
203	Maurice Cheeks	5.00	2.00
204	Julius Erving	40.00	20.00
205	Clemon Johnson	2.00	.75
206	George L. Johnson	2.00	.75
207	Bobby Jones	5.00	2.00
208	Clint Richardson	2.00	.75
209	Sedale Threatt	2.00	.75
210	Andrew Toney	4.00	1.50
211	Sam Williams	2.00	.75
212	Leon Wood XRC	5.00	2.00
213	Mel Turpin XRC	3.00	1.25
214	Ron Anderson XRC	3.00	1.25
215	John Bagley	2.00	.75
216	Johnny Davis	2.00	.75
217	World B.Free	3.00	1.25
218	Roy Hinson	2.00	.75
219	Phil Hubbard	2.00	.75
220	Edgar Jones	2.00	.75
221	Ben Poquette	2.00	.75
222	Lonnie Shelton	3.00	1.25
223	Mark West	2.00	.75
224	Kevin Williams	2.00	.75
225	Mark Eaton	3.00	1.25
226	Mitchell Anderson	2.00	.75
227	Thurl Bailey	2.00	.75
228	Adrian Dantley	6.00	3.00
229	Rickey Green	2.00	.75
230	Darrell Griffith	3.00	1.25
231	Rich Kelley	2.00	.75
232	Pace Mannion	2.00	.75
233	Billy Paultz	2.00	.75
234	Fred Roberts	2.00	.75
235	John Stockton XRC !	200.00	100.00
236	Jeff Wilkins	2.00	.75
237	Hakeem Olajuwon XRC !	225.00	100.00
238	Craig Ehlo XRC !	15.00	7.50
239	Lionel Hollins	2.00	.75
240	Allen Leavell	2.00	.75
241	Lewis Lloyd	2.00	.75
242	John Lucas	2.00	.75
243	Rodney McCray	3.00	1.25
244	Hank McDowell	2.00	.75
245	Larry Micheaux	2.00	.75
246	Jim Petersen XRC	3.00	1.25
247	Robert Reid	2.00	.75
248	Ralph Sampson	5.00	2.00
249	Mitchell Wiggins	2.00	.75
250	Mark Aguirre	5.00	2.00
251	Rolando Blackman	5.00	2.00
252	Wallace Bryant	2.00	.75
253	Brad Davis	4.00	1.50
254	Dale Ellis	6.00	3.00
255	Derek Harper	6.00	3.00
256	Kurt Nimphius	2.00	.75
257	Sam Perkins XRC	12.00	6.00
258	Charlie Sitton	2.00	.75
259	Tom Sluby	2.00	.75
260	Jay Vincent	2.00	.75
261	Isiah Thomas	25.00	10.00
262	Kent Benson	2.00	.75
263	Earl Cureton	2.00	.75
264	Vinnie Johnson	3.00	1.25
265	Bill Laimbeer	4.00	1.50
266	John Long	2.00	.75
267	Dan Roundfield	2.00	.75
268	Kelly Tripucka	2.00	.75
269	Terry Tyler	2.00	.75

#	Player		
270	Reggie Theus	4.00	1.50
271	Don Buse	2.00	.75
272	Larry Drew	2.00	.75
273	Eddie Johnson	4.00	1.50
274	Billy Knight	2.00	.75
275	Joe Meriweather	2.00	.75
276	Mark Olberding	2.00	.75
277	LaSalle Thompson	2.00	.75
278	Otis Thorpe XRC	9.00	4.00
279	Pete Verhoeven	2.00	.75
280	Mike Woodson	4.00	1.50
281	Julius Erving SPEC !	20.00	10.00
282	K.Abdul-Jabbar SPEC !	20.00	10.00
283	Dan Issel SPEC !	6.00	3.00
284	Bernard King SPEC !	4.00	1.50
285	Moses Malone SPEC !	8.00	4.00
286	Mark Eaton SPEC !	4.00	1.50
287	Isiah Thomas SPEC !	15.00	7.50
288	Michael Jordan SPEC !	350.00	200.00

1985-86 Star

ROBERT PARISH
Center - Boston Celtics

COMPLETE SET (172)	1400.00	900.00
COMP.76ERS (1-9)	100.00	50.00
COMP.PISTONS (10-17)	40.00	20.00
COMP.ROCKETS (18-25)	90.00	45.00
COMP.LAKERS SP (26-33)	200.00	100.00
COMP.SUNS (34-41)	20.00	8.00
COMP.HAWKS (42-49)	50.00	25.00
COMP.NUGGETS (50-57)	18.00	9.00
COMP.NETS (58-65)	18.00	9.00
COMP.SONICS (66-73)	18.00	9.00
COMP.KINGS (74-80)	18.00	9.00
COMP.CLIPPERS (88-94)	18.00	9.00
COMP.CELTICS GR. (95-102)	70.00	35.00
COMP.CELTICS WH. (95-102)	100.00	50.00
COMP.BLAZERS (103-109)	80.00	40.00
COMP.BULLETS (110-116)	18.00	9.00
COMP.BULLS (117-123)	800.00	500.00
COMP.BUCKS (124-130)	18.00	9.00
COMP.WARRIORS (131-137)	18.00	9.00
COMP.JAZZ (138-144)	90.00	50.00
COMP.SPURS (145-151)	18.00	9.00
COMP.CAVS (152-158)	18.00	9.00
COMP.MAVS (159-165)	25.00	10.00
COMP.KNICKS (166-172)	175.00	100.00
COMMON CARD (1-25/34-172)	2.00	.75
COMMON SP (26-33)	4.00	1.50
*OPENED TEAM SETS: .75X to 1.0X		

#	Player		
1	Maurice Cheeks !	6.00	3.00
2	Charles Barkley !	70.00	35.00
3	Julius Erving !	30.00	15.00
4	Clemon Johnson	2.00	.75
5	Bobby Jones !	4.00	1.50
6	Moses Malone !	8.00	3.00
7	Sedale Threatt !	2.00	.75
8	Andrew Toney	3.00	1.25
9	Leon Wood	3.00	1.25
10	Isiah Thomas UER	20.00	8.00
11	Kent Benson	2.00	.75
12	Earl Cureton	2.00	.75
13	Vinnie Johnson	3.00	1.25
14	Bill Laimbeer *	4.00	1.50
15	John Long	2.00	.75
16	Rick Mahorn	2.00	.75
17	Kelly Tripucka	2.00	.75
18	Hakeem Olajuwon !	75.00	35.00
19	Allen Leavell	2.00	.75
20	Lewis Lloyd	2.00	.75
21	John Lucas	2.00	.75
22	Rodney McCray	2.00	.75
23	Robert Reid	2.00	.75
24	Ralph Sampson	4.00	1.50
25	Mitchell Wiggins	2.00	.75
26	K.Abdul-Jabbar SP	35.00	20.00
27	Michael Cooper SP	8.00	4.00
28	Magic Johnson SP !	95.00	50.00
29	Mitch Kupchak	4.00	1.50
30	Maurice Lucas SP	4.00	1.50
31	Kurt Rambis SP	5.00	2.00
32	Byron Scott SP	8.00	4.00
33	James Worthy SP	15.00	6.00
34	Larry Nance	6.00	3.00
35	Alvan Adams	2.00	.75
36	Walter Davis	4.00	1.50
37	James Edwards	2.00	.75
38	Jay Humphries	2.00	.75
39	Charles Pittman	2.00	.75
40	Rick Robey	2.00	.75
41	Mike Sanders	2.00	.75
42	Dominique Wilkins	25.00	12.50
43	Scott Hastings	2.00	.75
44	Eddie Johnson	2.00	.75
45	Cliff Levingston	2.00	.75
46	Tree Rollins	2.00	.75
47	Doc Rivers UER	5.00	2.00
48	Kevin Willis XRC	18.00	9.00
49	Randy Wittman	2.00	.75
50	Alex English	7.00	3.50
51	Wayne Cooper	2.00	.75
52	T.R. Dunn	2.00	.75
53	Mike Evans	2.00	.75
54	Fat Lever	3.00	1.25
55	Calvin Natt	2.00	.75
56	Danny Schayes	4.00	1.50
57	Elston Turner	2.00	.75
58	Buck Williams	4.00	1.50
59	Otis Birdsong	2.00	.75
60	Darwin Cook	2.00	.75
61	Darryl Dawkins	4.00	1.50
62	Mike Gminski	2.00	.75
63	Mickey Johnson	2.00	.75
64	Mike O'Koren	2.00	.75
65	Micheal R. Richardson	2.00	.75
66	Tom Chambers	5.00	2.00
67	Gerald Henderson	2.00	.75
68	Tim McCormick	2.00	.75
69	Jack Sikma	4.00	1.50
70	Ricky Sobers	2.00	.75
71	Danny Vranes	2.00	.75
72	Al Wood	2.00	.75
73	Danny Young XRC	3.00	1.25
74	Reggie Theus	4.00	1.50
75	Larry Drew	2.00	.75
76	Eddie Johnson	4.00	1.50
77	Mark Olberding	2.00	.75
78	LaSalle Thompson	2.00	.75
79	Otis Thorpe	4.00	1.50
80	Mike Woodson	3.00	1.25
81	Clark Kellogg	4.00	1.50
82	Quinn Buckner	2.00	.75
83	Vern Fleming	2.00	.75
84	Bill Garnett	2.00	.75
85	Terence Stansbury	2.00	.75
86	Steve Stipanovich	2.00	.75
87	Herb Williams	2.00	.75
88	Marques Johnson	4.00	1.50
89	Michael Cage	4.00	1.50
90	Franklin Edwards	2.00	.75
91	Cedric Maxwell	2.00	.75
92	Derek Smith	3.00	1.25
93	Rory White	2.00	.75
94	Jamaal Wilkes	4.00	1.50
95G	Larry Bird Green	30.00	15.00
95W	Larry Bird White	80.00	40.00
96	Danny Ainge	10.00	5.00
97	Dennis Johnson	4.00	1.50
98	Kevin McHale	12.00	6.00
99	Robert Parish	8.00	4.00
100	Jerry Sichting	2.00	.75
101	Bill Walton	12.00	6.00
102	Scott Wedman	2.00	.75
103	Kiki Vandeweghe	4.00	1.50
104	Sam Bowie	4.00	1.50
105	Kenny Carr	2.00	.75
106	Clyde Drexler !	60.00	30.00
107	Jerome Kersey XRC	8.00	3.00
108	Jim Paxson	4.00	1.50
109	Mychal Thompson	4.00	1.50
110	Gus Williams	4.00	1.50
111	Darren Daye	2.00	.75
112	Jeff Malone	4.00	1.50
113	Tom McMillen	4.00	1.50
114	Cliff Robinson	2.00	.75
115	Dan Roundfield	2.00	.75
116	Jeff Ruland	2.00	.75
117	Michael Jordan !	750.00	450.00
118	Gene Banks	4.00	1.50
119	Dave Corzine	4.00	1.50
120	Quintin Dailey	2.00	.75
121	George Gervin	15.00	6.00
122	Jawann Oldham	4.00	1.50
123	Orlando Woolridge	4.00	1.50
124	Terry Cummings	4.00	1.50
125	Craig Hodges	2.00	.75
126	Alton Lister	2.00	.75
127	Paul Mokeski	2.00	.75
128	Sidney Moncrief	5.00	2.00
129	Ricky Pierce	4.00	1.50
130	Paul Pressey	2.00	.75
131	Purvis Short	2.00	.75
132	Joe Barry Carroll	2.00	.75
133	Lester Conner	2.00	.75
134	Sleepy Floyd	2.00	.75
135	Geoff Huston	2.00	.75
136	Larry Smith	2.00	.75
137	Jerome Whitehead	2.00	.75
138	Adrian Dantley	4.00	1.50
139	Mitchell Anderson	2.00	.75
140	Thurl Bailey	3.00	1.25
141	Mark Eaton	3.00	1.25
142	Rickey Green	2.00	.75
143	Darrell Griffith	3.00	1.25
144	John Stockton	75.00	40.00
145	Artis Gilmore	4.00	1.50
146	Marc Iavaroni	3.00	1.25
147	Steve Johnson	2.00	.75
148	Mike Mitchell	2.00	.75
149	Johnny Moore	2.00	.75
150	Alvin Robertson	2.00	.75
151	Jon Sundvold	2.00	.75
152	World B.Free	4.00	1.50
153	John Bagley	2.00	.75
154	Johnny Davis	2.00	.75
155	Roy Hinson	2.00	.75
156	Phil Hubbard	2.00	.75
157	Ben Poquette	2.00	.75
158	Mel Turpin	2.00	.75
159	Rolando Blackman	5.00	2.00
160	Mark Aguirre	4.00	1.50
161	Brad Davis	4.00	1.50
162	Dale Ellis	4.00	1.50
163	Derek Harper	6.00	3.00
164	Sam Perkins	6.00	3.00
165	Jay Vincent	2.00	.75
166	Patrick Ewing XRC !	165.00	80.00
167	Bill Cartwright	4.00	1.50
168	Pat Cummings	2.00	.75
169	Ernie Grunfeld	4.00	1.50
170	Rory Sparrow	2.00	.75
171	Trent Tucker	2.00	.75
172	Darrell Walker	3.00	1.25

1957-58 Topps

COMPLETE SET (80)	5500.00	4000.00
COMMON NON-DP (1-80)	40.00	25.00
COMMON DP	25.00	12.50
1 Nat Clifton RC DP !	250.00	150.00
2 George Yardley RC DP	70.00	35.00
3 Neil Johnston RC DP	55.00	30.00
4 Carl Braun DP	50.00	30.00
5 Bill Sharman RC DP !	125.00	75.00
6 George King RC DP	35.00	20.00
7 Kenny Sears RC DP	35.00	20.00
8 Dick Ricketts RC DP	35.00	20.00
9 Jack Nichols DP	25.00	15.00
10 Paul Arizin RC DP	100.00	60.00
11 Chuck Noble DP	25.00	15.00
12 Slater Martin RC DP	70.00	45.00
13 Dolph Schayes RC DP	70.00	45.00

❏ 14 Dick Atha DP	25.00	15.00
❏ 15 Frank Ramsey DP	90.00	55.00
❏ 16 Dick McGuire RC DP	55.00	35.00
❏ 17 Bob Cousy RC DP !	400.00	250.00
❏ 18 Larry Foust RC DP	35.00	20.00
❏ 19 Tom Heinsohn RC !	250.00	150.00
❏ 20 Bill Thieben DP	25.00	15.00
❏ 21 Don Meineke RC DP	35.00	20.00
❏ 22 Tom Marshall	40.00	25.00
❏ 23 Dick Garmaker	40.00	25.00
❏ 24 Bob Pettit RC QP !	150.00	90.00
❏ 25 Jim Krebs RC DP	35.00	20.00
❏ 26 Gene Shue RC DP	60.00	40.00
❏ 27 Ed Macauley RC DP	70.00	45.00
❏ 28 Vern Mikkelsen RC	100.00	60.00
❏ 29 Willie Naulls RC	60.00	40.00
❏ 30 Walter Dukes RC DP	45.00	30.00
❏ 31 Dave Piontek DP	25.00	15.00
❏ 32 John/Red Kerr DP	100.00	60.00
❏ 33 Larry Costello RC DP	50.00	30.00
❏ 34 Woody Sauldsberry RC RC DP	35.00	20.00
❏ 35 Ray Felix RC	45.00	30.00
❏ 36 Ernie Beck	40.00	25.00
❏ 37 Cliff Hagan RC	100.00	60.00
❏ 38 Guy Sparrow RC	25.00	15.00
❏ 39 Jim Loscutoff RC	60.00	40.00
❏ 40 Arnie Risen DP	45.00	30.00
❏ 41 Joe Graboski	40.00	25.00
❏ 42 Maurice Stokes RC DP!	100.00	60.00
❏ 43 Rod Hundley RC DP !	100.00	60.00
❏ 44 Tom Gola RC DP	80.00	50.00
❏ 45 Med Park RC	45.00	30.00
❏ 46 Mel Hutchins DP	25.00	15.00
❏ 47 Larry Friend DP	25.00	15.00
❏ 48 L.Rosenbluth RC DP	50.00	30.00
❏ 49 Walt Davis	40.00	25.00
❏ 50 Richie Regan RC	45.00	30.00
❏ 51 Frank Selvy RC DP	50.00	30.00
❏ 52 Art Spoelstra DP	25.00	15.00
❏ 53 Bob Hopkins RC	45.00	30.00
❏ 54 Earl Lloyd RC	50.00	30.00
❏ 55 Phil Jordan DP	25.00	15.00
❏ 56 Bob Houbregs RC DP	40.00	25.00
❏ 57 Lou Tsioropoulos DP	25.00	15.00
❏ 58 Ed Conlin RC	45.00	30.00
❏ 59 Al Bianchi RC	80.00	50.00
❏ 60 George Dempsey RC	45.00	30.00
❏ 61 Chuck Share	40.00	25.00
❏ 62 Harry Gallatin RC DP	50.00	30.00
❏ 63 Bob Harrison	40.00	25.00
❏ 64 Bob Burrow DP	25.00	15.00
❏ 65 Win Willfong DP	25.00	15.00
❏ 66 Jack McMahon RC DP	35.00	20.00
❏ 67 Jack George	40.00	25.00
❏ 68 Charlie Tyra DP	25.00	15.00
❏ 69 Ron Sobie	40.00	25.00
❏ 70 Jack Coleman	40.00	25.00
❏ 71 Jack Twyman RC DP	110.00	65.00
❏ 72 Paul Seymour RC	45.00	30.00
❏ 73 Jim Paxson RC DP UER	55.00	35.00
❏ 74 Bob Leonard RC	50.00	30.00
❏ 75 Andy Phillip	60.00	40.00
❏ 76 Joe Holup	40.00	25.00
❏ 77 Bill Russell RC !	1100.00	700.00
❏ 78 Clyde Lovellette RC DP	100.00	60.00
❏ 79 Ed Fleming DP	25.00	15.00
❏ 80 Dick Schnittker RC !	120.00	60.00

1969-70 Topps

❏ COMPLETE SET (99)	1800.00	1200.00
❏ 1 Wilt Chamberlain !	175.00	100.00
❏ 2 Gail Goodrich RC	50.00	30.00
❏ 3 Cazzie Russell RC	15.00	8.00
❏ 4 Darrall Imhoff RC	6.00	3.00
❏ 5 Bailey Howell	8.00	4.00
❏ 6 Lucius Allen RC	10.00	5.00
❏ 7 Tom Boerwinkle RC	6.00	3.00
❏ 8 Jimmy Walker RC	8.00	4.00
❏ 9 John Block RC	6.00	3.00
❏ 10 Nate Thurmond RC	35.00	20.00
❏ 11 Gary Gregor	4.00	2.50
❏ 12 Gus Johnson RC	20.00	12.00
❏ 13 Luther Rackley	4.00	2.50
❏ 14 Jon McGlocklin RC	6.00	3.00
❏ 15 Connie Hawkins RC	45.00	25.00
❏ 16 Johnny Egan	4.00	2.50
❏ 17 Jim Washington	4.00	2.50
❏ 18 Dick Barnett RC	8.00	4.00
❏ 19 Tom Meschery	8.00	4.00
❏ 20 John Havlicek RC !	120.00	60.00
❏ 21 Eddie Miles	4.00	2.50
❏ 22 Walt Wesley	6.00	3.00
❏ 23 Rick Adelman RC	8.00	4.00
❏ 24 Al Attles	8.00	4.00
❏ 25 Lew Alcindor RC !	350.00	200.00
❏ 26 Jack Marin RC	8.00	4.00
❏ 27 Walt Hazzard RC	12.00	6.00
❏ 28 Connie Dierking	4.00	2.50
❏ 29 Keith Erickson RC	12.00	6.00
❏ 30 Bob Rule RC	10.00	5.00
❏ 31 Dick Van Arsdale RC	12.00	6.00
❏ 32 Archie Clark RC	12.00	6.00
❏ 33 Terry Dischinger RC	4.00	2.50
❏ 34 Henry Finkel RC	4.00	2.50
❏ 35 Elgin Baylor	50.00	30.00
❏ 36 Ron Williams	4.00	2.50
❏ 37 Loy Petersen	4.00	2.50
❏ 38 Guy Rodgers	8.00	4.00
❏ 39 Toby Kimball	4.00	2.50
❏ 40 Billy Cunningham RC	40.00	15.00
❏ 41 Joe Caldwell RC	8.00	4.00
❏ 42 Leroy Ellis RC	6.00	3.00
❏ 43 Bill Bradley RC	100.00	50.00
❏ 44 Len Wilkens UER	30.00	18.00
❏ 45 Jerry Lucas RC	40.00	25.00
❏ 46 Neal Walk RC	6.00	3.00
❏ 47 Emmette Bryant RC	4.00	2.50
❏ 48 Bob Kauffman RC	4.00	2.50
❏ 49 Mel Counts RC	6.00	3.00
❏ 50 Oscar Robertson	50.00	20.00
❏ 51 Jim Barnett RC	8.00	4.00
❏ 52 Don Smith	4.00	2.50
❏ 53 Jim Davis	4.00	2.50
❏ 54 Walt Jones RC	6.00	3.00
❏ 55 Dave Bing RC	35.00	20.00
❏ 56 Wes Unseld RC	50.00	30.00
❏ 57 Joe Ellis	4.00	2.50
❏ 58 Jon Tresvant	4.00	2.50
❏ 59 Larry Siegfried RC	6.00	3.00
❏ 60 Willis Reed RC	40.00	15.00
❏ 61 Paul Silas RC	20.00	12.00
❏ 62 Bob Weiss RC	8.00	4.00
❏ 63 Willie McCarter	4.00	2.50
❏ 64 Don Kojis RC	4.00	2.50
❏ 65 Lou Hudson RC	20.00	12.00

❏ 66 Jim King	4.00	2.50
❏ 67 Luke Jackson RC	6.00	3.00
❏ 68 Len Chappell RC	4.00	2.50
❏ 69 Ray Scott	4.00	2.50
❏ 70 Jeff Mullins RC	8.00	4.00
❏ 71 Howie Komives	4.00	2.50
❏ 72 Tom Sanders RC	10.00	5.00
❏ 73 Dick Snyder	4.00	2.50
❏ 74 Dave Stallworth RC	6.00	3.00
❏ 75 Elvin Hayes RC	70.00	45.00
❏ 76 Art Harris	4.00	2.50
❏ 77 Don Ohl	6.00	3.00
❏ 78 Bob Love RC	50.00	30.00
❏ 79 Tom Van Arsdale RC	10.00	5.00
❏ 80 Earl Monroe RC	40.00	25.00
❏ 81 Greg Smith	4.00	2.50
❏ 82 Don Nelson RC	35.00	20.00
❏ 83 Happy Hairston RC	8.00	4.00
❏ 84 Hal Greer	12.00	6.00
❏ 85 Dave DeBusschere RC	40.00	25.00
❏ 86 Bill Bridges RC	8.00	4.00
❏ 87 Herm Gilliam RC	6.00	3.00
❏ 88 Jim Fox	4.00	2.50
❏ 89 Bob Boozer	6.00	3.00
❏ 90 Jerry West	80.00	40.00
❏ 91 Chet Walker RC	15.00	8.00
❏ 92 Flynn Robinson RC	6.00	3.00
❏ 93 Clyde Lee	4.00	2.50
❏ 94 Kevin Loughery RC	10.00	5.00
❏ 95 Walt Bellamy	10.00	5.00
❏ 96 Art Williams	4.00	2.50
❏ 97 Adrian Smith RC	6.00	3.00
❏ 98 Walt Frazier RC	60.00	25.00
❏ 99 Checklist 1-99	300.00	200.00

1970-71 Topps

❏ COMPLETE SET (175)	1200.00	700.00
❏ COMMON CARD (1-110)	2.50	1.50
❏ COMMON CARD (111-175)	3.00	2.00
❏ 1 Alcind/West/Hayes LL !	35.00	18.00
❏ 2 West/Alcin/Hayes LL SP	35.00	18.00
❏ 3 Green/Imhoff/Hudson LL	5.00	2.50
❏ 4 Rob/Walker/Mull LL! SP !	10.00	5.00
❏ 5 Hayes/Uns/Alcindor LL	25.00	15.00
❏ 6 Wilkens/Fraz/Hask LL SP	12.00	6.00
❏ 7 Bill Bradley	50.00	30.00
❏ 8 Ron Williams	2.50	1.50
❏ 9 Otto Moore	2.50	1.50
❏ 10 John Havlicek SP !	75.00	40.00
❏ 11 George Wilson RC	2.50	1.50
❏ 12 John Trapp	2.50	1.50
❏ 13 Pat Riley RC	60.00	35.00
❏ 14 Jim Washington	2.50	1.50
❏ 15 Bob Rule	4.00	2.00
❏ 16 Bob Weiss	4.00	2.00
❏ 17 Neil Johnson	2.50	1.50
❏ 18 Walt Bellamy	6.00	3.00
❏ 19 McCoy McLemore	2.50	1.50
❏ 20 Earl Monroe	15.00	7.50
❏ 21 Wally Anderzunas	2.50	1.50
❏ 22 Guy Rodgers	4.00	2.00
❏ 23 Rick Roberson	2.50	1.50
❏ 24 Checklist 1-110	40.00	20.00
❏ 25 Jimmy Walker	4.00	2.00
❏ 26 Mike Riordan RC	6.00	3.00
❏ 27 Henry Finkel	2.50	1.50
❏ 28 Joe Ellis	2.50	1.50
❏ 29 Mike Davis	2.50	1.50

❑ 30 Lou Hudson	6.00	3.00
❑ 31 Lucius Allen SP	8.00	4.00
❑ 32 Toby Kimball SP	6.00	3.00
❑ 33 Luke Jackson SP	6.00	3.00
❑ 34 Johnny Egan	2.50	1.50
❑ 35 Leroy Ellis SP	6.00	3.00
❑ 36 Jack Marin SP	8.00	4.00
❑ 37 Joe Caldwell SP	8.00	4.00
❑ 38 Keith Erickson	6.00	3.00
❑ 39 Don Smith	2.50	1.50
❑ 40 Flynn Robinson	4.00	2.00
❑ 41 Bob Boozer	2.50	1.50
❑ 42 Howie Komives	2.50	1.50
❑ 43 Dick Barnett	4.00	2.00
❑ 44 Stu Lantz RC	3.00	2.00
❑ 45 Dick Van Arsdale	6.00	3.00
❑ 46 Jerry Lucas	10.00	5.00
❑ 47 Don Chaney RC	10.00	5.00
❑ 48 Ray Scott	2.50	1.50
❑ 49 Dick Cunningham SP	8.00	4.00
❑ 50 Wilt Chamberlain	80.00	50.00
❑ 51 Kevin Loughery	4.00	2.00
❑ 52 Stan McKenzie	2.50	1.50
❑ 53 Fred Foster	2.50	1.50
❑ 54 Jim Davis	2.50	1.50
❑ 55 Walt Wesley	2.50	1.50
❑ 56 Bill Hewitt	2.50	1.50
❑ 57 Darrall Imhoff	2.50	1.50
❑ 58 John Block	2.50	1.50
❑ 59 Al Attles SP	8.00	4.00
❑ 60 Chet Walker	6.00	3.00
❑ 61 Luther Rackley	2.50	1.50
❑ 62 Jerry Chambers RC SP	8.00	4.00
❑ 63 Bob Dandridge RC	8.00	4.00
❑ 64 Dick Snyder	2.50	1.50
❑ 65 Elgin Baylor	30.00	18.00
❑ 66 Connie Dierking	2.50	1.50
❑ 67 Steve Kuberski RC	2.50	1.50
❑ 68 Tom Boerwinkle	2.50	1.50
❑ 69 Paul Silas	6.00	3.00
❑ 70 Elvin Hayes	30.00	18.00
❑ 71 Bill Bridges	4.00	2.00
❑ 72 Wes Unseld	15.00	7.50
❑ 73 Herm Gilliam	2.50	1.50
❑ 74 Bobby Smith RC SP	8.00	4.00
❑ 75 Lew Alcindor	80.00	50.00
❑ 76 Jeff Mullins	4.00	2.00
❑ 77 Happy Hairston	4.00	2.00
❑ 78 Dave Stallworth SP	6.00	3.00
❑ 79 Fred Hetzel	2.50	1.50
❑ 80 Len Wilkens SP	20.00	12.00
❑ 81 Johnny Green RC	6.00	3.00
❑ 82 Erwin Mueller	2.50	1.50
❑ 83 Wally Jones	4.00	2.00
❑ 84 Bob Love	8.00	4.00
❑ 85 Dick Garrett SP	2.50	1.50
❑ 86 Don Nelson SP	20.00	12.00
❑ 87 Neal Walk SP	6.00	3.00
❑ 88 Larry Siegfried	2.50	1.50
❑ 89 Gary Gregor	2.50	1.50
❑ 90 Nate Thurmond	8.00	4.00
❑ 91 John Warren	2.50	1.50
❑ 92 Gus Johnson	6.00	3.00
❑ 93 Gail Goodrich	15.00	7.50
❑ 94 Dorrie Murrey	2.50	1.50
❑ 95 Cazzie Russell SP	10.00	5.00
❑ 96 Terry Dischinger	2.50	1.50
❑ 97 Norm Van Lier RC SP	15.00	7.50
❑ 98 Jim Fox	2.50	1.50
❑ 99 Tom Meschery	2.50	1.50
❑ 100 Oscar Robertson	35.00	20.00
❑ 101A Checklist 111-175	30.00	15.00
❑ 101B Checklist 111-175	30.00	15.00
❑ 102 Rich Johnson	2.50	1.50
❑ 103 Mel Counts	4.00	2.00
❑ 104 Bill Hosket RC SP	6.00	3.00
❑ 105 Archie Clark	4.00	2.00
❑ 106 Walt Frazier AS	10.00	5.00
❑ 107 Jerry West AS	25.00	12.50
❑ 108 Billy Cunningham AS SP	10.00	5.00
❑ 109 Connie Hawkins AS	8.00	4.00
❑ 110 Willis Reed AS	8.00	4.00
❑ 111 Nate Thurmond AS	5.00	2.50
❑ 112 John Havlicek AS	30.00	18.00
❑ 113 Elgin Baylor AS	18.00	9.00
❑ 114 Oscar Robertson AS	20.00	12.00

❑ 115 Lou Hudson AS	4.00	2.00
❑ 116 Emmette Bryant	3.00	2.00
❑ 117 Greg Howard	3.00	2.00
❑ 118 Rick Adelman	5.00	2.50
❑ 119 Barry Clemens	3.00	2.00
❑ 120 Walt Frazier	30.00	18.00
❑ 121 Jim Barnes RC	3.00	2.00
❑ 122 Bernie Williams	3.00	2.00
❑ 123 Pete Maravich RC !	300.00	175.00
❑ 124 Matt Guokas SC	8.00	4.00
❑ 125 Dave Bing	12.00	6.00
❑ 126 John Tresvant	3.00	2.00
❑ 127 Shaler Halimon	3.00	2.00
❑ 128 Don Ohl	3.00	2.00
❑ 129 Fred Carter RC	6.00	3.00
❑ 130 Connie Hawkins	18.00	9.00
❑ 131 Jim King	3.00	2.00
❑ 132 Ed Manning RC	6.00	3.00
❑ 133 Adrian Smith	3.00	2.00
❑ 134 Walt Hazzard	6.00	3.00
❑ 135 Dave DeBusschere	15.00	7.50
❑ 136 Don Kojis	3.00	2.00
❑ 137 Calvin Murphy RC	35.00	18.00
❑ 138 Nate Bowman	3.00	2.00
❑ 139 Jon McGlocklin	5.00	2.50
❑ 140 Billy Cunningham	18.00	9.00
❑ 141 Willie McCarter	3.00	2.00
❑ 142 Jim Barnett	3.00	2.00
❑ 143 Jo Jo White RC	20.00	10.00
❑ 144 Clyde Lee	3.00	2.00
❑ 145 Tom Van Arsdale	6.00	3.00
❑ 146 Len Chappell	3.00	2.00
❑ 147 Lee Winfield	3.00	2.00
❑ 148 Jerry Sloan RC	20.00	10.00
❑ 149 Art Harris	3.00	2.00
❑ 150 Willis Reed	20.00	10.00
❑ 151 Art Williams	3.00	2.00
❑ 152 Don May	3.00	2.00
❑ 153 Loy Petersen	3.00	2.00
❑ 154 Dave Gambee	3.00	2.00
❑ 155 Hal Greer	10.00	5.00
❑ 156 Dave Newmark	3.00	2.00
❑ 157 Jimmy Collins	3.00	2.00
❑ 158 Bill Turner	3.00	2.00
❑ 159 Eddie Miles	3.00	2.00
❑ 160 Jerry West	50.00	30.00
❑ 161 Bob Quick	3.00	2.00
❑ 162 Fred Crawford	3.00	2.00
❑ 163 Tom Sanders	6.00	3.00
❑ 164 Dale Schlueter	3.00	2.00
❑ 165 Clem Haskins RC	12.00	6.00
❑ 166 Greg Smith	3.00	2.00
❑ 167 Rod Thorn RC	8.00	4.00
❑ 168 Playoff G1/W.Reed	10.00	5.00
❑ 169 Playoff G2/D.Garnett	5.00	2.50
❑ 170 Playoff G3/DeBussch	10.00	5.00
❑ 171 Playoff G4/J.West	18.00	9.00
❑ 172 Playoff G5/Bradley	18.00	9.00
❑ 173 Playoff G6/Wilt	18.00	9.00
❑ 174 Playoff G7/Frazier	12.00	6.00
❑ 175 Knicks Celebrate	20.00	10.00

1971-72 Topps

BILL BRADLEY
KNICKS FORWARD

❑ COMPLETE SET (233)	750.00	500.00
❑ COM. NBA CARD (1-144)	1.50	.75
❑ COM. ABA CARD (145-233)	2.00	1.00
❑ 1 Oscar Robertson !	40.00	20.00
❑ 2 Bill Bradley	30.00	15.00

❑ 3 Jim Fox	1.50	.75
❑ 4 John Johnson RC	2.00	1.00
❑ 5 Luke Jackson	2.00	1.00
❑ 6 Don May DP	1.50	.75
❑ 7 Kevin Loughery	2.00	1.00
❑ 8 Terry Dischinger	1.50	.75
❑ 9 Neal Walk	2.00	1.00
❑ 10 Elgin Baylor	25.00	12.50
❑ 11 Rick Adelman	2.00	1.00
❑ 12 Clyde Lee	1.50	.75
❑ 13 Jerry Chambers	1.50	.75
❑ 14 Fred Carter	2.00	1.00
❑ 15 Tom Boerwinkle DP	1.50	.75
❑ 16 John Block	1.50	.75
❑ 17 Dick Barnett	2.00	1.00
❑ 18 Henry Finkel	1.50	.75
❑ 19 Norm Van Lier	4.00	2.00
❑ 20 Spencer Haywood RC	15.00	7.50
❑ 21 George Johnson	1.50	.75
❑ 22 Bobby Lewis	1.50	.75
❑ 23 Bill Hewitt	1.50	.75
❑ 24 Walt Hazzard	4.00	2.00
❑ 25 Happy Hairston	2.00	1.00
❑ 26 George Wilson	1.50	.75
❑ 27 Lucius Allen	2.00	1.00
❑ 28 Jim Washington	1.50	.75
❑ 29 Nate Archibald RC !	25.00	12.50
❑ 30 Willis Reed	10.00	5.00
❑ 31 Erwin Mueller	1.50	.75
❑ 32 Art Harris	1.50	.75
❑ 33 Pete Cross	1.50	.75
❑ 34 Geoff Petrie RC	4.00	2.00
❑ 35 John Havlicek	30.00	15.00
❑ 36 Larry Siegfried	1.50	.75
❑ 37 John Tresvant DP	1.50	.75
❑ 38 Ron Williams	1.50	.75
❑ 39 Lamar Green DP	1.50	.75
❑ 40 Bob Rule DP	2.00	1.00
❑ 41 Jim McMillian RC	2.00	1.00
❑ 42 Wally Jones	2.00	1.00
❑ 43 Bob Boozer	1.50	.75
❑ 44 Eddie Miles	1.50	.75
❑ 45 Bob Love DP	5.00	2.50
❑ 46 Claude English	1.50	.75
❑ 47 Dave Cowens RC	40.00	20.00
❑ 48 Emmette Bryant	1.50	.75
❑ 49 Dave Stallworth	2.00	1.00
❑ 50 Jerry West	40.00	20.00
❑ 51 Joe Ellis	1.50	.75
❑ 52 Walt Wesley DP	1.50	.75
❑ 53 Howie Komives	1.50	.75
❑ 54 Paul Silas	4.00	2.00
❑ 55 Pete Maravich DP	40.00	20.00
❑ 56 Gary Gregor	1.50	.75
❑ 57 Sam Lacey RC	4.00	2.00
❑ 58 Calvin Murphy DP	6.00	3.00
❑ 59 Bob Dandridge	2.00	1.00
❑ 60 Hal Greer	4.00	2.00
❑ 61 Keith Erickson	2.00	1.00
❑ 62 Joe Cooke	1.50	.75
❑ 63 Bob Lanier RC	40.00	20.00
❑ 64 Don Kojis	1.50	.75
❑ 65 Walt Frazier	20.00	10.00
❑ 66 Chet Walker DP	4.00	2.00
❑ 67 Dick Garrett	1.50	.75
❑ 68 John Trapp	2.00	1.00
❑ 69 Jo Jo White	8.00	4.00
❑ 70 Wilt Chamberlain	50.00	25.00
❑ 71 Dave Sorenson	1.50	.75
❑ 72 Jim King	1.50	.75
❑ 73 Cazzie Russell	4.00	2.00
❑ 74 Jon McGlocklin	2.00	1.00
❑ 75 Tom Van Arsdale	2.00	1.00
❑ 76 Dale Schlueter	1.50	.75
❑ 77 Gus Johnson DP	4.00	2.00
❑ 78 Dave Bing	8.00	4.00
❑ 79 Billy Cunningham	10.00	5.00
❑ 80 Len Wilkens	10.00	5.00
❑ 81 Jerry Lucas DP	5.00	2.50
❑ 82 Don Chaney	4.00	2.00
❑ 83 McCoy McLemore	1.50	.75
❑ 84 Bob Kauffman DP	1.50	.75
❑ 85 Dick Van Arsdale	4.00	2.00
❑ 86 Johnny Green	2.00	1.00
❑ 87 Jerry Sloan	5.00	2.50
❑ 88 Luther Rackley DP	1.50	.75

❑ 89 Shaler Halimon	1.50	.75
❑ 90 Jimmy Walker	2.00	1.00
❑ 91 Rudy Tomjanovich RC	25.00	12.50
❑ 92 Levi Fontaine	1.50	.75
❑ 93 Bobby Smith	2.00	1.00
❑ 94 Bob Arnzen	1.50	.75
❑ 95 Wes Unseld DP	6.00	3.00
❑ 96 Clem Haskins DP	4.00	2.00
❑ 97 Jim Davis	1.50	.75
❑ 98 Steve Kuberski	1.50	.75
❑ 99 Mike Davis DP	1.50	.75
❑ 100 Lew Alcindor	50.00	30.00
❑ 101 Willie McCarter	1.50	.75
❑ 102 Charlie Paulk	1.50	.75
❑ 103 Lee Winfield	1.50	.75
❑ 104 Jim Barnett	1.50	.75
❑ 105 Connie Hawkins DP	8.00	4.00
❑ 106 Archie Clark DP	2.00	1.00
❑ 107 Dave DeBusschere	8.00	4.00
❑ 108 Stu Lantz DP	2.00	1.00
❑ 109 Don Smith	1.50	.75
❑ 110 Lou Hudson	4.00	2.00
❑ 111 Leroy Ellis	1.50	.75
❑ 112 Jack Marin	2.00	1.00
❑ 113 Matt Guokas	2.00	1.00
❑ 114 Don Nelson	6.00	3.00
❑ 115 Jeff Mullins DP	2.00	1.00
❑ 116 Walt Bellamy	6.00	3.00
❑ 117 Bob Quick	1.50	.75
❑ 118 John Warren	1.50	.75
❑ 119 Barry Clemens	1.50	.75
❑ 120 Elvin Hayes DP	10.00	5.00
❑ 121 Gail Goodrich	8.00	4.00
❑ 122 Ed Manning	2.00	1.00
❑ 123 Herm Gilliam DP	1.50	.75
❑ 124 Dennis Awtrey RC	2.00	1.00
❑ 125 John Hummer DP	1.50	.75
❑ 126 Mike Riordan	2.00	1.00
❑ 127 Mel Counts	1.50	.75
❑ 128 Bob Weiss DP	1.50	.75
❑ 129 Greg Smith DP	1.50	.75
❑ 130 Earl Monroe	10.00	5.00
❑ 131 Nate Thurmond DP	4.00	2.00
❑ 132 Bill Bridges DP	2.00	1.00
❑ 133 Playoffs G1/Alcindor	12.00	6.00
❑ 134 NBA Playoffs G2	3.00	1.50
❑ 135 NBA Playoffs G3	3.00	1.50
❑ 136 Playoffs G4/Oscar	8.00	4.00
❑ 137 NBA Champs/Oscar	15.00	7.50
❑ 138 Alcind/Hayes/Havl LL	20.00	12.00
❑ 139 Alcind/Havl/Hayes LL	20.00	12.00
❑ 140 Green/Alcind/Wilt LL	15.00	7.50
❑ 141 Walker/Oscar/Williams LL	5.00	2.50
❑ 142 Wilt/Hayes/Alcind LL	25.00	12.50
❑ 143 Van Lier/Oscar/West LL	12.00	6.00
❑ 144A NBA Checklist 1-144	18.00	9.00
❑ 144B NBA Checklist 1-144	18.00	9.00
❑ 145 ABA Checklist 145-233	18.00	9.00
❑ 146 Issel/Brisker/Scott LL	18.00	9.00
❑ 147 Issel/Barry/Brisker LL	12.00	6.00
❑ 148 ABA 2pt FG Pct Leaders	4.00	2.00
❑ 149 Barry/Carrier/Keller LL	10.00	5.00
❑ 150 ABA Rebound Leaders	4.00	2.00
❑ 151 ABA Assist Leaders	4.00	2.00
❑ 152 Larry Brown RC	20.00	10.00
❑ 153 Bob Bedell	2.00	1.00
❑ 154 Merv Jackson	2.00	1.00
❑ 155 Joe Caldwell	2.50	1.25
❑ 156 Billy Paultz RC	5.00	2.50
❑ 157 Les Hunter	2.50	1.25
❑ 158 Charlie Williams	2.00	1.00
❑ 159 Stew Johnson	2.00	1.00
❑ 160 Mack Calvin RC	5.00	2.50
❑ 161 Don Sidle	2.00	1.00
❑ 162 Mike Barrett	2.00	1.00
❑ 163 Tom Workman	2.00	1.00
❑ 164 Joe Hamilton	2.50	1.25
❑ 165 Zelmo Beaty RC	8.00	4.00
❑ 166 Dan Hester	2.00	1.00
❑ 167 Bob Verga	2.00	1.00
❑ 168 Wilbert Jones	2.00	1.00
❑ 169 Skeeter Swift	2.00	1.00
❑ 170 Rick Barry RC	50.00	30.00
❑ 171 Billy Keller RC	4.00	2.00
❑ 172 Ron Franz	2.00	1.00
❑ 173 Roland Taylor RC	2.50	1.25

❑ 174 Julian Hammond	2.00	1.00
❑ 175 Steve Jones RC	6.00	3.00
❑ 176 Gerald Govan	2.00	1.25
❑ 177 Darrell Carrier RC	2.50	1.25
❑ 178 Ron Boone RC	5.00	2.50
❑ 179 George Peeples	2.00	1.00
❑ 180 John Brisker	2.50	1.25
❑ 181 Doug Moe RC	6.00	3.00
❑ 182 Ollie Taylor	2.00	1.00
❑ 183 Bob Netolicky RC	2.50	1.25
❑ 184 Sam Robinson	2.00	1.00
❑ 185 James Jones	2.50	1.25
❑ 186 Julius Keye	2.50	1.25
❑ 187 Wayne Hightower	2.00	1.00
❑ 188 Warren Armstrong RC	2.50	1.25
❑ 189 Mike Lewis	2.00	1.00
❑ 190 Charlie Scott RC	8.00	4.00
❑ 191 Jim Ard	2.00	1.00
❑ 192 George Lehmann	2.00	1.00
❑ 193 Ira Harge	2.00	1.00
❑ 194 Willie Wise RC	5.00	2.50
❑ 195 Mel Daniels RC	8.00	4.00
❑ 196 Larry Cannon	2.00	1.00
❑ 197 Jim Eakins	2.50	1.25
❑ 198 Rich Jones	2.50	1.25
❑ 199 Bill Melchionni RC	4.00	2.00
❑ 200 Dan Issel RC	30.00	15.00
❑ 201 George Stone	2.00	1.00
❑ 202 George Thompson	2.00	1.00
❑ 203 Craig Raymond	2.00	1.00
❑ 204 Freddie Lewis RC	2.50	1.25
❑ 205 George Carter	2.50	1.25
❑ 206 Lonnie Wright	2.00	1.00
❑ 207 Cincy Powell	2.50	1.25
❑ 208 Larry Miller	2.50	1.25
❑ 209 Sonny Dove	2.00	1.00
❑ 210 Byron Beck RC	2.50	1.25
❑ 211 John Beasley	2.00	1.00
❑ 212 Lee Davis	2.00	1.00
❑ 213 Rick Mount RC	6.00	3.00
❑ 214 Walt Simon	2.00	1.00
❑ 215 Glen Combs	2.00	1.00
❑ 216 Neil Johnson	2.00	1.00
❑ 217 Manny Leaks	2.00	1.00
❑ 218 Chuck Williams	2.50	1.25
❑ 219 Warren Davis	2.00	1.00
❑ 220 Donnie Freeman RC	2.50	1.25
❑ 221 Randy Mahaffey	2.00	1.00
❑ 222 John Barnhill	2.00	1.00
❑ 223 Al Cueto	2.00	1.00
❑ 224 Louie Dampier RC	8.00	4.00
❑ 225 Roger Brown RC	5.00	2.50
❑ 226 Joe DePre	2.00	1.00
❑ 227 Ray Scott	2.00	1.00
❑ 228 Arvesta Kelly	2.00	1.00
❑ 229 Warren Williford	2.00	1.00
❑ 230 Larry Jones	2.50	1.25
❑ 231 Gene Moore	2.00	1.00
❑ 232 Ralph Simpson RC	2.50	1.25
❑ 233 Red Robbins RC !	5.00	2.50

1972-73 Topps

❑ COMPLETE SET (264)	800.00	500.00
❑ COM. NBA CARD (1-176)	1.00	.50
❑ COM. ABA CARD (177-264)	1.50	.75
❑ 1 Wilt Chamberlain !	60.00	40.00
❑ 2 Stan Love	1.00	.50
❑ 3 Geoff Petrie	1.50	.75

❑ 4 Curtis Perry RC	1.00	.50
❑ 5 Pete Maravich	35.00	20.00
❑ 6 Gus Johnson	3.00	1.50
❑ 7 Dave Cowens	15.00	7.50
❑ 8 Randy Smith RC	4.00	2.00
❑ 9 Matt Guokas	1.50	.75
❑ 10 Spencer Haywood	4.00	2.00
❑ 11 Jerry Sloan	3.00	1.50
❑ 12 Dave Sorenson	1.00	.50
❑ 13 Howie Komives	1.00	.50
❑ 14 Joe Ellis	1.00	.50
❑ 15 Jerry Lucas	5.00	2.50
❑ 16 Stu Lantz	1.50	.75
❑ 17 Bill Bridges	1.50	.75
❑ 18 Leroy Ellis	1.00	.50
❑ 19 Art Williams	1.00	.50
❑ 20 Sidney Wicks RC	8.00	4.00
❑ 21 Wes Unseld	6.00	3.00
❑ 22 Jim Washington	1.00	.50
❑ 23 Fred Hilton	1.00	.50
❑ 24 Curtis Rowe RC	1.50	.75
❑ 25 Oscar Robertson	20.00	10.00
❑ 26 Larry Steele RC	1.50	.75
❑ 27 Charlie Davis	1.00	.50
❑ 28 Nate Thurmond	5.00	2.50
❑ 29 Fred Carter	1.50	.75
❑ 30 Connie Hawkins	7.00	3.50
❑ 31 Calvin Murphy	5.00	2.50
❑ 32 Phil Jackson RC	40.00	25.00
❑ 33 Lee Winfield	1.00	.50
❑ 34 Jim Fox	1.00	.50
❑ 35 Dave Bing	6.00	3.00
❑ 36 Gary Gregor	1.00	.50
❑ 37 Mike Riordan	1.50	.75
❑ 38 George Trapp	1.00	.50
❑ 39 Mike Davis	1.00	.50
❑ 40 Bob Rule	1.50	.75
❑ 41 John Block	1.00	.50
❑ 42 Bob Dandridge	1.50	.75
❑ 43 John Johnson	1.50	.75
❑ 44 Rick Barry	18.00	9.00
❑ 45 Jo Jo White	4.00	2.00
❑ 46 Cliff Meely	1.00	.50
❑ 47 Charlie Scott	3.00	1.50
❑ 48 Johnny Green	1.50	.75
❑ 49 Pete Cross	1.00	.50
❑ 50 Gail Goodrich	6.00	3.00
❑ 51 Jim Davis	1.00	.50
❑ 52 Dick Barnett	1.50	.75
❑ 53 Bob Christian	1.00	.50
❑ 54 Jon McGlocklin	1.50	.75
❑ 55 Paul Silas	3.00	1.50
❑ 56 Hal Greer	3.00	1.50
❑ 57 Barry Clemens	1.00	.50
❑ 58 Nick Jones	1.00	.50
❑ 59 Cornell Warner	1.00	.50
❑ 60 Walt Frazier	10.00	5.00
❑ 61 Dorie Murrey	1.00	.50
❑ 62 Dick Cunningham	1.00	.50
❑ 63 Sam Lacey	1.50	.75
❑ 64 John Warren	1.00	.50
❑ 65 Tom Boerwinkle	1.00	.50
❑ 66 Fred Foster	1.00	.50
❑ 67 Mel Counts	1.00	.50
❑ 68 Toby Kimball	1.00	.50
❑ 69 Dale Schlueter	1.00	.50
❑ 70 Jack Marin	1.50	.75
❑ 71 Jim Barnett	1.00	.50
❑ 72 Clem Haskins	3.00	1.50
❑ 73 Earl Monroe	6.00	3.00
❑ 74 Tom Sanders	1.50	.75
❑ 75 Jerry West	25.00	12.50
❑ 76 Elmore Smith RC	1.50	.75
❑ 77 Don Adams	1.00	.50
❑ 78 Wally Jones	1.50	.75
❑ 79 Tom Van Arsdale	1.50	.75
❑ 80 Bob Lanier	20.00	10.00
❑ 81 Len Wilkens	8.00	4.00
❑ 82 Neal Walk	1.50	.75
❑ 83 Kevin Loughery	1.50	.75
❑ 84 Stan McKenzie	1.00	.50
❑ 85 Jeff Mullins	1.00	.50
❑ 86 Otto Moore	1.00	.50
❑ 87 John Tresvant	1.00	.50
❑ 88 Dean Meminger RC	1.00	.50
❑ 89 Jim McMillian	1.50	.75

#	Player		
90	Austin Carr RC	7.00	3.50
91	Clifford Ray RC	1.50	.75
92	Don Nelson	4.00	2.00
93	Mahdi Abdul-Rahman	1.50	.75
94	Willie Norwood	1.00	.50
95	Dick Van Arsdale	1.50	.75
96	Don May	1.00	.50
97	Walt Bellamy	4.00	2.00
98	Garfield Heard RC	4.00	2.00
99	Dave Wohl	1.00	.50
100	Kareem Abdul-Jabbar	30.00	15.00
101	Ron Knight	1.00	.50
102	Phil Chenier RC	4.00	2.00
103	Rudy Tomjanovich	8.00	4.00
104	Flynn Robinson	1.00	.50
105	Dave DeBusschere	6.00	3.00
106	Dennis Layton	1.00	.50
107	Bill Hewitt	1.00	.50
108	Dick Garrett	1.00	.50
109	Walt Wesley	1.00	.50
110	John Havlicek	25.00	12.50
111	Norm Van Lier	1.50	.75
112	Cazzie Russell	3.00	1.50
113	Herm Gilliam	1.00	.50
114	Greg Smith	1.00	.50
115	Nate Archibald	6.00	3.00
116	Don Kojis	1.00	.50
117	Rick Adelman	1.50	.75
118	Luke Jackson	1.50	.75
119	Lamar Green	1.00	.50
120	Archie Clark	1.50	.75
121	Happy Hairston	1.50	.75
122	Bill Bradley	20.00	10.00
123	Ron Williams	1.00	.50
124	Jimmy Walker	1.50	.75
125	Bob Kauffman	1.00	.50
126	Rick Roberson	1.00	.50
127	Howard Porter RC	1.50	.75
128	Mike Newlin RC	1.50	.75
129	Willis Reed	8.00	4.00
130	Lou Hudson	3.00	1.50
131	Don Chaney	3.00	1.50
132	Dave Stallworth	1.00	.50
133	Charlie Yelverton	1.00	.50
134	Ken Durrett	1.00	.50
135	John Brisker	1.50	.75
136	Dick Snyder	1.00	.50
137	Jim McDaniels	1.00	.50
138	Clyde Lee	1.00	.50
139	Dennis Awtrey UER	1.50	.75
140	Keith Erickson	1.50	.75
141	Bob Weiss	1.50	.75
142	Butch Beard RC	3.00	1.50
143	Terry Dischinger	1.00	.50
144	Pat Riley	18.00	9.00
145	Lucius Allen	1.50	.75
146	John Mengelt RC	1.50	.75
147	John Hummer	1.00	.50
148	Bob Love	5.00	2.50
149	Bobby Smith	1.50	.75
150	Elvin Hayes	10.00	5.00
151	Nate Williams	1.00	.50
152	Chet Walker	3.00	1.50
153	Steve Kuberski	1.00	.50
154	Playoffs G1 Monroe	3.00	1.50
155	NBA Playoffs G2	2.50	1.25
156	NBA Playoffs G3	2.50	1.25
157	NBA Playoffs G4	2.50	1.25
158	Playoffs G5/J.West	8.00	4.00
159	Champs Lakers/Wilt	10.00	5.00
160	NBA Checklist 1-176	16.00	8.00
161	John Havlicek AS	10.00	5.00
162	Spencer Haywood AS	2.00	1.00
163	Kareem Abdul-Jabbar AS	25.00	12.50
164	Jerry West AS	18.00	9.00
165	Walt Frazier AS	5.00	2.50
166	Bob Love AS	2.00	1.00
167	Billy Cunningham AS	4.00	2.00
168	Wilt Chamberlain AS	20.00	10.00
169	Nate Archibald AS	4.00	2.00
170	Archie Clark AS	2.00	1.00
171	Jabbar/Havl/Arch LL	14.00	7.00
172	Jabbar/Arch/Havl LL	14.00	7.00
173	Wilt/Jabbar/Bell LL	16.00	8.00
174	Marin/Murphy/Goodr LL	3.00	1.50
175	Wilt/Jabbar/Unseld LL	16.00	8.00
176	Wilkens/West/Arch LL	12.00	6.00
177	Roland Taylor	1.50	.75
178	Art Becker	1.50	.75
179	Mack Calvin	2.00	1.00
180	Artis Gilmore RC	20.00	10.00
181	Collis Jones	1.50	.75
182	John Roche RC	2.00	1.00
183	George McGinnis RC	14.00	7.00
184	Johnny Neumann	2.00	1.00
185	Willie Wise	2.00	1.00
186	Bernie Williams	1.50	.75
187	Byron Beck	2.00	1.00
188	Larry Miller	2.00	1.00
189	Cincy Powell	1.50	.75
190	Donnie Freeman	2.00	1.00
191	John Baum	1.50	.75
192	Billy Keller	2.00	1.00
193	Wilbert Jones	1.50	.75
194	Glen Combs	1.50	.75
195	Julius Erving RC	200.00	125.00
196	Al Smith	1.50	.75
197	George Carter	1.50	.75
198	Louie Dampier	3.00	1.50
199	Rich Jones	1.50	.75
200	Mel Daniels	3.00	1.50
201	Gene Moore	1.50	.75
202	Randy Denton	1.50	.75
203	Larry Jones	1.50	.75
204	Jim Ligon	1.50	.75
205	Warren Jabali	2.00	1.00
206	Joe Caldwell	2.00	1.00
207	Darrell Carrier	2.00	1.00
208	Gene Kennedy	1.50	.75
209	Ollie Taylor	1.50	.75
210	Roger Brown	2.00	1.00
211	George Lehmann	1.50	.75
212	Red Robbins	1.50	.75
213	Jim Eakins	2.00	1.00
214	Willie Long	1.50	.75
215	Billy Cunningham	8.00	4.00
216	Steve Jones	2.00	1.00
217	Les Hunter	1.50	.75
218	Billy Paultz	2.00	1.00
219	Freddie Lewis	2.00	1.00
220	Zelmo Beaty	2.00	1.00
221	George Thompson	1.50	.75
222	Neil Johnson	1.50	.75
223	Dave Robisch RC	2.00	1.00
224	Walt Simon	1.50	.75
225	Bill Melchionni	2.00	1.00
226	Wendell Ladner RC	2.00	1.00
227	Joe Hamilton	1.50	.75
228	Ron Netolicky	2.00	1.00
229	James Jones	2.00	1.00
230	Dan Issel	10.00	5.00
231	Charlie Williams	1.50	.75
232	Willie Sojourner	1.50	.75
233	Merv Jackson	1.50	.75
234	Mike Lewis	1.50	.75
235	Ralph Simpson	2.00	1.00
236	Darnell Hillman	2.00	1.00
237	Rick Mount	3.00	1.50
238	Gerald Govan	1.50	.75
239	Ron Boone	2.00	1.00
240	Tom Washington	1.50	.75
241	ABA Playoffs G1	2.50	1.25
242	Playoffs G2/Barry	5.00	2.50
243	Playoffs G3/McGinnis	4.00	2.00
244	Playoffs G4/Barry	5.00	2.50
245	ABA Playoffs G5	2.50	1.25
246	ABA Playoffs G6	2.50	1.25
247	ABA Champs: Pacers	3.00	1.50
248	ABA Checklist 177-264	16.00	8.00
249	Dan Issel AS	6.00	3.00
250	Rick Barry AS	8.00	4.00
251	Artis Gilmore AS	6.00	3.00
252	Donnie Freeman AS	2.50	1.25
253	Bill Melchionni AS	2.50	1.25
254	Willie Wise AS	2.50	1.25
255	Julius Erving AS	50.00	25.00
256	Zelmo Beaty AS	2.50	1.25
257	Ralph Simpson AS	2.50	1.25
258	Charlie Scott AS	2.50	1.25
259	Scott/Barry/Issel LL	8.00	4.00
260	Gilmore/Wash/Jones LL	4.00	2.00
261	ABA 3pt FG Pct.	2.50	1.25
262	Barry/Calvin/Jones LL	4.00	2.00
263	Gilmore/Erving/Dan LL	20.00	10.00
264	Melch/Brown/Damp LL	6.00	3.00

1973-74 Topps

HOUSTON ROCKETS
CALVIN MURPHY

#	Player		
	COMPLETE SET (264)	325.00	225.00
	COM. NBA CARD (1-176)	.50	.25
	COM. ABA CARD (177-264)	1.00	.50
1	Nate Archibald	10.00	5.00
2	Steve Kuberski	.50	.25
3	John Mengelt	.50	.25
4	Jim McMillian	1.00	.50
5	Nate Thurmond	4.00	2.00
6	Dave Wohl	.50	.25
7	John Brisker	.50	.25
8	Charlie Davis	.50	.25
9	Lamar Green	.50	.25
10	Walt Frazier	6.00	3.00
11	Bob Christian	.50	.25
12	Cornell Warner	.50	.25
13	Calvin Murphy	4.00	2.00
14	Dave Sorenson	.50	.25
15	Archie Clark	1.00	.50
16	Clifford Ray	.50	.25
17	Terry Driscoll	.50	.25
18	Matt Guokas	1.00	.50
19	Elmore Smith	.50	.25
20	John Havlicek	15.00	7.50
21	Pat Riley	8.00	4.00
22	George Trapp	.50	.25
23	Ron Williams	.50	.25
24	Jim Fox	.50	.25
25	Dick Van Arsdale	1.00	.50
26	John Tresvant	.50	.25
27	Rick Adelman	.50	.25
28	Eddie Mast	.50	.25
29	Jim Cleamons	1.00	.50
30	Dave DeBusschere	5.00	2.50
31	Norm Van Lier	.50	.25
32	Stan McKenzie	.50	.25
33	Bob Dandridge	1.00	.50
34	Leroy Ellis	.50	.25
35	Mike Riordan	1.00	.50
36	Fred Hilton	.50	.25
37	Toby Kimball	.50	.25
38	Jim Price	.50	.25
39	Willie Norwood	.50	.25
40	Dave Cowens	10.00	5.00
41	Cazzie Russell	1.00	.50
42	Lee Winfield	.50	.25
43	Connie Hawkins	5.00	2.50
44	Mike Newlin	1.00	.50
45	Chet Walker	1.00	.50
46	Walt Bellamy	4.00	2.00
47	John Johnson	1.00	.50
48	Henry Bibby RC	.50	.25
49	Bobby Smith	1.00	.50
50	Kareem Abdul-Jabbar	25.00	15.00
51	Mike Price	.50	.25
52	John Hummer	.50	.25
53	Kevin Porter RC	5.00	2.50
54	Nate Williams	.50	.25
55	Gail Goodrich	4.00	2.00
56	Fred Foster	.50	.25
57	Don Chaney	1.00	.50
58	Bud Stallworth	.50	.25
59	Clem Haskins	1.00	.50
60	Bob Love	3.00	1.50

❑ 61 Jimmy Walker	1.00	.50	❑ 147 Art Williams	.50	.25	❑ 233 Gerald Govan	1.50	.75
❑ 62 NBA Eastern Semis	1.00	.50	❑ 148 Curtis Perry	.50	.25	❑ 234 Erving/McG/Issel LL	10.00	5.00
❑ 63 NBA Eastern Semis	1.00	.50	❑ 149 Rich Rinaldi	.50	.25	❑ 235 ABA 2 Pt. Pct.	2.00	1.00
❑ 64 Western Semis/Wilt	8.00	4.00	❑ 150 Lou Hudson	1.00	.50	❑ 236 ABA 3 Pt. Pct.	2.00	1.00
❑ 65 NBA Western Semis	1.00	.50	❑ 151 Mel Counts	.50	.25	❑ 237 ABA F.T. Pct. Leaders	2.00	1.00
❑ 66 Eastern Finals/Reed	3.00	1.50	❑ 152 Jim McDaniels	.50	.25	❑ 238 Gilmore/Daniels/Paultz LL	3.00	1.50
❑ 67 NBA Western Finals	1.00	.50	❑ 153 ArchJabbar/Hayw LL	8.00	4.00	❑ 239 ABA Assist Leaders	2.00	1.00
❑ 68 Knicks Champs/Frazier	4.00	2.00	❑ 154 ArchJabbar/Hayw LL	8.00	4.00	❑ 240 Julius Erving	50.00	30.00
❑ 69 Larry Steele	1.00	.50	❑ 155 Witt/Guokas/Jabbar LL	12.00	6.00	❑ 241 Jimmy O'Brien	1.00	.50
❑ 70 Oscar Robertson	15.00	7.50	❑ 156 Barry/Murphy/Archibald LL	4.00	2.00	❑ 242 ABA Checklist 177-264	12.00	6.00
❑ 71 Phil Jackson	15.00	7.50	❑ 157 Witt/Thurm/Cowens LL	8.00	4.00	❑ 243 Johnny Neumann	1.00	.50
❑ 72 John Wetzel	.50	.25	❑ 158 Arch/Wilkens/Bing LL	4.00	2.00	❑ 244 Darnell Hillman	1.50	.75
❑ 73 Steve Patterson RC	1.00	.50	❑ 159 Don Smith	.50	.25	❑ 245 Willie Wise	1.50	.75
❑ 74 Manny Leaks	.50	.25	❑ 160 Sidney Wicks	3.00	1.50	❑ 246 Collis Jones	1.00	.50
❑ 75 Jeff Mullins	1.00	.50	❑ 161 Howie Komives	.50	.25	❑ 247 Ted McClain	1.00	.50
❑ 76 Stan Love	.50	.25	❑ 162 John Gianelli	.50	.25	❑ 248 George Irvine RC	1.00	.50
❑ 77 Dick Garrett	.50	.25	❑ 163 Jeff Halliburton	.50	.25	❑ 249 Bill Melchionni	1.50	.75
❑ 78 Don Nelson	4.00	2.00	❑ 164 Kennedy McIntosh	.50	.25	❑ 250 Artis Gilmore	6.00	3.00
❑ 79 Chris Ford RC	3.00	1.50	❑ 165 Len Wilkens	6.00	3.00	❑ 251 Willie Long	1.00	.50
❑ 80 Wilt Chamberlain	25.00	15.00	❑ 166 Corky Calhoun	.50	.25	❑ 252 Larry Miller	1.00	.50
❑ 81 Dennis Layton	.50	.25	❑ 167 Howard Porter	1.00	.50	❑ 253 Lee Davis	1.00	.50
❑ 82 Bill Bradley	15.00	7.50	❑ 168 Jo Jo White	3.00	1.50	❑ 254 Donnie Freeman	1.50	.75
❑ 83 Jerry Sloan	1.00	.50	❑ 169 John Block	.50	.25	❑ 255 Joe Caldwell	1.50	.75
❑ 84 Cliff Meely	.50	.25	❑ 170 Dave Bing	4.00	2.00	❑ 256 Bob Netolicky	1.50	.75
❑ 85 Sam Lacey	.50	.25	❑ 171 Joe Ellis	.50	.25	❑ 257 Bernie Williams	1.00	.50
❑ 86 Dick Snyder	.50	.25	❑ 172 Chuck Terry	.50	.25	❑ 258 Byron Beck	1.50	.75
❑ 87 Jim Washington	.50	.25	❑ 173 Randy Smith	1.00	.50	❑ 259 Jim Chones RC	3.00	1.50
❑ 88 Lucius Allen	1.00	.50	❑ 174 Bill Bridges	1.00	.50	❑ 260 James Jones AS1	1.50	.75
❑ 89 LaRue Martin	.50	.25	❑ 175 Geoff Petrie	1.00	.50	❑ 261 Wendell Ladner	1.00	.50
❑ 90 Rick Barry	8.00	4.00	❑ 176 Wes Unseld	4.00	2.00	❑ 262 Ollie Taylor	1.00	.50
❑ 91 Fred Boyd	.50	.25	❑ 177 Skeeter Swift	1.00	.50	❑ 263 Les Hunter	1.00	.50
❑ 92 Barry Clemens	.50	.25	❑ 178 Jim Eakins	1.50	.75	❑ 264 Billy Keller !	3.00	1.50
❑ 93 Dean Meminger	.50	.25	❑ 179 Steve Jones	1.50	.75			
❑ 94 Henry Finkel	.50	.25	❑ 180 George McGinnis	3.00	1.50			
❑ 95 Elvin Hayes	6.00	3.00	❑ 181 Al Smith	1.00	.50			
❑ 96 Stu Lantz	.50	.25	❑ 182 Tom Washington	1.00	.50			
❑ 97 Bill Hewitt	.50	.25	❑ 183 Louie Dampier	1.50	.75			
❑ 98 Neal Walk	.50	.25	❑ 184 Simmie Hill	1.00	.50			
❑ 99 Garfield Heard	1.00	.50	❑ 185 George Thompson	1.00	.50			
❑ 100 Jerry West	20.00	10.00	❑ 186 Cincy Powell	1.50	.75			
❑ 101 Otto Moore	.50	.25	❑ 187 Larry Jones	1.00	.50			
❑ 102 Don Kojis	.50	.25	❑ 188 Neil Johnson	1.00	.50			
❑ 103 Fred Brown RC	6.00	3.00	❑ 189 Tom Owens	1.00	.50			
❑ 104 Dwight Davis	.50	.25	❑ 190 Ralph Simpson AS2	1.50	.75			
❑ 105 Willis Reed	6.00	3.00	❑ 191 George Carter	1.00	.50			
❑ 106 Herm Gilliam	.50	.25	❑ 192 Rick Mount	1.50	.75			
❑ 107 Mickey Davis	.50	.25	❑ 193 Red Robbins	1.00	.50			
❑ 108 Jim Barnett	.50	.25	❑ 194 George Lehmann	1.00	.50			
❑ 109 Ollie Johnson	.50	.25	❑ 195 Mel Daniels	1.00	.50			
❑ 110 Bob Lanier	6.00	3.00	❑ 196 Bob Warren	1.00	.50			
❑ 111 Fred Carter	1.00	.50	❑ 197 Gene Kennedy	1.00	.50			
❑ 112 Paul Silas	3.00	1.50	❑ 198 Mike Barr	1.00	.50			
❑ 113 Phil Chenier	1.00	.50	❑ 199 Dave Robisch	1.00	.50			
❑ 114 Dennis Awtrey	.50	.25	❑ 200 Billy Cunningham	5.00	2.50			
❑ 115 Austin Carr	1.00	.50	❑ 201 John Roche	1.50	.75			
❑ 116 Bob Kauffman	.50	.25	❑ 202 ABA Western Semis	2.00	1.00			
❑ 117 Keith Erickson	1.00	.50	❑ 203 ABA Western Semis	2.00	1.00			
❑ 118 Walt Wesley	.50	.25	❑ 204 ABA Eastern Semis	2.00	1.00			
❑ 119 Steve Bracey	.50	.25	❑ 205 ABA Eastern Semis	2.00	1.00			
❑ 120 Spencer Haywood	3.00	1.50	❑ 206 ABA Western Finals	2.00	1.00			
❑ 121 NBA Checklist 1-176	12.00	6.00	❑ 207 Eastern Finals/Gilmore	3.00	1.50			
❑ 122 Jack Marin	1.00	.50	❑ 208 ABA Championship	2.00	1.00			
❑ 123 Jon McGlocklin	.50	.25	❑ 209 Glen Combs	1.00	.50			
❑ 124 Johnny Green	1.00	.50	❑ 210 Dan Issel	6.00	3.00			
❑ 125 Jerry Lucas	3.00	1.50	❑ 211 Randy Denton	1.00	.50			
❑ 126 Paul Westphal RC	20.00	10.00	❑ 212 Freddie Lewis	1.50	.75			
❑ 127 Curtis Rowe	1.00	.50	❑ 213 Stew Johnson	1.00	.50			
❑ 128 Mahdi Abdul-Rahman	1.00	.50	❑ 214 Roland Taylor	1.00	.50			
❑ 129 Lloyd Neal RC	.50	.25	❑ 215 Rich Jones	1.00	.50			
❑ 130 Pete Maravich	30.00	18.00	❑ 216 Billy Paultz	1.50	.75			
❑ 131 Don May	.50	.25	❑ 217 Ron Boone	1.50	.75			
❑ 132 Bob Weiss	1.00	.50	❑ 218 Walt Simon	1.00	.50			
❑ 133 Dave Stallworth	.50	.25	❑ 219 Mike Lewis	1.00	.50			
❑ 134 Dick Cunningham	.50	.25	❑ 220 Warren Jabali AS1	1.50	.75			
❑ 135 Bob McAdoo RC !	20.00	10.00	❑ 221 Wilbert Jones	1.00	.50			
❑ 136 Butch Beard	1.00	.50	❑ 222 Don Buse RC	1.50	.75			
❑ 137 Happy Hairston	1.00	.50	❑ 223 Gene Moore	1.00	.50			
❑ 138 Bob Rule	1.00	.50	❑ 224 Joe Hamilton	1.50	.75			
❑ 139 Don Adams	.50	.25	❑ 225 Zelmo Beaty	1.50	.75			
❑ 140 Charlie Scott	1.00	.50	❑ 226 Brian Taylor RC	1.50	.75			
❑ 141 Ron Riley	.50	.25	❑ 227 Julius Keye	1.00	.50			
❑ 142 Earl Monroe	4.00	2.00	❑ 228 Mike Gale RC	1.50	.75			
❑ 143 Clyde Lee	.50	.25	❑ 229 Warren Davis	1.00	.50			
❑ 144 Rick Roberson	.50	.25	❑ 230 Mack Calvin	1.50	.75			
❑ 145 Rudy Tomjanovich	6.00	3.00	❑ 231 Roger Brown	1.50	.75			
❑ 146 Tom Van Arsdale	1.00	.50	❑ 232 Chuck Williams	1.50	.75			

1974-75 Topps

❑ COMPLETE SET (264)	325.00	200.00
❑ COM. NBA CARD (1-176)	.50	.25
❑ COM. ABA CARD (177-264)	1.00	.50
❑ 1 Kareem Abdul-Jabbar !	30.00	15.00
❑ 2 Don May	.50	.25
❑ 3 Bernie Fryer RC	.50	.25
❑ 4 Don Adams	.50	.25
❑ 5 Herm Gilliam	.50	.25
❑ 6 Jim Chones	1.00	.50
❑ 7 Rick Adelman	1.00	.50
❑ 8 Randy Smith	1.00	.50
❑ 9 Paul Silas	3.00	1.50
❑ 10 Pete Maravich	25.00	12.50
❑ 11 Ron Behagen	.50	.25
❑ 12 Kevin Porter	1.00	.50
❑ 13 Bill Bridges	1.00	.50
❑ 14 Charles Johnson RC	.50	.25
❑ 15 Bob Love	1.00	.50
❑ 16 Henry Bibby	1.00	.50
❑ 17 Neal Walk	.50	.25
❑ 18 John Brisker	1.00	.50
❑ 19 Lucius Allen	.50	.25
❑ 20 Tom Van Arsdale	1.00	.50
❑ 21 Larry Steele	1.00	.50
❑ 22 Curtis Rowe	1.00	.50
❑ 23 Dean Meminger	.50	.25
❑ 24 Steve Patterson	.50	.25
❑ 25 Earl Monroe	3.00	1.50
❑ 26 Jack Marin	.50	.25
❑ 27 Jo Jo White	3.00	1.50
❑ 28 Rudy Tomjanovich	6.00	3.00
❑ 29 Otto Moore	.50	.25
❑ 30 Elvin Hayes	5.00	2.50
❑ 31 Pat Riley	8.00	4.00

#	Player		
32	Clyde Lee	.50	.25
33	Bob Weiss	.50	.25
34	Jim Fox	.50	.25
35	Charlie Scott	1.00	.50
36	Cliff Meely	.50	.25
37	Jon McGlocklin	.50	.25
38	Jim McMillian	1.00	.50
39	Bill Walton RC	50.00	30.00
40	Dave Bing	3.00	1.50
41	Jim Washington	.50	.25
42	Jim Cleamons	1.00	.50
43	Mel Davis	.50	.25
44	Garfield Heard	1.00	.50
45	Jimmy Walker	1.00	.50
46	Don Nelson	1.00	.50
47	Jim Barnett	.50	.25
48	Manny Leaks	.50	.25
49	Elmore Smith	1.00	.50
50	Rick Barry	6.00	3.00
51	Jerry Sloan	1.00	.50
52	John Hummer	.50	.25
53	Keith Erickson	1.00	.50
54	George E. Johnson	.50	.25
55	Oscar Robertson	12.00	6.00
56	Steve Mix RC	1.00	.50
57	Rick Roberson	.50	.25
58	John Mengelt	.50	.25
59	Dwight Jones RC	1.00	.50
60	Austin Carr	1.00	.50
61	Nick Weatherspoon RC	1.00	.50
62	Clem Haskins	1.00	.50
63	Don Kojis	.50	.25
64	Paul Westphal	3.00	1.50
65	Walt Bellamy	4.00	2.00
66	John Johnson	1.00	.50
67	Butch Beard	1.00	.50
68	Happy Hairston	1.00	.50
69	Tom Boerwinkle	.50	.25
70	Spencer Haywood	3.00	1.50
71	Gary Melchionni	.50	.25
72	Ed Ratleff RC	1.00	.50
73	Mickey Davis	.50	.25
74	Dennis Awtrey	.50	.25
75	Fred Carter	1.00	.50
76	George Trapp	.50	.25
77	John Wetzel	.50	.25
78	Bobby Smith	1.00	.50
79	John Gianelli	.50	.25
80	Bob McAdoo	6.00	3.00
81	Hawks TL/Maravich/Bell	6.00	3.00
82	Celtics TL/Havlicek	5.00	2.50
83	Buffalo Braves TL	1.00	.50
84	Bulls TL/Love/Walker	3.00	1.50
85	Cleveland Cavs TL	1.00	.50
86	Detroit Pistons TL	1.00	.50
87	Warriors TL/Barry	3.00	1.50
88	Houston Rockets TL	1.00	.50
89	Kansas City Omaha TL	1.00	.50
90	Lakers TL/Goodrich	3.00	1.50
91	Bucks TL/Jabbar/Oscar	12.00	6.00
92	New Orleans Jazz	1.00	.50
93	Knicks TL/Fraz/Brad/DeB	5.00	2.50
94	Philadelphia 76ers TL	1.00	.50
95	Phoenix Suns TL	1.00	.50
96	Trail Blazers TL	1.00	.50
97	Seattle Supersonics TL	1.00	.50
98	Capitol Bullets TL	1.00	.50
99	Sam Lacey	.50	.25
100	John Havlicek	10.00	5.00
101	Stu Lantz	.50	.25
102	Mike Riordan	.50	.25
103	Larry Jones	.50	.25
104	Connie Hawkins	4.00	2.00
105	Nate Thurmond	3.00	1.50
106	Dick Gibbs	.50	.25
107	Corky Calhoun	.50	.25
108	Dave Wohl	.50	.25
109	Cornell Warner	.50	.25
110	Geoff Petrie	1.00	.50
111	Leroy Ellis	1.00	.50
112	Chris Ford	1.00	.50
113	Bill Bradley	10.00	5.00
114	Clifford Ray	1.00	.50
115	Dick Snyder	.50	.25
116	Nate Williams	.50	.25
117	Matt Guokas	1.00	.50
118	Henry Finkel	.50	.25
119	Curtis Perry	.50	.25
120	Gail Goodrich	3.00	1.50
121	Wes Unseld	3.00	1.50
122	Howard Porter	.50	.25
123	Jeff Mullins	.50	.25
124	Mike Bantom RC	1.00	.50
125	Fred Brown	1.00	.50
126	Bob Dandridge	1.00	.50
127	Mike Newlin	1.00	.50
128	Greg Smith	.50	.25
129	Doug Collins RC	16.00	8.00
130	Lou Hudson	1.00	.50
131	Bob Lanier	5.00	2.50
132	Phil Jackson	10.00	5.00
133	Don Chaney	1.00	.50
134	Jim Brewer RC	1.00	.50
135	Ernie DiGregorio RC	3.00	1.50
136	Steve Kuberski	.50	.25
137	Jim Price	.50	.25
138	Mike D'Antoni	.50	.25
139	John Brown	.50	.25
140	Norm Van Lier	1.00	.50
141	NBA Checklist 1-176	10.00	5.00
142	Slick Watts RC	1.00	.50
143	Walt Wesley	.50	.25
144	McAd/Jabbar/Marav LL	12.00	6.00
145	McAd/Marav/Jabbar LL	12.00	6.00
146	McAd/Jabbar/Tomjan LL	10.00	5.00
147	NBA F.T. Pct. Leaders	1.00	.50
148	Hayes/Cowens/McAd LL	4.00	2.00
149	NBA Assist Leaders	1.00	.50
150	Walt Frazier	5.00	2.50
151	Cazzie Russell	1.00	.50
152	Calvin Murphy	3.00	1.50
153	Bob Kauffman	.50	.25
154	Fred Boyd	.50	.25
155	Dave Cowens	6.00	3.00
156	Willie Norwood	.50	.25
157	Lee Winfield	.50	.25
158	Dwight Davis	.50	.25
159	George T. Johnson	.50	.25
160	Dick Van Arsdale	1.00	.50
161	NBA Eastern Semis	1.00	.50
162	NBA Western Semis	.50	.25
163	NBA Div. Finals	1.00	.50
164	NBA Championship	1.50	.75
165	Phil Chenier	1.00	.50
166	Kermit Washington RC	1.00	.50
167	Dale Schlueter	.50	.25
168	John Block	.50	.25
169	Don Smith	.50	.25
170	Nate Archibald	4.00	2.00
171	Chet Walker	1.00	.50
172	Archie Clark	.50	.25
173	Kennedy McIntosh	.50	.25
174	George Thompson	.50	.25
175	Sidney Wicks	3.00	1.50
176	Jerry West	20.00	10.00
177	Dwight Lamar	1.00	.50
178	George Carter	1.50	.75
179	Wil Robinson	1.00	.50
180	Artis Gilmore	4.00	2.00
181	Brian Taylor	1.00	.50
182	Darnell Hillman	1.50	.75
183	Dave Robisch	1.50	.75
184	Gene Littles RC	1.50	.75
185	Willie Wise AS2	1.50	.75
186	James Silas RC	3.00	1.50
187	Caldwell Jones RC	1.50	.75
188	Roland Taylor	1.00	.50
189	Randy Denton	1.00	.50
190	Dan Issel	5.00	2.50
191	Mike Gale	1.00	.50
192	Mel Daniels	1.50	.75
193	Steve Jones	1.00	.50
194	Marv Roberts	1.00	.50
195	Ron Boone AS2	1.50	.75
196	George Gervin RC !	40.00	25.00
197	Flynn Robinson	1.00	.50
198	Cincy Powell	1.50	.75
199	Glen Combs	1.00	.50
200	Julius Erving UER	40.00	25.00
201	Billy Keller	1.50	.75
202	Willie Long	1.00	.50
203	ABA Checklist 177-264	10.00	5.00
204	Joe Caldwell	1.50	.75
205	Swen Nater RC	1.50	.75
206	Rick Mount	1.50	.75
207	Erving/McG/Issel LL	10.00	5.00
208	ABA Two-Point Field	2.00	1.00
209	ABA Three-Point Field	2.00	1.00
210	ABA Free Throw	2.00	1.00
211	Gil/McGinn/Jones LL	2.00	1.00
212	ABA Assist Leaders	2.00	1.00
213	Larry Miller	1.00	.50
214	Stew Johnson	1.00	.50
215	Larry Kenon RC	3.00	1.50
216	Joe Hamilton	1.50	.75
217	Gerald Govan	1.50	.75
218	Ralph Simpson	1.50	.75
219	George McGinnis	3.00	1.50
220	Carolina Cougars TL	2.00	1.00
221	Denver Nuggets TL	2.00	1.00
222	Indiana Pacers TL	2.00	1.00
223	Colonels TL/Issel	3.00	1.50
224	Memphis Sounds TL	2.00	1.00
225	Nets TL/Erving	10.00	5.00
226	Spurs TL/Gervin	6.00	3.00
227	San Diego Conq. TL	2.00	1.00
228	Utah Stars TL	2.00	1.00
229	Virginia Squires TL	2.00	1.00
230	Bird Averitt	1.00	.50
231	John Roche	1.00	.50
232	George Irvine	1.00	.50
233	John Williamson RC	1.50	.75
234	Billy Cunningham	4.00	2.00
235	Jimmy O'Brien	1.00	.50
236	Wilbert Jones	1.00	.50
237	Johnny Neumann	1.00	.50
238	Al Smith	1.00	.50
239	Roger Brown	1.50	.75
240	Chuck Williams	1.50	.75
241	Rich Jones	1.00	.50
242	Dave Twardzik RC	1.50	.75
243	Wendell Ladner	1.50	.75
244	Mack Calvin	1.50	.75
245	ABA Eastern Semis	2.00	1.00
246	ABA Western Semis	2.00	1.00
247	ABA Div. Finals	2.00	1.00
248	ABA Championships/Dr.J.	12.00	6.00
249	Ron Robinson	1.00	.50
250	Wilt Chamberlain	35.00	20.00
251	Zelmo Beaty	1.50	.75
252	Donnie Freeman	1.50	.75
253	Mike Green	1.50	.75
254	Louie Dampier AS2	1.50	.75
255	Tom Owens	1.00	.50
256	George Karl RC	10.00	5.00
257	Jim Eakins	1.50	.75
258	Travis Grant	1.50	.75
259	James Jones AS1	1.50	.75
260	Mike Jackson	1.00	.50
261	Billy Paultz	1.50	.75
262	Freddie Lewis	1.50	.75
263	Byron Beck !	3.00	1.50

1975-76 Topps

Bob Lanier

COMPLETE SET (330)		450.00	275.00
COM. NBA CARD (1-220)		.75	.35
COM. ABA CARD (221-330)		1.50	.75
1	McAd/Barry/Jabbar LL !	12.00	6.00
2	Nelson/Beard/Tomj LL	4.00	2.00

#	Card	Price 1	Price 2
3	Barry/Murphy/Bradley LL	5.00	2.50
4	Unseld/Cowens/Lacey LL	1.50	.75
5	Porter/Bing/Arch LL	1.50	.75
6	Barry/Frazier/Steele LL	4.00	2.00
7	Tom Van Arsdale	1.25	.60
8	Paul Silas	1.25	.60
9	Jerry Sloan	1.25	.60
10	Bob McAdoo	6.00	3.00
11	Dwight Davis	.75	.35
12	John Mengelt	.75	.35
13	George Johnson	.75	.35
14	Ed Ratleff	.75	.35
15	Nate Archibald	4.00	2.00
16	Elmore Smith	.75	.35
17	Bob Dandridge	1.25	.60
18	Louie Nelson RC	.75	.35
19	Neal Walk	.75	.35
20	Billy Cunningham	4.00	2.00
21	Gary Melchionni	.75	.35
22	Barry Clemens	.75	.35
23	Jimmy Jones	.75	.35
24	Tom Burleson RC	1.25	.60
25	Lou Hudson	1.25	.60
26	Henry Finkel	.75	.35
27	Jim McMillian	1.25	.60
28	Matt Guokas	1.25	.60
29	Fred Foster DP	.75	.35
30	Bob Lanier	5.00	2.50
31	Jimmy Walker	1.25	.60
32	Cliff Meely	.75	.35
33	Butch Beard	1.25	.60
34	Cazzie Russell	1.25	.60
35	Jon McGlocklin	.75	.35
36	Bernie Fryer	.75	.35
37	Bill Bradley	10.00	5.00
38	Fred Carter	1.25	.60
39	Dennis Awtrey DP	.75	.35
40	Sidney Wicks	1.25	.60
41	Fred Brown	1.25	.60
42	Rowland Garrett	.75	.35
43	Harm Gilliam	.75	.35
44	Don Nelson	1.25	.60
45	Ernie DiGregorio	1.25	.60
46	Jim Brewer	.75	.35
47	Chris Ford	1.25	.60
48	Nick Weatherspoon	.75	.35
49	Zaid Abdul-Aziz	.75	.35
50	Keith/Jamaal Wilkes RC	10.00	5.00
51	Ollie Johnson DP	.75	.35
52	Lucius Allen	1.25	.60
53	Mickey Davis	.75	.35
54	Otto Moore	.75	.35
55	Walt Frazier	5.00	2.50
56	Steve Mix	1.25	.60
57	Nate Hawthorne	.75	.35
58	Lloyd Neal	.75	.35
59	Don Watts	1.25	.60
60	Elvin Hayes	5.00	2.50
61	Checklist 1-110	8.00	4.00
62	Mike Sojourner	.75	.35
63	Randy Smith	1.25	.60
64	John Block DP	.75	.35
65	Charlie Scott	1.25	.60
66	Jim Chones	1.25	.60
67	Rick Adelman	1.25	.60
68	Curtis Rowe	.75	.35
69	Derrek Dickey RC	1.25	.60
70	Rudy Tomjanovich	5.00	2.50
71	Pat Riley	6.00	3.00
72	Cornell Warner	.75	.35
73	Earl Monroe	3.00	1.50
74	Allan Bristow RC	3.00	1.50
75	Pete Maravich DP	20.00	12.00
76	Curtis Perry	.75	.35
77	Bill Walton	20.00	12.00
78	Leonard Gray	.75	.35
79	Kevin Porter	1.25	.60
80	John Havlicek	10.00	5.00
81	Dwight Jones	.75	.35
82	Jack Marin	.75	.35
83	Dick Snyder	.75	.35
84	George Trapp	.75	.35
85	Nate Thurmond	3.00	1.50
86	Charles Johnson	.75	.35
87	Ron Riley	.75	.35
88	Stu Lantz	1.25	.60
89	Scott Wedman RC	1.25	.60
90	Kareem Abdul-Jabbar	20.00	12.00
91	Aaron James	.75	.35
92	Jim Barnett	.75	.35
93	Clyde Lee	.75	.35
94	Larry Steele	1.25	.60
95	Mike Riordan	.75	.35
96	Archie Clark	1.25	.60
97	Mike Bantom	.75	.35
98	Bob Kauffman	.75	.35
99	Kevin Stacom RC	.75	.35
100	Rick Barry	6.00	3.00
101	Ken Charles	.75	.35
102	Tom Boerwinkle	.75	.35
103	Mike Newlin	1.25	.60
104	Leroy Ellis	.75	.35
105	Austin Carr	1.25	.60
106	Ron Behagen	.75	.35
107	Jim Price	.75	.35
108	Bud Stallworth	.75	.35
109	Earl Williams	.75	.35
110	Gail Goodrich	3.00	1.50
111	Phil Jackson	6.00	3.00
112	Rod Derline	.75	.35
113	Keith Erickson	.75	.35
114	Phil Lumpkin	.75	.35
115	Wes Unseld	3.00	1.50
116	Atlanta Hawks TL	1.50	.75
117	Cowens/White TL	3.00	1.50
118	Buffalo Braves TL	3.00	1.50
119	Love/Walk/Thur TL	3.00	1.50
120	Cleveland Cavs TL	1.50	.75
121	Lanier/Bing TL	3.00	1.50
122	Rick Barry TL	3.00	1.50
123	Houston Rockets TL	2.00	1.00
124	Kansas City Kings TL	2.00	1.00
125	Los Angeles Lakers TL	1.50	.75
126	Kareem A.-Jabbar TL	8.00	4.00
127	Pete Maravich TL	10.00	5.00
128	Frazier/Bradley TL DP	2.00	1.00
129	Carl/Coll/Cunn TL DP	2.00	1.00
130	Phoenix Suns TL DP	1.50	.75
131	Portland Blazers TL DP	1.50	.75
132	Seattle Sonics TL	2.00	1.00
133	Hayes/Unseld TL	3.00	1.50
134	John Drew RC	1.25	.60
135	Jo Jo White	2.00	1.00
136	Garfield Heard	1.25	.60
137	Jim Cleamons	.75	.35
138	Howard Porter	1.25	.60
139	Phil Smith RC	1.25	.60
140	Bob Love	1.25	.60
141	John Gianelli DP	.75	.35
142	Larry McNeill RC	.75	.35
143	Brian Winters RC	3.00	1.50
144	George Thompson	.75	.35
145	Kevin Kunnert	.75	.35
146	Henry Bibby	1.25	.60
147	John Johnson	.75	.35
148	Doug Collins	4.00	2.00
149	John Brisker	.75	.35
150	Dick Van Arsdale	1.25	.60
151	Leonard Robinson RC	3.00	1.50
152	Dean Meminger	.75	.35
153	Phil Hankinson	.75	.35
154	Dale Schlueter	.75	.35
155	Norm Van Lier	1.25	.60
156	Campy Russell RC	3.00	1.50
157	Jeff Mullins	1.25	.60
158	Sam Lacey	.75	.35
159	Happy Hairston	1.25	.60
160	Dave Bing DP	3.00	1.50
161	Kevin Restani RC	.75	.35
162	Dave Wohl	.75	.35
163	E.C. Coleman	.75	.35
164	Jim Fox	.75	.35
165	Geoff Petrie	1.25	.60
166	Hawthorne Wingo DP UER	.75	.35
167	Fred Boyd	.75	.35
168	Willie Norwood	.75	.35
169	Bob Wilson	.75	.35
170	Dave Cowens	6.00	3.00
171	Tom Henderson RC	.75	.35
172	Jim Washington	.75	.35
173	Clem Haskins	1.25	.60
174	Jim Davis	.75	.35
175	Bobby Smith DP	.75	.35
176	Mike D'Antoni	.75	.35
177	Zelmo Beaty	1.25	.60
178	Gary Brokaw RC	.75	.35
179	Mel Davis	.75	.35
180	Calvin Murphy	3.00	1.50
181	Checklist 111-220 DP	8.00	4.00
182	Nate Williams	.75	.35
183	LaRue Martin	.75	.35
184	George McGinnis	3.00	1.50
185	Clifford Ray	.75	.35
186	Paul Westphal	4.00	2.00
187	Talvin Skinner	.75	.35
188	NBA Playoff Semis DP	1.50	.75
189	NBA Playoff Finals	1.50	.75
190	Phil Chenier AS2 DP	1.25	.60
191	John Brown	.75	.35
192	Lee Winfield	.75	.35
193	Steve Patterson	.75	.35
194	Charles Dudley	.75	.35
195	Connie Hawkins DP	3.00	1.50
196	Leon Benbow	.75	.35
197	Don Kojis	.75	.35
198	Ron Williams	.75	.35
199	Mel Counts	.75	.35
200	Spencer Haywood	3.00	1.50
201	Greg Jackson	.75	.35
202	Tom Kozelko DP	.75	.35
203	Atlanta Hawks	1.50	.75
204	Celtics Team CL	3.00	1.50
205	Buffalo Braves CL	1.50	.75
206	Bulls Team CL	3.00	1.50
207	Cleveland Cavs	1.50	.75
208	Detroit Pistons	1.50	.75
209	Golden State	1.50	.75
210	Houston Rockets	1.50	.75
211	Kansas City Kings DP	1.50	.75
212	Los Angeles Lakers DP	1.50	.75
213	Milwaukee Bucks	1.50	.75
214	New Orleans Jazz	1.50	.75
215	New York Knicks	1.50	.75
216	Philadelphia 76ers	1.50	.75
217	Phoenix Suns DP	1.50	.75
218	Portland Blazers	1.50	.75
219	Sonics Team/B.Russell	10.00	5.00
220	Washington Bullets	1.50	.75
221	McGin/Erving/Boone LL	8.00	4.00
222	Jones/Gilmore/Malone LL	8.00	4.00
223	ABA 3 Pt. Field Goal	2.00	1.00
224	ABA Free Throw	2.00	1.00
225	ABA Rebounds Leaders	2.00	1.00
226	ABA Assists Leaders	2.00	1.00
227	Mack Calvin	1.50	.75
228	Billy Knight RC	3.00	1.50
229	Bird Averitt	1.50	.75
230	George Carter	1.50	.75
231	Swen Nater	2.00	1.00
232	Steve Jones	2.00	1.00
233	George Gervin	20.00	10.00
234	Lee Davis	1.50	.75
235	Ron Boone AS1	2.00	1.00
236	Mike Jackson	1.50	.75
237	Kevin Joyce RC	1.50	.75
238	Marv Roberts	1.50	.75
239	Tom Owens	1.50	.75
240	Ralph Simpson	2.00	1.00
241	Gus Gerard	1.50	.75
242	Brian Taylor AS2	2.00	1.00
243	Rich Jones	1.50	.75
244	John Roche	1.50	.75
245	Travis Grant	2.00	1.00
246	Dave Twardzik	2.00	1.00
247	Mike Green	1.50	.75
248	Billy Keller	2.00	1.00
249	Stew Johnson	1.50	.75
250	Artis Gilmore	4.00	2.00
251	John Williamson	2.00	1.00
252	Marvin Barnes RC	4.00	2.00
253	James Silas	2.00	1.00
254	Moses Malone RC !	35.00	18.00
255	Willie Wise	2.00	1.00
256	Dwight Lamar	1.50	.75
257	Checklist 221-330	8.00	4.00
258	Byron Beck	2.00	1.00
259	Len Elmore RC	3.00	1.50
260	Dan Issel	5.00	2.50

❏ 261	Rick Mount	1.50	.75
❏ 262	Billy Paultz	2.00	1.00
❏ 263	Donnie Freeman	1.50	.75
❏ 264	George Adams	1.50	.75
❏ 265	Don Chaney	2.00	1.00
❏ 266	Randy Denton	1.50	.75
❏ 267	Don Washington	1.50	.75
❏ 268	Roland Taylor	1.50	.75
❏ 269	Charlie Edge	1.50	.75
❏ 270	Louie Dampier	2.00	1.00
❏ 271	Collis Jones	1.50	.75
❏ 272	Al Skinner RC	1.50	.75
❏ 273	Coby Dietrick	1.50	.75
❏ 274	Tim Bassett	1.50	.75
❏ 275	Freddie Lewis	2.00	1.00
❏ 276	Gerald Govan	1.50	.75
❏ 277	Ron Thomas	1.50	.75
❏ 278	Denver Nuggets TL	2.00	1.00
❏ 279	McGinnis/Keller TL	2.50	1.25
❏ 280	Gilmore/Dampier TL	2.50	1.25
❏ 281	Memphis Sounds TL	2.00	1.00
❏ 282	Julius Erving TL	15.00	6.00
❏ 283	Barnes/Lewis TL	2.50	1.25
❏ 284	George Gervin TL	5.00	2.50
❏ 285	San Diego Sails TL	2.00	1.00
❏ 286	Malone/Boone TL	8.00	4.00
❏ 287	Virginia Squires TL	2.00	1.00
❏ 288	Claude Terry	1.50	.75
❏ 289	Wilbert Jones	1.50	.75
❏ 290	Darnell Hillman	2.00	1.00
❏ 291	Bill Melchionni	2.00	1.00
❏ 292	Mel Daniels	2.00	1.00
❏ 293	Fly Williams RC	2.00	1.00
❏ 294	Larry Kenon	2.00	1.00
❏ 295	Red Robbins	2.00	1.00
❏ 296	Warren Jabali	2.00	1.00
❏ 297	Jim Eakins	2.00	1.00
❏ 298	Bobby Jones RC	12.00	6.00
❏ 299	Don Buse	2.00	1.00
❏ 300	Julius Erving	35.00	20.00
❏ 301	Billy Shepherd	1.50	.75
❏ 302	Maurice Lucas RC	6.00	3.00
❏ 303	George Karl	5.00	2.50
❏ 304	Jim Bradley	1.50	.75
❏ 305	Caldwell Jones	2.00	1.00
❏ 306	Al Smith	1.50	.75
❏ 307	Jan VanBredaKolff RC	2.00	1.00
❏ 308	Darrell Elston	1.50	.75
❏ 309	ABA Playoff Semifinals	2.00	1.00
❏ 310	Artis Gilmore PO	2.50	1.25
❏ 311	Ted McClain	1.50	.75
❏ 312	Willie Sojourner	1.50	.75
❏ 313	Bob Warren	1.50	.75
❏ 314	Bob Netolicky	2.00	1.00
❏ 315	Chuck Williams	1.50	.75
❏ 316	Gene Kennedy	1.50	.75
❏ 317	Jimmy O'Brien	1.50	.75
❏ 318	Dave Robisch	1.50	.75
❏ 319	Wali Jones	1.50	.75
❏ 320	George Irvine	1.50	.75
❏ 321	Denver Nuggets	2.00	1.00
❏ 322	Indiana Pacers	2.00	1.00
❏ 323	Kentucky Colonels	2.00	1.00
❏ 324	Memphis Sounds	2.00	1.00
❏ 325	New York Nets	2.00	1.00
❏ 326	St. Louis Spirits	2.00	1.00
❏ 327	San Antonio Spurs	2.00	1.00
❏ 328	San Diego Sails	2.00	1.00
❏ 329	Utah Stars	2.00	1.00
❏ 330	Squires Checklist !	4.00	2.00

1976-77 Topps

❏ COMPLETE SET (144)		375.00	200.00
❏ 1	Julius Erving !	60.00	30.00
❏ 2	Dick Snyder	1.75	.75
❏ 3	Paul Silas	2.50	1.25
❏ 4	Keith Erickson	1.75	.75
❏ 5	Wes Unseld	5.00	2.50
❏ 6	Butch Beard	2.50	1.25
❏ 7	Lloyd Neal	1.75	.75
❏ 8	Tom Henderson	1.75	.75
❏ 9	Jim McMillian	2.50	1.25
❏ 10	Bob Lanier	6.00	3.00
❏ 11	Junior Bridgeman RC	2.50	1.25
❏ 12	Corky Calhoun	1.75	.75
❏ 13	Billy Keller	2.50	1.25

DAVID THOMPSON

❏ 14	Mickey Johnson RC	1.75	.75
❏ 15	Fred Brown	2.50	1.25
❏ 16	Keith Wilkes	2.50	1.25
❏ 17	Louie Nelson	1.75	.75
❏ 18	Ed-Ratleff	1.75	.75
❏ 19	Billy Paultz	2.50	1.25
❏ 20	Nate Archibald	5.00	2.50
❏ 21	Steve Mix	2.50	1.25
❏ 22	Ralph Simpson	1.75	.75
❏ 23	Campy Russell	2.50	1.25
❏ 24	Charlie Scott	2.50	1.25
❏ 25	Artis Gilmore	5.00	2.50
❏ 26	Dick Van Arsdale	2.50	1.25
❏ 27	Phil Chenier	2.50	1.25
❏ 28	Spencer Haywood	5.00	2.50
❏ 29	Chris Ford	2.50	1.25
❏ 30	Dave Cowens	10.00	5.00
❏ 31	Sidney Wicks	2.50	1.25
❏ 32	Jim Price	1.75	.75
❏ 33	Dwight Jones	1.75	.75
❏ 34	Lucius Allen	1.75	.75
❏ 35	Marvin Barnes	2.50	1.25
❏ 36	Henry Bibby	2.50	1.25
❏ 37	Joe C.Meriweather RC	1.75	.75
❏ 38	Doug Collins	6.00	3.00
❏ 39	Garfield Heard	2.50	1.25
❏ 40	Randy Smith	2.50	1.25
❏ 41	Tom Burleson	2.50	1.25
❏ 42	Dave Twardzik	2.50	1.25
❏ 43	Bill Bradley	12.00	6.00
❏ 44	Calvin Murphy	5.00	2.50
❏ 45	Bob Love	2.50	1.25
❏ 46	Brian Winters	2.50	1.25
❏ 47	Glenn McDonald	1.75	.75
❏ 48	Checklist 1-144	30.00	15.00
❏ 49	Bird Averitt	1.75	.75
❏ 50	Rick Barry	10.00	5.00
❏ 51	Ticky Burden	1.75	.75
❏ 52	Rich Jones	1.75	.75
❏ 53	Austin Carr	2.50	1.25
❏ 54	Steve Kuberski	1.75	.75
❏ 55	Paul Westphal	2.50	1.25
❏ 56	Mike Riordan	1.75	.75
❏ 57	Bill Walton	25.00	15.00
❏ 58	Eric Money RC	1.75	.75
❏ 59	John Drew	2.50	1.25
❏ 60	Pete Maravich	45.00	25.00
❏ 61	John Shumate RC	2.50	1.25
❏ 62	Mack Calvin	2.50	1.25
❏ 63	Bruce Seals	1.75	.75
❏ 64	Walt Frazier	6.00	3.00
❏ 65	Elmore Smith	1.75	.75
❏ 66	Rudy Tomjanovich	6.00	3.00
❏ 67	Sam Lacey	1.75	.75
❏ 68	George Gervin	25.00	15.00
❏ 69	Gus Williams RC	5.00	2.50
❏ 70	George McGinnis	2.50	1.25
❏ 71	Len Elmore	1.75	.75
❏ 72	Jack Marin	1.75	.75
❏ 73	Brian Taylor	1.75	.75
❏ 74	Jim Brewer	1.75	.75
❏ 75	Adrians Adams RC	6.00	3.00
❏ 76	Dave Bing	5.00	2.50
❏ 77	Phil Jackson	10.00	5.00
❏ 78	Geoff Petrie	2.50	1.25
❏ 79	Mike Sojourner	1.75	.75
❏ 80	James Silas	2.50	1.25
❏ 81	Bob Dandridge	2.50	1.25

❏ 82	Ernie DiGregorio	2.50	1.25
❏ 83	Cazzie Russell	2.50	1.25
❏ 84	Kevin Porter	2.50	1.25
❏ 85	Tom Boerwinkle	1.75	.75
❏ 86	Darnell Hillman	2.50	1.25
❏ 87	Herm Gilliam	1.75	.75
❏ 88	Nate Williams	1.75	.75
❏ 89	Phil Smith	2.50	1.25
❏ 90	John Havlicek	15.00	7.50
❏ 91	Kevin Kunnert	1.75	.75
❏ 92	Jimmy Walker	2.50	1.25
❏ 93	Billy Cunningham	5.00	2.50
❏ 94	Dan Issel	6.00	3.00
❏ 95	Ron Boone	2.50	1.25
❏ 96	Lou Hudson	2.50	1.25
❏ 97	Jim Chones	2.50	1.25
❏ 98	Earl Monroe	5.00	2.50
❏ 99	Tom Van Arsdale	2.50	1.25
❏ 100	Kareem Abdul-Jabbar	40.00	20.00
❏ 101	Moses Malone	25.00	12.50
❏ 102	Ricky Sobers RC	1.75	.75
❏ 103	Swen Nater	2.50	1.25
❏ 104	Leonard Robinson	2.50	1.25
❏ 105	Don Watts	2.50	1.25
❏ 106	Otto Moore	1.75	.75
❏ 107	Maurice Lucas	2.50	1.25
❏ 108	Norm Van Lier	2.50	1.25
❏ 109	Clifford Ray	1.75	.75
❏ 110	David Thompson RC	40.00	20.00
❏ 111	Fred Carter	2.50	1.25
❏ 112	Caldwell Jones	2.50	1.25
❏ 113	John Williamson	2.50	1.25
❏ 114	Bobby Smith	2.50	1.25
❏ 115	Jo Jo White	2.50	1.25
❏ 116	Curtis Perry	1.75	.75
❏ 117	John Gianelli	1.75	.75
❏ 118	Curtis Rowe	1.75	.75
❏ 119	Lionel Hollins RC	2.50	1.25
❏ 120	Elvin Hayes	6.00	3.00
❏ 121	Ken Charles	1.75	.75
❏ 122	Dave Meyers RC	2.50	1.25
❏ 123	Jerry Sloan	2.50	1.25
❏ 124	Billy Knight	2.50	1.25
❏ 125	Gail Goodrich	2.50	1.25
❏ 126	K. Abdul-Jabbar AS	20.00	12.00
❏ 127	Julius Erving AS	25.00	15.00
❏ 128	George McGinnis AS	2.50	1.25
❏ 129	Nate Archibald AS	2.50	1.25
❏ 130	Pete Maravich AS	25.00	15.00
❏ 131	Dave Cowens AS	5.00	2.50
❏ 132	Rick Barry AS	5.00	2.50
❏ 133	Elvin Hayes AS	5.00	2.50
❏ 134	James Silas AS	2.00	1.00
❏ 135	Randy Smith AS	2.00	1.00
❏ 136	Leonard Gray	1.75	.75
❏ 137	Charles Johnson	1.75	.75
❏ 138	Ron Behagen	1.75	.75
❏ 139	Mike Newlin	2.50	1.25
❏ 140	Bob McAdoo	6.00	3.00
❏ 141	Mike Gale	1.75	.75
❏ 142	Scott Wedman	2.50	1.25
❏ 143	Lloyd Free RC	6.00	3.00
❏ 144	Bobby Jones !	8.00	4.00

1977-78 Topps

BULLS — ARTIS GILMORE

❏ COMPLETE SET (132)		100.00	50.00
❏ 1	Kareem Abdul-Jabbar !	15.00	7.50
❏ 2	Henry Bibby	.40	.15

☐ 3	Curtis Rowe	.30	.10
☐ 4	Norm Van Lier	.40	.15
☐ 5	Darnell Hillman	.40	.15
☐ 6	Earl Monroe	1.50	.60
☐ 7	Leonard Gray	.30	.10
☐ 8	Bird Averitt	.30	.10
☐ 9	Jim Brewer	.30	.10
☐ 10	Paul Westphal	1.00	.40
☐ 11	Bob Gross RC	.40	.15
☐ 12	Phil Smith	.30	.10
☐ 13	Dan Roundfield RC	.60	.25
☐ 14	Brian Taylor	.30	.10
☐ 15	Rudy Tomjanovich	2.00	1.00
☐ 16	Kevin Porter	.40	.15
☐ 17	Scott Wedman	.40	.15
☐ 18	Lloyd Free	.60	.25
☐ 19	Tom Boswell RC	.30	.10
☐ 20	Pete Maravich	15.00	7.50
☐ 21	Cliff Poindexter	.30	.10
☐ 22	Bubbles Hawkins	.40	.15
☐ 23	Kevin Grevey RC	1.25	.50
☐ 24	Ken Charles	.30	.10
☐ 25	Bob Dandridge	.40	.15
☐ 26	Lonnie Shelton RC	.40	.15
☐ 27	Don Chaney	.40	.15
☐ 28	Larry Kenon	.40	.15
☐ 29	Checklist 1-132		
☐ 30	Fred Brown	.40	.15
☐ 31	Dan Gianelli UER	.30	.10
☐ 32	Austin Carr	.40	.15
☐ 33	Keith/Jamaal Wilkes	.60	.25
☐ 34	Caldwell Jones	.40	.15
☐ 35	Jo Jo White	.60	.25
☐ 36	Scott May RC	1.25	.50
☐ 37	Mike Newlin	.30	.10
☐ 38	Mel Davis	.30	.10
☐ 39	Lionel Hollins	.60	.25
☐ 40	Elvin Hayes	2.50	1.25
☐ 41	Dan Issel	2.00	1.00
☐ 42	Ricky Sobers	.30	.10
☐ 43	Don Ford	.30	.10
☐ 44	John Williamson	.30	.10
☐ 45	Bob McAdoo	2.00	1.00
☐ 46	Geoff Petrie	.40	.15
☐ 47	M.L.Carr RC	2.00	.75
☐ 48	Brian Winters	.60	.25
☐ 49	Sam Lacey	.30	.10
☐ 50	George McGinnis	.60	.25
☐ 51	Don Watts	.40	.15
☐ 52	Sidney Wicks	.60	.25
☐ 53	Wilbur Holland	.30	.10
☐ 54	Tim Bassett	.30	.10
☐ 55	Phil Chenier	.40	.15
☐ 56	Adrian Dantley RC	8.00	4.00
☐ 57	Jim Chones	.30	.15
☐ 58	John Lucas RC	2.50	1.25
☐ 59	Cazzie Russell	.40	.15
☐ 60	David Thompson	5.00	2.50
☐ 61	Bob Lanier	2.00	1.00
☐ 62	Dave Twardzik	.40	.15
☐ 63	Wilbert Jones	.30	.10
☐ 64	Clifford Ray	.30	.10
☐ 65	Doug Collins	1.50	.60
☐ 66	Tom McMillen RC	2.50	1.25
☐ 67	Rich Kelley RC	.30	.10
☐ 68	Mike Bantom	.30	.10
☐ 69	Tom Boerwinkle	.30	.10
☐ 70	John Havlicek	6.00	3.00
☐ 71	Marvin Webster RC	.40	.15
☐ 72	Curtis Perry	.30	.10
☐ 73	George Gervin	8.00	4.00
☐ 74	Leonard Robinson	.60	.25
☐ 75	Wes Unseld	1.50	.60
☐ 76	Dave Meyers	.40	.15
☐ 77	Gail Goodrich	.60	.25
☐ 78	Richard Washington RC	.60	.25
☐ 79	Mike Gale	.30	.10
☐ 80	Maurice Lucas	.60	.25
☐ 81	Harvey Catchings RC	.40	.15
☐ 82	Randy Smith	.40	.15
☐ 83	Campy Russell	.40	.15
☐ 84	Kevin Kunnert	.30	.10
☐ 85	Lou Hudson	.40	.15
☐ 86	Mickey Johnson	.30	.10
☐ 87	Lucius Allen	.30	.10
☐ 88	Spencer Haywood	1.00	.40

☐ 89	Gus Williams	.60	.25
☐ 90	Dave Cowens	3.00	1.50
☐ 91	Al Skinner	.30	.10
☐ 92	Swen Nater	.30	.10
☐ 93	Tom Henderson	.30	.10
☐ 94	Don Buse	.40	.15
☐ 95	Alvan Adams	.60	.25
☐ 96	Mack Calvin	.40	.15
☐ 97	Tom Burleson	.30	.10
☐ 98	John Drew	.40	.15
☐ 99	Mike Green	.30	.10
☐ 100	Julius Erving	15.00	7.50
☐ 101	John Mengelt	.30	.10
☐ 102	Howard Porter	.40	.15
☐ 103	Billy Paultz	.40	.15
☐ 104	John Shumate	.40	.15
☐ 105	Calvin Murphy	1.50	.60
☐ 106	Elmore Smith	.30	.10
☐ 107	Jim McMillian	.30	.10
☐ 108	Kevin Stacom	.30	.10
☐ 109	Jan Van Breda Kolff	.30	.10
☐ 110	Billy Knight	.40	.15
☐ 111	Robert Parish RC !	25.00	10.00
☐ 112	Larry Wright	.30	.10
☐ 113	Bruce Seals	.30	.10
☐ 114	Junior Bridgeman	.40	.15
☐ 115	Artis Gilmore	1.50	.60
☐ 116	Steve Mix	.40	.15
☐ 117	Ron Lee	.30	.10
☐ 118	Bobby Jones	.60	.25
☐ 119	Ron Boone	.40	.15
☐ 120	Bill Walton	8.00	4.00
☐ 121	Chris Ford	.40	.15
☐ 122	Earl Tatum	.30	.10
☐ 123	E.C. Coleman	.30	.10
☐ 124	Moses Malone	6.00	3.00
☐ 125	Charlie Scott	.40	.15
☐ 126	Bobby Smith	.30	.10
☐ 127	Nate Archibald	1.50	.60
☐ 128	Mitch Kupchak RC	1.25	.50
☐ 129	Walt Frazier	2.50	1.25
☐ 130	Rick Barry	3.00	1.50
☐ 131	Ernie DiGregorio	.40	.15
☐ 132	Darryl Dawkins RC !	10.00	5.00

1978-79 Topps

☐ 1	Bill Walton !	10.00	5.00
☐ 2	Doug Collins	1.50	.60
☐ 3	Jamaal Wilkes	.75	.30
☐ 4	Wilbur Holland	.30	.10
☐ 5	Bob McAdoo	1.25	.50
☐ 6	Lucius Allen	.30	.10
☐ 7	Wes Unseld	.75	.30
☐ 8	Dave Meyers	.50	.20
☐ 9	Austin Carr	.50	.20
☐ 10	Walter Davis RC	7.00	3.50
☐ 11	John Williamson	.30	.10
☐ 12	E.C. Coleman	.30	.10
☐ 13	Calvin Murphy	1.00	.40
☐ 14	Bobby Jones	.75	.30
☐ 15	Chris Ford	.50	.20
☐ 16	Kermit Washington	.50	.20
☐ 17	Butch Beard	.50	.20
☐ 18	Steve Mix	.30	.10
☐ 19	Marvin Webster	.50	.20
☐ 20	George Gervin	6.00	3.00
☐ 21	Steve Hawes	.30	.10
☐ 22	Johnny Davis RC	.50	.20

☐ 23	Swen Nater	.30	.10
☐ 24	Lou Hudson	.50	.20
☐ 25	Elvin Hayes	1.50	.60
☐ 26	Nate Archibald	1.00	.40
☐ 27	James Edwards RC	3.00	1.50
☐ 28	Howard Porter	.50	.20
☐ 29	Quinn Buckner RC	1.25	.50
☐ 30	Leonard Robinson	.50	.20
☐ 31	Jim Cleamons	.30	.10
☐ 32	Campy Russell	.50	.20
☐ 33	Phil Smith	.30	.10
☐ 34	Darryl Dawkins	2.00	1.00
☐ 35	Don Buse	.50	.20
☐ 36	Mickey Johnson	.30	.10
☐ 37	Mike Gale	.30	.10
☐ 38	Moses Malone	4.00	2.00
☐ 39	Gus Williams	.75	.30
☐ 40	Dave Cowens	2.00	1.00
☐ 41	Bobby Wilkerson RC	.50	.20
☐ 42	Wilbert Jones	.30	.10
☐ 43	Charlie Scott	.50	.20
☐ 44	John Drew	.50	.20
☐ 45	Earl Monroe	1.25	.50
☐ 46	John Shumate	.50	.20
☐ 47	Earl Tatum	.30	.10
☐ 48	Mitch Kupchak	.50	.20
☐ 49	Ron Boone	.50	.20
☐ 50	Maurice Lucas	.75	.30
☐ 51	Louie Dampier	.50	.20
☐ 52	Aaron James	.30	.10
☐ 53	John Mengelt	.50	.20
☐ 54	Garfield Heard	.50	.20
☐ 55	George Johnson	.30	.10
☐ 56	Junior Bridgeman	.30	.10
☐ 57	Elmore Smith	.30	.10
☐ 58	Rudy Tomjanovich	1.50	.60
☐ 59	Fred Brown	.50	.20
☐ 60	Rick Barry	2.00	1.00
☐ 61	Dave Bing	1.25	.50
☐ 62	Anthony Roberts	.30	.10
☐ 63	Norm Nixon RC	2.00	1.00
☐ 64	Leon Douglas RC	.50	.20
☐ 65	Henry Bibby	.50	.20
☐ 66	Lonnie Shelton	.30	.10
☐ 67	Checklist 1-132	2.00	1.00
☐ 68	Tom Henderson	.30	.10
☐ 69	Dan Roundfield	.50	.20
☐ 70	Armond Hill RC	.50	.20
☐ 71	Larry Kenon	.50	.20
☐ 72	Billy Knight	.50	.20
☐ 73	Artis Gilmore	1.00	.40
☐ 74	Lionel Hollins	.50	.20
☐ 75	Bernard King RC	7.00	3.50
☐ 76	Brian Winters	.75	.30
☐ 77	Alvan Adams	.75	.30
☐ 78	Dennis Johnson RC	8.00	4.00
☐ 79	Scott Wedman	.30	.10
☐ 80	Pete Maravich	10.00	5.00
☐ 81	Dan Issel	1.50	.60
☐ 82	M.L. Carr	.75	.30
☐ 83	Walt Frazier	1.50	.60
☐ 84	Dwight Jones	.30	.10
☐ 85	Jo Jo White	.75	.30
☐ 86	Robert Parish	5.00	2.50
☐ 87	Charlie Criss RC	.50	.20
☐ 88	Jim McMillian	.30	.10
☐ 89	Chuck Williams	.30	.10
☐ 90	George McGinnis	.75	.30
☐ 91	Billy Paultz	.50	.20
☐ 92	Bob Dandridge	.50	.20
☐ 93	Ricky Sobers	.30	.10
☐ 94	Paul Silas	.50	.20
☐ 95	Gail Goodrich	.75	.30
☐ 96	Tim Bassett	.30	.10
☐ 97	Ron Lee	.30	.10
☐ 98	Bob Gross	.50	.20
☐ 99	Sam Lacey	.30	.10
☐ 100	David Thompson	3.00	1.50
☐ 101	John Gianelli	.30	.10
☐ 102	Norm Van Lier	.50	.20
☐ 103	Caldwell Jones	.50	.20
☐ 104	Eric Money	.30	.10
☐ 105	Jim Chones	.50	.20
☐ 106	John Lucas	1.00	.40
☐ 107	Spencer Haywood	.50	.20
☐ 108	Fast Eddie Johnson RC	.30	.10

☐ 109 Sidney Wicks	.75	.30
☐ 110 Kareem Abdul-Jabbar	8.00	4.00
☐ 111 Sonny Parker RC	.50	.20
☐ 112 Randy Smith	.30	.10
☐ 113 Kevin Grevey	.50	.20
☐ 114 Rich Kelley	.30	.10
☐ 115 Scott May	.50	.20
☐ 116 Lloyd Free	.75	.30
☐ 117 Jack Sikma RC	2.00	1.00
☐ 118 Kevin Porter	.50	.20
☐ 119 Darnell Hillman	.50	.20
☐ 120 Paul Westphal	1.00	.40
☐ 121 Richard Washington	.30	.10
☐ 122 Dave Twardzik	.50	.20
☐ 123 Mike Bantom	.30	.10
☐ 124 Mike Newlin	.30	.10
☐ 125 Bob Lanier	1.50	.60
☐ 126 Marques Johnson RC	4.00	2.00
☐ 127 Foots Walker RC	.50	.20
☐ 128 Cedric Maxwell RC	1.25	.50
☐ 129 Ray Williams RC	.50	.20
☐ 130 Julius Erving	10.00	5.00
☐ 131 Clifford Ray	.30	.10
☐ 132 Adrian Dantley !	3.00	1.50

1979-80 Topps

☐ COMPLETE SET (132)	80.00	40.00
☐ 1 George Gervin !	6.00	3.00
☐ 2 Mitch Kupchak	.40	.15
☐ 3 Henry Bibby	.40	.15
☐ 4 Bob Gross	.40	.15
☐ 5 Dave Cowens	2.00	1.00
☐ 6 Dennis Johnson	1.50	.60
☐ 7 Scott Wedman	.30	.10
☐ 8 Earl Monroe	1.25	.50
☐ 9 Mike Bantom	.30	.10
☐ 10 Kareem Abdul-Jabbar	8.00	4.00
☐ 11 Jo Jo White	.60	.25
☐ 12 Spencer Haywood	.60	.25
☐ 13 Kevin Porter	.40	.15
☐ 14 Bernard King	1.50	.60
☐ 15 Mike Newlin	.30	.10
☐ 16 Sidney Wicks	.60	.25
☐ 17 Dan Issel	1.25	.50
☐ 18 Tom Henderson	.30	.10
☐ 19 Jim Chones	.40	.15
☐ 20 Julius Erving	10.00	5.00
☐ 21 Brian Winters	.60	.25
☐ 22 Billy Paultz	.40	.15
☐ 23 Cedric Maxwell	.40	.15
☐ 24 Eddie Johnson	.30	.10
☐ 25 Artis Gilmore	.75	.30
☐ 26 Maurice Lucas	.60	.25
☐ 27 Gus Williams	.30	.10
☐ 28 Sam Lacey	.30	.10
☐ 29 Toby Knight	.30	.10
☐ 30 Paul Westphal	.60	.25
☐ 31 Alex English RC	8.00	4.00
☐ 32 Gail Goodrich	.60	.25
☐ 33 Caldwell Jones	.40	.15
☐ 34 Kevin Grevey	.40	.15
☐ 35 Jamaal Wilkes	.60	.25
☐ 36 Sonny Parker	.30	.10
☐ 37 John Gianelli	.30	.10
☐ 38 John Long RC	.40	.15
☐ 39 George Johnson	.30	.10
☐ 40 Lloyd Free 'AS2	.60	.25
☐ 41 Rudy Tomjanovich	1.25	.50

☐ 42 Foots Walker	.40	.15
☐ 43 Dan Roundfield	.40	.15
☐ 44 Reggie Theus RC	3.00	1.50
☐ 45 Bill Walton	3.00	1.50
☐ 46 Fred Brown	.40	.15
☐ 47 Darnell Hillman	.40	.15
☐ 48 Ray Williams	.30	.10
☐ 49 Larry Kenon	.40	.15
☐ 50 David Thompson	2.00	1.00
☐ 51 Billy Knight	.40	.15
☐ 52 Alvan Adams	.60	.25
☐ 53 Phil Smith	.30	.10
☐ 54 Adrian Dantley	1.25	.50
☐ 55 John Williamson	.40	.15
☐ 56 Campy Russell	.40	.15
☐ 57 Armond Hill	.30	.10
☐ 58 Bob Lanier	1.25	.50
☐ 59 Mickey Johnson	.30	.10
☐ 60 Pete Maravich	10.00	5.00
☐ 61 Nick Weatherspoon	.30	.10
☐ 62 Robert Reid RC	.60	.25
☐ 63 Mychal Thompson RC	1.50	.60
☐ 64 Doug Collins	1.00	.40
☐ 65 Wes Unseld	1.25	.50
☐ 66 Jack Sikma	.60	.25
☐ 67 Bobby Wilkerson	.30	.10
☐ 68 Bill Robinzine	.30	.10
☐ 69 Joe Meriweather	.30	.10
☐ 70 Marques Johnson	.40	.15
☐ 71 Ricky Sobers	.30	.10
☐ 72 Clifford Ray	.30	.10
☐ 73 Tim Bassett	.30	.10
☐ 74 James Silas	.40	.15
☐ 75 Bob McAdoo	.75	.30
☐ 76 Austin Carr	.40	.15
☐ 77 Don Ford	.30	.10
☐ 78 Steve Hawes	.30	.10
☐ 79 Ron Brewer RC	.30	.10
☐ 80 Walter Davis	1.00	.40
☐ 81 Calvin Murphy	.75	.30
☐ 82 Tom Boswell	.30	.10
☐ 83 Lonnie Shelton	.30	.10
☐ 84 Terry Tyler RC	.40	.15
☐ 85 Randy Smith	.30	.10
☐ 86 Rich Kelley	.30	.10
☐ 87 Otis Birdsong RC	.60	.25
☐ 88 Marvin Webster	.30	.10
☐ 89 Eric Money	.30	.10
☐ 90 Elvin Hayes	1.50	.60
☐ 91 Junior Bridgeman	.30	.10
☐ 92 Johnny Davis	.30	.10
☐ 93 Robert Parish	3.00	1.50
☐ 94 Eddie Jordan	.40	.15
☐ 95 Leonard Robinson	.40	.15
☐ 96 Rick Robey RC	.40	.15
☐ 97 Norm Nixon	.60	.25
☐ 98 Mark Olberding	.30	.10
☐ 99 Wilbur Holland	.30	.10
☐ 100 Moses Malone	3.00	1.50
☐ 101 Checklist 1-132	2.00	.75
☐ 102 Tom Owens	.30	.10
☐ 103 Phil Chenier	.40	.15
☐ 104 John Johnson	.30	.10
☐ 105 Darryl Dawkins	1.00	.40
☐ 106 Charlie Scott	.40	.15
☐ 107 M.L. Carr	.60	.25
☐ 108 Phil Ford RC	2.50	1.25
☐ 109 Swen Nater	.30	.10
☐ 110 Nate Archibald	1.25	.50
☐ 111 Aaron James	.30	.10
☐ 112 Jim Cleamons	.30	.10
☐ 113 James Edwards	.60	.25
☐ 114 Don Buse	.30	.10
☐ 115 Steve Mix	.30	.10
☐ 116 Charles Johnson	.30	.10
☐ 117 Elmore Smith	.30	.10
☐ 118 John Drew	.30	.10
☐ 119 Lou Hudson	.40	.15
☐ 120 Rick Barry	2.00	1.00
☐ 121 Kent Benson RC	.40	.15
☐ 122 Mike Gale	.30	.10
☐ 123 Jan Van Breda Kolff	.30	.10
☐ 124 Chris Ford	.40	.15
☐ 125 George McGinnis	.60	.25
☐ 126 Leon Douglas	.30	.10
☐ 127 John Lucas	.60	.25

☐ 128 Kermit Washington	.40	.15
☐ 129 Lionel Hollins	.40	.15
☐ 130 Bob Dandridge AS2	.40	.15
☐ 131 James McElroy	.30	.10
☐ 132 Bobby Jones !	1.50	.60

1980-81 Topps

☐ COMPLETE SET (176)	500.00	300.00
☐ 1 3/Erving/258 Brewer	5.00	2.50
☐ 2 7 Malone AS/185/Parish T	1.50	.60
☐ 3 12 Gus Williams AS	.60	.25
☐ 4 24/32/248 Elvin Hayes	1.00	.40
☐ 5 29 Dan Roundfield	.60	.25
☐ 6 34 Bird/Erving/Magic!	250.00	125.00
☐ 7 36 Cowens/166/Wilkes	1.00	.40
☐ 8 38 Maravich/264/194 DJ	6.00	3.00
☐ 9 40 Rick Robey	1.00	.40
☐ 10 47 Scott May	.30	.10
☐ 11 55 Don Ford	.30	.10
☐ 12 58 Campy Russell	.30	.10
☐ 13 60 Foots Walker	.30	.10
☐ 14 61/Jabbar AS/200 Natt	3.00	1.50
☐ 15 63 Jim Cleamons	.30	.10
☐ 16 69 Tom LaGarde	.30	.10
☐ 17 71 Jerome Whitehead	.60	.25
☐ 18 74 John Roche TL	.30	.10
☐ 19 75 English/2/68	1.25	.50
☐ 20 82 Terry Tyler TL	.30	.10
☐ 21 84 Kent Benson	.60	.25
☐ 22 86/Parish TL/126	1.50	.60
☐ 23 88/Erving AS/Sobers	3.00	1.50
☐ 24 90 Eric Money	.30	.10
☐ 25 95 Wayne Cooper	.30	.10
☐ 26 97 Parish/187/46	2.00	.75
☐ 27 98 Sonny Parker	.30	.10
☐ 28 105 Barry/122/48	1.00	.40
☐ 29 106 Allen Leavell	.30	.10
☐ 30 108/176 Cheeks TL/87	.60	.25
☐ 31 110 Robert Reid	.60	.25
☐ 32 111 Rudy Tomjanovich	.60	.25
☐ 33 112/28 Tree Rollins/15	.30	.10
☐ 34 115 Mike Bantom	.30	.10
☐ 35 116 Dudley Bradley	.30	.10
☐ 36 118 James Edwards	.30	.10
☐ 37 119 Mickey Johnson	.30	.10
☐ 38 120 Billy Knight	.60	.25
☐ 39 121 George McGinnis	.60	.25
☐ 40 124 Phil Ford TL	.30	.10
☐ 41 127 Phil Ford	.30	.10
☐ 42 131 Scott Wedman	.60	.25
☐ 43 132 Jabbar TL/Mitch/31	3.00	1.50
☐ 44 135 Jabbar/79/216	5.00	2.50
☐ 45 137 Coop/Malone TL/148	1.50	.60
☐ 46 140/Lanier AS/Walton	1.50	.60
☐ 47 141 Norm Nixon	.30	.10
☐ 48 143/30 Bird TL/Sikma	20.00	8.00
☐ 49 146/31 Bird TL/Brewer	15.00	7.50
☐ 50 147/133 Jabbar TL/207	3.00	1.50
☐ 51 149/262 Erving SD/62	3.00	1.50
☐ 52 151 Moncrief/260/220	3.00	1.50
☐ 53 156 George Johnson	.30	.10
☐ 54 158 Maurice Lucas	.60	.25
☐ 55 159 Mike Newlin	.30	.10
☐ 56 160 Roger Phegley	.30	.10
☐ 57 161 Cliff Robinson	.30	.10
☐ 58 162 Jan V.Breda Kolff	.60	.25
☐ 59 165/214/Gilmore	.30	.10
☐ 60 166 Cartwright/244/25	1.50	.60

❑ 61	168/14/Dantley	.30	.10
❑ 62	169 Joe Meriweather	.60	.25
❑ 63	170 Monroe/27/85	.60	.25
❑ 64	172 Marvin Webster	.60	.25
❑ 65	173 Ray Williams	.30	.10
❑ 66	178 Cheeks/Magic AS/237	12.00	6.00
❑ 67	183 Bobby Jones	1.00	.40
❑ 68	189/163/Issel	1.00	.40
❑ 69	190 Don Buse	.60	.25
❑ 70	191 Davis/Gervin AS/136	1.00	.40
❑ 71	192/Malone TL/64	1.00	.40
❑ 72	201 Tom Owens	.60	.25
❑ 73	208 Gervin/Issel TL/249	1.50	.60
❑ 74	217/263/107 Malone	1.50	.60
❑ 75	219 Swen Nater	.60	.25
❑ 76	221 Brian Taylor	.30	.10
❑ 77	228 Fred Brown	.30	.10
❑ 78	230/W.Davis AS/Archibald	1.00	.40
❑ 79	231 Lonnie Shelton	.60	.25
❑ 80	233 Gus Williams	.30	.10
❑ 81	236 Allan Bristow TL	.30	.10
❑ 82	238/109/Lanier	1.00	.40
❑ 83	241 Ben Poquette	1.00	.40
❑ 84	245 Greg Ballard	.30	.10
❑ 85	246 Rob Dandridge	.60	.25
❑ 86	250 Kevin Porter	.30	.10
❑ 87	251 Unseld/195/78	.60	.25
❑ 88	257 Hayes SD/144/McAdoo	.60	.25
❑ 89	3 Dan Roundfield	.60	.25
❑ 90	7 Malone AS/247/52	1.00	.40
❑ 91	12 Gus Williams	.30	.10
❑ 92	24 Steve Hawes	.30	.10
❑ 93	29 Dan Roundfield	.30	.10
❑ 94	34 Bird/Cartwright/23	40.00	20.00
❑ 95	36 Cowens/16/59	1.00	.40
❑ 96	38 Maravich/187/46	5.00	2.50
❑ 97	40 Rick Robey	.60	.25
❑ 98	47/30 Bird TL/Sikma	15.00	7.50
❑ 99	55 Don Ford	1.00	.40
❑ 100	58 Campy Russell	.60	.25
❑ 101	60 Foots Walker	.30	.10
❑ 102	61 Austin Carr	.30	.10
❑ 103	63 Jim Cleamons	.30	.10
❑ 104	69/109/Bob Lanier	1.00	.40
❑ 105	71 Jerome Whitehead	.60	.25
❑ 106	74/28 Tree Rollins/15	.30	.10
❑ 107	75 English/Malone TL/64	1.50	.60
❑ 108	82 Terry Tyler TL	.30	.10
❑ 109	84 Kent Benson	.60	.25
❑ 110	86 Phil Hubbard	.30	.10
❑ 111	88/18 Magic AS/237	10.00	5.00
❑ 112	90 Eric Money	.30	.10
❑ 113	95 Wayne Cooper	.30	.10
❑ 114	97 Parish/Malone TL/148	2.00	.75
❑ 115	98 Sonny Parker	.60	.25
❑ 116	105 Barry/123/54	1.00	.40
❑ 117	106 Allen Leavell	.60	.25
❑ 118	108 Calvin Murphy	.60	.25
❑ 119	110 Robert Reid	.60	.25
❑ 120	111 Rudy Tomjanovich	1.00	.40
❑ 121	112/264/D.Johnson	1.00	.40
❑ 122	115 Mike Bantom	.60	.25
❑ 123	116 Dudley Bradley	1.00	.40
❑ 124	118/Archibald TL/Hayes	1.25	.50
❑ 125	119 Mickey Johnson	1.00	.40
❑ 126	120 Billy Knight	.30	.10
❑ 127	121/Lanier AS/Walton	1.50	.60
❑ 128	124 Phil Ford TL	.60	.25
❑ 129	127 Phil Ford	.60	.25
❑ 130	131 Scott Wedman	.30	.10
❑ 131	132 Jabbar TL/Par.TL/126	4.00	2.00
❑ 132	135 Jabbar/253/167	5.00	2.50
❑ 133	137 M.Cooper/212/229	1.00	.40
❑ 134	140/214/Gilmore	.60	.25
❑ 135	141 Norm Nixon	.60	.25
❑ 136	143 Marq.Johnson TL	.30	.10
❑ 137	146/Erving AS/Sobers	3.00	1.50
❑ 138	147 Quinn Buckner	.60	.25
❑ 139	149 Marques Johnson	.30	.10
❑ 140	151 Moncrief/Jabb.TL/207	4.00	2.00
❑ 141	156 George Johnson	.30	.10
❑ 142	158/262 Erving SD/62	3.00	1.50
❑ 143	159 Mike Newlin	.60	.25
❑ 144	160 Roger Phegley	.30	.10
❑ 145	161 Cliff Robinson	.30	.10
❑ 146	162/Erving SD/139 Magic	35.00	17.50

❑ 147	165/185/Parish TL	1.00	.40
❑ 148	166 Cartwright/13/179	1.00	.40
❑ 149	168 Toby Knight	.60	.25
❑ 150	169 Joe Meriweather	.30	.10
❑ 151	170 Monroe/206/91	.30	.10
❑ 152	172 Marvin Webster	.60	.25
❑ 153	173 Ray Williams	.30	.10
❑ 154	178 Cheeks/Gervin AS/136	4.00	2.00
❑ 155	183 Bobby Jones	.60	.25
❑ 156	189/14/Dantley	.60	.25
❑ 157	190 Don Buse	.60	.25
❑ 158	191 Walter Davis	.60	.25
❑ 159	192/263/107 Malone	1.50	.60
❑ 160	201 Tom Owens	.60	.25
❑ 161	208 Gervin/53/223	1.50	.60
❑ 162	217/8 Jabbar AS/Natt	3.00	1.50
❑ 163	219 Swen Nater	.30	.10
❑ 164	221 Brian Taylor	.30	.10
❑ 165	228/31 Bird TL/Brewer	15.00	7.50
❑ 166	230/163/Issel	1.00	.40
❑ 167	231 Lonnie Shelton	.30	.10
❑ 168	233 Gus Williams	.60	.25
❑ 169	236 Allan Bristow TL	.30	.10
❑ 170	238 Tom Boswell	.30	.10
❑ 171	241/Cheeks TL/87	1.00	.40
❑ 172	245/W.Davis AS/Archibald	1.00	.40
❑ 173	246 Bob Dandridge	.30	.10
❑ 174	250 Kevin Porter	.30	.10
❑ 175	251 Unseld/67/5	1.00	.40
❑ 176	257 Hayes SD/Erving/258	5.00	2.50

1981-82 Topps

FORWARD
JULIUS ERVING
76ers

❑	COMPLETE SET (198)	80.00	40.00
❑	COMMON CARD (1-66)	.10	.02
❑	COMMON CARD (E67-E110)	.15	—
❑	COMMON CARD (MW67-MW110)	.15	.05
❑	COMMON CARD (W67-W110)	.15	.05
❑	TL (44-66)	.15	.05
❑ 1	John Drew	.20	.07
❑ 2	Dan Roundfield	.20	.07
❑ 3	Nate Archibald	.60	.25
❑ 4	Larry Bird	15.00	6.00
❑ 5	Cedric Maxwell	.20	.07
❑ 6	Robert Parish	1.50	.60
❑ 7	Artis Gilmore	.60	.25
❑ 8	Ricky Sobers	.10	.02
❑ 9	Mike Mitchell	.20	.07
❑ 10	Tom LaGarde	.10	.02
❑ 11	Dan Issel	.75	.30
❑ 12	David Thompson	.75	.30
❑ 13	Lloyd Free	.25	.08
❑ 14	Moses Malone	1.50	.60
❑ 15	Calvin Murphy	.25	.08
❑ 16	Johnny Davis	.10	.02
❑ 17	Otis Birdsong	.20	.07
❑ 18	Phil Ford	.20	.07
❑ 19	Scott Wedman	.20	.07
❑ 20	Kareem Abdul-Jabbar	4.00	1.50
❑ 21	Magic Johnson !	10.00	4.00
❑ 22	Norm Nixon	.25	.08
❑ 23	Jamaal Wilkes	.25	.08
❑ 24	Marques Johnson	.25	.08
❑ 25	Bob Lanier	.75	.30
❑ 26	Bill Cartwright	.50	.20
❑ 27	Michael Ray Richardson	.20	.07
❑ 28	Ray Williams	.20	.07
❑ 29	Darryl Dawkins	.25	.08
❑ 30	Julius Erving	4.00	1.50

❑ 31	Lionel Hollins	.10	.02
❑ 32	Bobby Jones	.25	.08
❑ 33	Walter Davis	.50	.20
❑ 34	Dennis Johnson	.50	.20
❑ 35	Leonard Robinson	.25	.08
❑ 36	Mychal Thompson	.25	.08
❑ 37	George Gervin	2.00	.75
❑ 38	Swen Nater	.10	.02
❑ 39	Jack Sikma	.25	.08
❑ 40	Adrian Dantley	.60	.25
❑ 41	Darrell Griffith RC	1.00	.40
❑ 42	Elvin Hayes	.75	.30
❑ 43	Fred Brown	.25	.08
❑ 44	Atlanta Hawks TL	.15	.05
❑ 45	Celtics TL/Bird/Arch	2.00	.75
❑ 46	Chicago Bulls TL	.25	.08
❑ 47	Cleveland Cavs TL	.15	.05
❑ 48	Dallas Mavericks TL	.15	.05
❑ 49	Denver Nuggets TL	.25	.08
❑ 50	Detroit Pistons TL	.15	.05
❑ 51	Golden State TL	.25	.08
❑ 52	Rockets TL/Malone	.40	.15
❑ 53	Indiana Pacers TL	.25	.08
❑ 54	Kansas City Kings TL	.15	.05
❑ 55	Lakers TL/Jabbar	1.25	.50
❑ 56	Milwaukee Bucks TL	.25	.08
❑ 57	New Jersey Nets TL	.15	.05
❑ 58	New York Knicks TL	.25	.08
❑ 59	76ers TL/Erving	1.25	.50
❑ 60	Phoenix Suns TL	.25	.08
❑ 61	Trail Blazers TL	.15	.05
❑ 62	San Antonio Spurs TL	.15	.05
❑ 63	San Diego Clippers TL	.15	.05
❑ 64	Seattle Sonics TL	.25	.08
❑ 65	Utah Jazz TL	.25	.08
❑ 66	Washington Bullets TL	.25	.08
❑ E67	Charlie Criss	.25	.08
❑ E68	Eddie Johnson	.15	.05
❑ E69	Wes Matthews	.15	.05
❑ E70	Tom McMillen	.40	.15
❑ E71	Tree Rollins	.40	.15
❑ E72	M.L. Carr	.25	.08
❑ E73	Chris Ford	.25	.08
❑ E74	Gerald Henderson RC	.40	.15
❑ E75	Kevin McHale RC !	20.00	8.00
❑ E76	Rick Robey	.25	.08
❑ E77	Darwin Cook RC	.15	.05
❑ E78	Mike Gminski RC	.75	.30
❑ E79	Maurice Lucas	.25	.08
❑ E80	Mike Newlin	.25	.08
❑ E81	Mike O'Koren RC	.25	.08
❑ E82	Steve Hawes	.25	.08
❑ E83	Foots Walker	.25	.08
❑ E84	Campy Russell	.25	.08
❑ E85	DeWayne Scales	.15	.05
❑ E86	Randy Smith	.25	.08
❑ E87	Marvin Webster	.25	.08
❑ E88	Sly Williams	.15	.05
❑ E89	Mike Woodson RC	.25	.08
❑ E90	Maurice Cheeks	1.50	.60
❑ E91	Caldwell Jones	.25	.08
❑ E92	Steve Mix	.25	.08
❑ E93A	Checklist 1-110 ERR	2.00	1.00
❑ E93B	Checklist 1-110 COR	.25	.08
❑ E94	Greg Ballard	.15	.05
❑ E95	Don Collins	.15	.05
❑ E96	Kevin Grevey	.25	.08
❑ E97	Mitch Kupchak	.25	.08
❑ E98	Rick Mahorn RC	.75	.30
❑ E99	Kevin Porter	.25	.08
❑ E100	Nate Archibald SA	.25	.08
❑ E101	Larry Bird SA	12.00	5.00
❑ E102	Bill Cartwright SA	.15	.05
❑ E103	Darryl Dawkins SA	.25	.08
❑ E104	Julius Erving SA	2.00	.75
❑ E105	Kevin Porter SA	.25	.08
❑ E106	Bobby Jones SA	.25	.08
❑ E107	Cedric Maxwell SA	.25	.08
❑ E108	Robert Parish SA	1.00	.40
❑ E109	M.R.Richardson SA	.25	.08
❑ E110	Dan Roundfield SA	.25	.08
❑ W67	T.R.Dunn RC	.15	.05
❑ W68	Alex English	1.50	.60
❑ W69	Billy McKinney RC	.25	.08
❑ W70	Dave Robisch	.25	.08
❑ W71	Joe Barry Carroll RC	.40	.15

❑ W72 Bernard King	1.00	.40
❑ W73 Sonny Parker	.15	.05
❑ W74 Purvis Short	.25	.08
❑ W75 Larry Smith RC	.40	.15
❑ W76 Jim Chones	.25	.08
❑ W77 Michael Cooper	.75	.30
❑ W78 Mark Landsberger	.15	.05
❑ W79 Alvan Adams	.25	.08
❑ W80 Jeff Cook	.15	.05
❑ W81 Rich Kelley	.15	.05
❑ W82 Kyle Macy RC	.40	.15
❑ W83 Billy Ray Bates RC	.40	.15
❑ W84 Bob Gross	.25	.08
❑ W85 Calvin Natt	.25	.08
❑ W86 Lonnie Shelton	.25	.08
❑ W87 Jim Paxson RC	.75	.30
❑ W88 Kelvin Ransey	.15	.05
❑ W89 Kermit Washington	.25	.08
❑ W90 Henry Bibby	.25	.08
❑ W91 Michael Brooks RC	.15	.05
❑ W92 Joe Bryant	.15	.05
❑ W93 Phil Smith	.15	.05
❑ W94 Brian Taylor	.15	.05
❑ W95 Freeman Williams	.25	.08
❑ W96 James Bailey	.15	.05
❑ W97 Checklist 1-110		
❑ W98 John Johnson	.15	.05
❑ W99 Vinnie Johnson	1.50	.60
❑ W100 Wally Walker RC	.25	.08
❑ W101 Paul Westphal	.25	.08
❑ W102 Allan Bristow	.25	.08
❑ W103 Wayne Cooper	.15	.05
❑ W104 Carl Nicks	.15	.05
❑ W105 Ben Poquette	.15	.05
❑ W106 Kar.Abdul-Jabbar SA	2.00	.75
❑ W107 Dan Issel SA	.50	.20
❑ W108 Dennis Johnson SA	.25	.08
❑ W109 Magic Johnson SA !	8.00	3.00
❑ W110 Jack Sikma SA	.25	.08
❑ MW67 David Greenwood	.25	.08
❑ MW68 Dwight Jones	.15	.05
❑ MW69 Reggie Theus	.25	.08
❑ MW70 Bobby Wilkerson	.15	.05
❑ MW71 Mike Bratz	.15	.05
❑ MW72 Kenny Carr	.15	.05
❑ MW73 Geoff Huston	.15	.05
❑ MW74 Bill Laimbeer RC	3.00	1.50
❑ MW75 Roger Phegley	.15	.05
❑ MW76 Checklist 1-110		
❑ MW77 Abdul Jeelani	.15	.05
❑ MW78 Bill Robinzine	.15	.05
❑ MW79 Jim Spanarkel	.15	.05
❑ MW80 Kent Benson	.25	.08
❑ MW81 Keith Herron	.15	.05
❑ MW82 Phil Hubbard	.15	.05
❑ MW83 John Long	.15	.05
❑ MW84 Terry Tyler	.15	.05
❑ MW85 Mike Dunleavy RC	.75	.30
❑ MW86 Tom Henderson	.15	.05
❑ MW87 Billy Paultz	.25	.08
❑ MW88 Robert Reid	.15	.05
❑ MW89 Mike Bantom	.15	.05
❑ MW90 James Edwards	.25	.08
❑ MW91 Billy Knight	.25	.08
❑ MW92 George McGinnis	.25	.08
❑ MW93 Louis Orr	.15	.05
❑ MW94 Ernie Grunfeld RC	.40	.15
❑ MW95 Reggie King	.15	.05
❑ MW96 Sam Lacey	.15	.05
❑ MW97 Junior Bridgeman	.25	.08
❑ MW98 Mickey Johnson	.25	.08
❑ MW99 Sidney Moncrief	.75	.30
❑ MW100 Brian Winters	.25	.08
❑ MW101 Dave Corzine RC	.15	.05
❑ MW102 Paul Griffin	.15	.05
❑ MW103 Johnny Moore RC	.25	.08
❑ MW104 Mark Olberding	.15	.05
❑ MW105 James Silas	.25	.08
❑ MW106 George Gervin SA	.75	.30
❑ MW107 Artis Gilmore SA	.25	.08
❑ MW108 Marques Johnson SA	.25	.08
❑ MW109 Bob Lanier SA	.50	.20
❑ MW110 Moses Malone SA	1.00	.40

1992-93 Topps

❑ COMPLETE SET (396)	15.00	6.00
❑ COMPLETE FACT. SET (408)	20.00	8.00
❑ COMPLETE SERIES 1 (198)	4.00	2.00
❑ COMPLETE SERIES 2 (198)	12.00	5.00
❑ 1 Larry Bird	.60	.25
❑ 2 Magic Johnson HL	.25	.08
❑ 3 Michael Jordan HL	1.00	.40
❑ 4 David Robinson HL	.15	.05
❑ 5 Johnny Newman	.05	.01
❑ 6 Mike Iuzzolino	.05	.01
❑ 7 Ken Norman	.05	.01
❑ 8 Chris Jackson	.05	.01
❑ 9 Duane Ferrell	.05	.01
❑ 10 Sean Elliott	.08	.01
❑ 11 Bernard King	.08	.01
❑ 12 Armon Gilliam	.05	.01
❑ 13 Reggie Williams	.05	.01
❑ 14 Steve Kerr	.08	.01
❑ 15 Anthony Bowie	.05	.01
❑ 16 Alton Lister	.05	.01
❑ 17 Dee Brown	.05	.01
❑ 18 Tom Chambers	.05	.01
❑ 19 Otis Thorpe	.08	.01
❑ 20 Karl Malone	.25	.08
❑ 21 Kenny Gattison	.05	.01
❑ 22 Lionel Simmons UER	.05	.01
❑ 23 Vern Fleming	.05	.01
❑ 24 John Paxson	.05	.01
❑ 25 Mitch Richmond	.15	.05
❑ 26 Danny Schayes	.05	.01
❑ 27 Derrick McKey	.05	.01
❑ 28 Mark Randall	.05	.01
❑ 29 Bill Laimbeer	.08	.01
❑ 30 Chris Morris	.05	.01
❑ 31 Alec Kessler	.05	.01
❑ 32 Vlade Divac	.08	.01
❑ 33 Rick Fox	.08	.01
❑ 34 Charles Shackleford	.05	.01
❑ 35 Dominique Wilkins	.15	.05
❑ 36 Sleepy Floyd	.05	.01
❑ 37 Doug West	.05	.01
❑ 38 Pete Chilcutt	.05	.01
❑ 39 Orlando Woolridge	.05	.01
❑ 40 Eric Leckner	.05	.01
❑ 41 Joe Kleine	.05	.01
❑ 42 Scott Skiles	.05	.01
❑ 43 Jerrod Mustaf	.05	.01
❑ 44 John Starks	.08	.01
❑ 45 Sedale Threatt	.05	.01
❑ 46 Doug Smith	.05	.01
❑ 47 Byron Scott	.08	.01
❑ 48 Willie Anderson	.05	.01
❑ 49 David Benoit	.05	.01
❑ 50 Scott Hastings	.05	.01
❑ 51 Terry Porter	.05	.01
❑ 52 Sidney Green	.05	.01
❑ 53 Danny Young	.05	.01
❑ 54 Magic Johnson	.50	.20
❑ 55 Brian Williams	.05	.01
❑ 56 Randy Wittman	.05	.01
❑ 57 Kevin McHale	.15	.05
❑ 58 Dana Barros	.05	.01
❑ 59 Thurl Bailey	.05	.01
❑ 60 Kevin Duckworth	.05	.01
❑ 61 John Williams	.05	.01
❑ 62 Willie Burton	.05	.01

❑ 63 Spud Webb	.08	.01
❑ 64 Detlef Schrempf	.08	.01
❑ 65 Sherman Douglas	.05	.01
❑ 66 Patrick Ewing	.15	.05
❑ 67 Michael Adams	.05	.01
❑ 68 Vernon Maxwell	.05	.01
❑ 69 Terrell Brandon	.15	.05
❑ 70 Terry Catledge	.05	.01
❑ 71 Mark Eaton	.05	.01
❑ 72 Tony Smith	.05	.01
❑ 73 B.J. Armstrong	.05	.01
❑ 74 Moses Malone	.15	.05
❑ 75 Anthony Bonner	.05	.01
❑ 76 George McCloud	.05	.01
❑ 77 Glen Rice	.15	.05
❑ 78 Jon Koncak	.05	.01
❑ 79 Michael Cage	.05	.01
❑ 80 Ron Harper	.08	.01
❑ 81 Tom Tolbert	.05	.01
❑ 82 Brad Sellers	.05	.01
❑ 83 Winston Garland	.05	.01
❑ 84 Negele Knight	.05	.01
❑ 85 Ricky Pierce	.05	.01
❑ 86 Mark Aguirre	.08	.01
❑ 87 Ron Anderson	.05	.01
❑ 88 Loy Vaught	.05	.01
❑ 89 Luc Longley	.08	.01
❑ 90 Jerry Reynolds	.05	.01
❑ 91 Terry Cummings	.08	.01
❑ 92 Rony Seikaly	.05	.01
❑ 93 Derek Harper	.08	.01
❑ 94 Cliff Robinson	.08	.01
❑ 95 Kenny Anderson	.15	.05
❑ 96 Chris Gatling	.05	.01
❑ 97 Stacey Augmon	.08	.01
❑ 98 Chris Corchiani	.05	.01
❑ 99 Pervis Ellison	.05	.01
❑ 100 Larry Bird AS	.30	.10
❑ 101 John Stockton AS	.08	.01
❑ 102 Clyde Drexler AS	.08	.01
❑ 103 Scottie Pippen AS	.25	.08
❑ 104 Reggie Lewis AS	.05	.01
❑ 105 Hakeem Olajuwon AS	.15	.05
❑ 106 David Robinson AS	.15	.05
❑ 107 Charles Barkley AS	.15	.05
❑ 108 James Worthy AS	.08	.01
❑ 109 Kevin Willis AS	.05	.01
❑ 110 Dikembe Mutombo AS	.15	.05
❑ 111 Joe Dumars AS	.08	.01
❑ 112 Jeff Hornacek AS UER	.05	.01
❑ 113 Mark Price AS	.05	.01
❑ 114 Michael Adams AS	.05	.01
❑ 115 Michael Jordan AS	1.00	.40
❑ 116 Brad Daugherty AS	.05	.01
❑ 117 Dennis Rodman AS	.15	.05
❑ 118 Isiah Thomas AS	.08	.01
❑ 119 Tim Hardaway AS	.15	.05
❑ 120 Chris Mullin AS	.08	.01
❑ 121 Patrick Ewing AS	.08	.01
❑ 122 Dan Majerle AS	.05	.01
❑ 123 Karl Malone AS	.15	.05
❑ 124 Otis Thorpe AS	.05	.01
❑ 125 Dominique Wilkins AS	.08	.01
❑ 126 Magic Johnson AS	.25	.08
❑ 127 Charles Oakley AS	.08	.01
❑ 128 Robert Pack AS	.05	.01
❑ 129 Billy Owens AS	.08	.01
❑ 130 Jeff Malone	.05	.01
❑ 131 Danny Ferry	.05	.01
❑ 132 Sam Bowie	.05	.01
❑ 133 Avery Johnson	.05	.01
❑ 134 Jayson Williams	.08	.01
❑ 135 Fred Roberts	.05	.01
❑ 136 Greg Sutton	.05	.01
❑ 137 Dennis Rodman	.30	.10
❑ 138 John Williams	.05	.01
❑ 139 Greg Dreiling	.05	.01
❑ 140 Rik Smits	.08	.01
❑ 141 Michael Jordan	2.00	.75
❑ 142 Nick Anderson	.08	.01
❑ 143 Jerome Kersey	.05	.01
❑ 144 Fat Lever	.05	.01
❑ 145 Tyrone Corbin	.05	.01
❑ 146 Robert Parish	.08	.01
❑ 147 Steve Smith	.20	.07
❑ 148 Chris Dudley	.05	.01

#	Player			#	Player			#	Player		
149	Antoine Carr	.05	.01	235	Mark Bryant	.05	.01	321	Anthony Avent RC	.05	.01
150	Elden Campbell	.08	.01	236	Lloyd Daniels RC	.05	.01	322	Matt Geiger RC	.08	.01
151	Randy White	.05	.01	237	Dale Davis	.05	.01	323	Duane Causwell	.05	.01
152	Felton Spencer	.05	.01	238	Jayson Williams	.08	.01	324	Horace Grant	.08	.01
153	Cedric Ceballos	.08	.01	239	Mike Sanders	.05	.01	325	Mark Jackson	.08	.01
154	Mark Macon	.05	.01	240	Mike Gminski	.05	.01	326	Dan Majerle	.08	.01
155	Jack Haley	.05	.01	241	William Bedford	.05	.01	327	Chuck Person	.05	.01
156	Bimbo Coles	.05	.01	242	Dell Curry	.05	.01	328	Buck Johnson	.05	.01
157	A.J. English	.05	.01	243	Gerald Paddio	.05	.01	329	Duane Cooper RC	.05	.01
158	Kendall Gill	.08	.01	244	Chris Smith RC	.05	.01	330	Rod Strickland	.15	.05
159	A.C. Green	.08	.01	245	Jud Buechler	.05	.01	331	Isiah Thomas	.15	.05
160	Mark West	.05	.01	246	Walter Palmer	.05	.01	332	Greg Kite	.05	.01
161	Benoit Benjamin	.05	.01	247	Larry Krystkowiak	.05	.01	333	Don MacLean RC	.05	.01
162	Tyrone Hill	.05	.01	248	Marcus Liberty	.05	.01	334	Christian Laettner RC	.30	.10
163	Larry Nance	.05	.01	249	Sam Mitchell	.05	.01	335	John Crotty RC	.05	.01
164	Gary Grant	.05	.01	250	Kiki Vandeweghe	.05	.01	336	Tracy Moore RC	.05	.01
165	Bill Cartwright	.05	.01	251	Vincent Askew	.05	.01	337	Hakeem Olajuwon	.25	.08
166	Greg Anthony	.05	.01	252	Travis Mays	.05	.01	338	Byron Houston RC	.05	.01
167	Jim Les	.05	.01	253	Charles Smith	.05	.01	339	Walter Bond RC	.05	.01
168	Johnny Dawkins	.05	.01	254	John Bagley	.05	.01	340	Brent Price RC	.08	.01
169	Alvin Robertson	.05	.01	255	James Worthy	.15	.05	341	Bryant Stith RC	.08	.01
170	Kenny Smith	.05	.01	256	Paul Pressey P/CO	.05	.01	342	Will Perdue	.05	.01
171	Gerald Glass	.05	.01	257	Rumeal Robinson	.05	.01	343	Jeff Hornacek	.08	.01
172	Harvey Grant	.05	.01	258	Tom Gugliotta RC	.50	.20	344	Adam Keefe RC	.05	.01
173	Paul Graham	.05	.01	259	Eric Anderson RC	.05	.01	345	Rafael Addison	.05	.01
174	Sam Perkins	.08	.01	260	Hersey Hawkins	.08	.01	346	Marlon Maxey RC	.05	.01
175	Manute Bol	.05	.01	261	Terry Davis	.05	.01	347	Joe Dumars	.15	.05
176	Muggsy Bogues	.08	.01	262	Rex Chapman	.05	.01	348	Jon Barry RC	.08	.01
177	Mike Brown	.05	.01	263	Chucky Brown	.05	.01	349	Marty Conlon	.05	.01
178	Donald Hodge	.05	.01	264	Danny Young	.05	.01	350	Alaa Abdelnaby	.05	.01
179	Dave Jamerson	.05	.01	265	Olden Polynice	.05	.01	351	Micheal Williams	.05	.01
180	Mookie Blaylock	.08	.01	266	Kevin Willis	.05	.01	352	Brad Daugherty	.05	.01
181	Randy Brown	.05	.01	267	Shawn Kemp	.30	.10	353	Tony Bennett RC	.05	.01
182	Todd Lichti	.05	.01	268	Mookie Blaylock	.08	.01	354	Clyde Drexler	.15	.05
183	Kevin Gamble	.05	.01	269	Malik Sealy RC	.08	.01	355	Rolando Blackman	.05	.01
184	Gary Payton	.30	.10	270	Charles Barkley	.25	.08	356	Tom Tolbert	.05	.01
185	Brian Shaw	.05	.01	271	Corey Williams RC	.05	.01	357	Sarunas Marciulionis	.05	.01
186	Grant Long	.05	.01	272	Stephen Howard RC	.05	.01	358	Jaren Jackson RC	.08	.01
187	Frank Brickowski	.05	.01	273	Keith Askins	.05	.01	359	Stacey King	.05	.01
188	Tim Hardaway	.20	.07	274	Matt Bullard	.05	.01	360	Danny Ainge	.08	.01
189	Danny Manning	.08	.01	275	John Battle	.05	.01	361	Dale Ellis	.05	.01
190	Kevin Johnson	.15	.05	276	Andrew Lang	.05	.01	362	Shaquille O'Neal RC	10.00	4.00
191	Craig Ehlo	.05	.01	277	David Robinson	.25	.08	363	Bob McCann RC	.05	.01
192	Dennis Scott	.08	.01	278	Harold Miner RC	.08	.01	364	Reggie Smith RC	.05	.01
193	Reggie Miller	.15	.05	279	Tracy Murray RC	.08	.01	365	Vinny Del Negro	.05	.01
194	Darrell Walker	.05	.01	280	Pooh Richardson	.05	.01	366	Robert Pack	.05	.01
195	Anthony Mason	.15	.05	281	Dikembe Mutombo	.20	.07	367	David Wood	.05	.01
196	Buck Williams	.08	.01	282	Wayman Tisdale	.05	.01	368	Rodney McCray	.05	.01
197	Checklist 1-99	.05	.01	283	Larry Johnson	.20	.07	369	Terry Mills	.05	.01
198	Checklist 100-198	.05	.01	284	Todd Day RC	.08	.01	370	Eric Murdock	.05	.01
199	Karl Malone 50P	.15	.05	285	Stanley Roberts	.05	.01	371	Alex Blackwell RC	.05	.01
200	Dominique Wilkins 50P	.08	.01	286	Randy Woods RC UER 272	.05	.01	372	Jay Humphries	.05	.01
201	Tom Chambers 50P	.05	.01	287	Avery Johnson	.05	.01	373	Eddie Lee Wilkins	.05	.01
202	Bernard King 50P	.05	.01	288	Anthony Peeler RC	.08	.01	374	James Edwards	.05	.01
203	Kiki Vandeweghe 50P	.05	.01	289	Mario Elie	.08	.01	375	Tim Kempton	.05	.01
204	Dale Ellis 50P	.05	.01	290	Doc Rivers	.08	.01	376	J.R. Reid	.05	.01
205	Michael Jordan 50P	1.00	.40	291	Blue Edwards	.05	.01	377	Sam Mack RC	.08	.01
206	Michael Adams 50P	.05	.01	292	Sean Rooks RC	.05	.01	378	Donald Royal	.05	.01
207	Charles Smith 50P	.05	.01	293	Xavier McDaniel	.05	.01	379	Mark Price	.05	.01
208	Moses Malone 50P	.08	.01	294	C.Weatherspoon RC	.15	.05	380	Mark Acres	.05	.01
209	Terry Cummings 50P	.05	.01	295	Morlon Wiley	.05	.01	381	Hubert Davis RC	.08	.01
210	Vernon Maxwell 50P	.05	.01	296	LaBradford Smith	.05	.01	382	Dave Johnson RC	.05	.01
211	Patrick Ewing 50P	.08	.01	297	Reggie Lewis	.08	.01	383	John Salley	.05	.01
212	Clyde Drexler 50P	.08	.01	298	Chris Mullin	.15	.05	384	Eddie Johnson	.05	.01
213	Kevin McHale 50P	.08	.01	299	Litterial Green RC	.05	.01	385	Brian Howard RC	.05	.01
214	Hakeem Olajuwon 50P	.15	.05	300	Elmore Spencer RC	.05	.01	386	Isaiah Morris RC	.05	.01
215	Reggie Miller 50P	.08	.01	301	John Stockton	.15	.05	387	Frank Johnson	.05	.01
216	Gary Grant 20A	.05	.01	302	Walt Williams RC	.15	.05	388	Rick Mahorn	.05	.01
217	Doc Rivers 20A	.05	.01	303	Anthony Avent RC	.05	.01	389	Scottie Pippen	.50	.20
218	Mark Price 20A	.05	.01	304	Gundars Vetra RC	.05	.01	390	Lee Mayberry RC	.05	.01
219	Isiah Thomas 20A	.08	.01	305	LaSalle Thompson	.05	.01	391	Tony Campbell	.05	.01
220	Nate McMillan 20A	.05	.01	306	Nate McMillan	.05	.01	392	Latrell Sprewell RC	1.25	.50
221	Fat Lever 20A	.05	.01	307	Steve Bardo RC	.05	.01	393	Alonzo Mourning RC	1.00	.40
222	Kevin Johnson 20A	.08	.01	308	Robert Horry RC	.15	.05	394	Robert Werdann RC	.05	.01
223	John Stockton 20A	.08	.01	309	Scott Williams	.05	.01	395	Checklist 199-297 UER	.05	.01
224	Scott Skiles 20A	.05	.01	310	Bo Kimble	.05	.01	396	Checklist 298-396	.05	.01
225	Kevin Brooks	.05	.01	311	Tree Rollins	.05	.01				
226	Bobby Phills RC	.15	.05	312	Tim Perry	.05	.01		**1993-94 Topps**		
227	Oliver Miller RC	.05	.01	313	Isaac Austin RC	.08	.01		COMPLETE SET (396)	20.00	10.00
228	John Williams	.05	.01	314	Tate George	.05	.01		COMPLETE FACT.SET (410)	25.00	12.50
229	Brad Lohaus	.05	.01	315	Kevin Lynch	.05	.01		COMPLETE SERIES 1 (198)	10.00	5.00
230	Derrick Coleman	.08	.01	316	Victor Alexander	.05	.01		COMPLETE SERIES 2 (198)	10.00	5.00
231	Ed Pinckney	.05	.01	317	Doug Overton	.05	.01	1	Charles Barkley HL	.25	.08
232	Trent Tucker	.05	.01	318	Tom Hammonds	.05	.01	2	Hakeem Olajuwon HL	.25	.08
233	Lance Blanks	.05	.01	319	LaPhonso Ellis RC	.15	.05	3	Shaquille O'Neal HL	.50	.20
234	Drazen Petrovic	.05	.01	320	Scott Brooks	.05	.01	4	Chris Jackson HL	.05	.01

❏ 5	Cliff Robinson HL	.05	.01
❏ 6	Donald Hodge	.05	.01
❏ 7	Victor Alexander	.05	.01
❏ 8	Chris Morris	.05	.01
❏ 9	Muggsy Bogues	.10	.02
❏ 10	Steve Smith UER	.25	.08
❏ 11	Dave Johnson	.05	.01
❏ 12	Tom Gugliotta	.25	.08
❏ 13	Doug Edwards RC	.05	.01
❏ 14	Vlade Divac	.10	.02
❏ 15	Corie Blount RC	.05	.01
❏ 16	Derek Harper	.10	.02
❏ 17	Matt Bullard	.05	.01
❏ 18	Terry Catledge	.05	.01
❏ 19	Mark Eaton	.05	.01
❏ 20	Mark Jackson	.10	.02
❏ 21	Terry Mills	.05	.01
❏ 22	Johnny Dawkins	.05	.01
❏ 23	Michael Jordan	3.00	1.25
❏ 24	Rick Fox UER	.05	.01
❏ 25	Charles Oakley	.10	.02
❏ 26	Derrick McKey	.05	.01
❏ 27	Christian Laettner	.10	.02
❏ 28	Todd Day	.05	.01
❏ 29	Danny Ferry	.05	.01
❏ 30	Kevin Johnson	.10	.02
❏ 31	Vinny Del Negro	.05	.01
❏ 32	Kevin Brooks	.05	.01
❏ 33	Pete Chilcutt	.05	.01
❏ 34	Larry Stewart	.05	.01
❏ 35	Dave Jamerson	.05	.01
❏ 36	Sidney Green	.05	.01
❏ 37	J.R. Reid	.05	.01
❏ 38	Jim Jackson	.10	.02
❏ 39	Micheal Williams UER	.05	.01
❏ 40	Rex Walters RC	.05	.01
❏ 41	Shawn Bradley RC	.25	.08
❏ 42	Jon Koncak	.05	.01
❏ 43	Byron Houston	.05	.01
❏ 44	Brian Shaw	.05	.01
❏ 45	Bill Cartwright	.05	.01
❏ 46	Jerome Kersey	.05	.01
❏ 47	Danny Schayes	.05	.01
❏ 48	Olden Polynice	.05	.01
❏ 49	Anthony Peeler	.05	.01
❏ 50	Nick Anderson 50	.05	.01
❏ 51	David Benoit	.05	.01
❏ 52	David Robinson 50P	.25	.08
❏ 53	Greg Kite	.05	.01
❏ 54	Gerald Paddio	.05	.01
❏ 55	Don MacLean	.05	.01
❏ 56	Randy Woods	.05	.01
❏ 57	Reggie Miller 50P	.10	.02
❏ 58	Kevin Gamble	.05	.01
❏ 59	Sean Green	.05	.01
❏ 60	Jeff Hornacek	.10	.02
❏ 61	John Starks	.10	.02
❏ 62	Gerald Wilkins	.05	.01
❏ 63	Jim Les	.05	.01
❏ 64	Michael Jordan 50P	1.50	.60
❏ 65	Alvin Robertson	.05	.01
❏ 66	Tim Kempton	.05	.01
❏ 67	Bryant Stith	.05	.01
❏ 68	Jeff Turner	.05	.01
❏ 69	Malik Sealy	.05	.01
❏ 70	Dell Curry	.05	.01
❏ 71	Brent Price	.05	.01
❏ 72	Kevin Lynch	.05	.01
❏ 73	Bimbo Coles	.05	.01
❏ 74	Larry Nance	.05	.01
❏ 75	Luther Wright RC	.05	.01
❏ 76	Willie Anderson	.05	.01
❏ 77	Dennis Rodman	.50	.20
❏ 78	Anthony Mason	.10	.02
❏ 79	Chris Gatling	.05	.01
❏ 80	Antoine Carr	.05	.01
❏ 81	Kevin Willis	.05	.01
❏ 82	Thurl Bailey	.05	.01
❏ 83	Reggie Williams	.05	.01
❏ 84	Rod Strickland	.10	.02
❏ 85	Rolando Blackman	.05	.01
❏ 86	Bobby Hurley RC	.10	.02
❏ 87	Jeff Malone	.05	.01
❏ 88	James Worthy	.25	.08
❏ 89	Alaa Abdelnaby	.05	.01
❏ 90	Duane Ferrell	.05	.01
❏ 91	Anthony Avent	.05	.01
❏ 92	Scottie Pippen	.75	.30
❏ 93	Ricky Pierce	.05	.01
❏ 94	P.J.Brown RC	.25	.08
❏ 95	Jeff Grayer	.05	.01
❏ 96	Jerrod Mustaf	.05	.01
❏ 97	Elmore Spencer	.05	.01
❏ 98	Walt Williams	.05	.01
❏ 99	Otis Thorpe	.10	.02
❏ 100	Patrick Ewing AS	.10	.02
❏ 101	Michael Jordan AS	1.50	.60
❏ 102	John Stockton AS	.10	.02
❏ 103	Dominique Wilkins AS	.10	.02
❏ 104	Charles Barkley AS	.25	.08
❏ 105	Lee Mayberry	.05	.01
❏ 106	James Edwards	.05	.01
❏ 107	Scott Brooks	.05	.01
❏ 108	John Battle	.05	.01
❏ 109	Kenny Gattison	.05	.01
❏ 110	Pooh Richardson	.05	.01
❏ 111	Rony Seikaly	.05	.01
❏ 112	Mahmoud Abdul-Rauf	.05	.01
❏ 113	Nick Anderson	.10	.02
❏ 114	Gundars Vetra	.05	.01
❏ 115	Joe Dumars AS	.10	.02
❏ 116	Hakeem Olajuwon AS	.25	.08
❏ 117	Scottie Pippen AS	.40	.15
❏ 118	Mark Price AS	.05	.01
❏ 119	Karl Malone AS	.25	.08
❏ 120	Michael Cage	.05	.01
❏ 121	Ed Pinckney	.05	.01
❏ 122	Jay Humphries	.05	.01
❏ 123	Dale Davis	.05	.01
❏ 124	Sean Rooks	.05	.01
❏ 125	Mookie Blaylock	.10	.02
❏ 126	Buck Williams	.05	.01
❏ 127	John Williams	.05	.01
❏ 128	Stacey King	.05	.01
❏ 129	Tim Perry	.05	.01
❏ 130	Tim Hardaway AS	.10	.02
❏ 131	Larry Johnson AS	.10	.02
❏ 132	Detlef Schrempf AS	.05	.01
❏ 133	Reggie Miller AS	.10	.02
❏ 134	Shaquille O'Neal AS	.50	.20
❏ 135	Dale Ellis	.05	.01
❏ 136	Duane Causwell	.05	.01
❏ 137	Rumeal Robinson	.05	.01
❏ 138	Billy Owens	.05	.01
❏ 139	Malcolm Mackey RC	.05	.01
❏ 140	Vernon Maxwell	.05	.01
❏ 141	LaPhonso Ellis	.05	.01
❏ 142	Robert Parish	.10	.02
❏ 143	LaBradford Smith	.05	.01
❏ 144	Charles Smith	.05	.01
❏ 145	Terry Porter	.05	.01
❏ 146	Elden Campbell	.05	.01
❏ 147	Bill Laimbeer	.05	.01
❏ 148	Chris Mills RC	.25	.08
❏ 149	Brad Lohaus	.05	.01
❏ 150	Jim Jackson ART	.05	.01
❏ 151	Tom Gugliotta ART	.05	.01
❏ 152	Shaquille O'Neal ART	.50	.20
❏ 153	Latrell Sprewell ART	.25	.08
❏ 154	Walt Williams ART	.05	.01
❏ 155	Gary Payton	.40	.15
❏ 156	Orlando Woolridge	.05	.01
❏ 157	Adam Keefe	.05	.01
❏ 158	Calbert Cheaney RC	.10	.02
❏ 159	Rick Mahorn	.05	.01
❏ 160	Robert Horry	.10	.02
❏ 161	John Salley	.05	.01
❏ 162	Sam Mitchell	.05	.01
❏ 163	Stanley Roberts	.05	.01
❏ 164	Clarence Weatherspoon	.05	.01
❏ 165	Anthony Bowie	.05	.01
❏ 166	Derrick Coleman	.10	.02
❏ 167	Negele Knight	.05	.01
❏ 168	Marlon Maxey	.05	.01
❏ 169	Spud Webb UER	.10	.02
❏ 170	Alonzo Mourning	.40	.15
❏ 171	Ervin Johnson RC	.10	.02
❏ 172	Sedale Threatt	.05	.01
❏ 173	Mark Macon	.05	.01
❏ 174	B.J. Armstrong	.05	.01
❏ 175	Harold Miner ART	.05	.01
❏ 176	Anthony Peeler ART	.05	.01
❏ 177	Alonzo Mourning ART	.25	.08
❏ 178	Christian Laettner ART	.05	.01
❏ 179	Clarence Weatherspoon ART	.05	.01
❏ 180	Dee Brown	.05	.01
❏ 181	Shaquille O'Neal	1.25	.50
❏ 182	Loy Vaught	.05	.01
❏ 183	Terrell Brandon	.10	.02
❏ 184	Lionel Simmons	.05	.01
❏ 185	Mark Aguirre	.05	.01
❏ 186	Danny Ainge	.10	.02
❏ 187	Reggie Miller	.25	.08
❏ 188	Terry Davis	.05	.01
❏ 189	Mark Bryant	.05	.01
❏ 190	Tyrone Corbin	.05	.01
❏ 191	Chris Mullin	.25	.08
❏ 192	Johnny Newman	.05	.01
❏ 193	Doug West	.05	.01
❏ 194	Keith Askins	.05	.01
❏ 195	Bo Kimble	.05	.01
❏ 196	Sean Elliott	.10	.02
❏ 197	Checklist 1-99 UER	.05	.01
❏ 198	Checklist 100-198	.05	.01
❏ 199	Michael Jordan FPM	1.50	.60
❏ 200	Patrick Ewing FPM	.10	.02
❏ 201	John Stockton FPM	.10	.02
❏ 202	Shawn Kemp FPM	.25	.08
❏ 203	Mark Price FPM	.05	.01
❏ 204	Charles Barkley FPM	.25	.08
❏ 205	Hakeem Olajuwon FPM	.25	.08
❏ 206	Clyde Drexler FPM	.10	.02
❏ 207	Kevin Johnson FPM	.05	.01
❏ 208	John Starks FPM	.05	.01
❏ 209	Chris Mullin FPM	.10	.02
❏ 210	Doc Rivers	.05	.02
❏ 211	Kenny Walker	.05	.01
❏ 212	Doug Christie	.10	.02
❏ 213	James Robinson RC	.05	.01
❏ 214	Larry Krystkowiak	.05	.01
❏ 215	Manute Bol	.05	.01
❏ 216	Carl Herrera	.05	.01
❏ 217	Paul Graham	.05	.01
❏ 218	Jud Buechler	.05	.01
❏ 219	Mike Brown	.05	.01
❏ 220	Tom Chambers	.05	.01
❏ 221	Kendall Gill	.10	.02
❏ 222	Kenny Anderson	.10	.02
❏ 223	Larry Johnson	.25	.08
❏ 224	Chris Webber RC	2.50	1.00
❏ 225	Randy White	.05	.01
❏ 226	Rik Smits	.10	.02
❏ 227	A.C. Green	.10	.02
❏ 228	David Robinson	.40	.15
❏ 229	Sean Elliott	.10	.02
❏ 230	Gary Grant	.05	.01
❏ 231	Dana Barros	.05	.01
❏ 232	Bobby Hurley	.10	.02
❏ 233	Blue Edwards	.05	.01
❏ 234	Tom Hammonds	.05	.01
❏ 235	Pete Myers	.05	.01
❏ 236	Acie Earl RC	.05	.01
❏ 237	Tony Smith	.05	.01
❏ 238	Bill Wennington	.05	.01
❏ 239	Andrew Lang	.05	.01
❏ 240	Ervin Johnson	.05	.01
❏ 241	Byron Scott	.10	.02
❏ 242	Eddie Johnson	.05	.01
❏ 243	Anthony Bonner	.05	.01
❏ 244	Luther Wright	.05	.01

245	LaSalle Thompson	.05	.01
246	Harold Miner	.05	.01
247	Chris Smith	.05	.01
248	John Williams	.05	.01
249	Clyde Drexler	.25	.08
250	Calbert Cheaney	.10	.02
251	Avery Johnson	.05	.01
252	Steve Kerr	.10	.02
253	Warren Kidd RC	.05	.01
254	Wayman Tisdale	.05	.01
255	Bob Martin RC	.05	.01
256	Popeye Jones RC	.05	.01
257	Jimmy Oliver	.05	.01
258	Kevin Edwards	.05	.01
259	Dan Majerle	.10	.02
260	Jon Barry	.05	.01
261	Allan Houston RC	1.00	.40
262	Dikembe Mutombo	.25	.08
263	Sleepy Floyd	.05	.01
264	George Lynch RC	.05	.01
265	Stacey Augmon UER	.05	.01
266	Hakeem Olajuwon	.40	.15
267	Scott Skiles	.05	.01
268	Detlef Schrempf	.10	.02
269	Brian Davis RC	.05	.01
270	Tracy Murray	.05	.01
271	Gheorghe Muresan RC	.25	.08
272	Terry Dehere RC	.05	.01
273	Terry Cummings	.05	.01
274	Keith Jennings	.05	.01
275	Tyrone Hill	.05	.01
276	Hersey Hawkins	.10	.02
277	Grant Long	.05	.01
278	Herb Williams	.05	.01
279	Karl Malone	.40	.15
280	Mitch Richmond	.25	.08
281	Derek Strong RC	.05	.01
282	Dino Radja RC	.05	.01
283	Jack Haley	.05	.01
284	Derek Harper	.10	.02
285	Dwayne Schintzius	.05	.01
286	Michael Curry RC	.05	.01
287	Rodney Rogers RC	.25	.08
288	Horace Grant	.10	.02
289	Oliver Miller	.05	.01
290	Luc Longley	.05	.01
291	Walter Bond	.05	.01
292	Dominique Wilkins	.25	.08
293	Vern Fleming	.05	.01
294	Mark Price	.05	.01
295	Mark Aguirre	.05	.01
296	Shawn Kemp	.40	.15
297	Pervis Ellison	.05	.01
298	Josh Grant RC	.05	.01
299	Scott Burrell RC	.25	.08
300	Patrick Ewing	.25	.08
301	Sam Cassell RC	1.00	.40
302	Nick Van Exel RC	.75	.30
303	Clifford Robinson	.10	.02
304	Frank Johnson	.05	.01
305	Matt Geiger	.05	.01
306	Vin Baker RC	.60	.25
307	Benoit Benjamin	.05	.01
308	Shawn Bradley	.25	.08
309	Chris Whitney RC	.05	.01
310	Eric Riley RC	.05	.01
311	Isiah Thomas	.25	.08
312	Jamal Mashburn RC	.60	.25
313	Xavier McDaniel	.05	.01
314	Mike Peplowski RC	.05	.01
315	Darnell Mee RC	.05	.01
316	Toni Kukoc RC	1.00	.40
317	Felton Spencer	.05	.01
318	Sam Bowie	.05	.01
319	Mario Elie	.05	.01
320	Tim Hardaway	.25	.08
321	Ken Norman	.05	.01
322	Isaiah Rider RC	.50	.20
323	Rex Chapman	.05	.01
324	Dennis Rodman	.50	.20
325	Derrick McKey	.05	.01
326	Corie Blount	.05	.01
327	Fat Lever	.05	.01
328	Ron Harper	.10	.02
329	Eric Anderson	.05	.01
330	Armon Gilliam	.05	.01
331	Lindsey Hunter RC	.25	.08
332	Eric Leckner	.05	.01
333	Chris Corchiani	.05	.01
334	Anfernee Hardaway RC	2.00	.75
335	Randy Brown	.05	.01
336	Sam Perkins	.10	.02
337	Glen Rice	.10	.02
338	Orlando Woolridge	.05	.01
339	Mike Gminski	.05	.01
340	Latrell Sprewell	.60	.25
341	Harvey Grant	.05	.01
342	Doug Smith	.05	.01
343	Kevin Duckworth	.05	.01
344	Cedric Ceballos	.10	.02
345	Chuck Person	.05	.01
346	Scott Haskin RC	.05	.01
347	Frank Brickowski	.05	.01
348	Scott Williams	.05	.01
349	Brad Daugherty	.05	.01
350	Willie Burton	.05	.01
351	Joe Dumars	.25	.08
352	Craig Ehlo	.05	.01
353	Lucious Harris RC	.05	.01
354	Danny Manning	.10	.02
355	Litteral Green	.05	.01
356	John Stockton	.25	.08
357	Nate McMillan	.05	.01
358	Greg Graham RC	.05	.01
359	Rex Walters	.05	.01
360	Lloyd Daniels	.05	.01
361	Antonio Harvey RC	.05	.01
362	Brian Williams	.05	.01
363	LeRon Ellis	.05	.01
364	Chris Dudley	.05	.01
365	Hubert Davis	.05	.01
366	Evers Burns RC	.05	.01
367	Sherman Douglas	.05	.01
368	Sarunas Marciulionis	.05	.01
369	Tom Tolbert	.05	.01
370	Robert Pack	.05	.01
371	Michael Adams	.05	.01
372	Negele Knight	.05	.01
373	Charles Barkley	.40	.15
374	Bryon Russell RC	.05	.01
375	Greg Anthony	.05	.01
376	Ken Williams	.05	.01
377	John Paxson	.05	.01
378	Corey Gaines	.05	.01
379	Eric Murdock	.05	.01
380	Kevin Thompson RC	.05	.01
381	Moses Malone	.25	.08
382	Kenny Smith	.05	.01
383	Dennis Scott	.05	.01
384	Michael Jordan FSL	1.50	.60
385	Hakeem Olajuwon FSL	.25	.08
386	Shaquille O'Neal FSL	.50	.20
387	David Robinson FSL	.25	.08
388	Derrick Coleman FSL	.05	.01
389	Karl Malone FSL	.25	.08
390	Patrick Ewing FSL	.10	.02
391	Scottie Pippen FSL	.40	.15
392	Dominique Wilkins FSL	.10	.02
393	Charles Barkley FSL	.25	.08
394	Larry Johnson FSL	.10	.02
395	Checklist	.05	.01
396	Checklist	.05	.01
NNO	Expired Finest Redempt.	1.00	.40

1994-95 Topps

	COMPLETE SET (396)	25.00	12.50
	COMPLETE SERIES 1 (198)	10.00	5.00
	COMPLETE SERIES 2 (198)	15.00	7.50
1	Patrick Ewing AS	.10	.02
2	Mookie Blaylock AS	.05	.01
3	Charles Oakley AS	.05	.01
4	Mark Price AS	.05	.01
5	John Starks AS	.05	.01
6	Dominique Wilkins AS	.10	.02
7	Horace Grant AS	.05	.01
8	Alonzo Mourning AS	.25	.08
9	B.J. Armstrong AS	.05	.01
10	Kenny Anderson AS	.05	.01
11	Scottie Pippen AS	.40	.15
12	Derrick Coleman AS	.05	.01
13	Shaquille O'Neal AS	.50	.20
14	Anfernee Hardaway AS	.40	.15
15	Isaiah Rider SPEC	.05	.01
16	John Williams	.05	.01
17	Todd Day	.05	.01
18	Dale Davis	.05	.01
19	Sean Rooks	.05	.01
20	George Lynch	.05	.01
21	Mitchell Butler	.05	.01
22	Stacey King	.05	.01
23	Sherman Douglas	.05	.01
24	Derrick McKey	.05	.01
25	Joe Dumars	.25	.08
26	Scott Brooks	.05	.01
27	Clarence Weatherspoon	.05	.01
28	Jayson Williams	.10	.02
29	Scottie Pippen	.75	.30
30	John Starks	.05	.01
31	Robert Pack	.05	.01
32	Donald Royal	.05	.01
33	Haywoode Workman	.05	.01
34	Greg Graham	.05	.01
35	Terry Cummings	.05	.01
36	Andrew Lang	.05	.01
37	Jason Kidd RC	2.50	1.00
38	Terry Mills	.05	.01
39	Alonzo Mourning	.30	.10
40	Shawn Kemp	.40	.15
41	Kevin Willis FTR	.05	.01
42	Kevin Willis	.05	.01
43	Armon Gilliam	.05	.01
44	Bobby Hurley	.05	.01
45	Jerome Kersey	.05	.01
46	Xavier McDaniel	.05	.01
47	Chris Webber	.60	.25
48	Chris Webber FR	.30	.10
49	Jeff Malone	.05	.01
50	Dikembe Mutombo SPEC	.05	.01
51	Dan Majerle SPEC	.05	.01
52	Dee Brown SPEC	.05	.01
53	John Stockton SPEC	.10	.02
54	Dennis Rodman SPEC	.25	.08
55	Eric Murdock SPEC	.05	.01
56	Glen Rice	.10	.02
57	Glen Rice FTR	.05	.01
58	Dino Radja	.05	.01
59	Billy Owens	.05	.01
60	Doc Rivers	.10	.02
61	Don MacLean	.05	.01
62	Lindsey Hunter	.10	.02
63	Sam Cassell	.25	.08
64	James Worthy	.25	.08
65	Christian Laettner	.10	.02
66	Wesley Person RC	.25	.08
67	Rich King	.05	.01
68	Jon Koncak	.05	.01
69	Muggsy Bogues	.10	.02
70	Jamal Mashburn	.25	.08
71	Gary Grant	.05	.01
72	Eric Murdock	.05	.01
73	Scott Burrell	.05	.01
74	Scott Burrell FTR	.05	.01
75	Anfernee Hardaway	.60	.25
76	Anfernee Hardaway FR	.30	.10
77	Yinka Dare RC	.05	.01
78	Anthony Avent	.05	.01
79	Jon Barry	.05	.01
80	Rodney Rogers	.05	.01
81	Chris Mills	.10	.02
82	Antonio Davis	.05	.01

☐ 83 Steve Smith	.10	.02	☐ 169 A.C. Green	.10	.02	☐ 255 Clyde Drexler	.25	.08
☐ 84 Buck Williams	.05	.01	☐ 170 Kendall Gill	.10	.02	☐ 256 Andres Guibert	.05	.01
☐ 85 Spud Webb	.05	.01	☐ 171 Kendall Gill FTR	.05	.01	☐ 257 Gheorghe Muresan	.05	.01
☐ 86 Stacey Augmon	.05	.01	☐ 172 Danny Ferry	.05	.01	☐ 258 Tom Hammonds	.05	.01
☐ 87 Allan Houston	.40	.15	☐ 173 Bryant Stith	.05	.01	☐ 259 Charles Barkley	.40	.15
☐ 88 Will Perdue	.05	.01	☐ 174 John Salley	.05	.01	☐ 260 Charles Barkley FR	.25	.08
☐ 89 Chris Gatling	.05	.01	☐ 175 Cedric Ceballos	.05	.01	☐ 261 Acie Earl	.05	.01
☐ 90 Danny Ainge	.05	.01	☐ 176 Derrick Coleman	.10	.02	☐ 262 Lamond Murray RC	.10	.02
☐ 91 Rick Mahorn	.05	.01	☐ 177 Tony Bennett	.05	.01	☐ 263 Dana Barros	.05	.01
☐ 92 Elmore Spencer	.05	.01	☐ 178 Kevin Duckworth	.05	.01	☐ 264 Greg Anthony	.05	.01
☐ 93 Vin Baker	.25	.08	☐ 179 Jay Humphries	.05	.01	☐ 265 Dan Majerle	.10	.02
☐ 94 Rex Chapman	.05	.01	☐ 180 Sean Elliott	.10	.02	☐ 266 Zan Tabak	.05	.01
☐ 95 Dale Ellis	.05	.01	☐ 181 Sam Perkins	.10	.02	☐ 267 Ricky Pierce	.05	.01
☐ 96 Doug Smith	.05	.01	☐ 182 Luc Longley	.05	.01	☐ 268 Eric Leckner	.05	.01
☐ 97 Tim Perry	.05	.01	☐ 183 Mitch Richmond AS	.10	.02	☐ 269 Duane Ferrell	.05	.01
☐ 98 Toni Kukoc	.40	.15	☐ 184 Clyde Drexler AS	.10	.02	☐ 270 Mark Price	.05	.01
☐ 99 Terry Dehere	.05	.01	☐ 185 Karl Malone AS	.25	.08	☐ 271 Anthony Peeler	.05	.01
☐ 100 Shaquille O'Neal PP	.50	.20	☐ 186 Shawn Kemp AS	.25	.08	☐ 272 Adam Keefe	.05	.01
☐ 101 Shawn Kemp PP	.25	.08	☐ 187 Hakeem Olajuwon AS	.25	.08	☐ 273 Rex Walters	.05	.01
☐ 102 Hakeem Olajuwon PP	.25	.08	☐ 188 Danny Manning AS	.05	.01	☐ 274 Scott Skiles	.05	.01
☐ 103 Derrick Coleman PP	.05	.01	☐ 189 Kevin Johnson AS	.05	.01	☐ 275 Glenn Robinson RC	.75	.30
☐ 104 Alonzo Mourning PP	.25	.08	☐ 190 John Stockton AS	.10	.02	☐ 276 Tony Dumas RC	.05	.01
☐ 105 Dikembe Mutombo PP	.05	.01	☐ 191 Latrell Sprewell AS	.25	.08	☐ 277 Elliot Perry	.05	.01
☐ 106 Chris Webber PP	.30	.10	☐ 192 Gary Payton AS	.25	.08	☐ 278 Bo Outlaw RC	.05	.01
☐ 107 Dennis Rodman PP	.25	.08	☐ 193 Clifford Robinson AS	.05	.01	☐ 279 Karl Malone	.40	.15
☐ 108 David Robinson PP	.25	.08	☐ 194 David Robinson AS	.25	.08	☐ 280 Karl Malone FR	.25	.08
☐ 109 Charles Barkley PP	.25	.08	☐ 195 Charles Barkley AS	.25	.08	☐ 281 Herb Williams	.05	.01
☐ 110 Brad Daugherty	.05	.01	☐ 196 Mark Price SPEC	.05	.01	☐ 282 Vincent Askew	.05	.01
☐ 111 Derek Harper	.05	.01	☐ 197 Checklist 1-99	.05	.01	☐ 283 Askia Jones RC	.05	.01
☐ 112 Detlef Schrempf	.10	.02	☐ 198 Checklist 100-198	.05	.01	☐ 284 Shawn Bradley	.05	.01
☐ 113 Harvey Grant	.05	.01	☐ 199 Patrick Ewing	.25	.08	☐ 285 Tim Hardaway	.25	.08
☐ 114 Vlade Divac	.05	.01	☐ 200 Patrick Ewing FR	.10	.02	☐ 286 Mark West	.05	.01
☐ 115 Isaiah Rider	.10	.02	☐ 201 Tracy Murray PP	.05	.01	☐ 287 Chuck Person	.05	.01
☐ 116 Mitch Richmond	.25	.08	☐ 202 Craig Ehlo PP	.05	.01	☐ 288 James Edwards	.05	.01
☐ 117 Tom Chambers	.05	.01	☐ 203 Nick Anderson PP	.05	.01	☐ 289 Antonio Lang RC	.05	.01
☐ 118 Kenny Gattison	.05	.01	☐ 204 John Starks PP	.05	.01	☐ 290 Dominique Wilkins	.25	.08
☐ 119 Kenny Gattison FTR	.05	.01	☐ 205 Rex Chapman PP	.05	.01	☐ 291 Khalid Reeves RC	.05	.01
☐ 120 Vernon Maxwell	.05	.01	☐ 206 Hersey Hawkins PP	.05	.01	☐ 292 Jamie Watson RC	.05	.01
☐ 121 Reggie Williams	.05	.01	☐ 207 Glen Rice PP	.05	.01	☐ 293 Darnell Mee	.05	.01
☐ 122 Chris Mullin	.25	.08	☐ 208 Jeff Malone PP	.05	.01	☐ 294 Brian Grant RC	.60	.25
☐ 123 Harold Miner	.05	.01	☐ 209 Dan Majerle PP	.05	.01	☐ 295 Hakeem Olajuwon	.40	.15
☐ 124 Harold Miner FTR	.05	.01	☐ 210 Chris Mullin PP	.10	.02	☐ 296 Dickey Simpkins RC	.05	.01
☐ 125 Calbert Cheaney	.05	.01	☐ 211 Grant Hill RC	1.25	.50	☐ 297 Tyrone Corbin	.05	.01
☐ 126 Randy Woods	.05	.01	☐ 212 Bobby Phills	.05	.01	☐ 298 David Wingate	.05	.01
☐ 127 Mike Gminski	.05	.01	☐ 213 Dennis Rodman	.50	.20	☐ 299 Shaquille O'Neal RC	1.25	.50
☐ 128 Willie Anderson	.05	.01	☐ 214 Doug West	.05	.01	☐ 300 Shaquille O'Neal FR	.50	.20
☐ 129 Mark Macon	.05	.01	☐ 215 Harold Ellis	.05	.01	☐ 301 B.J. Armstrong PP	.05	.01
☐ 130 Avery Johnson	.05	.01	☐ 216 Kevin Edwards	.05	.01	☐ 302 Mitch Richmond PP	.10	.02
☐ 131 Bimbo Coles	.05	.01	☐ 217 Lorenzo Williams	.05	.01	☐ 303 Jim Jackson PP	.05	.01
☐ 132 Kenny Smith	.05	.01	☐ 218 Rick Fox	.05	.01	☐ 304 Jeff Hornacek PP	.05	.01
☐ 133 Dennis Scott	.05	.01	☐ 219 Mookie Blaylock	.05	.01	☐ 305 Mark Price PP	.05	.01
☐ 134 Lionel Simmons	.05	.01	☐ 220 Mookie Blaylock FR	.05	.01	☐ 306 Kendall Gill PP	.05	.01
☐ 135 Nate McMillan	.05	.01	☐ 221 John Williams	.05	.01	☐ 307 Dale Ellis PP	.05	.01
☐ 136 Eric Montross RC	.05	.01	☐ 222 Keith Jennings	.05	.01	☐ 308 Vernon Maxwell PP	.05	.01
☐ 137 Sedale Threatt	.05	.01	☐ 223 Nick Van Exel	.25	.08	☐ 309 Joe Dumars PP	.10	.02
☐ 138 Kenny Anderson	.10	.02	☐ 224 Gary Payton	.40	.15	☐ 310 Reggie Miller PP	.10	.02
☐ 139 Micheal Williams	.05	.01	☐ 225 John Stockton	.25	.08	☐ 311 Geert Hammink	.05	.01
☐ 140 Grant Long	.05	.01	☐ 226 Ron Harper	.10	.02	☐ 312 Charles Smith	.05	.01
☐ 141 Grant Long FTR	.05	.01	☐ 227 Monty Williams RC	.05	.01	☐ 313 Bill Cartwright	.05	.01
☐ 142 Tyrone Corbin	.05	.01	☐ 228 Marty Conlon	.05	.01	☐ 314 Aaron McKie RC	.75	.30
☐ 143 Craig Ehlo	.05	.01	☐ 229 Hersey Hawkins	.10	.02	☐ 315 Tom Gugliotta	.10	.02
☐ 144 Gerald Wilkins	.05	.01	☐ 230 Rik Smits	.05	.01	☐ 316 P.J. Brown	.05	.01
☐ 145 LaPhonso Ellis	.05	.01	☐ 231 James Robinson	.05	.01	☐ 317 David Wesley	.05	.01
☐ 146 Reggie Miller	.25	.08	☐ 232 Malik Sealy	.05	.01	☐ 318 Felton Spencer	.05	.01
☐ 147 Tracy Murray	.05	.01	☐ 233 Sergei Bazarevich	.05	.01	☐ 319 Robert Horry	.10	.02
☐ 148 Victor Alexander	.05	.01	☐ 234 Brad Lohaus	.05	.01	☐ 320 Robert Horry FR	.05	.01
☐ 149 Victor Alexander FTR	.05	.01	☐ 235 Olden Polynice	.05	.01	☐ 321 Larry Krystkowiak	.05	.01
☐ 150 Clifford Robinson	.10	.02	☐ 236 Brian Williams	.05	.01	☐ 322 Eric Piatkowski RC	.05	.01
☐ 151 Anthony Mason FTR	.05	.01	☐ 237 Tyrone Hill	.05	.01	☐ 323 Anthony Bonner	.05	.01
☐ 152 Anthony Mason	.10	.02	☐ 238 Jim McIlvaine RC	.05	.01	☐ 324 Keith Askins	.05	.01
☐ 153 Jim Jackson	.10	.02	☐ 239 Latrell Sprewell	.25	.08	☐ 325 Mahmoud Abdul-Rauf	.05	.01
☐ 154 Jeff Hornacek	.10	.02	☐ 240 Latrell Sprewell FR	.05	.01	☐ 326 Darrin Hancock RC	.05	.01
☐ 155 Nick Anderson	.05	.01	☐ 241 Popeye Jones	.05	.01	☐ 327 Vern Fleming	.05	.01
☐ 156 Mike Brown	.05	.01	☐ 242 Scott Williams	.05	.01	☐ 328 Wayman Tisdale	.05	.01
☐ 157 Kevin Johnson	.10	.02	☐ 243 Eddie Jones	.60	.25	☐ 329 Sam Bowie	.05	.01
☐ 158 John Paxson	.05	.01	☐ 244 Moses Malone	.25	.08	☐ 330 Billy Owens	.05	.01
☐ 159 Loy Vaught	.05	.01	☐ 245 B.J. Armstrong	.05	.01	☐ 331 Donald Hodge	.05	.01
☐ 160 Carl Herrera	.05	.01	☐ 246 Jim Les	.05	.01	☐ 332 Derrick Alston RC	.05	.01
☐ 161 Shawn Bradley	.05	.01	☐ 247 Greg Grant	.05	.01	☐ 333 Doug Edwards	.05	.01
☐ 162 Hubert Davis	.05	.01	☐ 248 Lee Mayberry	.05	.01	☐ 334 Johnny Newman	.05	.01
☐ 163 David Benoit	.05	.01	☐ 249 Mark Jackson	.05	.01	☐ 335 Otis Thorpe	.10	.02
☐ 164 Dell Curry	.05	.01	☐ 250 Larry Johnson	.10	.02	☐ 336 Bill Curley RC	.05	.01
☐ 165 Dee Brown	.05	.01	☐ 251 Terrell Brandon	.10	.02	☐ 337 Michael Cage	.05	.01
☐ 166 LaSalle Thompson	.05	.01	☐ 252 Ledell Eackles	.05	.01	☐ 338 Chris Smith	.05	.01
☐ 167 Eddie Jones RC	1.25	.50	☐ 253 Yinka Dare	.05	.01	☐ 339 Dikembe Mutombo	.10	.02
☐ 168 Walt Williams	.05	.01	☐ 254 Dontonio Wingfield RC	.05	.01	☐ 340 Dikembe Mutombo FR	.05	.01

❑ 341 Duane Causwell	.05	.01
❑ 342 Sean Higgins	.05	.01
❑ 343 Steve Kerr	.05	.01
❑ 344 Eric Montross	.05	.01
❑ 345 Charles Oakley	.05	.01
❑ 346 Brooks Thompson RC	.05	.01
❑ 347 Rony Seikaly	.05	.01
❑ 348 Chris Dudley	.05	.01
❑ 349 Sharone Wright RC	.05	.01
❑ 350 Sarunas Marciulionis	.05	.01
❑ 351 Anthony Miller RC	.05	.01
❑ 352 Pooh Richardson	.05	.01
❑ 353 Byron Scott	.10	.02
❑ 354 Michael Adams	.05	.01
❑ 355 Ken Norman	.05	.01
❑ 356 Clifford Rozier RC	.05	.01
❑ 357 Tim Breaux	.05	.01
❑ 358 Derek Strong	.05	.01
❑ 359 David Robinson	.40	.15
❑ 360 David Robinson FR	.25	.08
❑ 361 Benoit Benjamin	.05	.01
❑ 362 Terry Porter	.05	.01
❑ 363 Ervin Johnson	.05	.01
❑ 364 Alaa Abdelnaby	.05	.01
❑ 365 Robert Parish	.10	.02
❑ 366 Mario Elie	.05	.01
❑ 367 Antonio Harvey	.05	.01
❑ 368 Charlie Ward RC	.25	.08
❑ 369 Kevin Gamble	.05	.01
❑ 370 Rod Strickland	.10	.02
❑ 371 Jason Kidd	1.25	.50
❑ 372 Oliver Miller	.05	.01
❑ 373 Eric Mobley RC	.05	.01
❑ 374 Brian Shaw	.05	.01
❑ 375 Horace Grant	.10	.02
❑ 376 Corie Blount	.05	.01
❑ 377 Sam Mitchell	.05	.01
❑ 378 Jalen Rose RC	1.00	.40
❑ 379 Elden Campbell	.05	.01
❑ 380 Elden Campbell FR	.05	.01
❑ 381 Donyell Marshall RC	.25	.08
❑ 382 Frank Brickowski	.05	.01
❑ 383 B.J. Tyler RC	.05	.01
❑ 384 Bryon Russell	.05	.01
❑ 385 Danny Manning	.10	.02
❑ 386 Manute Bol	.05	.01
❑ 387 Brent Price	.05	.01
❑ 388 J.R. Reid	.05	.01
❑ 389 Byron Houston	.05	.01
❑ 390 Blue Edwards	.05	.01
❑ 391 Adrian Caldwell	.05	.01
❑ 392 Wesley Person	.10	.02
❑ 393 Juwan Howard RC	.60	.25
❑ 394 Chris Morris	.05	.01
❑ 395 Checklist 199-296	.05	.01
❑ 396 Checklist 297-396	.05	.01

1995-96 Topps

❑ COMPLETE SET (291)	30.00	15.00
❑ COMPLETE SERIES 1 (181)	15.00	7.50
❑ COMPLETE SERIES 2 (110)	15.00	7.50
❑ 1 Michael Jordan AL	1.50	.60
❑ 2 Dennis Rodman AL	.15	.05
❑ 3 John Stockton AL	.50	.20
❑ 4 Michael Jordan AL	1.50	.60
❑ 5 David Robinson AL	.30	.10
❑ 6 Shaquille O'Neal AL	.50	.20
❑ 7 Hakeem Olajuwon LL	.30	.10

❑ 8 David Robinson LL	.30	.10
❑ 9 Karl Malone LL	.50	.20
❑ 10 Jamal Mashburn LL	.15	.05
❑ 11 Dennis Rodman LL	.15	.05
❑ 12 Dikembe Mutombo LL	.15	.05
❑ 13 Shaquille O'Neal LL	.50	.20
❑ 14 Patrick Ewing LL	.30	.10
❑ 15 Tyrone Hill LL	.15	.05
❑ 16 John Stockton LL	.50	.20
❑ 17 Kenny Anderson LL	.15	.05
❑ 18 Tim Hardaway LL	.15	.05
❑ 19 Rod Strickland LL	.15	.05
❑ 20 Muggsy Bogues LL	.15	.05
❑ 21 Scottie Pippen LL	.30	.10
❑ 22 Mookie Blaylock LL	.15	.05
❑ 23 Gary Payton LL	.30	.10
❑ 24 John Stockton LL	.50	.20
❑ 25 Nate McMillan LL	.15	.05
❑ 26 Dikembe Mutombo LL	.15	.05
❑ 27 Hakeem Olajuwon LL	.30	.10
❑ 28 Shawn Bradley LL	.15	.05
❑ 29 David Robinson LL	.30	.10
❑ 30 Alonzo Mourning LL	.15	.05
❑ 31 Reggie Miller	.50	.20
❑ 32 Karl Malone	.60	.25
❑ 33 Grant Hill	.60	.25
❑ 34 Charles Barkley	.60	.25
❑ 35 Cedric Ceballos	.15	.05
❑ 36 Gheorghe Muresan	.15	.05
❑ 37 Doug West	.15	.05
❑ 38 Tony Dumas	.15	.05
❑ 39 Kenny Gattison	.15	.05
❑ 40 Chris Mullin	.50	.20
❑ 41 Pervis Ellison	.15	.05
❑ 42 Vinny Del Negro	.15	.05
❑ 43 Mario Elie	.15	.05
❑ 44 Todd Day	.15	.05
❑ 45 Scottie Pippen	.75	.30
❑ 46 Buck Williams	.15	.05
❑ 47 P.J. Brown	.15	.05
❑ 48 Bimbo Coles	.15	.05
❑ 49 Terrell Brandon	.30	.10
❑ 50 Charles Oakley	.15	.05
❑ 51 Sam Perkins	.30	.10
❑ 52 Dale Ellis	.15	.05
❑ 53 Andrew Lang	.15	.05
❑ 54 Harold Ellis	.15	.05
❑ 55 Clarence Weatherspoon	.15	.05
❑ 56 Bill Curley	.15	.05
❑ 57 Robert Parish	.30	.10
❑ 58 David Benoit	.15	.05
❑ 59 Anthony Avent	.15	.05
❑ 60 Jamal Mashburn	.30	.10
❑ 61 Duane Ferrell	.15	.05
❑ 62 Elden Campbell	.15	.05
❑ 63 Rex Chapman	.15	.05
❑ 64 Wesley Person	.15	.05
❑ 65 Mitch Richmond	.30	.10
❑ 66 Micheal Williams	.15	.05
❑ 67 Clifford Rozier	.15	.05
❑ 68 Eric Montross	.15	.05
❑ 69 Dennis Rodman	.30	.10
❑ 70 Vin Baker	.30	.10
❑ 71 Tyrone Hill	.15	.05
❑ 72 Tyrone Corbin	.15	.05
❑ 73 Chris Dudley	.15	.05
❑ 74 Nate McMillan	.15	.05
❑ 75 Kenny Anderson	.30	.10
❑ 76 Monty Williams	.15	.05
❑ 77 Kenny Smith	.15	.05
❑ 78 Rodney Rogers	.15	.05
❑ 79 Corie Blount	.15	.05
❑ 80 Glen Rice	.30	.10
❑ 81 Walt Williams	.15	.05
❑ 82 Scott Williams	.15	.05
❑ 83 Michael Adams	.15	.05
❑ 84 Terry Mills	.15	.05
❑ 85 Horace Grant	.30	.10
❑ 86 Chuck Person	.15	.05
❑ 87 Adam Keefe	.15	.05
❑ 88 Scott Brooks	.15	.05
❑ 89 George Lynch	.15	.05
❑ 90 Kevin Johnson	.30	.10
❑ 91 Armon Gilliam	.15	.05
❑ 92 Greg Minor	.15	.05
❑ 93 Derrick McKey	.15	.05

❑ 94 Victor Alexander	.15	.05
❑ 95 B.J. Armstrong	.15	.05
❑ 96 Terry Dehere	.15	.05
❑ 97 Christian Laettner	.30	.10
❑ 98 Hubert Davis	.15	.05
❑ 99 Aaron McKie	.30	.10
❑ 100 Hakeem Olajuwon	.50	.20
❑ 101 Michael Cage	.15	.05
❑ 102 Grant Long	.15	.05
❑ 103 Calbert Cheaney	.15	.05
❑ 104 Olden Polynice	.15	.05
❑ 105 Sharone Wright	.15	.05
❑ 106 Lee Mayberry	.15	.05
❑ 107 Robert Pack	.15	.05
❑ 108 Loy Vaught	.15	.05
❑ 109 Khalid Reeves	.15	.05
❑ 110 Shawn Kemp	.30	.10
❑ 111 Lindsey Hunter	.15	.05
❑ 112 Dell Curry	.15	.05
❑ 113 Dan Majerle	.30	.10
❑ 114 Bryon Russell	.15	.05
❑ 115 John Starks	.30	.10
❑ 116 Roy Tarpley	.15	.05
❑ 117 Dale Davis	.15	.05
❑ 118 Nick Anderson	.15	.05
❑ 119 Rex Walters	.15	.05
❑ 120 Dominique Wilkins	.50	.20
❑ 121 Sam Cassell	.50	.20
❑ 122 Sean Elliott	.30	.10
❑ 123 B.J. Tyler	.15	.05
❑ 124 Eric Mobley	.15	.05
❑ 125 Toni Kukoc	.30	.10
❑ 126 Pooh Richardson	.15	.05
❑ 127 Isaiah Rider	.15	.05
❑ 128 Steve Smith	.30	.10
❑ 129 Chris Mills	.15	.05
❑ 130 Detlef Schrempf	.30	.10
❑ 131 Donyell Marshall	.30	.10
❑ 132 Eddie Jones	.60	.25
❑ 133 Otis Thorpe	.15	.05
❑ 134 Lionel Simmons	.15	.05
❑ 135 Jeff Hornacek	.15	.05
❑ 136 Jalen Rose	.60	.25
❑ 137 Kevin Willis	.30	.10
❑ 138 Don MacLean	.15	.05
❑ 139 Dee Brown	.15	.05
❑ 140 Glenn Robinson	.50	.20
❑ 141 Joe Kleine	.15	.05
❑ 142 Ron Harper	.30	.10
❑ 143 Antonio Davis	.15	.05
❑ 144 Jeff Malone	.15	.05
❑ 145 Joe Dumars	.50	.20
❑ 146 Jason Kidd	1.50	.60
❑ 147 J.R. Reid	.15	.05
❑ 148 Lamond Murray	.15	.05
❑ 149 Derrick Coleman	.15	.05
❑ 150 Alonzo Mourning	.30	.10
❑ 151 Clifford Robinson	.15	.05
❑ 152 Kendall Gill	.15	.05
❑ 153 Doug Christie	.30	.10
❑ 154 Stacey Augmon	.15	.05
❑ 155 Anfernee Hardaway	.50	.20
❑ 156 Mahmoud Abdul-Rauf	.15	.05
❑ 157 Latrell Sprewell	.50	.20
❑ 158 Mark Price	.30	.10
❑ 159 Brian Grant	.50	.20
❑ 160 Clyde Drexler	.50	.20
❑ 161 Juwan Howard	.50	.20
❑ 162 Tom Gugliotta	.15	.05
❑ 163 Nick Van Exel	.50	.20
❑ 164 Billy Owens	.15	.05
❑ 165 Brooks Thompson	.15	.05
❑ 166 Acie Earl	.15	.05
❑ 167 Ed Pinckney	.15	.05
❑ 168 Oliver Miller	.15	.05
❑ 169 John Salley	.15	.05
❑ 170 Jerome Kersey	.15	.05
❑ 171 Willie Anderson	.15	.05
❑ 172 Keith Jennings	.15	.05
❑ 173 Doug Smith	.15	.05
❑ 174 Gerald Wilkins	.15	.05
❑ 175 Byron Scott	.15	.05
❑ 176 Benoit Benjamin	.15	.05
❑ 177 Blue Edwards	.15	.05
❑ 178 Greg Anthony	.15	.05
❑ 179 Trevor Ruffin	.15	.05

☐ 180	Kenny Gattison	.15	.05
☐ 181	Checklist 1-181	.15	.05
☐ 182	Cherokee Parks RC	.15	.05
☐ 183	Kurt Thomas RC	.30	.10
☐ 184	Ervin Johnson	.15	.05
☐ 185	Chucky Brown	.15	.05
☐ 186	Luc Longley	.15	.05
☐ 187	Anthony Miller	.15	.05
☐ 188	Ed O'Bannon RC	.15	.05
☐ 189	Bobby Hurley	.15	.05
☐ 190	Dikembe Mutombo	.30	.10
☐ 191	Robert Horry	.30	.10
☐ 192	George Zidek RC	.15	.05
☐ 193	Rasheed Wallace RC	1.25	.50
☐ 194	Marty Conlon	.15	.05
☐ 195	A.C. Green	.30	.10
☐ 196	Mike Brown	.15	.05
☐ 197	Oliver Miller	.15	.05
☐ 198	Charles Smith	.15	.05
☐ 199	Eric Williams RC	.30	.10
☐ 200	Rik Smits	.30	.10
☐ 201	Donald Royal	.15	.05
☐ 202	Bryant Reeves RC	.50	.20
☐ 203	Danny Ferry	.15	.05
☐ 204	Brian Williams	.15	.05
☐ 205	Joe Smith RC	.75	.30
☐ 206	Gary Trent RC	.15	.05
☐ 207	Greg Ostertag RC	.15	.05
☐ 208	Ken Norman	.15	.05
☐ 209	Avery Johnson	.15	.05
☐ 210	Theo Ratliff RC	.60	.25
☐ 211	Corie Blount	.15	.05
☐ 212	Hersey Hawkins	.15	.05
☐ 213	Loren Meyer RC	.15	.05
☐ 214	Mario Bennett RC	.15	.05
☐ 215	Randolph Childress RC	.15	.05
☐ 216	Spud Webb	.30	.10
☐ 217	Popeye Jones	.15	.05
☐ 218	Shawn Respert RC	.15	.05
☐ 219	Malik Sealy	.15	.05
☐ 220	Dino Radja	.15	.05
☐ 221	James Robinson	.15	.05
☐ 222	David Vaughn	.15	.05
☐ 223	Michael Smith	.15	.05
☐ 224	Jamie Watson	.15	.05
☐ 225	LaPhonso Ellis	.15	.05
☐ 226	Kevin Gamble	.15	.05
☐ 227	Dennis Rodman	.30	.10
☐ 228	B.J. Armstrong	.15	.05
☐ 229	Jerry Stackhouse RC	1.50	.60
☐ 230	Muggsy Bogues	.30	.10
☐ 231	Lawrence Moten RC	.15	.05
☐ 232	Cory Alexander RC	.15	.05
☐ 233	Carlos Rogers	.15	.05
☐ 234	Tyus Edney RC	.15	.05
☐ 235	Doc Rivers	.30	.10
☐ 236	Antonio Harvey	.15	.05
☐ 237	Kevin Garnett RC	2.50	1.25
☐ 238	Derek Harper	.30	.10
☐ 239	Kevin Edwards	.15	.05
☐ 240	Chris Smith	.15	.05
☐ 241	Haywoode Workman	.15	.05
☐ 242	Bobby Phills	.15	.05
☐ 243	Sherrell Ford RC	.15	.05
☐ 244	Corliss Williamson RC	.50	.20
☐ 245	Shawn Bradley	.15	.05
☐ 246	Jason Caffey RC	.30	.10
☐ 247	Bryant Stith	.15	.05
☐ 248	Mark West	.15	.05
☐ 249	Dennis Scott	.15	.05
☐ 250	Jim Jackson	.15	.05
☐ 251	Travis Best RC	.15	.05
☐ 252	Sean Rooks	.15	.05
☐ 253	Yinka Dare	.15	.05
☐ 254	Felton Spencer	.15	.05
☐ 255	Vlade Divac	.30	.10
☐ 256	Michael Finley RC	1.25	.50
☐ 257	Damon Stoudamire RC	1.00	.40
☐ 258	Mark Bryant	.15	.05
☐ 259	Brent Barry RC	.50	.20
☐ 260	Rony Seikaly	.15	.05
☐ 261	Alan Henderson RC	.50	.20
☐ 262	Kendall Gill	.15	.05
☐ 263	Rex Chapman	.15	.05
☐ 264	Eric Murdock	.15	.05
☐ 265	Rodney Rogers	.15	.05

☐ 266	Greg Graham	.15	.05
☐ 267	Jayson Williams	.15	.05
☐ 268	Antonio McDyess RC	1.00	.40
☐ 269	Sedale Threatt	.15	.05
☐ 270	Danny Manning	.30	.10
☐ 271	Pete Chilcutt	.15	.05
☐ 272	Bob Sura RC	.30	.10
☐ 273	Dana Barros	.15	.05
☐ 274	Allan Houston	.30	.10
☐ 275	Tracy Murray	.15	.05
☐ 276	Anthony Mason	.30	.10
☐ 277	Michael Jordan	3.00	1.25
☐ 278	Patrick Ewing	.50	.20
☐ 279	Shaquille O'Neal	1.25	.50
☐ 280	Larry Johnson	.30	.10
☐ 281	Mark Jackson	.30	.10
☐ 282	Chris Webber	.60	.25
☐ 283	David Robinson	.50	.20
☐ 284	John Stockton	.60	.25
☐ 285	Mookie Blaylock	.15	.05
☐ 286	Mark Price	.15	.05
☐ 287	Tim Hardaway	.30	.10
☐ 288	Rod Strickland	.15	.05
☐ 289	Sherman Douglas	.15	.05
☐ 290	Gary Payton	.50	.20
☐ 291	Checklist (182-291)	.15	.05

1996-97 Topps

☐ COMPLETE SET (221)		30.00	15.00
☐ COMP.FACT.HOB.SET (227)		35.00	15.00
☐ COMPLETE SERIES 1 (110)		12.00	6.00
☐ COMPLETE SERIES 2 (111)		20.00	10.00
☐ 1	Patrick Ewing	.50	.20
☐ 2	Christian Laettner	.30	.10
☐ 3	Mahmoud Abdul-Rauf	.15	.05
☐ 4	Chris Webber	.50	.20
☐ 5	Jason Kidd	.75	.30
☐ 6	Clifford Rozier	.15	.05
☐ 7	Elden Campbell	.15	.05
☐ 8	Chuck Person	.15	.05
☐ 9	Jeff Hornacek	.30	.10
☐ 10	Rik Smits	.30	.10
☐ 11	Kurt Thomas	.30	.10
☐ 12	Rod Strickland	.15	.05
☐ 13	Kendall Gill	.15	.05
☐ 14	Brian Williams	.15	.05
☐ 15	Tom Gugliotta	.30	.10
☐ 16	Ron Harper	.30	.10
☐ 17	Eric Williams	.15	.05
☐ 18	A.C. Green	.30	.10
☐ 19	Scott Williams	.15	.05
☐ 20	Damon Stoudamire	.50	.20
☐ 21	Bryant Reeves	.15	.05
☐ 22	Bob Sura	.15	.05
☐ 23	Mitch Richmond	.30	.10
☐ 24	Larry Johnson	.30	.10
☐ 25	Vin Baker	.30	.10
☐ 26	Mark Bryant	.15	.05
☐ 27	Horace Grant	.15	.05
☐ 28	Allan Houston	.30	.10
☐ 29	Sam Perkins	.15	.05
☐ 30	Antonio McDyess	.30	.10
☐ 31	Rasheed Wallace	.60	.25
☐ 32	Malik Sealy	.15	.05
☐ 33	Scottie Pippen	.75	.30
☐ 34	Charles Barkley	.60	.25
☐ 35	Hakeem Olajuwon	.50	.20
☐ 36	John Starks	.30	.10

☐ 37	Byron Scott	.15	.05
☐ 38	Arvydas Sabonis	.30	.10
☐ 39	Vlade Divac	.15	.05
☐ 40	Joe Dumars	.50	.20
☐ 41	Danny Ferry	.15	.05
☐ 42	Jerry Stackhouse	.60	.25
☐ 43	B.J. Armstrong	.15	.05
☐ 44	Shawn Bradley	.15	.05
☐ 45	Kevin Garnett	1.00	.40
☐ 46	Dee Brown	.15	.05
☐ 47	Michael Smith	.15	.05
☐ 48	Doug Christie	.30	.10
☐ 49	Mark Jackson	.15	.05
☐ 50	Shawn Kemp	.30	.10
☐ 51	Sasha Danilovic	.15	.05
☐ 52	Nick Anderson	.15	.05
☐ 53	Matt Geiger	.15	.05
☐ 54	Charles Smith	.15	.05
☐ 55	Mookie Blaylock	.15	.05
☐ 56	Johnny Newman	.15	.05
☐ 57	George McCloud	.15	.05
☐ 58	Greg Ostertag	.15	.05
☐ 59	Reggie Williams	.15	.05
☐ 60	Brent Barry	.15	.05
☐ 61	Doug West	.15	.05
☐ 62	Donald Royal	.15	.05
☐ 63	Randy Brown	.15	.05
☐ 64	Vincent Askew	.15	.05
☐ 65	John Stockton	.50	.20
☐ 66	Joe Kleine	.15	.05
☐ 67	Keith Askins	.15	.05
☐ 68	Bobby Phills	.15	.05
☐ 69	Chris Mullin	.50	.20
☐ 70	Nick Van Exel	.50	.20
☐ 71	Rick Fox	.15	.05
☐ 72	Chicago Bulls - 72 Wins	1.50	.60
☐ 73	Shawn Respert	.15	.05
☐ 74	Hubert Davis	.15	.05
☐ 75	Jim Jackson	.15	.05
☐ 76	Olden Polynice	.15	.05
☐ 77	Gheorghe Muresan	.15	.05
☐ 78	Theo Ratliff	.30	.10
☐ 79	Khalid Reeves	.15	.05
☐ 80	David Robinson	.50	.20
☐ 81	Lawrence Moten	.15	.05
☐ 82	Sam Cassell	.50	.20
☐ 83	George Zidek	.15	.05
☐ 84	Sharone Wright	.15	.05
☐ 85	Clarence Weatherspoon	.15	.05
☐ 86	Alan Henderson	.15	.05
☐ 87	Chris Dudley	.15	.05
☐ 88	Ed O'Bannon	.15	.05
☐ 89	Calbert Cheaney	.15	.05
☐ 90	Cedric Ceballos	.15	.05
☐ 91	Michael Cage	.15	.05
☐ 92	Ervin Johnson	.15	.05
☐ 93	Gary Trent	.15	.05
☐ 94	Sherman Douglas	.15	.05
☐ 95	Joe Smith	.30	.10
☐ 96	Dale Davis	.15	.05
☐ 97	Tony Dumas	.15	.05
☐ 98	Muggsy Bogues	.15	.05
☐ 99	Toni Kukoc	.30	.10
☐ 100	Grant Hill	.50	.20
☐ 101	Michael Finley	.60	.25
☐ 102	Isaiah Rider	.30	.10
☐ 103	Bryant Stith	.15	.05
☐ 104	Pooh Richardson	.15	.05
☐ 105	Karl Malone	.50	.20
☐ 106	Brian Grant	.50	.20
☐ 107	Sean Elliott	.30	.10
☐ 108	Charles Oakley	.15	.05
☐ 109	Pervis Ellison	.15	.05
☐ 110	Anfernee Hardaway	.50	.20
☐ 111	Checklist SP	.50	.20
☐ 112	Dikembe Mutombo	.30	.10
☐ 113	Alonzo Mourning	.30	.10
☐ 114	Hubert Davis	.15	.05
☐ 115	Rony Seikaly	.15	.05
☐ 116	Danny Manning	.15	.05
☐ 117	Donyell Marshall	.30	.10
☐ 118	Gerald Wilkins	.15	.05
☐ 119	Ervin Johnson	.15	.05
☐ 120	Jalen Rose	.50	.20
☐ 121	Dino Radja	.15	.05
☐ 122	Glenn Robinson	.50	.20

123	John Stockton	.50	.20
124	Matt Maloney RC	.30	.10
125	Clifford Robinson	.15	.05
126	Steve Kerr	.30	.10
127	Nate McMillan	.15	.05
128	Shareef Abdur-Rahim RC	1.50	.60
129	Loy Vaught	.15	.05
130	Anthony Mason	.30	.10
131	Kevin Garnett	1.00	.40
132	Roy Rogers RC	.15	.05
133	Erick Dampier RC	.50	.20
134	Tyus Edney	.15	.05
135	Chris Mills	.15	.05
136	Cory Alexander	.15	.05
137	Juwan Howard	.30	.10
138	Kobe Bryant RC	10.00	4.00
139	Michael Jordan	3.00	1.25
140	Jayson Williams	.30	.10
141	Rod Strickland	.15	.05
142	Lorenzen Wright RC	.30	.10
143	Will Perdue	.15	.05
144	Derek Harper	.15	.05
145	Billy Owens	.15	.05
146	Antoine Walker RC	1.50	.60
147	P.J. Brown	.15	.05
148	Terrell Brandon	.30	.10
149	Larry Johnson	.30	.10
150	Steve Smith	.30	.10
151	Eddie Jones	.50	.20
152	Detlef Schrempf	.30	.10
153	Dale Ellis	.15	.05
154	Isaiah Rider	.30	.10
155	Tony Delk RC	.50	.20
156	Adrian Caldwell	.15	.05
157	Jamal Mashburn	.30	.10
158	Dennis Scott	.15	.05
159	Dana Barros	.15	.05
160	Martin Muursepp RC	.15	.05
161	Marcus Camby RC	.60	.25
162	Jerome Williams RC	.50	.20
163	Wesley Person	.15	.05
164	Luc Longley	.15	.05
165	Charlie Ward	.15	.05
166	Mark Jackson	.15	.05
167	Derrick Coleman	.30	.10
168	Dell Curry	.15	.05
169	Armon Gilliam	.15	.05
170	Vlade Divac	.15	.05
171	Allen Iverson RC	4.00	1.50
172	Vitaly Potapenko RC	.15	.05
173	Jon Koncak	.15	.05
174	Lindsey Hunter	.15	.05
175	Kevin Johnson	.30	.10
176	Dennis Rodman	.30	.10
177	Stephon Marbury RC	1.25	.50
178	Karl Malone	.50	.20
179	Charles Barkley	.60	.25
180	Popeye Jones	.15	.05
181	Samaki Walker RC	.15	.05
182	Steve Nash RC	4.00	1.50
183	Latrell Sprewell	.50	.20
184	Kenny Anderson	.15	.05
185	Tyrone Hill	.15	.05
186	Robert Pack	.15	.05
187	Greg Anthony	.15	.05
188	Derrick McKey	.15	.05
189	John Wallace RC	.50	.20
190	Bryon Russell	.15	.05
191	Jermaine O'Neal RC	1.50	.60
192	Clyde Drexler	.50	.20
193	Mahmoud Abdul-Rauf	.15	.05
194	Eric Montross	.15	.05
195	Allan Houston	.30	.10
196	Harvey Grant	.15	.05
197	Rodney Rogers	.15	.05
198	Kerry Kittles RC	.50	.20
199	Grant Hill	.50	.20
200	Lionel Simmons	.15	.05
201	Reggie Miller	.50	.20
202	Avery Johnson	.15	.05
203	LaPhonso Ellis	.15	.05
204	Brian Shaw	.15	.05
205	Priest Lauderdale RC	.15	.05
206	Derek Fisher RC	1.25	.50
207	Terry Porter	.15	.05
208	Todd Fuller RC	.15	.05
209	Hersey Hawkins	.30	.10
210	Tim Legler	.15	.05
211	Terry Dehere	.15	.05
212	Gary Payton	.50	.20
213	Joe Dumars	.50	.20
214	Don MacLean	.15	.05
215	Greg Minor	.15	.05
216	Tim Hardaway	.30	.10
217	Ray Allen RC	1.25	.60
218	Mario Elie	.15	.05
219	Brooks Thompson	.15	.05
220	Shaquille O'Neal	1.25	.50

1997-98 Topps

	COMPLETE SET (220)	30.00	15.00
	COMPLETE SERIES 1 (110)	10.00	5.00
	COMPLETE SERIES 2 (110)	20.00	10.00
1	Scottie Pippen	.75	.30
2	Nate McMillan	.15	.05
3	Byron Scott	.15	.05
4	Mark Davis	.15	.05
5	Rod Strickland	.15	.05
6	Brian Grant	.30	.10
7	Damon Stoudamire	.30	.10
8	John Stockton	.50	.20
9	Grant Long	.15	.05
10	Darrell Armstrong	.15	.05
11	Anthony Mason	.30	.10
12	Travis Best	.15	.05
13	Stephon Marbury	.60	.25
14	Jamal Mashburn	.30	.10
15	Detlef Schrempf	.30	.10
16	Terrell Brandon	.30	.10
17	Charles Barkley	.60	.25
18	Vin Baker	.30	.10
19	Gary Trent	.15	.05
20	Vinny Del Negro	.15	.05
21	Todd Day	.15	.05
22	Malik Sealy	.15	.05
23	Wesley Person	.15	.05
24	Reggie Miller	.50	.20
25	Dan Majerle	.30	.10
26	Todd Fuller	.15	.05
27	Juwan Howard	.30	.10
28	Clarence Weatherspoon	.15	.05
29	Grant Hill	.50	.20
30	John Williams	.15	.05
31	Ken Norman	.15	.05
32	Patrick Ewing	.50	.20
33	Bryon Russell	.15	.05
34	Tony Smith	.15	.05
35	Andrew Lang	.15	.05
36	Rony Seikaly	.15	.05
37	Billy Owens	.15	.05
38	Dino Radja	.15	.05
39	Chris Gatling	.15	.05
40	Dale Davis	.15	.05
41	Arvydas Sabonis	.30	.10
42	Chris Mills	.15	.05
43	A.C. Green	.30	.10
44	Tyrone Hill	.15	.05
45	Tracy Murray	.15	.05
46	David Robinson	.50	.20
47	Lee Mayberry	.15	.05
48	Jayson Williams	.15	.05
49	Jason Kidd	.75	.30
50	Bryant Stith	.15	.05
51	Latrell Sprewell	.50	.20
52	Brent Barry	.30	.10
53	Henry James	.15	.05
54	Allen Iverson	1.25	.50
55	Shandon Anderson	.15	.05
56	Mitch Richmond	.30	.10
57	Allan Houston	.30	.10
58	Ron Harper	.30	.10
59	Gheorghe Muresan	.15	.05
60	Vincent Askew	.15	.05
61	Ray Allen	.50	.20
62	Kenny Anderson	.30	.10
63	Dikembe Mutombo	.30	.10
64	Sam Perkins	.30	.10
65	Walt Williams	.15	.05
66	Chris Carr	.15	.05
67	Vlade Divac	.30	.10
68	LaPhonso Ellis	.15	.05
69	B.J. Armstrong	.15	.05
70	Jim Jackson	.15	.05
71	Clyde Drexler	.50	.20
72	Lindsey Hunter	.15	.05
73	Sasha Danilovic	.15	.05
74	Elden Campbell	.15	.05
75	Robert Pack	.15	.05
76	Dennis Scott	.15	.05
77	Will Perdue	.15	.05
78	Anthony Peeler	.15	.05
79	Steve Smith	.30	.10
80	Steve Kerr	.30	.10
81	Buck Williams	.15	.05
82	Terry Mills	.15	.05
83	Michael Smith	.15	.05
84	Adam Keefe	.15	.05
85	Kevin Willis	.30	.10
86	David Wesley	.15	.05
87	Muggsy Bogues	.30	.10
88	Bimbo Coles	.15	.05
89	Tom Gugliotta	.30	.10
90	Jermaine O'Neal	.75	.30
91	Cedric Ceballos	.15	.05
92	Shawn Kemp	.30	.10
93	Horace Grant	.30	.10
94	Shareef Abdur-Rahim	.75	.30
95	Robert Horry	.30	.10
96	Vitaly Potapenko	.15	.05
97	Pooh Richardson	.15	.05
98	Doug Christie	.30	.10
99	Voshon Lenard	.15	.05
100	Dominique Wilkins	.50	.20
101	Alonzo Mourning	.30	.10
102	Sam Cassell	.50	.20
103	Sherman Douglas	.15	.05
104	Shawn Bradley	.15	.05
105	Mark Jackson	.30	.10
106	Dennis Rodman	.30	.10
107	Charles Oakley	.30	.10
108	Matt Maloney	.15	.05
109	Shaquille O'Neal	1.25	.50
110	Checklist	.15	.05
111	Antonio McDyess	.30	.10
112	Bob Sura	.15	.05
113	Terrell Brandon	.30	.10
114	Tim Thomas RC	.75	.30
115	Tim Duncan RC	2.00	.75
116	Antonio Daniels RC	.50	.20
117	Bryant Reeves	.15	.05
118	Keith Van Horn RC	.60	.25
119	Loy Vaught	.15	.05
120	Rasheed Wallace	.50	.20
121	Bobby Jackson RC	.75	.30
122	Kevin Johnson	.30	.10
123	Michael Jordan	3.00	1.25
124	Ron Mercer RC	.50	.20
125	Tracy McGrady RC	3.00	1.25
126	Antoine Walker	.60	.25
127	Carlos Rogers	.15	.05
128	Isaac Austin	.15	.05
129	Mookie Blaylock	.15	.05
130	Rodrick Rhodes RC	.15	.05
131	Dennis Scott	.15	.05
132	Chris Mullin	.50	.20
133	P.J. Brown	.15	.05
134	Rex Chapman	.15	.05
135	Sean Elliott	.30	.10
136	Alan Henderson	.15	.05
137	Austin Croshere RC	.40	.15

1998-99 Topps

❏ 138	Nick Van Exel	.50	.20
❏ 139	Derek Strong	.15	.05
❏ 140	Glenn Robinson	.50	.20
❏ 141	Avery Johnson	.15	.05
❏ 142	Calbert Cheaney	.15	.05
❏ 143	Mahmoud Abdul-Rauf	.15	.05
❏ 144	Stojko Vrankovic	.15	.05
❏ 145	Chris Childs	.15	.05
❏ 146	Danny Manning	.30	.10
❏ 147	Jeff Hornacek	.30	.10
❏ 148	Kevin Garnett	1.00	.40
❏ 149	Joe Dumars	.50	.20
❏ 150	Johnny Taylor RC	.15	.05
❏ 151	Mark Price	.30	.10
❏ 152	Toni Kukoc	.30	.10
❏ 153	Erick Dampier	.30	.10
❏ 154	Lorenzen Wright	.15	.05
❏ 155	Matt Geiger	.15	.05
❏ 156	Tim Hardaway	.30	.10
❏ 157	Charles Smith RC	.15	.05
❏ 158	Hersey Hawkins	.15	.05
❏ 159	Michael Finley	.50	.20
❏ 160	Tyus Edney	.15	.05
❏ 161	Christian Laettner	.30	.10
❏ 162	Doug West	.15	.05
❏ 163	Jim Jackson	.15	.05
❏ 164	Larry Johnson	.30	.10
❏ 165	Vin Baker	.30	.10
❏ 166	Karl Malone	.50	.20
❏ 167	Kelvin Cato RC	.50	.20
❏ 168	Luc Longley	.15	.05
❏ 169	Dale Davis	.15	.05
❏ 170	Joe Smith	.30	.10
❏ 171	Kobe Bryant	2.00	.75
❏ 172	Scot Pollard RC	.30	.10
❏ 173	Derek Anderson RC	.50	.20
❏ 174	Erick Strickland RC	.30	.10
❏ 175	Olden Polynice	.15	.05
❏ 176	Chris Whitney	.15	.05
❏ 177	Anthony Parker RC	.15	.05
❏ 178	Armon Gilliam	.15	.05
❏ 179	Gary Payton	.50	.20
❏ 180	Glen Rice	.30	.10
❏ 181	Chauncey Billups RC	1.25	.50
❏ 182	Derek Fisher	.50	.20
❏ 183	John Starks	.30	.10
❏ 184	Mario Elie	.15	.05
❏ 185	Chris Webber	.50	.20
❏ 186	Shawn Kemp	.30	.10
❏ 187	Greg Ostertag	.15	.05
❏ 188	Olivier Saint-Jean RC	.15	.05
❏ 189	Eric Snow	.30	.10
❏ 190	Isaiah Rider	.30	.10
❏ 191	Paul Grant RC	.15	.05
❏ 192	Samaki Walker	.15	.05
❏ 193	Cory Alexander	.15	.05
❏ 194	Eddie Jones	.50	.20
❏ 195	John Thomas RC	.15	.05
❏ 196	Otis Thorpe	.15	.05
❏ 197	Rod Strickland	.15	.05
❏ 198	David Wesley	.15	.05
❏ 199	Jacque Vaughn RC	.30	.10
❏ 200	Rik Smits	.30	.10
❏ 201	Brevin Knight RC	.30	.10
❏ 202	Clifford Robinson	.15	.05
❏ 203	Hakeem Olajuwon	.50	.20
❏ 204	Jerry Stackhouse	.50	.20
❏ 205	Tyrone Hill	.15	.05
❏ 206	Kendall Gill	.15	.05
❏ 207	Marcus Camby	.50	.20
❏ 208	Tony Battie RC	.50	.20
❏ 209	Brent Price	.15	.05
❏ 210	Danny Fortson RC	.30	.10
❏ 211	Jerome Williams	.30	.10
❏ 212	Maurice Taylor RC	.40	.15
❏ 213	Brian Williams	.15	.05
❏ 214	Keith Booth RC	.15	.05
❏ 215	Nick Anderson	.15	.05
❏ 216	Travis Knight	.15	.05
❏ 217	Adonal Foyle RC	.30	.10
❏ 218	Anfernee Hardaway	.50	.20
❏ 219	Kerry Kittles	.50	.20
❏ 220	Checklist	.15	.05

❏	COMPLETE SET (220)	30.00	15.00
❏	COMPLETE SERIES 1 (110)	10.00	5.00
❏	COMPLETE SERIES 2 (110)	20.00	10.00
❏ 1	Scottie Pippen	.75	.30
❏ 2	Shareef Abdur-Rahim	.50	.20
❏ 3	Rod Strickland	.15	.05
❏ 4	Keith Van Horn	.50	.20
❏ 5	Ray Allen	.50	.20
❏ 6	Chris Mullin	.50	.20
❏ 7	Anthony Parker	.15	.05
❏ 8	Lindsey Hunter	.15	.05
❏ 9	Mario Elie	.15	.05
❏ 10	Jerry Stackhouse	.50	.20
❏ 11	Eldridge Recasner	.15	.05
❏ 12	Jeff Hornacek	.30	.10
❏ 13	Chris Webber	.50	.20
❏ 14	Lee Mayberry	.15	.05
❏ 15	Erick Strickland	.15	.05
❏ 16	Arvydas Sabonis	.30	.10
❏ 17	Tim Thomas	.30	.10
❏ 18	Luc Longley	.15	.05
❏ 19	Detlef Schrempf	.30	.10
❏ 20	Alonzo Mourning	.30	.10
❏ 21	Adonal Foyle	.15	.05
❏ 22	Tony Battie	.15	.05
❏ 23	Robert Horry	.30	.10
❏ 24	Derek Harper	.15	.05
❏ 25	Jamal Mashburn	.30	.10
❏ 26	Elliot Perry	.15	.05
❏ 27	Jalen Rose	.50	.20
❏ 28	Joe Smith	.30	.10
❏ 29	Henry James	.15	.05
❏ 30	Travis Knight	.15	.05
❏ 31	Tom Gugliotta	.15	.05
❏ 32	Chris Anstey	.15	.05
❏ 33	Antonio Daniels	.15	.05
❏ 34	Elden Campbell	.15	.05
❏ 35	Charlie Ward	.15	.05
❏ 36	Eddie Johnson	.15	.05
❏ 37	John Wallace	.15	.05
❏ 38	Antonio Davis	.15	.05
❏ 39	Antoine Walker	.50	.20
❏ 40	Patrick Ewing	.50	.20
❏ 41	Doug Christie	.30	.10
❏ 42	Andrew Lang	.15	.05
❏ 43	Joe Dumars	.50	.20
❏ 44	Jaren Jackson	.15	.05
❏ 45	Loy Vaught	.15	.05
❏ 46	Allan Houston	.30	.10
❏ 47	Mark Jackson	.30	.10
❏ 48	Tracy Murray	.15	.05
❏ 49	Tim Duncan	.75	.30
❏ 50	Micheal Williams	.15	.05
❏ 51	Steve Nash	.50	.20
❏ 52	Matt Maloney	.15	.05
❏ 53	Sam Cassell	.50	.20
❏ 54	Voshon Lenard	.15	.05
❏ 55	Dikembe Mutombo	.30	.10
❏ 56	Malik Sealy	.15	.05
❏ 57	Dell Curry	.15	.05
❏ 58	Stephon Marbury	.50	.20
❏ 59	Tariq Abdul-Wahad	.15	.05
❏ 60	Isaiah Rider	.30	.10
❏ 61	Kelvin Cato	.15	.05
❏ 62	LaPhonso Ellis	.15	.05
❏ 63	Jim Jackson	.15	.05

❏ 64	Greg Ostertag	.15	.05
❏ 65	Glenn Robinson	.30	.10
❏ 66	Chris Carr	.15	.05
❏ 67	Marcus Camby	.15	.05
❏ 68	Kobe Bryant	2.00	.75
❏ 69	Bobby Jackson	.30	.10
❏ 70	B.J. Armstrong	.15	.05
❏ 71	Alan Henderson	.15	.05
❏ 72	Terry Davis	.15	.05
❏ 73	John Stockton	.50	.20
❏ 74	Lamond Murray	.15	.05
❏ 75	Mark Price	.30	.10
❏ 76	Rex Chapman	.15	.05
❏ 77	Michael Jordan	3.00	1.25
❏ 78	Terry Cummings	.15	.05
❏ 79	Dan Majerle	.30	.10
❏ 80	Bo Outlaw	.15	.05
❏ 81	Michael Finley	.50	.20
❏ 82	Vin Baker	.30	.10
❏ 83	Clifford Robinson	.15	.05
❏ 84	Greg Anthony	.15	.05
❏ 85	Brevin Knight	.15	.05
❏ 86	Jacque Vaughn	.15	.05
❏ 87	Bobby Phills	.15	.05
❏ 88	Sherman Douglas	.15	.05
❏ 89	Kevin Johnson	.30	.10
❏ 90	Mahmoud Abdul-Rauf	.15	.05
❏ 91	Lorenzen Wright	.15	.05
❏ 92	Eric Williams	.15	.05
❏ 93	Will Perdue	.15	.05
❏ 94	Charles Barkley	.60	.25
❏ 95	Kendall Gill	.15	.05
❏ 96	Wesley Person	.15	.05
❏ 97	Buck Williams	.15	.05
❏ 98	Erick Dampier	.30	.10
❏ 99	Nate McMillan	.15	.05
❏ 100	Sean Elliott	.30	.10
❏ 101	Rasheed Wallace	.50	.20
❏ 102	Zydrunas Ilgauskas	.50	.20
❏ 103	Eddie Jones	.50	.20
❏ 104	Ron Mercer	.25	.10
❏ 105	Horace Grant	.15	.05
❏ 106	Corliss Williamson	.30	.10
❏ 107	Anthony Mason	.30	.10
❏ 108	Mookie Blaylock	.15	.05
❏ 109	Dennis Rodman	.30	.10
❏ 110	Checklist	.15	.05
❏ 111	Steve Smith	.15	.05
❏ 112	Cedric Henderson	.15	.05
❏ 113	Rael LaFrentz RC	.50	.20
❏ 114	Calbert Cheaney	.15	.05
❏ 115	Rik Smits	.30	.10
❏ 116	Rony Seikaly	.15	.05
❏ 117	Lawrence Funderburke	.15	.05
❏ 118	Ricky Davis RC	1.50	.60
❏ 119	Howard Eisley	.15	.05
❏ 120	Kenny Anderson	.30	.10
❏ 121	Corey Benjamin RC	.30	.10
❏ 122	Maurice Taylor	.25	.10
❏ 123	Eric Murdock	.15	.05
❏ 124	Derek Fisher	.50	.20
❏ 125	Kevin Garnett	1.00	.40
❏ 126	Walt Williams	.15	.05
❏ 127	Bryce Drew RC	.30	.10
❏ 128	A.C. Green	.30	.10
❏ 129	Ervin Johnson	.15	.05
❏ 130	Christian Laettner	.15	.05
❏ 131	Chauncey Billups	.30	.10
❏ 132	Hakeem Olajuwon	.50	.20
❏ 133	Al Harrington RC	.75	.30
❏ 134	Danny Manning	.15	.05
❏ 135	Paul Pierce RC	2.50	1.00
❏ 136	Terrell Brandon	.30	.10
❏ 137	Bob Sura	.15	.05
❏ 138	Chris Gatling	.15	.05
❏ 139	Donyell Marshall	.30	.10
❏ 140	Marcus Camby	.30	.10
❏ 141	Brian Skinner RC	.15	.05
❏ 142	Charles Oakley	.15	.05
❏ 143	Antawn Jamison RC	1.50	.60
❏ 144	Nazr Mohammed RC	.20	.07
❏ 145	Karl Malone	.50	.20
❏ 146	Chris Mills	.15	.05
❏ 147	Bison Dele	.15	.05
❏ 148	Gary Payton	.50	.20
❏ 149	Terry Porter	.15	.05

❏ 150	Tim Hardaway	.30	.10
❏ 151	Larry Hughes RC	1.00	.40
❏ 152	Derek Anderson	.40	.15
❏ 153	Jason Williams RC	1.25	.50
❏ 154	Dirk Nowitzki RC	5.00	2.00
❏ 155	Juwan Howard	.30	.10
❏ 156	Avery Johnson	.15	.05
❏ 157	Matt Harpring RC	.60	.25
❏ 158	Reggie Miller	.50	.20
❏ 159	Walter McCarty	.15	.05
❏ 160	Allen Iverson	1.00	.40
❏ 161	Felipe Lopez RC	.40	.15
❏ 162	Tracy McGrady	1.25	.50
❏ 163	Damon Stoudamire	.30	.10
❏ 164	Antonio McDyess	.30	.10
❏ 165	Grant Hill	.50	.20
❏ 166	Tyronn Lue RC	.40	.15
❏ 167	P.J. Brown	.15	.05
❏ 168	Antonio Daniels	.15	.05
❏ 169	Mitch Richmond	.30	.10
❏ 170	David Robinson	.50	.20
❏ 171	Shawn Bradley	.15	.05
❏ 172	Shandon Anderson	.15	.05
❏ 173	Chris Childs	.15	.05
❏ 174	Shawn Kemp	.30	.10
❏ 175	Shaquille O'Neal	1.25	.50
❏ 176	John Starks	.30	.10
❏ 177	Tyrone Hill	.15	.05
❏ 178	Jayson Williams	.15	.05
❏ 179	Anfernee Hardaway	.50	.20
❏ 180	Chris Webber	.50	.20
❏ 181	Don Reid	.15	.05
❏ 182	Stacey Augmon	.15	.05
❏ 183	Hersey Hawkins	.15	.05
❏ 184	Sam Mitchell	.15	.05
❏ 185	Jason Kidd	.75	.30
❏ 186	Nick Van Exel	.50	.20
❏ 187	Larry Johnson	.30	.10
❏ 188	Bryant Reeves	.15	.05
❏ 189	Glen Rice	.30	.10
❏ 190	Kerry Kittles	.15	.05
❏ 191	Toni Kukoc	.30	.10
❏ 192	Ron Harper	.30	.10
❏ 193	Bryon Russell	.15	.05
❏ 194	Vladimir Stepania RC	.15	.05
❏ 195	Michael Olowokandi RC	.30	.10
❏ 196	Mike Bibby RC	2.00	.75
❏ 197	Dale Ellis	.15	.05
❏ 198	Muggsy Bogues	.30	.10
❏ 199	Vince Carter RC	6.00	2.50
❏ 200	Robert Traylor RC	.30	.10
❏ 201	Peja Stojakovic RC	3.00	1.25
❏ 202	Aaron McKie	.30	.10
❏ 203	Hubert Davis	.15	.05
❏ 204	Dana Barros	.15	.05
❏ 205	Bonzi Wells RC	1.25	.50
❏ 206	Michael Doleac RC	.30	.10
❏ 207	Keon Clark RC	.50	.20
❏ 208	Michael Dickerson RC	.60	.25
❏ 209	Nick Anderson	.15	.05
❏ 210	Brent Price	.15	.05
❏ 211	Cherokee Parks	.15	.05
❏ 212	Sam Jacobson RC	.15	.05
❏ 213	Pat Garrity RC	.20	.07
❏ 214	Tyrone Corbin	.15	.05
❏ 215	David Wesley	.15	.05
❏ 216	Rodney Rogers	.15	.05
❏ 217	Dean Garrett	.15	.05
❏ 218	Roshown McLeod RC	.20	.07
❏ 219	Dale Davis	.30	.10
❏ 220	Checklist	.15	.05

1999-00 Topps

❏ COMPLETE SET (257)		60.00	30.00
❏ COMPLETE SERIES 1 (120)		25.00	12.50
❏ COMPLETE SERIES 2 (137)		35.00	17.50
❏ COMP.SERIES 1 w/o SP (110)		12.00	6.00
❏ COMP.SERIES 2 w/o SP (110)		10.00	5.00
❏ COMMON CARD (1-257)		.15	.05
❏ COMMON RC(111-120/231-248)		.50	.20
❏ COMMON USA (249-257)		.30	.10
❏ 1	Steve Smith	.30	.10
❏ 2	Ron Harper	.30	.10
❏ 3	Michael Dickerson	.30	.10
❏ 4	LaPhonso Ellis	.15	.05
❏ 5	Chris Webber	.50	.20

❏ 6	Jason Caffey	.15	.05
❏ 7	Bryon Russell	.15	.05
❏ 8	Bison Dele	.15	.05
❏ 9	Isaiah Rider	.15	.05
❏ 10	Dean Garrett	.15	.05
❏ 11	Eric Murdock	.15	.05
❏ 12	Juwan Howard	.30	.10
❏ 13	Latrell Sprewell	.50	.20
❏ 14	Jalen Rose	.50	.20
❏ 15	Larry Johnson	.30	.10
❏ 16	Eric Williams	.15	.05
❏ 17	Bryant Reeves	.15	.05
❏ 18	Tony Battie	.15	.05
❏ 19	Luc Longley	.15	.05
❏ 20	Gary Payton	.50	.20
❏ 21	Tariq Abdul-Wahad	.15	.05
❏ 22	Armen Gilliam UER	.15	.05
❏ 23	Shaquille O'Neal	1.25	.50
❏ 24	Gary Trent	.15	.05
❏ 25	John Stockton	.50	.20
❏ 26	Mark Jackson	.15	.05
❏ 27	Cherokee Parks	.15	.05
❏ 28	Michael Olowokandi	.15	.05
❏ 29	Rael LaFrentz	.30	.10
❏ 30	Dell Curry	.15	.05
❏ 31	Travis Best	.15	.05
❏ 32	Shawn Kemp	.30	.10
❏ 33	Voshon Lenard	.15	.05
❏ 34	Brian Grant	.30	.10
❏ 35	Alvin Williams	.15	.05
❏ 36	Derek Fisher	.50	.20
❏ 37	Allan Houston	.30	.10
❏ 38	Arvydas Sabonis	.30	.10
❏ 39	Terry Cummings	.15	.05
❏ 40	Dale Ellis	.15	.05
❏ 41	Maurice Taylor	.30	.10
❏ 42	Grant Hill	.50	.20
❏ 43	Anthony Mason	.15	.05
❏ 44	John Wallace	.15	.05
❏ 45	David Wesley	.15	.05
❏ 46	Nick Van Exel	.50	.20
❏ 47	Cuttino Mobley	.50	.20
❏ 48	Anfernee Hardaway	.50	.20
❏ 49	Terry Porter	.15	.05
❏ 50	Brent Barry	.30	.10
❏ 51	Derek Harper	.15	.05
❏ 52	Antoine Walker	.50	.20
❏ 53	Karl Malone	.50	.20
❏ 54	Ben Wallace	.30	.10
❏ 55	Vlade Divac	.30	.10
❏ 56	Sam Mitchell	.15	.05
❏ 57	Joe Smith	.30	.10
❏ 58	Shawn Bradley	.15	.05
❏ 59	Darrell Armstrong	.15	.05
❏ 60	Kenny Anderson	.30	.10
❏ 61	Jason Williams	.50	.20
❏ 62	Alonzo Mourning	.30	.10
❏ 63	Matt Harpring	.50	.20
❏ 64	Antonio Davis	.15	.05
❏ 65	Lindsey Hunter	.15	.05
❏ 66	Allen Iverson	1.00	.40
❏ 67	Mookie Blaylock	.15	.05
❏ 68	Wesley Person	.15	.05
❏ 69	Bobby Phills	.15	.05
❏ 70	Theo Ratliff	.30	.10
❏ 71	Antonio Davis	.15	.05
❏ 72	P.J. Brown	.15	.05
❏ 73	David Robinson	.50	.20

❏ 74	Sean Elliott	.30	.10
❏ 75	Zydrunas Ilgauskas	.30	.10
❏ 76	Kerry Kittles	.15	.05
❏ 77	Otis Thorpe	.30	.10
❏ 78	John Starks	.30	.10
❏ 79	Jaren Jackson	.15	.05
❏ 80	Hersey Hawkins	.30	.10
❏ 81	Glenn Robinson	.50	.20
❏ 82	Paul Pierce	.50	.20
❏ 83	Glen Rice	.30	.10
❏ 84	Charlie Ward	.15	.05
❏ 85	Dee Brown	.15	.05
❏ 86	Danny Fortson	.15	.05
❏ 87	Billy Owens	.15	.05
❏ 88	Jason Kidd	.75	.30
❏ 89	Brent Price	.15	.05
❏ 90	Don Reid	.15	.05
❏ 91	Mark Bryant	.15	.05
❏ 92	Vinny Del Negro	.15	.05
❏ 93	Stephon Marbury	.50	.20
❏ 94	Donyell Marshall	.30	.10
❏ 95	Jim Jackson	.15	.05
❏ 96	Horace Grant	.15	.05
❏ 97	Calbert Cheaney	.15	.05
❏ 98	Vince Carter	1.25	.50
❏ 99	Bobby Jackson	.30	.10
❏ 100	Alan Henderson	.15	.05
❏ 101	Mike Bibby	.50	.20
❏ 102	Cedric Henderson	.15	.05
❏ 103	Lamond Murray	.15	.05
❏ 104	A.C. Green	.30	.10
❏ 105	Hakeem Olajuwon	.50	.20
❏ 106	George Lynch	.15	.05
❏ 107	Kendall Gill	.15	.05
❏ 108	Rex Chapman	.15	.05
❏ 109	Eddie Jones	.50	.20
❏ 110	Kornel David RC	.15	.05
❏ 111	Jason Terry RC	2.00	.75
❏ 112	Corey Maggette RC	2.50	1.00
❏ 113	Ron Artest RC	1.50	.60
❏ 114	Richard Hamilton RC	2.50	1.00
❏ 115	Elton Brand RC	3.00	1.25
❏ 116	Baron Davis RC	5.00	2.00
❏ 117	Wally Szczerbiak RC	2.50	1.00
❏ 118	Steve Francis RC	3.00	1.25
❏ 119	James Posey RC	1.50	.60
❏ 120	Shawn Marion RC	3.00	1.25
❏ 121	Tim Duncan	1.00	.40
❏ 122	Danny Manning	.15	.05
❏ 123	Chris Mullin	.50	.20
❏ 124	Antawn Jamison	.75	.30
❏ 125	Kobe Bryant	2.00	.75
❏ 126	Matt Geiger	.15	.05
❏ 127	Rod Strickland	.15	.05
❏ 128	Howard Eisley	.15	.05
❏ 129	Steve Nash	.50	.20
❏ 130	Felipe Lopez	.15	.05
❏ 131	Ron Mercer	.30	.10
❏ 132	Ruben Patterson	.30	.10
❏ 133	Dana Barros	.15	.05
❏ 134	Dale Davis	.15	.05
❏ 135	Bo Outlaw	.15	.05
❏ 136	Shandon Anderson	.15	.05
❏ 137	Mitch Richmond	.30	.10
❏ 138	Doug Christie	.30	.10
❏ 139	Rasheed Wallace	.50	.20
❏ 140	Chris Childs	.15	.05
❏ 141	Jamal Mashburn	.30	.10
❏ 142	Terrell Brandon	.30	.10
❏ 143	Jamie Feick RC	.50	.20
❏ 144	Robert Traylor	.15	.05
❏ 145	Rick Fox	.15	.05
❏ 146	Charles Barkley	.60	.25
❏ 147	Tyrone Nesby RC	.15	.05
❏ 148	Jerry Stackhouse	.50	.20
❏ 149	Cedric Ceballos	.15	.05
❏ 150	Dikembe Mutombo	.30	.10
❏ 151	Anthony Peeler	.15	.05
❏ 152	Larry Hughes	.50	.20
❏ 153	Clifford Robinson	.15	.05
❏ 154	Corliss Williamson	.30	.10
❏ 155	Olden Polynice	.15	.05
❏ 156	Avery Johnson	.15	.05
❏ 157	Tracy Murray	.15	.05
❏ 158	Tom Gugliotta	.15	.05
❏ 159	Tim Thomas	.30	.10

160	Reggie Miller	.50	.20
161	Tim Hardaway	.30	.10
162	Dan Majerle	.30	.10
163	Will Perdue	.15	.05
164	Brevin Knight	.15	.05
165	Elden Campbell	.15	.05
166	Chris Gatling	.15	.05
167	Walter McCarty	.15	.05
168	Chauncey Billups	.30	.10
169	Chris Mills	.30	.10
170	Christian Laettner	.30	.10
171	Robert Pack	.15	.05
172	Rik Smits	.30	.10
173	Tyrone Hill	.15	.05
174	Damon Stoudamire	.30	.10
175	Nick Anderson	.15	.05
176	Peja Stojakovic	.60	.25
177	Vladimir Stepania	.15	.05
178	Tracy McGrady	1.25	.50
179	Adam Keefe	.15	.05
180	Shareef Abdur-Rahim	.50	.20
181	Isaac Austin	.15	.05
182	Mario Elie	.15	.05
183	Rashard Lewis	.50	.20
184	Scott Burrell	.15	.05
185	Othella Harrington	.15	.05
186	Eric Piatkowski	.30	.10
187	Bryant Stith	.15	.05
188	Michael Finley	.50	.20
189	Chris Crawford	.15	.05
190	Toni Kukoc	.30	.10
191	Danny Ferry	.15	.05
192	Erick Dampier	.30	.10
193	Clarence Weatherspoon	.15	.05
194	Bob Sura	.15	.05
195	Jayson Williams	.15	.05
196	Kurt Thomas	.30	.10
197	Greg Anthony	.15	.05
198	Rodney Rogers	.15	.05
199	Detlef Schrempf	.30	.10
200	Keith Van Horn	.50	.20
201	Robert Horry	.30	.10
202	Sam Cassell	.50	.20
203	Malik Sealy	.15	.05
204	Kelvin Cato	.15	.05
205	Antonio McDyess	.30	.10
206	Andrew DeClercq	.15	.05
207	Ricky Davis	.15	.05
208	Vitaly Potapenko	.15	.05
209	Loy Vaught	.15	.05
210	Kevin Garnett	1.00	.40
211	Eric Snow	.30	.10
212	Anfernee Hardaway	.50	.20
213	Vin Baker	.30	.10
214	Lawrence Funderburke	.15	.05
215	Jeff Hornacek	.30	.10
216	Doug West	.15	.05
217	Michael Doleac	.15	.05
218	Ray Allen	.50	.20
219	Derek Anderson	.30	.10
220	Jerome Williams	.15	.05
221	Derrick Coleman	.30	.10
222	Randy Brown	.15	.05
223	Patrick Ewing	.50	.20
224	Walt Williams	.15	.05
225	Charles Oakley	.15	.05
226	Steve Kerr	.30	.10
227	Muggsy Bogues	.30	.10
228	Kevin Willis	.15	.05
229	Marcus Camby	.30	.10
230	Scottie Pippen	.75	.30
231	Lamar Odom RC	2.50	1.00
232	Jonathan Bender RC	2.50	1.00
233	Andre Miller RC	2.50	1.00
234	Trajan Langdon RC	1.00	.40
235	A.Radojevic RC	.50	.20
236	William Avery RC	1.00	.40
237	Cal Bowdler RC	.75	.30
238	Quincy Lewis RC	.75	.30
239	Dion Glover RC	.75	.30
240	Jeff Foster RC	.75	.30
241	Kenny Thomas RC	1.00	.40
242	Devean George RC	1.25	.50
243	Tim James RC	.75	.30
244	Vonteego Cummings RC	1.00	.40
245	Jumaine Jones RC	1.00	.40
246	Scott Padgett RC	.75	.30
247	Adrian Griffin RC	.75	.30
248	Chris Herren RC	.50	.20
249	Allan Houston USA	.50	.20
250	Kevin Garnett USA	2.00	.75
251	Gary Payton USA	.50	.20
252	Steve Smith USA	.30	.10
253	Tim Hardaway USA	.50	.20
254	Tim Duncan USA	2.00	.75
255	Jason Kidd USA	1.50	.60
256	Tom Gugliotta USA	.30	.10
257	Vin Baker USA	.30	.10

2000-01 Topps

	COMPLETE SET (295)	80.00	40.00
	COMPLETE SERIES 1 (155)	60.00	30.00
	COMP.SERIES 1 w/o RC (130)	15.00	7.50
	COMPLETE SERIES 2 (140)	25.00	12.50
	COMP.SERIES 2 w/o RC (120)	15.00	7.50
	COMMON CARD (1-295)	1.00	.05
	COMMON RC (125-149/266-285)	1.00	.40
1	Elton Brand	.50	.20
2	Marcus Camby	.30	.10
3	Jalen Rose	.50	.20
4	Jamie Feick	.15	.05
5	Toni Kukoc	.30	.10
6	Todd MacCulloch	.15	.05
7	Mario Elie	.15	.05
8	Doug Christie	.30	.10
9	Sam Cassell	.50	.20
10	Shaquille O'Neal	1.25	.50
11	Larry Hughes	.30	.10
12	Jerry Stackhouse	.50	.20
13	Rick Fox	.30	.10
14	Clifford Robinson	.15	.05
15	Felipe Lopez	.15	.05
16	Dirk Nowitzki	.75	.30
17	Cuttino Mobley	.30	.10
18	Latrell Sprewell	.50	.20
19	Nick Anderson	.15	.05
20	Kevin Garnett	1.00	.40
21	Rik Smits	.30	.10
22	Jerome Williams	.15	.05
23	Chris Webber	.50	.20
24	Jason Terry	.50	.20
25	Elden Campbell	.15	.05
26	Kelvin Cato	.15	.05
27	Tyrone Nesby	.15	.05
28	Jonathan Bender	.30	.10
29	Otis Thorpe	.15	.05
30	Scottie Pippen	.75	.30
31	Radoslav Nesterovic	.30	.10
32	P.J. Brown	.15	.05
33	Reggie Miller	.50	.20
34	Andre Miller	.30	.10
35	Tariq Abdul-Wahad	.15	.05
36	Michael Doleac	.15	.05
37	Rashard Lewis	.30	.10
38	Jacque Vaughn	.15	.05
39	Larry Johnson	.30	.10
40	Steve Francis	.50	.20
41	Arvydas Sabonis	.30	.10
42	Jaren Jackson	.15	.05
43	Howard Eisley	.15	.05
44	Rod Strickland	.15	.05
45	Tim Thomas	.30	.10
46	Robert Horry	.30	.10
47	Kenny Thomas	.15	.05
48	Anthony Peeler	.15	.05
49	Darrell Armstrong	.15	.05
50	Vince Carter	1.25	.50
51	Othella Harrington	.15	.05
52	Derek Anderson	.30	.10
53	Anthony Carter	.30	.10
54	Scott Burrell	.15	.05
55	Ray Allen	.50	.20
56	Jason Kidd	.75	.30
57	Sean Elliott	.30	.10
58	Muggsy Bogues	.30	.10
59	LaPhonso Ellis	.15	.05
60	Tim Duncan	1.00	.40
61	Adrian Griffin	.15	.05
62	Wally Szczerbiak	.30	.10
63	Austin Croshere	.30	.10
64	Wesley Person	.15	.05
65	James Posey	.30	.10
66	Alan Henderson	.15	.05
67	Ruben Patterson	.30	.10
68	Jahidi White	.15	.05
69	Shawn Marion	.50	.20
70	Lamar Odom	.50	.20
71	Lindsey Hunter	.15	.05
72	Keon Clark	.30	.10
73	Gary Trent	.15	.05
74	Lamond Murray	.15	.05
75	Paul Pierce	.50	.20
76	Charlie Ward	.15	.05
77	Matt Geiger	.15	.05
78	Greg Anthony	.15	.05
79	Horace Grant	.30	.10
80	John Stockton	.50	.20
81	Peja Stojakovic	.30	.10
82	William Avery	.15	.05
83	Dan Majerle	.30	.10
84	Christian Laettner	.30	.10
85	Dana Barros	.15	.05
86	Corey Benjamin	.15	.05
87	Keith Van Horn	.50	.20
88	Patrick Ewing	.50	.20
89	Steve Smith	.30	.10
90	Antonio Davis	.15	.05
91	Samaki Walker	.15	.05
92	Mitch Richmond	.30	.10
93	Michael Olowokandi	.15	.05
94	Baron Davis	.50	.20
95	Dikembe Mutombo	.30	.10
96	Andrew DeClercq	.30	.10
97	Raef LaFrentz	.30	.10
98	Trajan Langdon	.30	.10
99	Ervin Johnson	.15	.05
100	Alonzo Mourning	.30	.10
101	Kendall Gill	.15	.05
102	George Lynch	.15	.05
103	Detlef Schrempf	.30	.10
104	Donyell Marshall	.30	.10
105	Bo Outlaw	.15	.05
106	Kenny Anderson	.30	.10
107	Eddie Robinson	.30	.10
108	Jermaine O'Neal	.50	.20
109	John Amaechi	.15	.05
110	Glen Rice	.30	.10
111	Vlade Divac	.30	.10
112	Vin Baker	.30	.10
113	Mike Bibby	.50	.20
114	Richard Hamilton	.30	.10
115	Mookie Blaylock	.15	.05
116	Vitaly Potapenko	.15	.05
117	Anthony Mason	.30	.10
118	Robert Pack	.15	.05
119	Vonteego Cummings	.15	.05
120	Michael Finley	.50	.20
121	Ron Artest	.30	.10
122	Tyrone Hill	.15	.05
123	Rodney Rogers	.15	.05
124	Quincy Lewis	.15	.05
125	Kenyon Martin RC	4.00	1.50
126	Stromile Swift RC	2.00	.75
127	Darius Miles RC	3.00	1.25
128	Marcus Fizer EXCH RC	1.00	.40
129	Mike Miller RC	3.00	1.25
130	DerMarr Johnson RC	1.00	.40
131	Chris Mihm RC	1.00	.40
132	Jamal Crawford EXCH RC	1.25	.50
133	Joel Przybilla RC	1.00	.40

☐ 134	Keyon Dooling RC	1.00	.40
☐ 135	Jerome Moiso EXCH RC	1.00	.40
☐ 136	Etan Thomas RC	1.00	.40
☐ 137	Courtney Alexander RC	1.00	.40
☐ 138	Mateen Cleaves EXCH RC	1.00	.40
☐ 139	Jason Collier RC	1.50	.60
☐ 140	Desmond Mason RC	1.00	.40
☐ 141	Quentin Richardson RC	3.00	1.25
☐ 142	Jamaal Magloire RC	1.00	.40
☐ 143	Speedy Claxton RC	1.00	.40
☐ 144	Morris Peterson EXCH RC	2.00	.75
☐ 145	Donnell Harvey EXCH RC	1.00	.40
☐ 146	DeShawn Stevenson RC	1.00	.40
☐ 147	Mamadou N'diaye RC	1.00	.40
☐ 148	Erick Barkley EXCH RC	1.00	.40
☐ 149	Mark Madsen RC	1.00	.40
☐ 150	Shaq/Iverson/G.Hill SL	.40	.15
☐ 151	Kidd/Cassell/Van Exel SL	.50	.20
☐ 152	Mutombo/Shaq/Duncan SL	.60	.25
☐ 153	E.Jones/Pierce/Armstrong SL	.10	.10
☐ 154	Mourning/Mutombo/Shaq SL	.50	.20
☐ 155	Team Championship SL	.75	.30
☐ 156	Jason Williams	.30	.10
☐ 157	David Robinson	.50	.20
☐ 158	Shammond Williams	.15	.05
☐ 159	Charles Oakley	.15	.05
☐ 160	Greg Ostertag	.15	.05
☐ 161	Juwan Howard	.30	.10
☐ 162	Antoine Walker	.50	.20
☐ 163	Alan Henderson	.15	.05
☐ 164	Eddie Jones	.50	.20
☐ 165	Allen Iverson	1.00	.40
☐ 166	Grant Hill	.50	.20
☐ 167	Terrell Brandon	.30	.10
☐ 168	Stephon Marbury	.50	.20
☐ 169	Jason Caffey	.15	.05
☐ 170	Sam Mitchell	.15	.05
☐ 171	Jamal Mashburn	.30	.10
☐ 172	Ron Harper	.30	.10
☐ 173	Eric Piatkowski	.30	.10
☐ 174	Sam Perkins	.30	.10
☐ 175	Walt Williams	.15	.05
☐ 176	Bob Sura	.15	.05
☐ 177	Michael Curry	.15	.05
☐ 178	Nick Van Exel	.50	.20
☐ 179	Danny Ferry	.15	.05
☐ 180	Randy Brown	.15	.05
☐ 181	Danny Fortson	.15	.05
☐ 182	Jim Jackson	.15	.05
☐ 183	Brad Miller	.50	.20
☐ 184	Shawn Bradley	.15	.05
☐ 185	Voshon Lenard	.15	.05
☐ 186	Erick Dampier	.30	.10
☐ 187	Mark Jackson	.15	.05
☐ 188	Maurice Taylor	.15	.05
☐ 189	Kobe Bryant	2.00	.75
☐ 190	Clarence Weatherspoon	.15	.05
☐ 191	Bobby Jackson	.30	.10
☐ 192	Eric Snow	.30	.10
☐ 193	Allan Houston	.30	.10
☐ 194	Kurt Thomas	.30	.10
☐ 195	Chauncey Billups	.30	.10
☐ 196	Tom Gugliotta	.15	.05
☐ 197	Theo Ratliff	.30	.10
☐ 198	Rasheed Wallace	.50	.20
☐ 199	Jon Barry	.15	.05
☐ 200	Malik Rose	.15	.05
☐ 201	Vernon Maxwell	.15	.05
☐ 202	Dee Brown	.15	.05
☐ 203	Bryon Russell	.15	.05
☐ 204	Brent Barry	.30	.10
☐ 205	Tracy McGrady	1.25	.50
☐ 206	Bryant Reeves	.15	.05
☐ 207	Isaac Austin	.15	.05
☐ 208	Damon Stoudamire	.30	.10
☐ 209	Anfernee Hardaway	.50	.20
☐ 210	Aaron McKie	.30	.10
☐ 211	Johnny Newman	.15	.05
☐ 212	Scott Williams	.15	.05
☐ 213	Brian Shaw	.15	.05
☐ 214	Corey Maggette	.30	.10
☐ 215	Travis Best	.15	.05
☐ 216	Hakeem Olajuwon	.50	.20
☐ 217	Antawn Jamison	.50	.20
☐ 218	John Starks	.30	.10
☐ 219	Antonio McDyess	.30	.10
☐ 220	Cedric Ceballos	.15	.05
☐ 221	Chris Carr	.15	.05
☐ 222	Roshown McLeod	.15	.05
☐ 223	Calbert Cheaney	.15	.05
☐ 224	Gary Payton	.50	.20
☐ 225	Karl Malone	.50	.20
☐ 226	Michael Dickerson	.30	.10
☐ 227	Tracy Murray	.15	.05
☐ 228	Chris Childs	.15	.05
☐ 229	Pat Garrity	.15	.05
☐ 230	Rex Chapman	.15	.05
☐ 231	Jumaine Jones	.30	.10
☐ 232	Fred Hoiberg	.15	.05
☐ 233	Bimbo Coles	.15	.05
☐ 234	Shawn Kemp	.30	.10
☐ 235	David Wesley	.15	.05
☐ 236	Tony Battie	.15	.05
☐ 237	Ron Mercer	.30	.10
☐ 238	John Wallace	.15	.05
☐ 239	Robert Traylor	.15	.05
☐ 240	Derrick Coleman	.15	.05
☐ 241	Steve Nash	.50	.20
☐ 242	Ben Wallace	.50	.20
☐ 243	Brian Skinner	.15	.05
☐ 244	Chris Gatling	.15	.05
☐ 245	Dale Davis	.15	.05
☐ 246	Joe Smith	.30	.10
☐ 247	Glenn Robinson	.50	.20
☐ 248	Kerry Kittles	.15	.05
☐ 249	Erick Strickland	.15	.05
☐ 250	Sam Cassell	.50	.20
☐ 251	Chucky Atkins	.15	.05
☐ 252	Brian Grant	.30	.10
☐ 253	Bonzi Wells	.30	.10
☐ 254	Corliss Williamson	.30	.10
☐ 255	Shareef Abdur-Rahim	.50	.20
☐ 256	Kevin Willis	.15	.05
☐ 257	Scott Padgett	.15	.05
☐ 258	Terry Porter	.15	.05
☐ 259	Tony Delk	.15	.05
☐ 260	Avery Johnson	.15	.05
☐ 261	Tim Hardaway	.30	.10
☐ 262	Derek Fisher	.50	.20
☐ 263	Isaiah Rider	.30	.10
☐ 264	Shandon Anderson	.15	.05
☐ 265	Adonal Foyle	.15	.05
☐ 266	Hidayet Turkoglu RC	2.50	1.00
☐ 267	Brian Cardinal RC	1.00	.40
☐ 268	Iakovos Tsakalidis RC	1.00	.40
☐ 269	Dalibor Bagaric RC	1.00	.40
☐ 270	Marko Jaric RC	1.00	.40
☐ 271	Dan Langhi RC	1.00	.40
☐ 272	A.J. Guyton RC	1.00	.40
☐ 273	Jake Voskuhl RC	1.00	.40
☐ 274	Khalid El-Amin RC	1.00	.40
☐ 275	Mike Smith RC	1.00	.40
☐ 276	Soumaila Samake RC	1.00	.40
☐ 277	Eddie House RC	1.00	.40
☐ 278	Eduardo Najera RC	1.50	.60
☐ 279	Lavor Postell RC	1.00	.40
☐ 280	Hanno Mottola RC	1.00	.40
☐ 281	Chris Carrawell RC	1.00	.40
☐ 282	Olumide Oyedeji RC	1.00	.40
☐ 283	Michael Redd RC	2.00	.75
☐ 284	Chris Porter RC	1.00	.40
☐ 285	Mark Karcher RC	1.00	.40
☐ 286	S.Francis/G.Payton SC	.50	.20
☐ 287	D.Miles/K.Garnett SC	.30	.12
☐ 288	L.Odom/Abdur-Rahim SC	.50	.20
☐ 289	T.Duncan/A.Mourning SC	.60	.20
☐ 290	E.Brand/K.Malone SC	.50	.20
☐ 291	L.Hughes/A.Iverson SC	.50	.20
☐ 292	K.Bryant/R.Miller SC	1.25	.50
☐ 293	V.Carter/G.Hill SC	.60	.20
☐ 294	T.McGrady/S.Pippen SC	1.00	.40
☐ 295	K.Martin/M.Camby SC	2.00	.75

2001-02 Topps

☐	COMPLETE SET (257)	80.00	40.00
☐	COMP. SET w/o RC (220)	30.00	15.00
☐	COMMON CARD (1-220)	.15	.05
☐	COMMON ROOKIE (221-256)	1.25	.50
☐ 1	Shaquille O'Neal	1.25	.50
☐ 2	Travis Best	.15	.05
☐ 3	Allen Iverson	1.00	.40
☐ 4	Shawn Marion	.50	.20

☐ 5	Rasheed Wallace	.50	.20
☐ 6	Antonio Daniels	.15	.05
☐ 7	Rashard Lewis	.30	.10
☐ 8	John Starks	.30	.10
☐ 9	Stromile Swift	.30	.10
☐ 10	Vince Carter	1.25	.50
☐ 11	George Lynch	.15	.05
☐ 12	Kendall Gill	.15	.05
☐ 13	Glen Rice	.30	.10
☐ 14	Glenn Robinson	.50	.20
☐ 15	Wally Szczerbiak	.30	.10
☐ 16	Rick Fox	.30	.10
☐ 17	Darius Miles	.50	.20
☐ 18	Jermaine O'Neal	.50	.20
☐ 19	Erick Dampier	.30	.10
☐ 20	Tracy McGrady	1.25	.50
☐ 21	Kevin Garnett	1.00	.40
☐ 22	Tim Thomas	.30	.10
☐ 23	Larry Hughes	.30	.10
☐ 24	Jerry Stackhouse	.50	.20
☐ 25	Voshon Lenard	.15	.05
☐ 26	Howard Eisley	.15	.05
☐ 27	Clarence Weatherspoon	.15	.05
☐ 28	Marcus Fizer	.30	.10
☐ 29	Elden Campbell	.15	.05
☐ 30	Tim Duncan	1.00	.40
☐ 31	Doug Christie	.30	.10
☐ 32	Keon Clark	.30	.10
☐ 33	Patrick Ewing	.50	.20
☐ 34	Hakeem Olajuwon	.50	.20
☐ 35	Stephen Jackson	.30	.10
☐ 36	Larry Johnson	.30	.10
☐ 37	Eric Snow	.30	.10
☐ 38	Tom Gugliotta	.15	.05
☐ 39	Scottie Pippen	.75	.30
☐ 40	Chris Webber	.50	.20
☐ 41	David Robinson	.50	.20
☐ 42	Elton Brand	.50	.20
☐ 43	Theo Ratliff	.30	.10
☐ 44	Paul Pierce	.50	.20
☐ 45	Jamal Mashburn	.30	.10
☐ 46	Eric Williams	.15	.05
☐ 47	DerMarr Johnson	.30	.10
☐ 48	Andre Miller	.30	.10
☐ 49	Dirk Nowitzki	.75	.30
☐ 50	Kobe Bryant	2.00	.75
☐ 51	Keyon Dooling	.30	.10
☐ 52	Brian Grant	.30	.10
☐ 53	Ervin Johnson	.15	.05
☐ 54	Anthony Peeler	.15	.05
☐ 55	Dikembe Mutombo	.30	.10
☐ 56	Steve Smith	.30	.10
☐ 57	Hidayet Turkoglu	.30	.10
☐ 58	Terry Porter	.15	.05
☐ 59	Lorenzen Wright	.15	.05
☐ 60	Jason Terry	.50	.20
☐ 61	Vitaly Potapenko	.15	.05
☐ 62	Derrick Coleman	.15	.05
☐ 63	Ron Artest	.30	.10
☐ 64	Chris Gatling	.15	.05
☐ 65	Chris Mihm	.15	.05
☐ 66	Reggie Miller	.50	.20
☐ 67	Lamar Odom	.50	.20
☐ 68	Ron Harper	.30	.10
☐ 69	Baron Davis	.50	.20
☐ 70	Brad Miller	.50	.20
☐ 71	Shawn Bradley	.15	.05
☐ 72	James Posey	.30	.10

73	Ben Wallace	.50	.20
74	Marc Jackson	.30	.10
75	Maurice Taylor	.30	.10
76	Aaron McKie	.30	.10
77	Grant Hill	.50	.20
78	Arvydas Sabonis	.30	.10
79	Peja Stojakovic	.50	.20
80	Jason Kidd	.75	.30
81	Vin Baker	.30	.10
82	Morris Peterson	.30	.10
83	Bryon Russell	.15	.05
84	Michael Dickerson	.30	.10
85	Christian Laettner	.30	.10
86	Jerome Williams	.15	.05
87	Desmond Mason	.30	.10
88	Sean Elliott	.30	.10
89	Marcus Camby	.30	.10
90	Stephon Marbury	.50	.20
91	Joel Przybilla	.30	.10
92	Alonzo Mourning	.30	.10
93	Brian Shaw	.15	.05
94	Austin Croshere	.30	.10
95	Mookie Blaylock	.15	.05
96	Mateen Cleaves	.30	.10
97	Nick Van Exel	.50	.20
98	Michael Finley	.50	.20
99	Jamal Crawford	.30	.10
100	Steve Francis	.50	.20
101	Tim Hardaway	.30	.10
102	Sam Cassell	.50	.20
103	Shammond Williams	.15	.05
104	DeShawn Stevenson	.30	.10
105	Bryant Reeves	.15	.05
106	Richard Hamilton	.30	.10
107	Antonio Davis	.15	.05
108	Brent Barry	.30	.10
109	Derek Anderson	.30	.10
110	Kenny Anderson	.30	.10
111	Brevin Knight	.15	.05
112	Tyrone Nesby	.15	.05
113	Erick Strickland	.15	.05
114	Jacque Vaughn	.15	.05
115	John Stockton	.50	.20
116	Alvin Williams	.15	.05
117	Speedy Claxton	.30	.10
118	Bo Outlaw	.15	.05
119	Jahidi White	.15	.05
120	Karl Malone	.50	.20
121	Charles Oakley	.15	.05
122	Malik Rose	.15	.05
123	Avery Johnson	.15	.05
124	Toni Kukoc	.30	.10
125	Bryant Stith	.15	.05
126	P.J. Brown	.15	.05
127	Ron Mercer	.30	.10
128	Lamond Murray	.15	.05
129	Steve Nash	.50	.20
130	Raef LaFrentz	.30	.10
131	Corliss Williamson	.30	.10
132	Danny Fortson	.15	.05
133	Chris Porter	.15	.05
134	Shandon Anderson	.15	.05
135	Jalen Rose	.50	.20
136	Corey Maggette	.30	.10
137	Horace Grant	.30	.10
138	Eddie Jones	.50	.20
139	Chauncey Billups	.30	.10
140	Ray Allen	.50	.20
141	Terrell Brandon	.30	.10
142	Keith Van Horn	.50	.20
143	Allan Houston	.30	.10
144	Mark Jackson	.30	.10
145	Pat Garrity	.15	.05
146	Anfernee Hardaway	.50	.20
147	Iakovos Tsakalidis	.15	.05
148	Damon Stoudamire	.30	.10
149	Bobby Jackson	.30	.10
150	Antawn Jamison	.50	.20
151	Kenny Thomas	.15	.05
152	Jonathan Bender	.30	.10
153	Jeff McInnis	.15	.05
154	Robert Horry	.30	.10
155	Anthony Mason	.30	.10
156	Lindsey Hunter	.15	.05
157	LaPhonso Ellis	.15	.05
158	Jamie Feick	.15	.05
159	Kurt Thomas	.30	.10
160	Gary Payton	.50	.20
161	Rod Strickland	.15	.05
162	Bonzi Wells	.30	.10
163	Scot Pollard	.15	.05
164	Raja Bell RC	1.25	.50
165	Rodney Rogers	.15	.05
166	John Amaechi	.15	.05
167	Darrell Armstrong	.15	.05
168	Aaron Williams	.15	.05
169	Latrell Sprewell	.50	.20
170	Radoslav Nesterovic	.30	.10
171	Anthony Carter	.30	.10
172	Quentin Richardson	.30	.10
173	Primoz Brezec RC	1.50	.60
174	Michael Olowokandi	.15	.05
175	Jason Williams	.30	.10
176	Ruben Patterson	.30	.10
177	Chris Childs	.15	.05
178	Greg Ostertag	.15	.05
179	Mike Bibby	.50	.20
180	Mitch Richmond	.30	.10
181	Donyell Marshall	.30	.10
182	Dale Davis	.30	.10
183	Tony Delk	.15	.05
184	Mike Miller	.50	.20
185	Charlie Ward	.15	.05
186	Kenyon Martin	.50	.20
187	Walt Williams	.15	.05
188	Al Harrington	.30	.10
189	Chucky Atkins	.15	.05
190	Kevin Willis	.15	.05
191	Juwan Howard	.30	.10
192	Jim Jackson	.15	.05
193	Antonio McDyess	.30	.10
194	Jamaal Magloire	.30	.10
195	Mark Blount	.15	.05
196	Fred Hoiberg	.15	.05
197	Nazr Mohammed	.15	.05
198	Antoine Walker	.50	.20
199	Wang Zhizhi	.50	.20
200	Shareef Abdur-Rahim	.50	.20
201	Chris Whitney	.15	.05
202	David Wesley	.15	.05
203	Matt Harpring	.50	.20
204	George McCloud	.15	.05
205	Joe Smith	.30	.10
206	Cuttino Mobley	.30	.10
207	Tyrone Hill	.15	.05
208	Clifford Robinson	.15	.05
209	Vlade Divac	.30	.10
210	Eddie Robinson	.30	.10
211	Michael Curry	.15	.05
212	Courtney Alexander	.30	.10
213	Grant Long	.15	.05
214	Dan Majerle	.30	.10
215	Points Leaders	.75	.30
216	Rebounds Leaders	.30	.10
217	Assists Leaders	.50	.20
218	Steals Leaders	.30	.10
219	Blocks Leaders	.30	.10
220	Team Championship	1.00	.40
221	Kwame Brown RC	3.00	1.25
222	Tyson Chandler RC	4.00	1.50
223	Pau Gasol RC	5.00	2.00
224	Eddy Curry RC	5.00	2.00
225	Jason Richardson RC	5.00	2.00
226	Shane Battier RC	2.50	1.00
227	Eddie Griffin RC	2.00	.75
228	DeSagana Diop RC	1.25	.50
229	Rodney Rogers RC	1.50	.60
230	Joe Johnson RC	4.00	1.50
231	Kedrick Brown RC	1.25	.50
232	Vladimir Radmanovic RC	1.25	.50
233	Richard Jefferson RC	4.00	1.50
234	Troy Murphy RC	2.50	1.00
235	Steven Hunter RC	1.25	.50
236	Kirk Haston RC	1.25	.50
237	Michael Bradley RC	1.25	.50
238	Jason Collins RC	1.25	.50
239	Zach Randolph RC	5.00	2.00
240	Brendan Haywood RC	1.50	.60
241	Joseph Forte RC	2.00	.75
242	Jeryl Sasser RC	1.25	.50
243	Brandon Armstrong RC	1.25	.50
244	Gerald Wallace RC	5.00	2.00
245	Samuel Dalembert RC	1.25	.50
246	Jamaal Tinsley RC	2.50	1.00
247	Tony Parker RC	6.00	2.50
248	Trenton Hassell RC	2.00	.75
249	Gilbert Arenas RC	12.00	5.00
250	Jeff Trepagnier RC	1.25	.50
251	Damone Brown RC	1.25	.50
252	Loren Woods RC	1.25	.50
253	Ousmane Cisse RC	1.25	.50
254	Ken Johnson RC	1.25	.50
255	Kenny Satterfield RC	1.25	.50
256	Alvin Jones RC	1.25	.50
257	Pau Gasol Preseason	12.00	5.00
TR-SC	S.O'Neal/K.Abdul-Jabbar	250.00	125.00
NNO	G.Arenas SPEC AU	60.00	25.00

2002-03 Topps

	COMPLETE SET (220)	80.00	40.00
	COMMON CARD (1-164)	.15	.05
	COMMON ROOKIE (185-220)	1.25	.50
1	Shaquille O'Neal	1.25	.50
2	Pau Gasol	.50	.20
3	Allen Iverson	1.00	.40
4	Tom Gugliotta	.15	.05
5	Rasheed Wallace	.50	.20
6	Peja Stojakovic	.50	.20
7	Jason Richardson	.50	.20
8	Rashard Lewis	.30	.10
9	Morris Peterson	.30	.10
10	Michael Jordan	4.00	1.50
11	Matt Harpring	.50	.20
12	Shareef Abdur-Rahim	.50	.20
13	Antoine Walker	.50	.20
14	Stephon Marbury	.50	.20
15	Jamal Mashburn	.30	.10
16	Eddy Curry	.50	.20
17	Jumaine Jones	.30	.10
18	Wang Zhizhi	.50	.20
19	James Posey	.30	.10
20	Jason Kidd	.75	.30
21	Jerry Stackhouse	.50	.20
22	Kenny Thomas	.15	.05
23	Ron Mercer	.30	.10
24	Jeff McInnis	.15	.05
25	Kobe Bryant	2.00	.75
26	Jason Williams	.30	.10
27	Eddie Jones	.50	.20
28	Anthony Mason	.30	.10
29	Kenyon Martin	.50	.20
30	Kevin Garnett	1.00	.40
31	Kurt Thomas	.30	.10
32	Karl Malone	.50	.20
33	Patrick Ewing	.50	.20
34	Antonio McDyess	.30	.10
35	Dirk Nowitzki	.75	.30
36	Wesley Person	.15	.05
37	Theo Ratliff	.30	.10
38	Jarron Collins	.15	.05
39	Horace Grant	.30	.10
40	Vince Carter	1.25	.50
41	Desmond Mason	.30	.10
42	Todd MacCulloch	.15	.05
43	Bobby Jackson	.30	.10
44	Vlade Divac	.30	.10
45	Keith Van Horn	.50	.20
46	Bo Outlaw	.15	.05
47	Eric Snow	.30	.10
48	Grant Hill	.50	.20

2003-04 Topps

❏ 49	Terrell Brandon	.30	.10
❏ 50	Tracy Mcgrady	1.25	.50
❏ 51	Tim Thomas	.30	.10
❏ 52	Loren Woods	.30	.10
❏ 53	Michael Redd	.50	.20
❏ 54	Stromile Swift	.30	.10
❏ 55	Dikembe Mutombo	.30	.10
❏ 56	Richard Jefferson	.30	.10
❏ 57	Glenn Robinson	.50	.20
❏ 58	Samaki Walker	.15	.05
❏ 59	Quentin Richardson	.30	.10
❏ 60	Elton Brand	.50	.20
❏ 61	Reggie Miller	.50	.20
❏ 62	Eddie Griffin	.30	.10
❏ 63	Gilbert Arenas	.50	.20
❏ 64	Zeljko Rebraca	.30	.10
❏ 65	Donnell Harvey	.15	.05
❏ 66	Juwan Howard	.30	.10
❏ 67	Nick Van Exel	.50	.20
❏ 68	Donyell Marshall	.30	.10
❏ 69	Tyson Chandler	.50	.20
❏ 70	Baron Davis	.50	.20
❏ 71	Nazr Mohammed	.15	.05
❏ 72	Marcus Camby	.30	.10
❏ 73	Jamaal Magloire	.15	.05
❏ 74	Marcus Fizer	.30	.10
❏ 75	Steve Francis	.50	.20
❏ 76	Aaron Mckie	.30	.10
❏ 77	Anfernee Hardaway	.50	.20
❏ 78	Scottie Pippen	.75	.30
❏ 79	Mike Bibby	.50	.20
❏ 80	Paul Pierce	.50	.20
❏ 81	Tony Delk	.15	.05
❏ 82	Kwame Brown	.30	.10
❏ 83	Andrei Kirilenko	.50	.20
❏ 84	Keon Clark	.30	.10
❏ 85	Alvin Williams	.15	.05
❏ 86	Brent Barry	.30	.10
❏ 87	David Robinson	.50	.20
❏ 88	Doug Christie	.30	.10
❏ 89	Derek Anderson	.30	.10
❏ 90	Chris Webber	.50	.20
❏ 91	Speedy Claxton	.30	.10
❏ 92	Robert Horry	.30	.10
❏ 93	Allan Houston	.30	.10
❏ 94	Kerry Kittles	.15	.05
❏ 95	Wally Szczerbiak	.30	.10
❏ 96	Jonathan Bender	.30	.10
❏ 97	Sam Cassell	.50	.20
❏ 98	Rod Strickland	.15	.05
❏ 99	Shane Battier	.50	.20
❏ 100	Tim Duncan	1.00	.40
❏ 101	Jermaine O'Neal	.50	.20
❏ 102	Cuttino Mobley	.30	.10
❏ 103	Danny Fortson	.15	.05
❏ 104	Clifford Robinson	.15	.05
❏ 105	Tim Hardaway	.30	.10
❏ 106	Steve Nash	.50	.20
❏ 107	Zydrunas Ilgauskas	.30	.10
❏ 108	Travis Best	.15	.05
❏ 109	Eddie Robinson	.15	.05
❏ 110	David Wesley	.15	.05
❏ 111	Kenny Anderson	.30	.10
❏ 112	DerMarr Johnson	.15	.05
❏ 113	Courtney Alexander	.15	.05
❏ 114	Brian Grant	.30	.10
❏ 115	Lorenzen Wright	.15	.05
❏ 116	Corliss Williamson	.30	.10
❏ 117	Malik Rose	.15	.05
❏ 118	Tony Parker	.50	.20
❏ 119	Vladimir Radmanovic	.30	.10
❏ 120	Hidayet Turkoglu	.30	.10
❏ 121	Damon Stoudamire	.30	.10
❏ 122	Brendan Haywood	.15	.05
❏ 123	Jalen Rose	.50	.20
❏ 124	Mike Miller	.50	.20
❏ 125	Derrick Coleman	.15	.05
❏ 126	Mark Jackson	.15	.05
❏ 127	Raef Lafrentz	.30	.10
❏ 128	Ben Wallace	.50	.20
❏ 129	Larry Hughes	.30	.10
❏ 130	Ray Allen	.50	.20
❏ 131	Gary Payton	.50	.20
❏ 132	P.J. Brown	.15	.05
❏ 133	Derek Fisher	.50	.20
❏ 134	Michael Olowokandi	.15	.05
❏ 135	Jamaal Tinsley	.50	.20
❏ 136	Moochie Norris	.15	.05
❏ 137	Chris Mihm	.15	.05
❏ 138	Antawn Jamison	.50	.20
❏ 139	Chucky Atkins	.15	.05
❏ 140	Mengke Bateer	.50	.20
❏ 141	Brad Miller	.50	.20
❏ 142	Michael Finley	.50	.20
❏ 143	Andre Miller	.30	.10
❏ 144	Michael Dickerson	.15	.05
❏ 145	Elden Campbell	.15	.05
❏ 146	Kedrick Brown	.30	.10
❏ 147	Jason Terry	.50	.20
❏ 148	Chris Whitney	.15	.05
❏ 149	Bryon Russell	.15	.05
❏ 150	Darius Miles	.50	.20
❏ 151	Latrell Sprewell	.50	.20
❏ 152	Darrell Armstrong	.15	.05
❏ 153	Joe Johnson	.50	.20
❏ 154	Bonzi Wells	.30	.10
❏ 155	Jim Jackson	.15	.05
❏ 156	Steve Smith	.30	.10
❏ 157	Vin Baker	.30	.10
❏ 158	Antonio Davis	.15	.05
❏ 159	John Stockton	.50	.20
❏ 160	Shawn Marion	.50	.20
❏ 161	Devean George	.30	.10
❏ 162	Clarence Weatherspoon	.15	.05
❏ 163	Rick Fox	.30	.10
❏ 164	Chauncey Billups	.30	.10
❏ 165	Joe Smith	.30	.10
❏ 166	Laphonso Ellis	.15	.05
❏ 167	Maurice Taylor	.15	.05
❏ 168	Lamond Murray	.15	.05
❏ 169	Lamar Odom	.50	.20
❏ 170	Toni Kukoc	.30	.10
❏ 171	Alonzo Mourning	.30	.10
❏ 172	Antonio Daniels	.15	.05
❏ 173	Troy Murphy	.30	.10
❏ 174	Hakeem Olajuwon	.50	.20
❏ 175	Richard Hamilton	.30	.10
❏ 176	Rodney Rogers	.15	.05
❏ 177	Ruben Patterson	.30	.10
❏ 178	Dale Davis	.30	.10
❏ 179	League Leaders	1.25	.50
❏ 180	League Leaders	.50	.20
❏ 181	League Leaders	.50	.20
❏ 182	League Leaders	.50	.20
❏ 183	League Leaders	.50	.20
❏ 184	Team Championship Card	1.50	.60
❏ 185	Yao Ming RC	15.00	6.00
❏ 186	Jay Williams RC	2.50	1.00
❏ 187	Mike Dunleavy RC	3.00	1.25
❏ 188	Drew Gooden RC	5.00	2.00
❏ 189	Nikoloz Tskitishvili RC	2.00	.75
❏ 190	DaJuan Wagner RC	3.00	1.25
❏ 191	Nene Hilario RC	2.50	1.00
❏ 192	Chris Wilcox RC	2.50	1.00
❏ 193	Amare Stoudemire RC	10.00	4.00
❏ 194	Caron Butler RC	4.00	1.50
❏ 195	Jared Jeffries RC	1.25	.50
❏ 196	Melvin Ely RC	1.50	.60
❏ 197	Marcus Haislip RC	1.25	.50
❏ 198	Fred Jones RC	2.00	.75
❏ 199	Bostjan Nachbar RC	1.50	.60
❏ 200	Jiri Welsch RC	1.25	.50
❏ 201	Juan Dixon RC	3.00	1.25
❏ 202	Curtis Borchardt RC	1.25	.50
❏ 203	Ryan Humphrey RC	1.25	.50
❏ 204	Kareem Rush RC	2.00	.75
❏ 205	Qyntel Woods RC	2.00	.75
❏ 206	Casey Jacobsen RC	1.25	.50
❏ 207	Tayshaun Prince RC	2.50	1.00
❏ 208	Frank Williams RC	1.25	.50
❏ 209	John Salmons RC	1.25	.50
❏ 210	Chris Jefferies ERR RC	1.50	.60
❏ 211	Sam Clancy RC	1.25	.50
❏ 212	Dan Gadzuric RC	1.25	.50
❏ 213	Matt Barnes RC	1.25	.50
❏ 214	Robert Archibald RC	1.25	.50
❏ 215	Vincent Yarbrough RC	1.25	.50
❏ 216	Dan Dickau RC	3.00	1.25
❏ 217	Carlos Boozer RC	4.00	1.50
❏ 218	Tito Maddox RC	1.25	.50
❏ 219	Chris Owens RC	1.25	.50
❏ 220	Ronald Murray RC	2.50	1.00

❏	COMPLETE SET (249)	60.00	25.00
❏	COMMON CARD (1-220)	.15	.60
❏	COMMON ROOKIE (221-249)	1.50	.60
❏ 1	Tracy McGrady	1.25	.50
❏ 2	DaJuan Wagner	.25	.10
❏ 3	Allen Iverson	1.00	.40
❏ 4	Chris Webber	.50	.20
❏ 5	Jason Kidd	.75	.30
❏ 6	Stephon Marbury	.50	.20
❏ 7	Jermaine O'Neal	.50	.20
❏ 8	Antoine Walker	.50	.20
❏ 9	Tony Parker	.50	.20
❏ 10	Mike Bibby	.50	.20
❏ 11	Yao Ming	1.50	.60
❏ 12	Walter McCarty	.15	.60
❏ 13	Steve Nash	.50	.20
❏ 14	Paul Pierce	.50	.20
❏ 15	Vince Carter	1.25	.50
❏ 16	Peja Stojakovic	.50	.20
❏ 17	Kenny Anderson	.25	.10
❏ 18	Kenyon Martin	.50	.20
❏ 19	Pau Gasol	.50	.20
❏ 20	Gary Payton	.50	.20
❏ 21	Tim Duncan	1.00	.40
❏ 22	Jay Williams	.25	.10
❏ 23	Jason Richardson	.50	.20
❏ 24	Andre Miller	.25	.10
❏ 25	Latrell Sprewell	.50	.20
❏ 26	Darius Miles	.50	.20
❏ 27	Richard Jefferson	.25	.10
❏ 28	Shawn Marion	.50	.20
❏ 29	Baron Davis	.50	.20
❏ 30	Ben Wallace	.50	.20
❏ 31	Reggie Miller	.50	.20
❏ 32	Karl Malone	.50	.20
❏ 33	Grant Hill	.50	.20
❏ 34	Shaquille O'Neal	1.25	.50
❏ 35	Steve Francis	.50	.20
❏ 36	Kobe Bryant	2.00	.75
❏ 37	Mike Dunleavy	.25	.10
❏ 38	Glenn Robinson	.50	.20
❏ 39	Allan Houston	.25	.10
❏ 40	Kevin Ollie	.15	.60
❏ 41	Dirk Nowitzki	.75	.30
❏ 42	Elton Brand	.50	.20
❏ 43	Juan Dixon	.25	.10
❏ 44	Brian Grant	.25	.10
❏ 45	Jason Terry	.50	.20
❏ 46	Richard Hamilton	.25	.10
❏ 47	Morris Peterson	.25	.10
❏ 48	Ray Allen	.50	.20
❏ 49	Scottie Pippen	.75	.30
❏ 50	David Robinson	.50	.20
❏ 51	Cuttino Mobley	.50	.20
❏ 52	Jerry Stackhouse	.50	.20
❏ 53	Marcus Camby	.25	.10
❏ 54	Jalen Rose	.50	.20
❏ 55	Dikembe Mutombo	.25	.10
❏ 56	P.J. Brown	.15	.60
❏ 57	Jumaine Jones	.25	.10
❏ 58	Shawn Bradley	.15	.60
❏ 59	Juwan Howard	.25	.10
❏ 60	Clifford Robinson	.15	.60
❏ 61	Antawn Jamison	.50	.20
❏ 62	Rael LaFrentz	.25	.10
❏ 63	Kareem Rush	.25	.10

□	#	Player		
□	64	LaPhonso Ellis	.15	.60
□	65	Toni Kukoc	.15	.60
□	66	Mike Miller	.25	.10
□	67	Aaron McKie	.25	.10
□	68	Tom Gugliotta	.15	.60
□	69	Dale Davis	.25	.10
□	70	Jared Jeffries	.15	.60
□	71	Alvin Williams	.15	.60
□	72	DeShawn Stevenson	.15	.60
□	73	Doug Christie	.15	.60
□	74	Troy Hudson	.15	.60
□	75	Jason Collins	.15	.60
□	76	Eddie Griffin	.25	.10
□	77	Vladimir Radmanovic	.15	.60
□	78	Michael Olowokandi	.15	.60
□	79	Michael Redd	.50	.20
□	80	Tim Thomas	.25	.10
□	81	Ron Mercer	.15	.60
□	82	Shareef Abdur-Rahim	.50	.20
□	83	Eduardo Najera	.25	.10
□	84	Jon Barry	.15	.60
□	85	Erick Dampier	.25	.10
□	86	Derek Fisher	.50	.20
□	87	Drew Gooden	.25	.10
□	88	Dan Gadzuric	.15	.60
□	89	Antonio McDyess	.25	.10
□	90	Derrick Coleman	.50	.20
□	91	Carlos Boozer	.50	.20
□	92	Rasheed Wallace	.50	.20
□	93	Antonio Davis	.15	.60
□	94	Kwame Brown	.25	.10
□	95	Manu Ginobili	.50	.20
□	96	Eric Williams	.15	.60
□	97	Trenton Hassell	.15	.60
□	98	Chris Whitney	.15	.60
□	99	Chauncey Billups	.25	.10
□	100	Kevin Garnett	1.00	.40
□	101	Marko Jaric	.25	.10
□	102	Rasual Butler	.25	.10
□	103	Gilbert Arenas	.50	.20
□	104	Keith Van Horn	.50	.20
□	105	Iakovos Tsakalidis	.15	.60
□	106	Ruben Patterson	.25	.10
□	107	Jarron Collins	.15	.60
□	108	Rodney White	.15	.60
□	109	Rashard Lewis	.50	.20
□	110	Malik Rose	.15	.60
□	111	Bobby Jackson	.25	.10
□	112	Brendan Haywood	.15	.60
□	113	Charlie Ward	.15	.60
□	114	Courtney Alexander	.25	.10
□	115	Kerry Kittles	.15	.60
□	116	Wally Szczerbiak	.25	.10
□	117	Darrell Armstrong	.15	.60
□	118	Anfernee Hardaway	.50	.20
□	119	Qyntel Woods	.15	.60
□	120	Quentin Richardson	.25	.10
□	121	Jonathan Bender	.25	.10
□	122	Robert Horry	.25	.10
□	123	Lorenzen Wright	.15	.60
□	124	Malik Allen	.15	.60
□	125	Sam Cassell	.50	.20
□	126	Joe Smith	.25	.10
□	127	Dion Glover	.15	.60
□	128	Jamal Crawford	.15	.60
□	129	Ricky Davis	.50	.20
□	130	Nikoloz Tskitishvili	.15	.60
□	131	Tyronn Lue	.15	.60
□	132	Scott Padgett	.15	.60
□	133	Jerome James	.15	.60
□	134	Hedo Turkoglu	.50	.20
□	135	Jamal Mashburn	.25	.10
□	136	Pat Burke	.15	.60
□	137	Joe Johnson	.25	.10
□	138	Anthony Peeler	.15	.60
□	139	Ron Artest	.25	.10
□	140	Theo Ratliff	.25	.10
□	141	Caron Butler	.50	.20
□	142	Anthony Mason	.25	.10
□	143	Vin Baker	.25	.10
□	144	Donyell Marshall	.25	.10
□	145	Nene	.25	.10
□	146	Chucky Atkins	.15	.60
□	147	Tyson Chandler	.50	.20
□	148	Jason Williams	.25	.10
□	149	Larry Hughes	.25	.10
□	150	Stephen Jackson	.15	.60
□	151	Kurt Thomas	.25	.10
□	152	Mehmet Okur	.15	.60
□	153	Amare Stoudemire	1.00	.40
□	154	Elden Campbell	.15	.60
□	155	Jamaal Tinsley	.50	.20
□	156	Chris Wilcox	.25	.10
□	157	Rick Fox	.25	.10
□	158	Gordan Giricek	.25	.10
□	159	Voshon Lenard	.15	.60
□	160	Brent Barry	.25	.10
□	161	Dan Dickau	.15	.60
□	162	Junior Harrington	.15	.60
□	163	Jiri Welsch	.25	.10
□	164	Vladimir Stepania	.15	.60
□	165	Brad Miller	.50	.20
□	166	Moochie Norris	.15	.60
□	167	Wesley Person	.15	.60
□	168	Greg Buckner	.15	.60
□	169	Bonzi Wells	.25	.10
□	170	Predrag Drobnjak	.15	.60
□	171	Andrei Kirilenko	.50	.20
□	172	Vlade Divac	.25	.10
□	173	Rodney Rogers	.15	.60
□	174	Kendall Gill	.15	.60
□	175	Kenny Thomas	.15	.60
□	176	Derek Anderson	.25	.10
□	177	Steve Smith	.25	.10
□	178	Christian Laettner	.25	.10
□	179	Tony Delk	.15	.60
□	180	Zydrunas Ilgauskas	.25	.10
□	181	James Posey	.25	.10
□	182	Tayshaun Prince	.25	.10
□	183	Devean George	.15	.60
□	184	Eddie Jones	.50	.20
□	185	Corey Maggette	.25	.10
□	186	Ira Newble	.15	.60
□	187	Shane Battier	.50	.20
□	188	Clarence Weatherspoon	.15	.60
□	189	Eric Snow	.25	.10
□	190	Damon Stoudamire	.25	.10
□	191	Keon Clark	.15	.60
□	192	Desmond Mason	.25	.10
□	193	Matt Harpring	.50	.20
□	194	Radoslav Nesterovic	.25	.10
□	195	Jamaal Magloire	.15	.60
□	196	Pat Garrity	.15	.60
□	197	Fred Jones	.15	.60
□	198	Tony Battie	.15	.60
□	199	Tyrone Hill	.15	.60
□	200	Adrian Griffin	.15	.60
□	201	Nick Van Exel	.50	.20
□	202	Shammond Williams	.15	.60
□	203	Corliss Williamson	.25	.10
□	204	Lamar Odom	.50	.20
□	205	Travis Best	.15	.60
□	206	Howard Eisley	.15	.60
□	207	Jerome Williams	.15	.60
□	208	David Wesley	.15	.60
□	209	Bostjan Nachbar	.15	.60
□	210	Marcus Fizer	.25	.10
□	211	Michael Finley	.50	.20
□	212	Troy Murphy	.50	.20
□	213	Adonal Foyle	.15	.60
□	214	Samaki Walker	.15	.60
□	215	Lucious Harris	.15	.60
□	216	Lindsey Hunter	.15	.60
□	217	Stromile Swift	.25	.10
□	218	Eddy Curry	.25	.10
□	219	Kelvin Cato	.15	.60
□	220	Chris Anderson	.15	.60
□	221	LeBron James RC	20.00	8.00
□	222	Darko Milicic EXCH.	3.00	1.25
□	223	Carmelo Anthony RC	10.00	4.00
□	224	Chris Bosh RC	6.00	2.50
□	225	Dwyane Wade RC	12.00	5.00
□	226	Chris Kaman RC	1.50	.60
□	227	Kirk Hinrich RC	3.00	1.25
□	228	T.J. Ford RC	2.50	1.00
□	229	Mike Sweetney RC	1.50	.60
□	230	Jarvis Hayes RC	1.50	.60
□	231	Mickael Pietrus RC	1.50	.60
□	232	Nick Collison RC	1.50	.60
□	233	Marcus Banks RC	1.50	.60
□	234	Luke Ridnour RC	2.50	1.00
□	235	Reece Gaines RC	1.50	.60
□	236	Troy Bell RC	2.00	.75
□	237	Zarko Cabarkapa RC	2.00	.75
□	238	David West RC	2.00	.75
□	239	Aleksandar Pavlovic RC	2.50	1.00
□	240	Dahntay Jones RC	1.50	.60
□	241	Boris Diaw RC	2.00	.75
□	242	Zoran Planinic RC	1.50	.60
□	243	Travis Outlaw RC	1.50	.60
□	244	Brian Cook RC	1.50	.60
□	245	Carlos Delfino RC	1.50	.60
□	246	Ndudi Ebi RC	1.50	.60
□	247	Kendrick Perkins RC	1.50	.60
□	248	Leandro Barbosa RC	2.50	1.00
□	249	Josh Howard RC	2.50	1.00

2004-05 Topps

□	#	Player		
□		COMPLETE SET (249)	50.00	20.00
□		COMMON CARD (1-220)	.15	.06
□		COMMON ROOKIE (221-249)	1.50	.60
□	1	Allen Iverson	1.00	.40
□	2	Eddy Curry	.25	.10
□	3	Stephon Marbury	.50	.20
□	4	Chris Bosh	.75	.30
□	5	Jason Kidd	.75	.30
□	6	Bonzi Wells	.25	.10
□	7	Fred Jones	.15	.06
□	8	Kobe Bryant	2.00	.75
□	9	Ben Wallace	.50	.20
□	10	Darrell Armstrong	.15	.06
□	11	Yao Ming	1.25	.50
□	12	Udonis Haslem	.25	.10
□	13	Nene	.25	.10
□	14	Michael Redd	.25	.10
□	15	Carmelo Anthony	1.50	.60
□	16	Gary Trent	.15	.06
□	17	Larry Hughes	.25	.10
□	18	Kareem Rush	.25	.10
□	19	Antonio McDyess	.25	.10
□	20	Drew Gooden	.25	.10
□	21	Kevin Garnett	1.00	.40
□	22	DeShawn Stevenson	.15	.06
□	23	LeBron James	3.00	1.25
□	24	Robert Horry	.25	.10
□	25	Shareef Abdur-Rahim	.25	.10
□	26	Antonio Daniels	.15	.06
□	27	Scottie Pippen	.75	.30
□	28	Mike Bibby	.50	.20
□	29	Joe Smith	.25	.10
□	30	Vince Carter	1.25	.50
□	31	Reggie Miller	.50	.20
□	32	Chris Wilcox	.25	.10
□	33	Rasheed Wallace	.50	.20
□	34	Paul Pierce	.50	.20
□	35	Tayshaun Prince	.25	.10
□	36	Raja Bell	.15	.06
□	37	Stephen Jackson	.15	.06
□	38	Eric Snow	.25	.10
□	39	Zydrunas Ilgauskas	.25	.10
□	40	Andre Miller	.25	.10
□	41	Dirk Nowitzki	.75	.30
□	42	Steve Francis	.50	.20
□	43	Ray Allen	.50	.20
□	44	Donyell Marshall	.50	.20
□	45	Pau Gasol	.50	.20
□	46	T.J. Ford	.25	.10
□	47	Andrei Kirilenko	.50	.20
□	48	Jamaal Tinsley	.25	.10
□	49	Earl Boykins	.25	.10

#	Player		
❏ 50	Tim Duncan	1.00	.40
❏ 51	Erick Dampier	.25	.10
❏ 52	Nazr Mohammed	.15	.06
❏ 53	Tim Thomas	.25	.10
❏ 54	Keyon Dooling	.15	.06
❏ 55	Jason Kapono	.25	.10
❏ 56	Kirk Hinrich	.50	.20
❏ 57	Aaron McKie	.25	.10
❏ 58	Brad Miller	.50	.20
❏ 59	Al Harrington	.25	.10
❏ 60	Gary Payton	.50	.20
❏ 61	Nick Van Exel	.50	.20
❏ 62	Cuttino Mobley	.25	.10
❏ 63	Marcus Camby	.25	.10
❏ 64	Desmond Mason	.25	.10
❏ 65	Boris Diaw	.15	.06
❏ 66	Kenyon Martin	.50	.20
❏ 67	Mike Miller	.50	.20
❏ 68	Dwyane Wade	1.50	.60
❏ 69	Allan Houston	.25	.10
❏ 70	Jermaine O'Neal	.50	.20
❏ 71	Travis Hansen	.15	.06
❏ 72	Qyntel Woods	.15	.06
❏ 73	Jamal Crawford	.25	.10
❏ 74	Bobby Jackson	.25	.10
❏ 75	Derrick Coleman	.15	.06
❏ 76	Brian Skinner	.15	.06
❏ 77	Elton Brand	.50	.20
❏ 78	Rodney Rogers	.15	.06
❏ 79	Zarko Cabarkapa	.25	.10
❏ 80	Mike Bibby	.50	.20
❏ 81	Jim Jackson	.15	.06
❏ 82	Kurt Thomas	.25	.10
❏ 83	Vin Baker	.25	.10
❏ 84	Rodney White	.15	.06
❏ 85	Gordan Giricek	.25	.10
❏ 86	Jamal Mashburn	.25	.10
❏ 87	Kenny Thomas	.15	.06
❏ 88	Antoine Walker	.50	.20
❏ 89	Rasho Nesterovic	.25	.10
❏ 90	Shawn Marion	.50	.20
❏ 91	Shane Battier	.50	.20
❏ 92	Marquis Daniels	.50	.20
❏ 93	Ruben Patterson	.15	.06
❏ 94	Michael Olowokandi	.15	.06
❏ 95	Bruce Bowen	.15	.06
❏ 96	Caron Butler	.50	.20
❏ 97	Corliss Williamson	.15	.06
❏ 98	Jeff Foster	.15	.06
❏ 99	Carlos Boozer	.50	.20
❏ 100	Tracy McGrady	1.25	.50
❏ 101	Stromile Swift	.25	.10
❏ 102	Keith Van Horn	.50	.20
❏ 103	Derek Fisher	.50	.20
❏ 104	Juwan Howard	.25	.10
❏ 105	Tony Parker	.50	.20
❏ 106	Jason Terry	.50	.20
❏ 107	Vlade Divac	.25	.10
❏ 108	Marcus Banks	.25	.10
❏ 109	Derek Anderson	.25	.10
❏ 110	Karl Malone	.50	.20
❏ 111	Baron Davis	.50	.20
❏ 112	Chris Crawford	.15	.06
❏ 113	Kwame Brown	.25	.10
❏ 114	Jiri Welsch	.25	.10
❏ 115	Maciej Lampe	.25	.10
❏ 116	Josh Howard	.25	.10
❏ 117	Luke Walton	.25	.10
❏ 118	John Salmons	.15	.06
❏ 119	David West	.25	.10
❏ 120	Amare Stoudemire	1.00	.40
❏ 121	Antawn Jamison	.50	.20
❏ 122	Clarence Weatherspoon	.25	.10
❏ 123	Aleksandar Pavlovic	.15	.06
❏ 124	Kerry Kittles	.15	.06
❏ 125	Rafer Alston	.15	.06
❏ 126	Jarvis Hayes	.25	.10
❏ 127	Toni Kukoc	.25	.10
❏ 128	Latrell Sprewell	.50	.20
❏ 129	Keith Bogans	.15	.06
❏ 130	Jason Richardson	.50	.20
❏ 131	Brent Barry	.25	.10
❏ 132	Darko Milicic	.25	.10
❏ 133	Peja Stojakovic	.50	.20
❏ 134	Jerome Williams	.15	.06
❏ 135	Malik Rose	.15	.06
❏ 136	Quentin Richardson	.25	.10
❏ 137	Wally Szczerbiak	.25	.10
❏ 138	Theo Ratliff	.25	.10
❏ 139	Gilbert Arenas	.50	.20
❏ 140	Richard Hamilton	.25	.10
❏ 141	Rashard Lewis	.50	.20
❏ 142	Joe Johnson	.25	.10
❏ 143	P.J. Brown	.15	.06
❏ 144	Jason Collins	.15	.06
❏ 145	Chauncey Billups	.25	.10
❏ 146	Raef LaFrentz	.15	.06
❏ 147	Mickael Pietrus	.25	.10
❏ 148	Lamar Odom	.50	.20
❏ 149	Vladimir Radmanovic	.15	.06
❏ 150	Chris Webber	.50	.20
❏ 151	Tony Delk	.15	.06
❏ 152	Troy Hudson	.15	.06
❏ 153	David Wesley	.15	.06
❏ 154	Juan Dixon	.25	.10
❏ 155	Darius Miles	.50	.20
❏ 156	Gerald Wallace	.25	.10
❏ 157	Jalen Rose	.50	.20
❏ 158	Charlie Ward	.15	.06
❏ 159	Michael Finley	.50	.20
❏ 160	Jonathan Bender	.15	.06
❏ 161	Lorenzen Wright	.15	.06
❏ 162	George Lynch	.15	.06
❏ 163	Leandro Barbosa	.25	.10
❏ 164	Dajuan Wagner	.25	.10
❏ 165	Francisco Elson	.15	.06
❏ 166	Jerry Stackhouse	.50	.20
❏ 167	Manu Ginobili	.50	.20
❏ 168	Chris Kaman	.25	.10
❏ 169	James Posey	.25	.10
❏ 170	Doug Christie	.25	.10
❏ 171	Zoran Planinic	.15	.06
❏ 172	Maurice Taylor	.15	.06
❏ 173	Carlos Arroyo	1.00	.40
❏ 174	Damon Stoudamire	.25	.10
❏ 175	Brian Cardinal	.15	.06
❏ 176	Devean George	.25	.10
❏ 177	Hedo Turkoglu	.50	.20
❏ 178	Anfernee Hardaway	.50	.20
❏ 179	Tony Battie	.15	.06
❏ 180	Steve Nash	.50	.20
❏ 181	Glenn Robinson	.50	.20
❏ 182	Morris Peterson	.25	.10
❏ 183	Luke Ridnour	.25	.10
❏ 184	Mehmet Okur	.15	.06
❏ 185	Eddie Jones	.50	.20
❏ 186	Tyronn Lue	.15	.06
❏ 187	Raul Lopez	.15	.06
❏ 188	Lucious Harris	.15	.06
❏ 189	Alvin Williams	.15	.06
❏ 190	Zach Randolph	.50	.20
❏ 191	Steve Blake	.15	.06
❏ 192	Marko Jaric	.15	.06
❏ 193	Anthony Peeler	.15	.06
❏ 194	Troy Murphy	.50	.20
❏ 195	Jamaal Magloire	.15	.06
❏ 196	Brandon Hunter	.15	.06
❏ 197	Jason Williams	.25	.10
❏ 198	Corey Maggette	.25	.10
❏ 199	Ron Artest	.50	.20
❏ 200	Shaquille O'Neal	1.25	.50
❏ 201	Richard Jefferson	.25	.10
❏ 202	Kelvin Cato	.15	.06
❏ 203	Mark Blount	.15	.06
❏ 204	Eric Williams	.15	.06
❏ 205	Sam Cassell	.25	.10
❏ 206	Voshon Lenard	.15	.06
❏ 207	Bob Sura	.15	.06
❏ 208	Speedy Claxton	.15	.06
❏ 209	Samuel Dalembert	.15	.06
❏ 210	Tyson Chandler	.50	.20
❏ 211	Brian Grant	.25	.10
❏ 212	Stanislav Medvedenko	.15	.06
❏ 213	Danny Fortson	.15	.06
❏ 214	Chucky Atkins	.15	.06
❏ 215	Matt Harpring	.50	.20
❏ 216	Trenton Hassell	.15	.06
❏ 217	Ronald Murray	.25	.10
❏ 218	Jeff McInnis	.15	.06
❏ 219	Primoz Brezec	.15	.06
❏ 220	Ricky Davis	.50	.20
❏ 221	Dwight Howard RC	6.00	2.50
❏ 222	Emeka Okafor RC	8.00	3.00
❏ 223	Ben Gordon RC	8.00	3.00
❏ 224	Shaun Livingston RC	3.00	1.25
❏ 225	Devin Harris RC	3.00	1.25
❏ 226	Josh Childress RC	2.50	1.00
❏ 227	Luol Deng RC	4.00	1.50
❏ 228	Rafael Araujo RC	1.50	.60
❏ 229	Andre Iguodala RC	5.00	2.00
❏ 230	Luke Jackson RC	1.50	.60
❏ 231	Andris Biedrins RC	4.00	1.50
❏ 232	Robert Swift RC	1.50	.60
❏ 233	Sebastian Telfair RC	2.00	.75
❏ 234	Kris Humphries RC	1.50	.60
❏ 235	Al Jefferson RC	2.50	1.00
❏ 236	Kirk Snyder RC	1.50	.60
❏ 237	Josh Smith RC	4.00	1.50
❏ 238	J.R. Smith RC	4.00	1.50
❏ 239	Dorell Wright RC	2.50	1.00
❏ 240	Jameer Nelson RC	3.00	1.25
❏ 241	Pavel Podkolzine RC	1.50	.60
❏ 242	Viktor Khryapa RC	1.50	.60
❏ 243	Sergei Monia RC	1.50	.60
❏ 244	Delonte West RC	3.00	1.25
❏ 245	Tony Allen RC	2.50	1.00
❏ 246	Kevin Martin RC	3.00	1.25
❏ 247	Sasha Vujacic RC	1.50	.60
❏ 248	Beno Udrih RC	2.50	1.00
❏ 249	David Harrison RC	1.50	.60

2005-06 Topps

❏	COMPLETE SET (255)	50.00	20.00
❏	COMMON CARD (1-220)	.15	.06
❏	SEMISTARS	.25	.10
❏	UNLISTED STARS	.50	.20
❏	COMMON ROOKIE (221-250)	2.00	.75
❏	COMMON CELEBRITY (251-255)	4.00	1.50
❏ 1	Grant Hill	.50	.20
❏ 2	Keith Van Horn	.25	.10
❏ 3	Quentin Richardson	.25	.10
❏ 4	Damon Jones	.25	.10
❏ 5	Lamar Odom	.50	.20
❏ 6	Jamal Crawford	.25	.10
❏ 7	Ben Gordon	1.00	.40
❏ 8	Zach Randolph	.50	.20
❏ 9	Rafer Alston	.15	.06
❏ 10	Gilbert Arenas	.50	.20
❏ 11	Yao Ming	1.25	.50
❏ 12	Cuttino Mobley	.25	.10
❏ 13	Josh Smith	.50	.20
❏ 14	Ray Allen	.50	.20
❏ 15	Vince Carter	1.25	.50
❏ 16	Kenyon Martin	.50	.20
❏ 17	Mark Blount	.15	.06
❏ 18	Carlos Arroyo	.75	.30
❏ 19	Lee Nailon	.15	.06
❏ 20	Bobby Simmons	.15	.06
❏ 21	Tim Duncan	1.00	.40
❏ 22	Michael Redd	.50	.20
❏ 23	Antawn Jamison	.50	.20
❏ 24	Matt Bonner	.15	.06
❏ 25	Shane Battier	.50	.20
❏ 26	Nick Van Exel	.50	.20
❏ 27	Jason Hart	.15	.06
❏ 28	Nene	.25	.10
❏ 29	Fred Jones	.25	.10
❏ 30	Baron Davis	.50	.20
❏ 31	Danny Fortson	.15	.06
❏ 32	Caron Butler	.25	.10

33	Allen Iverson	1.00	.40
34	Eddie Griffin	.15	.06
35	Jameer Nelson	.25	.10
36	Brent Barry	.25	.10
37	Zydrunas Ilgauskas	.25	.10
38	Jason Terry	.50	.20
39	Mike Dunleavy	.50	.20
40	Paul Pierce	.50	.20
41	Reggie Miller	.50	.20
42	Lorenzen Wright	.15	.06
43	Peja Stojakovic	.50	.20
44	Zaza Pachulia	.15	.06
45	Dan Dickau	.15	.06
46	Andre Iguodala	.50	.20
47	Andrei Kirilenko	.50	.20
48	Nenad Krstic	.25	.10
49	Damon Stoudamire	.25	.10
50	Emeka Okafor	.75	.30
51	Jalen Rose	.50	.20
52	Beno Udrih	.25	.10
53	Jared Jeffries	.15	.06
54	Ricky Davis	.25	.10
55	Jason Kidd	.75	.30
56	Eddy Curry	.25	.10
57	Chauncey Billups	.50	.20
58	Eric Snow	.25	.10
59	Derek Fisher	.50	.20
60	Amare Stoudemire	1.00	.40
61	Josh Childress	.25	.10
62	Juwan Howard	.15	.06
63	Mehmet Okur	.15	.06
64	Jerome Williams	.15	.06
65	Shaun Livingston	.50	.20
66	Stephen Jackson	.25	.10
67	Alonzo Mourning	.25	.10
68	J.R. Smith	.25	.10
69	Kobe Bryant	2.00	.75
70	Dwight Howard	.60	.25
71	Manu Ginobili	.50	.20
72	Kyle Korver	.50	.20
73	Reggie Evans	.15	.06
74	Shareef Abdur-Rahim	.50	.20
75	Rafael Araujo	.25	.10
76	Kirk Snyder	.15	.06
77	Jermaine O'Neal	.50	.20
78	Melvin Ely	.15	.06
79	Chris Kaman	.15	.06
80	Stephon Marbury	.50	.20
81	Joe Smith	.25	.10
82	Samuel Dalembert	.25	.10
83	Luke Ridnour	.25	.10
84	Sebastian Telfair	.25	.10
85	Larry Hughes	.25	.10
86	Tyson Chandler	.50	.20
87	Michael Finley	.50	.20
88	Drew Gooden	.25	.10
89	Marcus Camby	.15	.06
90	Dwyane Wade	1.50	.60
91	Troy Murphy	.50	.20
92	David Wesley	.15	.06
93	Stromile Swift	.25	.10
94	Clifford Robinson	.15	.06
95	Sam Cassell	.50	.20
96	Joe Johnson	.25	.10
97	Bobby Jackson	.25	.10
98	Derek Anderson	.25	.10
99	Rashard Lewis	.50	.20
100	Shaquille O'Neal	1.25	.50
101	Keith McLeod	.15	.06
102	Keith Bogans	.15	.06
103	Al Harrington	.25	.10
104	Anderson Varejao	.25	.10
105	Al Jefferson	.50	.20
106	Jerry Stackhouse	.50	.20
107	Chris Duhon	.25	.10
108	Earl Boykins	.25	.10
109	Tayshaun Prince	.50	.20
110	Carlos Boozer	.25	.10
111	Rasual Butler	.15	.06
112	Bonzi Wells	.25	.10
113	Chris Wilcox	.15	.06
114	Latrell Sprewell	.50	.20
115	Richard Jefferson	.25	.10
116	Toni Kukoc	.25	.10
117	Doug Christie	.25	.10
118	Brad Miller	.50	.20
119	Antonio Daniels	.15	.06
120	Richard Hamilton	.25	.10
121	Kevin Garnett	1.00	.40
122	Tony Parker	.50	.20
123	Mike Sweetney	.25	.10
124	Speedy Claxton	.15	.06
125	Udonis Haslem	.50	.20
126	Chucky Atkins	.15	.06
127	David Harrison	.15	.06
128	Jason Collier	.15	.06
129	Pau Gasol	.50	.20
130	Chris Webber	.50	.20
131	Kelvin Cato	.15	.06
132	Michael Olowokandi	.15	.06
133	Ben Wallace	.50	.20
134	Antoine Walker	.50	.20
135	Marquis Daniels	.25	.10
136	Ira Newble	.15	.06
137	Austin Croshere	.15	.06
138	Mike James	.15	.06
139	Michael Doleac	.15	.06
140	Carmelo Anthony	1.25	.50
141	Sasha Vujacic	.15	.06
142	Brian Cardinal	.25	.10
143	Ron Mercer	.15	.06
144	Tim Thomas	.25	.10
145	Juan Dixon	.15	.06
146	Rodney Rogers	.15	.06
147	Hedo Turkoglu	.25	.10
148	Nazr Mohammed	.15	.06
149	Gerald Wallace	.25	.10
150	Dirk Nowitzki	.75	.30
151	Tony Allen	.15	.06
152	Adonal Foyle	.15	.06
153	Corey Maggette	.25	.10
154	Rasheed Wallace	.50	.20
155	Andre Miller	.25	.10
156	Luol Deng	.50	.20
157	Mike Miller	.50	.20
158	Wally Szczerbiak	.25	.10
159	Maurice Williams	.15	.06
160	Chris Bosh	.25	.10
161	Jamaal Magloire	.15	.06
162	Leandro Barbosa	.15	.06
163	Kevin Martin	.25	.10
164	Jeff Foster	.15	.06
165	Nick Collison	.15	.06
166	Matt Harpring	.50	.20
167	Kirk Hinrich	.50	.20
168	Antonio McDyess	.25	.10
169	Josh Howard	.25	.10
170	Elton Brand	.50	.20
171	Kurt Thomas	.25	.10
172	Tyronn Lue	.15	.06
173	Bob Sura	.15	.06
174	Chris Mihm	.15	.06
175	Jason Williams	.25	.10
176	Jim Jackson	.25	.10
177	Brevin Knight	.15	.06
178	Eduardo Najera	.15	.06
179	Jeff McInnis	.15	.06
180	Jason Richardson	.25	.10
181	Vladimir Radmanovic	.15	.06
182	Jamaal Tinsley	.25	.10
183	Eddie Jones	.50	.20
184	P.J. Brown	.15	.06
185	Troy Hudson	.15	.06
186	Steve Francis	.50	.20
187	Marc Jackson	.15	.06
188	Kenny Thomas	.15	.06
189	Joel Przybilla	.15	.06
190	Steve Nash	.50	.20
191	Devin Brown	.15	.06
192	Donyell Marshall	.50	.20
193	Raja Bell	.15	.06
194	Brendan Haywood	.15	.06
195	Primoz Brezec	.15	.06
196	Gary Payton	.50	.20
197	Devin Harris	.50	.20
198	Predrag Drobnjak	.15	.06
199	Dikembe Mutombo	.50	.20
200	LeBron James	3.00	1.25
201	Marko Jaric	.25	.10
202	Mike Bibby	.50	.20
203	Desmond Mason	.25	.10
204	Morris Peterson	.15	.06
205	Jarvis Hayes	.15	.06
206	Bruce Bowen	.25	.10
207	Trevor Ariza	.25	.10
208	Raef LaFrentz	.15	.06
209	Brian Grant	.25	.10
210	Shawn Marion	.50	.20
211	Dan Gadzuric	.15	.06
212	Andres Nocioni	.25	.10
213	Tony Delk	.15	.06
214	Darius Miles	.50	.20
215	Gordan Giricek	.15	.06
216	Rasho Nesterovic	.15	.06
217	Jason Collins	.15	.06
218	Mickael Pietrus	.15	.06
219	Erick Dampier	.25	.10
220	Tracy McGrady	1.25	.50
221	Andrew Bogut RC	3.00	1.25
222	Marvin Williams RC	5.00	2.00
223	Deron Williams RC	8.00	3.00
224	Chris Paul RC	10.00	4.00
225	Raymond Felton RC	4.00	1.50
226	Martell Webster RC	2.00	.75
227	Charlie Villanueva RC	3.00	1.25
228	Channing Frye RC	3.00	1.25
229	Ike Diogu RC	3.00	1.25
230	Andrew Bynum RC	6.00	2.50
231	Fran Vazquez RC	2.00	.75
232	Daniel Ewing RC	3.00	1.25
233	Sean May RC	2.00	.75
234	Rashad McCants RC	4.00	1.50
235	Antoine Wright RC	2.00	.75
236	Joey Graham RC	2.00	.75
237	Danny Granger RC	1.50	.60
238	Gerald Green RC	6.00	2.50
239	Hakim Warrick RC	5.00	2.00
240	Julius Hodge RC	3.00	1.25
241	Nate Robinson RC	2.00	.75
242	Jarrett Jack RC	2.00	.75
243	Francisco Garcia RC	2.00	.75
244	Luther Head RC	3.00	1.25
245	Johan Petro RC	2.00	.75
246	Jason Maxiell RC	2.00	.75
247	Linas Kleiza RC	2.00	.75
248	Ryan Gomes RC	2.00	.75
249	Wayne Simien RC	3.00	1.25
250	David Lee RC	3.00	1.25
251	Shannon Elizabeth	4.00	1.50
252	Carmen Electra	4.00	1.50
253	Jenny McCarthy	4.00	1.50
254	Christie Brinkley	4.00	1.50
255	Jay-Z	4.00	1.50

2006-07 Topps

2 AMARE STOUDEMIRE

1	Elton Brand	.50	.20
2	Tim Duncan	1.00	.40
3	Chris Paul	1.25	.50
4	Joe Johnson	.30	.12
5	Chauncey Billups	.50	.20
6	Al Harrington	.15	.05
7	Andres Nocioni	.15	.05
8	Kobe Bryant	2.00	.75
9	Al Jefferson	.50	.20
10	Gerald Wallace	.50	.20
11	Jason Terry	.50	.20
12	Dwight Howard	.60	.25
13	Larry Hughes	.30	.12
14	Sebastian Telfair	.30	.12
15	Vince Carter	1.25	.50

#	Player		
16	Mike Bibby	.50	.20
17	Ben Gordon	1.00	.40
18	Desmond Mason	.15	.05
19	Eddie Jones	.15	.05
20	Raymond Felton	.60	.25
21	Paul Pierce	.50	.20
22	Eddy Curry	.30	.12
23	Jason Richardson	.50	.20
24	Rasheed Wallace	.50	.20
25	Andrew Bogut	.60	.25
26	Stromile Swift	.30	.12
27	Peja Stojakovic	.50	.20
28	Deron Williams	.50	.20
29	Kwame Brown	.30	.12
30	Michael Redd	.50	.20
31	Shawn Marion	.50	.20
32	Shaquille O'Neal	1.25	.50
33	Larry Bird	8.00	3.00
34	Ray Allen	.50	.20
35	Marko Jaric	.15	.05
36	Luther Head	.30	.12
37	Robert Horry	.30	.12
38	Jason Collins	.15	.05
39	Cuttino Mobley	.30	.12
40	Donyell Marshall	.15	.05
41	Dirk Nowitzki	.75	.30
42	Jermaine O'Neal	.50	.20
43	Kurt Thomas	.15	.05
44	Gerald Green	.60	.25
45	Marvin Williams	.60	.25
46	Bonzi Wells	.30	.12
47	Andrei Kirilenko	.50	.20
48	J.R. Smith	.30	.12
49	Baron Davis	.50	.20
50	Tracy McGrady	1.25	.50
51	Chris Kaman	.15	.05
52	Luol Deng	.50	.20
53	Emeka Okafor	.50	.20
54	Grant Hill	.50	.20
55	Amare Stoudemire	1.00	.40
56	Lamar Odom	.50	.20
57	Eric Snow	.15	.05
58	Ike Diogu	.30	.12
59	Alonzo Mourning	.15	.05
60	Maurice Evans	.15	.05
61	Marcus Camby	.15	.05
62	Bobby Simmons	.15	.05
63	Vladimir Radmanovic	.15	.05
64	Ryan Gomes	.25	.10
65	Fred Jones	.30	.12
66	Kirk Snyder	.15	.05
67	Flip Murray	.15	.05
68	T.J. Ford	.30	.12
69	DeSagana Diop	.15	.05
70	Josh Smith	.50	.20
71	Lorenzen Wright	.15	.05
72	Nate Robinson	.50	.20
73	Brendan Haywood	.15	.05
74	Darius Miles	.50	.20
75	Keith Van Horn	.15	.05
76	Johan Petro	.15	.05
77	Yao Ming	1.25	.50
78	Darko Milicic	.50	.20
79	Smush Parker	.15	.05
80	Sarunas Jasikevicius	.30	.12
81	Mike Dunleavy	.30	.12
82	Joey Graham	.30	.12
83	Jason Williams	.30	.12
84	Melvin Ely	.15	.05
85	Ricky Davis	.50	.20
86	Michael Finley	.50	.20
87	Steve Blake	.15	.05
88	Nenad Krstic	.30	.12
89	Earl Boykins	.15	.05
90	Richard Hamilton	.30	.12
91	Chris Duhon	.15	.05
92	Hakim Warrick	.30	.12
93	Wally Szczerbiak	.30	.12
94	Corey Maggette	.30	.12
95	Leandro Barbosa	.30	.12
96	Jamaal Tinsley	.30	.12
97	Kenyon Martin	.50	.20
98	Kyle Korver	.50	.20
99	Jason Kidd	.75	.30
100	Dwyane Wade	1.50	.60
101	Ben Wallace	.50	.20
102	Mike James	.15	.05
103	Josh Howard	.30	.12
104	Joe Smith	.30	.12
105	Josh Childress	.30	.12
106	Eddie Griffin	.15	.05
107	Richard Jefferson	.30	.12
108	Jalen Rose	.40	.15
109	Mickael Pietrus	.30	.12
110	Steve Nash	.50	.20
111	Juwan Howard	.30	.12
112	Drew Gooden	.30	.12
113	Eduardo Najera	.15	.05
114	Chris Mihm	.15	.05
115	Jose Calderon	.30	.12
116	Kevin Garnett	1.00	.40
117	Rafer Alston	.15	.05
118	Delonte West	.30	.12
119	Jamaal Magloire	.15	.05
120	Channing Frye	.30	.12
121	Andre Iguodala	.50	.20
122	Pau Gasol	.50	.20
123	LeBron James	3.00	1.25
124	Antonio Daniels	.15	.05
125	James Posey	.15	.05
126	Devean George	.30	.12
127	Linas Kleiza	.15	.05
128	Brian Cook	.15	.05
129	Sean May	.30	.12
130	Sam Cassell	.50	.20
131	Mehmet Okur	.30	.12
132	Bruce Bowen	.15	.05
133	Kirk Hinrich	.50	.20
134	Chris Wilcox	.15	.05
135	Brad Miller	.50	.20
136	Erick Dampier	.15	.05
137	Primoz Brezec	.15	.05
138	Derek Fisher	.30	.12
139	Antonio McDyess	.15	.05
140	Chris Bosh	.50	.20
141	Jamal Crawford	.15	.05
142	Mike Miller	.30	.12
143	Danny Granger	.50	.20
144	Quinton Ross	.15	.05
145	Manu Ginobili	.50	.20
146	Udonis Haslem	.50	.20
147	Marquis Daniels	.30	.12
148	Maurice Williams	.15	.05
149	Viktor Khryapa	.15	.05
150	Gilbert Arenas	.50	.20
151	Tony Parker	.50	.20
152	Carlos Boozer	.30	.12
153	Quentin Richardson	.30	.12
154	Clifford Robinson	.15	.05
155	Speedy Claxton	.15	.05
156	Charlie Villanueva	.50	.20
157	Rashard Lewis	.50	.20
158	DeShawn Stevenson	.15	.05
159	Boris Diaw	.30	.12
160	Francisco Garcia	.30	.12
161	Zaza Pachulia	.15	.05
162	Raja Bell	.15	.05
163	Juan Dixon	.15	.05
164	Shaun Livingston	.40	.15
165	Shareef Abdur-Rahim	.50	.20
166	Devin Harris	.50	.20
167	Brevin Knight	.15	.05
168	Troy Murphy	.50	.20
169	Antawn Jamison	.50	.20
170	Tyson Chandler	.50	.20
171	Stephen Jackson	.30	.12
172	Shane Battier	.50	.20
173	Chris Webber	.50	.20
174	Trenton Hassell	.15	.05
175	Devin Brown	.15	.05
176	Luke Ridnour	.30	.12
177	Joel Przybilla	.15	.05
178	David West	.15	.05
179	John Salmons	.15	.05
180	Nazr Mohammed	.15	.05
181	Caron Butler	.30	.12
182	Troy Hudson	.15	.05
183	Zydrunas Ilgauskas	.15	.05
184	David Wesley	.15	.05
185	Andre Miller	.30	.12
186	Nick Collison	.15	.05
187	Ron Artest	.30	.12
188	Samuel Dalembert	.15	.05
189	Tayshaun Prince	.50	.20
190	Jameer Nelson	.30	.12
191	Zach Randolph	.50	.20
192	Stephon Marbury	.50	.20
193	Steve Francis	.50	.20
194	Matt Harpring	.30	.12
195	Kevin Martin	.50	.20
196	Rashad McCants	.60	.25
197	Carmelo Anthony	1.00	.40
198	Morris Peterson	.30	.12
199	Etan Thomas	.15	.05
200	Allen Iverson	1.00	.40
201	Antoine Walker	.50	.20
202	Eddie House	.15	.05
203	Adrian Griffin	.15	.05
204	Salim Stoudamire	.30	.12
205	Raef LaFrentz	.15	.05
206	Jared Jeffries	.15	.05
207	Rasual Butler	.15	.05
208	Damon Jones	.30	.12
209	Chuck Hayes	.15	.05
210	James Singleton	.15	.05
211	Marcus Banks	.15	.05
212	P.J. Brown	.15	.05
213	Hedo Turkoglu	.30	.12
214	Jarrett Jack	.30	.12
215	Kendrick Perkins	.15	.05
217	Leon Powe RC	2.00	.75
219	Alexander Johnson RC	2.00	.75
220	Will Blalock RC	2.00	.75
221	Steve Novak RC	2.00	.75
222	Shawne Williams RC	2.50	1.00
223	Guillermo Diaz RC	2.00	.75
224	Mardy Collins RC	2.00	.75
225	Ryan Hollins RC	2.00	.75
226	Kyle Lowry RC	2.00	.75
227	Craig Smith RC	2.00	.75
228	Denham Brown RC	2.00	.75
229	Dee Brown RC	3.00	1.25
230	Daniel Gibson RC	5.00	2.00
233	Cedric Simmons RC	2.00	.75
234	P.J. Tucker RC	2.00	.75
235	Hassan Adams RC	2.50	1.00
236	Hilton Armstrong RC	2.00	.75
237	James Augustine RC	2.00	.75
238	Josh Boone RC	2.00	.75
239	James White RC	2.00	.75
242	Maurice Ager RC	2.00	.75
244	Paul Davis RC	2.00	.75
245	Jordan Farmar RC	4.00	1.50
247	Quincy Douby RC	2.00	.75
248	Ronnie Brewer RC	2.50	1.00
249	Rodney Carney RC	2.00	.75
251	Rajon Rondo RC	2.50	1.00
252	Rudy Gay RC	4.00	1.50
253	Paul Millsap RC	4.00	1.50
254	Saer Sene RC	2.00	.75
256	Allan Ray RC	2.00	.75
257	Thabo Sefolosha RC	3.00	1.25
258	Darius Washington RC	2.00	.75
259	Renaldo Balkman RC	2.00	.75
260	Mike Gansey RC	2.00	.75
261	Solomon Jones RC	2.00	.75
262	Bobby Jones RC	2.00	.75
263	David Noel RC	2.00	.75
264	Kevin Pittsnogle RC	2.00	.75
265	Shannon Brown RC	2.00	.75
216A	Adam Morrison RC	5.00	2.00
216B	Adam Morrison Draft RC	5.00	2.00
218A	Shelden Williams RC	2.50	1.00
218B	Shelden Williams Draft RC	2.50	1.00
231A	Tyrus Thomas RC	6.00	2.50
231B	Tyrus Thomas Draft RC	6.00	2.50
240A	Patrick O'Bryant RC	2.00	.75
240A	J.J. Redick RC	4.00	1.50
240B	J.J. Redick Draft RC	4.00	1.50
241A	LaMarcus Aldridge RC	5.00	2.00
241B	LaMarcus Aldridge Draft RC	5.00	2.00
243A	Marcus Williams RC	2.50	1.00
243B	Marcus Williams Draft RC	2.50	1.00
246A	Brandon Roy RC	6.00	2.50
246B	Brandon Roy Draft RC	6.00	2.50
250A	Randy Foye RC	4.00	1.50
250B	Randy Foye Draft RC	4.00	1.50
255A	Andrea Bargnani RC	5.00	2.00

☐ 255B Andrea Bargnani Draft RC 5.00 2.00
☐ 332B Patrick O'Bryant Draft RC 2.00 .75

2005-06 Topps Big Game

☐ COMMON CARD (1-110) 1.50 .60
☐ COMMON ROOKIE (111-141) 5.00 2.00
☐ COMMON CELEBRITY (142-146) 6.00 2.50
☐ 1 Vince Carter 6.00 2.50
☐ 2 Mehmet Okur 1.50 .60
☐ 3 Andre Iguodala 2.50 1.00
☐ 4 Baron Davis 2.50 1.00
☐ 5 Drew Gooden 1.50 .60
☐ 6 Yao Ming 6.00 2.50
☐ 7 Gary Payton 2.50 1.00
☐ 8 Shaun Livingston 2.50 1.00
☐ 9 Marcus Camby 1.50 .60
☐ 10 Ben Wallace 2.50 1.00
☐ 11 Mike Miller 2.50 1.00
☐ 12 Steve Francis 2.50 1.00
☐ 13 Sam Cassell 2.50 1.00
☐ 14 Gilbert Arenas 2.50 1.00
☐ 15 Chris Bosh 2.50 1.00
☐ 16 Jamaal Magloire 1.50 .60
☐ 17 Zach Randolph 2.50 1.00
☐ 18 Josh Childress 1.50 .60
☐ 19 Kirk Hinrich 2.50 1.00
☐ 20 Dirk Nowitzki 4.00 1.50
☐ 21 Trevor Ariza 1.50 .60
☐ 22 Primoz Brezec 1.50 .60
☐ 23 LeBron James 15.00 6.00
☐ 24 Vladimir Radmanovic 1.50 .60
☐ 25 Tim Duncan 5.00 2.00
☐ 26 Damon Jones 1.50 .60
☐ 27 Rasheed Wallace 2.50 1.00
☐ 28 Corey Maggette 1.50 .60
☐ 29 Stephen Jackson 1.50 .60
☐ 30 Amare Stoudemire 5.00 2.00
☐ 31 Jason Richardson 2.50 1.00
☐ 32 Brad Miller 2.50 1.00
☐ 33 Kenyon Martin 2.50 1.00
☐ 34 Paul Pierce 2.50 1.00
☐ 35 Lamar Odom 2.50 1.00
☐ 36 Marquis Daniels 1.50 .60
☐ 37 Shane Battier 2.50 1.00
☐ 38 Eddy Curry 1.50 .60
☐ 39 Michael Redd 2.50 1.00
☐ 40 Ray Allen 2.50 1.00
☐ 41 Latrell Sprewell 2.50 1.00
☐ 42 Rafer Alston 1.50 .60
☐ 43 Brendan Haywood 1.50 .60
☐ 44 Al Harrington 1.50 .60
☐ 45 Udonis Haslem 2.50 1.00
☐ 46 Chauncey Billups 2.50 1.00
☐ 47 Andrei Kirilenko 2.50 1.00
☐ 48 Chris Webber 2.50 1.00
☐ 49 Stephon Marbury 2.50 1.00
☐ 50 Emeka Okafor 4.00 1.50
☐ 51 Cuttino Mobley 1.50 .60
☐ 52 Shawn Marion 2.50 1.00
☐ 53 Jamaal Tinsley 1.50 .60
☐ 54 Nenad Krstic 1.50 .60
☐ 55 Bob Sura 1.50 .60
☐ 56 Manu Ginobili 2.50 1.00
☐ 57 Dan Dickau 1.50 .60
☐ 58 Wally Szczerbiak 1.50 .60
☐ 59 Mike Dunleavy 1.50 .60
☐ 60 Carmelo Anthony 5.00 2.00
☐ 61 Zydrunas Ilgauskas 1.50 .60
☐ 62 Elton Brand 2.50 1.00
☐ 63 Jamal Crawford 1.50 .60
☐ 64 Grant Hill 2.50 1.00
☐ 65 Ben Gordon 5.00 2.00
☐ 66 Rashard Lewis 2.50 1.00
☐ 67 Josh Howard 1.50 .60
☐ 68 Jalen Rose 2.50 1.00
☐ 69 Pau Gasol 2.50 1.00
☐ 70 Steve Nash 2.50 1.00
☐ 71 Larry Hughes 1.50 .60
☐ 72 J.R. Smith 1.50 .60
☐ 73 Jason Kidd 4.00 1.50
☐ 74 Mike Bibby 2.50 1.00
☐ 75 Josh Smith 1.50 .60
☐ 76 Richard Hamilton 2.50 1.00
☐ 77 Caron Butler 1.50 .60
☐ 78 Richard Jefferson 1.50 .60
☐ 79 Mike Sweetney 1.50 .60
☐ 80 Shaquille O'Neal 6.00 2.50
☐ 81 Dwight Howard 3.00 1.25
☐ 82 Allen Iverson 5.00 2.00
☐ 83 Luol Deng 2.50 1.00
☐ 84 Luke Ridnour 1.50 .60
☐ 85 Desmond Mason 1.50 .60
☐ 86 Gerald Wallace 1.50 .60
☐ 87 Carlos Boozer 1.50 .60
☐ 88 Antoine Walker 2.50 1.00
☐ 89 Tony Parker 2.50 1.00
☐ 90 Tracy McGrady 6.00 2.50
☐ 91 Jermaine O'Neal 2.50 1.00
☐ 92 Andre Miller 1.50 .60
☐ 93 Quentin Richardson 1.50 .60
☐ 94 Dwyane Wade 8.00 3.00
☐ 95 Kevin Garnett 5.00 2.00
☐ 96 Peja Stojakovic 2.50 1.00
☐ 97 Antawn Jamison 2.50 1.00
☐ 98 Devin Harris 2.50 1.00
☐ 99 Kobe Bryant 10.00 4.00
☐ 100 Sebastian Telfair 1.50 .60
☐ 101 Samuel Dalembert 1.50 .60
☐ 102 Darius Miles 2.50 1.00
☐ 103 Al Jefferson 2.50 1.00
☐ 104 Brevin Knight 1.50 .60
☐ 105 Anderson Varejao 2.50 1.00
☐ 106 Troy Murphy 2.50 1.00
☐ 107 Mike James 1.50 .60
☐ 108 Maurice Williams 1.50 .60
☐ 109 Robert Horry 1.50 .60
☐ 110 Bobby Simmons 1.50 .60
☐ 111 Andrew Bogut RC 6.00 2.50
☐ 112 Gerald Green RC 12.00 5.00
☐ 113 Raymond Felton RC 8.00 3.00
☐ 114 Francisco Garcia RC 5.00 2.00
☐ 115 Hakim Warrick RC 10.00 4.00
☐ 116 Jarrett Jack RC 5.00 2.00
☐ 117 Wayne Simien RC 6.00 2.50
☐ 118 Nate Robinson RC 6.00 2.50
☐ 119 Julius Hodge RC 6.00 2.50
☐ 120 Chris Paul RC 20.00 8.00
☐ 121 Rashad McCants RC 8.00 3.00
☐ 122 Ike Diogu RC 6.00 2.50
☐ 123 Antoine Wright RC 5.00 2.00
☐ 124 Luther Head RC 6.00 2.50
☐ 125 Ryan Gomes RC 5.00 2.00
☐ 126 David Lee RC 8.00 3.00
☐ 127 Andrew Bynum RC 15.00 6.00
☐ 128 Salim Stoudamire RC 6.00 2.50
☐ 129 Sean May RC 4.00 1.50
☐ 130 Deron Williams RC 15.00 6.00
☐ 131 Joey Graham RC 5.00 2.00
☐ 132 Fran Vazquez RC 5.00 2.00
☐ 133 Brandon Bass RC 5.00 2.00
☐ 134 Jason Maxiell RC 5.00 2.00
☐ 135 Charlie Villanueva RC 6.00 2.50
☐ 136 Daniel Ewing RC 6.00 2.50
☐ 137 Channing Frye RC 6.00 2.50
☐ 138 Chris Taft RC 5.00 2.00
☐ 139 Marvin Williams RC 10.00 4.00
☐ 140 Danny Granger RC 8.00 3.00
☐ 141 Travis Diener RC 5.00 2.00
☐ 142 Shannon Elizabeth 6.00 2.50
☐ 143 Jenny McCarthy 6.00 2.50
☐ 144 Christie Brinkley 6.00 2.50
☐ 145 Jay-Z 10.00 4.00
☐ 146 Carmen Electra 6.00 2.50

2006-07 Topps Big Game

☐ 1 Dirk Nowitzki 3.00 1.25
☐ 2 Tracy McGrady 5.00 2.00
☐ 3 Elton Brand 2.00 .75
☐ 4 Ricky Davis 2.00 .75
☐ 5 Marcus Camby .60 .25
☐ 6 Gilbert Arenas 2.00 .75
☐ 7 Channing Frye 1.25 .50
☐ 8 Chauncey Billups 2.00 .75
☐ 9 Shaquille O'Neal 5.00 2.00
☐ 10 Lamar Odom 2.00 .75
☐ 11 Pau Gasol 2.00 .75
☐ 12 Charlie Villanueva 2.00 .75
☐ 13 Larry Hughes 1.25 .50
☐ 14 Peja Stojakovic 2.00 .75
☐ 15 Andre Iguodala 2.00 .75
☐ 16 Vince Carter 5.00 2.00
☐ 17 Jason Terry 2.00 .75
☐ 18 Ron Artest 1.25 .50
☐ 19 Luke Ridnour 1.25 .50
☐ 20 Paul Pierce 2.00 .75
☐ 21 Michael Redd 2.00 .75
☐ 22 Rasheed Wallace 2.00 .75
☐ 23 Baron Davis 2.00 .75
☐ 24 Amare Stoudemire 4.00 1.50
☐ 25 Zach Randolph 2.00 .75
☐ 26 Yao Ming 5.00 2.00
☐ 27 Raymond Felton 2.50 1.00
☐ 28 Stephon Marbury 2.00 .75
☐ 29 Kirk Hinrich 2.00 .75
☐ 30 Andre Miller 1.25 .50
☐ 31 Jason Kidd 3.00 1.25
☐ 32 Tayshaun Prince 2.00 .75
☐ 33 Antoine Walker 2.00 .75
☐ 34 LeBron James 12.00 5.00
☐ 35 Brad Miller 2.00 .75
☐ 36 Tim Duncan 4.00 1.50
☐ 37 Jermaine O'Neal 2.00 .75
☐ 38 Josh Smith 2.00 .75
☐ 39 Gerald Wallace 2.00 .75
☐ 40 Delonte West 1.25 .50
☐ 41 Darius Miles 1.25 .50
☐ 42 Chris Paul 5.00 2.00
☐ 43 Mike Bibby 2.00 .75
☐ 44 Sam Cassell 2.00 .75
☐ 45 Josh Howard 1.25 .50
☐ 46 Allen Iverson 4.00 1.50
☐ 47 Jameer Nelson 1.25 .50
☐ 48 Mehmet Okur .60 .25
☐ 49 Shawn Marion 2.00 .75
☐ 50 Ray Allen 2.00 .75
☐ 51 Joe Johnson 1.25 .50
☐ 52 Richard Hamilton 1.25 .50
☐ 53 Richard Jefferson 1.25 .50
☐ 54 Kobe Bryant 8.00 3.00
☐ 55 Manu Ginobili 2.00 .75
☐ 56 Carmelo Anthony 4.00 1.50
☐ 57 Ben Gordon 4.00 1.50
☐ 58 Andrew Bogut 2.00 .75
☐ 59 Antawn Jamison 2.00 .75
☐ 60 Chris Bosh 2.00 .75
☐ 61 David West .60 .25
☐ 62 Steve Nash 2.00 .75
☐ 63 Ben Wallace 2.00 .75
☐ 64 Caron Butler 1.25 .50
☐ 65 Caron Butler 1.25 .50
☐ 66 Danny Granger 1.25 .50

#	Player		
67	Andrei Kirilenko	2.00	.75
68	Kevin Garnett	4.00	1.50
69	Dwyane Wade	6.00	2.50
70	Tony Parker	2.00	.75
71	Dwight Howard	2.50	1.00
72	Rashard Lewis	2.00	.75
73	Mike Miller	2.00	.75
74	Jason Richardson	2.00	.75
75	T.J. Ford	1.25	.50
76	J.J. Redick RC	8.00	3.00
77	Marcus Williams RC	5.00	2.00
78	Shelden Williams RC	5.00	2.00
79	Tyrus Thomas RC	12.00	5.00
80	LaMarcus Aldridge RC	10.00	4.00
81	Cedric Simmons RC	4.00	1.50
82	Saer Sene RC	4.00	1.50
83	Randy Foye RC	8.00	3.00
84	Patrick O'Bryant RC	4.00	1.50
85	Adam Morrison RC	10.00	4.00
86	Rudy Gay RC	8.00	3.00
87	Ronnie Brewer RC	5.00	2.00
88	Josh Boone RC	4.00	1.50
89	Maurice Ager RC	4.00	1.50
90	Shannon Brown RC	4.00	1.50
91	Renaldo Balkman RC	4.00	1.50
92	Thabo Sefolosha RC	6.00	2.50
93	Shawne Williams RC	5.00	2.00
94	Hilton Armstrong RC	4.00	1.50
95	Brandon Roy RC	12.00	5.00
96	Kyle Lowry RC	4.00	1.50
97	Steve Novak RC	4.00	1.50
98	Paul Davis RC	4.00	1.50
99	Solomon Jones RC	4.00	1.50
100	P.J. Tucker RC	4.00	1.50
101	Rajon Rondo RC	5.00	2.00
102	Dee Brown RC	6.00	2.50
103	Craig Smith RC	4.00	1.50
104	Bobby Jones RC	4.00	1.50
105	James White RC	4.00	1.50
106	Jordan Farmar RC	8.00	3.00
107	Mardy Collins RC	4.00	1.50
108	Quincy Douby RC	4.00	1.50
109	Rodney Carney RC	4.00	1.50
110	Andrea Bargnani RC	10.00	4.00

1996-97 Topps Chrome

#	Player		
	COMPLETE SET (220)	700.00	500.00
	COMMON CARD (1-220)	.50	.20
	COMMON RC	2.50	1.00
1	Patrick Ewing	1.50	.60
2	Christian Laettner	1.00	.40
3	Mahmoud Abdul-Rauf	.50	.20
4	Chris Webber	1.50	.60
5	Jason Kidd	2.50	1.00
6	Clifford Rozier	.50	.20
7	Elden Campbell	.50	.20
8	Chuck Person	.50	.20
9	Jeff Hornacek	1.00	.40
10	Rik Smits	1.00	.40
11	Kurt Thomas	1.00	.40
12	Rod Strickland	.50	.20
13	Kendall Gill	.50	.20
14	Brian Williams	.50	.20
15	Tom Gugliotta	.50	.20
16	Ron Harper	1.00	.40
17	Eric Williams	.50	.20
18	A.C. Green	1.00	.40
19	Scott Williams	.50	.20

#	Player		
20	Damon Stoudamire	1.50	.60
21	Bryant Reeves	.50	.20
22	Bob Sura	.50	.20
23	Mitch Richmond	1.00	.40
24	Larry Johnson	1.00	.40
25	Vin Baker	1.00	.40
26	Mark Bryant	.50	.20
27	Horace Grant	1.00	.40
28	Allan Houston	1.00	.40
29	Sam Perkins	1.00	.40
30	Antonio McDyess	1.00	.40
31	Rasheed Wallace	2.00	.75
32	Malik Sealy	.50	.20
33	Scottie Pippen	2.50	1.25
34	Charles Barkley	2.00	.75
35	Hakeem Olajuwon	1.50	.60
36	John Starks	.50	.20
37	Byron Scott	.50	.20
38	Arvydas Sabonis	1.00	.40
39	Vlade Divac	.50	.20
40	Joe Dumars	1.50	.60
41	Danny Ferry	.50	.20
42	Jerry Stackhouse	2.00	.75
43	B.J. Armstrong	.50	.20
44	Shawn Bradley	.50	.20
45	Kevin Garnett	4.00	1.50
46	Dee Brown	.50	.20
47	Michael Smith	.50	.20
48	Doug Christie	1.00	.40
49	Mark Jackson	.50	.20
50	Shawn Kemp	1.00	.40
51	Sasha Danilovic	.50	.20
52	Nick Anderson	.50	.20
53	Matt Geiger	.50	.20
54	Charles Smith	.50	.20
55	Mookie Blaylock	.50	.20
56	Johnny Newman	.50	.20
57	George McCloud	.50	.20
58	Greg Ostertag	.50	.20
59	Reggie Williams	.50	.20
60	Brent Barry	.50	.20
61	Doug West	.50	.20
62	Donald Royal	.50	.20
63	Randy Brown	.50	.20
64	Vincent Askew	.50	.20
65	John Stockton	1.50	.60
66	Joe Kleine	.50	.20
67	Keith Askins	.50	.20
68	Bobby Phills	.50	.20
69	Chris Mullin	1.50	.60
70	Nick Van Exel	1.50	.60
71	Rick Fox	.50	.20
72	Chicago Bulls - 72 Wins	4.00	1.50
73	Shawn Respert	.50	.20
74	Hubert Davis	.50	.20
75	Jim Jackson	.50	.20
76	Olden Polynice	.50	.20
77	Gheorghe Muresan	.50	.20
78	Theo Ratliff	1.00	.40
79	Khalid Reeves	.50	.20
80	David Robinson	1.50	.60
81	Lawrence Moten	.50	.20
82	Sam Cassell	1.50	.60
83	George Zidek	.50	.20
84	Sharone Wright	.50	.20
85	Clarence Weatherspoon	.50	.20
86	Alan Henderson	.50	.20
87	Chris Dudley	.50	.20
88	Ed O'Bannon	.50	.20
89	Calbert Cheaney	.50	.20
90	Cedric Ceballos	.50	.20
91	Michael Cage	.50	.20
92	Ervin Johnson	.50	.20
93	Gary Trent	.50	.20
94	Sherman Douglas	.50	.20
95	Joe Smith	1.00	.40
96	Dale Davis	.50	.20
97	Tony Dumas	.50	.20
98	Muggsy Bogues	.50	.20
99	Toni Kukoc	1.00	.40
100	Grant Hill	1.50	.60
101	Michael Finley	2.00	.75
102	Isaiah Rider	1.00	.40
103	Bryant Stith	.50	.20
104	Pooh Richardson	.50	.20
105	Karl Malone	1.50	.60

#	Player		
106	Brian Grant	1.50	.60
107	Sean Elliott	1.00	.40
108	Charles Oakley	.50	.20
109	Pervis Ellison	.50	.20
110	Anfernee Hardaway	1.50	.60
111	Checklist (1-220)	.50	.20
112	Dikembe Mutombo	1.00	.40
113	Alonzo Mourning	1.00	.40
114	Hubert Davis	.50	.20
115	Rony Seikaly	.50	.20
116	Danny Manning	1.00	.40
117	Donyell Marshall	1.00	.40
118	Gerald Wilkins	.50	.20
119	Ervin Johnson	.50	.20
120	Jalen Rose	1.50	.60
121	Dino Radja	.50	.20
122	Glenn Robinson	1.50	.60
123	John Stockton	1.50	.60
124	Matt Maloney RC	2.50	1.00
125	Clifford Robinson	.50	.20
126	Steve Kerr	1.00	.40
127	Nate McMillan	.50	.20
128	Shareef Abdur-Rahim RC	30.00	12.50
129	Loy Vaught	.50	.20
130	Anthony Mason	.50	.20
131	Kevin Garnett	4.00	1.50
132	Roy Rogers RC	2.50	1.00
133	Erick Dampier RC	5.00	2.00
134	Tyus Edney	.50	.20
135	Chris Mills	.50	.20
136	Cory Alexander	.50	.20
137	Juwan Howard	1.00	.40
138	Kobe Bryant RC	200.00	100.00
139	Michael Jordan	20.00	8.00
140	Jayson Williams	1.00	.40
141	Rod Strickland	.50	.20
142	Lorenzen Wright RC	3.00	1.25
143	Will Perdue	.50	.20
144	Derek Harper	.50	.20
145	Billy Owens	.50	.20
146	Antoine Walker RC	30.00	12.50
147	P.J. Brown	.50	.20
148	Terrell Brandon	1.00	.40
149	Larry Johnson	1.00	.40
150	Steve Smith	1.00	.40
151	Eddie Jones	1.50	.60
152	Detlef Schrempf	1.00	.40
153	Dale Ellis	.50	.20
154	Isaiah Rider	1.00	.40
155	Tony Delk RC	6.00	2.50
156	Adrian Caldwell	.50	.20
157	Jamal Mashburn	1.00	.40
158	Dennis Scott	.50	.20
159	Dana Barros	.50	.20
160	Martin Muursepp RC	2.50	1.00
161	Marcus Camby RC	12.00	5.00
162	Jerome Williams RC	8.00	3.00
163	Wesley Person	.50	.20
164	Luc Longley	.50	.20
165	Charlie Ward	.50	.20
166	Mark Jackson	.50	.20
167	Derrick Coleman	1.00	.40
168	Dell Curry	.50	.20
169	Armon Gilliam	.50	.20
170	Vlade Divac	.50	.20
171	Allen Iverson RC	60.00	25.00
172	Vitaly Potapenko RC	2.50	1.00
173	Jon Koncak	.50	.20
174	Lindsey Hunter	.50	.20
175	Kevin Johnson	1.00	.40
176	Dennis Rodman	1.50	.60
177	Stephon Marbury RC	30.00	12.50
178	Karl Malone	1.50	.60
179	Charles Barkley	2.00	.75
180	Popeye Jones	.50	.20
181	Samaki Walker RC	2.50	1.00
182	Steve Nash RC	60.00	30.00
183	Latrell Sprewell	1.50	.60
184	Kenny Anderson	.50	.20
185	Tyrone Hill	.50	.20
186	Robert Pack	.50	.20
187	Greg Anthony	.50	.20
188	Derrick McKey	.50	.20
189	John Wallace RC	5.00	2.00
190	Bryon Russell	.50	.20
191	Jermaine O'Neal RC	40.00	15.00

☐ 192	Clyde Drexler	1.50	.60
☐ 193	Mahmoud Abdul-Rauf	.50	.20
☐ 194	Eric Montross	.50	.20
☐ 195	Allan Houston	1.00	.40
☐ 196	Harvey Grant	.50	.20
☐ 197	Rodney Rogers	.50	.20
☐ 198	Kerry Kittles RC	5.00	2.00
☐ 199	Grant Hill	.50	.20
☐ 200	Lionel Simmons	.50	.20
☐ 201	Reggie Miller	1.50	.60
☐ 202	Avery Johnson	.50	.20
☐ 203	LaPhonso Ellis	.50	.20
☐ 204	Brian Shaw	.50	.20
☐ 205	Priest Lauderdale RC	2.50	1.00
☐ 206	Derek Fisher RC	20.00	8.00
☐ 207	Terry Porter	.50	.20
☐ 208	Todd Fuller RC	2.50	1.00
☐ 209	Hersey Hawkins	1.00	.40
☐ 210	Tim Legler	.50	.20
☐ 211	Terry Dehere	.50	.20
☐ 212	Gary Payton	1.50	.60
☐ 213	Joe Dumars	1.50	.60
☐ 214	Don MacLean	.50	.20
☐ 215	Greg Minor	.50	.20
☐ 216	Tim Hardaway	1.00	.40
☐ 217	Ray Allen RC	40.00	15.00
☐ 218	Mario Elie	.50	.20
☐ 219	Brooks Thompson	.50	.20
☐ 220	Shaquille O'Neal	4.00	1.50

1997-98 Topps Chrome

☐ COMPLETE SET (220)		120.00	60.00
☐ COMMON CARD (1-220)		.50	.20
☐ COMMON ROOKIE		1.50	.60
☐ 1	Scottie Pippen	2.50	1.00
☐ 2	Nate McMillan	.50	.20
☐ 3	Byron Scott	.50	.20
☐ 4	Mark Davis	.50	.20
☐ 5	Rod Strickland	.50	.20
☐ 6	Brian Grant	1.00	.40
☐ 7	Damon Stoudamire	1.00	.40
☐ 8	John Stockton	1.50	.60
☐ 9	Grant Long	.50	.20
☐ 10	Darrell Armstrong	.50	.20
☐ 11	Anthony Mason	1.00	.40
☐ 12	Travis Best	.50	.20
☐ 13	Stephon Marbury	2.00	.75
☐ 14	Jamal Mashburn	1.00	.40
☐ 15	Detlef Schrempf	1.00	.40
☐ 16	Terrell Brandon	1.00	.40
☐ 17	Charles Barkley	2.00	.75
☐ 18	Vin Baker	1.00	.40
☐ 19	Gary Trent	.50	.20
☐ 20	Vinny Del Negro	.50	.20
☐ 21	Todd Day	.50	.20
☐ 22	Malik Sealy	.50	.20
☐ 23	Wesley Person	.50	.20
☐ 24	Reggie Miller	1.50	.60
☐ 25	Dan Majerle	1.00	.40
☐ 26	Todd Fuller	.50	.20
☐ 27	Juwan Howard	1.00	.40
☐ 28	Clarence Weatherspoon	.50	.20
☐ 29	Grant Hill	1.50	.60
☐ 30	John Williams	.50	.20
☐ 31	Ken Norman	.50	.20
☐ 32	Patrick Ewing	1.50	.60
☐ 33	Bryon Russell	.50	.20
☐ 34	Tony Smith	.50	.20

☐ 35	Andrew Lang	.50	.20
☐ 36	Rony Seikaly	.50	.20
☐ 37	Billy Owens	.50	.20
☐ 38	Dino Radja	.50	.20
☐ 39	Chris Gatling	.50	.20
☐ 40	Dale Davis	.50	.20
☐ 41	Arvydas Sabonis	1.00	.40
☐ 42	Chris Mills	.50	.20
☐ 43	A.C. Green	1.00	.40
☐ 44	Tyrone Hill	.50	.20
☐ 45	Tracy Murray	.50	.20
☐ 46	David Robinson	1.50	.60
☐ 47	Lee Mayberry	.50	.20
☐ 48	Jayson Williams	.50	.20
☐ 49	Jason Kidd	2.50	1.00
☐ 50	Bryant Stith	.50	.20
☐ 51	CL/Bulls - Team of the 90s	4.00	1.50
☐ 52	Brent Barry	1.00	.40
☐ 53	Henry James	.50	.20
☐ 54	Allen Iverson	4.00	1.50
☐ 55	Shandon Anderson	.50	.20
☐ 56	Mitch Richmond	1.00	.40
☐ 57	Allan Houston	1.00	.40
☐ 58	Ron Harper	1.00	.40
☐ 59	Gheorghe Muresan	.50	.20
☐ 60	Vincent Askew	.50	.20
☐ 61	Ray Allen	1.50	.60
☐ 62	Kenny Anderson	1.00	.40
☐ 63	Dikembe Mutombo	1.00	.40
☐ 64	Sam Perkins	1.00	.40
☐ 65	Walt Williams	.50	.20
☐ 66	Chris Carr	.50	.20
☐ 67	Vlade Divac	1.00	.40
☐ 68	LaPhonso Ellis	.50	.20
☐ 69	B.J. Armstrong	.50	.20
☐ 70	Jim Jackson	.50	.20
☐ 71	Clyde Drexler	1.50	.60
☐ 72	Lindsey Hunter	.50	.20
☐ 73	Sasha Danilovic	.50	.20
☐ 74	Elden Campbell	.50	.20
☐ 75	Robert Pack	.50	.20
☐ 76	Dennis Scott	.50	.20
☐ 77	Will Perdue	.50	.20
☐ 78	Anthony Peeler	.50	.20
☐ 79	Steve Smith	1.00	.40
☐ 80	Steve Kerr	1.00	.40
☐ 81	Buck Williams	.50	.20
☐ 82	Terry Mills	.50	.20
☐ 83	Michael Smith	.50	.20
☐ 84	Adam Keefe	.50	.20
☐ 85	Kevin Willis	1.00	.40
☐ 86	David Wesley	.50	.20
☐ 87	Muggsy Bogues	1.00	.40
☐ 88	Bimbo Coles	.50	.20
☐ 89	Tom Gugliotta	1.00	.40
☐ 90	Jermaine O'Neal	2.50	1.00
☐ 91	Cedric Ceballos	.50	.20
☐ 92	Shawn Kemp	1.00	.40
☐ 93	Horace Grant	1.00	.40
☐ 94	Shareef Abdur-Rahim	2.50	1.00
☐ 95	Robert Horry	1.00	.40
☐ 96	Vitaly Potapenko	.50	.20
☐ 97	Pooh Richardson	.50	.20
☐ 98	Doug Christie	.50	.20
☐ 99	Voshon Lenard	.50	.20
☐ 100	Dominique Wilkins	1.50	.60
☐ 101	Alonzo Mourning	1.00	.40
☐ 102	Sam Cassell	1.50	.60
☐ 103	Sherman Douglas	.50	.20
☐ 104	Shawn Bradley	.50	.20
☐ 105	Mark Jackson	1.00	.40
☐ 106	Dennis Rodman	1.00	.40
☐ 107	Charles Oakley	1.00	.40
☐ 108	Matt Maloney	.50	.20
☐ 109	Shaquille O'Neal	4.00	1.50
☐ 110	CL/K.Malone MVP	1.50	.60
☐ 111	Antonio McDyess	1.00	.40
☐ 112	Bob Sura	.50	.20
☐ 113	Terrell Brandon	1.00	.40
☐ 114	Tim Thomas RC	8.00	3.00
☐ 115	Tim Duncan RC	30.00	12.50
☐ 116	Antonio Daniels RC	2.00	.75
☐ 117	Bryant Reeves	.50	.20
☐ 118	Keith Van Horn RC	6.00	2.50
☐ 119	Loy Vaught	.50	.20
☐ 120	Rasheed Wallace	1.50	.60

☐ 121	Bobby Jackson RC	5.00	2.00
☐ 122	Kevin Johnson	1.00	.40
☐ 123	Michael Jordan	12.00	5.00
☐ 124	Ron Mercer RC	4.00	1.50
☐ 125	Tracy McGrady RC	30.00	12.50
☐ 126	Antoine Walker	2.00	.75
☐ 127	Carlos Rogers	.50	.20
☐ 128	Isaac Austin	.50	.20
☐ 129	Mookie Blaylock	.50	.20
☐ 130	Rodrick Rhodes RC	1.50	.60
☐ 131	Dennis Scott	.50	.20
☐ 132	Chris Mullin	1.50	.60
☐ 133	P.J. Brown	.50	.20
☐ 134	Rex Chapman	.50	.20
☐ 135	Sean Elliott	1.00	.40
☐ 136	Alan Henderson	.50	.20
☐ 137	Austin Croshere RC	4.00	1.50
☐ 138	Nick Van Exel	1.50	.60
☐ 139	Derek Strong	.50	.20
☐ 140	Glenn Robinson	1.50	.60
☐ 141	Avery Johnson	.50	.20
☐ 142	Calbert Cheaney	.50	.20
☐ 143	Mahmoud Abdul-Rauf	.50	.20
☐ 144	Stojko Vrankovic	.50	.20
☐ 145	Chris Childs	.50	.20
☐ 146	Danny Manning	1.00	.40
☐ 147	Jeff Hornacek	1.00	.40
☐ 148	Kevin Garnett	3.00	1.25
☐ 149	Joe Dumars	1.50	.60
☐ 150	Johnny Taylor RC	1.50	.60
☐ 151	Mark Price	1.00	.40
☐ 152	Toni Kukoc	1.00	.40
☐ 153	Erick Dampier	1.00	.40
☐ 154	Lorenzen Wright	.50	.20
☐ 155	Matt Geiger	.50	.20
☐ 156	Tim Hardaway	1.00	.40
☐ 157	Charles Smith RC	1.50	.60
☐ 158	Hersey Hawkins	.50	.20
☐ 159	Michael Finley	1.50	.60
☐ 160	Tyus Edney	.50	.20
☐ 161	Christian Laettner	1.00	.40
☐ 162	Doug West	.50	.20
☐ 163	Jim Jackson	.50	.20
☐ 164	Larry Johnson	1.00	.40
☐ 165	Vin Baker	1.00	.40
☐ 166	Karl Malone	1.50	.60
☐ 167	Kelvin Cato RC	2.00	.75
☐ 168	Luc Longley	.50	.20
☐ 169	Dale Davis	.50	.20
☐ 170	Joe Smith	1.00	.40
☐ 171	Kobe Bryant	8.00	3.00
☐ 172	Scot Pollard RC	2.00	.75
☐ 173	Derek Anderson RC	4.00	1.50
☐ 174	Erick Strickland RC	2.00	.75
☐ 175	Olden Polynice	.50	.20
☐ 176	Chris Whitney	.50	.20
☐ 177	Anthony Parker RC	1.50	.60
☐ 178	Armon Gilliam	.50	.20
☐ 179	Gary Payton	1.50	.60
☐ 180	Glen Rice	1.00	.40
☐ 181	Chauncey Billups RC	8.00	3.00
☐ 182	Derek Fisher	1.50	.60
☐ 183	John Starks	1.00	.40
☐ 184	Mario Elie	.50	.20
☐ 185	Chris Webber	1.50	.60
☐ 186	Shawn Kemp	1.00	.40
☐ 187	Greg Ostertag	.50	.20
☐ 188	Olivier Saint-Jean RC	1.50	.60
☐ 189	Eric Snow	1.50	.60
☐ 190	Isaiah Rider	.50	.20
☐ 191	Paul Grant RC	1.50	.60
☐ 192	Samaki Walker	.50	.20
☐ 193	Cory Alexander	.50	.20
☐ 194	Eddie Jones	1.50	.60
☐ 195	John Thomas RC	1.50	.60
☐ 196	Otis Thorpe	.50	.20
☐ 197	Rod Strickland	.50	.20
☐ 198	David Wesley	.50	.20
☐ 199	Jacque Vaughn RC	2.00	.75
☐ 200	Rik Smits	1.00	.40
☐ 201	Brevin Knight RC	2.50	1.00
☐ 202	Clifford Robinson	.50	.20
☐ 203	Hakeem Olajuwon	1.50	.60
☐ 204	Jerry Stackhouse	1.50	.60
☐ 205	Tyrone Hill	.50	.20
☐ 206	Kendall Gill	.50	.20

207 Marcus Camby	1.50	.60
208 Tony Battie RC	2.00	.75
209 Brent Price	.50	.20
210 Danny Fortson RC	5.00	2.00
211 Jerome Williams	1.00	.40
212 Maurice Taylor RC	5.00	2.00
213 Brian Williams	.50	.20
214 Keith Booth RC	1.50	.60
215 Nick Anderson	.50	.20
216 Travis Knight	.50	.20
217 Adonal Foyle RC	2.00	.75
218 Anfernee Hardaway	1.50	.60
219 Kerry Kittles	1.50	.60
220 CL/D.Mutombo Def POY	.50	.20

1998-99 Topps Chrome

COMPLETE SET (220)	150.00	75.00
COMP.SET W/PREV (230)	200.00	100.00
COMMON CARD (1-235)	.40	.15
COMMON ROOKIE	1.00	.40
1 Scottie Pippen	2.00	.75
2 Shareef Abdur-Rahim	1.25	.50
3 Rod Strickland	.40	.15
4 Keith Van Horn	1.25	.50
5 Ray Allen	1.25	.50
6 Does not exist		
7 Anthony Parker	.40	.15
8 Lindsey Hunter	.40	.15
9 Mario Elie	.40	.15
10 Does not exist		
11 Eldridge Recasner	.40	.15
12 Jeff Hornacek	.75	.30
13 Chris Webber	1.25	.50
14 Lee Mayberry	.40	.15
15 Erick Strickland	.40	.15
16 Arvydas Sabonis	.75	.30
17 Tim Thomas	.75	.30
18 Luc Longley	.40	.15
19 Does not exist		
20 Alonzo Mourning	.75	.30
21 Adonal Foyle	.40	.15
22 Tony Battie	.40	.15
23 Robert Horry	.75	.30
25 Derek Harper	.40	.15
25 Jamal Mashburn	.75	.30
26 Elliott Perry	.40	.15
27 Jalen Rose	1.25	.50
28 Joe Smith	.75	.30
29 Henry James	.40	.15
30 Travis Knight	.40	.15
31 Tom Gugliotta	.40	.15
32 Chris Anstey	.40	.15
33 Antonio Daniels	.40	.15
34 Elden Campbell	.40	.15
35 Charlie Ward	.40	.15
36 Eddie Johnson	.40	.15
37 John Wallace	.40	.15
38 Antonio Davis	.40	.15
39 Antoine Walker	1.25	.50
40 Does not exist		
41 Doug Christie	.75	.30
42 Andrew Lang	.40	.15
43 Does not exist		
44 Jaren Jackson	.40	.15
45 Loy Vaught	.40	.15
46 Allan Houston	.75	.30
47 Mark Jackson	.75	.30
48 Tracy Murray	.40	.15
49 Tim Duncan	2.00	.75
50 Micheal Williams	.40	.15
51 Steve Nash	1.25	.50
52 Matt Maloney	.40	.15
53 Sam Cassell	1.25	.50
54 Voshon Lenard	.40	.15
55 Dikembe Mutombo	.75	.30
56 Malik Sealy	.40	.15
57 Dell Curry	.40	.15
58 Stephon Marbury	1.25	.50
59 Tariq Abdul-Wahad	.40	.15
60 Does not exist		
61 Kelvin Cato	.40	.15
62 LaPhonso Ellis	.40	.15
63 Jim Jackson	.40	.15
64 Greg Ostertag	.40	.15
65 Glenn Robinson	.75	.30
66 Chris Carr	.40	.15
67 Marcus Camby	.75	.30
68 Kobe Bryant	5.00	2.00
69 Bobby Jackson	.75	.30
70 B.J. Armstrong	.40	.15
71 Alan Henderson	.40	.15
72 Terry Davis	.40	.15
73 Does not exist		
74 Lamond Murray	.40	.15
75 Does not exist		
76 Rex Chapman	.40	.15
77 Does not exist		
78 Terry Cummings	.40	.15
79 Dan Majerle	.75	.30
80 Bo Outlaw	.40	.15
81 Does not exist		
82 Vin Baker	.75	.30
83 Clifford Robinson	.40	.15
84 Greg Anthony	.40	.15
85 Brevin Knight	.40	.15
86 Jacque Vaughn	.40	.15
87 Bobby Phills	.40	.15
88 Sherman Douglas	.40	.15
89 Does not exist		
90 Does not exist		
91 Lorenzen Wright	.40	.15
92 Eric Williams	.40	.15
93 Will Perdue	.40	.15
94 Charles Barkley	1.50	.60
95 Kendall Gill	.40	.15
96 Wesley Person	.40	.15
97 Does not exist		
98 Erick Dampier	.75	.30
99 Does not exist		
100 Does not exist		
101 Rasheed Wallace	1.25	.50
102 Zydrunas Ilgauskas	.75	.30
103 Eddie Jones	1.25	.50
104 Ron Mercer	.60	.25
105 Horace Grant	.75	.30
106 Corliss Williamson	.75	.30
107 Anthony Mason	.75	.30
108 Mookie Blaylock	.40	.15
109 Dennis Rodman	.75	.30
110 Checklist	.40	.15
111 Steve Smith	.75	.30
112 Cedric Henderson	.40	.15
113 Raef LaFrentz RC	3.00	1.25
114 Calbert Cheaney	.40	.15
115 Rik Smits	.75	.30
116 Rony Seikaly	.40	.15
117 Lawrence Funderburke	.40	.15
118 Ricky Davis RC	5.00	2.00
119 Howard Eisley	.40	.15
120 Kenny Anderson	.75	.30
121 Corey Benjamin RC	2.00	.75
122 Maurice Taylor	.60	.25
123 Eric Murdock	.40	.15
124 Derek Fisher	1.25	.50
125 Kevin Garnett	2.50	1.00
126 Walt Williams	.40	.15
127 Bryce Drew RC	2.00	.75
128 A.C. Green	.75	.30
129 Ervin Johnson	.40	.15
130 Christian Laettner	.40	.15
131 Chauncey Billups	.75	.30
132 Hakeem Olajuwon	1.25	.50
133 Al Harrington RC	4.00	1.50
134 Danny Manning	.40	.15
135 Paul Pierce RC	8.00	3.00
136 Terrell Brandon	.75	.30
137 Bob Sura	.40	.15
138 Chris Gatling	.40	.15
139 Donyell Marshall	.75	.30
140 Marcus Camby	.75	.30
141 Brian Skinner RC	2.00	.75
142 Charles Oakley	.40	.15
143 Antawn Jamison RC	5.00	2.00
144 Nazr Mohammed RC	1.00	.40
145 Karl Malone	1.25	.50
146 Chris Mills	.40	.15
147 Bison Dele	.40	.15
148 Gary Payton	1.25	.50
149 Terry Porter	.40	.15
150 Tim Hardaway	.75	.30
151 Larry Hughes RC	4.00	1.50
152 Derek Anderson	1.00	.40
153 Jason Williams RC	5.00	2.00
154 Dirk Nowitzki RC	15.00	6.00
155 Juwan Howard	.75	.30
156 Avery Johnson	.40	.15
157 Matt Harpring RC	2.50	1.00
158 Reggie Miller	1.25	.50
159 Walter McCarty	.40	.15
160 Allen Iverson	2.50	1.00
161 Felipe Lopez RC	2.00	.75
162 Tracy McGrady	3.00	1.25
163 Damon Stoudamire	.75	.30
164 Antonio McDyess	.75	.30
165 Grant Hill	1.25	.50
166 Tyronn Lue RC	2.00	.75
167 P.J. Brown	.40	.15
168 Antonio Daniels	.40	.15
169 Mitch Richmond	.75	.30
170 David Robinson	1.25	.50
171 Shawn Bradley	.40	.15
172 Shandon Anderson	.40	.15
173 Chris Childs	.40	.15
174 Shawn Kemp	.75	.30
175 Shaquille O'Neal	3.00	1.25
176 John Starks	.75	.30
177 Tyrone Hill	.40	.15
178 Jayson Williams	.40	.15
179 Anfernee Hardaway	1.25	.50
180 Chris Webber	1.25	.50
181 Don Reid	.40	.15
182 Stacey Augmon	.40	.15
183 Hersey Hawkins	.40	.15
184 Sam Mitchell	.40	.15
185 Jason Kidd	2.00	.75
186 Nick Van Exel	1.25	.50
187 Larry Johnson	.75	.30
188 Bryant Reeves	.40	.15
189 Glen Rice	.75	.30
190 Kerry Kittles	.75	.30
191 Toni Kukoc	.75	.30
192 Ron Harper	.75	.30
193 Bryon Russell	.40	.15
194 Vladimir Stepania RC	1.00	.40
195 Michael Olowokandi RC	2.00	.75
196 Mike Bibby RC	10.00	4.00
197 Dale Ellis	.40	.15
198 Muggsy Bogues	.75	.30
199 Vince Carter RC	25.00	10.00
200 Robert Traylor RC	2.00	.75
201 Peja Stojakovic RC	5.00	2.00
202 Aaron McKie	.75	.30
203 Hubert Davis	.40	.15
204 Dana Barros	.40	.15
205 Bonzi Wells RC	5.00	2.00
206 Michael Doleac RC	2.00	.75
207 Keon Clark RC	2.50	1.00
208 Michael Dickerson RC	3.00	1.25
209 Nick Anderson	.40	.15
210 Brent Price	.40	.15
211 Cherokee Parks	.40	.15
212 Sam Jacobson RC	1.00	.40
213 Pat Garrity RC	1.25	.50
214 Tyrone Corbin	.40	.15
215 David Wesley	.40	.15
216 Rodney Rogers	.40	.15
217 Dean Garrett	.40	.15
218 Roshown McLeod RC	1.25	.50
219 Dale Davis	.75	.30
220 Checklist	.40	.15

❏ 221 Scottie Pippen MO	1.25	.50
❏ 222 Antonio McDyess MO	.75	.30
❏ 223 Stephon Marbury MO	1.25	.50
❏ 224 Tom Gugliotta MO	.40	.15
❏ 225 Chris Webber MO	.75	.30
❏ 226 Latrell Sprewell MO	1.25	.50
❏ 227 Mitch Richmond MO	.75	.30
❏ 228 Joe Smith MO	.40	.15
❏ 229 John Starks MO	.40	.15
❏ 230 Charles Oakley MO	.40	.15
❏ 231 Dennis Rodman MO	.40	.15
❏ 232 Eddie Jones MO	1.25	.50
❏ 233 Nick Van Exel MO	.40	.15
❏ 234 Bobby Jackson MO	.75	.30
❏ 235 Glen Rice MO	.40	.15

1999-00 Topps Chrome

❏ COMMON CARD (1-257)	.30	.10
❏ COMMON USA (249-257)	.50	.20
❏ COMMON ROOKIE	1.25	.50
❏ 1 Steve Smith	.60	.25
❏ 2 Ron Harper	.60	.25
❏ 3 Michael Dickerson	.60	.25
❏ 4 LaPhonso Ellis	.30	.10
❏ 5 Chris Webber	1.00	.40
❏ 6 Jason Caffey	.30	.10
❏ 7 Bryon Russell	.30	.10
❏ 8 Bison Dele	.30	.10
❏ 9 Isaiah Rider	.30	.10
❏ 10 Dean Garrett	.30	.10
❏ 11 Eric Murdock	.30	.10
❏ 12 Juwan Howard	.60	.25
❏ 13 Latrell Sprewell	1.00	.40
❏ 14 Jalen Rose	1.00	.40
❏ 15 Larry Johnson	.60	.25
❏ 16 Eric Williams	.30	.10
❏ 17 Bryant Reeves	.30	.10
❏ 18 Tony Battie	.30	.10
❏ 19 Luc Longley	.30	.10
❏ 20 Gary Payton	1.00	.40
❏ 21 Tariq Abdul-Wahad	.30	.10
❏ 22 Armon Gilliam UER	.30	.10
❏ 23 Shaquille O'Neal	2.50	1.00
❏ 24 Gary Trent	.30	.10
❏ 25 John Stockton	1.00	.40
❏ 26 Mark Jackson	.60	.25
❏ 27 Cherokee Parks	.30	.10
❏ 28 Michael Olowokandi	.60	.25
❏ 29 Raef LaFrentz	.60	.25
❏ 30 Dell Curry	.30	.10
❏ 31 Travis Best	.30	.10
❏ 32 Shawn Kemp	.60	.25
❏ 33 Voshon Lenard	.30	.10
❏ 34 Brian Grant	.60	.25
❏ 35 Alvin Williams	.30	.10
❏ 36 Derek Fisher	1.00	.40
❏ 37 Allan Houston	.60	.25
❏ 38 Arvydas Sabonis	.30	.10
❏ 39 Terry Cummings	.30	.10
❏ 40 Dale Ellis	.30	.10
❏ 41 Maurice Taylor	.60	.25
❏ 42 Grant Hill	1.00	.40
❏ 43 Anthony Mason	.60	.25
❏ 44 John Wallace	.30	.10
❏ 45 David Wesley	.30	.10
❏ 46 Nick Van Exel	1.00	.40
❏ 47 Cuttino Mobley	1.00	.40
❏ 48 Anfernee Hardaway	1.00	.40

❏ 49 Terry Porter	.30	.10
❏ 50 Brent Barry	.60	.25
❏ 51 Derek Harper	.60	.25
❏ 52 Antoine Walker	1.00	.40
❏ 53 Karl Malone	1.00	.40
❏ 54 Ben Wallace	1.00	.40
❏ 55 Vlade Divac	.60	.25
❏ 56 Sam Mitchell	.30	.10
❏ 57 Joe Smith	.60	.25
❏ 58 Shawn Bradley	.30	.10
❏ 59 Darrell Armstrong	.30	.10
❏ 60 Kenny Anderson	.60	.25
❏ 61 Jason Williams	1.00	.40
❏ 62 Alonzo Mourning	.60	.25
❏ 63 Matt Harpring	1.00	.40
❏ 64 Antonio Davis	.30	.10
❏ 65 Lindsey Hunter	.30	.10
❏ 66 Allen Iverson	2.00	.75
❏ 67 Mookie Blaylock	.30	.10
❏ 68 Wesley Person	.30	.10
❏ 69 Bobby Phills	.30	.10
❏ 70 Theo Ratliff	.60	.25
❏ 71 Antonio Daniels	.30	.10
❏ 72 P.J. Brown	.30	.10
❏ 73 David Robinson	1.00	.40
❏ 74 Sean Elliott	.60	.25
❏ 75 Zydrunas Ilgauskas	.60	.25
❏ 76 Kerry Kittles	.30	.10
❏ 77 Otis Thorpe	.60	.25
❏ 78 John Starks	.60	.25
❏ 79 Jaren Jackson	.30	.10
❏ 80 Hersey Hawkins	.60	.25
❏ 81 Glenn Robinson	1.00	.40
❏ 82 Paul Pierce	1.00	.40
❏ 83 Glen Rice	.60	.25
❏ 84 Charlie Ward	.30	.10
❏ 85 Dee Brown	.30	.10
❏ 86 Danny Fortson	.30	.10
❏ 87 Billy Owens	.30	.10
❏ 88 Jason Kidd	1.50	.60
❏ 89 Brent Price	.30	.10
❏ 90 Don Reid	.30	.10
❏ 91 Mark Bryant	.30	.10
❏ 92 Vinny Del Negro	.30	.10
❏ 93 Stephon Marbury	1.00	.40
❏ 94 Donyell Marshall	.60	.25
❏ 95 Jim Jackson	.30	.10
❏ 96 Horace Grant	.60	.25
❏ 97 Calbert Cheaney	.30	.10
❏ 98 Vince Carter	2.50	1.00
❏ 99 Bobby Jackson	.60	.25
❏ 100 Alan Henderson	.30	.10
❏ 101 Mike Bibby	1.00	.40
❏ 102 Cedric Henderson	.30	.10
❏ 103 Lamond Murray	.30	.10
❏ 104 A.C. Green	.60	.25
❏ 105 Hakeem Olajuwon	1.00	.40
❏ 106 George Lynch	.30	.10
❏ 107 Kendall Gill	.30	.10
❏ 108 Rex Chapman	.30	.10
❏ 109 Eddie Jones	1.00	.40
❏ 110 Kornel David RC	.30	.10
❏ 111 Jason Terry RC	5.00	2.00
❏ 112 Corey Maggette RC	6.00	2.50
❏ 113 Ron Artest RC	4.00	1.50
❏ 114 Richard Hamilton RC	10.00	4.00
❏ 115 Elton Brand RC	8.00	3.00
❏ 116 Baron Davis RC	8.00	3.00
❏ 117 Wally Szczerbiak RC	6.00	2.50
❏ 118 Steve Francis RC	8.00	3.00
❏ 119 James Posey RC	4.00	1.50
❏ 120 Shawn Marion RC	8.00	3.00
❏ 121 Tim Duncan	2.00	.75
❏ 122 Danny Manning	.30	.10
❏ 123 Chris Mullin	1.00	.40
❏ 124 Antawn Jamison	1.50	.60
❏ 125 Kobe Bryant	4.00	1.50
❏ 126 Matt Geiger	.30	.10
❏ 127 Rod Strickland	.30	.10
❏ 128 Howard Eisley	.30	.10
❏ 129 Steve Nash	1.00	.40
❏ 130 Felipe Lopez	.30	.10
❏ 131 Ron Mercer	.60	.25
❏ 132 Ruben Patterson	.60	.25
❏ 133 Dana Barros	.30	.10
❏ 134 Dale Davis	.30	.10

❏ 135 Bo Outlaw	.30	.10
❏ 136 Shandon Anderson	.30	.10
❏ 137 Mitch Richmond	.60	.25
❏ 138 Doug Christie	.60	.25
❏ 139 Rasheed Wallace	1.00	.40
❏ 140 Chris Childs	.30	.10
❏ 141 Jamal Mashburn	.60	.25
❏ 142 Terrell Brandon	.60	.25
❏ 143 Jamie Feick RC	1.25	.50
❏ 144 Robert Traylor	.30	.10
❏ 145 Rick Fox	.60	.25
❏ 146 Charles Barkley	1.25	.50
❏ 147 Tyrone Nesby RC	1.25	.50
❏ 148 Jerry Stackhouse	1.00	.40
❏ 149 Cedric Ceballos	.30	.10
❏ 150 Dikembe Mutombo	.60	.25
❏ 151 Anthony Peeler	.30	.10
❏ 152 Larry Hughes	1.00	.40
❏ 153 Clifford Robinson	.30	.10
❏ 154 Corliss Williamson	.60	.25
❏ 155 Olden Polynice	.30	.10
❏ 156 Avery Johnson	.30	.10
❏ 157 Tracy Murray	.30	.10
❏ 158 Tom Gugliotta	.30	.10
❏ 159 Tim Thomas	.60	.25
❏ 160 Reggie Miller	1.00	.40
❏ 161 Tim Hardaway	.60	.25
❏ 162 Dan Majerle	.60	.25
❏ 163 Will Perdue	.30	.10
❏ 164 Brevin Knight	.30	.10
❏ 165 Elden Campbell	.30	.10
❏ 166 Chris Gatling	.30	.10
❏ 167 Walter McCarty	.30	.10
❏ 168 Chauncey Billups	.60	.25
❏ 169 Chris Mills	.30	.10
❏ 170 Christian Laettner	.60	.25
❏ 171 Robert Pack	.30	.10
❏ 172 Rik Smits	.60	.25
❏ 173 Tyrone Hill	.30	.10
❏ 174 Damon Stoudamire	.60	.25
❏ 175 Nick Anderson	.30	.10
❏ 176 Peja Stojakovic	1.25	.50
❏ 177 Vladimir Stepania	.30	.10
❏ 178 Tracy McGrady	2.50	1.00
❏ 179 Adam Keefe	.30	.10
❏ 180 Shareef Abdur-Rahim	1.00	.40
❏ 181 Isaac Austin	.30	.10
❏ 182 Mario Elie	.30	.10
❏ 183 Rashard Lewis	1.00	.40
❏ 184 Scott Burrell	.30	.10
❏ 185 Othella Harrington	.30	.10
❏ 186 Eric Piatkowski	.30	.25
❏ 187 Bryant Stith	.30	.10
❏ 188 Michael Finley	1.00	.40
❏ 189 Chris Crawford	.30	.10
❏ 190 Toni Kukoc	.60	.25
❏ 191 Danny Ferry	.30	.10
❏ 192 Erick Dampier	.60	.25
❏ 193 Clarence Weatherspoon	.30	.10
❏ 194 Bob Sura	.30	.10
❏ 195 Jayson Williams	.30	.10
❏ 196 Kurt Thomas	.60	.25
❏ 197 Greg Anthony	.30	.10
❏ 198 Rodney Rogers	.30	.10
❏ 199 Detlef Schrempf	.60	.25
❏ 200 Keith Van Horn	1.00	.40
❏ 201 Robert Horry	.60	.25
❏ 202 Sam Cassell	1.00	.40
❏ 203 Malik Sealy	.30	.10
❏ 204 Kelvin Cato	.30	.10
❏ 205 Antonio McDyess	.60	.25
❏ 206 Andrew DeClercq	.30	.10
❏ 207 Ricky Davis	.60	.25
❏ 208 Vitaly Potapenko	.30	.10
❏ 209 Loy Vaught	.30	.10
❏ 210 Kevin Garnett	2.00	.75
❏ 211 Eric Snow	.60	.25
❏ 212 Anfernee Hardaway	1.00	.40
❏ 213 Vin Baker	.60	.25
❏ 214 Lawrence Funderburke	.30	.10
❏ 215 Jeff Hornacek	.60	.25
❏ 216 Doug West	.30	.10
❏ 217 Michael Doleac	.30	.10
❏ 218 Ray Allen	1.00	.40
❏ 219 Derek Anderson	.60	.25
❏ 220 Jerome Williams	.30	.10

#	Player		
221	Derrick Coleman	.60	.25
222	Randy Brown	.30	.10
223	Patrick Ewing	1.00	.40
224	Walt Williams	.30	.10
225	Charles Oakley	.30	.10
226	Steve Kerr	.60	.25
227	Muggsy Bogues	.60	.25
228	Kevin Willis	.30	.10
229	Marcus Camby	.60	.25
230	Scottie Pippen	1.50	.60
231	Lamar Odom RC	6.00	2.50
232	Jonathan Bender RC	6.00	2.50
233	Andre Miller RC	6.00	2.50
234	Trajan Langdon RC	2.50	1.00
235	A.Radojevic RC	1.25	.50
236	William Avery RC	2.50	1.00
237	Cal Bowdler RC	2.00	.75
238	Quincy Lewis RC	2.00	.75
239	Dion Glover RC	2.00	.75
240	Jeff Foster RC	2.00	.75
241	Kenny Thomas RC	2.50	1.00
242	Devean George RC	3.00	1.25
243	Tim James RC	2.00	.75
244	Vonteego Cummings RC	2.50	1.00
245	Jumaine Jones RC	2.50	1.00
246	Scott Padgett RC	2.00	.75
247	Adrian Griffin RC	2.00	.75
248	Chris Herren RC	1.25	.50
249	Allan Houston USA	1.00	.40
250	Kevin Garnett USA	3.00	1.25
251	Gary Payton USA	1.00	.40
252	Steve Smith USA	.50	.20
253	Tim Hardaway USA	1.00	.40
254	Tim Duncan USA	3.00	1.25
255	Jason Kidd USA	2.50	1.00
256	Tom Gugliotta USA	.50	.20
257	Vin Baker USA	.50	.20

2000-01 Topps Chrome

#	Player		
	COMPLETE SET (200)	300.00	150.00
	COMPLETE SET w/o SP's (150)	40.00	15.00
	COMMON CARD (1-150)	.30	.10
	COMMON ROOKIE (151-200)	4.00	1.50
1	Elton Brand	1.00	.40
2	Marcus Camby	.60	.25
3	Jalen Rose	1.00	.40
4	Jamie Feick	.30	.10
5	Toni Kukoc	.60	.25
6	Doug Christie	.60	.25
7	Sam Cassell	1.00	.40
8	Shaquille O'Neal	2.50	1.00
9	Larry Hughes	.60	.25
10	Jerry Stackhouse	1.00	.40
11	Rick Fox	.60	.25
12	Clifford Robinson	.30	.10
13	Dirk Nowitzki	1.50	.60
14	Cuttino Mobley	.60	.25
15	Latrell Sprewell	1.00	.40
16	Kevin Garnett	2.00	.75
17	Jerome Williams	.30	.10
18	Chris Webber	1.00	.40
19	Jason Terry	1.00	.40
20	Elden Campbell	.30	.10
21	Jonathan Bender	.60	.25
22	Scottie Pippen	1.50	.60
23	Radoslav Nesterovic	.60	.25
24	Reggie Miller	1.00	.40
25	Andre Miller	.60	.25
26	Rashard Lewis	.60	.25
27	Larry Johnson	.60	.25
28	Steve Francis	1.00	.40
29	Rod Strickland	.30	.10
30	Tim Thomas	.60	.25
31	Robert Horry	.60	.25
32	Darrell Armstrong	.30	.10
33	Vince Carter	2.50	1.00
34	Othella Harrington	.60	.25
35	Derek Anderson	.60	.25
36	Anthony Carter	.60	.25
37	Ray Allen	1.00	.40
38	Jason Kidd	1.50	.60
39	Sean Elliott	.60	.25
40	Tim Duncan	2.00	.75
41	Adrian Griffin	.30	.10
42	Wally Szczerbiak	.60	.25
43	Austin Croshere	.60	.25
44	James Posey	.60	.25
45	Alan Henderson	.30	.10
46	Jahidi White	.30	.10
47	Shawn Marion	1.00	.40
48	Lamar Odom	.60	.25
49	Keon Clark	.60	.25
50	Lamond Murray	.30	.10
51	Paul Pierce	1.00	.40
52	Charlie Ward	.30	.10
53	Horace Grant	.60	.25
54	John Stockton	1.00	.40
55	Peja Stojakovic	.60	.25
56	Christian Laettner	.60	.25
57	Keith Van Horn	.60	.25
58	Patrick Ewing	1.00	.40
59	Steve Smith	.60	.25
60	Antonio Davis	.30	.10
61	Mitch Richmond	.60	.25
62	Michael Olowokandi	.30	.10
63	Baron Davis	1.00	.40
64	Dikembe Mutombo	.60	.25
65	Rael LaFrentz	.30	.10
66	Ervin Johnson	.30	.10
67	Alonzo Mourning	.60	.25
68	Kendall Gill	.30	.10
69	George Lynch	.30	.10
70	Donyell Marshall	.60	.25
71	Bo Outlaw	.30	.10
72	Kenny Anderson	.60	.25
73	John Amaechi	.30	.10
74	Vlade Divac	.60	.25
75	Vin Baker	.60	.25
76	Mike Bibby	1.00	.40
77	Richard Hamilton	.60	.25
78	Mookie Blaylock	.30	.10
79	Vitaly Potapenko	.30	.10
80	Anthony Mason	.60	.25
81	Vonteego Cummings	.30	.10
82	Michael Finley	.60	.25
83	Ron Artest	.60	.25
84	Rodney Rogers	.30	.10
85	Team Championship	2.00	.75
86	Jason Williams	.60	.25
87	David Robinson	1.00	.40
88	Charles Oakley	.30	.10
89	Juwan Howard	.60	.25
90	Antoine Walker	1.00	.40
91	Roshown McLeod	.30	.10
92	Eddie Jones	1.00	.40
93	Allen Iverson	2.00	.75
94	Grant Hill	1.00	.40
95	Terrell Brandon	.60	.25
96	Stephon Marbury	1.00	.40
97	Jamal Mashburn	.60	.25
98	Ron Harper	.60	.25
99	Jermaine O'Neal	1.00	.40
100	Nick Van Exel	1.00	.40
101	Danny Fortson	.30	.10
102	Jim Jackson	.30	.10
103	Brad Miller	1.00	.40
104	Shawn Bradley	.30	.10
105	Mark Jackson	.60	.25
106	Maurice Taylor	.30	.10
107	Kobe Bryant	4.00	1.50
108	Clarence Weatherspoon	.30	.10
109	Eric Snow	.60	.25
110	Allan Houston	.60	.25
111	Chauncey Billups	.60	.25
112	Tom Gugliotta	.30	.10
113	Theo Ratliff	.60	.25
114	Rasheed Wallace	1.00	.40
115	Glen Rice	.60	.25
116	Bryon Russell	.30	.10
117	Tracy McGrady	2.50	1.00
118	Bryant Reeves	.30	.10
119	Damon Stoudamire	.60	.25
120	Anfernee Hardaway	1.00	.40
121	Johnny Newman	.30	.10
122	Corey Maggette	.60	.25
123	Travis Best	.30	.10
124	Hakeem Olajuwon	1.00	.40
125	Antawn Jamison	1.00	.40
126	John Starks	.60	.25
127	Antonio McDyess	.60	.25
128	Gary Payton	1.00	.40
129	Karl Malone	1.00	.40
130	Michael Dickerson	.60	.25
131	Shawn Kemp	.60	.25
132	David Wesley	.30	.10
133	P.J. Brown	.30	.10
134	Ron Mercer	.60	.25
135	Robert Traylor	.30	.10
136	Derrick Coleman	.30	.10
137	Steve Nash	1.00	.40
138	Ben Wallace	1.00	.40
139	Brian Skinner	.30	.10
140	Chris Gatling	.30	.10
141	Dale Davis	.30	.10
142	Glenn Robinson	.60	.25
143	Chucky Atkins	.30	.10
144	Brian Grant	.60	.25
145	Corliss Williamson	.60	.25
146	Shareef Abdur-Rahim	1.00	.40
147	Avery Johnson	.30	.10
148	Tim Hardaway	.60	.25
149	Isaiah Rider	.60	.25
150	Shandon Anderson	.30	.10
151	Kenyon Martin RC	12.00	5.00
152	Stromile Swift RC	8.00	3.00
153	Darius Miles RC	15.00	6.00
154	Marcus Fizer RC	4.00	1.50
155	Mike Miller RC	12.00	5.00
156	DerMarr Johnson RC	4.00	1.50
157	Chris Mihm RC	4.00	1.50
158	Jamal Crawford RC	5.00	2.00
159	Joel Przybilla RC	4.00	1.50
160	Keyon Dooling RC	4.00	1.50
161	Jerome Moiso RC	4.00	1.50
162	Etan Thomas RC	4.00	1.50
163	Courtney Alexander RC	6.00	2.50
164	Mateen Cleaves RC	4.00	1.50
165	Jason Collier RC	5.00	2.00
166	Desmond Mason RC	4.00	1.50
167	Quentin Richardson RC	5.00	2.00
168	Jamaal Magloire RC	4.00	1.50
169	Speedy Claxton RC	4.00	1.50
170	Morris Peterson RC	6.00	2.50
171	Donnell Harvey RC	4.00	1.50
172	DeShawn Stevenson RC	4.00	1.50
173	Mamadou N'Diaye RC	4.00	1.50
174	Erick Barkley RC	4.00	1.50
175	Mark Madsen RC	4.00	1.50
176	Hidayet Turkoglu RC	6.00	2.50
177	Brian Cardinal RC	4.00	1.50
178	Iakovos Tsakalidis RC	4.00	1.50
179	Dalibor Bagaric RC	4.00	1.50
180	Dragan Tarlac RC	4.00	1.50
181	Dan Langhi RC	4.00	1.50
182	A.J. Guyton RC	4.00	1.50
183	Jake Voskuhl RC	4.00	1.50
184	Khalid El-Amin RC	4.00	1.50
185	Mike Smith RC	4.00	1.50
186	Soumaila Samake RC	4.00	1.50
187	Eddie House RC	4.00	1.50
188	Eduardo Najera RC	5.00	2.00
189	Lavor Postell RC	4.00	1.50
190	Hanno Mottola RC	4.00	1.50
191	Olumide Oyedeji RC	4.00	1.50
192	Michael Redd RC	10.00	4.00
193	Chris Porter RC	4.00	1.50
194	Jabari Smith RC	4.00	1.50
195	Marc Jackson RC	4.00	1.50
196	Stephen Jackson RC	5.00	2.00
197	Pepe Sanchez RC	4.00	1.50

2001-02 Topps Chrome

#	Player		
	COMP.SET w/o RC's (129)	60.00	30.00
	COMMON CARD (1-129)	.30	.10
	COMMON ROOKIE (130-165)	2.50	1.00
1	Shaquille O'Neal	2.50	1.00
2	Steve Nash	1.00	.40
3	Allen Iverson	2.00	.75
4	Shawn Marion	1.00	.40
5	Rasheed Wallace	1.00	.40
6	Antonio Daniels	.30	.10
7	Rashard Lewis	.60	.25
8	Raef LaFrentz	.60	.25
9	Stromile Swift	.60	.25
10	Vince Carter	2.50	1.00
11	Danny Fortson	.30	.10
12	Jalen Rose	1.00	.40
13	Glen Rice	.60	.25
14	Glenn Robinson	.60	.25
15	Wally Szczerbiak	.60	.25
16	Rick Fox	.60	.25
17	Darius Miles	1.00	.40
18	Jermaine O'Neal	1.00	.40
19	Eddie Jones	1.00	.40
20	Tracy McGrady	2.50	1.00
21	Kevin Garnett	2.00	.75
22	Tim Thomas	.60	.25
23	Larry Hughes	.60	.25
24	Jerry Stackhouse	1.00	.40
25	Ray Allen	1.00	.40
26	Terrell Brandon	.60	.25
27	Keith Van Horn	.60	.25
28	Marcus Fizer	.60	.25
29	Elden Campbell	.30	.10
30	Tim Duncan	2.00	.75
31	Doug Christie	.60	.25
32	Allan Houston	.60	.25
33	Patrick Ewing	1.00	.40
34	Hakeem Olajuwon	.60	.25
35	Anfernee Hardaway	1.00	.40
36	Larry Johnson	.60	.25
37	Eric Snow	.60	.25
38	Tom Gugliotta	.30	.10
39	Scottie Pippen	1.50	.60
40	Chris Webber	1.00	.40
41	David Robinson	1.00	.40
42	Elton Brand	1.00	.40
43	Theo Ratliff	.60	.25
44	Paul Pierce	1.00	.40
45	Jamal Mashburn	.60	.25
46	Damon Stoudamire	.60	.25
47	DerMarr Johnson	.60	.25
48	Andre Miller	.60	.25
49	Dirk Nowitzki	1.50	.60
50	Kobe Bryant	4.00	1.50
51	Keyon Dooling	.60	.25
52	Brian Grant	.60	.25
53	Antawn Jamison	1.00	.40
54	Jonathan Bender	.60	.25
55	Dikembe Mutombo	.60	.25
56	Steve Smith	.60	.25
57	Hidayet Turkoglu	.60	.25
58	Robert Horry	.60	.25
59	Kurt Thomas	.60	.25
60	Jason Terry	1.00	.40
61	Vitaly Potapenko	.30	.10
62	Gary Payton	1.00	.40
63	Bonzi Wells	.60	.25
64	Raja Bell RC	5.00	2.00
65	Chris Mihm	.60	.25
66	Reggie Miller	1.00	.40
67	Lamar Odom	1.00	.40
68	Darrell Armstrong	.30	.10
69	Baron Davis	1.00	.40
70	Aaron Williams	.30	.10
71	Latrell Sprewell	1.00	.40
72	James Posey	.60	.25
73	Ben Wallace	1.00	.40
74	Marc Jackson	.60	.25
75	Maurice Taylor	.60	.25
76	Aaron McKie	.60	.25
77	Grant Hill	1.00	.40
78	Anthony Carter	.60	.25
79	Peja Stojakovic	1.00	.40
80	Jason Kidd	1.50	.60
81	Vin Baker	.60	.25
82	Morris Peterson	.60	.25
83	Bryon Russell	.30	.10
84	Michael Dickerson	.60	.25
85	Quentin Richardson	.60	.25
86	Primoz Brezec RC	3.00	1.25
87	Desmond Mason	.60	.25
88	Jason Williams	.60	.25
89	Marcus Camby	.60	.25
90	Stephon Marbury	1.00	.40
91	Mike Bibby	1.00	.40
92	Alonzo Mourning	.60	.25
93	Mitch Richmond	.60	.25
94	Donyell Marshall	.60	.25
95	Michael Jordan	20.00	8.00
96	Mike Miller	1.00	.40
97	Nick Van Exel	1.00	.40
98	Michael Finley	1.00	.40
99	Jamal Crawford	.60	.25
100	Steve Francis	1.00	.40
101	Kenyon Martin	1.00	.40
102	Sam Cassell	1.00	.40
103	Chucky Atkins	.30	.10
104	Juwan Howard	.60	.25
105	Bryant Reeves	.30	.10
106	Richard Hamilton	.60	.25
107	Antonio Davis	.30	.10
108	Antonio McDyess	.60	.25
109	Derek Anderson	.60	.25
110	Kenny Anderson	.60	.25
111	Antoine Walker	1.00	.40
112	Wang ZhiZhi	1.00	.40
113	Shareef Abdur-Rahim	1.00	.40
114	Chris Whitney	.30	.10
115	John Stockton	1.00	.40
116	Alvin Williams	.30	.10
117	David Wesley	.30	.10
118	Joe Smith	.60	.25
119	Jahidi White	.30	.10
120	Karl Malone	1.00	.40
121	Cuttino Mobley	.60	.25
122	Tyrone Hill	.30	.10
123	Clifford Robinson	.60	.25
124	Toni Kukoc	.60	.25
125	Eddie Robinson	.60	.25
126	Courtney Alexander	.60	.25
127	Ron Mercer	.60	.25
128	Lamond Murray	.30	.10
129	Rodney Rogers	.30	.10
130	Tyson Chandler RC	6.00	2.50
131	Pau Gasol RC	8.00	3.00
132	Eddy Curry RC	6.00	2.50
133	Jason Richardson RC	6.00	2.50
134	Shane Battier RC	4.00	1.50
135	Eddie Griffin RC	3.00	1.25
136	DeSagana Diop RC	2.50	1.00
137	Rodney White RC	3.00	1.25
138	Joe Johnson RC	6.00	2.50
139	Kedrick Brown RC	2.50	1.00
140	Vladimir Radmanovic RC	3.00	1.25
141	Richard Jefferson RC	6.00	2.50
142	Troy Murphy RC	5.00	2.00
143	Steven Hunter RC	2.50	1.00
144	Kirk Haston RC	2.50	1.00
145	Michael Bradley RC	2.50	1.00
146	Jason Collins RC	2.50	1.00
147	Zach Randolph RC	8.00	3.00
148	Brendan Haywood RC	3.00	1.25
149	Joseph Forte RC	6.00	2.50
150	Jeryl Sasser RC	2.50	1.00
151	Brandon Armstrong RC	3.00	1.25
152	Gerald Wallace RC	6.00	2.50
153	Samuel Dalembert RC	2.50	1.00
154	Jamaal Tinsley RC	4.00	1.50
155	Tony Parker RC	10.00	4.00
156	Trenton Hassell RC	4.00	1.50
157	Gilbert Arenas RC	10.00	4.00
158	Jeff Trepagnier RC	2.50	1.00
159	Damone Brown RC	2.50	1.00
160	Loren Woods RC	2.50	1.00
161	Andrei Kirilenko RC	6.00	2.50
162	Zeljko Rebraca RC	2.50	1.00
163	Kenny Satterfield RC	2.50	1.00
164	Alvin Jones RC	2.50	1.00
165	Kwame Brown RC	4.00	1.50

2002-03 Topps Chrome

#	Player		
	COMPLETE SET (175)	180.00	75.00
	COMMON CARD (1-165)	.25	.10
	COMMON ROOKIE	4.00	1.50
1	Shaquille O'Neal	2.50	1.00
2	Pau Gasol	1.00	.40
3	Allen Iverson	2.00	.75
4	Tom Gugliotta	.25	.10
5	Rasheed Wallace	1.00	.40
6	Peja Stojakovic	1.00	.40
7	Jason Richardson	1.00	.40
8	Rashard Lewis	.60	.25
9	Morris Peterson	.60	.25
10	Michael Jordan	8.00	3.00
11	Matt Harpring	1.00	.40
12	Shareef Abdur-Rahim	1.00	.40
13	Antoine Walker	1.00	.40
14	Stephon Marbury	1.00	.40
15	Jamal Mashburn	.60	.25
16	Eddy Curry	1.00	.40
17	Jumaine Jones	.60	.25
18	Jason Kidd	1.50	.60
19	Jerry Stackhouse	1.00	.40
20	Kenny Thomas	.25	.10
21	Kobe Bryant	4.00	1.50
22	Jason Williams	.60	.25
23	Eddie Jones	1.00	.40
24	Kenyon Martin	1.00	.40
25	Kevin Garnett	1.50	.60
26	Kurt Thomas	.60	.25
27	Karl Malone	1.00	.40
28	Reggie Evans RC	4.00	1.50
29	Dirk Nowitzki	1.50	.60
30	Vince Carter	2.50	1.00
31	Desmond Mason	.60	.25
32	Todd MacCulloch	.25	.10
33	Grant Hill	1.00	.40
34	Terrell Brandon	.60	.25
35	Tracy McGrady	2.50	1.00
36	Tim Thomas	.60	.25
37	Loren Woods	.60	.25
38	Michael Redd	.60	.25
39	Stromile Swift	.60	.25
40	Dikembe Mutombo	.60	.25
41	Richard Jefferson	.60	.25
42	Glenn Robinson	1.00	.40
43	Quentin Richardson	.60	.25
44	Elton Brand	1.00	.40

❑ 45	Reggie Miller	1.00	.40
❑ 46	Eddie Griffin	.60	.25
❑ 47	Gilbert Arenas	1.00	.40
❑ 48	Zeljko Rebraca	.60	.25
❑ 49	Mark Jackson	.25	.10
❑ 50	Juwan Howard	.60	.25
❑ 51	Nick Van Exel	1.00	.40
❑ 52	Donyell Marshall	.60	.25
❑ 53	Tyson Chandler	1.00	.40
❑ 54	Baron Davis	1.00	.40
❑ 55	Nate Huffman RC	.25	.10
❑ 56	Jamaal Magloire	.25	.10
❑ 57	Marcus Fizer	.60	.25
❑ 58	Steve Francis	1.00	.40
❑ 59	Aaron McKie	.60	.25
❑ 60	Scottie Pippen	1.50	.60
❑ 61	Mike Bibby	1.00	.40
❑ 62	Paul Pierce	1.00	.40
❑ 63	Kwame Brown	.60	.25
❑ 64	Andrei Kirilenko	1.00	.40
❑ 65	Keon Clark	.60	.25
❑ 66	Alvin Williams	.25	.10
❑ 67	Brent Barry	.60	.25
❑ 68	Doug Christie	.60	.25
❑ 69	Chris Webber	1.00	.40
❑ 70	Robert Horry	.60	.25
❑ 71	Allan Houston	.60	.25
❑ 72	Kerry Kittles	.25	.10
❑ 73	Wally Szczerbiak	.60	.25
❑ 74	Jonathan Bender	.60	.25
❑ 75	Sam Cassell	1.00	.40
❑ 76	Rod Strickland	.25	.10
❑ 77	Shane Battier	1.00	.40
❑ 78	Tim Duncan	2.00	.75
❑ 79	Jermaine O'Neal	1.00	.40
❑ 80	Cuttino Mobley	.60	.25
❑ 81	Clifford Robinson	.25	.10
❑ 82	Steve Nash	1.00	.40
❑ 83	Demarr Johnson	.25	.10
❑ 84	Courtney Alexander	.60	.25
❑ 85	Corliss Williamson	.60	.25
❑ 86	Tony Parker	1.00	.40
❑ 87	Damon Stoudamire	.60	.25
❑ 88	Jalen Rose	1.00	.40
❑ 89	Mike Miller	1.00	.40
❑ 90	Raef Lafrentz	.25	.10
❑ 91	Ben Wallace	1.00	.40
❑ 92	Ray Allen	1.00	.40
❑ 93	Gary Payton	1.00	.40
❑ 94	Derek Fisher	.60	.25
❑ 95	Michael Olowokandi	.25	.10
❑ 96	Jamaal Tinsley	1.00	.40
❑ 97	Chris Mihm	.25	.10
❑ 98	Antawn Jamison	1.00	.40
❑ 99	Mengke Bateer	1.00	.40
❑ 100	Michael Finley	1.00	.40
❑ 101	Andre Miller	.60	.25
❑ 102	Elden Campbell	.25	.10
❑ 103	Kedrick Brown	.60	.25
❑ 104	Jason Terry	1.00	.40
❑ 105	Kenny Anderson	.60	.25
❑ 106	Darius Miles	1.00	.40
❑ 107	Latrell Sprewell	1.00	.40
❑ 108	Darrell Armstrong	.25	.10
❑ 109	Joe Johnson	1.00	.40
❑ 110	Bonzi Wells	.60	.25
❑ 111	LaPhonso Ellis	.25	.10
❑ 112	Steve Smith	.60	.25
❑ 113	Vin Baker	.60	.25
❑ 114	Antonio Davis	.25	.10
❑ 115	John Stockton	1.00	.40
❑ 116	Shawn Marion	1.00	.40
❑ 117	Devean George	.60	.25
❑ 118	Joe Smith	.60	.25
❑ 119	Sean Lampley	.25	.10
❑ 120	Lamar Odom	1.00	.40
❑ 121	Alonzo Mourning	.60	.25
❑ 122	Antonio Daniels	.25	.10
❑ 123	Troy Murphy	1.00	.40
❑ 124A	Manu Ginobili RC	20.00	8.00
❑ 124B	Manu Ginobili RC	20.00	8.00
❑ 125	Richard Hamilton	.60	.25
❑ 126	Amare Stoudemire RC	20.00	8.00
❑ 127	Carlos Boozer RC	8.00	3.00
❑ 128	Casey Jacobsen RC	4.00	1.50
❑ 129	Juaquin Hawkins RC	4.00	1.50

❑ 130	Pat Burke RC	4.00	1.50
❑ 131	Dan Dickau RC	4.00	1.50
❑ 132	Drew Gooden RC	8.00	3.00
❑ 133	Fred Jones RC	4.00	1.50
❑ 134	Jared Jeffries RC	4.00	1.50
❑ 135A	Jiri Welsch RC	4.00	1.50
❑ 135B	Jiri Welsch RC	4.00	1.50
❑ 136	Juan Dixon RC	6.00	2.50
❑ 137	Marcus Haislip RC	4.00	1.50
❑ 138	Melvin Ely RC	4.00	1.50
❑ 139A	Nene Hilario RC	5.00	2.00
❑ 139B	Nene Hilario RC	5.00	2.00
❑ 140	Qyntel Woods RC	4.00	1.50
❑ 141	Lonny Baxter RC	4.00	1.50
❑ 142	Ryan Humphrey RC	4.00	1.50
❑ 143	Smush Parker RC	6.00	2.50
❑ 144	Tayshaun Prince RC	5.00	2.00
❑ 145	Vincent Yarbrough RC	4.00	1.50
❑ 146A	Yao Ming RC	30.00	12.50
❑ 146B	Yao Ming RC	30.00	12.50
❑ 147	Pete Mickeal	.25	.10
❑ 148	Tamar Slay RC	4.00	1.50
❑ 149A	Efthimios Rentzias RC	4.00	1.50
❑ 149B	Efthimios Rentzias RC	4.00	1.50
❑ 150A	Igor Rakocevic RC	4.00	1.50
❑ 150B	Igor Rakocevic RC	4.00	1.50
❑ 151A	Gordan Giricek RC	5.00	2.00
❑ 151B	Gordan Giricek RC	5.00	2.00
❑ 152A	Nikoloz Tskitishvili RC	4.00	1.50
❑ 152B	Nikoloz Tskitishvili RC	4.00	1.50
❑ 153	Mike Dunleavy RC	6.00	2.50
❑ 154A	Marko Jaric RC	4.00	1.50
❑ 154B	Marko Jaric RC	4.00	1.50
❑ 155	Kareem Rush RC	5.00	2.00
❑ 156	John Salmons RC	4.00	1.50
❑ 157	Jay Williams RC	5.00	2.00
❑ 158	J.R. Bremer RC	4.00	1.50
❑ 159	Frank Williams RC	4.00	1.50
❑ 160	Adam Harrington RC	4.00	1.50
❑ 161	DaJuan Wagner RC	6.00	2.50
❑ 162	Chris Wilcox RC	5.00	2.00
❑ 163	Chris Jefferies RC	4.00	1.50
❑ 164	Caron Butler RC	8.00	3.00
❑ 165A	Bostjan Nachbar RC	4.00	1.50
❑ 165B	Bostjan Nachbar RC	4.00	1.50

2003-04 Topps Chrome

❑ COMP.SET w/o RC's (110)		50.00	20.00
❑ COMMON CARD (1-110)		.25	.10
❑ COMMON ROOKIE (111-165)		5.00	2.00
❑ B VERSION FOR CARDS 112, 121, 127			
129, 131, 132, 138, 140, 146, 147, 149, 154			
❑ CARD B VERSION NOT IN ENGLISH			
❑ 1	Tracy McGrady	2.50	1.00
❑ 2	Dajuan Wagner	.60	.25
❑ 3	Allen Iverson	2.00	.75
❑ 4	Chris Webber	1.00	.40
❑ 5	Jason Kidd	1.50	.60
❑ 6	Stephon Marbury	1.00	.40
❑ 7	Jermaine O'Neal	1.00	.40
❑ 8	Antoine Walker	1.00	.40
❑ 9	Tony Parker	1.00	.40
❑ 10	Mike Bibby	1.00	.40
❑ 11	Yao Ming	2.50	1.00
❑ 12	Bobby Jackson	.60	.25
❑ 13	Steve Nash	1.00	.40
❑ 14	Paul Pierce	1.00	.40
❑ 15	Vince Carter	2.50	1.00

❑ 16	Peja Stojakovic	1.00	.40
❑ 17	Wally Szczerbiak	.60	.25
❑ 18	Kenyon Martin	1.00	.40
❑ 19	Pau Gasol	1.00	.40
❑ 20	Gary Payton	1.00	.40
❑ 21	Tim Duncan	2.00	.75
❑ 22	Anfernee Hardaway	1.00	.40
❑ 23	Jason Richardson	1.00	.40
❑ 24	Andre Miller	.60	.25
❑ 25	Latrell Sprewell	1.00	.40
❑ 26	Darius Miles	1.00	.40
❑ 27	Richard Jefferson	.60	.25
❑ 28	Shawn Marion	1.00	.40
❑ 29	Baron Davis	1.00	.40
❑ 30	Ben Wallace	1.00	.40
❑ 31	Reggie Miller	1.00	.40
❑ 32	Karl Malone	1.00	.40
❑ 33	Jonathan Bender	.60	.25
❑ 34	Shaquille O'Neal	2.50	1.00
❑ 35	Steve Francis	1.00	.40
❑ 36	Kobe Bryant	4.00	1.50
❑ 37	Mike Dunleavy	1.00	.40
❑ 38	Glenn Robinson	1.00	.40
❑ 39	Allan Houston	.60	.25
❑ 40	Sam Cassell	1.00	.40
❑ 41	Dirk Nowitzki	1.50	.60
❑ 42	Elton Brand	1.00	.40
❑ 43	Joe Smith	.60	.25
❑ 44	Brian Grant	.60	.25
❑ 45	Jason Terry	1.00	.40
❑ 46	Richard Hamilton	.60	.25
❑ 47	Morris Peterson	.60	.25
❑ 48	Ray Allen	1.00	.40
❑ 49	Scottie Pippen	1.50	.60
❑ 50	Jamal Crawford	.60	.25
❑ 51	Cuttino Mobley	.60	.25
❑ 52	Jerry Stackhouse	1.00	.40
❑ 53	Marcus Camby	.60	.25
❑ 54	Jalen Rose	1.00	.40
❑ 55	Ricky Davis	1.00	.40
❑ 56	Jamal Mashburn	.60	.25
❑ 57	Ron Artest	.60	.25
❑ 58	Theo Ratliff	.60	.25
❑ 59	Juwan Howard	.60	.25
❑ 60	Caron Butler	1.00	.40
❑ 61	Antawn Jamison	.60	.25
❑ 62	Nene	.60	.25
❑ 63	Tyson Chandler	.60	.25
❑ 64	Jason Williams	.60	.25
❑ 65	Kurt Thomas	.60	.25
❑ 66	Mike Miller	1.00	.40
❑ 67	Amare Stoudemire	2.50	1.00
❑ 68	Jamaal Tinsley	1.00	.40
❑ 69	Brent Barry	.60	.25
❑ 70	Brad Miller	1.00	.40
❑ 71	Bonzi Wells	.60	.25
❑ 72	Andrei Kirilenko	1.00	.40
❑ 73	Kenny Thomas	.25	.10
❑ 74	Derek Anderson	.60	.25
❑ 75	Zydrunas Ilgauskas	.60	.25
❑ 76	Eddie Griffin	.60	.25
❑ 77	Tayshaun Prince	.60	.25
❑ 78	Michael Olowokandi	.25	.10
❑ 79	Michael Redd	1.00	.40
❑ 80	Tim Thomas	.60	.25
❑ 81	Eddie Jones	1.00	.40
❑ 82	Shareef Abdur-Rahim	1.00	.40
❑ 83	Corey Maggette	.60	.25
❑ 84	Eric Snow	.60	.25
❑ 85	Keon Clark	.60	.25
❑ 86	Desmond Mason	.60	.25
❑ 87	Drew Gooden	.60	.25
❑ 88	Matt Harpring	1.00	.40
❑ 89	Antonio McDyess	1.00	.40
❑ 90	Radoslav Nesterovic	.60	.25
❑ 91	Jamaal Magloire	.25	.10
❑ 92	Rasheed Wallace	1.00	.40
❑ 93	Antonio Davis	.25	.10
❑ 94	Kwame Brown	1.00	.40
❑ 95	Manu Ginobili	1.00	.40
❑ 96	Eric Williams	.25	.10
❑ 97	Nick Van Exel	1.00	.40
❑ 98	Lamar Odom	1.00	.40
❑ 99	Chauncey Billups	.60	.25
❑ 100	Kevin Garnett	2.00	.75
❑ 101	Marko Jaric	.60	.25

❏ 102	David Wesley	.25	.10
❏ 103	Gilbert Arenas	1.00	.40
❏ 104	Keith Van Horn	1.00	.40
❏ 105	Bostjan Nachbar	.25	.10
❏ 106	Michael Finley	1.00	.40
❏ 107	Troy Murphy	1.00	.40
❏ 108	Eddy Curry	.60	.25
❏ 109	Rashard Lewis	1.00	.40
❏ 110	Tony Battie	.25	.10
❏ 111	Lebron James RC	80.00	40.00
❏ 112A	Darko Milicic RC	10.00	4.00
❏ 112B	Darko Milicic	10.00	4.00
❏ 113	Carmelo Anthony RC	25.00	10.00
❏ 114	Chris Bosh RC	15.00	6.00
❏ 115	Dwyane Wade RC	40.00	15.00
❏ 116	Chris Kaman RC	5.00	2.00
❏ 117	Kirk Hinrich RC	10.00	4.00
❏ 118	T.J. Ford RC	8.00	3.00
❏ 119	Mike Sweetney RC	5.00	2.00
❏ 120	Jarvis Hayes RC	5.00	2.00
❏ 121A	Mickael Pietrus RC	5.00	2.00
❏ 121B	Mickael Pietrus	5.00	2.00
❏ 122	Nick Collison RC	5.00	2.00
❏ 123	Marcus Banks RC	5.00	2.00
❏ 124	Luke Ridnour RC	8.00	3.00
❏ 125	Reece Gaines RC	5.00	2.00
❏ 126	Troy Bell RC	5.00	2.00
❏ 127A	Zarko Cabarkapa RC	5.00	2.00
❏ 127B	Zarko Cabarkapa	5.00	2.00
❏ 128	David West RC	5.00	2.00
❏ 129A	Aleksandar Pavlovic RC	6.00	2.50
❏ 129B	Aleksandar Pavlovic	5.00	2.00
❏ 130	Dahntay Jones RC	5.00	2.00
❏ 131A	Boris Diaw RC	6.00	2.50
❏ 131B	Boris Diaw RC	5.00	2.00
❏ 132A	Zoran Planinic RC	5.00	2.00
❏ 132B	Zoran Planinic	5.00	2.00
❏ 133	Travis Outlaw RC	5.00	2.00
❏ 134	Brian Cook RC	5.00	2.00
❏ 135	Matt Carroll RC	5.00	2.00
❏ 136	Ndudi Ebi RC	5.00	2.00
❏ 137	Kendrick Perkins RC	5.00	2.00
❏ 138A	Leandro Barbosa RC	8.00	3.00
❏ 138B	Leandro Barbosa	8.00	3.00
❏ 139	Josh Howard RC	10.00	4.00
❏ 140A	Maciej Lampe RC	5.00	2.00
❏ 140B	Maciej Lampe	5.00	2.00
❏ 141	Jason Kapono RC	5.00	2.00
❏ 142	Luke Walton RC	6.00	2.50
❏ 143	Jerome Beasley RC	5.00	2.00
❏ 144	Travis Hansen RC	5.00	2.00
❏ 145	Steve Blake RC	5.00	2.00
❏ 146A	Slavko Vranes RC	5.00	2.00
❏ 146B	Slavko Vranes	5.00	2.00
❏ 147A	Francisco Elson RC	5.00	2.00
❏ 147B	Francisco Elson RC	5.00	2.00
❏ 148	Willie Green RC	5.00	2.00
❏ 149A	Zaur Pachulia RC	5.00	2.00
❏ 149B	Zaur Pachulia	5.00	2.00
❏ 150	Keith Bogans RC	5.00	2.00
❏ 151	Maurice Williams RC	5.00	1.50
❏ 152	James Jones RC	5.00	2.00
❏ 153	Kyle Korver RC	10.00	4.00
❏ 154A	Jon Stefansson RC	5.00	2.00
❏ 154B	Jon Stefansson	5.00	2.00
❏ 155	Brandon Hunter RC	5.00	2.00
❏ 156	Josh Moore RC	5.00	2.00
❏ 157	Torraye Braggs RC	5.00	2.00
❏ 158	Devin Brown RC	5.00	2.00
❏ 159	James Lang RC	5.00	2.00
❏ 160	Theron Smith RC	5.00	2.00
❏ 161	Linton Johnson RC	5.00	2.00
❏ 162	Marquis Daniels RC	12.00	5.00
❏ 163	Keith Mcleod RC	5.00	2.00
❏ 164	Udonis Haslem RC	5.00	2.00
❏ 165	Ben Handlogten RC	5.00	2.00

2004-05 Topps Chrome

❏	COMP.SET w/o RC's (165)	40.00	15.00
❏	COMMON CARD (1-165)	.25	.10
❏	COMMON ROOKIE (166-220)	4.00	1.50
❏ 1	Allen Iverson	2.00	.75
❏ 2	Eddy Curry	.60	.25
❏ 3	Stephon Marbury	1.00	.40
❏ 4	Chris Bosh	1.00	.40
❏ 5	Jason Kidd	1.50	.60

❏ 6	Baron Davis	1.00	.40
❏ 7	Kwame Brown	.60	.25
❏ 8	Kobe Bryant	4.00	1.50
❏ 9	Ben Wallace	1.00	.40
❏ 10	Josh Howard	.60	.25
❏ 11	Yao Ming	2.50	1.00
❏ 12	Luke Walton	.60	.25
❏ 13	Nene	.60	.25
❏ 14	Michael Redd	.60	.25
❏ 15	Carmelo Anthony	2.00	.75
❏ 16	Amare Stoudemire	2.00	.75
❏ 17	Jarvis Hayes	.60	.25
❏ 18	Toni Kukoc	.60	.25
❏ 19	Latrell Sprewell	1.00	.40
❏ 20	Jason Richardson	1.00	.40
❏ 21	Kevin Garnett	2.00	.75
❏ 22	Darko Milicic	.60	.25
❏ 23	LeBron James	6.00	2.50
❏ 24	Peja Stojakovic	1.00	.40
❏ 25	Wally Szczerbiak	.60	.25
❏ 26	Theo Ratliff	.60	.25
❏ 27	Gilbert Arenas	1.00	.40
❏ 28	Mike Dunleavy	.60	.25
❏ 29	Joe Smith	.60	.25
❏ 30	Vince Carter	2.50	1.00
❏ 31	Reggie Miller	1.00	.40
❏ 32	Chris Wilcox	.60	.25
❏ 33	Rasheed Wallace	1.00	.40
❏ 34	Paul Pierce	.60	.25
❏ 35	Tayshaun Prince	.60	.25
❏ 36	Richard Hamilton	.60	.25
❏ 37	Rashard Lewis	1.00	.40
❏ 38	Joe Johnson	.60	.25
❏ 39	Zydrunas Ilgauskas	.60	.25
❏ 40	Andre Miller	.60	.25
❏ 41	Dirk Nowitzki	1.50	.60
❏ 42	Chauncey Billups	.60	.25
❏ 43	Ray Allen	1.00	.40
❏ 44	Raef LaFrentz	.60	.25
❏ 45	Mickael Pietrus	.60	.25
❏ 46	T.J. Ford	.60	.25
❏ 47	Chris Webber	1.00	.40
❏ 48	Jamaal Tinsley	1.00	.40
❏ 49	Earl Boykins	.60	.25
❏ 50	Tim Duncan	2.00	.75
❏ 51	Troy Hudson	.25	.10
❏ 52	Juan Dixon	.60	.25
❏ 53	Tim Thomas	.60	.25
❏ 54	Darius Miles	1.00	.40
❏ 55	Jalen Rose	1.00	.40
❏ 56	Kirk Hinrich	1.00	.40
❏ 57	Michael Finley	1.00	.40
❏ 58	Brad Miller	1.00	.40
❏ 59	Jonathan Bender	.60	.25
❏ 60	Manu Ginobili	1.00	.40
❏ 61	Chris Kaman	.60	.25
❏ 62	Doug Christie	.60	.25
❏ 63	Marcus Camby	.60	.25
❏ 64	Desmond Mason	.60	.25
❏ 65	Boris Diaw	.25	.10
❏ 66	Maurice Taylor	.25	.10
❏ 67	Damon Stoudamire	.60	.25
❏ 68	Dwyane Wade	3.00	1.25
❏ 69	Allan Houston	.60	.25
❏ 70	Jermaine O'Neal	1.00	.40
❏ 71	Glenn Robinson	1.00	.40
❏ 72	Morris Peterson	.60	.25
❏ 73	Luke Ridnour	.60	.25

❏ 74	Bobby Jackson	.60	.25
❏ 75	Eddie Jones	1.00	.40
❏ 76	Alvin Williams	.25	.10
❏ 77	Elton Brand	1.00	.40
❏ 78	Zach Randolph	1.00	.40
❏ 79	Marko Jaric	.60	.25
❏ 80	Mike Bibby	1.00	.40
❏ 81	Jim Jackson	.25	.10
❏ 82	Kurt Thomas	.60	.25
❏ 83	Troy Murphy	1.00	.40
❏ 84	Rodney White	.25	.10
❏ 85	Jamaal Magloire	.25	.10
❏ 86	Jamal Mashburn	.60	.25
❏ 87	Kenny Thomas	.25	.10
❏ 88	Corey Maggette	.60	.25
❏ 89	Rasho Nesterovic	.60	.25
❏ 90	Shawn Marion	1.00	.40
❏ 91	Antonio Daniels	.25	.10
❏ 92	Marquis Daniels	1.00	.40
❏ 93	Richard Jefferson	.60	.25
❏ 94	Michael Olowokandi	.25	.10
❏ 95	Bruce Bowen	.25	.10
❏ 96	Mark Blount	.25	.10
❏ 97	Sam Cassell	.60	.25
❏ 98	Voshon Lenard	.25	.10
❏ 99	Speedy Claxton	.60	.25
❏ 100	Samuel Dalembert	.25	.10
❏ 101	Tyson Chandler	.60	.25
❏ 102	Keith Van Horn	1.00	.40
❏ 103	Udonis Haslem	.25	.10
❏ 104	Trenton Hassell	.25	.10
❏ 105	Tony Parker	1.00	.40
❏ 106	Ronald Murray	.25	.10
❏ 107	Jeff McInnis	.25	.10
❏ 108	Marcus Banks	.25	.10
❏ 109	Ricky Davis	1.00	.40
❏ 110	Karl Malone	1.00	.40
❏ 111	Bonzi Wells	.60	.25
❏ 112	Antonio McDyess	1.00	.40
❏ 113	Drew Gooden	.60	.25
❏ 114	Stephen Jackson	.60	.25
❏ 115	Eric Snow	.60	.25
❏ 116	Steve Francis	1.00	.40
❏ 117	Pau Gasol	1.00	.40
❏ 118	Andrei Kirilenko	1.00	.40
❏ 119	Erick Dampier	.60	.25
❏ 120	Jason Kapono	.60	.25
❏ 121	Al Harrington	.60	.25
❏ 122	Gary Payton	1.00	.40
❏ 123	Nick Van Exel	1.00	.40
❏ 124	Cuttino Mobley	.25	.10
❏ 125	Kenyon Martin	1.00	.40
❏ 126	Mike Miller	1.00	.40
❏ 127	Jamal Crawford	.60	.25
❏ 128	Kerry Kittles	.25	.10
❏ 129	Derrick Coleman	.25	.10
❏ 130	Gordan Giricek	.60	.25
❏ 131	Antoine Walker	1.00	.40
❏ 132	Shane Battier	1.00	.40
❏ 133	Caron Butler	1.00	.40
❏ 134	Corliss Williamson	.60	.25
❏ 135	Carlos Boozer	1.00	.40
❏ 136	Tracy McGrady	2.50	1.00
❏ 137	Stromile Swift	.60	.25
❏ 138	Derek Fisher	1.00	.40
❏ 139	Juwan Howard	.60	.25
❏ 140	Jason Terry	.60	.25
❏ 141	Vlade Divac	.60	.25
❏ 142	Antawn Jamison	1.00	.40
❏ 143	Aleksandar Pavlovic	.25	.10
❏ 144	Rafer Alston	.60	.25
❏ 145	Brent Barry	.25	.10
❏ 146	Quentin Richardson	.60	.25
❏ 147	Lamar Odom	1.00	.40
❏ 148	Gerald Wallace	.60	.25
❏ 149	Charlie Ward	.25	.10
❏ 150	Jerry Stackhouse	1.00	.40
❏ 151	Carlos Arroyo	1.50	.60
❏ 152	Hedo Turkoglu	.60	.25
❏ 153	Steve Nash	1.00	.40
❏ 154	Mehmet Okur	.25	.10
❏ 155	Tyronn Lue	.25	.10
❏ 156	Bob Sura	.25	.10
❏ 157	Jason Williams	.60	.25
❏ 158	Shaquille O'Neal	2.50	1.00
❏ 159	Kelvin Cato	.25	.10

160	Eric Williams	.25	.10
161	Brian Grant	.60	.25
162	Danny Fortson	.25	.10
163	Chucky Atkins	.25	.10
164	Matt Harpring	1.00	.40
165	Primoz Brezec	.25	.10
166	Dwight Howard RC	12.00	5.00
167	Emeka Okafor RC	15.00	6.00
168	Ben Gordon RC	15.00	6.00
169	Shaun Livingston RC	6.00	2.50
170	Devin Harris RC	8.00	3.00
171	Josh Childress RC	5.00	2.00
172	Luol Deng RC	8.00	3.00
173	Rafael Araujo RC	4.00	1.50
174	Andre Iguodala RC	10.00	4.00
175	Luke Jackson RC	4.00	1.50
176	Andris Biedrins RC	6.00	2.50
177	Robert Swift RC	4.00	1.50
178	Sebastian Telfair RC	4.00	1.50
179	Kris Humphries RC	4.00	1.50
180	Al Jefferson RC	10.00	4.00
181	Kirk Snyder RC	4.00	1.50
182	Josh Smith RC	8.00	3.00
183	J.R. Smith RC	8.00	3.00
184	Dorell Wright RC	6.00	2.50
185	Jameer Nelson RC	6.00	2.50
186	Pavel Podkolzine RC	4.00	1.50
187	Horace Jenkins RC	4.00	1.50
188	Luis Flores RC	4.00	1.50
189	Delonte West RC	8.00	3.00
190	Tony Allen RC	5.00	2.00
191	Kevin Martin RC	6.00	2.50
192	Sasha Vujacic RC	4.00	1.50
193	Beno Udrih RC	6.00	2.50
194	David Harrison RC	4.00	1.50
195	Yuta Tabuse RC	8.00	3.00
196	Peter John Ramos RC	4.00	1.50
197	Chris Duhon RC	6.00	2.50
198	Trevor Ariza RC	5.00	2.00
199	Bernard Robinson RC	4.00	1.50
200	Andre Emmett RC	4.00	1.50
201	Mario Kasun RC	4.00	1.50
202	Matt Freije RC	4.00	1.50
203	Maurice Evans RC	4.00	1.50
204	Erik Daniels RC	4.00	1.50
205	Lionel Chalmers RC	4.00	1.50
206	Jared Reiner RC	4.00	1.50
207	D.J. Mbenga RC	4.00	1.50
208	Antonio Burks RC	4.00	1.50
209	Justin Reed RC	4.00	1.50
210	Pape Sow RC	4.00	1.50
211	Jackson Vroman RC	4.00	1.50
212	Romain Sato RC	4.00	1.50
213	Nenad Krstic RC	5.00	2.00
214	Damien Wilkins RC	4.00	1.50
215	Arthur Johnson RC	4.00	1.50
216	Ibrahim Kutluay RC	4.00	1.50
217	Andres Nocioni RC	5.00	2.00
218	Josh Davis RC	4.00	1.50
219	Donta Smith RC	4.00	1.50
220	Anderson Varejao RC	5.00	2.00

2005-06 Topps Chrome

COMPLETE SET (274)		120.00	60.00
COMMON CARD (1-165)		.25	.10
SEMISTARS		.60	.25
UNLISTED STARS		1.00	.40
COMMON ROOKIE (166-215)		5.00	2.00

	COMMON CELEBRITY (216-220)	4.00	1.50
	COMMON NBDL (221-274)	2.50	1.00
1	Grant Hill	1.00	.40
2	Lamar Odom	1.00	.40
3	Jamal Crawford	.60	.25
4	Ben Gordon	2.00	.75
5	Zach Randolph	.60	.25
6	Chris Duhon	.60	.25
7	Gilbert Arenas	1.00	.40
8	Yao Ming	2.50	1.00
9	Josh Smith	1.00	.40
10	Ray Allen	1.00	.40
11	Vince Carter	2.50	1.00
12	Kenyon Martin	1.00	.40
13	Tim Duncan	2.00	.75
14	Michael Redd	1.00	.40
15	Antawn Jamison	1.00	.40
16	Shane Battier	1.00	.40
17	Baron Davis	1.00	.40
18	Allen Iverson	2.00	.75
19	Jameer Nelson	.60	.25
20	Brent Barry	.30	.10
21	Zydrunas Ilgauskas	.30	.10
22	Jason Terry	1.00	.40
23	Mike Dunleavy	.60	.25
24	Paul Pierce	1.00	.40
25	Peja Stojakovic	1.00	.40
26	Andre Iguodala	1.00	.40
27	Andrei Kirilenko	1.00	.40
28	Nenad Krstic	.60	.25
29	Emeka Okafor	1.50	.60
30	Jalen Rose	.75	.30
31	Ricky Davis	1.00	.40
32	Jason Kidd	1.50	.60
33	Chauncey Billups	1.00	.40
34	Amare Stoudemire	2.00	.75
35	Josh Childress	.60	.25
36	Mehmet Okur	.30	.10
37	Shaun Livingston	.75	.30
38	Bruce Bowen	.30	.10
39	J.R. Smith	.60	.25
40	Kobe Bryant	4.00	1.50
41	Dwight Howard	1.25	.50
42	Manu Ginobili	1.00	.40
43	Keith Van Horn	.60	.25
44	Stephon Marbury	1.00	.40
45	Samuel Dalembert	.30	.10
46	Luke Ridnour	.60	.25
47	Sebastian Telfair	.60	.25
48	Tyson Chandler	1.00	.40
49	Drew Gooden	.60	.25
50	Marcus Camby	.30	.10
51	Dwyane Wade	3.00	1.25
52	Troy Murphy	1.00	.40
53	Rashard Lewis	1.00	.40
54	Shaquille O'Neal	2.50	1.00
55	Al Harrington	.30	.10
56	Al Jefferson	1.00	.40
57	Earl Boykins	.30	.10
58	Tayshaun Prince	1.00	.40
59	Carlos Boozer	.60	.25
60	Richard Jefferson	.60	.25
61	Toni Kukoc	.30	.10
62	Brad Miller	1.00	.40
63	Richard Hamilton	.60	.25
64	Kevin Garnett	2.00	.75
65	Tony Parker	1.00	.40
66	Udonis Haslem	1.00	.40
67	Dikembe Mutombo	.60	.25
68	Pau Gasol	1.00	.40
69	Chris Webber	1.00	.40
70	Ben Wallace	1.00	.40
71	Carmelo Anthony	2.00	.75
72	Dirk Nowitzki	1.50	.60
73	Tony Allen	.60	.25
74	Corey Maggette	.60	.25
75	Rasheed Wallace	1.00	.40
76	Andre Miller	.60	.25
77	Luol Deng	1.00	.40
78	Mike Miller	1.00	.40
79	Wally Szczerbiak	.60	.25
80	Chris Bosh	1.00	.40
81	Marquis Daniels	.60	.25
82	Nick Collison	.30	.10
83	Matt Harpring	1.00	.40
84	Kirk Hinrich	1.00	.40
85	Josh Howard	.60	.25
86	Elton Brand	1.00	.40
87	Tyronn Lue	.30	.10
88	Bob Sura	.30	.10
89	Chris Mihm	.30	.10
90	Brevin Knight	.30	.10
91	Jason Richardson	1.00	.40
92	Vladimir Radmanovic	.30	.10
93	Eddie Griffin	.30	.10
94	P.J. Brown	.30	.10
95	Troy Hudson	.30	.10
96	Steve Francis	1.00	.40
97	Joel Przybilla	.30	.10
98	Steve Nash	1.00	.40
99	Brendan Haywood	.30	.10
100	Primoz Brezec	.30	.10
101	Devin Harris	1.00	.40
102	Lebron James	6.00	2.50
103	Mike Bibby	1.00	.40
104	Jared Jeffries	.30	.10
105	Morris Peterson	.60	.25
106	Trevor Ariza	.60	.25
107	Shawn Marion	1.00	.40
108	Andres Nocioni	.30	.10
109	Darius Miles	1.00	.40
110	Tracy Mcgrady	2.50	1.00
111	Stephen Jackson	.60	.25
112	Joe Johnson	.60	.25
113	Bonzi Wells	.60	.25
114	Damon Jones	.60	.25
115	Rafer Alston	.30	.10
116	Cuttino Mobley	.60	.25
117	Nick Van Exel	1.00	.40
118	Jason Hart	.30	.10
119	Fred Jones	.60	.25
120	Dan Dickau	.30	.10
121	Damon Stoudamire	.60	.25
122	Kirk Snyder	.30	.10
123	Larry Hughes	.60	.25
124	Michael Finley	1.00	.40
125	Sam Cassell	1.00	.40
126	Bobby Jackson	.30	.10
127	Austin Croshere	.30	.10
128	Kwame Brown	.60	.25
129	Doug Christie	.30	.10
130	Antonio Daniels	.30	.10
131	Eddy Curry	.60	.25
132	Mike James	.30	.10
133	Juan Dixon	.30	.10
134	Jason Williams	.60	.25
135	Jeff Mcinnis	.30	.10
136	Jamaal Tinsley	.60	.25
137	Derek Anderson	.60	.25
138	Devin Brown	.30	.10
139	Raja Bell	.30	.10
140	Gary Payton	1.00	.40
141	Marko Jaric	.30	.10
142	Ron Artest	1.00	.40
143	Zaza Pachulia	.30	.10
144	Jermaine O'Neal	1.00	.40
145	Quentin Richardson	.60	.25
146	Lee Nailon	.30	.10
147	Bobby Simmons	.30	.10
148	Caron Butler	.60	.25
149	Shareef Abdur-Rahim	1.00	.40
150	Stromile Swift	.60	.25
151	Rasual Butler	.30	.10
152	Mike Sweetney	.60	.25
153	Antoine Walker	1.00	.40
154	Eddie Jones	1.00	.40
155	David Harrison	.30	.10
156	Kurt Thomas	.30	.10
157	Donyell Marshall	.30	.10
158	Brian Grant	.30	.10
159	Desmond Mason	.30	.10
160	Tim Thomas	.30	.10
161	Marc Jackson	.30	.10
162	Chucky Atkins	.30	.10
163	Jeff Foster	.30	.10
164	Jamaal Magloire	.30	.10
165	Desagana Diop	.30	.10
166	Danny Granger RC	8.00	3.00
167	Hakim Warrick RC	10.00	4.00
168	Chris Paul RC	20.00	8.00
169	Marvin Williams RC	10.00	4.00
170	Ike Diogu RC	6.00	2.50

#	Player		
171	Wayne Simien RC	6.00	2.50
172	James Singleton RC	5.00	2.00
173	Robert Whaley RC	5.00	2.00
174	Arvydas Macijauskas RC	5.00	2.00
175	Linas Kleiza RC	5.00	2.00
176	Raymond Felton RC	10.00	4.00
177	Ersan Ilyasova RC	5.00	2.00
178	Jarrett Jack RC	5.00	2.00
179	Antoine Wright RC	5.00	2.00
180	David Lee RC	8.00	3.00
181	Esteban Batista RC	5.00	2.00
182	Sarunas Jasikevicius RC	6.00	2.50
183	Francisco Garcia RC	5.00	2.00
184	C.J. Miles RC	5.00	2.00
185	Ryan Gomes RC	5.00	2.00
186	Andrew Bynum RC	12.00	5.00
187	Sean May RC	6.00	2.00
188	Jose Calderon RC	5.00	2.00
189	Rashad Mccants RC	10.00	4.00
190	Johan Petro RC	5.00	2.00
191	Jason Maxiell RC	5.00	2.00
192	Martell Webster RC	5.00	2.00
193	Nate Robinson RC	8.00	3.00
194	Daniel Ewing RC	6.00	2.50
195	Fabricio Oberto RC	5.00	2.00
196	Travis Diener RC	5.00	2.00
197	Salim Stoudamire RC	5.00	2.00
198	Charlie Villanueva RC	8.00	3.00
199	Orien Greene RC	5.00	2.00
200	Deron Williams RC	15.00	6.00
201	Bracey Wright RC	5.00	2.00
202	Lawrence Roberts RC	5.00	2.00
203	Eddie Basden RC	5.00	2.00
204	Brandon Bass RC	5.00	2.00
205	Martynas Andriuskevicius RC	5.00	2.00
206	Channing Frye RC	6.00	2.50
207	Julius Hodge RC	6.00	2.50
208	Luther Head RC	6.00	2.50
209	Chris Taft RC	5.00	2.00
210	Andrew Bogut RC	10.00	4.00
211	Gerald Green RC	10.00	4.00
212	Joey Graham RC	5.00	2.00
213	Louis Williams RC	5.00	2.00
214	Yaroslav Korolev RC	5.00	2.00
215	Monta Ellis RC	10.00	4.00
216	Christie Brinkley	4.00	1.50
217	Jay-Z	4.00	1.50
218	Shannon Elizabeth	4.00	1.50
219	Carmen Electra	4.00	1.50
220	Jenny McCarthy	60.00	25.00
221	Joe Shipp DL RC	2.50	1.00
222	Dwayne Jones DL RC	2.50	1.00
223	Will Conroy DL RC	2.50	1.00
224	Darnell Miller DL RC	2.50	1.00
225	Will Bynum DL RC	2.50	1.00
226	Jamar Smith DL RC	2.50	1.00
227	Daryl Dorsey DL RC	2.50	1.00
228	Tony Bland DL RC	2.50	1.00
229	Hiram Fuller DL RC	2.50	1.00
230	Tyrone Sally DL RC	2.50	1.00
231	Clay Tucker DL RC	2.50	1.00
232	George Leach DL RC	2.50	1.00
233	Marcus Douthit DL RC	2.50	1.00
234	Carlos Hurt DL RC	2.50	1.00
235	Seamus Boxley DL RC	2.50	1.00
236	Ramel Curry DL RC	2.50	1.00
237	Andreas Glyniadakis DL RC	2.50	1.00
238	Kareem Reid DL RC	2.50	1.00
239	Austin Nichols DL RC	2.50	1.00
240	Chris Shumate DL RC	2.50	1.00
241	Brandon Robinson DL RC	2.50	1.00
242	Harvey Thomas DL RC	2.50	1.00
243	Desmon Farmer DL RC	2.50	1.00
244	Marcus Hill DL RC	2.50	1.00
245	Robb Dryden DL RC	2.50	1.00
246	Nate Daniels DL RC	2.50	1.00
247	James Lang DL RC	2.50	1.00
248	Anthony Terrell DL RC	2.50	1.00
249	Jeff Hagen DL RC	2.50	1.00
250	Kevin Owens DL RC	2.50	1.00
251	Myron Allen DL RC	2.50	1.00
252	Ayudeji Akindele DL RC	2.50	1.00
253	T.J. Cummings DL RC	2.50	1.00
254	Mike King DL RC	2.50	1.00
255	Otis George DL RC	2.50	1.00
256	Ezra Williams DL RC	2.50	1.00
257	Anthony Wilkins DL RC	2.50	1.00
258	Scott Merritt DL RC	2.50	1.00
259	Seth Doliboa DL RC	2.50	1.00
260	Anthony Fuqua DL RC	2.50	1.00
261	Malik Moore DL RC	2.50	1.00
262	Randall Orr DL RC	2.50	1.00
263	Ricky Shields DL RC	2.50	1.00
264	John Lucas DL RC	2.50	1.00
265	Butter Johnson DL RC	2.50	1.00
266	Isiah Victor DL RC	2.50	1.00
267	Roderick Riley DL RC	2.50	1.00
268	Bernard King DL RC	2.50	1.00
269	E.J. Rowland DL RC	2.50	1.00
270	Anthony Grundy DL RC	2.50	1.00
271	Brian Jackson DL RC	2.50	1.00
272	Keith Langford DL RC	2.50	1.00
273	Chuck Hayes DL RC	2.50	1.00
274	Jonathan Moore DL RC	2.50	1.00

2006-07 Topps Chrome

#	Player		
1	Elton Brand	1.00	.40
2	Tim Duncan	2.00	.75
3	Chris Paul	2.50	1.00
4	Joe Johnson	.60	.25
5	Chauncey Billups	1.00	.40
6	Andres Nocioni	.30	.12
7	Al Jefferson	1.00	.40
8	Gerald Wallace	1.00	.40
9	Jason Terry	1.00	.40
10	Dwight Howard	1.25	.50
11	Larry Hughes	.60	.25
12	Vince Carter	2.50	1.00
13	Mike Bibby	1.00	.40
14	Ben Gordon	2.00	.75
15	Desmond Mason	.30	.12
16	Raymond Felton	1.25	.50
17	Paul Pierce	1.00	.40
18	Jason Richardson	1.00	.40
19	Rasheed Wallace	1.00	.40
20	Leandro Barbosa	.60	.25
21	Deron Williams	1.00	.40
22	Kwame Brown	.60	.25
23	Josh Childress	.60	.25
24	Shawn Marion	1.00	.40
25	Shaquille O'Neal	2.50	1.00
26	Ray Allen	1.00	.40
27	Cuttino Mobley	.60	.25
28	Dirk Nowitzki	1.50	.60
29	Jermaine O'Neal	1.00	.40
30	Marvin Williams	1.25	.50
31	Eddy Curry	.60	.25
32	Andrei Kirilenko	1.00	.40
33	Baron Davis	1.00	.40
34	Tracy McGrady	2.50	1.00
35	Chris Kaman	.30	.12
36	Luol Deng	1.00	.40
37	Emeka Okafor	1.00	.40
38	Lamar Odom	1.00	.40
39	Alonzo Mourning	.60	.25
40	Marcus Camby	.30	.12
41	Ike Diogu	.60	.25
42	Josh Smith	1.00	.40
43	Nate Robinson	1.00	.40
44	Yao Ming	2.50	1.00
45	Darko Milicic	1.00	.40
46	Smush Parker	.30	.12
47	Mike Dunleavy	.60	.25
48	Ricky Davis	1.00	.40
49	Michael Finley	1.00	.40
50	Nenad Krstic	.60	.25
51	Earl Boykins	.30	.12
52	Richard Hamilton	.60	.25
53	Hakim Warrick	.60	.25
54	Corey Maggette	.60	.25
55	Kenyon Martin	1.00	.40
56	Jason Kidd	1.50	.60
57	Dwyane Wade	3.00	1.25
58	Josh Howard	.60	.25
59	Richard Jefferson	.60	.25
60	Steve Nash	1.00	.40
61	Drew Gooden	.60	.25
62	Kevin Garnett	2.00	.75
63	Delonte West	.60	.25
64	Channing Frye	.60	.25
65	Andre Iguodala	1.00	.40
66	Pau Gasol	1.00	.40
67	LeBron James	6.00	2.50
68	Sam Cassell	1.00	.40
69	Mehmet Okur	.30	.12
70	Bruce Bowen	.30	.12
71	Kirk Hinrich	1.00	.40
72	Chris Wilcox	.30	.12
73	Brad Miller	1.00	.40
74	Chris Bosh	1.00	.40
75	Jamal Crawford	.30	.12
76	Mike Miller	1.00	.40
77	Danny Granger	.60	.25
78	Manu Ginobili	1.00	.40
79	Udonis Haslem	1.00	.40
80	Gilbert Arenas	1.00	.40
81	Tony Parker	1.00	.40
82	Carlos Boozer	.60	.25
83	Rashard Lewis	1.00	.40
84	Boris Diaw	.60	.25
85	Shaun Livingston	.75	.30
86	Shareef Abdur-Rahim	1.00	.40
87	Devin Harris	1.00	.40
88	Brevin Knight	.30	.12
89	Troy Murphy	.60	.25
90	Antawn Jamison	1.00	.40
91	Stephen Jackson	.60	.25
92	Chris Webber	1.00	.40
93	Luke Ridnour	.60	.25
94	Joel Przybilla	.30	.12
95	David West	.30	.12
96	Caron Butler	.60	.25
97	Andre Miller	.60	.25
98	Ron Artest	1.00	.40
99	Samuel Dalembert	.30	.12
100	Tayshaun Prince	1.00	.40
101	Jameer Nelson	.60	.25
102	Zach Randolph	1.00	.40
103	Stephon Marbury	1.00	.40
104	Steve Francis	1.00	.40
105	Kevin Martin	1.00	.40
106	Carmelo Anthony	2.00	.75
107	Morris Peterson	.60	.25
108	Allen Iverson	2.00	.75
109	Antoine Walker	1.00	.40
110	Jarrett Jack	.60	.25
111	Ben Wallace	1.00	.40
112	Vladimir Radmanovic	.30	.12
113	Andrew Bogut	1.25	.50
114	Nazr Mohammed	.30	.12
115	Kirk Snyder	.30	.12
116	Marquis Daniels	.60	.25
117	T.J. Ford	.60	.25
118	Stromile Swift	.60	.25
119	Lorenzen Wright	.30	.12
120	Mike James	.30	.12
121	Amare Stoudemire	2.00	.75
122	Raef LaFrentz	.30	.12
123	Adrian Griffin	.30	.12
124	Maurice Evans	.30	.12
125	David Wesley	.30	.12
126	J.R. Smith	.60	.25
127	Ronald Murray	.30	.12
128	Shane Battier	1.00	.40
129	Kobe Bryant	4.00	1.50
130	Jamaal Magloire	.30	.12
131	Charlie Villanueva	1.00	.40
132	Tyson Chandler	1.00	.40
133	Eddie House	.30	.12
134	Marcus Banks	.30	.12

❑ 135	Derek Fisher	.60	.25
❑ 136	Bobby Simmons	.30	.12
❑ 137	Al Harrington	.30	.12
❑ 138	Speedy Claxton	.30	.12
❑ 139	Viktor Khryapa	.30	.12
❑ 140	Sean May	.60	.25
❑ 141	Devean George	.60	.25
❑ 142	Joe Smith	.60	.25
❑ 143	Peja Stojakovic	1.00	.40
❑ 144	DeShawn Stevenson	.30	.12
❑ 145	Fred Jones	.60	.25
❑ 146	P.J. Brown	.30	.12
❑ 147	Sebastian Telfair	.60	.25
❑ 148	Bonzi Wells	.60	.25
❑ 149	Michael Redd	1.00	.40
❑ 150	Jared Jeffries	.30	.12
❑ 151	Larry Bird	6.00	2.50
❑ 152	Dominique Wilkins	2.00	.75
❑ 153	Isiah Thomas	1.50	.60
❑ 154	Wilt Chamberlain	1.50	.60
❑ 155	Bill Walton	1.50	.60
❑ 156	Oscar Robertson	1.50	.60
❑ 157	Walt Frazier	1.50	.60
❑ 158	Elgin Baylor	1.50	.60
❑ 159	George Gervin	1.50	.60
❑ 160	Moses Malone	1.50	.60
❑ 161	Solomon Jones RC	3.00	1.25
❑ 162	Kyle Lowry RC	3.00	1.25
❑ 163	Maurice Ager RC	3.00	1.25
❑ 164	Patrick O'Bryant RC	3.00	1.25
❑ 165	Marcus Vinicius RC	3.00	1.25
❑ 166	Jorge Garbajosa RC	6.00	2.50
❑ 167	Josh Boone RC	3.00	1.25
❑ 168	Mardy Collins RC	3.00	1.25
❑ 169	Rodney Carney RC	3.00	1.25
❑ 170	P.J. Tucker RC	3.00	1.25
❑ 171	Shelden Williams RC	4.00	1.50
❑ 172	Ryan Hollins RC	3.00	1.25
❑ 173	Pops Mensah-Bonsu RC	3.00	1.25
❑ 174	Steve Novak RC	3.00	1.25
❑ 175	Paul Davis RC	3.00	1.25
❑ 176	David Noel RC	3.00	1.25
❑ 177	Marcus Williams RC	4.00	1.50
❑ 178	Renaldo Balkman RC	3.00	1.25
❑ 179	Quincy Douby RC	3.00	1.25
❑ 180	Andrea Bargnani RC	8.00	3.00
❑ 181	Chris Quinn RC	3.00	1.25
❑ 182	Thabo Sefolosha RC	5.00	2.00
❑ 183	LaMarcus Aldridge RC	8.00	3.00
❑ 184	Rudy Gay RC	6.00	2.50
❑ 185	Jordan Farmar RC	6.00	2.50
❑ 186	Damir Markota RC	3.00	1.25
❑ 187	Mile Ilic RC	3.00	1.25
❑ 188	James Augustine RC	3.00	1.25
❑ 189	Tyrus Thomas RC	10.00	4.00
❑ 190	Brandon Roy RC	10.00	4.00
❑ 191	Allan Ray RC	3.00	1.25
❑ 192	Shannon Brown RC	3.00	1.25
❑ 193	Will Blalock RC	3.00	1.25
❑ 194	James White RC	3.00	1.25
❑ 195	Adam Morrison RC	8.00	3.00
❑ 196	Craig Smith RC	3.00	1.25
❑ 197	Cedric Simmons RC	3.00	1.25
❑ 198	J.J. Redick RC	6.00	2.50
❑ 199	Sergio Rodriguez RC	3.00	1.25
❑ 200	Ronnie Brewer RC	4.00	1.50
❑ 201	Rajon Rondo RC	4.00	1.50
❑ 202	Daniel Gibson RC	8.00	3.00
❑ 203	Hassan Adams RC	4.00	1.50
❑ 204	Shawne Williams RC	4.00	1.50
❑ 205	Alexander Johnson RC	3.00	1.25
❑ 206	Randy Foye RC	6.00	2.50
❑ 207	Hilton Armstrong RC	3.00	1.25
❑ 208	Bobby Jones RC	3.00	1.25
❑ 209	Saer Sene RC	3.00	1.25
❑ 210	Dee Brown RC	5.00	2.00

2003-04 Topps Contemporary Collection

❑ COMMON ROOKIE (1-20)		8.00	3.00
❑ COMMON AU (21-30)		15.00	6.00
❑ COMMON CARD (31-130)		.75	.30
❑ COMMON AU (131-140)		9.00	3.00
❑ 1	LeBron James RC	60.00	25.00
❑ 2	Darko Milicic RC	12.00	5.00

❑ 3	Chris Bosh RC	20.00	8.00
❑ 4	Dwyane Wade RC	30.00	12.50
❑ 5	Chris Kaman RC	8.00	3.00
❑ 6	Kirk Hinrich RC	12.00	5.00
❑ 7	Jarvis Hayes RC	8.00	3.00
❑ 8	Mickael Pietrus RC	8.00	3.00
❑ 9	Luke Ridnour RC	10.00	4.00
❑ 10	David West RC	8.00	3.00
❑ 11	Aleksandar Pavlovic RC	10.00	4.00
❑ 12	Boris Diaw RC	.10.00	4.00
❑ 13	Zoran Planinic RC	8.00	3.00
❑ 14	Francisco Elson RC	8.00	3.00
❑ 15	Leandro Barbosa RC	12.00	5.00
❑ 16	Josh Howard RC	12.00	5.00
❑ 17	Luke Walton RC	8.00	3.00
❑ 18	Willie Green RC	8.00	3.00
❑ 19	Maurice Williams RC	8.00	3.00
❑ 20	Udonis Haslem RC	8.00	3.00
❑ 21	Reece Gaines AU RC	15.00	6.00
❑ 22	Carmelo Anthony AU RC	100.00	50.00
❑ 23	Zarko Cabarkapa AU RC	15.00	6.00
❑ 24	Troy Bell AU RC	15.00	6.00
❑ 25	Travis Outlaw AU RC	15.00	6.00
❑ 26	Marcus Banks AU RC	15.00	6.00
❑ 27	Kendrick Perkins AU RC	15.00	6.00
❑ 28	Dahntay Jones AU RC	15.00	6.00
❑ 29	T.J. Ford AU RC	40.00	15.00
❑ 30	Mike Sweetney AU RC	15.00	6.00
❑ 31	Jason Terry	2.50	1.00
❑ 32	Theo Ratliff	1.50	.60
❑ 33	Raef LaFrentz	1.50	.60
❑ 34	Eddy Curry	1.50	.60
❑ 35	Ricky Davis	2.50	1.00
❑ 36	Zydrunas Ilgauskas	1.50	.60
❑ 37	Darius Miles	2.50	1.00
❑ 38	Dirk Nowitzki	4.00	1.50
❑ 39	Steve Nash	2.50	1.00
❑ 40	Antawn Jamison	2.50	1.00
❑ 41	Antoine Walker	2.50	1.00
❑ 42	Andre Miller	1.50	.60
❑ 43	Nene	1.50	.60
❑ 44	Richard Hamilton	2.50	1.00
❑ 45	Ben Wallace	2.50	1.00
❑ 46	Jason Richardson	2.50	1.00
❑ 47	Nick Van Exel	2.50	1.00
❑ 48	Troy Murphy	2.50	1.00
❑ 49	Yao Ming	6.00	2.50
❑ 50	Steve Francis	2.50	1.00
❑ 51	Ron Artest	1.50	.60
❑ 52	Jermaine O'Neal	2.50	1.00
❑ 53	Al Harrington	1.50	.60
❑ 54	Marko Jaric	1.50	.60
❑ 55	Corey Maggette	1.50	.60
❑ 56	Kobe Bryant	10.00	4.00
❑ 57	Shaquille O'Neal	6.00	2.50
❑ 58	Devean George	1.50	.60
❑ 59	Gary Payton	2.50	1.00
❑ 60	Pau Gasol	2.50	1.00
❑ 61	Stromile Swift	1.50	.60
❑ 62	Mike Miller	2.50	1.00
❑ 63	Lamar Odom	2.50	1.00
❑ 64	Caron Butler	2.50	1.00
❑ 65	Eddie Jones	2.50	1.00
❑ 66	Brian Grant	1.50	.60
❑ 67	Desmond Mason	1.50	.60
❑ 68	Tim Thomas	1.50	.60
❑ 69	Michael Redd	2.50	1.00
❑ 70	Sam Cassell	2.50	1.00

❑ 71	Kevin Garnett	5.00	2.00
❑ 72	Latrell Sprewell	2.50	1.00
❑ 73	Michael Olowokandi	.75	.30
❑ 74	Wally Szczerbiak	1.50	.60
❑ 75	Richard Jefferson	1.50	.60
❑ 76	Kenyon Martin	2.50	1.00
❑ 77	Alonzo Mourning	1.50	.60
❑ 78	Baron Davis	2.50	1.00
❑ 79	Jamal Mashburn	1.50	.60
❑ 80	Allan Houston	1.50	.60
❑ 81	Keith Van Horn	2.50	1.00
❑ 82	Kurt Thomas	1.50	.60
❑ 83	Tracy McGrady	6.00	2.50
❑ 84	Juwan Howard	1.50	.60
❑ 85	Drew Gooden	1.50	.60
❑ 86	Allen Iverson	5.00	2.00
❑ 87	Glenn Robinson	2.50	1.00
❑ 88	Derrick Coleman	.75	.30
❑ 89	Stephon Marbury	2.50	1.00
❑ 90	Shawn Marion	2.50	1.00
❑ 91	Amare Stoudemire	5.00	2.00
❑ 92	Zach Randolph	2.50	1.00
❑ 93	Rasheed Wallace	2.50	1.00
❑ 94	Bonzi Wells	1.50	.60
❑ 95	Mike Bibby	2.50	1.00
❑ 96	Chris Webber	2.50	1.00
❑ 97	Brad Miller	2.50	1.00
❑ 98	Tim Duncan	5.00	2.00
❑ 99	Nesterovic	1.50	.60
❑ 100	Tony Parker	2.50	1.00
❑ 101	Manu Ginobili	2.50	1.00
❑ 102	Brent Barry	1.50	.60
❑ 103	Rashard Lewis	2.50	1.00
❑ 104	Ray Allen	2.50	1.00
❑ 105	Vince Carter	6.00	2.50
❑ 106	Jerome Williams	.75	.30
❑ 107	Carlos Arroyo	4.00	1.50
❑ 108	Matt Harpring	2.50	1.00
❑ 109	Andrei Kirilenko	2.50	1.00
❑ 110	Gilbert Arenas	2.50	1.00
❑ 111	Kwame Brown	1.50	.60
❑ 112	Jerry Stackhouse	2.50	1.00
❑ 113	Darrell Armstrong	.75	.30
❑ 114	Alvin Williams	.75	.30
❑ 115	Kelvin Cato	.75	.30
❑ 116	Stephen Jackson	.75	.30
❑ 117	Shareef Abdur-Rahim	2.50	1.00
❑ 118	Eric Williams	.75	.30
❑ 119	Tony Battie	.75	.30
❑ 120	Tyson Chandler	2.50	1.00
❑ 121	Scottie Pippen	4.00	1.50
❑ 122	Nikoloz Tskitishvili	.75	.30
❑ 123	Chauncey Billups	1.50	.60
❑ 124	Quentin Richardson	1.50	.60
❑ 125	Dikembe Mutombo	1.50	.60
❑ 126	Joe Smith	1.50	.60
❑ 127	Qyntel Woods	.75	.30
❑ 128	Dajuan Wagner	1.50	.60
❑ 129	Robert Horry	1.50	.60
❑ 130	Cuttino Mobley	1.50	.60
❑ 131	Bobby Jackson AU	15.00	6.00
❑ 132	Elton Brand AU	15.00	6.00
❑ 133	Peja Stojakovic AU	20.00	8.00
❑ 134	Jamal Crawford AU	15.00	6.00
❑ 135	Jalen Rose AU	15.00	6.00
❑ 136	Paul Pierce AU	30.00	12.50
❑ 137	Jason Kidd AU	30.00	12.50
❑ 138	Tayshaun Prince AU	15.00	6.00
❑ 139	Morris Peterson AU	15.00	6.00
❑ 140	Speedy Claxton AU	15.00	6.00

2005-06 Topps First Row

❑ COMP.SET (100)			
❑ COMMON CARD (1-100)		.40	.15
❑ COMMON ROOKIE (101-145)		6.00	2.50
❑ COMMON CELEBRITY (146-150)		10.00	4.00
❑ 1	Shaquille O'Neal	3.00	1.25
❑ 2	Marcus Camby	.40	.15
❑ 3	Caron Butler	.75	.30
❑ 4	Carlos Boozer	.75	.30
❑ 5	Peja Stojakovic	1.25	.50
❑ 6	Chris Webber	1.25	.50
❑ 7	Vince Carter	3.00	1.25
❑ 8	Bobby Simmons	.40	.15
❑ 9	Pau Gasol	1.25	.50
❑ 10	Stromile Swift	.75	.30

#	Player		
☐ 11	Carmelo Anthony	2.50	1.00
☐ 12	Drew Gooden	.75	.30
☐ 13	Al Harrington	.40	.15
☐ 14	Emeka Okafor	2.00	.75
☐ 15	Gilbert Arenas	1.25	.50
☐ 16	Tony Parker	1.25	.50
☐ 17	Steve Nash	1.25	.50
☐ 18	Jamal Crawford	.75	.30
☐ 19	Troy Hudson	.40	.15
☐ 20	Kobe Bryant	5.00	2.00
☐ 21	Tracy McGrady	3.00	1.25
☐ 22	Chauncey Billups	1.25	.50
☐ 23	Devin Harris	1.25	.50
☐ 24	Brevin Knight	.40	.15
☐ 25	Joe Johnson	.75	.30
☐ 26	Nenad Krstic	.75	.30
☐ 27	Primoz Brezec	.40	.15
☐ 28	Mehmet Okur	.40	.15
☐ 29	Shareef Abdur-Rahim	1.25	.50
☐ 30	Amare Stoudemire	2.50	1.00
☐ 31	Quentin Richardson	.75	.30
☐ 32	Kevin Garnett	2.50	1.00
☐ 33	Shane Battier	1.25	.50
☐ 34	Elton Brand	1.25	.50
☐ 35	Kenyon Martin	1.25	.50
☐ 36	LeBron James	8.00	3.00
☐ 37	Al Jefferson	1.25	.50
☐ 38	Jermaine O'Neal	1.25	.50
☐ 39	Ron Artest	.75	.30
☐ 40	Luke Ridnour	.75	.30
☐ 41	Sebastian Telfair	.75	.30
☐ 42	Steve Francis	1.25	.50
☐ 43	Jason Kidd	2.00	.75
☐ 44	Ben Wallace	1.25	.50
☐ 45	Mike Miller	1.25	.50
☐ 46	Jamaal Tinsley	.75	.30
☐ 47	Richard Hamilton	.75	.30
☐ 48	Jerry Stackhouse	1.25	.50
☐ 49	Kirk Hinrich	1.25	.50
☐ 50	Josh Childress	.75	.30
☐ 51	Jamaal Magloire	.40	.15
☐ 52	Yao Ming	3.00	1.25
☐ 53	Tyson Chandler	1.25	.50
☐ 54	Andrei Kirilenko	1.25	.50
☐ 55	Rashard Lewis	1.25	.50
☐ 56	Shawn Marion	1.25	.50
☐ 57	Grant Hill	1.25	.50
☐ 58	Wally Szczerbiak	.75	.30
☐ 59	Antoine Walker	1.25	.50
☐ 60	Corey Maggette	.75	.30
☐ 61	Rasheed Wallace	1.25	.50
☐ 62	Dirk Nowitzki	2.00	.75
☐ 63	Paul Pierce	1.25	.50
☐ 64	Tim Duncan	2.50	1.00
☐ 65	Desmond Mason	.40	.15
☐ 66	Ray Allen	1.25	.50
☐ 67	Mike Bibby	1.25	.50
☐ 68	Andre Iguodala	1.25	.50
☐ 69	J.R. Smith	.75	.30
☐ 70	Dwyane Wade	4.00	1.50
☐ 71	Shaun Livingston	1.00	.40
☐ 72	Jason Richardson	1.25	.50
☐ 73	Earl Boykins	.40	.15
☐ 74	Ben Gordon	2.50	1.00
☐ 75	Stephen Jackson	.75	.30
☐ 76	Samuel Dalembert	.40	.15
☐ 77	Kwame Brown	.75	.30
☐ 78	Zydrunas Ilgauskas	.40	.15
☐ 79	Antawn Jamison	1.25	.50
☐ 80	Chris Bosh	1.25	.50
☐ 81	Zach Randolph	1.25	.50
☐ 82	Dwight Howard	1.50	.60
☐ 83	Richard Jefferson	.75	.30
☐ 84	Udonis Haslem	1.25	.50
☐ 85	Lamar Odom	1.25	.50
☐ 86	Mike Dunleavy	.75	.30
☐ 87	Josh Howard	.75	.30
☐ 88	Luol Deng	1.25	.50
☐ 89	Josh Smith	1.25	.50
☐ 90	Jalen Rose	1.00	.40
☐ 91	Rafer Alston	.40	.15
☐ 92	Manu Ginobili	1.25	.50
☐ 93	Allen Iverson	2.50	1.00
☐ 94	Stephon Marbury	1.25	.50
☐ 95	Michael Redd	1.25	.50
☐ 96	Sam Cassell	1.25	.50
☐ 97	Baron Davis	1.25	.50
☐ 98	Andre Miller	.75	.30
☐ 99	Larry Hughes	.75	.30
☐ 100	Ricky Davis	1.25	.50
☐ 101	Nate Robinson RC	8.00	3.00
☐ 102	Danny Granger RC	8.00	3.00
☐ 103	Marvin Williams RC	10.00	4.00
☐ 104	Rashad McCants RC	10.00	4.00
☐ 105	Jarrett Jack RC	5.00	2.00
☐ 106	Andrew Bogut RC	10.00	4.00
☐ 107	Ike Diogu RC	6.00	2.50
☐ 108	Chris Paul RC	20.00	8.00
☐ 109	Julius Hodge RC	5.00	2.00
☐ 110	C.J. Miles RC	5.00	2.00
☐ 111	Francisco Garcia RC	6.00	2.50
☐ 112	Channing Frye RC	6.00	2.50
☐ 113	Deron Williams RC	15.00	6.00
☐ 114	Hakim Warrick RC	10.00	4.00
☐ 115	Salim Stoudamire RC	6.00	2.50
☐ 116	Raymond Felton RC	10.00	4.00
☐ 117	Joey Graham RC	5.00	2.00
☐ 118	Wayne Simien RC	6.00	2.50
☐ 119	David Lee RC	8.00	3.00
☐ 120	Luther Head RC	6.00	2.50
☐ 121	Andrew Bynum RC	12.00	5.00
☐ 122	Monta Ellis RC	10.00	4.00
☐ 123	Brandon Bass RC	5.00	2.00
☐ 124	Antoine Wright RC	5.00	2.00
☐ 125	Gerald Green RC	10.00	4.00
☐ 126	Charlie Villanueva RC	8.00	3.00
☐ 127	Chris Taft RC	5.00	2.00
☐ 128	Sarunas Jasikevicius RC	6.00	2.50
☐ 129	Sean May RC	6.00	2.50
☐ 130	Martell Webster RC	5.00	2.00
☐ 131	Yaroslav Korolev RC	5.00	2.00
☐ 132	Eddie Basden RC	5.00	2.00
☐ 133	Ersan Ilyasova RC	5.00	2.00
☐ 134	Martynas Andriuskevicius RC	5.00	2.00
☐ 135	Orien Greene RC	5.00	2.00
☐ 136	Johan Petro RC	5.00	2.00
☐ 137	Linas Kleiza RC	5.00	2.00
☐ 138	Daniel Ewing RC	6.00	2.50
☐ 139	Fabricio Oberto RC	5.00	2.00
☐ 140	Travis Diener RC	5.00	2.00
☐ 141	Ryan Gomes RC	5.00	2.00
☐ 142	Andray Blatche RC	5.00	2.00
☐ 143	Louis Williams RC	5.00	2.00
☐ 144	Jose Calderon RC	5.00	2.00
☐ 145	Robert Whaley RC	5.00	2.00
☐ 146	Jay-Z	10.00	4.00
☐ 147	Carmen Electra	10.00	4.00
☐ 148	Christie Brinkley	10.00	4.00
☐ 149	Shannon Elizabeth	10.00	4.00
☐ 150	Jenny McCarthy	10.00	4.00

2006-07 Topps Full Court

☐ 1	Vince Carter	2.00	.75
☐ 2	Josh Smith	.75	.30
☐ 3	Dwyane Wade	2.50	1.00
☐ 4	Lamar Odom	.75	.30
☐ 5	Jermaine O'Neal	.75	.30
☐ 6	Andrei Kirilenko	.75	.30
☐ 7	Rasheed Wallace	.75	.30
☐ 8	Manu Ginobili	.75	.30
☐ 9	Richard Hamilton	.50	.20
☐ 10	Tim Duncan	1.50	.60
☐ 11	Ricky Davis	.75	.30
☐ 12	Antoine Walker	.75	.30
☐ 13	Troy Murphy	.75	.30
☐ 14	Ray Allen	.75	.30
☐ 15	Ben Wallace	.75	.30
☐ 16	Dwight Howard	1.00	.40
☐ 17	Joe Johnson	.50	.20
☐ 18	Jason Kidd	1.25	.50
☐ 19	Michael Redd	.75	.30
☐ 20	Kobe Bryant	3.00	1.25
☐ 21	Al Harrington	.25	.10
☐ 22	Mehmet Okur	.25	.10
☐ 23	Danny Granger	.75	.30
☐ 24	Caron Butler	.50	.20
☐ 25	Elton Brand	.75	.30
☐ 26	Gilbert Arenas	.75	.30
☐ 27	Sam Cassell	.75	.30
☐ 28	Antawn Jamison	.75	.30
☐ 29	Carmelo Anthony	1.50	.60
☐ 30	Zach Randolph	.75	.30
☐ 31	Ben Gordon	1.50	.60
☐ 32	Andre Iguodala	.75	.30
☐ 33	Paul Pierce	.75	.30
☐ 34	Peja Stojakovic	.75	.30
☐ 35	Andrew Bogut	1.00	.40
☐ 36	Mike Miller	.75	.30
☐ 37	Mike James	.25	.10
☐ 38	Shaquille O'Neal	2.00	.75
☐ 39	Baron Davis	.75	.30
☐ 40	Jason Richardson	.75	.30
☐ 41	Rashard Lewis	.75	.30
☐ 42	Marcus Camby	.25	.10
☐ 43	Ron Artest	.50	.20
☐ 44	Larry Hughes	.50	.20
☐ 45	Allen Iverson	1.50	.60
☐ 46	Al Jefferson	.75	.30
☐ 47	Chris Paul	2.00	.75
☐ 48	Tony Parker	.75	.30
☐ 49	Pau Gasol	.75	.30
☐ 50	Kevin Garnett	1.50	.60
☐ 51	Richard Jefferson	.50	.20
☐ 52	Corey Maggette	.50	.20
☐ 53	Yao Ming	2.00	.75
☐ 54	T.J. Ford	.50	.20
☐ 55	Andre Miller	.50	.20
☐ 56	Mike Bibby	.75	.30
☐ 57	LeBron James	5.00	2.00
☐ 58	Chris Webber	.75	.30
☐ 59	Emeka Okafor	.75	.30
☐ 60	Tyson Chandler	.75	.30
☐ 61	Raymond Felton	1.00	.40
☐ 62	Channing Frye	.75	.30
☐ 63	Gerald Wallace	.75	.30
☐ 64	Stephon Marbury	.75	.30
☐ 65	Kirk Hinrich	.75	.30
☐ 66	Jameer Nelson	.50	.20
☐ 67	Charlie Villanueva	.75	.30
☐ 68	Smush Parker	.25	.10
☐ 69	Tracy McGrady	2.00	.75
☐ 70	Chris Bosh	.75	.30
☐ 71	Chauncey Billups	.75	.30
☐ 72	Brad Miller	.75	.30
☐ 73	Drew Gooden	.50	.20
☐ 74	Amare Stoudemire	1.50	.60
☐ 75	Dirk Nowitzki	1.25	.50
☐ 76	Shawn Marion	.75	.30
☐ 77	Jason Terry	.75	.30
☐ 78	Steve Nash	.75	.30
☐ 79	Josh Howard	.50	.20
☐ 80	Darius Miles	.75	.30
☐ 81	John Stockton	3.00	1.25

#	Player		
82	Wilt Chamberlain	10.00	4.00
83	Dennis Rodman	2.50	1.00
84	Karl Malone	3.00	1.25
85	Dominique Wilkins	3.00	1.25
86	Isiah Thomas	2.50	1.00
87	Earl Monroe	2.50	1.00
88	Hakeem Olajuwon	2.50	1.00
89	Clyde Drexler	2.50	1.00
90	George Gervin	2.50	1.00
91	Oscar Robertson	2.50	1.00
92	Rick Barry	2.50	1.00
93	Walt Frazier	2.50	1.00
94	Drazen Petrovic	3.00	1.25
95	Dan Majerle	2.50	1.00
96	Jerry West	3.00	1.25
97	Larry Bird	10.00	4.00
98	Moses Malone	2.50	1.00
99	Kareem Abdul-Jabbar	5.00	2.00
100	Bill Russell	6.00	2.50
101	Shelden Williams RC	5.00	2.00
102	Adam Morrison RC	10.00	4.00
103	Daniel Gibson RC	10.00	4.00
104	Mile Ilic RC	4.00	1.50
105	Jorge Garbajosa RC	8.00	3.00
106	David Noel RC	4.00	1.50
107	Hassan Adams RC	5.00	2.00
108	J.J. Redick RC	8.00	3.00
109	Brandon Roy RC	12.00	5.00
110	Damir Markota RC	4.00	1.50
111	Solomon Jones RC	4.00	1.50
112	Yakhouba Diawara RC	4.00	1.50
113	Maurice Ager RC	4.00	1.50
114	Steve Novak RC	4.00	1.50
115	Jordan Farmar RC	8.00	3.00
116	Randy Foye RC	8.00	3.00
117	Cedric Simmons RC	4.00	1.50
118	James Augustine RC	4.00	1.50
119	Sergio Rodriguez RC	4.00	1.50
120	P.J. Tucker RC	4.00	1.50
121	Rajon Rondo RC	5.00	2.00
122	Tyrus Thomas RC	12.00	5.00
123	Will Blalock RC	4.00	1.50
124	Shawne Williams RC	5.00	2.00
125	Rudy Gay RC	8.00	3.00
126	Craig Smith RC	4.00	1.50
127	Hilton Armstrong RC	4.00	1.50
128	Bobby Jones RC	4.00	1.50
129	Quincy Douby RC	4.00	1.50
130	Andrea Bargnani RC	10.00	4.00
131	Vassilis Spanoulis RC	4.00	1.50
132	Thabo Sefolosha RC	6.00	2.50
133	Pops Mensah-Bonsu RC	4.00	1.50
134	Paul Millsap RC	8.00	3.00
135	Kyle Lowry RC	4.00	1.50
136	Marcus Williams RC	5.00	2.00
137	Renaldo Balkman RC	4.00	1.50
138	Rodney Carney RC	4.00	1.50
139	Marcus Vinicius RC	4.00	1.50
140	Ronnie Brewer RC	5.00	2.00
141	Leon Powe RC	4.00	1.50
142	Shannon Brown RC	4.00	1.50
143	Patrick O'Bryant RC	4.00	1.50
144	Paul Davis RC	4.00	1.50
145	Alexander Johnson RC	4.00	1.50
146	Josh Boone RC	4.00	1.50
147	Mardy Collins RC	4.00	1.50
148	LaMarcus Aldridge RC	10.00	4.00
149	Saer Sene RC	4.00	1.50
150	Dee Brown RC	6.00	2.50

1995-96 Topps Gallery

	COMPLETE SET (144)	30.00	15.00
1	Shaquille O'Neal	2.00	.75
2	Shawn Kemp	.50	.20
3	Reggie Miller	.75	.30
4	Mitch Richmond	.50	.20
5	Grant Hill	1.00	.40
6	Magic Johnson	1.25	.50
7	Vin Baker	.50	.20
8	Charles Barkley	1.00	.40
9	Hakeem Olajuwon	.75	.30
10	Michael Jordan	6.00	3.00
11	Patrick Ewing	.75	.30
12	David Robinson	.75	.30
13	Alonzo Mourning	.50	.20
14	Karl Malone	1.00	.40

DENNIS RODMAN

#	Player		
15	Chris Webber	1.00	.40
16	Dikembe Mutombo	.50	.20
17	Larry Johnson	.50	.20
18	Jamal Mashburn	.50	.20
19	Anfernee Hardaway	.75	.30
20	Bryant Stith	.25	.08
21	Juwan Howard	.75	.30
22	Jason Kidd	2.50	1.00
23	Sharone Wright	.25	.08
24	Tom Gugliotta	.25	.08
25	Eric Montross	.25	.08
26	Allan Houston	.50	.20
27	Antonio Davis	.25	.08
28	Brian Grant	.75	.30
29	Terrell Brandon	.50	.20
30	Eddie Jones	1.00	.40
31	James Robinson	.25	.08
32	Wesley Person	.25	.08
33	Glenn Robinson	.75	.30
34	Donyell Marshall	.50	.20
35	Sam Cassell	.75	.30
36	Lamond Murray	.25	.08
37	Damon Stoudamire RC	1.50	.60
38	Tyus Edney RC	.25	.08
39	Jerry Stackhouse RC	2.50	1.00
40	Arvydas Sabonis RC	1.00	.40
41	Kevin Garnett RC	4.00	2.00
42	Brent Barry RC	.75	.30
43	Alan Henderson RC	.75	.30
44	Bryant Reeves RC	.25	.08
45	Shawn Respert RC	.25	.08
46	Michael Finley RC	2.00	.75
47	Gary Trent RC	.25	.08
48	Antonio McDyess RC	1.50	.60
49	George Zidek RC	.25	.08
50	Joe Smith RC	1.25	.50
51	Ed O'Bannon RC	.25	.08
52	Rasheed Wallace RC	2.00	.75
53	Eric Williams RC	.50	.20
54	Kurt Thomas RC	.50	.20
55	Mookie Blaylock	.25	.08
56	Robert Pack	.25	.08
57	Dana Barros	.25	.08
58	Eric Murdock	.25	.08
59	Glen Rice	.50	.20
60	John Stockton	1.00	.40
61	Scottie Pippen	1.25	.50
62	Oliver Miller	.25	.08
63	Tyrone Hill	.25	.08
64	Gary Payton	.75	.30
65	Jim Jackson	.25	.08
66	Avery Johnson	.25	.08
67	Mahmoud Abdul-Rauf	.25	.08
68	Olden Polynice	.25	.08
69	Joe Dumars	.75	.30
70	Rod Strickland	.25	.08
71	Chris Mullin	.75	.30
72	Kevin Johnson	.50	.20
73	Derrick Coleman	.25	.08
74	Clyde Drexler	.75	.30
75	Dale Davis	.25	.08
76	Horace Grant	.50	.20
77	Loy Vaught	.25	.08
78	Armon Gilliam	.25	.08
79	Nick Van Exel	.75	.30
80	Charles Oakley	.25	.08
81	Kevin Willis	.50	.20
82	Sherman Douglas	.25	.08

#	Player		
83	Isaiah Rider	.25	.08
84	Steve Smith	.50	.20
85	Dee Brown	.25	.08
86	Dell Curry	.25	.08
87	Calbert Cheaney	.25	.08
88	Greg Anthony	.25	.08
89	Jeff Hornacek	.50	.20
90	Dennis Rodman	.75	.30
91	Willie Anderson	.25	.08
92	Chris Mills	.25	.08
93	Hersey Hawkins	.25	.08
94	Popeye Jones	.25	.08
95	Chuck Person	.25	.08
96	Reggie Williams	.25	.08
97	A.C. Green	.50	.20
98	Otis Thorpe	.25	.08
99	Walt Williams	.25	.08
100	Latrell Sprewell	.75	.30
101	Buck Williams	.25	.08
102	Robert Horry	.50	.20
103	Clarence Weatherspoon	.25	.08
104	Dennis Scott	.25	.08
105	Rik Smits	.50	.20
106	Jayson Williams	.25	.08
107	Pooh Richardson	.25	.08
108	Anthony Mason	.50	.20
109	Cedric Ceballos	.25	.08
110	Billy Owens	.25	.08
111	Johnny Newman	.25	.08
112	Christian Laettner	.50	.20
113	Stacey Augmon	.25	.08
114	Chris Morris	.25	.08
115	Detlef Schrempf	.50	.20
116	Dino Radja	.25	.08
117	Sean Elliott	.25	.08
118	Muggsy Bogues	.50	.20
119	Toni Kukoc	.50	.20
120	Clifford Robinson	.25	.08
121	Bobby Hurley	.25	.08
122	Lorenzo Williams	.25	.08
123	Wayman Tisdale	.25	.08
124	Bobby Phills	.25	.08
125	Nick Anderson	.25	.08
126	LaPhonso Ellis	.25	.08
127	Scott Williams	.25	.08
128	Mark West	.25	.08
129	P.J. Brown	.25	.08
130	Tim Hardaway	.50	.20
131	Derek Harper	.50	.20
132	Mario Elie	.25	.08
133	Benoit Benjamin	.25	.08
134	Terry Porter	.25	.08
135	Derrick McKey	.25	.08
136	Bimbo Coles	.25	.08
137	John Salley	.25	.08
138	Malik Sealy	.25	.08
139	Byron Scott	.50	.20
140	Vlade Divac	.50	.20
141	Mark Price	.50	.20
142	Rony Seikaly	.25	.08
143	Mark Jackson	.50	.20
144	John Starks	.50	.20

1999-00 Topps Gallery

SCOTTIE PIPPEN

	COMPLETE SET (150)	60.00	30.00
	COMMON CARD (1-124)	.25	.08
	COMMON ROOKIE (125-150)	.50	.20
1	Gary Payton	.75	.30

#	Player		
2	Derek Anderson	.50	.20
3	Jalen Rose	.75	.30
4	Tim Hardaway	.50	.20
5	Jerry Stackhouse	.75	.30
6	Antonio McDyess	.50	.20
7	Paul Pierce	.75	.30
8	Reggie Miller	.75	.30
9	Maurice Taylor	.50	.20
10	Stephon Marbury	.75	.30
11	Terrell Brandon	.50	.20
12	Marcus Camby	.50	.20
13	Michael Doleac	.25	.08
14	Doug Christie	.50	.20
15	Brent Barry	.50	.20
16	John Stockton	.75	.30
17	Rod Strickland	.25	.08
18	Shareef Abdur-Rahim	.75	.30
19	Vin Baker	.50	.20
20	Jason Kidd	1.25	.50
21	Nick Anderson	.25	.08
22	Brian Grant	.50	.20
23	Chris Webber	.75	.30
24	Tariq Abdul-Wahad	.25	.08
25	Jason Williams	.75	.30
26	Joe Smith	.50	.20
27	Ray Allen	.75	.30
28	Glenn Robinson	.75	.30
29	Alonzo Mourning	.50	.20
30	Scottie Pippen	1.25	.50
31	Mookie Blaylock	.25	.08
32	Christian Laettner	.50	.20
33	Mark Jackson	.50	.20
34	Shawn Kemp	.50	.20
35	Anfernee Hardaway	.75	.30
36	Chris Mullin	.50	.20
37	Dennis Rodman	.50	.20
38	Lamond Murray	.25	.08
39	Jim Jackson	.25	.08
40	Shaquille O'Neal	2.00	.75
41	Randy Brown	.25	.08
42	Nick Van Exel	.75	.30
43	Robert Traylor	.25	.08
44	Vlade Divac	.50	.20
45	Karl Malone	.75	.30
46	Avery Johnson	.25	.08
47	Jayson Williams	.25	.08
48	Darrell Armstrong	.25	.08
49	Michael Olowokandi	.50	.20
50	Kevin Garnett	1.50	.60
51	Dirk Nowitzki	1.50	.60
52	Antawn Jamison	1.25	.50
53	Latrell Sprewell	.75	.30
54	Ruben Patterson	.50	.20
55	Vince Carter	2.00	.75
56	Michael Dickerson	.50	.20
57	Raef LaFrentz	.50	.20
58	Keith Van Horn	.75	.30
59	Tom Gugliotta	.25	.08
60	Allen Iverson	1.50	.60
61	Eric Snow	.50	.20
62	Kerry Kittles	.25	.08
63	Sam Cassell	.75	.30
64	Rik Smits	.50	.20
65	Isaiah Rider	.25	.08
66	Anthony Mason	.50	.20
67	Hersey Hawkins	.50	.20
68	Cuttino Mobley	.75	.30
69	Allan Houston	.50	.20
70	Kobe Bryant	3.00	1.25
71	Damon Stoudamire	.50	.20
72	Charles Oakley	.50	.20
73	Mike Bibby	.75	.30
74	David Robinson	.75	.30
75	Eddie Jones	.75	.30
76	Juwan Howard	.50	.20
77	Antoine Walker	.75	.30
78	Michael Finley	.75	.30
79	Larry Hughes	.75	.30
80	Charles Barkley	1.00	.40
81	Tracy McGrady	2.00	.75
82	Dikembe Mutombo	.50	.20
83	Rasheed Wallace	.75	.30
84	Jeff Hornacek	.50	.20
85	Patrick Ewing	.75	.30
86	P.J. Brown	.25	.08
87	Brevin Knight	.25	.08
88	Elden Campbell	.25	.08
89	Kenny Anderson	.50	.20
90	Grant Hill	.75	.30
91	Mitch Richmond	.50	.20
92	Steve Smith	.50	.20
93	Jamal Mashburn	.50	.20
94	Toni Kukoc	.50	.20
95	Hakeem Olajuwon	.75	.30
96	Ron Mercer	.50	.20
97	John Starks	.50	.20
98	Glen Rice	.50	.20
99	Cedric Ceballos	.25	.08
100	Tim Duncan	1.50	.60
101	Karl Malone MAS	.75	.30
102	Alonzo Mourning MAS	.50	.20
103	Gary Payton MAS	.50	.20
104	Scottie Pippen MAS	.75	.30
105	Shaquille O'Neal MAS	1.00	.40
106	Charles Barkley MAS	.75	.30
107	Grant Hill MAS	.50	.20
108	John Stockton MAS	.75	.30
109	Jason Kidd MAS	.75	.30
110	Reggie Miller MAS	.50	.20
111	Shawn Kemp MAS	.25	.08
112	Patrick Ewing MAS	.50	.20
113	Kevin Garnett ART	.75	.30
114	Vince Carter ART	1.00	.40
115	Kobe Bryant ART	1.50	.60
116	Chris Webber ART	.50	.20
117	Tracy McGrady ART	1.00	.40
118	Shareef Abdur-Rahim ART	.50	.20
119	Paul Pierce ART	.75	.30
120	Jason Williams ART	.50	.20
121	Tim Duncan ART	.75	.30
122	Eddie Jones ART	.75	.30
123	Allen Iverson ART	.75	.30
124	Stephon Marbury ART	.50	.20
125	Elton Brand RC	3.00	1.25
126	Lamar Odom RC	2.50	1.00
127	Steve Francis RC	3.00	1.25
128	Adrian Griffin RC	.75	.30
129	Wally Szczerbiak RC	2.50	1.00
130	Baron Davis RC	5.00	2.00
131	Richard Hamilton RC	2.50	1.00
132	Jonathan Bender RC	2.50	1.00
133	Andre Miller RC	2.50	1.00
134	Shawn Marion RC	3.00	1.25
135	Jason Terry RC	2.00	.75
136	Trajan Langdon RC	1.00	.40
137	Corey Maggette RC	2.50	1.00
138	William Avery RC	1.00	.40
139	Ron Artest RC	1.50	.60
140	Cal Bowdler RC	.75	.30
141	James Posey RC	1.50	.60
142	Quincy Lewis RC	.75	.30
143	Kenny Thomas RC	1.00	.40
144	Vonteego Cummings RC	1.00	.40
145	Todd MacCulloch RC	.75	.30
146	Anthony Carter RC	1.50	.60
147	A.Radojevic RC	.50	.20
148	Devean George RC	1.25	.50
149	Scott Padgett RC	.75	.30
150	Jumaine Jones RC	1.00	.40

2000-01 Topps Gallery

COMP.SET w/o RC's (125)	40.00	15.00
COMMON CARD (1-125)	.20	.07
COMMON ROOKIE (126-150)	3.00	1.25

#	Player		
1	Allen Iverson	1.25	.50
2	Terrell Brandon	.40	.15
3	Tracy McGrady	1.50	.60
4	Shawn Marion	.60	.25
5	Steve Smith	.40	.15
6	Avery Johnson	.20	.07
7	Gary Payton	.60	.25
8	Mark Jackson	.40	.15
9	Mike Bibby	.60	.25
10	Karl Malone	.60	.25
11	Kevin Garnett	1.25	.50
12	Tim Hardaway	.40	.15
13	Isaiah Rider	.20	.07
14	Corey Maggette	.40	.15
15	Vince Carter	1.50	.60
16	Vin Baker	.40	.15
17	Paul Pierce	.60	.25
18	Matt Harpring	.60	.25
19	Ron Artest	.60	.25
20	Kenny Anderson	.40	.15
21	Larry Hughes	.40	.15
22	Antonio McDyess	.40	.15
23	Shandon Anderson	.20	.07
24	Joe Smith	.40	.15
25	Jermaine O'Neal	.60	.25
26	Horace Grant	.40	.15
27	Ray Allen	.60	.25
28	Keith Van Horn	.60	.25
29	Darrell Armstrong	.20	.07
30	Shaquille O'Neal	1.50	.60
31	Reggie Miller	.60	.25
32	Allan Houston	.40	.15
33	Grant Hill	.60	.25
34	David Robinson	.60	.25
35	Clifford Robinson	.20	.07
36	Theo Ratliff	.40	.15
37	Rashard Lewis	.40	.15
38	Peja Stojakovic	.60	.25
39	Jason Kidd	1.00	.40
40	Latrell Sprewell	.60	.25
41	Stephon Marbury	.60	.25
42	Sam Cassell	.60	.25
43	Brian Grant	.40	.15
44	Jalen Rose	.60	.25
45	Antawn Jamison	.40	.15
46	Raef LaFrentz	.40	.15
47	Dirk Nowitzki	1.00	.40
48	Lamond Murray	.20	.07
49	Derrick Coleman	.20	.07
50	Steve Francis	.60	.25
51	Dikembe Mutombo	.40	.15
52	Elton Brand	.60	.25
53	Christian Laettner	.40	.15
54	Ben Wallace	.60	.25
55	Jim Jackson	.40	.15
56	Cuttino Mobley	.40	.15
57	Jonathan Bender	.40	.15
58	Anthony Mason	.20	.07
59	Tim Thomas	.40	.15
60	Lamar Odom	.60	.25
61	Glenn Robinson	.40	.15
62	Kendall Gill	.20	.07
63	Glen Rice	.40	.15
64	Anfernee Hardaway	.60	.25
65	Jason Williams	.40	.15
66	Shawn Kemp	.40	.15
67	Derek Anderson	.40	.15
68	Patrick Ewing	.60	.25
69	Shareef Abdur-Rahim	.60	.25
70	Tim Duncan	1.25	.50
71	Rod Strickland	.20	.07
72	Bryon Russell	.20	.07
73	Antonio Davis	.20	.07
74	Rasheed Wallace	.60	.25
75	Wally Szczerbiak	.40	.15
76	Eric Snow	.40	.15
77	Toni Kukoc	.40	.15
78	Michael Olowokandi	.20	.07
79	Hakeem Olajuwon	.60	.25
80	Kobe Bryant	2.50	1.00
81	Mookie Blaylock	.20	.07
82	Michael Finley	.60	.25
83	Jerry Stackhouse	.60	.25
84	Baron Davis	.60	.25
85	Jason Terry	.60	.25
86	Andre Miller	.40	.15

#	Player		
87	Antoine Walker	.60	.25
88	Jamal Mashburn	.40	.15
89	Nick Van Exel	.60	.25
90	Eddie Jones	.60	.25
91	Marcus Camby	.40	.15
92	Scottie Pippen	1.00	.40
93	John Stockton	.60	.25
94	Richard Hamilton	.40	.15
95	John Starks	.40	.15
96	Juwan Howard	.40	.15
97	Michael Dickerson	.40	.15
98	Ron Mercer	.40	.15
99	Chris Webber	.60	.25
100	Magic Johnson	3.00	1.25
101	Shaquille O'Neal MAS	1.50	.60
102	Tim Duncan MAS	1.25	.50
103	Chris Webber MAS	.40	.15
104	Grant Hill MAS	.60	.25
105	Kevin Garnett MAS	1.25	.50
106	Vince Carter MAS	1.50	.60
107	Gary Payton MAS	.60	.25
108	Jason Kidd MAS	1.00	.40
109	Kobe Bryant MAS	2.50	1.00
110	Karl Malone MAS	.60	.25
111	Scottie Pippen MAS	1.00	.40
112	Reggie Miller MAS	.60	.25
113	John Stockton MAS	.60	.25
114	Elton Brand ART	.60	.25
115	Tracy McGrady ART	1.50	.60
116	Steve Francis ART	.60	.25
117	Lamar Odom ART	.60	.25
118	Baron Davis ART	.60	.25
119	Andre Miller ART	.40	.15
120	Jonathan Bender ART	.40	.15
121	Paul Pierce ART	.60	.25
122	Jason Williams ART	.40	.15
123	Rashard Lewis ART	.40	.15
124	Larry Hughes ART	.40	.15
125	Shawn Marion ART	.60	.25
126	Kenyon Martin RC	10.00	4.00
127	Stromile Swift RC	5.00	2.00
128	Darius Miles RC	8.00	3.00
129	Marcus Fizer RC	3.00	1.25
130	Mike Miller RC	8.00	3.00
131	DerMarr Johnson RC	3.00	1.25
132	Chris Mihm RC	3.00	1.25
133	Jamal Crawford RC	4.00	1.50
134	Joel Przybilla RC	3.00	1.25
135	Keyon Dooling RC	4.00	1.50
136	Jerome Moiso RC	3.00	1.25
137	Etan Thomas RC	3.00	1.25
138	Courtney Alexander RC	3.00	1.25
139	Mateen Cleaves RC	3.00	1.25
140	Jason Collier RC	4.00	1.50
141	Hidayet Turkoglu RC	6.00	2.50
142	Desmond Mason RC	3.00	1.25
143	Quentin Richardson RC	6.00	2.50
144	Jamaal Magloire RC	3.00	1.25
145	Speedy Claxton RC	3.00	1.25
146	Morris Peterson RC	5.00	2.00
147	Donnell Harvey RC	3.00	1.25
148	DeShawn Stevenson RC	3.00	1.25
149	Stephen Jackson RC	5.00	2.00
150	Marc Jackson RC	3.00	1.25

1999-00 Topps Gold Label Class 1

	COMPLETE SET (100)	60.00	30.00
	COMMON CARD (1-85)	.30	.10
	COMMON ROOKIE (86-100)	.60	.25
1	Tim Duncan	2.00	.75
2	Steve Smith	.60	.25
3	Jeff Hornacek	.30	.10
4	Kevin Garnett	2.00	.75
5	Paul Pierce	1.00	.40
6	Doug Christie	.60	.25
7	Charles Barkley	1.25	.50
8	Nick Van Exel	1.00	.40
9	Shareef Abdur-Rahim	1.00	.40
10	Rod Strickland	.30	.10
11	Keith Van Horn	1.00	.40
12	Matt Harpring	1.00	.40
13	Randy Brown	.30	.10
14	Vin Baker	.60	.25
15	Mark Jackson	.60	.25
16	Latrell Sprewell	1.00	.40
17	Anthony Mason	.60	.25
18	Brian Grant	.60	.25
19	Brevin Knight	.30	.10
20	Elden Campbell	.30	.10
21	Allen Iverson	2.00	.75
22	Kobe Bryant	4.00	1.50
23	Antawn Jamison	1.50	.60
24	Lindsey Hunter	.30	.10
25	Eddie Jones	1.00	.40
26	Michael Finley	.60	.25
27	Juwan Howard	.60	.25
28	Antonio McDyess	.60	.25
29	David Robinson	1.00	.40
30	Karl Malone	1.00	.40
31	Jason Kidd	1.50	.60
32	Zydrunas Ilgauskas	.60	.25
33	Vince Carter	2.50	1.00
34	Maurice Taylor	.60	.25
35	Alonzo Mourning	.60	.25
36	Tim Thomas	.60	.25
37	Dikembe Mutombo	.60	.25
38	Grant Hill	1.00	.40
39	Jason Williams	1.00	.40
40	Scottie Pippen	1.50	.60
41	Stephon Marbury	1.00	.40
42	Reggie Miller	1.00	.40
43	Tyrone Nesby RC	.30	.10
44	Ron Mercer	.60	.25
45	Terrell Brandon	.60	.25
46	Darrell Armstrong	.30	.10
47	Larry Hughes	.60	.25
48	Alan Henderson	.30	.10
49	Ray Allen	1.00	.40
50	Rasheed Wallace	1.00	.40
51	Toni Kukoc	.60	.25
52	Patrick Ewing	1.00	.40
53	Tom Gugliotta	.30	.10
54	Chris Mills	.30	.10
55	Gary Payton	1.00	.40
56	Michael Olowokandi	.60	.25
57	Chris Mullin	1.00	.40
58	Shawn Kemp	.60	.25
59	Joe Smith	.60	.25
60	Steve Nash	1.00	.40
61	Gary Trent	.30	.10
62	Shaquille O'Neal	2.50	1.00
63	Kerry Kittles	.30	.10
64	Tim Hardaway	.60	.25
65	Glenn Robinson	1.00	.40
66	Damon Stoudamire	.60	.25
67	Anfernee Hardaway	1.00	.40
68	Vlade Divac	.60	.25
69	John Starks	.60	.25
70	Allan Houston	.60	.25
71	Jerry Stackhouse	1.00	.40
72	Avery Johnson	.30	.10
73	Glen Rice	.60	.25
74	Felipe Lopez	.30	.10
75	Clifford Robinson	.30	.10
76	Jamal Mashburn	.60	.25
77	Hakeem Olajuwon	1.00	.40
78	Matt Geiger	.30	.10
79	John Stockton	1.00	.40
80	Chauncey Billups	.60	.25
81	Chris Webber	1.00	.40
82	Antoine Walker	1.00	.40
83	Mike Bibby	1.00	.40

#	Player		
84	Tracy McGrady	2.50	1.00
85	Mitch Richmond	.60	.25
86	Elton Brand RC	4.00	1.50
87	Steve Francis RC	4.00	1.50
88	Baron Davis RC	5.00	2.00
89	Lamar Odom RC	3.00	1.25
90	Jonathan Bender RC	3.00	1.25
91	Wally Szczerbiak RC	3.00	1.25
92	Richard Hamilton RC	3.00	1.25
93	Andre Miller RC	3.00	1.25
94	Shawn Marion RC	4.00	1.50
95	Jason Terry RC	2.50	1.00
96	Trajan Langdon RC	1.25	.50
97	A.Radojevic RC	.60	.25
98	Corey Maggette RC	3.00	1.25
99	William Avery RC	1.25	.50
100	Cal Bowdler RC	1.00	.40

2000-01 Topps Gold Label Class 1

#	Player		
	COMPLETE SET w/o RC (80)	30.00	15.00
	COMMON CARD (1-80)	.30	.10
	COMMON ROOKIE (81-100)	4.00	1.50
1	Steve Francis	1.00	.40
2	Jalen Rose	1.00	.40
3	Allen Iverson	2.00	.75
4	Damon Stoudamire	.60	.25
5	David Robinson	1.00	.40
6	Bryon Russell	.30	.10
7	Toni Kukoc	.60	.25
8	Tracy McGrady	2.50	1.00
9	John Stockton	1.00	.40
10	Tim Duncan	2.00	.75
11	Hakeem Olajuwon	1.00	.40
12	Antoine Walker	1.00	.40
13	Dikembe Mutombo	.60	.25
14	Shawn Kemp	.60	.25
15	Ron Artest	.60	.25
16	Eddie Jones	1.00	.40
17	Dirk Nowitzki	1.50	.60
18	Nick Van Exel	1.00	.40
19	Grant Hill	1.00	.40
20	Antawn Jamison	.60	.25
21	Cuttino Mobley	.60	.25
22	Jonathan Bender	.60	.25
23	Maurice Taylor	.30	.10
24	Kobe Bryant	4.00	1.50
25	Tim Hardaway	.60	.25
26	Tim Thomas	.60	.25
27	Terrell Brandon	.60	.25
28	Marcus Camby	.60	.25
29	Keith Van Horn	1.00	.40
30	Shawn Marion	1.00	.40
31	Rasheed Wallace	1.00	.40
32	Corey Maggette	.60	.25
33	Jason Kidd	1.50	.60
34	Shaquille O'Neal	2.50	1.00
35	Rashard Lewis	.60	.25
36	Karl Malone	1.00	.40
37	Michael Dickerson	.60	.25
38	Richard Hamilton	.60	.25
39	Darrell Armstrong	.30	.10
40	Wally Szczerbiak	.60	.25
41	Glen Rice	.60	.25
42	Glenn Robinson	1.00	.40
43	Reggie Miller	1.00	.40
44	Alonzo Mourning	.60	.25

☐ 45	Larry Hughes	.60	.25
☐ 46	Antonio McDyess	.60	.25
☐ 47	Derrick Coleman	.30	.10
☐ 48	Brevin Knight	.30	.10
☐ 49	Jason Terry	1.00	.40
☐ 50	Elton Brand	1.00	.40
☐ 51	Latrell Sprewell	1.00	.40
☐ 52	Theo Ratliff	.60	.25
☐ 53	Scottie Pippen	1.50	.60
☐ 54	Jason Williams	.60	.25
☐ 55	Gary Payton	1.00	.40
☐ 56	Mitch Richmond	.60	.25
☐ 57	Vin Baker	.60	.25
☐ 58	Raef LaFrentz	.60	.25
☐ 59	Anfernee Hardaway	1.00	.40
☐ 60	Steve Smith	.60	.25
☐ 61	Stephon Marbury	1.00	.40
☐ 62	Vlade Divac	.60	.25
☐ 63	Jamal Mashburn	.60	.25
☐ 64	Jerome Williams	.30	.10
☐ 65	Patrick Ewing	1.00	.40
☐ 66	Lamar Odom	1.00	.40
☐ 67	Jerry Stackhouse	1.00	.40
☐ 68	Michael Finley	1.00	.40
☐ 69	Vince Carter	2.50	1.00
☐ 70	Andre Miller	.60	.25
☐ 71	Paul Pierce	1.00	.40
☐ 72	Baron Davis	1.00	.40
☐ 73	Derek Anderson	.60	.25
☐ 74	Chris Webber	1.00	.40
☐ 75	Ray Allen	1.00	.40
☐ 76	Kevin Garnett	2.00	.75
☐ 77	Allan Houston	.60	.25
☐ 78	Mike Bibby	1.00	.40
☐ 79	Shareef Abdur-Rahim	1.00	.40
☐ 80	Juwan Howard	.60	.25
☐ 81	Kenyon Martin RC	12.00	5.00
☐ 82	Stromile Swift RC	6.00	2.50
☐ 83	Darius Miles RC	10.00	4.00
☐ 84	Marcus Fizer RC	4.00	1.50
☐ 85	Mike Miller RC	10.00	4.00
☐ 86	DerMarr Johnson RC	4.00	1.50
☐ 87	Chris Mihm RC	4.00	1.50
☐ 88	Jamal Crawford RC	5.00	2.00
☐ 89	Joel Przybilla RC	4.00	1.50
☐ 90	Keyon Dooling RC	4.00	1.50
☐ 91	Jerome Moiso RC	4.00	1.50
☐ 92	Etan Thomas RC	4.00	1.50
☐ 93	Courtney Alexander RC	4.00	1.50
☐ 94	Mateen Cleaves RC	4.00	1.50
☐ 95	Jason Collier RC	5.00	2.00
☐ 96	Desmond Mason RC	4.00	1.50
☐ 97	Quentin Richardson RC	10.00	4.00
☐ 98	Jamaal Magloire RC	4.00	1.50
☐ 99	Speedy Claxton RC	4.00	1.50
☐ 100	Morris Peterson RC	6.00	2.50

2003-04 Topps Collection

☐ COMP.FACT.SET (265)		65.00	40.00
☐ COL.SINGLES: 4X TO 1X BASE TOPPS HI			
☐ COMMON ROOKIE (250-265)		1.50	.60
☐ 250	Maciej Lampe RC		
☐ 251	Luke Walton RC	2.00	.75
☐ 252	Maurice Williams RC	1.50	.60
☐ 253	Jason Kapono RC	1.50	.60
☐ 254	Travis Hansen RC	1.50	.60
☐ 255	Zaur Pachulia RC	1.50	.60
☐ 256	Willie Green RC	1.50	.60
☐ 257	James Jones RC	1.50	.60

☐ 258	Slavko Vranes RC	1.50	.60
☐ 259	Keith Bogans RC	1.50	.60
☐ 260	Steve Blake RC	1.50	.60
☐ 261	Carl English RC	1.50	.60
☐ 262	James Lang RC	1.50	.60
☐ 263	Brandon Hunter RC	1.50	.60
☐ 264	Kyle Korver RC	2.50	1.00
☐ 265	Devin Brown RC	1.50	.60

2000-01 Topps Heritage

KOBE BRYANT
LAKERS' GUARD

☐ COMPLETE SET w/o RC (197)		60.00	40.00
☐ COMMON CARD (1-233)		.30	.10
☐ COMMON ROOKIE (25-60)		3.00	1.25
☐ 1	Jason Kidd	1.50	.60
☐ 2	Allen Iverson	2.00	.75
☐ 3	Tracy McGrady	2.50	1.00
☐ 4	Tim Duncan	2.00	.75
☐ 5	Michael Finley	1.00	.40
☐ 6	Jason Williams	.60	.25
☐ 7	Kobe Bryant	4.00	1.50
☐ 8	Gary Payton	1.00	.40
☐ 9	Latrell Sprewell	1.00	.40
☐ 10	Antonio McDyess	.60	.25
☐ 11	Antoine Walker	1.00	.40
☐ 12	Steve Francis	1.00	.40
☐ 13	Elton Brand	1.00	.40
☐ 14	Larry Hughes	.60	.25
☐ 15	Shaquille O'Neal	2.50	1.00
☐ 16	Lamar Odom	1.00	.40
☐ 17	Kevin Garnett	2.00	.75
☐ 18	Vince Carter	2.50	1.00
☐ 19	Ray Allen	1.00	.40
☐ 20	Grant Hill	1.00	.40
☐ 21	Chris Webber	1.00	.40
☐ 22	Paul Pierce	1.00	.40
☐ 23	Shareef Abdur-Rahim	1.00	.40
☐ 24	Eddie Jones	1.00	.40
☐ 25	Kenyon Martin RC	15.00	6.00
☐ 26	Stromile Swift RC	8.00	3.00
☐ 27	Darius Miles RC	8.00	3.00
☐ 28	Marcus Fizer RC	3.00	1.25
☐ 29	Mike Miller RC	10.00	4.00
☐ 30	DerMarr Johnson RC	3.00	1.25
☐ 31	Chris Mihm RC	3.00	1.25
☐ 32	Jamal Crawford RC	4.00	1.50
☐ 33	Joel Przybilla RC	3.00	1.25
☐ 34	Keyon Dooling RC	3.00	1.25
☐ 35	Jerome Moiso RC	3.00	1.25
☐ 36	Etan Thomas RC	3.00	1.25
☐ 37	Courtney Alexander RC	3.00	1.25
☐ 38	Mateen Cleaves RC	3.00	1.25
☐ 39	Jason Collier RC	4.00	1.50
☐ 40	Hidayet Turkoglu RC	8.00	3.00
☐ 41	Desmond Mason RC	3.00	1.25
☐ 42	Quentin Richardson RC	8.00	3.00
☐ 43	Jamaal Magloire RC	3.00	1.25
☐ 44	Speedy Claxton RC	3.00	1.25
☐ 45	Morris Peterson RC	6.00	2.50
☐ 46	Donnell Harvey RC	3.00	1.25
☐ 47	DeShawn Stevenson RC	3.00	1.25
☐ 48	Dalibor Bagaric RC	3.00	1.25
☐ 49	Iakovos Tsakalidis RC	3.00	1.25
☐ 50	Mamadou N'Diaye RC	3.00	1.25
☐ 51	Erick Barkley RC	3.00	1.25
☐ 52	Mark Madsen RC	3.00	1.25
☐ 53	Dan Langhi RC	3.00	1.25
☐ 54	A.J. Guyton RC	3.00	1.25
☐ 55	Jake Voskuhl RC	3.00	1.25

☐ 56	Khalid El-Amin RC	3.00	1.25
☐ 57	Lavor Postell RC	3.00	1.25
☐ 58	Eduardo Najera RC	5.00	2.00
☐ 59	Michael Redd RC	8.00	3.00
☐ 60	Stephen Jackson RC	6.00	2.50
☐ 61	Andrew DeClercq	.30	.10
☐ 62	Darrell Armstrong	.30	.10
☐ 63	Al Harrington	.60	.25
☐ 64	Johnny Newman	.30	.10
☐ 65	Baron Davis	1.00	.40
☐ 66	Adrian Griffin	.30	.10
☐ 67	Anthony Mason	.60	.25
☐ 68	Ron Harper	.60	.25
☐ 69	Michael Olowokandi	.30	.10
☐ 70	Maurice Taylor	.30	.10
☐ 71	Travis Best	.30	.10
☐ 72	Chucky Atkins	.30	.10
☐ 73	Bob Sura	.30	.10
☐ 74	Jason Terry	1.00	.40
☐ 75	Ervin Johnson	.30	.10
☐ 76	Eric Snow	.60	.25
☐ 77	Shawn Bradley	.30	.10
☐ 78	Christian Laettner	.60	.25
☐ 79	Keith Van Horn	1.00	.40
☐ 80	Damon Stoudamire	.60	.25
☐ 81	Peja Stojakovic	1.00	.40
☐ 82	Clifford Robinson	.30	.10
☐ 83	Elden Campbell	.30	.10
☐ 84	Kenny Anderson	.60	.25
☐ 85	Patrick Ewing	1.00	.40
☐ 86	Mookie Blaylock	.30	.10
☐ 87	Brian Skinner	.30	.10
☐ 88	Rick Fox	.60	.25
☐ 89	Tim Hardaway	.60	.25
☐ 90	Brian Grant	.60	.25
☐ 91	Joe Smith	.60	.25
☐ 92	Kerry Kittles	.30	.10
☐ 93	Scottie Pippen	1.50	.60
☐ 94	Steve Smith	.60	.25
☐ 95	Sean Elliott	.60	.25
☐ 96	Rashard Lewis	.60	.25
☐ 97	Michael Dickerson	.60	.25
☐ 98	Rod Strickland	.30	.10
☐ 99	Sam Cassell	1.00	.40
☐ 100	Kareem Abdul-Jabbar	3.00	1.25
☐ 101	John Amaechi	.30	.10
☐ 102	Kendall Gill	.30	.10
☐ 103	Terrell Brandon	.60	.25
☐ 104	Dan Majerle	.60	.25
☐ 105	Mark Jackson	.30	.10
☐ 106	Hakeem Olajuwon	1.00	.40
☐ 107	Antawn Jamison	1.00	.40
☐ 108	Cedric Ceballos	.30	.10
☐ 109	Shandon Anderson	.30	.10
☐ 110	Gary Trent	.30	.10
☐ 111	Wesley Person	.30	.10
☐ 112	James Posey	.60	.25
☐ 113	David Wesley	.30	.10
☐ 114	Vitaly Potapenko	.30	.10
☐ 115	P.J. Brown	.30	.10
☐ 116	Alan Henderson	.30	.10
☐ 117	Terry Porter	.30	.10
☐ 118	Lindsey Hunter	.30	.10
☐ 119	Chauncey Billups	.60	.25
☐ 120	Doug Christie	.60	.25
☐ 121	Glen Rice	.60	.25
☐ 122	Jamie Feick	.30	.10
☐ 123	Tom Gugliotta	.30	.10
☐ 124	Arvydas Sabonis	.60	.25
☐ 125	Toni Kukoc	.60	.25
☐ 126	Shawn Marion	1.00	.40
☐ 127	Dale Davis	.30	.10
☐ 128	Corliss Williamson	.30	.10
☐ 129	Brent Barry	.60	.25
☐ 130	Shammond Williams	.30	.10
☐ 131	Nick Anderson	.30	.10
☐ 132	Charles Oakley	.30	.10
☐ 133	Shaquille O'Neal CHAMP	1.25	.50
☐ 134	Ron Harper CHAMP	.30	.10
☐ 135	Kobe Bryant CHAMP	2.00	.75
☐ 136	Shaquille O'Neal CHAMP	1.25	.50
☐ 137	L.A. Lakers CHAMP	1.00	.40
☐ 138	V.Carter/Iverson/J.Stack	1.25	.50
☐ 139	Iverson/G./V.Carter	1.00	.40
☐ 140	Mutombo/Mourning/D.Davis	1.00	.40
☐ 141	R.Miller/D.Arm/R.Allen	1.00	.40

142 Mutombo/Brand/Je.Williams	1.00	.40
143 S.Cassell/M.Jackson/E.Snow	1.00	.40
144 Checklist	.30	.10
145 Checklist	.30	.10
146 Shaq/K.Malone/Payton	2.00	.75
147 Shaq/K.Malone/Webber	1.50	.60
148 Shaq/Patterson/R.Wallace	.30	.10
149 Hornacek/Brandon/Stojakovic	.30	.10
150 Shaq/Garnett/Duncan	1.50	.60
151 Payton/Van Exel/Stockton	1.00	.40
152 Chris Whitney	.30	.10
153 Isaac Austin	.30	.10
154 Kevin Willis	.30	.10
155 Vin Baker	.60	.25
156 Avery Johnson	.30	.10
157 Rodney Rogers	.30	.10
158 Allan Houston	.60	.25
159 Austin Croshere	.60	.25
160 George Lynch	.30	.10
161 Howard Eisley	.30	.10
162 Jerome Williams	.30	.10
163 LaPhonso Ellis	.30	.10
164 Ron Mercer	.60	.25
165 Andre Miller	.60	.25
166 Tariq Abdul-Wahad	.30	.10
167 Donyell Marshall	.60	.25
168 Quincy Lewis	.30	.10
169 Mitch Richmond	.60	.25
170 Richard Hamilton	.60	.25
171 Bryant Reeves	.30	.10
172 Jim Jackson	.30	.10
173 David Robinson	1.00	.40
174 Derrick Coleman	.30	.10
175 Anthony Peeler	.30	.10
176 Theo Ratliff	.60	.25
177 Roshown McLeod	.30	.10
178 Ron Artest	.60	.25
179 Bryon Russell	.30	.10
180 Othella Harrington	.60	.25
181 Juwan Howard	.60	.25
182 Antonio Davis	.30	.10
183 Ruben Patterson	.60	.25
184 Shawn Kemp	.60	.25
185 Larry Johnson	.60	.25
186 Marcus Camby	.60	.25
187 Eric Piatkowski	.60	.25
188 Reggie Miller	1.00	.40
189 Anfernee Hardaway	1.00	.40
190 Kelvin Cato	.30	.10
191 Erick Dampier	.30	.10
192 Keon Clark	.60	.25
193 Dirk Nowitzki	1.50	.60
194 Robert Traylor	.30	.10
195 Lamond Murray	.30	.10
196 John Wallace	.30	.10
197 Robert Horry	.60	.25
198 Robert Pack	.30	.10
199 Jamal Mashburn	.60	.25
200 Corey Benjamin	.30	.10
201 Matt Harpring	1.00	.40
202 Nick Van Exel	1.00	.40
203 Vonteego Cummings	.30	.10
204 Ben Wallace	1.00	.40
205 Karl Malone	1.00	.40
206 Jonathan Bender	.60	.25
207 Cuttino Mobley	.60	.25
208 Isaiah Rider	.30	.10
209 Tyrone Nesby	.30	.10
210 Jermaine O'Neal	1.00	.40
211 Corey Maggette	.60	.25
212 Anthony Carter	.60	.25
213 Horace Grant	.60	.25
214 Tim Thomas	.60	.25
215 Wally Szczerbiak	.60	.25
216 Stephon Marbury	1.00	.40
217 Charlie Ward	.30	.10
218 Bo Outlaw	.30	.10
219 Matt Geiger	.30	.10
220 Vlade Divac	.60	.25
221 Rasheed Wallace	1.00	.40
222 Derek Anderson	.60	.25
223 John Stockton	1.00	.40
224 Dikembe Mutombo	.60	.25
225 John Starks	.60	.25
226 Mike Bibby	.50	.20
227 Jahidi White	.30	.10

228 Jalen Rose	1.00	.40
229 Glenn Robinson	1.00	.40
230 Brevin Knight	.30	.10
231 Jerry Stackhouse	1.00	.40
232 Rael LaFrentz	.60	.25
233 Brad Miller	1.00	.40

2001-02 Topps Heritage

TYSON CHANDLER

COMPLETE SET (264)	300.00	150.00
COMMON CARD (1-264)	.30	.10
COMMON ROOKIE	2.00	.75
1 Shaquille O'Neal	2.50	1.00
2 Jalen Rose	1.00	.40
3 Kwame Brown RC	4.00	1.50
4 Bryon Russell	.30	.10
5 Hakeem Olajuwon	.60	.25
6 Shammond Williams	.30	.10
7 Aaron Mckie	.60	.25
8 Anfernee Hardaway	1.00	.40
9 Dale Davis	.30	.10
10 Tracy McGrady	2.50	1.00
11 Speedy Claxton	.30	.10
12 Kurt Thomas	.60	.25
13 Keith Van Horn	.60	.25
14 Tyson Chandler RC	6.00	2.50
15 Andre Miller	.60	.25
16 Dirk Nowitzki	1.50	.60
17 Rael Lafrentz	.60	.25
18 Mateen Cleaves	.60	.25
19 Danny Fortson	.30	.10
20 Steve Francis	1.00	.40
21 Al Harrington	.60	.25
22 Keyon Dooling	.60	.25
23 Rick Fox	.60	.25
24 Michael Dickerson	.30	.10
25 Alonzo Mourning	.60	.25
26 Glenn Robinson	1.00	.40
27 Wally Szczerbiak	.60	.25
28 Todd MacCulloch	.30	.10
29 Shandon Anderson	.30	.10
30 Kobe Bryant	4.00	1.50
31 Tyrone Hill	.30	.10
32 Grant Hill	1.00	.40
33 Shawn Marion	.60	.25
34 Derek Anderson	.60	.25
35 Hidayet Turkoglu	.60	.25
36 David Robinson	1.00	.40
37 Gary Payton	1.00	.40
38 Alvin Williams	.30	.10
39 Pau Gasol RC	6.00	2.50
40 Tim Duncan	2.00	.75
41 Rashard Lewis	.60	.25
42 Antonio Davis	.30	.10
43 Donyell Marshall	.60	.25
44 Jahidi White	.30	.10
45 Shareef Abdur-Rahim	1.00	.40
46 Antoine Walker	1.00	.40
47 P.J. Brown	.30	.10
48 Eddie Robinson	.60	.25
49 Chris Mihm	.60	.25
50 Kevin Garnett	2.00	.75
51 Marcus Camby	.60	.25
52 Mike Miller	1.00	.40
53 Tony Delk	.30	.10
54 Mike Bibby	1.00	.40
55 Dikembe Mutombo	.60	.25
56 Eddy Curry RC	6.00	2.50
57 Shawn Bradley	.30	.10

58 James Posey	.60	.25
59 Jason Richardson RC	6.00	2.50
60 Jason Kidd	1.50	.60
61 Eddie Griffin RC	2.50	1.00
62 Larry Hughes	.60	.25
63 Ben Wallace	1.00	.40
64 Antonio McDyess	.60	.25
65 Tim Hardaway	.60	.25
66 Shawn Kemp	.60	.25
67 Bobby Jackson	.60	.25
68 Tom Gugliotta	.30	.10
69 Antawn Jamison	1.00	.40
70 Lamar Odom	1.00	.40
71 Jamaal Tinsley RC	3.00	1.25
72 Moochie Norris	.30	.10
73 Marc Jackson	.30	.10
74 Andrei Kirilenko RC	6.00	2.50
75 Wang Zhizhi	1.00	.40
76 Eric Snow	.60	.25
77 Rasheed Wallace	1.00	.40
78 Antonio Daniels	.30	.10
79 Vladimir Radmanovic RC	2.00	.75
80 Morris Peterson	.60	.25
81 Terry/Terry/Mutombo/Terry	1.00	.40
82 Pierce/Pllcio/Walkr/Walkr	.60	.25
83 Mash/Hawkins/Brwn/Davis	.60	.25
84 Brand/Hoiberg/Brand/Hoiberg	1.00	.40
85 Millr/Lngdn/Wthrspoon/Millr	.60	.25
86 Nowitz/Nash/Nowitz/Nash	1.00	.40
87 McDys/McCld/McDys/VnEx	.60	.25
88 Stack/Barros/Wllce/Stack	1.00	.40
89 Jmisn/Jcksn/Jmisn/Blaylck	1.00	.40
90 Frncis/Mobly/Fmcis/Frncis	.30	.10
91 Rose/Miller/O'Neal/Best	1.00	.40
92 Odm/Fisher/Odm/McInns	1.00	.40
93 Shaq/Penbrthy/Shaq/Kobe	1.50	.60
94 Rahim/Rahim/Rahim/Bibby	1.00	.40
95 Jones/Jones/Masn/Hrdawy	.60	.25
96 Robnsn/Allen/Jhnsn/Cassll	1.00	.40
97 Grntt/Brandn/Grntt/Brandn	1.25	.50
98 Mrbry/Newmn/Wllams/Mrbry	.60	.25
99 Deshawn Stevenson	.60	.25
100 Allen Iverson	2.00	.75
101 Jeryl Sasser RC	2.00	.75
102 Jason Terry	1.00	.40
103 Vitaly Potapenko	.30	.10
104 Elden Campbell	.30	.10
105 Jamal Crawford	.60	.25
106 Michael Finley	1.00	.40
107 Earl Watson RC	2.00	.75
108 Clifford Robinson	.30	.10
109 Chucky Atkins	.30	.10
110 Glen Rice	.60	.25
111 Jermaine O'Neal	1.00	.40
112 Jonathan Bender	.60	.25
113 Michael Olowokandi	.30	.10
114 Derek Fisher	.60	.25
115 Stromile Swift	.60	.25
116 Toni Kukoc	.60	.25
117 Samuel Dalembert RC	2.00	.75
118 Paul Pierce	1.00	.40
119 Jamal Mashburn	.60	.25
120 Ron Mercer	.60	.25
121 Lamond Murray	.30	.10
122 Steve Nash	1.00	.40
123 Nick Van Exel	1.00	.40
124 Desagana Diop RC	2.00	.75
125 Ron Artest	.60	.25
126 Marcus Fizer	.60	.25
127 Jumaine Jones	.60	.25
128 Corliss Williamson	.60	.25
129 Rodney White RC	2.50	1.00
130 Cuttino Mobley	.60	.25
131 Reggie Miller	1.00	.40
132 Austin Croshere	.60	.25
133 Jeff McInnis	.30	.10
134 Joe Johnson RC	6.00	2.50
135 Kedrick Brown RC	2.00	.75
136 Theo Ratliff	.60	.25
137 Laphonso Ellis	.30	.10
138 Ervin Johnson	.30	.10
139 Terrell Brandon	.60	.25
140 Chauncey Billups	.60	.25
141 Kenyon Martin	1.00	.40
142 Richard Jefferson RC	3.00	1.25
143 Howard Eisley	.30	.10

❑ 144	Stackhouse/Iverson/Shaq	1.25	.50
❑ 145	Iverson/Stackhouse/Shaq	1.50	.60
❑ 146	Shaq/Wells/Camby	1.00	.40
❑ 147	Miller/Houston/Christie	.60	.25
❑ 148	Mutombo/Wallace/Shaq	1.00	.40
❑ 149	Kidd/Stockton/Van Exel	1.00	.40
❑ 150	Vince Carter	2.50	1.00
❑ 151	Calvin Booth	.30	.10
❑ 152	Chris Whitney	.30	.10
❑ 153	John Amaechi	.30	.10
❑ 154	Keon Clark	.60	.25
❑ 155	Terry Porter	.30	.10
❑ 156	Doug Christie	.60	.25
❑ 157	Gerald Wallace RC	5.00	2.00
❑ 158	Zach Randolph RC	4.00	1.50
❑ 159	Iakovos Tsakalidis	.30	.10
❑ 160	Damone Brown RC	2.00	.75
❑ 161	Ivrsn/Miller/Grntt/Duncan	1.25	.50
❑ 162	Allen/T-Mac/Shaq/Smith	2.50	1.00
❑ 163	Mornig/Dvis/Wbber/Hrdway	1.00	.40
❑ 164	Houstn/Crtr/Nowitz/Malone	1.50	.60
❑ 165	Christian Laettner	.60	.25
❑ 166	John Starks	.60	.25
❑ 167	Jerome Williams	.30	.10
❑ 168	Brent Barry	.60	.25
❑ 169	Malik Rose	.30	.10
❑ 170	Vlade Divac	.60	.25
❑ 171	Damon Stoudamire	.60	.25
❑ 172	Rodney Rogers	.30	.10
❑ 173	Alvin Jones RC	2.50	1.00
❑ 174	Darrell Armstrong	.30	.10
❑ 175	Mark Jackson	.60	.25
❑ 176	Kerry Kittles ERR	.30	.10
❑ 177	Radoslav Nesterovic	.60	.25
❑ 178	Brandon Armstrong RC	2.00	.75
❑ 179	Joe Smith	.60	.25
❑ 180	Ray Allen	1.00	.40
❑ 181	Anthony Mason	.60	.25
❑ 182	Bryant Reeves	.30	.10
❑ 183	Jason Williams	.60	.25
❑ 184	Terence Morris RC	2.00	.75
❑ 185	Travis Best	.30	.10
❑ 186	Troy Murphy RC	4.00	1.50
❑ 187	Gilbert Arenas RC	8.00	3.00
❑ 188	Avery Johnson	.30	.10
❑ 189	Juwan Howard	.60	.25
❑ 190	Checklist	.30	.10
❑ 191	Courtney Alexander	.60	.25
❑ 192	John Stockton	1.00	.40
❑ 193	Vin Baker	.60	.25
❑ 194	Desmond Mason	.60	.25
❑ 195	Steve Smith	.60	.25
❑ 196	Steven Hunter RC	2.00	.75
❑ 197	Stephon Marbury	1.00	.40
❑ 198	Patrick Ewing	1.00	.40
❑ 199	Allan Houston	.60	.25
❑ 200	Karl Malone	1.00	.40
❑ 201	Peja Stojakovic	1.00	.40
❑ 202	Bonzi Wells	.60	.25
❑ 203	Latrell Sprewell	1.00	.40
❑ 204	Rafer Alston	.30	.10
❑ 205	Tony Parker RC	8.00	3.00
❑ 206	Michael Bradley RC	2.00	.75
❑ 207	Richard Hamilton	.60	.25
❑ 208	Zeljko Rebraca RC	2.00	.75
❑ 209	Joel Przybilla	.60	.25
❑ 210	Tim Thomas	.60	.25
❑ 211	Eddie House	.60	.25
❑ 212	Brian Grant	.60	.25
❑ 213	Lindsey Hunter	.30	.10
❑ 214	Corey Maggette	.60	.25
❑ 215	Shane Battier RC	3.00	1.25
❑ 216	Will Solomon	.30	.10
❑ 217	Mitch Richmond	.60	.25
❑ 218	Eddie Jones	1.00	.40
❑ 219	Elton Brand	1.00	.40
❑ 220	Quentin Richardson	.60	.25
❑ 221	Hustn/Houstn/Cmby/Ward	.60	.25
❑ 222	T-Mac/Armstrong/Outlw/Arm	1.00	.40
❑ 223	Ivrsn/Ivrsn/Hill/McKie	1.50	.60
❑ 224	Mrion/Kidd/Mrion/Kidd	1.00	.40
❑ 225	Wllce/Smth/Davis/Stoudmr	.60	.25
❑ 226	Wbbr/Smth/Wbbr/Wllams	1.00	.40
❑ 227	Duncn/Andrsn/Duncn/Drills	1.00	.40
❑ 228	Pytn/Williams/Ewing/Pytn	.60	.25
❑ 229	Cartr/Curry/Davis/Jackson	1.00	.40

❑ 230	Malon/Stock/Malon/Stock	1.00	.40
❑ 231	Hwrd/Whtny/White/Whtny	.60	.25
❑ 232	Brendan Haywood RC	2.50	1.00
❑ 233	Scottie Pippen	1.50	.60
❑ 234	Loren Woods RC	2.00	.75
❑ 235	Sam Cassell	1.00	.40
❑ 236	Anthony Carter	.60	.25
❑ 237	Raja Bell RC	2.00	.75
❑ 238	Robert Horry	.60	.25
❑ 239	Maurice Taylor	.60	.25
❑ 240	Zydrunas Ilgauskas	.60	.25
❑ 241	Derrick Coleman	.30	.10
❑ 242	Kenny Anderson	.60	.25
❑ 243	Joseph Forte RC	4.00	1.50
❑ 244	Baron Davis	1.00	.40
❑ 245	Nazr Mohammed	.30	.10
❑ 246	Ivrsn/Cartr/Duncn/Bradly	1.25	.50
❑ 247	Allen/Davis/Kobe/Divac	2.00	.75
❑ 248	Mtmb/Robnsn/Robnsn/Lue	1.00	.40
❑ 249	Bryant/Iverson	1.25	.50
❑ 250	Darius Miles	1.00	.40
❑ 251	Samaki Walker	.30	.10
❑ 252	Dermarr Johnson	.60	.25
❑ 253	David Wesley	.30	.10
❑ 254	Trenton Hassell RC	3.00	1.25
❑ 255	Jeff Trepagnier RC	2.00	.75
❑ 256	Jacque Vaughn	.30	.10
❑ 257	Kirk Haston RC	2.00	.75
❑ 258	Jamaal Magloire	.60	.25
❑ 259	Jason Collins RC	2.00	.75
❑ 260	Chris Webber	1.00	.40
❑ 261	Kenny Satterfield RC	2.00	.75
❑ 262	Horace Grant	.60	.25
❑ 263	Jerry Stackhouse	1.00	.40
❑ 264	Michael Jordan	15.00	6.00

2001-02 Topps High Topps

❑	COMPLETE SET (164)	800.00	400.00
❑	COMP.SET w/o SP's (105)	60.00	30.00
❑	COMMON CARD (1-105)	.30	.10
❑	COMMON AU (106-113)	12.00	5.00
❑	COMMON JSY (114-129)	10.00	4.00
❑	COMMON AU RC (130-140)	12.00	5.00
❑	COMMON JSY RC (141-153)	10.00	4.00
❑	COMMON ROOKIE (154-164)	4.00	1.50
❑ 1	Shaquille O'Neal	2.50	1.00
❑ 2	Reggie Miller	1.00	.40
❑ 3	Steve Francis	1.00	.40
❑ 4	Jerry Stackhouse	1.00	.40
❑ 5	Nick Van Exel	1.00	.40
❑ 6	Dirk Nowitzki	1.50	.60
❑ 7	Dikembe Mutombo	.60	.25
❑ 8	Terrell Brandon	.60	.25
❑ 9	Allan Houston	.60	.25
❑ 10	Kevin Garnett	2.00	.75
❑ 11	Eric Snow	.60	.25
❑ 12	Stephon Marbury	1.00	.40
❑ 13	Jalen Rose	1.00	.40
❑ 14	Rick Fox	.60	.25
❑ 15	Alonzo Mourning	.60	.25
❑ 16	Tim Thomas	.60	.25
❑ 17	Keith Van Horn	.60	.25
❑ 18	Glen Rice	.60	.25
❑ 19	Mike Miller	1.00	.40
❑ 20	Chris Webber	1.00	.40
❑ 21	Larry Hughes	.60	.25
❑ 22	Joe Smith	1.00	.40

❑ 23	Ron Mercer	.60	.25
❑ 24	Jamal Mashburn	.60	.25
❑ 25	Shareef Abdur-Rahim	1.00	.40
❑ 26	P.J. Brown	.30	.10
❑ 27	Ben Wallace	1.00	.40
❑ 28	Wang Zhizhi	1.00	.40
❑ 29	Jermaine O'Neal	1.00	.40
❑ 30	Lamar Odom	1.00	.40
❑ 31	Stromile Swift	.60	.25
❑ 32	Theo Ratliff	.60	.25
❑ 33	Patrick Ewing	1.00	.40
❑ 34	Antonio Davis	.30	.10
❑ 35	John Stockton	1.00	.40
❑ 36	Courtney Alexander	.60	.25
❑ 37	Alvin Williams	.30	.10
❑ 38	Rashard Lewis	.60	.25
❑ 39	Mike Bibby	1.00	.40
❑ 40	Scottie Pippen	1.50	.60
❑ 41	Anfernee Hardaway	1.00	.40
❑ 42	Marcus Camby	.60	.25
❑ 43	Glenn Robinson	.60	.25
❑ 44	Jason Williams	.60	.25
❑ 45	Horace Grant	.60	.25
❑ 46	Chris Mihm	.60	.25
❑ 47	Paul Pierce	1.00	.40
❑ 48	DerMarr Johnson	.60	.25
❑ 49	Steve Nash	1.00	.40
❑ 50	Vince Carter	2.50	1.00
❑ 51	Michael Jordan	15.00	6.00
❑ 52	Donyell Marshall	.60	.25
❑ 53	Desmond Mason	.60	.25
❑ 54	Tom Gugliotta	.30	.10
❑ 55	Hidayet Turkoglu	.60	.25
❑ 56	Grant Hill	1.00	.40
❑ 57	Kenyon Martin	1.00	.40
❑ 58	Wally Szczerbiak	.60	.25
❑ 59	Eddie Jones	1.00	.40
❑ 60	Kobe Bryant	4.00	1.50
❑ 61	Cuttino Mobley	.60	.25
❑ 62	Michael Dickerson	.60	.25
❑ 63	Clifford Robinson	.30	.10
❑ 64	Raef LaFrentz	.60	.25
❑ 65	Lamond Murray	.30	.10
❑ 66	Kenny Anderson	.60	.25
❑ 67	Antonio Daniels	.30	.10
❑ 68	Hakeem Olajuwon	.60	.25
❑ 69	Eddie Robinson	.60	.25
❑ 70	Karl Malone	1.00	.40
❑ 71	Richard Hamilton	.60	.25
❑ 72	Derek Anderson	.60	.25
❑ 73	Bonzi Wells	.60	.25
❑ 74	Darrell Armstrong	.30	.10
❑ 75	Gary Payton	1.00	.40
❑ 76	Bryon Russell	.30	.10
❑ 77	Steve Smith	.60	.25
❑ 78	Sam Cassell	1.00	.40
❑ 79	Brian Grant	.60	.25
❑ 80	Antoine Walker	1.00	.40
❑ 81	Marcus Fizer	.60	.25
❑ 82	Tim Duncan AN	2.00	.75
❑ 83	Chris Webber AN	.60	.25
❑ 84	Shaquille O'Neal AN	2.50	1.00
❑ 85	Allen Iverson AN	2.00	.75
❑ 86	Jason Kidd AN	1.50	.60
❑ 87	Kevin Garnett AN	2.00	.75
❑ 88	Vince Carter AN	2.50	1.00
❑ 89	Dikembe Mutombo AN	.60	.25
❑ 90	Kobe Bryant AN	4.00	1.50
❑ 91	Tracy McGrady AN	2.50	1.00
❑ 92	Allen Iverson SL	.60	.25
❑ 93	Dikembe Mutombo SL	.30	.10
❑ 94	Jason Kidd SL	1.00	.40
❑ 95	Allen Iverson SL	1.25	.50
❑ 96	Theo Ratliff SL	.30	.10
❑ 97	Shaquille O'Neal SL	1.50	.60
❑ 98	Reggie Miller SL	.60	.25
❑ 99	Antoine Walker SL	.60	.25
❑ 100	Michael Finley SL	.60	.25
❑ 101	Jason Kidd SL	1.00	.40
❑ 102	Shaquille O'Neal RTC	1.50	.60
❑ 103	Kobe Bryant RTC	2.50	1.00
❑ 104	Derek Fisher RTC	1.00	.40
❑ 105	Shaquille O'Neal RTC	1.50	.60
❑ 106	Shawn Marion AU	15.00	6.00
❑ 107	Antawn Jamison AU	20.00	8.00
❑ 108	Peja Stojakovic AU	40.00	15.00

#	Player		
109	Jason Terry AU	15.00	6.00
110	Aaron McKie AU	12.00	5.00
111	Keyon Dooling AU	12.00	5.00
112	Al Harrington AU	12.00	5.00
113	Chauncey Billups AU	12.00	5.00
114	Tim Duncan JSY	25.00	10.00
115	Tracy McGrady JSY	25.00	10.00
116	Jason Kidd JSY	20.00	8.00
117	Latrell Sprewell JSY	10.00	4.00
118	David Robinson JSY	25.00	10.00
119	Baron Davis JSY	12.00	4.00
120	Allen Iverson JSY	25.00	10.00
121	Ray Allen JSY	15.00	6.00
122	Rasheed Wallace JSY	10.00	4.00
123	Morris Peterson JSY	10.00	4.00
124	Darius Miles JSY	10.00	4.00
125	Marc Jackson JSY	10.00	4.00
126	Michael Finley JSY	10.00	4.00
127	Elton Brand JSY	10.00	4.00
128	Antonio McDyess JSY		
129	Andre Miller JSY	10.00	4.00
130	Kwame Brown AU RC	12.00	5.00
131	Eddy Curry AU RC	20.00	8.00
132	Loren Woods AU RC	12.00	5.00
133	Joe Johnson AU RC	25.00	10.00
134	R.Jefferson AU RC	20.00	8.00
135	Z.Randolph AU RC	25.00	10.00
136	B.Haywood AU RC	12.00	5.00
137	Gilbert Arenas AU RC	75.00	35.00
138	Damone Brown AU RC	12.00	5.00
139	K.Satterfield AU RC	12.00	5.00
140	V.Radmanovic AU RC	12.00	5.00
141	Eddie Griffin JSY RC	12.00	5.00
142	Shane Battier JSY RC	12.00	5.00
143	M.Bradley JSY RC	12.00	5.00
144	Gerald Wallace JSY RC	15.00	6.00
145	S.Dalembert JSY RC	10.00	4.00
146	Tyson Chandler JSY RC	12.00	5.00
147	Pau Gasol JSY RC	20.00	8.00
148	Steven Hunter JSY RC	10.00	4.00
149	Rodney White JSY RC	10.00	4.00
150	Jeryl Sasser JSY RC	10.00	4.00
151	B.Armstrong JSY RC	12.00	5.00
152	Jamaal Tinsley JSY RC	12.00	5.00
153	DeSagana Diop JSY RC	10.00	4.00
154	Jason Richardson RC	8.00	3.00
155	Kirk Haston RC	4.00	1.50
156	Joseph Forte RC	5.00	2.00
157	Jason Collins RC	4.00	1.50
158	Kedrick Brown RC	4.00	1.50
159	Troy Murphy RC	6.00	2.50
160	Tony Parker RC	12.00	5.00
161	Raja Bell RC	4.00	1.50
162	Jeff Trepagnier RC	4.00	1.50
163	Terence Morris RC	4.00	1.50
164	Zeljko Rebraca RC	4.00	1.50

2002-03 Topps Jersey Edition

ASTERISKS PERCIEVED AS SP VERSION

JEAD	Antonio Davis R UER	12.00	5.00
JEAFM	Aaron McKie R UER	12.00	5.00
JEAHO	Allan Houston H	12.00	5.00
JEAI	Allen Iverson R *	20.00	8.00
JEAIV	Allen Iverson H	15.00	6.00
JEAJ	Antawn Jamison R	12.00	5.00
JEAK	Andrei Kirilenko R	12.00	5.00
JEALM	Andre Miller R	12.00	5.00
JEAMG	Drew Gooden R	20.00	8.00
JEAMI	Andre Miller R	12.00	5.00
JEAS	A.Stoudemire R RC	40.00	15.00
JEAST	Amare Stoudemire R	40.00	
JEBD	Baron Davis R	12.00	5.00
JEBDA	Baron Davis H	12.00	5.00
JEBG	Brian Grant R	12.00	5.00
JEBW	Ben Wallace R	12.00	5.00
JEBWA	Ben Wallace H	12.00	5.00
JECA	Courtney Alexander R UER	12.00	5.00
JECB	Carlos Boozer R RC	25.00	10.00
JECBU	Caron Butler R UER	20.00	8.00
JECJ	Chris Jefferies H RC	12.00	5.00
JECM	Cuttino Mobley R	12.00	5.00
JECW	C.Wilcox R UER RC	15.00	6.00
JEDAS	Damon Stoudamire H	12.00	5.00
JEDD	Dan Dickau R RC	12.00	5.00
JEDDI	Dan Dickau H UER	12.00	5.00
JEDF	Derek Fisher R	12.00	5.00
JEDGO	Drew Gooden R	20.00	8.00
JEDJG	Devean George R	12.00	5.00
JEDLM	Darius Miles R	12.00	5.00
JEDMA	Donyell Marshall R UER	12.00	05.00
JEDN	Dirk Nowitzki R	15.00	6.00
JEDNO	Dirk Nowitzki H	15.00	6.00
JEDW	DaJuan Wagner R	15.00	6.00
JEDWA	DaJuan Wagner H RC	15.00	6.00
JEEB	Elton Brand R	12.00	5.00
JEEBR	Elton Brand H	12.00	5.00
JEEC	Eddy Curry R	12.00	5.00
JEECU	Eddy Curry H	12.00	5.00
JEEG	Eddie Griffin R UER	12.00	5.00
JEEJ	Eddie Jones R	12.00	5.00
JEECW	Elden Campbell R UER	12.00	5.00
JEFJ	Fred Jones R RC	12.00	5.00
JEGA	Gilbert Arenas R UER	12.00	5.00
JEGDW	Bonzi Wells R	12.00	5.00
JEGG	Gordan Giricek R RC	15.00	6.00
JEGRO	Glenn Robinson H	12.00	5.00
JEJAR	Jason Richardson R	12.00	5.00
JEJAT	Jason Terry R	12.00	5.00
JEJCB	Caron Butler R	20.00	8.00
JEJDM	Jamaal Magloire R UER	12.00	05.00
JEJH	Juwan Howard R	12.00	5.00
JEJHS	John Stockton R	12.00	5.00
JEJKI	Jason Kidd H	15.00	6.00
JEJM	Jamal Mashburn R	12.00	5.00
JEJMJ	Joe Johnson R	12.00	5.00
JEJO	Jermaine O'Neal H	12.00	5.00
JEJON	Jermaine O'Neal H	12.00	5.00
JEJOS	John Stockton H	12.00	5.00
JEJR	Jalen Rose H	12.00	5.00
JEJRI	Jason Richardson H	12.00	5.00
JEJRO	Jalen Rose H	12.00	5.00
JEJRS	John Salmons R RC	12.00	5.00
JEJS	Joe Smith R	12.00	5.00
JEJT	Jamaal Tinsley R	12.00	5.00
JEJWL	Jerome Williams H	12.00	5.00
JEKAM	Karl Malone R	12.00	5.00
JEKG	Kevin Garnett R	20.00	8.00
JEKGA	Kevin Garnett H	20.00	8.00
JEKMA	Karl Malone H	12.00	5.00
JEKR	Kareem Rush R RC	12.00	5.00
JEKRU	Kareem Rush H	15.00	6.00
JEKS	Kenny Satterfield R	12.00	5.00
JEKV	Keith Van Horn R	12.00	5.00
JEKVH	Keith Van Horn H	12.00	5.00
JELSP	Latrell Sprewell H	12.00	5.00
JEMAF	Marcus Fizer R	12.00	5.00
JEMD	Mike Dunleavy H RC	20.00	8.00
JEMF	Michael Finley R	12.00	5.00
JEMO	Mehmet Okur R	12.00	5.00
JEMOK	Mehmet Okur H RC	12.00	5.00
JEMP	Morris Peterson R UER	12.00	5.00
JENT	N.Tskitishvili R RC	12.00	5.00
JENTS	Nikoloz Tskitishvili H	12.00	5.00
JEPG	Pau Gasol H	12.00	5.00
JEPGA	Pau Gasol R	12.00	5.00
JEPP	Paul Pierce R	12.00	5.00
JEQR	Quentin Richardson R	12.00	5.00
JEQRI	Quentin Richardson H	12.00	5.00
JEQW	Qyntel Woods R RC	12.00	5.00
JEQWO	Qyntel Woods H RC	12.00	5.00
JERAO	Ron Artest R	12.00	5.00
JERAW	Rasheed Wallace R	12.00	5.00
JERB	Rasual Butler R RC	12.00	5.00
JERBU	Rasual Butler H	12.00	5.00
JERCH	Richard Hamilton R	12.00	5.00
JERHO	Robert Horry R	12.00	5.00
JERIH	Richard Hamilton H	12.00	5.00
JERM	Reggie Miller R	12.00	5.00
JERWA	Rasheed Wallace H	12.00	5.00
JESA	Shareef Abdur-Rahim R	12.00	5.00
JESCB	Shane Battier R	12.00	5.00
JESDM	Shawn Marion R	12.00	5.00
JESFR	Steve Francis R	12.00	5.00
JESM	Stephon Marbury R	12.00	5.00
JESMA	Shawn Marion R	12.00	5.00
JESN	Steve Nash R	12.00	5.00
JESNA	Steve Nash H *	12.00	5.00
JESO	Shaquille O'Neal R	25.00	10.00
JESON	Shaquille O'Neal H	25.00	10.00
JETC	Tyson Chandler R	12.00	5.00
JETCH	Tyson Chandler H	12.00	5.00
JETDU	Tim Duncan R	25.00	10.00
JETDU	Tim Duncan R	20.00	8.00
JETH	Troy Hudson R	12.00	5.00
JETML	Tracy McGrady R	25.00	10.00
JETPA	Tony Parker R	12.00	5.00
JETPR	Tayshaun Prince R RC	15.00	6.00
JEWS	Wally Szczerbiak R	12.00	5.00
JEWSZ	Wally Szczerbiak H	12.00	5.00
JEYM	Yao Ming R RC	80.00	40.00
NNO	Kidd/Parker EXCH		
NNO	Walker/Webber EXCH	20.00	8.00
NNO	Pierce/Allen EXCH		
NNO	Payton/Dixon EXCH	20.00	8.00
NNO	McGrady/Dunleavy EXCH		
NNO	Ginobili/Stojakovic EXCH	20.00	8.00

2003-04 Topps Jersey Edition

	COMMON CARD	8.00	3.00
	COMMON ROOKIE	8.00	3.00
	COMMON SS RC	10.00	4.00
AD	Antonio Davis	8.00	3.00
AH	Allan Houston	8.00	3.00
AI	Allen Iverson	12.00	5.00
AJ	Antawn Jamison	8.00	3.00
AK	Andrei Kirilenko	8.00	3.00
AM	Andre Miller	8.00	3.00
AP	Aleksandar Pavlovic RC	10.00	4.00
AS	Amare Stoudemire	12.00	5.00
BB	Brent Barry	8.00	3.00
BC	Brian Cook RC EXCH	8.00	3.00
BD	Baron Davis	8.00	3.00
BH	Brandon Hunter RC	8.00	3.00
BJ	Bobby Jackson	8.00	3.00
BM	Brad Miller	8.00	3.00
BW	Ben Wallace	8.00	3.00
CA	Carmelo Anthony SS RC	30.00	12.50
CB	Caron Butler	8.00	3.00
CK	Chris Kaman RC	8.00	3.00
CM	Corey Maggette	8.00	3.00
CW	Chris Webber EXCH	8.00	3.00
DC	Derrick Coleman EXCH	8.00	3.00
DG	Drew Gooden	8.00	3.00
DJ	Dahntay Jones RC	8.00	3.00
DM	Desmond Mason EXCH	8.00	3.00
DN	Dirk Nowitzki	10.00	4.00
DW	Dwyane Wade SS RC	40.00	15.00
EB	Elton Brand AU	20.00	8.00
EC	Eddy Curry	8.00	3.00
EG	Manu Ginobili	8.00	3.00

GA	Gilbert Arenas	8.00	3.00	CWI	Corliss Williamson	8.00	3.00	32	Shaquille O'Neal	2.50	1.00
GP	Gary Payton EXCH	8.00	3.00	DAM	Darko Milicic SS RC	20.00	8.00	33	Carlos Arroyo	1.50	.60
GR	Glenn Robinson	8.00	3.00	DCH	Doug Christie	8.00	3.00	34	Jamaal Tinsley	1.00	.40
HT	Hedo Turkoglu	8.00	3.00	DGE	Devean George	8.00	3.00	35	Luke Ridnour	.60	.25
JB	Jerome Beasley RC	8.00	3.00	DMI	Darius Miles	8.00	3.00	36	Kenny Anderson	.25	.10
JC	Jamal Crawford	8.00	3.00	DWA	DaJuan Wagner EXCH	8.00	3.00	37	Brad Miller	1.00	.40
JH	Juwan Howard	8.00	3.00	DWE	David West SS RC	10.00	4.00	38	Caron Butler	1.00	.40
JJ	James Jones RC	8.00	3.00	JHA	Jarvis Hayes RC	8.00	3.00	39	Troy Murphy	1.00	.40
JK	Jason Kidd	10.00	4.00	JHO	Josh Howard RC	12.00	5.00	40	Vince Carter	2.50	1.00
JM	Jamal Mashburn	8.00	3.00	JKA	Jason Kapono SS RC	10.00	4.00	41	Shane Battier	1.00	.40
JO	Jermaine O'Neal	8.00	3.00	JMA	Jamaal Magloire	8.00	3.00	42	Joe Johnson	.60	.25
JR	Jalen Rose	8.00	3.00	JRI	Jason Richardson	8.00	3.00	43	Jason Kapono	.60	.25
JS	Jerry Stackhouse	8.00	3.00	JSM	Joe Smith EXCH	8.00	3.00	44	Juwan Howard	.60	.25
JT	Jason Terry	8.00	3.00	JWI	Jerome Williams	8.00	3.00	45	Zydrunas Ilgauskas	.60	.25
JW	Jason Williams	8.00	3.00	KMA	Kenyon Martin	8.00	3.00	46	Jerry Stackhouse	1.00	.40
KB	Kwame Brown	8.00	3.00	KVH	Keith Van Horn	8.00	3.00	47	Jamaal Magloire	.25	.10
KC	Keon Clark	8.00	3.00	MBA	Marcus Banks RC	8.00	3.00	48	Steve Francis	1.00	.40
KG	Kevin Garnett	12.00	5.00	MJA	Marc Jackson	8.00	3.00	49	Kwame Brown	.60	.25
KH	Kirk Hinrich AU RC	50.00	25.00	MPI	Mickael Pietrus RC	8.00	3.00	50	Kevin Garnett	2.00	.75
KM	Karl Malone EXCH	8.00	3.00	NVE	Nick Van Exel	8.00	3.00	51	Shareef Abdur-Rahim	1.00	.40
KP	Kendrick Perkins RC	8.00	3.00	RAR	Ron Artest	8.00	3.00	52	Tony Parker	1.00	.40
KR	Kareem Rush SS RC	8.00	3.00	RHO	Robert Horry	8.00	3.00	53	Marcus Camby	.60	.25
KT	Kurt Thomas	8.00	3.00	RLO	Raul Lopez	8.00	3.00	54	Morris Peterson	.60	.25
LB	Leandro Barbosa SS RC	15.00	6.00	RMI	Reggie Miller	8.00	3.00	55	Antoine Walker	1.00	.40
LJ	Lebron James SS RC	80.00	30.00	SAR	Shareef Abdur-Rahim	8.00	3.00	56	Elton Brand	1.00	.40
LO	Lamar Odom	8.00	3.00	SBA	Shane Battier	8.00	3.00	57	Paul Pierce	1.00	.40
LR	Luke Ridnour AU RC	25.00	10.00	SCL	Speedy Claxton	8.00	3.00	58	Jason Kidd	1.50	.60
LS	Latrell Sprewell	8.00	3.00	SMA	Stephon Marbury	8.00	3.00	59	Gerald Wallace	.60	.25
LW	Luke Walton SS RC	12.00	5.00	TMU	Troy Murphy	8.00	3.00	60	Jason Williams	.60	.25
MB	Mike Bibby	8.00	3.00	TPR	Tayshaun Prince	8.00	3.00	61	Dwyane Wade	3.00	1.25
MC	Marcus Camby	8.00	3.00	ZPA	Zaur Pachulia RC	8.00	3.00	62	Amare Stoudemire	2.00	.75
MD	Mike Dunleavy	8.00	3.00					63	T.J. Ford	.60	.25
MJ	Marko Jaric	8.00	3.00		**2004-05 Topps Luxury**			64	Tyson Chandler	1.00	.40
MM	Mike Miller	8.00	3.00		**Box**			65	Alonzo Mourning	.60	.25
MO	Michael Olowokandi	8.00	3.00					66	Dirk Nowitzki	1.50	.60
MP	Morris Peterson	8.00	3.00					67	Allan Houston	.60	.25
MR	Michael Redd EXCH	8.00	3.00					68	Andre Miller	.60	.25
MS	Mike Sweetney SS RC	10.00	4.00					69	Glenn Robinson	1.00	.40
MT	Maurice Taylor	8.00	3.00					70	Richard Hamilton	.60	.25
MW	Maurice Williams RC	8.00	3.00					71	Darius Miles	1.00	.40
NE	Ndudi Ebi RC	8.00	3.00					72	Mike Dunleavy	.60	.25
NH	Nene	8.00	3.00					73	Mike Bibby	1.00	.40
PG	Pau Gasol	8.00	3.00					74	Tracy McGrady	2.50	1.00
PP	Paul Pierce	8.00	3.00					75	Manu Ginobili	1.00	.40
PS	Peja Stojakovic	8.00	3.00					76	Jermaine O'Neal	1.00	.40
QR	Quentin Richardson	8.00	3.00					77	Rashard Lewis	1.00	.40
QW	Qyntel Woods	8.00	3.00					78	Corey Maggette	.60	.25
RA	Ray Allen	8.00	3.00					79	Chris Bosh	1.00	.40
RD	Ricky Davis	8.00	3.00					80	Pau Gasol	1.00	.40
RG	Reece Gaines SS RC	10.00	4.00					81	Carlos Boozer	1.00	.40
RH	Richard Hamilton	8.00	3.00					82	Desmond Mason	.60	.25
RJ	Richard Jefferson	8.00	3.00					83	Antawn Jamison	1.00	.40
RL	Raef LaFrentz	8.00	3.00	COMMON CARD (1-100)		.25	.10	84	Sam Cassell	.60	.25
RL	Rashard Lewis	8.00	3.00	COMMON ROOKIE (101-130)		3.00	1.25	85	Al Harrington	.60	.25
RM	Ron Mercer	8.00	3.00	COMMON CARD (131-150)		3.00	1.25	86	Steve Nash	1.00	.40
RN	Radoslav Nesterovic	8.00	3.00	1	Andrei Kirilenko	1.00	.40	87	Ricky Davis	1.00	.40
RW	Rasheed Wallace	8.00	3.00	2	Peja Stojakovic	1.00	.40	88	Chris Andersen	.25	.10
SB	Steve Blake RC	8.00	3.00	3	Grant Hill	1.00	.40	89	Kirk Hinrich	1.00	.40
SC	Sam Cassell	8.00	3.00	4	Baron Davis	1.00	.40	90	Carmelo Anthony	2.00	.75
SF	Steve Francis	8.00	3.00	5	Wally Szczerbiak	.60	.25	91	Ron Mercer	.25	.10
SM	Shawn Marion	8.00	3.00	6	Ray Allen	1.00	.40	92	Ben Wallace	1.00	.40
SN	Steve Nash	8.00	3.00	7	Shawn Marion	1.00	.40	93	Josh Howard	.60	.25
SO	Shaquille O'Neal AU	80.00	40.00	8	Gilbert Arenas	1.00	.40	94	Reggie Miller	1.00	.40
SP	Scottie Pippen	10.00	4.00	9	Keith Van Horn	.60	.25	95	Chris Webber	1.00	.40
TB	Troy Bell RC	8.00	3.00	10	Eddie Jones	1.00	.40	96	Drew Gooden	.60	.25
TC	Tyson Chandler EXCH	8.00	3.00	11	Lamar Odom	1.00	.40	97	Michael Redd	1.00	.40
TD	Tim Duncan	12.00	5.00	12	Stephen Jackson	.60	.25	98	Allen Iverson	2.00	.75
TF	T.J. Ford AU RC EXCH	25.00	10.00	13	Rasheed Wallace	1.00	.40	99	Kobe Bryant	4.00	1.50
TM	Tracy McGrady	15.00	6.00	14	Steve Smith	.60	.25	100	Stephon Marbury	1.00	.40
TO	Travis Outlaw RC	8.00	3.00	15	Gary Payton	1.00	.40	101	Dwight Howard RC	8.00	3.00
TP	Tony Parker	8.00	3.00	16	Jason Terry	1.00	.40	102	Emeka Okafor RC	10.00	4.00
TR	Theo Ratliff	8.00	3.00	17	Eddy Curry	.60	.25	103	Ben Gordon RC	10.00	4.00
TS	Theron Smith RC	8.00	3.00	18	Yao Ming	2.50	1.00	104	Shaun Livingston RC	4.00	1.50
TT	Tim Thomas	8.00	3.00	19	Kenyon Martin	1.00	.40	105	Devin Harris RC	4.00	1.50
WG	Willie Green RC	8.00	3.00	20	Jason Richardson	1.00	.40	106	Josh Childress RC	3.00	1.25
YM	Yao Ming	15.00	6.00	21	Bonzi Wells	.60	.25	107	Luol Deng RC	5.00	2.00
ZC	Zarko Cabarkapa RC	8.00	3.00	22	Richard Jefferson	.60	.25	108	Rafael Araujo RC	3.00	1.25
ZI	Zydrunas Ilgauskas	8.00	3.00	23	LeBron James	6.00	2.50	109	Andre Iguodala RC	6.00	2.50
ZP	Zoran Planinic RC	8.00	3.00	24	Marko Jaric	.60	.25	110	Luke Jackson RC	3.00	1.25
ZR	Zach Randolph	8.00	3.00	25	Chauncey Billups	1.00	.40	111	Andris Biedrins RC	5.00	2.00
AHA	Al Harrington	8.00	3.00	26	Jamal Crawford	.60	.25	112	Robert Swift RC	3.00	1.25
BDR	Boris Diaw RC	10.00	4.00	27	Willie Green	.25	.10	113	Sebastian Telfair RC	2.50	1.00
CBI	Chauncey Billups	8.00	3.00	28	Zach Randolph	1.00	.40	114	Kris Humphries RC	3.00	1.25
CBO	Chris Bosh RC	20.00	8.00	29	Latrell Sprewell	1.00	.40	115	Al Jefferson RC	6.00	2.50
CBO	Carlos Boozer	8.00	3.00	30	Tim Duncan	2.00	.75	116	Kirk Snyder RC	3.00	1.25
CMO	Cuttino Mobley	8.00	3.00	31	Cuttino Mobley	.60	.25	117	Josh Smith RC	5.00	2.00

118 J.R. Smith RC	5.00	2.00
119 Dorell Wright RC	5.00	2.00
120 Jameer Nelson RC	4.00	1.50
121 Andres Nocioni RC	3.00	1.25
122 Kevin Martin RC	4.00	1.50
123 Tony Allen RC	3.00	1.25
124 Anderson Varejao RC	3.00	1.25
125 Nenad Krstic RC	3.00	1.25
126 Sasha Vujacic RC	3.00	1.25
127 David Harrison RC	3.00	1.25
128 Pavel Podkolzin RC	3.00	1.25
129 Trevor Ariza RC	3.00	1.25
130 Delonte West RC	3.00	1.25
131 Rick Barry	3.00	1.25
132 Elgin Baylor	4.00	1.50
133 Larry Bird	8.00	3.00
134 Bob Cousy	3.00	1.25
135 Bill Russell	6.00	2.50
136 Walt Frazier	3.00	1.25
137 George Gervin	5.00	2.00
138 John Havlicek	5.00	2.00
139 James Worthy	5.00	2.00
140 Wilt Chamberlain	6.00	2.50
141 Dave Cowens	3.00	1.25
142 Moses Malone	4.00	1.50
143 Kevin McHale	3.00	1.25
144 Earl Monroe	3.00	1.25
145 Pete Maravich	12.00	5.00
146 Willis Reed	3.00	1.25
147 Oscar Robertson	5.00	2.00
148 Isiah Thomas	5.00	2.00
149 Bill Walton	4.00	1.50
150 Kareem Abdul-Jabbar	5.00	2.00

2005-06 Topps Luxury Box

COMP.SET w/o SP's (100)	50.00	20.00
COMMON CARD (1-100)	.30	.10
COMMON ROOKIE (101-145)	3.00	1.25
COMMON CELEB. (146-150)	4.00	1.50
1 Dwyane Wade	3.00	1.25
2 Joe Johnson	.60	.25
3 Larry Hughes	.60	.25
4 Michael Finley	1.00	.40
5 Josh Howard	.60	.25
6 Kenyon Martin	1.00	.40
7 Jermaine O'Neal	1.00	.40
8 Luke Ridnour	.60	.25
9 Andre Iguodala	1.00	.40
10 Wally Szczerbiak	.60	.25
11 Yao Ming	2.50	1.00
12 Dwight Howard	1.25	.50
13 Ricky Davis	1.00	.40
14 Baron Davis	1.00	.40
15 Carmelo Anthony	2.00	.75
16 Pau Gasol	1.00	.40
17 Robert Horry	.60	.25
18 Andres Nocioni	.30	.10
19 Sam Cassell	1.00	.40
20 Shareef Abdur-Rahim	1.00	.40
21 Gerald Wallace	1.00	.40
22 Vince Carter	2.50	1.00
23 LeBron James	6.00	2.50
24 Richard Hamilton	.60	.25
25 Shawn Marion	1.00	.40
26 Stephon Marbury	1.00	.40
27 Chris Bosh	1.00	.40
28 Darius Miles	1.00	.40
29 Jamaal Magloire	.30	.10
30 Kevin Garnett	2.00	.75
31 Lamar Odom	1.00	.40
32 Shaquille O'Neal	2.50	1.00
33 Allen Iverson	2.00	.75
34 Paul Pierce	1.00	.40
35 Keith Van Horn	.60	.25
36 Damon Stoudamire	.60	.25
37 Jason Richardson	1.00	.40
38 Ben Gordon	2.00	.75
39 J.R. Smith	.60	.25
40 Brad Miller	1.00	.40
41 Dirk Nowitzki	1.50	.60
42 Bonzi Wells	.60	.25
43 Corey Maggette	.60	.25
44 Tracy McGrady	2.50	1.00
45 T.J. Ford	.60	.25
46 Steve Francis	1.00	.40
47 Bobby Simmons	.30	.10
48 Eddy Curry	.60	.25
49 Antawn Jamison	1.00	.40
50 Emeka Okafor	1.50	.60
51 Tim Duncan	2.00	.75
52 Chauncey Billups	1.00	.40
53 Kwame Brown	.60	.25
54 Ray Allen	1.00	.40
55 Jason Kidd	1.50	.60
56 Marcus Camby	.30	.10
57 Stephen Jackson	.60	.25
58 Rasheed Wallace	1.00	.40
59 Rashard Lewis	1.00	.40
60 Sebastian Telfair	.60	.25
61 Manu Ginobili	1.00	.40
62 Kurt Thomas	.30	.10
63 Jamal Crawford	.60	.25
64 Jamaal Tinsley	.60	.25
65 Donyell Marshall	.30	.10
66 Chris Webber	1.00	.40
67 Peja Stojakovic	1.00	.40
68 P.J. Brown	.30	.10
69 Nenad Krstic	.60	.25
70 Ben Wallace	1.00	.40
71 Grant Hill	1.00	.40
72 Elton Brand	1.00	.40
73 Zach Randolph	1.00	.40
74 Josh Smith	1.00	.40
75 Samuel Dalembert	.30	.10
76 Andre Miller	.60	.25
77 Al Jefferson	1.00	.40
78 Caron Butler	.60	.25
79 Shaun Livingston	.75	.30
80 Richard Jefferson	.60	.25
81 Rafer Alston	.30	.10
82 Antoine Walker	1.00	.40
83 Zydrunas Ilgauskas	.30	.10
84 Morris Peterson	.60	.25
85 Marko Jaric	.30	.10
86 Steve Nash	1.00	.40
87 Kirk Hinrich	1.00	.40
88 Kobe Bryant	4.00	1.50
89 Eddie Jones	.30	.10
90 Luol Deng	1.00	.40
91 Ron Artest	.60	.25
92 Desmond Mason	.30	.10
93 Jason Terry	1.00	.40
94 Andrei Kirilenko	1.00	.40
95 Michael Redd	1.00	.40
96 Mehmet Okur	.30	.10
97 Mike Dunleavy	.60	.25
98 Mike Bibby	1.00	.40
99 Amare Stoudemire	2.00	.75
100 Gilbert Arenas	1.00	.40
101 Daniel Ewing RC	4.00	1.50
102 Andray Blatche RC	3.00	1.25
103 Jose Calderon RC	8.00	3.00
104 Shavlik Randolph RC	3.00	1.25
105 Travis Diener RC	3.00	1.25
106 Brandon Bass RC	3.00	1.25
107 Fabricio Oberto RC	3.00	1.25
108 Ryan Gomes RC	3.00	1.25
109 Gerald Fitch RC	3.00	1.25
110 James Singleton RC	3.00	1.25
111 Deron Williams RC	10.00	4.00
112 Gerald Green RC	6.00	2.50
113 C.J. Miles RC	3.00	1.25
114 Chris Paul RC	12.00	5.00
115 Julius Hodge RC	4.00	1.50
116 Salim Stoudamire RC	4.00	1.50
117 Raymond Felton RC	6.00	2.50
118 Nate Robinson RC	5.00	2.00
119 Sarunas Jasikevicius RC	4.00	1.50
120 Monta Ellis RC	6.00	2.50
121 Jarrett Jack RC	3.00	1.25
122 Orien Greene RC	3.00	1.25
123 Rashad McCants RC	6.00	2.50
124 Francisco Garcia RC	4.00	1.50
125 Antoine Wright RC	3.00	1.25
126 Luther Head RC	4.00	1.50
127 Martell Webster RC	3.00	1.25
128 Eddie Basden RC	3.00	1.25
129 Marvin Williams RC	6.00	2.50
130 Danny Granger RC	5.00	2.00
131 Charlie Villanueva RC	5.00	2.00
132 Hakim Warrick RC	6.00	2.50
133 Ike Diogu RC	4.00	1.50
134 Wayne Simien RC	4.00	1.50
135 Yaroslav Korolev RC	3.00	1.25
136 David Lee RC	5.00	2.00
137 Sean May RC	4.00	1.50
138 Linas Kleiza RC	3.00	1.25
139 Joey Graham RC	3.00	1.25
140 Jason Maxiell RC	6.00	2.50
141 Channing Frye RC	4.00	1.50
142 Andrew Bynum RC	8.00	3.00
143 Martynas Andriuskevicius RC	3.00	1.25
145 Johan Petro RC	3.00	1.25
146 Christie Brinkley RC	4.00	1.50
147 Jenny McCarthy RC	4.00	1.50
148 Shannon Elizabeth RC	4.00	1.50
149 Carmen Electra RC	4.00	1.50
150 Jay-Z	4.00	1.50

2006-07 Topps Luxury Box

1 Chris Bosh	1.25	.50
2 Dirk Nowitzki	2.00	.75
3 Ben Wallace	1.25	.50
4 Mike Bibby	1.25	.50
5 Josh Howard	.75	.30
6 Vince Carter	3.00	1.25
7 Andrei Kirilenko	1.25	.50
8 Richard Hamilton	.75	.30
9 Tony Parker	1.25	.50
10 Dwyane Wade	4.00	1.50
11 Amare Stoudemire	2.50	1.00
12 Tim Duncan	2.50	1.00
13 Steve Nash	1.25	.50
14 Dwight Howard	1.50	.60
15 Carmelo Anthony	2.50	1.00
16 Pau Gasol	1.25	.50
17 Zach Randolph	1.25	.50
18 Kirk Hinrich	1.25	.50
19 Stephon Marbury	1.25	.50
20 Tracy McGrady	3.00	1.25
21 Kevin Garnett	2.50	1.00
22 Michael Redd	1.25	.50
23 LeBron James	8.00	3.00
24 Kobe Bryant	5.00	2.00
25 Jason Kidd	2.00	.75
26 Baron Davis	1.25	.50
27 Jermaine O'Neal	1.25	.50
28 Ray Allen	1.25	.50
29 Joe Johnson	.75	.30

❏ 30 Elton Brand	1.25	.50
❏ 31 Chris Paul	3.00	1.25
❏ 32 Shaquille O'Neal	3.00	1.25
❏ 33 Allen Iverson	2.50	1.00
❏ 34 Paul Pierce	1.25	.50
❏ 35 Chauncey Billups	1.25	.50
❏ 36 Gerald Wallace	1.25	.50
❏ 37 Jason Richardson	1.25	.50
❏ 38 Yao Ming	3.00	1.25
❏ 39 Andre Iguodala	1.25	.50
❏ 40 Gilbert Arenas	1.25	.50
❏ 41 Larry Bird	8.00	3.00
❏ 42 Isiah Thomas	2.00	.75
❏ 43 Dominique Wilkins	2.50	1.00
❏ 44 Moses Malone	2.00	.75
❏ 45 George Gervin	2.00	.75
❏ 46 Chris Mullin	2.00	.75
❏ 47 Karl Malone	2.50	1.00
❏ 48 Bob McAdoo	2.00	.75
❏ 49 James Worthy	2.00	.75
❏ 50 Walt Frazier	2.00	.75
❏ 51 J.J. Redick RC	6.00	2.50
❏ 52 Tyrus Thomas RC	10.00	4.00
❏ 53 Rodney Carney RC	3.00	1.25
❏ 54 Jorge Garbajosa RC	6.00	2.50
❏ 55 Shawne Williams RC	4.00	1.50
❏ 56 Renaldo Balkman RC	3.00	1.25
❏ 57 Chris Quinn RC	3.00	1.25
❏ 58 Solomon Jones RC	3.00	1.25
❏ 59 Maurice Ager RC	3.00	1.25
❏ 60 Rudy Gay RC	6.00	2.50
❏ 61 Hassan Adams RC	4.00	1.50
❏ 62 Sergio Rodriguez RC	3.00	1.25
❏ 63 Dee Brown RC	4.00	1.50
❏ 64 Saer Sene RC	3.00	1.25
❏ 65 Allan Ray RC	3.00	1.25
❏ 66 Damir Markota RC	3.00	1.25
❏ 67 Bobby Jones RC	3.00	1.25
❏ 68 Kyle Lowry RC	3.00	1.25
❏ 69 Cedric Simmons RC	3.00	1.25
❏ 70 LaMarcus Aldridge RC	8.00	3.00
❏ 71 Mardy Collins RC	3.00	1.25
❏ 72 Daniel Gibson RC	8.00	3.00
❏ 73 Patrick O'Bryant RC	3.00	1.25
❏ 74 Josh Boone RC	3.00	1.25
❏ 75 Paul Davis RC	3.00	1.25
❏ 76 Craig Smith RC	3.00	1.25
❏ 77 Andrea Bargnani RC	10.00	4.00
❏ 78 Alexander Johnson RC	3.00	1.25
❏ 79 James Augustine RC	3.00	1.25
❏ 80 Jordan Farmar RC	6.00	2.50
❏ 81 Marcus Vinicius RC	3.00	1.25
❏ 82 Ryan Hollins RC	3.00	1.25
❏ 83 Marcus Williams RC	4.00	1.50
❏ 84 Will Blalock RC	3.00	1.25
❏ 85 Shannon Brown RC	3.00	1.25
❏ 86 Pops Mensah-Bonsu RC	3.00	1.25
❏ 87 P.J. Tucker RC	3.00	1.25
❏ 88 Steve Novak RC	3.00	1.25
❏ 89 Quincy Douby RC	3.00	1.25
❏ 90 Rajon Rondo RC	4.00	1.50
❏ 91 David Noel RC	3.00	1.25
❏ 92 Mile Ilic RC	3.00	1.25
❏ 93 Ronnie Brewer RC	4.00	1.50
❏ 94 James White RC	3.00	1.25
❏ 95 Hilton Armstrong RC	3.00	1.25
❏ 96 Randy Foye RC	6.00	2.50
❏ 97 Shelden Williams RC	4.00	1.50
❏ 98 Thabo Sefolosha RC	5.00	2.00
❏ 99 Brandon Roy RC	10.00	4.00
❏ 100 Adam Morrison RC	8.00	3.00

2005-06 Topps NBA Collector Chips

❏ COMPLETE SET (110)	160.00	80.00
❏ COMMON CHIP (1-90)	2.00	.75
❏ 1 Al Harrington	2.00	.75
❏ 2 Josh Smith	2.00	.75
❏ 3 Josh Childress	2.00	.75
❏ 4 Paul Pierce	2.00	.75
❏ 5 Al Jefferson	2.00	.75
❏ 6 Antoine Walker	2.00	.75
❏ 7 Brevin Knight	2.00	.75
❏ 8 Primoz Brezec	2.00	.75
❏ 9 Emeka Okafor	2.00	.75

❏ 10 Luol Deng	2.00	.75
❏ 11 Kirk Hinrich	2.00	.75
❏ 12 Ben Gordon	2.50	1.00
❏ 13 Drew Gooden	2.00	.75
❏ 14 LeBron James	8.00	3.00
❏ 15 Anderson Varejao	2.00	.75
❏ 16 Dirk Nowitzki	2.00	.75
❏ 17 Michael Finley	2.00	.75
❏ 18 Josh Howard	2.00	.75
❏ 19 Carmelo Anthony	2.50	1.00
❏ 20 Andre Miller	2.00	.75
❏ 21 Kenyon Martin	2.00	.75
❏ 22 Ben Wallace	2.00	.75
❏ 23 Richard Hamilton	2.00	.75
❏ 24 Rasheed Wallace	2.00	.75
❏ 25 Troy Murphy	2.00	.75
❏ 26 Jason Richardson	2.00	.75
❏ 27 Baron Davis	2.00	.75
❏ 28 Tracy McGrady	3.00	1.25
❏ 29 Yao Ming	3.00	1.25
❏ 30 Bob Sura	2.00	.75
❏ 31 Jermaine O'Neal	2.00	.75
❏ 32 Stephen Jackson	2.00	.75
❏ 33 Ron Artest	2.00	.75
❏ 34 Elton Brand	2.00	.75
❏ 35 Shaun Livingston	2.00	.75
❏ 36 Corey Maggette	2.00	.75
❏ 37 Kobe Bryant	5.00	2.00
❏ 38 Caron Butler	2.00	.75
❏ 39 Lamar Odom	2.00	.75
❏ 40 Pau Gasol	2.00	.75
❏ 41 Shane Battier	2.00	.75
❏ 42 Mike Miller	2.00	.75
❏ 43 Dwyane Wade	4.00	1.50
❏ 44 Shaquille O'Neal	3.00	1.25
❏ 45 Udonis Haslem	2.00	.75
❏ 46 Maurice Williams	2.00	.75
❏ 47 Desmond Mason	2.00	.75
❏ 48 Michael Redd	2.00	.75
❏ 49 Wally Szczerbiak	2.00	.75
❏ 50 Latrell Sprewell	2.00	.75
❏ 51 Kevin Garnett	2.50	1.00
❏ 52 Vince Carter	3.00	1.25
❏ 53 Jason Kidd	2.00	.75
❏ 54 Richard Jefferson	2.00	.75
❏ 55 J.R. Smith	2.00	.75
❏ 56 Jamaal Magloire	2.00	.75
❏ 57 Dan Dickau	2.00	.75
❏ 58 Jamal Crawford	2.00	.75
❏ 59 Stephon Marbury	2.00	.75
❏ 60 Trevor Ariza	2.00	.75
❏ 61 Grant Hill	2.00	.75
❏ 62 Steve Francis	2.00	.75
❏ 63 Dwight Howard	2.00	.75
❏ 64 Allen Iverson	2.50	1.00
❏ 65 Andre Iguodala	2.00	.75
❏ 66 Chris Webber	2.00	.75
❏ 67 Shawn Marion	2.00	.75
❏ 68 Amare Stoudemire	2.50	1.00
❏ 69 Steve Nash	2.00	.75
❏ 70 Zach Randolph	2.00	.75
❏ 71 Sebastian Telfair	2.00	.75
❏ 72 Darius Miles	2.00	.75
❏ 73 Peja Stojakovic	2.00	.75
❏ 74 Brad Miller	2.00	.75
❏ 75 Mike Bibby	2.00	.75
❏ 76 Tony Parker	2.00	.75
❏ 77 Tim Duncan	2.50	1.00
❏ 78 Manu Ginobili	2.00	.75
❏ 79 Rashard Lewis	2.00	.75
❏ 80 Ray Allen	2.00	.75
❏ 81 Luke Ridnour	2.00	.75
❏ 82 Morris Peterson	2.00	.75

❏ 83 Chris Bosh	2.00	.75
❏ 84 Jalen Rose	2.00	.75
❏ 85 Carlos Boozer	2.00	.75
❏ 86 Mehmet Okur	2.00	.75
❏ 87 Andrei Kirilenko	2.00	.75
❏ 88 Gilbert Arenas	2.00	.75
❏ 89 Antawn Jamison	2.00	.75
❏ 90 Larry Hughes	2.00	.75
❏ 91 Andrew Bogut	4.00	1.50
❏ 92 Marvin Williams	5.00	2.00
❏ 93 Chris Paul	8.00	3.00
❏ 94 Deron Williams	5.00	2.00
❏ 95 Gerald Green	5.00	2.00
❏ 96 Wayne Simien	4.00	1.50
❏ 97 Antoine Wright	3.00	1.25
❏ 98 Martell Webster	3.00	1.25
❏ 99 Channing Frye	5.00	2.00
❏ 100 Charlie Villanueva	5.00	2.00
❏ 101 Danny Granger	3.00	1.25
❏ 102 Chris Taft	3.00	1.25
❏ 103 Raymond Felton	5.00	2.00
❏ 104 Monta Ellis	4.00	1.50
❏ 105 Sean May	3.00	1.25
❏ 106 Joey Graham	3.00	1.25
❏ 107 Rashad McCants	5.00	2.00
❏ 108 Hakim Warrick	4.00	1.50
❏ 109 Julius Hodge	3.00	1.25
❏ 110 Ike Diogu	3.00	1.25

2001-02 Topps Pristine

❏ COMPLETE SET (110)	500.00	25.00
❏ COMP.SET w/o SP's (50)	120.00	50.00
❏ COMMON CARD (1-50)	1.50	.60
❏ COMMON ROOKIE (51-110)	3.00	1.25
❏ 1 Allen Iverson	5.00	2.00
❏ 2 Shawn Marion	2.50	1.00
❏ 3 Baron Davis	2.50	1.00
❏ 4 Peja Stojakovic	2.50	1.00
❏ 5 Dirk Nowitzki	4.00	1.50
❏ 6 Michael Jordan	25.00	10.00
❏ 7 Dikembe Mutombo	1.50	.60
❏ 8 Antoine Walker	2.50	1.00
❏ 9 David Robinson	2.50	1.00
❏ 10 Tracy McGrady	6.00	2.50
❏ 11 Rasheed Wallace	2.50	1.00
❏ 12 Kenyon Martin	2.50	1.00
❏ 13 Glenn Robinson	1.50	.60
❏ 14 Shareef Abdur-Rahim	2.50	1.00
❏ 15 Lamar Odom	2.50	1.00
❏ 16 Alonzo Mourning	1.50	.60
❏ 17 Latrell Sprewell	2.50	1.00
❏ 18 Stephon Marbury	2.50	1.00
❏ 19 Chris Webber	2.50	1.00
❏ 20 Darius Miles	2.50	1.00
❏ 21 Tim Duncan	5.00	2.00
❏ 22 Antawn Jamison	2.50	1.00
❏ 23 Jason Kidd	4.00	1.50
❏ 24 John Stockton	2.50	1.00
❏ 25 Michael Finley	2.50	1.00
❏ 26 Eddie Jones	2.50	1.00
❏ 27 Jamal Mashburn	1.50	.60
❏ 28 Paul Pierce	2.50	1.00
❏ 29 Jason Terry	2.50	1.00
❏ 30 Kobe Bryant	10.00	4.00
❏ 31 Reggie Miller	2.50	1.00
❏ 32 Elton Brand	2.50	1.00
❏ 33 Antonio McDyess	1.50	.60
❏ 34 Ray Allen	2.50	1.00

❑ 35	Kevin Garnett	5.00	2.00
❑ 36	Allan Houston	1.50	.60
❑ 37	Grant Hill	2.50	1.00
❑ 38	Jalen Rose	2.50	1.00
❑ 39	Gary Payton	2.50	1.00
❑ 40	Vince Carter	6.00	2.50
❑ 41	Jerry Stackhouse	2.50	1.00
❑ 42	Karl Malone	2.50	1.00
❑ 43	Wang Zhizhi	2.50	1.00
❑ 44	Marcus Fizer	1.50	.60
❑ 45	Marcus Camby	1.50	.60
❑ 46	Andre Miller	1.50	.60
❑ 47	Jason Williams	1.50	.60
❑ 48	Hakeem Olajuwon	2.50	1.00
❑ 49	Shaquille O'Neal	6.00	2.50
❑ 50	Steve Francis	2.50	1.00
❑ 51	Eddie Griffin U	2.50	1.00
❑ 52	Eddie Griffin U	3.00	1.25
❑ 53	Eddie Griffin R	4.00	1.50
❑ 54	Kwame Brown C RC	3.00	1.25
❑ 55	Kwame Brown U	4.00	1.50
❑ 56	Kwame Brown R	5.00	2.00
❑ 57	Shane Battier C RC	3.00	1.25
❑ 58	Shane Battier U	4.00	1.50
❑ 59	Shane Battier R	5.00	2.00
❑ 60	Eddy Curry C RC	5.00	2.00
❑ 61	Eddy Curry U	6.00	2.50
❑ 62	Eddy Curry R	8.00	3.00
❑ 63	Tyson Chandler C RC	5.00	2.00
❑ 64	Tyson Chandler U	6.00	2.50
❑ 65	Tyson Chandler R	8.00	3.00
❑ 66	Rodney White C RC	3.00	1.25
❑ 67	Rodney White U	5.00	2.00
❑ 68	Rodney White R	6.00	2.50
❑ 69	J.Richardson C RC	5.00	2.00
❑ 70	Jason Richardson U	6.00	2.50
❑ 71	Jason Richardson R	8.00	3.00
❑ 72	Joe Johnson C RC	6.00	2.50
❑ 73	Joe Johnson U	4.00	1.50
❑ 74	Joe Johnson R	5.00	2.00
❑ 75	Pau Gasol C RC	6.00	2.50
❑ 76	Pau Gasol U	8.00	3.00
❑ 77	Pau Gasol R	10.00	4.00
❑ 78	Desagana Diop C RC	3.00	1.25
❑ 79	Desagana Diop U	4.00	1.50
❑ 80	Desagana Diop R	5.00	2.00
❑ 81	V.Radmanovic C RC	2.50	1.00
❑ 82	V.Radmanovic U	3.00	1.25
❑ 83	V.Radmanovic R	4.00	1.50
❑ 84	Troy Murphy C RC	3.00	1.25
❑ 85	Troy Murphy U	5.00	2.00
❑ 86	Troy Murphy R	6.00	2.50
❑ 87	Zach Randolph C RC	6.00	2.50
❑ 88	Zach Randolph U	8.00	3.00
❑ 89	Zach Randolph R	10.00	4.00
❑ 90	Jamaal Tinsley C RC	3.00	1.25
❑ 91	Jamaal Tinsley U	4.00	1.50
❑ 92	Jamaal Tinsley R	5.00	2.00
❑ 93	Richard Jefferson C RC	3.00	1.25
❑ 94	Richard Jefferson U	4.00	1.50
❑ 95	Richard Jefferson R	5.00	2.00
❑ 96	Loren Woods C RC	3.00	1.25
❑ 97	Loren Woods U	4.00	1.50
❑ 98	Loren Woods R	5.00	2.00
❑ 99	Joseph Forte C RC	5.00	2.00
❑ 100	Joseph Forte U	6.00	2.50
❑ 101	Joseph Forte R	8.00	3.00
❑ 102	Gerald Wallace C RC	5.00	2.00
❑ 103	Gerald Wallace U	6.00	2.50
❑ 104	Gerald Wallace R	8.00	3.00
❑ 105	Andrei Kirilenko C RC	5.00	2.00
❑ 106	Andrei Kirilenko U	6.00	2.50
❑ 107	Andrei Kirilenko R	8.00	3.00
❑ 108	Tony Parker C RC	8.00	3.00
❑ 109	Tony Parker U	10.00	4.00
❑ 110	Tony Parker R	12.00	5.00

2002-03 Topps Pristine

❑	COMMON CARD (1-50)	.50	.20
❑	COMMON ROOKIE (51-125)	4.00	1.50
❑ 1	Shaquille O'Neal	4.00	1.50
❑ 2	Steve Nash	1.50	.60
❑ 3	Vince Carter	4.00	1.50
❑ 4	Michael Jordan	12.00	5.00
❑ 5	Chris Webber	1.50	.60
❑ 6	Tim Duncan	3.00	1.25

❑ 7	Vladimir Radmanovic	1.00	.40
❑ 8	Kobe Bryant	6.00	2.50
❑ 9	Allan Houston	1.00	.40
❑ 10	Tracy McGrady	4.00	1.50
❑ 11	Allen Iverson	3.00	1.25
❑ 12	Scottie Pippen	2.50	1.00
❑ 13	Steve Francis	1.50	.60
❑ 14	Reggie Miller	1.50	.60
❑ 15	Antoine Walker	1.50	.60
❑ 16	Shawn Marion	1.50	.60
❑ 17	Wally Szczerbiak	1.00	.40
❑ 18	Elton Brand	1.50	.60
❑ 19	Jerry Stackhouse	1.50	.60
❑ 20	Andre Miller	1.00	.40
❑ 21	Gary Payton	1.50	.60
❑ 22	Richard Hamilton	1.00	.40
❑ 23	Pau Gasol	1.50	.60
❑ 24	Juwan Howard	1.00	.40
❑ 25	Jalen Rose	1.50	.60
❑ 26	Eddie Jones	1.50	.60
❑ 27	Baron Davis	1.50	.60
❑ 28	Darrell Armstrong	.50	.20
❑ 29	John Stockton	1.50	.60
❑ 30	Mike Bibby	1.50	.60
❑ 31	Eddy Curry	1.50	.60
❑ 32	Kevin Garnett	4.00	1.50
❑ 33	Dikembe Mutombo	1.00	.40
❑ 34	Jason Kidd	2.50	1.00
❑ 35	Clifford Robinson	.50	.20
❑ 36	Ray Allen	1.50	.60
❑ 37	Paul Pierce	1.50	.60
❑ 38	Shane Battier	1.50	.60
❑ 39	Kenyon Martin	1.50	.60
❑ 40	Rasheed Wallace	1.50	.60
❑ 41	Latrell Sprewell	1.50	.60
❑ 42	Cuttino Mobley	1.00	.40
❑ 43	Karl Malone	1.50	.60
❑ 44	Dirk Nowitzki	2.50	1.00
❑ 45	Antawn Jamison	1.50	.60
❑ 46	Elden Campbell	.50	.20
❑ 47	Lamar Odom	1.50	.60
❑ 48	Jason Richardson	1.50	.60
❑ 49	Jermaine O'Neal	1.50	.60
❑ 50	Shareef Abdur-Rahim	1.50	.60
❑ 51	Yao Ming C RC	40.00	15.00
❑ 52	Yao Ming U	40.00	15.00
❑ 53	Yao Ming R	80.00	30.00
❑ 54	Jay Williams C RC	6.00	2.50
❑ 55	Jay Williams U	8.00	3.00
❑ 56	Jay Williams R	15.00	6.00
❑ 57	Mike Dunleavy C RC	8.00	3.00
❑ 58	Mike Dunleavy U	10.00	4.00
❑ 59	Mike Dunleavy R	20.00	8.00
❑ 60	Drew Gooden C RC	12.00	5.00
❑ 61	Drew Gooden U	15.00	6.00
❑ 62	Drew Gooden R	30.00	12.50
❑ 63	Nikoloz Tskitishvili C RC	6.00	2.50
❑ 64	Nikoloz Tskitishvili U	8.00	3.00
❑ 65	Nikoloz Tskitishvili R	15.00	6.00
❑ 66	DaJuan Wagner C RC	8.00	3.00
❑ 67	DaJuan Wagner U	10.00	4.00
❑ 68	DaJuan Wagner R	20.00	8.00
❑ 69	Nene Hilario C RC	6.00	2.50
❑ 70	Nene Hilario U	8.00	3.00
❑ 71	Nene Hilario R	15.00	6.00
❑ 72	Chris Wilcox C RC	6.00	2.50
❑ 73	Chris Wilcox U	8.00	3.00
❑ 74	Chris Wilcox R	15.00	6.00

❑ 75	Amare Stoudemire C RC	25.00	10.00
❑ 75A	A.Stoudemire G.Ref ERR		
❑ 76	A.Stoudemire G.Ref U	30.00	12.50
❑ 77	Amare Stoudemire R	60.00	25.00
❑ 78	Caron Butler C RC	8.00	3.00
❑ 79	Caron Butler U	10.00	4.00
❑ 80	Caron Butler R	20.00	8.00
❑ 81	Jared Jeffries C RC	4.00	1.50
❑ 82	Jared Jeffries U	5.00	2.00
❑ 83	Jared Jeffries R	10.00	4.00
❑ 84	Melvin Ely C RC	4.00	1.50
❑ 85	Melvin Ely U	5.00	2.00
❑ 86	Melvin Ely R	10.00	4.00
❑ 87	Marcus Haislip C RC	4.00	1.50
❑ 88	Marcus Haislip U	5.00	2.00
❑ 89	Marcus Haislip R	10.00	4.00
❑ 90	Fred Jones C RC	4.00	1.50
❑ 91	Fred Jones U	5.00	2.00
❑ 92	Fred Jones R	10.00	4.00
❑ 93	Casey Jacobsen C RC	4.00	1.50
❑ 94	Casey Jacobsen U	4.00	1.50
❑ 95	Casey Jacobsen R	8.00	3.00
❑ 96	John Salmons C RC	4.00	1.50
❑ 97	John Salmons U	5.00	2.00
❑ 98	John Salmons R	10.00	4.00
❑ 99	Juan Dixon C RC	6.00	2.50
❑ 100	Juan Dixon U	8.00	3.00
❑ 101	Juan Dixon R	15.00	6.00
❑ 102	Chris Jefferies C RC	4.00	1.50
❑ 103	Chris Jefferies U	5.00	2.00
❑ 104	Chris Jefferies R	10.00	4.00
❑ 105	Ryan Humphrey C RC	4.00	1.50
❑ 106	Ryan Humphrey U	5.00	2.00
❑ 107	Ryan Humphrey R	10.00	4.00
❑ 108	Kareem Rush C RC	5.00	2.00
❑ 109	Kareem Rush U	6.00	2.50
❑ 110	Kareem Rush R	12.00	5.00
❑ 111	Qyntel Woods C RC	4.00	1.50
❑ 112	Qyntel Woods U	5.00	2.00
❑ 113	Qyntel Woods R	10.00	4.00
❑ 114	Frank Williams C RC	4.00	1.50
❑ 115	Frank Williams U	5.00	2.00
❑ 116	Frank Williams R	10.00	4.00
❑ 117	Tayshaun Prince C RC	4.00	1.50
❑ 118	Tayshaun Prince U	6.00	2.50
❑ 119	Tayshaun Prince R	12.00	5.00
❑ 120	Carlos Boozer C RC	8.00	3.00
❑ 121	Carlos Boozer U	10.00	4.00
❑ 122	Carlos Boozer R	20.00	8.00
❑ 123	Dan Dickau C RC	4.00	1.50
❑ 124	Dan Dickau U	5.00	2.00
❑ 125	Dan Dickau R	8.00	3.00

2003-04 Topps Pristine

❑	COMP.SET w/o RC's (100)	60.00	25.00
❑	COMMON CARD (1-100)	.40	.15
❑	COMMON ROOKIE (101-197)	5.00	2.00
❑ 1	Tracy McGrady	3.00	1.25
❑ 2	DaJuan Wagner	.75	.30
❑ 3	Allen Iverson	2.50	1.00
❑ 4	Chris Webber	1.25	.50
❑ 5	Jason Kidd	2.00	.75
❑ 6	Eddie Jones	1.25	.50
❑ 7	Jermaine O'Neal	1.25	.50
❑ 8	Kobe Bryant	5.00	2.00
❑ 9	Tony Parker	1.25	.50
❑ 10	Wally Szczerbiak	.75	.30
❑ 11	Yao Ming	3.00	1.25

#	Player		
12	Amare Stoudemire	2.50	1.00
13	Steve Nash	1.25	.50
14	Baron Davis	1.25	.50
15	Vince Carter	3.00	1.25
16	Peja Stojakovic	1.25	.50
17	Desmond Mason	.75	.30
18	Antoine Walker	1.25	.50
19	Steve Francis	1.25	.50
20	Gary Payton	1.25	.50
21	Tim Duncan	2.50	1.00
22	Jalen Rose	1.25	.50
23	Jason Richardson	1.25	.50
24	Andre Miller	.75	.30
25	Allan Houston	.75	.30
26	Ron Artest	.75	.30
27	Andrei Kirilenko	1.25	.50
28	Kenyon Martin	1.25	.50
29	Kevin Garnett	2.50	1.00
30	Rasheed Wallace	1.25	.50
31	Shawn Marion	1.25	.50
32	Karl Malone	1.25	.50
33	Antawn Jamison	1.25	.50
34	Shaquille O'Neal	3.00	1.25
35	Paul Pierce	1.25	.50
36	Nene	.75	.30
37	Ray Allen	1.25	.50
38	Bonzi Wells	.75	.30
39	Ben Wallace	1.25	.50
40	Jerry Stackhouse	1.25	.50
41	Dirk Nowitzki	2.00	.75
42	Elton Brand	1.25	.50
43	Pau Gasol	1.25	.50
44	Richard Hamilton	1.25	.50
45	Shareef Abdur-Rahim	1.25	.50
46	Jason Terry	1.25	.50
47	Jamal Mashburn	.75	.30
48	Latrell Sprewell	1.25	.50
49	Keith Van Horn	1.25	.50
50	Mike Miller	1.25	.50
51	Theo Ratliff	.75	.30
52	Scottie Pippen	2.00	.75
53	Nick Van Exel	1.25	.50
54	Chauncey Billups	.75	.30
55	Al Harrington	.75	.30
56	Corey Maggette	.75	.30
57	Shane Battier	1.25	.50
58	Tim Thomas	.75	.30
59	Darius Miles	1.25	.50
60	Alonzo Mourning	.75	.30
61	Jamaal Magloire	.40	.15
62	Antonio McDyess	.75	.30
63	Juwan Howard	.75	.30
64	Eric Snow	.75	.30
65	Anfernee Hardaway	1.25	.50
66	Tayshaun Prince	.75	.30
67	Derek Anderson	.75	.30
68	Mike Bibby	1.25	.50
69	Deshawn Stevenson	.40	.15
70	Kwame Brown	1.25	.50
71	Jerome Williams	.40	.15
72	Radoslav Nesterovic	.75	.30
73	Stephon Marbury	1.25	.50
74	P.J. Brown	.40	.15
75	Sam Cassell	1.25	.50
76	Kenny Thomas	.40	.15
77	Jason Williams	.75	.30
78	Jamaal Tinsley	1.25	.50
79	Nikoloz Tskitishvili	.40	.15
80	Michael Finley	1.25	.50
81	Jamal Crawford	.40	.15
82	Brent Barry	.75	.30
83	Gilbert Arenas	1.25	.50
84	Morris Peterson	.75	.30
85	Manu Ginobili	1.25	.50
86	Dale Davis	.75	.30
87	Aaron McKie	.75	.30
88	Richard Jefferson	.75	.30
89	Michael Redd	1.25	.50
90	Reggie Miller	1.25	.50
91	Cuttino Mobley	.75	.30
92	Marcus Camby	.75	.30
93	Tony Delk	.40	.15
94	Tyson Chandler	.75	.30
95	Caron Butler	1.25	.50
96	Kurt Thomas	.75	.30
97	Glenn Robinson	1.25	.50
98	Brad Miller	1.25	.50
99	Matt Harpring	1.25	.50
100	Alvin Williams	.40	.15
101	LeBron James C RC	50.00	20.00
102	LeBron James U	75.00	30.00
103	LeBron James R	100.00	40.00
104	Darko Milicic C RC	6.00	2.50
105	Darko Milicic U	10.00	4.00
106	Darko Milicic R	12.00	5.00
107	Carmelo Anthony C RC	20.00	8.00
108	Carmelo Anthony U	25.00	10.00
109	Carmelo Anthony R	30.00	12.50
110	Chris Bosh C RC	10.00	4.00
111	Chris Bosh U	12.00	5.00
112	Chris Bosh R	15.00	6.00
113	Dwyane Wade C RC	25.00	10.00
114	Dwyane Wade U	30.00	12.50
115	Dwyane Wade R	40.00	15.00
116	Chris Kaman C RC	5.00	2.00
117	Chris Kaman U	5.00	2.00
118	Chris Kaman R	5.00	2.00
119	Kirk Hinrich C RC	6.00	2.50
120	Kirk Hinrich U	10.00	4.00
121	Kirk Hinrich R	12.00	5.00
122	T.J. Ford C RC	5.00	2.00
123	T.J. Ford U	5.00	2.00
124	T.J. Ford R	12.00	5.00
125	Mike Sweetney C RC	5.00	2.00
126	Mike Sweetney U	8.00	3.00
127	Mike Sweetney R	10.00	4.00
128	Jarvis Hayes C RC	5.00	2.00
129	Jarvis Hayes U	8.00	3.00
130	Jarvis Hayes R	10.00	4.00
131	Mickael Pietrus C RC	5.00	2.00
132	Mickael Pietrus U	8.00	3.00
133	Mickael Pietrus R	10.00	4.00
134	Nick Collison C RC	5.00	2.00
135	Nick Collison U	6.00	2.50
136	Nick Collison R	8.00	3.00
137	Marcus Banks C RC	5.00	2.00
138	Marcus Banks U	8.00	3.00
139	Marcus Banks R	10.00	4.00
140	Luke Ridnour C RC	5.00	2.00
141	Luke Ridnour U	8.00	3.00
142	Luke Ridnour R	10.00	4.00
143	Reece Gaines C RC	5.00	2.00
144	Reece Gaines U	8.00	3.00
145	Reece Gaines R	10.00	4.00
146	Troy Bell C RC	5.00	2.00
147	Troy Bell U	8.00	3.00
148	Troy Bell R	10.00	4.00
149	Zarko Cabarkapa C RC	5.00	2.00
150	Zarko Cabarkapa U	8.00	3.00
151	Zarko Cabarkapa R	10.00	4.00
152	David West C RC	5.00	2.00
153	David West U	8.00	3.00
154	David West R	10.00	4.00
155	Aleksandar Pavlovic C RC	6.00	2.50
156	Aleksandar Pavlovic U	8.00	3.00
157	Aleksandar Pavlovic R	10.00	4.00
158	Dahntay Jones C RC	5.00	2.00
159	Dahntay Jones U	8.00	3.00
160	Dahntay Jones R	10.00	4.00
161	Boris Diaw C RC	6.00	2.50
162	Boris Diaw U	8.00	3.00
163	Boris Diaw R	10.00	4.00
164	Zoran Planinic C RC	5.00	2.00
165	Zoran Planinic U	8.00	3.00
166	Zoran Planinic R	10.00	4.00
167	Travis Outlaw C RC	5.00	2.00
168	Travis Outlaw U	8.00	3.00
169	Travis Outlaw R	10.00	4.00
170	Brian Cook C RC	5.00	2.00
171	Brian Cook U	8.00	3.00
172	Brian Cook R	10.00	4.00
173	Travis Hansen C RC	5.00	2.00
174	Travis Hansen U	8.00	3.00
175	Travis Hansen R	10.00	4.00
176	Ndudi Ebi C RC	5.00	2.00
177	Ndudi Ebi U	8.00	3.00
178	Ndudi Ebi R	10.00	4.00
179	Kendrick Perkins C RC	5.00	2.00
180	Kendrick Perkins U	8.00	3.00
181	Kendrick Perkins R	10.00	4.00
182	Leandro Barbosa C RC	8.00	3.00
183	Leandro Barbosa U	10.00	4.00
184	Leandro Barbosa R	12.00	5.00
185	Josh Howard C RC	8.00	3.00
186	Josh Howard U	10.00	4.00
187	Josh Howard R	12.00	5.00
188	Maciej Lampe C RC	5.00	2.00
189	Maciej Lampe U	8.00	3.00
190	Maciej Lampe R	10.00	4.00
191	Jason Kapono C RC	5.00	2.00
192	Jason Kapono U	8.00	3.00
193	Jason Kapono R	10.00	4.00
194	Luke Walton C RC	5.00	2.00
195	Luke Walton U	6.00	2.50
196	Luke Walton R	8.00	3.00
197	Jerome Beasley C RC	5.00	2.00
198	Jerome Beasley U	8.00	3.00
199	Jerome Beasley R	10.00	4.00

2004-05 Topps Pristine

COMPLETE SET (199)			
COMMON CARD (1-100)		.40	.15
COMMON ROOKIE (101-197)		4.00	1.50
1	Ben Wallace	1.25	.50
2	Michael Redd	1.25	.50
3	Dwyane Wade	4.00	1.50
4	Chris Webber	1.25	.50
5	Cuttino Mobley	.75	.30
6	Bonzi Wells	.75	.30
7	Rashard Lewis	1.25	.50
8	Kobe Bryant	5.00	2.00
9	Gilbert Arenas	1.25	.50
10	Jeff Foster	.40	.15
11	Yao Ming	3.00	1.25
12	Ricky Davis	1.25	.50
13	Glenn Robinson	1.25	.50
14	Chauncey Billups	.75	.30
15	Carmelo Anthony	2.50	1.00
16	Pau Gasol	1.25	.50
17	Erick Dampier	.40	.15
18	Jason Terry	1.25	.50
19	Corey Maggette	.75	.30
20	Zach Randolph	1.25	.50
21	Kevin Garnett	2.50	1.00
22	Steve Nash	1.25	.50
23	LeBron James	8.00	3.00
24	Andre Miller	.75	.30
25	Manu Ginobili	1.25	.50
26	Gordan Giricek	.75	.30
27	Juwan Howard	.75	.30
28	Brad Miller	1.25	.50
29	Al Harrington	.75	.30
30	Allen Iverson	2.50	1.00
31	Shawn Marion	1.25	.50
32	Elton Brand	1.25	.50
33	Steve Francis	1.25	.50
34	Shaquille O'Neal	3.00	1.25
35	Marcus Camby	.75	.30
36	Tyson Chandler	.75	.30
37	Dirk Nowitzki	2.00	.75
38	Damon Stoudamire	.75	.30
39	Richard Hamilton	.75	.30
40	Kurt Thomas	.75	.30
41	Paul Pierce	1.25	.50
42	Jarvis Hayes	.75	.30
43	Ray Allen	1.25	.50
44	Keith Van Horn	1.25	.50
45	Kirk Hinrich	1.25	.50
46	Caron Butler	.75	.30
47	Andrei Kirilenko	1.25	.50

#	Player		
48	Jamaal Magloire	.40	.15
49	Chris Kaman	.75	.30
50	Stephon Marbury	1.25	.50
51	Mike Miller	1.25	.50
52	Eddy Curry	.75	.30
53	Sam Cassell	1.25	.50
54	Vince Carter	3.00	1.25
55	Jason Kidd	2.00	.75
56	Desmond Mason	.75	.30
57	Nene	.75	.30
58	Gerald Wallace	.75	.30
59	Baron Davis	1.25	.50
60	Tim Duncan	2.50	1.00
61	Drew Gooden	.75	.30
62	Jason Williams	.75	.30
63	Eddie Jones	1.25	.50
64	Michael Finley	1.25	.50
65	Gary Payton	1.25	.50
66	Kenyon Martin	1.25	.50
67	Mike Bibby	1.25	.50
68	Jason Kapono	.75	.30
69	Allan Houston	.75	.30
70	Ron Artest	1.25	.50
71	Rasho Nesterovic	.75	.30
72	Kwame Brown	.75	.30
73	Wally Szczerbiak	.75	.30
74	Joe Johnson	.75	.30
75	Jamal Mashburn	.75	.30
76	Peja Stojakovic	1.25	.50
77	Lamar Odom	1.25	.50
78	Jalen Rose	1.25	.50
79	Mike Dunleavy	.75	.30
80	Rasheed Wallace	1.25	.50
81	Richard Jefferson	.75	.30
82	Luke Ridnour	.75	.30
83	Samuel Dalembert	.40	.15
84	Zydrunas Ilgauskas	.75	.30
85	Carlos Arroyo	2.00	.75
86	Primoz Brezec	.75	.30
87	Chris Bosh	1.25	.50
88	Antoine Walker	1.25	.50
89	Boris Diaw	.40	.15
90	Tracy McGrady	3.00	1.25
91	Amare Stoudemire	2.50	1.00
92	Karl Malone	1.25	.50
93	Jamal Crawford	.75	.30
94	Shareef Abdur-Rahim	1.25	.50
95	Jason Richardson	1.25	.50
96	Marcus Banks	.75	.30
97	Jermaine O'Neal	1.25	.50
98	Latrell Sprewell	1.25	.50
99	Tony Parker	1.25	.50
100	Carlos Boozer	1.25	.50
101	Dwight Howard C RC	12.00	5.00
102	Dwight Howard U	20.00	8.00
103	Dwight Howard R	25.00	10.00
104	Ben Gordon C RC	15.00	6.00
105	Ben Gordon U	30.00	12.50
106	Ben Gordon R	40.00	15.00
107	Devin Harris C RC	6.00	2.50
108	Devin Harris U	10.00	4.00
109	Devin Harris R	12.00	5.00
110	Rafael Araujo C RC	4.00	1.50
111	Rafael Araujo U	6.00	2.50
112	Rafael Araujo R	8.00	3.00
113	Luke Jackson C RC	4.00	1.50
114	Luke Jackson U	5.00	2.00
115	Luke Jackson R	6.00	2.50
116	Yuta Tabuse C RC	8.00	3.00
117	Yuta Tabuse U	12.00	5.00
118	Yuta Tabuse R	15.00	6.00
119	Kris Humphries C RC	4.00	1.50
120	Kris Humphries U	6.00	2.50
121	Kris Humphries R	8.00	3.00
122	Josh Smith C RC	8.00	3.00
123	Josh Smith U	12.00	5.00
124	Josh Smith R	15.00	6.00
125	Dorell Wright C RC	6.00	2.50
126	Dorell Wright U	8.00	3.00
127	Dorell Wright R	10.00	4.00
128	Jackson Vroman C RC	4.00	1.50
129	Jackson Vroman U	6.00	2.50
130	Jackson Vroman R	8.00	3.00
131	Sasha Vujacic C RC	4.00	1.50
132	Sasha Vujacic U	6.00	2.50
133	Sasha Vujacic R	8.00	3.00
134	David Harrison C RC	4.00	1.50
135	David Harrison U	6.00	2.50
136	David Harrison R	8.00	3.00
137	Blake Stepp C RC	4.00	1.50
138	Blake Stepp U	6.00	2.50
139	Blake Stepp R	8.00	3.00
140	Lionel Chalmers C RC	4.00	1.50
141	Lionel Chalmers U	6.00	2.50
142	Lionel Chalmers R	8.00	3.00
143	Delonte West C RC	6.00	3.00
144	Delonte West U	12.00	5.00
145	Delonte West R	15.00	6.00
146	Kevin Martin C RC	6.00	2.50
147	Kevin Martin U	8.00	3.00
148	Kevin Martin R	10.00	4.00
149	Robert Swift C RC	4.00	1.50
150	Robert Swift U	6.00	2.50
151	Robert Swift R	8.00	3.00
152	Trevor Ariza C RC	5.00	2.00
153	Trevor Ariza U	8.00	3.00
154	Trevor Ariza R	10.00	4.00
155	Peter John Ramos C RC	4.00	1.50
156	Peter John Ramos U	6.00	2.50
157	Peter John Ramos R	8.00	3.00
158	Anderson Varejao C RC	5.00	2.00
159	Anderson Varejao U	8.00	3.00
160	Anderson Varejao R	10.00	4.00
161	Andre Emmett C RC	4.00	1.50
162	Andre Emmett U	6.00	2.50
163	Andre Emmett R	8.00	3.00
164	Tony Allen C RC	5.00	2.00
165	Tony Allen U	8.00	3.00
166	Tony Allen R	10.00	4.00
167	Jameer Nelson C RC	6.00	2.50
168	Jameer Nelson U	12.00	5.00
169	Jameer Nelson R	15.00	6.00
170	J.R. Smith C RC	10.00	4.00
171	J.R. Smith U	15.00	6.00
172	J.R. Smith R	20.00	8.00
173	Kirk Snyder C RC	4.00	1.50
174	Kirk Snyder U	6.00	2.50
175	Kirk Snyder R	8.00	3.00
176	Al Jefferson C RC	10.00	4.00
177	Al Jefferson U	15.00	6.00
178	Al Jefferson R	20.00	8.00
179	Sebastian Telfair C RC	4.00	1.50
180	Sebastian Telfair U	8.00	3.00
181	Sebastian Telfair R	10.00	4.00
182	Andris Biedrins C RC	4.00	1.50
183	Andris Biedrins U	6.00	2.50
184	Andris Biedrins R	8.00	3.00
185	Andre Iguodala C RC	10.00	4.00
186	Andre Iguodala U	15.00	6.00
187	Andre Iguodala R	20.00	8.00
188	Luol Deng C RC	8.00	3.00
189	Luol Deng U	12.00	5.00
190	Luol Deng R	15.00	6.00
191	Josh Childress C RC	5.00	2.00
192	Josh Childress U	8.00	3.00
193	Josh Childress R	10.00	4.00
194	Shaun Livingston C RC	6.00	2.50
195	Shaun Livingston U	10.00	4.00
196	Shaun Livingston R	12.00	5.00
197	Emeka Okafor C RC	15.00	6.00
198	Emeka Okafor U	25.00	10.00
199	Emeka Okafor R	30.00	12.50

2005-06 Topps Pristine

COMP.SET w/o SP's	60.00	25.00
COMMON CARD (1-100)	.25	.10
SEMISTARS	.60	.25
UNLISTED STARS	1.00	.40
COMMON ROOKIE (101-130)	5.00	2.00
UNCOMMON RELIC (131-180)	8.00	3.00
SEMISTARS RELIC	8.00	3.00
UNLISTED STARS RELIC	8.00	3.00
RELIC PRINT RUN 500 SER.#'d SETS		
RARE AUTOGRAPH (181-205)	20.00	8.00
SEMISTARS AU	20.00	8.00
UNLISTED STARS AU	20.00	8.00
AUTO PRINT RUN 100 SER.#'d SETS		
UNLESS LISTED IN CHECKLIST		
SCARCE JSY AU (206-210)		
JSY AU PRINT RUN 50 SER.#'d SETS		

#	Player		
1	Ray Allen	1.00	.40
2	Cuttino Mobley	.60	.25
3	Sebastian Telfair	.60	.25
4	Dwight Howard	1.25	.50
5	Udonis Haslem	1.00	.40
6	Luol Deng	1.00	.40
7	Lamar Odom	1.00	.40
8	Paul Pierce	1.00	.40
9	Stephen Jackson	.60	.25
10	Mike Dunleavy	.60	.25
11	Andre Miller	.60	.25
12	Ben Gordon	2.00	.75
13	Caron Butler	.60	.25
14	Al Jefferson	1.00	.40
15	Jamaal Tinsley	.60	.25
16	Josh Childress	.60	.25
17	Larry Hughes	.60	.25
18	Andrei Kirilenko	1.00	.40
19	Brad Miller	1.00	.40
20	Steve Nash	1.00	.40
21	Grant Hill	1.00	.40
22	Samuel Dalembert	.60	.25
23	Quentin Richardson	.60	.25
24	Wally Szczerbiak	.60	.25
25	Desmond Mason	.60	.25
26	Dwyane Wade	3.00	1.25
27	Richard Hamilton	.60	.25
28	Shane Battier	1.00	.40
29	Chauncey Billups	1.00	.40
30	Shawn Marion	1.00	.40
31	Kenyon Martin	1.00	.40
32	Marquis Daniels	.60	.25
33	Al Harrington	.60	.25
34	Brendan Haywood	.25	.10
35	Mehmet Okur	.25	.10
36	Rafer Alston	.25	.10
37	Luke Ridnour	.60	.25
38	Tim Duncan	2.00	.75
39	Mike Miller	1.00	.40
40	Allen Iverson	2.00	.75
41	Jamal Crawford	.60	.25
42	J.R. Smith	.60	.25
43	Kevin Garnett	1.00	.40
44	Baron Davis	1.00	.40
45	Corey Maggette	.60	.25
46	Jermaine O'Neal	1.00	.40
47	Yao Ming	2.50	1.00
48	Pau Gasol	1.00	.40
49	Devin Harris	1.00	.40
50	Emeka Okafor	1.50	.60
51	Zydrunas Ilgauskas	.60	.25
52	Vladimir Radmanovic	.25	.10
53	Tracy McGrady	2.50	1.00
54	Steve Francis	1.00	.40
55	Stephon Marbury	1.00	.40
56	Shaun Livingston	1.00	.40
57	Sam Cassell	1.00	.40
58	Rasheed Wallace	1.00	.40
59	Primoz Brezec	.25	.10
60	Nenad Krstic	.60	.25
61	Mike Bibby	1.00	.40
62	Marcus Camby	.25	.10
63	LeBron James	6.00	2.50
64	Kobe Bryant	4.00	1.50
65	Josh Smith	.60	.25
66	Jason Richardson	1.00	.40
67	Jamaal Magloire	.25	.10
68	Gilbert Arenas	1.00	.40
69	Zach Randolph	.60	.25
70	Vince Carter	2.50	1.00

#	Player		
71	Tony Parker	1.00	.40
72	Shaquille O'Neal	2.50	1.00
73	Richard Jefferson	.60	.25
74	Rashard Lewis	1.00	.40
75	Peja Stojakovic	1.00	.40
76	Mike Sweetney	.60	.25
77	Elton Brand	1.00	.40
78	Drew Gooden	.60	.25
79	Chris Webber	1.00	.40
80	Carmelo Anthony	2.00	.75
81	Bobby Simmons	.25	.10
82	Bob Sura	.60	.25
83	Antoine Walker	1.00	.40
84	Andre Iguodala	1.00	.40
85	Michael Redd	1.00	.40
86	Manu Ginobili	1.00	.40
87	Latrell Sprewell	1.00	.40
88	Kirk Hinrich	1.00	.40
89	Josh Howard	.60	.25
90	Jason Kidd	1.50	.60
91	Jalen Rose	1.00	.40
92	Gerald Wallace	.60	.25
93	Eddy Curry	.60	.25
94	Dirk Nowitzki	1.50	.60
95	Joe Johnson	.60	.25
96	Chris Bosh	1.00	.40
97	Carlos Boozer	.60	.25
98	Ben Wallace	1.00	.40
99	Antawn Jamison	1.00	.40
100	Amare Stoudemire	2.00	.75
101	Andrew Bogut RC	6.00	2.50
102	Marvin Williams RC	10.00	4.00
103	Deron Williams RC	15.00	6.00
104	Chris Paul RC	20.00	8.00
105	Raymond Felton RC	8.00	3.00
106	Martell Webster RC	5.00	2.00
107	Charlie Villanueva RC	8.00	3.00
108	Channing Frye RC	6.00	2.50
109	Ike Diogu RC	6.00	2.50
110	Andrew Bynum RC	15.00	6.00
111	Monta Ellis RC	8.00	3.00
112	Yaroslav Korolev RC	5.00	2.00
113	Sean May RC	4.00	1.50
114	Rashad McCants RC	8.00	3.00
115	Antoine Wright RC	5.00	2.00
116	Joey Graham RC	5.00	2.00
117	Danny Granger RC	8.00	3.00
118	Gerald Green RC	12.00	5.00
119	Hakim Warrick RC	10.00	4.00
120	Julius Hodge RC	6.00	2.50
121	Nate Robinson RC	8.00	3.00
122	Jarrett Jack RC	5.00	2.00
123	Francisco Garcia RC	6.00	2.50
124	Luther Head RC	6.00	2.50
125	C.J. Miles RC	5.00	2.00
126	Salim Stoudamire RC	6.00	2.50
127	Sarunas Jasikevicius RC	6.00	2.50
128	Wayne Simien RC	6.00	2.50
129	David Lee RC	8.00	3.00
130	Jay-Z	8.00	3.00
131	Tim Duncan JSY	10.00	4.00
132	Ray Allen JSY	8.00	3.00
133	Grant Hill Warm	8.00	3.00
134	Dwyane Wade Shorts	15.00	6.00
135	Shawn Marion JSY	8.00	3.00
136	Jermaine O'Neal JSY	8.00	3.00
137	Emeka Okafor JSY	8.00	3.00
138	Tracy McGrady JSY	12.00	5.00
139	Chris Bosh Shorts	8.00	3.00
140	Dwight Howard JSY	8.00	3.00
141	Elton Brand JSY	8.00	3.00
142	Manu Ginobili JSY	8.00	3.00
143	Dirk Nowitzki JSY	8.00	3.00
144	Ben Wallace Warm	8.00	3.00
145	Steve Nash Warm	8.00	3.00
146	Allen Iverson Shirt	10.00	4.00
147	Kevin Garnett JSY	10.00	4.00
148	Corey Maggette JSY	8.00	3.00
149	Yao Ming JSY	12.00	5.00
150	Kobe Bryant Shorts	20.00	8.00
151	Rashad Wallace JSY	8.00	3.00
152	Ben Gordon JSY	10.00	4.00
153	Gilbert Arenas Shirt	8.00	3.00
154	Shaquille O'Neal Warm	12.00	5.00
155	Peja Stojakovic JSY	8.00	3.00
156	Carmelo Anthony JSY	10.00	4.00
157	Kirk Hinrich JSY	8.00	3.00
158	Paul Pierce Shirt	8.00	3.00
159	Antawn Jamison JSY	8.00	3.00
160	Amare Stoudemire Shirt	10.00	4.00
161	Sarunas Jasikevicius Shorts	8.00	3.00
162	Wayne Simien JSY	8.00	3.00
163	Channing Frye JSY	12.00	5.00
164	Antoine Wright JSY	8.00	3.00
165	Sean May JSY	6.00	2.50
166	Rashad McCants JSY	8.00	3.00
167	Julius Hodge JSY	8.00	3.00
168	Nate Robinson JSY	10.00	4.00
169	Jarrett Jack JSY	8.00	3.00
170	Francisco Garcia JSY	8.00	3.00
171	Charlie Villanueva JSY	10.00	4.00
172	Andrew Bogut JSY	10.00	4.00
173	David Lee JSY	8.00	3.00
174	Deron Williams JSY	15.00	6.00
175	Chris Paul JSY	25.00	10.00
176	Raymond Felton JSY	10.00	4.00
177	Martell Webster JSY	8.00	3.00
178	Danny Granger JSY	10.00	4.00
179	Gerald Green JSY	10.00	4.00
180	Hakim Warrick JSY	10.00	4.00
181	Shaun Livingston JSY	20.00	8.00
182	Danny Granger AU	25.00	10.00
183	Ryan Gomes AU	20.00	8.00
184	Jermaine O'Neal AU/75	25.00	10.00
185	George Gervin AU/60	30.00	12.50
186	Allen Iverson AU	200.00	100.00
187	Sean May AU	20.00	8.00
188	Andrew Bogut AU	30.00	12.50
189	Deron Williams AU	50.00	20.00
190	Stephon Marbury AU	25.00	10.00
191	Jason Kidd AU	30.00	12.50
192	Raymond Felton AU	30.00	12.50
193	Rashad McCants AU	30.00	12.50
194	Gerald Green AU	40.00	15.00
195	Andrew Bynum AU	50.00	20.00
196	Charlie Villanueva AU	40.00	15.00
197	Antoine Wright AU	20.00	8.00
198	Martell Webster AU	20.00	8.00
199	Francisco Garcia AU	20.00	8.00
200	Emeka Okafor AU	20.00	8.00
201	Hakim Warrick AU	30.00	12.50
202	Joey Graham AU	20.00	8.00
203	Julius Hodge AU	20.00	8.00
204	Ike Diogu AU	20.00	8.00
205	Johan Petro AU RC	20.00	8.00
206	Shaquille O'Neal JSY AU	80.00	40.00
207	Carmelo Anthony JSY AU		
208	Andrew Bogut AU		
209	Deron Williams AU	80.00	40.00
210	Jay-Z Jeans AU	150.00	75.00

2000-01 Topps Reserve

	COMPLETE SET (134)	300.00	150.00
	COMP.SET w/o SPs (100)	80.00	40.00
	COMMON CARD (1-100)	.40	.15
	COMMON ROOKIE/499	6.00	2.50
	COMMON ROOKIE/999	5.00	2.00
	COMMON ROOKIE/1499	4.00	1.50
1	Tim Duncan	2.50	1.00
2	Clifford Robinson	.40	.15
3	Allen Iverson	2.50	1.00
4	Marcus Camby	.75	.30
5	Chauncey Billups	.75	.30
6	Anthony Mason	.40	.15
7	Toni Kukoc	.75	.30
8	Tim Thomas	.75	.30
9	Corey Maggette	.75	.30
10	Steve Francis	1.25	.50
11	Larry Hughes	.75	.30
12	Jerome Williams	.40	.15
13	Reggie Miller	1.25	.50
14	Chris Gatling	.40	.15
15	Ron Artest	.40	.15
16	Derrick Coleman	.40	.15
17	Paul Pierce	1.25	.50
18	Dikembe Mutombo	.75	.30
19	Andre Miller	.75	.30
20	Gary Payton	1.25	.50
21	Kevin Garnett	2.50	1.00
22	Allan Houston	.75	.30
23	Rasheed Wallace	1.25	.50
24	Derek Anderson	.75	.30
25	Vin Baker	.75	.30
26	John Stockton	1.25	.50
27	Richard Hamilton	.75	.30
28	Mike Bibby	1.25	.50
29	Dale Davis	.40	.15
30	Vince Carter	3.00	1.25
31	Shawn Marion	1.25	.50
32	Karl Malone	1.25	.50
33	Patrick Ewing	1.25	.50
34	Shaquille O'Neal	3.00	1.25
35	Jermaine O'Neal	1.25	.50
36	Danny Fortson	.40	.15
37	Steve Nash	1.25	.50
38	Antoine Walker	1.25	.50
39	Jason Terry	1.25	.50
40	Vlade Divac	.75	.30
41	Avery Johnson	.40	.15
42	Elton Brand	1.25	.50
43	Mitch Richmond	.75	.30
44	Antonio Davis	.40	.15
45	Shawn Kemp	.75	.30
46	Anfernee Hardaway	1.25	.50
47	Kendall Gill	.40	.15
48	Glen Rice	.75	.30
49	Tim Hardaway	.75	.30
50	Tracy McGrady	3.00	1.25
51	Horace Grant	.75	.30
52	Hakeem Olajuwon	1.25	.50
53	Antawn Jamison	1.25	.50
54	Dirk Nowitzki	2.00	.75
55	Antonio McDyess	.75	.30
56	Michael Dickerson	.40	.15
57	Baron Davis	1.25	.50
58	Nick Van Exel	1.25	.50
59	Joe Smith	.75	.30
60	Kobe Bryant	5.00	2.00
61	Ray Allen	1.25	.50
62	Keith Van Horn	1.25	.50
63	Latrell Sprewell	1.25	.50
64	Jason Kidd	2.00	.75
65	Chris Webber	1.25	.50
66	David Robinson	1.25	.50
67	Mark Jackson	.75	.30
68	Bryon Russell	.40	.15
69	Lamar Odom	.75	.30
70	Maurice Taylor	.75	.30
71	Jonathan Bender	.75	.30
72	Raef LaFrentz	.75	.30
73	Sam Cassell	1.25	.50
74	Wally Szczerbiak	.75	.30
75	Grant Hill	1.25	.50
76	Theo Ratliff	.75	.30
77	Rashard Lewis	.75	.30
78	Darrell Armstrong	.40	.15
79	Glenn Robinson	1.25	.50
80	Stephon Marbury	1.25	.50
81	Michael Olowokandi	.40	.15
82	Isaiah Rider	.40	.15
83	Jalen Rose	1.25	.50
84	Cuttino Mobley	.75	.30
85	Jerry Stackhouse	1.25	.50
86	Jamal Mashburn	.75	.30
87	Kenny Anderson	.75	.30
88	Michael Finley	1.25	.50
89	Lamond Murray	.40	.15
90	Eddie Jones	1.25	.50
91	Eric Snow	.75	.30
92	Terrell Brandon	.75	.30

❏ 93	Jason Williams	.75	.30
❏ 94	Scottie Pippen	2.00	.75
❏ 95	Rod Strickland	.40	.15
❏ 96	Jim Jackson	.40	.15
❏ 97	Ron Mercer	.75	.30
❏ 98	Juwan Howard	.75	.30
❏ 99	Brian Grant	.75	.30
❏ 100	Shareef Abdur-Rahim	1.25	.50
❏ 101	Kenyon Martin/499 RC	20.00	8.00
❏ 102	Stromile Swift/999 RC	8.00	3.00
❏ 103	Darius Miles/1499 RC	10.00	4.00
❏ 104	Marcus Fizer/499 RC	6.00	2.50
❏ 105	Mike Miller/999 RC	12.00	5.00
❏ 106	DerMarr Johnson/1499 RC	4.00	1.50
❏ 107	Chris Mihm/499 RC	6.00	2.50
❏ 108	Jamal Crawford/999 RC	8.00	3.00
❏ 109	Joel Przybilla/1499 RC	4.00	1.50
❏ 110	Keyon Dooling/499 RC	6.00	2.50
❏ 111	Jerome Moiso/999 RC	5.00	2.00
❏ 112	Etan Thomas/1499 RC	4.00	1.50
❏ 113	Courtney Alexander/499 RC	6.00	2.50
❏ 114	Mateen Cleaves/999 RC	5.00	2.00
❏ 115	Jason Collier/1499 RC	5.00	2.00
❏ 116	Hidayet Turkoglu/499 RC	12.00	5.00
❏ 117	Desmond Mason/999 RC	5.00	2.00
❏ 118	Quentin Richardson/1499 RC	10.00	4.00
❏ 119	Jamaal Magloire/499 RC	6.00	2.50
❏ 120	Speedy Claxton/999 RC	5.00	2.00
❏ 121	Morris Peterson/1499 RC	8.00	3.00
❏ 122	Donnell Harvey/499 RC	6.00	2.50
❏ 123	DeShawn Stevenson/999 RC	5.00	2.00
❏ 124	Dalibor Bagaric/1499 RC	4.00	1.50
❏ 125	Iakovos Tsakalidis/499 RC	6.00	2.50
❏ 126	Mamadou N'Diaye/999 RC	5.00	2.00
❏ 127	Erick Barkley/1499 RC	4.00	1.50
❏ 128	Mark Madsen/499 RC	6.00	2.50
❏ 129	A.J. Guyton/999 RC	5.00	2.00
❏ 130	Khalid El-Amin/1499 RC	4.00	1.50
❏ 131	Lavor Postell/499 RC	6.00	2.50
❏ 132	Marc Jackson/999 RC	5.00	2.00
❏ 133	Stephen Jackson/1499 RC	6.00	2.50
❏ 134	Wang Zhizhi/1499 RC	10.00	4.00

2003-04 Topps Rookie Matrix

❏ COMP.SET w/o RC's (110)	30.00	12.50
❏ COMMON CARD (1-110)	.20	.08
❏ COMMON TRI-RC	3.00	1.25
❏ 1	Allen Iverson	1.50	.60
❏ 2	Andre Hardaway	.75	.30
❏ 3	Bonzi Wells	.50	.20
❏ 4	Bobby Jackson	.50	.20
❏ 5	Manu Ginobili	.75	.30
❏ 6	Andrei Kirilenko	.75	.30
❏ 7	Ray Allen	.75	.30
❏ 8	Kwame Brown	.50	.20
❏ 9	Jason Terry	.75	.30
❏ 10	Paul Pierce	.75	.30
❏ 11	Tyson Chandler	.75	.30
❏ 12	Darius Miles	.75	.30
❏ 13	Antoine Walker	.75	.30
❏ 14	Antawn Jamison	.75	.30
❏ 15	Steve Nash	.75	.30
❏ 16	Marcus Camby	.50	.20
❏ 17	Chauncey Billups	.50	.20
❏ 18	Jason Richardson	.75	.30
❏ 19	Cuttino Mobley	.50	.20
❏ 20	Yao Ming	2.00	.75

❏ 21	Ron Artest	.50	.20
❏ 22	Gary Payton	.75	.30
❏ 23	Jason Williams	.50	.20
❏ 24	Eddie Jones	.75	.30
❏ 25	Kevin Garnett	1.50	.60
❏ 26	Wally Szczerbiak	.50	.20
❏ 27	Kenyon Martin	.75	.30
❏ 28	Jamaal Magloire	.20	.08
❏ 29	Keith Van Horn	.75	.30
❏ 30	Tracy McGrady	2.00	.75
❏ 31	Glenn Robinson	.75	.30
❏ 32	Derek Anderson	.50	.20
❏ 33	Chris Webber	.75	.30
❏ 34	Tony Parker	.75	.30
❏ 35	Morris Peterson	.50	.20
❏ 36	Jerry Stackhouse	.75	.30
❏ 37	Theo Ratliff	.50	.20
❏ 38	Jalen Rose	.75	.30
❏ 39	Dajuan Wagner	.50	.20
❏ 40	Dirk Nowitzki	1.25	.50
❏ 41	Nikoloz Tskitishvili	.20	.08
❏ 42	Ben Wallace	.75	.30
❏ 43	Tayshaun Prince	.50	.20
❏ 44	Troy Murphy	.75	.30
❏ 45	Jamaal Tinsley	.75	.30
❏ 46	Corey Maggette	.50	.20
❏ 47	Karl Malone	.75	.30
❏ 48	Mike Miller	.75	.30
❏ 49	Lamar Odom	.75	.30
❏ 50	Shaquille O'Neal	2.00	.75
❏ 51	Michael Redd	.75	.30
❏ 52	Sam Cassell	.75	.30
❏ 53	Raef LaFrentz	.50	.20
❏ 54	Baron Davis	.75	.30
❏ 55	Allan Houston	.50	.20
❏ 56	Drew Gooden	.50	.20
❏ 57	Eric Snow	.50	.20
❏ 58	Stephon Marbury	.75	.30
❏ 59	Zach Randolph	.75	.30
❏ 60	Peja Stojakovic	.75	.30
❏ 61	Brent Barry	.50	.20
❏ 62	Radoslav Nesterovic	.50	.20
❏ 63	Antonio Davis	.20	.08
❏ 64	Gilbert Arenas	.75	.30
❏ 65	Shareef Abdur-Rahim	.75	.30
❏ 66	Scottie Pippen	1.25	.50
❏ 67	Ronald Murray	.50	.20
❏ 68	Zydrunas Ilgauskas	.50	.20
❏ 69	Nene	.50	.20
❏ 70	Steve Francis	.75	.30
❏ 71	Mike Dunleavy	.50	.20
❏ 72	Jermaine O'Neal	.75	.30
❏ 73	Elton Brand	.75	.30
❏ 74	Caron Butler	.75	.30
❏ 75	Kobe Bryant	3.00	1.25
❏ 76	Kenny Thomas	.20	.08
❏ 77	Joe Smith	.50	.20
❏ 78	Jason Kidd	1.25	.50
❏ 79	Antonio McDyess	.75	.30
❏ 80	Shawn Marion	.75	.30
❏ 81	Rasheed Wallace	.75	.30
❏ 82	Mike Bibby	.75	.30
❏ 83	Tim Thomas	.50	.20
❏ 84	Rashard Lewis	.75	.30
❏ 85	Vince Carter	2.00	.75
❏ 86	Matt Harpring	.75	.30
❏ 87	Ricky Davis	.75	.30
❏ 88	Michael Finley	.75	.30
❏ 89	Andre Miller	.50	.20
❏ 90	Pau Gasol	.75	.30
❏ 91	Dion Glover	.20	.08
❏ 92	Jamal Crawford	.50	.20
❏ 93	Richard Hamilton	.50	.20
❏ 94	Nick Van Exel	.75	.30
❏ 95	Maurice Taylor	.50	.20
❏ 96	Reggie Miller	.75	.30
❏ 97	Marko Jaric	.50	.20
❏ 98	Brian Grant	.50	.20
❏ 99	Desmond Mason	.75	.30
❏ 100	Tim Duncan	1.50	.60
❏ 101	Latrell Sprewell	.75	.30
❏ 102	Richard Jefferson	.50	.20
❏ 103	David Wesley	.20	.08
❏ 104	Kurt Thomas	.50	.20
❏ 105	Juwan Howard	.50	.20
❏ 106	Amare Stoudemire	1.50	.60

❏ 107	Brad Miller	.75	.30
❏ 108	Keon Clark	.50	.20
❏ 109	Pat Garrity	.20	.08
❏ 110	Jamal Mashburn	.50	.20
❏ AJF	Carmelo/Kaman/Ford	12.00	5.00
❏ AKM	Carmelo/Kaman/Darko	6.00	2.50
❏ AMB	Carmelo/Darko/Bosh	10.00	4.00
❏ AWB	Carmelo/Wade/Bosh	15.00	6.00
❏ BAH	Bosh/Carmelo/Hinrich	8.00	3.00
❏ BAJ	Bosh/Carmelo/LeBron	25.00	10.00
❏ BBG	Barbosa/Bell/Gaines	4.00	1.50
❏ BBR	Banks/Bell/Ridnour	3.00	1.25
❏ BCC	Bell/Zarko/Collison	3.00	1.25
❏ BCG	Bell/Collison/Gaines	3.00	1.25
❏ BCP	Barbosa/Zarko/Pavlovic	5.00	2.00
❏ BCP	Banks/Collison/Pietrus	3.00	1.25
❏ BHJ	Bosh/Hinrich/LeBron	10.00	4.00
❏ BJP	Bell/Jones/Planinic	3.00	1.25
❏ BKC	Beasley/Kapono/Cook	3.00	1.25
❏ BKS	Banks/Kaman/Sweetney	3.00	1.25
❏ BKW	Bosh/Kaman/Wade	8.00	3.00
❏ BPH	Banks/Pietrus/Hayes	3.00	1.25
❏ BPW	Barbosa/Pavlovic/Williams	5.00	2.00
❏ BRG	Banks/Ridnour/Gaines	3.00	1.25
❏ BWM	Bosh/Wade/Darko	10.00	4.00
❏ CEK	Cook/Ebi/Kapono	3.00	1.25
❏ CHB	Collison/Hayes/Banks	3.00	1.25
❏ CHC	Cook/Howard/Zarko	4.00	1.50
❏ CPD	Zarko/Pietrus/Diaw	3.00	1.25
❏ CPS	Collison/Pietrus/Sweetney	3.00	1.25
❏ CSH	Collison/Sweetney/Hayes	3.00	1.25
❏ CWC	Cook/West/Collison	3.00	1.25
❏ DPP	Diaw/Pavlovic/Planinic	5.00	2.00
❏ DPW	Diaw/Pavlovic/West	5.00	2.00
❏ EPW	Ebi/Perkins/West	3.00	1.25
❏ EWC	Ebi/West/Cook	3.00	1.25
❏ FAH	Ford/Carmelo/Hinrich	5.00	2.00
❏ FBH	Ford/Banks/Hinrich	3.00	1.25
❏ FBJ	Ford/Bosh/LeBron	8.00	3.00
❏ FBR	Ford/Banks/Ridnour	3.00	1.25
❏ FBW	Ford/Bosh/Wade	8.00	3.00
❏ FCH	Ford/Collison/Hinrich	3.00	1.25
❏ FGB	Ford/Gaines/Banks	2.50	1.00
❏ FKW	Ford/Kaman/Wade	5.00	2.00
❏ GBB	Gaines/Banks/Bell	3.00	1.25
❏ GBR	Gaines/Bell/Ridnour	3.00	1.25
❏ HAM	Hinrich/Carmelo/Darko	8.00	3.00
❏ HBM	Hinrich/Bosh/Darko	8.00	3.00
❏ HBS	Hayes/Banks/Sweetney	3.00	1.25
❏ HCJ	Howard/Cook/Jones	4.00	1.50
❏ HGP	Hayes/Gaines/Pietrus	3.00	1.25
❏ HJM	Hinrich/LeBron/Darko	8.00	3.00
❏ HKC	Hinrich/Kaman/Collison	3.00	1.25
❏ HLC	Howard/Lampe/Cook	3.00	1.25
❏ HLK	Howard/Lampe/Kapono	4.00	1.50
❏ HPR	Hayes/Peitrus/Ridnour	3.00	1.25
❏ HSL	Hayes/Sweetney/Lampe	3.00	1.25
❏ HSP	Hayes/Sweetney/Pietrus	3.00	1.25
❏ HWS	Hinrich/Wade/Sweetney	6.00	2.50
❏ JAW	LeBron/Carmelo/Wade	30.00	12.50
❏ JBM	LeBron/Bosh/Darko	10.00	4.00
❏ JHA	LeBron/Hinrich/Carmelo	15.00	6.00
❏ JKA	LeBron/Carmelo/Hinrich	12.00	5.00
❏ JMA	LeBron/Darko/Carmelo	20.00	8.00
❏ JMK	LeBron/Darko/Kaman	8.00	3.00
❏ JOB	Jones/Outlaw/Barbosa	4.00	1.50
❏ JWE	Jones/Walton/Ebi	3.00	1.25
❏ KCP	Kaman/Zarko/Perkins	3.00	1.25
❏ KEW	Kapono/Ebi/Williams	3.00	1.25
❏ KHW	Kaman/Hinrich/Wade	6.00	2.50
❏ KPH	Kaman/Pietrus/Hayes	3.00	1.25
❏ KSC	Kaman/Sweetney/Collison	3.00	1.25
❏ LBB	Lampe/Barbosa/Beasley	3.00	1.25
❏ LHC	Lampe/Howard/Zarko	4.00	1.50
❏ LSP	Lampe/Sweetney/Planinic	3.00	1.25
❏ MAF	Darko/Carmelo/Ford	5.00	2.00
❏ MBF	Darko/Bosh/Ford	4.00	1.50
❏ MFJ	Darko/Ford/LeBron	6.00	2.50
❏ MJW	Darko/LeBron/Wade	15.00	6.00
❏ OBD	Outlaw/Beasley/Darko	4.00	1.50
❏ OCB	Outlaw/Cook/Beasley	3.00	1.25
❏ OEJ	Outlaw/Ebi/Jones	3.00	1.25
❏ OPE	Outlaw/Perkins/Ebi	3.00	1.25
❏ PBE	Perkins/Beasley/Ebi	3.00	1.25
❏ PBG	Perkins/Banks/Gaines	3.00	1.25
❏ PBH	Pietrus/Bell/Hayes	3.00	1.25

PCH	Pietrus/Collison/Hayes	3.00	1.25
PCR	Pietrus/Collison/Ridnour	3.00	1.25
PCW	Perkins/Zarko/West	3.00	1.25
PDB	Planinic/Diaw/Barbosa	5.00	2.00
PJD	Pavlovic/Jones/Diaw	5.00	2.00
PLH	Perkins/Lampe/Howard	4.00	1.50
POP	Pavlovic/Outlaw/Planinic	4.00	1.50
PPC	Pietrus/Darko/Zarko	4.00	1.50
PSK	Pietrus/Sweetney/Kaman	3.00	1.25
PWO	Planinic/West/Outlaw	4.00	1.50
RFH	Ridnour/Ford/Hinrich	3.00	1.25
RHC	Ridnour/Hayes/Collison	3.00	1.25
SBC	Sweetney/Banks/Collison	3.00	1.25
SHK	Sweetney/Hayes/Kaman	3.00	1.25
SPB	Sweetney/Pietrus/Banks	3.00	1.25
WBH	Wade/Bosh/Hinrich	8.00	3.00
WBP	Williams/Barbosa/Planinic	4.00	1.50
WDJ	West/Diaw/Jones	4.00	1.50
WDP	Williams/Diaw/Planinic	3.00	1.50
WFH	Wade/Ford/Hinrich	5.00	2.00
WHL	Walton/Howard/Lampe	4.00	1.50
WHO	Walton/Outlaw/Howard	4.00	1.50
WJB	Wade/LeBron/Bosh	20.00	8.00
WKP	Walton/Kapono/Perkins	3.00	1.25
WKS	Wade/Kaman/Sweetney	6.00	2.50
WMA	Wade/Darko/Carmelo	15.00	6.00
WPJ	West/Pavlovic/Jones	4.00	1.50
WWB	Walton/Williams/Beasley	3.00	1.25

2000-01 Topps Stars

	COMPLETE SET (150)	60.00	30.00
	COMMON CARD (1-150)	.20	.07
	COMMON ROOKIE (101-125)	.60	.25
1	Elton Brand	.60	.25
2	Paul Pierce	.60	.25
3	Baron Davis	.60	.25
4	Corey Benjamin	.20	.07
5	Jason Kidd	1.00	.40
6	Stephon Marbury	.60	.25
7	Eric Snow	.40	.15
8	Joe Smith	.40	.15
9	Larry Hughes	.40	.15
10	Tim Duncan	1.25	.50
11	Theo Ratliff	.40	.15
12	Dikembe Mutombo	.40	.15
13	Tim Hardaway	.40	.15
14	Glenn Robinson	.60	.25
15	Grant Hill	.60	.25
16	Patrick Ewing	.60	.25
17	Ron Mercer	.40	.15
18	Ron Artest	.40	.15
19	Tom Gugliotta	.20	.07
20	Steve Smith	.40	.15
21	Vlade Divac	.40	.15
22	Rashard Lewis	.40	.15
23	Tracy McGrady	1.50	.60
24	Bryon Russell	.20	.07
25	Michael Dickerson	.40	.15
26	Juwan Howard	.40	.15
27	Damon Stoudamire	.60	.25
28	Hakeem Olajuwon	.60	.25
29	Antonio McDyess	.40	.15
30	Kobe Bryant	2.50	1.00
31	Lindsey Hunter	.20	.07
32	Magic Johnson	2.50	1.00
33	Alonzo Mourning	.40	.15
34	Kenny Anderson	.40	.15
35	Allan Houston	.40	.15
36	Keith Van Horn	.60	.25
37	Shawn Marion	.60	.25
38	David Robinson	.60	.25
39	Mitch Richmond	.40	.15
40	Shaquille O'Neal	1.50	.60
41	Gary Payton	.60	.25
42	Sean Elliott	.40	.15
43	Sam Cassell	.60	.25
44	Dale Davis	.20	.07
45	Derek Anderson	.40	.15
46	Jonathan Bender	.40	.15
47	Shandon Anderson	.20	.07
48	Rael LaFrentz	.40	.15
49	Michael Finley	.60	.25
50	Toni Kukoc	.40	.15
51	Anthony Mason	.40	.15
52	Jim Jackson	.20	.07
53	Glen Rice	.40	.15
54	Jalen Rose	.60	.25
55	Keon Clark	.40	.15
56	Anfernee Hardaway	.60	.25
57	Vin Baker	.40	.15
58	Shawn Kemp	.40	.15
59	John Stockton	.60	.25
60	Shareef Abdur-Rahim	.60	.25
61	Doug Christie	.40	.15
62	Lamond Murray	.20	.07
63	Scottie Pippen	1.00	.40
64	Darrell Armstrong	.20	.07
65	Marcus Camby	.40	.15
66	Wally Szczerbiak	.40	.15
67	Jamal Mashburn	.40	.15
68	Antonio Davis	.20	.07
69	Kevin Garnett	1.25	.50
70	Cuttino Mobley	.40	.15
71	Jerry Stackhouse	.60	.25
72	Cedric Ceballos	.20	.07
73	Nick Van Exel	.60	.25
74	Latrell Sprewell	.60	.25
75	Antoine Walker	.60	.25
76	Allen Iverson	1.25	.50
77	Antawn Jamison	.60	.25
78	Derrick Coleman	.20	.07
79	Jason Terry	.60	.25
80	Steve Francis	.60	.25
81	Reggie Miller	.60	.25
82	Rasheed Wallace	.60	.25
83	Chris Webber	.60	.25
84	Donyell Marshall	.40	.15
85	Ruben Patterson	.40	.15
86	Terrell Brandon	.40	.15
87	Mike Bibby	.60	.25
88	Richard Hamilton	.60	.25
89	Jason Williams	.40	.15
90	Corey Maggette	.40	.15
91	Kerry Kittles	.20	.07
92	Karl Malone	.60	.25
93	Rod Strickland	.20	.07
94	Eddie Jones	.60	.25
95	Maurice Taylor	.20	.07
96	Dirk Nowitzki	1.00	.40
97	Andre Miller	.40	.15
98	Lamar Odom	.60	.25
99	Ray Allen	.60	.25
100	Vince Carter	1.50	.60
101	Chris Mihm RC	.60	.25
102	Kenyon Martin RC	2.50	1.00
103	Stromile Swift RC	1.25	.50
104	Joel Przybilla RC	.60	.25
105	Marcus Fizer RC	.60	.25
106	Mike Miller RC	2.00	.75
107	Darius Miles RC	2.00	.75
108	Mark Madsen RC	.60	.25
109	Courtney Alexander RC	.60	.25
110	DeShawn Stevenson RC	.60	.25
111	DerMarr Johnson RC	.60	.25
112	Mamadou N'diaye RC	.60	.25
113	Mateen Cleaves RC	.60	.25
114	Morris Peterson RC	1.25	.50
115	Etan Thomas RC	.60	.25
116	Erick Barkley RC	.60	.25
117	Quentin Richardson RC	2.00	.75
118	Keyon Dooling RC	.60	.25
119	Jerome Moiso RC	.60	.25
120	Desmond Mason RC	.60	.25
121	Speedy Claxton RC	.60	.25
122	Jamaal Magloire RC	.60	.25
123	Donnell Harvey RC	.60	.25
124	Jamal Crawford RC	.75	.30
125	Jason Collier RC	.75	.30
126	Tim Duncan SPOT	.60	.25
127	Shaquille O'Neal SPOT	.60	.25
128	Vince Carter SPOT	.75	.30
129	Allen Iverson SPOT	.60	.25
130	Jason Kidd SPOT	.60	.25
131	Kevin Garnett SPOT	.60	.25
132	Gary Payton SPOT	.60	.25
133	Tracy McGrady SPOT	.60	.25
134	Jason Williams SPOT	.20	.07
135	Kobe Bryant SPOT	1.25	.50
136	Elton Brand SPOT	.40	.15
137	Ray Allen SPOT	.40	.15
138	Grant Hill SPOT	.60	.25
139	Chris Webber SPOT	.40	.15
140	Latrell Sprewell SPOT	.60	.25
141	Alonzo Mourning SPOT	.40	.15
142	Lamar Odom SPOT	.40	.15
143	Shareef Abdur-Rahim SPOT	.40	.15
144	Steve Francis SPOT	.60	.25
145	Magic Johnson SPOT	1.25	.50
146	Darius Miles SPOT	1.00	.40
147	Kenyon Martin SPOT	1.25	.50
148	Marcus Fizer SPOT	.60	.25
149	Mateen Cleaves SPOT	.60	.25
150	Stromile Swift SPOT	.60	.25

2005-06 Topps Style

	COMPLETE SET (165)	80.00	40.00
	COMMON CARD (1-130)	.40	.15
	COMMON ROOKIE (131-160)	3.00	1.25
	COMMON CELEBRITY (161-165)	5.00	2.00
1	Ben Wallace	1.25	.50
2	Joe Johnson	.75	.30
3	Luol Deng	1.25	.50
4	Morris Peterson	.75	.30
5	Jason Terry	1.25	.50
6	Carmelo Anthony	2.50	1.00
7	Mickey Mantle	8.00	3.00
8	Ron Artest	.75	.30
9	Elton Brand	1.25	.50
10	Chris Mihm	.40	.15
11	Shane Battier	1.25	.50
12	Speedy Claxton	.40	.15
13	Baron Davis	1.25	.50
14	Damon Stoudamire	.75	.30
15	Desmond Mason	.75	.30
16	Marko Jaric	.40	.15
17	Vince Carter	3.00	1.25
18	Sam Cassell	1.25	.50
19	J.R. Smith	.75	.30
20	Trevor Ariza	.75	.30
21	Quentin Richardson	.75	.30
22	Jamal Crawford	.75	.30
23	Dwight Howard	1.50	.60
24	Kyle Korver	1.25	.50
25	Steve Nash	1.25	.50
26	Amare Stoudemire	2.50	1.00
27	Zach Randolph	1.25	.50
28	Brad Miller	1.25	.50
29	Tim Duncan	2.50	1.00
30	Michael Finley	1.25	.50
31	Ray Allen	1.25	.50
32	Luke Ridnour	.75	.30
33	Andrei Kirilenko	1.25	.50

#	Player		
34	Tony Allen	.75	.30
35	Paul Pierce	1.25	.50
36	Al Jefferson	1.25	.50
37	Emeka Okafor	2.00	.75
38	Al Harrington	.40	.15
39	Ben Gordon	2.50	1.00
40	Andres Nocioni	.40	.15
41	Zydrunas Ilgauskas	.40	.15
42	Anderson Varejao	.75	.30
43	Keith Van Horn	.75	.30
44	Richard Hamilton	.75	.30
45	Stromile Swift	.75	.30
46	Dirk Nowitzki	2.00	.75
47	Stephen Jackson	.75	.30
48	Pau Gasol	1.25	.50
49	Lamar Odom	1.25	.50
50	Kobe Bryant	5.00	2.00
51	Shaquille O'Neal	3.00	1.25
52	Jason Williams	.75	.30
53	Dwyane Wade	4.00	1.50
54	Michael Redd	1.25	.50
55	Joe Smith	.75	.30
56	Troy Hudson	.40	.15
57	Jameer Nelson	.75	.30
58	Chris Webber	1.25	.50
59	Darius Miles	1.25	.50
60	Chris Wilcox	.40	.15
61	Rafer Alston	.40	.15
62	Kirk Hinrich	1.25	.50
63	Jalen Rose	1.00	.40
64	Matt Harpring	1.25	.50
65	Caron Butler	.75	.30
66	Shareef Abdur-Rahim	.75	.30
67	Josh Childress	.75	.30
68	Delonte West	.75	.30
69	Brevin Knight	.40	.15
70	Larry Hughes	.75	.30
71	Dikembe Mutombo	.75	.30
72	Kenyon Martin	1.25	.50
73	Earl Boykins	.40	.15
74	Tayshaun Prince	1.25	.50
75	Chauncey Billups	1.25	.50
76	Josh Smith	1.25	.50
77	Troy Murphy	.75	.30
78	Jermaine O'Neal	1.25	.50
79	Corey Maggette	.75	.30
80	Wally Szczerbiak	.75	.30
81	Richard Jefferson	.75	.30
82	Nenad Krstic	.75	.30
83	Jason Kidd	2.00	.75
84	Jamaal Magloire	.40	.15
85	Stephon Marbury	1.25	.50
86	Samuel Dalembert	.40	.15
87	Andre Iguodala	1.25	.50
88	Yao Ming	3.00	1.25
89	Kurt Thomas	.40	.15
90	Brendan Haywood	.40	.15
91	Peja Stojakovic	1.25	.50
92	Mike Bibby	1.25	.50
93	Tony Parker	1.25	.50
94	Manu Ginobili	1.25	.50
95	Rashard Lewis	1.25	.50
96	Mehmet Okur	.40	.15
97	Gilbert Arenas	1.25	.50
98	Antawn Jamison	1.25	.50
99	Ricky Davis	1.25	.50
100	Shawn Marion	1.25	.50
101	Melvin Ely	.40	.15
102	Tyson Chandler	1.25	.50
103	Jason Richardson	1.25	.50
104	Drew Gooden	.75	.30
105	Josh Howard	.75	.30
106	Marcus Camby	.40	.15
107	Jerry Stackhouse	1.25	.50
108	Andre Miller	.75	.30
109	Rasheed Wallace	1.25	.50
110	Mike Dunleavy	.75	.30
111	LeBron James	8.00	3.00
112	Allen Iverson	2.50	1.00
113	Tracy McGrady	3.00	1.25
114	Jamaal Tinsley	.75	.30
115	Cuttino Mobley	.75	.30
116	Kwame Brown	.75	.30
117	Derek Anderson	.75	.30
118	Eddie Jones	.40	.15
119	Antoine Walker	1.25	.50
120	Alonzo Mourning	.75	.30
121	Bobby Simmons	.40	.15
122	Kevin Garnett	2.50	1.00
123	P.J. Brown	.40	.15
124	Steve Francis	1.25	.50
125	Grant Hill	1.25	.50
126	Primoz Brezec	.40	.15
127	Mike Miller	1.25	.50
128	Sebastian Telfair	.75	.30
129	Chris Bosh	1.25	.50
130	Carlos Boozer	.75	.30
131	Andrew Bogut RC	6.00	2.50
132	Raymond Felton RC	6.00	2.50
133	Ike Diogu RC	4.00	1.50
134	Rashad McCants RC	6.00	2.50
135	Gerald Green RC	6.00	2.50
136	Jarrett Jack RC	3.00	1.25
137	Linas Kleiza RC	3.00	1.25
138	Brandon Bass RC	3.00	1.25
139	Marvin Williams RC	6.00	2.50
140	Martell Webster RC	3.00	1.25
141	Sarunas Jasikevicius RC	4.00	1.50
142	Antoine Wright RC	3.00	1.25
143	Hakim Warrick RC	6.00	2.50
144	Francisco Garcia RC	4.00	1.50
145	Wayne Simien RC	4.00	1.50
146	Monta Ellis RC	6.00	2.50
147	Deron Williams RC	10.00	4.00
148	Charlie Villanueva RC	5.00	2.00
149	Chris Taft RC	3.00	1.25
150	Joey Graham RC	3.00	1.25
151	Julius Hodge RC	4.00	1.50
152	Luther Head RC	4.00	1.50
153	David Lee RC	5.00	2.00
154	Chris Paul RC	12.00	5.00
155	Channing Frye RC	4.00	1.50
156	Sean May RC	4.00	1.50
157	Danny Granger RC	5.00	2.00
158	Nate Robinson RC	5.00	2.00
159	Jason Maxiell RC	3.00	1.25
160	Salim Stoudamire RC	4.00	1.50
161	Christie Brinkley	5.00	2.00
162	Carmen Electra	5.00	2.00
163	Shannon Elizabeth	5.00	2.00
164	Jenny McCarthy	5.00	2.00
165	Jay-Z	5.00	2.00

2001-02 Topps TCC

	COMPLETE SET (150)	80.00	30.00
	COMMON CARD	.20	.07
	COMMON ROOKIE (118-150)	1.00	.40
1	Shaquille O'Neal	1.50	.60
2	Jason Williams	.40	.15
3	Eddie Jones	.60	.25
4	Anthony Mason	.40	.15
5	Joe Smith	.40	.15
6	Kenyon Martin	.60	.25
7	Tracy McGrady	1.50	.60
8	Horace Grant	.40	.15
9	Andre Miller	.40	.15
10	Allen Iverson	1.25	.50
11	Shawn Marion	.60	.25
12	Derek Anderson	.40	.15
13	Chris Webber	.60	.25
14	Bruce Bowen	.20	.07
15	Alvin Williams	.20	.07
16	Brent Barry	.40	.15
17	Donyell Marshall	.40	.15
18	Richard Hamilton	.40	.15
19	Vlade Divac	.40	.15
20	Vince Carter	1.50	.60
21	Kevin Garnett	1.25	.50
22	Jason Terry	.60	.25
23	Antoine Walker	.60	.25
24	P.J. Brown	.20	.07
25	Baron Davis	.60	.25
26	Eddie Robinson	.40	.15
27	Chris Mihm	.40	.15
28	Michael Finley	.60	.25
29	Nick Van Exel	.60	.25
30	Steve Francis	.60	.25
31	Chucky Atkins	.20	.07
32	Raef LaFrentz	.40	.15
33	Antawn Jamison	.60	.25
34	Jalen Rose	.60	.25
35	Lamar Odom	.60	.25
36	Elton Brand	.60	.25
37	Derek Fisher	.60	.25
38	Alonzo Mourning	.40	.15
39	Ervin Johnson	.20	.07
40	Tim Duncan	1.25	.50
41	Kurt Thomas	.40	.15
42	Latrell Sprewell	.60	.25
43	Darrell Armstrong	.20	.07
44	Tom Gugliotta	.20	.07
45	Derrick Coleman	.20	.07
46	Dale Davis	.40	.15
47	David Robinson	.60	.25
48	Scottie Pippen	1.00	.40
49	Hakeem Olajuwon	.60	.25
50	Darius Miles	.60	.25
51	Greg Ostertag	.20	.07
52	Karl Malone	.60	.25
53	Morris Peterson	.40	.15
54	Shareef Abdur-Rahim	.60	.25
55	Dikembe Mutombo	.40	.15
56	Elden Campbell	.20	.07
57	Ron Mercer	.40	.15
58	Jumaine Jones	.40	.15
59	Wang ZhiZhi	.60	.25
60	Ray Allen	.60	.25
61	Marcus Camby	.40	.15
62	Jermaine O'Neal	.60	.25
63	Kenny Thomas	.20	.07
64	Danny Fortson	.20	.07
65	Ben Wallace	.60	.25
66	DeShawn Stevenson	.40	.15
67	Antonio Davis	.20	.07
68	Doug Christie	.40	.15
69	Rasheed Wallace	.60	.25
70	Stephon Marbury	.60	.25
71	Allan Houston	.40	.15
72	Kerry Kittles	.20	.07
73	Todd MacCulloch	.20	.07
74	Sam Cassell	.60	.25
75	Kobe Bryant	2.50	1.00
76	Aaron McKie	.40	.15
77	Terrell Brandon	.40	.15
78	Brian Grant	.40	.15
79	Michael Dickerson	.40	.15
80	Jerry Stackhouse	.60	.25
81	Antonio McDyess	.40	.15
82	Steve Nash	.60	.25
83	Paul Pierce	.60	.25
84	Jamal Mashburn	.40	.15
85	Toni Kukoc	.40	.15
86	James Posey	.40	.15
87	Larry Hughes	.40	.15
88	Cuttino Mobley	.40	.15
89	Jeff Foster	.20	.07
90	Jason Kidd	1.00	.40
91	Keith Van Horn	.60	.25
92	Mike Miller	.60	.25
93	Anfernee Hardaway	.60	.25
94	Bonzi Wells	.40	.15
95	Mike Bibby	.60	.25
96	Steve Smith	.40	.15
97	Gary Payton	.60	.25
98	John Stockton	.60	.25
99	Peja Stojakovic	.60	.25
100	Michael Jordan	12.00	5.00
101	Iakovos Tsakalidis	.20	.07
102	Mark Jackson	.40	.15
103	Wally Szczerbiak	.40	.15

❏ 104	Rod Strickland	.20	.07
❏ 105	Rick Fox	.40	.15
❏ 106	Glenn Robinson	.60	.25
❏ 107	Michael Olowokandi	.20	.07
❏ 108	Reggie Miller	.60	.25
❏ 109	Kelvin Cato	.20	.07
❏ 110	Clifford Robinson	.20	.07
❏ 111	Dirk Nowitzki	1.00	.40
❏ 112	Brad Miller	.60	.25
❏ 113	David Wesley	.20	.07
❏ 114	Kenny Anderson	.40	.15
❏ 115	Theo Ratliff	.40	.15
❏ 116	Rashard Lewis	.40	.15
❏ 117	Matt Harpring	.60	.25
❏ 118	Eddie Griffin RC	1.25	.50
❏ 119	Brendan Haywood RC	1.25	.50
❏ 120	Steven Hunter RC	1.00	.40
❏ 121	Jamaal Tinsley RC	1.50	.60
❏ 122	Jason Richardson RC	2.50	1.00
❏ 123	Tony Parker RC	4.00	1.50
❏ 124	Pau Gasol RC	3.00	1.25
❏ 125	Shane Battier RC	2.00	.75
❏ 126	Joe Johnson RC	2.50	1.00
❏ 127	Leon Smith RC	.40	.15
❏ 128	Mengke Bateer RC	2.50	1.00
❏ 129	Loren Woods RC	1.00	.40
❏ 130	Kwame Brown RC	1.50	.60
❏ 131	Tyson Chandler RC	2.50	1.00
❏ 132	Eddy Curry RC	2.50	1.00
❏ 133	Kedrick Brown RC	1.00	.40
❏ 134	Joseph Forte RC	2.50	1.00
❏ 135	Troy Murphy RC	2.00	.75
❏ 136	Richard Jefferson RC	1.50	.60
❏ 137	DeSagana Diop RC	1.00	.40
❏ 138	Vladimir Radmanovic RC	1.25	.50
❏ 139	Zach Randolph RC	3.00	1.25
❏ 140	Gerald Wallace RC	2.50	1.00
❏ 141	Brandon Armstrong RC	1.25	.50
❏ 142	Jeryl Sasser RC	1.00	.40
❏ 143	Rodney White RC	1.25	.50
❏ 144	Samuel Dalembert RC	1.00	.40
❏ 145	Jason Collins RC	1.00	.40
❏ 146	Michael Bradley RC	1.00	.40
❏ 147	Oscar Torres RC	1.00	.40
❏ 148	Zeljko Rebraca RC	1.00	.40
❏ 149	Andrei Kirilenko RC	2.50	1.00
❏ 150	Trenton Hassell RC	1.00	.40

2000 Topps Team USA

❏ COMPLETE SET (96)		30.00	12.50
❏ 1	T.Duncan 1/33/57/72	1.00	.40
❏ 2	J.Kidd 2/34/48/81	.60	.25
❏ 3	V.Baker 3/35/47/78	.40	.15
❏ 4	S.Smith 4/27/54/80	.20	.07
❏ 5	G.Hill 5/32/56/77	.60	.25
❏ 6	G.Payton 6/24/53/74	.60	.25
❏ 7	V.Carter 7/31/55/76	1.25	.50
❏ 8	R.Allen 8/28/50/75	.60	.25
❏ 9	K.Garnett 9/25/52/71	1.00	.40
❏ 10	T.Hardaway 10/26/58/73	.60	.25
❏ 11	A.Houston 11/30/49/70	.60	.25
❏ 12	A.Mourning 12/29/51/79	.60	.25
❏ 13	L.Leslie 13/36/63/83	2.00	.75
❏ 14	D.Staley 14/41/65/84	1.00	.40
❏ 15	K.Smith 15/44/60/87	1.00	.40
❏ 16	N.McCray 16/40/62/86	.60	.25
❏ 17	R.B-Holifield 17/36/66/90	1.00	.40
❏ 18	C.Holdsclaw 18/39/59/82	2.50	1.00
❏ 19	Y.Griffith 19/43/61/89	1.25	.50
❏ 20	T.Edwards 20/42/64/88	.75	.30
❏ 21	N.Williams 21/37/67/85	1.25	.50
❏ 22	D.Milton 22/45/68/91	.40	.15
❏ 23	K.Wolters 23/46/69/92	.60	.25
❏ 24	Gary Payton ST	.40	.15
❏ 25	Kevin Garnett ST	1.00	.40
❏ 26	Tim Hardaway ST	.40	.15
❏ 27	Steve Smith ST	.20	.07
❏ 28	Ray Allen ST	.40	.15
❏ 29	Alonzo Mourning ST	.40	.15
❏ 30	Allan Houston ST	.40	.15
❏ 31	Vince Carter ST	1.25	.50
❏ 32	Grant Hill ST	.40	.15
❏ 33	Tim Duncan ST	1.00	.40
❏ 34	Jason Kidd ST	.60	.25
❏ 35	Vin Baker ST	.40	.15
❏ 36	R.Bolton-Holifield ST	1.00	.40
❏ 37	Natalie Williams ST	1.25	.50
❏ 38	Lisa Leslie ST	2.00	.75
❏ 39	Chamique Holdsclaw ST	2.50	1.00
❏ 40	Nikki McCray ST	1.00	.40
❏ 41	Dawn Staley ST	1.00	.40
❏ 42	Teresa Edwards ST	.75	.30
❏ 43	Yolanda Griffith ST	1.25	.50
❏ 44	Katie Smith ST	1.00	.40
❏ 45	Delisha Milton ST	.40	.15
❏ 46	Kara Wolters ST	.60	.25
❏ 47	Vin Baker PAI	.40	.15
❏ 48	Jason Kidd PAI	.60	.25
❏ 49	Allan Houston PAI	.40	.15
❏ 50	Ray Allen PAI	.40	.15
❏ 51	Alonzo Mourning PAI	.40	.15
❏ 52	Kevin Garnett PAI	1.00	.40
❏ 53	Gary Payton PAI	.40	.15
❏ 54	Steve Smith PAI	.20	.07
❏ 55	Vince Carter PAI	1.25	.50
❏ 56	Grant Hill PAI	.40	.15
❏ 57	Tim Duncan PAI	1.00	.40
❏ 58	Tim Hardaway PAI	.40	.15
❏ 59	Chamique Holdsclaw PAI	2.50	1.00
❏ 60	Katie Smith PAI	1.00	.40
❏ 61	Yolanda Griffith PAI	1.25	.50
❏ 62	Nikki McCray PAI	1.00	.40
❏ 63	Lisa Leslie PAI	2.00	.75
❏ 64	Teresa Edwards PAI	.75	.30
❏ 65	Dawn Staley PAI	1.00	.40
❏ 66	R.Bolton-Holifield PAI	1.00	.40
❏ 67	Natalie Williams PAI	1.25	.50
❏ 68	Delisha Milton PAI	.40	.15
❏ 69	Kara Wolters PAI	.60	.25
❏ 70	Allan Houston QU	.40	.15
❏ 71	Kevin Garnett QU	1.00	.40
❏ 72	Tim Duncan QU	1.00	.40
❏ 73	Tim Hardaway QU	.40	.15
❏ 74	Gary Payton QU	.40	.15
❏ 75	Ray Allen QU	.40	.15
❏ 76	Vince Carter QU	1.25	.50
❏ 77	Grant Hill QU	.40	.15
❏ 78	Vin Baker QU	.40	.15
❏ 79	Alonzo Mourning QU	.40	.15
❏ 80	Steve Smith QU	.20	.07
❏ 81	Jason Kidd QU	.60	.25
❏ 82	Chamique Holdsclaw QU	2.50	1.00
❏ 83	Lisa Leslie QU	2.00	.75
❏ 84	Dawn Staley QU	1.00	.40
❏ 85	Natalie Williams QU	1.25	.50
❏ 86	Nikki McCray QU	1.00	.40
❏ 87	Katie Smith QU	1.00	.40
❏ 88	Teresa Edwards QU	.75	.30
❏ 89	Yolanda Griffith QU	1.25	.50
❏ 90	R.Bolton-Holifield QU	1.00	.40
❏ 91	Delisha Milton QU	.40	.15
❏ 92	Kara Wolters QU	.60	.25
❏ 93	Team USA Men's	1.00	.40
❏ 94	Team USA Women's	1.00	.40
❏ 95	Group Shot	1.50	.60
❏ 96	Checklist	.20	.07

2002-03 Topps Ten

❏ COMPLETE SET (150)		50.00	20.00
❏ COMMON CARD (1-121)		.20	.08
❏ COMMON ROOKIE (121-150)		2.00	.75
❏ 1	Allen Iverson	1.25	.50
❏ 2	Shaquille O'Neal	1.50	.60
❏ 3	Paul Pierce	.60	.25

❏ 4	Tracy McGrady	1.50	.60
❏ 5	Tim Duncan	1.25	.50
❏ 6	Kobe Bryant	2.50	1.00
❏ 7	Dirk Nowitzki	1.00	.40
❏ 8	Karl Malone	.60	.25
❏ 9	Antoine Walker	.60	.25
❏ 10	Gary Payton	.60	.25
❏ 11	Shaquille O'Neal	1.50	.60
❏ 12	Allen Iverson	1.25	.50
❏ 13	Tracy McGrady	1.50	.60
❏ 14	Kobe Bryant	2.50	1.00
❏ 15	Michael Jordan	5.00	2.00
❏ 16	Paul Pierce	.60	.25
❏ 17	Chris Webber	.60	.25
❏ 18	Tim Duncan	1.25	.50
❏ 19	Corliss Williamson	.40	.15
❏ 20	Dirk Nowitzki	1.00	.40
❏ 21	Ben Wallace	.60	.25
❏ 22	Tim Duncan	1.25	.50
❏ 23	Kevin Garnett	1.25	.50
❏ 24	Danny Fortson	.20	.08
❏ 25	Elton Brand	.60	.25
❏ 26	Dikembe Mutombo	.40	.15
❏ 27	Antoine O'Neal	.60	.25
❏ 28	Dirk Nowitzki	1.00	.40
❏ 29	Shawn Marion	.60	.25
❏ 30	P.J. Brown	.20	.08
❏ 31	Andre Miller	.40	.15
❏ 32	Jason Kidd	1.00	.40
❏ 33	Gary Payton	.60	.25
❏ 34	Baron Davis	.60	.25
❏ 35	Stephon Marbury	.60	.25
❏ 36	John Stockton	.60	.25
❏ 37	Jamaal Tinsley	.40	.15
❏ 38	Jason Williams	.40	.15
❏ 39	Steve Nash	.60	.25
❏ 40	Mark Jackson	.20	.08
❏ 41	Ben Wallace	.60	.25
❏ 42	Raef LaFrentz	.40	.15
❏ 43	Alonzo Mourning	.40	.15
❏ 44	Tim Duncan	1.25	.50
❏ 45	Dikembe Mutombo	.40	.15
❏ 46	Jermaine O'Neal	.60	.25
❏ 47	Erick Dampier	.40	.15
❏ 48	Adonal Foyle	.20	.08
❏ 49	Pau Gasol	.60	.25
❏ 50	Shaquille O'Neal	1.50	.60
❏ 51	Allen Iverson	1.25	.50
❏ 52	Ron Artest	.40	.15
❏ 53	Jason Kidd	1.00	.40
❏ 54	Baron Davis	.60	.25
❏ 55	Doug Christie	.40	.15
❏ 56	Darrell Armstrong	.20	.08
❏ 57	Karl Malone	.60	.25
❏ 58	Paul Pierce	.60	.25
❏ 59	Kenny Anderson	.40	.15
❏ 60	John Stockton	.60	.25
❏ 61	Shaquille O'Neal	1.50	.60
❏ 62	Elton Brand	.60	.25
❏ 63	Donyell Marshall	.40	.15
❏ 64	Paul Gasol	.60	.25
❏ 65	John Stockton	.60	.25
❏ 66	Alonzo Mourning	.40	.15
❏ 67	Ruben Patterson	.40	.15
❏ 68	Corliss Williamson	.40	.15
❏ 69	Tim Duncan	1.25	.50
❏ 70	Brent Barry	.40	.15
❏ 71	Steve Smith	.40	.15

❏ 72 Jon Barry	.20	.08
❏ 73 Eric Piatkowski	.40	.15
❏ 74 Wally Szczerbiak	.40	.15
❏ 75 Steve Nash	.60	.25
❏ 76 Hubert Davis	.20	.08
❏ 77 Tyronn Lue	.20	.08
❏ 78 Michael Redd	.60	.25
❏ 79 Wesley Person	.60	.25
❏ 80 Ray Allen	.60	.25
❏ 81 Reggie Miller	.60	.25
❏ 82 Richard Hamilton	.40	.15
❏ 83 Darrell Armstrong	.20	.08
❏ 84 Damon Stoudamire	.40	.15
❏ 85 Steve Nash	.60	.25
❏ 86 Chauncey Billups	.40	.15
❏ 87 Chris Whitney	.20	.08
❏ 88 Steve Smith	.40	.15
❏ 89 Peja Stojakovic	.60	.25
❏ 90 Troy Hudson	.20	.08
❏ 91 Allen Iverson	1.25	.50
❏ 92 Cuttino Mobley	.40	.15
❏ 93 Antoine Walker	.60	.25
❏ 94 Steve Francis	.60	.25
❏ 95 Latrell Sprewell	.60	.25
❏ 96 Tim Duncan	1.25	.50
❏ 97 Baron Davis	.60	.25
❏ 98 Paul Pierce	.60	.25
❏ 99 Gary Payton	.60	.25
❏ 100 Michael Finley	.60	.25
❏ 101 Tim Duncan	1.25	.50
❏ 102 Kevin Garnett	1.25	.50
❏ 103 Elton Brand	.60	.25
❏ 104 Jason Kidd	1.00	.40
❏ 105 Shawn Marion	.60	.25
❏ 106 Andre Miller	.40	.15
❏ 107 Shaquille O'Neal	1.50	.60
❏ 108 Jermaine O'Neal	.60	.25
❏ 109 Dirk Nowitzki	1.00	.40
❏ 110 Pau Gasol	.60	.25
❏ 111 Pau Gasol	.60	.25
❏ 112 Shane Battier	.60	.25
❏ 113 Jason Richardson	.60	.25
❏ 114 Gilbert Arenas	.60	.25
❏ 115 Andrei Kirilenko	.60	.25
❏ 116 Richard Jefferson	.40	.15
❏ 117 Jamaal Tinsley	.60	.25
❏ 118 Tony Parker	.60	.25
❏ 119 Eddie Griffin	.40	.15
❏ 120 Trenton Hassell	.40	.15
❏ 121 Jay Williams RC	3.00	1.25
❏ 122 DaJuan Wagner RC	4.00	1.50
❏ 123 Fred Jones RC	2.50	1.00
❏ 124 Jiri Welsch RC	2.00	.75
❏ 125 Juan Dixon RC	4.00	1.50
❏ 126 Kareem Rush RC	3.00	1.25
❏ 127 Casey Jacobsen RC	2.00	.75
❏ 128 Frank Williams RC	2.00	.75
❏ 129 John Salmons RC	2.00	.75
❏ 130 Dan Dickau RC	2.00	.75
❏ 131 Mike Dunleavy RC	4.00	1.50
❏ 132 Nikoloz Tskitishvili RC	2.50	1.00
❏ 133 Caron Butler RC	5.00	2.00
❏ 134 Jared Jeffries RC	2.00	.75
❏ 135 Bostjan Nachbar RC	2.00	.75
❏ 136 Ryan Humphrey RC	2.00	.75
❏ 137 Qyntel Woods RC	2.50	1.00
❏ 138 Tayshaun Prince RC	4.00	1.50
❏ 139 Chris Jefferies RC	2.00	.75
❏ 140 Vincent Yarbrough RC	2.00	.75
❏ 141 Yao Ming RC	20.00	8.00
❏ 142 Drew Gooden RC	6.00	2.50
❏ 143 Nene Hilario RC	3.00	1.25
❏ 144 Chris Wilcox RC	3.00	1.25
❏ 145 Amare Stoudemire RC	12.00	5.00
❏ 146 Melvin Ely RC	2.00	.75
❏ 147 Marcus Haislip RC	2.00	.75
❏ 148 Curtis Borchardt RC	2.00	.75
❏ 149 Robert Archibald RC	2.00	.75
❏ 150 Dan Gadzuric RC	2.00	.75

1999-00 Topps Tip-Off

❏ COMPLETE SET (132)	30.00	15.00
❏ 1 Steve Smith	.30	.10
❏ 2 Ron Harper	.30	.10
❏ 3 Michael Dickerson	.30	.10
❏ 4 LaPhonso Ellis	.15	.05

❏ 5 Chris Webber	.50	.20
❏ 6 Jason Caffey	.15	.05
❏ 7 Bryon Russell	.15	.05
❏ 8 Bison Dele	.15	.05
❏ 9 Isaiah Rider	.15	.05
❏ 10 Dean Garrett	.15	.05
❏ 11 Eric Murdock	.15	.05
❏ 12 Juwan Howard	.30	.10
❏ 13 Latrell Sprewell	.50	.20
❏ 14 Jalen Rose	.50	.20
❏ 15 Larry Johnson	.30	.10
❏ 16 Eric Williams	.15	.05
❏ 17 Bryant Reeves	.15	.05
❏ 18 Tony Battie	.15	.05
❏ 19 Luc Longley	.15	.05
❏ 20 Gary Payton	.50	.20
❏ 21 Tariq Abdul-Wahad	.15	.05
❏ 22 Armen Gilliam	.15	.05
❏ 23 Shaquille O'Neal	1.25	.50
❏ 24 Gary Trent	.15	.05
❏ 25 John Stockton	.50	.20
❏ 26 Mark Jackson	.30	.10
❏ 27 Cherokee Parks	.15	.05
❏ 28 Michael Olowokandi	.30	.10
❏ 29 Rael LaFrentz	.30	.10
❏ 30 Dell Curry	.15	.05
❏ 31 Travis Best	.15	.05
❏ 32 Shawn Kemp	.30	.10
❏ 33 Voshon Lenard	.15	.05
❏ 34 Brian Grant	.30	.10
❏ 35 Alvin Williams	.15	.05
❏ 36 Derek Fisher	.50	.20
❏ 37 Allan Houston	.30	.10
❏ 38 Arvydas Sabonis	.30	.10
❏ 39 Terry Cummings	.15	.05
❏ 40 Dale Ellis	.15	.05
❏ 41 Maurice Taylor	.30	.10
❏ 42 Grant Hill	.50	.20
❏ 43 Anthony Mason	.30	.10
❏ 44 John Wallace	.15	.05
❏ 45 David Wesley	.15	.05
❏ 46 Nick Van Exel	.50	.20
❏ 47 Cuttino Mobley	.50	.20
❏ 48 Anfernee Hardaway	.50	.20
❏ 49 Terry Porter	.15	.05
❏ 50 Brent Barry	.30	.10
❏ 51 Derek Harper	.30	.10
❏ 52 Antoine Walker	.50	.20
❏ 53 Karl Malone	.50	.20
❏ 54 Ben Wallace	.50	.20
❏ 55 Vlade Divac	.15	.05
❏ 56 Sam Mitchell	.15	.05
❏ 57 Joe Smith	.30	.10
❏ 58 Shawn Bradley	.15	.05
❏ 59 Darrell Armstrong	.15	.05
❏ 60 Kenny Anderson	.30	.10
❏ 61 Jason Williams	.50	.20
❏ 62 Alonzo Mourning	.30	.10
❏ 63 Matt Harpring	.50	.20
❏ 64 Antonio Davis	.15	.05
❏ 65 Lindsey Hunter	.15	.05
❏ 66 Allen Iverson	1.00	.40
❏ 67 Mookie Blaylock	.15	.05
❏ 68 Wesley Person	.15	.05
❏ 69 Bobby Phills	.15	.05
❏ 70 Theo Ratliff	.30	.10
❏ 71 Antonio Daniels	.15	.05
❏ 72 P.J. Brown	.15	.05

❏ 73 David Robinson	.50	.20
❏ 74 Sean Elliott	.30	.10
❏ 75 Zydrunas Ilgauskas	.30	.10
❏ 76 Kerry Kittles	.15	.05
❏ 77 Otis Thorpe	.30	.10
❏ 78 John Starks	.30	.10
❏ 79 Jaren Jackson	.15	.05
❏ 80 Hersey Hawkins	.30	.10
❏ 81 Glenn Robinson	.50	.20
❏ 82 Paul Pierce	.50	.20
❏ 83 Glen Rice	.30	.10
❏ 84 Charlie Ward	.15	.05
❏ 85 Dee Brown	.15	.05
❏ 86 Danny Fortson	.15	.05
❏ 87 Billy Owens	.15	.05
❏ 88 Jason Kidd	.75	.30
❏ 89 Brent Price	.15	.05
❏ 90 Don Reid	.15	.05
❏ 91 Mark Bryant	.15	.05
❏ 92 Vinny Del Negro	.15	.05
❏ 93 Stephon Marbury	.50	.20
❏ 94 Donyell Marshall	.30	.10
❏ 95 Jim Jackson	.15	.05
❏ 96 Horace Grant	.30	.10
❏ 97 Calbert Cheaney	.15	.05
❏ 98 Vince Carter	1.25	.50
❏ 99 Bobby Jackson	.30	.10
❏ 100 Alan Henderson	.15	.05
❏ 101 Mike Bibby	.50	.20
❏ 102 Cedric Henderson	.15	.05
❏ 103 Lamond Murray	.15	.05
❏ 104 A.C. Green	.30	.10
❏ 105 Hakeem Olajuwon	.50	.20
❏ 106 George Lynch	.15	.05
❏ 107 Kendall Gill	.15	.05
❏ 108 Rex Chapman	.15	.05
❏ 109 Eddie Jones	.50	.20
❏ 110 Kornel David RC	.15	.05
❏ 111 Jason Terry RC	2.00	.75
❏ 112 Corey Maggette RC	2.50	1.00
❏ 113 Ron Artest RC	1.50	.60
❏ 114 Richard Hamilton RC	2.50	1.00
❏ 115 Elton Brand RC	3.00	1.25
❏ 116 Baron Davis RC	5.00	2.00
❏ 117 Wally Szczerbiak RC	2.50	1.00
❏ 118 Steve Francis RC	3.00	1.25
❏ 119 James Posey RC	1.50	.60
❏ 120 Shawn Marion RC	3.00	1.25
❏ 121 Tim Duncan	1.00	.40
❏ 122 Danny Manning	.15	.05
❏ 123 Chris Mullin	.50	.20
❏ 124 Antawn Jamison	.75	.30
❏ 125 Kobe Bryant	2.00	.75
❏ 126 Matt Geiger	.15	.05
❏ 127 Rod Strickland	.15	.05
❏ 128 Howard Eisley	.15	.05
❏ 129 Steve Nash	.50	.20
❏ 130 Felipe Lopez	.15	.05
❏ 131 Ron Mercer	.30	.10
❏ 132 Checklist	.15	.05

2000-01 Topps Tip-Off

❏ COMPLETE SET (160)	60.00	30.00
❏ COMMON CARD (1-160)	.15	.05
❏ COMMON ROOKIE	.75	.30
❏ 1 Elton Brand	.50	.20
❏ 2 Marcus Camby	.30	.10
❏ 3 Jalen Rose	.50	.20

❑ 4 Jamie Feick	.15	.05
❑ 5 Toni Kukoc	.30	.10
❑ 6 Todd MacCulloch	.15	.05
❑ 7 Mario Elie	.15	.05
❑ 8 Doug Christie	.30	.10
❑ 9 Sam Cassell	.50	.20
❑ 10 Shaquille O'Neal	1.25	.50
❑ 11 Larry Hughes	.30	.10
❑ 12 Jerry Stackhouse	.50	.20
❑ 13 Rick Fox	.30	.10
❑ 14 Clifford Robinson	.15	.05
❑ 15 Felipe Lopez	.15	.05
❑ 16 Dirk Nowitzki	.75	.30
❑ 17 Cuttino Mobley	.30	.10
❑ 18 Latrell Sprewell	.50	.20
❑ 19 Nick Anderson	.15	.05
❑ 20 Kevin Garnett	1.00	.40
❑ 21 Rik Smits	.30	.10
❑ 22 Jerome Williams	.15	.05
❑ 23 Chris Webber	.50	.20
❑ 24 Jason Terry	.50	.20
❑ 25 Elden Campbell	.15	.05
❑ 26 Kelvin Cato	.15	.05
❑ 27 Tyrone Nesby	.15	.05
❑ 28 Jonathan Bender	.30	.10
❑ 29 Otis Thorpe	.15	.05
❑ 30 Scottie Pippen	.75	.30
❑ 31 Radoslav Nesterovic	.30	.10
❑ 32 P.J. Brown	.15	.05
❑ 33 Reggie Miller	.50	.20
❑ 34 Andre Miller	.30	.10
❑ 35 Tariq Abdul-Wahad	.15	.05
❑ 36 Michael Doleac	.15	.05
❑ 37 Rashard Lewis	.30	.10
❑ 38 Jacque Vaughn	.15	.05
❑ 39 Larry Johnson	.30	.10
❑ 40 Steve Francis	.50	.20
❑ 41 Arvydas Sabonis	.30	.10
❑ 42 Jaren Jackson	.15	.05
❑ 43 Howard Eisley	.15	.05
❑ 44 Rod Strickland	.15	.05
❑ 45 Tim Thomas	.30	.10
❑ 46 Robert Horry	.30	.10
❑ 47 Kenny Thomas	.15	.05
❑ 48 Anthony Peeler	.15	.05
❑ 49 Darrell Armstrong	.15	.05
❑ 50 Vince Carter	1.25	.50
❑ 51 Othella Harrington	.15	.05
❑ 52 Derek Anderson	.30	.10
❑ 53 Anthony Carter	.30	.10
❑ 54 Scott Burrell	.15	.05
❑ 55 Ray Allen	.50	.20
❑ 56 Jason Kidd	.75	.30
❑ 57 Sean Elliott	.30	.10
❑ 58 Muggsy Bogues	.30	.10
❑ 59 LaPhonso Ellis	.15	.05
❑ 60 Tim Duncan	1.00	.40
❑ 61 Adrian Griffin	.30	.10
❑ 62 Wally Szczerbiak	.30	.10
❑ 63 Austin Croshere	.30	.10
❑ 64 Wesley Person	.15	.05
❑ 65 James Posey	.30	.10
❑ 66 Alan Henderson	.15	.05
❑ 67 Ruben Patterson	.30	.10
❑ 68 Jahidi White	.15	.05
❑ 69 Shawn Marion	.50	.20
❑ 70 Lamar Odom	.50	.20
❑ 71 Lindsey Hunter	.15	.05
❑ 72 Keon Clark	.30	.10
❑ 73 Gary Trent	.15	.05
❑ 74 Lamond Murray	.15	.05
❑ 75 Paul Pierce	.50	.20
❑ 76 Charlie Ward	.15	.05
❑ 77 Matt Geiger	.15	.05
❑ 78 Greg Anthony	.15	.05
❑ 79 Horace Grant	.30	.10
❑ 80 John Stockton	.50	.20
❑ 81 Peja Stojakovic	.50	.20
❑ 82 William Avery	.15	.05
❑ 83 Dan Majerle	.30	.10
❑ 84 Christian Laettner	.30	.10
❑ 85 Dana Barros	.15	.05
❑ 86 Corey Benjamin	.15	.05
❑ 87 Keith Van Horn	.50	.20
❑ 88 Patrick Ewing	.50	.20
❑ 89 Steve Smith	.30	.10

❑ 90 Antonio Davis	.15	.05
❑ 91 Samaki Walker	.15	.05
❑ 92 Mitch Richmond	.30	.10
❑ 93 Michael Olowokandi	.15	.05
❑ 94 Baron Davis	.50	.20
❑ 95 Dikembe Mutombo	.30	.10
❑ 96 Andrew DeClercq	.15	.05
❑ 97 Raef LaFrentz	.30	.10
❑ 98 Trajan Langdon	.30	.10
❑ 99 Ervin Johnson	.15	.05
❑ 100 Alonzo Mourning	.30	.10
❑ 101 Kendall Gill	.15	.05
❑ 102 George Lynch	.15	.05
❑ 103 Detlef Schrempf	.30	.10
❑ 104 Donyell Marshall	.30	.10
❑ 105 Bo Outlaw	.15	.05
❑ 106 Kenny Anderson	.30	.10
❑ 107 Eddie Robinson	.30	.10
❑ 108 Jermaine O'Neal	.50	.20
❑ 109 John Amaechi	.15	.05
❑ 110 Glen Rice	.30	.10
❑ 111 Vlade Divac	.30	.10
❑ 112 Vin Baker	.30	.10
❑ 113 Mike Bibby	.50	.20
❑ 114 Richard Hamilton	.30	.10
❑ 115 Mookie Blaylock	.15	.05
❑ 116 Vitaly Potapenko	.15	.05
❑ 117 Anthony Mason	.30	.10
❑ 118 Robert Pack	.15	.05
❑ 119 Vonteego Cummings	.15	.05
❑ 120 Michael Finley	.50	.20
❑ 121 Ron Artest	.30	.10
❑ 122 Tyrone Hill	.15	.05
❑ 123 Rodney Rogers	.15	.05
❑ 124 Quincy Lewis	.15	.05
❑ 125 Kenyon Martin RC	3.00	1.25
❑ 126 Stromile Swift RC	1.50	.60
❑ 127 Darius Miles RC	2.50	1.00
❑ 128 Marcus Fizer RC	.75	.30
❑ 129 Mike Miller RC	2.50	1.00
❑ 130 DerMarr Johnson RC	.75	.30
❑ 131 Chris Mihm RC	.75	.30
❑ 132 Jamal Crawford RC	1.00	.40
❑ 133 Joel Przybilla RC	.75	.30
❑ 134 Keyon Dooling RC	.75	.30
❑ 135 Shaq/Iverson/G.Hill SL	.50	.20
❑ 136 Kidd/Van Exel/Cassell SL	.50	.20
❑ 137 Mutombo/Shaq/Duncan SL	.60	
❑ 138 E.Jones/Pierce/Armstrong SL	.30	.10
❑ 139 Mourning/Mutombo/Shaq SL	.50	.20
❑ 140 Team Championship SL	.75	.30
❑ 141 Kobe Bryant	2.00	.75
❑ 142 Stephon Marbury	.50	.20
❑ 143 Antoine Walker	.50	.20
❑ 144 Jason Williams	.30	.10
❑ 145 Shareef Abdur-Rahim	.50	.20
❑ 146 Gary Payton	.50	.20
❑ 147 Grant Hill	.50	.20
❑ 148 Allen Iverson	1.00	.40
❑ 149 Khalid El-Amin RC EXCH	1.00	.40
❑ 150 Chris Carrawell RC	.75	.30
❑ 151 Shaquille O'Neal CS	.60	.25
❑ 152 Allen Iverson CS	.50	.20
❑ 153 Kevin Garnett CS	.60	.25
❑ 154 Vince Carter CS	.60	.25
❑ 155 Tim Duncan CS	.50	.20
❑ 156 Karl Malone CS	.30	.10
❑ 157 Chris Webber CS	.30	.10
❑ 158 Latrell Sprewell CS	.30	.10
❑ 159 Alonzo Mourning CS	.30	.10
❑ 160 Checklist	.15	.05

2004-05 Topps Total

❑ COMPLETE SET (440)	50.00	20.00
❑ COMMON CARD (1-311)	.15	.06
❑ COMMON ROOKIE (312-360)	.75	.30
❑ COMMON COACH (361-420)	.50	.20
❑ COMMON MASCOT (421-440)	.75	.30
❑ 1 Antoine Walker	.50	.20
❑ 2 Paul Pierce	.50	.20
❑ 3 Tyson Chandler	.50	.20
❑ 4 Lebron James	3.00	1.25
❑ 5 Dirk Nowitzki	.75	.30
❑ 6 Carmelo Anthony	1.00	.40
❑ 7 Chauncey Billups	.25	.10
❑ 8 Juwan Howard	.25	.10

❑ 9 Eddie Gill	.15	.06
❑ 10 Elton Brand	.50	.20
❑ 11 Chucky Atkins	.15	.06
❑ 12 Shane Battier	.25	.10
❑ 13 Shaquille O'Neal	1.25	.50
❑ 14 T.J. Ford	.25	.10
❑ 15 Sam Cassell	.25	.10
❑ 16 Rodney Buford	.15	.06
❑ 17 David West	.15	.06
❑ 18 Stephon Marbury	.50	.20
❑ 19 Steve Francis	.50	.20
❑ 20 Samuel Dalembert	.15	.06
❑ 21 Steve Nash	.50	.20
❑ 22 Shareef Abdur-Rahim	.50	.20
❑ 23 Mike Bibby	.50	.20
❑ 24 Tim Duncan	1.00	.40
❑ 25 Ray Allen	.50	.20
❑ 26 Vince Carter	1.25	.50
❑ 27 Carlos Arroyo	.75	.30
❑ 28 Gilbert Arenas	.50	.20
❑ 29 Mark Blount	.15	.06
❑ 30 Primoz Brezec	.15	.06
❑ 31 Eddy Curry	.25	.10
❑ 32 Lucious Harris	.15	.06
❑ 33 Shawn Bradley	.15	.06
❑ 34 Earl Boykins	.25	.10
❑ 35 Elden Campbell	.15	.06
❑ 36 Calbert Cheaney	.15	.06
❑ 37 Jim Jackson	.15	.06
❑ 38 Jonathan Bender	.25	.10
❑ 39 Kobe Bryant	2.00	.75
❑ 40 Malik Allen	.15	.06
❑ 41 Dan Gadzuric	.15	.06
❑ 42 Eddie Griffin	.25	.10
❑ 43 Jason Collins	.15	.06
❑ 44 Chris Andersen	.15	.06
❑ 45 Marc Jackson	.15	.06
❑ 46 Leandro Barbosa	.25	.10
❑ 47 Derek Anderson	.25	.10
❑ 48 Doug Christie	.25	.10
❑ 49 Brent Barry	.25	.10
❑ 50 Nick Collison	.15	.06
❑ 51 Carlos Boozer	.50	.20
❑ 52 Steve Blake	.25	.10
❑ 53 Al Harrington	.25	.10
❑ 54 Melvin Ely	.15	.06
❑ 55 Zydrunas Ilgauskas	.25	.10
❑ 56 Erick Dampier	.25	.10
❑ 57 Marcus Camby	.25	.10
❑ 58 Derrick Coleman	.15	.06
❑ 59 Speedy Claxton	.15	.06
❑ 60 Tyronn Lue	.15	.06
❑ 61 Austin Croshere	.15	.06
❑ 62 Marko Jaric	.25	.10
❑ 63 Caron Butler	.50	.20
❑ 64 Pau Gasol	.50	.20
❑ 65 Christian Laettner	.25	.10
❑ 66 Daniel Santiago	.15	.06
❑ 67 Kevin Garnett	1.00	.40
❑ 68 Richard Jefferson	.50	.20
❑ 69 David Wesley	.15	.06
❑ 70 Vin Baker	.25	.10
❑ 71 Tony Battie	.15	.06
❑ 72 Allen Iverson	1.00	.40
❑ 73 Darius Miles	.50	.20
❑ 74 Bobby Jackson	.25	.10
❑ 75 Bruce Bowen	.15	.06
❑ 76 Antonio Daniels	.15	.06

#	Player			#	Player			#	Player		
77	Chris Bosh	.50	.20	163	Andre Miller	.25	.10	249	Zaza Pachulia	.25	.10
78	Gordan Giricek	.25	.10	164	Lindsey Hunter	.15	.06	250	Ervin Johnson	.15	.06
79	Kwame Brown	.25	.10	165	Adonal Foyle	.15	.06	251	Jabari Smith	.15	.06
80	Raef Lafrentz	.25	.10	166	Maurice Taylor	.15	.06	252	Nazr Mohammed	.15	.06
81	Jason Hart	.15	.06	167	Fred Jones	.15	.06	253	Andrew Declercq	.15	.06
82	Marquis Daniels	.50	.20	168	Corey Maggette	.25	.10	254	Kyle Korver	.25	.10
83	Francisco Elson	.15	.06	169	Brian Grant	.25	.10	255	Jake Voskuhl	.15	.06
84	Carlos Delfino	.15	.06	170	Bonzi Wells	.25	.10	256	Travis Outlaw	.15	.06
85	Dale Davis	.15	.06	171	Michael Redd	.50	.20	257	Vladimir Radmanovic	.15	.06
86	Tracy McGrady	1.25	.50	172	Latrell Sprewell	.50	.20	258	Lamond Murray	.15	.06
87	Jeff Foster	.15	.06	173	Steven Hunter	.15	.06	259	Jarron Collins	.15	.06
88	Chris Kaman	.25	.10	174	Rodney Rogers	.15	.06	260	Jared Jeffries	.15	.06
89	Brian Cook	.15	.06	175	Anfernee Hardaway	.50	.20	261	Jason Collier	.15	.06
90	Mike Miller	.50	.20	176	Pat Garrity	.15	.06	262	Tom Gugliotta	.15	.06
91	Rasual Butler	.15	.06	177	Brian Skinner	.15	.06	263	Gerald Wallace	.25	.10
92	Mike James	.15	.06	178	Zarko Cabarkapa	.25	.10	264	Eric Piatkowski	.15	.06
93	Trenton Hassell	.15	.06	179	Damon Stoudamire	.25	.10	265	Desagana Diop	.15	.06
94	Jason Kidd	.75	.30	180	Tony Parker	.50	.20	266	Alan Henderson	.15	.06
95	Lee Nailon	.15	.06	181	Ronald Murray	.15	.06	267	Greg Buckner	.15	.06
96	Jerome Williams	.15	.06	182	Alvin Williams	.15	.06	268	Ben Wallace	.50	.20
97	Stacey Augmon	.15	.06	183	Raul Lopez	.15	.06	269	Jason Richardson	.50	.20
98	Willie Green	.15	.06	184	Larry Hughes	.25	.10	270	Ryan Bowen	.15	.06
99	Amare Stoudemire	1.00	.40	185	Predrag Drobnjak	.15	.06	271	Mikki Moore	.15	.06
100	Ruben Patterson	.15	.06	186	Jiri Welsch	.25	.10	272	Brian Cardinal	.15	.06
101	Chris Webber	.50	.20	187	Robert Traylor	.15	.06	273	Maurice Williams	.15	.06
102	Manu Ginobili	.50	.20	188	Nene	.25	.10	274	Mark Madsen	.15	.06
103	Danny Fortson	.15	.06	189	Antonio McDyess	.50	.20	275	Jacque Vaughn	.15	.06
104	Donyell Marshall	.50	.20	190	Troy Murphy	.50	.20	276	George Lynch	.15	.06
105	Matt Harpring	.50	.20	191	Charlie Ward	.15	.06	277	Allan Houston	.25	.10
106	Juan Dixon	.25	.10	192	Reggie Miller	.50	.20	278	Aaron McKie	.25	.10
107	Boris Diaw	.15	.06	193	Bobby Simmons	.15	.06	279	Joe Johnson	.25	.10
108	Ricky Davis	.50	.20	194	Stanislav Medvedenko	.15	.06	280	Qyntel Woods	.15	.06
109	Eddie House	.15	.06	195	Jason Williams	.25	.10	281	Darius Songaila	.15	.06
110	Kirk Hinrich	.50	.20	196	Dwyane Wade	1.50	.60	282	Devin Brown	.15	.06
111	Jeff McInnis	.15	.06	197	Joe Smith	.25	.10	283	Mehmet Okur	.15	.06
112	Michael Finley	.50	.20	198	Wally Szczerbiak	.25	.10	284	Kenny Anderson	.15	.06
113	Voshon Lenard	.15	.06	199	Zoran Planinic	.15	.06	285	Jahidi White	.15	.06
114	Darvin Ham	.15	.06	200	Baron Davis	.50	.20	286	Jon Barry	.15	.06
115	Mike Dunleavy	.25	.10	201	Kurt Thomas	.25	.10	287	Drew Gooden	.25	.10
116	Dikembe Mutombo	.25	.10	202	Deshawn Stevenson	.15	.06	288	Wesley Person	.15	.06
117	Kerry Kittles	.15	.06	203	John Salmons	.15	.06	289	Rasheed Wallace	.50	.20
118	Vlade Divac	.25	.10	204	Maciej Lampe	.15	.06	290	Clifford Robinson	.15	.06
119	James Posey	.25	.10	205	Greg Ostertag	.15	.06	291	Bostjan Nachbar	.15	.06
120	Michael Doleac	.15	.06	206	Malik Rose	.15	.06	292	Scot Pollard	.15	.06
121	Toni Kukoc	.25	.10	207	Matt Bonner	.15	.06	293	Quinton Ross	.15	.06
122	Troy Hudson	.15	.06	208	Keith Mcleod	.15	.06	294	Luke Walton	.25	.10
123	Jamal Crawford	.25	.10	209	Antawn Jamison	.50	.20	295	Earl Watson	.15	.06
124	Grant Hill	.50	.20	210	Marcus Banks	.25	.10	296	Udonis Haslem	.15	.06
125	Corliss Williamson	.15	.06	211	Keith Bogans	.15	.06	297	Erick Strickland	.15	.06
126	Quentin Richardson	.25	.10	212	Antonio Davis	.15	.06	298	Eric Williams	.15	.06
127	Zach Randolph	.50	.20	213	Jerry Stackhouse	.50	.20	299	Junior Harrington	.15	.06
128	Peja Stojakovic	.50	.20	214	Nikoloz Tskitishvili	.15	.06	300	Moochie Norris	.15	.06
129	Robert Horry	.25	.10	215	Darko Milicic	.25	.10	301	Cuttino Mobley	.25	.10
130	Jerome James	.15	.06	216	Eduardo Najera	.25	.10	302	Shawn Marion	.50	.20
131	Morris Peterson	.25	.10	217	Yao Ming	1.25	.50	303	Richie Frahm	.15	.06
132	Jarvis Hayes	.25	.10	218	Jermaine O'Neal	.50	.20	304	Brad Miller	.50	.20
133	Tony Delk	.15	.06	219	Chris Wilcox	.25	.10	305	Michael Wilks	.15	.06
134	Jason Kapono	.15	.06	220	Lamar Odom	.50	.20	306	Rafer Alston	.15	.06
135	Adrian Griffin	.15	.06	221	Lorenzen Wright	.15	.06	307	Andrei Kirilenko	.50	.20
136	Aleksandar Pavlovic	.15	.06	222	Damon Jones	.15	.06	308	Etan Thomas	.15	.06
137	Kenyon Martin	.50	.20	223	Keith Van Horn	.25	.10	309	Ndudi Ebi	.15	.06
138	Richard Hamilton	.25	.10	224	Fred Holberg	.15	.06	310	Anthony Peeler	.15	.06
139	Derek Fisher	.50	.20	225	Brian Scalabrine	.15	.06	311	Pavel Podkolzine RC	.75	.30
140	Bob Sura	.15	.06	226	Jamaal Magloire	.25	.10	312	Lionel Chalmers RC	.75	.30
141	Stephen Jackson	.25	.10	227	Mike Sweetney	.25	.10	313	Andre Emmett RC	.75	.30
142	Devean George	.25	.10	228	Hedo Turkoglu	.50	.20	314	Trevor Ariza RC	.75	.30
143	Stromile Swift	.25	.10	229	Glenn Robinson	.50	.20	315	Dwight Howard RC	2.50	1.00
144	Keyon Dooling	.15	.06	230	Casey Jacobsen	.15	.06	316	Rafael Araujo RC	.75	.30
145	Desmond Mason	.25	.10	231	Nick Van Exel	.50	.20	317	Tony Allen RC	1.00	.40
146	Michael Olowokandi	.15	.06	232	Matt Barnes	.15	.06	318	Luol Deng RC	1.50	.60
147	Ron Mercer	.15	.06	233	Luke Ridnour	.25	.10	319	Jackson Vroman RC	.75	.30
148	P.J. Brown	.15	.06	234	Loren Woods	.15	.06	320	Josh Smith RC	1.50	.60
149	Tim Thomas	.25	.10	235	Raja Bell	.15	.06	321	Ben Gordon RC	4.00	1.50
150	Kelvin Cato	.15	.06	236	Walter McCarty	.15	.06	322	Luke Jackson RC	.75	.30
151	Kenny Thomas	.15	.06	237	Steve Smith	.25	.10	323	David Harrison RC	.75	.30
152	Theo Ratliff	.25	.10	238	Frank Williams	.15	.06	324	Nenad Krstic RC	1.00	.40
153	Rasho Nesterovic	.25	.10	239	Dajuan Wagner	.25	.10	325	J.R. Smith RC	1.00	.40
154	Rashard Lewis	.50	.20	240	Jason Terry	.50	.20	326	Kris Humphries RC	.75	.30
155	Jalen Rose	.50	.20	241	Rodney White	.15	.06	327	Al Jefferson RC	2.00	.75
156	Brendan Haywood	.15	.06	242	Tayshaun Prince	.25	.10	328	Devin Harris RC	1.25	.50
157	Kevin Willis	.15	.06	243	Mickael Pietrus	.25	.10	329	Shaun Livingston RC	1.25	.50
158	Gary Payton	.50	.20	244	Reece Gaines	.15	.06	330	Kaniel Dickens RC	1.50	.60
159	Brevin Knight	.15	.06	245	Jamaal Tinsley	.50	.20	331	Kevin Martin RC	1.25	.50
160	Othella Harrington	.15	.06	246	Zeljko Rebraca	.15	.06	332	Kirk Snyder RC	.75	.30
161	Eric Snow	.25	.10	247	Chris Mihm	.15	.06	333	Josh Childress RC	1.00	.40
162	Josh Howard	.25	.10	248	Eddie Jones	.50	.20	334	Erik Daniels RC	.75	.30

#	Player		
❑ 335	Bernard Robinson RC	.75	.30
❑ 336	Andres Nocioni RC	1.00	.40
❑ 337	D.J. Mbenga RC	.75	.30
❑ 338	Sebastian Telfair RC	.75	.30
❑ 339	Robert Swift RC	.75	.30
❑ 340	Royal Ivey RC	.75	.30
❑ 341	Anderson Varejao RC	1.00	.40
❑ 342	Romain Sato RC	.75	.30
❑ 343	Peter John Ramos RC	.75	.30
❑ 344	Chris Duhon RC	1.25	.50
❑ 345	Emeka Okafor RC	3.00	1.25
❑ 346	Matt Freije RC	.75	.30
❑ 347	Maurice Evans RC	.75	.30
❑ 348	Beno Udrih RC	1.00	.40
❑ 349	John Edwards RC	.75	.30
❑ 350	Sasha Vujacic RC	.75	.30
❑ 351	Dorell Wright RC	1.25	.50
❑ 352	Jameer Nelson RC	1.25	.50
❑ 353	Damien Wilkins RC	.75	.30
❑ 354	Pape Sow RC	.75	.30
❑ 355	Andris Biedrins RC	1.25	.50
❑ 356	Delonte West RC	.75	.30
❑ 357	Arthur Johnson RC	.75	.30
❑ 358	Antonio Burks RC	.75	.30
❑ 359	Andre Iguodala RC	2.00	.75
❑ 360	Ibrahim Kutluay RC	.75	.30
❑ 361	Mike Woodson CO	.50	.20
❑ 362	Larry Drew CO	.50	.20
❑ 363	Doc Rivers CO	1.00	.40
❑ 364	Tony Brown CO	.50	.20
❑ 365	Bernie Bickerstaff CO	.50	.20
❑ 366	Gary Brokaw CO	.50	.20
❑ 367	Scott Skiles CO	1.00	.40
❑ 368	Ron Adams CO	.50	.20
❑ 369	Paul Silas CO	.50	.20
❑ 370	Brendan Malone CO	.50	.20
❑ 371	Don Nelson CO	1.00	.40
❑ 372	Donn Nelson CO	.50	.20
❑ 373	Jeff Bzdelik CO	.50	.20
❑ 374	Michael Cooper CO	.50	.20
❑ 375	Larry Brown CO	1.25	.50
❑ 376	Dave Hanner CO	.50	.20
❑ 377	Mike Montgomery CO	1.00	.40
❑ 378	Terry Stotts CO	.50	.20
❑ 379	Jeff Van Gundy CO	1.00	.40
❑ 380	Tom Thibodeau CO	.50	.20
❑ 381	Rick Carlisle CO	.50	.20
❑ 382	Mike Brown CO	.50	.20
❑ 383	Mike Dunleavy Sr. CO	1.00	.40
❑ 384	Jim Eyen CO	.50	.20
❑ 385	Rudy Tomjanovich CO	1.00	.40
❑ 386	Frank Hamblen CO	.50	.20
❑ 387	Mike Fratello CO	1.00	.40
❑ 388	Eric Musselman CO	1.00	.40
❑ 389	Stan Van Gundy CO	1.00	.40
❑ 390	Bob Mcadoo CO	1.00	.40
❑ 391	Terry Porter CO	.50	.20
❑ 392	Mike Schuler CO	.50	.20
❑ 393	Flip Saunders CO	1.00	.40
❑ 394	Jerry Sichting CO	.50	.20
❑ 395	Lawrence Frank CO	1.00	.40
❑ 396	Brian Hill CO	.50	.20
❑ 397	Byron Scott CO	.50	.20
❑ 398	Darrell Walker CO	.50	.20
❑ 399	Lenny Wilkens CO	1.25	.50
❑ 400	Mark Aguirre CO	.50	.20
❑ 401	Johnny Davis CO	.50	.20
❑ 402	Paul Westhead CO	.50	.20
❑ 403	Jim O'Brien CO	1.00	.40
❑ 404	Lester Conner CO	.50	.20
❑ 405	Mike D'Antoni CO	1.00	.40
❑ 406	Marc Iavaroni CO	.50	.20
❑ 407	Maurice Cheeks CO	1.00	.40
❑ 408	Jim Lynam CO	.50	.20
❑ 409	Rick Adelman CO	1.00	.40
❑ 410	Elston Turner CO	.50	.20
❑ 411	Gregg Popovich CO	1.25	.50
❑ 412	P.J. Carlesimo CO	1.00	.40
❑ 413	Nate Mcmillan CO	.50	.20
❑ 414	Dwane Casey CO	.50	.20
❑ 415	Sam Mitchell CO	.50	.20
❑ 416	Alex English CO	1.00	.40
❑ 417	Jerry Sloan CO	1.00	.40
❑ 418	Phil Johnson CO	.50	.20
❑ 419	Eddie Jordan CO	.50	.20
❑ 420	Mike O'Koren CO	.50	.20

#	Mascot		
❑ 421	Harry The Hawk	.75	.30
❑ 422	Blaze	.75	.30
❑ 423	Benny Da Bull	.75	.30
❑ 424	Slamson	.75	.30
❑ 425	Champ	.75	.30
❑ 426	Rocky	.75	.30
❑ 427	Clutch	.75	.30
❑ 428	Squatch	.75	.30
❑ 429	Boomer	.75	.30
❑ 430	The Raptor	.75	.30
❑ 431	Super Grizz	.75	.30
❑ 432	G-Wiz	.75	.30
❑ 433	Crunch	.75	.30
❑ 434	Sly The Fox	.75	.30
❑ 435	Hip Hop	.75	.30
❑ 436	The Gorilla	.75	.30
❑ 437	Skyhawk	.75	.30
❑ 438	Turbo	.75	.30
❑ 439	Bowser	.75	.30
❑ 440	Da Bull	.75	.30

2005-06 Topps Total

❑ COMPLETE SET (440)	50.00	20.00
❑ COMMON CARD (1-360)	.15	.60
❑ COMMON ROOKIE (1-360)	.75	.30
❑ COMMON COACH (361-420)	.50	.20
❑ COMMON MASCOT (421-436)	.75	.30
❑ COMMON CELEBRITY (436-440)	1.00	.40

#	Player		
❑ 1	Josh Childress	.25	.10
❑ 2	Emeka Okafor	.75	.30
❑ 3	Luol Deng	.50	.20
❑ 4	Carmelo Anthony	1.00	.40
❑ 5	Carlos Arroyo	.75	.20
❑ 6	Shane Battier	.50	.20
❑ 7	Vince Carter	1.25	.50
❑ 8	Samuel Dalembert	.25	.10
❑ 9	Leandro Barbosa	.15	.60
❑ 10	Mike Bibby	.50	.20
❑ 11	Brent Barry	.25	.10
❑ 12	Ray Allen	.50	.20
❑ 13	Rafer Alston	.15	.60
❑ 14	Gilbert Arenas	.50	.20
❑ 15	Al Harrington	.25	.10
❑ 16	Primoz Brezec	.15	.60
❑ 17	Antonio Davis	.15	.60
❑ 18	Earl Boykins	.25	.10
❑ 19	Chauncey Billups	.50	.20
❑ 20	Antonio Burks	.15	.60
❑ 21	Jason Collins	.15	.60
❑ 22	P.J. Brown	.15	.60
❑ 23	Andre Iguodala	.50	.20
❑ 24	Bruce Bowen	.25	.10
❑ 25	Nick Collison	.15	.60
❑ 26	Rafael Araujo	.25	.10
❑ 27	Josh Smith	.50	.20
❑ 28	Melvin Ely	.15	.60
❑ 29	Ben Gordon	1.00	.40
❑ 30	Zydrunas Ilgauskas	.25	.10
❑ 31	Marcus Camby	.15	.60
❑ 32	Carlos Delfino	.15	.60
❑ 33	Mike James	.15	.60
❑ 34	Brian Cardinal	.25	.10
❑ 35	Udonis Haslem	.50	.20
❑ 36	Toni Kukoc	.25	.10
❑ 37	Kevin Garnett	1.00	.40
❑ 38	Richard Jefferson	.25	.10
❑ 39	Jamal Crawford	.25	.10
❑ 40	Allen Iverson	1.00	.40
❑ 41	Tim Duncan	1.00	.40
❑ 42	Danny Fortson	.15	.60
❑ 43	Chris Bosh	.50	.20
❑ 44	Ricky Davis	.50	.20
❑ 45	LeBron James	3.00	1.25
❑ 46	Devin Harris	.50	.20
❑ 47	Tracy McGrady	1.25	.50
❑ 48	Chris Kaman	.25	.10
❑ 49	Pau Gasol	.50	.20
❑ 50	Jamaal Magloire	.15	.60
❑ 51	Trenton Hassell	.15	.60
❑ 52	Jason Kidd	.75	.30
❑ 53	Speedy Claxton	.15	.60
❑ 54	Kevin Martin	.25	.10
❑ 55	Manu Ginobili	.50	.20
❑ 56	Rashard Lewis	.50	.20
❑ 57	Matt Harpring	.50	.20
❑ 58	Kenyon Martin	.50	.20
❑ 59	Al Jefferson	.50	.20
❑ 60	Josh Howard	.25	.10
❑ 61	Bob Sura	.25	.10
❑ 62	David Harrison	.15	.60
❑ 63	Shaun Livingston	.50	.20
❑ 64	Alonzo Mourning	.25	.10
❑ 65	Michael Redd	.50	.20
❑ 66	Mark Madsen	.15	.60
❑ 67	Brad Miller	.25	.10
❑ 68	Robert Horry	.25	.10
❑ 69	Luke Ridnour	.25	.10
❑ 70	Paul Pierce	.50	.20
❑ 71	Anderson Varejao	.25	.10
❑ 72	Dirk Nowitzki	.75	.30
❑ 73	Stephen Jackson	.25	.10
❑ 74	Corey Maggette	.25	.10
❑ 75	Shaquille O'Neal	1.25	.50
❑ 76	Joe Smith	.25	.10
❑ 77	Troy Hudson	.15	.60
❑ 78	Steve Francis	.50	.20
❑ 79	Shawn Marion	.50	.20
❑ 80	Ruben Patterson	.15	.60
❑ 81	Morris Peterson	.25	.10
❑ 82	Jarvis Hayes	.25	.10
❑ 83	Derek Fisher	.25	.10
❑ 84	Fred Jones	.25	.10
❑ 85	Chris Mihm	.15	.60
❑ 86	Stephon Marbury	.50	.20
❑ 87	Grant Hill	.50	.20
❑ 88	Steve Nash	.50	.20
❑ 89	Joel Przybilla	.15	.60
❑ 90	Jalen Rose	.50	.20
❑ 91	Brendan Haywood	.15	.60
❑ 92	Jerry Stackhouse	.50	.20
❑ 93	Adonal Foyle	.15	.60
❑ 94	Lamar Odom	.50	.20
❑ 95	Dwight Howard	.60	.25
❑ 96	Amare Stoudemire	1.00	.40
❑ 97	Zach Randolph	.50	.20
❑ 98	Peja Stojakovic	.50	.20
❑ 99	Mehmet Okur	.15	.60
❑ 100	Antawn Jamison	.50	.20
❑ 101	Jason Terry	.50	.20
❑ 102	Troy Murphy	.50	.20
❑ 103	Sasha Vujacic	.15	.60
❑ 104	Dwyane Wade	1.50	.60
❑ 105	Jameer Nelson	.25	.10
❑ 106	Jared Jeffries	.15	.60
❑ 107	J.R. Smith	.25	.10
❑ 108	Mike Sweetney	.15	.60
❑ 109	DeShawn Stevenson	.15	.60
❑ 110	Sebastian Telfair	.25	.10
❑ 111	Eddie Griffin	.15	.60
❑ 112	Tyronn Lue	.15	.60
❑ 113	Jon Barry	.15	.60
❑ 114	Eric Williams	.15	.60
❑ 115	Rasho Nesterovic	.15	.60
❑ 116	Keith Van Horn	.25	.10
❑ 117	Kenny Thomas	.15	.60
❑ 118	Chris Wilcox	.15	.60
❑ 119	Chris Webber	.50	.20
❑ 120	Nene	.25	.10
❑ 121	John Salmons	.15	.60
❑ 122	Chris Andersen	.15	.60
❑ 123	Lindsey Hunter	.15	.60
❑ 124	Matt Bonner	.15	.60
❑ 125	Darius Miles	.50	.20
❑ 126	Orien Greene RC	.75	.30

#	Player			#	Player			#	Player		
127	Jarron Collins	.15	.60	213	Tony Parker	.50	.20	299	Tyson Chandler	.50	.20
128	Trevor Ariza	.25	.10	214	Brian Skinner	.15	.60	300	Sarunas Jasikevicius RC	1.50	.60
129	Dan Gadzuric	.15	.60	215	Mike Dunleavy	.25	.10	301	Joey Graham RC	.75	.30
130	Loren Woods	.15	.60	216	Kris Humphries	.15	.60	302	Alan Anderson RC	.75	.30
131	Jason Richardson	.50	.20	217	Mark Blount	.15	.60	303	Steve Blake	.15	.60
132	Corliss Williamson	.15	.60	218	Marquis Daniels	.25	.10	304	Nikoloz Tsktishvili	.15	.60
133	Zeljko Rebraca	.15	.60	219	Tony Allen	.25	.10	305	Shareef Abdur-Rahim	.50	.20
134	Othella Harrington	.15	.60	220	Tony Battie	.15	.60	306	Sean May RC	1.50	.60
135	Theo Ratliff	.25	.10	221	Luther Head RC	2.00	.75	307	Julius Hodge RC	1.50	.60
136	David Wesley	.15	.60	222	Richie Frahm	.15	.60	308	Deron Williams RC	5.00	2.00
137	Bostjan Nachbar	.15	.60	223	Arvydas Macijauskas RC	.75	.30	309	Michael Ruffin	.15	.60
138	Eric Snow	.25	.10	224	Eddie Jones	.25	.10	310	Darius Songaila	.15	.60
139	Desmond Mason	.15	.60	225	Dan Dickau	.15	.60	311	Donyell Marshall	.15	.60
140	Dahntay Jones	.15	.60	226	Marko Jaric	.15	.60	312	Jermaine O'Neal	.50	.20
141	Andre Miller	.25	.10	227	Daniel Ewing RC	1.50	.60	313	Bracey Wright RC	.75	.30
142	Travis Outlaw	.15	.60	228	Keyon Dooling	.15	.60	314	Scot Pollard	.15	.60
143	Jim Jackson	.25	.10	229	James Posey	.15	.60	315	Linas Kleiza RC	.75	.30
144	Gordan Giricek	.15	.60	230	Earl Watson	.15	.60	316	Jerome James	.15	.60
145	Kelvin Cato	.15	.60	231	Juan Dixon	.15	.60	317	Brian Scalabrine	.15	.60
146	Michael Doleac	.15	.60	232	Rasual Butler	.15	.60	318	Tim Thomas	.15	.60
147	Lorenzen Wright	.15	.60	233	Bernard Robinson	.15	.60	319	Reggie Evans	.15	.60
148	Vladimir Radmanovic	.15	.60	234	Joe Johnson	.25	.10	320	Jason Maxiell RC	.75	.30
149	Maurice Evans	.15	.60	235	Antoine Walker	.50	.20	321	Jannero Pargo	.15	.60
150	Hedo Turkoglu	.25	.10	236	Andris Biedrins	.15	.60	322	Michael Finley	.50	.20
151	Ryan Bowen	.15	.60	237	Gary Payton	.50	.20	323	Ersan Ilyasova RC	.75	.30
152	Brevin Knight	.15	.60	238	Monta Ellis RC	1.50	.60	324	Robert Whaley RC	.75	.30
153	Jacque Vaughn	.15	.60	239	Quentin Richardson	.25	.10	325	Chris Taft RC	.75	.30
154	Tayshaun Prince	.50	.20	240	Martynas Andriuskevicius RC	.75	.30	326	Esteban Batista RC	.75	.30
155	Clifford Robinson	.15	.60	241	Kwame Brown	.25	.10	327	Louis Williams RC	.75	.30
156	Delonte West	.50	.20	242	Travis Diener RC	.75	.30	328	Austin Croshere	.15	.60
157	Zoran Planinic	.15	.60	243	Stromile Swift	.25	.10	329	Martell Webster RC	.75	.30
158	Slava Medvedenko	.15	.60	244	Wayne Simien RC	2.00	.75	330	Etan Thomas	.15	.60
159	Andres Nocioni	.25	.10	245	Zaza Pachulia	.15	.60	331	Brandon Bass RC	.75	.30
160	Kyle Korver	.50	.20	246	Andrew Bogut RC	2.00	.75	332	Ron Artest	.25	.10
161	Brian Cook	.15	.60	247	Marvin Williams RC	3.00	1.25	333	Gerald Fitch RC	.75	.30
162	Viktor Khryapa	.15	.60	248	David Lee RC	1.50	.60	334	Chucky Atkins	.15	.60
163	Malik Rose	.15	.60	249	Nate Robinson RC	2.50	1.00	335	Jonathan Bender	.15	.60
164	Elton Brand	.50	.20	250	Jason Williams	.25	.10	336	Boris Diaw	.25	.10
165	Gerald Wallace	.25	.10	251	Larry Hughes	.25	.10	337	Andray Blatche RC	.75	.30
166	Michael Bradley	.15	.60	252	Ike Diogu RC	1.50	.60	338	Jeff Foster	.15	.60
167	DerMarr Johnson	.15	.60	253	Marc Jackson	.15	.60	339	Andrew Bynum RC	5.00	2.00
168	Reece Gaines	.15	.60	254	Luke Jackson	.25	.10	340	Caron Butler	.25	.10
169	Mickael Pietrus	.15	.60	255	Lee Nailon	.15	.60	341	Danny Granger RC	2.00	.75
170	Donta Smith	.15	.60	256	T.J. Ford	.25	.10	342	Channing Frye RC	2.00	.75
171	Wally Szczerbiak	.25	.10	257	Shavlik Randolph RC	.75	.30	343	Antonio Daniels	.15	.60
172	Aleksandar Pavlovic	.15	.60	258	Eddie Basden RC	.75	.30	344	Brian Grant	.15	.60
173	Michael Olowokandi	.15	.60	259	Yaroslav Korolev RC	.75	.30	345	Steven Hunter	.15	.60
174	Jose Calderon RC	1.50	.60	260	James Jones	.15	.60	346	Chris Paul RC	6.00	2.50
175	Jiri Welsch	.15	.60	261	Raja Bell	.15	.60	347	Lawrence Roberts RC	.75	.30
176	Antonio McDyess	.25	.10	262	Salim Stoudamire RC	2.00	.75	348	Bobby Simmons	.15	.60
177	Andrei Kirilenko	.50	.20	263	Cuttino Mobley	.25	.10	349	Dijon Thompson RC	.75	.30
178	Nenad Krstic	.25	.10	264	Kurt Thomas	.25	.10	350	Von Wafer RC	.75	.30
179	Richard Hamilton	.25	.10	265	D.J. Mbenga	.15	.60	351	Damon Stoudamire	.25	.10
180	Stacey Augmon	.15	.60	266	Zarko Cabarkapa	.15	.60	352	Kevin Ollie	.15	.60
181	Kobe Bryant	2.00	.75	267	Bobby Jackson	.25	.10	353	Kirk Snyder	.15	.60
182	Erick Dampier	.15	.60	268	Rashad McCants RC	3.00	1.25	354	Hakim Warrick RC	3.00	1.25
183	Raef LaFrentz	.15	.60	269	Antoine Wright RC	.75	.30	355	Eddy Curry	.25	.10
184	Jackie Butler RC	.75	.30	270	Josh Powell RC	.75	.30	356	Aaron McKie	.25	.10
185	Ira Newble	.15	.60	271	Francisco Garcia RC	1.50	.60	357	Sam Cassell	.50	.20
186	Luke Walton	.25	.10	272	Robert Swift	.25	.10	358	Dorell Wright	.25	.10
187	Rasheed Wallace	.50	.20	273	Gerald Green RC	4.00	1.50	359	Scott Padgett	.15	.60
188	Alvin Williams	.15	.60	274	Peter John Ramos	.15	.60	360	Pat Garrity	.15	.60
189	Ben Wallace	.50	.20	275	Nick Van Exel	.50	.20	361	Mike Woodson	.50	.20
190	Chris Duhon	.25	.10	276	Jarrett Jack RC	.75	.30	362	Larry Drew	.50	.20
191	Maurice Williams	.15	.60	277	Ronnie Price RC	.75	.30	363	Doc Rivers	1.00	.40
192	Ronald Murray	.15	.60	278	Jamaal Tinsley	.15	.60	364	Tony Brown	.50	.20
193	Yao Ming	1.25	.50	279	Jake Voskuhl	.15	.60	365	Bernie Bickerstaff	.50	.20
194	Eduardo Najera	.15	.60	280	Devin Brown	.15	.60	366	Gary Brokaw	.50	.20
195	Nazr Mohammed	.15	.60	281	James Singleton RC	.75	.30	367	Scott Skiles	.50	.20
196	Devean George	.15	.60	282	C.J. Miles RC	.75	.30	368	Ron Adams	.50	.20
197	Kirk Hinrich	.50	.20	283	Charlie Villanueva RC	2.50	1.00	369	Mike Brown	.50	.20
198	Baron Davis	.50	.20	284	Jeff McInnis	.15	.60	370	Kenny Natt	.50	.20
199	Juwan Howard	.25	.10	285	Eddie House	.15	.60	371	Avery Johnson	.50	.20
200	Drew Gooden	.25	.10	286	Rawle Marshall RC	.75	.30	372	Del Harris	.50	.20
201	Carlos Boozer	.50	.20	287	Royal Ivey	.15	.60	373	George Karl	.50	.20
202	Tony Delk	.15	.60	288	Dikembe Mutombo	.25	.10	374	Scott Brooks	.50	.20
203	David West	.15	.60	289	Fabricio Oberto RC	.75	.30	375	Flip Saunders	1.00	.40
204	Keith Bogans	.15	.60	290	Damon Jones	.25	.10	376	Sid Lowe	.50	.20
205	Quinton Ross	.15	.60	291	Jason Hart	.15	.60	377	Mike Montgomery	.50	.20
206	Darrell Armstrong	.15	.60	292	Jumaine Jones	.15	.60	378	Mario Elie	.50	.20
207	Damien Wilkins	.15	.60	293	Greg Ostertag	.15	.60	379	Jeff Van Gundy	1.00	.40
208	Voshon Lenard	.15	.60	294	Ryan Gomes RC	.75	.30	380	Tom Thibodeau	.50	.20
209	Vitaly Potapenko	.15	.60	295	Derek Anderson	.25	.10	381	Rick Carlisle	.50	.20
210	Mike Miller	.50	.20	296	Raymond Felton RC	3.00	1.25	382	Kevin O'Neill	.50	.20
211	Beno Udrih	.25	.10	297	John Petro RC	.15	.60	383	Mike Dunleavy Sr.	1.00	.40
212	Darko Milicic	.25	.10	298	Bonzi Wells	.25	.10	384	Jim Eyen	.50	.20

#	Player		
385	Phil Jackson	2.00	.75
386	Frank Hamblen	.50	.20
387	Mike Fratello	1.00	.40
388	Eric Musselman	.50	.20
389	Pat Riley	1.25	.50
390	Bob McAdoo	.50	.20
391	Terry Stotts	.50	.20
392	Lester Conner	.50	.20
393	Dwane Casey	.50	.20
394	Johnny Davis	.50	.20
395	Lawrence Frank	.50	.20
396	Bill Cartwright	.50	.20
397	Byron Scott	.50	.20
398	Darrell Walker	.50	.20
399	Larry Brown	1.25	.50
400	Herb Williams	.50	.20
401	Brian Hill	.50	.20
402	Randy Ayers	.50	.20
403	Maurice Cheeks	1.00	.40
404	John Kuester	.50	.20
405	Mike D'Antoni	1.00	.40
406	Marc Iavaroni	.50	.20
407	Nate McMillan	.50	.20
408	Dean Demopoulos	.50	.20
409	Rick Adelman	.75	.30
410	Elston Turner	.50	.20
411	Gregg Popovich	1.00	.40
412	P.J. Carlesimo	1.00	.40
413	Bob Weiss	.50	.20
414	Jack Sikma	.50	.20
415	Sam Mitchell	.50	.20
416	Jim Todd	.50	.20
417	Jerry Sloan	.50	.20
418	Phil D. Johnson	.50	.20
419	Eddie Jordan	.50	.20
420	Mike O'Koren	.50	.20
421	The Gorilla	.75	.30
422	Rocky	.75	.30
423	Slamson	.75	.30
424	The Raptor	.75	.30
425	Squatch	.75	.30
426	Blaze	.75	.30
427	Crunch	.75	.30
428	Harry the Hawk	.75	.30
429	Champ	.75	.30
430	Hip Hop	.75	.30
431	Sly the Silver Fox	.75	.30
432	Benny the Bull	.75	.30
433	G-Wiz	.75	.30
434	Clutch	.75	.30
435	Boomer	.75	.30
436	Shannon Elizabeth	1.00	.40
437	Christie Brinkley	1.00	.40
438	Jenny McCarthy	1.00	.40
439	Carmen Electra	1.00	.40
440	Jay-Z	1.50	.60

2006-07 Topps Trademark Moves

#	Player		
1	Dwyane Wade	2.50	1.00
2	Richard Jefferson	.50	.20
3	Raymond Felton	1.00	.40
4	Ray Allen	.75	.30
5	Peja Stojakovic	.75	.30
6	Mike Miller	.75	.30
7	Mike Bibby	.75	.30
8	Marcus Camby	.25	.10
9	LeBron James	5.00	2.00

#	Player		
10	Joe Johnson	.50	.20
11	Corey Maggette	.50	.20
12	Charlie Villanueva	.75	.30
13	Caron Butler	.50	.20
14	Amare Stoudemire	1.50	.60
15	Vince Carter	2.00	.75
16	Tracy McGrady	2.00	.75
17	Shawn Marion	.75	.30
18	Ron Artest	.50	.20
19	Pau Gasol	.75	.30
20	Smush Parker	.25	.10
21	Josh Smith	.75	.30
22	Gilbert Arenas	.75	.30
23	Elton Brand	.75	.30
24	Dwight Howard	1.00	.40
25	Dirk Nowitzki	1.25	.50
26	Chris Bosh	.75	.30
27	Chauncey Billups	.75	.30
28	Ben Gordon	1.50	.60
29	Yao Ming	2.00	.75
30	Tyson Chandler	.50	.20
31	T.J. Ford	.50	.20
32	Steve Nash	.75	.30
33	Sam Cassell	.75	.30
34	Speedy Claxton	.25	.10
35	Manu Ginobili	.75	.30
36	Kevin Garnett	1.50	.60
37	Jason Terry	.75	.30
38	Jameer Nelson	.50	.20
39	Ben Wallace	.75	.30
40	Antoine Walker	.50	.20
41	Al Jefferson	.75	.30
42	Tim Duncan	1.50	.60
43	Richard Hamilton	.50	.20
44	Paul Pierce	.75	.30
45	Mike James	.25	.10
46	Martell Webster	.50	.20
47	Kobe Bryant	3.00	1.25
48	Kirk Hinrich	.75	.30
49	Josh Howard	.50	.20
50	Bobby Simmons	.25	.10
51	Channing Frye	.50	.20
52	Andrei Kirilenko	.75	.30
53	Allen Iverson	1.50	.60
54	Al Harrington	.25	.10
55	Zach Randolph	.75	.30
56	Tony Parker	.75	.30
57	Stephon Marbury	.75	.30
58	Shaquille O'Neal	2.00	.75
59	Ricky Davis	.75	.30
60	Lamar Odom	.75	.30
61	Emeka Okafor	.75	.30
62	Raja Bell	.25	.10
63	Deron Williams	.75	.30
64	Danny Granger	.50	.20
65	Baron Davis	.75	.30
66	Andre Miller	.50	.20
67	Andre Iguodala	.75	.30
68	Michael Redd	.75	.30
69	Rashard Lewis	.75	.30
70	Larry Hughes	.50	.20
71	Jermaine O'Neal	.75	.30
72	Jason Richardson	.75	.30
73	Jason Kidd	1.25	.50
74	Gerald Wallace	.75	.30
75	Leandro Barbosa	.50	.20
76	Chris Paul	2.00	.75
77	Carmelo Anthony	1.50	.60
78	Brad Miller	.75	.30
79	Antawn Jamison	.75	.30
80	Andrew Bogut	1.00	.40
81	Dominique Wilkins	1.50	.60
82	Larry Bird	5.00	2.00
83	Clyde Drexler	1.25	.50
84	Dennis Rodman	1.25	.50
85	Isiah Thomas	1.25	.50
86	Rick Barry	1.25	.50
87	Hakeem Olajuwon	1.25	.50
88	George Gervin	1.25	.50
89	Spud Webb	1.25	.50
90	Kareem Abdul-Jabbar	2.50	1.00
91	Oscar Robertson	1.25	.50
92	Earl Monroe	1.25	.50
93	Walt Frazier	1.25	.50
94	Moses Malone	1.25	.50
95	Wilt Chamberlain	5.00	2.00

#	Player		
96	Karl Malone	1.50	.60
97	Manute Bol	1.25	.50
98	Bill Walton	1.25	.50
99	Maurice Cheeks	1.25	.50
100	Bob Lanier	1.25	.50
101	Solomon Jones AU/149 RC	8.00	3.00
102	Kyle Lowry AU/149 RC	8.00	3.00
103	Maurice Ager AU/149 RC	8.00	3.00
104	Patrick O'Bryant AU/75 RC	10.00	4.00
105	Pops Mensah-Bonsu AU/149 RC	8.00	3.00
106	Marcus Vinicius AU/149 RC	8.00	3.00
107	Josh Boone AU/149 RC	12.00	5.00
108	Mardy Collins AU/149 RC	8.00	3.00
109	Rodney Carney AU/75 RC	10.00	4.00
110	P.J. Tucker AU/149 RC	10.00	4.00
111	Shelden Williams AU/75 RC	15.00	6.00
112	Ryan Hollins AU/149 RC	8.00	3.00
113	Sergio Rodriguez AU/149 RC EXCH	8.00	3.00
114	Steve Novak AU/149 RC	8.00	3.00
115	Paul Davis AU/149 RC	8.00	3.00
116	David Noel AU/149 RC	8.00	3.00
117	Marcus Williams AU/75 RC	15.00	6.00
118	Renaldo Balkman AU/75 RC	10.00	4.00
119	Quincy Douby AU/149 RC EXCH	8.00	3.00
120	Andrea Bargnani AU/75 RC	40.00	15.00
121	Chris Quinn AU/149 RC	8.00	3.00
122	Thabo Sefolosha AU/75 RC	20.00	8.00
123	Hassan Adams AU/149 RC	8.00	3.00
124	James White AU/149 RC	10.00	4.00
125	Jordan Farmar AU/75 RC	20.00	8.00
126	Damir Markota AU/149 RC	8.00	3.00
127	Mile Ilic AU/149 RC	8.00	3.00
128	James Augustine AU/149 RC	8.00	3.00
129	Paul Millsap AU/75 RC	15.00	6.00
130	Jorge Garbajosa AU/149 RC	12.00	5.00
131	Allan Ray AU/75 RC EXCH	10.00	4.00
132	Shannon Brown AU/149 RC	8.00	3.00
133	Will Blalock AU/149 RC	8.00	3.00
134	Vassilis Spanoulis AU/149 RC	8.00	3.00
135	Adam Morrison AU/75 RC	30.00	12.50
136	Craig Smith AU/149 RC	8.00	3.00
137	Cedric Simmons AU/149 RC	8.00	3.00
138	J.J. Redick AU/75 RC	30.00	12.50
139	Rookie Exchange		
140	Ronnie Brewer AU/75 RC	12.00	5.00
141	Rajon Rondo AU/149 RC	12.00	5.00
142	Daniel Gibson AU/149 RC	10.00	4.00
143	Mickael Gelabale AU/75 RC EXCH	10.00	4.00
144	Shawne Williams AU/75 RC	12.00	5.00
145	Alexander Johnson AU/149 RC	8.00	3.00
146	Randy Foye AU/75 RC	20.00	8.00
147	Hilton Armstrong AU RC		
148	Bobby Jones AU/149 RC	8.00	3.00
149	Saer Sene AU/149 RC	8.00	3.00
150	Dee Brown AU/75 RC		

2006-07 Topps Triple Threads

#	Player		
1	Amare Stoudemire	5.00	2.00
2	Dirk Nowitzki	4.00	1.50
3	Dwyane Wade	8.00	3.00
4	Allen Iverson	5.00	2.00
5	LeBron James	15.00	6.00
6	Tracy McGrady	6.00	2.50
7	Ben Wallace	2.50	1.00
8	Jason Richardson	2.50	1.00
9	Vince Carter	6.00	2.50

#	Player		
10	Joe Johnson	1.50	.60
11	Paul Pierce	2.50	1.00
12	Gerald Wallace	2.50	1.00
13	Elton Brand	2.50	1.00
14	Gilbert Arenas	2.50	1.00
15	Marcus Camby	.75	.30
16	Andrew Bogut	3.00	1.25
17	Stephon Marbury	2.50	1.00
18	Kevin Garnett	5.00	2.00
19	Al Harrington	.75	.30
20	Tim Duncan	5.00	2.00
21	Pau Gasol	2.50	1.00
22	Kobe Bryant	10.00	4.00
23	Dwight Howard	3.00	1.25
24	Jarrett Jack	1.50	.60
25	T.J. Ford	1.50	.60
26	Ron Artest	1.50	.60
27	Deron Williams	2.50	1.00
28	Rasheed Wallace	2.50	1.00
29	Shaquille O'Neal	6.00	2.50
30	Ray Allen	2.50	1.00
31	Peja Stojakovic	2.50	1.00
32	Jermaine O'Neal	2.50	1.00
33	Larry Hughes	2.50	1.00
34	Brad Miller	6.00	2.50
35	Caron Butler	2.50	1.00
36	Andre Miller	2.50	1.00
37	Kirk Hinrich	2.50	1.00
38	Andrei Kirilenko	1.50	.60
39	Charlie Villanueva	2.50	1.00
40	Sebastian Telfair	1.50	.60
41	Josh Howard	1.50	.60
42	Emeka Okafor	2.50	1.00
43	Danny Granger	2.50	1.00
44	Tony Parker	2.50	1.00
45	Zach Randolph	1.50	.60
46	Ricky Davis	2.50	1.00
47	Chris Webber	2.50	1.00
48	Mike Bibby	2.50	1.00
49	Troy Murphy	2.50	1.00
50	Josh Smith	2.50	1.00
51	Steve Nash	2.50	1.00
52	Chris Paul	6.00	2.50
53	Rashard Lewis	2.50	1.00
54	Ben Gordon	5.00	2.00
55	Mehmet Okur	1.50	.60
56	Chris Bosh	2.50	1.00
57	Drew Gooden	1.50	.60
58	Corey Maggette	2.50	1.00
59	Eddy Curry	2.50	1.00
60	Yao Ming	.75	.30
61	Al Jefferson	2.50	1.00
62	Smush Parker	1.50	.60
63	Jason Kidd	1.50	.60
64	Hakim Warrick	1.50	.60
65	Richard Hamilton	1.50	.60
66	Luke Ridnour	1.50	.60
67	Raymond Felton	3.00	1.25
68	Andre Iguodala	2.50	1.00
69	Jason Terry	2.50	1.00
70	Richard Jefferson	1.50	.60
71	Lamar Odom	2.50	1.00
72	Jameer Nelson	1.50	.60
73	Mike James	.75	.30
74	Antwan Jamison	2.50	1.00
75	Shaun Livingston	2.00	.75
76	Manu Ginobili	2.50	1.00
77	Antoine Walker	2.50	1.00
78	Desmond Mason	.75	.30
79	Channing Frye	1.50	.60
80	Morris Peterson	1.50	.60
81	Michael Redd	2.50	1.00
82	Shawn Marion	2.50	1.00
83	Bonzi Wells	1.50	.60
84	Chauncey Billups	6.00	2.50
85	Baron Davis	2.50	1.00
86	Carmelo Anthony	.75	.30
87	Brandon Roy RC	4.00	1.50
88	Rudy Gay RC	1.50	.60
89	Tyrus Thomas RC	12.00	5.00
90	LaMarcus Aldridge RC	10.00	4.00
91	Wilt Chamberlain	15.00	6.00
92	Larry Bird	15.00	6.00
93	Isiah Thomas	4.00	1.50
94	Bernard King	1.50	.60
95	Elgin Baylor	4.00	1.50
96	Oscar Robertson	4.00	1.50
97	Walt Frazier	4.00	1.50
98	Chris Mullin	4.00	1.50
99	Bill Laimbeer	4.00	1.50
100	George Gervin	4.00	1.50
101	Dee Brown JSY AU RC	20.00	8.00
102	Renaldo Balkman JSY AU RC	15.00	6.00
103	Maurice Ager JSY AU RC	15.00	6.00
104	Shelden Williams JSY AU RC	20.00	8.00
105	Rodney Carney JSY AU RC	15.00	6.00
106	J.J. Redick JSY AU RC	30.00	12.00
107	Hilton Armstrong JSY AU RC	15.00	6.00
108	Craig Smith JSY AU RC	15.00	6.00
109	Kyle Lowry JSY AU RC	15.00	6.00
110	Josh Boone JSY AU RC	15.00	6.00
111	Saer Sene JSY AU RC	15.00	6.00
112	Jorge Garbajosa JSY AU RC	30.00	12.00
113	Paul Davis JSY AU RC	15.00	6.00
114	Thabo Sefolosha JSY AU RC	25.00	10.00
115	Shannon Brown JSY AU RC	15.00	6.00
116	Bobby Jones JSY AU RC	15.00	6.00
117	Jordan Farmar JSY AU RC	30.00	12.00
118	Allan Ray JSY AU RC	15.00	6.00
119	Randy Foye JSY AU RC	30.00	12.00
120	Marcus Williams JSY AU RC	20.00	8.00
121	Adam Morrison JSY AU RC	40.00	15.00
122	Cedric Simmons JSY AU RC	15.00	6.00
123	Rajon Rondo JSY AU RC	20.00	8.00
124	Patrick O'Bryant JSY AU RC	15.00	6.00
125	Shawne Williams JSY AU RC	20.00	8.00
126	Mardy Collins JSY AU RC	15.00	6.00
127	Steve Novak JSY AU RC	15.00	6.00
128	Ronnie Brewer JSY AU RC	20.00	8.00
129	Quincy Douby JSY AU RC	15.00	6.00
130	Andrea Bargnani JSY AU RC	50.00	20.00

2006-07 Topps Turkey Red

1	Dwyane Wade SP	4.00	1.50
2	LeBron James	6.00	2.50
3	Allen Iverson SP	2.50	1.00
4	Sebastian Telfair	.60	.25
5	Bonzi Wells	.60	.25
6	Antwan Jamison	1.00	.40
7	Joe Johnson	.60	.25
8	DeSagana Diop	.30	.12
9	Stromile Swift	.30	.12
10	Shaun Livingston	.75	.30
11	Baron Davis	1.00	.40
12	Richard Hamilton	.60	.25
13	Andrei Kirilenko	.60	.25
14	Richard Jefferson	.60	.25
15	T.J. Ford	.60	.25
16	Luke Ridnour	.60	.25
17	Carlos Boozer	.60	.25
18	Al Jefferson	1.00	.40
19	Andrew Bogut SP	1.50	.60
20	Kobe Bryant	4.00	1.50
21	Tim Duncan	2.00	.75
22	Ben Gordon	2.00	.75
22B	Ben Gordon Ad	2.50	1.00
23	Stephen Jackson	.60	.25
24	Peja Stojakovic	1.00	.40
25	Mike Miller	1.00	.40
26	Ricky Davis SP	1.00	.40
27	Boris Diaw SP	.60	.25
28	Shareef Abdur-Rahim	1.00	.40
29	Caron Butler	.60	.25
30	Al Harrington	.30	.12
31	Ben Wallace SP	1.00	.40
32	Jason Richardson	1.00	.40
33	Channing Frye	.60	.25
34	Paul Pierce	1.00	.40
35	Andre Iguodala	1.00	.40
35B	Andre Iguodala Ad	.60	.25
36	Joey Graham	.60	.25
37	Corey Maggette	.60	.25
38	Sarunas Jasikevicius	.60	.25
39	Lamar Odom	1.00	.40
40	Shaquille O'Neal	2.50	1.00
40B	Shaquille O'Neal Ad	2.50	1.00
41	Larry Hughes	.60	.25
42	Darko Milicic SP	1.00	.40
43	Jerry Stackhouse	1.00	.40
44	Raymond Felton	1.25	.50
45	Nenad Krstic SP	.60	.25
46	Michael Redd	1.00	.40
47	Shane Battier	1.00	.40
48	Kevin Garnett	2.00	.75
49	Deron Williams	1.00	.40
50	Chris Paul SP	3.00	1.25
51	Rashard Lewis	1.00	.40
52	Kevin Martin SP	1.00	.40
53	Zach Randolph	1.00	.40
54	Jared Jeffries	.30	.12
55	Donyell Marshall	.30	.12
56	Josh Howard SP	.60	.25
57	Stephon Marbury	1.00	.40
58	Raja Bell	.30	.12
59	Tony Parker	1.00	.40
60	Dwight Howard	1.25	.50
61	Kirk Hinrich	1.00	.40
62	Emeka Okafor	1.00	.40
63	Zaza Pachulia	.30	.12
64	Troy Murphy	1.00	.40
65	Chris Duhon	.30	.12
65B	Chris Duhon Ad	.40	.15
66	Earl Boykins SP	.30	.12
67	Tracy McGrady	2.50	1.00
68	Hakim Warrick	.60	.25
69	Charlie Villanueva SP	1.00	.40
70	Jason Kidd	1.50	.60
71	Joel Przybilla SP	.30	.12
72	Antonio Daniels	.30	.12
73	Wally Szczerbiak	.60	.25
74	Drew Gooden	.60	.25
75	Antonio McDyess	.30	.12
76	Ray Allen SP	1.00	.40
77	Rashad McCants	1.25	.50
78	Eddy Curry	.60	.25
79	Chris Webber	1.00	.40
80	Yao Ming	3.00	1.25
81	Tyson Chandler	1.00	.40
82	Bobby Simmons	.30	.12
83	Jarrett Jack	.60	.25
84	Jameer Nelson SP	.60	.25
85	Luol Deng	1.00	.40
86	Kurt Thomas	.30	.12
87	Mickael Pietrus	.30	.12
88	Chris Bosh SP	1.00	.40
89	Devin Harris	1.00	.40
90	Jermaine O'Neal	1.00	.40
91	Luther Head	.60	.25
92	Elton Brand SP	1.00	.40
93	Antoine Walker	1.00	.40
94	Smush Parker	.30	.12
95	Nate Robinson SP	1.00	.40
96	Marvin Williams SP	1.50	.60
97	Primoz Brezec	.30	.12
98	Desmond Mason	.30	.12
99	Ron Artest SP	.60	.25
100	Jason Terry	1.00	.40
101	Mehmet Okur	.30	.12
102	Kenyon Martin	1.00	.40
103	Ike Diogu SP	.60	.25
104	Eddie Griffin	.30	.12
105	Amare Stoudemire	2.00	.75
106	Shawn Marion SP	.60	.25
107	Hedo Turkoglu	.60	.25
108	Chauncey Billups	1.00	.40
108B	Chauncey Billups Ad	1.00	.40
109	Rafer Alston	.30	.12
110	Dirk Nowitzki SP	2.00	.75
111	Steve Francis	1.00	.40

☐ 112	Mike Bibby	1.00	.40
☐ 113	Kirk Snyder	.30	.12
☐ 114	Luke Walton	.30	.12
☐ 114B	Luke Walton Ad	.30	.12
☐ 115	Maurice Williams	.30	.12
☐ 116	Nick Collison	.30	.12
☐ 117	Brendan Haywood	.30	.12
☐ 118	Delonte West SP	.60	.25
☐ 119	Mike Dunleavy	.60	.25
☐ 120	Vince Carter	2.50	1.00
☐ 120B	Vince Carter Ad	2.50	1.00
☐ 121	Juwan Howard	.60	.25
☐ 122	J.R. Smith	.60	.25
☐ 123	Gerald Wallace SP	1.00	.40
☐ 124	Cuttino Mobley	.60	.25
☐ 125	James Posey	.30	.12
☐ 126	Tayshaun Prince SP	1.00	.40
☐ 127	Anderson Varejao	.60	.25
☐ 128	Trenton Hassell	.30	.12
☐ 129	Matt Harpring	.60	.25
☐ 130	Gilbert Arenas SP	1.00	.40
☐ 131	Leandro Barbosa	.60	.25
☐ 132	Bruce Bowen	.30	.12
☐ 133	Morris Peterson	.30	.12
☐ 134	David West SP	.30	.12
☐ 135	Joe Smith	.60	.25
☐ 136	Rasheed Wallace	1.00	.40
☐ 137	Nene	.30	.12
☐ 138	Alonzo Mourning	.60	.25
☐ 139	Jamal Crawford	.30	.12
☐ 140	Carmelo Anthony SP	2.50	1.00
☐ 141	Brad Miller	1.00	.40
☐ 142	Tim Thomas	.30	.12
☐ 143	Jose Calderon	.60	.25
☐ 144	Sean May	.60	.25
☐ 145	Andres Nocioni SP	.30	.12
☐ 146	Samuel Dalembert	.30	.12
☐ 147	Chris Wilcox	.30	.12
☐ 148	Jason Williams	.30	.12
☐ 149	DeShawn Stevenson	.30	.12
☐ 150	Josh Smith SP	1.00	.40
☐ 151	Andre Miller	.60	.25
☐ 152	Michael Finley	1.00	.40
☐ 153	Marquis Daniels	.60	.25
☐ 154	Martell Webster	.60	.25
☐ 155	Brevin Knight	.30	.12
☐ 156	Steve Nash SP	1.00	.40
☐ 157	Vladimir Radmanovic	.30	.12
☐ 158	Speedy Claxton	.30	.12
☐ 158B	Speedy Claxton Ad	.30	.12
☐ 159	Darius Miles	1.00	.40
☐ 160	Pau Gasol SP	1.00	.40
☐ 161	Sam Cassell	1.00	.40
☐ 162	Nazr Mohammed	.30	.12
☐ 163	Shawn Marion	1.00	.40
☐ 164	Francisco Garcia	.30	.12
☐ 165	Kyle Korver	1.00	.40
☐ 166	Udonis Haslem	.30	.12
☐ 167	Manu Ginobili SP	1.00	.40
☐ 168	Zydrunas Ilgauskas	.60	.25
☐ 169	Eddie Jones	.30	.12
☐ 170	Danny Granger SP	.60	.25
☐ 171	Mike James	.30	.12
☐ 172	Ryan Gomes	.60	.25
☐ 173	Josh Childress	.60	.25
☐ 174	Marcus Camby	.30	.12
☐ 175	Chris Kaman SP	.30	.12
☐ 176	Brandon Roy RC	6.00	2.50
☐ 177	Kyle Lowry RC	4.00	1.50
☐ 178	Tyrus Thomas RC	5.00	2.00
☐ 179	Hilton Armstrong RC	2.50	1.00
☐ 180	LaMarcus Aldridge RC	5.00	2.00
☐ 181	Ronnie Brewer RC	5.00	2.00
☐ 182	Rajon Rondo RC	5.00	2.00
☐ 183	Marcus Vinicius RC	2.50	1.00
☐ 184	Solomon Jones RC	2.50	1.00
☐ 185	Leon Powe RC	2.50	1.00
☐ 186	Shawne Williams RC	3.00	1.25
☐ 187	Craig Smith RC	2.50	1.00
☐ 187B	Craig Smith Ad RC	2.50	1.00
☐ 188	Patrick O'Bryant RC	3.00	1.25
☐ 189	James Augustine RC	2.50	1.00
☐ 190	Maurice Ager RC	3.00	1.25
☐ 191	Quincy Douby RC	3.00	1.25
☐ 192	Rudy Gay RC	5.00	2.00
☐ 193	Thabo Sefolosha RC	3.00	1.25
☐ 194	Bobby Jones RC	2.50	1.00
☐ 195	Shelden Williams RC	3.00	1.25
☐ 195B	Shelden Williams Ad RC	3.00	1.25
☐ 196	Mile Ilic RC	2.50	1.00
☐ 197	Jorge Garbajosa RC	4.00	1.50
☐ 198	Cedric Simmons RC	2.50	1.00
☐ 199	Josh Boone RC	2.50	1.00
☐ 200	Adam Morrison RC	6.00	2.50
☐ 200B	Adam Morrison Ad RC	8.00	3.00
☐ 201	Marcus Williams RC	3.00	1.25
☐ 201B	Marcus Williams Ad RC	4.00	1.50
☐ 202	Steve Novak RC	2.50	1.00
☐ 203	Vassilis Spanoulis RC	2.50	1.00
☐ 204	Allan Ray RC	2.50	1.00
☐ 205	David Noel RC	2.50	1.00
☐ 206	Alexander Johnson RC	2.50	1.00
☐ 207	Mardy Collins RC	2.50	1.00
☐ 208	Dee Brown RC	4.00	1.50
☐ 209	P.J. Tucker RC	2.50	1.00
☐ 210	Paul Millsap RC	4.00	1.50
☐ 211	Paul Davis RC	2.50	1.00
☐ 212	Rodney Carney RC	3.00	1.25
☐ 212B	Rodney Carney Ad RC	3.00	1.25
☐ 213	Saer Sene RC	2.50	1.00
☐ 214	Renaldo Balkman RC	2.50	1.00
☐ 215	Ryan Hollins RC	2.50	1.00
☐ 216	Will Blalock RC	2.50	1.00
☐ 217	Mickael Gelabale RC		
☐ 218	Daniel Gibson RC	6.00	2.50
☐ 219	Hassan Adams RC	3.00	1.25
☐ 220	J.J. Redick RC	5.00	2.00
☐ 221	Jordan Farmar RC	5.00	2.00
☐ 221B	Jordan Farmar Ad RC	6.00	2.50
☐ 222	Randy Foye RC	6.00	2.50
☐ 223	Shannon Brown RC	3.00	1.25
☐ 224	Sergio Rodriguez RC	2.50	1.00
☐ 225	Andrea Bargnani RC	6.00	2.50
☐ 225B	Andrea Bargnani Ad RC	8.00	3.00
☐ 226	Larry Bird	10.00	4.00
☐ 227	George Gervin	2.50	1.00
☐ 228	Earl Monroe	2.50	1.00
☐ 229	Kareem Abdul-Jabbar	5.00	2.00
☐ 230	Wilt Chamberlain	10.00	4.00
☐ 231	Bill Walton	2.50	1.00
☐ 232	Isiah Thomas	2.50	1.00
☐ 233	Oscar Robertson	3.00	1.25
☐ 234	Pete Maravich	15.00	6.00
☐ 235	Bill Russell	6.00	2.50
☐ 236	James Worthy	2.50	1.00
☐ 237	Rick Barry	2.50	1.00
☐ 238	Walt Frazier	2.50	1.00
☐ 239	Elgin Baylor	2.50	1.00
☐ 240	Karl Malone	3.00	1.25
☐ 241	Connie Hawkins	2.50	1.00
☐ 242	Dennis Rodman	2.50	1.00
☐ 243	John Stockton	3.00	1.25
☐ 244	Jerry West	2.50	1.00
☐ 245	Bob Cousy	2.50	1.00
☐ 246	Hakeem Olajuwon	2.50	1.00
☐ 247	John Havlicek	2.50	1.00
☐ 248	Spencer Haywood	2.50	1.00
☐ 249	Moses Malone	2.50	1.00
☐ 250	Willis Reed	2.50	1.00
☐ 251	LeBron James CL	4.00	1.50
☐ 252	Shaquille O'Neal CL	1.50	.60
☐ 253	Dwyane Wade CL	2.00	.75
☐ 254	Y.Ming/T.McGrady CL	1.50	.60
☐ 255	Carmelo Anthony CL	1.25	.50
☐ 256	K.Garnett/D.Howard CL	2.00	.75
☐ 257	Nate Robinson CL	.50	.20
☐ 258	Kobe Bryant/Team CL	2.50	1.00
☐ 259	Larry Bird CL	5.00	2.00
☐ 260	S.Nash/K.Thomas CL	1.50	.60

2001-02 Topps Xpectations

☐	COMP.SET w/ SP's (145)	120.00	50.00
☐	COMMON CARD (1-151)	.25	.08
☐	COMMON ROOKIE (101-150)	2.00	.75
☐ 1	Baron Davis	.75	.30
☐ 2	Jason Terry	.75	.30
☐ 3	Paul Pierce	.75	.30
☐ 4	Ron Mercer	.50	.20
☐ 5	Dirk Nowitzki	1.25	.50
☐ 6	Marc Jackson	.50	.20
☐ 7	Cuttino Mobley	.50	.20
☐ 8	Al Harrington	.50	.20
☐ 9	Keyon Dooling	.50	.20
☐ 10	Mark Madsen	.50	.20
☐ 11	Jumaine Jones	.50	.20
☐ 12	Shawn Marion	.75	.30
☐ 13	Mike Bibby	.75	.30
☐ 14	Antonio Daniels	.25	.08
☐ 15	Vince Carter	2.00	.75
☐ 16	Stromile Swift	.50	.20
☐ 17	Courtney Alexander	.50	.20
☐ 18	Desmond Mason	.50	.20
☐ 19	Hidayet Turkoglu	.50	.20
☐ 20	Speedy Claxton	.50	.20
☐ 21	Lavor Postell	.50	.20
☐ 22	Chauncey Billups	.50	.20
☐ 23	Eddie House	.50	.20
☐ 24	Maurice Taylor	.25	.08
☐ 25	Lamar Odom	.75	.30
☐ 26	Antawn Jamison	.75	.30
☐ 27	Rael La'Frentz	.50	.20
☐ 28	Marcus Fizer	.50	.20
☐ 29	Chris Mihm	.50	.20
☐ 30	Eddie Robinson	.50	.20
☐ 31	Mark Blount	.25	.08
☐ 32	DerMarr Johnson	.50	.20
☐ 33	Wang Zhizhi	.75	.30
☐ 34	Danny Fortson	.25	.08
☐ 35	Elton Brand	.75	.30
☐ 36	Anthony Carter	.50	.20
☐ 37	Wally Szczerbiak	.50	.20
☐ 38	Mike Miller	.75	.30
☐ 39	Bonzi Wells	.50	.20
☐ 40	Tim Duncan	1.50	.60
☐ 41	Ruben Patterson	.50	.20
☐ 42	Keon Clark	.50	.20
☐ 43	Jason Williams	.50	.20
☐ 44	Richard Hamilton	.50	.20
☐ 45	Scott Padgett	.25	.08
☐ 46	Derek Anderson	.50	.20
☐ 47	Keith Van Horn	.75	.30
☐ 48	Tim Thomas	.50	.20
☐ 49	Jonathan Bender	.50	.20
☐ 50	Tracy McGrady	2.00	.75
☐ 51	Tyronn Lue	.25	.08
☐ 52	Austin Croshere	.50	.20
☐ 53	James Posey	.50	.20
☐ 54	Mateen Cleaves	.50	.20
☐ 55	Matt Harpring	.75	.30
☐ 56	Calvin Booth	.25	.08
☐ 57	Quentin Richardson	.50	.20
☐ 58	Joel Przybilla	.50	.20
☐ 59	Kenyon Martin	.75	.30
☐ 60	Iakovos Tsakalidis	.25	.08
☐ 61	Peja Stojakovic	.75	.30
☐ 62	Shammond Williams	.25	.08
☐ 63	Alvin Williams	.25	.08
☐ 64	Jahidi White	.50	.20
☐ 65	Morris Peterson	.50	.20
☐ 66	Larry Hughes	.50	.20
☐ 67	Andre Miller	.50	.20
☐ 68	Jamaal Magloire	.50	.20
☐ 69	Steve Francis	.75	.30
☐ 70	Todd MacCulloch	.25	.08
☐ 71	Rashard Lewis	.50	.20
☐ 72	Michael Dickerson	.50	.20
☐ 73	Nazr Mohammed	.25	.08
☐ 74	Jamal Crawford	.50	.20

❏ 75	Darius Miles	.75	.30
❏ 76	Allen Iverson	1.50	.60
❏ 77	Shaquille O'Neal	2.00	.75
❏ 78	Michael Finley	.75	.30
❏ 79	Antonio McDyess	.50	.20
❏ 80	Jerry Stackhouse	.75	.30
❏ 81	Chris Webber	.75	.30
❏ 82	Eddie Jones	.75	.30
❏ 83	Reggie Miller	.75	.30
❏ 84	Antoine Walker	.75	.30
❏ 85	Latrell Sprewell	.75	.30
❏ 86	Alonzo Mourning	.50	.20
❏ 87	Jalen Rose	.75	.30
❏ 88	Ray Allen	.75	.30
❏ 89	Gary Payton	.75	.30
❏ 90	Jason Kidd	1.25	.50
❏ 91	Stephon Marbury	.75	.30
❏ 92	Kobe Bryant	3.00	1.25
❏ 93	Grant Hill	.75	.30
❏ 94	Karl Malone	.75	.30
❏ 95	John Stockton	.75	.30
❏ 96	Anfernee Hardaway	.50	.20
❏ 97	Rasheed Wallace	.75	.30
❏ 98	Hakeem Olajuwon	.75	.30
❏ 99	Shareef Abdur-Rahim	.75	.30
❏ 100	Kevin Garnett	1.50	.60
❏ 101	Kwame Brown/250 RC	20.00	8.00
❏ 102	Tyson Chandler RC	5.00	2.00
❏ 103	Pau Gasol RC	6.00	2.50
❏ 104	Eddy Curry RC	5.00	2.00
❏ 105	Jason Richardson/250 RC	30.00	12.50
❏ 106	Shane Battier/250 RC	25.00	10.00
❏ 107	Eddie Griffin RC	2.50	1.00
❏ 108	DeSagana Diop RC	2.00	.75
❏ 109	Rodney White RC	2.50	1.00
❏ 110	Joe Johnson/250 RC	30.00	12.50
❏ 111	Kedrick Brown RC	2.00	.75
❏ 112	Vladimir Radmanovic RC	2.50	1.00
❏ 113	Richard Jefferson RC	5.00	2.00
❏ 114	Troy Murphy/250 RC	30.00	12.50
❏ 115	Steven Hunter RC	2.00	.75
❏ 116	Kirk Haston RC	2.00	.75
❏ 117	Michael Bradley RC	2.00	.75
❏ 118	Jason Collins RC	2.00	.75
❏ 119	Zach Randolph/250 RC	40.00	15.00
❏ 120	Brendan Haywood RC	2.00	.75
❏ 121	Joseph Forte RC	4.00	1.50
❏ 122	Jeryl Sasser RC	2.00	.75
❏ 123	Brandon Armstrong RC	2.50	1.00
❏ 124	Gerald Wallace RC	5.00	2.00
❏ 125	Samuel Dalembert RC	2.00	.75
❏ 126	Jamaal Tinsley RC	3.00	1.25
❏ 127	Tony Parker RC	8.00	3.00
❏ 128	Trenton Hassell RC	3.00	1.25
❏ 129	Gilbert Arenas RC	8.00	3.00
❏ 130	Raja Bell RC	2.00	.75
❏ 131	Will Solomon RC	2.00	.75
❏ 132	Terence Morris RC	2.00	.75
❏ 133	Brian Scalabrine RC	2.00	.75
❏ 134	Jeff Trepagnier RC	2.00	.75
❏ 135	Damone Brown RC	2.00	.75
❏ 136	Carlos Arroyo RC	15.00	6.00
❏ 137	Earl Watson RC	2.50	1.00
❏ 138	Jamison Brewer RC	2.00	.75
❏ 139	Bobby Simmons RC	2.00	.75
❏ 140	Andrei Kirilenko RC	5.00	2.00
❏ 141	Zeljko Rebraca RC	2.00	.75
❏ 142	Sean Lampley RC	2.00	.75
❏ 143	Loren Woods RC	2.00	.75
❏ 144	Alton Ford RC	2.50	1.00
❏ 145	Antonis Fotsis RC	2.00	.75
❏ 146	Charlie Bell RC	3.00	1.25
❏ 147	Ruben Boumtje-Boumtje RC	2.00	.75
❏ 148	Jarron Collins RC	2.00	.75
❏ 149	Kenny Satterfield RC	2.00	.75
❏ 150	Alvin Jones RC	2.00	.75
❏ 151	Michael Jordan	12.00	5.00

2002-03 Topps Xpectations

❏	COMPLETE SET (178)	300.00	125.00
❏	COMP.SET w/o SP's (100)	25.00	10.00
❏	COMMON CARD (1-100)	.20	.08
❏	COMMON ROOKIE (101-133)	2.50	1.00
❏	COMMON ROOKIE (134-153)	6.00	2.50

❏	COMMON CARD (154-178)	2.50	1.00
❏ 1	Darius Miles	.60	.25
❏ 2	Jason Williams	.40	.15
❏ 3	Speedy Claxton	.40	.15
❏ 4	Eduardo Najera	.20	.08
❏ 5	Chris Mihm	.20	.08
❏ 6	Eddie Robinson	.40	.15
❏ 7	Lee Nailon	.20	.08
❏ 8	Joseph Forte	.40	.15
❏ 9	Jason Terry	.60	.25
❏ 10	Vince Carter	1.50	.60
❏ 11	Matt Harpring	.60	.25
❏ 12	Bonzi Wells	.40	.15
❏ 13	Mike Bibby	.60	.25
❏ 14	Jerome James	.20	.08
❏ 15	Morris Peterson	.40	.15
❏ 16	Jarron Collins	.20	.08
❏ 17	Brendan Haywood	.40	.15
❏ 18	Dermarr Johnson	.20	.08
❏ 19	Kirk Haston	.40	.15
❏ 20	Paul Pierce	.60	.25
❏ 21	Eddy Curry	.60	.25
❏ 22	Ricky Davis	.40	.15
❏ 23	James Posey	.40	.15
❏ 24	Zeljko Rebraca	.40	.15
❏ 25	Jason Richardson	.60	.25
❏ 26	Ron Artest	.40	.15
❏ 27	Jonathan Bender	.40	.15
❏ 28	Elton Brand	.60	.25
❏ 29	Stromile Swift	.40	.15
❏ 30	Steve Francis	.60	.25
❏ 31	Devean George	.20	.08
❏ 32	Eddie House	.20	.08
❏ 33	Loren Woods	.40	.15
❏ 34	Richard Jefferson	.40	.15
❏ 35	Mike Miller	.60	.25
❏ 36	Joe Johnson	.60	.25
❏ 37	Zach Randolph	.60	.25
❏ 38	Peja Stojakovic	.60	.25
❏ 39	Predrag Drobnjak	.20	.08
❏ 40	Kwame Brown	.40	.15
❏ 41	DeShawn Stevenson	.20	.08
❏ 42	Desmond Mason	.40	.15
❏ 43	Stephen Jackson	.40	.15
❏ 44	Ruben Patterson	.20	.08
❏ 45	Samuel Dalembert	.20	.08
❏ 46	Pat Garrity	.20	.08
❏ 47	Jason Collins	.20	.08
❏ 48	Marc Jackson	.20	.08
❏ 49	Rafer Alston	.40	.15
❏ 50	Shawn Marion	.60	.25
❏ 51	Joel Przybilla	.20	.08
❏ 52	Shane Battier	.60	.25
❏ 53	Quentin Richardson	.40	.15
❏ 54	Jamaal Tinsley	.60	.25
❏ 55	Cuttino Mobley	.40	.15
❏ 56	Antwain Jamison	.40	.15
❏ 57	Chucky Atkins	.20	.08
❏ 58	Raef Lafrentz	.40	.15
❏ 59	Jumaine Jones	.40	.15
❏ 60	Dirk Nowitzki	1.00	.40
❏ 61	Marcus Fizer	.40	.15
❏ 62	Kedrick Brown	.40	.15
❏ 63	Nazr Mohammed	.20	.08
❏ 64	Jamaal Magloire	.20	.08
❏ 65	Tyson Chandler	.60	.25
❏ 66	Andre Miller	.40	.15
❏ 67	Wang Zhizhi	.60	.25

❏ 68	Mengke Bateer	.60	.25
❏ 69	Gilbert Arenas	.60	.25
❏ 70	Baron Davis	.60	.25
❏ 71	Lamar Odom	.60	.25
❏ 72	Mark Madsen	.20	.08
❏ 73	Pau Gasol	.60	.25
❏ 74	Anthony Carter	.40	.15
❏ 75	Wally Szczerbiak	.40	.15
❏ 76	Todd MacCulloch	.20	.08
❏ 77	Steven Hunter	.20	.08
❏ 78	Iakovos Tsakalidis	.20	.08
❏ 79	Ruben Boumtje-Boumtje	.20	.08
❏ 80	Gerald Wallace	.60	.25
❏ 81	Vladimir Radmanovic	.40	.15
❏ 82	Keon Clark	.40	.15
❏ 83	Andrei Kirilenko	.60	.25
❏ 84	Richard Hamilton	.40	.15
❏ 85	Trenton Hassell	.40	.15
❏ 86	Donnell Harvey	.20	.08
❏ 87	Rodney White	.40	.15
❏ 88	Troy Murphy	.40	.15
❏ 89	Terence Morris	.20	.08
❏ 90	Al Harrington	.40	.15
❏ 91	Michael Redd	.60	.25
❏ 92	Kenyon Martin	.60	.25
❏ 93	Lavor Postell	.20	.08
❏ 94	Jeryl Sasser	.20	.08
❏ 95	Hidayet Turkoglu	.60	.25
❏ 96	Tony Parker	.60	.25
❏ 97	Rashard Lewis	.40	.15
❏ 98	Michael Bradley	.40	.15
❏ 99	Courtney Alexander	.40	.15
❏ 100	Eddie Griffin	.40	.15
❏ 101	Yao Ming	15.00	6.00
❏ 102	Dan Gadzuric RC	2.50	1.00
❏ 103	Mike Dunleavy RC	4.00	1.50
❏ 104	Drew Gooden RC	6.00	2.50
❏ 105	Nikoloz Tskitishvili RC	2.50	1.00
❏ 106	Roger Mason RC	2.50	1.00
❏ 107	Nene Hilario RC	3.00	1.25
❏ 108	Chris Wilcox RC	3.00	1.25
❏ 109	Rod Grizzard RC	2.50	1.00
❏ 110	Chris Owens RC	2.50	1.00
❏ 111	Jared Jeffries RC	2.50	1.00
❏ 112	Efthimios Rentzias RC	2.50	1.00
❏ 113	Marcus Haislip RC	2.50	1.00
❏ 114	Fred Jones RC	2.50	1.00
❏ 115	Bostjan Nachbar RC	2.50	1.00
❏ 116	Jiri Welsch RC	2.50	1.00
❏ 117	Jannero Pargo RC	2.50	1.00
❏ 118	Curtis Borchardt RC	2.50	1.00
❏ 119	Ryan Humphrey RC	2.50	1.00
❏ 120	Raul Lopez RC	3.00	1.25
❏ 121	Cezary Trybanski RC	2.50	1.00
❏ 122	Predrag Savovic RC	2.50	1.00
❏ 123	Tayshaun Prince RC	3.00	1.25
❏ 124	Frank Williams RC	2.50	1.00
❏ 125	John Salmons RC	2.50	1.00
❏ 126	Chris Jefferies RC	2.50	1.00
❏ 127	Luke Recker RC	3.00	1.25
❏ 128	Tamar Slay RC	2.50	1.00
❏ 129	Matt Barnes RC	2.50	1.00
❏ 130	Rasual Butler RC	2.50	1.00
❏ 131	Vincent Yarbrough RC	2.50	1.00
❏ 132	Junior Harrington RC	2.50	1.00
❏ 133	Carlos Boozer RC	5.00	2.00
❏ 134	DaJuan Wagner/500 RC	10.00	4.00
❏ 135	Jay Williams/500 RC	8.00	3.00
❏ 136	Amare Stoudemire/500 RC	30.00	12.50
❏ 137	Caron Butler/500 RC	15.00	6.00
❏ 138	Melvin Ely/500 RC	6.00	2.50
❏ 139	Juan Dixon/500 RC	10.00	4.00
❏ 140	Kareem Rush/500 RC	8.00	3.00
❏ 141	Qyntel Woods/500 RC	2.50	1.00
❏ 142	Casey Jacobsen/500 RC	6.00	2.50
❏ 143	Robert Archibald/500 RC	6.00	2.50
❏ 144	Tito Maddox/500 RC	6.00	2.50
❏ 145	Ronald Murray/500 RC	8.00	3.00
❏ 146	Sam Clancy/500 RC	6.00	2.50
❏ 147	Dan Dickau/500 RC	2.50	1.00
❏ 148	Mehmet Okur/500 RC	8.00	3.00
❏ 149	Marko Jaric/500 RC	6.00	2.50
❏ 150	Gordan Giricek/500 RC	10.00	4.00
❏ 151	Manu Ginobili/500 RC	30.00	12.50
❏ 152	J.R. Bremer/500 RC	6.00	2.50
❏ 153	Corsley Edwards/500 RC	6.00	2.50

❏ 154 Michael Jordan XX	25.00	10.00
❏ 155 Allen Iverson XX	5.00	2.00
❏ 156 Shaquille O'Neal XX	6.00	2.50
❏ 157 Tim Duncan XX	5.00	2.00
❏ 158 Tracy McGrady XX	6.00	2.50
❏ 159 Kevin Garnett XX	5.00	2.00
❏ 160 Chris Webber XX	2.50	1.00
❏ 161 Alonzo Mourning XX	2.50	1.00
❏ 162 Antoine Walker XX	2.50	1.00
❏ 163 Latrell Sprewell XX	2.50	1.00
❏ 164 Eddie Jones XX	2.50	1.00
❏ 165 Kobe Bryant XX	10.00	4.00
❏ 166 Allan Houston XX	2.50	1.00
❏ 167 Ray Allen XX	2.50	1.00
❏ 168 Gary Payton XX	2.50	1.00
❏ 169 Antonio McDyess XX	6.00	2.50
❏ 170 Jason Kidd XX	4.00	1.50
❏ 171 Jerry Stackhouse XX	2.50	1.00
❏ 172 Stephon Marbury XX	2.50	1.00
❏ 173 Karl Malone XX	2.50	1.00
❏ 174 Reggie Miller XX	2.50	1.00
❏ 175 S.Abdur-Rahim XX	2.50	1.00
❏ 176 Rasheed Wallace XX	2.50	1.00
❏ 177 John Stockton XX	2.50	1.00
❏ 178 Grant Hill XX	2.50	1.00

1996-97 UD3

❏ COMPLETE SET (60)	50.00	30.00
❏ COMMON CARD (1-20)	.25	.08
❏ COMMON CARD (21-40)	.50	.20
❏ COMMON CARD (41-60)	.30	.10
❏ 1 Kerry Kittles RC	.75	.30
❏ 2 Stephon Marbury RC	2.00	.75
❏ 3 Jermaine O'Neal RC	2.50	1.00
❏ 4 Shareef Abdur-Rahim RC	2.50	1.00
❏ 5 Ray Allen RC	2.50	1.00
❏ 6 Antoine Walker RC	2.50	1.00
❏ 7 Erick Dampier RC	.75	.30
❏ 8 Walter McCarty RC	.25	.08
❏ 9 Todd Fuller RC	.25	.08
❏ 10 Tony Delk RC	.75	.30
❏ 11 Marcus Camby RC	1.00	.40
❏ 12 John Wallace RC	.75	.30
❏ 13 Vitaly Potapenko RC	.25	.08
❏ 14 Allen Iverson RC	4.00	1.50
❏ 15 Steve Nash RC	6.00	2.50
❏ 16 Derek Fisher RC	1.25	.50
❏ 17 Samaki Walker RC	.25	.08
❏ 18 Roy Rogers RC	.25	.08
❏ 19 Kobe Bryant RC	8.00	3.00
❏ 20 Lorenzen Wright RC	.50	.20
❏ 21 Kevin Garnett	3.00	1.25
❏ 22 Hakeem Olajuwon	.75	.30
❏ 23 Michael Jordan	10.00	4.00
❏ 24 John Stockton	.75	.30
❏ 25 Terrell Brandon	1.00	.40
❏ 26 Damon Stoudamire	.75	.30
❏ 27 Charles Barkley	2.00	.75
❏ 28 Dikembe Mutombo	1.00	.40
❏ 29 Gary Payton	.75	.30
❏ 30 Patrick Ewing	1.50	.60
❏ 31 Dennis Rodman	.50	.20
❏ 32 Joe Smith	1.00	.40
❏ 33 Grant Hill	.75	.30
❏ 34 Shaquille O'Neal	4.00	1.50
❏ 35 Kevin Johnson	1.00	.40
❏ 36 David Robinson	.75	.30
❏ 37 Juwan Howard	1.00	.40
❏ 38 Mitch Richmond	1.00	.40
❏ 39 Alonzo Mourning	1.00	.40
❏ 40 Reggie Miller	1.50	.60
❏ 41 Shawn Kemp	.50	.20
❏ 42 Scottie Pippen	1.50	.60
❏ 43 Kobe Bryant	8.00	3.00
❏ 44 Anfernee Hardaway	.75	.30
❏ 45 Brent Barry	.30	.10
❏ 46 Glenn Robinson	1.00	.40
❏ 47 Karl Malone	.75	.30
❏ 48 Chris Webber	.75	.30
❏ 49 Danny Manning	.50	.20
❏ 50 Antonio McDyess	.50	.20
❏ 51 Dominique Wilkins	1.00	.40
❏ 52 Vin Baker	.60	.25
❏ 53 Isaiah Rider	.60	.25
❏ 54 Eddie Jones	.75	.30
❏ 55 Glen Rice	.60	.25
❏ 56 Larry Johnson	.60	.25
❏ 57 Latrell Sprewell	.75	.30
❏ 58 Sean Elliott	.60	.25
❏ 59 Clyde Drexler	1.00	.40
❏ 60 Jerry Stackhouse	1.25	.50

1997-98 UD3

❏ COMPLETE SET (60)	50.00	25.00
❏ COMMON CARD (1-40)	.25	.08
❏ COMMON CARD (41-60)	.40	.15
❏ 1 Anfernee Hardaway JM	.75	.30
❏ 2 Alonzo Mourning JM	.50	.20
❏ 3 Grant Hill JM	.75	.30
❏ 4 Kerry Kittles JM	.75	.30
❏ 5 Latrell Sprewell JM	.75	.30
❏ 6 Rasheed Wallace JM	.75	.30
❏ 7 Jerry Stackhouse JM	.75	.30
❏ 8 Glen Rice JM	.50	.20
❏ 9 Marcus Camby JM	.75	.30
❏ 10 Scottie Pippen JM	1.25	.50
❏ 11 Patrick Ewing JM	.75	.30
❏ 12 Michael Finley JM	.75	.30
❏ 13 Karl Malone JM	.75	.30
❏ 14 Antonio McDyess JM	.50	.20
❏ 15 Michael Jordan JM	5.00	2.00
❏ 16 Clyde Drexler JM	.75	.30
❏ 17 Brent Barry JM	.50	.20
❏ 18 Glenn Robinson JM	.75	.30
❏ 19 Kobe Bryant JM	3.00	1.25
❏ 20 Reggie Miller JM	.75	.30
❏ 21 John Stockton JM	.75	.30
❏ 22 Gary Payton AS	.75	.30
❏ 23 Michael Jordan AS	5.00	2.00
❏ 24 Vin Baker AS	.50	.20
❏ 25 Karl Malone AS	.50	.20
❏ 26 Juwan Howard AS	.50	.20
❏ 27 Charles Barkley AS	1.00	.40
❏ 28 Jason Kidd AS	1.25	.50
❏ 29 Joe Dumars AS	.75	.30
❏ 30 Anfernee Hardaway AS	.50	.20
❏ 31 Mitch Richmond AS	.50	.20
❏ 32 Alonzo Mourning AS	.25	.08
❏ 33 Grant Hill AS	.75	.30
❏ 34 Shaquille O'Neal AS	2.00	.75
❏ 35 Scottie Pippen AS	1.25	.50
❏ 36 Reggie Miller AS	.75	.30
❏ 37 Hakeem Olajuwon AS	.50	.20
❏ 38 Tim Hardaway AS	.50	.20
❏ 39 David Robinson AS	.75	.30
❏ 40 Shawn Kemp AS	.50	.20
❏ 41 Allen Iverson BP	3.00	1.25
❏ 42 Stephon Marbury BP	1.50	.60
❏ 43 Dennis Rodman BP	.75	.30
❏ 44 Terrell Brandon BP	.75	.30
❏ 45 Michael Jordan BP	8.00	3.00
❏ 46 Kerry Kittles BP	1.25	.50
❏ 47 Hakeem Olajuwon BP	.75	.30
❏ 48 Loy Vaught BP	.40	.15
❏ 49 Antoine Walker BP	1.50	.60
❏ 50 Gary Payton BP	.75	.30
❏ 51 Kevin Johnson BP	.75	.30
❏ 52 Kevin Garnett BP	2.50	1.00
❏ 53 Shareef Abdur-Rahim BP	2.00	.75
❏ 54 Larry Johnson BP	.75	.30
❏ 55 Dikembe Mutombo BP	.40	.15
❏ 56 Chris Webber BP	.50	.20
❏ 57 Joe Smith BP	.75	.30
❏ 58 Kendall Gill BP	.40	.15
❏ 59 Kenny Anderson BP	.75	.30
❏ 60 Damon Stoudamire BP	.75	.30
❏ NNO Michael Jordan Promo		

2002-03 UD Authentics

Jason Kidd

❏ COMPLETE SET (132)	350.00	175.00
❏ COMP.SET w/o SPs (90)	40.00	15.00
❏ COMMON CARD (1-90)	.20	.08
❏ COMMON ROOKIE (91-123)	4.00	1.50
❏ COMMON ROOKIE (124-132)	12.00	5.00
❏ 1 Shareef Abdur-Rahim	.75	.30
❏ 2 Jason Terry	.75	.30
❏ 3 Glenn Robinson	.75	.30
❏ 4 Paul Pierce	.75	.30
❏ 5 Antoine Walker	.75	.30
❏ 6 Eric Williams	.20	.08
❏ 7 Kedrick Brown	.50	.20
❏ 8 Jalen Rose	.75	.30
❏ 9 Tyson Chandler	.75	.30
❏ 10 Eddy Curry	.75	.30
❏ 11 Darius Miles	.75	.30
❏ 12 Lamond Murray	.20	.08
❏ 13 Chris Mihm	.20	.08
❏ 14 Dirk Nowitzki	1.25	.50
❏ 15 Steve Nash	.75	.30
❏ 16 Michael Finley	.75	.30
❏ 17 Raef LaFrentz	.50	.20
❏ 18 James Posey	.50	.20
❏ 19 Juwan Howard	.50	.20
❏ 20 Jerry Stackhouse	.75	.30
❏ 21 Ben Wallace	.75	.30
❏ 22 Clifford Robinson	.20	.08
❏ 23 Jason Richardson	.75	.30
❏ 24 Antawn Jamison	.75	.30
❏ 25 Gilbert Arenas	.75	.30
❏ 26 Steve Francis	.75	.30
❏ 27 Eddie Griffin	.50	.20
❏ 28 Cuttino Mobley	.50	.20
❏ 29 Reggie Miller	.75	.30
❏ 30 Jamaal Tinsley	.75	.30
❏ 31 Jermaine O'Neal	.75	.30
❏ 32 Elton Brand	.75	.30
❏ 33 Lamar Odom	.75	.30
❏ 34 Andre Miller	.50	.20
❏ 35 Kobe Bryant	3.00	1.25
❏ 36 Shaquille O'Neal	2.00	.75
❏ 37 Derek Fisher	.75	.30
❏ 38 Devean George	.50	.20
❏ 39 Pau Gasol	.75	.30
❏ 40 Shane Battier	.75	.30

#	Player		
41	Alonzo Mourning	.50	.20
42	Brian Grant	.50	.20
43	Eddie Jones	.75	.30
44	Ray Allen	.75	.30
45	Tim Thomas	.50	.20
46	Kevin Garnett	1.50	.60
47	Wally Szczerbiak	.50	.20
48	Terrell Brandon	.50	.20
49	Jason Kidd	1.25	.50
50	Dikembe Mutombo	.50	.20
51	Richard Jefferson	.50	.20
52	Baron Davis	.75	.30
53	Jamal Mashburn	.50	.20
54	David Wesley	.20	.06
55	P.J. Brown	.20	.06
56	Latrell Sprewell	.75	.30
57	Allan Houston	.50	.20
58	Antonio McDyess	.50	.20
59	Tracy McGrady	2.00	.75
60	Mike Miller	.75	.30
61	Darrell Armstrong	.20	.06
62	Allen Iverson	1.50	.60
63	Keith Van Horn	.75	.30
64	Stephon Marbury	.75	.30
65	Shawn Marion	.75	.30
66	Anfernee Hardaway	.75	.30
67	Rasheed Wallace	.75	.30
68	Bonzi Wells	.50	.20
69	Scottie Pippen	1.25	.50
70	Chris Webber	.75	.30
71	Peja Stojakovic	.75	.30
72	Mike Bibby	.75	.30
73	Hidayet Turkoglu	.75	.30
74	Tim Duncan	1.50	.60
75	David Robinson	.75	.30
76	Tony Parker	.75	.30
77	Malik Rose	.20	.08
78	Gary Payton	.75	.30
79	Rashard Lewis	.50	.20
80	Desmond Mason	.50	.20
81	Brent Barry	.50	.20
82	Vince Carter	2.00	.75
83	Morris Peterson	.50	.20
84	Antonio Davis	.20	.08
85	Karl Malone	.75	.30
86	John Stockton	.75	.30
87	Andrei Kirilenko	.75	.30
88	Michael Jordan	6.00	2.50
89	Richard Hamilton	.75	.30
90	Kwame Brown	.50	.20
91	Efthimios Rentzias RC	4.00	1.50
92	Darius Songaila RC	4.00	1.50
93	Matt Barnes RC	4.00	1.50
94	Sam Clancy RC	4.00	1.50
95	Lonny Baxter RC	4.00	1.50
96	Manu Ginobili RC	20.00	8.00
97	Rod Grizzard RC	4.00	1.50
98	Tito Maddox RC	4.00	1.50
99	Predrag Savovic RC	4.00	1.50
100	Carlos Boozer RC	6.00	2.50
101	Dan Gadzuric RC	4.00	1.50
102	Vincent Yarbrough RC	4.00	1.50
103	Robert Archibald RC	4.00	1.50
104	Roger Mason RC	4.00	1.50
105	Steve Logan RC	4.00	1.50
106	Dan Dickau RC	4.00	1.50
107	Chris Jefferies RC	4.00	1.50
108	John Salmons RC	4.00	1.50
109	Frank Williams RC	4.00	1.50
110	Tayshaun Prince RC	5.00	2.00
111	Casey Jacobsen RC	4.00	1.50
112	Qyntel Woods RC	4.00	1.50
113	Kareem Rush RC	4.00	1.50
114	Ryan Humphrey RC	4.00	1.50
115	Curtis Borchardt RC	4.00	1.50
116	Juan Dixon RC	15.00	6.00
117	Jiri Welsch RC	4.00	1.50
118	Bostjan Nachbar RC	4.00	1.50
119	Fred Jones RC	4.00	1.50
120	Marcus Haislip RC	4.00	1.50
121	Melvin Ely RC	4.00	1.50
122	Jared Jeffries RC	4.00	1.50
123	Caron Butler RC	8.00	3.00
124	Amare Stoudemire RC	25.00	10.00
125	Chris Wilcox RC	12.00	5.00
126	Nene Hilario RC	12.00	5.00
127	DaJuan Wagner RC	12.00	5.00
128	Nikoloz Tskitishvili RC	12.00	5.00
129	Drew Gooden RC	15.00	6.00
130	Mike Dunleavy RC	12.00	5.00
131	Jay Williams RC	12.00	5.00
132	Yao Ming RC	40.00	15.00

1998-99 UD Choice Preview

#	Player		
	COMPLETE SET (55)	8.00	3.00
1	Dikembe Mutombo	.10	.02
3	Mookie Blaylock	.05	.01
7	Ron Mercer	.10	.02
9	Walter McCarty	.05	.01
13	Anthony Mason	.10	.02
14	Glen Rice	.10	.02
16	Toni Kukoc	.10	.02
23	Michael Jordan	2.00	.75
26	Zydrunas Ilgauskas	.10	.02
27	Cedric Henderson	.05	.01
29	Michael Finley	.15	.05
32	Hubert Davis	.05	.01
34	Bobby Jackson	.10	.02
37	Danny Fortson	.05	.01
41	Grant Hill	.15	.05
43	Jerome Williams	.05	.01
45	Erick Dampier	.10	.02
48	Donyell Marshall	.10	.02
50	Charles Barkley	.40	.15
51	Hakeem Olajuwon	.30	.10
56	Reggie Miller	.15	.05
60	Chris Mullin	.15	.05
64	Eric Piatkowski	.05	.01
65	Maurice Taylor	.10	.02
68	Shaquille O'Neal	.60	.25
69	Kobe Bryant	1.25	.50
74	Alonzo Mourning	.10	.02
75	Tim Hardaway	.10	.02
79	Ray Allen	.15	.05
80	Terrell Brandon	.10	.02
84	Stephon Marbury	.15	.05
85	Kevin Garnett	.60	.25
89	Keith Van Horn	.15	.05
90	Sam Cassell	.15	.05
95	Patrick Ewing	.15	.05
97	John Starks	.10	.02
100	Anfernee Hardaway	.15	.05
105	Nick Anderson	.05	.01
105	Allen Iverson	.60	.25
117	Jason Kidd	.40	.15
117	Isaiah Rider	.05	.01
118	Rasheed Wallace	.15	.05
121	Corliss Williamson	.10	.02
123	Billy Owens	.05	.01
126	Tim Duncan	.60	.25
127	Sean Elliott	.10	.02
131	Vin Baker	.10	.02
135	Gary Payton	.15	.05
137	Chauncey Billups	.15	.05
142	John Stockton	.15	.05
143	Karl Malone	.15	.05
148	Bryant Reeves	.05	.01
149	Shareef Abdur-Rahim	.15	.05
152	Harvey Grant	.05	.01
153	Juwan Howard	.10	.02

1998-99 UD Choice

#	Player		
	COMPLETE SET (200)	15.00	7.50
1	Dikembe Mutombo	.25	.08
2	Alan Henderson	.15	.05
3	Mookie Blaylock	.15	.05
4	Ed Gray	.15	.05
5	Eldridge Recasner	.15	.05
6	Kenny Anderson	.25	.08
7	Ron Mercer	.50	.10
8	Dana Barros	.15	.05
9	Walter McCarty	.15	.05
10	Travis Knight	.15	.05
11	Andrew DeClercq	.15	.05
12	David Wesley	.15	.05
13	Anthony Mason	.25	.08
14	Glen Rice	.25	.08
15	J.R. Reid	.15	.05
16	Bobby Phills	.15	.05
17	Dell Curry	.15	.05
18	Toni Kukoc	.25	.08
19	Randy Brown	.15	.05
20	Ron Harper	.25	.08
21	Keith Booth	.15	.05
22	Scott Burrell	.15	.05
23	Michael Jordan	2.50	1.00
24	Derek Anderson	.30	.12
25	Brevin Knight	.15	.05
26	Zydrunas Ilgauskas	.15	.05
27	Cedric Henderson	.15	.05
28	Vitaly Potapenko	.15	.05
29	Michael Finley	.40	.15
30	Erick Strickland	.15	.05
31	Shawn Bradley	.15	.05
32	Hubert Davis	.15	.05
33	Khalid Reeves	.15	.05
34	Bobby Jackson	.25	.08
35	Tony Battie	.15	.05
36	Bryant Stith	.15	.05
37	Danny Fortson	.15	.05
38	Dean Garrett	.15	.05
39	Eric Williams	.15	.05
40	Brian Williams	.15	.05
41	Grant Hill	.40	.15
42	Lindsey Hunter	.15	.05
43	Jerome Williams	.15	.05
44	Eric Montross	.15	.05
45	Erick Dampier	.15	.08
46	Muggsy Bogues	.25	.08
47	Tony Delk	.15	.05
48	Donyell Marshall	.25	.08
49	Bimbo Coles	.15	.05
50	Charles Barkley	.50	.20
51	Hakeem Olajuwon	.40	.15
52	Brent Price	.15	.05
53	Mario Elie	.15	.05
54	Rodrick Rhodes	.15	.05
55	Kevin Willis	.15	.05
56	Reggie Miller	.40	.15
57	Jalen Rose	.25	.08
58	Mark Jackson	.25	.08
59	Dale Davis	.15	.05
60	Chris Mullin	.40	.15
61	Derrick McKey	.15	.05
62	Lorenzan Wright	.15	.05
63	Rodney Rogers	.15	.05
64	Eric Piatkowski	.25	.08
65	Maurice Taylor	.20	.08

❑ 66	Isaac Austin	.15	.05
❑ 67	Corie Blount	.15	.05
❑ 68	Shaquille O'Neal	1.00	.40
❑ 69	Kobe Bryant	1.50	.60
❑ 70	Robert Horry	.25	.08
❑ 71	Sean Rooks	.15	.05
❑ 72	Derek Fisher	.40	.15
❑ 73	P.J. Brown	.15	.05
❑ 74	Alonzo Mourning	.25	.08
❑ 75	Tim Hardaway	.25	.08
❑ 76	Voshon Lenard	.15	.05
❑ 77	Dan Majerle	.25	.08
❑ 78	Ervin Johnson	.15	.05
❑ 79	Ray Allen	.40	.15
❑ 80	Terrell Brandon	.15	.05
❑ 81	Tyrone Hill	.15	.05
❑ 82	Elliot Perry	.15	.05
❑ 83	Anthony Peeler	.15	.05
❑ 84	Stephon Marbury	.40	.15
❑ 85	Kevin Garnett	.75	.30
❑ 86	Paul Grant	.15	.05
❑ 87	Chris Carr	.15	.05
❑ 88	Micheal Williams UER	.15	.05
❑ 89	Keith Van Horn	.40	.15
❑ 90	Sam Cassell	.40	.15
❑ 91	Kendall Gill	.15	.05
❑ 92	Chris Gatling	.15	.05
❑ 93	Kerry Kittles	.15	.05
❑ 94	Allan Houston	.25	.08
❑ 95	Patrick Ewing UER	.15	.05
❑ 96	Charles Oakley	.15	.05
❑ 97	John Starks	.15	.05
❑ 98	Charlie Ward	.15	.05
❑ 99	Chris Mills	.15	.05
❑ 100	Anfernee Hardaway	.40	.15
❑ 101	Nick Anderson	.15	.05
❑ 102	Mark Price	.15	.05
❑ 103	Horace Grant	.25	.08
❑ 104	David Benoit	.15	.05
❑ 105	Allen Iverson	.75	.30
❑ 106	Joe Smith	.25	.08
❑ 107	Tim Thomas	.25	.08
❑ 108	Brian Shaw	.15	.05
❑ 109	Aaron McKie	.25	.08
❑ 110	Jason Kidd	.60	.25
❑ 111	Danny Manning	.15	.05
❑ 112	Steve Nash	.40	.15
❑ 113	Rex Chapman	.15	.05
❑ 114	Dennis Scott	.15	.05
❑ 115	Antonio McDyess	.25	.08
❑ 116	Damon Stoudamire	.25	.08
❑ 117	Isaiah Rider	.15	.05
❑ 118	Rasheed Wallace	.40	.15
❑ 119	Kelvin Cato	.15	.05
❑ 120	Jermaine O'Neal	.40	.15
❑ 121	Corliss Williamson	.25	.08
❑ 122	Olden Polynice	.15	.05
❑ 123	Billy Owens	.15	.05
❑ 124	Lawrence Funderburke	.15	.05
❑ 125	Anthony Johnson	.15	.05
❑ 126	Tim Duncan	.60	.25
❑ 127	Sean Elliott	.25	.08
❑ 128	Avery Johnson	.15	.05
❑ 129	Vinny Del Negro	.15	.05
❑ 130	Monty Williams	.15	.05
❑ 131	Vin Baker	.25	.08
❑ 132	Hersey Hawkins	.15	.05
❑ 133	Nate McMillan	.15	.05
❑ 134	Detlef Schrempf	.25	.08
❑ 135	Gary Payton	.40	.15
❑ 136	Jim McIlvaine	.15	.05
❑ 137	Chauncey Billups	.25	.08
❑ 138	Doug Christie	.15	.05
❑ 139	John Wallace	.15	.05
❑ 140	Tracy McGrady	1.00	.40
❑ 141	Dee Brown	.15	.05
❑ 142	John Stockton	.40	.15
❑ 143	Karl Malone	.40	.15
❑ 144	Shandon Anderson	.15	.05
❑ 145	Jacque Vaughn	.15	.05
❑ 146	Bryon Russell	.15	.05
❑ 147	Lee Mayberry	.15	.05
❑ 148	Bryant Reeves	.15	.05
❑ 149	Shareef Abdur-Rahim	.40	.15
❑ 150	Michael Smith	.15	.05
❑ 151	Pete Chilcutt	.15	.05

❑ 152	Harvey Grant	.15	.05
❑ 153	Juwan Howard	.25	.08
❑ 154	Calbert Cheaney	.15	.05
❑ 155	Tracy Murray	.15	.05
❑ 156	Dikembe Mutombo FS	.15	.05
❑ 157	Antoine Walker FS	.40	.15
❑ 158	Glen Rice FS	.15	.05
❑ 159	Michael Jordan FS	1.25	.50
❑ 160	Wesley Person FS	.15	.05
❑ 161	Shawn Bradley FS	.15	.05
❑ 162	Dean Garrett FS	.15	.05
❑ 163	Jerry Stackhouse FS	.25	.08
❑ 164	Donyell Marshall FS	.25	.08
❑ 165	Hakeem Olajuwon FS	.25	.08
❑ 166	Chris Mullin FS	.25	.08
❑ 167	Isaac Austin FS	.15	.05
❑ 168	Shaquille O'Neal FS	.50	.20
❑ 169	Tim Hardaway FS	.25	.08
❑ 170	Glenn Robinson FS	.15	.05
❑ 171	Kevin Garnett FS	.40	.15
❑ 172	Keith Van Horn FS	.25	.08
❑ 173	Larry Johnson FS	.15	.05
❑ 174	Horace Grant FS	.15	.05
❑ 175	Derrick Coleman FS	.15	.05
❑ 176	Steve Nash FS	.25	.08
❑ 177	Arvydas Sabonis FS UER	.15	.05
❑ 178	Corliss Williamson FS	.15	.05
❑ 179	David Robinson FS	.40	.15
❑ 180	Vin Baker FS	.15	.05
❑ 181	Marcus Camby FS	.25	.08
❑ 182	John Stockton FS	.40	.15
❑ 183	Antonio Daniels FS	.15	.05
❑ 184	Rod Strickland FS	.15	.05
❑ 185	Michael Jordan FS	1.25	.50
❑ 186	Kobe Bryant YIR	.75	.30
❑ 187	Clyde Drexler YIR	.25	.08
❑ 188	Gary Payton YIR	.40	.15
❑ 189	Michael Jordan YIR	1.25	.50
❑ 190	D.Robinson/T.Duncan YIR	.30	.12
❑ 191	Attendance Record YIR	.15	.05
❑ 192	Karl Malone YIR	.40	.15
❑ 193	Dikembe Mutombo YIR	.15	.05
❑ 194	New Jersey Nets YIR	.40	.15
❑ 195	Ray Allen YIR	.40	.15
❑ 196	Michael Jordan YIR	1.25	.50
❑ 197	Los Angeles Lakers YIR	.75	.30
❑ 198	Michael Jordan YIR	1.25	.50
❑ 199	Michael Jordan CL	.60	.25
❑ 200	Michael Jordan CL	.60	.25

2002-03 UD Glass

❑ COMP.SET w/o SP's (90)		40.00	15.00
❑ COMMON CARD (1-90)		.25	.10
❑ COMMON (91-110)		12.00	5.00
❑ COMMON ROOKIE (111-120)		15.00	6.00
❑ COMMON ROOKIE (121-130)		10.00	4.00
❑ COMMON ROOKIE (131-150)		8.00	3.00
❑ 1	Shareef Abdur-Rahim	1.00	.40
❑ 2	Glenn Robinson	1.00	.40
❑ 3	Jason Terry	1.00	.40
❑ 4	Paul Pierce	1.00	.40
❑ 5	Antoine Walker	1.00	.40
❑ 6	Vin Baker	.60	.25
❑ 7	Jalen Rose	1.00	.40
❑ 8	Eddy Curry	1.00	.40
❑ 9	Tyson Chandler	1.00	.40
❑ 10	Darius Miles	1.00	.40
❑ 11	Ricky Davis	1.00	.40

❑ 12	Zydrunas Ilgauskas	.60	.25
❑ 13	Dirk Nowitzki	1.50	.60
❑ 14	Michael Finley	1.00	.40
❑ 15	Steve Nash	1.00	.40
❑ 16	Rael LaFrentz	.60	.25
❑ 17	Rodney White	.60	.25
❑ 18	Marcus Camby	.60	.25
❑ 19	Juwan Howard	.60	.25
❑ 20	Richard Hamilton	.60	.25
❑ 21	Ben Wallace	1.00	.40
❑ 22	Chauncey Billups	.60	.25
❑ 23	Jason Richardson	1.00	.40
❑ 24	Antawn Jamison	1.00	.40
❑ 25	Steve Francis	1.00	.40
❑ 26	Cuttino Mobley	.60	.25
❑ 27	Eddie Griffin	.60	.25
❑ 28	Jermaine O'Neal	1.00	.40
❑ 29	Reggie Miller	1.00	.40
❑ 30	Jamaal Tinsley	1.00	.40
❑ 31	Andre Miller	.60	.25
❑ 32	Elton Brand	1.00	.40
❑ 33	Quentin Richardson	.60	.25
❑ 34	Kobe Bryant	4.00	1.50
❑ 35	Shaquille O'Neal	2.50	1.00
❑ 36	Robert Horry	.60	.25
❑ 37	Pau Gasol	1.00	.40
❑ 38	Shane Battier	1.00	.40
❑ 39	Jason Williams	.60	.25
❑ 40	Eddie Jones	1.00	.40
❑ 41	Brian Grant	.60	.25
❑ 42	Malik Allen	.25	.10
❑ 43	Ray Allen	1.00	.40
❑ 44	Tim Thomas	.60	.25
❑ 45	Sam Cassell	1.00	.40
❑ 46	Kevin Garnett	2.00	.75
❑ 47	Wally Szczerbiak	.60	.25
❑ 48	Troy Hudson	.25	.10
❑ 49	Loren Woods	.60	.25
❑ 50	Jason Kidd	1.50	.60
❑ 51	Richard Jefferson	.60	.25
❑ 52	Kenyon Martin	1.00	.40
❑ 53	Baron Davis	1.00	.40
❑ 54	Jamal Mashburn	.60	.25
❑ 55	David Wesley	.25	.10
❑ 56	P.J. Brown	.25	.10
❑ 57	Allan Houston	.60	.25
❑ 58	Kurt Thomas	.60	.25
❑ 59	Latrell Sprewell	1.00	.40
❑ 60	Tracy McGrady	2.50	1.00
❑ 61	Mike Miller	1.00	.40
❑ 62	Grant Hill	1.00	.40
❑ 63	Allen Iverson	2.00	.75
❑ 64	Keith Van Horn	1.00	.40
❑ 65	Aaron McKie	.60	.25
❑ 66	Stephon Marbury	1.00	.40
❑ 67	Shawn Marion	1.00	.40
❑ 68	Anfernee Hardaway	1.00	.40
❑ 69	Rasheed Wallace	1.00	.40
❑ 70	Damon Stoudamire	.60	.25
❑ 71	Bonzi Wells	.60	.25
❑ 72	Chris Webber	1.00	.40
❑ 73	Mike Bibby	1.00	.40
❑ 74	Peja Stojakovic	1.00	.40
❑ 75	Hedo Turkoglu	1.00	.40
❑ 76	Tim Duncan	2.00	.75
❑ 77	David Robinson	1.00	.40
❑ 78	Tony Parker	1.00	.40
❑ 79	Gary Payton	1.00	.40
❑ 80	Rashard Lewis	.60	.25
❑ 81	Desmond Mason	.60	.25
❑ 82	Vince Carter	2.50	1.00
❑ 83	Antonio Davis	.25	.10
❑ 84	Morris Peterson	.60	.25
❑ 85	John Stockton	1.00	.40
❑ 86	Karl Malone	1.00	.40
❑ 87	Andrei Kirilenko	1.00	.40
❑ 88	Jerry Stackhouse	1.00	.40
❑ 89	Larry Hughes	.60	.25
❑ 90	Michael Jordan	8.00	3.00
❑ 91	Kobe Bryant CW	20.00	8.00
❑ 92	Paul Pierce CW	12.00	5.00
❑ 93	Chris Webber CW	12.00	5.00
❑ 94	Vince Carter CW	15.00	6.00
❑ 95	Tracy McGrady CW	15.00	6.00
❑ 96	Allen Iverson CW	15.00	6.00
❑ 97	Pau Gasol CW	12.00	5.00

98 Steve Francis CW	12.00	5.00
99 Jason Kidd CW	12.00	5.00
100 Dirk Nowitzki CW	12.00	5.00
101 Antoine Walker CW	12.00	5.00
102 Jason Richardson CW	12.00	5.00
103 Baron Davis CW	12.00	5.00
104 Elton Brand CW	12.00	5.00
105 Stephon Marbury CW	12.00	5.00
106 Ray Allen CW	12.00	5.00
107 Shaquille O'Neal CW	15.00	6.00
108 Kevin Garnett CW	15.00	6.00
109 Tim Duncan CW	15.00	6.00
110 Mike Bibby CW	12.00	5.00
111 Jay Williams RC	15.00	6.00
112 Yao Ming RC	120.00	60.00
113 Mike Dunleavy RC	25.00	10.00
114 Drew Gooden RC	30.00	12.50
115 Nikoloz Tskitishvili RC	15.00	6.00
116 DaJuan Wagner RC	20.00	8.00
117 Nene Hilario RC	20.00	8.00
118 Amare Stoudemire RC	80.00	40.00
119 Caron Butler RC	30.00	12.50
120 Manu Ginobili RC	60.00	25.00
121 Juaquin Hawkins RC	10.00	4.00
122 Kareem Rush RC	15.00	6.00
123 Jiri Welsch RC	10.00	4.00
124 Chris Wilcox RC	15.00	6.00
125 Tayshaun Prince RC	12.00	5.00
126 Qyntel Woods RC	10.00	4.00
127 Jared Jeffries RC	10.00	4.00
128 Gordan Giricek RC	15.00	6.00
129 Ryan Humphrey RC	10.00	4.00
130 Marko Jaric RC	8.00	3.00
131 Casey Jacobsen RC	8.00	3.00
132 Dan Dickau RC	8.00	3.00
133 Juan Dixon RC	10.00	4.00
134 Melvin Ely RC	8.00	3.00
135 Fred Jones RC	8.00	3.00
136 John Salmons RC	8.00	3.00
137 Marcus Haislip RC	8.00	3.00
138 Carlos Boozer RC	15.00	6.00
139 Chris Jefferies RC	8.00	3.00
140 Smush Parker RC	12.00	5.00
141 Vincent Yarbrough RC	8.00	3.00
142 Pat Burke RC	8.00	3.00
143 Lonny Baxter RC	8.00	3.00
144 Bostjan Nachbar RC	8.00	3.00
145 Rasual Butler RC	8.00	3.00
146 Ronald Murray RC	15.00	6.00
147 J.R. Bremer RC	8.00	3.00
148 Reggie Evans RC	8.00	3.00
149 Sam Clancy RC	8.00	3.00
150 Tamar Slay RC	8.00	3.00
NNO K.Bryant AF Promo	10.00	4.00

2003-04 UD Glass

COMP.SET w/o SP's (60).	35.00	17.50
COMMON CARD (1-60)	.40	.15
COMMON LEV.3 RC (61-80)	5.00	2.00
COMMON LEV.2 RC (81-90)	4.00	1.50
COMMON LEV.1 RC (91-100)	15.00	6.00
1 Shareef Abdur-Rahim	1.25	.50
2 Jason Terry	1.25	.50
3 Paul Pierce	1.25	.50
4 Antoine Walker	1.25	.50
5 Scottie Pippen	2.00	.75
6 Jalen Rose	1.25	.50
7 Darius Miles	1.25	.50
8 Dajuan Wagner	.75	.30
9 Dirk Nowitzki	2.00	.75
10 Steve Nash	1.25	.50
11 Michael Finley	1.25	.50
12 Andre Miller	.75	.30
13 Nene	.75	.30
14 Richard Hamilton	.75	.30
15 Ben Wallace	1.25	.50
16 Jason Richardson	1.25	.50
17 Nick Van Exel	1.25	.50
18 Steve Francis	1.25	.50
19 Yao Ming	3.00	1.25
20 Jermaine O'Neal	1.25	.50
21 Reggie Miller	1.25	.50
22 Elton Brand	1.25	.50
23 Corey Maggette	.75	.30
24 Kobe Bryant	5.00	2.00
25 Shaquille O'Neal	3.00	1.25
26 Gary Payton	1.25	.50
27 Pau Gasol	1.25	.50
28 Shane Battier	1.25	.50
29 Caron Butler	1.25	.50
30 Eddie Jones	1.25	.50
31 Desmond Mason	.75	.30
32 Michael Redd	1.25	.50
33 Kevin Garnett	2.50	1.00
34 Latrell Sprewell	1.25	.50
35 Jason Kidd	2.00	.75
36 Richard Jefferson	.75	.30
37 Baron Davis	1.25	.50
38 Jamal Mashburn	.75	.30
39 Allan Houston	.75	.30
40 Keith Van Horn	1.25	.50
41 Tracy McGrady	3.00	1.25
42 Juwan Howard	.75	.30
43 Allen Iverson	2.50	1.00
44 Glenn Robinson	1.25	.50
45 Amare Stoudemire	2.50	1.00
46 Stephon Marbury	1.25	.50
47 Rasheed Wallace	1.25	.50
48 Bonzi Wells	.75	.30
49 Chris Webber	1.25	.50
50 Mike Bibby	1.25	.50
51 Tim Duncan	2.50	1.00
52 Tony Parker	1.25	.50
53 Ray Allen	1.25	.50
54 Rashard Lewis	1.25	.50
55 Vince Carter	3.00	1.25
56 Antonio Davis	.40	.15
57 Andrei Kirilenko	1.25	.50
58 Jarron Collins	.40	.15
59 Gilbert Arenas	1.25	.50
60 Jerry Stackhouse	.75	.30
61 Kyle Korver RC	8.00	3.00
62 Travis Hansen RC	5.00	2.00
63 Willie Green RC	5.00	2.00
64 Keith Bogans RC	5.00	2.00
65 Theron Smith RC	5.00	2.00
66 Zaur Pachulia RC	5.00	2.00
67 Derrick Zimmerman RC	5.00	2.00
68 Jason Kapono RC	5.00	2.00
69 Steve Blake RC	5.00	2.00
70 Slavko Vranes RC	5.00	2.00
71 Jerome Beasley RC	5.00	2.00
72 Aleksandar Pavlovic RC	6.00	2.50
73 Boris Diaw RC	6.00	2.50
74 Kendrick Perkins RC	5.00	2.00
75 Leandro Barbosa RC	8.00	3.00
76 Josh Howard RC	8.00	3.00
77 Luke Walton RC	5.00	2.00
78 Maciej Lampe RC	5.00	2.00
79 Brian Cook RC	5.00	2.00
80 Zarko Cabarkapa RC	5.00	2.00
81 Travis Outlaw RC	8.00	3.00
82 Ndudi Ebi RC	8.00	3.00
83 David West RC	8.00	3.00
84 Reece Gaines RC	8.00	3.00
85 Dahntay Jones RC	8.00	3.00
86 Marcus Banks RC	8.00	3.00
87 Troy Bell RC	8.00	3.00
88 Luke Ridnour RC	8.00	3.00
89 Mickael Pietrus RC	8.00	3.00
90 Chris Kaman RC	8.00	3.00
91 Nick Collison RC	15.00	6.00
92 Mike Sweetney RC	15.00	6.00
93 Jarvis Hayes RC	15.00	6.00
94 T.J. Ford RC	15.00	6.00
95 Kirk Hinrich RC	20.00	8.00
96 Chris Bosh RC	30.00	12.50
97 Dwyane Wade RC	100.00	50.00
98 Carmelo Anthony RC	80.00	40.00
99 Darko Milicic RC	40.00	15.00
100 LeBron James RC	250.00	125.00

1998-99 UD Ionix

COMPLETE SET (80)	80.00	40.00
COMPLETE SET w/o MJ (60)	30.00	15.00
COMMON MJ (1-6/13)	4.00	1.50
COMMON CARD (7-60)	.25	.08
COMMON ROOKIE (61-80)	1.25	.50
1 Michael Jordan	4.00	1.50
2 Michael Jordan	4.00	1.50
3 Michael Jordan	4.00	1.50
4 Michael Jordan	4.00	1.50
5 Michael Jordan	4.00	1.50
6 Michael Jordan	4.00	1.50
7 Steve Smith	.50	.20
8 Dikembe Mutombo	.50	.20
9 Ron Mercer	.40	.15
10 Antoine Walker	.75	.30
11 Derrick Coleman	.25	.08
12 Glen Rice	.50	.20
13 Michael Jordan	4.00	1.50
14 Toni Kukoc	.50	.20
15 Derek Anderson	.60	.25
16 Shawn Kemp	.50	.20
17 Michael Finley	.75	.30
18 Steve Nash	.75	.30
19 Antonio McDyess	.50	.20
20 Nick Van Exel	.75	.30
21 Grant Hill	.75	.30
22 Jerry Stackhouse	.75	.30
23 Donyell Marshall	.50	.20
24 John Starks	.50	.20
25 Charles Barkley	1.00	.40
26 Hakeem Olajuwon	.75	.30
27 Scottie Pippen	1.25	.50
28 Reggie Miller	.75	.30
29 Rik Smits	.50	.20
30 Maurice Taylor	.40	.15
31 Kobe Bryant	3.00	1.25
32 Shaquille O'Neal	2.00	.75
33 Tim Hardaway	.50	.20
34 Alonzo Mourning	.50	.20
35 Ray Allen	.75	.30
36 Glenn Robinson	.50	.20
37 Stephon Marbury	.75	.30
38 Kevin Garnett	1.50	.60
39 Jayson Williams	.25	.08
40 Keith Van Horn	.75	.30
41 Patrick Ewing	.75	.30
42 Allan Houston	.50	.20
43 Anfernee Hardaway	.75	.30
44 Isaac Austin	.25	.08
45 Tim Thomas	.50	.20
46 Allen Iverson	1.50	.60
47 Tom Gugliotta	.25	.08
48 Jason Kidd	1.25	.50
49 Damon Stoudamire	.50	.20
50 Chris Webber	.75	.30
51 Tim Duncan	2.00	.75
52 David Robinson	.75	.30
53 Gary Payton	.75	.30
54 Vin Baker	.50	.20

☐ 55	Tracy McGrady	2.00	.75
☐ 56	John Stockton	.75	.30
☐ 57	Karl Malone	.75	.30
☐ 58	Shareef Abdur-Rahim	.75	.30
☐ 59	Juwan Howard	.50	.20
☐ 60	Mitch Richmond	.50	.20
☐ 61	Michael Olowokandi RC	2.00	.75
☐ 62	Mike Bibby RC	6.00	2.50
☐ 63	Raef LaFrentz RC	2.00	.75
☐ 64	Antawn Jamison RC	5.00	2.00
☐ 65	Vince Carter RC	12.00	5.00
☐ 66	Robert Traylor RC	1.25	.50
☐ 67	Jason Williams RC	4.00	1.50
☐ 68	Larry Hughes RC	4.00	1.50
☐ 69	Dirk Nowitzki RC	12.00	6.00
☐ 70	Paul Pierce RC	6.00	2.50
☐ 71	Cuttino Mobley RC	5.00	2.00
☐ 72	Corey Benjamin RC	1.25	.50
☐ 73	Peja Stojakovic RC	3.00	1.00
☐ 74	Michael Dickerson RC	2.50	1.00
☐ 75	Matt Harpring RC	2.00	.75
☐ 76	Rashard Lewis RC	6.00	2.50
☐ 77	Pat Garrity RC	1.25	.50
☐ 78	Roshown McLeod RC	1.25	.50
☐ 79	Ricky Davis RC	4.00	1.50
☐ 80	Felipe Lopez RC	1.50	.60
☐ J1A	Michael Jordan AU	6000.00	3000.00

1999-00 UD Ionix

☐ COMPLETE SET (90)		100.00	50.00
☐ COMPLETE SET w/o SP (60)		20.00	10.00
☐ COMMON CARD (1-60)		.25	.08
☐ COMMON ROOKIE (61-90)		1.25	.50
☐ 1	Dikembe Mutombo	.50	.20
☐ 2	Isaiah Rider	.25	.08
☐ 3	Antoine Walker	.75	.30
☐ 4	Paul Pierce	.75	.30
☐ 5	Eddie Jones	.75	.30
☐ 6	Anthony Mason	.50	.20
☐ 7	Toni Kukoc	.50	.20
☐ 8	Hersey Hawkins	.50	.20
☐ 9	Shawn Kemp	.50	.20
☐ 10	Lamond Murray	.25	.08
☐ 11	Michael Finley	.75	.30
☐ 12	Cedric Ceballos	.50	.20
☐ 13	Antonio McDyess	.50	.20
☐ 14	Ron Mercer	.50	.20
☐ 15	Grant Hill	.75	.30
☐ 16	Jerry Stackhouse	.75	.30
☐ 17	Antawn Jamison	1.25	.50
☐ 18	Mookie Blaylock	.25	.08
☐ 19	Charles Barkley	1.00	.40
☐ 20	Hakeem Olajuwon	.75	.30
☐ 21	Reggie Miller	.75	.30
☐ 22	Rik Smits	.50	.20
☐ 23	Maurice Taylor	.50	.20
☐ 24	Derek Anderson	.50	.20
☐ 25	Kobe Bryant	3.00	1.25
☐ 26	Shaquille O'Neal	2.00	.75
☐ 27	Tim Hardaway	.50	.20
☐ 28	Alonzo Mourning	.50	.20
☐ 29	Ray Allen	.75	.30
☐ 30	Glenn Robinson	.75	.30
☐ 31	Kevin Garnett	1.50	.60
☐ 32	Terrell Brandon	.50	.20
☐ 33	Stephon Marbury	.75	.30
☐ 34	Keith Van Horn	.75	.30
☐ 35	Allan Houston	.50	.20

☐ 36	Latrell Sprewell	.75	.30
☐ 37	Darrell Armstrong	.25	.08
☐ 38	Tariq Abdul-Wahad	.25	.08
☐ 39	Allen Iverson	1.50	.60
☐ 40	Larry Hughes	.75	.30
☐ 41	Anfernee Hardaway	.75	.30
☐ 42	Jason Kidd	1.25	.50
☐ 43	Tom Gugliotta	.25	.08
☐ 44	Scottie Pippen	1.25	.50
☐ 45	Damon Stoudamire	.50	.20
☐ 46	Rasheed Wallace	.75	.30
☐ 47	Jason Williams	.75	.30
☐ 48	Chris Webber	.75	.30
☐ 49	Tim Duncan	1.50	.60
☐ 50	David Robinson	.75	.30
☐ 51	Gary Payton	.75	.30
☐ 52	Vin Baker	.50	.20
☐ 53	Vince Carter	2.00	.75
☐ 54	Tracy McGrady	2.00	.75
☐ 55	Karl Malone	.75	.30
☐ 56	John Stockton	.75	.30
☐ 57	Mike Bibby	.75	.30
☐ 58	Shareef Abdur-Rahim	.75	.30
☐ 59	Mitch Richmond	.50	.20
☐ 60	Juwan Howard	.50	.20
☐ 61	Elton Brand RC	8.00	3.00
☐ 62	Steve Francis RC	8.00	3.00
☐ 63	Baron Davis RC	10.00	4.00
☐ 64	Lamar Odom RC	6.00	2.50
☐ 65	Jonathan Bender RC	6.00	2.50
☐ 66	Wally Szczerbiak RC	6.00	2.50
☐ 67	Richard Hamilton RC	6.00	2.50
☐ 68	Andre Miller RC	6.00	2.50
☐ 69	Shawn Marion RC	8.00	3.00
☐ 70	Jason Terry RC	5.00	2.00
☐ 71	Trajan Langdon RC	2.50	1.00
☐ 72	A.Radojevic RC	1.25	.50
☐ 73	Corey Maggette RC	6.00	2.50
☐ 74	William Avery RC	2.50	1.00
☐ 75	Ron Artest RC	4.00	1.50
☐ 76	Cal Bowdler RC	2.00	.75
☐ 77	James Posey RC	4.00	1.50
☐ 78	Quincy Lewis RC	2.00	.75
☐ 79	Dion Glover RC	2.00	.75
☐ 80	Jeff Foster RC	2.00	.75
☐ 81	Kenny Thomas RC	2.50	1.00
☐ 82	Devean George RC	3.00	1.25
☐ 83	Tim James RC	2.00	.75
☐ 84	Vonteego Cummings RC	2.50	1.00
☐ 85	Jumaine Jones RC	2.50	1.00
☐ 86	Scott Padgett RC	2.00	.75
☐ 87	Chucky Atkins RC	2.50	1.00
☐ 88	Adrian Griffin RC	2.00	.75
☐ 89	Todd MacCulloch RC	2.00	.75
☐ 90	Anthony Carter RC	4.00	1.50

2005-06 UD Portraits

☐ COMP.SET w/o SP's (100)		125.00	50.00
☐ COMMON CARD (1-100)		.60	.25
☐ COMMON ROOKIE (101-136)		6.00	2.50
☐ COMMON ROOKIE (137-142)		15.00	6.00
☐ 1	Al Harrington	1.50	.60
☐ 2	Al Jefferson	2.00	.75
☐ 3	Allen Iverson	4.00	1.50
☐ 4	Amare Stoudemire	4.00	1.50
☐ 5	Andre Iguodala	2.00	.75
☐ 6	Andre Miller	1.50	.60
☐ 7	Andrei Kirilenko	2.00	.75

☐ 8	Antawn Jamison	2.00	.75
☐ 9	Antoine Walker	2.00	.75
☐ 10	Baron Davis	2.00	.75
☐ 11	Ben Gordon	4.00	1.50
☐ 12	Ben Wallace	2.00	.75
☐ 13	Bob Sura	1.50	.60
☐ 14	Brevin Knight	.60	.25
☐ 15	Carlos Boozer	2.00	.75
☐ 16	Carmelo Anthony	4.00	1.50
☐ 17	Caron Butler	2.00	.75
☐ 18	Chauncey Billups	2.00	.75
☐ 19	Chris Bosh	2.00	.75
☐ 20	Chris Webber	2.00	.75
☐ 21	Corey Maggette	1.50	.60
☐ 22	Cuttino Mobley	1.50	.60
☐ 23	Damon Jones	1.50	.60
☐ 24	Dan Dickau	.60	.25
☐ 25	Desmond Mason	1.50	.60
☐ 26	Dirk Nowitzki	3.00	1.25
☐ 27	Donyell Marshall	.60	.25
☐ 28	Drew Gooden	1.50	.60
☐ 29	Dwight Howard	2.50	1.00
☐ 30	Dwyane Wade	6.00	2.50
☐ 31	Elton Brand	2.00	.75
☐ 32	Emeka Okafor	2.50	1.00
☐ 33	Gary Payton	2.00	.75
☐ 34	Gerald Wallace	1.50	.60
☐ 35	Gilbert Arenas	2.00	.75
☐ 36	Grant Hill	2.00	.75
☐ 37	J.R. Smith	1.50	.60
☐ 38	Jalen Rose	2.00	.75
☐ 39	Jamaal Magloire	.60	.25
☐ 40	Jamaal Tinsley	1.50	.60
☐ 41	Jamal Crawford	1.50	.60
☐ 42	Jameer Nelson	2.00	.75
☐ 43	Jason Kidd	3.00	1.25
☐ 44	Jason Richardson	2.00	.75
☐ 45	Jason Terry	2.00	.75
☐ 46	Jason Williams	1.50	.60
☐ 47	Jermaine O'Neal	2.00	.75
☐ 48	Joe Johnson	2.00	.75
☐ 49	Josh Childress	1.50	.60
☐ 50	Josh Howard	2.00	.75
☐ 51	Josh Smith	2.00	.75
☐ 52	Kenyon Martin	2.00	.75
☐ 53	Kevin Garnett	4.00	1.50
☐ 54	Kirk Hinrich	2.00	.75
☐ 55	Kobe Bryant	8.00	3.00
☐ 56	Kurt Thomas	1.50	.60
☐ 57	Kyle Korver	2.00	.75
☐ 58	Lamar Odom	2.00	.75
☐ 59	Larry Hughes	1.50	.60
☐ 60	Eddie Griffin	.60	.25
☐ 61	LeBron James	12.00	5.00
☐ 62	Luke Ridnour	1.50	.60
☐ 63	Luol Deng	2.00	.75
☐ 64	Manu Ginobili	2.00	.75
☐ 65	Marcus Camby	.60	.25
☐ 66	Maurice Williams	.60	.25
☐ 67	Michael Finley	2.00	.75
☐ 68	Michael Jordan	12.00	5.00
☐ 69	Michael Redd	2.00	.75
☐ 70	Mike Bibby	2.00	.75
☐ 71	Pau Gasol	2.00	.75
☐ 72	Paul Pierce	2.00	.75
☐ 73	Peja Stojakovic	2.00	.75
☐ 74	Raja Bell	.60	.25
☐ 75	Rashard Lewis	2.00	.75
☐ 76	Rasheed Wallace	2.00	.75
☐ 77	Ray Allen	2.00	.75
☐ 78	Richard Hamilton	1.50	.60
☐ 79	Richard Jefferson	1.50	.60
☐ 80	Ron Artest	1.50	.60
☐ 81	Sam Cassell	2.00	.75
☐ 82	Sebastian Telfair	1.50	.60
☐ 83	Shaquille O'Neal	5.00	2.00
☐ 84	Shareef Abdur-Rahim	2.00	.75
☐ 85	Shaun Livingston	2.00	.75
☐ 86	Shawn Marion	2.00	.75
☐ 87	Stephon Marbury	2.00	.75
☐ 88	Steve Francis	2.00	.75
☐ 89	Steve Nash	2.00	.75
☐ 90	Stromile Swift	1.50	.60
☐ 91	Tim Duncan	4.00	1.50
☐ 92	Tony Parker	2.00	.75
☐ 93	Tracy McGrady	5.00	2.00

❏ 94 Troy Murphy	2.00	.75
❏ 95 Tyronn Lue	.60	.25
❏ 96 Vince Carter	5.00	2.00
❏ 97 Vladimir Radmanovic	.60	.25
❏ 98 Yao Ming	5.00	2.00
❏ 99 Zach Randolph	2.00	.75
❏ 100 Zydrunas Ilgauskas	1.50	.60
❏ 101 Andray Blatche RC	6.00	2.50
❏ 102 Andrew Bynum RC	15.00	6.00
❏ 103 Antoine Wright RC	6.00	2.50
❏ 104 Brandon Bass RC	6.00	2.50
❏ 105 C.J. Miles RC	6.00	2.50
❏ 106 Channing Frye RC	6.00	2.50
❏ 107 Charlie Villanueva RC	8.00	3.00
❏ 108 Chris Taft RC	6.00	2.50
❏ 109 Daniel Ewing RC	6.00	2.50
❏ 110 Danny Granger RC	8.00	3.00
❏ 111 David Lee RC	8.00	3.00
❏ 112 Dijon Thompson RC	6.00	2.50
❏ 113 Ersan Ilyasova RC	6.00	2.50
❏ 114 Sarunas Jasikevicius RC	6.00	2.50
❏ 115 Francisco Garcia RC	6.00	2.50
❏ 116 Gerald Green RC	12.00	5.00
❏ 117 Hakim Warrick RC	10.00	4.00
❏ 118 Jose Calderon RC	6.00	2.50
❏ 119 Ike Diogu RC	6.00	2.50
❏ 120 Jarrett Jack RC	6.00	2.50
❏ 121 Jason Maxiell RC	6.00	2.50
❏ 122 Joey Graham RC	6.00	2.50
❏ 123 Julius Hodge RC	6.00	2.50
❏ 124 Linas Kleiza RC	6.00	2.50
❏ 125 Louis Williams RC	6.00	2.50
❏ 126 Luther Head RC	6.00	2.50
❏ 127 Martell Webster RC	6.00	2.50
❏ 128 Monta Ellis RC	10.00	4.00
❏ 129 Nate Robinson RC	8.00	3.00
❏ 130 Rashad McCants RC	8.00	3.00
❏ 131 James Singleton RC	6.00	2.50
❏ 132 Ryan Gomes RC	6.00	2.50
❏ 133 Salim Stoudamire RC	6.00	2.50
❏ 134 Travis Diener RC	6.00	2.50
❏ 135 Wayne Simien RC	6.00	2.50
❏ 136 Yaroslav Korolev RC	6.00	2.50
❏ 137 Andrew Bogut RC	10.00	4.00
❏ 138 Chris Paul RC	30.00	12.50
❏ 139 Deron Williams RC	25.00	10.00
❏ 140 Raymond Felton RC	15.00	6.00
❏ 141 Marvin Williams RC	15.00	6.00
❏ 142 Sean May RC	10.00	4.00

2000-01 UD Reserve

❏ COMP.SET w/o SP's (90)	25.00	10.00
❏ COMMON CARD (1-90)	.25	.08
❏ COMMON ROOKIE (91-120)	1.00	.40
❏ 1 Dikembe Mutombo	.25	.20
❏ 2 Jason Terry	.75	.30
❏ 3 Alan Henderson	.25	.08
❏ 4 Paul Pierce	.75	.30
❏ 5 Antoine Walker	.75	.30
❏ 6 Kenny Anderson	.50	.20
❏ 7 Derrick Coleman	.25	.08
❏ 8 Baron Davis	.75	.30
❏ 9 Jamal Mashburn	.50	.20
❏ 10 Elton Brand	.75	.30
❏ 11 Ron Mercer	.50	.20
❏ 12 Ron Artest	.50	.20
❏ 13 Lamond Murray	.25	.08
❏ 14 Andre Miller	.50	.20

❏ 15 Matt Harpring	.75	.30
❏ 16 Michael Finley	.75	.30
❏ 17 Dirk Nowitzki	1.25	.50
❏ 18 Steve Nash	.75	.30
❏ 19 Antonio McDyess	.50	.20
❏ 20 James Posey	.50	.20
❏ 21 Nick Van Exel	.25	.08
❏ 22 Jerry Stackhouse	.75	.30
❏ 23 Jerome Williams	.25	.08
❏ 24 Chucky Atkins	.25	.08
❏ 25 Antawn Jamison	.75	.30
❏ 26 Larry Hughes	.50	.20
❏ 27 Chris Mills	.25	.08
❏ 28 Steve Francis	.75	.30
❏ 29 Hakeem Olajuwon	.75	.30
❏ 30 Cuttino Mobley	.50	.20
❏ 31 Reggie Miller	.75	.30
❏ 32 Jalen Rose	.75	.30
❏ 33 Austin Croshere	.25	.08
❏ 34 Lamar Odom	.75	.30
❏ 35 Jeff McInnis	.25	.08
❏ 36 Corey Maggette	.50	.20
❏ 37 Shaquille O'Neal ™ Neal	2.00	.75
❏ 38 Kobe Bryant	3.00	1.25
❏ 39 Isaiah Rider	.50	.20
❏ 40 Horace Grant	.50	.20
❏ 41 Eddie Jones	.75	.30
❏ 42 Tim Hardaway	.50	.20
❏ 43 Brian Grant	.25	.20
❏ 44 Ray Allen	.75	.30
❏ 45 Tim Thomas	.50	.20
❏ 46 Glenn Robinson	.75	.30
❏ 47 Sam Cassell	.75	.30
❏ 48 Kevin Garnett	1.50	.60
❏ 49 Wally Szczerbiak	.50	.20
❏ 50 Terrell Brandon	.50	.20
❏ 51 Chauncey Billups	.75	.30
❏ 52 Stephon Marbury	.75	.30
❏ 53 Keith Van Horn	.75	.30
❏ 54 Kendall Gill	.25	.08
❏ 55 Latrell Sprewell	.75	.30
❏ 56 Marcus Camby	.50	.20
❏ 57 Allan Houston	.50	.20
❏ 58 Grant Hill	.75	.30
❏ 59 Tracy McGrady	2.00	.75
❏ 60 Darrell Armstrong	.25	.08
❏ 61 Allen Iverson	1.50	.60
❏ 62 Theo Ratliff	.50	.20
❏ 63 Toni Kukoc	.50	.20
❏ 64 Jason Kidd	1.25	.50
❏ 65 Clifford Robinson	.25	.08
❏ 66 Shawn Marion	.75	.30
❏ 67 Rasheed Wallace	.75	.30
❏ 68 Scottie Pippen	1.25	.50
❏ 69 Damon Stoudamire	.50	.20
❏ 70 Chris Webber	.75	.30
❏ 71 Jason Williams	.50	.20
❏ 72 Vlade Divac	.50	.20
❏ 73 Tim Duncan	1.50	.60
❏ 74 David Robinson	.75	.30
❏ 75 Derek Anderson	.50	.20
❏ 76 Gary Payton	.75	.30
❏ 77 Patrick Ewing	.75	.30
❏ 78 Rashard Lewis	.50	.20
❏ 79 Vince Carter	2.00	.75
❏ 80 Mark Jackson	.25	.08
❏ 81 Antonio Davis	.25	.08
❏ 82 Karl Malone	.75	.30
❏ 83 John Stockton	.75	.30
❏ 84 John Starks	.50	.20
❏ 85 Shareef Abdur-Rahim	.75	.30
❏ 86 Mike Bibby	.75	.30
❏ 87 Michael Dickerson	.50	.20
❏ 88 Mitch Richmond	.50	.20
❏ 89 Richard Hamilton	.50	.20
❏ 90 Juwan Howard	.50	.20
❏ 91 Kenyon Martin RC	3.00	1.25
❏ 92 Stromile Swift RC	2.00	.75
❏ 93 Darius Miles RC	2.50	1.00
❏ 94 Marcus Fizer RC	1.00	.40
❏ 95 Mike Miller RC	2.50	1.00
❏ 96 DerMarr Johnson RC	1.00	.40
❏ 97 Chris Mihm RC	1.00	.40
❏ 98 Jamal Crawford RC	1.25	.50
❏ 99 Joel Przybilla RC	1.00	.40
❏ 100 Keyon Dooling RC	1.00	.40

❏ 101 Jerome Moiso RC	1.00	.40
❏ 102 Etan Thomas RC	1.00	.40
❏ 103 Courtney Alexander RC	1.00	.40
❏ 104 Mateen Cleaves RC	1.00	.40
❏ 105 Hidayet Turkoglu RC	2.00	.75
❏ 106 Desmond Mason RC	1.00	.40
❏ 107 Quentin Richardson RC	2.50	1.00
❏ 108 Jamaal Magloire RC	1.00	.40
❏ 109 Speedy Claxton RC	1.00	.40
❏ 110 Morris Peterson RC	2.00	.75
❏ 111 Donnell Harvey RC	1.00	.40
❏ 112 DeShawn Stevenson RC	1.00	.40
❏ 113 Mamadou Nâ ™diaye RC	1.00	.40
❏ 114 Erick Barkley RC	1.00	.40
❏ 115 Mark Madsen RC	1.00	.40
❏ 116 Eduardo Najera RC	1.25	.50
❏ 117 Lavor Postell RC	1.00	.40
❏ 118 Hanno Mottola RC	1.00	.40
❏ 119 Stephen Jackson RC	1.50	.60
❏ 120 Marc Jackson RC	1.00	.40

2006-07 UD Reserve

❏ 1 Josh Childress	1.00	.40
❏ 2 Al Harrington	.50	.20
❏ 3 Joe Johnson	1.00	.40
❏ 4 Josh Smith	1.50	.60
❏ 5 Salim Stoudamire	1.00	.40
❏ 6 Marvin Williams	2.00	.75
❏ 7 Tony Allen	.50	.20
❏ 8 Dan Dickau	.50	.20
❏ 9 Al Jefferson	1.50	.60
❏ 10 Raef LaFrentz	.50	.20
❏ 11 Michael Olowokandi	.50	.20
❏ 12 Paul Pierce	1.50	.60
❏ 13 Wally Szczerbiak	1.00	.40
❏ 14 Brevin Knight	.50	.20
❏ 15 Raymond Felton	2.00	.75
❏ 16 Othella Harrington	.50	.20
❏ 17 Sean May	1.00	.40
❏ 18 Emeka Okafor	1.50	.60
❏ 19 Primoz Brezec	.50	.20
❏ 20 Gerald Wallace	1.50	.60
❏ 21 Tyson Chandler	1.50	.60
❏ 22 Michael Jordan	10.00	4.00
❏ 23 Luol Deng	1.50	.60
❏ 24 Chris Duhon	.50	.20
❏ 25 Ben Gordon	3.00	1.25
❏ 26 Kirk Hinrich	1.50	.60
❏ 27 Mike Sweetney	.50	.20
❏ 28 Drew Gooden	1.00	.40
❏ 29 Larry Hughes	1.00	.40
❏ 30 Zydrunas Ilgauskas	1.00	.40
❏ 31 LeBron James	10.00	4.00
❏ 32 Damon Jones	1.00	.40
❏ 33 Donyell Marshall	.50	.20
❏ 34 Anderson Varejao	1.00	.40
❏ 35 Erick Dampier	.50	.20
❏ 36 Marquis Daniels	1.00	.40
❏ 37 Devin Harris	1.50	.60
❏ 38 Josh Howard	1.00	.40
❏ 39 Dirk Nowitzki	2.50	1.00
❏ 40 Jerry Stackhouse	1.50	.60
❏ 41 Jason Terry	1.50	.60
❏ 42 Carmelo Anthony	3.00	1.25
❏ 43 Earl Boykins	.50	.20
❏ 44 Marcus Camby	.50	.20
❏ 45 Kenyon Martin	1.50	.60
❏ 46 Andre Miller	1.00	.40

#	Player		
47	Eduardo Najera	.50	.20
48	Nene	.50	.20
49	Chauncey Billups	1.50	.60
50	Richard Hamilton	1.00	.40
51	Lindsey Hunter	.50	.20
52	Antonio McDyess	.50	.20
53	Tayshaun Prince	1.50	.60
54	Ben Wallace	1.50	.60
55	Rasheed Wallace	1.50	.60
56	Baron Davis	1.50	.60
57	Ike Diogu	1.00	.40
58	Mike Dunleavy	1.00	.40
59	Derek Fisher	1.00	.40
60	Troy Murphy	1.50	.60
61	Mickael Pietrus	1.00	.40
62	Jason Richardson	1.50	.60
63	Rafer Alston	.50	.20
64	Luther Head	1.00	.40
65	Juwan Howard	1.00	.40
66	Tracy McGrady	4.00	1.50
67	Dikembe Mutombo	1.00	.40
68	Stromile Swift	1.00	.40
69	Yao Ming	4.00	1.50
70	Austin Croshere	.50	.20
71	Stephen Jackson	1.00	.40
72	Sarunas Jasikevicius	1.00	.40
73	Jermaine O'Neal	1.50	.60
74	Peja Stojakovic	1.50	.60
75	Jamaal Tinsley	1.00	.40
76	Elton Brand	1.50	.60
77	Sam Cassell	1.50	.60
78	Chris Kaman	.50	.20
79	Shaun Livingston	1.25	.50
80	Yaroslav Korolev	.50	.20
81	Cuttino Mobley	1.00	.40
82	Vladimir Radmanovic	.50	.20
83	Kwame Brown	1.00	.40
84	Kobe Bryant	6.00	2.50
85	Devean George	1.00	.40
86	Lamar Odom	1.50	.60
87	Ronny Turiaf	.50	.20
88	Sasha Vujacic	.50	.20
89	Luke Walton	.50	.20
90	Shane Battier	1.50	.60
91	Pau Gasol	1.50	.60
92	Bobby Jackson	.50	.20
93	Eddie Jones	.50	.20
94	Mike Miller	1.50	.60
95	Damon Stoudamire	1.00	.40
96	Hakim Warrick	1.00	.40
97	Alonzo Mourning	1.00	.40
98	Shaquille O'Neal	4.00	1.50
99	Gary Payton	1.50	.60
100	Wayne Simien	1.00	.40
101	Dwyane Wade	5.00	2.00
102	Antoine Walker	1.50	.60
103	Jason Williams	1.00	.40
104	Andrew Bogut	2.00	.75
105	T.J. Ford	1.00	.40
106	Jamaal Magloire	.50	.20
107	Michael Redd	1.50	.60
108	Bobby Simmons	.50	.20
109	Maurice Williams	.50	.20
110	Ricky Davis	1.50	.60
111	Kevin Garnett	3.00	1.25
112	Kelenna Azubuike	3.00	1.25
113	Trenton Hassell	.50	.20
114	Troy Hudson	.50	.20
115	Rashad McCants	2.00	.75
116	Vince Carter	4.00	1.50
117	Jason Collins	.50	.20
118	Richard Jefferson	1.00	.40
119	Jason Kidd	2.50	1.00
120	Nenad Krstic	1.00	.40
121	Jeff McInnis	.50	.20
122	Antoine Wright	.50	.20
123	P.J. Brown	.50	.20
124	Speedy Claxton	.50	.20
125	Desmond Mason	.50	.20
126	Chris Paul	4.00	1.50
127	J.R. Smith	1.00	.40
128	Kirk Snyder	.50	.20
129	David West	.50	.20
130	Jamal Crawford	.50	.20
131	Eddy Curry	1.00	.40
132	Channing Frye	1.00	.40
133	Stephon Marbury	1.50	.60
134	Quentin Richardson	1.00	.40
135	Nate Robinson	1.50	.60
136	David Lee	.50	.20
137	Carlos Arroyo	2.50	1.00
138	Tony Battie	.50	.20
139	Keyon Dooling	.50	.20
140	Grant Hill	1.50	.60
141	Dwight Howard	2.00	.75
142	Darko Milicic	1.50	.60
143	Jameer Nelson	1.00	.40
144	Samuel Dalembert	.50	.20
145	Steven Hunter	.50	.20
146	Andre Iguodala	1.50	.60
147	Allen Iverson	3.00	1.25
148	Kyle Korver	1.50	.60
149	Shavlik Randolph	.50	.20
150	Chris Webber	1.50	.60
151	Raja Bell	.50	.20
152	Boris Diaw	1.00	.40
153	Shawn Marion	1.50	.60
154	Steve Nash	1.50	.60
155	Amare Stoudemire	3.00	1.25
156	Kurt Thomas	.50	.20
157	Tim Thomas	.50	.20
158	Steve Blake	.50	.20
159	Juan Dixon	.50	.20
160	Zach Randolph	1.50	.60
161	Joel Przybilla	.50	.20
162	Sebastian Telfair	1.00	.40
163	Martell Webster	1.00	.40
164	Shareef Abdur-Rahim	1.50	.60
165	Ron Artest	1.00	.40
166	Mike Bibby	1.50	.60
167	Brad Miller	1.50	.60
168	Kenny Thomas	.50	.20
169	Bonzi Wells	1.00	.40
170	Bruce Bowen	.50	.20
171	Tim Duncan	3.00	1.25
172	Michael Finley	1.50	.60
173	Manu Ginobili	1.50	.60
174	Nazr Mohammed	.50	.20
175	Tony Parker	1.50	.60
176	Ray Allen	1.50	.60
177	Danny Fortson	.50	.20
178	Rashard Lewis	1.50	.60
179	Luke Ridnour	1.00	.40
180	Earl Watson	.50	.20
181	Chris Wilcox	.50	.20
182	Rafael Araujo	.50	.20
183	Chris Bosh	1.50	.60
184	Joey Graham	1.00	.40
185	Mike James	.50	.20
186	Morris Peterson	1.00	.40
187	Charlie Villanueva	1.50	.60
188	Carlos Boozer	1.00	.40
189	Matt Harpring	1.00	.40
190	Kris Humphries	.50	.20
191	Andrei Kirilenko	1.50	.60
192	C.J. Miles	.50	.20
193	Paul Millsap	5.00	2.00
194	Deron Williams	1.50	.60
195	Gilbert Arenas	1.50	.60
196	Andray Blatche	.50	.20
197	Caron Butler	1.00	.40
198	Antonio Daniels	.50	.20
199	Brendan Haywood	.50	.20
200	Antawn Jamison	1.50	.60
201	Andrea Bargnani RC	10.00	4.00
202	LaMarcus Aldridge RC	8.00	3.00
203	Adam Morrison RC	8.00	3.00
204	Tyrus Thomas RC	6.00	2.50
205	Shelden Williams RC	4.00	1.50
206	Brandon Roy RC	10.00	4.00
207	Randy Foye RC	6.00	2.50
208	Rudy Gay RC	6.00	2.50
209	Patrick O'Bryant RC	3.00	1.25
210	Saer Sene RC	3.00	1.25
211	J.J. Redick RC	6.00	2.50
212	Hilton Armstrong RC	3.00	1.25
213	Thabo Sefolosha RC	5.00	2.00
214	Ronnie Brewer RC	4.00	1.50
215	Cedric Simmons RC	3.00	1.25
216	Rodney Carney RC	3.00	1.25
217	Shawne Williams RC	4.00	1.50
218	Quincy Douby RC	3.00	1.25
219	Renaldo Balkman RC	3.00	1.25
220	Rajon Rondo RC	4.00	1.50
221	Marcus Williams RC	4.00	1.50
222	Josh Boone RC	3.00	1.25
223	Kyle Lowry RC	3.00	1.25
224	Shannon Brown RC	3.00	1.25
225	Jordan Farmar RC	6.00	2.50
226	Maurice Ager RC	3.00	1.25
227	Mardy Collins RC	3.00	1.25
228	Jorge Garbajosa RC	6.00	2.50
229	James White RC	3.00	1.25
230	Steve Novak RC	3.00	1.25
231	Solomon Jones RC	3.00	1.25
232	Paul Davis RC	3.00	1.25
233	P.J. Tucker RC	3.00	1.25
234	Craig Smith RC	3.00	1.25
235	Bobby Jones RC	3.00	1.25
236	David Noel RC	3.00	1.25
237	Vassilis Spanoulis RC	3.00	1.25
238	James Augustine RC	3.00	1.25
239	Daniel Gibson RC	8.00	3.00
240	Alexander Johnson RC	3.00	1.25

2000-01 Ultimate Collection

	COMMON CARD (1-60)	2.50	1.00
	COMMON ROOKIE	12.00	5.00
1	Dikembe Mutombo	4.00	1.50
2	Hanno Mottola RC	10.00	4.00
3	Paul Pierce	6.00	2.50
4	Antoine Walker	6.00	2.50
5	Derrick Coleman	2.50	1.00
6	Baron Davis	6.00	2.50
7	Elton Brand	6.00	2.50
8	Michael Jordan	50.00	20.00
9	Andre Miller	4.00	1.50
10	Chris Mihm RC	10.00	4.00
11	Michael Finley	6.00	2.50
12	Donnell Harvey RC	10.00	4.00
13	Antonio McDyess	4.00	1.50
14	Nick Van Exel	6.00	2.50
15	Jerry Stackhouse	6.00	2.50
16	Jerome Williams	2.50	1.00
17	Larry Hughes	4.00	1.50
18	Antawn Jamison	6.00	2.50
19	Steve Francis	6.00	2.50
20	Hakeem Olajuwon	6.00	2.50
21	Reggie Miller	6.00	2.50
22	Jalen Rose	6.00	2.50
23	Lamar Odom	6.00	2.50
24	Michael Olowokandi	2.50	1.00
25	Shaquille O'Neal	15.00	6.00
26	Kobe Bryant	25.00	10.00
27	Ron Harper	4.00	1.50
28	Alonzo Mourning	4.00	1.50
29	Eddie House RC	10.00	4.00
30	Glenn Robinson	6.00	2.50
31	Ray Allen	6.00	2.50
32	Kevin Garnett	12.00	5.00
33	Wally Szczerbiak	4.00	1.50
34	Terrell Brandon	4.00	1.50
35	Stephon Marbury	6.00	2.50
36	Keith Van Horn	4.00	1.50
37	Allan Houston	4.00	1.50
38	Latrell Sprewell	6.00	2.50
39	Grant Hill	6.00	2.50
40	Tracy McGrady	12.00	5.00
41	Allen Iverson	12.00	5.00

❏ 42	Toni Kukoc	4.00	1.50
❏ 43	Jason Kidd	10.00	4.00
❏ 44	Anfernee Hardaway	6.00	2.50
❏ 45	Scottie Pippen	10.00	4.00
❏ 46	Rasheed Wallace	6.00	2.50
❏ 47	Chris Webber	6.00	2.50
❏ 48	Jason Williams	4.00	1.50
❏ 50	Tim Duncan	12.00	5.00
❏ 50	David Robinson	6.00	2.50
❏ 51	Gary Payton	6.00	2.50
❏ 52	Rashard Lewis	4.00	1.50
❏ 53	Vince Carter	12.00	5.00
❏ 54	Morris Peterson RC	25.00	10.00
❏ 55	Karl Malone	6.00	2.50
❏ 56	John Stockton	6.00	2.50
❏ 57	Shareef Abdur-Rahim	6.00	2.50
❏ 58	Mike Bibby	6.00	2.50
❏ 59	Mike Smith RC	10.00	4.00
❏ 60	Richard Hamilton	4.00	1.50
❏ P1	Kenyon Martin SAMPLE		

2001-02 Ultimate Collection

❏ COMPLETE SET (90)		2500.00	1250.00
❏ COMP.SET w/o SP's (60)		500.00	250.00
❏ COMMON CARD (1-60)		2.50	1.00
❏ COMMON ROOKIE (61-70)		12.00	5.00
❏ COMMON ROOKIE (71-84)		20.00	8.00
❏ 1	Jason Terry	8.00	3.00
❏ 2	Shareef Abdur-Rahim	8.00	3.00
❏ 3	Paul Pierce	8.00	3.00
❏ 4	Antoine Walker	8.00	3.00
❏ 5	Baron Davis	8.00	3.00
❏ 6	Jamal Mashburn	5.00	2.00
❏ 7	Ron Mercer	5.00	2.00
❏ 8	Marcus Fizer	5.00	2.00
❏ 9	Andre Miller	5.00	2.00
❏ 10	Lamond Murray	2.50	1.00
❏ 11	Dirk Nowitzki	12.00	5.00
❏ 12	Michael Finley	8.00	3.00
❏ 13	Antonio McDyess	8.00	3.00
❏ 14	Nick Van Exel	8.00	3.00
❏ 15	Jerry Stackhouse	8.00	3.00
❏ 16	Zeljko Rebraca RC	20.00	8.00
❏ 17	Antawn Jamison	8.00	3.00
❏ 18	Larry Hughes	5.00	2.00
❏ 19	Steve Francis	8.00	3.00
❏ 20	Cuttino Mobley	5.00	2.00
❏ 21	Reggie Miller	8.00	3.00
❏ 22	Jalen Rose	8.00	3.00
❏ 23	Darius Miles	8.00	3.00
❏ 24	Quentin Richardson	5.00	2.00
❏ 25	Kobe Bryant	30.00	12.50
❏ 26	Shaquille O'Neal	20.00	8.00
❏ 27	Mitch Richmond	5.00	2.00
❏ 28	Stromile Swift	5.00	2.00
❏ 29	Jason Williams	5.00	2.00
❏ 30	Alonzo Mourning	5.00	2.00
❏ 31	Eddie Jones	8.00	3.00
❏ 32	Ray Allen	8.00	3.00
❏ 33	Glenn Robinson	5.00	2.00
❏ 34	Kevin Garnett	15.00	6.00
❏ 35	Terrell Brandon	5.00	2.00
❏ 36	Wally Szczerbiak	5.00	2.00
❏ 37	Jason Kidd	12.00	5.00
❏ 38	Kenyon Martin	8.00	3.00
❏ 39	Latrell Sprewell	8.00	3.00
❏ 40	Allan Houston	5.00	2.00

❏ 41	Tracy McGrady	20.00	8.00
❏ 42	Grant Hill	8.00	3.00
❏ 43	Allen Iverson	15.00	6.00
❏ 44	Dikembe Mutombo	5.00	2.00
❏ 45	Stephon Marbury	8.00	3.00
❏ 46	Anfernee Hardaway	8.00	3.00
❏ 47	Rasheed Wallace	8.00	3.00
❏ 48	Derek Anderson	5.00	2.00
❏ 49	Chris Webber	8.00	3.00
❏ 50	Peja Stojakovic	8.00	3.00
❏ 51	Tim Duncan	15.00	6.00
❏ 52	David Robinson	8.00	3.00
❏ 53	Rashard Lewis	5.00	2.00
❏ 54	Desmond Mason	5.00	2.00
❏ 55	Vince Carter	20.00	8.00
❏ 56	Morris Peterson	5.00	2.00
❏ 57	Karl Malone	8.00	3.00
❏ 58	John Stockton	8.00	3.00
❏ 59	Richard Hamilton	5.00	2.00
❏ 60	Michael Jordan	80.00	30.00
❏ 61	Andrei Kirilenko RC	30.00	12.50
❏ 62	Gilbert Arenas RC	60.00	25.00
❏ 63	Trenton Hassell RC	12.00	5.00
❏ 64	Tony Parker RC	40.00	15.00
❏ 65	Jamaal Tinsley RC	12.00	5.00
❏ 66	Samuel Dalembert RC	12.00	5.00
❏ 67	Gerald Wallace RC	30.00	12.50
❏ 68	Brandon Armstrong RC	12.00	5.00
❏ 69	Jeryl Sasser RC	12.00	5.00
❏ 70	Joseph Forte RC	20.00	8.00
❏ 71	Pau Gasol RC	100.00	50.00
❏ 72	Brendan Haywood RC	40.00	15.00
❏ 73	Zach Randolph RC	50.00	20.00
❏ 74	Jason Collins RC	20.00	8.00
❏ 75	Michael Bradley RC	20.00	8.00
❏ 76	Kirk Haston RC	20.00	8.00
❏ 77	Steven Hunter RC	20.00	8.00
❏ 78	Troy Murphy RC	40.00	15.00
❏ 79	Richard Jefferson RC	40.00	15.00
❏ 80	Vladimir Radmanovic RC	20.00	8.00
❏ 81	Kedrick Brown RC	20.00	8.00
❏ 82	Joe Johnson RC	40.00	15.00
❏ 83	DeSagana Diop RC	20.00	8.00
❏ 84	Shane Battier RC	30.00	12.50
❏ 85	Rodney White AU RC	20.00	8.00
❏ 86	Eddie Griffin AU RC	20.00	8.00
❏ 87	Jason Richardson AU RC	80.00	40.00
❏ 88	Eddy Curry AU RC	40.00	15.00
❏ 89	Tyson Chandler AU RC	40.00	15.00
❏ 90	Kwame Brown AU RC	40.00	15.00

2002-03 Ultimate Collection

❏ COMP.SET w/o SP's (67)		350.00	150.00
❏ COMMON CARD (1-67)		2.00	.75
❏ COMMON RC (68-79)		40.00	15.00
❏ COMMON ROOKIE (80-103)		20.00	8.00
❏ COMMON ROOKIE (104-120)		10.00	4.00
❏ 1	Shareef Abdur-Rahim	6.00	2.50
❏ 2	Glenn Robinson	6.00	2.50
❏ 3	Jason Terry	6.00	2.50
❏ 4	Paul Pierce	6.00	2.50
❏ 5	Antoine Walker	6.00	2.50
❏ 6	Vin Baker	4.00	1.50
❏ 7	Jalen Rose	6.00	2.50
❏ 8	Darius Miles	6.00	2.50
❏ 9	Dirk Nowitzki	10.00	4.00
❏ 10	Michael Finley	6.00	2.50

❏ 11	Steve Nash	6.00	2.50
❏ 12	Raef LaFrentz	4.00	1.50
❏ 13	Juwan Howard	4.00	1.50
❏ 14	Richard Hamilton	4.00	1.50
❏ 15	Chauncey Billups	4.00	1.50
❏ 16	Ben Wallace	6.00	2.50
❏ 17	Jason Richardson	6.00	2.50
❏ 18	Gilbert Arenas	6.00	2.50
❏ 19	Antawn Jamison	6.00	2.50
❏ 20	Steve Francis	6.00	2.50
❏ 21	Reggie Miller	6.00	2.50
❏ 22	Jamaal Tinsley	6.00	2.50
❏ 23	Jermaine O'Neal	6.00	2.50
❏ 24	Elton Brand	6.00	2.50
❏ 25	Andre Miller	4.00	1.50
❏ 26	Kobe Bryant	25.00	10.00
❏ 27	Shaquille O'Neal	15.00	6.00
❏ 28	Pau Gasol	6.00	2.50
❏ 29	Shane Battier	6.00	2.50
❏ 30	Eddie Jones	6.00	2.50
❏ 31	Brian Grant	4.00	1.50
❏ 32	Ray Allen	6.00	2.50
❏ 33	Kevin Garnett	12.00	5.00
❏ 34	Wally Szczerbiak	4.00	1.50
❏ 35	Troy Hudson	2.00	.75
❏ 36	Jason Kidd	10.00	4.00
❏ 37	Richard Jefferson	4.00	1.50
❏ 38	Kenyon Martin	6.00	2.50
❏ 39	Baron Davis	6.00	2.50
❏ 40	Jamal Mashburn	4.00	1.50
❏ 41	David Wesley	2.00	.75
❏ 42	P.J. Brown	2.00	.75
❏ 43	Allan Houston	4.00	1.50
❏ 44	Latrell Sprewell	6.00	2.50
❏ 45	Kurt Thomas	4.00	1.50
❏ 46	Tracy McGrady	15.00	6.00
❏ 47	Grant Hill	6.00	2.50
❏ 48	Allen Iverson	12.00	5.00
❏ 49	Stephon Marbury	6.00	2.50
❏ 50	Shawn Marion	6.00	2.50
❏ 51	Rasheed Wallace	6.00	2.50
❏ 52	Derek Anderson	4.00	1.50
❏ 53	Bonzi Wells	4.00	1.50
❏ 54	Chris Webber	6.00	2.50
❏ 55	Mike Bibby	6.00	2.50
❏ 56	Peja Stojakovic	6.00	2.50
❏ 57	Tim Duncan	12.00	5.00
❏ 58	David Robinson	6.00	2.50
❏ 59	Tony Parker	6.00	2.50
❏ 60	Gary Payton	6.00	2.50
❏ 61	Rashard Lewis	4.00	1.50
❏ 62	Desmond Mason	4.00	1.50
❏ 63	Vince Carter	15.00	6.00
❏ 64	Morris Peterson	4.00	1.50
❏ 65	Karl Malone	6.00	2.50
❏ 66	John Stockton	6.00	2.50
❏ 67	Michael Jordan	40.00	15.00
❏ 68	Chris Wilcox AU RC	50.00	20.00
❏ 69	Drew Gooden AU RC	120.00	60.00
❏ 70	M.Haislip AU RC EXCH	40.00	15.00
❏ 71	Melvin Ely AU RC	40.00	15.00
❏ 72	Jared Jeffries AU RC	40.00	15.00
❏ 73	Caron Butler AU RC	120.00	60.00
❏ 74	A.Stoudemire AU RC	300.00	200.00
❏ 75	Nene Hilario AU RC	80.00	40.00
❏ 76	DaJuan Wagner AU RC	100.00	50.00
❏ 77	N.Tskitishvili AU RC	50.00	20.00
❏ 78	Jay Williams AU RC	80.00	40.00
❏ 79	Yao Ming AU RC	500.00	250.00
❏ 80	Predrag Savovic RC	20.00	8.00
❏ 81	Igor Rakocevic RC	20.00	8.00
❏ 82	Sam Clancy RC	20.00	8.00
❏ 83	Ronald Murray RC	40.00	15.00
❏ 84	Tito Maddox RC	20.00	8.00
❏ 85	Carlos Boozer RC	40.00	15.00
❏ 86	Dan Gadzuric RC	20.00	8.00
❏ 87	Vincent Yarbrough RC	20.00	8.00
❏ 88	Robert Archibald RC	20.00	8.00
❏ 89	Roger Mason RC	20.00	8.00
❏ 90	Juaquin Hawkins RC	20.00	8.00
❏ 91	Chris Jefferies RC	20.00	8.00
❏ 92	John Salmons RC	20.00	8.00
❏ 93	Manu Ginobili RC	90.00	45.00
❏ 94	Tayshaun Prince RC	25.00	10.00
❏ 95	Casey Jacobsen RC	20.00	8.00
❏ 96	Qyntel Woods RC	20.00	8.00

97	Kareem Rush RC	20.00	8.00
98	Ryan Humphrey RC	20.00	8.00
99	Juan Dixon RC	25.00	10.00
100	Fred Jones RC	20.00	8.00
101	Jiri Welsch RC	20.00	8.00
102	Bostjan Nachbar RC	20.00	8.00
103	Marko Jaric	20.00	8.00
104	Gordan Giricek RC	12.00	5.00
105	Frank Williams RC	10.00	4.00
106	Pat Burke RC	10.00	4.00
107	Junior Harrington RC	10.00	4.00
108	Rasual Butler RC	10.00	4.00
109	Raul Lopez RC	10.00	4.00
110	Cezary Trybanski RC	10.00	4.00
111	Dan Dickau RC	10.00	4.00
112	Efthimios Rentzias RC	10.00	4.00
113	Mehmet Okur RC	10.00	4.00
114	Curtis Borchardt RC	10.00	4.00
115	J.R. Bremer RC	10.00	4.00
116	Lonny Baxter RC	10.00	4.00
117	Jamal Sampson RC	10.00	4.00
118	Tamar Slay RC	10.00	4.00
119	Jannero Pargo RC	10.00	4.00
120	Smush Parker RC	15.00	6.00

2003-04 Ultimate Collection

COMMON CARD (1-116)		2.00	.75
COMMON ROOKIE (117-126)		12.00	5.00
COMMON AU (127-164)		20.00	8.00
COMMON AU (165-190)		8.00	3.00
LIMITED PRINT RUN 25 SER.#'d SETS			
LIMITED NOT PRICED DUE TO SCARCITY			
LIM.BLACK SER.#'D TO ONE EXIST			
1	Dominique Wilkins	10.00	4.00
2	Jason Terry	6.00	2.50
3	Dion Glover	2.00	.75
4	Stephen Jackson	2.00	.75
5	Bill Russell	10.00	4.00
6	Paul Pierce	6.00	2.50
7	Larry Bird	12.00	5.00
8	Ricky Davis	6.00	2.50
9	Antonio Davis	4.00	1.50
10	Michael Jordan	25.00	10.00
11	Scottie Pippen	10.00	4.00
12	Tyson Chandler	6.00	2.50
13	Jeff McInnis	2.00	.75
14	Dajuan Wagner	4.00	1.50
15	Carlos Boozer	6.00	2.50
16	Zydrunas Ilgauskas	4.00	1.50
17	Dirk Nowitzki	10.00	4.00
18	Steve Nash	6.00	2.50
19	Antoine Walker	6.00	2.50
20	Michael Finley	6.00	2.50
21	Andre Miller	4.00	1.50
22	Nene	4.00	1.50
23	Nikoloz Tskitishvili	2.00	.75
24	Marcus Camby	4.00	1.50
25	Richard Hamilton	4.00	1.50
26	Ben Wallace	6.00	2.50
27	Chauncey Billups	4.00	1.50
28	Rasheed Wallace	6.00	2.50
29	Jason Richardson	6.00	2.50
30	Nick Van Exel	6.00	2.50
31	Speedy Claxton	2.00	.75
32	Mike Dunleavy	4.00	1.50
33	Yao Ming	15.00	6.00
34	Steve Francis	6.00	2.50
35	Cuttino Mobley	4.00	1.50
36	Jim Jackson	2.00	.75
37	Reggie Miller	6.00	2.50
38	Jermaine O'Neal	6.00	2.50
39	Ron Artest	4.00	1.50
40	Al Harrington	4.00	1.50
41	Elton Brand	6.00	2.50
42	Corey Maggette	4.00	1.50
43	Quentin Richardson	4.00	1.50
44	Chris Wilcox	4.00	1.50
45	Kobe Bryant	20.00	8.00
46	Shaquille O'Neal	15.00	6.00
47	Gary Payton	6.00	2.50
48	Karl Malone	6.00	2.50
49	Pau Gasol	6.00	2.50
50	Bonzi Wells	4.00	1.50
51	Mike Miller	6.00	2.50
52	Jason Williams	4.00	1.50
53	Caron Butler	6.00	2.50
54	Lamar Odom	6.00	2.50
55	Eddie Jones	6.00	2.50
56	Brian Grant	4.00	1.50
57	Desmond Mason	4.00	1.50
58	Oscar Robertson	10.00	4.00
59	Michael Redd	6.00	2.50
60	Toni Kukoc	4.00	1.50
61	Latrell Sprewell	6.00	2.50
62	Kevin Garnett	12.00	5.00
63	Wally Szczerbiak	4.00	1.50
64	Sam Cassell	6.00	2.50
65	Kenyon Martin	6.00	2.50
66	Jason Kidd	10.00	4.00
67	Richard Jefferson	6.00	2.50
68	Alonzo Mourning	4.00	1.50
69	Jamal Mashburn	4.00	1.50
70	David Wesley	2.00	.75
71	Baron Davis	6.00	2.50
72	Jamaal Magloire	2.00	.75
73	Allan Houston	4.00	1.50
74	Patrick Ewing	6.00	2.50
75	Stephon Marbury	6.00	2.50
76	Dikembe Mutombo	4.00	1.50
77	Tracy McGrady	15.00	-6.00
78	Drew Gooden	4.00	1.50
79	Juwan Howard	4.00	1.50
80	DeShawn Stevenson	2.00	.75
81	Julius Erving	10.00	4.00
82	Allen Iverson	12.00	5.00
83	Glenn Robinson	6.00	2.50
84	Eric Snow	4.00	1.50
85	Amare Stoudemire	15.00	6.00
86	Shawn Marion	6.00	2.50
87	Antonio McDyess	6.00	2.50
88	Joe Johnson	4.00	1.50
89	Shareef Abdur-Rahim	6.00	2.50
90	Derek Anderson	4.00	1.50
91	Damon Stoudamire	4.00	1.50
92	Zach Randolph	6.00	2.50
93	Mike Bibby	6.00	2.50
94	Chris Webber	6.00	2.50
95	Peja Stojakovic	6.00	2.50
96	Bobby Jackson	4.00	1.50
97	Manu Ginobili	6.00	2.50
98	Tim Duncan	12.00	5.00
99	Tony Parker	6.00	2.50
100	Radoslav Nesterovic	4.00	1.50
101	Rashard Lewis	6.00	2.50
102	Ray Allen	6.00	2.50
103	Vladimir Radmanovic	4.00	1.50
104	Brent Barry	4.00	1.50
105	Vince Carter	15.00	6.00
106	Morris Peterson	4.00	1.50
107	Jalen Rose	6.00	2.50
108	Donyell Marshall	4.00	1.50
109	John Stockton	6.00	2.50
110	Andrei Kirilenko	6.00	2.50
111	Matt Harpring	6.00	2.50
112	Carlos Arroyo	10.00	4.00
113	Gilbert Arenas	6.00	2.50
114	Jerry Stackhouse	6.00	2.50
115	Kwame Brown	6.00	2.50
116	Larry Hughes	4.00	1.50
117	T.J. Ford RC	15.00	6.00
118	Kirk Hinrich RC	20.00	8.00
119	Nick Collison RC	12.00	5.00
120	James Jones RC	12.00	5.00
121	Travis Hansen RC	12.00	5.00
122	Alex Garcia RC	12.00	5.00
123	Theron Smith RC	12.00	5.00
124	Francisco Elson RC	12.00	5.00
125	Jon Stefansson RC	12.00	5.00
126	Ronald Dupree RC	12.00	5.00
127	LeBron James AU RC	1000.00	600.00
128	Darko Milicic AU RC	120.00	60.00
129	Carmelo Anthony AU RC	400.00	200.00
130	Chris Bosh AU RC	150.00	75.00
131	Dwyane Wade AU RC	500.00	250.00
132	Chris Kaman AU RC	30.00	12.50
133	Jarvis Hayes AU RC	20.00	8.00
134	Mickael Pietrus AU RC	30.00	12.50
135	Dahntay Jones AU RC	20.00	8.00
136	Marcus Banks AU RC	20.00	8.00
137	Luke Ridnour AU RC	40.00	15.00
138	Reece Gaines AU RC	20.00	8.00
139	Troy Bell AU RC	20.00	8.00
140	Mike Sweetney AU RC	20.00	8.00
141	David West AU RC	25.00	10.00
142	Aleksandar Pavlovic AU RC	20.00	8.00
143	Steve Blake AU RC	30.00	12.50
144	Boris Diaw AU RC	75.00	35.00
145	Zoran Planinic AU RC	20.00	8.00
146	Travis Outlaw AU RC	20.00	8.00
147	Brian Cook AU RC	20.00	8.00
148	Jerome Beasley AU RC	20.00	8.00
149	Ndudi Ebi AU RC	20.00	8.00
150	Kendrick Perkins AU RC	20.00	8.00
151	Leandro Barbosa AU RC	60.00	25.00
152	Josh Howard AU RC	75.00	35.00
153	Maciej Lampe AU RC	20.00	8.00
154	Jason Kapono AU RC	25.00	10.00
155	Luke Walton AU RC	30.00	12.50
156	Kyle Korver AU RC	60.00	25.00
157	Zarko Cabarkapa AU RC	20.00	8.00
158	Zaur Pachulia AU RC	30.00	12.50
159	Maurice Williams AU RC	30.00	12.50
160	Brandon Hunter AU RC	20.00	8.00
161	Keith Bogans AU RC	20.00	8.00
162	Marquis Daniels AU RC	50.00	20.00
163	Willie Green AU RC	20.00	8.00
164	Udonis Haslem AU RC	40.00	15.00
165	Larry Bird US	15.00	6.00
166	Bill Russell US	12.00	5.00
167	Michael Jordan US	30.00	12.50
168	Steve Nash US	8.00	3.00
169	Michael Finley US	8.00	3.00
170	Ben Wallace US	8.00	3.00
171	Jason Richardson US	8.00	3.00
172	Yao Ming US	20.00	8.00
173	Reggie Miller US	8.00	3.00
174	Kobe Bryant US	25.00	10.00
175	Shaquille O'Neal US	20.00	8.00
176	Gary Payton US	8.00	3.00
177	Magic Johnson US	10.00	4.00
178	Pau Gasol US	8.00	3.00
179	Lamar Odom US	8.00	3.00
180	Oscar Robertson US	12.00	5.00
181	Kenyon Martin US	8.00	3.00
182	Baron Davis US	8.00	3.00
183	Julius Erving US	12.00	5.00
184	Amare Stoudemire US	20.00	8.00
185	Mike Bibby US	8.00	3.00
186	Tony Parker US	8.00	3.00
187	Rashard Lewis US	8.00	3.00
188	Vince Carter US	20.00	8.00
189	Andrei Kirilenko US	8.00	3.00
190	Gilbert Arenas US	8.00	3.00

2004-05 Ultimate Collection

COMMON CARD (1-116)		2.00	.75
COMMON ROOKIE (117-126)		10.00	4.00
COMMON AU RC (127-164)		25.00	10.00
1	Tyronn Lue	2.00	.75
2	Tony Delk	2.00	.75
3	Al Harrington	4.00	1.50
4	Paul Pierce	6.00	2.50
5	Antoine Walker	6.00	2.50
6	Bill Russell	10.00	4.00
7	Larry Bird	15.00	-6.00
8	Gerald Wallace	4.00	1.50
9	Jason Kapono	4.00	1.50

❏ 10 Primoz Brezec	4.00	1.50
❏ 11 Kirk Hinrich	6.00	2.50
❏ 12 Eddy Curry	4.00	1.50
❏ 13 Tyson Chandler	6.00	2.50
❏ 14 Michael Jordan	35.00	15.00
❏ 15 LeBron James	30.00	12.50
❏ 16 Drew Gooden	4.00	1.50
❏ 17 Jeff McInnis	2.00	.75
❏ 18 Zydrunas Ilgauskas	4.00	1.50
❏ 19 Dirk Nowitzki	10.00	4.00
❏ 20 Michael Finley	6.00	2.50
❏ 21 Josh Howard	4.00	1.50
❏ 22 Marquis Daniels	6.00	2.50
❏ 23 Carmelo Anthony	12.00	5.00
❏ 24 Kenyon Martin	6.00	2.50
❏ 25 Andre Miller	4.00	1.50
❏ 26 Nene	4.00	1.50
❏ 27 Ben Wallace	6.00	2.50
❏ 28 Richard Hamilton	4.00	1.50
❏ 29 Isiah Thomas	10.00	4.00
❏ 30 Chauncey Billups	4.00	1.50
❏ 31 Jason Richardson	6.00	2.50
❏ 32 Baron Davis	6.00	2.50
❏ 33 Derek Fisher	6.00	2.50
❏ 34 Tracy McGrady	15.00	6.00
❏ 35 Yao Ming	15.00	6.00
❏ 36 Hakeem Olajuwon	6.00	2.50
❏ 37 Jermaine O'Neal	6.00	2.50
❏ 38 Reggie Miller	6.00	2.50
❏ 39 Ron Artest	4.00	1.50
❏ 40 Stephen Jackson	2.00	.75
❏ 41 Elton Brand	6.00	2.50
❏ 42 Chris Kaman	4.00	1.50
❏ 43 Corey Maggette	4.00	1.50
❏ 44 Bobby Simmons	2.00	.75
❏ 45 Kobe Bryant	20.00	8.00
❏ 46 Magic Johnson	15.00	6.00
❏ 47 Wilt Chamberlain	10.00	4.00
❏ 48 Lamar Odom	6.00	2.50
❏ 49 Pau Gasol	6.00	2.50
❏ 50 Bonzi Wells	4.00	1.50
❏ 51 Jason Williams	4.00	1.50
❏ 52 Mike Miller	6.00	2.50
❏ 53 Shaquille O'Neal	15.00	6.00
❏ 54 Dwyane Wade	15.00	6.00
❏ 55 Eddie Jones	6.00	2.50
❏ 56 Udonis Haslem	2.00	.75
❏ 57 Oscar Robertson	10.00	4.00
❏ 58 Michael Redd	6.00	2.50
❏ 59 Desmond Mason	4.00	1.50
❏ 60 T.J. Ford	4.00	1.50
❏ 61 Kevin Garnett	12.00	5.00
❏ 62 Latrell Sprewell	6.00	2.50
❏ 63 Sam Cassell	6.00	2.50
❏ 64 Michael Olowokandi	2.00	.75
❏ 65 Jason Kidd	10.00	4.00
❏ 66 Richard Jefferson	4.00	1.50
❏ 67 Vince Carter	15.00	6.00
❏ 68 Ron Mercer	2.00	.75
❏ 69 Dan Dickau	2.00	.75
❏ 70 Jamaal Magloire	2.00	.75
❏ 71 P.J. Brown	2.00	.75
❏ 72 Lee Nailon	2.00	.75
❏ 73 Stephon Marbury	6.00	2.50
❏ 74 Allan Houston	4.00	1.50
❏ 75 Jamal Crawford	4.00	1.50
❏ 76 Bernard King	8.00	3.00
❏ 77 Steve Francis	6.00	2.50

❏ 78 Doug Christie	4.00	1.50
❏ 79 Grant Hill	6.00	2.50
❏ 80 Hedo Turkoglu	6.00	2.50
❏ 81 Allen Iverson	12.00	5.00
❏ 82 Julius Erving	10.00	4.00
❏ 83 Chris Webber	6.00	2.50
❏ 84 Kyle Korver	4.00	1.50
❏ 85 Amare Stoudemire	12.00	5.00
❏ 86 Steve Nash	6.00	2.50
❏ 87 Shawn Marion	6.00	2.50
❏ 88 Quentin Richardson	4.00	1.50
❏ 89 Shareef Abdur-Rahim	6.00	2.50
❏ 90 Darius Miles	6.00	2.50
❏ 91 Zach Randolph	6.00	2.50
❏ 92 Damon Stoudamire	4.00	1.50
❏ 93 Peja Stojakovic	6.00	2.50
❏ 94 Mike Bibby	6.00	2.50
❏ 95 Cuttino Mobley	4.00	1.50
❏ 96 Brad Miller	6.00	2.50
❏ 97 Tim Duncan	12.00	5.00
❏ 98 Manu Ginobili	6.00	2.50
❏ 99 Tony Parker	6.00	2.50
❏ 100 David Robinson	10.00	4.00
❏ 101 Ray Allen	6.00	2.50
❏ 102 Rashard Lewis	6.00	2.50
❏ 103 Ronald Murray	2.00	.75
❏ 104 Luke Ridnour	4.00	1.50
❏ 105 Rafer Alston	2.00	.75
❏ 106 Jalen Rose	6.00	2.50
❏ 107 Chris Bosh	6.00	2.50
❏ 108 Morris Peterson	4.00	1.50
❏ 109 Andrei Kirilenko	6.00	2.50
❏ 110 Carlos Boozer	6.00	2.50
❏ 111 John Stockton	10.00	4.00
❏ 112 Matt Harpring	6.00	2.50
❏ 113 Gilbert Arenas	6.00	2.50
❏ 114 Antawn Jamison	6.00	2.50
❏ 115 Jarvis Hayes	4.00	1.50
❏ 116 Larry Hughes	4.00	1.50
❏ 117 D.J. Mbenga RC	10.00	4.00
❏ 118 Damien Wilkins RC	10.00	4.00
❏ 119 Billy Thomas RC	10.00	4.00
❏ 120 Andre Barrett RC	10.00	4.00
❏ 121 Erik Daniels RC	10.00	4.00
❏ 122 Justin Reed RC	10.00	4.00
❏ 123 Viktor Khryapa RC	10.00	4.00
❏ 124 Mario Kasun RC	10.00	4.00
❏ 125 Luis Flores RC	10.00	4.00
❏ 126 Emeka Okafor RC	30.00	12.50
❏ 127 Dwight Howard AU RC	250.00	125.00
❏ 128 Ben Gordon AU RC	200.00	100.00
❏ 129 Shaun Livingston AU RC	40.00	15.00
❏ 130 Devin Harris AU RC	40.00	15.00
❏ 131 Josh Childress AU RC	30.00	12.50
❏ 132 Luol Deng AU RC	75.00	30.00
❏ 133 Rafael Araujo AU RC	25.00	10.00
❏ 134 Andre Iguodala AU RC	60.00	25.00
❏ 135 Luke Jackson AU RC	25.00	10.00
❏ 136 Andris Biedrins AU RC	40.00	15.00
❏ 137 Robert Swift AU RC	25.00	10.00
❏ 138 Sebastian Telfair AU RC	30.00	12.50
❏ 139 Kris Humphries AU RC	25.00	10.00
❏ 140 Al Jefferson AU RC	100.00	50.00
❏ 141 Kirk Snyder AU RC	25.00	10.00
❏ 142 Josh Smith AU RC	60.00	25.00
❏ 143 J.R. Smith AU RC	60.00	25.00
❏ 144 Dorell Wright AU RC	40.00	15.00
❏ 145 Jameer Nelson AU RC	40.00	15.00
❏ 146 Pavel Podkolzin AU RC	25.00	10.00
❏ 147 Delonte West AU RC	50.00	20.00
❏ 148 Tony Allen AU RC	30.00	12.50
❏ 149 Kevin Martin AU RC	40.00	15.00
❏ 150 Sasha Vujacic AU RC	25.00	10.00
❏ 151 Beno Udrih AU RC	30.00	12.50
❏ 152 David Harrison AU RC	25.00	10.00
❏ 153 Anderson Varejao AU RC	30.00	12.50
❏ 154 Jackson Vroman AU RC	25.00	10.00
❏ 155 Peter John Ramos AU RC	25.00	10.00
❏ 156 Lionel Chalmers AU RC	25.00	10.00
❏ 157 Donta Smith AU RC	25.00	10.00
❏ 158 Andre Emmett AU RC	25.00	10.00
❏ 159 Antonio Burks AU RC	25.00	10.00
❏ 160 Royal Ivey AU RC	25.00	10.00
❏ 161 Chris Duhon AU RC	30.00	12.50
❏ 162 Nenad Krstic AU RC	30.00	12.50
❏ 163 Trevor Ariza AU RC	30.00	12.50

❏ 164 Matt Freije AU RC	25.00	10.00
❏ 165 Bernard Robinson AU RC	25.00	10.00
❏ 166 Andres Nocioni AU RC	30.00	12.50
❏ 167 Pape Sow AU RC	25.00	10.00
❏ 168 Ha Seung-Jin AU RC	25.00	10.00

2005-06 Ultimate Collection

❏ COMMON CARD (1-130)	.75	.30
❏ COMMON ROOKIE (131-142)	8.00	3.00
❏ COMMON AU (143-183)	20.00	8.00
❏ 1 Josh Smith	2.50	1.00
❏ 2 Josh Childress	1.50	.60
❏ 3 Joe Johnson	1.50	.60
❏ 4 Al Harrington	.75	.30
❏ 5 Tony Allen	1.50	.60
❏ 6 Ricky Davis	2.50	1.00
❏ 7 Al Jefferson	2.50	1.00
❏ 8 Paul Pierce	2.50	1.00
❏ 9 Delonte West	1.50	.60
❏ 10 Brevin Knight	.75	.30
❏ 11 Emeka Okafor	4.00	1.50
❏ 12 Kareem Rush	.75	.30
❏ 13 Gerald Wallace	2.50	1.00
❏ 14 Tyson Chandler	2.50	1.00
❏ 15 Luol Deng	2.50	1.00
❏ 16 Michael Jordan	15.00	6.00
❏ 17 Ben Gordon	5.00	2.00
❏ 18 Kirk Hinrich	2.50	1.00
❏ 19 LeBron James	15.00	6.00
❏ 20 Drew Gooden	1.50	.60
❏ 21 Larry Hughes	1.50	.60
❏ 22 Donyell Marshall	.75	.30
❏ 23 Zydrunas Ilgauskas	.75	.30
❏ 24 Marquis Daniels	1.50	.60
❏ 25 Josh Howard	1.50	.60
❏ 26 Dirk Nowitzki	4.00	1.50
❏ 27 Jason Terry	2.50	1.00
❏ 28 Devin Harris	2.50	1.00
❏ 29 Carmelo Anthony	5.00	2.00
❏ 30 Marcus Camby	.75	.30
❏ 31 Nene	.75	.30
❏ 32 Kenyon Martin	2.50	1.00
❏ 33 Andre Miller	1.50	.60
❏ 34 Ben Wallace	2.50	1.00
❏ 35 Richard Hamilton	2.50	1.00
❏ 36 Tayshaun Prince	2.50	1.00
❏ 37 Chauncey Billups	2.50	1.00
❏ 38 Rasheed Wallace	2.50	1.00
❏ 39 Baron Davis	2.50	1.00
❏ 40 Mike Dunleavy	1.50	.60
❏ 41 Troy Murphy	2.50	1.00
❏ 42 Jason Richardson	2.50	1.00
❏ 43 Tracy McGrady	6.00	2.50
❏ 44 Yao Ming	6.00	2.50
❏ 45 Stromile Swift	1.50	.60
❏ 46 Juwan Howard	1.50	.60
❏ 47 Bob Sura	.75	.30
❏ 48 Ron Artest	1.50	.60
❏ 49 Stephen Jackson	1.50	.60
❏ 50 Jermaine O'Neal	2.50	1.00
❏ 51 Jamaal Tinsley	1.50	.60
❏ 52 Elton Brand	2.50	1.00
❏ 53 Corey Maggette	1.50	.60
❏ 54 Sam Cassell	1.50	.60
❏ 55 Shaun Livingston	2.00	.75
❏ 56 Cuttino Mobley	1.50	.60
❏ 57 Kobe Bryant	10.00	4.00

#	Player		
58	Kwame Brown	1.50	.60
59	Lamar Odom	2.50	1.00
60	Devean George	1.50	.60
61	Pau Gasol	2.50	1.00
62	Damon Stoudamire	1.50	.60
63	Eddie Jones	.75	.30
64	Bobby Jackson	.75	.30
65	Shaquille O'Neal	6.00	2.50
66	Gary Payton	2.50	1.00
67	Antoine Walker	2.50	1.00
68	Dwyane Wade	8.00	3.00
69	Jason Williams	1.50	.60
70	Jamaal Magloire	.75	.30
71	Michael Redd	2.50	1.00
72	Bobby Simmons	.75	.30
73	Maurice Williams	.75	.30
74	Kevin Garnett	5.00	2.00
75	Marko Jaric	.75	.30
76	Wally Szczerbiak	1.50	.60
77	Michael Olowokandi	.75	.30
78	Vince Carter	6.00	2.50
79	Richard Jefferson	1.50	.60
80	Jason Kidd	4.00	1.50
81	Jeff McInnis	.75	.30
82	J.R. Smith	1.50	.60
83	Desmond Mason	.75	.30
84	Speedy Claxton	.75	.30
85	David West	1.50	.60
86	Stephon Marbury	2.50	1.00
87	Jamal Crawford	1.50	.60
88	Quentin Richardson	1.50	.60
89	Eddy Curry	1.50	.60
90	Steve Francis	2.50	1.00
91	Grant Hill	2.50	1.00
92	Dwight Howard	3.00	1.25
93	Jameer Nelson	1.50	.60
94	Hedo Turkoglu	1.50	.60
95	Allen Iverson	5.00	2.00
96	Andre Iguodala	2.50	1.00
97	Kyle Korver	2.50	1.00
98	Chris Webber	2.50	1.00
99	Steve Nash	2.50	1.00
100	Shawn Marion	2.50	1.00
101	Amare Stoudemire	5.00	2.00
102	Kurt Thomas	.75	.30
103	Juan Dixon	.75	.30
104	Darius Miles	2.50	1.00
105	Zach Randolph	2.50	1.00
106	Sebastian Telfair	1.50	.60
107	Shareef Abdur-Rahim	2.50	1.00
108	Mike Bibby	2.50	1.00
109	Brad Miller	2.50	1.00
110	Peja Stojakovic	2.50	1.00
111	Tim Duncan	5.00	2.00
112	Manu Ginobili	2.50	1.00
113	Tony Parker	2.50	1.00
114	Michael Finley	2.50	1.00
115	Ray Allen	2.50	1.00
116	Rashard Lewis	2.50	1.00
117	Vladimir Radmanovic	.75	.30
118	Luke Ridnour	1.50	.60
119	Chris Bosh	2.50	1.00
120	Morris Peterson	1.50	.60
121	Jalen Rose	2.00	.75
122	Alvin Williams	.75	.30
123	Carlos Boozer	1.50	.60
124	Matt Harpring	2.50	1.00
125	Andrei Kirilenko	2.50	1.00
126	Mehmet Okur	.75	.30
127	Gilbert Arenas	2.50	1.00
128	Caron Butler	1.50	.60
129	Antawn Jamison	2.50	1.00
130	Brendan Haywood	.75	.30
131	Von Wafer RC	8.00	3.00
132	Bracey Wright RC	8.00	3.00
133	Ryan Gomes RC	8.00	3.00
134	Robert Whaley RC	8.00	3.00
135	Orien Greene RC	8.00	3.00
136	Dijon Thompson RC	8.00	3.00
137	Lawrence Roberts RC	8.00	3.00
138	Amir Johnson RC	8.00	3.00
139	John Lucas III RC	8.00	3.00
140	Chuck Hayes RC	8.00	3.00
141	Alex Acker RC	8.00	3.00
142	Fabricio Oberto RC	8.00	3.00
143	Andrew Bogut AU RC	40.00	15.00
144	Marvin Williams AU RC	60.00	25.00
145	Deron Williams AU RC	90.00	45.00
146	Chris Paul AU RC	200.00	100.00
147	Raymond Felton AU RC	50.00	20.00
148	Martell Webster AU RC	40.00	15.00
149	Charlie Villanueva AU RC	50.00	20.00
150	Channing Frye AU RC	20.00	8.00
151	Ike Diogu AU RC	30.00	12.50
152	Andrew Bynum AU RC	80.00	40.00
153	Yaroslav Korolev AU RC	15.00	6.00
154	Sean May AU RC	20.00	8.00
155	Rashad McCants AU RC	30.00	12.50
156	Antoine Wright AU RC EXCH	15.00	6.00
157	Joey Graham AU RC	15.00	6.00
158	Danny Granger AU RC	30.00	12.50
159	Gerald Green AU RC	100.00	50.00
160	Hakim Warrick AU RC	40.00	15.00
161	Julius Hodge AU RC	15.00	6.00
162	Nate Robinson AU RC	30.00	12.50
163	Jarrett Jack AU RC	15.00	6.00
164	Francisco Garcia AU RC	15.00	6.00
165	Luther Head AU RC	20.00	8.00
166	Johan Petro AU RC	15.00	6.00
167	Jason Maxiell AU RC	15.00	6.00
168	Linas Kleiza AU RC	15.00	6.00
169	Wayne Simien AU RC	12.00	5.00
170	David Lee AU RC	25.00	10.00
171	Salim Stoudamire AU RC	12.00	5.00
172	Daniel Ewing AU RC	15.00	6.00
173	Brandon Bass AU RC	15.00	6.00
174	C.J. Miles AU RC	15.00	6.00
175	Ersan Ilyasova AU RC	15.00	6.00
176	Travis Diener AU RC	15.00	6.00
177	Chris Taft AU RC EXCH	15.00	6.00
178	Martynas Andriuskevicius AU RC	15.00	6.00
179	Louis Williams AU RC	15.00	6.00
180	Monta Ellis AU RC	50.00	20.00
181	Andray Blatche AU RC EXCH	15.00	6.00
182	Sarunas Jasikevicius AU RC	15.006.00	
183	James Singleton AU RC	15.00	6.00

1999-00 Ultimate Victory

COMPLETE SET (150)		100.00	50.00
COMP. SET w/o RC (120)		60.00	30.00
COMMON CARD (1-90)		.30	.10
COMMON ROOKIE (121-150)		1.00	.40
COMMON MJ GH (91-120)		1.50	.60
1	Dikembe Mutombo	.60	.25
2	Alan Henderson	.30	.10
3	LaPhonso Ellis	.30	.10
4	Kenny Anderson	.60	.25
5	Antoine Walker	1.00	.40
6	Paul Pierce	1.00	.40
7	Elden Campbell	.30	.10
8	Eddie Jones	1.00	.40
9	David Wesley	.30	.10
10	Michael Jordan	5.00	2.00
11	Kornel David RC	.30	.10
12	Toni Kukoc	.60	.25
13	Shawn Kemp	.60	.25
14	Brevin Knight	.30	.10
15	Zydrunas Ilgauskas	.60	.25
16	Michael Finley	1.00	.40
17	Shawn Bradley	.30	.10
18	Dirk Nowitzki	2.00	.75
19	Antonio McDyess	.60	.25
20	Nick Van Exel	1.00	.40
21	Ron Mercer	.60	.25
22	Grant Hill	1.00	.40
23	Lindsey Hunter	.30	.10
24	Jerry Stackhouse	1.00	.40
25	John Starks	.60	.25
26	Antawn Jamison	1.50	.60
27	Mookie Blaylock	.30	.10
28	Hakeem Olajuwon	1.00	.40
29	Cuttino Mobley	1.00	.40
30	Charles Barkley	1.25	.50
31	Reggie Miller	1.00	.40
32	Rik Smits	.60	.25
33	Jalen Rose	.60	.25
34	Maurice Taylor	.60	.25
35	Tyrone Nesby RC	.30	.10
36	Michael Olowokandi	.60	.25
37	Kobe Bryant	4.00	1.50
38	Shaquille O'Neal	2.50	1.00
39	Glen Rice	.60	.25
40	Robert Horry	.60	.25
41	Tim Hardaway	.60	.25
42	Alonzo Mourning	.60	.25
43	Jamal Mashburn	.60	.25
44	Ray Allen	1.00	.40
45	Glenn Robinson	1.00	.40
46	Robert Traylor	.30	.10
47	Kevin Garnett	2.00	.75
48	Joe Smith	.60	.25
49	Bobby Jackson	.60	.25
50	Keith Van Horn	1.00	.40
51	Stephon Marbury	1.00	.40
52	Jayson Williams	.30	.10
53	Patrick Ewing	.60	.25
54	Allan Houston	.60	.25
55	Latrell Sprewell	1.00	.40
56	Marcus Camby	.60	.25
57	Darrell Armstrong	.30	.10
58	Matt Harpring	1.00	.40
59	Bo Outlaw	.30	.10
60	Allen Iverson	2.00	.75
61	Theo Ratliff	.60	.25
62	Larry Hughes	1.00	.40
63	Jason Kidd	1.50	.60
64	Tom Gugliotta	.30	.10
65	Anfernee Hardaway	1.00	.40
66	Scottie Pippen	1.50	.60
67	Damon Stoudamire	.60	.25
68	Brian Grant	.60	.25
69	Jason Williams	1.00	.40
70	Vlade Divac	.60	.25
71	Chris Webber	1.00	.40
72	Tim Duncan	2.00	.75
73	Sean Elliott	.60	.25
74	David Robinson	1.00	.40
75	Avery Johnson	.30	.10
76	Gary Payton	1.00	.40
77	Vin Baker	.60	.25
78	Brent Barry	.60	.25
79	Vince Carter	2.50	1.00
80	Doug Christie	.60	.25
81	Tracy McGrady	2.50	1.00
82	Karl Malone	1.00	.40
83	John Stockton	1.00	.40
84	Bryon Russell	.30	.10
85	Shareef Abdur-Rahim	1.00	.40
86	Mike Bibby	1.00	.40
87	Felipe Lopez	.30	.10
88	Juwan Howard	.60	.25
89	Rod Strickland	.30	.10
90	Mitch Richmond	.60	.25
91	Michael Jordan GH	1.50	.60
92	Michael Jordan GH	1.50	.60
93	Michael Jordan GH	1.50	.60
94	Michael Jordan GH	1.50	.60
95	Michael Jordan GH	1.50	.60
96	Michael Jordan GH	1.50	.60
97	Michael Jordan GH	1.50	.60
98	Michael Jordan GH	1.50	.60
99	Michael Jordan GH	1.50	.60
100	Michael Jordan GH	1.50	.60
101	Michael Jordan GH	1.50	.60
102	Michael Jordan GH	1.50	.60
103	Michael Jordan GH	1.50	.60
104	Michael Jordan GH	1.50	.60
105	Michael Jordan GH	1.50	.60
106	Michael Jordan GH	1.50	.60
107	Michael Jordan GH	1.50	.60

#	Player		
108	Michael Jordan GH	1.50	.60
109	Michael Jordan GH	1.50	.60
110	Michael Jordan GH	1.50	.60
111	Michael Jordan GH	1.50	.60
112	Michael Jordan GH	1.50	.60
113	Michael Jordan GH	1.50	.60
114	Michael Jordan GH	1.50	.60
115	Michael Jordan GH	1.50	.60
116	Michael Jordan GH	1.50	.60
117	Michael Jordan GH	1.50	.60
118	Michael Jordan GH	1.50	.60
119	Michael Jordan GH	1.50	.60
120	Michael Jordan GH	1.50	.60
121	Elton Brand RC	6.00	2.50
122	Steve Francis RC	6.00	2.50
123	Baron Davis RC	8.00	3.00
124	Lamar Odom RC	5.00	2.00
125	Jonathan Bender RC	3.00	1.25
126	Wally Szczerbiak RC	5.00	2.00
127	Richard Hamilton RC	5.00	2.00
128	Andre Miller RC	5.00	2.00
129	Shawn Marion RC	6.00	2.50
130	Jason Terry RC	4.00	1.50
131	Trajan Langdon RC	2.00	.75
132	A.Radojevic RC	1.00	.40
133	Corey Maggette RC	5.00	2.00
134	William Avery RC	2.00	.75
135	Ron Artest RC	3.00	1.25
136	Cal Bowdler RC	1.50	.60
137	James Posey RC	3.00	1.25
138	Quincy Lewis RC	1.50	.60
139	Dion Glover RC	1.50	.60
140	Jeff Foster RC	1.50	.60
141	Kenny Thomas RC	2.00	.75
142	Devean George RC	2.50	1.00
143	Tim James RC	1.50	.60
144	Vonteego Cummings RC	2.00	.75
145	Jumaine Jones RC	2.00	.75
146	Scott Padgett RC	1.50	.60
147	John Celestand RC	1.50	.60
148	Adrian Griffin RC	1.50	.60
149	Chris Herren RC	1.00	.40
150	Anthony Carter RC	3.00	1.25

2000-01 Ultimate Victory

#	Player		
	COMP.SET w/o SP (60)	25.00	12.50
	COMMON CARD (1-60)	.25	.08
	COMMON KOBE (61-75)	3.00	1.25
	COMMON KG (76-90)	3.00	1.25
	COMMON ROOKIE (91-120)	3.00	1.25
1	Dikembe Mutombo	.50	.20
2	Jim Jackson	.25	.08
3	Paul Pierce	.75	.30
4	Antoine Walker	.75	.30
5	Jamal Mashburn	.50	.20
6	Baron Davis	.75	.30
7	Elton Brand	.75	.30
8	Ron Artest	.50	.20
9	Lamond Murray	.25	.08
10	Andre Miller	.50	.20
11	Michael Finley	.75	.30
12	Dirk Nowitzki	1.25	.50
13	Antonio McDyess	.50	.20
14	Nick Van Exel	.75	.30
15	Jerry Stackhouse	.75	.30
16	Chucky Atkins	.25	.08
17	Antawn Jamison	.75	.30
18	Larry Hughes	.50	.20
19	Steve Francis	.75	.30
20	Hakeem Olajuwon	.75	.30
21	Reggie Miller	.75	.30
22	Jalen Rose	.75	.30
23	Lamar Odom	.75	.30
24	Corey Maggette	.50	.20
25	Shaquille O'Neal	2.00	.75
26	Kobe Bryant	3.00	1.25
27	Ron Harper	.50	.20
28	Tim Hardaway	.50	.20
29	Eddie Jones	.75	.30
30	Ray Allen	.75	.30
31	Tim Thomas	.50	.20
32	Kevin Garnett	1.50	.60
33	Wally Szczerbiak	.50	.20
34	Terrell Brandon	.50	.20
35	Stephon Marbury	.75	.30
36	Keith Van Horn	.75	.30
37	Allan Houston	.50	.20
38	Latrell Sprewell	.75	.30
39	Grant Hill	.75	.30
40	Tracy McGrady	2.00	.75
41	Allen Iverson	1.50	.60
42	Toni Kukoc	.50	.20
43	Jason Kidd	1.25	.50
44	Anfernee Hardaway	.75	.30
45	Scottie Pippen	1.25	.50
46	Rasheed Wallace	.75	.30
47	Jason Williams	.50	.20
48	Chris Webber	.75	.30
49	Tim Duncan	1.50	.60
50	David Robinson	.75	.30
51	Gary Payton	.75	.30
52	Rashard Lewis	.50	.20
53	Vince Carter	2.00	.75
54	Mark Jackson	.25	.08
55	Karl Malone	.75	.30
56	John Stockton	.75	.30
57	Shareef Abdur-Rahim	.75	.30
58	Mike Bibby	.75	.30
59	Mitch Richmond	.50	.20
60	Richard Hamilton	.50	.20
61	Kobe Bryant FLY	3.00	1.25
62	Kobe Bryant FLY	3.00	1.25
63	Kobe Bryant FLY	3.00	1.25
64	Kobe Bryant FLY	3.00	1.25
65	Kobe Bryant FLY	3.00	1.25
66	Kobe Bryant FLY	3.00	1.25
67	Kobe Bryant FLY	3.00	1.25
68	Kobe Bryant FLY	3.00	1.25
69	Kobe Bryant FLY	3.00	1.25
70	Kobe Bryant FLY	3.00	1.25
71	Kobe Bryant FLY	3.00	1.25
72	Kobe Bryant FLY	3.00	1.25
73	Kobe Bryant FLY	3.00	1.25
74	Kobe Bryant FLY	3.00	1.25
75	Kobe Bryant FLY	3.00	1.25
76	Kevin Garnett FLY	3.00	1.25
77	Kevin Garnett FLY	3.00	1.25
78	Kevin Garnett FLY	3.00	1.25
79	Kevin Garnett FLY	3.00	1.25
80	Kevin Garnett FLY	3.00	1.25
81	Kevin Garnett FLY	3.00	1.25
82	Kevin Garnett FLY	3.00	1.25
83	Kevin Garnett FLY	3.00	1.25
84	Kevin Garnett FLY	3.00	1.25
85	Kevin Garnett FLY	3.00	1.25
86	Kevin Garnett FLY	3.00	1.25
87	Kevin Garnett FLY	3.00	1.25
88	Kevin Garnett FLY	3.00	1.25
89	Kevin Garnett FLY	3.00	1.25
90	Kevin Garnett FLY	3.00	1.25
91	Kenyon Martin RC	12.00	5.00
92	Stromile Swift RC	6.00	2.50
93	Darius Miles RC	12.00	5.00
94	Marcus Fizer RC	3.00	1.25
95	Mike Miller RC	10.00	4.00
96	DerMarr Johnson RC	3.00	1.25
97	Chris Mihm RC	3.00	1.25
98	Jamal Crawford RC	4.00	1.50
99	Joel Przybilla RC	3.00	1.25
100	Keyon Dooling RC	3.00	1.25
101	Jerome Moiso RC	3.00	1.25
102	Etan Thomas RC	3.00	1.25
103	Courtney Alexander RC	4.00	1.50
104	Mateen Cleaves RC	3.00	1.25
105	Jason Collier RC	4.00	1.50
106	Hidayet Turkoglu RC	8.00	3.00
107	Desmond Mason RC	3.00	1.25
108	Quentin Richardson RC	8.00	3.00
109	Jamaal Magloire RC	3.00	1.25
110	Speedy Claxton RC	3.00	1.25
111	Morris Peterson RC	6.00	2.50
112	Donnell Harvey RC	3.00	1.25
113	DeShawn Stevenson RC	3.00	1.25
114	Mamadou N'Diaye RC	3.00	1.25
115	Erick Barkley RC	3.00	1.25
116	Mike Smith RC	3.00	1.25
117	Eddie House RC	3.00	1.25
118	Eduardo Najera RC	5.00	2.00
119	Jason Hart RC	3.00	1.25
120	Chris Porter RC	3.00	1.25

1992-93 Ultra

#	Player		
	COMPLETE SET (375)	30.00	15.00
	COMPLETE SERIES 1 (200)	15.00	7.50
	COMPLETE SERIES 2 (175)	15.00	7.50
	COMMON CARD (1-200)	.10	.02
	COMMON CARD (201-375)	.05	.01
1	Stacey Augmon	.10	.02
2	Duane Ferrell	.10	.02
3	Paul Graham	.10	.02
4	Blair Rasmussen	.10	.02
5	Rumeal Robinson	.10	.02
6	Dominique Wilkins	.50	.20
7	Kevin Willis	.10	.02
8	John Bagley	.10	.02
9	Dee Brown	.10	.02
10	Rick Fox	.25	.08
11	Kevin Gamble	.10	.02
12	Joe Kleine	.10	.02
13	Reggie Lewis	.25	.08
14	Kevin McHale	.50	.20
15	Robert Parish	.25	.08
16	Ed Pinckney	.10	.02
17	Muggsy Bogues	.25	.08
18	Dell Curry	.10	.02
19	Kenny Gattison	.10	.02
20	Kendall Gill	.25	.08
21	Larry Johnson	.60	.25
22	Johnny Newman	.10	.02
23	J.R. Reid	.10	.02
24	B.J.Armstrong	.10	.02
25	Bill Cartwright	.10	.02
26	Horace Grant	.25	.08
27	Michael Jordan	6.00	2.50
28	Stacey King	.10	.02
29	John Paxson	.10	.02
30	Will Perdue	.10	.02
31	Scottie Pippen	1.50	.60
32	Scott Williams	.10	.02
33	John Battle	.10	.02
34	Terrell Brandon	.50	.20
35	Brad Daugherty	.10	.02
36	Craig Ehlo	.10	.02
37	Larry Nance	.10	.02
38	Mark Price	.10	.02
39	Mike Sanders	.10	.02
40	John Williams	.10	.02
41	Terry Davis	.10	.02
42	Derek Harper	.25	.08
43	Donald Hodge	.10	.02
44	Mike Iuzzolino	.10	.02
45	Fat Lever	.10	.02

#	Player		
☐ 46	Doug Smith	.10	.02
☐ 47	Randy White	.10	.02
☐ 48	Winston Garland	.10	.02
☐ 49	Chris Jackson	.10	.02
☐ 50	Marcus Liberty	.10	.02
☐ 51	Todd Lichti	.10	.02
☐ 52	Mark Macon	.10	.02
☐ 53	Dikembe Mutombo	.60	.25
☐ 54	Reggie Williams	.10	.02
☐ 55	Mark Aguirre	.10	.02
☐ 56	Joe Dumars	.50	.20
☐ 57	Bill Laimbeer	.25	.08
☐ 58	Dennis Rodman	1.00	.40
☐ 59	Isiah Thomas	.50	.20
☐ 60	Darrell Walker	.10	.02
☐ 61	Orlando Woolridge	.10	.02
☐ 62	Victor Alexander	.10	.02
☐ 63	Chris Gatling	.10	.02
☐ 64	Tim Hardaway	.60	.25
☐ 65	Tyrone Hill	.10	.02
☐ 66	Sarunas Marciulionis	.10	.02
☐ 67	Chris Mullin	.50	.20
☐ 68	Billy Owens	.25	.08
☐ 69	Sleepy Floyd	.10	.02
☐ 70	Avery Johnson	.10	.02
☐ 71	Vernon Maxwell	.10	.02
☐ 72	Hakeem Olajuwon	.75	.30
☐ 73	Kenny Smith	.10	.02
☐ 74	Otis Thorpe	.25	.08
☐ 75	Dale Davis	.10	.02
☐ 76	Vern Fleming	.10	.02
☐ 77	George McCloud	.10	.02
☐ 78	Reggie Miller	.50	.20
☐ 79	Detlef Schrempf	.25	.08
☐ 80	Rik Smits	.25	.08
☐ 81	LaSalle Thompson	.10	.02
☐ 82	Gary Grant	.10	.02
☐ 83	Ron Harper	.25	.08
☐ 84	Mark Jackson	.25	.08
☐ 85	Danny Manning	.10	.02
☐ 86	Ken Norman	.10	.02
☐ 87	Stanley Roberts	.10	.02
☐ 88	Loy Vaught	.10	.02
☐ 89	Elden Campbell	.25	.08
☐ 90	Vlade Divac	.25	.08
☐ 91	A.C. Green	.25	.08
☐ 92	Sam Perkins	.25	.08
☐ 93	Byron Scott	.25	.08
☐ 94	Tony Smith	.10	.02
☐ 95	Sedale Threatt	.10	.02
☐ 96	James Worthy	.50	.20
☐ 97	Willie Burton	.10	.02
☐ 98	Bimbo Coles	.10	.02
☐ 99	Kevin Edwards	.10	.02
☐ 100	Grant Long	.10	.02
☐ 101	Glen Rice	.50	.20
☐ 102	Rony Seikaly	.10	.02
☐ 103	Brian Shaw	.10	.02
☐ 104	Steve Smith	.60	.25
☐ 105	Frank Brickowski	.10	.02
☐ 106	Moses Malone	.50	.20
☐ 107	Fred Roberts	.10	.02
☐ 108	Alvin Robertson	.10	.02
☐ 109	Thurl Bailey	.10	.02
☐ 110	Gerald Glass	.10	.02
☐ 111	Luc Longley	.25	.08
☐ 112	Felton Spencer	.10	.02
☐ 113	Doug West	.10	.02
☐ 114	Kenny Anderson	.50	.20
☐ 115	Mookie Blaylock	.25	.08
☐ 116	Sam Bowie	.10	.02
☐ 117	Derrick Coleman	.25	.08
☐ 118	Chris Dudley	.10	.02
☐ 119	Chris Morris	.10	.02
☐ 120	Drazen Petrovic	.25	.08
☐ 121	Greg Anthony	.10	.02
☐ 122	Patrick Ewing	.50	.20
☐ 123	Anthony Mason	.50	.20
☐ 124	Charles Oakley	.25	.08
☐ 125	Doc Rivers	.25	.08
☐ 126	Charles Smith	.10	.02
☐ 127	John Starks	.25	.08
☐ 128	Nick Anderson	.25	.08
☐ 129	Anthony Bowie	.10	.02
☐ 130	Terry Catledge	.10	.02
☐ 131	Jerry Reynolds	.10	.02
☐ 132	Dennis Scott	.25	.08
☐ 133	Scott Skiles	.10	.02
☐ 134	Brian Williams	.10	.02
☐ 135	Ron Anderson	.10	.02
☐ 136	Manute Bol	.10	.02
☐ 137	Johnny Dawkins	.10	.02
☐ 138	Armon Gilliam	.10	.02
☐ 139	Hersey Hawkins	.25	.08
☐ 140	Jeff Ruland	.10	.02
☐ 141	Charles Shackleford	.10	.02
☐ 142	Cedric Ceballos	.25	.08
☐ 143	Tom Chambers	.10	.02
☐ 144	Kevin Johnson	.50	.20
☐ 145	Negele Knight	.10	.02
☐ 146	Dan Majerle	.25	.08
☐ 147	Mark West	.10	.02
☐ 148	Mark Bryant	.10	.02
☐ 149	Clyde Drexler	.50	.20
☐ 150	Kevin Duckworth	.10	.02
☐ 151	Jerome Kersey	.10	.02
☐ 152	Robert Pack	.10	.02
☐ 153	Terry Porter	.10	.02
☐ 154	Cliff Robinson	.25	.08
☐ 155	Buck Williams	.25	.08
☐ 156	Anthony Bonner	.10	.02
☐ 157	Duane Causwell	.10	.02
☐ 158	Mitch Richmond	.50	.20
☐ 159	Lionel Simmons	.10	.02
☐ 160	Wayman Tisdale	.10	.02
☐ 161	Spud Webb	.25	.08
☐ 162	Willie Anderson	.10	.02
☐ 163	Antoine Carr	.10	.02
☐ 164	Terry Cummings	.25	.08
☐ 165	Sean Elliott	.25	.08
☐ 166	Sidney Green	.10	.02
☐ 167	David Robinson	.75	.30
☐ 168	Dana Barros	.10	.02
☐ 169	Benoit Benjamin	.10	.02
☐ 170	Michael Cage	.10	.02
☐ 171	Eddie Johnson	.10	.02
☐ 172	Shawn Kemp	1.00	.40
☐ 173	Derrick McKey	.10	.02
☐ 174	Nate McMillan	.10	.02
☐ 175	Gary Payton	1.00	.40
☐ 176	Ricky Pierce	.10	.02
☐ 177	David Benoit	.10	.02
☐ 178	Mike Brown	.10	.02
☐ 179	Tyrone Corbin	.10	.02
☐ 180	Mark Eaton	.10	.02
☐ 181	Jeff Malone	.10	.02
☐ 182	Karl Malone	.75	.30
☐ 183	John Stockton	.50	.20
☐ 184	Michael Adams	.10	.02
☐ 185	Ledell Eackles	.10	.02
☐ 186	Pervis Ellison -	.10	.02
☐ 187	A.J. English	.10	.02
☐ 188	Harvey Grant	.10	.02
☐ 189	Buck Johnson	.10	.02
☐ 190	LaBradford Smith	.10	.02
☐ 191	Larry Stewart	.10	.02
☐ 192	David Wingate	.10	.02
☐ 193	Alonzo Mourning RC	2.00	.75
☐ 194	Adam Keefe RC	.10	.02
☐ 195	Robert Horry RC	.50	.20
☐ 196	Anthony Peeler RC	.25	.08
☐ 197	Tracy Murray RC	.25	.08
☐ 198	Dave Johnson RC	.10	.02
☐ 199	Checklist 1-104	.10	.02
☐ 200	Checklist 105-200	.10	.02
☐ 201	David Robinson JS	.30	.10
☐ 202	Dikembe Mutombo JS	.30	.10
☐ 203	Otis Thorpe JS	.05	.01
☐ 204	Hakeem Olajuwon JS	.30	.10
☐ 205	Shawn Kemp JS	.50	.20
☐ 206	Charles Barkley JS	.30	.10
☐ 207	Pervis Ellison JS	.05	.01
☐ 208	Chris Morris JS	.05	.01
☐ 209	Brad Daugherty JS	.05	.01
☐ 210	Derrick Coleman JS	.05	.01
☐ 211	Tim Perry JS	.05	.01
☐ 212	Duane Causwell JS	.05	.01
☐ 213	Scottie Pippen JS	.50	.20
☐ 214	Robert Parish JS	.05	.01
☐ 215	Stacey Augmon JS	.05	.01
☐ 216	Michael Jordan JS	2.00	.75
☐ 217	Karl Malone JS	.30	.10
☐ 218	John Williams JS	.05	.01
☐ 219	Horace Grant JS	.05	.01
☐ 220	Orlando Woolridge JS	.05	.01
☐ 221	Mookie Blaylock	.15	.05
☐ 222	Greg Foster	.05	.01
☐ 223	Steve Henson	.05	.01
☐ 224	Adam Keefe	.05	.01
☐ 225	Jon Koncak	.05	.01
☐ 226	Travis Mays	.05	.01
☐ 227	Alaa Abdelnaby	.05	.01
☐ 228	Sherman Douglas	.05	.01
☐ 229	Xavier McDaniel	.05	.01
☐ 230	Marcus Webb RC	.05	.01
☐ 231	Tony Bennett RC	.05	.01
☐ 232	Mike Gminski	.05	.01
☐ 233	Kevin Lynch	.05	.01
☐ 234	Alonzo Mourning	.75	.30
☐ 235	David Wingate	.05	.01
☐ 236	Rodney McCray	.05	.01
☐ 237	Trent Tucker	.05	.01
☐ 238	Corey Williams RC	.05	.01
☐ 239	Danny Ferry	.05	.01
☐ 240	Jay Guidinger RC	.05	.01
☐ 241	Jerome Lane	.05	.01
☐ 242	Bobby Phills RC	.30	.10
☐ 243	Gerald Wilkins	.05	.01
☐ 244	Walter Bond RC	.05	.01
☐ 245	Dexter Cambridge RC	.05	.01
☐ 246	Radisav Curcic RC	.05	.01
☐ 247	Brian Howard RC	.05	.01
☐ 248	Tracy Moore RC	.05	.01
☐ 249	Sean Rooks RC	.05	.01
☐ 250	Kevin Brooks	.05	.01
☐ 251	LaPhonso Ellis RC	.30	.10
☐ 252	Scott Hastings	.05	.01
☐ 253	Robert Pack	.05	.01
☐ 254	Gary Plummer RC	.05	.01
☐ 255	Bryant Stith RC	.15	.05
☐ 256	Robert Werdann RC	.05	.01
☐ 257	Gerald Glass	.05	.01
☐ 258	Terry Mills	.05	.01
☐ 259	Olden Polynice	.05	.01
☐ 260	Danny Young	.05	.01
☐ 261	Jud Buechler	.05	.01
☐ 262	Jeff Grayer	.05	.01
☐ 263	Byron Houston RC	.05	.01
☐ 264	Keith Jennings RC	.05	.01
☐ 265	Ed Nealy	.05	.01
☐ 266	Latrell Sprewell RC	2.50	1.00
☐ 267	Scott Brooks	.05	.01
☐ 268	Matt Bullard	.05	.01
☐ 269	Winston Garland	.05	.01
☐ 270	Carl Herrera	.05	.01
☐ 271	Robert Horry	.30	.10
☐ 272	Tree Rollins	.05	.01
☐ 273	Greg Dreiling	.05	.01
☐ 274	Sean Green	.05	.01
☐ 275	Sam Mitchell	.05	.01
☐ 276	Pooh Richardson	.05	.01
☐ 277	Malik Sealy RC	.15	.05
☐ 278	Kenny Williams	.05	.01
☐ 279	Mark Jackson	.15	.05
☐ 280	Stanley Roberts	.05	.01
☐ 281	Elmore Spencer RC	.05	.01
☐ 282	Kiki Vandeweghe	.05	.01
☐ 283	John S. Williams	.05	.01
☐ 284	Randy Woods RC	.05	.01
☐ 285	Alex Blackwell RC	.05	.01
☐ 286	Duane Cooper RC	.05	.01
☐ 287	James Edwards	.05	.01
☐ 288	Jack Haley	.05	.01
☐ 289	Anthony Peeler	.15	.05
☐ 290	Keith Askins	.05	.01
☐ 291	Matt Geiger RC	.15	.05
☐ 292	Alec Kessler	.05	.01
☐ 293	Harold Miner RC w/Jordan	.15	.05
☐ 294	John Salley	.05	.01
☐ 295	Anthony Avent RC	.05	.01
☐ 296	Jon Barry RC	.15	.05
☐ 297	Todd Day RC	.15	.05
☐ 298	Blue Edwards	.05	.01
☐ 299	Brad Lohaus	.05	.01
☐ 300	Lee Mayberry RC	.05	.01
☐ 301	Eric Murdock	.05	.01
☐ 302	Danny Schayes	.05	.01
☐ 303	Lance Blanks	.05	.01

☐ 304 Christian Laettner RC	.60	.25
☐ 305 Marlon Maxey RC	.05	.01
☐ 306 Bob McCann RC	.05	.01
☐ 307 Chuck Person	.05	.01
☐ 308 Brad Sellers	.05	.01
☐ 309 Chris Smith RC	.05	.01
☐ 310 Gundars Vetra RC	.05	.01
☐ 311 Micheal Williams	.05	.01
☐ 312 Rafael Addison	.05	.01
☐ 313 Chucky Brown	.05	.01
☐ 314 Maurice Cheeks	.05	.01
☐ 315 Tate George	.05	.01
☐ 316 Rick Mahorn	.05	.01
☐ 317 Rumeal Robinson	.05	.01
☐ 318 Eric Anderson RC	.05	.01
☐ 319 Rolando Blackman	.05	.01
☐ 320 Tony Campbell	.05	.01
☐ 321 Hubert Davis RC	.15	.05
☐ 322 Doc Rivers	.15	.05
☐ 323 Charles Smith	.05	.01
☐ 324 Herb Williams	.05	.01
☐ 325 Litteral Green RC	.05	.01
☐ 326 Steve Kerr	.15	.05
☐ 327 Greg Kite	.05	.01
☐ 328 Shaquille O'Neal RC	10.00	4.00
☐ 329 Tom Tolbert	.05	.01
☐ 330 Jeff Turner	.05	.01
☐ 331 Greg Grant	.05	.01
☐ 332 Jeff Hornacek	.15	.05
☐ 333 Andrew Lang	.05	.01
☐ 334 Tim Perry	.05	.01
☐ 335 C'Weatherspoon RC	.30	.10
☐ 336 Danny Ainge	.15	.05
☐ 337 Charles Barkley	.50	.20
☐ 338 Richard Dumas RC	.05	.01
☐ 339 Frank Johnson	.05	.01
☐ 340 Tim Kempton	.05	.01
☐ 341 Oliver Miller RC	.15	.05
☐ 342 Jerrod Mustaf	.05	.01
☐ 343 Mario Elie	.15	.05
☐ 344 Dave Johnson	.05	.01
☐ 345 Tracy Murray	.15	.05
☐ 346 Rod Strickland	.30	.10
☐ 347 Randy Brown	.05	.01
☐ 348 Pete Chilcutt	.05	.01
☐ 349 Marty Conlon	.05	.01
☐ 350 Jim Les	.05	.01
☐ 351 Kurt Rambis	.05	.01
☐ 352 Walt Williams RC	.30	.10
☐ 353 Lloyd Daniels RC	.05	.01
☐ 354 Vinny Del Negro	.05	.01
☐ 355 Dale Ellis	.05	.01
☐ 356 Avery Johnson	.05	.01
☐ 357 Sam Mack RC	.15	.05
☐ 358 J.R. Reid	.05	.01
☐ 359 David Wood	.05	.01
☐ 360 Vincent Askew	.05	.01
☐ 361 Isaac Austin RC	.15	.05
☐ 362 John Crotty RC	.05	.01
☐ 363 Stephen Howard RC	.05	.01
☐ 364 Jay Humphries	.05	.01
☐ 365 Larry Krystkowiak	.05	.01
☐ 366 Rex Chapman	.05	.01
☐ 367 Tom Gugliotta RC	1.00	.40
☐ 368 Buck Johnson	.05	.01
☐ 369 Charles Jones	.05	.01
☐ 370 Don MacLean RC	.05	.01
☐ 371 Doug Overton	.05	.01
☐ 372 Brent Price RC	.15	.05
☐ 373 Checklist 201-266	.05	.01
☐ 374 Checklist 267-330	.05	.01
☐ 375 Checklist 331-375	.05	.01
☐ JS207 Pervis Ellison AU	25.00	10.00
☐ JS212 Duane Causwell AU	25.00	10.00
☐ JS215 Stacey Augmon AU	30.00	15.00
☐ NNO Jam Session Rank 1-10	2.50	1.00
☐ NNO Jam Session Rank 11-20	2.50	1.00

1993-94 Ultra

☐ COMPLETE SET (375)	30.00	15.00
☐ COMPLETE SERIES 1 (200)	15.00	7.50
☐ COMPLETE SERIES 2 (175)	15.00	7.50
☐ 1 Stacey Augmon	.05	.02
☐ 2 Mookie Blaylock	.15	.05
☐ 3 Doug Edwards RC	.05	.02
☐ 4 Duane Ferrell	.05	.02

☐ 5 Paul Graham	.05	.02
☐ 6 Adam Keefe	.05	.02
☐ 7 Dominique Wilkins	.30	.10
☐ 8 Kevin Willis	.05	.02
☐ 9 Alaa Abdelnaby	.05	.02
☐ 10 Dee Brown	.05	.02
☐ 11 Sherman Douglas	.05	.02
☐ 12 Rick Fox	.05	.02
☐ 13 Kevin Gamble	.05	.02
☐ 14 Xavier McDaniel	.05	.02
☐ 15 Robert Parish	.15	.05
☐ 16 Muggsy Bogues	.15	.05
☐ 17 Scott Burrell RC	.30	.10
☐ 18 Dell Curry	.05	.02
☐ 19 Kenny Gattison	.05	.02
☐ 20 Hersey Hawkins	.15	.05
☐ 21 Eddie Johnson	.05	.02
☐ 22 Larry Johnson	.15	.05
☐ 23 Alonzo Mourning	.50	.20
☐ 24 Johnny Newman	.05	.02
☐ 25 David Wingate	.05	.02
☐ 26 B.J. Armstrong	.05	.02
☐ 27 Corie Blount RC	.05	.02
☐ 28 Bill Cartwright	.05	.02
☐ 29 Horace Grant	.15	.05
☐ 30 Michael Jordan	4.00	1.50
☐ 31 Stacey King	.05	.02
☐ 32 John Paxson	.05	.02
☐ 33 Will Perdue	.05	.02
☐ 34 Scottie Pippen	1.00	.40
☐ 35 Terrell Brandon	.15	.05
☐ 36 Brad Daugherty	.05	.02
☐ 37 Danny Ferry	.05	.02
☐ 38 Chris Mills RC	.30	.10
☐ 39 Larry Nance	.05	.02
☐ 40 Mark Price	.05	.02
☐ 41 Gerald Wilkins	.05	.02
☐ 42 John Williams	.05	.02
☐ 43 Terry Davis	.05	.02
☐ 44 Derek Harper	.05	.02
☐ 45 Donald Hodge	.05	.02
☐ 46 Jim Jackson	.15	.05
☐ 47 Sean Rooks	.05	.02
☐ 48 Doug Smith	.05	.02
☐ 49 Mahmoud Abdul-Rauf	.05	.02
☐ 50 LaPhonso Ellis	.05	.02
☐ 51 Mark Macon	.05	.02
☐ 52 Dikembe Mutombo	.30	.10
☐ 53 Bryant Stith	.05	.02
☐ 54 Reggie Williams	.05	.02
☐ 55 Mark Aguirre	.05	.02
☐ 56 Joe Dumars	.30	.10
☐ 57 Bill Laimbeer	.05	.02
☐ 58 Terry Mills	.05	.02
☐ 59 Olden Polynice	.05	.02
☐ 60 Alvin Robertson	.05	.02
☐ 61 Sean Elliott	.15	.05
☐ 62 Isiah Thomas	.30	.10
☐ 63 Victor Alexander	.05	.02
☐ 64 Chris Gatling	.05	.02
☐ 65 Tim Hardaway	.30	.10
☐ 66 Byron Houston	.05	.02
☐ 67 Sarunas Marciulionis	.05	.02
☐ 68 Chris Mullin	.30	.10
☐ 69 Billy Owens	.05	.02
☐ 70 Latrell Sprewell	.75	.30
☐ 71 Matt Bullard	.05	.02
☐ 72 Sam Cassell RC	1.25	.50

☐ 73 Carl Herrera	.05	.02
☐ 74 Robert Horry	.15	.05
☐ 75 Vernon Maxwell	.05	.02
☐ 76 Hakeem Olajuwon	.50	.20
☐ 77 Kenny Smith	.05	.02
☐ 78 Otis Thorpe	.15	.05
☐ 79 Dale Davis	.05	.02
☐ 80 Vern Fleming	.05	.02
☐ 81 Reggie Miller	.30	.10
☐ 82 Sam Mitchell	.05	.02
☐ 83 Pooh Richardson	.05	.02
☐ 84 Detlef Schrempf	.15	.05
☐ 85 Rik Smits	.15	.05
☐ 86 Ron Harper	.15	.05
☐ 87 Mark Jackson	.15	.05
☐ 88 Danny Manning	.15	.05
☐ 89 Stanley Roberts	.05	.02
☐ 90 Loy Vaught	.05	.02
☐ 91 John Williams	.05	.02
☐ 92 Sam Bowie	.05	.02
☐ 93 Doug Christie	.15	.05
☐ 94 Vlade Divac	.15	.05
☐ 95 George Lynch RC	.05	.02
☐ 96 Anthony Peeler	.05	.02
☐ 97 James Worthy	.30	.10
☐ 98 Bimbo Coles	.05	.02
☐ 99 Grant Long	.05	.02
☐ 100 Harold Miner	.05	.02
☐ 101 Glen Rice	.15	.05
☐ 102 Rony Seikaly	.05	.02
☐ 103 Brian Shaw	.05	.02
☐ 104 Steve Smith	.30	.10
☐ 105 Anthony Avent	.05	.02
☐ 106 Vin Baker RC	.75	.30
☐ 107 Frank Brickowski	.05	.02
☐ 108 Todd Day	.05	.02
☐ 109 Blue Edwards	.05	.02
☐ 110 Lee Mayberry	.05	.02
☐ 111 Eric Murdock	.05	.02
☐ 112 Orlando Woolridge	.05	.02
☐ 113 Thurl Bailey	.05	.02
☐ 114 Christian Laettner	.15	.05
☐ 115 Chuck Person	.05	.02
☐ 116 Doug West	.05	.02
☐ 117 Micheal Williams	.05	.02
☐ 118 Kenny Anderson	.15	.05
☐ 119 Derrick Coleman	.15	.05
☐ 120 Rick Mahorn	.05	.02
☐ 121 Chris Morris	.05	.02
☐ 122 Rumeal Robinson	.05	.02
☐ 123 Rex Walters RC	.05	.02
☐ 124 Greg Anthony	.05	.02
☐ 125 Rolando Blackman	.05	.02
☐ 126 Hubert Davis	.05	.02
☐ 127 Patrick Ewing	.30	.10
☐ 128 Anthony Mason	.15	.05
☐ 129 Charles Oakley	.15	.05
☐ 130 Doc Rivers	.15	.05
☐ 131 Charles Smith	.05	.02
☐ 132 John Starks	.15	.05
☐ 133 Nick Anderson	.15	.05
☐ 134 Anthony Bowie	.05	.02
☐ 135 Shaquille O'Neal	1.50	.60
☐ 136 Dennis Scott	.05	.02
☐ 137 Scott Skiles	.05	.02
☐ 138 Jeff Turner	.05	.02
☐ 139 Shawn Bradley RC	.30	.10
☐ 140 Johnny Dawkins	.05	.02
☐ 141 Jeff Hornacek	.15	.05
☐ 142 Tim Perry	.05	.02
☐ 143 Clarence Weatherspoon	.15	.05
☐ 144 Danny Ainge	.15	.05
☐ 145 Charles Barkley	.50	.20
☐ 146 Cedric Ceballos	.15	.05
☐ 147 Kevin Johnson	.15	.05
☐ 148 Negele Knight	.05	.02
☐ 149 Malcolm Mackey RC	.05	.02
☐ 150 Dan Majerle	.15	.05
☐ 151 Oliver Miller	.05	.02
☐ 152 Mark West	.05	.02
☐ 153 Mark Bryant	.05	.02
☐ 154 Clyde Drexler	.30	.10
☐ 155 Jerome Kersey	.05	.02
☐ 156 Terry Porter	.05	.02
☐ 157 Cliff Robinson	.15	.05
☐ 158 Rod Strickland	.15	.05

❑ 159	Buck Williams	.05	.02
❑ 160	Duane Causwell	.05	.02
❑ 161	Bobby Hurley RC	.15	.05
❑ 162	Mitch Richmond	.30	.10
❑ 163	Lionel Simmons	.05	.02
❑ 164	Wayman Tisdale	.05	.02
❑ 165	Spud Webb	.15	.05
❑ 166	Walt Williams	.05	.02
❑ 167	Willie Anderson	.05	.02
❑ 168	Antoine Carr	.05	.02
❑ 169	Lloyd Daniels	.05	.02
❑ 170	Dennis Rodman	.60	.25
❑ 171	Dale Ellis	.05	.02
❑ 172	Avery Johnson	.05	.02
❑ 173	J.R. Reid	.05	.02
❑ 174	David Robinson	.50	.20
❑ 175	Michael Cage	.05	.02
❑ 176	Kendall Gill	.15	.05
❑ 177	Ervin Johnson RC	.15	.05
❑ 178	Shawn Kemp	.50	.20
❑ 179	Derrick McKey	.05	.02
❑ 180	Nate McMillan	.05	.02
❑ 181	Gary Payton	.50	.20
❑ 182	Sam Perkins	.15	.05
❑ 183	Ricky Pierce	.05	.02
❑ 184	David Benoit	.05	.02
❑ 185	Tyrone Corbin	.05	.02
❑ 186	Mark Eaton	.05	.02
❑ 187	Jay Humphries	.05	.02
❑ 188	Jeff Malone	.05	.02
❑ 189	Karl Malone	.50	.20
❑ 190	John Stockton	.30	.10
❑ 191	Luther Wright RC	.05	.02
❑ 192	Michael Adams	.05	.02
❑ 193	Calbert Cheaney RC	.15	.05
❑ 194	Pervis Ellison	.05	.02
❑ 195	Tom Gugliotta	.30	.10
❑ 196	Buck Johnson	.05	.02
❑ 197	LaBradford Smith	.05	.02
❑ 198	Larry Stewart	.05	.02
❑ 199	Checklist	.05	.02
❑ 200	Checklist	.05	.02
❑ 201	Doug Edwards	.05	.02
❑ 202	Craig Ehlo	.05	.02
❑ 203	Jon Koncak	.05	.02
❑ 204	Andrew Lang	.05	.02
❑ 205	Ennis Whatley	.05	.02
❑ 206	Chris Corchiani	.05	.02
❑ 207	Acie Earl RC	.05	.02
❑ 208	Jimmy Oliver	.05	.02
❑ 209	Ed Pinckney	.05	.02
❑ 210	Dino Radja RC	.30	.10
❑ 211	Matt Wenstrom RC	.05	.02
❑ 212	Tony Bennett	.05	.02
❑ 213	Scott Burrell	.30	.10
❑ 214	LeRon Ellis	.05	.02
❑ 215	Hersey Hawkins	.15	.05
❑ 216	Eddie Johnson	.05	.02
❑ 217	Rumeal Robinson	.05	.02
❑ 218	Corie Blount	.05	.02
❑ 219	Dave Johnson	.05	.02
❑ 220	Steve Kerr	.15	.05
❑ 221	Toni Kukoc RC	1.25	.50
❑ 222	Pete Myers	.05	.02
❑ 223	Bill Wennington	.05	.02
❑ 224	Scott Williams	.05	.02
❑ 225	John Battle	.05	.02
❑ 226	Tyrone Hill	.05	.02
❑ 227	Gerald Madkins RC	.05	.02
❑ 228	Chris Mills	.30	.10
❑ 229	Bobby Phills	.05	.02
❑ 230	Greg Dreiling	.05	.02
❑ 231	Lucious Harris RC	.05	.02
❑ 232	Popeye Jones RC	.05	.02
❑ 233	Tim Legler RC	.05	.02
❑ 234	Fat Lever	.05	.02
❑ 235	Jamal Mashburn RC	.75	.30
❑ 236	Tom Hammonds	.05	.02
❑ 237	Darnell Mee RC	.05	.02
❑ 238	Robert Pack	.05	.02
❑ 239	Rodney Rogers RC	.30	.10
❑ 240	Brian Williams	.05	.02
❑ 241	Greg Anderson	.05	.02
❑ 242	Sean Elliott	.15	.05
❑ 243	Allan Houston RC	1.25	.50
❑ 244	Lindsey Hunter RC	.30	.10

❑ 245	Mark Macon	.05	.02
❑ 246	David Wood	.05	.02
❑ 247	Jud Buechler	.05	.02
❑ 248	Josh Grant RC	.05	.02
❑ 249	Jeff Grayer	.05	.02
❑ 250	Keith Jennings	.05	.02
❑ 251	Avery Johnson	.05	.02
❑ 252	Chris Webber RC	3.00	1.25
❑ 253	Scott Brooks	.05	.02
❑ 254	Sam Cassell	.30	.10
❑ 255	Mario Elie	.05	.02
❑ 256	Richard Petruska RC	.05	.02
❑ 257	Eric Riley RC	.05	.02
❑ 258	Antonio Davis RC	.40	.15
❑ 259	Scott Haskin RC	.05	.02
❑ 260	Derrick McKey	.05	.02
❑ 261	Byron Scott	.15	.05
❑ 262	Malik Sealy	.05	.02
❑ 263	Kenny Williams	.05	.02
❑ 264	Haywoode Workman	.05	.02
❑ 265	Mark Aguirre	.05	.02
❑ 266	Terry Dehere RC	.05	.02
❑ 267	Harold Ellis RC	.05	.02
❑ 268	Gary Grant	.05	.02
❑ 269	Bob Martin RC	.05	.02
❑ 270	Elmore Spencer	.05	.02
❑ 271	Tom Tolbert	.05	.02
❑ 272	Sam Bowie	.05	.02
❑ 273	Elden Campbell	.05	.02
❑ 274	Antonio Harvey RC	.05	.02
❑ 275	George Lynch	.05	.02
❑ 276	Tony Smith	.05	.02
❑ 277	Sedale Threatt	.05	.02
❑ 278	Nick Van Exel RC	1.00	.40
❑ 279	Willie Burton	.05	.02
❑ 280	Matt Geiger	.05	.02
❑ 281	John Salley	.05	.02
❑ 282	Vin Baker	.40	.15
❑ 283	Jon Barry	.05	.02
❑ 284	Brad Lohaus	.05	.02
❑ 285	Ken Norman	.05	.02
❑ 286	Derek Strong RC	.05	.02
❑ 287	Mike Brown	.05	.02
❑ 288	Brian Davis RC	.05	.02
❑ 289	Tellis Frank	.05	.02
❑ 290	Luc Longley	.15	.05
❑ 291	Marlon Maxey	.05	.02
❑ 292	Isaiah Rider RC	.60	.25
❑ 293	Chris Smith	.05	.02
❑ 294	P.J.Brown RC	.30	.10
❑ 295	Kevin Edwards	.05	.02
❑ 296	Armon Gilliam	.05	.02
❑ 297	Johnny Newman	.05	.02
❑ 298	Rex Walters	.05	.02
❑ 299	David Wesley RC	.30	.10
❑ 300	Jayson Williams	.15	.05
❑ 301	Anthony Bonner	.05	.02
❑ 302	Derek Harper	.15	.05
❑ 303	Herb Williams	.05	.02
❑ 304	Litterial Green	.05	.02
❑ 305	Anfernee Hardaway RC	2.50	1.00
❑ 306	Greg Kite	.05	.02
❑ 307	Larry Krystkowiak	.05	.02
❑ 308	Keith Tower RC	.05	.02
❑ 309	Dana Barros	.05	.02
❑ 310	Shawn Bradley	.30	.10
❑ 311	Greg Graham RC	.05	.02
❑ 312	Sean Green	.05	.02
❑ 313	Warren Kidd RC	.05	.02
❑ 314	Eric Leckner	.05	.02
❑ 315	Moses Malone	.30	.10
❑ 316	Orlando Woolridge	.05	.02
❑ 317	Duane Cooper	.05	.02
❑ 318	Joe Courtney RC	.05	.02
❑ 319	A.C. Green	.15	.05
❑ 320	Frank Johnson	.05	.02
❑ 321	Joe Kleine	.05	.02
❑ 322	Chris Dudley	.05	.02
❑ 323	Harvey Grant	.05	.02
❑ 324	Jaren Jackson	.05	.02
❑ 325	Tracy Murray	.05	.02
❑ 326	James Robinson RC	.05	.02
❑ 327	Reggie Smith	.05	.02
❑ 328	Kevin Thompson RC	.05	.02
❑ 329	Randy Brown	.05	.02
❑ 330	Evers Burns RC	.05	.02

❑ 331	Pete Chilcutt	.05	.02
❑ 332	Bobby Hurley	.15	.05
❑ 333	Mike Peplowski RC	.05	.02
❑ 334	LaBradford Smith	.05	.02
❑ 335	Trevor Wilson	.05	.02
❑ 336	Terry Cummings	.05	.02
❑ 337	Vinny Del Negro	.05	.02
❑ 338	Sleepy Floyd	.05	.02
❑ 339	Negele Knight	.05	.02
❑ 340	Dennis Rodman	.60	.25
❑ 341	Chris Whitney RC	.05	.02
❑ 342	Vincent Askew	.05	.02
❑ 343	Kendall Gill	.15	.05
❑ 344	Ervin Johnson	.15	.05
❑ 345	Chris King RC	.05	.02
❑ 346	Detlef Schrempf	.15	.05
❑ 347	Walter Bond	.05	.02
❑ 348	Tom Chambers	.05	.02
❑ 349	John Crotty	.05	.02
❑ 350	Bryon Russell RC	.30	.10
❑ 351	Felton Spencer	.05	.02
❑ 352	Mitchell Butler RC	.05	.02
❑ 353	Rex Chapman	.05	.02
❑ 354	Calbert Cheaney	.15	.05
❑ 355	Kevin Duckworth	.05	.02
❑ 356	Don MacLean	.05	.02
❑ 357	Gheorghe Muresan RC	.30	.10
❑ 358	Doug Overton	.05	.02
❑ 359	Brent Price	.05	.02
❑ 360	Kenny Walker	.05	.02
❑ 361	Derrick Coleman USA	.05	.02
❑ 362	Joe Dumars USA	.15	.05
❑ 363	Tim Hardaway USA	.15	.05
❑ 364	Larry Johnson USA	.15	.05
❑ 365	Shawn Kemp USA	.40	.15
❑ 366	Dan Majerle USA	.05	.02
❑ 367	Alonzo Mourning USA	.30	.10
❑ 368	Mark Price USA	.05	.02
❑ 369	Steve Smith USA	.15	.05
❑ 370	Isiah Thomas USA	.15	.05
❑ 371	Dominique Wilkins USA	.15	.05
❑ 372	Don Nelson	.15	.05
❑ 373	Jamal Mashburn CL	.30	.10
❑ 374	Checklist	.05	.02
❑ 375	Checklist	.05	.02
❑ M1	Reggie Miller USA	.75	.30
❑ M2	Shaquille O'Neal USA	6.00	2.50
❑ M3	Team Checklist USA	2.00	.75

1994-95 Ultra

❑ COMPLETE SET (350)	35.00	17.50
❑ COMPLETE SERIES 1 (200)	20.00	10.00
❑ COMPLETE SERIES 2 (150)	15.00	7.50
❑ 1 Stacey Augmon	.10	.02
❑ 2 Mookie Blaylock	.10	.02
❑ 3 Craig Ehlo	.10	.02
❑ 4 Adam Keefe	.10	.02
❑ 5 Andrew Lang	.10	.02
❑ 6 Ken Norman	.10	.02
❑ 7 Kevin Willis	.10	.02
❑ 8 Dee Brown	.10	.02
❑ 9 Sherman Douglas	.10	.02
❑ 10 Acie Earl	.10	.02
❑ 11 Pervis Ellison	.10	.02
❑ 12 Rick Fox	.10	.02
❑ 13 Xavier McDaniel	.10	.02
❑ 14 Eric Montross RC	.10	.02
❑ 15 Dino Radja	.10	.02

#	Player		
❑ 16	Dominique Wilkins	.40	.15
❑ 17	Michael Adams	.10	.02
❑ 18	Muggsy Bogues	.15	.05
❑ 19	Dell Curry	.10	.02
❑ 20	Kenny Gattison	.10	.02
❑ 21	Hersey Hawkins	.15	.05
❑ 22	Larry Johnson	.15	.05
❑ 23	Alonzo Mourning	.50	.20
❑ 24	Robert Parish	.15	.05
❑ 25	B.J. Armstrong	.10	.02
❑ 26	Steve Kerr	.10	.02
❑ 27	Toni Kukoc	.60	.25
❑ 28	Luc Longley	.10	.02
❑ 29	Pete Myers	.10	.02
❑ 30	Will Perdue	.10	.02
❑ 31	Scottie Pippen	1.25	.50
❑ 32	Terrell Brandon	.15	.05
❑ 33	Brad Daugherty	.10	.02
❑ 34	Tyrone Hill	.10	.02
❑ 35	Chris Mills	.10	.02
❑ 36	Bobby Phills	.10	.02
❑ 37	Mark Price	.10	.02
❑ 38	Gerald Wilkins	.10	.02
❑ 39	John Williams	.10	.02
❑ 40	Terry Davis	.10	.02
❑ 41	Jim Jackson	.15	.05
❑ 42	Popeye Jones	.10	.02
❑ 43	Jason Kidd RC	4.00	1.50
❑ 44	Jamal Mashburn	.40	.15
❑ 45	Sean Rooks	.10	.02
❑ 46	Doug Smith	.10	.02
❑ 47	Mahmoud Abdul-Rauf	.10	.02
❑ 48	LaPhonso Ellis	.10	.02
❑ 49	Dikembe Mutombo	.15	.05
❑ 50	Robert Pack	.10	.02
❑ 51	Rodney Rogers	.10	.02
❑ 52	Bryant Stith	.10	.02
❑ 53	Brian Williams	.10	.02
❑ 54	Reggie Williams	.10	.02
❑ 55	Greg Anderson	.10	.02
❑ 56	Joe Dumars	.40	.15
❑ 57	Allan Houston	.60	.25
❑ 58	Lindsey Hunter	.15	.05
❑ 59	Terry Mills	.10	.02
❑ 60	Tim Hardaway	.40	.15
❑ 61	Chris Mullin	.40	.15
❑ 62	Billy Owens	.10	.02
❑ 63	Latrell Sprewell	.40	.15
❑ 64	Chris Webber	1.00	.40
❑ 65	Sam Cassell	.40	.15
❑ 66	Carl Herrera	.10	.02
❑ 67	Robert Horry	.15	.05
❑ 68	Vernon Maxwell	.10	.02
❑ 69	Hakeem Olajuwon	.60	.25
❑ 70	Kenny Smith	.10	.02
❑ 71	Otis Thorpe	.10	.02
❑ 72	Antonio Davis	.10	.02
❑ 73	Dale Davis	.10	.02
❑ 74	Mark Jackson	.10	.02
❑ 75	Derrick McKey	.10	.02
❑ 76	Reggie Miller	.40	.15
❑ 77	Byron Scott	.15	.05
❑ 78	Rik Smits	.10	.02
❑ 79	Haywoode Workman	.10	.02
❑ 80	Gary Grant	.10	.02
❑ 81	Ron Harper	.15	.05
❑ 82	Elmore Spencer	.10	.02
❑ 83	Loy Vaught	.10	.02
❑ 84	Elden Campbell	.10	.02
❑ 85	Doug Christie	.15	.05
❑ 86	Vlade Divac	.10	.02
❑ 87	Eddie Jones RC	2.00	.75
❑ 88	George Lynch	.10	.02
❑ 89	Anthony Peeler	.10	.02
❑ 90	Sedale Threatt	.10	.02
❑ 91	Nick Van Exel	.40	.15
❑ 92	James Worthy	.40	.15
❑ 93	Bimbo Coles	.10	.02
❑ 94	Matt Geiger	.10	.02
❑ 95	Grant Long	.10	.02
❑ 96	Harold Miner	.10	.02
❑ 97	Glen Rice	.15	.05
❑ 98	John Salley	.10	.02
❑ 99	Rony Seikaly	.10	.02
❑ 100	Brian Shaw	.10	.02
❑ 101	Steve Smith	.15	.05
❑ 102	Vin Baker	.40	.15
❑ 103	Jon Barry	.10	.02
❑ 104	Todd Day	.10	.02
❑ 105	Lee Mayberry	.10	.02
❑ 106	Eric Murdock	.10	.02
❑ 107	Thurl Bailey	.10	.02
❑ 108	Stacey King	.10	.02
❑ 109	Christian Laettner	.15	.05
❑ 110	Isaiah Rider	.15	.05
❑ 111	Chris Smith	.10	.02
❑ 112	Doug West	.10	.02
❑ 113	Micheal Williams	.10	.02
❑ 114	Kenny Anderson	.15	.05
❑ 115	Benoit Benjamin	.10	.02
❑ 116	P.J. Brown	.10	.02
❑ 117	Derrick Coleman	.15	.05
❑ 118	Yinka Dare RC	.10	.02
❑ 119	Kevin Edwards	.10	.02
❑ 120	Armon Gilliam	.10	.02
❑ 121	Chris Morris	.10	.02
❑ 122	Greg Anthony	.10	.02
❑ 123	Anthony Bonner	.10	.02
❑ 124	Hubert Davis	.10	.02
❑ 125	Patrick Ewing	.40	.15
❑ 126	Derek Harper	.10	.02
❑ 127	Anthony Mason	.15	.05
❑ 128	Charles Oakley	.10	.02
❑ 129	Doc Rivers	.15	.05
❑ 130	John Starks	.10	.02
❑ 131	Nick Anderson	.10	.02
❑ 132	Anthony Avent	.10	.02
❑ 133	Anthony Bowie	.10	.02
❑ 134	Anfernee Hardaway	1.00	.40
❑ 135	Shaquille O'Neal	2.00	.75
❑ 136	Dennis Scott	.10	.02
❑ 137	Jeff Turner	.10	.02
❑ 138	Dana Barros	.10	.02
❑ 139	Shawn Bradley	.10	.02
❑ 140	Greg Graham	.10	.02
❑ 141	Jeff Malone	.10	.02
❑ 142	Tim Perry	.10	.02
❑ 143	Clarence Weatherspoon	.10	.02
❑ 144	Scott Williams	.10	.02
❑ 145	Danny Ainge	.10	.02
❑ 146	Charles Barkley	.60	.25
❑ 147	Cedric Ceballos	.10	.02
❑ 148	A.C. Green	.15	.05
❑ 149	Frank Johnson	.10	.02
❑ 150	Kevin Johnson	.15	.05
❑ 151	Dan Majerle	.15	.05
❑ 152	Oliver Miller	.10	.02
❑ 153	Wesley Person RC	.40	.15
❑ 154	Mark Bryant	.10	.02
❑ 155	Clyde Drexler	.40	.15
❑ 156	Harvey Grant	.10	.02
❑ 157	Jerome Kersey	.10	.02
❑ 158	Tracy Murray	.10	.02
❑ 159	Terry Porter	.10	.02
❑ 160	Clifford Robinson	.15	.05
❑ 161	James Robinson	.10	.02
❑ 162	Rod Strickland	.10	.02
❑ 163	Buck Williams	.10	.02
❑ 164	Duane Causwell	.10	.02
❑ 165	Olden Polynice	.10	.02
❑ 166	Mitch Richmond	.40	.15
❑ 167	Lionel Simmons	.10	.02
❑ 168	Walt Williams	.10	.02
❑ 169	Willie Anderson	.10	.02
❑ 170	Terry Cummings	.15	.05
❑ 171	Sean Elliott	.15	.05
❑ 172	Avery Johnson	.10	.02
❑ 173	J.R. Reid	.10	.02
❑ 174	David Robinson	.60	.25
❑ 175	Dennis Rodman	.75	.30
❑ 176	Kendall Gill	.15	.05
❑ 177	Shawn Kemp	.60	.25
❑ 178	Nate McMillan	.10	.02
❑ 179	Gary Payton	.60	.25
❑ 180	Sam Perkins	.15	.05
❑ 181	Detlef Schrempf	.15	.05
❑ 182	David Benoit	.10	.02
❑ 183	Tyrone Corbin	.10	.02
❑ 184	Jeff Hornacek	.15	.05
❑ 185	Jay Humphries	.10	.02
❑ 186	Karl Malone	.60	.25
❑ 187	Bryon Russell	.10	.02
❑ 188	Felton Spencer	.10	.02
❑ 189	John Stockton	.40	.15
❑ 190	Mitchell Butler	.10	.02
❑ 191	Rex Chapman	.10	.02
❑ 192	Calbert Cheaney	.10	.02
❑ 193	Kevin Duckworth	.10	.02
❑ 194	Tom Gugliotta	.15	.05
❑ 195	Don MacLean	.10	.02
❑ 196	Gheorghe Muresan	.10	.02
❑ 197	Scott Skiles	.10	.02
❑ 198	Checklist	.10	.02
❑ 199	Checklist	.10	.02
❑ 200	Checklist	.10	.02
❑ 201	Tyrone Corbin	.10	.02
❑ 202	Doug Edwards	.10	.02
❑ 203	Jim Les	.10	.02
❑ 204	Grant Long	.10	.02
❑ 205	Ken Norman	.10	.02
❑ 206	Steve Smith	.15	.05
❑ 207	Blue Edwards	.10	.02
❑ 208	Greg Minor RC	.10	.02
❑ 209	Eric Montross	.10	.02
❑ 210	Derek Strong	.10	.02
❑ 211	David Wesley	.10	.02
❑ 212	Tony Bennett	.10	.02
❑ 213	Scott Burrell	.10	.02
❑ 214	Darrin Hancock	.10	.02
❑ 215	Greg Sutton	.10	.02
❑ 216	Corie Blount	.10	.02
❑ 217	Jud Buechler	.10	.02
❑ 218	Ron Harper	.15	.05
❑ 219	Larry Krystkowiak	.10	.02
❑ 220	Dickey Simpkins RC	.10	.02
❑ 221	Bill Wennington	.10	.02
❑ 222	Michael Cage	.10	.02
❑ 223	Tony Campbell	.10	.02
❑ 224	Steve Colter	.10	.02
❑ 225	Greg Dreiling	.10	.02
❑ 226	Danny Ferry	.10	.02
❑ 227	Tony Dumas RC	.10	.02
❑ 228	Lucious Harris	.10	.02
❑ 229	Donald Hodge	.10	.02
❑ 230	Jason Kidd	2.00	.75
❑ 231	Lorenzo Williams	.10	.02
❑ 232	Dale Ellis	.10	.02
❑ 233	Tom Hammonds	.10	.02
❑ 234	Jalen Rose RC	1.50	.60
❑ 235	Reggie Slater	.10	.02
❑ 236	Rafael Addison	.10	.02
❑ 237	Bill Curley RC	.10	.02
❑ 238	Johnny Dawkins	.10	.02
❑ 239	Grant Hill RC	2.00	.75
❑ 240	Eric Leckner	.10	.02
❑ 241	Mark Macon	.10	.02
❑ 242	Oliver Miller	.10	.02
❑ 243	Mark West	.10	.02
❑ 244	Victor Alexander	.10	.02
❑ 245	Chris Gatling	.10	.02
❑ 246	Tom Gugliotta	.15	.05
❑ 247	Keith Jennings	.10	.02
❑ 248	Ricky Pierce	.10	.02
❑ 249	Carlos Rogers RC	.10	.02
❑ 250	Clifford Rozier RC	.10	.02
❑ 251	Rony Seikaly	.10	.02
❑ 252	David Wood	.10	.02
❑ 253	Tim Breaux	.10	.02
❑ 254	Scott Brooks	.10	.02
❑ 255	Zan Tabak	.10	.02
❑ 256	Duane Ferrell	.10	.02
❑ 257	Mark Jackson	.10	.02
❑ 258	Sam Mitchell	.10	.02
❑ 259	John Williams	.10	.02
❑ 260	Terry Dehere	.10	.02
❑ 261	Harold Ellis	.10	.02
❑ 262	Matt Fish	.10	.02
❑ 263	Tony Massenburg	.10	.02
❑ 264	Lamond Murray RC	.15	.05
❑ 265	Bo Outlaw RC	.10	.02
❑ 266	Eric Piatkowski RC	.10	.02
❑ 267	Pooh Richardson	.10	.02
❑ 268	Malik Sealy	.10	.02
❑ 269	Randy Woods	.10	.02
❑ 270	Sam Bowie	.10	.02
❑ 271	Cedric Ceballos	.10	.02
❑ 272	Antonio Harvey	.10	.02
❑ 273	Eddie Jones	1.00	.40

274 Anthony Miller RC	.10	.02
275 Tony Smith	.10	.02
276 Ledell Eackles	.10	.02
277 Kevin Gamble	.10	.02
278 Brad Lohaus	.10	.02
279 Billy Owens	.10	.02
280 Khalid Reeves RC	.10	.02
281 Kevin Willis	.10	.02
282 Marty Conlon	.10	.02
283 Alton Lister	.10	.02
284 Eric Mobley RC	.10	.02
285 Johnny Newman	.10	.02
286 Ed Pinckney	.10	.02
287 Glenn Robinson RC	1.25	.50
288 Howard Eisley	.10	.02
289 Winston Garland	.10	.02
290 Andres Guibert	.10	.02
291 Donyell Marshall RC	.40	.15
292 Sean Rooks	.10	.02
293 Yinka Dare	.10	.02
294 Sleepy Floyd	.10	.02
295 Sean Higgins	.10	.02
296 Rex Walters	.10	.02
297 Jayson Williams	.10	.05
298 Charles Smith	.10	.02
299 Charlie Ward RC	.40	.15
300 Herb Williams	.10	.02
301 Monty Williams RC	.10	.02
302 Horace Grant	.15	.05
303 Geert Hammink	.10	.02
304 Tree Rollins	.10	.02
305 Donald Royal	.10	.02
306 Brian Shaw	.10	.02
307 Brooks Thompson RC	.10	.02
308 Derrick Alston RC	.10	.02
309 Willie Burton	.10	.02
310 Jaren Jackson	.10	.02
311 B.J.Tyler RC	.10	.02
312 Scott Williams	.10	.02
313 Sharone Wright RC	.10	.02
314 Joe Kleine	.10	.02
315 Danny Manning	.15	.05
316 Elliot Perry	.10	.02
317 Wesley Person	.15	.05
318 Trevor Ruffin RC	.10	.02
319 Danny Schayes	.10	.02
320 Wayman Tisdale	.10	.02
321 Chris Dudley	.10	.02
322 James Edwards	.10	.02
323 Alaa Abdelnaby	.10	.02
324 Randy Brown	.10	.02
325 Brian Grant RC	1.00	.40
326 Bobby Hurley	.10	.02
327 Michael Smith RC	.10	.02
328 Henry Turner	.10	.02
329 Trevor Wilson	.10	.02
330 Vinny Del Negro	.10	.02
331 Moses Malone	.40	.15
332 Julius Nwosu	.10	.02
333 Chuck Person	.10	.02
334 Chris Whitney	.10	.02
335 Vincent Askew	.10	.02
336 Bill Cartwright	.10	.02
337 Ervin Johnson	.10	.02
338 Sarunas Marciulionis	.10	.02
339 Antoine Carr	.10	.02
340 Tom Chambers	.10	.02
341 John Crotty	.10	.02
342 Jamie Watson RC	.10	.02
343 Juwan Howard RC	1.00	.40
344 Jim McIlvaine	.10	.02
345 Doug Overton	.10	.02
346 Scott Skiles	.10	.02
347 Anthony Tucker RC	.10	.02
348 Chris Webber	1.00	.40
349 Checklist	.10	.02
350 Checklist	.10	.02

1995-96 Ultra

COMPLETE SET (350)	40.00	20.00
COMPLETE SERIES 1 (200)	20.00	10.00
COMPLETE SERIES 2 (150)	20.00	10.00
1 Stacey Augmon	.25	.08
2 Mookie Blaylock	.25	.08
3 Craig Ehlo	.25	.08
4 Andrew Lang	.25	.08
5 Grant Long	.25	.08
6 Ken Norman	.25	.08
7 Steve Smith	.50	.20
8 Spud Webb	.50	.20
9 Dee Brown	.25	.08
10 Sherman Douglas	.25	.08
11 Pervis Ellison	.25	.08
12 Rick Fox	.50	.20
13 Eric Montross	.25	.08
14 Dino Radja	.25	.08
15 David Wesley	.25	.08
16 Dominique Wilkins	.75	.30
17 Muggsy Bogues	.50	.20
18 Scott Burrell	.25	.08
19 Dell Curry	.25	.08
20 Kendall Gill	.25	.08
21 Larry Johnson	.50	.20
22 Alonzo Mourning	.50	.20
23 Robert Parish	.50	.20
24 Ron Harper	.50	.20
25 Michael Jordan	5.00	2.00
26 Toni Kukoc	.50	.20
27 Will Perdue	.25	.08
28 Scottie Pippen	1.25	.50
29 Terrell Brandon	.50	.20
30 Michael Cage	.25	.08
31 Tyrone Hill	.25	.08
32 Chris Mills	.25	.08
33 Bobby Phills	.25	.08
34 Mark Price	.50	.20
35 John Williams	.25	.08
36 Lucious Harris	.25	.08
37 Jim Jackson	.50	.20
38 Popeye Jones	.25	.08
39 Jason Kidd	2.50	1.00
40 Jamal Mashburn	.50	.20
41 George McCloud	.25	.08
42 Roy Tarpley	.25	.08
43 Lorenzo Williams	.25	.08
44 Mahmoud Abdul-Rauf	.25	.08
45 Dikembe Mutombo	.50	.20
46 Robert Pack	.25	.08
47 Jalen Rose	1.00	.40
48 Bryant Stith	.25	.08
49 Brian Williams	.25	.08
50 Reggie Williams	.25	.08
51 Joe Dumars	.75	.30
52 Grant Hill	1.00	.40
53 Allan Houston	.50	.20
54 Lindsey Hunter	.25	.08
55 Terry Mills	.25	.08
56 Mark West	.25	.08
57 Chris Gatling	.25	.08
58 Tim Hardaway	.50	.20
59 Donyell Marshall	.50	.20
60 Chris Mullin	.75	.30
61 Carlos Rogers	.25	.08
62 Clifford Rozier	.25	.08
63 Rony Seikaly	.25	.08
64 Latrell Sprewell	.75	.30
65 Sam Cassell	.25	.08
66 Clyde Drexler	.75	.30
67 Mario Elie	.25	.08
68 Carl Herrera	.25	.08
69 Robert Horry	.50	.20
70 Hakeem Olajuwon	.75	.30
71 Kenny Smith	.25	.08
72 Antonio Davis	.25	.08
73 Dale Davis	.25	.08
74 Mark Jackson	.50	.20
75 Derrick McKey	.25	.08
76 Reggie Miller	.75	.30
77 Rik Smits	.50	.20
78 Terry Dehere	.25	.08
79 Lamond Murray	.25	.08
80 Bo Outlaw	.25	.08
81 Pooh Richardson	.25	.08
82 Rodney Rogers	.25	.08
83 Malik Sealy	.25	.08
84 Loy Vaught	.25	.08
85 Sam Bowie	.25	.08
86 Elden Campbell	.25	.08
87 Cedric Ceballos	.25	.08
88 Vlade Divac	.50	.20
89 Eddie Jones	1.00	.40
90 Anthony Peeler	.25	.08
91 Sedale Threatt	.25	.08
92 Nick Van Exel	.75	.30
93 Rex Chapman	.25	.08
94 Bimbo Coles	.25	.08
95 Matt Geiger	.25	.08
96 Billy Owens	.25	.08
97 Khalid Reeves	.25	.08
98 Glen Rice	.50	.20
99 Kevin Willis	.50	.20
100 Vin Baker	.50	.20
101 Marty Conlon	.25	.08
102 Todd Day	.25	.08
103 Eric Murdock	.25	.08
104 Glenn Robinson	.75	.30
105 Winston Garland	.25	.08
106 Tom Gugliotta	.25	.08
107 Christian Laettner	.50	.20
108 Isaiah Rider	.25	.08
109 Sean Rooks	.25	.08
110 Doug West	.25	.08
111 Kenny Anderson	.50	.20
112 P.J. Brown	.25	.08
113 Derrick Coleman	.25	.08
114 Armon Gilliam	.25	.08
115 Chris Morris	.25	.08
116 Anthony Bonner	.25	.08
117 Patrick Ewing	.75	.30
118 Derek Harper	.50	.20
119 Anthony Mason	.50	.20
120 Charles Oakley	.25	.08
121 Charles Smith	.25	.08
122 John Starks	.50	.20
123 Nick Anderson	.25	.08
124 Horace Grant	.50	.20
125 Anfernee Hardaway	.75	.30
126 Shaquille O'Neal	2.00	.75
127 Donald Royal	.25	.08
128 Dennis Scott	.25	.08
129 Brian Shaw	.25	.08
130 Derrick Alston	.25	.08
131 Dana Barros	.25	.08
132 Shawn Bradley	.25	.08
133 Willie Burton	.25	.08
134 Jeff Malone	.25	.08
135 Clarence Weatherspoon	.25	.08
136 Scott Williams	.25	.08
137 Sharone Wright	.25	.08
138 Danny Ainge	.25	.08
139 Charles Barkley	1.00	.40
140 A.C. Green	.50	.20
141 Kevin Johnson	.50	.20
142 Dan Majerle	.50	.20
143 Danny Manning	.25	.08
144 Elliot Perry	.25	.08
145 Wesley Person	.25	.08
146 Wayman Tisdale	.25	.08
147 Chris Dudley	.25	.08
148 Harvey Grant	.25	.08
149 Aaron McKie	.50	.20
150 Terry Porter	.25	.08
151 Clifford Robinson	.25	.08
152 Rod Strickland	.25	.08
153 Otis Thorpe	.25	.08
154 Buck Williams	.25	.08
155 Brian Grant	.75	.30
156 Bobby Hurley	.25	.08
157 Olden Polynice	.25	.08
158 Mitch Richmond	.50	.20

#	Player		
159	Michael Smith	.25	.08
160	Walt Williams	.25	.08
161	Vinny Del Negro	.25	.08
162	Sean Elliott	.50	.20
163	Avery Johnson	.25	.08
164	Chuck Person	.25	.08
165	J.R. Reid	.25	.08
166	Doc Rivers	.50	.20
167	David Robinson	.75	.30
168	Dennis Rodman	.75	.30
169	Vincent Askew	.25	.08
170	Hersey Hawkins	.25	.08
171	Shawn Kemp	.50	.20
172	Sarunas Marciulionis	.25	.08
173	Nate McMillan	.25	.08
174	Gary Payton	.75	.30
175	Sam Perkins	.50	.20
176	Detlef Schrempf	.50	.20
177	B.J. Armstrong	.25	.08
178	Jerome Kersey	.25	.08
179	Tony Massenburg	.25	.08
180	Oliver Miller	.25	.08
181	John Salley	.25	.08
182	David Benoit	.25	.08
183	Antoine Carr	.25	.08
184	Jeff Hornacek	.50	.20
185	Karl Malone	1.00	.40
186	Felton Spencer	.25	.08
187	John Stockton	1.00	.40
188	Greg Anthony	.25	.08
189	Benoit Benjamin	.25	.08
190	Byron Scott	.25	.08
191	Calbert Cheaney	.25	.08
192	Juwan Howard	.75	.30
193	Don MacLean	.25	.08
194	Gheorghe Muresan	.25	.08
195	Doug Overton	.25	.08
196	Scott Skiles	.25	.08
197	Chris Webber	1.00	.40
198	Checklist (1-94)	.25	.08
199	Checklist (95-190)	.25	.08
200	Checklist (191-290)	.25	.08
201	Stacey Augmon	.25	.08
202	Mookie Blaylock	.25	.08
203	Grant Long	.25	.08
204	Steve Smith	.50	.20
205	Dana Barros	.25	.08
206	Kendall Gill	.25	.08
207	Khalid Reeves	.25	.08
208	Glen Rice	.50	.20
209	Luc Longley	.25	.08
210	Dennis Rodman	1.00	.40
211	Dan Majerle	.50	.20
212	Tony Dumas	.25	.08
213	Elmore Spencer	.25	.08
214	Otis Thorpe	.25	.08
215	B.J. Armstrong	.25	.08
216	Sam Cassell	.75	.30
217	Clyde Drexler	.75	.30
218	Robert Horry	.50	.20
219	Hakeem Olajuwon	.75	.30
220	Eddie Johnson	.25	.08
221	Ricky Pierce	.25	.08
222	Eric Piatkowski	.25	.08
223	Rodney Rogers	.25	.08
224	Brian Williams	.25	.08
225	George Lynch	.25	.08
226	Alonzo Mourning	.50	.20
227	Benoit Benjamin	.25	.08
228	Terry Porter	.25	.08
229	Shawn Bradley	.25	.08
230	Kevin Edwards	.25	.08
231	Jayson Williams	.25	.08
232	Charlie Ward	.25	.08
233	Jon Koncak	.25	.08
234	Derrick Coleman	.25	.08
235	Richard Dumas	.25	.08
236	Vernon Maxwell	.25	.08
237	John Williams	.25	.08
238	Dontonio Wingfield	.25	.08
239	Tyrone Corbin	.25	.08
240	Will Perdue	.25	.08
241	Shawn Kemp	.50	.20
242	Gary Payton	.75	.30
243	Sam Perkins	.50	.20
244	Detlef Schrempf	.50	.20
245	Chris Morris	.25	.08
246	Robert Pack	.25	.08
247	Willie Anderson EXP	.25	.08
248	Oliver Miller EXP	.25	.08
249	Tracy Murray EXP	.25	.08
250	Alvin Robertson EXP	.25	.08
251	Carlos Rogers EXP	.25	.08
252	John Salley EXP	.25	.08
253	Damon Stoudamire EXP	1.00	.40
254	Zan Tabak EXP	.25	.08
255	Greg Anthony EXP	.25	.08
256	Blue Edwards EXP	.25	.08
257	Kenny Gattison EXP	.25	.08
258	Chris King EXP	.25	.08
259	Lawrence Moten EXP	.25	.08
260	Eric Murdock EXP	.25	.08
261	Bryant Reeves EXP	.50	.20
262	Byron Scott EXP	.25	.08
263	Cory Alexander RC	.25	.08
264	Brent Barry RC	.75	.30
265	Mario Bennett RC	.25	.08
266	Travis Best RC	.25	.08
267	Junior Burrough RC	.25	.08
268	Jason Caffey RC	.50	.20
269	Randolph Childress RC	.25	.08
270	Sasha Danilovic RC	.25	.08
271	Tyus Edney RC	.25	.08
272	Michael Finley RC	3.00	1.25
273	Sherrell Ford RC	.25	.08
274	Kevin Garnett RC	4.00	2.00
275	Alan Henderson RC	.75	.30
276	Donny Marshall RC	.25	.08
277	Antonio McDyess RC	1.50	.60
278	Loren Meyer RC	.25	.08
279	Lawrence Moten RC	.25	.08
280	Ed O'Bannon RC	.25	.08
281	Greg Ostertag RC	.25	.08
282	Cherokee Parks RC	.25	.08
283	Theo Ratliff RC	1.00	.40
284	Bryant Reeves RC	.75	.30
285	Shawn Respert RC	.25	.08
286	Lou Roe RC	.25	.08
287	Arvydas Sabonis RC	1.00	.40
288	Joe Smith RC	.25	.08
289	Jerry Stackhouse RC	2.50	1.00
290	Damon Stoudamire RC	1.50	.60
291	Bob Sura RC	.50	.20
292	Kurt Thomas RC	.50	.20
293	Gary Trent RC	.25	.08
294	David Vaughn RC	.25	.08
295	Rasheed Wallace RC	2.00	.75
296	Eric Williams RC	.50	.20
297	Corliss Williamson RC	.75	.30
298	George Zidek RC	.25	.08
299	Mahmoud Abdul-Rauf ENC	.25	.08
300	Kenny Anderson ENC	.25	.08
301	Vin Baker ENC	.25	.08
302	Charles Barkley ENC	.75	.30
303	Mookie Blaylock ENC	.25	.08
304	Cedric Ceballos ENC	.25	.08
305	Vlade Divac ENC	.25	.08
306	Clyde Drexler ENC	.50	.20
307	Joe Dumars ENC	.50	.20
308	Sean Elliott ENC	.25	.08
309	Patrick Ewing ENC	.50	.20
310	Anfernee Hardaway ENC	.50	.20
311	Tim Hardaway ENC	.25	.08
312	Grant Hill ENC	.75	.30
313	Tyrone Hill ENC	.25	.08
314	Robert Horry ENC	.25	.08
315	Juwan Howard ENC	.50	.20
316	Jim Jackson ENC	.25	.08
317	Kevin Johnson ENC	.25	.08
318	Larry Johnson ENC	.25	.08
319	Eddie Jones ENC	.75	.30
320	Shawn Kemp ENC	.50	.20
321	Jason Kidd ENC	1.25	.50
322	Christian Laettner ENC	.25	.08
323	Karl Malone ENC	.75	.30
324	Jamal Mashburn ENC	.25	.08
325	Reggie Miller ENC	.50	.20
326	Alonzo Mourning ENC	.25	.08
327	Dikembe Mutombo ENC	.25	.08
328	Hakeem Olajuwon ENC	.50	.20
329	Gary Payton ENC	.50	.20
330	Scottie Pippen ENC	.50	.20
331	Dino Radja ENC	.25	.08
332	Glen Rice ENC	.25	.08
333	Mitch Richmond ENC	.25	.08
334	Clifford Robinson ENC	.25	.08
335	David Robinson ENC	.50	.20
336	Glenn Robinson ENC	.50	.20
337	Dennis Rodman ENC	.75	.30
338	Carlos Rogers ENC	.25	.08
339	Detlef Schrempf ENC	.25	.08
340	Byron Scott ENC	.25	.08
341	Rik Smits ENC	.25	.08
342	Latrell Sprewell ENC	.75	.30
343	John Stockton ENC	.75	.30
344	Nick Van Exel ENC	.50	.20
345	Loy Vaught ENC	.25	.08
346	Clarence Weatherspoon ENC	.25	.08
347	Chris Webber ENC	.75	.30
348	Kevin Willis ENC	.25	.08
349	Checklist (299-298)	.25	.08
350	Checklist (299-350/inserts)	.25	.08

1996-97 Ultra

	COMPLETE SET (300)	50.00	25.00
	COMPLETE SERIES 1 (150)	35.00	17.50
	COMPLETE SERIES 2 (150)	15.00	7.50
1	Mookie Blaylock	.25	.08
2	Alan Henderson	.25	.08
3	Christian Laettner	.50	.20
4	Dikembe Mutombo	.50	.20
5	Steve Smith	.50	.20
6	Dana Barros	.25	.08
7	Rick Fox	.25	.08
8	Dino Radja	.25	.08
9	Antoine Walker RC	2.00	.75
10	Eric Williams	.25	.08
11	Dell Curry	.25	.08
12	Tony Delk RC	.75	.30
13	Matt Geiger	.25	.08
14	Glen Rice	.50	.20
15	Ron Harper	.50	.20
16	Michael Jordan	5.00	2.00
17	Toni Kukoc	.50	.20
18	Scottie Pippen	1.25	.50
19	Dennis Rodman	.50	.20
20	Terrell Brandon	.50	.20
21	Chris Mills	.25	.08
22	Bobby Phills	.25	.08
23	Bob Sura	.25	.08
24	Jim Jackson	.25	.08
25	Jason Kidd	1.25	.50
26	Jamal Mashburn	.50	.20
27	George McCloud	.25	.08
28	Samaki Walker RC	.25	.08
29	LaPhonso Ellis	.25	.08
30	Antonio McDyess	.50	.20
31	Bryant Stith	.25	.08
32	Joe Dumars	.75	.30
33	Grant Hill	.75	.30
34	Theo Ratliff	.50	.20
35	Otis Thorpe	.25	.08
36	Chris Mullin	.75	.30
37	Joe Smith	.50	.20
38	Latrell Sprewell	.75	.30
39	Charles Barkley	1.00	.40
40	Clyde Drexler	.75	.30
41	Mario Elie	.25	.08
42	Hakeem Olajuwon	.75	.30
43	Erick Dampier RC	.75	.30

#	Player		
44	Dale Davis	.25	.08
45	Derrick McKey	.25	.08
46	Reggie Miller	.75	.30
47	Rik Smits	.50	.20
48	Brent Barry	.25	.08
49	Malik Sealy	.25	.08
50	Loy Vaught	.25	.08
51	Lorenzen Wright RC	.50	.20
52	Kobe Bryant RC	12.00	5.00
53	Cedric Ceballos	.25	.08
54	Eddie Jones	.75	.30
55	Shaquille O'Neal	2.00	.75
56	Nick Van Exel	.75	.30
57	Tim Hardaway	.50	.20
58	Alonzo Mourning	.50	.20
59	Kurt Thomas	.50	.20
60	Ray Allen RC	2.50	1.00
61	Vin Baker	.50	.20
62	Sherman Douglas	.25	.08
63	Glenn Robinson	.75	.30
64	Kevin Garnett	1.50	.60
65	Tom Gugliotta	.25	.08
66	Stephon Marbury RC	2.00	.75
67	Doug West	.25	.08
68	Shawn Bradley	.25	.08
69	Kendall Gill	.25	.08
70	Kerry Kittles RC	.75	.30
71	Ed O'Bannon	.25	.08
72	Patrick Ewing	.75	.30
73	Larry Johnson	.50	.20
74	Charles Oakley	.25	.08
75	John Starks	.25	.08
76	John Wallace RC	.75	.30
77	Nick Anderson	.25	.08
78	Horace Grant	.50	.20
79	Anfernee Hardaway	.75	.30
80	Dennis Scott	.25	.08
81	Derrick Coleman	.50	.20
82	Allen Iverson RC	8.00	3.00
83	Jerry Stackhouse	1.00	.40
84	Clarence Weatherspoon	.25	.08
85	Michael Finley	1.00	.40
86	Kevin Johnson	.50	.20
87	Steve Nash RC	5.00	2.00
88	Wesley Person	.25	.08
89	Jermaine O'Neal RC	2.50	1.00
90	Clifford Robinson	.25	.08
91	Arvydas Sabonis	.50	.20
92	Gary Trent	.25	.08
93	Tyus Edney	.25	.08
94	Brian Grant	.75	.30
95	Olden Polynice	.25	.08
96	Mitch Richmond	.50	.20
97	Corliss Williamson	.25	.08
98	Vinny Del Negro	.25	.08
99	Sean Elliott	.50	.20
100	Avery Johnson	.25	.08
101	David Robinson	.75	.30
102	Hersey Hawkins	.50	.20
103	Shawn Kemp	.75	.30
104	Gary Payton	.75	.30
105	Sam Perkins	.50	.20
106	Detlef Schrempf	.50	.20
107	Marcus Camby RC	1.00	.40
108	Doug Christie	.50	.20
109	Damon Stoudamire	.75	.30
110	Sharone Wright	.25	.08
111	Jeff Hornacek	.25	.08
112	Karl Malone	.75	.30
113	Chris Morris	.25	.08
114	Bryon Russell	.25	.08
115	John Stockton	.75	.30
116	Shareef Abdur-Rahim RC	2.50	1.00
117	Greg Anthony	.25	.08
118	Blue Edwards	.25	.08
119	Bryant Reeves	.25	.08
120	Calbert Cheaney	.25	.08
121	Juwan Howard	.50	.20
122	Gheorghe Muresan	.25	.08
123	Chris Webber	.75	.30
124	Vin Baker RE	.25	.08
125	Charles Barkley OTB	.75	.30
126	Kevin Garnett OTB	.75	.30
127	Juwan Howard OTB	.25	.08
128	Larry Johnson OTB	.25	.08
129	Shawn Kemp OTB	.75	.30
130	Karl Malone OTB	.75	.30
131	Anthony Mason OTB	.25	.08
132	Antonio McDyess OTB	.50	.20
133	Alonzo Mourning OTB	.25	.08
134	Hakeem Olajuwon OTB	.50	.20
135	Shaquille O'Neal OTB	.75	.30
136	David Robinson OTB	.50	.20
137	Dennis Rodman OTB	.75	.30
138	Joe Smith OTB	.25	.08
139	Mookie Blaylock UE	.25	.08
140	Terrell Brandon UE	.25	.08
141	Anfernee Hardaway UE	.50	.20
142	Grant Hill UE	.50	.20
143	Michael Jordan UE	2.50	1.00
144	Jason Kidd UE	.50	.20
145	Gary Payton UE	.50	.20
146	Jerry Stackhouse UE	.75	.30
147	Damon Stoudamire UE	.50	.20
148	H.Olajuwon/D.Robinson ME	.75	.30
149	Checklist	.25	.08
150	Checklist	.25	.08
151	Tyrone Corbin	.25	.08
152	Priest Lauderdale RC	.25	.08
153	Dikembe Mutombo	.50	.20
154	Eldridge Recasner RC	.25	.08
155	Todd Day	.25	.08
156	Greg Minor	.25	.08
157	David Wesley	.25	.08
158	Vlade Divac	.25	.08
159	Anthony Mason	.50	.20
160	Malik Rose RC	.25	.08
161	Jason Caffey	.25	.08
162	Steve Kerr	.50	.20
163	Luc Longley	.25	.08
164	Danny Ferry	.25	.08
165	Tyrone Hill	.25	.08
166	Vitaly Potapenko RC	.25	.08
167	Sam Cassell	.75	.30
168	Michael Finley	1.00	.40
169	Chris Gatling	.25	.08
170	A.C. Green	.50	.20
171	Oliver Miller	.25	.08
172	Eric Montross	.25	.08
173	Dale Ellis	.25	.08
174	Mark Jackson	.25	.08
175	Ervin Johnson	.25	.08
176	Sarunas Marciulionis	.25	.08
177	Stacey Augmon	.25	.08
178	Joe Dumars	.75	.30
179	Grant Hill	.75	.30
180	Lindsey Hunter	.25	.08
181	Grant Long	.25	.08
182	Terry Mills	.25	.08
183	Otis Thorpe	.25	.08
184	Jerome Williams RC	.75	.30
185	Todd Fuller RC	.25	.08
186	Ray Owes RC	.25	.08
187	Mark Price	.50	.20
188	Felton Spencer	.25	.08
189	Charles Barkley	1.00	.40
190	Emanual Davis RC	.25	.08
191	Othella Harrington RC	.75	.30
192	Matt Maloney RC	.50	.20
193	Brent Price	.25	.08
194	Kevin Willis	.25	.08
195	Travis Best	.25	.08
196	Antonio Davis	.25	.08
197	Jalen Rose	.75	.30
198	Pooh Richardson	.25	.08
199	Stanley Roberts	.25	.08
200	Rodney Rogers	.25	.08
201	Elden Campbell	.25	.08
202	Derek Fisher RC	1.25	.50
203	Travis Knight RC	.25	.08
204	Shaquille O'Neal	2.00	.75
205	Byron Scott	.25	.08
206	Sasha Danilovic	.25	.08
207	Dan Majerle	.25	.08
208	Martin Muursepp RC	.25	.08
209	Amrom Gilliam	.25	.08
210	Andrew Lang	.25	.08
211	Johnny Newman	.25	.08
212	Kevin Garnett	1.50	.60
213	Tom Gugliotta	.25	.08
214	Shane Heal RC	.25	.08
215	Stojko Vrankovic	.25	.08
216	Robert Pack	.25	.08
217	Khalid Reeves	.25	.08
218	Jayson Williams	.50	.20
219	Chris Childs	.25	.08
220	Allan Houston	.50	.20
221	Larry Johnson	.50	.20
222	Walter McCarty RC	.25	.08
223	Charlie Ward	.25	.08
224	Brian Evans RC	.25	.08
225	Amal McCaskill RC	.25	.08
226	Rony Seikaly	.25	.08
227	Gerald Wilkins	.25	.08
228	Mark Davis	.25	.08
229	Lucious Harris	.25	.08
230	Don MacLean	.25	.08
231	Cedric Ceballos	.25	.08
232	Rex Chapman	.25	.08
233	Jason Kidd	1.25	.50
234	Danny Manning	.50	.20
235	Kenny Anderson	.25	.08
236	Aaron McKie	.50	.20
237	Isaiah Rider	.50	.20
238	Rasheed Wallace	1.00	.40
239	Mahmoud Abdul-Rauf	.25	.08
240	Billy Owens	.25	.08
241	Michael Smith	.25	.08
242	Vernon Maxwell	.25	.08
243	Charles Smith	.25	.08
244	Dominique Wilkins	.75	.30
245	Craig Ehlo	.25	.08
246	Jim McIlvaine	.25	.08
247	Nate McMillan	.25	.08
248	Hubert Davis	.25	.08
249	Carlos Rogers	.25	.08
250	Zan Tabak	.25	.08
251	Walt Williams	.25	.08
252	Jeff Hornacek	.50	.20
253	Karl Malone	.75	.30
254	Greg Ostertag	.25	.08
255	Bryon Russell	.25	.08
256	John Stockton	.75	.30
257	George Lynch	.25	.08
258	Lawrence Moten	.25	.08
259	Anthony Peeler	.25	.08
260	Roy Rogers RC	.25	.08
261	Tracy Murray	.25	.08
262	Rod Strickland	.25	.08
263	Ben Wallace RC	5.00	2.00
264	Shareef Abdur-Rahim RE	1.25	.50
265	Ray Allen RE	1.50	.60
266	Kobe Bryant RE	6.00	2.50
267	Marcus Camby RE	.50	.20
268	Erick Dampier RE	.25	.08
269	Tony Delk RE	.50	.20
270	Allen Iverson RE	2.00	.75
271	Kerry Kittles RE	.75	.30
272	Stephon Marbury RE	1.50	.60
273	Steve Nash RE	1.00	.40
274	Jermaine O'Neal RE	2.00	.75
275	Antoine Walker RE	1.50	.60
276	Samaki Walker RE	.25	.08
277	John Wallace RE	.50	.20
278	Lorenzen Wright RE	.25	.08
279	Anfernee Hardaway SU	.50	.20
280	Michael Jordan SU	2.50	1.00
281	Jason Kidd SU	.50	.20
282	Hakeem Olajuwon SU	.50	.20
283	Gary Payton SU	.50	.20
284	Mitch Richmond SU	.25	.08
285	David Robinson SU	.50	.20
286	John Stockton SU	.75	.30
287	Damon Stoudamire SU	.50	.20
288	Chris Webber SU	.75	.30
289	Clyde Drexler PG	.75	.30
290	Kevin Garnett PG	.75	.30
291	Grant Hill PG	.75	.30
292	Shawn Kemp PG	.75	.30
293	Karl Malone PG	.75	.30
294	Antonio McDyess PG	.50	.20
295	Alonzo Mourning PG	.25	.08
296	Shaquille O'Neal PG	.75	.30
297	Scottie Pippen PG	.75	.30
298	Jerry Stackhouse PG	.75	.30
299	Checklist (151-263)	.25	.08
300	Checklist (264-300/inserts)	.25	.08
NNO	Jerry Stackhouse Promo	3.00	1.25

1997-98 Ultra

❏ COMPLETE SET (275)		100.00	50.00
❏ COMPLETE SERIES 1 (150)		50.00	25.00
❏ COMPLETE SERIES 2 (125)		50.00	25.00
❏ COMMON CARD (1-275)		.25	.08
❏ COMMON ROOKIE (124-148)		1.00	.40
❏ 1 Kobe Bryant		3.00	1.25
❏ 2 Charles Barkley		1.00	.40
❏ 3 Joe Dumars		.75	.30
❏ 4 Wesley Person		.25	.08
❏ 5 Walt Williams		.25	.08
❏ 6 Vlade Divac		.50	.20
❏ 7 Mookie Blaylock		.25	.08
❏ 8 Jason Kidd		1.25	.50
❏ 9 Ron Harper		.25	.08
❏ 10 Sherman Douglas		.25	.08
❏ 11 Cedric Ceballos		.25	.08
❏ 12 Karl Malone		.75	.30
❏ 13 Antonio McDyess		.50	.20
❏ 14 Steve Kerr		.50	.20
❏ 15 Matt Maloney		.25	.08
❏ 16 Glenn Robinson		.75	.30
❏ 17 Rony Seikaly		.25	.08
❏ 18 Derrick Coleman		.25	.08
❏ 19 Jermaine O'Neal		1.25	.50
❏ 20 Scott Burrell		.25	.08
❏ 21 Glen Rice		.50	.20
❏ 22 Dale Ellis		.25	.08
❏ 23 Michael Jordan		5.00	2.00
❏ 24 Anfernee Hardaway		.75	.30
❏ 25 Bryon Russell		.25	.08
❏ 26 Toni Kukoc		.50	.20
❏ 27 Theo Ratliff		.25	.08
❏ 28 Tom Gugliotta		.50	.20
❏ 29 Dennis Rodman		.75	.30
❏ 30 John Stockton		.75	.30
❏ 31 Priest Lauderdale		.25	.08
❏ 32 Luc Longley		.25	.08
❏ 33 Grant Hill		.75	.30
❏ 34 Antonio Davis		.25	.08
❏ 35 Eddie Jones		.75	.30
❏ 36 Nick Anderson		.25	.08
❏ 37 Shareef Abdur-Rahim		1.25	.50
❏ 38 Stephon Marbury		1.00	.40
❏ 39 Todd Day		.25	.08
❏ 40 Tim Hardaway		.50	.20
❏ 41 Avery Johnson		.25	.08
❏ 42 Sam Perkins		.25	.08
❏ 43 Dikembe Mutombo		.50	.20
❏ 44 Bo Outlaw		.25	.08
❏ 45 Mitch Richmond		.50	.20
❏ 46 Bryant Reeves		.25	.08
❏ 47 P.J. Brown		.25	.08
❏ 48 Steve Smith		.50	.20
❏ 49 Martin Muursepp		.25	.08
❏ 50 Jamal Mashburn		.50	.20
❏ 51 Kendall Gill		.25	.08
❏ 52 Vinny Del Negro		.25	.08
❏ 53 Roy Rogers		.25	.08
❏ 54 Khalid Reeves		.25	.08
❏ 55 Scottie Pippen		1.25	.50
❏ 56 Joe Smith		.50	.20
❏ 57 Mark Jackson		.25	.08
❏ 58 Voshon Lenard		.25	.08
❏ 59 Dan Majerle		.25	.08
❏ 60 Alonzo Mourning		.50	.20
❏ 61 Kerry Kittles		.75	.30
❏ 62 Chris Childs		.25	.08
❏ 63 Patrick Ewing		.75	.30
❏ 64 Allan Houston		.75	.30
❏ 65 Marcus Camby		.75	.30
❏ 66 Christian Laettner		.50	.20
❏ 67 Loy Vaught		.25	.08
❏ 68 Jayson Williams		.25	.08
❏ 69 Avery Johnson		.25	.08
❏ 70 Damon Stoudamire		.50	.20
❏ 71 Kevin Johnson		.50	.20
❏ 72 Gheorghe Muresan		.25	.08
❏ 73 Reggie Miller		.75	.30
❏ 74 John Wallace		.25	.08
❏ 75 Terrell Brandon		.50	.20
❏ 76 Dale Davis		.25	.08
❏ 77 Latrell Sprewell		.75	.30
❏ 78 Lorenzen Wright		.25	.08
❏ 79 Rod Strickland		.25	.08
❏ 80 Kenny Anderson		.50	.20
❏ 81 Anthony Mason		.50	.20
❏ 82 Hakeem Olajuwon		.75	.30
❏ 83 Kevin Garnett		1.50	.60
❏ 84 Isaiah Rider		.50	.20
❏ 85 Mark Price		.50	.20
❏ 86 Shawn Bradley		.25	.08
❏ 87 Vin Baker		.50	.20
❏ 88 Steve Nash		.75	.30
❏ 89 Jeff Hornacek		.50	.20
❏ 90 Tony Delk		.25	.08
❏ 91 Horace Grant		.50	.20
❏ 92 Othella Harrington		.25	.08
❏ 93 Arvydas Sabonis		.50	.20
❏ 94 Antoine Walker		1.00	.40
❏ 95 Todd Fuller		.25	.08
❏ 96 John Starks		.50	.20
❏ 97 Olden Polynice		.25	.08
❏ 98 Sean Elliott		.50	.20
❏ 99 Travis Best		.25	.08
❏ 100 Chris Gatling		.25	.08
❏ 101 Derek Harper		.50	.20
❏ 102 LaPhonso Ellis		.25	.08
❏ 103 Dean Garrett		.25	.08
❏ 104 Hersey Hawkins		.25	.08
❏ 105 Jerry Stackhouse		.75	.30
❏ 106 Ray Allen		.75	.30
❏ 107 Allen Iverson		2.00	.75
❏ 108 Chris Webber		.75	.30
❏ 109 Robert Pack		.25	.08
❏ 110 Gary Payton		.75	.30
❏ 111 Mario Elie		.25	.08
❏ 112 Dell Curry		.25	.08
❏ 113 Lindsey Hunter		.25	.08
❏ 114 Robert Horry		.50	.20
❏ 115 David Robinson		.75	.30
❏ 116 Kevin Willis		.50	.20
❏ 117 Tyrone Hill		.25	.08
❏ 118 Vitaly Potapenko		.25	.08
❏ 119 Clyde Drexler		.75	.30
❏ 120 Derek Fisher		.75	.30
❏ 121 Detlef Schrempf		.50	.20
❏ 122 Gary Trent		.25	.08
❏ 123 Danny Ferry		.25	.08
❏ 124 Derek Anderson RC		4.00	1.50
❏ 125 Chris Anstey RC		1.00	.40
❏ 126 Tony Battle RC		2.00	.75
❏ 127 Chauncey Billups RC		8.00	3.00
❏ 128 Kelvin Cato RC		2.00	.75
❏ 129 Austin Croshere RC		3.00	1.25
❏ 130 Antonio Daniels RC		2.00	.75
❏ 131 Tim Duncan RC !		15.00	6.00
❏ 132 Danny Fortson RC		2.50	1.00
❏ 133 Adonal Foyle RC		1.50	.60
❏ 134 Paul Grant RC		1.00	.40
❏ 135 Ed Gray RC		1.00	.40
❏ 136 Bobby Jackson RC		3.00	1.25
❏ 137 Brevin Knight RC		2.50	1.00
❏ 138 Tracy McGrady RC		20.00	8.00
❏ 139 Ron Mercer RC		4.00	1.50
❏ 140 Anthony Parker RC		1.00	.40
❏ 141 Scot Pollard RC		1.50	.60
❏ 142 Rodrick Rhodes RC		1.00	.40
❏ 143 Olivier Saint-Jean RC		1.00	.40
❏ 144 Maurice Taylor RC		3.00	1.25
❏ 145 Johnny Taylor RC		1.00	.40
❏ 146 Tim Thomas RC		6.00	2.50
❏ 147 Keith Van Horn RC		5.00	2.00
❏ 148 Jacque Vaughn RC		1.50	.60
❏ 149 Checklist		.25	.08
❏ 150 Checklist		.25	.08
❏ 151 Scott Burrell		.25	.08
❏ 152 Brian Williams		.25	.08
❏ 153 Terry Mills		.25	.08
❏ 154 Jim Jackson		.25	.08
❏ 155 Michael Finley		.75	.30
❏ 156 Jeff Nordgaard RC		.25	.08
❏ 157 Carl Herrera		.25	.08
❏ 158 Otis Thorpe		.25	.08
❏ 159 Wesley Person		.25	.08
❏ 160 Tyrone Hill		.25	.08
❏ 161 Charles O'Bannon RC		.25	.08
❏ 162 Greg Anthony		.25	.08
❏ 163 Rusty LaRue RC		.25	.08
❏ 164 David Wesley		.25	.08
❏ 165 Chris Garner RC		.25	.08
❏ 166 George McCloud		.25	.08
❏ 167 Mark Price		.50	.20
❏ 168 God Shammgod RC		.25	.08
❏ 169 Isaac Austin		.25	.08
❏ 170 Alan Henderson		.25	.08
❏ 171 Eric Washington RC		.75	.30
❏ 172 Darrell Armstrong		.25	.08
❏ 173 Calbert Cheaney		.25	.08
❏ 174 Cedric Henderson RC		.25	.08
❏ 175 Bryant Stith		.25	.08
❏ 176 Sean Rooks		.25	.08
❏ 177 Chris Mills		.25	.08
❏ 178 Eldridge Recasner		.25	.08
❏ 179 Priest Lauderdale		.25	.08
❏ 180 Rick Fox		.50	.20
❏ 181 Keith Closs RC		.25	.08
❏ 182 Chris Dudley		.25	.08
❏ 183 Lawrence Funderburke RC		.50	.20
❏ 184 Michael Stewart RC		.25	.08
❏ 185 Alvin Williams RC		1.00	.40
❏ 186 Adam Keefe		.25	.08
❏ 187 Chauncey Billups		.60	.25
❏ 188 Jon Barry		.25	.08
❏ 189 Bobby Jackson		.50	.20
❏ 190 Sam Cassell		.75	.30
❏ 191 Dee Brown		.25	.08
❏ 192 Travis Knight		.25	.08
❏ 193 Dean Garrett		.25	.08
❏ 194 David Benoit		.25	.08
❏ 195 Chris Morris		.25	.08
❏ 196 Bubba Wells RC		.25	.08
❏ 197 James Robinson		.25	.08
❏ 198 Anthony Johnson RC		.25	.08
❏ 199 Dennis Scott		.25	.08
❏ 200 DeJuan Wheat RC		.25	.08
❏ 201 Rodney Rogers		.25	.08
❏ 202 Tariq Abdul-Wahad		.25	.08
❏ 203 Cherokee Parks		.25	.08
❏ 204 Jacque Vaughn		.25	.08
❏ 205 Cory Alexander		.25	.08
❏ 206 Kevin Ollie RC		.25	.08
❏ 207 George Lynch		.25	.08
❏ 208 Lamond Murray		.25	.08
❏ 209 Jud Buechler		.25	.08
❏ 210 Erick Dampier		.50	.20
❏ 211 Malcolm Huckaby RC		.25	.08
❏ 212 Chris Webber		.75	.30
❏ 213 Chris Crawford RC		.25	.08
❏ 214 J.R. Reid		.25	.08
❏ 215 Eddie Johnson		.25	.08
❏ 216 Nick Van Exel		.75	.30
❏ 217 Antonio McDyess		.50	.20
❏ 218 David Wingate		.25	.08
❏ 219 Malik Sealy		.25	.08
❏ 220 Bo Outlaw		.25	.08
❏ 221 Serge Zwikker RC		.25	.08
❏ 222 Bobby Phills		.25	.08
❏ 223 Shea Seals RC		.25	.08
❏ 224 Clifford Robinson		.25	.08
❏ 225 Zydrunas Ilgauskas		.50	.20
❏ 226 John Thomas RC		.25	.08
❏ 227 Rik Smits		.50	.20
❏ 228 Rasheed Wallace		.75	.30
❏ 229 John Wallace		.25	.08
❏ 230 Bob Sura		.25	.08
❏ 231 Ervin Johnson		.25	.08
❏ 232 Keith Booth RC		.25	.08
❏ 233 Chuck Person		.25	.08

#	Player		
234	Brian Shaw	.25	.08
235	Todd Day	.25	.08
236	Clarence Weatherspoon	.25	.08
237	Charlie Ward	.25	.08
238	Rod Strickland	.25	.08
239	Shawn Kemp	.50	.20
240	Terrell Brandon	.50	.20
241	Corey Beck RC	.25	.08
242	Vin Baker	.50	.20
243	Fred Hoiberg	.25	.08
244	Chris Mullin	.75	.30
245	Brian Grant	.50	.20
246	Derek Anderson	1.00	.40
247	Zan Tabak	.25	.08
248	Charles Smith RC	.25	.08
249	Shareef Abdur-Rahim GRE	2.50	1.00
250	Ray Allen GRE	1.50	.60
251	Charles Barkley GRE	2.00	.75
252	Kobe Bryant GRE	6.00	2.50
253	Marcus Camby GRE	1.50	.60
254	Anfernee Hardaway GRE	1.50	.60
255	Grant Hill GRE	1.50	.60
256	Juwan Howard GRE	.75	.30
257	Allen Iverson GRE	4.00	1.50
259	Michael Jordan GRE	10.00	4.00
260	Shawn Kemp GRE	1.00	.40
261	Kerry Kittles GRE	1.50	.60
262	Karl Malone GRE	1.50	.60
263	Stephon Marbury GRE	2.00	.75
264	Hakeem Olajuwon GRE	1.50	.60
265	Shaquille O'Neal GRE	3.00	1.25
266	Gary Payton GRE	1.50	.60
267	Scottie Pippen GRE	2.50	1.00
268	David Robinson GRE	1.50	.60
269	Dennis Rodman GRE	1.00	.40
270	Joe Smith GRE	1.00	.40
271	Jerry Stackhouse GRE	1.00	.40
272	Damon Stoudamire GRE	1.00	.40
273	Antoine Walker GRE	2.00	.75
274	Checklist	.25	.08
275	Checklist	.25	.08
NNO	Jerry Stackhouse Promo	2.00	.75

1998-99 Ultra

#	Player		
	COMPLETE SET (125)	100.00	50.00
	COMPLETE SET w/o SP (100)	25.00	12.50
	COMMON CARD (1-100)	.25	.08
	COMMON ROOKIE (101-125)	.50	.20
1	Keith Van Horn	.75	.30
1B	K.Van Horn Promo	.75	.30
2	Antonio Daniels	.25	.08
3	Patrick Ewing	.75	.30
4	Alonzo Mourning	.50	.20
5	Isaac Austin	.25	.08
6	Bryant Reeves	.25	.08
7	Dennis Scott	.25	.08
8	Damon Stoudamire	.50	.20
9	Kenny Anderson	.50	.20
10	Mookie Blaylock	.25	.08
11	Mitch Richmond	.50	.20
12	Jalen Rose	.75	.30
13	Vin Baker	.50	.20
14	Donyell Marshall	.50	.20
15	Bryon Russell	.25	.08
16	Rasheed Wallace	.75	.30
17	Allan Houston	.50	.20
18	Shawn Kemp	.50	.20
19	Nick Van Exel	.75	.30
20	Theo Ratliff	.50	.20
21	Jayson Williams	.25	.08
22	Chauncey Billups	.50	.20
23	Brent Barry	.50	.20
24	David Wesley	.25	.08
25	Joe Dumars	.75	.30
26	Marcus Camby	.50	.20
27	Juwan Howard	.50	.20
28	Brevin Knight	.25	.08
29	Reggie Miller	.75	.30
30	Ray Allen	.75	.30
31	Michael Finley	.75	.30
32	Tom Gugliotta	.25	.08
33	Allen Iverson	1.50	.60
34	Toni Kukoc	.50	.20
35	Tim Thomas	.50	.20
36	Jeff Hornacek	.50	.20
37	Bobby Jackson	.50	.20
38	Bo Outlaw	.25	.08
39	Steve Smith	.50	.20
40	Terrell Brandon	.50	.20
41	Glen Rice	.50	.20
42	Rik Smits	.25	.08
43	Calbert Cheaney	.25	.08
44	Stephon Marbury	.75	.30
45	Glenn Robinson	.50	.20
46	Corliss Williamson	.50	.20
47	Larry Johnson	.50	.20
48	Antonio McDyess	.50	.20
49	Detlef Schrempf	.50	.20
50	Jerry Stackhouse	.75	.30
51	Doug Christie	.50	.20
52	Eddie Jones	.75	.30
53	Karl Malone	.75	.30
54	Anthony Mason	.50	.20
55	Tim Duncan	1.25	.50
56	Christian Laettner	.50	.20
57	Isaiah Rider	.25	.08
58	Shawn Bradley	.25	.08
59	Jim Jackson	.25	.08
60	Mark Jackson	.25	.08
61	Kobe Bryant	3.00	1.25
62	Zydrunas Ilgauskas	.50	.20
63	Ron Mercer	.40	.15
64	Hersey Hawkins	.25	.08
65	John Wallace	.25	.08
66	Avery Johnson	.25	.08
67	Dikembe Mutombo	.50	.20
68	Hakeem Olajuwon	.75	.30
69	Tony Battie	.25	.08
70	Jason Kidd	1.25	.50
71	Latrell Sprewell	.75	.30
72	Kevin Garnett	1.50	.60
73	Voshon Lenard	.25	.08
74	Gary Payton	.75	.30
75	Cherokee Parks	.25	.08
76	Antoine Walker	.75	.30
77	Anthony Johnson	.25	.08
78	Danny Fortson	.25	.08
79	Grant Hill	.75	.30
80	Dennis Rodman	.50	.20
81	Arvydas Sabonis	.50	.20
82	Tracy McGrady	2.00	.75
83	David Robinson	.75	.30
84	Tariq Abdul-Wahad	.25	.08
85	Michael Jordan	5.00	2.00
86	Maurice Taylor	.40	.15
87	Cedric Ceballos	.25	.08
88	Anfernee Hardaway	.75	.30
89	John Stockton	.75	.30
90	Shareef Abdur-Rahim	.75	.30
91	Tim Hardaway	.50	.20
92	Shaquille O'Neal	2.00	.75
93	Rodney Rogers	.25	.08
94	Derek Anderson	.60	.25
95	Kendall Gill	.25	.08
96	Rod Strickland	.25	.08
97	Charles Barkley	1.00	.40
98	Chris Webber	.75	.30
99	Scottie Pippen	1.25	.50
100	Raef LaFrentz RC	2.00	.75
101	Ricky Davis RC	4.00	1.50
102	Robert Traylor RC	.50	.20
103	Roshown McLeod RC	.60	.25
105	Tyronn Lue RC	1.50	.60
106	Vince Carter RC	12.00	5.00
107	Miles Simon RC	.50	.20
108	Paul Pierce RC	6.00	2.50
109	Pat Garrity RC	.60	.25
110	Nazr Mohammed RC	.60	.25
111	Mike Bibby RC	6.00	2.50
112	Michael Dickerson RC	2.50	1.00
113	Michael Doleac RC	1.25	.50
114	Matt Harpring RC	2.00	.75
115	Larry Hughes RC	4.00	1.50
116	Keon Clark RC	2.00	.75
117	Felipe Lopez RC	1.50	.60
118	Dirk Nowitzki RC	12.00	6.00
119	Corey Benjamin RC	1.25	.50
120	Bryce Drew RC	1.25	.50
121	Brian Skinner RC	1.25	.50
122	Bonzi Wells RC	5.00	2.00
123	Antawn Jamison RC	6.00	2.50
124	Al Harrington RC	3.00	1.25
125	Michael Olowokandi RC	2.00	.75

1999-00 Ultra

#	Player		
	COMPLETE SET (150)	100.00	50.00
	COMPLETE SET w/o RC (125)	25.00	12.50
	COMMON CARD (1-125)	.25	.08
	COMMON ROOKIE (126-150)	1.00	.40
1	Vince Carter	2.00	.75
2	Randell Jackson	.25	.08
3	Ray Allen	.75	.30
4	Corliss Williamson	.25	.20
5	Darrell Armstrong	.25	.20
6	Charles Oakley	.25	.08
7	Tyrone Nesby RC	.25	.08
8	Eddie Jones	.75	.30
9	Kerry Kittles	.25	.08
10	Jason Williams	.75	.30
11	Elden Campbell	.25	.08
12	Mookie Blaylock	.25	.08
13	Brent Barry	.50	.20
14	Mark Jackson	.50	.20
15	Tim Hardaway	.50	.20
16	Kendall Gill	.25	.08
17	Larry Johnson	.50	.20
18	Eric Snow	.50	.20
19	Raef LaFrentz	.50	.20
20	Allen Iverson	1.50	.60
21	Kenny Anderson	.50	.20
22	John Starks	.50	.20
23	Isaiah Rider	.25	.08
24	Tariq Abdul-Wahad	.25	.08
25	Vitaly Potapenko	.25	.08
26	Patrick Ewing	.75	.30
27	Mitch Richmond	.50	.20
28	Steve Nash	.75	.30
29	Dickey Simpkins	.25	.08
30	Grant Hill	.75	.30
31	Matt Geiger	.25	.08
32	John Stockton	.75	.30
33	Jayson Williams	.25	.08
34	Reggie Miller	.75	.30
35	Eric Piatkowski	.50	.20
36	Jason Kidd	1.25	.50
37	Allan Houston	.50	.20
38	Christian Laettner	.50	.20
39	Marcus Camby	.50	.20
40	Shaquille O'Neal	2.00	.75
41	Derek Anderson	.50	.20

#	Player		
42	Gary Trent	.25	.08
43	Vin Baker	.50	.20
44	Alonzo Mourning	.50	.20
45	Latrell Sprewell	.75	.30
46	Rod Strickland	.25	.08
47	Bobby Jackson	.50	.20
48	Karl Malone	.75	.30
49	Mario Elie	.25	.08
50	Kobe Bryant	3.00	1.25
51	Clifford Robinson	.25	.08
52	Jamal Mashburn	.50	.20
53	Dirk Nowitzki	1.50	.60
54	Rik Smits	.50	.20
55	Doug Christie	.50	.20
56	Ricky Davis	.50	.20
57	Jalen Rose	.75	.30
58	Michael Olowokandi	.50	.20
59	Cedric Ceballos	.25	.08
60	Ron Mercer	.50	.20
61	Brevin Knight	.25	.08
62	Rashard Lewis	.75	.30
63	Detlef Schrempf	.50	.20
64	Keith Van Horn	.75	.30
64B	K.Van Horn Promo	.75	.30
65	Nick Anderson	.25	.08
66	Jon Hughes	.75	.30
67	Antonio McDyess	.50	.20
68	Terrell Brandon	.50	.20
69	Felipe Lopez	.25	.08
70	Scottie Pippen	1.25	.50
71	Erick Dampier	.50	.20
72	Arvydas Sabonis	.50	.20
73	Brian Grant	.50	.20
74	Nick Van Exel	.75	.30
75	Bryon Russell	.25	.08
76	Danny Fortson	.25	.08
77	Avery Johnson	.25	.08
78	Jerry Stackhouse	.75	.30
79	Robert Traylor	.25	.08
80	Tim Duncan	1.50	.40
81	Lindsey Hunter	.25	.08
82	Tyronn Lue	.50	.20
83	Michael Finley	.75	.30
84	Dikembe Mutombo	.50	.20
85	Zydrunas Ilgauskas	.50	.20
86	Pat Garrity	.25	.08
87	Damon Stoudamire	.50	.20
88	Shareef Abdur-Rahim	.75	.30
89	Matt Harpring	.75	.30
90	Michael Dickerson	.50	.20
91	Steve Smith	.50	.20
92	Bison Dele	.25	.08
93	Glenn Robinson	.75	.30
94	Antawn Jamison	1.25	.50
95	Glen Rice	.50	.20
96	Vlade Divac	.50	.20
97	Vladimir Stepania	.25	.08
98	Kornel David RC	.50	.20
99	Shawn Kemp	.50	.20
100	Kevin Garnett	1.50	.60
101	Tim Thomas	.50	.20
102	Mike Bibby	.75	.30
103	Maurice Taylor	.50	.20
104	Gary Payton	.75	.30
105	Voshon Lenard	.25	.08
106	Theo Ratliff	.50	.20
107	Hakeem Olajuwon	.75	.30
108	Joe Smith	.50	.20
109	Toni Kukoc	.50	.20
110	Stephon Marbury	.75	.30
111	Anthony Mason	.50	.20
112	Anfernee Hardaway	.75	.30
113	Juwan Howard	.50	.20
114	Charles Barkley	1.00	.40
115	Antoine Walker	.75	.30
116	Donyell Marshall	.50	.20
117	Tom Gugliotta	.25	.08
118	Rasheed Wallace	.75	.30
119	Tracy McGrady	2.00	.75
120	Paul Pierce	.75	.30
121	Sean Elliott	.50	.20
122	Bryant Reeves	.25	.08
123	Michael Doleac	.25	.08
124	Chris Webber	.75	.30
125	David Robinson	.75	.30
126	Steve Francis RC	6.00	2.50
127	Elton Brand RC	6.00	2.50
128	Wally Szczerbiak RC	5.00	2.00
129	Richard Hamilton RC	5.00	2.00
130	Shawn Marion RC	6.00	2.50
131	Trajan Langdon RC	2.00	.75
132	Corey Maggette RC	5.00	2.00
133	Dion Glover RC	1.50	.60
134	James Posey RC	3.00	1.25
135	Lamar Odom RC	5.00	2.00
136	A.Radojevic RC	1.00	.40
137	Cal Bowdler RC	1.50	.60
138	Scott Padgett RC	1.50	.60
139	Jumaine Jones RC	2.00	.75
140	Jonathan Bender RC	5.00	2.00
141	Tim James RC	1.50	.60
142	Jason Terry RC	4.00	1.50
143	Quincy Lewis RC	1.50	.60
144	William Avery RC	2.00	.75
145	Galen Young RC	1.00	.40
146	Ron Artest RC	3.00	1.25
147	Kenny Thomas RC	2.00	.75
148	Devean George RC	2.50	1.00
149	Andre Miller RC	5.00	2.00
150	Baron Davis RC	8.00	3.00

2000-01 Ultra

COMPLETE SET w/o RC (200)		40.00	20.00
COMMON CARD (1-200)		.25	.08
COMMON ROOKIE (201-225)		2.00	.75
1	Vince Carter	2.00	.75
2	Antawn Jamison	.75	.30
3	Shaquille O'Neal	2.00	.75
4	Paul Pierce	.75	.30
5	Antonio McDyess	.50	.20
6	Scott Burrell	.25	.08
7	Elton Brand	.75	.30
8	Lamar Odom	.75	.30
9	Nick Van Exel	.75	.30
10	Kobe Bryant	3.00	1.25
11	Reggie Miller	.75	.30
12	Sam Cassell	.75	.30
13	Darrell Armstrong	.25	.08
14	Rasheed Wallace	.75	.30
15	Charles Oakley	.25	.08
16	David Wesley	.25	.08
17	Al Harrington	.50	.20
18	Latrell Sprewell	.75	.30
19	Rick Brunson	.50	.20
20	Steve Smith	.50	.20
21	Antonio Davis	.25	.08
22	Michael Finley	.75	.30
23	Shandon Anderson	.25	.08
24	Danny Fortson	.25	.08
25	Kerry Kittles	.50	.20
26	Anfernee Hardaway	.75	.30
27	Vin Baker	.50	.20
28	Calvin Booth	.25	.08
29	Haywoode Workman	.25	.08
30	Dickey Simpkins	.25	.08
31	Jerome Williams	.25	.08
32	Ron Artest	.50	.20
33	Dennis Scott	.25	.08
34	Ron Mercer	.50	.20
35	Chris Webber	.75	.30
36	Bryon Russell	.25	.08
37	Dale Davis	.25	.08
38	Dirk Nowitzki	1.25	.50
39	Steve Francis	.75	.30
40	Glen Rice	.50	.20
41	Stephon Marbury	.75	.30
42	Jason Kidd	1.25	.50
43	Brent Barry	.25	.08
44	Richard Hamilton	.50	.20
45	Antoine Walker	.75	.30
46	Gary Trent	.25	.08
47	Cuttino Mobley	.50	.20
48	P.J. Brown	.25	.08
49	Elliot Perry	.25	.08
50	Shawn Marion	.75	.30
51	Horace Grant	.50	.20
52	Juwan Howard	.50	.20
53	Elden Campbell	.25	.08
54	Erick Strickland	.25	.08
55	Hakeem Olajuwon	.75	.30
56	Anthony Carter	.50	.20
57	Keith Van Horn	.75	.30
58	Clifford Robinson	.25	.08
59	Ruben Patterson	.50	.20
60	Mitch Richmond	.50	.20
61	Jason Terry	.75	.30
62	Andre Miller	.50	.20
63	Vonteego Cummings	.25	.08
64	Joe Smith	.50	.20
65	Toni Kukoc	.50	.20
66	Sean Elliott	.50	.20
67	Michael Dickerson	.50	.20
68	Derrick Coleman	.25	.08
69	Shawn Bradley	.25	.08
70	Kenny Thomas	.25	.08
71	Tim Hardaway	.50	.20
72	Rex Chapman	.25	.08
73	Gary Payton	.75	.30
74	Jahidi White	.25	.08
75	Baron Davis	.75	.30
76	Chauncey Billups	.50	.20
77	Moochie Norris	.25	.08
78	Dan Majerle	.50	.20
79	Marcus Camby	.50	.20
80	Rodney Rogers	.25	.08
81	Rashard Lewis	.50	.20
82	Laron Profit	.25	.08
83	Ricky Davis	.50	.20
84	Keon Clark	.25	.08
85	Anthony Miller	.25	.08
86	Jamal Mashburn	.50	.20
87	Chris Childs	.25	.08
88	Brian Grant	.50	.20
89	Muggsy Bogues	.25	.08
90	Randy Brown	.25	.08
91	Tariq Abdul-Wahad	.25	.08
92	Lindsey Hunter	.25	.08
93	Rik Smits	.50	.20
94	Glenn Robinson	.75	.30
95	Michael Doleac	.25	.08
96	Quincy Lewis	.25	.08
97	Grant Hill	.75	.30
98	Jalen Rose	.75	.30
99	Ervin Johnson	.25	.08
100	Chucky Atkins	.25	.08
101	Jermaine O'Neal	.75	.30
102	Howard Eisley	.25	.08
103	Kenny Anderson	.50	.20
104	Lamond Murray	.25	.08
105	Adonal Foyle	.25	.08
106	Derek Fisher	.75	.30
107	Wally Szczerbiak	.50	.20
108	Todd MacCulloch	.25	.08
109	Avery Johnson	.25	.08
110	Othella Harrington	.25	.08
111	Tony Battie	.25	.08
112	Bob Sura	.25	.08
113	Larry Hughes	.50	.20
114	Rick Fox	.50	.20
115	Travis Best	.25	.08
116	Theo Ratliff	.50	.20
117	David Robinson	.75	.30
118	Felipe Lopez	.25	.08
119	John Amaechi	.25	.08
120	George Lynch	.25	.08
121	Christian Laettner	.50	.20
122	Derek Anderson	.50	.20
123	Tim Thomas	.50	.20
124	Matt Harpring	.50	.20
125	Nick Anderson	.25	.08

#	Player		
126	Karl Malone	.75	.30
127	Dion Glover	.25	.08
128	Wesley Person	.25	.08
129	Mikki Moore	.25	.08
130	Michael Olowokandi	.25	.08
131	William Avery	.25	.08
132	Bo Outlaw	.25	.08
133	Jason Williams	.50	.20
134	John Stockton	.75	.30
135	Adrian Griffin	.25	.08
136	Hubert Davis	.25	.08
137	Donyell Marshall	.50	.20
138	Travis Knight	.25	.08
139	Kendall Gill	.25	.08
140	Tom Gugliotta	.25	.08
141	Malik Rose	.25	.08
142	Isaac Austin	.25	.08
143	Alan Henderson	.25	.08
144	Shawn Kemp	.50	.20
145	Terry Mills	.25	.08
146	Maurice Taylor	.25	.08
147	Terrell Brandon	.50	.20
148	Matt Geiger	.25	.08
149	Corliss Williamson	.50	.20
150	Jacque Vaughn	.25	.08
151	Dikembe Mutombo	.50	.20
152	Trajan Langdon	.50	.20
153	Jason Caffey	.25	.08
154	Tyrone Nesby	.25	.08
155	Bobby Jackson	.50	.20
156	Allen Iverson	1.50	.60
157	Mario Elie	.25	.08
158	Mike Bibby	.75	.30
159	Robert Horry	.50	.20
160	James Posey	.50	.20
161	Mark Jackson	.25	.08
162	Ray Allen	.75	.30
163	Charlie Ward	.25	.08
164	Damon Stoudamire	.50	.20
165	Tracy McGrady	2.00	.75
166	Bimbo Coles	.25	.08
167	Chucky Brown	.25	.08
168	Jerry Stackhouse	.75	.30
169	Greg Ostertag	.25	.08
170	Radoslav Nesterovic	.50	.20
171	Corey Maggette	.50	.20
172	Vlade Divac	.50	.20
173	Scott Padgett	.25	.08
174	Anthony Mason	.50	.20
175	Raef LaFrentz	.50	.20
176	Austin Croshere	.25	.08
177	Mark Strickland	.25	.08
178	Allan Houston	.50	.20
179	Arvydas Sabonis	.50	.20
180	Doug Christie	.50	.20
181	Jim Jackson	.25	.08
182	Brevin Knight	.25	.08
183	Mookie Blaylock	.25	.08
184	Chris Herren	.25	.08
185	Kevin Garnett	1.50	.60
186	Tyrone Hill	.25	.08
187	Tim Duncan	1.50	.60
188	Eddie Jones	.75	.30
189	Shareef Abdur-Rahim	.75	.30
190	Jonathan Bender	.50	.20
191	Alonzo Mourning	.50	.20
192	Patrick Ewing	.75	.30
193	Scottie Pippen	1.25	.50
194	Scot Pollard	.25	.08
195	Cedric Ceballos	.25	.08
196	Clarence Weatherspoon	.25	.08
197	Jamie Feick	.25	.08
198	Eric Snow	.50	.20
199	Ron Harper	.25	.08
200	Bryant Reeves	.25	.08
201	Chris Mihm RC	2.00	.75
202	Joel Przybilla RC	2.00	.75
203	Kenyon Martin RC	8.00	3.00
204	Stromile Swift RC	4.00	1.50
205	Etan Thomas RC	2.00	.75
206	Jason Collier RC	3.00	1.25
207	Marcus Fizer RC	2.00	.75
208	Mateen Cleaves RC	2.00	.75
209	Dan Langhi RC	2.00	.75
210	Mike Miller RC	6.00	2.50
211	Jabari Smith RC	2.00	.75
212	Hanno Mottola RC	2.00	.75
213	Chris Porter RC	2.00	.75
214	Desmond Mason RC	2.00	.75
215	Erick Barkley RC	2.00	.75
216	Donnell Harvey RC	2.00	.75
217	DerMarr Johnson RC	2.00	.75
218	Jerome Moiso RC	2.00	.75
219	Quentin Richardson RC	6.00	2.50
220	Courtney Alexander RC	4.00	1.50
221	Michael Redd RC	4.00	1.50
222	Morris Peterson RC	4.00	1.50
223	Darius Miles RC	6.00	2.50
224	Jamal Crawford RC	2.50	1.00
225	Keyon Dooling RC	2.50	1.00

2001-02 Ultra

COMP.SET w/o SP's (150)		40.00	20.00
COMP.UPDATE SET (6)		40.00	15.00
COMMON CARD (1-150)		.25	.08
COMMON ROOKIE (151-175)		3.00	1.25
151-175 PRINT RUN 2222 SERIAL #'d SETS			
COMMON UPDATE (1U-6U)		3.00	1.25
1	Vince Carter	2.00	.75
2	Allen Iverson	1.50	.60
3	Jerry Stackhouse	.75	.30
4	Travis Best	.25	.08
5	Eddie Jones	.75	.30
6	Felipe Lopez	.25	.08
7	Antonio Daniels	.25	.08
8	A.J. Guyton	.25	.08
9	Quentin Richardson	.50	.20
10	Charlie Ward	.25	.08
11	Ron Mercer	.50	.20
12	Shandon Anderson	.25	.08
13	Antawn Jamison	.75	.30
14	Darius Miles	.75	.30
15	Anthony Mason	.50	.20
16	Latrell Sprewell	.75	.30
17	Scottie Pippen	1.25	.50
18	Shammond Williams	.25	.08
19	P.J. Brown	.25	.08
20	Dirk Nowitzki	1.25	.50
21	Mateen Cleaves	.50	.20
22	Tim Hardaway	.50	.20
23	Christian Laettner	.50	.20
24	Toni Kukoc	.50	.20
25	Bob Sura	.25	.08
26	Kobe Bryant	3.00	1.25
27	Wally Szczerbiak	.50	.20
28	Darrell Armstrong	.25	.08
29	Chris Webber	.75	.30
30	David Wesley	.25	.08
31	Michael Finley	.75	.30
32	Jermaine O'Neal	.75	.30
33	Jason Kidd	1.25	.50
34	Tony Delk	.25	.08
35	Avery Johnson	.25	.08
36	Elden Campbell	.25	.08
37	Lamond Murray	.25	.08
38	Ben Wallace	.75	.30
39	Jalen Rose	.75	.30
40	Michael Dickerson	.50	.20
41	Shawn Marion	.75	.30
42	Jahidi White	.25	.08
43	Jamal Mashburn	.50	.20
44	Trajan Langdon	.50	.20
45	Reggie Miller	.75	.30
46	Stromile Swift	.50	.20
47	Keith Van Horn	.75	.30
48	Tom Gugliotta	.25	.08
49	Brent Barry	.50	.20
50	Courtney Alexander	.50	.20
51	Antonio McDyess	.50	.20
52	Robert Horry	.50	.20
53	Ervin Johnson	.25	.08
54	Speedy Claxton	.50	.20
55	Bryon Russell	.25	.08
56	Baron Davis	.75	.30
57	Robert Traylor	.25	.08
58	Chucky Atkins	.25	.08
59	Stephon Marbury	.75	.30
60	Desmond Mason	.50	.20
61	Tyrone Nesby	.25	.08
62	Brevin Knight	.25	.08
63	Kenyon Martin	.75	.30
64	Jumaine Jones	.50	.20
65	Rashard Lewis	.50	.20
66	Kenny Anderson	.50	.20
67	Andre Miller	.50	.20
68	Joe Smith	.50	.20
69	Kelvin Cato	.25	.08
70	Jason Williams	.50	.20
71	Marcus Camby	.50	.20
72	Eric Snow	.50	.20
73	Gary Payton	.75	.30
74	Robert Pack	.25	.08
75	Brian Cardinal	.50	.20
76	Sam Cassell	.75	.30
77	Allan Houston	.50	.20
78	Anfernee Hardaway	.50	.20
79	Morris Peterson	.50	.20
80	Chris Mihm	.50	.20
81	Elton Brand	.75	.30
82	Glenn Robinson	.75	.30
83	Damon Stoudamire	.50	.20
84	Alvin Williams	.25	.08
85	Paul Pierce	.75	.30
86	James Posey	.50	.20
87	Cuttino Mobley	.50	.20
88	Tim Thomas	.50	.20
89	Dikembe Mutombo	.50	.20
90	Tim Duncan	1.50	.60
91	John Starks	.50	.20
92	Antoine Walker	.75	.30
93	Moochie Norris	.25	.08
94	Dalibor Bagaric	.25	.08
95	Ray Allen	.75	.30
96	David Robinson	.75	.30
97	Shareef Abdur-Rahim	.75	.30
98	Wang Zhizhi	.75	.30
99	Chris Porter	.25	.08
100	Chauncey Billups	.50	.20
101	Tracy McGrady	2.00	.75
102	Michael Jordan	12.00	5.00
103	Jerome Williams	.25	.08
104	Jason Terry	.75	.30
105	Calvin Booth	.25	.08
106	Shaquille O'Neal	2.00	.75
107	Kevin Garnett	1.50	.60
108	Doug Christie	.50	.20
109	Karl Malone	.75	.30
110	Steve Nash	.75	.30
111	Austin Croshere	.50	.20
112	Alonzo Mourning	.50	.20
113	Dan Majerle	.50	.20
114	Malik Rose	.25	.08
115	Richard Hamilton	.50	.20
116	DerMarr Johnson	.50	.20
117	Raef LaFrentz	.50	.20
118	Derek Fisher	.50	.20
119	Vlade Divac	.50	.20
120	John Stockton	.75	.30
121	Dion Glover	.25	.08
122	Voshon Lenard	.25	.08
123	Steve Francis	.75	.30
124	Darvin Ham	.25	.08
125	Aaron McKie	.50	.20
126	Peja Stojakovic	.75	.30
127	Ron Artest	.50	.20
128	Keyon Dooling	.50	.20
129	Anthony Carter	.50	.20
130	Kurt Thomas	.50	.20
131	Rasheed Wallace	.75	.30
132	Theo Ratliff	.50	.20

#	Player		
133	Eric Piatkowski	.50	.20
134	Terrell Brandon	.50	.20
135	Mike Miller	.75	.30
136	Mike Bibby	.75	.30
137	Antonio Davis	.25	.08
138	Lamar Odom	.75	.30
139	Eddie House	.50	.20
140	Nick Van Exel	.75	.30
141	Rick Fox	.50	.20
142	Juwan Howard	.50	.20
143	Hidayet Turkoglu	.50	.20
144	Donyell Marshall	.50	.20
145	Marcus Fizer	.50	.20
146	Larry Hughes	.50	.20
147	Steve Smith	.50	.20
148	Brian Grant	.50	.20
149	Grant Hill	.75	.30
150	Derek Anderson	.50	.20
151	Kwame Brown RC	4.00	1.50
152	Eddie Griffin RC	3.00	1.25
153	Eddy Curry RC	6.00	2.50
154	Jamaal Tinsley RC	5.00	2.00
155	Jason Richardson RC	6.00	2.50
156	Shane Battier RC	5.00	2.00
157	Troy Murphy RC	5.00	2.00
158	Richard Jefferson RC	6.00	2.50
159	DeSagana Diop RC	3.00	1.25
160	Tyson Chandler RC	6.00	2.50
161	Joe Johnson RC	6.00	2.50
162	Zach Randolph RC	8.00	3.00
163	Andrei Kirilenko RC	6.00	2.50
164	Loren Woods RC	3.00	1.25
165	Jason Collins RC	3.00	1.25
166	Rodney White RC	4.00	1.50
167	Jeryl Sasser RC	3.00	1.25
168	Kirk Haston RC	3.00	1.25
169	Pau Gasol RC	8.00	3.00
170	Kedrick Brown RC	3.00	1.25
171	Steven Hunter RC	3.00	1.25
172	Michael Bradley RC	3.00	1.25
173	Joseph Forte RC	5.00	2.00
174	Brandon Armstrong RC	3.00	1.25
175	Primoz Brezec RC	4.00	1.50
1U	Gerald Wallace RC	6.00	2.50
2U	Tony Parker RC	30.00	4.00
3U	Vladimir Radmanovic RC	3.00	1.25
4U	Trenton Hassell RC	15.00	1.50
5U	Zeljko Rebraca RC	3.00	1.25
6U	Oscar Torres RC	3.00	1.25

2002-03 Ultra

COMPLETE SET (210)	250.00	100.00	
COMP.SET w/o RC's (180)	50.00	20.00	
COMMON CARD (1-180)	.25	.08	
COMMON ROOKIE (181-210)	3.00	1.25	
1	Vince Carter	2.00	.75
2	Ben Wallace	.75	.30
3	Tim Thomas	.50	.20
4	Eric Snow	.50	.20
5	Peja Stojakovic	.75	.30
6	Andrei Kirilenko	.75	.30
7	Dion Glover	.25	.08
8	James Posey	.50	.20
9	Kenny Thomas	.25	.08
10	Michael Dickerson	.25	.08
11	Charlie Ward	.25	.08
12	Gary Payton	.75	.30
13	Eddy Curry	.75	.30
14	Rick Fox	.50	.20
15	Joel Przybilla	.25	.08
16	Aaron McKie	.50	.20
17	Hidayet Turkoglu	.75	.30
18	Jarron Collins	.25	.08
19	Jason Collins	.25	.08
20	Nick Van Exel	.75	.30
21	Reggie Miller	.75	.30
22	Devean George	.50	.20
23	Michael Jordan	6.00	2.50
24	Tony Parker	.75	.30
25	Robert Horry	.50	.20
26	Wally Szczerbiak	.50	.20
27	Dikembe Mutombo	.50	.20
28	Scot Pollard	.25	.08
29	Darrell Armstrong	.25	.08
30	Jalen Rose	.75	.30
31	Antawn Jamison	1.00	.40
32	Anfernee Hardaway	.75	.30
33	Paul Pierce	.75	.30
34	Juwan Howard	.50	.20
35	Eddie Griffin	.50	.20
36	Shane Battier	.75	.30
37	Shandon Anderson	.25	.08
38	Vladimir Radmanovic	.50	.20
39	DerMarr Johnson	.25	.08
40	Antonio McDyess	.50	.20
41	Cuttino Mobley	.50	.20
42	Stromile Swift	.50	.20
43	Tracy McGrady	2.00	.75
44	Charles Smith	.25	.08
45	Shawn Marion	.75	.30
46	P.J. Brown	.25	.08
47	Wang Zhizhi	.75	.30
48	Austin Croshere	.25	.08
49	Ervin Johnson	.25	.08
50	Jason Kidd	1.25	.50
51	Tom Gugliotta	.25	.08
52	Jamal Crawford	.25	.08
53	Toni Kukoc	.50	.20
54	Mengke Bateer	.75	.30
55	Moochie Norris	.25	.08
56	Jason Williams	.50	.20
57	Mike Miller	.75	.30
58	Steve Smith	.50	.20
59	Shareef Abdur-Rahim	.75	.30
60	Michael Finley	.75	.30
61	Jermaine O'Neal	.75	.30
62	Mark Madsen	.25	.08
63	Troy Hudson	.25	.08
64	David Robinson	.75	.30
65	Corliss Williamson	.50	.20
66	Rodney Rogers	.25	.08
67	Derek Fisher	.75	.30
68	Anthony Carter	.50	.20
69	Allan Houston	.50	.20
70	Desmond Mason	.50	.20
71	Brendan Haywood	.50	.20
72	Tony Delk	.25	.08
73	Ryan Bowen	.25	.08
74	Danny Fortson	.25	.08
75	Alonzo Mourning	.75	.30
76	Latrell Sprewell	.75	.30
77	Rashard Lewis	.50	.20
78	Courtney Alexander	.50	.20
79	Marcus Fizer	.50	.20
80	Jason Richardson	.75	.30
81	Terrell Brandon	.50	.20
82	Allen Iverson	1.50	.60
83	Vlade Divac	.50	.20
84	Jahidi White	.25	.08
85	Eric Piatkowski	.50	.20
86	Marc Jackson	.50	.20
87	Pat Garrity	.25	.08
88	Tim Duncan	1.50	.60
89	Kwame Brown	.50	.20
90	Andre Miller	.50	.20
91	Troy Murphy	.50	.20
92	John Stockton	.75	.30
93	Kenny Anderson	.50	.20
94	Chris Mihm	.25	.08
95	Larry Hughes	.50	.20
96	Lamar Odom	.75	.30
97	Brian Grant	.50	.20
98	Marcus Camby	.50	.20
99	Mike Bibby	.75	.30
100	Joseph Forte	.50	.20
101	Lamond Murray	.25	.08
102	Darius Miles	.75	.30
103	Eddie Jones	.75	.30
104	Aaron Williams	.25	.08
105	Derek Anderson	.50	.20
106	Karl Malone	.75	.30
107	Jon Barry	.25	.08
108	Tony Battie	.25	.08
109	Jumaine Jones	.50	.20
110	Corey Maggette	.50	.20
111	Eddie House	.50	.20
112	Theo Ratliff	.50	.20
113	Scottie Pippen	1.25	.50
114	Hakeem Olajuwon	.75	.30
115	Antoine Walker	.75	.30
116	Tim Hardaway	.75	.30
117	Steve Francis	.75	.30
118	Lorenzen Wright	.25	.08
119	Howard Eisley	.25	.08
120	Brent Barry	.50	.20
121	Baron Davis	.75	.30
122	Michael Doleac	.25	.08
123	Quentin Richardson	.50	.20
124	LaPhonso Ellis	.25	.08
125	Richard Jefferson	.50	.20
126	Damon Stoudamire	.50	.20
127	Alvin Williams	.25	.08
128	Chucky Atkins	.25	.08
129	Jamal Mashburn	.50	.20
130	Wesley Person	.25	.08
131	Elton Brand	.75	.30
132	Ray Allen	.75	.30
133	Kerry Kittles	.25	.08
134	Rasheed Wallace	.75	.30
135	Antonio Davis	.25	.08
136	David Wesley	.25	.08
137	Dirk Nowitzki	1.25	.50
138	Rodney White	.50	.20
139	Jamaal Tinsley	.75	.30
140	Sam Cassell	.75	.30
141	Keith Van Horn	.50	.20
142	Ruben Patterson	.25	.08
143	Jerome Williams	.25	.08
144	Jason Terry	.75	.30
145	Eduardo Najera	.50	.20
146	Maurice Taylor	.25	.08
147	Pau Gasol	.75	.30
148	Grant Hill	.75	.30
149	Antonio Daniels	.25	.08
150	George Lynch	.25	.08
151	Steve Nash	.75	.30
152	Al Harrington	.50	.20
153	Anthony Mason	.50	.20
154	Kenyon Martin	.75	.30
155	Bonzi Wells	.50	.20
156	Morris Peterson	.50	.20
157	Eddie Robinson	.50	.20
158	Kevin Garnett	1.50	.60
159	Chris Webber	.75	.30
160	John Amaechi	.25	.08
161	Kobe Bryant	3.00	1.25
162	Joe Smith	.75	.30
163	Speedy Claxton	.50	.20
164	Doug Christie	.50	.20
165	Richard Hamilton	.50	.20
166	Tyson Chandler	.75	.30
167	Gilbert Arenas	.75	.30
168	Stephon Marbury	.75	.30
169	Jamaal Magloire	.25	.08
170	Rael LaFrentz	.50	.20
171	Ron Mercer	.50	.20
172	Glenn Robinson	.75	.30
173	Chauncey Billups	.50	.20
174	Iakovos Tsakalidis	.25	.08
175	Vin Baker	.50	.20
176	Joe Johnson	.75	.30
177	Jerry Stackhouse	.75	.30
178	Shaquille O'Neal	2.00	.75
179	Derrick Coleman	.25	.08
180	Bryon Russell	.25	.08
181	Yao Ming RC	25.00	10.00
181B	Rookie Exchange		
182	Jay Williams RC	5.00	2.00
183	Drew Gooden RC	8.00	3.00
184	DaJuan Wagner RC	6.00	2.50

☐ 185	Qyntel Woods RC	3.00	1.25
☐ 186	Rookie Exchange	4.00	1.50
☐ 187	Curtis Borchardt RC	3.00	1.25
☐ 188	Rookie Exchange	3.00	1.25
☐ 189	Caron Butler RC	8.00	3.00
☐ 190	Nene Hilario RC	5.00	2.00
☐ 191	Jared Jeffries RC	4.00	1.50
☐ 192	Mike Dunleavy RC	6.00	2.50
☐ 193	Kareem Rush RC	4.00	1.50
☐ 194	Amare Stoudemire RC	15.00	6.00
☐ 194B	Rookie Exchange		
☐ 195	Rookie Exchange	3.00	1.25
☐ 196	Rookie Exchange	4.00	1.50
☐ 197	Jiri Welsch RC	3.00	1.25
☐ 198	Frank Williams RC	3.00	1.25
☐ 199	John Salmons RC	3.00	1.25
☐ 200	Gordan Giricek RC	5.00	2.00
☐ 200B	Rookie Exchange		
☐ 201	Ryan Humphrey RC	3.00	1.25
☐ 201B	Rookie Exchange		
☐ 202	Casey Jacobsen RC	3.00	1.25
☐ 203	Carlos Boozer RC	8.00	3.00
☐ 203B	Rookie Exchange		
☐ 204	Manu Ginobili RC	10.00	4.00
☐ 204B	Rookie Exchange		
☐ 205	Bostjan Nachbar RC	3.00	1.25
☐ 206	Fred Jones RC	4.00	1.50
☐ 207	Dan Dickau RC	3.00	1.25
☐ 208	Tayshaun Prince RC	5.00	2.00
☐ 208B	Rookie Exchange		
☐ 209	Rookie Exchange	5.00	2.00
☐ 210	Juan Dixon RC	6.00	2.50

2003-04 Ultra

☐	COMP. SET w/o SP's	30.00	12.50
☐	COMMON CARD (1-170)	.20	.08
☐	COMMON L13 RC (171-183)	10.00	4.00
☐	COMMON ROOKIE (184-195)	4.00	1.50
☐ 1	Yao Ming	2.00	.75
☐ 2	DeShawn Stevenson	.20	.08
☐ 3	Malik Rose	.20	.08
☐ 4	DaJuan Wagner	.50	.20
☐ 5	Troy Murphy	.75	.30
☐ 6	Caron Butler	.75	.30
☐ 7	Radoslav Nesterovic	.50	.20
☐ 8	Joe Johnson	.50	.20
☐ 9	Al Harrington	.50	.20
☐ 10	Carlos Boozer	.75	.30
☐ 11	Morris Peterson	.50	.20
☐ 12	Malik Allen	.20	.08
☐ 13	Kurt Thomas	.50	.20
☐ 14	Derek Anderson	.50	.20
☐ 15	Zydrunas Ilgauskas	.50	.20
☐ 16	Jason Richardson	.75	.30
☐ 17	Brian Grant	.50	.20
☐ 18	Allan Houston	.50	.20
☐ 19	Bonzi Wells	.50	.20
☐ 20	Stephen Jackson	.50	.20
☐ 21	Eddy Curry	.75	.30
☐ 22	Tayshaun Prince	.75	.30
☐ 23	Brad Miller	.75	.30
☐ 24	Chris Swift	.20	.08
☐ 25	Kendall Gill	.20	.08
☐ 26	Vladimir Radmanovic	.20	.08
☐ 27	Theo Ratliff	.50	.20
☐ 28	Nick Van Exel	.75	.30
☐ 29	Marko Jaric	.20	.08
☐ 30	Jason Collins	.20	.08
☐ 31	Darrell Armstrong	.20	.08
☐ 32	Vlade Divac	.50	.20
☐ 33	Juan Dixon	.50	.20
☐ 34	Calbert Cheaney	.20	.08
☐ 35	Tyson Chandler	.75	.30
☐ 36	Chauncey Billups	.50	.20
☐ 37	Reggie Miller	.75	.30
☐ 38	Mike Miller	.75	.30
☐ 39	Marc Jackson	.50	.20
☐ 40	Casey Jacobsen	.20	.08
☐ 41	Ray Allen	.75	.30
☐ 42	Mehmet Okur	.20	.08
☐ 43	Jermaine O'Neal	.75	.30
☐ 44	Lorenzen Wright	.20	.08
☐ 45	Wally Szczerbiak	.50	.20
☐ 46	Anfernee Hardaway	.75	.30
☐ 47	Matt Harpring	.75	.30
☐ 48	Jay Williams	.50	.20
☐ 49	Corliss Williamson	.50	.20
☐ 50	Jamaal Tinsley	.75	.30
☐ 51	Shane Battier	.75	.30
☐ 52	Kevin Garnett	1.50	.60
☐ 53	Shawn Marion	.75	.30
☐ 54	Alvin Williams	.20	.08
☐ 55	Juwan Howard	.50	.20
☐ 56	Shaquille O'Neal	2.00	.75
☐ 57	Jamal Mashburn	.50	.20
☐ 58	Kenny Thomas	.20	.08
☐ 59	Tim Duncan	1.50	.60
☐ 60	Predrag Drobnjak	.20	.08
☐ 61	Jalen Rose	.75	.30
☐ 62	Ben Wallace	.75	.30
☐ 63	James Posey	.50	.20
☐ 64	Pau Gasol	.75	.30
☐ 65	Michael Redd	.75	.30
☐ 66	Amare Stoudemire	1.50	.60
☐ 67	Karl Malone	.75	.30
☐ 68	Richard Hamilton	.50	.20
☐ 69	Eddie Griffin	.20	.08
☐ 70	Robert Horry	.50	.20
☐ 71	Tim Thomas	.50	.20
☐ 72	Eric Snow	.50	.20
☐ 73	Brent Barry	.50	.20
☐ 74	Jamal Crawford	.20	.08
☐ 75	Nikoloz Tskitishvili	.20	.08
☐ 76	Bostjan Nachbar	.20	.08
☐ 77	Devean George	.20	.08
☐ 78	Dan Gadzuric	.20	.08
☐ 79	Brian Skinner	.20	.08
☐ 80	Cuttino Mobley	.50	.20
☐ 81	Desmond Mason	.20	.08
☐ 82	Othella Harrington	.20	.08
☐ 83	Chris Webber	.75	.30
☐ 84	Dirk Nowitzki	1.25	.50
☐ 85	Steve Francis	.75	.30
☐ 86	Gary Payton	.75	.30
☐ 87	Howard Eisley	.20	.08
☐ 88	Zach Randolph	.75	.30
☐ 89	Sam Cassell	.75	.30
☐ 90	Tony Battie	.20	.08
☐ 91	Shammond Williams	.20	.08
☐ 92	Rick Fox	.50	.20
☐ 93	David Wesley	.20	.08
☐ 94	Frank Williams	.20	.08
☐ 95	Tony Delk	.20	.08
☐ 96	Troy Hudson	.20	.08
☐ 97	Donnell Harvey	.20	.08
☐ 98	Derek Fisher	.75	.30
☐ 99	Jamaal Magloire	.20	.08
☐ 100	Keith Van Horn	.75	.30
☐ 101	Tony Parker	.75	.30
☐ 102	Rashard Lewis	.75	.30
☐ 103	Shareef Abdur-Rahim	.75	.30
☐ 104	Michael Finley	.75	.30
☐ 105	Jason Kidd	1.25	.50
☐ 106	Drew Gooden	.50	.20
☐ 107	Mike Bibby	.75	.30
☐ 108	Jerry Stackhouse	.75	.30
☐ 109	Chris Jefferies	.20	.08
☐ 110	Glenn Robinson	.75	.30
☐ 111	Shawn Bradley	.20	.08
☐ 112	Corey Maggette	.50	.20
☐ 113	Richard Jefferson	.50	.20
☐ 114	Gordan Giricek	.20	.08
☐ 115	Bobby Jackson	.50	.20
☐ 116	Larry Hughes	.50	.20
☐ 117	Scott Padgett	.20	.08
☐ 118	Gilbert Arenas	.75	.30
☐ 119	Ron Artest	.50	.20
☐ 120	Jason Williams	.50	.20
☐ 121	Eric Williams	.20	.08
☐ 122	Stephon Marbury	.75	.30
☐ 123	Vince Carter	2.00	.75
☐ 124	Jason Terry	.75	.30
☐ 125	Raef LaFrentz	.50	.20
☐ 126	Michael Olowokandi	.20	.08
☐ 127	Kerry Kittles	.20	.08
☐ 128	Pat Garrity	.20	.08
☐ 129	Peja Stojakovic	.75	.30
☐ 130	Jared Jeffries	.20	.08
☐ 131	Antonio Davis	.20	.08
☐ 132	Rodney White	.20	.08
☐ 133	Kobe Bryant	3.00	1.25
☐ 134	Baron Davis	.75	.30
☐ 135	Derrick Coleman	.20	.08
☐ 136	Walter McCarty	.20	.08
☐ 137	Bruce Bowen	.20	.08
☐ 138	Mike Dunleavy	.50	.20
☐ 139	Rasual Butler	.50	.20
☐ 140	Latrell Sprewell	.75	.30
☐ 141	Rasheed Wallace	.75	.30
☐ 142	Andrei Kirilenko	.75	.30
☐ 143	Dan Dickau	.20	.08
☐ 144	Steve Nash	.75	.30
☐ 145	Elton Brand	.75	.30
☐ 146	Kenyon Martin	.75	.30
☐ 147	Jeryl Sasser	.20	.08
☐ 148	Doug Christie	.50	.20
☐ 149	Kwame Brown	.50	.20
☐ 150	Ricky Davis	.50	.20
☐ 151	Antawn Jamison	.75	.30
☐ 152	Travis Best	.20	.08
☐ 153	Courtney Alexander	.20	.08
☐ 154	Scottie Pippen	1.25	.50
☐ 155	Jerome Williams	.20	.08
☐ 156	Quentin Richardson	.50	.20
☐ 157	Lucious Harris	.20	.08
☐ 158	Allen Iverson	1.50	.60
☐ 159	Manu Ginobili	.75	.30
☐ 160	Bryon Russell	.20	.08
☐ 161	Paul Pierce	.75	.30
☐ 162	Nene	.50	.20
☐ 163	Darius Miles	.75	.30
☐ 164	Earl Boykins	.50	.20
☐ 165	Eddie Jones	.75	.30
☐ 166	P.J. Brown	.20	.08
☐ 167	Qyntel Woods	.20	.08
☐ 168	Andre Miller	.50	.20
☐ 169	Tracy McGrady	2.00	.75
☐ 170	Antoine Walker	.75	.30
☐ 171	LeBron James L13 RC	175.00	100.00
☐ 172	Darko Milicic L13 RC	30.00	12.50
☐ 173	Carmelo Anthony L13 RC	50.00	20.00
☐ 174	Chris Bosh L13 RC	30.00	12.50
☐ 175	Dwyane Wade L13 RC	60.00	30.00
☐ 176	Chris Kaman L13 RC	10.00	4.00
☐ 177	Lucky 13 Exchange	25.00	10.00
☐ 178	T.J. Ford L13 RC	12.00	5.00
☐ 179	Mike Sweetney L13 RC	10.00	4.00
☐ 180	Lucky 13 Exchange	10.00	4.00
☐ 181	Mickael Pietrus L13 RC	12.00	5.00
☐ 182	Nick Collison L13 RC	10.00	4.00
☐ 183	Marcus Banks L13 RC	10.00	4.00
☐ 184	Luke Ridnour RC	5.00	2.00
☐ 185	Troy Bell RC	4.00	1.50
☐ 186	Zarko Cabarkapa RC	4.00	1.50
☐ 187	David West RC	4.00	1.50
☐ 188	Sofoklis Schortsanitis RC	5.00	2.00
☐ 189	Travis Outlaw RC	4.00	1.50
☐ 190	Leandro Barbosa RC	6.00	2.50
☐ 191	Josh Howard RC	6.00	2.50
☐ 192	Maciej Lampe RC	4.00	1.50
☐ 193	Luke Walton RC	4.00	1.50
☐ 194	Travis Hansen RC	4.00	1.50
☐ 195	Rick Rickert RC	4.00	1.50

2004-05 Ultra

☐	COMP. SET w/o RC's (175)	40.00	15.00
☐	COMMON CARD (1-175)	.20	.08
☐	COMMON ROOKIE (189-199)	4.00	1.50
☐	COMMON RC UPDATE (200U-219U)	5.00	2.00
☐	AT THE RATE OF TWO PER BOX		

#	Player		
☐ 1	Ben Wallace	.75	.30
☐ 2	Chris Kaman	.50	.20
☐ 3	Steve Nash	.75	.30
☐ 4	Al Harrington	.50	.20
☐ 5	T.J. Ford	.50	.20
☐ 6	Jason Collins	.20	.08
☐ 7	Theo Ratliff	.20	.20
☐ 8	Kobe Bryant	3.00	1.25
☐ 9	Kirk Hinrich	.75	.30
☐ 10	Darko Milicic	.50	.20
☐ 11	Karl Malone	.75	.30
☐ 12	Michael Olowokandi	.20	.08
☐ 13	Frank Williams	.20	.08
☐ 14	Vlade Divac	.50	.20
☐ 15	Vince Carter	2.00	.75
☐ 16	Eddy Curry	.50	.20
☐ 17	Chris Van Horn	.75	.30
☐ 18	Chris Wilcox	.50	.20
☐ 19	Tim Thomas	.50	.20
☐ 20	Shareef Abdur-Rahim	.75	.30
☐ 21	Carlos Arroyo	1.25	.50
☐ 22	Jason Collier	.20	.08
☐ 23	Voshon Lenard	.20	.08
☐ 24	Reggie Miller	.75	.30
☐ 25	Dan Gadzuric	.20	.08
☐ 26	David Wesley	.20	.08
☐ 27	Vladimir Radmanovic	.20	.08
☐ 28	Derek Anderson	.50	.20
☐ 29	Zydrunas Ilgauskas	.50	.20
☐ 30	Nick Van Exel	.75	.30
☐ 31	Stromile Swift	.50	.20
☐ 32	Kerry Kittles	.20	.08
☐ 33	Zaza Pachulia	.50	.20
☐ 34	Brad Miller	.75	.30
☐ 35	Jerry Stackhouse	.75	.30
☐ 36	Jason Terry	.75	.30
☐ 37	Earl Boykins	.50	.20
☐ 38	Jermaine O'Neal	.75	.30
☐ 39	Joe Smith	.50	.20
☐ 40	Jamaal Magloire	.20	.08
☐ 41	Zarko Cabarkapa	.20	.08
☐ 42	Ronald Murray	.20	.08
☐ 43	Bob Sura	.20	.08
☐ 44	Andre Miller	.50	.20
☐ 45	Jamaal Tinsley	.75	.30
☐ 46	Michael Redd	.50	.20
☐ 47	Baron Davis	.75	.30
☐ 48	Amare Stoudemire	1.50	.60
☐ 49	Rashard Lewis	.75	.30
☐ 50	Jiri Welsch	.50	.20
☐ 51	Marcus Camby	.50	.20
☐ 52	Ron Artest	.50	.20
☐ 53	Eddie Jones	.75	.30
☐ 54	Darrell Armstrong	.20	.08
☐ 55	Shawn Marion	.75	.30
☐ 56	Brent Barry	.50	.20
☐ 57	Michael Finley	.75	.30
☐ 58	Jim Jackson	.20	.08
☐ 59	Jason Williams	.50	.20
☐ 60	Kenyon Martin	.75	.30
☐ 61	Kyle Korver	.50	.20
☐ 62	Marquis Daniels	.75	.30
☐ 63	Chucky Atkins	.20	.08
☐ 64	Nene	.50	.20
☐ 65	Marko Jaric	.50	.20
☐ 66	Dwyane Wade	2.50	1.00
☐ 67	P.J. Brown	.20	.08
☐ 68	Casey Jacobsen	.20	.08
☐ 69	Morris Peterson	.50	.20
☐ 70	Ricky Davis	.75	.30
☐ 71	Tayshaun Prince	.50	.20
☐ 72	Corey Maggette	.50	.20
☐ 73	Udonis Haslem	.50	.20
☐ 74	Kurt Thomas	.50	.20
☐ 75	Leandro Barbosa	.50	.20
☐ 76	Alvin Williams	.20	.08
☐ 77	Mark Blount	.20	.08
☐ 78	Chauncey Billups	.50	.20
☐ 79	Boris Diaw	.50	.20
☐ 80	Brian Grant	.50	.20
☐ 81	Allan Houston	.50	.20
☐ 82	Joe Johnson	.50	.20
☐ 83	Donyell Marshall	.75	.30
☐ 84	Jamal Crawford	.50	.20
☐ 85	Jason Richardson	.75	.30
☐ 86	Gary Payton	.75	.30
☐ 87	Nazr Mohammed	.20	.08
☐ 88	Mike Bibby	.75	.30
☐ 89	Jalen Rose	.75	.30
☐ 90	Scottie Pippen	1.25	.50
☐ 91	Speedy Claxton	.50	.20
☐ 92	Devean George	.50	.20
☐ 93	Sam Cassell	.75	.30
☐ 94	Mike Sweetney	.50	.20
☐ 95	Chris Webber	.75	.30
☐ 96	Chris Bosh	.75	.30
☐ 97	Antoine Walker	.75	.30
☐ 98	Cuttino Mobley	.50	.20
☐ 99	Caron Butler	.75	.30
☐ 100	John Salmons	.20	.08
☐ 101	Bruce Bowen	.20	.08
☐ 102	Josh Howard	.50	.20
☐ 103	Steve Francis	.75	.30
☐ 104	Lamar Odom	.75	.30
☐ 105	Troy Hudson	.20	.08
☐ 106	Allen Iverson	1.50	.60
☐ 107	Dajuan Wagner	.50	.20
☐ 108	Erick Dampier	.20	.08
☐ 109	Luke Walton	.50	.20
☐ 110	Aaron Williams	.20	.08
☐ 111	Juwan Howard	.50	.20
☐ 112	Bobby Jackson	.50	.20
☐ 113	Andrei Kirilenko	.75	.30
☐ 114	LeBron James	5.00	2.00
☐ 115	Brian Cardinal	.20	.08
☐ 116	Mike Miller	.75	.30
☐ 117	Tracy McGrady	2.00	.75
☐ 118	Doug Christie	.50	.20
☐ 119	Larry Hughes	.50	.20
☐ 120	Stephen Jackson	.20	.08
☐ 121	Carmelo Anthony	1.50	.60
☐ 122	Fred Jones	.20	.08
☐ 123	Desmond Mason	.50	.20
☐ 124	Jamal Mashburn	.50	.20
☐ 125	Ray Allen	.75	.30
☐ 126	Jeff McInnis	.20	.08
☐ 127	Yao Ming	2.00	.75
☐ 128	Bonzi Wells	.50	.20
☐ 129	Richard Jefferson	.50	.20
☐ 130	Kenny Thomas	.20	.08
☐ 131	Hedo Turkoglu	.75	.30
☐ 132	Kwame Brown	.50	.20
☐ 133	Dirk Nowitzki	1.25	.50
☐ 134	Maurice Taylor	.20	.08
☐ 135	Pau Gasol	.75	.30
☐ 136	Jason Kidd	1.25	.50
☐ 137	Samuel Dalembert	.20	.08
☐ 138	Tim Duncan	1.50	.60
☐ 139	Gilbert Arenas	.75	.30
☐ 140	Tony Parker	.75	.30
☐ 141	Tyson Chandler	.50	.20
☐ 142	Richard Hamilton	.50	.20
☐ 143	Shaquille O'Neal	2.00	.75
☐ 144	Stephon Marbury	.75	.30
☐ 145	Damon Stoudamire	.50	.20
☐ 146	Gordan Giricek	.50	.20
☐ 147	Latrell Sprewell	.75	.30
☐ 148	Carlos Boozer	.75	.30
☐ 149	Mike Dunleavy	.50	.20
☐ 150	Luke Ridnour	.50	.20
☐ 151	DeShawn Stevenson	.20	.08
☐ 152	Peja Stojakovic	.75	.30
☐ 153	Juan Dixon	.50	.20
☐ 154	Marcus Banks	.50	.20
☐ 155	Rasheed Wallace	.75	.30
☐ 156	Quentin Richardson	.50	.20
☐ 157	Wally Szczerbiak	.50	.20
☐ 158	Keith Bogans	.20	.08
☐ 159	Darius Miles	.75	.30
☐ 160	Matt Harpring	.75	.30
☐ 161	Antawn Jamison	.75	.30
☐ 162	Kelvin Cato	.20	.08
☐ 163	James Posey	.50	.20
☐ 164	Willie Green	.20	.08
☐ 165	Rasho Nesterovic	.50	.20
☐ 166	Jarvis Hayes	.50	.20
☐ 167	Paul Pierce	.75	.30
☐ 168	Mehmet Okur	.20	.08
☐ 169	Elton Brand	.75	.30
☐ 170	Kevin Garnett	1.50	.60
☐ 171	Drew Gooden	.50	.20
☐ 172	Zach Randolph	.75	.30
☐ 173	Raul Lopez	.20	.08
☐ 174	Manu Ginobili	.75	.30
☐ 175	Raja Bell	.20	.08
☐ 176	Dwight Howard L13 RC	30.00	12.50
☐ 177	Emeka Okafor L13 EXCH	40.00	15.00
☐ 178	Ben Gordon L13 RC	50.00	20.00
☐ 179	Shaun Livingston L13 RC	15.00	6.00
☐ 180	Devin Harris L13 RC	15.00	6.00
☐ 181	Josh Childress L13 RC	12.00	5.00
☐ 182	Luol Deng L13 RC	20.00	8.00
☐ 183	Rafael Araujo L13 RC	10.00	4.00
☐ 184	Andre Iguodala L13 RC	25.00	10.00
☐ 185	Luke Jackson L13 RC	10.00	4.00
☐ 186	Andris Biedrins L13 RC	20.00	8.00
☐ 187	Robert Swift L13 RC	10.00	4.00
☐ 188	Sebastian Telfair L13 RC	10.00	4.00
☐ 189	Kris Humphries RC	4.00	1.50
☐ 190	Al Jefferson RC	8.00	3.00
☐ 191	Kirk Snyder RC	4.00	1.50
☐ 192	Josh Smith RC	8.00	3.00
☐ 193	J.R. Smith RC	6.00	2.50
☐ 194	Dorell Wright RC	6.00	2.50
☐ 195	Jameer Nelson RC	5.00	2.00
☐ 196	Pavel Podkolzine RC	4.00	1.50
☐ 197	Ha Seung-Jin RC	4.00	1.50
☐ 198	Sasha Vujacic RC	4.00	1.50
☐ 199	Anderson Varejao RC	5.00	2.00
☐ 200U	Bernard Robinson RC	5.00	2.00
☐ 201U	Andres Nocioni RC	6.00	2.50
☐ 202U	Delonte West RC	5.00	2.00
☐ 203U	Tony Allen RC	8.00	3.00
☐ 204U	Kevin Martin RC	10.00	4.00
☐ 205U	Beno Udrih RC	6.00	2.50
☐ 206U	David Harrison RC	5.00	2.00
☐ 207U	Jackson Vroman RC	5.00	2.00
☐ 208U	Peter John Ramos RC	5.00	2.00
☐ 209U	Lionel Chalmers RC	5.00	2.00
☐ 210U	Donta Smith RC	5.00	2.00
☐ 211U	Andre Emmett RC	5.00	2.00
☐ 212U	Antonio Burks RC	5.00	2.00
☐ 213U	Royal Ivey RC	5.00	2.00
☐ 214U	Chris Duhon RC	6.00	2.50
☐ 215U	Damien Wilkins RC	5.00	2.00
☐ 216U	Justin Reed RC	5.00	2.00
☐ 217U	Trevor Ariza RC	6.00	2.50
☐ 218U	Tim Pickett RC	5.00	2.00
☐ 219U	Yuta Tabuse RC	15.00	6.00

2006-07 Ultra

#	Player		
❏ 1	Josh Childress	.50	.20
❏ 2	Al Harrington	.25	.10
❏ 3	Joe Johnson	.50	.20
❏ 4	Tyronn Lue	.25	.10
❏ 5	Josh Smith	.75	.30
❏ 6	Tony Allen	.50	.20
❏ 7	Dan Dickau	.25	.10
❏ 8	Al Jefferson	.75	.30
❏ 9	Paul Pierce	.75	.30
❏ 10	Wally Szczerbiak	.50	.20
❏ 11	Raef LaFrentz	.25	.10
❏ 12	Primoz Brezec	.25	.10
❏ 13	Brevin Knight	.25	.10
❏ 14	Emeka Okafor	.75	.30
❏ 15	Kareem Rush	.25	.10
❏ 16	Gerald Wallace	.75	.30
❏ 17	Bernard Robinson	.25	.10
❏ 18	Tyson Chandler	.75	.30
❏ 19	Luol Deng	.75	.30
❏ 20	Chris Duhon	.25	.10
❏ 21	Ben Gordon	1.50	.60
❏ 22	Kirk Hinrich	.75	.30
❏ 23	Drew Gooden	.50	.20
❏ 24	Larry Hughes	.50	.20
❏ 25	Zydrunas Ilgauskas	.25	.10
❏ 26	LeBron James	5.00	2.00
❏ 27	Luke Jackson	.25	.10
❏ 28	Anderson Varejao	.25	.10
❏ 29	Erick Dampier	.25	.10
❏ 30	Marquis Daniels	.50	.20
❏ 31	Devin Harris	.75	.30
❏ 32	Josh Howard	.50	.20
❏ 33	Dirk Nowitzki	1.25	.50
❏ 34	Jason Terry	.75	.30
❏ 35	Carmelo Anthony	1.50	.60
❏ 36	Earl Boykins	.25	.10
❏ 37	Marcus Camby	.25	.10
❏ 38	Kenyon Martin	.75	.30
❏ 39	Andre Miller	.25	.10
❏ 40	Eduardo Najera	.25	.10
❏ 41	Chauncey Billups	.75	.30
❏ 42	Richard Hamilton	.50	.20
❏ 43	Antonio McDyess	.25	.10
❏ 44	Tayshaun Prince	.75	.30
❏ 45	Ben Wallace	.75	.30
❏ 46	Rasheed Wallace	.75	.30
❏ 47	Baron Davis	.75	.30
❏ 48	Mike Dunleavy	.50	.20
❏ 49	Derek Fisher	.50	.20
❏ 50	Troy Murphy	.75	.30
❏ 51	Jason Richardson	.75	.30
❏ 52	Rafer Alston	.25	.10
❏ 53	Juwan Howard	.50	.20
❏ 54	Tracy McGrady	2.00	.75
❏ 55	Stromile Swift	.50	.20
❏ 56	David Wesley	.25	.10
❏ 57	Yao Ming	2.00	.75
❏ 58	Austin Croshere	.25	.10
❏ 59	Stephen Jackson	.50	.20
❏ 60	Jermaine O'Neal	.75	.30
❏ 61	Peja Stojakovic	.75	.30
❏ 62	Jamaal Tinsley	.50	.20
❏ 63	Elton Brand	.75	.30
❏ 64	Sam Cassell	.75	.30
❏ 65	Chris Kaman	.25	.10
❏ 66	Shaun Livingston	.60	.25
❏ 67	Corey Maggette	.50	.20
❏ 68	Cuttino Mobley	.50	.20
❏ 69	Kwame Brown	.50	.20
❏ 70	Kobe Bryant	3.00	1.25
❏ 71	Devean George	.25	.10
❏ 72	Lamar Odom	.75	.30
❏ 73	Smush Parker	.25	.10
❏ 74	Luke Walton	.25	.10
❏ 75	Shane Battier	.75	.30
❏ 76	Pau Gasol	.75	.30
❏ 77	Bobby Jackson	.25	.10
❏ 78	Mike Miller	.75	.30
❏ 79	Damon Stoudamire	.25	.10
❏ 80	Alonzo Mourning	.50	.20
❏ 81	Shaquille O'Neal	2.00	.75
❏ 82	Gary Payton	.75	.30
❏ 83	Dwyane Wade	2.50	1.00
❏ 84	Antoine Walker	.75	.30
❏ 85	Jason Williams	.50	.20
❏ 86	T.J. Ford	.50	.20
❏ 87	Jamaal Magloire	.25	.10
❏ 88	Michael Redd	.75	.30
❏ 89	Bobby Simmons	.25	.10
❏ 90	Maurice Williams	.25	.10
❏ 91	Mark Blount	.25	.10
❏ 92	Ricky Davis	.75	.30
❏ 93	Kevin Garnett	1.50	.60
❏ 94	Eddie Griffin	.25	.10
❏ 95	Trenton Hassell	.25	.10
❏ 96	Troy Hudson	.25	.10
❏ 97	Vince Carter	2.00	.75
❏ 98	Jason Collins	.25	.10
❏ 99	Richard Jefferson	.50	.20
❏ 100	Jason Kidd	1.25	.50
❏ 101	Jeff McInnis	.25	.10
❏ 102	Antoine Wright	.25	.10
❏ 103	P.J. Brown	.25	.10
❏ 104	Speedy Claxton	.25	.10
❏ 105	Marc Jackson	.25	.10
❏ 106	Desmond Mason	.25	.10
❏ 107	J.R. Smith	.50	.20
❏ 108	Eddy Curry	.50	.20
❏ 109	Steve Francis	.75	.30
❏ 110	Stephon Marbury	.75	.30
❏ 111	Quentin Richardson	.25	.10
❏ 112	Jalen Rose	.60	.25
❏ 113	Maurice Taylor	.25	.10
❏ 114	Carlos Arroyo	1.25	.50
❏ 115	Grant Hill	.75	.30
❏ 116	Dwight Howard	1.00	.40
❏ 117	Darko Milicic	.75	.30
❏ 118	Jameer Nelson	.50	.20
❏ 119	DeShawn Stevenson	.25	.10
❏ 120	Samuel Dalembert	.25	.10
❏ 121	Steven Hunter	.25	.10
❏ 122	Andre Iguodala	.75	.30
❏ 123	Allen Iverson	1.50	.60
❏ 124	Kyle Korver	.75	.30
❏ 125	Chris Webber	.75	.30
❏ 126	Raja Bell	.25	.10
❏ 127	Boris Diaw	.50	.20
❏ 128	Shawn Marion	.75	.30
❏ 129	Steve Nash	.75	.30
❏ 130	Amare Stoudemire	1.50	.60
❏ 131	Kurt Thomas	.25	.10
❏ 132	Darius Miles	.75	.30
❏ 133	Joel Przybilla	.25	.10
❏ 134	Zach Randolph	.75	.30
❏ 135	Ha Seung-Jin	.25	.10
❏ 136	Sebastian Telfair	.75	.30
❏ 137	Shareef Abdur-Rahim	.75	.30
❏ 138	Ron Artest	.75	.30
❏ 139	Mike Bibby	.75	.30
❏ 140	Brad Miller	.75	.30
❏ 141	Vitaly Potapenko	.25	.10
❏ 142	Bruce Bowen	.25	.10
❏ 143	Tim Duncan	1.50	.60
❏ 144	Michael Finley	.75	.30
❏ 145	Manu Ginobili	.75	.30
❏ 146	Robert Horry	.50	.20
❏ 147	Tony Parker	.75	.30
❏ 148	Ray Allen	.75	.30
❏ 149	Rashard Lewis	.75	.30
❏ 150	Luke Ridnour	.50	.20
❏ 151	Robert Swift	.25	.10
❏ 152	Earl Watson	.25	.10
❏ 153	Chris Wilcox	.25	.10
❏ 154	Rafael Araujo	.25	.10
❏ 155	Chris Bosh	.75	.30
❏ 156	Jose Calderon	.50	.20
❏ 157	Mike James	.25	.10
❏ 158	Morris Peterson	.50	.20
❏ 159	Pape Sow	.25	.10
❏ 160	Carlos Boozer	.50	.20
❏ 161	Gordan Giricek	.25	.10
❏ 162	Kris Humphries	.25	.10
❏ 163	Andrei Kirilenko	.75	.30
❏ 164	Mehmet Okur	.25	.10
❏ 165	Greg Ostertag	.25	.10
❏ 166	Gilbert Arenas	.75	.30
❏ 167	Calvin Booth	.25	.10
❏ 168	Caron Butler	.50	.20
❏ 169	Antonio Daniels	.25	.10
❏ 170	Antawn Jamison	.75	.30
❏ 171	Andrew Bogut L14 Ret	2.50	1.00
❏ 172	Marvin Williams L14 Ret	2.50	1.00
❏ 173	Deron Williams L14 Ret	2.00	.75
❏ 174	Chris Paul L14 Ret	5.00	2.00
❏ 175	Raymond Felton L14 Ret	2.50	1.00
❏ 176	Martell Webster L14 Ret	1.25	.50
❏ 177	Charlie Villanueva L14 Ret	2.00	.75
❏ 178	Channing Frye L14 Ret	1.25	.50
❏ 179	Ike Diogu L14 Ret	1.25	.50
❏ 180	Andrew Bynum L14 Ret	1.25	.50
❏ 181	Yaroslav Korolev L14 Ret	1.25	.50
❏ 182	Sean May L14 Ret	1.25	.50
❏ 183	Rashad McCants L14 Ret	2.50	1.00
❏ 184	Antoine Wright L14 Ret	1.25	.50
❏ 185	Nate Robinson WP Ret	2.00	.75
❏ 186	Luther Head WP Ret	1.25	.50
❏ 187	Joey Graham WP Ret	1.25	.50
❏ 188	Johan Petro WP Ret	1.25	.50
❏ 189	Wayne Simien WP Ret	1.25	.50
❏ 190	David Lee WP Ret	1.25	.50
❏ 191	Salim Stoudamire WP Ret	1.25	.50
❏ 192	Travis Diener WP Ret	1.25	.50
❏ 193	Monta Ellis WP Ret	1.25	.50
❏ 194	Martynas Andruskevicius WP Ret	1.25	.50
❏ 195	Chuck Hayes WP Ret	1.25	.50
❏ 196	Danny Granger WP Ret	1.25	.50
❏ 197	Sarunas Jasikevicius WP Ret	1.25	.50
❏ 198	Francisco Garcia WP Ret	1.25	.50
❏ 199	Jarrett Jack WP Ret	1.25	.50
❏ 200	Jose Calderon WP Ret	1.25	.50
❏ 201	Andrea Bargnani L14/500 RC	25.00	10.00
❏ 202	LaMarcus Aldridge L14/500 RC	25.00	10.00
❏ 203	Adam Morrison L14/500 RC	25.00	10.00
❏ 204	Tyrus Thomas L14/500 RC	30.00	12.00
❏ 205	Shelden Williams L14/500 RC	12.00	5.00
❏ 206	Brandon Roy L14/500 RC	30.00	12.00
❏ 207	Randy Foye L14/500 RC	20.00	8.00
❏ 208	Rudy Gay L14/500 RC	20.00	8.00
❏ 209	Patrick O'Bryant L14/500 RC	10.00	4.00
❏ 210	Saer Sene L14/500 RC	10.00	4.00
❏ 211	J.J. Redick L14/500 RC	20.00	8.00
❏ 212	Hilton Armstrong L14/500 RC	10.00	4.00
❏ 213	Thabo Sefolosha L14/500 RC	15.00	6.00
❏ 214	Ronnie Brewer L14/500 RC	12.00	5.00
❏ 215	Allan Ray WP RC	2.50	1.00
❏ 216	Leon Powe WP RC	2.50	1.00
❏ 217	Joel Freeland WP RC	2.50	1.00
❏ 218	Shawne Williams WP RC	3.00	1.25
❏ 219	Kevin Pittsnogle WP RC	2.50	1.00
❏ 220	Shannon Brown WP RC	2.50	1.00
❏ 221	Kyle Lowry WP RC	2.50	1.00
❏ 222	Mardy Collins WP RC	2.50	1.00
❏ 223	Rodney Carney WP RC	2.50	1.00
❏ 224	Maurice Ager WP RC	2.50	1.00
❏ 225	Quincy Douby WP RC	2.50	1.00
❏ 226	Rajon Rondo WP RC	3.00	1.25
❏ 227	Jordan Farmar WP RC	5.00	2.00
❏ 228	Marcus Williams WP RC	3.00	1.25
❏ 229	Josh Boone WP RC	2.50	1.00
❏ 230	Solomon Jones WP RC	2.50	1.00
❏ 231	Denham Brown WP RC	2.50	1.00
❏ 232	Renaldo Balkman WP RC	2.50	1.00
❏ 233	Will Blalock WP RC	2.50	1.00
❏ 234	Bobby Jones WP RC	2.50	1.00
❏ 235	Steve Novak WP RC	2.50	1.00
❏ 236	James Augustine WP RC	2.50	1.00
❏ 237	Dee Brown WP RC	4.00	1.50
❏ 238	Hassan Adams WP RC	3.00	1.25
❏ 239	Alexander Johnson WP RC	2.50	1.00
❏ 240	Cedric Simmons WP RC	2.50	1.00
❏ 241	James White WP RC	2.50	1.00
❏ 242	Paul Davis WP RC	2.50	1.00
❏ 243	P.J. Tucker WP RC	2.50	1.00
❏ 244	Ryan Hollins WP RC	2.50	1.00

1999 Ultra WNBA

#			
	COMPLETE SET (125)	100.00	50.00
	COMPLETE SET w/o SP (100)	20.00	8.00
	COMMON CARD (1-100)	.80	.30
	COMMON SP (101-125)	4.00	1.50
❏ 1	Sheryl Swoopes	5.00	2.00
❏ 2	Christy Smith	.80	.30
❏ 3	Nikki McCray	1.50	.60
❏ 4	Coquese Washington RC	.80	.30
❏ 5	Vickie Johnson	.80	.30
❏ 6	Toni Foster	.80	.30
❏ 7	Allison Feaster	.80	.30
❏ 8	Penny Toler	.80	.30

☐ 9	Brandy Reed RC	2.50	1.00
☐ 10	Yolanda Moore	.80	.30
☐ 11	Lisa Leslie	3.00	1.25
☐ 12	Kisha Ford	.80	.30
☐ 13	Merlakia Jones	.80	.30
☐ 14	Umeki Webb	.80	.30
☐ 15	Tora Suber	.80	.30
☐ 16	Octavia Blue RC	.80	.30
☐ 17	Bridget Pettis	.80	.30
☐ 18	LaTonya Johnson RC	.80	.30
☐ 19	A.Santos de Oliveria RC	.80	.30
☐ 20	Tia Paschal	.80	.30
☐ 21	Jennifer Gillom	1.50	.60
☐ 22	Wanda Guyton	.80	.30
☐ 23	Franthea Price RC	.80	.30
☐ 24	Andrea Kuklova	.80	.30
☐ 25	Vicky Bullett	.80	.30
☐ 26	Dena Head	.80	.30
☐ 27	Isabelle Fijalkowski	.80	.30
☐ 28	Michelle Edwards	1.50	.60
☐ 29	Pamela McGee	.80	.30
☐ 30	Elisabeth Cabrian RC	.80	.30
☐ 31	Olympia Scott-Richardson	.80	.30
☐ 32	Murriel Page	.80	.30
☐ 33	Korie Hlede RC	.80	.30
☐ 34	Andrea Stinson	1.50	.60
☐ 35	Kristie Harrower RC	.80	.30
☐ 36	Kym Hampton	.80	.30
☐ 37	Gergana Branzova RC	.80	.30
☐ 38	Teresa Weatherspoon	2.50	1.00
☐ 39	Rebecca Lobo	2.50	1.00
☐ 40	Michelle Timms	2.50	1.00
☐ 41	Tamecka Dixon	.80	.30
☐ 42	Tina Thompson	2.50	1.00
☐ 43	Janice Braxton	.80	.30
☐ 44	Elena Baranova	1.50	.60
☐ 45	Adrienne Johnson RC	.80	.30
☐ 46	Adia Barnes RC	.80	.30
☐ 47	Elaine Powell RC	.80	.30
☐ 48	Lady Hardmon	.80	.30
☐ 49	Kim Perrot	2.50	1.00
☐ 50	Marlies Askamp RC	.80	.30
☐ 51	Deborah Carter	.80	.30
☐ 52	Sandy Brondello RC	3.00	1.25
☐ 53	Heidi Burge	.80	.30
☐ 54	Janeth Arcain	.80	.30
☐ 55	Rushia Brown	.80	.30
☐ 56	Suzie McConnell-Serio	.80	.30
☐ 57	Penny Moore	.80	.30
☐ 58	Margo Dydek	.80	.30
☐ 59	Angie Potthoff RC	.80	.30
☐ 60	Monica Lamb RC	.80	.30
☐ 61	Jamila Wideman	.80	.30
☐ 62	Ticha Penicheiro	3.00	1.25
☐ 63	Andrea Congreaves	.80	.30
☐ 64	Rachael Sporn RC	.80	.30
☐ 65	Chantel Tremitiere RC	.80	.30
☐ 66	Carla McGhee RC	.80	.30
☐ 67	Kim Williams	.80	.30
☐ 68	Tangela Smith RC	.80	.30
☐ 69	Quacy Barnes	.80	.30
☐ 70	Sue Wicks	.80	.30
☐ 71	Tracy Reid RC	.80	.30
☐ 72	Linda Burgess	.80	.30
☐ 73	Razija Brcaninovic RC	.80	.30
☐ 74	Sharon Manning	.80	.30
☐ 75	Tammy Jackson	.80	.30
☐ 76	Rita Williams	.80	.30
☐ 77	Carla Porter RC	.80	.30
☐ 78	Michelle Griffiths RC	.80	.30
☐ 79	Eva Nemcova	1.50	.60
☐ 80	Sophia Witherspoon	.80	.30
☐ 81	Sonja Tate RC	.80	.30
☐ 82	Cynthia Cooper	5.00	2.00
☐ 83	Wendy Palmer	1.50	.60
☐ 84	Ruthie Bolton-Holifield	2.50	1.00
☐ 85	Tammi Reiss	.80	.30
☐ 86	Katrina Colleton RC	.80	.30
☐ 87	Cindy Brown	.80	.30
☐ 88	Latasha Byears	.80	.30
☐ 89	Mwadi Mabika	.80	.30
☐ 90	Rhonda Mapp	.80	.30
☐ 91	Tina Thompson AW	.80	.30
☐ 92	Sheryl Swoopes AW	2.50	1.00
☐ 93	Jennifer Gillom AW	.80	.30
☐ 94	Cynthia Cooper AW	2.50	1.00
☐ 95	Suzie McConnell Serio AW	.80	.30
☐ 96	Cindy Brown AW	.80	.30
☐ 97	Eva Nemcova AW	.80	.30
☐ 98	Lisa Leslie AW	1.50	.60
☐ 99	Andrea Stinson AW	.80	.30
☐ 100	Teresa Weatherspoon AW	1.50	.60
☐ 101	Dawn Staley RC	6.00	2.50
☐ 102	Chamique Holdsclaw RC	40.00	15.00
☐ 103	Katrina Fokl RC	4.00	1.50
☐ 104	Nykesha Sales RC	5.00	2.50
☐ 105	Natalie Williams RC	8.00	3.00
☐ 106	Yolanda Griffith RC	10.00	4.00
☐ 107	Crystal Robinson RC	4.00	1.50
☐ 108	Edna Campbell RC	4.00	1.50
☐ 109	Tari Phillips RC	4.00	1.50
☐ 110	Tonya Edwards RC	4.00	1.50
☐ 111	Debbie Black RC	4.00	1.50
☐ 112	Kate Starbird RC	5.00	2.50
☐ 113	Adrienne Goodson RC	4.00	1.50
☐ 114	Sheri Sam RC	4.00	1.50
☐ 115	DeLisha Milton RC	4.00	1.50
☐ 116	Shannon Johnson RC	4.00	1.50
☐ 117	Katie Smith RC	6.00	2.50
☐ 118	Kara Wolters RC	4.00	1.50
☐ 119	Jennifer Azzi RC	6.00	2.50
☐ 120	Michele VanGorp RC	4.00	1.50
☐ 121	S.White-McCarty RC	6.00	3.00
☐ 122	Ukari Figgs RC	4.00	1.50
☐ 123	Val Whiting RC	4.00	1.50
☐ 124	Mery Andrade RC	4.00	1.50
☐ 125	Charlotte Smith RC	4.00	1.50

2000 Ultra WNBA

☐	COMPLETE SET (150)	70.00	35.00
☐	COMPLETE SET w/o SP (125)	40.00	20.00
☐	COMMON CARD (1-125)	.60	.25
☐	COMMON CARD (126-150)	2.00	.75
☐ 1	Cynthia Cooper	4.00	1.50
☐ 2	Chamique Holdsclaw	4.00	1.50
☐ 3	Lisa Leslie	2.50	1.00
☐ 4	Anna DeForge RC	.60	.25
☐ 5	Stephanie McCarty	1.25	.50
☐ 6	Katrina Colleton	.60	.25
☐ 7	Clarisse Machanguana RC	.60	.25
☐ 8	Adrienne Goodson	.60	.25
☐ 9	Charlotte Smith	.60	.25
☐ 10	DeLisha Milton	.60	.25
☐ 11	Janeth Arcain	.60	.25
☐ 12	Donna Harrington RC	.60	.25
☐ 13	Michele Timms	2.00	.75
☐ 14	Charmin Smith RC	.60	.25
☐ 15	Tricia Bader RC	.60	.25
☐ 16	Vickie Johnson	.60	.25
☐ 17	Monica Lamb	.60	.25
☐ 18	Dawn Staley	2.00	.75
☐ 19	Ruthie Bolton-Holifield	2.00	.75
☐ 20	Jennifer Azzi	2.00	.75
☐ 21	Becky Hammon RC	10.00	4.00
☐ 22	Latasha Byears	.60	.25
☐ 23	Lisa Harrison RC	.60	.25
☐ 24	Jennifer Rizzotti RC	4.00	1.50
☐ 25	Yolanda Griffith	2.00	.75
☐ 26	Tracy Henderson RC	.60	.25
☐ 27	Sophia Witherspoon	.60	.25
☐ 28	Sheryl Swoopes	4.00	1.50
☐ 29	Korie Hlede	.60	.25
☐ 30	Shannon Johnson	.60	.25
☐ 31	Chasity Melvin RC	1.50	.60
☐ 32	Tamika Whitmore RC	.60	.25
☐ 33	Tina Thompson	2.00	.75
☐ 34	Kedra Holland-Corn RC	2.00	.75
☐ 35	Markita Aldridge RC	.60	.25
☐ 36	Daina Ivanyi RC	.60	.25
☐ 37	Ticha Penicheiro	1.25	.50
☐ 38	Quacy Barnes	.60	.25
☐ 39	Ukari Figgs	.60	.25
☐ 40	Andrea Lloyd Curry RC	.60	.25
☐ 41	Tammy Jackson	.60	.25
☐ 42	Nikki McCray	1.25	.50
☐ 43	Kate Starbird	2.00	.75
☐ 44	Andrea Nagy RC	2.00	.75
☐ 45	Bridget Pettis	.60	.25
☐ 46	Eva Nemcova	1.25	.50
☐ 47	Tangela Smith	.60	.25
☐ 48	Astou Ndiaye-Diatta RC	.60	.25
☐ 49	Tamecka Dixon	.60	.25
☐ 50	Taj McWilliams RC	2.00	.75
☐ 51	Kristin Folkl	.60	.25
☐ 52	Amanda Wilson RC	.60	.25
☐ 53	Chantel Tremitiere	.60	.25
☐ 54	Dominique Canty RC	4.00	1.50
☐ 55	Allison Feaster	.60	.25
☐ 56	Angie Potthoff	.60	.25
☐ 57	Nykesha Sales	.60	.25
☐ 58	Rhonda Mapp	.60	.25
☐ 59	Murriel Page	.60	.25
☐ 60	Maria Stepanova	.60	.25
☐ 61	Katie Smith	2.00	.75
☐ 62	Michelle Edwards	1.25	.50
☐ 63	Venus Lacy RC	2.00	.75
☐ 64	Adrienne Johnson	.60	.25
☐ 65	Rita Williams	.60	.25
☐ 66	Andrea Stinson	1.25	.50
☐ 67	La'Keshia Frett RC	.60	.25
☐ 68	Jennifer Gillom	1.25	.50
☐ 69	LaTonya Johnson	.60	.25
☐ 70	Joy Holmes-Harris RC	.60	.25
☐ 71	Rushia Brown	.60	.25
☐ 72	Michelle Campbell RC	.60	.25
☐ 73	Angie Braziel RC	.60	.25
☐ 74	Crystal Robinson	.60	.25
☐ 75	Alicia Thompson	.60	.25
☐ 76	Suzie McConnell-Serio	.60	.25
☐ 77	Tanja Kostic RC	.60	.25
☐ 78	Amaya Valdemoro RC	.60	.25
☐ 79	Sue Wicks	.60	.25
☐ 80	Sonja Tate	.60	.25
☐ 81	Natalie Williams	2.00	.75
☐ 82	Mery Andrade	.60	.25
☐ 83	Tracy Reid	.60	.25
☐ 84	Olympia Scott-Richardson	.60	.25
☐ 85	Rebecca Lobo	2.00	.75
☐ 86	Margo Dydek	.60	.25
☐ 87	Sonja Henning RC	3.00	1.25
☐ 88	Vicky Bullett	.60	.25
☐ 89	Mwadi Mabika	.60	.25
☐ 90	Linda Burgess	.60	.25
☐ 91	Merlakia Jones	.60	.25
☐ 92	Umeki Webb	.60	.25
☐ 93	Niesa Johnson RC	.60	.25
☐ 94	Texlan Quinney RC	.60	.25
☐ 95	Teresa Weatherspoon	2.00	.75
☐ 96	Wendy Palmer	1.25	.50
☐ 97	Brandy Reed	.60	.25
☐ 98	Oksana Zakaluzhnaya RC	.60	.25
☐ 99	Sharon Manning	.60	.25

#	Player		
❏ 100	Kara Wolters	.60	.25
❏ 101	Keisha Anderson RC	.60	.25
❏ 102	Edna Campbell	.60	.25
❏ 103	DeMya Walker RC	.60	.25
❏ 104	Michele VanGorp	.60	.25
❏ 105	Coquese Washington	.60	.25
❏ 106	Marlies Askamp	.60	.25
❏ 107	Michelle Marciniak RC	1.50	.60
❏ 108	Angela Aycock RC	.60	.25
❏ 109	Tari Phillips	.60	.25
❏ 110	Sylvia Crawley RC	.60	.25
❏ 111	Tonya Edwards	.60	.25
❏ 112	Monica Maxwell RC	.60	.25
❏ 113	Beth Cunningham RC	.60	.25
❏ 114	Debbie Black	.60	.25
❏ 115	Shalonda Enis RC	.60	.25
❏ 116	Naomi Mulitauaopele RC	.60	.25
❏ 117	Jamila Wideman	.60	.25
❏ 118	Shanele Stires RC	.60	.25
❏ 119	Alisa Burras RC	.60	.25
❏ 120	Gordana Grubin RC	.60	.25
❏ 121	Elaine Powell	.60	.25
❏ 122	Tausha Mills RC	.60	.25
❏ 123	Katy Steding RC	.60	.25
❏ 124	Jannon Roland RC	.60	.25
❏ 125	Jessie Hicks	.60	.25
❏ 126	Ann Wauters RC	4.00	1.50
❏ 127	Edwina Brown RC	2.00	.75
❏ 128	Grace Daley RC	2.00	.75
❏ 129	Helen Darling RC	2.00	.75
❏ 130	Summer Erb RC	4.00	1.50
❏ 131	Kamila Vodichkova RC	2.00	.75
❏ 132	Tamicha Jackson RC	2.00	.75
❏ 133	Betty Lennox RC	10.00	4.00
❏ 134	Maylana Martin RC	2.00	.75
❏ 135	Lynn Pride RC	2.00	.75
❏ 136	Paige Sauer RC	2.00	.75
❏ 137	Madinah Slaise RC	2.00	.75
❏ 138	Stacey Thomas RC	2.00	.75
❏ 139	Cintia Dos Santos RC	2.00	.75
❏ 140	Milena Flores RC	2.00	.75
❏ 141	Rhonda Banchero RC	2.00	.75
❏ 142	Jameka Jones RC	2.00	.75
❏ 143	Jessica Bibby RC	2.00	.75
❏ 144	Adrain Williams RC	2.00	.75
❏ 145	Olga Firsova RC	3.00	1.25
❏ 146	Usha Gilmore RC	2.50	1.00
❏ 147	Shantia Owens RC	2.00	.75
❏ 148	Jurgita Streimikyte RC	2.00	.75
❏ 149	Katrina Hibbert RC	2.00	.75
❏ 150	Tonya Washington RC	2.00	.75

2001 Ultra WNBA

❏	COMPLETE SET (150)	160.00	80.00
❏	COMMON CARD	.80	.30
❏	COMMON CO (110-123)	2.00	.75
❏	COMMON ROOKIE (124-150)	6.00	2.50
❏ 1	Betty Lennox	1.50	.60
❏ 2	Ukari Figgs	.80	.30
❏ 3	Tangela Smith	.80	.30
❏ 4	Sue Wicks	.80	.30
❏ 5	Marla Brumfield RC	1.50	.60
❏ 6	Maria Stepanova	.80	.30
❏ 7	Murriel Page	.80	.30
❏ 8	Michele Timms	2.50	1.00
❏ 9	Janeth Arcain	.80	.30
❏ 10	Lisa Harrison	.80	.30
❏ 11	Tausha Mills	.80	.30
❏ 12	Sheri Sam	.80	.30

#	Player		
❏ 13	Sonja Henning	.80	.30
❏ 14	Adrienne Johnson	.80	.30
❏ 15	Mwadi Mabika	.80	.30
❏ 16	Chasity Melvin	.80	.30
❏ 17	Allison Feaster	.80	.30
❏ 18	Monica Maxwell	.80	.30
❏ 19	Katie Smith	2.50	1.00
❏ 20	Stacey Thomas	.80	.30
❏ 21	Robin Threatt-Elliott RC	1.50	.60
❏ 22	Jennifer Azzi	2.50	1.00
❏ 23	Shannon Johnson	.80	.30
❏ 24	Rhonda Mapp	.80	.30
❏ 25	Eva Nemcova	1.50	.60
❏ 26	Edwina Brown	.80	.30
❏ 27	Margo Dydek	.80	.30
❏ 28	Ann Wauters	1.50	.60
❏ 29	Nicky McCrimmon RC	.80	.30
❏ 30	Dominique Canty	.80	.30
❏ 31	Adrienne Goodson	.80	.30
❏ 32	Taj McWilliams-Franklin	.80	.30
❏ 33	DeLisha Milton	.80	.30
❏ 34	Mery Andrade	.80	.30
❏ 35	Yolanda Griffith	2.50	1.00
❏ 36	Tari Phillips	.80	.30
❏ 37	Rita Williams	.80	.30
❏ 38	Marlies Askamp	.80	.30
❏ 39	Korie Hlede	.80	.30
❏ 40	Tamecka Jackson	.80	.30
❏ 41	Elaine Powell	.80	.30
❏ 42	Elena Baranova	1.50	.60
❏ 43	Astou Ndiaye-Diatta	.80	.30
❏ 44	Nykesha Sales	.80	.30
❏ 45	Natalie Williams	2.50	1.00
❏ 46	Debbie Black	.80	.30
❏ 47	Vicky Bullett	.80	.30
❏ 48	Michelle Cleary RC	1.50	.60
❏ 49	Wendy Palmer	1.50	.60
❏ 50	Tully Bevilaqua RC	1.50	.60
❏ 51	Helen Darling	.80	.30
❏ 52	Katy Steding	.80	.30
❏ 53	Sheryl Swoopes	5.00	2.00
❏ 54	Kristin Folkl	.80	.30
❏ 55	Lady Hardmon	.80	.30
❏ 56	Jennifer Rizzotti	1.50	.60
❏ 57	Adrain Williams	.80	.30
❏ 58	Tricia Bader Binford	.80	.30
❏ 59	Kedra Holland-Corn	.80	.30
❏ 60	Crystal Robinson	.80	.30
❏ 61	Ann Wauters	.80	.30
❏ 62	Rushia Brown	.80	.30
❏ 63	Tamecka Dixon	.80	.30
❏ 64	Ticha Penicheiro	1.50	.60
❏ 65	Teresa Weatherspoon	2.50	1.00
❏ 66	Edna Campbell	.80	.30
❏ 67	Sylvia Crawley	.80	.30
❏ 68	Shalonda Enis	.80	.30
❏ 69	Andrea Lloyd-Curry	.80	.30
❏ 70	Tina Thompson	2.50	1.00
❏ 71	Michelle Edwards	1.50	.60
❏ 72	Stephanie McCarty	1.50	.60
❏ 73	Shantia Owens	.80	.30
❏ 74	Shanele Stires	.80	.30
❏ 75	DeMya Walker	.80	.30
❏ 76	Quacy Barnes	.80	.30
❏ 77	Cintia Dos Santos	.80	.30
❏ 78	Merlakia Jones	.80	.30
❏ 79	Lisa Leslie	3.00	1.25
❏ 80	Grace Daley	.80	.30
❏ 81	Jamie Redd RC	1.50	.60
❏ 82	Charlotte Smith	.80	.30
❏ 83	Jurgita Streimikyte	.80	.30
❏ 84	Sophia Witherspoon	.80	.30
❏ 85	Ruthie Bolton-Holifield	2.50	1.00
❏ 86	Vickie Johnson	.80	.30
❏ 87	Andrea Stinson	1.50	.60
❏ 88	Texlan Quinney	.80	.30
❏ 89	Tammy Jackson	.80	.30
❏ 90	Andrea Nagy	.80	.30
❏ 91	Andrea Riley	.80	.30
❏ 92	Umeki Webb	.80	.30
❏ 93	Andrea Garner	.80	.30
❏ 94	Maylana Martin	.80	.30
❏ 95	Vanessa Nygaard	.80	.30
❏ 96	Kamila Vodichkova	.80	.30
❏ 97	Coquese Washington	.80	.30
❏ 98	Jennifer Gillom	1.50	.60

#	Player		
❏ 99	Nikki McCray	1.50	.60
❏ 100	Tracy Reid	.80	.30
❏ 101	Elena Tornikidou RC	1.50	.60
❏ 102	Becky Hammon	1.50	.60
❏ 103	Dawn Staley	2.50	1.00
❏ 104	Alicia Thompson	.80	.30
❏ 105	Tiffany Travis RC	1.50	.60
❏ 106	Sandy Brondello	2.50	1.00
❏ 107	Tonya Edwards	.80	.30
❏ 108	Chamique Holdsclaw	5.00	2.00
❏ 109	Olympia Scott-Richardson	.80	.30
❏ 110	Anne Donovan CO	2.00	.75
❏ 111	Brian Alger CO	2.00	.75
❏ 112	Lin Dunn CO	2.00	.75
❏ 113	Van Chancellor CO	2.00	.75
❏ 114	Nell Fortner CO	2.00	.75
❏ 115	Michael Cooper CO	2.00	.75
❏ 116	Ron Rothstein CO	2.00	.75
❏ 117	Richie Adubato CO	2.00	.75
❏ 118	Cynthia Cooper CO	5.00	2.00
❏ 119	Linda Hargrove CO	2.00	.75
❏ 120	Fred Williams CO	2.00	.75
❏ 121	Dan Hughes CO	2.00	.75
❏ 122	Carolyn Peck CO	2.00	.75
❏ 123	Sonny Allen CO	2.00	.75
❏ 124	Brooke Wyckoff RC	25.00	10.00
❏ 125	Jackie Stiles RC	100.00	50.00
❏ 126	Svetlana Abrosimova RC	10.00	4.00
❏ 127	Tamika Catchings RC	8.00	3.00
❏ 128	Katie Douglas RC	10.00	4.00
❏ 129	Lauren Jackson RC	60.00	25.00
❏ 130	Shea Ralph RC	8.00	3.00
❏ 131	Ruth Riley RC	10.00	4.00
❏ 132	Kelly Miller RC	6.00	2.50
❏ 133	Marie Ferdinand RC	6.00	2.50
❏ 134	Tammy Sutton-Brown RC	6.00	2.50
❏ 135	Camille Cooper RC	6.00	2.50
❏ 136	Janell Burse RC	6.00	2.50
❏ 137	LaQuanda Barksdale RC	6.00	2.50
❏ 138	Niele Ivey RC	6.00	2.50
❏ 139	Coco Miller RC	6.00	2.50
❏ 140	Deanna Nolan RC	6.00	2.50
❏ 141	Penny Taylor RC	6.00	2.50
❏ 142	Kristen Veal RC	8.00	3.00
❏ 143	Kelly Schumacher RC	6.00	2.50
❏ 144	Amanda Lassiter RC	6.00	2.50
❏ 145	Semeka Randall RC	6.00	2.50
❏ 146	Jenny Mowe RC	6.00	2.50
❏ 147	Georgia Schweitzer RC	6.00	2.50
❏ 148	Jae Kingi RC	6.00	2.50
❏ 149	Erin Buescher RC	6.00	2.50
❏ 150	Michaela Pavlickova RC	6.00	2.50
❏ NNO	Cynthia Cooper AU/350	80.00	40.00

2002 Ultra WNBA

❏	COMPLETE SET (120)	200.00	75.00
❏	COMP.SET w/o SP's (100)	40.00	15.00
❏	COMMON CARD (1-99)	.80	.30
❏	COMMON ROOKIE (100-120)	6.00	2.50
❏ 1	Jackie Stiles	5.00	2.00
❏ 2	Sheryl Swoopes	4.00	1.50
❏ 3	Katie Smith	2.50	1.00
❏ 4	Sophia Witherspoon	.80	.30
❏ 5	Natalie Williams	2.50	1.00
❏ 6	Trisha Stafford-Odom	.80	.30
❏ 7	Lynn Pride	.80	.30
❏ 8	Ruthie Bolton-Holifield	2.50	1.00
❏ 9	Coquese Washington	.80	.30

☐ 10	Erin Buescher	.80	.30
☐ 11	Tully Bevilaqua	.80	.30
☐ 12	Deanna Nolan	.80	.30
☐ 13	Kristen Rasmussen	.80	.30
☐ 14	Bridget Pettis	.80	.30
☐ 15	Marie Ferdinand	.80	.30
☐ 16	Andrea Stinson	1.50	.60
☐ 17	Olympia Scott-Richardson	.80	.30
☐ 18	Teresa Weatherspoon	2.50	1.00
☐ 19	Edna Campbell	.80	.30
☐ 20	Elena Tornikidou	.80	.30
☐ 21	Elena Baranova	1.50	.60
☐ 22	Kristen Veal	.80	.30
☐ 23	Margo Dydek	.80	.30
☐ 24	Wendy Palmer	1.50	.60
☐ 25	Sandy Brondello	1.50	.60
☐ 26	Lisa Harrison	.80	.30
☐ 27	Korie Hlede	.80	.30
☐ 28	Astou Ndiaye-Diatta	.80	.30
☐ 29	Sheri Sam	.80	.30
☐ 30	Trisha Fallon	.80	.30
☐ 31	Chamique Holdsclaw	4.00	1.50
☐ 32	Chasity Melvin	.80	.30
☐ 33	Mwadi Mabika	.80	.30
☐ 34	Shannon Johnson	.80	.30
☐ 35	Kamila Vodichkova	.80	.30
☐ 36	Edwina Brown	.80	.30
☐ 37	Ruth Riley	.80	.30
☐ 38	Maria Stepanova	.80	.30
☐ 39	Coco Miller	.80	.30
☐ 40	Eva Nemcova	1.50	.60
☐ 41	DeLisha Milton	.80	.30
☐ 42	Jennifer Gillom	1.50	.60
☐ 43	Vicky Bullett	.80	.30
☐ 44	Penny Taylor	.80	.30
☐ 45	Rhonda Mapp	.80	.30
☐ 46	Tawona Alehaleem	.80	.30
☐ 47	Murriel Page	.80	.30
☐ 48	Tamika Catchings	.80	.30
☐ 49	Sue Wicks	.80	.30
☐ 50	Ticha Penicheiro	1.50	.60
☐ 51	Tammy Jackson	.80	.30
☐ 52	Rebecca Lobo	2.50	1.00
☐ 53	Yolanda Griffith	2.50	1.00
☐ 54	Ann Wauters	1.50	.60
☐ 55	Latasha Byears	.80	.30
☐ 56	Katie Douglas	.80	.30
☐ 57	Sonja Henning	.80	.30
☐ 58	Rushia Brown	.80	.30
☐ 59	Ukari Figgs	.80	.30
☐ 60	Elaine Powell	.80	.30
☐ 61	Jennifer Azzi	2.50	1.00
☐ 62	Allison Feaster	.80	.30
☐ 63	Rita Williams	.80	.30
☐ 64	Tangela Smith	.80	.30
☐ 65	Tari Phillips	.80	.30
☐ 66	Shalonda Enis	.80	.30
☐ 67	Alicia Thompson	.80	.30
☐ 68	Crystal Robinson	.80	.30
☐ 69	Lauren Jackson	2.50	1.00
☐ 70	Jae Kingi	.80	.30
☐ 71	Marla Brumfield	.80	.30
☐ 72	Dawn Staley	2.50	1.00
☐ 73	Adrienne Goodson	.80	.30
☐ 74	Clarisse Machanguana	.80	.30
☐ 75	Nikki McCray	1.50	.60
☐ 76	Becky Hammon	1.50	.60
☐ 77	Semeka Randall	.80	.30
☐ 78	Merlakia Jones	.80	.30
☐ 79	Tamecka Dixon	.80	.30
☐ 80	Taj McWilliams-Franklin	.80	.30
☐ 81	Jamie Redd	.80	.30
☐ 82	Amanda Lassiter	.80	.30
☐ 83	Maylana Martin	.80	.30
☐ 84	Tamicha Jackson	.80	.30
☐ 85	Tammy Sutton-Brown	.80	.30
☐ 86	Jurgita Streimikyte	.80	.30
☐ 87	Vickie Johnson	.80	.30
☐ 88	Kedra Holland-Corn	.80	.30
☐ 89	Janeth Arcain	.80	.30
☐ 90	Betty Lennox	1.50	.60
☐ 91	Kristin Folkl	.80	.30
☐ 92	Helen Luz	.80	.30
☐ 93	Kelly Miller	.80	.30
☐ 94	Lisa Leslie	4.00	1.50
☐ 95	Nykesha Sales	.80	.30
☐ 96	Simone Edwards	.80	.30
☐ 97	Tina Thompson	2.50	1.00
☐ 98	Svetlana Abrosimova	.80	.30
☐ 99	Sylvia Crawley	.80	.30
☐ 100	Annie Burgess RC	2.50	1.00
☐ 101	Rookie Exchange	50.00	20.00
☐ 102	Rookie Exchange	15.00	6.00
☐ 103	Rookie Exchange	20.00	8.00
☐ 104	Rookie Exchange	15.00	6.00
☐ 105	Rookie Exchange	12.00	5.00
☐ 106	Rookie Exchange	12.00	5.00
☐ 107	Rookie Exchange	10.00	4.00
☐ 108	Rookie Exchange	6.00	2.50
☐ 109	Rookie Exchange	8.00	3.00
☐ 110	Rookie Exchange	15.00	6.00
☐ 111	Rookie Exchange	6.00	2.50
☐ 112	Rookie Exchange	6.00	2.50
☐ 113	Rookie Exchange	6.00	2.50
☐ 114	Rookie Exchange	6.00	2.50
☐ 115	Rookie Exchange	6.00	2.50
☐ 116	Rookie Exchange	6.00	2.50
☐ 117	Rookie Exchange	6.00	2.50
☐ 118	Rookie Exchange	6.00	2.50
☐ 119	Rookie Exchange	6.00	2.50
☐ 120	Rookie Exchange	6.00	2.50

2003 Ultra WNBA

	COMP.SET w/o SP's (105)	30.00	12.50
	COMMON CARD (1-105)	.40	.15
	COMMON ROOKIE (106-120)	5.00	2.00
☐ 1	Sue Bird	6.00	2.50
☐ 2	Kelly Schumacher	.40	.15
☐ 3	Tamika Williams	.40	.15
☐ 4	Rebecca Lobo	2.50	1.00
☐ 5	Stacey Thomas	.40	.15
☐ 6	Lisa Leslie	4.00	1.50
☐ 7	Adrain Williams	.40	.15
☐ 8	Helen Luz	.40	.15
☐ 9	Rushia Brown	.40	.15
☐ 10	Bridget Pettis	.40	.15
☐ 11	Annie Burgess	.40	.15
☐ 12	Allison Feaster	.40	.15
☐ 13	Sylvia Crawley	.40	.15
☐ 14	Svetlana Abrosimova	.40	.15
☐ 15	Jessie Hicks	.40	.15
☐ 16	Dominique Canty	.40	.15
☐ 17	Michele VanGorp	.40	.15
☐ 18	Yolanda Griffith	2.00	.75
☐ 19	Dawn Staley	2.00	.75
☐ 20	Shalonda Enis	.40	.15
☐ 21	Katie Smith	2.00	.75
☐ 22	Brooke Wyckoff	.75	.30
☐ 23	Adrienne Goodson	.40	.15
☐ 24	Erin Buescher	.40	.15
☐ 25	Sonja Henning	.40	.15
☐ 26	Betty Lennox	.75	.30
☐ 27	Wendy Palmer	1.50	.60
☐ 28	Semeka Randall	.40	.15
☐ 29	Charlotte Smith-Taylor	.40	.15
☐ 30	Tully Bevilaqua	.75	.30
☐ 31	DeLisha Milton	.40	.15
☐ 32	Katie Douglas	.75	.30
☐ 33	Natalie Williams	2.50	1.00
☐ 34	Kayte Christensen	.40	.15
☐ 35	Janeth Arcain	1.50	.60
☐ 36	Vickie Johnson	1.50	.60
☐ 37	Kamila Vodichkova	.40	.15
☐ 38	Kelly Miller	.40	.15
☐ 39	Grace Daley	.40	.15
☐ 40	Nicky McCrimmon	.40	.15
☐ 41	Taj McWilliams-Franklin	.40	.15
☐ 42	LaTonya Johnson	.75	.30
☐ 43	Jackie Stiles	2.50	1.00
☐ 44	Rita Williams	.75	.30
☐ 45	Tamecka Dixon	2.00	.75
☐ 46	Nykesha Sales	1.50	.60
☐ 47	Murriel Page	.40	.15
☐ 48	Marie Ferdinand	.40	.15
☐ 49	Penny Taylor	2.50	1.00
☐ 50	Tina Thompson	2.00	.75
☐ 51	Anna DeForge	.40	.15
☐ 52	Ruth Riley	.75	.30
☐ 53	Stacey Dales-Schuman	1.50	.60
☐ 54	Merlakia Jones	.75	.30
☐ 55	Nikki Teasley	.40	.15
☐ 56	Ticha Penicheiro	1.50	.60
☐ 57	Lindsey Yamasaki	.40	.15
☐ 58	Chasity Melvin	.40	.15
☐ 59	Mwadi Mabika	1.50	.60
☐ 60	Alisa Burras	.40	.15
☐ 61	Tonya Washington	.40	.15
☐ 62	Michelle Snow	.40	.15
☐ 63	Tari Phillips	2.00	.75
☐ 64	Simone Edwards	.40	.15
☐ 65	Sheryl Swoopes	5.00	2.00
☐ 66	Crystal Robinson	.75	.30
☐ 67	Adia Barnes	.40	.15
☐ 68	DeMya Walker	.40	.15
☐ 69	Lynn Pride	.40	.15
☐ 70	Ruthie Bolton-Holifield	1.50	.60
☐ 71	Sandy Brondello	1.50	.60
☐ 72	Debbie Black	.40	.15
☐ 73	Sheri Sam	.40	.15
☐ 74	Kedra Holland-Corn	.75	.30
☐ 75	Andrea Stinson	1.50	.60
☐ 76	Tamika Catchings	2.00	.75
☐ 77	Georgia Schweitzer	.40	.15
☐ 78	Shannon Johnson	.75	.30
☐ 79	Jennifer Azzi	2.00	.75
☐ 80	Deanna Nolan	.40	.15
☐ 81	Teresa Weatherspoon	2.50	1.00
☐ 82	Tangela Smith	.40	.15
☐ 83	Ukari Figgs	.40	.15
☐ 84	Becky Hammon	.75	.30
☐ 85	Lauren Jackson	1.50	.60
☐ 86	LaQuanda Quick	.40	.15
☐ 87	Jennifer Rizzotti	.75	.30
☐ 88	Tamicha Jackson	.75	.30
☐ 89	Asjha Jones	.40	.15
☐ 90	Margo Dydek	.40	.15
☐ 91	Swintayla Cash	.40	.15
☐ 92	Kristi Harrower	.40	.15
☐ 93	Edna Campbell	.40	.15
☐ 94	Deanna Jackson	.40	.15
☐ 95	Nikki McCray	.75	.30
☐ 96	Cynthia Cooper	5.00	2.00
☐ 97	Jennifer Gillom	.75	.30
☐ 98	Coco Miller	.40	.15
☐ 99	Ayana Walker	.40	.15
☐ 100	Tamika Whitmore	.75	.30
☐ 101	Tammy Sutton-Brown	.75	.30
☐ 102	Edwina Brown	.40	.15
☐ 103	Coquese Washington	.40	.15
☐ 104	Lisa Harrison	.40	.15
☐ 105	Chamique Holdsclaw	5.00	2.00
☐ 106	LaToya Thomas RC	5.00	2.00
☐ 107	Plenette Pierson RC	5.00	2.00
☐ 108	Coretta Brown RC	5.00	2.00
☐ 109	Sun-Min Jung RC	6.00	2.50
☐ 110	Kara Lawson RC	15.00	6.00
☐ 111	Gwen Jackson RC	6.00	2.50
☐ 112	Cheryl Ford RC	12.00	5.00
☐ 113	Courtney Coleman RC	5.00	2.00
☐ 114	Chantelle Anderson RC	5.00	2.00
☐ 115	Shaquala Williams RC	5.00	2.00
☐ 116	Tamara Bowie RC	5.00	2.00
☐ 117	Teresa Edwards RC	12.00	5.00
☐ 118	Aiysha Smith RC	6.00	2.50
☐ 119	Petra Ujhelyi RC	5.00	2.00
☐ 120	Allison Curtin RC	6.00	2.50

2004 Ultra WNBA

❏ COMPLETE SET (110)		80.00	30.00
❏ COMP.SET w/o SP's (90)		20.00	8.00
❏ COMMON CARD (1-90)		.20	.08
❏ COMMON ROOKIE (91-110)		5.00	2.00
❏ 1 Tamika Catchings		.75	.30
❏ 2 Sheri Sam		.20	.08
❏ 3 Ruthie Bolton		.75	.30
❏ 4 Chamique Holdsclaw		3.00	1.25
❏ 5 Michelle Snow		.20	.08
❏ 6 Crystal Robinson		.20	.08
❏ 7 Betty Lennox		.50	.20
❏ 8 Dominique Canty		.20	.08
❏ 9 Vickie Johnson		.20	.08
❏ 10 Margo Dydek		2.00	.75
❏ 11 Charlotte Smith-Taylor		.20	.08
❏ 12 Katie Smith		2.00	.75
❏ 13 Shannon Johnson		.20	.08
❏ 14 Teresa Weatherspoon		.75	.30
❏ 15 Natalie Williams		.75	.30
❏ 16 Yolanda Griffith		.75	.30
❏ 17 Adia Barnes		.20	.08
❏ 18 Andrea Stinson		.50	.20
❏ 19 Michele Van Gorp		.20	.08
❏ 20 Kara Lawson		.20	.08
❏ 21 Tammy Sutton-Brown		.20	.08
❏ 22 Svetlana Abrosimova		.20	.08
❏ 23 Chantelle Anderson		.20	.08
❏ 24 Tynesha Lewis		.20	.08
❏ 25 Tamika Williams		.20	.08
❏ 26 LaToya Thomas		.20	.08
❏ 27 Edna Campbell		.20	.08
❏ 28 Lisa Leslie		4.00	1.50
❏ 29 Kayte Christensen		.20	.08
❏ 30 Stacey Dales-Schuman		.20	.08
❏ 31 Wendy Palmer		.50	.20
❏ 32 Swin Cash		1.50	.60
❏ 33 Jessie Hicks		.20	.08
❏ 34 Katie Douglas		.20	.08
❏ 35 Mwadi Mabika		.20	.08
❏ 36 Adrienne Goodson		.20	.08
❏ 37 Taj McWilliams-Franklin		.50	.20
❏ 38 Slobodanka Tuvic		.20	.08
❏ 39 Semeka Randall		.20	.08
❏ 40 Kelly Miller		.20	.08
❏ 41 Tamika Whitmore		.20	.08
❏ 42 Tully Bevilaqua		.20	.08
❏ 43 Sheryl Swoopes		4.00	1.50
❏ 44 Becky Hammon		.50	.20
❏ 45 Sue Bird		5.00	2.00
❏ 46 Debbie Black		.20	.08
❏ 47 DeLisha Milton-Jones		.20	.08
❏ 48 Adrain Williams		.20	.08
❏ 49 Asjha Jones		.20	.08
❏ 50 Janell Burse		.20	.08
❏ 51 Tamecka Dixon		.20	.08
❏ 52 Penny Taylor		.20	.08
❏ 53 Coco Miller		.20	.08
❏ 54 Cheryl Ford		.75	.30
❏ 55 Deanna Jackson		.20	.08
❏ 56 DeMya Walker		.20	.08
❏ 57 Kamila Vodichkova		.20	.08
❏ 58 Deanna Nolan		.20	.08
❏ 59 Allison Feaster		.20	.08
❏ 60 Plenette Pierson		.20	.08
❏ 61 Lauren Jackson		2.00	.75
❏ 62 Dawn Staley		.75	.30
❏ 63 Nykesha Sales		1.00	.40
❏ 64 Tangela Smith		.20	.08
❏ 65 Aiysha Smith		.20	.08
❏ 66 Ruth Riley		.75	.30
❏ 67 Nikki McCray		.50	.20
❏ 68 Nikki Teasley		.20	.08
❏ 69 Chasity Melvin		.20	.08
❏ 70 Merlakia Jones		.20	.08
❏ 71 Coretta Brown		.20	.08
❏ 72 Anna DeForge		.20	.08
❏ 73 Murriel Page		.20	.08
❏ 74 Tina Thompson		.75	.30
❏ 75 Tari Phillips		.50	.20
❏ 76 Gwen Jackson		.20	.08
❏ 77 Ayana Walker		.20	.08
❏ 78 Kelly Schumacher		.20	.08
❏ 79 Ticha Penicheiro		1.25	.50
❏ 80 Simone Edwards		.20	.08
❏ 81 Kedra Holland-Corn		.50	.20
❏ 82 K.B. Sharp RC		.20	.08
❏ 83 LaQuanda Quick		.50	.20
❏ 84 Barbara Farris		.20	.08
❏ 85 Stephanie White		.50	.20
❏ 86 Tamicha Jackson		.50	.20
❏ 87 Elena Baranova		1.00	.40
❏ 88 Elaine Powell		.20	.08
❏ 89 Teresa Edwards		.20	.08
❏ 90 Marie Ferdinand		.20	.08
❏ 91 Diana Taurasi RC		30.00	12.50
❏ 92 Alana Beard RC		10.00	4.00
❏ 93 Nicole Powell RC		6.00	2.50
❏ 94 Lindsay Whalen RC		15.00	6.00
❏ 95 Shameka Christon RC		10.00	4.00
❏ 96 Nicole Ohlde RC		6.00	2.50
❏ 97 Vanessa Hayden RC		6.00	2.50
❏ 98 Chandi Jones RC		6.00	2.50
❏ 99 Ebony Hoffman RC		8.00	3.00
❏ 100 Rebekkah Brunson RC		5.00	2.00
❏ 101 Iciss Tillis RC		5.00	2.00
❏ 102 Christi Thomas RC		5.00	2.00
❏ 103 Shereka Wright RC		5.00	2.00
❏ 104 Ashley Robinson RC		5.00	2.00
❏ 105 Kaayla Chones RC		5.00	2.00
❏ 106 Jessica Brungo RC		6.00	2.50
❏ 107 Kelly Mazzante RC		10.00	4.00
❏ 108 Catrina Frierson RC		5.00	2.00
❏ 109 Bethany Donaphin RC		5.00	2.00
❏ 110 Agnieszka Bibrzycka RC		5.00	2.00

1991-92 Upper Deck

❏ COMPLETE SET (500)		20.00	10.00
❏ COMPLETE FACT.SET (500)		20.00	10.00
❏ COMPLETE SERIES 1 (400)		12.00	6.00
❏ COMMON CARD (1-400)		.05	.01
❏ COMPLETE SERIES 2 (100)		8.00	4.00
❏ COMMON CARD (401-500)		.10	.02
❏ 1 S.Augmon/R.Monroe CL		.05	.01
❏ 2 Larry Johnson RC		1.00	.40
❏ 3 Dikembe Mutombo RC		1.00	.40
❏ 4 Steve Smith RC		1.00	.40
❏ 5 Stacey Augmon RC		.25	.08
❏ 6 Terrell Brandon RC		.75	.30
❏ 7 Greg Anthony RC		.25	.08
❏ 8 Rich King RC		.05	.01
❏ 9 Chris Gatling RC		.25	.08
❏ 10 Victor Alexander RC		.05	.01
❏ 11 John Turner RC		.05	.01
❏ 12 Eric Murdock RC		.05	.01
❏ 13 Mark Randall RC		.05	.01
❏ 14 Rodney Monroe RC		.05	.01
❏ 15 Myron Brown		.05	.01
❏ 16 Mike Iuzzolino RC		.05	.01
❏ 17 Chris Corchiani RC		.05	.01
❏ 18 Elliot Perry RC		.10	.02
❏ 19 Jimmy Oliver RC		.05	.01
❏ 20 Doug Overton RC		.05	.01
❏ 21 Steve Hood UER		.05	.01
❏ 22 Michael Jordan SCHOOL		.75	.30
❏ 23 Kevin Johnson School		.10	.02
❏ 24 Kurk Lee		.05	.01
❏ 25 Sean Higgins RC		.05	.01
❏ 26 Morlon Wiley		.05	.01
❏ 27 Derek Smith		.05	.01
❏ 28 Kenny Payne		.05	.01
❏ 29 Magic Johnson SPEC		.40	.15
❏ 30 L.Bird/C.Person CC		.25	.08
❏ 31 K.Malone/C.Barkley CC		.25	.08
❏ 32 K.Johnson/Stockton CC		.10	.02
❏ 33 H.Olajuwon/P.Ewing CC		.25	.08
❏ 34 M.Johnson/M.Jordan CC		1.00	.40
❏ 35 Derrick Coleman ART		.05	.01
❏ 36 Lionel Simmons ART		.05	.01
❏ 37 Dee Brown ART		.05	.01
❏ 38 Dennis Scott ART		.05	.01
❏ 39 Kendall Gill ART		.05	.01
❏ 40 Winston Garland		.05	.01
❏ 41 Danny Young		.05	.01
❏ 42 Rick Mahorn		.05	.01
❏ 43 Michael Adams		.05	.01
❏ 44 Michael Jordan		3.00	1.50
❏ 45 Magic Johnson		.75	.30
❏ 46 Doc Rivers		.10	.02
❏ 47 Moses Malone		.25	.08
❏ 48 Michael Jordan AS CL		1.50	.60
❏ 49 James Worthy AS		.10	.02
❏ 50 Tim Hardaway AS		.25	.08
❏ 51 Karl Malone AS		.25	.08
❏ 52 John Stockton AS		.10	.02
❏ 53 Clyde Drexler AS		.10	.02
❏ 54 Terry Porter AS		.05	.01
❏ 55 Kevin Duckworth AS		.05	.01
❏ 56 Tom Chambers AS		.05	.01
❏ 57 Magic Johnson AS		.40	.15
❏ 58 David Robinson AS		.25	.08
❏ 59 Kevin Johnson AS		.10	.02
❏ 60 Chris Mullin AS		.05	.01
❏ 61 Joe Dumars AS		.10	.02
❏ 62 Kevin McHale AS		.05	.01
❏ 63 Brad Daugherty AS		.05	.01
❏ 64 Alvin Robertson AS		.05	.01
❏ 65 Bernard King AS		.05	.01
❏ 66 Dominique Wilkins AS		.10	.02
❏ 67 Ricky Pierce AS		.05	.01
❏ 68 Patrick Ewing AS		.10	.02
❏ 69 Michael Jordan AS		1.50	.60
❏ 70 Charles Barkley AS		.25	.08
❏ 71 Hersey Hawkins AS		.05	.01
❏ 72 Robert Parish AS		.05	.01
❏ 73 Alvin Robertson TC		.05	.01
❏ 74 Bernard King TC		.05	.01
❏ 75 Michael Jordan TC		1.50	.60
❏ 76 Brad Daugherty TC		.05	.01
❏ 77 Larry Bird TC		.50	.20
❏ 78 Ron Harper TC		.05	.01
❏ 79 Dominique Wilkins TC		.10	.02
❏ 80 Rony Seikaly TC		.05	.01
❏ 81 Rex Chapman TC		.05	.01
❏ 82 Mark Eaton TC		.05	.01
❏ 83 Lionel Simmons TC		.05	.01
❏ 84 Gerald Wilkins TC		.05	.01
❏ 85 James Worthy TC		.10	.02
❏ 86 Scott Skiles TC		.05	.01
❏ 87 Rolando Blackman TC		.05	.01
❏ 88 Derrick Coleman TC		.05	.01
❏ 89 Chris Jackson TC		.05	.01
❏ 90 Reggie Miller TC		.10	.02
❏ 91 Isiah Thomas TC		.10	.02
❏ 92 Hakeem Olajuwon TC		.25	.08
❏ 93 Hersey Hawkins TC		.05	.01
❏ 94 David Robinson TC		.25	.08
❏ 95 Tom Chambers TC		.05	.01
❏ 96 Shawn Kemp TC		.25	.08
❏ 97 Pooh Richardson TC		.05	.01
❏ 98 Clyde Drexler TC		.10	.02

#	Player		
❑ 99	Chris Mullin TC	.10	.02
❑ 100	Checklist 1-100	.05	.01
❑ 101	John Shasky	.05	.01
❑ 102	Dana Barros	.05	.01
❑ 103	Stojko Vrankovic	.05	.01
❑ 104	Larry Drew	.05	.01
❑ 105	Randy White	.05	.01
❑ 106	Dave Corzine	.05	.01
❑ 107	Joe Kleine	.05	.01
❑ 108	Lance Blanks	.05	.01
❑ 109	Rodney McCray	.05	.01
❑ 110	Sedale Threatt	.05	.01
❑ 111	Ken Norman	.05	.01
❑ 112	Rickey Green	.05	.01
❑ 113	Andy Toolson	.05	.01
❑ 114	Bo Kimble	.05	.01
❑ 115	Mark West	.05	.01
❑ 116	Mark Eaton	.05	.01
❑ 117	John Paxson	.05	.01
❑ 118	Mike Brown	.05	.01
❑ 119	Brian Oliver	.05	.01
❑ 120	Will Perdue	.05	.01
❑ 121	Michael Smith	.05	.01
❑ 122	Sherman Douglas	.05	.01
❑ 123	Reggie Lewis	.10	.02
❑ 124	James Donaldson	.05	.01
❑ 125	Scottie Pippen	.75	.30
❑ 126	Elden Campbell	.10	.02
❑ 127	Michael Cage	.05	.01
❑ 128	Tony Smith	.05	.01
❑ 129	Ed Pinckney	.05	.01
❑ 130	Keith Askins RC	.05	.01
❑ 131	Darrell Griffith	.05	.01
❑ 132	Vinnie Johnson	.05	.01
❑ 133	Ron Harper	.10	.02
❑ 134	Andre Turner	.05	.01
❑ 135	Jeff Hornacek	.10	.02
❑ 136	John Stockton	.25	.08
❑ 137	Derek Harper	.10	.02
❑ 138	Loy Vaught	.05	.01
❑ 139	Thurl Bailey	.05	.01
❑ 140	Olden Polynice	.05	.01
❑ 141	Kevin Edwards	.05	.01
❑ 142	Byron Scott	.10	.02
❑ 143	Dee Brown	.05	.01
❑ 144	Sam Perkins	.10	.02
❑ 145	Rony Seikaly	.05	.01
❑ 146	James Worthy	.25	.08
❑ 147	Glen Rice	.25	.08
❑ 148	Craig Hodges	.05	.01
❑ 149	Bimbo Coles	.05	.01
❑ 150	Mychal Thompson	.05	.01
❑ 151	Xavier McDaniel	.05	.01
❑ 152	Roy Tarpley	.05	.01
❑ 153	Gary Payton	.60	.25
❑ 154	Rolando Blackman	.05	.01
❑ 155	Hersey Hawkins	.10	.02
❑ 156	Ricky Pierce	.05	.01
❑ 157	Fat Lever	.05	.01
❑ 158	Andrew Lang	.05	.01
❑ 159	Benoit Benjamin	.05	.01
❑ 160	Cedric Ceballos	.10	.02
❑ 161	Charles Smith	.05	.01
❑ 162	Jeff Martin	.05	.01
❑ 163	Robert Parish	.10	.02
❑ 164	Danny Manning	.10	.02
❑ 165	Mark Aguirre	.05	.01
❑ 166	Jeff Malone	.05	.01
❑ 167	Bill Laimbeer	.10	.02
❑ 168	Willie Burton	.05	.01
❑ 169	Dennis Hopson	.05	.01
❑ 170	Kevin Gamble	.05	.01
❑ 171	Terry Teagle	.05	.01
❑ 172	Dan Majerle	.10	.02
❑ 173	Shawn Kemp	.50	.25
❑ 174	Tom Chambers	.05	.01
❑ 175	Vlade Divac	.10	.02
❑ 176	Johnny Dawkins	.05	.01
❑ 177	A.C. Green	.10	.02
❑ 178	Manute Bol	.05	.01
❑ 179	Terry Davis	.05	.01
❑ 180	Ron Anderson	.05	.01
❑ 181	Horace Grant	.10	.02
❑ 182	Stacey King	.05	.01
❑ 183	William Bedford	.05	.01
❑ 184	B.J. Armstrong	.05	.01
❑ 185	Dennis Rodman	.50	.20
❑ 186	Nate McMillan	.05	.01
❑ 187	Cliff Levingston	.05	.01
❑ 188	Quintin Dailey	.05	.01
❑ 189	Bill Cartwright	.05	.01
❑ 190	John Salley	.05	.01
❑ 191	Jayson Williams	.25	.08
❑ 192	Grant Long	.05	.01
❑ 193	Negele Knight	.05	.01
❑ 194	Alec Kessler	.05	.01
❑ 195	Gary Grant	.05	.01
❑ 196	Billy Thompson	.05	.01
❑ 197	Delaney Rudd	.05	.01
❑ 198	Alan Ogg	.05	.01
❑ 199	Blue Edwards	.05	.01
❑ 200	Checklist 101-200	.05	.01
❑ 201	Mark Acres	.05	.01
❑ 202	Craig Ehlo	.05	.01
❑ 203	Anthony Cook	.05	.01
❑ 204	Eric Leckner	.05	.01
❑ 205	Terry Catledge	.05	.01
❑ 206	Reggie Williams	.05	.01
❑ 207	Greg Kite	.05	.01
❑ 208	Steve Kerr	.10	.02
❑ 209	Kenny Battle	.05	.01
❑ 210	John Morton	.05	.01
❑ 211	Kenny Williams	.05	.01
❑ 212	Mark Jackson	.10	.02
❑ 213	Alaa Abdelnaby	.05	.01
❑ 214	Rod Strickland	.25	.08
❑ 215	Micheal Williams	.05	.01
❑ 216	Kevin Duckworth	.05	.01
❑ 217	David Wingate	.05	.01
❑ 218	LaSalle Thompson	.05	.01
❑ 219	John Starks RC	.25	.08
❑ 220	Clifford Robinson	.10	.02
❑ 221	Jeff Grayer	.05	.01
❑ 222	Marcus Liberty	.05	.01
❑ 223	Larry Nance	.10	.02
❑ 224	Michael Ansley	.05	.01
❑ 225	Kevin McHale	.10	.02
❑ 226	Scott Skiles	.05	.01
❑ 227	Darnell Valentine	.05	.01
❑ 228	Nick Anderson	.10	.02
❑ 229	Brad Davis	.05	.01
❑ 230	Gerald Paddio	.05	.01
❑ 231	Sam Bowie	.05	.01
❑ 232	Sam Vincent	.05	.01
❑ 233	George McCloud	.05	.01
❑ 234	Gerald Wilkins	.05	.01
❑ 235	Mookie Blaylock	.10	.02
❑ 236	Jon Koncak	.05	.01
❑ 237	Danny Ferry	.05	.01
❑ 238	Vern Fleming	.05	.01
❑ 239	Mark Price	.10	.02
❑ 240	Sidney Moncrief	.05	.01
❑ 241	Jay Humphries	.05	.01
❑ 242	Muggsy Bogues	.10	.02
❑ 243	Tim Hardaway	.40	.15
❑ 244	Alvin Robertson	.05	.01
❑ 245	Chris Mullin	.25	.08
❑ 246	Pooh Richardson	.05	.01
❑ 247	Winston Bennett	.05	.01
❑ 248	Kelvin Upshaw	.05	.01
❑ 249	John Williams	.05	.01
❑ 250	Steve Alford	.05	.01
❑ 251	Spud Webb	.10	.02
❑ 252	Sleepy Floyd	.05	.01
❑ 253	Chuck Person	.05	.01
❑ 254	Hakeem Olajuwon	.40	.15
❑ 255	Dominique Wilkins	.25	.08
❑ 256	Reggie Miller	.25	.08
❑ 257	Dennis Scott	.10	.02
❑ 258	Charles Oakley	.10	.02
❑ 259	Sidney Green	.05	.01
❑ 260	Detlef Schrempf	.10	.02
❑ 261	Rod Higgins	.05	.01
❑ 262	J.R. Reid	.05	.01
❑ 263	Tyrone Hill	.10	.02
❑ 264	Reggie Theus	.05	.01
❑ 265	Mitch Richmond	.25	.08
❑ 266	Dale Ellis	.10	.02
❑ 267	Terry Cummings	.05	.01
❑ 268	Johnny Newman	.05	.01
❑ 269	Doug West	.05	.01
❑ 270	Jim Petersen	.05	.01
❑ 271	Otis Thorpe	.10	.02
❑ 272	John Williams	.05	.01
❑ 273	Kennard Winchester RC	.05	.01
❑ 274	Duane Ferrell	.05	.01
❑ 275	Vernon Maxwell	.05	.01
❑ 276	Kenny Smith	.05	.01
❑ 277	Jerome Kersey	.05	.01
❑ 278	Kevin Willis	.05	.01
❑ 279	Danny Ainge	.10	.02
❑ 280	Larry Smith	.05	.01
❑ 281	Maurice Cheeks	.05	.01
❑ 282	Willie Anderson	.05	.01
❑ 283	Tom Tolbert	.05	.01
❑ 284	Jerrod Mustaf	.05	.01
❑ 285	Randolph Keys	.05	.01
❑ 286	Jerry Reynolds	.05	.01
❑ 287	Sean Elliott	.10	.02
❑ 288	Otis Smith	.05	.01
❑ 289	Terry Mills RC	.25	.08
❑ 290	Kelly Tripucka	.05	.01
❑ 291	Jon Sundvold	.05	.01
❑ 292	Rumeal Robinson	.05	.01
❑ 293	Fred Roberts	.05	.01
❑ 294	Rik Smits	.10	.02
❑ 295	Jerome Lane	.05	.01
❑ 296	Dave Jamerson	.05	.01
❑ 297	Joe Wolf	.05	.01
❑ 298	David Wood RC	.05	.01
❑ 299	Todd Lichti	.05	.01
❑ 300	Checklist 201-300	.05	.01
❑ 301	Randy Breuer	.05	.01
❑ 302	Buck Johnson	.05	.01
❑ 303	Scott Brooks	.05	.01
❑ 304	Jeff Turner	.05	.01
❑ 305	Felton Spencer	.05	.01
❑ 306	Greg Dreiling	.05	.01
❑ 307	Gerald Glass	.05	.01
❑ 308	Tony Brown	.05	.01
❑ 309	Sam Mitchell	.05	.01
❑ 310	Adrian Caldwell	.05	.01
❑ 311	Chris Dudley	.05	.01
❑ 312	Blair Rasmussen	.05	.01
❑ 313	Antoine Carr	.05	.01
❑ 314	Greg Anderson	.05	.01
❑ 315	Drazen Petrovic	.10	.02
❑ 316	Alton Lister	.05	.01
❑ 317	Jack Haley	.05	.01
❑ 318	Bobby Hansen	.05	.01
❑ 319	Chris Jackson	.05	.01
❑ 320	Herb Williams	.05	.01
❑ 321	Kendall Gill	.10	.02
❑ 322	Tyrone Corbin	.05	.01
❑ 323	Kiki Vandeweghe	.05	.01
❑ 324	David Robinson	.50	.20
❑ 325	Rex Chapman	.10	.02
❑ 326	Tony Campbell	.05	.01
❑ 327	Dell Curry	.05	.01
❑ 328	Charles Jones	.05	.01
❑ 329	Kenny Gattison	.05	.01
❑ 330	Haywoode Workman RC	.10	.02
❑ 331	Travis Mays	.05	.01
❑ 332	Derrick Coleman	.25	.08
❑ 333	Isiah Thomas	.25	.08
❑ 334	Jud Buechler	.05	.01
❑ 335	Joe Dumars	.25	.08
❑ 336	Tate George	.05	.01
❑ 337	Mike Sanders	.05	.01
❑ 338	James Edwards	.05	.01
❑ 339	Chris Morris	.05	.01
❑ 340	Scott Hastings	.05	.01
❑ 341	Trent Tucker	.05	.01
❑ 342	Harvey Grant	.05	.01
❑ 343	Patrick Ewing	.25	.08
❑ 344	Larry Bird	1.00	.40
❑ 345	Charles Barkley	.40	.15
❑ 346	Brian Shaw	.05	.01
❑ 347	Kenny Walker	.05	.01
❑ 348	Danny Schayes	.05	.01
❑ 349	Tom Hammonds	.05	.01
❑ 350	Frank Brickowski	.05	.01
❑ 351	Terry Porter	.05	.01
❑ 352	Orlando Woolridge	.05	.01
❑ 353	Buck Williams	.05	.01
❑ 354	Sarunas Marciulionis	.05	.01
❑ 355	Karl Malone	.40	.15
❑ 356	Kevin Johnson	.25	.08

357 Clyde Drexler	.25	.08
358 Duane Causwell	.05	.01
359 Paul Pressey	.05	.01
360 Jim Les RC	.05	.01
361 Derrick McKey	.05	.01
362 Scott Williams RC	.05	.01
363 Mark Alarie	.05	.01
364 Brad Daugherty	.05	.01
365 Bernard King	.05	.01
366 Steve Henson	.05	.01
367 Darrell Walker	.05	.01
368 Larry Krystkowiak	.05	.01
369 Henry James UER	.05	.01
370 Jack Sikma	.05	.01
371 Eddie Johnson	.10	.02
372 Wayman Tisdale	.05	.01
373 Joe Barry Carroll	.05	.01
374 David Greenwood	.05	.01
375 Lionel Simmons	.05	.01
376 Dwayne Schintzius	.05	.01
377 Tod Murphy	.05	.01
378 Wayne Cooper	.05	.01
379 Anthony Bonner	.05	.01
380 Walter Davis	.05	.01
381 Lester Conner	.05	.01
382 Ledell Eackles	.05	.01
383 Brad Lohaus	.05	.01
384 Derrick Gervin	.05	.01
385 Pervis Ellison	.05	.01
386 Tim McCormick	.05	.01
387 A.J. English	.05	.01
388 John Battle	.05	.01
389 Roy Hinson	.05	.01
390 Armon Gilliam	.05	.01
391 Kurt Rambis	.05	.01
392 Mark Bryant	.05	.01
393 Chucky Brown	.05	.01
394 Avery Johnson	.10	.02
395 Rory Sparrow	.05	.01
396 Mario Elie RC	.25	.08
397 Ralph Sampson	.05	.01
398 Mike Gminski	.05	.01
399 Bill Wennington	.05	.01
400 Checklist 301-400	.05	.01
401 David Wingate	.10	.02
402 Moses Malone	.50	.20
403 Darrell Walker	.10	.02
404 Antoine Carr	.10	.02
405 Charles Shackleford	.10	.02
406 Orlando Woolridge	.10	.02
407 Robert Pack RC	.25	.08
408 Bobby Hansen	.10	.02
409 Dale Davis RC	.50	.20
410 Vincent Askew RC	.10	.02
411 Alexander Volkov	.10	.02
412 Dwayne Schintzius	.10	.02
413 Tim Perry	.10	.02
414 Tyrone Corbin	.10	.02
415 Pete Chilcutt RC	.10	.02
416 James Edwards	.10	.02
417 Jerrod Mustaf	.10	.02
418 Thurl Bailey	.10	.02
419 Spud Webb	.25	.08
420 Doc Rivers	.25	.08
421 Sean Green RC	.10	.02
422 Walter Davis	.10	.02
423 Terry Davis	.10	.02
424 John Battle	.10	.02
425 Vinnie Johnson	.10	.02
426 Sherman Douglas	.10	.02
427 Kevin Brooks RC	.10	.02
428 Greg Sutton	.10	.02
429 Rafael Addison RC	.10	.02
430 Anthony Mason RC	1.00	.40
431 Paul Graham RC	.10	.02
432 Anthony Frederick RC	.10	.02
433 Dennis Hopson	.10	.02
434 Rory Sparrow	.10	.02
435 Michael Adams	.10	.02
436 Kevin Lynch RC	.10	.02
437 Randy Brown RC	.10	.02
438 L.Johnson/B.Owens TP CL	.25	.08
439 Stacey Augmon TP	.10	.02
440 Larry Stewart RC TP	.10	.02
441 Terrell Brandon TP	.50	.20
442 Billy Owens TP RC	.10	.02

443 Rick Fox TP RC	.25	.08
444 Kenny Anderson TP RC	1.00	.40
445 Larry Johnson TP	.50	.20
446 Dikembe Mutombo TP	.50	.20
447 Steve Smith TP	.50	.20
448 Greg Anthony TP	.25	.08
449 East All-Star CL	.25	.08
450 West All-Star CL	.25	.08
451 Isiah Thomas AS w/Magic	.50	.20
452 Michael Jordan AS	3.00	1.25
453 Scottie Pippen AS	.75	.30
454 Charles Barkley AS	.50	.20
455 Patrick Ewing AS	.25	.08
456 Michael Adams AS	.10	.02
457 Dennis Rodman AS	.50	.20
458 Reggie Lewis AS	.10	.02
459 Joe Dumars AS	.25	.08
460 Mark Price AS	.10	.02
461 Brad Daugherty AS	.10	.02
462 Kevin Willis AS	.10	.02
463 Clyde Drexler AS	.25	.08
464 Magic Johnson AS	.75	.30
465 Chris Mullin AS	.25	.08
466 Karl Malone AS	.50	.20
467 David Robinson AS	.50	.20
468 Tim Hardaway AS	.50	.20
469 Jeff Hornacek AS	.10	.02
470 John Stockton AS	.25	.08
471 Dikembe Mutombo AS	.25	.08
472 Hakeem Olajuwon AS	.50	.20
473 James Worthy AS	.25	.08
474 Otis Thorpe AS	.10	.02
475 Dan Majerle AS	.10	.02
476 Cedric Ceballos SD CL	.10	.02
477 Nick Anderson SD	.10	.02
478 Stacey Augmon SD	.25	.08
479 Cedric Ceballos SD	.10	.02
480 Larry Johnson SD	.50	.20
481 Shawn Kemp SD	.60	.25
482 John Starks SD	.25	.08
483 Doug West SD	.10	.02
484 Craig Hodges	.10	.02
485 LaBradford Smith RC	.10	.02
486 Winston Garland	.10	.02
487 David Benoit RC	.25	.08
488 John Bagley	.10	.02
489 Mark Macon RC	.10	.02
490 Mitch Richmond	.25	.08
491 Luc Longley RC	.25	.08
492 Sedale Threatt	.10	.02
493 Doug Smith RC	.10	.02
494 Travis Mays	.10	.02
495 Xavier McDaniel	.10	.02
496 Brian Shaw	.10	.02
497 Stanley Roberts RC	.10	.02
498 Blair Rasmussen	.10	.02
499 Brian Williams RC	.50	.20
500 Checklist Card	.10	.02

1992-93 Upper Deck

COMPLETE SET (514)	80.00	40.00
COMPLETE LO SERIES (311)	20.00	10.00
COMPLETE HI SERIES (203)	60.00	30.00
1 Shaquille O'Neal SP RC!	40.00	15.00
1A Draft Trade Card	.30	.10
1B Shaquille O'Neal TRADE	20.00	8.00
1AX Draft Trade Stamped	.30	.10
2 Alonzo Mourning RC	2.00	.75

3 Christian Laettner RC	.60	.25
4 LaPhonso Ellis RC	.30	.10
5 C.Weatherspoon RC	.30	.10
6 Adam Keefe RC	.15	.05
7 Robert Horry RC	.30	.10
8 Harold Miner RC	.15	.05
9 Bryant Stith RC	.15	.05
10 Malik Sealy RC	.15	.05
11 Anthony Peeler RC	.15	.05
12 Randy Woods RC	.05	.01
13 Tracy Murray RC	.15	.05
14 Tom Gugliotta RC	1.00	.40
15 Hubert Davis RC	.15	.05
16 Don MacLean RC	.05	.01
17 Lee Mayberry RC	.05	.01
18 Corey Williams RC	.05	.01
19 Sean Rooks RC	.05	.01
20 Todd Day RC	.15	.05
21 B.Stith/L.Ellis CL	.30	.10
22 Jeff Hornacek	.05	.01
23 Michael Jordan	4.00	1.50
24 John Salley	.05	.01
25 Andre Turner	.05	.01
26 Charles Barkley	.50	.20
27 Anthony Frederick	.05	.01
28 Mario Elie	.15	.05
29 Olden Polynice	.05	.01
30 Rodney Monroe	.05	.01
31 Tim Perry	.05	.01
32 Doug Christie SP RC	1.00	.40
32A Magic Johnson SP	2.00	.75
33 Jim Jackson SP RC	2.50	1.00
33A Larry Bird SP	2.50	1.00
34 Randy White	.05	.01
35 Frank Brickowski TC	.05	.01
36 Michael Adams TC	.05	.01
37 Scottie Pippen TC	.50	.20
38 Mark Price TC	.05	.01
39 Robert Parish TC	.05	.01
40 Danny Manning TC	.05	.01
41 Kevin Willis TC	.05	.01
42 Glen Rice TC	.15	.05
43 Kendall Gill TC	.05	.01
44 Karl Malone TC	.30	.10
45 Mitch Richmond TC	.30	.10
46 Patrick Ewing TC	.30	.10
47 Sam Perkins TC	.05	.01
48 Dennis Scott TC	.05	.01
49 Derek Harper TC	.05	.01
50 Drazen Petrovic TC	.05	.01
51 Reggie Williams TC	.05	.01
52 Rik Smits TC	.05	.01
53 Joe Dumars TC	.15	.05
54 Otis Thorpe TC	.05	.01
55 Johnny Dawkins TC	.05	.01
56 Sean Elliott TC	.05	.01
57 Kevin Johnson TC	.15	.05
58 Ricky Pierce TC	.05	.01
59 Doug West TC	.05	.01
60 Terry Porter TC	.05	.01
61 Tim Hardaway TC	.30	.10
62 M.Jordan/S.Pippen ST	1.00	.40
63 K.Gill/L.Johnson ST	.30	.10
64 T.Chambers/K.Johnson ST	.15	.05
65 T.Hardaway/C.Mullin ST	.05	.01
66 K.Malone/J.Stockton ST	.30	.10
67 Michael Jordan MVP	2.00	.75
68 Stacey Augmon 6 MIL	.05	.01
69 Bob Lanier	.15	.05
70 Alaa Abdelnaby	.05	.01
71 Andrew Lang	.05	.01
72 Larry Krystkowiak	.05	.01
73 Gerald Wilkins	.05	.01
74 Rod Strickland	.30	.10
75 Danny Ainge	.15	.05
76 Chris Corchiani	.05	.01
77 Jeff Grayer	.05	.01
78 Eric Murdock	.05	.01
79 Rex Chapman	.05	.01
80 LaBradford Smith	.05	.01
81 Jay Humphries	.05	.01
82 David Robinson	.50	.20
83 William Bedford	.05	.01
84 James Edwards	.05	.01
85 Danny Schayes	.05	.01
86 Lloyd Daniels RC	.05	.01

❑ 87	Blue Edwards	.05	.01
❑ 88	Dale Ellis	.05	.01
❑ 89	Rolando Blackman	.05	.01
❑ 90	Form Checklist 1	.30	.10
❑ 91	Rik Smits	.15	.05
❑ 92	Terry Davis	.05	.01
❑ 93	Bill Cartwright	.05	.01
❑ 94	Avery Johnson	.05	.01
❑ 95	Micheal Williams	.05	.01
❑ 96	Spud Webb	.15	.05
❑ 97	Benoit Benjamin	.05	.01
❑ 98	Derek Harper	.15	.05
❑ 99	Matt Bullard	.05	.01
❑ 100A	Tyrone Corbin ERR Heat	1.00	.40
❑ 100B	Tyrone Corbin COR Jazz	.05	.01
❑ 101	Doc Rivers	.15	.05
❑ 102	Tony Smith	.05	.01
❑ 103	Doug West	.05	.01
❑ 104	Kevin Duckworth	.05	.01
❑ 105	Luc Longley	.15	.05
❑ 106	Antoine Carr	.05	.01
❑ 107	Cliff Robinson	.15	.05
❑ 108	Grant Long	.05	.01
❑ 109	Terry Porter	.05	.01
❑ 110A	Steve Smith ERR Jazz	4.00	1.50
❑ 110B	Steve Smith COR	.40	.15
❑ 111	Brian Williams	.05	.01
❑ 112	Karl Malone	.50	.20
❑ 113	Reggie Williams	.05	.01
❑ 114	Tom Chambers	.05	.01
❑ 115	Winston Garland	.05	.01
❑ 116	John Stockton	.30	.10
❑ 117	Chris Jackson	.05	.01
❑ 118	Mike Brown	.05	.01
❑ 119	Kevin Johnson	.30	.10
❑ 120	Reggie Lewis	.15	.05
❑ 121	Bimbo Coles	.05	.01
❑ 122	Drazen Petrovic	.05	.01
❑ 123	Reggie Miller	.30	.10
❑ 124	Derrick Coleman	.15	.05
❑ 125	Chuck Person	.05	.01
❑ 126	Glen Rice	.30	.10
❑ 127	Kenny Anderson	.30	.10
❑ 128	Willie Burton	.05	.01
❑ 129	Chris Morris	.05	.01
❑ 130	Patrick Ewing	.30	.10
❑ 131	Sean Elliott	.15	.05
❑ 132	Clyde Drexler	.30	.10
❑ 133	Scottie Pippen	1.00	.40
❑ 134	Pooh Richardson	.05	.01
❑ 135	Horace Grant	.15	.05
❑ 136	Hakeem Olajuwon	.50	.20
❑ 137	John Paxson	.05	.01
❑ 138	Kendall Gill	.15	.05
❑ 139	Michael Adams	.05	.01
❑ 140	Otis Thorpe	.15	.05
❑ 141	Dennis Scott	.05	.01
❑ 142	Stacey Augmon	.15	.05
❑ 143	Robert Pack	.05	.01
❑ 144	Kevin Willis	.05	.01
❑ 145	Jerome Kersey	.05	.01
❑ 146	Paul Graham	.05	.01
❑ 147	Stanley Roberts	.05	.01
❑ 148	Dominique Wilkins	.30	.10
❑ 149	Scott Skiles	.05	.01
❑ 150	Rumeal Robinson	.05	.01
❑ 151	Mookie Blaylock	.15	.05
❑ 152	Elden Campbell	.15	.05
❑ 153	Chris Dudley	.05	.01
❑ 154	Sedale Threatt	.05	.01
❑ 155	Tate George	.05	.01
❑ 156	James Worthy	.30	.10
❑ 157	B.J. Armstrong	.05	.01
❑ 158	Gary Payton	.60	.25
❑ 159	Ledell Eackles	.05	.01
❑ 160	Sam Perkins	.15	.05
❑ 161	Nick Anderson	.15	.05
❑ 162	Mitch Richmond	.30	.10
❑ 163	Buck Willis	.15	.05
❑ 164	Blair Rasmussen	.05	.01
❑ 165	Vern Fleming	.05	.01
❑ 166	Duane Ferrell	.05	.01
❑ 167	George McCloud	.05	.01
❑ 168	Terry Cummings	.15	.05
❑ 169	Detlef Schrempf	.15	.05
❑ 170	Willie Anderson	.05	.01
❑ 171	Scott Williams	.05	.01
❑ 172	Vernon Maxwell	.05	.01
❑ 173	Todd Lichti	.05	.01
❑ 174	David Benoit	.05	.01
❑ 175	Marcus Liberty	.05	.01
❑ 176	Kenny Smith	.05	.01
❑ 177	Dan Majerle	.15	.05
❑ 178	Jeff Malone	.05	.01
❑ 179	Robert Parish	.15	.05
❑ 180	Mark Eaton	.05	.01
❑ 181	Rony Seikaly	.05	.01
❑ 182	Tony Campbell	.05	.01
❑ 183	Kevin McHale	.30	.10
❑ 184	Thurl Bailey	.05	.01
❑ 185	Kevin Edwards	.05	.01
❑ 186	Gerald Glass	.05	.01
❑ 187	Hersey Hawkins	.15	.05
❑ 188	Sam Mitchell	.05	.01
❑ 189	Brian Shaw	.05	.01
❑ 190	Felton Spencer	.05	.01
❑ 191	Mark Macon	.05	.01
❑ 192	Jerry Reynolds	.05	.01
❑ 193	Dale Davis	.05	.01
❑ 194	Sleepy Floyd	.05	.01
❑ 195	A.C. Green	.15	.05
❑ 196	Terry Catledge	.05	.01
❑ 197	Byron Scott	.15	.05
❑ 198	Sam Bowie	.05	.01
❑ 199	Vlade Divac	.15	.05
❑ 200	Form Checklist 2	.30	.10
❑ 201	Brad Lohaus	.05	.01
❑ 202	Johnny Newman	.05	.01
❑ 203	Gary Grant	.05	.01
❑ 204	Sidney Green	.05	.01
❑ 205	Frank Brickowski	.05	.01
❑ 206	Anthony Bowie	.05	.01
❑ 207	Duane Causwell	.05	.01
❑ 208	A.J. English	.05	.01
❑ 209	Mark Aguirre	.05	.01
❑ 210	Jon Koncak	.05	.01
❑ 211	Kevin Gamble	.05	.01
❑ 212	Craig Ehlo	.05	.01
❑ 213	Herb Williams	.15	.05
❑ 214	Cedric Ceballos	.15	.05
❑ 215	Mark Jackson	.05	.01
❑ 216	John Bagley	.05	.01
❑ 217	Ron Anderson	.05	.01
❑ 218	John Battle	.05	.01
❑ 219	Kevin Lynch	.05	.01
❑ 220	Donald Hodge	.05	.01
❑ 221	Chris Gatling	.05	.01
❑ 222	Muggsy Bogues	.15	.05
❑ 223	Bill Laimbeer	.15	.05
❑ 224	Anthony Bonner	.05	.01
❑ 225	Fred Roberts	.05	.01
❑ 226	Larry Stewart	.05	.01
❑ 227	Darrell Walker	.05	.01
❑ 228	Larry Smith	.05	.01
❑ 229	Billy Owens	.15	.05
❑ 230	Vinnie Johnson	.05	.01
❑ 231	Johnny Dawkins	.05	.01
❑ 232	Rick Fox	.15	.05
❑ 233	Travis Mays	.05	.01
❑ 234	Mark Price	.15	.05
❑ 235	Derrick McKey	.05	.01
❑ 236	Greg Anthony	.05	.01
❑ 237	Doug Smith	.05	.01
❑ 238	Alec Kessler	.05	.01
❑ 239	Anthony Mason	.30	.10
❑ 240	Shawn Kemp	.60	.25
❑ 241	Jim Les	.05	.01
❑ 242	Dennis Rodman	.60	.25
❑ 243	Lionel Simmons	.05	.01
❑ 244	Pervis Ellison	.05	.01
❑ 245	Terrell Brandon	.30	.10
❑ 246	Mark Bryant	.05	.01
❑ 247	Brad Daugherty	.05	.01
❑ 248	Scott Brooks	.05	.01
❑ 249	Sarunas Marciulionis	.05	.01
❑ 250	Danny Ferry	.05	.01
❑ 251	Loy Vaught	.05	.01
❑ 252	Dee Brown	.05	.01
❑ 253	Alvin Robertson	.05	.01
❑ 254	Charles Smith	.05	.01
❑ 255	Dikembe Mutombo	.40	.15
❑ 256	Greg Kite	.05	.01
❑ 257	Ed Pinckney	.05	.01
❑ 258	Ron Harper	.15	.05
❑ 259	Elliot Perry	.05	.01
❑ 260	Rafael Addison	.05	.01
❑ 261	Tim Hardaway	.40	.15
❑ 262	Randy Brown	.05	.01
❑ 263	Isiah Thomas	.30	.10
❑ 264	Victor Alexander	.05	.01
❑ 265	Wayman Tisdale	.05	.01
❑ 266	Harvey Grant	.05	.01
❑ 267	Mike Iuzzolino	.05	.01
❑ 268	Joe Dumars	.30	.10
❑ 269	Xavier McDaniel	.05	.01
❑ 270	Jeff Sanders	.05	.01
❑ 271	Danny Manning	.15	.05
❑ 272	Jayson Williams	.15	.05
❑ 273	Ricky Pierce	.05	.01
❑ 274	Will Perdue	.05	.01
❑ 275	Dana Barros	.05	.01
❑ 276	Randy Breuer	.05	.01
❑ 277	Manute Bol	.05	.01
❑ 278	Negele McCray	.05	.01
❑ 279	Rodney McCray	.05	.01
❑ 280	Greg Sutton	.05	.01
❑ 281	Larry Nance	.05	.01
❑ 282	John Starks	.15	.05
❑ 283	Pete Chilcutt	.05	.01
❑ 284	Kenny Gattison	.05	.01
❑ 285	Stacey King	.05	.01
❑ 286	Bernard King	.05	.01
❑ 287	Larry Johnson	.40	.15
❑ 288	John Williams	.05	.01
❑ 289	Dell Curry	.05	.01
❑ 290	Orlando Woolridge	.05	.01
❑ 291	Nate McMillan	.05	.01
❑ 292	Terry Mills	.05	.01
❑ 293	Sherman Douglas	.05	.01
❑ 294	Charles Shackleford	.05	.01
❑ 295	Ken Norman	.05	.01
❑ 296	LaSalle Thompson	.05	.01
❑ 297	Chris Mullin	.30	.10
❑ 298	Eddie Johnson	.05	.01
❑ 299	Armon Gilliam	.05	.01
❑ 300	Michael Cage	.05	.01
❑ 301	Moses Malone	.30	.10
❑ 302	Charles Oakley	.15	.05
❑ 303	David Wingate	.05	.01
❑ 304	Steve Kerr	.05	.01
❑ 305	Tyrone Hill	.05	.01
❑ 306	Mark West	.05	.01
❑ 307	Fat Lever	.05	.01
❑ 308	J.R. Reid	.05	.01
❑ 309	Ed Nealy	.05	.01
❑ 310	Form Checklist 3	.30	.10
❑ 311	Alaa Abdelnaby	.05	.01
❑ 312	Stacey Augmon	.15	.05
❑ 313	Anthony Avent RC	.05	.01
❑ 314	Walter Bond RC	.05	.01
❑ 315	Byron Houston RC	.05	.01
❑ 316	Rick Mahorn	.05	.01
❑ 317	Sam Mitchell	.05	.01
❑ 318	Mookie Blaylock	.15	.05
❑ 319	Lance Blanks	.05	.01
❑ 320	John Williams	.05	.01
❑ 321	Rolando Blackman	.05	.01
❑ 322	Danny Ainge	.15	.05
❑ 323	Gerald Glass	.05	.01
❑ 324	Robert Pack	.05	.01
❑ 325	Oliver Miller RC	.05	.01
❑ 326	Charles Smith	.05	.01
❑ 327	Duane Ferrell	.05	.01
❑ 328	Pooh Richardson	.05	.01
❑ 329	Scott Brooks	.05	.01
❑ 330	Walt Williams RC	.30	.10
❑ 331	Andrew Lang	.05	.01
❑ 332	Eric Murdock	.05	.01
❑ 333	Vinny Del Negro	.05	.01
❑ 334	Charles Barkley	.50	.20
❑ 335	James Edwards	.05	.01
❑ 336	Xavier McDaniel	.05	.01
❑ 337	Paul Graham	.05	.01
❑ 338	David Wingate	.05	.01
❑ 339	Richard Dumas RC	.05	.01
❑ 340	Jay Humphries	.05	.01
❑ 341	Mark Jackson	.15	.05
❑ 342	John Salley	.05	.01

☐ 343	Jon Koncak	.05	.01
☐ 344	Rodney McCray	.05	.01
☐ 345	Chuck Person	.05	.01
☐ 346	Mario Elie	.15	.05
☐ 347	Frank Johnson	.05	.01
☐ 348	Rumeal Robinson	.05	.01
☐ 349	Terry Mills	.05	.01
☐ 350	Kevin Willis TFC	.05	.01
☐ 351	Dee Brown TFC	.05	.01
☐ 352	Muggsy Bogues TFC	.05	.01
☐ 353	B.J. Armstrong TFC	.05	.01
☐ 354	Larry Nance TFC	.05	.01
☐ 355	Doug Smith TFC	.05	.01
☐ 356	Robert Pack TFC	.05	.01
☐ 357	Joe Dumars TFC	.15	.05
☐ 358	Saramas Marciulionis TFC	.05	.01
☐ 359	Kenny Smith TFC	.05	.01
☐ 360	Pooh Richardson TFC	.05	.01
☐ 361	Mark Jackson TFC	.05	.01
☐ 362	Sedale Threatt TFC	.05	.01
☐ 363	Grant Long TFC	.05	.01
☐ 364	Eric Murdock TFC	.05	.01
☐ 365	Doug West TFC	.05	.01
☐ 366	Kenny Anderson TFC	.15	.05
☐ 367	Anthony Mason TFC	.15	.05
☐ 368	Nick Anderson TFC	.05	.01
☐ 369	Jeff Hornacek TFC	.05	.01
☐ 370	Dan Majerle TFC	.05	.01
☐ 371	Cliff Robinson TFC	.05	.01
☐ 372	Lionel Simmons TFC	.05	.01
☐ 373	Dale Ellis TFC	.05	.01
☐ 374	Gary Payton TFC	.30	.10
☐ 375	David Benoit TFC	.05	.01
☐ 376	Harvey Grant TFC	.05	.01
☐ 377	Buck Johnson	.05	.01
☐ 378	Brian Howard RC	.05	.01
☐ 379	Travis Mays	.05	.01
☐ 380	Jud Buechler	.05	.01
☐ 381	Matt Geiger RC	.15	.05
☐ 382	Bob McCann RC	.05	.01
☐ 383	Cedric Ceballos	.15	.05
☐ 384	Rod Strickland	.30	.10
☐ 385	Kiki Vandeweghe	.05	.01
☐ 386	Latrell Sprewell RC	2.50	1.00
☐ 387	Larry Krystkowiak	.05	.01
☐ 388	Dale Ellis	.05	.01
☐ 389	Trent Tucker	.05	.01
☐ 390	Negele Knight	.05	.01
☐ 391	Stanley Roberts	.05	.01
☐ 392	Tony Campbell	.05	.01
☐ 393	Tim Perry	.05	.01
☐ 394	Doug Overton	.05	.01
☐ 395	Dan Majerle	.15	.05
☐ 396	Duane Cooper RC	.05	.01
☐ 397	Kevin Willis	.05	.01
☐ 398	Micheal Williams	.05	.01
☐ 399	Avery Johnson	.05	.01
☐ 400	Dominique Wilkins	.30	.10
☐ 401	Chris Smith RC	.05	.01
☐ 402	Blair Rasmussen	.05	.01
☐ 403	Jeff Hornacek	.15	.05
☐ 404	Blue Edwards	.05	.01
☐ 405	Olden Polynice	.05	.01
☐ 406	Jeff Grayer	.05	.01
☐ 407	Tony Bennett RC	.05	.01
☐ 408	Don MacLean	.05	.01
☐ 409	Tom Chambers	.05	.01
☐ 410	Keith Jennings RC	.05	.01
☐ 411	Gerald Wilkins	.05	.01
☐ 412	Kennard Winchester	.05	.01
☐ 413	Doc Rivers	.15	.05
☐ 414	Brent Price RC	.15	.05
☐ 415	Mark West	.05	.01
☐ 416	J.R. Reid	.05	.01
☐ 417	Jon Barry RC	.15	.05
☐ 418	Kevin Johnson	.30	.10
☐ 419	Form Checklist	.05	.01
☐ 420	Form Checklist	.05	.01
☐ 421	Daugh/Price/Nance AS CL	.05	.01
☐ 422	Scottie Pippen AS	.50	.20
☐ 423	Larry Johnson AS	.30	.10
☐ 424	Shaquille O'Neal AS	2.50	1.00
☐ 425	Michael Jordan AS	2.00	.75
☐ 426	Isiah Thomas AS	.15	.05
☐ 427	Brad Daugherty AS	.05	.01
☐ 428	Joe Dumars AS	.15	.05
☐ 429	Patrick Ewing AS	.15	.05
☐ 430	Larry Nance AS	.05	.01
☐ 431	Mark Price AS	.05	.01
☐ 432	Detlef Schrempf AS	.05	.01
☐ 433	Dominique Wilkins AS	.15	.05
☐ 434	Karl Malone AS	.30	.10
☐ 435	Charles Barkley AS	.30	.10
☐ 436	David Robinson AS	.30	.10
☐ 437	John Stockton AS	.15	.05
☐ 438	Clyde Drexler AS	.15	.05
☐ 439	Sean Elliott AS	.05	.01
☐ 440	Tim Hardaway AS	.30	.10
☐ 441	Shawn Kemp AS	.30	.10
☐ 442	Dan Majerle AS	.05	.01
☐ 443	Danny Manning AS	.05	.01
☐ 444	Hakeem Olajuwon AS	.30	.10
☐ 445	Terry Porter AS	.05	.01
☐ 446	Harold Miner FACE	.15	.05
☐ 447	David Benoit FACE	.05	.01
☐ 448	Cedric Ceballos FACE	.05	.01
☐ 449	Chris Jackson FACE	.05	.01
☐ 450	Tim Perry FACE	.05	.01
☐ 451	Kenny Smith FACE	.05	.01
☐ 452	Clar.Weatherspoon FACE	.30	.10
☐ 453A	M.Jordan FACE 85 ERR	15.00	6.00
☐ 453B	M.Jordan FACE 87 COR	2.00	.75
☐ 454A	D.Wilkins FACE 87 ERR	2.00	.75
☐ 454B	D.Wilkins FACE 85 COR	.30	.10
☐ 455	D.Cooper/A.Peeler TP CL	.05	.01
☐ 456	Adam Keefe TP	.05	.01
☐ 457	Alonzo Mourning TP	.50	.20
☐ 458	Jim Jackson TP	.50	.20
☐ 459	Sean Rooks TP	.05	.01
☐ 460	LaPhonso Ellis TP	.15	.05
☐ 461	Bryant Stith TP	.05	.01
☐ 462	Byron Houston TP	.05	.01
☐ 463	Latrell Sprewell TP	.30	.10
☐ 464	Robert Horry TP	.15	.05
☐ 465	Malik Sealy TP	.05	.01
☐ 466	Doug Christie TP	.30	.10
☐ 467	Duane Cooper TP	.05	.01
☐ 468	Anthony Peeler TP	.05	.01
☐ 469	Harold Miner TP	.05	.01
☐ 470	Todd Day TP	.05	.01
☐ 471	Lee Mayberry TP	.05	.01
☐ 472	Christian Laettner TP	.30	.10
☐ 473	Hubert Davis TP	.05	.01
☐ 474	Shaquille O'Neal TP	2.50	1.00
☐ 475	Clarence Weatherspoon TP	.05	.01
☐ 476	Richard Dumas TP	.30	.10
☐ 477	Oliver Miller TP	.05	.01
☐ 478	Tracy Murray TP	.05	.01
☐ 479	Walt Williams TP	.15	.05
☐ 480	Lloyd Daniels TP	.05	.01
☐ 481	Tom Gugliotta TP	.30	.10
☐ 482	Brent Price TP	.05	.01
☐ 483	Mark Aguirre TP	.05	.01
☐ 484	Frank Brickowski GF	.05	.01
☐ 485	Derrick Coleman GF	.05	.01
☐ 486	Clyde Drexler GF	.15	.05
☐ 487	Harvey Grant GF	.05	.01
☐ 488	Michael Jordan GF	2.00	.75
☐ 489	Karl Malone GF	.30	.10
☐ 490	Xavier McDaniel GF	.05	.01
☐ 491	Drazen Petrovic GF	.05	.01
☐ 492	John Starks GF	.05	.01
☐ 493	Robert Parish GF	.05	.01
☐ 494	Christian Laettner GF	.30	.10
☐ 495	Ron Harper GF	.05	.01
☐ 496	David Robinson GF	.30	.10
☐ 497	John Salley GF	.05	.01
☐ 498	B.Daugherty/M.Price ST	.05	.01
☐ 499	D.Mutombo/C.Jackson ST	.30	.10
☐ 500	I.Thomas/J.Dumars ST	.30	.10
☐ 501	H.Olajuwon/Thorpe ST	.30	.10
☐ 502	D.Coleman/D.Petrovic ST	.15	.05
☐ 503	T.Porter/C.Drexler ST	.05	.01
☐ 504	Lionel Simmons ST	.15	.05
☐ 505	D.Robinson/S.Elliott ST	.30	.10
☐ 506	Michael Jordan FAN	2.00	.75
☐ 507	Larry Bird FAN	.60	.25
☐ 508	Karl Malone FAN	.30	.10
☐ 509	Dikembe Mutombo FAN	.30	.10
☐ 510	L.Bird/M.Jordan FAN	1.00	.40
☐ SP1	L.Bird/M.Johnson Retire	3.00	1.25
☐ SP2	D.Wilkins/M.Jordan 20K	6.00	2.50

☐ COMPLETE SET (510)	30.00	15.00
☐ COMPLETE SERIES 1 (255)	15.00	7.50
☐ COMPLETE SERIES 2 (255)	15.00	7.50
☐ 1 Muggsy Bogues	.05	.01
☐ 2 Kenny Anderson	.15	.05
☐ 3 Dell Curry	.05	.01
☐ 4 Charles Smith	.05	.01
☐ 5 Chuck Person	.05	.01
☐ 6 Chucky Brown	.05	.01
☐ 7 Kevin Johnson	.15	.05
☐ 8 Winston Garland	.05	.01
☐ 9 John Salley	.05	.01
☐ 10 Dale Ellis	.05	.01
☐ 11 Otis Thorpe	.15	.05
☐ 12 John Stockton	.30	.10
☐ 13 Kendall Gill	.15	.05
☐ 14 Randy White	.05	.01
☐ 15 Mark Jackson	.05	.01
☐ 16 Vlade Divac	.15	.05
☐ 17 Scott Skiles	.05	.01
☐ 18 Xavier McDaniel	.15	.05
☐ 19 Jeff Hornacek	.05	.01
☐ 20 Stanley Roberts	.05	.01
☐ 21 Harold Miner	.05	.01
☐ 22 Terrel Brandon	.15	.05
☐ 23 Michael Jordan	4.00	1.50
☐ 24 Jim Jackson	.15	.05
☐ 25 Keith Askins	.05	.01
☐ 26 Corey Williams	.05	.01
☐ 27 David Benoit	.05	.01
☐ 28 Charles Oakley	.15	.05
☐ 29 Michael Adams	.05	.01
☐ 30 Clarence Weatherspoon	.05	.01
☐ 31 Jon Koncak	.05	.01
☐ 32 Gerald Wilkins	.05	.01
☐ 33 Anthony Bowie	.05	.01
☐ 34 Willie Burton	.05	.01
☐ 35 Stacey Augmon	.15	.05
☐ 36 Doc Rivers	.05	.01
☐ 37 Luc Longley	.15	.05
☐ 38 Dee Brown	.05	.01
☐ 39 Litterial Green	.05	.01
☐ 40 Dan Majerle	.15	.05
☐ 41 Doug West	.05	.01
☐ 42 Joe Dumars	.30	.10
☐ 43 Dennis Scott	.05	.01
☐ 44 Mahmoud Abdul-Rauf	.05	.01
☐ 45 Mark Eaton	.05	.01
☐ 46 Danny Ferry	.05	.01
☐ 47 Kenny Smith	.05	.01
☐ 48 Ron Harper	.15	.05
☐ 49 Adam Keefe	.05	.01
☐ 50 David Robinson	.50	.20
☐ 51 John Starks	.15	.05
☐ 52 Jeff Malone	.05	.01
☐ 53 Vern Fleming	.05	.01
☐ 54 Olden Polynice	.05	.01
☐ 55 Dikembe Mutombo	.30	.10
☐ 56 Chris Morris	.05	.01
☐ 57 Sean Rooks	.05	.01
☐ 58 Richard Dumas	.05	.01
☐ 59 J.R. Reid	.05	.01
☐ 60 Brad Daugherty	.05	.01
☐ 61 Blue Edwards	.05	.01
☐ 62 Mark Macon	.05	.01
☐ 63 Latrell Sprewell	.75	.30

#	Player			#	Player			#	Player		
64	Mitch Richmond	.30	.10	150	Dino Radja RC	.05	.01	236	Gugliotta/Adams SKED	.15	.05
65	David Wingate	.05	.01	151	Johnny Dawkins	.05	.01	237	Michael Jordan SM	2.00	.75
66	LaSalle Thompson	.05	.01	152	Tim Legler RC	.05	.01	238	Clyde Drexler SM	.15	.05
67	Sedale Threatt	.05	.01	153	Bill Laimbeer	.05	.01	239	Tim Hardaway SM	.15	.05
68	Larry Krystkowiak	.05	.01	154	Glen Rice	.15	.05	240	Dominique Wilkins SM	.15	.05
69	John Paxson	.05	.01	155	Bill Cartwright	.05	.01	241	Brad Daugherty SM	.05	.01
70	Frank Brickowski	.05	.01	156	Luther Wright RC	.05	.01	242	Chris Mullin SM	.15	.05
71	Duane Causwell	.05	.01	157	Rex Walters RC	.05	.01	243	Kenny Anderson SM	.05	.01
72	Fred Roberts	.05	.01	158	Doug Edwards RC	.05	.01	244	Patrick Ewing SM	.15	.05
73	Rod Strickland	.15	.05	159	George Lynch RC	.05	.01	245	Isiah Thomas SM	.15	.05
74	Willie Anderson	.05	.01	160	Chris Mills RC	.30	.10	246	Dikembe Mutombo SM	.15	.05
75	Thurl Bailey	.05	.01	161	Sam Cassell RC	1.25	.50	247	Danny Manning SM	.05	.01
76	Ricky Pierce	.05	.01	162	Nick Van Exel RC	1.00	.40	248	David Robinson SM	.30	.10
77	Todd Day	.05	.01	163	Shawn Bradley RC	.30	.10	249	Karl Malone SM	.30	.10
78	Hot Rod Williams	.05	.01	164	Calbert Cheaney RC	.15	.05	250	James Worthy SM	.15	.05
79	Danny Ainge	.15	.05	165	Corie Blount RC	.05	.01	251	Shawn Kemp SM	.30	.10
80	Mark West	.05	.01	166	Michael Jordan SL	2.00	.75	252	Checklist 1-64	.05	.01
81	Marcus Liberty	.05	.01	167	Dennis Rodman SL	.30	.10	253	Checklist 65-128	.05	.01
82	Keith Jennings	.05	.01	168	John Stockton SL	.15	.05	254	Checklist 129-192	.05	.01
83	Derrick Coleman	.15	.05	169	B.J. Armstrong SL	.05	.01	255	Checklist 193-255	.05	.01
84	Larry Stewart	.05	.01	170	Hakeem Olajuwon SL	.30	.10	256	Patrick Ewing	.30	.10
85	Tracy Murray	.05	.01	171	Michael Jordan SL	2.00	.75	257	B.J. Armstrong	.05	.01
86	Robert Horry	.15	.05	172	Cedric Ceballos SL	.05	.01	258	Oliver Miller	.05	.01
87	Derek Harper	.15	.05	173	Mark Price SL	.05	.01	259	Jud Buechler	.05	.01
88	Scott Hastings	.05	.01	174	Charles Barkley SL	.30	.10	260	Pooh Richardson	.05	.01
89	Sam Perkins	.15	.05	175	Clifford Robinson SL	.05	.01	261	Victor Alexander	.05	.01
90	Clyde Drexler	.30	.10	176	Hakeem Olajuwon SL	.30	.10	262	Kevin Gamble	.05	.01
91	Brent Price	.05	.01	177	Shaquille O'Neal SL	.60	.25	263	Doug Smith	.05	.01
92	Chris Mullin	.30	.10	178	R.Miller/C.Oakley PO	.15	.05	264	Isiah Thomas	.30	.10
93	Rafael Addison	.05	.01	179	1st Round: Hornets 3&	.05	.01	265	Doug Christie	.15	.05
94	Tyrone Corbin	.05	.01	180	M.Jordan/S.Augmon PO	1.00	.40	266	Mark Bryant	.05	.01
95	Sarunas Marciulionis	.05	.01	181	Brad Daugherty PO	.05	.01	267	Lloyd Daniels	.05	.01
96	Antoine Carr	.05	.01	182	O.Miller/B.Scott PO	.05	.01	268	Micheal Williams	.05	.01
97	Tony Bennett	.05	.01	183	D.Robinson/Elliott PO	.30	.10	269	Nick Anderson	.15	.05
98	Sam Mitchell	.05	.01	184	1st Round: Rockets 3&	.05	.01	270	Tom Gugliotta	.30	.10
99	Lionel Simmons	.05	.01	185	1st Round: Sonics	.05	.01	271	Kenny Gattison	.05	.01
100	Tim Perry	.05	.01	186	A.Mason/P.Ewing	.30	.10	272	Vernon Maxwell	.05	.01
101	Horace Grant	.15	.05	187	M.Jordan/G.Wilkins PO	1.00	.40	273	Terry Cummings	.05	.01
102	Tom Hammonds	.05	.01	188	Oliver Miller PO	.05	.01	274	Karl Malone	.50	.20
103	Walter Bond	.05	.01	189	West Semis: Sonics 4&	.30	.10	275	Rick Fox	.05	.01
104	Detlef Schrempf	.15	.05	190	East Finals: Bulls 4&	.05	.01	276	Matt Bullard	.05	.01
105	Terry Porter	.05	.01	191	K.Johnson PO	.15	.05	277	Johnny Newman	.05	.01
106	Danny Schayes	.05	.01	192	Dan Majerle PO	.05	.01	278	Mark Price	.05	.01
107	Rumeal Robinson	.05	.01	193	Michael Jordan PO	2.00	.75	279	Mookie Blaylock	.15	.05
108	Gerald Glass	.05	.01	194	L.Johnson/Bogues PO	.05	.01	280	Charles Barkley	.50	.20
109	Mike Gminski	.05	.01	195	Miller ties Playoffs	.15	.05	281	Larry Nance	.05	.01
110	Terry Mills	.05	.01	196	Bulls and Knicks	.30	.10	282	Walt Williams	.05	.01
111	Loy Vaught	.05	.01	197	C.Barkley PO	.30	.10	283	Brian Shaw	.05	.01
112	Jim Les	.05	.01	198	Michael Jordan FIN	2.00	.75	284	Robert Parish	.15	.05
113	Byron Houston	.05	.01	199	Scottie Pippen FIN	.50	.20	285	Pervis Ellison	.05	.01
114	Randy Brown	.05	.01	200	Kevin Johnson G3	.05	.01	286	Spud Webb	.15	.05
115	Anthony Avent	.05	.01	201	Michael Jordan FIN	2.00	.75	287	Hakeem Olajuwon	.50	.20
116	Donald Hodge	.05	.01	202	Richard Dumas FIN	.05	.01	288	Jerome Kersey	.05	.01
117	Kevin Willis	.05	.01	203	Horace Grant G6	.05	.01	289	Carl Herrera	.05	.01
118	Robert Pack	.05	.01	204	Michael Jordan FIN	2.00	.75	290	Dominique Wilkins	.30	.10
119	Dale Davis	.05	.01	205	S.Pippen/C.Barkley FIN	.30	.10	291	Billy Owens	.05	.01
120	Grant Long	.05	.01	206	John Paxson	.05	.01	292	Greg Anthony	.05	.01
121	Anthony Bonner	.05	.01	207	B.J. Armstrong	.05	.01	293	Nate McMillan	.05	.01
122	Chris Smith	.05	.01	208	1992-93 Bulls	.05	.01	294	Christian Laettner	.15	.05
123	Elden Campbell	.05	.01	209	1992-93 Suns	.05	.01	295	Gary Payton	.50	.20
124	Cliff Robinson	.15	.05	210	Atlanta Hawks Sked	.05	.01	296	Steve Smith	.30	.10
125	Sherman Douglas	.05	.01	211	Boston Celtics Sked	.05	.01	297	Anthony Mason	.15	.05
126	Alvin Robertson	.05	.01	212	Charlotte Hornets Sked	.05	.01	298	Sean Rooks	.05	.01
127	Rolando Blackman	.05	.01	213	M.Jordan/Group SKED	1.00	.40	299	Toni Kukoc	1.25	.50
128	Malik Sealy	.05	.01	214	Cleveland Cavaliers	.05	.01	300	Shaquille O'Neal	1.50	.60
129	Ed Pinckney	.05	.01	215	J.Jackson/S.Rooks SKED	.05	.01	301	Jay Humphries	.05	.01
130	Anthony Peeler	.05	.01	216	Denver Nuggets Sked	.15	.05	302	Sleepy Floyd	.05	.01
131	Scott Brooks	.05	.01	217	Detroit Pistons Sked	.05	.01	303	Bimbo Coles	.05	.01
132	Rik Smits	.15	.05	218	Golden State Warriors	.05	.01	304	John Battle	.05	.01
133	Derrick McKey	.05	.01	219	H.Olajuwon/Group SKED	.30	.10	305	Shawn Kemp	.50	.20
134	Alaa Abdelnaby	.05	.01	220	Indiana Pacers Sked	.05	.01	306	Scott Williams	.05	.01
135	Rex Chapman	.05	.01	221	L.A. Clippers Sked	.05	.01	307	Wayman Tisdale	.05	.01
136	Tony Campbell	.05	.01	222	L.A. Lakers Sked	.05	.01	308	Rony Seikaly	.05	.01
137	John Williams	.05	.01	223	Smith/Miner/Seik SKED	.15	.05	309	Reggie Miller	.30	.10
138	Vincent Askew	.05	.01	224	Milwaukee Bucks Sked	.05	.01	310	Scottie Pippen	1.00	.40
139	LaBradford Smith	.05	.01	225	Minnesota Timberwolves	.05	.01	311	Chris Webber RC	3.00	1.25
140	Vinny Del Negro	.05	.01	226	New Jersey Nets Sked	.05	.01	312	Trevor Wilson	.05	.01
141	Darrell Walker	.05	.01	227	New York Knicks Sked	.05	.01	313	Derek Strong RC	.05	.01
142	James Worthy	.30	.10	228	S.O'Neal/Group SKED	.40	.15	314	Bobby Hurley RC	.15	.05
143	Jeff Turner	.05	.01	229	Philadelphia 76ers	.05	.01	315	Herb Williams	.05	.01
144	Duane Ferrell	.05	.01	230	C.Barkley/Group SKED	.30	.10	316	Rex Walters	.05	.01
145	Larry Smith	.05	.01	231	Portland Trail Blazers	.05	.01	317	Doug Edwards	.05	.01
146	Eddie Johnson	.05	.01	232	Sacramento Kings Sked	.05	.01	318	Ken Williams	.05	.01
147	Chris Gatling	.05	.01	233	D.Robinson/Group SKED	.30	.10	319	Jon Barry	.05	.01
148	Buck Williams	.05	.01	234	S.Kemp/G.Payton SKED	.15	.05	320	Joe Courtney RC	.05	.01
149	Donald Royal	.05	.01	235	Utah Jazz Sked	.05	.01	321	Ervin Johnson RC	.15	.05

#	Player		
322	Sam Cassell	.30	.10
323	Tim Hardaway	.30	.10
324	Ed Stokes	.05	.01
325	Steve Kerr	.15	.05
326	Doug Overton	.05	.01
327	Reggie Williams	.05	.01
328	Avery Johnson	.05	.01
329	Stacey King	.05	.01
330	Vin Baker RC	.75	.30
331	Greg Kite	.05	.01
332	Michael Cage	.05	.01
333	Alonzo Mourning	.50	.20
334	Acie Earl RC	.05	.01
335	Terry Dehere RC	.05	.01
336	Negele Knight	.05	.01
337	Gerald Madkins RC	.05	.01
338	Lindsey Hunter RC	.30	.10
339	Luther Wright	.05	.01
340	Mike Peplowski RC	.05	.01
341	Dino Radja	.05	.01
342	Danny Manning	.15	.05
343	Chris Mills	.30	.10
344	Kevin Lynch	.05	.01
345	Shawn Bradley	.30	.10
346	Evers Burns RC	.05	.01
347	Rodney Rogers RC	.30	.10
348	Cedric Ceballos	.15	.05
349	Warren Kidd RC	.05	.01
350	Darnell Mee RC	.05	.01
351	Matt Geiger	.05	.01
352	Jamal Mashburn RC	.75	.30
353	Antonio Davis RC	.40	.15
354	Calbert Cheaney	.15	.05
355	George Lynch	.05	.01
356	Derrick McKey	.05	.01
357	Jerry Reynolds	.05	.01
358	Don MacLean	.05	.01
359	Scott Haskin RC	.05	.01
360	Malcolm Mackey RC	.05	.01
361	Isaiah Rider RC	.60	.25
362	Detlef Schrempf	.15	.05
363	Josh Grant RC	.05	.01
364	Richard Petruska	.05	.01
365	Larry Johnson	.30	.10
366	Richard Petruska RC	.05	.01
367	Ken Norman	.05	.01
368	Anthony Cook	.05	.01
369	James Robinson RC	.05	.01
370	Kevin Duckworth	.05	.01
371	Chris Whitney RC	.05	.01
372	Moses Malone	.30	.10
373	Nick Van Exel	.50	.20
374	Scott Burrell RC	.30	.10
375	Harvey Grant	.05	.01
376	Benoit Benjamin	.05	.01
377	Henry James	.05	.01
378	Craig Ehlo	.05	.01
379	Ennis Whatley	.05	.01
380	Sean Green	.05	.01
381	Eric Murdock	.05	.01
382	Anfernee Hardaway RC	2.50	1.00
383	Gheorghe Muresan RC	.30	.10
384	Kendall Gill	.15	.05
385	David Wood	.05	.01
386	Mario Elie	.05	.01
387	Chris Corchiani	.05	.01
388	Greg Graham RC	.05	.01
389	Hersey Hawkins	.15	.05
390	Mark Aguirre	.05	.01
391	LaPhonso Ellis	.05	.01
392	Anthony Bonner	.05	.01
393	Lucious Harris RC	.05	.01
394	Andrew Lang	.05	.01
395	Chris Dudley	.05	.01
396	Dennis Rodman	.60	.25
397	Larry Krystkowiak	.05	.01
398	A.C. Green	.15	.05
399	Eddie Johnson	.05	.01
400	Kevin Edwards	.05	.01
401	Tyrone Hill	.05	.01
402	Greg Anderson	.05	.01
403	P.J.Brown RC	.30	.10
404	Dana Barros	.05	.01
405	Allan Houston RC	1.25	.50
406	Mike Brown	.05	.01
407	Lee Mayberry	.05	.01

#	Player		
408	Fat Lever	.05	.01
409	Tony Smith	.05	.01
410	Tom Chambers	.05	.01
411	Manute Bol	.05	.01
412	Joe Kleine	.05	.01
413	Bryant Stith	.05	.01
414	Eric Riley RC	.05	.01
415	Jo Jo English RC	.05	.01
416	Sean Elliott	.15	.05
417	Sam Bowie	.05	.01
418	Armon Gilliam	.05	.01
419	Brian Williams	.05	.01
420	Popeye Jones RC	.05	.01
421	Dennis Rodman	.30	.10
422	Karl Malone	.30	.10
423	Tom Gugliotta EB	.15	.05
424	Kevin Willis EB	.05	.01
425	Hakeem Olajuwon EB	.30	.10
426	Charles Oakley EB	.05	.01
427	Clarence Weatherspoon EB	.05	.01
428	Derrick Coleman EB	.05	.01
429	Buck Williams EB	.05	.01
430	Christian Laettner EB	.05	.01
431	Dikembe Mutombo EB	.15	.05
432	Rony Seikaly EB	.05	.01
433	Brad Daugherty EB	.05	.01
434	Horace Grant EB	.05	.01
435	Larry Johnson EB	.15	.05
436	Dee Brown EB	.05	.01
437	Muggsy Bogues BT	.05	.01
438	Michael Jordan BT	2.00	.75
439	Tim Hardaway BT	.15	.05
440	Micheal Williams BT	.05	.01
441	Gary Payton BT	.30	.10
442	Mookie Blaylock BT	.06	.01
443	Doc Rivers BT	.05	.01
444	Kenny Smith BT	.05	.01
445	John Stockton BT	.15	.05
446	Alvin Robertson BT	.05	.01
447	Mark Jackson BT	.05	.01
448	Kenny Anderson BT	.05	.01
449	Scottie Pippen BT	.50	.20
450	Isiah Thomas BT	.15	.05
451	Mark Price BT	.05	.01
452	Latrell Sprewell BT	.30	.10
453	Sedale Threatt BT	.05	.01
454	Nick Anderson BT	.05	.01
455	Rod Strickland BT	.05	.01
456	Oliver Miller GI	.05	.01
457	J.Worthy/V.Divac GI	.05	.01
458	Robert Horry GI	.05	.01
459	Rockets Shot-Around GI	.05	.01
460	Rooks/Jackson/Legler GI	.05	.01
461	Mitch Richmond GI	.15	.05
462	Chris Morris GI	.05	.01
463	M.Jackson/G.Grant GI	.05	.01
464	David Robinson GI	.30	.10
465	Danny Ainge GI	.05	.01
466	Michael Jordan SKL	2.00	.75
467	Dominique Wilkins SKL	.15	.05
468	Alonzo Mourning SKL	.30	.10
469	Shaquille O'Neal SKL	.60	.25
470	Tim Hardaway SL	.15	.05
471	Patrick Ewing SL	.15	.05
472	Kevin Johnson SL	.05	.01
473	Clyde Drexler SKL	.15	.05
474	David Robinson SKL	.30	.10
475	Shawn Kemp SKL	.30	.10
476	Dee Brown SL	.05	.01
477	Jim Jackson SKL	.05	.01
478	John Stockton SKL	.15	.05
479	Robert Horry SL	.05	.01
480	Glen Rice SL	.05	.01
481	Micheal Williams SIS	.05	.01
482	G.Lynch/T.Dehere CL	.05	.01
483	Chris Webber CL	1.50	.60
484	Anfernee Hardaway TP	1.25	.50
485	Shawn Bradley TP	.15	.05
486	Jamal Mashburn TP	.30	.10
487	Calbert Cheaney TP	.05	.01
488	Isaiah Rider TP	.30	.10
489	Bobby Hurley TP	.05	.01
490	Vin Baker TP	.30	.10
491	Rodney Rogers TP	.15	.05
492	Lindsey Hunter TP	.15	.05
493	Allan Houston TP	.30	.10
494	Terry Dehere TP	.05	.01
495	George Lynch TP	.05	.01
496	Toni Kukoc TP	.30	.10
497	Nick Van Exel TP	.30	.10
498	Charles Barkley MO	.05	.01
499	A.C. Green MO	.05	.01
500	Dan Majerle MO	.05	.01
501	Jerrod Mustaf MO	.05	.01
502	Kevin Johnson MO	.05	.01
503	Negele Knight MO	.05	.01
504	Danny Ainge MO	.05	.01
505	Oliver Miller MO	.05	.01
506	Joe Courtney MO	.05	.01
507	Checklist	.05	.01
508	Checklist	.05	.01
509	Checklist	.05	.01
510	Checklist	.05	.01
SP3	M.Jordan/W.Chamberlain	8.00	3.00
SP4	Chicago Bulls Third	8.00	3.00

1994-95 Upper Deck

❏ COMPLETE SET (360)	45.00	22.50
❏ COMPLETE SERIES 1 (180)	25.00	12.50
❏ COMPLETE SERIES 2 (180)	20.00	10.00
❏ 1 Chris Webber ART	.50	.20
❏ 2 Anfernee Hardaway ART	.50	.20
❏ 3 Vin Baker ART	.15	.05
❏ 4 Jamal Mashburn ART	.15	.05
❏ 5 Isaiah Rider ART	.10	.02
❏ 6 Dino Radja ART	.10	.02
❏ 7 Nick Van Exel ART	.15	.05
❏ 8 Shawn Bradley ART	.10	.02
❏ 9 Toni Kukoc ART	.10	.02
❏ 10 Lindsey Hunter ART	.40	.15
❏ 11 Scottie Pippen AN	.60	.25
❏ 12 Karl Malone AN	.40	.15
❏ 13 Hakeem Olajuwon AN	.40	.15
❏ 14 John Stockton AN	.15	.05
❏ 15 Latrell Sprewell AN	.40	.15
❏ 16 Shawn Kemp AN	.40	.15
❏ 17 Charles Barkley AN	.40	.15
❏ 18 David Robinson AN	.40	.15
❏ 19 Mitch Richmond AN	.10	.02
❏ 20 Kevin Johnson AN	.10	.05
❏ 21 Derrick Coleman AN	.10	.02
❏ 22 Dominique Wilkins AN	.15	.05
❏ 23 Shaquille O'Neal AN	.75	.30
❏ 24 Mark Price AN	.10	.02
❏ 25 Gary Payton AN	.40	.15
❏ 26 Dan Majerle AN	.15	.05
❏ 27 Vernon Maxwell AN	.10	.02
❏ 28 Matt Geiger	.10	.02
❏ 29 Jeff Turner	.10	.02
❏ 30 Vinny Del Negro	.10	.02
❏ 31 B.J. Armstrong	.10	.02
❏ 32 Chris Gatling	.10	.02
❏ 33 Tony Smith	.10	.02
❏ 34 Doug West	.10	.02
❏ 35 Clyde Drexler	.40	.15
❏ 36 Keith Jennings	.10	.02
❏ 37 Steve Smith	.15	.05
❏ 38 Kendall Gill	.10	.02
❏ 39 Bob Martin	.10	.02
❏ 40 Calbert Cheaney	.15	.05
❏ 41 Terrell Brandon	.15	.05
❏ 42 Pete Chilcutt	.10	.02
❏ 43 Avery Johnson	.10	.02
❏ 44 Tom Gugliotta	.15	.05

#	Player			#	Player			#	Player		
45	LaBradford Smith	.10	.02	131	Jim Jackson	.15	.05	217	Doug Smith	.10	.02
46	Sedale Threatt	.10	.02	132	Dikembe Mutombo	.15	.05	218	Danny Manning	.15	.05
47	Chris Smith	.10	.02	133	Terry Porter	.10	.02	219	Otis Thorpe	.10	.02
48	Kevin Edwards	.10	.02	134	Mario Elie	.10	.02	220	Mark Price	.10	.02
49	Lucious Harris	.10	.02	135	Vlade Divac	.10	.02	221	Victor Alexander	.10	.02
50	Tim Perry	.10	.02	136	Robert Horry	.15	.05	222	Brent Price	.10	.02
51	Lloyd Daniels	.10	.02	137	Popeye Jones	.10	.02	223	Howard Eisley RC	.10	.02
52	Dee Brown	.10	.02	138	Brad Lohaus	.10	.02	224	Chris Mullin	.40	.15
53	Sean Elliott	.15	.05	139	Anthony Bonner	.10	.02	225	Nick Van Exel	.40	.15
54	Tim Hardaway	.40	.15	140	Doug Christie	.15	.05	226	Xavier McDaniel	.10	.02
55	Christian Laettner	.15	.05	141	Rony Seikaly	.10	.02	227	Khalid Reeves RC	.10	.02
56	Bo Outlaw RC	.10	.02	142	Allan Houston	.60	.25	228	Anfernee Hardaway	1.00	.40
57	Kevin Johnson	.15	.05	143	Tyrone Hill	.10	.02	229	B.J Tyler RC	.10	.02
58	Duane Ferrell	.10	.02	144	Latrell Sprewell	.40	.15	230	Elmore Spencer	.10	.02
59	Jo Jo English	.10	.02	145	Andres Guibert	.10	.02	231	Rick Fox	.10	.02
60	Stanley Roberts	.10	.02	146	Dominique Wilkins	.40	.15	232	Alonzo Mourning	.50	.20
61	Kevin Willis	.10	.02	147	Jon Barry	.10	.02	233	Hakeem Olajuwon	.60	.25
62	Dana Barros	.10	.02	148	Tracy Murray	.10	.02	234	Blue Edwards	.10	.02
63	Gheorghe Muresan	.10	.02	149	Mike Peplowski	.10	.02	235	P.J. Brown	.10	.02
64	Vern Fleming	.10	.02	150	Mike Brown	.10	.02	236	Ron Harper	.15	.05
65	Anthony Peeler	.10	.02	151	Cedric Ceballos	.15	.05	237	Isaiah Rider	.15	.05
66	Negele Knight	.10	.02	152	Stacey King	.10	.02	238	Eric Mobley RC	.10	.02
67	Harold Ellis	.10	.02	153	Trevor Wilson	.10	.02	239	Brian Williams	.10	.02
68	Vincent Askew	.10	.02	154	Anthony Avent	.10	.02	240	Eric Piatkowski RC	.10	.02
69	Ennis Whatley	.10	.02	155	Horace Grant	.15	.05	241	Karl Malone	.60	.25
70	Elden Campbell	.10	.02	156	Bill Curley RC	.10	.02	242	Wayman Tisdale	.10	.02
71	Sherman Douglas	.10	.02	157	Grant Hill RC	2.00	.75	243	Sarunas Marciulionis	.10	.02
72	Luc Longley	.10	.02	158	Charlie Ward RC	.40	.15	244	Sean Rooks	.10	.02
73	Lorenzo Williams	.10	.02	159	Jalen Rose RC	1.50	.60	245	Ricky Pierce	.10	.02
74	Jay Humphries	.10	.02	160	Jason Kidd RC	4.00	1.50	246	Don MacLean	.10	.02
75	Chris King	.10	.02	161	Yinka Dare RC	.10	.02	247	Aaron McKie RC	.75	.30
76	Tyrone Corbin	.10	.02	162	Eric Montross RC	.10	.02	248	Kenny Gattison	.10	.02
77	Bobby Hurley	.10	.02	163	Donyell Marshall RC	.40	.15	249	Derek Harper	.10	.02
78	Dell Curry	.10	.02	164	Tony Dumas RC	.10	.02	250	Michael Smith RC	.10	.02
79	Dino Radja	.10	.02	165	Wesley Person RC	.40	.15	251	John Williams	.10	.02
80	A.C. Green	.15	.05	166	Eddie Jones RC	2.00	.75	252	Pooh Richardson	.10	.02
81	Craig Ehlo	.10	.02	167	Tim Hardaway USA	.15	.05	253	Sergei Bazarevich	.10	.02
82	Gary Payton	.60	.25	168	Isiah Thomas USA	.15	.05	254	Brian Grant RC	1.00	.40
83	Sleepy Floyd	.10	.02	169	Joe Dumars USA	.15	.05	255	Ed Pinckney	.10	.02
84	Rodney Rogers	.10	.02	170	Mark Price USA	.10	.02	256	Ken Norman	.10	.02
85	Brian Shaw	.10	.02	171	Derrick Coleman USA	.10	.02	257	Marty Conlon	.10	.02
86	Kevin Gamble	.10	.02	172	Shawn Kemp USA	.40	.15	258	Matt Fish	.10	.02
87	John Stockton	.40	.15	173	Steve Smith USA	.10	.02	259	Darrin Hancock RC	.10	.02
88	Hersey Hawkins	.15	.05	174	Dan Majerle USA	.10	.02	260	Mahmoud Abdul-Rauf	.10	.02
89	Johnny Newman	.10	.02	175	Reggie Miller USA	.15	.05	261	Roy Tarpley	.10	.02
90	Larry Johnson	.15	.05	176	Kevin Johnson USA	.10	.02	262	Chris Morris	.10	.02
91	Robert Pack	.10	.02	177	Dominique Wilkins USA	.15	.05	263	Sharone Wright RC	.10	.02
92	Willie Burton	.10	.02	178	Shaquille O'Neal USA	.75	.30	264	Jamal Mashburn	.40	.15
93	Bobby Phills	.10	.02	179	Alonzo Mourning USA	.15	.05	265	John Starks	.15	.05
94	David Benoit	.10	.02	180	Larry Johnson USA	.10	.02	266	Rod Strickland	.15	.05
95	Harold Miner	.10	.02	181	Brian Grant DA	.15	.05	267	Adam Keefe	.10	.02
96	David Robinson	.60	.25	182	Darrin Hancock DA	.10	.02	268	Scott Burrell	.10	.02
97	Nate McMillan	.10	.02	183	Grant Hill DA	.75	.30	269	Eric Riley	.10	.02
98	Chris Mills	.15	.05	184	Jalen Rose DA	.75	.30	270	Sam Perkins	.15	.05
99	Hubert Davis	.10	.02	185	Lamond Murray DA	.10	.02	271	Stacey Augmon	.10	.02
100	Shaquille O'Neal	2.00	.75	186	Jason Kidd DA	1.50	.60	272	Kevin Willis	.10	.02
101	Loy Vaught	.10	.02	187	Donyell Marshall DA	.15	.05	273	Lamond Murray RC	.15	.05
102	Kenny Smith	.10	.02	188	Eddie Jones DA	1.00	.40	274	Derrick Coleman	.15	.05
103	Terry Dehere	.10	.02	189	Eric Montross DA	.10	.02	275	Scott Skiles	.10	.02
104	Carl Herrera	.10	.02	190	Khalid Reeves DA	.10	.02	276	Buck Williams	.10	.02
105	LaPhonso Ellis	.10	.02	191	Sharone Wright DA	.10	.02	277	Sam Cassell	.40	.15
106	Armon Gilliam	.10	.02	192	Wesley Person DA	.15	.05	278	Rik Smits	.10	.02
107	Greg Graham	.10	.02	193	Glenn Robinson DA	.60	.25	279	Dennis Rodman	.75	.30
108	Eric Murdock	.10	.02	194	Carlos Rogers DA	.10	.02	280	Olden Polynice	.10	.02
109	Ron Harper	.15	.05	195	Aaron McKie DA	.15	.05	281	Glenn Robinson RC	1.25	.50
110	Andrew Lang	.10	.02	196	Juwan Howard DA	.75	.30	282	Clarence Weatherspoon	.10	.02
111	Johnny Dawkins	.10	.02	197	Charlie Ward DA	.15	.05	283	Monty Williams RC	.10	.02
112	David Wingate	.10	.02	198	Brooks Thompson DA	.10	.02	284	Terry Mills	.10	.02
113	Tom Hammonds	.10	.02	199	Tony Massenburg	.10	.02	285	Oliver Miller	.10	.02
114	Brad Daugherty	.10	.02	200	James Robinson	.10	.02	286	Dennis Scott	.10	.02
115	Charles Smith	.10	.02	201	Dickey Simpkins RC	.10	.02	287	Micheal Williams	.10	.02
116	Dale Ellis	.10	.02	202	Johnny Newman	.10	.02	288	Moses Malone	.40	.15
117	Bryant Stith	.10	.02	203	Joe Kleine	.10	.02	289	Donald Royal	.10	.02
118	Lindsey Hunter	.15	.05	204	Bill Wennington	.10	.02	290	Mark Jackson	.10	.02
119	Patrick Ewing	.40	.15	205	Sean Higgins	.10	.02	291	Walt Williams	.10	.02
120	Kenny Anderson	.15	.05	206	Larry Krystkowiak	.10	.02	292	Bimbo Coles	.10	.02
121	Charles Barkley	.60	.25	207	Winston Garland	.10	.02	293	Derrick Alston RC	.10	.02
122	Harvey Grant	.10	.02	208	Muggsy Bogues	.15	.05	294	Scott Williams	.10	.02
123	Anthony Bowie	.10	.02	209	Charles Oakley	.10	.02	295	Acie Earl	.10	.02
124	Shawn Kemp	.60	.25	210	Vin Baker	.40	.15	296	Jeff Hornacek	.15	.05
125	Lee Mayberry	.10	.02	211	Malik Sealy	.10	.02	297	Kevin Duckworth	.10	.02
126	Reggie Miller	.40	.15	212	Willie Anderson	.10	.02	298	Dontonio Wingfield RC	.10	.02
127	Scottie Pippen	1.25	.50	213	Dale Davis	.10	.02	299	Danny Ferry	.10	.02
128	Spud Webb	.10	.02	214	Grant Long	.10	.02	300	Mark West	.10	.02
129	Antonio Davis	.10	.02	215	Danny Ainge	.15	.05	301	Jayson Williams	.15	.05
130	Greg Anderson	.10	.02	216	Toni Kukoc	.60	.25	302	David Wesley	.10	.02

❏ 303	Jim McIlvaine RC	.10	.02
❏ 304	Michael Adams	.10	.02
❏ 305	Greg Minor RC	.10	.02
❏ 306	Jeff Malone	.10	.02
❏ 307	Pervis Ellison	.10	.02
❏ 308	Clifford Rozier RC	.10	.02
❏ 309	Billy Owens	.10	.02
❏ 310	Duane Causwell	.10	.02
❏ 311	Rex Chapman	.10	.02
❏ 312	Detlef Schrempf	.15	.05
❏ 313	Mitch Richmond	.40	.15
❏ 314	Carlos Rogers RC	.10	.02
❏ 315	Byron Scott	.15	.05
❏ 316	Dwayne Morton	.10	.02
❏ 317	Bill Cartwright	.10	.02
❏ 318	J.R. Reid	.10	.02
❏ 319	Derrick McKey	.10	.02
❏ 320	Jamie Watson RC	.10	.02
❏ 321	Mookie Blaylock	.10	.02
❏ 322	Chris Webber	1.00	.40
❏ 323	Joe Dumars	.40	.15
❏ 324	Shawn Bradley	.10	.02
❏ 325	Chuck Person	.10	.02
❏ 326	Haywoode Workman	.10	.02
❏ 327	Benoit Benjamin	.10	.02
❏ 328	Will Perdue	.10	.02
❏ 329	Sam Mitchell	.10	.02
❏ 330	George Lynch	.10	.02
❏ 331	Juwan Howard RC	1.00	.40
❏ 332	Robert Parish	.15	.05
❏ 333	Glen Rice	.15	.05
❏ 334	Michael Cage	.10	.02
❏ 335	Brooks Thompson RC	.10	.02
❏ 336	Rony Seikaly	.10	.02
❏ 337	Steve Kerr	.10	.02
❏ 338	Anthony Miller RC	.10	.02
❏ 339	Nick Anderson	.10	.02
❏ 340	Clifford Robinson	.15	.05
❏ 341	Todd Day	.10	.02
❏ 342	Jon Koncak	.10	.02
❏ 343	Felton Spencer	.10	.02
❏ 344	Willie Burton	.10	.02
❏ 345	Ledell Eackles	.10	.02
❏ 346	Anthony Mason	.15	.05
❏ 347	Derek Strong	.10	.02
❏ 348	Reggie Williams	.10	.02
❏ 349	Johnny Newman	.10	.02
❏ 350	Terry Cummings	.10	.02
❏ 351	Anthony Tucker RC	.10	.02
❏ 352	Junior Bridgeman	.10	.02
❏ 353	Jerry West TN	.40	.15
❏ 354	Harvey Catchings TN	.10	.02
❏ 355	John Lucas TN	.15	.05
❏ 356	Bill Bradley TN	.15	.05
❏ 357	Bill Walton TN	.15	.05
❏ 358	Don Nelson TN	.15	.05
❏ 359	Michael Jordan TN	2.50	1.00
❏ 360	Tom(Satch) Sanders	.10	.02

1995-96 Upper Deck

❏	COMPLETE SET (360)	50.00	25.00
❏	COMPLETE SERIES 1 (180)	20.00	10.00
❏	COMPLETE SERIES 2 (180)	30.00	15.00
❏ 1	Eddie Jones	1.00	.40
❏ 2	Hubert Davis	.25	.08
❏ 3	Latrell Sprewell	.75	.30
❏ 4	Stacey Augmon	.25	.08
❏ 5	Mario Elie	.25	.08

❏ 6	Tyrone Hill	.25	.08
❏ 7	Dikembe Mutombo	.50	.20
❏ 8	Antonio Davis	.25	.08
❏ 9	Horace Grant	.50	.20
❏ 10	Ken Norman	.25	.08
❏ 11	Aaron McKie	.50	.20
❏ 12	Vinny Del Negro	.25	.08
❏ 13	Glenn Robinson	.75	.30
❏ 14	Allan Houston	.50	.20
❏ 15	Bryon Russell	.25	.08
❏ 16	Tony Dumas	.25	.08
❏ 17	Gary Payton	.75	.30
❏ 18	Rik Smits	.50	.20
❏ 19	Dino Radja	.25	.08
❏ 20	Robert Pack	.25	.08
❏ 21	Calbert Cheaney	.25	.08
❏ 22	Clarence Weatherspoon	.25	.08
❏ 23	Michael Jordan	5.00	2.00
❏ 24	Felton Spencer	.25	.08
❏ 25	J.R. Reid	.25	.08
❏ 26	Cedric Ceballos	.25	.08
❏ 27	Dan Majerle	.50	.20
❏ 28	Donald Hodge	.25	.08
❏ 29	Nate McMillan	.25	.08
❏ 30	Bimbo Coles	.25	.08
❏ 31	Mitch Richmond	.50	.20
❏ 32	Scott Brooks	.25	.08
❏ 33	Patrick Ewing	.75	.30
❏ 34	Carl Herrera	.25	.08
❏ 35	Rick Fox	.50	.20
❏ 36	James Robinson	.25	.08
❏ 37	Donald Royal	.25	.08
❏ 38	Joe Dumars	.75	.30
❏ 39	Rony Seikaly	.25	.08
❏ 40	Dennis Rodman	.50	.20
❏ 41	Muggsy Bogues	.50	.20
❏ 42	Gheorghe Muresan	.25	.08
❏ 43	Ervin Johnson	.25	.08
❏ 44	Todd Day	.25	.08
❏ 45	Rex Walters	.25	.08
❏ 46	Terrell Brandon	.50	.20
❏ 47	Wesley Person	.50	.20
❏ 48	Terry Dehere	.25	.08
❏ 49	Steve Smith	.50	.20
❏ 50	Brian Grant	.75	.30
❏ 51	Eric Piatkowski	.25	.08
❏ 52	Lindsey Hunter	.25	.08
❏ 53	Chris Webber	.75	.30
❏ 54	Antoine Carr	.25	.08
❏ 55	Chris Dudley	.25	.08
❏ 56	Clyde Drexler	.75	.30
❏ 57	P.J. Brown	.25	.08
❏ 58	Kevin Willis	.50	.20
❏ 59	Jeff Turner	.25	.08
❏ 60	Sean Elliott	.50	.20
❏ 61	Kevin Johnson	.50	.20
❏ 62	Scott Skiles	.25	.08
❏ 63	Charles Smith	.25	.08
❏ 64	Danny Ferry	.25	.08
❏ 65	Danny Ferry	.25	.08
❏ 66	Detlef Schrempf	.50	.20
❏ 67	Shawn Bradley	.25	.08
❏ 68	Isaiah Rider	.50	.20
❏ 69	Karl Malone	1.00	.40
❏ 70	Will Perdue	.25	.08
❏ 71	Terry Mills	.25	.08
❏ 72	Glen Rice	.50	.20
❏ 73	Tim Breaux	.25	.08
❏ 74	Malik Sealy	.25	.08
❏ 75	Walt Williams	.25	.08
❏ 76	Bobby Phills	.25	.08
❏ 77	Anthony Avent	.25	.08
❏ 78	Jamal Mashburn	.50	.20
❏ 79	Vlade Divac	.50	.20
❏ 80	Reggie Williams	.25	.08
❏ 81	Xavier McDaniel	.25	.08
❏ 82	Avery Johnson	.25	.08
❏ 83	Derek Harper	.50	.20
❏ 84	Don MacLean	.25	.08
❏ 85	Tom Gugliotta	.50	.20
❏ 86	Craig Ehlo	.25	.08
❏ 87	Robert Horry	.50	.20
❏ 88	Kevin Edwards	.25	.08
❏ 89	Chuck Person	.25	.08
❏ 90	Sharone Wright	.25	.08
❏ 91	Steve Kerr	.50	.20

❏ 92	Marty Conlon	.25	.08
❏ 93	Jalen Rose	1.00	.40
❏ 94	Bryant Reeves RC	.75	.30
❏ 95	Shaquille O'Neal	2.00	.75
❏ 96	David Wesley	.25	.08
❏ 97	Chris Mills	.25	.08
❏ 98	Rod Strickland	.25	.08
❏ 99	Pooh Richardson	.25	.08
❏ 100	Sam Perkins	.50	.20
❏ 101	Dell Curry	.25	.08
❏ 102	David Benoit	.25	.08
❏ 103	Christian Laettner	.50	.20
❏ 104	Duane Causwell	.25	.08
❏ 105	Jason Kidd	2.50	1.00
❏ 106	Mark West	.25	.08
❏ 107	Lee Mayberry	.25	.08
❏ 108	John Salley	.25	.08
❏ 109	Jeff Malone	.25	.08
❏ 110	George Zidek RC	.25	.08
❏ 111	Kenny Smith	.25	.08
❏ 112	George Lynch	.25	.08
❏ 113	Toni Kukoc	.50	.20
❏ 114	A.C. Green	.50	.20
❏ 115	Kenny Anderson	.50	.20
❏ 116	Robert Parish	.50	.20
❏ 117	Chris Mullin	.75	.30
❏ 118	Loy Vaught	.25	.08
❏ 119	Olden Polynice	.25	.08
❏ 120	Clifford Robinson	.25	.08
❏ 121	Eric Mobley	.25	.08
❏ 122	Doug West	.25	.08
❏ 123	Sam Cassell	.75	.30
❏ 124	Nick Anderson	.25	.08
❏ 125	Matt Geiger	.25	.08
❏ 126	Elden Campbell	.25	.08
❏ 127	Alonzo Mourning	.50	.20
❏ 128	Bryant Stith	.25	.08
❏ 129	Mark Jackson	.50	.20
❏ 130	Cherokee Parks RC	.25	.08
❏ 131	Shawn Respert RC	.25	.08
❏ 132	Alan Henderson RC	.75	.30
❏ 133	Jerry Stackhouse RC	2.50	1.00
❏ 134	Rasheed Wallace RC	2.00	.75
❏ 135	Antonio McDyess RC	1.50	.60
❏ 136	Charles Barkley ROO	.75	.30
❏ 137	Michael Jordan ROO	2.50	1.00
❏ 138	Hakeem Olajuwon ROO	.50	.20
❏ 139	Joe Dumars ROO	.50	.20
❏ 140	Patrick Ewing ROO	.50	.20
❏ 141	A.C. Green ROO	.25	.08
❏ 142	Karl Malone ROO	.75	.30
❏ 143	Detlef Schrempf ROO	.25	.08
❏ 144	Chuck Person ROO	.25	.08
❏ 145	Muggsy Bogues ROO	.25	.08
❏ 146	Horace Grant ROO	.25	.08
❏ 147	Mark Jackson ROO	.25	.08
❏ 148	Kevin Johnson ROO	.25	.08
❏ 149	Mitch Richmond ROO	.25	.08
❏ 150	Rik Smits ROO	.25	.08
❏ 151	Nick Anderson ROO	.25	.08
❏ 152	Tim Hardaway ROO	.25	.08
❏ 153	Shawn Kemp ROO	.50	.20
❏ 154	David Robinson ROO	.50	.20
❏ 155	Jason Kidd ROO	1.25	.50
❏ 156	Grant Hill ART	.75	.30
❏ 157	Glenn Robinson ART	.50	.20
❏ 158	Eddie Jones ART	.75	.30
❏ 159	Brian Grant ART	.50	.20
❏ 160	Juwan Howard ART	.50	.20
❏ 161	Eric Montross ART	.25	.08
❏ 162	Wesley Person ART	.25	.08
❏ 163	Jalen Rose ART	.75	.30
❏ 164	Donyell Marshall ART	.50	.20
❏ 165	Sharone Wright ART	.25	.08
❏ 166	Karl Malone AN	.75	.30
❏ 167	Scottie Pippen AN	.50	.20
❏ 168	David Robinson AN	.50	.20
❏ 169	John Stockton AN	.75	.30
❏ 170	Anfernee Hardaway AN	.50	.20
❏ 171	Charles Barkley AN	.75	.30
❏ 172	Shawn Kemp AN	.50	.20
❏ 173	Shaquille O'Neal AN	.75	.30
❏ 174	Gary Payton AN	.50	.20
❏ 175	Mitch Richmond AN	.25	.08
❏ 176	Dennis Rodman AN	.50	.20
❏ 177	Detlef Schrempf AN	.25	.08

#	Player		
178	Hakeem Olajuwon AN	.50	.20
179	Reggie Miller AN	.50	.20
180	Clyde Drexler AN	.50	.20
181	Hakeem Olajuwon	.75	.30
182	Vin Baker	.50	.20
183	Jeff Hornacek	.50	.20
184	Popeye Jones	.25	.08
185	Sedale Threatt	.25	.08
186	Scottie Pippen	1.25	.50
187	Terry Porter	.50	.20
188	Dan Majerle	.50	.20
189	Clifford Rozier	.25	.08
190	Greg Minor	.25	.08
191	Dennis Scott	.25	.08
192	Hersey Hawkins	.25	.08
193	Chris Gatling	.25	.08
194	Charles Oakley	.25	.08
195	Dale Davis	.25	.08
196	Robert Pack	.25	.08
197	Lamond Murray	.25	.08
198	Mookie Blaylock	.25	.08
199	Dickey Simpkins	.25	.08
200	Kevin Gamble	.25	.08
201	Lorenzo Williams	.25	.08
202	Scott Burrell	.25	.08
203	Armon Gilliam	.25	.08
204	Doc Rivers	.50	.20
205	Blue Edwards	.25	.08
206	Billy Owens	.25	.08
207	Juwan Howard	.75	.30
208	Harvey Grant	.25	.08
209	Richard Dumas	.25	.08
210	Anthony Peeler	.25	.08
211	Matt Geiger	.25	.08
212	Lucious Harris	.25	.08
213	Grant Long	.25	.08
214	Sasha Danilovic RC	.25	.08
215	Chris Morris	.25	.08
216	Donyell Marshall	.50	.20
217	Alonzo Mourning	.50	.20
218	John Stockton	1.00	.40
219	Khalid Reeves	.25	.08
220	Mahmoud Abdul-Rauf	.25	.08
221	Sean Rooks	.25	.08
222	Shawn Kemp	.50	.20
223	John Williams	.25	.08
224	Dee Brown	.25	.08
225	Jim Jackson	.25	.08
226	Harold Miner	.25	.08
227	B.J. Armstrong	.25	.08
228	Elliot Perry	.25	.08
229	Anthony Miller	.25	.08
230	Donny Marshall RC	.25	.08
231	Tyrone Corbin	.25	.08
232	Anthony Mason	.50	.20
233	Grant Hill	1.00	.40
234	Buck Williams	.25	.08
235	Brian Shaw	.25	.08
236	Dale Ellis	.25	.08
237	Magic Johnson	1.25	.50
238	Eric Montross	.25	.08
239	Rex Chapman	.25	.08
240	Otis Thorpe	.25	.08
241	Tracy Murray	.25	.08
242	Sarunas Marciulionis	.25	.08
243	Luc Longley	.25	.08
244	Elmore Spencer	.25	.08
245	Terry Cummings	.25	.08
246	Sam Mitchell	.25	.08
247	Terrence Rencher RC	.25	.08
248	Byron Houston	.25	.08
249	Pervis Ellison	.25	.08
250	Carlos Rogers	.25	.08
251	Kendall Gill	.25	.08
252	Sherrell Ford RC	.25	.08
253	Michael Finley RC	3.00	1.25
254	Kurt Thomas RC	.50	.20
255	Joe Smith RC	1.25	.50
256	Bobby Hurley	.25	.08
257	Greg Anthony	.25	.08
258	Willie Anderson	.25	.08
259	Theo Ratliff RC	1.00	.40
260	Duane Ferrell	.25	.08
261	Antonio Harvey	.25	.08
262	Gary Grant	.25	.08
263	Brian Williams	.25	.08

#	Player		
264	Danny Manning	.50	.20
265	Micheal Williams	.25	.08
266	Dennis Rodman	.50	.20
267	Arvydas Sabonis RC	1.00	.40
268	Don MacLean	.25	.08
269	Keith Askins	.25	.08
270	Reggie Miller	.75	.30
271	Ed Pinckney	.25	.08
272	Bob Sura RC	.50	.20
273	Kevin Garnett RC	5.00	2.50
274	Byron Scott	.25	.08
275	Mario Bennett RC	.25	.08
276	Junior Burrough RC	.25	.08
277	Anfernee Hardaway	.75	.30
278	George McCloud	.25	.08
279	Loren Meyer RC	.25	.08
280	Ed O'Bannon RC	.25	.08
281	Lawrence Moten RC	.25	.08
282	Dana Barros	.25	.08
283	Damon Stoudamire RC	1.50	.60
284	Eric Williams RC	.50	.20
285	Wayman Tisdale	.25	.08
286	Rodney Rogers	.25	.08
287	Sherman Douglas	.25	.08
288	Greg Ostertag RC	.25	.08
289	Alvin Robertson	.25	.08
290	Tim Legler	.25	.08
291	Zan Tabak	.25	.08
292	Gary Trent RC	.25	.08
293	Haywoode Workman	.25	.08
294	Charles Barkley	1.00	.40
295	Derrick Coleman	.25	.08
296	Ricky Pierce	.25	.08
297	Benoit Benjamin	.25	.08
298	Larry Johnson	.50	.20
299	Travis Best RC	.25	.08
300	Jason Caffey RC	.50	.20
301	Cory Alexander RC	.25	.08
302	Nick Van Exel	.75	.30
303	Corliss Williamson RC	.75	.30
304	Eric Murdock	.25	.08
305	Tyus Edney RC	.25	.08
306	Lou Roe RC	.25	.08
307	John Salley	.25	.08
308	Spud Webb	.50	.20
309	Brent Barry RC	.75	.30
310	David Robinson	.75	.30
311	Glen Rice	.50	.20
312	Chris King	.25	.08
313	David Vaughn RC	.25	.08
314	Kenny Gattison	.25	.08
315	Randolph Childress RC	.25	.08
316	Anfernee Hardaway USA	.50	.20
317	Grant Hill USA	.75	.30
318	Karl Malone USA	.75	.30
319	Reggie Miller USA	.50	.20
320	Hakeem Olajuwon USA	.50	.20
321	Shaquille O'Neal USA	.75	.30
322	Scottie Pippen USA	.50	.20
323	David Robinson USA	.50	.20
324	Glenn Robinson USA	.50	.20
325	John Stockton USA	.75	.30
326	Cedric Ceballos I95	.25	.08
327	Shaquille O'Neal I95	.75	.30
328	Glenn Robinson I95	.50	.20
329	Shawn Kemp I95	.25	.08
330	Nick Anderson I95	.25	.08
331	Shawn Bradley I95	.25	.08
332	Orlando's Magic I95	.25	.08
333	1995 NBA Finals I95	.50	.20
334	NBA Expansion I95	.25	.08
335	Michael Jordan I95	2.50	1.00
336	N.Van Exel/O.Cannon MA	.25	.08
337	M.Jordan/D.Hanson MA	1.25	.50
338	S.Pippen/J.Von Oy MA	.75	.30
339	M.Johnson/C.Sheen MA	1.25	.50
340	J.Kidd/C.Reid MA	.75	.30
341	M.Jordan/Q.Latifah MA	1.25	.50
342	C.Barkley/D.Johnson MA	.75	.30
343	Olajuwon/C.Bernsen MA	.75	.30
344	Ahmad Rashad MA	.25	.08
345	Willow Bay MA	.25	.08
346	Mark Curry MA	.75	.30
347	Horace Grant SJ	.50	.20
348	Juwan Howard SJ	.50	.20
349	David Robinson SJ	.50	.20

#	Player		
350	Reggie Miller SJ	.50	.20
351	Brian Grant SJ	.50	.20
352	Michael Jordan SJ	2.50	1.00
353	Cedric Ceballos SJ	.25	.08
354	Blue Edwards SJ	.25	.08
355	Acie Earl SJ	.25	.08
356	Dennis Rodman SJ	.25	.08
357	Shawn Kemp SJ	.25	.08
358	Jerry Stackhouse SJ	1.25	.50
359	Jamal Mashburn SJ	.25	.08
360	Antonio McDyess SJ	.75	.30

1996-97 Upper Deck

	COMPLETE SET (360)	50.00	25.00
	COMPLETE SERIES 1 (180)	30.00	15.00
	COMPLETE SERIES 2 (180)	20.00	10.00
1	Mookie Blaylock	.25	.08
2	Alan Henderson	.25	.08
3	Christian Laettner	.50	.20
4	Ken Norman	.25	.08
5	Dee Brown	.25	.08
6	Todd Day	.25	.08
7	Rick Fox	.25	.08
8	Dino Radja	.25	.08
9	Dana Barros	.25	.08
10	Eric Williams	.25	.08
11	Scott Burrell	.25	.08
12	Dell Curry	.25	.08
13	Matt Geiger	.25	.08
14	Glen Rice	.50	.20
15	Ron Harper	.50	.20
16	Michael Jordan	5.00	2.00
17	Luc Longley	.25	.08
18	Toni Kukoc	.50	.20
19	Dennis Rodman	.50	.20
20	Danny Ferry	.25	.08
21	Tyrone Hill	.25	.08
22	Bobby Phills	.25	.08
23	Bob Sura	.25	.08
24	Tony Dumas	.25	.08
25	George McCloud	.25	.08
26	Jim Jackson	.25	.08
27	Jamal Mashburn	.50	.20
28	Loren Meyer	.25	.08
29	Dale Ellis	.25	.08
30	LaPhonso Ellis	.25	.08
31	Tom Hammonds	.25	.08
32	Antonio McDyess	.50	.20
33	Joe Dumars	.75	.30
34	Grant Hill	.75	.30
35	Lindsey Hunter	.25	.08
36	Terry Mills	.25	.08
37	Theo Ratliff	.50	.20
38	B.J. Armstrong	.25	.08
39	Donyell Marshall	.50	.20
40	Chris Mullin	.75	.30
41	Rony Seikaly	.25	.08
42	Joe Smith	.50	.20
43	Sam Cassell	.75	.30
44	Clyde Drexler	.75	.30
45	Mario Elie	.25	.08
46	Robert Horry	.50	.20
47	Travis Best	.25	.08
48	Antonio Davis	.25	.08
49	Dale Davis	.25	.08
50	Eddie Johnson	.25	.08
51	Derrick McKey	.25	.08
52	Reggie Miller	.75	.30

#	Player		
53	Brent Barry	.25	.08
54	Lamond Murray	.25	.08
55	Eric Piatkowski	.50	.20
56	Rodney Rogers	.25	.08
57	Loy Vaught	.25	.08
58	Kobe Bryant RC	10.00	4.00
59	Eddie Jones	.75	.30
60	Elden Campbell	.25	.08
61	Shaquille O'Neal	2.00	.75
62	Nick Van Exel	.75	.30
63	Keith Askins	.25	.08
64	Rex Chapman	.25	.08
65	Sasha Danilovic	.25	.08
66	Alonzo Mourning	.50	.20
67	Kurt Thomas	.50	.20
68	Tim Hardaway	.50	.20
69	Ray Allen RC	2.50	1.00
70	Johnny Newman	.25	.08
71	Shawn Respert	.25	.08
72	Glenn Robinson	.75	.30
73	Tom Gugliotta	.25	.08
74	Stephon Marbury RC	2.00	.75
75	Terry Porter	.25	.08
76	Doug West	.25	.08
77	Shawn Bradley	.25	.08
78	Kevin Edwards	.25	.08
79	Vern Fleming	.25	.08
80	Ed O'Bannon	.25	.08
81	Jayson Williams	.50	.20
82	John Starks	.50	.20
83	Patrick Ewing	.75	.30
84	Charlie Ward	.25	.08
85	Nick Anderson	.25	.08
86	Anfernee Hardaway	.75	.30
87	Jon Koncak	.25	.08
88	Donald Royal	.25	.08
89	Brian Shaw	.25	.08
90	Derrick Coleman	.50	.20
91	Allen Iverson RC	5.00	2.00
92	Jerry Stackhouse	1.00	.40
93	Clarence Weatherspoon	.25	.08
94	Charles Barkley	1.00	.40
95	Kevin Johnson	.50	.20
96	Danny Manning	.50	.20
97	Elliot Perry	.25	.08
98	Wayman Tisdale	.25	.08
99	Randolph Childress	.25	.08
100	Aaron McKie	.50	.20
101	Arvydas Sabonis	.50	.20
102	Gary Trent	.25	.08
103	Chris Dudley	.25	.08
104	Tyus Edney	.25	.08
105	Brian Grant	.75	.30
106	Bobby Hurley	.25	.08
107	Olden Polynice	.25	.08
108	Corliss Williamson	.50	.20
109	Vinny Del Negro	.25	.08
110	Avery Johnson	.25	.08
111	Will Perdue	.25	.08
112	David Robinson	.75	.30
113	Hersey Hawkins	.50	.20
114	Shawn Kemp	.50	.20
115	Nate McMillan	.25	.08
116	Detlef Schrempf	.50	.20
117	Gary Payton	.75	.30
118	Marcus Camby RC	1.00	.40
119	Zan Tabak	.25	.08
120	Damon Stoudamire	.75	.30
121	Carlos Rogers	.25	.08
122	Sharone Wright	.25	.08
123	Antoine Carr	.25	.08
124	Jeff Hornacek	.50	.20
125	Adam Keefe	.25	.08
126	Chris Morris	.25	.08
127	John Stockton	.75	.30
128	Blue Edwards	.25	.08
129	Shareef Abdur-Rahim RC	2.50	1.00
130	Bryant Reeves	.25	.08
131	Roy Rogers RC	.25	.08
132	Calbert Cheaney	.25	.08
133	Tim Legler	.25	.08
134	Gheorghe Muresan	.25	.08
135	Chris Webber	.75	.30
136	Mutombo/Blaylock/Smith BW	.75	.30
137	Barros/Radja/Williams BW	.25	.08
138	Rice/Geiger/Divac BW	.75	.30
139	Jordan/Pip/Rodman BW	2.00	.75
140	Brandon/Ferry/Hill BW	.50	.20
141	Kidd/Mash/Jackson BW	.50	.20
142	L.Ellis/McDyess/Jackson BW	.25	.08
143	Dumars/Hill/Augmon BW	.75	.30
144	Smith/Sprewell/Mullin BW	.75	.30
145	Olaj/Drexler/Barkley BW	.75	.30
146	R.Miller/Best/Smits BW	.50	.20
147	B.Barry/Murray/Rogers BW	.25	.08
148	O'Neal/Jones/Bryant BW	1.50	.60
149	ZO/Hardaway/Danilovic BW	.75	.30
150	Baker/Robinson/Douglas BW	.75	.30
151	Garnett/Gug/Parks BW	.75	.30
152	Bradley/Gill/O'Bannon BW	.50	.20
153	Ewing/Houston/L.Johnson BW	.75	.30
154	Hardaway/Scott/Grant BW	.50	.20
155	Stack/W'spoon/Cole BW	.50	.20
156	K.Johnson/Manning/Finley BW	.50	.20
157	Robinson/Rider/Sabonis BW	.50	.20
158	Richmond/Grant/Owens BW	.50	.20
159	D.Rob/Elliott/Johnson BW	.75	.30
160	Kemp/Payton/Schrem BW	.50	.20
161	Stoud/Tabak/Wright BW	.75	.30
162	Stockton/Malone/Hornacek BW	.75	.30
163	Reeves/Rahim/Edwards BW	.75	.30
164	Howard/Muresan/Web BW	.75	.30
165	Michael Jordan GP	2.50	1.00
166	Corliss Williamson GP	.25	.08
167	Dell Curry GP	.25	.08
168	John Starks GP	.25	.08
169	Dennis Rodman GP	.75	.30
170	C.Webber/L.Sprewell GP	.75	.30
171	Cedric Ceballos GP	.25	.08
172	Theo Ratliff GP	.25	.08
173	Anfernee Hardaway GP	.75	.30
174	Grant Hill GP	.75	.30
175	Alonzo Mourning GP	.25	.08
176	Shawn Kemp GP	.25	.08
177	Jason Kidd GP	.75	.30
178	Avery Johnson GP	.25	.08
179	Gary Payton GP	.50	.20
180	Michael Jordan CL	.75	.30
181	Priest Lauderdale RC	.25	.08
182	Dikembe Mutombo	.50	.20
183	Eldridge Recasner RC	.25	.08
184	Steve Smith	.50	.20
185	Pervis Ellison	.25	.08
186	Greg Minor	.25	.08
187	Antoine Walker RC	2.50	1.00
188	David Wesley	.25	.08
189	Muggsy Bogues	.25	.08
190	Tony Delk RC	.75	.30
191	Vlade Divac	.25	.08
192	Anthony Mason	.25	.08
193	George Zidek	.25	.08
194	Jason Caffey	.25	.08
195	Steve Kerr	.50	.20
196	Robert Parish	.50	.20
197	Scottie Pippen	1.25	.50
198	Terrell Brandon	.50	.20
199	Antonio Lang	.25	.08
200	Chris Mills	.25	.08
201	Vitaly Potapenko RC	.25	.08
202	Mark West	.25	.08
203	Chris Gatling	.25	.08
204	Derek Harper	.25	.08
205	Sam Cassell	.75	.30
206	Eric Montross	.25	.08
207	Samaki Walker RC	.25	.08
208	Mark Jackson	.25	.08
209	Ervin Johnson	.25	.08
210	Sarunas Marciulionis	.25	.08
211	Ricky Pierce	.25	.08
212	Bryant Stith	.25	.08
213	Stacey Augmon	.25	.08
214	Grant Long	.25	.08
215	Rick Mahorn	.25	.08
216	Otis Thorpe	.25	.08
217	Jerome Williams RC	.25	.08
218	Bimbo Coles	.25	.08
219	Todd Fuller RC	.25	.08
220	Mark Price	.50	.20
221	Felton Spencer	.25	.08
222	Latrell Sprewell	.75	.30
223	Charles Barkley	1.00	.40
224	Othella Harrington RC	.75	.30
225	Hakeem Olajuwon	.75	.30
226	Matt Maloney RC	.50	.20
227	Kevin Willis	.25	.08
228	Erick Dampier RC	.75	.30
229	Duane Ferrell	.25	.08
230	Jalen Rose	.75	.30
231	Rik Smits	.50	.20
232	Terry Dehere	.25	.08
233	Bo Outlaw	.25	.08
234	Pooh Richardson	.25	.08
235	Malik Sealy	.25	.08
236	Lorenzen Wright RC	.50	.20
237	Cedric Ceballos	.25	.08
238	Derek Fisher RC	1.25	.50
239	Travis Knight RC	.25	.08
240	Sean Rooks	.25	.08
241	Byron Scott	.25	.08
242	P.J. Brown	.25	.08
243	Voshon Lenard RC	.50	.20
244	Dan Majerle	.50	.20
245	Martin Muursepp RC	.25	.08
246	Gary Grant	.25	.08
247	Vin Baker	.50	.20
248	Armon Gilliam	.25	.08
249	Andrew Lang	.25	.08
250	Elliot Perry	.25	.08
251	Kevin Garnett	1.50	.60
252	Shane Heal RC	.25	.08
253	Cherokee Parks	.25	.08
254	Stojko Vrankovic	.25	.08
255	Kendall Gill	.25	.08
256	Kerry Kittles RC	.75	.30
257	Xavier McDaniel	.25	.08
258	Robert Pack	.25	.08
259	Chris Childs	.25	.08
260	Allan Houston	.50	.20
261	Larry Johnson	.50	.20
262	Dontae' Jones RC	.25	.08
263	Walter McCarty RC	.25	.08
264	Charles Oakley	.25	.08
265	John Wallace RC	.75	.30
266	Buck Williams	.25	.08
267	Brian Evans RC	.25	.08
268	Horace Grant	.25	.08
269	Dennis Scott	.25	.08
270	Rony Seikaly	.25	.08
271	Michael Cage	.25	.08
272	Lucious Harris	.25	.08
273	Don MacLean	.25	.08
274	Mark Davis	.25	.08
275	Jason Kidd	1.25	.50
276	Michael Finley	1.00	.40
277	A.C. Green	.50	.20
278	Robert Horry	.50	.20
279	Steve Nash RC	5.00	2.00
280	Wesley Person	.25	.08
281	Kenny Anderson	.25	.08
282	Aleksandar Djordjevic RC	.25	.08
283	Jermaine O'Neal RC	2.50	1.00
284	Isaiah Rider	.50	.20
285	Clifford Robinson	.25	.08
286	Rasheed Wallace	1.00	.40
287	Mahmoud Abdul-Rauf	.25	.08
288	Billy Owens	.25	.08
289	Mitch Richmond	.50	.20
290	Michael Smith	.25	.08
291	Cory Alexander	.25	.08
292	Sean Elliott	.25	.08
293	Vernon Maxwell	.25	.08
294	Dominique Wilkins	.75	.30
295	Craig Ehlo	.25	.08
296	Jim McIlvaine	.25	.08
297	Sam Perkins	.50	.20
298	Steve Scheffler RC	.25	.08
299	Hubert Davis	.25	.08
300	Popeye Jones	.25	.08
301	Donald Whiteside RC	.25	.08
302	Walt Williams	.25	.08
303	Karl Malone	.75	.30
304	Greg Ostertag	.25	.08
305	Bryon Russell	.25	.08
306	Jamie Watson	.25	.08
307	Greg Anthony	.25	.08
308	George Lynch	.25	.08
309	Lawrence Moten	.25	.08

#	Player		
311	Anthony Peeler	.25	.08
312	Juwan Howard	.50	.20
313	Tracy Murray	.25	.08
314	Rod Strickland	.25	.08
315	Harvey Grant	.25	.08
316	Charles Barkley DN	.75	.30
317	Clyde Drexler DN	.50	.20
318	Dikembe Mutombo DN	.25	.08
319	Larry Johnson DN	.25	.08
320	Shaquille O'Neal DN	.75	.30
321	Mookie Blaylock DN	.25	.08
322	Tim Hardaway DN	.25	.08
323	Dennis Rodman DN	.25	.08
324	Dan Majerle DN	.25	.08
325	Stacey Augmon DN	.25	.08
326	Kenny Anderson DN	.25	.08
327	Kenny Anderson DN	.25	.08
328	Mahmoud Abdul-Rauf DN	.25	.08
329	Chris Webber DN	.75	.30
330	Dominique Wilkins DN	.50	.20
331	Dikembe Mutombo WD	.25	.08
332	Dana Barros WD	.25	.08
333	Glen Rice WD	.25	.08
334	Dennis Rodman WD	.25	.08
335	Terrell Brandon WD	.25	.08
336	Jason Kidd WD	.75	.30
337	Antonio McDyess WD	.50	.20
338	Grant Hill WD	.75	.30
339	Joe Smith WD	.25	.08
340	Charles Barkley WD	.75	.30
341	Reggie Miller WD	.50	.20
342	Brent Barry WD	.25	.08
343	Shaquille O'Neal WD	.75	.30
344	Alonzo Mourning WD	.25	.08
345	Glenn Robinson WD	.25	.08
346	Stephon Marbury WD	1.50	.60
347	Kerry Kittles WD	.75	.30
348	Patrick Ewing WD	.50	.20
349	Anfernee Hardaway WD	.50	.20
350	Allen Iverson WD	2.00	.75
351	Danny Manning WD	.25	.08
352	Arvydas Sabonis WD	.25	.08
353	Mitch Richmond WD	.25	.08
354	David Robinson WD	.50	.20
355	Shawn Kemp WD	.75	.30
356	Marcus Camby WD	.50	.20
357	Karl Malone WD	.75	.30
358	Shareef Abdur-Rahim WD	1.25	.50
359	Gheorghe Muresan WD	.25	.08
360	Checklist	.25	.08

1997-98 Upper Deck

COMPLETE SET (360)		50.00	30.00
COMPLETE SERIES 1 (180)		25.00	15.00
COMPLETE SERIES 2 (180)		25.00	15.00
1	Steve Smith	.50	.20
2	Christian Laettner	.50	.20
3	Alan Henderson	.25	.08
4	Dikembe Mutombo	.50	.20
5	Dana Barros	.25	.08
6	Antoine Walker	1.00	.40
7	Dee Brown	.25	.08
8	Eric Williams	.25	.08
9	Muggsy Bogues	.25	.08
10	Dell Curry	.25	.08
11	Vlade Divac	.50	.20
12	Anthony Mason	.50	.20
13	Glen Rice	.50	.20
14	Jason Caffey	.25	.08
15	Steve Kerr	.50	.20
16	Toni Kukoc	.50	.20
17	Luc Longley	.25	.08
18	Michael Jordan	5.00	2.00
19	Terrell Brandon	.50	.20
20	Danny Ferry	.25	.08
21	Tyrone Hill	.25	.08
22	Derek Anderson RC	1.00	.40
23	Bob Sura	.25	.08
24	Shawn Bradley	.25	.08
25	Michael Finley	.75	.30
26	Ed O'Bannon	.25	.08
27	Robert Pack	.25	.08
28	Samaki Walker	.25	.08
29	LaPhonso Ellis	.25	.08
30	Tony Battie RC	.75	.30
31	Antonio McDyess	.50	.20
32	Bryant Stith	.25	.08
33	Randolph Childress	.25	.08
34	Grant Hill	.75	.30
35	Lindsey Hunter	.25	.08
36	Grant Long	.25	.08
37	Theo Ratliff	.25	.08
38	B.J. Armstrong	.25	.08
39	Adonal Foyle RC	.50	.20
40	Mark Price	.50	.20
41	Felton Spencer	.25	.08
42	Latrell Sprewell	.75	.30
43	Clyde Drexler	.75	.30
44	Mario Elie	.25	.08
45	Hakeem Olajuwon	.75	.30
46	Brent Price	.25	.08
47	Kevin Willis	.50	.20
48	Erick Dampier	.50	.20
49	Antonio Davis	.25	.08
50	Dale Davis	.25	.08
51	Mark Jackson	.25	.08
52	Rik Smits	.50	.20
53	Brent Barry	.50	.20
54	Lamond Murray	.25	.08
55	Eric Piatkowski	.25	.08
56	Loy Vaught	.25	.08
57	Lorenzen Wright	.25	.08
58	Kobe Bryant	3.00	1.25
59	Derek Campbell	.25	.08
60	Derek Fisher	.75	.30
61	Eddie Jones	.75	.30
62	Nick Van Exel	.75	.30
63	Keith Askins	.25	.08
64	Isaac Austin	.25	.08
65	P.J. Brown	.25	.08
66	Tim Hardaway	.50	.20
67	Alonzo Mourning	.50	.20
68	Ray Allen	.75	.30
69	Vin Baker	.50	.20
70	Sherman Douglas	.25	.08
71	Armon Gilliam	.25	.08
72	Elliot Perry	.25	.08
73	Chris Carr	.25	.08
74	Tom Gugliotta	.50	.20
75	Kevin Garnett	1.50	.60
76	Doug West	.25	.08
77	Keith Van Horn RC	1.00	.40
78	Chris Gatling	.25	.08
79	Kendall Gill	.25	.08
80	Kerry Kittles	.75	.30
81	Jayson Williams	.25	.08
82	Chris Childs	.25	.08
83	Allan Houston	.50	.20
84	Larry Johnson	.50	.20
85	Charles Oakley	.50	.20
86	John Starks	.50	.20
87	Horace Grant	.50	.20
88	Anfernee Hardaway	.75	.30
89	Dennis Scott	.25	.08
90	Rony Seikaly	.25	.08
91	Brian Shaw	.25	.08
92	Derrick Coleman	.25	.08
93	Allen Iverson	2.00	.75
94	Tim Thomas RC	1.25	.50
95	Scott Williams	.25	.08
96	Cedric Ceballos	.25	.08
97	Kevin Johnson	.50	.20
98	Loren Meyer	.25	.08
99	Steve Nash	.75	.30
100	Wesley Person	.25	.08
101	Kenny Anderson	.50	.20
102	Jermaine O'Neal	1.25	.50
103	Isaiah Rider	.50	.20
104	Arvydas Sabonis	.50	.20
105	Gary Trent	.25	.08
106	Mahmoud Abdul-Rauf	.25	.08
107	Billy Owens	.25	.08
108	Olden Polynice	.25	.08
109	Mitch Richmond	.50	.20
110	Michael Smith	.25	.08
111	Cory Alexander	.25	.08
112	Vinny Del Negro	.25	.08
113	Carl Herrera	.25	.08
114	Tim Duncan RC	6.00	2.50
115	Hersey Hawkins	.25	.08
116	Shawn Kemp	.50	.20
117	Nate McMillan	.25	.08
118	Sam Perkins	.25	.08
119	Detlef Schrempf	.50	.20
120	Doug Christie	.25	.08
121	Popeye Jones	.25	.08
122	Carlos Rogers	.25	.08
123	Damon Stoudamire	.50	.20
124	Adam Keefe	.25	.08
125	Chris Morris	.25	.08
126	Greg Ostertag	.25	.08
127	John Stockton	.75	.30
128	Shareef Abdur-Rahim	1.25	.50
129	George Lynch	.25	.08
130	Lee Mayberry	.25	.08
131	Anthony Peeler	.25	.08
132	Calbert Cheaney	.25	.08
133	Tracy Murray	.25	.08
134	Rod Strickland	.25	.08
135	Chris Webber	.75	.30
136	Christian Laettner JAM	.25	.08
137	Eric Williams JAM	.25	.08
138	Vlade Divac JAM	.25	.08
139	Michael Jordan JAM	2.50	1.00
140	Tyrone Hill JAM	.25	.08
141	Michael Finley JAM	.50	.20
142	Tom Hammonds JAM	.25	.08
143	Theo Ratliff JAM	.25	.08
144	Latrell Sprewell JAM	.75	.30
145	Hakeem Olajuwon JAM	.50	.20
146	Reggie Miller JAM	.50	.20
147	Rodney Rogers JAM	.25	.08
148	Eddie Jones JAM	.50	.20
149	Jamal Mashburn JAM	.50	.20
150	Glenn Robinson JAM	.50	.20
151	Chris Carr JAM	.25	.08
152	Kendall Gill JAM	.25	.08
153	John Starks JAM	.25	.08
154	Anfernee Hardaway JAM	.50	.20
155	Derrick Coleman JAM	.25	.08
156	Cedric Ceballos JAM	.25	.08
157	Rasheed Wallace JAM	.25	.08
158	Corliss Williamson JAM	.25	.08
159	Sean Elliott JAM	.50	.20
160	Shawn Kemp JAM	.50	.20
161	Doug Christie JAM	.25	.08
162	Karl Malone JAM	.75	.30
163	Bryant Reeves JAM	.25	.08
164	Gheorghe Muresan JAM	.25	.08
165	Michael Jordan JAM	2.50	1.00
166	Dikembe Mutombo CP	.25	.08
167	Glen Rice CP	.25	.08
168	Mitch Richmond CP	.25	.08
169	Juwan Howard CP	.25	.08
170	Clyde Drexler CP	.50	.20
171	Terrell Brandon CP	.25	.08
172	Jerry Stackhouse CP	.50	.20
173	Damon Stoudamire CP	.25	.08
174	Jayson Williams CP	.25	.08
175	P.J. Brown CP	.25	.08
176	Anfernee Hardaway CP	.25	.08
177	Vin Baker CP	.25	.08
178	LaPhonso Ellis CP	.25	.08
179	Shawn Kemp CP	.25	.08
180	Checklist	.25	.08
181	Mookie Blaylock	.25	.08
182	Tyrone Corbin	.25	.08
183	Chucky Brown	.25	.08
184	Ed Gray RC	.25	.08
185	Chauncey Billups RC	2.00	.75

186	Tyus Edney	.25	.08
187	Travis Knight	.25	.08
188	Ron Mercer RC	.75	.30
189	Walter McCarty	.25	.08
190	B.J. Armstrong	.25	.08
191	Matt Geiger	.25	.08
192	Bobby Phills	.25	.08
193	David Wesley	.25	.08
194	Keith Booth RC	.25	.08
195	Randy Brown	.25	.08
196	Ron Harper	.50	.20
197	Scottie Pippen	1.25	.50
198	Dennis Rodman	.50	.20
199	Zydrunas Ilgauskas	.50	.20
200	Brevin Knight RC	.50	.20
201	Shawn Kemp	.50	.20
202	Vitaly Potapenko	.25	.08
203	Wesley Person	.25	.08
204	Erick Strickland RC	.50	.20
205	A.C. Green	.50	.20
206	Khalid Reeves	.25	.08
207	Hubert Davis	.25	.08
208	Dennis Scott	.25	.08
209	Danny Fortson RC	.50	.20
210	Bobby Jackson RC	1.25	.50
211	Eric Williams	.25	.08
212	Dean Garrett	.25	.08
213	Priest Lauderdale	.25	.08
214	Joe Dumars	.75	.30
215	Aaron McKie	.25	.08
216	Scot Pollard RC	.50	.20
217	Brian Williams	.25	.08
218	Malik Sealy	.25	.08
219	Duane Ferrell	.25	.08
220	Erick Dampier	.25	.08
221	Todd Fuller	.25	.08
222	Donyell Marshall	.50	.20
223	Joe Smith	.50	.20
224	Charles Barkley	1.00	.40
225	Matt Bullard	.25	.08
226	Othella Harrington	.25	.08
227	Rodrick Rhodes RC	.25	.08
228	Eddie Johnson	.25	.08
229	Matt Maloney	.25	.08
230	Travis Best	.25	.08
231	Reggie Miller	.75	.30
232	Chris Mullin	.75	.30
233	Fred Hoiberg	.25	.08
234	Austin Croshere RC	.60	.25
235	Keith Closs RC	.25	.08
236	Darrick Martin	.25	.08
237	Pooh Richardson	.25	.08
238	Rodney Rogers	.25	.08
239	Maurice Taylor RC	.60	.25
240	Robert Horry	.50	.20
241	Rick Fox	.25	.08
242	Shaquille O'Neal	2.00	.75
243	Corie Blount	.25	.08
244	Charles Smith RC	.60	.25
245	Voshon Lenard	.25	.08
246	Eric Murdock	.25	.08
247	Dan Majerle	.50	.20
248	Terry Mills	.25	.08
249	Terrell Brandon	.50	.20
250	Tyrone Hill	.25	.08
251	Ervin Johnson	.25	.08
252	Glenn Robinson	.75	.30
253	Terry Porter	.25	.08
254	Paul Grant RC	.25	.08
255	Stephon Marbury	1.00	.40
256	Sam Mitchell	.25	.08
257	Cherokee Parks	.25	.08
258	Sam Cassell	.75	.30
259	David Benoit	.25	.08
260	Kevin Edwards	.25	.08
261	Don MacLean	.25	.08
262	Patrick Ewing	.75	.30
263	Herb Williams	.25	.08
264	John Starks	.50	.20
265	Chris Mills	.25	.08
266	Chris Dudley	.25	.08
267	Darrell Armstrong	.25	.08
268	Nick Anderson	.25	.08
269	Derek Harper	.25	.08
270	Johnny Taylor RC	.25	.08
271	Mark Price	.50	.20

272	Clarence Weatherspoon	.25	.08
273	Jerry Stackhouse	.75	.30
274	Eric Montross	.25	.08
275	Anthony Parker RC	.25	.08
276	Antonio McDyess	.50	.20
277	Clifford Robinson	.25	.08
278	Jason Kidd	1.25	.50
279	Danny Manning	.50	.20
280	Rex Chapman	.25	.08
281	Stacey Augmon	.25	.08
282	Kelvin Cato RC	.75	.30
283	Brian Grant	.50	.20
284	Rasheed Wallace	.75	.30
285	Lawrence Funderburke RC	.50	.20
286	Anthony Johnson	.25	.08
287	Tariq Abdul-Wahad RC	.50	.20
288	Corliss Williamson	.25	.08
289	Sean Elliott	.50	.20
290	Avery Johnson	.25	.08
291	David Robinson	.75	.30
292	Will Perdue	.25	.08
293	Greg Anthony	.25	.08
294	Jim McIlvaine	.25	.08
295	Dale Ellis	.25	.08
296	Gary Payton	.75	.30
297	Aaron Williams	.25	.08
298	Marcus Camby	.75	.30
299	John Wallace	.25	.08
300	Tracy McGrady RC	4.00	1.50
301	Walt Williams	.25	.08
302	Shandon Anderson	.25	.08
303	Antoine Carr	.25	.08
304	Jeff Hornacek	.50	.20
305	Karl Malone	.75	.30
306	Bryon Russell	.25	.08
307	Jacque Vaughn RC	.50	.20
308	Antonio Daniels RC	.75	.30
309	Blue Edwards	.25	.08
310	Bryant Reeves	.25	.08
311	Otis Thorpe	.25	.08
312	Harvey Grant	.25	.08
313	Terry Davis	.25	.08
314	Juwan Howard	.50	.20
315	Gheorghe Muresan	.25	.08
316	Michael Jordan A	2.50	1.00
317	Allen Iverson OT	.75	.30
318	Karl Malone OT	.75	.30
319	Glen Rice OT	.25	.08
320	Dikembe Mutombo OT	.25	.08
321	Grant Hill OT	.50	.20
322	Hakeem Olajuwon OT	.50	.20
323	Stephon Marbury OT	.75	.30
324	Anfernee Hardaway OT	.50	.20
325	Eddie Jones OT	.50	.20
326	Mitch Richmond OT	.25	.08
327	Kevin Johnson OT	.25	.08
328	Kevin Garnett OT	.75	.30
329	Shareef Abdur-Rahim OT	.60	.25
330	Damon Stoudamire OT	.25	.08
331	Atlanta Hawks DM	.25	.08
332	Boston Celtics DM	.25	.08
333	Charlotte Hornets DM	.50	.20
334	Chicago Bulls DM	1.00	.40
335	Cleveland Cavaliers DM	.50	.20
336	Dallas Mavericks DM	.50	.20
337	Denver Nuggets DM	.75	.30
338	Detroit Pistons DM	.75	.30
339	Golden State Warriors DM	.75	.30
340	Houston Rockets DM	.50	.20
341	Indiana Pacers DM	.50	.20
342	Los Angeles Clippers DM	.25	.08
343	Los Angeles Lakers DM	.60	.25
344	Miami Heat DM	.75	.30
345	Milwaukee Bucks DM	.50	.20
346	Minnesota Timberwolves DM	.30	.12
347	New Jersey Nets DM	.50	.20
348	New York Knicks DM	.75	.30
349	Orlando Magic DM	.75	.30
350	Philadelphia 76ers DM	.30	.12
351	Phoenix Suns DM	.50	.20
352	Portland Trail Blazers DM	.25	.08
353	Sacramento Kings DM	.50	.20
354	San Antonio Spurs DM	.40	.15
355	Seattle Sonics DM	.75	.30
356	Toronto Raptors DM	.50	.20
357	Utah Jazz DM	.50	.20

358	Vancouver Grizzlies DM	.25	.08
359	Washington Wizards DM	.75	.30
360	Checklist	.25	.08
NNO	M.Jordan Red Audio	25.00	10.00
NNO	M.Jordan Black Audio	10.00	4.00

1998-99 Upper Deck

COMPLETE SET (355)		180.00	90.00
COMPLETE SERIES 1 (175)		100.00	50.00
COMPLETE SERIES 2 (180)		80.00	40.00
COMMON CARD (1-311)		.25	.08
COMMON ROOKIE (312-333)		.60	.25
COMMON JORDAN (230A-W)		3.00	1.25
COMMON HS SUBSET		.75	.30
COMMON TN SUBSET		1.00	.40
1	Mookie Blaylock	.25	.08
2	Ed Gray	.25	.08
3	Dikembe Mutombo	.50	.20
4	Steve Smith	.50	.20
5	D.Mutombo/S.Smith HS	.75	.30
6	Kenny Anderson	.50	.20
7	Dana Barros	.25	.08
8	Travis Knight	.25	.08
9	Walter McCarty	.25	.08
10	Ron Mercer	.40	.15
11	Greg Minor	.25	.08
12	A.Walker/R.Mercer HS	.60	.25
13	B.J. Armstrong	.25	.08
14	David Wesley	.25	.08
15	Anthony Mason	.50	.20
16	Glen Rice	.50	.20
17	J.R. Reid	.25	.08
18	Bobby Phills	.25	.08
19	G.Rice/A.Mason HS	.75	.30
20	Ron Harper	.50	.20
21	Toni Kukoc	.50	.20
22	Scottie Pippen	1.25	.50
23	Michael Jordan	5.00	2.00
24	Dennis Rodman	.50	.20
25	M.Jordan/S.Pippen HS	10.00	5.00
26	M.Jordan/M.Jordan HS	12.00	6.00
27	Shawn Kemp	.50	.20
28	Zydrunas Ilgauskas	.50	.20
29	Cedric Henderson	.25	.08
30	Vitaly Potapenko	.25	.08
31	Derek Anderson	.60	.25
32	S.Kemp/Z.Ilgauskas HS	1.25	.50
33	Shawn Bradley	.25	.08
34	Khalid Reeves	.25	.08
35	Robert Pack	.25	.08
36	Michael Finley	.75	.30
37	Erick Strickland	.25	.08
38	M.Finley/S.Bradley HS	1.00	.40
39	Bryant Stith	.25	.08
40	Dean Garrett	.25	.08
41	Eric Williams	.25	.08
42	Bobby Jackson	.50	.20
43	Danny Fortson	.25	.08
44	L.Ellis/B.Stith HS	.75	.30
45	Grant Hill	.75	.30
46	Lindsey Hunter	.25	.08
47	Brian Williams	.25	.08
48	Scot Pollard	.25	.08
49	G.Hill/B.Williams HS	.75	.30
50	Donyell Marshall	.50	.20
51	Tony Delk	.25	.08
52	Erick Dampier	.25	.08
53	Felton Spencer	.25	.08

#	Player		
☐ 54	Bimbo Coles	.25	.08
☐ 55	Muggsy Bogues	.50	.20
☐ 56	D.Marshall/M.Bogues HS	.75	.30
☐ 57	Charles Barkley	1.00	.40
☐ 58	Brent Price	.25	.08
☐ 59	Hakeem Olajuwon	.75	.30
☐ 60	Rodrick Rhodes	.25	.08
☐ 61	C.Barkley/H.Olaj HS	2.00	.75
☐ 62	Dale Davis	.50	.20
☐ 63	Antonio Davis	.25	.08
☐ 64	Chris Mullin	.75	.30
☐ 65	Jalen Rose	.75	.30
☐ 66	Reggie Miller	.75	.30
☐ 67	Mark Jackson	.50	.20
☐ 68	R.Miller/M.Jackson HS	1.25	.50
☐ 69	Rodney Rogers	.25	.08
☐ 70	Lamond Murray	.25	.08
☐ 71	Eric Piatkowski	.50	.20
☐ 72	Lorenzen Wright	.25	.08
☐ 73	Maurice Taylor	.40	.15
☐ 74	M.Taylor/L.Murray HS	.60	.25
☐ 75	Kobe Bryant	3.00	1.25
☐ 76	Shaquille O'Neal	2.00	.75
☐ 77	Derek Fisher	.75	.30
☐ 78	Elden Campbell	.25	.08
☐ 79	Corie Blount	.25	.08
☐ 80	S.O'Neal/K.Bryant HS	8.00	3.00
☐ 81	Jamal Mashburn	.50	.20
☐ 82	Alonzo Mourning	.50	.20
☐ 83	Tim Hardaway	.50	.20
☐ 84	Voshon Lenard	.25	.08
☐ 85	A.Mourning/T.Hard HS	1.25	.50
☐ 86	Ray Allen	.75	.30
☐ 87	Terrell Brandon	.25	.08
☐ 88	Elliot Perry	.25	.08
☐ 89	Ervin Johnson	.25	.08
☐ 90	R.Allen/G.Robinson HS	.75	.30
☐ 91	Micheal Williams	.25	.08
☐ 92	Anthony Peeler	.25	.08
☐ 93	Chris Carr	.25	.08
☐ 94	Kevin Garnett	1.50	.60
☐ 95	K.Garnett/S.Marbury HS	3.00	1.25
☐ 96	Keith Van Horn	.75	.30
☐ 97	Kerry Kittles	.25	.08
☐ 98	Kendall Gill	.25	.08
☐ 99	Sam Cassell	.75	.30
☐ 100	Chris Gatling	.25	.08
☐ 101	K.Van Horn/Cassell HS	1.00	.40
☐ 102	Patrick Ewing	.75	.30
☐ 103	John Starks	.50	.20
☐ 104	Allan Houston	.50	.20
☐ 105	Chris Mills	.25	.08
☐ 106	Chris Childs	.25	.08
☐ 107	Charlie Ward	.25	.08
☐ 108	P.Ewing/J.Starks HS	1.25	.50
☐ 109	Anfernee Hardaway	.75	.30
☐ 110	Horace Grant	.50	.20
☐ 111	Nick Anderson	.25	.08
☐ 112	Johnny Taylor	.25	.08
☐ 113	A.Hardaway/H.Grant HS	2.00	.75
☐ 114	Allen Iverson	1.50	.60
☐ 115	Scott Williams	.25	.08
☐ 116	Tim Thomas	.50	.20
☐ 117	Brian Shaw	.25	.08
☐ 118	Anthony Parker	.25	.08
☐ 119	A.Iverson/T.Thomas HS	2.00	.75
☐ 120	Jason Kidd	1.25	.50
☐ 121	Rex Chapman	.25	.08
☐ 122	Danny Manning	.25	.08
☐ 123	J.Kidd/D.Manning HS	2.50	1.00
☐ 124	Rasheed Wallace	.75	.30
☐ 125	Walt Williams	.25	.08
☐ 126	Kelvin Cato	.25	.08
☐ 127	Arvydas Sabonis	.50	.20
☐ 128	Brian Grant	.50	.20
☐ 129	R.Wallace/I.Rider HS	.75	.30
☐ 130	Tariq Abdul-Wahad	.25	.08
☐ 131	Corliss Williamson	.50	.20
☐ 132	Olden Polynice	.25	.08
☐ 133	Chris Robinson	.25	.08
☐ 134	T.Abdul-Wahad/O.Polynice HS	.75	.30
☐ 135	Tim Duncan	1.25	.50
☐ 136	Avery Johnson	.25	.08
☐ 137	David Robinson	.75	.30
☐ 138	Monty Williams	.25	.08
☐ 139	T.Duncan/D.Rob HS	2.50	1.00
☐ 140	Vin Baker	.50	.20
☐ 141	Hersey Hawkins	.25	.08
☐ 142	Detlef Schrempf	.50	.20
☐ 143	Jim McIlvaine	.25	.08
☐ 144	G.Payton/V.Baker HS	1.00	.40
☐ 145	Chauncey Billups	.50	.20
☐ 146	Tracy McGrady	2.00	.75
☐ 147	John Wallace	.25	.08
☐ 148	Doug Christie	.50	.20
☐ 149	Dee Brown	.25	.08
☐ 150	T.McGrady/C.Billups HS	1.50	.60
☐ 151	Karl Malone	.75	.30
☐ 152	John Stockton	.75	.30
☐ 153	Adam Keefe	.25	.08
☐ 154	Howard Eisley	.25	.08
☐ 155	K.Malone/J.Stockton HS	.75	.30
☐ 156	Bryant Reeves	.25	.08
☐ 157	Lee Mayberry	.25	.08
☐ 158	Michael Smith	.25	.08
☐ 159	Abdur-Rahim/Reeves HS	2.00	.75
☐ 160	Juwan Howard	.50	.20
☐ 161	Calbert Cheaney	.25	.08
☐ 162	Tracy Murray	.25	.08
☐ 163	J.Howard/C.Cheaney HS	.75	.30
☐ 164	Shaquille O'Neal TN	4.00	1.50
☐ 165	Maurice Taylor TN	.75	.30
☐ 166	Stephon Marbury TN	.75	.30
☐ 167	Tracy McGrady TN	4.00	1.50
☐ 168	Antoine Walker TN	1.25	.50
☐ 169	Michael Jordan TN	10.00	5.00
☐ 170	Keith Van Horn TN	.75	.30
☐ 171	S.Abdur-Rahim TN	2.00	.75
☐ 172	Kobe Bryant TN	6.00	2.50
☐ 173	Gary Payton TN	1.50	.60
☐ 174	Michael Jordan CL	1.00	.40
☐ 175	Michael Jordan CL	1.00	.40
☐ 176	Kevin Johnson	.50	.20
☐ 177	Glenn Robinson	.50	.20
☐ 178	Antoine Walker	.75	.30
☐ 179	Jerry Stackhouse	.75	.30
☐ 180	Mark Price	.50	.20
☐ 181	Stephon Marbury	.75	.30
☐ 182	Shareef Abdur-Rahim	.75	.30
☐ 183	Wesley Person	.25	.08
☐ 184	Keith Booth	.25	.08
☐ 185	Sean Elliott	.50	.20
☐ 186	Alan Henderson	.25	.08
☐ 187	Bryon Russell	.25	.08
☐ 188	Jermaine O'Neal	.75	.30
☐ 189	Steve Nash	.75	.30
☐ 190	Eldridge Recasner	.25	.08
☐ 191	Damon Stoudamire	.50	.20
☐ 192	Dell Curry	.25	.08
☐ 193	Michael Stewart	.25	.08
☐ 194	Bruce Bowen RC	.50	.20
☐ 195	Steve Kerr	.50	.20
☐ 196	Dale Ellis	.25	.08
☐ 197	Shandon Anderson	.25	.08
☐ 198	Larry Johnson	.50	.20
☐ 199	Chris Webber	.75	.30
☐ 200	Matt Geiger	.25	.08
☐ 201	Chris Anstey	.25	.08
☐ 202	Loy Vaught	.25	.08
☐ 203	Aaron McKie	.50	.20
☐ 204	A.C. Green	.50	.20
☐ 205	Bo Outlaw	.25	.08
☐ 206	Antonio McDyess	.50	.20
☐ 207	Priest Lauderdale	.25	.08
☐ 208	Greg Ostertag	.25	.08
☐ 209	Dan Majerle	.50	.20
☐ 210	Johnny Newman	.25	.08
☐ 211	Tyrone Corbin	.25	.08
☐ 212	Pervis Ellison	.25	.08
☐ 213	Shawnelle Scott	.25	.08
☐ 214	Travis Best	.25	.08
☐ 215	Stacey Augmon	.25	.08
☐ 216	Brevin Knight	.50	.20
☐ 217	Jerome Williams	.25	.08
☐ 218	Terry Mills	.25	.08
☐ 219	Matt Maloney	.25	.08
☐ 220	Dennis Scott	.25	.08
☐ 221	John Thomas	.25	.08
☐ 222	Nick Van Exel	.75	.30
☐ 223	Duane Ferrell	.25	.08
☐ 224	Chris Whitney	.25	.08
☐ 225	Luc Longley	.25	.08
☐ 226	Robert Horry	.50	.20
☐ 227	Clifford Robinson	.25	.08
☐ 228	Samaki Walker	.25	.08
☐ 229	Derrick McKey	.25	.08
☐ 230A	Michael Jordan	3.00	1.25
☐ 230B	Michael Jordan	3.00	1.25
☐ 230C	Michael Jordan	3.00	1.25
☐ 230D	Michael Jordan	3.00	1.25
☐ 230E	Michael Jordan	3.00	1.25
☐ 230F	Michael Jordan	3.00	1.25
☐ 230G	Michael Jordan	3.00	1.25
☐ 230H	Michael Jordan	3.00	1.25
☐ 230I	Michael Jordan	3.00	1.25
☐ 230J	Michael Jordan	3.00	1.25
☐ 230K	Michael Jordan	3.00	1.25
☐ 230L	Michael Jordan	3.00	1.25
☐ 230M	Michael Jordan	3.00	1.25
☐ 230N	Michael Jordan	3.00	1.25
☐ 230O	Michael Jordan	3.00	1.25
☐ 230P	Michael Jordan	3.00	1.25
☐ 230Q	Michael Jordan	3.00	1.25
☐ 230R	Michael Jordan	3.00	1.25
☐ 230S	Michael Jordan	3.00	1.25
☐ 230T	Michael Jordan	3.00	1.25
☐ 230U	Michael Jordan	3.00	1.25
☐ 230V	Michael Jordan	3.00	1.25
☐ 230W	Michael Jordan	3.00	1.25
☐ 231	Armon Gilliam	.25	.08
☐ 232	Andrew DeClercq	.25	.08
☐ 233	Stojko Vrankovic	.25	.08
☐ 234	Jayson Williams	.25	.08
☐ 235	Vinny Del Negro	.25	.08
☐ 236	Theo Ratliff	.50	.20
☐ 237	Othella Harrington	.25	.08
☐ 238	Mitch Richmond	.50	.20
☐ 239	Vlade Divac	.50	.20
☐ 240	Duane Causwell	.25	.08
☐ 241	Todd Fuller	.25	.08
☐ 242	Tom Gugliotta	.50	.20
☐ 243	LaPhonso Ellis	.25	.08
☐ 244	Brian Evans	.25	.08
☐ 245	Jason Caffey	.25	.08
☐ 246	Pooh Richardson	.25	.08
☐ 247	George Lynch	.25	.08
☐ 248	Bill Wennington	.25	.08
☐ 249	Rik Smits	.50	.20
☐ 250	Kevin Willis	.25	.08
☐ 251	Mario Elie	.25	.08
☐ 252	Austin Croshere	.60	.25
☐ 253	Sharone Wright	.25	.08
☐ 254	Danny Ferry	.25	.08
☐ 255	Jacque Vaughn	.25	.08
☐ 256	Adonal Foyle	.25	.08
☐ 257	Billy Owens	.25	.08
☐ 258	Randy Brown	.25	.08
☐ 259	Joe Smith	.50	.20
☐ 260	Joe Dumars	.75	.30
☐ 261	Sean Rooks	.25	.08
☐ 262	Eric Montross	.25	.08
☐ 263	Hubert Davis	.25	.08
☐ 264	Gary Payton	.75	.30
☐ 265	Tyrone Hill	.25	.08
☐ 266	John Crotty	.25	.08
☐ 267	P.J. Brown	.25	.08
☐ 268	Michael Cage	.25	.08
☐ 269	Scott Burrell	.25	.08
☐ 270	Marcus Camby	.50	.20
☐ 271	Rod Strickland	.25	.08
☐ 272	Jim Jackson	.25	.08
☐ 273	Corey Beck	.25	.08
☐ 274	James Robinson	.25	.08
☐ 275	Cedric Ceballos	.25	.08
☐ 276	Charles Oakley	.25	.08
☐ 277	Anthony Johnson	.25	.08
☐ 278	Bob Sura	.25	.08
☐ 279	Isaiah Rider	.50	.20
☐ 280	Jeff Hornacek	.50	.20
☐ 281	Rony Seikaly	.25	.08
☐ 282	Charles Smith	.25	.08
☐ 283	Eddie Jones	.75	.30
☐ 284	Lucious Harris	.25	.08
☐ 285	Andrew Lang	.25	.08
☐ 286	Terry Cummings	.25	.08
☐ 287	Keith Closs	.25	.08
☐ 288	Chris Anstey	.25	.08
☐ 289	Clarence Weatherspoon	.25	.08

290	Michael Jordan H99	2.50	1.00
291	Shawn Kemp H99	.50	.20
292	Tracy McGrady H99	1.00	.40
293	Glen Rice H99	.25	.08
294	David Robinson H99	.75	.30
295	Antonio McDyess H99	.50	.20
296	Vin Baker H99	.25	.08
297	Juwan Howard H99	.25	.08
298	Ron Mercer H99	.40	.15
299	Michael Finley H99	.50	.20
300	Scottie Pippen H99	.60	.25
301	Tim Thomas H99	.50	.20
302	Rasheed Wallace H99	.50	.20
303	Alonzo Mourning H99	.50	.20
304	Dikembe Mutombo H99	.25	.08
305	Derek Anderson H99	.40	.15
306	Ray Allen H99	.75	.30
307	Patrick Ewing H99	.50	.20
308	Sean Elliott H99	.25	.08
309	Shaquille O'Neal H99	1.00	.40
310	Michael Jordan CL	1.00	.40
311	Michael Jordan CL	1.00	.40
312	Michael Olowokandi RC	2.50	1.00
313	Mike Bibby RC	8.00	3.00
314	Raef LaFrentz RC	2.50	1.00
315	Antawn Jamison RC	8.00	3.00
316	Vince Carter RC	15.00	6.00
317	Robert Traylor RC	1.50	.60
318	Jason Williams RC	6.00	2.50
319	Larry Hughes RC	5.00	2.00
320	Dirk Nowitzki RC	15.00	6.00
321	Paul Pierce RC	8.00	3.00
322	Bonzi Wells RC	6.00	2.50
323	Michael Doleac RC	1.50	.60
324	Keon Clark RC	2.50	1.00
325	Michael Dickerson RC	3.00	1.25
326	Matt Harpring RC	2.50	1.00
327	Bryce Drew RC	1.50	.60
328	Pat Garrity RC	.75	.30
329	Roshown McLeod RC	.60	.25
330	Ricky Davis RC	5.00	2.00
331	Peja Stojakovic RC	6.00	2.50
332	Felipe Lopez RC	2.00	.75
333	Al Harrington RC	4.00	1.50
UDX	M.Jordan Retires	3.00	1.25

1999-00 Upper Deck

COMPLETE SET (360)	180.00	90.00
COMPLETE SERIES 1 (180)	120.00	60.00
COMPLETE SERIES 2 (180)	60.00	30.00
COMP.SERIES 1 w/o RC (155)	50.00	25.00
COMP.SERIES 2 w/o SP (133)	10.00	5.00
COMMON CARD (1-133/181-315)	.25	.08
COMMON MJ (134-153)	2.50	1.00
COMMON (156-180/316-360)	.40	.10

1	Roshown McLeod	.25	.08
2	Dikembe Mutombo	.50	.20
3	Alan Henderson	.25	.08
4	LaPhonso Ellis	.25	.08
5	Chris Crawford	.25	.08
6	Kenny Anderson	.50	.20
7	Antoine Walker	.75	.30
8	Paul Pierce	.75	.30
9	Vitaly Potapenko	.25	.08
10	Dana Barros	.25	.08
11	Elden Campbell	.25	.08
12	Eddie Jones	.75	.30
13	David Wesley	.25	.08
14	Derrick Coleman	.50	.20
15	Ricky Davis	.50	.20
16	Corey Benjamin	.25	.08
17	Randy Brown	.25	.08
18	Kornel David RC	.50	.20
19	Toni Kukoc	.50	.20
20	Keith Booth	.25	.08
21	Shawn Kemp	.50	.20
22	Wesley Person	.25	.08
23	Brevin Knight	.25	.08
24	Bob Sura	.25	.08
25	Zydrunas Ilgauskas	.50	.20
26	Michael Finley	.75	.30
27	Shawn Bradley	.25	.08
28	Dirk Nowitzki	1.50	.60
29	Steve Nash	.75	.30
30	Antonio McDyess	.50	.20
31	Nick Van Exel	.50	.20
32	Chauncey Billups	.50	.20
33	Bryant Stith	.25	.08
34	Raef LaFrentz	.50	.20
35	Grant Hill	.75	.30
36	Lindsey Hunter	.25	.08
37	Bison Dele	.25	.08
38	Jerry Stackhouse	.75	.30
39	John Starks	.50	.20
40	Antawn Jamison	1.25	.50
41	Erick Dampier	.50	.20
42	Jason Caffey	.25	.08
43	Hakeem Olajuwon	.75	.30
44	Scottie Pippen	1.25	.50
45	Cuttino Mobley	.75	.30
46	Charles Barkley	1.00	.40
47	Bryce Drew	.25	.08
48	Reggie Miller	.75	.30
49	Jalen Rose	.75	.30
50	Mark Jackson	.50	.20
51	Dale Davis	.25	.08
52	Chris Mullin	.50	.20
53	Maurice Taylor	.50	.20
54	Tyrone Nesby RC	.25	.08
55	Michael Olowokandi	.50	.20
56	Eric Piatkowski	.25	.08
57	Troy Hudson RC	.25	.08
58	Kobe Bryant	3.00	1.25
59	Shaquille O'Neal	2.00	.75
60	Glen Rice	.50	.20
61	Robert Horry	.50	.20
62	Tim Hardaway	.50	.20
63	Alonzo Mourning	.50	.20
64	P.J. Brown	.25	.08
65	Dan Majerle	.50	.20
66	Ray Allen	.75	.30
67	Glenn Robinson	.75	.30
68	Sam Cassell	.75	.30
69	Robert Traylor	.25	.08
70	Kevin Garnett	1.50	.60
71	Sam Mitchell	.25	.08
72	Dean Garrett	.25	.08
73	Bobby Jackson	.50	.20
74	Radoslav Nesterovic RC	1.00	.40
75	Keith Van Horn	.75	.30
76	Stephon Marbury	.75	.30
77	Kendall Gill	.25	.08
78	Scott Burrell	.25	.08
79	Patrick Ewing	.75	.30
80	Allan Houston	.50	.20
81	Latrell Sprewell	.75	.30
82	Larry Johnson	.50	.20
83	Marcus Camby	.50	.20
84	Darrell Armstrong	.25	.08
85	Derek Strong	.25	.08
86	Matt Harpring	.75	.30
87	Michael Doleac	.25	.08
88	Bo Outlaw	.25	.08
89	Allen Iverson	1.50	.60
90	Theo Ratliff	.50	.20
91	Larry Hughes	.75	.30
92	Eric Snow	.50	.20
93	Jason Kidd	1.25	.50
94	Clifford Robinson	.25	.08
95	Tom Gugliotta	.25	.08
96	Luc Longley	.25	.08
97	Rasheed Wallace	.75	.30
98	Arvydas Sabonis	.50	.20
99	Damon Stoudamire	.50	.20
100	Brian Grant	.50	.20
101	Jason Williams	.75	.30
102	Vlade Divac	.50	.20
103	Peja Stojakovic	1.00	.40
104	Lawrence Funderburke	.25	.08
105	Tim Duncan	1.50	.60
106	Sean Elliott	.25	.08
107	David Robinson	.75	.30
108	Mario Elie	.25	.08
109	Avery Johnson	.25	.08
110	Gary Payton	.75	.30
111	Vin Baker	.50	.20
112	Rashard Lewis	.75	.30
113	Jelani McCoy	.25	.08
114	Vladimir Stepania	.25	.08
115	Vince Carter	2.00	.75
116	Doug Christie	.50	.20
117	Kevin Willis	.25	.08
118	Dee Brown	.25	.08
119	John Thomas	.25	.08
120	Karl Malone	.75	.30
121	John Stockton	.75	.30
122	Howard Eisley	.25	.08
123	Bryon Russell	.25	.08
124	Greg Ostertag	.25	.08
125	Shareef Abdur-Rahim	.75	.30
126	Mike Bibby	.75	.30
127	Felipe Lopez	.25	.08
128	Cherokee Parks	.25	.08
129	Juwan Howard	.50	.20
130	Rod Strickland	.25	.08
131	Chris Whitney	.25	.08
132	Tracy Murray	.25	.08
133	Jahidi White	.25	.08
134	Michael Jordan AIR	2.50	1.00
135	Michael Jordan AIR	2.50	1.00
136	Michael Jordan AIR	2.50	1.00
137	Michael Jordan AIR	2.50	1.00
138	Michael Jordan AIR	2.50	1.00
139	Michael Jordan AIR	2.50	1.00
140	Michael Jordan AIR	2.50	1.00
141	Michael Jordan AIR	2.50	1.00
142	Michael Jordan AIR	2.50	1.00
143	Michael Jordan AIR	2.50	1.00
144	Michael Jordan AIR	2.50	1.00
145	Michael Jordan AIR	2.50	1.00
146	Michael Jordan AIR	2.50	1.00
147	Michael Jordan AIR	2.50	1.00
148	Michael Jordan AIR	2.50	1.00
149	Michael Jordan AIR	2.50	1.00
150	Michael Jordan AIR	2.50	1.00
151	Michael Jordan AIR	2.50	1.00
152	Michael Jordan AIR	2.50	1.00
153	Michael Jordan AIR	2.50	1.00
154	Michael Jordan CL	1.00	.40
155	Michael Jordan CL	1.00	.40
156	Elton Brand RC	6.00	2.50
157	Steve Francis RC	6.00	2.50
158	Baron Davis RC	8.00	3.00
159	Lamar Odom RC	5.00	2.00
160	Jonathan Bender RC	5.00	2.00
161	Wally Szczerbiak RC	5.00	2.00
162	Richard Hamilton RC	5.00	2.00
163	Andre Miller RC	5.00	2.00
164	Shawn Marion RC	6.00	2.50
165	Jason Terry RC	4.00	1.50
166	Trajan Langdon RC	2.00	.75
167	Kenny Thomas RC	2.00	.75
168	Corey Maggette RC	5.00	2.00
169	William Avery RC	2.00	.75
170	Jumaine Jones RC	1.25	.50
171	Ron Artest RC	3.00	1.25
172	Cal Bowdler RC	1.50	.60
173	James Posey RC	3.00	1.25
174	Quincy Lewis RC	1.50	.60
175	Vonteego Cummings RC	2.00	.75
176	Dion Glover RC	1.50	.60
177	Jeff Foster RC	1.50	.60
178	Devean George RC	2.50	1.00
179	Evan Eschmeyer RC	1.00	.40
180	Tim James RC	1.50	.60
181	Jim Jackson	.25	.08
182	Isaiah Rider	.25	.08
183	Lorenzen Wright	.25	.08
184	Bimbo Coles	.25	.08
185	Anthony Johnson	.25	.08

#	Player		
186	Calbert Cheaney	.25	.08
187	Pervis Ellison	.25	.08
188	Walter McCarty	.25	.08
189	Eric Williams	.25	.08
190	Tony Battie	.25	.08
191	Anthony Mason	.50	.20
192	Bobby Phills	.25	.08
193	Todd Fuller	.25	.08
194	Brad Miller	.75	.30
195	Eldridge Recasner	.25	.08
196	Chris Anstey	.25	.08
197	Fred Hoiberg	.25	.08
198	Hersey Hawkins	.50	.20
199	Will Perdue	.25	.08
200	Mark Bryant	.25	.08
201	Lamond Murray	.25	.08
202	Cedric Henderson	.25	.08
203	Andrew DeClercq	.25	.08
204	Danny Ferry	.25	.08
205	Erick Strickland	.25	.08
206	Cedric Ceballos	.25	.08
207	Hubert Davis	.25	.08
208	Robert Pack	.25	.08
209	Gary Trent	.25	.08
210	Ron Mercer	.50	.20
211	George McCloud	.25	.08
212	Roy Rogers	.25	.08
213	Keon Clark	.25	.20
214	Terry Mills	.25	.08
215	Michael Curry	.25	.08
216	Christian Laettner	.50	.20
217	Jerome Williams	.25	.08
218	Loy Vaught	.25	.08
219	Jud Buechler	.25	.08
220	Mookie Blaylock	.25	.08
221	Terry Cummings	.25	.08
222	Donyell Marshall	.50	.20
223	Chris Mills	.25	.08
224	Adonal Foyle	.25	.08
225	Shandon Anderson	.25	.08
226	Kelvin Cato	.25	.08
227	Walt Williams	.25	.08
228	Al Harrington	.75	.30
229	Rik Smits	.50	.20
230	Derrick McKey	.25	.08
231	Sam Perkins	.25	.20
232	Austin Croshere	.50	.20
233	Derek Anderson	.50	.20
234	Keith Closs	.25	.08
235	Eric Murdock	.25	.08
236	Brian Skinner	.25	.08
237	Charles Jones	.25	.08
238	Ron Harper	.50	.20
239	Derek Fisher	.75	.30
240	Rick Fox	.50	.20
241	A.C. Green	.50	.20
242	Jamal Mashburn	.50	.20
243	Mark Strickland	.25	.08
244	Rex Walters	.25	.08
245	Clarence Weatherspoon	.25	.08
246	Ervin Johnson	.25	.08
247	J.R. Reid	.25	.08
248	Dale Ellis	.25	.08
249	Danny Manning	.25	.08
250	Tim Thomas	.50	.20
251	Terrell Brandon	.50	.20
252	Malik Sealy	.25	.08
253	Joe Smith	.50	.20
254	Anthony Peeler	.25	.08
255	Jayson Williams	.25	.08
256	Jamie Feick RC	1.00	.40
257	Kerry Kittles	.25	.08
258	Johnny Newman	.25	.08
259	Chris Childs	.25	.08
260	Kurt Thomas	.50	.20
261	Charlie Ward	.25	.08
262	Chris Dudley	.25	.08
263	John Wallace	.25	.08
264	Tariq Abdul-Wahad	.25	.08
265	John Amaechi RC	1.00	.40
266	Chris Gatling	.25	.08
267	Monty Williams	.25	.08
268	Ben Wallace	.75	.30
269	George Lynch	.25	.08
270	Tyrone Hill	.25	.08
271	Billy Owens	.25	.08
272	Anfernee Hardaway	.75	.30
273	Rex Chapman	.25	.08
274	Oliver Miller	.25	.08
275	Rodney Rogers	.25	.08
276	Randy Livingston	.25	.08
277	Scottie Pippen	1.25	.50
278	Detlef Schrempf	.50	.20
279	Steve Smith	.50	.20
280	Jermaine O'Neal	.75	.30
281	Bonzi Wells	.75	.30
282	Chris Webber	.75	.30
283	Nick Anderson	.25	.08
284	Darrick Martin	.25	.08
285	Corliss Williamson	.50	.20
286	Samaki Walker	.25	.08
287	Terry Porter	.25	.08
288	Malik Rose	.25	.08
289	Jaren Jackson	.25	.08
290	Antonio Daniels	.25	.08
291	Steve Kerr	.50	.20
292	Brent Barry	.50	.20
293	Horace Grant	.50	.20
294	Vernon Maxwell	.25	.08
295	Ruben Patterson	.50	.20
296	Shammond Williams	.25	.08
297	Antonio Davis	.25	.08
298	Tracy McGrady	2.00	.75
299	Dell Curry	.25	.08
300	Charles Oakley	.25	.08
301	Muggsy Bogues	.50	.20
302	Jeff Hornacek	.50	.20
303	Adam Keefe	.25	.08
304	Olden Polynice	.25	.08
305	Doug West	.25	.08
306	Michael Dickerson	.50	.20
307	Othella Harrington	.25	.08
308	Bryant Reeves	.25	.08
309	Brent Price	.25	.08
310	Mitch Richmond	.50	.20
311	Aaron Williams	.25	.08
312	Isaac Austin	.25	.08
313	Michael Smith	.25	.08
314	Michael Jordan CL	1.00	.40
315	Kevin Garnett CL	.50	.20
316	Elton Brand	3.00	1.25
317	Steve Francis	4.00	1.50
318	Baron Davis	2.50	1.00
319	Lamar Odom	2.50	1.00
320	Jonathan Bender	2.50	1.00
321	Wally Szczerbiak	2.50	1.00
322	Richard Hamilton	2.00	.75
323	Andre Miller	2.50	1.00
324	Shawn Marion	3.00	1.25
325	Jason Terry	.75	.30
326	Trajan Langdon	1.25	.50
327	A.Radojevic RC	1.00	.40
328	Corey Maggette	2.50	1.00
329	William Avery	1.25	.50
330	Ron Artest	1.25	.50
331	Cal Bowdler	1.25	.50
332	James Posey	1.25	.50
333	Quincy Lewis	1.25	.50
334	Dion Glover	1.25	.50
335	Jeff Foster	1.00	.40
336	Kenny Thomas	1.25	.50
337	Devean George	.75	.30
338	Tim James	1.25	.50
339	Vonteego Cummings	1.25	.50
340	Jumaine Jones	2.00	.75
341	Scott Padgett RC	1.50	.60
342	John Celestand RC	1.50	.60
343	Adrian Griffin RC	1.50	.60
344	Michael Ruffin RC	1.25	.50
345	Chris Herren RC	1.00	.40
346	Evan Eschmeyer	.75	.30
347	Eddie Robinson RC	3.00	1.25
348	Obinna Ekezie RC	1.25	.50
349	Laron Profit RC	1.50	.60
350	Jermaine Jackson RC	1.00	.40
351	Lazaro Borrell RC	1.00	.40
352	Chucky Atkins RC	2.00	.75
353	Ryan Robertson RC	1.25	.50
354	Todd MacCulloch RC	1.50	.60
355	Rafer Alston RC	2.00	.75
356	Mirsad Turkcan RC	1.00	.40
357	Anthony Carter RC	3.00	1.25

#	Player		
358	Ryan Bowen RC	1.00	.40
359	Rodney Buford RC	1.00	.40
360	Tim Young RC	1.00	.40

1999-00 Upper Deck MJ Master Collection

COMP.FACT SET (23)		400.00	200.00
COMMON CARD (1-23)		30.00	15.00

2000-01 Upper Deck

COMPLETE SET (445)		200.00	100.00
COMPLETE SERIES 1 (245)		120.00	60.00
COMPLETE SER.1 w/o RC (200)		40.00	20.00
COMPLETE SERIES 2 (200)		80.00	40.00
COMMON CARD (1-445)		.25	.08
COMMON ROOKIE		.75	.30
1	Dikembe Mutombo	.50	.20
2	Jim Jackson	.25	.08
3	Alan Henderson	.25	.08
4	Jason Terry	.75	.30
5	Roshown McLeod	.25	.08
6	Lorenzen Wright	.25	.08
7	Paul Pierce	.75	.30
8	Antoine Walker	.75	.30
9	Vitaly Potapenko	.25	.08
10	Kenny Anderson	.50	.20
11	Tony Battie	.25	.08
12	Adrian Griffin	.25	.08
13	Eric Williams	.25	.08
14	Derrick Coleman	.25	.08
15	David Wesley	.25	.08
16	Baron Davis	.75	.30
17	Elden Campbell	.25	.20
18	Jamal Mashburn	.50	.20
19	Eddie Robinson	.50	.20
20	Elton Brand	.75	.30
21	Chris Carr	.25	.08
22	Ron Artest	.50	.20
23	Michael Ruffin	.25	.08
24	Fred Hoiberg	.25	.08
25	Corey Benjamin	.25	.08
26	Shawn Kemp	.50	.20
27	Lamond Murray	.25	.08
28	Andre Miller	.50	.20
29	Cedric Henderson	.25	.08
30	Wesley Person	.25	.08
31	Brevin Knight	.25	.08
32	Mark Bryant	.25	.08
33	Michael Finley	.75	.30
34	Cedric Ceballos	.25	.08

#	Player		
35	Dirk Nowitzki	1.25	.50
36	Hubert Davis	.25	.08
37	Steve Nash	.75	.30
38	Gary Trent	.25	.08
39	Antonio McDyess	.50	.20
40	James Posey	.50	.20
41	Nick Van Exel	.75	.30
42	Raef LaFrentz	.50	.20
43	George McCloud	.25	.08
44	Keon Clark	.50	.20
45	Jerry Stackhouse	.75	.30
46	Christian Laettner	.50	.20
47	Loy Vaught	.25	.08
48	Jerome Williams	.25	.08
49	Michael Curry	.25	.08
50	Lindsey Hunter	.25	.08
51	Antawn Jamison	.75	.30
52	Larry Hughes	.50	.20
53	Chris Mills	.25	.08
54	Donyell Marshall	.50	.20
55	Mookie Blaylock	.25	.08
56	Vonteego Cummings	.25	.08
57	Erick Dampier	.50	.20
58	Steve Francis	.75	.30
59	Shandon Anderson	.25	.08
60	Hakeem Olajuwon	.75	.30
61	Walt Williams	.25	.08
62	Kenny Thomas	.25	.08
63	Kelvin Cato	.25	.08
64	Cuttino Mobley	.50	.20
65	Reggie Miller	.75	.30
66	Jalen Rose	.75	.30
67	Austin Croshere	.50	.20
68	Dale Davis	.25	.08
69	Travis Best	.25	.08
70	Jonathan Bender	.50	.20
71	Al Harrington	.50	.20
72	Lamar Odom	.75	.30
73	Tyrone Nesby	.25	.08
74	Michael Olowokandi	.25	.08
75	Brian Skinner	.25	.08
76	Eric Piatkowski	.50	.20
77	Keith Closs	.25	.08
78	Shaquille O'Neal	2.00	.75
79	Ron Harper	.50	.20
80	Kobe Bryant	3.00	1.25
81	Rick Fox	.50	.20
82	Robert Horry	.50	.20
83	Derek Fisher	.75	.30
84	Devean George	.50	.20
85	Alonzo Mourning	.50	.20
86	Eddie Jones	.75	.30
87	Anthony Carter	.75	.30
88	Bruce Bowen	.25	.08
89	Clarence Weatherspoon	.25	.08
90	Tim Hardaway	.50	.20
91	Ray Allen	.75	.30
92	Tim Thomas	.50	.20
93	Glenn Robinson	.75	.30
94	Scott Williams	.25	.08
95	Sam Cassell	.75	.30
96	Ervin Johnson	.25	.08
97	Darvin Ham	.25	.08
98	Kevin Garnett	1.50	.60
99	Wally Szczerbiak	.50	.20
100	Terrell Brandon	.50	.20
101	Joe Smith	.50	.20
102	Radoslav Nesterovic	.25	.08
103	William Avery	.25	.08
104	Stephon Marbury	.75	.30
105	Kerry Kittles	.25	.08
106	Keith Van Horn	.75	.30
107	Lucious Harris	.25	.08
108	Jamie Feick	.25	.08
109	Johnny Newman	.25	.08
110	Patrick Ewing	.75	.30
111	Latrell Sprewell	.75	.30
112	Marcus Camby	.50	.20
113	Larry Johnson	.50	.20
114	Charlie Ward	.25	.08
115	Allan Houston	.50	.20
116	Chris Childs	.25	.08
117	Grant Hill	.75	.30
118	John Amaechi	.25	.08
119	Tracy McGrady	2.00	.75
120	Michael Doleac	.25	.08
121	Darrell Armstrong	.25	.08
122	Bo Outlaw	.25	.08
123	Allen Iverson	1.50	.60
124	Theo Ratliff	.50	.20
125	Matt Geiger	.25	.08
126	Tyrone Hill	.25	.08
127	George Lynch	.25	.08
128	Toni Kukoc	.50	.20
129	Jason Kidd	1.25	.50
130	Rodney Rogers	.25	.08
131	Anfernee Hardaway	.75	.30
132	Clifford Robinson	.25	.08
133	Tom Gugliotta	.25	.08
134	Shawn Marion	.75	.30
135	Luc Longley	.25	.08
136	Rasheed Wallace	.75	.30
137	Scottie Pippen	1.25	.50
138	Arvydas Sabonis	.50	.20
139	Steve Smith	.50	.20
140	Damon Stoudamire	.50	.20
141	Bonzi Wells	.50	.20
142	Jermaine O'Neal	.75	.30
143	Chris Webber	.75	.30
144	Jason Williams	.50	.20
145	Nick Anderson	.25	.08
146	Vlade Divac	.50	.20
147	Peja Stojakovic	.75	.30
148	Jon Barry	.25	.08
149	Corliss Williamson	.50	.20
150	Tim Duncan	1.50	.60
151	David Robinson	.75	.30
152	Terry Porter	.25	.08
153	Malik Rose	.25	.08
154	Steve Kerr	.50	.20
155	Avery Johnson	.25	.08
156	Gary Payton	.75	.30
157	Brent Barry	.50	.20
158	Vin Baker	.50	.20
159	Rashard Lewis	.50	.20
160	Ruben Patterson	.50	.20
161	Shammond Williams	.25	.08
162	Vince Carter	2.00	.75
163	Dell Curry	.25	.08
164	Doug Christie	.50	.20
165	Antonio Davis	.25	.08
166	Kevin Willis	.25	.08
167	Charles Oakley	.25	.08
168	Karl Malone	.75	.30
169	John Stockton	.75	.30
170	Bryon Russell	.25	.08
171	Olden Polynice	.25	.08
172	Quincy Lewis	.25	.08
173	Scott Padgett	.25	.08
174	Shareef Abdur-Rahim	.75	.30
175	Mike Bibby	.75	.30
176	Michael Dickerson	.50	.20
177	Bryant Reeves	.25	.08
178	Othella Harrington	.25	.08
179	Grant Long	.25	.08
180	Mitch Richmond	.50	.20
181	Richard Hamilton	.50	.20
182	Juwan Howard	.50	.20
183	Rod Strickland	.25	.08
184	Tracy Murray	.25	.08
185	Chris Whitney	.25	.08
186	Kobe Bryant Y3K	.75	.30
187	Kobe Bryant Y3K	.75	.30
188	Kobe Bryant Y3K	.75	.30
189	Kobe Bryant Y3K	.75	.30
190	Kobe Bryant Y3K	.75	.30
191	Kevin Garnett Y3K	.75	.30
192	Kevin Garnett Y3K	.75	.30
193	Kevin Garnett Y3K	.75	.30
194	Kevin Garnett Y3K	.75	.30
195	Kevin Garnett Y3K	.75	.30
196	Kenyon Martin Y3K	.75	.30
197	Kenyon Martin Y3K	.75	.30
198	Kenyon Martin Y3K	.75	.30
199	Kenyon Martin Y3K	.75	.30
200	Kenyon Martin Y3K	.75	.30
201	Kenyon Martin RC	5.00	2.00
202	Stromile Swift RC	2.50	1.00
203	Chris Mihm RC	.75	.30
204	Marcus Fizer RC	.75	.30
205	Darius Miles RC	4.00	1.50
206	Joel Przybilla RC	.75	.30
207	Mike Miller RC	4.00	1.50
208	Courtney Alexander RC	.75	.30
209	DerMarr Johnson RC	.75	.30
210	Iakovos Tsakalidis RC	.75	.30
211	Jerome Moiso RC	.75	.30
212	Keyon Dooling RC	.75	.30
213	Erick Barkley RC	.75	.30
214	Jason Collier RC	1.25	.50
215	Jamaal Magloire RC	.75	.30
216	DeShawn Stevenson RC	.75	.30
217	Hidayet Turkoglu RC	3.00	1.25
218	Morris Peterson RC	2.50	1.00
219	Jamal Crawford RC	1.00	.40
220	Etan Thomas RC	.75	.30
221	Quentin Richardson RC	3.00	1.25
222	Mateen Cleaves RC	.75	.30
223	Chris Carrawell RC	.75	.30
224	Corey Hightower RC	.75	.30
225	Donnell Harvey RC	.75	.30
226	Mark Madsen RC	.75	.30
227	Jake Voskuhl RC	.75	.30
228	Soumaila Samake RC	.75	.30
229	Mamadou N'diaye RC	.75	.30
230	Dan Langhi RC	.75	.30
231	Hanno Mottola RC	.75	.30
232	Olumide Oyedeji RC	.75	.30
233	Jason Hart RC	.75	.30
234	Mike Smith RC	.75	.30
235	Chris Porter RC	.75	.30
236	Jabari Smith RC	.75	.30
237	Desmond Mason RC	.75	.30
238	Eddie House RC	.75	.30
239	A.J. Guyton RC	.75	.30
240	Speedy Claxton RC	.75	.30
241	Lavor Postell RC	.75	.30
242	Khalid El-Amin RC	.75	.30
243	Pepe Sanchez RC	.75	.30
244	Eduardo Najera RC	2.00	.75
245	Michael Redd RC	2.00	.75
246	DerMarr Johnson	1.25	.50
247	Hanno Mottola	.75	.30
248	Dion Glover	.25	.08
249	Matt Maloney	.25	.08
250	Jason Terry	.75	.30
251	Jerome Moiso	.75	.30
252	Bryant Stith	.25	.08
253	Randy Brown	.25	.08
254	Mark Blount	.25	.08
255	Chris Herren	.25	.08
256	Jamal Mashburn	.50	.20
257	P.J. Brown	.25	.08
258	Lee Nailon	.25	.08
259	Jamaal Magloire	1.00	.40
260	Otis Thorpe	.25	.08
261	Ron Mercer	.50	.20
262	Marcus Fizer	1.50	.60
263	Jamal Crawford	.75	.30
264	A.J. Guyton	1.00	.40
265	Dalibor Bagaric RC	.25	.08
266	Chris Mihm	.50	.20
267	Robert Traylor	.25	.08
268	Matt Harpring	.75	.30
269	Clarence Weatherspoon	.25	.08
270	Bimbo Coles	.25	.08
271	Elan Thomas	.75	.30
272	Courtney Alexander	1.25	.50
273	Donnell Harvey	.25	.08
274	Eduardo Najera	1.00	.40
275	Christian Laettner	.50	.20
276	Mamadou N'Diaye	.50	.20
277	Tariq Abdul-Wahad	.25	.08
278	Voshon Lenard	.25	.08
279	Robert Pack	.25	.08
280	Tracy Murray	.25	.08
281	Mateen Cleaves	.75	.30
282	Ben Wallace	.75	.30
283	Chucky Atkins	.25	.08
284	Billy Owens	.25	.08
285	Brian Cardinal RC	.75	.30
286	Chris Porter	1.50	.60
287	Bob Sura	.25	.08
288	Vinny Del Negro	.25	.08
289	Marc Jackson RC	4.00	1.50
290	Danny Fortson	.25	.08
291	Jason Collier	.75	.30
292	Maurice Taylor	.25	.08

❑ 293	Dan Langhi	.75	.30
❑ 294	Carlos Rogers	.25	.08
❑ 295	Moochie Norris	.25	.08
❑ 296	Jermaine O'Neal	.75	.30
❑ 297	Derrick McKey	.25	.08
❑ 298	Sam Perkins	.50	.20
❑ 299	Zan Tabak	.25	.08
❑ 300	Jeff Foster	.25	.08
❑ 301	Corey Maggette	.50	.20
❑ 302	Darius Miles	2.00	.75
❑ 303	Keyon Dooling	.75	.30
❑ 304	Quentin Richardson	1.50	.60
❑ 305	Jeff McInnis	.25	.08
❑ 306	Isaiah Rider	.50	.20
❑ 307	Mark Madsen	.75	.30
❑ 308	Mike Penberthy RC	3.00	1.25
❑ 309	Brian Shaw	.25	.08
❑ 310	Horace Grant	.50	.20
❑ 311	Eddie Jones	.75	.30
❑ 312	Brian Grant	.50	.20
❑ 313	Anthony Mason	.50	.20
❑ 314	Duane Causwell	.25	.08
❑ 315	Eddie House	1.25	.50
❑ 316	Lindsey Hunter	.25	.08
❑ 317	Jason Caffey	.25	.08
❑ 318	Joel Przybilla	.75	.30
❑ 319	Michael Redd	1.50	.60
❑ 320	Rafer Alston	.25	.08
❑ 321	Chauncey Billups	.50	.20
❑ 322	LaPhonso Ellis	.25	.08
❑ 323	Sam Mitchell	.25	.08
❑ 324	Dean Garrett	.25	.08
❑ 325	Tom Hammonds	.25	.08
❑ 326	Kenyon Martin	2.50	1.00
❑ 327	Soumaila Samake	.25	.08
❑ 328	Aaron Williams	.25	.08
❑ 329	Kendall Gill	.25	.08
❑ 330	Stephen Jackson RC	2.50	1.00
❑ 331	Lavor Postell	.75	.30
❑ 332	Pete Mickeal RC	.75	.30
❑ 333	Kurt Thomas	.50	.20
❑ 334	Erick Strickland	.25	.08
❑ 335	Glen Rice	.50	.20
❑ 336	Grant Hill	.75	.30
❑ 337	Tracy McGrady	2.00	.75
❑ 338	Pat Garrity	.25	.08
❑ 339	Troy Hudson	.25	.08
❑ 340	Mike Miller	2.00	.75
❑ 341	Speedy Claxton	.75	.30
❑ 342	Eric Snow	.50	.20
❑ 343	Pepe Sanchez	.75	.30
❑ 344	Aaron McKie	.50	.20
❑ 345	Nazr Mohammed	.25	.08
❑ 346	Ruben Garces RC	.75	.30
❑ 347	Daniel Santiago RC	2.00	.75
❑ 348	Tony Delk	.25	.08
❑ 349	Paul McPherson RC	2.00	.75
❑ 350	Iakovos Tsakalidis	.50	.20
❑ 351	Dale Davis	.25	.08
❑ 352	Shawn Kemp	.50	.20
❑ 353	Erick Barkley	1.00	.40
❑ 354	Greg Anthony	.25	.08
❑ 355	Stacey Augmon	.25	.08
❑ 356	Bobby Jackson	.50	.20
❑ 357	Hidayet Turkoglu	1.50	.60
❑ 358	Jabari Smith	.50	.20
❑ 359	Doug Christie	.50	.20
❑ 360	Darrick Martin	.25	.08
❑ 361	Sean Elliott	.50	.20
❑ 362	Jaren Jackson	.25	.08
❑ 363	Samaki Walker	.25	.08
❑ 364	Derek Anderson	.50	.20
❑ 365	Antonio Daniels	.25	.08
❑ 366	Patrick Ewing	.75	.30
❑ 367	Desmond Mason	.75	.30
❑ 368	Jelani McCoy	.25	.08
❑ 369	Ruben Wolkowyski RC	1.00	.40
❑ 370	Emanual Davis	.25	.08
❑ 371	Mark Jackson	.50	.20
❑ 372	Morris Peterson	1.50	.60
❑ 373	Muggsy Bogues	.50	.20
❑ 374	Alvin Williams	.25	.08
❑ 375	Corliss Williamson	.50	.20
❑ 376	John Starks	.50	.20
❑ 377	Danny Manning	.50	.20
❑ 378	DeShawn Stevenson	.75	.30

❑ 379	Donyell Marshall	.50	.20
❑ 380	David Benoit	.25	.08
❑ 381	Isaac Austin	.25	.08
❑ 382	Mahmoud Abdul-Rauf	.25	.08
❑ 383	Stromile Swift	.75	.30
❑ 384	Kevin Edwards	.25	.08
❑ 385	Brent Price	.25	.08
❑ 386	Popeye Jones	.25	.08
❑ 387	Mike Smith RC	1.00	.40
❑ 388	Jahidi White	.25	.08
❑ 389	Laron Profit	.25	.08
❑ 390	Felipe Lopez	.25	.08
❑ 391	Dikembe Mutombo MVP	.50	.20
❑ 392	Paul Pierce MVP	.50	.20
❑ 393	Derrick Coleman MVP	.25	.08
❑ 394	Elton Brand MVP	.75	.30
❑ 395	Andre Miller MVP	.50	.20
❑ 396	Michael Finley MVP	.50	.20
❑ 397	Antonio McDyess MVP	.50	.20
❑ 398	Jerry Stackhouse MVP	.50	.20
❑ 399	Larry Hughes MVP	.25	.08
❑ 400	Steve Francis MVP	.75	.30
❑ 401	Reggie Miller MVP	.50	.20
❑ 402	Lamar Odom MVP	.50	.20
❑ 403	Shaquille O'Neal MVP	1.00	.40
❑ 404	Tim Hardaway MVP	.25	.08
❑ 405	Ray Allen MVP	.50	.20
❑ 406	Kevin Garnett MVP	.75	.30
❑ 407	Stephon Marbury MVP	.50	.20
❑ 408	Allan Houston MVP	.50	.20
❑ 409	Grant Hill MVP	.50	.20
❑ 410	Allen Iverson MVP	.75	.30
❑ 411	Jason Kidd MVP	.75	.30
❑ 412	Rasheed Wallace MVP	.50	.20
❑ 413	Chris Webber MVP	.50	.20
❑ 414	Tim Duncan MVP	.75	.30
❑ 415	Gary Payton MVP	.75	.30
❑ 416	Vince Carter MVP	1.00	.40
❑ 417	Karl Malone MVP	.75	.30
❑ 418	Shareef Abdur-Rahim MVP	.50	.20
❑ 419	Mitch Richmond MVP	.25	.08
❑ 420	Kobe Bryant MVP	1.50	.60
❑ 421	Mateen Cleaves ROC	.75	.30
❑ 422	Speedy Claxton ROC	.75	.30
❑ 423	Courtney Alexander ROC	.60	.25
❑ 424	Desmond Mason ROC	.75	.30
❑ 425	Mike Miller ROC	.75	.30
❑ 426	DerMarr Johnson ROC	.75	.30
❑ 427	Chris Mihm ROC	.50	.20
❑ 428	Jamal Crawford ROC	.75	.30
❑ 429	Joel Przybilla ROC	.75	.30
❑ 430	Keyon Dooling ROC	.75	.30
❑ 431	Kobe Bryant PR	.75	.30
❑ 432	Kobe Bryant PR	.75	.30
❑ 433	Kobe Bryant PR	.75	.30
❑ 434	Kobe Bryant PR	.75	.30
❑ 435	Kobe Bryant PR	.75	.30
❑ 436	Kobe Bryant PR	.75	.30
❑ 437	Kobe Bryant PR	.75	.30
❑ 438	Kobe Bryant PR	.75	.30
❑ 439	Kobe Bryant PR	.75	.30
❑ 440	Kobe Bryant PR	.75	.30
❑ 441	Kobe Bryant PR	.75	.30
❑ 442	Kobe Bryant PR	.75	.30
❑ 443	Kobe Bryant PR	.75	.30
❑ 444	Kobe Bryant PR	.75	.30
❑ 445	Kobe Bryant PR	.75	.30
❑ CL1	Checklist	.25	.08
❑ CL1	Checklist	.25	.08
❑ CL2	Checklist	.25	.08
❑ CL2	Checklist	.25	.08
❑ CL3	Checklist	.25	.08
❑ CL3	Checklist	.25	.08

2001-02 Upper Deck

❑ COMP.SET w/o SP's (360)	120.00	60.00
❑ COMPLETE SER.1 (225)	200.00	100.00
❑ COMP.SER 1 w/o SP's (180)	40.00	20.00
❑ COMPLETE SER.2 (225)	200.00	100.00
❑ COMP.SER 2 w/o SP's (180)	80.00	40.00
❑ COMMON CARD (1-405)	.25	.08
❑ COMMON ROOKIE (181-225)	2.00	.75
❑ COMMON CARD (406A-450B)	.50	.20
❑ SEMISTARS 406-450	1.00	.40
❑ UNLISTED STARS 406-450	1.50	.60
❑ COMMON ROOKIE (406A-417B)	3.00	1.25

❑ 406B-450B NOT INCLUDED IN SET PRICES

❑ 1	Jason Terry	.75	.30
❑ 2	Toni Kukoc	.50	.20
❑ 3	Alan Henderson	.25	.08
❑ 4	Theo Ratliff	.50	.20
❑ 5	Shareef Abdur-Rahim	.75	.30
❑ 6	DerMarr Johnson	.50	.20
❑ 7	Paul Pierce	.75	.30
❑ 8	Antoine Walker	.75	.30
❑ 9	Kenny Anderson	.50	.20
❑ 10	Vitaly Potapenko	.25	.08
❑ 11	Eric Williams	.25	.08
❑ 12	Jamal Mashburn	.50	.20
❑ 13	Baron Davis	.75	.30
❑ 14	David Wesley	.25	.08
❑ 15	P.J. Brown	.25	.08
❑ 16	Elden Campbell	.25	.08
❑ 17	Jamaal Magloire	.50	.20
❑ 18	Lee Nailon	.25	.08
❑ 19	A.J. Guyton	.50	.20
❑ 20	Ron Mercer	.50	.20
❑ 21	Jamal Crawford	.25	.08
❑ 22	Fred Hoiberg	.25	.08
❑ 23	Marcus Fizer	.50	.20
❑ 24	Ron Artest	.50	.20
❑ 25	Lamond Murray	.25	.08
❑ 26	Andre Miller	.50	.20
❑ 27	Jim Jackson	.25	.08
❑ 28	Chris Mihm	.50	.20
❑ 29	Trajan Langdon	.25	.08
❑ 30	Chris Gatling	.25	.08
❑ 31	Michael Finley	.75	.30
❑ 32	Dirk Nowitzki	1.25	.50
❑ 33	Steve Nash	.75	.30
❑ 34	Juwan Howard	.50	.20
❑ 35	Wang Zhizhi	.75	.30
❑ 36	Eduardo Najera	.50	.20
❑ 37	Shawn Bradley	.25	.08
❑ 38	Antonio McDyess	.50	.20
❑ 39	Nick Van Exel	.75	.30
❑ 40	Raef LaFrentz	.50	.20
❑ 41	James Posey	.50	.20
❑ 42	Voshon Lenard	.25	.08
❑ 43	Ben Wallace	.75	.30
❑ 44	Jerry Stackhouse	.75	.30
❑ 45	Corliss Williamson	.50	.20
❑ 46	Chucky Atkins	.25	.08
❑ 47	Michael Curry	.25	.08
❑ 48	Dana Barros	.25	.08
❑ 49	Antawn Jamison	.75	.30
❑ 50	Larry Hughes	.50	.20
❑ 51	Bob Sura	.25	.08
❑ 52	Marc Jackson	.50	.20
❑ 53	Chris Porter	.25	.08
❑ 54	Vonteego Cummings	.25	.08
❑ 55	Steve Francis	.75	.30
❑ 56	Cuttino Mobley	.50	.20
❑ 57	Maurice Taylor	.50	.20
❑ 58	Kenny Thomas	.25	.08
❑ 59	Moochie Norris	.25	.08
❑ 60	Walt Williams	.25	.08
❑ 61	Reggie Miller	.75	.30
❑ 62	Jalen Rose	.75	.30
❑ 63	Jermaine Oâ„¢Neal	.75	.30
❑ 64	Austin Croshere	.25	.08
❑ 65	Travis Best	.25	.08
❑ 66	Jonathan Bender	.50	.20
❑ 67	Eric Piatkowski	.50	.20

#	Player		
☐ 68	Darius Miles	.75	.30
☐ 69	Lamar Odom	.75	.30
☐ 70	Quentin Richardson	.50	.20
☐ 71	Corey Maggette	.50	.20
☐ 72	Elton Brand	.75	.30
☐ 73	Jeff McInnis	.25	.08
☐ 74	Kobe Bryant	3.00	1.25
☐ 75	Shaquille O'™Neal	2.00	.75
☐ 76	Derek Fisher	.75	.30
☐ 77	Rick Fox	.50	.20
☐ 78	Mitch Richmond	.50	.20
☐ 79	Ron Harper	.50	.20
☐ 80	Brian Shaw	.25	.08
☐ 81	Stromile Swift	.50	.20
☐ 82	Michael Dickerson	.50	.20
☐ 83	Jason Williams	.50	.20
☐ 84	Grant Long	.25	.08
☐ 85	Bryant Reeves	.25	.08
☐ 86	Alonzo Mourning	.50	.20
☐ 87	Eddie Jones	.75	.30
☐ 88	Brian Grant	.50	.20
☐ 89	Anthony Mason	.50	.20
☐ 90	LaPhonso Ellis	.25	.08
☐ 91	Anthony Carter	.50	.20
☐ 92	Jason Caffey	.25	.08
☐ 93	Ray Allen	.75	.30
☐ 94	Glenn Robinson	.75	.30
☐ 95	Sam Cassell	.75	.30
☐ 96	Tim Thomas	.50	.20
☐ 97	Ervin Johnson	.25	.08
☐ 98	Joel Przybilla	.25	.08
☐ 99	Kevin Garnett	1.50	.60
☐ 100	Terrell Brandon	.50	.20
☐ 101	Wally Szczerbiak	.50	.20
☐ 102	Felipe Lopez	.25	.08
☐ 103	Chauncey Billups	.50	.20
☐ 104	Anthony Peeler	.25	.08
☐ 105	Kenyon Martin	.75	.30
☐ 106	Keith Van Horn	.75	.30
☐ 107	Jamie Feick	.25	.08
☐ 108	Aaron Williams	.25	.08
☐ 109	Lucious Harris	.25	.08
☐ 110	Jason Kidd	1.25	.50
☐ 111	Latrell Sprewell	.75	.30
☐ 112	Allan Houston	.50	.20
☐ 113	Marcus Camby	.50	.20
☐ 114	Mark Jackson	.25	.08
☐ 115	Othella Harrington	.25	.08
☐ 116	Kurt Thomas	.50	.20
☐ 117	Tracy McGrady	2.00	.75
☐ 118	Mike Miller	.75	.30
☐ 119	Darrell Armstrong	.25	.08
☐ 120	Grant Hill	.75	.30
☐ 121	Pat Garrity	.25	.08
☐ 122	Bo Outlaw	.25	.08
☐ 123	Allen Iverson	1.50	.60
☐ 124	Dikembe Mutombo	.50	.20
☐ 125	Aaron McKie	.50	.20
☐ 126	Matt Geiger	.25	.08
☐ 127	Eric Snow	.50	.20
☐ 128	George Lynch	.25	.08
☐ 129	Raja Bell RC	2.00	.75
☐ 130	Shawn Marion	.75	.30
☐ 131	Tom Gugliotta	.25	.08
☐ 132	Rodney Rogers	.25	.08
☐ 133	Anfernee Hardaway	.75	.30
☐ 134	Tony Delk	.25	.08
☐ 135	Stephon Marbury	.75	.30
☐ 136	Rasheed Wallace	.75	.30
☐ 137	Damon Stoudamire	.50	.20
☐ 138	Rod Strickland	.25	.08
☐ 139	Dale Davis	.50	.20
☐ 140	Scottie Pippen	1.25	.50
☐ 141	Bonzi Wells	.50	.20
☐ 142	Peja Stojakovic	.75	.30
☐ 143	Chris Webber	.75	.30
☐ 144	Doug Christie	.50	.20
☐ 145	Mike Bibby	.75	.30
☐ 146	Hidayet Turkoglu	.50	.20
☐ 147	Scot Pollard	.25	.08
☐ 148	Vlade Divac	.50	.20
☐ 149	Tim Duncan	1.50	.60
☐ 150	David Robinson	.75	.30
☐ 151	Antonio Daniels	.25	.08
☐ 152	Danny Ferry	.25	.08
☐ 153	Malik Rose	.25	.08
☐ 154	Terry Porter	.25	.08
☐ 155	Rashard Lewis	.25	.08
☐ 156	Gary Payton	.75	.30
☐ 157	Brent Barry	.25	.08
☐ 158	Vin Baker	.50	.20
☐ 159	Desmond Mason	.50	.20
☐ 160	Shammond Williams	.25	.08
☐ 161	Vince Carter	2.00	.75
☐ 162	Antonio Davis	.25	.08
☐ 163	Morris Peterson	.50	.20
☐ 164	Keon Clark	.25	.08
☐ 165	Chris Childs	.25	.08
☐ 166	Alvin Williams	.25	.08
☐ 167	Karl Malone	.75	.30
☐ 168	John Stockton	.75	.30
☐ 169	Donyell Marshall	.25	.08
☐ 170	John Starks	.50	.20
☐ 171	Bryon Russell	.25	.08
☐ 172	David Benoit	.25	.08
☐ 173	DeShawn Stevenson	.50	.20
☐ 174	Richard Hamilton	.50	.20
☐ 175	Jahidi White	.25	.08
☐ 176	Courtney Alexander	.50	.20
☐ 177	Chris Whitney	.25	.08
☐ 178	Michael Jordan	10.00	4.00
☐ 179	Kobe Bryant CL	.75	.30
☐ 180	Kevin Garnett CL	.75	.30
☐ 181	Sean Lampley RC	2.00	.75
☐ 182	Andrei Kirilenko RC	6.00	2.50
☐ 183	Brandon Armstrong RC	2.50	1.00
☐ 184	Gerald Wallace RC	6.00	2.50
☐ 185	Tony Parker RC	10.00	4.00
☐ 186	Jeryl Sasser RC	2.00	.75
☐ 187	Alton Ford RC	3.00	1.25
☐ 188	Kenny Satterfield RC	2.00	.75
☐ 189	Will Solomon RC	2.00	.75
☐ 190	Earl Watson RC	3.00	1.25
☐ 191	Michael Wright RC	2.00	.75
☐ 192	Samuel Dalembert RC	2.00	.75
☐ 193	Ousmane Cisse RC	2.00	.75
☐ 194	R.Bourntje-Bourntje RC	2.00	.75
☐ 195	Damone Brown RC	2.00	.75
☐ 196	Jarron Collins RC	2.00	.75
☐ 197	Terence Morris RC	2.00	.75
☐ 198	Pau Gasol RC	8.00	3.00
☐ 199	Trenton Hassell RC	4.00	1.50
☐ 200	Kirk Haston RC	2.00	.75
☐ 201	Brian Scalabrine RC	2.00	.75
☐ 202	Gilbert Arenas RC	8.00	3.00
☐ 203	Jeff Trepagnier RC	2.00	.75
☐ 204	Joseph Forte RC	5.00	2.00
☐ 205	Steven Hunter RC	2.00	.75
☐ 206	Omar Cook RC	2.00	.75
☐ 207	Jason Collins RC	2.00	.75
☐ 208	Kedrick Brown RC	2.00	.75
☐ 209	Michael Bradley RC	2.00	.75
☐ 210	Zach Randolph RC	8.00	3.00
☐ 211	Richard Jefferson RC	6.00	2.50
☐ 212	Jamaal Tinsley RC	4.00	1.50
☐ 213	Vladimir Radmanovic RC	3.00	1.25
☐ 214	Brendan Haywood RC	3.00	1.25
☐ 215	Troy Murphy RC	5.00	2.00
☐ 216	DeSagana Diop RC	2.00	.75
☐ 217	Jason Richardson RC	6.00	2.50
☐ 218	Joe Johnson RC	6.00	2.50
☐ 219	Rodney White RC	3.00	1.25
☐ 220	Loren Woods RC	2.00	.75
☐ 221	Tyson Chandler RC	6.00	2.50
☐ 222	Eddy Curry RC	6.00	2.50
☐ 223	Shane Battier RC	4.00	1.50
☐ 224	Eddie Griffin RC	5.00	2.00
☐ 225	Kwame Brown RC	4.00	1.50
☐ 226	Shareef Abdur-Rahim	.75	.30
☐ 227	Nazr Mohammed	.25	.08
☐ 228	Hanno Mottola	.25	.08
☐ 229	Emanual Davis	.25	.08
☐ 230	Dion Glover	.25	.08
☐ 231	Chris Crawford	.25	.08
☐ 232	Mark Blount	.25	.08
☐ 233	Joe Johnson	4.00	1.50
☐ 234	Milt Palacio	.25	.08
☐ 235	Kedrick Brown	.75	.30
☐ 236	Tony Battie	.25	.08
☐ 237	Erick Strickland	.25	.08
☐ 238	Kirk Haston	1.00	.40
☐ 239	Stacey Augmon	.25	.08
☐ 240	Matt Bullard	.25	.08
☐ 241	Bryce Drew	.25	.08
☐ 242	Jerome Moiso	.50	.20
☐ 243	Robert Traylor	.25	.08
☐ 244	Tyson Chandler	3.00	1.25
☐ 245	Eddy Curry	3.00	1.25
☐ 246	Charles Oakley	.25	.08
☐ 247	Brad Miller	.75	.30
☐ 248	Kevin Ollie	.25	.08
☐ 249	Trenton Hassell	2.00	.75
☐ 250	Ricky Davis	.50	.20
☐ 251	Jumaine Jones	.50	.20
☐ 252	DeSagana Diop	1.00	.40
☐ 253	Bryant Stith	.25	.08
☐ 254	Jeff Trepagnier	1.00	.40
☐ 255	Michael Doleac	.25	.08
☐ 256	Tim Hardaway	.75	.30
☐ 257	Danny Manning	.25	.08
☐ 258	Johnny Newman	.25	.08
☐ 259	Adrian Griffin	.25	.08
☐ 260	Greg Buckner	.25	.08
☐ 261	Donnell Harvey	.25	.08
☐ 262	Evan Eschmeyer	.25	.08
☐ 263	Avery Johnson	.25	.08
☐ 264	Kenny Satterfield	1.00	.40
☐ 265	Scott Williams	.25	.08
☐ 266	Tariq Abdul-Wahad	.25	.08
☐ 267	George McCloud	.25	.08
☐ 268	Clifford Robinson	.25	.08
☐ 269	Jon Barry	.25	.08
☐ 270	Brian Cardinal	.25	.08
☐ 271	Rodney White	1.50	.60
☐ 272	Mikki Moore	.25	.08
☐ 273	Victor Alexander	.25	.08
☐ 274	Jason Richardson	3.00	1.25
☐ 275	Adonal Foyle	.25	.08
☐ 276	Troy Murphy	2.50	1.00
☐ 277	Chris Mills	.25	.08
☐ 278	Gilbert Arenas	2.00	.75
☐ 279	Erick Dampier	.50	.20
☐ 280	Glen Rice	.50	.20
☐ 281	Eddie Griffin	1.50	.60
☐ 282	Kevin Willis	.25	.08
☐ 283	Terence Morris	1.00	.40
☐ 284	Kelvin Cato	.25	.08
☐ 285	Dan Langhi	.50	.20
☐ 286	Jason Collier	.25	.08
☐ 287	Jamaal Tinsley	2.00	.75
☐ 288	Carlos Rogers	.25	.08
☐ 289	Jeff Foster	.25	.08
☐ 290	Al Harrington	.50	.20
☐ 291	Bruno Sundov	.25	.08
☐ 292	Elton Brand	.75	.30
☐ 293	Keyon Dooling	.50	.20
☐ 294	Michael Olowokandi	.50	.20
☐ 295	Obinna Ekezie	.25	.08
☐ 296	Earl Boykins	.25	.08
☐ 297	Harold Jamison	.25	.08
☐ 298	Sean Rooks	.25	.08
☐ 299	Lindsey Hunter	.25	.08
☐ 300	Samaki Walker	.25	.08
☐ 301	Mitch Richmond	.50	.20
☐ 302	Stanislav Medvedenko	.25	.08
☐ 303	Devean George	.50	.20
☐ 304	Robert Horry	.50	.20
☐ 305	Jelani McCoy	.25	.08
☐ 306	Pau Gasol	4.00	1.50
☐ 307	Shane Battier	2.50	1.00
☐ 308	Jason Williams	.50	.20
☐ 309	Isaac Austin	.25	.08
☐ 310	Will Solomon	.25	.08
☐ 311	Lorenzen Wright	.25	.08
☐ 312	Kendall Gill	.25	.08
☐ 313	LaPhonso Ellis	.25	.08
☐ 314	Sean Marks	.25	.08
☐ 315	Rod Strickland	.25	.08
☐ 316	Jim Jackson	.25	.08
☐ 317	Eddie House	.50	.20
☐ 318	Jason Caffey	.25	.08
☐ 319	Rafer Alston	.25	.08
☐ 320	Anthony Mason	.50	.20
☐ 321	Mark Pope	.25	.08
☐ 322	Michael Redd	.75	.30
☐ 323	Darvin Ham	.25	.08
☐ 324	Joe Smith	.50	.20
☐ 325	William Avery	.25	.08

#	Player		
❏ 326	Sam Mitchell	.25	.08
❏ 327	Loren Woods	1.00	.40
❏ 328	Dean Garrett	.25	.08
❏ 329	Gary Trent	.25	.08
❏ 330	Jason Kidd	1.25	.50
❏ 331	Todd MacCulloch	.25	.08
❏ 332	Richard Jefferson	3.00	1.25
❏ 333	Brandon Armstrong	1.25	.50
❏ 334	Jason Collins	1.00	.40
❏ 335	Kerry Kittles	.50	.20
❏ 336	Shandon Anderson	.25	.08
❏ 337	Howard Eisley	.25	.08
❏ 338	Charlie Ward	.25	.08
❏ 339	Lavor Postell	.50	.20
❏ 340	Clarence Weatherspoon	.25	.08
❏ 341	Travis Knight	.25	.08
❏ 342	Horace Grant	.50	.20
❏ 343	Steven Hunter	1.00	.40
❏ 344	Patrick Ewing	.75	.30
❏ 345	Jeryl Sasser	1.00	.40
❏ 346	Don Reid	.25	.08
❏ 347	Troy Hudson	.25	.08
❏ 348	Speedy Claxton	.50	.20
❏ 349	Derrick Coleman	.25	.08
❏ 350	Damone Brown	1.00	.40
❏ 351	Samuel Dalembert	.75	.30
❏ 352	Vonteego Cummings	.25	.08
❏ 353	Matt Harpring	.75	.30
❏ 354	Corie Blount	.25	.08
❏ 355	Stephon Marbury	.75	.30
❏ 356	Dan Majerle	.50	.20
❏ 357	Jake Voskuhl	.50	.20
❏ 358	Alton Ford	1.50	.60
❏ 359	Iakovos Tsakalidis	.25	.08
❏ 360	John Wallace	.25	.08
❏ 361	Derek Anderson	.50	.20
❏ 362	Erick Barkley	.25	.08
❏ 363	R.Boumtje-Boumtje	2.00	.75
❏ 364	Zach Randolph	4.00	1.50
❏ 365	Steve Kerr	.50	.20
❏ 366	Shawn Kemp	.50	.20
❏ 367	Mateen Cleaves	.50	.20
❏ 368	Bobby Jackson	.25	.08
❏ 369	Mike Bibby	.75	.30
❏ 370	Gerald Wallace	3.00	1.25
❏ 371	Jabari Smith	.50	.20
❏ 372	Lawrence Funderburke	.25	.08
❏ 373	Brent Price	.25	.08
❏ 374	Bruce Bowen	.25	.08
❏ 375	Stephen Jackson	.50	.20
❏ 376	Tony Parker	5.00	2.00
❏ 377	Steve Smith	.50	.20
❏ 378	Cherokee Parks	.25	.08
❏ 379	Mark Bryant	.25	.08
❏ 380	Jerome James	.25	.08
❏ 381	Earl Watson	1.50	.60
❏ 382	Vladimir Radmanovic	1.50	.60
❏ 383	Art Long	.25	.08
❏ 384	Calvin Booth	.25	.08
❏ 385	Olumide Oyedeji	.25	.08
❏ 386	Jerome Williams	.25	.08
❏ 387	Hakeem Olajuwon	.75	.30
❏ 388	Dell Curry	.25	.08
❏ 389	Michael Bradley	1.00	.40
❏ 390	Tracy Murray	.25	.08
❏ 391	Eric Montross	.25	.08
❏ 392	John Amaechi	.25	.08
❏ 393	John Crotty	.25	.08
❏ 394	Scott Padgett	.25	.08
❏ 395	Andrei Kirilenko	3.00	1.25
❏ 396	Jarron Collins	1.00	.40
❏ 397	Quincy Lewis	.25	.08
❏ 398	Kwame Brown	2.00	.75
❏ 399	Christian Laettner	.50	.20
❏ 400	Tyrone Nesby	.25	.08
❏ 401	Brendan Haywood	2.00	.75
❏ 402	Tyronn Lue	.25	.08
❏ 403	Michael Jordan	10.00	4.00
❏ 404	Kobe Bryant CL	.50	.20

#	Player		
❏ 405	Michael Jordan CL	4.00	1.50
❏ 406A	Zeljko Rebraca RC	3.00	1.25
❏ 406B	Zeljko Rebraca RC	3.00	1.25
❏ 407A	Jamison Brewer RC	3.00	1.25
❏ 407B	Jamison Brewer RC	3.00	1.25
❏ 408A	Shawn Marion	1.50	.60
❏ 408B	Shawn Marion	1.50	.60
❏ 409A	Primoz Brezec RC	4.00	1.50
❏ 409B	Primoz Brezec RC	4.00	1.50
❏ 410A	Antonis Fotsis RC	3.00	1.25
❏ 410B	Antonis Fotsis RC	3.00	1.25
❏ 411A	Bobby Simmons RC	3.00	1.25
❏ 411B	Bobby Simmons RC	3.00	1.25
❏ 412A	Malik Allen RC	3.00	1.25
❏ 412B	Malik Allen RC	3.00	1.25
❏ 413A	Ratko Varda RC	3.00	1.25
❏ 413B	Ratko Varda RC	3.00	1.25
❏ 414A	Tierre Brown RC	3.00	1.25
❏ 414B	Tierre Brown RC	3.00	1.25
❏ 415A	Norm Richardson RC	3.00	1.25
❏ 415B	Norm Richardson RC	3.00	1.25
❏ 416A	Oscar Torres RC	3.00	1.25
❏ 416B	Oscar Torres RC	3.00	1.25
❏ 417A	Chris Anderson RC	3.00	1.25
❏ 417B	Chris Anderson RC	3.00	1.25
❏ 418A	Peja Stojakovic	1.50	.60
❏ 418B	Peja Stojakovic	1.50	.60
❏ 419A	Dirk Nowitzki	2.50	1.00
❏ 419B	Dirk Nowitzki	2.50	1.00
❏ 420A	Shareef Abdur-Rahim	1.50	.60
❏ 420B	Shareef Abdur-Rahim	1.50	.60
❏ 421A	Kenny Anderson	.50	.20
❏ 421B	Kenny Anderson	.50	.20
❏ 422A	Jamal Mashburn	1.00	.40
❏ 422B	Jamal Mashburn	1.00	.40
❏ 423A	Charles Oakley	.50	.20
❏ 423B	Charles Oakley	.50	.20
❏ 424A	Andre Miller	1.00	.40
❏ 424B	Andre Miller	1.00	.40
❏ 425A	Michael Finley	1.50	.60
❏ 425B	Michael Finley	1.50	.60
❏ 426A	Tim Hardaway	1.50	.60
❏ 426B	Tim Hardaway	1.50	.60
❏ 427A	Nick Van Exel	1.50	.60
❏ 427B	Nick Van Exel	1.50	.60
❏ 428A	Jerry Stackhouse	1.50	.60
❏ 428B	Jerry Stackhouse	1.50	.60
❏ 429A	Mookie Blaylock	.50	.20
❏ 429B	Mookie Blaylock	.50	.20
❏ 430A	Glen Rice	1.00	.40
❏ 430B	Glen Rice	1.00	.40
❏ 431A	Reggie Miller	1.50	.60
❏ 431B	Reggie Miller	1.50	.60
❏ 432A	Elton Brand	1.50	.60
❏ 432B	Elton Brand	1.50	.60
❏ 433A	Kobe Bryant	6.00	2.50
❏ 433B	Kobe Bryant	6.00	2.50
❏ 434A	Jason Williams	1.00	.40
❏ 434B	Jason Williams	1.00	.40
❏ 435A	Eddie Jones	1.50	.60
❏ 435B	Eddie Jones	1.50	.60
❏ 436A	Alonzo Mourning	1.00	.40
❏ 436B	Alonzo Mourning	1.00	.40
❏ 437A	Glenn Robinson	1.00	.40
❏ 437B	Glenn Robinson	1.00	.40
❏ 438A	Kevin Garnett	3.00	1.25
❏ 438B	Kevin Garnett	3.00	1.25
❏ 439A	Jason Kidd	2.50	1.00
❏ 439B	Jason Kidd	2.50	1.00
❏ 440A	Latrell Sprewell	.75	.30
❏ 440B	Latrell Sprewell	.75	.30
❏ 441A	Grant Hill	1.50	.60
❏ 441B	Grant Hill	1.50	.60
❏ 442A	Dikembe Mutombo	1.50	.60
❏ 442B	Dikembe Mutombo	1.50	.60
❏ 443A	Anfernee Hardaway	1.50	.60
❏ 443B	Anfernee Hardaway	1.50	.60
❏ 444A	Scottie Pippen	2.50	1.00
❏ 444B	Scottie Pippen	2.50	1.00

#	Player		
❏ 445A	Mike Bibby	1.50	.60
❏ 445B	Mike Bibby	1.50	.60
❏ 446A	David Robinson	1.50	.60
❏ 446B	David Robinson	1.50	.60
❏ 447A	Gary Payton	1.50	.60
❏ 447B	Gary Payton	1.50	.60
❏ 448A	Vince Carter	4.00	1.50
❏ 448B	Vince Carter	4.00	1.50
❏ 449A	John Stockton	.75	.30
❏ 449B	John Stockton	.75	.30
❏ 450A	Michael Jordan	20.00	8.00
❏ 450B	Michael Jordan	20.00	8.00
❏ NNO	M.Jordan Buyback EXCH		

2001-02 Upper Deck
Michael Jordan Buybacks

❏ 100 CARDS INSERTED INTO UD PACKS
❏ A1   M.Jordan 93-4UD#23/10

2002-03 Upper Deck

❏	COMPLETE SER.1 (210)	160.00	80.00
❏	COMPLETE SER. 2 (220)	40.00	20.00
❏	COMP.SER.1 w/o SP's (180)	40.00	15.00
❏	COMMON CARD (1-420)	.20	.08
❏	COMMON ROOKIE	3.00	1.25
❏ 1	Shareef Abdur-Rahim	.75	.30
❏ 2	Jason Terry	.75	.30
❏ 3	Glenn Robinson	.75	.30
❏ 4	Nazr Mohammed	.20	.08
❏ 5	DerMarr Johnson	.20	.08
❏ 6	Dion Glover	.20	.08
❏ 7	Paul Pierce	.75	.30
❏ 8	Antoine Walker	.75	.30
❏ 9	Vin Baker	.20	.08
❏ 10	Eric Williams	.20	.08
❏ 11	Tony Delk	.20	.08
❏ 12	Kedrick Brown	.50	.20
❏ 13	Jalen Rose	.75	.30
❏ 14	Eddy Curry	.75	.30
❏ 15	Tyson Chandler	.75	.30
❏ 16	Jamal Crawford	.20	.08
❏ 17	Marcus Fizer	.50	.20
❏ 18	Trenton Hassell	.50	.20
❏ 19	Zydrunas Ilgauskas	.50	.20
❏ 20	Tyrone Hill	.20	.08
❏ 21	Darius Miles	.50	.20
❏ 22	Chris Mihm	.20	.08
❏ 23	Ricky Davis	.50	.20
❏ 24	Jumaine Jones	.50	.20
❏ 25	Dirk Nowitzki	1.25	.50
❏ 26	Michael Finley	.75	.30
❏ 27	Steve Nash	.75	.30
❏ 28	Raef LaFrentz	.50	.20
❏ 29	Nick Van Exel	.75	.30
❏ 30	Adrian Griffin	.20	.08
❏ 31	Wang Zhizhi	.75	.30
❏ 32	Marcus Camby	.50	.20
❏ 33	Juwan Howard	.50	.20
❏ 34	James Posey	.50	.20
❏ 35	Donnell Harvey	.20	.08
❏ 36	Ryan Bowen	.20	.08
❏ 37	Zeljko Rebraca	.50	.20

#	Player		
38	Ben Wallace	.75	.30
39	Clifford Robinson	.20	.08
40	Corliss Williamson	.50	.20
41	Chucky Atkins	.20	.08
42	Michael Curry	.20	.08
43	Jason Richardson	.75	.30
44	Antawn Jamison	.75	.30
45	Troy Murphy	.50	.20
46	Gilbert Arenas	.75	.30
47	Danny Fortson	.20	.08
48	Steve Francis	.75	.30
49	Eddie Griffin	.50	.20
50	Cuttino Mobley	.50	.20
51	Kenny Thomas	.20	.08
52	Moochie Norris	.20	.08
53	Kelvin Cato	.20	.08
54	Reggie Miller	.75	.30
55	Jermaine O'Neal	.75	.30
56	Ron Mercer	.50	.20
57	Austin Croshere	.20	.08
58	Ron Artest	.50	.20
59	Jamaal Tinsley	.75	.30
60	Elton Brand	.75	.30
61	Andre Miller	.50	.20
62	Lamar Odom	.75	.30
63	Michael Olowokandi	.20	.08
64	Quentin Richardson	.50	.20
65	Corey Maggette	.50	.20
66	Kobe Bryant	3.00	1.25
67	Shaquille O'Neal	2.00	.75
68	Rick Fox	.50	.20
69	Robert Horry	.50	.20
70	Devean George	.50	.20
71	Samaki Walker	.20	.08
72	Brian Shaw	.20	.08
73	Pau Gasol	.75	.30
74	Jason Williams	.50	.20
75	Shane Battier	.75	.30
76	Stromile Swift	.50	.20
77	Lorenzen Wright	.20	.08
78	LaPhonso Ellis	.20	.08
79	Eddie Jones	.75	.30
80	Brian Grant	.50	.20
81	Vladimir Stepania	.20	.08
82	Eddie House	.20	.08
83	Anthony Carter	.50	.20
84	Ray Allen	.75	.30
85	Sam Cassell	.75	.30
86	Tim Thomas	.50	.20
87	Toni Kukoc	.50	.20
88	Jason Caffey	.20	.08
89	Anthony Mason	.50	.20
90	Joel Przybilla	.20	.08
91	Kevin Garnett	1.50	.60
92	Wally Szczerbiak	.50	.20
93	Terrell Brandon	.50	.20
94	Joe Smith	.50	.20
95	Felipe Lopez	.20	.08
96	Anthony Peeler	.20	.08
97	Radoslav Nesterovic	.50	.20
98	Jason Kidd	1.25	.50
99	Kenyon Martin	.75	.30
100	Dikembe Mutombo	.50	.20
101	Richard Jefferson	.50	.20
102	Kerry Kittles	.20	.08
103	Lucious Harris	.20	.08
104	Jason Collins	.20	.08
105	Baron Davis	.75	.30
106	Jamal Mashburn	.50	.20
107	Elden Campbell	.20	.08
108	David Wesley	.20	.08
109	P.J. Brown	.20	.08
110	Lee Nailon	.20	.08
111	Latrell Sprewell	.75	.30
112	Allan Houston	.50	.20
113	Kurt Thomas	.50	.20
114	Antonio McDyess	.50	.20
115	Othella Harrington	.20	.08
116	Clarence Weatherspoon	.20	.08
117	Tracy McGrady	2.00	.75
118	Mike Miller	.75	.30
119	Darrell Armstrong	.20	.08
120	Grant Hill	.75	.30
121	Pat Garrity	.20	.08
122	Steven Hunter	.20	.08
123	Allen Iverson	1.50	.60
124	Keith Van Horn	.75	.30
125	Aaron McKie	.50	.20
126	Eric Snow	.50	.20
127	Derrick Coleman	.20	.08
128	Samuel Dalembert	.20	.08
129	Stephon Marbury	.75	.30
130	Shawn Marion	.75	.30
131	Joe Johnson	.50	.20
132	Tom Gugliotta	.20	.08
133	Anfernee Hardaway	.75	.30
134	Iakovos Tsakalidis	.20	.08
135	Rasheed Wallace	.75	.30
136	Bonzi Wells	.50	.20
137	Damon Stoudamire	.50	.20
138	Scottie Pippen	1.25	.50
139	Derek Anderson	.50	.20
140	Ruben Patterson	.20	.08
141	Dale Davis	.50	.20
142	Mike Bibby	.75	.30
143	Chris Webber	.75	.30
144	Peja Stojakovic	.75	.30
145	Doug Christie	.50	.20
146	Hidayet Turkoglu	.75	.30
147	Vlade Divac	.50	.20
148	Scot Pollard	.20	.08
149	Tim Duncan	1.50	.60
150	David Robinson	.75	.30
151	Tony Parker	.75	.30
152	Malik Rose	.20	.08
153	Steve Smith	.50	.20
154	Bruce Bowen	.20	.08
155	Danny Ferry	.20	.08
156	Gary Payton	.75	.30
157	Rashard Lewis	.50	.20
158	Brent Barry	.20	.08
159	Kenny Anderson	.50	.20
160	Desmond Mason	.50	.20
161	Predrag Drobnjak	.20	.08
162	Vince Carter	2.00	.75
163	Morris Peterson	.50	.20
164	Antonio Davis	.20	.08
165	Alvin Williams	.20	.08
166	Jerome Williams	.20	.08
167	Michael Bradley	.50	.20
168	Karl Malone	.75	.30
169	John Stockton	.75	.30
170	John Amaechi	.20	.08
171	Andrei Kirilenko	.75	.30
172	Greg Ostertag	.20	.08
173	Jarron Collins	.20	.08
174	DeShawn Stevenson	.20	.08
175	Christian Laettner	.50	.20
176	Brendan Haywood	.50	.20
177	Chris Whitney	.20	.08
178	Tyronn Lue	.20	.08
179	Kwame Brown	.50	.20
180	Michael Jordan	6.00	2.50
181	Jay Williams RC	4.00	1.50
182	Juan Dixon RC	5.00	2.00
183	Vincent Yarbrough RC	3.00	1.25
184	Casey Jacobsen RC	3.00	1.25
185	Chris Wilcox RC	4.00	1.50
186	John Salmons RC	3.00	1.25
187	Marcus Haislip RC	3.00	1.25
188	Robert Archibald RC	3.00	1.25
189	Jared Jeffries RC	3.00	1.25
190	Nikoloz Tskitishvili RC	4.00	1.50
191	Kareem Rush RC	4.00	1.50
192	Fred Jones RC	4.00	1.50
193	Caron Butler RC	6.00	2.50
194	Chris Jefferies RC	3.00	1.25
195	Ryan Humphrey RC	3.00	1.25
196	Frank Williams RC	3.00	1.25
197	DaJuan Wagner RC	5.00	2.00
198	Bostjan Nachbar RC	3.00	1.25
199	Mike Dunleavy RC	5.00	2.00
200	Roger Mason RC	3.00	1.25
201	Nene Hilario RC	4.00	1.50
202	Melvin Ely RC	3.00	1.25
203	Tayshaun Prince RC	5.00	2.00
204	Dan Dickau RC	3.00	1.25
205	Qyntel Woods RC	4.00	1.50
206	Curtis Borchardt RC	3.00	1.25
207	Amare Stoudemire RC	12.00	5.00
208	Drew Gooden RC	8.00	3.00
210	Yao Ming RC	20.00	8.00
211	Glenn Robinson	.75	.30
212	Theo Ratliff	.50	.20
213	Emanual Davis	.20	.08
214	Dan Dickau	2.00	.75
215	Alan Henderson	.20	.08
216	Chris Crawford	.20	.08
217	Darvin Ham	.20	.08
218	Ira Newble	.20	.08
219	Vin Baker	.50	.20
220	Shammond Williams	.20	.08
221	Tony Battie	.20	.08
222	Walter McCarty	.20	.08
223	Bruno Sundov	.20	.08
224	Ruben Wolkowyski	.20	.08
225	Eddie Robinson	.50	.20
226	Jay Williams	3.00	1.25
227	Fred Hoiberg	.20	.08
228	Donyell Marshall	.50	.20
229	Roger Mason	1.50	.60
230	Darius Miles	.75	.30
231	Michael Stewart	.20	.08
232	Tyrone Hill	.20	.08
233	DaJuan Wagner	3.00	1.25
234	DeSagana Diop	.50	.20
235	Bimbo Coles	.20	.08
236	Milt Palacio	.20	.08
237	Avery Johnson	.20	.08
238	Evan Eschmeyer	.20	.08
239	Raja Bell	.20	.08
240	Shawn Bradley	.20	.08
241	Walt Williams	.20	.08
242	Eduardo Najera	.50	.20
243	Marcus Camby	.50	.20
244	Chris Whitney	.20	.08
245	Nikoloz Tskitishvili	2.00	.75
246	Kenny Satterfield	.20	.08
247	Nene Hilario	2.00	.75
248	Mark Blount	.20	.08
249	Richard Hamilton	.50	.20
250	Chauncey Billups	.50	.20
251	Tayshaun Prince	2.50	1.00
252	Don Reid	.20	.08
253	Jon Barry	.20	.08
254	Hubert Davis	.20	.08
255	Pepe Sanchez	.20	.08
256	Chris Mills	.20	.08
257	Bob Sura	.20	.08
258	Mike Dunleavy	2.50	1.00
259	Jiri Welsch	1.50	.60
260	Adonal Foyle	.20	.08
261	Erick Dampier	.50	.20
262	Maurice Taylor	.20	.08
263	Glen Rice	.50	.20
264	Yao Ming	8.00	3.00
265	Bostjan Nachbar	1.50	.60
266	Jason Collier	.20	.08
267	Terence Morris	.20	.08
268	Jonathan Bender	.50	.20
269	Jeff Foster	.20	.08
270	Fred Jones	2.00	.75
271	Al Harrington	.50	.20
272	Brad Miller	.75	.30
273	Jamison Brewer	.20	.08
274	Erick Strickland	.20	.08
275	Andre Miller	.50	.20
276	Melvin Ely	1.50	.60
277	Keyon Dooling	.20	.08
278	Chris Wilcox	2.00	.75
279	Eric Piatkowski	.20	.08
280	Sean Rooks	.20	.08
281	Wang Zhi Zhi	.75	.30
282	Mark Madsen	.20	.08
283	Kareem Rush	2.00	.75
284	Stanislav Medvedenko	.20	.08
285	Derek Fisher	.75	.30
286	Tracy Murray	.20	.08
287	Michael Dickerson	.20	.08
288	Wesley Person	.20	.08
289	Drew Gooden	4.00	1.50
290	Robert Archibald	.20	.08
291	Brevin Knight	.20	.08
292	Mike James	.20	.08
293	LaPhonso Ellis	.20	.08
294	Caron Butler	3.00	1.25
295	Malik Allen	.20	.08

❑ 296	Travis Best	.20	.08	❑ 382	Curtis Borchardt	1.50	.60	❑ 25	Eddy Curry	.50	.20
❑ 297	Alonzo Mourning	.50	.20	❑ 383	Mark Jackson	.20	.08	❑ 26	Trenton Hassell	.50	.20
❑ 298	Toni Kukoc	.50	.20	❑ 384	Scott Padgett	.20	.08	❑ 27	Michael Jordan	5.00	2.00
❑ 299	Michael Redd	.75	.30	❑ 385	Jerry Stackhouse	.50	.20	❑ 28	Tyson Chandler	.75	.30
❑ 300	Marcus Haislip	1.50	.60	❑ 386	Jared Jeffries	.50	.20	❑ 29	Jay Williams	.50	.20
❑ 301	Ervin Johnson	.20	.08	❑ 387	Larry Hughes	.50	.20	❑ 30	Scottie Pippen	1.25	.50
❑ 302	Kevin Ollie	.20	.08	❑ 388	Juan Dixon	2.50	1.00	❑ 31	Eddie Robinson	.50	.20
❑ 303	Troy Hudson	.20	.08	❑ 389	Bryon Russell	.20	.08	❑ 32	Lonny Baxter	.20	.08
❑ 304	Marc Jackson	.50	.20	❑ 390	Etan Thomas	.20	.08	❑ 33	Darius Miles	.75	.30
❑ 305	Gary Trent	.20	.08	❑ 391	Efthimios Rentzias RC	3.00	1.25	❑ 34	DeSagana Diop	.50	.20
❑ 306	Kendall Gill	.20	.08	❑ 392	Manu Ginobili RC	10.00	4.00	❑ 35	Ricky Davis	.75	.30
❑ 307	Loren Woods	.50	.20	❑ 393	Juaquin Hawkins RC	3.00	1.25	❑ 36	Chris Mihm	.20	.08
❑ 308	Dikembe Mutombo	.50	.20	❑ 394	Rasual Butler RC	3.00	1.25	❑ 37	Carlos Boozer	.20	.08
❑ 309	Anthony Johnson	.20	.08	❑ 395	Ronald Murray RC	5.00	2.00	❑ 38	Michael Stewart	.20	.08
❑ 310	Rodney Rogers	.20	.08	❑ 396	Igor Rakocevic RC	3.00	1.25	❑ 39	Zydrunas Ilgauskas	.50	.20
❑ 311	Brandon Armstrong	.50	.20	❑ 397	Tito Maddox RC	3.00	1.25	❑ 40	Dajuan Wagner	.50	.20
❑ 312	Brian Scalabrine	.20	.08	❑ 398	Mike Batiste RC	3.00	1.25	❑ 41	J.R. Bremer	.20	.08
❑ 313	Aaron Williams	.20	.08	❑ 399	Sam Clancy RC	3.00	1.25	❑ 42	Kevin Ollie	.20	.08
❑ 314	Courtney Alexander	.50	.20	❑ 400	Tamar Slay RC	3.00	1.25	❑ 43	Dirk Nowitzki	1.25	.50
❑ 315	Kirk Haston	.50	.20	❑ 401	Lonny Baxter RC	3.00	1.25	❑ 44	Antawn Jamison	.75	.30
❑ 316	George Lynch	.20	.08	❑ 402	Marko Jaric	3.00	1.25	❑ 45	Shawn Bradley	.20	.08
❑ 317	Stacey Augmon	.20	.08	❑ 403	Dan Gadzuric RC	3.00	1.25	❑ 46	Raef LaFrentz	.50	.20
❑ 318	Robert Traylor	.20	.08	❑ 404	Jannero Pargo RC	3.00	1.25	❑ 47	Eduardo Najera	.50	.20
❑ 319	Jamaal Magloire	.20	.08	❑ 405	Pat Burke RC	3.00	1.25	❑ 48	Travis Best	.20	.08
❑ 320	Lee Nailon	.20	.08	❑ 406	Smush Parker RC	5.00	2.00	❑ 49	Danny Fortson	.20	.08
❑ 321	Frank Williams	1.50	.60	❑ 407	Reggie Evans RC	3.00	1.25	❑ 50	Michael Finley	.75	.30
❑ 322	Michael Doleac	.20	.08	❑ 408	Gordan Giricek RC	3.00	1.25	❑ 51	Jiri Welsch	.20	.08
❑ 323	Shandon Anderson	.20	.08	❑ 409	Mehmet Okur RC	3.00	1.25	❑ 52	Steve Nash	.75	.30
❑ 324	Howard Eisley	.20	.08	❑ 410	Jamal Sampson RC	3.00	1.25	❑ 53	Marcus Camby	.50	.20
❑ 325	Travis Knight	.20	.08	❑ 411	Raul Lopez RC	3.00	1.25	❑ 54	Chris Anderson	.20	.08
❑ 326	Lavor Postell	.20	.08	❑ 412	Predrag Savovic RC	3.00	1.25	❑ 55	Rodney White	.20	.08
❑ 327	Charlie Ward	.20	.08	❑ 413	Carlos Boozer RC	6.00	2.50	❑ 56	Vincent Yarbrough	.20	.08
❑ 328	Mark Pope	.20	.08	❑ 414	Ken Johnson RC	3.00	1.25	❑ 57	Nikoloz Tskitishvili	.20	.08
❑ 329	Olumide Oyedeji	.20	.08	❑ 415	Cezary Trybanski RC	3.00	1.25	❑ 58	Nene	.50	.20
❑ 330	Shawn Kemp	.20	.08	❑ 416	Mike Wilks RC	3.00	1.25	❑ 59	Andre Miller	.50	.20
❑ 331	Jacque Vaughn	.20	.08	❑ 417	J.R. Bremer RC	3.00	1.25	❑ 60	Earl Boykins	.50	.20
❑ 332	Ryan Humphrey	1.50	.60	❑ 418	Junior Harrington RC	3.00	1.25	❑ 61	Ryan Bowen	.20	.08
❑ 333	Andrew DeClercq	.20	.08	❑ 419	Nate Huffman RC	3.00	1.25	❑ 62	Ben Wallace	.75	.30
❑ 334	Jeryl Sasser	.20	.08	❑ 420	Michael Jordan	6.00	2.50	❑ 63	Tayshaun Prince	.50	.20
❑ 335	Keith Van Horn	.75	.30					❑ 64	Richard Hamilton	.50	.20
❑ 336	Todd MacCulloch	.20	.08		**2003-04 Upper Deck**			❑ 65	Mehmet Okur	.20	.08
❑ 337	Monty Williams	.20	.08					❑ 66	Bob Sura	.20	.08
❑ 338	John Salmons	.20	.08					❑ 67	Chucky Atkins	.20	.08
❑ 339	Brian Skinner	.20	.08					❑ 68	Chauncey Billups	.50	.20
❑ 340	Mark Bryant	.20	.08					❑ 69	Elden Campbell	.20	.08
❑ 341	Greg Buckner	.20	.08					❑ 70	Corliss Williamson	.50	.20
❑ 342	Bo Outlaw	.20	.08					❑ 71	Zeljko Rebraca	.20	.08
❑ 343	Amare Stoudemire	6.00	2.50					❑ 72	Jason Richardson	.75	.30
❑ 344	Casey Jacobsen	1.25	.50					❑ 73	Popeye Jones	.20	.08
❑ 345	Alton Ford	.50	.20					❑ 74	Clifford Robinson	.20	.08
❑ 346	Scott Williams	.20	.08					❑ 75	Mike Dunleavy	.50	.20
❑ 347	Dan Langhi	.20	.08					❑ 76	Troy Murphy	.75	.30
❑ 348	Arvydas Sabonis	.20	.08					❑ 77	Speedy Claxton	.20	.08
❑ 349	Antonio Daniels	.20	.08					❑ 78	Erick Dampier	.50	.20
❑ 350	Jeff McInnis	.20	.08					❑ 79	Nick Van Exel	.75	.30
❑ 351	Qyntel Woods	2.00	.75					❑ 80	Avery Johnson	.20	.08
❑ 352	Zach Randolph	.75	.30					❑ 81	Adonal Foyle	.20	.08
❑ 353	Ruben Boumtje-Boumtje	.20	.08					❑ 82	Pepe Sanchez	.20	.08
❑ 354	Chris Dudley	.20	.08	❑ COMP.SER.1 w/o SP's (300)		40.00	20.00	❑ 83	Steve Francis	.75	.30
❑ 355	Charles Smith	.20	.08	❑ COMMON CARD (1-300)		.20	.08	❑ 84	Glen Rice	.50	.20
❑ 356	Keon Clark	.50	.20	❑ COMMON ROOKIE (301-342)		3.00	1.25	❑ 85	Eddie Griffin	.50	.20
❑ 357	Bobby Jackson	.50	.20	❑ 1	Shareef Abdur-Rahim	.75	.30	❑ 86	Moochie Norris	.20	.08
❑ 358	Mateen Cleaves	.50	.20	❑ 2	Alan Henderson	.20	.08	❑ 87	Maurice Taylor	.20	.08
❑ 359	Gerald Wallace	.50	.20	❑ 3	Dan Dickau	.20	.08	❑ 88	Kelvin Cato	.20	.08
❑ 360	Lawrence Funderburke	.20	.08	❑ 4	Theo Ratliff	.50	.20	❑ 89	Jason Collier	.20	.08
❑ 361	Speedy Claxton	.20	.08	❑ 5	Terrell Brandon	.20	.08	❑ 90	Cuttino Mobley	.50	.20
❑ 362	Stephen Jackson	.50	.20	❑ 6	Darvin Ham	.20	.08	❑ 91	Yao Ming	2.00	.75
❑ 363	Kevin Willis	.20	.08	❑ 7	Nazr Mohammed	.20	.08	❑ 92	Eric Piatkowski	.50	.20
❑ 364	Steve Kerr	.20	.08	❑ 8	Jason Terry	.50	.20	❑ 93	Bostjan Nachbar	.20	.08
❑ 365	Mengke Bateer	.20	.08	❑ 9	Dion Glover	.20	.08	❑ 94	Adrian Griffin	.20	.08
❑ 366	Kenny Anderson	.50	.20	❑ 10	Chris Crawford	.20	.08	❑ 95	Reggie Miller	.75	.30
❑ 367	Vladimir Radmanovic	.50	.20	❑ 11	Paul Pierce	.75	.30	❑ 96	Fred Jones	.50	.20
❑ 368	Joseph Forte	.50	.20	❑ 12	Antoine Walker	.75	.30	❑ 97	Scot Pollard	.20	.08
❑ 369	Jerome James	.20	.08	❑ 13	Eric Williams	.20	.08	❑ 98	Jamaal Tinsley	.50	.20
❑ 370	Vitaly Potapenko	.20	.08	❑ 14	Kedrick Brown	.20	.08	❑ 99	Al Harrington	.50	.20
❑ 371	Calvin Booth	.20	.08	❑ 15	Tony Battie	.20	.08	❑ 100	Jonathan Bender	.50	.20
❑ 372	Ansu Sesay	.20	.08	❑ 16	Vin Baker	.50	.20	❑ 101	Primoz Brezec	.20	.08
❑ 373	Voshon Lenard	.20	.08	❑ 17	Mark Blount	.20	.08	❑ 102	Ron Artest	.50	.20
❑ 374	Lindsey Hunter	.20	.08	❑ 18	Tony Delk	.20	.08	❑ 103	Jermaine O'Neal	.75	.30
❑ 375	Mamadou N'diaye	.20	.08	❑ 19	Walter McCarty	.20	.08	❑ 104	Kenny Anderson	.50	.20
❑ 376	Chris Jefferies	.20	.08	❑ 20	Jumaine Jones	.50	.20	❑ 105	Jeff Foster	.20	.08
❑ 377	Jelani McCoy	.20	.08	❑ 21	Jalen Rose	.75	.30	❑ 106	Austin Croshere	.20	.08
❑ 378	Lamond Murray	.20	.08	❑ 22	Marcus Fizer	.20	.08	❑ 107	Elton Brand	.75	.30
❑ 379	Eric Montross	.20	.08	❑ 23	Jamal Crawford	.20	.08	❑ 108	Tremaine Fowlkes	.20	.08
❑ 380	Matt Harpring	.75	.30	❑ 24	Donyell Marshall	.50	.20	❑ 109	Quentin Richardson	.50	.20
❑ 381	Calbert Cheaney	.20	.08					❑ 110	Melvin Ely	.20	.08

#	Player		
❏ 111	Marko Jaric	.50	.20
❏ 112	Chris Wilcox	.20	.08
❏ 113	Wang Zhizhi	.75	.30
❏ 114	Corey Maggette	.50	.20
❏ 115	Keyon Dooling	.20	.08
❏ 116	Kobe Bryant	3.00	1.25
❏ 117	Shaquille O'Neal	2.00	.75
❏ 118	Slava Medvedenko	.20	.08
❏ 119	Gary Payton	.75	.30
❏ 120	Jannero Pargo	.20	.08
❏ 121	Kareem Rush	.20	.08
❏ 122	Karl Malone	.75	.30
❏ 123	Derek Fisher	.50	.20
❏ 124	Rick Fox	.50	.20
❏ 125	Devean George	.20	.08
❏ 126	Pau Gasol	.75	.30
❏ 127	Jason Williams	.50	.20
❏ 128	Stromile Swift	.50	.20
❏ 129	Wesley Person	.20	.08
❏ 130	Michael Dickerson	.20	.08
❏ 131	Lorenzen Wright	.20	.08
❏ 132	Earl Watson	.20	.08
❏ 133	Mike Miller	.75	.30
❏ 134	Shane Battier	.75	.30
❏ 135	Eddie Jones	.75	.30
❏ 136	Rasual Butler	.20	.08
❏ 137	Caron Butler	.75	.30
❏ 138	Brian Grant	.50	.20
❏ 139	Lamar Odom	.75	.30
❏ 140	Malik Allen	.20	.08
❏ 141	Ken Johnson	.20	.08
❏ 142	Samaki Walker	.20	.08
❏ 143	Sean Lampley	.20	.08
❏ 144	Vladimir Stepania	.20	.08
❏ 145	Erick Strickland	.20	.08
❏ 146	Toni Kukoc	.50	.20
❏ 147	Joel Przybilla	.20	.08
❏ 148	Tim Thomas	.50	.20
❏ 149	Dan Gadzuric	.20	.08
❏ 150	Joe Smith	.50	.20
❏ 151	Michael Redd	.75	.30
❏ 152	Desmond Mason	.50	.20
❏ 153	Brian Skinner	.20	.08
❏ 154	Kevin Garnett	1.50	.60
❏ 155	Michael Olowokandi	.20	.08
❏ 156	Troy Hudson	.20	.08
❏ 157	Latrell Sprewell	.75	.30
❏ 158	Wally Szczerbiak	.50	.20
❏ 159	Sam Cassell	.75	.30
❏ 160	Fred Hoiberg	.20	.08
❏ 161	Ervin Johnson	.20	.08
❏ 162	Mark Madsen	.20	.08
❏ 163	Gary Trent	.20	.08
❏ 164	Jason Kidd	1.25	.50
❏ 165	Dikembe Mutombo	.50	.20
❏ 166	Lucious Harris	.20	.08
❏ 167	Kerry Kittles	.20	.08
❏ 168	Brandon Armstrong	.20	.08
❏ 169	Jason Collins	.20	.08
❏ 170	Alonzo Mourning	.50	.20
❏ 171	Kenyon Martin	.75	.30
❏ 172	Richard Jefferson	.50	.20
❏ 173	Rodney Rogers	.20	.08
❏ 174	Aaron Williams	.20	.08
❏ 175	Jamal Mashburn	.50	.20
❏ 176	David Wesley	.20	.08
❏ 177	Kirk Haston	.20	.08
❏ 178	Courtney Alexander	.50	.20
❏ 179	Darrell Armstrong	.20	.08
❏ 180	Robert Traylor	.20	.08
❏ 181	George Lynch	.20	.08
❏ 182	Jamaal Magloire	.20	.08
❏ 183	Baron Davis	.75	.30
❏ 184	P.J. Brown	.20	.08
❏ 185	Sean Rooks	.20	.08
❏ 186	Stacey Augmon	.20	.08
❏ 187	Allan Houston	.50	.20
❏ 188	Antonio McDyess	.50	.20
❏ 189	Clarence Weatherspoon	.20	.08
❏ 190	Kurt Thomas	.50	.20
❏ 191	Shandon Anderson	.20	.08
❏ 192	Keith Van Horn	.75	.30
❏ 193	Michael Doleac	.20	.08
❏ 194	Othella Harrington	.20	.08
❏ 195	Charlie Ward	.20	.08
❏ 196	Lee Nailon	.20	.08
❏ 197	Tracy McGrady	2.00	.75
❏ 198	Pat Garrity	.20	.08
❏ 199	Grant Hill	.75	.30
❏ 200	Gordan Giricek	.50	.20
❏ 201	Steven Hunter	.20	.08
❏ 202	Jeryl Sasser	.20	.08
❏ 203	Andrew DeClercq	.20	.08
❏ 204	Juwan Howard	.50	.20
❏ 205	Tyronn Lue	.20	.08
❏ 206	Drew Gooden	.50	.20
❏ 207	Marc Jackson	.50	.20
❏ 208	Aaron McKie	.50	.20
❏ 209	Derrick Coleman	.50	.20
❏ 210	Eric Snow	.50	.20
❏ 211	Glenn Robinson	.75	.30
❏ 212	Greg Buckner	.20	.08
❏ 213	Allen Iverson	1.50	.60
❏ 214	Kenny Thomas	.20	.08
❏ 215	Sam Clancy	.20	.08
❏ 216	Monty Williams	.20	.08
❏ 217	Stephon Marbury	.75	.30
❏ 218	Shawn Marion	.75	.30
❏ 219	Joe Johnson	.50	.20
❏ 220	Bo Outlaw	.20	.08
❏ 221	Amare Stoudemire	1.50	.60
❏ 222	Casey Jacobsen	.20	.08
❏ 223	Tom Gugliotta	.20	.08
❏ 224	Scott Williams	.20	.08
❏ 225	Jake Tsakalidis	.20	.08
❏ 226	Damon Stoudamire	.50	.20
❏ 227	Arvydas Sabonis	.20	.08
❏ 228	Zach Randolph	.75	.30
❏ 229	Ruben Patterson	.50	.20
❏ 230	Derek Anderson	.50	.20
❏ 231	Dale Davis	.50	.20
❏ 232	Bonzi Wells	.50	.20
❏ 233	Rasheed Wallace	.75	.30
❏ 234	Jeff McInnis	.20	.08
❏ 235	Qyntel Woods	.20	.08
❏ 236	Chris Webber	.75	.30
❏ 237	Doug Christie	.50	.20
❏ 238	Vlade Divac	.50	.20
❏ 239	Bobby Jackson	.50	.20
❏ 240	Lawrence Funderburke	.20	.08
❏ 241	Peja Stojakovic	.75	.30
❏ 242	Gerald Wallace	.50	.20
❏ 243	Brad Miller	.75	.30
❏ 244	Mike Bibby	.75	.30
❏ 245	Anthony Peeler	.20	.08
❏ 246	Jim Jackson	.20	.08
❏ 247	David Robinson	.75	.30
❏ 248	Ron Mercer	.20	.08
❏ 249	Tony Parker	.75	.30
❏ 250	Malik Rose	.20	.08
❏ 251	Kevin Willis	.20	.08
❏ 252	Manu Ginobili	.75	.30
❏ 253	Bruce Bowen	.20	.08
❏ 254	Hedo Turkoglu	.75	.30
❏ 255	Tim Duncan	1.50	.60
❏ 256	Robert Horry	.50	.20
❏ 257	Radoslav Nesterovic	.50	.20
❏ 258	Ray Allen	.75	.30
❏ 259	Rashard Lewis	.75	.30
❏ 260	Reggie Evans	.20	.08
❏ 261	Brent Barry	.50	.20
❏ 262	Ronald Murray	.20	.08
❏ 263	Vladimir Radmanovic	.20	.08
❏ 264	Predrag Drobnjak	.20	.08
❏ 265	Antonio Daniels	.20	.08
❏ 266	Vitaly Potapenko	.20	.08
❏ 267	Calvin Booth	.20	.08
❏ 268	Vince Carter	2.00	.75
❏ 269	Chris Jefferies	.20	.08
❏ 270	Mengke Bateer	.20	.08
❏ 271	Alvin Williams	.20	.08
❏ 272	Jerome Williams	.20	.08
❏ 273	Michael Bradley	.20	.08
❏ 274	Lamond Murray	.20	.08
❏ 275	Antonio Davis	.20	.08
❏ 276	Morris Peterson	.50	.20
❏ 277	Jerome Moiso	.20	.08
❏ 278	Carlos Arroyo	1.25	.50
❏ 279	Matt Harpring	.75	.30
❏ 280	Andrei Kirilenko	.75	.30
❏ 281	Jarron Collins	.20	.08
❏ 282	Greg Ostertag	.20	.08
❏ 283	Curtis Borchardt	.20	.08
❏ 284	DeShawn Stevenson	.20	.08
❏ 285	Keon Clark	.50	.20
❏ 286	John Amaechi	.20	.08
❏ 287	Raul Lopez	.20	.08
❏ 288	Jerry Stackhouse	.75	.30
❏ 289	Kwame Brown	.75	.30
❏ 290	Larry Hughes	.50	.20
❏ 291	Brendan Haywood	.20	.08
❏ 292	Juan Dixon	.50	.20
❏ 293	Bryon Russell	.20	.08
❏ 294	Christian Laettner	.50	.20
❏ 295	Jahidi White	.20	.08
❏ 296	Jared Jeffries	.20	.08
❏ 297	Gilbert Arenas	.75	.30
❏ 298	Kobe Bryant CL	1.50	.60
❏ 299	Michael Jordan CL	2.50	1.00
❏ 300	Michael Jordan CL	2.50	1.00
❏ 301	LeBron James RC	40.00	15.00
❏ 302	Darko Milicic RC	6.00	2.50
❏ 303	Carmelo Anthony RC	12.00	5.00
❏ 304	Chris Bosh RC	8.00	3.00
❏ 305	Dwyane Wade RC	15.00	6.00
❏ 306	Chris Kaman RC	3.00	1.25
❏ 307	Kirk Hinrich RC	5.00	2.00
❏ 308	T.J. Ford RC	4.00	1.50
❏ 309	Mike Sweetney RC	3.00	1.25
❏ 310	Jarvis Hayes RC	3.00	1.25
❏ 311	Mickael Pietrus RC	3.00	1.25
❏ 312	Nick Collison RC	3.00	1.25
❏ 313	Marcus Banks RC	3.00	1.25
❏ 314	Luke Ridnour RC	4.00	1.50
❏ 315	Reece Gaines RC	3.00	1.25
❏ 316	Troy Bell RC	3.00	1.25
❏ 317	Zarko Cabarkapa RC	3.00	1.25
❏ 318	David West RC	3.00	1.25
❏ 319	Aleksandar Pavlovic RC	4.00	1.50
❏ 320	Dahntay Jones RC	3.00	1.25
❏ 321	Boris Diaw RC	4.00	1.50
❏ 322	Zoran Planinic RC	3.00	1.25
❏ 323	Travis Outlaw RC	3.00	1.25
❏ 324	Brian Cook RC	3.00	1.25
❏ 325	Kirk Penney RC	3.00	1.25
❏ 326	Ndudi Ebi RC	3.00	1.25
❏ 327	Kendrick Perkins RC	3.00	1.25
❏ 328	Leandro Barbosa RC	5.00	2.00
❏ 329	Josh Howard RC	5.00	2.00
❏ 330	Maciej Lampe RC	3.00	1.25
❏ 331	Jason Kapono RC	3.00	1.25
❏ 332	Luke Walton RC	3.00	1.25
❏ 333	Jerome Beasley RC	3.00	1.25
❏ 334	Brandon Hunter RC	3.00	1.25
❏ 335	Kyle Korver RC	5.00	2.00
❏ 336	Travis Hansen RC	3.00	1.25
❏ 337	Steve Blake RC	3.00	1.25
❏ 338	Slavko Vranes RC	3.00	1.25
❏ 339	Zaur Pachulia RC	3.00	1.25
❏ 340	Keith Bogans RC	3.00	1.25
❏ 341	Willie Green RC	3.00	1.25
❏ 342	Maurice Williams RC	3.00	1.25

2004-05 Upper Deck

❏ COMP.SET w/o SP's (200)	40.00	20.00
❏ COMMON CARD (1-200)	.20	.08
❏ COMMON ROOKIE (201-220)	3.00	1.25
❏ COMMON ROOKIE (221-220)		
❏ 1 Antoine Walker	.75	.30
❏ 2 Boris Diaw	.20	.08

#	Player		
3	Al Harrington	.50	.20
4	Tony Delk	.20	.08
5	Jason Collier	.20	.08
6	Chris Crawford	.20	.08
7	Ricky Davis	.75	.30
8	Paul Pierce	.75	.30
9	Jiri Welsch	.50	.20
10	Gary Payton	.75	.30
11	Rick Fox	.50	.20
12	Mark Blount	.20	.08
13	Adrian Griffin	.20	.08
14	Tyson Chandler	.75	.30
15	Eddy Curry	.50	.20
16	Kirk Hinrich	.75	.30
17	Scottie Pippen	1.00	.40
18	Jannero Pargo	.20	.08
19	Antonio Davis	.20	.08
20	Gerald Wallace	.50	.20
21	Eddie House	.20	.08
22	Steve Smith	.50	.20
23	Brandon Hunter	.20	.08
24	Theron Smith	.20	.08
25	Jahidi White	.20	.08
26	LeBron James	5.00	2.00
27	DeSagana Diop	.20	.08
28	Zydrunas Ilgauskas	.50	.20
29	Dajuan Wagner	.50	.20
30	Jeff McInnis	.20	.08
31	Eric Snow	.50	.20
32	Dirk Nowitzki	1.00	.40
33	Jason Terry	.75	.30
34	Michael Finley	.75	.30
35	Jerry Stackhouse	.75	.30
36	Erick Dampier	.50	.20
37	Josh Howard	.50	.20
38	Marquis Daniels	.75	.30
39	Carmelo Anthony	1.50	.60
40	Nene	.20	.08
41	Andre Miller	.50	.20
42	Earl Boykins	.50	.20
43	Marcus Camby	.50	.20
44	Voshon Lenard	.20	.08
45	Kenyon Martin	.75	.30
46	Richard Hamilton	.50	.20
47	Chauncey Billups	.50	.20
48	Rasheed Wallace	.75	.30
49	Tayshaun Prince	.50	.20
50	Ben Wallace	.75	.30
51	Antonio McDyess	.75	.30
52	Carlos Delfino	.20	.08
53	Jason Richardson	.75	.30
54	Dale Davis	.20	.08
55	Adonal Foyle	.20	.08
56	Mickael Pietrus	.50	.20
57	Mike Dunleavy	.50	.20
58	Speedy Claxton	.20	.08
59	Derek Fisher	.75	.30
60	Yao Ming	2.00	.75
61	Jim Jackson	.20	.08
62	Tracy McGrady	2.00	.75
63	Maurice Taylor	.20	.08
64	Juwan Howard	.50	.20
65	Tyronn Lue	.20	.08
66	Dikembe Mutombo	.50	.20
67	Reggie Miller	.75	.30
68	Stephen Jackson	.20	.08
69	Jermaine O'Neal	.75	.30
70	Jamaal Tinsley	.75	.30
71	Ron Artest	.50	.20
72	Fred Jones	.20	.08
73	Jonathan Bender	.50	.20
74	Kerry Kittles	.20	.08
75	Chris Kaman	.50	.20
76	Elton Brand	.75	.30
77	Marko Jaric	.50	.20
78	Corey Maggette	.50	.20
79	Bobby Simmons	.20	.08
80	Chris Wilcox	.50	.20
81	Lamar Odom	.75	.30
82	Karl Malone	.75	.30
83	Kobe Bryant	3.00	1.25
84	Kareem Rush	.50	.20
85	Caron Butler	.50	.20
86	Devean George	.20	.08
87	Vlade Divac	.50	.20
88	Pau Gasol	.75	.30
89	Bonzi Wells	.50	.20
90	Mike Miller	.75	.30
91	Jason Williams	.50	.20
92	Shane Battier	.75	.30
93	James Posey	.50	.20
94	Stromile Swift	.50	.20
95	Shaquille O'Neal	2.00	.75
96	Dwyane Wade	2.50	1.00
97	Eddie Jones	.75	.30
98	Wang Zhizhi	.75	.30
99	Rasual Butler	.20	.08
100	Malik Allen	.20	.08
101	Udonis Haslem	.20	.08
102	Michael Redd	.50	.20
103	T.J. Ford	.50	.20
104	Keith Van Horn	.75	.30
105	Toni Kukoc	.50	.20
106	Desmond Mason	.50	.20
107	Mike James	.20	.08
108	Joe Smith	.50	.20
109	Kevin Garnett	1.50	.60
110	Michael Olowokandi	.20	.08
111	Sam Cassell	.75	.30
112	Troy Hudson	.20	.08
113	Latrell Sprewell	.75	.30
114	Fred Hoiberg	.20	.08
115	Wally Szczerbiak	.50	.20
116	Richard Jefferson	.50	.20
117	Alonzo Mourning	.50	.20
118	Jason Kidd	1.00	.40
119	Jacque Vaughn	.20	.08
120	Jason Collins	.20	.08
121	Aaron Williams	.20	.08
122	Zoran Planinic	.20	.08
123	Jamaal Magloire	.50	.20
124	P.J. Brown	.20	.08
125	Baron Davis	.75	.30
126	Darrell Armstrong	.20	.08
127	Jamal Mashburn	.50	.20
128	Rodney Rogers	.20	.08
129	David Wesley	.20	.08
130	Allan Houston	.50	.20
131	Jamal Crawford	.50	.20
132	Stephon Marbury	.75	.30
133	Tim Thomas	.50	.20
134	Anfernee Hardaway	.75	.30
135	Kurt Thomas	.50	.20
136	Mike Sweetney	.50	.20
137	Tony Battie	.20	.08
138	DeShawn Stevenson	.20	.08
139	Steve Francis	.75	.30
140	Cuttino Mobley	.50	.20
141	Hedo Turkoglu	.75	.30
142	Keith Bogans	.20	.08
143	Samuel Dalembert	.20	.08
144	Kenny Thomas	.20	.08
145	Allen Iverson	1.50	.60
146	Aaron McKie	.50	.20
147	Glenn Robinson	.75	.30
148	Willie Green	.20	.08
149	Corliss Williamson	.50	.20
150	Shawn Marion	.75	.30
151	Leandro Barbosa	.20	.08
152	Amare Stoudemire	1.50	.60
153	Quentin Richardson	.50	.20
154	Joe Johnson	.50	.20
155	Steve Nash	.75	.30
156	Damon Stoudamire	.50	.20
157	Theo Ratliff	.50	.20
158	Shareef Abdur-Rahim	.75	.30
159	Derek Anderson	.50	.20
160	Zach Randolph	.75	.30
161	Nick Van Exel	.75	.30
162	Darius Miles	.75	.30
163	Mike Bibby	.75	.30
164	Brad Miller	.75	.30
165	Peja Stojakovic	.75	.30
166	Bobby Jackson	.50	.20
167	Chris Webber	.75	.30
168	Darius Songaila	.20	.08
169	Doug Christie	.50	.20
170	Manu Ginobili	.75	.30
171	Brent Barry	.50	.20
172	Tony Parker	.75	.30
173	Malik Rose	.20	.08
174	Tim Duncan	1.50	.60
175	Radoslav Nesterovic	.50	.20
176	Bruce Bowen	.20	.08
177	Rashard Lewis	.75	.30
178	Vladimir Radmanovic	.20	.08
179	Ray Allen	.75	.30
180	Antonio Daniels	.20	.08
181	Ronald Murray	.20	.08
182	Luke Ridnour	.50	.20
183	Vince Carter	2.00	.75
184	Donyell Marshall	.75	.30
185	Chris Bosh	.75	.30
186	Morris Peterson	.50	.20
187	Jalen Rose	.75	.30
188	Rafer Alston	.50	.20
189	Carlos Arroyo	1.00	.40
190	Matt Harpring	.75	.30
191	Andrei Kirilenko	.75	.30
192	Carlos Boozer	.75	.30
193	Gordan Giricek	.50	.20
194	Mehmet Okur	.20	.08
195	Antawn Jamison	.75	.30
196	Larry Hughes	.50	.20
197	Gilbert Arenas	.75	.30
198	Kwame Brown	.50	.20
199	Jarvis Hayes	.50	.20
200	Juan Dixon	.50	.20
201	Rafael Araujo RC	3.00	1.25
202	Luke Jackson RC	3.00	1.25
203	Andris Biedrins RC	5.00	2.00
204	Robert Swift RC	3.00	1.25
205	Kris Humphries RC	3.00	1.25
206	Al Jefferson RC	8.00	3.00
207	Kirk Snyder RC	3.00	1.25
208	J.R. Smith RC	8.00	3.00
209	Dorell Wright RC	5.00	2.00
210	Jameer Nelson RC	6.00	2.50
211	Pavel Podkolzine RC	3.00	1.25
212	Viktor Khryapa RC	3.00	1.25
213	Sergei Monia RC	3.00	1.25
214	Delonte West RC	6.00	2.50
215	Tony Allen RC	4.00	1.50
216	Kevin Martin RC	5.00	2.00
217	Sasha Vujacic RC	3.00	1.25
218	Beno Udrih RC	5.00	2.00
219	David Harrison RC	3.00	1.25
220	Chris Duhon RC	5.00	2.00
221	Josh Smith SP RC	8.00	3.00
222	Sebastian Telfair SP RC	4.00	1.50
223	Andre Iguodala SP RC	10.00	4.00
224	Dwight Howard SP RC	12.00	5.00
225	Emeka Okafor SP RC	15.00	6.00
226	Ben Gordon SP RC	15.00	6.00
227	Shaun Livingston SP RC	6.00	2.50
228	Devin Harris SP RC	6.00	2.50
229	Josh Childress SP RC	5.00	2.00
230	Luol Deng SP RC	8.00	3.00

2004-05 Upper Deck Immaculate Glossy

#	Player
1	Antoine Walker
2	Boris Diaw
3	Al Harrington
4	Tony Delk
5	Jason Collier

- ❑ 6 Chris Crawford
- ❑ 7 Ricky Davis
- ❑ 8 Paul Pierce
- ❑ 9 Jiri Welsch
- ❑ 10 Gary Payton
- ❑ 11 Rick Fox
- ❑ 12 Mark Blount
- ❑ 13 Adrian Griffin
- ❑ 14 Tyson Chandler
- ❑ 15 Eddy Curry
- ❑ 16 Kirk Hinrich
- ❑ 17 Scottie Pippen
- ❑ 18 Jannero Pargo
- ❑ 19 Antonio Davis
- ❑ 20 Gerald Wallace
- ❑ 21 Eddie House
- ❑ 22 Steve Smith
- ❑ 23 Brandon Hunter
- ❑ 24 Theron Smith
- ❑ 25 Jahidi White
- ❑ 26 LeBron James
- ❑ 27 DeSagana Diop
- ❑ 28 Zydrunas Ilgauskas
- ❑ 29 Dajuan Wagner
- ❑ 30 Jeff McInnis
- ❑ 31 Eric Snow
- ❑ 32 Dirk Nowitzki
- ❑ 33 Jason Terry
- ❑ 34 Michael Finley
- ❑ 35 Jerry Stackhouse
- ❑ 36 Erick Dampier
- ❑ 37 Josh Howard
- ❑ 38 Marquis Daniels
- ❑ 39 Carmelo Anthony
- ❑ 40 Nene
- ❑ 41 Andre Miller
- ❑ 42 Earl Boykins
- ❑ 43 Marcus Camby
- ❑ 44 Voshon Lenard
- ❑ 45 Kenyon Martin
- ❑ 46 Richard Hamilton
- ❑ 47 Chauncey Billups
- ❑ 48 Rasheed Wallace
- ❑ 49 Tayshaun Prince
- ❑ 50 Ben Wallace
- ❑ 51 Antonio McDyess
- ❑ 52 Carlos Delfino
- ❑ 53 Jason Richardson
- ❑ 54 Dale Davis
- ❑ 55 Adonal Foyle
- ❑ 56 Mickael Pietrus
- ❑ 57 Mike Dunleavy
- ❑ 58 Speedy Claxton
- ❑ 59 Derek Fisher
- ❑ 60 Yao Ming
- ❑ 61 Jim Jackson
- ❑ 62 Tracy McGrady
- ❑ 63 Maurice Taylor
- ❑ 64 Juwan Howard
- ❑ 65 Tyronn Lue
- ❑ 66 Dikembe Mutombo
- ❑ 67 Reggie Miller
- ❑ 68 Stephen Jackson
- ❑ 69 Jermaine O'Neal
- ❑ 70 Jamaal Tinsley
- ❑ 71 Ron Artest
- ❑ 72 Fred Jones
- ❑ 73 Jonathan Bender
- ❑ 74 Kerry Kittles
- ❑ 75 Chris Kaman
- ❑ 76 Elton Brand
- ❑ 77 Marko Jaric
- ❑ 78 Corey Maggette
- ❑ 79 Bobby Simmons
- ❑ 80 Chris Wilcox
- ❑ 81 Lamar Odom
- ❑ 82 Karl Malone
- ❑ 83 Kobe Bryant
- ❑ 84 Kareem Rush
- ❑ 85 Caron Butler
- ❑ 86 Devean George
- ❑ 87 Vlade Divac
- ❑ 88 Pau Gasol
- ❑ 89 Bonzi Wells
- ❑ 90 Mike Miller
- ❑ 91 Jason Williams

- ❑ 92 Shane Battier
- ❑ 93 James Posey
- ❑ 94 Stromile Swift
- ❑ 95 Shaquille O'Neal
- ❑ 96 Dwyane Wade
- ❑ 97 Eddie Jones
- ❑ 98 Wang Zhizhi
- ❑ 99 Rasual Butler
- ❑ 100 Malik Allen
- ❑ 101 Udonis Haslem
- ❑ 102 Michael Redd
- ❑ 103 T.J. Ford
- ❑ 104 Keith Van Horn
- ❑ 105 Toni Kukoc
- ❑ 106 Desmond Mason
- ❑ 107 Mike James
- ❑ 108 Joe Smith
- ❑ 109 Kevin Garnett
- ❑ 110 Michael Olowokandi
- ❑ 111 Sam Cassell
- ❑ 112 Troy Hudson
- ❑ 113 Latrell Sprewell
- ❑ 114 Fred Hoiberg
- ❑ 115 Wally Szczerbiak
- ❑ 116 Richard Jefferson
- ❑ 117 Alonzo Mourning
- ❑ 118 Jason Kidd
- ❑ 119 Jacque Vaughn
- ❑ 120 Jason Collins
- ❑ 121 Aaron Williams
- ❑ 122 Zoran Planinic
- ❑ 123 Jamaal Magloire
- ❑ 124 P.J. Brown
- ❑ 125 Baron Davis
- ❑ 126 Darrell Armstrong
- ❑ 127 Jamal Mashburn
- ❑ 128 Rodney Rogers
- ❑ 129 David Wesley
- ❑ 130 Allan Houston
- ❑ 131 Jamal Crawford
- ❑ 132 Stephon Marbury
- ❑ 133 Tim Thomas
- ❑ 134 Anfernee Hardaway
- ❑ 135 Kurt Thomas
- ❑ 136 Mike Sweetney
- ❑ 137 Tony Battie
- ❑ 138 DeShawn Stevenson
- ❑ 139 Steve Francis
- ❑ 140 Cuttino Mobley
- ❑ 141 Hedo Turkoglu
- ❑ 142 Keith Bogans
- ❑ 143 Samuel Dalembert
- ❑ 144 Kenny Thomas
- ❑ 145 Allen Iverson
- ❑ 146 Aaron McKie
- ❑ 147 Glenn Robinson
- ❑ 148 Willie Green
- ❑ 149 Corliss Williamson
- ❑ 150 Shawn Marion
- ❑ 151 Leandro Barbosa
- ❑ 152 Amare Stoudemire
- ❑ 153 Quentin Richardson
- ❑ 154 Joe Johnson
- ❑ 155 Steve Nash
- ❑ 156 Damon Stoudamire
- ❑ 157 Theo Ratliff
- ❑ 158 Shareef Abdur-Rahim
- ❑ 159 Derek Anderson
- ❑ 160 Zach Randolph
- ❑ 161 Nick Van Exel
- ❑ 162 Darius Miles
- ❑ 163 Mike Bibby
- ❑ 164 Brad Miller
- ❑ 165 Peja Stojakovic
- ❑ 166 Bobby Jackson
- ❑ 167 Chris Webber
- ❑ 168 Darius Songaila
- ❑ 169 Doug Christie
- ❑ 170 Manu Ginobili
- ❑ 171 Brent Barry
- ❑ 172 Tony Parker
- ❑ 173 Malik Rose
- ❑ 174 Tim Duncan
- ❑ 175 Radoslav Nesterovic
- ❑ 176 Bruce Bowen
- ❑ 177 Rashard Lewis

- ❑ 178 Vladimir Radmanovic
- ❑ 179 Ray Allen
- ❑ 180 Antonio Daniels
- ❑ 181 Ronald Murray
- ❑ 182 Luke Ridnour
- ❑ 183 Vince Carter
- ❑ 184 Donyell Marshall
- ❑ 185 Chris Bosh
- ❑ 186 Morris Peterson
- ❑ 187 Jalen Rose
- ❑ 188 Rafer Alston
- ❑ 189 Carlos Arroyo
- ❑ 190 Matt Harpring
- ❑ 191 Andrei Kirilenko
- ❑ 192 Carlos Boozer
- ❑ 193 Gordan Giricek
- ❑ 194 Mehmet Okur
- ❑ 195 Antawn Jamison
- ❑ 196 Larry Hughes
- ❑ 197 Gilbert Arenas
- ❑ 198 Kwame Brown
- ❑ 199 Jarvis Hayes
- ❑ 200 Juan Dixon
- ❑ 201 Rafael Araujo
- ❑ 202 Luke Jackson
- ❑ 203 Andris Biedrins
- ❑ 204 Robert Swift
- ❑ 205 Kris Humphries
- ❑ 206 Al Jefferson
- ❑ 207 Kirk Snyder
- ❑ 208 J.R. Smith
- ❑ 209 Dorell Wright
- ❑ 210 Jameer Nelson
- ❑ 211 Pavel Podkolzine
- ❑ 212 Viktor Khryapa
- ❑ 213 Sergei Monia
- ❑ 214 Delonte West
- ❑ 215 Tony Allen
- ❑ 216 Kevin Martin
- ❑ 217 Sasha Vujacic
- ❑ 218 Beno Udrih
- ❑ 219 David Harrison
- ❑ 220 Chris Duhon
- ❑ 221 Josh Smith
- ❑ 222 Sebastian Telfair
- ❑ 223 Andre Iguodala
- ❑ 224 Dwight Howard
- ❑ 225 Emeka Okafor
- ❑ 226 Ben Gordon
- ❑ 227 Shaun Livingston
- ❑ 228 Devin Harris
- ❑ 229 Josh Childress
- ❑ 230 Luol Deng

2005-06 Upper Deck

❑ COMP.SET w/o SP's (200)	40.00	20.00
❑ COMMON CARD (1-200)	.20	.08
❑ COMMON ROOKIE (201-220)	3.00	1.25
❑ 1 Josh Childress	.50	.20
❑ 2 Josh Smith	.75	.30
❑ 3 Al Harrington	.50	.20
❑ 4 Tyronn Lue	.20	.08
❑ 5 Boris Diaw	.20	.08
❑ 6 Tony Delk	.20	.08
❑ 7 Paul Pierce	.75	.30
❑ 8 Antoine Walker	.75	.30
❑ 9 Gary Payton	.75	.30
❑ 10 Al Jefferson	.75	.30

#	Player		
❑ 11	Tony Allen	.50	.20
❑ 12	Ricky Davis	.75	.30
❑ 13	Delonte West	.75	.30
❑ 14	Emeka Okafor	1.25	.50
❑ 15	Primoz Brezec	.20	.08
❑ 16	Kareem Rush	.20	.08
❑ 17	Gerald Wallace	.50	.20
❑ 18	Brevin Knight	.20	.08
❑ 19	Jason Kapono	.20	.08
❑ 20	Kirk Hinrich	.75	.30
❑ 21	Ben Gordon	1.50	.60
❑ 22	Eddy Curry	.50	.20
❑ 23	Michael Jordan	5.00	2.00
❑ 24	Andres Nocioni	.50	.20
❑ 25	Chris Duhon	.50	.20
❑ 26	Luol Deng	.75	.30
❑ 27	LeBron James	5.00	2.00
❑ 28	Zydrunas Ilgauskas	.50	.20
❑ 30	Drew Gooden	.50	.20
❑ 30	Jeff McInnis	.20	.08
❑ 31	Dajuan Wagner	.20	.08
❑ 32	Larry Hughes	.50	.20
❑ 33	Robert Traylor	.20	.08
❑ 34	Dirk Nowitzki	1.25	.50
❑ 35	Michael Finley	.75	.30
❑ 36	Jerry Stackhouse	.75	.30
❑ 37	Josh Howard	.50	.20
❑ 38	Marquis Daniels	.50	.20
❑ 39	Devin Harris	.75	.30
❑ 40	Jason Terry	.75	.30
❑ 41	Carmelo Anthony	1.50	.60
❑ 42	Kenyon Martin	.75	.30
❑ 43	Andre Miller	.50	.20
❑ 44	Earl Boykins	.50	.20
❑ 45	Nene	.50	.20
❑ 46	Marcus Camby	.20	.08
❑ 47	Ben Wallace	.75	.30
❑ 48	Richard Hamilton	.50	.20
❑ 49	Chauncey Billups	.75	.30
❑ 50	Rasheed Wallace	.75	.30
❑ 51	Tayshaun Prince	.75	.30
❑ 52	Carlos Arroyo	1.25	.50
❑ 53	Antonio McDyess	.50	.20
❑ 54	Jason Richardson	.75	.30
❑ 55	Baron Davis	.75	.30
❑ 56	Troy Murphy	.75	.30
❑ 57	Mickael Pietrus	.20	.08
❑ 58	Derek Fisher	.75	.30
❑ 59	Mike Dunleavy	.50	.20
❑ 60	Yao Ming	2.00	.75
❑ 61	Tracy McGrady	2.00	.75
❑ 62	David Wesley	.20	.08
❑ 63	Bob Sura	.50	.20
❑ 64	Mike James	.20	.08
❑ 65	Jon Barry	.20	.08
❑ 66	Jermaine O'Neal	.75	.30
❑ 67	Ron Artest	.50	.20
❑ 68	Stephen Jackson	.50	.20
❑ 69	Jamaal Tinsley	.50	.20
❑ 70	Dale Davis	.20	.08
❑ 71	Anthony Johnson	.20	.08
❑ 72	Elton Brand	.75	.30
❑ 73	Corey Maggette	.50	.20
❑ 74	Bobby Simmons	.20	.08
❑ 75	Marko Jaric	.20	.08
❑ 76	Shaun Livingston	.75	.30
❑ 77	Chris Kaman	.50	.20
❑ 78	Chris Wilcox	.20	.08
❑ 79	Kobe Bryant	3.00	1.25
❑ 80	Caron Butler	.50	.20
❑ 81	Lamar Odom	.75	.30
❑ 82	Chucky Atkins	.20	.08
❑ 83	Brian Cook	.20	.08
❑ 84	Devean George	.20	.08
❑ 85	Sasha Vujacic	.20	.08
❑ 86	Pau Gasol	.75	.30
❑ 87	Mike Miller	.75	.30
❑ 88	Jason Williams	.50	.20
❑ 89	Shane Battier	.75	.30
❑ 90	Bonzi Wells	.20	.08
❑ 91	James Posey	.20	.08
❑ 92	Stromile Swift	.50	.20
❑ 93	Shaquille O'Neal	2.00	.75
❑ 94	Dwyane Wade	2.50	1.00
❑ 95	Eddie Jones	.50	.20
❑ 96	Udonis Haslem	.75	.30
❑ 97	Damon Jones	.50	.20
❑ 98	Alonzo Mourning	.50	.20
❑ 99	Keyon Dooling	.20	.08
❑ 100	Michael Redd	.75	.30
❑ 101	Desmond Mason	.50	.20
❑ 102	Maurice Williams	.20	.08
❑ 103	Joe Smith	.20	.08
❑ 104	Toni Kukoc	.50	.20
❑ 105	Dan Gadzuric	.20	.08
❑ 106	T.J. Ford	.50	.20
❑ 107	Kevin Garnett	1.50	.60
❑ 108	Sam Cassell	.75	.30
❑ 109	Latrell Sprewell	.75	.30
❑ 110	Wally Szczerbiak	.50	.20
❑ 111	Troy Hudson	.20	.08
❑ 112	Eddie Griffin	.20	.08
❑ 113	Jason Kidd	1.25	.50
❑ 114	Richard Jefferson	.50	.20
❑ 115	Vince Carter	2.00	.75
❑ 116	Nenad Krstic	.50	.20
❑ 117	Scott Padgett	.20	.08
❑ 118	Jason Collins	.20	.08
❑ 119	Jamaal Magloire	.20	.08
❑ 120	J.R. Smith	.50	.20
❑ 121	Speedy Claxton	.20	.08
❑ 122	Lee Nailon	.20	.08
❑ 123	P.J. Brown	.20	.08
❑ 124	Chris Andersen	.20	.08
❑ 125	Stephon Marbury	.75	.30
❑ 126	Jamal Crawford	.50	.20
❑ 127	Allan Houston	.50	.20
❑ 128	Trevor Ariza	.50	.20
❑ 129	Quentin Richardson	.50	.20
❑ 130	Tim Thomas	.20	.08
❑ 131	Michael Sweetney	.20	.08
❑ 132	Dwight Howard	1.00	.40
❑ 133	Steve Francis	.75	.30
❑ 134	Grant Hill	.75	.30
❑ 135	Jameer Nelson	.50	.20
❑ 136	Hedo Turkoglu	.50	.20
❑ 137	Doug Christie	.50	.20
❑ 138	DeShawn Stevenson	.20	.08
❑ 139	Allen Iverson	1.50	.60
❑ 140	Chris Webber	.75	.30
❑ 141	Andre Iguodala	.50	.20
❑ 142	Samuel Dalembert	.50	.20
❑ 143	Kyle Korver	.75	.30
❑ 144	Willie Green	.20	.08
❑ 145	Marc Jackson	.20	.08
❑ 146	Steve Nash	.75	.30
❑ 147	Amare Stoudemire	1.50	.60
❑ 148	Joe Johnson	.50	.20
❑ 149	Shawn Marion	.75	.30
❑ 150	Kurt Thomas	.50	.20
❑ 151	Jim Jackson	.20	.08
❑ 152	Leandro Barbosa	.20	.08
❑ 153	Damon Stoudamire	.50	.20
❑ 154	Shareef Abdur-Rahim	.75	.30
❑ 155	Zach Randolph	.75	.30
❑ 156	Darius Miles	.75	.30
❑ 157	Sebastian Telfair	.50	.20
❑ 158	Theo Ratliff	.50	.20
❑ 159	Nick Van Exel	.75	.30
❑ 160	Peja Stojakovic	.75	.30
❑ 161	Mike Bibby	.75	.30
❑ 162	Brad Miller	.75	.30
❑ 163	Cuttino Mobley	.50	.20
❑ 164	Bobby Jackson	.20	.08
❑ 165	Kenny Thomas	.20	.08
❑ 166	Corliss Williamson	.20	.08
❑ 167	Tim Duncan	1.50	.60
❑ 168	Tony Parker	.75	.30
❑ 169	Manu Ginobili	.75	.30
❑ 170	Robert Horry	.50	.20
❑ 171	Beno Udrih	.50	.20
❑ 172	Nazr Mohammed	.20	.08
❑ 173	Brent Barry	.50	.20
❑ 174	Ray Allen	.75	.30
❑ 175	Rashard Lewis	.75	.30
❑ 176	Ronald Murray	.20	.08
❑ 177	Luke Ridnour	.50	.20
❑ 178	Vladimir Radmanovic	.20	.08
❑ 179	Antonio Daniels	.20	.08
❑ 180	Danny Fortson	.20	.08
❑ 181	Chris Bosh	.75	.30
❑ 182	Donyell Marshall	.20	.08
❑ 183	Jalen Rose	.75	.30
❑ 184	Morris Peterson	.20	.08
❑ 185	Rafer Alston	.20	.08
❑ 186	Matt Bonner	.20	.08
❑ 187	Aaron Williams	.20	.08
❑ 188	Andrei Kirilenko	.75	.30
❑ 189	Carlos Boozer	.50	.20
❑ 190	Matt Harpring	.75	.30
❑ 191	Keith McLeod	.20	.08
❑ 192	Raja Bell	.20	.08
❑ 193	Raul Lopez	.20	.08
❑ 194	Gordan Giricek	.20	.08
❑ 195	Gilbert Arenas	.75	.30
❑ 196	Antawn Jamison	.75	.30
❑ 197	Jarvis Hayes	.50	.20
❑ 198	Brendan Haywood	.20	.08
❑ 199	Juan Dixon	.20	.08
❑ 200	Etan Thomas	.20	.08
❑ 201	Daniel Ewing RC	3.00	1.25
❑ 202	Nate Robinson RC	5.00	2.00
❑ 203	C.J. Miles RC	3.00	1.25
❑ 204	Salim Stoudamire RC	5.00	2.00
❑ 205	Francisco Garcia RC	4.00	1.50
❑ 206	Julius Hodge RC	4.00	1.50
❑ 207	Andrew Bynum RC	12.00	5.00
❑ 208	Joey Graham RC	3.00	1.25
❑ 209	Johan Petro RC	3.00	1.25
❑ 210	Luther Head RC	5.00	2.00
❑ 211	Channing Frye RC	5.00	2.00
❑ 212	Sean May RC	3.00	1.25
❑ 213	Wayne Simien RC	3.00	1.25
❑ 214	Antoine Wright RC	3.00	1.25
❑ 215	Ike Diogu RC	4.00	1.50
❑ 216	Jarrett Jack RC	3.00	1.25
❑ 217	Jason Maxiell RC	3.00	1.25
❑ 218	David Lee RC	5.00	2.00
❑ 219	Travis Diener RC	3.00	1.25
❑ 220	Danny Granger RC	5.00	2.00
❑ 221	Charlie Villanueva SP RC	8.00	3.00
❑ 222	Hakim Warrick SP RC	12.00	5.00
❑ 223	Rashad McCants SP RC	10.00	4.00
❑ 224	Raymond Felton SP RC	10.00	4.00
❑ 225	Martell Webster SP RC	3.00	1.25
❑ 226	Gerald Green SP RC	15.00	6.00
❑ 227	Deron Williams SP RC	15.00	6.00
❑ 228	Andrew Bogut SP RC	8.00	3.00
❑ 229	Marvin Williams SP RC	12.00	5.00
❑ 230	Chris Paul SP RC	25.00	10.00

2006-07 Upper Deck

#	Player		
❑ 1	Josh Childress	.50	.20
❑ 2	Al Harrington	.25	.10
❑ 3	Joe Johnson	.50	.20
❑ 4	Josh Smith	.75	.30
❑ 5	Salim Stoudamire	.50	.20
❑ 6	Marvin Williams	1.00	.40
❑ 7	Tony Allen	.25	.10
❑ 8	Dan Dickau	.25	.10
❑ 9	Al Jefferson	.75	.30
❑ 10	Raef LaFrentz	.25	.10
❑ 11	Michael Olowokandi	.25	.10
❑ 12	Paul Pierce	.75	.30
❑ 13	Wally Szczerbiak	.50	.20
❑ 14	Alan Anderson	.25	.10
❑ 15	Raymond Felton	1.00	.40
❑ 16	Othella Harrington	.25	.10
❑ 17	Sean May	.50	.20
❑ 18	Emeka Okafor	.75	.30

#	Player		
❏ 19	Primoz Brezec	.25	.10
❏ 20	Gerald Wallace	.75	.30
❏ 21	Tyson Chandler	.75	.30
❏ 22	Michael Jordan	5.00	2.00
❏ 23	Luol Deng	.75	.30
❏ 24	Chris Duhon	.25	.10
❏ 25	Ben Gordon	1.50	.60
❏ 26	Kirk Hinrich	.75	.30
❏ 27	Mike Sweetney	.25	.10
❏ 28	Drew Gooden	.50	.20
❏ 29	Larry Hughes	.50	.20
❏ 30	Zydrunas Ilgauskas	.50	.20
❏ 31	LeBron James	·5.00	2.00
❏ 32	Damon Jones	.25	.10
❏ 33	Donyell Marshall	.25	.10
❏ 34	Anderson Varejao	.50	.20
❏ 35	Erick Dampier	.25	.10
❏ 36	Marquis Daniels	.50	.20
❏ 37	Devin Harris	.75	.30
❏ 38	Josh Howard	.50	.20
❏ 39	Dirk Nowitzki	1.25	.50
❏ 40	Jerry Stackhouse	.75	.30
❏ 41	Jason Terry	.75	.30
❏ 42	Carmelo Anthony	1.50	.60
❏ 43	Earl Boykins	.25	.10
❏ 44	Marcus Camby	.25	.10
❏ 45	Kenyon Martin	.75	.30
❏ 46	Andre Miller	.50	.20
❏ 47	Eduardo Najera	.25	.10
❏ 48	Nene	.25	.10
❏ 49	Chauncey Billups	.75	.30
❏ 50	Richard Hamilton	.50	.20
❏ 51	Lindsey Hunter	.25	.10
❏ 52	Antonio McDyess	.25	.10
❏ 53	Tayshaun Prince	.75	.30
❏ 54	Ben Wallace	.75	.30
❏ 55	Rasheed Wallace	.75	.30
❏ 56	Baron Davis	.75	.30
❏ 57	Ike Diogu	.50	.20
❏ 58	Mike Dunleavy	.50	.20
❏ 59	Derek Fisher	.50	.20
❏ 60	Troy Murphy	.50	.20
❏ 61	Mickael Pietrus	.50	.20
❏ 62	Jason Richardson	.75	.30
❏ 63	Rafer Alston	.25	.10
❏ 64	Luther Head	.50	.20
❏ 65	Juwan Howard	.50	.20
❏ 66	Tracy McGrady	2.00	.75
❏ 67	Dikembe Mutombo	.50	.20
❏ 68	Stromile Swift	.50	.20
❏ 69	Yao Ming	2.00	.75
❏ 70	Austin Croshere	.25	.10
❏ 71	Stephen Jackson	.50	.20
❏ 72	Sarunas Jasikevicius	.50	.20
❏ 73	Jermaine O'Neal	.75	.30
❏ 74	Peja Stojakovic	.75	.30
❏ 75	Jamaal Tinsley	.50	.20
❏ 76	Elton Brand	.75	.30
❏ 77	Sam Cassell	.75	.30
❏ 78	Chris Kaman	.25	.10
❏ 79	Shaun Livingston	.60	.25
❏ 80	Corey Maggette	.50	.20
❏ 81	Cuttino Mobley	.50	.20
❏ 82	Vladimir Radmanovic	.25	.10
❏ 83	Kwame Brown	.50	.20
❏ 84	Kobe Bryant	3.00	1.25
❏ 85	Devean George	.50	.20
❏ 86	Lamar Odom	.75	.30
❏ 87	Ronny Turiaf	.25	.10
❏ 88	Sasha Vujacic	.25	.10
❏ 89	Luke Walton	.25	.10
❏ 90	Shane Battier	.75	.30
❏ 91	Pau Gasol	.75	.30
❏ 92	Bobby Jackson	.25	.10
❏ 93	Eddie Jones	.25	.10
❏ 94	Mike Miller	.75	.30
❏ 95	Damon Stoudamire	.25	.10
❏ 96	Hakim Warrick	.50	.20
❏ 97	Alonzo Mourning	.50	.20
❏ 98	Shaquille O'Neal	2.00	.75
❏ 99	Gary Payton	.75	.30
❏ 100	Wayne Simien	.50	.20
❏ 101	Dwyane Wade	2.50	1.00
❏ 102	Antoine Walker	.75	.30
❏ 103	Jason Williams	.50	.20
❏ 104	Andrew Bogut	1.00	.40
❏ 105	T.J. Ford	.50	.20
❏ 106	Jamaal Magloire	.25	.10
❏ 107	Michael Redd	.75	.30
❏ 108	Bobby Simmons	.25	.10
❏ 109	Maurice Williams	.25	.10
❏ 110	Ricky Davis	.75	.30
❏ 111	Kevin Garnett	1.50	.60
❏ 112	Eddie Griffin	.25	.10
❏ 113	Trenton Hassell	.25	.10
❏ 114	Troy Hudson	.25	.10
❏ 115	Rashad McCants	1.00	.40
❏ 116	Vince Carter	2.00	.75
❏ 117	Jason Collins	.25	.10
❏ 118	Richard Jefferson	.50	.20
❏ 119	Jason Kidd	1.25	.50
❏ 120	Nenad Krstic	.25	.10
❏ 121	Jeff McInnis	.25	.10
❏ 122	Antoine Wright	.25	.10
❏ 123	P.J. Brown	.25	.10
❏ 124	Speedy Claxton	.25	.10
❏ 125	Desmond Mason	.25	.10
❏ 126	Chris Paul	2.00	.75
❏ 127	J.R. Smith	.50	.20
❏ 128	Kirk Snyder	.25	.10
❏ 129	David West	.25	.10
❏ 130	Jamal Crawford	.25	.10
❏ 131	Steve Francis	.75	.30
❏ 132	Channing Frye	.50	.20
❏ 133	Stephon Marbury	.75	.30
❏ 134	Quentin Richardson	.50	.20
❏ 135	Nate Robinson	.75	.30
❏ 136	Maurice Taylor	.25	.10
❏ 137	Carlos Arroyo	1.25	.50
❏ 138	Tony Battie	.25	.10
❏ 139	Keyon Dooling	.25	.10
❏ 140	Grant Hill	.75	.30
❏ 141	Dwight Howard	1.00	.40
❏ 142	Darko Milicic	.75	.30
❏ 143	Jameer Nelson	.50	.20
❏ 144	Samuel Dalembert	.25	.10
❏ 145	Steven Hunter	.25	.10
❏ 146	Andre Iguodala	.75	.30
❏ 147	Allen Iverson	1.50	.60
❏ 148	Kyle Korver	.75	.30
❏ 149	Shavlik Randolph	.25	.10
❏ 150	Chris Webber	.75	.30
❏ 151	Raja Bell	.25	.10
❏ 152	Boris Diaw	.50	.20
❏ 153	Shawn Marion	.75	.30
❏ 154	Steve Nash	.75	.30
❏ 155	Amare Stoudemire	1.50	.60
❏ 156	Kurt Thomas	.25	.10
❏ 157	Tim Thomas	.25	.10
❏ 158	Steve Blake	.25	.10
❏ 159	Juan Dixon	.25	.10
❏ 160	Zach Randolph	.75	.30
❏ 161	Ha Seung-Jin	.25	.10
❏ 162	Sebastian Telfair	.50	.20
❏ 163	Martell Webster	.50	.20
❏ 164	Shareef Abdur-Rahim	.75	.30
❏ 165	Ron Artest	.75	.30
❏ 166	Mike Bibby	.75	.30
❏ 167	Brad Miller	.75	.30
❏ 168	Kenny Thomas	.25	.10
❏ 169	Bonzi Wells	.50	.20
❏ 170	Bruce Bowen	.25	.10
❏ 171	Tim Duncan	1.50	.60
❏ 172	Michael Finley	.75	.30
❏ 173	Manu Ginobili	.75	.30
❏ 174	Nazr Mohammed	.25	.10
❏ 175	Tony Parker	.75	.30
❏ 176	Ray Allen	.75	.30
❏ 177	Danny Fortson	.25	.10
❏ 178	Rashard Lewis	.75	.30
❏ 179	Luke Ridnour	.50	.20
❏ 180	Earl Watson	.25	.10
❏ 181	Chris Wilcox	.25	.10
❏ 182	Rafael Araujo	.25	.10
❏ 183	Chris Bosh	.75	.30
❏ 184	Joey Graham	.50	.20
❏ 185	Mike James	.25	.10
❏ 186	Morris Peterson	.50	.20
❏ 187	Charlie Villanueva	.75	.30
❏ 188	Carlos Boozer	.50	.20
❏ 189	Matt Harpring	.50	.20
❏ 190	Kris Humphries	.25	.10
❏ 191	Andrei Kirilenko	.75	.30
❏ 192	C.J. Miles	.25	.10
❏ 193	Chris Taft	.25	.10
❏ 194	Deron Williams	.75	.30
❏ 195	Gilbert Arenas	.75	.30
❏ 196	Andray Blatche	.25	.10
❏ 197	Caron Butler	.50	.20
❏ 198	Antonio Daniels	.25	.10
❏ 199	Brendan Haywood	.25	.10
❏ 200	Antawn Jamison	.75	.30
❏ 201	Andrea Bargnani RC	6.00	2.50
❏ 202	LaMarcus Aldridge RC	5.00	2.00
❏ 203	Adam Morrison RC	6.00	2.50
❏ 204	Tyrus Thomas RC	4.00	1.50
❏ 205	Shelden Williams RC	4.00	1.50
❏ 206	Brandon Roy RC	6.00	2.50
❏ 207	Randy Foye RC	6.00	2.50
❏ 208	Rudy Gay RC	5.00	2.00
❏ 209	Patrick O'Bryant RC	3.00	1.25
❏ 210	Saer Sene RC	2.50	1.00
❏ 211	J.J. Redick RC	5.00	2.00
❏ 212	Hilton Armstrong RC	3.00	1.25
❏ 213	Thabo Sefolosha RC	3.00	1.25
❏ 214	Ronnie Brewer RC	5.00	2.00
❏ 215	Cedric Simmons RC	2.50	1.00
❏ 216	Rodney Carney RC	3.00	1.25
❏ 217	Shawne Williams RC	3.00	1.25
❏ 218	Quincy Douby RC	2.50	1.00
❏ 219	Renaldo Balkman RC	2.50	1.00
❏ 220	Rajon Rondo RC	5.00	2.00
❏ 221	Marcus Williams RC	3.00	1.25
❏ 222	Josh Boone RC	2.50	1.00
❏ 223	Kyle Lowry RC	4.00	1.50
❏ 224	Shannon Brown RC	4.00	1.50
❏ 225	Jordan Farmar RC	4.00	1.50
❏ 226	Maurice Ager RC	3.00	1.25
❏ 227	Mardy Collins RC	2.50	1.00
❏ 228	Jorge Garbajosa RC	4.00	1.50
❏ 229	James White RC	2.50	1.00
❏ 230	Steve Novak RC	2.50	1.00
❏ 231	Solomon Jones RC	2.50	1.00
❏ 232	Paul Davis RC	2.50	1.00
❏ 233	P.J. Tucker RC	2.50	1.00
❏ 234	Craig Smith RC	2.50	1.00
❏ 235	Bobby Jones RC	2.50	1.00
❏ 236	David Noel RC	2.50	1.00
❏ 237	Denham Brown RC	2.50	1.00
❏ 238	James Augustine RC	2.50	1.00
❏ 239	Daniel Gibson RC	6.00	2.50
❏ 240	Alexander Johnson RC	2.50	1.00

2004 Upper Deck All-Star Game

LeBron James

❏	COMPLETE SET (10)	150.00	75.00
❏ BO	Chris Bosh	8.00	3.00
❏ LJ1	LeBron James	30.00	12.50
❏ LJ2	LeBron James	30.00	12.50
❏ LJ3	LeBron James	30.00	12.50
❏ LJ4	LeBron James	30.00	12.50
❏ LJ5	LeBron James	30.00	12.50
❏ CA	Carmelo Anthony	10.00	4.00
❏ GP	Gary Payton	8.00	3.00
❏ KB	Kobe Bryant	12.00	5.00
❏ MJ	Michael Jordan	15.00	6.00
❏ SZMJ	M.Jordan S.Zone Sample	12.00	5.00

2004-05 Upper Deck All-Star Lineup

☐ COMMON CARD (1-90)	.20	.08
☐ COMMON ROOKIE (91-132)	2.00	.75
☐ 1 Jason Terry	.60	.25
☐ 2 Al Harrington	.40	.15
☐ 3 Boris Diaw	.20	.08
☐ 4 Paul Pierce	.60	.25
☐ 5 Ricky Davis	.60	.25
☐ 6 Jiri Welsch	.40	.15
☐ 7 Marcus Fizer	.40	.15
☐ 8 Gerald Wallace	.40	.15
☐ 9 Jahidi White	.20	.08
☐ 10 Eddy Curry	.40	.15
☐ 11 Kirk Hinrich	.60	.25
☐ 12 Jamal Crawford	.40	.15
☐ 13 LeBron James	4.00	1.50
☐ 14 Dajuan Wagner	.40	.15
☐ 15 Jeff McInnis	.20	.08
☐ 16 Dirk Nowitzki	1.00	.40
☐ 17 Antoine Walker	.60	.25
☐ 18 Michael Finley	.60	.25
☐ 19 Carmelo Anthony	1.00	.40
☐ 20 Andre Miller	.40	.15
☐ 21 Kenyon Martin	.60	.25
☐ 22 Chauncey Billups	.40	.15
☐ 23 Rasheed Wallace	.60	.25
☐ 24 Ben Wallace	.60	.25
☐ 25 Erick Dampier	.40	.15
☐ 26 Jason Richardson	.60	.25
☐ 27 Mike Dunleavy	.40	.15
☐ 28 Yao Ming	1.50	.60
☐ 29 Tracy McGrady	1.50	.60
☐ 30 Juwan Howard	.40	.15
☐ 31 Jermaine O'Neal	.60	.25
☐ 32 Reggie Miller	.60	.25
☐ 33 Ron Artest	.40	.15
☐ 34 Elton Brand	.60	.25
☐ 35 Corey Maggette	.40	.15
☐ 36 Quentin Richardson	.40	.15
☐ 37 Kobe Bryant	3.00	1.25
☐ 38 Gary Payton	.60	.25
☐ 39 Lamar Odom	.60	.25
☐ 40 Pau Gasol	.60	.25
☐ 41 Jason Williams	.40	.15
☐ 42 Bonzi Wells	.40	.15
☐ 43 Shaquille O'Neal	1.50	.60
☐ 44 Dwyane Wade	1.50	.60
☐ 45 Eddie Jones	.60	.25
☐ 46 Michael Redd	.60	.25
☐ 47 Desmond Mason	.40	.15
☐ 48 T.J. Ford	.40	.15
☐ 49 Latrell Sprewell	.60	.25
☐ 50 Kevin Garnett	1.25	.50
☐ 51 Sam Cassell	.60	.25
☐ 52 Richard Jefferson	.40	.15
☐ 53 Kerry Kittles	.20	.08
☐ 54 Jason Kidd	1.00	.40
☐ 55 Jamal Mashburn	.40	.15
☐ 56 Baron Davis	.60	.25

☐ 57 Jamaal Magloire	.20	.08
☐ 58 Allan Houston	.40	.15
☐ 59 Kurt Thomas	.40	.15
☐ 60 Stephon Marbury	.60	.25
☐ 61 Cuttino Mobley	.40	.15
☐ 62 Drew Gooden	.40	.15
☐ 63 Steve Francis	.60	.25
☐ 64 Glenn Robinson	.60	.25
☐ 65 Allen Iverson	1.25	.50
☐ 66 Samuel Dalembert	.20	.08
☐ 67 Amare Stoudemire	1.25	.50
☐ 68 Steve Nash	.60	.25
☐ 69 Shawn Marion	.60	.25
☐ 70 Shareef Abdur-Rahim	.60	.25
☐ 71 Damon Stoudamire	.40	.15
☐ 72 Zach Randolph	.60	.25
☐ 73 Peja Stojakovic	.60	.25
☐ 74 Chris Webber	.60	.25
☐ 75 Mike Bibby	.60	.25
☐ 76 Tony Parker	.60	.25
☐ 77 Tim Duncan	1.25	.50
☐ 78 Manu Ginobili	.60	.25
☐ 79 Ronald Murray	.20	.08
☐ 80 Ray Allen	.60	.25
☐ 81 Rashard Lewis	.60	.25
☐ 82 Chris Bosh	.60	.25
☐ 83 Vince Carter	1.50	.60
☐ 84 Jalen Rose	.60	.25
☐ 85 Andrei Kirilenko	.60	.25
☐ 86 Carlos Boozer	.60	.25
☐ 87 Carlos Arroyo	1.00	.40
☐ 88 Gilbert Arenas	.60	.25
☐ 89 Jarvis Hayes	.40	.15
☐ 90 Antawn Jamison	.60	.25
☐ 91 Emeka Okafor RC	8.00	3.00
☐ 92 Dwight Howard RC	6.00	2.50
☐ 93 Shaun Livingston RC	4.00	1.50
☐ 94 Luol Deng RC	4.00	1.50
☐ 95 Ben Gordon RC	8.00	3.00
☐ 96 Devin Harris RC	3.00	1.25
☐ 97 Andre Iguodala RC	5.00	2.00
☐ 98 Andris Biedrins RC	4.00	1.50
☐ 99 Josh Childress RC	2.50	1.00
☐ 100 Josh Smith RC	4.00	1.50
☐ 101 Jameer Nelson RC	3.00	1.25
☐ 102 J.R. Smith RC	4.00	1.50
☐ 103 Sergei Monia RC	2.00	.75
☐ 104 Sebastian Telfair RC	2.00	.75
☐ 105 Pavel Podkolzine RC	2.00	.75
☐ 106 Luke Jackson RC	2.00	.75
☐ 107 Dorell Wright RC	3.00	1.25
☐ 108 Robert Swift RC	2.00	.75
☐ 109 Anderson Varejao RC	2.50	1.00
☐ 110 Sasha Vujacic RC	2.00	.75
☐ 111 Rafael Araujo RC	2.00	.75
☐ 112 Al Jefferson RC	5.00	2.00
☐ 113 Kris Humphries RC	2.00	.75
☐ 114 Kirk Snyder RC	2.00	.75
☐ 115 Darius Rice RC	2.00	.75
☐ 116 Beno Udrih RC	3.00	1.25
☐ 117 Viktor Khryapa RC	2.00	.75
☐ 118 David Harrison RC	2.00	.75
☐ 119 Trevor Ariza RC	2.50	1.00
☐ 120 Ha Seung-Jin RC	2.00	.75
☐ 121 Kevin Martin RC	3.00	1.25
☐ 122 Delonte West RC	4.00	1.50
☐ 123 Rickey Paulding RC	2.00	.75
☐ 124 Chris Duhon RC	3.00	1.25
☐ 125 Tony Allen RC	2.50	1.00
☐ 126 Donta Smith RC	2.00	.75
☐ 127 Andre Emmett RC	2.00	.75
☐ 128 Royal Ivey RC	2.00	.75
☐ 129 Matt Freije RC	2.00	.75
☐ 130 Romain Sato RC	2.00	.75
☐ 131 Antonio Burks RC	2.00	.75
☐ 132 Lionel Chalmers RC	2.00	.75

2005-06 Upper Deck LeBron James

☐ COMPLETE SET (45)	40.00	15.00
☐ COMMON CARD (LJ1-LJ45)	3.00	1.25

2005-06 Upper Deck Michael Jordan

☐ COMPLETE SET (45)	60.00	25.00
☐ COMMON CARD (MJ1-MJ45)	4.00	1.50

2005-06 Upper Deck Michael Jordan/LeBron James

☐ COMLETE SET (10)	40.00	15.00
☐ COMMON CARD	8.00	3.00

1999 Upper Deck Century Legends

☐ COMPLETE SET (89)	40.00	20.00
☐ COMMON CARD (1-80)	.20	.07
☐ COMMON MJ (81-90)	2.00	.75
☐ 1 Michael Jordan	4.00	1.50
☐ 2 Bill Russell	1.00	.40
☐ 3 Wilt Chamberlain	1.00	.40
☐ 4 George Mikan	1.00	.40
☐ 5 Oscar Robertson	.75	.30
☐ 6 Does not exist		
☐ 7 Larry Bird	2.50	1.00
☐ 8 Karl Malone	.60	.25
☐ 9 Elgin Baylor	.60	.25

❏ 10	Kareem Abdul-Jabbar	1.00 .40
❏ 11	Jerry West	.75 .30
❏ 12	Bob Cousy	.60 .25
❏ 13	Julius Erving	1.00 .40
❏ 14	Hakeem Olajuwon	.60 .25
❏ 15	John Havlicek	.75 .30
❏ 16	John Stockton	.60 .25
❏ 17	Rick Barry	.40 .15
❏ 18	Moses Malone	.60 .25
❏ 19	Nate Thurmond	.20 .07
❏ 20	Bob Pettit	.40 .15
❏ 21	Pete Maravich	.75 .30
❏ 22	Willis Reed	.40 .15
❏ 23	Isiah Thomas	.60 .25
❏ 24	Dolph Schayes	.20 .15
❏ 25	Walt Frazier	.60 .25
❏ 26	Wes Unseld	.20 .07
❏ 27	Bill Sharman	.20 .07
❏ 28	George Gervin	.60 .25
❏ 29	Hal Greer	.20 .07
❏ 30	Dave DeBusschere	.20 .07
❏ 31	Earl Monroe	.60 .25
❏ 32	Kevin McHale	.60 .25
❏ 33	Charles Barkley	.75 .30
❏ 34	Elvin Hayes	.40 .15
❏ 35	Scottie Pippen	1.00 .40
❏ 36	Jerry Lucas	.20 .07
❏ 37	Dave Bing	.20 .07
❏ 38	Lenny Wilkens	.40 .15
❏ 39	Paul Arizin	.20 .07
❏ 40	Nate Archibald	.60 .25
❏ 41	James Worthy	.60 .25
❏ 42	Patrick Ewing	.60 .25
❏ 43	Billy Cunningham	.20 .07
❏ 44	Sam Jones	.20 .07
❏ 45	Dave Cowens	.40 .15
❏ 46	Robert Parish	.60 .25
❏ 47	Bill Walton	.60 .25
❏ 48	Shaquille O'Neal	1.50 .60
❏ 49	David Robinson	.60 .25
❏ 50	Dominique Wilkins	.40 .15
❏ 51	Kobe Bryant	2.50 1.00
❏ 52	Vince Carter	1.50 .60
❏ 53	Paul Pierce	.75 .30
❏ 54	Allen Iverson	1.25 .50
❏ 55	Stephon Marbury	.60 .25
❏ 56	Mike Bibby	.60 .25
❏ 57	Jason Williams	.60 .25
❏ 58	Kevin Garnett	1.25 .50
❏ 59	Tim Duncan	1.25 .50
❏ 60	Antawn Jamison	.60 .25
❏ 61	Antoine Walker	.60 .25
❏ 62	Shareef Abdur-Rahim	.60 .25
❏ 63	Michael Olowokandi	.40 .15
❏ 64	Robert Traylor	.20 .07
❏ 65	Keith Van Horn	.60 .25
❏ 66	Shaquille O'Neal	1.50 .60
❏ 67	Ray Allen	.60 .25
❏ 68	Gary Payton	.60 .25
❏ 69	Raef LaFrentz	.40 .15
❏ 70	Grant Hill	.60 .25
❏ 71	Anfernee Hardaway	.60 .25
❏ 72	Maurice Taylor	.40 .15
❏ 73	Ron Mercer	.40 .15
❏ 74	Michael Finley	.60 .25
❏ 75	Jason Kidd	1.00 .40
❏ 76	Allan Houston	.40 .15
❏ 77	Damon Stoudamire	.40 .15

❏ 78	Antonio McDyess	.40 .15
❏ 79	Eddie Jones	.60 .25
❏ 80	Michael Dickerson	.40 .15
❏ 81	Michael Jordan	2.00 .75
❏ 82	Michael Jordan	2.00 .75
❏ 83	Michael Jordan	2.00 .75
❏ 84	Michael Jordan	2.00 .75
❏ 85	Michael Jordan	2.00 .75
❏ 86	Michael Jordan	2.00 .75
❏ 87	Michael Jordan	2.00 .75
❏ 88	Michael Jordan	2.00 .75
❏ 89	Michael Jordan	2.00 .75
❏ 90	Michael Jordan	2.00 .75
❏ S1	Michael Jordan	5.00 2.00

2000 Upper Deck Century Legends

❏	COMPLETE SET (90)	25.00 10.00
❏	COMMON CARD (1-90)	.20 .07
❏	COMMON MJ (66-71/81-90)	1.50 .60
❏ 1	Michael Jordan	4.00 1.50
❏ 2	Magic Johnson	2.00 .75
❏ 3	Larry Bird	2.50 1.00
❏ 4	Bob Cousy	.60 .25
❏ 5	Bill Russell	1.00 .40
❏ 6	Julius Erving	1.00 .40
❏ 7	Nate Archibald	.60 .25
❏ 8	Oscar Robertson	.75 .30
❏ 9	Elgin Baylor	.60 .25
❏ 10	Jo Jo White	.20 .07
❏ 11	Hal Greer	.20 .07
❏ 12	Clyde Drexler	.60 .25
❏ 13	Wilt Chamberlain	1.00 .40
❏ 14	Walt Bellamy	.20 .07
❏ 15	Walt Frazier	.60 .25
❏ 16	Earl Monroe	.60 .25
❏ 17	John Havlicek	.75 .30
❏ 18	George Mikan	1.00 .40
❏ 19	George Karl	.40 .15
❏ 20	Tom Heinsohn	.20 .07
❏ 21	Kareem Abdul-Jabbar	1.00 .40
❏ 22	Bill Sharman	.20 .07
❏ 23	Elvin Hayes	.40 .15
❏ 24	Rick Barry	.60 .25
❏ 25	Paul Silas	.40 .15
❏ 26	Mitch Kupchak	.20 .07
❏ 27	Dave Cowens	.40 .15
❏ 28	Nate Thurmond	.20 .07
❏ 29	Dave DeBusschere	.20 .07
❏ 30	Jerry Lucas	.20 .07
❏ 31	Bill Walton	.60 .25
❏ 32	Jerry West	.60 .25
❏ 33	David Thompson	.20 .07
❏ 34	Spencer Haywood	.20 .07
❏ 35	Moses Malone	.60 .25
❏ 36	Alex English	.20 .07
❏ 37	Willis Reed	.40 .15
❏ 38	George Gervin	.60 .25
❏ 39	Dolph Schayes	.40 .15
❏ 40	Wes Unseld	.20 .07
❏ 41	Bob Lanier	.20 .07
❏ 42	James Worthy	.60 .25
❏ 43	Maurice Lucas	.20 .07
❏ 44	Pete Maravich	.75 .30
❏ 45	Isiah Thomas	.60 .25
❏ 46	Robert Parish	.60 .25
❏ 47	Dominique Wilkins	.60 .25
❏ 48	Walter Davis	.20 .07

❏ 49	Bob Pettit	.40 .15
❏ 50	Kevin McHale	.60 .25
❏ 51	Julius Erving HD	.60 .25
❏ 52	Dominique Wilkins HD	.40 .15
❏ 53	George Gervin HD	.40 .15
❏ 54	Kareem Abdul-Jabbar HD	.60 .25
❏ 55	Clyde Drexler HD	.40 .15
❏ 56	David Thompson HD	.20 .07
❏ 57	Walter Davis HD	.20 .07
❏ 58	James Worthy HD	.40 .15
❏ 59	Moses Malone HD	.40 .15
❏ 60	Bob Lanier HD	.20 .07
❏ 61	Robert Parish HD	.40 .15
❏ 62	Maurice Lucas HD	.20 .07
❏ 63	Wes Unseld HD	.20 .07
❏ 64	Ron Boone HD	.20 .07
❏ 65	Larry Nance HD	.20 .07
❏ 66	Michael Jordan HD	1.50 .60
❏ 67	Michael Jordan HD	1.50 .60
❏ 68	Michael Jordan HD	1.50 .60
❏ 69	Michael Jordan HD	1.50 .60
❏ 70	Michael Jordan HD	1.50 .60
❏ 71	Michael Jordan UDT	1.50 .60
❏ 72	Wilt Chamberlain UDT	.60 .25
❏ 73	Magic Johnson UDT	1.00 .40
❏ 74	Julius Erving UDT	.60 .25
❏ 75	Larry Bird UDT	1.25 .50
❏ 76	Bill Russell UDT	.60 .25
❏ 77	Jerry West UDT	.60 .25
❏ 78	Oscar Robertson UDT	.60 .25
❏ 79	John Havlicek UDT	.60 .25
❏ 80	Elgin Baylor UDT	.40 .15
❏ 81	Michael Jordan TB	1.50 .60
❏ 82	Michael Jordan TB	1.50 .60
❏ 83	Michael Jordan TB	1.50 .60
❏ 84	Michael Jordan TB	1.50 .60
❏ 85	Michael Jordan TB	1.50 .60
❏ 86	Michael Jordan TB	1.50 .60
❏ 87	Michael Jordan TB	1.50 .60
❏ 88	Michael Jordan TB	1.50 .60
❏ 89	Michael Jordan TB	1.50 .60
❏ 90	Michael Jordan TB	1.50 .60

2002-03 Upper Deck Championship Drive

❏	COMP.SET w/o SP's (100)	40.00 15.00
❏	COMMON CARD (1-100)	.25 .10
❏	COMMON JSY RC (101-130)	10.00 4.00
❏	COMMON ROOKIE (131-155)	5.00 2.00
❏ 1	Shareef Abdur-Rahim	1.00 .40
❏ 2	Glenn Robinson	1.00 .40
❏ 3	Jason Terry	1.00 .40
❏ 4	Dion Glover	.25 .10
❏ 5	Antoine Walker	1.00 .40
❏ 6	Paul Pierce	1.00 .40
❏ 7	Vin Baker	.60 .25
❏ 8	Kedrick Brown	.25 .10
❏ 9	Jalen Rose	1.00 .40
❏ 10	Tyson Chandler	1.00 .40
❏ 11	Eddy Curry	1.00 .40
❏ 12	Darius Miles	1.00 .40
❏ 13	Ricky Davis	1.00 .40
❏ 14	Zydrunas Ilgauskas	1.00 .40
❏ 15	Dirk Nowitzki	1.50 .60
❏ 16	Michael Finley	1.00 .40
❏ 17	Steve Nash	1.00 .40
❏ 18	Raef LaFrentz	.25 .10
❏ 19	Nick Van Exel	1.00 .40

❑ 20 James Posey	.60	.25
❑ 21 Juwan Howard	.60	.25
❑ 22 Chauncey Billups	.60	.25
❑ 23 Ben Wallace	1.00	.40
❑ 24 Richard Hamilton	.60	.25
❑ 25 Jason Richardson	1.00	.40
❑ 26 Antawn Jamison	1.00	.40
❑ 27 Gilbert Arenas	1.00	.40
❑ 28 Steve Francis	1.00	.40
❑ 29 Cuttino Mobley	.60	.25
❑ 30 Eddie Griffin	.60	.25
❑ 31 Reggie Miller	1.00	.40
❑ 32 Jermaine O'Neal	1.00	.40
❑ 33 Jamaal Tinsley	1.00	.40
❑ 34 Ron Mercer	.60	.25
❑ 35 Elton Brand	1.00	.40
❑ 36 Andre Miller	.60	.25
❑ 37 Kobe Bryant	4.00	1.50
❑ 38 Shaquille O'Neal	2.50	1.00
❑ 39 Rick Fox	.60	.25
❑ 40 Devean George	.60	.25
❑ 41 Pau Gasol	1.00	.40
❑ 42 Shane Battier	1.00	.40
❑ 43 Jason Williams	.60	.25
❑ 44 Eddie Jones	1.00	.40
❑ 45 Brian Grant	.60	.25
❑ 46 Anthony Carter	.60	.25
❑ 47 Ray Allen	1.00	.40
❑ 48 Tim Thomas	.60	.25
❑ 49 Kevin Garnett	2.00	.75
❑ 50 Terrell Brandon	.60	.25
❑ 51 Wally Szczerbiak	.60	.25
❑ 52 Joe Smith	.60	.25
❑ 53 Jason Kidd	1.50	.60
❑ 54 Richard Jefferson	.60	.25
❑ 55 Dikembe Mutombo	.60	.25
❑ 56 Kenyon Martin	1.00	.40
❑ 57 Baron Davis	1.00	.40
❑ 58 Jamal Mashburn	.60	.25
❑ 59 David Wesley	.25	.10
❑ 60 P.J. Brown	.25	.10
❑ 61 Courtney Alexander	.60	.25
❑ 62 Latrell Sprewell	1.00	.40
❑ 63 Allan Houston	.60	.25
❑ 64 Kurt Thomas	.60	.25
❑ 65 Antonio McDyess	.60	.25
❑ 66 Tracy McGrady	2.50	1.00
❑ 67 Mike Miller	1.00	.40
❑ 68 Grant Hill	1.00	.40
❑ 69 Allen Iverson	2.00	.75
❑ 70 Keith Van Horn	1.00	.40
❑ 71 Shawn Marion	1.00	.40
❑ 72 Stephon Marbury	1.00	.40
❑ 73 Anfernee Hardaway	1.00	.40
❑ 74 Rasheed Wallace	1.00	.40
❑ 75 Bonzi Wells	.60	.25
❑ 76 Scottie Pippen	1.50	.60
❑ 77 Mike Bibby	1.00	.40
❑ 78 Peja Stojakovic	1.00	.40
❑ 79 Chris Webber	1.00	.40
❑ 80 Hidayet Turkoglu	1.00	.40
❑ 81 Vlade Divac	.60	.25
❑ 82 Tim Duncan	2.00	.75
❑ 83 David Robinson	1.00	.40
❑ 84 Tony Parker	1.00	.40
❑ 85 Malik Rose	.25	.10
❑ 86 Gary Payton	1.00	.40
❑ 87 Rashard Lewis	.60	.25
❑ 88 Brent Barry	.60	.25
❑ 89 Desmond Mason	.60	.25
❑ 90 Vladimir Radmanovic	.60	.25
❑ 91 Vince Carter	2.50	1.00
❑ 92 Morris Peterson	.60	.25
❑ 93 Antonio Davis	.25	.10
❑ 94 Karl Malone	1.00	.40
❑ 95 John Stockton	1.00	.40
❑ 96 Andrei Kirilenko	1.00	.40
❑ 97 Matt Harpring	1.00	.40
❑ 98 Jerry Stackhouse	1.00	.40
❑ 99 Larry Hughes	.60	.25
❑ 100 Michael Jordan	6.00	2.50
❑ 101 Juan Dixon JSY RC	15.00	10.00
❑ 102 Carlos Boozer JSY RC	20.00	8.00
❑ 103 Dan Gadzuric JSY RC	10.00	4.00
❑ 104 V.Yarbrough JSY RC	10.00	4.00
❑ 105 R.Archibald JSY RC	10.00	4.00

❑ 106 Roger Mason JSY RC	10.00	4.00
❑ 107 Ronald Murray JSY RC	15.00	6.00
❑ 108 Chris Jefferies JSY RC	10.00	4.00
❑ 109 John Salmons JSY RC	10.00	4.00
❑ 110 P.Savovic JSY RC	10.00	4.00
❑ 111 Tayshaun Prince JSY RC	12.00	5.00
❑ 112 Casey Jacobsen JSY RC	10.00	4.00
❑ 113 Qyntel Woods JSY RC	10.00	4.00
❑ 114 Kareem Rush JSY RC	12.00	5.00
❑ 115 Ryan Humphrey JSY RC	10.00	4.00
❑ 116 Sam Clancy JSY RC	10.00	4.00
❑ 117 Lonny Baxter JSY RC	10.00	4.00
❑ 118 Fred Jones JSY RC	10.00	4.00
❑ 119 Marcus Haislip JSY RC	10.00	4.00
❑ 120 Melvin Ely JSY RC	10.00	4.00
❑ 121 Jared Jeffries JSY RC	10.00	4.00
❑ 122 Caron Butler JSY RC	20.00	8.00
❑ 123 A.Stoudemire JSY RC	50.00	20.00
❑ 124 Chris Wilcox JSY RC	12.00	5.00
❑ 125 Nene Hilario JSY RC	12.00	5.00
❑ 126 DaJuan Wagner JSY RC	15.00	6.00
❑ 127 N.Tskitishvili JSY RC	10.00	4.00
❑ 128 Drew Gooden JSY RC	25.00	10.00
❑ 129 Jay Williams JSY RC	12.00	5.00
❑ 130 Yao Ming JSY RC	80.00	40.00
❑ 131 Manu Ginobili RC	15.00	6.00
❑ 132 Efthimios Rentzias RC	5.00	2.00
❑ 133 Juaquin Hawkins RC	5.00	2.00
❑ 134 Marko Jaric RC	5.00	2.00
❑ 135 Dan Dickau RC	5.00	2.00
❑ 136 Frank Williams RC	5.00	2.00
❑ 137 Curtis Borchardt RC	5.00	2.00
❑ 138 Mike Dunleavy RC	8.00	3.00
❑ 139 Smush Parker RC	8.00	3.00
❑ 140 Tito Maddox RC	5.00	2.00
❑ 141 Jannero Pargo RC	5.00	2.00
❑ 142 Jiri Welsch RC	5.00	2.00
❑ 143 Bostjan Nachbar RC	5.00	2.00
❑ 144 Rasual Butler RC	5.00	2.00
❑ 145 Gordan Giricek RC	6.00	2.50
❑ 146 Igor Rakocevic RC	5.00	2.00
❑ 147 Tamar Slay RC	5.00	2.00
❑ 148 Junior Harrington RC	5.00	2.00
❑ 149 Nate Huffman RC	5.00	2.00
❑ 150 Jamal Sampson RC	5.00	2.00
❑ 151 Reggie Evans RC	5.00	2.00
❑ 152 Cezary Trybanski RC	5.00	2.00
❑ 153 Pat Burke RC	5.00	2.00
❑ 154 J.R. Bremer RC	5.00	2.00
❑ 155 Mehmet Okur RC	5.00	2.00

2003 Upper Deck City Heights LeBron James

❑ ONE PER 03-04 UD EXCHANGE CARD		
❑ NNO LeBron James	15.00	6.00

1997-98 Upper Deck Diamond Vision

❑ COMPLETE SET (29)	125.00	75.00
❑ 1 Dikembe Mutombo	3.00	1.25
❑ 2 Dana Barros	1.50	.60
❑ 3 Glen Rice	3.00	1.25
❑ 4 Michael Jordan	25.00	10.00
❑ 5 Terrell Brandon	3.00	1.25
❑ 6 Michael Finley	4.00	1.50
❑ 7 Antonio McDyess	3.00	1.25
❑ 8 Grant Hill	4.00	1.50

❑ 9 Latrell Sprewell	4.00	1.50
❑ 10 Hakeem Olajuwon	4.00	1.50
❑ 11 Reggie Miller	4.00	1.50
❑ 12 Loy Vaught	1.50	.60
❑ 13 Shaquille O'Neal	12.00	5.00
❑ 14 Alonzo Mourning	3.00	1.25
❑ 15 Vin Baker	3.00	1.25
❑ 16 Kevin Garnett	10.00	4.00
❑ 17 Kerry Kittles	4.00	1.50
❑ 18 Patrick Ewing	4.00	1.50
❑ 19 Anfernee Hardaway	4.00	1.50
❑ 20 Allen Iverson	12.00	5.00
❑ 21 Jason Kidd	8.00	3.00
❑ 22 Isaiah Rider	3.00	1.25
❑ 23 Mitch Richmond	3.00	1.25
❑ 24 David Robinson	4.00	1.50
❑ 25 Gary Payton	4.00	1.50
❑ 26 Damon Stoudamire	3.00	1.25
❑ 27 Karl Malone	4.00	1.50
❑ 28 Shareef Abdur-Rahim	8.00	3.00
❑ 29 Chris Webber	4.00	1.50

1998-99 Upper Deck Encore

❑ COMPLETE SET (150)	120.00	60.00
❑ COMMON CARD (1-90)	.25	.08
❑ COMMON MJ (91-113)	3.00	1.25
❑ COMMON ROOKIE (114-143)	.60	.25
❑ COMMON BONUS (144-150)	1.25	.50
❑ 1 Mookie Blaylock	.25	.08
❑ 2 Dikembe Mutombo	.50	.20
❑ 3 Steve Smith	.50	.20
❑ 4 Kenny Anderson	.50	.20
❑ 5 Antoine Walker	.75	.30
❑ 6 Ron Mercer	.40	.15
❑ 7 David Wesley	.25	.08
❑ 8 Eiden Campbell	.25	.08
❑ 9 Eddie Jones	.75	.30
❑ 10 Ron Harper	.25	.08
❑ 11 Toni Kukoc	.50	.20
❑ 12 Brent Barry	.50	.20
❑ 13 Shawn Kemp	.75	.30
❑ 14 Brevin Knight	.25	.08
❑ 15 Derek Anderson	.60	.25
❑ 16 Shawn Bradley	.25	.08
❑ 17 Robert Pack	.25	.08
❑ 18 Michael Finley	.75	.30
❑ 19 Antonio McDyess	.50	.20
❑ 20 Nick Van Exel	.75	.30
❑ 21 Danny Fortson	.25	.08

#	Player		
22	Grant Hill	.75	.30
23	Jerry Stackhouse	.75	.30
24	Bison Dele	.25	.08
25	Donyell Marshall	.25	.08
26	Tony Delk	.25	.08
27	Erick Dampier	.50	.20
28	John Starks	.50	.20
29	Charles Barkley	1.00	.40
30	Hakeem Olajuwon	.75	.30
31	Othella Harrington	.25	.08
32	Scottie Pippen	1.25	.50
33	Rik Smits	.50	.20
34	Reggie Miller	.75	.30
35	Mark Jackson	.50	.20
36	Rodney Rogers	.25	.08
37	Lamond Murray	.25	.08
38	Maurice Taylor	.40	.15
39	Kobe Bryant	3.00	1.25
40	Shaquille O'Neal	2.00	.75
41	Derek Fisher	.75	.30
42	Glen Rice	.50	.20
43	Jamal Mashburn	.50	.20
44	Alonzo Mourning	.50	.20
45	Tim Hardaway	.50	.20
46	Ray Allen	.75	.30
47	Vinny Del Negro	.25	.08
48	Glenn Robinson	.50	.20
49	Joe Smith	.50	.20
50	Terrell Brandon	.50	.20
51	Kevin Garnett	1.50	.60
52	Keith Van Horn	.75	.30
53	Stephon Marbury	.75	.30
54	Jayson Williams	.25	.08
55	Patrick Ewing	.75	.30
56	Allan Houston	.50	.20
57	Latrell Sprewell	.75	.30
58	Anfernee Hardaway	.75	.30
59	Horace Grant	.50	.20
60	Nick Anderson	.25	.08
61	Allen Iverson	1.50	.60
62	Matt Geiger	.25	.08
63	Theo Ratliff	.50	.20
64	Jason Kidd	1.25	.50
65	Rex Chapman	.25	.08
66	Tom Gugliotta	.50	.20
67	Rasheed Wallace	.75	.30
68	Arvydas Sabonis	.50	.20
69	Damon Stoudamire	.50	.20
70	Vlade Divac	.50	.20
71	Corliss Williamson	.50	.20
72	Chris Webber	.75	.30
73	Tim Duncan	1.25	.50
74	Sean Elliott	.50	.20
75	David Robinson	.75	.30
76	Vin Baker	.50	.20
77	Gary Payton	.75	.30
78	Detlef Schrempf	.50	.20
79	Tracy McGrady	2.00	.75
80	John Wallace	.25	.08
81	Doug Christie	.50	.20
82	Karl Malone	.75	.30
83	John Stockton	.75	.30
84	Jeff Hornacek	.50	.20
85	Bryant Reeves	.25	.08
86	Michael Smith	.25	.08
87	Shareef Abdur-Rahim	.75	.30
88	Juwan Howard	.50	.20
89	Rod Strickland	.25	.08
90	Mitch Richmond	.50	.20
91	Michael Jordan	3.00	1.25
92	Michael Jordan	3.00	1.25
93	Michael Jordan	3.00	1.25
94	Michael Jordan	3.00	1.25
95	Michael Jordan	3.00	1.25
96	Michael Jordan	3.00	1.25
97	Michael Jordan	3.00	1.25
98	Michael Jordan	3.00	1.25
99	Michael Jordan	3.00	1.25
100	Michael Jordan	3.00	1.25
101	Michael Jordan	3.00	1.25
102	Michael Jordan	3.00	1.25
103	Michael Jordan	3.00	1.25
104	Michael Jordan	3.00	1.25
105	Michael Jordan	3.00	1.25
106	Michael Jordan	3.00	1.25
107	Michael Jordan	3.00	1.25

#	Player		
108	Michael Jordan	3.00	1.25
109	Michael Jordan	3.00	1.25
110	Michael Jordan	3.00	1.25
111	Michael Jordan	3.00	1.25
112	Michael Jordan	3.00	1.25
113	Michael Jordan	3.00	1.25
114	Michael Olowokandi RC	2.50	1.00
115	Mike Bibby RC	8.00	3.00
116	Raef LaFrentz RC	2.50	1.00
117	Antawn Jamison RC	6.00	2.50
118	Vince Carter RC	15.00	6.00
119	Robert Traylor RC	1.50	.60
120	Jason Williams RC	6.00	2.50
121	Larry Hughes RC	5.00	2.00
122	Dirk Nowitzki RC	15.00	6.00
123	Paul Pierce RC	10.00	4.00
124	Michael Doleac RC	1.50	.60
125	Keon Clark RC	2.50	1.00
126	Michael Dickerson RC	3.00	1.25
127	Matt Harpring RC	2.50	1.00
128	Bryce Drew RC	1.50	.60
129	Pat Garrity RC	.75	.30
130	Roshown McLeod RC	.75	.30
131	Ricky Davis RC	5.00	2.00
132	Peja Stojakovic RC	6.00	2.50
133	Felipe Lopez RC	2.00	.75
134	Al Harrington RC	4.00	1.50
135	Ruben Patterson RC	3.00	1.25
136	Cuttino Mobley RC	8.00	3.00
137	Tyronn Lue RC	1.00	.40
138	Brian Skinner RC	1.50	.60
139	Nazr Mohammed RC	.75	.30
140	Toby Bailey RC	.60	.25
141	Casey Shaw RC	.60	.25
142	Corey Benjamin RC	1.50	.60
143	Rashard Lewis RC	6.00	2.50
144	Jason Williams BON	3.00	1.25
145	Paul Pierce BON	5.00	2.00
146	Vince Carter BON	10.00	4.00
147	Antawn Jamison BON	4.00	1.50
148	Raef LaFrentz BON		
149	Mike Bibby BON	4.00	1.50
150	Michael Olowokandi BON	1.25	.50
MJ	Michael Jordan AU	2000.00	1000.00

1999-00 Upper Deck Encore

COMPLETE SET (120)		150.00	75.00
COMPLETE SET w/o RC (90)		25.00	12.50
COMMON CARD (1-90)		.25	.08
COMMON ROOKIE (91-120)		1.50	.60
1	Dikembe Mutombo	.50	.20
2	Alan Henderson	.25	.08
3	Isaiah Rider	.25	.08
4	Kenny Anderson	.50	.20
5	Antoine Walker	.75	.30
6	Paul Pierce	.75	.30
7	Elden Campbell	.25	.08
8	Eddie Jones	.75	.30
9	David Wesley	.25	.08
10	Hersey Hawkins	.50	.20
11	Randy Brown	.25	.08
12	Toni Kukoc	.50	.20
13	Shawn Kemp	.50	.20
14	Bob Sura	.25	.08
15	Michael Finley	.75	.30
16	Dirk Nowitzki	1.50	.60
17	Gary Trent	.25	.08

#	Player		
18	Antonio McDyess	.50	.20
19	Nick Van Exel	.75	.30
20	Raef LaFrentz	.50	.20
21	Christian Laettner	.50	.20
22	Grant Hill	.75	.30
23	Lindsey Hunter	.25	.08
24	Jerry Stackhouse	.75	.30
25	John Starks	.50	.20
26	Antawn Jamison	1.25	.50
27	Tony Farmer	.25	.08
28	Hakeem Olajuwon	.75	.30
29	Cuttino Mobley	.75	.30
30	Charles Barkley	1.00	.40
31	Reggie Miller	.75	.30
32	Jalen Rose	.75	.30
33	Mark Jackson	.50	.20
34	Maurice Taylor	.50	.20
35	Derek Anderson	.50	.20
36	Michael Olowokandi	.50	.20
37	Kobe Bryant	3.00	1.25
38	Shaquille O'Neal	2.00	.75
39	Glen Rice	.50	.20
40	Tim Hardaway	.50	.20
41	Alonzo Mourning	.50	.20
42	Ray Allen	.75	.30
43	Glenn Robinson	.75	.30
44	Sam Cassell	.75	.30
45	Tim Thomas	.50	.20
46	Kevin Garnett	1.50	.60
47	Terrell Brandon	.50	.20
48	Keith Van Horn	.75	.30
49	Stephon Marbury	.75	.30
50	Kendall Gill	.25	.08
51	Patrick Ewing	.75	.30
52	Allan Houston	.50	.20
53	Latrell Sprewell	.75	.30
54	Darrell Armstrong	.25	.08
55	John Amaechi RC	.75	.30
56	Michael Doleac	.25	.08
57	Allen Iverson	1.50	.60
58	Theo Ratliff	.50	.20
59	Larry Hughes	.75	.30
60	Jason Kidd	1.25	.50
61	Tom Gugliotta	.25	.08
62	Anfernee Hardaway	.75	.30
63	Rasheed Wallace	.75	.30
64	Steve Smith	.50	.20
65	Damon Stoudamire	.50	.20
66	Scottie Pippen	1.25	.50
67	Corliss Williamson	.25	.08
68	Jason Williams	.75	.30
69	Vlade Divac	.50	.20
70	Chris Webber	.75	.30
71	Tim Duncan	1.50	.60
72	David Robinson	.75	.30
73	Avery Johnson	.25	.08
74	Mario Elie	.25	.08
75	Gary Payton	.75	.30
76	Vin Baker	.50	.20
77	Ruben Patterson	.50	.20
78	Brent Barry	.50	.20
79	Vince Carter	2.00	.75
80	Antonio Davis	.25	.08
81	Tracy McGrady	2.00	.75
82	Karl Malone	.75	.30
83	John Stockton	.75	.30
84	Bryon Russell	.25	.08
85	Shareef Abdur-Rahim	.75	.30
86	Mike Bibby	.75	.30
87	Othella Harrington	.25	.08
88	Juwan Howard	.50	.20
89	Rod Strickland	.25	.08
90	Mitch Richmond	.50	.20
91	Elton Brand RC	10.00	4.00
92	Steve Francis RC	12.00	5.00
93	Baron Davis RC	12.00	5.00
94	Lamar Odom RC	8.00	3.00
95	Jonathan Bender RC	8.00	3.00
96	Wally Szczerbiak RC	8.00	3.00
97	Richard Hamilton RC	8.00	3.00
98	Andre Miller RC	8.00	3.00
99	Shawn Marion RC	10.00	4.00
100	Jason Terry RC	6.00	2.50
101	Trajan Langdon RC	3.00	1.25
102	Kenny Thomas RC	3.00	1.25
103	Corey Maggette RC	8.00	3.00

❏ 104	William Avery RC	3.00	1.25
❏ 105	Ron Artest RC	5.00	2.00
❏ 106	A.Radojevic RC	1.50	.60
❏ 107	James Posey RC	2.50	1.00
❏ 108	Quincy Lewis RC	1.50	.60
❏ 109	Vonteego Cummings RC	3.00	1.25
❏ 110	Jeff Foster RC	2.50	1.00
❏ 111	Dion Glover RC	2.50	1.00
❏ 112	Devean George RC	4.00	1.50
❏ 113	Evan Eschmeyer RC	1.50	.60
❏ 114	Tim James RC	2.50	1.00
❏ 115	Adrian Griffin RC	2.50	1.00
❏ 116	Anthony Carter RC	5.00	2.00
❏ 117	Obinna Ekezie RC	2.00	.75
❏ 118	Todd MacCulloch RC	2.50	1.00
❏ 119	Chucky Atkins RC	3.00	1.25
❏ 120	Lazaro Borrell RC	1.50	.60

2000-01 Upper Deck Encore

❏ COMPLETE SET w/o RC's		25.00	10.00
❏ COMMON CARD (1-135)		.25	.08
❏ COMMON ROOKIE (136-165)		3.00	1.25
❏ 1	Brevin Knight	.25	.08
❏ 2	Lorenzen Wright	.25	.08
❏ 3	Alan Henderson	.25	.08
❏ 4	Jason Terry	.75	.30
❏ 5	Paul Pierce	.75	.30
❏ 6	Antoine Walker	.75	.30
❏ 7	Kenny Anderson	.50	.20
❏ 8	Tony Battie	.25	.08
❏ 9	Adrian Griffin	.25	.08
❏ 10	Derrick Coleman	.25	.08
❏ 11	David Wesley	.25	.08
❏ 12	Baron Davis	.75	.30
❏ 13	Elden Campbell	.25	.08
❏ 14	Jamal Mashburn	.50	.20
❏ 15	Elton Brand	.75	.30
❏ 16	Ron Mercer	.50	.20
❏ 17	Ron Artest	.50	.20
❏ 18	Michael Ruffin	.50	.20
❏ 19	Lamond Murray	.25	.08
❏ 20	Andre Miller	.50	.20
❏ 21	Matt Harpring	.75	.30
❏ 22	Jim Jackson	.25	.08
❏ 23	Michael Finley	.75	.30
❏ 24	Dirk Nowitzki	1.25	.50
❏ 25	Steve Nash	.75	.30
❏ 26	Howard Eisley	.25	.08
❏ 27	Antonio McDyess	.50	.20
❏ 28	James Posey	.50	.20
❏ 29	Nick Van Exel	.25	.08
❏ 30	Raef LaFrentz	.50	.20
❏ 31	Voshon Lenard	.25	.08
❏ 32	Jerry Stackhouse	.75	.30
❏ 33	Ben Wallace	.75	.30
❏ 34	Michael Curry	.25	.08
❏ 35	Joe Smith	.50	.20
❏ 36	Chucky Atkins	.25	.08
❏ 37	Antawn Jamison	.75	.30
❏ 38	Larry Hughes	.50	.20
❏ 39	Chris Mills	.25	.08
❏ 40	Mookie Blaylock	.25	.08
❏ 41	Vonteego Cummings	.25	.08
❏ 42	Steve Francis	.75	.30
❏ 43	Maurice Taylor	.25	.08
❏ 44	Hakeem Olajuwon	.75	.30
❏ 45	Walt Williams	.25	.08

❏ 46	Cuttino Mobley	.50	.20
❏ 47	Reggie Miller	.75	.30
❏ 48	Jalen Rose	.75	.30
❏ 49	Austin Croshere	.50	.20
❏ 50	Travis Best	.25	.08
❏ 51	Jermaine O&™Neal	.75	.30
❏ 52	Lamar Odom	.75	.30
❏ 53	Jeff McInnis	.25	.08
❏ 54	Michael Olowokandi	.25	.08
❏ 55	Brian Skinner	.25	.08
❏ 56	Corey Maggette	.50	.20
❏ 57	Shaquille O&™Neal	2.00	.75
❏ 58	Ron Harper	.50	.20
❏ 59	Kobe Bryant	4.00	1.50
❏ 60	Robert Horry	.50	.20
❏ 61	Isaiah Rider	.50	.20
❏ 62	Eddie Jones	.75	.30
❏ 63	Anthony Carter	.50	.20
❏ 64	Tim Hardaway	.50	.20
❏ 65	Brian Grant	.50	.20
❏ 66	Anthony Mason	.50	.20
❏ 67	Ray Allen	.75	.30
❏ 68	Tim Thomas	.50	.20
❏ 69	Glenn Robinson	.75	.30
❏ 70	Sam Cassell	.75	.30
❏ 71	Lindsey Hunter	.25	.08
❏ 72	Kevin Garnett	1.50	.60
❏ 73	Wally Szczerbiak	.50	.20
❏ 74	Terrell Brandon	.50	.20
❏ 75	Chauncey Billups	.75	.30
❏ 76	Stephon Marbury	.75	.30
❏ 77	Keith Van Horn	.75	.30
❏ 78	Lucious Harris	.25	.08
❏ 79	Kendall Gill	.25	.08
❏ 80	Latrell Sprewell	.75	.30
❏ 81	Marcus Camby	.50	.20
❏ 82	Larry Johnson	.50	.20
❏ 83	Allan Houston	.50	.20
❏ 84	Glen Rice	.50	.20
❏ 85	Grant Hill	.75	.30
❏ 86	Tracy McGrady	2.00	.75
❏ 87	John Amaechi	.25	.08
❏ 88	Darrell Armstrong	.25	.08
❏ 89	Allen Iverson	1.50	.50
❏ 90	Dikembe Mutombo	.50	.20
❏ 91	George Lynch	.25	.08
❏ 92	Aaron McKie	.50	.20
❏ 93	Eric Snow	.50	.20
❏ 94	Jason Kidd	1.25	.50
❏ 95	Tony Delk	.25	.08
❏ 96	Clifford Robinson	.25	.08
❏ 97	Tom Gugliotta	.25	.08
❏ 98	Shawn Marion	.75	.30
❏ 99	Rasheed Wallace	.75	.30
❏ 100	Scottie Pippen	1.25	.50
❏ 101	Steve Smith	.50	.20
❏ 102	Damon Stoudamire	.50	.20
❏ 103	Bonzi Wells	.50	.20
❏ 104	Chris Webber	.75	.30
❏ 105	Jason Williams	.75	.30
❏ 106	Peja Stojakovic	.75	.30
❏ 107	Vlade Divac	.50	.20
❏ 108	Doug Christie	.50	.20
❏ 109	Tim Duncan	1.50	.60
❏ 110	David Robinson	.75	.30
❏ 111	Derek Anderson	.50	.20
❏ 112	Antonio Daniels	.25	.08
❏ 113	Sean Elliott	.50	.20
❏ 114	Gary Payton	.75	.30
❏ 115	Patrick Ewing	.75	.30
❏ 116	Vin Baker	.50	.20
❏ 117	Rashard Lewis	.75	.30
❏ 118	Vince Carter	2.00	.75
❏ 119	Alvin Williams	.25	.08
❏ 120	Antonio Davis	.25	.08
❏ 121	Charles Oakley	.25	.08
❏ 122	Karl Malone	.75	.30
❏ 123	John Stockton	.75	.30
❏ 124	Bryon Russell	.25	.08
❏ 125	John Starks	.50	.20
❏ 126	Shareef Abdur-Rahim	.50	.20
❏ 127	Mike Bibby	.75	.30
❏ 128	Michael Dickerson	.50	.20
❏ 129	Grant Long	.25	.08
❏ 130	Mitch Richmond	.50	.20
❏ 131	Richard Hamilton	.50	.20

❏ 132	Chris Whitney	.25	.08
❏ 133	Jahidi White	.25	.08
❏ 134	Checklist 1	.25	.08
❏ 135	Checklist 2	.25	.08
❏ 136	Kenyon Martin RC	10.00	4.00
❏ 137	Stromile Swift RC	6.00	2.50
❏ 138	Chris Mihm RC	3.00	1.25
❏ 139	Marcus Fizer RC	3.00	1.25
❏ 140	Darius Miles RC	8.00	3.00
❏ 141	Joel Przybilla RC	3.00	1.25
❏ 142	Mike Miller RC	8.00	3.00
❏ 143	Courtney Alexander RC	3.00	1.25
❏ 144	DerMarr Johnson RC	3.00	1.25
❏ 145	Stephen Jackson RC	5.00	2.00
❏ 146	Jerome Moiso RC	3.00	1.25
❏ 147	Keyon Dooling RC	3.00	1.25
❏ 148	Erick Barkley RC	3.00	1.25
❏ 149	Jason Collier RC	4.00	1.50
❏ 150	Jamaal Magloire RC	3.00	1.25
❏ 151	DeShawn Stevenson RC	3.00	1.25
❏ 152	Hidayet Turkoglu RC	6.00	2.50
❏ 153	Morris Peterson RC	6.00	2.50
❏ 154	Jamal Crawford RC	4.00	1.50
❏ 155	Etan Thomas RC	3.00	1.25
❏ 156	Quentin Richardson RC	8.00	3.00
❏ 157	Mateen Cleaves RC	3.00	1.25
❏ 158	Donnell Harvey RC	3.00	1.25
❏ 159	Mark Madsen RC	3.00	1.25
❏ 160	Desmond Mason RC	3.00	1.25
❏ 161	Speedy Claxton RC	3.00	1.25
❏ 162	Hanno Mottola RC	3.00	1.25
❏ 163	Mamadou Nã™diaye RC	3.00	1.25
❏ 164	Eduardo Najera RC	4.00	1.50
❏ 165	Khalid El-Amin RC	3.00	1.25

2005-06 Upper Deck ESPN

❏ COMPLETE SET (132)		40.00	15.00
❏ COMP.SET w/o SP's (90)		15.00	6.00
❏ COMMON CARD (1-90)		.15	.06
❏ COMMON ROOKIE (91-132)		2.00	.75
❏ 1	Josh Childress	.25	.10
❏ 2	Josh Smith	.50	.20
❏ 3	Al Harrington	.25	.10
❏ 4	Antoine Walker	.50	.20
❏ 5	Ricky Davis	.50	.20
❏ 6	Paul Pierce	.50	.20
❏ 7	Kareem Rush	.15	.06
❏ 8	Emeka Okafor	.75	.30
❏ 9	Gerald Wallace	.25	.10
❏ 10	Eddy Curry	.25	.10
❏ 11	Kirk Hinrich	.50	.20
❏ 12	Ben Gordon	1.00	.40
❏ 13	Drew Gooden	.25	.10
❏ 14	LeBron James	3.00	1.25
❏ 15	Zydrunas Ilgauskas	.25	.10
❏ 16	Dirk Nowitzki	.75	.30
❏ 17	Jason Terry	.50	.20
❏ 18	Josh Howard	.25	.10
❏ 19	Carmelo Anthony	1.00	.40
❏ 20	Kenyon Martin	.50	.20
❏ 21	Andre Miller	.25	.10
❏ 22	Ben Wallace	.50	.20
❏ 23	Chauncey Billups	.50	.20
❏ 24	Richard Hamilton	.25	.10
❏ 25	Troy Murphy	.50	.20
❏ 26	Jason Richardson	.50	.20
❏ 27	Baron Davis	.50	.20
❏ 28	Tracy McGrady	1.25	.50

29	Yao Ming	1.25	.50
30	Juwan Howard	.25	.10
31	Jermaine O'Neal	.50	.20
32	Reggie Miller	.50	.20
33	Ron Artest	.25	.10
34	Corey Maggette	.25	.10
35	Elton Brand	.50	.20
36	Bobby Simmons	.15	.06
37	Caron Butler	.25	.10
38	Kobe Bryant	2.00	.75
39	Lamar Odom	.50	.20
40	Mike Miller	.50	.20
41	Jason Williams	.25	.10
42	Pau Gasol	.25	.10
43	Dwyane Wade	1.50	.60
44	Eddie Jones	.25	.10
45	Shaquille O'Neal	1.25	.50
46	Desmond Mason	.25	.10
47	Maurice Williams	.15	.06
48	Michael Redd	.50	.20
49	Kevin Garnett	1.00	.40
50	Latrell Sprewell	.50	.20
51	Sam Cassell	.50	.20
52	Vince Carter	1.25	.50
53	Jason Kidd	.75	.30
54	Richard Jefferson	.25	.10
55	Dan Dickau	.15	.06
56	Jamaal Magloire	.15	.06
57	J.R. Smith	.25	.10
58	Jamal Crawford	.25	.10
59	Stephon Marbury	.25	.10
60	Allan Houston	.25	.10
61	Dwight Howard	.60	.25
62	Grant Hill	.50	.20
63	Steve Francis	.50	.20
64	Allen Iverson	1.00	.40
65	Andre Iguodala	1.00	.40
66	Chris Webber	.50	.20
67	Amare Stoudemire	1.00	.40
68	Shawn Marion	.50	.20
69	Steve Nash	.50	.20
70	Damon Stoudamire	.25	.10
71	Shareef Abdur-Rahim	.50	.20
72	Zach Randolph	.50	.20
73	Brad Miller	.50	.20
74	Mike Bibby	.50	.20
75	Peja Stojakovic	.50	.20
76	Manu Ginobili	.50	.20
77	Tim Duncan	1.00	.40
78	Tony Parker	.50	.20
79	Rashard Lewis	.50	.20
80	Ray Allen	.50	.20
81	Luke Ridnour	.25	.10
82	Rafer Alston	.25	.10
83	Jalen Rose	.50	.20
84	Chris Bosh	.50	.20
85	Andrei Kirilenko	.50	.20
86	Carlos Boozer	.25	.10
87	Matt Harpring	.50	.20
88	Antawn Jamison	.50	.20
89	Gilbert Arenas	.50	.20
90	Larry Hughes	.25	.10
91	Chris Taft RC	2.00	.75
92	Marvin Williams RC	6.00	2.50
93	Chris Paul RC	12.00	5.00
94	Andrew Bogut RC	5.00	2.00
95	Martynas Andriuskevicius RC	2.00	.75
96	Louis Williams RC	2.00	.75
97	C.J. Miles RC	2.00	.75
98	Gerald Green RC	8.00	3.00
99	Rashad McCants RC	5.00	2.00
100	Sarunas Jasikevicius RC	4.00	1.50
101	Andrew Bynum RC	10.00	4.00
102	Raymond Felton RC	5.00	2.00
103	Hakim Warrick RC	6.00	2.50
104	Deron Williams RC	10.00	4.00
105	Daniel Ewing RC	4.00	1.50
106	Martell Webster RC	2.00	.75
107	Johan Petro RC	2.00	.75
108	Travis Diener RC	2.00	.75
109	Joey Graham RC	2.00	.75
110	Antoine Wright RC	2.00	.75
111	Ersan Ilyasova RC	2.00	.75
112	Jason Maxiell RC	2.00	.75
113	Linas Kleiza RC	2.00	.75
114	Jarrett Jack RC	2.00	.75
115	Danny Granger RC	1.50	.60
116	Monta Ellis RC	3.00	1.25
117	Francisco Garcia RC	2.00	.75
118	Ryan Gomes RC	2.00	.75
119	Wayne Simien RC	4.00	1.50
120	Von Wafer RC	2.00	.75
121	Dijon Thompson RC	2.00	.75
122	Nate Robinson RC	2.00	.75
123	Bracey Wright RC	4.00	1.50
124	Andray Blatche RC	2.00	.75
125	Channing Frye RC	4.00	1.50
126	Salim Stoudamire RC	4.00	1.50
127	Luther Head RC	4.00	1.50
128	Julius Hodge RC	4.00	1.50
129	David Lee RC	3.00	1.25
130	Ike Diogu RC	4.00	1.50
131	Sean May RC	2.50	1.00
132	Brandon Bass RC	2.00	.75

2002-03 Upper Deck Finite

	COMP.SET w/o SP's (100)	40.00	15.00
	COMMON CARD (1-100)	.40	.15
	181-200 NOT PRICED DUE TO SCARCITY		
	COMMON ROOKIE (201-221)	5.00	2.00
	COMMON ROOKIE (222-233)	4.00	1.50
	COMMON ROOKIE (234-242)	15.00	6.00
1	Shareef Abdur-Rahim	1.25	.50
2	Theo Ratliff	.75	.30
3	Glenn Robinson	1.25	.50
4	Jason Terry	1.25	.50
5	Vin Baker	.75	.30
6	Kedrick Brown	.75	.30
7	Paul Pierce	1.25	.50
8	Antoine Walker	1.25	.50
9	Tyson Chandler	1.25	.50
10	Eddy Curry	1.25	.50
11	Jalen Rose	1.25	.50
12	Chris Mihm	.40	.15
13	Darius Miles	1.25	.50
14	Ricky Davis	.75	.30
15	Michael Finley	1.25	.50
16	Rael LaFrentz	.75	.30
17	Steve Nash	1.25	.50
18	Dirk Nowitzki	2.00	.75
19	Nick Van Exel	1.25	.50
20	Marcus Camby	.75	.30
21	Juwan Howard	.75	.30
22	James Posey	.75	.30
23	Chauncey Billups	.75	.30
24	Richard Hamilton	.75	.30
25	Ben Wallace	1.25	.50
26	Clifford Robinson	.40	.15
27	Gilbert Arenas	1.25	.50
28	Antawn Jamison	1.25	.50
29	Jason Richardson	1.25	.50
30	Eddie Griffin	.75	.30
31	Steve Francis	1.25	.50
32	Cuttino Mobley	.75	.30
33	Reggie Miller	1.25	.50
34	Jermaine O'Neal	1.25	.50
35	Jamaal Tinsley	1.25	.50
36	Ron Mercer	.75	.30
37	Elton Brand	1.25	.50
38	Andre Miller	.75	.30
39	Lamar Odom	1.25	.50
40	Kobe Bryant	6.00	2.50
41	Rick Fox	.75	.30
42	Devean George	.75	.30
43	Shaquille O'Neal	3.00	1.25
44	Shane Battier	1.25	.50
45	Pau Gasol	1.25	.50
46	Jason Williams	.75	.30
47	LaPhonso Ellis	.40	.15
48	Eddie Jones	1.25	.50
49	Brian Grant	.75	.30
50	Ray Allen	1.25	.50
51	Tim Thomas	.75	.30
52	Sam Cassell	1.25	.50
53	Terrell Brandon	.75	.30
54	Kevin Garnett	3.00	1.25
55	Wally Szczerbiak	.75	.30
56	Marc Jackson	.75	.30
57	Richard Jefferson	.75	.30
58	Jason Kidd	1.50	.60
59	Kenyon Martin	1.25	.50
60	Kerry Kittles	.40	.15
61	Baron Davis	1.25	.50
62	Jamal Mashburn	.75	.30
63	David Wesley	.40	.15
64	P.J. Brown	.40	.15
65	Latrell Sprewell	1.25	.50
66	Antonio McDyess	.75	.30
67	Allan Houston	.75	.30
68	Tracy McGrady	4.00	1.50
69	Mike Miller	1.25	.50
70	Darrell Armstrong	.40	.15
71	Allen Iverson	2.50	1.00
72	Aaron McKie	.75	.30
73	Keith Van Horn	1.25	.50
74	Stephon Marbury	1.25	.50
75	Shawn Marion	1.25	.50
76	Anfernee Hardaway	1.25	.50
77	Rasheed Wallace	1.25	.50
78	Bonzi Wells	.75	.30
79	Scottie Pippen	2.00	.75
80	Mike Bibby	1.25	.50
81	Peja Stojakovic	1.25	.50
82	Chris Webber	1.25	.50
83	Hidayet Turkoglu	1.25	.50
84	Tim Duncan	3.00	1.25
85	David Robinson	1.25	.50
86	Tony Parker	1.25	.50
87	Malik Rose	.40	.15
88	Gary Payton	1.25	.50
89	Rashard Lewis	.75	.30
90	Brent Barry	.75	.30
91	Desmond Mason	.75	.30
92	Vince Carter	3.00	1.25
93	Morris Peterson	.75	.30
94	Antonio Davis	.40	.15
95	Karl Malone	1.25	.50
96	John Stockton	1.25	.50
97	Andrei Kirilenko	1.25	.50
98	Kwame Brown	.75	.30
99	Jerry Stackhouse	1.25	.50
100	Michael Jordan	12.00	5.00
101	Kobe Bryant MF	12.00	5.00
102	Eddie Griffin MF	.75	.30
103	Shawn Marion MF	2.50	1.00
104	Richard Jefferson MF	1.50	.60
105	Jermaine O'Neal MF	2.50	.75
106	Allan Houston MF	1.50	.60
107	Shane Battier MF	3.00	1.25
108	Hidayet Turkoglu MF	2.50	1.00
109	Michael Finley MF	2.50	1.00
110	Jamaal Mashburn MF	1.50	.60
111	Rashard Lewis MF	1.50	.60
112	Tyson Chandler MF	2.50	1.00
113	Terrell Brandon MF	1.50	.60
114	Antonio Davis MF	1.00	.40
115	Jamaal Tinsley MF	2.50	1.00
116	Tony Parker MF	3.00	1.25
117	Ray Allen MF	2.00	.75
118	Rasheed Wallace MF	2.00	.75
119	Cuttino Mobley MF	1.50	.60
120	Jason Terry MF	1.50	.60
121	Mike Miller MF	2.50	1.00
122	Jalen Rose MF	2.50	1.00
123	Morris Peterson MF	1.25	.50
124	Ricky Davis MF	1.50	.60
125	Peja Stojakovic MF	2.50	1.00
126	Gary Payton MF	2.50	1.00
127	Andrei Kirilenko MF	2.00	.75

#	Player		
❏ 128	Tim Duncan MF	6.00	2.50
❏ 129	Anfernee Hardaway MF	2.50	1.00
❏ 130	Shaquille O'Neal MF	6.00	2.50
❏ 131	Latrell Sprewell MF	1.25	.50
❏ 132	Shareef Abdur-Rahim MF	2.50	-1.00
❏ 133	Steve Nash MF	2.50	1.00
❏ 134	Lamar Odom MF	2.50	1.00
❏ 135	Antawn Jamison MF	2.50	1.00
❏ 136	Reggie Miller MF	2.00	.75
❏ 137	Tim Thomas MF	1.50	.60
❏ 138	Eddy Curry MF	2.00	.75
❏ 139	Jason Williams MF	1.50	.60
❏ 140	John Stockton MF	2.50	.75
❏ 141	Ben Wallace MF	1.50	.60
❏ 142	Bonzi Wells MF	1.50	.60
❏ 143	David Robinson MF	2.50	1.00
❏ 144	Stephon Marbury MF	2.50	1.00
❏ 145	Vince Carter MF	6.00	2.50
❏ 146	James Posey MF	1.50	.60
❏ 147	Wally Szczerbiak MF	1.50	.60
❏ 148	Eddie Jones MF	2.50	1.00
❏ 149	Scottie Pippen MF	10.00	4.00
❏ 150	Michael Jordan MF	25.00	10.00
❏ 151	Kobe Bryant PP	30.00	12.50
❏ 152	Pau Gasol PP	5.00	2.00
❏ 153	Tim Duncan PP	15.00	6.00
❏ 154	Karl Malone PP	6.00	2.50
❏ 155	Allan Houston PP	4.00	1.50
❏ 156	Steve Nash PP	6.00	2.50
❏ 157	Shawn Marion PP	6.00	2.50
❏ 158	Jamal Mashburn PP	4.00	1.50
❏ 159	Shaquille O'Neal PP	15.00	6.00
❏ 160	Reggie Miller PP	6.00	2.50
❏ 161	Latrell Sprewell PP	1.25	.50
❏ 162	Peja Stojakovic PP	6.00	2.50
❏ 163	Jalen Rose PP	6.00	2.50
❏ 164	Kenyon Martin PP	6.00	2.50
❏ 165	Baron Davis PP	6.00	2.50
❏ 166	Ray Allen PP	6.00	2.50
❏ 167	Vince Carter PP	15.00	6.00
❏ 168	Rashard Lewis PP	4.00	1.50
❏ 169	Steve Francis PP		
❏ 170	Jermaine O'Neal PP		
❏ 171	Shane Battier PP	8.00	3.00
❏ 172	Shareef Abdur-Rahim PP	6.00	2.50
❏ 173	Michael Finley PP	6.00	2.50
❏ 174	John Stockton PP	6.00	2.50
❏ 175	Jamaal Tinsley PP	4.00	1.50
❏ 176	Wally Szczerbiak PP	4.00	1.50
❏ 177	Antawn Jamison PP	6.00	2.50
❏ 178	Richard Jefferson PP	4.00	1.50
❏ 179	Rasheed Wallace PP	6.00	2.50
❏ 180	Michael Jordan PP	60.00	25.00
❏ 181	Kobe Bryant FC		
❏ 182	Paul Pierce FC		
❏ 183	Nikoloz Tskitishvili FC		
❏ 184	Kareem Rush FC		
❏ 185	Jason Kidd FC		
❏ 186	Dominique Wilkins FC		
❏ 187	Kevin Garnett FC		
❏ 188	Antoine Walker FC		
❏ 189	Jay Williams FC		
❏ 190	DaJuan Wagner FC		
❏ 191	Caron Butler FC		
❏ 192	Mike Bibby FC		
❏ 193	Mike Miller FC		
❏ 194	Tyson Chandler FC		
❏ 195	Drew Gooden FC		
❏ 196	Kenyon Martin FC		
❏ 197	Marcus Fizer FC		
❏ 198	Nene Hilario FC		
❏ 199	Yao Ming FC		
❏ 200	Michael Jordan FC		
❏ 201	Manu Ginobili RC	4.00	1.50
❏ 202	Dan Dickau RC	4.00	1.50
❏ 203	Tito Maddox RC	4.00	1.50
❏ 204	Predrag Savovic RC	4.00	1.50
❏ 205	Robert Archibald RC	4.00	1.50
❏ 206	Frank Williams RC	4.00	1.50
❏ 207	Ronald Murray RC	5.00	2.00
❏ 208	Lonny Baxter RC	4.00	1.50
❏ 209	Efthimios Rentzias RC	4.00	1.50
❏ 210	Vincent Yarbrough RC	4.00	1.50
❏ 211	Gordan Giricek RC	5.00	2.00
❏ 212	Carlos Boozer RC	8.00	3.00
❏ 213	John Salmons RC	4.00	1.50

#	Player		
❏ 214	Manu Ginobili RC	15.00	6.00
❏ 215	Roger Mason Jr. RC	4.00	1.50
❏ 216	Chris Jefferies RC	4.00	1.50
❏ 217	Sam Clancy RC	4.00	1.50
❏ 218	Rasual Butler RC	4.00	1.50
❏ 219	Dan Gadzuric RC	4.00	1.50
❏ 220	Tayshaun Prince RC	8.00	3.00
❏ 221	Casey Jacobsen RC	4.00	1.50
❏ 222	Qyntel Woods RC	4.00	1.50
❏ 223	Jiri Welsch RC	4.00	1.50
❏ 224	Curtis Borchardt RC	4.00	1.50
❏ 225	Marcus Haislip RC	4.00	1.50
❏ 226	Kareem Rush RC	5.00	2.00
❏ 227	Fred Jones RC	5.00	2.00
❏ 228	Caron Butler RC	8.00	3.00
❏ 229	Juan Dixon RC	6.00	2.50
❏ 230	Ryan Humphrey RC	4.00	1.50
❏ 231	Melvin Ely RC	4.00	1.50
❏ 232	Bostjan Nachbar RC	4.00	1.50
❏ 233	Jared Jeffries RC	4.00	1.50
❏ 234	Jay Williams RC	12.00	5.00
❏ 235	Nikoloz Tskitishvili RC	4.00	1.50
❏ 236	Chris Wilcox RC	4.00	1.50
❏ 237	Drew Gooden RC	25.00	10.00
❏ 238	Amare Stoudemire RC	60.00	25.00
❏ 239	DaJuan Wagner RC	15.00	6.00
❏ 240	Nene Hilario RC	4.00	1.50
❏ 241	Mike Dunleavy RC	15.00	6.00
❏ 242	Yao Ming RC	80.00	40.00

2003-04 Upper Deck Finite

❏	COMMON ODD (1-200)	.40	.15
❏	COMMON EVEN (1-200)	.60	.25
❏	COMMON ROOKIE (201-228)	5.00	2.00
❏	COMMON ROOKIE (229-236)	6.00	2.50
❏	COMMON ROOKIE (237-242)	20.00	8.00
❏	COMMON MAJ.FACT.(243-292)	3.00	1.25
❏	COMMON PROM.POW.(293-322)	5.00	2.00
❏	COMMON FIRST CLS.(323-342)	20.00	8.00
❏ 1	Shareef Abdur-Rahim	1.25	.50
❏ 2	Dominique Wilkins	2.00	.75
❏ 3	Theo Ratliff	.75	.30
❏ 4	Dan Dickau	.60	.25
❏ 5	Jason Terry	1.25	.50
❏ 6	Dion Glover	.60	.25
❏ 7	Alan Henderson	.40	.15
❏ 8	Paul Pierce	2.00	.75
❏ 9	Larry Bird	10.00	4.00
❏ 10	Raef LaFrentz	1.25	.50
❏ 11	Robert Parish	2.50	1.00
❏ 12	Jiri Welsch	1.25	.50
❏ 13	John Havlicek	2.50	1.00
❏ 14	Vin Baker	1.25	.50
❏ 15	Jamal Crawford	.40	.15
❏ 16	Michael Jordan	12.00	5.00
❏ 17	Scottie Pippen	2.00	.75
❏ 18	Reggie Theus	2.00	.75
❏ 19	Jalen Rose	1.25	.50
❏ 20	Tyson Chandler	2.00	.75
❏ 21	Eddy Curry	1.25	.50
❏ 22	Dajuan Wagner	1.25	.50
❏ 23	Lenny Wilkens	2.00	.75
❏ 24	Carlos Boozer	2.00	.75
❏ 25	World B. Free	1.50	.60
❏ 26	Darius Miles	2.00	.75
❏ 27	Craig Ehlo	1.25	.50
❏ 28	Ricky Davis	2.00	.75

#	Player		
❏ 29	Dirk Nowitzki	2.00	.75
❏ 30	Rolando Blackman	2.00	.75
❏ 31	Steve Nash	1.25	.50
❏ 32	Tony Delk	.60	.25
❏ 33	Antawn Jamison	1.25	.50
❏ 34	Antoine Walker	2.00	.75
❏ 35	Michael Finley	1.25	.50
❏ 36	Andre Miller	1.25	.50
❏ 37	David Thompson	2.00	.75
❏ 38	Nene	1.25	.50
❏ 39	Dan Issel	1.25	.50
❏ 40	Nikoloz Tskitishvili	.60	.25
❏ 41	Alex English	1.50	.60
❏ 42	Earl Boykins	1.25	.50
❏ 43	Richard Hamilton	.75	.30
❏ 44	Mehmet Okur	.60	.25
❏ 45	Ben Wallace	1.25	.50
❏ 46	Bob Lanier	2.50	1.00
❏ 47	Chauncey Billups	.75	.30
❏ 48	Dave Bing	2.00	.75
❏ 49	Tayshaun Prince	.75	.30
❏ 50	Nick Van Exel	2.00	.75
❏ 51	Erick Dampier	.75	.30
❏ 52	Jason Richardson	2.00	.75
❏ 53	Joe Barry Carroll	1.25	.50
❏ 54	Mike Dunleavy	1.25	.50
❏ 55	Wilt Chamberlain	5.00	2.00
❏ 56	Troy Murphy	2.00	.75
❏ 57	Steve Francis	1.25	.50
❏ 58	Maurice Taylor	2.00	.75
❏ 59	Yao Ming	3.00	1.25
❏ 60	Robert Reid	2.00	.75
❏ 61	Cuttino Mobley	.75	.30
❏ 62	Moses Malone	2.00	.75
❏ 63	Eddie Griffin	.75	.30
❏ 64	Jermaine O'Neal	2.00	.75
❏ 65	George McGinnis	1.25	.50
❏ 66	Reggie Miller	2.00	.75
❏ 67	Clark Kellogg	1.25	.50
❏ 68	Jamaal Tinsley	2.00	.75
❏ 69	Al Harrington	.75	.30
❏ 70	Ron Artest	2.00	.75
❏ 71	Elton Brand	1.25	.50
❏ 72	Corey Maggette	1.25	.50
❏ 73	Chris Wilcox	.40	.15
❏ 74	Quentin Richardson	1.25	.50
❏ 75	Bill Walton	2.50	1.00
❏ 76	Marko Jaric	.60	.25
❏ 77	Kobe Bryant	5.00	2.00
❏ 78	Kareem Abdul-Jabbar	4.00	1.50
❏ 79	Shaquille O'Neal	3.00	1.25
❏ 80	Michael Cooper	2.00	.75
❏ 81	Gary Payton	1.25	.50
❏ 82	James Worthy	2.50	1.00
❏ 83	Karl Malone	1.25	.50
❏ 84	Pau Gasol	2.00	.75
❏ 85	Michael Dickerson	.40	.15
❏ 86	Mike Miller	2.00	.75
❏ 87	Brevin Knight	.40	.15
❏ 88	Shane Battier	2.00	.75
❏ 89	Stromile Swift	.40	.15
❏ 90	Jason Williams	1.25	.50
❏ 91	Caron Butler	1.25	.50
❏ 92	Samaki Walker	.60	.25
❏ 93	Eddie Jones	1.25	.50
❏ 94	Rasual Butler	.60	.25
❏ 95	Brian Grant	.75	.30
❏ 96	Loren Woods	.60	.25
❏ 97	Lamar Odom	1.25	.50
❏ 98	Desmond Mason	1.25	.50
❏ 99	Sidney Moncrief	1.25	.50
❏ 100	Toni Kukoc	1.25	.50
❏ 101	Oscar Robertson	3.00	1.25
❏ 102	Michael Redd	2.00	.75
❏ 103	Terry Cummings	1.25	.50
❏ 104	Tim Thomas	1.25	.50
❏ 105	Kevin Garnett	2.50	1.00
❏ 106	Troy Hudson	.60	.25
❏ 107	Sam Cassell	1.25	.50
❏ 108	Latrell Sprewell	1.25	.50
❏ 109	Michael Olowokandi	.40	.15
❏ 110	Wally Szczerbiak	1.25	.50
❏ 111	Jason Kidd	2.00	.75
❏ 112	Otis Birdsong	2.00	.75
❏ 113	Kenyon Martin	1.25	.50
❏ 114	Albert King	2.00	.75

#	Player		
❏ 115	Richard Jefferson	.75	.30
❏ 116	Kerry Kittles	.60	.25
❏ 117	Alonzo Mourning	.75	.30
❏ 118	Baron Davis	2.00	.75
❏ 119	Darrell Armstrong	.40	.15
❏ 120	Jamal Mashburn	1.25	.50
❏ 121	P.J. Brown	.40	.15
❏ 122	David Wesley	.60	.25
❏ 123	Courtney Alexander	.75	.30
❏ 124	Jamaal Magloire	.60	.25
❏ 125	Allan Houston	.75	.30
❏ 126	Willis Reed	2.50	1.00
❏ 127	Keith Van Horn	1.25	.50
❏ 128	Walt Frazier	2.50	1.00
❏ 129	Antonio McDyess	.75	.30
❏ 130	Earl Monroe	2.50	1.00
❏ 131	Kurt Thomas	.75	.30
❏ 132	Tracy McGrady	5.00	2.00
❏ 133	Pat Garrity	.40	.15
❏ 134	Grant Hill	2.00	.75
❏ 135	Tyronn Lue	.40	.15
❏ 136	Drew Gooden	1.25	.50
❏ 137	Juwan Howard	.75	.30
❏ 138	Gordan Giricek	1.25	.50
❏ 139	Allen Iverson	3.00	1.25
❏ 140	Julius Erving	5.00	2.00
❏ 141	Glenn Robinson	.75	.30
❏ 142	Maurice Cheeks	2.50	1.00
❏ 143	Aaron McKie	.75	.30
❏ 144	Billy Cunningham	2.00	.75
❏ 145	Eric Snow	.75	.30
❏ 146	Stephon Marbury	2.00	.75
❏ 147	Kevin Johnson	1.25	.50
❏ 148	Amare Stoudemire	4.00	1.50
❏ 149	Larry Nance	1.25	.50
❏ 150	Shawn Marion	2.00	.75
❏ 151	Walter Davis	1.25	.50
❏ 152	Anfernee Hardaway	2.00	.75
❏ 153	Rasheed Wallace	1.25	.50
❏ 154	Zach Randolph	2.00	.75
❏ 155	Derek Anderson	.75	.30
❏ 156	Dale Davis	.60	.25
❏ 157	Bonzi Wells	.75	.30
❏ 158	Jim Paxson	2.00	.75
❏ 159	Damon Stoudamire	.75	.30
❏ 160	Chris Webber	2.00	.75
❏ 161	Vlade Divac	.75	.30
❏ 162	Mike Bibby	2.00	.75
❏ 163	Bobby Jackson	.75	.30
❏ 164	Peja Stojakovic	2.00	.75
❏ 165	Doug Christie	.75	.30
❏ 166	Brad Miller	2.00	.75
❏ 167	Tim Duncan	2.50	1.00
❏ 168	Radoslav Nesterovic	1.25	.50
❏ 169	Tony Parker	1.25	.50
❏ 170	George Gervin	2.50	1.00
❏ 171	Manu Ginobili	1.25	.50
❏ 172	Artis Gilmore	2.00	.75
❏ 173	Ron Mercer	.40	.15
❏ 174	Ray Allen	2.00	.75
❏ 175	Spencer Haywood	1.25	.50
❏ 176	Rashard Lewis	2.00	.75
❏ 177	Fred Brown	1.25	.50
❏ 178	Vladimir Radmanovic	.60	.25
❏ 179	Jack Sikma	1.25	.50
❏ 180	Brent Barry	2.00	.75
❏ 181	Vince Carter	3.00	1.25
❏ 182	Antonio Davis	.60	.25
❏ 183	Morris Peterson	.75	.30
❏ 184	Alvin Williams	.60	.25
❏ 185	Chris Jefferies	.40	.15
❏ 186	Jerome Williams	.60	.25
❏ 187	Andrei Kirilenko	1.25	.50
❏ 188	Pete Maravich	12.00	5.00
❏ 189	Matt Harpring	1.25	.50
❏ 190	Mark Eaton	2.00	.75
❏ 191	Jarron Collins	.40	.15
❏ 192	Greg Ostertag	.60	.25
❏ 193	Carlos Arroyo	8.00	3.00
❏ 194	Jerry Stackhouse	2.00	.75
❏ 195	Wes Unseld	1.25	.50
❏ 196	Gilbert Arenas	2.00	.75
❏ 197	Larry Hughes	.75	.30
❏ 198	Kwame Brown	1.25	.50
❏ 199	Jeff Malone	1.25	.50
❏ 200	Jared Jeffries	.60	.25
❏ 201	Aleksandar Pavlovic RC	6.00	2.50
❏ 202	James Lang RC	5.00	2.00
❏ 203	Jason Kapono RC	5.00	2.00
❏ 204	Luke Walton RC	5.00	2.00
❏ 205	Jerome Beasley RC	5.00	2.00
❏ 206	Willie Green RC	5.00	2.00
❏ 207	Steve Blake RC	5.00	2.00
❏ 208	Slavko Vranes RC	5.00	2.00
❏ 209	Zaur Pachulia RC	5.00	2.00
❏ 210	Travis Hansen RC	5.00	2.00
❏ 211	Keith Bogans RC	5.00	2.00
❏ 212	Kyle Korver RC	5.00	2.00
❏ 213	Brandon Hunter RC	5.00	2.00
❏ 214	James Jones RC	5.00	2.00
❏ 215	Josh Howard RC	8.00	3.00
❏ 216	Leandro Barbosa RC	5.00	2.00
❏ 217	Kendrick Perkins RC	5.00	2.00
❏ 218	Ndudi Ebi RC	5.00	2.00
❏ 219	Brian Cook RC	5.00	2.00
❏ 220	Travis Outlaw RC	5.00	2.00
❏ 221	Zoran Planinic RC	5.00	2.00
❏ 222	Dahntay Jones RC	5.00	2.00
❏ 223	Boris Diaw RC	6.00	2.50
❏ 224	Zarko Cabarkapa RC	5.00	2.00
❏ 225	Troy Bell RC	5.00	2.00
❏ 226	Reece Gaines RC	5.00	2.00
❏ 227	Luke Ridnour RC	6.00	2.50
❏ 228	Chris Kaman RC	5.00	2.00
❏ 229	Marcus Banks RC	5.00	2.00
❏ 230	Maciej Lampe RC	6.00	2.50
❏ 231	David West RC	5.00	2.00
❏ 232	Mickael Pietrus RC	6.00	2.50
❏ 233	Jarvis Hayes RC	.60	.25
❏ 234	Mike Sweetney RC	6.00	2.50
❏ 235	Kirk Hinrich RC	10.00	4.00
❏ 236	Chris Bosh RC	15.00	6.00
❏ 237	Nick Collison RC	5.00	2.00
❏ 238	T.J. Ford RC	25.00	10.00
❏ 239	Dwyane Wade RC	80.00	40.00
❏ 240	Carmelo Anthony RC	100.00	50.00
❏ 241	Darko Milicic RC	30.00	12.50
❏ 242	LeBron James RC	300.00	150.00
❏ 243	Michael Jordan MF	15.00	6.00
❏ 244	Kobe Bryant MF	10.00	4.00
❏ 245	Michael Finley MF	3.00	1.25
❏ 246	Andrei Kirilenko MF	3.00	1.25
❏ 247	Desmond Mason MF	3.00	1.25
❏ 248	Kenyon Martin MF	3.00	1.25
❏ 249	Shaquille O'Neal MF	6.00	2.50
❏ 250	Jamal Mashburn MF	3.00	1.25
❏ 251	Jason Terry MF	3.00	1.25
❏ 252	Andre Miller MF	3.00	1.25
❏ 253	Keith Van Horn MF	3.00	1.25
❏ 254	Derek Anderson MF	3.00	1.25
❏ 255	Stephon Marbury MF	3.00	1.25
❏ 256	Glenn Robinson MF	3.00	1.25
❏ 257	Richard Hamilton MF	3.00	1.25
❏ 258	Lamar Odom MF	3.00	1.25
❏ 259	Bonzi Wells MF	3.00	1.25
❏ 260	Wally Szczerbiak MF	3.00	1.25
❏ 261	Alonzo Mourning MF	3.00	1.25
❏ 262	Gilbert Arenas MF	3.00	1.25
❏ 263	Mike Bibby MF	3.00	1.25
❏ 264	Antawn Jamison MF	3.00	1.25
❏ 265	Tony Parker MF	3.00	1.25
❏ 266	Reggie Miller MF	3.00	1.25
❏ 267	Vince Carter MF	6.00	2.50
❏ 268	Richard Jefferson MF	3.00	1.25
❏ 269	Nene MF	3.00	1.25
❏ 270	Grant Hill MF	3.00	1.25
❏ 271	Rashard Lewis MF	3.00	1.25
❏ 272	Shawn Marion MF	3.00	1.25
❏ 273	Morris Peterson MF	3.00	1.25
❏ 274	Chauncey Billups MF	3.00	1.25
❏ 275	Eddie Jones MF	3.00	1.25
❏ 276	Raef LaFrentz MF	3.00	1.25
❏ 277	Jerry Stackhouse MF	3.00	1.25
❏ 278	Pau Gasol MF	3.00	1.25
❏ 279	Darius Miles MF	3.00	1.25
❏ 280	Nick Van Exel MF	3.00	1.25
❏ 281	Gary Payton MF	3.00	1.25
❏ 282	Peja Stojakovic MF	3.00	1.25
❏ 283	Karl Malone MF	3.00	1.25
❏ 284	Michael Miller MF	3.00	1.25
❏ 285	Caron Butler MF	3.00	1.25
❏ 286	Cuttino Mobley MF	3.00	1.25
❏ 287	Zach Randolph MF	3.00	1.25
❏ 288	Scottie Pippen MF	4.00	1.50
❏ 289	Gordan Giricek MF	3.00	1.25
❏ 290	Ben Wallace MF	3.00	1.25
❏ 291	Manu Ginobili MF	3.00	1.25
❏ 292	Vladimir Radmanovic MF	3.00	1.25
❏ 293	Michael Jordan FC	25.00	10.00
❏ 294	Kobe Bryant FC	15.00	6.00
❏ 295	Vince Carter FC	10.00	4.00
❏ 296	Steve Nash FC	5.00	2.00
❏ 297	Shaquille O'Neal FC	10.00	4.00
❏ 298	Amare Stoudemire FC	8.00	3.00
❏ 299	Tracy McGrady FC	10.00	4.00
❏ 300	Gary Payton FC	5.00	2.00
❏ 301	Chris Bosh FC	8.00	3.00
❏ 302	Michael Finley FC	5.00	2.00
❏ 303	Caron Butler FC	5.00	2.00
❏ 304	Jarvis Hayes FC	5.00	2.50
❏ 305	Ben Wallace FC	5.00	2.00
❏ 306	Allan Houston FC	5.00	2.00
❏ 307	Mike Bibby FC	5.00	2.00
❏ 308	Antoine Walker FC	5.00	2.00
❏ 309	Dajuan Wagner FC	5.00	2.00
❏ 310	Kevin Garnett FC	8.00	3.00
❏ 311	Mickael Pietrus FC	5.00	2.00
❏ 312	Baron Davis FC	5.00	2.00
❏ 313	Paul Pierce FC	5.00	2.00
❏ 314	Rasheed Wallace FC	5.00	2.00
❏ 315	Chris Webber FC	5.00	2.00
❏ 316	Jermaine O'Neal FC	5.00	2.00
❏ 317	Shareef Abdur-Rahim FC	5.00	2.00
❏ 318	Ray Allen FC	5.00	2.00
❏ 319	Peja Stojakovic FC	5.00	2.00
❏ 320	Tim Duncan FC	8.00	3.00
❏ 321	Gilbert Arenas FC	5.00	2.00
❏ 322	Jason Richardson FC	5.00	2.00
❏ 323	Dwyane Wade FC	60.00	30.00
❏ 324	Gary Payton FC	20.00	8.00
❏ 325	Karl Malone FC	20.00	8.00
❏ 326	Jason Kidd FC	25.00	10.00
❏ 327	Darko Milicic FC	30.00	12.50
❏ 328	Steve Francis FC	20.00	8.00
❏ 329	Vince Carter FC	40.00	15.00
❏ 330	Elton Brand FC	20.00	8.00
❏ 331	Amare Stoudemire FC	40.00	15.00
❏ 332	Shaquille O'Neal FC	40.00	15.00
❏ 333	Carmelo Anthony FC	60.00	25.00
❏ 334	Tracy McGrady FC	40.00	15.00
❏ 335	Tim Duncan FC	40.00	15.00
❏ 336	Chris Webber FC	20.00	8.00
❏ 337	Allen Iverson FC	40.00	15.00
❏ 338	Dirk Nowitzki FC	30.00	12.50
❏ 339	Kevin Garnett FC	40.00	15.00
❏ 340	Kobe Bryant FC	50.00	20.00
❏ 341	LeBron James FC	300.00	150.00
❏ 342	Michael Jordan FC	100.00	50.00

2001-02 Upper Deck Flight Team

❏ COMPLETE SET (240)	600.00	250.00
❏ COMP.SET w/o SP's (90)	40.00	20.00
❏ COMMON CARD (1-90)	.25	.08
❏ COMMON ROOKIE (91-120)	2.00	.75
❏ COMMON ROOKIE (121-134)	2.50	1.00
❏ COMMON ROOKIE (135-140)	6.00	2.50
❏ 1 Michael Jordan	12.00	5.00
❏ 2 Dirk Nowitzki		.50
❏ 3 Antawn Jamison	.75	.30

❏ 4 Latrell Sprewell	.75	.30
❏ 5 Peja Stojakovic	.75	.30
❏ 6 Dikembe Mutombo	.50	.20
❏ 7 Jason Williams	.50	.20
❏ 8 Kobe Bryant	3.00	1.25
❏ 9 Baron Davis	.75	.30
❏ 10 Wally Szczerbiak	.50	.20
❏ 11 Reggie Miller	.75	.30
❏ 12 Marcus Fizer	.50	.20
❏ 13 Desmond Mason	.50	.20
❏ 14 Glenn Robinson	.75	.30
❏ 15 Vince Carter	2.00	.75
❏ 16 James Posey	.50	.20
❏ 17 Darius Miles	.75	.30
❏ 18 Jason Kidd	1.25	.50
❏ 19 Anfernee Hardaway	.75	.30
❏ 20 Karl Malone	.75	.30
❏ 21 Kevin Garnett	1.50	.60
❏ 22 Shareef Abdur-Rahim	.75	.30
❏ 23 Steve Francis	.75	.30
❏ 24 Paul Pierce	.75	.30
❏ 25 Mike Miller	.75	.30
❏ 26 Tim Duncan	1.50	.60
❏ 27 Derek Anderson	.50	.20
❏ 28 Eddie Jones	.75	.30
❏ 29 Keith Van Horn	.75	.30
❏ 30 Chris Mihm	.50	.20
❏ 31 Clifford Robinson	.25	.08
❏ 32 Gary Payton	.75	.30
❏ 33 Courtney Alexander	.50	.20
❏ 34 Shaquille O'Neal	2.00	.75
❏ 35 Tim Thomas	.50	.20
❏ 36 Raef LaFrentz	.50	.20
❏ 37 Stromile Swift	.50	.20
❏ 38 Stephon Marbury	.75	.30
❏ 39 Morris Peterson	.50	.20
❏ 40 Donyell Marshall	.50	.20
❏ 41 Kenny Thomas	.25	.08
❏ 42 Juwan Howard	.50	.20
❏ 43 Tracy McGrady	2.00	.75
❏ 44 Kenny Anderson	.50	.20
❏ 45 Larry Hughes	.50	.20
❏ 46 Allan Houston	.50	.20
❏ 47 Chris Webber	.75	.30
❏ 48 Andre Miller	.50	.20
❏ 49 Corey Maggette	.50	.20
❏ 50 Sam Cassell	.75	.30
❏ 51 Steve Smith	.50	.20
❏ 52 Jamal Mashburn	.50	.20
❏ 53 Al Harrington	.50	.20
❏ 54 Brian Grant	.50	.20
❏ 55 Rasheed Wallace	.75	.30
❏ 56 Rick Fox	.75	.30
❏ 57 Jason Terry	.75	.30
❏ 58 Rashard Lewis	.75	.30
❏ 59 Joe Smith	.50	.20
❏ 60 Michael Dickerson	.50	.20
❏ 61 Michael Finley	.75	.30
❏ 62 Danny Fortson	.25	.08
❏ 63 Allen Iverson	1.50	.60
❏ 64 Richard Hamilton	.50	.20
❏ 65 Antonio McDyess	.50	.20
❏ 66 David Wesley	.25	.08
❏ 67 Ben Wallace	.75	.30
❏ 68 Mike Bibby	.75	.30
❏ 69 Antonio Davis	.25	.08
❏ 70 Cuttino Mobley	.50	.20
❏ 71 Lamond Murray	.25	.08
❏ 72 Antoine Walker	.75	.30
❏ 73 Jermaine O'Neal	.75	.30
❏ 74 Alonzo Mourning	.50	.20
❏ 75 Shawn Marion	.75	.30
❏ 76 John Stockton	.75	.30
❏ 77 Marcus Camby	.50	.20
❏ 78 Derek Fisher	.75	.30
❏ 79 DerMarr Johnson	.50	.20
❏ 80 Aaron McKie	.50	.20
❏ 81 David Robinson	.75	.30
❏ 82 Steve Nash	.75	.30
❏ 83 Ray Allen	.75	.30
❏ 84 Elton Brand	.75	.30
❏ 85 Kenyon Martin	.75	.30
❏ 86 Bonzi Wells	.75	.30
❏ 87 Grant Hill	.75	.30
❏ 88 Terrell Brandon	.50	.20
❏ 89 Toni Kukoc	.50	.20

❏ 90 Jerry Stackhouse	.75	.30
❏ 91A Tierre Brown RC	2.00	.75
❏ 91B Tierre Brown RC	2.00	.75
❏ 91C Tierre Brown RC	2.00	.75
❏ 92A Jamison Brewer RC	2.00	.75
❏ 92B Jamison Brewer RC	2.00	.75
❏ 92C Jamison Brewer RC	2.00	.75
❏ 93A Antonis Fotsis RC	2.00	.75
❏ 93B Antonis Fotsis RC	2.00	.75
❏ 93C Antonis Fotsis RC	2.00	.75
❏ 94A Mike James RC	2.00	.75
❏ 94B Mike James RC	2.00	.75
❏ 94C Mike James RC	2.00	.75
❏ 95A Primoz Brezec RC	2.50	1.00
❏ 95B Primoz Brezec RC	2.50	1.00
❏ 95C Primoz Brezec RC	2.50	1.00
❏ 96A Jeryl Sasser RC	2.00	.75
❏ 96B Jeryl Sasser RC	2.00	.75
❏ 96C Jeryl Sasser RC	2.00	.75
❏ 97A DeSagana Diop RC	2.00	.75
❏ 97B DeSagana Diop RC	2.00	.75
❏ 97C DeSagana Diop RC	2.00	.75
❏ 98A Mengke Bateer RC	2.00	.75
❏ 98B Mengke Bateer RC	2.00	.75
❏ 98C Mengke Bateer RC	2.00	.75
❏ 99A Gerald Wallace RC	4.00	1.50
❏ 99B Gerald Wallace RC	4.00	1.50
❏ 99C Gerald Wallace RC	4.00	1.50
❏ 100A Kenny Satterfield RC	2.00	.75
❏ 100B Kenny Satterfield RC	2.00	.75
❏ 100C Kenny Satterfield RC	2.00	.75
❏ 101A R.Boumtje-Boumtje RC	2.00	.75
❏ 101B R.Boumtje-Boumtje RC	2.00	.75
❏ 101C R.Boumtje-Boumtje RC	2.00	.75
❏ 102A Brian Scalabrine RC	2.00	.75
❏ 102B Brian Scalabrine RC	2.00	.75
❏ 102C Brian Scalabrine RC	2.00	.75
❏ 103A Oscar Torres RC	2.00	.75
❏ 103B Oscar Torres RC	2.00	.75
❏ 103C Oscar Torres RC	2.00	.75
❏ 104A Jarron Collins RC	2.00	.75
❏ 104B Jarron Collins RC	2.00	.75
❏ 104C Jarron Collins RC	2.00	.75
❏ 105A Jeff Trepagnier RC	2.00	.75
❏ 105B Jeff Trepagnier RC	2.00	.75
❏ 105C Jeff Trepagnier RC	2.00	.75
❏ 106A Brendan Haywood RC	2.50	1.00
❏ 106B Brendan Haywood RC	2.50	1.00
❏ 106C Brendan Haywood RC	2.50	1.00
❏ 107A Vladimir Radmanovic RC	2.50	1.00
❏ 107B Vladimir Radmanovic RC	2.50	1.00
❏ 107C Vladimir Radmanovic RC	2.50	1.00
❏ 108A Loren Woods RC	2.00	.75
❏ 108B Loren Woods RC	2.00	.75
❏ 108C Loren Woods RC	2.00	.75
❏ 109A Terence Morris RC	2.00	.75
❏ 109B Terence Morris RC	2.00	.75
❏ 109C Terence Morris RC	2.00	.75
❏ 110A Kirk Haston RC	2.00	.75
❏ 110B Kirk Haston RC	2.00	.75
❏ 110C Kirk Haston RC	2.00	.75
❏ 111A Earl Watson RC	2.00	.75
❏ 111B Earl Watson RC	2.00	.75
❏ 111C Earl Watson RC	2.00	.75
❏ 112A Brandon Armstrong RC	2.50	1.00
❏ 112B Brandon Armstrong RC	2.50	1.00
❏ 112C Brandon Armstrong RC	2.50	1.00
❏ 113A Zach Randolph RC	6.00	2.50
❏ 113B Zach Randolph RC	6.00	2.50
❏ 113C Zach Randolph RC	6.00	2.50
❏ 114A Bobby Simmons RC	2.00	.75
❏ 114B Bobby Simmons RC	2.00	.75
❏ 114C Bobby Simmons RC	2.00	.75
❏ 115A Alton Ford RC	2.00	.75
❏ 115B Alton Ford RC	2.00	.75
❏ 115C Alton Ford RC	2.00	.75
❏ 116A Predrag Drobnjak RC	2.50	1.00
❏ 116B Predrag Drobnjak RC	2.50	1.00
❏ 116C Predrag Drobnjak RC	2.50	1.00
❏ 117A Michael Bradley RC	2.50	1.00
❏ 117B Michael Bradley RC	2.50	1.00
❏ 117C Michael Bradley RC	2.50	1.00
❏ 118A Samuel Dalembert RC	2.50	1.00
❏ 118B Samuel Dalembert RC	2.50	1.00
❏ 118C Samuel Dalembert RC	2.50	1.00
❏ 119A Gilbert Arenas RC	5.00	2.00

❏ 119B Gilbert Arenas RC	5.00	2.00
❏ 119C Gilbert Arenas RC	5.00	2.00
❏ 120A Kedrick Brown RC	2.00	.75
❏ 120B Kedrick Brown RC	2.00	.75
❏ 120C Kedrick Brown RC	2.00	.75
❏ 121A Trenton Hassell RC	4.00	1.50
❏ 121B Trenton Hassell RC	4.00	1.50
❏ 121C Trenton Hassell RC	4.00	1.50
❏ 122A Zeljko Rebraca RC	2.50	1.00
❏ 122B Zeljko Rebraca RC	2.50	1.00
❏ 122C Zeljko Rebraca RC	2.50	1.00
❏ 123A Jason Collins RC	2.50	1.00
❏ 123B Jason Collins RC	2.50	1.00
❏ 123C Jason Collins RC	2.50	1.00
❏ 124A Will Solomon RC	2.50	1.00
❏ 124B Will Solomon RC	2.50	1.00
❏ 124C Will Solomon RC	2.50	1.00
❏ 125A Joseph Forte RC	6.00	2.50
❏ 125B Joseph Forte RC	6.00	2.50
❏ 125C Joseph Forte RC	6.00	2.50
❏ 126A Steven Hunter RC	2.50	1.00
❏ 126B Steven Hunter RC	2.50	1.00
❏ 126C Steven Hunter RC	2.50	1.00
❏ 127A Eddy Curry RC	6.00	2.50
❏ 127B Eddy Curry RC	6.00	2.50
❏ 127C Eddy Curry RC	6.00	2.50
❏ 128A Troy Murphy RC	5.00	2.00
❏ 128B Troy Murphy RC	5.00	2.00
❏ 128C Troy Murphy RC	5.00	2.00
❏ 129A Shane Battier RC	4.00	1.50
❏ 129B Shane Battier RC	4.00	1.50
❏ 129C Shane Battier RC	4.00	1.50
❏ 130A Tyson Chandler RC	8.00	3.00
❏ 130B Tyson Chandler RC	8.00	3.00
❏ 130C Tyson Chandler RC	8.00	3.00
❏ 131A Joe Johnson RC	6.00	2.50
❏ 131B Joe Johnson RC	6.00	2.50
❏ 131C Joe Johnson RC	6.00	2.50
❏ 132A Richard Jefferson RC	4.00	1.50
❏ 132B Richard Jefferson RC	4.00	1.50
❏ 132C Richard Jefferson RC	4.00	1.50
❏ 133A Eddie Griffin RC	3.00	1.25
❏ 133A Eddie Griffin RC	3.00	1.25
❏ 133B Eddie Griffin RC	3.00	1.25
❏ 134B Rodney White RC	3.00	1.25
❏ 134C Rodney White RC	3.00	1.25
❏ 135A Andrei Kirilenko RC	8.00	3.00
❏ 135B Andrei Kirilenko RC	8.00	3.00
❏ 135C Andrei Kirilenko RC	8.00	3.00
❏ 136A Tony Parker RC	12.00	5.00
❏ 136B Tony Parker RC	12.00	5.00
❏ 136C Tony Parker RC	12.00	5.00
❏ 137A Jamaal Tinsley RC	6.00	2.50
❏ 137B Jamaal Tinsley RC	6.00	2.50
❏ 137C Jamaal Tinsley RC	6.00	2.50
❏ 138A Pau Gasol RC	10.00	4.00
❏ 138B Pau Gasol RC	10.00	4.00
❏ 138C Pau Gasol RC	10.00	4.00
❏ 139A Jason Richardson RC	8.00	3.00
❏ 139B Jason Richardson RC	8.00	3.00
❏ 139C Jason Richardson RC	8.00	3.00
❏ 140A Kwame Brown RC	6.00	2.50
❏ 140B Kwame Brown RC	6.00	2.50
❏ 140C Kwame Brown RC	6.00	2.50

2002-03 Upper Deck Generations

	COMP.SET w/o SP's (150)	60.00	25.00
	COMMON CARD (1-50)	.20	.08
	COMMON ROOKIE (51-92)	4.00	1.50
	COMMON CARD (93-192)	.75	.30
	COMMON CARD (193-234)	4.00	1.50
1	Shareef Abdur-Rahim	.75	.30
2	Paul Pierce	.75	.30
3	Antoine Walker	.75	.30
4	Jalen Rose	.75	.30
5	Tyson Chandler	.75	.30
6	Darius Miles	.75	.30
7	Dirk Nowitzki	1.25	.50
8	Steve Nash	.75	.30
9	James Posey	.50	.20
10	Richard Hamilton	.50	.20
11	Ben Wallace	.75	.30
12	Antawn Jamison	.75	.30
13	Jason Richardson	.75	.30
14	Steve Francis	.75	.30
15	Eddie Griffin	.50	.20
16	Reggie Miller	.75	.30
17	Jamaal Tinsley	.75	.30
18	Elton Brand	.75	.30
19	Andre Miller	.50	.20
20	Kobe Bryant	3.00	1.25
21	Shaquille O'Neal	2.00	.75
22	Pau Gasol	.75	.30
23	Shane Battier	.75	.30
24	Alonzo Mourning	.50	.20
25	Ray Allen	.75	.30
26	Kevin Garnett	1.50	.60
27	Wally Szczerbiak	.50	.20
28	Jason Kidd	1.25	.50
29	Kenyon Martin	.75	.30
30	Jamal Mashburn	.50	.20
31	Baron Davis	.75	.30
32	Latrell Sprewell	.75	.30
33	Tracy McGrady	2.00	.75
34	Allen Iverson	1.50	.60
35	Stephon Marbury	.75	.30
36	Shawn Marion	.75	.30
37	Rasheed Wallace	.75	.30
38	Bonzi Wells	.50	.20
39	Chris Webber	.75	.30
40	Mike Bibby	.75	.30
41	Tim Duncan	1.50	.60
42	Tony Parker	.75	.30
43	Gary Payton	.75	.30
44	Rashard Lewis	.50	.20
45	Vince Carter	2.00	.75
46	Morris Peterson	.50	.20
47	Karl Malone	.75	.30
48	John Stockton	.75	.30
49	Michael Jordan	8.00	3.00
50	Jerry Stackhouse	.75	.30
51	Yao Ming RC	25.00	10.00
52	Jay Williams RC	5.00	2.00
53	Mike Dunleavy RC	6.00	2.50
54	Drew Gooden RC	10.00	4.00
55	Nikoloz Tskitishvili RC	4.00	1.50
56	DaJuan Wagner RC	6.00	2.50
57	Nene Hilario RC	5.00	2.00
58	Chris Wilcox RC	5.00	2.00
59	Amare Stoudemire RC	15.00	6.00
60	Caron Butler RC	8.00	3.00
61	Jared Jeffries RC	4.00	1.50
62	Melvin Ely RC	4.00	1.50
63	Marcus Haislip RC	4.00	1.50
64	Fred Jones RC	4.00	1.50
65	Bostjan Nachbar RC	4.00	1.50
66	Jiri Welsch RC	4.00	1.50
67	Juan Dixon RC	6.00	2.50
68	Curtis Borchardt RC	4.00	1.50
69	Ryan Humphrey RC	4.00	1.50
70	Kareem Rush RC	5.00	2.00
71	Qyntel Woods RC	4.00	1.50
72	Casey Jacobsen RC	4.00	1.50
73	Tayshaun Prince RC	5.00	2.00
74	Predrag Savovic RC	4.00	1.50
75	Frank Williams RC	4.00	1.50
76	John Salmons RC	4.00	1.50
77	Chris Jefferies RC	4.00	1.50
78	Dan Dickau RC	4.00	1.50
79	Marcus Taylor RC	5.00	2.00
80	Roger Mason RC	4.00	1.50
81	Robert Archibald RC	4.00	1.50
82	Vincent Yarbrough RC	4.00	1.50
83	Dan Gadzuric RC	4.00	1.50
84	Carlos Boozer RC	8.00	3.00
85	Tito Maddox RC	4.00	1.50
86	Rod Grizzard RC	4.00	1.50
87	Ronald Murray RC	6.00	2.50
88	Marko Jaric	4.00	1.50
89	Lonny Baxter RC	4.00	1.50
90	Sam Clancy RC	4.00	1.50
91	Matt Barnes RC	4.00	1.50
92	Jamal Sampson RC	4.00	1.50
93	Oscar Robertson	2.00	.75
94	Moses Malone	1.25	.50
95	Earl Monroe	.75	.30
96	Pete Maravich	3.00	1.25
97	Artis Gilmore	.75	.30
98	Julius Erving	3.00	1.25
99	Nate Archibald	.75	.30
100	Wes Unseld	.75	.30
101	Willis Reed	.75	.30
102	Jo Jo White	.75	.30
103	Isiah Thomas	1.25	.50
104	Bill Sharman	.75	.30
105	Wilt Chamberlain	2.00	.75
106	Bob Cousy	1.25	.50
107	Tom Heinsohn	.75	.30
108	Terry Cummings	.75	.30
109	John Havlicek	1.50	.60
110	Bob Pettit	.75	.30
111	Drazen Petrovic	.75	.30
112	Dan Roundfield	.75	.30
113	David Thompson	.75	.30
114	Bobby Jones	.75	.30
115	Clyde Lovellette	.75	.30
116	Rick Barry	1.25	.50
117	K.C. Jones	.75	.30
118	Lionel Hollins	.75	.30
119	Bob Lanier	.75	.30
120	Al Attles	.75	.30
121	Jack Sikma	.75	.30
122	George McGinnis	.75	.30
123	Quinn Buckner	.75	.30
124	Magic Johnson	3.00	1.25
125	Larry Bird	4.00	1.50
126	Cliff Hagan	.75	.30
127	Jerry Lucas	.75	.30
128	Ricky Pierce	.75	.30
129	Walter Davis	.75	.30
130	Danny Ainge	.75	.30
131	Reggie Theus	.75	.30
132	Darryl Dawkins	1.25	.50
133	Tom Chambers	.75	.30
134	M.L. Carr	.75	.30
135	Kelly Tripucka	.75	.30
136	George Gervin	.75	.30
137	Robert Parish	1.25	.50
138	Mitch Kupchak	.75	.30
139	Lou Hudson	.75	.30
140	Bill Cartwright	.75	.30
141	Lafayette Lever	.75	.30
142	Kevin Loughery	.75	.30
143	Hal Greer	.75	.30
144	Jamaal Wilkes	.75	.30
145	Alvan Adams	.75	.30
146	Thomas Sanders	.75	.30
147	Cazzie Russell	1.25	.50
148	Austin Carr	.75	.30
149	Gail Goodrich	.75	.30
150	Billy Knight	.75	.30
151	Dave Bing	.75	.30
152	Bill Walton	2.00	.75
153	Sam Jones	.75	.30
154	Swen Nater	.75	.30
155	Bobby Dandridge	.75	.30
156	Junior Bridgeman	.75	.30
157	Paul Silas	1.25	.50
158	John Kerr	.75	.30
159	Phil Chenier	.75	.30
160	Alex English	.75	.30
161	Geoff Petrie	.75	.30
162	Walt Bellamy	.75	.30
163	Don Nelson	.75	.30
164	Byron Scott	.75	.30
165	Harvey Catchings	.75	.30
166	Edward Macauley	.75	.30
167	John Drew	.75	.30
168	Detlef Schrempf	.75	.30
169	Rolando Blackman	.75	.30
170	Dave DeBusschere	1.25	.50
171	Marvin Barnes	.75	.30
172	Elgin Baylor	1.25	.50
173	Cedric Maxwell	.75	.30
174	Vern Mikkelsen	.75	.30
175	Larry Brown	.75	.30
176	Rick Mahorn	.75	.30
177	Dolph Schayes	.75	.30
178	Kevin McHale	1.50	.60
179	Clark Kellogg	.75	.30
180	Otis Birdsong	.75	.30
181	Michael Cooper	.75	.30
182	Mike Dunleavy	.75	.30
183	Spencer Haywood	.75	.30
184	Larry Nance	.75	.30
185	Maurice Lucas	.75	.30
186	Fred Brown	.75	.30
187	Jerry West	1.50	.60
188	Joe Barry Carroll	.75	.30
189	Dave Cowens	.75	.30
190	Sidney Moncrief	1.25	.50
191	Kiki Vandeweghe	.75	.30
192	Walt Frazier	1.50	.60
193	Y.Ming/W.Chamberlain	15.00	6.00
194	J.Williams/J.Erving	6.00	2.50
195	D.Gooden/J.Havlicek	10.00	4.00
196	N.Tskitishvili/K.McHale	4.00	1.50
197	D.Wagner/O.Robertson	4.00	1.50
198	H.Nilario/K.Vandeweghe	4.00	1.50
199	Chris Wilcox	4.00	1.50
200	A.Stoudamire/G.McGinnis	15.00	6.00
201	C.Butler/W.Reed	8.00	3.00
202	J.Jeffries/L.Bird	6.00	2.50
203	M.Ely/E.Baylor	4.00	1.50
204	M.Haislip/K.Abdul-Jabbar	4.00	1.50
205	F.Jones/K.C.Jones	4.00	1.50
206	Bostjan Nachbar	4.00	1.50
207	Jiri Welsch	4.00	1.50
208	Juan Dixon	6.00	2.50
209	Curtis Borchardt	4.00	1.50
210	R.Humphrey/B.Lanier	4.00	1.50
211	K.Rush/W.Frazier	5.00	2.00
212	Q.Woods/J.Wilkes	4.00	1.50
213	J.Jacobsen/T.Chambers	4.00	1.50
214	T.Prince/B.Scott	5.00	2.00
215	P.Savovic/D.Petrovic	4.00	1.50
216	Frank Williams	4.00	1.50
217	J.Salmons/E.Baylor	4.00	1.50
218	C.Jefferies/W.Davis	4.00	1.50
219	Dan Dickau	4.00	1.50
220	M.Taylor/O.Robertson	4.00	1.50
221	R.Mason/J.White	4.00	1.50
222	R.Archibald/S.Moncrief	4.00	1.50
223	V.Yarbrough/E.Monroe	4.00	1.50
224	D.Gadzuric/B.Walton	4.00	1.50
225	C.Boozer/R.Parish	8.00	3.00
226	Tito Maddox	4.00	1.50
227	R.Grizzard/G.Gervin	4.00	1.50
228	R.Murray/I.Lever	4.00	1.50
229	Marko Jaric	4.00	1.50
230	Lonny Baxter	4.00	1.50
231	S.Clancy/W.Unseld	4.00	1.50
232	Matt Barnes	4.00	1.50
233	Jamal Sampson	4.00	1.50
234	J.Sampson/M.Dunleavy	4.00	1.50

1999-00 Upper Deck Gold Reserve

	COMPLETE SET (270)	120.00	60.00
	COMPLETE SET w/o SP's (240)	40.00	20.00
	COMMON CARD (1-240)	.25	.08
	COMMON ROOKIE (241-270)	1.50	.60
1	Roshown McLeod	.25	.08
2	Dikembe Mutombo	.50	.20
3	Alan Henderson	.25	.08
4	Chris Crawford	.25	.08
5	Jim Jackson	.25	.08
6	Isaiah Rider	.25	.08
7	Lorenzen Wright	.25	.08
8	Bimbo Coles	.25	.08
9	Kenny Anderson	.50	.20
10	Antoine Walker	.75	.30
11	Paul Pierce	.75	.30

#	Player		
❏ 12	Vitaly Potapenko	.25	.08
❏ 13	Dana Barros	.25	.08
❏ 14	Calbert Cheaney	.25	.08
❏ 15	Pervis Ellison	.25	.08
❏ 16	Eric Williams	.25	.08
❏ 17	Tony Battie	.25	.08
❏ 18	Elden Campbell	.25	.08
❏ 19	Eddie Jones	.75	.30
❏ 20	David Wesley	.25	.08
❏ 21	Derrick Coleman	.50	.20
❏ 22	Ricky Davis	.50	.20
❏ 23	Anthony Mason	.50	.20
❏ 24	Todd Fuller	.25	.08
❏ 25	Brad Miller	.75	.30
❏ 26	Corey Benjamin	.25	.08
❏ 27	Randy Brown	.25	.08
❏ 28	Dickey Simpkins	.25	.08
❏ 29	Toni Kukoc	.50	.20
❏ 30	Fred Hoiberg	.25	.08
❏ 31	Hersey Hawkins	.50	.20
❏ 32	Will Perdue	.25	.08
❏ 33	Chris Anstey	.25	.08
❏ 34	Shawn Kemp	.50	.20
❏ 35	Wesley Person	.25	.08
❏ 36	Brevin Knight	.25	.08
❏ 37	Bob Sura	.25	.08
❏ 38	Danny Ferry	.25	.08
❏ 39	Lamond Murray	.25	.08
❏ 40	Cedric Henderson	.25	.08
❏ 41	Andrew DeClercq	.25	.08
❏ 42	Michael Finley	.75	.30
❏ 43	Shawn Bradley	.25	.08
❏ 44	Dirk Nowitzki	1.50	.60
❏ 45	Erick Strickland	.25	.08
❏ 46	Cedric Ceballos	.25	.08
❏ 47	Hubert Davis	.25	.08
❏ 48	Robert Pack	.25	.08
❏ 49	Gary Trent	.25	.08
❏ 50	Antonio McDyess	.50	.20
❏ 51	Nick Van Exel	.75	.30
❏ 52	Chauncey Billups	.50	.20
❏ 53	Bryant Stith	.25	.08
❏ 54	Raef LaFrentz	.50	.20
❏ 55	Ron Mercer	.50	.20
❏ 56	George McCloud	.25	.08
❏ 57	Roy Rogers	.25	.08
❏ 58	Keon Clark	.50	.20
❏ 59	Grant Hill	.75	.30
❏ 60	Lindsey Hunter	.25	.08
❏ 61	Jerry Stackhouse	.75	.30
❏ 62	Terry Mills	.25	.08
❏ 63	Michael Curry	.25	.08
❏ 64	Christian Laettner	.50	.20
❏ 65	Jerome Williams	.25	.08
❏ 66	Loy Vaught	.25	.08
❏ 67	John Starks	.50	.20
❏ 68	Antawn Jamison	1.25	.50
❏ 69	Erick Dampier	.50	.20
❏ 70	Jason Caffey	.25	.08
❏ 71	Terry Cummings	.25	.08
❏ 72	Donyell Marshall	.50	.20
❏ 73	Chris Mills	.25	.08
❏ 74	Tony Farmer	.25	.08
❏ 75	Adonal Foyle	.25	.08
❏ 76	Hakeem Olajuwon	.75	.30
❏ 77	Cuttino Mobley	.75	.30
❏ 78	Charles Barkley	1.00	.40
❏ 79	Bryce Drew	.25	.08
❏ 80	Shandon Anderson	.25	.08
❏ 81	Kelvin Cato	.25	.08
❏ 82	Walt Williams	.25	.08
❏ 83	Carlos Rogers	.25	.08
❏ 84	Reggie Miller	.75	.30
❏ 85	Jalen Rose	.75	.30
❏ 86	Mark Jackson	.50	.20
❏ 87	Dale Davis	.25	.08
❏ 88	Chris Mullin	.75	.30
❏ 89	Al Harrington	.75	.30
❏ 90	Rik Smits	.50	.20
❏ 91	Sam Perkins	.25	.08
❏ 92	Austin Croshere	.25	.08
❏ 93	Maurice Taylor	.50	.20
❏ 94	Tyrone Nesby RC	.25	.08
❏ 95	Michael Olowokandi	.50	.20
❏ 96	Eric Piatkowski	.50	.20
❏ 97	Troy Hudson	.25	.08
❏ 98	Derek Anderson	.50	.20
❏ 99	Eric Murdock	.25	.08
❏ 100	Brian Skinner	.25	.08
❏ 101	Kobe Bryant	3.00	1.25
❏ 102	Shaquille O'Neal ™	2.00	.75
❏ 103	Glen Rice	.50	.20
❏ 104	Robert Horry	.25	.08
❏ 105	Ron Harper	.50	.20
❏ 106	Derek Fisher	.75	.30
❏ 107	Rick Fox	.50	.20
❏ 108	A.C. Green	.50	.20
❏ 109	Tim Hardaway	.50	.20
❏ 110	Alonzo Mourning	.50	.20
❏ 111	P.J. Brown	.25	.08
❏ 112	Dan Majerle	.50	.20
❏ 113	Jamal Mashburn	.50	.20
❏ 114	Voshon Lenard	.25	.08
❏ 115	Clarence Weatherspoon	.25	.08
❏ 116	Rex Walters	.25	.08
❏ 117	Ray Allen	.75	.30
❏ 118	Glenn Robinson	.75	.30
❏ 119	Sam Cassell	.75	.30
❏ 120	Robert Traylor	.25	.08
❏ 121	J.R. Reid	.25	.08
❏ 122	Ervin Johnson	.25	.08
❏ 123	Danny Manning	.25	.08
❏ 124	Tim Thomas	.50	.20
❏ 125	Kevin Garnett	1.50	.60
❏ 126	Sam Mitchell	.25	.08
❏ 127	Dean Garrett	.25	.08
❏ 128	Bobby Jackson	.50	.20
❏ 129	Radoslav Nesterovic	.50	.20
❏ 130	Terrell Brandon	.50	.20
❏ 131	Joe Smith	.50	.20
❏ 132	Anthony Peeler	.25	.08
❏ 133	Keith Van Horn	.75	.30
❏ 134	Stephon Marbury	.75	.30
❏ 135	Kendall Gill	.25	.08
❏ 136	Scott Burrell	.25	.08
❏ 137	Jayson Williams	.50	.20
❏ 138	Jamie Feick RC	.25	.08
❏ 139	Kerry Kittles	.25	.08
❏ 140	Johnny Newman	.25	.08
❏ 141	Patrick Ewing	.75	.30
❏ 142	Allan Houston	.50	.20
❏ 143	Latrell Sprewell	.75	.30
❏ 144	Larry Johnson	.50	.20
❏ 145	Marcus Camby	.50	.20
❏ 146	Chris Childs	.25	.08
❏ 147	Kurt Thomas	.50	.20
❏ 148	Charlie Ward	.25	.08
❏ 149	Darrell Armstrong	.25	.08
❏ 150	Matt Harpring	.75	.30
❏ 151	Michael Doleac	.25	.08
❏ 152	Bo Outlaw	.25	.08
❏ 153	Tariq Abdul-Wahad	.25	.08
❏ 154	John Amaechi RC	.75	.30
❏ 155	Ben Wallace	.75	.30
❏ 156	Monty Williams	.25	.08
❏ 157	Allen Iverson	1.50	.60
❏ 158	Theo Ratliff	.50	.20
❏ 159	Larry Hughes	.75	.30
❏ 160	Eric Snow	.50	.20
❏ 161	George Lynch	.25	.08
❏ 162	Tyrone Hill	.25	.08
❏ 163	Billy Owens	.25	.08
❏ 164	Aaron McKie	.50	.20
❏ 165	Jason Kidd	1.25	.50
❏ 166	Clifford Robinson	.25	.08
❏ 167	Tom Gugliotta	.25	.08
❏ 168	Luc Longley	.25	.08
❏ 169	Anfernee Hardaway	.75	.30
❏ 170	Rex Chapman	.25	.08
❏ 171	Oliver Miller	.25	.08
❏ 172	Rodney Rogers	.25	.08
❏ 173	Rasheed Wallace	.75	.30
❏ 174	Arvydas Sabonis	.50	.20
❏ 175	Damon Stoudamire	.50	.20
❏ 176	Brian Grant	.50	.20
❏ 177	Scottie Pippen	1.25	.50
❏ 178	Detlef Schrempf	.50	.20
❏ 179	Steve Smith	.50	.20
❏ 180	Jermaine O'Neal	.75	.30
❏ 181	Bonzi Wells	.75	.30
❏ 182	Jason Williams	.75	.30
❏ 183	Vlade Divac	.50	.20
❏ 184	Peja Stojakovic	1.00	.40
❏ 185	Lawrence Funderburke	.25	.08
❏ 186	Chris Webber	.75	.30
❏ 187	Nick Anderson	.25	.08
❏ 188	Darrick Martin	.25	.08
❏ 189	Corliss Williamson	.50	.20
❏ 190	Tim Duncan	1.50	.60
❏ 191	Sean Elliott	.25	.08
❏ 192	David Robinson	.75	.30
❏ 193	Mario Elie	.25	.08
❏ 194	Avery Johnson	.25	.08
❏ 195	Terry Porter	.25	.08
❏ 196	Malik Rose	.25	.08
❏ 197	Jaren Jackson	.25	.08
❏ 198	Gary Payton	.75	.30
❏ 199	Vin Baker	.50	.20
❏ 200	Rashard Lewis	.75	.30
❏ 201	Jelani McCoy	.25	.08
❏ 202	Brent Barry	.50	.20
❏ 203	Horace Grant	.50	.20
❏ 204	Vernon Maxwell UER	.25	.08
❏ 205	Ruben Patterson	.50	.20
❏ 206	Vince Carter	2.00	.75
❏ 207	Doug Christie	.25	.08
❏ 208	Kevin Willis	.25	.08
❏ 209	Dee Brown	.25	.08
❏ 210	Antonio Davis	.25	.08
❏ 211	Tracy McGrady	2.00	.75
❏ 212	Dell Curry	.25	.08
❏ 213	Charles Oakley	.25	.08
❏ 214	Karl Malone	.75	.30
❏ 215	John Stockton	.75	.30
❏ 216	Howard Eisley	.25	.08
❏ 217	Bryon Russell	.25	.08
❏ 218	Greg Ostertag	.25	.08
❏ 219	Jeff Hornacek	.50	.20
❏ 220	Olden Polynice	.25	.08
❏ 221	Adam Keefe	.25	.08
❏ 222	Shareef Abdur-Rahim	.75	.30
❏ 223	Mike Bibby	.75	.30
❏ 224	Felipe Lopez	.25	.08
❏ 225	Cherokee Parks	.25	.08
❏ 226	Michael Dickerson	.50	.20
❏ 227	Othella Harrington	.25	.08
❏ 228	Bryant Reeves	.25	.08
❏ 229	Brent Price	.25	.08
❏ 230	Michael Smith	.25	.08
❏ 231	Juwan Howard	.50	.20
❏ 232	Rod Strickland	.25	.08
❏ 233	Chris Whitney	.25	.08
❏ 234	Tracy Murray	.25	.08
❏ 235	Mitch Richmond	.50	.20
❏ 236	Aaron Williams	.25	.08
❏ 237	Isaac Austin	.25	.08
❏ 238	Kobe Bryant CL	.75	.30
❏ 239	Michael Jordan CL	1.00	.40
❏ 240	Kevin Garnett CL	.75	.30
❏ 241	Elton Brand RC	10.00	4.00
❏ 242	Steve Francis RC	10.00	4.00
❏ 243	Baron Davis RC	12.00	5.00
❏ 244	Lamar Odom RC	8.00	3.00
❏ 245	Jonathan Bender RC	8.00	3.00
❏ 246	Wally Szczerbiak RC	8.00	3.00
❏ 247	Richard Hamilton RC	8.00	3.00
❏ 248	Andre Miller RC	8.00	3.00
❏ 249	Shawn Marion RC	10.00	4.00
❏ 250	Jason Terry RC	6.00	2.50
❏ 251	Trajan Langdon RC	3.00	1.25

❑ 252	A.Radojevic RC	1.50	.60
❑ 253	Corey Maggette RC	8.00	3.00
❑ 254	William Avery RC	3.00	1.25
❑ 255	Ron Artest RC	5.00	2.00
❑ 256	Cal Bowdler RC	2.50	1.00
❑ 257	James Posey RC	5.00	2.00
❑ 258	Quincy Lewis RC	2.50	1.00
❑ 259	Dion Glover RC	2.50	1.00
❑ 260	Jeff Foster RC	2.60	1.00
❑ 261	Kenny Thomas RC	3.00	1.25
❑ 262	Devean George RC	4.00	1.50
❑ 263	Tim James RC	2.50	1.00
❑ 264	Vonteego Cummings RC	3.00	1.25
❑ 265	Jumaine Jones RC	3.00	1.25
❑ 266	Scott Padgett RC	2.50	1.00
❑ 267	Rodney Buford RC	1.50	.60
❑ 268	Adrian Griffin RC	2.50	1.00
❑ 269	Anthony Carter RC	5.00	2.00
❑ 270	Eddie Robinson RC	5.00	2.00

1998 Upper Deck Hardcourt

❑	COMPLETE SET (90)	75.00	40.00
❑ 1	Kobe Bryant	8.00	3.00
❑ 2	Donyell Marshall	1.50	.60
❑ 3	Bryant Reeves	.60	.25
❑ 4	Keith Van Horn	2.00	.75
❑ 5	David Robinson	2.00	.75
❑ 6	Nick Anderson	.60	.25
❑ 7	Nick Van Exel	2.00	.75
❑ 8	David Wesley	.60	.25
❑ 9	Alonzo Mourning	1.50	.60
❑ 10	Shawn Kemp	1.50	.60
❑ 11	Maurice Taylor	1.25	.50
❑ 12	Kenny Anderson	1.50	.60
❑ 13	Jason Kidd	3.00	1.25
❑ 14	Marcus Camby	1.50	.60
❑ 15	Tim Hardaway	1.50	.60
❑ 16	Damon Stoudamire	1.50	.60
❑ 17	Detlef Schrempf	1.50	.60
❑ 18	Dikembe Mutombo	1.50	.60
❑ 19	Charles Barkley	2.50	1.00
❑ 20	Ray Allen	2.00	.75
❑ 21	Ron Mercer	1.25	.50
❑ 22	Shawn Bradley	.60	.25
❑ 23	Michael Jordan	10.00	4.00
❑ 23A	Michael Jordan Spec.	20.00	8.00
❑ 24	Antonio McDyess	1.50	.60
❑ 25	Stephon Marbury	2.00	.75
❑ 26	Rik Smits	1.50	.60
❑ 27	Michael Stewart	.60	.25
❑ 28	Steve Smith	1.50	.60
❑ 29	Glenn Robinson	1.50	.60
❑ 30	Chris Webber	2.00	.75
❑ 31	Antoine Walker	2.00	.75
❑ 32	Eddie Jones	2.00	.75
❑ 33	Mitch Richmond	1.50	.60
❑ 34	Kevin Garnett	4.00	1.50
❑ 35	Grant Hill	2.00	.75
❑ 36	John Stockton	2.00	.75
❑ 37	Allan Houston	1.50	.60
❑ 38	Bobby Jackson	1.50	.60
❑ 39	Sam Cassell	2.00	.75
❑ 40	Allen Iverson	4.00	1.50
❑ 41	LaPhonso Ellis	.60	.25
❑ 42	Lorenzen Wright	.60	.25
❑ 43	Gary Payton	2.00	.75
❑ 44	Patrick Ewing	2.00	.75

❑ 45	Scottie Pippen	3.00	1.25
❑ 46	Hakeem Olajuwon	2.00	.75
❑ 47	Glen Rice	1.50	.60
❑ 48	Antonio Daniels	.60	.25
❑ 49	Jayson Williams	.60	.25
❑ 50	Juwan Howard	1.50	.60
❑ 51	Reggie Miller	2.00	.75
❑ 52	Joe Smith	1.50	.60
❑ 53	Shaquille O'Neal	5.00	2.00
❑ 54	Dennis Rodman	1.50	.60
❑ 55	Vin Baker	1.50	.60
❑ 56	Rod Strickland	.60	.25
❑ 57	Anfernee Hardaway	2.00	.75
❑ 58	Zydrunas Ilgauskas	1.50	.60
❑ 59	Chris Mullin	2.00	.75
❑ 60	Rasheed Wallace	2.00	.75
❑ 61	Shareef Abdur-Rahim	2.00	.75
❑ 62	Tom Gugliotta	.60	.25
❑ 63	Tim Duncan	3.00	1.25
❑ 64	Michael Finley	2.00	.75
❑ 65	Jim Jackson	.60	.25
❑ 66	Chauncey Billups	1.50	.60
❑ 67	Jerry Stackhouse	2.00	.75
❑ 68	Jeff Hornacek	1.50	.60
❑ 69	Clyde Drexler	2.00	.75
❑ 70	Karl Malone	2.00	.75
❑ 71	Tim Duncan RE	1.50	.60
❑ 72	Keith Van Horn RE	1.50	.60
❑ 73	Chauncey Billups RE	1.50	.60
❑ 74	Antonio Daniels RE	.60	.25
❑ 75	Tony Battie RE	.60	.25
❑ 76	Ron Mercer RE	1.25	.50
❑ 77	Tim Thomas RE	1.50	.60
❑ 78	Tracy McGrady RE	5.00	2.00
❑ 79	Danny Fortson RE	.60	.25
❑ 80	Derek Anderson RE	1.50	.60
❑ 81	Maurice Taylor RE	1.25	.50
❑ 82	Kelvin Cato RE	.60	.25
❑ 83	Brevin Knight RE	.60	.25
❑ 84	Bobby Jackson RE	.60	.25
❑ 85	Rodrick Rhodes RE	.60	.25
❑ 86	Anthony Johnson RE	.60	.25
❑ 87	Cedric Henderson RE	.60	.25
❑ 88	Chris Anstey RE	.60	.25
❑ 89	Michael Stewart RE	.60	.25
❑ 90	Zydrunas Ilgauskas RE	.60	.25
❑ NNO	Michael Jordan Jumbo	10.00	4.00

1999-00 Upper Deck Hardcourt

❑	COMPLETE SET (90)	100.00	50.00
❑	COMPLETE SET w/o RC (60)	25.00	12.50
❑	COMMON CARD (1-60)	.30	.10
❑	COMMON ROOKIE 61-90	1.00	.40
❑ 1	Dikembe Mutombo	.60	.25
❑ 2	Alan Henderson	.30	.10
❑ 3	Antoine Walker	1.00	.40
❑ 4	Paul Pierce	1.00	.40
❑ 5	Eddie Jones	1.00	.40
❑ 6	Elden Campbell	.30	.10
❑ 7	Toni Kukoc	.60	.25
❑ 8	Randy Brown	.30	.10
❑ 9	Shawn Kemp	.60	.25
❑ 10	Brevin Knight	.30	.10
❑ 11	Michael Finley	1.00	.40
❑ 12	Dirk Nowitzki	2.00	.75
❑ 13	Antonio McDyess	.60	.25
❑ 14	Nick Van Exel	1.00	.40

❑ 15	Grant Hill	1.00	.40
❑ 16	Jerry Stackhouse	1.00	.40
❑ 17	Antawn Jamison	1.50	.60
❑ 18	John Starks	.60	.25
❑ 19	Hakeem Olajuwon	1.00	.40
❑ 20	Scottie Pippen	1.50	.60
❑ 21	Reggie Miller	1.00	.40
❑ 22	Jalen Rose	1.00	.40
❑ 23	Maurice Taylor	.60	.25
❑ 24	Michael Olowokandi	.60	.25
❑ 25	Shaquille O'Neal	2.50	1.00
❑ 26	Kobe Bryant	4.00	1.50
❑ 27	Tim Hardaway	.60	.25
❑ 28	Alonzo Mourning	.60	.25
❑ 29	Glenn Robinson	1.00	.40
❑ 30	Ray Allen	1.00	.40
❑ 31	Kevin Garnett	2.00	.75
❑ 32	Terrell Brandon	.60	.25
❑ 33	Stephon Marbury	1.00	.40
❑ 34	Keith Van Horn	1.00	.40
❑ 35	Latrell Sprewell	1.00	.40
❑ 36	Allan Houston	.60	.25
❑ 37	Patrick Ewing	1.00	.40
❑ 38	Darrell Armstrong	.30	.10
❑ 39	Bo Outlaw	.30	.10
❑ 40	Allen Iverson	2.00	.75
❑ 41	Larry Hughes	1.00	.40
❑ 42	Jason Kidd	1.50	.60
❑ 43	Tom Gugliotta	.30	.10
❑ 44	Brian Grant	.60	.25
❑ 45	Damon Stoudamire	.60	.25
❑ 46	Jason Williams	1.00	.40
❑ 47	Vlade Divac	.60	.25
❑ 48	Tim Duncan	2.00	.75
❑ 49	David Robinson	1.00	.40
❑ 50	Avery Johnson	.30	.10
❑ 51	Gary Payton	1.00	.40
❑ 52	Vin Baker	.60	.25
❑ 53	Vince Carter	2.50	1.00
❑ 54	Tracy McGrady	2.50	1.00
❑ 55	Karl Malone	1.00	.40
❑ 56	John Stockton	1.00	.40
❑ 57	Shareef Abdur-Rahim	1.00	.40
❑ 58	Mike Bibby	1.00	.40
❑ 59	Juwan Howard	.60	.25
❑ 60	Mitch Richmond	.60	.25
❑ 61	Elton Brand RC	6.00	2.50
❑ 62	Jason Terry RC	4.00	1.50
❑ 63	Kenny Thomas RC	2.00	.75
❑ 64	Jonathan Bender RC	5.00	2.00
❑ 65	A.Radojevic RC	1.00	.40
❑ 66	Galen Young RC	1.00	.40
❑ 67	Baron Davis RC	8.00	3.00
❑ 68	Corey Maggette RC	5.00	2.00
❑ 69	Dion Glover RC	1.50	.60
❑ 70	Scott Padgett RC	1.50	.60
❑ 71	Steve Francis RC	6.00	2.50
❑ 72	Richard Hamilton RC	5.00	2.00
❑ 73	James Posey RC	3.00	1.25
❑ 74	Jumaine Jones RC	2.00	.75
❑ 75	Chris Herren RC	1.00	.40
❑ 76	Andre Miller RC	5.00	2.00
❑ 77	Lamar Odom RC	5.00	2.00
❑ 78	Wally Szczerbiak RC	5.00	2.00
❑ 79	William Avery RC	2.00	.75
❑ 80	Devean George RC	2.50	1.00
❑ 81	Trajan Langdon RC	2.00	.75
❑ 82	Cal Bowdler RC	1.50	.60
❑ 83	Kris Clack RC	1.00	.40
❑ 84	Tim James RC	1.50	.60
❑ 85	Shawn Marion RC	6.00	2.50
❑ 86	Ryan Robertson RC	1.25	.50
❑ 87	Quincy Lewis RC	1.50	.60
❑ 88	Vonteego Cummings RC	2.00	.75
❑ 89	Obinna Ekezie RC	1.25	.50
❑ 90	Jeff Foster RC	1.50	.60
❑ GF1	M.Jordan Floor	1200.00	600.00
❑ GF6	W.Chamberlain Floor	200.00	80.00

2000-01 Upper Deck Hardcourt

❑	COMPLETE SET w/o RC (60)	25.00	10.00
❑	COMMON CARD (1-60)	.25	.08
❑	COMMON ROOKIE (61-102)	4.00	1.50
❑ 1	Dikembe Mutombo	.50	.20

#	Player		
❏ 2	Jason Terry	.75	.30
❏ 3	Antoine Walker	.75	.30
❏ 4	Paul Pierce	.75	.30
❏ 5	Eddie Jones	.75	.30
❏ 6	Baron Davis	.75	.30
❏ 7	Elton Brand	.75	.30
❏ 8	Ron Artest	.50	.20
❏ 9	Andre Miller	.50	.20
❏ 10	Shawn Kemp	.50	.20
❏ 11	Dirk Nowitzki	1.25	.50
❏ 12	Michael Finley	.75	.30
❏ 13	Antonio McDyess	.50	.20
❏ 14	Nick Van Exel	.75	.30
❏ 15	Grant Hill	.75	.30
❏ 16	Jerry Stackhouse	.75	.30
❏ 17	Antawn Jamison	.75	.30
❏ 18	Larry Hughes	.50	.20
❏ 19	Steve Francis	.75	.30
❏ 20	Hakeem Olajuwon	.75	.30
❏ 21	Reggie Miller	.75	.30
❏ 22	Jalen Rose	.75	.30
❏ 23	Lamar Odom	.75	.30
❏ 24	Eric Piatkowski	.50	.20
❏ 25	Shaquille O'Neal	2.00	.75
❏ 26	Kobe Bryant	3.00	1.25
❏ 27	Alonzo Mourning	.50	.20
❏ 28	Jamal Mashburn	.50	.20
❏ 29	Ray Allen	.75	.30
❏ 30	Glenn Robinson	.75	.30
❏ 31	Kevin Garnett	1.50	.60
❏ 32	Wally Szczerbiak	.50	.20
❏ 33	Keith Van Horn	.75	.30
❏ 34	Stephon Marbury	.75	.30
❏ 35	Allan Houston	.50	.20
❏ 36	Latrell Sprewell	.75	.30
❏ 37	Darrell Armstrong	.25	.08
❏ 38	Ron Mercer	.50	.20
❏ 39	Allen Iverson	1.50	.60
❏ 40	Toni Kukoc	.50	.20
❏ 41	Jason Kidd	1.25	.50
❏ 42	Anfernee Hardaway	.75	.30
❏ 43	Shawn Marion	.75	.30
❏ 44	Scottie Pippen	1.25	.50
❏ 45	Damon Stoudamire	.50	.20
❏ 46	Chris Webber	.75	.30
❏ 47	Jason Williams	.50	.20
❏ 48	Tim Duncan	1.50	.60
❏ 49	David Robinson	.75	.30
❏ 50	Gary Payton	.75	.30
❏ 51	Vin Baker	.50	.20
❏ 52	Rashard Lewis	.50	.20
❏ 53	Tracy McGrady	2.00	.75
❏ 54	Vince Carter	2.00	.75
❏ 55	Karl Malone	.75	.30
❏ 56	John Stockton	.75	.30
❏ 57	Shareef Abdur-Rahim	.75	.30
❏ 58	Mike Bibby	.75	.30
❏ 59	Mitch Richmond	.50	.20
❏ 60	Richard Hamilton	.50	.20
❏ 61	Kenyon Martin RC	20.00	8.00
❏ 62	Marcus Fizer RC	4.00	1.50
❏ 63	Chris Mihm RC	4.00	1.50
❏ 64	Chris Porter RC	4.00	1.50
❏ 65	Stromile Swift RC	8.00	3.00
❏ 66	Morris Peterson RC	8.00	3.00
❏ 67	Quentin Richardson RC	10.00	4.00
❏ 68	Courtney Alexander RC	5.00	2.00
❏ 69	Scoonie Penn RC	4.00	1.50
❏ 70	Mateen Cleaves RC	4.00	1.50
❏ 71	Erick Barkley RC	4.00	1.50
❏ 72	A.J. Guyton RC	4.00	1.50
❏ 73	Darius Miles RC	15.00	6.00
❏ 74	DerMarr Johnson RC	4.00	1.50
❏ 75	Hidayet Turkoglu RC	8.00	3.00
❏ 76	Hanno Mottola RC	4.00	1.50
❏ 77	Mike Miller RC	8.00	3.00
❏ 78	Desmond Mason RC	4.00	1.50
❏ 79	Mark Madsen RC	4.00	1.50
❏ 80	Eduardo Najera RC	6.00	2.50
❏ 81	Speedy Claxton RC	4.00	1.50
❏ 82	Joel Przybilla RC	4.00	1.50
❏ 83	Brian Cardinal RC	4.00	1.50
❏ 84	Khalid El-Amin RC	4.00	1.50
❏ 85	Etan Thomas RC	4.00	1.50
❏ 86	Corey Hightower RC	4.00	1.50
❏ 87	Dan Langhi RC	4.00	1.50
❏ 88	Michael Redd RC	6.00	2.50
❏ 89	Pete Mickeal RC	4.00	1.50
❏ 90	Mamadou N'diaye RC	4.00	1.50
❏ 91	Jerome Moiso RC	4.00	1.50
❏ 92	Chris Carrawell RC	4.00	1.50
❏ 93	Jason Collier RC	5.00	2.00
❏ 94	Keyon Dooling RC	4.00	1.50
❏ 95	Mark Karcher RC	4.00	1.50
❏ 96	Jamaal Magloire RC	4.00	1.50
❏ 97	Jason Hart RC	4.00	1.50
❏ 98	Jabari Smith RC	4.00	1.50
❏ 99	Donnell Harvey RC	4.00	1.50
❏ 100	Lavor Postell RC	4.00	1.50
❏ 101	Eddie House RC	4.00	1.50
❏ 102	Dan McClintock RC	4.00	1.50

2001-02 Upper Deck Hardcourt

#	Player		
❏	COMP.SET w/o SP's (90)	50.00	25.00
❏	COMMON CARD (1-121)	.30	.10
❏	COMMON ROOKIE (101-110)	5.00	2.00
❏	COMMON ROOKIE (111-120)	12.00	5.00
❏ 1	Jason Terry	1.00	.40
❏ 2	DerMarr Johnson	.60	.25
❏ 3	Toni Kukoc	.60	.25
❏ 4	Antoine Walker	1.00	.40
❏ 5	Paul Pierce	1.00	.40
❏ 6	Kenny Anderson	.60	.25
❏ 7	Jamal Mashburn	.60	.25
❏ 8	Baron Davis	1.00	.40
❏ 9	David Wesley	.30	.10
❏ 10	Ron Artest	1.00	.40
❏ 11	Jamal Crawford	.60	.25
❏ 12	Ron Mercer	.60	.25
❏ 13	Andre Miller	.60	.25
❏ 14	Lamond Murray	.30	.10
❏ 15	Matt Harpring	1.00	.40
❏ 16	Michael Finley	1.00	.40
❏ 17	Dirk Nowitzki	1.50	.60
❏ 18	Steve Nash	.60	.25
❏ 19	Antonio McDyess	.60	.25
❏ 20	Nick Van Exel	1.00	.40
❏ 21	James Posey	.60	.25
❏ 22	Jerry Stackhouse	1.00	.40
❏ 23	Chucky Atkins	.30	.10
❏ 24	Mateen Cleaves	.60	.25
❏ 25	Antawn Jamison	1.00	.40
❏ 26	Larry Hughes	.60	.25
❏ 27	Marc Jackson	.60	.25
❏ 28	Steve Francis	1.00	.40
❏ 29	Maurice Taylor	.60	.25
❏ 30	Cuttino Mobley	.60	.25
❏ 31	Reggie Miller	1.00	.40
❏ 32	Jalen Rose	1.00	.40
❏ 33	Jermaine O'Neal	1.00	.40
❏ 34	Darius Miles	1.00	.40
❏ 35	Lamar Odom	1.00	.40
❏ 36	Elton Brand	1.00	.40
❏ 37	Kobe Bryant	4.00	1.50
❏ 38	Shaquille O'Neal	2.50	1.00
❏ 39	Derek Fisher	1.00	.40
❏ 40	Robert Horry	.60	.25
❏ 41	Alonzo Mourning	.60	.25
❏ 42	Eddie Jones	1.00	.40
❏ 43	Brian Grant	.60	.25
❏ 44	Anthony Mason	.60	.25
❏ 45	Ray Allen	1.00	.40
❏ 46	Glenn Robinson	1.00	.40
❏ 47	Tim Thomas	.60	.25
❏ 48	Kevin Garnett	2.00	.75
❏ 49	Wally Szczerbiak	.60	.25
❏ 50	Terrell Brandon	.60	.25
❏ 51	Anthony Peeler	.30	.10
❏ 52	Jason Kidd	1.50	.60
❏ 53	Kenyon Martin	1.00	.40
❏ 54	Stephen Jackson	.60	.25
❏ 55	Latrell Sprewell	1.00	.40
❏ 56	Allan Houston	.60	.25
❏ 57	Glen Rice	.60	.25
❏ 58	Tracy McGrady	2.50	1.00
❏ 59	Darrell Armstrong	.30	.10
❏ 60	Mike Miller	1.00	.40
❏ 61	Allen Iverson	2.00	.75
❏ 62	Dikembe Mutombo	.60	.25
❏ 63	Aaron McKie	.60	.25
❏ 64	Stephon Marbury	1.00	.40
❏ 65	Shawn Marion	1.00	.40
❏ 66	Tom Gugliotta	.30	.10
❏ 67	Rasheed Wallace	1.00	.40
❏ 68	Scottie Pippen	1.50	.60
❏ 69	Damon Stoudamire	.60	.25
❏ 70	Chris Webber	1.00	.40
❏ 71	Mike Bibby	1.00	.40
❏ 72	Peja Stojakovic	1.00	.40
❏ 73	Tim Duncan	2.00	.75
❏ 74	David Robinson	1.00	.40
❏ 75	Derek Anderson	.60	.25
❏ 76	Gary Payton	1.00	.40
❏ 77	Rashard Lewis	.60	.25
❏ 78	Desmond Mason	.60	.25
❏ 79	Vince Carter	2.50	1.00
❏ 80	Morris Peterson	.60	.25
❏ 81	Antonio Davis	.30	.10
❏ 82	Karl Malone	1.00	.40
❏ 83	John Stockton	1.00	.40
❏ 84	Donyell Marshall	.60	.25
❏ 85	Bryant Reeves	.30	.10
❏ 86	Jason Williams	.60	.25
❏ 87	Stromile Swift	.60	.25
❏ 88	Richard Hamilton	.60	.25
❏ 89	Courtney Alexander	.60	.25
❏ 90	Chris Whitney	.30	.10
❏ 91A	Kenny Satterfield ON RC	4.00	1.50
❏ 92A	Jeff Trepagnier ON RC	4.00	1.50
❏ 93A	Michael Wright ON RC	4.00	1.50
❏ 94A	Terence Morris ON RC	4.00	1.50
❏ 95A	Omar Cook ON RC	4.00	1.50
❏ 96A	Gilbert Arenas ON RC	15.00	6.00
❏ 97A	Joseph Forte ON RC	5.00	2.00
❏ 98A	Jamaal Tinsley ON RC	6.00	2.50
❏ 99A	Samuel Dalembert ON RC	4.00	1.50
❏ 100A	Gerald Wallace ON RC	8.00	3.00
❏ 101A	Brendan Haywood ON RC	6.00	2.50
❏ 102A	Richard Jefferson ON RC	12.00	5.00
❏ 103A	Michael Bradley ON RC	5.00	2.00
❏ 104A	Loren Woods ON RC	5.00	2.00
❏ 105A	Jeryl Sasser ON RC	5.00	2.00
❏ 106A	Jason Collins ON RC	5.00	2.00
❏ 107A	Kirk Haston ON RC	4.00	1.50
❏ 108A	Steven Hunter ON RC	5.00	2.00
❏ 109A	Troy Murphy ON RC	5.00	2.00
❏ 110A	Vladimir Radmanovic ON RC	5.00	2.00
❏ 111A	Rodney White ON RC	12.00	5.00
❏ 112A	Kedrick Brown ON RC	12.00	5.00
❏ 113A	Joe Johnson ON RC	15.00	6.00
❏ 114A	Eddie Griffin ON RC	12.00	5.00

☐ 115A Shane Battier ON RC	12.00	5.00
☐ 116A Eddy Curry ON RC	20.00	8.00
☐ 117A Jason Richardson ON RC	20.00	8.00
☐ 118A DeSagana Diop ON RC	20.00	8.00
☐ 119A Tyson Chandler ON RC	20.00	8.00
☐ 120A Kwame Brown ON RC	12.00	6.00
☐ 121 Michael Jordan	15.00	6.00

2002-03 Upper Deck Hardcourt

☐ COMP.SET w/o SP's (90)	50.00	20.00
☐ COMMON CARD (1-90)	.30	.10
☐ COMMON ROOKIE (91-120)	3.00	1.25
☐ COMMON ROOKIE (121-135)	4.00	1.50
☐ 1 Shareef Abdur-Rahim	1.00	.40
☐ 2 Glenn Robinson	1.00	.40
☐ 3 Jason Terry	1.00	.40
☐ 4 Antoine Walker	1.00	.40
☐ 5 Paul Pierce	1.00	.40
☐ 6 Kedrick Brown	.60	.25
☐ 7 Jalen Rose	1.00	.40
☐ 8 Eddy Curry	1.00	.40
☐ 9 Tyson Chandler	1.00	.40
☐ 10 Marcus Fizer	.60	.25
☐ 11 Lamond Murray	.30	.10
☐ 12 Darius Miles	1.00	.40
☐ 13 Chris Mihm	.30	.10
☐ 14 Dirk Nowitzki	1.50	.60
☐ 15 Michael Finley	.60	.25
☐ 16 Steve Nash	1.00	.40
☐ 17 James Posey	.60	.25
☐ 18 Juwan Howard	.60	.25
☐ 19 Kenny Satterfield	.30	.10
☐ 20 Jerry Stackhouse	1.00	.40
☐ 21 Clifford Robinson	.30	.10
☐ 22 Ben Wallace	1.00	.40
☐ 23 Antawn Jamison	1.00	.40
☐ 24 Jason Richardson	1.00	.40
☐ 25 Gilbert Arenas	1.00	.40
☐ 26 Steve Francis	1.00	.40
☐ 27 Cuttino Mobley	.60	.25
☐ 28 Eddie Griffin	.60	.25
☐ 29 Reggie Miller	1.00	.40
☐ 30 Jermaine O'Neal	1.00	.40
☐ 31 Jamaal Tinsley	1.00	.40
☐ 32 Elton Brand	1.00	.40
☐ 33 Andre Miller	.60	.25
☐ 34 Lamar Odom	1.00	.40
☐ 35 Kobe Bryant	4.00	1.50
☐ 36 Shaquille O'Neal	2.50	1.00
☐ 37 Derek Fisher	1.00	.40
☐ 38 Devean George	.60	.25
☐ 39 Pau Gasol	1.00	.40
☐ 40 Jason Williams	.60	.25
☐ 41 Shane Battier	1.00	.40
☐ 42 Alonzo Mourning	.60	.25
☐ 43 Eddie Jones	1.00	.40
☐ 44 Brian Grant	.60	.25
☐ 45 Ray Allen	1.00	.40
☐ 46 Tim Thomas	.60	.25
☐ 47 Sam Cassell	1.00	.40
☐ 48 Kevin Garnett	2.00	.75
☐ 49 Wally Szczerbiak	.60	.25
☐ 50 Terrell Brandon	.60	.25
☐ 51 Jason Kidd	1.50	.60
☐ 52 Richard Jefferson	.60	.25
☐ 53 Dikembe Mutombo	.60	.25
☐ 54 Jamal Mashburn	.60	.25

☐ 55 Baron Davis	1.00	.40
☐ 56 David Wesley	.30	.10
☐ 57 Allan Houston	.60	.25
☐ 58 Latrell Sprewell	1.00	.40
☐ 59 Antonio McDyess	.60	.25
☐ 60 Tracy McGrady	2.50	1.00
☐ 61 Mike Miller	1.00	.40
☐ 62 Darrell Armstrong	.30	.10
☐ 63 Allen Iverson	2.00	.75
☐ 64 Keith Van Horn	1.00	.40
☐ 65 Aaron McKie	.60	.25
☐ 66 Stephon Marbury	1.00	.40
☐ 67 Shawn Marion	1.00	.40
☐ 68 Anfernee Hardaway	1.00	.40
☐ 69 Rasheed Wallace	1.00	.40
☐ 70 Damon Stoudamire	.60	.25
☐ 71 Scottie Pippen	1.50	.60
☐ 72 Chris Webber	1.00	.40
☐ 73 Mike Bibby	1.00	.40
☐ 74 Peja Stojakovic	1.00	.40
☐ 75 Tim Duncan	2.00	.75
☐ 76 David Robinson	1.00	.40
☐ 77 Tony Parker	1.00	.40
☐ 78 Gary Payton	1.00	.40
☐ 79 Rashard Lewis	.60	.25
☐ 80 Desmond Mason	.60	.25
☐ 81 Vince Carter	2.50	1.00
☐ 82 Morris Peterson	.60	.25
☐ 83 Antonio Davis	.30	.10
☐ 84 Karl Malone	1.00	.40
☐ 85 John Stockton	1.00	.40
☐ 86 Andrei Kirilenko	1.00	.40
☐ 87 Richard Hamilton	.60	.25
☐ 88 Michael Jordan	8.00	3.00
☐ 89 Chris Whitney	.30	.10
☐ 90 Kwame Brown	.60	.25
☐ 91 Efthimios Rentzias RC	2.50	1.00
☐ 92 Marko Jaric	2.50	1.00
☐ 93 Jiri Welsch RC	2.50	1.00
☐ 94 Carlos Boozer RC	6.00	2.50
☐ 95 Fred Jones RC	3.00	1.25
☐ 96 Sam Clancy RC	2.50	1.00
☐ 97 Predrag Savovic RC	2.50	1.00
☐ 98 Frank Williams RC	2.50	1.00
☐ 99 Rod Grizzard RC	2.50	1.00
☐ 100 Casey Jacobsen RC	2.50	1.00
☐ 101 Jamal Sampson RC	2.50	1.00
☐ 102 Lonny Baxter RC	2.50	1.00
☐ 103 Darius Songaila RC	2.50	1.00
☐ 104 Tito Maddox RC	2.50	1.00
☐ 105 Chris Owens RC	2.50	1.00
☐ 106 Juan Dixon RC	5.00	2.00
☐ 107 Chris Jefferies RC	2.50	1.00
☐ 108 Dan Dickau RC	2.50	1.00
☐ 109 Manu Ginobili RC	12.00	5.00
☐ 110 Tamar Slay RC	3.00	1.25
☐ 111 Matt Barnes RC	2.50	1.00
☐ 112 Vincent Yarbrough RC	2.50	1.00
☐ 113 Bostjan Nachbar RC	2.50	1.00
☐ 114 Dan Gadzuric RC	2.50	1.00
☐ 115 Robert Archibald RC	2.50	1.00
☐ 116 Ryan Humphrey RC	2.50	1.00
☐ 117 Tayshaun Prince RC	4.00	1.50
☐ 118 John Salmons RC	2.50	1.00
☐ 119 Steve Logan RC	2.50	1.00
☐ 120 Melvin Ely RC	2.50	1.00
☐ 121 Nikoloz Tskitishvili RC	4.00	1.50
☐ 122 Qyntel Woods RC	4.00	1.50
☐ 123 Marcus Haislip RC	3.00	1.25
☐ 124 Nene Hilario RC	5.00	2.00
☐ 125 Amare Stoudemire RC	15.00	6.00
☐ 126 Jared Jeffries RC	4.00	1.50
☐ 127 Kareem Rush RC	5.00	2.00
☐ 128 Chris Wilcox RC	5.00	2.00
☐ 129 Curtis Borchardt RC	3.00	1.25
☐ 130 Drew Gooden RC	12.00	5.00
☐ 131 Mike Dunleavy RC	8.00	3.00
☐ 132 DaJuan Wagner RC	8.00	3.00
☐ 133 Caron Butler RC	10.00	4.00
☐ 134 Yao Ming RC	40.00	15.00
☐ 135 Jay Williams RC	6.00	2.50

2003-04 Upper Deck Hardcourt

☐ COMP.SET w/o SP's (90)	40.00	15.00
☐ COMMON CARD (1-90)	.20	.08
☐ COMMON ROOKIE (91-126)	5.00	2.00
☐ COMMON ROOKIE (127-132)	12.00	5.00
☐ 1 Shareef Abdur-Rahim	.75	.30
☐ 2 Jason Terry	.75	.30
☐ 3 Glenn Robinson	.75	.30
☐ 4 Paul Pierce	.75	.30
☐ 5 Antoine Walker	.75	.30
☐ 6 Vin Baker	.50	.20
☐ 7 Jalen Rose	.75	.30
☐ 8 Tyson Chandler	.75	.30
☐ 9 Michael Jordan	5.00	2.00
☐ 10 DaJuan Wagner	.50	.20
☐ 11 Ricky Davis	.75	.30
☐ 12 Darius Miles	.75	.30
☐ 13 Dirk Nowitzki	1.25	.50
☐ 14 Michael Finley	.75	.30
☐ 15 Steve Nash	.50	.20
☐ 16 Nene	.50	.20
☐ 17 Marcus Camby	.50	.20
☐ 18 Nikoloz Tskitishvili	.20	.08
☐ 19 Richard Hamilton	.50	.20
☐ 20 Ben Wallace	.75	.30
☐ 21 Tayshaun Prince	.50	.20
☐ 22 Antawn Jamison	.75	.30
☐ 23 Jason Richardson	.75	.30
☐ 24 Gilbert Arenas	.75	.30
☐ 25 Steve Francis	.75	.30
☐ 26 Yao Ming	2.00	.75
☐ 27 Eddie Griffin	.50	.20
☐ 28 Reggie Miller	.75	.30
☐ 29 Jamaal Tinsley	.50	.20
☐ 30 Jermaine O'Neal	.75	.30
☐ 31 Elton Brand	.50	.20
☐ 32 Andre Miller	.50	.20
☐ 33 Lamar Odom	.75	.30
☐ 34 Kobe Bryant	3.00	1.25
☐ 35 Gary Payton	.75	.30
☐ 36 Shaquille O'Neal	2.00	.75
☐ 37 Karl Malone	.75	.30
☐ 38 Pau Gasol	.75	.30
☐ 39 Shane Battier	.75	.30
☐ 40 Mike Miller	.75	.30
☐ 41 Eddie Jones	.75	.30
☐ 42 Rasual Butler	.50	.20
☐ 43 Caron Butler	.75	.30
☐ 44 Michael Redd	.75	.30
☐ 45 Joe Smith	.50	.20
☐ 46 Desmond Mason	.50	.20
☐ 47 Kevin Garnett	1.50	.60
☐ 48 Wally Szczerbiak	.50	.20
☐ 49 Sam Cassell	.50	.20
☐ 50 Jason Kidd	1.25	.50
☐ 51 Richard Jefferson	.50	.20
☐ 52 Alonzo Mourning	.50	.20
☐ 53 Baron Davis	.50	.20
☐ 54 Jamal Mashburn	.20	.08
☐ 55 Jamaal Magloire	.20	.08
☐ 56 Allan Houston	.50	.20
☐ 57 Antonio McDyess	.50	.20
☐ 58 Latrell Sprewell	.75	.30
☐ 59 Tracy McGrady	2.00	.75
☐ 60 Grant Hill	.75	.30
☐ 61 Drew Gooden	.50	.20

#	Player		
62	Allen Iverson	1.50	.60
63	Keith Van Horn	.75	.30
64	Kenny Thomas	.20	.08
65	Stephon Marbury	.75	.30
66	Shawn Marion	.75	.30
67	Amare Stoudemire	1.50	.60
68	Rasheed Wallace	.75	.30
69	Bonzi Wells	.50	.20
70	Damon Stoudamire	.50	.20
71	Chris Webber	.75	.30
72	Mike Bibby	.75	.30
73	Peja Stojakovic	.75	.30
74	Bobby Jackson	.50	.20
75	Tim Duncan	1.50	.60
76	David Robinson	.75	.30
77	Tony Parker	.75	.30
78	Manu Ginobili	.75	.30
79	Ray Allen	.75	.30
80	Rashard Lewis	.75	.30
81	Reggie Evans	.20	.08
82	Vince Carter	2.00	.75
83	Morris Peterson	.50	.20
84	Antonio Davis	.20	.08
85	Matt Harpring	.75	.30
86	John Stockton	.75	.30
87	Andrei Kirilenko	.75	.30
88	Jerry Stackhouse	.75	.30
89	Kwame Brown	.50	.20
90	Larry Hughes	.50	.20
91	Kirk Hinrich RC	8.00	3.00
92	T.J. Ford RC	6.00	2.50
93	Mike Sweetney RC	5.00	2.00
94	Jarvis Hayes RC	5.00	2.00
95	Mickael Pietrus RC	5.00	2.00
96	Nick Collison RC	5.00	2.00
97	Marcus Banks RC	5.00	2.00
98	Luke Ridnour RC	6.00	2.50
99	Reece Gaines RC	5.00	2.00
100	Troy Bell RC	5.00	2.00
101	Zarko Cabarkapa RC	5.00	2.00
102	David West RC	5.00	2.00
103	Aleksandar Pavlovic RC	6.00	2.50
104	Dahntay Jones RC	5.00	2.00
105	Boris Diaw RC	6.00	2.50
106	Zoran Planinic RC	5.00	2.00
107	Travis Outlaw RC	5.00	2.00
108	Brian Cook RC	5.00	2.00
109	Carlos Delfino RC	5.00	2.00
110	Ndudi Ebi RC	5.00	2.00
111	Kendrick Perkins RC	5.00	2.00
112	Leandro Barbosa RC	8.00	3.00
113	Josh Howard RC	8.00	3.00
114	Maciej Lampe RC	5.00	2.00
115	Jason Kapono RC	5.00	2.00
116	Luke Walton RC	5.00	2.00
117	Jerome Beasley RC	5.00	2.00
118	Sofoklis Schortsanitis RC	6.00	2.50
119	Kyle Korver RC	8.00	3.00
120	Travis Hansen RC	5.00	2.00
121	Steve Blake RC	5.00	2.00
122	Slavko Vranes RC	5.00	2.00
123	Zaur Pachulia RC	5.00	2.00
124	Keith Bogans RC	5.00	2.00
125	Matt Bonner RC	5.00	2.00
126	Maurice Williams RC	5.00	2.00
127	Chris Kaman RC	12.00	5.00
128	Dwyane Wade RC	40.00	15.00
129	Chris Bosh RC	20.00	8.00
130	Carmelo Anthony RC	30.00	12.50
131	Darko Milicic RC	12.00	5.00
132	LeBron James RC	80.00	40.00

2004-05 Upper Deck Hardcourt

#	Player		
	COMP.SET w/o SP's (90)	40.00	15.00
	COMMON CARD (1-90)	.20	.08
	COMMON ROOKIE (91-96)	8.00	3.00
	COMMON ROOKIE (97-132)	5.00	2.00
1	Boris Diaw	.40	.15
2	Antoine Walker	.75	.30
3	Al Harrington	.50	.20
4	Jiri Welsch	.50	.20
5	Paul Pierce	.75	.30
6	Ricky Davis	.75	.30
7	Gerald Wallace	.50	.20

#	Player		
8	Eddie House	.20	.08
9	Jason Kapono	.50	.20
10	Tyson Chandler	.75	.30
11	Eddy Curry	.75	.30
12	Kirk Hinrich	.75	.30
13	Jeff McInnis	.20	.08
14	Dajuan Wagner	.50	.20
15	LeBron James	5.00	2.00
16	Michael Finley	.75	.30
17	Dirk Nowitzki	1.25	.50
18	Marquis Daniels	.75	.30
19	Kenyon Martin	.75	.30
20	Carmelo Anthony	1.50	.60
21	Nene	.50	.20
22	Ben Wallace	.75	.30
23	Richard Hamilton	.50	.20
24	Rasheed Wallace	.50	.20
25	Mike Dunleavy	.50	.20
26	Jason Richardson	.75	.30
27	Tracy McGrady	2.00	.75
28	Tyronn Lue	.20	.08
29	Yao Ming	2.00	.75
30	Jermaine O'Neal	.75	.30
31	Reggie Miller	.75	.30
32	Stephen Jackson	.50	.20
33	Corey Maggette	.50	.20
34	Elton Brand	.75	.30
35	Marko Jaric	.50	.20
36	Karl Malone	.75	.30
37	Kobe Bryant	3.00	1.25
38	Lamar Odom	.75	.30
39	James Posey	.50	.20
40	Mike Miller	.75	.30
41	Pau Gasol	.75	.30
42	Dwyane Wade	2.50	1.00
43	Eddie Jones	.50	.20
44	Shaquille O'Neal	2.00	.75
45	Desmond Mason	.50	.20
46	Michael Redd	.75	.30
47	T.J. Ford	.50	.20
48	Kevin Garnett	1.50	.60
49	Latrell Sprewell	.75	.30
50	Sam Cassell	.75	.30
51	Jason Kidd	1.25	.50
52	Aaron Williams	.20	.08
53	Richard Jefferson	.75	.30
54	Baron Davis	.75	.30
55	Jamaal Magloire	.20	.08
56	Jamal Mashburn	.50	.20
57	Allan Houston	.50	.20
58	Jamal Crawford	.50	.20
59	Jamal Crawford	.50	.20
60	Stephon Marbury	.75	.30
61	Steve Francis	.75	.30
62	Steve Francis	.75	.30
63	Cuttino Mobley	.50	.20
64	Allen Iverson	1.50	.60
65	Glenn Robinson	.75	.30
66	Kenny Thomas	.20	.08
67	Amare Stoudemire	1.50	.60
68	Quentin Richardson	.50	.20
69	Shawn Marion	.75	.30
70	Darius Miles	.75	.30
71	Shareef Abdur-Rahim	.75	.30
72	Zach Randolph	.75	.30
73	Chris Webber	.75	.30
74	Mike Bibby	.75	.30
75	Peja Stojakovic	.75	.30

#	Player		
76	Manu Ginobili	.75	.30
77	Tim Duncan	1.50	.60
78	Tony Parker	.75	.30
79	Rashard Lewis	.75	.30
80	Ray Allen	.75	.30
81	Ronald Murray	.20	.08
82	Chris Bosh	.75	.30
83	Jalen Rose	.75	.30
84	Vince Carter	2.00	.75
85	Andrei Kirilenko	.75	.30
86	Carlos Arroyo	1.25	.50
87	Carlos Boozer	.75	.30
88	Gilbert Arenas	.75	.30
89	Jarvis Hayes	.50	.20
90	Antawn Jamison	.75	.30
91	Dwight Howard RC	20.00	8.00
92	Emeka Okafor RC	25.00	10.00
93	Ben Gordon RC	25.00	10.00
94	Shaun Livingston RC	10.00	4.00
95	Devin Harris RC	10.00	4.00
96	Josh Childress RC	8.00	3.00
97	Luol Deng RC	10.00	4.00
98	Andre Iguodala RC	12.00	5.00
99	Luke Jackson RC	8.00	3.00
100	Andris Biedrins RC	10.00	4.00
101	Sebastian Telfair RC	5.00	2.00
102	Josh Smith RC	12.00	5.00
103	Rafael Araujo RC	5.00	2.00
104	Robert Swift RC	8.00	3.00
105	Kris Humphries RC	8.00	3.00
106	Al Jefferson RC	12.00	5.00
107	Kirk Snyder RC	8.00	3.00
108	J.R. Smith RC	10.00	4.00
109	Dorell Wright RC	8.00	3.00
110	Jameer Nelson RC	8.00	3.00
111	Pavel Podkolzine RC	8.00	3.00
112	Justin Reed RC	8.00	3.00
113	Sergei Monia RC	8.00	3.00
114	Delonte West RC	10.00	4.00
115	Tony Allen RC	6.00	2.50
116	Kevin Martin RC	10.00	4.00
117	Sasha Vujacic RC	5.00	2.00
118	Beno Udrih RC	12.00	5.00
119	David Harrison RC	8.00	3.00
120	Anderson Varejao RC	10.00	4.00
121	Jackson Vroman RC	8.00	3.00
122	Peter John Ramos RC	8.00	3.00
123	Lionel Chalmers RC	8.00	3.00
124	Donta Smith RC	8.00	3.00
125	Andre Emmett RC	8.00	3.00
126	Antonio Burks RC	8.00	3.00
127	Royal Ivey RC	8.00	3.00
128	Chris Duhon RC	8.00	3.00
129	Trevor Ariza RC	10.00	4.00
130	Ha Seung-Jin RC	8.00	3.00
131	Romain Sato RC	8.00	3.00
132	Rickey Paulding RC	8.00	3.00

2005-06 Upper Deck Hardcourt

#	Player		
	COMP.SET w/o SP's (90)	40.00	15.00
	COMMON CARD (1-90)	.20	.08
	COMMON ROOKIE (91-140)	5.00	2.00
1	Tony Delk	.20	.08
2	Josh Smith	.75	.30
3	Al Harrington	.50	.20
4	Antoine Walker	.75	.30
5	Gary Payton	.75	.30

#	Player		
6	Paul Pierce	.75	.30
7	Kareem Rush	.20	.08
8	Emeka Okafor	1.25	.50
9	Primoz Brezec	.20	.08
10	Eddy Curry	.50	.20
11	Kirk Hinrich	.75	.30
12	Ben Gordon	1.50	.60
13	Drew Gooden	.50	.20
14	LeBron James	5.00	2.00
15	Zydrunas Ilgauskas	.50	.20
16	Dirk Nowitzki	1.25	.50
17	Jason Terry	.75	.30
18	Jerry Stackhouse	.75	.30
19	Carmelo Anthony	1.50	.60
20	Kenyon Martin	.75	.30
21	Earl Boykins	.50	.20
22	Ben Wallace	.75	.30
23	Chauncey Billups	.75	.30
24	Richard Hamilton	.50	.20
25	Troy Murphy	.75	.30
26	Jason Richardson	.75	.30
27	Baron Davis	.75	.30
28	Tracy McGrady	2.00	.75
29	Yao Ming	2.00	.75
30	Juwan Howard	.50	.20
31	Jermaine O'Neal	.75	.30
32	Stephen Jackson	.50	.20
33	Ron Artest	.50	.20
34	Corey Maggette	.50	.20
35	Elton Brand	.75	.30
36	Bobby Simmons	.20	.08
37	Caron Butler	.50	.20
38	Kobe Bryant	3.00	1.25
39	Lamar Odom	.75	.30
40	Mike Miller	.75	.30
41	Jason Williams	.50	.20
42	Pau Gasol	.75	.30
43	Dwyane Wade	2.50	1.00
44	Eddie Jones	.75	.30
45	Shaquille O'Neal	2.00	.75
46	Desmond Mason	.20	.08
47	Maurice Williams	.20	.08
48	Michael Redd	.75	.30
49	Kevin Garnett	1.50	.60
50	Latrell Sprewell	.75	.30
51	Sam Cassell	.75	.30
52	Vince Carter	2.00	.75
53	Jason Kidd	1.25	.50
54	Richard Jefferson	.50	.20
55	Dan Dickau	.20	.08
56	Jamaal Magloire	.20	.08
57	J.R. Smith	.50	.20
58	Jamal Crawford	.50	.20
59	Stephon Marbury	.75	.30
60	Allan Houston	.50	.20
61	Dwight Howard	1.00	.40
62	Grant Hill	.75	.30
63	Steve Francis	.75	.30
64	Allen Iverson	1.50	.60
65	Andre Iguodala	.75	.30
66	Chris Webber	.75	.30
67	Amare Stoudemire	1.50	.60
68	Shawn Marion	.75	.30
69	Steve Nash	.75	.30
70	Damon Stoudamire	.50	.20
71	Shareef Abdur-Rahim	.75	.30
72	Zach Randolph	.75	.30
73	Mike Bibby	.75	.30
74	Peja Stojakovic	.75	.30
75	Brad Miller	.75	.30
76	Manu Ginobili	.75	.30
77	Tim Duncan	1.50	.60
78	Tony Parker	.75	.30
79	Rashard Lewis	.75	.30
80	Ray Allen	.75	.30
81	Ronald Murray	.20	.08
82	Rafer Alston	.50	.20
83	Jalen Rose	.75	.30
84	Chris Bosh	.75	.30
85	Andrei Kirilenko	.75	.30
86	Carlos Boozer	.50	.20
87	Matt Harpring	.75	.30
88	Antawn Jamison	.75	.30
89	Gilbert Arenas	.75	.30
90	Larry Hughes	.50	.20
91	Linas Kleiza RC	5.00	2.00

#	Player		
92	Julius Hodge RC	6.00	2.50
93	David Lee RC	8.00	3.00
94	Sarunas Jasikevicius RC	8.00	3.00
95	Jason Maxiell RC	5.00	2.00
96	Luther Head RC	8.00	3.00
97	Brandon Bass RC	5.00	2.00
98	Ricky Sanchez RC	5.00	2.00
99	Ersan Ilyasova RC	5.00	2.00
100	Andray Blatche RC	5.00	2.00
101	Sean May RC	5.00	2.00
102	Ike Diogu RC	6.00	2.50
103	Nate Robinson RC	8.00	3.00
104	Bracey Wright RC	5.00	2.00
105	Daniel Ewing RC	5.00	2.00
106	Salim Stoudamire RC	6.00	2.50
107	Dijon Thompson RC	5.00	2.00
108	Danny Granger RC	8.00	3.00
109	Raymond Felton RC	10.00	4.00
110	Louis Williams RC	5.00	2.00
111	Channing Frye RC	8.00	3.00
112	Francisco Garcia RC	6.00	2.50
113	Ryan Gomes RC	5.00	2.00
114	Travis Diener RC	5.00	2.00
115	Jarrett Jack RC	5.00	2.00
116	Von Wafer RC	5.00	2.00
117	C.J. Miles RC	5.00	2.00
118	Lawrence Roberts RC	5.00	2.00
119	Amir Johnson RC	5.00	2.00
120	Monta Ellis RC	8.00	3.00
121	Martell Webster RC	5.00	2.00
122	Johan Petro RC	5.00	2.00
123	Andrew Bynum RC	20.00	8.00
124	Martynas Andriuskevicius RC	5.00	2.00
125	Charlie Villanueva RC	8.00	3.00
126	Andrew Wright RC	5.00	2.00
127	Joey Graham RC	5.00	2.00
128	Wayne Simien RC	8.00	3.00
129	Hakim Warrick RC	12.00	5.00
130	Gerald Green RC	15.00	6.00
131	Marvin Williams RC	12.00	5.00
132	Deron Williams RC	20.00	8.00
133	Rashad McCants RC	10.00	4.00
134	Yaroslav Korolev RC	5.00	2.00
135	Chris Taft RC	5.00	2.00
136	Chris Paul RC	25.00	10.00
137	Andrew Bogut RC	8.00	3.00

2006-07 Upper Deck Hardcourt

#	Player		
1	Joe Johnson	.50	.20
2	Salim Stoudamire	.50	.20
3	Marvin Williams	1.00	.40
4	Dan Dickau	.25	.10
5	Paul Pierce	.75	.30
6	Wally Szczerbiak	.50	.20
7	Raymond Felton	1.00	.40
8	Emeka Okafor	.75	.30
9	Gerald Wallace	.75	.30
10	Tyson Chandler	.75	.30
11	Luol Deng	.75	.30
12	Ben Gordon	1.50	.60
13	Michael Jordan	5.00	2.00
14	Drew Gooden	.50	.20
15	Larry Hughes	.50	.20
16	Zydrunas Ilgauskas	.25	.10
17	LeBron James	5.00	2.00
18	Erick Dampier	.25	.10
19	Devin Harris	.75	.30

#	Player		
20	Dirk Nowitzki	1.25	.50
21	Jason Terry	.75	.30
22	Carmelo Anthony	1.50	.60
23	Earl Boykins	.25	.10
24	Marcus Camby	.25	.10
25	Kenyon Martin	.75	.30
26	Chauncey Billups	.75	.30
27	Richard Hamilton	.50	.20
28	Antonio McDyess	.25	.10
29	Ben Wallace	.75	.30
30	Baron Davis	.75	.30
31	Derek Fisher	.50	.20
32	Troy Murphy	.75	.30
33	Jason Richardson	.75	.30
34	Luther Head	.50	.20
35	Tracy McGrady	2.00	.75
36	Yao Ming	2.00	.75
37	Danny Granger	.50	.20
38	Jermaine O'Neal	.75	.30
39	Peja Stojakovic	.75	.30
40	Elton Brand	.75	.30
41	Sam Cassell	.75	.30
42	Chris Kaman	.25	.10
43	Shaun Livingston	.60	.25
44	Kwame Brown	.50	.20
45	Kobe Bryant	3.00	1.25
46	Andrew Bynum	.50	.20
47	Shane Battier	.75	.30
48	Pau Gasol	.75	.30
49	Mike Miller	.75	.30
50	Hakim Warrick	.50	.20
51	Shaquille O'Neal	2.00	.75
52	Dwyane Wade	2.50	1.00
53	Jason Williams	.50	.20
54	Andrew Bogut	1.00	.40
55	T.J. Ford	.50	.20
56	Jamaal Magloire	.25	.10
57	Michael Redd	.75	.30
58	Ricky Davis	.75	.30
59	Kevin Garnett	1.50	.60
60	Rashad McCants	1.00	.40
61	Vince Carter	2.00	.75
62	Richard Jefferson	.50	.20
63	Jason Kidd	1.25	.50
64	Desmond Mason	.25	.10
65	Chris Paul	2.00	.75
66	Tim Duncan	1.50	.60
67	J.R. Smith	.50	.20
67	Jamal Crawford	.25	.10
68	Channing Frye	.50	.20
69	Stephon Marbury	.75	.30
70	Quentin Richardson	.50	.20
71	Dwight Howard	1.00	.40
72	Darko Milicic	.75	.30
73	Jameer Nelson	.50	.20
74	Andre Iguodala	.75	.30
75	Allen Iverson	1.50	.60
76	Chris Webber	.75	.30
77	Shawn Marion	.75	.30
78	Steve Nash	.75	.30
79	Amare Stoudemire	1.50	.60
80	Zach Randolph	.75	.30
81	Sebastian Telfair	.50	.20
82	Martell Webster	.50	.20
83	Ron Artest	.50	.20
84	Mike Bibby	.75	.30
85	Brad Miller	.75	.30
86	Tim Duncan	1.50	.60
87	Manu Ginobili	.75	.30
88	Tony Parker	.75	.30
89	Ray Allen	.75	.30
90	Danny Fortson	.25	.10
91	Rashard Lewis	.75	.30
92	Chris Bosh	.75	.30
93	Joey Graham	.50	.20
94	Charlie Villanueva	.75	.30
95	Carlos Boozer	.75	.30
96	Andrei Kirilenko	.75	.30
97	Deron Williams	.75	.30
98	Gilbert Arenas	.75	.30
99	Caron Butler	.50	.20
100	Antawn Jamison	.75	.30
101	Adam Morrison RC	10.00	4.00
102	Randy Foye RC	8.00	3.00
103	Rudy Gay RC	8.00	3.00
104	Patrick O'Bryant RC	4.00	1.50
105	Saer Sene RC	4.00	1.50

❏ 106	J.J. Redick RC	8.00	3.00
❏ 107	Hilton Armstrong RC	4.00	1.50
❏ 108	Thabo Sefolosha RC	6.00	2.50
❏ 109	Cedric Simmons RC	4.00	1.50
❏ 110	Shawne Williams RC	5.00	2.00
❏ 111	Tarence Kinsey RC	4.00	1.50
❏ 112	Quincy Douby RC	4.00	1.50
❏ 113	Renaldo Balkman RC	4.00	1.50
❏ 114	Josh Boone RC	4.00	1.50
❏ 115	Kyle Lowry RC	4.00	1.50
❏ 116	Shannon Brown RC	4.00	1.50
❏ 117	Jordan Farmar RC	8.00	3.00
❏ 118	Joel Freeland RC	4.00	1.50
❏ 119	Paul Davis RC	4.00	1.50
❏ 120	P.J. Tucker RC	4.00	1.50
❏ 121	Craig Smith RC	4.00	1.50
❏ 122	Bobby Jones RC	4.00	1.50
❏ 123	David Noel RC	4.00	1.50
❏ 124	Denham Brown RC	4.00	1.50
❏ 125	James Augustine RC	4.00	1.50
❏ 126	Daniel Gibson RC	10.00	4.00
❏ 127	Allan Ray RC	4.00	1.50
❏ 128	Alexander Johnson RC	4.00	1.50
❏ 129	Dee Brown RC	6.00	2.50
❏ 130	Paul Millsap RC	8.00	3.00
❏ 131	Leon Powe RC	4.00	1.50
❏ 132	Ryan Hollins RC	4.00	1.50
❏ 133	Mike Gansey RC	4.00	1.50
❏ 134	Hassan Adams RC	5.00	2.00
❏ 135	Will Blalock RC	4.00	1.50
❏ 136	A.Bargnani AU EXCH	30.00	12.50
❏ 137	LaMarcus Aldridge AU RC	30.00	12.50
❏ 138	Tyrus Thomas AU RC	40.00	15.00
❏ 139	Shelden Williams AU RC	20.00	8.00
❏ 140	Brandon Roy AU RC	60.00	30.00
❏ 141	Ronnie Brewer AU RC	15.00	6.00
❏ 142	Rodney Carney AU RC	15.00	6.00
❏ 143	Rajon Rondo AU RC	40.00	20.00
❏ 144	Marcus Williams AU RC EXCH	25.00	10.00
❏ 145	Kevin Pittsnogle AU RC	20.00	8.00
❏ 146	Maurice Ager AU RC	15.00	6.00
❏ 147	Mardy Collins AU RC	20.00	8.00
❏ 148	James White AU RC	15.00	6.00
❏ 149	Steve Novak AU RC	20.00	8.00
❏ 150	Solomon Jones AU RC	15.00	6.00

1999-00 Upper Deck HoloGrFX

❏	COMPLETE SET (90)	60.00	30.00
❏	COMPLETE SET w/o SP's (60)	20.00	10.00
❏	COMMON CARD (1-60)	.25	.08
❏	COMMON ROOKIE (61-90)	.60	.25
❏ 1	Dikembe Mutombo	.50	.20
❏ 2	Alan Henderson	.25	.08
❏ 3	Antoine Walker	.75	.30
❏ 4	Paul Pierce	.75	.30
❏ 5	Eddie Jones	.75	.30
❏ 6	David Wesley	.25	.08
❏ 7	Dickey Simpkins	.25	.08
❏ 8	Toni Kukoc	.50	.20
❏ 9	Shawn Kemp	.50	.20
❏ 10	Zydrunas Ilgauskas	.50	.20
❏ 11	Michael Finley	.75	.30
❏ 12	Cedric Ceballos	.25	.08
❏ 13	Antonio McDyess	.50	.20
❏ 14	Nick Van Exel	.75	.30
❏ 15	Grant Hill	.75	.30
❏ 16	Bison Dele	.25	.08
❏ 17	Jerry Stackhouse	.75	.30
❏ 18	Antawn Jamison	1.25	.50
❏ 19	John Starks	.50	.20
❏ 20	Scottie Pippen	1.25	.50
❏ 21	Charles Barkley	1.00	.40
❏ 22	Hakeem Olajuwon	.75	.30
❏ 23	Reggie Miller	.75	.30
❏ 24	Rik Smits	.50	.20
❏ 25	Michael Olowokandi	.50	.20
❏ 26	Maurice Taylor	.50	.20
❏ 27	Shaquille O'Neal	2.00	.75
❏ 28	Kobe Bryant	3.00	1.25
❏ 29	Tim Hardaway	.50	.20
❏ 30	Alonzo Mourning	.50	.20
❏ 31	Ray Allen	.75	.30
❏ 32	Glenn Robinson	.75	.30
❏ 33	Kevin Garnett	1.50	.60
❏ 34	Terrell Brandon	.50	.20
❏ 35	Stephon Marbury	.75	.30
❏ 36	Keith Van Horn	.75	.30
❏ 37	Allan Houston	.50	.20
❏ 38	Latrell Sprewell	.75	.30
❏ 39	Bo Outlaw	.25	.08
❏ 40	Darrell Armstrong	.25	.08
❏ 41	Allen Iverson	1.50	.60
❏ 42	Larry Hughes	.75	.30
❏ 43	Jason Kidd	1.25	.50
❏ 44	Tom Gugliotta	.25	.08
❏ 45	Damon Stoudamire	.50	.20
❏ 46	Rasheed Wallace	.50	.20
❏ 47	Jason Williams	.75	.30
❏ 48	Chris Webber	.75	.30
❏ 49	Tim Duncan	1.50	.60
❏ 50	David Robinson	.75	.30
❏ 51	Gary Payton	.75	.30
❏ 52	Vin Baker	.50	.20
❏ 53	Vince Carter	2.00	.75
❏ 54	Tracy McGrady	2.00	.75
❏ 55	John Stockton	.75	.30
❏ 56	Karl Malone	.75	.30
❏ 57	Mike Bibby	.75	.30
❏ 58	Shareef Abdur-Rahim	.75	.30
❏ 59	Juwan Howard	.50	.20
❏ 60	Mitch Richmond	.50	.20
❏ 61	Elton Brand RC	4.00	1.50
❏ 62	Lamar Odom RC	3.00	1.25
❏ 63	Kenny Thomas RC	1.25	.50
❏ 64	Scott Padgett RC	1.00	.40
❏ 65	Trajan Langdon RC	1.25	.50
❏ 66	James Posey RC	2.00	.75
❏ 67	Shawn Marion RC	4.00	1.50
❏ 68	Chris Herren RC	.60	.25
❏ 69	Tim James RC	1.00	.40
❏ 70	Evan Eschmeyer RC	.60	.25
❏ 71	Corey Maggette RC	3.00	1.25
❏ 72	Richard Hamilton RC	3.00	1.25
❏ 73	Baron Davis RC	5.00	2.00
❏ 74	Galen Young RC	.60	.25
❏ 75	Dion Glover RC	1.00	.40
❏ 76	Jumaine Jones RC	1.25	.50
❏ 77	Wally Szczerbiak RC	3.00	1.25
❏ 78	Andre Miller RC	3.00	1.25
❏ 79	Devean George RC	1.50	.60
❏ 80	Obinna Ekezie RC	.75	.30
❏ 81	Steve Francis RC	4.00	1.50
❏ 82	Jason Terry RC	2.50	1.00
❏ 83	Quincy Lewis RC	1.00	.40
❏ 84	Ryan Robertson RC	.75	.30
❏ 85	William Avery RC	1.25	.50
❏ 86	A.Radojevic RC	.60	.25
❏ 87	Jonathan Bender RC	2.00	.75
❏ 88	Cal Bowdler RC	1.00	.40
❏ 89	Vonteego Cummings RC	1.25	.50
❏ 90	Jeff Foster RC	1.00	.40

2001-02 Upper Deck Honor Roll

❏	COMPLETE SET (130)	350.00	125.00
❏	COMP.SET w/o SP's (90)	40.00	20.00
❏	COMMON CARD (1-90)	.25	.08
❏	COMMON ROOKIE (91-120)	3.00	1.25
❏	COMMON JSY (121-130)	12.00	5.00
❏ 1	Shareef Abdur-Rahim	.75	.30
❏ 2	Jason Terry	.75	.30
❏ 3	Dion Glover	.25	.08
❏ 4	Paul Pierce	.75	.30
❏ 5	Antoine Walker	.75	.30
❏ 6	Kenny Anderson	.50	.20
❏ 7	Baron Davis	.75	.30
❏ 8	Jamal Mashburn	.50	.20
❏ 9	David Wesley	.25	.08
❏ 10	Ron Mercer	.50	.20
❏ 11	Brad Miller	.75	.30
❏ 12	Andre Miller	.50	.20
❏ 13	Lamond Murray	.25	.08
❏ 14	Chris Mihm	.50	.20
❏ 15	Michael Finley	.75	.30
❏ 16	Dirk Nowitzki	1.25	.50
❏ 17	Steve Nash	.75	.30
❏ 18	Juwan Howard	.50	.20
❏ 19	Nick Van Exel	.75	.30
❏ 20	Raef LaFrentz	.50	.20
❏ 21	Antonio McDyess	.50	.20
❏ 22	James Posey	.50	.20
❏ 23	Jerry Stackhouse	.75	.30
❏ 24	Clifford Robinson	.25	.08
❏ 25	Ben Wallace	.75	.30
❏ 26	Antawn Jamison	.75	.30
❏ 27	Larry Hughes	.50	.20
❏ 28	Steve Francis	.75	.30
❏ 29	Cuttino Mobley	.50	.20
❏ 30	Glen Rice	.75	.30
❏ 31	Reggie Miller	.75	.30
❏ 32	Jalen Rose	.75	.30
❏ 33	Jermaine O'Neal	.75	.30
❏ 34	Darius Miles	.75	.30
❏ 35	Elton Brand	.75	.30
❏ 36	Lamar Odom	.75	.30
❏ 37	Corey Maggette	.50	.20
❏ 38	Kobe Bryant	3.00	1.25
❏ 39	Shaquille O'Neal	2.00	.75
❏ 40	Rick Fox	.50	.20
❏ 41	Lindsey Hunter	.25	.08
❏ 42	Stromile Swift	.50	.20
❏ 43	Jason Williams	.50	.20
❏ 44	Alonzo Mourning	.50	.20
❏ 45	Eddie Jones	.75	.30
❏ 46	Anthony Carter	.50	.20
❏ 47	Brian Grant	.50	.20
❏ 48	Ray Allen	.75	.30
❏ 49	Glenn Robinson	.75	.30
❏ 50	Sam Cassell	.75	.30
❏ 51	Kevin Garnett	1.50	.60
❏ 52	Terrell Brandon	.50	.20
❏ 53	Wally Szczerbiak	.50	.20
❏ 54	Joe Smith	.50	.20
❏ 55	Jason Kidd	1.25	.50
❏ 56	Kenyon Martin	.75	.30
❏ 57	Allan Houston	.50	.20
❏ 58	Latrell Sprewell	.75	.30
❏ 59	Marcus Camby	.50	.20
❏ 60	Mark Jackson	.50	.20
❏ 61	Tracy McGrady	2.00	.75
❏ 62	Grant Hill	.75	.30
❏ 63	Mike Miller	.75	.30
❏ 64	Allen Iverson	1.50	.60
❏ 65	Dikembe Mutombo	.50	.20
❏ 66	Aaron McKie	.50	.20
❏ 67	Stephon Marbury	.75	.30
❏ 68	Shawn Marion	.75	.30
❏ 69	Anfernee Hardaway	.75	.30
❏ 70	Tom Gugliotta	.25	.08
❏ 71	Rasheed Wallace	.75	.30

❑ 72 Damon Stoudamire	.50	.20
❑ 73 Derek Anderson	.50	.20
❑ 74 Chris Webber	.75	.30
❑ 75 Mike Bibby	.75	.30
❑ 76 Peja Stojakovic	.75	.30
❑ 77 Tim Duncan	1.50	.60
❑ 78 David Robinson	.75	.30
❑ 79 Steve Smith	.50	.20
❑ 80 Gary Payton	.75	.30
❑ 81 Rashard Lewis	.50	.20
❑ 82 Desmond Mason	.50	.20
❑ 83 Vince Carter	2.00	.75
❑ 84 Morris Peterson	.50	.20
❑ 85 Antonio Davis	.25	.08
❑ 86 Karl Malone	.75	.30
❑ 87 John Stockton	.75	.30
❑ 88 Donyell Marshall	.50	.20
❑ 89 Richard Hamilton	.50	.20
❑ 90 Michael Jordan	12.00	5.00
❑ 91 Andrei Kirilenko RC	6.00	2.50
❑ 92 Gilbert Arenas RC	12.00	5.00
❑ 93 Earl Watson RC	3.00	1.25
❑ 94 Terence Morris RC	3.00	1.25
❑ 95 Kedrick Brown RC	3.00	1.25
❑ 96 Zach Randolph RC	8.00	3.00
❑ 97 Joe Johnson RC	6.00	2.50
❑ 98 Brandon Armstrong RC	3.00	1.25
❑ 99 DeSagana Diop RC	3.00	1.25
❑ 100 Joseph Forte RC	6.00	2.50
❑ 101 Brendan Haywood RC	4.00	1.50
❑ 102 Samuel Dalembert RC	3.00	1.25
❑ 103 Jason Collins RC	3.00	1.25
❑ 104 Michael Bradley RC	3.00	1.25
❑ 105 Gerald Wallace RC	6.00	2.50
❑ 106 Tierre Brown RC	3.00	1.25
❑ 107 Troy Murphy RC	5.00	2.00
❑ 108 Alton Ford RC	3.00	1.25
❑ 109 Vladimir Radmanovic RC	3.00	1.25
❑ 110 Ruben Boumtje-Boumtje RC	3.00	1.25
❑ 111 Bobby Simmons RC	3.00	1.25
❑ 112 Oscar Torres RC	3.00	1.25
❑ 113 Jeryl Sasser RC	3.00	1.25
❑ 114 Loren Woods RC	3.00	1.25
❑ 115 Shane Battier RC	4.00	1.50
❑ 116 Jamison Brewer RC	3.00	1.25
❑ 117 Richard Jefferson RC	4.00	1.50
❑ 118 Pau Gasol RC	8.00	3.00
❑ 119 Damone Brown RC	3.00	1.25
❑ 120 Rodney White RC	4.00	1.50
❑ 121 Kw.Brown RC/Garnett JSY	20.00	8.00
❑ 122 Chandler RC/Miles JSY	12.00	5.00
❑ 123 Curry RC/Malone JSY	25.00	10.00
❑ 124 Richardson RC/Kobe JSY	30.00	12.50
❑ 125 Parker RC/Kidd JSY	40.00	15.00
❑ 126 Griffin RC/A.Hardaway JSY	12.00	5.00
❑ 127 Haston RC/Mash JSY	12.00	5.00
❑ 128 Tinsley RC/A.Miller JSY	8.00	3.00
❑ 129 Hassell RC/Fizer JSY	8.00	3.00
❑ 130 Hunter RC/T-Mac JSY	20.00	8.00

2002-03 Upper Deck Honor Roll

❑ COMP.SET w/o SP's (90)	30.00	12.50
❑ COMMON CARD (1-90)	.20	.08
❑ COMMON JSY (91-105)	8.00	3.00
❑ COMMON ROOKIE (106-135)	5.00	2.00
❑ 1 Glenn Robinson	.75	.30
❑ 2 Shareef Abdur-Rahim	.75	.30

❑ 3 Jason Terry	.75	.30
❑ 4 Paul Pierce	.75	.30
❑ 5 Antoine Walker	.75	.30
❑ 6 Tony Delk	.20	.08
❑ 7 Jalen Rose	.75	.30
❑ 8 Tyson Chandler	.75	.30
❑ 9 Eddy Curry	.75	.30
❑ 10 Darius Miles	.75	.30
❑ 11 Zydrunas Ilgauskas	.50	.20
❑ 12 Ricky Davis	.75	.30
❑ 13 Dirk Nowitzki	1.25	.50
❑ 14 Michael Finley	.75	.30
❑ 15 Steve Nash	.75	.30
❑ 16 Raef LaFrentz	.50	.20
❑ 17 Eduardo Najera	.20	.08
❑ 18 Rodney White	.50	.20
❑ 19 Juwan Howard	.50	.20
❑ 20 Chris Whitney	.20	.08
❑ 21 Ben Wallace	.75	.30
❑ 22 Richard Hamilton	.50	.20
❑ 23 Chauncey Billups	.50	.20
❑ 24 Chucky Atkins	.20	.08
❑ 25 Jason Richardson	.75	.30
❑ 26 Antawn Jamison	.75	.30
❑ 27 Gilbert Arenas	.75	.30
❑ 28 Steve Francis	.75	.30
❑ 29 Cuttino Mobley	.50	.20
❑ 30 Jermaine O'Neal	.75	.30
❑ 31 Reggie Miller	.75	.30
❑ 32 Jamaal Tinsley	.75	.30
❑ 33 Andre Miller	.50	.20
❑ 34 Elton Brand	.75	.30
❑ 35 Quentin Richardson	.50	.20
❑ 36 Shaquille O'Neal	2.00	.75
❑ 37 Kobe Bryant	3.00	1.25
❑ 38 Robert Horry	.75	.30
❑ 39 Shane Battier	.75	.30
❑ 40 Pau Gasol	.75	.30
❑ 41 Stromile Swift	.50	.20
❑ 42 Eddie Jones	.75	.30
❑ 43 Brian Grant	.50	.20
❑ 44 Malik Allen	.20	.08
❑ 45 Ray Allen	.75	.30
❑ 46 Tim Thomas	.50	.20
❑ 47 Kevin Garnett	1.50	.60
❑ 48 Wally Szczerbiak	.50	.20
❑ 49 Jason Kidd	1.25	.50
❑ 50 Kenyon Martin	.75	.30
❑ 51 Richard Jefferson	.50	.20
❑ 52 Baron Davis	.75	.30
❑ 53 Jamal Mashburn	.50	.20
❑ 54 David Wesley	.20	.08
❑ 55 P.J. Brown	.20	.08
❑ 56 Allan Houston	.50	.20
❑ 57 Latrell Sprewell	.75	.30
❑ 58 Kurt Thomas	.50	.20
❑ 59 Tracy McGrady	2.00	.75
❑ 60 Grant Hill	.75	.30
❑ 61 Mike Miller	.75	.30
❑ 62 Allen Iverson	1.50	.60
❑ 63 Keith Van Horn	.50	.20
❑ 64 Aaron McKie	.50	.20
❑ 65 Shawn Marion	.75	.30
❑ 66 Stephon Marbury	.75	.30
❑ 67 Rasheed Wallace	.75	.30
❑ 68 Derek Anderson	.50	.20
❑ 69 Bonzi Wells	.50	.20
❑ 70 Mike Bibby	.75	.30
❑ 71 Chris Webber	.75	.30
❑ 72 Peja Stojakovic	.75	.30
❑ 73 Hedo Turkoglu	.75	.30
❑ 74 Tim Duncan	1.50	.60
❑ 75 David Robinson	.75	.30
❑ 76 Tony Parker	.75	.30
❑ 77 Gary Payton	.75	.30
❑ 78 Rashard Lewis	.50	.20
❑ 79 Brent Barry	.50	.20
❑ 80 Desmond Mason	.50	.20
❑ 81 Vince Carter	2.00	.75
❑ 82 Antonio Davis	.20	.08
❑ 83 Morris Peterson	.50	.20
❑ 84 John Stockton	.75	.30
❑ 85 Karl Malone	.75	.30
❑ 86 Andrei Kirilenko	.50	.20
❑ 87 Matt Harpring	.75	.30
❑ 88 Jerry Stackhouse	.75	.30

❑ 89 Kwame Brown	.50	.20
❑ 90 Michael Jordan	6.00	2.50
❑ 91 R.Humphrey JSY RC	8.00	3.00
❑ 92 Juan Dixon JSY RC	12.00	5.00
❑ 93 Fred Jones JSY RC	8.00	3.00
❑ 94 Marcus Haislip JSY RC	8.00	3.00
❑ 95 Melvin Ely JSY RC	8.00	3.00
❑ 96 Jared Jeffries JSY RC	10.00	4.00
❑ 97 Caron Butler JSY RC	15.00	6.00
❑ 98 A.Stoudemire JSY RC	40.00	15.00
❑ 99 Chris Wilcox JSY RC	10.00	4.00
❑ 100 Nene Hilario JSY RC	8.00	3.00
❑ 101 Dajuan Wagner JSY RC	10.00	4.00
❑ 102 N.Tskitishvili JSY RC	8.00	3.00
❑ 103 Drew Gooden JSY RC	15.00	6.00
❑ 104 Jay Williams JSY RC	10.00	4.00
❑ 105 Yao Ming JSY RC	60.00	25.00
❑ 106 Mike Dunleavy RC	8.00	3.00
❑ 107 Bostjan Nachbar RC	5.00	2.00
❑ 108 Jiri Welsch RC	5.00	2.00
❑ 109 Rasual Butler RC	5.00	2.00
❑ 110 Kareem Rush RC	6.00	2.50
❑ 111 Qyntel Woods RC	5.00	2.00
❑ 112 Casey Jacobsen RC	5.00	2.00
❑ 113 Tayshaun Prince RC	6.00	2.50
❑ 114 Frank Williams RC	5.00	2.00
❑ 115 John Salmons RC	5.00	2.00
❑ 116 Chris Jefferies RC	5.00	2.00
❑ 117 Dan Dickau RC	5.00	2.00
❑ 118 Juaquin Hawkins RC	5.00	2.00
❑ 119 Roger Mason RC	5.00	2.00
❑ 120 Robert Archibald RC	5.00	2.00
❑ 121 Vincent Yarbrough RC	5.00	2.00
❑ 122 Dan Gadzuric RC	5.00	2.00
❑ 123 Carlos Boozer RC	10.00	4.00
❑ 124 Tito Maddox RC	5.00	2.00
❑ 125 Gordan Giricek RC	5.00	2.00
❑ 126 Ronald Murray RC	8.00	3.00
❑ 127 Lonny Baxter RC	5.00	2.00
❑ 128 Pat Burke RC	5.00	2.00
❑ 129 Manu Ginobili RC	20.00	8.00
❑ 130 Predrag Savovic RC	5.00	2.00
❑ 131 Marko Jaric	5.00	2.00
❑ 132 Efthimios Rentzias RC	5.00	2.00
❑ 133 J.R. Bremer RC	5.00	2.00
❑ 134 Igor Rakocevic RC	5.00	2.00
❑ 135 Tamar Slay RC	5.00	2.00

2003-04 Upper Deck Honor Roll

❑ COMP.SET w/o SP's (90)	40.00	15.00
❑ COMMON ROOKIE (91-105)	4.00	1.50
❑ COMMON JSY RC (106-130)	10.00	4.00
JSY RC SWATCHES ARE EVENT WORN		
❑ 8 Scottie Pippen	1.25	.50
❑ 9 Jamal Crawford	.50	.20
❑ 10 Dajuan Wagner	.50	.20
❑ 11 Ricky Davis	.75	.30
❑ 12 Darius Miles	.75	.30
❑ 13 Dirk Nowitzki	1.25	.30
❑ 14 Antoine Walker	.75	.30
❑ 15 Steve Nash	.75	.30
❑ 16 Michael Finley	.75	.30
❑ 17 Nikoloz Tskitishvili	.20	.08
❑ 18 Andre Miller	.50	.20
❑ 19 Nene	.50	.20
❑ 20 Chauncey Billups	.50	.20
❑ 21 Richard Hamilton	.50	.20

#	Player		
❑ 22	Ben Wallace	.75	.30
❑ 23	Clifford Robinson	.20	.08
❑ 24	Jason Richardson	.75	.30
❑ 25	Mike Dunleavy	.50	.20
❑ 26	Yao Ming	2.00	.75
❑ 27	Cuttino Mobley	.50	.20
❑ 28	Steve Francis	.75	.30
❑ 29	Jermaine O'Neal	.75	.30
❑ 30	Reggie Miller	.75	.30
❑ 31	Al Harrington	.75	.20
❑ 32	Elton Brand	.75	.30
❑ 33	Corey Maggette	.50	.20
❑ 34	Quentin Richardson	.50	.20
❑ 35	Kobe Bryant	3.00	1.25
❑ 36	Karl Malone	.75	.30
❑ 37	Gary Payton	.75	.30
❑ 38	Shaquille O'Neal	2.00	.75
❑ 39	Pau Gasol	.75	.30
❑ 40	Jason Williams	.50	.20
❑ 41	Mike Miller	.75	.30
❑ 42	Lamar Odom	.75	.30
❑ 43	Eddie Jones	.75	.30
❑ 44	Caron Butler	.75	.30
❑ 45	Michael Redd	.75	.30
❑ 46	Desmond Mason	.50	.20
❑ 47	Tim Thomas	.50	.20
❑ 48	Latrell Sprewell	.75	.30
❑ 49	Kevin Garnett	1.50	.60
❑ 50	Wally Szczerbiak	.50	.20
❑ 51	Richard Jefferson	.50	.20
❑ 52	Kenyon Martin	.75	.30
❑ 53	Jason Kidd	1.25	.50
❑ 54	Jamal Mashburn	.50	.20
❑ 55	Baron Davis	.75	.30
❑ 56	Jamaal Magloire	.20	.08
❑ 57	Allan Houston	.50	.20
❑ 58	Antonio McDyess	.75	.30
❑ 59	Keith Van Horn	.75	.30
❑ 60	Grant Hill	.75	.30
❑ 61	Drew Gooden	.50	.20
❑ 62	Tracy McGrady	2.00	.75
❑ 63	Glenn Robinson	.75	.30
❑ 64	Allen Iverson	1.50	.60
❑ 65	Eric Snow	.50	.20
❑ 66	Amare Stoudemire	1.50	.60
❑ 67	Stephon Marbury	.75	.30
❑ 68	Shawn Marion	.75	.30
❑ 69	Derek Anderson	.50	.20
❑ 70	Damon Stoudamire	.50	.20
❑ 71	Rasheed Wallace	.75	.30
❑ 72	Peja Stojakovic	.75	.30
❑ 73	Chris Webber	.75	.30
❑ 74	Mike Bibby	.75	.30
❑ 75	Bobby Jackson	.50	.20
❑ 76	Tony Parker	.75	.30
❑ 77	Tim Duncan	1.50	.60
❑ 78	Manu Ginobili	.75	.30
❑ 79	Vladimir Radmanovic	.20	.08
❑ 80	Ray Allen	.75	.30
❑ 81	Rashard Lewis	.75	.30
❑ 82	Morris Peterson	.50	.20
❑ 83	Vince Carter	2.00	.75
❑ 84	Jalen Rose	.75	.30
❑ 85	Andrei Kirilenko	.75	.30
❑ 86	Matt Harpring	.75	.30
❑ 87	Greg Ostertag	.20	.08
❑ 88	Gilbert Arenas	.75	.30
❑ 89	Larry Hughes	.50	.20
❑ 90	Jerry Stackhouse	.75	.30
❑ 91	Kirk Hinrich RC	6.00	2.50
❑ 92	T.J. Ford RC	5.00	2.00
❑ 93	Nick Collison RC	4.00	1.50
❑ 94	Kendrick Perkins RC	4.00	1.50
❑ 95	Leandro Barbosa RC	6.00	2.50
❑ 96	Josh Howard RC	6.00	2.50
❑ 97	Jason Kapono RC	4.00	1.50
❑ 98	Jerome Beasley RC	4.00	1.50
❑ 99	Travis Hansen RC	4.00	1.50
❑ 100	Steve Blake RC	4.00	1.50
❑ 101	Willie Green RC	4.00	1.50
❑ 102	Zaur Pachulia RC	4.00	1.50
❑ 103	Keith Bogans RC	4.00	1.50
❑ 104	Kyle Korver RC	6.00	2.50
❑ 105	Brandon Hunter RC	4.00	1.50
❑ 106	LeBron James JSY RC	120.00	60.00
❑ 107	Darko Milicic JSY RC	15.00	6.00
❑ 108	Carmelo Anthony JSY RC	40.00	15.00
❑ 109	Chris Bosh JSY RC	25.00	10.00
❑ 110	Dwyane Wade JSY RC	50.00	20.00
❑ 111	Chris Kaman JSY RC	10.00	4.00
❑ 112	Mike Sweetney JSY RC	10.00	4.00
❑ 113	Jarvis Hayes JSY RC	10.00	4.00
❑ 114	Mickael Pietrus JSY RC	10.00	4.00
❑ 115	Marcus Banks JSY RC	10.00	4.00
❑ 116	Luke Ridnour JSY RC	12.00	5.00
❑ 117	Reece Gaines JSY RC	10.00	4.00
❑ 118	Troy Bell JSY RC	10.00	4.00
❑ 119	Z.Cabarkapa JSY RC	10.00	4.00
❑ 120	David West JSY RC	10.00	4.00
❑ 121	A.Pavlovic JSY RC	12.00	5.00
❑ 122	Dahntay Jones JSY RC	10.00	4.00
❑ 123	Boris Diaw JSY RC	12.00	5.00
❑ 124	Zoran Planinic JSY RC	10.00	4.00
❑ 125	Travis Outlaw JSY RC	10.00	4.00
❑ 126	Brian Cook JSY RC	10.00	4.00
❑ 127	Ndudi Ebi JSY RC	10.00	4.00
❑ 128	Maciej Lampe JSY RC	10.00	4.00
❑ 129	Slavko Vranes JSY RC	10.00	4.00
❑ 130	Luke Walton JSY RC	12.00	5.00

2001-02 Upper Deck Inspirations

❑	COMP. SET w/o SP's (90)	40.00	15.00
❑	COMMON CARD (1-90)	.25	.08
❑	COMMON ROOKIE (91-103)	6.00	2.50
❑	COMMON ROOKIE (104-109)	80.00	40.00
❑	COMMON ROOKIE (110-116)	20.00	8.00
❑	COMMON ROOKIE (117-124)	12.00	5.00
❑	COMMON ROOKIE (125-134)	15.00	6.00
❑	COMMON ROOKIE (135-140)	20.00	8.00
❑	COMMON XRC (141-152)	5.00	2.00
❑	COMMON XRC (153-164)	6.00	2.50
❑	COMMON XRC (165-176)	8.00	3.00
❑	COMMON XRC (177-182)		

#	Player		
❑ 1	Shareef Abdur-Rahim	.75	.30
❑ 2	Jason Terry	.75	.30
❑ 3	Dion Glover	.25	.08
❑ 4	Antoine Walker	.75	.30
❑ 5	Paul Pierce	.75	.30
❑ 6	Larry Bird	2.50	1.00
❑ 7	Baron Davis	.75	.30
❑ 8	Jamal Mashburn	.50	.20
❑ 9	David Wesley	.25	.08
❑ 10	Elden Campbell	.25	.08
❑ 11	Jalen Rose	.75	.30
❑ 12	Marcus Fizer	.50	.20
❑ 13	Andre Miller	.50	.20
❑ 14	Lamond Murray	.25	.08
❑ 15	Chris Mihm	.50	.20
❑ 16	Dirk Nowitzki	1.25	.50
❑ 17	Steve Nash	.75	.30
❑ 18	Michael Finley	.75	.30
❑ 19	Nick Van Exel	.75	.30
❑ 20	Raef LaFrentz	.50	.20
❑ 21	Antonio McDyess	.50	.20
❑ 22	Juwan Howard	.50	.20
❑ 23	Tim Hardaway	.50	.20
❑ 24	James Posey	.50	.20
❑ 25	Jerry Stackhouse	.75	.30
❑ 26	Ben Wallace	.75	.30
❑ 27	Isaih Thomas	1.25	.50
❑ 28	Antawn Jamison	.75	.30
❑ 29	Larry Hughes	.50	.20
❑ 30	Steve Francis	.75	.30
❑ 31	Moses Malone	1.00	.40
❑ 32	Reggie Miller	.75	.30
❑ 33	Jermaine O'Neal	.75	.30
❑ 34	Elton Brand	.75	.30
❑ 35	Darius Miles	.75	.30
❑ 36	Lamar Odom	.75	.30
❑ 37	Quentin Richardson	.50	.20
❑ 38	Kobe Bryant	3.00	1.25
❑ 39	Shaquille O'Neal	2.00	.75
❑ 40	Derek Fisher	.75	.30
❑ 41	Devean George	.50	.20
❑ 42	Stromile Swift	.50	.20
❑ 43	Jason Williams	.50	.20
❑ 44	Alonzo Mourning	.75	.30
❑ 45	Eddie Jones	.75	.30
❑ 46	Anthony Carter	.50	.20
❑ 47	Ray Allen	.75	.30
❑ 48	Sam Cassell	.75	.30
❑ 49	Glenn Robinson	.75	.30
❑ 50	Tim Thomas	.50	.20
❑ 51	Oscar Robertson	1.00	.40
❑ 52	Kevin Garnett	1.50	.60
❑ 53	Wally Szczerbiak	.50	.20
❑ 54	Terrell Brandon	.50	.20
❑ 55	Chauncey Billups	.50	.20
❑ 56	Jason Kidd	1.25	.50
❑ 57	Kenyon Martin	.75	.30
❑ 58	Latrell Sprewell	.75	.30
❑ 59	Allan Houston	.50	.20
❑ 60	Marcus Camby	.50	.20
❑ 61	Kurt Thomas	.50	.20
❑ 62	Grant Hill	.75	.30
❑ 63	Mike Miller	.75	.30
❑ 64	Tracy McGrady	2.00	.75
❑ 65	Allen Iverson	1.50	.60
❑ 66	Julius Erving	2.00	.75
❑ 67	Bobby Jones	.25	.08
❑ 68	Stephon Marbury	.75	.30
❑ 69	Shawn Marion	.75	.30
❑ 70	Anfernee Hardaway	.75	.30
❑ 71	Rasheed Wallace	.75	.30
❑ 72	Bill Walton	1.00	.40
❑ 73	Chris Webber	.75	.30
❑ 74	Peja Stojakovic	.75	.30
❑ 75	Mike Bibby	.75	.30
❑ 76	Tim Duncan	1.50	.60
❑ 77	David Robinson	.75	.30
❑ 78	George Gervin	1.00	.40
❑ 79	Gary Payton	.75	.30
❑ 80	Rashard Lewis	.75	.30
❑ 81	Desmond Mason	.50	.20
❑ 82	Vince Carter	2.00	.75
❑ 83	Morris Peterson	.75	.30
❑ 84	Antonio Davis	.25	.08
❑ 85	Hakeem Olajuwon	1.00	.40
❑ 86	Karl Malone	.75	.30
❑ 87	John Stockton	.75	.30
❑ 88	Donyell Marshall	.50	.20
❑ 89	Richard Hamilton	.50	.20
❑ 90	Michael Jordan	10.00	4.00
❑ 91	Z.Rebraca RC/S.O'Neal	6.00	2.50
❑ 92	O.Robertson/O.Torres RC	6.00	2.50
❑ 93	R.Miller/J.Brewer RC	6.00	2.50
❑ 94	P.Stojak/P.Drobnjak RC	6.00	2.50
❑ 95	M.Bateer RC/W.Zhi-Zhi	5.00	2.00
❑ 96	J.West/W.Solomon RC	6.00	2.50
❑ 97	T.Duncan/M.Allen RC	6.00	2.50
❑ 98	W.Frazier/D.Brown RC	6.00	2.50
❑ 99	S.Marion/A.Ford RC	6.00	2.50
❑ 100	T.Kukoc/A.Fotsis RC	6.00	2.50
❑ 101	B.Walton/Z.Randolph RC	15.00	6.00
❑ 102	S.Marbury/J.Crispin RC	6.00	2.50
❑ 103	W.Unseld/B.Simmons RC	6.00	2.50
❑ 104	J.Kidd AU/J.Tinsley RC	30.00	12.50
❑ 105	K.Garnett AU/P.Gasol RC	50.00	20.00
❑ 106	K.Bryant AU/S.Battier RC	60.00	25.00
❑ 107	Carter/J.Trepagnier AU RC	30.00	12.50
❑ 108	J.Erving/Kw.Brown AU RC	30.00	12.50
❑ 109	T.Duncan/E.Curry AU RC	40.00	15.00
❑ 110	Odom AU/E.Griffin AU RC	25.00	10.00
❑ 111	Alexndr AU/Watson AU RC	15.00	6.00
❑ 112	MoPete AU/Arenas AU RC	60.00	25.00
❑ 113	Martin AU/Scalabrine AU	20.00	8.00
❑ 114	Chandler AU RC/Fizer AU	30.00	12.50
❑ 115	Mggtte AU/Boumtje AU RC	15.00	6.00
❑ 116	Jr.Collins AU RC/Madsen AU	15.00	6.00

❏ 117	V.Carter/J.Forte JSY RC	15.00	6.00
❏ 118	Jamison/Murphy JSY SP RC	25.00	10.00
❏ 119	Martin/Armstrong JSY RC	12.00	5.00
❏ 120	Francis/T.Morris JSY RC	12.00	5.00
❏ 121	G.Hill/S.Hunter JSY RC	12.00	5.00
❏ 122	Mourng/Radmnov JSY RC	12.00	5.00
❏ 123	Haywood JSY RC/Shaq	20.00	8.00
❏ 124	Dalmbrt JSY RC/M.Malone	12.00	5.00
❏ 125	Szczerbiak/P.Brezec RC	20.00	8.00
❏ 126	P.Stojakovic/M.Bradley RC	15.00	6.00
❏ 127	A.Hardaway/J.Johnson RC	15.00	6.00
❏ 128	L.Woods RC/T.Ratliff	15.00	6.00
❏ 129	C.Webber/G.Wallace RC	12.00	5.00
❏ 130	A.Walker/Ke.Brown RC	15.00	6.00
❏ 131	B.Davis/J.Brewer RC	20.00	8.00
❏ 132	D.Nowitzki/A.Kirilenko RC	25.00	10.00
❏ 133	J.Smith/A.Ford RC	15.00	6.00
❏ 134	J.Stockton/J.Crispin RC	15.00	6.00
❏ 135	K.Malone/R.White RC	20.00	8.00
❏ 136	T.McGrady/J.Sasser RC	40.00	15.00
❏ 137	E.Brand/Jas.Collins RC	20.00	8.00
❏ 138	K.Bryant/R.Jefferson RC	80.00	40.00
❏ 139	A.Iverson/T.Parker RC	50.00	20.00
❏ 140	Jordan/J.Richardson RC	120.00	60.00
❏ 141	Ronald Murray XRC	8.00	3.00
❏ 141T	Draft Pick #42 EXCH		
❏ 142	Pat Burke XRC	5.00	2.00
❏ 142T	Draft Pick #41 EXCH		
❏ 143	Manu Ginobili XRC	35.00	15.00
❏ 143T	Draft Pick #40 EXCH		
❏ 144	Gordan Giricek XRC	3.00	
❏ 144T	Draft Pick #39 EXCH		
❏ 145	Tito Maddox XRC	5.00	2.00
❏ 145T	Draft Pick #38 EXCH		
❏ 146	Tamar Slay XRC	2.00	
❏ 146T	Draft Pick #37 EXCH		
❏ 147	Rasual Butler XRC	5.00	2.00
❏ 147T	Draft Pick #36 EXCH		
❏ 148	Carlos Boozer XRC	12.00	5.00
❏ 148T	Draft Pick #35 EXCH		
❏ 149	Dan Gadzuric XRC	5.00	2.00
❏ 149T	Draft Pick #34 EXCH		
❏ 150	Vincent Yarbrough XRC	3.00	
❏ 150T	Draft Pick #33 EXCH		
❏ 151	Robert Archibald XRC	5.00	2.00
❏ 151T	Draft Pick #32 EXCH		
❏ 152	Roger Mason XRC	5.00	2.00
❏ 152T	Draft Pick #31 EXCH		
❏ 153	Jamal Sampson XRC	6.00	2.50
❏ 153T	Draft Pick #30 EXCH		
❏ 154	Sam Clancy XRC	6.00	2.50
❏ 154T	Draft Pick #29 EXCH		
❏ 155	Dan Dickau XRC	6.00	2.50
❏ 155T	Draft Pick #28 EXCH		
❏ 156	Chris Jefferies XRC	6.00	2.50
❏ 156T	Draft Pick #27 EXCH		
❏ 157	John Salmons XRC	6.00	2.50
❏ 157T	Draft Pick #26 EXCH		
❏ 158	Frank Williams XRC	6.00	2.50
❏ 158T	Draft Pick #25 EXCH		
❏ 159	Lonny Baxter XRC	6.00	2.50
❏ 159T	Draft Pick #24 EXCH		
❏ 160	Tayshaun Prince XRC	6.00	2.50
❏ 160T	Draft Pick #23 EXCH		
❏ 161	Casey Jacobsen XRC	6.00	2.50
❏ 161T	Draft Pick #22 EXCH		
❏ 162	Qyntel Woods XRC	6.00	2.50
❏ 162T	Draft Pick #21 EXCH		
❏ 163	Kareem Rush XRC	6.00	2.50
❏ 163T	Draft Pick #20 EXCH		
❏ 164	Ryan Humphrey XRC	6.00	2.50
❏ 164T	Draft Pick #19 EXCH		
❏ 165	Curtis Borchardt XRC	8.00	3.00
❏ 165T	Draft Pick #18 EXCH		
❏ 166	Juan Dixon XRC	15.00	6.00
❏ 166T	Draft Pick #17 EXCH		
❏ 167	Jiri Welsch XRC	8.00	3.00
❏ 167T	Draft Pick #16 EXCH		
❏ 168	Bostjan Nachbar XRC		
❏ 168T	Draft Pick #15 EXCH		
❏ 169	Fred Jones XRC	8.00	3.00
❏ 169T	Draft Pick #14 EXCH		
❏ 170	Marcus Haislip XRC	8.00	3.00
❏ 170T	Draft Pick #13 EXCH		
❏ 171	Melvin Ely XRC	8.00	3.00
❏ 171T	Draft Pick #12 EXCH		

❏ 172	Jared Jeffries XRC		
❏ 172T	Draft Pick #11 EXCH		
❏ 173	Caron Butler XRC	15.00	6.00
❏ 173T	Draft Pick #10 EXCH		
❏ 174	Amare Stoudemire XRC	25.00	10.00
❏ 174T	Draft Pick #9 EXCH		
❏ 175	Chris Wilcox XRC	10.00	4.00
❏ 175T	Draft Pick #8 EXCH		
❏ 176	Nene Hilario XRC	10.00	4.00
❏ 176T	Draft Pick #7 EXCH		
❏ 177	Dajuan Wagner XRC	30.00	12.50
❏ 177T	Draft Pick #6 EXCH		
❏ 178	Nikoloz Tskitishvili XRC		
❏ 178T	Draft Pick #5 EXCH		
❏ 179	Drew Gooden XRC		
❏ 179T	Draft Pick #4 EXCH		
❏ 180	Mike Dunleavy XRC	25.00	10.00
❏ 180T	Draft Pick #3 EXCH		
❏ 181	Jay Williams XRC	30.00	12.50
❏ 181T	Draft Pick #2 EXCH		
❏ 182	Yao Ming XRC	80.00	40.00
❏ 182T	Draft Pick #1 EXCH		

2002-03 Upper Deck Inspirations

❏	COMP.SET w/o SP's (90)	30.00	12.50
❏	COMMON CARD (1-90)	.20	.08
❏	COMMON ROOKIE (91-104)	5.00	2.00
❏	COMMON ROOKIE (105-110)	15.00	6.00
❏	COMMON ROOKIE (111-127)	10.00	4.00
❏	111-127 PER.RUN 1500 SER.#'d SETS		
❏	111-127 DUAL JERSEY CARDS		
❏	COMMON ROOKIE (128-133)	25.00	10.00
❏	128-133 PER.RUN 275 SER.#'d SETS		
❏	128-133 DUAL AUTOGRAPH CARDS		
❏	COMMON ROOKIE (134-139)	15.00	6.00
❏	134-139 PER.RUN 1600 SER.#'d SETS		
❏	134-139 DUAL AUTOGRAPH CARDS		
❏	COMMON ROOKIE (140-149)	20.00	8.00
❏	140-149 PER.RUN 1600 SER.#'d SETS		
❏	140-149 ROOKIE AUTOGRAPH ONLY		
❏	COMMON DRAFT (156-161)	20.00	8.00
❏	156-161 PER.RUN 499 SER.#'d SETS		
❏	COMMON DRAFT (162-167)	12.00	5.00
❏	162-167 PER.RUN 799 SER.#'d SETS		
❏	COMMON DRAFT (168-175)	8.00	3.00
❏	168-175 PER.RUN 1499 SER.#'d SETS		
❏	COMMON DRAFT (176-197)	6.00	2.50
❏	176-197 PER.RUN 2999 SER.#'d SETS		
❏ 1	Shareef Abdur-Rahim	.75	.30
❏ 2	Jason Terry	.75	.30
❏ 3	Glenn Robinson	.75	.30
❏ 4	Paul Pierce	.75	.30
❏ 5	Antoine Walker	.75	.30
❏ 6	Bill Russell	1.50	.60
❏ 7	Vin Baker	.50	.20
❏ 8	Jalen Rose	.75	.30
❏ 9	Tyson Chandler	.75	.30
❏ 10	Eddy Curry	.75	.30
❏ 11	Ricky Davis	.75	.30
❏ 12	Zydrunas Ilgauskas	.50	.20
❏ 13	Darius Miles	.75	.30
❏ 14	Dirk Nowitzki	1.25	.50
❏ 15	Michael Finley	.75	.30
❏ 16	Steve Nash	.75	.30
❏ 17	Nick Van Exel	.75	.30
❏ 18	Rodney White	.50	.20
❏ 19	Juwan Howard	.50	.20

❏ 20	Richard Hamilton	.50	.20
❏ 21	Ben Wallace	.75	.30
❏ 22	Isiah Thomas	1.50	.60
❏ 23	Antawn Jamison	.75	.30
❏ 24	Jason Richardson	.75	.30
❏ 25	Gilbert Arenas	.75	.30
❏ 26	Steve Francis	.75	.30
❏ 27	Eddie Griffin	.50	.20
❏ 28	Cuttino Mobley	.50	.20
❏ 29	Reggie Miller	.75	.30
❏ 30	Jamaal Tinsley	.75	.30
❏ 31	Jermaine O'Neal	.75	.30
❏ 32	Elton Brand	.75	.30
❏ 33	Andre Miller	.50	.20
❏ 34	Lamar Odom	.75	.30
❏ 35	Kobe Bryant	3.00	1.25
❏ 36	Shaquille O'Neal	2.00	.75
❏ 37	Wilt Chamberlain	2.50	1.00
❏ 38	Derek Fisher	.75	.30
❏ 39	Pau Gasol	.75	.30
❏ 40	Shane Battier	.75	.30
❏ 41	Stromile Swift	.50	.20
❏ 42	Eddie Jones	.75	.30
❏ 43	Alonzo Mourning	.50	.20
❏ 44	Travis Best	.20	.08
❏ 45	Gary Payton	.75	.30
❏ 46	Sam Cassell	.75	.30
❏ 47	Desmond Mason	.50	.20
❏ 48	Kevin Garnett	1.50	.60
❏ 49	Wally Szczerbiak	.50	.20
❏ 50	Joe Smith	.50	.20
❏ 51	Jason Kidd	1.25	.50
❏ 52	Richard Jefferson	.50	.20
❏ 53	Kenyon Martin	.75	.30
❏ 54	Baron Davis	.75	.30
❏ 55	Jamal Mashburn	.50	.20
❏ 56	David Wesley	.20	.08
❏ 57	Allan Houston	.50	.20
❏ 58	Antonio McDyess	.50	.20
❏ 59	Latrell Sprewell	.75	.30
❏ 60	Tracy McGrady	2.00	.75
❏ 61	Grant Hill	.75	.30
❏ 62	Pat Garrity	.20	.08
❏ 63	Allen Iverson	1.50	.60
❏ 64	Julius Erving	2.00	.75
❏ 65	Stephon Marbury	.75	.30
❏ 66	Shawn Marion	.75	.30
❏ 67	Anfernee Hardaway	.75	.30
❏ 68	Rasheed Wallace	.75	.30
❏ 69	Derek Anderson	.50	.20
❏ 70	Scottie Pippen	1.25	.50
❏ 71	Chris Webber	.75	.30
❏ 72	Mike Bibby	.75	.30
❏ 73	Peja Stojakovic	.75	.30
❏ 74	Hedo Turkoglu	.50	.20
❏ 75	Tim Duncan	1.50	.60
❏ 76	David Robinson	.75	.30
❏ 77	Tony Parker	.75	.30
❏ 78	Ray Allen	.75	.30
❏ 79	Rashard Lewis	.75	.30
❏ 80	Brent Barry	.50	.20
❏ 81	Voshon Lenard	.20	.08
❏ 82	Vince Carter	2.00	.75
❏ 83	Morris Peterson	.50	.20
❏ 84	Antonio Davis	.20	.08
❏ 85	Karl Malone	.75	.30
❏ 86	John Stockton	.75	.30
❏ 87	Andrei Kirilenko	.75	.30
❏ 88	Jerry Stackhouse	.75	.30
❏ 89	Michael Jordan	6.00	2.50
❏ 90	Kwame Brown	.50	.20
❏ 91	Mason RC/Jordan	6.00	2.50
❏ 92	Harrington RC/English	5.00	2.00
❏ 93	Dunleavy RC/R.Barry	6.00	2.50
❏ 94	Archibald RC/Swift	5.00	2.00
❏ 95	Maddox RC/Francis	4.00	1.50
❏ 96	Hawkins RC/M.Malone	5.00	2.00
❏ 97	Batiste RC/Jas.Williams	5.00	2.00
❏ 98	K.Johnson RC/Mourning	5.00	2.00
❏ 99	S.Parker RC/D.Miles	8.00	3.00
❏ 100	P.Burke RC/S.O'Neal	5.00	2.00
❏ 101	R.Lopez RC/J.Stockton	5.00	2.00
❏ 102	C.Owens RC/S.Battier	5.00	2.00
❏ 103	M.Wilks RC/E.Boykins	5.00	2.00
❏ 104	Rigadeau RC/Nowitzki	5.00	2.00
❏ 105	Butler JSY RC/Garnett JSY	25.00	10.00

No.	Card	Hi	Lo
106	Wagner JSY RC/Iversn JSY	25.00	10.00
107	Rush JSY RC/Bryant JSY	30.00	12.50
108	Hilario JSY RC/Duncan JSY	25.00	10.00
109	Ely JSY RC/E.Brand JSY	15.00	6.00
110	Hmphry JSY RC/T-Mac JSY	20.00	8.00
111	M.Jaric JSY/A.Miller JSY	10.00	4.00
112	Jones JSY RC/Miller JSY	10.00	4.00
113	Baxter JSY RC/Smith JSY	10.00	4.00
114	Bremer JSY RC/Pierce JSY	10.00	4.00
115	Boozer JSY RC/Hill JSY	20.00	8.00
116	Savovic JSY RC/Divac JSY	10.00	4.00
117	Okur JSY RC/Turkoglu JSY	10.00	4.00
118	Pargo JSY RC/Fisher JSY	10.00	4.00
119	Trybnski JSY RC/Swift JSY	10.00	4.00
120	Murray JSY RC/Lewis JSY	15.00	6.00
121	Evans JSY RC/Allen JSY	10.00	4.00
122	Butler JSY RC/Jones JSY	10.00	4.00
123	Smpsn JSY RC/A-Rahim JSY	10.00	4.00
124	Rakocv JSY RC/Bmdn JSY	10.00	4.00
125	Slay JSY RC/Jefferson JSY	10.00	4.00
126	E.Rentz JSY RC/V.Hom JSY	8.00	3.00
127	Yarbr JSY RC/Howard JSY	10.00	4.00
128A	JayWill AU RC/Kobe AU	150.00	75.00
128B	JayWill AU RC/Jordan AU	400.00	200.00
129	Gooden AU RC/Garnett AU	60.00	25.00
130	A.Stout AU RC/Marion AU	100.00	50.00
131	Tskitishv AU RC/Peja AU	20.00	8.00
132	Ming AU RC/Zhizhi AU	100.00	50.00
133	Dixon AU RC/Kidd AU	40.00	15.00
134	Jeffries AU RC/Stack AU	15.00	6.00
135	Haislip AU/K-Mart AU EXCH	15.00	6.00
136	Welsch AU RC/J-Rich AU	15.00	6.00
137	Salmons AU RC/Wallace AU	15.00	6.00
138	Ginobili AU RC/Parker AU	60.00	30.00
139	Dickau AU RC/Bibby AU	10.00	4.00
140	Clancy AU RC/J.Erving	10.00	4.00
141	Q.Woods AU EXCH	10.00	4.00
142	F.Williams AU EXCH	10.00	4.00
143	Jacobsen AU RC/Hardaway	10.00	4.00
144	Nachbar AU RC/Duncan	10.00	4.00
145	Gadzuric AU RC/S.O'Neal	10.00	4.00
146	Giricek AU RC/McGrady	12.00	5.00
147	Borchardt AU RC/Malone	10.00	4.00
148	Prince AU RC/Walker	15.00	6.00
149	Wilcox AU RC/Carter	10.00	4.00
150	W.Chamberlain/Y.Ming		
151	B.Russell/A.Stoudemire		
152	J.Erving/J.Williams		
153	L.Bird/M.Ginobili		
154	M.Jordan/D.Wagner		
155	K.Bryant/C.Butler		
156A	LeBron James XRC	200.00	100.00
156B	Draft Pick #1		
157A	Darko Milicic XRC	20.00	8.00
157B	Draft Pick #2		
158A	Carmelo Anthony XRC	60.00	25.00
158B	Draft Pick #3		
159A	Chris Bosh XRC	30.00	12.50
159B	Draft Pick #4		
160A	Dwyane Wade XRC	50.00	20.00
160B	Draft Pick #5		
161A	Chris Kaman XRC	20.00	8.00
161B	Draft Pick #6		
162A	Kirk Hinrich XRC	20.00	8.00
162B	Draft Pick #7		
163A	T.J. Ford XRC	25.00	10.00
163B	Draft Pick #8		
164A	Mike Sweetney XRC	12.00	5.00
164B	Draft Pick #9		
165A	Jarvis Hayes XRC	12.00	5.00
165B	Draft Pick #10		
166A	Mickael Pietrus XRC	12.00	5.00
166B	Draft Pick #11		
167A	Nick Collison XRC	12.00	5.00
167B	Draft Pick #12		
168A	Marcus Banks XRC	8.00	3.00
168B	Draft Pick #13		
169A	Luke Ridnour XRC	10.00	4.00
169B	Draft Pick #14		
170A	Reece Gaines XRC	8.00	3.00
170B	Draft Pick #15		
171A	Troy Bell XRC	8.00	3.00
171B	Draft Pick #16		
172A	Zarko Cabarkapa XRC	8.00	3.00
172B	Draft Pick #17		
173A	David West XRC	8.00	3.00
173B	Draft Pick #18		
174A	Aleksandar Pavlovic XRC	8.00	3.00
174B	Draft Pick #19		
175A	Dahntay Jones XRC	8.00	3.00
175B	Draft Pick #20		
176A	Boris Diaw XRC	6.00	2.50
176B	Draft Pick #21		
177A	Zoran Planinic XRC	6.00	2.50
177B	Draft Pick #22		
178A	Travis Outlaw XRC	6.00	2.50
178B	Draft Pick #23		
179A	Brian Cook XRC	6.00	2.50
179B	Draft Pick #24		
180A	Carlos Delfino XRC	6.00	2.50
180B	Draft Pick #25		
181A	Ndudi Ebi XRC	6.00	2.50
181B	Draft Pick #26		
182A	Kendrick Perkins XRC	6.00	2.50
182B	Draft Pick #27		
183A	Leandro Barbosa XRC	10.00	4.00
183B	Draft Pick #28		
184A	Josh Howard XRC	10.00	4.00
184B	Draft Pick #29		
185A	Maciej Lampe XRC	6.00	2.50
185B	Draft Pick #30		
186A	Jason Kapono XRC	6.00	2.50
186B	Draft Pick #31	6.00	2.50
187B	Draft Pick #32	6.00	2.50
188B	Draft Pick #33	6.00	2.50
189B	Draft Pick #34	6.00	2.50
190A	Luke Walton XRC	6.00	2.50
190B	Draft Pick #35		
191A	Jerome Beasley XRC	6.00	2.50
191B	Draft Pick #36		
192A	Travis Hansen XRC	6.00	2.50
192B	Draft Pick #37		
193A	Steve Blake XRC	6.00	2.50
193B	Draft Pick #38		
194A	Slavko Vranes XRC	6.00	2.50
194B	Draft Pick #39		
195A	Keith Bogans XRC	6.00	2.50
195B	Draft Pick #40		
196A	Willie Green XRC	6.00	2.50
196B	Draft Pick #41		
197A	Zaur Pachulia XRC	6.00	2.50
197B	Draft Pick #42		

2000 Upper Deck Lakers Master Collection

No.	Card	Hi	Lo
	COMPLETE SET (25)	400.00	200.00
1	Magic Johnson	60.00	25.00
2	Wilt Chamberlain	50.00	20.00
3	Kareem Abdul-Jabbar	40.00	15.00
4	Jerry West	25.00	10.00
5	Elgin Baylor	15.00	6.00
6	James Worthy	15.00	6.00
7	Byron Scott	12.00	5.00
8	Kurt Rambis	10.00	4.00
9	Michael Cooper	10.00	4.00
10	Norm Nixon	10.00	4.00
11	Gail Goodrich	10.00	4.00
12	Jamaal Wilkes	10.00	4.00
13	A.C. Green	10.00	4.00
14	Kobe Bryant	80.00	30.00
15	Shaquille O'Neal	80.00	30.00
16	Kobe Bryant	10.00	4.00
17	Derek Fisher	10.00-	4.00
18	Robert Horry	10.00	4.00

2001-02 Upper Deck Legends

No.	Card	Hi	Lo
	COMP.SET w/o SP's (90)	25.00	10.00
	COMMON CARD	.20	.07
	SEMISTARS	.40	.15
	COMMON ROOKIE (91-110)	4.00	1.50
	COMMON ROOKIE (111-125)	10.00	4.00
	NOTE CARDS READ 2000-01		
1	Michael Jordan	4.00	1.50
2	Wilt Chamberlain	1.00	.40
3	Karl Malone	.60	.25
4	Steve Francis	.60	.25
5	George McGinnis	.40	.15
6	Julius Erving	1.00	.40
7	Alonzo Mourning	.40	.15
8	Kobe Bryant	2.50	1.00
9	Glen Rice	.40	.15
10	Mitch Kupchak	.20	.07
11	Isiah Thomas	.60	.25
12	Rick Barry	.60	.25
13	Moses Malone	.60	.25
14	Larry Bird	2.50	1.00
15	Vince Carter	1.50	.60
16	Jamaal Wilkes	.40	.15
17	John Havlicek	.75	.30
18	Elgin Baylor	.60	.25
19	Dave Bing	.40	.15
20	Steve Smith	.20	.07
21	Kevin Garnett	1.25	.50
22	Hakeem Olajuwon	.60	.25
23	Walt Bellamy	.20	.07
24	Kevin McHale	.60	.25
25	Kareem Abdul-Jabbar	1.00	.40
26	Chris Webber	.60	.25
27	Tom Heinsohn	.20	.07
28	Walt Frazier	.60	.25
29	Ron Boone	.40	.15
30	Gary Payton	.60	.25
31	Wes Unseld	.20	.07
32	Magic Johnson	2.00	.75
33	David Thompson	.20	.07
34	Maurice Lucas	.20	.07
35	Paul Pierce	.60	.25
36	Dikembe Mutombo	.40	.15
37	Gail Goodrich	.40	.15
38	Bob Lanier	.20	.07
39	Chris Mullin	.20	.07
40	Allen Iverson	1.25	.50
41	Sam Jones	.20	.07
42	James Worthy	.60	.25
43	Cedric Maxwell	.20	.07
44	George Gervin	.60	.25
45	Earl Monroe	.60	.25
46	Lenny Wilkens	.40	.15
47	Tracy McGrady	1.50	.60
48	Walter Davis	.20	.07
49	Stephon Marbury	.60	.25
50	Bob Cousy	.60	.25
51	Spencer Haywood	.20	.07
52	Dave Cowens	.40	.15

❏ 53	Scottie Pippen	1.00	.75
❏ 54	Hal Greer	.20	.07
❏ 55	Kiki Vandeweghe	.40	.15
❏ 56	Paul Silas	.40	.15
❏ 57	Elton Brand	.40	.15
❏ 58	John Stockton	.60	.25
❏ 59	Shareef Abdur-Rahim	.60	.25
❏ 60	Reggie Miller	.60	.25
❏ 61	Nate Thurmond	.20	.07
❏ 62	Billy Cunningham	.20	.07
❏ 63	Patrick Ewing	.60	.25
❏ 64	Nate Archibald	.60	.25
❏ 65	Tim Duncan	1.25	.50
❏ 66	Lafayette Lever	.40	.15
❏ 67	Willis Reed	.40	.15
❏ 68	Ray Allen	.60	.25
❏ 69	Jo Jo White	.20	.07
❏ 70	Pete Maravich	.75	.30
❏ 71	Grant Hill	.60	.25
❏ 72	Jerry West	.60	.25
❏ 73	George Karl	.40	.15
❏ 74	Bill Sharman	.20	.07
❏ 75	Dave DeBusschere	.20	.07
❏ 76	Tim Hardaway	.40	.15
❏ 77	Bill Walton	.60	.25
❏ 78	Jerry Lucas	.20	.07
❏ 79	Antonio McDyess	.40	.15
❏ 80	Robert Parish	.60	.25
❏ 81	Shaquille O'Neal	1.50	.60
❏ 82	Bill Russell	1.00	.40
❏ 83	Clyde Drexler	.60	.25
❏ 84	Dolph Schayes	.20	.07
❏ 85	K.C. Jones	.20	.07
❏ 86	Bob Pettit	.40	.15
❏ 87	Jason Kidd	1.00	.40
❏ 88	Mitch Richmond	.40	.15
❏ 89	Oscar Robertson	.75	.30
❏ 90	David Robinson	.60	.25
❏ 91	Bobby Simmons RC	4.00	1.50
❏ 92	Jamison Brewer RC	4.00	1.50
❏ 93	Earl Watson RC	4.00	1.50
❏ 94	Kenny Satterfield RC	4.00	1.50
❏ 95	Zeljko Rebraca RC	4.00	1.50
❏ 96	Damone Brown RC	4.00	1.50
❏ 97	R.Boumtje-Boumtje RC	4.00	1.50
❏ 98	Brian Scalabrine RC	4.00	1.50
❏ 99	Terence Morris RC	4.00	1.50
❏ 100	Willie Solomon RC	4.00	1.50
❏ 101	Primoz Brezec RC	5.00	2.00
❏ 102	Gilbert Arenas RC	20.00	8.00
❏ 103	Trenton Hassell RC	6.00	2.50
❏ 104	Loren Woods RC	4.00	1.50
❏ 105	Troy Parker RC	15.00	6.00
❏ 106	Jamaal Tinsley RC	6.00	2.50
❏ 107	Samuel Dalembert RC	4.00	1.50
❏ 108	Gerald Wallace RC	10.00	4.00
❏ 109	Andrei Kirilenko RC	12.00	5.00
❏ 110	Brandon Armstrong RC	6.00	2.50
❏ 111	Jeryl Sasser RC	10.00	4.00
❏ 112	Joseph Forte RC	12.00	5.00
❏ 113	Brendan Haywood RC	12.00	5.00
❏ 114	Zach Randolph RC	20.00	8.00
❏ 115	Jason Collins RC	10.00	4.00
❏ 116	Michael Bradley RC	10.00	4.00
❏ 117	Kirk Haston RC	10.00	4.00
❏ 118	Steven Hunter RC	10.00	4.00
❏ 119	Troy Murphy RC	15.00	6.00
❏ 120	Richard Jefferson RC	12.00	5.00
❏ 121	Vladimir Radmanovic RC	10.00	4.00
❏ 122	Kedrick Brown RC	10.00	4.00
❏ 123	Joe Johnson RC	20.00	8.00
❏ 124	Rodney White RC	12.00	5.00
❏ 125	DeSagana Diop RC	10.00	4.00
❏ 126	Eddie Griffin RC	12.00	5.00
❏ 127	Shane Battier RC	12.00	5.00
❏ 128	Jason Richardson RC	20.00	8.00
❏ 129	Eddy Curry RC	25.00	10.00
❏ 130	Pau Gasol RC	30.00	12.50
❏ 131	Tyson Chandler RC	20.00	8.00
❏ 132	Kwame Brown RC	15.00	6.00

2003-04 Upper Deck Legends

❏ COMP.SET w/o SP's (90)		30.00	12.50
❏ COMMON CARD (1-90)		.20	.08

❏ COMMON ROOKIE (91-125)	5.00	2.00
❏ COMMON ROOKIE (126-135)	6.00	2.50
❏ COMMON DRAFT (136-150)	8.00	3.00
❏ 1	Bob Sura	.20	.08
❏ 2	Stephen Jackson	.20	.08
❏ 3	Jason Terry	.50	.20
❏ 4	Ricky Davis	.75	.30
❏ 5	Jiri Welsch	.50	.20
❏ 6	Paul Pierce	.75	.30
❏ 7	Eddy Curry	.75	.30
❏ 8	Jamal Crawford	.50	.20
❏ 9	Tyson Chandler	.75	.30
❏ 10	Dajuan Wagner	.50	.20
❏ 11	Carlos Boozer	.75	.30
❏ 12	Zydrunas Ilgauskas	.50	.20
❏ 13	Dirk Nowitzki	1.25	.50
❏ 14	Antoine Walker	.75	.30
❏ 15	Steve Nash	.75	.30
❏ 16	Michael Finley	.75	.30
❏ 17	Jon Barry	.20	.08
❏ 18	Andre Miller	.50	.20
❏ 19	Nene	.50	.20
❏ 20	Rasheed Wallace	.75	.30
❏ 21	Richard Hamilton	.50	.20
❏ 22	Ben Wallace	.75	.30
❏ 23	Erick Dampier	.50	.20
❏ 24	Jason Richardson	.75	.30
❏ 25	Nick Van Exel	.75	.30
❏ 26	Yao Ming	2.00	.75
❏ 27	Cuttino Mobley	.50	.20
❏ 28	Steve Francis	.75	.30
❏ 29	Jermaine O'Neal	.75	.30
❏ 30	Reggie Miller	.75	.30
❏ 31	Ron Artest	.50	.20
❏ 32	Elton Brand	.75	.30
❏ 33	Corey Maggette	.50	.20
❏ 34	Quentin Richardson	.50	.20
❏ 35	Kobe Bryant	3.00	1.25
❏ 36	Karl Malone	.75	.30
❏ 37	Gary Payton	.75	.30
❏ 38	Shaquille O'Neal	2.00	.75
❏ 39	Pau Gasol	.75	.30
❏ 40	Bonzi Wells	.50	.20
❏ 41	Mike Miller	.75	.30
❏ 42	Lamar Odom	.75	.30
❏ 43	Eddie Jones	.75	.30
❏ 44	Caron Butler	.75	.30
❏ 45	Keith Van Horn	.75	.30
❏ 46	Desmond Mason	.50	.20
❏ 47	Michael Redd	.75	.30
❏ 48	Latrell Sprewell	.75	.30
❏ 49	Kevin Garnett	1.50	.60
❏ 50	Sam Cassell	.75	.30
❏ 51	Richard Jefferson	.50	.20
❏ 52	Kenyon Martin	.75	.30
❏ 53	Jason Kidd	1.25	.50
❏ 54	Jamal Mashburn	.50	.20
❏ 55	Baron Davis	.75	.30
❏ 56	David Wesley	.20	.08
❏ 57	Allan Houston	.50	.20
❏ 58	Stephon Marbury	.75	.30
❏ 59	Kurt Thomas	.50	.20
❏ 60	Juwan Howard	.20	.20
❏ 61	Drew Gooden	.50	.20
❏ 62	Tracy McGrady	2.00	.75
❏ 63	Zendon Hamilton	1.00	.40
❏ 64	Allen Iverson	1.50	.60
❏ 65	Eric Snow	.50	.20

❏ 66	Amare Stoudemire	1.50	.60
❏ 67	Joe Johnson	.50	.20
❏ 68	Shawn Marion	.75	.30
❏ 69	Zach Randolph	.75	.30
❏ 70	Darius Miles	.75	.30
❏ 71	Shareef Abdur-Rahim	.75	.30
❏ 72	Peja Stojakovic	.75	.30
❏ 73	Chris Webber	.75	.30
❏ 74	Mike Bibby	.75	.30
❏ 75	Brad Miller	.75	.30
❏ 76	Tony Parker	.75	.30
❏ 77	Tim Duncan	1.50	.60
❏ 78	Manu Ginobili	.75	.30
❏ 79	Ronald Murray	.20	.08
❏ 80	Ray Allen	.75	.30
❏ 81	Rashard Lewis	.75	.30
❏ 82	Donyell Marshall	.75	.30
❏ 83	Vince Carter	2.00	.75
❏ 84	Jalen Rose	.75	.30
❏ 85	Andrei Kirilenko	.75	.30
❏ 86	Matt Harpring	.75	.30
❏ 87	Carlos Arroyo	1.25	.50
❏ 88	Gilbert Arenas	.75	.30
❏ 89	Larry Hughes	.50	.20
❏ 90	Jerry Stackhouse	.75	.30
❏ 91	Devin Brown RC	5.00	2.00
❏ 92	Ronald Dupree RC	5.00	2.00
❏ 93	Alex Garcia RC	5.00	2.00
❏ 94	Udonis Haslem RC	5.00	2.00
❏ 95	Maurice Williams RC	5.00	2.00
❏ 96	Brandon Hunter RC	5.00	2.00
❏ 97	Keith Bogans RC	5.00	2.00
❏ 98	Willie Green RC	5.00	2.00
❏ 99	Zaza Pachulia RC	5.00	2.00
❏ 100	Zarko Cabarkapa RC	5.00	2.00
❏ 101	Kyle Korver RC	8.00	3.00
❏ 102	Luke Walton RC	5.00	2.00
❏ 103	Maciej Lampe RC	5.00	2.00
❏ 104	Josh Howard RC	8.00	3.00
❏ 105	Kendrick Perkins RC	5.00	2.00
❏ 106	Ndudi Ebi RC	5.00	2.00
❏ 107	Jerome Beasley RC	5.00	2.00
❏ 108	Brian Cook RC	5.00	2.00
❏ 109	Travis Outlaw RC	5.00	2.00
❏ 110	Zoran Planinic RC	5.00	2.00
❏ 111	Boris Diaw RC	6.00	2.50
❏ 112	Steve Blake RC	5.00	2.00
❏ 113	Aleksandar Pavlovic RC	6.00	2.50
❏ 114	David West RC	5.00	2.00
❏ 115	Mike Sweetney RC	5.00	2.00
❏ 116	Troy Bell RC	5.00	2.00
❏ 117	Reece Gaines RC	5.00	2.00
❏ 118	Marcus Banks RC	5.00	2.00
❏ 119	Dahntay Jones RC	5.00	2.00
❏ 120	Chris Kaman RC	5.00	2.00
❏ 121	Mickael Pietrus RC	5.00	2.00
❏ 122	Luke Ridnour RC	6.00	2.50
❏ 123	Jason Kapono RC	5.00	2.00
❏ 124	Marquis Daniels RC	8.00	3.00
❏ 125	Travis Hansen RC	5.00	2.00
❏ 126	Leandro Barbosa RC	10.00	4.00
❏ 127	Nick Collison RC	6.00	2.50
❏ 128	Kirk Hinrich RC	12.00	5.00
❏ 129	T.J. Ford RC	10.00	4.00
❏ 130	Jarvis Hayes RC	6.00	2.50
❏ 131	Dwyane Wade RC	25.00	10.00
❏ 132	Chris Bosh RC	15.00	6.00
❏ 133	Carmelo Anthony RC	20.00	8.00
❏ 134	Darko Milicic RC	12.00	5.00
❏ 135	LeBron James RC	60.00	25.00
❏ 136	Draft Pick #1 EXCH	50.00	20.00
❏ 137	Draft Pick #2 EXCH	50.00	20.00
❏ 138	Draft Pick #3 EXCH	25.00	10.00
❏ 139	Draft Pick #4 EXCH	25.00	10.00
❏ 140	Draft Pick #5 EXCH	15.00	6.00
❏ 141	Draft Pick #6 EXCH	17.00	7.00
❏ 142	Draft Pick #7 EXCH	12.00	5.00
❏ 143	Draft Pick #8 EXCH	10.00	4.00
❏ 144	Andre Iguodala	8.00	3.00
❏ 145	Draft Pick #10 EXCH	12.00	5.00
❏ 146	Draft Pick #11 EXCH	8.00	3.00
❏ 147	Draft Pick #12 EXCH	8.00	3.00
❏ 148	Draft Pick #13 EXCH	15.00	6.00
❏ 149	Draft Pick #14 EXCH	10.00	4.00
❏ 150	Draft Pick #15 EXCH	10.00	4.00

2003 Upper Deck LeBron James Box Set

❑ COMPLETE SET (30)	40.00	15.00
❑ COMMON JAMES (1-30)	2.00	.75
❑ COMMON JUMBO (LJ1-LJ2)	2.00	.75
❑ AU's NOT PRICED DUE TO SCARCITY		

2001-02 Upper Deck MJ's Back

❑ COMMON CARD (MJ1-MJ90)	4.00	1.50

1999-00 Upper Deck MVP

❑ COMPLETE SET (220)	40.00	20.00
❑ COMMON CARD (1-178)	.15	.05
❑ COMMON ROOKIE (209-218)	.75	.30
❑ COMMON MJ (179-208)	1.50	.60
❑ 1 Dikembe Mutombo	.30	.10
❑ 2 Steve Smith	.15	.05
❑ 3 Mookie Blaylock	.15	.05
❑ 4 Alan Henderson	.15	.05
❑ 5 LaPhonso Ellis	.15	.05
❑ 6 Grant Long	.15	.05
❑ 7 Kenny Anderson	.30	.10
❑ 8 Antoine Walker	.50	.20
❑ 9 Ron Mercer	.30	.10
❑ 10 Paul Pierce	.50	.20
❑ 11 Vitaly Potapenko	.15	.05
❑ 12 Dana Barros	.15	.05
❑ 13 Elden Campbell	.15	.05
❑ 14 Eddie Jones	.50	.20
❑ 15 David Wesley	.15	.05
❑ 16 Bobby Phills	.15	.05
❑ 17 Derrick Coleman	.30	.10
❑ 18 Ricky Davis	.30	.10
❑ 19 Toni Kukoc	.30	.10
❑ 20 Brent Barry	.15	.05
❑ 21 Ron Harper	.30	.10
❑ 22 Kornel David RC	.15	.05
❑ 23 Mark Bryant	.15	.05
❑ 24 Dickey Simpkins	.15	.05
❑ 25 Shawn Kemp	.30	.10
❑ 26 Derek Anderson	.30	.10
❑ 27 Brevin Knight	.15	.05
❑ 28 Andrew DeClercq	.15	.05
❑ 29 Zydrunas Ilgauskas	.30	.10
❑ 30 Cedric Henderson	.15	.05
❑ 31 Shawn Bradley	.15	.05
❑ 32 A.C. Green	.30	.10
❑ 33 Gary Trent	.15	.05
❑ 34 Michael Finley	.60	.20
❑ 35 Dirk Nowitzki	1.00	.40
❑ 36 Steve Nash	.50	.20
❑ 37 Antonio McDyess	.30	.10
❑ 38 Nick Van Exel	.50	.20
❑ 39 Chauncey Billups	.30	.10
❑ 40 Danny Fortson	.15	.05
❑ 41 Eric Washington	.15	.05
❑ 42 Raef LaFrentz	.30	.10
❑ 43 Grant Hill	.50	.20
❑ 44 Bison Dele	.15	.05
❑ 45 Lindsey Hunter	.15	.05
❑ 46 Jerry Stackhouse	.50	.20
❑ 47 Don Reid	.15	.05
❑ 48 Christian Laettner	.30	.10
❑ 49 John Starks	.30	.10
❑ 50 Antawn Jamison	.75	.30
❑ 51 Erick Dampier	.30	.10
❑ 52 Donyell Marshall	.15	.05
❑ 53 Chris Mills	.15	.05
❑ 54 Bimbo Coles	.15	.05
❑ 55 Charles Barkley	.75	.30
❑ 56 Hakeem Olajuwon	.50	.20
❑ 57 Scottie Pippen	.75	.30
❑ 58 Othella Harrington	.15	.05
❑ 59 Bryce Drew	.15	.05
❑ 60 Michael Dickerson	.30	.10
❑ 61 Rik Smits	.30	.10
❑ 62 Reggie Miller	.50	.20
❑ 63 Mark Jackson	.30	.10
❑ 64 Antonio Davis	.15	.05
❑ 65 Jalen Rose	.50	.20
❑ 66 Dale Davis	.15	.05
❑ 67 Chris Mullin	.50	.20
❑ 68 Maurice Taylor	.30	.10
❑ 69 Lamond Murray	.15	.05
❑ 70 Rodney Rogers	.15	.05
❑ 71 Darrick Martin	.15	.05
❑ 72 Michael Olowokandi	.30	.10
❑ 73 Tyrone Nesby RC	.15	.05
❑ 74 Kobe Bryant	2.00	.75
❑ 75 Shaquille O'Neal	1.25	.50
❑ 76 Robert Horry	.30	.10
❑ 77 Glen Rice	.30	.10
❑ 78 J.R. Reid	.15	.05
❑ 79 Rick Fox	.30	.10
❑ 80 Derek Fisher	.50	.20
❑ 81 Tim Hardaway	.30	.10
❑ 82 Alonzo Mourning	.30	.10
❑ 83 Jamal Mashburn	.30	.10
❑ 84 P.J. Brown	.15	.05
❑ 85 Terry Porter	.15	.05
❑ 86 Dan Majerle	.30	.10
❑ 87 Ray Allen	.50	.20
❑ 88 Vinny Del Negro	.15	.05
❑ 89 Glenn Robinson	.30	.10
❑ 90 Dell Curry	.15	.05
❑ 91 Sam Cassell	.30	.10
❑ 92 Robert Traylor	.15	.05
❑ 93 Kevin Garnett	1.00	.40
❑ 94 Terrell Brandon	.30	.10
❑ 95 Joe Smith	.30	.10
❑ 96 Sam Mitchell	.15	.05
❑ 97 Anthony Peeler	.15	.05
❑ 98 Bobby Jackson	.30	.10
❑ 99 Keith Van Horn	.50	.20
❑ 100 Stephon Marbury	.50	.20
❑ 101 Jayson Williams	.15	.05
❑ 102 Kendall Gill	.15	.05
❑ 103 Kerry Kittles	.15	.05
❑ 104 Scott Burrell	.15	.05
❑ 105 Patrick Ewing	.50	.20
❑ 106 Allan Houston	.30	.10
❑ 107 Latrell Sprewell	.50	.20
❑ 108 Larry Johnson	.30	.10
❑ 109 Marcus Camby	.30	.10
❑ 110 Charlie Ward	.15	.05
❑ 111 Anfernee Hardaway	.50	.20
❑ 112 Darrell Armstrong	.15	.05
❑ 113 Nick Anderson	.15	.05
❑ 114 Horace Grant	.30	.10
❑ 115 Isaac Austin	.15	.05
❑ 116 Matt Harpring	.50	.20
❑ 117 Michael Doleac	.15	.05
❑ 118 Allen Iverson	1.00	.40
❑ 119 Theo Ratliff	.30	.10
❑ 120 Matt Geiger	.15	.05
❑ 121 Larry Hughes	.50	.20
❑ 122 Tyrone Hill	.15	.05
❑ 123 George Lynch	.15	.05
❑ 124 Jason Kidd	.75	.30
❑ 125 Tom Gugliotta	.15	.05
❑ 126 Rex Chapman	.15	.05
❑ 127 Clifford Robinson	.15	.05
❑ 128 Luc Longley	.15	.05
❑ 129 Danny Manning	.15	.05
❑ 130 Rasheed Wallace	.50	.20
❑ 131 Arvydas Sabonis	.30	.10
❑ 132 Damon Stoudamire	.30	.10
❑ 133 Brian Grant	.30	.10
❑ 134 Isaiah Rider	.15	.05
❑ 135 Walt Williams	.15	.05
❑ 136 Jim Jackson	.15	.05
❑ 137 Jason Williams	.50	.20
❑ 138 Vlade Divac	.30	.10
❑ 139 Chris Webber	.50	.20
❑ 140 Corliss Williamson	.30	.10
❑ 141 Peja Stojakovic	.60	.25
❑ 142 Tariq Abdul-Wahad	.15	.05
❑ 143 Tim Duncan	1.00	.40
❑ 144 Sean Elliott	.15	.05
❑ 145 David Robinson	.50	.20
❑ 146 Mario Elie	.15	.05
❑ 147 Avery Johnson	.15	.05
❑ 148 Steve Kerr	.30	.10
❑ 149 Gary Payton	.50	.20
❑ 150 Vin Baker	.30	.10
❑ 151 Detlef Schrempf	.30	.10
❑ 152 Hersey Hawkins	.30	.10
❑ 153 Dale Ellis	.15	.05
❑ 154 Olden Polynice	.15	.05
❑ 155 Vince Carter	1.25	.50
❑ 156 John Wallace	.15	.05
❑ 157 Doug Christie	.30	.10
❑ 158 Tracy McGrady	1.25	.50
❑ 159 Kevin Willis	.15	.05
❑ 160 Charles Oakley	.15	.05
❑ 161 Karl Malone	.50	.20
❑ 162 John Stockton	.50	.20
❑ 163 Jeff Hornacek	.30	.10
❑ 164 Bryon Russell	.15	.05
❑ 165 Howard Eisley	.15	.05
❑ 166 Shandon Anderson	.15	.05
❑ 167 Shareef Abdur-Rahim	.50	.20
❑ 168 Mike Bibby	.50	.20
❑ 169 Bryant Reeves	.15	.05
❑ 170 Felipe Lopez	.15	.05
❑ 171 Cherokee Parks	.15	.05
❑ 172 Michael Smith	.15	.05
❑ 173 Juwan Howard	.30	.10
❑ 174 Rod Strickland	.15	.05
❑ 175 Mitch Richmond	.30	.10
❑ 176 Otis Thorpe	.30	.10
❑ 177 Calbert Cheaney	.15	.05
❑ 178 Tracy Murray	.15	.05
❑ 179 Michael Jordan	1.50	.60
❑ 180 Michael Jordan	1.50	.60
❑ 181 Michael Jordan	1.50	.60
❑ 182 Michael Jordan	1.50	.60
❑ 183 Michael Jordan	1.50	.60
❑ 184 Michael Jordan	1.50	.60
❑ 185 Michael Jordan	1.50	.60
❑ 186 Michael Jordan	1.50	.60

#	Player		
❑ 187	Michael Jordan	1.50	.60
❑ 188	Michael Jordan	1.50	.60
❑ 189	Michael Jordan	1.50	.60
❑ 190	Michael Jordan	1.50	.60
❑ 191	Michael Jordan	1.50	.60
❑ 192	Michael Jordan	1.50	.60
❑ 193	Michael Jordan	1.50	.60
❑ 194	Michael Jordan	1.50	.60
❑ 195	Michael Jordan	1.50	.60
❑ 196	Michael Jordan	1.50	.60
❑ 197	Michael Jordan	1.50	.60
❑ 198	Michael Jordan	1.50	.60
❑ 199	Michael Jordan	1.50	.60
❑ 200	Michael Jordan	1.50	.60
❑ 201	Michael Jordan	1.50	.60
❑ 202	Michael Jordan	1.50	.60
❑ 203	Michael Jordan	1.50	.60
❑ 204	Michael Jordan	1.50	.60
❑ 205	Michael Jordan	1.50	.60
❑ 206	Michael Jordan	1.50	.60
❑ 207	Michael Jordan	1.50	.60
❑ 208	Michael Jordan	1.50	.60
❑ 209	Elton Brand RC	1.50	.60
❑ 210	Steve Francis RC	1.50	.60
❑ 211	Baron Davis RC	3.00	1.25
❑ 212	Wally Szczerbiak RC	1.25	.50
❑ 213	Richard Hamilton RC	1.25	.50
❑ 214	Andre Miller RC	1.25	.50
❑ 215	Jason Terry RC	1.00	.40
❑ 216	Corey Maggette RC	1.25	.50
❑ 217	Shawn Marion RC	1.50	.60
❑ 218	Lamar Odom RC	1.25	.50
❑ 219	M.Jordan CL	1.00	.40
❑ 220	M.Jordan CL	1.00	.40

2000-01 Upper Deck MVP

#	Player		
❑	COMPLETE SET (220)	40.00	20.00
❑	COMMON CARD (1-190)	.15	.05
❑	COMMON ROOKIE (191-220)	.40	.15
❑ 1	Dikembe Mutombo	.30	.10
❑ 2	Jason Terry	.50	.20
❑ 3	Jim Jackson	.15	.05
❑ 4	Alan Henderson	.15	.05
❑ 5	Roshown McLeod	.15	.05
❑ 6	Bimbo Coles	.15	.05
❑ 7	Lorenzen Wright	.15	.05
❑ 8	Antoine Walker	.50	.20
❑ 9	Paul Pierce	.50	.20
❑ 10	Kenny Anderson	.30	.10
❑ 11	Adrian Griffin	.15	.05
❑ 12	Vitaly Potapenko	.15	.05
❑ 13	Dana Barros	.15	.05
❑ 14	Eric Williams	.15	.05
❑ 15	Eddie Jones	.50	.20
❑ 16	Eddie Robinson	.30	.10
❑ 17	Ricky Davis	.30	.10
❑ 18	Elden Campbell	.15	.05
❑ 19	Derrick Coleman	.15	.05
❑ 20	David Wesley	.15	.05
❑ 21	Baron Davis	.50	.20
❑ 22	Elton Brand	.50	.20
❑ 23	Ron Artest	.30	.10
❑ 24	Hersey Hawkins	.15	.05
❑ 25	Chris Carr	.15	.05
❑ 26	Corey Benjamin	.15	.05
❑ 27	Will Perdue	.15	.05
❑ 28	Andre Miller	.30	.10
❑ 29	Shawn Kemp	.30	.10
❑ 30	Wesley Person	.15	.05
❑ 31	Lamond Murray	.15	.05
❑ 32	Bob Sura	.15	.05
❑ 33	Andrew DeClercq	.15	.05
❑ 34	Dirk Nowitzki	.15	.05
❑ 35	Michael Finley	.50	.20
❑ 36	Cedric Ceballos	.15	.05
❑ 37	Shawn Bradley	.15	.05
❑ 38	Erick Strickland	.15	.05
❑ 39	Hubert Davis	.15	.05
❑ 40	Antonio McDyess	.30	.10
❑ 41	Raef LaFrentz	.30	.10
❑ 42	Keon Clark	.30	.10
❑ 43	Nick Van Exel	.50	.20
❑ 44	James Posey	.30	.10
❑ 45	Chris Gatling	.15	.05
❑ 46	George McCloud	.15	.05
❑ 47	Grant Hill	.50	.20
❑ 48	Jerry Stackhouse	.50	.20
❑ 49	Lindsey Hunter	.15	.05
❑ 50	Christian Laettner	.30	.10
❑ 51	Jerome Williams	.15	.05
❑ 52	Terry Mills	.15	.05
❑ 53	Antawn Jamison	.50	.20
❑ 54	Donyell Marshall	.30	.10
❑ 55	Chris Mills	.15	.05
❑ 56	Larry Hughes	.30	.10
❑ 57	Mookie Blaylock	.15	.05
❑ 58	Vonteego Cummings	.15	.05
❑ 59	Steve Francis	.50	.20
❑ 60	Shandon Anderson	.15	.05
❑ 61	Cuttino Mobley	.30	.10
❑ 62	Hakeem Olajuwon	.50	.20
❑ 63	Walt Williams	.15	.05
❑ 64	Kelvin Cato	.15	.05
❑ 65	Reggie Miller	.50	.20
❑ 66	Austin Croshere	.30	.10
❑ 67	Rik Smits	.30	.10
❑ 68	Jalen Rose	.50	.20
❑ 69	Dale Davis	.15	.05
❑ 70	Jonathan Bender	.30	.10
❑ 71	Michael Olowokandi	.15	.05
❑ 72	Lamar Odom	.50	.20
❑ 73	Tyrone Nesby	.15	.05
❑ 74	Eldrick Bohannon RC	.15	.05
❑ 75	Eric Piatkowski	.15	.05
❑ 76	Shaquille O'Neal	1.25	.50
❑ 77	Kobe Bryant	2.00	.75
❑ 78	Robert Horry	.30	.10
❑ 79	Ron Harper	.30	.10
❑ 80	Rick Fox	.30	.10
❑ 81	Derek Fisher	.50	.20
❑ 82	Devean George	.30	.10
❑ 83	Alonzo Mourning	.30	.10
❑ 84	Clarence Weatherspoon	.15	.05
❑ 85	Anthony Carter	.30	.10
❑ 86	P.J. Brown	.15	.05
❑ 87	Tim Hardaway	.30	.10
❑ 88	Jamal Mashburn	.30	.10
❑ 89	Voshon Lenard	.15	.05
❑ 90	Ray Allen	.50	.20
❑ 91	Glenn Robinson	.50	.20
❑ 92	Tim Thomas	.30	.10
❑ 93	Sam Cassell	.50	.20
❑ 94	Robert Traylor	.15	.05
❑ 95	Ervin Johnson	.15	.05
❑ 96	Danny Manning	.15	.05
❑ 97	Kevin Garnett	1.00	.40
❑ 98	Wally Szczerbiak	.30	.10
❑ 99	Terrell Brandon	.30	.10
❑ 100	William Avery	.15	.05
❑ 101	Anthony Peeler	.15	.05
❑ 102	Radoslav Nesterovic	.30	.10
❑ 103	Dean Garrett	.15	.05
❑ 104	Keith Van Horn	.50	.20
❑ 105	Kerry Kittles	.15	.05
❑ 106	Stephon Marbury	.50	.20
❑ 107	Evan Eschmeyer	.15	.05
❑ 108	Jim McIlvaine	.15	.05
❑ 109	Lucious Harris	.15	.05
❑ 110	Jamie Feick	.15	.05
❑ 111	Allan Houston	.30	.10
❑ 112	Latrell Sprewell	.50	.20
❑ 113	Patrick Ewing	.50	.20
❑ 114	Chris Childs	.15	.05
❑ 115	Marcus Camby	.30	.10
❑ 116	Charlie Ward	.15	.05
❑ 117	Larry Johnson	.30	.10
❑ 118	Darrell Armstrong	.15	.05
❑ 119	Corey Maggette	.30	.10
❑ 120	Ron Mercer	.30	.10
❑ 121	Pat Garrity	.15	.05
❑ 122	Chucky Atkins	.15	.05
❑ 123	Ben Wallace	.50	.20
❑ 124	Michael Doleac	.15	.05
❑ 125	Allen Iverson	1.00	.40
❑ 126	Matt Geiger	.15	.05
❑ 127	Eric Snow	.30	.10
❑ 128	Toni Kukoc	.30	.10
❑ 129	Theo Ratliff	.30	.10
❑ 130	George Lynch	.15	.05
❑ 131	Jason Kidd	.75	.30
❑ 132	Tom Gugliotta	.15	.05
❑ 133	Rodney Rogers	.15	.05
❑ 134	Shawn Marion	.50	.20
❑ 135	Clifford Robinson	.15	.05
❑ 136	Kevin Johnson	.30	.10
❑ 137	Anfernee Hardaway	.50	.20
❑ 138	Scottie Pippen	.75	.30
❑ 139	Damon Stoudamire	.30	.10
❑ 140	Arvydas Sabonis	.30	.10
❑ 141	Jermaine O'Neal	.50	.20
❑ 142	Bonzi Wells	.30	.10
❑ 143	Rasheed Wallace	.50	.20
❑ 144	Detlef Schrempf	.30	.10
❑ 145	Chris Webber	.50	.20
❑ 146	Vlade Divac	.30	.10
❑ 147	Peja Stojakovic	.50	.20
❑ 148	Jason Williams	.30	.10
❑ 149	Corliss Williamson	.30	.10
❑ 150	Nick Anderson	.15	.05
❑ 151	Jon Barry	.15	.05
❑ 152	Tim Duncan	1.00	.40
❑ 153	David Robinson	.50	.20
❑ 154	Avery Johnson	.15	.05
❑ 155	Terry Porter	.15	.05
❑ 156	Mario Elie	.15	.05
❑ 157	Jaren Jackson	.15	.05
❑ 158	Steve Kerr	.30	.10
❑ 159	Gary Payton	.50	.20
❑ 160	Vin Baker	.30	.10
❑ 161	Brent Barry	.30	.10
❑ 162	Horace Grant	.30	.10
❑ 163	Ruben Patterson	.30	.10
❑ 164	Rashard Lewis	.30	.10
❑ 165	Tracy McGrady	1.50	.60
❑ 166	Charles Oakley	.15	.05
❑ 167	Doug Christie	.30	.10
❑ 168	Antonio Davis	.15	.05
❑ 169	Vince Carter	1.25	.50
❑ 170	Kevin Willis	.15	.05
❑ 171	Karl Malone	.50	.20
❑ 172	John Stockton	.50	.20
❑ 173	Bryon Russell	.15	.05
❑ 174	Quincy Lewis	.15	.05
❑ 175	Olden Polynice	.15	.05
❑ 176	Jacque Vaughn	.15	.05
❑ 177	Shareef Abdur-Rahim	.50	.20
❑ 178	Michael Dickerson	.30	.10
❑ 179	Bryant Reeves	.15	.05
❑ 180	Mike Bibby	.50	.20
❑ 181	Othella Harrington	.15	.05
❑ 182	Felipe Lopez	.15	.05
❑ 183	Mitch Richmond	.30	.10
❑ 184	Richard Hamilton	.30	.10
❑ 185	Jahidi White	.15	.05
❑ 186	Aaron Williams	.15	.05
❑ 187	Juwan Howard	.30	.10
❑ 188	Rod Strickland	.15	.05
❑ 189	Kobe Bryant CL	1.00	.40
❑ 190	Kevin Garnett CL	.50	.20
❑ 191	Kenyon Martin RC	1.50	.60
❑ 192	Marcus Fizer RC	.40	.15
❑ 193	Chris Mihm RC	.40	.15
❑ 194	Stromile Swift RC	.75	.30
❑ 195	Morris Peterson RC	.75	.30
❑ 196	Quentin Richardson RC	1.25	.50
❑ 197	Courtney Alexander RC	.40	.15
❑ 198	Scoonie Penn RC	.40	.15
❑ 199	Mateen Cleaves RC	.40	.15
❑ 200	Erick Barkley RC	.40	.15
❑ 201	A.J. Guyton RC	.40	.15

❏ 202	Darius Miles RC	1.25	.50
❏ 203	DerMarr Johnson RC	.40	.15
❏ 204	Jerome Moiso RC	.40	.15
❏ 205	Jamaal Magloire RC	.40	.15
❏ 206	Hanno Mottola RC	.40	.15
❏ 207	Mike Miller RC	1.25	.50
❏ 209	Desmond Mason RC	.40	.15
❏ 210	Eduardo Najera RC	.60	.25
❏ 211	Speedy Claxton RC	.40	.15
❏ 212	Joel Przybilla RC	.40	.15
❏ 213	Mark Madsen RC	.40	.15
❏ 214	Khalid El-Amin RC	.40	.15
❏ 215	Etan Thomas RC	.40	.15
❏ 216	Jason Collier RC	.60	.25
❏ 217	Jason Hart RC	.40	.15
❏ 218	Michael Redd RC	1.25	.50
❏ 219	Keyon Dooling RC	.40	.15
❏ 220	Mamadou N'diaye RC	.40	.15

2001-02 Upper Deck MVP

❏ COMPLETE SET (220)		40.00	20.00
❏ COMMON CARD		.15	.05
❏ COMMON ROOKIE		1.00	.40
❏ 1	Jason Terry	.50	.20
❏ 3	Toni Kukoc	.30	.10
❏ 4	Hanno Mottola	.30	.10
❏ 5	Theo Ratliff	.30	.10
❏ 6	DerMarr Johnson	.30	.10
❏ 7	Paul Pierce	.50	.20
❏ 8	Antoine Walker	.50	.20
❏ 10	Kenny Anderson	.30	.10
❏ 13	Jamal Mashburn	.30	.10
❏ 15	Baron Davis	.50	.20
❏ 18	Jamaal Magloire	.30	.10
❏ 19	Eddie Robinson	.30	.10
❏ 20	Elton Brand	.50	.20
❏ 21	Ron Mercer	.30	.10
❏ 23	Jamal Crawford	.30	.10
❏ 24	Ron Artest	.30	.10
❏ 25	Marcus Fizer	.30	.10
❏ 26	Andre Miller	.30	.10
❏ 30	Matt Harpring	.50	.20
❏ 32	Michael Finley	.50	.20
❏ 33	Steve Nash	.50	.20
❏ 34	Dirk Nowitzki	.75	.30
❏ 35	Juwan Howard	.30	.10
❏ 37	Eduardo Najera	.30	.10
❏ 38	Wang Zhizhi	.30	.10
❏ 39	Antonio McDyess	.50	.20
❏ 40	Nick Van Exel	.50	.20
❏ 41	Rael LaFrentz	.30	.10
❏ 42	James Posey	.30	.10
❏ 45	Jerry Stackhouse	.50	.20
❏ 47	Corliss Williamson	.30	.10
❏ 48	Joe Smith	.30	.10
❏ 49	Mateen Cleaves	.30	.10
❏ 50	Ben Wallace	.50	.20
❏ 51	Antawn Jamison	.50	.20
❏ 52	Marc Jackson	.30	.10
❏ 53	Larry Hughes	.30	.10
❏ 55	Chris Porter	.30	.10
❏ 57	Steve Francis	.50	.20
❏ 58	Hakeem Olajuwon	.50	.20
❏ 59	Cuttino Mobley	.30	.10
❏ 60	Maurice Taylor	.30	.10
❏ 63	Moochie Norris	.15	.05
❏ 64	Reggie Miller	.50	.20

❏ 65	Jalen Rose	.50	.20
❏ 66	Jermaine O'Neal	.50	.20
❏ 67	Austin Croshere	.30	.10
❏ 69	Al Harrington	.30	.10
❏ 70	Jonathan Bender	.30	.10
❏ 71	Darius Miles	.50	.20
❏ 72	Corey Maggette	.30	.10
❏ 73	Lamar Odom	.50	.20
❏ 74	Quentin Richardson	.30	.10
❏ 75	Keyon Dooling	.30	.10
❏ 77	Eric Piatkowski	.30	.10
❏ 78	Kobe Bryant	2.00	.75
❏ 79	Shaquille O'Neal	1.25	.50
❏ 80	Rick Fox	.30	.10
❏ 81	Derek Fisher	.50	.20
❏ 82	Robert Horry	.30	.10
❏ 83	Ron Harper	.30	.10
❏ 85	Alonzo Mourning	.30	.10
❏ 86	Eddie Jones	.50	.20
❏ 87	Tim Hardaway	.30	.10
❏ 88	Anthony Mason	.30	.10
❏ 89	Brian Grant	.30	.10
❏ 90	Anthony Carter	.30	.10
❏ 92	Ray Allen	.50	.20
❏ 93	Glenn Robinson	.50	.20
❏ 94	Sam Cassell	.30	.10
❏ 95	Tim Thomas	.30	.10
❏ 97	Joel Przybilla	.30	.10
❏ 98	Kevin Garnett	1.00	.40
❏ 99	Terrell Brandon	.30	.10
❏ 100	Wally Szczerbiak	.30	.10
❏ 101	Chauncey Billups	.30	.10
❏ 104	Stephon Marbury	.50	.20
❏ 105	Keith Van Horn	.50	.20
❏ 106	Kenyon Martin	.50	.20
❏ 109	Stephen Jackson	.30	.10
❏ 110	Latrell Sprewell	.50	.20
❏ 111	Allan Houston	.30	.10
❏ 112	Marcus Camby	.30	.10
❏ 113	Mark Jackson	.30	.10
❏ 114	Glen Rice	.30	.10
❏ 115	Kurt Thomas	.30	.10
❏ 116	Tracy McGrady	1.25	.50
❏ 117	Mike Miller	.50	.20
❏ 119	Grant Hill	.50	.20
❏ 122	Allen Iverson	1.00	.40
❏ 123	Dikembe Mutombo	.30	.10
❏ 124	Aaron McKie	.30	.10
❏ 126	George Lynch	.15	.05
❏ 127	Eric Snow	.30	.10
❏ 129	Jason Kidd	.75	.30
❏ 130	Shawn Marion	.50	.20
❏ 134	Anfernee Hardaway	.50	.20
❏ 135	Rasheed Wallace	.50	.20
❏ 136	Damon Stoudamire	.30	.10
❏ 137	Arvydas Sabonis	.30	.10
❏ 138	Scottie Pippen	.75	.30
❏ 139	Steve Smith	.30	.10
❏ 141	Bonzi Wells	.30	.10
❏ 142	Jason Williams	.30	.10
❏ 143	Chris Webber	.50	.20
❏ 144	Peja Stojakovic	.50	.20
❏ 145	Doug Christie	.30	.10
❏ 147	Hidayet Turkoglu	.30	.10
❏ 148	Vlade Divac	.30	.10
❏ 149	Tim Duncan	1.00	.40
❏ 150	David Robinson	.50	.20
❏ 152	Sean Elliott	.30	.10
❏ 153	Derek Anderson	.30	.10
❏ 156	Gary Payton	.50	.20
❏ 157	Rashard Lewis	.30	.10
❏ 158	Patrick Ewing	.50	.20
❏ 159	Vin Baker	.30	.10
❏ 161	Desmond Mason	.30	.10
❏ 162	Vince Carter	1.25	.50
❏ 163	Morris Peterson	.30	.10
❏ 170	Karl Malone	.50	.20
❏ 171	John Stockton	.50	.20
❏ 172	Donyell Marshall	.30	.10
❏ 173	John Starks	.30	.10
❏ 177	Shareef Abdur-Rahim	.50	.20
❏ 178	Mike Bibby	.50	.20
❏ 179	Michael Dickerson	.30	.10
❏ 182	Stromile Swift	.30	.10
❏ 183	Richard Hamilton	.30	.10
❏ 187	Courtney Alexander	.30	.10

❏ 188	Christian Laettner	.30	.10
❏ 189	Kobe Bryant CL	1.00	.40
❏ 190	Kevin Garnett CL	.50	.20
❏ 193	Tyson Chandler RC	2.00	.75
❏ 197	Eddie Griffin RC	1.00	.40
❏ 198	Zach Randolph RC	2.50	1.00
❏ 199	Eddy Curry RC	2.50	1.00
❏ 201	Gerald Wallace RC	1.50	.60
❏ 202	Jamaal Tinsley RC	1.50	.60
❏ 205	Jarron Collins RC	1.25	.50
❏ 209	Jason Richardson RC	2.50	1.00
❏ 211	Gilbert Arenas RC	6.00	2.50
❏ 215	Rodney White RC	1.25	.50
❏ 216	Joe Johnson RC	2.00	.75
❏ 217	Richard Jefferson RC	2.00	.75
❏ 218	Kwame Brown RC	1.50	.60

2002-03 Upper Deck MVP

❏ COMPLETE SET (220)		50.00	20.00
❏ COMMON ROOKIE (191-220)		1.25	.50
❏ 1	Shareef Abdur-Rahim	.50	.20
❏ 2	Jason Terry	.50	.20
❏ 3	Toni Kukoc	.30	.10
❏ 4	DerMarr Johnson	.15	.05
❏ 5	Nazr Mohammed	.15	.05
❏ 6	Theo Ratliff	.30	.10
❏ 7	Dion Glover	.15	.05
❏ 8	Paul Pierce	.50	.20
❏ 9	Antoine Walker	.50	.20
❏ 10	Kenny Anderson	.30	.10
❏ 11	Tony Delk	.15	.05
❏ 12	Eric Williams	.15	.05
❏ 13	Rodney Rogers	.15	.05
❏ 14	Jamal Mashburn	.30	.10
❏ 15	Baron Davis	.50	.20
❏ 16	David Wesley	.15	.05
❏ 17	Elden Campbell	.15	.05
❏ 18	P.J. Brown	.15	.05
❏ 19	Jamaal Magloire	.15	.05
❏ 20	Stacey Augmon	.15	.05
❏ 21	Jalen Rose	.50	.20
❏ 22	Marcus Fizer	.30	.10
❏ 23	Tyson Chandler	.30	.10
❏ 24	Trenton Hassell	.30	.10
❏ 25	Eddy Curry	.50	.20
❏ 26	Travis Best	.15	.05
❏ 27	Andre Miller	.30	.10
❏ 28	Lamond Murray	.15	.05
❏ 29	Ricky Davis	.30	.10
❏ 30	Zydrunas Ilgauskas	.30	.10
❏ 31	Jumaine Jones	.15	.05
❏ 32	Chris Mihm	.15	.05
❏ 33	Dirk Nowitzki	.75	.30
❏ 34	Michael Finley	.50	.20
❏ 35	Steve Nash	.50	.20
❏ 36	Nick Van Exel	.50	.20
❏ 37	Rael LaFrentz	.30	.10
❏ 38	Adrian Griffin	.15	.05
❏ 39	Avery Johnson	.15	.05
❏ 40	Marcus Camby	.30	.10
❏ 41	Juwan Howard	.30	.10
❏ 42	James Posey	.30	.10
❏ 43	Ryan Bowen	.15	.05
❏ 44	Donnell Harvey	.15	.05
❏ 45	Voshon Lenard	.15	.05
❏ 46	Jerry Stackhouse	.50	.20
❏ 47	Clifford Robinson	.15	.05
❏ 48	Chucky Atkins	.15	.05

#	Player		
☐ 49	Ben Wallace	.50	.20
☐ 50	Jon Barry	.15	.05
☐ 51	Corliss Williamson	.30	.10
☐ 52	Antawn Jamison	.50	.20
☐ 53	Jason Richardson	.50	.20
☐ 54	Danny Fortson	.15	.05
☐ 55	Gilbert Arenas	.50	.20
☐ 56	Bob Sura	.15	.05
☐ 57	Troy Murphy	.30	.10
☐ 58	Steve Francis	.50	.20
☐ 59	Cuttino Mobley	.30	.10
☐ 60	Eddie Griffin	.30	.10
☐ 61	Kenny Thomas	.15	.05
☐ 62	Moochie Norris	.15	.05
☐ 63	Kelvin Cato	.15	.05
☐ 64	Glen Rice	.50	.20
☐ 65	Reggie Miller	.50	.20
☐ 66	Jermaine O'Neal	.50	.20
☐ 67	Ron Mercer	.30	.10
☐ 68	Jamaal Tinsley	.30	.20
☐ 69	Al Harrington	.30	.10
☐ 70	Ron Artest	.30	.10
☐ 71	Austin Croshere	.15	.05
☐ 72	Elton Brand	.50	.20
☐ 73	Darius Miles	.50	.20
☐ 74	Lamar Odom	.50	.20
☐ 75	Quentin Richardson	.30	.10
☐ 76	Corey Maggette	.30	.10
☐ 77	Jeff McInnis	.15	.05
☐ 78	Michael Olowokandi	.15	.05
☐ 79	Kobe Bryant	2.00	.75
☐ 80	Shaquille O'Neal	1.25	.50
☐ 81	Derek Fisher	.30	.10
☐ 82	Rick Fox	.30	.10
☐ 83	Robert Horry	.30	.10
☐ 84	Devean George	.30	.10
☐ 85	Samaki Walker	.15	.05
☐ 86	Pau Gasol	.50	.20
☐ 87	Jason Williams	.30	.10
☐ 88	Shane Battier	.30	.10
☐ 89	Stromile Swift	.30	.10
☐ 90	Lorenzen Wright	.15	.05
☐ 91	Tony Massenburg	.15	.05
☐ 92	Eddie Jones	.50	.20
☐ 93	Alonzo Mourning	.30	.10
☐ 94	Brian Grant	.30	.10
☐ 95	Anthony Carter	.30	.10
☐ 96	LaPhonso Ellis	.15	.05
☐ 97	Jim Jackson	.15	.05
☐ 98	Ray Allen	.50	.20
☐ 99	Glenn Robinson	.50	.20
☐ 100	Sam Cassell	.50	.20
☐ 101	Tim Thomas	.30	.10
☐ 102	Anthony Mason	.30	.10
☐ 103	Joel Przybilla	.15	.05
☐ 104	Ervin Johnson	.15	.05
☐ 105	Kevin Garnett	1.00	.40
☐ 106	Wally Szczerbiak	.30	.10
☐ 107	Chauncey Billups	.30	.10
☐ 108	Terrell Brandon	.30	.10
☐ 109	Marc Jackson	.15	.05
☐ 110	Joe Smith	.30	.10
☐ 111	Jason Kidd	.75	.30
☐ 112	Keith Van Horn	.50	.20
☐ 113	Kenyon Martin	.50	.20
☐ 114	Kerry Kittles	.15	.05
☐ 115	Richard Jefferson	.30	.10
☐ 116	Jason Collins	.15	.05
☐ 117	Todd MacCulloch	.15	.05
☐ 118	Allan Houston	.30	.10
☐ 119	Latrell Sprewell	.50	.20
☐ 120	Kurt Thomas	.30	.10
☐ 121	Antonio McDyess	.30	.10
☐ 122	Othella Harrington	.15	.05
☐ 123	Clarence Weatherspoon	.15	.05
☐ 124	Tracy McGrady	1.25	.50
☐ 125	Mike Miller	.50	.20
☐ 126	Darrell Armstrong	.15	.05
☐ 127	Grant Hill	.50	.20
☐ 128	Horace Grant	.30	.10
☐ 129	Steven Hunter	.15	.05
☐ 130	Allen Iverson	1.00	.40
☐ 131	Dikembe Mutombo	.30	.10
☐ 132	Aaron McKie	.30	.10
☐ 133	Derrick Coleman	.15	.05
☐ 134	Eric Snow	.30	.10
☐ 135	Matt Harpring	.50	.20
☐ 136	Stephon Marbury	.50	.20
☐ 137	Shawn Marion	.50	.20
☐ 138	Joe Johnson	.50	.20
☐ 139	Anfernee Hardaway	.50	.20
☐ 140	Iakovos Tsakalidis	.15	.05
☐ 141	Tom Gugliotta	.15	.05
☐ 142	Bo Outlaw	.15	.05
☐ 143	Rasheed Wallace	.50	.20
☐ 144	Damon Stoudamire	.30	.10
☐ 145	Scottie Pippen	.75	.30
☐ 146	Ruben Patterson	.30	.10
☐ 147	Derek Anderson	.30	.10
☐ 148	Dale Davis	.30	.10
☐ 149	Bonzi Wells	.30	.10
☐ 150	Chris Webber	.50	.20
☐ 151	Peja Stojakovic	.50	.20
☐ 152	Mike Bibby	.50	.20
☐ 153	Doug Christie	.30	.10
☐ 154	Vlade Divac	.30	.10
☐ 155	Bobby Jackson	.30	.10
☐ 156	Hidayet Turkoglu	.50	.20
☐ 157	Tim Duncan	1.00	.40
☐ 158	David Robinson	.50	.20
☐ 159	Steve Smith	.30	.10
☐ 160	Tony Parker	.50	.20
☐ 161	Antonio Daniels	.15	.05
☐ 162	Charles Smith	.15	.05
☐ 163	Bruce Bowen	.15	.05
☐ 164	Gary Payton	.50	.20
☐ 165	Rashard Lewis	.30	.10
☐ 166	Vin Baker	.30	.10
☐ 167	Brent Barry	.30	.10
☐ 168	Desmond Mason	.30	.10
☐ 169	Vladimir Radmanovic	.30	.10
☐ 170	Vince Carter	1.25	.50
☐ 171	Morris Peterson	.30	.10
☐ 172	Antonio Davis	.15	.05
☐ 173	Hakeem Olajuwon	.50	.20
☐ 174	Alvin Williams	.15	.05
☐ 175	Jerome Williams	.15	.05
☐ 176	Keon Clark	.30	.10
☐ 177	Karl Malone	.50	.20
☐ 178	John Stockton	.50	.20
☐ 179	Donyell Marshall	.30	.10
☐ 180	Andrei Kirilenko	.50	.20
☐ 181	Bryon Russell	.15	.05
☐ 182	Jarron Collins	.15	.05
☐ 183	DeShawn Stevenson	.15	.05
☐ 184	Michael Jordan	4.00	1.50
☐ 185	Richard Hamilton	.30	.10
☐ 186	Kwame Brown	.30	.10
☐ 187	Chris Whitney	.15	.05
☐ 188	Tyronn Lue	.15	.05
☐ 189	Brendan Haywood	.30	.10
☐ 190	Jahidi White	.15	.05
☐ 191	DaJuan Wagner RC	2.00	.75
☐ 192	Jay Williams RC	1.50	.60
☐ 193	Yao Ming RC	10.00	4.00
☐ 194	Drew Gooden RC	4.00	1.50
☐ 195	Chris Jefferies RC	1.25	.50
☐ 196	Casey Jacobsen RC	1.25	.50
☐ 197	Juan Dixon RC	2.00	.75
☐ 198	Melvin Ely RC	1.25	.50
☐ 199	Curtis Borchardt RC	1.25	.50
☐ 200	John Salmons RC	1.25	.50
☐ 201	Carlos Boozer RC	2.50	1.00
☐ 202	Fred Jones RC	1.25	.50
☐ 203	Frank Williams RC	1.25	.50
☐ 204	Jamaal Sampson RC	1.25	.50
☐ 205	Dan Dickau RC	1.25	.50
☐ 206	Marcus Haislip RC	1.25	.50
☐ 207	Jared Jeffries RC	1.25	.50
☐ 208	Amare Stoudemire RC	6.00	2.50
☐ 209	Caron Butler RC	2.50	1.00
☐ 210	Qyntel Woods RC	1.25	.50
☐ 211	Kareem Rush RC	1.50	.60
☐ 212	Ryan Humphrey RC	1.25	.50
☐ 213	Jiri Welsch RC	1.25	.50
☐ 214	Mike Dunleavy RC	5.00	2.00
☐ 215	Tayshaun Prince RC	1.50	.60
☐ 216	Nene Hilario RC	2.00	.75
☐ 217	Nikoloz Tskitishvili RC	1.25	.50
☐ 218	Bostjan Nachbar RC	1.25	.50
☐ 219	Efthimios Rentzias RC	1.25	.50
☐ 220	Rod Grizzard RC	1.25	.50

2003-04 Upper Deck MVP

☐	COMP.SET w/o SP's		
☐	COMMON ROOKIE (201-230)	1.50	.60
☐	BLACK NOT PRICED DUE TO SCARCITY		
	*GOLD SINGLES: 8X TO 20X BASE CARD HI		
	*GOLD RC's: 4X TO 10X BASE CARD HI		
	*SILVER SINGLES: .75X TO 2X BASE CARD HI		
☐ 1	Shareef Abdur-Rahim	.50	.20
☐ 2	Jason Terry	.50	.20
☐ 3	Terrell Brandon	.15	.06
☐ 4	Alan Henderson	.15	.06
☐ 5	Dan Dickau	.15	.06
☐ 6	Theo Ratliff	.25	.10
☐ 7	Dion Glover	.15	.06
☐ 8	Paul Pierce	.50	.20
☐ 9	Antoine Walker	.50	.20
☐ 10	Eric Williams	.15	.06
☐ 11	Tony Delk	.15	.06
☐ 12	J.R. Bremer	.15	.06
☐ 13	Vin Baker	.25	.10
☐ 14	Jalen Rose	.50	.20
☐ 15	Marcus Fizer	.15	.06
☐ 16	Tyson Chandler	.50	.20
☐ 17	Jamal Crawford	.15	.06
☐ 18	Eddy Curry	.25	.10
☐ 19	Scottie Pippen	.75	.30
☐ 20	Darius Miles	.50	.20
☐ 21	Dajuan Wagner	.25	.10
☐ 22	Ricky Davis	.50	.20
☐ 23	Zydrunas Ilgauskas	.25	.10
☐ 24	Carlos Boozer	.50	.20
☐ 25	Chris Mihm	.15	.06
☐ 26	Dirk Nowitzki	.75	.30
☐ 27	Michael Finley	.50	.20
☐ 28	Steve Nash	.50	.20
☐ 29	Nick Van Exel	.50	.20
☐ 30	Raef LaFrentz	.25	.10
☐ 31	Eduardo Najera	.25	.10
☐ 32	Shawn Bradley	.15	.06
☐ 33	Marcus Camby	.25	.10
☐ 34	Vincent Yarbrough	.15	.06
☐ 35	Rodney White	.15	.06
☐ 36	Nene Hilario	.50	.20
☐ 37	Nikoloz Tskitishvili	.15	.06
☐ 38	Shammond Williams	.15	.06
☐ 39	Richard Hamilton	.25	.10
☐ 40	Clifford Robinson	.15	.06
☐ 41	Chauncey Billups	.25	.10
☐ 42	Ben Wallace	.50	.20
☐ 43	Elden Campbell	.15	.06
☐ 44	Corliss Williamson	.25	.10
☐ 45	Antawn Jamison	.50	.20
☐ 46	Jason Richardson	.50	.20
☐ 47	Danny Fortson	.15	.06
☐ 48	Mike Dunleavy	.25	.10
☐ 49	Speedy Claxton	.15	.06
☐ 50	Troy Murphy	.50	.20
☐ 51	Steve Francis	.25	.10
☐ 52	Cuttino Mobley	.25	.10
☐ 53	Eddie Griffin	.15	.06
☐ 54	Yao Ming	1.25	.50
☐ 55	Maurice Taylor	.15	.06
☐ 56	Kelvin Cato	.15	.06
☐ 57	Glen Rice	.50	.20
☐ 58	Reggie Miller	.50	.20
☐ 59	Jermaine Oá ™Neal	.50	.20

□			
□ 60	Scot Pollard	.15	.06
□ 61	Jamaal Tinsley	.50	.20
□ 62	Al Harrington	.25	.10
□ 63	Ron Artest	.25	.10
□ 64	Danny Ferry	.15	.06
□ 65	Elton Brand	.50	.20
□ 66	Andre Miller	.25	.10
□ 67	Lamar Odom	.50	.20
□ 68	Quentin Richardson	.25	.10
□ 69	Corey Maggette	.25	.10
□ 70	Chris Wilcox	.25	.10
□ 71	Marko Jaric	.25	.10
□ 72	Kobe Bryant	2.00	.75
□ 73	Shaquille Oâ ™Neal	1.25	.50
□ 74	Derek Fisher	.50	.20
□ 75	Karl Malone	.50	.20
□ 76	Gary Payton	.50	.20
□ 77	Devean George	.25	.10
□ 78	Kareem Rush	.25	.10
□ 79	Pau Gasol	.50	.20
□ 80	Jason Williams	.25	.10
□ 81	Shane Battier	.50	.20
□ 82	Stromile Swift	.25	.10
□ 83	Lorenzen Wright	.15	.06
□ 84	Mike Miller	.50	.20
□ 85	Eddie Jones	.50	.20
□ 86	Ken Johnson	.15	.06
□ 87	Brian Grant	.25	.10
□ 88	Anthony Carter	.25	.10
□ 89	Rasual Butler	.25	.10
□ 90	Caron Butler	.50	.20
□ 91	Marcus Haislip	.15	.06
□ 92	Toni Kukoc	.25	.10
□ 93	Joe Smith	.25	.10
□ 94	Tim Thomas	.25	.10
□ 95	Anthony Mason	.25	.10
□ 96	Joel Przybilla	.15	.06
□ 97	Desmond Mason	.25	.10
□ 98	Kevin Garnett	1.00	.40
□ 99	Wally Szczerbiak	.25	.10
□ 100	Troy Hudson	.15	.06
□ 101	Michael Olowokandi	.15	.06
□ 102	Kendall Gill	.15	.06
□ 103	Sam Cassell	.50	.20
□ 104	Jason Kidd	.75	.30
□ 105	Kenyon Martin	.50	.20
□ 106	Alonzo Mourning	.25	.10
□ 107	Kerry Kittles	.15	.06
□ 108	Richard Jefferson	.25	.10
□ 109	Jason Collins	.15	.06
□ 110	Dikembe Mutombo	.25	.10
□ 111	Jamal Mashburn	.25	.10
□ 112	Baron Davis	.50	.20
□ 113	David Wesley	.15	.06
□ 114	Kenny Anderson	.25	.10
□ 115	P.J. Brown	.15	.06
□ 116	Jamaal Magloire	.15	.06
□ 117	George Lynch	.15	.06
□ 118	Courtney Alexander	.25	.10
□ 119	Allan Houston	.25	.10
□ 120	Keith Van Horn	.50	.20
□ 121	Kurt Thomas	.25	.10
□ 122	Antonio McDyess	.25	.10
□ 123	Othella Harrington	.15	.06
□ 124	Clarence Weatherspoon	.15	.06
□ 125	Tracy McGrady	1.25	.50
□ 126	Drew Gooden	.25	.10
□ 127	Tyronn Lue	.15	.06
□ 128	Pat Garrity	.15	.06
□ 129	Grant Hill	.50	.20
□ 130	Gordan Giricek	.25	.10
□ 131	Juwan Howard	.25	.10
□ 132	Allen Iverson	1.00	.40
□ 133	Glenn Robinson	.25	.10
□ 134	Aaron McKie	.15	.06
□ 135	Derrick Coleman	.15	.06
□ 136	Eric Snow	.25	.10
□ 137	Kenny Thomas	.15	.06
□ 138	Stephon Marbury	.50	.20
□ 139	Shawn Marion	.50	.20
□ 140	Joe Johnson	.25	.10
□ 141	Anfernee Hardaway	.50	.20
□ 142	Amare Stoudemire	1.00	.40
□ 143	Casey Jacqbsen	.15	.06
□ 144	Tom Gugliotta	.15	.06
□ 145	Bo Outlaw	.15	.06

□			
□ 146	Rasheed Wallace	.50	.20
□ 147	Damon Stoudamire	.25	.10
□ 148	Jeff McInnis	.15	.06
□ 149	Ruben Patterson	.25	.10
□ 150	Derek Anderson	.25	.10
□ 151	Dale Davis	.15	.06
□ 152	Bonzi Wells	.25	.10
□ 153	Chris Webber	.50	.20
□ 154	Peja Stojakovic	.50	.20
□ 155	Mike Bibby	.50	.20
□ 156	Doug Christie	.25	.10
□ 157	Vlade Divac	.25	.10
□ 158	Bobby Jackson	.25	.10
□ 159	Brad Miller	.50	.20
□ 160	Keon Clark	.25	.10
□ 161	Tim Duncan	1.00	.40
□ 162	David Robinson	.50	.20
□ 163	Steve Smith	.25	.10
□ 164	Tony Parker	.50	.20
□ 165	Hedo Turkoglu	.50	.20
□ 166	Radoslav Nesterovic	.25	.10
□ 167	Manu Ginobili	.50	.20
□ 168	Ron Mercer	.15	.06
□ 169	Ray Allen	.50	.20
□ 170	Rashard Lewis	.50	.20
□ 171	Antonio Daniels	.15	.06
□ 172	Brent Barry	.25	.10
□ 173	Predrag Drobnjak	.15	.06
□ 174	Vladimir Radmanovic	.15	.06
□ 175	Vince Carter	1.00	.40
□ 176	Morris Peterson	.25	.10
□ 177	Antonio Davis	.15	.06
□ 178	Chris Jefferies	.15	.06
□ 179	Lindsey Hunter	.15	.06
□ 180	Alvin Williams	.15	.06
□ 181	Jerome Williams	.15	.06
□ 182	Jerome Moiso	.15	.06
□ 183	Greg Ostertag	.15	.06
□ 184	John Stockton	.50	.20
□ 185	Matt Harpring	.50	.20
□ 186	Andrei Kirilenko	.50	.20
□ 187	Calbert Cheaney	.15	.06
□ 188	Jarron Collins	.15	.06
□ 189	DeShawn Stevenson	.15	.06
□ 190	Michael Jordan	3.00	1.25
□ 191	Jerry Stackhouse	.50	.20
□ 192	Kwame Brown	.25	.10
□ 193	Larry Hughes	.25	.10
□ 194	Gilbert Arenas	.50	.20
□ 195	Brendan Haywood	.15	.06
□ 196	Juan Dixon	.25	.10
□ 197	Jahidi White	.15	.06
□ 198	Etan Thomas	.15	.06
□ 199	Michael Jordan - Checklist	2.00	.75
□ 200	Michael Jordan - Checklist	2.00	.75
□ 201	LeBron James RC	15.00	6.00
□ 202	Darko Milicic RC	2.50	1.00
□ 203	Carmelo Anthony RC	8.00	3.00
□ 204	Chris Bosh RC	3.00	1.25
□ 205	Dwyane Wade RC	6.00	2.50
□ 206	Chris Kaman RC	1.50	.60
□ 207	Kirk Hinrich RC	2.50	1.00
□ 208	T.J. Ford RC	2.00	.75
□ 209	Mike Sweetney RC	1.50	.60
□ 210	Jarvis Hayes RC	1.50	.60
□ 211	Mickael Pietrus RC	1.50	.60
□ 212	Nick Collison RC	1.50	.60
□ 213	Marcus Banks RC	1.50	.60
□ 214	Luke Ridnour RC	2.00	.75
□ 215	Reece Gaines RC	1.50	.60
□ 216	Troy Bell RC	1.50	.60
□ 217	Zarko Cabarkapa RC	1.50	.60
□ 218	David West RC	1.50	.60
□ 219	Aleksandar Pavlovic RC	2.00	.75
□ 220	Dahntay Jones RC	1.50	.60
□ 221	Boris Diaw-Riffiod RC	2.00	.75
□ 222	Zoran Planinic RC	1.50	.60
□ 223	Travis Outlaw RC	1.50	.60
□ 224	Brian Cook RC	1.50	.60
□ 225	Carlos Delfino RC	1.50	.60
□ 226	Ndudi Ebi RC	1.50	.60
□ 227	Kendrick Perkins RC	1.50	.60
□ 228	Leandro Barbosa RC	2.50	1.00
□ 229	Josh Howard RC	2.50	1.00
□ 230	Maciej Lampe RC	1.50	.60

1998-99 Upper Deck Ovation

□			
□	COMPLETE SET (80)	120.00	60.00
□	COMPLETE SET w/o RC (70)	40.00	20.00
□	COMMON CARD (1-70)	.40	.15
□	COMMON ROOKIE (71-80)	1.50	.60
□ 1	Steve Smith	.75	.30
□ 2	Dikembe Mutombo	.75	.30
□ 3	Antoine Walker	1.25	.50
□ 4	Ron Mercer	.60	.25
□ 5	Glen Rice	.75	.30
□ 6	Bobby Phills	.40	.15
□ 7	Michael Jordan	8.00	4.00
□ 8	Toni Kukoc	.75	.30
□ 9	Dennis Rodman	.75	.30
□ 10	Scottie Pippen	2.00	.75
□ 11	Shawn Kemp	.75	.30
□ 12	Derek Anderson	1.00	.40
□ 13	Brevin Knight	.40	.15
□ 14	Michael Finley	1.25	.50
□ 15	Shawn Bradley	.40	.15
□ 16	LaPhonso Ellis	.40	.15
□ 17	Bobby Jackson	.75	.30
□ 18	Grant Hill	1.25	.50
□ 19	Jerry Stackhouse	1.25	.50
□ 20	Donyell Marshall	.75	.30
□ 21	Erick Dampier	.75	.30
□ 22	Hakeem Olajuwon	1.25	.50
□ 23	Charles Barkley	1.50	.60
□ 24	Reggie Miller	1.25	.50
□ 25	Chris Mullin	1.25	.50
□ 26	Rik Smits	.75	.30
□ 27	Maurice Taylor	.60	.25
□ 28	Lorenzen Wright	.40	.15
□ 29	Kobe Bryant	5.00	2.00
□ 30	Eddie Jones	1.25	.50
□ 31	Shaquille O'Neal	3.00	1.25
□ 32	Alonzo Mourning	.75	.30
□ 33	Tim Hardaway	.75	.30
□ 34	Jamal Mashburn	.75	.30
□ 35	Ray Allen	1.25	.50
□ 36	Terrell Brandon	.75	.30
□ 37	Glenn Robinson	.75	.30
□ 38	Kevin Garnett	4.00	1.50
□ 39	Tom Gugliotta	.40	.15
□ 40	Stephon Marbury	1.25	.50
□ 41	Keith Van Horn	1.25	.50
□ 42	Kerry Kittles	.40	.15
□ 43	Jayson Williams	.40	.15
□ 44	Patrick Ewing	1.25	.50
□ 45	Allan Houston	.75	.30
□ 46	Larry Johnson	.75	.30
□ 47	Anfernee Hardaway	1.25	.50
□ 48	Nick Anderson	.40	.15
□ 49	Allen Iverson	2.50	1.00
□ 50	Joe Smith	.75	.30
□ 51	Tim Thomas	.75	.30
□ 52	Jason Kidd	2.00	.75
□ 53	Antonio McDyess	.75	.30
□ 54	Damon Stoudamire	.75	.30
□ 55	Isaiah Rider	.40	.15
□ 56	Rasheed Wallace	1.25	.50
□ 57	Tariq Abdul-Wahad	.40	.15
□ 58	Corliss Williamson	.75	.30
□ 59	Tim Duncan	2.00	.75
□ 60	David Robinson	1.25	.50
□ 61	Vin Baker	.75	.30

#	Player		
62	Gary Payton	1.25	.50
63	Chauncey Billups	.75	.30
64	Tracy McGrady	3.00	1.25
65	Karl Malone	1.25	.50
66	John Stockton	1.25	.50
67	Shareef Abdur-Rahim	1.25	.50
68	Bryant Reeves	.40	.15
69	Juwan Howard	.75	.30
70	Rod Strickland	.40	.15
71	Michael Olowokandi RC	1.50	.60
72	Mike Bibby RC	6.00	2.50
73	Raef LaFrentz RC	2.00	.75
74	Antawn Jamison RC	5.00	2.00
75	Vince Carter RC	15.00	6.00
76	Robert Traylor RC	1.50	.60
77	Jason Williams RC	4.00	1.50
78	Larry Hughes RC	4.00	1.50
79	Dirk Nowitzki RC	12.00	5.00
80	Paul Pierce RC	6.00	2.50
BK1	M.Jordan Ball/90	1500.00	1000.00

1999-00 Upper Deck Ovation

#	Player		
	COMPLETE SET (90)	100.00	50.00
	COMPLETE SET w/o RC (60)	25.00	12.50
	COMMON CARD (1-60)	.30	.10
	COMMON ROOKIE (61-90)	1.00	.40
1	Dikembe Mutombo	.60	.25
2	Alan Henderson	.30	.10
3	Antoine Walker	1.00	.40
4	Paul Pierce	1.00	.40
5	David Wesley	.30	.10
6	Eddie Jones	1.00	.40
7	Toni Kukoc	.60	.25
8	Randy Brown	.30	.10
9	Shawn Kemp	.60	.25
10	Zydrunas Ilgauskas	.60	.25
11	Michael Finley	1.00	.40
12	Dirk Nowitzki	2.00	.75
13	Nick Van Exel	1.00	.40
14	Antonio McDyess	.60	.25
15	Grant Hill	1.00	.40
16	Jerry Stackhouse	1.00	.40
17	Antawn Jamison	1.50	.60
18	John Starks	.60	.25
19	Hakeem Olajuwon	1.00	.40
20	Charles Barkley	1.25	.50
21	Cuttino Mobley	.60	.25
22	Reggie Miller	1.00	.40
23	Rik Smits	.60	.25
24	Maurice Taylor	.60	.25
25	Michael Olowokandi	.60	.25
26	Kobe Bryant	4.00	1.50
27	Shaquille O'Neal	2.50	1.00
28	Tim Hardaway	.60	.25
29	Alonzo Mourning	.60	.25
30	Glenn Robinson	1.00	.40
31	Ray Allen	1.00	.40
32	Kevin Garnett	2.00	.75
33	Joe Smith	.60	.25
34	Stephon Marbury	1.00	.40
35	Keith Van Horn	1.00	.40
36	Patrick Ewing	1.00	.40
37	Latrell Sprewell	1.00	.40
38	Darrell Armstrong	.30	.10
39	Bo Outlaw	.30	.10
40	Allen Iverson	2.00	.75
41	Larry Hughes	1.00	.40
42	Jason Kidd	1.50	.60
43	Anfernee Hardaway	1.00	.40
44	Brian Grant	.60	.25
45	Damon Stoudamire	.60	.25
46	Jason Williams	1.00	.40
47	Chris Webber	1.00	.40
48	Tim Duncan	2.00	.75
49	David Robinson	1.00	.40
50	Sean Elliott	.60	.25
51	Gary Payton	1.00	.40
52	Vin Baker	.60	.25
53	Vince Carter	2.50	1.00
54	Tracy McGrady	2.50	1.00
55	Karl Malone	1.00	.40
56	John Stockton	1.00	.40
57	Shareef Abdur-Rahim	1.00	.40
58	Mike Bibby	1.00	.40
59	Juwan Howard	.60	.25
60	Mitch Richmond	.60	.25
61	Elton Brand RC	6.00	2.50
62	Steve Francis RC	6.00	2.50
63	Baron Davis RC	8.00	3.00
64	Lamar Odom RC	5.00	2.00
65	Jonathan Bender RC	3.00	1.25
66	Wally Szczerbiak RC	5.00	2.00
67	Richard Hamilton RC	5.00	2.00
68	Andre Miller RC	5.00	2.00
69	Shawn Marion RC	6.00	2.50
70	Jason Terry RC	4.00	1.50
71	Trajan Langdon RC	2.00	.75
72	A.Radojevic RC	1.00	.40
73	Corey Maggette RC	5.00	2.00
74	William Avery RC	2.00	.75
75	Galen Young RC	1.00	.40
76	Chris Herren RC	1.00	.40
77	Cal Bowdler RC	1.50	.60
78	James Posey RC	3.00	1.25
79	Quincy Lewis RC	1.50	.60
80	Dion Glover RC	1.50	.60
81	Jeff Foster RC	1.50	.60
82	Kenny Thomas RC	2.00	.75
83	Devean George RC	2.50	1.00
84	Tim James RC	1.50	.60
85	Vonteego Cummings RC	2.00	.75
86	Jumaine Jones RC	2.00	.75
87	Scott Padgett RC	2.00	.75
88	Obinna Ekezie RC	1.25	.50
89	Ryan Robertson RC	1.25	.50
90	Evan Eschmeyer RC	1.00	.40
MJ-S	M.Jordan AU/23		

2000-01 Upper Deck Ovation

#	Player		
	COMPLETE SET w/o RC (60)	25.00	12.50
	COMMON CARD (1-60)	.25	.08
	COMMON ROOKIE (61-90)	3.00	1.25
1	Dikembe Mutombo	.50	.20
2	Jim Jackson	.25	.08
3	Paul Pierce	.75	.30
4	Antoine Walker	.75	.30
5	Derrick Coleman	.25	.08
6	Baron Davis	.75	.30
7	Elton Brand	.75	.30
8	Ron Artest	.50	.20
9	Lamond Murray	.25	.08
10	Andre Miller	.50	.20
11	Michael Finley	.50	.20
12	Dirk Nowitzki	1.25	.50
13	Antonio McDyess	.50	.20
14	Nick Van Exel	.75	.30
15	Jerry Stackhouse	.75	.30
16	Jerome Williams	.25	.08
17	Larry Hughes	.50	.20
18	Antawn Jamison	.75	.30
19	Steve Francis	.75	.30
20	Hakeem Olajuwon	.75	.30
21	Reggie Miller	.75	.30
22	Jalen Rose	.75	.30
23	Lamar Odom	.75	.30
24	Michael Olowokandi	.25	.08
25	Shaquille O'Neal	2.00	.75
26	Kobe Bryant	3.00	1.25
27	Alonzo Mourning	.50	.20
28	Anthony Carter	.50	.20
29	Ray Allen	.75	.30
30	Tim Thomas	.50	.20
31	Kevin Garnett	1.50	.60
32	Wally Szczerbiak	.50	.20
33	Stephon Marbury	.75	.30
34	Keith Van Horn	.75	.30
35	Allan Houston	.50	.20
36	Latrell Sprewell	.75	.30
37	Grant Hill	.75	.30
38	Tracy McGrady	2.00	.75
39	Allen Iverson	1.50	.60
40	Toni Kukoc	.50	.20
41	Jason Kidd	1.25	.50
42	Anfernee Hardaway	.75	.30
43	Rasheed Wallace	.50	.20
44	Scottie Pippen	1.25	.50
45	Damon Stoudamire	.50	.20
46	Chris Webber	.75	.30
47	Jason Williams	.50	.20
48	Tim Duncan	1.50	.60
49	David Robinson	.75	.30
50	Gary Payton	.75	.30
51	Brent Barry	.50	.20
52	Rashard Lewis	.50	.20
53	Vince Carter	2.00	.75
54	Antonio Davis	.25	.08
55	Karl Malone	.75	.30
56	John Stockton	.75	.30
57	Shareef Abdur-Rahim	.75	.30
58	Mike Bibby	.75	.30
59	Mitch Richmond	.50	.20
60	Richard Hamilton	.50	.20
61	Kenyon Martin RC	12.00	5.00
62	Stromile Swift RC	6.00	2.50
63	Darius Miles RC	10.00	4.00
64	Marcus Fizer RC	3.00	1.25
65	Mike Miller RC	10.00	4.00
66	DerMarr Johnson RC	3.00	1.25
67	Chris Mihm RC	3.00	1.25
68	Jamal Crawford RC	4.00	1.50
69	Joel Przybilla RC	3.00	1.25
70	Keyon Dooling RC	3.00	1.25
71	Jerome Moiso RC	3.00	1.25
72	Etan Thomas RC	3.00	1.25
73	Courtney Alexander RC	4.00	1.50
74	Mateen Cleaves RC	3.00	1.25
75	Jason Collier RC	4.00	1.50
76	Hidayet Turkoglu RC	8.00	3.00
77	Desmond Mason RC	3.00	1.25
78	Quentin Richardson RC	8.00	3.00
79	Jamaal Magloire RC	3.00	1.25
80	Speedy Claxton RC	3.00	1.25
81	Morris Peterson RC	6.00	2.50
82	Donnell Harvey RC	3.00	1.25
83	DeShawn Stevenson RC	3.00	1.25
84	Mamadou N'Diaye RC	3.00	1.25
85	Erick Barkley RC	3.00	1.25
86	Mark Madsen RC	3.00	1.25
87	A.J. Guyton RC	3.00	1.25
88	Khalid El-Amin RC	3.00	1.25
89	Eddie House RC	3.00	1.25
90	Chris Porter RC	3.00	1.25

2001-02 Upper Deck Ovation

	COMP.SET w/o SP's (90)	40.00	20.00
	COMMON CARD (1-90)	.25	.08
	COMMON ROOKIE (91-110)	2.50	1.00
	COMMON ROOKIE (111-120)	6.00	2.50

❏ 1	Jason Terry	.75	.30
❏ 2	DerMarr Johnson	.50	.20
❏ 3	Shareef Abdur-Rahim	.75	.30
❏ 4	Paul Pierce	.75	.30
❏ 5	Antoine Walker	.75	.30
❏ 6	Kenny Anderson	.50	.20
❏ 7	Jamal Mashburn	.50	.20
❏ 8	David Wesley	.25	.08
❏ 9	Baron Davis	.75	.30
❏ 10	Ron Mercer	.50	.20
❏ 11	Marcus Fizer	.50	.20
❏ 12	Ron Artest	.50	.20
❏ 13	Andre Miller	.50	.20
❏ 14	Lamond Murray	.25	.08
❏ 15	Chris Mihm	.50	.20
❏ 16	Michael Finley	.75	.30
❏ 17	Steve Nash	.75	.30
❏ 18	Dirk Nowitzki	1.25	.50
❏ 19	Antonio McDyess	.50	.30
❏ 20	Nick Van Exel	.75	.30
❏ 21	Raef LaFrentz	.50	.20
❏ 22	Jerry Stackhouse	.75	.30
❏ 23	Chucky Atkins	.25	.08
❏ 24	Corliss Williamson	.50	.20
❏ 25	Antawn Jamison	.75	.30
❏ 26	Chris Porter	.50	.20
❏ 27	Larry Hughes	.50	.20
❏ 28	Steve Francis	.75	.30
❏ 29	Cuttino Mobley	.50	.20
❏ 30	Maurice Taylor	.50	.20
❏ 31	Reggie Miller	.75	.30
❏ 32	Jalen Rose	.75	.30
❏ 33	Jermaine Oâ„¢Neal	.75	.30
❏ 34	Darius Miles	.75	.30
❏ 35	Corey Maggette	.50	.20
❏ 36	Lamar Odom	.75	.30
❏ 37	Elton Brand	.75	.30
❏ 38	Kobe Bryant	3.00	1.25
❏ 39	Shaquille Oâ„¢Neal	2.00	.75
❏ 40	Rick Fox	.75	.30
❏ 41	Derek Fisher	.75	.30
❏ 42	Stromile Swift	.50	.20
❏ 43	Michael Dickerson	.50	.20
❏ 44	Jason Williams	.50	.20
❏ 45	Alonzo Mourning	.75	.30
❏ 46	Eddie Jones	.75	.30
❏ 47	Anthony Carter	.50	.20
❏ 48	Ray Allen	.75	.30
❏ 49	Glenn Robinson	.75	.30
❏ 50	Sam Cassell	.75	.30
❏ 51	Kevin Garnett	1.50	.60
❏ 52	Terrell Brandon	.50	.20
❏ 53	Wally Szczerbiak	.50	.20
❏ 54	Joe Smith	.50	.20
❏ 55	Kenyon Martin	.75	.30
❏ 56	Keith Van Horn	.75	.30
❏ 57	Jason Kidd	1.25	.50
❏ 58	Latrell Sprewell	.75	.30
❏ 59	Allan Houston	.50	.20
❏ 60	Marcus Camby	.50	.20
❏ 61	Tracy McGrady	2.00	.75
❏ 62	Mike Miller	.75	.30
❏ 63	Grant Hill	.75	.30
❏ 64	Allen Iverson	1.50	.60
❏ 65	Dikembe Mutombo	.50	.20
❏ 66	Aaron McKie	.50	.20
❏ 67	Stephon Marbury	.75	.30
❏ 68	Shawn Marion	.75	.30
❏ 69	Tom Gugliotta	.25	.08
❏ 70	Rasheed Wallace	.75	.30
❏ 71	Damon Stoudamire	.50	.20
❏ 72	Bonzi Wells	.50	.20
❏ 73	Chris Webber	.75	.30
❏ 74	Peja Stojakovic	.75	.30
❏ 75	Mike Bibby	.75	.30
❏ 76	Tim Duncan	1.50	.60
❏ 77	David Robinson	.75	.30
❏ 78	Antonio Daniels	.25	.08
❏ 79	Gary Payton	.75	.30
❏ 80	Rashard Lewis	.50	.20
❏ 81	Desmond Mason	.50	.20
❏ 82	Vince Carter	2.00	.75
❏ 83	Morris Peterson	.50	.20
❏ 84	Antonio Davis	.25	.08
❏ 85	Karl Malone	.75	.30
❏ 86	John Stockton	.75	.30
❏ 87	Donyell Marshall	.50	.20
❏ 88	Richard Hamilton	.50	.20
❏ 89	Courtney Alexander	.50	.20
❏ 90	Michael Jordan	15.00	6.00
❏ 91A	Jeff Trepagnier P RC	2.50	1.00
❏ 91B	Jeff Trepagnier S RC	2.50	1.00
❏ 91C	Jeff Trepagnier SR RC	2.50	1.00
❏ 92A	Pau Gasol P RC	10.00	4.00
❏ 92B	Pau Gasol S RC	10.00	4.00
❏ 92C	Pau Gasol SR RC	10.00	4.00
❏ 93A	Will Solomon P RC	2.50	1.00
❏ 93B	Will Solomon S RC	2.50	1.00
❏ 93C	Will Solomon SP RC	2.50	1.00
❏ 94A	Gilbert Arenas P RC	10.00	4.00
❏ 94B	Gilbert Arenas S RC	10.00	4.00
❏ 94C	Gilbert Arenas SR RC	10.00	4.00
❏ 95A	Andrei Kirilenko P RC	10.00	4.00
❏ 95B	Andrei Kirilenko S RC	10.00	4.00
❏ 95C	Andrei Kirilenko SR RC	10.00	4.00
❏ 96A	Jamaal Tinsley P RC	5.00	2.00
❏ 96B	Jamaal Tinsley S RC	5.00	2.00
❏ 96C	Jamaal Tinsley SR RC	5.00	2.00
❏ 97A	Samuel Dalembert P RC	2.50	1.00
❏ 97B	Samuel Dalembert S RC	2.50	1.00
❏ 97C	Samuel Dalembert SR RC	2.50	1.00
❏ 98A	Gerald Wallace P RC	8.00	3.00
❏ 98B	Gerald Wallace S RC	8.00	3.00
❏ 98C	Gerald Wallace SR RC	8.00	3.00
❏ 99A	B.Armstrong P RC	3.00	1.25
❏ 99B	B.Armstrong S RC	3.00	1.25
❏ 99C	B.Armstrong SR RC	3.00	1.25
❏ 100A	Jeryl Sasser P RC	2.50	1.00
❏ 100B	Jeryl Sasser S RC	2.50	1.00
❏ 100C	Jeryl Sasser SR RC	2.50	1.00
❏ 101A	Joseph Forte P RC	6.00	2.50
❏ 101B	Joseph Forte S RC	6.00	2.50
❏ 101C	Joseph Forte SR RC	6.00	2.50
❏ 102A	B.Haywood P RC	3.00	1.25
❏ 102B	B.Haywood S RC	3.00	1.25
❏ 102C	B.Haywood SR RC	3.00	1.25
❏ 103A	Z.Randolph P RC	10.00	4.00
❏ 103B	Z.Randolph S RC	10.00	4.00
❏ 103C	Z.Randolph SR RC	10.00	4.00
❏ 104A	Jason Collins P RC	2.50	1.00
❏ 104B	Jason Collins S RC	2.50	1.00
❏ 104C	Jason Collins SR RC	2.50	1.00
❏ 105A	Michael Bradley P RC	2.50	1.00
❏ 105B	Michael Bradley S RC	2.50	1.00
❏ 105C	Michael Bradley SR RC	2.50	1.00
❏ 106A	Kirk Haston P RC	2.50	1.00
❏ 106B	Kirk Haston S RC	2.50	1.00
❏ 106C	Kirk Haston S RC	2.50	1.00
❏ 107A	Steven Hunter P RC	2.50	1.00
❏ 107B	Steven Hunter S RC	2.50	1.00
❏ 107C	Steven Hunter SR RC	2.50	1.00
❏ 108A	Troy Murphy P RC	6.00	2.50
❏ 108B	Troy Murphy S RC	6.00	2.50
❏ 108C	Troy Murphy SR RC	6.00	2.50
❏ 109A	R.Jefferson P RC	8.00	3.00
❏ 109B	R.Jefferson S RC	8.00	3.00
❏ 109C	R.Jefferson SR RC	8.00	3.00
❏ 110A	V.Radmanovic P RC	4.00	1.50
❏ 110B	V.Radmanovic S RC	4.00	1.50
❏ 110C	V.Radmanovic SR RC	4.00	1.50
❏ 111A	Kedrick Brown P RC	6.00	2.50
❏ 111B	Kedrick Brown S RC	6.00	2.50
❏ 111C	Kedrick Brown SR RC	6.00	2.50
❏ 112A	Joe Johnson P RC	12.00	5.00
❏ 112B	Joe Johnson S RC	12.00	5.00
❏ 112C	Joe Johnson SR RC	12.00	5.00
❏ 113A	Rodney White P RC	8.00	3.00
❏ 113B	Rodney White S RC	8.00	3.00
❏ 113C	Rodney White SR RC	8.00	3.00
❏ 114A	DeSagana Diop P RC	6.00	2.50
❏ 114B	DeSagana Diop S RC	6.00	2.50
❏ 114C	DeSagana Diop SR RC	6.00	2.50
❏ 115A	Eddie Griffin P RC	6.00	2.50
❏ 115B	Eddie Griffin S RC	6.00	2.50
❏ 115C	Eddie Griffin SR RC	6.00	2.50
❏ 116A	Shane Battier P RC	8.00	3.00
❏ 116B	Shane Battier S RC	8.00	3.00
❏ 116C	Shane Battier SR RC	8.00	3.00
❏ 117A	J.Richardson P RC	12.00	5.00
❏ 117B	J.Richardson S RC	12.00	5.00
❏ 117C	J.Richardson SR RC	12.00	5.00
❏ 118A	Eddy Curry P RC	12.00	5.00
❏ 118B	Eddy Curry S RC	12.00	5.00
❏ 118C	Eddy Curry SR RC	12.00	5.00
❏ 119A	Tyson Chandler P RC	10.00	4.00
❏ 119B	Tyson Chandler S RC	10.00	4.00
❏ 119C	Tyson Chandler SR RC	10.00	4.00
❏ 120A	Kwame Brown P RC	8.00	3.00
❏ 120B	Kwame Brown S RC	8.00	3.00
❏ 120C	Kwame Brown SR RC	8.00	3.00

2002-03 Upper Deck Ovation

❏ COMP.SET w/o SP's (90)		50.00	20.00
❏ COMMON CARD (1-90)		.25	.08
❏ COMMON ROOKIE (100-119)		6.00	2.50
❏ COMMON ROOKIE (120-134)		8.00	3.00
❏ 1	Shareef Abdur-Rahim	.75	.30
❏ 2	Jason Terry	.75	.30
❏ 3	Glenn Robinson	.75	.30
❏ 4	Paul Pierce	.75	.30
❏ 5	Antoine Walker	.75	.30
❏ 6	Vin Baker	.50	.20
❏ 7	Jalen Rose	.75	.30
❏ 8	Tyson Chandler	.75	.30
❏ 9	Eddy Curry	.75	.30
❏ 10	Marcus Fizer	.50	.20
❏ 11	Darius Miles	.75	.30
❏ 12	Lamond Murray	.25	.08
❏ 13	Chris Mihm	.25	.08
❏ 14	Dirk Nowitzki	1.25	.50
❏ 15	Michael Finley	.75	.30
❏ 16	Steve Nash	.75	.30
❏ 17	Marcus Camby	.50	.20
❏ 18	Juwan Howard	.50	.20
❏ 19	James Posey	.50	.20
❏ 20	Jerry Stackhouse	.75	.30
❏ 21	Ben Wallace	.75	.30
❏ 22	Clifford Robinson	.25	.08
❏ 23	Antawn Jamison	.75	.30
❏ 24	Jason Richardson	.75	.30
❏ 25	Gilbert Arenas	.75	.30
❏ 26	Steve Francis	.75	.30
❏ 27	Eddie Griffin	.50	.20
❏ 28	Cuttino Mobley	.50	.20
❏ 29	Jermaine O'Neal	.75	.30
❏ 30	Reggie Miller	.75	.30
❏ 31	Jamaal Tinsley	.75	.30
❏ 32	Elton Brand	.75	.30
❏ 33	Andre Miller	.50	.20
❏ 34	Lamar Odom	.75	.30
❏ 35	Kobe Bryant	3.00	1.25

#	Player		
36	Shaquille O'Neal	2.00	.75
37	Derek Fisher	.75	.30
38	Devean George	.50	.20
39	Pau Gasol	.75	.30
40	Shane Battier	.75	.30
41	Jason Williams	.50	.20
42	Alonzo Mourning	.50	.20
43	Eddie Jones	.75	.30
44	Brian Grant	.50	.20
45	Ray Allen	.75	.30
46	Tim Thomas	.50	.20
47	Sam Cassell	.75	.30
48	Kevin Garnett	1.50	.60
49	Wally Szczerbiak	.50	.20
50	Terrell Brandon	.50	.20
51	Jason Kidd	1.25	.50
52	Kenyon Martin	.75	.30
53	Richard Jefferson	.50	.20
54	Jamal Mashburn	.50	.20
55	Baron Davis	.75	.30
56	David Wesley	.25	.08
57	Latrell Sprewell	.75	.30
58	Allan Houston	.50	.20
59	Antonio McDyess	.50	.20
60	Tracy McGrady	2.00	.75
61	Mike Miller	.75	.30
62	Darrell Armstrong	.25	.08
63	Allen Iverson	1.50	.60
64	Eric Snow	.50	.20
65	Aaron McKie	.50	.20
66	Stephon Marbury	.75	.30
67	Shawn Marion	.75	.30
68	Anfernee Hardaway	.75	.30
69	Rasheed Wallace	.75	.30
70	Bonzi Wells	.50	.20
71	Scottie Pippen	1.25	.50
72	Chris Webber	.75	.30
73	Mike Bibby	.75	.30
74	Peja Stojakovic	.75	.30
75	Tim Duncan	1.50	.60
76	David Robinson	.75	.30
77	Tony Parker	.75	.30
78	Gary Payton	.75	.30
79	Rashard Lewis	.50	.20
80	Desmond Mason	.50	.20
81	Vince Carter	2.00	.75
82	Morris Peterson	.50	.20
83	Antonio Davis	.25	.08
84	Karl Malone	.75	.30
85	John Stockton	.75	.30
86	Andrei Kirilenko	.75	.30
87	Michael Jordan	8.00	3.00
88	Richard Hamilton	.50	.20
89	Chris Whitney	.25	.08
90	Kwame Brown	.50	.20
91	Kevin Garnett/2999	8.00	3.00
92	Kevin Garnett/2999	8.00	3.00
93	Kevin Garnett/2999	8.00	3.00
94	Kobe Bryant/1999	10.00	4.00
95	Kobe Bryant/1999	10.00	4.00
96	Kobe Bryant/1999	10.00	4.00
97	Michael Jordan/499	50.00	20.00
98	Michael Jordan/499	50.00	20.00
99	Michael Jordan/499	50.00	20.00
100	Fred Jones RC	8.00	3.00
101	Jamal Sampson RC	6.00	2.50
102	John Salmons RC	6.00	2.50
103	Jiri Welsch RC	6.00	2.50
104	Dan Gadzuric RC	6.00	2.50
105	Vincent Yarbrough RC	6.00	2.50
106	Juan Dixon RC	12.00	5.00
107	Efthimios Rentzias RC	6.00	2.50
108	Predrag Savovic RC	6.00	2.50
109	Rod Grizzard RC	6.00	2.50
110	Bostjan Nachbar RC	6.00	2.50
111	Marko Jaric RC	6.00	2.50
112	Tayshaun Prince RC	10.00	4.00
113	Chris Jefferies RC	6.00	2.50
114	Casey Jacobsen RC	6.00	2.50
115	Carlos Boozer RC	15.00	6.00
116	Frank Williams RC	8.00	3.00
117	Dan Dickau RC	8.00	3.00
118	Ryan Humphrey RC	6.00	2.50
119	Melvin Ely RC	6.00	2.50
120	Nene Hilario RC	8.00	3.00
121	Nikoloz Tskitishvili RC	8.00	3.00

#	Player		
122	Marcus Haislip RC	8.00	3.00
123	Qyntel Woods RC	8.00	3.00
124	Caron Butler RC	20.00	8.00
125	Amare Stoudemire RC	40.00	15.00
126	Curtis Borchardt RC	8.00	3.00
127	Chris Wilcox RC	12.00	5.00
128	Drew Gooden RC	20.00	8.00
129	Jared Jeffries RC	10.00	4.00
130	Kareem Rush RC	12.00	5.00
131	Mike Dunleavy RC	10.00	4.00
132	Yao Ming RC	60.00	25.00
133	DaJuan Wagner RC	15.00	6.00
134	Jay Williams RC	12.00	5.00

2006-07 Upper Deck Ovation

#	Player		
1	Joe Johnson	.60	.25
2	Marvin Williams	1.25	.50
3	Paul Pierce	1.00	.40
4	Wally Szczerbiak	.60	.25
5	Raymond Felton	1.25	.50
6	Emeka Okafor	1.00	.40
7	Gerald Wallace	1.00	.40
8	Tyson Chandler	1.00	.40
9	Ben Gordon	2.00	.75
10	Michael Jordan	6.00	2.50
11	Drew Gooden	.60	.25
12	Zydrunas Ilgauskas	.30	.12
13	LeBron James	6.00	2.50
14	Devin Harris	1.00	.40
15	Dirk Nowitzki	1.50	.60
16	Jason Terry	1.00	.40
17	Carmelo Anthony	2.00	.75
18	Marcus Camby	.30	.12
19	Kenyon Martin	1.00	.40
20	Chauncey Billups	1.00	.40
21	Richard Hamilton	.60	.25
22	Ben Wallace	1.00	.40
23	Baron Davis	1.00	.40
24	Jason Richardson	1.00	.40
25	Luther Head	.60	.25
26	Tracy McGrady	2.50	1.00
27	Yao Ming	2.50	1.00
28	Austin Croshere	.30	.12
29	Jermaine O'Neal	1.00	.40
30	Peja Stojakovic	1.00	.40
31	Elton Brand	1.00	.40
32	Sam Cassell	1.00	.40
33	Cuttino Mobley	.60	.25
34	Kwame Brown	.60	.25
35	Kobe Bryant	4.00	1.50
36	Lamar Odom	1.00	.40
37	Pau Gasol	1.00	.40
38	Mike Miller	1.00	.40
39	Damon Stoudamire	.60	.25
40	Shaquille O'Neal	2.50	1.00
41	Dwyane Wade	3.00	1.25
42	Wayne Simien	.60	.25
43	Andrew Bogut	1.25	.50
44	T.J. Ford	.60	.25
45	Michael Redd	1.00	.40
46	Ricky Davis	.60	.25
47	Kevin Garnett	2.00	.75
48	Mark McCants	1.25	.50
49	Vince Carter	2.50	1.00
50	Richard Jefferson	.60	.25
51	Jason Kidd	1.50	.60
52	Desmond Mason	.30	.12

#	Player		
53	Chris Paul	2.50	1.00
54	J.R. Smith	.60	.25
55	Steve Francis	1.00	.40
56	Stephon Marbury	1.00	.40
57	Nate Robinson	2.50	1.00
58	Dwight Howard	1.25	.50
59	Darko Milicic	1.00	.40
60	Jameer Nelson	.60	.25
61	Andre Iguodala	1.00	.40
62	Allen Iverson	2.00	.75
63	Chris Webber	1.00	.40
64	Boris Diaw	.60	.25
65	Shawn Marion	1.00	.40
66	Steve Nash	1.00	.40
67	Zach Randolph	1.00	.40
68	Sebastian Telfair	.60	.25
69	Ron Artest	.60	.25
70	Mike Bibby	1.00	.40
71	Bonzi Wells	.60	.25
72	Tim Duncan	2.00	.75
73	Manu Ginobili	1.00	.40
74	Tony Parker	1.00	.40
75	Ray Allen	1.00	.40
76	Rashard Lewis	1.00	.40
77	Luke Ridnour	.60	.25
78	Chris Bosh	1.00	.40
79	Joey Graham	1.50	.60
80	Charlie Villanueva	1.00	.40
81	Carlos Boozer	.60	.25
82	Andrei Kirilenko	1.00	.40
83	Gilbert Arenas	1.00	.40
84	Antawn Jamison	1.00	.40
85	Josh Childress	.60	.25
86	Al Jefferson	1.00	.40
87	Derek Fisher	.60	.25
88	Juan Dixon	.30	.12
89	Deron Williams	1.00	.40
90	Caron Butler	.60	.25
91	Tyrus Thomas RC	6.00	2.50
92	Adam Morrison RC	10.00	4.00
93	LaMarcus Aldridge RC	8.00	3.00
94	Rudy Gay RC	8.00	3.00
95	Andrea Bargnani RC	10.00	4.00
96	Rodney Carney RC	5.00	2.00
97	Will Blalock RC	4.00	1.50
98	Brandon Roy RC	10.00	4.00
99	Patrick O'Bryant RC	5.00	2.00
100	Randy Foye RC	10.00	4.00
101	Ronnie Brewer RC	8.00	3.00
102	Mardy Collins RC	4.00	1.50
103	Shelden Williams RC	6.00	2.50
104	J.J. Redick RC	8.00	3.00
105	Hilton Armstrong RC	4.00	1.50
106	Marcus Williams RC	5.00	2.00
107	Rajon Rondo RC	8.00	3.00
108	Cedric Simmons RC	4.00	1.50
109	Alexander Johnson RC	4.00	1.50
110	Jordan Farmar RC	5.00	2.00
111	Maurice Ager RC	4.00	1.50
112	Renaldo Balkman RC	4.00	1.50
113	Leon Powe RC	4.00	1.50
114	Saer Sene RC	4.00	1.50
115	Paul Millsap RC	6.00	2.50
116	Josh Boone RC	4.00	1.50
117	Steve Novak RC	4.00	1.50
118	Daniel Gibson RC	10.00	4.00
119	Hassan Adams RC	5.00	2.00
120	Kyle Lowry RC	6.00	2.50
121	James White RC	4.00	1.50
122	Dee Brown RC	6.00	2.50
123	Shawne Williams RC	5.00	2.00
124	P.J. Tucker RC	4.00	1.50
125	Craig Smith RC	4.00	1.50
126	Paul Davis RC	4.00	1.50
127	Solomon Jones RC	4.00	1.50
128	Denham Brown RC	4.00	1.50
129	Thabo Sefolosha RC	5.00	2.00
130	Quincy Douby RC	4.00	1.50
131	Joel Freeland RC	4.00	1.50
132	Ryan Hollins RC	4.00	1.50

2003-04 Upper Deck Phenomenal Beginning LeBron James

- ❑ COMPLETE SET
- ❑ COMMON CARD (1-20)

2001-02 Upper Deck Playmakers

❑	COMPLETE SET (145)	200.00	100.00
❑	COMP.SET w/o SP's (100)	40.00	20.00
❑	COMMON CARD (1-100)	.25	.08
❑	COMMON ROOKIE (101-130)	2.50	1.00
❑	COMMON ROOKIE (131-145)	5.00	2.00
❑ 1	Shareef Abdur-Rahim	.75	.30
❑ 2	Dion Glover	.25	.08
❑ 3	Jason Terry	.75	.30
❑ 4	Toni Kukoc	.50	.20
❑ 5	Theo Ratliff	.50	.20
❑ 6	Paul Pierce	.75	.30
❑ 7	Antoine Walker	.75	.30
❑ 8	Baron Davis	.75	.30
❑ 9	Jamal Mashburn	.50	.20
❑ 10	Ron Mercer	.50	.20
❑ 11	Brad Miller	.75	.30
❑ 12	Marcus Fizer	.50	.20
❑ 13	Andre Miller	.50	.20
❑ 14	Chris Mihm	.50	.20
❑ 15	Lamond Murray	.25	.08
❑ 16	Michael Finley	.75	.30
❑ 17	Dirk Nowitzki	1.25	.50
❑ 18	Steve Nash	.75	.30
❑ 19	Tim Hardaway	.50	.20
❑ 20	Antonio McDyess	.50	.20
❑ 21	Nick Van Exel	.75	.30
❑ 22	Raef LaFrentz	.50	.20
❑ 23	Jerry Stackhouse	.75	.30
❑ 24	Clifford Robinson	.25	.08
❑ 25	Ben Wallace	.75	.30
❑ 26	Antawn Jamison	.75	.30
❑ 27	Larry Hughes	.50	.20
❑ 28	Danny Fortson	.25	.08
❑ 29	Steve Francis	.75	.30
❑ 30	Cuttino Mobley	.50	.20
❑ 31	Kenny Thomas	.25	.08
❑ 32	Jalen Rose	.75	.30
❑ 33	Reggie Miller	.75	.30
❑ 34	Jermaine O'Neal	.75	.30
❑ 35	Darius Miles	.75	.30

❑ 36	Elton Brand	.75	.30
❑ 37	Corey Maggette	.50	.20
❑ 38	Quentin Richardson	.50	.20
❑ 39	Kobe Bryant	3.00	1.25
❑ 40	Shaquille O'Neal	2.00	.75
❑ 41	Mitch Richmond	.50	.20
❑ 42	Derek Fisher	.75	.30
❑ 43	Lindsey Hunter	.25	.08
❑ 44	Stromile Swift	.50	.20
❑ 45	Jason Williams	.50	.20
❑ 46	Michael Dickerson	.50	.20
❑ 47	Eddie Jones	.75	.30
❑ 48	Alonzo Mourning	.50	.20
❑ 49	Anthony Carter	.50	.20
❑ 50	Brian Grant	.50	.20
❑ 51	Glenn Robinson	.75	.30
❑ 52	Ray Allen	.75	.30
❑ 53	Sam Cassell	.75	.30
❑ 54	Tim Thomas	.50	.20
❑ 55	Anthony Mason	.50	.20
❑ 56	Kevin Garnett	1.50	.60
❑ 57	Wally Szczerbiak	.50	.20
❑ 58	Terrell Brandon	.50	.20
❑ 59	Joe Smith	.50	.20
❑ 60	Jason Kidd	1.25	.50
❑ 61	Kenyon Martin	.75	.30
❑ 62	Allan Houston	.50	.20
❑ 63	Latrell Sprewell	.75	.30
❑ 64	Marcus Camby	.50	.20
❑ 65	Mark Jackson	.50	.20
❑ 66	Kurt Thomas	.50	.20
❑ 67	Tracy McGrady	2.00	.75
❑ 68	Grant Hill	.75	.30
❑ 69	Mike Miller	.75	.30
❑ 70	Allen Iverson	1.50	.60
❑ 71	Dikembe Mutombo	.50	.20
❑ 72	Aaron McKie	.50	.20
❑ 73	Stephon Marbury	.75	.30
❑ 74	Shawn Marion	.75	.30
❑ 75	Anfernee Hardaway	.75	.30
❑ 76	Tom Gugliotta	.25	.08
❑ 77	Rasheed Wallace	.75	.30
❑ 78	Derek Anderson	.50	.20
❑ 79	Bonzi Wells	.50	.20
❑ 80	Chris Webber	.75	.30
❑ 81	Peja Stojakovic	.75	.30
❑ 82	Mike Bibby	.75	.30
❑ 83	Doug Christie	.50	.20
❑ 84	Tim Duncan	1.50	.60
❑ 85	David Robinson	.75	.30
❑ 86	Antonio Daniels	.25	.08
❑ 87	Steve Smith	.50	.20
❑ 88	Gary Payton	.75	.30
❑ 89	Rashard Lewis	.50	.20
❑ 90	Desmond Mason	.50	.20
❑ 91	Vince Carter	2.00	.75
❑ 92	Morris Peterson	.50	.20
❑ 93	Antonio Davis	.25	.08
❑ 94	Hakeem Olajuwon	.75	.30
❑ 95	Karl Malone	.75	.30
❑ 96	John Stockton	.75	.30
❑ 97	Donyell Marshall	.50	.20
❑ 98	Michael Jordan	12.00	5.00
❑ 99	Courtney Alexander	.50	.20
❑ 100	Richard Hamilton	.50	.20
❑ 101	Jeryl Sasser RC	2.50	1.00
❑ 102	DeSagana Diop RC	2.50	1.00
❑ 103	Alvin Jones RC	2.50	1.00
❑ 104	Gerald Wallace RC	5.00	2.00
❑ 105	Kenny Satterfield RC	2.50	1.00
❑ 106	Ruben Boumtje-Boumtje RC	2.50	1.00
❑ 107	Brian Scalabrine RC	2.50	1.00
❑ 108	Oscar Torres RC	2.50	1.00
❑ 109	Jarron Collins RC	2.50	1.00
❑ 110	Jeff Trepagnier RC	2.50	1.00
❑ 111	Brendan Haywood RC	3.00	1.25
❑ 112	Vladimir Radmanovic RC	2.50	1.00
❑ 113	Loren Woods RC	2.50	1.00
❑ 114	Terence Morris RC	2.50	1.00
❑ 115	Kirk Haston RC	2.50	1.00
❑ 116	Earl Watson RC	2.50	1.00
❑ 117	Brandon Armstrong RC	2.50	1.00
❑ 118	Zach Randolph RC	6.00	2.50
❑ 119	Bobby Simmons RC	2.50	1.00
❑ 120	Alton Ford RC	2.50	1.00
❑ 121	Trenton Hassell RC	3.00	1.25

❑ 122	Damone Brown RC	2.50	1.00
❑ 123	Michael Bradley RC	2.50	1.00
❑ 124	Zeljko Rebraca RC	2.50	1.00
❑ 125	Jason Collins RC	2.50	1.00
❑ 126	Samuel Dalembert RC	2.50	1.00
❑ 127	Gilbert Arenas RC	10.00	4.00
❑ 128	Willie Solomon RC	2.50	1.00
❑ 129	Joseph Forte RC	5.00	2.00
❑ 130	Steven Hunter RC	2.50	1.00
❑ 131	Andrei Kirilenko RC	8.00	3.00
❑ 132	Eddy Curry RC	8.00	3.00
❑ 133	Tony Parker RC	12.00	5.00
❑ 134	Troy Murphy RC	5.00	2.00
❑ 135	Shane Battier RC	5.00	2.00
❑ 136	Kedrick Brown RC	5.00	2.00
❑ 137	Tyson Chandler RC	8.00	3.00
❑ 138	Jamaal Tinsley RC	5.00	2.00
❑ 139	Pau Gasol RC	10.00	4.00
❑ 140	Joe Johnson RC	15.00	6.00
❑ 141	Jason Richardson RC	8.00	3.00
❑ 142	Richard Jefferson RC	4.00	1.50
❑ 143	Eddie Griffin RC	4.00	1.50
❑ 144	Rodney White RC	5.00	2.00
❑ 145	Kwame Brown RC	5.00	2.00

2004-05 Upper Deck Pro Sigs

❑	COMP.SET w/o SP's	20.00	8.00
❑	COMMON CARD (1-90)	.20	.08
❑	COMMON ROOKIE (91-120)	2.50	1.00
❑ 1	Antoine Walker	.60	.25
❑ 2	Al Harrington	.40	.15
❑ 3	Boris Diaw	.20	.08
❑ 4	Paul Pierce	.60	.25
❑ 5	Ricky Davis	.60	.25
❑ 6	Gary Payton	.60	.25
❑ 7	Jahidi White	.20	.08
❑ 8	Jason Kapono	.40	.15
❑ 9	Gerald Wallace	.40	.15
❑ 10	Eddy Curry	.40	.15
❑ 11	Kirk Hinrich	.60	.25
❑ 12	Tyson Chandler	.60	.25
❑ 13	LeBron James	4.00	1.50
❑ 14	Dajuan Wagner	.40	.15
❑ 15	Drew Gooden	.40	.15
❑ 16	Dirk Nowitzki	1.00	.40
❑ 17	Michael Finley	.60	.25
❑ 18	Jerry Stackhouse	.60	.25
❑ 19	Carmelo Anthony	1.25	.50
❑ 20	Andre Miller	.40	.15
❑ 21	Kenyon Martin	.60	.25
❑ 22	Chauncey Billups	.40	.15
❑ 23	Rasheed Wallace	.60	.25
❑ 24	Ben Wallace	.60	.25
❑ 25	Derek Fisher	.60	.25
❑ 26	Jason Richardson	.60	.25
❑ 27	Mike Dunleavy	.40	.15
❑ 28	Yao Ming	2.00	.75
❑ 29	Jim Jackson	.20	.08
❑ 30	Tracy McGrady	2.00	.75
❑ 31	Jermaine O'Neal	.60	.25
❑ 32	Reggie Miller	.60	.25
❑ 33	Ron Artest	.40	.15
❑ 34	Elton Brand	.60	.25
❑ 35	Corey Maggette	.40	.15
❑ 36	Kerry Kittles	.20	.08
❑ 37	Kobe Bryant	2.50	1.00
❑ 38	Chris Mihm	.20	.08

#	Player		
39	Lamar Odom	.60	.25
40	Pau Gasol	.60	.25
41	Jason Williams	.40	.15
42	Bonzi Wells	.40	.15
43	Shaquille O'Neal	2.00	.75
44	Dwyane Wade	2.00	.75
45	Eddie Jones	.60	.25
46	Michael Redd	.40	.15
47	Desmond Mason	.40	.15
48	T.J. Ford	.40	.15
49	Latrell Sprewell	.60	.25
50	Kevin Garnett	1.25	.50
51	Sam Cassell	.60	.25
52	Richard Jefferson	.40	.15
53	Aaron Williams	.20	.08
54	Jason Kidd	1.00	.40
55	Jamal Mashburn	.40	.15
56	Baron Davis	.60	.25
57	Jamaal Magloire	.20	.08
58	Allan Houston	.40	.15
59	Jamal Crawford	.40	.15
60	Stephon Marbury	.60	.25
61	Cuttino Mobley	.40	.15
62	Kelvin Cato	.20	.08
63	Steve Francis	.60	.25
64	Glenn Robinson	.60	.25
65	Allen Iverson	1.25	.50
66	Samuel Dalembert	.20	.08
67	Amare Stoudemire	1.25	.50
68	Steve Nash	.60	.25
69	Shawn Marion	.60	.25
70	Shareef Abdur-Rahim	.60	.25
71	Damon Stoudamire	.40	.15
72	Zach Randolph	.60	.25
73	Peja Stojakovic	.60	.25
74	Chris Webber	.60	.25
75	Mike Bibby	.60	.25
76	Tony Parker	.60	.25
77	Tim Duncan	1.50	.60
78	Manu Ginobili	.60	.25
79	Ronald Murray	.20	.08
80	Ray Allen	.60	.25
81	Rashard Lewis	.60	.25
82	Chris Bosh	.60	.25
83	Vince Carter	2.00	.75
84	Jalen Rose	.60	.25
85	Andrei Kirilenko	.60	.25
86	Carlos Boozer	.60	.25
87	Carlos Arroyo	1.00	.40
88	Gilbert Arenas	.60	.25
89	Jarvis Hayes	.40	.15
90	Antawn Jamison	.60	.25
91	Dwight Howard RC	8.00	3.00
92	Emeka Okafor RC	10.00	4.00
93	Ben Gordon RC	10.00	4.00
94	Shaun Livingston RC	4.00	1.50
95	Devin Harris RC	4.00	1.50
96	Josh Childress RC	3.00	1.25
97	Luol Deng RC	5.00	2.00
98	Rafael Araujo RC	2.50	1.00
99	Andre Iguodala RC	6.00	2.50
100	Luke Jackson RC	2.50	1.00
101	Andris Biedrins RC	5.00	2.00
102	Robert Swift RC	2.50	1.00
103	Sebastian Telfair RC	5.00	2.00
104	Kris Humphries RC	2.50	1.00
105	Al Jefferson RC	6.00	2.50
106	Kirk Snyder RC	2.50	1.00
107	Josh Smith RC	5.00	2.00
108	J.R. Smith RC	5.00	2.00
109	Dorell Wright RC	4.00	1.50
110	Jameer Nelson RC	4.00	1.50
111	Pavel Podkolzine RC	2.50	1.00
112	Viktor Khryapa RC	2.50	1.00
113	Sergei Monia RC	2.50	1.00
114	Delonte West RC	3.00	1.25
115	Tony Allen RC	3.00	1.25
116	Kevin Martin RC	4.00	1.50
117	Sasha Vujacic RC	2.50	1.00
118	Beno Udrih RC	4.00	1.50
119	David Harrison RC	2.50	1.00
120	Lionel Chalmers RC	2.50	1.00

2000-01 Upper Deck Pros and Prospects

#	Player		
	COMPLETE SET (120)	250.00	125.00
	COMP.SET w/o RC (90)	25.00	10.00
	COMMON CARD (1-90)	.25	.08
	COMMON ROOKIE (91-120)	5.00	2.00
1	Dikembe Mutombo	.50	.20
2	Alan Henderson	.25	.08
3	Jim Jackson	.25	.08
4	Paul Pierce	.75	.30
5	Kenny Anderson	.50	.20
6	Antoine Walker	.75	.30
7	Baron Davis	.75	.30
8	Derrick Coleman	.25	.08
9	David Wesley	.25	.08
10	Elton Brand	.75	.30
11	Ron Artest	.50	.20
12	Hersey Hawkins	.25	.08
13	Andre Miller	.50	.20
14	Lamond Murray	.25	.08
15	Shawn Kemp	.50	.20
16	Michael Finley	.75	.30
17	Dirk Nowitzki	1.25	.50
18	Cedric Ceballos	.25	.08
19	Antonio McDyess	.50	.20
20	Nick Van Exel	.75	.30
21	Rael LaFrentz	.50	.20
22	Christian Laettner	.50	.20
23	Jerry Stackhouse	.75	.30
24	Lindsey Hunter	.25	.08
25	Antawn Jamison	.75	.30
26	Larry Hughes	.50	.20
27	Chris Mills	.25	.08
28	Steve Francis	.75	.30
29	Hakeem Olajuwon	.75	.30
30	Shandon Anderson	.25	.08
31	Reggie Miller	.75	.30
32	Jonathan Bender	.50	.20
33	Jalen Rose	.75	.30
34	Lamar Odom	.75	.30
35	Michael Olowokandi	.25	.08
36	Tyrone Nesby	.25	.08
37	Kobe Bryant	3.00	1.25
38	Shaquille O'Neal	2.00	.75
39	Ron Harper	.50	.20
40	Robert Horry	.50	.20
41	Alonzo Mourning	.50	.20
42	P.J. Brown	.25	.08
43	Jamal Mashburn	.50	.20
44	Ray Allen	.75	.30
45	Glenn Robinson	.75	.30
46	Sam Cassell	.75	.30
47	Kevin Garnett	1.50	.60
48	Wally Szczerbiak	.50	.20
49	Terrell Brandon	.25	.08
50	William Avery	.25	.08
51	Stephon Marbury	.75	.30
52	Keith Van Horn	.75	.30
53	Kerry Kittles	.25	.08
54	Latrell Sprewell	.75	.30
55	Allan Houston	.50	.20
56	Patrick Ewing	.75	.30
57	Darrell Armstrong	.25	.08
58	Pat Garrity	.25	.08
59	Michael Doleac	.25	.08
60	Allen Iverson	1.50	.60
61	Theo Ratliff	.50	.20
62	Tyrone Hill	.25	.08
63	Jason Kidd	1.25	.50
64	Anfernee Hardaway	.75	.30
65	Shawn Marion	.75	.30
66	Scottie Pippen	1.25	.50
67	Rasheed Wallace	.75	.30
68	Damon Stoudamire	.50	.20
69	Bonzi Wells	.50	.20
70	Chris Webber	.75	.30
71	Peja Stojakovic	.75	.30
72	Jason Williams	.50	.20
73	Tim Duncan	1.50	.60
74	David Robinson	.75	.30
75	Terry Porter	.25	.08
76	Gary Payton	.75	.30
77	Rashard Lewis	.50	.20
78	Vin Baker	.50	.20
79	Vince Carter	2.00	.75
80	Doug Christie	.50	.20
81	Antonio Davis	.25	.08
82	Karl Malone	.75	.30
83	John Stockton	.75	.30
84	Bryon Russell	.25	.08
85	Shareef Abdur-Rahim	.75	.30
86	Mike Bibby	.75	.30
87	Michael Dickerson	.50	.20
88	Mitch Richmond	.50	.20
89	Richard Hamilton	.50	.20
90	Juwan Howard	.50	.20
91	Kenyon Martin JSY RC	40.00	20.00
92	Stromile Swift RC	10.00	4.00
93	Darius Miles RC	15.00	6.00
94	Marcus Fizer JSY RC	5.00	2.00
95	Mike Miller RC	15.00	6.00
96	DerMarr Johnson RC	5.00	2.00
97	Chris Mihm RC	5.00	2.00
98	Chris Porter RC	5.00	2.00
99	Joel Przybilla RC	5.00	2.00
100	Keyon Dooling RC	5.00	2.00
101	Jerome Moiso RC	5.00	2.00
102	Etan Thomas RC	5.00	2.00
103	Courtney Alexander RC	5.00	2.00
104	Mateen Cleaves RC	5.00	2.00
105	Jason Collier RC	8.00	3.00
106	Dan Langhi RC	5.00	2.00
107	Desmond Mason RC	5.00	2.00
108	Quentin Richardson RC	12.00	5.00
109	Jamaal Magloire RC	5.00	2.00
110	Speedy Claxton RC	5.00	2.00
111	Morris Peterson RC	10.00	4.00
112	Donnell Harvey RC	5.00	2.00
113	Hanno Mottola RC	5.00	2.00
114	Mamadou N'diaye RC	5.00	2.00
115	Erick Barkley RC	5.00	2.00
116	Mark Madsen RC	5.00	2.00
117	A.J. Guyton RC	5.00	2.00
118	Khalid El-Amin RC	5.00	2.00
119	Lavor Postell RC	5.00	2.00
120	Eddie House RC	5.00	2.00

2001-02 Upper Deck Pros and Prospects

#	Player		
	COMP.SET w/o SP's (90)	25.00	10.00
	COMMON CARD (1-90)	.25	.08
	COMMON ROOKIE (91-125)	6.00	2.50
	COMMON ROOKIE (126-171)	20.00	8.00
1	Jason Terry	.75	.30
2	Toni Kukoc	.50	.20

☐ 3	DerMarr Johnson	.50	.20
☐ 4	Paul Pierce	.75	.30
☐ 5	Antoine Walker	.75	.30
☐ 6	Kenny Anderson	.50	.20
☐ 7	Jamal Mashburn	.50	.20
☐ 8	Baron Davis	.75	.30
☐ 9	David Wesley	.25	.08
☐ 10	Elton Brand	.75	.30
☐ 11	Ron Mercer	.50	.20
☐ 12	Jamal Crawford	.50	.20
☐ 13	Andre Miller	.50	.20
☐ 14	Lamond Murray	.25	.08
☐ 15	Chris Mihm	.50	.20
☐ 16	Michael Finley	.75	.30
☐ 17	Wang ZhiZhi	.75	.30
☐ 18	Dirk Nowitzki	1.25	.50
☐ 19	Antonio McDyess	.50	.20
☐ 20	Nick Van Exel	.75	.30
☐ 21	Raef LaFrentz	.50	.20
☐ 22	Jerry Stackhouse	.75	.30
☐ 23	Joe Smith	.50	.20
☐ 24	Mateen Cleaves	.50	.20
☐ 25	Antawn Jamison	.75	.30
☐ 26	Marc Jackson	.50	.20
☐ 27	Larry Hughes	.50	.20
☐ 28	Steve Francis	.75	.30
☐ 29	Maurice Taylor	.50	.20
☐ 30	Hakeem Olajuwon	.75	.30
☐ 31	Reggie Miller	.75	.30
☐ 32	Jermaine O'Neal	.75	.30
☐ 33	Jalen Rose	.75	.30
☐ 34	Lamar Odom	.75	.30
☐ 35	Darius Miles	.75	.30
☐ 36	Quentin Richardson	.50	.20
☐ 37	Kobe Bryant	3.00	1.25
☐ 38	Shaquille O'Neal	2.00	.75
☐ 39	Derek Fisher	.75	.30
☐ 40	Rick Fox	.50	.20
☐ 41	Alonzo Mourning	.50	.20
☐ 42	Eddie Jones	.75	.30
☐ 43	Tim Hardaway	.50	.20
☐ 44	Brian Grant	.50	.20
☐ 45	Ray Allen	.75	.30
☐ 46	Glenn Robinson	.75	.30
☐ 47	Tim Thomas	.50	.20
☐ 48	Kevin Garnett	1.50	.60
☐ 49	Terrell Brandon	.50	.20
☐ 50	Wally Szczerbiak	.50	.20
☐ 51	Chauncey Billups	.75	.30
☐ 52	Stephon Marbury	.75	.30
☐ 53	Kenyon Martin	.75	.30
☐ 54	Keith Van Horn	.75	.30
☐ 55	Allan Houston	.75	.30
☐ 56	Latrell Sprewell	.75	.30
☐ 57	Glen Rice	.50	.20
☐ 58	Tracy McGrady	2.00	.75
☐ 59	Mike Miller	.75	.30
☐ 60	Darrell Armstrong	.25	.08
☐ 61	Allen Iverson	1.50	.60
☐ 62	Dikembe Mutombo	.50	.20
☐ 63	Aaron McKie	.50	.20
☐ 64	Jason Kidd	1.25	.50
☐ 65	Shawn Marion	.75	.30
☐ 66	Tom Gugliotta	.25	.08
☐ 67	Rasheed Wallace	.75	.30
☐ 68	Damon Stoudamire	.50	.20
☐ 69	Scottie Pippen	1.25	.50
☐ 70	Peja Stojakovic	.75	.30
☐ 71	Jason Williams	.50	.20
☐ 72	Chris Webber	.75	.30
☐ 73	Tim Duncan	1.50	.60
☐ 74	Derek Anderson	.50	.20
☐ 75	David Robinson	.75	.30
☐ 76	Gary Payton	.75	.30
☐ 77	Rashard Lewis	.50	.20
☐ 78	Desmond Mason	.75	.30
☐ 79	Vince Carter	2.00	.75
☐ 80	Morris Peterson	.50	.20
☐ 81	Antonio Davis	.25	.08
☐ 82	Karl Malone	.75	.30
☐ 83	John Stockton	.75	.30
☐ 84	Donyell Marshall	.50	.20
☐ 85	Shareef Abdur-Rahim	.75	.30
☐ 86	Mike Bibby	.75	.30
☐ 87	Stromile Swift	.50	.20
☐ 88	Richard Hamilton	.50	.20
☐ 89	Courtney Alexander	.50	.20
☐ 90	Chris Whitney	.25	.08
☐ 91	Ruben Boumtje-Boumtje RC	6.00	2.50
☐ 92	Sean Lampley RC	6.00*	2.50
☐ 93	Ken Johnson RC	8.00	3.00
☐ 94	Earl Watson RC	8.00	3.00
☐ 95	Jamaal Tinsley RC	15.00	6.00
☐ 96	Damone Brown RC	8.00	3.00
☐ 97	Michael Wright RC	8.00	3.00
☐ 98	Alvin Jones RC	6.00	2.50
☐ 99	Omar Cook RC	8.00	3.00
☐ 100	Jarron Collins RC	10.00	4.00
☐ 101	Brian Scalabrine RC	8.00	3.00
☐ 102	Jeryl Sasser RC	12.00	5.00
☐ 103	Samuel Dalembert RC	6.00	2.50
☐ 104	Terence Morris RC	8.00	3.00
☐ 105	Will Solomon RC	8.00	3.00
☐ 106	Kirk Haston RC	12.00	5.00
☐ 107	Richard Jefferson RC	20.00	8.00
☐ 108	Jason Collins RC	8.00	3.00
☐ 109	Troy Murphy RC	12.00	5.00
☐ 110	Gerald Wallace RC	12.00	5.00
☐ 111	Shane Battier RC	10.00	4.00
☐ 112	Jeff Trepagnier RC	12.00	5.00
☐ 113	Brandon Armstrong RC	8.00	3.00
☐ 114	Loren Woods RC	6.00	2.50
☐ 115	Joseph Forte RC	8.00	3.00
☐ 116	Michael Bradley RC	6.00	2.50
☐ 117	Joe Johnson RC	15.00	6.00
☐ 118	Gilbert Arenas RC	50.00	25.00
☐ 119	Ousmane Cisse RC	6.00	2.50
☐ 120	Kenny Satterfield RC	6.00	2.50
☐ 121	Vladimir Radmanovic RC	8.00	3.00
☐ 122	DeSagana Diop RC	6.00	2.50
☐ 123	Kedrick Brown RC	6.00	2.50
☐ 124	Trenton Hassell RC	10.00	4.00
☐ 125	Steven Hunter RC	6.00	2.50
☐ 126	Rodney White RC	20.00	8.00
☐ 127	Eddy Curry RC	30.00	12.50
☐ 128	Jason Richardson RC	30.00	12.50
☐ 129	Tyson Chandler RC	20.00	8.00
☐ 130	Eddie Griffin RC	20.00	8.00
☐ 131	Kwame Brown RC	15.00	6.00

2004-05 Upper Deck R-Class

☐	COMPLETE SET (132)	50.00	20.00
☐	COMP.SET w/o RC's (90)	20.00	8.00
☐	COMMON CARD (1-90)	.20	.08
☐	COMMON ROOKIE (91-132)	1.50	.60
☐ 1	Antoine Walker	.60	.25
☐ 2	Al Harrington	.40	.15
☐ 3	Boris Diaw	.20	.08
☐ 4	Paul Pierce	.60	.25
☐ 5	Gary Payton	.60	.25
☐ 6	Jiri Welsch	.40	.15
☐ 7	Gerald Wallace	.40	.15
☐ 8	Jason Kapono	.40	.15
☐ 9	Brandon Hunter	.20	.08
☐ 10	Eddy Curry	.40	.15
☐ 11	Kirk Hinrich	.60	.25
☐ 12	Tyson Chandler	.40	.15
☐ 13	LeBron James	4.00	1.50
☐ 14	Dajuan Wagner	.40	.15
☐ 15	Zydrunas Ilgauskas	.40	.15
☐ 16	Dirk Nowitzki	1.00	.40
☐ 17	Michael Finley	.60	.25
☐ 18	Jason Terry	.60	.25
☐ 19	Andre Miller	.40	.15
☐ 20	Carmelo Anthony	1.25	.50
☐ 21	Kenyon Martin	.60	.25
☐ 22	Chauncey Billups	.40	.15
☐ 23	Rasheed Wallace	.60	.25
☐ 24	Ben Wallace	.60	.25
☐ 25	Speedy Claxton	.20	.08
☐ 26	Jason Richardson	.60	.25
☐ 27	Mike Dunleavy	.40	.15
☐ 28	Yao Ming	1.50	.60
☐ 29	Tracy McGrady	1.50	.60
☐ 30	Juwan Howard	.40	.15
☐ 31	Jermaine O'Neal	.60	.25
☐ 32	Reggie Miller	.60	.25
☐ 33	Ron Artest	.60	.25
☐ 34	Elton Brand	.60	.25
☐ 35	Corey Maggette	.40	.15
☐ 36	Marko Jaric	.40	.15
☐ 37	Kobe Bryant	2.50	1.00
☐ 38	Devean George	.40	.15
☐ 39	Lamar Odom	.60	.25
☐ 40	Pau Gasol	.60	.25
☐ 41	Jason Williams	.40	.15
☐ 42	Bonzi Wells	.40	.15
☐ 43	Shaquille O'Neal	1.50	.60
☐ 44	Dwyane Wade	2.00	.75
☐ 45	Eddie Jones	.60	.25
☐ 46	Michael Redd	.40	.15
☐ 47	Desmond Mason	.40	.15
☐ 48	T.J. Ford	.40	.15
☐ 49	Latrell Sprewell	.60	.25
☐ 50	Kevin Garnett	1.50	.60
☐ 51	Sam Cassell	.60	.25
☐ 52	Richard Jefferson	.40	.15
☐ 53	Aaron Williams	.20	.08
☐ 54	Jason Kidd	1.00	.40
☐ 55	Jamal Mashburn	.40	.15
☐ 56	Baron Davis	.60	.25
☐ 57	Jamaal Magloire	.20	.08
☐ 58	Allan Houston	.40	.15
☐ 59	Jamal Crawford	.40	.15
☐ 60	Stephon Marbury	.60	.25
☐ 61	Steve Francis	.60	.25
☐ 62	Kelvin Cato	.20	.08
☐ 63	Cuttino Mobley	.40	.15
☐ 64	Glenn Robinson	.60	.25
☐ 65	Allen Iverson	1.25	.50
☐ 66	Willie Green	.20	.08
☐ 67	Amare Stoudemire	1.25	.50
☐ 68	Quentin Richardson	.40	.15
☐ 69	Steve Nash	.60	.25
☐ 70	Shareef Abdur-Rahim	.60	.25
☐ 71	Damon Stoudamire	.40	.15
☐ 72	Zach Randolph	.60	.25
☐ 73	Peja Stojakovic	.60	.25
☐ 74	Chris Webber	.60	.25
☐ 75	Mike Bibby	.60	.25
☐ 76	Tony Parker	.60	.25
☐ 77	Tim Duncan	1.25	.50
☐ 78	Manu Ginobili	.60	.25
☐ 79	Ronald Murray	.20	.08
☐ 80	Ray Allen	.60	.25
☐ 81	Rashard Lewis	.60	.25
☐ 82	Chris Bosh	.60	.25
☐ 83	Vince Carter	1.50	.60
☐ 84	Jalen Rose	.60	.25
☐ 85	Andrei Kirilenko	.60	.25
☐ 86	Carlos Boozer	.60	.25
☐ 87	Carlos Arroyo	1.00	.40
☐ 88	Gilbert Arenas	.60	.25
☐ 89	Jarvis Hayes	.40	.15
☐ 90	Antawn Jamison	.60	.25
☐ 91	Dwight Howard RC	5.00	2.00
☐ 92	Emeka Okafor RC	6.00	2.50
☐ 93	Ben Gordon RC	6.00	2.50
☐ 94	Shaun Livingston RC	2.50	1.00
☐ 95	Devin Harris RC	2.50	1.00
☐ 96	Josh Childress RC	2.00	.75
☐ 97	Luol Deng RC	1.50	.60
☐ 98	Andre Iguodala RC	4.00	1.50
☐ 99	Luke Jackson RC	1.50	.60
☐ 100	Andris Biedrins RC	2.50	1.00
☐ 101	Sebastian Telfair RC	1.50	.60
☐ 102	Josh Smith RC	3.00	1.25
☐ 103	Rafael Araujo RC	1.50	.60
☐ 104	Robert Swift RC	1.50	.60

❏ 105 Kris Humphries RC	1.50	.60
❏ 106 Al Jefferson RC	4.00	1.50
❏ 107 Kirk Snyder RC	1.50	.60
❏ 108 J.R. Smith RC	3.00	1.25
❏ 109 Dorell Wright RC	2.50	1.00
❏ 110 Jameer Nelson RC	2.50	1.00
❏ 111 Pavel Podkolzine RC	1.50	.60
❏ 112 Bernard Robinson RC	1.50	.60
❏ 113 Yuta Tabuse RC	3.00	1.25
❏ 114 Delonte West RC	3.00	1.25
❏ 115 Tony Allen RC	2.00	.75
❏ 116 Kevin Martin RC	2.50	1.00
❏ 117 Sasha Vujacic RC	1.50	.60
❏ 118 Beno Udrih RC	2.50	1.00
❏ 119 David Harrison RC	1.50	.60
❏ 120 Anderson Varejao RC	2.00	.75
❏ 121 Jackson Vroman RC	1.50	.60
❏ 122 Peter John Ramos RC	1.50	.60
❏ 123 Lionel Chalmers RC	1.50	.60
❏ 124 Donta Smith RC	1.50	.60
❏ 125 Andre Emmett RC	1.50	.60
❏ 126 Antonio Burks RC	1.50	.60
❏ 127 Royal Ivey RC	1.50	.60
❏ 128 Chris Duhon RC	2.50	1.00
❏ 129 Trevor Ariza RC	2.00	.75
❏ 130 Tim Pickett RC	1.50	.60
❏ 131 Romain Sato RC	1.50	.60
❏ 132 Nenad Krstic RC	2.00	.75

1999-00 Upper Deck Retro

❏ COMPLETE SET (110)	40.00	20.00
❏ COMMON CARD (1-95)	.20	.07
❏ COMMON ROOKIE (96-110)	.50	.20
❏ 1 Michael Jordan	4.00	1.50
❏ 2 John Havlicek	.75	.30
❏ 3 Antawn Jamison	1.00	.40
❏ 4 Chris Webber	.60	.25
❏ 5 Maurice Taylor	.40	.15
❏ 6 Kevin Garnett	1.25	.50
❏ 7 Walter Davis	.20	.07
❏ 8 Kobe Bryant	2.50	1.00
❏ 9 Tim Duncan	1.25	.50
❏ 10 Karl Malone	.60	.25
❏ 11 Larry Bird	2.00	.75
❏ 12 Juwan Howard	.40	.15
❏ 13 Bill Walton	.60	.25
❏ 14 Bob Cousy	.60	.25
❏ 15 Dave DeBusschere	.20	.07
❏ 16 Toni Kukoc	.40	.15
❏ 17 Allan Houston	.40	.15
❏ 18 Grant Hill	.60	.25
❏ 19 Rik Smits	.40	.15
❏ 20 Glenn Robinson	.60	.25
❏ 21 Dave Cowens	.40	.15
❏ 22 Isaac Austin	.20	.07
❏ 23 Derek Anderson	.40	.15
❏ 24 Tracy McGrady	1.50	.60
❏ 25 Nate Thurmond	.20	.07
❏ 26 Dikembe Mutombo	.40	.15
❏ 27 Oscar Robertson	.75	.30
❏ 28 Antonio McDyess	.40	.15
❏ 29 Jamaal Wilkes	.20	.07
❏ 30 Eddie Jones	.60	.25
❏ 31 Nick Van Exel	.60	.25
❏ 32 Reggie Miller	.60	.25
❏ 33 David Thompson	.20	.07
❏ 34 Ray Allen	.60	.25

❏ 35 Anfernee Hardaway	.60	.25
❏ 36 Brian Grant	.40	.15
❏ 37 Allen Iverson	1.25	.50
❏ 38 Vince Carter	1.50	.60
❏ 39 Mitch Richmond	.40	.15
❏ 40 Kareem Abdul-Jabbar	1.00	.40
❏ 41 Alonzo Mourning	.40	.15
❏ 42 Jonathan Bender RC	.75	.30
❏ 43 Scottie Pippen	1.00	.40
❏ 44 George Gervin	.60	.25
❏ 45 Shawn Kemp	.40	.15
❏ 46 Dave Bing	.20	.07
❏ 47 John Starks	.40	.15
❏ 48 Earl Monroe	.60	.25
❏ 49 Stephon Marbury	.60	.25
❏ 50 Cedric Maxwell	.20	.07
❏ 51 Tom Gugliotta	.20	.07
❏ 52 David Robinson	.60	.25
❏ 53 Shareef Abdur-Rahim	.60	.25
❏ 54 Elvin Hayes	.40	.15
❏ 55 Wilt Chamberlain	1.00	.40
❏ 56 Willis Reed	.40	.15
❏ 57 Kevin McHale	.60	.25
❏ 58 Elden Campbell	.20	.07
❏ 59 Steve Smith	.40	.15
❏ 60 Brent Barry	.40	.15
❏ 61 Jerry Stackhouse	.60	.25
❏ 62 Otis Birdsong	.20	.07
❏ 63 Michael Olowokandi	.40	.15
❏ 64 Joe Smith	.40	.15
❏ 65 Tim Thomas	.40	.15
❏ 66 Rick Barry	.40	.15
❏ 67 Jason Williams	.60	.25
❏ 68 Julius Erving	1.00	.40
❏ 69 John Stockton	.60	.25
❏ 70 Cal Bowdler RC	.60	.25
❏ 71 Nate Archibald	.60	.25
❏ 72 Elgin Baylor	.60	.25
❏ 73 Ron Mercer	.40	.15
❏ 74 Damon Stoudamire	.40	.15
❏ 75 Jerry West	.60	.25
❏ 76 Michael Finley	.60	.25
❏ 77 Charles Barkley	.75	.30
❏ 78 Shaquille O'Neal	1.50	.60
❏ 79 Paul Pierce	.60	.25
❏ 80 Keith Van Horn	.60	.25
❏ 81 Jason Kidd	1.00	.40
❏ 82 Gary Payton	.60	.25
❏ 83 James Worthy	.60	.25
❏ 84 Mike Bibby	.60	.25
❏ 85 Bill Russell	1.00	.40
❏ 86 Wes Unseld	.20	.07
❏ 87 Robert Parish	.60	.25
❏ 88 Walt Frazier	.60	.25
❏ 89 Antoine Walker	.60	.25
❏ 90 Steve Nash	.60	.25
❏ 91 Moses Malone	.60	.25
❏ 92 Hakeem Olajuwon	.60	.25
❏ 93 Tim Hardaway	.40	.15
❏ 94 Patrick Ewing	.60	.25
❏ 95 Vin Baker	.40	.15
❏ 96 Trajan Langdon RC	.60	.25
❏ 97 Ron Artest RC	1.00	.40
❏ 98 James Posey RC	1.00	.40
❏ 99 Shawn Marion RC	2.00	.75
❏ 100 Jumaine Jones RC	.75	.30
❏ 101 William Avery RC	.60	.25
❏ 102 Corey Maggette RC	1.50	.60
❏ 103 Andre Miller RC	1.50	.60
❏ 104 Jason Terry RC	1.25	.50
❏ 105 Wally Szczerbiak RC	1.50	.60
❏ 106 Richard Hamilton RC	1.50	.60
❏ 107 Elton Brand RC	2.00	.75
❏ 108 Baron Davis RC	3.00	1.25
❏ 109 Steve Francis RC	2.00	.75
❏ 110 Lamar Odom RC	1.50	.60

2004-05 Upper Deck Rivals Box Set

❏ COMPLETE SET (30)	20.00	8.00
❏ COMMON LEBRON (1-13)	.50	.60
❏ COMMON CARMELO (14-26)	.75	.30
❏ COMMON DUAL (27-30)	1.00	.40
❏ AUTO'S NOT PRICED DUE TO SCARCITY		
❏ KCLJ L.James Jumbo	3.00	1.25

2005-06 Upper Deck Rookie Debut

❏ COMPLETE SET (150)	80.00	40.00
❏ COMP SET w/o RC's (100)	40.00	15.00
❏ COMMON CARD (1-100)	.20	.08
❏ SEMISTARS	.50	.20
❏ UNLISTED STARS	.75	.30
❏ COMMON ROOKIE (101-150)	4.00	1.50
❏ 101-150 RC STATED ODDS 1:3		
❏ 1 Tony Delk	.20	.08
❏ 2 Josh Smith	.75	.30
❏ 3 Al Harrington	.50	.20
❏ 4 Antoine Walker	.75	.30
❏ 5 Ricky Davis	.75	.30
❏ 6 Paul Pierce	.75	.30
❏ 7 Kareem Rush	.20	.08
❏ 8 Emeka Okafor	1.25	.50
❏ 9 Primoz Brezec	.20	.08
❏ 10 Eddy Curry	.50	.20
❏ 11 Kirk Hinrich	.75	.30
❏ 12 Ben Gordon	1.50	.60
❏ 13 Luol Deng	.75	.30
❏ 14 Drew Gooden	.50	.20
❏ 15 LeBron James	5.00	2.00
❏ 16 Zydrunas Ilgauskas	.50	.20
❏ 17 Dirk Nowitzki	1.25	.50
❏ 18 Jason Terry	.75	.30
❏ 19 Josh Howard	.50	.20
❏ 20 Michael Finley	.75	.30
❏ 21 Carmelo Anthony	1.50	.60
❏ 22 Kenyon Martin	.75	.30
❏ 23 Andre Miller	.50	.20
❏ 24 Earl Boykins	.50	.20
❏ 25 Ben Wallace	.75	.30
❏ 26 Chauncey Billups	.75	.30
❏ 27 Richard Hamilton	.50	.20
❏ 28 Tayshaun Prince	.75	.30
❏ 29 Troy Murphy	.50	.20
❏ 30 Jason Richardson	.75	.30
❏ 31 Baron Davis	.75	.30
❏ 32 Tracy McGrady	2.00	.75
❏ 33 Yao Ming	2.00	.75
❏ 34 Juwan Howard	.50	.20
❏ 35 Jermaine O'Neal	.75	.30
❏ 36 Stephen Jackson	.20	.08
❏ 37 Ron Artest	.50	.20
❏ 38 Corey Maggette	.50	.20
❏ 39 Elton Brand	.75	.30
❏ 40 Bobby Simmons	.20	.08

#	Player		
41	Caron Butler	.50	.20
42	Kobe Bryant	3.00	1.25
43	Lamar Odom	.75	.30
44	Mike Miller	.75	.30
45	Jason Williams	.50	.20
46	Pau Gasol	.75	.30
47	Stromile Swift	.50	.20
48	Dwyane Wade	2.50	1.00
49	Eddie Jones	.50	.20
50	Shaquille O'Neal	2.00	.75
51	Desmond Mason	.50	.20
52	Maurice Williams	.20	.08
53	Michael Redd	.75	.30
54	Kevin Garnett	1.50	.60
55	Latrell Sprewell	.75	.30
56	Sam Cassell	.75	.30
57	Vince Carter	2.00	.75
58	Jason Kidd	1.25	.50
59	Richard Jefferson	.50	.20
60	Dan Dickau	.20	.08
61	Jamaal Magloire	.20	.08
62	J.R. Smith	.50	.20
63	Jamal Crawford	.50	.20
64	Stephon Marbury	.75	.30
65	Allan Houston	.50	.20
66	Dwight Howard	1.00	.40
67	Grant Hill	.75	.30
68	Steve Francis	.75	.30
69	Allen Iverson	1.50	.60
70	Andre Iguodala	.75	.30
71	Chris Webber	.75	.30
72	Kyle Korver	.75	.30
73	Amare Stoudemire	1.50	.60
74	Shawn Marion	.75	.30
75	Steve Nash	.75	.30
76	Quentin Richardson	.50	.20
77	Damon Stoudamire	.50	.20
78	Shareef Abdur-Rahim	.75	.30
79	Zach Randolph	.75	.30
80	Brad Miller	.75	.30
81	Mike Bibby	.75	.30
82	Peja Stojakovic	.75	.30
83	Cuttino Mobley	.50	.20
84	Manu Ginobili	.75	.30
85	Tim Duncan	1.50	.60
86	Tony Parker	.75	.30
87	Rashard Lewis	.75	.30
88	Ray Allen	.75	.30
89	Luke Ridnour	.50	.20
90	Vladimir Radmanovic	.20	.08
91	Rafer Alston	.20	.08
92	Jalen Rose	.75	.30
93	Chris Bosh	.75	.30
94	Andrei Kirilenko	.75	.30
95	Carlos Boozer	.50	.20
96	Matt Harpring	.75	.30
97	Antawn Jamison	.75	.30
98	Gilbert Arenas	.75	.30
99	Larry Hughes	.50	.20
100	Jarvis Hayes	.20	.08
101	Andrew Bogut RC	5.00	2.00
102	Chris Taft RC	4.00	1.50
103	Chris Paul RC	15.00	6.00
104	Martynas Andriuskevicius RC	4.00	1.50
105	Amir Johnson RC	4.00	1.50
106	Andrew Bynum RC	10.00	4.00
107	Gerald Green RC	10.00	4.00
108	Rashad McCants RC	6.00	2.50
109	Fran Vazquez RC	4.00	1.50
110	Ike Diogu RC	5.00	2.00
111	Raymond Felton RC	6.00	2.50
112	Hakim Warrick RC	8.00	3.00
113	Deron Williams RC	12.00	5.00
114	Daniel Ewing RC	5.00	2.00
115	Sean May RC	3.00	10.25
116	Johan Petro RC	4.00	1.50
117	Erazem Lorbek RC	4.00	1.50
118	Joey Graham RC	4.00	1.50
119	Antoine Wright RC	4.00	1.50
120	Ronny Turiaf RC	5.00	2.00
121	Linas Kleiza RC	4.00	1.50
122	Alex Acker RC	4.00	1.50
123	Jarrett Jack RC	4.00	1.50
124	Danny Granger RC	5.00	2.00
125	Francisco Garcia RC	4.00	1.50
126	Ryan Gomes RC	4.00	1.50
127	Wayne Simien RC	5.00	2.00
128	Robert Whaley RC	4.00	1.50
129	Dijon Thompson RC	4.00	1.50
130	Nate Robinson RC	4.00	1.50
131	Brandon Bass RC	4.00	1.50
132	Andray Blatche RC	4.00	1.50
133	Channing Frye RC	5.00	2.00
134	Salim Stoudamire RC	5.00	2.00
135	Luther Head RC	5.00	2.00
136	Julius Hodge RC	5.00	2.00
137	David Lee RC	6.00	2.50
138	Travis Diener RC	4.00	1.50
139	Marvin Williams RC	8.00	3.00
140	Lawrence Roberts RC	4.00	1.50
141	C.J. Miles RC	4.00	1.50
142	Ricky Sanchez RC	4.00	1.50
143	Bracey Wright RC	5.00	2.00
144	Jason Maxiell RC	4.00	1.50
145	Uros Slokar RC	4.00	1.50
146	Martell Webster RC	4.00	1.50
147	Orien Greene RC	4.00	1.50
148	Charlie Villanueva RC	5.00	2.00
149	Monta Ellis RC	6.00	2.50
150	Von Wafer RC	4.00	1.50

2006-07 Upper Deck Rookie Debut

#	Player		
1	Josh Childress	.40	.15
2	Joe Johnson	.40	.15
3	Marvin Williams	.75	.30
4	Gerald Green	.75	.30
5	Al Jefferson	.60	.25
6	Paul Pierce	.60	.25
7	Raymond Felton	.75	.30
8	Emeka Okafor	.60	.25
9	Gerald Wallace	.60	.25
10	Tyson Chandler	.60	.25
11	Luol Deng	.60	.25
12	Ben Gordon	1.25	.50
13	Larry Hughes	.40	.15
14	Zydrunas Ilgauskas	.20	.07
15	LeBron James	4.00	1.50
16	Devin Harris	.60	.25
17	Josh Howard	.40	.15
18	Dirk Nowitzki	1.00	.40
19	Jason Terry	.60	.25
20	Carmelo Anthony	1.25	.50
21	Marcus Camby	.20	.07
22	Kenyon Martin	.60	.25
23	Chauncey Billups	.60	.25
24	Richard Hamilton	.40	.15
25	Tayshaun Prince	.60	.25
26	Ben Wallace	.60	.25
27	Baron Davis	.60	.25
28	Troy Murphy	.60	.25
29	Jason Richardson	.60	.25
30	Rafer Alston	.20	.07
31	Tracy McGrady	1.50	.60
32	Stromile Swift	.40	.15
33	Yao Ming	1.50	.60
34	Jermaine O'Neal	.60	.25
35	Peja Stojakovic	.60	.25
36	Jamaal Tinsley	.40	.15
37	Elton Brand	.60	.25
38	Sam Cassell	.60	.25
39	Chris Kaman	.20	.07
40	Kobe Bryant	2.50	1.00
41	Devean George	.40	.15
42	Ronny Turiaf	.20	.07
43	Pau Gasol	.60	.25
44	Mike Miller	.60	.25
45	Damon Stoudamire	.40	.15
46	Shaquille O'Neal	1.50	.60
47	Gary Payton	.60	.25
48	Dwyane Wade	2.00	.75
49	Andrew Bogut	.75	.30
50	T.J. Ford	.40	.15
51	Jamaal Magloire	.20	.07
52	Michael Redd	.60	.25
53	Ricky Davis	.60	.25
54	Kevin Garnett	1.25	.50
55	Rashad McCants	.75	.30
56	Vince Carter	1.50	.60
57	Richard Jefferson	.40	.15
58	Jason Kidd	1.00	.40
59	P.J. Brown	.20	.07
60	Desmond Mason	.20	.07
61	Chris Paul	1.25	.50
62	J.R. Smith	.40	.15
63	Steve Francis	.60	.25
64	Channing Frye	.40	.15
65	Stephon Marbury	.60	.25
66	Nate Robinson	1.50	.60
67	Grant Hill	.60	.25
68	Dwight Howard	.75	.30
69	Jameer Nelson	.40	.15
70	Darko Milicic	.60	.25
71	Andre Iguodala	.60	.25
72	Allen Iverson	1.25	.50
73	Kyle Korver	.60	.25
74	Chris Webber	.60	.25
75	Boris Diaw	.40	.15
76	Shawn Marion	.60	.25
77	Steve Nash	.60	.25
78	Amare Stoudemire	1.25	.50
79	Juan Dixon	.20	.07
80	Joel Przybilla	.20	.07
81	Sebastian Telfair	.40	.15
82	Shareef Abdur-Rahim	.60	.25
83	Ron Artest	.40	.15
84	Mike Bibby	.60	.25
85	Tim Duncan	1.25	.50
86	Manu Ginobili	.60	.25
87	Robert Horry	.40	.15
88	Tony Parker	.60	.25
89	Ray Allen	.60	.25
90	Rashard Lewis	.60	.25
91	Luke Ridnour	.40	.15
92	Chris Bosh	.60	.25
93	Jose Calderon	.40	.15
94	Charlie Villanueva	.40	.15
95	Carlos Boozer	.40	.15
96	Andrei Kirilenko	.60	.25
97	Deron Williams	.60	.25
98	Gilbert Arenas	.60	.25
99	Antawn Jamison	.60	.25
100	Caron Butler	.40	.15
101	Tyrus Thomas RC	5.00	2.00
102	Adam Morrison RC	4.00	1.50
103	LaMarcus Aldridge RC	4.00	1.50
104	Rudy Gay RC	3.00	1.25
105	Andrea Bargnani RC	4.00	1.50
106	Rodney Carney RC	1.50	.60
107	Mike Gansey RC	1.50	.60
108	Brandon Roy RC	5.00	2.00
109	Patrick O'Bryant RC	1.50	.60
110	Randy Foye RC	3.00	1.25
111	Ronnie Brewer RC	2.00	.75
112	Mardy Collins RC	1.50	.60
113	Shelden Williams RC	2.00	.75
114	J.J. Redick RC	3.00	1.25
115	Hilton Armstrong RC	1.50	.60
116	Marcus Williams RC	2.00	.75
117	Rajon Rondo RC	2.00	.75
118	Cedric Simmons RC	1.50	.60
119	Ryan Hollins RC	1.50	.60
120	Jordan Farmar RC	3.00	1.25
121	Maurice Ager RC	1.50	.60
122	Renaldo Balkman RC	1.50	.60
123	Leon Powe RC	1.50	.60
124	Solomon Jones RC	1.50	.60
125	Bobby Jones RC	1.50	.60
126	Josh Boone RC	1.50	.60
127	Saer Sene RC	1.50	.60

❏ 128 Daniel Gibson RC	4.00	1.50	
❏ 129 Hassan Adams RC	2.00	.75	
❏ 130 Kyle Lowry RC	1.50	.60	
❏ 131 Shannon Brown RC	1.50	.60	
❏ 132 Dee Brown RC	2.50	1.00	
❏ 133 Shawne Williams RC	2.00	.75	
❏ 134 P.J. Tucker RC	1.50	.60	
❏ 135 Craig Smith RC	1.50	.60	
❏ 136 Paul Davis RC	1.50	.60	
❏ 137 Allan Ray RC	1.50	.60	
❏ 138 Denham Brown RC	1.50	.60	
❏ 139 Chris Quinn RC	1.50	.60	
❏ 140 Joel Freeland RC	1.50	.60	
❏ 141 James Augustine RC	1.50	.60	
❏ 142 Thabo Sefolosha RC	2.50	1.00	
❏ 143 Quincy Douby RC	1.50	.60	
❏ 144 James White RC	1.50	.60	
❏ 145 David Noel RC	1.50	.60	
❏ 146 Steve Novak RC	1.50	.60	

2003-04 Upper Deck Rookie Exclusives

❏ COMPLETE SET (60)	30.00	12.50
❏ COMMON ROOKIE (1-30)	1.00	.40
❏ COMMON CARD (31-60)	.20	.08
❏ 1 LeBron James RC	10.00	4.00
❏ 2 Darko Milicic RC	1.50	.60
❏ 3 Carmelo Anthony RC	4.00	1.50
❏ 4 Chris Bosh RC	2.50	1.00
❏ 5 Dwyane Wade RC	4.00	1.50
❏ 6 Chris Kaman RC	1.00	.40
❏ 7 Jarvis Hayes RC	1.00	.40
❏ 8 Mickael Pietrus RC	1.00	.40
❏ 9 Marcus Banks RC	1.00	.40
❏ 10 Luke Ridnour RC	1.25	.50
❏ 11 Reece Gaines RC	1.00	.40
❏ 12 Troy Bell RC	1.00	.40
❏ 13 Zarko Cabarkapa RC	1.00	.40
❏ 14 David West RC	1.00	.40
❏ 15 Aleksandar Pavlovic RC	1.25	.50
❏ 16 Dahntay Jones RC	1.00	.40
❏ 17 Boris Diaw RC	1.25	.50
❏ 18 Zoran Planinic RC	1.00	.40
❏ 19 Travis Outlaw RC	1.00	.40
❏ 20 Brian Cook RC	1.00	.40
❏ 21 Ndudi Ebi RC	1.00	.40
❏ 22 Kendrick Perkins RC	1.00	.40
❏ 23 Leandro Barbosa RC	1.50	.60
❏ 24 Josh Howard RC	1.50	.60
❏ 25 Maciej Lampe RC	1.00	.40
❏ 26 Jason Kapono RC	1.00	.40
❏ 27 Luke Walton RC	1.25	.50
❏ 28 Travis Hansen RC	1.00	.40
❏ 29 Steve Blake RC	1.00	.40
❏ 30 Slavko Vranes RC	1.00	.40
❏ 31 Darius Miles	1.00	.40
❏ 32 Tony Parker	1.00	.40
❏ 33 Chauncey Billups	1.00	.40
❏ 34 Carlos Boozer	1.00	.40
❏ 35 Richard Hamilton	1.00	.40
❏ 36 Jamaal Tinsley	1.00	.40
❏ 37 Tracy McGrady	1.50	.60
❏ 38 Manu Ginobili	1.00	.40
❏ 39 Andre Miller	1.00	.40
❏ 40 Richard Jefferson	1.00	.40
❏ 41 Paul Pierce	1.00	.40
❏ 42 Peja Stojakovic	1.00	.40
❏ 43 Jason Richardson	1.00	.40
❏ 44 Shawn Marion	1.00	.40
❏ 45 Antawn Jamison	1.00	.40
❏ 46 Reggie Evans	1.00	.40
❏ 47 Earl Boykins	1.00	.40
❏ 48 Corey Maggette	1.00	.40
❏ 49 Cuttino Mobley	1.00	.40
❏ 50 Shane Battier	1.00	.40
❏ 51 Shareef Abdur-Rahim	1.00	.40
❏ 52 Chris Wilcox	1.00	.40
❏ 53 Steve Francis	1.00	.40
❏ 54 Mike Bibby	1.00	.40
❏ 55 Morris Peterson	1.00	.40
❏ 56 Nene	1.00	.40
❏ 57 Juan Dixon	1.00	.40
❏ 58 Yao Ming	1.50	.60
❏ 59 Kobe Bryant	2.50	1.00
❏ 60 Michael Jordan	5.00	2.00

1993-94 Upper Deck SE

❏ COMPLETE SET (225)	15.00	7.50
❏ 1 Scottie Pippen	1.00	.40
❏ 2 Todd Day	.05	.01
❏ 3 Detlef Schrempf	.15	.05
❏ 4 Chris Webber RC	3.00	1.25
❏ 5 Michael Adams	.05	.01
❏ 6 Loy Vaught	.05	.01
❏ 7 Doug West	.05	.01
❏ 8 A.C. Green	.15	.05
❏ 9 Anthony Mason	.15	.05
❏ 10 Clyde Drexler	.30	.10
❏ 11 Popeye Jones RC	.05	.01
❏ 12 Vlade Divac	.15	.05
❏ 13 Armon Gilliam	.05	.01
❏ 14 Hersey Hawkins	.15	.05
❏ 15 Dennis Scott	.05	.01
❏ 16 Bimbo Coles	.05	.01
❏ 17 Blue Edwards	.05	.01
❏ 18 Negele Knight	.05	.01
❏ 19 Dale Davis	.05	.01
❏ 20 Isiah Thomas	.30	.10
❏ 21 Latrell Sprewell	.75	.30
❏ 22 Kenny Smith	.05	.01
❏ 23 Bryant Stith	.05	.01
❏ 24 Terry Porter	.05	.01
❏ 25 Spud Webb	.15	.05
❏ 26 John Battle	.05	.01
❏ 27 Jeff Malone	.05	.01
❏ 28 Olden Polynice	.05	.01
❏ 29 Kevin Willis	.05	.01
❏ 30 Robert Parish	.15	.05
❏ 31 Kevin Johnson	.15	.05
❏ 32 Shaquille O'Neal	1.50	.60
❏ 33 Willie Anderson	.05	.01
❏ 34 Micheal Williams	.05	.01
❏ 35 Steve Smith	.30	.10
❏ 36 Rik Smits	.15	.05
❏ 37 Pete Myers	.05	.01
❏ 38 Oliver Miller	.05	.01
❏ 39 Eddie Johnson	.05	.01
❏ 40 Calbert Cheaney RC	.15	.05
❏ 41 Vernon Maxwell	.05	.01
❏ 42 James Worthy	.30	.10
❏ 43 Dino Radja RC	.05	.01
❏ 44 Derrick Coleman	.15	.05
❏ 45 Reggie Williams	.05	.01
❏ 46 Dale Ellis	.05	.01
❏ 47 Clifford Robinson	.15	.05
❏ 48 Doug Christie	.15	.05
❏ 49 Ricky Pierce	.05	.01
❏ 50 Sean Elliott	.15	.05
❏ 51 Anfernee Hardaway RC	2.50	1.00
❏ 52 Dana Barros	.05	.01
❏ 53 Reggie Miller	.30	.10
❏ 54 Brian Williams	.05	.01
❏ 55 Otis Thorpe	.15	.05
❏ 56 Jerome Kersey	.05	.01
❏ 57 Larry Johnson	.30	.10
❏ 58 Rex Chapman	.05	.01
❏ 59 Kevin Edwards	.05	.01
❏ 60 Nate McMillan	.05	.01
❏ 61 Chris Mullin	.30	.10
❏ 62 Bill Cartwright	.05	.01
❏ 63 Dennis Rodman	.60	.25
❏ 64 Pooh Richardson	.05	.01
❏ 65 Tyrone Hill	.05	.01
❏ 66 Scott Brooks	.05	.01
❏ 67 Brad Daugherty	.05	.01
❏ 68 Joe Dumars	.30	.10
❏ 69 Vin Baker RC	.75	.30
❏ 70 Rod Strickland	.15	.05
❏ 71 Tom Chambers	.05	.01
❏ 72 Charles Oakley	.15	.05
❏ 73 Craig Ehlo	.05	.01
❏ 74 LaPhonso Ellis	.05	.01
❏ 75 Kevin Gamble	.05	.01
❏ 76 Shawn Bradley RC	.30	.10
❏ 77 Kendall Gill	.15	.05
❏ 78 Hakeem Olajuwon	.50	.20
❏ 79 Nick Anderson	.15	.05
❏ 80 Anthony Peeler	.05	.01
❏ 81 Wayman Tisdale	.05	.01
❏ 82 Danny Manning	.15	.05
❏ 83 John Starks	.15	.05
❏ 84 Jeff Hornacek	.15	.05
❏ 85 Victor Alexander	.05	.01
❏ 86 Mitch Richmond	.30	.10
❏ 87 Mookie Blaylock	.15	.05
❏ 88 Harvey Grant	.05	.01
❏ 89 Doug Smith	.05	.01
❏ 90 John Stockton	.30	.10
❏ 91 Charles Barkley	.50	.20
❏ 92 Gerald Wilkins	.05	.01
❏ 93 Mario Elie	.05	.01
❏ 94 Ken Norman	.05	.01
❏ 95 B.J. Armstrong	.05	.01
❏ 96 John Williams	.05	.01
❏ 97 Rony Seikaly	.05	.01
❏ 98 Sean Rooks	.05	.01
❏ 99 Shawn Kemp	.50	.20
❏ 100 Danny Ainge	.15	.05
❏ 101 Terry Mills	.05	.01
❏ 102 Doc Rivers	.15	.05
❏ 103 Chuck Person	.05	.01
❏ 104 Sam Cassell RC	1.25	.50
❏ 105 Kevin Duckworth	.05	.01
❏ 106 Dan Majerle	.15	.05
❏ 107 Mark Jackson	.05	.01
❏ 108 Steve Kerr	.15	.05
❏ 109 Sam Perkins	.15	.05
❏ 110 Clarence Weatherspoon	.05	.01
❏ 111 Felton Spencer	.05	.01
❏ 112 Greg Anthony	.05	.01
❏ 113 Pete Chilcutt	.05	.01
❏ 114 Malik Sealy	.05	.01
❏ 115 Horace Grant	.15	.05
❏ 116 Chris Morris	.05	.01
❏ 117 Xavier McDaniel	.05	.01
❏ 118 Lionel Simmons	.05	.01
❏ 119 Dell Curry	.05	.01
❏ 120 Moses Malone	.30	.10
❏ 121 Lindsey Hunter RC	.30	.10
❏ 122 Buck Williams	.05	.01
❏ 123 Mahmoud Abdul-Rauf	.05	.01
❏ 124 Rumeal Robinson	.05	.01
❏ 125 Chris Mills RC	.30	.10
❏ 126 Scott Skiles	.05	.01
❏ 127 Derrick McKey	.05	.01
❏ 128 Avery Johnson	.05	.01
❏ 129 Harold Miner	.05	.01
❏ 130 Frank Brickowski	.05	.01
❏ 131 Gary Payton	.50	.20
❏ 132 Don MacLean	.05	.01
❏ 133 Thurl Bailey	.05	.01
❏ 134 Nick Van Exel RC	1.00	.40

135 Matt Geiger	.05	.01
136 Stacey Augmon	.05	.01
137 Sedale Threatt	.05	.01
138 Patrick Ewing	.30	.10
139 Tyrone Corbin	.05	.01
140 Jim Jackson	.15	.05
141 Christian Laettner	.15	.05
142 Robert Horry	.15	.05
143 J.R. Reid	.05	.01
144 Eric Murdock	.05	.01
145 Alonzo Mourning	.50	.20
146 Sherman Douglas	.05	.01
147 Tom Gugliotta	.30	.10
148 Glen Rice	.15	.05
149 Mark Price	.05	.01
150 Dikembe Mutombo	.30	.10
151 Derek Harper	.15	.05
152 Karl Malone	.50	.20
153 Byron Scott	.15	.05
154 Reggie Jordan RC	.05	.01
155 Dominique Wilkins	.30	.10
156 Bobby Hurley RC	.15	.05
157 Ron Harper	.15	.05
158 Bryon Russell RC	.30	.10
159 Frank Johnson	.05	.01
160 Toni Kukoc RC	1.25	.50
161 Lloyd Daniels	.05	.01
162 Jeff Turner	.05	.01
163 Muggsy Bogues	.15	.05
164 Chris Gatling	.05	.01
165 Kenny Anderson	.15	.05
166 Elmore Spencer	.05	.01
167 Jamal Mashburn RC	.75	.30
168 Tim Perry	.05	.01
169 Antonio Davis RC	.40	.15
170 Isaiah Rider RC	.60	.25
171 Dee Brown	.05	.01
172 Walt Williams	.05	.01
173 Elden Campbell	.05	.01
174 Benoit Benjamin	.05	.01
175 Billy Owens	.05	.01
176 Andrew Lang	.05	.01
177 David Robinson	.50	.20
178 Checklist 1	.05	.01
179 Checklist 2	.05	.01
180 Checklist 3	.05	.01
181 Shawn Bradley ASW	.15	.05
182 Calbert Cheaney ASW	.05	.01
183 Toni Kukoc ASW	.30	.10
184 Popeye Jones ASW	.05	.01
185 Lindsey Hunter ASW	.15	.05
186 Chris Webber ASW	1.50	.60
187 Bryon Russell ASW	.15	.05
188 A.Hardaway ASW	1.25	.50
189 Nick Van Exel ASW	.30	.10
190 P.J.Brown ASW	.15	.05
191 Isaiah Rider ASW	.30	.10
192 Chris Mills ASW	.15	.05
193 Antonio Davis ASW	.15	.05
194 Jamal Mashburn ASW	.30	.10
195 Dino Radja ASW	.05	.01
196 Sam Cassell ASW	.30	.10
197 Isaiah Rider ASW SD	.30	.10
198 Mark Price LDS	.05	.01
199 Stacey Augmon TH	.05	.01
200 Celtics Team TH	.05	.01
201 Eddie Johnson TH	.05	.01
202 Scottie Pippen TH	.50	.20
203 Brad Daugherty TH	.05	.01
204 Jamal Mashburn TH	.30	.10
205 Dikembe Mutombo TH	.15	.05
206 Lindsey Hunter TH	.15	.05
207 Chris Webber TH	1.00	.40
208 Rockets Team TH	.05	.01
209 Derrick McKey TH	.05	.01
210 Danny Manning TH	.05	.01
211 Doug Christie TH	.15	.05
212 Glen Rice TH	.05	.01
213 Day/Norman/Barry/Baker T	.05	.01
214 Isaiah Rider TH	.30	.10
215 Kenny Anderson TH	.05	.01
216 Patrick Ewing TH	.15	.05
217 Anfernee Hardaway TH	.75	.30
218 Moses Malone TH	.15	.05
219 Kevin Johnson TH	.05	.01
220 Clifford Robinson TH	.05	.01
221 Wayman Tisdale TH	.05	.01
222 David Robinson TH	.30	.10
223 Sonics Team TH	.05	.01
224 John Stockton TH	.15	.05
225 Don MacLean TH	.05	.01
JK1 Johnny Kilroy	4.00	1.50
MJR1 M.Jordan Retirement	8.00	3.00

2000-01 Upper Deck Slam

COMPLETE SET w/o RC (60)	20.00	10.00
COMMON CARD (1-60)	.25	.08
COMMON RC/2500 (61-100)	1.25	.50
1 Dikembe Mutombo	.50	.20
2 Jim Jackson	.25	.08
3 Paul Pierce	.75	.30
4 Antoine Walker	.75	.30
5 Eddie Jones	.75	.30
6 Baron Davis	.75	.30
7 Derrick Coleman	.25	.08
8 Elton Brand	.75	.30
9 Ron Artest	.50	.20
10 Andre Miller	.50	.20
11 Shawn Kemp	.50	.20
12 Michael Finley	.75	.30
13 Dirk Nowitzki	1.25	.50
14 Antonio McDyess	.50	.20
15 James Posey	.50	.20
16 Jerry Stackhouse	.75	.30
17 Jerome Williams	.25	.08
18 Larry Hughes	.50	.20
19 Antawn Jamison	.75	.30
20 Steve Francis	.75	.30
21 Hakeem Olajuwon	.75	.30
22 Reggie Miller	.75	.30
23 Jalen Rose	.75	.30
24 Lamar Odom	.75	.30
25 Michael Olowokandi	.25	.08
26 Shaquille O'Neal	2.00	.75
27 Kobe Bryant	3.00	1.25
28 Alonzo Mourning	.50	.20
29 Jamal Mashburn	.50	.20
30 Ray Allen	.75	.30
31 Glenn Robinson	.50	.20
32 Kevin Garnett	1.50	.60
33 Wally Szczerbiak	.50	.20
34 Stephon Marbury	.75	.30
35 Keith Van Horn	.75	.30
36 Latrell Sprewell	.75	.30
37 Allan Houston	.50	.20
38 Darrell Armstrong	.25	.08
39 Ron Mercer	.50	.20
40 Allen Iverson	1.50	.60
41 Toni Kukoc	.50	.20
42 Jason Kidd	1.25	.50
43 Anfernee Hardaway	.75	.30
44 Shawn Marion	.75	.30
45 Scottie Pippen	1.25	.50
46 Rasheed Wallace	.75	.30
47 Chris Webber	.75	.30
48 Vlade Divac	.50	.20
49 Tim Duncan	1.50	.60
50 David Robinson	.75	.30
51 Gary Payton	.75	.30
52 Rashard Lewis	.50	.20
53 Vince Carter	2.00	.75
54 Doug Christie	.50	.20
55 Karl Malone	.75	.30
56 Bryon Russell	.25	.08
57 Shareef Abdur-Rahim	.75	.30
58 Michael Dickerson	.50	.20
59 Juwan Howard	.50	.20
60 Richard Hamilton	.50	.20
61 Jerome Moiso RC	1.25	.50
62 Etan Thomas RC	1.25	.50
63 Courtney Alexander RC	1.25	.50
64 Mateen Cleaves RC	1.25	.50
65 Jason Collier RC	2.00	.75
66 Hidayet Turkoglu RC	12.00	5.00
67 Desmond Mason RC	1.25	.50
68 Quentin Richardson RC	5.00	2.00
69 Jamaal Magloire RC	1.25	.50
70 Speedy Claxton RC	1.25	.50
71 Morris Peterson RC	3.00	1.25
72 Donnell Harvey RC	1.25	.50
73 Ira Newble RC	1.25	.50
74 Mamadou N'diaye RC	1.25	.50
75 Erick Barkley RC	1.25	.50
76 Mark Madsen RC	1.25	.50
77 Dan Langhi RC	1.25	.50
78 A.J. Guyton RC	1.25	.50
79 Olumide Oyedeji RC	6.00	2.50
80 Eddie House RC	6.00	2.50
81 Eduardo Najera RC	8.00	3.00
82 Lavor Postell RC	6.00	2.50
83 Hanno Mottola RC	1.25	.50
84 Chris Carrawell RC	1.25	.50
85 Michael Redd RC	10.00	4.00
86 Jabari Smith RC	6.00	2.50
87 Jason Hart RC	6.00	2.50
88 Corey Hightower RC	1.25	.50
89 Chris Porter RC	1.25	.50
90 Justin Love RC	6.00	2.50
91 Kenyon Martin RC	6.00	2.50
92 Stromile Swift RC	3.00	1.25
93 Darius Miles RC	5.00	2.00
94 Marcus Fizer RC	1.25	.50
95 Mike Miller RC	5.00	2.00
96 DerMarr Johnson RC	1.25	.50
97 Chris Mihm RC	1.25	.50
98 Jamal Crawford RC	1.50	.60
99 Joel Przybilla RC	1.25	.50
100 Keyon Dooling RC	1.25	.50
P21 Kevin Garnett	2.50	1.00

2005-06 Upper Deck Slam

COMPLETE SET (120)	40.00	15.00
COMP.SET w/o SP's	15.00	6.00
COMMON CARD (1-90)	.15	.06
COMMON ROOKIE (91-120)	1.50	.60
1 Tony Delk	.15	.06
2 Josh Smith	.50	.20
3 Al Harrington	.20	.08
4 Antoine Walker	.50	.20
5 Gary Payton	.50	.20
6 Paul Pierce	.50	.20
7 Kareem Rush	.15	.06
8 Emeka Okafor	.75	.30
9 Primoz Brezec	.15	.06
10 Eddy Curry	.20	.08
11 Kirk Hinrich	.50	.20
12 Ben Gordon	1.00	.40
13 Drew Gooden	.20	.08
14 LeBron James	3.00	1.25
15 Zydrunas Ilgauskas	.20	.08
16 Dirk Nowitzki	.75	.30
17 Jason Terry	.50	.20

#	Player		
18	Michael Finley	.50	.20
19	Carmelo Anthony	1.00	.40
20	Kenyon Martin	.50	.20
21	Earl Boykins	.20	.08
22	Ben Wallace	.50	.20
23	Richard Hamilton	.20	.08
25	Troy Murphy	.20	.08
26	Jason Richardson	.50	.20
27	Baron Davis	.50	.20
28	Tracy McGrady	1.25	.50
29	Yao Ming	1.25	.50
30	Juwan Howard	.20	.08
31	Jermaine O'Neal	.50	.20
32	Stephen Jackson	.20	.08
33	Ron Artest	.20	.08
34	Corey Maggette	.20	.08
35	Elton Brand	.50	.20
36	Bobby Simmons	.15	.06
37	Caron Butler	.20	.08
38	Kobe Bryant	2.00	.75
39	Lamar Odom	.50	.20
40	Mike Miller	.50	.20
41	Jason Williams	.20	.08
42	Pau Gasol	.50	.20
43	Dwyane Wade	1.50	.60
44	Eddie Jones	.20	.08
45	Shaquille O'Neal	1.25	.50
46	Desmond Mason	.20	.08
47	Maurice Williams	.15	.06
48	Michael Redd	.50	.20
49	Kevin Garnett	1.00	.40
50	Latrell Sprewell	.20	.08
51	Sam Cassell	.50	.20
52	Vince Carter	1.25	.50
53	Jason Kidd	.75	.30
54	Richard Jefferson	.20	.08
55	Dan Dickau	.15	.06
56	Jamaal Magloire	.15	.06
57	J.R. Smith	.20	.08
58	Jamal Crawford	.20	.08
59	Stephon Marbury	.50	.20
60	Allan Houston	.20	.08
61	Dwight Howard	.60	.25
62	Grant Hill	.50	.20
63	Steve Francis	.50	.20
64	Allen Iverson	1.00	.40
65	Andre Iguodala	.50	.20
66	Chris Webber	.50	.20
67	Amare Stoudemire	1.00	.40
68	Shawn Marion	.50	.20
69	Steve Nash	.50	.20
70	Damon Stoudamire	.20	.08
71	Shareef Abdur-Rahim	.20	.08
72	Zach Randolph	.50	.20
73	Mike Bibby	.50	.20
74	Peja Stojakovic	.50	.20
75	Brad Miller	.50	.20
76	Manu Ginobili	.50	.20
77	Tim Duncan	1.00	.40
78	Tony Parker	.50	.20
79	Rashard Lewis	.50	.20
80	Ray Allen	.50	.20
81	Ronald Murray	.15	.06
82	Rafer Alston	.15	.06
83	Jalen Rose	.50	.20
84	Chris Bosh	.50	.20
85	Andrei Kirilenko	.50	.20
86	Carlos Boozer	.50	.20
87	Matt Harpring	.50	.20
88	Antawn Jamison	.50	.20
89	Gilbert Arenas	.50	.20
90	Larry Hughes	.20	.08
91	Andrew Bogut RC	2.50	1.00
92	Martynas Andriuskevicius RC	1.50	.60
93	Chris Paul RC	8.00	3.00
94	Deron Williams RC	6.00	2.50
95	Luther Head RC	2.50	1.00
96	Chris Taft RC	1.50	.60
97	David Lee RC	2.50	1.00
98	Gerald Green RC	5.00	2.00
99	Andrew Bynum RC	6.00	2.50
100	Rashad McCants RC	4.00	1.50
101	Raymond Felton RC	4.00	1.50
102	Danny Granger RC	2.00	.75
103	Johan Petro RC	1.50	.60
104	Antoine Wright RC	1.50	.60
105	Channing Frye RC	2.50	1.00
106	Joey Graham RC	1.50	.60
107	Wayne Simien RC	2.50	1.00
108	Monta Ellis RC	2.50	1.00
109	Charlie Villanueva RC	2.50	1.00
110	Martell Webster RC	1.50	.60
111	C.J. Miles RC	1.50	.60
112	Hakim Warrick RC	4.00	1.50
113	Ike Diogu RC	2.50	1.00
114	Jarrett Jack RC	1.50	.60
115	Nate Robinson RC	1.50	.60
116	Francisco Garcia RC	1.50	.60
117	Sarunas Jasikevicius RC	2.50	1.00
118	Salim Stoudamire RC	2.50	1.00
119	Marvin Williams RC	4.00	1.50
120	Sean May RC	2.00	.75

2003 UD Top Prospects LeBron James Promos

COMPLETE SET (3)	25.00	10.00
COMMON CARD (P1-P3)	10.00	4.00

2003-04 Upper Deck Standing O

COMP.SET w/o SP's		40.00	15.00
COMMON ROOKIE (85-126)		4.00	1.50
*DIECUT SINGLES: .75X TO 2X BASE HI			
*EMBOSS RC's: .6X TO 1.5X BASE HI			
1	Shareef Abdur-Rahim	.75	.30
2	Jason Terry	.75	.30
3	Theo Ratliff	.50	.20
4	Paul Pierce	.75	.30
5	Antoine Walker	.75	.30
6	Vin Baker	.50	.20
7	Jalen Rose	.75	.30
8	Tyson Chandler	.75	.30
9	Michael Jordan	5.00	2.00
10	Dajuan Wagner	.50	.20
11	Zydrunas Ilgauskas	.50	.20
12	Darius Miles	.75	.30
13	Dirk Nowitzki	1.25	.50
14	Michael Finley	.75	.30
15	Steve Nash	.75	.30
16	Nene	.50	.20
17	Rodney White	.20	.08
18	Richard Hamilton	.50	.20
19	Ben Wallace	.75	.30
20	Chauncey Billups	.50	.20
21	Nick Van Exel	.75	.30
22	Jason Richardson	.75	.30
23	Mike Dunleavy	.50	.20
24	Steve Francis	.75	.30
25	Yao Ming	2.00	.75
26	Cuttino Mobley	.50	.20
27	Reggie Miller	.75	.30
28	Jamaal Tinsley	.75	.30
29	Jermaine O'™Neal	.75	.30
30	Elton Brand	.75	.30
31	Corey Maggette	.50	.20
32	Quentin Richardson	.50	.20
33	Kobe Bryant	3.00	1.25
34	Shaquille O'™Neal	2.00	.75
35	Gary Payton	.75	.30
36	Karl Malone	.75	.30
37	Pau Gasol	.75	.30
38	Mike Miller	.75	.30
39	Eddie Jones	.75	.30
40	Brian Grant	.50	.20
41	Caron Butler	.75	.30
42	Michael Redd	.75	.30
43	Joe Smith	.50	.20
44	Desmond Mason	.50	.20
45	Kevin Garnett	1.50	.60
46	Latrell Sprewell	.75	.30
47	Sam Cassell	.75	.30
48	Jason Kidd	1.25	.50
49	Richard Jefferson	.50	.20
50	Alonzo Mourning	.50	.20
51	Baron Davis	.75	.30
52	Jamal Mashburn	.50	.20
53	Jamaal Magloire	.20	.08
54	Allan Houston	.50	.20
55	Antonio McDyess	.50	.20
56	Keith Van Horn	.75	.30
57	Tracy McGrady	2.00	.75
58	Juwan Howard	.50	.20
59	Drew Gooden	.50	.20
60	Allen Iverson	1.50	.60
61	Glenn Robinson	.50	.20
62	Stephon Marbury	.75	.30
63	Shawn Marion	.75	.30
64	Amare Stoudemire	1.50	.60
65	Rasheed Wallace	.75	.30
66	Bonzi Wells	.50	.20
67	Chris Webber	.75	.30
68	Mike Bibby	.75	.30
69	Peja Stojakovic	.75	.30
70	Tim Duncan	1.50	.60
71	David Robinson	.75	.30
72	Tony Parker	.75	.30
73	Ray Allen	.75	.30
74	Rashard Lewis	.75	.30
75	Reggie Evans	.20	.08
76	Vince Carter	2.00	.75
77	Morris Peterson	.50	.20
78	Antonio Davis	.20	.08
79	Jarron Collins	.20	.08
80	John Stockton	.75	.30
81	Andrei Kirilenko	.75	.30
82	Jerry Stackhouse	.75	.30
83	Gilbert Arenas	.75	.30
84	Larry Hughes	.50	.20
85	LeBron James RC	50.00	20.00
86	Darko Milicic RC	6.00	2.50
87	Carmelo Anthony RC	15.00	6.00
88	Chris Bosh RC	10.00	4.00
89	Dwyane Wade RC	20.00	8.00
90	Chris Kaman RC	4.00	1.50
91	Kirk Hinrich RC	6.00	2.50
92	T.J. Ford RC	5.00	2.00
93	Mike Sweetney RC	4.00	1.50
94	Jarvis Hayes RC	4.00	1.50
95	Mickael Pietrus RC	4.00	1.50
96	Nick Collison RC	4.00	1.50
97	Marcus Banks RC	4.00	1.50
98	Luke Ridnour RC	5.00	2.00
99	Reece Gaines RC	4.00	1.50
100	Troy Bell RC	4.00	1.50
101	Zarko Cabarkapa RC	4.00	1.50
102	David West RC	5.00	2.00
103	Aleksandar Pavlovic RC	5.00	2.00
104	Dahntay Jones RC	4.00	1.50
105	Boris Diaw RC	5.00	2.00
106	Zoran Planinic RC	4.00	1.50

❏ 107	Travis Outlaw RC	4.00	1.50
❏ 108	Brian Cook RC	4.00	1.50
❏ 109	Carlos Delfino RC	4.00	1.50
❏ 110	Ndudi Ebi RC	4.00	1.50
❏ 111	Kendrick Perkins RC	4.00	1.50
❏ 112	Leandro Barbosa RC	6.00	2.50
❏ 113	Josh Howard RC	6.00	2.50
❏ 114	Maciej Lampe RC	4.00	1.50
❏ 115	Jason Kapono RC	4.00	1.50
❏ 116	Luke Walton RC	4.00	1.50
❏ 117	Jerome Beasley RC	4.00	1.50
❏ 118	Willie Green RC	4.00	1.50
❏ 119	Kyle Korver RC	6.00	2.50
❏ 120	Travis Hansen RC	4.00	1.50
❏ 121	Steve Blake RC	4.00	1.50
❏ 122	Slavko Vranes RC	4.00	1.50
❏ 123	Zaur Pachulia RC	4.00	1.50
❏ 124	Keith Bogans RC	4.00	1.50
❏ 125	Theron Smith RC	4.00	1.50
❏ 126	Brandon Hunter RC	4.00	1.50

2001-02 Upper Deck Sweet Shot

❏	COMP. SET w/o SP's	40.00	20.00
❏	COMMON CARD (1-90)	.25	.08
❏	COMMON ROOKIE (91-110)	5.00	2.00
❏	COMMON ROOKIE (110-120)	6.00	2.50
❏ 1	Jason Terry	.75	.30
❏ 2	Shareef Abdur-Rahim	.75	.30
❏ 3	Toni Kukoc	.50	.20
❏ 4	Paul Pierce	.75	.30
❏ 5	Antoine Walker	.75	.30
❏ 6	Kenny Anderson	.50	.20
❏ 7	Baron Davis	.50	.20
❏ 8	Jamal Mashburn	.50	.20
❏ 9	David Wesley	.25	.08
❏ 10	Ron Mercer	.50	.20
❏ 11	Ron Artest	.50	.20
❏ 12	A.J. Guyton	.50	.20
❏ 13	Andre Miller	.50	.20
❏ 14	Lamond Murray	.25	.08
❏ 15	Chris Mihm	.50	.20
❏ 16	Michael Finley	.75	.30
❏ 17	Dirk Nowitzki	1.25	.50
❏ 18	Steve Nash	.75	.30
❏ 19	Antonio McDyess	.50	.20
❏ 20	Nick Van Exel	.75	.30
❏ 21	Raef LaFrentz	.50	.20
❏ 22	Jerry Stackhouse	.75	.30
❏ 23	Chucky Atkins	.25	.08
❏ 24	Corliss Williamson	.50	.20
❏ 25	Antawn Jamison	.75	.30
❏ 26	Marc Jackson	.50	.20
❏ 27	Larry Hughes	.50	.20
❏ 28	Steve Francis	.75	.30
❏ 29	Cuttino Mobley	.50	.20
❏ 30	Maurice Taylor	.50	.20
❏ 31	Reggie Miller	.75	.30
❏ 32	Jalen Rose	.75	.30
❏ 33	Jermaine O'Neal	.75	.30
❏ 34	Darius Miles	.75	.30
❏ 35	Elton Brand	.75	.30
❏ 36	Corey Maggette	.50	.20
❏ 37	Quentin Richardson	.50	.20
❏ 38	Kobe Bryant	3.00	1.25
❏ 39	Shaquille O'Neal	2.00	.75
❏ 40	Rick Fox	.50	.20
❏ 41	Derek Fisher	.75	.30
❏ 42	Stromile Swift	.50	.20
❏ 43	Jason Williams	.50	.20
❏ 44	Michael Dickerson	.50	.20
❏ 45	Alonzo Mourning	.50	.20
❏ 46	Eddie Jones	.75	.30
❏ 47	Anthony Carter	.50	.20
❏ 48	Glenn Robinson	.75	.30
❏ 49	Ray Allen	.75	.30
❏ 50	Sam Cassell	.75	.30
❏ 51	Kevin Garnett	1.50	.60
❏ 52	Chauncey Billups	.50	.20
❏ 53	Terrell Brandon	.50	.20
❏ 54	Joe Smith	.50	.20
❏ 55	Kenyon Martin	.75	.30
❏ 56	Keith Van Horn	.50	.20
❏ 57	Jason Kidd	1.25	.50
❏ 58	Latrell Sprewell	.75	.30
❏ 59	Allan Houston	.50	.20
❏ 60	Marcus Camby	.50	.20
❏ 61	Tracy McGrady	2.00	.75
❏ 62	Mike Miller	.75	.30
❏ 63	Grant Hill	.75	.30
❏ 64	Allen Iverson	1.50	.60
❏ 65	Dikembe Mutombo	.50	.20
❏ 66	Aaron McKie	.50	.20
❏ 67	Stephon Marbury	.75	.30
❏ 68	Shawn Marion	.75	.30
❏ 69	Tom Gugliotta	.25	.08
❏ 70	Rasheed Wallace	.75	.30
❏ 71	Damon Stoudamire	.50	.20
❏ 72	Bonzi Wells	.50	.20
❏ 73	Chris Webber	.75	.30
❏ 74	Peja Stojakovic	.75	.30
❏ 75	Mike Bibby	.75	.30
❏ 76	Tim Duncan	1.50	.60
❏ 77	David Robinson	.75	.30
❏ 78	Antonio Daniels	.25	.08
❏ 79	Gary Payton	.75	.30
❏ 80	Rashard Lewis	.50	.20
❏ 81	Desmond Mason	.50	.20
❏ 82	Vince Carter	2.00	.75
❏ 83	Morris Peterson	.50	.20
❏ 84	Antonio Davis	.25	.08
❏ 85	Karl Malone	.75	.30
❏ 86	John Stockton	.75	.30
❏ 87	Donyell Marshall	.50	.20
❏ 88	Richard Hamilton	.50	.20
❏ 89	Courtney Alexander	.50	.20
❏ 90	Michael Jordan	15.00	6.00
❏ 91	Zach Randolph	12.00	5.00
❏ 92	Troy Murphy	10.00	4.00
❏ 93	Michael Bradley RC	5.00	2.00
❏ 94	Vladimir Radmanovic RC	6.00	2.00
❏ 95	Kirk Haston RC	5.00	2.00
❏ 96	Joseph Forte RC	10.00	4.00
❏ 97	Jamaal Tinsley RC	8.00	3.00
❏ 98	Jason Collins RC	5.00	2.00
❏ 99	Brendan Haywood RC	6.00	2.50
❏ 100	Richard Jefferson RC	12.00	5.00
❏ 101	Gerald Wallace RC	12.00	5.00
❏ 102	Jeryl Sasser RC	5.00	2.00
❏ 103	Samuel Dalembert RC	5.00	2.00
❏ 104	Tony Parker RC	20.00	8.00
❏ 105	Kedrick Brown RC	5.00	2.00
❏ 106	Brandon Armstrong RC	6.00	2.50
❏ 107	Steven Hunter RC	5.00	2.00
❏ 108	Andrei Kirilenko RC	15.00	6.00
❏ 109	Primoz Brezec RC	6.00	2.50
❏ 110	Terence Morris RC	5.00	2.00
❏ 111	Eddie Griffin RC	8.00	3.00
❏ 112	DeSagana Diop RC	6.00	2.50
❏ 113	Tyson Chandler RC	15.00	6.00
❏ 114	Joe Johnson RC	15.00	6.00
❏ 115	Rodney White RC	10.00	4.00
❏ 116	Eddy Curry RC	20.00	8.00
❏ 117	Shane Battier RC	10.00	4.00
❏ 118	Jason Richardson RC	20.00	8.00
❏ 119	Kwame Brown RC	12.00	5.00
❏ 120	Pau Gasol RC	20.00	8.00

2002-03 Upper Deck Sweet Shot

❏	COMP. SET w/o SP's (90)	40.00	15.00
❏	COMMON ROOKIE (91-123)	8.00	3.00
❏	COMMON ROOKIE (124-132)	20.00	8.00

❏ 1	Shareef Abdur-Rahim	.75	.30
❏ 2	Jason Terry	.75	.30
❏ 3	Glenn Robinson	.75	.30
❏ 4	Paul Pierce	.75	.30
❏ 5	Antoine Walker	.75	.30
❏ 6	Kedrick Brown	.50	.20
❏ 7	Vin Baker	.50	.20
❏ 8	Jalen Rose	.75	.30
❏ 9	Eddy Curry	.75	.30
❏ 10	Tyson Chandler	.75	.30
❏ 11	Zydrunas Ilgauskas	.50	.20
❏ 12	Chris Mihm	.20	.08
❏ 13	Darius Miles	.75	.30
❏ 14	Dirk Nowitzki	1.25	.50
❏ 15	Michael Finley	.75	.30
❏ 16	Steve Nash	.75	.30
❏ 17	Raef LaFrentz	.50	.20
❏ 18	James Posey	.50	.20
❏ 19	Juwan Howard	.50	.20
❏ 20	Richard Hamilton	.50	.20
❏ 21	Ben Wallace	.75	.30
❏ 22	Chauncey Billups	.50	.20
❏ 23	Jason Richardson	.75	.30
❏ 24	Antawn Jamison	.75	.30
❏ 25	Steve Francis	.75	.30
❏ 26	Eddie Griffin	.50	.20
❏ 27	Cuttino Mobley	.50	.20
❏ 28	Reggie Miller	.75	.30
❏ 29	Jamaal Tinsley	.75	.30
❏ 30	Jermaine O'Neal	.75	.30
❏ 31	Elton Brand	.75	.30
❏ 32	Lamar Odom	.75	.30
❏ 33	Andre Miller	.50	.20
❏ 34	Kobe Bryant	3.00	1.25
❏ 35	Shaquille O'Neal	2.00	.75
❏ 36	Devean George	.50	.20
❏ 37	Pau Gasol	.75	.30
❏ 38	Shane Battier	.75	.30
❏ 39	Jason Williams	.50	.20
❏ 40	Eddie House	.20	.08
❏ 41	Eddie Jones	.75	.30
❏ 42	Brian Grant	.50	.20
❏ 43	Ray Allen	.75	.30
❏ 44	Tim Thomas	.50	.20
❏ 45	Kevin Garnett	2.00	.75
❏ 46	Terrell Brandon	.50	.20
❏ 47	Wally Szczerbiak	.50	.20
❏ 48	Joe Smith	.50	.20
❏ 49	Jason Kidd	1.25	.50
❏ 50	Richard Jefferson	.50	.20
❏ 51	Kenyon Martin	.75	.30
❏ 52	Dikembe Mutombo	.50	.20
❏ 53	Jamal Mashburn	.50	.20
❏ 54	Baron Davis	.75	.30
❏ 55	David Wesley	.20	.08
❏ 56	Allan Houston	.50	.20
❏ 57	Antonio McDyess	.50	.20
❏ 58	Latrell Sprewell	.75	.30
❏ 59	Tracy McGrady	2.00	.75
❏ 60	Mike Miller	.75	.30
❏ 61	Darrell Armstrong	.20	.08
❏ 62	Allen Iverson	1.50	.60
❏ 63	Keith Van Horn	.75	.30
❏ 64	Stephon Marbury	.75	.30
❏ 65	Shawn Marion	.75	.30
❏ 66	Anfernee Hardaway	.75	.30
❏ 67	Rasheed Wallace	.75	.30
❏ 68	Bonzi Wells	.50	.20

□	#	Player		
□	69	Scottie Pippen	1.25	.50
□	70	Chris Webber	.75	.30
□	71	Mike Bibby	.75	.30
□	72	Peja Stojakovic	.75	.30
□	73	Hidayet Turkoglu	.50	.20
□	74	Tim Duncan	1.50	.60
□	75	David Robinson	.75	.30
□	76	Tony Parker	.75	.30
□	77	Steve Smith	.50	.20
□	78	Gary Payton	.75	.30
□	79	Rashard Lewis	.50	.20
□	80	Desmond Mason	.50	.20
□	81	Brent Barry	.50	.20
□	82	Vince Carter	2.00	.75
□	83	Morris Peterson	.50	.20
□	84	Antonio Davis	.20	.08
□	85	Karl Malone	.75	.30
□	86	John Stockton	.75	.30
□	87	Andrei Kirilenko	.75	.30
□	88	Jerry Stackhouse	.75	.30
□	89	Michael Jordan	6.00	2.50
□	90	Kwame Brown	.50	.20
□	91	Efthimios Rentzias RC	8.00	3.00
□	92	Marko Jaric	8.00	3.00
□	93	Rasual Butler RC	8.00	3.00
□	94	Predrag Savovic RC	10.00	4.00
□	95	Sam Clancy RC	8.00	3.00
□	96	Lonny Baxter RC	8.00	3.00
□	97	Raul Lopez RC	8.00	3.00
□	98	Rod Grizzard RC	8.00	3.00
□	99	Tito Maddox RC	8.00	3.00
□	100	Carlos Boozer RC	25.00	10.00
□	101	Dan Gadzuric RC	8.00	3.00
□	102	Vincent Yarbrough RC	8.00	3.00
□	103	Robert Archibald RC	8.00	3.00
□	104	Roger Mason RC	8.00	3.00
□	105	Ronald Murray RC	12.00	5.00
□	106	Dan Dickau RC	8.00	3.00
□	107	Chris Jefferies RC	10.00	4.00
□	108	John Salmons RC	8.00	3.00
□	109	Frank Williams RC	10.00	4.00
□	110	Tayshaun Prince RC	15.00	6.00
□	111	Casey Jacobsen RC	8.00	3.00
□	112	Qyntel Woods RC	12.00	5.00
□	113	Kareem Rush RC	15.00	6.00
□	114	Ryan Humphrey RC	8.00	3.00
□	115	Curtis Borchardt RC	8.00	3.00
□	116	Juan Dixon RC	20.00	8.00
□	117	Jiri Welsch RC	8.00	3.00
□	118	Bostjan Nachbar RC	10.00	4.00
□	119	Fred Jones RC	12.00	5.00
□	120	Marcus Haislip RC	8.00	3.00
□	121	Melvin Ely RC	10.00	4.00
□	122	Jared Jeffries RC	10.00	4.00
□	123	Caron Butler RC	30.00	12.50
□	124	Amare Stoudemire RC	60.00	25.00
□	125	Chris Wilcox RC	20.00	8.00
□	126	Nene Hilario RC	20.00	8.00
□	127	DaJuan Wagner RC	25.00	10.00
□	128	Nikoloz Tskitishvili RC	20.00	8.00
□	129	Drew Gooden RC	40.00	15.00
□	130	Mike Dunleavy RC	25.00	10.00
□	131	Jay Williams RC	20.00	8.00
□	132	Yao Ming RC	120.00	60.00

2003-04 Upper Deck Sweet Shot

□	#	Player		
□		COMP.SET w/o SP's (90)	40.00	15.00
□		COMMON CARD (1-90)	.20	.08
□		COMMON ROOKIE (91-96)	20.00	8.00
□		COMMON ROOKIE (97-132)	10.00	4.00
□		COMMON JORDAN (133-144)	25.00	10.00
□	1	Shareef Abdur-Rahim	.75	.30
□	2	Jason Terry	.75	.30
□	3	Theo Ratliff	.50	.20
□	4	Paul Pierce	.75	.30
□	5	Antoine Walker	.75	.30
□	6	Vin Baker	.50	.20
□	7	Jalen Rose	.75	.30
□	8	Tyson Chandler	.75	.30
□	9	Jay Williams	.50	.20
□	10	Dajuan Wagner	.50	.20
□	11	Zydrunas Ilgauskas	.50	.20
□	12	Darius Miles	.75	.30
□	13	Dirk Nowitzki	1.25	.50
□	14	Antawn Jamison	.75	.30
□	15	Steve Nash	.75	.30
□	16	Nene Hilario	.50	.20
□	17	Marcus Camby	.50	.20
□	18	Andre Miller	.50	.20
□	19	Richard Hamilton	.75	.30
□	20	Ben Wallace	.75	.30
□	21	Chauncey Billups	.50	.20
□	22	Nick Van Exel	.75	.30
□	23	Jason Richardson	.75	.30
□	24	Erick Dampier	.50	.20
□	25	Steve Francis	.75	.30
□	26	Yao Ming	2.00	.75
□	27	Cuttino Mobley	.50	.20
□	28	Reggie Miller	.75	.30
□	29	Jamaal Tinsley	.75	.30
□	30	Jermaine O'Neal	.75	.30
□	31	Elton Brand	.75	.30
□	32	Corey Maggette	.50	.20
□	33	Mark Jaric	.50	.20
□	34	Kobe Bryant	3.00	1.25
□	35	Gary Payton	.75	.30
□	36	Shaquille O'Neal	2.00	.75
□	37	Karl Malone	.75	.30
□	38	Pau Gasol	.75	.30
□	39	Shane Battier	.75	.30
□	40	Mike Miller	.75	.30
□	41	Eddie Jones	.75	.30
□	42	Lamar Odom	.75	.30
□	43	Caron Butler	.75	.30
□	44	Michael Redd	.75	.30
□	45	Joe Smith	.50	.20
□	46	Desmond Mason	.50	.20
□	47	Kevin Garnett	1.50	.60
□	48	Wally Szczerbiak	.50	.20
□	49	Latrell Sprewell	.75	.30
□	50	Jason Kidd	1.25	.50
□	51	Richard Jefferson	.50	.20
□	52	Kenyon Martin	.75	.30
□	53	Baron Davis	.75	.30
□	54	Jamal Mashburn	.50	.20
□	55	David Wesley	.20	.08
□	56	Allan Houston	.50	.20
□	57	Antonio McDyess	.50	.20
□	58	Keith Van Horn	.75	.30
□	59	Tracy McGrady	2.00	.75
□	60	Grant Hill	.75	.30
□	61	Drew Gooden	.50	.20
□	62	Allen Iverson	1.50	.60
□	63	Does Not Exist		
□	64	Eric Snow	.50	.20
□	64A	Glenn Robinson	.75	.30
□	65	Stephon Marbury	.75	.30
□	66	Shawn Marion	.75	.30
□	67	Amare Stoudemire	1.50	.60
□	68	Rasheed Wallace	.75	.30
□	69	Bonzi Wells	.50	.20
□	70	Damon Stoudamire	.50	.20
□	71	Chris Webber	.75	.30
□	72	Mike Bibby	.75	.30
□	73	Peja Stojakovic	.75	.30
□	74	Vlade Divac	.50	.20
□	75	Tim Duncan	1.50	.60
□	76	David Robinson	.75	.30
□	77	Tony Parker	.75	.30
□	78	Manu Ginobili	.75	.30
□	79	Ray Allen	.75	.30
□	80	Rashard Lewis	.75	.30

□	#	Player		
□	81	Vladimir Radmanovic	.20	.08
□	82	Vince Carter	2.00	.75
□	83	Morris Peterson	.50	.20
□	84	Antonio Davis	.20	.08
□	85	Keon Clark	.20	.08
□	86	John Stockton	.75	.30
□	87	Andrei Kirilenko	.75	.30
□	88	Jerry Stackhouse	.75	.30
□	89	Kwame Brown	.50	.20
□	90	Larry Hughes	.50	.20
□	91	LeBron James RC	150.00	75.00
□	92	Darko Milicic RC	25.00	10.00
□	93	Carmelo Anthony RC	50.00	20.00
□	94	Chris Bosh RC	40.00	15.00
□	95	Dwyane Wade RC	50.00	20.00
□	96	Chris Kaman RC	20.00	8.00
□	97	Kirk Hinrich RC	20.00	8.00
□	98	T.J. Ford RC	12.00	5.00
□	99	Mike Sweetney RC	10.00	4.00
□	100	Jarvis Hayes RC	20.00	8.00
□	101	Mickael Pietrus RC	10.00	4.00
□	102	Nick Collison RC	10.00	4.00
□	103	Marcus Banks RC	10.00	4.00
□	104	Luke Ridnour RC	15.00	6.00
□	105	Reece Gaines RC	10.00	4.00
□	106	Troy Bell RC	10.00	4.00
□	107	Zarko Cabarkapa RC	10.00	4.00
□	108	David West RC	10.00	4.00
□	109	Aleksandar Pavlovic RC	12.00	5.00
□	110	Dahntay Jones RC	10.00	4.00
□	111	Boris Diaw RC	12.00	5.00
□	112	Zoran Planinic RC	10.00	4.00
□	113	Travis Outlaw RC	10.00	4.00
□	114	Brian Cook RC	10.00	4.00
□	115	Carlos Delfino RC	10.00	4.00
□	116	Ndudi Ebi RC	10.00	4.00
□	117	Kendrick Perkins RC	10.00	4.00
□	118	Leandro Barbosa RC	15.00	6.00
□	119	Josh Howard RC	15.00	6.00
□	120	Jason Kapono RC	10.00	4.00
□	121	Luke Walton RC	12.00	5.00
□	122	Jerome Beasley RC	10.00	4.00
□	123	Kyle Korver RC	15.00	6.00
□	124	Maciej Lampe RC	10.00	4.00
□	125	Travis Hansen RC	10.00	4.00
□	126	Steve Blake RC	10.00	4.00
□	127	Willie Green RC	10.00	4.00
□	128	Slavko Vranes RC	10.00	4.00
□	129	Keith Bogans RC	10.00	4.00
□	130	Maurice Williams RC	10.00	4.00
□	131	Matt Bonner RC	10.00	4.00
□	132	Zaur Pachulia RC	10.00	4.00

2004-05 Upper Deck Sweet Shot

□	#	Player		
□		COMP.SET w/o SP's (90)	40.00	15.00
□		COMMON CARD (1-90)	.20	.08
□		COMMON ROOKIE (91-130)	5.00	2.00
□		COMMON ROOKIE (131-136)	10.00	4.00
□	1	Antoine Walker	.75	.30
□	2	Al Harrington	.50	.20
□	3	Boris Diaw	.20	.08
□	4	Paul Pierce	.75	.30
□	5	Ricky Davis	.50	.20
□	6	Gary Payton	.75	.30
□	7	Gerald Wallace	.50	.20
□	8	Jason Kapono	.20	.08

#	Player		
9	Jahidi White	.20	.08
10	Eddy Curry	.50	.20
11	Kirk Hinrich	.75	.30
12	Antonio Davis	.20	.08
13	LeBron James	5.00	2.00
14	Dajuan Wagner	.50	.20
15	Jeff McInnis	.20	.08
16	Dirk Nowitzki	1.25	.50
17	Michael Finley	.75	.30
18	Jerry Stackhouse	.75	.30
19	Kenyon Martin	.75	.30
20	Andre Miller	.50	.20
21	Carmelo Anthony	1.50	.60
22	Chauncey Billups	.50	.20
23	Rasheed Wallace	.75	.30
24	Ben Wallace	.75	.30
25	Derek Fisher	.75	.30
26	Jason Richardson	.75	.30
27	Mike Dunleavy	.50	.20
28	Yao Ming	2.00	.75
29	Tracy McGrady	2.00	.75
30	Juwan Howard	.50	.20
31	Jermaine O'Neal	.75	.30
32	Reggie Miller	.75	.30
33	Ron Artest	.50	.20
34	Elton Brand	.75	.30
35	Corey Maggette	.50	.20
36	Marko Jaric	.50	.20
37	Kobe Bryant	3.00	1.25
38	Karl Malone	.75	.30
39	Lamar Odom	.75	.30
40	Pau Gasol	.75	.30
41	Jason Williams	.50	.20
42	Bonzi Wells	.50	.20
43	Shaquille O'Neal	2.00	.75
44	Dwyane Wade	2.50	1.00
45	Eddie Jones	.75	.30
46	Michael Redd	.50	.20
47	Desmond Mason	.50	.20
48	T.J. Ford	.50	.20
49	Latrell Sprewell	.75	.30
50	Kevin Garnett	1.25	.60
51	Sam Cassell	.75	.30
52	Aaron Williams	.20	.08
53	Richard Jefferson	.75	.30
54	Jason Kidd	1.25	.50
55	Jamal Mashburn	.50	.20
56	Baron Davis	.75	.30
57	Jamaal Magloire	.20	.08
58	Allan Houston	.50	.20
59	Jamal Crawford	.50	.20
60	Stephon Marbury	.75	.30
61	Keith Bogans	.20	.08
62	Cuttino Mobley	.50	.20
63	Steve Francis	.75	.30
64	Glenn Robinson	.75	.30
65	Allen Iverson	1.50	.60
66	Kenny Thomas	.20	.08
67	Amare Stoudemire	1.50	.60
68	Steve Nash	.75	.30
69	Quentin Richardson	.50	.20
70	Shareef Abdur-Rahim	.75	.30
71	Damon Stoudamire	.50	.20
72	Zach Randolph	.75	.30
73	Peja Stojakovic	.75	.30
74	Chris Webber	.75	.30
75	Mike Bibby	.75	.30
76	Tony Parker	.75	.30
77	Tim Duncan	1.50	.60
78	Manu Ginobili	.75	.30
79	Ronald Murray	.20	.08
80	Ray Allen	.75	.30
81	Rashard Lewis	.75	.30
82	Chris Bosh	.75	.30
83	Vince Carter	2.00	.75
84	Jalen Rose	.75	.30
85	Andrei Kirilenko	.75	.30
86	Matt Harpring	.75	.30
87	Carlos Boozer	.75	.30
88	Gilbert Arenas	.75	.30
89	Jarvis Hayes	.50	.20
90	Antawn Jamison	.75	.30
91	Anderson Varejao RC	6.00	2.50
92	Jackson Vroman RC	5.00	2.00
93	Peter John Ramos RC	5.00	2.00
94	Lionel Chalmers RC	5.00	2.00
95	Donta Smith RC	5.00	2.00
96	Andre Emmett RC	5.00	2.00
97	Antonio Burks RC	5.00	2.00
98	Royal Ivey RC	5.00	2.00
99	Chris Duhon RC	8.00	3.00
100	Albert Miralles RC	5.00	2.00
101	Justin Reed RC	5.00	2.00
102	David Young RC	5.00	2.00
103	Trevor Ariza RC	6.00	2.50
104	Luol Deng RC	10.00	4.00
105	Rafael Araujo RC	5.00	2.00
106	Andre Iguodala RC	12.00	5.00
107	Luke Jackson RC	5.00	2.00
108	Andris Biedrins RC	8.00	3.00
109	Robert Swift RC	5.00	2.00
110	Sebastian Telfair RC	5.00	2.00
111	Kris Humphries RC	5.00	2.00
112	Al Jefferson RC	12.00	5.00
113	Kirk Snyder RC	5.00	2.00
114	Josh Smith RC	10.00	4.00
115	J.R. Smith RC	10.00	4.00
116	Dorell Wright RC	8.00	3.00
117	Jameer Nelson RC	8.00	3.00
118	Pavel Podkolzine RC	5.00	2.00
119	Viktor Khryapa RC	5.00	2.00
120	Sergei Monia RC	5.00	2.00
121	Nenad Krstic RC	6.00	2.50
122	Tim Pickett RC	5.00	2.00
123	Bernard Robinson RC	5.00	2.00
124	Yuta Tabuse RC	10.00	4.00
125	Delonte West RC	10.00	4.00
126	Tony Allen RC	6.00	2.50
127	Kevin Martin RC	8.00	3.00
128	Sasha Vujacic RC	5.00	2.00
129	Beno Udrih RC	8.00	3.00
130	David Harrison RC	5.00	2.00
131	Dwight Howard RC	25.00	10.00
132	Emeka Okafor RC	30.00	12.50
133	Ben Gordon RC	30.00	12.50
134	Shaun Livingston RC	12.00	5.00
135	Devin Harris RC	12.00	5.00
136	Josh Childress RC	10.00	4.00

2005-06 Upper Deck Sweet Shot

COMP.SET w/o SP's	40.00	15.00
COMMON CARD (1-100)	.25	.10
COMMON ROOKIE (101-142)	6.00	2.50
COMMON ROOKIE (143-150)	12.00	5.00
1	Al Harrington	.60	.25
2	Josh Smith	1.00	.40
3	Josh Childress	.60	.25
4	Tyronn Lue	.25	.10
5	Paul Pierce	1.00	.40
6	Antoine Walker	1.00	.40
7	Gary Payton	1.00	.40
8	Al Jefferson	1.00	.40
9	Emeka Okafor	1.50	.60
10	Primoz Brezec	.25	.10
11	Gerald Wallace	.60	.25
12	Michael Jordan	6.00	2.50
13	Ben Gordon	2.00	.75
14	Luol Deng	1.00	.40
15	Kirk Hinrich	1.00	.40
16	LeBron James	6.00	2.50
17	Luke Jackson	.60	.25
18	Drew Gooden	.60	.25
19	Larry Hughes	.60	.25
20	Dirk Nowitzki	1.50	.60
21	Jason Terry	1.00	.40
22	Michael Finley	1.00	.40
23	Jerry Stackhouse	1.00	.40
24	Andre Miller	.60	.25
25	Carmelo Anthony	2.00	.75
26	Kenyon Martin	1.00	.40
27	Earl Boykins	.60	.25
28	Rasheed Wallace	1.00	.40
29	Ben Wallace	1.00	.40
30	Richard Hamilton	.60	.25
31	Chauncey Billups	1.00	.40
32	Baron Davis	1.00	.40
33	Derek Fisher	1.00	.40
34	Jason Richardson	1.00	.40
35	Tracy McGrady	2.50	1.00
36	Yao Ming	2.50	1.00
37	Juwan Howard	.60	.25
38	Jermaine O'Neal	1.00	.40
39	Ron Artest	.60	.25
40	Jamaal Tinsley	.60	.25
41	Corey Maggette	.60	.25
42	Elton Brand	1.00	.40
43	Shaun Livingston	1.00	.40
44	Kobe Bryant	4.00	1.50
45	Brian Cook	.25	.10
46	Lamar Odom	1.00	.40
47	Mike Miller	1.00	.40
48	Pau Gasol	1.00	.40
49	Shane Battier	1.00	.40
50	Shaquille O'Neal	2.50	1.00
51	Dwyane Wade	3.00	1.25
52	Udonis Haslem	1.00	.40
53	Joe Smith	.60	.25
54	Michael Redd	1.00	.40
55	Desmond Mason	.60	.25
56	Kevin Garnett	2.00	.75
57	Wally Szczerbiak	.60	.25
58	Sam Cassell	1.00	.40
59	Vince Carter	2.50	1.00
60	Jason Kidd	1.50	.60
61	Richard Jefferson	.60	.25
62	Jamaal Magloire	.25	.10
63	J.R. Smith	.60	.25
64	Speedy Claxton	.25	.10
65	Allan Houston	.60	.25
66	Stephon Marbury	1.00	.40
67	Jamal Crawford	.60	.25
68	Dwight Howard	1.25	.50
69	Grant Hill	1.00	.40
70	Jameer Nelson	.60	.25
71	Steve Francis	1.00	.40
72	Allen Iverson	2.00	.75
73	Andre Iguodala	1.00	.40
74	Chris Webber	1.00	.40
75	Kyle Korver	1.00	.40
76	Amare Stoudemire	2.00	.75
77	Steve Nash	1.00	.40
78	Quentin Richardson	.60	.25
79	Shawn Marion	1.00	.40
80	Damon Stoudamire	.60	.25
81	Zach Randolph	.60	.25
82	Sebastian Telfair	1.00	.40
83	Peja Stojakovic	1.00	.40
84	Mike Bibby	1.00	.40
85	Cuttino Mobley	.60	.25
86	Manu Ginobili	1.00	.40
87	Tim Duncan	2.00	.75
88	Tony Parker	1.00	.40
89	Ray Allen	1.00	.40
90	Rashard Lewis	1.00	.40
91	Luke Ridnour	.60	.25
92	Ronald Murray	.25	.10
93	Chris Bosh	1.00	.40
94	Morris Peterson	.25	.10
95	Jalen Rose	1.00	.40
96	Andrei Kirilenko	1.00	.40
97	Raul Lopez	.25	.10
98	Carlos Boozer	1.00	.40
99	Antawn Jamison	1.00	.40
100	Gilbert Arenas	1.00	.40
101	Ike Diogu RC	6.00	2.50
102	Julius Hodge RC	6.00	2.50
103	David Lee RC	10.00	4.00
104	Linas Kleiza RC	6.00	2.50
105	Jason Maxiell RC	6.00	2.50

❏ 106	Luther Head RC	6.00	2.50
❏ 107	Jose Calderon RC	6.00	2.50
❏ 108	Brandon Bass RC	6.00	2.50
❏ 109	Ricky Sanchez RC	6.00	2.50
❏ 110	Andray Blatche RC	6.00	2.50
❏ 111	Sean May RC	5.00	2.00
❏ 112	Travis Diener RC	6.00	2.50
❏ 113	Nate Robinson RC	8.00	3.00
❏ 114	Von Wafer RC	6.00	2.50
❏ 115	James Singleton RC	6.00	2.50
❏ 116	Daniel Ewing RC	6.00	2.50
❏ 117	Salim Stoudamire RC	6.00	2.50
❏ 118	Dijon Thompson RC	6.00	2.50
❏ 119	Danny Granger RC	8.00	3.00
❏ 120	Will Bynum RC	6.00	2.50
❏ 121	Louis Williams RC	6.00	2.50
❏ 122	Channing Frye RC	6.00	2.50
❏ 123	Francisco Garcia RC	6.00	2.50
❏ 124	Ryan Gomes RC	6.00	2.50
❏ 125	Ronnie Price RC	6.00	2.50
❏ 126	Jarrett Jack RC	6.00	2.50
❏ 127	Alan Anderson RC	6.00	2.50
❏ 128	Ersan Ilyasova RC	6.00	2.50
❏ 129	C.J. Miles RC	6.00	2.50
❏ 130	Arvydas Macijauskas RC	6.00	2.50
❏ 131	Bracey Wright RC	6.00	2.50
❏ 132	Monta Ellis RC	10.00	4.00
❏ 133	Chris Taft RC	6.00	2.50
❏ 134	Johan Petro RC	6.00	2.50
❏ 135	Yaroslav Korolev RC	6.00	2.50
❏ 136	Andrew Bynum RC	15.00	6.00
❏ 137	Martynas Andriuskevicius RC	6.00	2.50
❏ 138	Charlie Villanueva RC	8.00	3.00
❏ 139	Antoine Wright RC	6.00	2.50
❏ 140	Joey Graham RC	6.00	2.50
❏ 141	Wayne Simien RC	6.00	2.50
❏ 142	Hakim Warrick RC	10.00	4.00
❏ 143	Gerald Green RC	20.00	8.00
❏ 144	Marvin Williams RC	15.00	6.00
❏ 145	Deron Williams RC	25.00	10.00
❏ 146	Rashad McCants RC	15.00	6.00
❏ 147	Raymond Felton RC	15.00	6.00
❏ 148	Martell Webster RC	12.00	5.00
❏ 149	Chris Paul RC	30.00	12.50
❏ 150	Andrew Bogut RC	10.00	4.00

2006-07 Upper Deck Sweet Shot

❏ 1	Josh Childress	.60	.25
❏ 2	Joe Johnson	.60	.25
❏ 3	Marvin Williams	1.25	.50
❏ 4	Al Jefferson	1.00	.40
❏ 5	Paul Pierce	1.00	.40
❏ 6	Wally Szczerbiak	.60	.25
❏ 7	Raymond Felton	1.25	.50
❏ 8	Emeka Okafor	1.00	.40
❏ 9	Gerald Wallace	1.00	.40
❏ 10	Ben Gordon	2.00	.75
❏ 11	Kirk Hinrich	1.00	.40
❏ 12	Michael Jordan	6.00	2.50
❏ 13	Larry Hughes	.60	.25
❏ 14	Zydrunas Ilgauskas	.30	.12
❏ 15	LeBron James	6.00	2.50
❏ 16	Marquis Daniels	.60	.25
❏ 17	Dirk Nowitzki	1.50	.60
❏ 18	Jason Terry	1.00	.40
❏ 19	Carmelo Anthony	2.00	.75
❏ 20	Marcus Camby	.30	.12

❏ 21	Kenyon Martin	1.00	.40
❏ 22	Chauncey Billups	1.00	.40
❏ 23	Richard Hamilton	.60	.25
❏ 24	Ben Wallace	1.00	.40
❏ 25	Baron Davis	1.00	.40
❏ 26	Mike Dunleavy	.60	.25
❏ 27	Jason Richardson	1.00	.40
❏ 28	Rafer Alston	.30	.12
❏ 29	Tracy McGrady	2.50	1.00
❏ 30	Yao Ming	2.50	1.00
❏ 31	Austin Croshere	.30	.12
❏ 32	Jermaine O'Neal	1.00	.40
❏ 33	Peja Stojakovic	1.00	.40
❏ 34	Elton Brand	1.00	.40
❏ 35	Sam Cassell	1.00	.40
❏ 36	Shaun Livingston	.75	.30
❏ 37	Kwame Brown	.60	.25
❏ 38	Kobe Bryant	4.00	1.50
❏ 39	Lamar Odom	1.00	.40
❏ 40	Pau Gasol	1.00	.40
❏ 41	Bobby Jackson	.30	.12
❏ 42	Hakim Warrick	.60	.25
❏ 43	Shaquille O'Neal	2.50	1.00
❏ 44	Dwyane Wade	3.00	1.25
❏ 45	Jason Williams	.60	.25
❏ 46	Andrew Bogut	1.25	.50
❏ 47	T.J. Ford	.60	.25
❏ 48	Jamaal Magloire	.30	.12
❏ 49	Ricky Davis	1.00	.40
❏ 50	Kevin Garnett	2.00	.75
❏ 51	Rashad McCants	1.25	.50
❏ 52	Vince Carter	2.50	1.00
❏ 53	Richard Jefferson	.60	.25
❏ 54	Jason Kidd	1.50	.60
❏ 55	Desmond Mason	.30	.12
❏ 56	Chris Paul	2.50	1.00
❏ 57	J.R. Smith	.60	.25
❏ 58	Channing Frye	.60	.25
❏ 59	Stephon Marbury	1.00	.40
❏ 60	Quentin Richardson	.60	.25
❏ 61	Carlos Arroyo	1.50	.60
❏ 62	Dwight Howard	1.25	.50
❏ 63	Darko Milicic	1.00	.40
❏ 64	Andre Iguodala	1.00	.40
❏ 65	Allen Iverson	2.00	.75
❏ 66	Chris Webber	1.00	.40
❏ 67	Boris Diaw	.60	.25
❏ 68	Shawn Marion	1.00	.40
❏ 69	Steve Nash	1.00	.40
❏ 70	Juan Dixon	.30	.12
❏ 71	Zach Randolph	1.00	.40
❏ 72	Sebastian Telfair	.60	.25
❏ 73	Ron Artest	.60	.25
❏ 74	Mike Bibby	1.00	.40
❏ 75	Brad Miller	1.00	.40
❏ 76	Tim Duncan	2.00	.75
❏ 77	Manu Ginobili	1.00	.40
❏ 78	Tony Parker	1.00	.40
❏ 79	Ray Allen	1.00	.40
❏ 80	Rashard Lewis	1.00	.40
❏ 81	Luke Ridnour	.60	.25
❏ 82	Chris Bosh	1.00	.40
❏ 83	Joey Graham	.60	.25
❏ 84	Charlie Villanueva	1.00	.40
❏ 85	Carlos Boozer	.60	.25
❏ 86	Andrei Kirilenko	1.00	.40
❏ 87	Deron Williams	1.00	.40
❏ 88	Gilbert Arenas	1.00	.40
❏ 89	Caron Butler	.60	.25
❏ 90	Antawn Jamison	1.00	.40
❏ 91	David Noel AU RC	12.00	5.00
❏ 92	James Augustine AU RC	12.00	5.00
❏ 93	Kyle Lowry AU RC	12.00	5.00
❏ 94	Bobby Jones AU RC	12.00	5.00
❏ 95	Solomon Jones AU RC	12.00	5.00
❏ 96	Craig Smith AU RC	12.00	5.00
❏ 97	Josh Boone AU RC	12.00	5.00
❏ 98	Jordan Farmar AU RC	30.00	12.50
❏ 99	Marcus Williams AU RC	25.00	10.00
❏ 100	Hassan Adams AU RC	15.00	6.00
❏ 101	Dee Brown AU RC	20.00	8.00
❏ 102	Denham Brown AU RC	12.00	5.00
❏ 103	Steve Novak AU RC	12.00	5.00
❏ 104	James White AU RC	12.00	5.00
❏ 105	Daniel Gibson AU RC	30.00	12.50
❏ 106	Renaldo Balkman AU RC	12.00	5.00

❏ 107	P.J. Tucker AU RC	12.00	5.00
❏ 108	Saer Sene AU RC	12.00	5.00
❏ 109	Thabo Sefolosha AU RC	20.00	8.00
❏ 110	Maurice Ager AU RC	12.00	5.00
❏ 111	Rajon Rondo AU RC	15.00	6.00
❏ 112	Shawne Williams AU RC	15.00	6.00
❏ 113	Mardy Collins AU RC	12.00	5.00
❏ 114	Paul Davis AU RC	12.00	5.00
❏ 115	Quincy Douby AU RC	12.00	5.00
❏ 121	Rodney Carney AU RC	15.00	6.00
❏ 122	Randy Foye AU RC	30.00	12.00
❏ 123	Ronnie Brewer AU RC	20.00	8.00
❏ 124	Cedric Simmons AU RC	12.00	5.00
❏ 128	Rudy Gay AU RC	30.00	12.00
❏ 129	Shelden Williams AU RC	20.00	8.00
❏ 130	Patrick O'Bryant AU RC	15.00	6.00
❏ 131	Hilton Armstrong AU RC	15.00	6.00
❏ 133	Adam Morrison AU RC	30.00	12.00
❏ 134	J.J. Redick RC	25.00	10.00
❏ 135	Alexander Johnson RC	12.00	5.00
❏ 136	Damir Markota RC	12.00	5.00
❏ 137	Leon Powe RC	12.00	5.00
❏ 138	Ryan Hollins RC	12.00	5.00
❏ 139	Tarence Kinsey RC	12.00	5.00
❏ 140	Jorge Garbajosa RC	25.00	10.00

2004-05 Upper Deck Trilogy

❏	COMP.SET w/o SP's (100)	150.00	60.00
❏	COMMON CARD (1-100)	2.50	1.00
❏	COMMON ROOKIE (101-140)	8.00	3.00
❏	COMMON ROOKIE (141-150)	10.00	4.00
❏ 1	Antoine Walker	2.50	1.25
❏ 2	Al Harrington	2.50	1.25
❏ 3	Boris Diaw	2.50	1.00
❏ 4	Paul Pierce	3.00	1.25
❏ 5	Ricky Davis	3.00	1.25
❏ 6	Gary Payton	2.50	1.25
❏ 7	Gerald Wallace	2.50	1.00
❏ 8	Emeka Okafor RC	12.00	5.00
❏ 9	Keith Bogans	2.50	1.00
❏ 10	Eddy Curry	2.50	1.25
❏ 11	Kirk Hinrich	4.00	1.50
❏ 12	Michael Jordan	12.00	5.00
❏ 13	LeBron James	12.00	5.00
❏ 14	Dajuan Wagner	2.50	1.00
❏ 15	Jeff McInnis	2.50	1.25
❏ 16	Drew Gooden	2.50	1.00
❏ 17	Dirk Nowitzki	4.00	1.50
❏ 18	Michael Finley	3.00	1.25
❏ 19	Jerry Stackhouse	3.00	1.25
❏ 20	Jason Terry	3.00	1.25
❏ 21	Kenyon Martin	3.00	1.25
❏ 22	Andre Miller	2.50	1.00
❏ 23	Carmelo Anthony	4.00	1.50
❏ 24	Nene	2.50	1.00
❏ 25	Chauncey Billups	2.50	1.00
❏ 26	Rasheed Wallace	3.00	1.25
❏ 27	Ben Wallace	2.50	1.00
❏ 28	Richard Hamilton	2.50	1.00
❏ 29	Derek Fisher	3.00	1.25
❏ 30	Jason Richardson	3.00	1.25
❏ 31	Mike Dunleavy	2.50	1.00
❏ 32	Yao Ming	5.00	2.00
❏ 33	Tracy McGrady	5.00	2.00
❏ 34	Juwan Howard	2.50	1.00
❏ 35	Jermaine O'Neal	3.00	1.25
❏ 36	Reggie Miller	3.00	1.25

#	Player		
37	Ron Artest	2.50	1.00
38	Jamaal Tinsley	3.00	1.00
39	Elton Brand	3.00	1.25
40	Corey Maggette	2.50	1.00
41	Marko Jaric	2.50	1.00
42	Kerry Kittles	2.50	1.00
43	Kobe Bryant	8.00	3.00
44	Caron Butler	2.50	1.00
45	Lamar Odom	3.00	1.25
46	Brian Cook	2.50	1.00
47	Pau Gasol	3.00	1.25
48	Jason Williams	2.50	1.00
49	Bonzi Wells	2.50	1.00
50	Shaquille O'Neal	5.00	2.00
51	Dwyane Wade	6.00	2.50
52	Eddie Jones	3.00	1.25
53	Michael Redd	2.50	1.00
54	Desmond Mason	2.50	1.00
55	Maurice Williams	2.50	1.00
56	Latrell Sprewell	3.00	1.25
57	Kevin Garnett	4.00	1.50
58	Sam Cassell	2.50	1.00
59	Troy Hudson	2.50	1.00
60	Vince Carter	5.00	2.00
61	Richard Jefferson	2.50	1.00
62	Jason Kidd	4.00	1.50
63	P.J. Brown	2.50	1.00
64	Baron Davis	3.00	1.25
65	Jamaal Magloire	2.50	1.00
66	Allan Houston	2.50	1.00
67	Jamal Crawford	2.50	1.00
68	Stephon Marbury	3.00	1.25
69	Grant Hill	3.00	1.25
70	Cuttino Mobley	2.50	1.00
71	Steve Francis	3.00	1.25
72	Glenn Robinson	3.00	1.25
73	Allen Iverson	4.00	1.50
74	Willie Green	2.50	1.00
75	Amare Stoudemire	4.00	1.50
76	Steve Nash	3.00	1.25
77	Quentin Richardson	2.50	1.00
78	Shawn Marion	3.00	1.25
79	Shareef Abdur-Rahim	3.00	1.25
80	Damon Stoudamire	2.50	1.00
81	Zach Randolph	3.00	1.25
82	Darius Miles	3.00	1.25
83	Peja Stojakovic	3.00	1.25
84	Chris Webber	3.00	1.25
85	Mike Bibby	3.00	1.25
86	Tony Parker	3.00	1.25
87	Tim Duncan	4.00	1.50
88	Manu Ginobili	3.00	1.25
89	Ronald Murray	2.50	1.00
90	Ray Allen	3.00	1.25
91	Rashard Lewis	3.00	1.25
92	Chris Bosh	3.00	1.25
93	Rafer Alston	2.50	1.00
94	Jalen Rose	3.00	1.25
95	Andrei Kirilenko	3.00	1.25
96	Carlos Arroyo	4.00	1.50
97	Carlos Boozer	3.00	1.25
98	Gilbert Arenas	3.00	1.25
99	Jarvis Hayes	2.50	1.00
100	Antawn Jamison	3.00	1.25
101	Rafael Araujo RC	8.00	3.00
102	Luke Jackson RC	8.00	3.00
103	Andris Biedrins RC	12.00	5.00
104	Robert Swift RC	8.00	3.00
105	Kris Humphries RC	8.00	3.00
106	Al Jefferson RC	20.00	8.00
107	Kirk Snyder RC	8.00	3.00
108	Josh Smith RC	15.00	6.00
109	Dorell Wright RC	12.00	5.00
110	Jameer Nelson RC	12.00	5.00
111	Pavel Podkolzine RC	8.00	3.00
112	Andres Nocioni RC	10.00	4.00
113	Luis Flores RC	8.00	3.00
114	Delonte West RC	15.00	6.00
115	Tony Allen RC	10.00	4.00
116	Kevin Martin RC	12.00	5.00
117	Sasha Vujacic RC	8.00	3.00
118	Beno Udrih RC	12.00	5.00
119	David Harrison RC	8.00	3.00
120	Anderson Varejao RC	10.00	4.00
121	Jackson Vroman RC	8.00	3.00
122	Peter John Ramos RC	8.00	3.00
123	Lionel Chalmers RC	8.00	3.00
124	Donta Smith RC	8.00	3.00
125	Andre Emmett RC	8.00	3.00
126	Antonio Burks RC	8.00	3.00
127	Royal Ivey RC	8.00	3.00
128	Chris Duhon RC	12.00	5.00
129	Nenad Krstic RC	10.00	4.00
130	Justin Reed RC	8.00	3.00
131	Pape Sow RC	8.00	3.00
132	Trevor Ariza RC	10.00	4.00
133	Tim Pickett RC	8.00	3.00
134	Bernard Robinson RC	8.00	3.00
135	John Edwards RC	8.00	3.00
136	Damien Wilkins RC	8.00	3.00
137	Romain Sato RC	8.00	3.00
138	Matt Freije RC	8.00	3.00
139	D.J. Mbenga RC	8.00	3.00
140	Yuta Tabuse RC	15.00	6.00
141	Dwight Howard RC	30.00	12.50
142	Emeka Okafor RC	40.00	15.00
143	Ben Gordon RC	50.00	20.00
144	Shaun Livingston RC	15.00	6.00
145	Devin Harris RC	15.00	6.00
146	Josh Childress RC	10.00	4.00
147	Luol Deng RC	25.00	10.00
148	Andre Iguodala RC	20.00	8.00
149	Sebastian Telfair RC	12.00	5.00
150	J.R. Smith RC	15.00	6.00

2005-06 Upper Deck Trilogy

	COMP.SET w/o SP's (90)	60.00	25.00
	COMMON CARD (1-90)	1.50	.60
	COMMON ROOKIE (91-130)	8.00	3.00
	COMMON ROOKIE (131-140)	10.00	4.00
1	Josh Smith	2.50	1.00
2	Josh Childress	1.50	.60
3	Al Harrington	.75	.30
4	Paul Pierce	2.50	1.00
5	Ricky Davis	2.50	1.00
6	Al Jefferson	2.50	1.00
7	Emeka Okafor	4.00	1.50
8	Gerald Wallace	2.50	1.00
9	Kareem Rush	.75	.30
10	Michael Jordan	15.00	6.00
11	Luol Deng	2.50	1.00
12	Ben Gordon	5.00	2.00
13	LeBron James	15.00	6.00
14	Larry Hughes	1.50	.60
15	Donyell Marshall	.75	.30
16	Dirk Nowitzki	4.00	1.50
17	Josh Howard	1.50	.60
18	Jason Terry	2.50	1.00
19	Carmelo Anthony	5.00	2.00
20	Kenyon Martin	2.50	1.00
21	Andre Miller	1.50	.60
22	Chauncey Billups	2.50	1.00
23	Richard Hamilton	1.50	.60
24	Ben Wallace	2.50	1.00
25	Jason Richardson	2.50	1.00
26	Baron Davis	2.50	1.00
27	Troy Murphy	2.50	1.00
28	Yao Ming	6.00	2.50
29	Tracy McGrady	6.00	2.50
30	Stromile Swift	1.50	.60
31	Ron Artest	1.50	.60
32	Jermaine O'Neal	2.50	1.00
33	Fred Jones	1.50	.60
34	Elton Brand	2.50	1.00
35	Shaun Livingston	2.00	.75
36	Corey Maggette	1.50	.60
37	Kobe Bryant	10.00	4.00
38	Kwame Brown	1.50	.60
39	Lamar Odom	2.50	1.00
40	Pau Gasol	2.50	1.00
41	Shane Battier	2.50	1.00
42	Mike Miller	2.50	1.00
43	Shaquille O'Neal	6.00	2.50
44	Dwyane Wade	8.00	3.00
45	Udonis Haslem	2.50	1.00
46	Michael Redd	2.50	1.00
47	Maurice Williams	.75	.30
48	Desmond Mason	.75	.30
49	Kevin Garnett	5.00	2.00
50	Wally Szczerbiak	1.50	.60
51	Marko Jaric	.75	.30
52	Jason Kidd	4.00	1.50
53	Vince Carter	6.00	2.50
54	Richard Jefferson	1.50	.60
55	Jamaal Magloire	.75	.30
56	J.R. Smith	1.50	.60
57	Speedy Claxton	.75	.30
58	Stephon Marbury	2.50	1.00
59	Jamal Crawford	1.50	.60
60	Quentin Richardson	1.50	.60
61	Steve Francis	2.50	1.00
62	Dwight Howard	3.00	1.25
63	Grant Hill	2.50	1.00
64	Allen Iverson	5.00	2.00
65	Kyle Korver	2.50	1.00
66	Chris Webber	2.50	1.00
67	Steve Nash	2.50	1.00
68	Amare Stoudemire	5.00	2.00
69	Shawn Marion	2.50	1.00
70	Sebastian Telfair	1.50	.60
71	Zach Randolph	2.50	1.00
72	Travis Outlaw	.75	.30
73	Peja Stojakovic	2.50	1.00
74	Mike Bibby	2.50	1.00
75	Brad Miller	2.50	1.00
76	Tim Duncan	5.00	2.00
77	Manu Ginobili	2.50	1.00
78	Tony Parker	2.50	1.00
79	Ray Allen	2.50	1.00
80	Rashard Lewis	2.50	1.00
81	Luke Ridnour	1.50	.60
82	Chris Bosh	2.50	1.00
83	Morris Peterson	1.50	.60
84	Jalen Rose	2.00	.75
85	Carlos Boozer	1.50	.60
86	Matt Harpring	2.50	1.00
87	Andrei Kirilenko	2.50	1.00
88	Antawn Jamison	2.50	1.00
89	Gilbert Arenas	2.50	1.00
90	Caron Butler	1.50	.60
91	Sarunas Jasikevicius RC	10.00	4.00
92	Alex Acker RC	6.00	2.50
93	Amir Johnson RC	6.00	3.00
94	Lawrence Roberts RC	8.00	3.00
95	Dijon Thompson RC	6.00	2.50
96	Orien Greene RC	8.00	3.00
97	Robert Whaley RC	8.00	3.00
98	Ryan Gomes RC	8.00	3.00
99	Andray Blatche RC	8.00	3.00
100	Yaroslav Korolev RC	8.00	3.00
101	Bracey Wright RC	8.00	3.00
102	Louis Williams RC	8.00	3.00
103	Martynas Andriuskevicius RC	8.00	3.00
104	Chris Taft RC	8.00	3.00
105	Monta Ellis RC	15.00	6.00
106	Von Wafer RC	6.00	2.50
107	Travis Diener RC	8.00	3.00
108	Ersan Ilyasova RC	8.00	3.00
109	Arvydas Macijauskas RC	8.00	3.00
110	C.J. Miles RC	8.00	3.00
111	Brandon Bass RC	8.00	3.00
112	Daniel Ewing RC	10.00	4.00
113	Salim Stoudamire RC	10.00	4.00
114	David Lee RC	12.00	5.00
115	Wayne Simien RC	10.00	4.00
116	Jason Maxiell RC	8.00	3.00
117	Johan Petro RC	8.00	3.00
118	Luther Head RC	10.00	4.00
119	Francisco Garcia RC	10.00	4.00

❑ 120	Jarrett Jack RC	8.00	3.00
❑ 121	Nate Robinson RC	12.00	5.00
❑ 122	Julius Hodge RC	10.00	4.00
❑ 123	Hakim Warrick RC	15.00	6.00
❑ 124	Gerald Green RC	15.00	6.00
❑ 125	Danny Granger RC	12.00	5.00
❑ 126	Joey Graham RC	8.00	3.00
❑ 127	Antoine Wright RC	8.00	3.00
❑ 128	Rashad McCants RC	15.00	6.00
❑ 129	Sean May RC	10.00	4.00
❑ 130	Linas Kleiza RC	8.00	3.00
❑ 131	Andrew Bynum RC	25.00	10.00
❑ 132	Ike Diogu RC	12.00	5.00
❑ 133	Channing Frye RC	12.00	5.00
❑ 134	Charlie Villanueva RC	16.00	6.00
❑ 135	Martell Webster RC	10.00	4.00
❑ 136	Raymond Felton RC	20.00	8.00
❑ 137	Chris Paul RC	60.00	25.00
❑ 138	Deron Williams RC	30.00	12.00
❑ 139	Marvin Williams RC	20.00	8.00
❑ 140	Andrew Bogut RC	20.00	8.00

2006-07 Upper Deck Trilogy

❑ 1	Joe Johnson	1.25	.50
❑ 2	Marvin Williams	2.50	1.00
❑ 3	Paul Pierce	2.00	.75
❑ 4	Wally Szczerbiak	1.25	.50
❑ 5	Emeka Okafor	2.00	.75
❑ 6	Raymond Felton	2.50	1.00
❑ 7	Ben Wallace	2.00	.75
❑ 8	Kirk Hinrich	2.00	.75
❑ 9	Ben Gordon	4.00	1.50
❑ 10	LeBron James	12.00	5.00
❑ 11	Larry Hughes	1.25	.50
❑ 12	Dirk Nowitzki	3.00	1.25
❑ 13	Jason Terry	2.00	.75
❑ 14	Carmelo Anthony	4.00	1.50
❑ 15	Andre Miller	1.25	.50
❑ 16	Chauncey Billups	2.00	.75
❑ 17	Richard Hamilton	1.25	.50
❑ 18	Jason Richardson	2.00	.75
❑ 19	Baron Davis	2.00	.75
❑ 20	Yao Ming	5.00	2.00
❑ 21	Tracy McGrady	5.00	2.00
❑ 22	Jermaine O'Neal	2.00	.75
❑ 23	Al Harrington	.60	.25
❑ 24	Elton Brand	2.00	.75
❑ 25	Sam Cassell	2.00	.75
❑ 26	Kobe Bryant	8.00	3.00
❑ 27	Lamar Odom	2.00	.75
❑ 28	Pau Gasol	2.00	.75
❑ 29	Dwyane Wade	6.00	2.50
❑ 30	Shaquille O'Neal	5.00	2.00
❑ 31	Michael Redd	2.00	.75
❑ 32	Andrew Bogut	2.50	1.00
❑ 33	Kevin Garnett	4.00	1.50
❑ 34	Mike James	.60	.25
❑ 35	Vince Carter	5.00	2.00
❑ 36	Jason Kidd	3.00	1.25
❑ 37	Richard Jefferson	1.25	.50
❑ 38	Chris Paul	5.00	2.00
❑ 39	David West	.60	.25
❑ 40	Stephon Marbury	2.00	.75
❑ 41	Steve Francis	2.00	.75
❑ 42	Dwight Howard	2.50	1.00
❑ 43	Jameer Nelson	1.25	.50
❑ 44	Allen Iverson	4.00	1.50
❑ 45	Chris Webber	2.00	.75
❑ 46	Steve Nash	2.00	.75
❑ 47	Shawn Marion	2.00	.75
❑ 48	Zach Randolph	2.00	.75
❑ 49	Mike Bibby	2.00	.75
❑ 50	Ron Artest	1.25	.50
❑ 51	Tim Duncan	4.00	1.50
❑ 52	Tony Parker	2.00	.75
❑ 53	Ray Allen	2.00	.75
❑ 54	Rashard Lewis	2.00	.75
❑ 55	Chris Bosh	2.00	.75
❑ 56	T.J. Ford	1.25	.50
❑ 57	Mehmet Okur	.60	.25
❑ 58	Andrei Kirilenko	2.00	.75
❑ 59	Gilbert Arenas	2.00	.75
❑ 60	Antawn Jamison	2.00	.75
❑ 61	Childress/Claxton/Smith	2.00	.75
❑ 62	Jefferson/West/Telfair	2.00	.75
❑ 63	Wallace/Brezec/Knight	2.00	.75
❑ 64	Nocioni/Deng/Brown	3.00	1.25
❑ 65	Gooden/Ilgauskas/Marshall	2.00	.75
❑ 66	Howard/Stackhouse/Harris	3.00	1.25
❑ 67	Martin/Camby/Smith	3.00	1.25
❑ 68	Wallace/Prince/Mohammed	3.00	1.25
❑ 69	Murphy/Dunleavy/Diogu	2.00	.75
❑ 70	Alston/Battier/Wells	2.00	.75
❑ 71	Granger/Tinsley/Dunleavy	2.00	.75
❑ 72	Kaman/Maggette/Livingston	2.00	.75
❑ 73	Parker/Radmanovic/Brown	3.00	1.25
❑ 74	Miller/Stoudamire/Warrick	2.00	.75
❑ 75	Walker/Haslem/Williams	3.00	1.25
❑ 76	Villanueva/Patterson/Williams	2.00	.75
❑ 77	Davis/Hassell/Blount	2.00	.75
❑ 78	Krstic/Collins/Robinson	2.00	.75
❑ 79	Chandler/Stojakovic/Mason	2.00	.75
❑ 80	Curry/Crawford/Frye	2.00	.75
❑ 81	Milicic/Turkoglu/Hill	2.50	1.00
❑ 82	Iguodala/Korver/Dalembert	2.00	.75
❑ 83	Stoudemire/Diaw/Bell	3.00	1.25
❑ 84	Jack/Randolph/Webster	2.00	.75
❑ 85	Miller/Abdur-Rahim/Martin	2.50	1.00
❑ 86	Ginobili/Finley/Bowen	4.00	1.50
❑ 87	Ridnour/Wilcox/Collison	2.00	.75
❑ 88	Peterson/Graham/Calderon	2.00	.75
❑ 89	Boozer/Williams/Giricek	2.00	.75
❑ 90	Butler/Thomas/Stevenson	2.00	.75
❑ 91	Shelden Williams RC	10.00	4.00
❑ 92	Tyrus Thomas RC	25.00	10.00
❑ 93	Rudy Gay RC	15.00	6.00
❑ 94	Randy Foye RC	15.00	6.00
❑ 95	Rodney Carney RC	8.00	3.00
❑ 96	LaMarcus Aldridge RC	20.00	8.00
❑ 97	Brandon Roy RC	25.00	10.00
❑ 98	Andrea Bargnani RC	25.00	10.00
❑ 99	Solomon Jones RC	5.00	2.00
❑ 100	Rajon Rondo RC	6.00	2.50
❑ 101	Allan Ray RC	5.00	2.00
❑ 102	Thabo Sefolosha RC	8.00	3.00
❑ 103	Shannon Brown RC	5.00	2.00
❑ 104	Maurice Ager RC	5.00	2.00
❑ 105	Patrick O'Bryant RC	5.00	2.00
❑ 106	Steve Novak RC	5.00	2.00
❑ 107	Shawne Williams RC	6.00	2.50
❑ 108	Paul Davis RC	5.00	2.00
❑ 109	Jordan Farmar RC	10.00	4.00
❑ 110	Kyle Lowry RC	5.00	2.00
❑ 111	David Noel RC	5.00	2.00
❑ 112	Craig Smith RC	5.00	2.00
❑ 113	Marcus Williams RC	6.00	2.50
❑ 114	Josh Boone RC	5.00	2.00
❑ 115	Hilton Armstrong RC	5.00	2.00
❑ 116	Cedric Simmons RC	5.00	2.00
❑ 117	Renaldo Balkman RC	5.00	2.00
❑ 118	Mardy Collins RC	5.00	2.00
❑ 119	Bobby Jones RC	5.00	2.00
❑ 120	Quincy Douby RC	5.00	2.00
❑ 121	Saer Sene RC	5.00	2.00
❑ 122	P.J. Tucker RC	5.00	2.00
❑ 123	Jorge Garbajosa RC	10.00	4.00
❑ 124	Ronnie Brewer RC	6.00	2.50
❑ 125	Dee Brown RC	6.00	2.50
❑ 126	Leon Powe RC	5.00	2.00
❑ 127	Ryan Hollins RC	5.00	2.00
❑ 128	Adam Morrison RC	10.00	5.00
❑ 129	Daniel Gibson RC	12.00	5.00
❑ 130	Pops Mensah-Bonsu RC	5.00	2.00
❑ 131	Yakhouba Diawara RC	5.00	2.00
❑ 132	Will Blalock RC	5.00	2.00
❑ 133	Alexander Johnson RC	5.00	2.00
❑ 134	Damir Markota RC	5.00	2.00
❑ 135	Hassan Adams RC	6.00	2.50
❑ 136	Marcus Vinicius RC	5.00	2.00
❑ 137	James Augustine RC	5.00	2.00
❑ 138	J.J. Redick RC	10.00	4.00
❑ 139	Sergio Rodriguez RC	5.00	2.00
❑ 140	Paul Millsap RC	10.00	4.00

2003-04 Upper Deck Triple Dimensions

❑	COMP.SET w/o SP's (90)	30.00	12.50
❑	COMMON CARD (1-90)	.20	.08
❑	COMMON ROOKIE (91-126)	5.00	2.00
❑ 1	Jason Terry	.75	.30
❑ 2	Theo Ratliff	.75	.20
❑ 3	Shareef Abdur-Rahim	.75	.20
❑ 4	Raef LaFrentz	.50	.20
❑ 5	Vin Baker	.50	.20
❑ 6	Paul Pierce	.75	.30
❑ 7	Eddy Curry	.50	.20
❑ 8	Tyson Chandler	.75	.30
❑ 9	Antonio Davis	.20	.08
❑ 10	Dajuan Wagner	.50	.20
❑ 11	Zydrunas Ilgauskas	.50	.20
❑ 12	Carlos Boozer	.75	.30
❑ 13	Steve Nash	.75	.30
❑ 14	Antoine Walker	.75	.30
❑ 15	Dirk Nowitzki	1.25	.50
❑ 16	Michael Finley	.75	.30
❑ 17	Andre Miller	.50	.20
❑ 18	Nene	.50	.20
❑ 19	Earl Boykins	.75	.30
❑ 20	Ben Wallace	.75	.30
❑ 21	Chauncey Billups	.50	.20
❑ 22	Richard Hamilton	.50	.20
❑ 23	Mike Dunleavy	.50	.20
❑ 24	Jason Richardson	.75	.30
❑ 25	Nick Van Exel	.75	.30
❑ 26	Cuttino Mobley	.50	.20
❑ 27	Yao Ming	2.00	.75
❑ 28	Steve Francis	.75	.30
❑ 29	Reggie Miller	.75	.30
❑ 30	Jamaal Tinsley	.75	.30
❑ 31	Jermaine O'Neal	.75	.30
❑ 32	Corey Maggette	.50	.20
❑ 33	Elton Brand	.75	.30
❑ 34	Quentin Richardson	.50	.20
❑ 35	Shaquille O'Neal	.75	.30
❑ 36	Kobe Bryant	3.00	1.25
❑ 37	Karl Malone	.75	.30
❑ 38	Gary Payton	.75	.30
❑ 39	Mike Miller	.75	.30
❑ 40	Pau Gasol	.75	.30
❑ 41	Shane Battier	.75	.30
❑ 42	Eddie Jones	.75	.30
❑ 43	Caron Butler	.75	.30
❑ 44	Lamar Odom	.75	.30
❑ 45	Desmond Mason	.50	.20
❑ 46	Tim Thomas	.50	.20
❑ 47	Michael Redd	.75	.30
❑ 48	Latrell Sprewell	.75	.30
❑ 49	Kevin Garnett	1.50	.60
❑ 50	Wally Szczerbiak	.50	.20
❑ 51	Kenyon Martin	.75	.30
❑ 52	Jason Kidd	1.25	.50

❏ 53	Richard Jefferson	.50	.20
❏ 54	Jamal Mashburn	.50	.20
❏ 55	Baron Davis	.75	.30
❏ 56	Jamaal Magloire	.20	.08
❏ 57	Stephon Marbury	.75	.30
❏ 58	Allan Houston	.50	.20
❏ 59	Keith Van Horn	.75	.30
❏ 60	Drew Gooden	.50	.20
❏ 61	Tracy McGrady	2.00	.75
❏ 62	Gordan Giricek	.50	.20
❏ 63	Glenn Robinson	.75	.30
❏ 64	Allen Iverson	1.50	.60
❏ 65	Eric Snow	.50	.20
❏ 66	Antonio McDyess	.50	.20
❏ 67	Amare Stoudemire	2.00	.75
❏ 68	Shawn Marion	.75	.30
❏ 69	Zach Randolph	.75	.30
❏ 70	Rasheed Wallace	.75	.30
❏ 71	Damon Stoudamire	.50	.20
❏ 72	Mike Bibby	.75	.30
❏ 73	Chris Webber	.75	.30
❏ 74	Peja Stojakovic	.75	.30
❏ 75	Brad Miller	.75	.30
❏ 76	Tony Parker	.75	.30
❏ 77	Tim Duncan	1.50	.60
❏ 78	Manu Ginobili	.75	.30
❏ 79	Rashard Lewis	.75	.30
❏ 80	Ray Allen	.75	.30
❏ 81	Vladimir Radmanovic	.20	.08
❏ 82	Morris Peterson	.50	.20
❏ 83	Vince Carter	2.00	.75
❏ 84	Jalen Rose	.75	.30
❏ 85	Andrei Kirilenko	.75	.30
❏ 86	Matt Harpring	.75	.30
❏ 87	Carlos Arroyo	1.25	.50
❏ 88	Jerry Stackhouse	.75	.30
❏ 89	Gilbert Arenas	.75	.30
❏ 90	Larry Hughes	.75	.30
❏ 91	Udonis Haslem RC	5.00	2.00
❏ 92	Brandon Hunter RC	5.00	2.00
❏ 93	Maurice Williams RC	5.00	2.00
❏ 94	Keith Bogans RC	5.00	2.00
❏ 95	Zaur Pachulia RC	5.00	2.00
❏ 96	Willie Green RC	5.00	2.00
❏ 97	Kyle Korver RC	8.00	3.00
❏ 98	James Jones RC	5.00	2.00
❏ 99	Steve Blake RC	5.00	2.00
❏ 100	Travis Hansen RC	5.00	2.00
❏ 101	Jerome Beasley RC	5.00	2.00
❏ 102	Luke Walton RC	5.00	2.00
❏ 103	Jason Kapono RC	5.00	2.00
❏ 104	Maciej Lampe RC	5.00	2.00
❏ 105	Josh Howard RC	8.00	3.00
❏ 106	Leandro Barbosa RC	8.00	3.00
❏ 107	Kendrick Perkins RC	5.00	2.00
❏ 108	Ndudi Ebi RC	5.00	2.00
❏ 109	Brian Cook RC	5.00	2.00
❏ 110	Travis Outlaw RC	5.00	2.00
❏ 111	Zoran Planinic RC	5.00	2.00
❏ 112	Boris Diaw RC	6.00	2.50
❏ 113	Dahntay Jones RC	5.00	2.00
❏ 114	Aleksandar Pavlovic RC	6.00	2.50
❏ 115	David West RC	5.00	2.00
❏ 116	Zarko Cabarkapa RC	5.00	2.00
❏ 117	Troy Bell RC	5.00	2.00
❏ 118	Reece Gaines RC	5.00	2.00
❏ 119	Luke Ridnour RC	6.00	2.50
❏ 120	Marcus Banks RC	5.00	2.00
❏ 121	Nick Collison RC	5.00	2.00
❏ 122	Mickael Pietrus RC	5.00	2.00
❏ 123	Mike Sweetney RC	5.00	2.00
❏ 124	Chris Kaman RC	5.00	2.00
❏ 125	T.J. Ford RC	6.00	2.50
❏ 126	Kirk Hinrich RC	8.00	3.00
❏ 127	Jarvis Hayes RC	5.00	2.00
❏ 128	Dwyane Wade RC	30.00	12.50
❏ 129	Chris Bosh RC	15.00	6.00
❏ 130	Carmelo Anthony RC	25.00	10.00
❏ 131	Darko Milicic RC	12.00	5.00
❏ 132	LeBron James RC	80.00	30.00

1999-00 Upper Deck Victory

❏ COMPLETE SET (440)	60.00	35.00
❏ COMMON CARD (1-380)	.15	.05

TIM DUNCAN
Guard / Forward Color

❏	COMMON ROOKIE (431-440)	1.00	.40
❏	COMMON MJ HITS (381-430)	1.00	.40
❏ 1	Dikembe Mutombo CL	.15	.05
❏ 2	Steve Smith	.25	.08
❏ 3	Dikembe Mutombo	.25	.08
❏ 4	Ed Gray	.15	.05
❏ 5	Alan Henderson	.15	.05
❏ 6	LaPhonso Ellis	.15	.05
❏ 7	Roshown McLeod	.15	.05
❏ 8	Bimbo Coles	.15	.05
❏ 9	Chris Crawford	.15	.05
❏ 10	Anthony Johnson	.15	.05
❏ 11	Antoine Walker CL	.25	.08
❏ 12	Kenny Anderson	.25	.08
❏ 13	Antoine Walker	.40	.15
❏ 14	Greg Minor	.15	.05
❏ 15	Tony Battie	.15	.05
❏ 16	Ron Mercer	.25	.08
❏ 17	Paul Pierce	.40	.15
❏ 18	Vitaly Potapenko	.15	.05
❏ 19	Dana Barros	.15	.05
❏ 20	Walter McCarty	.15	.05
❏ 21	Elden Campbell CL	.15	.05
❏ 22	Elden Campbell	.15	.05
❏ 23	Eddie Jones	.40	.15
❏ 24	David Wesley	.15	.05
❏ 25	Bobby Phills	.15	.05
❏ 26	Derrick Coleman	.25	.08
❏ 27	Anthony Mason	.25	.08
❏ 28	Brad Miller	.15	.05
❏ 29	Eldridge Recasner	.15	.05
❏ 30	Ricky Davis	.25	.08
❏ 31	Toni Kukoc CL	.15	.05
❏ 32	Michael Jordan	2.50	1.00
❏ 33	Brent Barry	.25	.08
❏ 34	Randy Brown	.15	.05
❏ 35	Keith Booth	.15	.05
❏ 36	Kornel David RC	.15	.05
❏ 37	Mark Bryant	.15	.05
❏ 38	Toni Kukoc	.25	.08
❏ 39	Rusty LaRue	.15	.05
❏ 40	Brevin Knight CL	.15	.05
❏ 41	Shawn Kemp	.25	.08
❏ 42	Wesley Person	.15	.05
❏ 43	Johnny Newman	.15	.05
❏ 44	Derek Anderson	.25	.08
❏ 45	Brevin Knight	.15	.05
❏ 46	Bob Sura	.15	.05
❏ 47	Andrew DeClercq	.15	.05
❏ 48	Zydrunas Ilgauskas	.25	.08
❏ 49	Danny Ferry	.15	.05
❏ 50	Steve Nash CL	.25	.08
❏ 51	Michael Finley	.40	.15
❏ 52	Robert Pack	.15	.05
❏ 53	Shawn Bradley	.15	.05
❏ 54	John Williams	.15	.05
❏ 55	Hubert Davis	.15	.05
❏ 56	Dirk Nowitzki	.75	.30
❏ 57	Steve Nash	.40	.15
❏ 58	Chris Anstey	.15	.05
❏ 59	Erick Strickland	.15	.05
❏ 60	Robert Pack	.15	.05
❏ 61	Antonio McDyess	.25	.08
❏ 62	Nick Van Exel	.40	.15
❏ 63	Bryant Stith	.15	.05
❏ 64	Chauncey Billups	.25	.08
❏ 65	Danny Fortson	.15	.05
❏ 66	Eric Williams	.15	.05

❏ 67	Eric Washington	.15	.05
❏ 68	Raef LaFrentz	.25	.08
❏ 69	Johnny Taylor	.15	.05
❏ 70	Jerry Stackhouse CL	.25	.08
❏ 71	Grant Hill	.40	.15
❏ 72	Lindsey Hunter	.15	.05
❏ 73	Bison Dele	.15	.05
❏ 74	Loy Vaught	.15	.05
❏ 75	Jerome Williams	.15	.05
❏ 76	Jerry Stackhouse	.40	.15
❏ 77	Christian Laettner	.25	.08
❏ 78	Jud Buechler	.15	.05
❏ 79	Don Reid	.15	.05
❏ 80	Antawn Jamison CL	.40	.15
❏ 81	John Starks	.25	.08
❏ 82	Antawn Jamison	.60	.25
❏ 83	Adonal Foyle	.15	.05
❏ 84	Jason Caffey	.15	.05
❏ 85	Donyell Marshall	.15	.05
❏ 86	Chris Mills	.15	.05
❏ 87	Tony Delk	.15	.05
❏ 88	Mookie Blaylock	.15	.05
❏ 89	Charles Barkley CL	.40	.15
❏ 90	Hakeem Olajuwon	.40	.15
❏ 91	Scottie Pippen	.60	.25
❏ 92	Charles Barkley	.50	.20
❏ 93	Bryce Drew	.15	.05
❏ 94	Cuttino Mobley	.40	.15
❏ 95	Othella Harrington	.15	.05
❏ 96	Matt Maloney	.15	.05
❏ 97	Michael Dickerson	.25	.08
❏ 98	Matt Bullard	.15	.05
❏ 99	Jalen Rose CL	.25	.08
❏ 100	Reggie Miller	.40	.15
❏ 101	Rik Smits	.25	.08
❏ 102	Jalen Rose	.40	.15
❏ 103	Antonio Davis	.15	.05
❏ 104	Mark Jackson	.25	.08
❏ 105	Sam Perkins	.15	.05
❏ 106	Travis Best	.15	.05
❏ 107	Dale Davis	.15	.05
❏ 108	Chris Mullin	.40	.15
❏ 109	Michael Olowokandi CL	.15	.05
❏ 110	Maurice Taylor	.25	.08
❏ 111	Tyrone Nesby RC	.15	.05
❏ 112	Lamond Murray	.15	.05
❏ 113	Darrick Martin	.15	.05
❏ 114	Michael Olowokandi	.25	.08
❏ 115	Rodney Rogers	.15	.05
❏ 116	Eric Piatkowski	.15	.05
❏ 117	Lorenzen Wright	.15	.05
❏ 118	Brian Skinner	.15	.05
❏ 119	Kobe Bryant CL	.75	.30
❏ 120	Kobe Bryant	1.50	.60
❏ 121	Shaquille O'Neal	1.00	.40
❏ 122	Derek Fisher	.40	.15
❏ 123	Tyronn Lue	.25	.08
❏ 124	Travis Knight	.15	.05
❏ 125	Glen Rice	.25	.08
❏ 126	Derek Harper	.25	.08
❏ 127	Robert Horry	.25	.08
❏ 128	Rick Fox	.25	.08
❏ 129	Tim Hardaway CL	.15	.05
❏ 130	Tim Hardaway	.25	.08
❏ 131	Alonzo Mourning	.25	.08
❏ 132	Keith Askins	.15	.05
❏ 133	Jamal Mashburn	.25	.08
❏ 134	P.J. Brown	.15	.05
❏ 135	Clarence Weatherspoon	.15	.05
❏ 136	Terry Porter	.15	.05
❏ 137	Dan Majerle	.25	.08
❏ 138	Voshon Lenard	.15	.05
❏ 139	Ray Allen CL	.25	.08
❏ 140	Ray Allen	.40	.15
❏ 141	Vinny Del Negro	.15	.05
❏ 142	Glenn Robinson	.40	.15
❏ 143	Dell Curry	.15	.05
❏ 144	Sam Cassell	.40	.15
❏ 145	Haywoode Workman	.15	.05
❏ 146	Armon Gilliam	.15	.05
❏ 147	Robert Traylor	.15	.05
❏ 148	Chris Gatling	.15	.05
❏ 149	Kevin Garnett CL	.40	.15
❏ 150	Kevin Garnett	.75	.30
❏ 151	Malik Sealy	.15	.05
❏ 152	Radoslav Nesterovic	.25	.08

#	Player			#	Player			#	Player		
153	Joe Smith	.25	.08	239	Detlef Schrempf	.25	.08	325	David Robinson DD	.25	.08
154	Sam Mitchell	.15	.05	240	Hersey Hawkins	.25	.08	326	Vin Baker DD	.15	.05
155	Dean Garrett	.15	.05	241	Dale Ellis	.15	.05	327	Vince Carter DD	.50	.20
156	Anthony Peeler	.15	.05	242	Rashard Lewis	.40	.15	328	Bryon Russell DD	.15	.05
157	Tom Hammonds	.15	.05	243	Billy Owens	.15	.05	329	Felipe Lopez DD	.15	.05
158	Bobby Jackson	.25	.08	244	Aaron Williams	.15	.05	330	Juwan Howard DD	.15	.05
159	Jayson Williams CL	.15	.05	245	Vince Carter CL	.50	.50	331	Michael Jordan DD	1.25	.50
160	Keith Van Horn	.40	.15	246	Vince Carter	1.00	.40	332	Jason Kidd CC	.25	.08
161	Stephon Marbury	.40	.15	247	John Wallace	.15	.05	333	Rod Strickland CC	.15	.05
162	Jayson Williams	.15	.05	248	Doug Christie	.25	.08	334	Stephon Marbury CC	.25	.08
163	Kendall Gill	.15	.05	249	Tracy McGrady	1.00	.40	335	Gary Payton CC	.25	.08
164	Kerry Kittles	.15	.05	250	Kevin Willis	.15	.05	336	Mark Jackson CC	.15	.05
165	Jamie Feick CL	.15	.05	251	Michael Stewart	.15	.05	337	John Stockton CC	.25	.08
166	Scott Burrell	.15	.05	252	Dee Brown	.15	.05	338	Brevin Knight CC	.15	.05
167	Lucious Harris	.15	.05	253	John Thomas	.15	.05	339	Bobby Jackson CC	.15	.05
168	Marcus Camby CL	.15	.05	254	Alvin Williams	.15	.05	340	Nick Van Exel CC	.15	.05
169	Patrick Ewing	.40	.15	255	Karl Malone CL	.40	.15	341	Tim Hardaway CC	.25	.08
170	Allan Houston	.25	.08	256	Karl Malone	.40	.15	342	Darrell Armstrong CC	.15	.05
171	Latrell Sprewell	.40	.15	257	John Stockton	.40	.15	343	Avery Johnson CC	.15	.05
172	Kurt Thomas	.25	.08	258	Jacque Vaughn	.15	.05	344	Mike Bibby CC	.25	.08
173	Larry Johnson	.25	.08	259	Bryon Russell	.15	.05	345	Damon Stoudamire CC	.15	.05
174	Chris Childs	.15	.05	260	Howard Eisley	.15	.05	346	Jason Williams CC	.25	.08
175	Marcus Camby	.25	.08	261	Greg Ostertag	.15	.05	347	Allen Iverson PC	.40	.15
176	Charlie Ward	.15	.05	262	Adam Keefe	.15	.05	348	Kobe Bryant PC	.75	.30
177	Chris Dudley	.15	.05	263	Todd Fuller	.15	.05	349	Karl Malone PC	.40	.15
178	Bo Outlaw CL	.15	.05	264	Mike Bibby CL	.25	.08	350	Keith Van Horn PC	.40	.15
179	Anfernee Hardaway	.40	.15	265	Shareef Abdur-Rahim	.40	.15	351	Kevin Garnett PC	.40	.15
180	Darrell Armstrong	.15	.05	266	Mike Bibby	.40	.15	352	Antoine Walker PC	.25	.08
181	Nick Anderson	.15	.05	267	Bryant Reeves	.15	.05	353	Tim Duncan PC	.50	.20
182	Horace Grant	.25	.08	268	Felipe Lopez	.15	.05	354	Scottie Pippen PC	.25	.08
183	Isaac Austin	.15	.05	269	Cherokee Parks	.15	.05	355	Paul Pierce PC	.40	.15
184	Matt Harpring	.40	.15	270	Michael Smith	.15	.05	356	Michael Finley PC	.25	.08
185	Michael Doleac	.15	.05	271	Tony Massenburg	.15	.05	357	Shaquille O'Neal PC	.50	.20
186	Bo Outlaw	.15	.05	272	Rodrick Rhodes	.15	.05	358	Grant Hill PC	.25	.08
187	Allen Iverson CL	.15	.05	273	Juwan Howard CL	.15	.05	359	Jason Williams PC	.25	.08
188	Allen Iverson	.75	.30	274	Juwan Howard	.25	.08	360	Antonio McDyess PC	.15	.05
189	Theo Ratliff	.25	.08	275	Rod Strickland	.25	.08	361	Shareef Abdur-Rahim PC	.25	.08
190	Matt Geiger	.15	.05	276	Mitch Richmond	.25	.08	362	Allen Iverson SC	.40	.15
191	Larry Hughes	.40	.15	277	Otis Thorpe	.15	.05	363	Shaquille O'Neal SC	.50	.20
192	Tyrone Hill	.15	.05	278	Calbert Cheaney	.15	.05	364	Karl Malone SC	.40	.15
193	George Lynch	.15	.05	279	Tracy Murray	.15	.05	365	Shareef Abdur-Rahim SC	.25	.08
194	Eric Snow	.25	.08	280	Ben Wallace	.15	.05	366	Keith Van Horn SC	.40	.15
195	Aaron McKie	.25	.08	281	Terry Davis	.15	.05	367	Tim Duncan SC	.50	.20
196	Harvey Grant	.15	.05	282	Michael Jordan RF	1.25	.50	368	Gary Payton SC	.25	.08
197	Jason Kidd CL	.25	.08	283	Reggie Miller RF	.25	.08	369	Stephon Marbury SC	.25	.08
198	Jason Kidd	.60	.25	284	Dikembe Mutombo RF	.15	.05	370	Antonio McDyess SC	.25	.08
199	Tom Gugliotta	.25	.08	285	Patrick Ewing RF	.25	.08	371	Grant Hill SC	.25	.08
200	Rex Chapman	.15	.05	286	Allan Houston RF	.25	.08	372	Kevin Garnett SC	.40	.15
201	Clifford Robinson	.15	.05	287	Danny Manning RF	.15	.05	373	Shawn Kemp SC	.15	.05
202	Luc Longley	.15	.05	288	Jalen Rose RF	.25	.08	374	Kobe Bryant SC	.75	.30
203	Danny Manning	.15	.05	289	Rasheed Wallace RF	.25	.08	375	Michael Finley SC	.25	.08
204	Pat Garrity	.15	.05	290	Jerry Stackhouse RF	.25	.08	376	Vince Carter SC	.50	.20
205	George McCloud	.15	.05	291	Damon Stoudamire RF	.15	.05	377	Checklist	.15	.05
206	Toby Bailey	.15	.05	292	Kenny Anderson RF	.15	.05	378	Checklist	.15	.05
207	Brian Grant CL	.15	.05	293	Shawn Kemp RF	.15	.05	379	Checklist	.15	.05
208	Rasheed Wallace	.40	.15	294	Vlade Divac RF	.15	.05	380	Checklist	.15	.05
209	Arvydas Sabonis	.25	.08	295	Larry Johnson RF	.15	.05	381	Michael Jordan GH	1.00	.40
210	Damon Stoudamire	.25	.08	296	Jamal Mashburn RF	.15	.05	382	Michael Jordan GH	1.00	.40
211	Brian Grant	.25	.08	297	Ron Harper RF	.15	.05	383	Michael Jordan GH	1.00	.40
212	Isaiah Rider	.15	.05	298	Steve Smith RF	.15	.05	384	Michael Jordan GH	1.00	.40
213	Walt Williams	.15	.05	299	Kendall Gill RF	.15	.05	385	Michael Jordan GH	1.00	.40
214	Jim Jackson	.15	.05	300	Chris Mullin RF	.25	.08	386	Michael Jordan GH	1.00	.40
215	Greg Anthony	.15	.05	301	Robert Horry RF	.15	.05	387	Michael Jordan GH	1.00	.40
216	Stacey Augmon	.15	.05	302	Dikembe Mutombo DD	.15	.05	388	Michael Jordan GH	1.00	.40
217	Vlade Divac CL	.15	.05	303	Ron Mercer DD	.25	.08	389	Michael Jordan GH	1.00	.40
218	Jason Williams	.40	.15	304	Eddie Jones DD	.25	.08	390	Michael Jordan GH	1.00	.40
219	Vlade Divac	.25	.08	305	Toni Kukoc DD	.15	.05	391	Michael Jordan GH	1.00	.40
220	Chris Webber	.40	.15	306	Derek Anderson DD	.15	.05	392	Michael Jordan GH	1.00	.40
221	Nick Anderson	.15	.05	307	Shawn Bradley DD	.15	.05	393	Michael Jordan GH	1.00	.40
222	Peja Stojakovic	.50	.20	308	Danny Fortson DD	.15	.05	394	Michael Jordan GH	1.00	.40
223	Tariq Abdul-Wahad	.15	.05	309	Brian Dele DD	.15	.05	395	Michael Jordan GH	1.00	.40
224	Vernon Maxwell	.15	.05	310	Antawn Jamison DD	.40	.15	396	Michael Jordan GH	1.00	.40
225	Lawrence Funderburke	.15	.05	311	Scottie Pippen DD	.25	.08	397	Michael Jordan GH	1.00	.40
226	Jon Barry	.15	.05	312	Reggie Miller DD	.25	.08	398	Michael Jordan GH	1.00	.40
227	David Robinson CL	.25	.08	313	Maurice Taylor DD	.15	.05	399	Michael Jordan GH	1.00	.40
228	Tim Duncan	.75	.30	314	Glen Rice DD	.15	.05	400	Michael Jordan GH	1.00	.40
229	Sean Elliott	.25	.08	315	Alonzo Mourning DD	.25	.08	401	Michael Jordan GH	1.00	.40
230	David Robinson	.40	.15	316	Glenn Robinson DD	.25	.08	402	Michael Jordan GH	1.00	.40
231	Mario Elie	.15	.05	317	Anthony Peeler DD	.15	.05	403	Michael Jordan GH	1.00	.40
232	Avery Johnson	.15	.05	318	Kerry Kittles DD	.15	.05	404	Michael Jordan GH	1.00	.40
233	Steve Kerr	.25	.08	319	Latrell Sprewell DD	.40	.15	405	Michael Jordan GH	1.00	.40
234	Malik Rose	.15	.05	320	Darrell Armstrong DD	.15	.05	406	Michael Jordan GH	1.00	.40
235	Jim Jackson	.15	.05	321	Larry Hughes DD	.25	.08	407	Michael Jordan GH	1.00	.40
236	Vin Baker CL	.15	.05	322	Tom Gugliotta DD	.15	.05	408	Michael Jordan GH	1.00	.40
237	Gary Payton	.40	.15	323	Brian Grant DD	.15	.05	409	Michael Jordan GH	1.00	.40
238	Vin Baker	.25	.08	324	Chris Webber DD	.25	.08	410	Michael Jordan GH	1.00	.40

#	Player		
411	Michael Jordan GH	1.00	.40
412	Michael Jordan GH	1.00	.40
413	Michael Jordan GH	1.00	.40
414	Michael Jordan GH	1.00	.40
415	Michael Jordan GH	1.00	.40
416	Michael Jordan GH	1.00	.40
417	Michael Jordan GH	1.00	.40
418	Michael Jordan GH	1.00	.40
419	Michael Jordan GH	1.00	.40
420	Michael Jordan GH	1.00	.40
421	Michael Jordan GH	1.00	.40
422	Michael Jordan GH	1.00	.40
423	Michael Jordan GH	1.00	.40
424	Michael Jordan GH	1.00	.40
425	Michael Jordan GH	1.00	.40
426	Michael Jordan GH	1.00	.40
427	Michael Jordan GH	1.00	.40
428	Michael Jordan GH	1.00	.40
429	Michael Jordan GH	1.00	.40
430	Michael Jordan GH	1.00	.40
431	Elton Brand RC	2.00	.75
432	Steve Francis RC	2.00	.75
433	Baron Davis RC	3.00	1.25
434	Lamar Odom RC	1.50	.60
435	Wally Szczerbiak RC	1.50	.60
436	Richard Hamilton RC	1.50	.60
437	Andre Miller RC	1.50	.60
438	Shawn Marion RC	2.00	.75
439	Jason Terry RC	1.25	.50
440	Corey Maggette RC	1.50	.60

2000-01 Upper Deck Victory

#	Player		
	COMPLETE SET (330)	60.00	30.00
	COMMON CARD (1-260)	.15	.05
	COMMON KOBE (281-305)	.60	.25
	COMMON KG (306-330)	.50	.20
	COMMON ROOKIE (261-280)	.60	.25
1	Dikembe Mutombo	.25	.08
2	Jim Jackson	.15	.05
3	Jason Terry	.40	.15
4	Roshown McLeod	.15	.05
5	Alan Henderson	.15	.05
6	Bimbo Coles	.15	.05
7	Dion Glover	.15	.05
8	Lorenzen Wright	.15	.05
9	Paul Pierce	.40	.15
10	Kenny Anderson	.25	.08
11	Antoine Walker	.40	.15
12	Adrian Griffin	.15	.05
13	Vitaly Potapenko	.15	.05
14	Dana Barros	.15	.05
15	Eric Williams	.15	.05
16	Calbert Cheaney	.15	.05
17	Derrick Coleman	.15	.05
18	Eddie Jones	.40	.15
19	Anthony Mason	.25	.08
20	Elden Campbell	.15	.05
21	Eddie Robinson	.25	.08
22	David Wesley	.15	.05
23	Baron Davis	.40	.15
24	Ricky Davis	.25	.08
25	Elton Brand	.40	.15
26	Ron Artest	.25	.08
27	Chris Carr	.15	.05
28	Fred Hoiberg	.15	.05
29	Hersey Hawkins	.15	.05
30	Dickey Simpkins	.15	.05
31	Corey Benjamin	.15	.05
32	Matt Maloney	.15	.05
33	Shawn Kemp	.25	.08
34	Lamond Murray	.15	.05
35	Wesley Person	.15	.05
36	Andre Miller	.25	.08
37	Bob Sura	.15	.05
38	Andrew DeClercq	.15	.05
39	Brevin Knight	.15	.05
40	Earl Boykins RC	2.00	.75
41	Michael Finley	.40	.15
42	Dirk Nowitzki	.60	.25
43	Cedric Ceballos	.15	.05
44	Robert Pack	.15	.05
45	Erick Strickland	.15	.05
46	Sean Rooks	.15	.05
47	Shawn Bradley	.15	.05
48	Steve Nash	.40	.15
49	Antonio McDyess	.25	.08
50	Nick Van Exel	.40	.15
51	Keon Clark	.25	.08
52	Raef LaFrentz	.25	.08
53	James Posey	.25	.08
54	Chris Gatling	.15	.05
55	George McCloud	.15	.05
56	Bryant Stith	.15	.05
57	Jerry Stackhouse	.40	.15
58	Lindsey Hunter	.15	.05
59	Christian Laettner	.25	.08
60	Jerome Williams	.15	.05
61	Michael Curry	.15	.05
62	Loy Vaught	.15	.05
63	Eric Montross	.15	.05
64	Grant Hill	.40	.15
65	Antawn Jamison	.40	.15
66	Chris Mills	.15	.05
67	Vonteego Cummings	.15	.05
68	Larry Hughes	.25	.08
69	Donyell Marshall	.25	.08
70	Mookie Blaylock	.15	.05
71	Erick Dampier	.25	.08
72	Jason Caffey	.15	.05
73	Steve Francis	.40	.15
74	Shandon Anderson	.15	.05
75	Hakeem Olajuwon	.40	.15
76	Walt Williams	.15	.05
77	Kenny Thomas	.15	.05
78	Carlos Rogers	.15	.05
79	Bryce Drew	.15	.05
80	Kelvin Cato	.15	.05
81	Reggie Miller	.40	.15
82	Austin Croshere	.25	.08
83	Rik Smits	.25	.08
84	Jalen Rose	.40	.15
85	Dale Davis	.15	.05
86	Jonathan Bender	.25	.08
87	Travis Best	.15	.05
88	Chris Mullin	.40	.15
89	Lamar Odom	.40	.15
90	Tyrone Nesby	.15	.05
91	Michael Olowokandi	.15	.05
92	Eric Piatkowski	.25	.08
93	Jeff McInnis	.15	.05
94	Brian Skinner	.15	.05
95	Pete Chilcutt	.15	.05
96	Eric Murdock	.15	.05
97	Shaquille O'Neal	1.00	.40
98	Kobe Bryant	1.50	.60
99	Ron Harper	.25	.08
100	Robert Horry	.25	.08
101	Rick Fox	.25	.08
102	Derek Fisher	.40	.15
103	Tyronn Lue	.25	.08
104	Devean George	.25	.08
105	Alonzo Mourning	.25	.08
106	Jamal Mashburn	.25	.08
107	Anthony Carter	.25	.08
108	P.J. Brown	.15	.05
109	Clarence Weatherspoon	.15	.05
110	Otis Thorpe	.15	.05
111	Voshon Lenard	.15	.05
112	Tim Hardaway	.25	.08
113	Ray Allen	.40	.15
114	Glenn Robinson	.40	.15
115	Sam Cassell	.40	.15
116	Robert Traylor	.15	.05
117	Ervin Johnson	.15	.05
118	Scott Williams	.15	.05
119	Tim Thomas	.25	.08
120	Vinny Del Negro	.15	.05
121	Kevin Garnett	.75	.30
122	Wally Szczerbiak	.25	.08
123	Terrell Brandon	.25	.08
124	Dean Garrett	.15	.05
125	William Avery	.15	.05
126	Sam Mitchell	.15	.05
127	Radoslav Nesterovic	.25	.08
128	Anthony Peeler	.15	.05
129	Stephon Marbury	.40	.15
130	Keith Van Horn	.40	.15
131	Kerry Kittles	.15	.05
132	Lucious Harris	.15	.05
133	Evan Eschmeyer	.15	.05
134	Jamie Feick	.15	.05
135	Jim McIlvaine	.15	.05
136	Kendall Gill	.15	.05
137	Allan Houston	.25	.08
138	Marcus Camby	.25	.08
139	Latrell Sprewell	.40	.15
140	Patrick Ewing	.40	.15
141	Larry Johnson	.25	.08
142	Charlie Ward	.15	.05
143	Chris Childs	.15	.05
144	John Wallace	.15	.05
145	Darrell Armstrong	.15	.05
146	Corey Maggette	.25	.08
147	Pat Garrity	.15	.05
148	John Amaechi	.15	.05
149	Matt Harpring	.40	.15
150	Michael Doleac	.15	.05
151	Ron Mercer	.25	.08
152	Chucky Atkins	.15	.05
153	Allen Iverson	.75	.30
154	Matt Geiger	.15	.05
155	Eric Snow	.15	.05
156	Tyrone Hill	.15	.05
157	Theo Ratliff	.15	.05
158	George Lynch	.15	.05
159	Kevin Ollie	.15	.05
160	Toni Kukoc	.25	.08
161	Jason Kidd	.60	.25
162	Anfernee Hardaway	.40	.15
163	Rodney Rogers	.15	.05
164	Shawn Marion	.40	.15
165	Clifford Robinson	.15	.05
166	Tom Gugliotta	.15	.05
167	Luc Longley	.15	.05
168	Randy Livingston	.15	.05
169	Scottie Pippen	.60	.25
170	Steve Smith	.25	.08
171	Damon Stoudamire	.25	.08
172	Bonzi Wells	.25	.08
173	Jermaine O'Neal	.40	.15
174	Arvydas Sabonis	.25	.08
175	Rasheed Wallace	.40	.15
176	Detlef Schrempf	.25	.08
177	Jason Williams	.25	.08
178	Chris Webber	.40	.15
179	Peja Stojakovic	.40	.15
180	Vlade Divac	.25	.08
181	Lawrence Funderburke	.15	.05
182	Tony Delk	.15	.05
183	Jon Barry	.15	.05
184	Tim Duncan	.75	.30
185	Sean Elliott	.25	.08
186	Terry Porter	.15	.05
187	David Robinson	.40	.15
188	Samaki Walker	.15	.05
189	Malik Rose	.15	.05
190	Jaren Jackson	.15	.05
191	Steve Kerr	.25	.08
192	Gary Payton	.40	.15
193	Brent Barry	.25	.08
194	Vin Baker	.25	.08
195	Horace Grant	.25	.08
196	Ruben Patterson	.15	.05
197	Vernon Maxwell	.15	.05
198	Shammond Williams	.15	.05
199	Rashard Lewis	.25	.08
200	Tracy McGrady	1.00	.40
201	Charles Oakley	.15	.05
202	Doug Christie	.25	.08

#	Player		
203	Antonio Davis	.15	.05
204	Vince Carter	1.00	.40
205	Kevin Willis	.15	.05
206	Dell Curry	.15	.05
207	Dee Brown	.15	.05
208	Karl Malone	.40	.15
209	John Stockton	.40	.15
210	Bryon Russell	.15	.05
211	Olden Polynice	.15	.05
212	Jacque Vaughn	.15	.05
213	Greg Ostertag	.15	.05
214	Quincy Lewis	.15	.05
215	Armon Gilliam	.15	.05
216	Shareef Abdur-Rahim	.40	.15
217	Michael Dickerson	.25	.08
218	Mike Bibby	.40	.15
219	Bryant Reeves	.15	.05
220	Othella Harrington	.15	.05
221	Grant Long	.15	.05
222	Felipe Lopez	.15	.05
223	Obinna Ekezie	.15	.05
224	Mitch Richmond	.25	.08
225	Richard Hamilton	.25	.08
226	Tracy Murray	.15	.05
227	Jahidi White	.15	.05
228	Aaron Williams	.15	.05
229	Juwan Howard	.25	.08
230	Rod Strickland	.15	.05
231	Isaac Austin	.15	.05
232	Dikembe Mutombo VL	.15	.05
233	Antoine Walker VL	.25	.08
234	Derrick Coleman VL	.15	.05
235	Elton Brand VL	.25	.08
236	Shawn Kemp VL	.15	.05
237	Michael Finley VL	.25	.08
238	Antonio McDyess VL	.25	.08
239	Grant Hill VL	.25	.08
240	Antawn Jamison VL	.40	.15
241	Steve Francis VL	.25	.08
242	Jalen Rose VL	.25	.08
243	Lamar Odom VL	.25	.08
244	Shaquille O'Neal VL	.50	.20
245	Alonzo Mourning VL	.25	.08
246	Ray Allen VL	.25	.08
247	Kevin Garnett VL	.40	.15
248	Stephon Marbury VL	.25	.08
249	Allan Houston VL	.25	.08
250	Darrell Armstrong VL	.15	.05
251	Allen Iverson VL	.40	.15
252	Jason Kidd VL	.40	.15
253	Rasheed Wallace VL	.25	.08
254	Chris Webber VL	.25	.08
255	Tim Duncan VL	.40	.15
256	Gary Payton VL	.40	.15
257	Vince Carter VL	.50	.20
258	Karl Malone VL	.25	.08
259	Shareef Abdur-Rahim VL	.25	.08
260	Mitch Richmond VL	.15	.05
261	Kenyon Martin RC	2.50	1.00
262	Marcus Fizer RC	.60	.25
263	Chris Mihm RC	.60	.25
264	Stromile Swift RC	1.25	.50
265	Keyon Dooling RC	.60	.25
266	Morris Peterson RC	1.25	.50
267	Quentin Richardson RC	2.00	.75
268	Courtney Alexander RC	.60	.25
269	Desmond Mason RC	.60	.25
270	Mateen Cleaves RC	.60	.25
271	A.J. Guyton RC	.60	.25
272	Darius Miles RC	2.00	.75
273	DerMarr Johnson RC	.60	.25
274	Joel Przybilla RC	.60	.25
275	Hanno Mottola RC	.60	.25
276	Mike Miller RC	2.00	.75
277	Donnell Harvey RC	.60	.25
278	Speedy Claxton RC	.60	.25
279	Khalid El-Amin RC	.60	.25
280	Kobe Bryant FLY	.60	.25
281	Kobe Bryant FLY	.60	.25
282	Kobe Bryant FLY	.60	.25
283	Kobe Bryant FLY	.60	.25
284	Kobe Bryant FLY	.60	.25
285	Kobe Bryant FLY	.60	.25
286	Kobe Bryant FLY	.60	.25
287	Kobe Bryant FLY	.60	.25
288	Kobe Bryant FLY	.60	.25
289	Kobe Bryant FLY	.60	.25
290	Kobe Bryant FLY	.60	.25
291	Kobe Bryant FLY	.60	.25
292	Kobe Bryant FLY	.60	.25
293	Kobe Bryant FLY	.60	.25
294	Kobe Bryant FLY	.60	.25
295	Kobe Bryant FLY	.60	.25
296	Kobe Bryant FLY	.60	.25
297	Kobe Bryant FLY	.60	.25
298	Kobe Bryant FLY	.60	.25
299	Kobe Bryant FLY	.60	.25
300	Kobe Bryant FLY	.60	.25
301	Kobe Bryant FLY	.60	.25
302	Kobe Bryant FLY	.60	.25
303	Kobe Bryant FLY	.60	.25
304	Kobe Bryant FLY	.60	.25
305	Kobe Bryant FLY	.60	.25
306	Kevin Garnett FLY	.50	.20
307	Kevin Garnett FLY	.50	.20
308	Kevin Garnett FLY	.50	.20
309	Kevin Garnett FLY	.50	.20
310	Kevin Garnett FLY	.50	.20
311	Kevin Garnett FLY	.50	.20
312	Kevin Garnett FLY	.50	.20
313	Kevin Garnett FLY	.50	.20
314	Kevin Garnett FLY	.50	.20
315	Kevin Garnett FLY	.50	.20
316	Kevin Garnett FLY	.50	.20
317	Kevin Garnett FLY	.50	.20
318	Kevin Garnett FLY	.50	.20
319	Kevin Garnett FLY	.50	.20
320	Kevin Garnett FLY	.50	.20
321	Kevin Garnett FLY	.50	.20
322	Kevin Garnett FLY	.50	.20
323	Kevin Garnett FLY	.50	.20
324	Kevin Garnett FLY	.50	.20
325	Kevin Garnett FLY	.50	.20
326	Kevin Garnett FLY	.50	.20
327	Kevin Garnett FLY	.50	.20
328	Kevin Garnett FLY	.50	.20
329	Kevin Garnett FLY	.50	.20
330	Kevin Garnett FLY	.50	.20

2003-04 Upper Deck Victory

#	Player		
	COMP.SET w/o SP's (100)	15.00	6.00
	COMMON ROOKIE (101-181)	1.50	.60
	COMMON POD (182-201)	1.00	.40
1	Shareef Abdur-Rahim	.25	.10
2	Jason Terry	.25	.10
3	Glenn Robinson	.25	.10
4	Paul Pierce	.25	.10
5	Antoine Walker	.25	.10
6	J.R.Bremer	.10	.02
7	Vin Baker	.20	.08
8	Jalen Rose	.20	.08
9	Tyson Chandler	.25	.10
10	Eddy Curry	.25	.10
11	Jay Williams	.20	.08
12	DaJuan Wagner	.20	.08
13	Ricky Davis	.25	.10
14	Zydrunas Ilgauskas	.20	.08
15	Darius Miles	.25	.10
16	Dirk Nowitzki	.50	.20
17A	Michael Finley	.25	.10
17B	Jermaine O'Neal	.25	.10
18	Steve Nash	.25	.10
19	Nick Van Exel	.25	.10
20	Rodney White	.10	.02
21	Juwan Howard	.20	.08
22	Marcus Camby	.20	.08
23	Nene Hilario	.20	.08
24	Richard Hamilton	.20	.08
25	Ben Wallace	.25	.10
26	Cliff Robinson	.10	.02
27	Antawn Jamison	.25	.10
28	Jason Richardson	.25	.10
29	Gilbert Arenas	.25	.10
30	Mike Dunleavy	.20	.08
31	Steve Francis	.25	.10
32	Eddie Griffin	.20	.08
33	Cuttino Mobley	.20	.08
34	Yao Ming	1.50	.60
35	Reggie Miller	.25	.10
36	Jamaal Tinsley	.25	.10
37	Does Not Exist		
38	Elton Brand	.25	.10
39	Andre Miller	.20	.08
40	Lamar Odom	.25	.10
41	Kobe Bryant	1.25	.50
42	Shaquille O'Neal	.75	.30
43	Derek Fisher	.25	.10
44	Pau Gasol	.25	.10
45	Shane Battier	.25	.10
46	Mike Miller	.25	.10
47	Eddie Jones	.25	.10
48	Alonzo Mourning	.20	.08
49	Caron Butler	.25	.10
50	Gary Payton	.25	.10
51	Desmond Mason	.20	.08
52	Sam Cassell	.25	.10
53	Toni Kukoc	.20	.08
54	Kevin Garnett	.60	.25
55	Wally Szczerbiak	.20	.08
56	Joe Smith	.20	.08
57	Jason Kidd	.50	.20
58	Richard Jefferson	.20	.08
59	Kenyon Martin	.25	.10
60	Baron Davis	.25	.10
61	Jamal Mashburn	.20	.08
62	Jamaal Magloire	.10	.02
63	Allan Houston	.20	.08
64	Antonio McDyess	.20	.08
65	Latrell Sprewell	.25	.10
66	Tracy McGrady	1.00	.40
67	Grant Hill	.25	.10
68	Drew Gooden	.20	.08
69	Gordan Giricek	.20	.08
70	Allen Iverson	.60	.25
71	Keth Van Horn	.25	.10
72	Aaron McKie	.20	.08
73	Stephon Marbury	.25	.10
74	Shawn Marion	.25	.10
75	Anfernee Hardaway	.25	.10
76	Amare Stoudemire	.60	.25
77	Rasheed Wallace	.25	.10
78	Derek Anderson	.20	.08
79	Scottie Pippen	.50	.20
80	Chris Webber	.25	.10
81	Mike Bibby	.25	.10
82	Peja Stojakovic	.25	.10
83	Hedo Turkoglu	.25	.10
84	Tim Duncan	.60	.25
85	David Robinson	.25	.10
86	Tony Parker	.25	.10
87	Manu Ginobili	.25	.10
88	Ray Allen	.25	.10
89	Rashard Lewis	.25	.10
90	Reggie Evans	.10	.02
91	Alvin Williams	.10	.02
92	Vince Carter	.75	.30
93	Morris Peterson	.20	.08
94	Antonio Davis	.10	.02
95	Karl Malone	.25	.10
96	John Stockton	.25	.10
97	Andrei Kirilenko	.25	.10
98	Jerry Stackhouse	.25	.10
99	Kwame Brown	.20	.08
100	Michael Jordan	3.00	1.25
101	Lebron James SP RC	15.00	6.00
102	Darko Milicic RC	2.00	.75
103	Carmelo Anthony RC	6.00	2.50
104	Chris Bosh RC	5.00	2.00
105	Dwyane Wade RC	6.00	2.50

#	Card	Hi	Lo
106	Chris Kaman RC	1.50	.60
107	Kirk Hinrich RC	2.50	1.00
108	T.J. Ford RC	2.00	.75
109	Mike Sweetney RC	1.50	.60
110	Jarvis Hayes RC	1.50	.60
111	Mickael Pietrus RC	1.50	.60
112	Nick Collison RC	1.50	.60
113	Marcus Banks RC	1.50	.60
114	Luke Ridnour RC	2.00	.75
115	Reece Gaines RC	1.50	.60
116	Troy Bell RC	1.50	.60
117	Zarko Cabarkapa RC	1.50	.60
118	David West RC	1.50	.60
119	Aleksandar Pavlovic RC	2.00	.75
120	Dahntay Jones RC	1.50	.60
121	Boris Diaw RC	2.00	.75
122	Zoran Planinic RC	1.50	.60
123	Travis Outlaw RC	1.50	.60
124	Brian Cook RC	1.50	.60
125	Carlos Delfino RC	1.50	.60
126	Ndudi Ebi RC	1.50	.60
127	Kendrick Perkins RC	1.50	.60
129	Leandro Barbosa RC	2.50	1.00
129	Josh Howard RC	2.00	.75
134	Maciej Lampe RC	2.00	.75
134	Michael Jordan AS	10.00	4.00
135	Kobe Bryant AS	5.00	2.00
136	Kevin Garnett AS	3.00	1.25
137	Yao Ming AS	3.00	1.25
138	Vince Carter AS	3.00	1.25
139	Dirk Nowitzki AS	2.00	.75
140	Antoine Walker AS	1.00	.40
141	Chris Webber AS		
142	Ben Wallace AS	1.00	.40
143	Tracy McGrady AS	3.00	1.25
144	Jason Kidd AS	2.00	.75
145	Steve Francis AS		
146	Gary Payton AS	1.00	.40
147	Peja Stojakovic AS	1.00	.40
148	Brad Miller AS	1.25	.50
149	Shawn Marion AS	1.00	.40
150	Zydrunas Ilgauskas AS	.75	.30
151	Stephon Marbury AS	1.00	.40
152	Jermaine O'Neal AS	1.00	.40
153	Desmond Mason AS	.75	.30
155	Jason Richardson AS		
155	Tony Parker AS	1.00	.40
156	Tim Duncan AS	2.50	1.00
157	Jamal Mashburn AS	1.00	.40
158	Allen Iverson AS	2.50	1.00
159	Shaquille O'Neal AS	3.00	1.25
160	Paul Pierce AS	1.00	.40
161	Steve Nash AS	1.00	.40
162	Michael Jordan CS	10.00	4.00
163	Mike Bibby CS	1.00	.40
164	Jay Williams CS	.75	.30
165	Richard Hamilton CS	.75	.30
166	Jerry Stackhouse CS	1.00	.40
167	Peja Stojakovic CS	1.00	.40
168	Reggie Miller CS	1.00	.40
169	Robert Horry CS	1.00	.40
170	Tim Duncan CS	2.50	1.00
171	Jalen Rose CS	1.00	.40
172	Jason Richardson CS	2.00	.75
173	Allen Iverson CS	2.50	1.00
174	Tracy McGrady CS	3.00	1.25
175	Paul Pierce CS	1.00	.40
176	Dirk Nowitzki CS	1.00	.40
177	Baron Davis CS	1.00	.40
178	Latrell Sprewell CS	1.00	.40
179	John Stockton CS	1.00	.40
180	Ray Allen CS	1.00	.40
181	Kobe Bryant CS	5.00	2.00
182	Mike Bibby POD	1.00	.40
183	Earl Boykins POD	1.00	.40
184	John Stockton POD	1.00	.40
185	Alvin Williams POD	1.00	.40
186	Darrell Armstrong POD	1.00	.40
187	Tony Parker POD	1.00	.40
188	Gary Payton POD	1.00	.40
189	Jalen Rose POD	1.00	.40
190	Jason Williams POD	1.00	.40
191	Derek Fisher POD	1.00	.40
192	Steve Nash POD	1.00	.40
193	Jamaal Tinsley POD	1.00	.40
194	Andre Miller POD	1.00	.40
195	Baron Davis POD	1.00	.40
196	Steve Francis POD	1.00	.40
197	DaJuan Wagner POD	1.00	.40
198	Stephon Marbury POD	1.00	.40
199	Jason Kidd POD	2.00	.75
200	Chauncey Billups POD	1.00	.40
201	Jay Williams POD	1.00	.40
202	Allen Iverson AKA	4.00	1.50
203	Steve Francis AKA	3.00	1.25
204	Kenyon Martin AKA	1.50	.60
205	Vince Carter AKA	3.00	1.25
206	Lebron James AKA	10.00	4.00
207	Julius Erving AKA	1.50	.60
208	Tracy McGrady AKA	5.00	2.00
209	Jason Richardson AKA	3.00	1.25
210	Earvin Johnson AKA	4.00	1.50
211	Michael Jordan AKA	15.00	6.00
212	Michael Jordan AKA	15.00	6.00
213	Kobe Bryant MJ	8.00	3.00
214	Richard Jefferson MJ	1.25	.50
215	Desmond Mason MJ	1.25	.50
216	Vince Carter MJ	5.00	2.00
217	Amare Stoudemire MJ	4.00	1.50
218	Yao Ming MJ	5.00	2.00
219	Elton Brand MJ	1.50	.60
220	Kevin Garnett MJ	4.00	1.50
221	Shaquille O'Neal MJ	5.00	2.00
222	Lebron James HR	15.00	6.00
223	Kobe Bryant HR	10.00	4.00
224	Richard Jefferson HR	1.50	.60
225	Yao Ming HR	6.00	2.50
226	Amare Stoudemire HR	1.50	.60
227	Michael Jordan FL	12.00	5.00
228	Michael Jordan FL	12.00	5.00
229	Michael Jordan FL	12.00	5.00
230	Michael Jordan FL	12.00	5.00
231	Michael Jordan FL	12.00	5.00
232	Michael Jordan FL	12.00	5.00
233	Michael Jordan FL	12.00	5.00

2005 WNBA

MINNESOTA LYNX
KATIE SMITH

#	Card	Hi	Lo
	COMPLETE SET (110)	30.00	12.50
	COMMON CARD	.20	.08
1	Seattle Storm TC	5.00	2.00
2	LaToya Thomas	.20	.08
3	Crystal Robinson	.20	.08
4	Chasity Melvin	.20	.08
5	Dawn Staley	1.50	.60
6	Svetlana Abrosimova	.75	.30
7	Houston Comets TC	1.50	.60
8	Wendy Palmer-Daniel	1.00	.40
9	Betty Lennox	1.00	.40
10	Lisa Leslie	2.00	.75
11	Margo Dydek	.20	.08
12	Vickie Johnson	.20	.08
13	Charlotte Sting TC	1.50	.60
14	Ayana Walker	.20	.08
15	Shannon Johnson	1.50	.60
16	Tangela Smith	.50	.20
17	Michelle Snow	.75	.30
18	Chandi Jones	.50	.20
19	Adrienne Goodson	.20	.08
20	Lauren Jackson	4.00	1.50
21	Elaine Powell	.20	.08
22	Minnesota Lynx TC	2.00	.75
23	La'Keshia Frett	.20	.08
24	Allison Feaster	.20	.08
25	Lindsay Whalen	.20	.08
26	DeMya Walker	.20	.08
27	Tamecka Dixon	.20	.08
28	Kelly Miller	.20	.08
29	San Antonio Silver Stars TC	1.50	.60
30	Tina Thompson	1.50	.60
31	Tamika Williams	.75	.30
32	Doneeka Hodges RC	2.00	.75
33	Kelly Mazzante	.20	.08
34	Shameka Christon	.20	.08
35	Sheryl Swoopes	2.00	.75
36	Nicole Powell	.20	.08
37	Indiana Fever TC	1.50	.60
38	Alicia Thompson	.20	.08
39	Kristen Rasmussen	.20	.08
40	Diana Taurasi	4.00	1.50
41	Elena Baranova	1.50	.60
42	Taj McWilliams-Franklin	.50	.20
43	Nakia Sanford RC	1.00	.40
44	Tamika Whitmore	.20	.08
45	Katie Smith	2.00	.75
46	Phoenix Mercury TC	1.50	.60
47	Tully Bevilaqua	.20	.08
48	Tari Phillips	.20	.08
49	Charlotte Smith-Taylor	.20	.08
50	Sue Bird	5.00	2.00
51	Natalie Williams	2.00	.75
52	Connecticut Sun TC	2.00	.75
53	Bernadette Ngoyisa RC	1.00	.40
54	Anna DeForge	.20	.08
55	Becky Hammon	4.00	1.50
56	Sacramento Monarchs TC	2.00	.75
57	Mwadi Mabika	.20	.08
58	Asjha Jones	1.25	.50
59	Kamila Vodichkova	.50	.20
60	Yolanda Griffith	1.50	.60
61	Deanna Jackson	.20	.08
62	Le'Coe Willingham RC	1.00	.40
63	Gwen Jackson	.20	.08
64	Erin Buescher	.20	.08
65	Alana Beard	.75	.30
66	New York Liberty TC	2.50	1.00
67	Helen Darling	.20	.08
68	Dominique Canty	.20	.08
69	Marie Ferdinand	.20	.08
70	Tamika Catchings	1.50	.60
71	Kara Lawson	.20	.08
72	Vanessa Hayden	.20	.08
73	Nikki McCray	1.25	.50
74	Washington Mystics TC	1.50	.60
75	Ruth Riley	1.00	.40
76	Penny Taylor	.20	.08
77	Ticha Penicheiro	1.25	.50
78	Katie Douglas	.50	.20
79	Janeth Arcain	.20	.08
80	Swin Cash	1.50	.60
81	Kelly Schumacher	.20	.08
82	Detroit Shock TC	1.50	.60
83	Plenette Pierson	.20	.08
84	Sheri Sam	.75	.30
85	Chamique Holdsclaw	3.00	1.25
86	Delisha Milton-Jones	.20	.08
87	Nicole Ohlde	.20	.08
88	Edna Campbell	.20	.08
89	Tammy Sutton-Brown	.50	.20
90	Nikki Teasley	1.25	.50
91	Ann Wauters	.50	.20
92	Janell Burse	.20	.08
93	Kristi Harrower	.20	.08
94	Murriel Page	.20	.08
95	Cheryl Ford	.50	.20
96	Christi Thomas	.20	.08
97	Brooke Wyckoff	.75	.30
98	Barbara Farris	.20	.08
99	Mandisa Stevenson RC	1.00	.40
100	Nykesha Sales	1.50	.60
101	Jurgita Streimikyte	.20	.08
102	Amber Jacobs RC	1.00	.40
103	Coco Miller	.50	.20
104	Iziane Castro Marques	.20	.08
105	Deanna Nolan	.20	.08
106	Los Angeles	2.00	.75
107	Rebekkah Brunson	.20	.08
108	Checklist 1	.20	.08
109	Checklist 2	.20	.08
110	Checklist 3	.20	.08

P1 Diana Taurasi Promo	6.00	2.50
P1A Becky Hammon Binder	10.00	4.00

2005 WNBA Promo Sheet

NNO Promo Sheet	10.00	4.00

1996-97 Z-Force

COMPLETE SET (200)	40.00	20.00
COMPLETE SERIES 1 (100)	20.00	10.00
COMPLETE SERIES 2 (100)	20.00	10.00
1 Mookie Blaylock	.20	.07
2 Alan Henderson	.20	.07
3 Christian Laettner	.40	.15
4 Steve Smith	.40	.15
5 Rick Fox	.20	.07
6 Dino Radja	.20	.07
7 Eric Williams	.20	.07
8 Muggsy Bogues	.20	.07
9 Larry Johnson	.40	.15
10 Glen Rice	.40	.15
11 Michael Jordan	4.00	1.50
12 Toni Kukoc	.40	.15
13 Scottie Pippen	1.00	.40
14 Dennis Rodman	.40	.15
15 Terrell Brandon	.40	.15
16 Bobby Phills	.20	.07
17 Bob Sura	.20	.07
18 Jim Jackson	.20	.07
19 Jason Kidd	1.00	.40
20 Jamal Mashburn	.40	.15
21 George McCloud	.20	.07
22 Mahmoud Abdul-Rauf	.20	.07
23 Antonio McDyess	.40	.15
24 Dikembe Mutombo	.40	.15
25 Joe Dumars	.60	.25
26 Grant Hill	.60	.25
27 Allan Houston	.40	.15
28 Otis Thorpe	.20	.07
29 Chris Mullin	.60	.25
30 Joe Smith	.40	.15
31 Latrell Sprewell	.40	.15
32 Sam Cassell	.60	.25
33 Clyde Drexler	.60	.25
34 Robert Horry	.40	.15
35 Hakeem Olajuwon	.60	.25
36 Travis Best	.20	.07
37 Dale Davis	.20	.07
38 Reggie Miller	.60	.25
39 Rik Smits	.40	.15
40 Brent Barry	.20	.07
41 Loy Vaught	.20	.07
42 Brian Williams	.40	.15
43 Cedric Ceballos	.20	.07
44 Eddie Jones	.60	.25
45 Nick Van Exel	.60	.25
46 Tim Hardaway	.40	.15
47 Alonzo Mourning	.40	.15
48 Kurt Thomas	.40	.15
49 Walt Williams	.20	.07
50 Vin Baker	.40	.15
51 Glenn Robinson	.40	.15
52 Kevin Garnett	1.25	.50
53 Tom Gugliotta	.20	.07
54 Isaiah Rider	.40	.15
55 Shawn Bradley	.20	.07
56 Chris Childs	.20	.07
57 Jayson Williams	.40	.15
58 Patrick Ewing	.60	.25
59 Anthony Mason	.40	.15
60 Charles Oakley	.20	.07
61 Nick Anderson	.20	.07
62 Horace Grant	.40	.15
63 Anfernee Hardaway	.60	.25
64 Shaquille O'Neal	1.50	.60
65 Dennis Scott	.20	.07
66 Jerry Stackhouse	.75	.30
67 Clarence Weatherspoon	.20	.07
68 Charles Barkley	.75	.30
69 Michael Finley	.75	.30
70 Kevin Johnson	.40	.15
71 Clifford Robinson	.20	.07
72 Arvydas Sabonis	.40	.15
73 Rod Strickland	.20	.07
74 Tyus Edney	.20	.07
75 Brian Grant	.60	.25
76 Billy Owens	.20	.07
77 Mitch Richmond	.40	.15
78 Vinny Del Negro	.20	.07
79 Sean Elliott	.40	.15
80 Avery Johnson	.20	.07
81 David Robinson	.60	.25
82 Hersey Hawkins	.40	.15
83 Shawn Kemp	.60	.25
84 Gary Payton	.60	.25
85 Detlef Schrempf	.40	.15
86 Doug Christie	.40	.15
87 Damon Stoudamire	.60	.25
88 Sharone Wright	.20	.07
89 Jeff Hornacek	.40	.15
90 Karl Malone	.60	.25
91 John Stockton	.60	.25
92 Greg Anthony	.20	.07
93 Bryant Reeves	.40	.15
94 Byron Scott	.20	.07
95 Juwan Howard	.40	.15
96 Gheorghe Muresan	.20	.07
97 Rasheed Wallace	.75	.30
98 Chris Webber	.60	.25
99 Checklist	.20	.07
100 Checklist	.20	.07
101 Dikembe Mutombo	.40	.15
102 Dee Brown	.20	.07
103 Dell Curry	.20	.07
104 Vlade Divac	.20	.07
105 Anthony Mason	.40	.15
106 Robert Parish	.40	.15
107 Oliver Miller	.20	.07
108 Eric Montross	.20	.07
109 Ervin Johnson	.20	.07
110 Stacey Augmon	.20	.07
111 Charles Barkley	.75	.30
112 Jalen Rose	.60	.25
113 Rodney Rogers	.20	.07
114 Shaquille O'Neal	1.50	.60
115 Dan Majerle	.40	.15
116 Kendall Gill	.20	.07
117 Khalid Reeves	.20	.07
118 Allan Houston	.40	.15
119 Larry Johnson	.40	.15
120 John Starks	.40	.15
121 Rony Seikaly	.20	.07
122 Gerald Wilkins	.20	.07
123 Michael Cage	.20	.07
124 Derrick Coleman	.20	.15
125 Sam Cassell	.60	.25
126 Danny Manning	.40	.15
127 Robert Horry	.40	.15
128 Kenny Anderson	.20	.07
129 Isaiah Rider	.40	.15
130 Rasheed Wallace	.75	.30
131 Mahmoud Abdul-Rauf	.20	.07
132 Vernon Maxwell	.20	.07
133 Dominique Wilkins	.60	.25
134 Hubert Davis	.20	.07
135 Popeye Jones	.20	.07
136 Anthony Peeler	.20	.07
137 Tracy Murray	.20	.07
138 Rod Strickland	.20	.07
139 Shareef Abdur-Rahim RC	2.00	.75
140 Ray Allen RC	2.00	.75
141 Shandon Anderson RC	.40	.15
142 Kobe Bryant RC	8.00	3.00
143 Marcus Camby RC	.75	.30
144 Erick Dampier RC	.60	.25
145 Emanual Davis RC	.20	.07
146 Tony Delk RC	.60	.25
147 Todd Fuller RC	.20	.07
148 Darvin Ham RC	.20	.07
149 Othella Harrington RC	.20	.07
150 Shane Heal RC	.20	.07
151 Allen Iverson RC	3.00	1.25
152 Dontae' Jones RC	.20	.07
153 Kerry Kittles RC	.60	.25
154 Priest Lauderdale RC	.20	.07
155 Matt Maloney RC	.40	.15
156 Stephon Marbury RC	1.50	.60
157 Walter McCarty RC	.20	.07
158 Steve Nash RC	5.00	2.00
159 Jermaine O'Neal RC	2.00	.75
160 Ray Owes RC	.20	.07
161 Vitaly Potapenko RC	.20	.07
162 Roy Rogers RC	.20	.07
163 Antoine Walker RC	2.00	.75
164 Samaki Walker RC	.20	.07
165 Ben Wallace RC	4.00	1.50
166 John Wallace RC	.60	.25
167 Jerome Williams RC	.60	.25
168 Lorenzen Wright RC	.40	.15
169 Vin Baker ZUP	.20	.07
170 Charles Barkley ZUP	.60	.25
171 Patrick Ewing ZUP	.40	.15
172 Michael Finley ZUP	.60	.25
173 Kevin Garnett ZUP	.60	.25
174 Anfernee Hardaway ZUP	.40	.15
175 Grant Hill ZUP	.60	.25
176 Juwan Howard ZUP	.20	.07
177 Jim Jackson ZUP	.20	.07
178 Eddie Jones ZUP	.40	.15
179 Michael Jordan ZUP	2.00	.75
180 Shawn Kemp ZUP	.20	.07
181 Jason Kidd ZUP	.60	.25
182 Karl Malone ZUP	.20	.07
183 Antonio McDyess ZUP	.60	.25
184 Reggie Miller ZUP	.40	.15
185 Alonzo Mourning ZUP	.40	.15
186 Hakeem Olajuwon ZUP	.40	.15
187 Shaquille O'Neal ZUP	.60	.25
188 Gary Payton ZUP	.40	.15
189 Mitch Richmond ZUP	.20	.07
190 Clifford Robinson ZUP	.20	.07
191 David Robinson ZUP	.40	.15
192 Glenn Robinson ZUP	.20	.15
193 Dennis Rodman ZUP	.20	.07
194 Joe Smith ZUP	.20	.07
195 Jerry Stackhouse ZUP	.60	.25
196 John Stockton ZUP	.40	.15
197 Damon Stoudamire ZUP	.40	.15
198 Chris Webber ZUP	.60	.25
199 Checklist	.20	.07
200 Checklist	.20	.07
NNO Grant Hill Promo	2.00	.75
NNO Grant Hill Total 2 (100)		
NNO G.Hill/J.Stackhouse Promo	2.00	.75

1997-98 Z-Force

COMPLETE SET (210)	25.00	12.50
COMPLETE SERIES 1 (110)	10.00	5.00
COMPLETE SERIES 2 (100)	15.00	7.50
1 Anfernee Hardaway	.50	.25
2 Mitch Richmond	.30	.10
3 Stephon Marbury	.60	.25
4 Charles Barkley	.60	.25

5	Juwan Howard	.30	.10
6	Avery Johnson	.15	.05
7	Rex Chapman	.15	.05
8	Antoine Walker	.60	.25
9	Nick Van Exel	.50	.20
10	Tim Hardaway	.30	.10
11	Clarence Weatherspoon	.15	.05
12	John Stockton	.50	.20
13	Glenn Robinson	.50	.20
14	Anthony Mason	.30	.10
15	Latrell Sprewell	.50	.20
16	Kendall Gill	.15	.05
17	Terry Mills	.15	.05
18	Mookie Blaylock	.15	.05
19	Michael Finley	.50	.20
20	Gary Payton	.50	.20
21	Kevin Garnett	1.00	.40
22	Clyde Drexler	.50	.20
23	Michael Jordan	3.00	1.25
24	Antonio McDyess	.30	.10
25	Nick Anderson	.15	.05
26	Patrick Ewing	.50	.20
27	Anthony Peeler	.15	.05
28	Doug Christie	.30	.10
29	Bobby Phills	.15	.05
30	Kerry Kittles	.50	.20
31	Reggie Miller	.50	.20
32	Karl Malone	.50	.20
33	Grant Hill	1.25	.50
34	Shaquille O'Neal	1.25	.50
35	Loy Vaught	.15	.05
36	Kenny Anderson	.30	.10
37	Wesley Person	.15	.05
38	Jamal Mashburn	.30	.10
39	Christian Laettner	.30	.10
40	Shawn Kemp	.30	.10
41	Glen Rice	.30	.10
42	Vin Baker	.30	.10
43	Popeye Jones	.15	.05
44	Derrick Coleman	.15	.05
45	Rik Smits	.30	.10
46	Dale Ellis	.15	.05
47	Rod Strickland	.15	.05
48	Mark Price	.30	.10
49	Toni Kukoc	.30	.10
50	David Robinson	.50	.20
51	John Wallace	.15	.05
52	Samaki Walker	.15	.05
53	Shareef Abdur-Rahim	.75	.30
54	Rodney Rogers	.15	.05
55	Dikembe Mutombo	.30	.10
56	Rony Seikaly	.15	.05
57	Matt Maloney	.15	.05
58	Chris Webber	.50	.20
59	Robert Horry	.30	.10
60	Rasheed Wallace	.50	.20
61	Jeff Hornacek	.30	.10
62	Walt Williams	.15	.05
63	Detlef Schrempf	.30	.10
64	Dan Majerle	.30	.10
65	Dell Curry	.15	.05
66	Scottie Pippen	.75	.30
67	Greg Anthony	.15	.05
68	Mahmoud Abdul-Rauf	.15	.05
69	Cedric Ceballos	.15	.05
70	Terrell Brandon	.30	.10
71	Arvydas Sabonis	.30	.10
72	Malik Sealy	.15	.05
73	Dean Garrett	.15	.05
74	Joe Dumars	.50	.20
75	Joe Smith	.30	.10
76	Shawn Bradley	.15	.05
77	Gheorghe Muresan	.15	.05
78	Dale Davis	.15	.05
79	Bryant Stith	.15	.05
80	Lorenzen Wright	.15	.05
81	Chris Childs	.15	.05
82	Bryon Russell	.15	.05
83	Steve Smith	.30	.10
84	Jerry Stackhouse	.50	.20
85	Hersey Hawkins	.15	.05
86	Ray Allen	.50	.20
87	Dominique Wilkins	.50	.20
88	Kobe Bryant	2.00	.75
89	Tom Gugliotta	.30	.10
90	Dennis Scott	.15	.05
91	Dennis Rodman	.30	.10
92	Bryant Reeves	.15	.05
93	Vlade Divac	.30	.10
94	Jason Kidd	.75	.30
95	Mario Elie	.15	.05
96	Lindsey Hunter	.15	.05
97	Olden Polynice	.15	.05
98	Allan Houston	.30	.10
99	Alonzo Mourning	.30	.10
100	Allen Iverson	1.25	.50
101	LaPhonso Ellis	.15	.05
102	Bob Sura	.15	.05
103	Chris Mullin	.50	.20
104	Sam Cassell	.50	.20
105	Eric Williams	.15	.05
106	Antonio Davis	.15	.05
107	Marcus Camby	.50	.20
108	Isaiah Rider	.30	.10
109	Checklist (Hawks/Suns)	.15	.05
110	Checklist (TrailBlazers/Wizards/Inserts)	.15	.05
111	Tim Duncan RC	2.00	.75
112	Joe Smith	.30	.10
113	Shawn Kemp	.30	.10
114	Terry Mills	.15	.05
115	Jacque Vaughn RC	.50	.20
116	Ron Mercer RC	.50	.20
117	Brian Williams	.15	.05
118	Rik Smits	.30	.10
119	Eric Williams	.15	.05
120	Tim Thomas RC	.75	.30
121	Damon Stoudamire	.30	.10
122	God Shammgod RC	.15	.05
123	Tyrone Hill	.15	.05
124	Elden Campbell	.15	.05
125	Keith Van Horn RC	.60	.25
126	Brian Grant	.30	.10
127	Antonio McDyess	.30	.10
128	Darrell Armstrong	.15	.05
129	Sam Perkins	.30	.10
130	Chris Mills	.15	.05
131	Reggie Miller	.50	.20
132	Chris Gatling	.15	.05
133	Ed Gray RC	.15	.05
134	Hakeem Olajuwon	.50	.20
135	Chris Webber	.50	.20
136	Kendall Gill	.15	.05
137	Wesley Person	.15	.05
138	Derrick Coleman	.15	.05
139	Dana Barros	.15	.05
140	Dennis Scott	.15	.05
141	Paul Grant RC	.15	.05
142	Scott Burrell	.15	.05
143	Does not Exist		
144	Austin Croshere RC	.40	.15
145	Maurice Taylor RC	.40	.15
146	Kevin Johnson	.30	.10
147	Tony Battie RC	.50	.20
148	Tariq Abdul-Wahad RC	.30	.10
149	Johnny Taylor RC	.15	.05
150	Allen Iverson	1.25	.50
151	Terrell Brandon	.30	.10
152	Derek Anderson RC	.50	.20
153	Calbert Cheaney	.15	.05
154	Jayson Williams	.15	.05
155	Rick Fox	.30	.10
156	John Thomas RC	.15	.05
157	David Wesley	.15	.05
158	Bobby Jackson RC	1.00	.40
159	Kelvin Cato RC	.50	.20
160	Vinny Del Negro	.15	.05
161	Adonal Foyle RC	.30	.10
162	Larry Johnson	.30	.10
163	Brevin Knight RC	.30	.10
164	Rod Strickland	.15	.05
165	Rodrick Rhodes RC	.15	.05
166	Scot Pollard RC	.30	.10
167	Sam Cassell	.50	.20
168	Jerry Stackhouse	.50	.20
169	Mark Jackson	.30	.10
170	John Wallace	.15	.05
171	Horace Grant	.30	.10
172A	Vin Baker	.30	.10
172B	Tracy McGrady RC ERR	2.50	1.00
173	Eddie Jones	.50	.20
174	Kerry Kittles	.50	.20
175	Antonio Daniels RC	.50	.20
176	Alan Henderson	.15	.05
177	Searl Elliott	.30	.10
178	John Starks	.30	.10
179	Chauncey Billups RC	1.25	.50
180	Juwan Howard	.30	.10
181	Bobby Phills	.15	.05
182	Latrell Sprewell	.50	.20
183	Jim Jackson	.15	.05
184	Danny Fortson RC	.30	.10
185	Zydrunas Ilgauskas	.30	.10
186	Clifford Robinson	.15	.05
187	Chris Mullin	.30	.10
188	Greg Ostertag	.15	.05
189	Antoine Walker ZUP	.50	.20
190	Michael Jordan ZUP	1.50	.60
191	Scottie Pippen ZUP	.40	.15
192	Dennis Rodman ZUP	.15	.05
193	Grant Hill ZUP	.30	.10
194	Clyde Drexler ZUP	.30	.10
195	Kobe Bryant ZUP	1.00	.40
196	Shaquille O'Neal ZUP	.50	.20
197	Alonzo Mourning ZUP	.30	.10
198	Ray Allen ZUP	.30	.10
199	Kevin Garnett ZUP	.50	.20
200	Stephon Marbury ZUP	.50	.20
201	Anfernee Hardaway ZUP	.30	.10
202	Jason Kidd ZUP	.40	.15
203	David Robinson ZUP	.30	.10
204	Gary Payton ZUP	.30	.10
205	Marcus Camby ZUP	.30	.10
206	Karl Malone ZUP	.50	.20
207	John Stockton ZUP	.50	.20
208	S.Abdur-Rahim ZUP	.40	.15
209	Charles Barkley CL	.50	.20
210	Gary Payton CL	.30	.10

Acknowledgments

Each year we refine the process of developing the most accurate and up-to-date information for this book. We believe this year's price guide is our best yet. Thanks again to all the contributors nationwide (listed below) as well as our staff here in Dallas.

Those who have worked closely with us on this and many other books, have again proven themselves invaluable in every aspect of producing this book: Rich Altman, Randy Archer, Mike Aronstein, Jerry Bell, Chris Benjamin, Mike Blaisdell, Bill Bossert (Mid-Atlantic Coin Exchange), Todd Crosner (California Sports Card Exchange), Bud Darland, Bill and Diane Dodge, Rick Donohoo, Willie Erving, Fleer (Tim Franz), Gervise Ford, Steve Freedman, Larry and Jeff Fritsch, Jim Galusha, Dick Gariepy, Dick Gilkeson, Mike and Howard Gordon, Sally Grace, Oscar Gracia, George Grauer, John Greenwald, Jess Guffey, George Henn, Mike Hersh, John Inouye, Steven Judd, Edward J. Kabala, Judy Kaye, Lon Levitan, Lew Lipset, Dave Lucey, Paul Marchant, Brian Marcy (Scottsdale Baseball Cards), Dr. John McCue, Mike Mosier (Columbia City Collectibles Co.), Clark Muldavin, B.A. Murry, Steven Panet, Earl N. Petersen, J.C. (Boo) Phillips, Jack Pollard, Racing Champions (Bill Surdock), Pat Quinn, Henry M. Reizes, Gavin Riley, Rotman Productions, John Rumierz, Kevin Savage and Pat Blandford (Sports Gallery), Mike Schechter (MSA), Dan Sherlock, Bill Shonscheck, Glen J. Sidler, John Spalding, Spanky's, Nigel Spill (Oldies and Goodies), Rob Springs, Murvin Sterling, Dan Stickney, Steve Taft, Ed Taylor, Lee Temanson, Topps (Clay Luraschi), Upper Deck (Jake Gonzales), Bill Vizas, Bill Wesslund (Portland Sports Card Co.), Jim Woods, Kit Young, Robert Zanze, Bill Zimpleman, and Dean Zindler.

Many other individuals have provided price input, illustrative material, checklist verifications, errata, and/or background information. At the risk of inadvertently overlooking or omitting these many contributors, we should like to personally thank Joseph Abram, Darren Adams, Harry and Angela Agens, Brett Allen, Alan Applegate, Randy Archer, Jeremy Bachman, Fran Bailey, Dean Bedell, Bubba Bennett, Eric Berger, Stanley Bernstein, Mike Blair, Andrew Bosarge, Naed Bou, David Bowlby, Gary Boyd, Terry Boyd, Nelson Brewart, Ray Bright, Britt Britton, Jacey Buel, Terry Bunt, David Cadelina, Danny Cariseo, Sally Carves, Tom Cavalierre, Garrett Chan, Lance Churchill, Craig Coddling, H. William Cook, Dave Cooper, Ron Cornell, Paul Czuchna, Jeff Daniels, Robert DeSalvatore, Robert Dichiara, Pat Dorsey, Joe Drelich, Brad Drummond, Charles Easterday Jr., Al Eng, Brad Engelhardt, Darrell Ereth, F&F Fast Break Cards, Gary Farbstein, Anthony Fernando, Joe Filas, Tom Freeman, Bob Frye, Alex and Chris Gala, Greg George, Pete George, Arthur Goyette, Dina Gray, Bob Grissett, Jess Guffey, Simon Gutis, Steve Hart, John Haupt, Sol Hauptman, Brian Headrick, Steven Hecht, Rod Heffem, Kevin Heffner, Stephen Hils, Neil Hoppenworth, Bill Huggins, Wendell Hunter, Frank Hurtado, Brett Hyle, John Inouye, Brian Jaccoma, Mike Jardina, David Johnson, Craig Jones, Carmen Jordan, Loyd Jungling, Nick Kardoulias, Scott Kashner, Glenn Kasnuba, Jan Kemplin, Kal Kenfield, John Kilian, Tim Kirk, John Klassnik, Steve (DJ) Kluback, Mike Knoll, Don Knutsen, Mike Kolhhas, Bob and Bryan Kornfeld, George Kruk, Tom Kummer, Tim Landis, Jeff La Scala, Howard Lau, John Law, Ed Lim, Neil Lopez, Kendall Loyd, Fernando Mercado, Bruce Margulies, Scott Martinez, Bill McAvoy, Chris Merrill, Robert Merrill, Blake Meyer, Chad Meyer, Mark Meyer, Midwest Sports Cards, Jeff Mimick, Jeff Monaco, Jeff Morris, Michael Olsen, Don Olson Jr., Glenn Olson, Arto Paladian, Michael Parker, Jeff Patton, Jeff Prillaman, Paul Purves, Don Ras, Ron Resling, Carson Ritchey, Brent Ruland, Erik Runge, Mark Samarin, Bob Santos, Eric Shilito, Masa Shinohara, Bob Shurtleff, Sam Sliheet, Doug Smith, Doug Spooner, Dan Statman, Geoff Stevers, Brad Stiles, Andy Stoltz, Nick Teresi, Jim Tripodi, Rob Veres, Bill Vizas, Kevin Vo, Mark Watson, Brian Wentz, Brian White, Doc White, Jeff Wiedenfeld, Mike Wiggins, Douglas Wilding, Steve Yeh, Zario Zigler, and Mark Zubrensky.

Every year we make active solicitations for expert input. We are particularly appreciative of help (however extensive or cursory) provided for this volume. We receive many inquiries, comments, and questions regarding material within this book. In fact, each and every one is read and digested. Time constraints, however, prevent us from personally replying. But keep sharing your knowledge. Your letters and input are part of the "big picture" of hobby information we can pass along to readers in our books and magazines. Even though we cannot respond to each letter, you are making significant contributions to the hobby through your interest and comments.

The effort to continually refine and improve this book also involves a growing number of people and types of expertise on our home team. Our company boasts a substantial Sports Data Publishing team, which strengthens our ability to provide comprehensive analysis of the marketplace. Sports Data Publishing capably handled numerous technical details and provided able assistance and leadership in the preparation of this edition.

Our basketball analysts played a major part in compiling this year's book, traveling thousands of miles during the past year to attend sports card shows and visit card shops around the United States and Canada. The Beckett basketball specialist is Keith Hower (price guide editor). His gathering information, entering sets, pricing analysis, and careful proofreading were key contributions to the accuracy of this annual.

Also, key contributor to endless hours of information gathering, pricing, and analysis was Rich Klein.